D1222513

CHILTON®

GENERAL MOTORS
SERVICE MANUAL
2012 EDITION
VOLUME II

CENGAGE
Learning®

Australia • Brazil • Japan • Korea • Mexico • Singapore • Spain • United Kingdom • United States

CHILTON®
General Motors Service Manual
2010 Edition
Volume II

Vice President,
Technology Professional
Business Unit:
  Gregory L. Clayton

Publisher,
Technology Professional
Business Unit:
  David Koontz

Director of Marketing:
  Beth A. Lutz

Senior Production Director:
  Wendy Troeger

Production Manager:
  Sherondra Thedford

Marketing Manager:
  Jennifer Barbic

Marketing Coordinator:
  Rachael Torres

Editorial Assistant:
  Lisa Staib

Chilton Content Specialist:
  Paula Baillie

Graphical Designer:
  Melinda Possinger

Art Director:
  Benj Gleeksman

Sr. Content Project Manager:
  Mike Tubbert

Senior Editors:
  Eugene F. Hannon, Jr., A.S.E.
  Ryan Lee Price
  Richard J. Rivele
  Christine L. Sheeky

Editors:
  Dennis Bailey
  David G. Olson

Printed in the United States of America
1 2 3 4 5 6 7 17 16 15 14 13 12

For product information and technology assistance, contact us at
Professional & Career Group Customer Support, 1-800-648-7450.
For permission to use material from this text or product,
submit all requests online at
www.cengage.com/permissions.
Further permissions questions can be e-mailed to
permissionrequest@cengage.com.

ISBN-13: 978-1-4354-6170-3
ISBN-10: 1-4354-6170-3
ISSN: 2160-8199

Chilton
5 Maxwell Drive
Clifton Park, NY 12065-2919
USA

Cengage Learning is a leading provider of customized learning solutions with office locations around the globe, including Singapore, the United Kingdom, Australia, Mexico, Brazil, and Japan. Locate your local office at: **international.cengage.com/region**

Cengage Learning products are represented in Canada by Nelson Education, Ltd.

NOTICE TO THE READER

Publisher does not warrant or guarantee any of the products described herein or perform any independent analysis in connection with any of the product information contained herein. Publisher does not assume, and expressly disclaims, any obligation to obtain and include information other than that provided to it by the manufacturer.

The reader is expressly warned to consider and adopt all safety precautions that might be indicated by the activities described herein and to avoid all potential hazards. By following the instructions contained herein, the reader willingly assumes all risks in connection with such instructions.

The publisher makes no representations or warranties of any kind, including but not limited to, the warranties of fitness for particular purpose or merchantability, nor are any such representations implied with respect to the material set forth herein, and the publisher takes no responsibility with respect to such material. The publisher shall not be liable for any special, consequential, or exemplary damages resulting, in whole or part, from the readers' use of, or reliance upon, this material.

Table of Contents

Sections

10   Cruze

11   Equinox, Terrain

12   Express, Savana

13   G6

14   HHR

15   Impala

16   Lacrosse

17   Lucerne

DTC   Diagnostic Trouble Codes

Model Index

Model	Section No.	Model	Section No.	Model	Section No.
C			**G**		**S**
Cruze	10-1	G6	13-1	Savana	12-1
E			**H**		**T**
Equinox	11-1	HHR	14-1	Terrain	11-1
Express	12-1		**I**		
		Impala	15-1		
			L		
		Lucerne	17-1		

USING THIS INFORMATION

Organization

To find where a particular model section or procedure is located, look in the Table of Contents. Main topics are listed with the page number on which they may be found. Following the main topics is an alphabetical listing of all of the procedures within the section and their page numbers.

Manufacturer and Model Coverage

This product covers 2010-2011 General Motors models that are produced in sufficient quantities to warrant coverage, and which have technical content available from the vehicle manufacturers before our publication date. Although this information is as complete as possible at the time of publication, some manufacturers may make changes which cannot be included here. While striving for total accuracy, the publisher cannot assume responsibility for any errors, changes, or omissions that may occur in the compilation of this data.

Part Numbers and Special Tools

Part numbers and special tools are recommended by the publisher and vehicle manufacturer to perform specific jobs. Before substituting any part or tool for the one recommended, you must be completely satisfied that neither your personal safety, nor the performance of the vehicle will be endangered.

ACKNOWLEDGEMENT

Portions of materials contained herein have been reprinted under license from General Motors Company, Service and Parts Operations License Agreement #1110757.

PRECAUTIONS

Before servicing any vehicle, please be sure to read all of the following precautions, which deal with personal safety, prevention of component damage, and important points to take into consideration when servicing a motor vehicle:

• Always wear safety glasses or goggles when drilling, cutting, grinding or prying.

• Steel-toed work shoes should be worn when working with heavy parts. Pockets should not be used for carrying tools. A slip or fall can drive a screwdriver into your body.

• Work surfaces, including tools and the floor should be kept clean of grease, oil or other slippery material.

• When working around moving parts, don't wear loose clothing. Long hair should be tied back under a hat or cap, or in a hair net.

• Always use tools only for the purpose for which they were designed. Never pry with a screwdriver.

• Keep a fire extinguisher and first aid kit handy.

• Always properly support the vehicle with approved stands or lift.

• Always have adequate ventilation when working with chemicals or hazardous material.

• Carbon monoxide is colorless, odorless and dangerous. If it is necessary to operate the engine with vehicle in a closed area such as a garage, always use an exhaust collector to vent the exhaust gases outside the closed area.

• When draining coolant, keep in mind that small children and some pets are attracted by ethylene glycol antifreeze, and are quite likely to drink any left in an open container, or in puddles on the ground. This will prove fatal in sufficient quantity. Always drain the coolant into a sealable container.

• To avoid personal injury, do not remove the coolant pressure relief cap while the engine is operating or hot. The cooling system is under pressure; steam and hot liquid can come out forcefully when the cap is loosened slightly. Failure to follow these instructions may result in personal injury. The coolant must be recovered in a suitable, clean container for reuse. If the coolant is contaminated it must be recycled or disposed of correctly.

• When carrying out maintenance on the starting system be aware that heavy gauge leads are connected directly to the battery. Make sure the protective caps are in place when maintenance is completed. Failure to follow these instructions may result in personal injury.

• Do not remove any part of the engine emission control system. Operating the engine without the engine emission control system will reduce fuel economy and engine ventilation. This will weaken engine performance and shorten engine life. It is also a violation of Federal law.

• Due to environmental concerns, when the air conditioning system is drained, the refrigerant must be collected using refrigerant recovery/recycling equipment. Federal law requires that refrigerant be recovered into appropriate recovery equipment and the process be conducted by qualified technicians who have been certified by an approved organization, such as MACS, ASI, etc. Use of a recovery machine dedicated to the appropriate refrigerant is necessary to reduce the possibility of oil and refrigerant incompatibility concerns. Refer to the instructions provided by the equipment manufacturer when removing refrigerant from or charging the air conditioning system.

• Always disconnect the battery ground when working on or around the electrical system.

• Batteries contain sulfuric acid. Avoid contact with skin, eyes, or clothing. Also, shield your eyes when working near batteries to protect against possible splashing of the acid solution. In case of acid contact with skin or eyes, flush immediately with water for a minimum of 15 minutes and get prompt medical attention. If acid is swallowed, call a physician immediately. Failure to follow these instructions may result in personal injury.

• Batteries normally produce explosive gases. Therefore, do not allow flames, sparks or lighted substances to come near the battery. When charging or working near a battery, always shield your face and protect your eyes. Always provide ventilation. Failure to follow these instructions may result in personal injury.

• When lifting a battery, excessive pressure on the end walls could cause acid to spew through the vent caps, resulting in personal injury, damage to the vehicle or battery. Lift with a battery carrier or with your hands on opposite corners. Failure to follow these instructions may result in personal injury.

• Observe all applicable safety precautions when working around fuel. Whenever servicing the fuel system, always work in a well-ventilated area. Do not allow fuel spray or vapors to come in contact with a spark, open flame, or excessive heat (a hot drop light, for example). Keep a dry chemical fire extinguisher near the work area. Always keep fuel in a container specifically designed for fuel storage; also, always properly seal fuel containers to avoid the possibility of fire or explosion. Do not smoke or carry lighted tobacco or open flame of any type when working on or near any fuel-related components.

• Fuel injection systems often remain pressurized, even after the engine has been turned OFF. The fuel system pressure must be relieved before disconnecting any fuel lines. Failure to do so may result in fire and/or personal injury.

• The evaporative emissions system contains fuel vapor and condensed fuel vapor. Although not present in large quantities, it still presents the danger of explosion or fire. Disconnect the battery ground cable from the battery to minimize the possibility of an electrical spark occurring, possibly causing a fire or explosion if fuel vapor or liquid fuel is present in the area. Failure to follow these instructions can result in personal injury.

• The EPA warns that prolonged contact with used engine oil may cause a number of skin disorders, including cancer! You should make every effort to minimize your exposure to used engine oil. Protective gloves should be worn when changing oil. Wash your hands and any other exposed skin areas as soon as possible after exposure to used engine oil. Soap and water, or waterless hand cleaner should be used.

• Some vehicles are equipped with an air bag system, often referred to as a Supplemental Restraint System (SRS) or Supplemental Inflatable Restraint (SIR) system. The system must be disabled before performing service on or around system components, steering column, instrument panel components, wiring and sensors. Failure to follow safety and disabling procedures could result in accidental air bag deployment, possible personal injury and unnecessary system repairs.

• Always wear safety goggles when working with, or around, the air bag system. When carrying a non-deployed air bag, be sure the bag and trim cover are pointed away from your body. When placing a non-deployed air bag on a work surface, always face the bag and trim cover upward, away from the surface. This will reduce the motion of the module if it is accidentally deployed.

• Electronic modules are sensitive to electrical charges. The ABS module can be damaged if exposed to these charges.

• Brake pads and shoes may contain asbestos, which has been determined to be a cancer-causing agent. Never clean brake surfaces with compressed air. Avoid inhaling brake dust. Clean all brake surfaces with a commercially available brake cleaning fluid.

• When replacing brake pads, shoes, discs or drums, replace them as complete axle sets.

• When servicing drum brakes, disassemble and assemble one side at a time, leaving the remaining side intact for reference.

• Brake fluid often contains polyglycol ethers and polyglycols. Avoid contact with the eyes and wash your hands thoroughly after handling brake fluid. If you do get brake fluid in your eyes, flush your eyes with clean, running water for 15 minutes. If eye irritation persists, or if you have taken brake fluid internally, immediately seek medical assistance.

• Clean, high quality brake fluid from a sealed container is essential to the safe and proper operation of the brake system. You should always buy the correct type of brake fluid for your vehicle. If the brake fluid becomes contaminated, completely flush the system with new fluid. Never reuse any brake fluid. Any brake fluid that is removed from the system should be discarded. Also, do not allow any brake fluid to come in contact with a painted or plastic surface; it will damage the paint.

• Never operate the engine without the proper amount and type of engine oil; doing so will result in severe engine damage.

• Timing belt maintenance is extremely important! Many models utilize an interference-type, non-freewheeling engine. If the timing belt breaks, the valves in the cylinder head may strike the pistons, causing potentially serious (also time-consuming and expensive) engine damage.

• Disconnecting the negative battery cable on some vehicles may interfere with the functions of the on-board computer system(s) and may require the computer to undergo a relearning process once the negative battery cable is reconnected.

• Steering and suspension fasteners are critical parts because they affect performance of vital components and systems and their failure can result in major service expense. They must be replaced with the same grade or part number or an equivalent part if replacement is necessary. Do not use a replacement part of lesser quality or substitute design. Torque values must be used as specified during reassembly.

CHEVROLET

Cruze

BRAKES 10-10

**ANTI-LOCK BRAKE
SYSTEM (ABS) 10-10**
General Information.................10-10
   Precautions........................10-10
Speed Sensors 10-10
   Removal & Installation........10-10
**BLEEDING THE BRAKE
SYSTEM 10-12**
Bleeding Procedure..................10-12
   Bleeding Procedure 10-12
   Bleeding the ABS System ...10-14
   Brake Line Bleeding............10-14
   Fluid Fill Procedure 10-15
   Master Cylinder
   Bleeding 10-14
FRONT DISC BRAKES 10-16
Brake Caliper..........................10-16
   Removal & Installation........10-16
Disc Brake Pads 10-17
   Removal & Installation........10-17
PARKING BRAKE.............10-22
Parking Brake Cables 10-22
   Adjustment 10-22
Parking Brake Shoes 10-22
   Removal & Installation........10-22
REAR DISC BRAKES 10-18
Brake Caliper..........................10-18
   Removal & Installation........10-18
Disc Brake Pads 10-19
   Removal & Installation........10-19
REAR DRUM BRAKES........10-20
Brake Drum 10-20
   Removal & Installation........10-20
Brake Shoes 10-21
   Adjustment 10-21
   Removal & Installation........10-21

CHASSIS ELECTRICAL 10-23

**AIR BAG (SUPPLEMENTAL
RESTRAINT SYSTEM) 10-23**
General Information.................10-23
   Arming the System 10-24
   Clockspring Centering........10-24
   Disarming the System........10-23
   Service Precautions 10-23

DRIVE TRAIN 10-25

Clutch....................................10-26
   Bleeding 10-27
   Fluid Fill Procedure 10-28
   Removal & Installation........10-26
Front Halfshaft.......................10-28
   Removal & Installation........10-28
Manual Transaxle Assembly....10-25
   Removal & Installation........10-25
Manual Transaxle Fluid 10-26
   Drain and Refill 10-26

ENGINE COOLING 10-31

Charge Air Cooler 10-31
   Removal & Installation........10-31
Engine Coolant........................10-32
   Bleeding 10-34
   Drain & Refill Procedure.....10-32
   Flushing..........................10-34
Engine Fan 10-34
   Removal & Installation........10-34
Radiator.................................10-36
   Removal & Installation........10-36
Thermostat 10-37
   Removal & Installation........10-37
Water Pump 10-38
   Removal & Installation........10-38

ENGINE ELECTRICAL 10-39

BATTERY SYSTEM............10-39
Battery...................................10-39
   Battery Reconnect/
   Relearn Procedure 10-40
   Removal & Installation........10-39
CHARGING SYSTEM 10-41
Alternator 10-41
   Removal & Installation........10-41
IGNITION SYSTEM 10-43
Firing Order............................10-43
Ignition Coil 10-43
   Removal & Installation........10-43
Ignition Timing 10-44
   Adjustment 10-44
Spark Plugs............................10-44
   Removal & Installation........10-44

STARTING SYSTEM 10-44

Starter 10-44
   Removal & Installation........10-44

ENGINE MECHANICAL......10-45

Accessory Drive Belts 10-45
   Accessory Belt Routing.......10-45
   Adjustment 10-45
   Inspection 10-45
   Removal & Installation........10-45
Air Cleaner 10-47
   Filter/Element
   Replacement 10-48
   Removal & Installation........10-47
Camshaft and Valve Lifters......10-49
   Inspection 10-49
   Removal & Installation........10-49
Camshaft Position Actuator
   Adjuster 10-52
   Removal & Installation........10-52
Catalytic Converter 10-53
   Removal & Installation........10-53
Crankshaft Damper (Balancer)...10-56
   Removal & Installation........10-56
Crankshaft Front Seal..............10-58
   Removal & Installation........10-58
Cylinder Head 10-59
   Removal & Installation........10-59
Engine Oil & Filter 10-66
   Replacement 10-66
Exhaust Manifold 10-67
   Removal & Installation........10-67
Flywheel/Flexplate...................10-68
   Removal & Installation........10-68
Intake Manifold 10-69
   Removal & Installation........10-69
Oil Pan 10-72
   Removal & Installation........10-72
Oil Pump................................10-74
   Inspection 10-76
   Removal & Installation........10-74
Piston and Ring.......................10-76
   Positioning 10-76
Rear Main Seal 10-77
   Removal & Installation........10-77
Timing Belt & Sprockets 10-79
   Removal & Installation........10-79

Timing Belt Front Cover 10-78
    Removal & Installation........10-78
Timing Belt Rear Cover 10-81
    Removal & Installation........10-81
Timing Chain & Sprockets 10-85
    Removal & Installation........10-85
Timing Chain Front Cover.......10-81
    Removal & Installation........10-81
Turbocharger 10-86
    Removal & Installation........10-86
Valve Covers 10-88
    Removal & Installation........10-88
Valve Lash 10-90
    Adjustment 10-90

ENGINE PERFORMANCE & EMISSION CONTROLS 10-90

Camshaft Position (CMP)
    Sensor 10-90
    Location 10-90
    Removal & Installation........10-90
Component Locations 10-90
Crankshaft Position (CKP)
    Sensor 10-94
    Location 10-94
    Removal & Installation........10-95
Engine Control Module
    (ECM) 10-95
    Location 10-95
    Removal & Installation........10-95
Engine Coolant Temperature
    (ECT) Sensor 10-96
    Location 10-96
    Removal & Installation........10-97
Heated Oxygen (HO2S)
    Sensor 10-97
    Location 10-97
    Removal & Installation........10-97
Intake Air Temperature (IAT)
    Sensor 10-98
    Location 10-98
    Removal & Installation........10-98
Knock Sensor (KS)................10-99
    Location 10-99
    Removal & Installation........10-99
Manifold Absolute Pressure
    (MAP) Sensor 10-99
    Location 10-99
    Removal & Installation........10-99
Mass Air Flow (MAF)
    Sensor 10-100
    Location 10-100
    Removal & Installation......10-100
Throttle Position Sensor
    (TPS) 10-100

Location...........................10-100
    Removal & Installation......10-100
Vehicle Speed Sensor
    (VSS) 10-100
    Location 10-100
    Removal & Installation......10-101

FUEL.........................10-101

GASOLINE FUEL INJECTION SYSTEM.....................10-101
Fuel Filter 10-101
    Removal & Installation......10-101
Fuel Injectors 10-101
    Removal & Installation......10-101
Fuel Pump Module...............10-103
    Removal & Installation......10-103
Fuel System Service
    Precautions 10-101
Fuel Tank............................10-104
    Draining.........................10-104
    Removal & Installation......10-104
Idle Speed 10-105
    Adjustment 10-105
Relieving Fuel System
    Pressure.........................10-101
Throttle Body......................10-105
    Removal & Installation......10-105

HEATING & AIR CONDITIONING SYSTEM..10-106

Blower Motor 10-106
    Removal & Installation......10-106
Heater Core 10-106
    Removal & Installation......10-106

PRECAUTIONS..............10-10

SPECIFICATIONS AND MAINTENANCE CHARTS.....10-3

Additional Maintenance
    Services - Normal 10-9
Additional Maintenance
    Services - Severe 10-9
Brake Specifications.................10-7
Camshaft Specifications............10-5
Capacities 10-4
Crankshaft and Connecting
    Rod Specifications...............10-5
Engine and Vehicle
    Identification 10-3
Engine Tune-Up
    Specifications 10-3
Fluid Specifications...................10-4

General Engine Specifications...10-3
Maintenance I and II Service
    Schedules 10-8
Piston and Ring
    Specifications 10-5
Tire, Wheel and Ball Joint
    Specifications 10-7
Torque Specifications.................10-6
Valve Specifications 10-4
Wheel Alignment......................10-6

STEERING 10-107

Power Steering Assist
    Motor......................10-107
    Removal & Installation......10-107
Power Steering Gear................10-108
    Removal & Installation......10-108

SUSPENSION...............10-111

FRONT SUSPENSION 10-111
Control Links 10-111
    Removal & Installation......10-111
Lower Ball Joint 10-111
    Removal & Installation......10-111
Lower Control Arm................10-111
    Control Arm Bushing
        Replacement 10-112
    Removal & Installation......10-111
Stabilizer Bar 10-112
    Removal & Installation......10-112
Steering Knuckle 10-113
    Removal & Installation......10-113
Strut & Spring Assembly 10-114
    Overhaul 10-114
    Removal & Installation......10-114
Wheel Bearings 10-115
    Adjustment 10-115
    Removal & Installation......10-115
REAR SUSPENSION 10-116
Coil Spring...........................10-116
    Removal & Installation......10-116
Equalizer Beam.....................10-117
    Removal & Installation......10-117
Shock Absorber.....................10-119
    Removal & Installation......10-119
Stabilizer Bar 10-119
    Removal & Installation......10-119
Wheel Bearings 10-119
    Adjustment 10-119
    Removal & Installation......10-119

SPECIFICATIONS AND MAINTENANCE CHARTS

ENGINE AND VEHICLE IDENTIFICATION

Engine							Model Year	
Code ①	Liters (cc)	Cu. In.	Cyl.	Fuel Sys.	Engine Type	Eng. Mfg.	Code ②	Year
9	1.4	83.2	4	MFI	DOHC	GM	B	2011
H	1.8	109.6	4	MFI	DOHC	GM		

MFI: Multiport Fuel Injection

DOHC: Double Overhead Camshafts

① 8th position of VIN

② 10th position of VIN

25742_CRUZ_C0001

GENERAL ENGINE SPECIFICATIONS

All measurements are given in inches.

Year	Model	Engine Displacement Liters	Engine ID/VIN	Fuel System Type	Net Horsepower @ rpm	Net Torque @ rpm (ft. lbs.)	Bore x Stroke (in.)	Compression Ratio	Oil Pressure @ rpm
2011	Cruze (except LS)	1.4	9	MFI	138@4,900	148@1,850	2.85 x 3.30	9.5:1	55-94 psi @3,000-3,500
	Cruze LS	1.8	H	MFI	136@6,300	123@3,800	3.17 x 3.47	10.5:1	19 psi @idle

25742_CRUZ_C0002

ENGINE TUNE-UP SPECIFICATIONS

Year	Engine Displacement Liters	Engine ID/VIN	Spark Plug Gap (in.)	Ignition Timing (deg.) MT	Ignition Timing (deg.) AT	Fuel Pump (psi)	Idle Speed (rpm) MT	Idle Speed (rpm) AT	Valve Clearance Intake	Valve Clearance Exhaust
2011	1.4	9	0.0335 -0.0374	①	①	40-47	②	②	HYD	HYD
	1.8	H	0.028	①	①	40-47	②	②	HYD	HYD

NOTE: The Vehicle Emission Control Information label often reflects specification changes made during production.

The label figures must be used if they differ from those in this chart.

HYD: Hydraulic

① Ignition timing is controlled by the ECM and is not adjustable

② Idle speed is controlled by the ECM and is not adjustable

25742_CRUZ_C0003

CAPACITIES

Year	Model	Engine Displacement Liters	Engine ID/VIN	Engine Oil with Filter (qts.)	Transaxle (pts.) Auto.	Transaxle (pts.) Manual	Drive Axle (pts.) Front	Drive Axle (pts.) Rear	Transfer Case (pts.)	Fuel Tank (gal.)	Cooling System (qts.)
2011	Cruze (except LS)	1.4	9	4.3	16.9	4.6	N/A	N/A	N/A	①	6.6
	Cruze LS	1.8	H	4.8	16.9	4.6	N/A	N/A	N/A	15.6	5.9

NOTE: All capacities are approximate. Add fluid gradually and ensure a proper fluid level is obtained.

N/A: Not Applicable

① Except ECO model with manual transmission: 15.6 gallons
   ECO model with manual transmission: 12.6 gallons

25742_CRUZ_C0004

FLUID SPECIFICATIONS

Year	Model	Engine Disp. Liters	Engine Oil	Manual Trans.	Auto. Trans.	Drive Axle Front	Drive Axle Rear	Power Steering Fluid	Brake Master Cylinder	Cooling System
2011	Cruze (except LS)	1.4	5W-30	Castrol BOT 0402	DEXRON®-VI ATF	N/A	N/A	N/A	DOT 3	DEX-COOL® Coolant
	Cruze LS	1.8	5W-30	Castrol BOT 0402	DEXRON®-VI ATF	N/A	N/A	N/A	DOT 3	DEX-COOL® Coolant

DOT: Department Of Transportation

N/A: Not Applicable

25742_CRUZ_C0005

VALVE SPECIFICATIONS

Year	Engine Displacement Liters	Engine ID/VIN	Seat Angle (deg.)	Face Angle (deg.)	Spring Test Pressure (lbs. @ in.)	Spring Free-Length (in.)	Spring Installed Height (in.)	Stem-to-Guide Clearance (in.) Intake	Stem-to-Guide Clearance (in.) Exhaust	Stem Diameter (in.) Intake	Stem Diameter (in.) Exhaust
2011	1.4	9	①	NS	NS	1.575	1.181	0.0010-0.0022	0.0015-0.0030	0.1949-0.1955	0.1941-0.1947
	1.8	H	②	③	NS	1.650	1.380	0.0008-0.0021	0.0014-0.0026	0.1955-0.1961	0.1949-0.1955

NS: Not Specified

① Cylinder head valve seat angle: 90° 30`

② Cylinder head valve seat angle: 90° (-0.5°)

③ Valve seat angle on valve disk: 90°40' (+/-15')

25742_CRUZ_C0006

CAMSHAFT SPECIFICATIONS
All measurements in inches unless noted

Year	Engine Displacement Liters	Engine Code/VIN	Journal Diameter	Brg. Oil Clearance	Shaft End-play	Runout	Journal Bore	Lobe Height Intake	Lobe Height Exhaust
2011	1.4	9	NS	NS	NS	NS	NS	NS	NS
	1.8	H	NS	NS	NS	NS	NS	NS	NS

NS: Not Specified

25742_CRUZ_C0007

CRANKSHAFT AND CONNECTING ROD SPECIFICATIONS
All measurements are given in inches.

Year	Engine Displacement Liters	Engine ID/VIN	Crankshaft Main Brg. Journal Dia.	Main Brg. Oil Clearance	Shaft End-play	Thrust on No.	Connecting Rod Journal Diameter	Oil Clearance	Side Clearance
2011	1.4	9	1.9687-1.9692	0.0003-0.0012	0.0040-0.0080	3	1.6918-1.6924	0.0005-0.0024	NS
	1.8	H	2.1650-2.1660	0.0002-0.0024	0.0040-0.0080	3	1.6920-1.6930	0.0007-0.0028	NS

NS: Not Specified

25742_CRUZ_C0008

PISTON AND RING SPECIFICATIONS
All measurements are given in inches.

Year	Engine Displacement Liters	Engine ID/VIN	Piston Clearance	Ring Gap Top Compression	Ring Gap Bottom Compression	Ring Gap Oil Control	Ring Side Clearance Top Compression	Ring Side Clearance Bottom Compression	Ring Side Clearance Oil Control
2011	1.4	9	0.0010-0.0022	0.0098-0.0157	0.0157-0.0236	0.0098-0.0295	0.0010-0.0028	0.0010-0.0028	0.0016-0.0047
	1.8	H	0.0011-0.0021	0.0079-0.0158	0.0158-0.0237	0.0098-0.0295	0.0016-0.0032	0.0012-0.0028	0.0012-0.0051

25742_CRUZ_C0009

TORQUE SPECIFICATIONS
All readings in ft. lbs.

Year	Engine Disp. Liters	Engine ID/VIN	Cylinder Head Bolts	Main Bearing Bolts	Rod Bearing Bolts	Crankshaft Damper Bolts	Flywheel Bolts	Manifold		Spark Plugs	Oil Pan Drain Plug
								Intake	Exhaust		
2011	1.4	9	①	②	③	④	⑤	15	16	18	10
	1.8	H	⑥	⑦	⑧	⑨	⑩	15	15	18	10

① Step 1: 26 ft. lbs.
   Step 2: Plus 180 degrees
② M6 bolts Step 1: 89 inch lbs.
   M6 bolts Step 2: Plus 60 degrees
   M6 bolts Step 3: Plus 15 degrees
   M8 bolts Step 1: 18 ft. lbs.
   M8 bolts Step 2: Plus 60 degrees
   M8 bolts Step 3: Plus 15 degrees

③ Step 1: 18 ft. lbs.
   Step 2: Plus 45 degrees
④ Step 1: 111 ft. lbs.
   Step 2: Plus 45 degrees
   Step 3: Plus 15 degrees
⑤ Step 1: 44 ft. lbs.
   Step 2: Plus 45 degrees
   Step 3: Plus 15 degrees

⑥ Step 1: 18 ft. lbs.
   Step 2: Plus 90 degrees
   Step 3: Plus 90 degrees
   Step 4: Plus 90 degrees
   Step 5: Plus 45 degrees
⑦ Step 1: 37 ft. lbs.
   Step 2: Plus 45 degrees
   Step 3: Plus 15 degrees

⑧ Step 1: 26 ft. lbs.
   Step 2: Plus 45 degrees
   Step 3: Plus 15 degrees
⑨ Step 1: 70 ft. lbs.
   Step 2: Plus 45 degrees
   Step 3: Plus 15 degrees
⑩ Step 1: 26 ft. lbs.
   Step 2: Plus 30 degrees
   Step 3: Plus 15 degrees

25742_CRUZ_C0010

WHEEL ALIGNMENT

Year	Model		Caster		Camber		Toe-in (in.)
			Range (+/-Deg.)	Preferred Setting (Deg.)	Range (+/-Deg.)	Preferred Setting (Deg.)	
2011	Cruze (all models)	F	0.75	0.00	0.75	0.00	0.20 +/- 0.20
		R	N/A	N/A	0.75	0.00	0.05 +/- 0.40

N/A: Not Applicable

25742_CRUZ_C0011

TIRE, WHEEL AND BALL JOINT SPECIFICATIONS

Year	Model	OEM Tires Standard	OEM Tires Optional	Tire Pressures (psi) Front	Tire Pressures (psi) Rear	Wheel Size	Ball Joint Inspection	Lug Nut (ft. lbs.)
2011	Cruze 1LT	P215/60R16	NA	①	①	16 inch	②	103
	Cruze 2LT	P215/60R16	P225/50R17	①	①	16/17 inch	②	103
	Cruze LTZ	P225/45R18	NA	①	①	18 inch	②	103
	Cruze ECO	P215/55R17	NA	①	①	17 inch	②	103
	Cruze LS	P215/60R16	NA	①	①	16 inch	②	103

OEM: Original Equipment Manufacturer

PSI: Pounds Per Square Inch

NA: Information not available

① Always refer to the owner's manual and/or vehicle label

② Check for smooth rotation of the ball stud and for any damage to the ball stud or dust cover. If damage is found, replace the lower control arm.

25742_CRUZ_C0012

BRAKE SPECIFICATIONS

All measurements in inches unless noted

Year	Model		Brake Disc Original Thickness	Brake Disc Minimum Thickness	Brake Disc Max. Runout	Brake Drum Diameter Original Inside Diameter	Brake Drum Diameter Max. Wear Limit	Brake Drum Diameter Maximum Machine Diameter	Minimum Pad/Lining Thickness Front	Minimum Pad/Lining Thickness Rear	Brake Caliper Bracket Bolts (ft. lbs.)	Brake Caliper Guide Pin Bolts (ft. lbs.)
2011	Cruze 1LT	F	1.024	0.905	0.002	N/A	N/A	N/A	0.078	N/A	①	21
		R	N/A	N/A	N/A	10	10.078	N/S	N/A	0.063	N/A	N/A
	Cruze 2LT	F	1.024	0.905	0.002	N/A	N/A	N/A	0.078	N/A	①	21
		R	0.472	0.393	0.002	10	10.078	N/S	N/A	0.063	①	21
	Cruze LTZ	F	1.024	0.905	0.002	N/A	N/A	N/A	0.078	N/A	①	21
		R	0.472	0.393	0.002	N/A	N/A	N/A	N/A	0.078	①	21
	Cruze ECO	F	1.024	0.905	0.002	N/A	N/A	N/A	0.078	N/A	①	21
		R	N/A	N/A	N/A	10	10.078	N/S	N/A	0.063	N/A	N/A
	Cruze LS	F	1.024	0.905	0.002	N/A	N/A	N/A	0.078	N/A	①	21
		R	N/A	N/A	N/A	10	10.078	N/S	N/A	0.063	N/A	N/A

F: Front

R: Rear

N/A: Not Applicable

N/S: Not Specified

① Step 1: 74 ft. lbs.

  Step 2: Plus 60-75 degrees

25742_CRUZ_C0013

MAINTENANCE I AND II SERVICE SCHEDULES
CRUZE

When the CHANGE ENGINE OIL light appears, certain services and inspections are required.

Required services are described as Maintenance I and Maintenance II.

The first service of a vehicle should be Maintenance I, and the second service should be Maintenance II.

Alternate between the 2 services thereafter. However, in some cases, Maintenance II may be required more often.

Maintenance I: Use Maintenance I if the CHANGE ENGINE OIL light comes on within 10 months since the vehicle was purchased or, if Maintenance II was performed.

Maintenance II: Use Maintenance II if the previous service performed was Maintenance I. Always use Maintenance II whenever the CHANGE ENGINE OIL light comes on 10 months or more since the last service, or, if the CHANGE ENGINE OIL light has not come on at all for one year.

Service Item	Maintenance I	Maintenance II
Change the engine oil and filter.	✓	✓
Reset the oil life system.	✓	✓
Visually inspect the vehicle for leaks or damage. A fluid loss in the vehicle system could indicate a problem. Inspect, repair and add fluid to the system if necessary.	✓	✓
Inspect the engine air cleaner filter. If necessary, replace the filter.	✓	✓
Rotate the tires. Inspect the tire inflation pressures and the tire wear.	✓	✓
Visually inspect the brake lines and hoses for proper hook-up, binding, leaks, cracks, chafing, etc. Inspect the disc brake pads for wear and the rotors for surface condition. Inspect the drum brake linings for wear or cracks. Inspect other brake parts, including drums, wheel cylinders, calipers, parking brake, etc. Inspect the parking brake adjustment.	✓	✓
Inspect engine coolant and windshield washer fluid levels. Add fluid as needed.	✓	✓
Inspect the suspension and steering components. Inspect the front and rear suspension and the steering system for damaged, loose or missing parts, or signs of wear. Inspect the power steering lines and the hoses for proper hook-up, binding, leaks, cracks, chafing, etc.	—	✓
Visually inspect the coolant hoses and replace the hoses if they are cracked, swollen or deteriorated. Inspect all pipes, fittings and clamps; replace with GM parts as needed. To help ensure proper operation, a pressure test of the cooling system and pressure cap and cleaning the outside of the radiator and air conditioning condenser is recommended at least once a year.	—	✓
Ensure the safety belt reminder light and all the belts, buckles, latch plates, retractors and anchorages are working properly. Look for any other loose or damaged safety belt system parts. If you see anything that might keep a safety belt system from working correctly, repair or replaced the damaged part. Replace torn or frayed safety belts, refer to Operational and Functional Checks in Seat Belts. Inspect for any opened or broken air bag coverings, and repair or replace as needed. The air bag system does require regular maintenance.	—	✓
Lubricate the body components.	—	✓
Lubricate all key lock cylinders, hood latch assemblies, secondary latches, pivots, spring anchor and release pawl, hood and door hinges, rear folding seats and liftgate hinges. Frequent lubrication may be required when exposed to a corrosive environment, refer to Fluid and Lubricant Recommendations . Applying dielectric silicone grease GM P/N 12345579 (Canadian P/N 1974984) or equivalent on the weatherstrips with a clean cloth.	—	✓
Inspect the transaxle fluid level and add fluid as needed.	—	✓
Inspect the wiper blades and replace as necessary	✓	✓
Inspect the throttle system.	—	✓
Replace the passenger compartment air filter.	—	✓

To reset the CHANGE ENGINE OIL light:

1. Turn the ignition key to the ON/RUN position with the engine OFF.
2. Press and release the stem in the lower center of the instrument cluster until the OIL LIFE message is displayed.
3. Once the alternating OIL LIFE and RESET messages appear, press and hold the stem until several beeps sound.
   This confirms that the oil life system has been reset to 100 percent.
4. Turn the ignition key to the OFF position.
   If the CHANGE ENGINE OIL message comes back on when the vehicle is started, the engine oil life system has not been reset. Repeat the procedure.

ADDITIONAL MAINTENANCE SERVICES - NORMAL
CRUZE

TO BE SERVICED	TYPE OF SERVICE	VEHICLE MILEAGE INTERVAL (x1000)					
		25	50	75	100	125	150
Engine coolant	Replace						✓
Air cleaner filter	Replace		✓		✓		✓
Automatic transaxle fluid	Replace				✓		
Spark plugs	Replace				✓		
Exhaust system & heat shields	Service/ Inspect	✓	✓	✓	✓	✓	✓
Cooling system hoses and clamps	Service/ Inspect	✓	✓	✓	✓	✓	✓
Fuel system	Inspect	✓	✓	✓	✓	✓	✓
Accessory drive belt	Replace						✓
Evaporative control system	Inspect		✓		✓		✓
Manual transmission fluid	Replace						✓
Passenger compartment air cleaner	Replace	✓	✓	✓	✓	✓	✓
Timing belt (1.8L)	Replace				✓		

25742_CRUZ_C0015

ADDITIONAL MAINTENANCE SERVICES - SEVERE
CRUZE

TO BE SERVICED	TYPE OF SERVICE	VEHICLE MILEAGE INTERVAL (x1000)					
		25	50	75	100	125	150
Engine coolant	Replace						✓
Air cleaner filter	Replace	✓	✓	✓	✓	✓	✓
Automatic transaxle fluid	Replace		✓		✓		✓
Spark plugs	Replace				✓		
Exhaust system & heat shields	Service/ Inspect	✓	✓	✓	✓	✓	✓
Cooling system hoses and clamps	Service/ Inspect	✓	✓	✓	✓	✓	✓
Fuel system	Inspect	✓	✓	✓	✓	✓	✓
Accessory drive belt	Inspect						✓
Evaporative control system	Inspect		✓		✓		✓
Manual transmission fluid	Replace		✓		✓		✓
Timing belt (1.8L)	Replace				✓		
Passenger compartment air cleaner	Replace	✓	✓	✓	✓	✓	✓

25742_CRUZ_C0016

PRECAUTIONS

Before servicing any vehicle, please be sure to read all of the following precautions, which deal with personal safety, prevention of component damage, and important points to take into consideration when servicing a motor vehicle:

• Never open, service or drain the radiator or cooling system when the engine is hot; serious burns can occur from the steam and hot coolant.

• Observe all applicable safety precautions when working around fuel. Whenever servicing the fuel system, always work in a well-ventilated area. Do not allow fuel spray or vapors to come in contact with a spark, open flame, or excessive heat (a hot drop light, for example). Keep a dry chemical fire extinguisher near the work area. Always keep fuel in a container specifically designed for fuel storage; also, always properly seal fuel containers to avoid the possibility of fire or explosion. Refer to the additional fuel system precautions later in this section.

• Fuel injection systems often remain pressurized, even after the engine has been turned **OFF**. The fuel system pressure must be relieved before disconnecting any fuel lines. Failure to do so may result in fire and/or personal injury.

• Brake fluid often contains polyglycol ethers and polyglycols. Avoid contact with the eyes and wash your hands thoroughly after handling brake fluid. If you do get brake fluid in your eyes, flush your eyes with clean, running water for 15 minutes. If eye irritation persists, or if you have taken

brake fluid internally, IMMEDIATELY seek medical assistance.

• The EPA warns that prolonged contact with used engine oil may cause a number of skin disorders, including cancer. You should make every effort to minimize your exposure to used engine oil. Protective gloves should be worn when changing oil. Wash your hands and any other exposed skin areas as soon as possible after exposure to used engine oil. Soap and water, or waterless hand cleaner should be used.

• All new vehicles are now equipped with an air bag system, often referred to as a Supplemental Restraint System (SRS) or Supplemental Inflatable Restraint (SIR) system. The system must be disabled before performing service on or around system components, steering column, instrument panel components, wiring and sensors. Failure to follow safety and disabling procedures could result in accidental air bag deployment, possible personal injury and unnecessary system repairs.

• Always wear safety goggles when working with, or around, the air bag system. When carrying a non-deployed air bag, be sure the bag and trim cover are pointed away from your body. When placing a non-deployed air bag on a work surface, always face the bag and trim cover upward, away from the surface. This will reduce the motion of the module if it is accidentally deployed. Refer to the additional air bag system precautions later in this section.

• Clean, high quality brake fluid from a sealed container is essential to the safe and

proper operation of the brake system. You should always buy the correct type of brake fluid for your vehicle. If the brake fluid becomes contaminated, completely flush the system with new fluid. Never reuse any brake fluid. Any brake fluid that is removed from the system should be discarded. Also, do not allow any brake fluid to come in contact with a painted surface; it will damage the paint.

• Never operate the engine without the proper amount and type of engine oil; doing so WILL result in severe engine damage.

• Timing belt maintenance is extremely important. Many models utilize an interference-type, non-freewheeling engine. If the timing belt breaks, the valves in the cylinder head may strike the pistons, causing potentially serious (also time-consuming and expensive) engine damage. Refer to the maintenance interval charts for the recommended replacement interval for the timing belt, and to the timing belt section for belt replacement and inspection.

• Disconnecting the negative battery cable on some vehicles may interfere with the functions of the on-board computer system(s) and may require the computer to undergo a relearning process once the negative battery cable is reconnected.

• When servicing drum brakes, only disassemble and assemble one side at a time, leaving the remaining side intact for reference.

• Only an MVAC-trained, EPA-certified automotive technician should service the air conditioning system or its components.

BRAKES

GENERAL INFORMATION

PRECAUTIONS

• Certain components within the ABS system are not intended to be serviced or repaired individually.

• Do not use rubber hoses or other parts not specifically specified for and ABS system. When using repair kits, replace all parts included in the kit. Partial or incorrect repair may lead to functional problems and require the replacement of components.

• Lubricate rubber parts with clean, fresh brake fluid to ease assembly. Do not use shop air to clean parts; damage to rubber components may result.

• Use only DOT 3 brake fluid from an unopened container.

• If any hydraulic component or line is removed or replaced, it may be necessary to bleed the entire system.

• A clean repair area is essential. Always clean the reservoir and cap thoroughly before removing the cap. The slightest amount of dirt in the fluid may plug an orifice and impair the system function. Perform repairs after components have been thoroughly cleaned; use only denatured alcohol to clean components. Do not allow ABS components to come into contact with any substance containing mineral oil; this includes used shop rags.

• The Anti-Lock control unit is a microprocessor similar to other computer units in the vehicle. Ensure that the ignition switch is **OFF** before removing or installing

ANTI-LOCK BRAKE SYSTEM (ABS)

controller harnesses. Avoid static electricity discharge at or near the controller.

• If any arc welding is to be done on the vehicle, the control unit should be unplugged before welding operations begin.

SPEED SENSORS

REMOVAL & INSTALLATION

Front Speed Sensor

See Figure 1.

1. Before servicing the vehicle, refer to the Precautions Section.
2. Raise and safely support the vehicle.
3. Remove the wheel and tire.
4. Remove the wheel speed sensor screw from the steering knuckle.

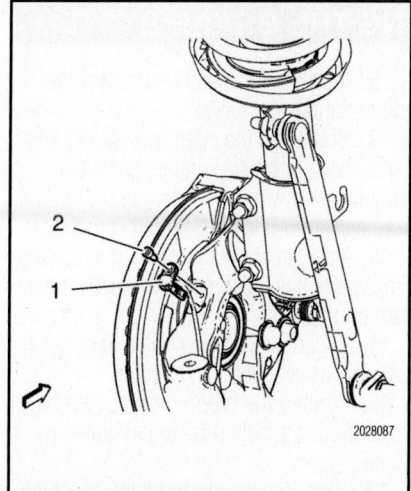

Fig. 1 Front wheel speed sensor location (1) and sensor screw (2)

5. Remove the wheel speed sensor.

6. Remove the wiring harness retainers from the frame.

7. Disconnect the electrical connector.

8. Remove wheel speed sensor from the vehicle.

To install:

9. Install the wheel speed sensor to the vehicle.

10. Connect the electrical connector.

11. Install the wiring harness retainers to the frame.

12. Install the wheel speed sensor to the steering knuckle.

13. Install the wheel speed sensor screw and tighten to 80 inch lbs. (9 Nm).

14. Install the tire and wheel assembly. Tighten the wheel nuts in a star pattern to 103 ft. lbs. (140 Nm).

Rear Speed Sensor

Disc Brakes

See Figure 2.

1. Before servicing the vehicle, refer to the Precautions Section.

2. Raise and safely support the vehicle.

3. Remove the tire and wheel assembly.

4. Remove rear wheelhouse panel liner.

5. Remove the wheel speed sensor screw.

6. Remove the wheel speed sensor.

7. Remove the wiring harness from the bracket.

8. Remove the wiring harness retainers from the brake hose.

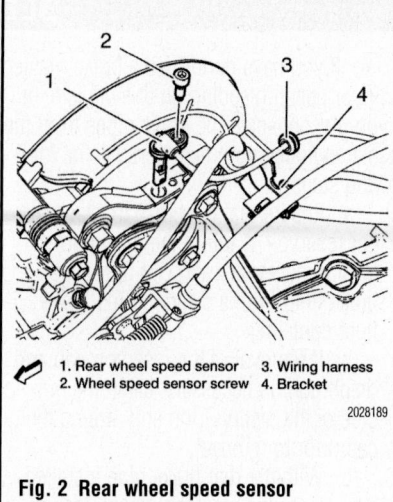

1. Rear wheel speed sensor
2. Wheel speed sensor screw
3. Wiring harness
4. Bracket

Fig. 2 Rear wheel speed sensor location—disc brakes

9. Remove the wiring harness from the body retainer.

10. Replace the body retainer.

11. Disconnect the electrical connector.

12. Remove wheel speed sensor from the vehicle.

To install:

13. Install the wheel speed sensor to the vehicle.

14. Connect the electrical connector.

15. Install the wiring harness retainers to the TOP SIDE of brake hose, using the marking points of the old wiring harness.

16. Install the wiring harness to the NEW body retainer.

17. Install the wheel speed sensor.

18. Install the wiring harness at the bracket.

19. Install the wheel speed sensor screw and tighten to 53 inch lbs. (6 Nm).

20. Check the correct installation position of the wiring harness. The wiring harness MUST be routed on top of the brake hose. If necessary adjust retainers to the marking positions on the brake hose.

21. Apply tension to the wiring harness between the retainers for the correct routing.

22. Push down the brake hose by hand, to assure the correct installation position.

23. Install the rear wheelhouse panel liner. Tighten the rear wheelhouse panel liner screws and nuts to 23 inch lbs. (3 Nm).

24. Install the tire and wheel assembly. Tighten the wheel nuts in a star pattern to 103 ft. lbs. (140 Nm).

Drum Brakes

See Figure 3.

1. Before servicing the vehicle, refer to the Precautions Section.

2. Raise and safely support the vehicle.

3. Remove the tire and wheel assembly.

4. Remove rear wheelhouse panel liner.

5. Remove the rear brake hose from the wheel cylinder and the rear backing plate.

6. Remove the wheel speed sensor screw.

7. Remove wheel speed sensor.

8. Remove the wiring harness from the bracket.

9. Disconnect the electrical connector.

10. Remove the wheel speed sensor from the vehicle.

To install:

11. Install the wheel speed sensor to the vehicle.

12. Connect the electrical connector.

13. Install the wheel speed sensor to vehicle.

14. Install the wiring harness at the bracket.

15. Install the wheel speed sensor screw and tighten to 80 inch lbs. (9 Nm).

16. Install the rear brake hose to the wheel cylinder and the rear backing plate.

17. Install the rear wheelhouse panel liner. Tighten the rear wheelhouse panel liner screws and nuts to 23 inch lbs. (3 Nm).

18. Install the tire and wheel assembly. Tighten the wheel nuts in a star pattern to 103 ft. lbs. (140 Nm).

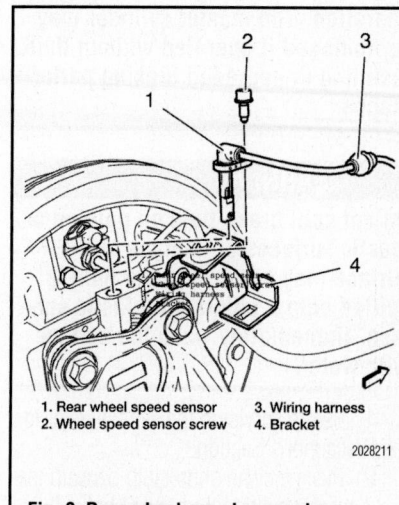

1. Rear wheel speed sensor
2. Wheel speed sensor screw
3. Wiring harness
4. Bracket

Fig. 3 Rear wheel speed sensor location—drum brakes

BRAKES

BLEEDING PROCEDURE

BLEEDING PROCEDURE

Manual Bleeding

✳✳ WARNING

Do not use any fluid other than clean brake fluid meeting manufacturer's specification. Additionally, do not use brake fluid that has been previously drained. Following these instructions will help prevent system contamination, brake component damage, and the risk of serious personal injury.

✳✳ CAUTION

Brake fluid contains polyglycol ethers and polyglycols. Avoid contact with the eyes. Wash hands thoroughly after handling. If brake fluid contacts the eyes, flush the eyes for 15 minutes with cold running water. Get medical attention if irritation persists. If taken internally, drink water and induce vomiting. Get medical attention immediately. Failure to follow these instructions may result in personal injury.

✳✳ WARNING

Do not allow the brake master cylinder to run dry during the bleeding operation. The master cylinder may be damaged if operated without fluid, resulting in degraded braking performance.

✳✳ WARNING

Do not spill brake fluid on painted or plastic surfaces or damage to the surface may occur. If brake fluid is spilled onto a painted or plastic surface, immediately wash the surface with water.

1. Before servicing the vehicle, refer to the Precautions Section.

2. Place a clean shop cloth beneath the brake master cylinder to prevent brake fluid spills.

3. With the ignition OFF and the brakes cool, apply the brakes 3–5 times, or until the brake pedal effort increases significantly, in order to deplete the brake booster power reserve.

4. If you have performed a brake master cylinder bench bleeding on this vehicle, or if you disconnected the brake pipes from the master cylinder, you must perform the following steps:

    a. Ensure that the brake master cylinder reservoir is full to the maximum-fill level. If necessary add GM approved brake fluid from a clean, sealed brake fluid container.

    b. If removal of the reservoir cap and diaphragm is necessary, clean the outside of the reservoir on and around the cap prior to removal.

    c. With the rear brake pipe installed securely to the master cylinder, loosen and separate the front brake pipe from the front port of the brake master cylinder.

    d. Allow a small amount of brake fluid to gravity bleed from the open port of the master cylinder.

    e. Reconnect the brake pipe to the master cylinder port and tighten securely.

    f. Have an assistant slowly depress the brake pedal fully and maintain steady pressure on the pedal.

    g. Loosen the same brake pipe to purge air from the open port of the master cylinder.

    h. Tighten the brake pipe, then have the assistant slowly release the brake pedal.

    i. Wait 15 seconds and then repeat the above steps until all air is purged from the same port of the master cylinder.

    j. With the front brake pipe installed securely to the master cylinder, after all air has been purged from the front port of the master cylinder, loosen and separate the rear brake pipe from the master cylinder, then repeat the above steps.

    k. After completing the final master cylinder port bleeding procedure, ensure that both of the brake pipe-to-master cylinder fittings are properly tightened.

5. Fill the brake master cylinder reservoir with GM approved brake fluid from a clean, sealed brake fluid container. Ensure that the brake master cylinder reservoir remains at least half-full during this bleeding procedure. Add fluid as needed to maintain the proper level.

6. Clean the outside of the reservoir on and around the reservoir cap prior to removing the cap and diaphragm.

7. Install a proper box-end wrench onto the RIGHT REAR wheel hydraulic circuit bleeder valve.

8. Install a transparent hose over the end of the bleeder valve.

9. Submerge the open end of the transparent hose into a transparent container partially filled with GM approved brake fluid from a clean, sealed brake fluid container.

10. Have an assistant slowly depress the brake pedal fully and maintain steady pressure on the pedal.

11. Loosen the bleeder valve to purge air from the wheel hydraulic circuit.

12. Tighten the bleeder valve, then have the assistant slowly release the brake pedal.

13. Wait 15 seconds and then repeat the steps until all air is purged from the same wheel hydraulic circuit.

14. With the right rear wheel hydraulic circuit bleeder valve tightened securely, after all air has been purged from the right rear hydraulic circuit install a proper box-end wrench onto the LEFT REAR wheel hydraulic circuit bleeder valve.

15. Install a transparent hose over the end of the bleeder valve and then repeat the bleeding procedure as it was performed on the RIGHT REAR.

16. Using the following sequence, bleed each hydraulic circuit bleeder valve:

    a. Right rear
    b. Left rear
    c. Right front
    d. Left front

17. After completing the final wheel hydraulic circuit bleeding procedure, ensure that each of the 4 wheel hydraulic circuit bleeder valves are properly tightened.

18. Fill the brake master cylinder reservoir to the maximum-fill level with GM approved brake fluid from a clean, sealed brake fluid container.

19. Slowly depress and release the brake pedal. Observe the feel of the brake pedal.

20. If the brake pedal feels spongy, repeat the bleeding procedure again. If the brake pedal still feels spongy after repeating the bleeding procedure, perform the following steps:

    a. Inspect the brake system for external leaks.

    b. Pressure bleed the hydraulic brake system in order to purge any air that may still be trapped in the system.

21. Turn the ignition key ON, with the engine OFF. Check to see if the brake system warning lamp remains illuminated.

✳✳ CAUTION

If the brake system warning lamp remains illuminated, DO NOT allow

the vehicle to be driven until it is diagnosed and repaired.

22. If the brake system warning lamp remains illuminated, perform a diagnostic check of the brake system.

Pressure Bleeding

※※ WARNING

Do not use any fluid other than clean brake fluid meeting manufacturer's specification. Additionally, do not use brake fluid that has been previously drained. Following these instructions will help prevent system contamination, brake component damage, and the risk of serious personal injury.

※※ CAUTION

Brake fluid contains polyglycol ethers and polyglycols. Avoid contact with the eyes. Wash hands thoroughly after handling. If brake fluid contacts the eyes, flush the eyes for 15 minutes with cold running water. Get medical attention if irritation persists. If taken internally, drink water and induce vomiting. Get medical attention immediately. Failure to follow these instructions may result in personal injury.

※※ WARNING

Do not allow the brake master cylinder to run dry during the bleeding operation. The master cylinder may be damaged if operated without fluid, resulting in degraded braking performance.

※※ WARNING

Do not spill brake fluid on painted or plastic surfaces or damage to the surface may occur. If brake fluid is spilled onto a painted or plastic surface, immediately wash the surface with water.

1. Before servicing the vehicle, refer to the Precautions Section.

➡The transaxle must be in the PARK position, the power button in the OFF position, and the brakes not applied to ensure the brake modulator and High Pressure Accumulator (HPA) pressure relief occurs. This process will take approximately 1 to 3 minutes.

2. Place the transaxle in PARK.

3. Place the power button in the OFF position.

4. Remove the Remote Keyless Entry (RKE) transmitter and close all of the vehicle doors.

5. Place a clean shop cloth beneath the brake master cylinder to prevent brake fluid spills.

6. With the power button OFF and the brakes cool, apply the brakes 3–5 times, or until the brake pedal effort increases significantly, in order to deplete the brake booster power reserve.

7. If you have performed a brake master cylinder bench bleeding on this vehicle, or if you disconnected the brake pipes from the master cylinder, you must perform the following steps:

a. Ensure that the brake master cylinder reservoir is full to the maximum-fill level. If necessary add Delco Supreme 11®, GM P/N 12377967 (Canadian P/N 992667), or equivalent DOT-3 brake fluid from a clean, sealed brake fluid container.

b. If removal of the reservoir cap and diaphragm is necessary, clean the outside of the reservoir on and around the cap prior to removal.

c. With the rear brake pipe installed securely to the master cylinder, loosen and separate the front brake pipe from the front port of the brake master cylinder.

d. Allow a small amount of brake fluid to gravity bleed from the open port of the master cylinder.

e. Reconnect the brake pipe to the master cylinder port and tighten securely.

f. Have an assistant slowly depress the brake pedal fully and maintain steady pressure on the pedal.

g. Loosen the same brake pipe to purge air from the open port of the master cylinder.

h. Tighten the brake pipe, then have the assistant slowly release the brake pedal.

i. Wait 15 seconds and then repeat the above steps until all air is purged from the same port of the master cylinder.

j. With the front brake pipe installed securely to the master cylinder, after all air has been purged from the front port of the master cylinder, loosen and separate the rear brake pipe from the master cylinder and then repeat the above bleeding steps.

k. After completing the final master cylinder port bleeding procedure, ensure

that both of the brake pipe-to-master cylinder fittings are properly tightened.

8. Fill the brake master cylinder reservoir to the maximum-fill level with Delco Supreme 11®, GM P/N 12377967 (Canadian P/N 992667), or equivalent DOT-3 brake fluid from a clean, sealed brake fluid container.

9. Clean the outside of the reservoir on and around the reservoir cap prior to removing the cap and diaphragm.

10. Install a suitable brake fluid reservoir adapter to the brake master cylinder reservoir.

11. Check the brake fluid level in the suitable brake pressure bleeder. Add Delco Supreme 11®, or equivalent DOT-3 brake fluid from a clean, sealed brake fluid container as necessary to bring the level to approximately the half-full point.

12. Connect the suitable brake pressure bleeder to a suitable brake fluid reservoir adapter.

13. Charge the brake pressure bleeder air tank to 25–30 psi (175–205 kPa).

14. Open the brake pressure bleeder fluid tank valve to allow pressurized brake fluid to enter the brake system.

15. Wait approximately 30 seconds, then inspect the entire hydraulic brake system in order to ensure that there are no existing external brake fluid leaks.

➡Any brake fluid leaks identified require repair prior to completing this procedure.

16. Install a proper box-end wrench onto the RIGHT REAR wheel hydraulic circuit bleeder valve.

17. Install a transparent hose over the end of the bleeder valve.

18. Submerge the open end of the transparent hose into a transparent container partially filled with DOT-3 brake fluid from a clean, sealed brake fluid container.

19. Loosen the bleeder valve to purge air from the wheel hydraulic circuit. Allow fluid to flow until air bubbles stop flowing from the bleeder, then tighten the bleeder valve.

20. With the right rear wheel hydraulic circuit bleeder valve tightened securely, after all air has been purged from the right rear hydraulic circuit, install a proper box-end wrench onto the LEFT REAR wheel hydraulic circuit bleeder valve.

21. Install a transparent hose over the end of the bleeder valve and then repeat the bleeding steps.

22. Using the following sequence, bleed each hydraulic circuit bleeder valve:

a. Right rear
b. Left rear

c. Right front
d. Left front

23. After completing the final wheel hydraulic circuit bleeding procedure, ensure that each of the 4 wheel hydraulic circuit bleeder valves are properly tightened.

24. Close the brake pressure fluid tank valve and then disconnect the brake pressure bleeder from the brake fluid reservoir adapter.

25. Remove the brake fluid reservoir adapter from the brake master cylinder reservoir.

26. Fill the brake master cylinder reservoir to the maximum-fill level with Delco Supreme 11®, GM P/N 12377967 (Canadian P/N 992667), or equivalent DOT-3 brake fluid from a clean, sealed brake fluid container.

27. Slowly depress and release the brake pedal. Observe the feel of the brake pedal.

28. If the brake pedal feels spongy perform the following steps:

a. Inspect the brake system for external leaks.

b. Using a scan tool, perform the antilock brake system automated bleeding procedure to remove any air that may have been trapped in the Brake Pressure Modulator Valve (BPMV).

29. Turn the power button ON, with the engine OFF. Check to see if the brake system warning lamp remains illuminated.

❊❊ CAUTION

If the brake system warning lamp remains illuminated, DO NOT allow the vehicle to be driven until it is diagnosed and repaired.

30. If the brake system warning lamp remains illuminated, perform a diagnostic check of the brake system.

MASTER CYLINDER BLEEDING

❊❊ WARNING

Do not use any fluid other than clean brake fluid meeting manufacturer's specification. Additionally, do not use brake fluid that has been previously drained. Following these instructions will help prevent system contamination, brake component damage, and the risk of serious personal injury.

❊❊ CAUTION

Brake fluid contains polyglycol ethers and polyglycols. Avoid contact with the eyes. Wash hands thoroughly after

handling. **If brake fluid contacts the eyes, flush the eyes for 15 minutes with cold running water. Get medical attention if irritation persists. If taken internally, drink water and induce vomiting. Get medical attention immediately. Failure to follow these instructions may result in personal injury.**

❊❊ WARNING

Do not allow the brake master cylinder to run dry during the bleeding operation. The master cylinder may be damaged if operated without fluid, resulting in degraded braking performance.

❊❊ WARNING

Do not spill brake fluid on painted or plastic surfaces or damage to the surface may occur. If brake fluid is spilled onto a painted or plastic surface, immediately wash the surface with water.

➡When the brake master cylinder has been installed new or the system has been emptied or partially emptied, it must be primed to prevent air from entering the system.

➡If you have performed a brake master cylinder bench bleeding on this vehicle, or if you disconnected the brake pipes from the master cylinder, you must perform the following steps.

1. Before servicing the vehicle, refer to the Precautions Section.

2. Ensure that the brake master cylinder reservoir is full to the maximum-fill level. If necessary add Delco Supreme 11®, GM P/N 12377967 (Canadian P/N 992667), or equivalent DOT-3 brake fluid from a clean, sealed brake fluid container.

3. If removal of the reservoir cap and diaphragm is necessary, clean the outside of the reservoir on and around the cap prior to removal.

4. With the rear brake pipe installed securely to the master cylinder, loosen and separate the front brake pipe from the front port of the brake master cylinder.

5. Allow a small amount of brake fluid to gravity bleed from the open port of the master cylinder.

6. Reconnect the brake pipe to the master cylinder port and tighten securely.

7. Have an assistant slowly depress the brake pedal fully and maintain steady pressure on the pedal.

8. Loosen the same brake pipe to purge air from the open port of the master cylinder.

9. Tighten the brake pipe, then have the assistant slowly release the brake pedal.

10. Wait 15 seconds and then repeat the above steps until all air is purged from the same port of the master cylinder.

11. With the front brake pipe installed securely to the master cylinder, after all air has been purged from the front port of the master cylinder, loosen and separate the rear brake pipe from the master cylinder and then repeat the above bleeding steps.

12. After completing the final master cylinder port bleeding procedure, ensure that both of the brake pipe-to-master cylinder fittings are properly tightened.

13. Fill the brake master cylinder reservoir to the maximum-fill level with Delco Supreme 11®, GM P/N 12377967 (Canadian P/N 992667), or equivalent DOT-3 brake fluid from a clean, sealed brake fluid container.

14. Slowly depress and release the brake pedal. Observe the feel of the brake pedal.

15. If the brake pedal feels spongy perform the following steps:

a. Inspect the brake system for external leaks.

b. Using a scan tool, perform the antilock brake system automated bleeding procedure to remove any air that may have been trapped in the Brake Pressure Modulator Valve (BPMV).

16. Turn the power button ON, with the engine OFF. Check to see if the brake system warning lamp remains illuminated.

❊❊ CAUTION

If the brake system warning lamp remains illuminated, DO NOT allow the vehicle to be driven until it is diagnosed and repaired.

17. If the brake system warning lamp remains illuminated, perform a diagnostic check of the brake system.

BRAKE LINE BLEEDING

Refer to Bleeding Procedure, Manual Bleeding or Pressure Bleeding.

BLEEDING THE ABS SYSTEM

❊❊ WARNING

Do not use any fluid other than clean brake fluid meeting manufacturer's specification. Additionally, do not use brake fluid that has been previously drained. Following these

instructions will help prevent system contamination, brake component damage, and the risk of serious personal injury.

❊❊ CAUTION

Brake fluid contains polyglycol ethers and polyglycols. Avoid contact with the eyes. Wash hands thoroughly after handling. If brake fluid contacts the eyes, flush the eyes for 15 minutes with cold running water. Get medical attention if irritation persists. If taken internally, drink water and induce vomiting. Get medical attention immediately. Failure to follow these instructions may result in personal injury.

❊❊ WARNING

Do not allow the brake master cylinder to run dry during the bleeding operation. Master cylinder may be damaged if operated without fluid, resulting in degraded braking performance.

❊❊ WARNING

Do not spill brake fluid on painted or plastic surfaces or damage to the surface may occur. If brake fluid is spilled onto a painted or plastic surface, immediately wash the surface with water.

➡ Before performing the ABS Automated Bleed Procedure, first perform a pressure bleed of the base brake system. Refer to Bleeding Procedure in this section. The automated bleed procedure is recommended when one of the following conditions exist:

- Base brake system bleeding does not achieve the desired pedal height or feel
- Extreme loss of brake fluid has occurred
- Air ingestion is suspected in the secondary circuits of the brake modulator assembly

➡ The ABS Automated Bleed Procedure uses a scan tool to cycle the system solenoid valves and run the pump in order to purge any air from the secondary circuits. These circuits are normally closed off, and are only opened during system initialization at vehicle start up and during ABS operation. The automated bleed procedure opens these secondary circuits and allows any air trapped in these circuits to flow out toward the brake corners.

❊❊ WARNING

The Auto Bleed Procedure may be terminated at any time during the process by pressing the EXIT button. No further Scan Tool prompts pertaining to the Auto Bleed procedure will be given. After exiting the bleed procedure, relieve bleed pressure and disconnect bleed equipment per manufacturer's instructions. Failure to properly relieve pressure may result in spilled brake fluid causing damage to components and painted surfaces.

1. Before servicing the vehicle, refer to the Precautions Section.
2. Raise and safely support the vehicle.
3. Remove all four tire and wheel assemblies.
4. Inspect the brake system for leaks and visual damage. Repair or replace components as needed.
5. Lower the vehicle.
6. Inspect the battery state of charge.
7. Install a scan tool.
8. Turn the ignition ON, with the engine OFF.
9. With the scan tool, establish communications with the ABS system. Select Control Functions. Select Automated Bleed from the Control Functions menu.
10. Raise and support the vehicle.
11. Following the directions given on the scan tool, pressure bleed the base brake system. Refer to Bleeding Procedure, Pressure Bleeding.
12. Follow the scan tool directions until the desired brake pedal height is achieved.
13. If the bleed procedure is aborted, a malfunction exists. Perform the following steps before resuming the bleed procedure:
    a. If a DTC is detected, refer to the Diagnostic Trouble Code (DTC) list.
    b. If the brake pedal feels spongy, perform the conventional brake bleed procedure again. Refer to Bleeding Procedure.
14. When the desired pedal height is achieved, press the brake pedal to inspect for firmness.
15. Lower the vehicle.
16. Remove the scan tool.
17. Install the tire and wheel assemblies.
18. Inspect the brake fluid level. Refer to Fluid Fill Procedure.
19. Road test the vehicle while inspecting that the pedal remains high and firm.

FLUID FILL PROCEDURE

❊❊ WARNING

Do not use any fluid other than clean brake fluid meeting manufacturer's specification. Additionally, do not use brake fluid that has been previously drained. Following these instructions will help prevent system contamination, brake component damage, and the risk of serious personal injury.

❊❊ CAUTION

Brake fluid contains polyglycol ethers and polyglycols. Avoid contact with the eyes. Wash hands thoroughly after handling. If brake fluid contacts the eyes, flush the eyes for 15 minutes with cold running water. Get medical attention if irritation persists. If taken internally, drink water and induce vomiting. Get medical attention immediately. Failure to follow these instructions may result in personal injury.

❊❊ WARNING

Do not allow the brake master cylinder to run dry during a bleeding operation. Master cylinder may be damaged if operated without fluid, resulting in degraded braking performance.

❊❊ WARNING

Do not spill brake fluid on painted or plastic surfaces or damage to the surface may occur. If brake fluid is spilled onto a painted or plastic surface, immediately wash the surface with water.

1. Before servicing the vehicle, refer to the Precautions Section.
2. Visually inspect the brake fluid level through the brake master cylinder auxiliary reservoir.
3. If the brake fluid level is at or below the half-full point during routine fluid checks, the brake system should be inspected for wear and possible brake fluid leaks.
4. If the brake fluid level is at or below the half-full point during routine fluid checks, and an inspection of the brake system did not reveal wear or brake fluid leaks, the brake fluid may be topped-off up to the maximum-fill level.

5. If brake system service was just completed, the brake fluid may be topped-off up to the maximum-fill level.

6. If the brake fluid level is above the half-full point, adding brake fluid is not recommended under normal conditions.

7. If brake fluid is to be added to the master cylinder auxiliary reservoir, clean the outside of the reservoir on and around the reservoir cap prior to removing the cap and diaphragm.

BRAKES

✳✳ CAUTION

Dust and dirt accumulating on brake parts during normal use may contain asbestos fibers from production or aftermarket brake linings. Breathing excessive concentrations of asbestos fibers can cause serious bodily harm. Exercise care when servicing brake parts. Do not sand or grind brake lining unless equipment used is designed to contain the dust residue. Do not clean brake parts with compressed air or by dry brushing. Cleaning should be done by dampening the brake components with a fine mist of water, then wiping the brake components clean with a dampened cloth. Dispose of cloth and all residue containing asbestos fibers in an impermeable container with the appropriate label. Follow practices prescribed by the Occupational Safety and Health Administration (OSHA) and the Environmental Protection Agency (EPA) for the handling, processing, and disposing of dust or debris that may contain asbestos fibers.

BRAKE CALIPER

REMOVAL & INSTALLATION
See Figure 4.

✳✳ WARNING

Do not use any fluid other than clean brake fluid meeting manufacturer's specification. Additionally, do not use brake fluid that has been previously drained. Following these instructions will help prevent system contamination, brake component damage, and the risk of serious personal injury.

✳✳ CAUTION

Brake fluid contains polyglycol ethers and polyglycols. Avoid contact with the eyes. Wash hands thoroughly after handling. If brake fluid contacts the eyes, flush the eyes for 15 minutes with cold running water. Get medical attention if irritation per- sists. If taken internally, drink water and induce vomiting. Get medical attention immediately. Failure to follow these instructions may result in personal injury.

✳✳ WARNING

Do not spill brake fluid on painted or plastic surfaces or damage to the surface may occur. If brake fluid is spilled onto a painted or plastic surface, immediately wash the surface with water.

✳✳ CAUTION

Use of eye goggles is necessary to prevent personal injury.

1. Before servicing the vehicle, refer to the Precautions Section.

2. Inspect the fluid level in the brake master cylinder reservoir.

3. If the brake fluid level is midway between the maximum-full point and the minimum allowable level, no brake fluid needs to be removed from the reservoir before proceeding.

4. If the brake fluid level is higher than midway between the maximum-full point and the minimum allowable level, remove brake fluid to the midway point before proceeding.

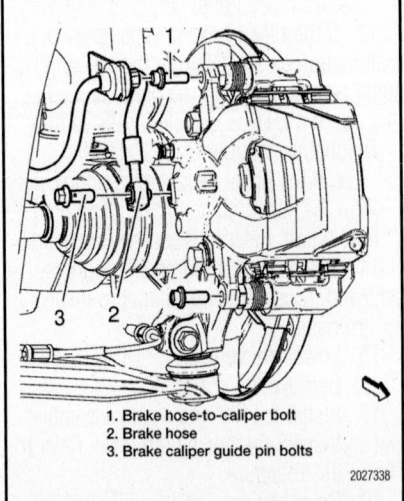

1. Brake hose-to-caliper bolt
2. Brake hose
3. Brake caliper guide pin bolts

2027338

Fig. 4 Removing the front brake caliper

FRONT DISC BRAKES

5. Raise and safely support the vehicle.

6. Remove the tire and wheel assembly.

7. Remove the brake hose-to-caliper bolt from the brake caliper.

8. Remove the brake hose from the brake caliper.

9. Remove and discard the copper brake hose washers. These washers may be stuck to the brake caliper and/or the brake hose end.

10. Cap or plug the opening in the brake caliper and the brake hose to prevent fluid loss and contamination.

11. Remove the brake caliper guide pin bolts.

12. Remove the brake caliper from the caliper bracket.

To install:

13. Inspect the brake caliper guide pins for freedom of movement, and inspect the condition of the guide pin boots. Move the guide pins inboard and outboard within the bracket bores, without disengaging the slides from the boots, and observe for the following:

- Restricted caliper guide pin movement
- Looseness in the brake caliper mounting bracket
- Seized or binding caliper guide pins
- Split or torn boots

14. If any of the conditions listed are found, the brake caliper guide pins and/or boots require replacement.

15. Install the brake caliper to the brake caliper bracket.

➡**Do not reuse the brake hose washers.**

16. Install NEW copper brake hose washers to the brake hose-to-caliper bolt and to the brake hose.

17. Install the brake caliper guide pin bolts and tighten to 21 ft. lbs. (28 Nm).

18. Remove the caps or plugs from the brake caliper opening and the brake hose.

19. Install the brake hose to the caliper.

20. Install brake hose-to-caliper bolt to the caliper and tighten to 30 ft. lbs. (40 Nm).

21. Bleed the hydraulic brake system. Refer to Bleeding Procedure.

22. Install the tire and wheel assembly. Tighten the wheel nuts in a star pattern to 103 ft. lbs. (140 Nm).

23. Lower the vehicle.

24. With the engine OFF, gradually apply the brake pedal to approximately ⅔ of its travel distance.

25. Slowly release the brake pedal.

26. Wait 15 seconds and then repeat until a firm brake pedal is obtained. This will properly seat the brake caliper piston and brake pads.

DISC BRAKE PADS

REMOVAL & INSTALLATION

See Figures 5 through 7.

> ✳✳ **WARNING**
>
> **Do not use any fluid other than clean brake fluid meeting manufacturer's specification. Additionally, do not use brake fluid that has been previously drained. Following these instructions will help prevent system contamination, brake component damage, and the risk of serious personal injury.**

> ✳✳ **CAUTION**
>
> **Brake fluid contains polyglycol ethers and polyglycols. Avoid contact with the eyes. Wash hands thoroughly after handling. If brake fluid contacts the eyes, flush the eyes for 15 minutes with cold running water. Get medical attention if irritation persists. If taken internally, drink water and induce vomiting. Get medical attention immediately. Failure to follow these instructions may result in personal injury.**

> ✳✳ **WARNING**
>
> **Do not spill brake fluid on painted or plastic surfaces or damage to the surface may occur. If brake fluid is spilled onto a painted or plastic surface, immediately wash the surface with water.**

> ✳✳ **CAUTION**
>
> **Use of eye goggles is necessary to prevent personal injury.**

1. Before servicing the vehicle, refer to the Precautions Section.

2. Inspect the fluid level in the brake master cylinder reservoir.

3. If the brake fluid level is midway between the maximum-full point and the minimum allowable level, no brake fluid needs to be removed from the reservoir before proceeding.

4. If the brake fluid level is higher than midway between the maximum-full point and the minimum allowable level, remove brake fluid to the midway point before proceeding.

5. Raise and safely support the vehicle.

6. Remove the tire and wheel assembly.

7. Remove the brake caliper lower guide pin bolt.

8. Without disconnecting the hydraulic brake flexible hose, pivot the caliper upward and secure the caliper with heavy mechanics wire, or equivalent.

9. Remove the brake pads from the caliper mounting bracket.

10. Push the disc brake caliper piston into the caliper bore using a disc brake piston installation tool.

11. Remove the brake pad retainer springs from the caliper bracket.

12. Thoroughly clean the brake pad hardware mating surfaces of the caliper bracket of any debris and corrosion.

To install:

13. Inspect the brake caliper guide pins for freedom of movement and inspect the condition of the guide pin boots. Move the guide pins inboard and outboard within the bracket bores, without disengaging the slides from the boots, and observe for the following:

- Restricted caliper guide pin movement
- Looseness in the brake caliper mounting bracket
- Seized or binding caliper guide pins
- Split or torn boots

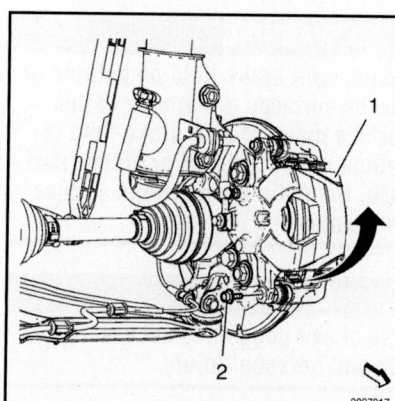

Fig. 5 Remove the brake caliper lower guide pin bolt (2) and pivot the caliper (1) upward

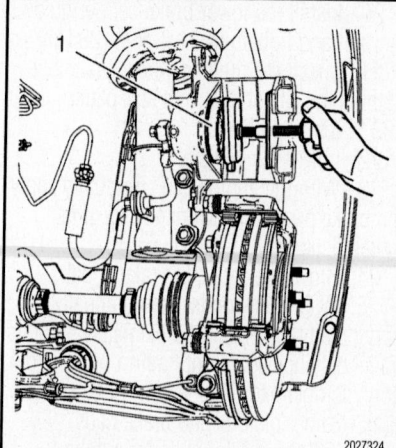

Fig. 6 Push the disc brake caliper piston (1) into the caliper bore using a disc brake piston installation tool

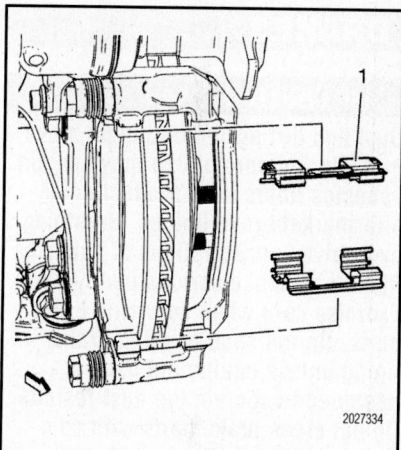

Fig. 7 Remove the brake pad retainer springs (1) from the caliper bracket

14. If any of the conditions listed are found, the brake caliper guide pins and/or boots require replacement.

15. Ensure the brake pad hardware mating surfaces are clean.

16. Install the brake pad retainer springs to the brake caliper bracket.

17. Apply a thin coat of high temperature silicone lube to the brake pad retainers.

➡ **The wear sensor equipped disc brake pad must be mounted inboard of the rotor with the leading edge of the sensor facing the brake rotor during forward wheel rotation, or at the top of the pad when installed in vehicle position.**

18. Install the brake pads to the caliper bracket.

19. Remove the support, and rotate the brake caliper into position over the disc brake pads and to the caliper mounting bracket.

20. Install the lower brake caliper guide pin bolt and tighten to 21 ft. lbs. (28 Nm).

21. Install the tire and wheel assembly. Tighten the wheel nuts in a star pattern to 103 ft. lbs. (140 Nm).

22. Lower the vehicle.

23. With the engine OFF, gradually apply the brake pedal approximately ⅔ of its travel distance.

24. Slowly release the brake pedal.

25. Wait 15 seconds, then gradually apply the brake pedal approximately ⅔ of its travel distance again until a firm brake pedal apply is obtained. This will properly seat the brake caliper pistons and brake pads.

26. Fill the master cylinder auxiliary reservoir to the proper level.

27. Burnish the brake pads and the brake rotor.

❋❋ CAUTION

Road test a vehicle under safe conditions and while obeying all traffic laws. Do not attempt any maneuvers that could jeopardize vehicle control. Failure to adhere to these precautions could lead to serious personal injury and vehicle damage.

➡ Burnishing the brake pads and brake rotors is necessary in order to ensure that the braking surfaces are properly prepared after service has been performed on the disc brake system. This procedure should be performed whenever the disc brake rotors have been refinished or replaced, and/or whenever the disc brake pads have been replaced.

a. Select a smooth road with little or no traffic.

b. Accelerate the vehicle to 30 mph (48 km/h).

❋❋ WARNING

Use care to avoid overheating the brakes while performing this step.

c. Using moderate to firm pressure, apply the brakes to bring the vehicle to a stop. Do not allow the brakes to lock.

d. Repeat until approximately 20 stops have been completed. Allow sufficient cooling periods between stops in order to properly burnish the brake pads and rotors.

BRAKES   REAR DISC BRAKES

❋❋ CAUTION

Dust and dirt accumulating on brake parts during normal use may contain asbestos fibers from production or aftermarket brake linings. Breathing excessive concentrations of asbestos fibers can cause serious bodily harm. Exercise care when servicing brake parts. Do not sand or grind brake lining unless equipment used is designed to contain the dust residue. Do not clean brake parts with compressed air or by dry brushing. Cleaning should be done by dampening the brake components with a fine mist of water, then wiping the brake components clean with a dampened cloth. Dispose of cloth and all residue containing asbestos fibers in an impermeable container with the appropriate label. Follow practices prescribed by the Occupational Safety and Health Administration (OSHA) and the Environmental Protection Agency (EPA) for the handling, processing, and disposing of dust or debris that may contain asbestos fibers.

BRAKE CALIPER

REMOVAL & INSTALLATION
See Figures 8 and 9.

❋❋ WARNING

Do not use any fluid other than clean brake fluid meeting manufacturer's specification. Additionally, do not use brake fluid that has been previously drained. Following these instructions will help prevent system contamination, brake component damage, and the risk of serious personal injury.

❋❋ CAUTION

Brake fluid contains polyglycol ethers and polyglycols. Avoid contact with the eyes. Wash hands thoroughly after handling. If brake fluid contacts the eyes, flush the eyes for 15 minutes with cold running water. Get medical attention if irritation persists. If taken internally, drink water and induce vomiting. Get medical attention immediately. Failure to follow these instructions may result in personal injury.

❋❋ WARNING

Do not spill brake fluid on painted or plastic surfaces or damage to the surface may occur. If brake fluid is spilled onto a painted or plastic surface, immediately wash the surface with water.

❋❋ CAUTION

Use of eye goggles is necessary to prevent personal injury.

1. Before servicing the vehicle, refer to the Precautions Section.

2. Inspect the fluid level in the brake master cylinder reservoir.

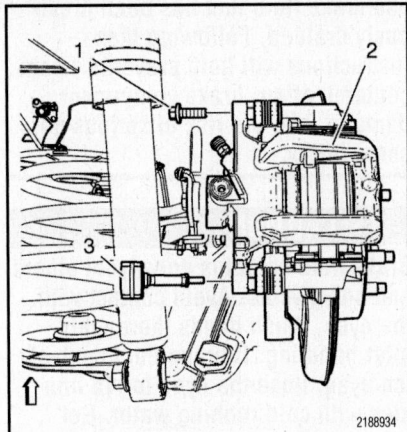

Fig. 8 View of the rear brake caliper (2), upper brake caliper pin bolt (1), and the brake caliper vibration dampener (3)—models with vibration dampener

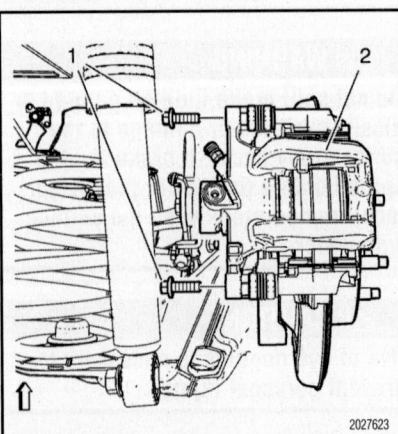

Fig. 9 View of the brake caliper (2) and brake caliper pin bolts (1)—models without vibration dampener

3. If the brake fluid level is midway between the maximum-full point and the minimum allowable level, no brake fluid needs to be removed from the reservoir before proceeding.

4. If the brake fluid level is higher than midway between the maximum-full point and the minimum allowable level, remove brake fluid to the midway point before proceeding.

5. Raise and safely support the vehicle.

6. Remove the tire and wheel assembly.

7. Remove the brake hose to caliper bolt from the brake caliper.

8. Remove the brake hose from the brake caliper.

9. Remove and discard the 2 copper brake hose gaskets. These gaskets may be stuck to the brake caliper and/or the brake hose end.

10. Cap or plug the opening in the brake caliper and the brake hose to prevent fluid loss and contamination.

11. Remove the upper brake caliper pin bolt.

12. Remove the brake caliper vibration dampener or lower caliper pin bolt.

13. Remove the park brake cable from the rear parking brake lever.

14. Remove the brake caliper from the brake caliper bracket.

To install:

15. Inspect the caliper slide boots for cuts, tears, or deterioration. If damaged, replace the slides and boots.

16. Install the brake caliper to the brake caliper bracket.

17. Install the upper brake caliper pin bolt and tighten to 20 ft. lbs. (28 Nm).

18. Install the brake caliper vibration dampener, or lower caliper pin bolt, and tighten to 20 ft. lbs. (28 Nm).

19. Install the park brake cable to the rear parking brake lever.

20. Remove the caps or plugs from the brake caliper opening and the brake hose.

➡**DO NOT reuse the copper brake hose gaskets.**

21. Install NEW copper brake hose gaskets to the brake hose-to-caliper bolt and to the brake hose.

22. Install the brake hose and the brake hose-to-caliper bolt to the brake caliper and tighten the bolt to 30 ft. lbs. (40 Nm).

23. Bleed the hydraulic brake system. Refer to Bleeding Procedure.

24. With the engine OFF, gradually apply the brake pedal to approximately ⅔ of its travel distance.

25. Slowly release the brake pedal.

26. Wait 15 seconds, then repeat steps until a firm brake pedal is obtained. This will properly seat the brake caliper pistons and brake pads.

27. Install the tire and wheel assembly. Tighten the wheel nuts in a star pattern to 103 ft. lbs. (140 Nm).

28. Lower the vehicle.

29. Apply and release the park brake lever 4 times.

DISC BRAKE PADS

REMOVAL & INSTALLATION

See Figures 8 through 11.

✳✳ WARNING

Do not use any fluid other than clean brake fluid meeting manufacturer's specification. Additionally, do not use brake fluid that has been previously drained. Following these instructions will help prevent system contamination, brake component damage, and the risk of serious personal injury.

✳✳ CAUTION

Brake fluid contains polyglycol ethers and polyglycols. Avoid contact with the eyes. Wash hands thoroughly after handling. If brake fluid contacts the eyes, flush the eyes for 15 minutes with cold running water. Get medical attention if irritation persists. If taken internally, drink water and induce vomiting. Get medical attention immediately. Failure to follow these instructions may result in personal injury.

✳✳ WARNING

Do not spill brake fluid on painted or plastic surfaces or damage to the surface may occur. If brake fluid is spilled onto a painted or plastic surface, immediately wash the surface with water.

✳✳ CAUTION

Use of eye goggles is necessary to prevent personal injury.

1. Before servicing the vehicle, refer to the Precautions Section.

2. Inspect the fluid level in the brake master cylinder reservoir.

3. If the brake fluid level is midway between the maximum-full point and the

minimum allowable level, no brake fluid needs to be removed from the reservoir before proceeding.

4. If the brake fluid level is higher than midway between the maximum-full point and the minimum allowable level, remove brake fluid to the midway point before proceeding.

5. Raise and safely support the vehicle.

6. Remove the tire and wheel assembly.

7. Remove the brake caliper mass dampener, if equipped, or the brake caliper lower pin bolt.

✳✳ WARNING

Support the brake caliper with heavy mechanic wire, or equivalent, whenever it is separated from its mount and the hydraulic flexible brake hose is still connected. Failure to support the caliper in this manner will cause the flexible brake hose to bear the weight of the caliper, which may cause damage to the brake hose and in turn may cause a brake fluid leak.

8. Without disconnecting the hydraulic brake flexible hose, pivot the caliper upward and secure the caliper with heavy mechanics wire, or equivalent.

9. Mark the brake caliper piston position to the brake caliper.

10. Remove the brake pads from the caliper mounting bracket.

11. Remove the brake pad retainer springs from the caliper bracket.

12. Thoroughly clean the brake pad hardware mating surfaces of the caliper bracket, of any debris and corrosion.

To install:

13. Inspect the brake caliper guide pins for freedom of movement, and inspect the condition of the guide pin boots. Move the

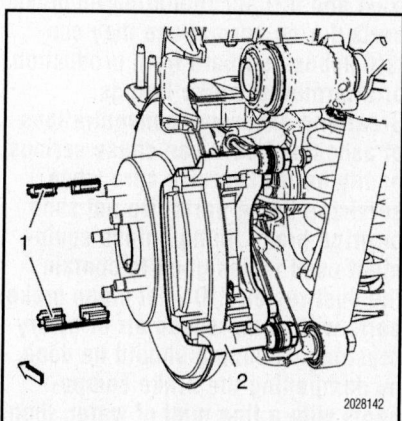

Fig. 10 Remove the brake pad retainer springs (1) from the caliper bracket (2)

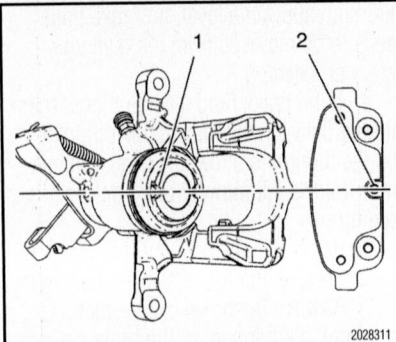

Fig. 11 Rotate the brake caliper piston (1) into the brake caliper bore. Align the notch on the brake caliper piston with the pin (2) on the disc brake pad

guide pins inboard and outboard within the bracket bores, without disengaging the slides from the boots, and observe for the following:

- Restricted caliper guide pin movement
- Looseness in the brake caliper mounting bracket
- Seized or binding caliper guide pins
- Split or torn boots.

14. If any of the conditions listed are found, the brake caliper guide pins and/or boots require replacement.

15. Ensure the brake pad hardware mating surfaces are clean.

16. Install the brake pad retainer springs to the brake caliper bracket and apply a thin coat of high temperature silicone lube to the brake pad retainers.

➡The wear sensor equipped disc brake pad must be mounted inboard of the rotor with the leading edge of the sensor facing the brake rotor during forward wheel rotation, or at the top of the pad when installed in vehicle position.

17. Install the brake pads to the caliper bracket.

18. Rotate the brake caliper piston into the brake caliper bore.

19. Align the notch on the brake caliper piston with the pin on the disc brake pad.

20. Remove the support, and rotate the brake caliper into position over the disc brake pads and to the caliper mounting bracket.

21. Install the lower brake caliper mass dampener, if equipped, or the lower caliper pin bolt. Tighten to 20 inch lbs. (28 Nm).

22. Install the tire and wheel assembly. Tighten the wheel nuts in a star pattern to 103 ft. lbs. (140 Nm).

23. Lower the vehicle.

24. With the engine OFF, gradually apply the brake pedal approximately ⅔ of its travel distance.

25. Slowly release the brake pedal.

26. Wait 15 seconds, then gradually apply the brake pedal approximately ⅔ of its travel distance again until a firm brake pedal apply is obtained. This will properly seat the brake caliper pistons and brake pads.

27. Fill the master cylinder reservoir to the proper level.

28. Burnish the brake pads and the brake rotor.

✳✳ CAUTION

Road test a vehicle under safe conditions and while obeying all traffic laws. Do not attempt any maneuvers that could jeopardize vehicle control. Failure to adhere to these precautions could lead to serious personal injury and vehicle damage.

➡Burnishing the brake pads and brake rotors is necessary in order to ensure that the braking surfaces are properly prepared after service has been performed on the disc brake system. This procedure should be performed whenever the disc brake rotors have been refinished or replaced, and/or whenever the disc brake pads have been replaced.

a. Select a smooth road with little or no traffic.

b. Accelerate the vehicle to 30 mph (48 km/h).

✳✳ WARNING

Use care to avoid overheating the brakes while performing this step.

c. Using moderate to firm pressure, apply the brakes to bring the vehicle to a stop. Do not allow the brakes to lock.

d. Repeat until approximately 20 stops have been completed. Allow sufficient cooling periods between stops in order to properly burnish the brake pads and rotors.

BRAKES

✳✳ CAUTION

Dust and dirt accumulating on brake parts during normal use may contain asbestos fibers from production or aftermarket brake linings. Breathing excessive concentrations of asbestos fibers can cause serious bodily harm. Exercise care when servicing brake parts. Do not sand or grind brake lining unless equipment used is designed to contain the dust residue. Do not clean brake parts with compressed air or by dry brushing. Cleaning should be done by dampening the brake components with a fine mist of water, then wiping the brake components clean with a dampened cloth. Dispose of cloth and all residue containing asbestos fibers in an impermeable container with the appropriate label. Follow practices prescribed by the Occupational Safety and Health Administration (OSHA) and the Environmental Protection Agency (EPA) for the handling, processing, and disposing of dust or debris that may contain asbestos fibers.

BRAKE DRUM

REMOVAL & INSTALLATION

See Figure 12.

Special Tools
- CH 41013 Rotor Resurfacing Kit
- CH 42450-A Wheel Hub Resurfacing Kit

REAR DRUM BRAKES

✳✳ CAUTION

Do not breathe dust or use compressed air to blow dust from storage containers or friction components. Remove dust using government-approved techniques. Friction component dust may be a cancer and lung disease hazard. Exposure to potentially hazardous components may occur if dusts are created during repair of friction components, such as brake pads and clutch discs. Exposure may also cause irritation to skin, eyes and respiratory tract, and may cause allergic reactions and/or may lead to other chronic health effects. If irritation persists, seek medical attention or advice. Failure to follow these

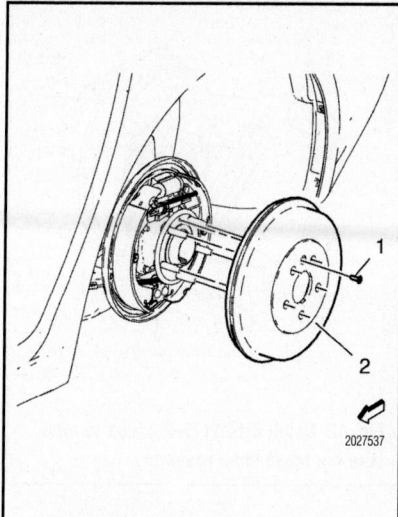

Fig. 12 Remove the brake drum screw (1) and the brake drum (2)

instructions may result in serious personal injury.

1. Before servicing the vehicle, refer to the Precautions Section.
2. Check to ensure that the park brake is fully released.
3. Raise and safely support the vehicle.
4. Remove the rear tire and wheel assembly.
5. Remove the brake drum screw.
6. Remove the brake drum.

To install:

7. If the brake drum is to be reinstalled to the vehicle, use the CH 41013 resurfacer, or equivalent, to clean any rust or corrosion from the hub/flange mating surface of the brake drum.
8. To clean any rust or corrosion from the hub/flange mating surface of the brake drum, use the CH 42450-A resurfacer, or equivalent, to clean the wheel hub flange.
9. If installing a new brake drum, use denatured alcohol or an equivalent approved brake cleaner and a clean shop towel to remove the protective coating from the friction surface of the drum.
10. Adjust the drum brakes. Refer to Brake Shoes, Adjustment.
11. Install the drum brake.
12. Install drum brake screw and tighten to 62 inch lbs. (7 Nm).
13. Install the tire and wheel assembly. Tighten the wheel nuts in a star pattern to 103 ft. lbs. (140 Nm).
14. Lower the vehicle.
15. Apply the brakes approximately 3 times in order to seat and center the brake shoes within the drum.

BRAKE SHOES

REMOVAL & INSTALLATION

See Figure 13.

Special Tool
- CH 346 Mounting Tool

✳✳ CAUTION

Do not breathe dust or use compressed air to blow dust from storage containers or friction components. Remove dust using government-approved techniques. Friction component dust may be a cancer and lung disease hazard. Exposure to potentially hazardous components may occur if dusts are created during repair of friction components, such as brake pads and clutch discs. Exposure may also cause irritation to skin, eyes and respiratory tract, and may cause allergic reactions and/or may lead to other chronic health effects. If irritation persists, seek medical attention or advice. Failure to follow these instructions may result in serious personal injury.

1. Before servicing the vehicle, refer to the Precautions Section.
2. Raise and safely support the vehicle.
3. Remove the tire and wheel assembly. Refer to Tire and Wheel Removal and Installation.
4. Remove the brake drum. Refer to Brake Drum, removal & installation.

✳✳ WARNING

Do not over stretch the adjuster spring. Damage can occur if the spring is over stretched.

5. Remove the adjuster spring. Disengage the adjuster spring hook end from the tab on the adjuster actuator lever, then release the spring from the brake shoe web hole.
6. Release the adjuster actuator lever from the adjuster assembly. Remove the adjuster assembly.
7. Remove the brake shoe springs, using the CH 346 mounting tool to twist spring caps.
8. Remove the brake shoes.
9. Remove the lower spring from front brake shoe.
10. Remove the parking brake cable from the parking brake lever.

To install:

11. Install the adjuster assembly to the adjuster actuator lever. Turn in the adjuster as far as possible.

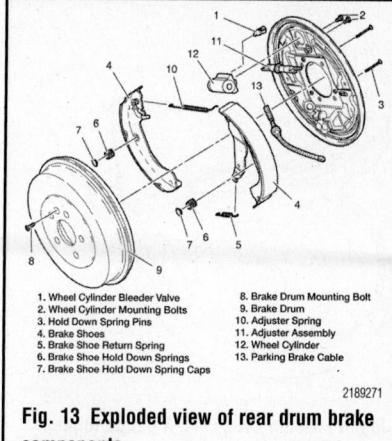

1. Wheel Cylinder Bleeder Valve
2. Wheel Cylinder Mounting Bolts
3. Hold Down Spring Pins
4. Brake Shoes
5. Brake Shoe Return Spring
6. Brake Shoe Hold Down Springs
7. Brake Shoe Hold Down Spring Caps
8. Brake Drum Mounting Bolt
9. Brake Drum
10. Adjuster Spring
11. Adjuster Assembly
12. Wheel Cylinder
13. Parking Brake Cable

Fig. 13 Exploded view of rear drum brake components

12. Install the parking brake cable to the parking brake lever.
13. Install the lower spring to front brake shoe.
14. Install the brake shoes.
15. Install the brake shoe springs, using the CH 346 mounting tool to twist spring caps.
16. Install the adjuster spring. Ensure that the loop end of the spring fully engages the tab on the actuator lever.
17. Install the brake drum. Refer to Brake Drum, removal & installation.
18. Install the tire and wheel assembly. Tighten the wheel nuts in a star pattern to 103 ft. lbs. (140 Nm).
19. Lower the vehicle.

ADJUSTMENT

See Figures 14 and 15.

Special Tool
- CH-21177-A Drum to Brake Shoe Clearance Gauge

✳✳ CAUTION

Do not breathe dust or use compressed air to blow dust from storage containers or friction components. Remove dust using government-approved techniques. Friction component dust may be a cancer and lung disease hazard. Exposure to potentially hazardous components may occur if dusts are created during repair of friction components, such as brake pads and clutch discs. Exposure may also cause irritation to skin, eyes and respiratory tract, and may cause allergic reactions and/or may lead to other chronic health effects. If irritation persists, seek medical attention or advice. Failure to follow these instructions may result in serious personal injury.

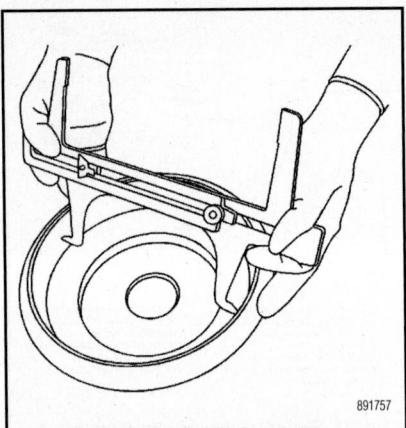

Fig. 14 Using CH-21177-A gauge to measure the brake drum inside diameter

1. Before servicing the vehicle, refer to the Precautions Section.

2. Ensure the park brake lever is in the fully released position.

3. Raise and safely support the vehicle.

4. Remove the tire and wheel assembly.

5. Remove the brake drum. Refer to Brake Drum, removal & installation.

6. Position the CH-21177-A gauge to the widest point of the brake drum inside diameter.

7. Firmly hand tighten the set screw on the CH-21177-A gauge.

8. Remove the CH-21177-A gauge from the brake drum and position it over the corresponding brake shoe assembly at its widest point.

9. While holding the CH-21177-A gauge in position, insert a proper feeler gauge between one side of the CH-21177-A gauge, and the corresponding brake shoe lining.

- The brake shoe lining-to-drum clearance should measure: 0.016–0.035 inch (0.4–0.9mm)

10. Rotate the brake shoe adjuster screw until the brake shoe linings contact the CH-21177-A gauge and the feeler gauge.

11. Repeat the above steps for the opposite brake drum and brake shoe assembly.

12. Install the brake drum. Refer to Brake Drum, removal & installation.

13. Install the tire and wheel assembly. Tighten the wheel nuts in a star pattern to 103 ft. lbs. (140 Nm).

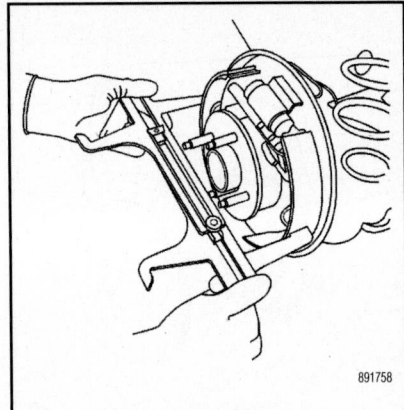

Fig. 15 Using CH-21177-A gauge to measure the brake shoe assembly

14. Lower vehicle.

15. Apply the brake pedal at least 10 times. Verify the clicking sound of the adjuster assembly is not audible from either brake drum.

16. Adjust the park brake. Refer to Parking Brake Cables, Adjustment.

17. Lower the vehicle.

BRAKES

PARKING BRAKE CABLES

ADJUSTMENT

✳ CAUTION

Do not breathe dust or use compressed air to blow dust from storage containers or friction components. Remove dust using government-approved techniques. Friction component dust may be a cancer and lung disease hazard. Exposure to potentially hazardous components may occur if dusts are created during repair of friction components, such as brake pads and clutch discs. Exposure may also cause irritation to skin, eyes and respiratory tract, and may cause allergic reactions and/or may lead to other chronic health effects. If irritation persists, seek medical attention or advice. Failure to follow these instructions may result in serious personal injury.

➡This vehicle utilizes a self-tensioning, or self-adjusting park brake cable system. The park brake system does not require adjustment under normal operating conditions. The tension on the park brake cables can be disabled and enabled when necessary during service of the disc brake and/or the park brake system.

1. Before servicing the vehicle, refer to the Precautions Section.

2. Apply and fully release the park brake several times. Verify that the park brake lever releases completely.

3. Turn ON the ignition. Verify the red BRAKE warning lamp is not illuminated.

4. If the red BRAKE warning lamp is illuminated, verify the following:

a. The park brake lever is in the fully released position and against the stop.

b. There is no slack in the park brake cables.

5. Turn OFF the ignition.

6. Raise and safely support the vehicle.

7. With the park brake lever fully released, check the park brake levers on the rear calipers. The levers should be against the stops on the caliper housings. If the levers are not against the stops, binding may exist.

8. Fully apply and release the park brake lever 3–5 times in order for the cable

PARKING BRAKE

tensioner to take up any slack in the park brake cables.

9. Fully apply the park brake lever, a firm lever should be obtained by depressing the lever less than one full stroke.

10. Attempt to rotate the rear tire and wheel assemblies. There should be no rotation forward or rearward.

11. Fully release the park brake lever.

12. Verify the park brake is released by rotating the rear tire and wheel assemblies. The rear tire and wheel assemblies should rotate freely and exhibit no brake drag.

13. Lower the vehicle.

PARKING BRAKE SHOES

REMOVAL & INSTALLATION

On vehicles equipped with rear drum brakes, the parking brakes utilize the regular service brakes. Refer to Rear Drum Brakes, Brake Shoes, removal & installation.

On vehicles equipped with rear disc brakes, the parking brakes utilize the regular service brake pads. Refer to Rear Disc Brakes, Disc Brake Pads, removal & installation.

CHASSIS ELECTRICAL   AIR BAG (SUPPLEMENTAL RESTRAINT SYSTEM)

GENERAL INFORMATION

✳✳ CAUTION

These vehicles are equipped with an air bag system. The system must be disarmed before performing service on, or around, system components, the steering column, instrument panel components, wiring and sensors. Failure to follow the safety precautions and the disarming procedure could result in accidental air bag deployment, possible injury and unnecessary system repairs.

SERVICE PRECAUTIONS

Disconnect and isolate the battery negative cable before beginning any airbag system component diagnosis, testing, removal, or installation procedures. Allow system capacitor to discharge for two minutes before beginning any component service. This will disable the airbag system. Failure to disable the airbag system may result in accidental airbag deployment, personal injury, or death.

Do not place an intact undeployed airbag face down on a solid surface. The airbag will propel into the air if accidentally deployed and may result in personal injury or death.

When carrying or handling an undeployed airbag, the trim side (face) of the airbag should be pointing away from the body to minimize possibility of injury if accidental deployment occurs. Failure to do this may result in personal injury or death.

Replace airbag system components with OEM replacement parts. Substitute parts may appear interchangeable, but internal differences may result in inferior occupant protection. Failure to do so may result in occupant personal injury or death.

Wear safety glasses, rubber gloves, and long sleeved clothing when cleaning powder residue from vehicle after an airbag deployment. Powder residue emitted from a deployed airbag can cause skin irritation. Flush affected area with cool water if irritation is experienced. If nasal or throat irritation is experienced, exit the vehicle for fresh air until the irritation ceases. If irritation continues, see a physician.

Do not use a replacement airbag that is not in the original packaging. This may result in improper deployment, personal injury, or death.

The factory installed fasteners, screws and bolts used to fasten airbag components have a special coating and are specifically designed for the airbag system. Do not use substitute fasteners. Use only original equipment fasteners listed in the parts catalog when fastener replacement is required.

During, and following, any child restraint anchor service, due to impact event or vehicle repair, carefully inspect all mounting hardware, tether straps, and anchors for proper installation, operation, or damage. If a child restraint anchor is found damaged in any way, the anchor must be replaced. Failure to do this may result in personal injury or death.

Deployed and non-deployed airbags may or may not have live pyrotechnic material within the airbag inflator.

Do not dispose of driver/passenger/curtain airbags or seat belt tensioners unless you are sure of complete deployment. Refer to the Hazardous Substance Control System for proper disposal.

Dispose of deployed airbags and tensioners consistent with state, provincial, local, and federal regulations.

After any airbag component testing or service, do not connect the battery negative cable. Personal injury or death may result if the system test is not performed first.

If the vehicle is equipped with the Occupant Classification System (OCS), do not connect the battery negative cable before performing the OCS Verification Test using the scan tool and the appropriate diagnostic information. Personal injury or death may result if the system test is not performed properly.

Never replace both the Occupant Restraint Controller (ORC) and the Occupant Classification Module (OCM) at the same time. If both require replacement, replace one, then perform the Airbag System test before replacing the other.

Both the ORC and the OCM store Occupant Classification System (OCS) calibration data, which they transfer to one another when one of them is replaced. If both are replaced at the same time, an irreversible fault will be set in both modules and the OCS may malfunction and cause personal injury or death.

If equipped with OCS, the Seat Weight Sensor is a sensitive, calibrated unit and must be handled carefully. Do not drop or handle roughly. If dropped or

damaged, replace with another sensor. Failure to do so may result in occupant injury or death.

If equipped with OCS, the front passenger seat must be handled carefully as well. When removing the seat, be careful when setting on floor not to drop. If dropped, the sensor may be inoperative, could result in occupant injury, or possibly death.

If equipped with OCS, when the passenger front seat is on the floor, no one should sit in the front passenger seat. This uneven force may damage the sensing ability of the seat weight sensors. If sat on and damaged, the sensor may be inoperative, could result in occupant injury, or possibly death.

DISARMING THE SYSTEM

✳✳ CAUTION

When performing service on or near the SIR components or the SIR wiring, the SIR system must be disabled. Failure to observe the correct procedure could cause deployment of the SIR components. Serious injury can occur. Failure to observe the correct procedure could also result in unnecessary SIR system repairs.

✳✳ CAUTION

The inflatable restraint Sensing and Diagnostic Module (SDM) maintains a reserved energy supply. The reserved energy supply provides deployment power for the air bags if the SDM loses battery power during a collision. Deployment power is available for as much as 1 minute after disconnecting the vehicle power. Waiting 1 minute before working on the system after disabling the SIR system prevents deployment of the air bags from the reserved energy supply.

Disarming Procedure—Air Bag Fuse

1. Before servicing the vehicle, refer to the Precautions Section.

2. Turn the steering wheel so that the vehicle wheels are pointing straight ahead.

3. Place the ignition in the OFF position.

❋❋ CAUTION

The inflatable restraint Sensing and Diagnostic Module (SDM) may have more than one fused power input. To ensure there is no unwanted SIR deployment, personal injury, or unnecessary SIR system repairs, remove all fuses supplying power to the SDM. With all SDM fuses removed and the ignition switch in the ON position, the AIR BAG warning indicator illuminates. This is a normal operation, and does not indicate a SIR system malfunction.

4. Locate and remove the fuse(s) supplying power to the SDM.

5. Wait 1 minute before working on the system.

Disarming Procedure—Negative Battery Cable

1. Before servicing the vehicle, refer to the Precautions Section.

2. Turn the steering wheel so that the vehicles wheels are pointing straight ahead.

3. Place the ignition in the OFF position.

4. Disconnect the negative battery cable from the battery.

5. Wait 1 minute before working on system.

ARMING THE SYSTEM

❋❋ CAUTION

When performing service on or near the SIR components or the SIR wiring, the SIR system must be disabled. Failure to observe the correct procedure could cause deployment of the SIR components. Serious injury can occur. Failure to observe the correct procedure could also result in unnecessary SIR system repairs.

❋❋ CAUTION

The inflatable restraint Sensing and Diagnostic Module (SDM) maintains a reserved energy supply. The reserved energy supply provides deployment

power for the air bags if the SDM loses battery power during a collision. Deployment power is available for as much as 1 minute after disconnecting the vehicle power. Waiting 1 minute before working on the system after disabling the SIR system prevents deployment of the air bags from the reserved energy supply.

Arming Procedure—Air Bag Fuse

1. Before servicing the vehicle, refer to the Precautions Section.

2. Place the ignition in the OFF position.

3. Install the fuse(s) supplying power to the inflatable restraint Sensing and Diagnostic Module (SDM).

4. Turn the ignition switch to the ON position. The AIR BAG indicator will flash then turn OFF.

Arming Procedure—Negative Battery Cable

1. Before servicing the vehicle, refer to the Precautions Section.

2. Place the ignition in the OFF position.

3. Connect the negative battery cable to the battery. Refer to Battery, removal & installation.

4. Turn the ignition switch to the ON position. The AIR BAG indicator will flash then turn OFF.

CLOCKSPRING CENTERING

See Figures 16 and 17.

❋❋ WARNING

The new SIR coil assembly will be centered. Improper alignment of the SIR coil assembly may damage the unit, causing an inflatable restraint malfunction.

1. Before servicing the vehicle, refer to the Precautions Section.

2. Verify the following conditions before centering the Supplemental Inflatable Restraint (SIR) steering wheel module coil:

   a. The wheels on the vehicle are straight ahead.

   b. The centering mark of the steering shaft is in the 6 o'clock position.

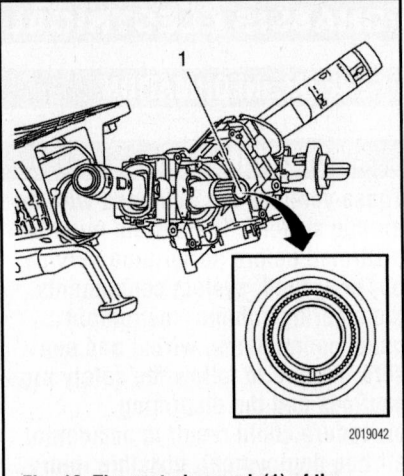

Fig. 16 The centering mark (1) of the steering shaft must be in the 6 o'clock position

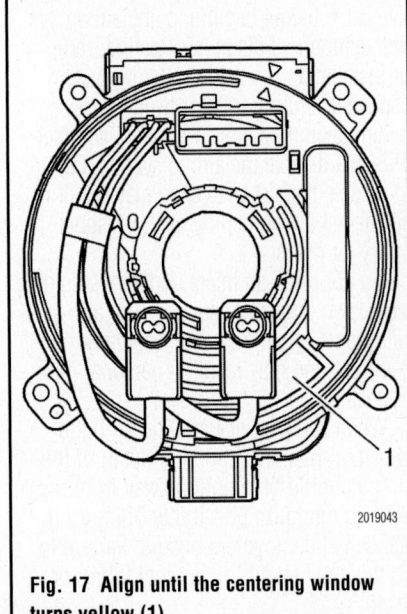

Fig. 17 Align until the centering window turns yellow (1)

3. Turn the lobe of the clock spring clockwise until the coil ribbon stops. Do not force.

4. Turn the lobe of the clock spring counterclockwise approximately 3 turns to the Neutral position.

5. Properly align until the centering window turns yellow. This indicates the CENTER position.

DRIVE TRAIN

MANUAL TRANSAXLE ASSEMBLY

REMOVAL & INSTALLATION

See Figures 18 through 22.

1. Before servicing the vehicle, refer to the Precautions Section.

2. Disconnect the negative battery cable.

3. Remove the battery. Refer to Battery, removal & installation.

4. Remove the battery tray.

5. Remove the transaxle shift lever cable from transaxle.

6. Disconnect the electrical connector from the backup lamp switch.

➡**Before disconnecting the clutch actuator cylinder front pipe, remove the clutch/brake fluid from the reservoir tank.**

7. Remove the clutch actuator cylinder front pipe retainer.

8. Disconnect the clutch actuator cylinder front pipe from the clutch actuator cylinder pipe elbow.

9. Unclip the wire harness from the transaxle.

10. Remove the 3 upper transaxle bolts from the engine.

11. Remove the drivetrain and front suspension frame.

12. Remove the transaxle front mount from the transaxle. Remove the 2 bolts.

13. Remove the transaxle mount bracket bolts and the rear transaxle mount bracket.

14. Drain the transaxle fluid.

15. Remove the halfshafts. Refer to Front Halfshafts, removal & installation.

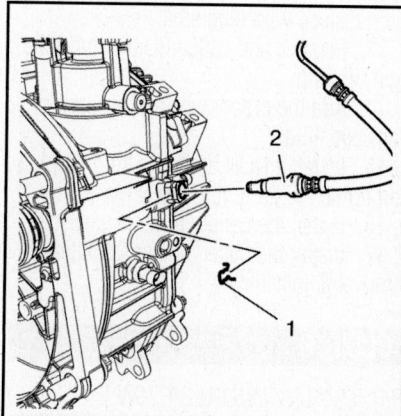

Fig. 18 Remove the clutch actuator cylinder front pipe retainer (1) and disconnect the clutch actuator cylinder front pipe (2)

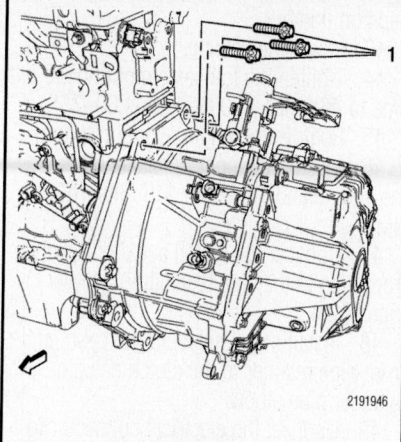

Fig. 19 Remove the 3 upper transaxle bolts from the engine (1)

16. Lower the vehicle.

17. Remove and DISCARD the transaxle mount bolts from transaxle mount bracket.

18. Lower the engine and the transaxle on the left hand side with the engine support fixture.

19. Remove the transaxle mount bracket-left side from the transaxle. Remove the 3 transaxle mount bracket bolts.

20. Raise the vehicle.

21. Using suitable straps or chains, secure the transaxle to a suitable transmission jack.

22. Remove the 4 transaxle lower bolts

23. Remove the transaxle lower bolt and nut

24. Install a NEW oil drain plug and tighten to 15 ft. lbs. (20 Nm).

25. Remove the remaining lower transaxle bolts.

26. Separate the transaxle from the engine.

27. Lower the transaxle from the vehicle.

To install:

28. Raise the transaxle with the transmission jack and position the transaxle to the engine.

29. Install the transaxle lower bolt and tighten to 44 ft. lbs. (60 Nm).

30. Remove the transmission jack.

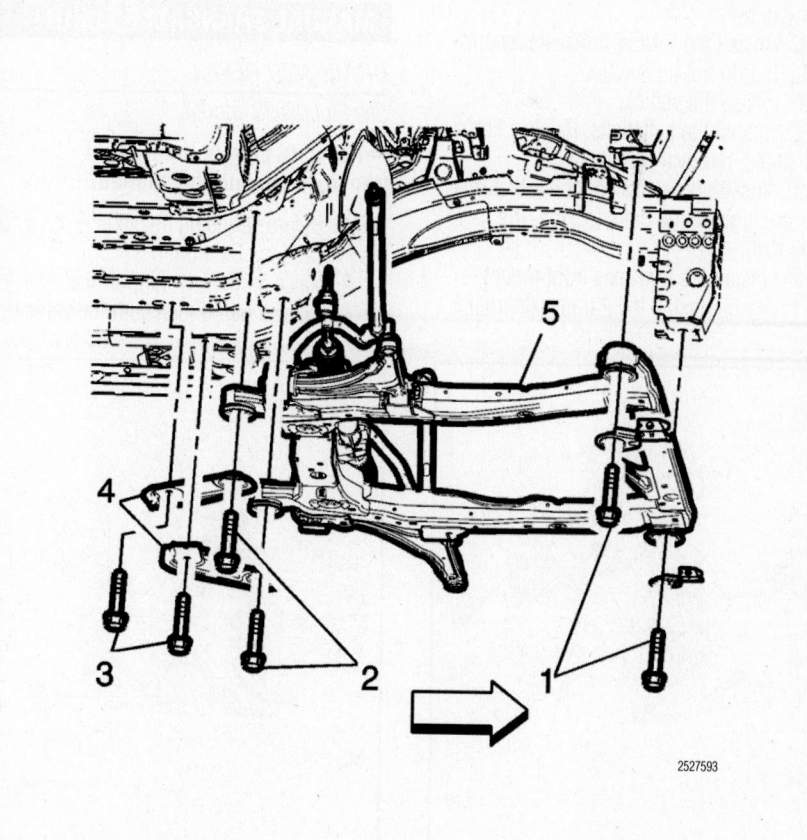

Fig. 20 View of drivetrain and front suspension frame removal

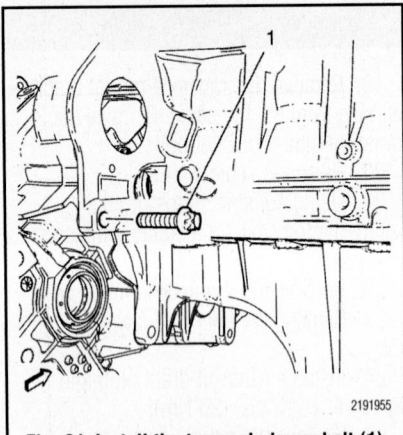

Fig. 21 Install the transaxle lower bolt (1)

31. Install 3 transaxle lower bolts and tighten to 32 ft. lbs. (40 Nm).

32. Install transaxle bolt and tighten to 44 ft. lbs. (60 Nm).

33. Install transaxle lower bolt and nut and tighten to 32 ft. lbs. (40 Nm).

34. Lower the vehicle.

35. Install the transaxle mount bracket-left side. Install the 3 transaxle mount bracket bolts and tighten to 74 ft. lbs. (100 Nm).

36. Raise the engine and the transaxle on the left hand side with the engine support fixture.

37. Install the 3 NEW transaxle mount bolts, but do not tighten yet.

38. Raise the vehicle.

39. Install the halfshafts. Refer to Front Halfshafts, removal & installation.

40. Install the transaxle mount bracket-rear and tighten the bolts to 74 ft. lbs. (100 Nm).

41. Install the transaxle front mount to the transaxle. Install the 2 transaxle front

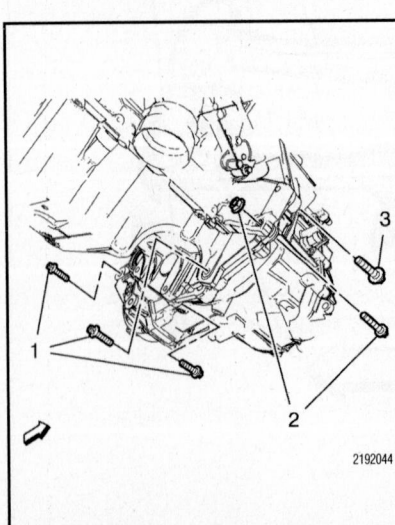

Fig. 22 Tighten the transaxle bolts as illustrated

mount bolts and tighten to 74 ft. lbs. (100 Nm).

42. Install the drivetrain and front suspension frame.

43. Lower the vehicle.

44. Tighten the transaxle mount bolts left side to 46 ft. lbs. (50 Nm), plus 60–75°.

45. Remove the engine support fixture.

46. Install the upper transaxle bolts to the engine and tighten to 44 ft. lbs. (60 Nm).

47. Connect the clutch actuator cylinder front pipe to the clutch actuator cylinder pipe elbow.

48. Install the clutch actuator cylinder front pipe retainer to the clutch actuator cylinder pipe elbow.

49. Connect the electrical connector to the backup lamp switch.

50. Install the transaxle shift lever cable to transaxle.

51. Adjust the shift lever and selector lever cables, as needed.

52. Bleed the clutch hydraulic system.

53. Inspect the transaxle fluid level.

54. Install the battery tray.

55. Install and connect the battery. Refer to Battery, removal & installation.

56. Road test the vehicle.

MANUAL TRANSAXLE FLUID

DRAIN AND REFILL

See Figures 23 and 24.

➡ **The fluid plug at the front of transaxle may not be opened.**

1. Before servicing the vehicle, refer to the Precautions Section.

2. Raise and safely support the vehicle.

3. Place a pan underneath the vehicle.

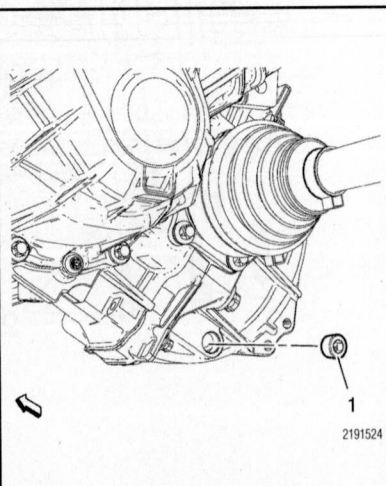

Fig. 23 Manual transaxle drain plug location (1)

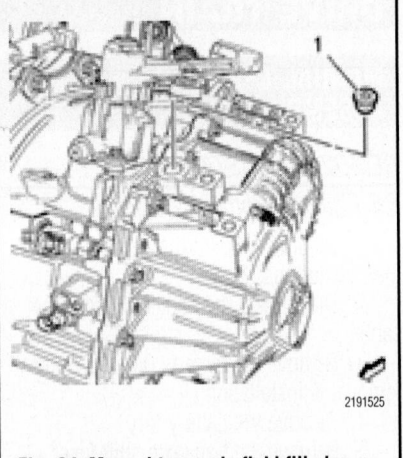

Fig. 24 Manual transaxle fluid fill plug location (1)

4. Clean away all dirt and debris from the transaxle fluid drain plug area.

5. Remove and DISCARD the transaxle fluid drain plug.

6. Let the transaxle fluid run out for 10 minutes.

To install:

7. Apply thread sealant to the NEW transaxle fluid drain plug.

8. Re-cut the transaxle drain hole threads.

➡ **Service may offer plugs that are not microencapsulated. If this is the case apply thread lock agent to the plug. If the fastener is microencapsulated, install a NEW transaxle fluid drain plug. DO NOT reuse the old plug.**

9. Install a NEW transaxle fluid drain plug and tighten to 15 ft. lbs. (20 Nm).

10. Lower the vehicle.

11. Remove the battery tray.

12. Clean away all dirt and debris from the transaxle fluid plug area.

13. Remove and DISCARD the transaxle fluid fill plug.

14. Add the proper type and amount of transaxle fluid.

15. Install a NEW transaxle fluid fill plug and tighten to 22 ft. lbs. (30 Nm).

16. Install the battery tray.

17. Install the battery. Refer to Battery, removal & installation.

CLUTCH

REMOVAL & INSTALLATION

See Figures 25 through 27.

Special Tools

• DT-6263 Remover / Installer, or equivalent

1. Before servicing the vehicle, refer to the Precautions Section.

2. Remove the transaxle. Refer to Manual Transaxle Assembly, removal & installation.

3. Remove 6 clutch pressure plate bolts. Discard the bolts.

4. Remove clutch pressure plate and driven plate.

➡**Clutch pressure plate and driven plates contaminated by foreign bodies (oil, cleaning agent etc.) have to be replaced. Check clutch driven plate for damage and friction rust in the hub profile and replace if necessary. Do not clean clutch pressure plate and driven plate with a high pressure cleaner or component washing machine.**

5. Inspect the clutch pressure plate and driven plate and replace if necessary. Inspect for:
- Excessive wear
- Burned friction surface

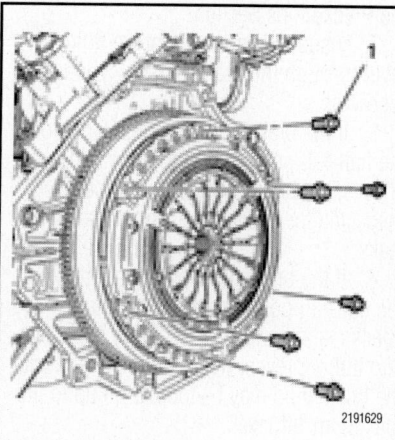
2191629

Fig. 25 Remove the clutch pressure plate bolts (1)

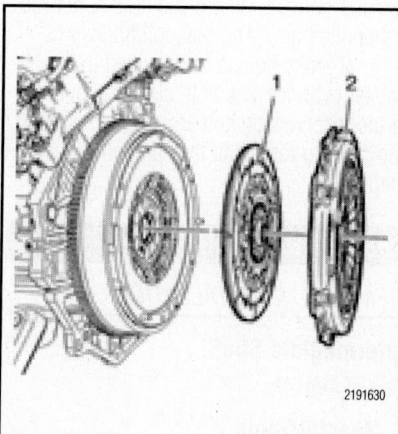
2191630

Fig. 26 View of the clutch pressure plate (2) and driven plate (1)

- Oil on friction surface
- Damaged spline hub
- Damaged springs

6. Inspect projection of lining at the clutch lining rivets.

➡**The clutch driven plate has to be replaced if the lining projection is less than 0.020 inch (0.5mm).**

7. Slide the clutch driven plate onto the transaxle input shaft and check for easy movement.

To install:

8. Clean the 6 threads in the flywheel for fastening the clutch pressure plate.

➡**The clutch driven plate must be installed so that the lettering on the hub faces the transaxle.**

9. Install the driven plate and clutch pressure plate.

➡**To prevent damage to the spring fangs of the pressure plate use DT-6263 remover / installer or equivalent to remove and install the clutch pressure plate. Note the different lengths of the brackets for attaching the DT-6263 to lower engine block.**

❈❈ WARNING

The DT-6263 remover / installer or equivalent may only be attached to the engine block and not to the oil pan.

10. Attach the DT-6263 or equivalent to the engine block. Do not tighten the bolts yet.

11. Install the 4 bolts to the engine block.

12. Attach the DT-6263-27 center guide or a fitting equivalent to the DT-6263-30 centering drift.

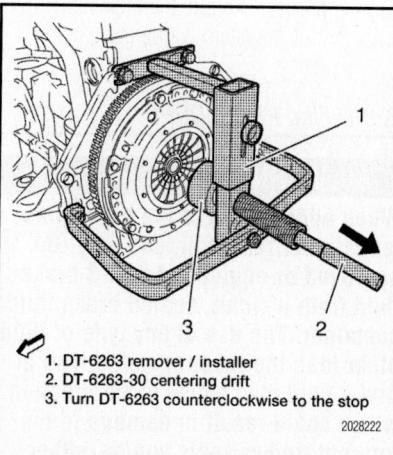

1. DT-6263 remover / installer
2. DT-6263-30 centering drift
3. Turn DT-6263 counterclockwise to the stop
2028222

Fig. 27 View of the DT-6263 remover / installer attached to the engine block

13. Fasten the DT-6263 remover / installer.

a. Align the DT-6263 or equivalent to center.

b. Insert DT-6263-30 centering drift or equivalent in conjunction with the clutch center guide through DT-6263 into the clutch pressure plate and crankshaft center.

c. Tighten the knurled wheel.

d. Tighten the bolt.

e. Tighten the 4 bolts of the DT-6263 or equivalent to the engine block.

14. Preload the clutch springs using the DT-6263 or equivalent.

a. Move the DT-6263 or equivalent so that it rests against the spring tangs of the clutch pressure plate.

b. Turn the DT-6263 or equivalent clockwise to the stop.

15. Install 6 NEW clutch pressure plate bolts and tighten crosswise to 21 ft. lbs. (28 Nm).

16. Remove DT-6263 or equivalent from the engine block.

a. Turn DT-6263 or equivalent counterclockwise to the stop.

b. Remove DT-6263-30 centering drift or equivalent in conjunction with the clutch center guide.

c. Remove the 4 bolts of the DT-6263 or equivalent from the engine block.

17. Install the transaxle. Refer to Manual Transaxle Assembly, removal & installation.

BLEEDING

See Figure 28.

❈❈ WARNING

Do not use any fluid other than clean brake fluid meeting manufacturer's specification. Additionally, do not use brake fluid that has been previously drained. Following these instructions will help prevent system contamination, brake component damage, and the risk of serious personal injury.

❈❈ CAUTION

Brake fluid contains polyglycol ethers and polyglycols. Avoid contact with the eyes. Wash hands thoroughly after handling. If brake fluid contacts the eyes, flush the eyes for 15 minutes with cold running water. Get medical attention if irritation persists. If taken internally, drink water and induce vomiting. Get medical attention immediately. Failure to follow these instructions may result in personal injury.

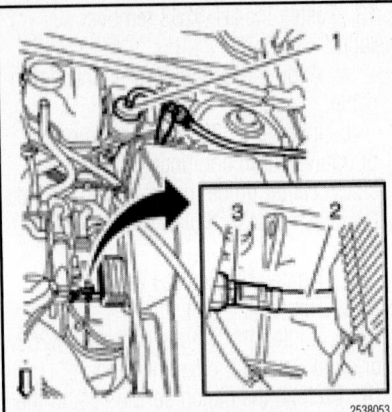

Fig. 28 Attach a brake bleeder to the system with a screw adapter (1), bleeder hose (2), and bleeder valve (3)

✳✳ WARNING

Do not spill brake fluid on painted or plastic surfaces or damage to the surface may occur. If brake fluid is spilled onto a painted or plastic surface, immediately wash the surface with water.

➡ Only use brake fluid DOT 3. The hydraulic clutch actuation must be bled from "below," i.e. from the bleeder valve. A brake bleeder must be used for this purpose. Manual bleeding is no longer permissible. Observe manufacturer's instructions before using brake bleeder. The brake bleeder must be set to an operating pressure of approximately 2 bar.

1. Before servicing the vehicle, refer to the Precautions Section.
2. Attach a brake bleeder.
   a. Screw the adapter for the corresponding brake bleeder onto the brake fluid reservoir. Insert the hose end in a suitable brake fluid collecting basin.
   b. Disconnect the valve cap from the bleeder valve.
   c. Connect the bleeder hose to the bleeder valve.
3. Bleed the clutch.
   a. Switch on the brake bleeder.
   b. Open the bleeder valve 2–3 turns.
   c. Bleed until brake fluid escapes without bubbles at the hose.
   d. Close the bleeder valve hand tight.
4. Detach the brake bleeder.
   a. Detach the adapter from the brake fluid reservoir.
   b. Push the valve cap onto the bleeder valve to protect the bleeder valve.

➡ The following operational stages must be undertaken to fill the pressure line between the transaxle housing and the central release. When bleeding, ensure that the brake fluid reservoir is always filled up sufficiently and does not run dry.

5. Bleed the pressure line between the transaxle housing and the central release.
   a. Press and hold the clutch pedal.
   b. Open the bleeder valve until air or air/brake fluid mixture emerges.
   c. Close the bleeder valve hand tight. Do not close the bleeder valve too fast.
   d. Release the clutch pedal as far as the stop at normal speed.
   e. Wait approximately 5 seconds.
   f. Repeat this bleeding process 4 times.
   g. Tighten the bleeder valve.
   h. Detach the bleeder hose.
   i. Push the valve cap on to the bleeder valve to protect the bleeder valve.
6. Connect the bleeder hose to the bleeder valve, place the free end in a suitable connecting container.
7. Top up brake fluid reservoir.
   a. Fill the brake fluid reservoir up to "MAX" marking.
   b. Install the brake fluid reservoir.
8. Check the actuation pressure of the clutch pedal.
9. Check shifting for ease of movement with the vehicle stationary, with the engine running and with the clutch disengaged.
10. Road test the vehicle to ensure proper operation.
    • Undertake a road test using varying RPM ranges and frequent gear changes, bring the vehicle to operating temperature during this process. Ensure the brake and clutch system is operating correctly.

FLUID FILL PROCEDURE

✳✳ WARNING

When adding fluid to the brake master cylinder reservoir, use only GM approved or equivalent DOT-3 brake fluid from a clean, sealed brake fluid container. The use of any type of fluid other than the recommended type of brake fluid may cause contamination which could result in damage to the internal rubber seals and/or rubber linings of hydraulic brake system components.

✳✳ CAUTION

Brake fluid contains polyglycol ethers and polyglycols. Avoid contact with the eyes. Wash hands thoroughly after handling. If brake fluid contacts the eyes, flush the eyes for 15 minutes with cold running water. Get medical attention if irritation persists. If taken internally, drink water and induce vomiting. Get medical attention immediately. Failure to follow these instructions may result in personal injury.

✳✳ WARNING

Do not spill brake fluid on painted or plastic surfaces or damage to the surface may occur. If brake fluid is spilled onto a painted or plastic surface, immediately wash the surface with water.

1. Before servicing the vehicle, refer to the Precautions Section.
2. Visually inspect the brake fluid level through the brake master cylinder reservoir.
3. If the brake fluid level is at or below the half-full point during routine fluid checks, the brake system should be inspected for wear and possible brake fluid leaks.
4. If the brake fluid level is at or below the half-full point during routine fluid checks, and an inspection of the brake system did not reveal wear or brake fluid leaks, the brake fluid may be topped-off up to the maximum-fill level.
5. If brake system service was just completed, the brake fluid may be topped-off up to the maximum-fill level.
6. If the brake fluid level is above the half-full point, adding brake fluid is not recommended under normal conditions.
7. If brake fluid is to be added to the master cylinder reservoir, clean the outside of the reservoir on and around the reservoir cap prior to removing the cap and diaphragm.

FRONT HALFSHAFT

REMOVAL & INSTALLATION

Intermediate Shaft
See Figure 29.

Special Tools
• DT-6332 Seal Protector
1. Before servicing the vehicle, refer to the Precautions Section.

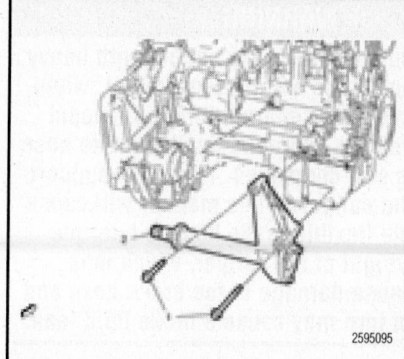

Fig. 29 View of intermediate shaft and bracket assembly (2) and bracket bolts (1)

2. Remove the right side halfshaft. Refer to Front Halfshaft, Right Side Halfshaft, removal & installation.

3. Remove the 3 intermediate shaft bracket bolts.

4. Remove and DISCARD the O-ring. DO NOT re-use, replace with NEW only.

To install:

5. To install, reverse the removal procedure.

➡The DT-6332 protector must be installed into the differential output shaft seal prior to installation of the intermediate shaft.

6. Tighten the 3 intermediate shaft bracket bolts to 43 ft. lbs. (58 Nm).

7. Check the transaxle fluid level.

Left Side Halfshaft

See Figures 30 through 33.

Special Tools

- CH-313 Slide Hammer
- CH-6003 Axle Shaft Remover
- DT-6332 Seal Protector
- DT-29794 Axle Shaft Remover Extension
- CH-49400 Hub Spindle Remover

❋❋ WARNING

To prevent personal injury and/or component damage, do not allow the weight of the vehicle to load the front wheels, or attempt to operate the vehicle, when the wheel drive shaft(s) or wheel drive shaft nut(s) are removed. To do so may cause the inner bearing race to separate, resulting in damage to brake and suspension components and loss of vehicle control.

❋❋ WARNING

Wheel drive shaft boots, seals and clamps should be protected from

sharp objects any time service is performed on or near the wheel drive shaft(s). Damage to the boot(s), the seal(s) or the clamp(s) may cause lubricant to leak from the joint and lead to increased noise and possible failure of the wheel drive shaft.

1. Before servicing the vehicle, refer to the Precautions Section.

2. Raise and safely support the vehicle.

3. Remove the tire and wheel assembly.

4. Insert a drift or punch in the cooling fins of the brake rotor.

5. Rotate the brake rotor until the drift or punch contacts the brake caliper mounting bracket.

6. Using a breaker bar, loosen the wheel drive shaft nut.

7. Remove and DISCARD the wheel drive shaft nut from the wheel drive shaft.

8. Using the CH-49400 remover, separate the brake rotor and wheel bearing/hub assembly.

9. Remove the outer tie rod assembly from the steering knuckle.

10. Remove the ball joint from the steering knuckle.

❋❋ WARNING

The wheel drive shaft seal protector must be installed into the differential output shaft seal prior to removing and installing the wheel drive shaft. Failure to install the wheel drive shaft seal protector may cause the splines of the wheel drive shaft to cut the differential output seal.

11. Install the DT-6332 protector into the differential output shaft seal.

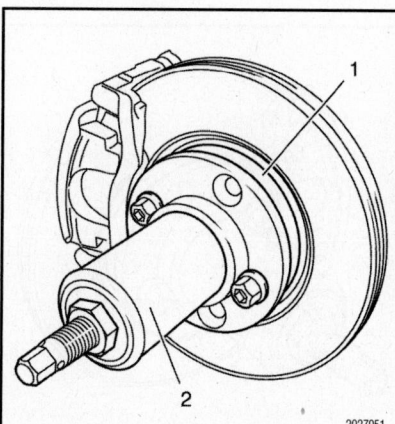

Fig. 30 Using the CH-49400 remover (2), separate the brake rotor and wheel bearing/hub assembly (1)

12. Using the CH-313 hammer with CH-6003 remover along with DT-29794 extension to remove the wheel drive shaft from the vehicle.

➡If there is no washer on the wheel drive shaft, install a NEW washer.

13. Remove and discard the washer from the wheel drive shaft. DO NOT re-use the washer, replace with NEW only.

To install:

14. Install a NEW washer to the wheel drive shaft.

❋❋ WARNING

In order to prevent lubricant leaks, use care when installing the wheel drive shaft to the differential. Do not damage the oil seal. Replace the oil seal if it becomes nicked, distorted, or otherwise damaged.

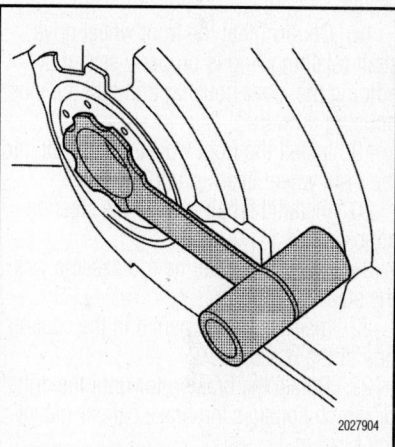

Fig. 31 Install the DT-6332 protector into the differential output shaft seal

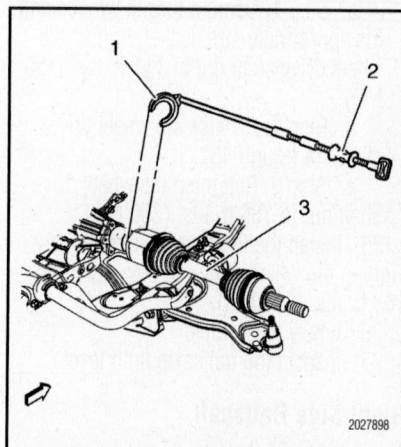

Fig. 32 Using the CH-313 hammer (2) with CH-6003 remover (1) along with DT-29794 extension to remove the wheel drive shaft (3) from the vehicle

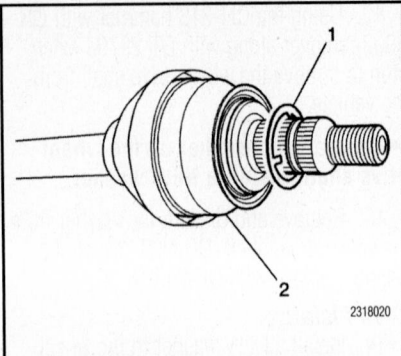

Fig. 33 Install a NEW washer (1) to the wheel drive shaft (2)

15. Carefully install the wheel drive shaft into the differential until the splines are past the DT-6332 protector.

16. Remove the DT-6332 protector from the differential output shaft seal.

17. Install the wheel drive shaft into the differential until the retaining ring is fully seated.

18. Confirm that the front wheel drive shaft retaining ring is properly seated by holding the inner housing and pull the inner housing outward

19. Install the front wheel drive shaft into the front wheel bearing/hub.

20. Install the ball joint to the steering knuckle.

21. Install the outer tie rod assembly at the steering knuckle.

22. Insert a drift or punch in the cooling fins of the brake rotor.

23. Rotate the brake rotor until the drift or punch contacts the brake caliper mounting bracket.

24. Install the NEW wheel drive shaft nut to the wheel drive shaft and tighten in 3 passes.

   a. Step 1: Using a torque wrench and the appropriate size socket, tighten the wheel drive shaft nut to 111 ft. lbs. (150 Nm).

   b. Step 2: Release the wheel drive shaft nut trough 45°.

   c. Step 3: Retighten the wheel drive shaft nut to 185 ft. lbs. (250 Nm).

25. Install the tire and wheel assembly. Tighten the wheel nuts in a star pattern to 103 ft. lbs. (140 Nm).

26. Lower the vehicle.

27. Inspect the transaxle fluid level.

Right Side Halfshaft

See Figures 34 through 37.

Special Tools
- CH-313 Slide Hammer
- CH-6003 Axle Shaft Remover
- DT-6332 Seal Protector

- DT-29794 Axle Shaft Remover Extension
- CH-49400 Hub Spindle Remover

✳✳ WARNING

To prevent personal injury and/or component damage, do not allow the weight of the vehicle to load the front wheels, or attempt to operate the vehicle, when the wheel drive shaft(s) or wheel drive shaft nut(s) are removed. To do so may cause the inner bearing race to separate, resulting in damage to brake and suspension components and loss of vehicle control.

✳✳ WARNING

Wheel drive shaft boots, seals and clamps should be protected from sharp objects any time service is performed on or near the wheel drive shaft(s). Damage to the boot(s), the seal(s) or the clamp(s) may cause lubricant to leak from the joint and lead to increased noise and possible failure of the wheel drive shaft.

1. Before servicing the vehicle, refer to the Precautions Section.

2. Raise and suitably support the vehicle.

3. Remove the tire and wheel assembly.

4. Insert a drift or punch in the cooling fins of the brake rotor.

5. Rotate the brake rotor until the drift or punch contacts the brake caliper mounting bracket.

6. Using a breaker bar, loosen the wheel drive shaft nut.

7. Remove and DISCARD the wheel drive shaft nut from the wheel drive shaft.

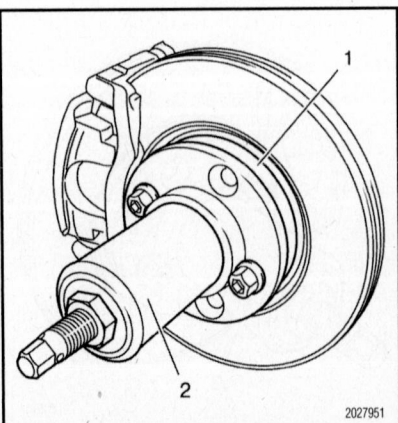

Fig. 34 Using the CH-49400 remover (2), separate the brake rotor and wheel bearing/hub assembly (1)

✳✳ WARNING

Support the brake caliper with heavy mechanic wire, or equivalent, whenever it is separated from its mount and the hydraulic flexible brake hose is still connected. Failure to support the caliper in this manner will cause the flexible brake hose to bear the weight of the caliper, which may cause damage to the brake hose and in turn may cause a brake fluid leak.

8. Using the CH-49400 remover, separate the brake rotor and wheel bearing/hub assembly.

9. Remove the outer tie rod assembly from the steering knuckle.

10. Remove the ball joint from the steering knuckle.

✳✳ WARNING

The wheel drive shaft seal protector must be installed into the differential output shaft seal prior to removing and installing the wheel drive shaft. Failure to install the wheel drive shaft seal protector as indicated may cause the splines of the wheel drive shaft to cut the differential output seal.

➥ **The DT-6332 protector not needed for vehicles with an intermediate shaft.**

11. Install the DT-6332 protector into the differential output shaft seal.

12. Using the CH-313 hammer with CH-6003 remover along with DT-29794 extension and remove the wheel drive shaft from the vehicle.

➥ **If there is no washer on the wheel drive shaft, install a NEW washer.**

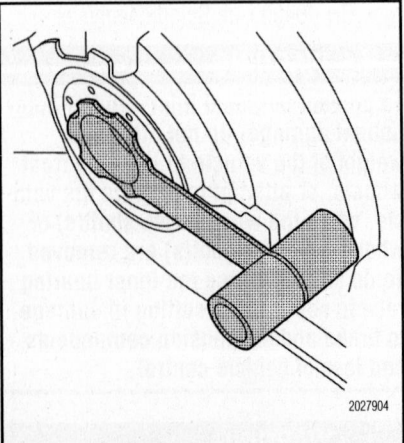

Fig. 35 Install the DT-6332 protector into the differential output shaft seal

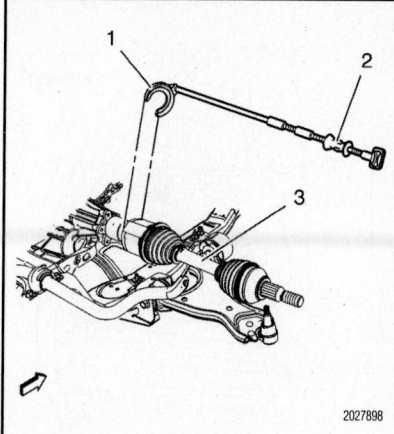

Fig. 36 Using the CH-313 hammer (2) with CH-6003 remover (1) along with DT-29794 extension to remove the wheel drive shaft (3) from the vehicle

13. Remove and discard the washer from the wheel drive shaft. DO NOT re-use the washer, replace with NEW only.

To install:

14. Install a NEW washer to the wheel drive shaft.

✹✹ WARNING

In order to prevent lubricant leaks, use care when installing the wheel drive shaft to the differential. Do not damage the oil seal. Replace the oil seal if it becomes nicked, distorted, or otherwise damaged.

15. Carefully install the wheel drive shaft into the differential until the splines are past the DT-6332 protector.

16. Remove the DT-6332 protector from the differential output shaft seal.

17. Install the wheel drive shaft into the differential until the retaining ring is fully seated.

18. Confirm that the front wheel drive shaft retaining ring is properly seated by holding the inner housing and pull the inner housing outward.

19. Install the front wheel drive shaft into the front wheel bearing/hub.

20. Install the ball joint to the steering knuckle.

21. Install the outer tie rod assembly at the steering knuckle.

22. Insert a drift or punch in the cooling fins of the brake rotor.

23. Rotate the brake rotor until the drift or punch contacts the brake caliper mounting bracket.

24. Install the NEW wheel drive shaft nut to the wheel drive shaft tighten in 3 passes.

25. Install the NEW wheel drive shaft nut to the wheel drive shaft and tighten in 3 passes.

    a. Step 1: Using a torque wrench and the appropriate size socket, tighten the wheel drive shaft nut to 111 ft. lbs. (150 Nm).

    b. Step 2: Release the wheel drive shaft nut trough 45°.

    c. Step 3: Retighten the wheel drive shaft nut to 185 ft. lbs. (250 Nm).

26. Install the tire and wheel assembly. Tighten the wheel nuts in a star pattern to 103 ft. lbs. (140 Nm).

27. Lower the vehicle.

28. Inspect the transaxle fluid level.

ENGINE COOLING

CHARGE AIR COOLER

REMOVAL & INSTALLATION

1.4L Engine

See Figures 37 through 40.

1. Before servicing the vehicle, refer to the Precautions Section.

2. Disconnect the battery negative cable. Refer to Battery, removal & installation.

3. Remove the front bumper fascia.

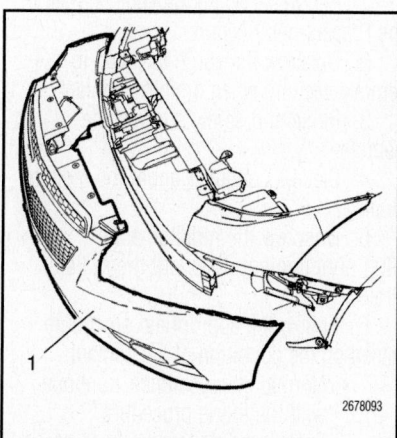

Fig. 37 View of front bumper fascia removal

4. Remove the radiator upper air seal.

5. Remove the left and right side radiator air baffles.

6. Loosen the charge air cooler inlet air hose clamp.

7. Remove the charge air cooler inlet air hose from the turbocharger.

8. Unlock the charge air cooler inlet air hose quick connector.

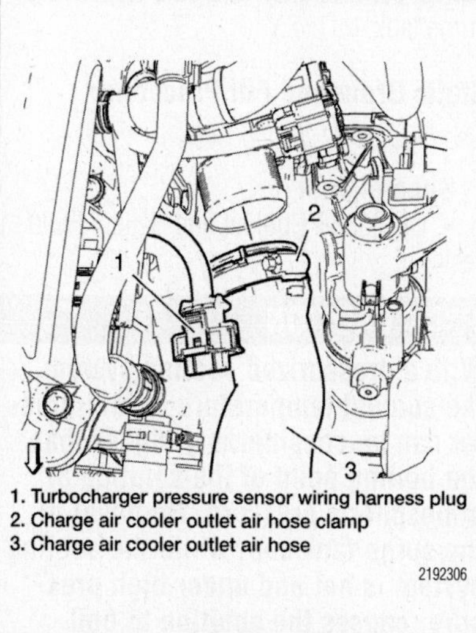

1. Turbocharger pressure sensor wiring harness plug
2. Charge air cooler outlet air hose clamp
3. Charge air cooler outlet air hose

Fig. 38 Remove the charge air cooler outlet air hose from the charge air cooler

9. Remove the charger air cooler inlet air hose.

10. Disconnect the turbocharger pressure sensor wiring harness plug.

11. Loosen the charge air cooler outlet air hose clamp.

12. Remove the charge air cooler outlet air hose from the throttle body.

13. Unclip the radiator inlet hose from the charge air cooler outlet air hose.

14. Remove the charge air cooler outlet air hose from the charge air cooler.

15. For automatic transaxle models:

    a. Unclip the transaxle fluid cooler from the radiator.

    b. Reposition the transaxle fluid cooler away from the radiator and secure.

16. Unclip the air conditioning condenser from the charge air cooler.

17. Reposition the air conditioning condenser forward and below the front bumper impact bar.

18. Unclip the charge air cooler from the radiator.

19. Lift the charge air cooler up and away from the radiator.

To install:

20. Clip the chevarge air cooler to the radiator.

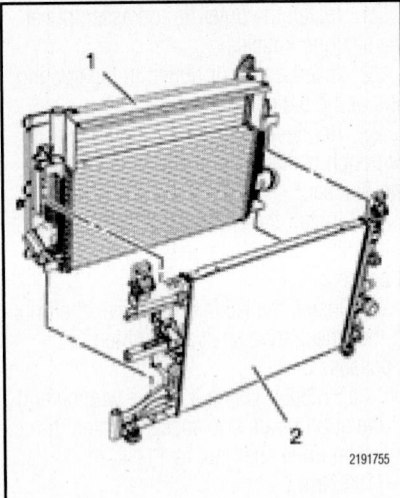

Fig. 39 Unclip the air conditioning condenser (2) from the charge air cooler (1)

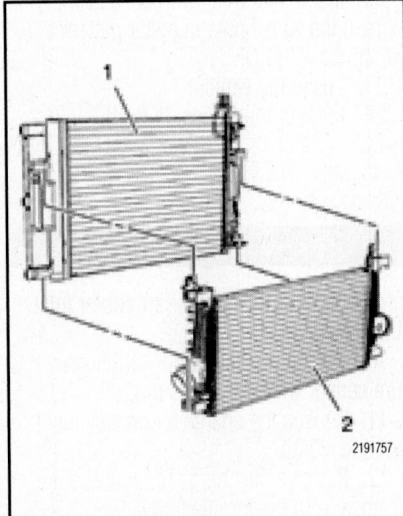

Fig. 40 Lift the charge air cooler (2) up and away from the radiator (1)

21. Clip the air conditioning condenser to the charge air cooler.

22. Clip the transaxle fluid cooler to the radiator.

23. Install the charge air cooler inlet air hose to the charge air cooler until it engages audibly.

24. Install the charge air cooler inlet air hose to the turbocharger.

25. Install and tighten the charge air cooler inlet air hose clamp.

26. Clip in the radiator inlet hose to the charge air cooler outlet air hose.

27. Install the charge air cooler outlet air hose to the charge air cooler.

28. Install the charge air cooler outlet air hose to the throttle body.

29. Install and tighten the charge air cooler outlet air hose clamp.

30. Connect the turbocharger pressure sensor wiring harness plug.

31. Install the left and right side radiator air baffles.

32. Install the radiator upper air seal.

33. Install the front bumper fascia.

34. Connect battery negative cable. Refer to Battery, removal & installation.

ENGINE COOLANT

DRAIN & REFILL PROCEDURE

❊❊ CAUTION

Always allow the engine to cool before opening the cooling system. Do not unscrew the coolant pressure relief cap when the engine is operating or the cooling system is hot. The cooling system is under pressure; steam and hot liquid can come out forcefully when the cap is loosened slightly. Failure to follow these instructions may result in serious personal injury.

➡ **The coolant must be recovered in a suitable, clean container for reuse. If the coolant is contaminated, it must be recycled or disposed of correctly. Using contaminated coolant may result in damage to the engine or cooling system components.**

➡ **The addition of stop leak pellets may darken engine coolant.**

Engine coolant provides boil protection, corrosion protection, freeze protection, and cooling efficiency to the engine and cooling components. In order to obtain these protections, maintain the engine coolant at the correct concentration and fluid level in the surge tank.

Static Drain and Fill Procedure

See Figures 41 through 43.

Special Tool
• GE-26568 Coolant and Battery Fluid Tester

❊❊ CAUTION

With a pressurized cooling system, the coolant temperature in the radiator can be considerably higher than the boiling point of the solution at atmospheric pressure. Removal of the surge tank cap, while the cooling system is hot and under high pressure, causes the solution to boil instantaneously with explosive force. This will cause the solution to spew

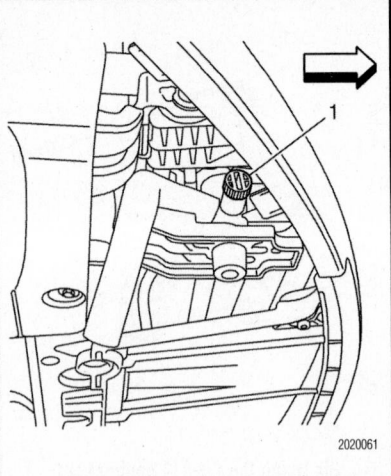

Fig. 41 Unscrew the radiator drain plug (1) until coolant flows out the radiator drain

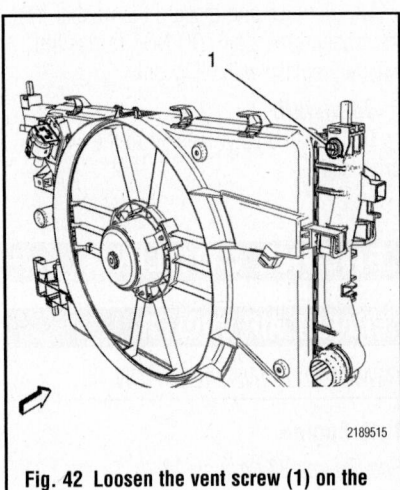

Fig. 42 Loosen the vent screw (1) on the radiator

out over the engine, the fenders, and the person removing the cap. Serious bodily injury may result.

1. Before servicing the vehicle, refer to the Precautions Section.

2. Unscrew the surge tank cap to remove vacuum when draining coolant.

3. Raise and safely support the vehicle.

4. Place a container under the radiator drain.

5. Unscrew the radiator drain plug until coolant flows out the radiator drain.

6. Follow the appropriate procedure based on the condition of the coolant:
   • Normal in appearance, continue with the filling procedure
   • Discolored, follow the flush procedure. Refer to Flushing procedure in this section.

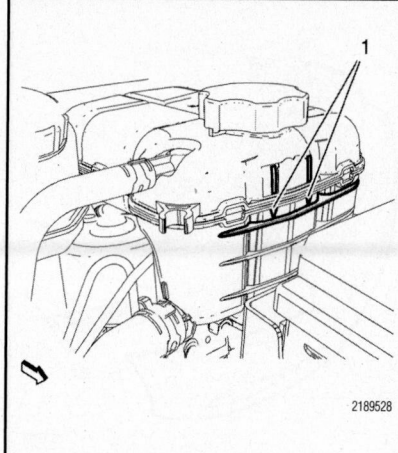

Fig. 43 Check the coolant level and fill to the "COLD" mark if necessary (1)

To fill:

7. Close the radiator drain plug.
8. Lower the vehicle. The vehicle should be level.
9. Loosen the vent screw on the radiator.

➡**Close vent screw when coolant begins to flow from the vent screw.**

10. Add a mixture of 50/50 DEX-COOL® antifreeze and clean drinkable water to the bottom line of the bleed nozzle on the coolant surge tank.
11. When the coolant level stabilizes, add enough coolant to reach the bottom line of the down pipe hole.
12. Start the Engine. After the engine starts, verify that the coolant level reaches the bottom line of the down pipe hole.
13. Install the surge tank cap.
14. Warm up the engine. Run at 2,500 RPM until the engine cooling fan turns ON.

➡**If the heater core has been replaced, let the engine run for 2 minutes at 2,000–2,500 RPM. This ensures complete venting of the cooling system.**

15. Turn the engine OFF and allow the engine to cool down.
16. Remove the surge tank cap.
17. Check the coolant level and fill to the "COLD" mark if necessary.

➡**After a test drive let the engine cool down again and check the coolant level. Adjust the coolant level to the "COLD" mark if necessary.**

18. Inspect the concentration of the engine coolant, using GE-26568 tester.
19. Install the surge tank cap.
20. Rinse away any excess coolant from the engine and the engine compartment.

Drain and Fill Using Coolant Refill Tool

See Figures 41, 44 and 45.

Special Tools
- GE-26568 Coolant and Battery Fluid Tester
- GE-42401-A Radiator Pressure Adapter
- GE-47716 Vac-N-Fill® Coolant Refill Tool

✴✴ WARNING

With a pressurized cooling system, the coolant temperature in the radiator can be considerably higher than the boiling point of the solution at atmospheric pressure. Removal of the surge tank cap, while the cooling system is hot and under high pressure, causes the solution to boil instantaneously with explosive force. This will cause the solution to spew out over the engine, the fenders, and the person removing the cap. Serious bodily injury may result.

1. Before servicing the vehicle, refer to the Precautions Section.
2. Unscrew the surge tank cap to remove vacuum when draining coolant.
3. Raise and safely support the vehicle.
4. Place a container under the radiator drain.
5. Unscrew the radiator drain plug until coolant flows out the radiator drain.
6. Follow the appropriate procedure based on the condition of the coolant:
   - Normal in appearance, continue with the filling procedure
   - Discolored, follow the flush procedure. Refer to Flushing procedure in this section.

To fill:

✴✴ WARNING

The procedure below must be followed. Improper coolant level could result in a low or high coolant level condition, causing engine damage.

7. Close the radiator drain cock by hand.

➡**To prevent boiling of the coolant/water mixture in the vehicle's cooling system, do not apply vacuum to a cooling system above 120° F (49° C). The tool will not operate properly when the coolant is boiling.**

8. Install GE-42401-2 adapter into the surge tank fill neck.

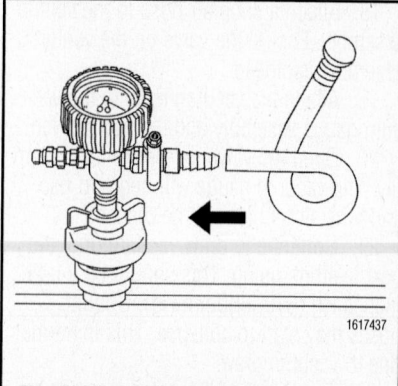

Fig. 44 Attach the vacuum gauge assembly to the Vac N Fill cap

9. Install GE-42401-3 adapter to the surge tank fill neck.
10. Attach the Vac N Fill cap to the GE-42401-3 adapter.
11. Attach the vacuum gauge assembly to the Vac N Fill cap.
12. Attach the fill hose to the barb fitting on the vacuum gauge assembly.
13. Ensure that the valve is closed.

➡**Use a 50/50 mixture of DEX-COOL® antifreeze and clean, drinkable water. Always use more coolant than necessary. This will eliminate air from being drawn into the cooling system.**

14. Pour the coolant mixture into the graduated reservoir.
15. Place the fill hose in the graduated reservoir.

➡**Prior to installing the vacuum tank onto the graduated reservoir, ensure that the drain valve located on the bottom of the tank is closed.**

16. Install the vacuum tank on the graduated reservoir with the fill hose routed through the cut-out area in the vacuum tank.
17. Attach the venturi assembly to the vacuum tank.

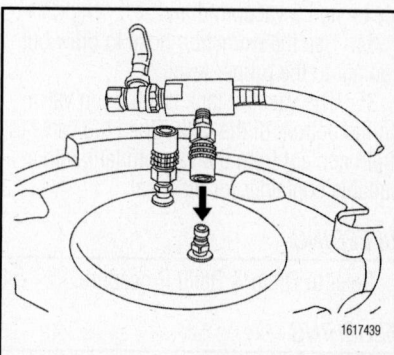

Fig. 45 Attach the venturi assembly to the vacuum tank

18. Attach a shop air hose to the venturi assembly. Ensure the valve on the venturi assembly is closed.

19. Attach the vacuum hose to the vacuum gauge assembly and the vacuum tank.

20. Open the valve on the venturi assembly. The vacuum gauge will begin to rise and a hissing noise will be present.

21. Continue to draw vacuum until the needle stops rising. This should be 24–26 inches Hg (610–660mm Hg). Cooling hoses may start to collapse. This is normal due to vacuum draw.

22. To aid in the fill process, position the graduated reservoir above the coolant fill port.

23. Slowly open the valve on the vacuum gauge assembly. When the coolant reaches the top of the fill hose, close the valve. This will eliminate air from the fill hose.

24. Close the valve on the venturi assembly.

25. If there is a suspected leak in the cooling system, allow the system to stabilize under vacuum and monitor for vacuum loss.

26. Open the valve on the vacuum gauge assembly. The vacuum gauge will drop as coolant is drawn into the system.

27. Once the vacuum gauge reaches zero, close the valve on the vacuum gauge assembly and repeat the above steps.

28. Detach the Vac N Fill cap from the vehicle's coolant fill port.

29. Add coolant to the system as necessary.

30. Inspect the concentration of the coolant mixture, using the GE-26568 tester.

➡After filling the cooling system, the extraction hose can be used to remove excess coolant to achieve the proper coolant level.

31. Detach the vacuum hose from the vacuum gauge assembly.

32. Attach the extraction hose to the vacuum hose.

33. Open the valve on the venturi assembly to start a vacuum draw.

34. Use the extraction hose to draw out coolant to the proper level.

35. The vacuum tank has a drain valve on the bottom of the tank. Open the valve to drain coolant from the vacuum tank into a suitable container for disposal.

BLEEDING

Refer to Drain & Refill Procedure.

FLUSHING

➡Do not use a chemical flush. Store used coolant in the proper manner, such as in a used engine coolant holding tank. Do not pour used coolant down a drain. Ethylene glycol antifreeze is a very toxic chemical. Do not dispose of coolant into the sewer system or ground water.

➡Various methods and equipment can be used to flush the cooling system. If special equipment is used, such as a back flusher, follow the manufacturer's instruction. However, always remove the thermostat before back flushing the system.

1. Before servicing the vehicle, refer to the Precautions Section.

2. Apply the parking brake.

3. Drain the coolant. Refer to Drain & Refill Procedure.

4. Fill the coolant system with clean drinkable water. Refer to Drain & Refill Procedure.

5. Start the engine and run at 2,000 RPM until the thermostat opens.

6. Turn OFF the engine.

7. Drain the coolant system. Refer to Drain & Refill Procedure.

8. Repeat the above procedure until the water from the coolant system is colorless.

9. Drain the coolant system. Refer to Drain & Refill Procedure.

10. Add 1.0 gallon (3.8 liters) of concentrated antifreeze since there will be some water in the system.

11. Add a mixture of 50/50 antifreeze and clean drinkable water until the level stabilizes at the weld seam on the surge tank. Refer to Drain & Refill Procedure.

ENGINE FAN

REMOVAL & INSTALLATION

See Figures 46 through 51.

➡It is not necessary to remove the hood latches and wiring clips from the front end upper tie bar for this procedure.

1. Before servicing the vehicle, refer to the Precautions Section.

2. Remove the front bumper fascia.

3. Remove the radiator support bracket.

4. Remove the radiator grille reinforcement support.

5. Remove and reposition the front end upper tie bar rearward.

6. Disconnect the battery negative cable. Refer to Battery, removal & installation.

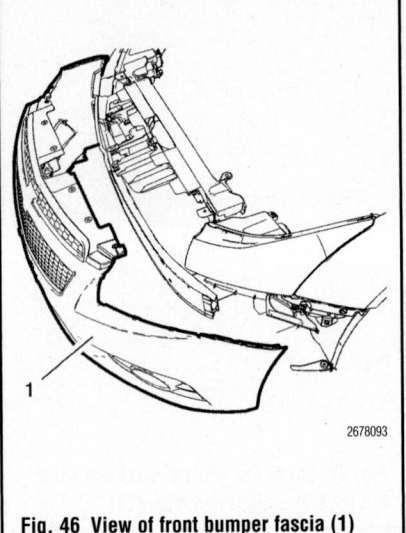

2678093

Fig. 46 View of front bumper fascia (1) removal

7. Remove the radiator upper air seal.

8. Remove the left and right side radiator air baffles.

9. Position the radiator assembly forward for engine coolant fan shroud access.

10. Disconnect the engine coolant fan resistor wiring harness connector and remove the ground cable nut.

11. Remove the wiring harness and clips.

12. Unclip the engine coolant fan shroud from the four mounting points shown.

13. Remove the engine coolant fan shroud.

   a. Slide the engine coolant fan shroud toward the right side of the vehicle.

   b. Lift the left hand side of the engine coolant fan shroud up.

   c. Remove the engine coolant fan shroud from the vehicle.

14. Remove the engine coolant fan resistor by unclipping the retainer clip.

15. Unclip the engine coolant fan resistor wiring harness from the shroud.

16. Remove the 3 engine coolant fan engine bolts from the engine coolant fan.

17. Remove the engine coolant fan.

To install:

18. Install the engine coolant fan.

19. Install the 3 engine coolant fan engine bolts to the engine coolant fan and tighten.

20. Clip in the engine coolant fan resistor wiring harness (arrows) to the shroud.

21. Install the engine coolant fan resistor by clipping the retainer clip.

22. Install the engine coolant fan shroud.

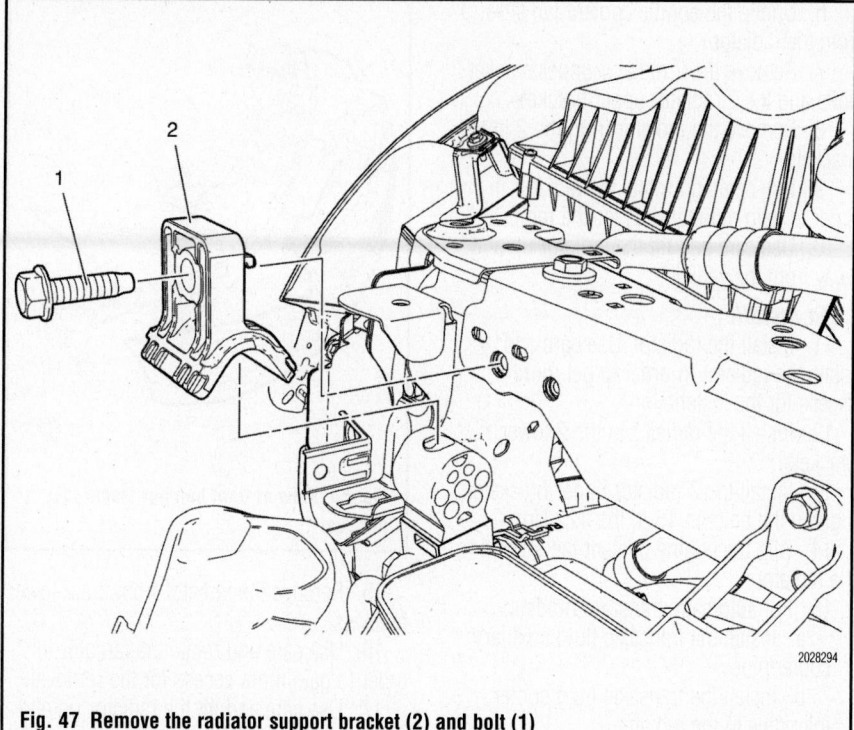

Fig. 47 Remove the radiator support bracket (2) and bolt (1)

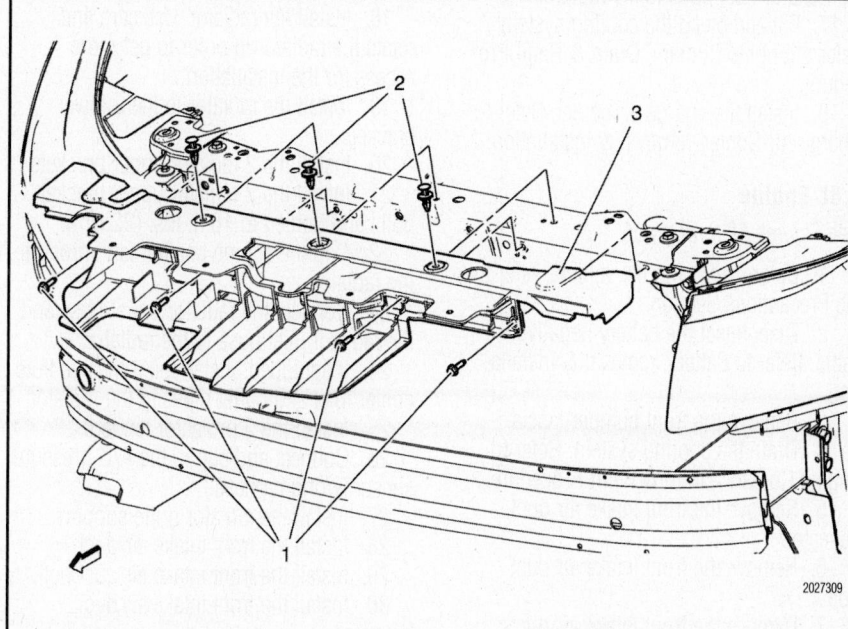

Fig. 48 Remove the radiator grille reinforcement support (3), support retainers (2), and bolts (1)

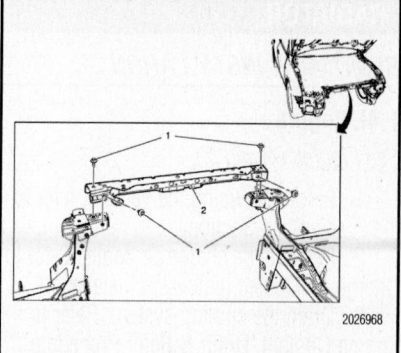

Fig. 49 Remove the bolts (1) and reposition the front end upper tie bar (2)

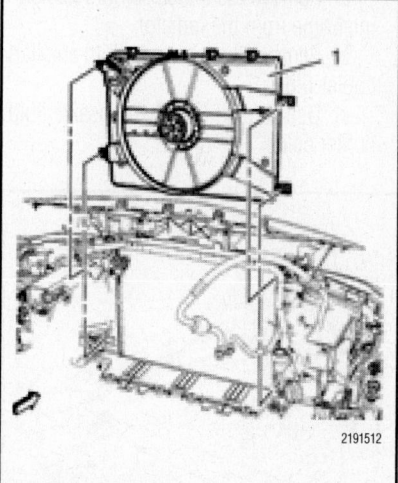

Fig. 50 Remove the engine coolant fan shroud (1)

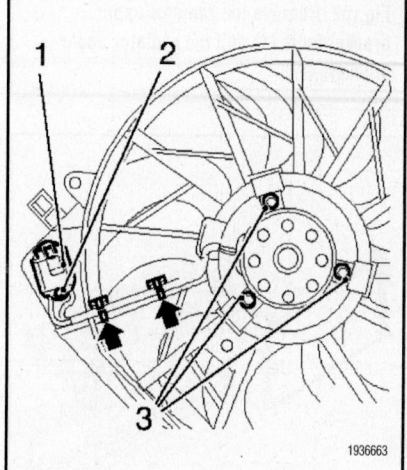

Fig. 51 Unclip the retainer clip (2) and remove the engine coolant fan resistor (1). Remove the 3 engine coolant fan engine bolts (3) and remove the engine coolant fan

a. Lower the right hand side of the engine coolant fan shroud behind the radiator.

b. Slide the engine coolant fan shroud toward the left side of the vehicle.

23. Clip in the engine coolant fan shroud to the four mounting points.

24. Connect the engine coolant fan resistor wiring harness connector.

25. Install the wiring harness and clips.

26. Install the front end upper tie bar.

27. Install the left and right side radiator air baffles.

28. Install the radiator upper air seal.

29. Connect battery negative cable. Refer to Battery, removal & installation.

RADIATOR

REMOVAL & INSTALLATION

1.4L Engine

See Figures 52 and 53.

1. Before servicing the vehicle, refer to the Precautions Section.

2. Remove the charge air cooler. Refer to Charge Air Cooler, removal & installation.

3. Drain the cooling system. Refer to Engine Coolant, Drain & Refill Procedure.

4. Disconnect the radiator outlet hose and the radiator inlet hose from the radiator.

5. For automatic transaxle models:

a. Remove the transaxle fluid cooler inlet pipe from the radiator.

b. Remove the transaxle fluid auxiliary cooler pipe.

c. Use care and lay the transaxle fluid cooler aside.

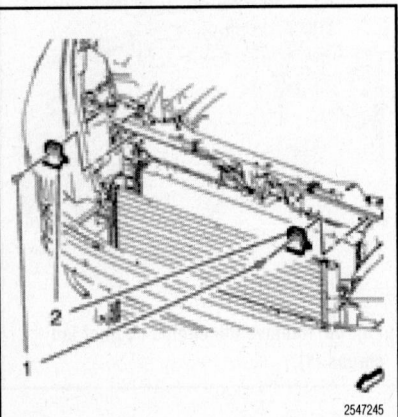

Fig. 52 Remove the radiator upper bracket bolts (1) and the radiator upper brackets (2)

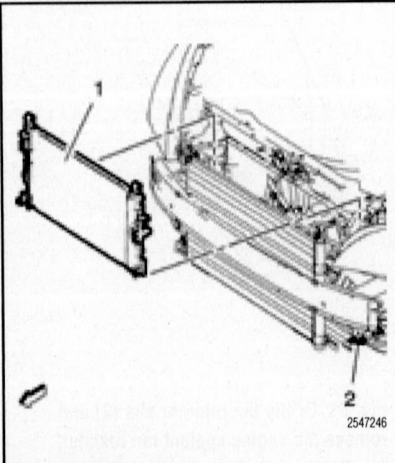

Fig. 53 Remove the radiator (1) from the lower brackets (2)

6. Unclip the engine coolant fan shroud from the radiator.

7. Remove the 2 radiator upper bracket bolts and the 2 radiator upper brackets.

8. Remove the radiator from the 2 lower brackets.

9. Use care and rotate the radiator in order to gain more access for the removal.

10. Use care and lift the radiator up and away from the vehicle.

To install:

11. Install the radiator. Use care and rotate the radiator in order to get more access for the installation.

12. Install the radiator to the 2 lower brackets.

13. Install the 2 radiator upper brackets. Tighten the bolts to 16 ft. lbs. (22 Nm).

14. Clip the engine coolant fan shroud to the radiator.

15. For automatic transaxle models:

a. Install the transaxle fluid auxiliary cooler pipe.

b. Install the transaxle fluid cooler inlet pipe to the radiator.

16. Connect the radiator outlet hose and the radiator inlet hose to the radiator.

17. Fill and bleed the cooling system. Refer to Engine Coolant, Drain & Refill Procedure.

18. Install the charge air cooler. Refer to Charge Air Cooler, removal & installation.

1.8L Engine

See Figures 52 through 55.

1. Before servicing the vehicle, refer to the Precautions Section.

2. Disconnect the battery negative cable. Refer to Battery, removal & installation.

3. Remove the front bumper fascia.

4. Drain the cooling system. Refer to Engine Coolant, Drain & Refill Procedure.

5. Remove the front intake air duct deflector.

6. Remove the front intake air duct bolt.

7. Remove the front intake air duct.

8. Remove the radiator grille support.

9. Disconnect and unclip the A/C pressure sensor wiring harness.

10. Remove the 2 protector fenders.

11. Disconnect the radiator outlet hose and the radiator inlet hose from the radiator.

12. If equipped, remove the transaxle fluid cooler inlet and outlet pipes from the radiator.

13. Unclip the engine coolant fan shroud from the radiator.

14. Remove the 2 radiator upper bracket bolts and the 2 radiator upper brackets.

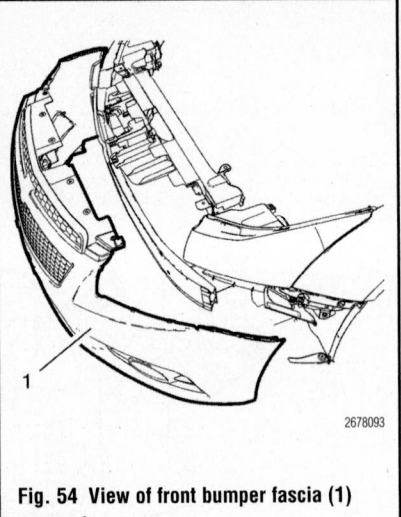

Fig. 54 View of front bumper fascia (1) removal

15. Remove the radiator from the 2 lower brackets.

16. Use care and rotate the radiator in order to gain more access for the removal.

17. Use care and lift the radiator up and away from the vehicle.

To install:

18. Install the radiator. Use care and rotate the radiator in order to get more access for the installation.

19. Install the radiator to the 2 lower brackets.

20. Install the 2 radiator upper brackets.

21. Install the 2 radiator upper bracket bolts and tighten to 16 ft. lbs. (22 Nm).

22. Clip the engine coolant fan shroud to the radiator.

23. Connect the radiator outlet hose and the radiator inlet hose to the radiator.

24. If equipped, install the transaxle fluid cooler inlet and outlet pipes to the radiator.

25. Install the 2 protector fenders.

26. Connect and clip in the A/C pressure sensor wiring harness.

27. Install the radiator grille support.

28. Install the front intake air duct.

29. Install the front intake air duct bolt.

30. Install the front intake air duct deflector.

31. Install the front bumper fascia.

32. Connect the battery negative cable. Refer to Battery, removal & installation.

33. Fill and bleed the cooling system. Refer to Engine Coolant, Drain & Refill Procedure.

THERMOSTAT

REMOVAL & INSTALLATION

1.4L Engine

See Figure 56.

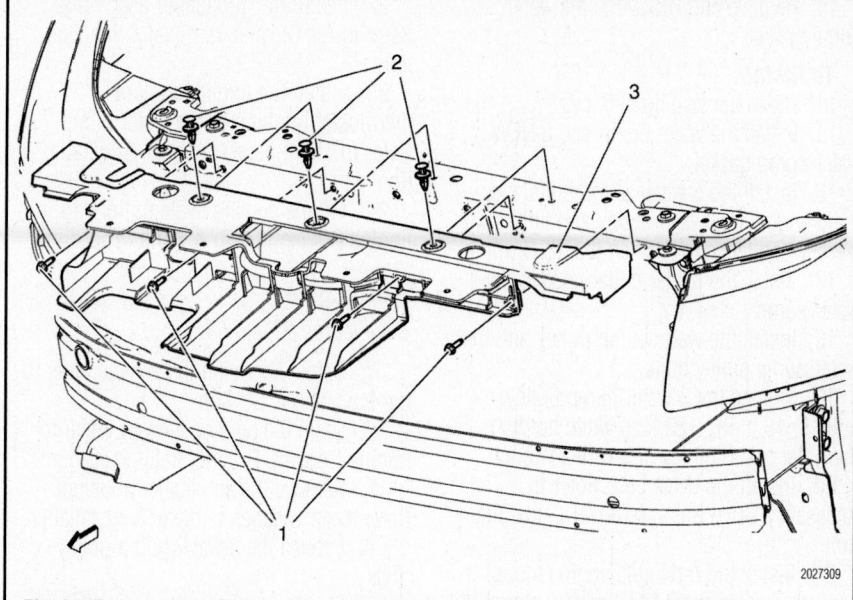

Fig. 55 Remove the radiator grille reinforcement support (3), support retainers (2), and bolts (1)

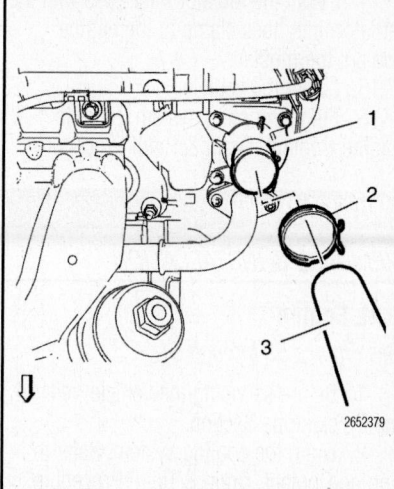

Fig. 57 Loosen the radiator inlet hose clamp (2) and remove the radiator inlet hose (3) from the engine coolant thermostat (1)

➡The thermostat is a regular part of the thermostat housing.

1. Before servicing the vehicle, refer to the Precautions Section.
2. Drain the cooling system. Refer to Engine Coolant, Drain & Refill Procedure.
3. Remove the air cleaner outlet duct.
4. Disconnect the positive crankcase ventilation pipe from the turbocharger.
5. Remove the radiator outlet hose from the engine coolant thermostat housing.
6. Disconnect the engine coolant temperature sensor wiring harness connector.
7. Remove the engine oil cooler outlet hose clamp.
8. Remove the engine oil cooler outlet hose from the engine coolant thermostat housing.
9. Remove the 3 engine coolant thermostat housing bolts.
10. Remove the engine coolant thermostat housing and the seal ring.

To install:
11. Clean the sealing surfaces.
12. Install the engine coolant thermostat housing along with a NEW seal ring.
13. Install the 3 engine coolant thermostat housing bolts and tighten to 71 inch lbs. (8 Nm).
14. Install the engine oil cooler outlet hose to the engine coolant thermostat housing.
15. Install the engine oil cooler outlet hose clamp.
16. Connect the engine coolant temperature sensor wiring harness connector.
17. Install the radiator outlet hose to the engine coolant thermostat housing.

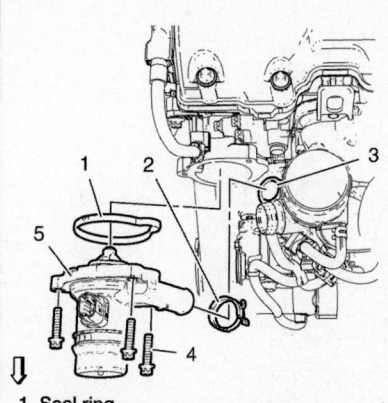

1. Seal ring
2. Engine oil cooler outlet hose clamp
3. Engine oil cooler outlet hose
4. Engine coolant thermostat housing bolts
5. Engine coolant thermostat housing

Fig. 56 Engine coolant thermostat housing removal

18. Connect the positive crankcase ventilation pipe to the turbocharger.
19. Install the air cleaner outlet duct.
20. Fill the cooling system. Refer to Engine Coolant, Drain & Refill Procedure.

1.8L Engine
See Figures 57 and 58.

❈❈ **WARNING**

Use care when performing this procedure. Use of excessive force may damage the coolant thermostat.

1. Before servicing the vehicle, refer to the Precautions Section.
2. Raise and safely support the vehicle.
3. Place a drain pan below the vehicle.
4. Drain the cooling system. Refer to Engine Coolant, Drain & Refill Procedure.
5. Loosen the radiator inlet hose clamp.
6. Remove the radiator inlet hose from the engine coolant thermostat.
7. Remove the 4 engine coolant thermostat bolts.
8. Remove the engine coolant thermostat assembly.
9. Remove the engine coolant seal.

To install:
10. Clean the engine coolant sealing surfaces.
11. Install the engine coolant seal.
12. Install the engine coolant thermostat assembly.
13. Install the 4 engine coolant thermostat bolts and tighten to 71 inch lbs. (8 Nm).

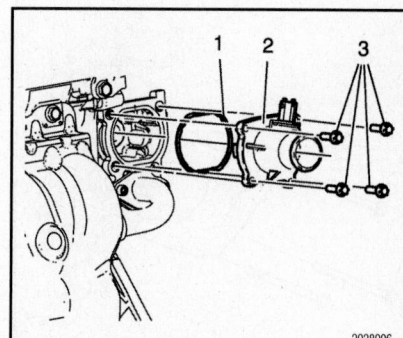

Fig. 58 Remove the engine coolant thermostat bolts (3), thermostat assembly (2), and coolant seal (1)

14. Install the radiator inlet hose with the radiator inlet hose clamp to the engine coolant thermostat.

15. Lower the vehicle.

16. Fill the cooling system. Refer to Engine Coolant, Drain & Refill Procedure.

WATER PUMP

REMOVAL & INSTALLATION

1.4L Engine

See Figures 59 through 61.

1. Before servicing the vehicle, refer to the Precautions Section.

2. Drain the cooling system. Refer to Engine Coolant, Drain & Refill Procedure.

3. Remove the engine coolant thermostat housing from the water pump. Refer to Thermostat, removal & installation.

4. Remove the air cleaner assembly. Refer to Air Cleaner, removal & installation.

5. Remove the right side engine mount bracket.

6. Remove the drive belt. Refer to Accessory Drive Belts, removal & installation.

7. Loosen the 3 water pump pulley bolts while holding the water pump pulley hub with a wrench.

8. Remove the 3 water pump pulley bolts.

9. Remove the water pump pulley.

10. Remove the heater outlet hose from the water pump.

11. Remove the 5 water pump bolts and the 5 long engine front cover bolts.

➡ **The bolts are not identical and must be kept in the order of their removal for ease of installation.**

12. Remove the water pump.

13. Remove and DISCARD the water pump gasket.

To install:

14. Clean the sealing surfaces.

15. Install the water pump and a NEW water pump gasket.

16. Install the 5 water pump bolts and the 5 engine front cover bolts and tighten in a cross sequence to 71 inch lbs. (8 Nm).

17. Install the heater outlet hose to the water pump.

18. Install the water pump pulley and the water pump pulley bolts.

19. Tighten the 3 water pump pulley bolts to 16 ft. lbs. (22 Nm) while holding the water pump pulley hub with a wrench.

20. Install the drive belt. Refer to Accessory Drive Belts, removal & installation.

21. Install the right side engine mount bracket. Tighten the 3 NEW engine mount bracket bolts to 45 ft. lbs. (60 Nm), plus 45–60°.

22. Install the air cleaner assembly. Refer to Air Cleaner, removal & installation.

23. Install the engine coolant thermostat housing to the water pump. Refer to Thermostat, removal & installation.

24. Fill the cooling system. Refer to Engine Coolant, Drain & Refill Procedure.

1.8L Engine

See Figures 62 and 63.

1. Before servicing the vehicle, refer to the Precautions Section.

2. Drain the cooling system. Refer to Engine Coolant, Drain & Refill Procedure.

3. Remove the air cleaner housing. Refer to Air Cleaner, removal & installation.

4. Loosen the 3 water pump pulley bolts.

➡ **Use the crankshaft balancer bolt for a counterhold.**

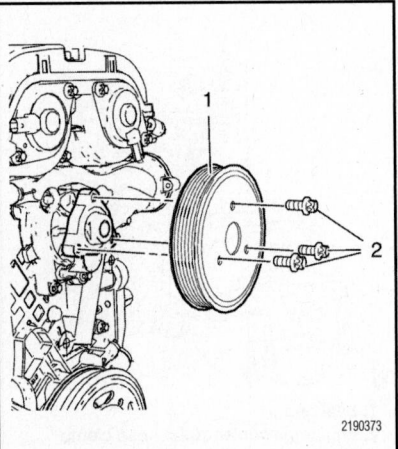

Fig. 60 View of water pump pulley (1) and pulley bolts (2)—1.4L engine

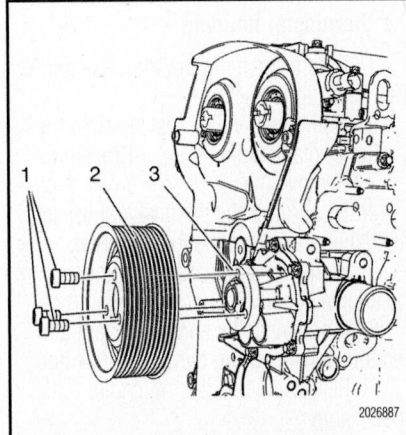

Fig. 62 View of water pump pulley (2), bolts (1), and water pump (3)—1.8L engine

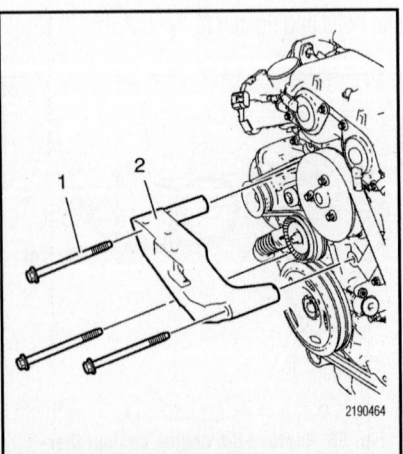

Fig. 59 View of right side engine mount bracket (2) and bolts (1)—1.4L engine

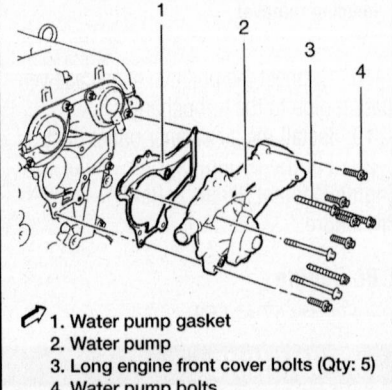

1. Water pump gasket
2. Water pump
3. Long engine front cover bolts (Qty: 5)
4. Water pump bolts

Fig. 61 Exploded view of water pump—1.4L engine

Fig. 63 Removing the water pump (1) and bolts (2)—1.8L engine

5. Remove the drive belt. Refer to Accessory Drive Belts, removal & installation.

6. Remove the 3 water pump pulley bolts.

7. Remove the water pump pulley from the water pump.

8. Remove the 5 water pump bolts.

9. Remove the water pump.

10. Remove and DISCARD the water pump seal ring.

To install:

11. Clean the 5 water pump threads.

12. Clean the water pump sealing surface.

13. Insert a NEW water pump seal ring.

14. Install the water pump.

15. Install the 5 water pump bolts and tighten to 71 inch lbs. (8 Nm).

16. Install the water pump pulley to the water pump.

17. Install the 3 water pump pulley bolts.

18. Install the drive belt. Refer to Accessory Drive Belts, removal & installation.

19. Tighten the 3 water pump pulley bolts to 15 ft. lbs. (20 Nm).

20. Install the air cleaner housing. Refer to Air Cleaner, removal & installation.

21. Refill the cooling system. Refer to Engine Coolant, Drain & Refill Procedure.

ENGINE ELECTRICAL

BATTERY SYSTEM

BATTERY

REMOVAL & INSTALLATION

See Figures 64 through 68.

1. Before servicing the vehicle, refer to the Precautions Section.

2. Turn on the radio and record all of the radio station presets.

3. Ensure that all of the lamps and accessories are turned OFF.

4. Turn the ignition Off and remove the ignition key.

5. Remove the battery cover.

❋❋ WARNING

Mind the 3 battery cover retainer clips (arrows). The battery cover could be damaged if the retainer clips are not fully unlocked.

6. Remove the battery negative cable from the battery.

7. Unlock the retaining tab on the battery fuse box cover.

8. Use a suitable screwdriver to unlock the clip through the window.

➡**Pull the battery fuse box housing. DO NOT pull the flap.**

9. Open the battery fuse box cover.

10. Remove the battery hold down retainer nut.

11. Remove the battery hold down retainer.

12. Remove the battery positive cable to starter cable nut.

13. Remove the battery positive cable to starter cable.

14. Loosen the 2 battery positive plate nuts.

15. Loosen the battery positive cable nut.

16. Remove the battery positive cable.

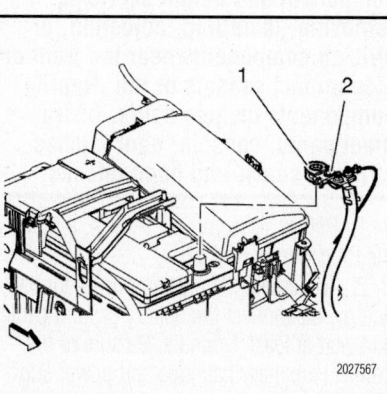

Fig. 65 Loosen the nut (2) and remove the battery negative cable (1) from the battery

17. Unclip the battery fuse block retainer clips from the battery and remove the battery fuse block along with the battery positive cable.

18. Unclip the battery tray protector retainer from battery tray.

19. Remove the battery tray protector by moving rearward.

20. Move the battery forward and lift to remove.

To install:

21. Install the battery and move rearward until it rests against the battery tray.

22. Install the battery tray protector to the battery tray and move it forward until the retainer engages with the battery tray.

23. Align the rear side of the battery fuse box exactly to the rear side of the battery.

24. Install the battery positive cable to the battery.

25. Tighten the battery positive cable nut to 40 inch lbs. (5 Nm).

26. Tighten the 2 battery positive plate nuts to 106 inch lbs. (12 Nm).

27. Install the battery positive cable-to-starter cable.

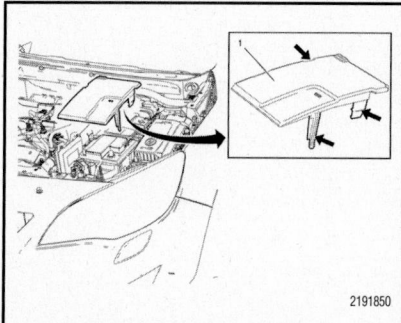

Fig. 64 Battery cover (1) removal

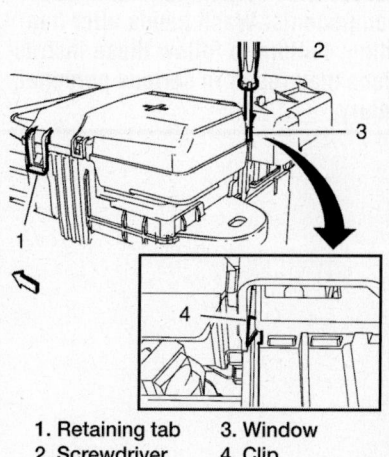

1. Retaining tab 3. Window
2. Screwdriver 4. Clip

Fig. 66 Unlock the retaining tab on the battery fuse box cover

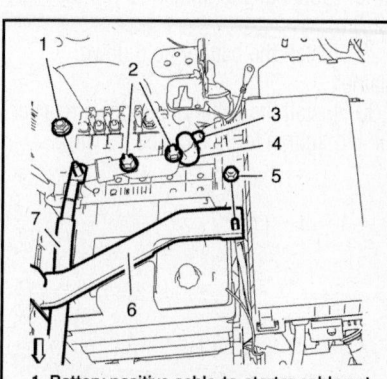

1. Battery positive cable-to-starter cable nut
2. Battery positive plate nuts
3. Battery positive cable nut
4. Battery positive cable
5. Battery hold down retainer nut
6. Battery hold down retainer
7. Battery positive cable-to-starter cable

Fig. 67 Removing the battery hold down and cables

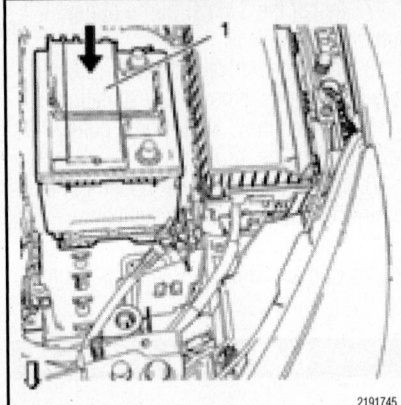

Fig. 68 Move the battery (1) forward, in the direction of the arrow, and lift to remove

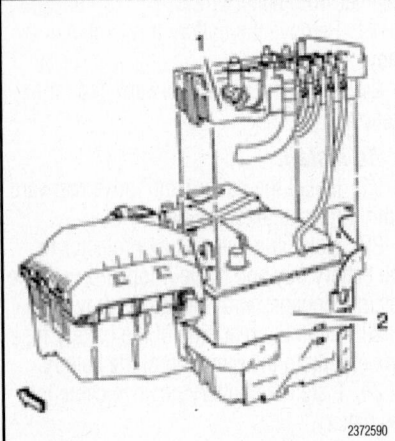

Fig. 69 Align the rear side of the battery fuse box (1) exactly to the rear side of the battery (2)

28. Install the battery positive cable-to-starter cable nut and tighten to 106 inch lbs. (12 Nm).

29. Install the battery hold down retainer.

30. Install the battery hold down retainer nut and tighten to 80 inch lbs. (9 Nm).

31. Close the battery fuse box cover and lock the retaining tabs.

32. Install the battery negative cable to the battery.

33. Fasten the battery negative cable nut and tighten the nut to 40 inch lbs. (5 Nm).

34. Install the battery cover.

35. Insert the ignition key and turn the ignition to the ON position.

36. Program the volatile memory. Refer to Battery Reconnect/Relearn Procedure.

37. Program all of the radio station presets and set the radio clock to the current time.

BATTERY RECONNECT/RELEARN PROCEDURE

> **✳ CAUTION**
>
> **Always deplete the backup power supply before repairing or installing any new front or side air bag Supplemental Restraint System (SRS) component and before servicing, removing, installing, adjusting, or striking components near the front or side impact sensors or the. Nearby components include doors, instrument panel, console, door latches, strikers, seats, and hood latches.**

1. Before servicing the vehicle, refer to the Precautions Section.

2. To deplete the backup power supply energy, disconnect the battery ground cable and wait at least 1 minute. Be sure to disconnect auxiliary batteries and power supplies (if equipped).

> **✳ CAUTION**
>
> **Battery posts, terminals and related accessories contain lead and lead components. Wash hands after handling. Failure to follow these instructions may result in serious personal injury.**

3. When the battery (or ECM) is disconnected and connected, some abnormal drive symptoms may occur while the vehicle relearns its adaptive strategy. The charging system set point may also vary. The vehicle may need to be driven to relearn its strategy.

Electric Window Lifters

1. Before servicing the vehicle, refer to the Precautions Section.

2. Move all the windows to the topmost position and hold the switch pressed down for 2 seconds.

Sliding Sunroof

1. Before servicing the vehicle, refer to the Precautions Section.

2. Move the sliding roof to the respective end stops to recalibrate the sensors.

Initialize Steering Angle Sensor (Vehicles without ESP and with Electric Power Steering)

> **✳ CAUTION**
>
> **For vehicles with Electric Power Steering (EPS) and without a vehicle stability enhancement program, the steering angle sensor MUST always be initialized after the battery has been disconnected. Failure to initialize the steering angle sensor could limit the operation of the EPS system and result in personal injury.**

1. Before servicing the vehicle, refer to the Precautions Section.

2. To ensure proper initialization of the EPS system, do the following:

   a. The engine should be on with the vehicle stationary.

   b. Turn the steering wheel counterclockwise until it stops.

   c. Turn the steering wheel clockwise until it stops.

ENGINE ELECTRICAL

CHARGING SYSTEM

ALTERNATOR

REMOVAL & INSTALLATION

1.4L Engine

See Figures 70 and 71.

1. Before servicing the vehicle, refer to the Precautions Section.
2. Disconnect the battery negative cable. Refer to Battery, removal & installation.
3. Raise and safely support the vehicle.
4. Disconnect the alternator wiring harness connector.
5. Remove the alternator positive cable nut.
6. Remove the alternator positive cable.
7. Lower the vehicle.
8. Remove the drive belt tensioner. Refer to Drive Belt Tensioner, removal & installation.
9. Remove the 2 alternator bolts.
10. Remove the alternator from above.

To install:

11. Install the alternator from above.
12. Install the 2 alternator bolts and tighten to 26 ft. lbs. (35 Nm).
13. Install the drive belt tensioner. Refer to Drive Belt Tensioner, removal & installation.
14. Raise and safely support the vehicle.
15. Connect the alternator wiring harness connector.
16. Install the alternator positive cable.
17. Install the alternator positive cable nut and tighten to 13 ft. lbs. (17 Nm).
18. Lower the vehicle.

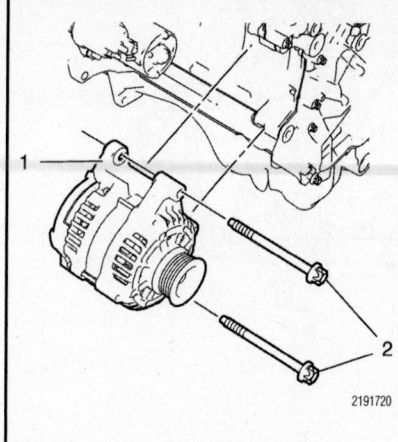

Fig. 71 Remove the alternator bolts (2) and the alternator (1)—1.4L engine

19. Connect the battery negative cable. Refer to Battery, removal & installation.

Drive Belt Tensioner

See Figures 72 through 76.

1. Before servicing the vehicle, refer to the Precautions Section.
2. Remove the air cleaner assembly. Refer to Air Cleaner, removal & installation.
3. Install an engine lifter to the right engine lift bracket and apply tension to the engine lifter chain in order to support the engine.
4. Remove and DISCARD the 3 engine mount-to-engine mount bracket bolts and the 3 washers.
5. Remove the 2 engine mount-to-body bolts and the engine mount nut.

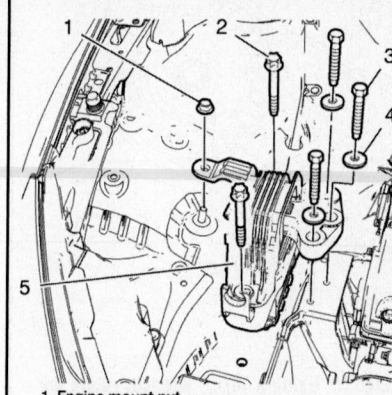

1. Engine mount nut
2. Engine mount-to-body bolts
3. Engine mount-to-engine mount bracket bolts
4. Washers
5. Engine mount

Fig. 73 Remove the engine mount—1.4L engine

6. Remove the engine mount.
7. Remove and DISCARD the 3 engine mount bracket bolts.
8. Remove the engine mount bracket.
9. Using a Torx® wrench, rotate the drive belt tensioner pulley bolt until the bore aligns with the bore in the engine front cover.
10. Install a suitable punch through the drive belt tensioner bore to the engine front cover bore to fix the tensioner in position.
11. Remove the drive belt.
12. Move the drive belt tensioner until the punch can be removed and remove the punch from the engine front cover bore and drive belt tensioner bore.

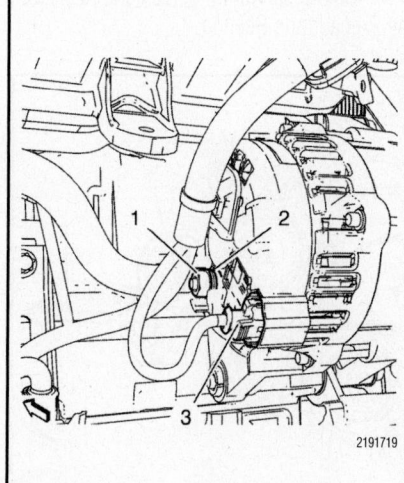

Fig. 70 Alternator connections shown—1.4L engine

Fig. 72 Install an engine lifter (1) to the right engine lift bracket—1.4L engine

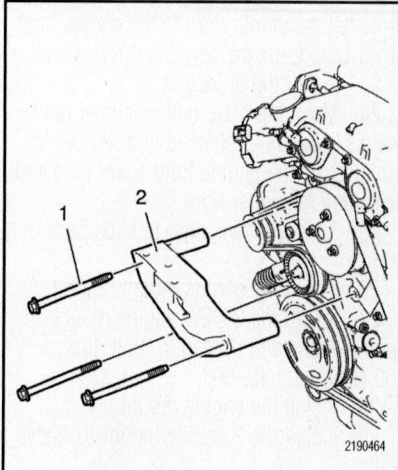

Fig. 74 Remove engine mount bracket bolts (1) and the engine mount bracket (2)—1.4L engine

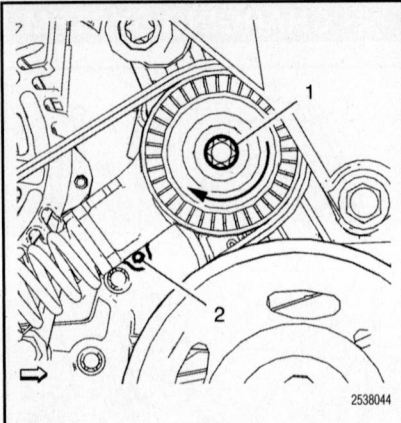

Fig. 75 Using a Torx® wrench, rotate the drive belt tensioner pulley bolt (1) in the direction shown until the bore (2) aligns with the bore in the engine front cover—1.4L engine

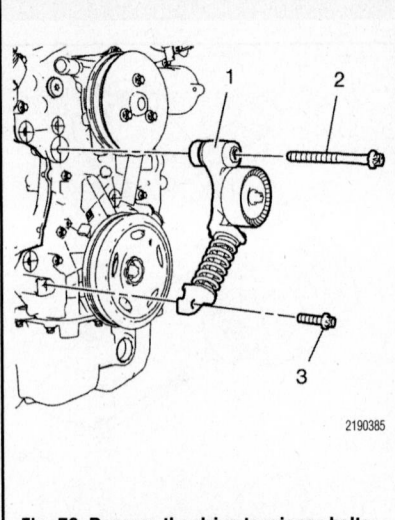

Fig. 76 Remove the drive tensioner bolts (2, 3) and drive belt tensioner (1)

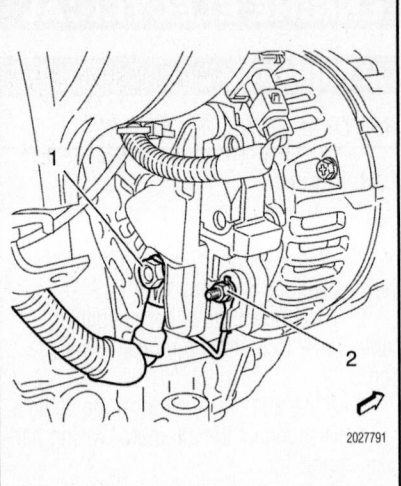

Fig. 77 Remove the alternator wiring harness nut (2) and positive cable nut (1)—1.8L engine

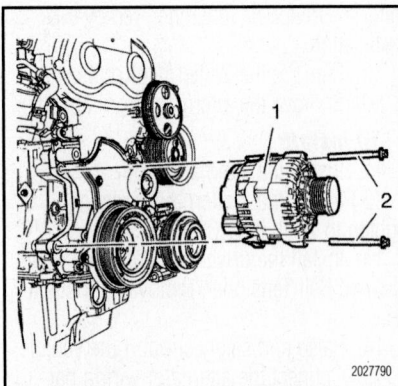

Fig. 78 Remove the alternator bolts (2) and the alternator (1)—1.8L engine

13. Remove the upper drive belt tensioner bolt.

14. Remove the lower drive belt tensioner bolt.

15. Remove the drive belt tensioner.

To install:

16. Install the drive belt tensioner.

17. Install the lower drive belt tensioner bolt.

18. Install the upper drive belt tensioner bolt.

19. Tighten the lower drive belt tensioner bolt to 16 ft. lbs. (22 Nm).

20. Tighten the upper drive belt tensioner bolt to 41 ft. lbs. (55 Nm).

21. Using a Torx® wrench, rotate the drive belt tensioner pulley bolt in the direction shown until the bore aligns with the bore in the engine front cover.

22. Install a suitable punch through the drive belt tensioner bore to the engine front cover bore to fix the tensioner in position.

23. Install the drive belt.

24. Move the drive belt tensioner until the punch can be removed and remove the punch from the engine front cover bore and drive belt tensioner bore.

25. Allow the tensioner to slide back slowly.

26. Install the engine mount bracket.

27. Install the 3 NEW engine mount bracket bolts and tighten to 45 ft. lbs. (60 Nm), plus 45–60°.

28. Install the engine mount.

29. Install the 2 engine mount-to-body bolts.

30. Install the engine mount nut.

31. Install the 3 NEW engine mount-to-engine mount bracket bolts and the 3 washers.

32. Tighten the 2 engine mount-to-body bolts and the engine mount nut to 46 ft. lbs. (62 Nm).

33. Tighten the 3 engine mount-to-engine mount bracket bolts to 37 ft. lbs. (50 Nm), plus 60–70°.

34. Remove the engine lifter from the right engine lift bracket.

35. Install the air cleaner assembly. Refer to Air Cleaner, removal & installation.

1.8L Engine

See Figures 77 and 78.

1. Before servicing the vehicle, refer to the Precautions Section.

2. Disconnect the battery negative cable. Refer to Battery, removal & installation.

3. Remove the alternator and air conditioning compressor belt. Refer to Accessory Drive Belts, removal & installation.

4. Remove the alternator wiring harness nut.

5. Remove the alternator positive cable nut.

6. Remove the 2 alternator bolts.

7. Remove the alternator.

To install:

8. Install the alternator.

9. Install the 2 alternator bolts and tighten to 26 ft. lbs. (35 Nm).

10. Install the alternator wiring harness nut and tighten to 15 ft. lbs. (20 Nm).

11. Install the alternator positive cable nut and tighten to 62 inch lbs. (7 Nm).

12. Install the alternator and air conditioning compressor belt. Refer to Accessory Drive Belts, removal & installation.

13. Connect the battery negative cable. Refer to Battery, removal & installation.

Drive Belt Tensioner

See Figure 79.

1. Before servicing the vehicle, refer to the Precautions Section.

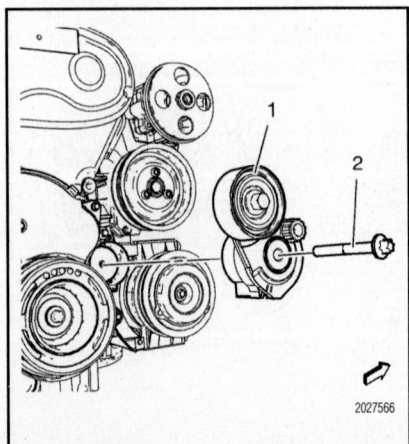

Fig. 79 Remove the drive belt tensioner bolt (2) and the drive belt tensioner (1)

2. Remove the alternator and air conditioning compressor belt. Refer to Accessory Drive Belts, removal & installation.

3. Remove the drive belt tensioner bolt.

4. Remove the drive belt tensioner.

To install:

5. Clean the drive belt tensioner threads.

6. Install the drive belt tensioner.

7. Install the drive belt tensioner

bolt and tighten to 41 inch lbs. (55 Nm).

8. Install the alternator and air conditioning compressor belt. Refer to Accessory Drive Belts, removal & installation.

ENGINE ELECTRICAL

IGNITION SYSTEM

FIRING ORDER

1.4L and 1.8L Engine firing order: 1–3–4–2

IGNITION COIL

REMOVAL & INSTALLATION

1.4L Engine

See Figures 80 through 83.

Special Tools

• EN-6009 Remover and Installer Ignition Module

1. Before servicing the vehicle, refer to the Precautions Section.

2. Remove the engine sight shield.

3. Disconnect the ignition coil wiring harness plug from the ignition coil.

4. Remove the 2 ignition coil bolts.

5. Install EN-6009 remover/installer to the ignition coil.

6. Remove the ignition coil.

To install:

7. Install the ignition coil.

8. Remove EN-6009 remover from the ignition coil.

9. Install the 2 ignition coil bolts and tighten to 71 inch lbs. (8 Nm).

10. Connect the ignition coil wiring harness plug to the ignition coil.

11. Install the engine sight shield.

1.8L Engine

See Figures 80, 84 and 85.

Special Tools

• EN-6009 Remover and Installer Ignition Module

1. Before servicing the vehicle, refer to the Precautions Section.

2. Remove the engine wiring harness guide from the cylinder head.

3. Disconnect the ignition coil plug.

➡**Note the arrow on the cover.**

4. Remove the cover of the ignition coil in the direction of the arrow.

5. Remove the 2 ignition coil bolts.

6. Install the EN-6009 remover/installer.

7. Remove the ignition coil.

8. Remove the EN-6009 remover/installer.

To install:

9. Install the EN-6009 remover/installer.

10. Install the ignition coil.

11. Remove the EN-6009 remover/installer.

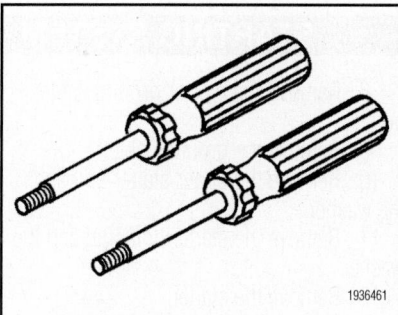

Fig. 80 View of Special Tool: EN-6009 Remover and Installer Ignition Module

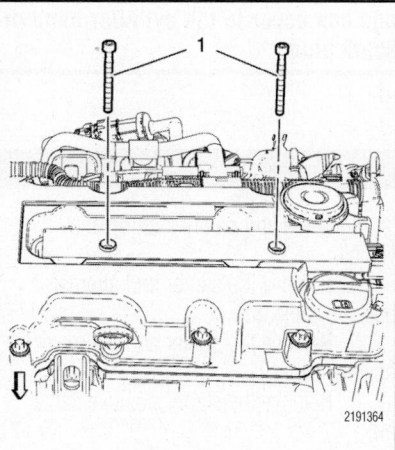

Fig. 82 Remove the 2 ignition coil bolts (1)—1.4L engine

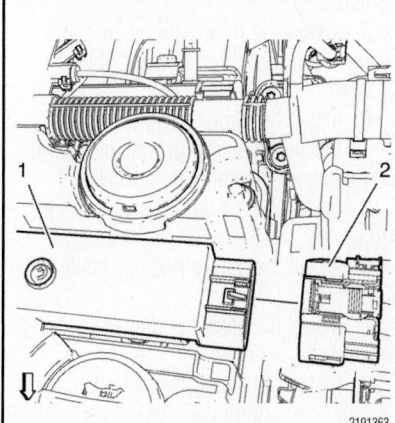

Fig. 81 Disconnect the ignition coil wiring harness plug (2) from the ignition coil (1)—1.4L engine

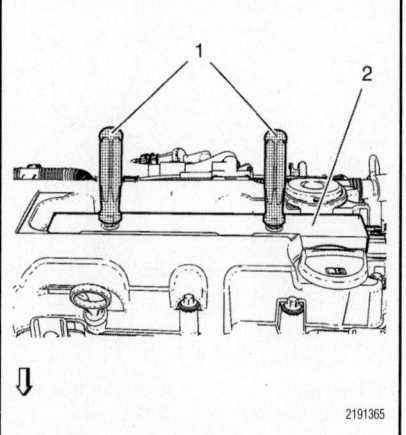

Fig. 83 Using Special Tool, EN-6009 remover/installer (1), to remove the ignition coil (2)—1.4L engine

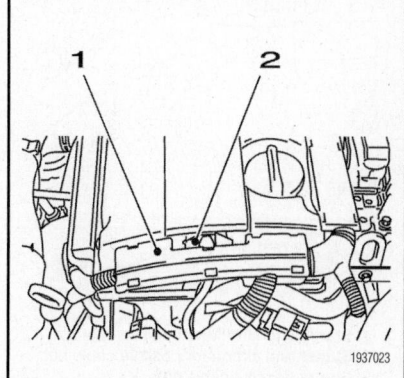

Fig. 84 Remove the engine wiring harness guide (1) from the cylinder head and disconnect the ignition coil plug (2)—1.8L engine

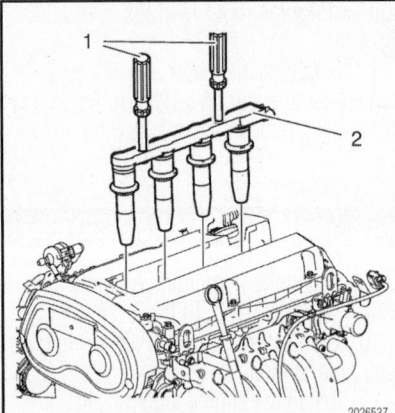

Fig. 85 Using Special Tool, EN-6009 remover/installer (1), to remove the ignition coil (2)—1.8L engine

12. Install the 2 ignition coil bolts and tighten to 71 inch lbs. (8 Nm).
13. Install the ignition coil cover in the direction of the arrow.
14. Connect the ignition coil plug.
15. Install the engine wiring harness guide at the cylinder head.

IGNITION TIMING

ADJUSTMENT

The ignition timing is controlled by the Engine Control Module (ECM). No adjustment is necessary.

SPARK PLUGS

REMOVAL & INSTALLATION

See Figure 86.

1. Before servicing the vehicle, refer to the Precautions Section.
2. With the 1.4L engine: remove the engine sight shield.
3. Remove the ignition coil. Refer to Ignition Coil, removal & installation.

✳✳ WARNING

Only use hand tools when removing or installing the spark plugs, or damage can occur to the cylinder head or spark plug.

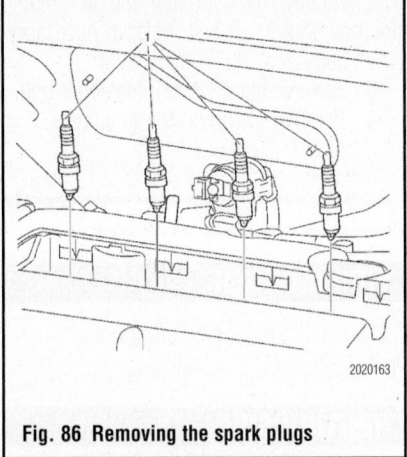

Fig. 86 Removing the spark plugs

4. Use compressed air to remove any foreign material in the spark plug wells prior to removing the spark plugs.
5. Remove the spark plugs.

To install:

6. Installation is the reverse of the removal procedure.
7. Tighten the spark plugs to 18 ft. lbs. (25 Nm).

ENGINE ELECTRICAL

STARTER

REMOVAL & INSTALLATION

1.4L Engine

See Figures 87 and 88.

1. Before servicing the vehicle, refer to the Precautions Section.
2. Disconnect the battery negative cable. Refer to Battery, removal & installation.

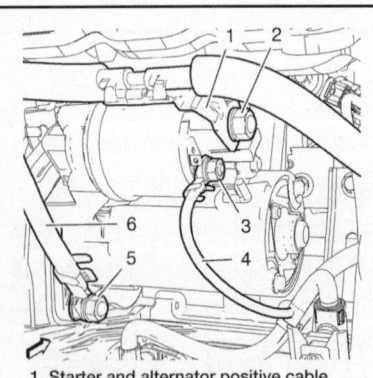

1. Starter and alternator positive cable
2. Starter and alternator positive cable nut
3. Starter positive cable nut
4. Starter positive cable
5. Starter ground cable nut
6. Ground cable

Fig. 87 View of starter electrical connections—1.4L engine

3. Raise and safely support the vehicle.
4. Remove the starter and alternator positive cable nut.
5. Remove the starter and alternator positive cable.
6. Remove the starter positive cable nut.
7. Remove the starter positive cable from the starter.

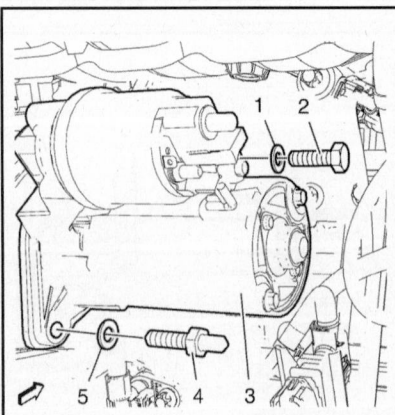

1. Washer
2. Upper starter bolt
3. Starter
4. Starter bolt stud
5. Washer

Fig. 88 Starter bolt location—1.4L engine

STARTING SYSTEM

8. Remove the starter ground cable nut.
9. Remove the ground cable.
10. Remove the upper starter bolt and the washer.
11. Remove the starter bolt stud and the washer.
12. Remove the starter.

To install:

13. Install the starter.
14. Install the washer and the starter bolt stud and tighten to 18 ft. lbs. (25 Nm).
15. Install the upper starter bolt and the washer and tighten to 18 ft. lbs. (25 Nm).
16. Install the ground cable.
17. Install the starter ground cable nut and tighten to 111 inch lbs. (13 Nm).
18. Install the starter positive cable to starter.
19. Install the starter positive cable nut and tighten.
20. Install the starter and alternator positive cable.
21. Install the starter and alternator positive cable nut and tighten to 111 inch lbs. (13 Nm).
22. Lower the vehicle.
23. Connect the battery negative cable. Refer to Battery, removal & installation.

1.8L Engine

See Figures 89 and 90.

1. Before servicing the vehicle, refer to the Precautions Section.

2. Disconnect the negative cable from the battery. Refer to Battery, removal & installation.

3. Remove the air cleaner outlet duct. Refer to Air Cleaner, removal & installation.

4. Raise and safely support the vehicle.

5. Remove the 2 intake manifold brace bolts.

6. Remove the intake manifold brace.

7. Remove the starter and alternator positive cable nut.

8. Remove the starter and alternator positive cable.

9. Remove the starter positive cable nut and the positive cable.

10. Remove the starter negative cable nut and the negative cable.

11. Remove the starter stud and the starter bolt.

12. Remove the starter.

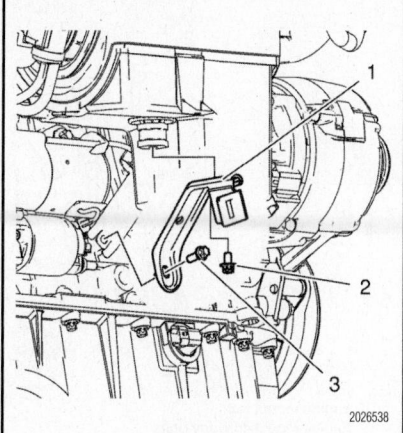

Fig. 89 Removing the intake manifold brace (1) and brace bolts (2, 3)—1.8L engine

To install:

13. Installation is the reverse of the removal procedure.

14. Install the starter.

15. Tighten the starter bolt to 18 ft. lbs. (25 Nm).

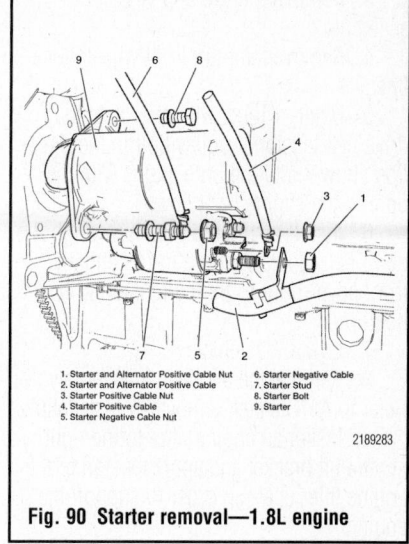

1. Starter and Alternator Positive Cable Nut
2. Starter and Alternator Positive Cable
3. Starter Positive Cable Nut
4. Starter Positive Cable
5. Starter Negative Cable Nut
6. Starter Negative Cable
7. Starter Stud
8. Starter Bolt
9. Starter

Fig. 90 Starter removal—1.8L engine

16. Tighten the starter stud to 18 ft. lbs. (25 Nm).

17. Tighten the starter negative cable nut to 111 inch lbs. (13 Nm).

18. Tighten the starter and alternator positive cable nut to 111 inch lbs. (13 Nm).

ENGINE MECHANICAL

➡ Disconnecting the negative battery cable may interfere with the functions of the on board computer systems and may require the computer to undergo a relearning process, once the negative battery cable is reconnected.

ACCESSORY DRIVE BELTS

ACCESSORY BELT ROUTING

1.4L Engine

See Figure 91.

1.8L Engine

See Figure 92.

INSPECTION

Inspect the drive belt for signs of glazing or cracking. A glazed belt will be perfectly smooth from slippage, while a good belt will have a slight texture of fabric visible. Cracks will usually start at the inner edge of the belt and run outward. All worn or damaged drive belts should be replaced immediately.

ADJUSTMENT

Accessory belt tension is automatically maintained by a spring-loaded tensioner. No adjustment is necessary.

REMOVAL & INSTALLATION

1.4L Engine

See Figures 93 through 97.

1. Before servicing the vehicle, refer to the Precautions Section.

2. Raise and safely support the vehicle.

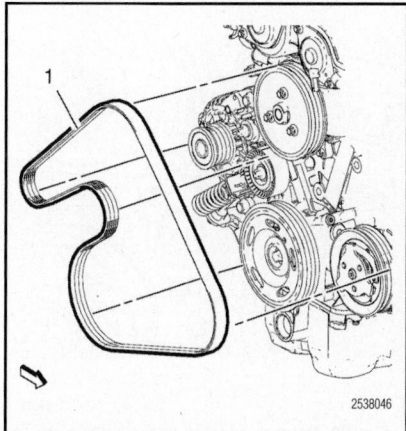

Fig. 91 Accessory drive belt (1) routing—1.4L engine

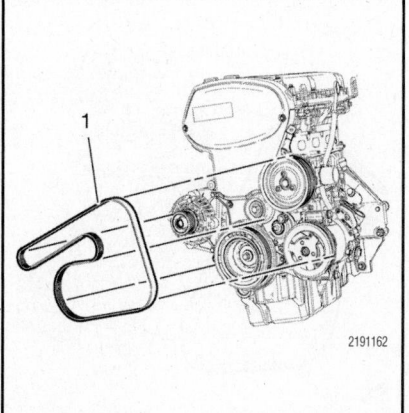

Fig. 92 Accessory drive belt (1) routing—1.8L engine

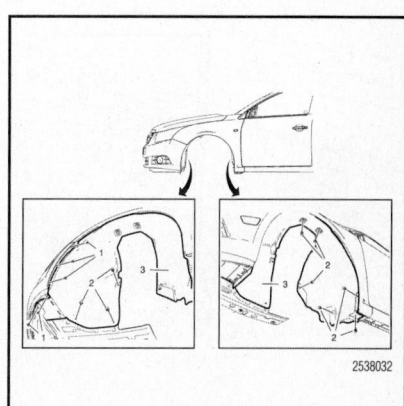

Fig. 93 View of front wheelhouse liner (3), plastic retainers (2), and liner screws (3)

3. Remove the tire and wheel assembly.

4. Remove the right front wheelhouse liner.

5. Using a Torx® wrench, rotate the drive belt tensioner pulley bolt in the direction shown until the bore aligns with the bore in the engine front cover.

6. Install a suitable punch through the drive belt tensioner bore to the engine front cover bore to fix the tensioner in position.

7. Lower the vehicle.

8. Remove the air cleaner assembly. Refer to Air Cleaner, removal & installation.

9. Install an engine lifter to the right engine lift bracket and apply tension to the engine lifter chain in order to support the engine.

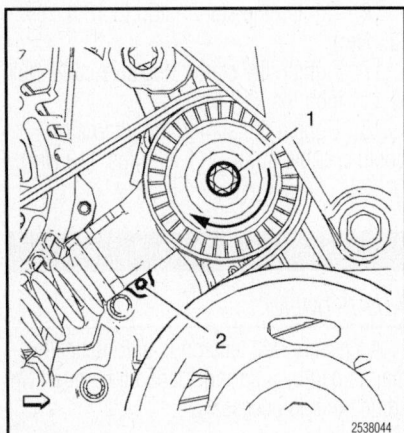

Fig. 94 Using a Torx® wrench, rotate the drive belt tensioner pulley bolt (1) in the direction shown until the bore (2) aligns with the bore in the engine front cover

Fig. 95 Install an engine lifter (1) to the right engine lift bracket and apply tension to the engine lifter chain in order to support the engine

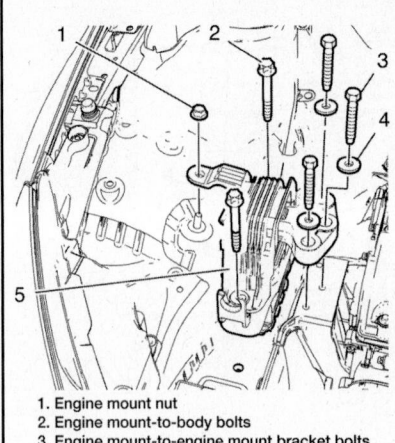

1. Engine mount nut
2. Engine mount-to-body bolts
3. Engine mount-to-engine mount bracket bolts
4. Washers
5. Engine mount

Fig. 96 Removing the engine mount

10. Remove and DISCARD the 3 engine mount-to-engine mount bracket bolts and the 3 washers.

11. Remove the 2 engine mount-to-body bolts and the engine mount nut.

12. Remove the engine mount.

13. Remove the drive belt.

To install:

14. Install the drive belt according to the shown routing.

15. Install the engine mount.

16. Install the 2 engine mount-to-body bolts.

17. Install the engine mount nut.

18. Install the 3 NEW engine mount-to-engine mount bracket bolts and the 3 washers.

19. Tighten the 2 engine mount-to-body bolts and the engine mount nut to 46 ft. lbs. (62 Nm).

20. Tighten the 3 engine mount-to-

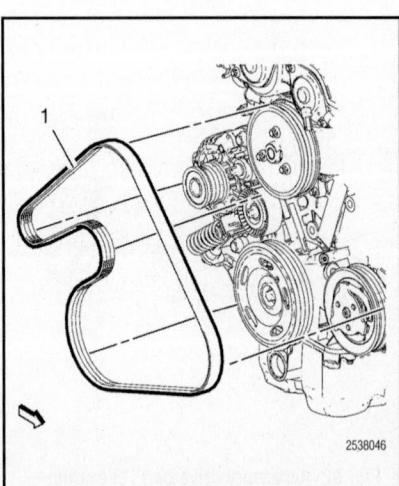

Fig. 97 Removing the drive belt (1)

engine mount bracket bolts to 37 ft. lbs. (50 Nm), plus 60–70°.

21. Remove the engine lifter from right engine lift bracket.

22. Install the air cleaner assembly. Refer to Air Cleaner, removal & installation.

23. Raise the vehicle.

24. Using a Torx® wrench, rotate the drive belt tensioner pulley bolt in the direction shown until the punch can be removed.

25. Remove the punch from the engine front cover bore and the drive belt tensioner bore.

26. Allow the tensioner to slide back slowly.

27. Install the right front wheelhouse liner.

28. Lower the vehicle.

1.8L Engine

See Figures 98 through 101.

Special Tools

• EN 6349 Locking Pin

1. Before servicing the vehicle, refer to the Precautions Section.

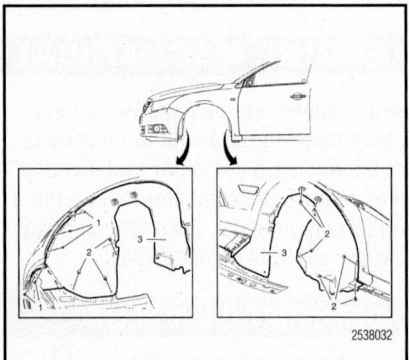

Fig. 98 View of front wheelhouse liner (3), plastic retainers (2), and liner screws (3)

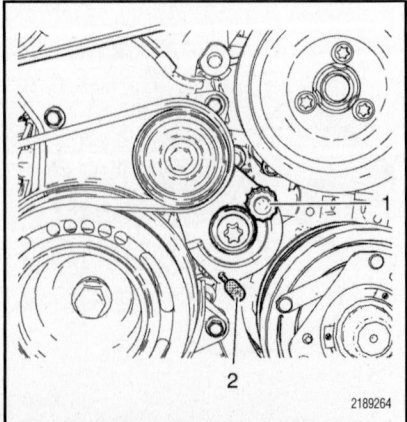

Fig. 99 Release tension to the drive belt tensioner by rotating counterclockwise (1) and lock with EN 6349 pin (2)

2. Raise and safely support the vehicle.

3. Remove the right front wheelhouse liner.

4. Release tension to the drive belt tensioner by rotating counterclockwise and lock with EN 6349 pin.

5. Remove the drive belt.

To install:

6. Install the drive belt.

➡**Ensure that the drive belt is aligned on the alternator pulley, crankshaft balancer, drive belt tensioner water pump pulley, and A/C compressor. The drive belt must lie on the water pump pulley between the flanges shown.**

7. Check the position of the drive belt.

8. Release tension to the tensioner by rotating counterclockwise.

➡**Allow the tensioner to slide back slowly.**

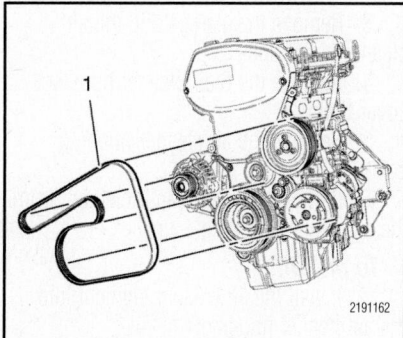

Fig. 100 Accessory drive belt (1) routing—1.8L engine

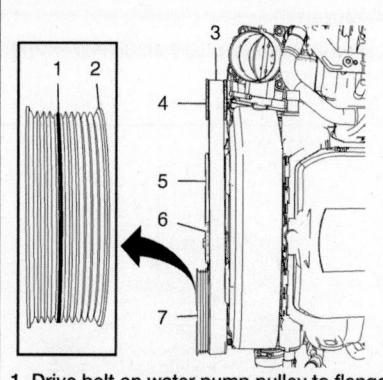

1. Drive belt on water pump pulley to flange
2. Drive belt on water pump pulley to flange
3. Position of the drive belt
4. Alternator pulley
5. Crankshaft balancer
6. Drive belt tensioner
7. Water pump pulley and A/C compressor

Fig. 101 Check the position of the drive belt during installation

9. Remove EN 6349 pin.

10. Apply tension to the tensioner clockwise.

11. Install the right front wheelhouse liner.

12. Lower the vehicle.

AIR CLEANER

REMOVAL & INSTALLATION

1.4L Engine

See Figure 102.

1. Before servicing the vehicle, refer to the Precautions Section.

2. Loosen the clamp and remove the air cleaner outlet duct from air cleaner assembly.

3. Disconnect the mass air flow sensor wiring harness plug from the mass air flow sensor and unclip it from the retainer clip.

4. Remove the air cleaner assembly.

5. Installation is the reverse of the removal procedure.

1.8L Engine

See Figures 103 through 105.

1. Before servicing the vehicle, refer to the Precautions Section.

2. Disconnect the intake air temperature sensor wiring harness plug.

➡**Any time service is being performed which requires removal of the air cleaner assembly, always cover the throttle body opening. This will prevent any foreign material from entering the engine.**

3. Remove the clamps and the air cleaner outlet duct.

4. Unclip the air cleaner inlet duct.

5. Unclip the drain hose, if equipped.

6. Remove the air cleaner assembly.

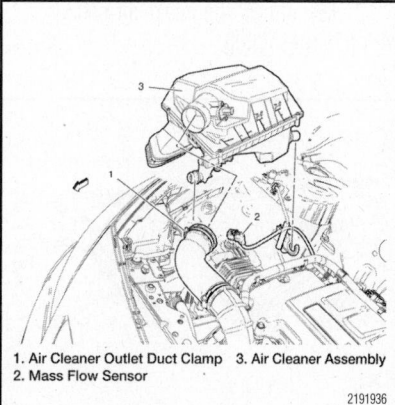

1. Air Cleaner Outlet Duct Clamp   3. Air Cleaner Assembly
2. Mass Flow Sensor

Fig. 102 Air cleaner assembly removal— 1.4L engine

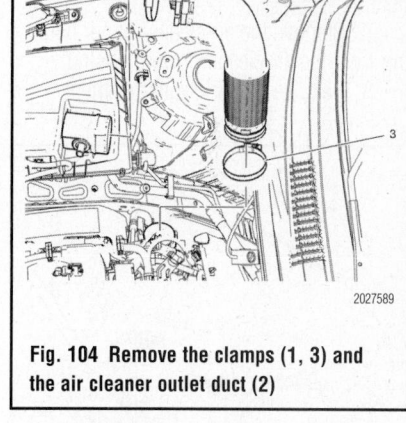

Fig. 103 Disconnect the intake air temperature sensor wiring harness plug (1)

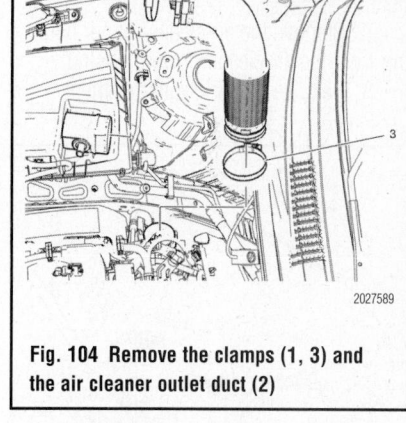

Fig. 104 Remove the clamps (1, 3) and the air cleaner outlet duct (2)

To install:

7. Install the air cleaner assembly.

8. Clip in the drain hose, if equipped.

9. Clip in the air cleaner inlet duct.

10. Install the clamps and the air cleaner outlet duct. Tighten the clamps to 31 inch lbs. (4 Nm).

11. Connect the intake air temperature sensor wiring harness plug.

12. Close the hood.

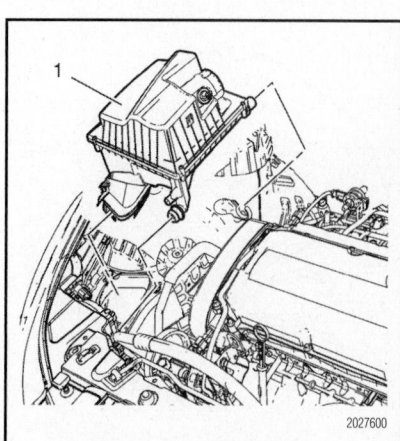

Fig. 105 Removing the air cleaner assembly (1)—1.8L engine

FILTER/ELEMENT REPLACEMENT

1.4L Engine

See Figures 106 through 108.

1. Before servicing the vehicle, refer to the Precautions Section.

2. Disconnect the mass air flow sensor wiring harness plug from the mass air flow sensor.

3. Unclip the mass air flow sensor wiring harness retainer clip from the air cleaner housing.

4. Remove the air cleaner outlet duct clamp.

5. Remove the air cleaner outlet duct from air cleaner housing.

6. Remove the 5 air cleaner housing bolts.

7. Remove the air cleaner upper housing from the air cleaner lower housing.

8. Remove the air cleaner element.

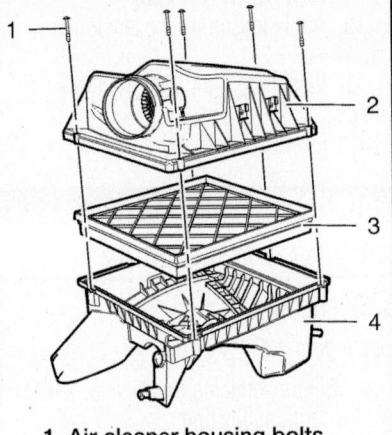

1. Air cleaner housing bolts
2. Air cleaner upper housing
3. Air cleaner element
4. Air cleaner lower housing

Fig. 108 Exploded view of air cleaner assembly

To install:

9. Install the air cleaner element.

10. Install the air cleaner upper housing to the air cleaner lower housing.

11. Install the 5 air cleaner housing bolts.

12. Install the air cleaner outlet duct to the air cleaner housing.

13. Install the air cleaner outlet duct clamp.

14. Clip in the mass air flow sensor wiring harness retainer clip to the air cleaner housing.

15. Connect the mass air flow sensor wiring harness plug to the mass air flow sensor.

1.8L Engine

See Figures 109 through 111.

1. Before servicing the vehicle, refer to the Precautions Section.

2. Disconnect the intake air sensor wiring harness plug.

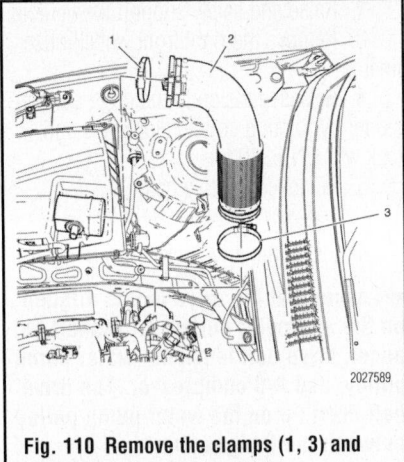

Fig. 110 Remove the clamps (1, 3) and the air cleaner outlet duct (2)

➡ **Any time service is being performed which requires removal of the air cleaner assembly, always cover the throttle body opening. This will prevent any foreign material from entering the engine.**

3. Remove the clamps and the air cleaner outlet duct.

4. Remove the 6 air cleaner housing cover bolts.

5. Remove the air cleaner housing cover.

6. Remove the air cleaner element from the air cleaner housing.

To install:

7. Install the air cleaner element into the air cleaner housing.

8. Install the air cleaner housing cover.

9. Install the 6 air cleaner housing cover bolts and tighten to 44 inch lbs. (5 Nm).

10. Install the clamps and the air cleaner outlet duct. Tighten the clamps to 31 inch lbs. (4 Nm).

11. Connect the intake air sensor wiring harness plug.

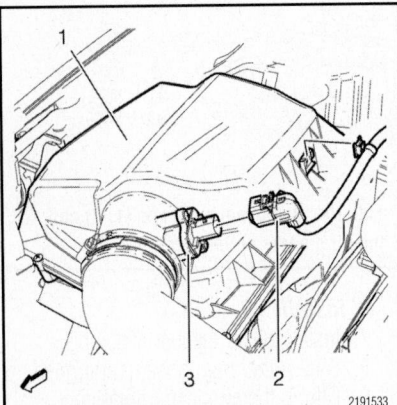

Fig. 106 Disconnect the mass air flow sensor wiring harness plug (2) from the mass air flow sensor (3) and unclip the wiring harness retainer clip from the air cleaner housing (1)

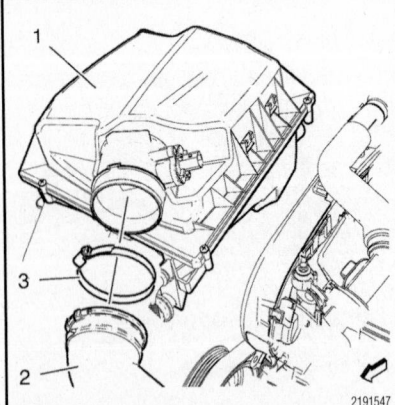

Fig. 107 Remove the air cleaner outlet duct clamp (3) and outlet duct (2) from air cleaner housing (1)

Fig. 109 Disconnect the intake air sensor wiring harness plug (1)

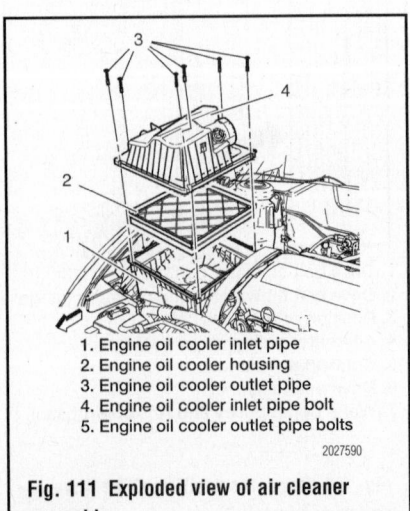

1. Engine oil cooler inlet pipe
2. Engine oil cooler housing
3. Engine oil cooler outlet pipe
4. Engine oil cooler inlet pipe bolt
5. Engine oil cooler outlet pipe bolts

Fig. 111 Exploded view of air cleaner assembly

CAMSHAFT AND VALVE LIFTERS

INSPECTION

Camshaft Bearing Journal Diameter

1. Before servicing the vehicle, refer to the Precautions Section.
2. Measure each camshaft journal diameter in 2 directions.
3. Compare the measurements with specifications.

Camshaft End Play

1. Before servicing the vehicle, refer to the Precautions Section.
2. Using the Dial Indicator Gauge with Holding Fixture, measure the camshaft end play.
3. Position the camshaft to the rear of the cylinder head.
4. Zero the Dial Indicator Gauge.
5. Move the camshaft to the front of the cylinder head. Note and record the camshaft end play.
   a. If camshaft end play exceeds specifications, install a new camshaft and recheck end play.
   b. If camshaft end play exceeds specification after camshaft installation, install a new cylinder head.

Camshaft Journal To Bearing Clearance

1. Before servicing the vehicle, refer to the Precautions Section.

➡**The camshaft journals must meet specifications before checking camshaft journal clearance.**

2. Measure each camshaft bearing in 2 directions.
3. Subtract the camshaft journal diameter from the camshaft bearing diameter to determine bearing oil clearance.

Camshaft Lobe Lift

1. Before servicing the vehicle, refer to the Precautions Section.
2. Use the Dial Indicator Gauge with Holding Fixture to measure camshaft intake/exhaust lobe lift.
3. Rotate the camshaft and subtract the lowest Dial Indicator Gauge reading from the highest Dial Indicator Gauge reading to figure the camshaft lobe lift.

Camshaft Runout

1. Before servicing the vehicle, refer to the Precautions Section.

➡**Camshaft journals must be within specifications before checking runout.**

2. Using the Dial Indicator Gauge with Holding Fixture, measure the camshaft runout.
3. Rotate the camshaft and subtract the lowest Dial Indicator Gauge reading from the highest Dial Indicator Gauge reading.

Camshaft Surface

1. Before servicing the vehicle, refer to the Precautions Section.
2. Inspect camshaft lobes for pitting or damage in the contact area. Minor pitting is acceptable outside the contact area.

REMOVAL & INSTALLATION

1.4L Engine

Intake Camshaft

See Figures 112 through 114.

1. Before servicing the vehicle, refer to the Precautions Section.
2. Remove the camshaft intake sprocket. Refer to Timing Chain & Sprockets, removal & installation.
3. Remove the camshaft bearing cap bolts in a spiral sequence one turn at a time until there is no spring tension pushing on the camshaft.

➡**Mind the markings on the camshaft bearing caps to ensure they will be installed in the same position.**

4. Remove the 10 camshaft bearing cap bolts.
5. Remove the 5 camshaft bearing caps.
6. Remove the intake camshaft.

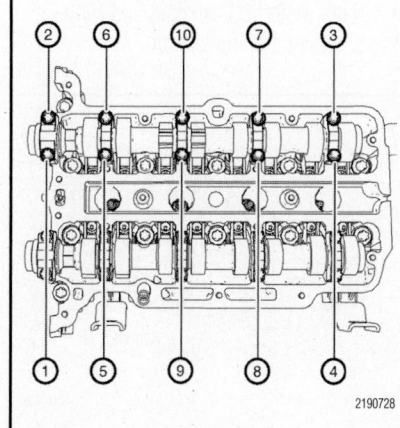

Fig. 112 Intake camshaft bearing cap bolt removal sequence

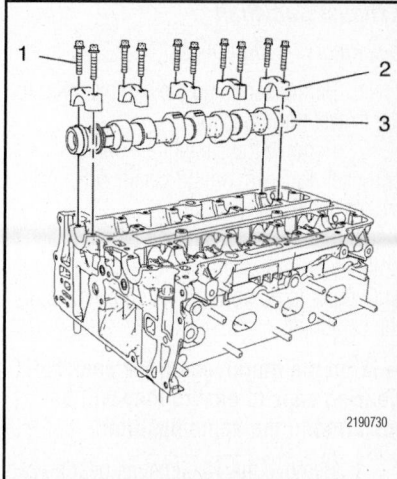

Fig. 113 Removing the intake camshaft (3), bearing caps (2), and bolts (1)

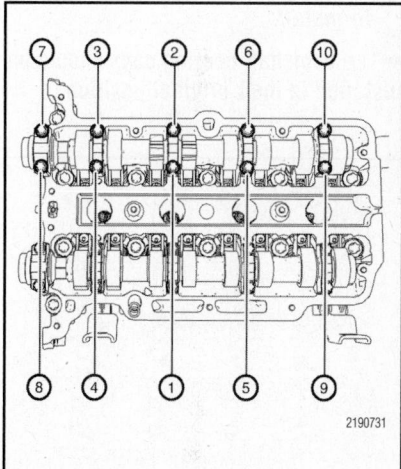

Fig. 114 Intake camshaft bearing cap bolt tightening sequence

To install:

➡**The camshaft bearing caps should be installed in their original position.**

7. Lubricate the camshaft and camshaft bearing caps with engine oil.
8. Install the intake camshaft.
9. Install the 5 camshaft bearing caps.
10. Install the 10 camshaft bearing cap bolts and hand tighten.

✳✳ WARNING

Tighten the camshaft bearing cap bolts one turn a time to avoid shape distortion of the camshaft.

11. Tighten the camshaft bearing cap bolts one turn at a time in a spiral sequence to 71 inch lbs. (8 Nm).
12. Install the camshaft intake sprocket. Refer to Timing Chain & Sprockets, removal & installation.

Exhaust Camshaft

See Figures 115 through 117.

1. Before servicing the vehicle, refer to the Precautions Section.

2. Remove the camshaft exhaust sprocket. Refer to Timing Chain & Sprockets, removal & installation.

3. Remove the camshaft bearing cap bolts in a spiral sequence one turn at a time until there is no spring tension pushing on the camshaft.

➡**Mind the markings on the camshaft bearing caps to ensure they will be installed in the same position.**

4. Remove the 10 camshaft bearing cap bolts.

5. Remove the 5 camshaft bearing caps.

6. Remove the exhaust camshaft.

To install:

➡**The camshaft bearing caps should be installed in their original position.**

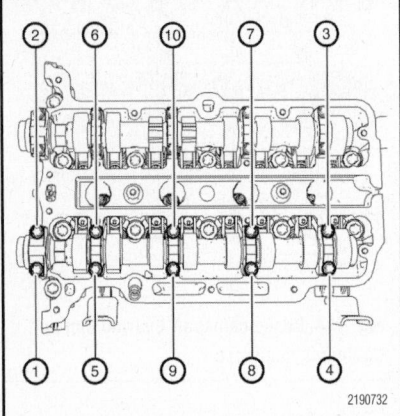

Fig. 115 Intake camshaft bearing cap bolt removal sequence

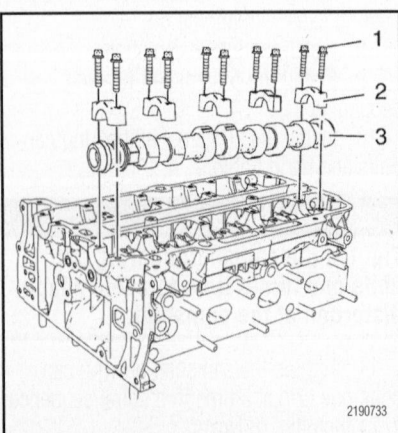

Fig. 116 Removing the exhaust camshaft (3), bearing caps (2), and bolts (1)

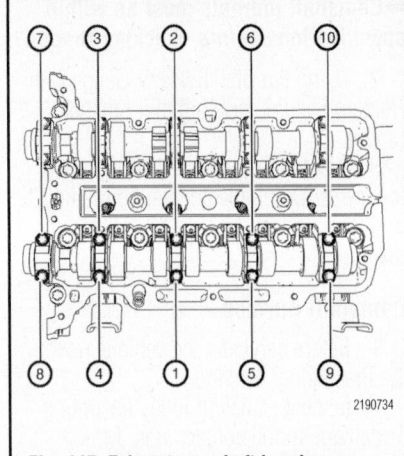

Fig. 117 Exhaust camshaft bearing cap bolt tightening sequence

7. Lubricate the camshaft and camshaft bearing caps with engine oil.

8. Install the exhaust camshaft.

9. Install the 5 camshaft bearing caps.

10. Install the 10 camshaft bearing cap bolts and hand tighten.

❊❊ WARNING

Tighten the camshaft bearing cap bolts one turn a time to avoid shape distortion of the camshaft.

11. Tighten the camshaft bearing cap bolts one turn at a time in a spiral sequence to 71 inch lbs. (8 Nm).

12. Install the camshaft exhaust sprocket. Refer to Timing Chain & Sprockets, removal & installation.

Valve Lifters

See Figures 118 and 119.

1. Before servicing the vehicle, refer to the Precautions Section.

2. Remove the intake and exhaust camshafts. Refer to Camshaft and Valve Lifters, removal & installation.

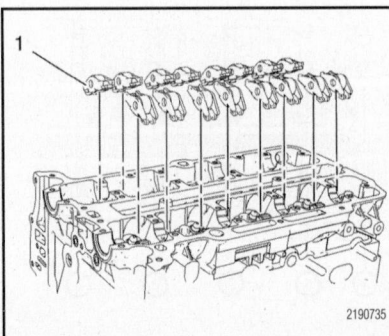

Fig. 118 Remove the 16 hydraulic valve lash adjuster arms (1)

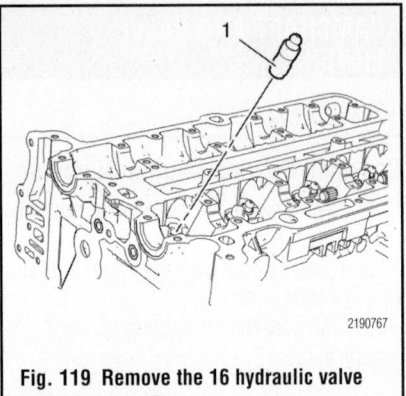

Fig. 119 Remove the 16 hydraulic valve lash adjusters (1)

➡**Mind the installation position of the hydraulic valve lash adjuster arms.**

3. Remove the 16 hydraulic valve lash adjuster arms.

➡**Mind the installation position of the hydraulic valve lash adjusters.**

4. Remove the 16 hydraulic valve lash adjusters.

To install:

5. Lubricate the hydraulic valve lash adjusters with engine oil.

6. Install the 16 hydraulic valve lash adjusters.

➡**Hydraulic valve lash adjuster arms should be installed in their original position**

7. Lubricate the hydraulic valve lash adjuster arms with engine oil.

8. Install the 16 hydraulic valve lash adjuster arms.

9. Install the intake and exhaust camshafts. Refer to Camshaft and Valve Lifters, removal & installation.

1.8L Engine

See Figures 120 through 122.

Special Tools

- EN-6340 Camshaft Adjuster Locking Tool
- EN-6628-A Camshaft Locking Tool
- EN-45059 Angle Meter

1. Before servicing the vehicle, refer to the Precautions Section.

2. Remove the camshaft adjuster. Refer to Camshaft Position Actuator Adjuster, removal & installation.

3. Remove the rear timing belt cover. Refer to Timing Belt Rear Cover, removal & installation.

4. Remove intake and exhaust camshaft position sensors. Refer to Camshaft Position (CMP) Sensor, removal & installation.

5. Remove the EN-6628-A locking tool.

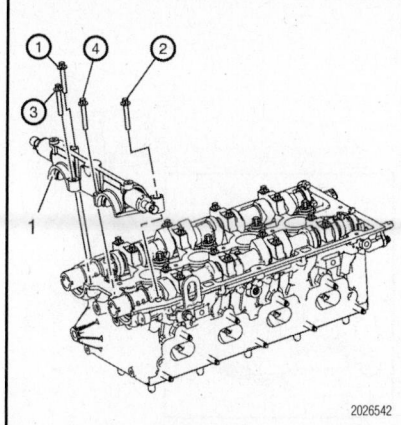

Fig. 120 Removal sequence for camshaft bearing cap bolts and first camshaft bearing cap (1)

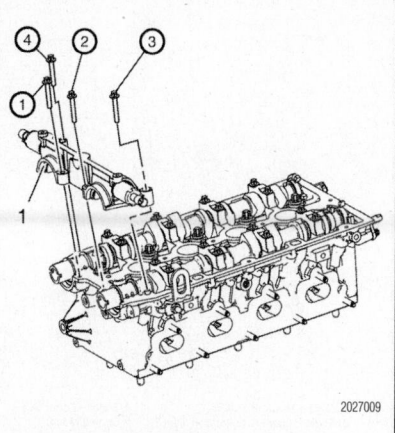

Fig. 121 Installation sequence for camshaft bearing cap bolts and first camshaft bearing cap (1)

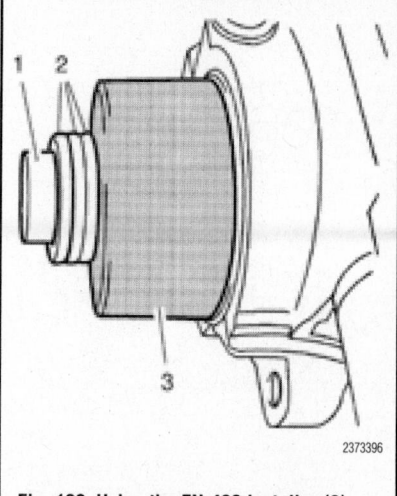

Fig. 122 Using the EN-422 installer (3) and camshaft sprocket bolt (1) in conjunction with shims (2)

6. Counterhold at the hexagon portion of the camshaft.

7. Remove the 4 camshaft bearing cap bolts in sequence.

➡**Release the bearing support by striking it gently with a plastic hammer.**

8. Remove the first camshaft bearing cap.

9. Loosen the 8 exhaust camshaft bearing cap bolts working from outside to inside in a spiral in steps of ½ up to 1 turn.

10. Remove the 8 exhaust camshaft bearing cap bolts.

➡**Mark the camshaft bearing caps before removal.**

11. Remove the 4 exhaust camshaft bearing caps from the cylinder head.

12. Remove the exhaust camshaft.

13. Loosen the 8 intake camshaft bearing cap bolts working from outside to inside in a spiral in steps of ½ up to 1 turn.

14. Remove the 8 intake camshaft bearing cap bolts.

➡**Mark the camshaft bearing caps before removal.**

15. Remove the 4 intake camshaft bearing caps from the cylinder head.

16. Remove the intake camshaft.

17. Detach the seal rings from the camshafts.

To install:

18. Lubricate the intake camshaft with clean engine oil and install.

➡**Note the identification marking on the camshaft bearing cover.**

19. Install the 4 intake camshaft bearing covers.

20. Install the 8 intake camshaft bearing

cover bolts and tighten in a spiral from the inside to the outside to 71 inch lbs. (8 Nm).

21. Lubricate the exhaust camshaft with clean engine oil and install.

➡**Note the identification marking on the camshaft bearing cover.**

22. Install the 4 exhaust camshaft bearing covers.

23. Install the 8 exhaust camshaft bearing cover bolts and tighten in a spiral from the inside to the outside to 71 inch lbs. (8 Nm).

24. Clean the sealing surfaces of the first camshaft bearing support and the cylinder head with a suitable tool.

25. Clean oil duct from any sealant residue.

➡**The sealing surfaces must be free from oil and grease. It is essential to ensure that no sealant is applied outside sealing areas. The grooves adjacent to the sealing surfaces must remain free from sealant.**

26. Apply surface sealant to sealing surfaces of the first camshaft bearing cap thinly and evenly.

27. Position the first camshaft bearing cap on the cylinder block and tighten the bolts approximately to 18 inch lbs. (2 Nm).

➡**Make certain that no sealant reaches the camshafts.**

28. Install the first camshaft bearing cap.

29. Install the first camshaft bearing cap bolts and tighten in sequence to 71 inch lbs. (8 Nm).

30. Install 2 NEW sealing rings to the camshafts.

31. Tighten the seal ring with EN-422 installer on the camshaft until this is in contact with the cylinder head.

32. To install, use the camshaft sprocket bolt in conjunction with shims with a total thickness of approximately 0.394 inch (10mm).

33. Remove the EN-422 installer.

34. Turn the intake camshaft against the direction of engine rotation.

35. Install EN-6628-A locking tool.

36. Turn the exhaust camshaft in the direction of rotation of the engine.

37. Install EN-6628-A locking tool.

38. Install the intake and exhaust camshaft position sensors. Refer to Camshaft Position (CMP) Sensor, removal & installation.

39. Install the rear timing belt cover. Refer to Timing Belt Rear Cover, removal & installation.

40. Install the camshaft adjuster. Refer to Camshaft Position Actuator Adjuster, removal & installation.

41. Install the timing belt. Refer to Timing Belt & Sprockets, removal & installation.

42. Install the drive belt tensioner. Refer to Alternator, Drive Belt Tensioner, removal & installation.

43. Install the camshaft cover. Refer to Valve Covers, removal & installation.

44. Install the air cleaner housing. Refer to Air Cleaner, removal & installation.

Valve Lifters

See Figure 123.

Special Tool
• EN-845 Suction Device

1. Before servicing the vehicle, refer to the Precautions Section.

2. Remove the camshafts. Refer to Camshaft and Lifters, removal & installation.

Fig. 123 View of valve lifter (1) removal—1.8L engine

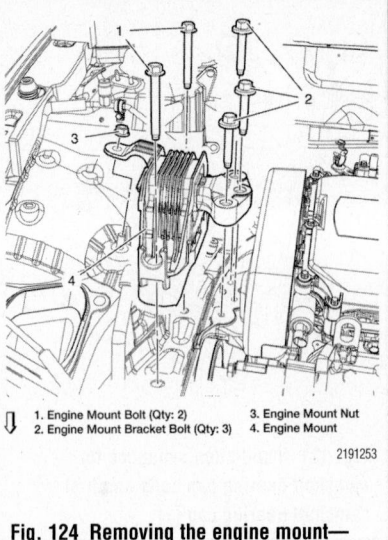

1. Engine Mount Bolt (Qty: 2)
2. Engine Mount Bracket Bolt (Qty: 3)
3. Engine Mount Nut
4. Engine Mount

Fig. 124 Removing the engine mount— 1.8L engine

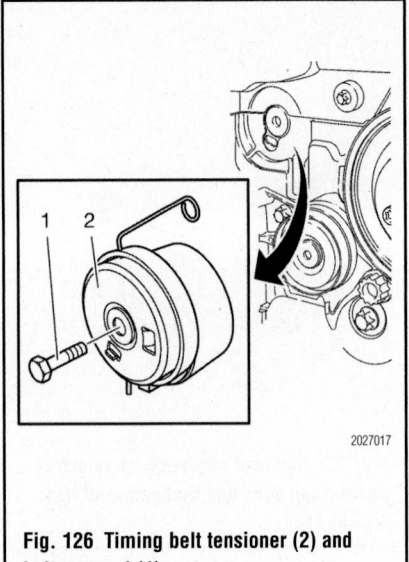

Fig. 126 Timing belt tensioner (2) and bolt removal (1)

➡**Mark the location of each component.**

3. Remove the 16 valve lifters, using the EN-845 suction device.

To install:

➡**Observe the correct location of components.**

4. Coat the sliding surfaces with NEW engine oil.

5. Install the 16 valve lifters, using the EN-845 suction device.

6. Install the camshafts. Refer to Camshaft and Lifters, removal & installation.

CAMSHAFT POSITION ACTUATOR ADJUSTER

REMOVAL & INSTALLATION

1.8L Engine

See Figures 124 through 130.

Special Tools
- EN-6340 Camshaft Adjuster Locking Tool
- EN-6628-A Camshaft Locking Tool
- EN-45059 Angle Meter

1. Before servicing the vehicle, refer to the Precautions Section.

2. Remove the air cleaner housing. Refer to Air Cleaner, removal & installation.

3. Remove the camshaft cover. Refer to Valve Covers, removal & installation.

4. Remove the drive belt tensioner. Refer to Alternator, Drive Belt Tensioner, removal & installation.

5. Remove the timing belt. Refer to Timing Belt & Sprockets, removal & installation.

6. Remove and DISCARD the timing belt idler pulley bolt.

7. Remove the timing belt idler pulley.

8. Using the EN-45059 meter and the crankshaft balancer bolt, set the crankshaft in the direction of engine rotation to 60° before Top Dead Center (TDC).

9. Remove the crankshaft sprocket.

10. Lower the vehicle.

11. Support the engine. Install a suitable engine lifting device. Install a suitable cable at the 3 engine lift brackets and at the engine lifting device.

12. Remove the engine mount bolts and the engine mount.

13. Remove the engine mount bracket bolts and the engine mount bracket.

14. Remove the center front timing belt cover. Refer to Timing Belt Front Cover, removal & installation.

15. Remove the tensioner bolt.

➡**Some engine oil will run out of the camshaft and the camshaft position actuator adjuster. That is the reason for**

the removal of the whole timing assembly.

16. Remove the timing belt tensioner.

17. Turn the camshaft by the hexagon until the groove on the end of the camshafts is horizontal.

18. Install the EN-6628-A locking tool.

19. Raise and safely support the vehicle.

20. Place a collecting basin underneath the vehicle.

21. Remove the camshaft position actuator adjuster closure bolt of the intake camshaft position actuator adjuster and/or the exhaust camshaft position actuator adjuster.

22. Remove and DISCARD the intake camshaft position actuator adjuster bolt and/or the exhaust camshaft position actuator adjuster bolt.

➡**A second person is required. Counterhold against the hexagon of corresponding camshaft with an open-ended wrench.**

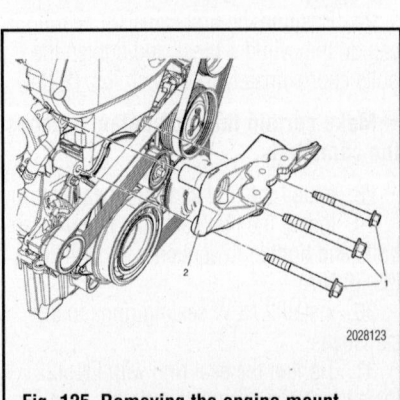

Fig. 125 Removing the engine mount bracket (2) and bolts (1)—1.8L engine

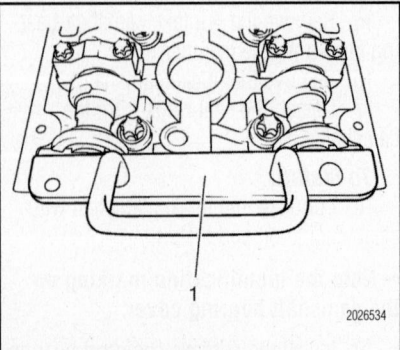

Fig. 127 EN-6628-A locking tool (1) shown installed

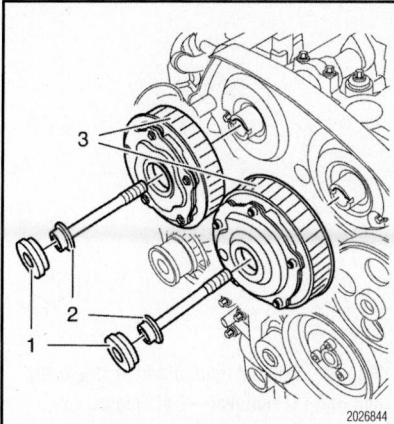

Fig. 128 View of intake and exhaust camshaft position actuator adjusters (3), closure bolts (1), and actuator adjuster bolts (2)

23. Remove the intake and exhaust camshaft position actuator adjusters.

To install:

24. Install the intake and exhaust camshaft position actuator adjusters.

25. Install NEW intake and exhaust camshaft position actuator adjuster bolts.

26. Install the EN-6340 locking tool into the camshaft position actuator adjusters.

➡**The spot type marking on the intake camshaft position actuator adjuster does not correspond to the groove of EN-6340-left during this process, but must be somewhat above.**

   a. Install the EN-6340-left locking tool in the camshaft position actuator adjusters as shown.

➡**The spot type marking on the exhaust camshaft position actuator adjuster must correspond to the groove on EN-6340-right.**

   b. Install the EN-6340-right locking tool in the camshaft position actuator adjusters.

➡**A second person is required to counterhold at the camshaft hexagon.**

27. Tighten the intake and exhaust camshaft position actuator adjuster bolts using EN-45059 meter, or equivalent.
   a. Step 1: Tighten to 48 ft. lbs. (65 Nm).
   b. Step 2: Tighten 120°.
   c. Step 3: Tighten an additional 15°.

➡**Install a NEW seal ring.**

28. Install the camshaft closure bolts and tighten to 22 ft. lbs. (30 Nm).

29. Remove the EN-6628-A locking tool.

30. Clean the timing belt tensioner threads.

31. Install the timing belt tensioner and tighten the NEW timing belt tensioner bolt to 15 ft. lbs. (20 Nm).

32. Install the timing belt center front cover. Refer to Timing Belt Front Cover, removal & installation.

33. Install the engine mount bracket and the bolts. Tighten the bolts to 45 ft. lbs. (60 Nm), plus 45–60°.

34. Install the engine mount into position.

35. Tighten the engine mount bolts to 46 ft. lbs. (62 Nm).

36. Tighten the NEW engine mount bracket bolts to 37 ft. lbs. (50 Nm), plus 60–75°.

37. Tighten the engine mount nut to 46 ft. lbs. (62 Nm).

38. Raise the vehicle.

➡**When installing the crankshaft sprocket, the cam and the groove must align.**

39. Install the crankshaft sprocket.

40. Set the crankshaft, in the direction of engine rotation, to TDC. Use the crankshaft balancer bolt.

41. Clean the timing belt idler pulley threads.

42. Install the timing belt idler pulley and the NEW bolt with screw locking compound.

43. Tighten the NEW bolt to 18 ft. lbs. (25 Nm).

44. Install the timing belt. Refer to Timing Belt & Sprockets, removal & installation.

45. Install the drive belt tensioner. Refer to Alternator, Drive Belt Tensioner, removal & installation.

46. Install the camshaft cover. Refer to Valve Covers, removal & installation.

47. Install the air cleaner housing. Refer to Air Cleaner, removal & installation.

CATALYTIC CONVERTER

REMOVAL & INSTALLATION

1.4L Engine

Catalytic Converter—2
See Figure 131.

❊❊ CAUTION

In order to avoid being burned, do not service the exhaust system while it is still hot. Service the system when it is cool.

❊❊ CAUTION

Always wear protective goggles and gloves when removing exhaust parts as falling rust and sharp edges from worn exhaust components could result in serious personal injury.

❊❊ WARNING

Do not bend the exhaust flex pipe more than 10° in any direction. Bending of more than 10° or twisting in a range of plus or minus 0.5° will damage the exhaust flex de-coupler.

1. Before servicing the vehicle, refer to the Precautions Section.

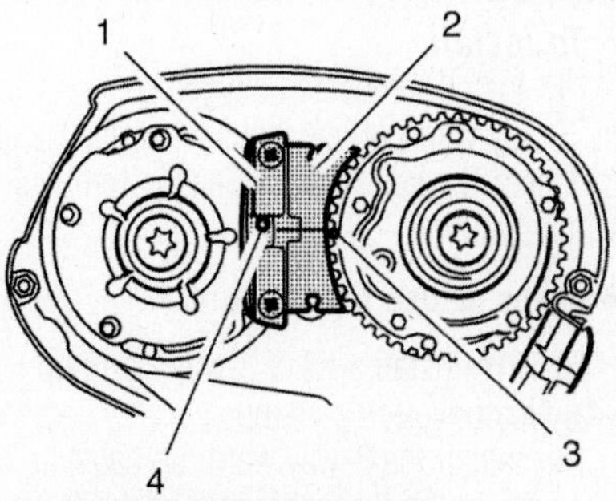

1. EN-6340-left locking tool
2. EN-6340-right locking tool
3. Spot type marking on the exhaust camshaft position actuator adjuster
4. Spot type marking on the intake camshaft position actuator adjuster

Fig. 129 EN-6340 locking tool shown installed into the camshaft position actuator adjusters

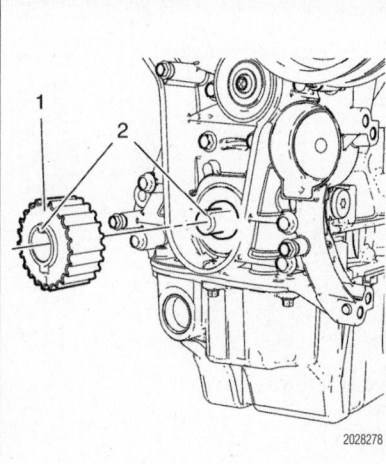

Fig. 130 Install the crankshaft sprocket (1) making sure the cam and the groove is aligned (2)

2. Raise and safely support the vehicle.

3. Disconnect the heated oxygen sensor wiring harness plug.

4. Remove and discard the catalytic converter-to-exhaust front pipe nuts.

5. Remove and discard the exhaust front pipe-to-exhaust muffler nuts.

6. Support the exhaust muffler with a suitable jack.

7. Remove the exhaust pipe front hanger bracket bolts

8. Remove the exhaust front pipe assembly with the catalytic converter.

To install:

9. Installation is the reverse of the removal procedure.

10. Tighten the heated oxygen sensor to 31 ft. lbs. (42 Nm).

11. Tighten the exhaust pipe front hanger insulator nuts to 13 ft. lbs. (17 Nm).

12. Tighten the exhaust pipe front hanger bracket bolts to 16 ft. lbs. (22 Nm).

13. Tighten the NEW drivetrain and front suspension frame support M10 bolts to 44 ft. lbs. (60 Nm), plus 30–45°.

14. Tighten the NEW catalytic converter-to-exhaust front pipe gasket to 16 ft. lbs. (22 Nm).

15. Tighten the NEW exhaust front pipe-to-exhaust muffler nuts to 13 ft. lbs. (17 Nm).

Warm Up 3-Way Catalytic Converter

See Figures 132 through 136.

> **✳✳ CAUTION**
>
> **In order to avoid being burned, do not service the exhaust system while it is still hot. Service the system when it is cool.**

> **✳✳ CAUTION**
>
> **Always wear protective goggles and gloves when removing exhaust parts as falling rust and sharp edges from worn exhaust components could result in serious personal injury.**

> **✳✳ WARNING**
>
> **Do not bend the exhaust flex pipe more than 10° in any direction. Bending of more than 10° or twisting in a range of plus or minus 0.5° will damage the exhaust flex de-coupler.**

1. Before servicing the vehicle, refer to the Precautions Section.

2. Disconnect battery negative cable. Refer to Battery, removal & installation.

3. Disconnect the heated oxygen sensor 1 wiring harness connector. Refer to Heated Oxygen (HO2S) Sensor, removal & installation.

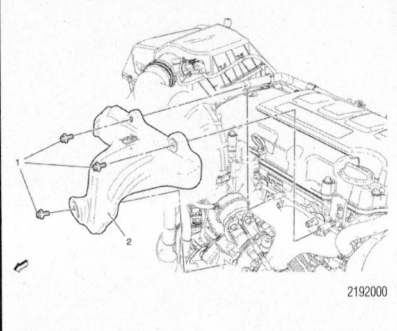

Fig. 132 Exhaust manifold heat shield (2) and bolt (1) removal—1.4L engine

4. Remove the exhaust manifold heat shield.

5. Loosen the 3-way warm up catalytic converter V-clamp bolt so that the 3-way warm up catalytic converter V-clamp can be removed from catalytic converter-to-turbocharger flange.

6. Raise and safely support the vehicle.

7. If equipped, remove the front compartment insulator.

8. Remove the 3 catalytic converter flange nuts.

9. Remove the catalytic converter from the 3-way warm up catalytic converter and hang aside.

10. Remove the catalytic converter gasket.

11. Remove the 3-way warm up catalytic converter bracket nuts and.

12. Remove the 3-way warm up catalytic converter and the 3-way warm up catalytic converter-to-turbocharger seal ring.

13. Remove the heated oxygen sensor 1 from the 3-way warm up catalytic converter. Refer to Heated Oxygen (HO2S) Sensor, removal & installation.

To install:

14. Install the heated oxygen sensor 1 to the 3-way warm up catalytic converter. Refer to Heated Oxygen (HO2S) Sensor, removal & installation.

➡**Never re-use the V-clamp.**

15. Pre-install a NEW 3-way warm up catalytic converter V-clamp.

16. Install the 3-way warm up catalytic converter to the turbocharger and the 3-way warm up catalytic converter brackets. Install a NEW 3-way warm up catalytic converter to turbocharger seal ring.

17. Install and hand-tighten the 3-way warm up catalytic converter bracket nuts.

18. Lower the vehicle.

19. Install the 3-way warm up catalytic converter V-clamp to the catalytic converter-to-turbocharger flange.

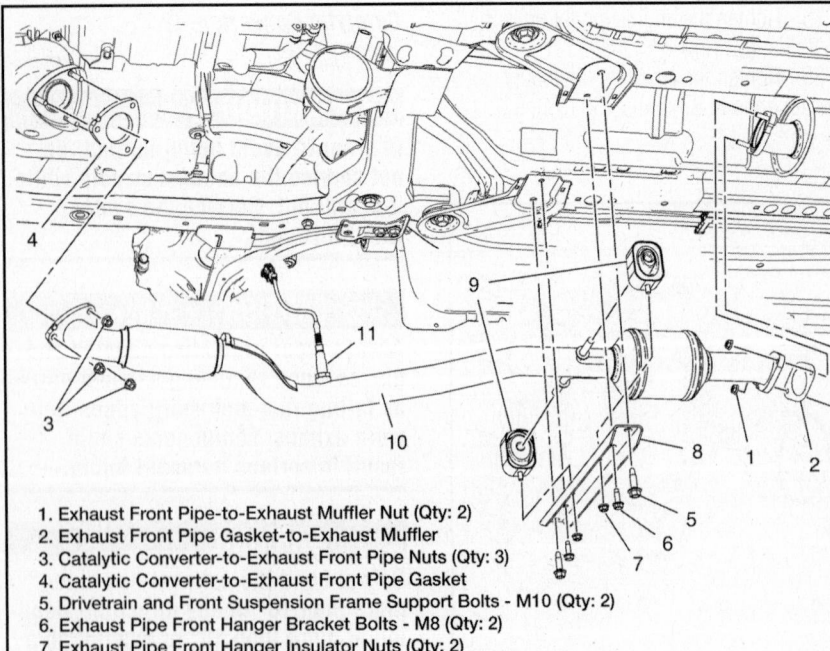

1. Exhaust Front Pipe-to-Exhaust Muffler Nut (Qty: 2)
2. Exhaust Front Pipe Gasket-to-Exhaust Muffler
3. Catalytic Converter-to-Exhaust Front Pipe Nuts (Qty: 3)
4. Catalytic Converter-to-Exhaust Front Pipe Gasket
5. Drivetrain and Front Suspension Frame Support Bolts - M10 (Qty: 2)
6. Exhaust Pipe Front Hanger Bracket Bolts - M8 (Qty: 2)
7. Exhaust Pipe Front Hanger Insulator Nuts (Qty: 2)
8. Exhaust Pipe Front Hanger Bracket
9. Exhaust Muffler Insulator (Qty: 2)
10. Exhaust Front Pipe Assembly
11. Heated Oxygen Sensor

Fig. 131 Exploded view of catalytic converter—1.4L engine

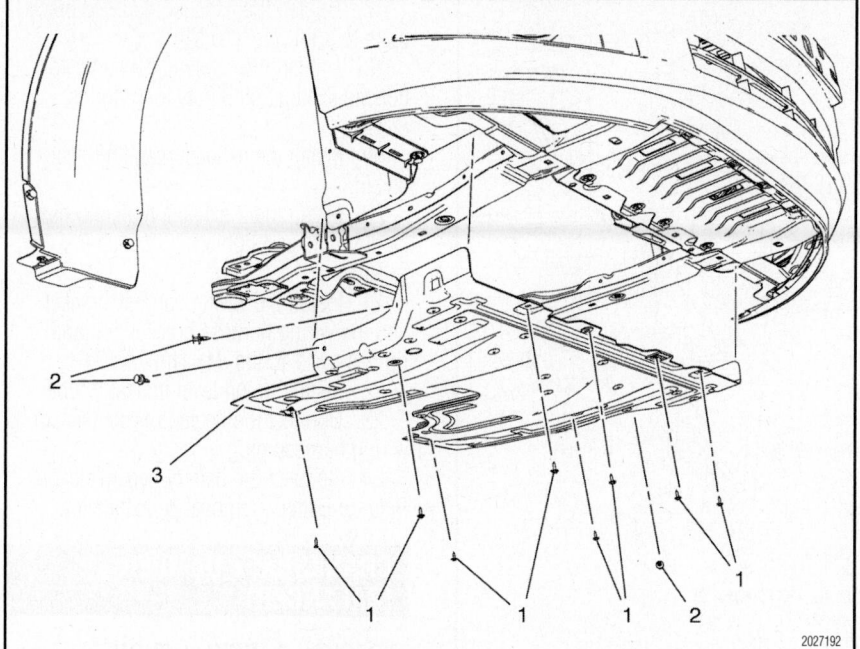

Fig. 133 Removing the front compartment insulator (3), plastic retainers (2), and screws (1)

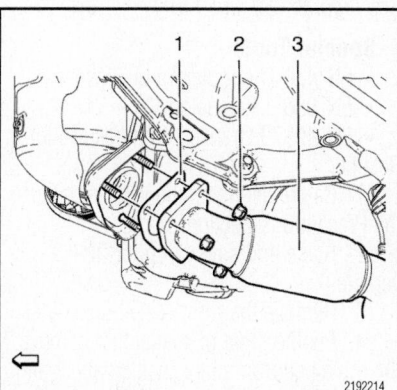

Fig. 134 Remove catalytic converter flange nuts (2), the catalytic converter (3), and gasket (1)

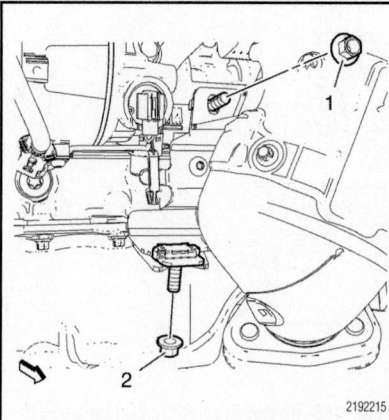

Fig. 135 Location of 3-way warm up catalytic converter bracket nuts (1) and (2)

20. The 3-way warm up catalytic converter V-clamp should be installed in the proper position.

21. Hand-tighten the 3-way warm up catalytic converter V-clamp.

22. Raise and safely support the vehicle.

23. Tighten the 3-way catalytic converter bracket nuts to 16 ft. lbs. (22 Nm).

24. Install the catalytic converter and a NEW catalytic converter gasket to the 3-way warm up catalytic converter.

25. Install the 3 catalytic converter flange nuts and tighten to 16 ft. lbs. (22 Nm).

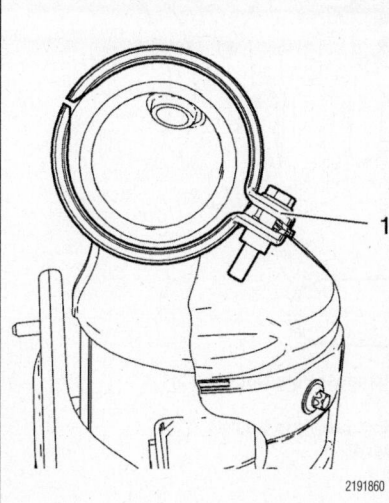

Fig. 136 The V-clamp should be installed to the 3-way warm up catalytic converter in the position shown

26. Install the engine front compartment insulator, if equipped.

27. Lower the vehicle.

28. Tighten the 3-way catalytic converter V-clamp bolt to 115 inch lbs. (13 Nm).

29. Install the exhaust manifold heat shield. Tighten the bolts to 71 inch lbs. (8 Nm).

30. Connect the heated oxygen sensor 1 wiring harness plug.

31. Connect battery negative cable. Refer to Battery, removal & installation.

1.8L Engine

See Figures 137 and 138.

> ❊❊ **CAUTION**
>
> **In order to avoid being burned, do not service the exhaust system while it is still hot. Service the system when it is cool.**

> ❊❊ **CAUTION**
>
> **Always wear protective goggles and gloves when removing exhaust parts as falling rust and sharp edges from worn exhaust components could result in serious personal injury.**

1. Before servicing the vehicle, refer to the Precautions Section.

2. Disconnect the battery negative cable. Refer to Battery, removal & installation.

3. Disconnect the heated oxygen sensor wiring harness plug.

4. Remove the oil level indicator tube.

5. Remove the wiring harness bracket bolt and the wiring harness bracket.

6. Remove the 2 exhaust manifold heat shield bolts.

7. Remove the exhaust manifold heat shield.

8. Remove the catalytic converter-to-flexible exhaust pipe nuts.

9. Remove the exhaust manifold brace bolts.

10. Remove the heated oxygen sensor.

11. Remove the catalytic converter-to-cylinder head nuts.

12. Remove the catalytic converter.

To install:

13. Installation is the reverse of the removal procedure.

14. Install the catalytic converter-to-cylinder head gasket.

15. Tighten the catalytic converter-to-cylinder head nuts to 15 ft. lbs. (20 Nm).

16. Tighten the heated oxygen sensor to 31 ft. lbs. (42 Nm).

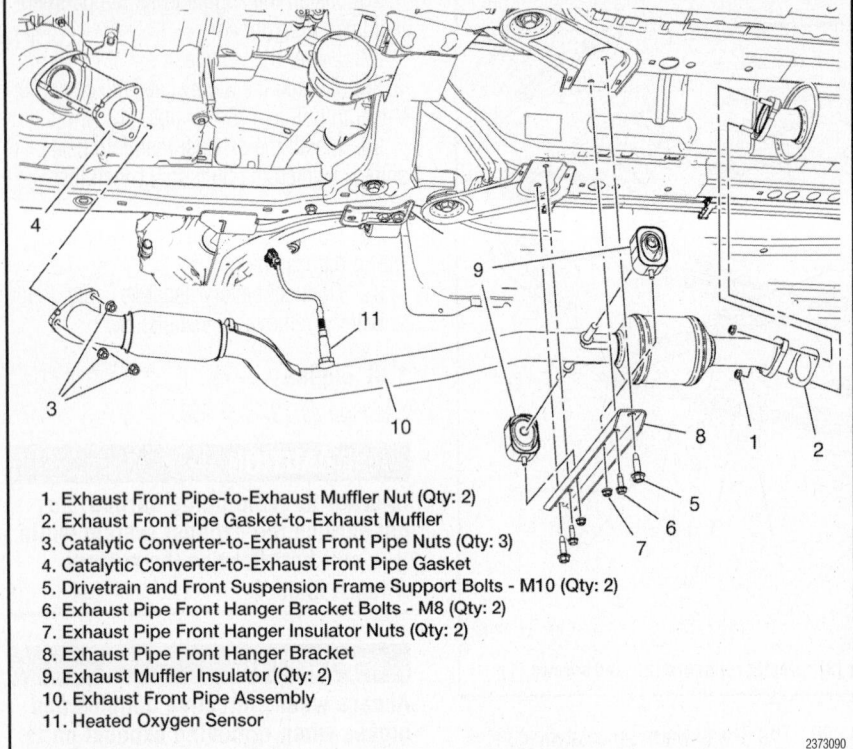

1. Exhaust Front Pipe-to-Exhaust Muffler Nut (Qty: 2)
2. Exhaust Front Pipe Gasket-to-Exhaust Muffler
3. Catalytic Converter-to-Exhaust Front Pipe Nuts (Qty: 3)
4. Catalytic Converter-to-Exhaust Front Pipe Gasket
5. Drivetrain and Front Suspension Frame Support Bolts - M10 (Qty: 2)
6. Exhaust Pipe Front Hanger Bracket Bolts - M8 (Qty: 2)
7. Exhaust Pipe Front Hanger Insulator Nuts (Qty: 2)
8. Exhaust Pipe Front Hanger Bracket
9. Exhaust Muffler Insulator (Qty: 2)
10. Exhaust Front Pipe Assembly
11. Heated Oxygen Sensor

2373090

Fig. 137 Exhaust manifold heat shield removal—1.8L engine

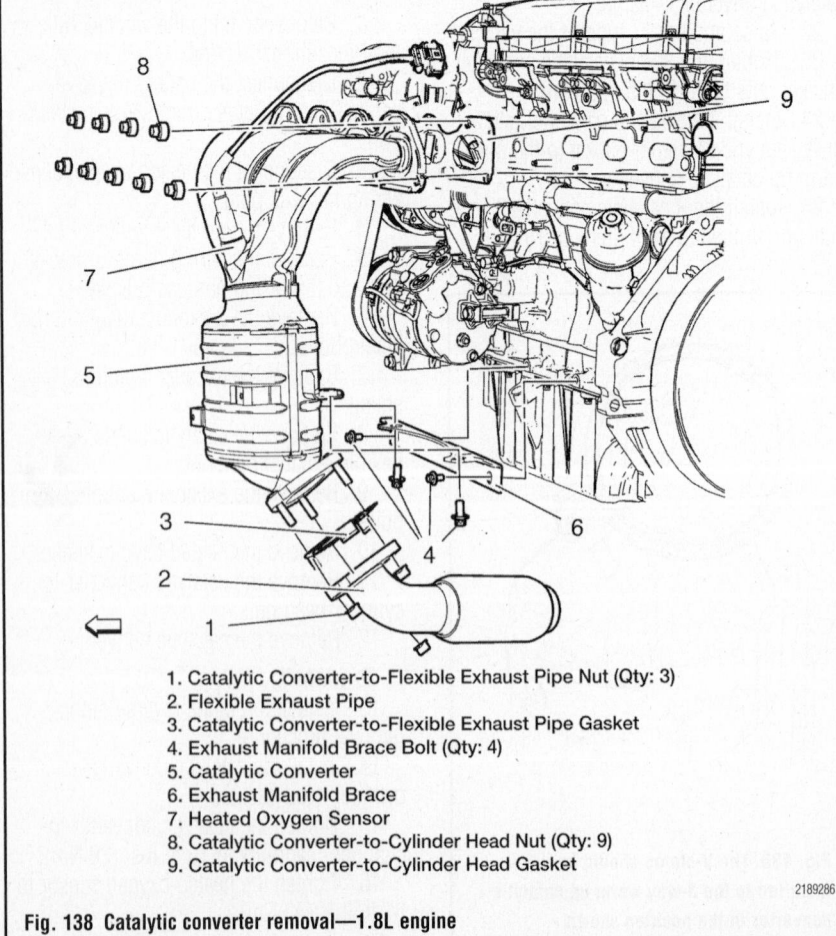

1. Catalytic Converter-to-Flexible Exhaust Pipe Nut (Qty: 3)
2. Flexible Exhaust Pipe
3. Catalytic Converter-to-Flexible Exhaust Pipe Gasket
4. Exhaust Manifold Brace Bolt (Qty: 4)
5. Catalytic Converter
6. Exhaust Manifold Brace
7. Heated Oxygen Sensor
8. Catalytic Converter-to-Cylinder Head Nut (Qty: 9)
9. Catalytic Converter-to-Cylinder Head Gasket

2189286

Fig. 138 Catalytic converter removal—1.8L engine

17. Tighten the exhaust manifold brace bolts to 15 ft. lbs. (20 Nm).

18. Tighten the catalytic converter-to-flexible exhaust pipe nuts to 16 ft. lbs. (22 Nm).

19. Install the exhaust manifold heat shield.

20. Install the 2 exhaust manifold heat shield bolts and tighten to 71 inch lbs. (8 Nm).

21. Install the wiring harness bracket and the wiring harness bracket bolt and tighten to 11 ft. lbs. (15 Nm).

22. Install the oil level indicator tube.

23. Connect the heated oxygen sensor wiring harness plug.

24. Connect the battery negative cable. Refer to Battery, removal & installation.

CRANKSHAFT DAMPER (BALANCER)

REMOVAL & INSTALLATION

1.4L Engine

See Figures 139 and 140.

Special Tools

- EN-470-B Angular Torque Wrench
- EN-956-1 Extension
- EN-49979 Crankshaft Shock Mount Retainer

1. Before servicing the vehicle, refer to the Precautions Section.

2. Raise and safely support the vehicle.

3. Remove the right wheelhouse liner.

4. Fix the drive belt tensioner, remove the drive belt from crankshaft balancer and lay aside. Refer to Accessory Drive Belts, removal & installation.

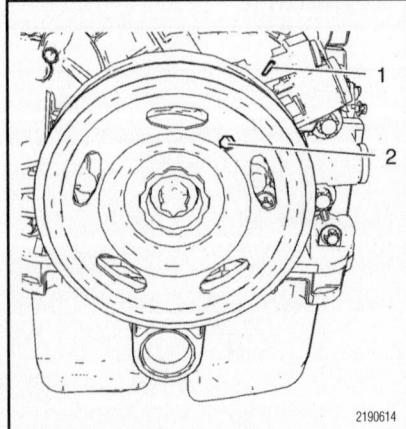

2190614

Fig. 139 Rotate the engine clockwise until the bore (2) in the crankshaft balancer aligns with the mark (1) on the engine front cover

5. Rotate the engine clockwise until the bore in the crankshaft balancer aligns with the mark on the engine front cover.

6. Install EN-49979 crankshaft shock mount retainer to EN-956-1 extension.

7. Loosen the crankshaft balancer bolt while fixing the crankshaft balancer with EN-49979 crankshaft shock mount retainer and EN-956-1 extension.

8. Remove and DISCARD the crankshaft balancer bolt.

9. Remove the crankshaft balancer.

To install:

10. Install the crankshaft balancer carefully by pressing into position.

11. Measure the distance between the crankshaft balancer and the mark on the engine front cover. The distance should be 0.22 inch (5.5mm).

➡**Never re-use the crankshaft balancer bolt.**

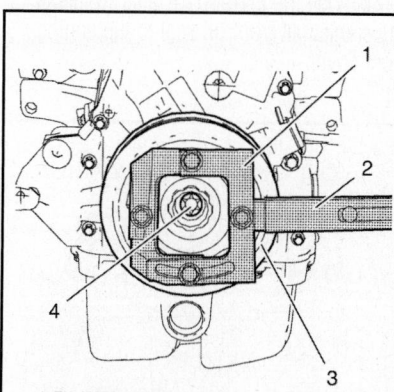

1. EN-49979 crankshaft shock mount retainer
2. EN-956-1 extension
3. Crankshaft balancer bolt
4. Crankshaft balancer

Fig. 140 Rotate the engine clockwise until the bore in the crankshaft balancer aligns with the mark on the engine front cover

12. Install a NEW crankshaft balancer bolt.

13. Tighten the crankshaft balancer bolt while fixing the crankshaft balancer with EN-49979 crankshaft shock mount retainer and EN-956-1 extension. Use EN-470-B wrench, or equivalent, to check the torque.

a. Step 1: Tighten to 111 ft. lbs. (150 Nm).

b. Step 2: Tighten an additional 60°.

14. Install the drive belt to the crankshaft balancer and remove the fixing pin. Refer to Accessory Drive Belts, removal & installation.

15. Install the right wheelhouse liner.

16. Lower the vehicle.

17. Check and correct engine oil level.

1.8L Engine

With Automatic Transaxle

See Figures 141 and 142.

Special Tools
- EN-6625 Crankshaft Locking Device
- EN-45059 Angle Meter

1. Before servicing the vehicle, refer to the Precautions Section.

2. Raise and safely support the vehicle.

3. Remove the right front wheelhouse liner.

4. Remove the drive belt. Refer to Accessory Drive Belts, removal & installation.

5. Remove the bolt from engine block.

6. Install the EN-6625 locking device to lock the crankshaft.

7. Install the bolt back into engine block.

8. Remove and DISCARD the crankshaft balancer bolt.

9. Remove the crankshaft balancer.

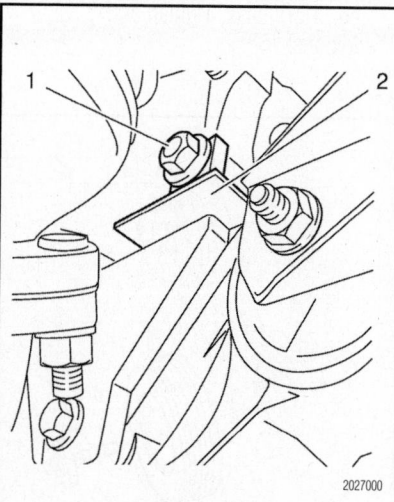

Fig. 141 Install EN-6625 locking device (2) to lock the crankshaft then reinstall the bolt (1) into engine block

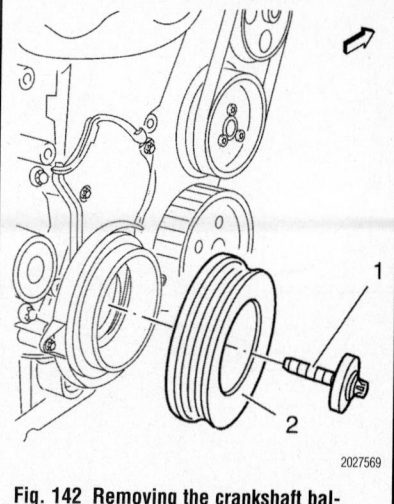

Fig. 142 Removing the crankshaft balancer bolt (1) and the crankshaft balancer (2)

To install:

10. Install the crankshaft balancer.

11. Install a NEW crankshaft balancer bolt and tighten in 3 passes using the EN-45059 meter:

12. First pass: Tighten to 70 ft. lbs. (95 Nm).

a. Second pass: Tighten an additional 45°.

b. Third pass. Tighten and additional 15°.

13. Remove the bolt and the EN-6625 locking device to unlock the crankshaft.

14. Install the bolt to the engine block and tighten to 33 ft. lbs. (45 Nm).

15. Install the drive belt. Refer to Accessory Drive Belts, removal & installation.

16. Install the right front wheelhouse liner.

17. Lower the vehicle.

With Manual Transaxle

See Figures 143 through 146.

Special Tools
- EN-6625 Crankshaft Locking Device
- EN-45059 Angle Meter

1. Before servicing the vehicle, refer to the Precautions Section.

2. Raise and safely support the vehicle.

3. Remove the right front wheelhouse liner.

4. Remove the drive belt. Refer to Accessory Drive Belts, removal & installation.

5. If equipped, remove the front compartment insulator.

6. Remove the transaxle front mount bolts.

7. Remove the transaxle front mount.

8. Remove the bolted connection.

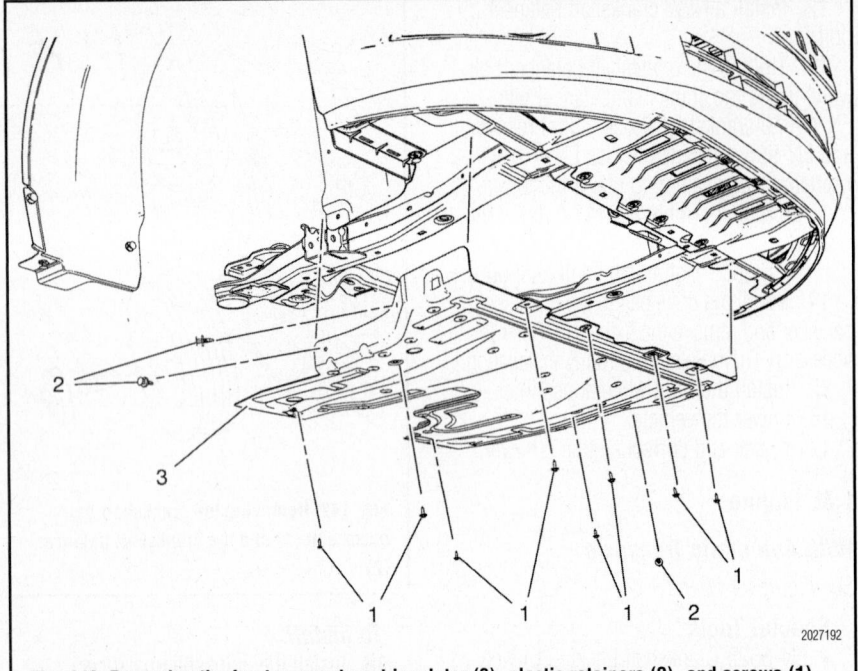

Fig. 143 Removing the front compartment insulator (3), plastic retainers (2), and screws (1)

16. Remove the bolted connection and the EN-6625 locking device to unlock the crankshaft.

17. Install the bolt to the engine block and tighten to 30 ft. lbs. (40 Nm).

18. Install the transaxle front mount.

19. Install the transaxle front mount bolts and tighten to 74 ft. lbs. (100 Nm).

20. If equipped, install the front compartment insulator. Tighten the screws to 27 inch lbs. (3 Nm).

21. Install the drive belt. Refer to Accessory Drive Belts, removal & installation.

22. Install the right front wheelhouse liner.

23. Lower the vehicle.

CRANKSHAFT FRONT SEAL

REMOVAL & INSTALLATION

1.4L Engine

See Figures 147 and 148.

Special Tools
- EN-960 Installer
- EN-45000 Remover Oil seal

1. Before servicing the vehicle, refer to the Precautions Section.

2. Remove the crankshaft balancer. Refer to Crankshaft Damper (Balancer), removal & installation.

3. Place a collecting basin underneath.

4. Using the EN-45000 remover, remove the crankshaft front oil seal from the engine front cover.

To install:

5. Install a NEW crankshaft front oil seal to the EN-960 installer.

6. Use the EN-960 installer to install the crankshaft front oil seal to the engine front cover.

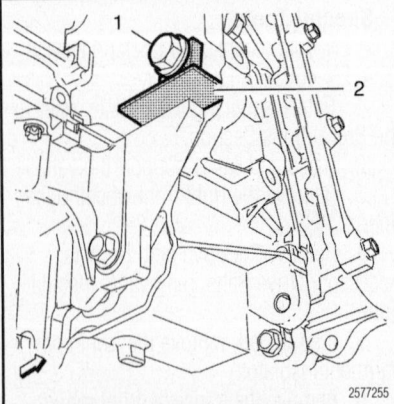

Fig. 144 Removing the transaxle front mount (2) and bolts (1, 3)

9. Install the EN-6625 locking device to lock the crankshaft.

10. Install the bolted connection.

11. Remove and DISCARD the crankshaft balancer bolt.

12. Remove the crankshaft balancer.

To install:

13. Install the crankshaft balancer.

14. Install a NEW crankshaft balancer bolt and tighten in 3 passes using the EN-45059 meter:

15. First pass: Tighten to 70 ft. lbs. (95 Nm).

  a. Second pass: Tighten an additional 45°.

  b. Third pass: Tighten and additional 15°.

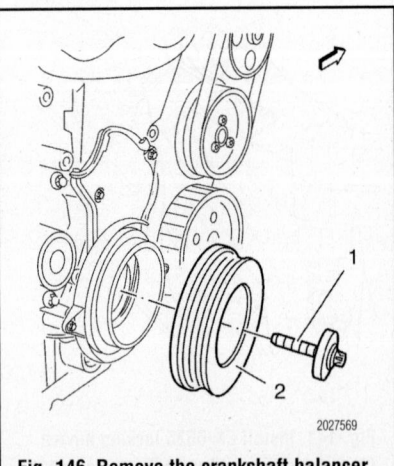

Fig. 146 Remove the crankshaft balancer bolt (1) and the crankshaft balancer (2)

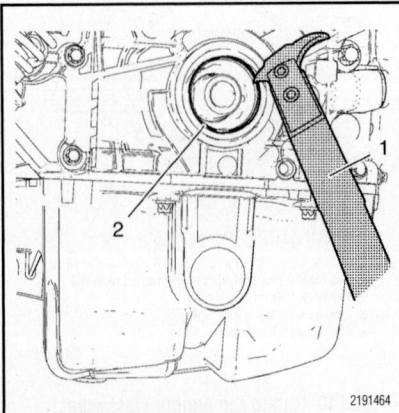

Fig. 147 Using the EN-45000 remover (1), remove the crankshaft front oil seal (2) from engine front cover

Fig. 145 Install the EN-6625 locking device (2) to lock the crankshaft and reinstall the bolted connection (1)

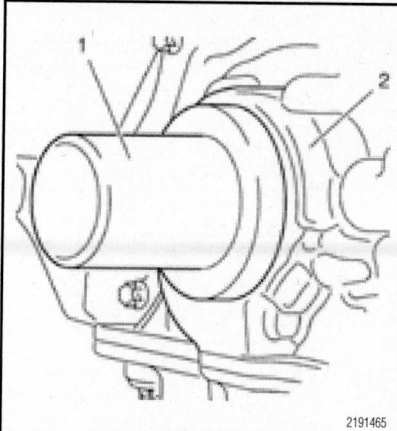

Fig. 148 Using the EN-960 installer (1) to install the crankshaft front oil seal to the engine front cover (2)

7. Ensure that the crankshaft front oil seal is flush with the engine front cover.
8. Install the crankshaft balancer. Refer to Crankshaft Damper (Balancer), removal & installation.
9. Remove the collecting basin.
10. Check and correct the engine oil level.

1.8L Engine

See Figures 149 through 152.

Special Tools
- EN-45000 Remover
- EN-6351 Mounting Sleeves

1. Before servicing the vehicle, refer to the Precautions Section.
2. Remove the timing belt. Refer to Timing Belt & Sprockets, removal & installation.
3. Raise and safely support the vehicle.
4. Remove the crankshaft sprocket.
5. Using the EN-45000 remover, remove the crankshaft front oil seal from the crankshaft.

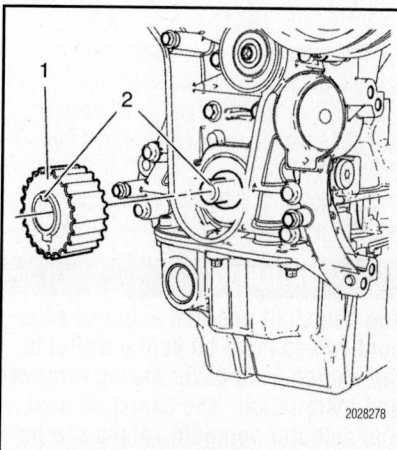

Fig. 149 Crankshaft sprocket (1) showing cam and groove alignment (2)

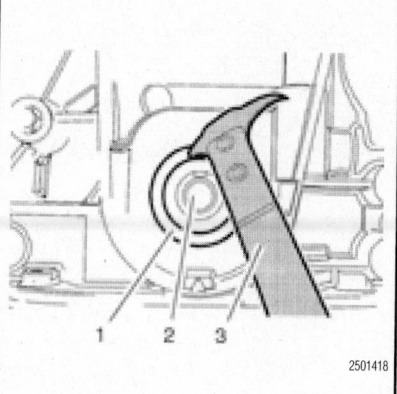

Fig. 150 Using the EN-45000 remover (3), remove the crankshaft front oil seal (1) from the crankshaft (2)

To install:

> ☀☀ **WARNING**
>
> **Clean the crankshaft sealing surface with a clean, lint-free towel. Inspect the lead-in edge of the crankshaft for burrs/sharp edges that could damage the rear main oil seal. Remove the burrs/sharp edges with a crocus cloth before proceeding.**

6. Slide the EN-6351 sleeves protective sleeve onto the crankshaft journal.
7. Slide the crankshaft front oil seal over the protective sleeve on the crankshaft journal.
8. Remove the protective sleeve, and using the EN-6351 sleeves, press the seal ring into the pump housing.
9. Use the crankshaft drive gear bolt and washer to press in the crankshaft front oil seal.

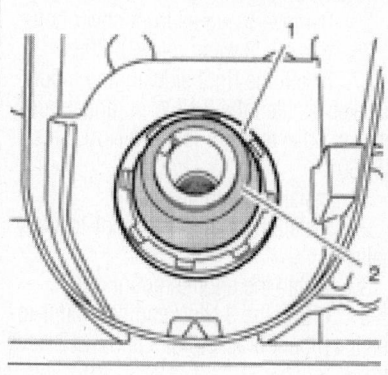

Fig. 151 Slide the EN-6351 (2) protective sleeve onto the crankshaft journal and slide the crankshaft front oil seal (1) over the protective sleeve

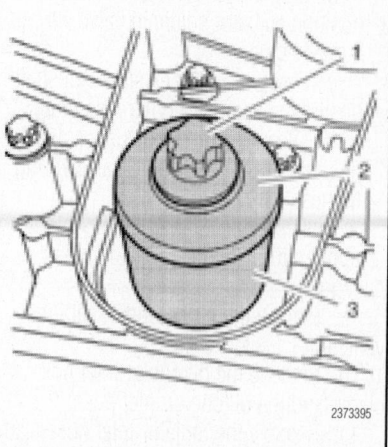

Fig. 152 Using the EN-6351 sleeves (3), press the seal ring into the pump housing. Use the crankshaft drive gear bolt (1) and washer (2) to press in the crankshaft front oil seal

10. Install the crankshaft sprocket.
11. Lower the vehicle.
12. Install the timing belt. Refer to Timing Belt & Sprockets, removal & installation.

CYLINDER HEAD

REMOVAL & INSTALLATION

1.4L Engine

See Figures 153 through 173.

Special Tools
- EN-470-B Angular Torque Wrench
- EN-953-A Fixing Tool
- EN-955-1 Fixing Pin from EN-955 Kit
- EN-952 Fixing Pin
- EN-953-A Fixing Tool
- EN-49977-100 Fixation Sensor Discs

1. Before servicing the vehicle, refer to the Precautions Section.
2. Disconnect the battery negative cable. Refer to Battery, removal & installation.
3. Remove the engine sight shield.
4. Remove the air cleaner assembly along with the air cleaner outlet duct. Refer to Air Cleaner, removal & installation.
5. Remove the positive crankcase ventilation pipe.
6. Remove the intake manifold. Refer to Intake Manifold, removal & installation.
7. Remove the turbocharger. Refer to Turbocharger, removal & installation.
8. Remove the engine control module wiring harness from camshaft cover:
   a. Disconnect the intake camshaft position sensor wiring harness plug.

b. Disconnect the intake camshaft position actuator solenoid valve wiring harness plug.

c. Disconnect the exhaust camshaft position sensor wiring harness plug.

d. Disconnect the exhaust camshaft position actuator solenoid valve wiring harness plug.

e. Disconnect the engine coolant temperature sensor wiring harness plug.

9. Place a drain pan underneath the vehicle.

10. Remove the oil cooler inlet hose clamp and the oil cooler inlet hose.

11. Remove the radiator inlet hose clamp and the radiator inlet hose.

12. Remove the engine coolant air bleed hose.

13. Disconnect the engine coolant temperature sensor wiring harness plug.

Fig. 153 Install an engine lifter (1) to the right engine lift bracket and apply tension to support the engine

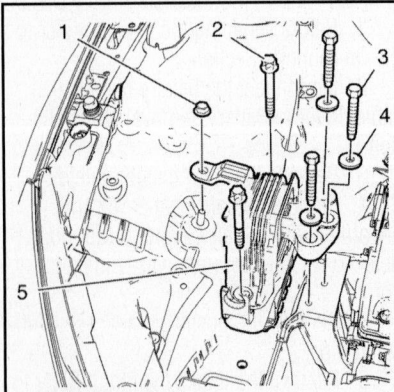

1. Engine mount nut
2. Engine mount-to-body bolts
3. Engine mount-to-engine mount bracket bolts
4. Washers
5. Engine mount

2191341

Fig. 154 Right side engine mount removal—1.4L engine

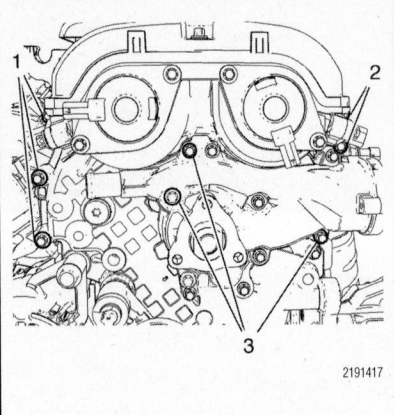

Fig. 155 Remove 5 engine front cover bolts (1, 2) and 3 water pump bolts (3)

14. Remove the heater inlet hose from the water outlet.

15. Remove the ground cable bolt and the ground cable from the engine.

16. Unclip the radiator outlet hose quick connector clamp.

17. Remove the radiator outlet hose from the engine coolant thermostat housing.

18. Install an engine lifter to the right engine lift bracket and apply tension to the engine lifter chain in order to support the engine.

19. Remove and DISCARD the 3 engine mount-to-engine mount bracket bolts and the 3 washers.

20. Remove the 2 engine mount-to-body bolts and the engine mount nut.

21. Remove the engine mount.

22. Remove the drive belt. Refer to Accessory Drive Belts, removal & installation.

23. Remove the drive belt. Refer to Accessory Drive Belts, removal & installation.

24. Remove the water pump pulley. Refer to Water Pump, removal & installation.

25. Remove 5 engine front cover bolts.

26. Remove 3 water pump bolts.

27. Install the right side engine mount bracket. Tighten the 3 NEW engine mount bracket bolts to 45 ft. lbs. (60 Nm), plus 45–60°.

28. Install the engine mount.

29. Install the 2 engine mount-to-body bolts.

30. Install the engine mount nut.

31. Install the 3 NEW engine mount-to-engine mount bracket bolts and the 3 washers.

32. Tighten the 2 engine mount-to-body bolts and the engine mount nut to 46 ft. lbs. (62 Nm).

33. Tighten the 3 engine mount-to-engine mount bracket bolts to 37 ft. lbs. (50 Nm), plus 60–70°.

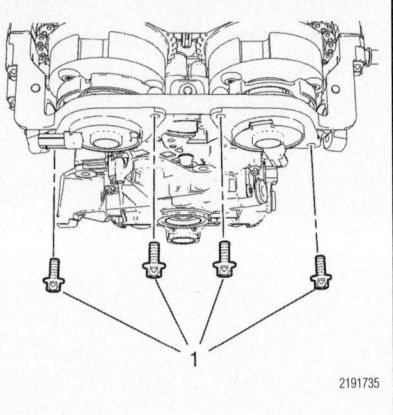

Fig. 156 Remove the 4 camshaft position actuator solenoid valve bolts (1)

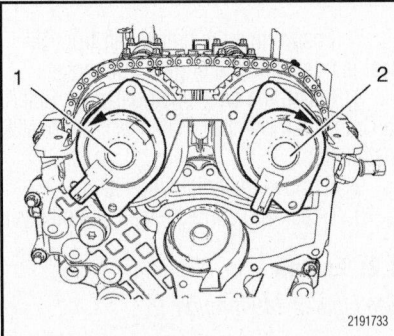

Fig. 157 Move the intake camshaft position actuator solenoid valve (1) counterclockwise to the position shown. Move the exhaust camshaft position actuator solenoid valve (2) clockwise to the position shown

34. Remove the ignition coil. Refer to Ignition Coil, removal & installation.

35. Remove the camshaft cover. Refer to Valve Covers, removal & installation.

36. Set the engine to Top Dead Center (TDC) in the direction of engine rotation to TDC. Use the crankshaft balancer bolt.

37. Remove the 4 camshaft position actuator solenoid valve bolts.

38. Move the intake camshaft position actuator solenoid valve carefully counterclockwise.

39. Move the exhaust camshaft position actuator solenoid valve carefully clockwise.

✳✳ WARNING

The camshaft position actuator solenoid valves must be kept parallel to the engine front cover during removal and installation. The camshaft position actuator solenoid valves can be damaged if they become wedged or stuck during this process.

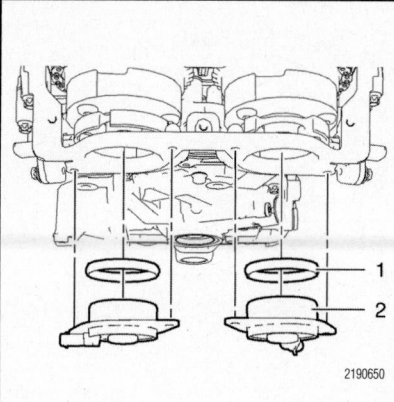

Fig. 158 Removing the 2 camshaft position actuator solenoid valves (2) and the seal rings (1)

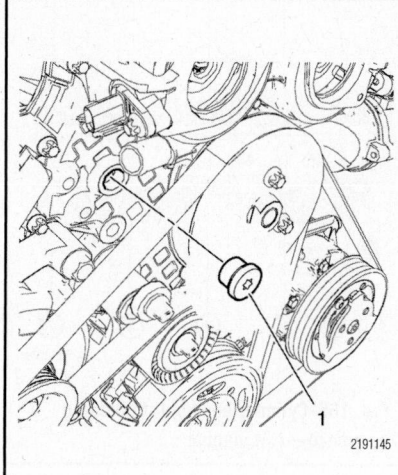

Fig. 159 Remove the timing chain tensioner plug (1) from the engine front cover

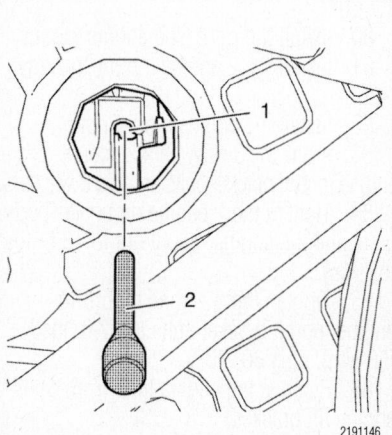

Fig. 160 Install EN-955-1 pin (2) to the timing chain tensioner bore (1) to secure it in place

40. Carefully remove the 2 camshaft position actuator solenoid valves and the seal rings.

41. Remove the timing chain tensioner plug from the engine front cover.

➡**Remove and reinstall the EN-953-A fixing tool for this step.**

42. Install a wrench to the hexagon of the intake camshaft and rotate it clockwise to apply tension to the timing chain and hold.

43. Install EN-955-1 pin to the timing chain tensioner bore to secure it in place.

44. Remove the wrench from the intake camshaft.

45. Remove 2 upper timing chain guide bolts.

46. Remove upper timing chain guide.

47. Loosen the intake camshaft sprocket bolt while holding the hexagon of intake camshaft sprocket with a wrench.

48. Loosen the exhaust camshaft sprocket bolt while holding with a wrench.

49. Remove the 2 camshaft sprocket bolts and the 2 camshaft position exciter wheels.

50. Remove the 2 camshaft sprockets along with the timing chain and place it in the engine front cover.

51. Loosen the 12 cylinder head bolts in sequence. Use the following procedure:

   a. Step 1: Loosen the cylinder head bolts 90°.

   b. Step 2: Loosen the cylinder head bolts 180°.

   c. Step 3: Remove and DISCARD the 12 cylinder head bolts.

52. Move the cylinder head assembly slightly in the direction of the transaxle.

➡**Mind the timing chain tensioner and the timing chain guide pin. A second technician is required.**

53. Remove the cylinder head assembly.

54. Remove the cylinder head gasket.

55. Remove the assembly parts from cylinder head, as necessary:

   a. Remove the EN-953-A fixing tool.

   b. Remove the engine coolant thermostat housing. Refer to Thermostat, removal & installation.

   c. Remove the water outlet.

   d. Remove the intake and exhaust camshafts. Refer to Camshaft and Valve Lifters, removal & installation.

   e. Remove the hydraulic valve lash adjuster arms.

   f. Remove the hydraulic valve lash adjusters.

   g. Remove the 3 engine lift brackets.

To install:

56. Install the cylinder head assembly parts, as necessary:

   a. Install the 3 engine lift brackets.

   b. Install the 3 engine lift bracket bolts and tighten to 16 ft. lbs. (22 Nm).

   c. Install the hydraulic valve lash adjusters.

   d. Install the hydraulic valve lash adjuster arms.

   e. Install the intake and exhaust camshafts. Refer to Camshaft and Valve Lifters, removal & installation.

   f. Install the water outlet.

   g. Install the engine coolant thermostat housing. Refer to Thermostat, removal & installation.

➡**Adjust the camshafts using the hexagon and a wrench.**

   h. Install the EN-953-A fixing tool.

57. Cut the 2 elastomer sealing lips from engine front cover gasket.

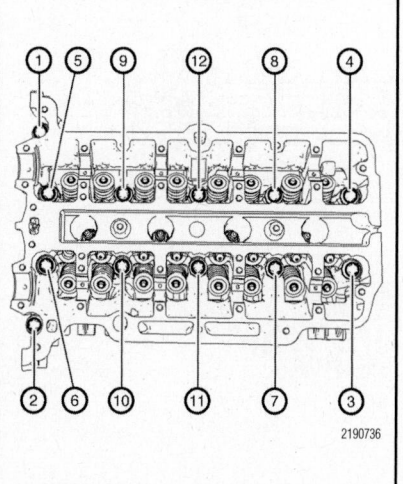

Fig. 161 Cylinder head bolt loosening sequence—1.4L engine

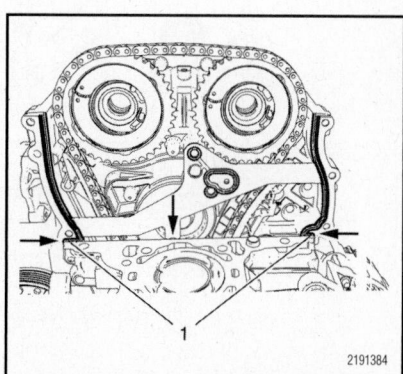

Fig. 162 Cut the 2 elastomer sealing lips (1) from engine front cover gasket and bend at arrows

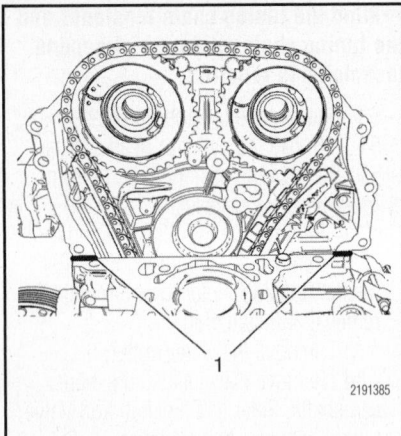

Fig. 163 Apply sealing compound to the shown areas (1)

58. Bend down the engine front cover gasket at the predetermined breaking points.

59. Clean sealing surfaces of engine front cover and engine block from grease and old gasket material.

60. Inspect cylinder block and cylinder head for flatness.

➡ **The thickness of the sealing bead should be 0.08 inch (2mm).**

61. Apply sealing compound to the area shown.

➡ **Mind the marking on the cylinder head gasket for top side.**

62. Install the cylinder head gasket to the engine block.

63. Install 2 engine front cover bolts in order to guide the NEW upper engine front cover gasket.

64. Install the NEW upper engine front cover gasket.

➡ **A second technician is required.**

65. Guide the timing chain guide pin to the timing chain guide and the timing chain tensioner with the installed fixing pin through the timing chain tensioner plug bore in engine front cover.

66. Install the cylinder head.

67. Loosely install 12 NEW cylinder head bolts.

68. Adjust the cylinder head to the engine front cover. Use a rubber mallet.

69. Locate the engine front cover-to-cylinder head by installing 3 bolts.

70. Tighten the 3 bolts to 71 inch lbs. (8 Nm).

71. Tighten the cylinder head bolts in the sequence:

   a. Step 1: Tighten the cylinder head bolts to 26 ft. lbs. (35 Nm).

   b. Step 2: Tighten the cylinder head bolts an additional 180°. Use EN-470-B wrench, or equivalent.

72. Loosen the 3 bolts from engine front cover.

73. Install the 5 remaining bolts to engine front cover and water pump.

74. Tighten the 5 engine front cover bolts and the 3 water pump bolts to 71 inch lbs. (8 Nm).

75. Remove the engine mount bracket.

76. Install the water pump pulley and the water pump pulley bolts.

77. Tighten the 3 water pump pulley bolts to 16 ft. lbs. (22 Nm) while holding the water pump pulley hub with a wrench.

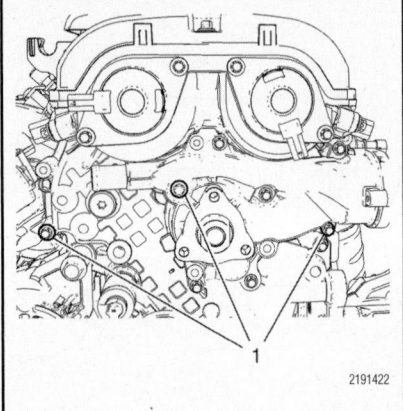

Fig. 165 Locate the engine front cover-to-cylinder head by installing 3 bolts (1)

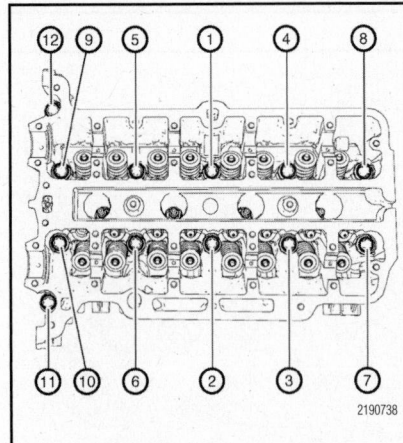

Fig. 166 Cylinder head bolt tightening sequence—1.4L engine

78. Install the drive belt. Refer to Accessory Drive Belts, removal & installation.

79. Install the right side engine mount bracket. Tighten the 3 NEW engine mount bracket bolts to 45 ft. lbs. (60 Nm), plus 45–60°.

80. Install the right side engine mount.

81. Install the 2 engine mount-to-body bolts.

82. Install the engine mount nut.

83. Install the 3 NEW engine mount-to-engine mount bracket bolts and the 3 washers.

84. Tighten the 2 engine mount-to-body bolts and the engine mount nut to 46 ft. lbs. (62 Nm).

85. Tighten the 3 engine mount-to-engine mount bracket bolts to 37 ft. lbs. (50 Nm), plus 60–70°.

86. Remove the engine lifter from right engine lift bracket.

87. Install the 2 camshaft sprockets along with the timing chain.

➡ **Camshaft position exciter wheels should stay rotatable.**

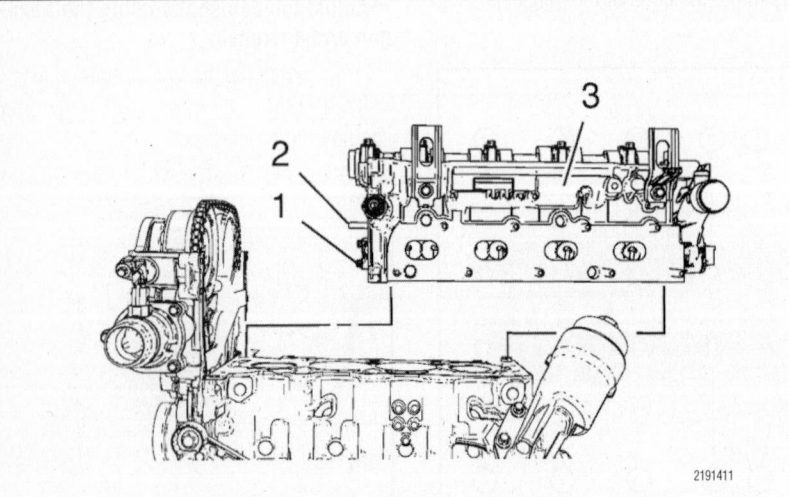

Fig. 164 Guide the timing chain guide pin (2) to the timing chain guide and the timing chain tensioner (1) with the installed fixing pin through the timing chain tensioner plug bore in engine front cover and install the cylinder head (3)

Fig. 167 Install the 2 camshaft position exciter wheels (1) and the 2 camshaft sprocket bolts (2)

88. Install the 2 camshaft position exciter wheels and the 2 camshaft sprocket bolts.

89. Remove the crankshaft bearing cap tie plate hole plug and the seal ring.

> **✳✳ WARNING**
>
> **To ensure proper crankshaft Top Dead Center (TDC) alignment, the retention pin should fit easily through the bore in the crankshaft tie plate and into the crankshaft. Binding of the retention pin could affect proper engine timing.**

90. Install the EN-952 fixing pin to hold the crankshaft in TDC position.

91. Loosen the intake camshaft sprocket bolt while holding the hexagon of the intake camshaft with a wrench until the camshaft position exciter wheel is clearly rotatable.

92. Loosen the exhaust camshaft sprocket bolt while holding the hexagon of the exhaust camshaft with a wrench until the

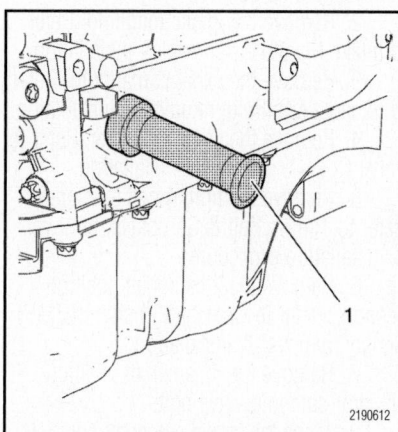

Fig. 168 Install the EN-952 fixing pin (1) to hold the crankshaft in TDC position

camshaft position exciter wheel is clearly rotatable.

➡ **The fixing tool should be installed completely to both camshaft grooves without high effort.**

93. Adjust the camshafts so that the EN-953-A fixing tool can be installed.

94. Remove the 2 upper timing chain guide bolts, if installed.

95. Remove the upper timing chain guide, if installed.

➡ **Push the fixing tool in the direction of the arrow to ensure it engages without clearance.**

96. Install the EN-49977-200 fixing tool and adjust the gearing of the fixing tool so it engages with the intake camshaft sprocket gearing.

97. Tighten the 2 fastening bolts of the

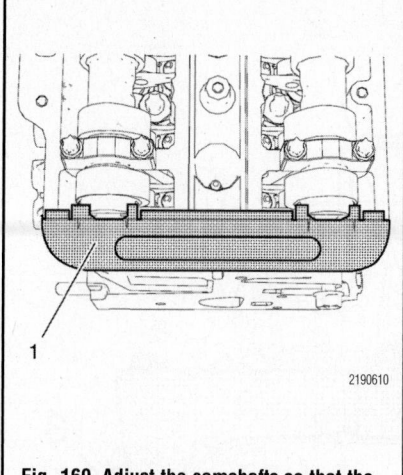

Fig. 169 Adjust the camshafts so that the EN-953-A fixing tool (1) can be installed

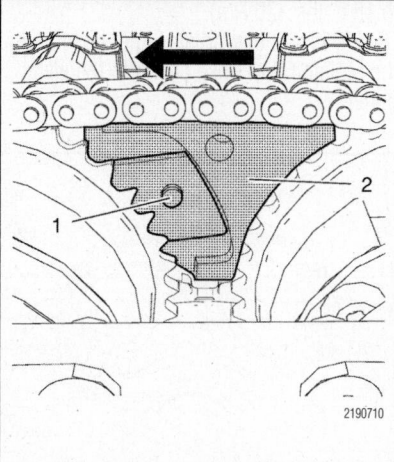

Fig. 170 Install the EN-49977-200 fixing tool (2) and adjust the gearing of the fixing tool so it engages with the intake camshaft sprocket gearing (1)

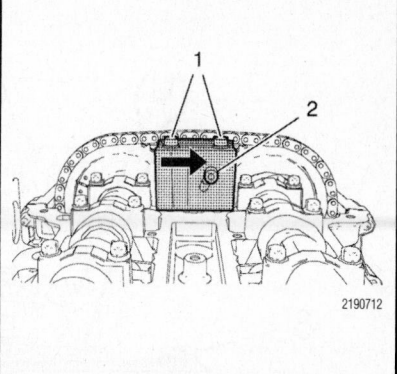

Fig. 171 Tighten the 2 fastening bolts (1) of the EN-49977-200 fixing tool while pushing the fixing tool in direction of the arrow, then tighten the adjuster bolt (2)

EN-49977-200 fixing tool while pushing the fixing tool in direction of the arrow.

98. Tighten the adjuster bolt.

> **✳✳ WARNING**
>
> **A wrong installation position is possible. Make sure that the fixation tool is installed without clearance to the cylinder head in areas and.**

99. Install the EN-49977-100 fixation to find and hold the camshaft position exciter wheels in the correct position.

100. Tighten the 2 fastening bolts of the EN-49977-100 fixation.

101. Tighten the intake camshaft sprocket bolt while holding the hexagon:
 a. Step 1: Tighten to 37 ft. lbs. (50 Nm).
 b. Step 2: Tighten an additional 60°.

102. Tighten the exhaust camshaft sprocket bolt while holding the hexagon:
 a. Step 1: Tighten to 37 ft. lbs. (50 Nm).
 b. Step 2: Tighten an additional 60°.

103. Remove the EN-49977-100 fixation and the EN-49977-200 fixing tool.

104. Install the upper timing chain guide.

105. Install the 2 upper timing chain guide bolts and tighten to 71 inch lbs. (8 Nm).

106. Remove the EN-953-A fixing tool.

107. Remove the EN-952 fixing pin.

108. Rotate the crankshaft for 720° and check the engine timing again. Repeat the adjustment procedure if necessary.

109. Install the crankshaft bearing cap tie plate hole plug and seal ring and tighten to 30 ft. lbs. (40 Nm).

110. Install the front compartment insulator.

111. Install the right front wheelhouse liner.

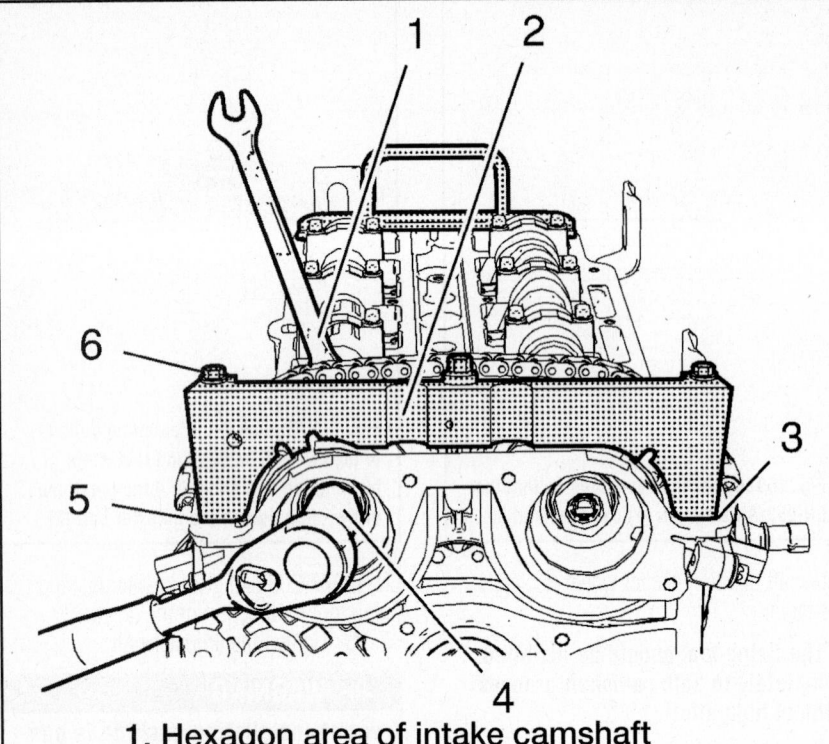

1. Hexagon area of intake camshaft
2. EN-49977-100 fixation
3. Cylinder head no clearance area
4. Intake camshaft sprocket bolt
5. Cylinder head no clearance area
6. Fastening bolts of the EN-49977-100

2190709

Fig. 172 Special tools used while tightening camshaft sprocket bolts

※※ WARNING

The camshaft position actuator solenoid valves must be kept parallel to the engine front cover during removal and installation. The camshaft position actuator solenoid valves can be damaged if they become wedged or stuck during this process.

112. Install the 2 camshaft position actuator solenoid valves and the 2 seal rings by carefully and evenly pressing.

113. Install the 4 camshaft position actuator solenoid valve bolts and tighten to 71 inch lbs. (8 Nm).

114. The 2 camshaft position actuator solenoid valves should be installed in the correct position.

115. Install the camshaft cover. Refer to Valve Covers, removal & installation.

116. Install the ignition coil. Refer to Ignition Coil, removal & installation.

117. Remove all special tools for timing chain adjustment and install and tighten the timing chain tensioner plug.

118. Connect radiator outlet hose to engine coolant thermostat housing. Clip quick connector.

119. Install the ground cable and the ground cable bolt to the engine and tighten to 15 ft. lbs. (20 Nm).

120. Install the radiator inlet hose and the radiator inlet hose clamp to the water outlet.

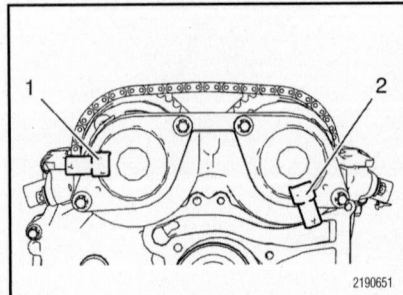

2190651

Fig. 173 The 2 camshaft position actuator solenoid valves should be installed in the position as shown (1) and (2)

121. Install the oil cooler inlet hose and the oil cooler inlet hose clamp to the water outlet.

122. Connect the engine coolant air bleed hose to the water outlet.

123. Connect the engine coolant temperature sensor wiring harness plug.

124. Install the heater inlet hose to the water outlet.

125. Install the engine control module wiring harness to the camshaft cover:

   a. Connect the engine coolant temperature sensor wiring harness plug.

   b. Connect the exhaust camshaft position actuator solenoid valve wiring harness plug.

   c. Connect the exhaust camshaft position sensor wiring harness plug.

   d. Connect the intake camshaft position actuator solenoid valve wiring harness plug.

   e. Connect the intake camshaft position sensor wiring harness plug.

126. Install the turbocharger. Refer to Turbocharger, removal & installation.

127. Install the intake manifold. Refer to Intake Manifold, removal & installation.

128. Install the air cleaner assembly in compound with the air cleaner outlet duct. Refer to Air Cleaner, removal & installation.

129. Install the engine sight shield.

130. Connect the battery negative cable. Refer to Battery, removal & installation.

131. Fill the engine coolant with the proper amount and type of fluid. Refer to Engine Coolant, Drain & Refill Procedure.

132. Check and correct the engine oil as necessary.

1.8L Engine

See Figures 174 through 179.

Special Tools

- EN-45059 Torque Angle Sensor Kit

1. Before servicing the vehicle, refer to the Precautions Section.

2. Remove the intake manifold. Refer to Intake Manifold, removal & installation.

3. Remove the exhaust manifold. Refer to Exhaust Manifold, removal & installation.

4. Remove the camshaft cover. Refer to Valve Covers, removal & installation.

5. Remove the timing belt tensioner. Refer to Timing Belt & Sprockets, removal & installation procedure.

6. Remove the 2 camshaft position sensors. Refer to Camshaft Position (CMP) Sensor, removal & installation.

7. Remove the 4 camshaft position actuator solenoid valve bolts.

8. Move the intake camshaft position actuator solenoid valve carefully counter-clockwise.

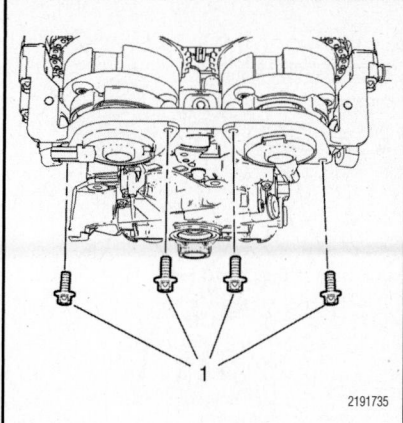

Fig. 174 Remove the 4 camshaft position actuator solenoid valve bolts (1)

9. Move the exhaust camshaft position actuator solenoid valve carefully clockwise.

⁂ WARNING

The camshaft position actuator solenoid valves must be kept parallel to the engine front cover during removal and installation. The camshaft position actuator solenoid valves can be damaged if they become wedged or stuck during this process.

10. Carefully remove the 2 camshaft position actuator solenoid valves and the seal rings.

11. Remove the 2 camshaft position actuator adjusters. Refer to Camshaft Position Actuator Adjuster, removal & installation.

12. Remove the timing belt rear cover. Refer to Timing Belt Rear Cover, removal & installation.

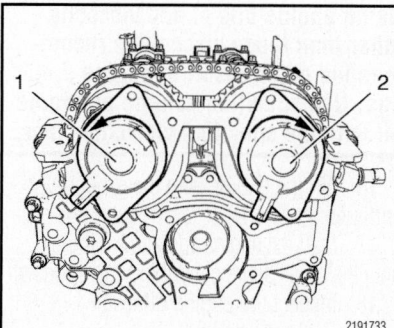

Fig. 175 Move the intake camshaft position actuator solenoid valve (1) counterclockwise to the position shown. Move the exhaust camshaft position actuator solenoid valve (2) clockwise to the position shown

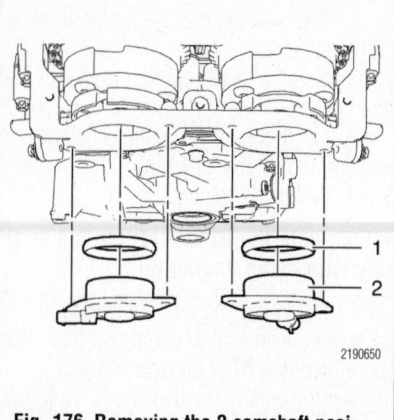

Fig. 176 Removing the 2 camshaft position actuator solenoid valves (2) and the seal rings (1)

13. Remove engine coolant thermostat housing. Refer to Thermostat, removal & installation.

14. Loosen the 10 cylinder head bolts in sequence.

   a. Step 1: Loosen the 10 bolts 90°.

   b. Step 2: Loosen the 10 bolts 180°.

   c. Remove the 10 cylinder head bolts.

15. Remove and DISCARD the cylinder head.

16. Remove and Discard the cylinder head gasket.

To install:

17. Clean the sealing surfaces.

18. Inspect for cylinder head and cylinder block for flatness.

19. Install a NEW cylinder head gasket.

20. Install the cylinder head.

21. Install 10 NEW cylinder head bolts in sequence using the EN-45059 sensor kit, or equivalent:

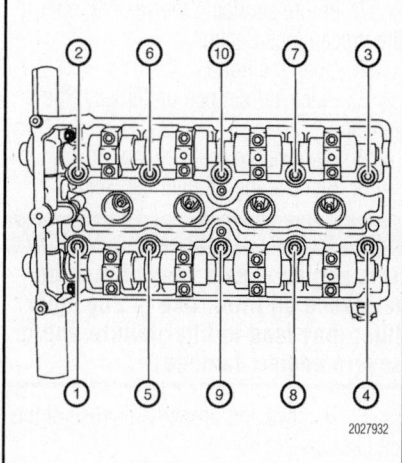

Fig. 177 Cylinder head bolt loosening sequence—1.8L engine

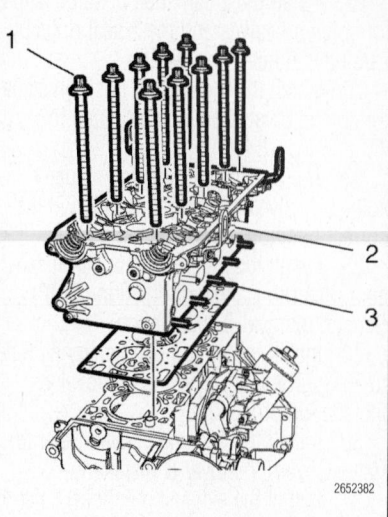

Fig. 178 Exploded view of cylinder head (2), bolts (1), and gasket (3)—1.8L engine

   a. First pass: Tighten to 18 ft. lbs. (25 Nm).

   b. Second pass: Tighten 90°.

   c. Third pass: Tighten 90°.

   d. Fourth pass: Tighten 90°.

   e. Fifth pass: Tighten 45°.

22. Install engine coolant thermostat housing. Refer to Thermostat, removal & installation.

23. Install the timing belt rear cover. Refer to Timing Belt Rear Cover, removal & installation.

24. Install the camshaft position actuator adjuster. Refer to Camshaft Position Actuator Adjuster, removal & installation.

⁂ WARNING

The camshaft position actuator solenoid valves must be kept parallel to the engine front cover during removal and installation. The camshaft position actuator solenoid valves can be damaged if they become wedged or stuck during this process.

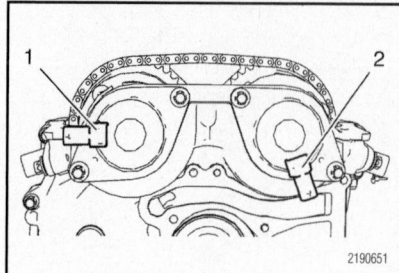

Fig. 179 The 2 camshaft position actuator solenoid valves should be installed in the position as shown (1) and (2)

25. Install the 2 camshaft position actuator solenoid valves and the 2 seal rings by carefully and evenly pressing.

26. Install the 4 camshaft position actuator solenoid valve bolts and tighten to 71 inch lbs. (8 Nm).

27. The 2 camshaft position actuator solenoid valves should be installed in the correct position.

28. Install the 2 camshaft position sensors. Refer to Camshaft Position (CMP) Sensor, removal & installation.

29. Install the timing belt tensioner. Refer to Timing Belt & Sprockets, removal & installation procedure.

30. Install the camshaft cover. Refer to Valve Covers, removal & installation.

31. Install the exhaust manifold. Refer to Exhaust Manifold, removal & installation.

32. Install the intake manifold. Refer to Intake Manifold, removal & installation.

33. Fill the engine coolant with the proper amount and type of fluid. Refer to Engine Coolant, Drain & Refill Procedure.

34. Check and correct the engine oil as necessary.

ENGINE OIL & FILTER

REPLACEMENT

1.4L Engine

See Figure 180.

1. Before servicing the vehicle, refer to the Precautions Section.

2. Open the hood.

3. Place a drain pan below the vehicle.

4. Remove the engine oil filter cap in compound with the engine oil filter cap seal ring and the oil filter element.

5. Raise and safely support the vehicle.

6. Remove the oil pan drain plug and allow the oil to drain into the drain pan.

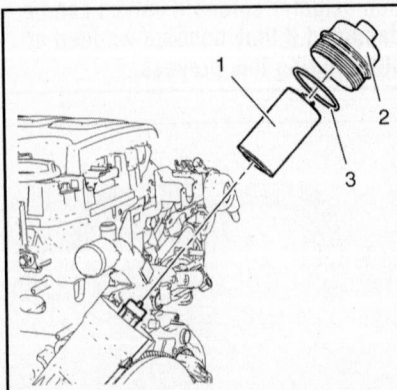

2190433

Fig. 180 View of the engine oil filter cap (2), engine oil filter cap seal ring (3), and the oil filter element (1)—1.4L engine

To install:

7. Clean the oil pan drain plug threads in the oil pan.

8. Install a NEW seal ring to the oil pan drain plug.

9. Install the oil pan drain plug and tighten to 10 ft. lbs. (14 Nm).

10. Lower the vehicle.

➡ **Lubricate the NEW oil filter cap seal ring with clean engine oil.**

11. Install the engine oil filter cap in compound with a NEW engine oil filter cap seal ring and a NEW oil filter element. Tighten the engine oil filter cap to 18 ft. lbs. (25 Nm).

❋❋ WARNING

Over-tightening the oil filter cap may cause damage to the oil filter cap resulting in an oil leak.

❋❋ WARNING

Using engine oils of any viscosity other than those viscosities recommended could result in engine damage.

➡ **Do not overfill the engine with engine oil.**

12. Fill the engine with the proper type and amount of NEW engine oil.

13. Start the engine and allow it to run until the oil pressure control indicator goes off.

14. Inspect the engine oil level.

15. Close the hood.

16. Reset the service interval indicator. Refer to Oil Life System Resetting.

1.8L Engine

See Figure 181.

1. Before servicing the vehicle, refer to the Precautions Section.

2. Open the hood.

3. Place a drain pan underneath the vehicle.

4. Remove the oil filter cap.

5. Remove the oil filter cap seal.

❋❋ WARNING

This engine uses a special high performance oil filter. Use of any other filter may lead to filter failure and/or severe engine damage.

6. Remove and properly dispose of the oil filter insert.

7. Raise and safely support the vehicle.

8. Remove the oil pan drain plug and allow the oil to drain into the drain pan.

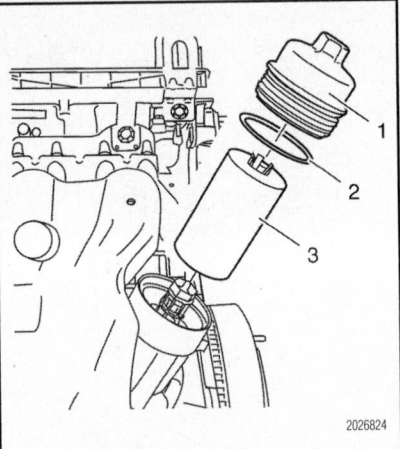

2026824

Fig. 181 View of the oil filter cap (1), oil filter cap seal (2), and oil filter insert (3)—1.8L engine

To install:

9. Clean the oil drain plug threads and the threads in the oil pan.

10. Install a NEW seal to the oil drain plug.

11. Install the oil drain bolt to the oil pan and tighten to 10 ft. lbs. (14 Nm).

12. Lower the vehicle.

13. Install the NEW oil filter insert.

➡ **Coat the seal ring with NEW engine oil.**

14. Install the NEW oil filter cap seal

❋❋ WARNING

Over-tightening the oil filter cap may cause damage to the oil filter cap resulting in an oil leak.

15. Install the oil filter cap and tighten to 18 ft. lbs. (25 Nm).

❋❋ WARNING

Using engine oils of any viscosity other than those viscosities recommended could result in engine damage. Use specified volume of engine oil with the specified viscosity class.

16. Fill the engine with the proper type and amount of oil.

17. Start the engine and allow it to run until the oil pressure control indicator goes off.

18. Inspect the engine oil level.

19. Close the hood

20. Reset the service interval indicator. Refer to Oil Life System Resetting.

Oil Life System Resetting

Description

The engine oil life system lets you know when to change the engine oil and filter.

Based on driving conditions, the interval at which an engine oil and filter change will be indicated can vary considerably. How to display the remaining oil duration is described in the Owner's Manual under Instruments and controls.

For the oil life system to work properly, the system must be reset every time the oil is changed. When the system has calculated that oil life has been diminished, it will indicate that an oil change is necessary.

The up level display will indicate CHANGE ENGINE OIL SOON. The low level display will indicate a certain code which is referenced in the Owner's Manual.

The engine oil and filter must be changed within one week or 300 miles (500 km).

It is possible that, if the vehicle is driven under the best conditions, the oil life system may not indicate that an oil change is necessary for over a year. However, the engine oil and filter must be changed by 18,640 miles (30,000 km), but at least once a year and at this time the system must be reset.

Remember to reset the oil life system whenever the oil and filter is changed.

Manual Oil Life System Reset

1. Before servicing the vehicle, refer to the Precautions Section.
2. Turn the ignition ON.
3. Push the Menu button on the turn signal switch.
4. Use the adjustment wheel and select the menu—Vehicle Information System.
5. Use the adjustment wheel and select the menu—Oil Life System.
6. Push the SET/CLR button on the turn signal switch and push the brake pedal at same time.

Automatic Oil Life System Reset

1. Before servicing the vehicle, refer to the Precautions Section.
2. Turn the ignition ON.
3. Connect a scan tool.
4. Select Module Diagnosis.
5. Select Engine Control Module.
6. Select Configuration/Reset function.
7. Select Engine Oil System Reset.
8. Push the Enter button to run the function.
9. Confirm that the procedure was executed successfully.
   a. Turn the ignition OFF and confirm.
   b. Turn the ignition ON and confirm.
10. Repeat the procedure if reset was incomplete.

EXHAUST MANIFOLD

REMOVAL & INSTALLATION

1.4L Engine

Refer to Turbocharger, removal & installation.

1.8L Engine

See Figures 182 and 183.

> ※ **CAUTION**
>
> **In order to avoid being burned, do not service the exhaust system while it is still hot. Service the system when it is cool.**

> ※ **CAUTION**
>
> **Always wear protective goggles and gloves when removing exhaust parts as falling rust and sharp edges from worn exhaust components could result in serious personal injury.**

1. Before servicing the vehicle, refer to the Precautions Section.
2. Disconnect the battery negative cable. Refer to Battery, removal & installation.
3. Disconnect the heated oxygen sensor wiring harness plug.
4. Remove the oil dipstick.

➡ **If the engine oil level is at maximum, some oil may emerge when drawing out the oil dipstick guide tube.**

5. Place a drain pan underneath the vehicle.
6. Remove the oil level indicator tube bolt.
7. Remove the oil level indicator tube and the oil level indicator seal.

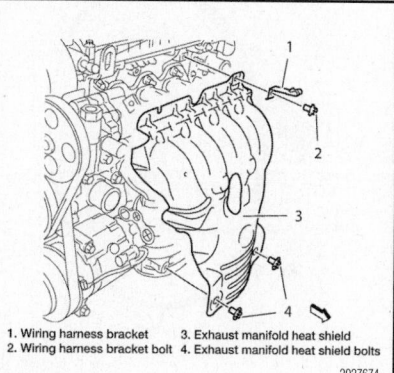

1. Wiring harness bracket
2. Wiring harness bracket bolt
3. Exhaust manifold heat shield
4. Exhaust manifold heat shield bolts

2027674

Fig. 182 Catalytic converter heat shield removal

8. Remove the wiring harness bracket bolt and the wiring harness bracket.
9. Remove the 2 exhaust manifold heat shield bolts.
10. Remove the exhaust manifold heat shield.
11. Remove the catalytic converter-to-flexible exhaust pipe nuts.
12. Remove the flexible exhaust pipe.
13. Remove the catalytic converter-to-flexible exhaust pipe gasket.
14. Remove the exhaust manifold brace bolts.
15. Remove the heated oxygen sensor. Refer to Heated Oxygen (HO2S) Sensor, removal & installation.
16. Remove the catalytic converter/exhaust manifold-to-cylinder head nuts.
17. Remove the catalytic converter-to-cylinder head gasket.

To install:

18. Install the catalytic converter-to-cylinder head gasket.
19. Install the catalytic converter/exhaust manifold-to-cylinder head nuts. Tighten to 15 ft. lbs. (20 Nm).
20. Install the heated oxygen sensor. Tighten to 31 ft. lbs. (42 Nm). Refer to Heated Oxygen (HO2S) Sensor, removal & installation for more information.
21. Install the exhaust manifold brace bolts. Tighten to 15 ft. lbs. (20 Nm).
22. Install the catalytic converter-to-flexible exhaust pipe gasket.
23. Install the flexible exhaust pipe.
24. Install the catalytic converter-to-flexible exhaust pipe nuts. Tighten to 16 ft. lbs. (22 Nm).
25. Install the exhaust manifold heat shield.
26. Install the 2 exhaust manifold heat shield bolts and tighten to 71 inch lbs. (8 Nm).
27. Install the wiring harness bracket and the wiring harness bracket bolt and tighten to 11 ft. lbs. (15 Nm).
28. Install the oil level indicator tube.
29. Install a NEW oil level indicator tube gasket.
30. Install the oil level indicator tube bolt and tighten to 11 ft. lbs. (15 Nm).
31. Install the oil dipstick.
32. Connect the heated oxygen sensor wiring harness plug.
33. Connect the battery negative cable. Refer to Battery, removal & installation.

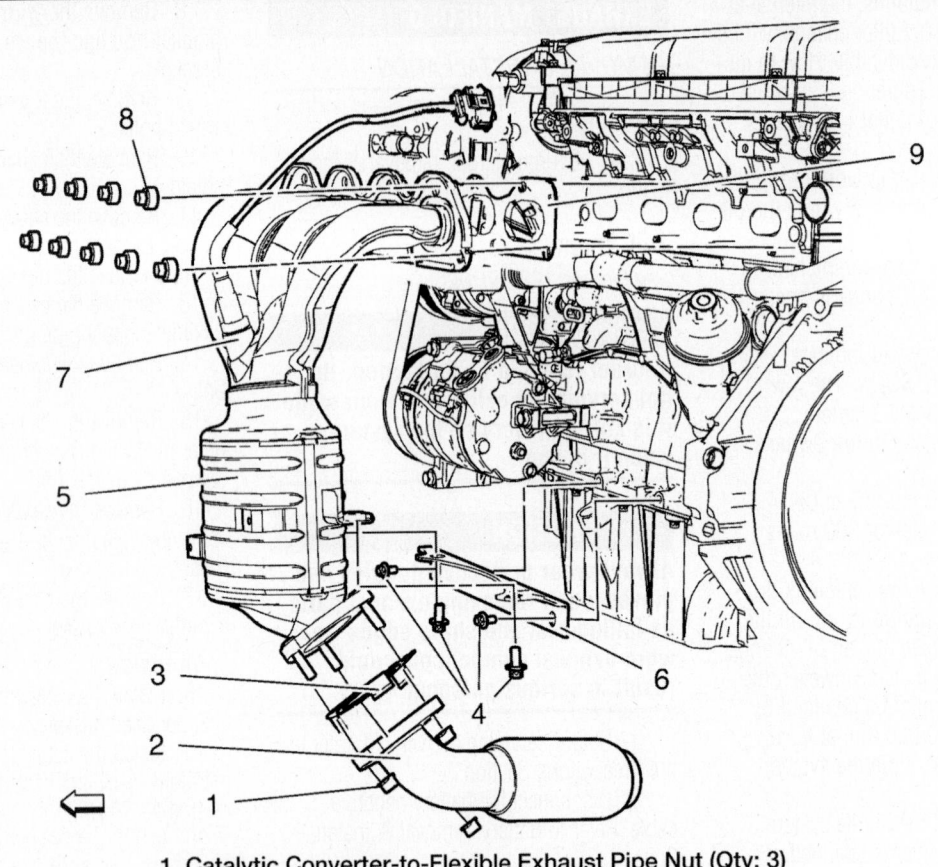

1. Catalytic Converter-to-Flexible Exhaust Pipe Nut (Qty: 3)
2. Flexible Exhaust Pipe
3. Catalytic Converter-to-Flexible Exhaust Pipe Gasket
4. Exhaust Manifold Brace Bolt (Qty: 4)
5. Catalytic Converter
6. Exhaust Manifold Brace
7. Heated Oxygen Sensor
8. Catalytic Converter-to-Cylinder Head Nut (Qty: 9)
9. Catalytic Converter-to-Cylinder Head Gasket

Fig. 183 Exploded view of exhaust manifold—1.8L engine

FLYWHEEL/FLEXPLATE

REMOVAL & INSTALLATION

1.4L Engine

With Automatic Transaxle

See Figure 184.

Special Tools
- EN-470-B Angular Torque Wrench
- EN-652 Flywheel Holder

1. Before servicing the vehicle, refer to the Precautions Section.
2. Remove the automatic transaxle.
3. Install EN-652 flywheel holder in order to fix the automatic transaxle flexplate.
4. Remove and DISCARD the 6 automatic transaxle flexplate bolts.
5. Remove the automatic transaxle flexplate.

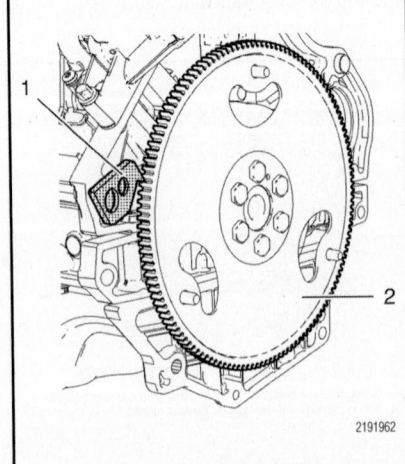

Fig. 184 Using EN-652 flywheel holder (1) to fix the automatic transaxle flexplate (2)

To install:

6. Clean the 6 screw bores. Rework if necessary.
7. Install the automatic transaxle flexplate.
8. Install 6 NEW automatic transaxle flexplate bolts.
9. Install EN-652 flywheel holder in order to fix the automatic transaxle flexplate.
10. Tighten the 6 automatic transaxle flexplate bolts in a cross sequence:
    a. Step 1: Tighten to 26 ft. lbs. (35 Nm).
    b. Step 2: Tighten 30°.
    c. Step 3: Tighten an additional 15°.
11. Install automatic transaxle.

With Manual Transaxle

See Figure 185.

Special Tools
- EN-470-B Angular Torque Wrench
- EN-652 Flywheel Holder

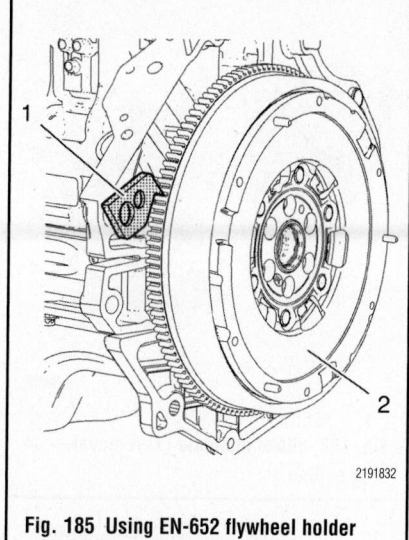

Fig. 185 Using EN-652 flywheel holder (1) to fix the engine flywheel (2)

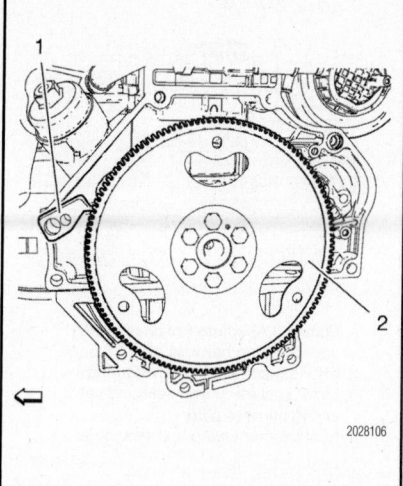

Fig. 186 Using EN-652 flexplate holder (1) to fix the automatic transaxle flexplate (2)

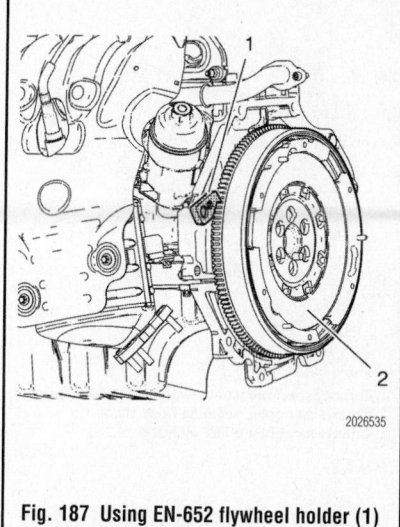

Fig. 187 Using EN-652 flywheel holder (1) to fix the flywheel (2)

1. Before servicing the vehicle, refer to the Precautions Section.

2. Remove the clutch pressure and driven plate from the engine flywheel. Refer to Clutch, removal & installation.

3. Install EN-652 flywheel holder in order to fix the engine flywheel.

4. Remove and DISCARD the 6 engine flywheel bolts.

5. Remove the engine flywheel.

To install:

6. Clean the 6 screw bores. Rework if necessary.

7. Install the engine flywheel.

8. Install 6 NEW engine flywheel bolts.

9. Install EN-652 flywheel holder in order to fix the engine flywheel.

10. Tighten the 6 engine flywheel bolts in a cross sequence:

    a. Step 1: Tighten to 44 ft. lbs. (60 Nm).

    b. Step 2: Tighten 45°.

    c. Step 3: Tighten an additional 15°.

11. Install the clutch pressure and driven plate. Refer to Clutch, removal & installation.

12. Install the manual transaxle. Refer to Manual Transaxle Assembly, removal & installation.

1.8L Engine

With Automatic Transaxle

See Figure 186.

Special Tools

• EN-652 Automatic Transaxle Flexplate Holder

1. Before servicing the vehicle, refer to the Precautions Section.

2. Install the EN-652 holder to hold the automatic transaxle flexplate.

3. Loosen the 6 automatic transaxle flexplate bolts.

4. Remove the EN-652 holder.

5. Remove the 6 automatic transaxle flexplate bolts.

6. Remove the automatic transaxle flexplate.

To install:

7. Clean the automatic transaxle flexplate bolt threads.

8. Install the automatic transaxle flexplate and the EN-652 holder.

9. Install the 6 NEW automatic transaxle flexplate bolts and tighten in a crisscross manner:

    • Tighten to 44 ft. lbs. (60 Nm), plus or minus 5°.

10. Remove the EN-652 holder.

With Manual Transaxle

See Figure 187.

Special Tools

• EN-652 Flywheel Holder
• EN-45059 Torque Angle Sensor Kit

1. Before servicing the vehicle, refer to the Precautions Section.

2. Install the EN-652 holder to lock the flywheel via the starter ring gear.

3. Loosen the 6 flywheel bolts.

4. Remove the EN-652 holder.

5. Remove and DISCARD the 6 flywheel bolts.

6. Remove the flywheel.

To install:

7. Clean the threads in the crankshaft.

8. Install the flywheel.

9. Install the EN-652 holder.

10. Install the 6 NEW flywheel bolts and tighten using the EN-45059 sensor kit:

    a. Step 1: Tighten to 26 ft. lbs. (35 Nm).

    b. Step 2: Tighten 30°.

    c. Step 3: Tighten an additional 15°.

11. Remove the EN-652 holder.

INTAKE MANIFOLD

REMOVAL & INSTALLATION

1.4L Engine

See Figures 188 through 192.

Special Tools

• EN-34730-91 Pressure Tester

1. Before servicing the vehicle, refer to the Precautions Section.

2. Disconnect the battery negative cable. Refer to Battery, removal & installation.

3. Remove the engine sight shield.

4. Unclip the heater outlet hose from retainer clip.

5. Unclip the engine control module wiring harness from 2 retainer clips.

6. Disconnect the turbocharger pressure sensor wiring harness plug.

7. Loosen the charge air cooler outlet air hose clamp.

8. Remove the charge air cooler outlet air hose from the throttle body.

9. Remove the front bumper fascia.

10. Unclip the radiator inlet hose from the charge air cooler outlet air hose.

11. Remove the charge air cooler outlet air hose from the charge air cooler.

12. Disconnect the throttle body wiring harness plug.

13. Disconnect the evaporative emission canister purge solenoid valve wiring harness plug.

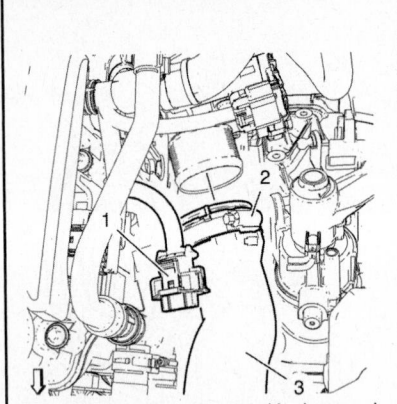

1. Turbocharger pressure sensor wiring harness plug
2. Charge air cooler outlet air hose clamp
3. Charge air cooler outlet air hose

2192306

Fig. 188 View of charge air cooler outlet air hose (3), turbocharger pressure sensor wiring harness plug (1), and charge air cooler outlet air hose clamp (2)

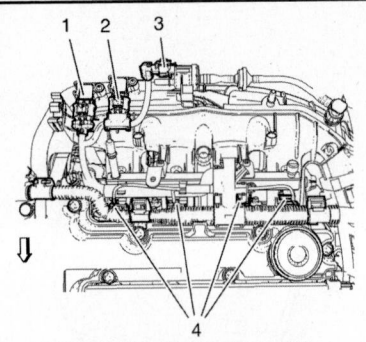

1. Manifold Absolute Pressure (MAP) sensor wiring harness plug
2. MAP sensor wiring harness plug
3. EVAP canister purge solenoid valve wiring harness plug
4. Fuel injector wiring harness plugs

2192265

Fig. 190 Make note of the installed position of the manifold absolute pressure sensor wiring harness plugs to ensure they will be connected in their original position

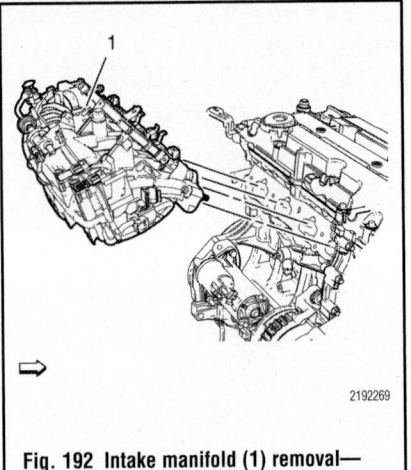

2192269

Fig. 192 Intake manifold (1) removal—1.4L engine

23. Disconnect the positive crankcase ventilation pipe from the intake manifold.

24. Disconnect the fuel ventilation pipe from the evaporative emission canister purge solenoid valve.

25. Unclip the fuel ventilation pipe from the retainer clip.

26. Disconnect the brake booster vacuum pipe from intake manifold.

➡ **The intake manifold bolts remain in intake manifold. Note the installation of the fuel rail ground strap for proper installation.**

27. Remove the 6 intake manifold bolts.

28. Remove the intake manifold.

29. Remove and DISCARD the intake manifold gasket.

30. Remove the assembly parts from the intake manifold as necessary.

To install:

31. Install the assembly parts to the intake manifold as necessary.

32. Clean the sealing surfaces.

33. Install the intake manifold along with a NEW intake manifold gasket.

➡ **Install the fuel rail ground strap to the appropriate intake manifold bolt.**

34. Install the 6 intake manifold bolts and tighten to 15 ft. lbs. (20 Nm).

35. Connect the fuel ventilation pipe to the evaporative emission canister purge solenoid valve.

36. Clip in the fuel ventilation pipe to the retainer clip.

37. Connect the positive crankcase ventilation pipe to the intake manifold.

38. Connect the fuel feed pipe to the fuel rail.

39. Clip in the fuel feed pipe to retainer clip.

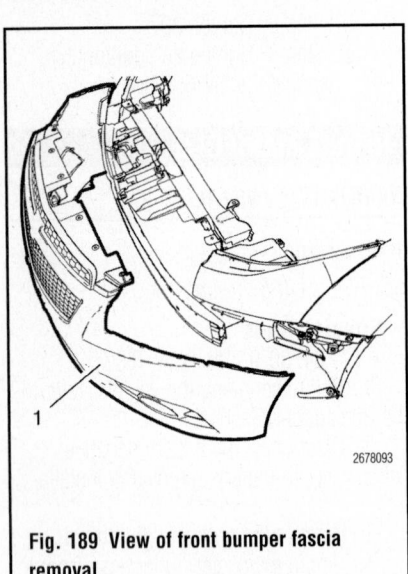

2678093

Fig. 189 View of front bumper fascia removal

➡ **Make note of the installed position of the manifold absolute pressure sensor wiring harness plugs to ensure they will be connected in their original position.**

14. Disconnect the 2 manifold absolute pressure sensor wiring harness plugs and.

15. Disconnect the 4 fuel injector wiring harness plugs.

16. Unclip the engine control module wiring harness from the camshaft cover.

17. Disconnect the turbocharger wastegate regulator solenoid valve wiring harness plug.

18. Unclip the engine control module wiring harness from the 2 intake manifold retainer clips and from 2 the fuel injection rail retainer clips.

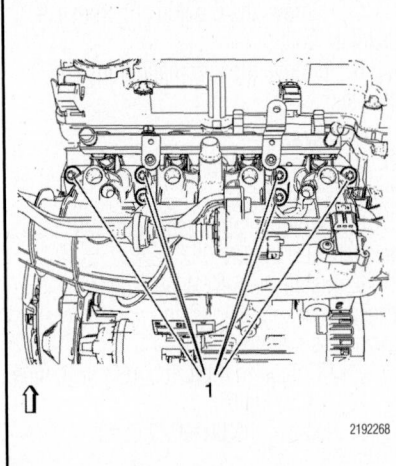

2192268

Fig. 191 View of intake manifold bolts (1)—1.4L engine

✳✳ CAUTION

Gasoline or gasoline vapors are highly flammable. A fire could occur if an ignition source is present. Never drain or store gasoline or diesel fuel in an open container, due to the possibility of fire or explosion. Have a dry chemical (Class B) fire extinguisher nearby.

19. Remove fuel injector rail cap.

20. Relieve the fuel system pressure. Use EN-34730-91 pressure tester, or equivalent.

21. Disconnect the fuel feed pipe from the fuel rail.

22. Unclip the fuel feed pipe from the retainer clip.

40. Connect the brake booster vacuum pipe to the intake manifold.

41. Install fuel injector rail cap.

42. Connect the turbocharger wastegate regulator solenoid valve wiring harness plug.

43. Clip in the engine control module wiring harness to 2 intake manifold retainer clips and from 2 fuel injection rail retainer clips.

44. Clip in the engine control module wiring harness to the camshaft cover.

45. Connect the 4 fuel injector wiring harness plugs.

46. Connect the 2 manifold absolute pressure sensor wiring harness plugs and.

47. Connect the evaporative emission canister purge solenoid valve wiring harness plug.

48. Connect the throttle body wiring harness plug.

49. Clip in the radiator inlet hose to the charge air cooler outlet air hose.

50. Install the charge air cooler outlet air hose to the charge air cooler.

51. Install the front bumper fascia.

52. Install the charge air cooler outlet air hose to the throttle body.

53. Install and tighten the charger air cooler outlet air hose clamp.

54. Connect the turbocharger pressure sensor wiring harness plug.

55. Clip in the heater outlet hose to retainer clip.

56. Clip in the engine control module wiring harness to 2 retainer clips.

57. Install the engine sight shield.

58. Connect the battery negative cable. Refer to Battery, removal & installation.

1.8L Engine

See Figure 193.

> **⁑ CAUTION**
>
> **Gasoline or gasoline vapors are highly flammable. A fire could occur if an ignition source is present. Never drain or store gasoline or diesel fuel in an open container, due to the possibility of fire or explosion. Have a dry chemical (Class B) fire extinguisher nearby.**

> **⁑ CAUTION**
>
> **Always wear safety goggles when working with fuel in order to protect the eyes from fuel splash.**

> **⁑ CAUTION**
>
> **In order to reduce the risk of fire and personal injury observe the following items:**

- Replace all nylon fuel pipes that are nicked, scratched or damaged during installation, do not attempt to repair the sections of the nylon fuel pipes
- Do not hammer directly on the fuel harness body clips when installing new fuel pipes. Damage to the nylon pipes may result in a fuel leak
- Always cover nylon vapor pipes with a wet towel before using a torch near them. Also, never expose the vehicle to temperatures higher than 239°F (115°C) for more than one hour, or more than 194°F (90°C) for any extended period
- Apply a few drops of clean engine oil to the male pipe ends before connecting fuel pipe fittings. This will ensure proper reconnection and prevent a possible fuel leak. (During normal operation, the O-rings located in the female connector will swell and may prevent proper reconnection if not lubricated)

1. Before servicing the vehicle, refer to the Precautions Section.

2. Remove the air cleaner outlet duct. Refer to Air Cleaner, removal & installation.

3. Raise and safely support the vehicle.

4. Place a drain pan underneath the vehicle.

5. Remove the 2 intake manifold brace bolts.

6. Remove and disconnect the wiring harness plug from the heated oxygen sensor 1.

7. Remove the intake manifold brace.

8. Remove the evaporative emission canister purge solenoid valve.

9. Unclip the fuel feed pipe from the fuel feed pipe clip.

10. Release the fuel feed pipe from the multiport fuel injection fuel rail and remove the fuel feed pipe.

11. Close the fuel feed pipe with a suitable cap.

12. Remove the positive crankcase ventilation tube from throttle body and the camshaft cover.

13. Remove the throttle body assembly. Refer to Throttle Body, removal & installation.

14. Disconnect the manifold absolute pressure sensor wiring harness plug.

15. Remove the clamp and remove the throttle body heater inlet hose from throttle body.

16. Disconnect the throttle body heater outlet hose from the throttle body.

17. Remove the engine management wiring harness and the fuel injectors wiring harness.

18. Remove the 2 multiport fuel injection fuel rail bolts.

19. Remove the multiport fuel injection fuel rail and the fuel injectors from the intake manifold.

20. Remove the 4 multiport fuel injector seals.

21. Disconnect the booster vacuum pipe from the intake manifold.

22. Remove the 7 intake manifold bolts.

23. Remove the intake manifold.

24. Remove the intake manifold gaskets from the intake manifold.

25. Remove the manifold absolute pressure sensor bolt.

26. Remove the manifold absolute pressure sensor from the intake manifold.

27. Remove the rubber bracket from intake manifold.

To install:

28. Clean the intake manifold mating surfaces.

29. Inspect the intake manifold for damage.

30. Inspect the intake manifold for cracks near metallic inserts.

31. Inspect the crankcase ventilation passages in the intake manifold face for blockage.

32. Clean the crankcase ventilation passages with compressed air if necessary. Use a maximum of 25 psi (172 kPa) of air pressure.

33. Clean the throttle body sealing surface.

34. Clean the intake manifold-to-cylinder head sealing surface.

35. Replace the intake manifold as necessary.

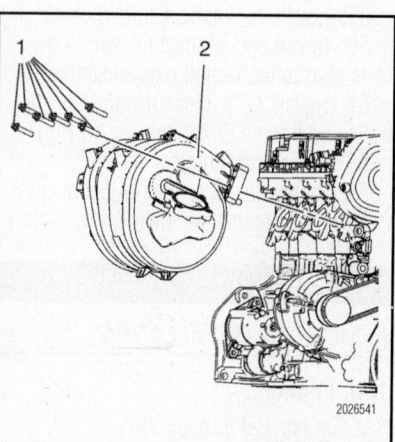

Fig. 193 Intake manifold (2) and bolt (1) removal—1.8L engine

36. Install the rubber bracket to intake manifold.

37. Install the manifold absolute pressure sensor to the intake manifold.

38. Install the manifold absolute pressure sensor bolt and tighten to 53 inch lbs. (6 Nm).

39. Install the NEW gaskets to the intake manifold.

40. Install the intake manifold and the 7 intake manifold bolts and tighten to 15 ft. lbs. (20 Nm).

41. Connect the booster vacuum pipe to the intake manifold.

42. Install the 4 multiport fuel injector seals.

43. Install the multiport fuel injection fuel rail and the fuel injectors to the intake manifold.

44. Install the 2 multiport fuel injection fuel rail bolts and tighten to 71 inch lbs. (8 Nm).

45. Connect the throttle body heater outlet hose to the throttle body.

46. Install the throttle body heater inlet hose to the throttle body and install the clamp.

47. Connect the manifold absolute pressure sensor wiring harness plug.

48. Install the engine management wiring harness and the fuel injectors wiring harness.

49. Install the positive crankcase ventilation tube to the throttle body and to the camshaft cover.

50. Install the throttle body assembly. Refer to Throttle Body, removal & installation.

51. Install the evaporative emission canister purge solenoid valve.

52. Remove the cap from fuel feed pipe.

53. Install the fuel feed pipe to the multiport fuel injection fuel rail.

54. Clip the fuel feed pipe to the fuel feed pipe clip.

55. Install the intake manifold brace.

56. Install and connect the wiring harness plug to the heated oxygen sensor 1.

57. Install the 2 intake manifold brace bolts and tighten to 71 inch lbs. (8 Nm).

58. Lower the vehicle.

59. Install the air cleaner outlet duct. Refer to Air Cleaner, removal & installation.

OIL PAN

REMOVAL & INSTALLATION

1.4L Engine

See Figures 194 through 197.

Special Tools
• EN-49980 Guidance Pins

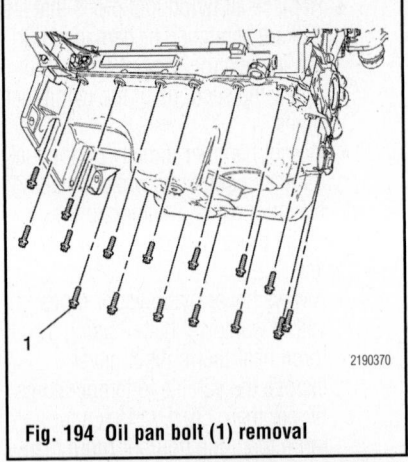

Fig. 194 Oil pan bolt (1) removal

※※ CAUTION

Wear safety glasses when using compressed air in order to prevent eye injury.

※※ WARNING

To ensure proper engine lubrication, clean clogged or contaminated oil galleries in an approved solvent and with compressed air. Failure to clean oil galleries may cause engine damage.

1. Before servicing the vehicle, refer to the Precautions Section.

2. Raise and safely support the vehicle.

3. Drain the engine oil. Refer to Engine Oil & Filter, Replacement.

4. Remove the catalytic converter. Refer to Catalytic Converter, removal & installation.

5. Remove the warm up 3-way catalytic converter. Refer to Warm Up 3-Way Catalytic Converter, removal & installation.

6. Remove the engine oil heater, if equipped.

7. Remove the transaxle-to-oil pan bolts.

• With manual transaxle: remove 3 bolts
• With automatic transaxle: remove 2 bolts

8. Remove the 16 oil pan bolts.

※※ WARNING

Pry the oil pan carefully in order to prevent damage to the transaxle case or the oil pan sealing surfaces.

9. Position a prying tool to the area shown, and gently pry the oil pan loose.

10. Remove the oil pan.

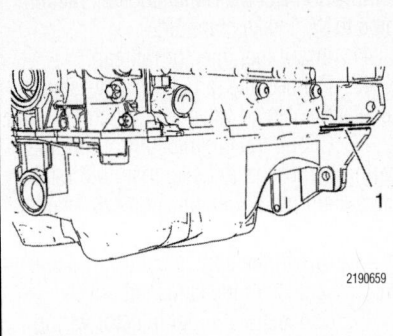

Fig. 195 Position a prying tool to the area (1) shown, and gently pry the oil pan loose

To install:

11. Clean the sealing surface of the crankshaft bearing cap tie plate and the groove in the engine front cover. Remove old gasket material, oil, dirt, and grease.

12. If the oil pan is being reused, clean and inspect before installation:

a. Clean the oil suction gallery with compressed air. Be sure to remove all dirt and old gasket material from the suction gallery.

b. Remove all remaining old gasket material from sealing surface and screw bores.

c. Clean the sealing surfaces from dirt and grease.

d. Inspect the sealing surface for cracks and damage.

13. Install the 2 EN-49980 pins to the proper oil pan screw bores.

➡**The sealing bead should be applied close to the inner edge of the oil pan. Take care that the oil suction gallery will not get contaminated with sealing compound or dirt. The thickness of the**

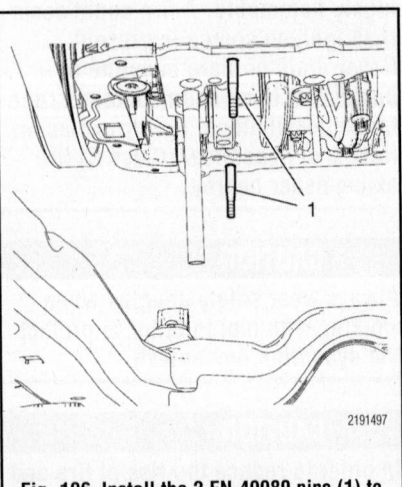

Fig. 196 Install the 2 EN-49980 pins (1) to the shown oil pan screw bores

sealing bead should be 0.08 inch (2mm).

14. Apply sealing compound to the oil pan.

15. Apply sealing compound to the groove of the engine front cover.

➡**The complete installation procedure of the oil pan should not take longer than 10 minutes.**

16. Apply sealing compound around the screw bore of the crankshaft bearing cap tie plate.

❊❊ WARNING

Use care when installing the oil pan to prevent disruption of the sealing bead. The sealing bead should remain consistent until the oil pan is mated with the engine. An inconsistent sealing bead can cause an insufficient seal and result in engine damage.

17. Lay the oil pan on the drive train and front suspension frame.

18. Hang in the oil pan to the crankshaft balancer.

19. Guide the oil pan with the 2 EN-49980 pins and the equivalent screw bores to the engine.

20. Secure the oil pan with 4 oil pan bolts.

21. Remove the 2 EN-49980 pins.

22. Install the remaining 12 oil pan bolts and hand tighten to approximately 18 inch lbs. (2 Nm).

23. Install the transaxle-to-oil pan bolts.

• With manual transaxle: Tighten the 3 bolts to 30 ft. lbs. (40 Nm)

• With automatic transaxle: Tighten the 2 bolts to 30 ft. lbs. (40 Nm)

24. Tighten the 16 oil pan bolts to 89 inch lbs. (10 Nm).

25. Install the engine oil heater, if equipped.

26. Install the warm up 3-way catalytic converter. Refer to Warm Up 3-Way Catalytic Converter, removal & installation.

27. Install the catalytic converter. Refer to Catalytic Converter, removal & installation.

28. Lower the vehicle.

29. Fill engine with the proper type and amount of oil.

1.8L Engine

See Figures 198 through 200.

1. Before servicing the vehicle, refer to the Precautions Section.

2. Raise and safely support the vehicle.

3. Place a collecting basin underneath the vehicle.

4. Remove the oil drain bolt.

5. Collect the engine oil.

6. Install the NEW seal ring and the oil drain bolt. Tighten the bolt to 10 ft. lbs. (14 Nm).

7. Lower the vehicle.

8. Remove the oil level indicator tube.

9. Raise the vehicle.

10. Remove the right front wheelhouse liner.

11. Remove the engine oil heater.

12. Remove the exhaust front pipe.

13. Remove the 3 oil pan bolts from the transaxle.

➡**Remove the oil pan evenly all the way around with a suitable tool.**

❊❊ WARNING

To prevent damage to the oil screen, ensure that the oil screen remains in the oil pan. If the oil screen gets caught on the cylinder block, push it into the oil pan.

14. Remove the 15 oil pan bolts and remove the oil pan.

To install:

15. Clean the sealing surfaces.

16. Apply an approximate 0.14 inch (3.5mm) thick bead of oil pan sealant to the joints of on the cylinder block.

➡**The assembly time including torque check must take no longer than 10 minutes.**

17. Apply an approximate 0.14 inch (3.5mm) thick bead of oil pan sealant to the oil pan.

18. Install the 15 oil pan bolts to the oil pan and tighten to 89 inch lbs. (10 Nm).

19. Install the 3 oil pan bolts to the transaxle and tighten to 30 ft. lbs. (40 Nm).

20. Install the exhaust front pipe.

21. Install the engine oil heater. Tighten the bolt to 30 ft. lbs. (40 Nm).

22. Install the right front wheelhouse liner.

23. Lower the vehicle.

24. Install the oil level indicator tube. Tighten the bolt to 11 ft. lbs. (15 Nm).

25. Fill engine with the proper type and amount of oil.

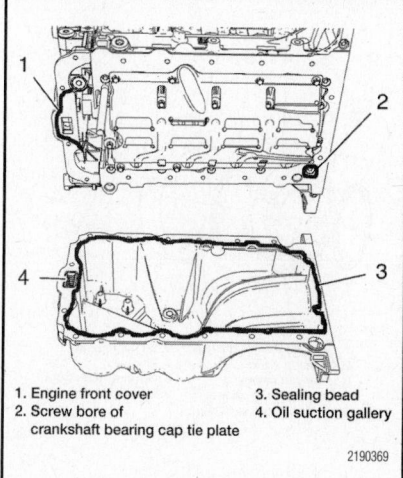

1. Engine front cover
2. Screw bore of crankshaft bearing cap tie plate
3. Sealing bead
4. Oil suction gallery

2190369

Fig. 197 Oil pan sealing compound application area shown

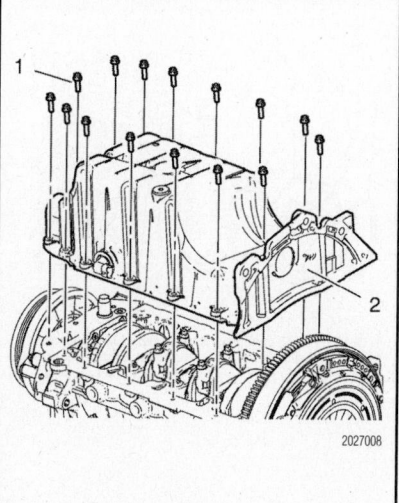

2027008

Fig. 198 Remove the 15 oil pan bolts (1) and remove the oil pan (2)

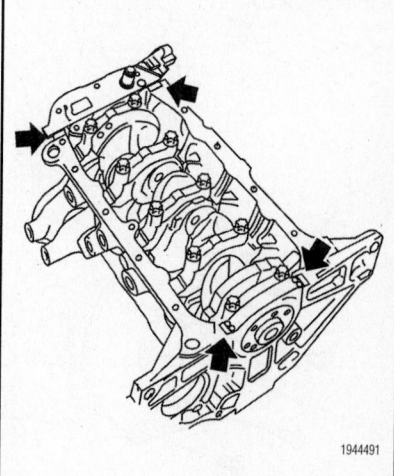

1944491

Fig. 199 Apply oil pan sealant to the cylinder block joints (arrows)

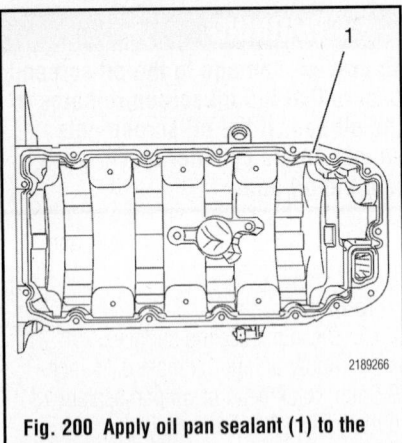

Fig. 200 Apply oil pan sealant (1) to the oil pan as illustrated

OIL PUMP

REMOVAL & INSTALLATION

1.4L Engine

See Figures 201 through 207.

1. Before servicing the vehicle, refer to the Precautions Section.
2. Measure the oil pressure and compare with the specified values.
3. Remove the engine front cover. Refer to Timing Chain Front Cover, removal & installation.
4. Remove the 8 oil pump cover bolts.
5. Remove the oil pump cover.

> ❋❋ **CAUTION**
>
> **Before removing the spring, cover the spring with a towel to prevent the spring from flying and possibly causing damage or personal injury.**

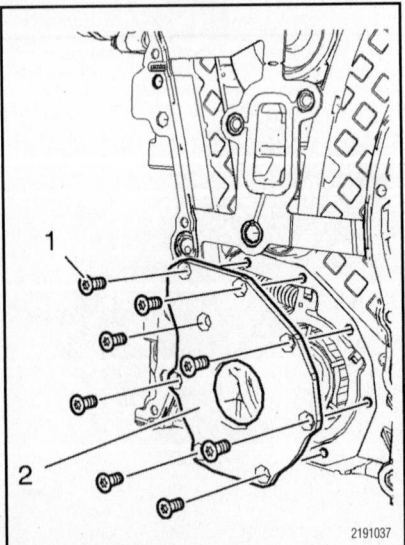

Fig. 201 Oil pump cover bolts (1) and the oil pump cover (2) removal

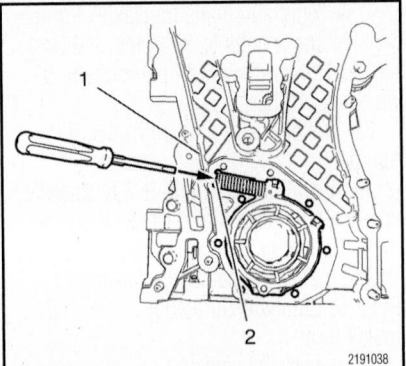

Fig. 202 Use a screwdriver between the oil pump slide spring windings (2) but protect the engine front cover edge (1)

➡ **Use a screwdriver between the oil pump slide spring windings, but protect the engine front cover edge with a suitable piece of plastic.**

6. Compress the oil pump slide spring with a screw driver and remove the oil pump slide spring in compound with the oil pump slide spring pin.

➡ **Mind the installation position of the oil pump components.**

7. Remove the oil pump components in the following order:
   a. Outer oil pump vane ring.
   b. Oil pump vane rotor and the 7 oil pump vanes.
   c. Inner oil pump vane ring.
   d. Oil pump slide and the 2 oil pump slide seals with the 2 oil pump slide seal springs.

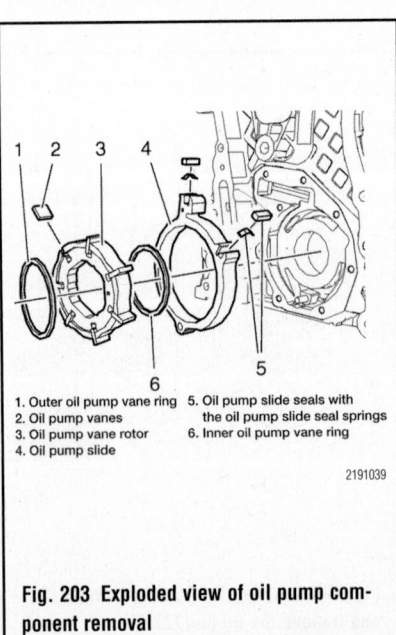

1. Outer oil pump vane ring
2. Oil pump vanes
3. Oil pump vane rotor
4. Oil pump slide
5. Oil pump slide seals with the oil pump slide seal springs
6. Inner oil pump vane ring

Fig. 203 Exploded view of oil pump component removal

To install:

8. Clean and inspect the oil pump. Refer to Inspection in this section.

➡ **Oil pump slide spring pin and oil pump slide spring, as well as slide seal and slide seal spring can be ordered as single parts. All other oil pump components can only be ordered as a replacement kit.**

9. Install the oil pan components in the following order:

➡ **The bore in the oil pump slide must fit smooth-running and without clearance to the oil pump slide pivot pin.**

   a. Install the oil pump slide.
   b. Install the inner oil pump vane ring.

➡ **Mind the installation position of the oil pump vane rotor. The mark must point to direction of the oil pump cover.**

   c. Install the oil pump vane rotor.

➡ **Mind the localized flattening on the oil pump vanes caused by the oil pump vane rings. The localized flattening must point to the oil pump vane rotor.**

   d. Install the 7 oil pump vanes.
   e. Install the outer oil pump vane ring.

10. Install the 2 oil pump slide seals and the 2 oil pump slide seal springs to the 2 grooves of the oil pump slide.
11. Protect the engine front cover edge with a suitable piece of plastic.

➡ **The length of the removed oil pump slide spring should be 3.012 inches**

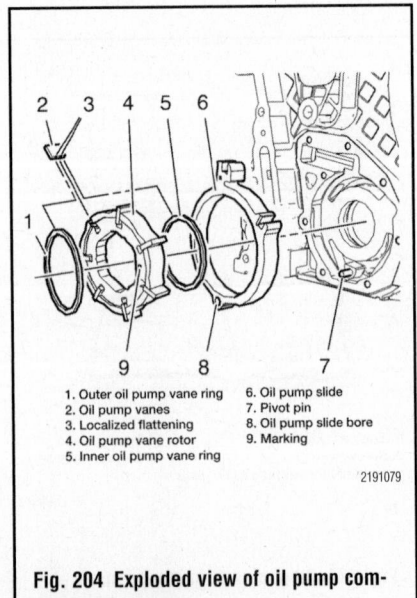

1. Outer oil pump vane ring
2. Oil pump vanes
3. Localized flattening
4. Oil pump vane rotor
5. Inner oil pump vane ring
6. Oil pump slide
7. Pivot pin
8. Oil pump slide bore
9. Marking

Fig. 204 Exploded view of oil pump component installation

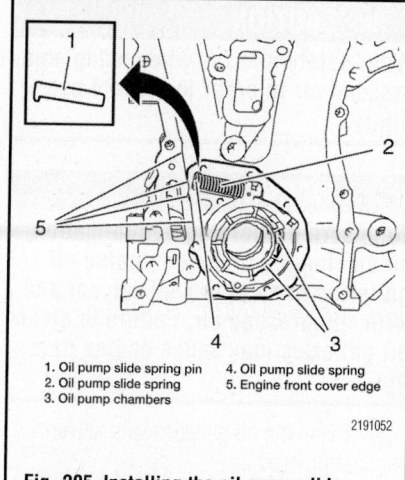

1. Oil pump slide spring pin
2. Oil pump slide spring
3. Oil pump chambers
4. Oil pump slide spring
5. Engine front cover edge

2191052

Fig. 205 Installing the oil pump slide spring mechanism

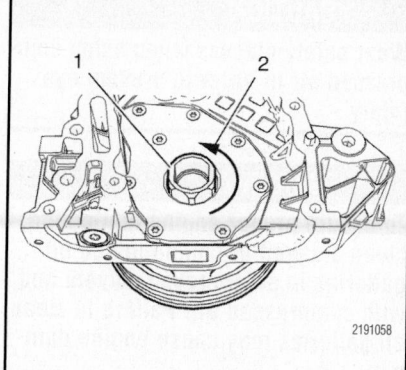
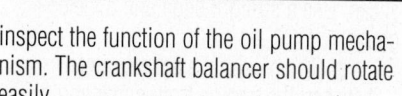

2191058

Fig. 207 Install the crankshaft balancer (1) and rotate in the direction shown (2) to inspect the function of the oil pump mechanism

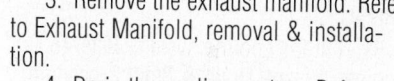

1. Engine front cover seal
2. Engine front cover bolts
3. Engine front cover bolts
4. Engine front cover

2027688

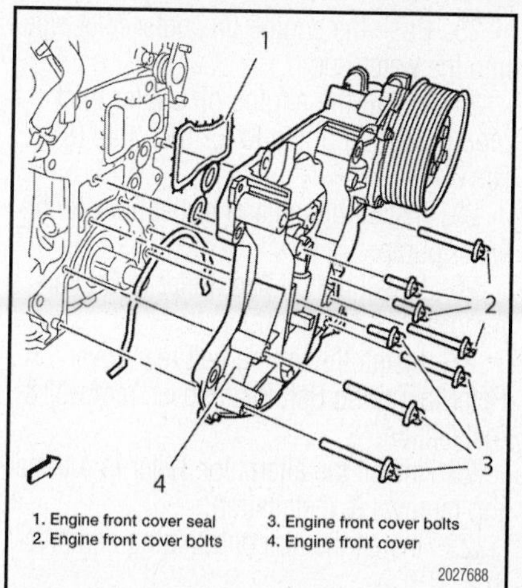

Fig. 209 Engine front cover and oil pump removal

(76.5mm) for suction engines and 2.402 inches (61mm) for turbo engines.

12. Install the oil pump slide spring pin in compound with the oil pump slide spring. Use a screwdriver to compress the oil pump slide spring. The flat side of oil pump slide spring pin must face upwards.

13. Lubricate the oil pump vanes, the oil pump vane rotor, the oil pump slide spring, and the chambers with engine oil.

14. Inspect the oil pump slide spring mechanism for proper function.

15. Measure the oil pump axial and radial clearances and compare with the specified values. Refer to Inspection in this section.

16. Install the oil pump cover and the 8 oil pump cover bolts.

17. Tighten the oil pump cover bolts in a sequence to 71 inch lbs. (8 Nm).

18. Install the crankshaft balancer and rotate in the specified direction in order to

inspect the function of the oil pump mechanism. The crankshaft balancer should rotate easily.

19. Remove the timing chain and replace the engine front cover gasket. Refer to Timing Chain & Sprockets, removal & installation.

20. Install the timing chain. Refer to Timing Chain & Sprockets, removal & installation.

21. Install the engine front cover. Refer to Timing Chain Front Cover, removal & installation.

22. Measure the oil pressure and compare with the specified values.

1.8L Engine

See Figures 208 and 209.

The oil pump body is within the engine front cover.

1. Before servicing the vehicle, refer to the Precautions Section.

2. Disconnect the negative battery cable. Refer to Battery, removal & installation.

3. Remove the exhaust manifold. Refer to Exhaust Manifold, removal & installation.

4. Drain the cooling system. Refer to Engine Coolant, Drain & Refill Procedure.

5. Remove the air conditioning compressor.

6. Remove the alternator. Refer to Alternator, removal & installation.

7. Remove the timing belt rear cover. Refer to Timing Belt Rear Cover, removal & installation.

8. Remove the oil pan. Refer to Oil Pan, removal & installation.

9. Remove the radiator outlet hose from the water pump.

10. Remove the engine oil cooler inlet pipe bolt.

11. Push the engine oil cooler inlet pipe into the engine oil cooler housing.

12. Remove the 2 engine oil cooler outlet pipe bolts from the water pump.

13. Push the engine oil cooler outlet pipe into the engine oil cooler housing.

14. Remove the 8 engine front cover bolts.

15. Remove the engine front cover and oil pump.

16. Remove the engine front cover seal.

To install:

17. Clean sealing surface.

18. Install a NEW engine front cover seal.

19. Install the engine front cover.

20. Install the 8 engine front cover bolts and tighten to 15 ft. lbs. (20 Nm).

21. Push the engine oil cooler outlet pipe to the water pump.

22. Install the engine oil cooler outlet pipe bolts and tighten to 71 inch lbs. (8 Nm).

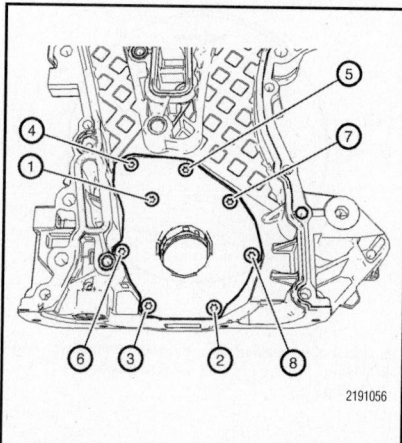

2191056

Fig. 206 Oil pump cover bolt tightening sequence shown

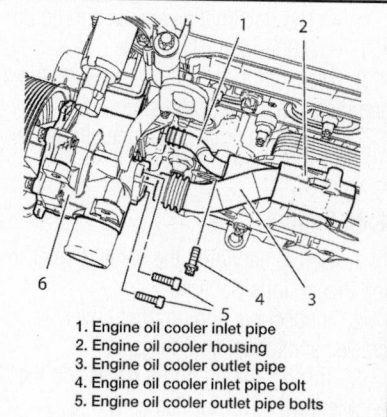

1. Engine oil cooler inlet pipe
2. Engine oil cooler housing
3. Engine oil cooler outlet pipe
4. Engine oil cooler inlet pipe bolt
5. Engine oil cooler outlet pipe bolts

2027690

Fig. 208 View of engine oil cooler pipes and housing

23. Push the engine oil cooler inlet pipe into the water pump.

24. Install the engine oil cooler inlet pipe bolt and tighten to 71 inch lbs. (8 Nm).

25. Install the radiator outlet hose to the water pump.

26. Install the oil pan. Refer to Oil Pan, removal & installation.

27. Install the timing belt rear cover. Refer to Timing Belt Rear Cover, removal & installation.

28. Install the alternator. Refer to Alternator, removal & installation.

29. Install the air conditioning compressor.

30. Install the exhaust manifold. Refer to Exhaust Manifold, removal & installation.

31. Connect the negative battery cable. Refer to Battery, removal & installation.

32. Fill the cooling system. Refer to Engine Coolant, Drain & Refill Procedure.

INSPECTION

1.4L Engine

See Figure 210.

1. Before servicing the vehicle, refer to the Precautions Section.

2. Inspect the engine front cover for cracks, scratches, and damage.

3. Inspect the oil pump cover and the engine front cover for flatness.

4. Inspect the oil pump vanes, the oil pump vane rotor, the oil pump vane rings, and the oil pump slide for localized flatting.

5. Inspect the oil pump slide pivot pin for firm seat.

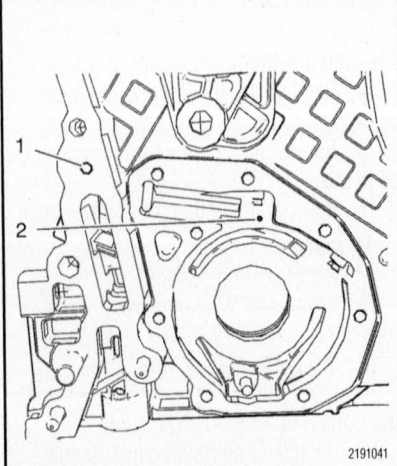

Fig. 210 Clean the oil galleries with solvent and compressed air. Blow compressed air from bore (2) to bore (1)

※ CAUTION

Wear safety glasses when using compressed air in order to prevent eye injury.

※ WARNING

To ensure proper engine lubrication, clean clogged or contaminated oil galleries in an approved solvent and with compressed air. Failure to clean oil galleries may cause engine damage.

6. Clean the oil galleries with solvent and compressed air.

7. With the oil pump components installed, measure the oil pump axial clearances. Use a straight edge and a feeler gauge.

a. The maximal axial clearance between the engine front cover and oil pump vane rotor should be 0.004 inch (0.1mm).

b. The maximal axial clearance between the engine front cover and oil pump vane should be 0.0035 inch (0.09mm).

c. The maximal axial clearance between the engine front cover and oil pump vane ring should be 0.016 inch (0.4mm).

d. The maximal axial clearance between the engine front cover and oil pump slide should be 0.0031 inch (0.08mm).

e. The maximal axial clearance between the engine front cover and oil pump slide seal should be 0.0035 inch (0.09mm).

8. Using a feeler gauge, measure the oil pump radial clearance. Measure the clearance between oil pump vane rotor and oil pump vane.

- The maximal clearance should be 0.002 inch (0.05mm)

9. Measure the clearance between the oil pump vane and oil pump slide.

- The maximal clearance should be 0.008 inch (0.2mm)

1.8L Engine

1. Before servicing the vehicle, refer to the Precautions Section.

2. Inspect the engine front cover for cracks, scratches, and damage.

3. Inspect the oil pump cover and the engine front cover for flatness.

4. Inspect the oil pump vanes, the oil pump vane rotor, and the oil pump vane rings for localized flatting.

※ CAUTION

Wear safety glasses when using compressed air in order to prevent eye injury.

※ WARNING

To ensure proper engine lubrication, clean clogged or contaminated oil galleries in an approved solvent and with compressed air. Failure to clean oil galleries may cause engine damage.

5. Clean the oil galleries with solvent and compressed air.

6. Remove the external rotor with the internal rotor.

7. Visually inspect the components.

8. Install the external and the internal rotors.

9. Inspect the axial clearance of the rotors in respect to the control unit housing upper edge.

- Permissible measurement is 0.00079–0.00228 inch (0.02–0.058mm)

PISTON AND RING

POSITIONING

1.4L Engine

See Figures 211 and 212.

1.8L Engine

See Figure 213.

Install the piston rings with TOP markings pointing upwards.

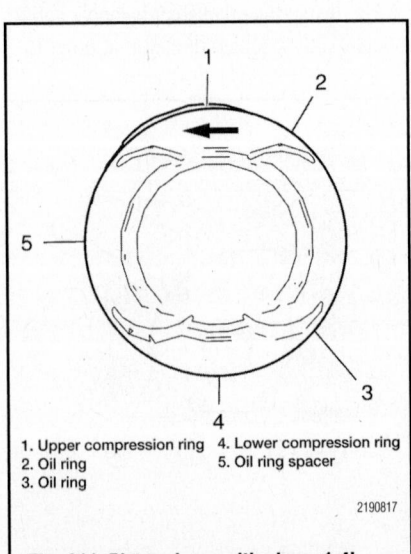

1. Upper compression ring
2. Oil ring
3. Oil ring
4. Lower compression ring
5. Oil ring spacer

Fig. 211 Piston ring positioning—1.4L engine

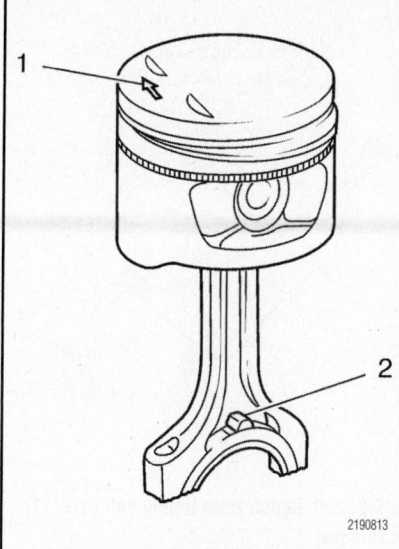

Fig. 212 Arrow (1) on the piston head must point to the timing side. Markings on the connecting rods (2) must point to the transaxle side—1.4L engine

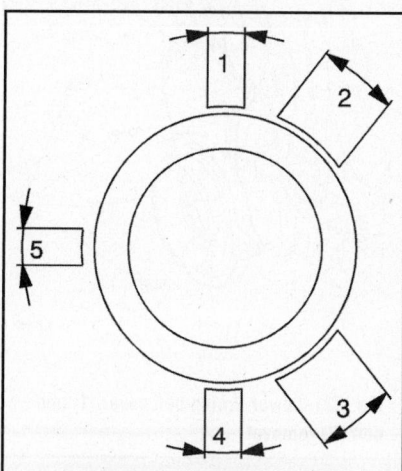

1. First piston ring (right-hand ring)
2. Second piston ring (minute ring)
3. Interim ring of oil scraper ring
4. Steel band ring of oil scraper ring
5. Steel band ring of oil scraper ring

Fig. 213 Piston ring positioning—1.8L engine

REAR MAIN SEAL

REMOVAL & INSTALLATION

1.4L Engine

See Figures 214 and 215.

Special Tools
- EN-658-1 Installer
- EN-235-6 Installer

1. Before servicing the vehicle, refer to the Precautions Section.

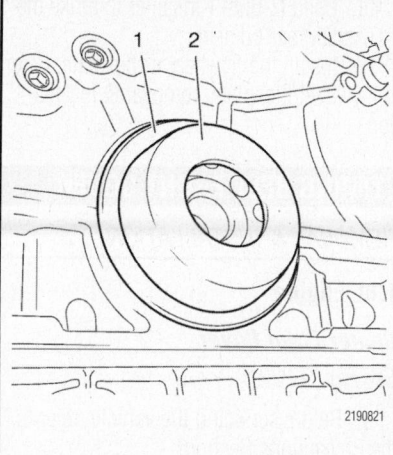

Fig. 214 Install the crankshaft rear oil seal (1) with EN-235-6 installer (2)

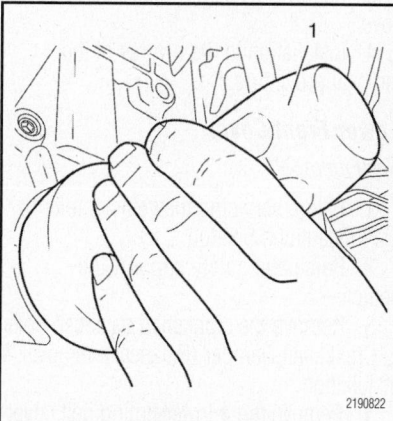

Fig. 215 Use EN-658-1 installer (1) to strike the crankshaft rear oil seal

2. Remove the flywheel or flexplate. Refer to Flywheel/Flexplate, removal & installation.
3. Place a collecting basin underneath the vehicle.
4. Remove the crankshaft rear oil seal.

To install:

5. Install the crankshaft rear oil seal with EN-235-6 installer.
6. Use EN-658-1 installer to strike the crankshaft rear oil seal.
7. Remove the collecting basin.
8. Install the flywheel or flexplate. Refer to Flywheel/Flexplate, removal & installation.

1.8L Engine

See Figures 216 through 219.

Special Tools
- EN-328-B Pin Remover
- EN-6624 Remover
- EN-658-1 Installer
- EN-235-6 Installer

✶✶ WARNING

Do not allow the crankshaft encoder wheel to come into contact with external magnetic fields or sharp metal objects. Do not drop the crankshaft encoder wheel. Do not damage the rubberized encoder track. Failure to follow these precautions may cause damage to the component.

1. Before servicing the vehicle, refer to the Precautions Section.
2. Remove the flywheel or flexplate. Refer to Flywheel/Flexplate, removal & installation.
3. Remove the crankshaft position sensor bolt.
4. Remove the crankshaft position sensor from the crankshaft rear oil seal housing.
5. Remove the crankshaft rear oil seal housing.
6. Remove the plastic ring with a screwdriver

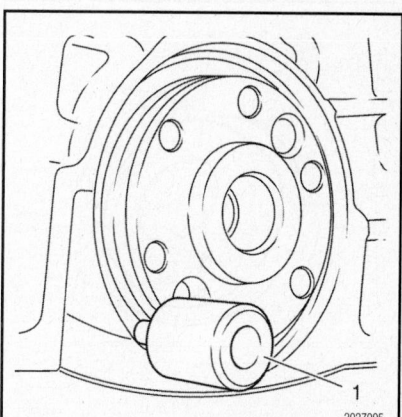

Fig. 216 Install EN-6624 remover (1) to the crankshaft rear oil seal and tighten the bolt

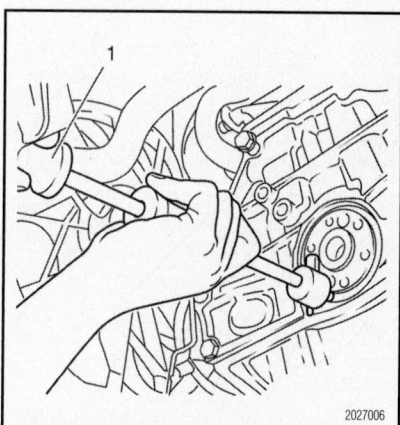

Fig. 217 Install the EN-328-B remover (1) to EN-6624 remover (2) and remove the crankshaft rear oil seal

→The diameter of the hole must not exceed 0.079 inch (2mm). If the diameter of the hole exceeds specifications, the bolt of EN-6624 remover will not be able to grip.

7. Only make a hole at the 5 o'clock and 7 o'clock positions, these are the only positions where is a cavity behind the seal ring.

8. Using a suitable tool, such as a scribe, make a hole in the crankshaft rear oil seal. Position the scribe at the outer edge of the crankshaft rear oil seal.

9. Remove the seal ring.

a. Install EN-6624 remover to the crankshaft rear oil seal and tighten the bolt.

b. Install the EN-328-B remover to EN-6624 remover and remove the crankshaft rear oil seal.

To install:

10. Install the crankshaft rear oil seal with EN-235-6 installer.

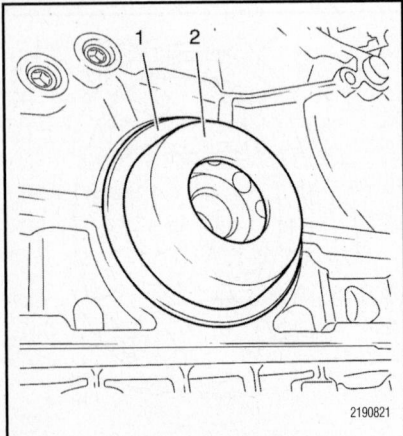

Fig. 218 Install the crankshaft rear oil seal (1) with EN-235-6 installer (2)

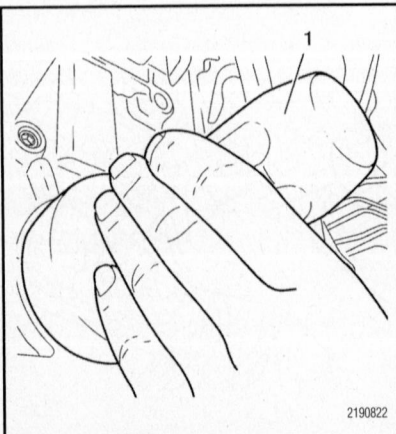

Fig. 219 Use EN-658-1 installer (1) to strike the crankshaft rear oil seal

11. Use EN-658-1 installer to strike the crankshaft rear oil seal.

12. Install the flywheel or flexplate. Refer to Flywheel/Flexplate, removal & installation.

TIMING BELT FRONT COVER

REMOVAL & INSTALLATION

1.8L Engine

Center Front Cover

See Figure 220.

1. Before servicing the vehicle, refer to the Precautions Section.

2. Remove the center front timing belt cover from the rear timing belt cover at 2 locations.

3. Remove the center front timing belt cover.

4. Installation is the reverse of the removal procedure.

Lower Front Cover

See Figure 221.

1. Before servicing the vehicle, refer to the Precautions Section.

2. Raise and safely support the vehicle.

3. Remove the crankshaft balancer. Refer to Crankshaft Damper (Balancer), removal & installation.

4. Remove the 4 lower timing belt cover bolts.

5. Remove the lower timing belt cover.

To install:

6. Install the lower timing belt cover.

7. Install the 4 lower timing belt cover bolts and tighten to 53 inch lbs. (6 Nm).

8. Install the crankshaft balancer. Refer to Crankshaft Damper (Balancer), removal & installation.

9. Lower the vehicle.

Upper Front Cover

See Figure 222.

1. Before servicing the vehicle, refer to the Precautions Section.

2. Remove the 2 timing belt upper front cover bolts.

3. Remove the timing belt upper front cover.

To install:

4. Install the timing belt upper front cover.

5. Install the 2 timing belt upper front cover bolts and tighten to 53 inch lbs. (6 Nm).

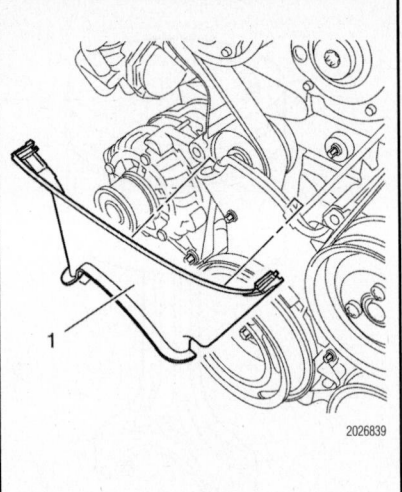

Fig. 220 Center front timing belt cover (1) removal

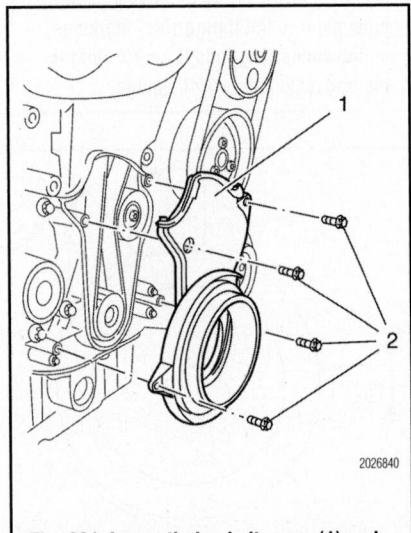

Fig. 221 Lower timing belt cover (1) and bolt (2) removal

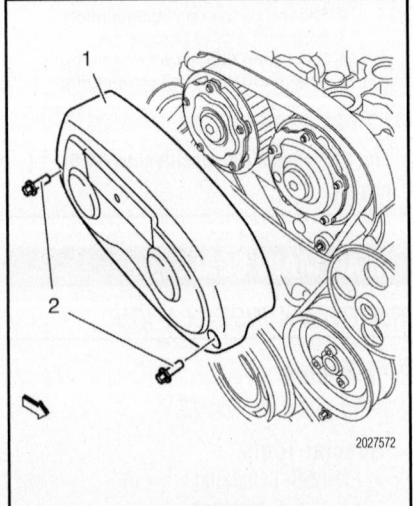

Fig. 222 View of timing belt upper front cover (1) cover bolts (2)

TIMING BELT & SPROCKETS

REMOVAL & INSTALLATION

1.8L Engine

See Figures 223 through 229.

Special Tools
- EN-6333 Timing Belt Tensioner Locking Pin
- EN-6340 Camshaft Locking Tool
- EN-6625 Crankshaft Locking Device
- EN-45059 Angle Meter

1. Before servicing the vehicle, refer to the Precautions Section.

2. Remove the air cleaner assembly. Refer to Air Cleaner, removal & installation.

3. Remove the timing belt upper front cover. Refer to Timing Belt Front Cover, removal & installation.

4. Raise and safely support the vehicle.

5. Remove the right front wheelhouse liner.

6. Remove the drive belt tensioner. Refer to Alternator, Drive Belt Tensioner, removal & installation.

7. If equipped, remove the front compartment insulator.

8. Set the engine to Top Dead Center (TDC).

9. With manual transaxle:

   a. Remove the transaxle front mount bolts.

   b. Remove the transaxle front mount.

   c. Remove the bolted connection.

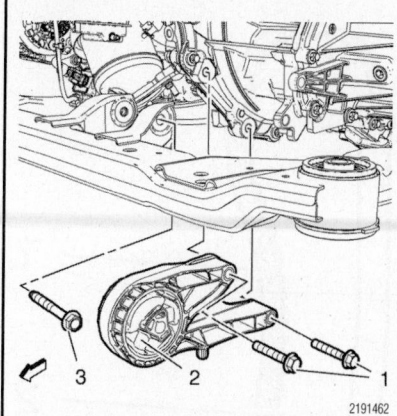

Fig. 224 Removing the transaxle front mount (2) and bolts (1, 3)—manual transaxle

10. With automatic transaxle, remove the bolt.

11. Install EN-6625 locking device to block the crankshaft.

12. Install the bolt or bolted connection as illustrated.

13. Remove and DISCARD the crankshaft balancer bolt.

14. Remove the 4 lower timing belt cover bolts and the lower timing belt cover. Refer to Timing Belt Front Cover, removal & installation.

15. Lower the vehicle.

➡ **The left half of the EN-6340 locking tool can be recognized by the marking LEFT, on the tool.**

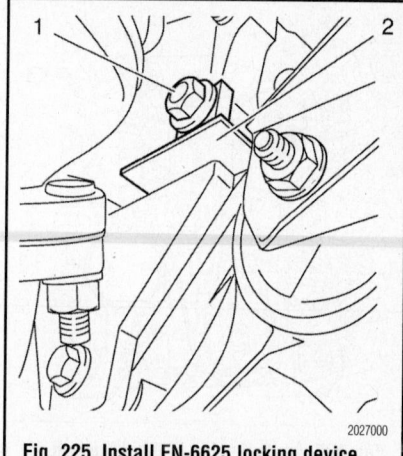

Fig. 225 Install EN-6625 locking device (2) to block the crankshaft and install the bolt or bolted connection (1)

16. Prepare the left half of the EN-6340 locking tool.

   a. Remove the 2 bolts.

   b. Remove the front panel from the EN-6340 locking tool-left.

17. Install the EN-6340 locking tool into the camshaft adjusters.

➡ **The spot type marking on the intake camshaft adjuster does not correspond to the groove of EN-6340-left during this process, but must be somewhat above.**

   a. Install the EN-6340 locking tool-left in the camshaft adjusters.

➡ **The spot type marking on the exhaust camshaft adjuster must correspond to the groove on EN-6340-right.**

   b. Install EN-6340 locking tool-right in the camshaft adjusters.

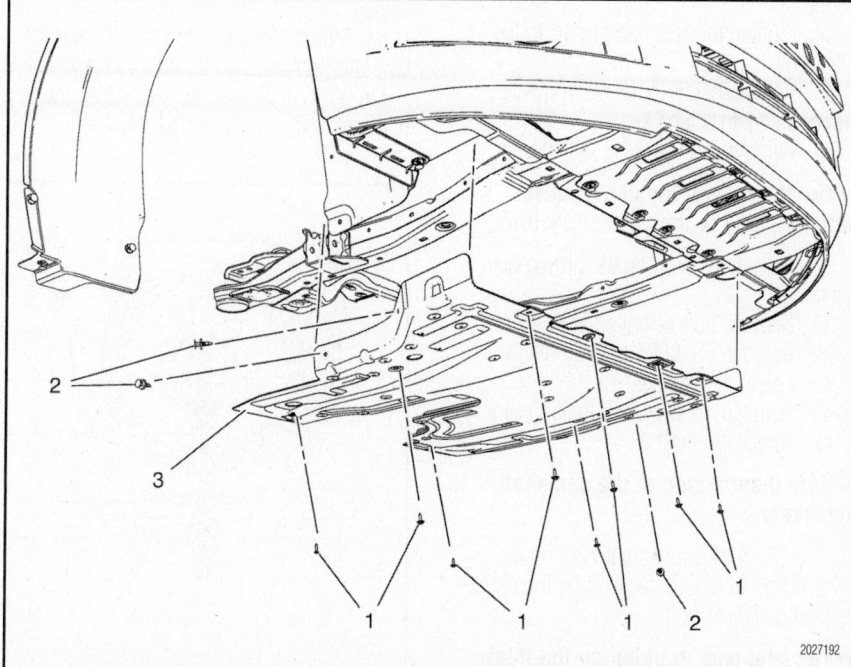

Fig. 223 Removing the front compartment insulator (3), plastic retainers (2), and screws (1)

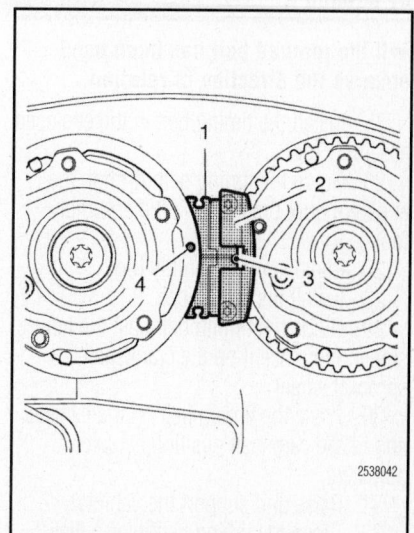

Fig. 226 EN-6340 locking tool shown installed

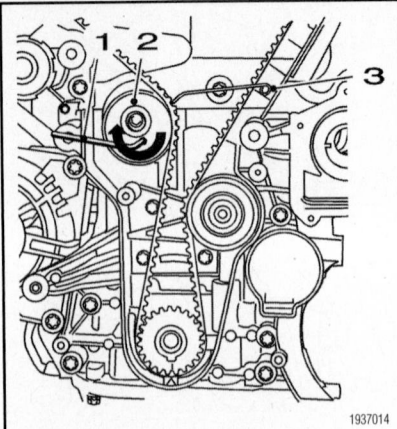

Fig. 227 Apply tension to the drive belt tensioner (2) in the direction of the arrow, using an Allen® key (1), then install the EN-6333 locking pin (3)

1937014

18. Remove EN-6340 locking tool.
19. Raise and safely support the vehicle.
20. Apply tension to the drive belt tensioner in the direction of the arrow, using an Allen® key.
21. Install the EN-6333 locking pin.
22. Remove and DISCARD the timing belt idler pulley bolt.
23. Remove the timing belt idler pulley.
24. Remove the timing belt and sprockets as needed.

To install:

※※ WARNING

Threading the timing belt through the engine mount bracket is only permissible in conjunction with the assembly tool supplied with NEW timing belts or otherwise it is possible to damage the toothed belt at this stage by kinking it.

➡ **If the toothed belt has been used, observe the direction of rotation.**

25. Install the timing belt in the enclosed assembly tool.
26. Guide the timing belt through the engine mount bracket with the assembly tool.
27. Remove the assembly tool.
28. Install the timing belt.
29. Guide the timing belt past the tensioner and place it on the crankshaft sprocket wheel.
30. Place the timing belt on the exhaust and intake camshaft position actuator adjusters.
31. Raise and support the vehicle.
32. Clean the timing belt idler pulley threads.
33. Install the timing belt idler pulley

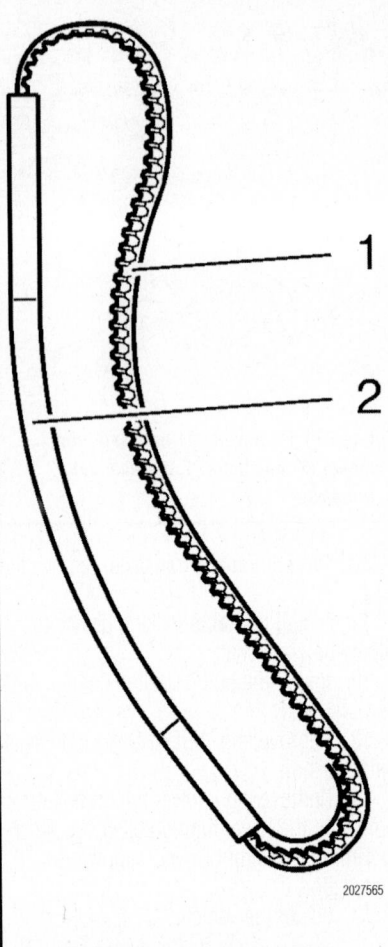

Fig. 228 Use the assembly tool (2) for timing belt (1) installation

2027565

and the NEW bolt with screw locking compound.
34. Tighten the NEW bolt to 18 ft. lbs. (25 Nm).
35. Apply tension to the drive belt tensioner using an Allen® key.
36. Remove the EN-6333 locking pin.

➡ **The timing belt tensioner moves automatically to the correct position.**

37. Release tension on the timing belt tensioner.
38. Remove bolt or bolted connection.
39. Remove EN-6625 locking device.
40. Lower the vehicle.
41. Remove the EN-6340 locking tool.
42. Check the timing:

➡ **Note the marking at the camshaft sprockets.**

a. Turn the crankshaft 720° in the direction of engine rotation by the crankshaft balancer bolt.

➡ **The spot type marking on the intake camshaft adjuster does not correspond**

to the groove of EN-6340-left during this process, but must be somewhat above.

b. Install EN-6340-left locking tool into the camshaft adjusters.

➡ **The spot type marking on the exhaust camshaft adjuster must correspond to the groove on EN-6340-right.**

c. Install EN-6340-right locking tool into the camshaft adjusters as done during the removal procedure.
43. Remove the EN-6340 locking tool.
44. Raise and safely support the vehicle.

➡ **The timing belt drive gear and oil pump housing must align.**

45. Control the crankshaft balancer position.
46. Install EN-6625 locking device to block the crankshaft.
47. Install the bolt or bolted connection.
48. Install the lower timing belt cover.
49. Install the 4 lower timing belt cover bolts and tighten to 53 inch lbs. (6 Nm).
50. Install the crankshaft balancer.
51. Install a NEW crankshaft balancer bolt and tighten using the EN-45059 meter, or equivalent:
a. First step: Tighten to 70 ft. lbs. (95 Nm).
b. Second step: Tighten 45°.
c. Third step: Tighten an additional 15°.
52. Remove the bolt or bolted connection.
53. Remove the EN-6625 locking device.
54. With automatic transaxle, install the bolt and tighten to 33 ft. lbs. (45 Nm).
55. With manual transaxle, install the bolt and tighten to 32 ft. lbs. (40 Nm).

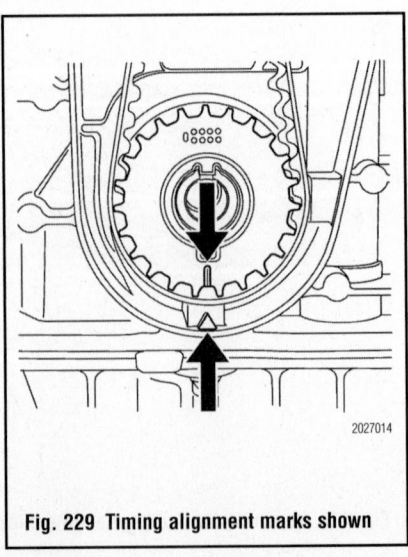

2027014

Fig. 229 Timing alignment marks shown

56. Install the drive belt tensioner. Refer to Alternator, Drive Belt Tensioner, removal & installation.

57. Install the right front wheelhouse liner.

58. Lower the vehicle.

59. Remove the EN-6340 locking tool.

60. Install the timing belt upper front cover. Refer to Timing Belt Front Cover, removal & installation.

61. Install the air cleaner assembly. Refer to Air Cleaner, removal & installation.

TIMING BELT REAR COVER

REMOVAL & INSTALLATION

1.8L Engine

See Figure 230.

1. Before servicing the vehicle, refer to the Precautions Section.

2. Remove the camshaft position actuator adjuster. Refer to Camshaft Position Actuator Adjuster, removal & installation.

3. Remove the timing belt tensioner. Refer to Timing Belt & Sprockets, removal & installation procedure.

4. Remove the 4 timing belt rear cover bolts.

➡**Oil can escape. Use a cloth, rag, or paper to keep the oil away from all timing components.**

5. Remove the timing belt rear cover.

To install:

6. Clean the 4 timing belt rear cover threads.

7. Apply locking compound to the 4 NEW timing belt rear cover bolts.

➡**If the cover is contaminated with oil, it must be cleaned.**

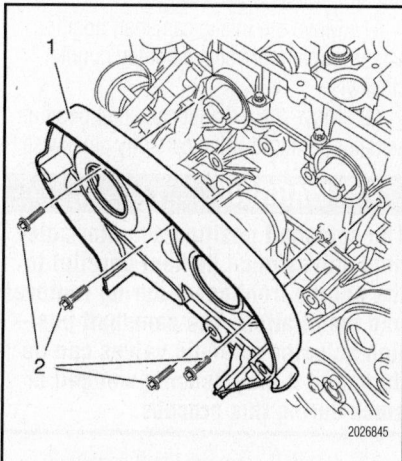

Fig. 230 Timing belt rear cover (1) and bolt (2) removal—1.8L engine

8. Install the timing belt rear cover.

9. Install the 4 timing belt rear cover bolts and tighten to 53 inch lbs. (6 Nm).

10. Install the timing belt tensioner. Refer to Timing Belt & Sprockets, removal & installation procedure.

11. Install the camshaft position actuator adjuster. Refer to Camshaft Position Actuator Adjuster, removal & installation.

TIMING CHAIN FRONT COVER

REMOVAL & INSTALLATION

1.4L Engine

See Figures 231 through 246.

Special Tools
- EN-952 Fixing Pin
- EN-953-A Fixing Tool
- EN-49977-100 Transmitter Disc Fixation

1. Before servicing the vehicle, refer to the Precautions Section.

2. Disconnect the battery negative cable. Refer to Battery, removal & installation.

3. Remove the ignition coil. Refer to Ignition Coil, removal & installation.

4. Remove the camshaft cover. Refer to Valve Covers, removal & installation.

5. Remove the right front wheelhouse liner.

6. Remove the front compartment insulator.

7. Rotate the engine clockwise until the bore in the crankshaft balancer aligns with the mark on the engine front cover.

8. Examine that the camshaft grooves are visible. If the camshaft grooves are not visible, rotate the crankshaft 360°.

9. Remove the crankshaft bearing cap tie plate hole plug and the seal ring.

⁑ WARNING

To ensure proper crankshaft TDC alignment, the retention pin should fit easily through the bore in the crankshaft tie plate and into the crankshaft. Binding of the retention pin could affect proper engine timing.

10. Install EN-952 fixing pin to hold the crankshaft in TDC position.

➡**The fixing tool should be installed completely to the camshaft grooves without high effort.**

11. Install EN-953-A fixing tool to the camshafts.

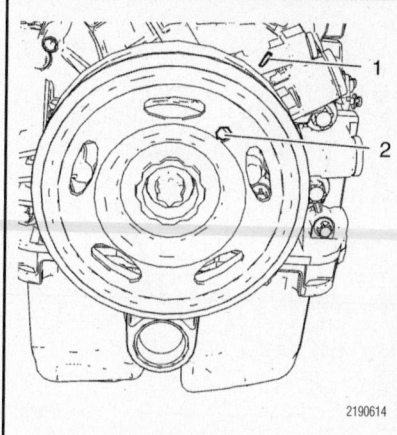

Fig. 231 Rotate the engine clockwise until the bore (2) in the crankshaft balancer aligns with the mark (1) on the engine front cover

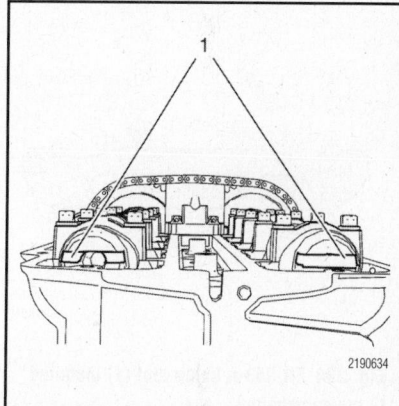

Fig. 232 The camshaft grooves (1) should be as shown to be at TDC

➡**A wrong installation position is possible in the next procedure. Make sure that the fixation tool is installed without clearance to the cylinder head in areas and.**

12. Install EN-49977-100 transmitter disc fixation to inspect the correct position of the camshaft position exciter wheels.

13. Tighten the bolts of EN-49977-100 transmitter disc fixation.

14. Remove EN-49977-100 transmitter disc fixation.

15. Remove EN-953-A fixing tool.

16. Remove EN-952 fixing pin.

17. Install the crankshaft bearing cap tie plate hole plug and seal ring and tighten to 30 ft. lbs. (40 Nm).

18. Raise and safely support the vehicle.

19. Remove the front compartment insulator.

20. Remove the right front wheelhouse liner.

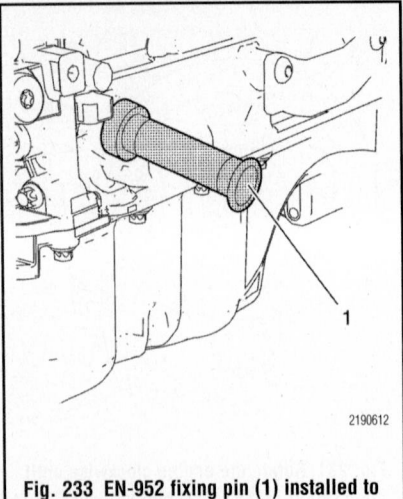

Fig. 233 EN-952 fixing pin (1) installed to hold the crankshaft in TDC position

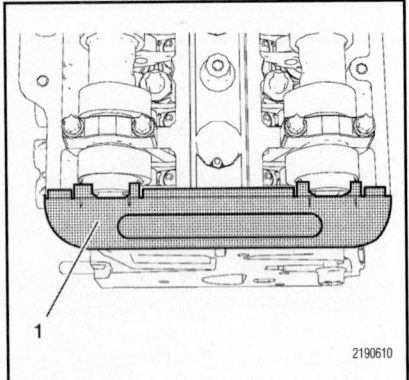

Fig. 234 EN-953-A fixing tool (1) installed to the camshafts

21. Disconnect all electrical connectors from the alternator. Refer to Alternator, removal & installation.

22. Fix the drive belt tensioner and remove the drive belt from crankshaft balancer, drive belt tensioner, and air conditioning compressor. Refer to Accessory Drive Belts, removal & installation.

23. Disconnect the air conditioning compressor wiring harness plug.

24. Unclip the air conditioning compressor wiring harness from the 2 retainer clips.

➡**Do not remove the air conditioning compressor and condenser hose from air conditioning compressor.**

25. Remove the air conditioning compressor from the air conditioning compressor bracket and hang aside.

26. Remove the 3 air conditioning compressor bracket bolts.

27. Remove the air conditioning compressor bracket.

28. Place a collecting basin underneath the vehicle.

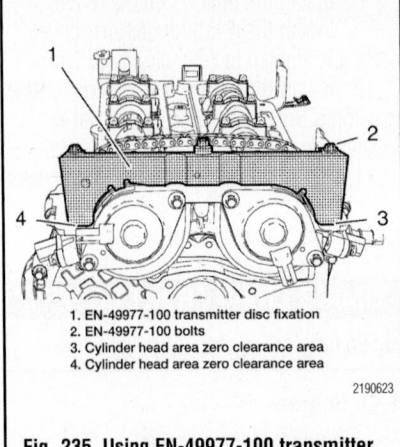

1. EN-49977-100 transmitter disc fixation
2. EN-49977-100 bolts
3. Cylinder head area zero clearance area
4. Cylinder head area zero clearance area

Fig. 235 Using EN-49977-100 transmitter disc fixation to inspect the correct position of the camshaft position exciter wheels

29. Remove the crankshaft balancer. Refer to Crankshaft Damper (Balancer), removal & installation.

30. Remove the oil pan. Refer to Oil Pan, removal & installation.

31. Lower the vehicle.

32. Install an engine lifter to the right engine lift bracket and apply tension to the engine lifter chain in order to support the engine.

33. Remove and DISCARD the 3 engine mount-to-engine mount bracket bolts and the 3 washers.

34. Remove the 2 engine mount-to-body bolts and the engine mount nut.

35. Remove the engine mount.

36. Remove the right side engine mount bracket.

37. Remove the drive belt tensioner. Refer to Alternator, Drive Belt Tensioner, removal & installation.

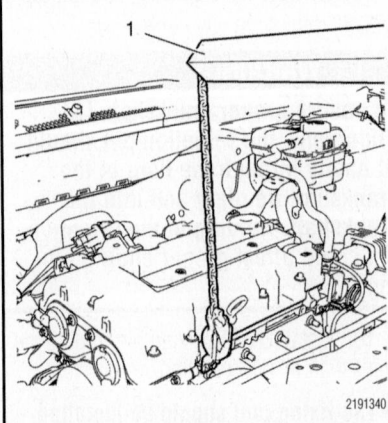

Fig. 236 Install an engine lifter (1) to the right engine lift bracket and apply tension to the engine lifter chain in order to support the engine

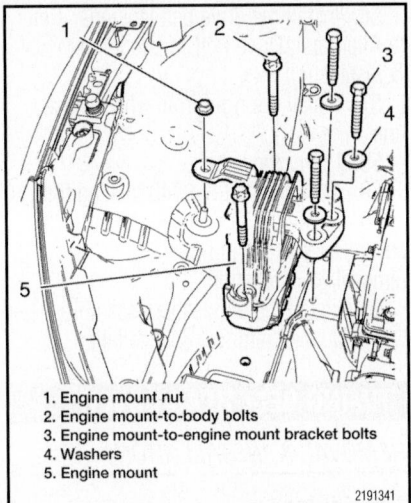

1. Engine mount nut
2. Engine mount-to-body bolts
3. Engine mount-to-engine mount bracket bolts
4. Washers
5. Engine mount

Fig. 237 Removing the engine mount

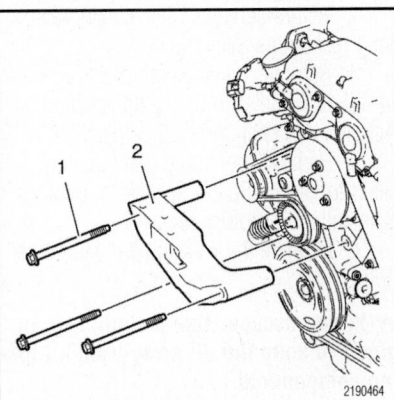

Fig. 238 View of right side engine mount bracket (2) and bolts (1)—1.4L engine

38. Remove the alternator from above. Refer to Alternator, removal & installation.

39. Remove the water pump pulley and the water pump. Refer to Water Pump, removal & installation.

40. Remove the 4 camshaft position actuator solenoid valve bolts.

41. Move the intake camshaft position actuator solenoid valve carefully counterclockwise.

42. Move the exhaust camshaft position actuator solenoid valve carefully clockwise.

✳✳ WARNING

The camshaft position actuator solenoid valves must be kept parallel to the engine front cover during removal and installation. The camshaft position actuator solenoid valves can be damaged if they become wedged or stuck during this process.

43. Carefully remove the 2 camshaft position actuator solenoid valves and the seal rings.

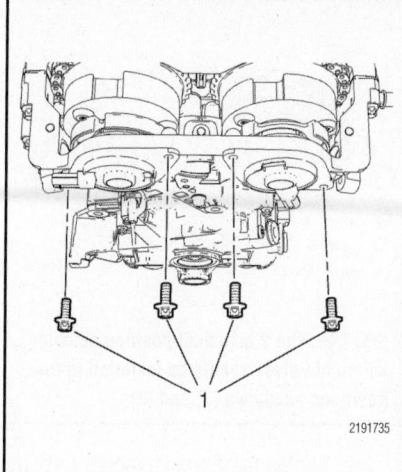

Fig. 239 Remove the 4 camshaft position actuator solenoid valve bolts (1)

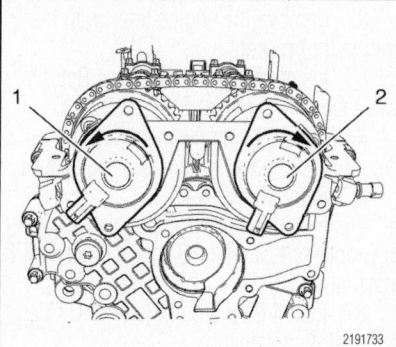

Fig. 240 Move the intake camshaft position actuator solenoid valve (1) counterclockwise to the position shown. Move the exhaust camshaft position actuator solenoid valve (2) clockwise to the position shown

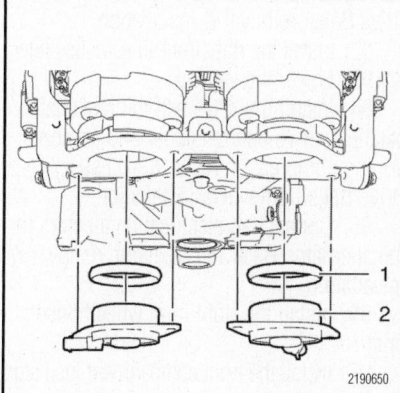

Fig. 241 Removing the 2 camshaft position actuator solenoid valves (2) and the seal rings (1)

44. Remove the camshaft position sensors. Refer to Camshaft Position (CMP) Sensor, removal & installation.

45. Loosen the camshaft sprocket bolts until the camshaft position exciter wheels freely rotate.

46. Remove the 13 M6 engine front cover bolts.

47. Remove the 2 M10 engine front cover bolts.

48. Remove the engine front cover.

➡**Removal of the timing chain is necessary to get access to the engine front cover gasket.**

49. Remove the camshaft timing chain. Refer to Timing Chain & Sprockets, removal & installation.

50. Remove the engine front cover gasket.

To install:

51. Install the crankshaft front oil seal, if necessary.

52. Install the oil pressure relief valve, if necessary. Tighten to 37 ft. lbs. (50 Nm).

53. Install the exhaust camshaft position sensor and the seal ring. Tighten the bolt to 53 ft. lbs. (6 Nm).

54. Install the intake camshaft position sensor and the seal ring. Tighten the bolt to 53 ft. lbs. (6 Nm).

55. Clean the engine front cover sealing surfaces on engine block and cylinder head.

➡**The thickness of the sealing bead should be 0.079 inch (2mm).**

56. Apply sealing compound to the appropriate areas and.

57. Install a NEW engine front cover gasket.

58. Install the timing chain. Refer to Timing Chain & Sprockets, removal & installation.

➡**Mind the guide sleeves when installing the engine front cover. The complete installation procedure of the engine front cover should not take longer than 10 minutes.**

59. Install the engine front cover.

60. Install the 13 M6 engine front cover bolts.

61. Install the 2 M10 engine front cover bolts.

62. Tighten the 13 M6 engine front cover bolts to 71 inch lbs. (8 Nm).

63. Tighten the 2 M10 engine front cover bolts to 26 ft. lbs. (35 Nm).

➡**The engine should be adjusted and fixed in TDC position.**

64. Tighten the camshaft sprockets, install the upper timing chain guide and

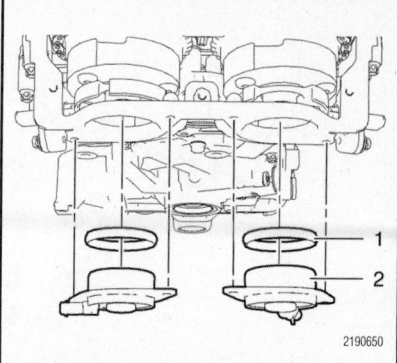

Fig. 242 Remove the M6 engine front cover bolts (1), the M10 engine front cover bolts (2), and the engine front cover (3)

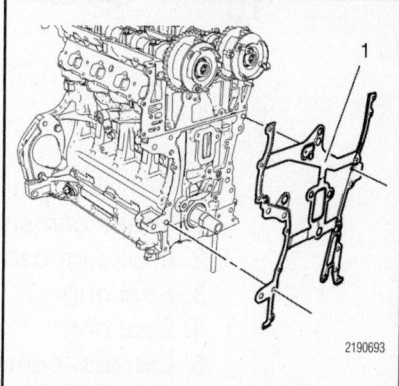

Fig. 243 Engine front cover gasket (1) removal

remove all special tools. Refer to Timing Chain & Sprockets, removal & installation.

65. Install the camshaft position sensors. Refer to Camshaft Position (CMP) Sensor, removal & installation.

✳ WARNING

The camshaft position actuator solenoid valves must be kept parallel to the engine front cover during removal and installation. The camshaft position actuator solenoid valves can be damaged if they become wedged or stuck during this process.

66. Install the 2 camshaft position actuator solenoid valves and the 2 seal rings by carefully and evenly pressing.

67. Install the 4 camshaft position actuator solenoid valve bolts and tighten to 71 inch lbs. (8 Nm).

68. The 2 camshaft position actuator solenoid valves should be installed in the correct positions.

69. Install the water pump and the water pump pulley. Refer to Water Pump, removal & installation.

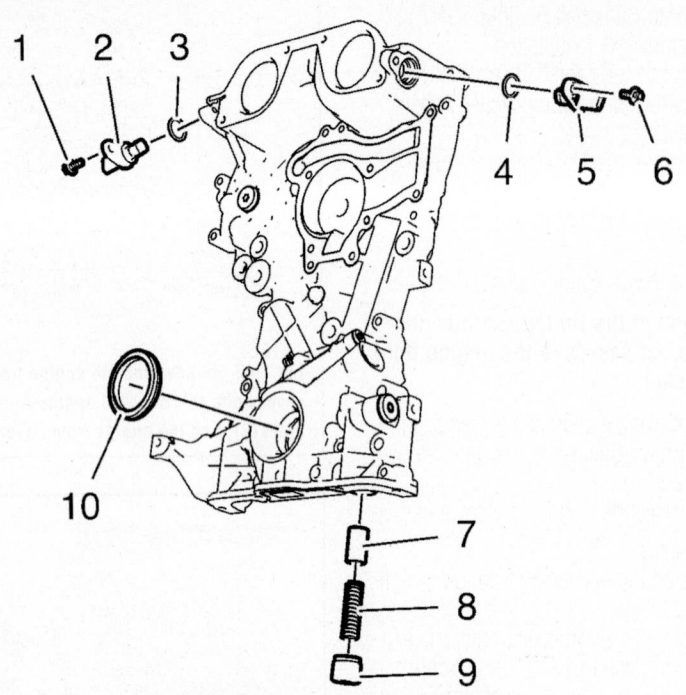

1. Intake camshaft sensor bolt
2. Intake camshaft position sensor
3. Seal ring
4. Seal ring
5. Exhaust camshaft position sensor
6. Exhaust camshaft sensor bolt
7. Oil pressure relief valve part
8. Oil pressure relief valve part
9. Oil pressure relief valve part
10. Crankshaft front oil seal

Fig. 244 Exploded view of engine front cover—1.4L engine

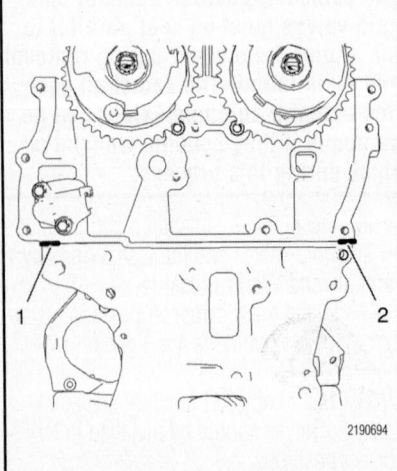

Fig. 245 Apply sealing compound to the areas shown (1) and (2)

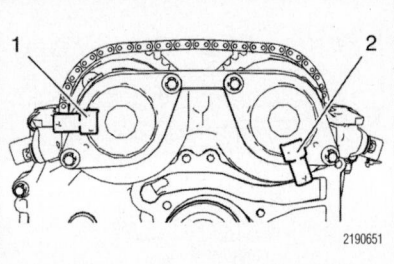

Fig. 246 The 2 camshaft position actuator solenoid valves should be installed in the positions as shown (1) and (2)

70. Install the alternator from above. Refer to Alternator, removal & installation.

71. Install the drive belt tensioner. Refer to Alternator, Drive Belt Tensioner, removal & installation.

72. Install the engine mount bracket.

73. Install the 3 NEW engine mount bracket bolts and tighten to 45 ft. lbs. (60 Nm), plus 45–60°.

74. Remove the engine lifter from the right engine lift bracket.

75. Loosely install the drive belt to the water pump pulley and alternator pulley.

76. Install the engine mount.

77. Install the 2 engine mount-to-body bolts.

78. Install the engine mount nut.

79. Install the 3 NEW engine mount-to-engine mount bracket bolts and the 3 washers.

80. Tighten the 2 engine mount-to-body bolts and the engine mount nut to 46 ft. lbs. (62 Nm).

81. Tighten the 3 engine mount-to-engine mount bracket bolts to 37 ft. lbs. (50 Nm), plus 60–70°.

82. Remove the engine lifter from the engine lift bracket.

83. Install the camshaft cover. Refer to Valve Covers, removal & installation.

84. Install the air cleaner assembly. Refer to Air Cleaner, removal & installation.

85. Raise the vehicle.

86. Install the crankshaft balancer. Refer to Crankshaft Damper (Balancer), removal & installation.

87. Install the oil pan. Refer to Oil Pan, removal & installation.

88. Install the air conditioning compressor and power steering pump bracket.

89. Install the 3 air conditioning compressor bracket bolts and tighten to 16 ft. lbs. (22 Nm).

90. Install the air conditioning compressor-to-air conditioning compressor bracket.

91. Install the drive belt to crankshaft balancer, drive belt tensioner and air conditioning compressor. Refer to Accessory Drive Belts, removal & installation.

92. Install the right front wheelhouse liner.

93. Lower the vehicle.

94. Install the drive belt to crankshaft balancer, drive belt tensioner and air conditioning compressor. Refer to Accessory Drive Belts, removal & installation.

95. Connect all electrical connectors to the alternator. Refer to Alternator, removal & installation.

96. Install the right front wheelhouse liner.

97. Install the front compartment insulator.

98. Lower the vehicle.

99. Connect the battery negative cable. Refer to Battery, removal & installation.

100. Fill the engine with the proper type and amount of engine oil.

TIMING CHAIN & SPROCKETS

REMOVAL & INSTALLATION

1.4L Engine

See Figures 247 through 252.

Special Tools

• EN-955-1 Fixing Pin from EN-955 Kit

1. Before servicing the vehicle, refer to the Precautions Section.

2. Remove the engine front cover with oil pump. Refer to Timing Chain Front Cover, removal & installation.

➡**If EN-955-1 fixing pin cannot be inserted, compress the timing chain tensioner further with the aid of a flat-bladed tool to allow complete insertion of the pin.**

3. Push the timing chain in direction to the timing chain tensioner and secure the tensioner with EN-955-1 fixing pin.

4. Remove the 2 upper timing chain guide bolts.

5. Remove the upper timing chain guide.

6. Remove the 2 timing chain guide right side bolts.

7. Remove the timing chain guide right side.

8. Remove the timing chain tensioner shoe bolt.

9. Remove the timing chain tensioner shoe.

10. Remove the timing chain along with the crankshaft sprocket.

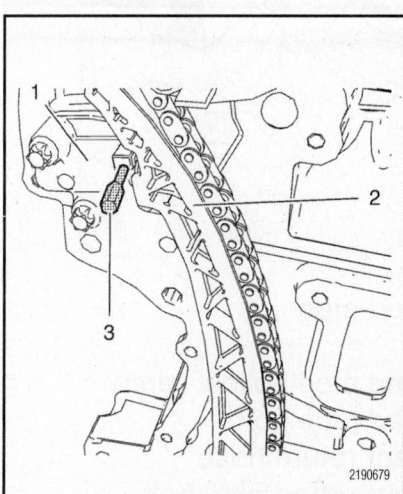

Fig. 247 Push the timing chain (2) in the direction of the timing chain tensioner (1) and secure the tensioner with EN-955-1 fixing pin (3)

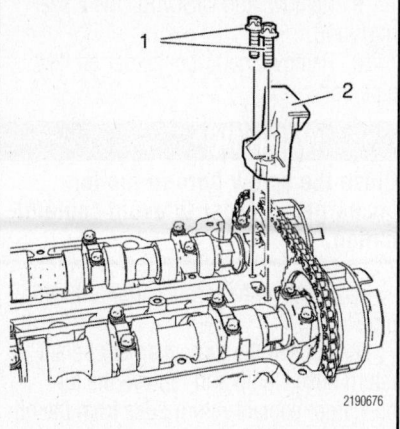

Fig. 248 Remove the upper timing chain guide (2) and bolts (1)

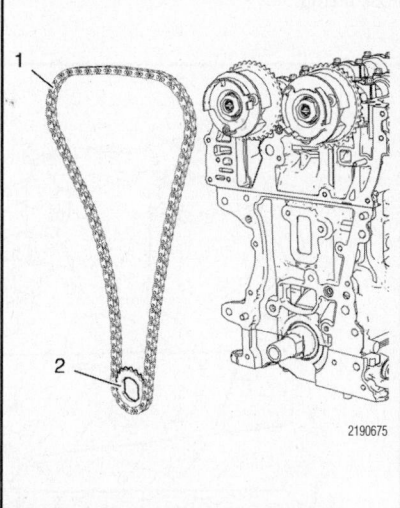

Fig. 249 Remove the timing chain (1) along with the crankshaft sprocket (2)

11. Remove the engine front cover gasket.

To install:

12. Clean the engine front cover sealing surfaces on the engine block and the cylinder head.

➡**The thickness of the sealing bead should be 0.079 inch (2mm).**

13. Apply sealing compound to the appropriate areas.

14. Install the engine front cover gasket.

15. Install the timing chain along with the crankshaft sprocket.

16. Install the timing chain tensioner shoe.

17. Install the timing chain tensioner shoe bolt and tighten to 15 ft. lbs. (20 Nm).

18. Install the timing chain guide right side.

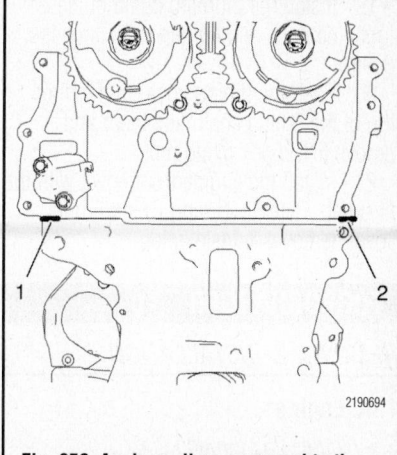

Fig. 250 Apply sealing compound to the areas shown (1) and (2)

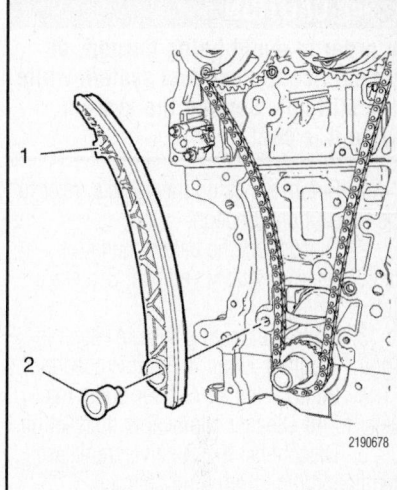

Fig. 251 Install the timing chain tensioner shoe (1) shoe bolt (2)

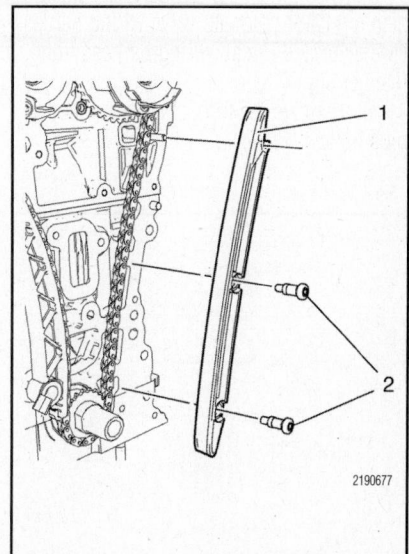

Fig. 252 Install the timing chain guide right side (1) and bolts (2)

19. Install the 2 timing chain guide right side bolts and tighten to 71 inch lbs. (8 Nm).

20. Push the timing chain in the direction of the timing chain tensioner and remove EN-955-1 fixing pin.

21. Install the engine front cover with the oil pump. Refer to Timing Chain Front Cover, removal & installation.

TURBOCHARGER

REMOVAL & INSTALLATION

1.4L Engine

See Figures 253 through 260.

Special Tools
- EN-49942 Holding Wrench

✳✳ CAUTION

In order to avoid being burned, do not service the exhaust system while it is still hot. Service the system when it is cool.

1. Before servicing the vehicle, refer to the Precautions Section.

2. Disconnect the battery negative cable. Refer to Battery, removal & installation.

3. Drain the cooling system. Refer to Engine Coolant, Drain & Refill Procedure.

4. Remove the air cleaner outlet duct. Refer to Air Cleaner, removal & installation.

5. Disconnect the positive crankcase ventilation pipe from turbocharger.

6. Remove the exhaust manifold heat shield bolts and the exhaust manifold heat shield.

7. Disconnect the turbocharger wastegate regulator solenoid valve wiring harness connector and unclip wiring harness from retainer clip.

8. Remove the turbocharger oil feed pipe hollow screw.

9. Remove and DISCARD the 2 seal rings and.

10. Remove the turbocharger oil feed pipe bolt.

✳✳ WARNING

Close the screw bore in the turbocharger in order to avoid contamination.

11. Remove the turbocharger oil feed pipe.

12. Loosen the turbocharger coolant return hose clamp and remove the turbocharger coolant return hose from the oil cooler inlet pipe.

13. Remove the turbocharger coolant return pipe bolt.

14. Loosen the charge air cooler inlet air hose clamp.

15. Remove the charge air cooler inlet air hose from the turbocharger.

16. Remove the front bumper fascia.

17. Unlock the charge air cooler inlet air hose quick connector.

18. Remove the charge air cooler inlet air hose.

19. Install the EN-49942 holding wrench to the turbocharger coolant feed pipe. Guide a ratchet wrench along with an extension through EN-49942 holding wrench to the turbocharger coolant feed pipe hollow screw.

✳✳ WARNING

The EN-49942 holding wrench should be installed to turbocharger coolant feed pipe avoid twisting the turbocharger coolant feed pipe during the loosening procedure.

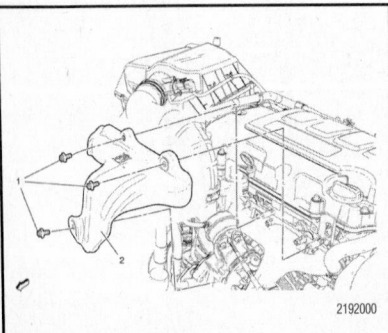

Fig. 253 View of exhaust manifold heat shield (2) and bolts (1)

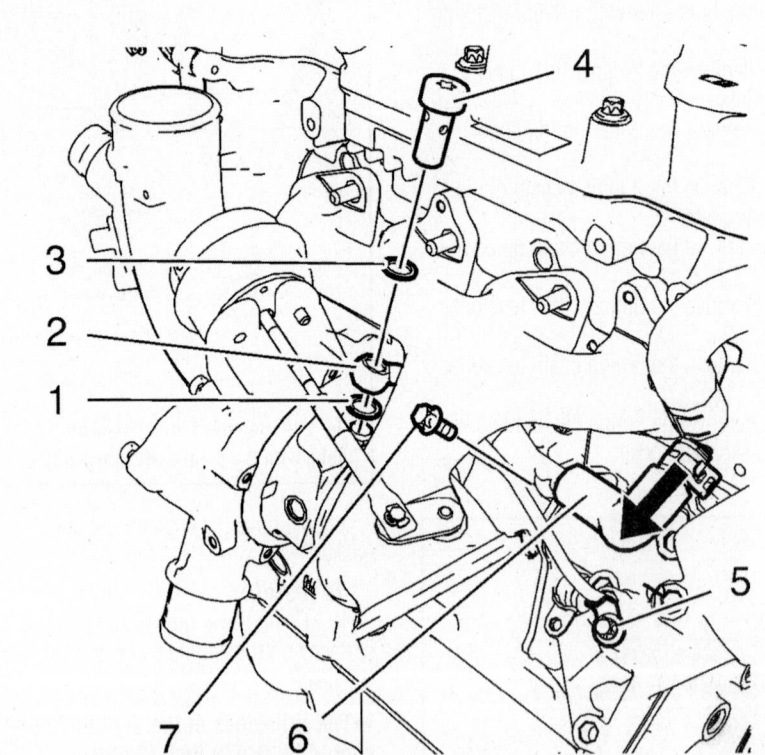

1. Seal ring
2. Turbocharger oil feed pipe
3. Seal ring
4. Turbocharger oil feed pipe hollow screw
5. Turbocharger oil feed pipe bolt
6. Turbocharger coolant return hose
7. Turbocharger coolant return pipe bolt

Fig. 254 Removing the turbocharger oil feed components

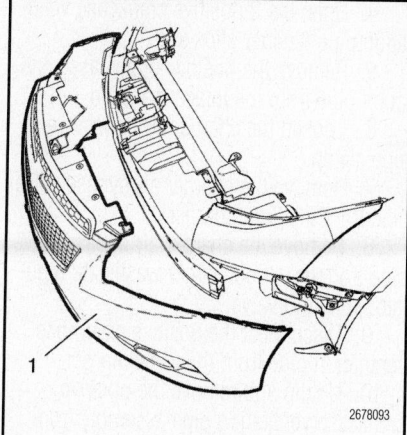

Fig. 255 View of front bumper fascia removal

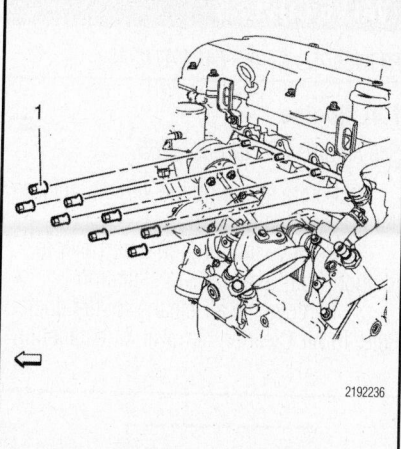

Fig. 257 Remove the 8 turbocharger nuts (1)

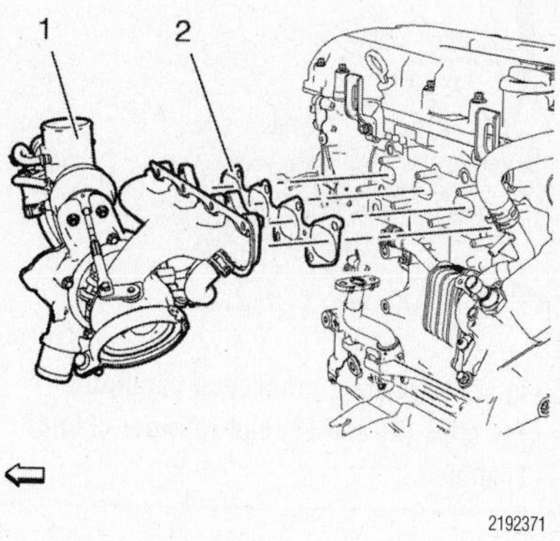

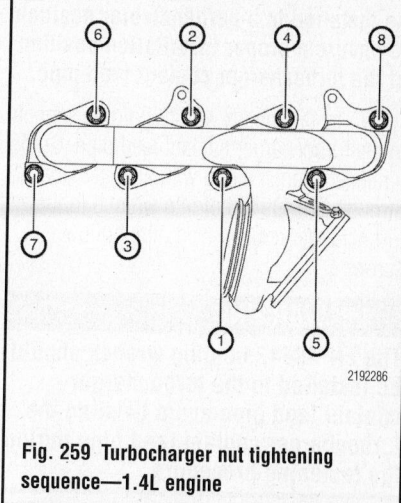

Fig. 259 Turbocharger nut tightening sequence—1.4L engine

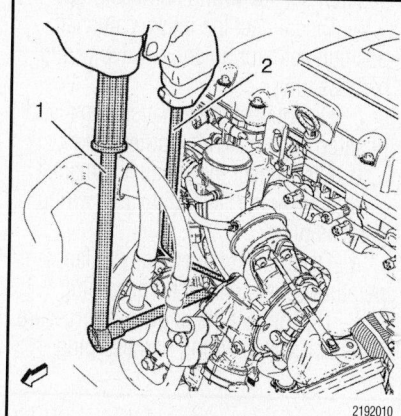

Fig. 256 Install the EN-49942 holding wrench (2) to the turbocharger coolant feed pipe. Guide a ratchet wrench (1) along with an extension through EN-49942 holding wrench to the turbocharger coolant feed pipe hollow screw

20. Remove the turbocharger coolant feed pipe hollow screw with a ratchet wrench and extension.

21. Remove and DISCARD the 2 seal rings.

22. Remove the warm up 3-way catalytic converter. Refer to Catalytic Converter, Warm Up 3-Way Catalytic Converter, removal & installation.

23. Remove the 2 turbocharger oil return pipe bolts and the oil return pipe from the turbocharger.

24. Remove and DISCARD the gasket.

25. Remove and DISCARD the 8 turbocharger nuts.

26. Remove the turbocharger assembly.

27. Remove and DISCARD the turbocharger gasket.

28. Remove the assembly parts from the turbocharger as necessary.

Fig. 258 Turbocharger assembly (1) and gasket (2) removal

To install:

29. Install the assembly parts to the turbocharger as necessary.

30. Clean the sealing surfaces.

31. Install a NEW turbocharger gasket.

32. Install the turbocharger assembly.

> ※※ **WARNING**
>
> **This component is equipped with torque-to-yield fasteners. Install NEW torque-to-yield fasteners when installing this component. Failure to replace the torque-to-yield fasteners could cause damage to the vehicle or component.**

33. Install the 8 NEW turbocharger nuts.

34. Tighten the 8 turbocharger nuts in sequence to 71 inch lbs. (8 Nm).

35. Repeat the tightening procedure to ensure a proper fastening of the turbocharger nuts.

36. Install a NEW gasket and the 2 turbocharger oil return pipe bolts and tighten to 71 inch lbs. (8 Nm).

37. Install the warm up 3-way catalytic converter. Refer to Catalytic Converter, Warm Up 3-Way Catalytic Converter, removal & installation.

38. Install the turbocharger coolant feed pipe to the engine block:

a. Install a NEW seal ring to the turbocharger coolant feed pipe hollow screw.

b. Install the turbocharger coolant feed pipe hollow screw along with the seal ring to the turbocharger coolant feed pipe.

c. Install a NEW seal ring to the turbocharger coolant feed pipe hollow screw.

d. Install the turbocharger coolant feed pipe hollow screw along with the turbocharger coolant feed pipe and the 2 seal rings to the engine.

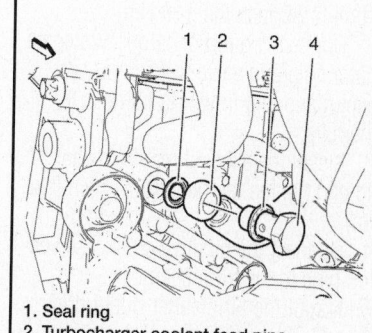

1. Seal ring
2. Turbocharger coolant feed pipe
3. Seal ring
4. Turbocharger coolant feed pipe hollow screw

Fig. 260 Turbocharger coolant feed pipe installation

→The EN-49942 holding wrench should be installed in a perpendicular position to ensure a proper installation position of the turbocharger coolant feed pipe.

39. Install the EN-49942 holding wrench to the turbocharger coolant feed pipe. Guide a ratchet wrench along with an extension through EN-49942 holding wrench to the turbocharger coolant feed pipe hollow screw.

✳✳ WARNING

The EN-49942 holding wrench should be installed to the turbocharger coolant feed pipe avoid twisting the turbocharger coolant feed pipe during the fastening procedure.

40. Tighten the turbocharger coolant feed pipe hollow screw with a ratchet wrench and extension to 22 ft. lbs. (30 Nm).

41. Install the charger air cooler inlet air hose to the charge air cooler. There should be an audible sound when it engages.

42. Install the front bumper fascia.

43. Install the charger air cooler inlet air hose to the turbocharger.

44. Install and tighten the charger air cooler inlet air hose clamp.

45. Install the turbocharger coolant return pipe bolt and tighten to 71 inch lbs. (8 Nm).

46. Install the turbocharger coolant return hose to the oil cooler inlet pipe.

47. Install the turbocharger coolant return hose clamp.

48. Install the turbocharger oil feed pipe to the oil cooler and the turbocharger.

49. Install the turbocharger oil feed pipe bolt.

50. Install the turbocharger oil feed pipe hollow screw along with the 2 NEW seal rings and tighten to 22 ft. lbs. (30 Nm).

51. Tighten the turbocharger oil feed pipe bolt to 89 inch lbs. (10 Nm).

52. Connect the turbocharger wastegate regulator solenoid valve wiring harness connector and clip in wiring harness to retainer clip.

53. Install the exhaust manifold heat shield and tighten the bolts to 71 inch lbs. (8 Nm).

54. Connect the positive crankcase ventilation pipe to the turbocharger.

55. Install the air cleaner outlet duct. Refer to Air Cleaner, removal & installation.

56. Connect the battery negative cable. Refer to Battery, removal & installation.

57. Fill the cooling system. Refer to Cooling System Draining and Filling.

VALVE COVERS

REMOVAL & INSTALLATION

1.4L Engine

See Figures 261 through 265.

1. Before servicing the vehicle, refer to the Precautions Section.

2. Remove the ignition coil. Refer to Ignition Coil, removal & installation.

3. Remove the air cleaner outlet duct. Refer to Air Cleaner, removal & installation.

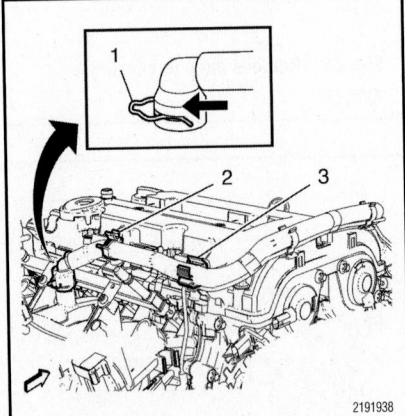

Fig. 261 Positive crankcase ventilation pipe clips (2) and (3) and retainer clamp (1) shown

4. Open the 2 positive crankcase ventilation pipe retainer clips and.

5. Remove the positive crankcase ventilation pipe from the intake manifold.

6. Loosen the charger air bypass valve pipe clamp.

7. Remove the charger air bypass valve pipe from the turbocharger.

8. Remove the charger air bypass valve pipe from the turbocharger wastegate regulator solenoid valve.

9. Disconnect the positive crankcase ventilation pipe from the turbocharger.

10. Unclip and remove the positive crankcase ventilation pipe assembly from the camshaft cover retainer clips.

11. Remove engine control module wiring harness from camshaft cover.

a. Disconnect the intake camshaft position sensor wiring harness plug.

b. Disconnect the intake camshaft position actuator solenoid valve wiring harness plug.

c. Disconnect the exhaust camshaft position sensor wiring harness plug.

d. Disconnect the exhaust camshaft position actuator solenoid valve wiring harness plug.

e. Disconnect the engine coolant temperature sensor wiring harness plug.

f. Disconnect the engine oil pressure indicator switch wiring harness plug.

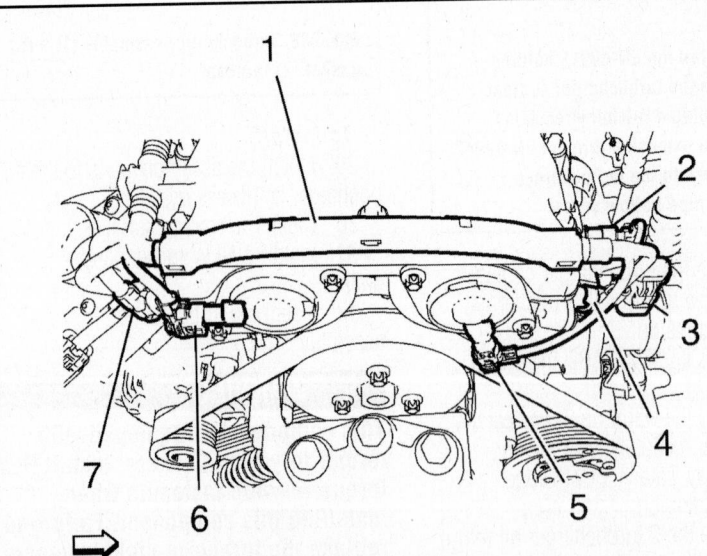

1. Engine control module wiring harness
2. Engine oil pressure indicator switch wiring harness plug
3. Engine coolant temperature sensor wiring harness plug
4. Exhaust camshaft position sensor wiring harness plug
5. Exhaust camshaft position actuator solenoid valve wiring harness plug
6. Intake camshaft position actuator solenoid valve wiring harness plug
7. Intake camshaft position sensor wiring harness plug

Fig. 262 Removing the engine control module wiring harness from the camshaft cover

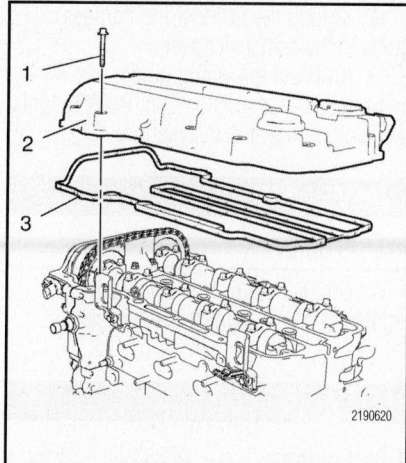

Fig. 263 Camshaft (valve) cover (2), cover gasket (3), and bolts (1) shown

g. Unclip the engine control module wiring harness plug from the camshaft cover and lay aside.

12. Remove the oil level indicator.

13. Remove the 15 camshaft cover bolts.

14. Remove the camshaft cover and the camshaft cover gasket.

To install:

15. Clean the sealing surfaces.

➡**The thickness of the sealing bead should be 0.079 inch (2mm).**

16. Apply sealing compound to the appropriate areas.

➡**The installation procedure should not take longer than 10 minutes.**

17. Install the camshaft cover and a NEW gasket.

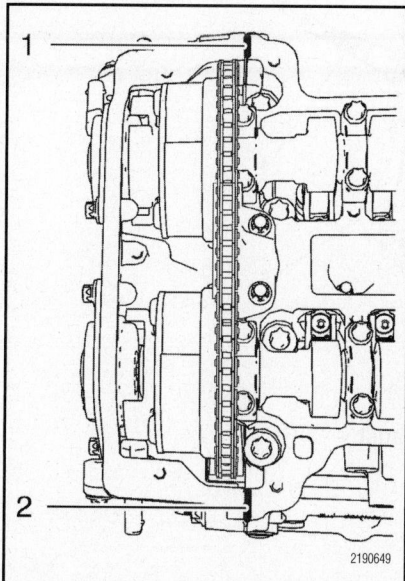

Fig. 264 Apply sealing compound to the indicated areas (1) and (2)

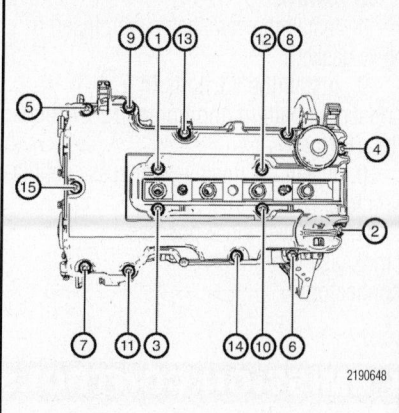

Fig. 265 Camshaft cover bolt tightening sequence—1.4L engine

18. Install the 15 camshaft cover bolts.

19. Tighten the 15 camshaft cover bolts in a sequence to 71 inch lbs. (8 Nm).

20. Install the engine control module wiring harness to the camshaft cover.

a. Clip the engine control module wiring harness plug to the camshaft cover.

b. Connect the intake camshaft position sensor wiring harness plug.

c. Connect the intake camshaft position actuator solenoid valve wiring harness plug.

d. Connect the exhaust camshaft position sensor wiring harness plug.

e. Connect the exhaust camshaft position actuator solenoid valve wiring harness plug.

f. Connect the engine coolant temperature sensor wiring harness plug.

g. Connect the engine oil pressure indicator switch wiring harness plug.

21. Install the ignition coil. Refer to Ignition Coil, removal & installation.

22. Install the positive crankcase ventilation pipe assembly to the camshaft cover retainer clips.

23. Connect the positive crankcase ventilation pipe to turbocharger.

24. Install the charger air bypass valve pipe to turbo charger wastegate regulator solenoid valve.

25. Install the charger air bypass valve pipe to turbocharger.

26. Fasten the charger air bypass valve pipe clamp.

27. Install the positive crankcase ventilation pipe to the intake manifold and fix with retainer clamp.

28. Clip in the positive crankcase ventilation pipe to the 2 retainer clips.

29. Install the air cleaner outlet duct. Refer to Air Cleaner, removal & installation.

30. Check and correct engine oil level.

1.8L Engine

See Figures 266 through 268.

1. Before servicing the vehicle, refer to the Precautions Section.

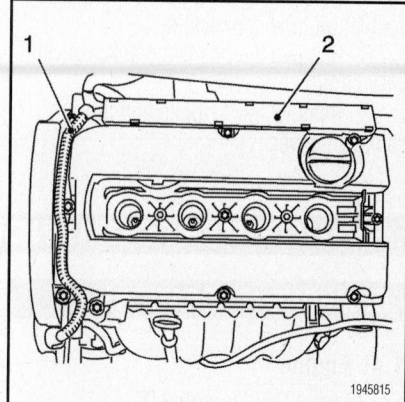

Fig. 266 Unclip the ECM wiring harness guide (1) from the camshaft cover and disconnect the wiring guide (2)

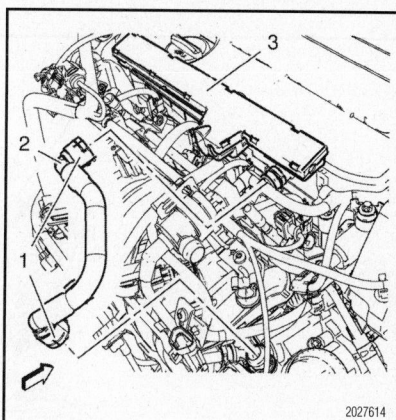

Fig. 267 View of the positive crankcase ventilation tube (2), positive crankcase ventilation tube connectors (1), and the ECM wiring harness guide (3)

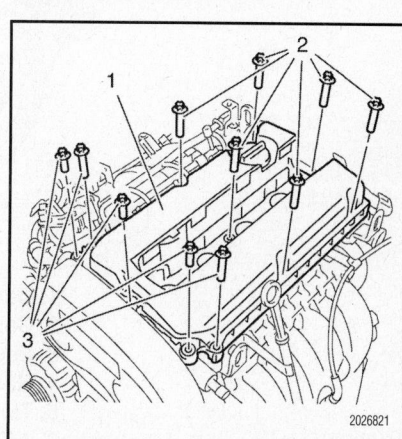

Fig. 268 Remove the bolts (2, 3) and the camshaft cover (1)—1.8L engine

2. Remove the ignition coil. Refer to Ignition Coil, removal & installation.

3. Unclip the ECM wiring harness guide from the camshaft (valve) cover.

4. Disconnect the wiring guide.

5. Disconnect the 2 positive crankcase ventilation tube connectors.

6. Remove the positive crankcase ventilation tube.

7. Remove the 11 bolts and the camshaft cover.

To install:

8. Install the camshaft cover. Insert a NEW gasket.

9. Install the 11 bolts in a crisscross pattern and tighten to 71 inch lbs. (8 Nm).

10. Install the positive crankcase ventilation tube.

11. Connect the 2 positive crankcase ventilation tube connectors.

12. Clip in the ECM wiring harness guide to the camshaft cover.

13. Connect the wiring guide.

14. Install the ignition coil. Refer to Ignition Coil, removal & installation.

VALVE LASH

ADJUSTMENT

All engines utilize hydraulic lash adjusters; no adjustment is necessary.

ENGINE PERFORMANCE & EMISSION CONTROLS

COMPONENT LOCATIONS

1.4L Engine
See Figures 269 through 271.

1.8L Engine
See Figures 272 through 275.

CAMSHAFT POSITION (CMP) SENSOR

LOCATION

1.4L Engine
See Figure 276.

Refer to the accompanying illustration.

1.8L Engine
See Figure 277.

Refer to the accompanying illustration.

REMOVAL & INSTALLATION

1.4L Engine
See Figure 276.

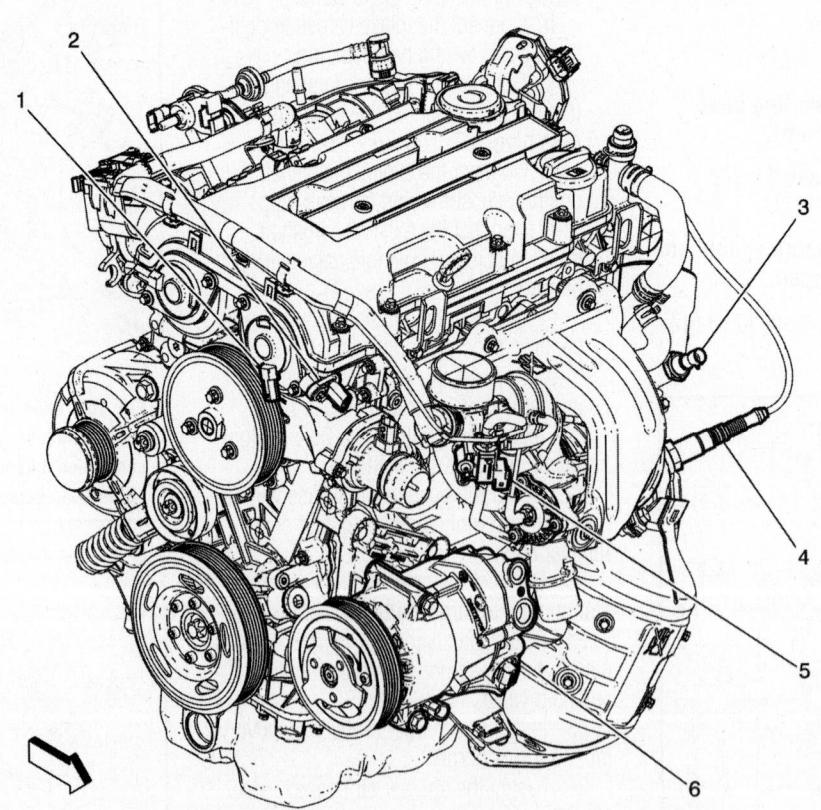

1. Camshaft Position Actuator Solenoid Valve - Exhaust
2. Camshaft Position Sensor - Exhaust
3. Engine Oil Pressure Switch
4. Heated Oxygen Sensor 1
5. Turbocharger Wastegate Solenoid Valve
6. A/C Compressor Solenoid Valve

2309762

Fig. 269 Engine and emission control component locations (right front)—1.4L engine

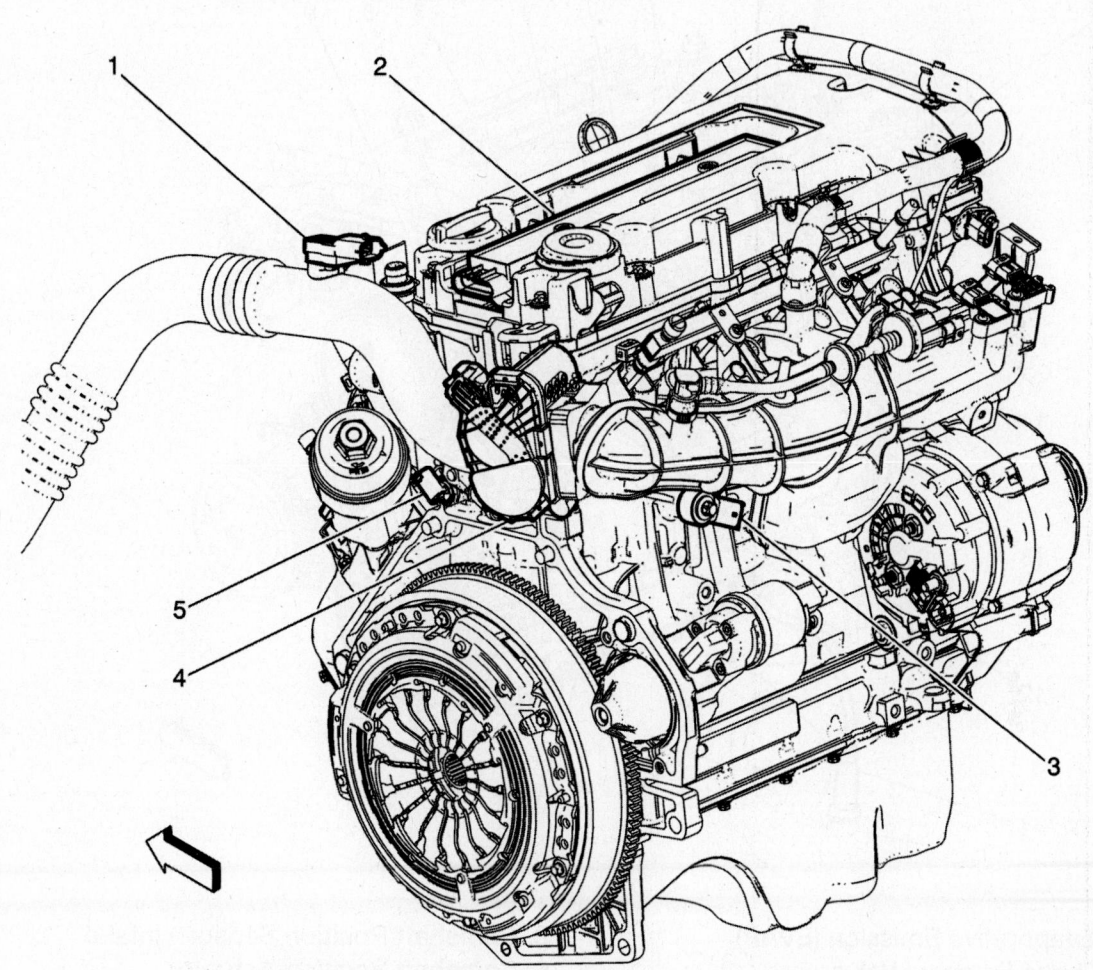

1. Intake Manifold Pressure and Air Temperature Sensor
2. Ignition Coil
3. Knock Sensor
4. Throttle Body
5. Engine Coolant Temperature Sensor 1

2309756

Fig. 270 Engine and emission control component locations (left rear)—1.4L engine

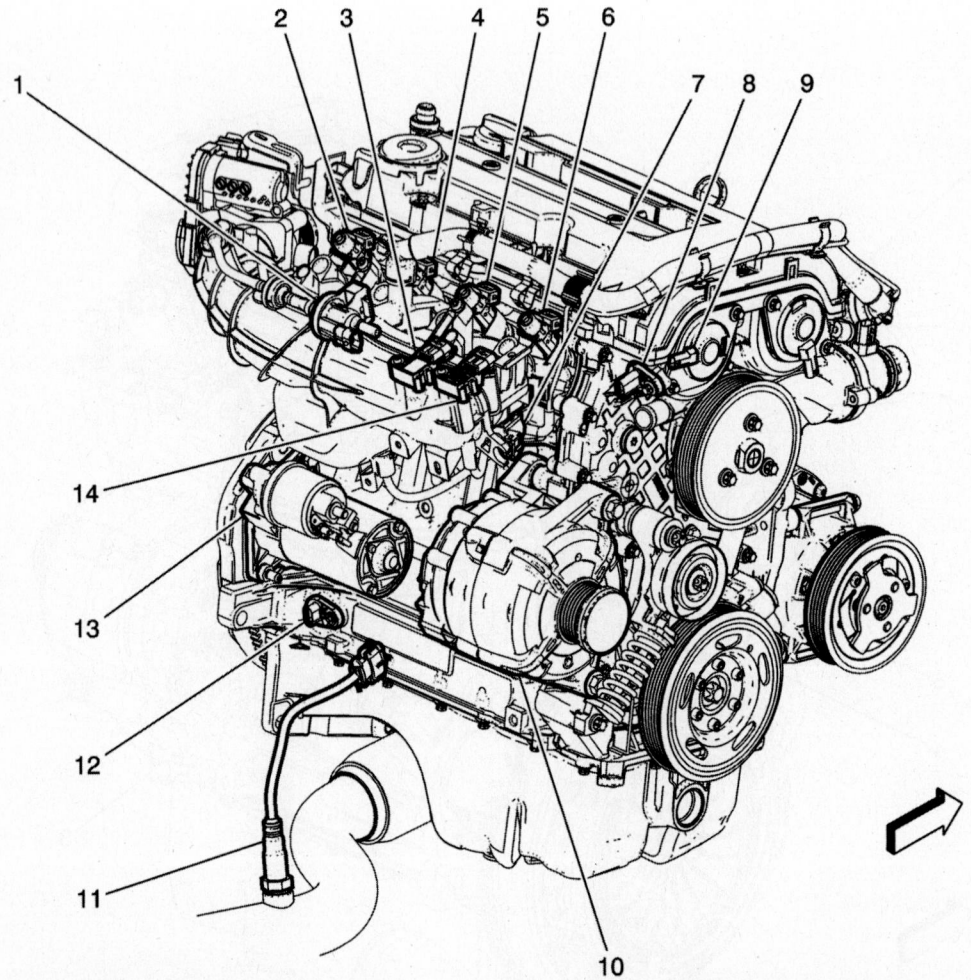

Fig. 271 Engine and emission control component locations (right rear)—1.4L engine

1. Evaporative Emission (EVAP) Purge Solenoid Valve
2. Fuel Injector 4
3. Manifold Absolute Pressure Sensor
4. Fuel Injector 3
5. Fuel Injector 2
6. Fuel Injector 1
7. Turbocharger Wastegate Solenoid Valve
8. Camshaft Position Sensor - Intake
9. Camshaft Position Actuator Solenoid Valve - Intake
10. Alternator
11. Heated Oxygen Sensor 2
12. Crankshaft Position (CKP) Sensor
13. Starter Motor
14. Barometric Pressure (BARO) Sensor

2309773

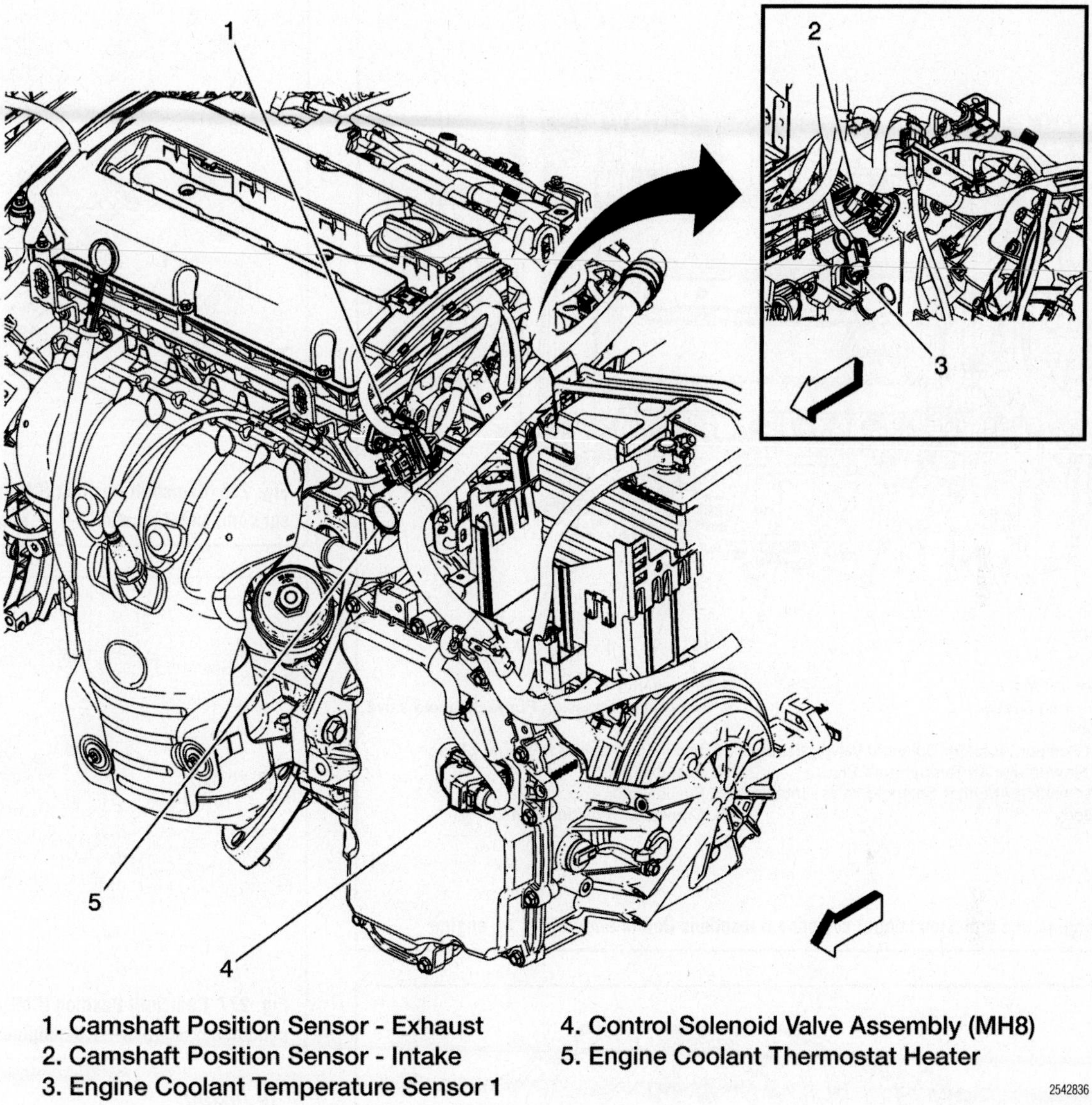

1. Camshaft Position Sensor - Exhaust
2. Camshaft Position Sensor - Intake
3. Engine Coolant Temperature Sensor 1
4. Control Solenoid Valve Assembly (MH8)
5. Engine Coolant Thermostat Heater

2542836

Fig. 272 Engine and emission control component locations (left front)—1.8L engine

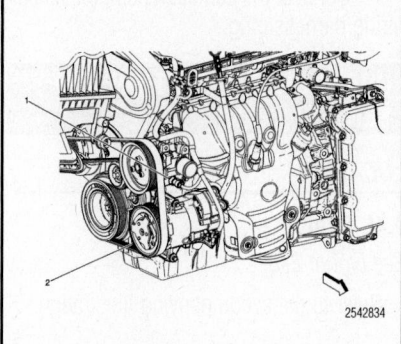

Fig. 273 Engine and emission control component locations (right front)—1.8L engine

➡**Graphic shows the exhaust camshaft position sensor. Use the same procedure for the intake camshaft position sensor.**

1. Before servicing the vehicle, refer to the Precautions Section.

2. Disconnect the camshaft position sensor wiring harness plug.

3. Remove the camshaft position sensor bolt.

4. Remove the camshaft position sensor and the seal ring.

To install:

5. Install the camshaft position sensor and the seal ring.

6. Install the camshaft position sensor bolt and tighten to 71 inch lbs. (8 Nm).

7. Connect the camshaft position sensor wiring harness plug.

8. After replacement of a camshaft position sensor, use a scan tool to speed up the learn function.

1.8L Engine

See Figure 277.

1. Before servicing the vehicle, refer to the Precautions Section.

2. Disconnect the camshaft position sensor wiring harness plug.

3. Remove the camshaft position sensor bolt.

4. Remove the camshaft position sensor and the seal ring.

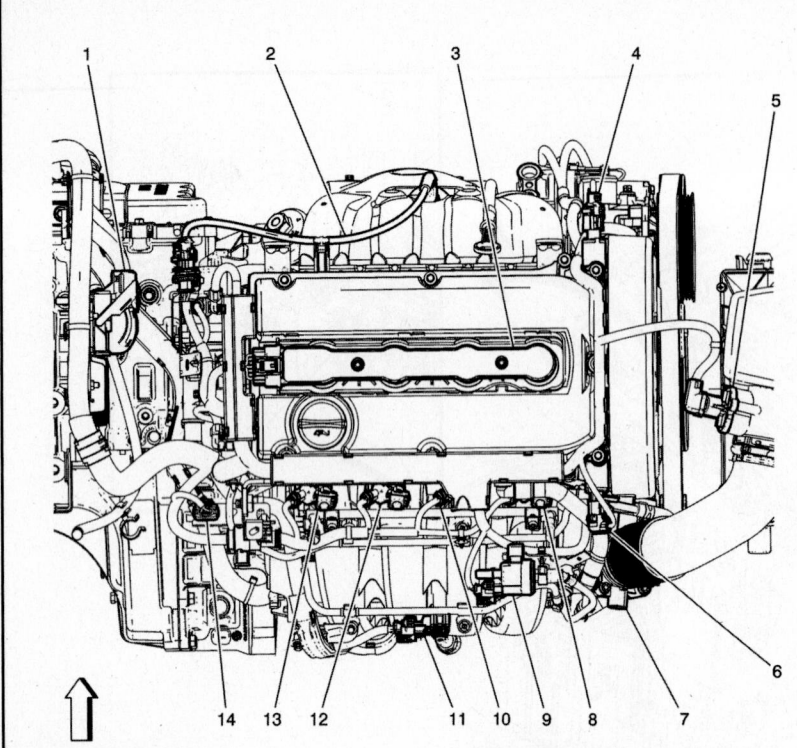

Fig. 274 Engine and emission control component locations (top of engine)—1.8L engine

1. Engine Control Module
2. Heated Oxygen Sensor 1
3. Ignition Coil
4. Camshaft Position Actuator Solenoid Valve - Exhaust
5. Mass Air Flow/Intake Air Temperature Sensor
6. Camshaft Position Actuator Solenoid Valve - Intake
7. Throttle Body
8. Fuel Injector 1
9. Evaporative Emission Purge Solenoid Valve
10. Fuel Injector 2
11. Manifold Absolute Pressure Sensor
12. Fuel Injector 3
13. Fuel Injector 4
14. Crankshaft Position Sensor

2542828

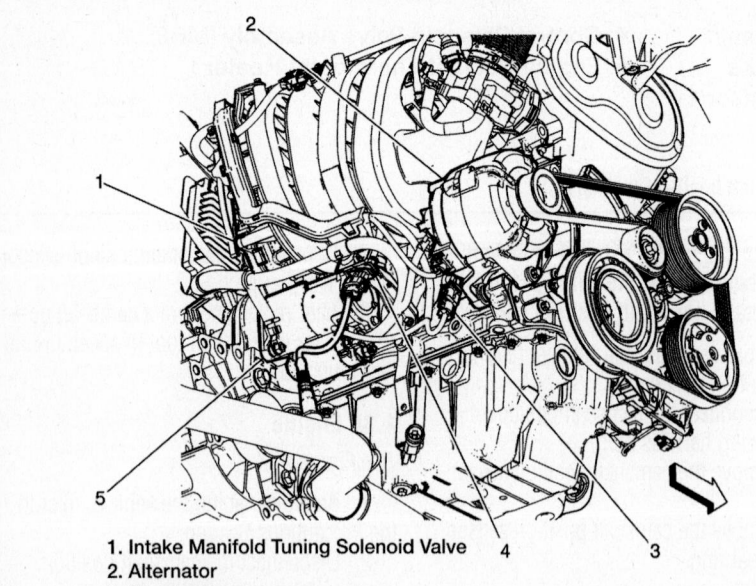

1. Intake Manifold Tuning Solenoid Valve
2. Alternator
3. Knock Sensor
4. Heated Oxygen Sensor 2
5. Starter Motor

2542838

Fig. 275 Engine and emission control component locations (right rear of engine)—1.8L engine

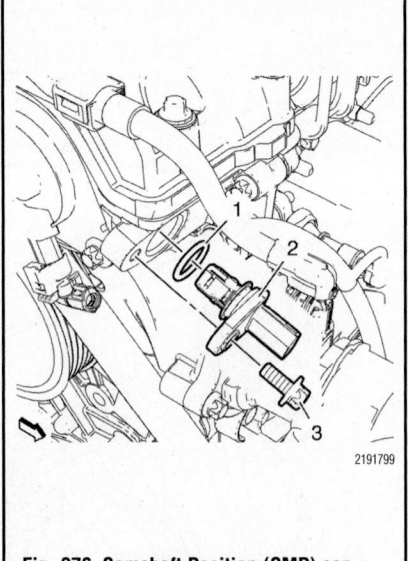

2191799

Fig. 276 Camshaft Position (CMP) sensor component location—1.4L engine

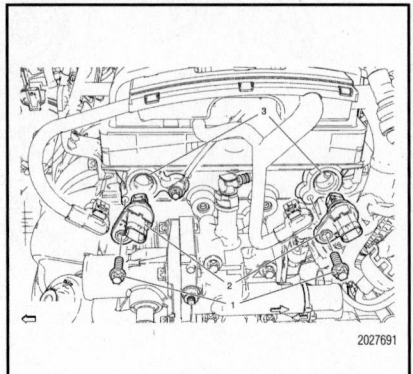

2027691

Fig. 277 Camshaft Position (CMP) sensor component location—1.8L engine

To install:

5. Install the camshaft position sensor and the seal ring.

6. Install the camshaft position sensor bolt and tighten to 53 inch lbs. (6 Nm).

7. Connect the camshaft position sensor wiring harness plug.

CRANKSHAFT POSITION (CKP) SENSOR

LOCATION

1.4L Engine

See Figure 278.

Refer to the accompanying illustration.

1.8L Engine

See Figure 279.

Refer to the accompanying illustration.

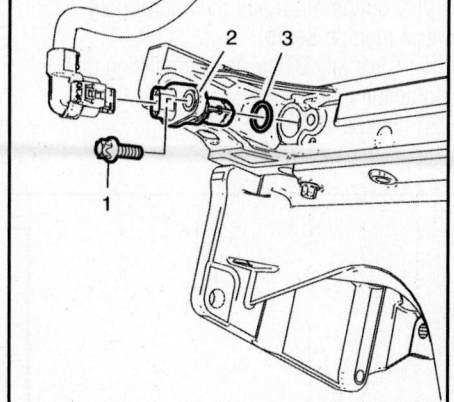

1. Crankshaft Position Sensor Bolt
2. Crankshaft Position Sensor
3. Crankshaft Position Sensor Seal Ring

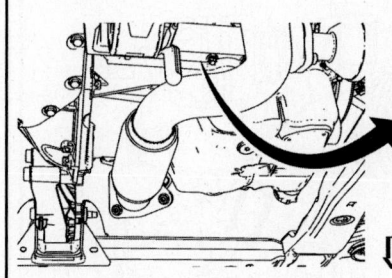

Fig. 278 Crankshaft Position (CKP) sensor component location—1.4L engine

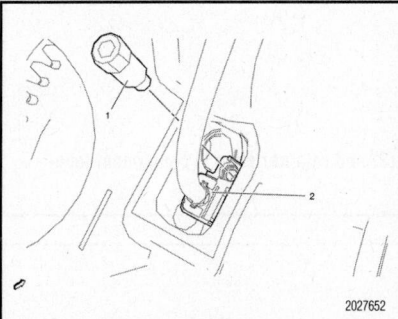

Fig. 279 Crankshaft Position (CKP) sensor (2) and fastener (1) component location— 1.8L engine

REMOVAL & INSTALLATION

1.4L Engine

See Figure 278.

1. Before servicing the vehicle, refer to the Precautions Section.
2. Raise and safely support the vehicle.
3. Disconnect the electrical connector from the Crankshaft Position (CKP) sensor.
4. Remove the CKP sensor bolt.
5. Remove the CKP sensor.

To install:

6. Install the CKP sensor with the seal ring and tighten the bolt to 71 inch lbs. (8 Nm).

7. Connect the electrical connector to the CKP sensor.
8. After replacement of CKP sensor, use a scan tool to speed up the learn function.

1.8L Engine

See Figure 279.

1. Before servicing the vehicle, refer to the Precautions Section.
2. Remove the starter motor. Refer to Starter, removal & installation.
3. Disconnect the electrical connector from the Crankshaft Position (CKP) sensor.
4. Remove the CKP sensor bolt.
5. Remove the CKP sensor.

To install:

6. Install the CKP sensor with the seal ring and tighten the bolt to 40 inch lbs. (5 Nm).
7. Connect the electrical connector to the CKP sensor.
8. Install the starter motor. Refer to Starter, removal & installation.
9. After replacement of CKP sensor, use a scan tool to speed up the learn function.

ENGINE CONTROL MODULE (ECM)

LOCATION

See Figure 280.

Refer to the accompanying illustration.

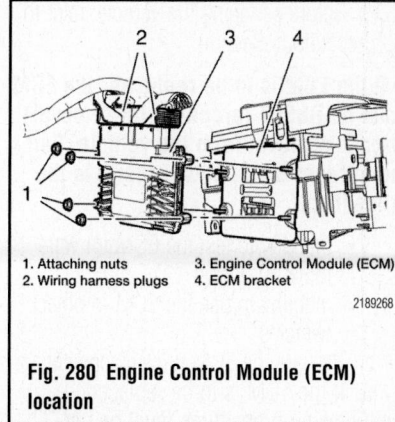

1. Attaching nuts
2. Wiring harness plugs
3. Engine Control Module (ECM)
4. ECM bracket

Fig. 280 Engine Control Module (ECM) location

REMOVAL & INSTALLATION

See Figure 280.

Note the following precautions before starting this procedure:

• Turn the ignition OFF when installing or removing the control module connectors and disconnecting or reconnecting the power to the control module (battery cable, Powertrain Control Module (PCM)/Engine Control Module (ECM)/Transaxle Control Module (TCM) pigtail, control module fuse, jumper cables, etc.) in order to prevent internal control module damage.

• Control module damage may result when the metal case contacts battery voltage. DO NOT contact the control module metal case with battery voltage when servicing a control module, using battery booster cables, or when charging the vehicle battery.

• In order to prevent any possible electrostatic discharge damage to the control module, do not touch the connector pins or the soldered components on the circuit board.

• Remove any debris from around the control module connector surfaces before servicing the control module. Inspect the control module connector gaskets when diagnosing or replacing the control module. Ensure that the gaskets are installed correctly. The gaskets prevent contaminant intrusion into the control module.

• The replacement control module must be programmed.

➡**It is necessary to record the remaining engine oil life. If the replacement module is not programmed with the remaining engine oil life, the engine oil life will default to 100 percent. If the replacement module is not programmed with the remaining engine oil life, the engine oil will need to be changed at 3,000 miles (5,000 km) from the last engine oil change.**

1. Before servicing the vehicle, refer to the Precautions Section.

➡ **If the ECM is to be replaced, the ECM must be RESET (prepared for removal) prior to removal from the vehicle. Failing to reset the ECM will result in the following:**

- Inability to test the ECM for warranty purposes
- Inability to use the ECM in other vehicles

2. Prepare the ECM for replacement.

3. If the ECM is to be replaced, the following procedures must be performed:

a. Connect a scan tool to the vehicle and access the Service Programming System (SPS).

➡ **The Prepare Control Module for Removal function can only be performed when communication with the old control module is still possible.**

b. Before removing the old control module, perform the SPS function Prepare Control Module for Removal.

4. Using a scan tool, retrieve the percentage of remaining engine oil. Record the remaining engine oil life.

5. Disconnect the battery negative cable. Refer to Battery, removal & installation.

6. Disconnect the 2 wiring harness plugs from the Engine Control Module (ECM).

7. Unclip the ECM bracket from the battery tray.

8. Remove the 4 nuts.

9. Remove the ECM from the ECM bracket.

To install:

10. Install the ECM to the ECM bracket.

11. Install the 4 nuts and tighten to 80 inch lbs. (9 Nm).

12. Clip the ECM bracket to the battery tray.

13. Connect the 2 wiring harness plug to the ECM.

14. Connect the battery negative cable. Refer to Battery, removal & installation.

15. Program the ECM.

16. Using a scan tool, perform the SPS function Engine Control Module Programming and follow the on-screen instructions.

17. Perform the SPS Function Immobilizer Learn.

18. Perform the SPS function Engine Control Module Configuration and Setup and follow the on-screen

instructions. On the screen Control Module Configuration and Setup Function(s), select both control module Configuration/Reconfiguration and the appropriate control module Setup.

19. Clear any DTCs after completing the programming procedure.

20. Start and idle the engine.

ENGINE COOLANT TEMPERATURE (ECT) SENSOR

LOCATION

See Figures 281 through 283.

Refer to the accompanying illustrations.

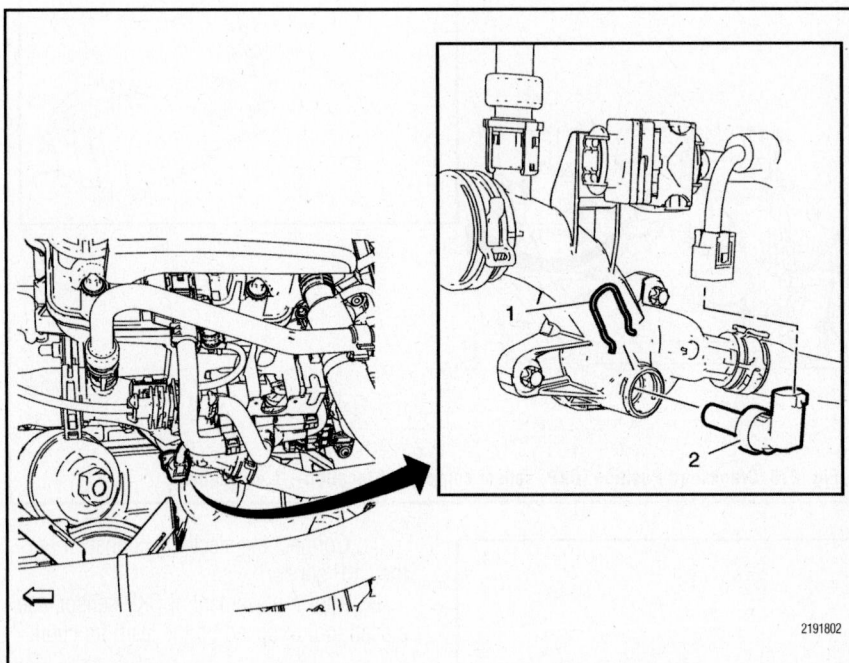

Fig. 281 Engine Coolant Temperature (ECT) sensor (2) and retainer clip (1) component locations (in water outlet)—1.4L engine

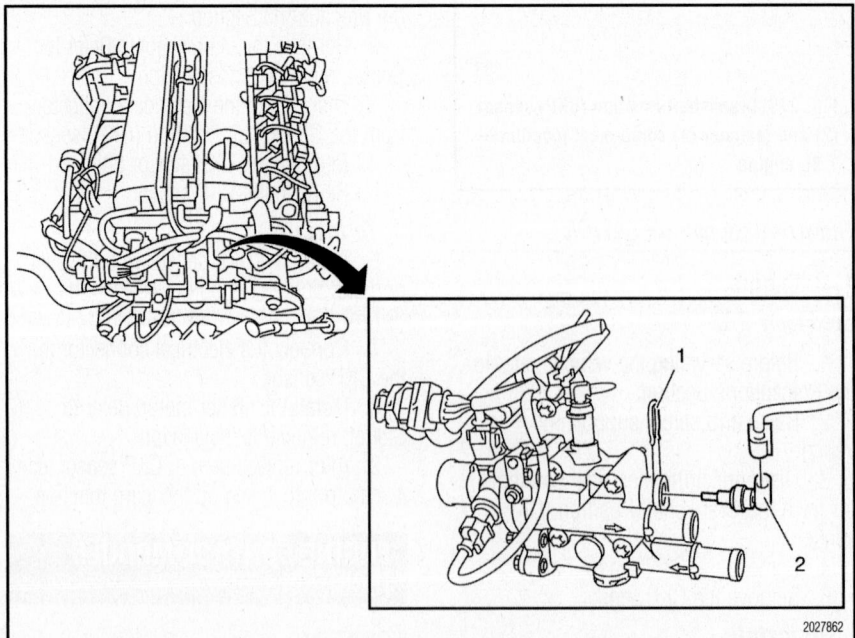

Fig. 282 Engine Coolant Temperature (ECT) sensor (2) and retainer clip (1) component locations (in thermostat housing)—1.8L engine

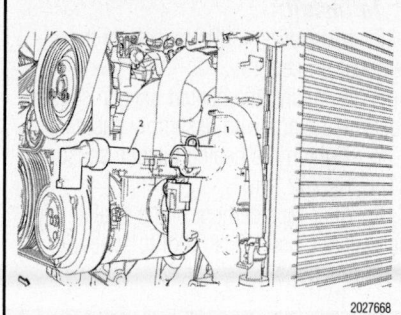

Fig. 283 Engine Coolant Temperature (ECT) sensor (2) and retaining clamp (1) component locations (in radiator)—1.4L and 1.8L engines

REMOVAL & INSTALLATION

1.4L Engine

In Water Outlet

See Figure 281.

> ※※ **CAUTION**
>
> **Allow sufficient time for the engine to cool before removing the ECT sensor. A hot engine may cause an excessive coolant loss or a personal injury.**

1. Before servicing the vehicle, refer to the Precautions Section.
2. Drain the cooling system. Refer to Engine Coolant, Drain & Refill Procedure.
3. Disconnect the ECT sensor electrical connector.
4. Remove the retainer clip.
5. Remove the ECT sensor from the water outlet.
6. Installation is the reverse of the removal procedure.

1.8L Engine

In Thermostat Housing

See Figure 282.

> ※※ **CAUTION**
>
> **Allow sufficient time for the engine to cool before removing the ECT sensor. A hot engine may cause an excessive coolant loss or a personal injury.**

1. Before servicing the vehicle, refer to the Precautions Section.
2. Drain the cooling system. Refer to Engine Coolant, Drain & Refill Procedure.
3. Disconnect the ECT sensor electrical connector.
4. Remove the retainer clip.
5. Remove the ECT sensor from the thermostat housing.

6. Installation is the reverse of the removal procedure.

1.4L and 1.8L Engines

In Radiator

See Figure 283.

1. Before servicing the vehicle, refer to the Precautions Section.
2. Drain the cooling system. Refer to Engine Coolant, Drain & Refill Procedure.
3. Disconnect the electrical connector.
4. Disconnect the retaining clamp.
5. Remove the ECT sensor from the radiator.
6. Installation is the reverse of the removal procedure.

HEATED OXYGEN (HO2S) SENSOR

LOCATION

See Figures 284 through 286.

Refer to the accompanying illustrations.

REMOVAL & INSTALLATION

1.4L Engine

See Figures 287 and 288.

Special Tools
- EN-48259 Installer/Remover

> ※※ **CAUTION**
>
> **In order to avoid being burned, do not service the exhaust system while it is still hot. Service the system when it is cool.**

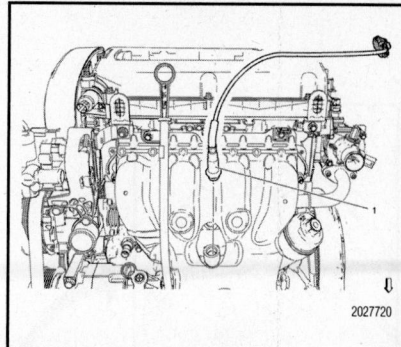

Fig. 285 Heated Oxygen (HO2S) sensor-1 location (1)—1.8L engine

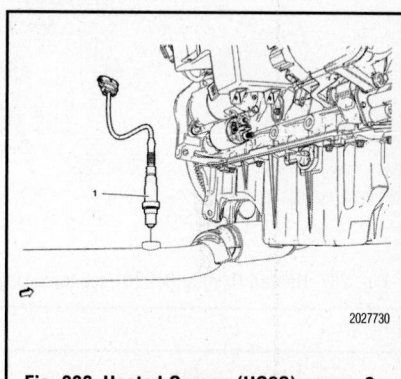

Fig. 286 Heated Oxygen (HO2S) sensor-2 location (1)—1.4L and 1.8L engines

1. Before servicing the vehicle, refer to the Precautions Section.
2. Disconnect the battery negative cable. Refer to Battery, removal & installation.
3. Remove the wiring harness from the retainer clip.
4. Disconnect the electrical connector.

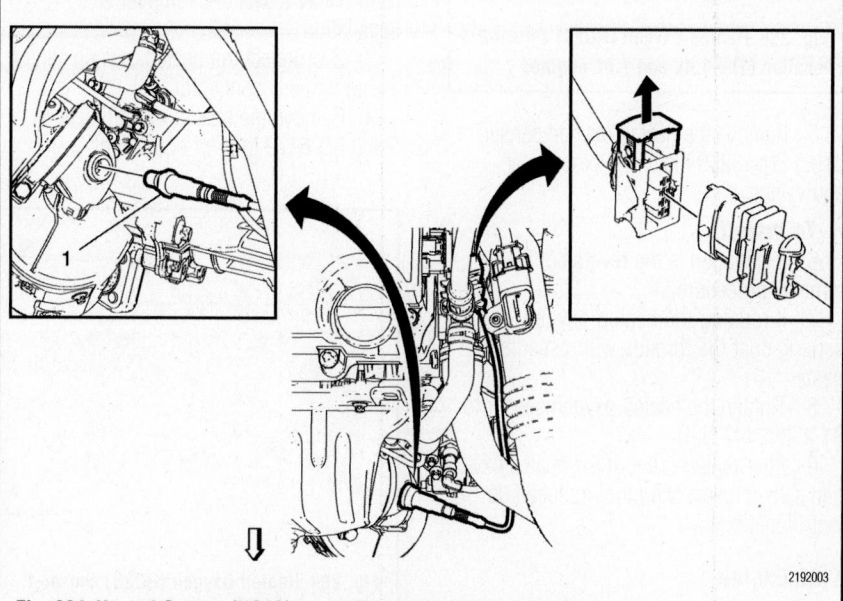

Fig. 284 Heated Oxygen (HO2S) sensor-1 location (1)—1.4L engine

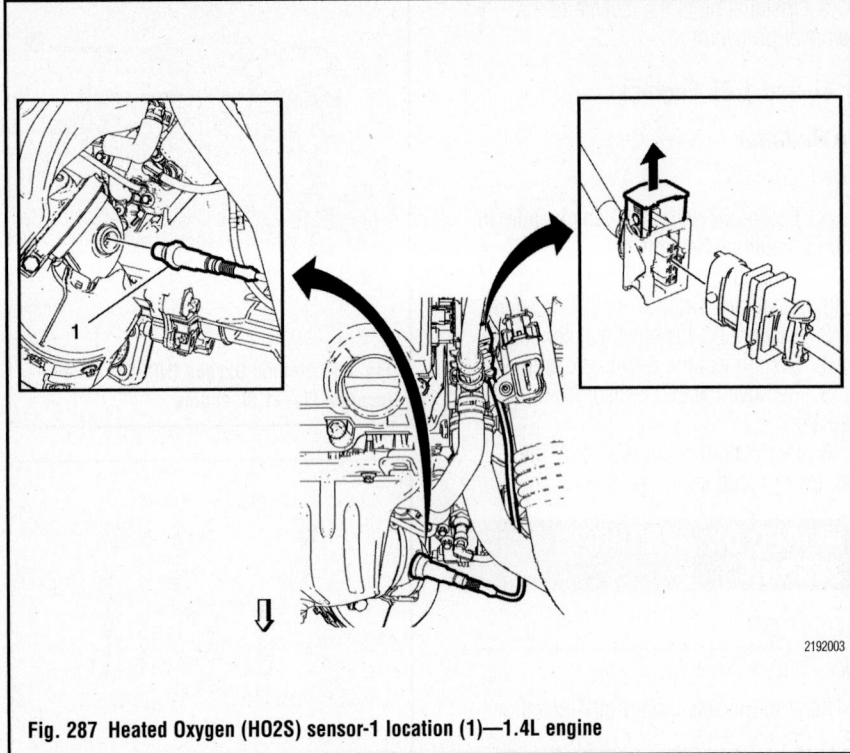

Fig. 287 Heated Oxygen (HO2S) sensor-1 location (1)—1.4L engine

Fig. 288 Heated Oxygen (HO2S) sensor-2 location (1)—1.4L and 1.8L engines

5. Remove the heated oxygen sensor using EN-48259 Installer/Remover, or equivalent.

To install:

6. Installation is the reverse of the removal procedure.

7. If reusing the heated oxygen sensor, coat the threads with assembly paste.

8. Tighten the heated oxygen sensor to 31 ft. lbs. (42 Nm).

9. After replacement of the heated oxygen sensor, use a scan tool to speed up learn functions.

1.8L Engine

See Figures 288 and 289.

Special Tools

- EN-6179 Heated Oxygen Sensor Remover/Installer

※※ CAUTION

In order to avoid being burned, do not service the exhaust system while it is still hot. Service the system when it is cool.

1. Before servicing the vehicle, refer to the Precautions Section.

2. Disconnect the battery negative cable. Refer to Battery, removal & installation.

3. Disconnect the heated oxygen sensor wiring harness connector.

4. Remove the heated oxygen sensor using EN-6179 tool, or equivalent.

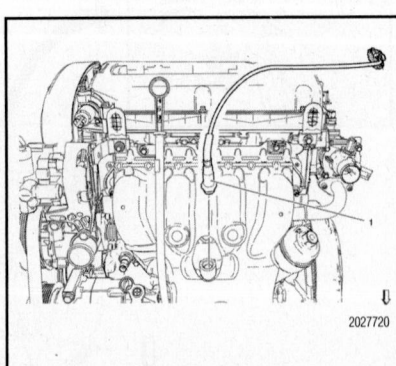

Fig. 289 Heated Oxygen (HO2S) sensor-1 location (1)—1.8L engine

To install:

5. Installation is the reverse of the removal procedure.

6. If reusing the heated oxygen sensor, coat the threads with assembly paste.

7. Tighten the heated oxygen sensor to 31 ft. lbs. (42 Nm).

8. After replacement of the heated oxygen sensor, use a scan tool to speed up learn functions.

INTAKE AIR TEMPERATURE (IAT) SENSOR

LOCATION

1.4L Engine

See Figure 290.

Refer to the accompanying illustration.

1.8L Engine

See Figure 291.

Refer to the accompanying illustration.

REMOVAL & INSTALLATION

1.4L Engine

See Figure 290.

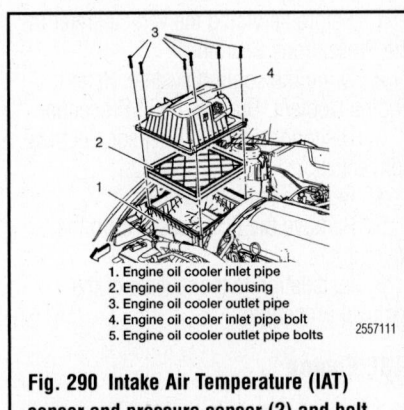

1. Engine oil cooler inlet pipe
2. Engine oil cooler housing
3. Engine oil cooler outlet pipe
4. Engine oil cooler inlet pipe bolt
5. Engine oil cooler outlet pipe bolts

Fig. 290 Intake Air Temperature (IAT) sensor and pressure sensor (2) and bolt (1) location—1.4L engine

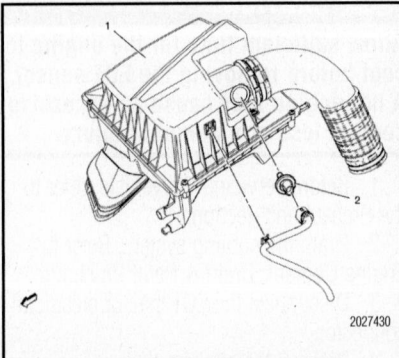

Fig. 291 Intake Air Temperature (IAT) sensor (1) and clip (2) location—1.8L engine

1. Before servicing the vehicle, refer to the Precautions Section.

2. Disconnect the electrical connector from the Intake Air Temperature (IAT) sensor and pressure sensor.

3. Remove the IAT attaching bolt and the IAT sensor.

4. Installation is the reverse of the removal procedure.

1.8L Engine

See Figure 291.

✳✳ WARNING

Any time service is being performed which requires removal of the air cleaner assembly, always cover the throttle body opening. This will prevent any foreign material from entering the engine.

1. Before servicing the vehicle, refer to the Precautions Section.

2. Disconnect the electrical connector from the Intake Air Temperature (IAT) sensor.

3. Remove the IAT sensor clip and the IAT sensor.

4. Installation is the reverse of the removal procedure.

KNOCK SENSOR (KS)

LOCATION

1.4L Engine

See Figure 292.

Refer to the accompanying illustration.

1.8L Engine

See Figure 293.

Refer to the accompanying illustration.

2191811

Fig. 292 Knock Sensor (KS) (2) and bolt (1) location—1.4L engine

REMOVAL & INSTALLATION

1.4L Engine

See Figure 292.

1. Before servicing the vehicle, refer to the Precautions Section.

2. Disconnect the negative cable from the battery. Refer to Battery, removal & installation.

3. Raise and safely support the vehicle.

4. Disconnect the knock sensor electrical connector.

➥ **DO NOT mistake the knock sensor electrical connector with the alternator electrical connector.**

5. Remove the knock sensor bolt and the knock sensor.

6. Installation is the reverse of the removal procedure.

7. Tighten the knock sensor bolt to 18 ft. lbs. (25 Nm).

1.8L Engine

See Figure 293.

1. Before servicing the vehicle, refer to the Precautions Section.

2. Disconnect the negative cable from the battery. Refer to Battery, removal & installation.

3. Remove the 2 intake manifold bracket bolts.

4. Unclip the wiring harness.

5. Remove the intake manifold bracket.

6. Remove the sensor bolt.

7. Disconnect the wiring harness plug.

8. Remove the knock sensor from the bracket.

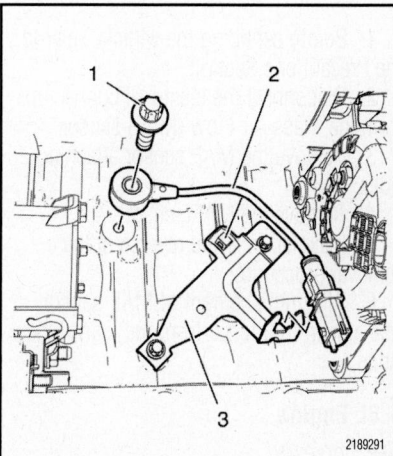

2189291

Fig. 293 Knock Sensor (KS) (2), bolt (1), and bracket (3) locations—1.8L engine

To install:

9. Install the knock sensor to the bracket.

10. Install the sensor bolt and tighten to 15 ft. lbs. (20 Nm).

11. Connect the wiring harness plug.

12. Install the intake manifold bracket.

13. Clip in the wiring harness.

14. Install the 2 intake manifold bracket bolts and tighten to 71 inch lbs. (8 Nm).

15. Connect the negative cable to the battery. Refer to Battery, removal & installation.

MANIFOLD ABSOLUTE PRESSURE (MAP) SENSOR

LOCATION

1.4L Engine

See Figure 294.

Refer to the accompanying illustration.

1.8L Engine

See Figure 295.

Refer to the accompanying illustration.

REMOVAL & INSTALLATION

1.4L Engine

See Figure 294.

1. Before servicing the vehicle, refer to the Precautions Section.

2. Disconnect the electrical connector from the Manifold Absolute Pressure (MAP) sensor.

3. Remove the MAP sensor bolt and the MAP sensor.

4. Installation is the reverse of the removal procedure.

5. After replacement of the MAP sensor, use a scan tool to speed up the learn process.

1.8L Engine

See Figure 295.

1. Before servicing the vehicle, refer to the Precautions Section.

2. Disconnect the electrical connector from the Manifold Absolute Pressure (MAP) sensor.

3. Remove the MAP sensor bolt and the MAP sensor.

4. Installation is the reverse of the removal procedure.

5. Tighten the MAP sensor bolt to 53 inch lbs. (6 Nm).

6. After replacement of the MAP sensor, use a scan tool to speed up the learn process.

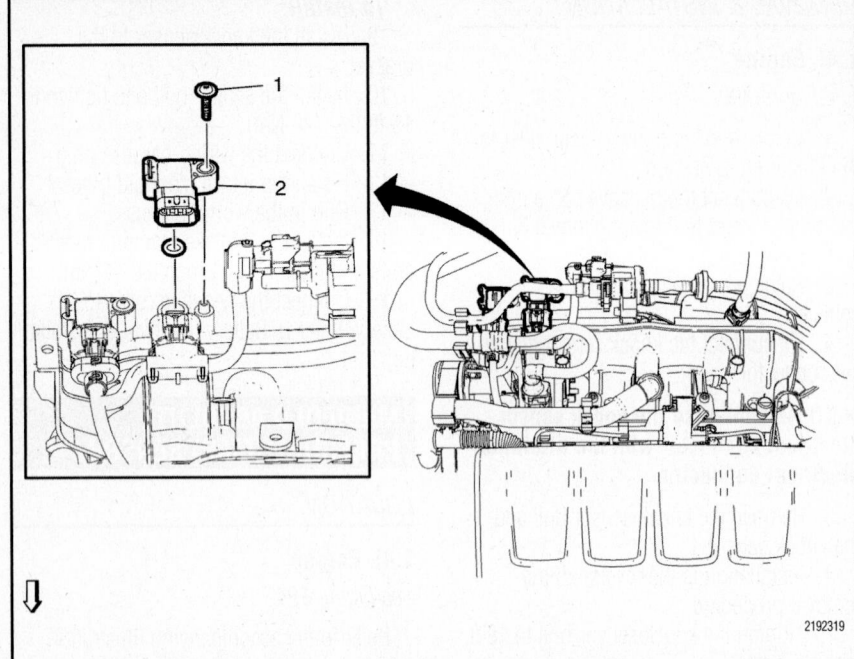

Fig. 294 Manifold Absolute Pressure (MAP) sensor (2) and bolt (1) location—1.4L engine

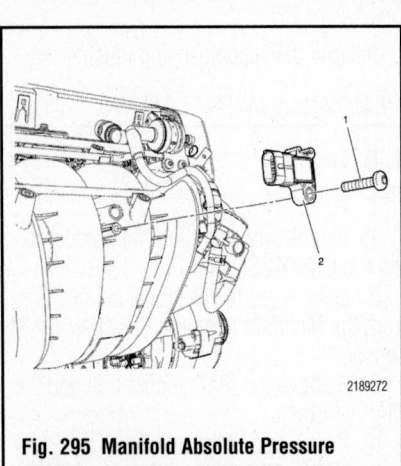

Fig. 295 Manifold Absolute Pressure (MAP) sensor (2) and bolt (1) location— 1.8L engine

MASS AIR FLOW (MAF) SENSOR

LOCATION

1.4L Engine

See Figure 296.

Refer to the accompanying illustration.

1.8L Engine

See Figure 297.

Refer to the accompanying illustration.

REMOVAL & INSTALLATION

1.4L Engine

See Figure 296.

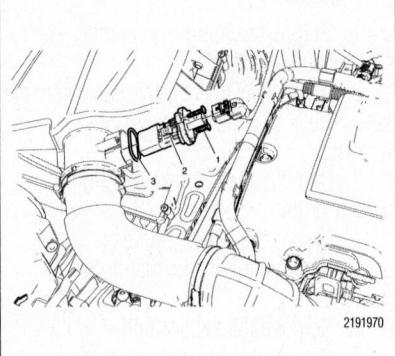

Fig. 296 Mass Air Flow (MAF) sensor (2), bolts (1), and seal ring (3) locations— 1.4L engine

1. Before servicing the vehicle, refer to the Precautions Section.
2. Disconnect the electrical connector from the Mass Air Flow (MAF) sensor.
3. Remove the MAF sensor attaching bolts.
4. Remove the MAF sensor.
5. Installation is the reverse of the removal procedure.
6. After replacement of MAF sensor, use a scan tool to perform the learn functions.

1.8L Engine

See Figure 297.

1. Before servicing the vehicle, refer to the Precautions Section.

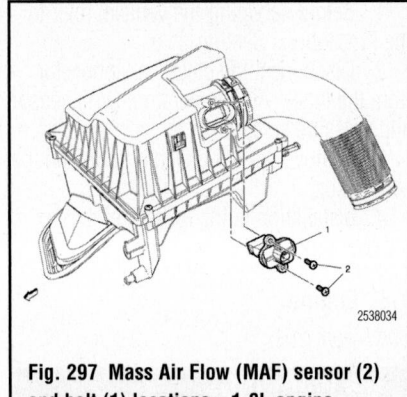

Fig. 297 Mass Air Flow (MAF) sensor (2) and bolt (1) locations—1.8L engine

2. Disconnect the electrical connector from the Mass Air Flow (MAF) sensor.
3. Remove the MAF sensor attaching bolts.
4. Remove the MAF sensor.
5. Installation is the reverse of the removal procedure.
6. After replacement of MAF sensor, use a scan tool to perform the learn functions.

THROTTLE POSITION SENSOR (TPS)

LOCATION

The Throttle Position (TP) sensor is located on the throttle body.

REMOVAL & INSTALLATION

The Throttle Position Sensor (TPS) is integral to the electronic throttle body. Refer to Throttle Body, removal & installation.

VEHICLE SPEED SENSOR (VSS)

LOCATION

See Figure 298.

Refer to the accompanying illustration.

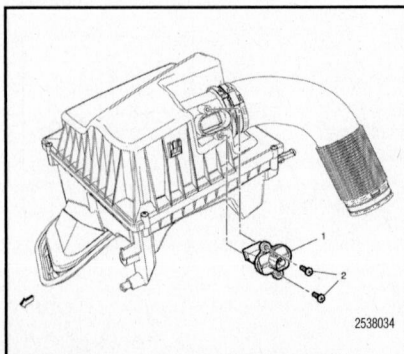

Fig. 298 Output and input speed sensor locations

REMOVAL & INSTALLATION

See Figure 298.

1. Before servicing the vehicle, refer to the Precautions Section.

2. Disconnect the sensor electrical connection.

3. Remove the sensor bolt.

➡**Compress the locking tabs on the plug to release it from the case and to avoid damaging the retainers.**

4. Remove the sensor.

5. Discard the seals. They are not reusable.

6. Installation is the reverse of the removal procedure.

7. Tighten the sensor bolts to 80 inch lbs. (9 Nm).

FUEL   **GASOLINE FUEL INJECTION SYSTEM**

FUEL SYSTEM SERVICE PRECAUTIONS

Safety is the most important factor when performing not only fuel system maintenance but any type of maintenance. Failure to conduct maintenance and repairs in a safe manner may result in serious personal injury or death. Maintenance and testing of the vehicle's fuel system components can be accomplished safely and effectively by adhering to the following rules and guidelines.

• To avoid the possibility of fire and personal injury, always disconnect the negative battery cable unless the repair or test procedure requires that battery voltage be applied.

• Always relieve the fuel system pressure prior to disconnecting any fuel system component (injector, fuel rail, pressure regulator, etc.), fitting or fuel line connection. Exercise extreme caution whenever relieving fuel system pressure to avoid exposing skin, face and eyes to fuel spray. Please be advised that fuel under pressure may penetrate the skin or any part of the body that it contacts.

• Always place a shop towel or cloth around the fitting or connection prior to loosening to absorb any excess fuel due to spillage. Ensure that all fuel spillage (should it occur) is quickly removed from engine surfaces. Ensure that all fuel soaked cloths or towels are deposited into a suitable waste container.

• Always keep a dry chemical (Class B) fire extinguisher near the work area.

• Do not allow fuel spray or fuel vapors to come into contact with a spark or open flame.

• Always use a back-up wrench when loosening and tightening fuel line connection fittings. This will prevent unnecessary stress and torsion to fuel line piping.

• Always replace worn fuel fitting O-rings with new Do not substitute fuel hose or equivalent where fuel pipe is installed.

Before servicing the vehicle, make sure to also refer to the precautions in the beginning of this section as well.

RELIEVING FUEL SYSTEM PRESSURE

See Figure 299.

Special Tools
• EN-34730-91 Pressure Tester

> ❊❊ **CAUTION**
>
> **Gasoline or gasoline vapors are highly flammable. A fire could occur if an ignition source is present. Never drain or store gasoline or diesel fuel in an open container, due to the possibility of fire or explosion. Have a dry chemical (Class B) fire extinguisher nearby.**

> ❊❊ **CAUTION**
>
> **Relieve the fuel system pressure before servicing fuel system components in order to reduce the risk of fire and personal injury.**

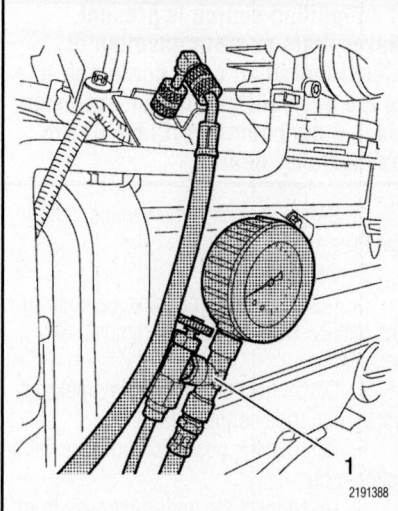

2191388

Fig. 299 Relieving fuel pressure using the EN-34730-91 Pressure Tester (1)

> ❊❊ **CAUTION**
>
> **Remove the fuel tank cap and relieve the fuel system pressure before servicing the fuel system in order to reduce the risk of personal injury. After you relieve the fuel system pressure, a small amount of fuel may be released when servicing the fuel lines, the fuel injection pump, or the connections. In order to reduce the risk of personal injury, cover the fuel system components with a shop towel before disconnection. This will catch any fuel that may leak out. Place the towel in an approved container when the disconnection is complete.**

1. Before servicing the vehicle, refer to the Precautions Section.

2. Disconnect the battery. Refer to Battery, removal & installation.

3. Remove the protective cap from the test connection or fuel injector rail cap.

4. Relieve the fuel pressure, using the EN-34730-91 Pressure Tester.

FUEL FILTER

REMOVAL & INSTALLATION

A lifetime fuel filter is serviced as part of the fuel pump module. Refer to Fuel Pump Module, removal & installation.

FUEL INJECTORS

REMOVAL & INSTALLATION

1.4L Engine
See Figures 300 and 301.

> ❊❊ **CAUTION**
>
> **Gasoline or gasoline vapors are highly flammable. A fire could occur if an ignition source is present. Never drain or store gasoline or diesel fuel in an open container, due to the possibility of fire or explosion. Have a dry chemical (Class B) fire extinguisher nearby.**

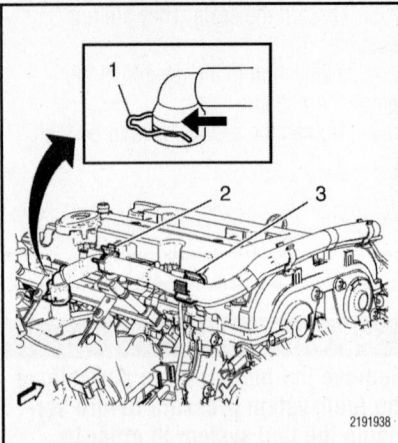

Fig. 300 Positive crankcase ventilation pipe clips (2) and (3) and retainer clamp (1) shown

1. Before servicing the vehicle, refer to the Precautions Section.

2. Disconnect the battery negative cable. Refer to Battery, removal & installation.

3. Remove the engine sight shield.

4. Remove the fuel feed pipe from the fuel injection fuel rail.

5. Relieve the fuel pressure. Refer to Relieving Fuel System Pressure.

6. Disconnect the fuel feed pipe connector from the fuel injector rail.

7. Remove the positive crankcase ventilation pipe from the intake manifold.

8. Disconnect the 4 fuel injector wiring harness plugs.

9. Unclip the ECM wiring harness from the retainer clips and the camshaft cover.

10. Remove the ground cable nut and the ground cable.

11. Remove the 2 fuel injection fuel rail bolts.

12. Remove the fuel injection fuel rail assembly and the 4 fuel injector seal rings.

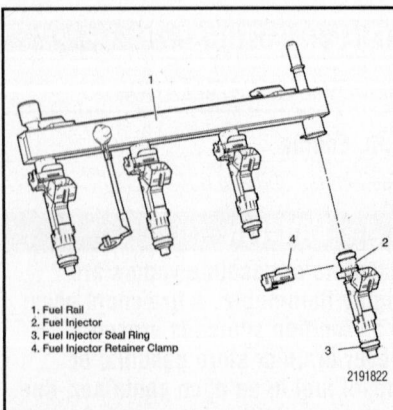

1. Fuel Rail
2. Fuel Injector
3. Fuel Injector Seal Ring
4. Fuel Injector Retainer Clamp

Fig. 301 Installing fuel injectors to fuel rail—1.4L engine

13. Remove the fuel injector retainer rings.

14. Remove the fuel injectors from the fuel rail assembly.

To install:

➡ **Lubricate the 4 NEW fuel injector seal rings with clean engine oil.**

15. Install fuel injector seal rings.

16. Install the fuel injectors to the fuel rail and attach the retainer ring.

17. Install the fuel injection fuel rail assembly to the intake manifold.

18. Install the 2 fuel injection fuel rail bolts and tighten to 62 inch lbs. (7 Nm).

19. Install the ground cable and the ground cable nut and tighten.

20. Connect the 4 fuel injector wiring harness plugs.

21. Clip the ECM wiring harness to the retainer clip and the camshaft cover.

22. Install the positive crankcase ventilation pipe to the intake manifold.

23. Install the fuel feed pipe to the fuel injection fuel rail.

24. Install the engine sight shield.

25. Connect the battery negative cable. Refer to Battery, removal & installation.

1.8L Engine

See Figures 302 through 304.

Special Tools
- CH-48027 Fuel Pressure Gauge
- CH-41769 Fuel Line Disconnect Tool Set

❋❋ CAUTION

Gasoline or gasoline vapors are highly flammable. A fire could occur if an ignition source is present. Never drain or store gasoline or diesel fuel in an open container, due to the possibility of fire or explosion. Have a dry chemical (Class B) fire extinguisher nearby.

1. Before servicing the vehicle, refer to the Precautions Section.

2. Open the hood.

3. Disconnect the negative cable from the battery. Refer to Battery, removal & installation.

4. Disconnect the 2 positive crankcase ventilation tube connectors.

5. Remove the positive crankcase ventilation tube.

6. Disconnect the wiring harness from:
- The evaporative emission purge valve
- The fuel injectors

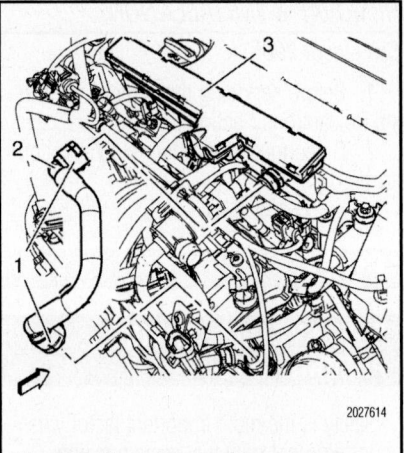

Fig. 302 View of the positive crankcase ventilation tube (2), positive crankcase ventilation tube connectors (1), and the ECM wiring harness guide (3)

- The manifold absolute pressure sensor

7. Place a drain pan underneath the vehicle.

8. Relieve the fuel pressure. Refer to Relieving Fuel System Pressure.

9. Disconnect the quick-release fitting of the fuel feed pipe with CH-41769 tool set.

10. Install a suitable cap to the fuel feed pipe.

11. Remove the 2 evaporative emission canister purge solenoid valve bracket bolts.

12. Remove the evaporative emission canister purge solenoid valve bracket from the intake manifold.

13. Remove the 2 multiport fuel injection fuel rail bolts.

14. Remove the multiport fuel injection fuel rail with the fuel injectors from the intake manifold.

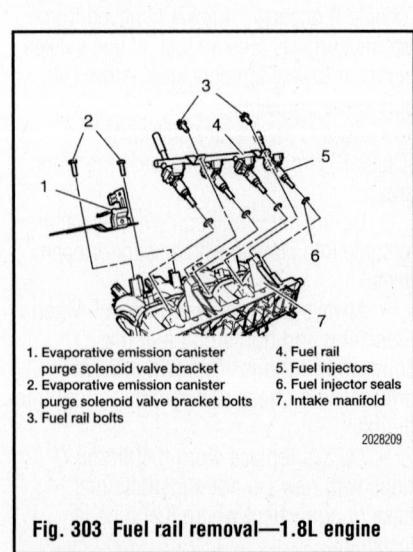

1. Evaporative emission canister purge solenoid valve bracket
2. Evaporative emission canister purge solenoid valve bracket bolts
3. Fuel rail bolts
4. Fuel rail
5. Fuel injectors
6. Fuel injector seals
7. Intake manifold

Fig. 303 Fuel rail removal—1.8L engine

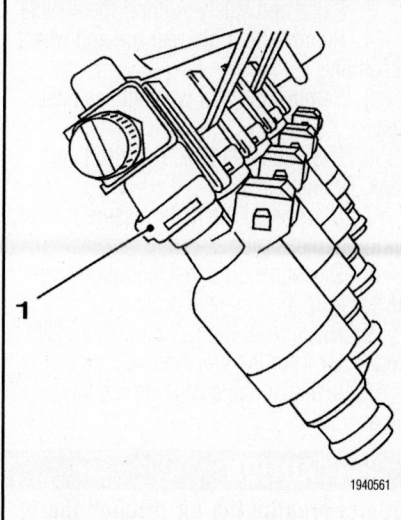

Fig. 304 Remove the fuel injector retainer (1) and fuel injector from the fuel rail

15. Remove the 4 fuel injector seals.
16. Remove the fuel injector retainers.
17. Remove the fuel injectors.

To install:
18. Install the fuel injectors.

➡**Install NEW fuel injector seals, coat the multiport fuel injector seals with silicone grease.**

19. Install the fuel injector retainer.
20. Install the 4 NEW fuel injector seals.
21. Install the multiport fuel injection fuel rail and the fuel injectors to the intake manifold.
22. Install the 2 multiport fuel injection fuel rail bolts and tighten to 71 inch lbs. (8 Nm).
23. Install the evaporative emission canister purge solenoid valve bracket to the intake manifold. Tighten the bracket bolts to 71 inch lbs. (8 Nm).
24. Remove the cap from the fuel feed pipe.
25. Connect the quick-release fitting to the fuel feed pipe.
26. Connect the wiring harness to:
   • The evaporative emission purge valve
   • The fuel injectors
   • The manifold absolute pressure sensor
27. Install the positive crankcase ventilation tube.
28. Connect the 2 positive crankcase ventilation tube connectors.
29. Connect the negative cable from the battery. Refer to Battery, removal & installation.

FUEL PUMP MODULE

REMOVAL & INSTALLATION

See Figures 305 through 307.

Special Tools
• CH-45722 Fuel Sender Lock Ring Wrench
1. Before servicing the vehicle, refer to the Precautions Section.
2. Remove the fuel tank. Refer to Fuel Tank, removal & installation.
3. Disconnect the fuel tank vent pipe and the fuel feed pipe from the fuel tank fuel pump module.
4. Disconnect the fuel tank fuel pump module wiring harness from the fuel tank fuel pump module.
5. Close the fuel feed pipe and the fuel tank vent feed pipe with suitable caps.

✳✳ WARNING

Do NOT use impact tools. Significant force will be required to release the lock ring. The use of a hammer and screwdriver is not recommended. Secure the fuel tank in order to prevent fuel tank rotation.

6. Using the CH-45722 wrench and a long breaker-bar, rotate the fuel pump module lock ring in a counterclockwise direction in order to unlock the lock ring.
7. Remove the fuel tank fuel pump module lock ring.
8. Remove the fuel tank fuel pump module.
9. Remove and DISCARD the fuel pump module seal.

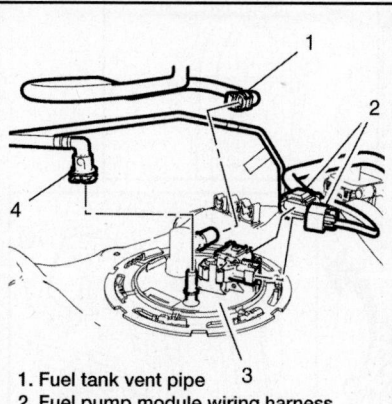

1. Fuel tank vent pipe
2. Fuel pump module wiring harness
3. Fuel pump module
4. Fuel feed pipe

Fig. 305 Fuel pump module connections illustrated

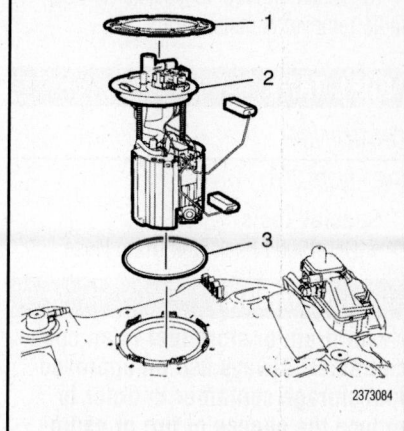

Fig. 306 View of fuel tank fuel pump module lock ring (1), fuel pump module (2), and fuel pump module seal (3)

To install:
10. Install a NEW fuel tank module seal.
11. Install the fuel tank fuel pump module.
12. Install the fuel pump module lock ring.
13. Make sure that the fuel tank fuel pump module aligns with the fuel tank line marking.
14. Using the CH-45722 wrench and a long breaker-bar, rotate the lock ring in a clockwise direction in order to lock the lock ring.
15. Connect the fuel tank fuel pump module wiring harness to the fuel tank fuel pump module.
16. Remove the caps from the fuel feed pipe and the fuel tank vent feed pipe.
17. Connect the fuel tank vent pipe and the fuel feed pipe to the fuel tank fuel pump module.

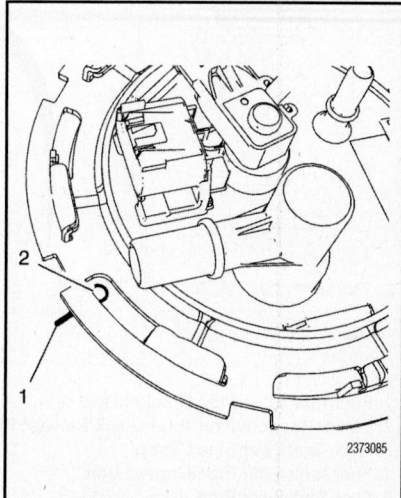

Fig. 307 Make sure the fuel tank fuel pump module (2) aligns with the fuel tank line marking (1)

18. Install the fuel tank. Refer to Fuel Tank, removal & installation.

FUEL TANK

DRAINING

See Figure 308.

Special Tools
- CH-45004 Fuel Tank Drain Hose

❈❈ CAUTION

Never drain or store fuel in an open container. Always use an approved fuel storage container in order to reduce the chance of fire or explosion.

❈❈ CAUTION

Gasoline or gasoline vapors are highly flammable. A fire could occur if an ignition source is present. Never drain or store gasoline or diesel fuel in an open container, due to the possibility of fire or explosion. Have a dry chemical (Class B) fire extinguisher nearby. Failure to follow these precautions may result in personal injury.

❈❈ CAUTION

Always wear safety goggles when working with fuel in order to protect the eyes from fuel splash.

1. Before servicing the vehicle, refer to the Precautions Section.
2. Disconnect the battery negative cable. Refer to Battery, removal & installation.
3. Remove the fuel fill cap.
4. Raise and safely support the vehicle.
5. Remove the rear wheelhouse panel liner.
6. Disconnect the electrical connector from the fuel tank filler door lock actuator.
7. Unclip the 4 clips and remove the fuel tank filler pipe housing.

➡**Push the fuel tank filler door lock actuator locking rod into the closed position.**

8. Remove the fuel tank filler bracket bolts, pipe clamp, and the fuel tank filler pipe.
9. Insert the CH-45004 drain hose into the fuel tank until the hose reaches the bottom of the fuel tank.
10. Use a hand or air-operated pump device in order to drain as much fuel as possible.
11. When fuel tank draining is complete, install the removed components in the reverse order of the removal procedure.

REMOVAL & INSTALLATION

See Figures 309 and 310.

1. Before servicing the vehicle, refer to the Precautions Section.
2. Disconnect the battery negative cable. Refer to Battery, removal & installation.

3. Raise and safely support the vehicle.
4. Remove the right rear tire and wheel assembly.
5. Remove the rear wheelhouse panel liner.
6. Drain the fuel tank. Refer to Fuel Tank, Draining.
7. Disconnect the fuel pressure sensor wiring harness plug.
8. Disconnect the fuel feed pipe connector from the fuel feed pipe.
9. Disconnect the fuel tank vent pipe connector from the fuel tank vent pipe.
10. Install suitable caps on the fuel pipes.

❈❈ CAUTION

Do not breathe the air through the EVAP component tubes or hoses. The fuel vapors inside the EVAP components may cause personal injury.

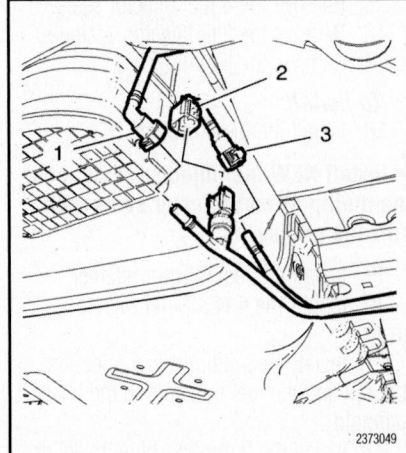

Fig. 309 Location of fuel pressure sensor wiring harness plug (2), fuel feed pipe connector (1), fuel tank vent pipe connector (3)

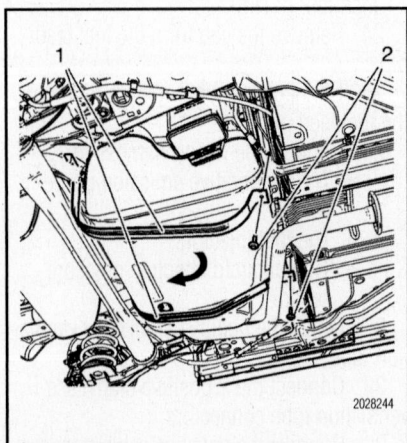

Fig. 310 Removing the fuel tank strap bolts (2) and fuel tank straps (1)

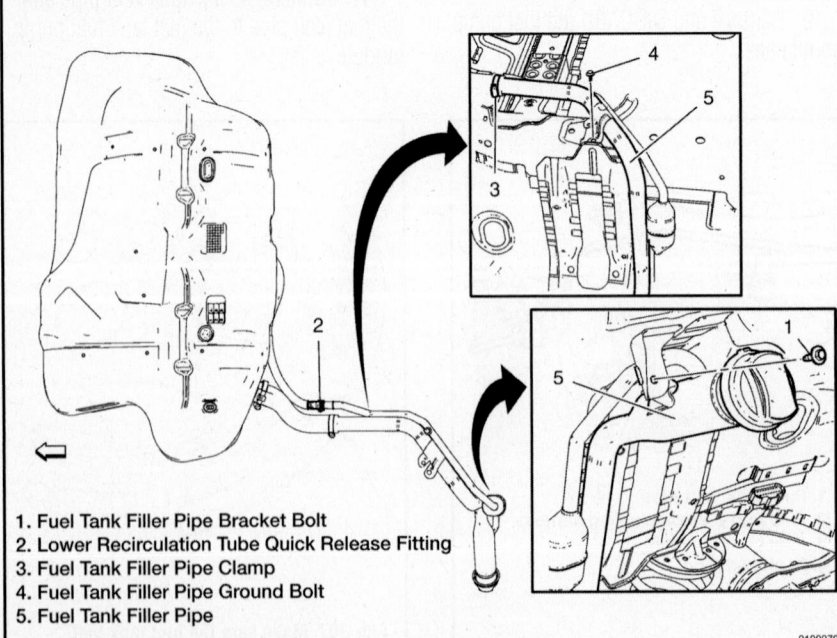

1. Fuel Tank Filler Pipe Bracket Bolt
2. Lower Recirculation Tube Quick Release Fitting
3. Fuel Tank Filler Pipe Clamp
4. Fuel Tank Filler Pipe Ground Bolt
5. Fuel Tank Filler Pipe

Fig. 308 View of fuel tank and fuel tank filler pipe components

11. Loosen the fuel tank filler hose clamp.

12. Remove the fuel tank filler hose from the fuel tank filler pipe.

13. Disconnect the fuel tank filler vent pipe connector from the fuel tank filler vent pipe.

14. Plug the fuel tank filler vent pipe with a suitable cap.

15. Disconnect the fuel tank wiring harness inline connector and unclip the wiring harness from 2 retainer clips.

16. Place a suitable adjustable jack under the fuel tank.

17. Remove the 2 fuel tank strap bolts.

18. Remove the 2 fuel tank straps.

➡**A second technician is required.**

19. Remove the fuel tank.

To install:

➡**A second technician is required.**

20. Install the fuel tank.

21. Install the 2 fuel tank straps.

22. Install the 2 fuel tank strap bolts and tighten to 16 ft. lbs. (22 Nm).

23. Install the fuel tank filler hose to the fuel tank filler pipe.

24. Tighten the fuel tank filler hose clamp.

25. Remove the cap from the fuel tank filler vent pipe.

26. Connect the fuel tank filler vent pipe connector to the fuel tank filler vent pipe.

27. Connect the fuel tank wiring harness inline connector and clip in the wiring harness to 2 retainer clips.

28. Remove the caps from the fuel pipes.

29. Connect the fuel tank vent pipe connector to the fuel tank vent pipe.

30. Connect the fuel feed pipe connector to the fuel feed pipe.

31. Connect the fuel pressure sensor wiring harness plug.

32. Lower the vehicle.

33. Install the rear wheelhouse panel liner.

34. Install the right rear tire and wheel assembly.

35. Lower the vehicle.

36. Connect the battery negative cable. Refer to Battery, removal & installation.

IDLE SPEED

ADJUSTMENT

The idle speed is controlled by the Engine Control Module (ECM). No adjustment is necessary.

THROTTLE BODY

REMOVAL & INSTALLATION

1.4L Engine

See Figure 311.

1. Before servicing the vehicle, refer to the Precautions Section.

2. Disconnect the throttle body wiring harness plug.

3. Remove the charge air cooler outlet air hose from the throttle body.

4. Remove the 4 throttle body bolts.

5. Remove the throttle body along with the throttle body seal ring.

To install:

6. Install the throttle body along with a NEW throttle body seal ring.

7. Install the 4 throttle body bolts and tighten to 71 inch lbs. (8 Nm).

8. Install the charge air cooler outlet air hose to the throttle body.

9. Connect the throttle body wiring harness plug.

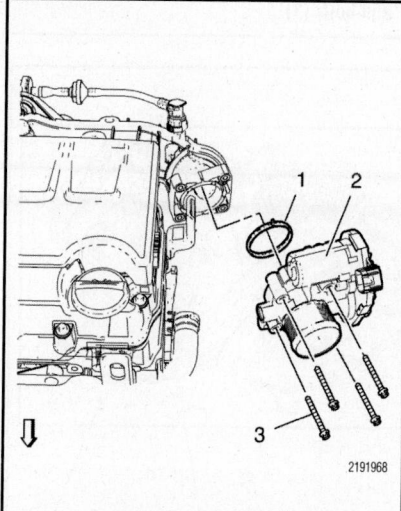

Fig. 311 View of throttle body (2), seal ring (1), and throttle body bolts (3)—1.4L engine

1.8L Engine

See Figure 312.

1. Before servicing the vehicle, refer to the Precautions Section.

2. Remove the air cleaner outlet duct. Refer to Air Cleaner, removal & installation.

3. Disconnect the wiring harness plug.

4. Disconnect the positive crankcase ventilation pipe.

5. Place a collecting basin underneath the vehicle.

6. Disconnect the throttle body heater outlet pipe.

7. Disconnect the throttle body heater inlet pipe.

8. Remove the 4 throttle body bolts.

9. Remove the throttle body.

10. Remove and DISCARD the throttle body gasket.

To install:

11. Install a NEW throttle body gasket.

12. Install the throttle body.

13. Install the 4 throttle body bolts and tighten to 71 inch lbs. (8 Nm).

14. Connect the throttle body heater inlet pipe.

15. Connect the throttle body heater outlet pipe.

16. Connect the positive crankcase ventilation pipe.

17. Connect the wiring harness plug.

18. Install the air cleaner outlet duct. Refer to Air Cleaner, removal & installation.

19. Reset the fuel trim using a scan tool.

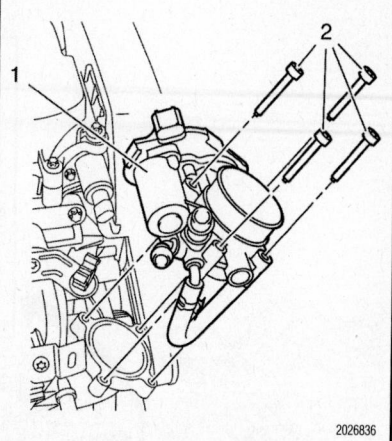

Fig. 312 View of throttle body (1) and attaching bolts (2)—1.8L engine

HEATING & AIR CONDITIONING SYSTEM

BLOWER MOTOR

REMOVAL & INSTALLATION

See Figures 313 through 316.

1. Before servicing the vehicle, refer to the Precautions Section.
2. Remove the instrument panel insulator panel.
3. Remove the inflatable restraint instrument panel lower module, if equipped.
4. Remove the instrument panel outer trim cover on the right side.

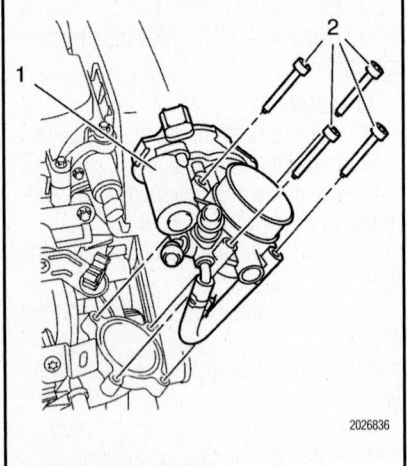

Fig. 313 View of instrument panel compartment (2) and fastening screws (1)

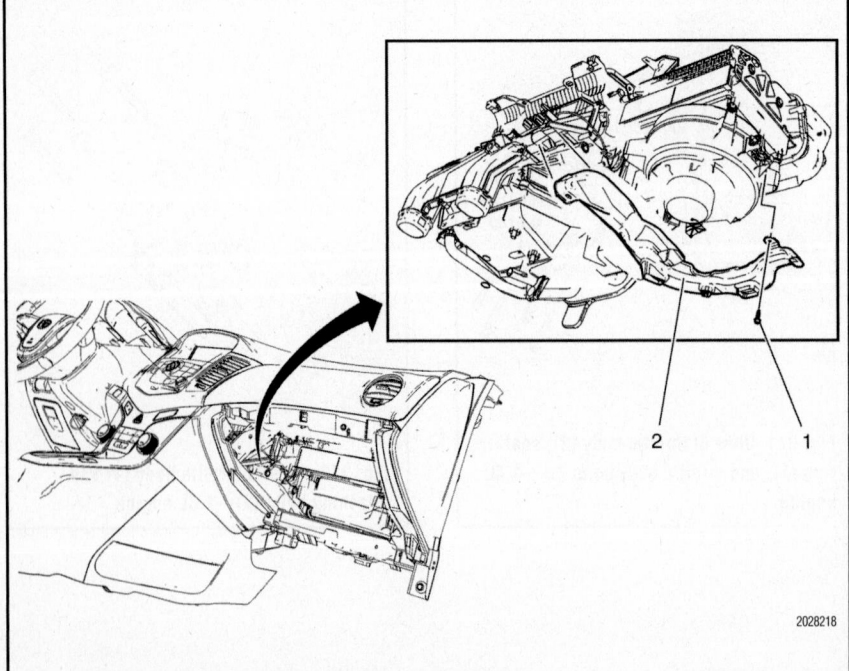

Fig. 314 View of floor air outlet duct (2) and fasteners (1)

5. Remove the right floor air outlet duct.
6. Remove the blower motor wire harness connector.
7. Remove the blower motor cup bolts.
8. Remove the blower motor cup from the blower motor.
9. Remove the blower motor bolts.
10. Remove the blower motor from the heater case.

To install:

11. Install the blower motor to the heater case.

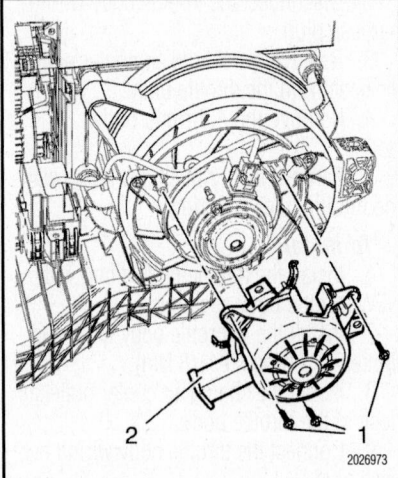

Fig. 315 View of blower motor cup (2) and bolts (1)

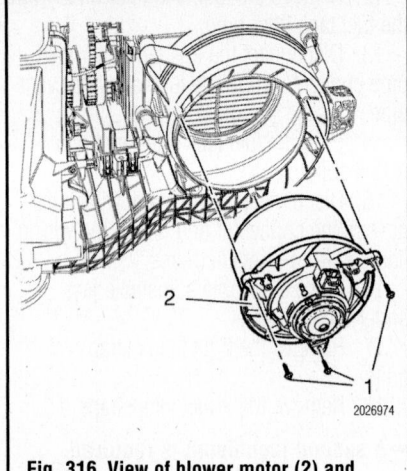

Fig. 316 View of blower motor (2) and mounting bolts (1)

12. Install the blower motor bolts and tighten to 40 inch lbs. (5 Nm).
13. Install the motor blower cup to the blower motor.
14. Install the blower motor cup bolts and tighten to 23 inch lbs. (3 Nm).
15. Install the blower motor wire harness connector.
16. Install the right floor air outlet duct and tighten the bolt to 22 inch lbs. (3 Nm).
17. Install the instrument panel compartment. Tighten the screws to 22 inch lbs. (3Nm).

HEATER CORE

REMOVAL & INSTALLATION

See Figures 317 and 318.

✳✳ CAUTION

These vehicles are equipped with an air bag system. The system must be disarmed before performing service on, or around, system components, the steering column, instrument panel components, wiring and sensors. Failure to follow the safety precautions and the disarming procedure could result in accidental air bag deployment, possible injury and unnecessary system repairs.

1. Before servicing the vehicle, refer to the Precautions Section.
2. Disable the SIR system. Refer to Chassis Electrical, Air Bag (Supplemental Restraint System), Disarming the System.
3. Drain the cooling system. Refer to Engine Coolant, Drain & Refill Procedure.

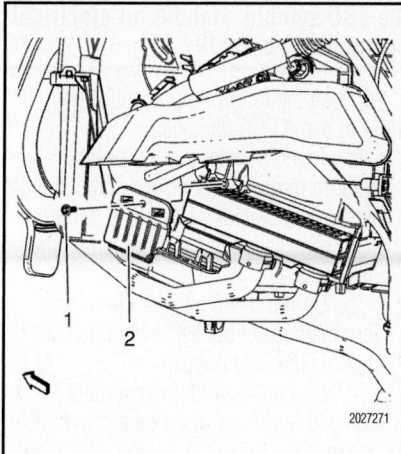

Fig. 317 Remove the heater core cover bolt (1) and the heater core cover (2)

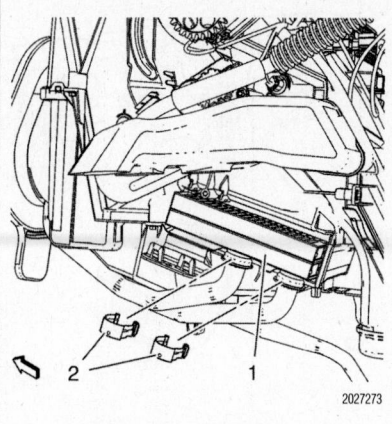

Fig. 318 View of heater core (1), heater core clamps (2), and heater core tubes (3)

4. Remove the instrument panel lower trim pad cover.

5. Disconnect the electrical connector from the inflatable restraint instrument panel lower module.

6. Remove the fasteners and the inflatable restraint instrument panel lower module.

7. Remove the instrument panel lower trim panel.

8. Remove the instrument panel side bolt.

9. Remove the heater core cover bolt and the heater core cover.

10. Remove the 2 heater core clamps.

11. Remove the 2 heater core tubes.

12. Remove the heater core.

13. Change the 2 heater core tube sealing rings.

To install:

14. Install the heater core.

15. Install the 2 heater core tubes.

16. Tighten the 2 heater core clamps.

17. Install the heater core cover bolt and heater core cover.

18. Install instrument panel side bolt.

19. Install the instrument panel lower trim panel.

20. Install the inflatable restraint instrument panel lower module on the driver's side. Tighten the module fasteners to 89 inch lbs. (10 Nm).

21. Fill the cooling system. Refer to Engine Coolant, Drain & Refill Procedure.

22. Enable the SIR system. Refer to Chassis Electrical, Air Bag (Supplemental Restraint System), Arming the System.

STEERING

POWER STEERING ASSIST MOTOR

REMOVAL & INSTALLATION

See Figure 319.

✳✳ WARNING

Electrostatic Discharge (ESD) can damage many solid-state electrical components. ESD susceptible components may or may not be labeled with the ESD symbol. Handle all electrical components carefully.

1. Use the following precautions in order to avoid ESD damage:

   a. Touch a metal ground point in order to remove your body's static charge before servicing any electronic component; especially after sliding across the vehicle seat.

   b. Do not touch exposed terminals. Terminals may connect to circuits susceptible the ESD damage.

   c. Do not allow tools to contact exposed terminals when servicing connectors.

   d. Do not remove components from their protective packaging until required to do so.

   e. Avoid the following actions unless required by the diagnostic procedure:

   - Jumpering or grounding of the components or connectors
   - Connecting test equipment probes to components or connectors. Connect the ground lead first when using test probes

   f. Ground the protective packaging of any component before opening. Do not rest solid-state components on metal workbenches, or on top of TVs, radios, or other electrical devices.

2. Before servicing the vehicle, refer to the Precautions Section.

3. Capture the data from the old power steering assist motor using a scan tool.

4. Disconnect the negative battery cable. Refer to Battery, removal & installation.

5. Carefully disconnect the electrical connectors of the electric power steering.

6. Remove the 2 upper bolts of the power assist motor from above in the engine compartment.

7. Remove the lowest bolt from below the vehicle.

8. Remove the power steering assist motor from the vehicle.

To install:

9. DISCARD the drive boot and use NEW ONLY.

10. Install the drive boot to the assist motor armature.

11. Align the drive boot on the assist motor armature to the steering gear.

12. DISCARD the O-ring and use NEW ONLY.

13. Lubricate the O-ring. Place the O-ring correctly in the groove on the motor housing.

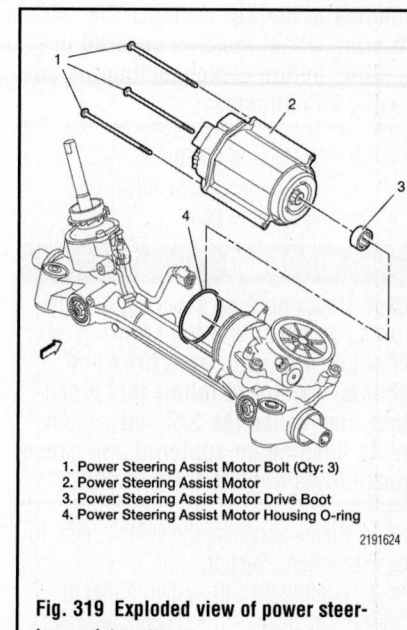

1. Power Steering Assist Motor Bolt (Qty: 3)
2. Power Steering Assist Motor
3. Power Steering Assist Motor Drive Boot
4. Power Steering Assist Motor Housing O-ring

Fig. 319 Exploded view of power steering assist motor

> **⁂⁂ WARNING**
>
> This component is equipped with torque-to-yield fasteners. Install a NEW torque-to-yield fastener when installing this component. Failure to replace the torque-to-yield fastener could cause damage to the vehicle or component.

14. Install the power steering assist motor with NEW bolts and tighten to 71 inch lbs. (8 Nm).

15. Attach all electrical connections.

16. Connect the battery negative cable. Refer to Battery, removal & installation.

17. Transfer the data from the old assist motor to the new power steering assist motor. Refer to Power Steering Control Module Programming and Setup.

18. Calibrate the steering angle sensor and learn the softend stops. Refer to Power Steering Control Module Calibration.

POWER STEERING GEAR

REMOVAL & INSTALLATION

See Figures 320 through 323.

Special Tools
- EN-45059 Angle Meter

> **⁂⁂ WARNING**
>
> With the wheels of the vehicle facing straight ahead, secure the steering wheel utilizing a steering column anti-rotation pin, steering column lock, or a strap to prevent rotation. Locking of the steering column will prevent damage and a possible malfunction of the SIR system. The steering wheel must be secured in position before disconnecting the following components:
>
> - The steering column
> - The intermediate shaft(s)
> - The steering gear

> **⁂⁂ WARNING**
>
> After disconnecting steering components, do not rotate the steering wheel or move the front tires and wheels. Failure to follow this procedure may cause the SIR coil assembly to become un-centered and cause possible damage to the SIR coil.

1. Before servicing the vehicle, refer to the Precautions Section.

2. Disable the SIR system. Refer to Chassis Electrical, Air Bag (Supplemental Restraint System), Disarming the System.

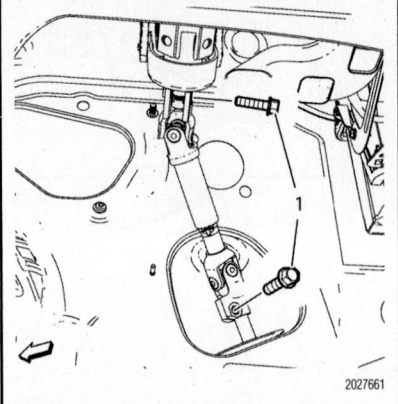

Fig. 320 Removing the upper and lower intermediate steering shaft bolts (1)

3. Disconnect the battery. Refer to Battery, removal & installation.

4. Turn the front wheels to the straight forward position and secure the steering wheel from moving.

5. Remove the upper intermediate steering shaft bolt.

6. Remove and DISCARD the lower intermediate steering shaft bolts.

7. Remove the intermediate steering shaft.

8. Raise and safely support the vehicle.

9. Perform the following steps in order to gain access to the steering gear.

   a. Remove the front tire and wheel assemblies.

   b. Remove the exhaust front pipe.

   c. Remove the front compartment splash shield.

   d. Remove the engine shield, if equipped.

   e. Remove the front compartment insulator, if equipped.

   f. Disconnect the 2 steering linkage outer tie rods from the 2 steering knuckles.

   g. Disconnect the 2 stabilizer shaft links.

   h. Remove the transaxle mount bracket bolts.

   i. Support the drivetrain and front suspension frame.

   j. Remove the rear frame bolts.

   k. Remove the frame reinforcement bolts and the frame reinforcements.

   l. Lower the drivetrain and front suspension frame 2 inches (55mm).

> **⁂⁂ WARNING**
>
> Electrostatic Discharge (ESD) can damage many solid-state electrical components. ESD susceptible components may or may not be labeled with

the ESD symbol. Handle all electrical components carefully.

10. Use the following precautions in order to avoid ESD damage:

   a. Touch a metal ground point in order to remove your body's static charge before servicing any electronic component; especially after sliding across the vehicle seat.

   b. Do not touch exposed terminals. Terminals may connect to circuits susceptible the ESD damage.

   c. Do not allow tools to contact exposed terminals when servicing connectors.

   d. Do not remove components from their protective packaging until required to do so.

   e. Avoid the following actions unless required by the diagnostic procedure:

   - Jumpering or grounding of the components or connectors
   - Connecting test equipment probes to components or connectors. Connect the ground lead first when using test probes

   f. Ground the protective packaging of any component before opening. Do not rest solid-state components on metal workbenches, or on top of TVs, radios, or other electrical devices.

➡ **Connector latches may be difficult to access.**

11. Disconnect the electrical connectors.

12. Use a suitable tool in order to carefully disconnect the 2 wiring harness plugs from the steering gear.

13. Remove the 2 wiring harness bracket bolts.

14. Remove the bracket.

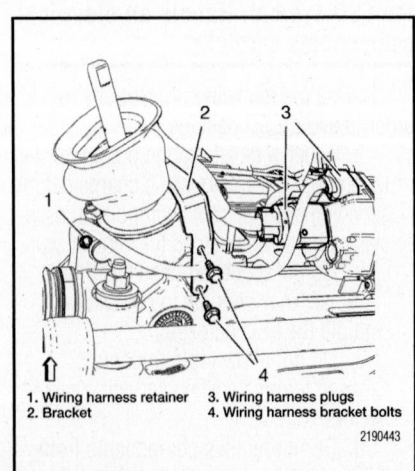

1. Wiring harness retainer
2. Bracket
3. Wiring harness plugs
4. Wiring harness bracket bolts

Fig. 321 Steering gear electrical connector locations

15. Disconnect the wiring harness retainer from the steering gear.

16. Remove and DISCARD the 2 right stabilizer shaft insulator clamp bolts.

17. Reposition the stabilizer shaft in order to gain clearance for the steering gear.

18. Remove and DISCARD the 2 steering gear bolts and the nuts from front suspension frame.

19. Carefully remove the steering gear through the right front wheel house.

To install:

✳✳ WARNING

Ensure that the steering column dash seal is installed properly onto the steering gear rack pinion housing. The sealing lip MUST rest on lower steering column cover surface evenly. To ease installation of the seal, apply liquid soap to the sealing lip. After installation, verify that the seal lip does not protrude into the vehicle's interior. Improper installation could result in poor sealing performance and water intrusion into the vehicle.

➡**Ensure the wiring routing is correct.**

20. Carefully install the steering gear through the right front wheel house and position the steering gear on the frame.

✳✳ WARNING

This component is equipped with torque-to-yield fasteners. Install a NEW torque-to-yield fastener when installing this component. Failure to replace the torque-to-yield fastener could cause damage to the vehicle or component.

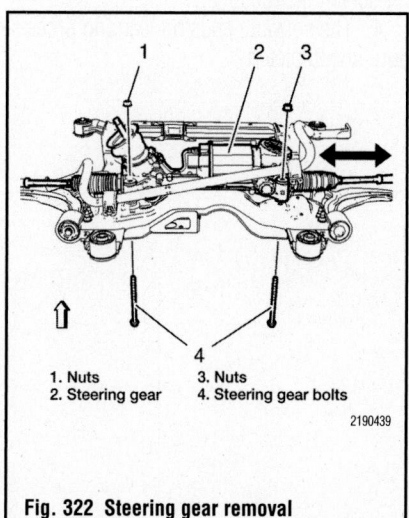

1. Nuts
2. Steering gear
3. Nuts
4. Steering gear bolts

2190439

Fig. 322 Steering gear removal

21. Install the 2 NEW steering gear bolts and the 2 NEW nuts and tighten to 81 ft. lbs. (110 Nm).

22. Use the EN-45059 sensor in order to tighten the steering gear bolts and nuts an additional 150–160°.

23. Install the wiring harness bracket.

24. Install the 2 wiring harness bracket bolts and tighten to 80 inch lbs. (9 Nm).

25. Connect the wiring harness retainer to steering gear.

26. Connect the 2 wiring harness plugs to the steering gear.

27. Connect the electrical connectors.

28. Position the stabilizer shaft and the bracket onto the suspension frame.

29. Install the NEW right stabilizer shaft insulator clamp bolts and tighten to 16 ft. lbs. (22 Nm).

30. Use the EN-45059 sensor in order to tighten the NEW right stabilizer shaft insulator clamp bolts an additional 30°.

31. Perform the following steps.

　a. Position the drivetrain and front suspension frame in the vehicle.

　b. Install the frame reinforcements and the frame reinforcement bolts.

　c. Install the rear frame bolts.

　d. Install the transaxle mount bracket bolts.

　e. Connect the 2 stabilizer shaft links.

　f. Connect the 2 steering linkage outer tie rods to the 2 steering knuckles.

　g. Install the front compartment insulator, if equipped.

　h. Install the engine shield, if equipped.

　i. Install the front compartment splash shield.

　j. Install the exhaust front pipe.

　k. Install the front tire and wheel assemblies.

32. Lower the vehicle.

33. Install the intermediate steering shaft.

34. Push the upper universal joint onto the steering column carefully.

35. Push down the lower universal joint onto the steering gear pinion.

36. Insert the lower bolt with thread lock compound.

➡**The recess of the splines in the universal joint must align precisely with the recess of the splines on the steering pinion. The bore in the universal joint must align with the groove on the steering pinion.**

37. Push the universal joint onto the steering pinion carefully.

38. Apply thread lock adhesive to the upper shaft bolt.

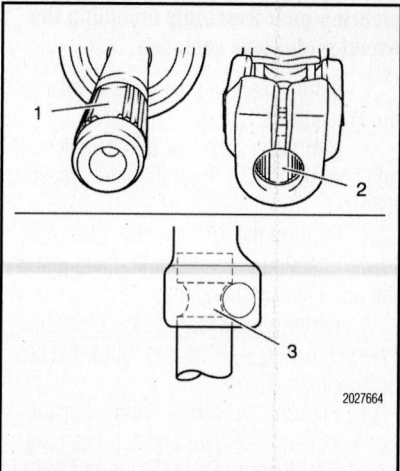

2027664

Fig. 323 The recess (2) of the splines in the universal joint must align precisely with the recess (1) of the splines on the steering pinion. The bore in the universal joint must align with the groove on the steering pinion (3)

39. Install the upper intermediate steering shaft bolt. Tighten the bolt to 25 ft. lbs. (34 Nm).

✳✳ WARNING

This component is equipped with torque-to-yield fasteners. Install a NEW torque-to-yield fastener when installing this component. Failure to replace the torque-to-yield fastener could cause damage to the vehicle or component.

40. Install the NEW lower intermediate steering shaft bolt. Tighten the bolt to 18 ft. lbs. (25 Nm), plus 180°.

41. Center the steering angle sensor using a scan tool.

42. Connect the battery. Refer to Battery, removal & installation.

43. Measure and adjust the front toe alignment.

44. Program the power steering control module. Refer to Power Steering Control Module Programming and Setup.

45. Center the steering angle sensor and learn the software end stops. Refer to Power Steering Control Module Calibration.

Power Steering Control Module Programming and Setup

Do not program or reprogram the electronic power steering control module unless directed by a service procedure or a service bulletin.

➡**This procedure applies to reprogramming of the existing steering gear or the initial programming if the complete**

steering gear assembly including the assist motor was replaced.

1. Before servicing the vehicle, refer to the Precautions Section.

2. Connect a scan tool to the vehicle and access Service Programming System (SPS).

3. Perform the SPS function Electronic Power Steering—Programming and follow the on-screen instructions.

4. Perform the SPS function Electronic Power Steering—Setup and follow the on-screen instructions.

5. Perform the Steering Angle Sensor Centering and Software Endstop Learning procedure. Refer to Power Steering Control Module Calibration.

6. Clear DTCs after completing the programming and setup procedures.

Power Steering Control Module Replacement

During the procedures below, critical data is retrieved from vehicle components and stored in the scan tool computer's hard drive. This data is needed during the programming and setup sequences. Ensure the same scan tool is used and capable of reading, storing, and writing the vehicle's system data.

1. Before servicing the vehicle, refer to the Precautions Section.

2. Connect a scan tool to the vehicle and access Service Programming System (SPS).

➡ **The next step copies the worm gear wear counter data from the power steering control module PRIOR to the module's removal and stores it on the scan tool computer's hard drive. AFTER completing the step, the power steering control module can be removed and replaced.**

3. Perform the SPS function Electronic Power Steering—Prepare Control Module for Removal and follow the on-screen instructions.

4. Replace the Power Steering Assist Motor containing the Power Steering Control Module.

➡ **The next two steps will transfer the vehicle's critical data, including the worm gear wear counter data saved earlier, back to the vehicle components.**

5. With the Power Steering Assist Motor replaced and reconnected, using the same scan tool, perform the SPS function Electronic Power Steering—Programming and follow the on-screen instructions.

6. Perform the SPS function Electronic Power Steering—Setup and follow the on-screen instructions.

7. Perform the Steering Angle Sensor Centering and Software Endstop Learning procedure. Refer to Power Steering Control Module Calibration.

8. Clear DTCs after completing the programming and setup procedures.

Power Steering Control Module Calibration

✳✳ CAUTION

An inaccurate or not centered steering angle sensor could limit the operation of the Electric Power Steering (EPS) and result in personal injury.

Centering of the steering angle sensor and software endstop learning might be required after certain service procedures are performed. Some of these procedures are as follows:

- Steering angle sensor replacement
- Steering gear replacement
- Power steering assist motor replacement
- Steering column replacement
- Steering linkage inner tie rod replacement
- Steering linkage outer tie rod replacement

➡ **It is necessary to perform the steering angle sensor centering BEFORE the software endstop learning.**

Steering Angle Sensor Centering

The following conditions should be met: Front axle measured and set, engine running, vehicle speed 0 MPH (0 km/h), and the internal steering angle sensor is activated.

1. Before servicing the vehicle, refer to the Precautions Section.

2. Using the steering wheel, align the front wheels in the center forward position.

3. Using a scan tool, perform the Configuration/Reset Functions, Steering Wheel Angle Sensor Centering procedure.

4. Steer from the center position slowly 90° to the left.

5. Steer slowly back to the center position and then slowly 90° to the right.

6. Steer slowly back to the center position.

7. Perform the steering movements again.

8. The centering procedure is completed.

Software Endstop Learning

The following conditions should be met: Front axle measured and set, vehicle speed 0 MPH (0 km/h), internal steering angle sensor is calibrated or external steering angle sensor sends a valid CAN signal.

1. Before servicing the vehicle, refer to the Precautions Section.

2. Using a scan tool, perform the Configuration/Reset Functions, Power Steering Softstops Reset procedure and follow the on-screen instructions.

3. Using a scan tool, perform the Configuration/Reset Functions, Power Steering Softstops Learn procedure and follow the on-screen instructions.

4. The software endstop learning procedure is completed.

CONTROL LINKS

REMOVAL & INSTALLATION

See Figure 324.

1. Before servicing the vehicle, refer to the Precautions Section.
2. Raise and safely support the vehicle.
3. Remove the tire and wheel assembly.
4. Using the proper size Allen® wrench, hold the stabilizer shaft link ball stud while removing the stabilizer shaft nut.
5. Remove and discard the nut. DO NOT re-use the nut, replace with NEW only.
6. Remove the stabilizer shaft control link.

To install:

❊❊ WARNING

This component is equipped with torque-to-yield fasteners. Install a NEW torque-to-yield fastener when installing this component. Failure to replace the torque-to-yield fastener could cause damage to the vehicle or component.

7. Installation is the reverse of the removal procedure.
8. Tighten the stabilizer shaft link nuts to 48 ft. lbs. (65 Nm).

LOWER BALL JOINT

REMOVAL & INSTALLATION

Clean and inspect the ball joint seal for cuts or tears. If the ball joint seal is damaged, replace the lower control arm. Refer to Lower Control Arm, removal & installation.

LOWER CONTROL ARM

REMOVAL & INSTALLATION

See Figures 325 and 326.

Special Tools
- EN-45059 Torque Angle Sensor Kit

1. Before servicing the vehicle, refer to the Precautions Section.
2. Raise and safely support the vehicle.
3. Remove the tire and wheel.
4. If equipped, remove the front compartment insulator.
5. Remove the wheel speed sensor wiring harness from the control arm and steering knuckle.
6. Remove the lower ball joint-to-knuckle nut and bolt. DISCARD the bolt.

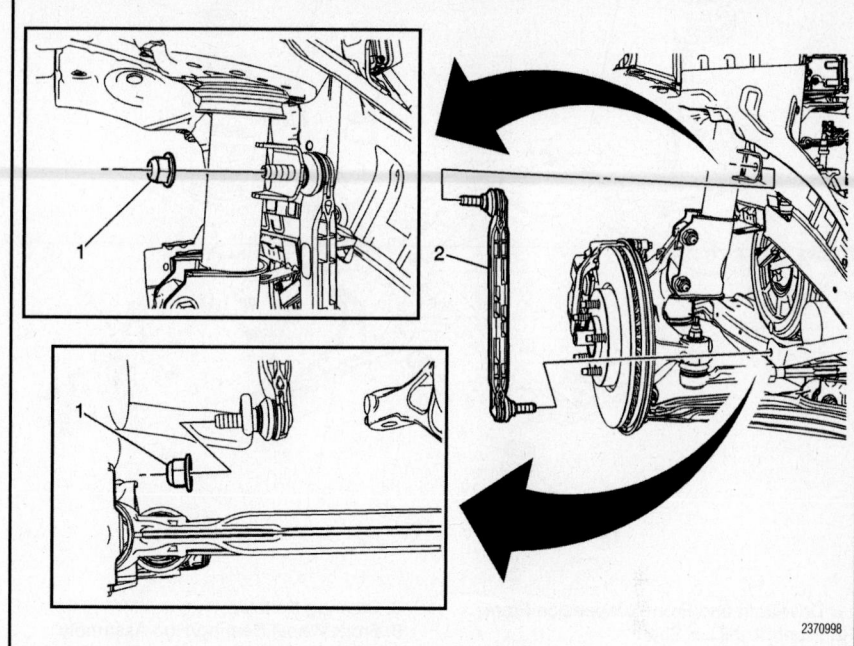

Fig. 324 View of stabilizer shaft control link (2) and nuts (1)

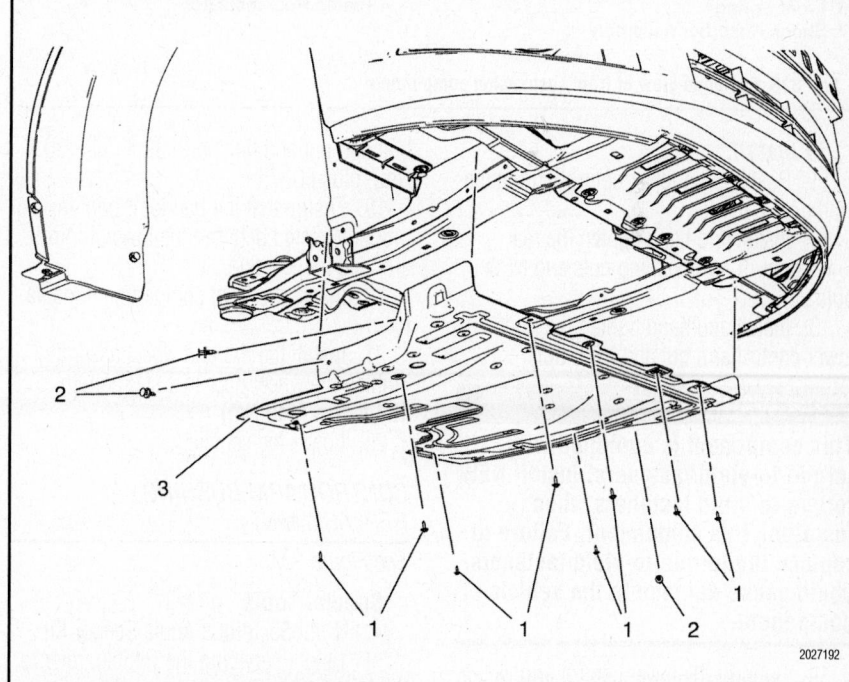

Fig. 325 Removing the front compartment insulator (3), plastic retainers (2), and screws (1)

❊❊ WARNING

Do not pry in such a way that the ball joint seal is contacted. Damage to the seal may result.

7. Separate the lower control arm from the knuckle.

8. Remove the front lower control arm nut and bolt. DISCARD the bolt.
9. Remove the rear lower control arm bushing nuts and bolts. DISCARD the bolts.
10. Remove the lower control arm from the front frame.

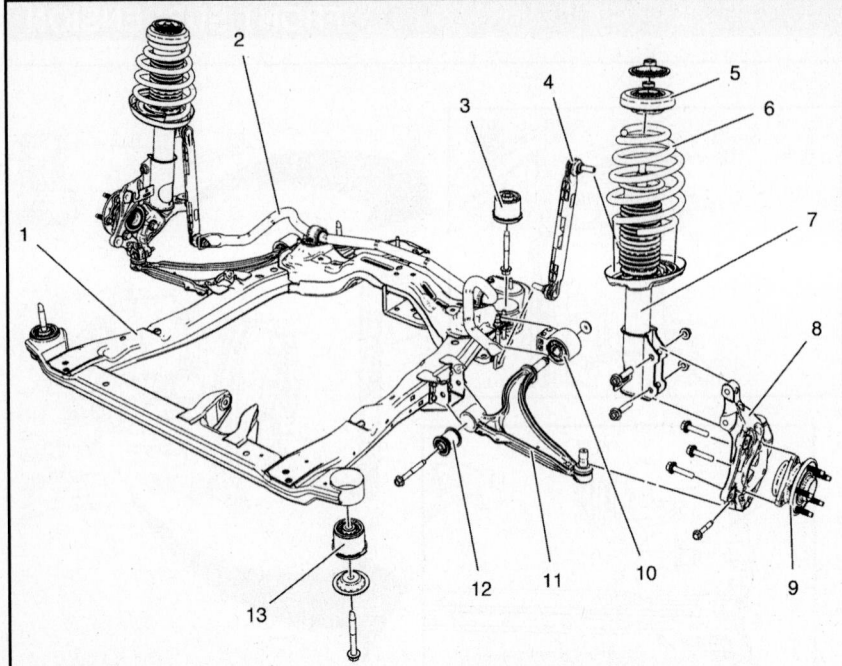

1. Drivetrain and Front Suspension Frame
2. Front Stabilizer Shaft
3. Drivetrain and Front Suspension Frame Rear Insulator
4. Front Stabilizer Shaft Link
5. Front Suspension Strut Insulator Assembly
6. Front Spring
7. Shock Absorber Assembly
8. Steering Knuckle
9. Front Wheel Bearing/Hub Assembly
10. Front Lower Control Arm Rear Bushing
11. Front Lower Control Arm
12. Front Lower Control Arm Bushing
13. Drivetrain and Front Suspension Frame Rear Insulator

2028235

Fig. 326 Exploded view of front suspension components

To install:

11. Position the lower control arm in the cradle.

12. Install and hand tighten the rear lower control arm bushing nuts and NEW bolts.

13. Install and hand tighten the front lower control arm nut and NEW bolt.

✳✳ WARNING

This component is equipped with torque-to-yield fasteners. Install NEW torque-to-yield fasteners when installing this component. Failure to replace the torque-to-yield fasteners could cause damage to the vehicle or component.

14. Support the lower control arm with a hydraulic jack and lift the control arm to the proper trim height inspection. Use the EN-45059 Torque Angle Sensor Kit, or equivalent, to tighten the bolts and nuts.

15. Tighten the front lower control arm bolt to 52 ft. lbs. (70 Nm), plus 75–90°.

16. Tighten the rear bushing-to-frame bolts to 52 ft. lbs. (70 Nm), plus 90°.

17. Remove the hydraulic jack.

18. Install the NEW ball joint to knuckle bolt and nut and tighten to 22 ft. lbs. (30 Nm), plus 60–75°.

19. Ensure that the ball joint boot is properly seated between the lower control arm and the knuckle.

20. Install the front compartment insulator.

21. Install the tire and wheel assembly. Tighten the wheel nuts in a star pattern to 103 ft. lbs. (140 Nm).

22. Lower the vehicle.

CONTROL ARM BUSHING REPLACEMENT

See Figure 327.

Special Tools
• EN-45059 Torque Angle Sensor Kit

1. Before servicing the vehicle, refer to the Precautions Section.

2. Raise and support the vehicle.

3. Remove the tire and wheel.

4. Remove the front compartment insulator.

5. Remove the lower control arm. Refer to Lower Control Arm, removal & installation.

6. Remove the bushing bolt and the lower control arm bushing.

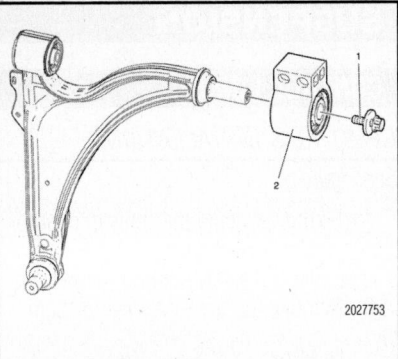

Fig. 327 Lower control arm rear bushing (2) and bushing bolt (1)

To install:

✳✳ WARNING

This component is equipped with torque-to-yield fasteners. Install NEW torque-to-yield fasteners when installing this component. Failure to replace the torque-to-yield fasteners could cause damage to the vehicle or component.

7. Install and hand tighten the NEW bushing bolt. Do NOT reuse an old bolt.

8. Install the lower control arm to the vehicle. Refer to Lower Control Arm, removal & installation.

9. Support the lower control arm with a hydraulic jack and lift the control arm into the neutral position.

10. Tighten the lower control arm bushing bolt to 41 ft. lbs. (55 Nm), plus 45–60°.

STABILIZER BAR

REMOVAL & INSTALLATION

See Figure 328.

1. Before servicing the vehicle, refer to the Precautions Section.

2. Raise and safely support the vehicle.

3. Remove the stabilizer shaft (bar) link from the stabilizer shaft. Refer to Control Links, removal & installation.

4. Lower the drivetrain and front suspension frame assembly.

5. Lower the front suspension frame assembly enough to gain access to the stabilizer shaft insulator bolts.

6. Remove the stabilizer shaft insulator clamp bolts.

7. Remove the stabilizer shaft from the vehicle.

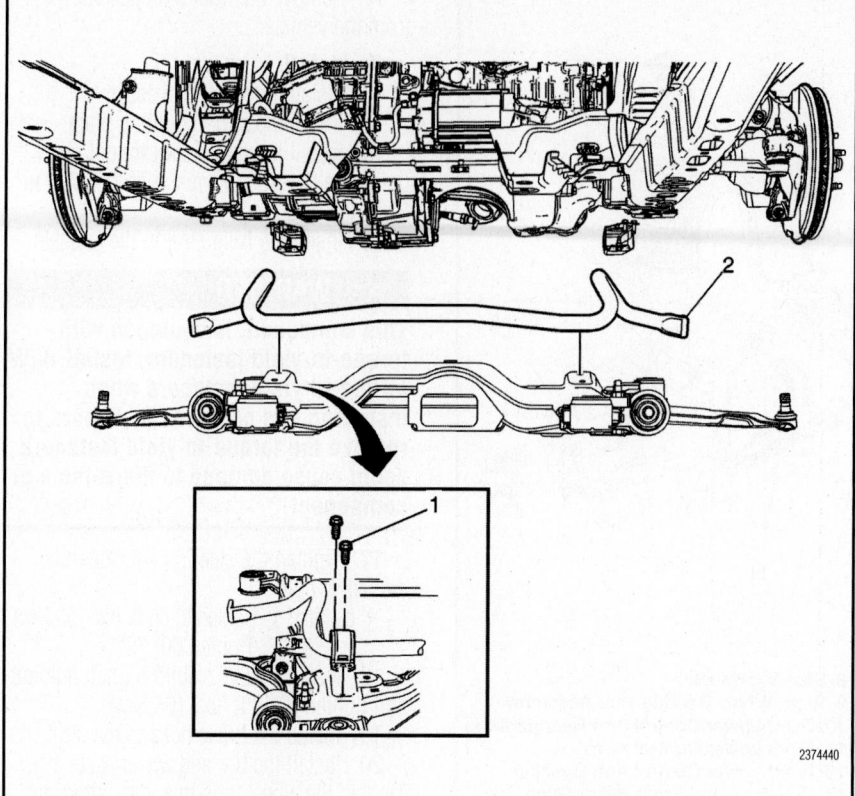

Fig. 328 View of front stabilizer shaft (2) and insulator clamp bolts (1)

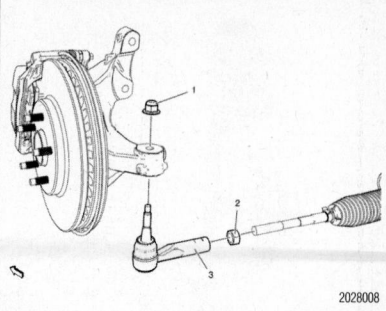

Fig. 329 View of steering linkage outer tie rod (3), outer tie rod nut (1), and steering linkage inner tie rod nut (2)

14. Remove the steering knuckle bolts and nuts and the steering knuckle.

To install:

✳✳ WARNING

This component is equipped with torque-to-yield fasteners. Install NEW torque-to-yield fasteners when installing this component. Failure to replace the torque-to-yield fasteners could cause damage to the vehicle or component.

15. Installation is the reverse of the removal procedure.

16. Install the steering knuckle using NEW bolts and nuts. Tighten to 66 ft. lbs. (90 Nm), plus 60–70°.

17. Install the steering linkage outer tie rod.

18. During the installation, align the match marks.

19. Do not tighten the nut during the installation. Tighten the nut after adjusting the front toe.

20. Install a NEW steering linkage outer tie rod nut. Do NOT reuse old nut. Tighten to 26 ft. lbs. (35 Nm).

21. Inspect the steering linkage inner tie rod for bent or damaged threads.

22. Clean the tapered surface of the steering knuckle.

23. After the installation, measure and adjust the front toe.

24. Position the front brake shield and front wheel bearing/hub assembly in the steering knuckle.

✳✳ WARNING

This component is equipped with torque-to-yield fasteners. Install NEW torque-to-yield fasteners when installing this component. Failure to replace the torque-to-yield fasteners could cause damage to the vehicle or component.

To install:

✳✳ WARNING

This component is equipped with torque-to-yield fasteners. Install NEW torque-to-yield fasteners when installing this component. Failure to replace the torque-to-yield fasteners could cause damage to the vehicle or component.

➡**The stabilizer shaft insulator and the clamps are serviced with the stabilizer shaft. They are not serviced separately.**

8. Install the stabilizer shaft and tighten the insulator bolts:
   a. Step 1: Tighten to 16 ft. lbs. (22 Nm).
   b. Step 2: Tighten an additional 40°.

STEERING KNUCKLE

REMOVAL & INSTALLATION

See Figures 329 and 330.

Special Tools
- EN-45059 Torque Angle Sensor Kit
- CH-24319-B Steering Linkage and Tie Rod Puller

1. Before servicing the vehicle, refer to the Precautions Section.

2. Raise and safely support the vehicle.

3. Matchmark front end components before removal.

4. Remove the brake rotor.

5. Remove the wheel speed sensor screw.

6. Remove the wheel speed sensor from the steering knuckle.

7. Remove the wheel drive shaft from the front wheel bearing/hub. Refer to Front Halfshaft, removal & installation.

8. Remove and DISCARD the front wheel bearing/hub bolts.

9. Remove the front wheel bearing/hub and front brake shield from the steering knuckle.

10. Use paint in order to place match marks on the steering linkage inner tie rod nut and on the steering linkage inner tie rod.

11. Remove and discard the steering linkage outer tie rod nut.

✳✳ WARNING

Do not free the ball stud by using a pickle fork or a wedge-type tool. Damage to the seal or bushing may result.

12. Use the CH-24319-B puller in order to separate the steering linkage outer tie rod from the steering knuckle.

13. Separate the control arm ball joint from the steering knuckle. Refer to Lower Control Arm, removal & installation.

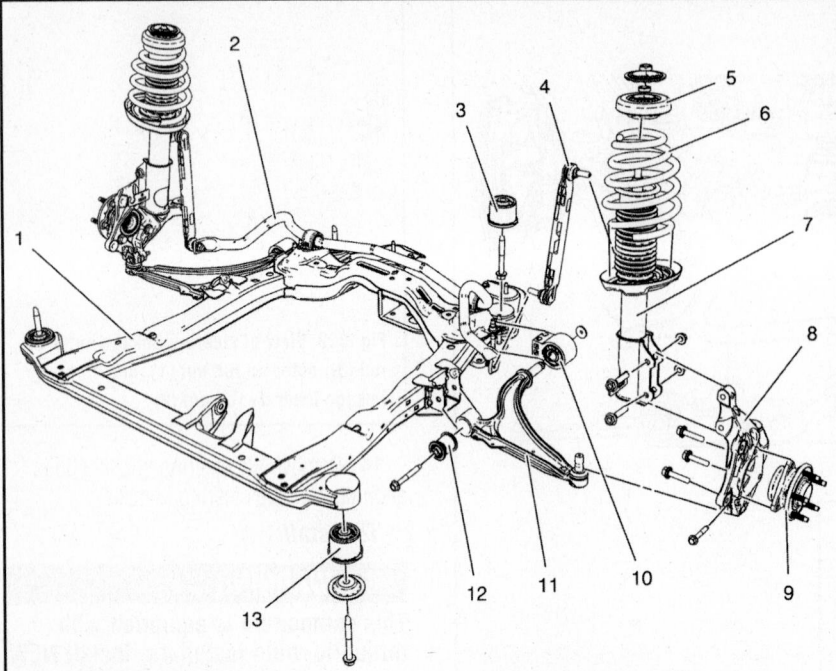

1. Drivetrain and Front Suspension Frame
2. Front Stabilizer Shaft
3. Drivetrain and Front Suspension Frame Rear Insulator
4. Front Stabilizer Shaft Link
5. Front Suspension Strut Insulator Assembly
6. Front Spring
7. Shock Absorber Assembly
8. Steering Knuckle
9. Front Wheel Bearing/Hub Assembly
10. Front Lower Control Arm Rear Bushing
11. Front Lower Control Arm
12. Front Lower Control Arm Bushing
13. Drivetrain and Front Suspension Frame Rear Insulator

2028235

Fig. 330 Exploded view of front suspension components

25. Install the NEW front wheel bearing/hub bolts.

26. Tighten the bearing/hub bolts in 3 steps. Use the EN-45059 angle meter.

    a. Step 1: Tighten to 66 ft. lbs. (90 Nm).

    b. Step 2: Tighten 60°.

    c. Step 3: Tighten and additional 15°.

27. Install the wheel drive shaft at the front wheel bearing/hub. Refer to Front Halfshaft, removal & installation.

28. Install the wheel speed sensor to the steering knuckle.

29. Install the wheel speed sensor screw and tighten to 53 ft. lbs. (6 Nm).

30. Install the brake rotor.

31. Lower the vehicle.

STRUT & SPRING ASSEMBLY

REMOVAL & INSTALLATION

See Figures 330 and 331.

Special Tools

• CH-49375 Wrench

1. Before servicing the vehicle, refer to the Precautions Section.

2. Raise and safely support the vehicle.

3. Remove the tire and wheel assembly.

4. Separate the brake hose from the shock absorber.

5. Remove the steering knuckle nuts and bolts. DISCARD the bolts.

6. Remove and DISCARD the stabilizer shaft link nut from the front strut.

7. Lower the vehicle.

8. Open the hood.

9. Remove the upper strut mount nut, using the CH-49375 wrench.

10. Remove the strut mounting plate.

11. Separate the front strut from the knuckle.

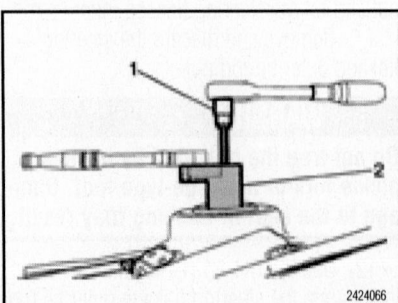

2424066

Fig. 331 Using the CH-49375 wrench (2) and special tool (1) to remove the strut mounting plate

12. Remove the front strut assembly from the vehicle.

To install:

13. Install the front strut assembly.

14. Install the strut mounting plate.

15. Install the upper strut mount nut, using the CH-49375 wrench and tighten to 34 ft. lbs. (45 Nm).

16. Insert the front strut in the knuckle.

> ※※ **WARNING**
>
> **This component is equipped with torque-to-yield fasteners. Install NEW torque-to-yield fasteners when installing this component. Failure to replace the torque-to-yield fasteners could cause damage to the vehicle or component.**

17. Tighten the steering knuckle nuts and NEW bolts:

    a. Step 1: Tighten to 66 ft. lbs. (90 Nm).

    b. Step 2: Tighten 60–75°.

18. Install a NEW stabilizer shaft link nut and tighten to 48 ft. lbs. (65 Nm).

19. Install the brake hose to the strut.

20. Install the tire and wheel assembly. Tighten the wheel nuts in a star pattern to 103 ft. lbs. (140 Nm).

21. Lower the vehicle.

22. Check the front camber alignment specifications.

OVERHAUL

See Figures 332 through 334.

Special Tools

• CH 6066 Strut Spring Compressor
• CH 35669 Wrench

1. Before servicing the vehicle, refer to the Precautions Section.

2. Remove the front suspension strut from the vehicle. Refer to Strut & Spring Assembly, removal & installation.

3. Install the front suspension strut in the CH 6066 compressor.

➡**The spring is compressed when the strut moves freely.**

4. Using the CH 6066 compressor, compress the front spring.

5. Using a Torx® bit and the CH 35669 wrench, remove the front suspension strut nut.

6. Remove the front suspension strut from the CH 6066 compressor.

7. Remove the front suspension strut mount and the front spring from the CH 6066 compressor.

To assemble:

8. Install the front spring and front suspension strut mount to the CH 6066 compressor.

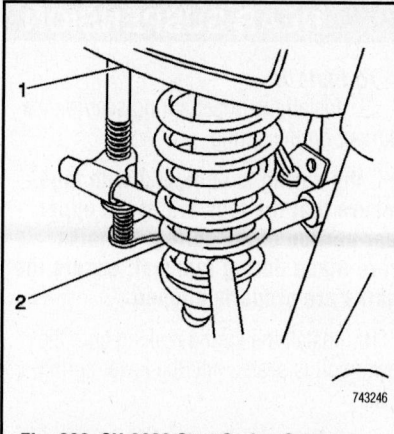

Fig. 332 CH 6066 Strut Spring Compressor (1) installed to the front suspension strut (2)

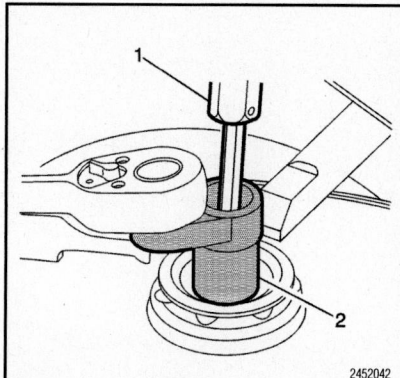

Fig. 333 Using a Torx® bit (1) and the CH 35669 wrench (2) to remove the front suspension strut nut

9. Using the CH 6066 compressor, compress the front spring.

10. Hand tighten the front suspension strut nut.

11. Using the CH 35669 wrench and the Torx® bit, tighten the front suspension strut nut to 52 ft. lbs. (70 Nm).

12. Remove the front suspension strut from the CH 6066 compressor.

13. Install the front suspension strut to

the vehicle. Refer to Strut & Spring Assembly, removal & installation.

WHEEL BEARINGS

REMOVAL & INSTALLATION
See Figure 330.

Special Tools
• EN-45059 Torque Angle Sensor Kit

1. Before servicing the vehicle, refer to the Precautions Section.

2. Raise and safely support the vehicle.

3. Remove the front brake rotor.

4. Remove the wheel speed sensor screw.

5. Remove the wheel speed sensor from the steering knuckle.

6. Remove the wheel drive shaft from the front wheel bearing/hub. Refer to Front Halfshaft, removal & installation.

7. Remove and DISCARD the front wheel bearing/hub bolts.

8. Remove the front wheel bearing/hub and front brake shield from the steering knuckle.

To install:

9. Position the front brake shield and front wheel bearing/hub assembly in the steering knuckle.

❋❋ WARNING

This component is equipped with torque-to-yield fasteners. Install NEW torque-to-yield fasteners when installing this component. Failure to replace the torque-to-yield fasteners could cause damage to the vehicle or component.

10. Install the NEW front wheel bearing/hub bolts.

11. Tighten the bearing/hub bolts in 3 steps. Use the EN-45059 angle meter, or equivalent.

   a. Step 1: Tighten to 66 ft. lbs. (90 Nm).

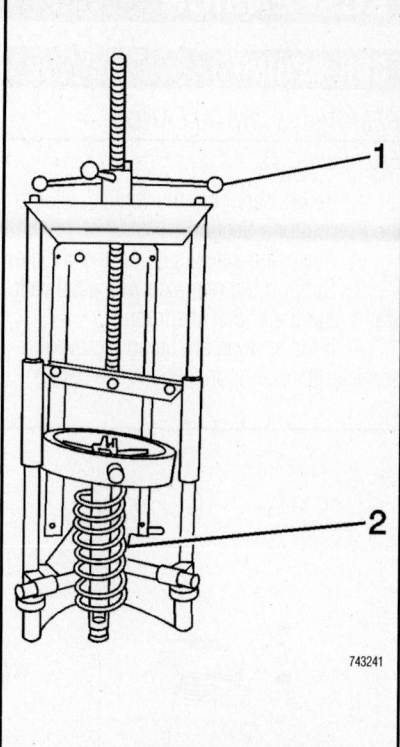

Fig. 334 Removing the front suspension strut (2) from the CH 6066 compressor (1)

   b. Step 2: Tighten 60°.

   c. Step 3: Tighten an additional 15°.

12. Install the wheel drive shaft at the front wheel bearing/hub. Refer to Front Halfshaft, removal & installation.

13. Install the wheel speed sensor to the steering knuckle.

14. Install the wheel speed sensor screw and tighten to 53 inch lbs. (6 Nm).

15. Install the brake rotor.

16. Lower the vehicle.

ADJUSTMENT

The wheel bearings are sealed at the factory and do not require any adjustment or maintenance.

COIL SPRING

REMOVAL & INSTALLATION

See Figure 335.

1. Before servicing the vehicle, refer to the Precautions Section.
2. Raise and safely support the vehicle.
3. Support the rear axle with a tall jack stand near the shock absorber.
4. If the springs are being removed to service other components and the spring tags are missing, mark the position of the rear spring to ensure proper installation.
5. Remove the lower shock absorber bolts. Refer to Shock Absorber, removal & installation.
6. Using the tall jack stands, slowly lower the rear axle in order to remove tension from the rear springs.
7. Remove the spring.
8. Remove the upper spring seat/jounce bumper from the spring, while leaving the lower spring seat on the axle.

To install:

9. Install the upper spring seat/jounce bumper on the spring.

➡ **If the spring is equipped with tags, ensure that the tags are at the upper rear portion of the spring. If marks were made during removal, ensure the marks are properly aligned.**

10. Install the spring making sure the lower coil is seated into the lower spring seat.

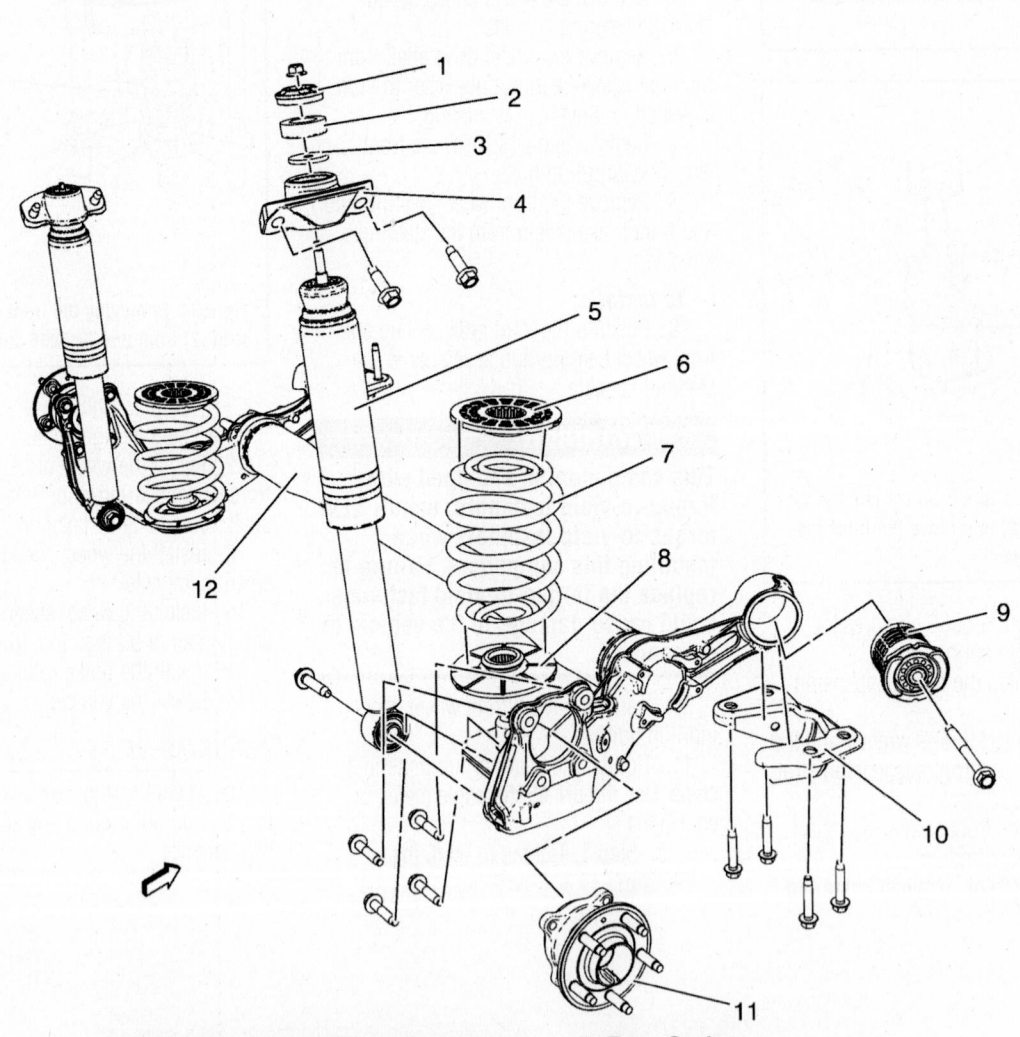

1. Rear Shock Absorber Upper Mount
2. Rear Shock Absorber Upper Mount
3. Rear Shock Absorber Upper Mount
4. Rear Shock Absorber Upper Mount
5. Shock Absorber Assembly
6. Upper Dumping Ring
7. Rear Spring
8. Lower Dumping Ring
9. Rear Axle Bushing
10. Rear Axle Bracket
11. Rear Wheel Bearing
12. Rear Axle

2028261

Fig. 335 Exploded view of rear suspension components

11. Using the jack stands, raise the rear axle in order to compress the rear springs.

12. Install the lower shock absorber bolts. Refer to Shock Absorber, removal & installation.

13. Lower the vehicle.

EQUALIZER BEAM

REMOVAL & INSTALLATION

Equalizer Beam Center Link

See Figures 336 and 337.

Special Tools

• EN-45059 Torque Angle Sensor Kit

1. Before servicing the vehicle, refer to the Precautions Section.

2. Raise and safely support the vehicle.

3. Remove the tire and wheel assemblies.

4. Remove and DISCARD the exhaust front pipe-to exhaust rear muffler nuts.

5. Remove the rear exhaust pipe from the flange.

6. DISCARD the flange gasket.

➡There may be additional attachment points, depending on the powertrain in the vehicle.

7. Loosen the rear exhaust muffler from the suspension points.

8. Lower and support the exhaust as required.

9. Remove the 3 rivets from the equalizer beam center link heat shield.

10. Remove and DISCARD the right equalizer beam link inner bolt and nut from the equalizer beam center link.

11. Lower and support the equalizer beam link as required.

12. Remove and DISCARD the left equalizer beam link inner bolt and nut from the equalizer beam center link.

13. Lower and support the equalizer beam link as required.

➡Remember the correct installation position of components.

14. Push down the rear muffler, remove and discard the equalizer beam center link bolt and nut from the equalizer beam center link.

15. Remove the equalizer beam center link from the vehicle.

To install:

16. Install the equalizer beam center link to the vehicle.

17. Using the lift table, raise the axle to the proper trim height specification by measuring the vertical distance between the center of the wheel hub and top of the wheel opening.

• Trim height specification: 15.2 inches (385mm)

✺✺ WARNING

This component is equipped with torque-to-yield fasteners. Install NEW torque-to-yield fasteners when installing this component. Failure to replace the torque-to-yield fasteners could cause damage to the vehicle or component.

➡Remember the correct installation position from the removal.

18. Push down the rear muffler and install the equalizer beam center link bolt and nut to the equalizer beam center link and tighten to 30 ft. lbs. (70 Nm), plus 45–60°.

19. Remove the support from the equalizer beam link.

20. Install the NEW left equalizer beam link inner bolt and nut to the equalizer beam center link and tighten to 30 ft. lbs. (40 Nm), plus 60°.

21. Remove the support from the equalizer beam link.

22. Install the NEW right equalizer beam link inner bolt and nut to the equalizer beam center link and tighten to 30 ft. lbs. (40 Nm), plus 60°.

23. Install the 3 rivets to the equalizer beam center link heat shield.

➡There may be additional attachment points, depending on the powertrain in the vehicle.

24. Install the rear exhaust muffler to the suspension points.

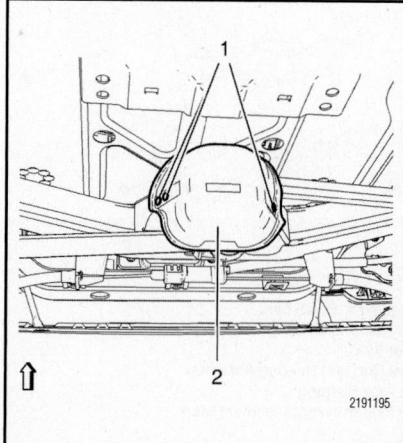

2191195

Fig. 336 Remove the 3 rivets (1) from the equalizer beam center link heat shield (2)

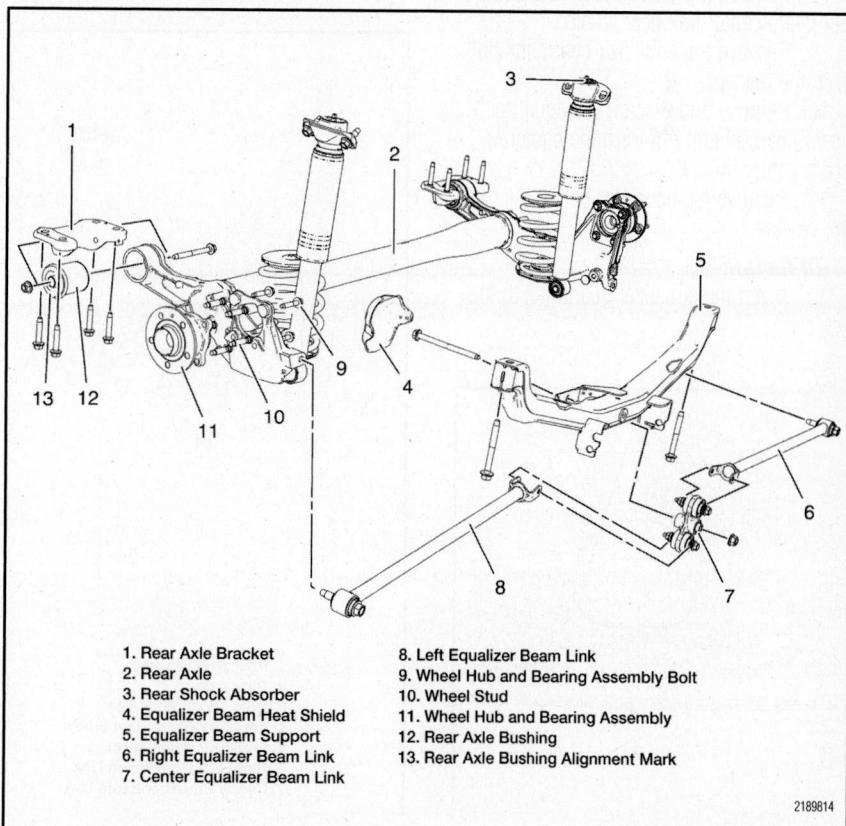

1. Rear Axle Bracket
2. Rear Axle
3. Rear Shock Absorber
4. Equalizer Beam Heat Shield
5. Equalizer Beam Support
6. Right Equalizer Beam Link
7. Center Equalizer Beam Link
8. Left Equalizer Beam Link
9. Wheel Hub and Bearing Assembly Bolt
10. Wheel Stud
11. Wheel Hub and Bearing Assembly
12. Rear Axle Bushing
13. Rear Axle Bushing Alignment Mark

2189814

Fig. 337 Exploded view of rear suspension components—with equalizer beam (Watt linkage)

25. Install the NEW flange gasket.
26. Install the rear exhaust pipe to the flange.
27. Install NEW exhaust front pipe-to-exhaust rear muffler nuts and tighten to 13 ft. lbs. (17 Nm).
28. Install the tire and wheel assembly. Tighten the wheel nuts in a star pattern to 103 ft. lbs. (140 Nm).
29. Lower the vehicle.

Equalizer Beam Link—Left Side

See Figures 338 and 339.

Special Tools

- EN-45059 Angle Sensor Kit

1. Before servicing the vehicle, refer to the Precautions Section.
2. Raise and safely support the vehicle.
3. Remove the tire and wheel assemblies.
4. Remove and DISCARD exhaust front pipe to exhaust rear muffler nuts.
5. Remove rear exhaust pipe from flange.
6. DISCARD flange gasket.

➡There may be additional attachment points, depending on the powertrain in the vehicle.

7. Loosen rear exhaust muffler from suspension points.
8. Remove the 3 rivets from the equalizer beam center link heat shield.
9. Remove the equalizer beam link bolt from the rear axle.
10. Remove and discard the equalizer beam link bolt and nut from the equalizer beam center link.
11. Remove the equalizer beam link from the vehicle.

To install:

12. Insert the equalizer beam link to the vehicle.

➡The next step must be followed in order to achieve correct rear axle joint alignment.

13. Using the lift table, raise the axle to the proper trim height specification by measuring the vertical distance between the center of the wheel hub and top of the wheel opening.
    - Trim height specification: 15.2 inches (385mm)

⁂ WARNING

This component is equipped with torque-to-yield fasteners. Install NEW torque-to-yield fasteners when installing this component. Failure to replace the torque-to-yield fasteners could cause damage to the vehicle or component.

14. Install the NEW equalizer beam link bolt and nut to the equalizer beam center link and tighten to 30 ft. lbs. (40 Nm), plus 60°, using the EN-45059 angle meter, or equivalent.
15. Install the equalizer beam link bolt to the rear axle and tighten to 118 ft. lbs. (160 Nm).
16. Install the tire and wheel assembly. Tighten the wheel nuts in a star pattern to 103 ft. lbs. (140 Nm).
17. Install 3 rivets to equalizer beam center link heat shield.

➡There may be additional attachment points, depending on the powertrain in the vehicle.

18. Install the rear exhaust muffler to the suspension points.
19. Install the NEW flange gasket.
20. Install the rear exhaust pipe to the flange.
21. Install the NEW exhaust front pipe-to-exhaust rear muffler nuts and tighten to 13 ft. lbs. (17 Nm).
22. Lower the vehicle.

Equalizer Beam Link—Right Side

See Figures 338 and 339.

Special Tools

- EN-45059 Angle Sensor Kit

1. Before servicing the vehicle, refer to the Precautions Section.
2. Raise and safely support the vehicle.
3. Remove the tire and wheel assemblies.
4. Remove the 3 rivets from the equalizer beam center link heat shield.
5. Remove the equalizer beam link bolt from the rear axle.

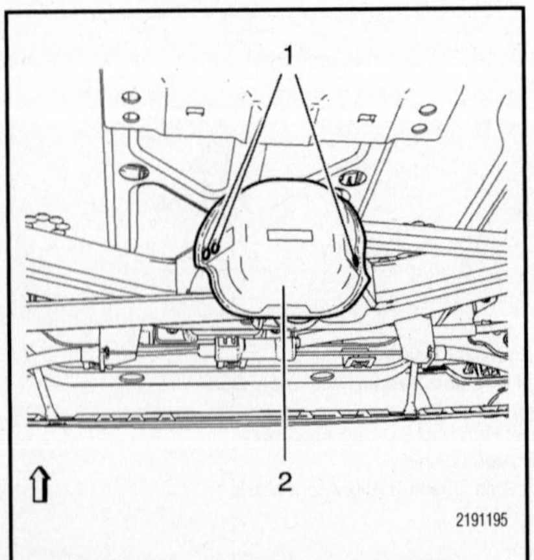
1
2
2191195

Fig. 338 Remove the 3 rivets (1) from the equalizer beam center link heat shield (2)

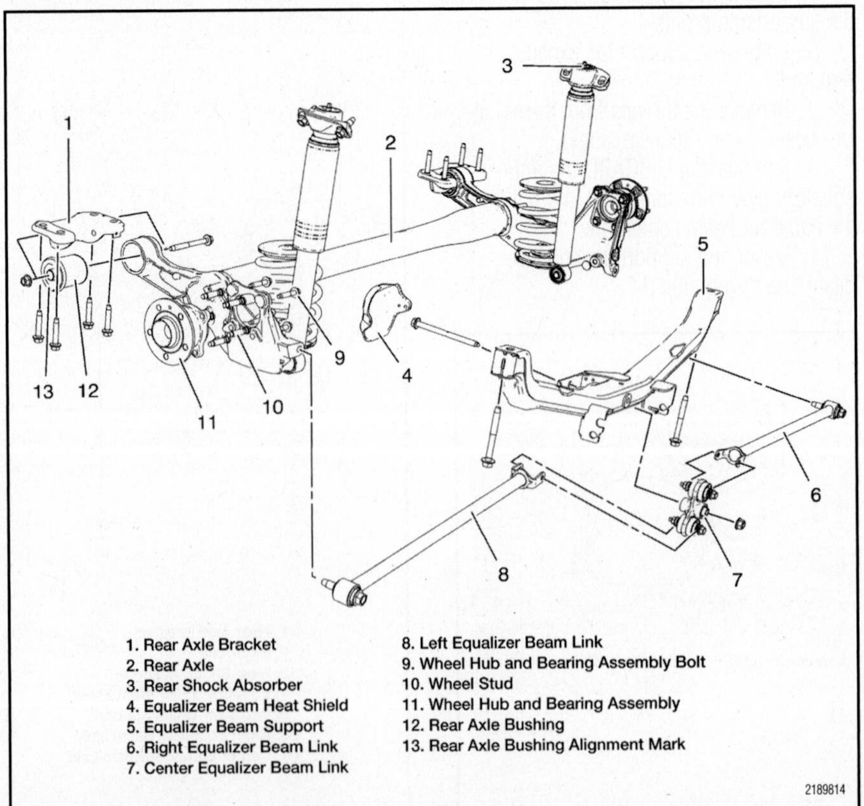
1
2
3
4
5
6
7
8
9
10
11
12
13
1. Rear Axle Bracket
2. Rear Axle
3. Rear Shock Absorber
4. Equalizer Beam Heat Shield
5. Equalizer Beam Support
6. Right Equalizer Beam Link
7. Center Equalizer Beam Link
8. Left Equalizer Beam Link
9. Wheel Hub and Bearing Assembly Bolt
10. Wheel Stud
11. Wheel Hub and Bearing Assembly
12. Rear Axle Bushing
13. Rear Axle Bushing Alignment Mark
2189814

Fig. 339 Exploded view of rear suspension components—with equalizer beam (Watt linkage)

6. Remove and DISCARD the equalizer beam link bolt and nut from the equalizer beam center link.

7. Remove the equalizer beam link from the vehicle.

To install:

8. Insert the equalizer beam link to the vehicle.

➡ **The next step must be followed in order to achieve correct rear axle joint alignment.**

9. Using the lift table, raise the axle to the proper trim height specification by measuring the vertical distance between the center of the wheel hub and top of the wheel opening.

- Trim height specification: 15.2 inches (385mm)

✳✳ WARNING

This component is equipped with torque-to-yield fasteners. Install NEW torque-to-yield fasteners when installing this component. Failure to replace the torque-to-yield fasteners could cause damage to the vehicle or component.

10. Install the NEW equalizer beam link bolt and nut to the equalizer beam center link and tighten to 30 ft. lbs. (40 Nm), plus 60°, using the EN-45059 angle meter, or equivalent.

11. Install and hand tighten the equalizer beam link bolt to the rear axle and tighten to 118 ft. lbs. (160 Nm).

12. Install the tire and wheel assembly. Tighten the wheel nuts in a star pattern to 103 ft. lbs. (140 Nm).

13. Lower the vehicle to ground.

14. Install 3 rivets to equalizer beam center link heat shield.

15. Lower the vehicle.

SHOCK ABSORBER

REMOVAL & INSTALLATION

See Figure 340.

Special Tools

- EN-45059 Torque Angle Sensor Kit

1. Before servicing the vehicle, refer to the Precautions Section.

2. Raise and safely support the vehicle.

3. Remove the tire and wheel assembly.

4. Support the rear axle with a suitable jack stand.

5. Remove the rear shock absorber upper and lower bolts and DISCARD.

6. Remove the rear shock absorber from the vehicle.

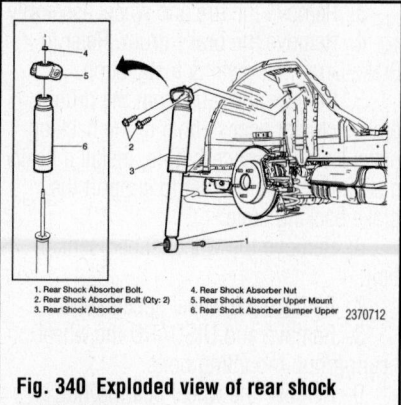

1. Rear Shock Absorber Bolt.
2. Rear Shock Absorber Bolt (Qty: 2)
3. Rear Shock Absorber
4. Rear Shock Absorber Nut
5. Rear Shock Absorber Upper Mount
6. Rear Shock Absorber Bumper Upper   2370712

Fig. 340 Exploded view of rear shock installation

To install:

✳✳ WARNING

This component is equipped with torque-to-yield fasteners. Install NEW torque-to-yield fasteners when installing this component. Failure to replace the torque-to-yield fasteners could cause damage to the vehicle or component.

7. Install the shock absorber to the vehicle.

8. Install NEW bolts. Do NOT reuse old bolts.

9. Support the front of the vehicle and raise the rear axle to the proper trim height specifications.

10. Tighten the lower rear shock absorber bolt:

　a. Step 1: Tighten to 111 ft. lbs. (150 Nm).

　b. Step 2: Tighten 60–70°.

11. Tighten the upper rear shock absorber bolts to 74 ft. lbs. (100 Nm).

12. Tighten the rear shock absorber nut to 15 ft. lbs. (20 Nm).

13. Install the tire and wheel assembly. Tighten the wheel nuts in a star pattern to 103 ft. lbs. (140 Nm).

STABILIZER BAR

REMOVAL & INSTALLATION

Refer to Equalizer Beam, removal & installation.

WHEEL BEARINGS

REMOVAL & INSTALLATION

With Disc Brakes

See Figures 341 and 342.

Special Tools

- EN 45059 Torque Angle Sensor Kit

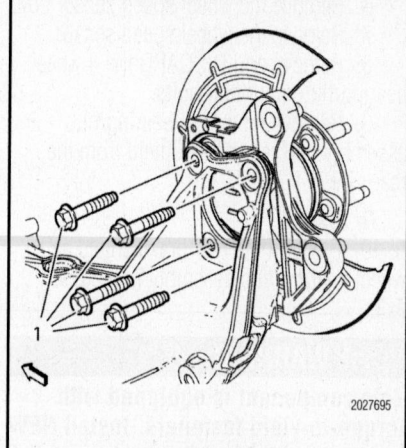

Fig. 341 Remove the 4 wheel bearing/hub mounting bolts (1)—disc brakes

1. Before servicing the vehicle, refer to the Precautions Section.

2. Raise and safely support the vehicle.

3. Remove the tire and wheel assembly.

4. Without disconnecting the hydraulic brake flex hose, remove and support the rear brake caliper and bracket as an assembly.

5. Remove the rear brake rotor.

✳✳ WARNING

Support the brake caliper with heavy mechanics wire, or equivalent, whenever it is separated from its mount and the hydraulic flexible brake hose is still connected. Failure to support the caliper in this manner will cause the flexible brake hose to bear the weight of the caliper, which may cause damage to the brake hose and in turn may cause a brake fluid leak.

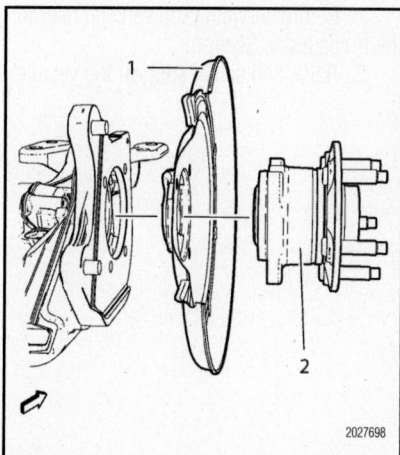

Fig. 342 Wheel bearing/hub assembly (2) and rear brake shield (1) removal—disc brakes

6. Remove the wheel speed sensor bolt.

7. Remove the wheel speed sensor.

8. Remove and DISCARD the 4 wheel bearing/hub mounting bolts.

9. Remove the wheel bearing/hub assembly and rear brake shield from the rear axle.

To install:

10. Position the rear brake shield and wheel bearing/hub assembly in the rear axle.

> **⚹⚹ WARNING**
>
> **This component is equipped with torque-to-yield fasteners. Install NEW torque-to-yield fasteners when installing this component. Failure to replace the torque-to-yield fasteners could cause damage to the vehicle or component.**

11. Install the 4 NEW wheel bearing/hub mounting bolts and tighten to 37 ft. lbs. (50 Nm), plus 40°, using the EN 45059 angle meter, or equivalent. Tighten the bolts evenly, in a cross-pattern.

12. Install the wheel speed sensor.

13. Install the wheel speed sensor bolt and tighten to 53 inch lbs. (6 Nm).

14. Install the brake rotor.

15. Install the brake caliper and bracket as an assembly. Refer to Brake Caliper, removal & installation.

16. Install the tire and wheel assembly. Tighten the wheel nuts in a star pattern to 103 ft. lbs. (140 Nm).

17. Lower the vehicle.

With Drum Brakes

See Figures 343 and 344.

Special Tools

- EN 45059 Torque Angle Sensor Kit

1. Before servicing the vehicle, refer to the Precautions Section.

2. Raise and safely support the vehicle.

3. Remove the tire and wheel assembly.

4. Remove the brake drum. Refer to Brake Drum, removal & installation.

5. Remove the plug from the drum brake actuator access hole in the backing plate. Using the access hole, install a heavy mechanics wire in order to support the brake backing plate.

6. Remove the wheel speed sensor bolt.

7. Remove the wheel speed sensor.

8. Remove and DISCARD the wheel bearing/hub mounting bolts.

9. Remove the wheel bearing/hub assembly from the rear axle assembly and brake backing plate.

To install:

10. Install the wheel bearing/hub assembly to the brake backing plate and the rear axle assembly.

> **⚹⚹ WARNING**
>
> **This component is equipped with torque-to-yield fasteners. Install NEW torque-to-yield fasteners when installing this component. Failure to replace the torque-to-yield fasteners could cause damage to the vehicle or component.**

11. Install the NEW wheel bearing/hub mounting bolts and tighten to 37 ft. lbs. (50 Nm), plus 40°, using the EN 45059 kit, or equivalent. Tighten the bolts evenly, in a cross-pattern.

12. Install the wheel speed sensor. Tighten the bolt to 54 inch lbs. (6 Nm).

13. Remove the mechanics wire supporting the brake backing plate.

14. Install the plug to the drum brake actuator access hole in the backing plate.

15. Install the brake drum. Refer to Brake Drum, removal & installation.

16. Install the tire and wheel assembly. Tighten the wheel nuts in a star pattern to 103 ft. lbs. (140 Nm).

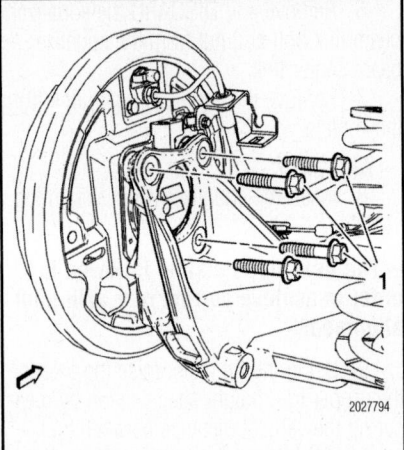

Fig. 343 Remove the 4 wheel bearing/hub mounting bolts (1)—drum brakes

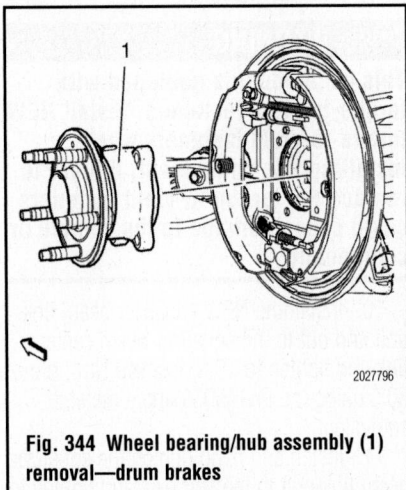

Fig. 344 Wheel bearing/hub assembly (1) removal—drum brakes

17. Remove the support and lower the vehicle.

ADJUSTMENT

The rear hub/bearing assembly is a sealed assembly, which requires no periodic maintenance and cannot be serviced. If the hub/bearing assembly becomes worn or damaged, the entire unit must be replaced.

CHEVROLET AND GMC

11

Equinox • Terrain

BRAKES 11-11

ANTI-LOCK BRAKE SYSTEM (ABS)...........................11-11
General Information.................11-11
  Precautions...........................11-11
Speed Sensors 11-11
  Removal & Installation........11-11
BLEEDING THE BRAKE SYSTEM 11-12
Brake System Bleeding............11-12
  ABS System Automated Bleed 11-12
  Fluid Fill Procedure 11-15
  Hydraulic System Manual Bleeding 11-13
  Hydraulic System Pressure Bleeding 11-13
  Master Cylinder Bleeding 11-14
FRONT DISC BRAKES 11-15
Brake Caliper...........................11-15
  Removal & Installation........11-15
Brake Pad & Rotor Burnishing 11-17
  Burnishing Procedure.........11-17
Disc Brake Pads 11-15
  Removal & Installation........11-15
Disc Brake Rotors....................11-16
  Removal & Installation........11-16
PARKING BRAKE..............11-18
Parking Brake Actuator............11-19
  Removal & Installation........11-19
Parking Brake Adjustment........11-18
  Adjustment 11-18
Parking Brake Shoes 11-19
  Removal & Installation........11-19
REAR DISC BRAKES 11-17
Brake Caliper...........................11-17
  Removal & Installation........11-17
Disc Brake Pads 11-17
  Removal & Installation........11-17
Disc Brake Rotors....................11-18
  Removal & Installation........11-18

CHASSIS ELECTRICAL 11-20

AIR BAG (SUPPLEMENTAL RESTRAINT SYSTEM) 11-20
General Information.................11-20
  Arming the System 11-22
  Clockspring Centering........11-22
  Disarming the System.........11-21
  Service Precautions 11-20

DRIVE TRAIN 11-22

Automatic Transaxle Fluid 11-22
  Drain & Refill......................11-22
Automatic Transaxle Shift Cable 11-22
  Adjustment 11-22
Differential Assembly 11-23
  Removal & Installation........11-23
Differential Fluid.....................11-23
  Drain & Refill......................11-23
Front Wheel Drive Shafts 11-23
  Removal & Installation........11-23
Intermediate Shaft 11-24
  Removal & Installation........11-24
Propeller Shaft 11-24
  Removal & Installation........11-24
Rear Wheel Drive Shaft 11-24
  Removal & Installation........11-24
Transfer Case 11-25
  Removal & Installation........11-25

ENGINE COOLING 11-26

Engine Coolant........................11-26
  Drain & Refill Procedure.....11-26
  Flushing..............................11-26
Engine Fan 11-26
  Removal & Installation........11-26
Radiator...................................11-27
  Removal & Installation........11-27
Thermostat 11-27
  Removal & Installation........11-27
Water Pump 11-28
  Removal & Installation........11-28

ENGINE ELECTRICAL 11-29

BATTERY SYSTEM............11-29
Battery.....................................11-29
  Removal & Installation........11-29
CHARGING SYSTEM 11-29
Alternator (Generator)..............11-29
  Removal & Installation........11-29
IGNITION SYSTEM 11-30
Firing Order.............................11-30
Ignition Coil 11-30
  Removal & Installation........11-30
Ignition Timing 11-30
  Adjustment 11-30
Spark Plugs.............................11-30
  Removal & Installation........11-30
STARTING SYSTEM 11-30
Starter 11-30
  Removal & Installation........11-30

ENGINE MECHANICAL......11-31

Accessory Drive Belts 11-31
  Accessory Belt Routing.......11-31
  Adjustment 11-31
  Removal & Installation........11-31
Air Cleaner 11-31
  Filter/Element Replacement 11-31
  Removal & Installation........11-31
Camshaft..................................11-33
  Removal & Installation........11-33
Camshaft & Valve Lifters.........11-31
  Removal & Installation........11-31
Camshaft Position Actuator 11-34
  Removal & Installation........11-34
Catalytic Converter 11-39
  Removal & Installation........11-39
Crankshaft Balancer 11-40
  Removal & Installation........11-40
Crankshaft Front Seal..............11-40
  Removal & Installation........11-40
Cylinder Head 11-40
  Removal & Installation........11-40

Engine Oil & Filter 11-43
  Replacement 11-43
Exhaust Manifold 11-43
  Removal & Installation.......11-43
Intake Manifold 11-44
  Removal & Installation.......11-44
Oil Pan 11-45
  Removal & Installation.......11-45
Oil Pump 11-46
  Removal & Installation.......11-46
Piston & Ring 11-46
  Positioning 11-46
Rear Main Seal 11-46
  Removal & Installation.......11-46
Timing Chain & Sprockets 11-47
  Removal & Installation.......11-47
Timing Chain Front Cover.......11-47
  Removal & Installation.......11-47
Valve Covers (Camshaft
  Covers) 11-51
  Removal & Installation.......11-51
Valve Lash............................11-52
  Adjustment 11-52

ENGINE PERFORMANCE & EMISSION CONTROLS 11-53

Accelerator Pedal Position
  (APP) Sensor 11-53
  Location.............................11-53
  Removal & Installation.......11-53
Camshaft Position (CMP)
  Sensor 11-53
  Location.............................11-53
  Removal & Installation.......11-53
Crankshaft Position (CKP)
  Sensor 11-54
  Location.............................11-54
  Removal & Installation.......11-54
Electronic Control Module
  (ECM) 11-55
  Location.............................11-55
  Removal & Installation.......11-55
Engine Coolant Temperature
  (ECT) Sensor 11-56
  Location.............................11-56
  Removal & Installation.......11-56
Evaporative Emission Control
  (EVAP) Canister 11-56
  Location.............................11-56
  Removal & Installation.......11-56
Evaporative Emission Control
  (EVAP) Canister Purge
  Solenoid.............................11-56
  Location.............................11-56
  Removal & Installation.......11-56

Evaporative Emission Control
  (EVAP) Canister Vent
  Solenoid.............................11-57
  Location.............................11-57
  Removal & Installation.......11-57
Fuel Pressure (FP) Sensor 11-57
  Location.............................11-57
  Removal & Installation.......11-57
Heated Oxygen (HO2S)
  Sensor 11-57
  Location.............................11-57
  Removal & Installation.......11-58
Intake Air Temperature (IAT)
  Sensor 11-58
Knock Sensor (KS)................11-58
  Location.............................11-58
  Removal & Installation.......11-58
Manifold Absolute Pressure
  (MAP) Sensor 11-59
  Location.............................11-59
  Removal & Installation.......11-59
Mass Air Flow (MAF)
  Sensor/Intake Air Temperature
  (IAT) Sensor 11-60
  Location.............................11-60
  Removal & Installation.......11-60
Throttle Inlet Absolute
  Pressure (TIAP) Sensor.........11-60
  Location.............................11-60
  Removal & Installation.......11-60

FUEL SYSTEM 11-60

GASOLINE FUEL INJECTION SYSTEM 11-60
Fuel Pump............................11-61
  Removal & Installation.......11-61
Fuel Rail & Injectors 11-60
  Removal & Installation.......11-60
Fuel System Service
  Precautions 11-60
Fuel Tank.............................11-62
  Draining............................11-62
  Removal & Installation.......11-63
Idle Speed 11-64
  Adjustment 11-64
Relieving Fuel System
  Pressure 11-60
Throttle Body.......................11-64
  Removal & Installation.......11-64
Throttle Learn Procedure.........11-64
  Learn Procedure
  (performed After the
  ECM is Flashed
  or Replaced) 11-64

Reset Procedure
  (performed After the
  Throttle Body is Cleaned
  or Replaced) 11-64

HEATING & AIR CONDITIONING SYSTEM 11-64

Blower Motor 11-64
  Removal & Installation.......11-64
Blower Motor Control
  Module...............................11-64
  Removal & Installation.......11-64
Condenser............................11-64
  Removal & Installation.......11-64
Evaporator Core 11-64
  Removal & Installation.......11-64
Heater Core 11-65
  Removal & Installation.......11-65
HVAC Module 11-65
  Removal & Installation.......11-65
Thermal Expansion Valve
  (TXV) 11-65
  Removal & Installation.......11-65

PRECAUTIONS...............11-11

SPECIFICATIONS AND MAINTENANCE CHARTS.....11-4

Additional Maintenance
  Services-Normal 11-10
Additional Maintenance
  Services-Severe 11-10
Brake Specifications 11-8
Camshaft Specifications............11-6
Capacities 11-5
Crankshaft & Connecting
  Rod Specifications 11-6
Engine and Vehicle
  Identification 11-4
Engine Tune-Up
  Specifications 11-4
Fluid Specifications.................11-5
General Engine
  Specifications 11-4
Maintenance I and II Service
  Schedules 11-9
Piston & Ring
  Specifications 11-6
Tire, Wheel & Ball Joint
  Specifications 11-8
Torque Specifications 11-7
Valve Specifications 11-5
Wheel Alignment 11-7

STEERING...................11-66

Power Steering Assist
Motor......................11-66
Removal &
Installation...................11-66
Power Steering Control
Module........................11-66
Power Steering Control
Module Calibration...........11-67
Power Steering Control
Module
Reprogramming...............11-66
Programming & Setup........11-66
Replacement...................11-66
Power Steering Gear..............11-67
Removal & Installation........11-67
Power Steering Pump.............11-68
Bleeding...........................11-69
Removal & Installation........11-68

SUSPENSION...............11-69

FRONT SUSPENSION........11-69
Lower Ball Joint.....................11-69
Removal & Installation........11-69
Lower Control Arm.................11-69
Removal & Installation........11-69
MacPherson Strut..................11-70
Overhaul..........................11-70
Removal & Installation........11-70
Stabilizer Bar.......................11-70
Removal & Installation........11-70
Stabilizer Bar Link.................11-71
Removal & Installation........11-71
Steering Knuckle...................11-71
Removal &
Installation...................11-71
Wheel Bearing & Hub.............11-71
Removal &
Installation...................11-71

REAR SUSPENSION..........11-72
Adjustment Link.....................11-72
Removal & Installation........11-72
Coil Spring..........................11-72
Removal & Installation........11-72
Knuckle.............................11-72
Removal & Installation........11-72
Lower Control Arm.................11-73
Removal & Installation........11-73
Shock Absorber.....................11-73
Removal & Installation........11-73
Stabilizer Bar.......................11-73
Removal & Installation........11-73
Stabilizer Bar Link.................11-73
Removal & Installation........11-73
Trailing Arm.........................11-74
Removal & Installation........11-74
Upper Control Arm.................11-74
Removal & Installation........11-74
Wheel Bearing & Hub.............11-74
Removal & Installation........11-74

SPECIFICATIONS AND MAINTENANCE CHARTS

ENGINE AND VEHICLE IDENTIFICATION

Engine							Model Year	
Code ①	Liters (cc)	Cu. In.	Cyl.	Fuel Sys.	Engine Type	Eng. Mfg.	Code ②	Year
C	2.4 (2400)	146	4	SIDI	DOHC	GM	A	2010
5	3.0 (3000)	183	6	SIDI	DOHC	GM	B	2011

① 8th position of VIN

② 10th position of VIN

25742_EQUI_C0001

GENERAL ENGINE SPECIFICATIONS

All measurements are given in inches.

Year	Model	Engine Displacement Liters	Engine ID/VIN	Fuel System Type	Net Horsepower @ rpm	Net Torque @ rpm (ft. lbs.)	Bore x Stroke (in.)	Compression Ratio	Oil Pressure psi@ rpm
2010	Equinox	2.4	C	SIDI	182@6700	172@4900	3.46x3.86	10:01	30-70@1000
	Terrain	2.4	C	SIDI	182@6700	172@4900	3.46x3.86	10:01	30-70@1000
	Terrain	3.0	5	SIDI	264@6950	222@5100	3.50x3.16	11.7:1	20@2000
2011	Equinox	2.4	C	SIDI	182@6700	172@4900	3.46x3.86	10:01	30-70@1000
	Terrain	2.4	C	SIDI	182@6700	172@4900	3.46x3.86	10:01	30-70@1000
	Terrain	3.0	5	SIDI	264@6950	222@5100	3.50x3.16	11.7:1	20@2000

25742_EQUI_C0002

ENGINE TUNE-UP SPECIFICATIONS

Year	Engine Displacement Liters	Engine ID/VIN	Spark Plug Gap (in.)	Ignition Timing (deg.) MT	AT	Fuel Pump (psi)	Idle Speed (rpm) MT	AT	Valve Clearance Intake	Exhaust
2010	2.4	C	0.035	—	①	N/A	—	①	②	②
	2.4	C	0.035	—	①	N/A	—	①	②	②
	3.0	5	0.043	—	①	N/A	—	①	②	②
2011	2.4	C	0.035	—	①	N/A	—	①	②	②
	2.4	C	0.035	—	①	N/A	—	①	②	②
	3.0	5	0.043	—	①	N/A	—	①	②	②

N/A: Information not available.

① Ignition timing and idle speed are computer controlled; therefore, it is not manually adjustable.

② Valve clearance is controlled by the hydraulic lifters.

25742_EQUI_C0003

CAPACITIES

Year	Model	Engine Displacement Liters	Engine ID/VIN	Engine Oil with Filter (qts.)	Trans. (pts.) Auto.	Manual	Drive Axle (pts.) Rear	Transfer Case (pts.)	Fuel Tank (gal.)	Cooling System (qts.)
2010	Equinox	2.4	C	5.0	8.4-12.6 ①	—	1.056	1.7	18.8	8.2
	Terrain	2.4	C	5.0	8.4-12.6 ①	—	1.056	1.7	18.8	8.2
	Terrain	3.0	5	6.0	8.4-12.6 ①	—	1.056	1.7	20.9	10.8
2011	Equinox	2.4	C	5.0	8.4-12.6 ①	—	1.056	1.7	18.8	8.2
	Terrain	2.4	C	5.0	8.4-12.6 ①	—	1.056	1.7	18.8	8.2
	Terrain	3.0	5	6.0	8.4-12.6 ①	—	1.056	1.7	20.9	10.8

NOTE: All capacities are approximate. Add fluid gradually and ensure a proper fluid level is obtained.

① Specification given is for fluid change (drain & refill); at overhaul, total capacity is 17.0-18.0 pts.

25742_EQUI_C0004

FLUID SPECIFICATIONS

Year	Model	Engine Displacement Liters	Engine Oil	Auto. Trans.	Drive Axle Rear	Transfer Case	Power Steering Fluid	Brake Master Cylinder	Cooling System
2010	Equinox	2.4	①	①	①	①	①	①	①
	Terrain	2.4	①	①	①	①	①	①	①
	Terrain	3.0	①	①	①	①	①	①	①
2011	Equinox	2.4	①	①	①	①	①	①	①
	Terrain	2.4	①	①	①	①	①	①	①
	Terrain	3.0	①	①	①	①	①	①	①

DOT: Department Of Transportation

① The Recommended Fluids and Lubricants information will be found in the Owner's Manual. Refer to the Maintenance Schedule subsection of the Owner's Manual

25742_EQUI_C0005

VALVE SPECIFICATIONS

Year	Engine Displacement Liters	Engine ID/VIN	Seat Angle (deg.)	Face Angle (deg.)	Closed Spring Test Pressure (lbs. @ in.)	Spring Free-Length (in.)	Spring Installed Height (in.)	Stem-to-Guide Clearance (in.) Intake	Exhaust	Stem Diameter (in.) Intake	Exhaust
2010	2.4	C	45	45	55-61@1.28	1.63-1.74	1.279	0.0012-0.0022	0.0020-0.0026	0.2344-0.2355	0.2337-0.2343
	3.0	5	45	44.25	56-61@1.378	0.945	1.378	0.0010-0.0026	0.0014-0.0030	0.2344-0.2352	0.2341-0.2348
2011	2.4	C	45	45	55-61@1.28	1.63-1.74	1.279	0.0012-0.0022	0.0020-0.0026	0.2344-0.2355	0.2337-0.2343
	3.0	5	45	44.25	56-61@1.378	0.945	1.378	0.0010-0.0026	0.0014-0.0030	0.2344-0.2352	0.2341-0.2348

25742_EQUI_C0006

CAMSHAFT SPECIFICATIONS

All measurements in inches unless noted

Year	Engine Displacement Liters	Engine Code/VIN	Journal Diameter	Brg. Oil Clearance	Shaft End-play	Runout	Journal Bore	Lobe Height Intake	Lobe Height Exhaust
2010	2.4	C	1.0604-1.0614	N/A	0.0016-0.0057	N/A	N/A	N/A	N/A
	3.0	5	①	0.0016-0.0033	0.0018-0.0085	②	3.5036-3.5042	1.6687-1.6805	1.6715-1.6833
2011	2.4	C	1.0604-1.0614	N/A	0.0016-0.0057	N/A	N/A	N/A	N/A
	3.0	5	①	0.0016-0.0033	0.0018-0.0085	②	3.5036-3.5042	1.6687-1.6805	1.6715-1.6833

N/A: Information not available.

① Front journal diameter: 1.3754-1.3764 in.

   Middle & rear (no. 2-4) diameter: 1.0605-1.0614 in.

② Front & rear journals (no. 1 & 4): 0.0010 in.

   Middle journals (no. 2 & 3): 0.0020 in.

25742_EQUI_C0007

CRANKSHAFT AND CONNECTING ROD SPECIFICATIONS

All measurements are given in inches.

Year	Engine Displacement Liters	Engine ID/VIN	Crankshaft Main Brg. Journal Dia.	Crankshaft Main Brg. Oil Clearance	Crankshaft Shaft End-play	Crankshaft Thrust on No.	Connecting Rod Journal Diameter	Connecting Rod Oil Clearance	Connecting Rod Side Clearance
2010	2.4	C	2.2044-2.2051	0.0012-0.0026	0.0012-0.0150	2	1.9291-1.9297	0.0011-0.0029	0.0028-0.0146
	3.0	5	2.6772	0.0004-0.0024	0.0039-0.0130	3	2.2044-2.2050	0.0004-0.0028	0.0037-0.0140
2011	2.4	C	2.2044-2.2051	0.0012-0.0026	0.0012-0.0150	2	1.9291-1.9297	0.0011-0.0029	0.0028-0.0146
	3.0	5	2.6772	0.0004-0.0024	0.0039-0.0130	3	2.2044-2.2050	0.0004-0.0028	0.0037-0.0140

25742_EQUI_C0008

PISTON AND RING SPECIFICATIONS

All measurements are given in inches.

Year	Engine Displacement Liters	Engine ID/VIN	Piston Clearance	Ring Gap Top Compression	Ring Gap Bottom Compression	Ring Gap Oil Control	Ring Side Clearance Top Compression	Ring Side Clearance Bottom Compression	Ring Side Clearance Oil Control
2010	2.4	C	0.0004-0.0016	0.006-0.012	0.008-0.018	0.006-0.026	0.0015-0.0031	0.0012-0.0030	0.0023-0.0081
	3.0	5	0.0008-0.0013	0.0059-0.0118	0.0110-0.0189	0.0059-0.0236	0.0012-0.0026	0.0006-0.0024	0.0012-0.0669
2011	2.4	C	0.0004-0.0016	0.006-0.012	0.008-0.018	0.006-0.026	0.0015-0.0031	0.0012-0.0030	0.0023-0.0081
	3.0	5	0.0008-0.0013	0.0059-0.0118	0.0110-0.0189	0.0059-0.0236	0.0012-0.0026	0.0006-0.0024	0.0012-0.0669

25742_EQUI_C0009

TORQUE SPECIFICATIONS
All readings in ft. lbs.

Year	Engine Disp. Liters	Engine ID/VIN	Cylinder Head Bolts	Main Bearing Bolts	Rod Bearing Bolts	Crankshaft Damper Bolts	Flywheel Bolts	Manifold Intake	Manifold Exhaust	Spark Plugs	Oil Pan Drain Plug
2010	2.4	C	①	②	③	④	⑤	⑥	⑦	15	18
	3.0	5	⑧	⑨	⑩	⑪	⑫	18	⑬	13	18
2011	2.4	C	①	②	③	④	⑤	⑥	⑦	15	18
	3.0	5	⑧	⑨	⑩	⑪	⑫	18	⑬	13	18

NOTE: Consult "Engine Mechanical" section for applicable tightening sequence illustrations.

① First pass: 22 ft. lbs.

Final pass: additional 155 degrees.

② First pass: 15 ft. lbs.

Final pass: additional 70 degrees.

Lower crankcase perimeter bolts: 18 ft. lbs.

③ First pass: 18 ft. lbs.

Final pass: additional 100 degrees.

④ First pass: 74 ft. lbs.

Final pass: additional 125 degrees.

⑤ First pass: 39 ft. lbs.

Final pass: additional 25 degrees.

⑥ All bolts and nuts, except to cylinder head stud: 89 inch lbs.

Intake manifold to cylinder head stud: 53 ft. lbs.

⑦ Exhaust manifold to cylinder head nut (2 passes): 124 inch lbs.

Exhaust manifold to cylinder head stud: 11 ft. lbs.

⑧ M8 bolts, first pass: 11 ft. lbs.

M8 bolts, Final pass: additional 75 degrees.

M11 bolts, first pass: 22 ft. lbs.

M11 bolts, final pass: additional 150 degrees.

⑨ Inner bolts, first pass: 15 ft. lbs.

Inner bolts, final pass: additional 80 degrees.

Outer bolts, first pass: 11 ft. lbs.

Outer bolts, final pass: additional 110 degrees.

Side bolts, first pass: 22 ft. lbs.

Side bolts, final pass: additional 60 degrees.

⑩ First pass: 22 ft. lbs.

Second pass (counterclockwise): back off to zero.

Third pass: 18 ft. lbs.

Final pass: additional 110 degrees.

⑪ First pass: 74 ft. lbs.

Final pass: additional 150 degrees.

⑫ First pass: 22 ft. lbs.

Final pass: additional 45 degrees.

⑬ Bolts: 15 ft. lbs.

Heat shield bolts: 89 inch lbs.

Studs: 53 inch lbs.

25742_EQUI_C0010

WHEEL ALIGNMENT

Year	Model		Caster Range (+/-Deg.)	Caster Preferred Setting (Deg.)	Camber Range (+/-Deg.)	Camber Preferred Setting (Deg.)	Toe-in (in.)
2010	Equinox	F	0.75	2.45	0.75	-0.40	0.20
		R	—	—	0.75	-0.50	0.10
	Terrain	F	0.75	2.45	0.75	-0.40	0.20
		R	—	—	0.75	-0.50	0.10
2011	Equinox	F	0.75	2.45	0.75	-0.40	0.20
		R	—	—	0.75	-0.50	0.10
	Terrain	F	0.75	2.45	0.75	-0.40	0.20
		R	—	—	0.75	-0.50	0.10

F: Front

R: Rear

25742_EQUI_C0011

TIRE, WHEEL AND BALL JOINT SPECIFICATIONS

Year	Model	OEM Tires Standard	OEM Tires Optional	Tire Pressures (psi) Front	Tire Pressures (psi) Rear	Wheel Size	Ball Joint Inspection	Lug Nut (ft. lbs.)
2010	Equinox	225/65R17	①	②	②	17	③	140
	Terrain	225/65R17	①	②	②	17	③	140
2011	Equinox	225/65R17	①	②	②	17	③	140
	Terrain	225/65R17	①	②	②	17	③	140

OEM: Original Equipment Manufacturer

PSI: Pounds Per Square Inch

NA: Information not available

① Optional sizes available: 235/55R18, 255/45R19, 255/40R20

② Consult label on driver's door jamb for applicable pressures.

③ Using dial gauge, if movement at ball joint is more than 0.02 in. (0.5 mm), replace ball joint.

25742_EQUI_C0012

BRAKE SPECIFICATIONS
All measurements in inches unless noted

Year	Model		Brake Disc Original Thickness	Brake Disc Minimum Thickness	Brake Disc Max. Runout	Minimum Pad/Lining Thickness Front	Minimum Pad/Lining Thickness Rear	Brake Caliper Bracket Bolts (ft. lbs.)	Brake Caliper Mounting Bolts (ft. lbs.)
2010	Equinox	Front	N/A	1.06	0.002	0.080	—	140	20
		Rear	N/A	0.72	0.002	—	0.080	92	20
	Terrain	Front	N/A	1.06	0.002	0.080	—	140	20
		Rear	N/A	0.72	0.002	—	0.080	92	20
2011	Equinox	Front	N/A	1.06	0.002	0.080	—	140	20
		Rear	N/A	0.72	0.002	—	0.080	92	20
	Terrain	Front	N/A	1.06	0.002	0.080	—	140	20
		Rear	N/A	0.72	0.002	—	0.080	92	20

F: Front

R: Rear

N/A: Information not available

25742_EQUI_C0013

MAINTENANCE I AND II SERVICE SCHEDULES
EQUINOX, TORRENT, TERRAIN

When the CHANGE ENGINE OIL light appears, certain services and inspections are required.

Required services are described as Maintenance I and Maintenance II.

The first service of a vehicle should be Maintenance I, and the second service should be Maintenance II.

Alternate between the 2 services thereafter. However, in some cases, Maintenance II may be required more often.

Maintenance I: Use Maintenance I if the CHANGE ENGINE OIL light comes on within 10 months since the vehicle was purchased or, if Maintenance II was performed.

Maintenance II: Use Maintenance II if the previous service performed was Maintenance I. Always use Maintenance II whenever the CHANGE ENGINE OIL light comes on 10 months or more since the last service, or, if the CHANGE ENGINE OIL light has not come on at all for one year.

Service Item	Maintenance I	Maintenance II
Change the engine oil and filter.	✓	✓
Reset the oil life system.	✓	✓
Visually inspect the vehicle for leaks or damage. A fluid loss in the vehicle system could indicate a problem. Inspect, repair and add fluid to the system if necessary.	✓	✓
Inspect the engine air cleaner filter. If necessary, replace the filter.	✓	✓
Rotate the tires. Inspect the tire inflation pressures and the tire wear.	✓	✓
Visually inspect the brake lines and hoses for proper hook-up, binding, leaks, cracks, chafing, etc. Inspect the disc brake pads for wear and the rotors for surface condition. Inspect the drum brake linings for wear or cracks. Inspect other brake parts, including drums, wheel cylinders, calipers, parking brake, etc. Inspect the parking brake adjustment.	✓	✓
Inspect engine coolant and windshield washer fluid levels. Add fluid as needed.	✓	✓
Inspect the suspension and steering components. Inspect the front and rear suspension and the steering system for damaged, loose or missing parts, or signs of wear. Inspect the power steering lines and the hoses for proper hook-up, binding, leaks, cracks,	—	✓
Ensure the safety belt reminder light and all the belts, buckles, latch plates, retractors and anchorages are working properly. Look for any other loose or damaged safety belt system parts. If you see anything that might keep a safety belt system from working correctly, repair or replaced the damaged part. Replace torn or frayed safety belts, refer to Operational and Functional Checks in Seat Belts. Inspect for any opened or broken air bag coverings, and repair or replace as needed. The air bag system does require regular maintenance.	—	✓
Visually inspect the coolant hoses and replace the hoses if they are cracked, swollen or deteriorated. Inspect all pipes, fittings and clamps; replace with GM parts as needed. To help ensure proper operation, a pressure test of the cooling system and pressure cap and cleaning the outside of the radiator and air conditioning condenser is recommended at least once a year.	—	✓
Inspect the front and rear suspension and the steering system for damaged, loose or missing parts, or signs of wear. Inspect power steering lines and hoses for proper hook-up, binding, leaks, cracks, chafing, etc.	—	✓
Inspect the throttle system for interference or binding and for damaged or missing parts. Replace the parts as needed. Replace any components that have high effort or excessive wear. Do not lubricate the accelerator or the cruise control cables.	—	✓

To reset the CHANGE ENGINE OIL light:

1. Turn the ignition key to the ON/RUN position with the engine OFF.
2. Press and release the stem in the lower center of the instrument cluster until the OIL LIFE message is displayed.
3. Once the alternating OIL LIFE and RESET messages appear, press and hold the stem until several beeps sound.
    This confirms that the oil life system has been reset to 100 percent.
4. Turn the ignition key to the OFF position.
    If the CHANGE ENGINE OIL message comes back on when the vehicle is started, the engine oil life system has not been reset. Repeat the procedure.

ADDITIONAL MAINTENANCE SERVICES - NORMAL
EQUINOX, TORRENT, TERRAIN

TO BE SERVICED	TYPE OF SERVICE	VEHICLE MILEAGE INTERVAL (x1000)					
		25	50	75	100	125	150
Engine coolant	Replace						✓
Air cleaner filter	Replace		✓		✓		✓
Automatic transmision fluid & filter	Replace				✓		
Spark plugs	Replace				✓		
Transfer case fluid	Replace				✓		
Exhaust system & heat shields	Service/ Inspect	✓	✓	✓	✓	✓	✓
Cooling system hoses and clamps	Service/ Inspect	✓	✓	✓	✓	✓	✓
Fuel system	Inspect	✓	✓	✓	✓	✓	✓
Accessory drive belt	Replace						✓
Evaporative control system	Inspect		✓		✓		✓
Passenger compartment air filter	Replace	✓	✓	✓	✓	✓	✓

25742_EQUI_C0015

ADDITIONAL MAINTENANCE SERVICES - SEVERE
EQUINOX, TORRENT, TERRAIN

TO BE SERVICED	TYPE OF SERVICE	VEHICLE MILEAGE INTERVAL (x1000)					
		25	50	75	100	125	150
Engine coolant	Replace						✓
Air cleaner filter	Replace	✓	✓	✓	✓	✓	✓
Automatic transaxle fluid	Replace		✓		✓		✓
Spark plugs	Replace				✓		✓
Transfer case fluid	Replace		✓		✓		✓
Exhaust system & heat shields	Service/ Inspect	✓	✓	✓	✓	✓	✓
Cooling system hoses and clamps	Service/ Inspect	✓	✓	✓	✓	✓	✓
Fuel system	Inspect	✓	✓	✓	✓	✓	✓
Accessory drive belt	Replace						✓
Evaporative control system	Inspect		✓		✓		✓
Passenger compartment air filter	Replace	✓	✓	✓	✓	✓	✓

25742_EQUI_C0016

PRECAUTIONS

Before servicing any vehicle, please be sure to read all of the following precautions, which deal with personal safety, prevention of component damage, and important points to take into consideration when servicing a motor vehicle:

• Never open, service or drain the radiator or cooling system when the engine is hot; serious burns can occur from the steam and hot coolant.

• Observe all applicable safety precautions when working around fuel. Whenever servicing the fuel system, always work in a well-ventilated area. Do not allow fuel spray or vapors to come in contact with a spark, open flame, or excessive heat (a hot drop light, for example). Keep a dry chemical fire extinguisher near the work area. Always keep fuel in a container specifically designed for fuel storage; also, always properly seal fuel containers to avoid the possibility of fire or explosion. Refer to the additional fuel system precautions later in this section.

• Fuel injection systems often remain pressurized, even after the engine has been turned **OFF**. The fuel system pressure must be relieved before disconnecting any fuel lines. Failure to do so may result in fire and/or personal injury.

• Brake fluid often contains polyglycol ethers and polyglycols. Avoid contact with the eyes and wash your hands thoroughly after handling brake fluid. If you do get brake fluid in your eyes, flush your eyes with clean, running water for 15 minutes. If eye irritation persists, or if you have taken brake fluid internally, IMMEDIATELY seek medical assistance.

• The EPA warns that prolonged contact with used engine oil may cause a number of skin disorders, including cancer. You should make every effort to minimize your exposure to used engine oil. Protective gloves should be worn when changing oil. Wash your hands and any other exposed skin areas as soon as possible after exposure to used engine oil. Soap and water, or waterless hand cleaner should be used.

• All new vehicles are now equipped with an air bag system, often referred to as a Supplemental Restraint System (SRS) or Supplemental Inflatable Restraint (SIR) system. The system must be disabled before performing service on or around system components, steering column, instrument panel components, wiring and sensors. Failure to follow safety and disabling procedures could result in accidental air bag deployment, possible personal injury and unnecessary system repairs.

• Always wear safety goggles when working with, or around, the air bag system. When carrying a non-deployed air bag, be sure the bag and trim cover are pointed away from your body. When placing a non-deployed air bag on a work surface, always face the bag and trim cover upward, away from the surface. This will reduce the motion of the module if it is accidentally deployed. Refer to the additional air bag system precautions later in this section.

• Clean, high quality brake fluid from a sealed container is essential to the safe and proper operation of the brake system. You should always buy the correct type of brake fluid for your vehicle. If the brake fluid becomes contaminated, completely flush the system with new fluid. Never reuse any brake fluid. Any brake fluid that is removed from the system should be discarded. Also, do not allow any brake fluid to come in contact with a painted surface; it will damage the paint.

• Never operate the engine without the proper amount and type of engine oil; doing so WILL result in severe engine damage.

• Timing belt maintenance is extremely important. Many models utilize an interference-type, non-freewheeling engine. If the timing belt breaks, the valves in the cylinder head may strike the pistons, causing potentially serious (also time-consuming and expensive) engine damage. Refer to the maintenance interval charts for the recommended replacement interval for the timing belt, and to the timing belt section for belt replacement and inspection.

• Disconnecting the negative battery cable on some vehicles may interfere with the functions of the on-board computer system(s) and may require the computer to undergo a relearning process once the negative battery cable is reconnected.

• When servicing drum brakes, only disassemble and assemble one side at a time, leaving the remaining side intact for reference.

• Only an MVAC-trained, EPA-certified automotive technician should service the air conditioning system or its components.

BRAKES

ANTI-LOCK BRAKE SYSTEM (ABS)

GENERAL INFORMATION

PRECAUTIONS

• Certain components within the ABS system are not intended to be serviced or repaired individually.

• Do not use rubber hoses or other parts not specifically specified for and ABS system. When using repair kits, replace all parts included in the kit. Partial or incorrect repair may lead to functional problems and require the replacement of components.

• Lubricate rubber parts with clean, fresh brake fluid to ease assembly. Do not use shop air to clean parts; damage to rubber components may result.

• Use only DOT 3 brake fluid from an unopened container.

• If any hydraulic component or line is removed or replaced, it may be necessary to bleed the entire system.

• A clean repair area is essential. Always clean the reservoir and cap thoroughly before removing the cap. The slightest amount of dirt in the fluid may plug an orifice and impair the system function. Perform repairs after components have been thoroughly cleaned; use only denatured alcohol to clean components. Do not allow ABS components to come into contact with any substance containing mineral oil; this includes used shop rags.

• The Anti-Lock control unit is a microprocessor similar to other computer units in the vehicle. Ensure that the ignition switch is **OFF** before removing or installing controller harnesses. Avoid static electricity discharge at or near the controller.

• If any arc welding is to be done on the vehicle, the control unit should be unplugged before welding operations begin.

SPEED SENSORS

REMOVAL & INSTALLATION

Front

See Figure 1.

1. Raise and support the vehicle.
2. Remove the tire and wheel assembly.
3. Disconnect the wheel speed sensor electrical connector.
4. Remove the front brake hose bracket nut.
5. Release the front wheel speed sensor harness from the retainers on the front brake hose.

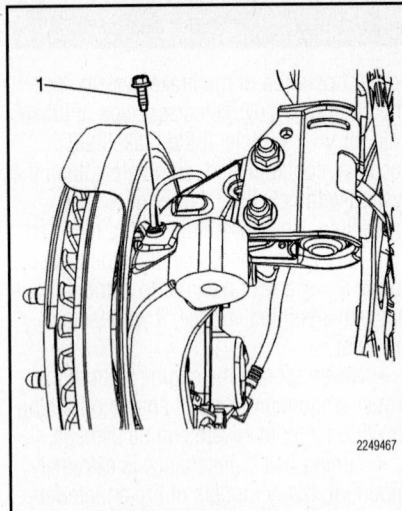

Fig. 1 Removing the front wheel speed sensor bolt (1)

6. Remove the wheel speed sensor bolt.

7. Remove the wheel speed sensor by pulling the sensor straight upward from the steering knuckle.

To install:

8. Install the wheel speed sensor to the steering knuckle.

9. Install the wheel speed sensor bolt and tighten to 89 inch lbs. (10 Nm).

10. Install the front brake hose bracket nut and tighten to 89 inch lbs. (10 Nm).

11. Connect the wheel speed sensor electrical connector.

12. Install the front wheel speed sensor harness to the retainers on the front brake hose.

13. Install the tire and wheel assembly.

Rear

See Figure 2.

1. Raise and support the vehicle.

2. Remove the tire and wheel.

3. Remove the park brake shoes. See "Parking Brake" in this section.

4. Remove the wheel speed sensor electrical connector, the sensor bolt and the wheel speed sensor.

   a. Release the wheel speed sensor electrical harness grommet from the backing plate.

   b. Route the wheel speed sensor electrical harness through the backing plate.

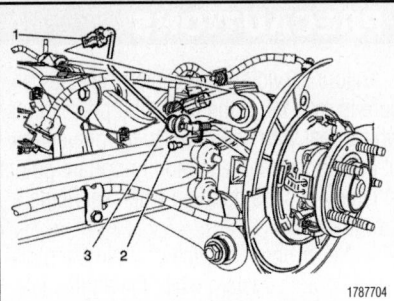

Fig. 2 Remove the wheel speed sensor electrical connector (1), the sensor bolt (2) and the wheel speed sensor(3).

To install:

5. Route the wheel speed sensor electrical harness through the backing plate.

6. Reposition the grommet.

7. Install the wheel speed sensor, the sensor bolt and the wheel speed sensor electrical connector. Tighten bolt to 89 inch lbs. (10 Nm).

8. Install the parking brake shoes.

9. Install the tire and wheel. Torque the wheel nuts, in a criss-cross pattern, to 140 ft. lbs. (190 Nm).

BRAKES

BLEEDING THE BRAKE SYSTEM

BRAKE SYSTEM BLEEDING

ABS SYSTEM AUTOMATED BLEED

1. Before performing the antilock brake system (ABS) Automated Bleed Procedure, first perform a manual or pressure bleed of the base brake system. Refer to Hydraulic Brake System Bleeding. The automated bleed procedure is recommended when one of the following conditions exist:

- Base brake system bleeding does not achieve the desired pedal height or feel
- Extreme loss of brake fluid has occurred
- Air ingestion is suspected in the secondary circuits of the brake modulator assembly

➡The ABS Automated Bleed Procedure uses a scan tool to cycle the system solenoid valves and run the pump in order to purge any air from the secondary circuits. These circuits are normally closed off, and are only opened during system initialization at vehicle start up and during ABS operation. The automated bleed procedure opens these secondary circuits and allows

any air trapped in these circuits to flow out toward the brake corners.

Automated Bleed Procedure

✳✳ CAUTION

The Auto Bleed Procedure may be terminated at any time during the process by pressing the EXIT button. No further Scan Tool prompts pertaining to the Auto Bleed procedure will be given. After exiting the bleed procedure, relieve bleed pressure and disconnect bleed equipment per manufacturer's instructions. Failure to properly relieve pressure may result in spilled brake fluid causing damage to components and painted surfaces.

1. Raise and support the vehicle.

2. Remove all 4 tire and wheel assemblies.

3. Inspect the brake system for leaks and visual damage. Repair or replace components as needed.

4. Lower the vehicle.

5. Inspect the battery state of charge.

6. Install a scan tool.

7. Turn the ignition ON, with the engine OFF.

8. With the scan tool, establish communications with the ABS system. Select "Special Functions". Select "Automated Bleed" from the Special Functions menu.

9. Raise and support the vehicle.

10. Following the directions given on the scan tool, pressure bleed the base brake system. Refer to "Hydraulic Brake System Bleeding".

11. Follow the scan tool directions until the desired brake pedal height is achieved.

12. If the bleed procedure is aborted, a malfunction exists. Perform the following steps before resuming the bleed procedure:

   a. If a DTC is detected, refer to applicable Diagnostic Trouble Code (DTC) List and diagnose the appropriate DTC.

   b. If the brake pedal feels spongy, perform the conventional brake bleed procedure again. Refer to "Hydraulic Brake System Bleeding".

13. When the desired pedal height is achieved, press the brake pedal to inspect for firmness.

14. Lower the vehicle.

15. Remove the scan tool.

16. Install the tire and wheel assemblies.

17. Inspect the brake fluid level.

18. Road test the vehicle while inspecting that the pedal remains high and firm.

HYDRAULIC SYSTEM MANUAL BLEEDING

1. Place a clean shop cloth beneath the brake master cylinder to prevent brake fluid spills.

2. With the ignition OFF and the brakes cool, apply the brakes 3–5 times, or until the brake pedal effort increases significantly, in order to deplete the brake booster power reserve.

3. If you have performed a brake master cylinder bench bleeding on this vehicle, or if you disconnected the brake pipes from the master cylinder, you must perform the following steps:

   a. Ensure that the brake master cylinder reservoir is full to the maximum-fill level.

   b. If necessary, add GM approved brake fluid from a clean, sealed brake fluid container.

4. If removal of the reservoir cap and diaphragm is necessary, clean the outside of the reservoir on and around the cap prior to removal.

5. With the rear brake pipe installed securely to the master cylinder, loosen and separate the front brake pipe from the front port of the brake master cylinder.

6. Allow a small amount of brake fluid to gravity bleed from the open port of the master cylinder.

7. Reconnect the brake pipe to the master cylinder port and tighten securely.

8. Have an assistant slowly depress the brake pedal fully and maintain steady pressure on the pedal.

9. Loosen the same brake pipe to purge air from the open port of the master cylinder.

10. Tighten the brake pipe, then have the assistant slowly release the brake pedal.

11. Wait 15 seconds, then repeat above steps until all air is purged from the same port of the master cylinder.

12. With the front brake pipe installed securely to the master cylinder, after all air has been purged from the front port of the master cylinder, loosen and separate the rear brake pipe from the master cylinder, then repeat above steps.

13. After completing the final master cylinder port bleeding procedure, ensure that both of the brake pipe-to-master cylinder fittings are properly tightened.

14. Fill the brake master cylinder reservoir with GM approved brake fluid from a clean, sealed brake fluid container. Ensure that the brake master cylinder reservoir remains at least half-full during this bleeding procedure. Add fluid as needed to maintain the proper level.

15. Clean the outside of the reservoir on and around the reservoir cap prior to removing the cap and diaphragm.

16. Install a proper box-end wrench onto the RIGHT REAR wheel hydraulic circuit bleeder valve.

17. Install a transparent hose over the end of the bleeder valve.

18. Submerge the open end of the transparent hose into a transparent container partially filled with GM approved brake fluid from a clean, sealed brake fluid container.

19. Have an assistant slowly depress the brake pedal fully and maintain steady pressure on the pedal.

20. Loosen the bleeder valve to purge air from the wheel hydraulic circuit.

21. Tighten the bleeder valve, then have the assistant slowly release the brake pedal.

22. Wait 15 seconds, then repeat above steps until all air is purged from the same wheel hydraulic circuit.

23. With the right rear wheel hydraulic circuit bleeder valve tightened securely, after all air has been purged from the right rear hydraulic circuit, install a proper box-end wrench onto the LEFT FRONT wheel hydraulic circuit bleeder valve.

24. Install a transparent hose over the end of the bleeder valve, then repeat previous steps.

25. With the left front wheel hydraulic circuit bleeder valve tightened securely, after all air has been purged from the left front hydraulic circuit, install a proper box-end wrench onto the LEFT REAR wheel hydraulic circuit bleeder valve.

26. Install a transparent hose over the end of the bleeder valve, then repeat previous steps.

27. With the left rear wheel hydraulic circuit bleeder valve tightened securely, after all air has been purged from the left rear hydraulic circuit, install a proper box-end wrench onto the RIGHT FRONT wheel hydraulic circuit bleeder valve.

28. Install a transparent hose over the end of the bleeder valve, then previous repeat steps.

29. After completing the final wheel hydraulic circuit bleeding procedure, ensure that each of the 4 wheel hydraulic circuit bleeder valves are properly tightened.

30. Fill the brake master cylinder reservoir to the maximum-fill level with GM approved brake fluid from a clean, sealed brake fluid container.

31. Slowly depress and release the brake pedal. Observe the feel of the brake pedal.

➡**If it is determined that air was inducted into the system upstream of the ABS modulator prior to servicing, the "Antilock Brake System Automated Bleed" must be performed.**

32. If the brake pedal feels spongy, repeat the bleeding procedure again. If the brake pedal still feels spongy after repeating the bleeding procedure, perform the following steps:

   a. Inspect the brake system for external leaks.

   b. Pressure bleed the hydraulic brake system in order to purge any air that may still be trapped in the system.

33. Turn the ignition key ON, with the engine OFF. Check to see if the brake system warning lamp remains illuminated.

❋❋ CAUTION

DO NOT allow the vehicle to be driven until it is diagnosed and repaired.

34. If the brake system warning lamp remains illuminated, perform further diagnosis on this circuit.

HYDRAULIC SYSTEM PRESSURE BLEEDING

1. Place a clean shop cloth beneath the brake master cylinder to prevent brake fluid spills.

2. With the ignition OFF and the brakes cool, apply the brakes 3–5 times, or until the brake pedal effort increases significantly, in order to deplete the brake booster power reserve.

3. If you have performed a brake master cylinder bench bleeding on this vehicle, or if you disconnected the brake pipes from the master cylinder, you must perform the following step:

   a. Ensure that the brake master cylinder reservoir is full to the maximum-fill level. If necessary, add GM approved brake fluid from a clean, sealed brake fluid container.

   b. If removal of the reservoir cap and diaphragm is necessary, clean the outside of the reservoir on and around the cap prior to removal.

   c. With the rear brake pipe installed securely to the master cylinder, loosen and separate the front brake pipe from the front port of the brake master cylinder.

d. Allow a small amount of brake fluid to gravity bleed from the open port of the master cylinder.

e. Reconnect the brake pipe to the master cylinder port and tighten securely.

f. Have an assistant slowly depress the brake pedal fully and maintain steady pressure on the pedal.

g. Loosen the same brake pipe to purge air from the open port of the master cylinder.

h. Tighten the brake pipe, then have the assistant slowly release the brake pedal.

i. Wait 15 seconds, then repeat applicable steps until all air is purged from the same port of the master cylinder.

j. With the front brake pipe installed securely to the master cylinder, after all air has been purged from the front port of the master cylinder, loosen and separate the rear brake pipe from the master cylinder, then repeat previous steps.

k. After completing the final master cylinder port bleeding procedure, ensure that both of the brake pipe-to-master cylinder fittings are properly tightened.

➡ **Clean the outside of the reservoir on and around the reservoir cap prior to removing the cap and diaphragm.**

4. Fill the brake master cylinder reservoir to the maximum-fill level with GM approved brake fluid from a clean, sealed brake fluid container.

5. Install an appropriate brake pressure bleeder adapter to the brake master cylinder reservoir.

6. Check the brake fluid level in the brake pressure bleeder. Add GM approved brake fluid from a clean, sealed brake fluid container as necessary to bring the level to approximately the half-full point.

7. Connect the brake pressure bleeder to the brake pressure bleeder adapter.

8. Charge the brake pressure bleeder air tank to 25–30 psi.

9. Open the brake pressure bleeder fluid tank valve to allow pressurized brake fluid to enter the brake system.

10. Wait approximately 30 seconds, then inspect the entire hydraulic brake system in order to ensure that there are no existing external brake fluid leaks.

11. Any brake fluid leaks identified require repair prior to completing this procedure.

12. Install a proper box-end wrench onto the RIGHT REAR wheel hydraulic circuit bleeder valve.

13. Install a transparent hose over the end of the bleeder valve.

14. Submerge the open end of the transparent hose into a transparent container partially filled with GM approved brake fluid from a clean, sealed brake fluid container.

15. Loosen the bleeder valve to purge air from the wheel hydraulic circuit. Allow fluid to flow until air bubbles stop flowing from the bleeder, then tighten the bleeder valve.

16. With the right rear wheel hydraulic circuit bleeder valve tightened securely, after all air has been purged from the right rear hydraulic circuit, install a proper box-end wrench onto the LEFT FRONT wheel hydraulic circuit bleeder valve.

17. Install a transparent hose over the end of the bleeder valve, then repeat previous steps.

18. With the left front wheel hydraulic circuit bleeder valve tightened securely, after all air has been purged from the left front hydraulic circuit, install a proper box-end wrench onto the LEFT REAR wheel hydraulic circuit bleeder valve.

19. Install a transparent hose over the end of the bleeder valve, then repeat previous steps.

20. With the left rear wheel hydraulic circuit bleeder valve tightened securely, after all air has been purged from the left rear hydraulic circuit, install a proper box-end wrench onto the RIGHT FRONT wheel hydraulic circuit bleeder valve

21. Install a transparent hose over the end of the bleeder valve, then repeat applicable steps.

22. After completing the final wheel hydraulic circuit bleeding procedure, ensure that each of the 4 wheel hydraulic circuit bleeder valves are properly tightened.

23. Close the brake pressure bleeder fluid tank valve, then disconnect the brake pressure bleeder from the brake pressure bleeder adapter.

24. Remove the brake pressure bleeder adapter from the brake master cylinder reservoir.

25. Fill the brake master cylinder reservoir to the maximum-fill level with GM approved brake fluid from a clean, sealed brake fluid container.

26. Slowly depress and release the brake pedal. Observe the feel of the brake pedal.

➡ **If it is determined that air was inducted into the system upstream of the ABS modulator prior to servicing, the "Antilock Brake System Automated Bleed" must be performed.**

27. If the brake pedal feels spongy, perform the following steps:

a. Inspect the brake system for external leaks.

b. Using a scan tool, perform the antilock brake system automated bleeding procedure to remove any air that may have been trapped in the brake pressure modulator valve (BPMV). Refer to "Antilock Brake System Automated Bleed".

28. Turn the ignition key ON, with the engine OFF. Check to see if the brake system warning lamp remains illuminated.

❄❄ CAUTION

DO NOT allow the vehicle to be driven until it is diagnosed and repaired.

29. If the brake system warning lamp remains illuminated, perform further diagnosis on this circuit.

MASTER CYLINDER BLEEDING

Bench Bleeding

See Figure 3.

1. With master cylinder removed from vehicle, secure the mounting flange of the brake master cylinder in a bench vise so that the rear of the primary piston is accessible.

2. Remove the master cylinder reservoir cap and diaphragm.

3. Install suitable fittings to the master cylinder ports that match the type of flare seat required and also provide for hose attachment.

4. Install transparent hoses to the fittings installed to the master cylinder ports, then route the hoses into the master cylinder reservoir.

5. Fill the master cylinder reservoir to at least the half-way point with GM approved brake fluid from a clean, sealed brake fluid container.

6. Ensure that the ends of the transparent hoses running into the master cylinder reservoir are fully submerged in the brake fluid.

7. Using a smooth, round-ended tool, depress and release the primary piston as far as it will travel, a depth of about 1 in. (25 mm), several times. Observe the flow of fluid coming from the ports.

8. As air is bled from the primary and secondary pistons, the effort required to depress the primary piston will increase and the amount of travel will decrease.

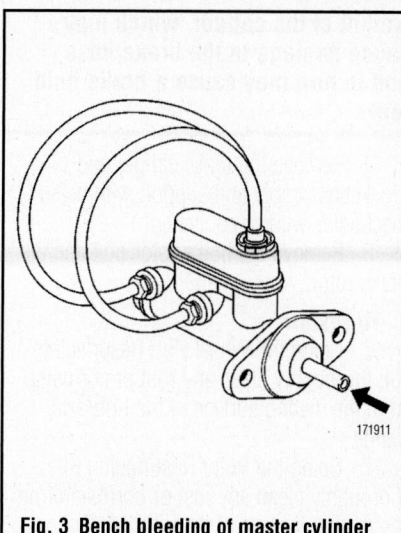

Fig. 3 Bench bleeding of master cylinder

9. Continue to depress and release the primary piston until fluid flows freely from the ports with no evidence of air bubbles.

10. Remove the transparent hoses from the master cylinder reservoir.

11. Install the master cylinder reservoir cap and diaphragm.

12. Remove the fittings with the transparent hoses from the master cylinder ports. Wrap the master cylinder with a clean shop cloth to prevent brake fluid spills.

13. Remove the master cylinder from the vise.

FLUID FILL PROCEDURE

1. Visually inspect the brake fluid level through the brake master cylinder reservoir.

2. If the brake fluid level is at or below the half-full point during routine fluid checks, the brake system should be inspected for wear and possible brake fluid leaks.

3. If the brake fluid level is at or below the half-full point during routine fluid checks, and an inspection of the brake system did not reveal wear or brake fluid leaks, the brake fluid may be topped-off up to the maximum-fill level.

4. If brake system service was just completed, the brake fluid may be topped-off up to the maximum-fill level.

5. If the brake fluid level is above the half-full point, adding brake fluid is not recommended under normal conditions.

6. If brake fluid is to be added to the master cylinder reservoir, clean the outside of the reservoir on and around the reservoir cap prior to removing the cap and diaphragm. Use only GM approved brake fluid from a clean, sealed brake fluid container.

BRAKES

✳✳ CAUTION

Dust and dirt accumulating on brake parts during normal use may contain asbestos fibers from production or aftermarket brake linings. Breathing excessive concentrations of asbestos fibers can cause serious bodily harm. Exercise care when servicing brake parts. Do not sand or grind brake lining unless equipment used is designed to contain the dust residue. Do not clean brake parts with compressed air or by dry brushing. Cleaning should be done by dampening the brake components with a fine mist of water, then wiping the brake components clean with a dampened cloth. Dispose of cloth and all residue containing asbestos fibers in an impermeable container with the appropriate label. Follow practices prescribed by the Occupational Safety and Health Administration (OSHA) and the Environmental Protection Agency (EPA) for the handling, processing, and disposing of dust or debris that may contain asbestos fibers.

BRAKE CALIPER

REMOVAL & INSTALLATION

See Figure 4.

1. Raise and support the vehicle.
2. Remove the tire and wheel assembly.

3. Remove the brake hose fitting bolt at the caliper.

➡**Do not reuse the brake hose fitting gaskets.**

4. Remove and discard the brake hose fitting gaskets from the brake hose fitting.

5. Cap the brake hose fitting to prevent brake fluid loss and contamination.

✳✳ CAUTION

DO NOT use any air tools to remove or install the guide pin bolts. Use hand tools ONLY. Install an open end wrench to hold the caliper guide pin in line with the brake caliper while removing or installing the caliper

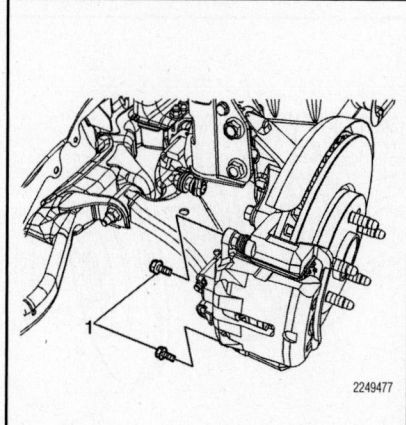

Fig. 4 Removing the brake caliper guide pin bolts (1)

FRONT DISC BRAKES

guide pin bolt. DO NOT allow the open end wrench to come in contact with the brake caliper. Allowing the open end wrench to come in contact with the brake caliper will cause a pulsation when the brakes are applied.

6. Using a backup wrench to hold the brake caliper guide pin stationary, remove the brake caliper guide pin bolts.

7. Remove the brake caliper.

To install:

8. Install the brake caliper.

9. Hold the brake caliper guide pin stationary and install the brake caliper guide pin bolts and tighten to 20 ft. lbs. (27 Nm).

10. Assemble the brake hose fitting bolt and the new brake hose fitting gaskets to the front brake hose fitting.

11. Install the brake hose assembly and tighten the brake hose fitting bolt to 30 ft. lbs. (40 Nm).

12. Bleed the hydraulic brake system, as described in this section.

13. Install the tire and wheel assembly.

DISC BRAKE PADS

REMOVAL & INSTALLATION

See Figure 5.

1. Inspect the fluid level in the brake master cylinder reservoir. If the brake fluid level is midway between the maximum-full

point and the minimum allowable level, no brake fluid needs to be removed before proceeding. If the brake fluid level is higher than midway between the maximum-full point and the minimum allowable level, remove brake fluid to the midway point before proceeding.

2. Raise and support the vehicle.

3. Remove the tire and wheel assembly.

4. Place a large C-clamp over the brake caliper body and against the outer brake pad.

5. Using the C-clamp, compress the brake caliper piston fully into the brake caliper bore.

❊❊ CAUTION

DO NOT use any air tools to remove or install the guide pin bolts. Use hand tools ONLY. Install an open end wrench to hold the caliper guide pin in line with the brake caliper while removing or installing the caliper guide pin bolt. DO NOT allow the open end wrench to come in contact with the brake caliper. Allowing the open end wrench to come in contact with the brake caliper will cause a pulsation when the brakes are applied.

6. Using a backup wrench to hold the brake caliper guide pin stationary, remove the lower brake caliper guide pin bolt. Pivot the brake caliper upward.

7. Note the location of the brake pad wear sensor for correct installation.

8. Remove the inner brake pad and the outer brake pad.

9. Remove the upper and lower brake pad springs. If installing new brake pads, discard the springs.

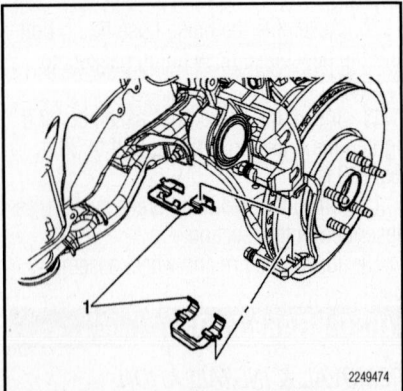

Fig. 5 Remove the upper and lower brake pad springs (1). If installing new brake pads, discard the eqrings.

To install:

10. Install the upper and lower brake pad springs.

11. Install the inner brake pad and the outer brake pad, noting the proper location of the wear sensor.

Pivot the brake caliper to the installed position.

12. Using a backup wrench to hold the brake caliper guide pin stationary, install the lower brake caliper guide pin bolt and tighten to 20 ft. lbs. (27 Nm).

13. Install the tire and wheel assembly.

14. With the engine OFF, gradually apply the brake pedal to approximately 2/3 of its travel distance.

Slowly release the brake pedal.

15. Wait 15 seconds, then repeat previous steps until a firm brake pedal is obtained. This will properly seat the brake caliper piston and brake pads.

16. Fill the master cylinder reservoir.

17. Burnish the brake pads and rotors. Refer to "Brake Pad & Rotor Burnishing".

DISC BRAKE ROTORS

REMOVAL & INSTALLATION

See Figure 6.

1. Raise and support the vehicle.
2. Remove the tire and wheel assembly.
3. Remove the brake caliper bracket bolts.

❊❊ CAUTION

Support the brake caliper with heavy mechanic wire, or equivalent, whenever it is separated from its mount and the hydraulic flexible brake hose is still connected. Failure to support the caliper in this manner will cause the flexible brake hose to bear the

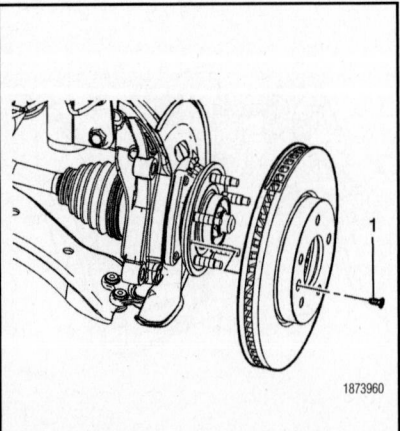

Fig. 6 Removing brake rotor and bolt(s) (1)

weight of the caliper, which may cause damage to the brake hose and in turn may cause a brake fluid leak.

4. Remove the brake caliper and bracket assembly and support with heavy mechanics wire or equivalent.

5. Remove the brake rotor bolt and the brake rotor.

To install:

6. Using the Wheel Hub Resurfacing Kit, thoroughly clean any rust or corrosion from the mating surface of the hub/axle flange.

7. Using the Rotor Resurfacing Kit, thoroughly clean any rust or corrosion from the mating surface of the rotor to the hub/axle flange.

8. Install the brake rotor.

9. Install the brake rotor bolt and tighten to 80 inch lbs. (9 Nm).

10. Position the brake caliper and bracket assembly to the vehicle.

➡️**If reusing the caliper bracket bolts the threads of the caliper bracket bolts and the threads of the knuckle mounting holes must be free of residue and debris prior to application of threadlocker in order to ensure proper adhesion and fastener retention.**

11. Prepare the bolts and the threaded holes for assembly:

a. Thoroughly clean the residue from the bolt threads by using denatured alcohol or equivalent and allow to dry.

b. Thoroughly clean the residue from the threaded holes by using denatured alcohol or equivalent and allow to dry.

12. Apply threadlocker (GM P/N 12345493, or equivalent), to 2/3 of the threaded length of the lower caliper bracket bolts. Ensure there are no gaps in the threadlocker along the length of the filled area of the bolts.

13. Ensure there are no gaps in the threadlocker along the length of the filled area of the bolts.

14. Allow the threadlocker to cure approximately 10 minutes before installation.

15. Install the brake caliper bracket bolts and tighten to 140 ft. lbs. (190 Nm).

16. Install the tire and wheel assembly.

17. Burnish the brake pads and rotors. Refer to "Brake Pad & Rotor Burnishing".

BRAKE PAD & ROTOR BURNISHING

BURNISHING PROCEDURE

➡Burnishing the brake pads and brake rotors is necessary in order to ensure that the braking surfaces are properly prepared after service has been performed on the disc brake system.

➡This procedure should be performed whenever the disc brake rotors have been refinished or replaced, and/or whenever the disc brake pads have been replaced.

1. Select a smooth road with little or no traffic.
2. Accelerate the vehicle to 30 mph.

➡Use care to avoid overheating the brakes while performing this step.

3. Using moderate to firm pressure, apply the brakes to bring the vehicle to a stop. Do not allow the brakes to lock.
4. Repeat steps until approximately 20 stops have been completed. Allow sufficient cooling periods between stops in order to properly burnish the brake pads and rotors.

BRAKES

❊❊ CAUTION

Dust and dirt accumulating on brake parts during normal use may contain asbestos fibers from production or aftermarket brake linings. Breathing excessive concentrations of asbestos fibers can cause serious bodily harm. Exercise care when servicing brake parts. Do not sand or grind brake lining unless equipment used is designed to contain the dust residue. Do not clean brake parts with compressed air or by dry brushing. Cleaning should be done by dampening the brake components with a fine mist of water, then wiping the brake components clean with a dampened cloth. Dispose of cloth and all residue containing asbestos fibers in an impermeable container with the appropriate label. Follow practices prescribed by the Occupational Safety and Health Administration (OSHA) and the Environmental Protection Agency (EPA) for the handling, processing, and disposing of dust or debris that may contain asbestos fibers.

BRAKE CALIPER

REMOVAL & INSTALLATION
See Figure 7.

1. Raise and support the vehicle.
2. Remove the tire and wheel assembly.
3. Remove the brake hose fitting bolt and remove the brake hose fitting from the brake caliper.

➡Do not reuse the brake hose fitting gaskets.

4. Remove and discard the brake hose fitting gaskets.
5. Cap the brake hose fitting to prevent brake fluid loss and contamination.

❊❊ CAUTION

DO NOT use any air tools to remove or install the guide pin bolts. Use hand tools ONLY. Install an open end wrench to hold the caliper guide pin in line with the brake caliper while removing or installing the caliper guide pin bolt. DO NOT allow the open end wrench to come in contact with the brake caliper. Allowing the open end wrench to come in contact with the brake caliper will cause a pulsation when the brakes are applied.

6. Hold the brake caliper guide pin stationary and remove the brake caliper guide pin bolts.
7. Remove the brake caliper.

To install:
8. Install the brake caliper.
9. Hold the brake caliper guide pin stationary and install the brake caliper guide pin bolts and tighten to 20 ft. lbs. (27 Nm).
10. Assemble the brake hose fitting bolt to the brake hose fitting with new brake hose fitting gaskets.

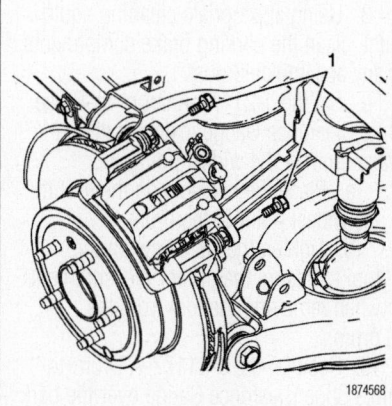

Fig. 7 Hold the brake caliper guide pin stationary and remove the brake caliper guide pin bolts (1).

REAR DISC BRAKES

11. Install the brake hose assembly to the brake caliper and tighten the brake hose fitting bolt to 38 ft. lbs. (52 Nm).
12. Bleed the hydraulic brake system.
13. Install the tire and wheel assembly.

DISC BRAKE PADS

REMOVAL & INSTALLATION

1. Inspect the fluid level in the brake master cylinder reservoir.
   a. If the brake fluid level is midway between the maximum-full point and the minimum allowable level, no brake fluid needs to be removed before proceeding.
   b. If the brake fluid level is higher than midway between the maximum-full point and the minimum allowable level, remove brake fluid to the midway point before proceeding.
2. Raise and support the vehicle.
3. Remove the tire and wheel assembly.

❊❊ CAUTION

DO NOT use any air tools to remove or install the guide pin bolts. Use hand tools ONLY. Install an open end wrench to hold the caliper guide pin in line with the brake caliper while removing or installing the caliper guide pin bolt. DO NOT allow the open end wrench to come in contact with the brake caliper. Allowing the open end wrench to come in contact with the brake caliper will cause a pulsation when the brakes are applied.

4. Hold the brake caliper guide pin stationary and remove the lower brake caliper guide pin bolt.
5. Pivot the brake caliper upward.
6. Place a block of wood or an old brake pad against the brake caliper pistons.
7. Using a brake pad spreader tool or equivalent, fully seat the caliper piston in the caliper bore.
8. Note the location of the brake pad wear sensor for correct installation.

9. Remove the outer brake pad and the inner brake pad.

10. Remove the upper and lower brake pad springs.

➡ **If installing new brake pads, discard the springs.**

To install:

➡ **If installing new brake pads, install new springs.**

11. Install the upper and lower brake pad springs.

12. Install the outer brake pad and the inner brake pad, making sure the wear sensor is in proper location.

13. Pivot the brake caliper to the installed position.

14. Using a backup wrench to hold the brake caliper guide pin stationary, install the lower brake caliper guide pin bolt and tighten to 20 ft. lbs. (27 Nm).

15. Install the tire and wheel assembly.

16. With the engine OFF, gradually apply the brake pedal to approximately 2/3 of its travel distance.

17. Slowly release the brake pedal. Wait 15 seconds, then repeat previous steps until a firm brake pedal is obtained. This will properly seat the brake caliper pistons and brake pads.

18. Fill the master cylinder reservoir.

19. Burnish the brake pads and rotors. See procedure under "Front Disc Brakes" section.

DISC BRAKE ROTORS

REMOVAL & INSTALLATION

1. Raise and support the vehicle.
2. Remove the tire and wheel assembly.
3. Remove the brake caliper bracket bolts.
4. Remove the brake caliper and bracket assembly and support with heavy mechanics wire or equivalent.
5. Remove the brake rotor bolt and the brake rotor.
6. If the brake rotor is difficult to remove, remove the park brake shoe adjuster access plug on the face of the brake rotor to gain access to the park brake adjuster and loosen the park brake shoe adjuster.

To install:

7. Using the J-42450-A Wheel Hub Resurfacing Kit, thoroughly clean any rust or corrosion from the mating surface of the hub/axle flange.

8. Using the J-41013 Rotor Resurfacing Kit, thoroughly clean any rust or corrosion from the mating surface of the rotor to the hub/axle flange.

9. Install the brake rotor.

10. Install the brake rotor bolt and tighten to 89 inch lbs. (10 Nm).

11. Position the brake caliper and bracket assembly to the vehicle.

➡ **If reusing the caliper bracket bolts the threads of the caliper bracket bolts**

and the threads of the knuckle mounting holes must be free of residue and debris prior to application of threadlocker in order to ensure proper adhesion and fastener retention.

12. Prepare the bolts and the threaded holes for assembly:

a. Thoroughly clean the residue from the bolt threads by using denatured alcohol or equivalent and allow to dry.

b. Thoroughly clean the residue from the threaded holes by using denatured alcohol or equivalent and allow to dry.

c. Apply threadlocker GM P/N 12345493 (Canada P/N 10953488), or equivalent to 2/3 of the threaded length of the lower caliper bracket bolts. Ensure there are no gaps in the threadlocker along the length of the filled area of the bolts.

d. Ensure there are no gaps in the threadlocker along the length of the filled area of the bolts.

13. Allow the threadlocker to cure approximately 10 minutes before installation.

14. Install the brake caliper bracket bolts and tighten to 92 ft. lbs. (125 Nm).

15. If necessary, adjust the park brake. Refer to "Parking Brake Adjustment" in this section.

16. Install the tire and wheel assembly.

17. Burnish the brake pads and rotors. Refer to "Brake Pad and Rotor Burnishing" under "Front Disc Brakes".

BRAKES

PARKING BRAKE ADJUSTMENT

ADJUSTMENT

See Figures 8 through 10.

1. Apply and fully release the park brake.

2. Verify that the park brake pedal releases completely.

3. Turn ON the ignition. Verify the BRAKE indicator lamp is off. If the BRAKE indicator lamp is on, ensure the park brake pedal is in release mode and has fully returned to the stop. Remove the slack in the front park brake cable by pulling downward on the cable.

4. Raise and support the vehicle.

5. Remove the rear tire and wheel assemblies.

6. Loosen the locknut at the park brake cable equalizer to relieve tension on the park brake system.

7. Remove the rear brake rotors. Refer to "Brake Rotors" under "Rear Disc Brakes".

8. Using appropriate cleaning equipment, clean the parking brake components of any accumulated dust.

9. Set the J-21177-A Drum-to-Brake Shoe Clearance Gauge inside of the park brake drum at the widest point.

a. Place the contacts on the tool to the widest point of the drum.

b. Tighten the set screw on the tool to ensure the proper measurement when removing the tool from the drum.

10. Position the J-21177-A Drum-to-Brake Shoe Clearance Gauge over the park brake shoe at the widest point.

11. Turn the adjuster screw until the park brake shoe just contacts the J-21177-A Drum-to-Brake Shoe Clearance Gauge.

PARKING BRAKE

12. Repeat steps for the opposite side.

13. Install the rear brake rotors.

14. Install the rear tire and wheel assemblies.

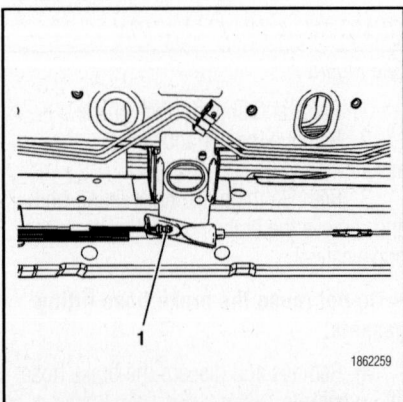

Fig. 8 Loosen the locknut (1) at the park brake cable equalizer to relieve tension on the park brake system.

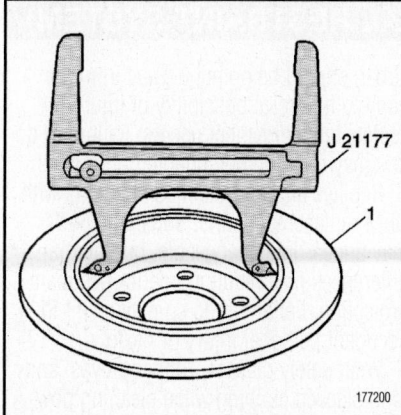

Fig. 9 Set the J-21177-A Drum-to-Brake Shoe Clearance Gauge inside of the park brake drum (1) at the widest point.

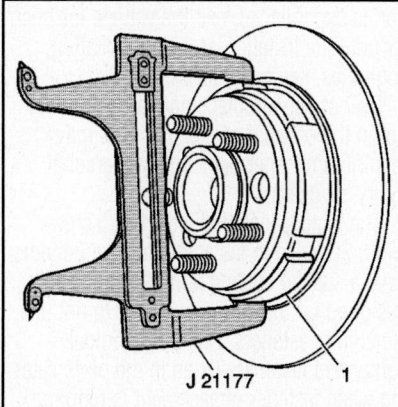

Fig. 10 Position the J-21177-A Drum-to-Brake Shoe Clearance Gauge over the park brake shoe (1) at the widest point.

15. Adjust the park brake by turning the locknut at the equalizer while spinning both rear wheels. When either rear wheel starts to drag, back off the locknut one full turn.

16. Lower the vehicle to curb height.

17. Apply the park brake, then inspect for rotation of the rear wheels. If the rear wheels rotate during this inspection, then readjust the park brake shoes.

18. Release the park brake. Verify the rear wheels rotate freely.

19. Lower the vehicle.

PARKING BRAKE ACTUATOR

REMOVAL & INSTALLATION

See Figure 11.

1. Raise and support the vehicle.
2. Remove the tire and wheel.
3. Remove the park brake shoes. Refer to "Parking Brake Shoes".
4. Disconnect the park brake cable eye from the actuator lever.

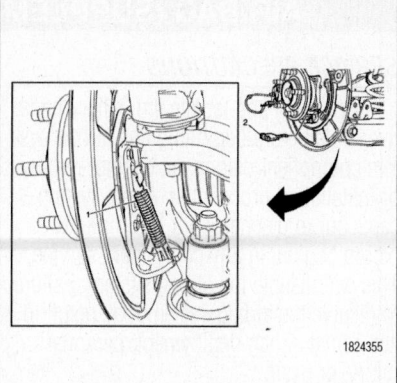

Fig. 11 Disconnect the park brake cable eye (1) from the actuator lever. Remove the parking brake actuator (2).

5. Remove the parking brake actuator.

To install:

6. Installation is the reverse of the removal procedure.
7. Adjust the park brake. Refer to "Parking Brake Adjustment".

PARKING BRAKE SHOES

REMOVAL & INSTALLATION

See Figure 12.

1. Raise and support the vehicle.
2. Remove the rear tire and wheel assembly.

3. Remove the rear brake rotor.
4. Compress and rotate the parking brake shoe hold down spring 1/4 turn to release.
5. Remove the parking brake shoe hold down spring pins.
6. Using the J-38400 brake shoe spanner and spring remover, remove the adjuster spring.
7. Clean the adjuster screw threads and apply high temperature grease to the adjuster screw.
8. Using the J-38400 brake shoe spanner and spring remover, remove the return spring.
9. Remove the parking brake shoe(s).

To install:

10. Installation is the reverse of the removal procedure. Note the following:

a. Use denatured alcohol to clean brake dust or grease from the park brake shoes and hardware.

b. If reinstalling the park brake shoes, note the location of the park brake shoes for installation.

c. Apply a small amount of high temperature silicone grease to the brake shoe and backing plate contact points.

d. Adjust the parking brake, as described in this section.

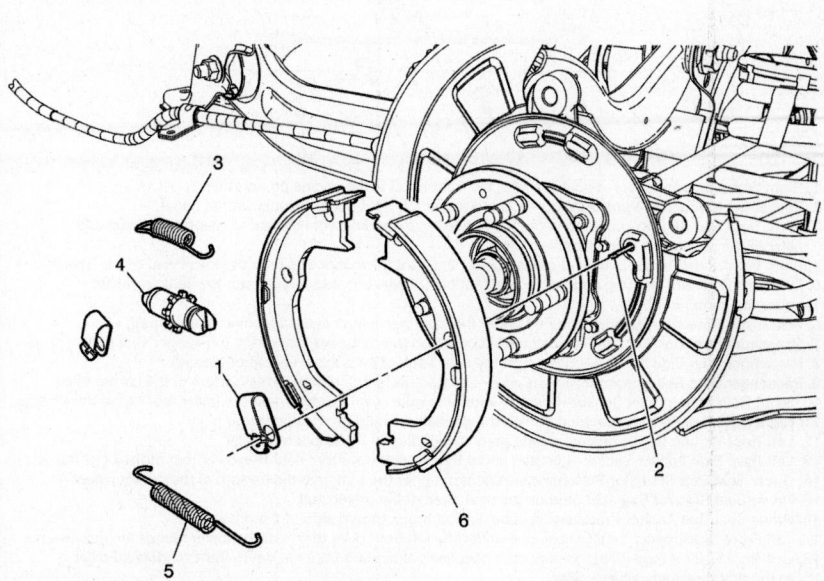

1. Park Brake Shoe Hold Down Spring (Qty: 2)
2. Park Brake Shoe Hold Down Spring Pin (Qty: 2)
3. Park Brake Shoe Adjuster Spring
4. Park Brake Shoe Adjuster Screw
5. Park Brake Shoe Return Spring
6. Park Brake Shoe (Qty: 2)

Fig. 12 Exploded view of the parking brake assembly

CHASSIS ELECTRICAL   AIR BAG (SUPPLEMENTAL RESTRAINT SYSTEM)

GENERAL INFORMATION

See Figure 13.

✳✳ CAUTION

These vehicles are equipped with an air bag system. The system must be disarmed before performing service on, or around, system components, the steering column, instrument panel components, wiring and sensors. Failure to follow the safety precautions and the disarming procedure could result in accidental air bag deployment, possible injury and unnecessary system repairs.

SERVICE PRECAUTIONS

Disconnect and isolate the battery negative cable before beginning any airbag system component diagnosis, testing, removal, or installation procedures. Allow system capacitor to discharge for two minutes before beginning any component service. This will disable the airbag system. Failure to disable the airbag system may result in accidental airbag deployment, personal injury, or death.

Do not place an intact undeployed airbag face down on a solid surface. The airbag will propel into the air if accidentally deployed and may result in personal injury or death.

When carrying or handling an undeployed airbag, the trim side (face) of the airbag should be pointing away from the body to minimize possibility of injury if accidental deployment occurs. Failure to do this may result in personal injury or death.

Replace airbag system components with OEM replacement parts. Substitute parts may appear interchangeable, but internal differences may result in inferior occupant protection. Failure to do so may result in occupant personal injury or death.

Wear safety glasses, rubber gloves, and long sleeved clothing when cleaning powder residue from vehicle after an airbag deployment. Powder residue emitted from a deployed airbag can cause skin irritation. Flush affected area with cool water if irritation is experienced. If nasal or throat irritation is experienced, exit the vehicle for fresh air until the irritation ceases. If irritation continues, see a physician.

Do not use a replacement airbag that is not in the original packaging. This may result in improper deployment, personal injury, or death.

The factory installed fasteners, screws and bolts used to fasten airbag components have a special coating and are specifically designed for the airbag system. Do not use substitute fasteners. Use only original equipment fasteners listed in the parts catalog when fastener replacement is required.

During, and following, any child restraint anchor service, due to impact event or vehicle repair, carefully inspect all mounting hardware, tether straps, and anchors for proper installation, operation, or damage. If a child restraint anchor is found damaged in any way, the anchor must be replaced. Failure to do this may result in personal injury or death.

Deployed and non-deployed airbags may or may not have live pyrotechnic material within the airbag inflator.

Do not dispose of driver/passenger/curtain airbags or seat belt tensioners unless you are sure of complete deployment. Refer to the Hazardous Substance Control System for proper disposal.

Dispose of deployed airbags and tensioners consistent with state, provincial, local, and federal regulations.

After any airbag component testing or service, do not connect the battery negative cable. Personal injury or death may result if the system test is not performed first.

If the vehicle is equipped with the Occupant Classification System (OCS), do not connect the battery negative cable before performing the OCS Verification Test using the scan tool and the appropriate diagnostic

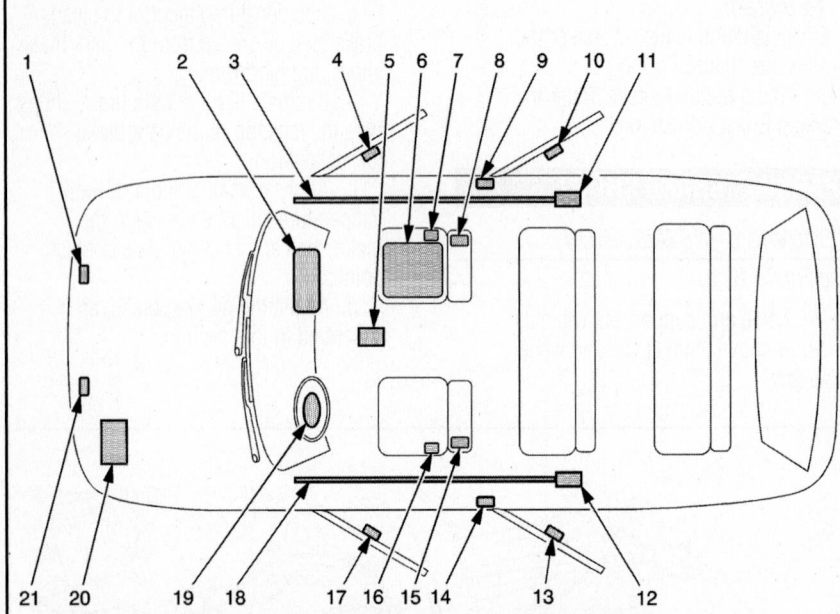

1. Right Front Impact Sensor--Located under the front hood in the engine compartment
2. Passenger Instrument Panel Air Bag--Located at the top right under the instrument panel
3. Right Roof Rail Air Bag--Located under the headliner, extending from the passenger front windshield pillar to the passenger rear windshield pillar
4. Right Front Side Impact Sensor--Located under the right front door trim near the lower rear of the door frame
5. Inflatable Restraint Sensing and Diagnostic Module (SDM)--Located underneath the vehicle carpet under the center console
6. Passenger Presence System--Located under the front passenger sear trim cover (if equipped)
7. Passenger Seat Belt Anchor Pretensioner--Located on the outboard side of the passenger seat (if equipped)
8. Passenger Seat Side Air Bag--Located on the seat back of passenger seat (if equipped)
9. Passenger Seat Belt Retractor Pretensioner--Located under the trim near the bottom of the center pillar
10. Right Rear Side Impact Sensor--Located under the right rear door trim near the lower rear of the door frame
11. Right Roof Rail Air Bag--Located behind the garnish molding on the upper rear pillar
12. Left Roof Rail Air Bag--Located behind garnish molding on the upper rear pillar
13. Left Rear Side Impact Sensor--Located under the left rear door trim near the lower rear of the door frame
14. Driver Seat Belt Retractor Pretensioner--Located under the trim near the bottom of the center pillar
15. Driver Seat Side Air Bag--Located on the seat back of the driver seat
16. Driver Seat Belt Anchor Pretensioner--Located on the outboard side of the driver seat
17. Left Front Side Impact Sensor--Located under the left front door trim near the lower rear of the door frame
18. Left Roof Rail Air Bag--Located under the headliner, extending from the driver front windshield pillar to the driver rear windshield pillar
19. Driver Steering Wheel Air Bag--Located on the steering wheel
20. Vehicle Battery--Located at the front left of the engine compartment.
21. Left Front Impact Sensor--Located under the front hood in the engine compartment

2322630

Fig. 13 Showing the location of supplemental restraint system components

information. Personal injury or death may result if the system test is not performed properly.

Never replace both the Occupant Restraint Controller (ORC) and the Occupant Classification Module (OCM) at the same time. If both require replacement, replace one, then perform the Airbag System test before replacing the other.

Both the ORC and the OCM store Occupant Classification System (OCS) calibration data, which they transfer to one another when one of them is replaced. If both are replaced at the same time, an irreversible fault will be set in both modules and the OCS may malfunction and cause personal injury or death.

If equipped with OCS, the Seat Weight Sensor is a sensitive, calibrated unit and must be handled carefully. Do not drop or handle roughly. If dropped or damaged, replace with another sensor. Failure to do so may result in occupant injury or death.

If equipped with OCS, the front passenger seat must be handled carefully as well. When removing the seat, be careful when setting on floor not to drop. If dropped, the sensor may be inoperative, could result in occupant injury, or possibly death.

If equipped with OCS, when the passenger front seat is on the floor, no one should sit in the front passenger seat. This uneven force may damage the sensing ability of the seat weight sensors. If sat on and damaged, the sensor may be inoperative, could result in occupant injury, or possibly death.

DISARMING THE SYSTEM

Prior to air bag disabling, determine the reason for disabling the system and follow the applicable procedure:

1. If the vehicle was involved in an accident with an air bag deployment: disconnect the negative battery cable(s)

2. When performing SIR diagnostics: follow the appropriate SIR service manual diagnostic procedure(s).

3. When moving, removing or replacing an SIR component or a component attached to an SIR component: disconnect the negative battery cable(s).

4. If the vehicle is suspected of having shorted electrical wires: disconnect the negative battery cable(s).

5. When performing electrical diagnosis on components other than the SIR system:

remove the SIR/Airbag fuse(s) when indicated by the diagnostic procedure to disable the SIR system.

➡**DTCs will be lost when the negative battery cable is disconnected.**

Disabling Procedure—Air Bag Fuse

See Figure 14.

1. Turn the steering wheel so that the vehicles wheels are pointing straight ahead.
2. Place the ignition in the OFF position.

✳✳ WARNING

The Sensing and Diagnostic Module (SDM) may have more than one fused power input. To ensure there is no unwanted SIR deployment, personal injury, or unnecessary SIR system repairs, remove all fuses supplying power to the SDM. With all SDM fuses removed and the ignition switch in the ON position, the AIR BAG warning indicator illuminates. This is normal operation, and does not indicate a SIR system malfunction.

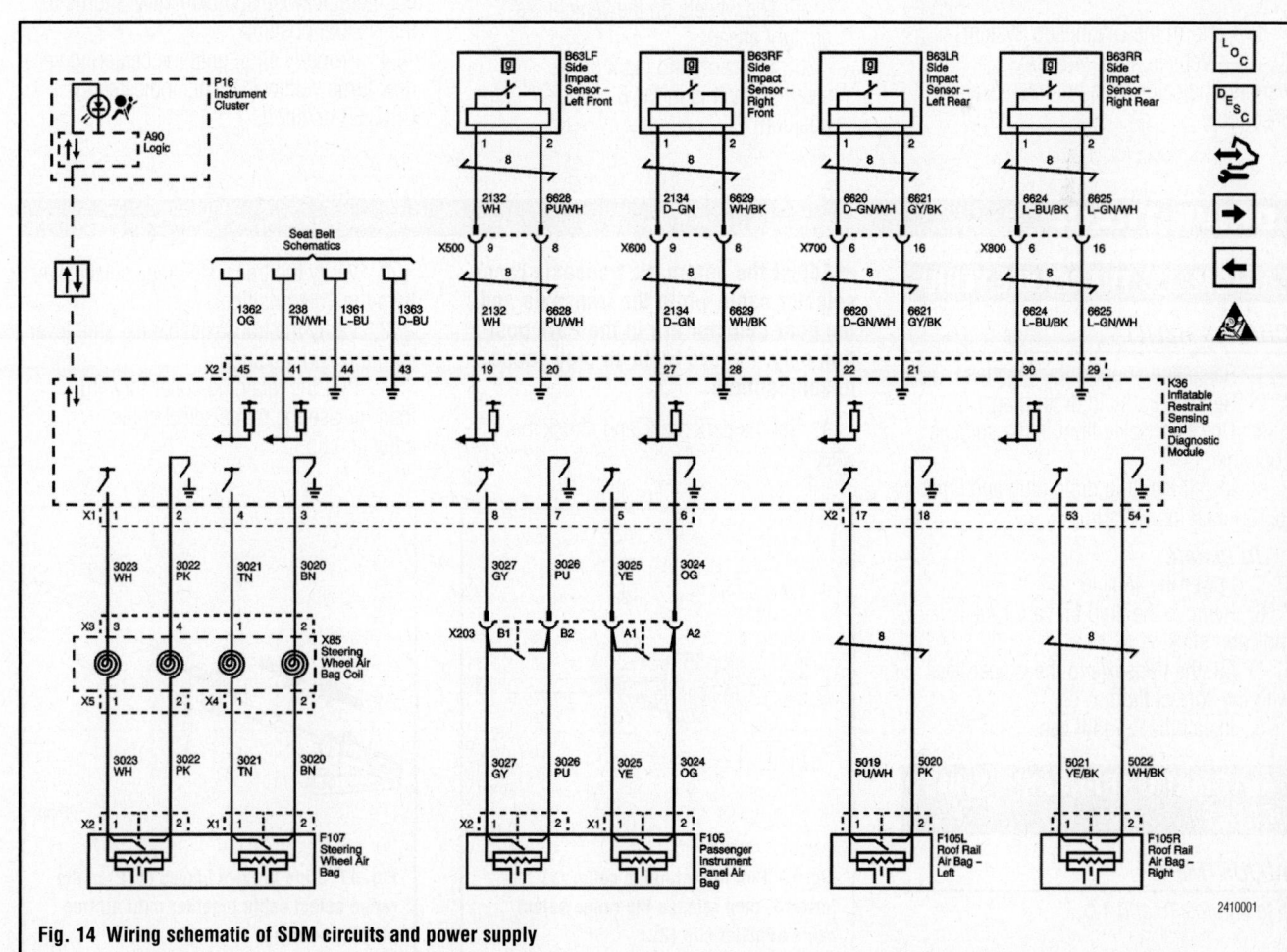

Fig. 14 Wiring schematic of SDM circuits and power supply

2410001

3. Locate and remove the fuse(s) supplying power to the SDM.

4. Wait 1 minute before working on the system.

Disabling Procedure—Negative Battery Cable

1. Turn the steering wheel so that the vehicles wheels are pointing straight ahead.

2. Place the ignition in the OFF position.

3. Disconnect the negative battery cable from the battery.

4. Wait 1 minute before working on system.

ARMING THE SYSTEM

Enabling Procedure—Air Bag Fuse

1. Place the ignition in the OFF position.

2. Install the fuse(s) supplying power to the SDM.

3. Turn the ignition switch to the ON position. The AIR BAG indicator will flash then turn OFF.

4. Perform the Diagnostic System Check—Vehicle, if the AIR BAG warning indicator does not operate as described.

Enabling Procedure—Negative Battery Cable

1. Place the ignition in the OFF position.

2. Connect the negative battery cable to the battery.

3. Turn the ignition switch to the ON position. The AIR BAG indicator will flash then turn OFF.

4. Perform the Diagnostic System Check—Vehicle, if the AIR BAG warning indicator does not operate as described.

CLOCKSPRING CENTERING

See Figure 15.

❈❈ CAUTION

The new SIR coil assembly will be centered. Improper alignment of the SIR coil assembly may damage the unit, causing an inflatable restraint malfunction.

1. Verify the following conditions before centering the supplemental inflatable restraint (SIR) steering wheel module coil:

   a. The wheels on the vehicle are straight ahead.

   b. The centering mark of the steering shaft is in the 6 o'clock position.

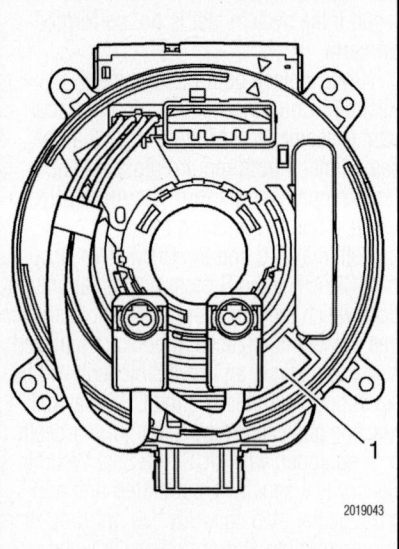

Fig. 15 Properly align until the centering window turns yellow (1). This indicates the CENTER position.

2. Turn the lobe of the clock spring clockwise until the coil ribbon stops. Do not force.

3. Turn the lobe of the clock spring counterclockwise approximately 3 turns to the Neutral position.

4. Properly align until the centering window turns yellow (1). This indicates the CENTER position.

DRIVE TRAIN

AUTOMATIC TRANSAXLE FLUID

DRAIN & REFILL

1. Raise and support the vehicle.

2. Remove the fluid drain plug.

3. Drain transaxle fluid into a suitable container.

4. Install the fluid drain plug and tighten to 106 inch lbs. (12 Nm).

To install:

5. Lower the vehicle.

6. Remove the fluid fill cap/level indicator stick.

7. Fill the transaxle to the proper level with the correct fluid.

8. Install the fluid fill cap.

AUTOMATIC TRANSAXLE SHIFT CABLE

ADJUSTMENT

See Figures 16 and 17.

➡**Adjust the automatic transaxle range selector cable while the transaxle and the gear selector are in the Park position only. Failure to do so may cause misadjustment.**

1. Set the park brake and chock the wheels.

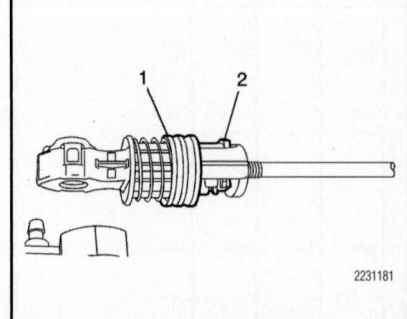

Fig. 16 Pull the retaining collar (1) forward, then release the range select cable adjuster clip (2).

2. Verify the transaxle range select lever is in the Park position.

3. Verify the transaxle manual shift lever is in the Park position.

4. Pull the retaining collar forward, then release the range select cable adjuster clip.

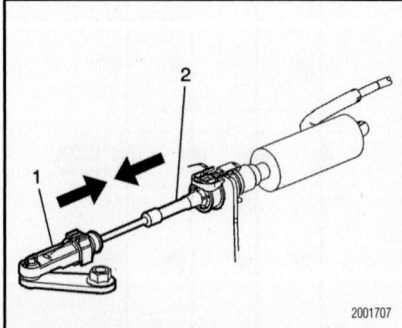

Fig. 17 Slide the two halves (1, 2) of the range select cable together until all free play is removed.

5. Slide the two halves of the range select cable together until all free play is removed.

6. Depress the adjuster clip locking the adjuster clip completely, then release the retaining collar.

7. Pull both halves of the range select cable in opposite directions to verify the cable adjuster is secured.

8. Check the transaxle range select lever in all gear selections for proper operation.

DIFFERENTIAL ASSEMBLY

REMOVAL & INSTALLATION

See Figures 18 and 19.

1. Raise and support the vehicle.
2. Drain the rear differential, if needed.
3. Remove the spare tire.
4. Remove the exhaust system.
5. Remove the rear wheel drive shafts.
6. Remove the propeller shaft from the vehicle, as described in this section.
7. Support the rear differential with a transmission jack stand.

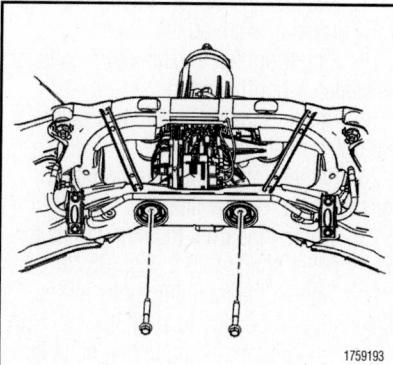

Fig. 18 Remove the rear differential support bushing bolts.

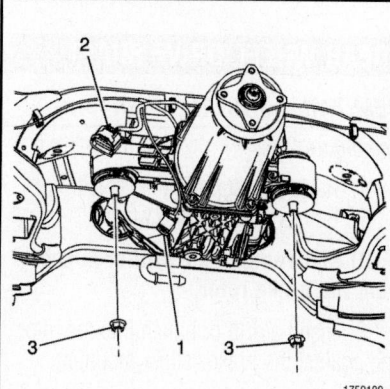

Fig. 19 Removing the small (1) and large (2) control module connector at the differential (3).

8. Remove the rear differential support bushing bolts.

9. Remove the front mounting nuts for the rear differential.

10. Lower the rear differential to gain access rear differential clutch control module.

11. Remove the small electrical connector from the control module.

12. Remove the large electrical connector from the control module.

13. Remove the rear differential assembly from the vehicle.

To install:

14. When positioning the rear differential assembly in the rear cradle, leave enough room to access the clutch control module.

15. If replacing the clutch control module, the new module must be programmed.

➡**Programming requires use of specialized data and instructions; consult a local service agent for programming.**

16. Position the rear differential assembly in the rear cradle.

17. Install the small and large electrical connectors.

18. Install the front mounting nuts and tighten first by hand.

19. Install the rear differential support bushing bolts and tighten first by hand.

20. Raise the rear differential assembly into place.

21. Tighten the front mounting nuts to 90 ft. lbs. (122 Nm).

22. Tighten the rear differential support bushing bolts to 139 ft. lbs. (188 Nm).

23. Remove the transmission jack stand.

24. Install the propeller shaft.

25. Install the rear wheel drive shafts.

26. Install the exhaust system.

27. Install the spare tire.

28. Fill the rear differential assembly with fluid, if drained.

29. Lower the vehicle.

DIFFERENTIAL FLUID

DRAIN & REFILL

1. Raise vehicle.
2. Remove differential oil drain plug and drain oil into suitable container.
3. Install drain plug and tighten to 29 ft. lbs. (39 Nm).
4. Fill differential oil through fill plug opening until fluid reaches bottom edge of fill plug opening.
5. Install and tighten fill plug to 29 ft. lbs. (39 Nm).

FRONT WHEEL DRIVE SHAFTS

REMOVAL & INSTALLATION

See Figure 20.

1. Raise and support the vehicle.
2. Remove the tire and wheel assembly.
3. Insert a punch or a drift in the cooling fins of the brake rotor. Rotate the brake rotor until it rest against the brake caliper mounting bracket. Using a breaker bar and the proper size socket, loosen the wheel drive shaft nut. Remove the wheel drive shaft nut and discard.
4. Using the J 42129 puller, separate the wheel drive shaft from the wheel hub.

➡**For the following steps, see "FRONT SUSPENSION" section, as applicable.**

5. Separate the stabilizer link from the lower control arm.
6. Separate the outer tie rod end from the knuckle.
7. Separate the lower control arm from the knuckle.

➡**The front axle shaft seal must be replaced once the wheel drive shaft has been removed. Replace with new only. DO NOT reuse the front axle shaft seal.**

8. Using the J 2619-01 hammer and the J 45341 tool, remove the wheel drive shaft from the vehicle. Remove the front axle shaft seal.

To install:

9. Install the new front axle shaft seal.
10. Insert the J 44394-A protector into the transaxle.

➡**The following service procedure is for vehicles equipped with an intermediate shaft.**

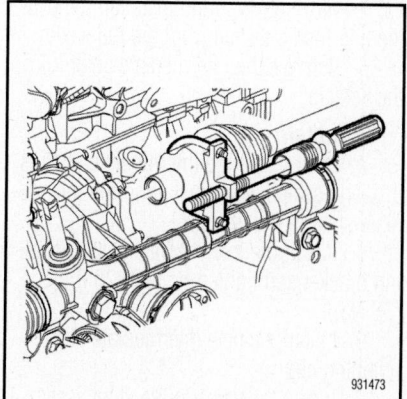

Fig. 20 Using the J 2619-01 hammer and the J 45341 tool, remove the wheel drive shaft from the vehicle.

11. For the right wheel drive shaft, apply a very small amount of grease to the splines of the wheel drive shaft inner joint.

12. Install the wheel drive shaft until the splines pass the oil seal.

13. Remove the J 44394-A protector from the oil seal.

14. Install the wheel drive shaft in the knuckle.

15. Hand install a new wheel drive shaft spindle nut.

16. Install the lower ball to the steering knuckle. Tighten ball joint nut to 30 ft. lbs. (40 Nm).

17. Install the lower link to the stabilizer bar. Tighten lower link nut to 63 ft. lbs. (85 Nm).

18. Install the tie rod end to the steering knuckle. Tighten tie rod end nut to 44 ft. lbs. (60 Nm).

19. Hand start the wheel drive shaft nut. Insert a drift or punch in the brake rotor cooling fins. Rotate the brake rotor until it rest against the brake caliper mounting bracket. Using a torque wrench and the proper size socket, tighten the wheel drive shaft nut to 151 ft. lbs. (205 Nm).

20. Install the tire and wheel assembly.

21. Lower the vehicle.

22. Inspect the transaxle fluid level.

INTERMEDIATE SHAFT

REMOVAL & INSTALLATION

See Figures 21 and 22.

1. Raise and support the vehicle.

2. Remove the wheel drive shaft assembly, as described in this section.

3. Remove the retaining clip for the intermediate shaft. Discard the clip.

4. Remove the mounting bolts for the intermediate shaft and support bracket.

5. Using the J 2619-01 hammer and the J 44467 remover and installer, remove the intermediate shaft from the transaxle.

6. Remove the intermediate shaft from the vehicle.

To install:

7. Ensure that the intermediate shaft is properly seated when installing the intermediate shaft in the vehicle.

8. Install the intermediate shaft mounting bracket and tighten bolts to 26 ft. lbs. (35 Nm).

9. Install the new intermediate shaft retaining clip.

10. Install the wheel drive shaft assembly, as described in this section.

11. Remove the support and lower the vehicle.

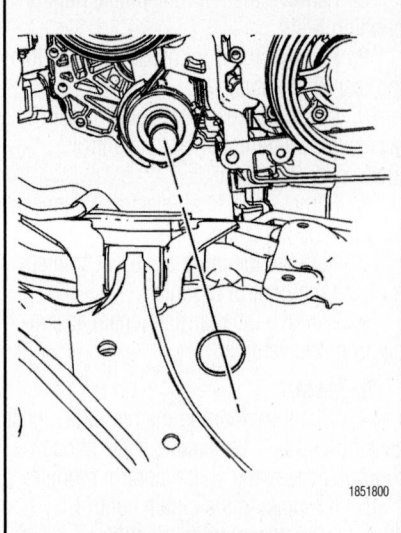

Fig. 21 Remove and discard the intermediate shaft retaining clip

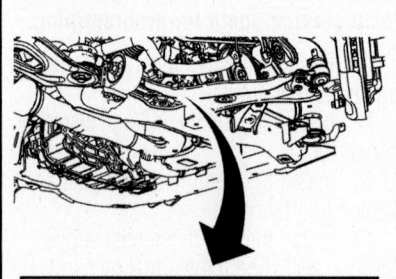

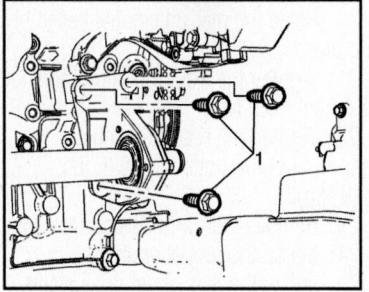

Fig. 22 Remove the mounting bolts (1) for the intermediate shaft and support bracket.

PROPELLER SHAFT

REMOVAL & INSTALLATION

1. Place the transaxle in neutral.

2. Raise and support the vehicle.

3. Mark the relationship of the propeller shaft to the rear differential drive flange and the transfer case.

4. Support the propeller shaft at the rear differential.

5. Remove the mounting bolts for the propeller shaft at the rear differential drive flange.

6. Support propeller shaft at the transfer case.

7. Remove the mounting bolts for the propeller shaft at the transfer case.

8. Support the propeller shaft at the center support bearing.

9. Remove the mounting bolts for the center support bearing.

10. With the aid of an assistant, remove the propeller shaft from the vehicle.

To install:

11. Thoroughly clean the mounting bolts for center bearing and the front and rear propeller shaft flanges.

12. Apply threadlocker, GM P/N 89021297 or equivalent, to the bolt threads.

13. With the aid of an assistant, position the propeller shaft on the supports.

14. Align the reference marks on the front and rear of the propeller shaft to the transfer case and rear differential.

15. Position the propeller shaft on the transfer case output flange.

16. Finger tighten the mounting bolts for the propeller shaft at the transfer case output flange.

17. Position the center support bearing of the propeller shaft on the vehicle.

18. Finger tighten the mounting bolts for the center support bearing.

19. Position the propeller shaft on the rear differential drive flange.

20. Finger tighten the rear mounting bolts for the propeller shaft.

21. Tighten the front mounting bolts for the propeller shaft to 25 ft. lbs. (35 Nm).

22. Tighten the mounting bolts for the center support bearing to 19 ft. lbs. (25 Nm).

23. Tighten the rear mounting bolts for the propeller shaft yoke to rear drive axle to 37 ft. lbs. (50 Nm).

24. Remove the supports for the propeller shaft.

25. Lower the vehicle.

REAR WHEEL DRIVE SHAFT

REMOVAL & INSTALLATION

See Figure 23.

1. Raise and support the vehicle.

2. Remove the tire and wheel.

➡**DO NOT remove the drift or punch from the brake rotor.**

3. Insert a drift or punch into the rotor and against the brake caliper mounting bracket.

4. Using the appropriate tool, loosen the wheel drive shaft nut.

5. Remove and discard the wheel drive shaft nut.

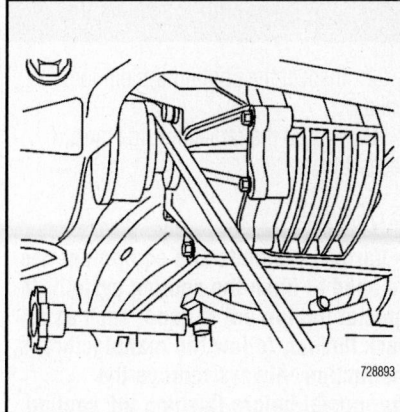

Fig. 23 Using a suitable tool, carefully release the wheel drive shaft from the rear differential carrier.

6. Rotate the brake rotor until the drift or punch is against the brake caliper mounting bracket.

7. Using the J 42129, disengage the wheel drive shaft from the wheel hub/bearing.

8. Remove the rear suspension knuckle. See "REAR SUSPENSION" section.

9. Using a suitable tool, carefully release the wheel drive shaft from the rear differential carrier.

➡**Because of the design of the inner seal wheel drive shaft seal, the seal will be removed at the same time the wheel drive shaft is. Replace the seal, DO NOT re-use the seal.**

10. Remove the wheel drive shaft from the vehicle.

11. Remove the wheel drive seal.

12. Remove and discard the retaining ring from the tripod.

To install:

13. Install the new retaining clip on the tripod.

14. Install the new wheel drive shaft seal.

➡**When installing the wheel drive shaft, you will notice a slight resistance. This is the wheel drive shaft seal. A snap or click should be heard when the wheel drive shaft is fully seated.**

15. Install the wheel drive shaft.

16. Install the rear suspension knuckle.

17. Hand install a new wheel drive shaft nut.

18. Insert a drift or punch into the rotor and against the brake caliper mounting bracket.

19. Tighten the wheel drive shaft nut to 151 ft. lbs. (205 Nm).

20. Install the tire and wheel assembly.

21. Remove the support and lower the vehicle.

TRANSFER CASE

REMOVAL & INSTALLATION

See Figures 24 and 25.

1. Raise and support the vehicle.
2. Drain the transfer case fluid.
3. Remove the propeller shaft. See "Propeller Shaft" in this section.
4. Remove the right wheel drive shaft. See "Drive Shafts" in this section.
5. Remove the catalytic converter.
6. Remove the transfer case brace.
7. Remove the transfer case mounting bracket.
8. Support the transaxle with a jackstand.
9. Remove the rear transaxle mount and bracket.
10. Remove the bolts securing the transfer case to the transaxle.
11. Remove the transfer case from the transaxle.
12. Remove the transfer case to transaxle O-ring for 2.4L engine or the gasket for 3.0L engine.
13. If replacing the transfer case, remove the transfer case heat shield, if equipped.

To install:

14. If removed, install the transfer case heat shield.

15. Install a NEW the transfer case to transaxle O-ring for 2.4L engine or new gasket for 3.0L engine.

16. Lube the O-ring with light coating of automatic transaxle fluid.

17. Install the transfer case to the transaxle.

18. Install the bolts securing the transfer case to the transaxle and tighten the bolts to 37 ft. lbs. (50 Nm).

19. Install the rear transaxle mount bracket to the transaxle. Tighten the bolts as follows:

- FWD bracket-to-transaxle side bolt: 37 ft. lbs. (50 Nm)
- FWD 3 bracket through bolts: 81 ft. lbs. (110 Nm).
- AWD, all bolts: 37 ft. lbs. (50 Nm).

20. Remove the jackstand supporting the transaxle.

21. For 2.4L engine vehicles, install the transfer case brace. Tighten bolts in specified sequential order to 37 ft. lbs. (50 Nm):

   a. Lightly install all fasteners.
   b. Torque fastener "5" first.
   c. Torque fasteners "1, "2" and "3".
   d. Torque fastener "4" last.

22. For 3.0L engine vehicles, install the transfer case brace. Tighten bolts in specified sequential order and per following bolt torques:

- Bolts "1": 37ft. lbs. (50 Nm)
- Bolts "2": 37ft. lbs. (50 Nm)
- Bolts "3": 17 ft. lbs. (23 Nm)

23. Install the catalytic converter.
24. Install the right wheel drive shaft.
25. Install the propeller shaft.
26. Fill the transfer case with fluid.
27. Lower the vehicle.

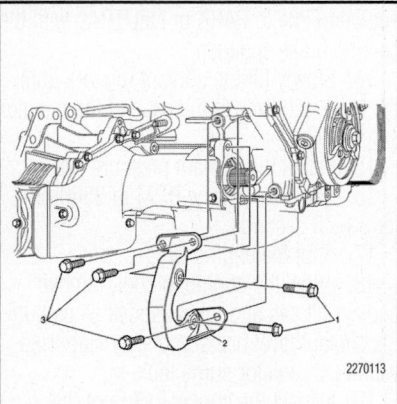

Fig. 24 Showing bolt tightening sequence (5-1-2-3-4) for transfer case brace (4)—2.4L engine models

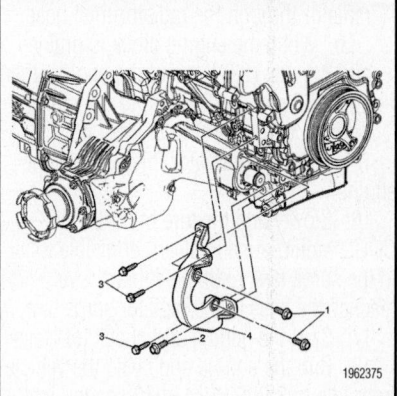

Fig. 25 Showing bolt tightening sequence (1-2-3) for transfer case brace (4)—3.0L engine models

ENGINE COOLING

ENGINE COOLANT

DRAIN & REFILL PROCEDURE

2.4L Engine

1. Remove the coolant pressure cap from the radiator surge tank.
2. Raise and support the vehicle.
3. Place a drain pan under the drain cock.

Loosen the radiator drain cock (located at the lower side of the radiator).

4. Drain the cooling system.
5. If a complete block drain is required, place a drain pan under the water pump drain.
6. Remove the water pump drain plug.
7. Drain the cooling system.
8. Inspect the coolant.
9. Follow the appropriate procedure based on the condition of the coolant.

➡**The procedure below must be followed. Improper coolant level could result in a low or high coolant level condition, causing engine damage.**

10. Tighten the radiator drain cock.
11. Install the water pump drain plug and tighten to 89 inch lbs. (10 Nm) if removed during the draining process.
12. Lower the vehicle.
13. Remove radiator inlet hose at the engine.
14. Slowly add mixture of 50/50 DEX-COOL® antifreeze and clean, drinkable water to the engine and radiator. Fill the cooling system as indicated below:

   a. When the engine block is not drained, add 1.85 qts. (1.75 liters) to the radiator through the radiator inlet hose.

   b. When the engine block is drained, add 2.1 qts. (2.0 liters to the engine, then add 1.85 qts. (1.75 liters) to the radiator through the radiator inlet hose.

15. Install the radiator inlet hose at the engine.
16. Slowly add mixture of 50/50 DEX-COOL® antifreeze and clean, drinkable water to the surge tank until the coolant level reaches the base of the radiator surge tank.
17. Start the engine and check for leaks.
18. Run the engine and cycle the vehicle from idle to 3,000 RPM in 30 second intervals until the engine cooling fan comes ON, the engine cooling fan turns ON at approximately 216°F (102°C). Repeat this process twice before the engine is turned OFF.
19. Return the engine to idle, and idle for 30 seconds, then turn the engine OFF.

20. Allow the vehicle to cool, before adding additional coolant.

➡**The level in the surge tank will return into the cold fill range once the vehicle cools.**

21. Add additional coolant to the surge tank until the level is approximately 13 mm (0.5 in) above the surge tank seam.
22. Install the coolant surge tank cap.

3.0L Engine

1. Remove the coolant pressure cap from the radiator surge tank.
2. Raise and support the vehicle.
3. Place a drain pan under the drain cock.
4. Loosen the radiator drain cock.
5. Drain the cooling system.
6. Lower the vehicle.
7. Inspect the coolant.

✳✳ CAUTION

The procedure below must be followed. Improper coolant level could result in a low or high coolant level condition, causing engine damage.

8. Raise and support the vehicle.
9. Tighten the radiator drain cock.
10. Lower the vehicle.
11. Slowly fill the radiator with a 50/50 coolant mixture until the coolant level reaches the base of the radiator surge tank.
12. Allow 30 seconds for the coolant level to stabilize and continue to fill the coolant filler neck until the level stabilizes for at least 2 minutes.
13. Start the engine and allow to the engine to idle in PARK or NEUTRAL with the parking brake engaged.
14. Slowly fill the coolant mixture until the level stabilizes at the base of the radiator surge tank.
15. Install the coolant pressure cap.
16. Raise the engine RPM to 2500rpm for 30–40 seconds.
17. Shut the engine OFF.
18. Allow the engine to cool, remove coolant fill cap and repeat above steps until the coolant level has completely stabilized within the radiator surge tank.
19. Inspect the concentration of the engine coolant using the J 26568 Coolant and Battery Fluid Tester.
20. Inspect and if necessary, fill the coolant reservoir bottle as necessary.
21. Rinse away any excess coolant from the engine and the engine compartment.

22. Inspect the cooling system for leaks.
23. Top off the radiator surge tank, if necessary.

FLUSHING

➡**Various methods and equipment can be used to flush the cooling system. If special equipment is used, such as a back flusher, follow the manufacturer's instruction. Always remove the thermostat before flushing the cooling system.**

When the cooling system becomes contaminated, the cooling system should be flushed thoroughly to remove the contaminants before the engine is seriously damaged.

1. Drain the cooling system.
2. Remove the surge tank.
3. Clean and flush the surge tank with clean, drinkable water.
4. Install the surge tank.
5. Follow the drain and fill procedure using only clean, drinkable water.
6. Run the engine for 20 minutes.
7. Stop the engine.
8. Drain the cooling system.
9. Repeat the procedure if necessary, until the fluid is nearly colorless.
10. Fill the cooling system.

ENGINE FAN

REMOVAL & INSTALLATION

2.4L Engine
See Figures 26 and 27.

1. Reposition radiator. See "Radiator" in this section.
2. Unclip transmission cooler lines from shroud.

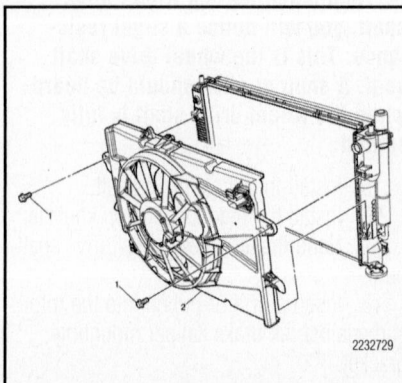

2232729

Fig. 26 Removing the engine fan shroud screws (1) and shroud (2)—2.4L engine

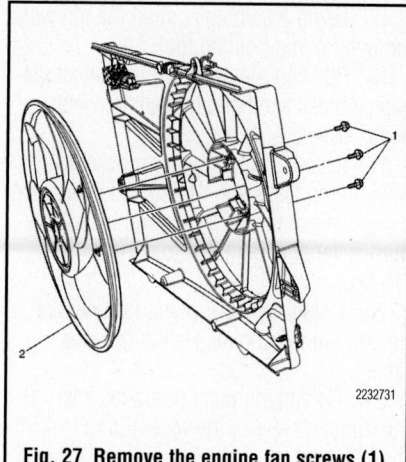

Fig. 27 Remove the engine fan screws (1) and fan (2)—2.4L engine

3. Unclip air conditioning lines from shroud.

4. Disconnect engine coolant fan motor and resistor electrical connectors.

5. Remove the 2 shroud retaining screws and remove the shroud.

6. Remove the 3 cooling fan to shroud screws and remove the fan.

7. Installation is the reverse of the removal procedure.

3.0L Engine

See Figures 28 through 30.

1. Remove the front bumper fascia support.

2. Remove the radiator inlet hose from radiator.

3. Remove the compressor hose from the condenser.

4. Remove the upper transmission cooler lines from radiator.

5. Remove the radiator mounting bolts and brackets.

6. Unclip transmission cooler lines from shroud.

7. Unclip air conditioning lines from shroud.

8. Disconnect engine coolant fan motor electrical connector.

9. Position radiator towards front of vehicle.

10. Remove the fan shroud to radiator screws and remove the shroud.

11. Remove the fan shroud to fan screws and remove the fan.

12. Installation is the reverse of the removal procedure.

RADIATOR

REMOVAL & INSTALLATION

1. Drain the cooling system.
2. Remove radiator hose inlet.

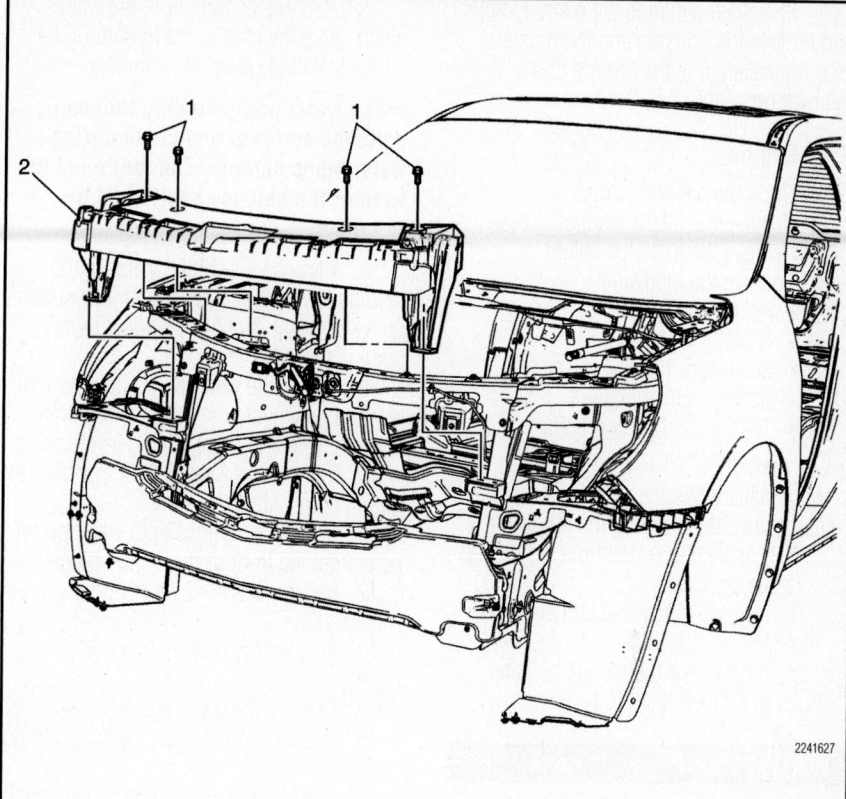

Fig. 28 Remove the front bumper fascia support screws (1) and support (2)—3.0L engine

3. Remove radiator hose outlet.

4. Remove the condenser.

5. Remove the engine coolant fan shroud.

6. Disconnect transmission oil cooler lines from radiator.

7. Remove upper radiator bracket fasteners and brackets and remove the radiator.

8. Installation is the reverse of the removal procedure.

THERMOSTAT

REMOVAL & INSTALLATION

2.4L Engine

1. Raise the vehicle by its full height.
2. Draining the cooling system.
3. Lower the vehicle.
4. Disconnect the engine coolant outlet hose and the radiator surge tank outlet hose, from the thermostat housing.

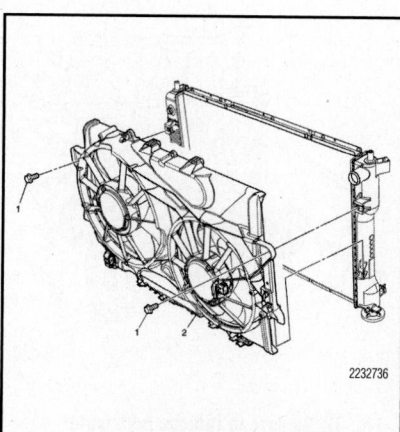

Fig. 29 Remove the engine fan shroud screws (1) and shroud (2)—3.0L engine

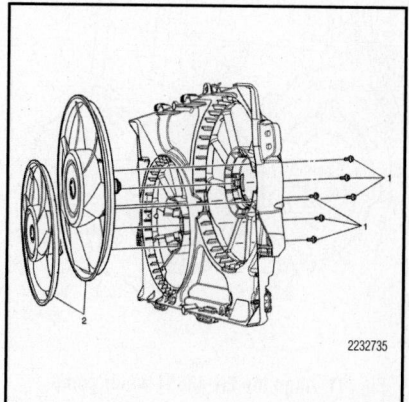

Fig. 30 Remove the engine fan screws (1) and fans (2)—3.0L engine

5. Remove the thermostat housing bolts and remove the housing and thermostat.

6. Installation is the reverse of the removal procedure.

3.0L Engine

1. Drain the cooling system.
2. Remove the intake manifold cover.
3. Remove the fuel pipe shield.
4. Remove the following:
   - Heater outlet hose
   - Heater inlet hose
   - Surge tank hose
   - Radiator outlet hose
   - Thermostat housing bolts

To install:

5. Installation is the reverse of the removal procedure, noting the following:

a. Ensure thermostat housing mating surfaces are clean.

b. Replace the gasket and any worn hoses.

c. Tighten the thermostat housing bolts to 88 inch lbs. (10 Nm).

WATER PUMP

REMOVAL & INSTALLATION

2.4L Engine

See Figures 31 and 32.

1. Remove the air cleaner assembly.
2. Remove the intake manifold cover.
3. If equipped, remove the coolant heater.
4. Remove the catalytic converter.
5. Remove the engine coolant thermostat housing.
6. Remove the water pump cover, fasteners and gasket from the engine front cover.

7. Drain the coolant from the water pump using the plug at the bottom of the pump. Install the plug when finished.

➡**The water pump holding tool supports the sprocket and chain during water pump service. The tool must be used or the balance shaft must be re-timed.**

8. Align the EN-43651 water pump holding tool with the threads on the water pump sprocket. Tighten the water pump holding tool fasteners.

9. Secure the water pump holding tool with the previously removed water pump cover fasteners into the engine front cover.

10. Remove the water pump sprocket to water pump fasteners.

11. Be sure to remove both water pump bolts from the front of the engine block.

12. Remove the front water pump fasteners.

13. Remove the rear water pump fasteners.

14. Remove the water pump.

15. If replacing the water pump cover, do the following:

a. Remove the water pump rear cover fasteners.

b. Separate the water pump cover from the water pump.

c. Remove and discard the water pump O-ring seal.

To install:

16. If replacing the water pump cover, install a new O-ring to the water pump and tighten the fasteners to 18 ft. lbs. (25 Nm).

➡**A guide pin can be created to aid in water pump alignment. Use a M 6 m x 6 mm x 50.8 mm stud (2 in). Thread the pin into the water pump sprocket.**

17. Using a guide pin, align the pin with the water pump holding tool.

18. Position the water pump against the engine block and hand tighten the water pump fasteners.

19. Install 2 water pump sprocket to water pump fasteners. After the fasteners are snug, remove the guide pin and install the third fastener and tighten to 89 inch lbs. (10 Nm).

20. Install the water pump fasteners at the front of the engine. Hand tighten at this time.

21. Tighten the water pump fasteners at the front and rear of the water pump to 18 ft. lbs. (25 Nm).

22. Remove the water pump cover fasteners from the engine front cover and water pump holding tool.

23. Remove the EN-43651 water pump holding tool from the water pump sprocket.

24. Install the water pump access plate gasket and fasteners and tighten to 89 inch lbs. (10 Nm).

25. If equipped, install the coolant heater.

26. Install the following:
   - Engine coolant thermostat housing
   - Catalytic converter
   - Intake manifold cover
   - Air cleaner assembly.

27. Refill the coolant system.

3.0L Engine

See Figure 33.

1. Drain the cooling system.
2. Remove the generator drive belt.

Fig. 31 Align the EN-43651 water pump holding tool (1) with the threads on the water pump sprocket (3). Tighten the water pump holding tool fasteners (2).

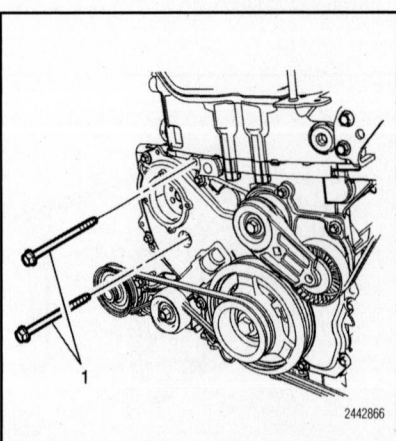

Fig. 32 Be sure to remove both water pump bolts (1) from the front of the engine block.

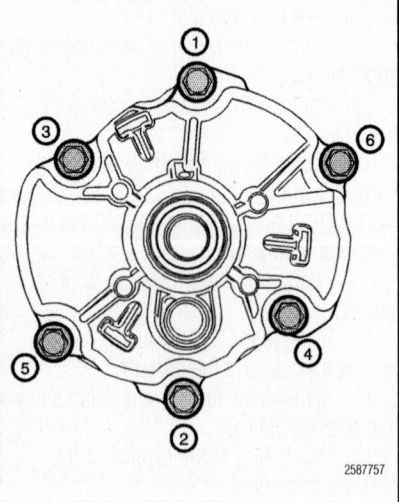

Fig. 33 Tighten the water pump bolts, in sequence shown, to 106 inch lbs. (12 Nm). Then, tighten the water pump bolts a second pass in sequence to this same torque value.

3. Use the EN 46104 water pump pulley holder to retain the pulley and remove the water pump pulley bolts. Remove the water pump pulley.

4. Remove the water pump bolts and remove the water pump.

5. Remove and discard the water pump seal.

6. Carefully clean the water pump sealing surfaces.

To install:

7. Install a new water pump seal and install the water pump.

8. Hand tighten the water pump bolts.

9. Tighten the water pump bolts, in sequence shown, to 106 inch lbs. (12 Nm). Then, tighten the water pump bolts a second pass in sequence to this same torque value.

10. Install the water pump pulley and the water pump pulley bolts.

11. Use the EN 46104 water pump pulley holder to hold the pulley.

12. Install the water pump pulley bolts and tighten to 106 inch lbs. (12 Nm).

13. Install the generator drive belt.

14. Fill the cooling system.

ENGINE ELECTRICAL | BATTERY SYSTEM

BATTERY

REMOVAL & INSTALLATION

See Figure 34.

1. Disconnect the negative battery cable.

2. Reposition the engine control module bracket/battery hold-down retainer.

3. Remove the positive battery cable from the battery post.

4. Remove the remaining battery components in the order shown.

To install:

5. Installation is the reverse of the removal procedure.

6. Tighten the battery retainer bracket bolt to 16 ft. lbs. (22 Nm).

7. Tighten the battery retainer bracket nut to 80 inch lbs. (9 Nm).

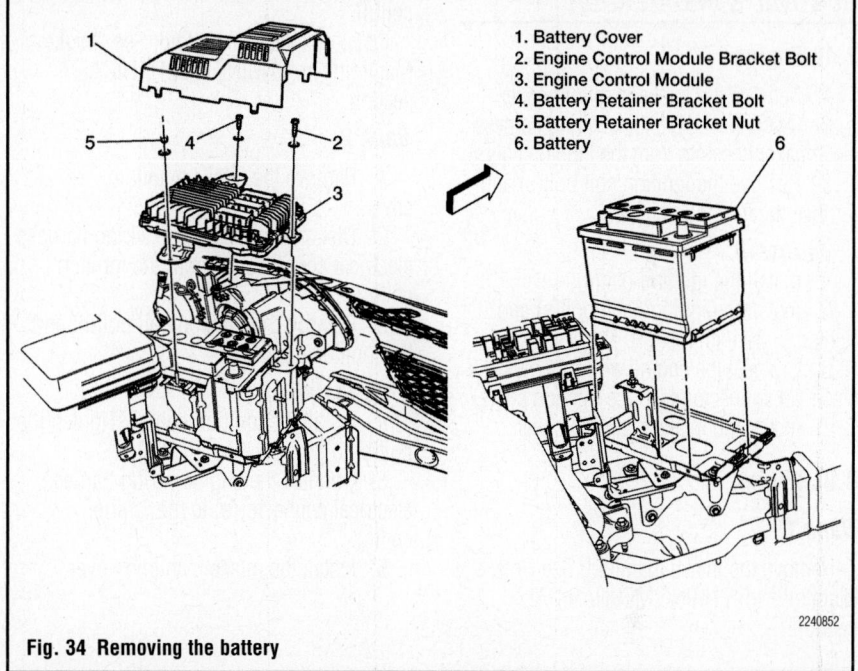

1. Battery Cover
2. Engine Control Module Bracket Bolt
3. Engine Control Module
4. Battery Retainer Bracket Bolt
5. Battery Retainer Bracket Nut
6. Battery

2240852

Fig. 34 Removing the battery

ENGINE ELECTRICAL | CHARGING SYSTEM

ALTERNATOR (GENERATOR)

REMOVAL & INSTALLATION

2.4L Engine

1. Disconnect the negative battery cable.

2. Remove the generator drive belt.

3. Disconnect the electrical connector from the generator.

4. Remove the generator mounting bolts and remove the generator.

5. Installation is the reverse of the removal procedure.

6. Tighten the generator mounting bolts to 16 ft. lbs. (22 Nm).

3.0L Engine

1. Disconnect the negative battery cable.

2. Reposition the positive battery cable boot at the generator terminal.

3. Disconnect the engine harness electrical connector from the generator.

4. Remove the positive battery cable nut at the generator.

5. Remove the positive battery cable terminal from the generator.

6. Remove the drive belt.

7. Remove the idler pulley bolt and idler pulley.

8. Remove the generator bolts.

➡**When removing the generator from the vehicle, it may be necessary to maneuver the generator to remove it from the vehicle.**

9. Remove the generator.

To install:

10. Position the generator to the engine.

11. Loosely install the generator bolts.

12. Install the idler pulley.

13. Tighten the generator bolts to 37 ft. lbs. (50 Nm).

14. Install the drive belt.

15. Connect the engine harness electrical connector to the generator.

16. Install the positive battery cable terminal to the generator.

17. Install the positive battery cable nut at the generator and tighten to 15 ft. lbs. (20 Nm).

18. Position the positive battery cable boot at the generator terminal.

19. Connect the negative battery cable.

ENGINE ELECTRICAL

IGNITION SYSTEM

FIRING ORDER

2.4L Engine

1–3–4–2

3.0L Engine

1–2–3–4–5–6

IGNITION COIL

REMOVAL & INSTALLATION

2.4L Engine

1. Remove the intake manifold cover.
2. Disconnect the engine wiring harness electrical connectors from the ignition coil(s).
3. Remove the ignition coil bolt(s) and remove the ignition coil(s).

To install:

4. Install the ignition coil(s).
5. Install the ignition coil bolt(s) and tighten to 89 inch lbs. (10 Nm).
6. Connect the engine wiring harness electrical connector(s) to the ignition coil(s).
7. Install the intake manifold cover.

3.0L Engine

Bank 1

Remove the intake manifold. See "Intake Manifold" in "ENGINE MECHANICAL" section.

Disconnect the engine wiring harness electrical connector(s) from the ignition coil(s).

Remove the ignition coil bolt(s).

Remove the ignition coil(s).

To install:

Install the ignition coil(s).

Install the ignition coil bolt(s) and tighten the bolt(s) to 89 inch lbs. (10 Nm).

Connect the engine wiring harness electrical connector(s) to the ignition coil(s).

Install the intake manifold. See "Intake Manifold" in "ENGINE MECHANICAL" section.

Bank 2

1. Remove the intake manifold cover.
2. Disconnect the engine wiring harness electrical connector(s) from the ignition coil(s).
3. Remove the ignition coil bolt(s) and the ignition coil(s).

To install:

4. Install the ignition coil(s). Tighten the bolt(s) to 89 inch lbs. (10 Nm).
5. Connect the engine wiring harness electrical connector(s) to the ignition coil(s).
6. Install the intake manifold cover.

IGNITION TIMING

ADJUSTMENT

➡**Ignition timing is computer controlled and is not manually adjustable.**

SPARK PLUGS

REMOVAL & INSTALLATION

1. Remove the ignition coil(s), as described in this section.

➡**Make sure that any water and/or debris is blown out of the spark plug holes prior to removing the spark plugs.**

2. Remove the spark plugs using a 5/8 inch spark plug socket.

To install:

✳✳ CAUTION

Do not coat spark plug threads with anti-seize compound. If anti-seize compound is used and spark plugs are over-torqued, damage to the cylinder head threads may result.

3. Check the spark plug gap, it should be 0.040 in. (1.0 mm).
4. Install the spark plugs. Tighten the plugs to 15 ft. lbs. (20 Nm).
5. Install the ignition coil(s).

ENGINE ELECTRICAL

STARTING SYSTEM

STARTER

REMOVAL & INSTALLATION

2.4L Engine

1. Disconnect the negative battery cable.
2. Remove the power vacuum brake booster pump. See "BRAKES" section.
3. Raise and support the vehicle.
4. Disconnect the engine harness connector from the starter.
5. Remove the starter solenoid terminal nut.
6. Remove the positive battery cable terminal from the starter.
7. Remove the starter solenoid wire terminal from the starter.
8. Remove the starter bolts and remove the starter.

To install:

9. Position the starter to the engine.

10. Install the starter bolts and tighten to 30 ft. lbs. (40 Nm).
11. Install the starter solenoid wire terminal to the starter.
12. Install the positive battery cable terminal to the starter Ensure that the anti-rotational tab is correctly located into the indexing slot.
13. Install the starter solenoid terminal nut and tighten to 13 ft. lbs. (17 Nm).
14. Connect the engine harness connector to the starter.
15. Install the power vacuum brake booster pump.
16. Lower the vehicle.
17. Connect the negative battery cable.

3.0L Engine

1. Disconnect the battery negative cable.
2. Remove the heat shield from the starter.
3. Disconnect the knock sensor connector.

4. Disconnect and remove the bank 1 sensor 2 oxygen sensor after the left catalytic converter.
5. Remove the battery positive nut and the engine harness connector from the starter solenoid.
6. Remove the starter motor bolts and the starter motor.

To install:

7. Install the starter motor and tighten the mounting bolts to 43 ft. lbs. (58 Nm).
8. Install the battery positive cable and engine harness connector to the starter. Tighten the battery positive cable nut to 18 ft. lbs. (25 Nm).
9. Install the engine harness connector to the starter solenoid.
10. Install the starter heat shield.
11. Connect the knock sensor connector.
12. Install and connect the bank 1 sensor 2 oxygen sensor.
13. Connect the battery negative cable.

ENGINE MECHANICAL

➡Disconnecting the negative battery cable may interfere with the functions of the on board computer systems and may require the computer to undergo a relearning process, once the negative battery cable is reconnected.

ACCESSORY DRIVE BELTS

ACCESSORY BELT ROUTING

See Figures 35 and 36.

ADJUSTMENT

➡Drive belt uses an automatic tensioner to maintain belt tightness. No manual adjustment is required.

REMOVAL & INSTALLATION

1. Remove the right engine splash shield.
2. Use the proper tool to rotate the drive belt tensioner and relieve pressure on the belt.
3. Remove the drive belt from the pulleys and tensioner.
4. Clean and inspect the drive belt surfaces of all the pulleys.
5. Inspect the drive belt for correct alignment.
6. Installation is the reverse of the removal procedure.

AIR CLEANER

REMOVAL & INSTALLATION

1. Remove the air cleaner outlet duct.
2. On 3.0L engine, remove throttle inlet absolute pressure sensor and MAF sensor.
3. Remove the retaining bolts.

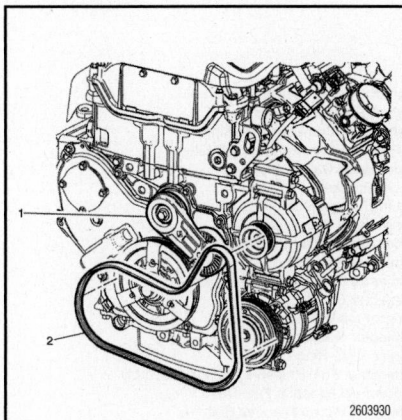

Fig. 35 Showing accessory drive belt (1) routing and tensioner (2)—2.4L engine

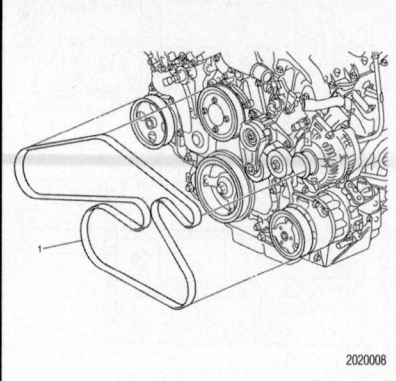

Fig. 36 Showing accessory drive belt (1) routing—3.0L engine

4. Disconnect any electrical connections as air cleaner assembly is removed.
5. Installation is the reverse of the removal procedure.

FILTER/ELEMENT REPLACEMENT

1. Remove air cleaner outlet duct from housing.
2. Remove top cover retaining screws and remove cover.
3. Remove and replace filter.

CAMSHAFT & VALVE LIFTERS

REMOVAL & INSTALLATION

2.4L Engine

See Figures 37 through 42.

1. Remove the rear lift bracket.
2. Remove the front lift bracket.
3. Remove the ignition coils. See "ENGINE ELECTRICAL" section.
4. Remove the camshaft housing cover plate from the front of the engine.

➡On DO NOT remove the PCV hose from the camshaft cover. If damage to the hose or connectors is present, the cover must be replaced.

5. Remove the camshaft cover assembly.
6. Remove and discard the camshaft cover gasket, camshaft cover grommets, and camshaft cover bolts if they are serviced with the grommet.
7. Remove the camshaft position actuator (intake or exhaust, as applicable). See "Camshaft Position Actuator" in this section.
8. Remove the fuel pump (intake camshaft).
9. Remove the camshaft position actua-

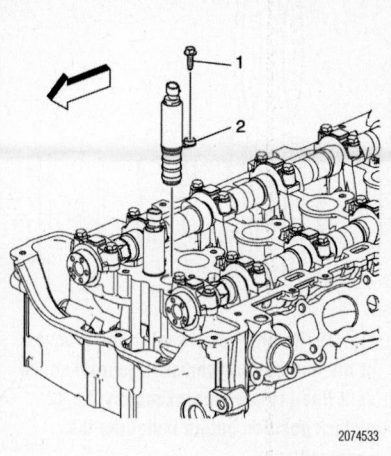

Fig. 37 Remove the camshaft position actuator solenoid valve bolt (1) and valve (2)—intake shown; exhaust similar

tor solenoid valve bolt and valve (intake or exhaust, as applicable).
10. For intake, remove the rear cylinder head intake camshaft cover plate.
11. For intake, remove the intake camshaft bearing rear cap bolts and cap.

➡Remove each bolt on each cap one turn at a time until there is no spring tension pushing on the camshaft. Mark camshaft caps to ensure they are installed in the same position.

12. Remove the camshaft cap bolts, caps, and intake and/or exhaust camshaft.

➡Keep all of the roller finger followers and hydraulic lash adjusters in order so

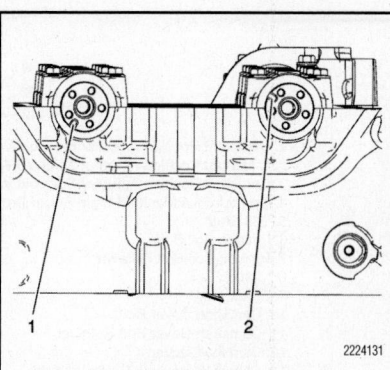

Fig. 38 When installing the camshafts, ensure the intake camshaft notch is in the 10 o'clock position (2) and the exhaust camshaft notch is in the 7 o'clock position (1). The number 1 piston should be at top dead center (TDC), crankshaft key at 12 o'clock.

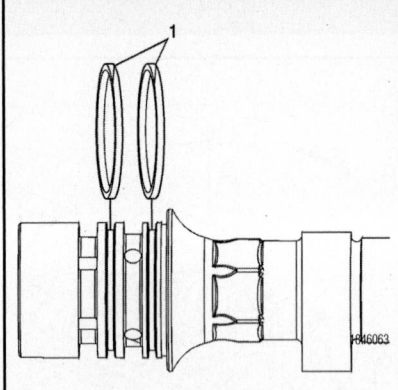

Fig. 39 Rotate the oil seal in the groove of the number one camshaft journal so the split line (1) is at approximately the 12 o'clock position before installing the camshaft caps.

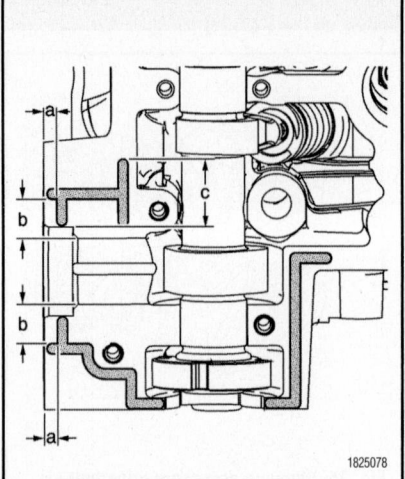

Fig. 40 Showing locations of sealer to camshaft

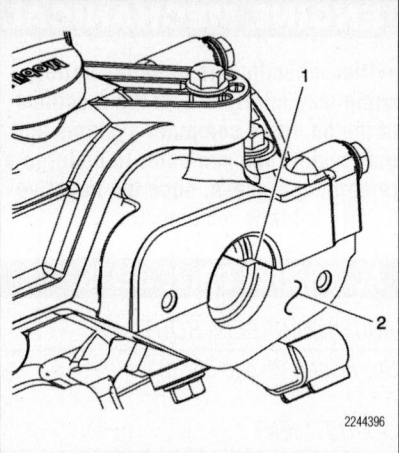

Fig. 41 Remove all excess sealing material from the fuel pump roller lifter bore (1), and ensure the bore is free of debris.

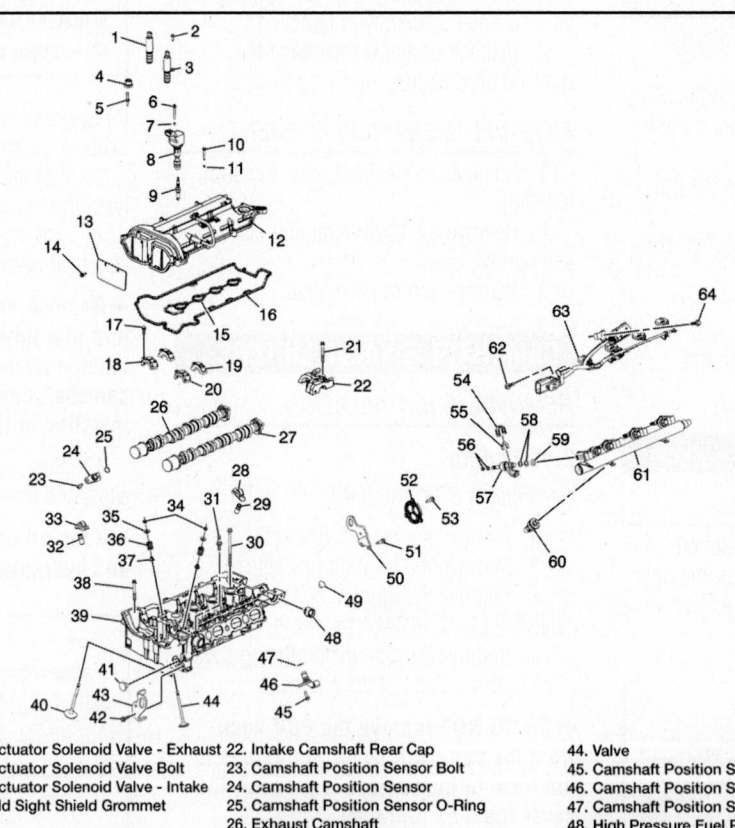

1. Camshaft Position Actuator Solenoid Valve - Exhaust
2. Camshaft Position Actuator Solenoid Valve Bolt
3. Camshaft Position Actuator Solenoid Valve - Intake
4. Upper Intake Manifold Sight Shield Grommet
5. Ball Stud
6. Ignition Coil Bolt
7. Ignition Coil Bolt Retainer
8. Ignition Coil
9. Spark Plug
10. Camshaft Cover Bolt
11. Camshaft Cover Bolt Retainer
12. Camshaft Cover
13. Camshaft Housing Cover Insulator
14. Camshaft Housing Cover Insulator Bolt
15. Camshaft Cover Seal
16. Camshaft Cover Seal
17. Camshaft Bearing Cap Bolt
18. Camshaft Bearing Front Cap
19. Camshaft Bearing Cap
20. Camshaft Bearing Front Cap
21. Camshaft Rear Cap Bolt
22. Intake Camshaft Rear Cap
23. Camshaft Position Sensor Bolt
24. Camshaft Position Sensor
25. Camshaft Position Sensor O-Ring
26. Exhaust Camshaft
27. Intake Camshaft
28. Roller Finger Follower
29. Hydraulic Lash Adjuster
30. Cylinder Head Bolt
31. Engine Coolant Air Bleed Fitting
32. Hydraulic Lash Adjuster
33. Roller Finger Follower
34. Valve Keys
35. Valve Spring Retainer
36. Valve Spring
37. Valve Stem Seal
38. Small Cylinder Head Bolt
39. Cylinder Head
40. Valve
41. Timing Chain Guide Bolt Access Hole Plug
42. Front Lift Bracket Bolt
43. Front Lift Bracket
44. Valve
45. Camshaft Position Sensor Bolt
46. Camshaft Position Sensor
47. Camshaft Position Sensor O-Ring
48. High Pressure Fuel Pump Roller Lifter
49. Cylinder Head Gallery Plug
50. Rear Lift Bracket
51. Rear Lift Bracket Bolt
52. Cylinder Head Cover Plate
53. Cylinder Head Cover Plate Bolt
54. Fuel Injector Retainer
55. Fuel Injector Bushing
56. Fuel Injector Seal
57. Multiport Fuel Injector
58. Fuel Injector Spacer
59. Fuel Injector O-Ring
60. Fuel Injection Fuel Pressure Sensor Assembly
61. Multiport Fuel Injection Fuel Rail
62. Fuel Injector Wiring Harness Bolt
63. Fuel Injector Wiring Harness
64. Fuel Injector Wiring Harness Bolt

Fig. 42 Exploded view of the cylinder head components—2.4L engine

that they can be reinstalled in their respective locations.

13. Remove the camshaft roller finger followers.

14. Remove the hydraulic lash adjusters.

To install:

15. Install the hydraulic lash adjusters into their bores in the cylinder head.

16. Lubricate the hydraulic lash adjusters. Lubricate the valve tips.

➡**Used roller followers must be returned to the original position on the camshaft. If the camshaft is being replaced, the roller followers actuated by the camshaft must also be replaced.**

17. Position the roller followers on the tip of the valve stem and on the lash adjuster. Lubricate roller followers.

➡**The engine is timed top-dead center exhaust stroke.**

18. When installing the camshafts, ensure the intake camshaft notch is in the 10 o'clock position and the exhaust camshaft notch is in the 7 o'clock position. The number 1 piston should be at top dead center (TDC), crankshaft key at 12 o'clock.

19. Set the camshaft on top of the roller followers in the camshaft bearing journals and lubricate.

20. Rotate the oil seal in the groove of the number one camshaft journal so the split line is at approximately the 12 o'clock position before installing the camshaft caps.

➡**The number 1 cylinder must be at top dead center (TDC), crankshaft keyway at the 12 o'clock position.**

21. Install the intake camshaft with the notch on the front at approximately the 10 o'clock position.

22. Install the exhaust camshaft with the notch on the front at approximately the 7 o'clock position.

23. Install the camshaft caps and hand start the camshaft cap bolts. Tighten the camshaft cap bolts in increments of 3 turns until they are seated. Tighten the camshaft caps to 89 inch lbs. (10 Nm).

24. It is critical during installation to ensure the bearing rear cap and cylinder head alignment is correct and the mating surfaces are flush:

   a. Ensure that all sealing material has been removed from the components, and the sealing surfaces are clean and free of contamination prior to applying the sealer.

   b. Install and align the rear cap within 20 minutes of applying the sealer.

➡**Apply the sealer to all locations centrally locating the bead on the rail.**

25. Run bead to 5.0 mm, dimension a, as shown.

26. Where the cap ends on the perimeter rail, extend bead approximately 4.0 mm beyond edge of cap.

27. Run bead, dimension c, 32 mm from the edge of the cylinder head as shown.

28. Run beads, dimension b, 20 mm from edge of cylinder head as shown.

29. Apply a 2.5 mm bead of sealer to the cylinder head at the number 6 intake camshaft rear cap mating surface.

30. For the intake camshaft, install the number 6 intake camshaft rear cap:

   a. Tighten the cap bolts evenly to 44 inch lbs. (5 Nm).

   b. Tighten the cap bolts evenly to 89 inch lbs. (10 Nm).

   c. Back the cap bolts out 120 degrees.

   d. Tighten the cap bolts evenly a final pass to 89 inch lbs. (10 Nm).

31. Remove all excess sealing material from the fuel pump roller lifter bore, and ensure the bore is free of debris. Do not allow any excess sealing material to remain within the cylinder head or on any sealing surface.

32. Remove all excess sealing material from the fuel pump assembly sealing surface.

33. Verify the seal on the cylinder head cover plate is intact and in good condition. Ensure that the cover plate sealing surface is clean and free of excess sealing material. Install the rear cylinder head cover plate and tighten the bolts to 89 inch lbs. (10 Nm).

34. Install the intake and/or exhaust camshaft position actuator solenoid valve. Tighten the solenoid valve bolt to 89 inch lbs. (10 Nm).

35. Install the camshaft position actuator. See "Camshaft Position Actuator" in this section.

36. For intake camshaft, install the fuel pump.

CAMSHAFT

REMOVAL & INSTALLATION

3.0L Engine

See Figures 43 and 44.

1. Remove the intake manifold. See "Intake Manifold" in this section.

2. Remove the fuel pump from the cylinder head. See "FUEL SYSTEMS" section.

3. Remove the left bank camshaft cover.

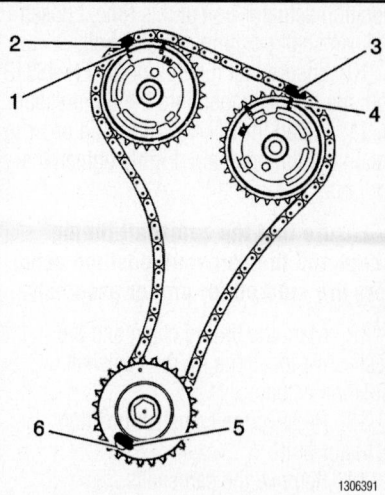

Fig. 43 Mark the timing chain and the respective locations on the camshaft position actuators (1-4)—items 5 and 6 apply only for full timing chain removal—right side shown; left side similar

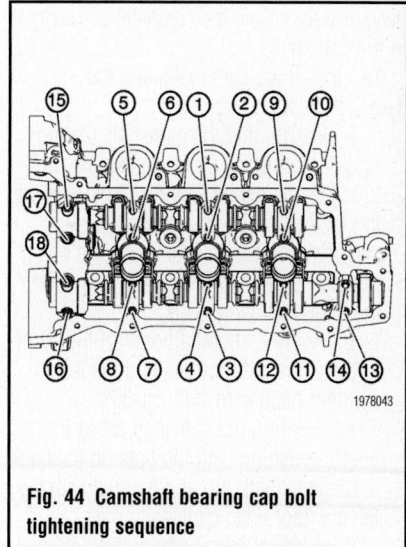

Fig. 44 Camshaft bearing cap bolt tightening sequence

4. Remove the camshaft sensors. See "ENGINE PERFORMANCE & EMISSION CONTROLS" section.

5. Remove the camshaft position actuator solenoid.

6. Remove the camshaft position actuator. See "Camshaft Position Actuator" in this section.

7. Remove the crankshaft balancer. See "Crankshaft Balancer" in this section.

8. Rotate the crankshaft with the EN-46111 socket until the camshafts are in a neutral (low tension) position. Check that the camshaft flats are parallel with the camshaft cover rail.

9. Use an open-end wrench at the camshaft hex to prevent camshaft/engine rotation. DO NOT remove the camshaft

position actuator bolt at this time. Loosen the camshaft position actuator bolt.

10. Ensure that the tips of the EN-48313 tool are fully engaged into the timing chain.

11. Install the EN-48313 tool in order to retain the timing chain. Firmly tighten the tool nuts.

➡**Ensure that the camshaft timing chain and the camshaft position actuators are marked for proper assembly.**

12. Mark the timing chain and the respective locations on the camshaft position actuators (1-4).

13. Remove the camshaft position actuator bolt.

14. Remove the camshafts.

To install:

15. Ensure that the marks on the camshaft position actuator and the timing chain (1-4) are aligned.

16. DO NOT tighten the camshaft position actuator bolt at this time.

17. Locate the camshafts to the cylinder head and assemble the camshaft actuators to the camshafts.

18. Install the camshafts and the camshaft bearing caps.

a. Ensure that the camshaft sealing rings are in place in the camshaft grooves. Camshaft sealing rings must be in place below the surface of the camshaft journal in order to avoid being pinched between the cylinder head and the camshaft caps.

b. Apply a liberal amount of lubricant to the camshaft journals and the left cylinder head camshaft carriers.

c. Position the camshaft lobes in a neutral position with the flats on the back of the camshafts up and parallel with the left cylinder head camshaft cover rail.

d. Apply a liberal amount of lubricant to the camshaft bearing caps.

e. Install and tighten the bearing cap bolts, in sequence, to 89inch lbs. (10 Nm).

19. Remove the EN-46108 tool.

20. Use an open-end wrench at the camshaft hex to prevent camshaft/engine rotation.

21. Install and tighten the camshaft position actuators.

22. Install the intake camshaft position actuator solenoid.

23. Install the camshaft sensors. See "ENGINE PERFORMANCE & EMISSION CONTROLS" section.

24. Install the crankshaft balancer. See "Crankshaft Balancer" in this section.

25. Install the camshaft cover.

26. Install the fuel pump to the cylinder head.

27. Install the intake manifold. See "Intake Manifold" in this section.

CAMSHAFT POSITION ACTUATOR

REMOVAL & INSTALLATION

2.4L Engine

See Figures 45 through 50.

1. Remove the air cleaner assembly.
2. Remove the camshaft cover.
3. Remove the spark plugs.
4. Remove the engine splash shield.
5. Rotate the crankshaft clockwise and install the EN-48953 retention tool.
6. Install the camshaft actuator retainer bolts and tighten to 89 inch lbs. (10 Nm).
7. Use a wrench on the camshaft flats to hold the camshaft. Loosen, but DO NOT remove the intake or exhaust camshaft actuator bolt.
8. Remove the EN-48953 locking tool.
9. Clean the timing chain and gears with solvent.

➡**Ensure the timing chain and the camshaft position actuators are marked for proper assembly.**

10. Mark the intake and exhaust camshaft actuators and the respective locations on the timing chain.

11. Remove the upper timing chain guide bolts and guide.

12. Remove the timing chain tensioner.

a. The camshaft actuator should not rotate during the removal or installation.

b. Ensure the tips of the tool are fully engaged into the timing chain. The retention tool rod can be used on the

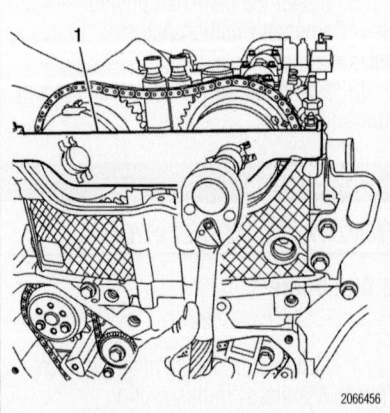

Fig. 45 Rotate the crankshaft clockwise and install the EN-48953 retention tool (1).

back side of the chain to ensure the teeth from the retention tool are engaged.

13. Install the EN-48749 retention tool to the intake and exhaust side of the timing chain.

14. Remove and discard the intake or exhaust camshaft actuator bolt.

15. Rotate the opposite camshaft clockwise slightly to take the tension off of the timing chain on the actuator of the side being serviced.

16. Remove the intake or exhaust camshaft actuator from the camshaft while also removing the actuator with its timing chain sprocket.

To install:

➡**Ensure that the alignment mark made previously on the intake**

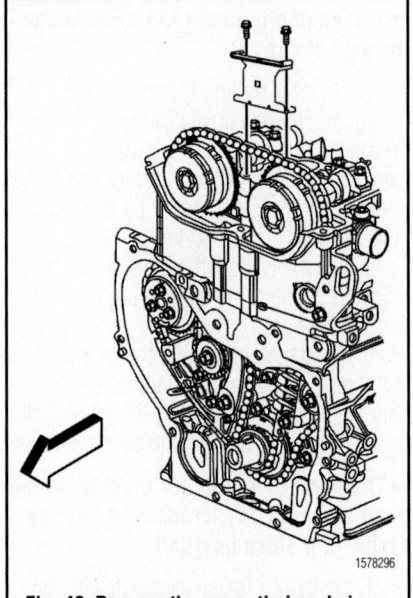

Fig. 46 Remove the upper timing chain guide bolts and guide.

Fig. 47 Remove the timing chain tensioner.

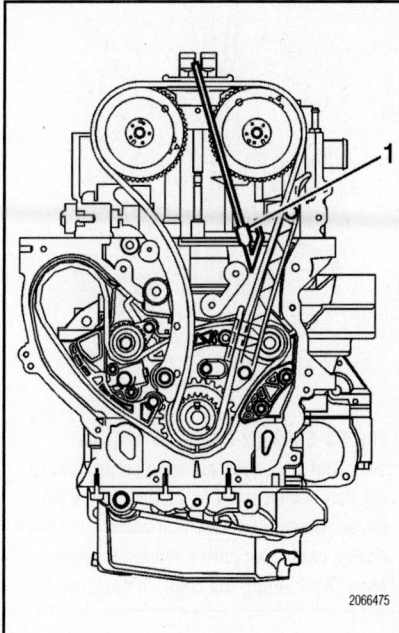

Fig. 48 Install the EN-48749 retention tool (1) to the intake side of the timing chain.

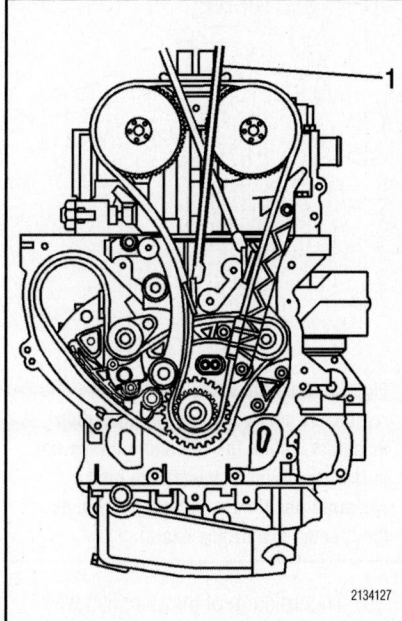

Fig. 49 Install the EN-48749 retention tool (1) to the exhaust side of the timing chain.

camshaft actuator is still aligned properly with the mark on the timing chain.

17. If replacing the actuator, transfer mark made on old actuator to the new actuator.

18. Install the timing chain onto the camshaft actuator.

19. Align the camshaft actuator alignment mark made previously with the timing chain mark and install the actuator onto the

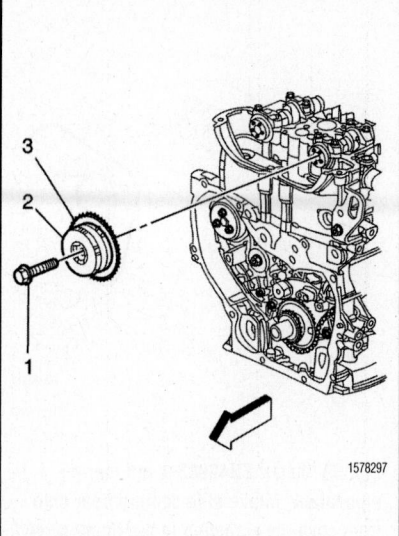

Fig. 50 Remove and discard the intake or exhaust camshaft actuator bolt (2), remove the actuator (3), with the timing chain sprocket (1).

camshaft rotating the opposite camshaft clockwise, if required.

20. Install a NEW camshaft actuator bolt until snug.

21. Remove the timing chain retention tool from the intake or exhaust side of the timing chain.

➡**Ensure that the alignment mark previously on the intake camshaft actuator is still aligned properly with the timing chain. If the mark made previously on the intake camshaft actuator is not aligned properly, refer to "Timing Chain, Sprocket & Tensioner" in this section.**

22. Remove the timing chain retention tool from the timing chain.

⚹⚹ **CAUTION**

Failure to reset the tensioner will allow the tensioner to over-extend, limiting the timing chain life.

23. Reset and install the timing chain tensioner.

24. Install the EN-48953 retention tool.

25. Install the camshaft actuator retention tool bolts and tighten to 89 inch lbs. (10 Nm).

26. Tighten the NEW camshaft actuator bolt to 20 ft. lbs. (30 Nm), plus an additional 100 degrees, using the EN-45059 meter, or equivalent. Use a wrench on the camshaft flats to hold the camshaft while tightening the fastener.

27. Remove the EN-48953 retention tool.

28. Install the upper timing chain guide and bolts and tighten to 89 inch lbs. (10 Nm).

29. Install the spark plugs.

30. Install the camshaft cover.

31. Install the engine splash shield.

32. Install the air cleaner assembly.

3.0L Engine

Bank 1

See Figures 51 through 55.

1. Remove the camshaft cover.

2. Remove the camshaft position actuator solenoid valve solenoid—intake and the intake camshaft position sensor. See "ENGINE PERFORMANCE & EMISSION CONTROLS" section.

3. Remove the camshaft position actuator solenoid valve solenoid—exhaust and the exhaust camshaft position sensor. See "ENGINE PERFORMANCE & EMISSION CONTROLS" section.

4. Rotate engine clockwise using crankshaft dampener retaining bolt until the flats at the rear ends of the camshafts are pointing up. This puts the camshafts on "base circle" and will reduce their tendency to rotate from valve spring pressure when the camshaft position actuators/drive chains are removed.

➡**Do NOT remove or back out the camshaft position actuator bolt(s) significantly, simply break them loose from their fully-torqued position. The position actuators must stay firmly attached until the retaining tools are in place, but they should be broken loose while the chain is still tight and in position.**

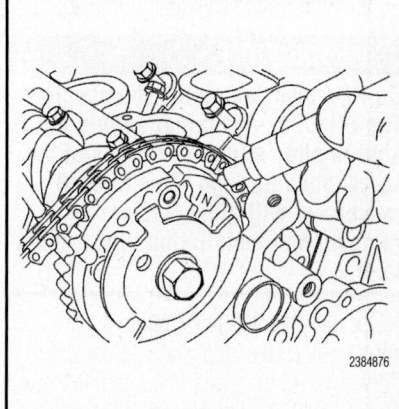

Fig. 51 Mark the position of the timing chain to each camshaft position actuator—intake shown; exhaust similar

Fig. 52 Remove the camshaft front cap (1).

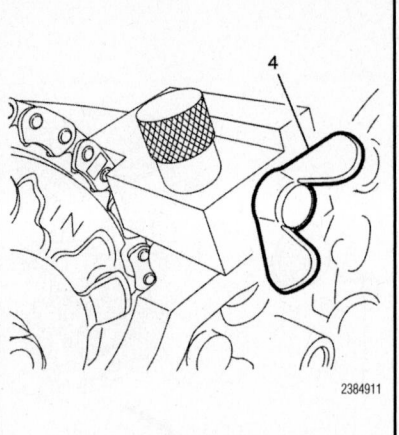

Fig. 53 Install EN49982-1 retainer, or equivalent, intake side chain holder onto front cover by screwing in the thumbscrew (2) on the EN49982-1 retainer finger-tight.

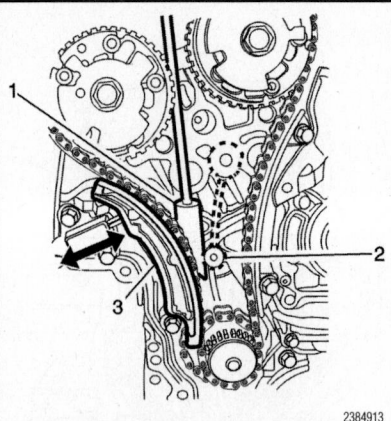

Fig. 54 EN49982-2 retainer installed such that it wedges between an internal rib (2) that is cast into the inside of the front cover (shown in dotted line above) and the timing chain and spring-loaded tensioner shoe (3), holding the chain in position.

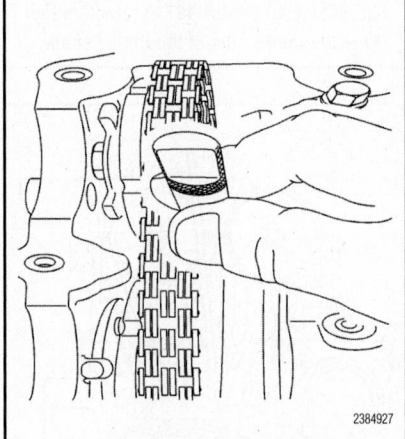

Fig. 55 Once the wedge portion of retainer is below the camshaft position actuators, rotate the retainer until the flat in the handle faces toward the intake camshaft position actuator. This orients the "teeth" toward the chain.

5. Loosen intake and/or exhaust camshaft position actuator retaining bolts, depending on which camshaft position actuator and/or camshaft you will be servicing. If servicing both camshaft position actuators and/or camshafts, loosen both bolts.

➡ Be certain to clearly mark the position of the chain to the camshaft position actuator(s). Though the engine does not need to be set to a specific timing mark before starting the procedure, the relationship of the chain to the actuator(s) is critical and must be reestablished on assembly.

6. Mark the position of the chain to the intake camshaft position actuator, then the exhaust actuator.
7. Remove camshaft front cap bolts.

➡ Do NOT remove or loosen any other camshaft bearing caps at this time, even if you intend to eventually remove the camshaft.

8. Remove the camshaft front cap.

✳✳ CAUTION

Do NOT overtighten the thumbscrew. The EN49982-1 retainer should be able to slide slightly via the slot the screw goes through. This fore/aft movement will allow easier removal and installation of the chain later.

9. Install EN49982-1 retainer, or equivalent, intake side chain holder onto front cover by screwing in the thumbscrew on the EN49982-1 retainer finger-tight.
10. Tighten wing nut so retainer closes over and firmly grasps timing chain.

➡ The engine front cover is removed for clarity in the following graphics, but is NOT required to be removed to perform the procedure.

➡ EN49982-2 retainer will be installed in the following steps such that it wedges between an internal rib that is cast into the inside of the front cover (shown in dotted line above) and the timing chain and spring-loaded tensioner shoe, holding the chain in position. The wedge will be left in place during the cam position actuator and/or camshaft service.

11. Insert the EN49982-2 retainer between the two camshaft position actuators with the "teeth" on the retainer facing toward the front cover.
12. Once the wedge portion of retainer is below the camshaft position actuators, rotate the retainer until the flat in the handle faces toward the intake camshaft position actuator. This orients the "teeth" toward the chain.

✳✳ CAUTION

Do not try to force the wedge into position, simply ensure it is loosely engaged in the timing chain and in the correct overall position.

13. Drop the wedge down until it begins to engage the timing chain and the belt internal rib.
14. Using a 20 mm wrench on the cast hexagonal portion of the exhaust camshaft, rotate the camshaft toward the intake camshaft while pushing down on the handle of the EN49982-2 retainer.

15. This rotation of the camshaft will compress the tensioner shoe against the spring force of the tensioner, opening up a gap between the chain and the internal rib in the front cover. The wedge will then drop into this gap. You will feel a distinct click as the teeth engage the chain.

✳✳ CAUTION

Be sure the EN49982-2 is captured firmly as described before continuing. This is critical to ensuring the camshaft drive chains stay properly timed.

16. Release the force on the wrench, allowing the spring tension to close the tensioner shoe against the wedge portion of retainer. You should be able to lightly tug on the retainer and it should stay in position. Repeat previous steps if necessary to re-insert the retainer until you are certain it is in position and will stay in position.

17. With retainer in position and with the 20 mm wrench removed, there should now be some slack in the timing drive chain as indicated in the graphics shown.

❊❊ CAUTION

Do not pry against the face of the camshaft position actuators or the position actuator retaining bolt.

18. Position a screwdriver or small pry bar between a camshaft cap and camshaft lobe. Carefully move/pry the camshafts as far as possible toward the rear/flywheel end of the engine.

❊❊ CAUTION

Do not move or disturb the EN49982 retainer components after their installation or the timing chains may be lost inside the front cover.

19. The retainer tools should be in position and they must be left in position during the servicing of the camshaft position actuator(s) and/or camshaft(s).

20. Remove and capture the plastic thrust washers (behind the camshaft position actuator sprocket). Ensure the plastic thrust washer does not fall into the front cover area:

   a. To remove the intake camshaft position actuator, remove the loosened retaining bolt. To remove only the exhaust camshaft position actuator, skip the steps for removing the intake camshaft position actuator. However, the retainer MUST be installed as discussed even if the intake side will not be serviced or the timing of the camshaft chains will be lost.

   b. Slide the camshaft position actuator forward and off the end of the intake camshaft. The slot in the retainer will allow the tool to move forward enough to disengage the camshaft position actuator from the front of the camshaft. Remove the plastic thrust washer when removing the camshaft position actuator from the end of the camshaft.

   c. Tilt the camshaft position actuator forward and out/away from the engine.

➡ **DO NOT remove the EN49982 retainers. They are holding the cam chains to**
maintain their properly-timed positions.

21. Allow the chain to rest on the retainer tools in position during service.

To install:

22. Install plastic camshaft position actuator thrust washer between cylinder head face and camshaft position actuator on assembly.

23. It may help to carefully pry the camshaft forward and to move the EN49982-1 retainer backward via the slot to reengage the position actuator to the camshaft. The dowel pin on the camshaft position actuator must be aligned with the slot in the camshaft nose for reassembly.

➡ **Ensure plastic thrust washer is in place before installing the actuator.**

24. Install the intake camshaft position actuator first by inserting the actuator between the timing chain and front cover. Tilt the actuator in and engage the chain while aligning the marks you made on the chain and position actuator.

25. Ensure the camshaft position actuator fits snugly to the end of the camshaft.

26. Install the intake camshaft position actuator retaining bolt, and lightly tighten the bolt to hold the camshaft actuator in place. DO NOT torque at this time.

27. Install the exhaust camshaft position actuator retaining bolt, and lightly tighten the bolt to hold the camshaft actuator in place. DO NOT torque at this time.

28. Double-check that the marks on both the intake and exhaust camshaft position actuators to ensure that they are aligned with their respective paint marks on the chain.

29. Using a 20 mm wrench on the cast hexagonal portion of the exhaust camshaft, rotate the camshaft clockwise while pulling up on the handle of the EN49982-2 retainer.

30. Remove EN49982-2 retainer.

31. Release the pressure on the wrench. The timing chain should now be tight and should lose the slack the wedge was providing.

➡ **Double-check the marks on the camshaft position actuators and chains to ensure they are correct.**

32. Torque one or both camshaft position actuator retaining bolts to 43 ft. lbs. (58 Nm).

33. Unscrew the wing nut on EN49982-1 retainer to release timing chain, and then remove retainer from the front cover by unscrewing the thumbscrew.

34. Install camshaft front cap and bolts.
Tighten the camshaft front cap bolts to 89 inch lbs. (10 Nm).

35. Install the camshaft position actuator solenoid valve solenoids and camshaft position sensors.

36. Install the camshaft cover.

Bank 2

See Figures 56 through 60.

1. Remove the intake manifold. See "Intake Manifold" in this section.

2. Remove the left camshaft cover.

3. Remove the left intake and exhaust camshaft position sensors.

4. Remove the left intake and exhaust camshaft position actuator solenoids.

➡ **Rotate the crankshaft balancer bolt in a clockwise direction ONLY.**

5. Rotate the crankshaft balancer using the balancer bolt until the camshafts are in a neutral (low tension) position. The camshafts will be parallel with the camshaft cover rail.

➡ **Ensure that the camshaft timing chain and the camshaft position actuators are marked for proper assembly.**

6. Use a paint stick to create an alignment mark on one of the timing chain links (2) and the adjacent tooth on the exhaust camshaft position actuator (1).

7. Use a paint stick to create an alignment mark on one of the timing chain links (3) and the adjacent tooth on the intake camshaft position actuator (4).

8. Use an open end wrench on the hex cast into the left intake and exhaust camshafts and rotate the camshafts toward each other in order to create slack in the chain between the actuators.

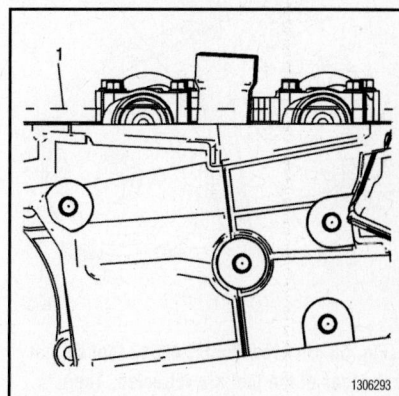
1306293

Fig. 56 Rotate the crankshaft balancer using the balancer bolt until the camshafts are in a neutral (low tension) position. The camshafts will be parallel with the camshaft cover rail (1).

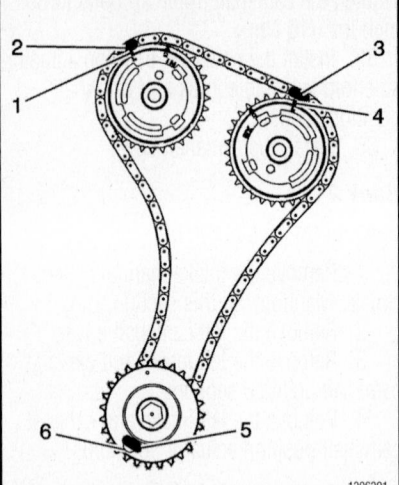

Fig. 57 Use a paint stick to make alignment marks on chain links (2, 3) of the exhaust and intake camshaft position actuators (1, 4)—items 5 and 6 apply only to complete timing chain removal.

9. Unscrew the EN-48313 tool so that the legs of the tool are retracted. Then, insert the tool between the camshaft actuators, rearward of the timing chain until the bottom line that is scribed in the body of the tool is adjacent to the top surface of the cylinder head. This is the approximate installed position.

➡ **The engine front cover is removed for clarity in the following graphics, but NOT required to perform the procedure.**

10. Ensure that the feet on the legs of the tool are facing the front of the engine.

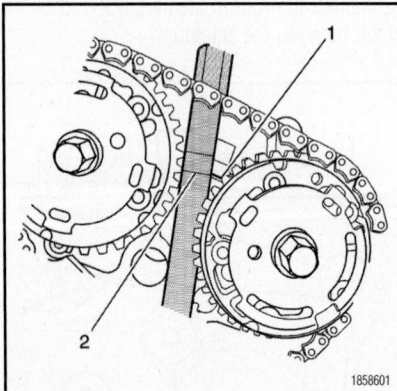

Fig. 58 Unscrew the EN-48313 tool so that the legs of the tool are retracted. Then, insert the tool between the camshaft actuators, rearward of the timing chain until the bottom line that is scribed in the body of the tool (2) is adjacent to the top surface of the cylinder head (1). This is the approximate installed position.

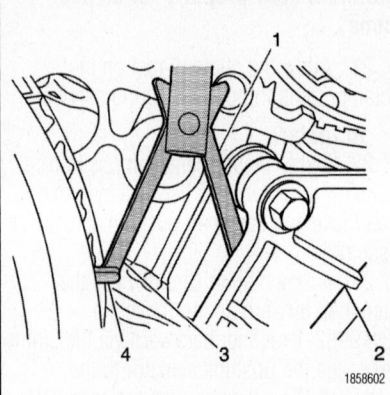

Fig. 59 Ensure that the feet (4) on the legs of the tool are facing the front of the engine. Partially expand the legs (1, 3) of the EN-48313 tool by turning the T-shaped handle clockwise. Insert the leg of the tool (1) behind the timing chain guide (2). Continue expanding the tool until the legs (1, 3) contact the timing chain.

Partially expand the legs of the EN-48313 tool by turning the T-shaped handle clockwise. Insert the leg of the tool behind the timing chain guide. Continue expanding the tool until the legs contact the timing chain. Do not tighten at this time.

11. Ensure that the foot of the EN-48313 tool is engaged into one of the link pockets to prevent tool slippage during tightening of the tool. Hand tighten the tool.

12. Use an open end wrench on the hex cast into the left intake and exhaust camshafts and rotate the camshafts toward

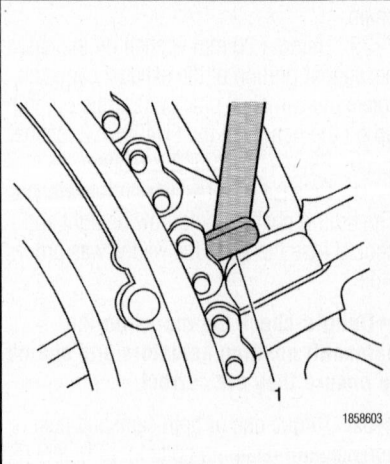

Fig. 60 Ensure that the foot (1) of the EN-48313 tool is engaged into one of the link pockets to prevent tool slippage during tightening of the tool. Hand tighten the tool.

each other in order to create slack in the chain between the actuators.

13. The tool is now properly installed to hold the timing chain in position.

14. Use an open end wrench on the hex cast into the camshaft in order to prevent engine rotation when loosening the camshaft position actuator bolt.

   a. If replacing the exhaust camshaft position actuator, then remove the bolt and the actuator.

   b. If replacing the intake camshaft position actuator, then remove the bolt and the actuator.

   c. If removing both the exhaust and intake camshaft actuators, the timing chain can be draped over the EN-48313 tool once the actuators have been removed.

15. Rotate the actuator in order to align the opening in the actuator reluctor wheel with the cam sensor boss in the front cover, to allow actuator removal.

16. Remove the camshaft thrust washer.

To install:

17. Ensure that the camshaft timing chain and the camshaft position actuators are marked for proper assembly.

18. Align the exhaust and intake camshaft actuator alignment paint marks to the timing chain alignment marks made during disassembly.

19. Position the exhaust camshaft actuator to the camshaft and install the actuator bolt hand tight. Remove the EN-48313 tool.

➡ **The camshaft position actuator will vary depending on application.**

➡ **Camshaft thrust washers must be installed on all 2010–11 applications when servicing the camshaft position actuators. Do not install washers on 2009 applications if they are not already present.**

20. Ensure the proper camshaft thrust washer is used. Use a 0.063 in. (1.6 mm) thrust washer on applications that have 5 attaching screws on the back side of the camshaft position actuator. Use a 0.043 in. (1.1 mm) thick thrust washer with yellow speckles on applications that have 4 attaching screws on the back side of the camshaft position actuator.

21. Install the thrust washer, if applicable.

22. If the exhaust and/or intake camshaft position actuator has been replaced, then tighten the bolt to 43 ft. lbs. (58 Nm).

23. Install the left intake and exhaust camshaft position actuator solenoids.

24. Install the left intake and exhaust camshaft position sensors.

25. Install the left camshaft cover.
26. Install the intake manifold.

CATALYTIC CONVERTER

REMOVAL & INSTALLATION

2.4L Engine

1. Raise and support the vehicle.
2. Remove the exhaust manifold heat shield.
3. Remove the catalytic converter brace.
4. Remove the oxygen sensor after the catalytic converter.
5. Remove the exhaust manifold nuts at the flange.
6. Remove the exhaust muffler nuts.
7. Remove the catalytic converter bracket clamp nut.
8. Remove the exhaust insulator hanger.
9. Remove and discard the seal and gasket.
10. Remove the catalytic converter.

To install:

11. Install the catalytic converter to position and install a new gasket and seal.
12. Install the exhaust insulator hanger.
13. Install the catalytic converter bracket clamp nut and tighten to 37 ft. lbs. (50 Nm).
14. Install the exhaust muffler nuts and tighten to 30 ft. lbs. (40 Nm).
15. Install the exhaust manifold nuts at the flange and tighten to 37 ft. lbs. (50 Nm).

3.0L Engine

Both Sides

1. Remove the catalytic converter heat shield.
2. Remove the exhaust flexible pipe.
3. Remove the catalytic converter nuts.

❊❊ CAUTION

To prevent damage to the exhaust manifold flange or stud, make sure the flange is fully seated before tightening.

4. Disconnect the oxygen sensor electrical connector.
5. Replace the exhaust front pipe nuts and the gasket with new ones.
6. Remove the catalytic converter.

To install:

7. Install the catalytic converter.
8. Clean and inspect the studs on the engine cylinder head, replace as necessary.
9. Verify that the studs are fully seated. Stud collar should touch the surface of the engine cylinder head.

10. During installation, tighten nuts in a criss-cross pattern, in two steps:
   • First Pass: 15 ft. lbs. (20 Nm)
   • Second Pass: 34 ft. lbs. (46 Nm)
11. Discard the old gasket and use a new one on installation.
12. If replacing catalytic converter, transfer oxygen sensor.
13. Install the exhaust flexible pipe.
14. Install the catalytic converter heat shield.

❊❊ CAUTION

Improperly installed and/or leaking exhaust manifold gaskets may affect vehicle emissions and/or On-Board Diagnostics (OBD) II system performance.

CRANKSHAFT BALANCER

REMOVAL & INSTALLATION

2.4L Engine

1. Remove the drive belt. See "Accessory Drive Belt".
2. Use EN-38122-A holder, or equivalent, to prevent the crankshaft from rotating while loosening the crankshaft balancer bolt.
3. Remove and discard the crankshaft balancer bolt and remove the washer and crankshaft balancer.

To install:

4. Position the crankshaft balancer.
5. Install washer and a NEW crankshaft balancer bolt.
6. Use the EN-38122-A holder to hold the crankshaft balancer in order to prevent the balancer from rotating while tightening the bolt.
7. Tighten the crankshaft balancer bolt to 74 ft. lbs. (100 Nm), plus an additional 125 degrees, using the EN-45059 meter.
8. Install the drive belt. See "Accessory Drive Belt".

3.0L Engine

See Figures 61 through 62.

1. Remove the drive belt. See "Accessory Drive Belt".
2. Install a suitable engine support mechanism, to hold the engine in place from above.
3. Remove the starter. See "ENGINE ELECTRICAL" section.
4. Install the EN-46106 tool through the starter mounting hole, to lock the flywheel.
5. Using engine support fixture, lower engine approximately two inches.

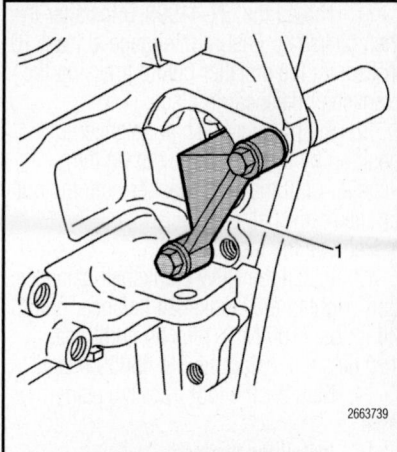

Fig. 61 Install the EN-46106 tool (1) through the starter mounting hole.

Fig. 62 Install a 3-jaw puller (3) and EN-38416-2 button (2) in the nose of the crankshaft and remove the crankshaft balancer (1).

6. Remove the crankshaft balancer bolt. Discard the bolt.
7. Install a 3-jaw puller and EN-38416-2 button in the nose of the crankshaft and remove the crankshaft balancer.
8. Install a 3-jaw puller (3) and EN-38416-2 button (2) in the nose of the crankshaft and remove the crankshaft balancer (1).

➡️**Tighten the center bolt of the puller in order to pull the crankshaft balancer off of the crankshaft.**

To install:

❊❊ CAUTION

Do not lubricate the crankshaft front oil seal or crankshaft balancer sealing surfaces. The crankshaft balancer is installed into a dry seal.

9. Apply lubricant to the inside of the crankshaft balancer hub bore.
10. Place the crankshaft balancer in position on the crankshaft.

11. Thread the EN-41998-B installer in the crankshaft. Ensure to engage at least 10 threads of the installer before pressing the crankshaft balancer in place.

12. Push the crankshaft balancer into position by tightening the nut on the installer until the large washer bottoms out on the crankshaft end.

Remove the installer tool.

13. Install the NEW crankshaft balancer bolt. Tighten the crankshaft balancer bolt to 74 ft. lbs. (100 Nm), plus an additional 150 degrees, using the EN-45059 meter.

14. Remove the tool from the starter hole.

15. Install the starter.

16. Install the drive belt.

17. Remove the engine support fixture.

CRANKSHAFT FRONT SEAL

REMOVAL & INSTALLATION

2.4L Engine

1. Remove the crankshaft balancer. See "Crankshaft Balancer" in this section.

2. Use a flat-bladed tool to remove the seal from the front cover.

✳✳ CAUTION

Use care not to scratch the seal bore surface.

3. Installation is the reverse of the removal procedure.

3.0L Engine

1. Remove the crankshaft balancer. See "Crankshaft Balancer" in this section.

2. Using EN-45000 seal remover, or equivalent, remove the crankshaft oil seal.

To install:

➡**Do not lubricate the crankshaft front oil seal or the crankshaft balancer sealing surfaces.**

3. Use the EN-29184 installer, or equivalent, to install the crankshaft front oil seal.

4. Install the crankshaft balancer.

CYLINDER HEAD

REMOVAL & INSTALLATION

2.4L Engine

See Figures 63 through 71.

1. Drain the cooling system.

2. Remove the exhaust manifold. See "Exhaust Manifold" in this section.

3. Remove the intake manifold. See "Intake Manifold" in this section.

4. Remove the fuel pump. See "FUEL SYSTEM" section.

5. Reposition the radiator surge tank air bleed hose clamp and remove the radiator surge tank air bleed hose from the cylinder head.

6. Reposition the radiator inlet hose clamp and remove the radiator inlet hose from the cylinder head.

7. Mark and disconnect all electrical connectors as necessary.

8. Remove the camshaft cover.

9. Remove the purge solenoid and bracket. See "ENGINE PERFORMANCE & EMISSION CONTROLS" section.

10. Remove the upper timing chain guide bolts and guide.

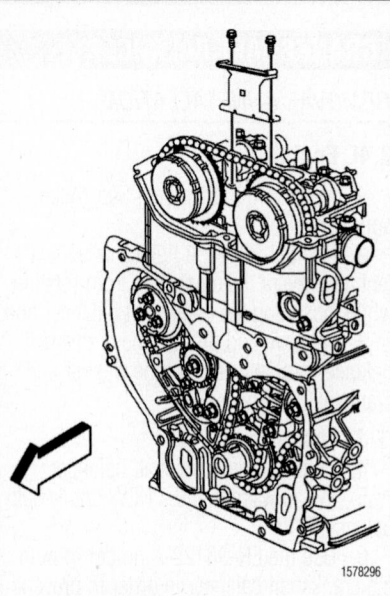

Fig. 63 Remove the upper timing chain guide bolts (1) and guide (2).

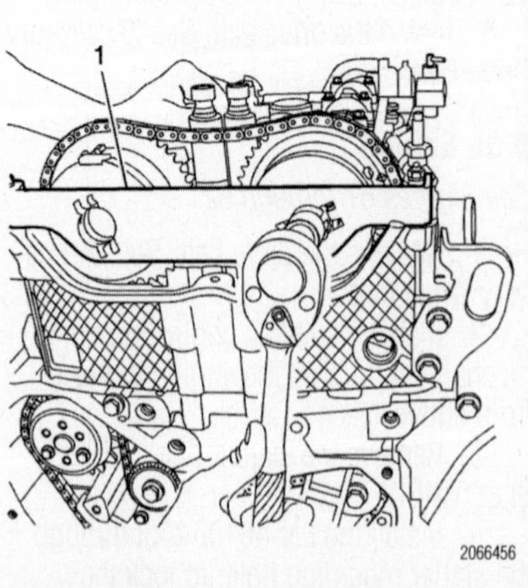

Fig. 64 Rotate the intake camshaft clockwise and install the EN-48953 locking tool (1) to the actuators.

11. If the intake camshaft actuator is moving independently of the camshaft, this means the camshaft is not locked to the actuator. Rotate the camshaft counterclockwise while the holding tool is installed and this will lock the camshaft to the actuator.

12. Ensure the timing chain and the camshaft position actuators are marked for proper assembly.

13. Rotate the intake camshaft clockwise and install the EN-48953 locking tool to the actuators.

14. Install the camshaft actuator retainer bolts and tighten to 89 inch lbs. (10 Nm).

15. Clean the timing chain and gears with solvent.

16. Mark the timing gear sprockets and the timing chain. It is recommended that the paint marks are located in the 12 o'clock position.

17. Use a 24 mm wrench on the hex flats of the camshaft to prevent camshaft rotation.

18. Loosen, but do not remove the intake and exhaust camshaft actuator bolts.

19. Remove the EN-48953 locking tool.

20. Remove the timing chain tensioner.

21. Install the EN-48749 retention tool to the intake side of the timing chain. Ensure the tips of the retention tool are fully engaged into the timing chain. The retention tool rod can be used on the back side of the chain to ensure the teeth from the retention tool are engaged.

✳✳ CAUTION

The camshaft actuators should not rotate during the removal or installation.

22. Install another EN-48749 retention tool to the exhaust side of the timing chain.

Fig. 65 Remove the timing chain tensioner.

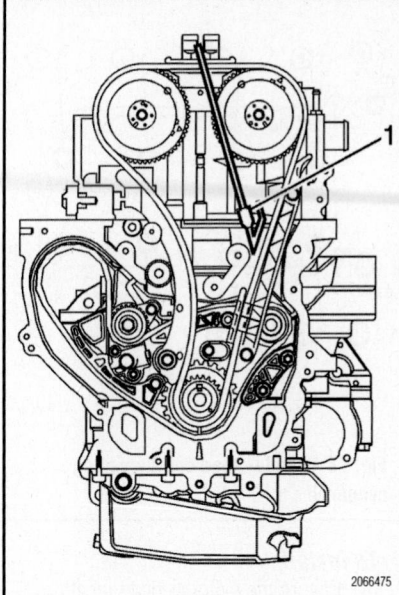

Fig. 66 Install the EN-48749 retention tool (1) to the intake side of the timing chain.

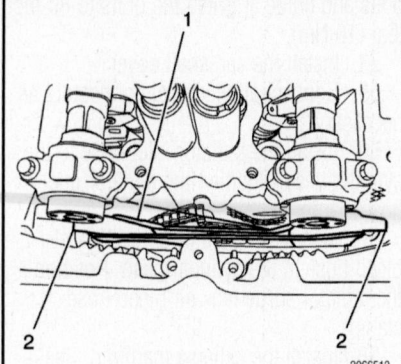

Fig. 68 Install a rubber band (1) around the top of the upper timing chain guides (2) in order to pull the guides together.

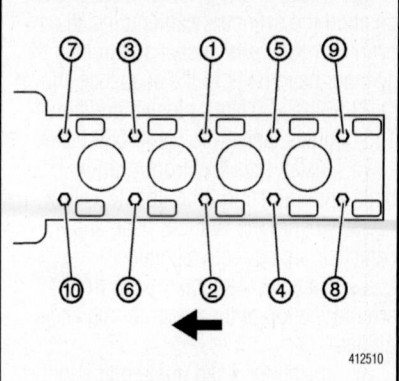

Fig. 70 Cylinder head bolt tightening sequence

23. Remove and discard the exhaust camshaft actuator bolt, and remove the exhaust camshaft actuator from the camshaft while also removing the actuator from the timing chain.

24. Repeat for the intake camshaft actuator.

25. Mark a line on the cylinder head in a straight line relationship to the camshaft actuator notch on each camshaft.

26. Remove the fixed timing chain guide access plug.

27. Remove the fixed guide upper bolt.

28. Install a rubber band around the top of the upper timing chain guides in order to pull the guides together.

29. Remove the cylinder head bolts in the sequence shown. Discard the bolts.

30. Remove the cylinder head and gasket.

31. Clean all of the gasket surfaces. Use the following steps when cleaning the cylinder head and cylinder block surfaces:

   a. Use a razor blade gasket scraper to clean the cylinder head and cylinder block gasket surfaces. Do not scratch or gouge either surface.

   b. DO NOT use any other method or technique to clean these gasket surfaces.

   c. Use a NEW razor blade on the cylinder head and a NEW blade on the cylinder block.

   d. Be careful not to gouge or scratch the gasket surfaces. DO NOT gouge or scrape the combustion chamber surfaces.

The feel of the gasket surface is important, not the appearance. There will be indentations from the gasket left in the cylinder head after all of the gasket material is removed. These small indentations will be filled in by the NEW gasket.

   e. Hold the razor blade as parallel to the gasket surface as possible.

   f. Clean the old sealer/lube and any dirt from around the bolt holes. Clean the bolts holes with a nylon bristle brush.

   g. When cleaning the cylinder head bolt holes use suitable commercial spray liquid solvent and compressed air from an extended-tip blow gun in order to reach the bottom of the holes.

32. If replacing the cylinder head, transfer all parts as necessary.

To install:

➡ **DO NOT use any sealing material.**

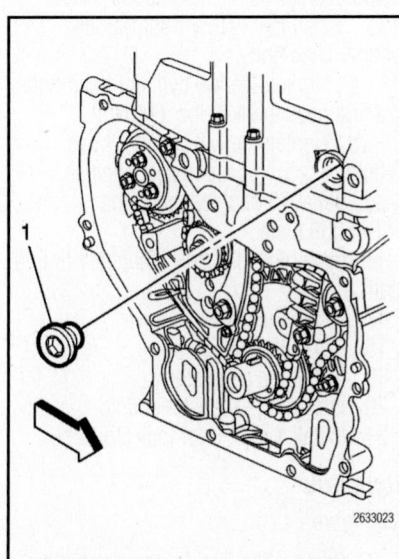

Fig. 67 Remove the fixed timing chain guide access plug (1).

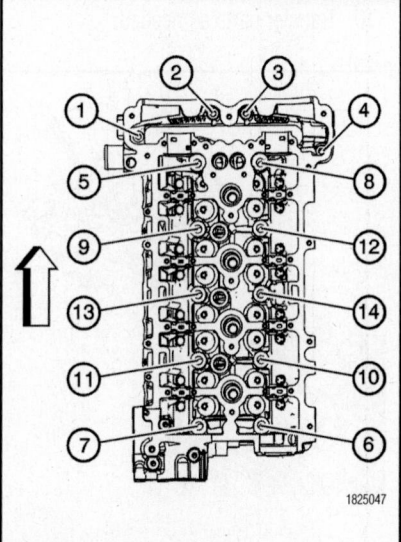

Fig. 69 Cylinder head bolt loosening sequence

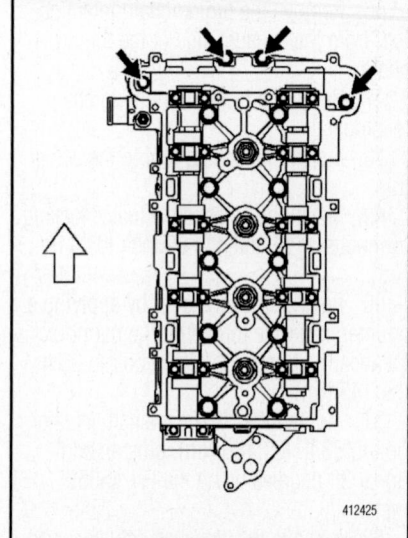

Fig. 71 Install the NEW front cylinder head bolts and tighten to 26 ft. lbs. (35 Nm).

33. Install a new cylinder head gasket, position the cylinder head and install new cylinder head bolts. Install and tighten the cylinder head bolts in the sequence shown to 22 ft. lbs. (30 Nm), plus an additional 155 degrees, using the EN-45059 meter.

34. Install the NEW front cylinder head bolts and tighten to 26 ft. lbs. (35 Nm).

35. Ensure the cylinder head and the camshaft are correctly aligned.

36. Remove the rubber band from around the top of the upper timing chain guides.

37. Install the fixed guide bolt into the cylinder bolt and tighten to 106 inch lbs. (12 Nm).

38. Apply sealant compound to thread and install the timing chain guide bolt access hole plug.

39. Install the fixed timing chain guide access plug. Tighten the chain guide plug to 59 ft. lbs. (90 Nm).

➡**Ensure that the alignment mark made previously on the respective camshaft actuator is still aligned properly with the mark on the timing chain.**

40. Install the timing chain onto the intake camshaft actuator.

41. Align the intake camshaft actuator alignment mark made previously with the timing chain mark and install the actuator onto the camshaft.

42. Install a NEW intake camshaft actuator bolt until snug.

43. Remove the timing chain retention tool from the intake side of the timing chain.

44. Install the timing chain onto the exhaust camshaft actuator.

45. Repeat the previous five steps for the exhaust camshaft actuator.

46. Remove the timing chain retention tool from the exhaust side of the timing chain.

47. Reset and install the timing chain tensioner.

48. Install the locking tool to the actuators.

49. Install the camshaft actuator locking tool bolts and tighten to 89 inch lbs. (10 Nm).

50. Release the tensioner by applying a counterclockwise torque on the harmonic balancer bolt and tighten the bolt to 33 ft. lbs. (45 Nm).

51. Tighten the NEW camshaft actuator bolt to 63 ft. lbs. (85 Nm), plus an additional 30 degrees using the EN-45059 meter.

52. Remove the camshaft actuator locking tool.

53. Install the upper timing chain guide

bolts and guide. Tighten the bolts to 89 inch lbs. (10 Nm).

54. Install the camshaft cover.

55. Connect all electrical connectors as necessary.

56. Install the radiator inlet hose to the cylinder head. Position the radiator inlet hose clamp.

57. Install the radiator surge tank air bleed hose to the cylinder head. Position the radiator surge tank air bleed hose clamp.

58. Install the exhaust manifold. See "Exhaust Manifold" in this section.

59. Install the intake manifold. See "Intake Manifold" in this section.

60. Fill the cooling system.

3.0L Engine

Left Side

See Figures 72 and 73.

1. Remove the left bank secondary timing chain. See "Timing Chain & Sprockets" in this section.

2. Remove the fuel pump. See "FUEL SYSTEM" section.

3. Remove the catalytic converter. See "Catalytic Converter" in this section.

4. Remove the oil level indicator tube.

5. Remove the 2 front M8 left cylinder head bolts, the left cylinder head bolts, and the left cylinder head.

6. Remove the ground wire bolt and ground wire.

7. Disconnect and reposition harness as necessary.

8. Remove and discard the left cylinder head gasket.

9. Clean and inspect the cylinder head and the engine block sealing surfaces.

10. Transfer parts as needed.

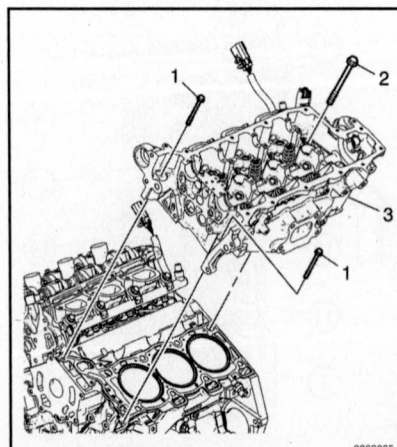

Fig. 72 Removing cylinder head bolts (1, 2) and cylinder head (3)

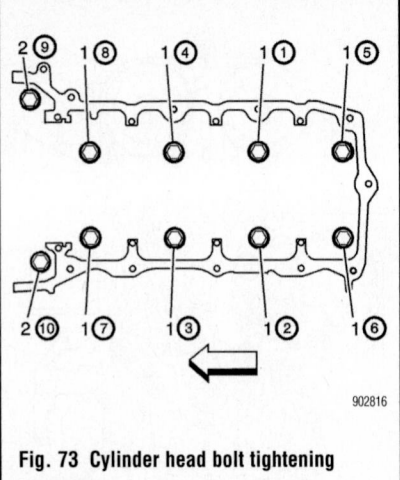

Fig. 73 Cylinder head bolt tightening sequence

To install:

11. Ensure the cylinder head locating pins are securely mounted in the cylinder block deck face.

12. Install a NEW left cylinder head gasket using the deck face locating pins for retention.

13. Align the left cylinder head with the deck face locating pins. Place the left cylinder head in position on the deck face.

➡**DO NOT allow oil on the cylinder head bolt bosses. DO NOT reuse the old cylinder head bolts.**

14. Install the NEW M11 cylinder head bolts.

   a. Tighten the M11 cylinder head bolts a first pass in sequence to 22 ft. lbs. (30 Nm).

   b. Tighten the M11 cylinder head bolts a second pass in sequence an additional 150 degrees using the J-45059 meter.

15. Install the 2 NEW front M8 left cylinder head bolts.

   a. Tighten the M8 cylinder head bolts a first pass to 11 ft. lbs. (15 Nm).

   b. Tighten the M8 cylinder head bolts a second pass in sequence an additional 75 degrees using the J-45059 meter.

16. Install the left bank secondary timing chain.

17. Install the camshaft cover.

18. Install the fuel pump.

19. Install the generator.

20. Install the exhaust manifold.

21. Install the oil level indicator tube.

Right Side

See Figure 74.

1. Remove the bank secondary timing chain. See "Timing Chain & Sprockets" in this section.

2. Remove the power brake booster pump aside.

3. Remove the catalytic converter.

4. Remove the cylinder head bolts and the cylinder head.

5. Remove ground wire and harness and position aside.

6. Remove and discard the cylinder head gasket.

7. Clean and inspect the cylinder head and the engine block sealing surfaces.

8. Disassemble the cylinder head if needed.

9. Transfer parts as needed.

To install:

10. Ensure the cylinder head locating pins are securely mounted in the cylinder block deck face.

11. Install a NEW cylinder head gasket, using the deck face locating pins for retention.

12. Align the cylinder head with the deck face locating pins. Place the cylinder head in position on the deck face.

❋❋ CAUTION

DO NOT allow oil on the cylinder head bolt bosses. DO NOT reuse the old cylinder head bolts.

13. Install the NEW M11 cylinder head bolts.

   a. Tighten the M11 cylinder head bolts a first pass in sequence to 22 ft. lbs. (30 Nm).

   b. Tighten the M11 cylinder head bolts a second pass in sequence an additional 150 degrees, using the J-45059 meter.

14. Install the NEW M8 cylinder head bolt.

   a. Tighten the M8 cylinder head bolt a first pass to 11 ft. lbs. (15 Nm).

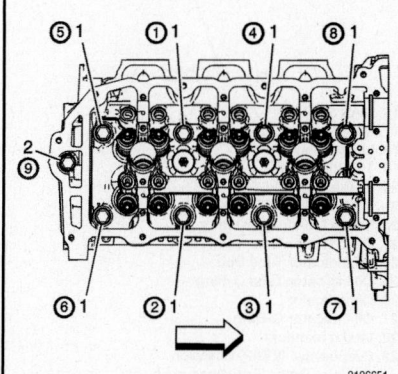

Fig. 74 Cylinder head bolt tightening sequence for M11 bolts (1) and for M8 bolts (2)

   b. Tighten the M8 cylinder head bolt a second pass an additional 75 degrees using the J-45059 meter.

15. Install the bank secondary timing chain.

16. Install the exhaust manifold.

17. Install the camshaft cover.

ENGINE OIL & FILTER

REPLACEMENT

2.4L Engine

1. Place a collecting pan underneath the oil filter.

2. Use a proper wrench to remove the oil filter cap and seal.

❋❋ CAUTION

This engine uses a special high performance oil filter. Use of any other filter may lead to filter failure and/or severe engine damage.

3. Remove and properly dispose of the oil filter insert.

4. Raise the vehicle.

5. Place a collecting pan underneath the oil drain plug.

6. Remove the oil drain plug and seal and drain oil.

To install:

7. Clean the oil drain plug thread and the thread in the oil pan.

8. Install a NEW seal to the oil drain plug. Tighten to 18 ft. lbs. (25 Nm).

9. Lower the vehicle.

❋❋ CAUTION

Over torquing the oil filter cap may cause damage to the oil filter cap resulting in an oil leak.

10. Coat the oil filter seal with NEW engine oil.

11. Use proper wrench to install a NEW oil filter and a NEW seal and tighten the oil filter cap to 16 ft. lbs. (22 Nm).

❋❋ CAUTION

Using engine oils of any viscosity other than those viscosities recommended could result in engine damage.

12. Start the engine and allow it to run until the oil pressure control indicator goes off. Inspect the engine oil level.

13. Fill with NEW engine oil.

14. Reset the service interval indicator.

3.0L Engine

1. Raise and support the vehicle.

2. Place a drain pan under the oil pan drain plug.

3. Remove the oil pan drain plug. Allow the oil to drain completely.

4. Install the oil pan drain plug and tighten to 15 ft. lbs. (20 Nm).

5. Place the drain pan under the oil filter. Remove the oil filter. Allow the oil to drain completely.

To install:

6. Lubricate the NEW oil filter gasket with clean engine oil.

7. Tighten the oil filter to 22 ft. lbs. (30 Nm).

8. Lower the vehicle.

9. Refill the engine oil.

10. Start the engine and inspect for leaks.

EXHAUST MANIFOLD

REMOVAL & INSTALLATION

2.4L Engine

See Figure 75.

1. Remove the catalytic converter.

2. Remove the exhaust manifold heated oxygen sensor. See "ENGINE PERFORMANCE & EMISSION CONTROLS" section.

3. Remove 10 exhaust manifold nuts.

4. Remove exhaust manifold and gasket. Discard gasket.

To install:

5. Install new exhaust manifold gasket, position manifold and install and tighten new nuts to 10 ft. lbs. (14 Nm), working from the center outward.

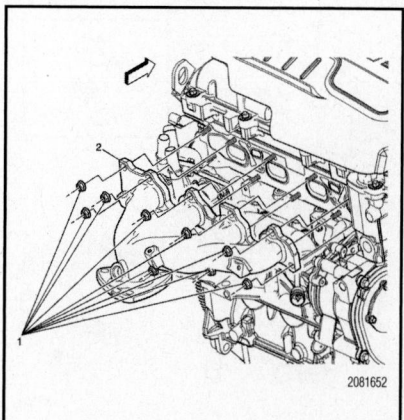

Fig. 75 Exhaust manifold retaining bolt locations

3.0L Engine

➡This engine does not use a separate exhaust manifold. See "Catalytic Converter" in this section.

INTAKE MANIFOLD

REMOVAL & INSTALLATION

2.4L Engine

See Figures 76 through 79.

1. Recover the A/C system.
2. Relieve the fuel system pressure. See "FUEL SYSTEM" section.
3. Remove the air cleaner outlet duct.

✳✳ CAUTION

Never attempt to remove the intake manifold from a hot engine, allow the engine to cool to ambient temperature. The intake manifold can be damaged if it is removed when the engine is hot.

4. Remove the oil fill cap.
5. Remove the intake manifold cover.
6. Remove the evaporative (EVAP) emission canister valve tube from the intake manifold and reposition.
7. Remove the MAP sensor electrical connector.
8. Remove the throttle body. See "FUEL SYSTEM" section.
9. Remove the fuel pump cover and insulator.

➡The low pressure fuel pipe used is model dependent.

10. Disconnect and reposition the low pressure fuel feed pipe from the fuel pump.

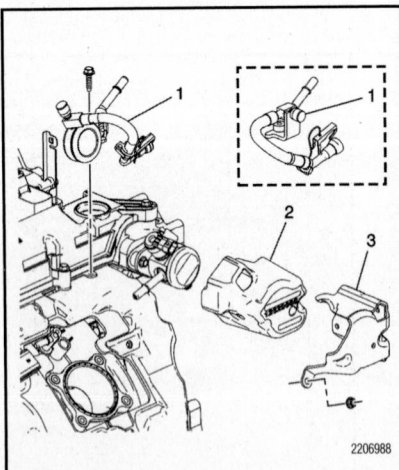

Fig. 76 Remove the fuel pump cover (3) and insulator (2)

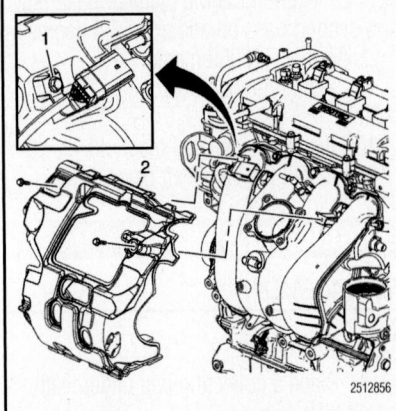

Fig. 77 Remove the fuel rail harness connector bracket bolt (1) and intake manifold insulator bolt. Remove the intake manifold insulator (2).

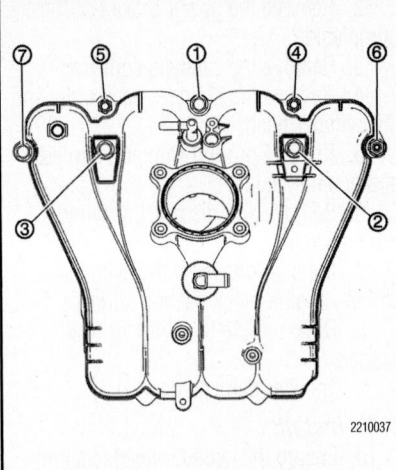

Fig. 79 Tighten the bolts (2) and nuts (1) in sequence to 89 inch lbs. (10 Nm).

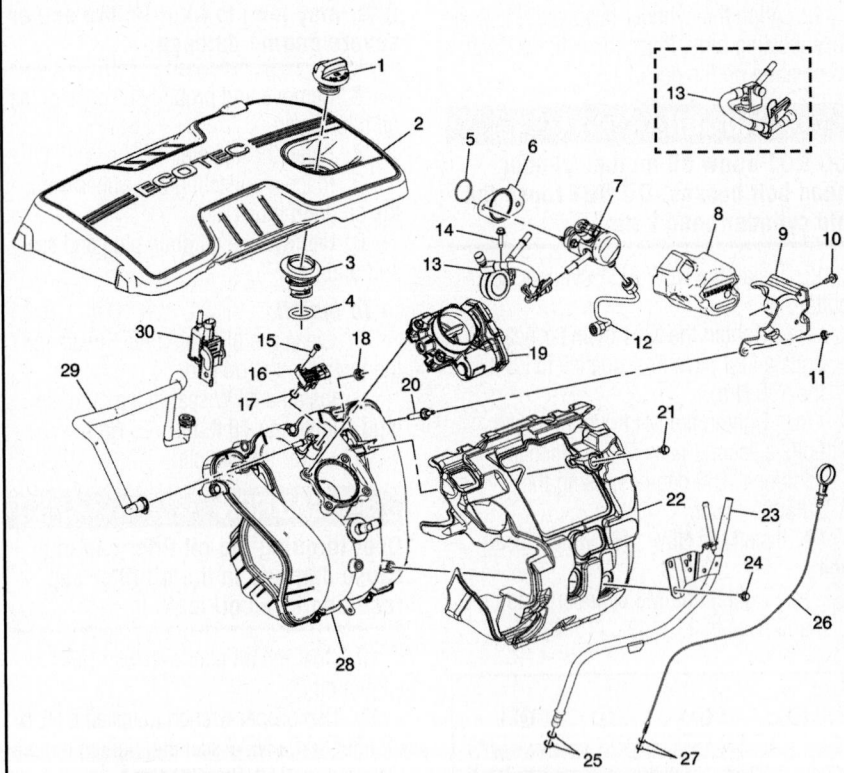

1. Oil Fill Cap
2. Intake Manifold Cover
3. Oil Fill Tube Assembly
4. Oil Fill Cap O-Ring
5. Fuel Pump Housing Seal
6. Fuel Pump Gasket
7. Fuel Pump Assembly
8. Fuel Pump Insulator
9. Fuel Pump Cover
10. Fuel Pump Cover Bolt
11. Fuel Pump Cover Nut
12. Fuel Feed Intermediate Pipe
13. Low Pressure Fuel Pipe Assembly, model dependent
14. Low Pressure Fuel Pipe Assembly Bolt
15. Manifold Absolute Pressure (MAP) Sensor Bolt
16. MAP Sensor
17. MAP Sensor O-Ring
18. Intake Manifold Nut
19. Throttle Body
20. Intake Manifold Stud
21. Intake Manifold Insulator Bolt
22. Intake Manifold Insulator
23. Oil Indicator Tube
24. Oil Indicator Tube Bolt
25. Oil Indicator Tube O-Ring
26. Oil Indicator
27. Oil Indicator O-Ring
28. Intake Manifold
29. Evaporative (EVAP) Emission Canister Purge Tube Assembly
30. EVAP Emission Canister Purge Solenoid Valve

Fig. 78 Exploded view of intake manifold and related components—2.4L engine

11. Remove the fuel rail harness connector bracket bolt and intake manifold insulator bolt. Remove the intake manifold insulator.

12. Remove the A/C line nut and line from the compressor and reposition the line to the side.

➡**Removing studs allows the intake manifold to be removed without removing the fuel pump.**

13. Remove the intake manifold retaining nuts, studs, and bolts. Remove the intake manifold.

14. Disconnect electrical connectors as necessary.

15. Transfer parts as necessary.

16. If reusing the intake manifold, clean and inspect as necessary.

To install:

17. Position the intake manifold and hand start the bolts.

18. Install the intake manifold studs and tighten to 53 inch lbs. (6 Nm).

19. Tighten the bolts and nuts in sequence to 89 inch lbs. (10 Nm).

20. Install the intake manifold insulator. Install the insulator bolts and tighten to 89 inch lbs. (10 Nm).

21. Install the fuel rail harness connector bracket to the intake manifold. Tighten the bracket bolt to 89 inch lbs. (10 Nm).

22. Install new seal washers to the compressor hose. Install the compressor hose to the compressor. Install the compressor hose nut to the compressor and tighten the nut to 16 ft. lbs. (22 Nm).

23. Connect the engine harness electrical connector as necessary.

24. Install the fuel pump insulator and cover.

25. Install the low pressure fuel pipe assembly, if equipped.

26. Install a new throttle body gasket. Install the throttle body. See "FUEL SYSTEM" section.

27. Install the EVAP canister valve tube. Connect the MAP sensor electrical connector.

28. Install the intake manifold cover onto the camshaft cover ball studs.

29. Install the oil fill cap.

30. Recharge the A/C system.

31. Install the air cleaner assembly.

3.0L Engine

1. Remove the power steering fluid reservoir upper bracket only.

2. Remove the power brake booster vacuum check valve and hose.

3. Remove the coolant air bleed pipe.

4. Remove the intake manifold cover.

5. Disconnect and remove the positive crankcase ventilation (PCV) tube from the intake manifold and right camshaft cover.

6. Remove the evaporative emission (EVAP) hose from the intake manifold and EVAP solenoid.

7. Remove the fuel pipe shield.

8. Unclip wire harnesses as necessary.

9. Remove the intake manifold bolts. Remove the intake manifold assembly. Remove and discard the intake manifold gasket.

10. Clean the intake manifold mating surfaces.

To install:

11. Install the NEW intake manifold gasket. Install the intake manifold assembly. Install the intake manifold bolts and tighten in sequence shown to 17 ft. lbs. (23 Nm).

12. Tighten the intake manifold bolts a second pass in sequence to 17 ft. lbs. (23 Nm).

13. Install the fuel pipe shield.

14. Connect the EVAP hose to the upper intake manifold and EVAP solenoid.

15. Connect the PCV tube assembly to the upper intake manifold and the right camshaft cover.

16. Install coolant hose.

17. Install intake manifold cover.

18. Install the coolant air bleed pipe.

19. Install the power steering fluid reservoir upper bracket.

20. Install the power brake booster vacuum check valve and hose.

OIL PAN

REMOVAL & INSTALLATION

2.4L Engine

See Figures 80 through 82.

1. Remove the drive belt. See "Accessory Drive Belt" in this section.

2. Remove the oil level indicator tube.

3. Raise and support the vehicle.

4. Loosen the upper air conditioning (A/C) compressor bolts. Remove the lower A/C compressor bolt.

5. Remove the lower 2 power brake booster pump bolts. Reposition the pump away from the oil pan.

6. Place a suitable drain pan under the oil pan drain plug. Remove the oil pan drain plug. Drain the engine oil. Reinstall the oil pan drain plug until snug.

7. Remove the 4 oil pan to transaxle bolts, then remove the oil pan bolts.

8. Remove the oil pan. Remove any old oil pan sealant.

To install:

9. Ensure that the oil pan and the sealing surface on the lower crankcase are free of all oil and debris.

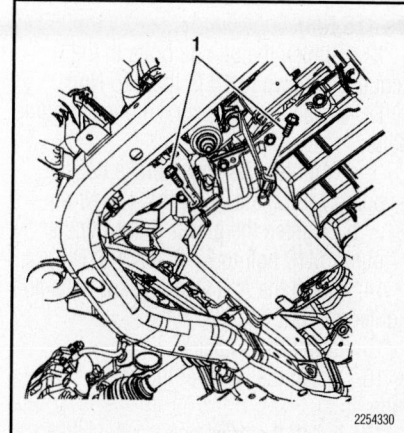

Fig. 80 Remove the lower 2 power brake booster pump bolts (1). Reposition the pump away from the oil pan.

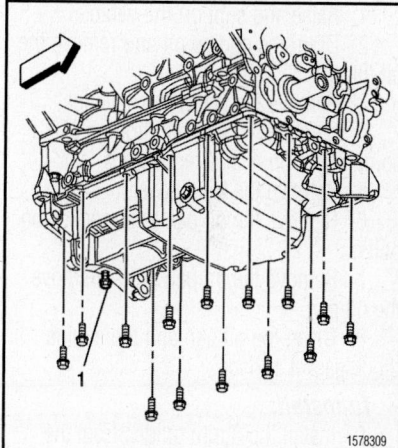

Fig. 81 Remove the 4 oil pan to transaxle bolts, then remove the oil pan bolts (1).

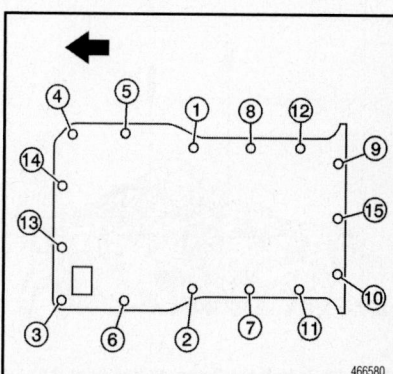

Fig. 82 Tighten the oil pan bolts in the sequence shown to 18 ft. lbs. (25 Nm).

10. Apply a 2 mm bead of sealant around the perimeter of the oil pan and the oil suction port opening.

➡**DO NOT over apply the sealant. More than a 2 mm bead is not required.**

11. Install the oil pan. Install the 4 oil pan to transaxle bolts and tighten to 55 ft. lbs. (75 Nm).

12. Tighten the oil pan bolts in the sequence shown to 18 ft. lbs. (25 Nm).

13. Install the power brake booster pump bolts:

   a. Tighten the power brake booster pump M8 bolt to 16 ft. lbs. (22 Nm).

   b. Tighten the power brake booster pump M10 bolt to 37 ft. lbs. (50 Nm).

14. Install the A/C Compressor bolts and tighten to 15 ft. lbs. (20 Nm).

15. Lower the vehicle.

16. Install the oil level indicator tube.

17. Install the drive belt.

18. Fill the engine oil to the proper level.

3.0L Engine

See Figures 83 and 84.

1. Raise and support the vehicle.

2. Drain the engine oil and remove the oil filter.

3. Remove the catalytic converter.

4. Remove the air conditioning (A/C) compressor bolts and reposition.

5. Remove the front cover.

6. Remove the oil pan to transmission bolts.

7. Remove the oil pan bolts. Remove the oil pan.

8. Clean the oil pan and the engine block gasket surface.

To install:

9. Install the 8 mm guides from the EN-46109 set into the center oil pan rail bolt hole on each side of the engine block.

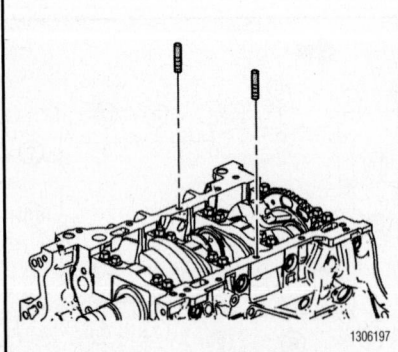

Fig. 83 Install the 8 mm guides from the EN-46109 set into the center oil pan rail bolt hole on each side of the engine block.

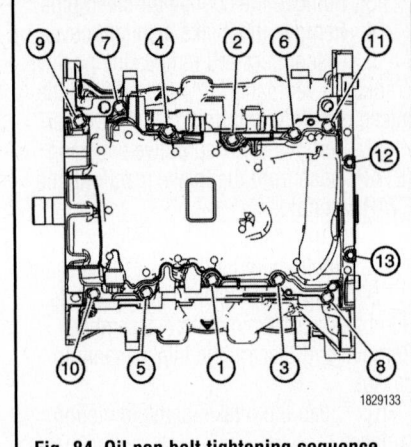

Fig. 84 Oil pan bolt tightening sequence

10. Place a 3 mm bead of RTV sealant on the block pan rail and the crankshaft rear oil seal housing.

11. Position the oil pan onto the block.

12. Remove the EN-46109 set 8 mm guides from the engine block.

13. Loosely install the oil pan bolts.

14. Tighten the oil pan bolts in sequence:

   • The 8mm bolts (1–11) to 17 ft. lbs. (23 Nm).

   • The 6mm bolts (12, 13) to 89 inch lbs. (10 Nm).

15. Install engine front cover.

16. Install the air conditioning (A/C) compressor.

17. Install the catalytic converter.

18. Lower the vehicle.

19. Refill the engine oil.

OIL PUMP

REMOVAL & INSTALLATION

2.4L Engine

➡**Manufacturer does not provide a specific removal and installation procedure for this component.**

3.0L Engine

See Figure 85.

1. Remove the primary timing chain. See "Timing Chain & Sprockets" in this section.

2. Remove the crankshaft sprocket.

3. Remove the oil pump bolts and the oil pump.

To install:

4. Install the oil pump and bolts.

5. Install the crankshaft sprocket.

6. Install the primary timing chain. See "Timing Chain & Sprockets" in this section.

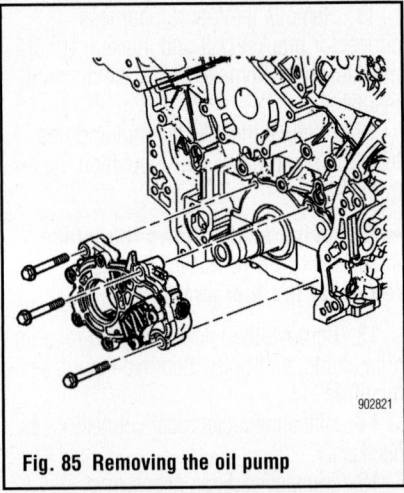

Fig. 85 Removing the oil pump

PISTON & RING

POSITIONING

2.4L Engine

See Figure 86.

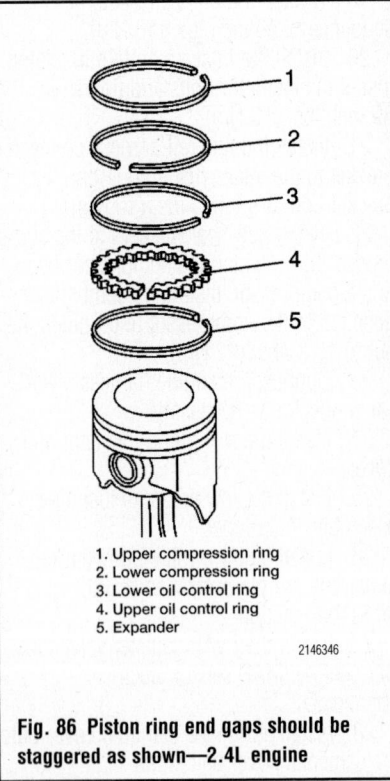

1. Upper compression ring
2. Lower compression ring
3. Lower oil control ring
4. Upper oil control ring
5. Expander

Fig. 86 Piston ring end gaps should be staggered as shown—2.4L engine

3.0L Engine

See Figure 87.

REAR MAIN SEAL

REMOVAL & INSTALLATION

2.4L Engine

See Figure 88.

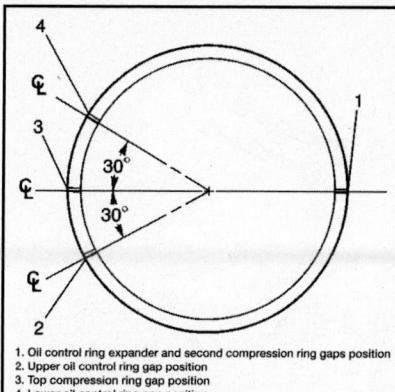

Fig. 87 Piston ring end gaps should be arranged as shown—3.0L engine

1. Oil control ring expander and second compression ring gaps position
2. Upper oil control ring gap position
3. Top compression ring gap position
4. Lower oil control ring gap position

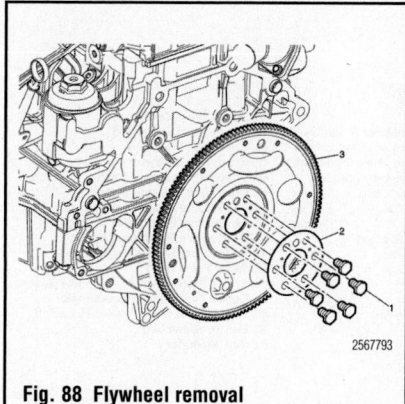

Fig. 88 Flywheel removal

1. Remove the transaxle.
2. Remove the flywheel.
3. Use a suitable tool to remove the oil seal from the rear crankshaft bore.
4. Installation is the reverse of the removal procedure.

3.0L Engine

1. Remove the automatic transaxle.
2. Remove the engine flywheel.
3. Remove the oil pan. See "Oil Pan" in this section.
4. Remove the crankshaft rear oil seal and housing.

To install:

5. Install the crankshaft rear oil seal and housing.
6. Install the oil pan.
7. Install the engine flywheel.
8. Install the automatic transaxle.

TIMING CHAIN FRONT COVER

REMOVAL & INSTALLATION

2.4L Engine

1. Remove the engine mount bracket,

2. Remove the drive belt tensioner.
3. Remove the crankshaft balancer. See "Crankshaft Balancer" in this section.
4. Disconnect the oxygen sensor harness from the front cover and reposition.
5. Remove the engine front cover to water pump bolt.
6. Raise and suitably support the vehicle.
7. Remove the engine front cover bolts.
8. Remove the engine front cover.
9. Remove and discard the engine front cover gasket.

To install:

10. Install a NEW engine front cover gasket to the dowel pins.
11. Install the engine front cover.
12. Install the engine front cover bolts and tighten to 18 ft. lbs. (25 Nm).
13. Lower the vehicle.
14. Install the engine front cover to water pump bolt and tighten to 18 ft. lbs. (25 Nm).
15. Reposition the oxygen sensor harness to the front cover.
16. Install the crankshaft balancer.
17. Install the drive belt tensioner.
18. Install the engine mount bracket.

3.0L Engine

1. Remove the intake manifold. See "Intake Manifold" in this section.
2. Remove the camshaft covers.
3. Drain the engine coolant.
4. Disconnect the purge vent hose from the water outlet.
5. Remove the water outlet with the radiator hose and reposition aside.
6. Remove the crankshaft balancer. See "Crankshaft Balancer" in this section.
7. Remove the camshaft position sensors. See "ENGINE PERFORMANCE & EMISSION CONTROLS" section.
8. Remove the generator. See "ENGINE ELECTRICAL" section.
9. Remove the water pump pulley only.
10. Remove the drive belt tensioner.
11. Remove the camshaft position actuator solenoid valves from the front cover.
12. There are a total of 22 M8 bolts that must be removed and 3 optional M12 bolts that may need to be removed before the front cover will separate from the engine block.
13. Remove the engine front cover with the water pump.
14. Carefully clean the engine front cover sealing surfaces.

➥Insert a piece of cardboard between the oil pan front and the oil pump in order to prevent any contaminants from falling into the oil pan.

15. Use compressed air in order to remove any engine coolant from the engine cooling passages and from the top of the oil pan scraper.

To install:

16. Use the EN-46109 pins in order to install the engine front cover.
17. Install the camshaft position actuator solenoid valves to the front cover.
18. Install the camshaft position sensors. See "ENGINE PERFORMANCE & EMISSION CONTROLS" section.
19. Install the crankshaft balancer. See "Crankshaft Balancer" in this section.
20. Install the generator bracket with the generator and the belt tensioner. See "ENGINE ELECTRICAL" section.
21. Install the water outlet. Install the purge vent hose to the water outlet.
22. Fill the cooling system.
23. Install the water pump pulley.
24. Install the drive belt tensioner.
25. Install the camshaft covers.
26. Install the intake manifold. See "Intake Manifold" in this section.
27. Fill the cooling system.

TIMING CHAIN & SPROCKETS

REMOVAL & INSTALLATION

2.4L Engine

See Figures 89 through 99.

1. Remove the camshaft cover.
2. Remove the number 1 cylinder spark plug.
3. Rotate the crankshaft in the engine rotational direction clockwise, until the number 1 piston is at top dead center (TDC) on the exhaust stroke.
4. Remove the engine front cover. See "Timing Chain Front Cover" in this section.
5. Remove the upper timing chain guide bolts and guide.

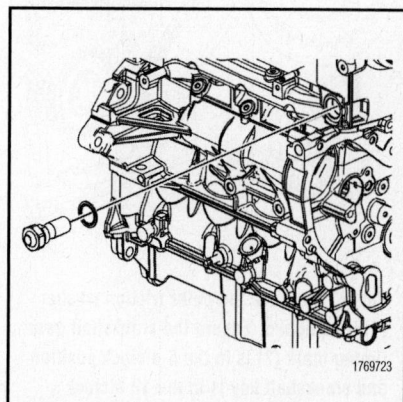

Fig. 89 Remove the timing chain tensioner

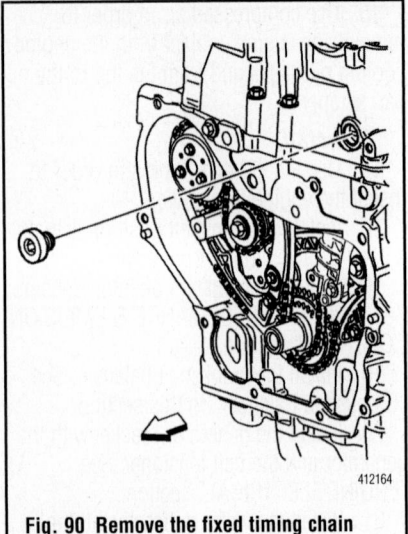

Fig. 90 Remove the fixed timing chain guide access plug.

➡️The timing chain tensioner must be removed to unload chain tension before the timing chain is removed. If it is not, the timing chain will become cocked and it will be difficult to remove.

6. Remove the timing chain tensioner.

7. Install a 24 mm wrench on the hex on the exhaust camshaft in order to hold the camshaft.

8. Remove and discard the exhaust camshaft actuator bolt. Remove the exhaust camshaft actuator from the camshaft and timing chain.

9. Remove the timing chain tensioner guide bolt and guide.

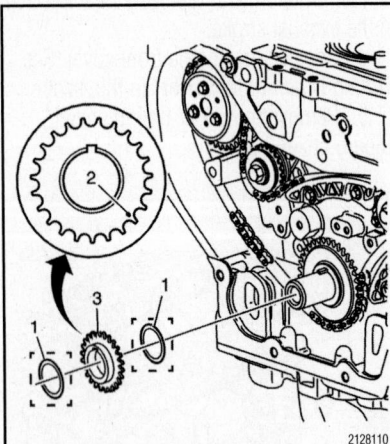

Fig. 91 Remove the outer friction washer (1) if equipped. Ensure the crankshaft gear timing mark (2) is in the 5 o'clock position and crankshaft key is in the 12 o'clock position. Remove the crankshaft sprocket (3). Remove the inner friction washer (1).

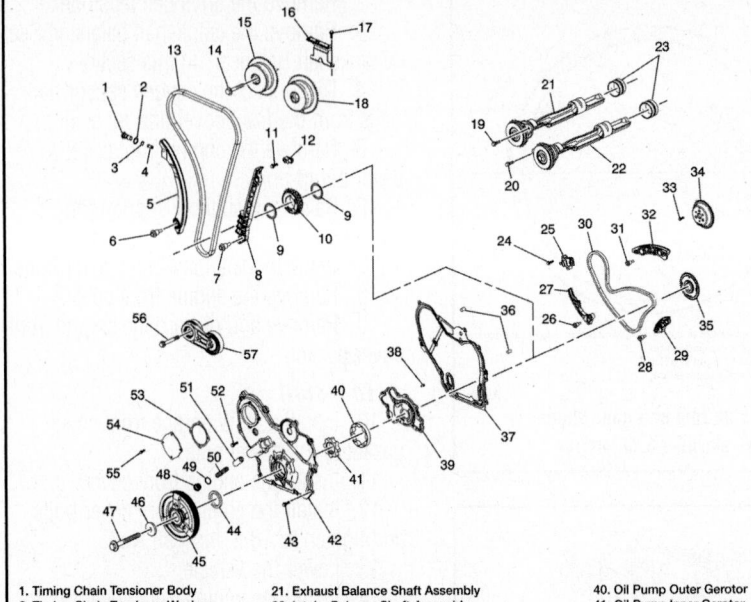

1. Timing Chain Tensioner Body
2. Timing Chain Tensioner Washer
3. Timing Chain Tensioner O-Ring Seal
4. Timing Chain Tensioner Plunger
5. Adjustable Timing Chain Guide
6. Adjustable Timing Chain Guide Bolt
7. Fixed Timing Chain Guide Bolt
8. Fixed Timing Chain Guide
9. Friction Washer
10. Timing Chain Drive Sprocket
11. Timing Chain Oil Nozzle Bolt
12. Timing Chain Oil Nozzle
13. Timing Chain
14. Camshaft Position Actuator Bolt
15. Exhaust Camshaft Position Actuator
16. Upper Timing Chain Guide
17. Upper Timing Chain Guide Bolt
18. Intake Camshaft Position Actuator
19. Exhaust Balance Shaft Assembly Bolt
20. Intake Balance Shaft Assembly Bolt
21. Exhaust Balance Shaft Assembly
22. Intake Balance Shaft Assembly
23. Balance Shaft Rear Bearing
24. Balance Shaft Drive Chain Tensioner Assembly Bolt
25. Balance Shaft Drive Chain Tensioner Assembly
26. Adjustable Balance Shaft Drive Chain Guide Bolt
27. Adjustable Balance Shaft Drive Chain Guide
28. Balance Shaft Drive Chain Guide Bolt
29. Balance Shaft Drive Chain Guide
30. Balance Shaft Drive Chain
31. Balance Shaft Drive Chain Guide Bolt
32. Balance Shaft Drive Chain Guide
33. Water Pump Drive Sprocket Bolt
34. Water Pump Drive Sprocket
35. Balance Shaft Drive Sprocket
36. Engine Front Cover Alignment Pins
37. Engine Front Cover Gasket
38. Oil Pump Cover Bolt
39. Oil Pump Cover
40. Oil Pump Outer Gerotor
41. Oil Pump Inner Gerotor
42. Engine Front Cover
43. Engine Front Cover Bolt
44. Crankshaft Front Seal
45. Crankshaft Balancer
46. Crankshaft Balancer Washer
47. Crankshaft Balancer Bolt
48. Oil Pressure Relief Valve Plug
49. Oil Pressure Relief Valve O-Ring Seal
50. Oil Pressure Relief Valve Spring
51. Oil Pressure Relief Valve Plunger
52. Water Pump Bolt
53. Engine Front Cover Access Plate Gasket
54. Engine Front Cover Access Plate
55. Engine Front Cover Access Plate Bolt
56. Belt Tensioner Bolt
57. Belt Tensioner

Fig. 92 Exploded view of the timing chain and components

10. Remove the fixed timing chain guide access plug.

11. Remove the fixed timing chain guide bolts and guide.

12. Install a 24 mm wrench on the hex on the intake camshaft in order to hold the camshaft.

13. Remove and discard the intake camshaft actuator bolt.

14. Remove the intake camshaft actuator and the timing chain through the top of the cylinder head.

➡️Ecotec 4 cylinder engines with SIDI-Direct Injection, the lower timing chain

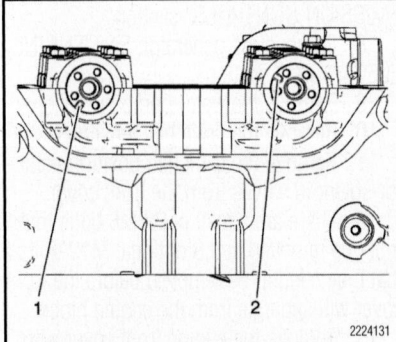

Fig. 93 When installing the camshafts, ensure the intake camshaft notch is in the 10 o'clock position (2) and the exhaust camshaft notch is in the 7 o'clock position (1). The number 1 piston should be at top dead center (TDC), crankshaft key at 12 o'clock.

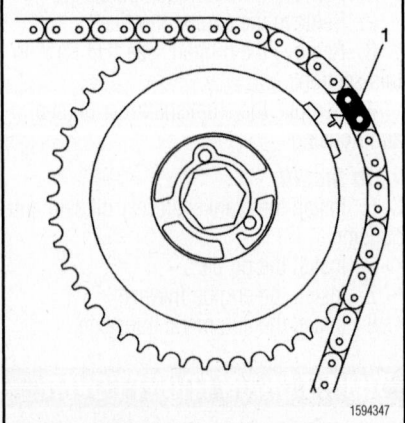

Fig. 94 Assemble the intake camshaft actuator into the timing chain with the timing mark lined up with the uniquely colored link.

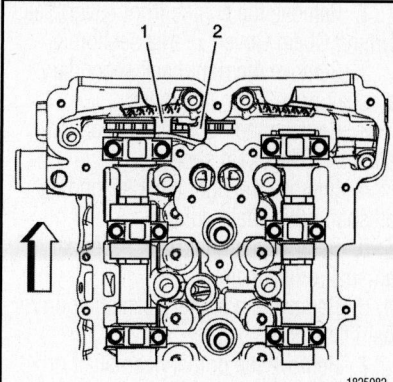

Fig. 95 Lower the timing chain through the opening in the cylinder head. Use care to ensure that the chain goes around both sides of the cylinder block bosses (1, 2). Install the intake camshaft actuator onto the intake camshaft while aligning the dowel pin into the camshaft slot.

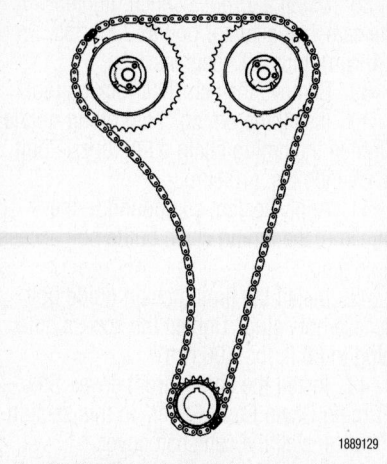

Fig. 96 Verify that all of the colored links and the appropriate timing marks are still aligned. If they are not aligned, repeat the portion of the procedure necessary to align the timing marks.

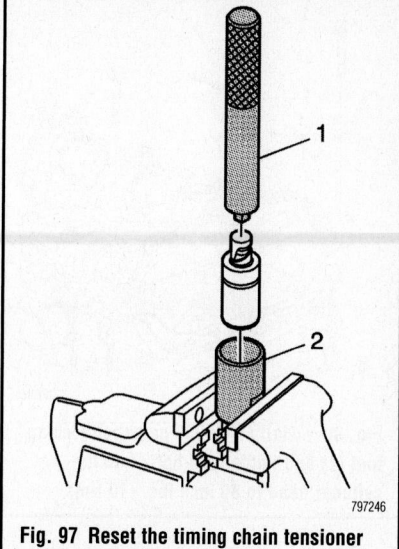

Fig. 97 Reset the timing chain tensioner with tools EN-45027-1 (1) and EN-45027-2 (2).

crank gear may be equipped with a second spacing washer installed in front of the lower timing chain crank gear. The outer spacer/washer is in between the crank/balancer pulley and the lower timing gear and may remain in place when the pulley is removed. The spacer/washer has a dot/mark on its surface that may be mistaken for the lower timing mark. If applicable, the washer must be removed in order to view the correct timing mark on the lower crank gear.

15. Remove the outer friction washer if equipped. Ensure the crankshaft gear timing mark is in the 5 o'clock position and crankshaft key is in the 12 o'clock position. Remove the crankshaft sprocket. Remove the inner friction washer.

To install:

16. When installing the camshafts, ensure the intake camshaft notch is in the 10 o'clock position and the exhaust camshaft notch is in the 7 o'clock position. The number 1 piston should be at top dead center (TDC), crankshaft key at 12 o'clock.

17. Install the inner friction washer. Install the crankshaft sprocket with the timing mark is in the 5 o'clock position and facing outward. Install the outer friction washer, if equipped.

➡There are 3 colored links on the timing chain. Two links are of matching color, and 1 link is of a unique color. Use the following procedure to line up the links with the actuators. Orient the chain so that the colored links are visible.

➡Always use new actuator bolts.

18. Assemble the intake camshaft actuator into the timing chain with the timing mark lined up with the uniquely colored link.

19. Lower the timing chain through the opening in the cylinder head. Use care to ensure that the chain goes around both sides of the cylinder block bosses. Install the intake camshaft actuator onto the intake camshaft while aligning the dowel pin into the camshaft slot.

20. Hand tighten the new intake camshaft actuator bolt.

21. Route the timing chain around the crankshaft sprocket and line up the first matching colored link with the timing mark on the crankshaft sprocket, in approximately the 5 o'clock position.

22. Install the friction washer, if applicable.

23. Rotate the crankshaft clockwise to remove all chain slack. Do not rotate the intake camshaft.

24. Install the adjustable timing chain guide down through the opening in the cylinder head and install the adjustable timing chain bolt. Tighten the adjustable timing chain guide bolt to 89 inch lbs. (10 Nm).

➡Always install NEW actuator bolts.

25. Install the exhaust camshaft actuator into the timing chain with the timing mark lined up with the second matching colored link.

26. Install the exhaust camshaft actuator onto the exhaust camshaft, aligning the dowel pin into the camshaft slot.

27. Use 24 mm open ended wrench, rotate the exhaust camshaft approximately

45 degrees until the dowel pin in the camshaft actuator goes into the camshaft slot.

28. When the actuator seats on the cam, tighten the new exhaust camshaft actuator bolt hand tight.

29. Verify that all of the colored links and the appropriate timing marks are still aligned. If they are not aligned, repeat the portion of the procedure necessary to align the timing marks.

30. Install the fixed timing chain guide and bolts. Tighten the fixed timing chain guide bolts to 89 inch lbs. (10 Nm).

31. Install the upper timing chain guide and bolts. Tighten the upper timing chain guide bolts to 89 inch lbs. (10 Nm).

32. Reset the timing chain tensioner by performing the following steps:

   a. Remove the snap ring.

   b. Remove the piston assembly from the body of the timing chain tensioner.

   c. Install the EN-45027-2 tool (2) into a vise.

   d. Install the notch end of the piston assembly into the EN-45027-2 tool (2).

   e. Using the EN-45027-1 tool (1), turn the ratchet cylinder into the piston.

   f. Reinstall the piston assembly into the body of the tensioner.

   g. Install the snap ring.

33. Inspect the timing chain tensioner seal for damage. If damaged, replace the seal.

34. Inspect to ensure all dirt and debris is removed from the timing chain tensioner threaded hole in the cylinder head.

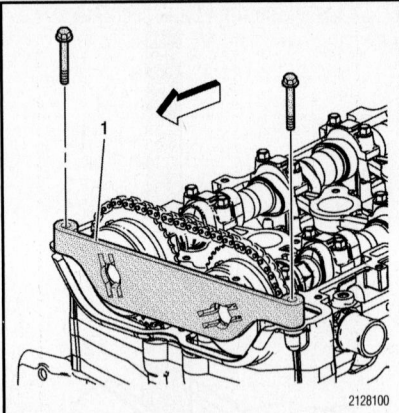

Fig. 98 Install EN-48953 camshaft locking tool (1) and tighten the bolts into the cylinder head to 89 inch lbs. (10 Nm).

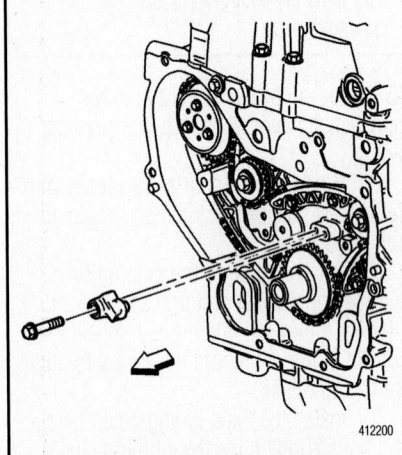

Fig. 99 Install the timing chain oiling nozzle. Tighten the timing chain oiling nozzle bolt to 89 inch lbs. (10 Nm).

✳✳ CAUTION

Ensure the timing chain tensioner seal is centered throughout the torque procedure to eliminate the possibility of an oil leak.

35. Install the timing chain tensioner assembly. Tighten the timing chain tensioner to 55 ft. lbs. (75 Nm).

➡ **The timing chain tensioner is released by compressing it 2 mm (0.079 in), which will release the locking mechanism in the ratchet.**

36. To release the timing chain tensioner, use a suitable tool with a rubber tip on the end. Feed the tool down through the cam drive chest to rest on the cam chain. Then give a sharp jolt diagonally downwards to release the tensioner.

37. Install EN-48953 camshaft locking tool and tighten the bolts into the cylinder head to 89 inch lbs. (10 Nm).

38. Using a torque wrench, tighten the camshaft actuator bolt to 22 ft. lbs. (30 Nm), plus 100 degrees.

39. Remove the camshaft locking tool.

40. Install the timing chain oiling nozzle. Tighten the timing chain oiling nozzle bolt to 89 inch lbs. (10 Nm).

41. Apply sealant compound to the thread of the timing chain guide bolt access hole plug.

42. Install the timing chain guide bolt access hole plug. Tighten the access hole plug to 66 ft. lbs. (90 Nm).

43. Install the engine front cover. See "Timing Chain Front Cover" in this section.

44. Install the camshaft cover.

45. Install the number 1 cylinder spark plug.

3.0L Engine

Primary Camshaft Timing Chain & Sprockets

See Figure 100.

1. Remove the engine front cover. See "Timing Chain Cover" in this section.

2. Remove the right bank secondary camshaft drive chain tensioner.

3. Remove the right bank secondary camshaft drive chain shoe.

4. Remove the right bank secondary camshaft drive chain guide.

5. Remove the right bank secondary camshaft drive chain.

6. Remove the primary camshaft drive chain tensioner.

7. Remove the primary camshaft drive chain upper guide.

8. Remove the primary camshaft timing chain.

To install:

➡ **When other components are indicated, refer to those component headings within this section and/or refer to the exploded view illustration of the timing chain components.**

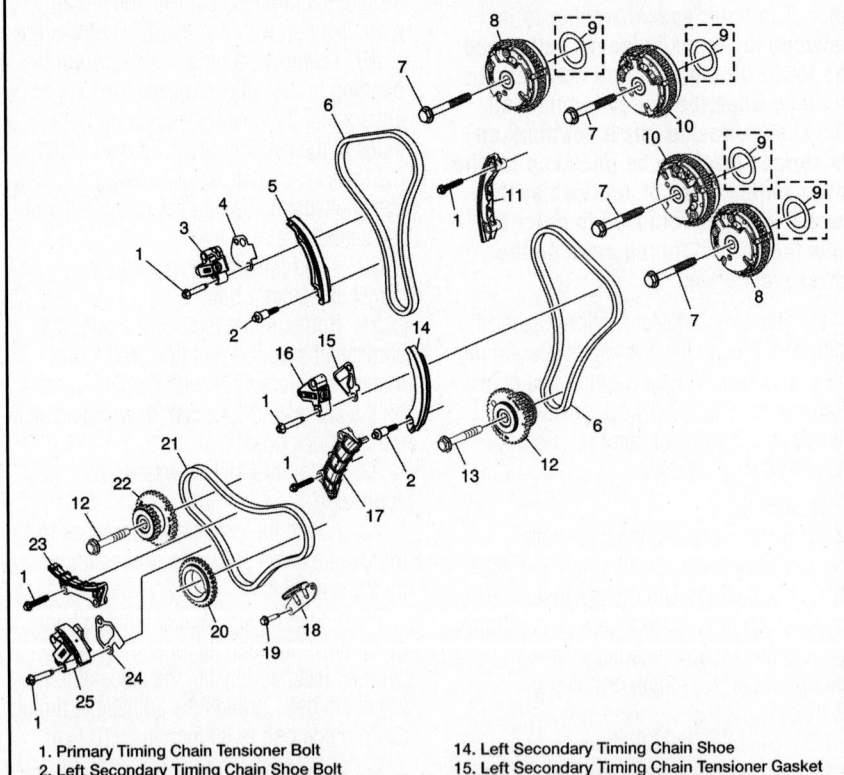

1. Primary Timing Chain Tensioner Bolt
2. Left Secondary Timing Chain Shoe Bolt
3. Right Secondary Timing Chain Tensioner
4. Right Secondary Timing Chain Tensioner Gasket
5. Right Secondary Timing Chain Shoe
6. Secondary Timing Chain
7. Camshaft Position Actuator Bolt
8. Exhaust Camshaft Position Actuator
9. Camshaft Position Actuator Thrust Washer
10. Intake Camshaft Position Actuator
11. Right Secondary Timing Chain Guide
12. Left Camshaft Intermediate Drive Shaft Sprocket
13. Camshaft Intermediate Drive Shaft Sprocket Bolt
14. Left Secondary Timing Chain Shoe
15. Left Secondary Timing Chain Tensioner Gasket
16. Left Secondary Timing Chain Tensioner
17. Left Secondary Timing Chain Guide
18. Lower Primary Timing Chain Guide
19. Lower Primary Timing Chain Guide Bolt
20. Crankshaft Sprocket
21. Primary Timing Chain
22. Right Camshaft Intermediate Drive Shaft Sprocket
23. Upper Primary Timing Chain Guide
24. Primary Timing Chain Tensioner Gasket
25. Primary Timing Chain Tensioner

Fig. 100 Exploded view of the timing chain components—3.0L engine

9. Install the primary camshaft timing chain.

10. Install the primary upper camshaft drive chain guide.

11. Install the primary camshaft drive chain tensioner.

12. Install the right bank secondary camshaft drive chain.

13. Install the right bank secondary camshaft drive chain guide.

14. Install the right bank secondary camshaft drive chain shoe.

15. Install the right bank secondary camshaft drive chain tensioner.

16. Install the engine front cover. See "Timing Chain Cover" in this section.

Secondary Camshaft Intermediate Drive Chain Replacement - Left Side

1. Remove the engine front cover. See "Timing Chain Cover" in this section.

2. Remove the right bank secondary camshaft drive chain tensioner.

3. Remove the right bank secondary camshaft drive chain shoe.

4. Remove the right bank secondary camshaft drive chain guide.

5. Remove the right bank secondary camshaft drive chain.

6. Remove the primary camshaft drive chain tensioner.

7. Remove the primary upper camshaft drive chain guide.

8. Remove the primary camshaft drive chain.

9. Remove the right bank camshaft intermediate drive chain idler.

10. Remove the left bank secondary camshaft drive chain tensioner.

11. Remove the left bank secondary camshaft drive chain shoe.

12. Remove the left bank secondary camshaft drive chain guide.

13. Remove the left bank camshaft intermediate drive chain idler.

14. Remove the left bank secondary camshaft drive chain.

15. Clean and inspect all of the camshaft timing drive components.

To install:

➡**When other components are indicated, refer to those component headings within this section and/or refer to the exploded view illustration of the timing chain components.**

16. Install the left bank secondary camshaft drive chain.

17. Install the left bank camshaft intermediate drive chain idler.

18. Install the left bank secondary camshaft drive chain guide.

19. Install the left bank secondary camshaft drive chain shoe.

20. Install the left bank secondary camshaft drive chain tensioner.

21. Install the right bank camshaft intermediate drive chain idler.

22. Install the primary camshaft drive chain.

23. Install the primary upper camshaft drive chain guide.

24. Install the primary camshaft drive chain tensioner.

25. Install the right bank secondary camshaft drive chain.

26. Install the right bank secondary camshaft drive chain guide.

27. Install the right bank secondary camshaft drive chain shoe.

28. Install the right bank secondary camshaft drive chain tensioner.

29. Install the engine front cover.

Secondary Camshaft Intermediate Drive Chain Replacement - Right Side

1. Remove the engine front cover. See "Timing Chain Cover" in this section.

2. Remove the right bank secondary camshaft drive chain tensioner.

3. Remove the right bank secondary camshaft drive chain shoe.

4. Remove the right bank secondary camshaft drive chain guide.

5. Remove the right bank secondary camshaft drive chain.

To install:

➡**When other components are indicated, refer to those component headings within this section and/or refer to the exploded view illustration of the timing chain components.**

6. Ensure the stage 1 camshaft timing is correct. Follow the left bank secondary camshaft drive chain replacement procedures to reset the camshaft timing. Refer to "Secondary Camshaft Intermediate Drive Chain Replacement—Left Side" in this section.

➡**Setting the camshaft timing is necessary whenever the camshaft drive system has been disturbed such that the relationship between any chain and sprocket has been lost. Even when only one sprocket is involved, multiple crankshaft rotations will not produce conditions where correct timing can be confirmed.**

7. Install the right bank secondary camshaft drive chain and guide.

8. Install the right bank secondary camshaft drive chain shoe.

9. Install the right bank secondary camshaft drive chain tensioner.

10. Install the engine front cover. See "Timing Chain Cover" in this section.

VALVE COVERS (CAMSHAFT COVERS)

REMOVAL & INSTALLATION

2.4L Engine

See Figure 101.

1. Remove the air cleaner outlet duct.

2. Remove the ignition coils. See "ENGINE ELECTRICAL" section.

3. Remove the intake and exhaust camshaft position actuator solenoid valves.

4. Remove the camshaft cover fasteners.

5. Remove the camshaft cover.

6. Do not reuse camshaft gasket. Also use a new gasket when removing or replacing camshaft cover.

7. Remove ignition coil wiring harness clips from the camshaft cover.

8. Remove the fuel line bracket from the camshaft cover.

9. Transfer components as necessary.

To install:

10. Installation is the reverse of the removal procedure.

11. Tighten the camshaft cover fasteners to 89 inch lbs. (10 Nm).

3.0L Engine

See Figures 102 through 105.

➡**This procedure is the same for the left or right side camshaft cover, except where indicated.**

1. Remove the ignition coils. See "ENGINE ELECTRICAL" section.

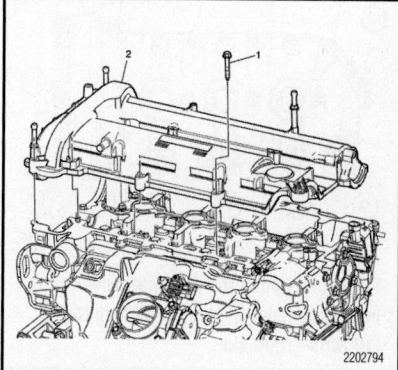

2202794

Fig. 101 Removing the camshaft cover—2.4L engine

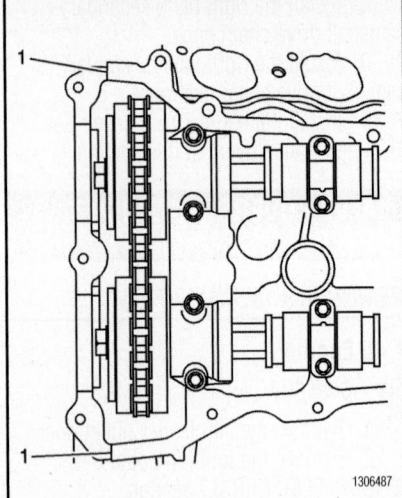

Fig. 102 Place a bead 8 mm in diameter by 4 mm in height of RTV sealant equivalent, on the engine front cover split lines (1).

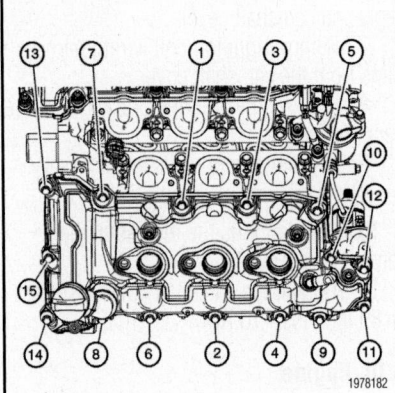

Fig. 103 Tighten the camshaft cover bolts, in the sequence shown, to 89 inch lbs. (10 Nm)—left side

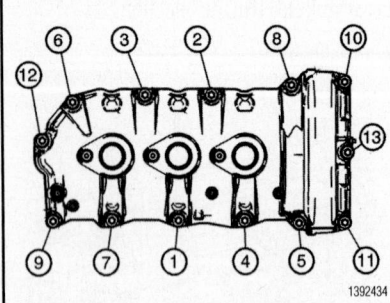

Fig. 104 Tighten the camshaft cover bolts, in the sequence shown, to 89 inch lbs. (10 Nm)—right side

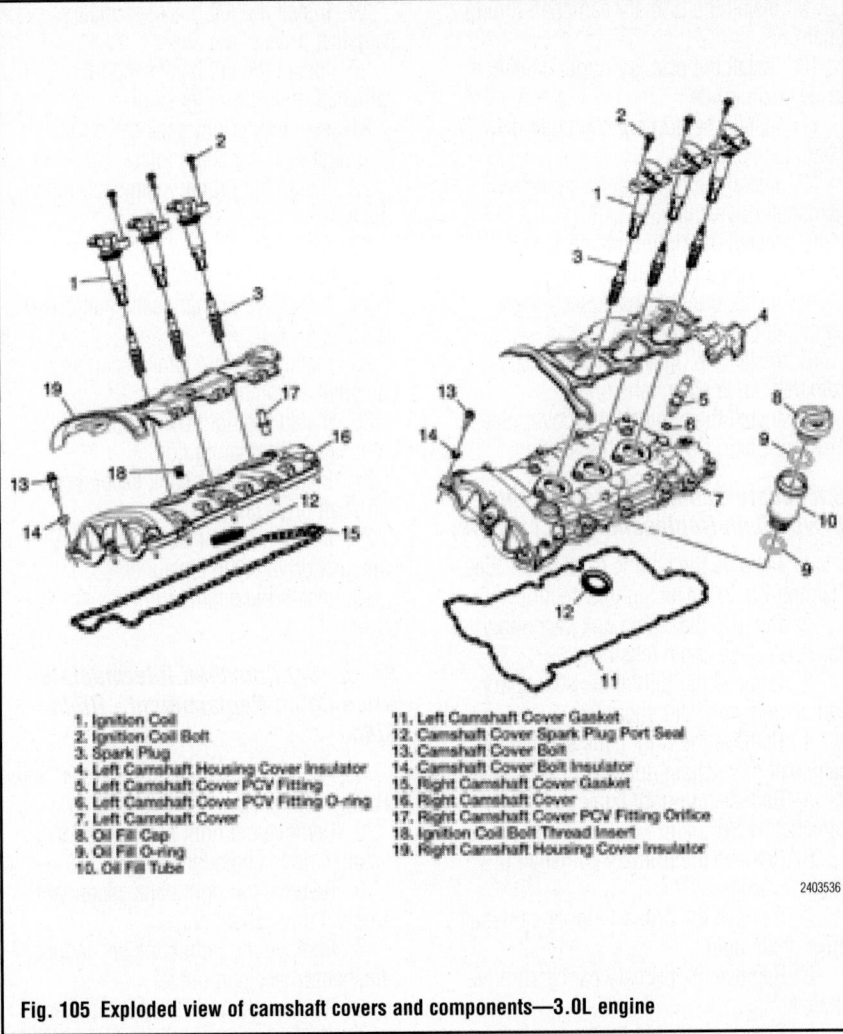

1. Ignition Coil
2. Ignition Coil Bolt
3. Spark Plug
4. Left Camshaft Housing Cover Insulator
5. Left Camshaft Cover PCV Fitting
6. Left Camshaft Cover PCV Fitting O-ring
7. Left Camshaft Cover
8. Oil Fill Cap
9. Oil Fill O-ring
10. Oil Fill Tube
11. Left Camshaft Cover Gasket
12. Camshaft Cover Spark Plug Port Seal
13. Camshaft Cover Bolt
14. Camshaft Cover Bolt Insulator
15. Right Camshaft Cover Gasket
16. Right Camshaft Cover
17. Right Camshaft Cover PCV Fitting Orifice
18. Ignition Coil Bolt Thread Insert
19. Right Camshaft Housing Cover Insulator

Fig. 105 Exploded view of camshaft covers and components—3.0L engine

2. Disconnect and remove the engine harness from the camshaft cover.

3. For left side cover, remove the intake manifold. See "Intake Manifold" in this section.

4. Remove the camshaft cover bolts.

5. Remove the camshaft cover from the cylinder head.

6. Clean the mating surfaces of the cylinder head and the camshaft cover.

7. Install the EN-46101 guide (protective plug) onto the spark plug tubes of the cylinder head.

To install:

8. Install new camshaft cover bolt grommets prior to installing the camshaft cover bolts.

9. Place a bead 8 mm in diameter by 4 mm in height of RTV sealant equivalent, on the engine front cover split lines.

10. Place the camshaft cover into position onto the cylinder head. Loosely install the left camshaft cover bolts.

11. Tighten the camshaft cover bolts, in the sequence shown, to 89 inch lbs. (10 Nm).

12. Connect and install the engine harness to the camshaft cover.

13. For the left side, install the intake manifold. See "Intake Manifold" in this section.

14. Remove the EN-46101 guide from the spark plug tubes of the cylinder head.

15. Install the ignition coils.

VALVE LASH

ADJUSTMENT

➡Valve clearance is automatically adjusted by the hydraulic valve lifters. No manual adjustment is required.

ENGINE PERFORMANCE & EMISSION CONTROLS

ACCELERATOR PEDAL POSITION (APP) SENSOR

LOCATION

See Figure 106.

Refer to the accompanying illustration.

REMOVAL & INSTALLATION

1. Remove the LH instrument panel insulator.
2. Remove the Communication Interface Module.
3. Remove the APP sensor bolts.
4. Remove the APP sensor.
5. Disconnect the electrical connector.
6. Installation is the reverse of the removal procedure.

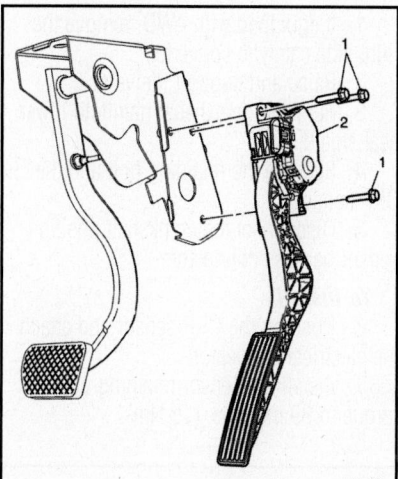

Fig. 106 Accelerator pedal and APP sensor bolts (1) and sensor (2)—2.4L & 3.0L engine

CAMSHAFT POSITION (CMP) SENSOR

LOCATION

See Figures 107 through 112.

Refer to the accompanying illustrations for sensor location.

REMOVAL & INSTALLATION

2.4L Engine

Intake

1. Remove the fuel pump cover.
2. Remove the CMP sensor bolt and remove the sensor.
3. Disconnect the electrical connector.

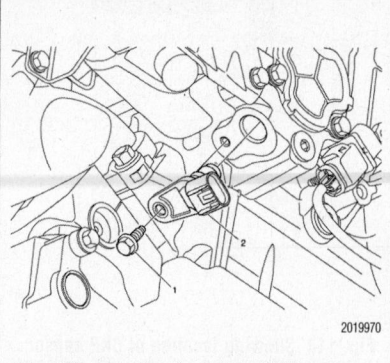

Fig. 107 Showing the intake CMP sensor (2) and bolt (1)—2.4L engine

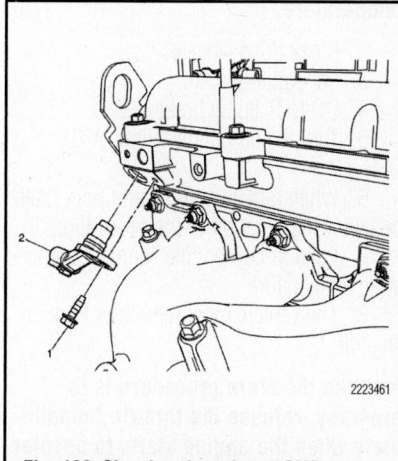

Fig. 108 Showing the exhaust CMP sensor (2) and bolt (1)—2.4L engine

4. Installation is the reverse of the removal procedure.
5. Tighten retainer bolt to 89 inch lbs. (10 Nm).

Exhaust

1. Remove the intake manifold cover.
2. Remove the CMP sensor bolt and remove the sensor.
3. Disconnect the electrical connector.
4. Installation is the reverse of the removal procedure.
5. Lube the sensor O-ring with clean engine oil.
6. Tighten retainer bolt to 89 inch lbs. (10 Nm).

3.0L Engine

Intake or Exhaust CMP Sensor— Right Side (Bank 1)

1. Remove air cleaner outlet duct.
2. Remove CMP sensor bolt and remove sensor.

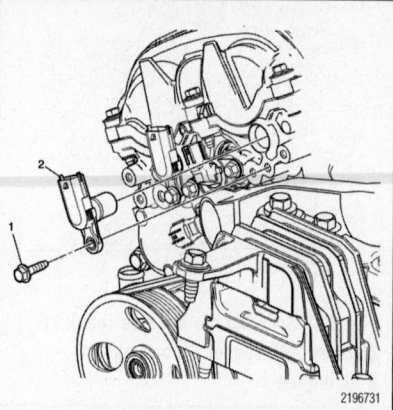

Fig. 109 Showing the right side (bank 1) intake CMP sensor (2) and bolt (1)—3.0L engine

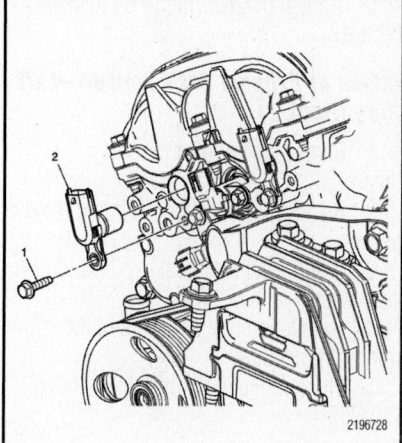

Fig. 110 Showing the right side (bank 1) exhaust CMP sensor (2) and bolt (1)— 3.0L engine

Fig. 111 Showing the left side (bank 2) intake CMP sensor (2) and bolt (1)—3.0L engine

Fig. 112 Showing the left side (bank 2) exhaust CMP sensor (2) and bolt (1)—3.0L engine

3. Disconnect electrical connector.

4. Installation is the reverse of the removal procedure.

5. Tighten retainer bolt to 89 inch lbs. (10 Nm).

Intake or Exhaust CMP Sensor—Left Side (Bank 2)

1. Remove the engine mount bracket.

2. Remove CMP sensor bolt and remove sensor.

3. Disconnect electrical connector.

4. Installation is the reverse of the removal procedure.

5. Tighten retainer bolt to 89 inch lbs. (10 Nm).

CRANKSHAFT POSITION (CKP) SENSOR

LOCATION

See Figures 113 and 114.

Refer to the accompanying illustrations for sensor location.

REMOVAL & INSTALLATION

2.4L Engine

1. Remove the CKP sensor retaining bolt.

2. Remove the sensor and disconnect the electrical connector.

3. Installation is the reverse of the removal procedure.

4. Tighten retaining bolt to 89 inch lbs. (10 Nm).

Crankshaft Position System Variation Learn—2.4L Engine

1. Close the hood.

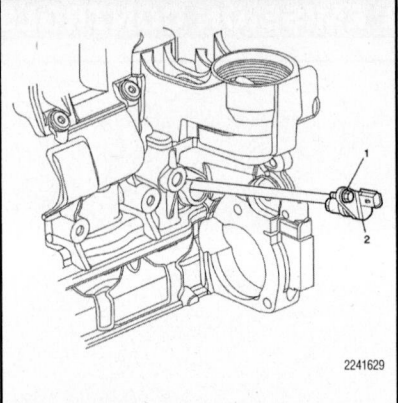

Fig. 113 Showing location of CKP sensor (1)—2.4L engine

➡ **The engine must be at operating temperature.**

2. Block drive wheels.

3. Set parking brake.

4. DO NOT apply brake pedal.

5. Turn the air conditioning (A/C) OFF.

6. When directed, apply and hold brake pedal for the duration of the procedure.

7. Ignition ON, engine running at operating temperature.

8. The vehicle must remain in Park or Neutral.

➡ **While the learn procedure is in progress, release the throttle immediately when the engine starts to decelerate. The engine control is returned to the operator and the engine responds**

to throttle position after the learn procedure is complete.

9. Accelerate to wide open throttle (WOT) and release when the fuel cut-off occurs.

10. The scan tool should display "Learn In Progress" and then "Learn Successful".

11. Verify DTC P0315 ran and passed "This Ignition Cycle".

12. If DTC P0315 failed or did not run "This Ignition Cycle", or another DTC is present, refer to appropriate DTC list and chart.

13. Once the Crankshaft Position Variation Learn procedure has successfully completed, and in order to store the crankshaft position variation values in the ECM, turn OFF the ignition and verify all vehicle systems are OFF. This may take up to 2 minutes.

3.0L Engine

1. If equipped with AWD, remove the right side catalytic converter.

2. Raise and support the vehicle.

3. Remove the exhaust manifold lower heat shield

4. Remove the retaining bolt and the CKP sensor.

5. Disconnect the crankshaft position sensor harness connector.

To install:

6. Position the CKP sensor and attach the electrical connector.

7. Install the sensor retaining bolt and torque to 89 inch lbs. (10 Nm).

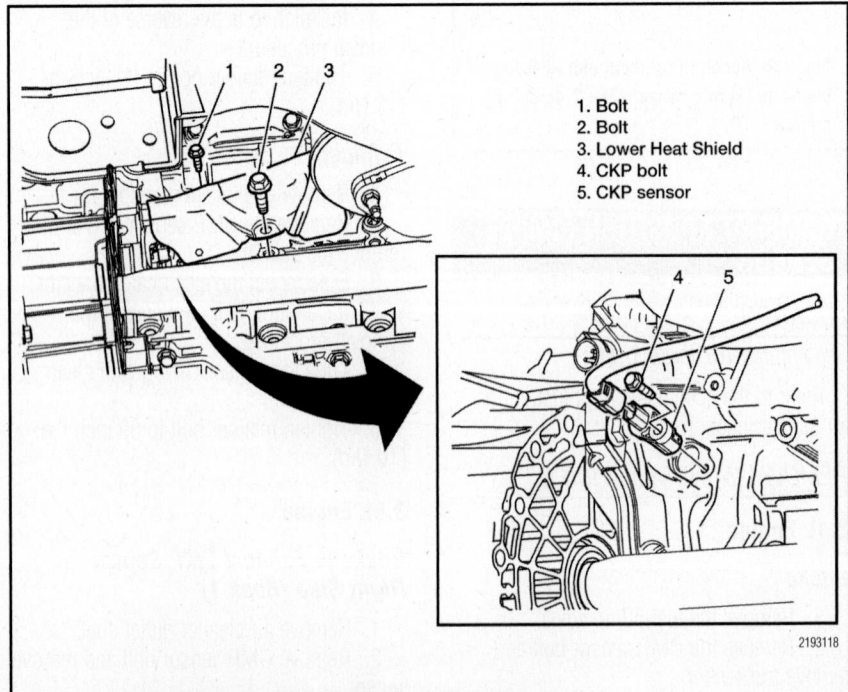

1. Bolt
2. Bolt
3. Lower Heat Shield
4. CKP bolt
5. CKP sensor

Fig. 114 Showing location of CKP sensor (1)—3.0L engine

8. Install the exhaust manifold lower heat shield.

9. Lower the vehicle.

10. Install the right side catalytic converter, if equipped.

Crankshaft Position System Variation Learn—3.0L Engine

➡The Crankshaft Position Variation Learn procedure is also required when the following service procedures have been performed, regardless of whether DTC P0315 is set:

- An engine replacement
- An engine control module (ECM) replacement
- A crankshaft balancer replacement
- A crankshaft replacement
- A crankshaft position sensor replacement
- Any engine repairs which disturb the crankshaft to crankshaft position sensor relationship.

➡The ECM monitors certain component signals to determine if all the conditions are met to continue with the Crankshaft Position Variation Learn procedure.

1. With ignition ON, observe the DTC information with a scan tool. Verify no other DTCs are set, except DTCs P0300-P0304, or P0315.

2. If DTCs are set, except DTCs P0300-P0304, or P0315, refer to appropriate DTC list and chart for further diagnosis.

3. Select the Crankshaft Position Variation Learn Procedure with a scan tool and perform the following:

a. Close the hood.

➡The engine must be at operating temperature.

b. Block drive wheels.

c. Set parking brake.

d. DO NOT apply brake pedal.

e. Turn the air conditioning (A/C) OFF.

f. When directed, apply and hold brake pedal for the duration of the procedure.

g. Ignition ON, engine running at operating temperature.

h. The vehicle must remain in Park or Neutral.

➡While the learn procedure is in progress, release the throttle immediately when the engine starts to decelerate. The engine control is returned to the operator and the engine responds

to throttle position after the learn procedure is complete.

i. Accelerate to wide open throttle (WOT) and release when the fuel cut-off occurs.

4. The scan tool should display "Learn In Progress" and then "Learn Successful".

5. Verify DTC P0315 ran and passed "This Ignition Cycle".

6. If DTC P0315 failed or did not run "This Ignition Cycle", or another DTC is present, refer to appropriate DTC list and chart.

7. Once the Crankshaft Position Variation Learn procedure has successfully completed, and in order to store the crankshaft position variation values in the ECM, turn OFF the ignition and verify all vehicle systems are OFF. This may take up to 2 minutes.

ELECTRONIC CONTROL MODULE (ECM)

LOCATION

See Figures 115 and 116.

Refer to the accompanying illustrations for location.

REMOVAL & INSTALLATION

❊❊ CAUTION

Turn the ignition OFF when installing or removing the control module connectors and disconnecting or reconnecting the power to the control module (battery cable, powertrain control module (PCM)/engine control module (ECM)/transaxle control module (TCM) pigtail, control module fuse, jumper cables, etc.) in order to prevent internal control module damage.

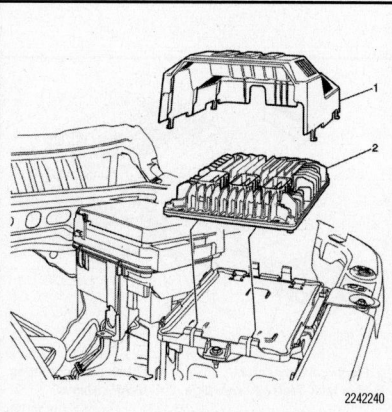

Fig. 115 Showing location of ECM—2.4L engine

❊❊ CAUTION

Control module damage may result when the metal case contacts battery voltage. DO NOT contact the control module metal case with battery voltage when servicing a control module, using battery booster cables, or when charging the vehicle battery. Observe the following:

- In order to prevent any possible electrostatic discharge damage to the control module, do not touch the connector pins or the soldered components on the circuit board.
- Remove any debris from around the control module connector surfaces before servicing the control module. Inspect the control module connector gaskets when diagnosing or replacing the control module. Ensure that the gaskets are installed correctly. The gaskets prevent contaminant intrusion into the control module.
- The replacement control module must be programmed.

❊❊ CAUTION

In order to prevent any possible electrostatic discharge damage to the ECM, do not touch the connector pins.

1. Disconnect the negative battery cable.

2. Release the plastic retaining tabs.

3. Disconnect the electrical connectors.

4. If replacing ECM, reprogram the ECM. Refer to appropriate service outlet or use updated aftermarket scan tool and software.

a. It is necessary to record the remaining engine oil life. If the

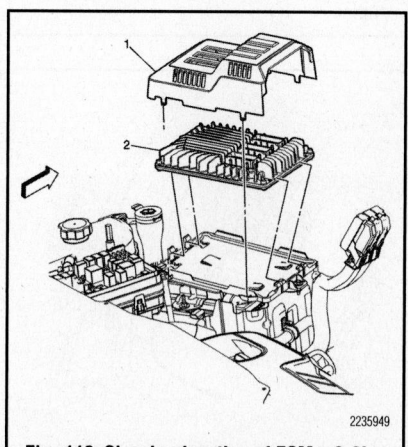

Fig. 116 Showing location of ECM—3.0L engine

replacement module is not programmed with the remaining engine oil life, the engine oil life will default to 100 percent. If the replacement module is not programmed with the remaining engine oil life, the engine oil will need to be changed at 3000 mi. from the last engine oil change.

b. It is necessary to record the remaining automatic transmission fluid life. If the replacement module is not programmed with the remaining automatic transmission fluid life, the automatic transmission fluid life will default to 100 percent. If the replacement module is not programmed with the remaining automatic transmission fluid life, the automatic transmission fluid will need to be changed at 50,000 mi. from the last automatic transmission fluid change.

ENGINE COOLANT TEMPERATURE (ECT) SENSOR

LOCATION

See Figures 117 and 118.

Refer to the accompanying illustrations for sensor location.

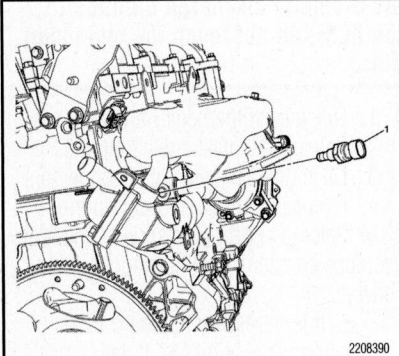

Fig. 117 Location of ECT sensor (1)—2.4L engine

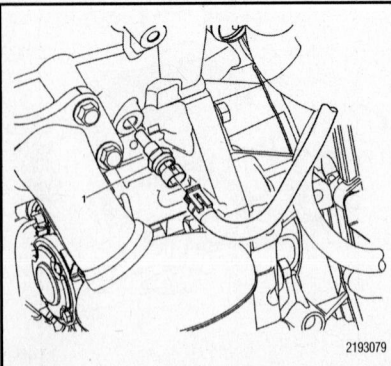

Fig. 118 Location of ECT sensor (1)—3.0L engine

REMOVAL & INSTALLATION

1. On 3.0L, reposition sensor heat shield.
2. Remove the ECT sensor bolt.
3. Remove the ECT sensor and detach the electrical connector.
4. Installation is the reverse of the removal procedure.
5. Tighten retaining bolt to 15 ft. lbs. (20 Nm).

EVAPORATIVE EMISSION CONTROL (EVAP) CANISTER

LOCATION

See Figure 119.

Refer to the accompanying illustration.

REMOVAL & INSTALLATION

The EVAP emissions canister is located under the center of the vehicle. It has 3 EVAP line connections:
- The EVAP fresh air
- The EVAP vent
- The EVAP purge

1. Raise and support the vehicle.
2. Clean all fuel pipe connections and surrounding areas before disconnecting the fuel pipes to avoid contamination of the fuel system.
3. Disconnect the EVAP canister fresh air hose/pipe from the fuel tank fresh air hose/pipe.
4. Disconnect the EVAP canister vent hose/pipe from the EVAP canister.
5. Disconnect the EVAP canister purge hose/pipe from the EVAP canister.
6. Remove the EVAP canister-to-underbody nuts.
7. Lower the EVAP canister.
8. Disconnect the EVAP vent solenoid electrical connector.
9. Remove the EVAP canister from the vehicle.

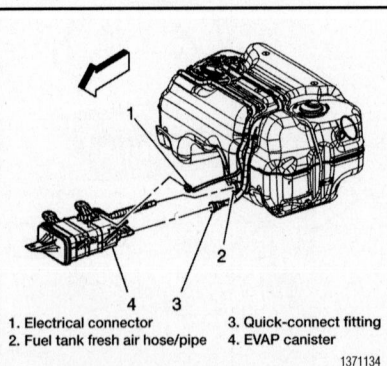

1. Electrical connector
2. Fuel tank fresh air hose/pipe
3. Quick-connect fitting
4. EVAP canister

Fig. 119 Showing the EVAP canister location

To install:

10. Connect the EVAP vent solenoid electrical connector.
11. Install the EVAP canister to the underbody of the vehicle.
12. Install the EVAP canister-to-underbody nuts. Tighten the nuts to 80 inch lbs. (9 Nm).
13. Connect the EVAP canister purge hose/pipe to the EVAP canister.
14. Connect the EVAP canister vent hose/pipe to the EVAP canister.
15. Connect the EVAP canister fresh air hose/pipe to the fuel tank fresh air hose/pipe.
16. Lower the vehicle.

EVAPORATIVE EMISSION CONTROL (EVAP) CANISTER PURGE SOLENOID

LOCATION

See Figures 120 and 121.

Refer to the accompanying illustrations for location.

REMOVAL & INSTALLATION

2.4L Engine

1. Remove the intake manifold cover.
2. Disconnect the evaporative emission pipes.
3. Remove EVAP canister purge solenoid bolt.
4. Remove solenoid.
5. Disconnect the electrical connector.
6. Installation is the reverse of the removal procedure.
7. Tighten retaining bolt to 18 ft. lbs. (25 Nm).

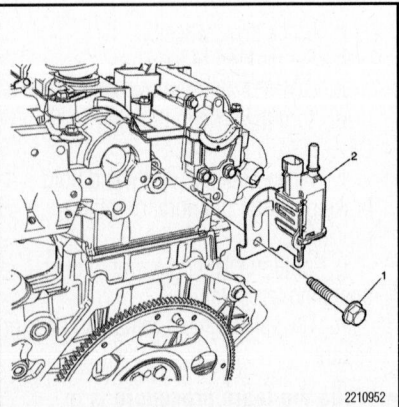

Fig. 120 Removing EVAP canister purge solenoid bolt (1) and solenoid (2)—2.4L engine

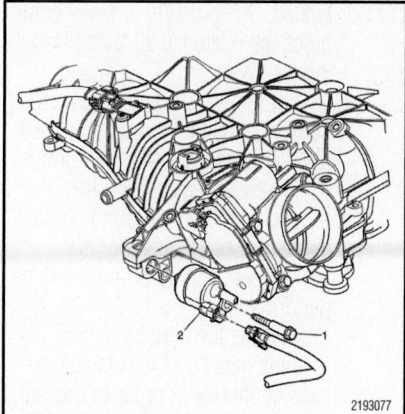

Fig. 121 Removing EVAP canister purge solenoid (2) and retaining bolt (1)—3.0L engine

3.0L Engine

1. Remove the intake manifold cover.
2. Remove the solenoid retaining bolt.
3. Remove the EVAP solenoid valve.
4. Disconnect the EVAP canister purge solenoid harness connector.
5. Installation is the reverse of the removal procedure.
6. Install a NEW O-ring.
7. Tighten retaining bolt to 89 inch lbs. (10 Nm).

EVAPORATIVE EMISSION CONTROL (EVAP) CANISTER VENT SOLENOID

LOCATION

See Figure 122.

Refer to the accompanying illustration for location.

REMOVAL & INSTALLATION

1. Remove the evaporative emission (EVAP) canister, as described in this section.

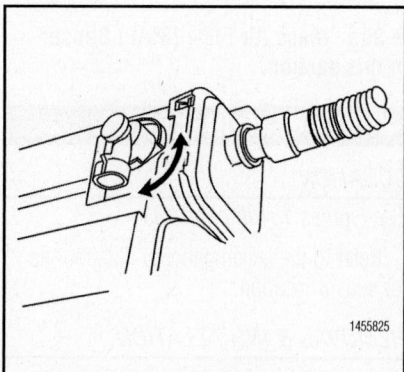

Fig. 122 Removing EVAP canister vent solenoid—2.4L & 3.0L engine

2. Rotate the EVAP canister vent valve counterclockwise to release from the locked position.
3. Remove the vent valve from the EVAP canister.

To install:

4. Insert the EVAP canister vent solenoid valve into the EVAP canister, with the valve aligned to the released position.
5. Rotate vent valve clockwise to secure into the locked position.
6. Install the EVAP canister.

FUEL PRESSURE (FP) SENSOR

LOCATION

See Figures 123 and 124.

Refer to the accompanying illustrations for sensor location.

REMOVAL & INSTALLATION

1. Relieve the fuel system pressure. See "FUEL SYSTEMS" section.
2. Raise and suitably support the vehicle.
3. Disconnect the body wiring harness electrical connector from the fuel pressure sensor.
4. Wrap a shop towel around the fuel pressure sensor fitting in order to absorb any fuel that may leak out.
5. Remove the fuel pressure sensor from the fuel line.
6. Remove and discard the fuel pressure sensor O-ring seal.

To install:

7. Lubricate a NEW fuel pressure sensor O-ring seal with clean engine oil.
8. Install the NEW fuel pressure sensor O-ring seal onto the fuel line fitting.

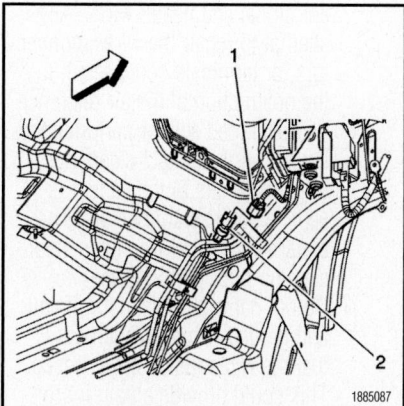

Fig. 123 Location of Fuel Pressure (FP) sensor (2) and electrical connector (1)—2.4L engine

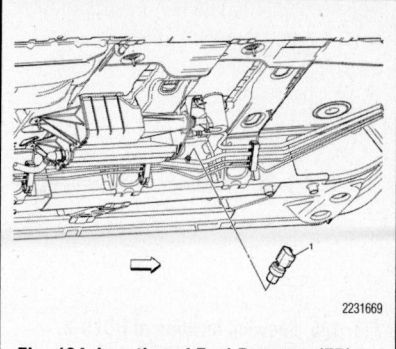

Fig. 124 Location of Fuel Pressure (FP) sensor (1)—3.0L engine

9. Install the fuel pressure sensor to the fuel line. Tighten the sensor to 11 ft. lbs. (15 Nm).
10. Connect the body wiring harness electrical connector to the fuel pressure sensor.
11. Lower the vehicle.
12. Use the following procedure in order to inspect for leaks:
   a. Turn the ignition ON, with the engine OFF, for 2 seconds.
   b. Turn the ignition OFF for 10 seconds.
   c. Turn the ignition ON, with the engine OFF.
   d. Inspect for fuel leaks.

HEATED OXYGEN (HO2S) SENSOR

LOCATION

See Figures 125 through 130.

Refer to the accompanying illustrations for sensor location.

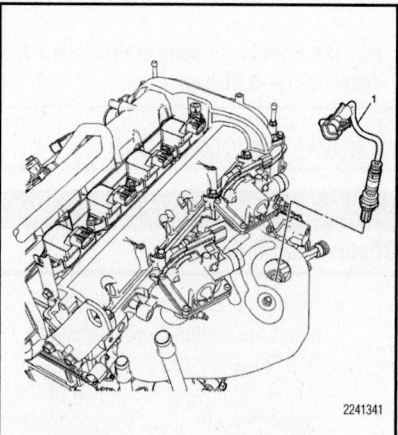

Fig. 125 Showing location of HO2S-1 (1)—2.4L engine

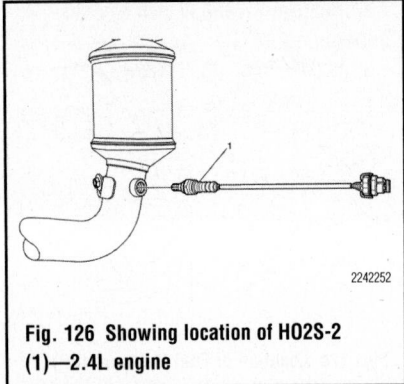

Fig. 126 Showing location of HO2S-2 (1)—2.4L engine

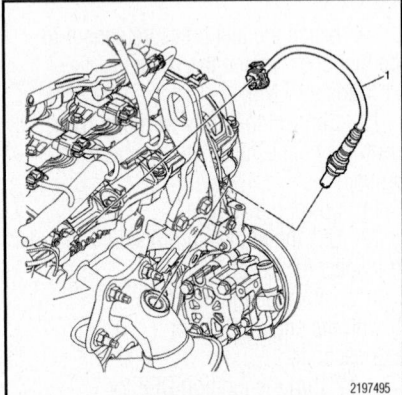

Fig. 127 Showing location of HO2S Bank 1 Sensor 1 (1)—3.0L engine

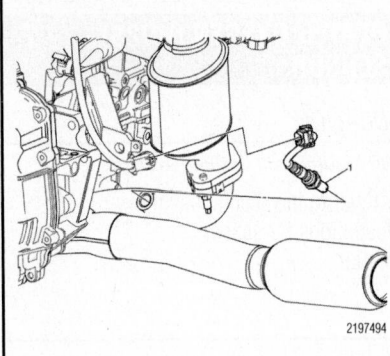

Fig. 128 Showing location of HO2S Bank 1 Sensor 2 (1)—3.0L engine

REMOVAL & INSTALLATION

❈❈ WARNING

Observe the following:

- Do not remove the pigtail from either the heated oxygen sensor (HO2S) or the oxygen sensor (O2S). Removing the pigtail or the connector will affect sensor operation.
- Handle the oxygen sensor carefully. Do not drop the HO2S. Keep the

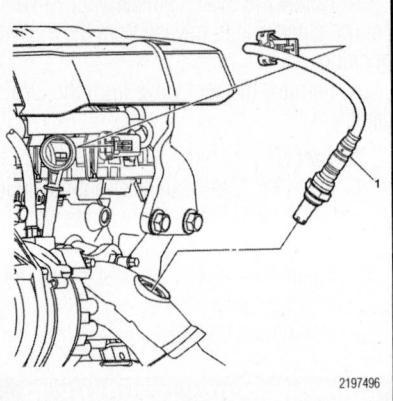

Fig. 129 Showing location of HO2S Bank 2 Sensor 1 (1)—3.0L engine

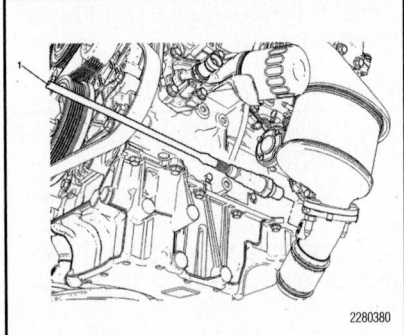

Fig. 130 Showing location of HO2S Bank 2 Sensor 2 (1)—3.0L engine

in-line electrical connector and the louvered end free of grease, dirt, or other contaminants. Do not use cleaning solvents of any type.
- Do not repair the wiring, connector or terminals. Replace the oxygen sensor if the pigtail wiring, connector, or terminal is damaged.
- This external clean air reference is obtained by way of the oxygen sensor signal and heater wires. Any attempt to repair the wires, connectors, or terminals could result in the obstruction of the air reference and degraded sensor performance.
- Do not apply contact cleaner or other materials to the sensor or vehicle harness connectors. These materials may get into the sensor causing poor performance.
- Do not damage the sensor pigtail and harness wires in such a way that the wires inside are exposed. This could provide a path for foreign materials to enter the sensor and cause performance problems.
- Ensure the sensor or vehicle lead wires are not bent sharply or

kinked. Sharp bends or kinks could block the reference air path through the lead wire.
- Do not remove or defeat the oxygen sensor ground wire, where applicable. Vehicles that utilize the ground wired sensor may rely on this ground as the only ground contact to the sensor. Removal of the ground wire will cause poor engine performance.
- Ensure that the peripheral seal remains intact on the vehicle harness connector in order to prevent damage due to water intrusion. The engine harness may be repaired using Packard's Crimp and Splice Seals Terminal Repair Kit. Under no circumstances should repairs be soldered since this could result in the air reference being obstructed.

1. Remove the intake manifold cover.
2. Disconnect the heated oxygen sensor harness connector.
3. If reinstalling the old sensor, coat the threads with anti-seize compound.

➡**A special anti-seize compound is used in the HO2S threads. The compound consists of liquid graphic and glass beads. The graphic tends to burn away, but the glass beads remain, making the sensor easier to remove. New, or service replacement sensors already have the compound applied to the threads. If the sensor is removed from an exhaust component and if for any reason the sensor is to be reinstalled, the threads must have anti-seize compound applied before reinstallation.**

4. When installing the sensor, tighten to 31 ft. lbs. (42 Nm).

INTAKE AIR TEMPERATURE (IAT) SENSOR

➡**See "Mass Air Flow (MAF) Sensor" in this section.**

KNOCK SENSOR (KS)

LOCATION

See Figures 131 through 133.

Refer to the accompanying illustrations for sensor location.

REMOVAL & INSTALLATION

2.4L Engine

1. Remove Knock Sensor (KS) retaining bolt.

2. Remove KS and detach electrical connector.

3. Installation is the reverse of the removal procedure.

4. Tighten retaining bolt to 17 ft. lbs. (23 Nm).

3.0L Engine

Bank 1

1. If equipped with AWD, remove the right side catalytic converter.

2. Raise and support the vehicle.

3. Remove the exhaust manifold lower heat shield

4. Remove the retaining bolt and the Knock Sensor (KS).

5. Disconnect the Crankshaft Position (CKP) sensor harness connector.

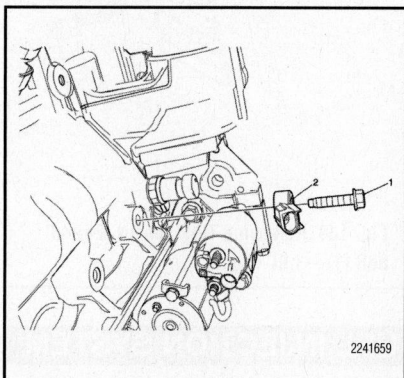

Fig. 131 Location of Knock Sensor (2) and retaining bolt (1)—2.4L engine

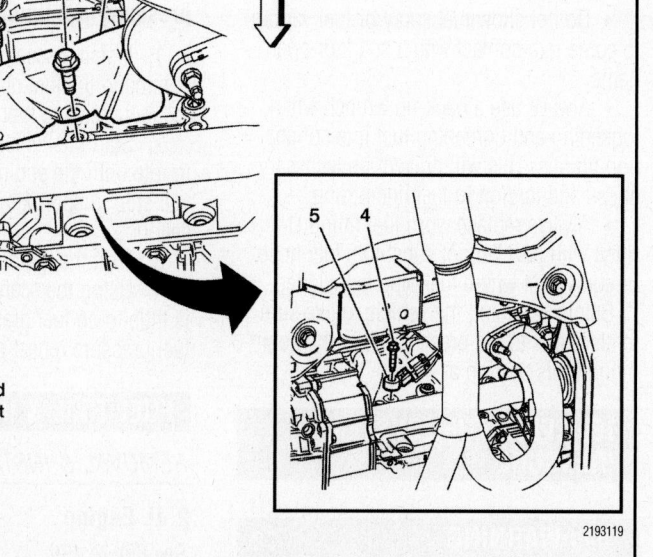

1. Bolt
2. Bolt
3. Lower Heat Shield
4. Knock sensor bolt
5. Knock sensor

Fig. 132 Location of Knock Sensor for Bank 1—3.0L engine

To install:

6. Position the KS and attach the electrical connector.

7. Install the sensor retaining bolt and torque to 17 ft. lbs. (23 Nm).

8. Install the exhaust manifold lower heat shield.

9. Lower the vehicle.

10. Install the right side catalytic converter, if equipped.

Bank 2

1. Remove Knock Sensor (KS) retaining bolt.

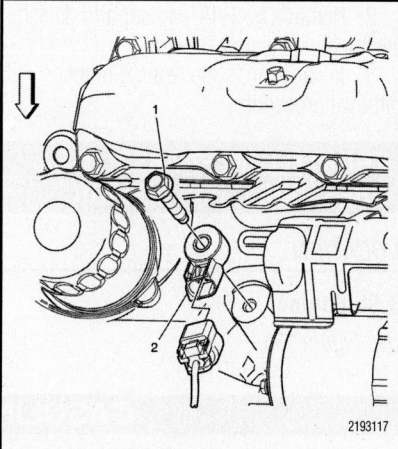

Fig. 133 Location of Knock Sensor for Bank 2—3.0L engine

2. Remove KS and detach electrical connector.

3. Installation is the reverse of the removal procedure.

4. Tighten retaining bolt to 17 ft. lbs. (23 Nm).

MANIFOLD ABSOLUTE PRESSURE (MAP) SENSOR

LOCATION

See Figures 134 and 135.

Refer to the accompanying illustrations for sensor location.

REMOVAL & INSTALLATION

1. Remove the air cleaner resonator.

2. Remove MAP sensor retaining bolt.

3. Remove MAP sensor and detach electrical connector.

4. Installation is the reverse of the removal procedure.

5. Tighten MAP sensor bolt to 35 inch lbs. (4 Nm).

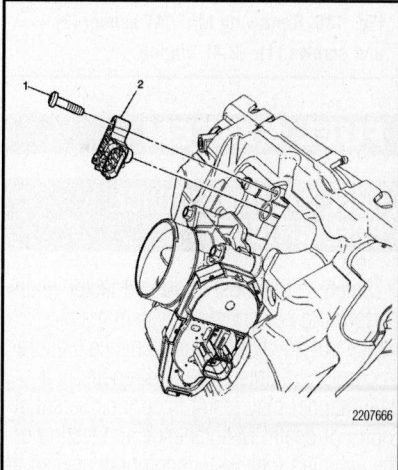

Fig. 134 Location of MAP sensor (1) and retaining bolt (2)—2.4L engine

Fig. 135 Location of MAP sensor (1) and retaining bolt (2)—3.0L engine

MASS AIR FLOW (MAF) SENSOR/INTAKE AIR TEMPERATURE (IAT) SENSOR

LOCATION

See Figures 136 and 137.

Refer to the accompanying illustrations for sensor location.

REMOVAL & INSTALLATION

1. Remove MAF/IAT sensor retaining screws.

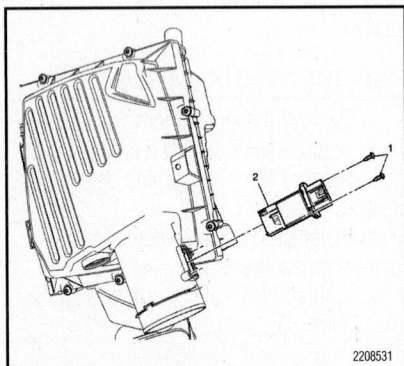

Fig. 136 Removing MAF/IAT sensor (2) and screws (1)—2.4L engine

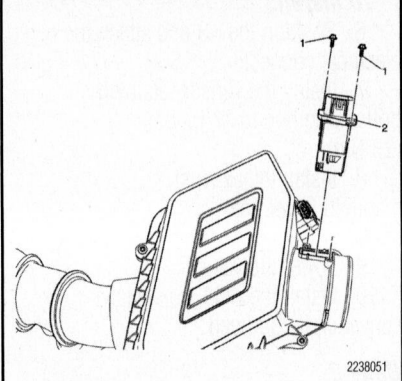

Fig. 137 Removing MAF/IAT sensor (2) and screws (1)—3.0L engine

2. Remove MAF/IAT sensor and detach electrical connector.
3. Installation is the reverse of the removal procedure.

THROTTLE INLET ABSOLUTE PRESSURE (TIAP) SENSOR

LOCATION

3.0L Engine
See Figure 138.

REMOVAL & INSTALLATION

3.0L Engine

1. Remove sensor retaining bolt.
2. Remove TIAP sensor and detach electrical connector.
3. Installation is the reverse of the removal procedure.

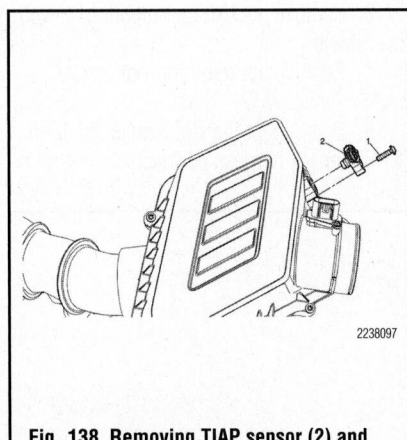

Fig. 138 Removing TIAP sensor (2) and bolt (1)—3.0L engine

FUEL SYSTEM

GASOLINE FUEL INJECTION SYSTEM

FUEL SYSTEM SERVICE PRECAUTIONS

Safety is the most important factor when performing not only fuel system maintenance but any type of maintenance. Failure to conduct maintenance and repairs in a safe manner may result in serious personal injury or death. Maintenance and testing of the vehicle's fuel system components can be accomplished safely and effectively by adhering to the following rules and guidelines.

• To avoid the possibility of fire and personal injury, always disconnect the negative battery cable unless the repair or test procedure requires that battery voltage be applied.

• Always relieve the fuel system pressure prior to disconnecting any fuel system component (injector, fuel rail, pressure regulator, etc.), fitting or fuel line connection. Exercise extreme caution whenever relieving fuel system pressure to avoid exposing skin, face and eyes to fuel spray. Please be advised that fuel under pressure may penetrate the skin or any part of the body that it contacts.

• Always place a shop towel or cloth around the fitting or connection prior to

loosening to absorb any excess fuel due to spillage. Ensure that all fuel spillage (should it occur) is quickly removed from engine surfaces. Ensure that all fuel soaked cloths or towels are deposited into a suitable waste container.

• Always keep a dry chemical (Class B) fire extinguisher near the work area.

• Do not allow fuel spray or fuel vapors to come into contact with a spark or open flame.

• Always use a back-up wrench when loosening and tightening fuel line connection fittings. This will prevent unnecessary stress and torsion to fuel line piping.

• Always replace worn fuel fitting O-rings with new Do not substitute fuel hose or equivalent where fuel pipe is installed.

Before servicing the vehicle, make sure to also refer to the precautions in the beginning of this section as well.

RELIEVING FUEL SYSTEM PRESSURE

✳✳ WARNING

Fuel that flows out at high pressure can cause serious injury to the skin and eyes. ALWAYS depressurize the fuel system before removing components that are under high fuel pressure.

➡**If a scan tool is not available, WAIT at LEAST 2 hours after the engine has been run, before removing the high pressure fuel line.**

1. Install a scan tool to the vehicle and command the fuel pump relay OFF, allowing the low pressure fuel pump to shut off.
2. Start the vehicle and allow the engine to idle until the engine stops. The engine will stop in approximately 20-30 seconds.
3. Turn the ignition OFF.
4. Using the scan tool, verify that there is little to no fuel pressure, if there still is fuel pressure repeat previous steps.

FUEL RAIL & INJECTORS

REMOVAL & INSTALLATION

2.4L Engine
See Figure 139.

1. Relieve the fuel system pressure.

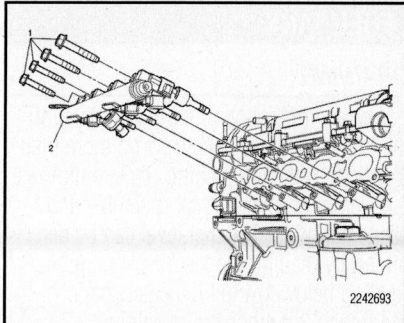

Fig. 139 Removing retainers (1) and fuel rail and injectors (2)—2.4L engine

2. Remove the intake manifold. See "Intake Manifold" in "ENGINE MECHANICAL" section.

3. Remove the fuel feed intermediate pipe.

4. Remove fuel injection fuel rail fasteners.

5. Disconnect the electrical connector.

6. Remove the fuel rail and injectors as an assembly.

7. Installation is the reverse of the removal procedure.

8. Tighten the fuel rail fasteners to 18 ft. lbs. (25 Nm).

3.0L Engine

1. Relieve the fuel system pressure.

2. Remove the fuel pipe shield.

3. Remove the intake manifold. See "ENGINE MECHANICAL" section.

4. Remove the fuel feed intermediate pipe.

5. Remove the foam insulator from the fuel rails.

6. Remove the cylinder head. See "ENGINE MECHANICAL" section.

7. Remove the bolts from the bank 2 fuel rail.

8. Remove the bank 1 fuel rail and injectors as an assembly.

9. Disconnect the bank 1 fuel injector electrical connections.

10. If the bank 2 fuel rail or injectors are being serviced, remove them.

11. Disconnect the bank 2 fuel injector and fuel pressure sensor electrical connections.

➡**The direct fuel injectors must be rebuilt whenever the injector has been released from the fuel rail or cylinder head.**

12. It is necessary to rebuild the fuel injectors.

To install:

13. Clean the fuel injector bores using EN-47909 kit.

14. Ensure that the fuel injectors have been properly rebuilt and lubricated.

15. Connect the bank 2 fuel injector and fuel pressure sensor electrical connections.

16. Position the bank 2 fuel rail and evenly hand tighten the 2 outer fuel rail bolts to seat the injectors into the injector bores. Remove the bolts.

17. Connect the bank 1 fuel injector electrical connections.

18. Position the bank 1 fuel rail and evenly hand tighten the 2 outer fuel rail bolts to seat the injectors into the injector bores.

19. Start and hand tighten the remaining fuel rail bolts.

20. Tighten the bank 1 and bank 2 fuel rail bolts to 89 inch lbs. (10 Nm).

21. Replace any wire harness tie straps cut from the fuel rails.

22. Install the cylinder head.

23. Install the fuel feed intermediate pipe.

24. Inspect for fuel leaks using the following procedure:

   a. Turn ON the ignition, with the engine OFF for 2 seconds.

   b. Turn OFF the ignition, for 10 seconds.

   c. Turn ON the ignition, with the engine OFF.

   d. Inspect for fuel leaks.

➡**Before installing the foam insulator, remove any remaining fuel from the injector well.**

25. Install the foam insulator to the fuel rails.

26. Install the intake manifold. See "Intake Manifold" in "ENGINE MECHANICAL" section.

27. Install the fuel pipe shield.

28. Install the low side fuel pressure service port cap.

FUEL PUMP

REMOVAL & INSTALLATION

2.4L Engine

See Figure 140.

1. Relieve the low and high side fuel system pressure. See "Relieving Fuel System Pressure" in this section.

2. Remove the intake manifold. See "Intake Manifold" in "ENGINE MECHANICAL" section.

3. Disconnect the engine wiring harness electrical connector from the high pressure fuel pump.

4. Remove the low pressure feed pipe.

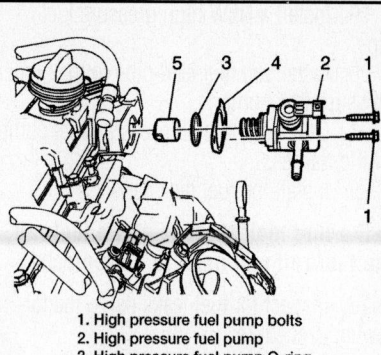

1. High pressure fuel pump bolts
2. High pressure fuel pump
3. High pressure fuel pump O-ring
4. Gasket
5. High pressure fuel pump roller lifter

Fig. 140 Removing the fuel pump—2.4L engine

5. Remove the high pressure pipe. Discard this pipe.

6. Remove and discard the high pressure fuel pump bolts.

7. Remove the high pressure fuel pump.

8. Remove and discard the high pressure fuel pump O-ring.

9. Remove and discard the high pressure fuel pump gasket.

10. Remove the high pressure fuel pump roller lifter.

To install:

➡**The camshaft must be in the base circle position before the high pressure fuel pump is installed.**

11. Use the EN-48896 alignment gauge to ensure that the camshaft lobe is in the base circle position. At base circle the tool will be flush with the head.

12. Lubricate the high pressure fuel pump cylinder head bore and roller lifter with camshaft prelube (GM P/N 12345501 or equivalent).

➡**The high pressure fuel pump gasket has a retaining feature to hold the pump retaining bolts in place.**

13. Install the high pressure fuel pump roller lifter.

14. Install a NEW high pressure fuel pump O-ring.

15. Position the NEW high pressure fuel pump gasket and bolts to the fuel pump.

16. Install the high pressure fuel pump. Force will be required while hand tightening the bolts.

17. Tighten the high pressure fuel pump retaining bolts to 11 ft. lbs. (15 Nm).

18. Ensure the high pressure fuel pump and fuel rail fittings are clean prior to assembly.

19. Install a NEW high pressure fuel pipe.

20. Install the fuel feed pipe to the high pressure fuel pump.

21. Connect the high pressure fuel pump wiring harness.

22. Install the fuel tank cap.

➡ **If a fuel leak accrues at the fuel rail, the fuel rail will need to be replaced.**

23. Inspect for fuel leaks using the following procedure:

    a. Turn ON the ignition, with the engine OFF for 2 seconds.

    b. Turn OFF the ignition, for 10 seconds.

    c. Turn ON the ignition, with the engine OFF.

    d. Inspect for fuel leaks.

24. Install the pressure relief cap to the fuel feed pipe.

25. Install the high pressure fuel pump cover.

3.0L Engine

See Figure 141.

1. Relieve the low and high side fuel system pressure. See "Relieving Fuel System Pressure" in this section.

2. Remove the high pressure fuel pump shield.

3. Disconnect the engine wiring harness electrical connector from the high pressure fuel pump.

4. Remove the low pressure feed pipe.

5. Remove the high pressure pipe. Discard the pipe.

6. Remove and discard the high pressure fuel pump bolts.

7. Remove the high pressure fuel pump.

8. Remove and discard the high pressure fuel pump O-ring.

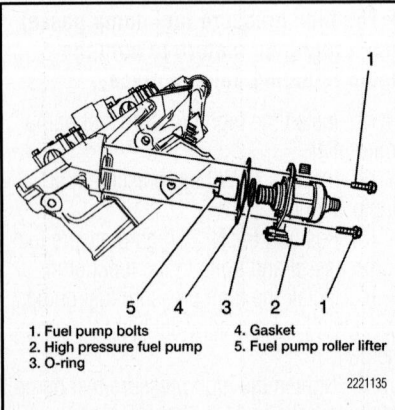

1. Fuel pump bolts
2. High pressure fuel pump
3. O-ring
4. Gasket
5. Fuel pump roller lifter

2221135

Fig. 141 Exploded view of the high pressure fuel pump

9. Remove and discard the high pressure fuel pump gasket.

10. Remove the high pressure fuel pump roller lifter.

To install:

➡ **The camshaft must be in the base circle position before the high pressure fuel pump is installed.**

11. Use the EN-48896 alignment gauge to ensure that the camshaft lobe is in the base circle position. At base circle the tool will be flush with the head.

12. Lubricate the high pressure fuel pump cylinder head bore and roller lifter with camshaft prelube.

➡ **The high pressure fuel pump gasket has a retaining feature to hold the pump retaining bolts in place.**

13. Install the high pressure fuel pump roller lifter.

14. Install a NEW high pressure fuel pump O-ring.

15. Position the NEW high pressure fuel pump gasket and bolts to the fuel pump.

16. Install the high pressure fuel pump. Force will be required while hand tightening the bolts.

17. Tighten the high pressure fuel pump retaining bolts to 11 ft. lbs. (15 Nm).

18. Ensure the high pressure fuel pump and fuel rail fittings are clean prior to assembly.

19. Install a NEW high pressure fuel pipe.

20. Install the fuel feed pipe to the high pressure fuel pump.

21. Connect the high pressure fuel pump wiring harness.

22. Install the fuel tank cap.

➡ **If a fuel leak accrues at the fuel rail, the fuel rail will need to be replaced.**

23. Inspect for fuel leaks using the following procedure:

    a. Turn ON the ignition, with the engine OFF for 2 seconds.

    b. Turn OFF the ignition, for 10 seconds.

    c. Turn ON the ignition, with the engine OFF.

    d. Inspect for fuel leaks.

24. Install the pressure relief cap to the fuel feed pipe.

25. Install the intake manifold. See "Intake Manifold" in "ENGINE MECHANICAL" section.

26. Install the high pressure fuel pump shield.

FUEL TANK

DRAINING

For any operation requiring removal of the fuel tank, there should be no more than 3 gallons of fuel remaining. This minimizes the weight of the fuel tank assembly and eases handling. The fuel level can be determined by reading the fuel level gauge. A reading below 1/4 full indicates that no more than 3 gallons are remaining.

Using The Fuel Pump

※ WARNING

Do not allow smoking or the use of open flames in the area where work on the fuel or EVAP system is taking place. Anytime work is being done on the fuel system, disconnect the negative battery cable, except for those tests where battery voltage is required.

※ CAUTION

Never drain or store fuel in an open container due to the possibility of fire or explosion.

➡ **Using the fuel pump to drain the tank is the easiest procedure if the fuel pump is operable. The fuel can be pumped out with the vehicle on the ground or on a hoist.**

On The Ground

※ WARNING

Fuel supply lines will remain pressurized for long periods of time after the engine is shutdown. This pressure must be relieved before servicing the fuel system.

1. Relieve the fuel system pressure.

2. Wrap a shop cloth around the fitting and have an approved container available to collect any fuel.

3. Disconnect the fuel feed quick connect fitting from the fuel rail.

4. Install the 3/8 in. x 1/4 in. fitting into the fuel feed quick connect fitting.

5. Connect a suitable drain hose to the other end of the adapter and connect the drain hose to a certified fuel handling cart.

6. Connect a scan tool to the vehicle diagnostic connector and turn the ignition ON.

7. Energize the fuel pump using the scan tool.

8. Pump out the fuel until no more than 1/4 tank of fuel remains.

On The Hoist

1. Connect a scan tool to the vehicle diagnostic connector and turn the ignition ON.

2. Relieve the fuel system pressure.

3. Ensure that the vehicle is properly supported and squarely positioned. To help avoid personal injury when a vehicle is on a hoist, provide additional support for the vehicle on the opposite end from which the components are being removed.

4. Raise the vehicle on a hoist to a comfortable working height, keeping the scan tool outside of the vehicle and accessible from under the car.

5. Wrap a shop cloth around the fitting and have an approved container available to collect any fuel.

6. Disconnect the fuel tank fuel feed line quick connect fitting from the chassis fuel feed pipe.

7. Install the 3/8 in. x 1/4 in. fitting into the fuel feed quick connect fitting.

8. Connect a suitable drain hose to the other end of the adapter and connect the drain hose to a certified fuel handling cart.

9. Energize the fuel pump using the scan tool.

10. Pump out the fuel until no more than 1/4 tank of fuel remains.

Siphoning The Fuel Tank

1. If the fuel pump is inoperative, the tank can be drained by siphoning from the tank. A suitable means is through the fuel fill pipe with the correct type and stiffness of tubing.

2. Disconnect the negative battery cable.

3. Open the fuel fill door and remove the gas cap.

✻ CAUTION

Do not attempt to insert any other type of siphon hose or tube into the fuel filler pipe. The design of the inlet check valve at the end of the fuel filler tube restricts the insertion of a hose and, most importantly, prevents the removal of this hose. If the siphon hose becomes stuck in the check valve, the fuel filler pipe will not be able to be removed from the fuel tank without damage to the fill pipe or fuel tank.

4. Insert the siphon hose guide/funnel into the fuel fill pipe opening.

➡ **The siphon hose will reach the bottom of the tank on the primary side only, within about 10 in. of the end fitting and tag. When connecting the siphon hose to another length of hose that is connected to the drain tank, DO NOT insert the siphon hose into the fill pipe funnel past the tag at the fitting end. If inserted too far, the upper portion of the siphon hose may pass through the check valve cage and then jam on attempted removal.**

5. Insert the hose into the guide funnel and into the fuel fill pipe. Some resistance may be encountered when the tip of the siphon hose reaches the inlet check valve. Repeated probing may be necessary to slide the hose tip through the check valve cage.

➡ **The fuel flow rate from the siphon hose will range from 0.3 gal./min up to 1.0 gal./min, depending on whether it is gravity siphoned or with an air-powered pump.**

6. Begin the fuel siphoning process. Place the fuel into an approved fuel container.

7. Remove the siphon hose from the fuel fill pipe after draining is complete.

REMOVAL & INSTALLATION

1. Ensure that the fuel level in the tank is less than 1/4 full. If necessary, drain the fuel tank to at least this level.

✻ WARNING

Fuel supply lines will remain pressurized for long periods of time after the engine is shutdown. This pressure must be relieved before servicing the fuel system.

2. Relieve the fuel system pressure.

3. Disconnect the negative battery cable.

4. Raise and support the vehicle.

5. Remove the exhaust system.

6. If equipped with AWD, remove the propeller shaft.

7. Disconnect the canister vent valve electrical connectors.

8. Disconnect the vent hose from the canister filter.

9. Disconnect the fuel tank vent pipe from the evaporative emission canister.

10. Clean all fuel pipe connections and surrounding areas before disconnecting the fuel pipes to avoid contamination of the fuel system.

11. Disconnect the chassis fuel supply line from the fuel tank.

12. Disconnect the fuel filler tube, EVAP vent hose, and fresh air hose from the fuel tank.

13. Disconnect the fuel tank electrical connector and remove the electrical connector retainer from the rear frame.

✻ CAUTION

Do not bend the fuel tank straps. Bending the fuel tank straps may cause damage to the straps.

➡ **Do not lower the rear frame. It is not necessary to lower the rear frame for fuel tank removal.**

14. Support the fuel tank using a suitable jack.

15. Remove the fuel tank strap nuts, and lower the fuel tank straps.

16. Lower the fuel tank from the underbody of the vehicle.

17. If replacing the fuel tank, remove the fuel tank module assemblies.

18. If replacing the fuel tank, remove the heat shield, hoses and wiring harness, and transfer to the new tank.

To install:

19. If previously removed, install the fuel tank module assemblies.

20. Using an adjustable jack, slowly raise and reposition the fuel tank in order to install the tank to the vehicle.

21. Install the fuel tank straps and the fuel tank strap-to-body nuts and tighten to 15 ft. lbs. (20 Nm).

22. Connect the fuel tank electrical connector and install the electrical connector retainer to the rear frame.

23. Connect the EVAP vent, and fresh air hoses to the fuel tank.

24. Connect the fuel filler tube to the fuel tank. Tighten the fuel filler tube clamp.

25. Connect the chassis fuel supply line to the fuel tank.

26. Connect the fuel tank vent pipe to the evaporative emission canister.

27. Connect the vent hose to the canister filter.

28. Connect the canister vent valve electrical connector.

29. Install the propeller shaft, if equipped with AWD.

30. Install the exhaust system.

31. Lower the vehicle.

32. Fill the fuel tank with gasoline.

33. Connect the negative battery cable.

34. Prime the fuel system:

a. Cycle the ignition ON for 5 seconds and then OFF for 10 seconds.

b. Repeat the previous step twice.

c. Crank the engine until it starts. The maximum starter motor cranking time is 20 seconds.

d. If the engine does not start, repeat these steps.

IDLE SPEED

ADJUSTMENT

➡ **The idle speed is computer controlled, therefore no manual adjustment is required.**

THROTTLE BODY

REMOVAL & INSTALLATION

1. On 2.4L, remove the outlet duct.
2. On 3.0L, remove the manifold cover.
3. Remove the throttle body assembly fasteners.
4. Remove the throttle body assembly.
5. Disconnect the electrical connector.
6. Installation is the reverse of the removal procedure.
7. Use a NEW throttle body O-ring.
8. Tighten the retaining bolts to 89 inch lbs. (10 Nm).
9. Perform the throttle learn procedure. Refer to "Throttle/Idle Learn".

THROTTLE LEARN PROCEDURE

RESET PROCEDURE (PERFORMED AFTER THE THROTTLE BODY IS CLEANED OR REPLACED)

1. Ignition ON, engine OFF, perform the Idle Learn Reset in Module Setup with a scan tool.
2. Start the engine and monitor the TB Idle Airflow Compensation parameter. The TB Idle Airflow Compensation value should equal 0 percent and the engine should be idling at a normal idle speed.
3. Clear the DTCs and return to the diagnostic that referred you here.

LEARN PROCEDURE (PERFORMED AFTER THE ECM IS FLASHED OR REPLACED)

➡ **Do NOT perform this procedure if DTCs are set.**

1. Start and idle the engine for 3 minutes.
2. With a scan tool, monitor the Desired Idle Speed and the actual Engine Speed.

3. The ECM will start to learn the new idle cells and Desired Idle Speed should start to decrease.
4. Ignition OFF for 60 seconds.
5. Start and idle the engine for 3 minutes.
6. After the 3 minute run time the engine should be idling normal.
7. During the drive cycle the check engine light may come on with idle speed DTCs. If idle speed codes are set, clear codes so the ECM can continue to learn.

   a. If the engine idle speed has not been learned the vehicle will need to be driven at speeds above 44 mph with several decelerations and extended idles.

8. After the drive cycle, the engine should be idling normally.

   a. If the engine idle speed has not been learned, turn OFF the ignition for 60 seconds and repeat previous step.

9. Once the engine speed has returned to normal, clear DTCs and return to the original diagnostic.

HEATING & AIR CONDITIONING SYSTEM

BLOWER MOTOR CONTROL MODULE

REMOVAL & INSTALLATION

See Figure 142

1. Remove the RH instrument panel insulator panel.
2. Disconnect the heater and blower and air conditioning control module electrical connectors.
3. Remove the blower motor control module.
4. Installation is the reverse of the removal procedure.

BLOWER MOTOR

REMOVAL & INSTALLATION

See Figure 143.

1. Remove the RH instrument panel (I/P) insulator panel.
2. Disconnect the blower motor electrical connector.
3. Remove the blower motor fasteners.
4. Remove the blower motor.
5. Installation is the reverse of the removal procedure.

CONDENSER

REMOVAL & INSTALLATION

1. Recover the refrigerant.
2. Remove the radiator air lower baffle and deflector.
3. Remove the radiator air upper baffle and deflector.
4. Remove the air conditioning compressor hose.
5. Remove the air conditioning condenser and air conditioning evaporator tube.
6. Remove the condenser bolts.
7. Remove the condenser.
8. Installation is the reverse of the removal procedure.
9. Add the specified amount of polyalkylene glycol (PAG) oil to the condenser.

EVAPORATOR CORE

REMOVAL & INSTALLATION

See Figure 144.

1. Remove the thermal expansion valve.
2. Remove the HVAC module, as described in this section.
3. Remove the heater core, as described in this section.
4. Disconnect the HVAC module electrical connectors.
5. Remove the HVAC case screws.

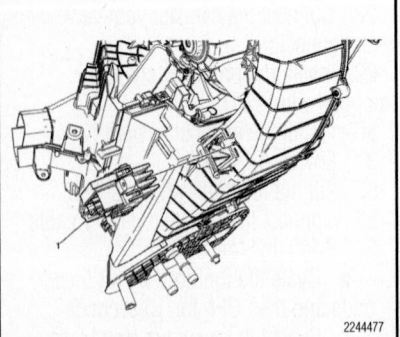

2244477

Fig. 142 Removing the blower motor control module (1)

2244404

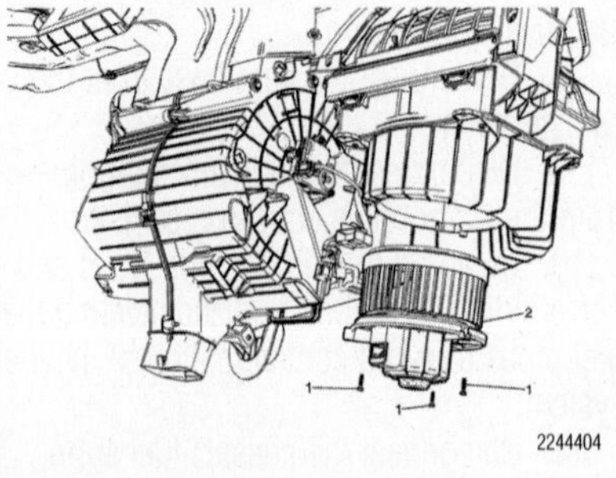

Fig. 143 Removing the blower motor (2) and retaining screws (1)

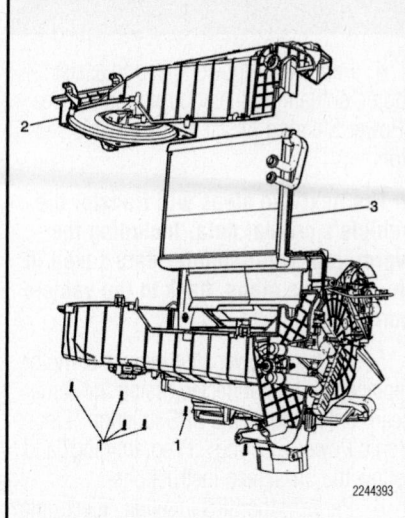

Fig. 144 Removing the fasteners (1), evaporator housing (2), and evaporator core (3)

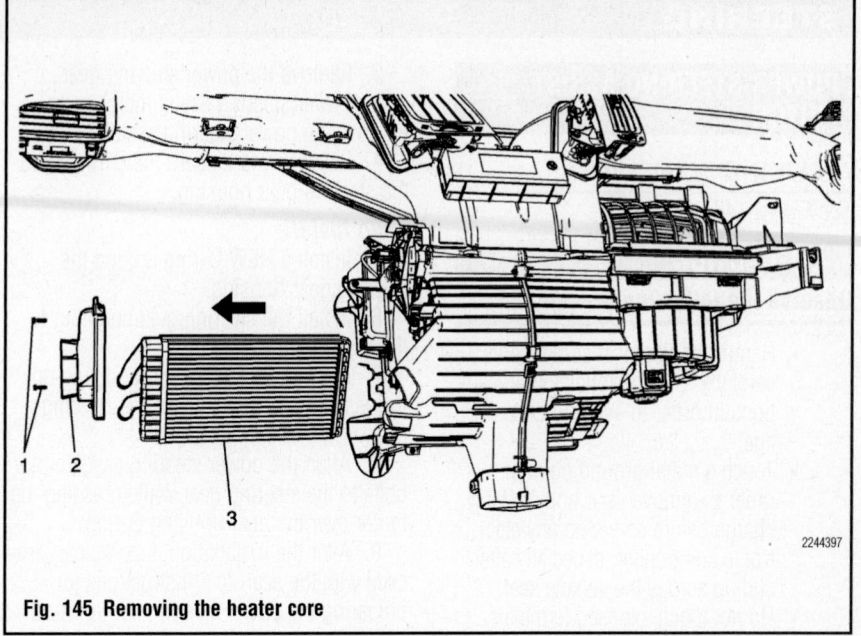

Fig. 145 Removing the heater core

6. Remove the upper evaporator case.
7. Remove the evaporator core.
8. Installation is the reverse of the removal procedure.

HEATER CORE

REMOVAL & INSTALLATION

See Figure 145.

1. Remove the heater and air conditioning evaporator and blower module. See "HVAC Module" in this section.
2. Remove the heater core cap fasteners and remove the heater core cap.
3. Remove the heater core.
4. Installation is the reverse of the removal procedure.

HVAC MODULE

REMOVAL & INSTALLATION

See Figure 146.

1. Remove the intake manifold sight shield.
2. Recover the refrigerant.
3. Remove the heater inlet hose from the heater core tube.
4. Remove the heater outlet hose from the heater core tube.
5. Remove the evaporator hose assembly from the thermal expansion valve.
6. Remove the instrument panel carrier.
7. Remove the HVAC module fasteners.
8. Remove the HVAC module, with the aid of an assistant.
9. Installation is the reverse of the removal procedure.
10. Recharge the A/C system.

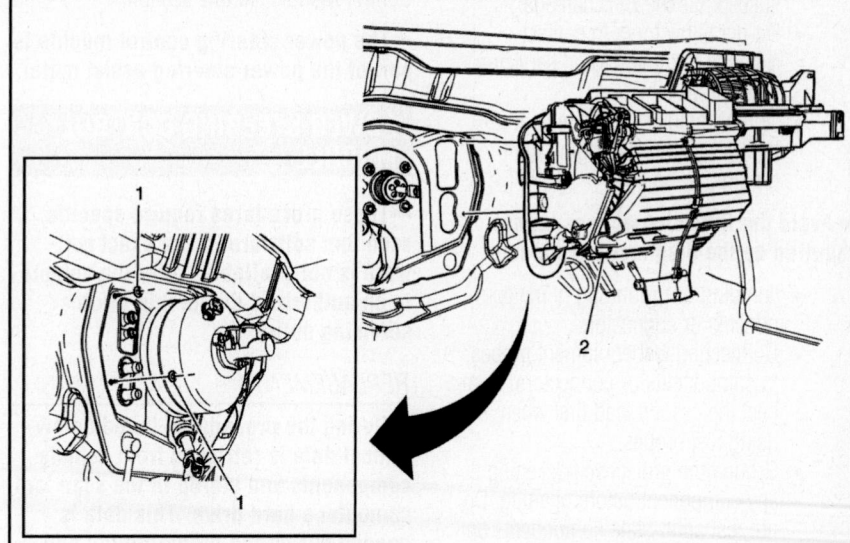

Fig. 146 Removing the HVAC module fasteners (1) and module (2)

THERMAL EXPANSION VALVE (TXV)

REMOVAL & INSTALLATION

See Figure 147.

1. Recover the refrigerant.
2. Remove the air conditioning condenser and air conditioning evaporator tube from the expansion valve.
3. Remove the thermal expansion valve bolts.
4. Remove the Thermal Expansion Valve.
5. Remove and discard the sealing washers.
6. Installation is the reverse of the removal procedure.

7. Tighten valve bolts to 41 inch lbs. (5 Nm).
8. Use new sealing washers.

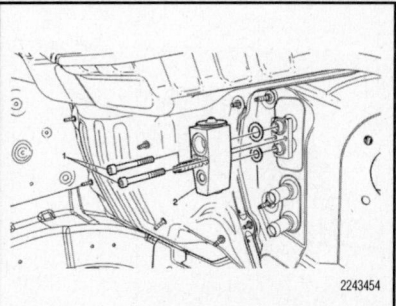

Fig. 147 Removing the TXV screws (1) and TXV (2)

STEERING

POWER STEERING ASSIST MOTOR

REMOVAL & INSTALLATION

See Figure 148.

❄❄ CAUTION

Observe the following precautions:

- Handle all electrical components carefully. Use the following precautions in order to avoid ESD damage:
- Touch a metal ground point in order to remove your body's static charge before servicing any electronic component; especially after sliding across the vehicle seat.
- Do not touch exposed terminals. Terminals may connect to circuits susceptible the ESD damage.
- Do not allow tools to contact exposed terminals when servicing connectors.
- Do not remove components from their protective packaging until required to do so.

➡**Avoid the following actions unless required by the diagnostic procedure:**

- Jumping or grounding of the components or connectors.
- Connecting test equipment probes to components or connectors. Connect the ground lead first when using test probes.
- Ground the protective packaging of any component before opening. Do not rest solid-state components on metal workbenches, or on top of TVs, radios, or other electrical devices.

1. Prepare the power steering control module for removal.

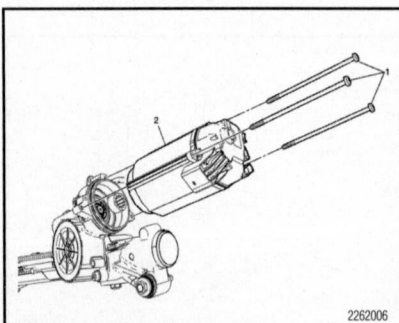

Fig. 148 Removing power steering assist motor

2. Remove the power steering gear.
3. Power steering assist motor bolts. Remove the power steering assist motor.
4. Remove and discard the O-ring from the steering gear housing.

To install:
5. Install a NEW O-ring around the steering gear housing.
6. Install the steering gear coupling to the assist motor armature.
7. Align the steering gear coupling on the assist motor armature to the steering gear.
8. Align the power steering assist motor bolts to the steering gear while pressing the motor over the gear housing O-ring.
9. After the installation is complete, proceed with the scan tool instructions for preparing the power steering control module for removal. Refer to "Power Steering Control Module" in this section.

➡**The power steering control module is part of the power steering assist motor.**

POWER STEERING CONTROL MODULE

➡**These procedures require specific scan tool software. If the exact software is not available, refer the vehicle to an authorized dealership or other servicing outlet.**

REPLACEMENT

➡**During the procedures listed below, critical data is retrieved from vehicle components and stored in the scan tool computer's hard drive. This data is needed during the programming and setup sequences.**

1. Ensure the same scan tool is used and capable of reading, storing, and writing the vehicle's system data.
2. Connect a scan tool to the vehicle and access Service Programming System (SPS).

➡**The next step copies the worm gear wear counter data from the power steering control module PRIOR to the module's removal and stores it on the scan tool computer's hard drive. AFTER completing the next step, the power steering control module can now be removed and replaced.**

3. Perform the SPS function "Electronic Power Steering - Prepare Control Module for Removal" and follow the on-screen instructions.

4. Replace the power steering assist motor, containing the control module. See "Power Steering Assist Motor" in this section.

➡**The next two steps will transfer the vehicle's critical data, including the worm gear wear counter data saved in the previous steps, back to the vehicle components.**

5. With the power steering assist motor replaced and reconnected, using the same scan tool, perform the SPS function "Electronic Power Steering - Programming" and follow the on-screen instructions.
6. Perform the SPS function "Electronic Power Steering - Setup" and follow the on-screen instructions.
7. Perform the "Steering Angle Sensor Centering and Software Endstop Learning" procedure.
8. Clear DTCs after completing the programming and setup procedures.

PROGRAMMING & SETUP

➡**The following service procedures require either a programming or a setup event performed for a complete repair.**

➡**The electronic power steering control module is part of the power steering assist motor assembly and is electronically paired with the steering gear's sensors.**

1. If the complete steering gear including the assist motor assembly was replaced, or for reprogramming of an existing power steering system without replacement, refer to the "Power Steering Control Module Reprogramming" instructions in this article.
2. If only the Power Steering Assist Motor assembly is replaced, follow the Power Steering Assist Motor" replacement instructions.

POWER STEERING CONTROL MODULE REPROGRAMMING

❄❄ CAUTION

Do not program or reprogram the electronic power steering control module unless directed by a service procedure or a service bulletin.

This procedure applies to reprogramming of the existing steering gear or the initial programming if the complete steering gear assembly including the assist motor was replaced. If only the power steering control module is replaced, follow the "Power Steering Control Module Replacement" instructions above.

1. Connect a scan tool to the vehicle and access SPS.

2. Perform the SPS function "Electronic Power Steering - Programming" and follow the on-screen instructions.

3. Perform the SPS function "Electronic Power Steering - Setup" and follow the on-screen instructions.

4. Perform the "Steering Angle Sensor Centering and Software Endstop Learning" procedure.

5. Clear DTCs after completing the programming and setup procedures.

POWER STEERING CONTROL MODULE CALIBRATION

Steering Angle Sensor Centering and Software Endstop Learning

✳✳ WARNING

An inaccurate or not centered steering angle sensor could limit the operation of the electric power steering (EPS) and result in personal injury.

Centering of the steering angle sensor and software endstop learning might be required after certain service procedures are performed. Some of these procedures are as follows:

- Steering angle sensor replacement
- Steering gear replacement
- Power steering assist motor replacement
- Steering column replacement
- Steering linkage inner tie rod replacement
- Steering linkage outer tie rod replacement

➡**It is necessary to perform the steering angle sensor centering BEFORE the software endstop learning.**

Steering Angle Sensor Centering

The centering procedure of the internal steering angle sensor (w/o electronic stability program) can be completed with the following steps:

Conditions:—Front axle measured and set, engine running, vehicle speed 0 MPH, internal steering angle sensor is activated.

1. Using the steering wheel, align the front wheels in the center forward position.

2. Using a scan tool, perform the "Configuration/Reset Functions, Steering Wheel Angle Sensor Centering" procedure.

3. Steer from the center position slowly 90° to the left.

4. Steer slowly back to the center position and then slowly 90° to the right.

5. Steer slowly back to the center position.

6. Perform the steering movements again.

7. Centering procedure is completed.

Software Endstop Learning

The software endstop learning procedure can be completed with the following steps:

Conditions:—Front axle measured and set, vehicle speed 0 MPH, internal steering angle sensor is calibrated or external steering angle sensor sends a valid CAN signal.

1. Using a scan tool, perform the "Configuration/Reset Functions, Power Steering Softstops Reset" procedure and follow the on-screen instructions.

2. Using a scan tool, perform the "Configuration/Reset Functions, Power Steering Softstops Learn" procedure and follow the on-screen instructions.

3. Software endstop learning procedure is completed.

POWER STEERING GEAR

REMOVAL & INSTALLATION

2.4L Engine
See Figure 149.

✳✳ CAUTION

Electrostatic discharge (ESD) can damage many solid-state electrical components. ESD susceptible

components may or may not be labeled with the ESD symbol. Handle all electrical components carefully. Use the following precautions in order to avoid ESD damage:

- Touch a metal ground point in order to remove your body's static charge before servicing any electronic component; especially after sliding across the vehicle seat.
- Do not touch exposed terminals. Terminals may connect to circuits susceptible the ESD damage.
- Do not allow tools to contact exposed terminals when servicing connectors.
- Do not remove components from their protective packaging until required to do so.
- Avoid the following actions unless required by the diagnostic procedure:
- Jumping or grounding of the components or connectors.
- Connecting test equipment probes to components or connectors. Connect the ground lead first when using test probes.
- Ground the protective packaging of any component before opening. Do not rest solid-state components on metal workbenches, or on top of TVs, radios, or other electrical devices.

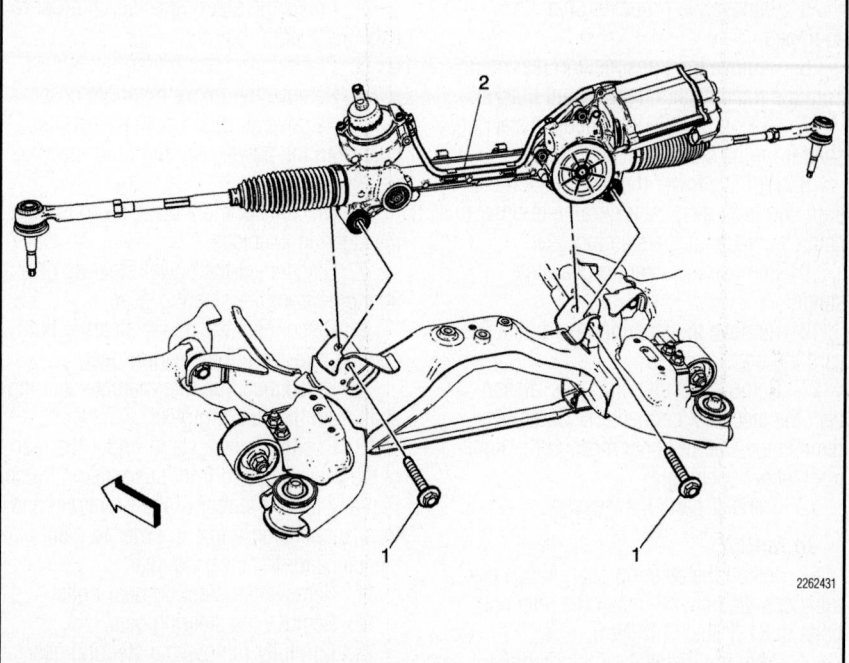

2262431

Fig. 149 Removing the power steering gear bolts (1) and gear (2)—2.4L engine

⚹⚹ CAUTION

With wheels of the vehicle facing straight ahead, secure the steering wheel utilizing steering column anti-rotation pin, steering column lock, or a strap to prevent rotation. Locking of the steering column will prevent damage and a possible malfunction of the SIR system. The steering wheel must be secured in position before disconnecting the following components:

- The steering column
- The intermediate shaft(s)
- The steering gear
- After disconnecting these components, do not rotate the steering wheel or move the front tires and wheels. Failure to follow this procedure may cause the SIR coil assembly to become un-centered and cause possible damage to the SIR coil. If you think the SIR coil has became un-centered, refer to your specific SIR coil's centering procedure to re-center SIR Coil.

1. With the front wheels in the straight ahead position, turn the ignition switch to the OFF position and remove the key from the ignition lock cylinder. Rotate the steering wheel in order to LOCK the steering column.

2. Raise and support the vehicle.

3. Disconnect the outer tie rod ends from the steering knuckles.

4. Remove the catalytic converter.

5. Remove the propeller shaft, if equipped.

6. Remove the transmission rear mount from the transmission rear mount bracket.

7. Disconnect the intermediate steering shaft from the steering gear.

8. Partially lower the rear of the drivetrain and front suspension frame in order to gain clearance for the steering gear.

9. Remove the steering gear heat shield.

10. Remove the steering gear bolts. Discard the bolts.

11. Remove the steering gear. Disconnect the electrical connectors. Carefully remove the steering gear through the right front wheel opening.

12. Transfer parts if necessary.

To install:

13. Install the steering gear. Attach electrical connectors and install the retaining bolts to 81 ft. lbs. (110 Nm).

14. After the installation is complete, measure and adjust the front toe.

➡The power steering control module is part of the power steering assist motor.

3.0L Engine

⚹⚹ CAUTION

With wheels of the vehicle facing straight ahead, secure the steering wheel utilizing steering column anti-rotation pin, steering column lock, or a strap to prevent rotation. Locking of the steering column will prevent damage and a possible malfunction of the SIR system. The steering wheel must be secured in position before disconnecting the following components:

- The steering column
- The intermediate shaft(s)
- The steering gear

⚹⚹ CAUTION

After disconnecting these components, do not rotate the steering wheel or move the front tires and wheels. Failure to follow this procedure may cause the SIR coil assembly to become un-centered and cause possible damage to the SIR coil. If you think the SIR coil has became un-centered, refer to your specific SIR coil's centering procedure to re-center SIR Coil.

1. With the front wheels in the straight ahead position, turn the ignition switch to the OFF position and remove the key from the ignition lock cylinder.

2. Rotate the steering wheel in order to lock the steering column.

3. Place drain pans under the vehicle.

4. Remove the intake manifold cover.

5. Remove as much power steering fluid from the power steering fluid reservoir as possible.

6. Disconnect the 2 outer tie rods from the steering knuckles.

7. Disconnect the power steering gear inlet pipe from the steering gear.

8. Disconnect the power steering fluid cooling pipe from the steering gear.

9. Disconnect the intermediate steering shaft from the steering gear.

10. Position a jack stand under the rear of the drivetrain and front suspension frame. Partially lower the rear of the drivetrain and front suspension frame in order to gain clearance for the steering gear.

11. Remove the steering gear bolts.

12. Remove the steering gear.

13. Carefully remove the steering gear through the left front wheel opening.

To install:

14. Install the steering gear and use NEW steering gear bolts. Tighten the bolts to 81 ft. lbs. (110 Nm).

15. Connect the intermediate steering shaft. Tighten the bolts to 27 ft. lbs. (36 Nm).

16. Connect the cooling pipe and inlet pipe to the steering gear.

17. Install the steering gear tie rod ends to the steering knuckles. Tighten the ball joint nuts to 44 ft. lbs. (60 Nm).

18. Install the intake manifold cover.

19. After the installation is complete, fill and bleed the power steering system.

20. Clean any excess power steering fluid from the vehicle.

21. Measure and adjust the front toe.

POWER STEERING PUMP

REMOVAL & INSTALLATION

2.4L Engine

➡Manufacturer does not provide a specific removal and installation procedure for this component.

3.0L Engine

See Figure 150.

1. Place drain pans under the vehicle.

2. Remove the intake manifold cover.

3. Remove as much power steering fluid from the upper power steering fluid reservoir as possible.

4. Remove the right front tire and wheel assembly.

5. Remove the drive belt from the power steering pump pulley only.

6. Remove the power steering fluid reservoir outlet hose by disconnecting the power steering fluid reservoir outlet hose from the lower power steering fluid reservoir.

7. Remove the power steering fluid cooling pipe by disconnecting the power steering fluid cooling pipe from the lower power steering fluid reservoir.

8. Remove the power steering gear inlet hose by disconnecting the power steering gear inlet hose from the power steering pump.

9. Remove the power steering pump bolts.

10. Note the bolt locations for installation. The left side bolt has a spacer.

11. Remove the power steering pump bolt spacer.

12. Remove the power steering pump through the right front wheel well opening.

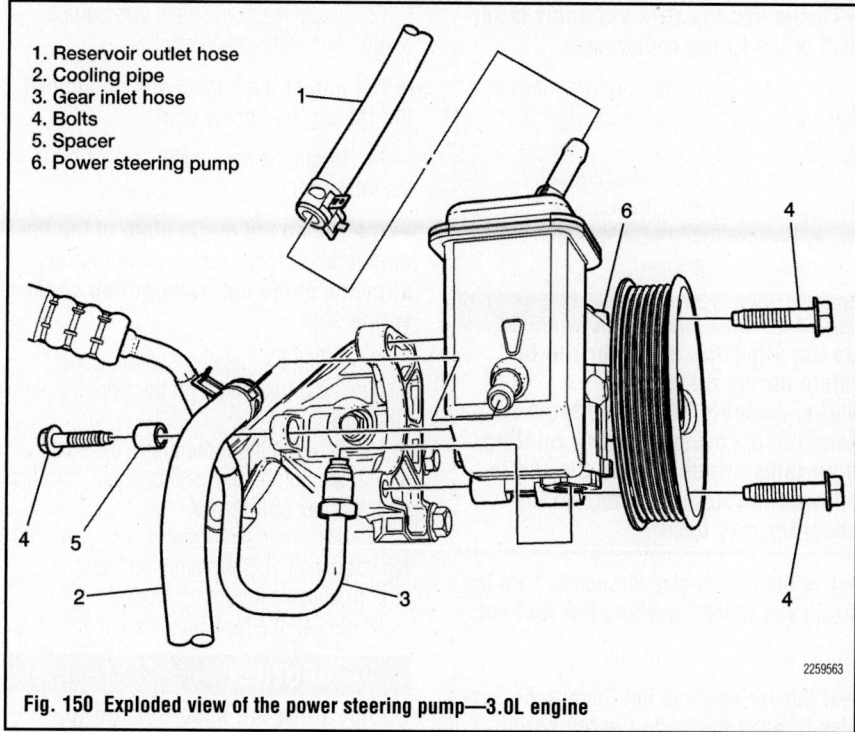

1. Reservoir outlet hose
2. Cooling pipe
3. Gear inlet hose
4. Bolts
5. Spacer
6. Power steering pump

2259563

Fig. 150 Exploded view of the power steering pump—3.0L engine

To install:

13. If necessary, transfer the power steering pump pulley.

14. Install the pump and tighten the mounting bolts to 17 ft. lbs. (23 Nm).

15. Transfer the lower power steering fluid reservoir.

16. Fill and bleed the power steering system.

17. Clean any excess power steering fluid from the vehicle.

BLEEDING

→Use clean, new power steering fluid only.

→Hoses touching the frame, body or engine may cause system noise.

Ensure the hoses do not touch any other part of the vehicle.

→Loose connections may not leak, but could allow air into the steering system. Ensure all hose connections are tight.

→Maintain the power steering fluid level throughout the bleeding procedure.

1. Fill the power steering fluid reservoir with fluid to the minimum system level, the FULL COLD level, or the middle of the hash mark on the cap stick fluid level indicator, as applicable.

2. Raise the vehicle until the front wheels are off the ground.

3. With the key in the ON position and with the engine OFF, turn the steering wheel from stop to stop 12 times.

4. If the vehicle is equipped with longer length power steering hoses, turn the steering wheel from stop to stop 15 to 20 times.

5. Verify the power steering fluid level.

6. Start the engine. Rotate the steering wheel from left to right. Inspect the power steering system for signs of cavitation or fluid aeration, like pump noise or whining.

7. Verify the fluid level. Repeat the bleed procedure, if necessary.

8. Lower the vehicle.

SUSPENSION

FRONT SUSPENSION

LOWER BALL JOINT

REMOVAL & INSTALLATION

1. Remove the lower control arm, as described in this section.

2. Place the control arm in a vise or suitable holding device.

3. Remove the ball joint rivets using the following procedure:

    a. Drill through the rivets using a 8 mm (5/16 in) drill bit.

    b. Enlarge the hole using a 12 mm (31/64 in) drill bit.

    c. Remove any remaining burs from the control arm.

4. Remove the ball joint from the control arm. Note the position of the ball joint for reassembly.

To install:

→The control arm must be clean and free of debris.

5. Install the ball joint to the control arm.

→Only use hardware provided with the new ball joint. The bolts must be installed with the bolt head on top of the ball joint.

6. Install the ball joint to control arm bolts and tighten the bolts/nuts to 50 ft. lbs. (68 Nm).

7. Install the lower control arm.

LOWER CONTROL ARM

REMOVAL & INSTALLATION

1. Raise and support the vehicle.

2. Remove the wheel and tire assembly.

3. Remove the lower ball joint stud cotter pin. Discard the cotter pin.

4. Loosen the ball stud nut until the nut is level with the top of the ball stud.

5. Using an appropriate tool (J-42188-B, or equivalent), separate the lower control arm from the steering knuckle.

6. Remove the lower ball joint stud nut.

7. Remove the control arm-to-frame front bolt and nut. Discard the bolt and nut.

8. Remove the control arm-to-frame rear bolts and nuts. Discard the bolts and nuts.

9. Remove the control arm.

To install:

10. Position the control arm to the cradle/frame.

11. Install new control arm-to-frame rear bolts and nuts and tighten to 52 ft. lbs. (70 Nm).

12. Install a new arm-to-frame front bolt and nut. Tighten as follows:

    a. For vehicles equipped RPO FE2, tighten the bolts and nuts and tighten to 140 ft. lbs. (190 Nm).

b. For vehicles equipped RPO FE3, tighten the bolts and nuts and tighten to 107 ft. lbs. (145 Nm).

13. Position the control arm ball stud into the steering knuckle and install the nut. Tighten the nut to 30 ft. lbs. (40 Nm).

➡**Do not loosen the castle nut, only tighten to align the ball stud slot. Ensure that the cotter pin ends do not contact the antilock brake system (ABS) sensor harness or drive axle.**

14. Continue to tighten the nut only enough to align the castle nut slots with the ball stud, install a new cotter pin.

15. Install the wheel and tire assembly.

16. Verify front end alignment.

17. Lower the vehicle.

MACPHERSON STRUT

REMOVAL & INSTALLATION

1. Remove the 3 upper strut mount bolts.

2. Raise and support the vehicle.

3. Remove the wheel and tire assembly.

4. Remove the brake hose bracket bolt from the strut assembly.

5. Remove the stabilizer link nut and separate the link from the strut assembly.

6. Remove the lower strut bolts and nuts.

7. Remove the strut assembly from the vehicle.

To install:

8. Position the strut assembly to the vehicle.

9. Install the 3 upper strut mount bolts and tighten to 18 ft. lbs. (25 Nm).

10. Install the lower strut bolts and nuts and tighten to 148 ft. lbs. (200 Nm).

11. Inspect the stabilizer link seals for damage prior to installation. Replace as required.

➡**Do not allow the stabilizer link ball stud to rotate while installing the link nut.**

12. Position the stabilizer link to the strut and install the nut and tighten the nut to 48 ft. lbs. (65 Nm).

13. Position the brake hose bracket to the strut assembly and install the bolt and tighten to 11 ft. lbs. (15 Nm).

14. Install the wheel and tire.

15. Lower the vehicle.

16. Perform a wheel alignment.

OVERHAUL

1. Position the strut assembly in a suitable compressor (J-45400, or equivalent).

➡**Ensure that the strut assembly is vertical in the spring compressor.**

2. Adjust the upper and lower legs so that they are properly positioned on the spring.

3. Compress the spring enough to unload the upper strut mount.

4. Remove the front suspension strut nut cover, if equipped.

✳✳ CAUTION

Do not allow the absorber rod to rotate during disassembly/reassembly. Use hand tools to keep the absorber rod from rotating. If air tools are used, and the rod is allowed to rotate, damage to the absorber may occur.

➡**Use the proper size wrench to hold the strut shaft while loosening the strut nut.**

5. Remove the strut nut.

➡**If the spring does not have to be serviced, leave the spring in the spring compressor.**

6. Lower the strut from the front spring.

✳✳ CAUTION

Do not handle the top mount assembly by the plastic portion. Handle the top mount assembly by the metal portion when removing/installing the top mount from/to the strut assembly. Holding the top mount assembly by the plastic portion may loosen the snap fit of the bearing components and cause the bearing to fall apart.

➡**If any of the strut components are found to have signs of excessive wear or are damaged, replace those components.**

7. Remove the front suspension strut mount, bearing, upper insulator.

8. Remove the front suspension strut and the dust shield and bumper from the front spring.

9. Remove the front spring if needed.

Reassembly:

10. Position the front spring in the compressor, if removed.

➡**Ensure that the strut assembly is vertical in the spring compressor.**

11. Adjust the upper and lower legs so that they are properly positioned on the spring.

12. Compress the spring enough to install the other front suspension strut components.

13. Install the dust shield and bumper on the front suspension strut.

➡**The end of the spring sits up against the tab on the spring seat.**

14. Install the front suspension strut in the front spring.

➡**The flat on the metal plate of the top mount assembly must face the same direction of the anti-rotation tab on the spring seat.**

15. Install the upper insulator, upper bearing, and the mount on the front suspension strut.

16. Position the mount onto the strut shaft and align the flat 180 degrees from flat on the upper spring seat.

17. Assemble the upper spring seat onto the strut shaft and align the flat with the strut to knuckle mounting bracket.

18. Install the front suspension strut nut.

✳✳ CAUTION

Do not allow the absorber rod to rotate during disassembly/reassembly. Use hand tools to keep the absorber rod from rotating. If air tools are used, and the rod is allowed to rotate, damage to the absorber may occur.

19. Using a proper socket and a torque wrench, tighten the front suspension strut nut to 55 ft. lbs. (75 Nm).

20. Release the tension on the compressor tool.

21. Remove the strut assembly.

STABILIZER BAR

REMOVAL & INSTALLATION

See Figures 151 and 152.

1. Raise and support the vehicle.

2. Remove the tire and wheel assembly.

3. Remove the engine front splash shield.

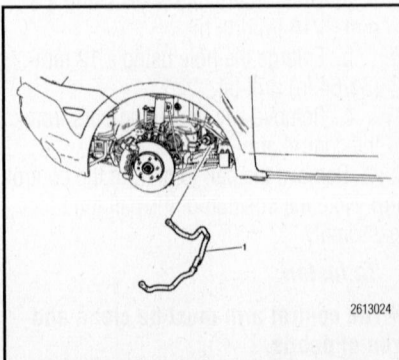

Fig. 151 Removing the stabilizer bar (1)

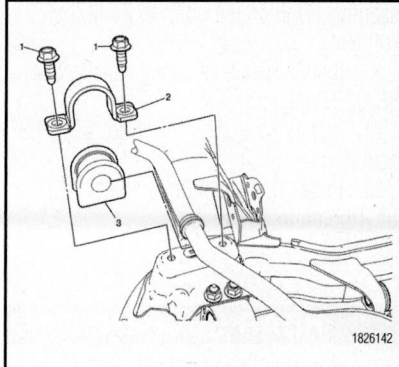

Fig. 152 Removing the stabilizer bar bolts (1), clamp (2) and insulator (3)

4. Remove the stabilizer bar as follows:
   a. Remove the outer tie rod end from the steering knuckle.
   b. Remove the stabilizer link from the stabilizer bar.
   c. Remove the stabilizer bar insulators.
   d. Remove the stabilizer bar through the left wheel opening.

To install:

5. Position the stabilizer bar to the vehicle.
6. Install the insulators and tighten the clamp bolts to 37 ft. lbs. (50 Nm).
7. Attach the stabilizer link, as described below.
8. Connect the outer tie rod ends to the steering knuckle. Tighten the new nuts to 47 ft. lbs. (60 Nm).
9. Install the splash shield.
10. Install the tire and wheel assembly.

STABILIZER BAR LINK

REMOVAL & INSTALLATION

See Figure 153.

1. Raise the vehicle.
2. Remove the front wheel and tire assembly.
3. Remove the upper stabilizer bar link nut at the steering knuckle connection. Use the proper size Allen wrench to keep the stabilizer link ball stud from rotate while removing or installing the nut.
4. Remove the lower stabilizer bar link nut. Use the proper size Allen wrench to keep the stabilizer link ball stud from rotate while removing or installing the nut.
5. Remove the stabilizer bar link.

To install:

6. Position the stabilizer bar link to the mounting.
7. Install and tighten the stabilizer bar link lower nut to 63 ft. lbs. (85 Nm).

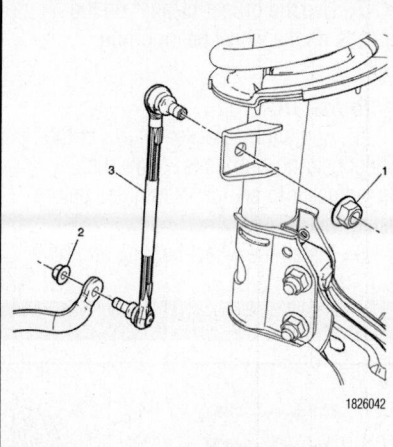

Fig. 153 Showing the stabilizer bar link mounting nuts (1, 2) and the link (3)

8. Install and tighten the stabilizer bar link upper nut to 55 ft. lbs. (75 Nm).
9. Install the front wheel and tire assembly.

STEERING KNUCKLE

REMOVAL & INSTALLATION

1. Raise and support the vehicle.
2. Remove the tire and wheel.
3. Remove the wheel bearing and hub assembly. See "Wheel Bearing & Hub" in this section.

➡**Do not allow the stabilizer link ball stud to rotate while removing the link nut.**

4. Remove the nut and separate the stabilizer link from the strut assembly.
5. Loosen the steering knuckle to strut bolts and nuts.
6. Remove and discard the lower ball joint cotter pin.
7. Loosen the ball stud nut, until level with the top of the ball stud.
8. Using the an appropriate tool (J-42188-B or equivalent), separate the lower ball joint from the steering knuckle.
9. Remove the lower ball joint nut and separate from the knuckle.

✳✳ CAUTION

Do not free the ball stud by using a pickle fork or a wedge-type tool. Damage to the seal or bushing may result.

10. Remove the outer tie rod end from the knuckle.
11. Remove the steering knuckle to strut bolts and nuts. Remove the steering knuckle from the vehicle.

To install:

12. Position the steering knuckle to strut assembly.
13. Loosely install the strut to steering knuckle bolts and nuts.
14. Position the lower ball joint stud into the steering knuckle.
15. Install the ball stud nut and tighten to 30 ft. lbs. (40 Nm).
16. Tighten the strut to steering knuckle bolts and nuts to 133 ft. lbs. (180 Nm).

➡**Do not loosen the castle nut for cotter pin installation.**

17. Tighten the castle nut enough to allow for cotter pin installation.

✳✳ CAUTION

The cotter pin must not contact the wheel speed sensor or drive axle.

18. Install the outer tie rod end to the knuckle.

➡**Do not allow the stabilizer link ball stud to rotate while installing the link nut.**

19. Position the stabilizer bar link to the strut assembly and install the nut. Tighten the nut to 48 ft. lbs. (65 Nm).
20. Install the wheel bearing/hub assembly.
21. Install the tire and wheel.
22. Lower the vehicle.
23. Perform a wheel alignment.

WHEEL BEARING & HUB

REMOVAL & INSTALLATION

See Figure 154.

1. Raise and support the vehicle.
2. Remove the tire and wheel.
3. Remove the wheel drive shaft nut.
4. Remove the brake rotor. See "BRAKES" section.

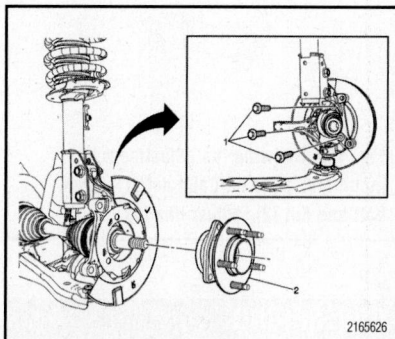

Fig. 154 Removing the wheel bearing and hub assembly bolts (1) and the hub assembly (2)

5. Remove the wheel speed sensor. See "BRAKES" section.

6. Remove the wheel nearing and hub assembly bolts.

➡ **If removing the wheel bearing/hub assembly to service other components, support the wheel drive shaft with mechanics wire.**

7. Use the proper cleaner on the threads on the wheel bearing/hub bolts.

To install:

8. Apply threadlocker on 2/3 of the wheel bearing/hub bolts. Allow the threadlocker to set for 10 minutes before using.

9. Install the wheel bearing and hub assembly. Tighten the bolts to 74 ft. lbs. (100 Nm).

10. Install the wheel speed sensor. See "BRAKES" section.

11. Install the brake rotor. See "BRAKES" section.

12. Install the wheel drive shaft nut. Tighten to 151 ft. lbs. (205 Nm).

SUSPENSION

ADJUSTMENT LINK

REMOVAL & INSTALLATION

See Figure 155.

1. Raise the vehicle.
2. Remove the rear wheel and tire assembly.
3. Remove the outer adjustment link to knuckle bolt and nut.
4. Remove the inner support to adjustment link bolt and nut.
5. Remove the adjustment link.

To install:

6. Position the adjustment link and install the inner support to adjustment link bolt and nut. Tighten to 118 ft. lbs. (160 Nm).
7. Install the outer adjustment link to knuckle bolt and nut. Tighten to 118 ft. lbs. (160 Nm).
8. Check rear alignment.

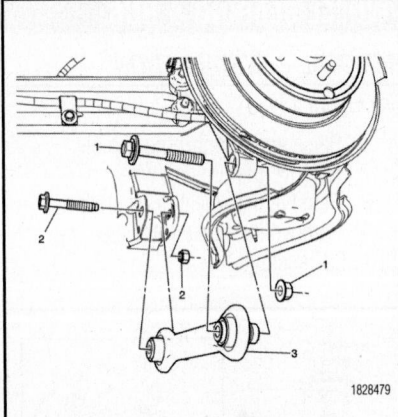

Fig. 155 Showing the adjustment link mounting: outer bolt and nut (1), inner bolt and nut (2), adjust link (3)

COIL SPRING

REMOVAL & INSTALLATION

See Figures 156 and 157.

1. Raise and support the vehicle.

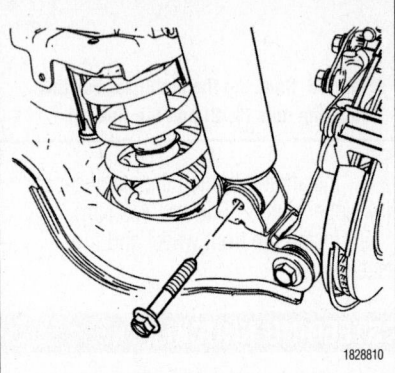

Fig. 156 Loosen the lower control arm to support frame nut and bolt.

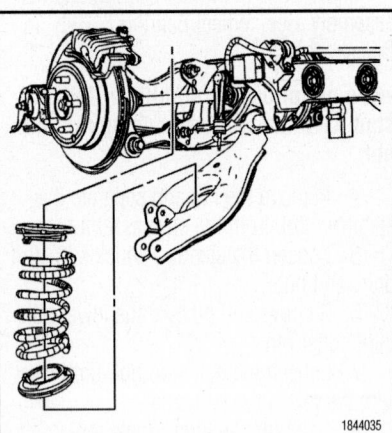

Fig. 157 Remove the coil spring and insulators.

2. Remove the rear tire and wheel assembly.
3. Remove the stabilizer bar link.
4. Position a jackstand underneath the lower control arm.
5. Raise the jackstand slightly to compress the coil spring.
6. Remove the lower shock bolt and nut.
7. Loosen the lower control arm to support frame nut and bolt.
8. Remove the lower control arm to knuckle nut and bolt.

REAR SUSPENSION

9. Slowly lower the control arm in order to unload the coil spring.
10. Remove the coil spring and insulators.

To install:

11. Inspect the coil spring upper and lower insulators, if damage exists replace the insulators.
12. If no damage exists, transfer the existing components.
13. Position the spring with the rubber insulators into the vehicle.
14. Raise the jackstand to compress the spring.
15. Position the lower control arm to the knuckle and install the nut and bolt and tighten the bolt/nut to 118 ft. lbs. (160 Nm).
16. Tighten the lower control arm to support nut and bolt to 81 ft. lbs. (110 Nm).
17. Install the shock to the lower control arm nut and bolt and tighten to 81 ft. lbs. (110 Nm).
18. Remove the jackstand from under the vehicle.
19. Install the stabilizer bar link as described in this section.
20. Install the rear tire and wheel assembly.
21. Lower the vehicle.

KNUCKLE

REMOVAL & INSTALLATION

1. Raise and support the vehicle.
2. Remove the tire and wheel.
3. Disconnect the rear park brake cable from the park brake actuator.
4. Remove the park brake cable from the mounting bracket

➡ **Support the brake caliper with heavy mechanic wire, or equivalent, whenever it is separated from its mount and the hydraulic flexible brake hose is still connected. Failure to support the caliper in this manner will cause the flexible brake hose to bear the weight of the caliper, which may cause damage to the brake hose and in turn may cause a brake fluid leak.**

5. Remove the brake caliper and bracket as an assembly and support it with heavy mechanics wire or equivalent.

6. Remove the wheel bearing and hub assembly.

7. Remove the upper control arm to knuckle bolt and nut.

8. Remove the lower control arm to knuckle bolt and nut.

9. Remove the toe link to knuckle bolt and nut.

10. Remove the 3 trailing arm to knuckle bolts.

11. Remove the knuckle from the vehicle.

To install:

12. Install the knuckle to the lower control arm. Loosely install the bolt and nut.

13. Install the knuckle to the upper control arm. Loosely install the bolt and nut.

14. Install the knuckle to the toe link. Loosely install the bolt and nut.

15. Apply an approved threadlocker the knuckle bolts.

16. Install the 3 trailing arm to knuckle bolts and hand tighten the bolts and nuts. Tighten the bolts and nuts in the following sequence:

  a. Tighten the knuckle to lower control arm bolt and nut to 118 ft. lbs. (160 Nm).

  b. Tighten the knuckle to upper control arm bolt and nut to 118 ft. lbs. (160 Nm).

  c. Tighten the knuckle to toe link bolt and nut to 118 ft. lbs. (160 Nm).

  d. Tighten the 3 trailing arm to knuckle bolts to 110 ft. lbs. (150 Nm).

17. Install the wheel bearing and hub assembly. See "Wheel Bearing & Hub" in this section.

18. Remove the supporting wire and position the brake caliper and bracket assemblies back onto the knuckles.

19. Connect the rear park brake cable through the mounting bracket and onto the park brake actuator.

20. Install the tire and wheel.

21. Lower the vehicle.

22. Perform a vehicle wheel alignment.

LOWER CONTROL ARM

REMOVAL & INSTALLATION

1. Raise and support the vehicle.

2. Remove the rear tire and wheel assembly.

3. Remove the stabilizer bar link.

4. Position a jackstand underneath the lower control arm.

5. Raise the jackstand slightly to compress the coil spring.

6. Remove the lower shock bolt and nut.

7. Loosen the lower control arm to support frame nut and bolt.

8. Remove the lower control arm to knuckle nut and bolt.

9. Slowly lower the control arm in order to unload the coil spring.

10. Remove the coil spring.

11. Remove the jackstand.

12. Remove the lower control arm to support frame nut and bolt. Remove the lower control arm.

To install:

13. Inspect the coil spring upper and lower insulators, if damage exists replace the insulators.

14. Position the lower control arm to the support frame and loosely install the nut and bolt.

15. Position the jackstand under the lower control arm.

16. Position the spring with the rubber insulators into the vehicle.

17. Raise the jackstand to compress the spring.

18. Position the lower control arm to the knuckle and install the nut and bolt and tighten to 118 ft. lbs. (160 Nm).

19. Tighten the lower control arm to support nut and bolt to 81 ft. lbs. (110 Nm).

20. Install the shock to the lower control arm nut and bolt and tighten to 81 ft. lbs. (110 Nm).

21. Remove the jackstand from under the vehicle.

22. Install the stabilizer bar link. See "Stabilizer Bar Link" in this section.

23. Install the rear tire and wheel assembly.

24. Lower the vehicle.

25. Check the rear alignment.

STABILIZER BAR

REMOVAL & INSTALLATION

1. Raise and support the vehicle.

2. Lower the rear suspension support enough to gain access to the stabilizer bar.

3. Remove the rear stabilizer bar:

  a. Remove the stabilizer links from the stabilizer shaft.

  b. Remove stabilizer shaft insulators.

4. Installation is the reverse of the removal procedure.

STABILIZER BAR LINK

REMOVAL & INSTALLATION

1. Raise and support the vehicle.

2. Remove the rear tire and wheel assembly.

3. Loosen the stabilizer shaft clamp bolts.

➡ **Use a 90 degree bend TORX® bit to hold the ball stud when loosening or tightening the nut.**

4. Remove the stabilizer link to stabilizer shaft nut.

5. When disconnecting the stabilizer link, hold the link with a wrench to prevent turning.

6. Remove the stabilizer link to lower control arm nut.

7. Remove the stabilizer link from the vehicle.

To install:

8. Position the stabilizer link through the lower control arm.

9. Install the stabilizer link to lower control arm nut and tighten to 11 ft. lbs. (15 Nm).

10. Install the stabilizer link to stabilizer shaft nut and tighten to 37 ft. lbs. (50 Nm).

11. Tighten the loose stabilizer shaft clamp bolts to 52 ft. lbs. (70 Nm).

12. Install the rear tire and wheel assembly.

13. Lower the vehicle.

SHOCK ABSORBER

REMOVAL & INSTALLATION

1. Raise and support the vehicle.

2. Remove the rear tire and wheel assembly.

3. Using the proper jackstand, support the lower control arm or the knuckle.

4. Remove the lower shock bolt.

5. Remove the rear wheel house from the vehicle.

6. Remove the upper shock bolt.

7. Remove the shock from the vehicle.

To install:

8. Position the shock to the vehicle.

9. Install the upper shock bolt and tighten to 81 ft. lbs. (110 Nm).

10. Install the lower shock bolt and tighten to 81 ft. lbs. (110 Nm).

11. Remove the jack stand from the lower control arm or the knuckle.

12. Install the rear wheel house in the vehicle.

13. Install the rear tire and wheel assembly.

14. Lower the vehicle.

TRAILING ARM

REMOVAL & INSTALLATION

See Figure 158.

1. Raise and support the vehicle.
2. Remove the tire and wheel.
3. Remove the park brake cable bolt from the trailing arm and from the frame.
4. Remove the trailing arm bracket to body bolts.
5. Remove the trailing arm bushing to bracket nut and bolt.
6. Remove the trailing arm to knuckle bolts.
7. Remove the trailing arm.

To install:

8. Position the trailing arm to the vehicle.
9. Install the trailing arm to knuckle bolts and tighten to 81 ft. lbs. (110 Nm).
10. Position the trailing arm bracket to the trailing arm.
11. Loosely install the trailing arm bushing to bracket nut and bolt.
12. Install the trail arm bracket.
13. Tighten the trailing arm bushing to bracket nut and bolt to 118 ft. lbs. (160 Nm).
14. Install the park brake cable bolt to trailing arm and to the frame.
15. Install the tire and wheel.
16. Lower the vehicle.

UPPER CONTROL ARM

REMOVAL & INSTALLATION

See Figures 159 and 160.

1. Raise and support the vehicle.
2. Remove the rear tire and wheel assembly.
3. Disconnect the antilock brake system (ABS) brake wiring harness from the upper control arm.
4. Remove the rear brake hose routing nut and bolt.
5. Remove the upper control arm to knuckle nut and bolt.
6. Remove the upper control to support cam nut and bolt.
7. Remove the upper control arm.

To install:

8. Position the upper control arm to the knuckle. Loosely install the upper control arm to knuckle nut and bolt.
9. Install the upper control to support bolt and cam nut.
10. Tighten the upper control arm to knuckle nut and bolt to 118 ft. lbs. (160 Nm).
11. Tighten the upper control arm to support bolt to 121 ft. lbs. (164 Nm).
12. Install the rear brake hose routing nut and bolt and tighten to 106 inch lbs. (12 Nm).
13. Connect the ABS brake wiring harness to the upper control arm.

14. Install the rear tire and wheel assembly.
15. Lower the vehicle.
16. Check the rear alignment.

WHEEL BEARING & HUB

REMOVAL & INSTALLATION

1. Raise and support the vehicle.
2. Remove the tire and wheel.
3. Remove the brake caliper bracket.
4. Remove the brake rotor. See "BRAKE" section.
5. Remove the wheel drive shaft retaining nut, if equipped.
6. Remove the rear wheel bearing and hub bolts.
7. Remove the rear wheel bearing and hub assembly.
8. Disconnect the electrical connector for the wheel speed sensor.

To install:

9. Use the proper cleaner to the thread of the bolts.
10. Apply thread locker to the wheel bearing and hub bolts. Allow the threadlocker to set for 10 minutes before using.
11. Tighten the hub bolts to 52 ft. lbs. (70 Nm).
12. If replacing the wheel bearing, transfer the wheel speed sensor.

Fig. 158 Removing trailing arm to knuckle bolts (1)

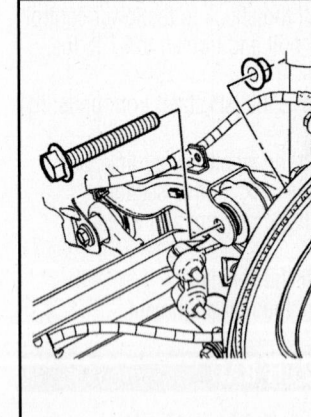

Fig. 159 Remove the upper control arm to knuckle nut and bolt.

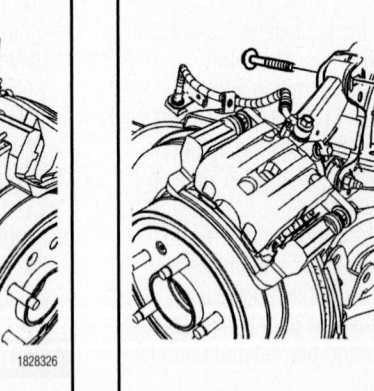

Fig. 160 Remove the upper control to support cam nut and bolt.

CHEVROLET AND GMC

12

Express • Savana

BRAKES 12-15

ANTI-LOCK BRAKE SYSTEM (ABS)..........................**12-15**
General Information.................12-15
  Precautions........................12-15
Wheel Speed Sensor
(WSS) 12-15
  Removal & Installation........12-15
BLEEDING THE BRAKE SYSTEM **12-1**
Bleeding Procedure.................12-17
  Bleeding the ABS
  System 12-18
  Fluid Fill Procedure............12-18
  Hydraulic Brake System
  Bleeding (Manual)............12-17
  Master Cylinder Bench
  Bleeding 12-17
FRONT DISC BRAKES **12-19**
Brake Caliper.........................12-19
  Removal & Installation........12-19
Disc Brake Pads 12-20
  Removal & Installation........12-20
PARKING BRAKE..............**12-26**
Parking Brake.........................12-26
  Adjustment 12-26
Parking Brake Shoes 12-26
  Removal &
  Installation........................12-26
REAR DISC BRAKES **12-22**
Brake Caliper.........................12-22
  Removal & Installation........12-22
Disc Brake Pads 12-24
  Removal & Installation........12-24

CHASSIS ELECTRICAL **12-29**

AIR BAG (SUPPLEMENTAL RESTRAINT SYSTEM) **12-29**
General Information.................12-29
  Arming the System/SIR
  Enabling 12-30
  Disarming the System/SIR
  Disabling 12-30
  Service Precautions 12-29
  Steering Wheel Module
  Coil/Centering 12-30

DRIVE TRAIN **12-31**

Automatic Transmission Fluid,
Fluid Pan and/or Filter
  Replacement 12-31
  4-speed Transmission 12-31
  6-speed Transmission 12-32
Front Axle Inner Shaft Seal
and Bearing..........................12-34
  Removal & Installation........12-34
Front Differential Drive Pinion
Gear Bearing Cup Seal..........12-36
  Installation 12-36
Front Driveshaft/Propeller
Shaft....................................12-35
  Removal & Installation........12-35
Rear Axle Fluid......................12-37
  Differential Oil
  Replacement 12-37
Rear Axle Housing..................12-37
  Removal & Installation........12-37
Rear Axle Hub Bearing Cup,
and/or Seal 12-38
  Removal & Installation........12-38
Rear Axle Shaft Seal and/or
Bearing 12-38
  Removal & Installation........12-38
Rear Drive Pinion Flange/Yoke
and/or Seal 12-40
  Removal & Installation........12-40
Rear Driveshaft 12-41
  Removal & Installation........12-41
Transfer Case Assembly 12-33
  Removal & Installation........12-33
Wheel Driveshaft 12-35
  Removal & Installation........12-35

ENGINE COOLING **12-43**

Engine Coolant.......................12-43
  Drain & Refill Procedure.....12-43
  Flushing............................12-44
Engine Fan 12-44
  Removal & Installation........12-44
Radiator.................................12-45
  Removal & Installation........12-45
Thermostat 12-46
  Removal & Installation........12-46

Water Pump 12-48
  Removal & Installation........12-48

ENGINE ELECTRICAL **12-51**

BATTERY SYSTEM............**12-51**
Battery...................................12-51
  Battery Disconnect/
  Connect 12-51
  Removal & Installation........12-51
CHARGING SYSTEM **12-52**
Alternator/ Generator 12-52
  Removal & Installation........12-52
IGNITION SYSTEM **12-53**
Firing Order............................12-53
Ignition Coil 12-53
  Removal & Installation........12-53
Ignition Timing........................12-55
  Adjustment 12-55
Spark Plugs............................12-55
  Removal & Installation........12-55
STARTING SYSTEM **12-56**
Starter 12-56
  Removal & Installation........12-56

ENGINE MECHANICAL **12-58**

Accessory Drive Belts 12-58
  Accessory Belt Routing.......12-58
  Adjustment 12-59
  Inspection 12-58
  Removal & Installation........12-59
Air Cleaner Assembly..............12-61
  Filter/Element
  Replacement 12-61
  Removal & Installation........12-61
Camshaft and Valve Lifters......12-62
  Cleaning & Inspection 12-62
  Removal & Installation........12-63
Catalytic Converter 12-67
  Removal & Installation........12-67
Crankshaft Front Oil Seal 12-69
  Removal & Installation........12-69
Crankshaft Rear Oil Seal 12-70
  Removal & Installation........12-70
Cylinder Head 12-71
  Removal & Installation........12-71
Engine Oil & Filter 12-75
  Replacement 12-75

Exhaust Manifold 12-76
 Removal & Installation....12-76
Intake Manifold 12-79
 Removal & Installation....12-79
Oil Pan 12-81
 Removal & Installation.......12-81
Oil Pump 12-85
 Cleaning and Inspection 12-85
 Removal & Installation.......12-86
Piston and Ring......................12-88
 Positioning 12-88
Timing Chain, Sprocket and
 Tensioner 12-88
 Removal & Installation.......12-88
Turbocharger 12-92
 Removal & Installation.......12-92
Valve Lash 12-95
 Adjustment 12-95
Valve Rocker Arm Covers........12-93
 Removal & Installation.......12-93

ENGINE PERFORMANCE & EMISSION CONTROLS 12-96

Camshaft Position (CMP)
 Sensor 12-96
 Removal & Installation........12-96
Crankshaft Position (CKP)
 Sensor 12-97
 Removal & Installation........12-97
Electronic Control Module
 (ECM) 12-99
 Removal & Installation........12-99
Engine Coolant Temperature
 (ECT) Sensor 12-101
 Removal & Installation......12-101
Heated Oxygen (HO2S)
 Sensor 12-102
 Removal & Installation......12-102
Input and Output Speed
 Sensors 12-105
 Removal & Installation......12-105
Intake Air Temperature (IAT)
 Sensor 2 12-105
 Removal & Installation......12-105
Knock Sensor (KS)................12-105
 Removal & Installation......12-105
Manifold Absolute Pressure
 (MAP) Sensor 12-107
 Removal & Installation......12-107
Mass Air Flow (MAF) Sensor
 with Intake Air Temperature
 (IAT) Sensor.......................12-107
 Removal & Installation......12-107
Vehicle Speed Sensor
 (VSS) 12-108
 Removal & Installation......12-108

FUEL.........................12-109

DIESEL FUEL INJECTION SYSTEM....................12-114
Fuel Filter 12-114
 Removal & Installation......12-114
 Water-in-fuel Draining 12-114
Fuel High Pressure Pipe 12-114
 Removal & Installation......12-114
Fuel Pressure Regulator 12-118
 Removal & Installation......12-118
Fuel Pump.............................12-117
 Removal & Installation......12-117
Fuel System Service
 Precautions 12-114
Glow Plugs...........................12-118
 Removal & Installation......12-118
Injection Pump 12-118
 Removal & Installation......12-118
Injection Timing 12-114
 Adjustment 12-114
Injectors 12-115
 Removal & Installation......12-115

GASOLINE FUEL INJECTION SYSTEM....................12-109
Fuel Filter 12-109
 Removal & Installation......12-109
Fuel Injectors 12-109
 Removal & Installation......12-109
Fuel Pressure Relief 12-109
Fuel System Service
 Precautions 12-109
Fuel Tank..............................12-110
 Draining.............................12-110
 Removal & Installation......12-111
Idle Speed 12-113
 Adjustment 12-113
Throttle Body Assembly 12-113
 Removal & Installation......12-113

HEATING & AIR CONDITIONING SYSTEM....................12-120

Blower Motor 12-120
 Removal & Installation......12-120
Heater Core 12-120
 Removal & Installation......12-120

PRECAUTIONS..............12-14

SPECIFICATIONS AND MAINTENANCE CHARTS.....12-3

Additional Maintenance
 Services-Normal 12-13
Additional Maintenance
 Services-Severe 12-13

Brake Specifications................12-10
Camshaft Specifications 12-6
Capacities 12-4
Crankshaft and Connecting
 Rod Specifications 12-6
Engine and Vehicle
 Identification 12-3
Engine Tune-Up
 Specifications 12-4
Fluid Specifications..................12-5
General Engine
 Specifications 12-3
Maintenance I and II
 Service Schedules............12-11,12
Piston and Ring
 Specifications 12-7
Tire, Wheel and Ball Joint
 Specifications 12-9
Torque Specifications..............12-8
Valve Specifications 12-5
Wheel Alignment......................12-9

STEERING 12-121

Power Steering Gear..............12-121
 Removal & Installation......12-121
Power Steering Pump............12-124
 Bleeding 12-127
 Checking and Adding
 Power Steering Fluid 12-127
 Removal & Installation......12-124

SUSPENSION...............12-128

FRONT SUSPENSION.......12-128
Lower Ball Joint 12-128
 Removal & Installation......12-128
Lower Control Arm................12-128
 Removal & Installation......12-128
Spring 12-128
 Removal & Installation......12-128
Stabilizer Shaft 12-129
 Removal & Installation......12-129
Steering Knuckle 12-129
 Removal & Installation......12-129
Upper Control Arm................12-130
 Removal & Installation......12-130
Wheel Bearings 12-131
 Removal & Installation......12-131
REAR SUSPENSION 12-132
Leaf Spring...........................12-132
 Removal & Installation......12-132
Stabilizer Shaft 12-133
 Removal & Installation......12-133

SPECIFICATIONS AND MAINTENANCE CHARTS

ENGINE AND VEHICLE IDENTIFICATION

	Engine						Model Year	
Code ①	Liters (cc)	Cu. In.	Cyl.	Fuel Sys.	Type	Fuel	Code ②	Year
A	4.8 (4800)	293	V8	SFI	L20	gas/alc	A	2010
G	6.0 (6000)	364	V8	SFI	L96	gas/alc	B	2011
L	6.6 (6600)	402	V8	DI	LGH	diesel		
4	5.3 (5300)	325	V8	SFI	LMF	gas/alc		
6	6.6 (6600)	402	V8	DPI	LMM	diesel		
X	4.3 (4300)	262	V6	MFI	LU3	gas		
8	6.6 (6600)	402	V8	DI	LML	diesel		

① 8th position of VIN

② 10th position of VIN

DI Direct Injection

DPI Diesel Port Fuel Injection

MFI Multi-Port Fuel Injection

SFI Sequential Fuel Injection

Gas/alc Vehicle designed to use either E85 ethanol blend or gas

Diesel Vehicle designed to use either diesel or up to 20% biodiesel fuel

25742_EXPR_C0001

GENERAL ENGINE SPECIFICATIONS

All measurements are given in inches.

Year	Models	Engine Displacement Liters (cc)	Engine ID/VIN	Fuel System Type	Bore x Stroke (inches)	Com-pression Ratio	Oil Pressure @ rpm
2010	Express, Savana	6.6 (6600)	LMM/6	DPI	4.0551 x 3.8976	16.8:1	28 psi @ 1800
2010-11	Express, Savana	4.3 (4300)	LU3/X	MFI	4.012 x 3.480	9.2:1	18 psi @ 2000
	Express, Savana	4.8 (4800)	L20/A	SFI	3.779-3.78 x 3.27	9.08:1	18 psig @ 2000
	Express, Savana	5.3 (5300)	LMF/4	SFI	3.779-3.78 x 3.622	9.95:1	18 psig @ 2000
	Express, Savana	6.0 (6000)	L96/G	SFI	4.0007-4.0017 x 3.622	9.67:1	18 psig @ 2000
	Express, Savana	6.6 (6600)	LGH/L	DI	4.0551 x 3.8976	16.8:1	28 psi @ 1800

DI Direct Injection

DPI Diesel Port Fuel Injection

MFI Multi-Port Fuel Injection

SFI Sequential Fuel Injection

25742_EXPR_C0002

ENGINE TUNE-UP SPECIFICATIONS

Year	Engine Disp. Liters	Engine ID/VIN	Spark Plug Gap (inches)	Spark Plug Wire Resistance (ohms)	Idle Speed (rpm)	Valve Stem-to-Guide Clearance Production Intake	Production Exhaust	Service Intake	Service Exhaust
2010	6.6	LMM/6	diesel		680	0.0012-0.0025	0.0015-0.0028	0.0079	0.0079
2010-11	4.3	LU3/X	0.06	397-1,337	TAC	0.0010-0.0027	0.0010-0.0027	0.0010-0.0037	0.0010-0.0037
	4.8	L20/A	0.04	397-1,337	TAC	0.001-0.0026	0.001-0.0026	0.0037	0.0037
	5.6	LMF/4	0.04	397-1,337	TAC	0.001-0.0026	0.001-0.0026	0.0037	0.0037
	6.0	L96/G	0.04	397-1,337	TAC	0.001-0.0026	0.001-0.0026	0.0037	0.0037
	6.6	LGH/L	diesel		680	0.0012-0.0025	0.0015-0.0028	0.0079	0.0079
2011	6.0	LC8/B	0.04	397-1,337	TAC	0.001-0.0026	0.001-0.0026	0.0037	0.0037

NOTE: The Vehicle Emission Control Information label often reflects specification changes made during production.

The label figures must be used if they differ from those in this chart.

The Engine Control Module (ECM) primarily collects information from the crankshaft position (CKP) and camshaft position (CMP) sensors to control the sequence, dwell, and timing of the spark.

TAC For the non-diesel engines, the Engine Control Module (ECM) controls idle speed through the Throttle Actuator Control (TAC).

25742_EXPR_C0003

CAPACITIES

Year	Model	Engine Disp. Liters	Engine ID/VIN	Engine Oil with Filter (qts.)	Transmission (pts.) Auto.	Drive Axle (pts.) Front	Drive Axle (pts.) Rear	Transfer Case (pts.)	Fuel Tank (gal.)	Cooling System (qts.)
2010	Express/Savana	4.3	LU3/X	4.6	①	2.54	②	3.0	③	④
	Express/Savana	4.8	L20/A	6.0	①	2.54	②	3.0	③	⑤
	Express/Savana	5.3	LMF/4	6.0	①	2.54	②	3.0	③	⑤
	Express/Savana	6.0	L96/G	6.0	①	2.54	②	3.0	③	⑤
	Express/Savana	6.6	LMM/6, LGH/L	10.0	①	2.54	②	3.0	③	⑥
2011	Express/Savana	4.3	LU3/X	4.6	①	2.54	②	3.0	③	④
	Express/Savana	4.8	L20/A	6.0	①	2.54	②	3.0	③	⑤
	Express/Savana	5.3	LMF/4	6.0	①	2.54	②	3.0	③	⑤
	Express/Savana	6.0	L96/G	6.0	①	2.54	②	3.0	③	⑤
	Express/Savana	6.6	LMM/6, LGH/L	10.0	①	2.54	②	3.0	③	⑥

NOTE: All capacities are approximate. Add fluid gradually and ensure a proper fluid level is obtained.

① 4L60E transmission:

Drain & refill (pan & filter): 10 pts.

Overhaul: 22 pts.

6L90 transmission:

Drain & refill (pan & filter): 12.6 pts.

Overhaul: 21 pts.

② 8.6 inch: 4.3 pts

9.5 inch: 5.5 pts

9.75 inch: 6.26 pts.

10.5/10.75 inch: 6.62 pts.

③ Passenger/cargo: 31 gal.

Cab/chassis, 33 gal.

Optional tank, 57 gal.

④ With rear heat: 13 qts.

Without rear heat: 10 qts.

⑤ With rear heat: 15.4 qts.

Without rear heat: 12.4 qts.

⑥ With front heat or A/C:

With FOH: 21.1 qts

Without FOH: 22.1 qts.

With front and Rear heat or A/C:

With FOH: 22.7 qts.

Without FOH: 23.7 qts.

25742_EXPR_C0004

FLUID SPECIFICATIONS

Year	Models	Engine Oil	Auto. Trans.	Drive Axle Front & Rear	Transfer Case	Power Steering Fluid	Brake Master Cylinder	Cooling System
2010	All	SAE 5W-30	DEXRON®-VI	①	DEXRON®-VI	GM PS Fluid	DOT 3	DEX-COOL
2011	All	SAE 5W-30	DEXRON®-VI	①	DEXRON®-VI	GM PS Fluid	DOT 3	DEX-COOL

DOT: Department Of Transpotation
① SAE 75W-90 Synthetic Lubricant

25742_EXPR_C0005

VALVE SPECIFICATIONS

Year	Engine Displacement Liters	Engine ID/VIN	Angle (deg.) Seat	Angle (deg.) Face	Spring Free-Length (inches)	Spring Installed Height (inches)	Valve Stem (inches) -to-Guide Clearance	Valve Stem Diameter Production	Valve Stem Diameter Service
2010	4.3	LU3/X	45	45	2.020	1.670-1.700	0.0010-0.0037 ②	NA	NA
	4.8, 5.3, 6.0	L20/A, LMF/4, L96/G	46	45	2.08	1.800	0.0037	0.313-0.3140	0.3130
	6.6	LMM/6, LGH/L	46	45	2.2283 ①	1.6142*	0.0079	NA	0.280
2011	4.3	LU3/X	45	45	2.020	1.670-1.700	0.0010-0.0037 ②	NA	NA
	4.8, 5.3, 6.0	L20/A, LMF/4, L96/G	46	45	2.08	1.800	0.0037	0.313-0.3140	0.3130
	6.6	LMM/6, LGH/L	46	45	2.2283 ①	1.6142*	0.0079	NA	0.280

NA: Not available
① Production
② Service

25742_EXPR_C0006

CAMSHAFT SPECIFICATIONS

All measurements in inches unless noted

Year	Engine Displacement Liters	Engine ID/VIN	Journal Diameter	Bearing Diameter	Shaft End-play	Runout	Journal Out-of-Round	Lobe Height Intake	Lobe Height Exhaust
2010	4.3	LU3/X	1.8677-1.8696	NA	0.0010-0.0090	0.0039	0.0003	0.2704	0.2793
	4.8, 6.0	L20/A, LMF/4	2.165-2.166	2.1678-2.1688	0.001-0.012	0.0020 ①	0.001	0.283	0.283
	5.3	L96/G	2.165-2.166	2.1678-2.1688	0.001-0.012	0.0020 ①	0.001	0.274	0.281
	6.6	LMM/6, LGH/L	2.3984 ②	2.4043 ② (inside diam.)	0.0079 ②	0.0020 ②	NA	0.2863 ③	0.2326 ③
2011	4.3	LU3/X	1.8677-1.8696	NA	0.0010-0.0090	0.0039	0.0003	0.2704	0.2793
	4.8, 6.0	L20/A, LMF/4	2.165-2.166	2.1678-2.1688	0.001-0.012	0.0020 ①	0.001	0.283	0.283
	5.3	L96/G	2.165-2.166	2.1678-2.1688	0.001-0.012	0.0020 ①	0.001	0.274	0.281
	6.6	LMM/6, LGH/L	2.3984 ②	2.4043 ② (inside diam.)	0.0079 ②	0.0020 ②	NA	0.2863 ③	0.2326 ③

NA Not available
① Measured at the intermediate journals
② Service limit
③ Production

25742_EXPR_C0007

CRANKSHAFT AND CONNECTING ROD SPECIFICATIONS

All measurements are given in inches.

Year	Engine Displacement Liters	Engine ID/VIN	Crankshaft Main Brg. Journal Dia.	Crankshaft Main Brg. Oil Clearance	Crankshaft Shaft End-play	Crankshaft Bore Out of-Round	Connecting Rod Journal Diameter	Connecting Rod Side Clearance
2010	4.3	LU3/X	①	②	0.002-0.0080	0.002	2.2487-2.2497	0.006-0.017
	4.8, 5.3, 6.0	L20/A, L96/G, LMF/4	2.558 ③	0.0010-0.0025 ③	0.0015-0.0078	0.002	2.0987	0.00433-0.0200
	6.6	LMM/6, LGH/L	3.1453	0.0055	0.0213 ③	NA	2.4756 ③	0.0213 ③
2011	4.3	LU3/X	①	②	0.002-0.0080	0.002	2.2487-2.2497	0.006-0.017
	4.8, 5.3, 6.0	L20/A, L96/G, LMF/4	2.558 ③	0.0010-0.0025 ③	0.0015-0.0078	0.002	2.0987	0.00433-0.0200
	6.6	LMM/6, LGH/L	3.1453	0.0055	0.0213 ③	NA	2.4756 ③	0.0213 ③

NA Not available
① No. 1: 2.4488-2.4495
  No. 2 & 3: 2.4485-2.4494
  No. 4: 2.4480-2.4489
② No. 1: 0.0010-0.0020 (service limit)
  No. 2 & 3: 0.0010-0.0020 (service limit)
  No. 4: 0.0010-0.0025 (service limit)
③ Service Limit

25742_EXPR_C0008

PISTON AND RING SPECIFICATIONS

All measurements are service limits except as noted and are given in inches.

Year	Engine Disp. Liters	Engine ID/VIN	Piston-to-Bore Clearance	Ring End Gap (Service Limit)			Ring-to-Groove Clearance (Service Limit)		
				First Compression	Second Compression	Oil Control	First Compression	Second Compression	Oil Control
2010	4.3	LU3/X	0.0029	0.010-0.020	0.015-0.0310	0.0002-0.0035	0.0012-0.0033	0.0012-0.0033	0.0030-0.0079
	4.8, 6.0	L20/A, LMF/4	0.0028 ①	0.0090-0.0196 ②	0.0173-0.0300 ②	0.007-0.032 ②	0.00157-0.0034	0.00157-0.0031	0.0005-0.0078
	5.3	L96/G	0.0028 ①	0.0079-0.0181	0.0146-0.0295	0.0086-0.0331	0.0016-0.0033	0.0014-0.0031	0.0005-0.0079
	6.6	LMM/6, LGH/L	0.0035-0.0047 ③	0.0539	0.0531	0.0472	0.0102	0.0039	0.0047
2011	4.3	LU3/X	0.0029	0.010-0.020	0.015-0.0310	0.0002-0.0035	0.0012-0.0033	0.0012-0.0033	0.0030-0.0079
	4.8, 6.0	L20/A, LMF/4	0.0028 ①	0.0090-0.0196 ②	0.0173-0.0300 ②	0.007-0.032 ②	0.00157-0.0034	0.00157-0.0031	0.0005-0.0078
	5.3	L96/G	0.0028 ①	0.0079-0.0181	0.0146-0.0295	0.0086-0.0331	0.0016-0.0033	0.0014-0.0031	0.0005-0.0079
	6.6	LMM/6, LGH/L	0.0035-0.0047 ③	0.0539	0.0531	0.0472	0.0102	0.0039	0.0047

① Service limit with skirt coating worn off

② Measured in cylinder bore

③ Production value; measurement not available for 2010 LGH

25742_EXPR_C0009

TORQUE SPECIFICATIONS
All readings in ft. lbs.

Year	Engine Displacement Liters	Cylinder Head Bolts	Main Bearing Bolts	Rod Bearing Bolts	Crankshaft Damper Bolts	Flywheel Bolts	Manifold Intake *	Manifold Exhaust	Spark Plugs	Oil Pan Drain Plug
2010	4.3	①	77	②	70	74	③	④	11	18
	4.8	⑤	⑥	⑦	⑧	⑨	⑩	⑪	11	18
	5.3	⑤	⑥	⑦	⑧	⑨	⑩	⑪	11	18
	6.0	⑤	⑥	⑦	⑧	⑨	⑩	⑪	11	18
	6.6	⑫	⑬	⑭	⑮	⑯	18	⑰	—	62
2011	4.3	①	77	②	70	74	③	④	11	18
	4.8	⑤	⑥	⑦	⑧	⑨	⑩	⑪	11	18
	5.3	⑤	⑥	⑦	⑧	⑨	⑩	⑪	11	18
	6.0	⑤	⑥	⑦	⑧	⑨	⑩	⑪	11	18
	6.6	⑫	⑬	⑭	⑮	⑯	18	⑰	—	62

* NOTE: Applies to Lower Manifold only.

① Step 1: 22 ft. lbs.

Step 2:

Short bolt: Plus 55 degrees

Medium bolt: Plus 65 degrees

Long bolt: Plus 75 degrees

② 15 ft. lbs. plus 100 degrees

③ Lower intake manifold:

Step 1: 27 inch lbs.

Step 2: 106 inch lbs.

Step 3: 11 ft. lbs.

Upper manifold bolts:

Step 1: 44 inch lbs.

Step 2: 80 inch lbs.

④ Tighten bolts to 12 ft. lbs.

Retorque to 22 ft. lbs.

⑤ M11 bolts Step 1: 22 ft. lbs.

M11 bolts Step 2: 90 degrees

M11 bolts Step 3: 70 degrees

M8 bolts: 22 ft. lbs.

⑥ Inner bolts:

Step 1: 15 ft. lbs.

Step 2: 80 degrees

Side Bolts: 18 ft. lbs.

Outer bolts:

Step 1: 15 ft. lbs.

Step 2: 51 degrees

⑦ Step 1: 15 ft. lbs.

Step 2: 85 degrees

⑧ First pass: 111

Second pass: loosen 360 degrees

Third pass: 37

Fourth pass: 280 degrees

⑨ Step 1: 15 ft. lbs.

Step 2: 37 ft. lbs.

Step 3: 74 ft. lbs.

⑩ Step 1: 44 inch lbs.

Step 2: 89 inch lbs.

⑪ Step 1: 11 ft. lbs.

Step 2: 15 ft. lbs.

⑫ M12 bolts: Step 1: 37 ft. lbs.

Step 2: 59 ft. lbs.

Step 3: Plus 60 degrees

Step 4: Plus 90 degrees

⑬ Step 1: 74 ft. lbs.

Step 2: Plus 90 degrees

⑭ Step 1: 47 ft. lbs.

Step 2: Plus 30 degrees

Step 3: Plus 30 degrees

⑮ 1st pass: 74 ft. lbs.

2nd pass: Plus 105 degrees

⑯ Step 1: 58 ft. lbs.

Step 2: Plus 60 degrees

Step 3: Plus 60 degrees

⑰ First pass: 42 ft. lbs.

Four center bolts an additional pass

25742_EXPR_C0010

WHEEL ALIGNMENT

Year	Series	Model	Caster Range (+/-Deg.)	Caster Preferred Setting (Deg.)	Camber Range (+/-Deg.)	Camber Preferred Setting (Deg.)	Toe-in (Deg.)
2010	1500 w/ 6200, 7200 & 2500 w/ 7300 GVW	2WD/AWD	1.00	L +4.20 R +4.50	0.50	+0.15	0.10+/-0.20
	2500 w/ 8500, 8600 &3500 w/ 8600, 9600 GVW	2WD	1.00	L +4.60 R +5.00	0.50	+0.25	0.10+/-0.20
	3500 w/10000,11,000 11, 500, 12,000 & 12,300 GVW	2WD	1.00	L +4.60 R +4.90	0.50	+0.25	0.10+/-0.20
2011	1500 w/ 6200, 7200 & 2500 w/ 7300 GVW	2WD/AWD	1.00	L +4.20 R +4.50	0.50	+0.15	0.10+/-0.20
	2500 w/ 8500, 8600 &3500 w/ 8600, 9600 GVW	2WD	1.00	L +4.60 R +5.00	0.50	+0.25	0.10+/-0.20
	3500 w/10000,11,000 11, 500, 12,000 & 12,300 GVW	2WD	1.00	L +4.60 R +4.90	0.50	+0.25	0.10+/-0.20

25742_EXPR_C0011

TIRE, WHEEL AND BALL JOINT SPECIFICATIONS

Year	Models	OEM Tires	Tire Pressure Front/Rear	Tire Pressure Indicator Sensor Nut	Wheel Size	Ball Joint Retaining Nut Lower	Ball Joint Retaining Nut Upper	Ball Joint Inspection	Lug Nut (ft. lbs.)
2010	Express, Savana	①	①	62 inch lbs.	①	74 ft. lbs.	37 ft. lbs.	②	140
2011	Express, Savana	①	①	62 inch lbs.	①	74 ft. lbs.	37 ft. lbs.	②	140

OEM: Original Equipment Manufacturer

① See tire placard on driver's side door.

② Clean and inspect the ball joint seal for cuts or tears. If the ball joint seal is damaged, replace the ball joint or the appropriate control arm as applicable for this ve

25742_EXPR_C0012

BRAKE SPECIFICATIONS

All measurements in inches unless noted

| Year | Model | | Brake Disc | | | Brake Drum Diameter | | | | Brake Caliper | |
			Original Thickness	Minimum Thickness	Maximum Runout	Original Inside Diameter	Max. Wear Limit	Max. Machine Diameter	Minimum Lining Thickness	Bracket Bolts (ft. lbs.)	Mounting Bolts (ft. lbs.)
2010	Express	F	①	②	0.005	—	—	—	—	③	④
		R	⑤	⑥	0.005	—	—	—	—	⑦	⑧
	Savana	F	①	②	0.005	—	—	—	—	③	④
		R	⑤	⑥	0.005	—	—	—	—	⑦	⑧
2011	Express	F	①	②	0.005	—	—	—	—	③	④
		R	⑤	⑥	0.005	—	—	—	—	⑦	⑧
	Savana	F	①	②	0.005	—	—	—	—	③	④
		R	⑤	⑥	0.005	—	—	—	—	⑦	⑧

NA: Not Available

① JH5: 1.142
  JH6: 1.496
  JH7: 1.496
② JH5: 1.102
  JH6: 1.457
  JH7: 1.457
③ JH5: 129
  JH6, JH7: 221
④ All 80
⑤ JH5: 1.181
  JH6: 1.142
  JH7: 1.181

⑥ JH5: 1.142
  JH6: 1.102
  JH7: 1.142
⑦ JH5: 148 single rear wheel
  JH6: 123 single rear wheel
  JH7: 123 single rear wheel
  All 221 dual rear wheel
⑧ JH5: 25 single rear wheel
  JH6: 53 single rear wheel
  JH7: 53 single rear wheel
  All 45 dual rear wheel

25742_EXPR_C0013

MAINTENANCE I AND II SERVICE SCHEDULES
EXPRESS, SAVANA

When the CHANGE ENGINE OIL light appears, certain services and inspections are required.

Required services are described as Maintenance I and Maintenance II.

The first service of a vehicle should be Maintenance I, and the second service should be Maintenance II.

Alternate between the 2 services thereafter. However, in some cases, Maintenance II may be required more often.

Maintenance I: Use Maintenance I if the CHANGE ENGINE OIL light comes on within 10 months since the vehicle was purchased or, if Maintenance II was performed.

Maintenance II: Use Maintenance II if the previous service performed was Maintenance I. Always use Maintenance II whenever the CHANGE ENGINE OIL light comes on 10 months or more since the last service, or, if the CHANGE ENGINE OIL light has not come on at all for one year.

Service Item	Maintenance I	Maintenance II
Change engine oil and filter, lubricate chassis components. Reset oil life system.	✓	✓
Lubricate the front suspension, steering linkage, rear driveline center splines (van models), and parking brake cable guides. Control arm ball joints on pickup models require lubrication but should not be lubricated unless their temperature is -12°C (10°F) or higher, or they could be damaged. Vehicles used under severe commercial operating conditions require lubrication on a regular basis every 5 000 km/3,000 miles.	✓	✓
Restraint system component check.	✓	✓
Rotate the tires. Inspect the tire inflation pressures and the tire wear. Tires should be rotated every 12 000 km/7,500 miles.	✓	✓
Fluids visual leak check (or every 12 months, whichever occurs first). A leak in any system must be repaired and the fluid level checked.	✓	✓
Engine cooling system inspection. Visual inspection of Coolant, hoses, pipes, fittings, clamps and replacement, if needed.	✓	✓
Windshield washer fluid level check.	✓	✓
Engine air cleaner filter inspection.	✓	✓
Add diesel exhaust fluid. (Diesel Engines)	✓	✓
Body component lubrication. Lubricate all key lock cylinders, body door hinges, hood latch assembly, secondary latch, pivots, spring anchor, release pawl, fuel door hinge, locks, latches, and any folding or moving seat hardware. Pickup models: Lubricate tailgate hinges, tailgate linkage, tailgate handle pivot points, and latch bolt. Van models: Lubricate hood hinges and rear compartment hinges. See Recommended Fluids and Lubricants. More frequent lubrication may be required when the vehicle is exposed to a corrosive environment. Applying silicone grease on weatherstrips with a clean cloth makes them last longer, seal better, and not stick or squeak.	—	✓
Steering and suspension inspection. Visually inspect front and rear suspension and steering system for damaged, loose, or missing parts, signs of wear or lack of lubrication. Inspect power steering lines and hoses for proper hook-up, binding, leaks, cracks, chafing, etc. Pickup models: Visually check constant velocity joints, rubber boots, and axle seals for leaks	—	✓
Inspect the transmission fluid level and add fluid as needed.	✓	✓
Brake system inspection (or every 12 months, whichever occurs first).	✓	✓
Windshield wiper blade inspection for wear, cracking, or contamination and windshield and wiper blade cleaning, if contaminated.	✓	✓
Fuel system inspection for damage or leaks.	—	✓
Gas engines check all exhaust system components. Diesel engines check the DPF pressure lines, and nearby heat shields inspection for loose or damaged components. Check to be sure that mud or dirt is not caked on the exhaust system, especially in the area of the diesel particulate filter and tailpipe. Clean the area as needed.	—	✓

25742_EXPR_C0014

MAINTENANCE I AND II SERVICE SCHEDULES
EXPRESS, SAVANA

When the CHANGE ENGINE OIL light appears, certain services and inspections are required.

Required services are described as Maintenance I and Maintenance II.

The first service of a vehicle should be Maintenance I, and the second service should be Maintenance II.

Alternate between the 2 services thereafter. However, in some cases, Maintenance II may be required more often.

Maintenance I: Use Maintenance I if the CHANGE ENGINE OIL light comes on within 10 months since the vehicle was purchased or, if Maintenance II was performed.

Maintenance II: Use Maintenance II if the previous service performed was Maintenance I. Always use Maintenance II whenever the CHANGE ENGINE OIL light comes on 10 months or more since the last service, or, if the CHANGE ENGINE OIL light has not come on at all for one year.

Service Item	Maintenance I	Maintenance II
Air intake system check. Check the air intake system installation to assure that gaskets are properly sealed and that all hose connections, fasteners, and other components are tight. Also check to be sure that the air cleaner housing is properly seated and the cover fits tightly. Tighten connections and fasteners or replace damaged parts as necessary.	—	✓
Fuel filter service (Diesel Engines). This vehicle has a CHANGE FUEL FILTER message in the Driver Information Center (DIC) to tell you when to replace the fuel filter. See Fuel System Messages. Change the fuel filter a minimum of once every two years. The PERCENT FUEL FILTER LIFE REMAINING message may be used to decide if the filter should be changed during routine vehicle service.	—	✓
Inspect the throttle system.	—	✓

To reset the CHANGE ENGINE OIL light:

1. Turn the ignition key to the ON/RUN position with the engine OFF.
2. Press and release the stem in the lower center of the instrument cluster until the OIL LIFE message is displayed.
3. Once the alternating OIL LIFE and RESET messages appear, press and hold the stem until several beeps sound.
   This confirms that the oil life system has been reset to 100 percent.
4. Turn the ignition key to the OFF position.
   If the CHANGE ENGINE OIL message comes back on when the vehicle is started, the engine oil life system has not been reset. Repeat the procedure.

25742_EXPR_C0015

ADDITIONAL MAINTENANCE SERVICES - NORMAL
EXPRESS, SAVANA

TO BE SERVICED	TYPE OF SERVICE	VEHICLE MILEAGE INTERVAL (x1000)					
		25	50	75	100	125	150
Engine coolant	Replace						✓
Air cleaner filter	Replace		✓		✓		✓
Automatic transmisison fluid & filter	Replace				✓		
Spark plugs (Gas engines)	Replace				✓		
Exhaust system & heat shields	Service/ Inspect	✓	✓	✓	✓	✓	✓
Cooling system hoses and clamps	Service/ Inspect	✓	✓	✓	✓	✓	✓
Fuel system	Inspect	✓	✓	✓	✓	✓	✓
Accessory drive belt	Replace						✓
Evaporative control system	Inspect		✓		✓		✓
Transfer case fluid	Replace				✓		

25742_EXPR_C0016

ADDITIONAL MAINTENANCE SERVICES - SEVERE
EXPRESS, SAVANA

TO BE SERVICED	TYPE OF SERVICE	VEHICLE MILEAGE INTERVAL (x1000)					
		25	50	75	100	125	150
Engine coolant	Replace						✓
Air cleaner filter	Replace	✓	✓	✓	✓	✓	✓
Automatic transmisison fluid & filter	Replace		✓		✓		✓
Spark plugs (Gas engines)	Replace				✓		
Exhaust system & heat shields	Service/ Inspect	✓	✓	✓	✓	✓	✓
Cooling system hoses and clamps	Service/ Inspect	✓	✓	✓	✓	✓	✓
Fuel system	Inspect	✓	✓	✓	✓	✓	✓
Accessory drive belt	Inspect						✓
Evaporative control system	Inspect		✓		✓		✓
Transfer case fluid	Replace		✓		✓		✓

25742_EXPR_C0017

PRECAUTIONS

Before servicing any vehicle, please be sure to read all of the following precautions, which deal with personal safety, prevention of component damage, and important points to take into consideration when servicing a motor vehicle:

• Never open, service or drain the radiator or cooling system when the engine is hot; serious burns can occur from the steam and hot coolant.

• Observe all applicable safety precautions when working around fuel. Whenever servicing the fuel system, always work in a well-ventilated area. Do not allow fuel spray or vapors to come in contact with a spark, open flame, or excessive heat (a hot drop light, for example). Keep a dry chemical fire extinguisher near the work area. Always keep fuel in a container specifically designed for fuel storage; also, always properly seal fuel containers to avoid the possibility of fire or explosion. Refer to the additional fuel system precautions later in this section.

• Fuel injection systems often remain pressurized, even after the engine has been turned **OFF**. Relive the fuel system pressure before disconnecting any fuel lines. Failure to relieve the fuel system pressure may result in fire and/or personal injury.

• Brake fluid often contains polyglycol ethers and polyglycols. Avoid contact with the eyes and wash your hands thoroughly after handling brake fluid. If you do get brake fluid in your eyes, flush your eyes with clean, running water for 15 minutes. If eye irritation persists, or if you have taken brake fluid internally, IMMEDIATELY seek medical assistance.

• The EPA warns that prolonged contact with used engine oil may cause a number of skin disorders, including cancer. You should make every effort to minimize your exposure to used engine oil. Protective gloves should be worn when changing oil. Wash your hands and any other exposed skin areas as soon as possible after exposure to used engine oil. Soap and water, or waterless hand cleaner should be used.

• This vehicle is equipped with Air Bags, which are also called Supplemental Inflatable Restraints. Refer to the "Warnings" in Dangers, Warnings and Cautions in the Air

Bag/Supplemental Inflatable Restraint section. Refer to Air Bag/Supplemental Inflatable Restraint component and wiring location views before performing a service on or around Supplemental Inflatable Restraint components or wiring. If you fail to follow "Dangers", "Warnings" and "Cautions," you could cause air bag deployment, personal injury, or otherwise unnecessary repairs. In order to help avoid accidental air bag deployment and personal injury, whenever you service a vehicle that requires repair of the Air Bag/Supplemental Inflatable Restraint and another vehicle system, we recommend that you first repair the Air Bag/Supplemental Inflatable Restraint, then go on to the other system.

• Always wear safety goggles when working with, or around, the air bag system. When carrying a non-deployed air bag, be sure the bag and trim cover are pointed away from your body. When placing a non-deployed air bag on a work surface, always face the bag and trim cover upward, away from the surface. This will reduce the motion of the module if it is accidentally deployed. Refer to the additional air bag system precautions later in this section.

• Clean, high quality brake fluid from a sealed container is essential to the safe and proper operation of the brake system. You should always buy the correct type of brake fluid for your vehicle. If the brake fluid becomes contaminated, completely flush the system with new fluid. Never reuse any brake fluid. Any brake fluid that is removed from the system should be discarded. Also, do not allow any brake fluid to come in contact with a painted surface; it will damage the paint.

• Never operate the engine without the proper amount and type of engine oil; doing so WILL result in severe engine damage.

• Timing belt maintenance is extremely important. Many models utilize an interference-type, non-freewheeling engine. If the timing belt breaks, the valves in the cylinder head may strike the pistons, causing potentially serious (also time-consuming and expensive) engine damage. Refer to the maintenance interval charts for the recommended replacement interval for the timing

belt, and to the timing belt section for belt replacement and inspection.

• Disconnecting the negative battery cable on some vehicles may interfere with the functions of the on-board computer system(s) and may require the computer to undergo a relearning process once the negative battery cable is reconnected. Refer to Battery Negative Cable Disconnect/Connect in the Engine Electrical section in the Engine Electrical section.

✳✳ WARNING

Battery Disconnect Warning—Unless directed otherwise, the ignition and start switch must be in the OFF or LOCK position, and all electrical loads must be OFF before servicing any electrical component. Disconnect the negative battery cable to prevent an electrical spark should a tool or equipment come in contact with an exposed electrical terminal. Failure to follow these precautions may result in personal injury and/or damage to the vehicle or its components.

For Vehicles equipped with OnStar® (UE1) with Back Up Battery:

The Back Up Battery is a redundant power supply to allow limited OnStar® functionality in the event of a main vehicle battery power disruption to the VCIM (OnStar® module). Do not disconnect the main vehicle battery or remove the OnStar® fuse with the ignition key in any position other than OFF. Retained accessory power (RAP) should be allowed to time out or be disabled (simply opening the driver door should disable RAP) before disconnecting power. Disconnecting power to the OnStar® module in any way while the ignition is On or with RAP activated may cause activation of the OnStar® Back-Up Battery (BUB) system and will discharge and permanently damage the back-up battery. Once the Back-Up Battery is activated it will stay on until it has completely discharged. The BUB is not rechargeable and once activated the BUB must be replaced.

• Only an MVAC-trained, EPA-certified automotive technician should service the air conditioning system or its components.

BRAKES ANTI-LOCK BRAKE SYSTEM (ABS)

GENERAL INFORMATION

PRECAUTIONS

ABS Precautions

Note the following ABS precautions:
• Certain components within the ABS system are not intended to be serviced or repaired individually.
• Do not use rubber hoses or other parts not specifically specified for and ABS system. When using repair kits, replace all parts included in the kit. Partial or incorrect repair may lead to functional problems and require the replacement of components.
• Lubricate rubber parts with clean, fresh brake fluid to ease assembly. Do not use shop air to clean parts; damage to rubber components may result.
• Use only DOT 3 brake fluid from an unopened container.
• If any hydraulic component or line is removed or replaced, it may be necessary to bleed the entire system.
• A clean repair area is essential. Always clean the reservoir and cap thoroughly before removing the cap. The slightest amount of dirt in the fluid may plug an orifice and impair the system function. Perform repairs after components have been thoroughly cleaned; use only denatured alcohol to clean components. Do not allow ABS components to come into contact with any substance containing mineral oil; this includes used shop rags.
• The Anti-Lock control unit is a microprocessor similar to other computer units in the vehicle. Ensure that the ignition switch is **OFF** before removing or installing controller harnesses. Avoid static electricity discharge at or near the controller.
• If any arc welding is to be done on the vehicle, unplug the control unit before welding operations begin.

General Brake Precautions

Avoid taking the following actions when you service wheel brake parts:
• Do not grind brake linings.
• Do not sand brake linings.
• Do not clean wheel brake parts with a dry brush or with compressed air.
Some models or aftermarket brake parts may contain asbestos fibers which can become airborne in dust. Breathing dust with asbestos fibers may cause serious bodily harm. Use a water-dampened cloth in order to remove any dust on brake parts. Use commercial equipment to perform this washing function. These wet methods prevent fibers from becoming airborne.

✳ WARNING

Brake fluid may irritate eyes and skin. In case of contact, take the following actions:

• Eye contact—rinse thoroughly with water.
• Skin contact—wash with soap and water.
• If ingested—consult a physician immediately.

✳ WARNING

Use only Delco Supreme 11, GM P/N 12377967 (Canadian P/N 992667), or equivalent DOT 3 brake fluid from a clean, sealed container. Do not use fluid from an open container that may be contaminated with water. Improper or contaminated fluid could result in damage to components, or loss of braking, with possible injury. The use of any type of fluid other than the recommended type of brake fluid, may cause contamination which could result in damage to the internal rubber seals and/or rubber linings of hydraulic brake system components.

✳ CAUTION

When filling the master cylinder, use only Delco Supreme 11, GM P/N 12377967 (Canadian P/N 992667), or equivalent DOT 3 brake fluid. Do not use a container which has been used for petroleum based fluids, or a container which is wet with water. Petroleum based fluids will cause swelling and distortion of rubber parts in the hydraulic brake system, and water will mix with brake fluid, lowering the boiling point. Keep all fluid containers capped to prevent contamination.

✳ CAUTION

Brake fluid will damage electrical connections and painted surfaces. Use shop cloths, suitable containers, and fender covers to prevent brake fluid from contacting these areas. Always re-seal and wipe off brake fluid containers to prevent spills.

✳ CAUTION

Avoid spilling brake fluid on any of the vehicle's painted surfaces, wiring, cables or electrical connectors. Brake fluid will damage paint and electrical connections. If any fluid is spilled on the vehicle, immediately flush the area with water to minimize the potential for damage.

✳ CAUTION

Power steering fluid, engine oil, brake fluid, or any mineral based fluids cannot be mixed. If brake seals contact power steering fluid or steering seals contact brake fluid, seal damage will result.

➡ Note the following:

• Do not reuse the brake fluid collected during the hydraulic brake system bleeding.
• Always store brake fluid in a closed container.
• Reseal brake fluid containers immediately after use.
• Do not use brake fluid left in an open container.
• Do not use brake fluid left in an improperly sealed container.
• Do not use the following fluids in the hydraulic brake system: Power steering fluid, Automatic transmission fluid, DOT 5 silicone hydraulic brake fluid.

WHEEL SPEED SENSOR (WSS)

REMOVAL & INSTALLATION

Front

See Figures 1 through 4.

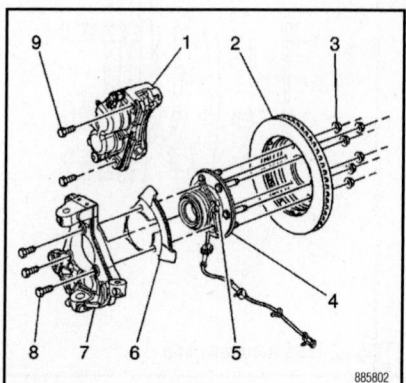

Fig. 1 Brake rotor (2), 1500 Series shown

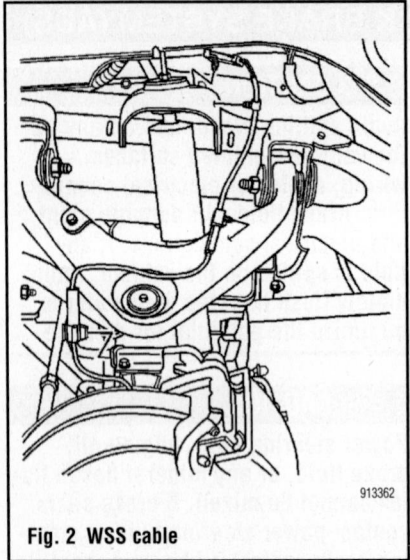

913362

Fig. 2 WSS cable

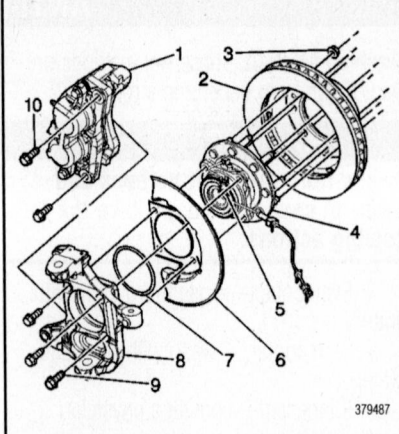

379487

Fig. 4 The hub/bearing assembly (4) and wheel speed sensor (5), the 2500/3500 Series shown

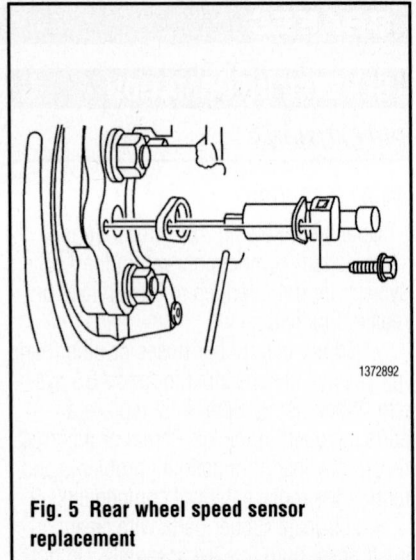

1372892

Fig. 5 Rear wheel speed sensor replacement

1. Raise and support the vehicle.
2. Remove the tire and wheel.
3. Remove the brake rotor (2) shown on the 1500 Series.
4. Remove the wheel speed sensor (WSS) cable mounting clip from the knuckle.
5. Remove the WSS cable mounting clip from the upper control arm.
6. Remove the WSS cable mounting clip from the frame attachment point.
7. Remove the WSS cable electrical connector.
8. Remove the WSS mounting bolt.

✲✲ CAUTION

Carefully remove the sensor by pulling it straight out of the bore. DO NOT use a screwdriver, or other device to pry the sensor out of the

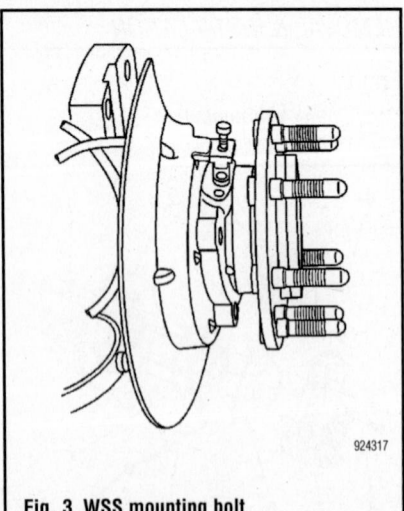

924317

Fig. 3 WSS mounting bolt

bore. Prying will cause the sensor body to break off in the bore. Remove the wheel speed sensor (5) from the hub/bearing assembly (4) shown on the 2500/3500 Series.

To install:

9. Plug the WSS bore to prevent debris from falling into the hub.
10. Use a wire brush or equivalent to clean the WSS mounting surface on the hub and to remove any rust or corrosion.
11. Apply a thin layer of wheel bearing lubricant, GM P/N 01051344 to the hub surface and the sensor O-ring prior to sensor installation.
12. Install the WSS into the hub/bearing assembly. Ensure that the sensor is seated flat against the hub.
13. Install the WSS mounting bolt and tighten to 13 ft. lbs. (18 Nm).
14. Install the WSS cable mounting clip to the knuckle.
15. Install the WSS cable mounting clip to the upper control arm.
16. Install the WSS cable mounting clip to the frame attachment point.
17. Connect the WSS cable electrical connector.
18. Install the brake rotor.
19. Install the tire and wheel.

Rear

See Figure 5.

1. Raise the vehicle.
2. For the left rear sensor, remove the leaf spring anchor plate.
3. Disconnect the electrical connector.

4. Remove the wheel speed sensor retaining bolt.
5. Remove the wheel speed sensor and spacer block.

To install:

6. Install the spacer block and the wheel speed sensor.
7. Install the wheel speed sensor retaining bolt and tighten to 124 inch lbs. (14 Nm).
8. Connect the electrical connector.
9. For the left rear sensor, install the leaf spring anchor plate.
10. Lower the vehicle.
11. Perform a low speed test to ensure the wheel speed sensor is functioning properly:

a. Start the engine and allow it to idle.

b. If the ABS indicator or the traction assist indicator remains illuminated, DO NOT drive the vehicle until it is diagnosed and repaired. Check the wheel speed sensor electrical connector to ensure it is not damaged and is installed properly. If the lamp remains illuminated, diagnose and repair the problem.

c. Select a smooth, dry, clean, and level road or large lot that is as free of traffic and obstacles as possible.

d. Drive the vehicle and maintain a speed of at least 16 km/h (10 mph) for at least 5 seconds.

e. Stop the vehicle and check to see if the ABS indicator or the traction assist indicator is illuminated.

f. If an indicator is illuminated, diagnose and repair the problem.

BLEEDING PROCEDURE

HYDRAULIC BRAKE SYSTEM BLEEDING (MANUAL)

❊❊ WARNING

Refer to the Brake Section Precautions

1. Place a clean shop cloth beneath the brake master cylinder to prevent brake fluid spills.

2. With the ignition OFF and the brakes cool, apply the brakes 3-5 times, or until the brake pedal effort increases significantly, in order to deplete the brake booster power reserve.

3. If you have performed a brake master cylinder bench bleeding on this vehicle, or if you disconnected the brake pipes from the master cylinder, you must perform the following steps:

   a. Ensure that the brake master cylinder reservoir is full to the maximum-fill level. If necessary add Delco Supreme 11®, GM P/N 12377967 (Canadian P/N 992667), or equivalent DOT-3 brake fluid from a clean, sealed brake fluid container.

   b. If you need to remove the reservoir cap and diaphragm, clean the outside of the reservoir on and around the cap before removing it.

   c. With the rear brake pipe installed securely to the master cylinder, loosen and separate the front brake pipe from the front port of the brake master cylinder.

   d. Allow a small amount of brake fluid to gravity bleed from the open port of the master cylinder.

   e. Reconnect the brake pipe to the master cylinder port and tighten securely.

   f. Have an assistant slowly depress the brake pedal fully and maintain steady pressure on the pedal.

   g. Loosen the same brake pipe to purge air from the open port of the master cylinder.

   h. Tighten the brake pipe, then have the assistant slowly release the brake pedal.

   i. Wait 15 seconds, then repeat steps 3 –7 until all air is purged from the same port of the master cylinder.

   j. With the front brake pipe installed securely to the master cylinder—after all air has been purged from the front port of the master cylinder—loosen and sepa-

rate the rear brake pipe from the master cylinder, then repeat steps 3 –8.

   k. After completing the final master cylinder port bleeding procedure, properly tighten both of the brake pipe-to-master cylinder fittings.

4. Fill the brake master cylinder reservoir with Delco Supreme 11®, GM P/N 12377967 (Canadian P/N 992667), or an equivalent DOT-3 brake fluid from a clean, sealed brake fluid container. Ensure that the brake master cylinder reservoir remains at least half-full during this bleeding procedure. Add fluid as needed to maintain the proper level.

5. Clean the outside of the reservoir on and around the reservoir cap prior to removing the cap and diaphragm.

6. Install a proper box-end wrench onto the RIGHT REAR wheel hydraulic circuit bleeder valve.

7. Install a transparent hose over the end of the bleeder valve.

8. Submerge the open end of the transparent hose into a transparent container partially filled with Delco Supreme 11®, GM P/N 12377967 (Canadian P/N 992667), or equivalent DOT-3 brake fluid from a clean, sealed brake fluid container.

9. Have an assistant slowly depress the brake pedal fully and maintain steady pressure on the pedal.

10. Loosen the bleeder valve to purge air from the wheel hydraulic circuit.

11. Tighten the bleeder valve, then have the assistant slowly release the brake pedal.

12. Wait 15 seconds, then repeat steps 8 –10 until all air is purged from the same wheel hydraulic circuit.

13. With the right rear wheel hydraulic circuit bleeder valve tightened securely, after all air has been purged from the right rear hydraulic circuit, install a proper box-end wrench onto the LEFT REAR wheel hydraulic circuit bleeder valve.

14. Install a transparent hose over the end of the bleeder valve, then repeat steps 7 –11.

With the left rear wheel hydraulic circuit bleeder valve tightened securely, after all air has been purged from the left rear hydraulic circuit, install a proper box-end wrench onto the RIGHT FRONT wheel hydraulic circuit bleeder valve.

15. Install a transparent hose over the end of the bleeder valve, then repeat steps 7 –11.

16. With the right front wheel hydraulic circuit bleeder valve tightened securely, after all air has been purged from the right front

hydraulic circuit, install a proper box-end wrench onto the LEFT FRONT wheel hydraulic circuit bleeder valve.

17. Install a transparent hose over the end of the bleeder valve, then repeat steps 7 –11.

18. After completing the final wheel hydraulic circuit bleeding procedure, properly tighten each of the four wheel hydraulic circuit bleeder valves.

19. Fill the brake master cylinder reservoir to the maximum-fill level.

20. Slowly depress and release the brake pedal. Observe the feel of the brake pedal.

21. If the brake pedal feels spongy, repeat the bleeding procedure again. If the brake pedal still feels spongy after repeating the bleeding procedure, perform the following steps:

   a. Inspect the brake system for external leaks.

   b. Pressure bleed the hydraulic brake system in order to purge any air that may still be trapped in the system.

22. Turn the ignition key ON, with the engine OFF. Check to see if the brake system warning lamp remains illuminated.

➡**If the brake system warning lamp remains illuminated, DO NOT allow the vehicle to be driven until it is diagnosed and repaired.**

MASTER CYLINDER BENCH BLEEDING

❊❊ WARNING

Refer to the Brakes Precautions.

1. Secure the mounting flange of the brake master cylinder in a bench vise so that the rear of the primary piston is accessible.

2. Remove the master cylinder reservoir cap and diaphragm.

3. Install suitable fittings to the master cylinder ports that match the type of flare seat required and also provide for hose attachment.

4. Install transparent hoses to the fittings installed to the master cylinder ports, then route the hoses into the master cylinder reservoir.

5. Fill the master cylinder reservoir to at least the half-way point with Delco Supreme 11® (GM P/N 12377967, Canadian P/N 992667) or an equivalent DOT-3 brake fluid from a clean, sealed brake fluid container.

6. Ensure that the ends of the transparent hoses running into the master cylinder reservoir are fully submerged in the brake fluid.

7. Using a smooth, round-ended tool, depress and release the primary piston as far as it will travel, a depth of about 1 inch (25 mm), several times. Observe the flow of fluid coming from the ports.

8. As air bleeds from the primary and secondary pistons, the effort required to depress the primary piston will increase and the amount of travel will decrease.

9. Continue to depress and release the primary piston until fluid flows freely from the ports with no evidence of air bubbles.

10. Remove the transparent hoses from the master cylinder reservoir.

11. Install the master cylinder reservoir cap and diaphragm.

12. Remove the fittings with the transparent hoses from the master cylinder ports. Wrap the master cylinder with a clean shop cloth to prevent brake fluid spills.

13. Remove the master cylinder from the vise.

BLEEDING THE ABS SYSTEM

✳✳ WARNING

Refer to the Brakes Precautions.

➡**Before performing the ABS Automated Bleed Procedure, first perform a manual or pressure bleed of the base hydraulic brake system.**

➡**The automated bleed procedure must be performed when a new brake pressure modulator valve (BPMV) is installed, because the secondary circuits of the new BPMV are not prefilled with brake fluid. The automated bleed procedure is recommended when one of the following conditions exists:**

    a. Base brake system bleeding does not achieve the desired pedal height or feel

    b. Extreme loss of brake fluid has occurred

    c. Air ingestion is suspected in the secondary circuits of the brake modulator assembly

The ABS Automated Bleed Procedure uses a scan tool to cycle the system solenoid valves and run the pump in order to purge any air from the secondary circuits. These circuits are normally closed off, and are only opened during system initialization at vehicle start up and during ABS operation. The automated bleed procedure opens

these secondary circuits and allows any air trapped in these circuits to flow out away from the brake modulator assembly, which is then forced out at the brake corners by the pressure bleeder.

Automated Bleed Procedure

✳✳ CAUTION

Terminate the Auto Bleed Procedure at any time during the process by pressing the EXIT button. No further Scan Tool prompts pertaining to the Auto Bleed procedure will be given. After exiting the bleed procedure, relieve bleed pressure and disconnect bleed equipment per the manufacturer's instructions. Failure to properly relieve pressure may result in spilled brake fluid causing damage to components and painted surfaces.

1. Raise and support the vehicle.

2. Remove the tire and wheel assemblies.

3. Inspect the brake system for leaks and visual damage. Repair or replace components as needed.

4. Lower the vehicle.

5. Prepare the brake bleeding equipment and the vehicle for a pressure bleed of the base hydraulic brake system.

6. Inspect the battery state of charge.

7. Install a scan tool.

8. Turn the ignition ON, with the engine OFF.

9. With the scan tool, perform the following steps:

    a. Select Diagnostics

    b. Select the appropriate vehicle information

    c. Select Chassis

    d. Select Electronic Brake Control Module (EBCM)

    e. Select Special Functions

    f. Select Automated Bleed

10. With an assistant ready, raise and support the vehicle.

11. Apply the brake pedal when instructed, using moderate effort.

    • Ensure the pedal remains applied until instructed to release by the scan tool.

    • Do not exceed the time period allowed by the scan tool for having the bleeder valves open.

    • The bleed sequence for each corner is as follows:

    • 1. Left front, 2. Right front, 3. Right rear, 4. Left rear

12. Perform the automated bleed procedure as instructed by the scan tool.

13. If the automated bleed procedure aborts, a malfunction exists. Diagnose any DTCs.

14. After you complete the automated bleed procedure, press and hold the brake pedal to inspect for pedal firmness.

15. If the brake pedal feels spongy, repeat the bleed procedure completely.

16. Remove the scan tool.

17. Install the tire and wheel assemblies.

18. Lower the vehicle.

19. Adjust the brake fluid level.

20. Road test the vehicle while confirming the brake pedal remains high and firm.

FLUID FILL PROCEDURE

✳✳ CAUTION

When adding fluid to the brake master cylinder reservoir, use only Delco Supreme 11®, GM P/N 12377967 (Canadian P/N 992667), or equivalent DOT-3 brake fluid from a clean, sealed brake fluid container. The use of any type of fluid other than the recommended type of brake fluid, may cause contamination which could result in damage to the internal rubber seals and/or rubber linings of hydraulic brake system components.

✳✳ CAUTION

Refer to the Brake Fluid Damage to Electrical Connections Caution in the Precautions section.

1. Visually inspect the brake fluid level through the brake master cylinder reservoir.

2. If the brake fluid level is at or below the half-full point during routine fluid checks, inspect the brake system for wear and possible brake fluid leaks.

3. If the brake fluid level is at or below the half-full point during routine fluid checks, and an inspection of the brake system did not reveal wear or brake fluid leaks, the brake fluid may be topped-off up to the maximum-fill level.

4. If brake system service was just completed, the brake fluid may be topped-off up to the maximum-fill level.

5. If the brake fluid level is above the half-full point, adding brake fluid is not recommended under normal conditions.

6. If brake fluid is to be added to the master cylinder reservoir, clean the outside of the reservoir on and around the reservoir cap prior to removing the cap and diaphragm.

❋❋ CAUTION

Dust and dirt accumulating on brake parts during normal use may contain asbestos fibers from production or aftermarket brake linings. Breathing excessive concentrations of asbestos fibers can cause serious bodily harm. Exercise care when servicing brake parts. Do not sand or grind brake lining unless equipment used is designed to contain the dust residue. Do not clean brake parts with compressed air or by dry brushing. To clean, dampen the brake components with a fine mist of water, then wipe the brake components clean with a damp cloth. Dispose of the cloth and all residue containing asbestos fibers in an impermeable container with the appropriate label. Follow practices prescribed by the Occupational Safety and Health Administration (OSHA) and the Environmental Protection Agency (EPA) for the handling, processing, and disposing of dust or debris that may contain asbestos fibers.

BRAKE CALIPER

REMOVAL & INSTALLATION

JH5 Brake Hydraulic Power, 4 Wheel Disc, 7,200 lbs

See Figures 6 through 9.

❋❋ WARNING

Refer to the Brakes Precautions.

1. Inspect the fluid level in the brake master cylinder reservoir.
2. If the brake fluid level is midway between the maximum-full point and the minimum allowable level, no brake fluid needs to be removed from the reservoir before proceeding.
3. If the brake fluid level is higher than midway between the maximum-full point and the minimum allowable level, remove brake fluid to the midway point before proceeding.
4. Raise and support the vehicle.
5. Remove the tire and wheel assembly.
6. If installing the original brake rotor, mark the relationship of the brake rotor to the hub.
7. Compress the brake caliper pistons.
   a. Install 2 large C-clamps over the top of the caliper housing and against the back of the outboard brake pad.

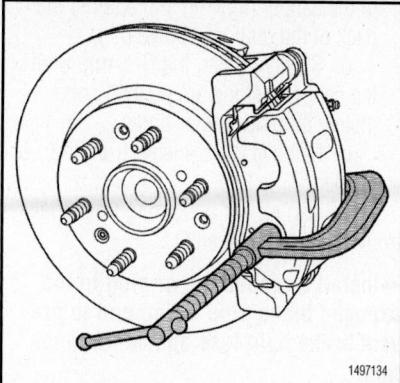

Fig. 6 Compress the brake caliper pistons

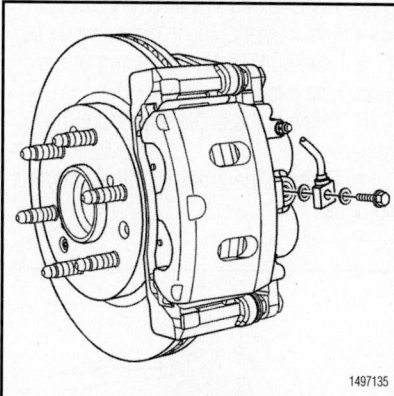

Fig. 7 Brake hose-to-caliper bolt

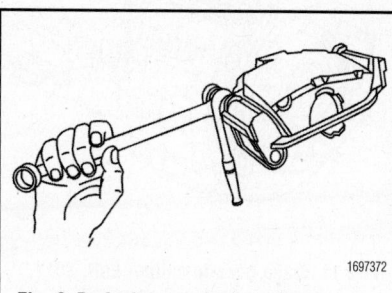

Fig. 8 Brake hose on brake caliper

b. Slowly tighten the C-clamps until the caliper pistons are pushed completely into the caliper bores.
   c. Remove the C-clamps from the caliper.
8. Clean all dirt and foreign material from the brake caliper.

➡**Cap or plug the brake hose to prevent brake fluid loss and contamination.**

9. Remove the brake hose-to-caliper bolt.

➡**Ensure the washers are not still attached to the brake hose or the brake caliper.**

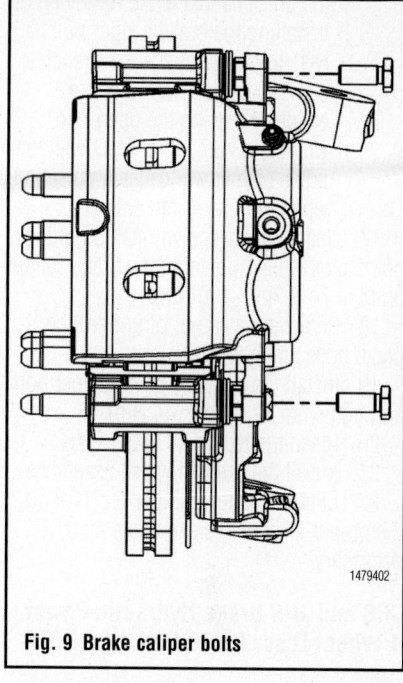

Fig. 9 Brake caliper bolts

10. Remove and discard the 2 copper brake hose gaskets.
11. Remove the brake hose from the brake caliper.

❋❋ WARNING

DO NOT use any air tools to remove or install the brake caliper bolts. Use hand tools ONLY.

➡**Install an open-end wrench to hold the caliper guide pin in line with the brake caliper while removing or installing the brake caliper bolt. DO NOT allow the open-end wrench to come in contact with the brake caliper. Allowing the open-end wrench to come in contact with the brake caliper will cause a pulsation when the brakes are applied.**

12. Using an open-end wrench to hold the guide pin, loosen the brake caliper bolts.
13. Remove the brake caliper bolts.
14. Remove the brake caliper from the mounting bracket.

To install:
15. Install the caliper to the caliper bracket.
16. Install the brake caliper bolts.

➡**DO NOT use any air tools to remove or install the brake caliper bolts. Use hand tools ONLY.**

- Install an open-end wrench to hold the caliper guide pin in line with the brake caliper while removing or installing the brake caliper bolt. DO NOT allow the open-end wrench to come in contact with the brake caliper. Allowing the open-end wrench to come in contact with the brake caliper will cause a pulsation when the brakes are applied.

17. Use an open-end wrench to hold the guide pins while tightening the brake caliper bolts to 74 ft. lbs. (100 Nm).

18. Remove the cap or plug from the brake hose fitting end.

19. Install the brake hose-to-caliper bolt and tighten to 32 ft. lbs. (44 Nm).

20. Bleed the hydraulic brake system.

21. Install the tire and wheel assembly.

22. Fill the master cylinder reservoir to the proper level with clean brake fluid, if necessary.

JH6 and JH9 Brake Hydraulic Power, 4 Wheel Disc, 9,900 lbs and 14,050 lbs

See Figures 10 through 12.

✳✳ WARNING

Refer to the Brakes Precautions.

1. Inspect the fluid level in the brake master cylinder reservoir.

2. If the brake fluid level is midway between the maximum-full point and the minimum allowable level, no brake fluid needs to be removed from the reservoir before proceeding.

3. If the brake fluid level is higher than midway between the maximum-full point and the minimum allowable level, remove brake fluid to the midway point before proceeding.

4. Raise and support the vehicle.

5. Remove the tire and wheel assembly.

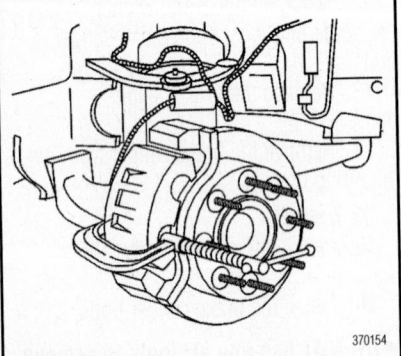

Fig. 10 Compress the brake caliper pistons

370154

6. Compress the brake caliper pistons.
   a. Install a large C-clamp over the top of the caliper housing and against the back of the outboard brake pad.
   b. Slowly tighten the C-clamp until the caliper pistons are pushed completely into the caliper bores.
   c. Remove the C-clamp from the caliper.

7. Clean all dirt and foreign material from the brake hose end.

➡**Install a rubber cap or plug to the exposed brake pipe fitting end to prevent brake fluid loss and contamination.**

8. Remove the brake hose-to-caliper bolt from the brake caliper.

9. Remove and discard the 2 copper brake hose gaskets. These gaskets may be stuck to the brake caliper housing or the brake hose end.

10. Remove the brake hose from the caliper.

11. Remove the 2 brake caliper mounting bolts.

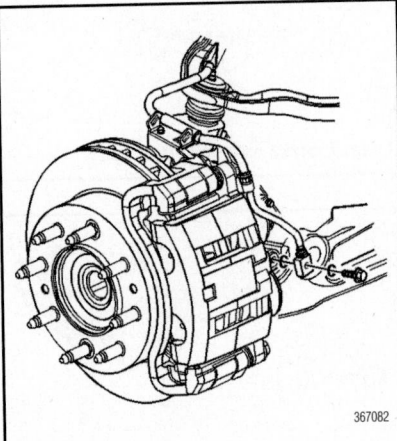

Fig. 11 Brake hose-to-caliper bolt, 2011 model shown

367082

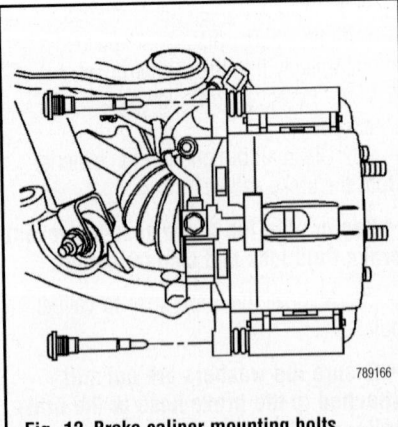

Fig. 12 Brake caliper mounting bolts

789166

✳✳ CAUTION

Danger: Do not depress the brake pedal with the brake rotors/calipers and/or the brake discs removed. It may damage the brake system. If brake system damage occurs and is not repaired, vehicle damage and/or personal injury or death may result.

12. Remove the brake caliper from the brake caliper mounting bracket.

To install:

13. Install the brake caliper to the brake caliper mounting bracket.

14. Perform the following procedure before installing the caliper mounting bolts:
   a. Remove all traces of the original adhesive patch.
   b. Clean the threads of the bolt with brake parts cleaner or the equivalent and allow the bolt threads to dry.
   c. Apply thread locker GM P/N 12345493 (Canadian P/N 10953488) to the threads of the bolt.

15. Install the 2 brake caliper mounting bolts and tighten to 80 ft. lbs. (108 Nm).

16. Remove the rubber cap or plug from the exposed brake hose fitting end.

➡**Install 2 new copper brake hose gaskets.**

17. Assemble the 2 new copper brake hose gaskets and the brake hose to caliper bolt to the brake hose.

18. Install the brake hose to caliper bolt to the brake caliper and tighten to 32 ft. lbs. (44 Nm).

19. Bleed the hydraulic brake system.

20. Install the tire and wheel assembly.

21. Lower the vehicle.

22. Fill the master cylinder reservoir to the proper level with clean brake fluid.

DISC BRAKE PADS

REMOVAL & INSTALLATION

JH5 Brake Hydraulic Power, 4 Wheel Disc, 7,200 lbs

See Figures 13 through 15.

✳✳ WARNING

Refer to the Brakes Precautions.

1. Inspect the fluid level in the brake master cylinder reservoir.

2. If the brake fluid level is midway between the maximum-full point and the minimum allowable level, no brake fluid needs to be removed from the reservoir before proceeding.

3. If the brake fluid level is higher than midway between the maximum-full point and the minimum allowable level, remove brake fluid to the midway point before proceeding.

4. Raise and support the vehicle.

5. Remove the tire and wheel assembly.

6. Compress the brake caliper pistons.

a. Install 2 large C-clamps over the top of the caliper housing and against the back of the outboard brake pad.

b. Slowly tighten the C-clamps until the caliper pistons are pushed completely into the caliper bores.

c. Remove the C-clamps from the caliper.

➡**DO NOT use any air tools to remove or install the brake caliper bolts. Use hand tools ONLY.**

• Install an open-end wrench to hold the caliper guide pin in line with the brake caliper while removing or installing the brake caliper bolt. DO NOT allow the open-end wrench to come in contact with the brake caliper. Allowing the open-end wrench to come in contact with the

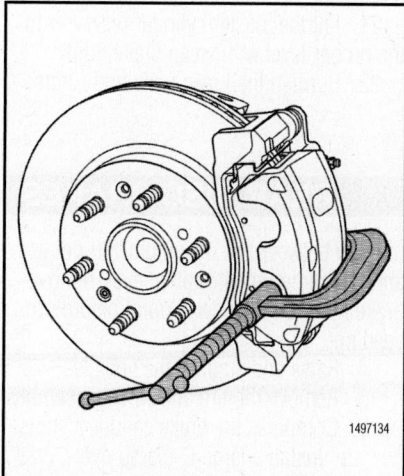

Fig. 13 Compress the brake caliper pistons

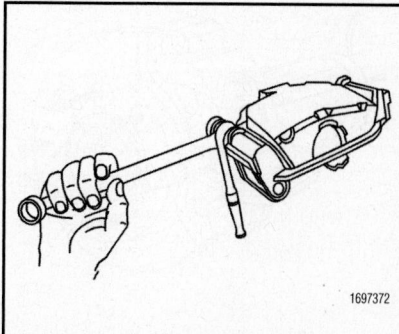

Fig. 14 Brake caliper guide pin bolts

brake caliper will cause a pulsation when the brakes are applied.

7. Using an open-end wrench to hold the guide pin, loosen the brake caliper bolts.

8. Using an open end wrench to hold the guide pin, loosen the brake caliper guide pin bolt.

9. Remove the lower brake caliper guide pin bolt (1).

✳✳ CAUTION

Support the brake caliper with heavy mechanic wire, or equivalent, whenever it is separated from its mount and the hydraulic flexible brake hose is still connected. Failure to support the caliper in this manner will cause the flexible brake hose to bear the weight of the caliper, which may cause damage to the brake hose and in turn may cause a brake fluid leak.

➡**DO NOT disconnect the flexible brake hose from the brake caliper.**

10. Rotate the brake caliper (2) upward until it rests on the brake caliper mounting bracket and support with heavy mechanics wire or an equivalent.

➡**If installing the original brake pads, mark the position of the inner and outer brake pads for proper installation.**

11. Remove the brake pads (3).

➡**If installing the original brake pads and spring clips, mark the position of the pads and spring clips for proper installation. If installing new brake pads, install new pad spring clips. Do not reuse the old brake pad spring clips with new brake pads.**

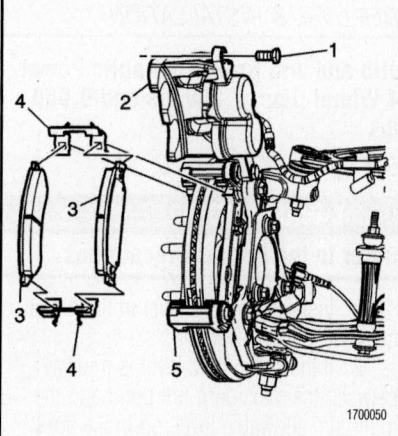

Fig. 15 Lower brake caliper guide pin bolt (1), caliper (2), pins (3), pad spring clips (4), and mounting bracket (5)

12. Remove the brake pad spring clips (4) from the mounting bracket (5).

13. Thoroughly clean the pad hardware mating surfaces of the caliper bracket of any corrosion or debris with denatured alcohol and allow the mating surfaces to dry.

➡**Use care when cleaning the brake caliper pistons to avoid damaging the piston dust seals.**

If installing new brake pads, thoroughly clean the brake caliper piston faces and caliper housing to brake pad contact surfaces of all disc brake pad insulator adhesive residue with denatured alcohol and allow the piston faces to dry.

To install:

14. Apply a very thin coating of high temperature silicone brake lubricant to the pad mating surfaces of the caliper bracket only.

15. Install the spring clips to the mounting bracket.

a. Install the NEW spring clips if replacing the brake pads.

b. Install the original spring clips in their original position if installing the original brake pads.

16. If installing new brake pads, remove the adhesive backing paper from the brake pad insulators.

➡**If installing the original brake pads, position the brake pads as marked during the removal procedure.**

17. Install the brake pads.

18. Rotate the brake caliper into the proper position on the mounting bracket.

➡**DO NOT use any air tools to remove or tighten the guide pin bolts. Use hand tools ONLY.**

➡**Install an open-end wrench to hold the caliper guide pin in line with the caliper while removing or installing the caliper. DO NOT allow the wrench to come in contact with the brake caliper. Allowing the wrench to come in contact with the brake caliper will cause a pulsation when the brakes are applied.**

19. Use an open-end wrench to hold the caliper guide pin while tightening the brake caliper guide pin bolt to 74 ft. lbs. (100 Nm).

20. Install the tire and wheel assembly.

21. Lower the vehicle.

22. With the engine OFF, gradually apply the brake pedal to approximately 2/3 of its travel distance.

23. Slowly release the brake pedal.

24. Wait 15 seconds, then repeat steps 9–10 until a firm pedal is obtained to properly seat the brake caliper pistons and pads.

25. Fill the brake master cylinder reservoir to the proper level with clean brake fluid, if necessary.

26. Firmly apply and maintain pressure on the brake pedal for 30 seconds to seat the brake pad insulators to the brake caliper pistons and caliper housing. Repeat this step 1 additional time.

27. Burnish the brake pads and rotors.

JH6 and JH9 Brake Hydraulic Power, 4 Wheel Disc, 9,900 lbs and 14,050 lbs

See Figure 16.

✳✳ WARNING

Refer to the Brakes Precautions.

1. Inspect the fluid level in the brake master cylinder reservoir.

2. If the brake fluid level is midway between the maximum-full point and the minimum allowable level, no brake fluid needs to be removed from the reservoir before proceeding.

3. If the brake fluid level is higher than midway between the maximum-full point and the minimum allowable level, remove brake fluid to the midway point before proceeding.

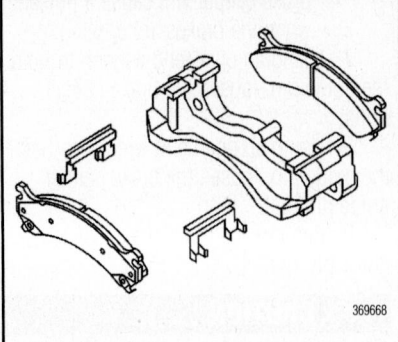

Fig. 16 Front disc brake pad replacement components

4. Raise and support the vehicle.
5. Remove the tire and wheel assembly.
6. Inspect the caliper operation.

✳✳ CAUTION

Support the brake caliper with heavy mechanic wire, or an equivalent, whenever it is separated from its mount and the hydraulic flexible brake hose is still connected. Failure to support the caliper in this manner will cause the flexible brake hose to bear the weight of the caliper, which may cause damage to the brake hose and in turn may cause a brake fluid leak.

7. Remove the caliper from the mounting bracket and support the caliper with

heavy mechanic wire or an equivalent. DO NOT disconnect the hydraulic brake flexible hose from the caliper.

8. Remove the brake pads from the caliper mounting bracket.

9. Remove and discard the anti-rattle clips from the brake caliper mounting bracket.

10. Inspect the caliper and mounting bracket.

To install:

11. Install new anti-rattle clips to the inside ends of the caliper mounting bracket.

12. Install the brake pads to the caliper mounting bracket.

13. Place the new pads in the same orientation as noted during removal.

14. Install the brake caliper.

15. Install the tire and wheel assembly.

16. Remove the safety stands.

17. Lower the vehicle.

18. With the engine OFF, gradually apply the brake pedal to approximately 2/3 of its travel distance.

19. Slowly release the brake pedal.

20. Wait 15 seconds, then repeat steps 8–9 until a firm pedal is obtained. This will properly seat the brake caliper pistons and brake pads.

21. Fill the master cylinder reservoir to the proper level with clean brake fluid.

22. Burnish the brake pads and rotors.

BRAKES

✳✳ CAUTION

Dust and dirt accumulating on brake parts during normal use may contain asbestos fibers from production or aftermarket brake linings. Breathing excessive concentrations of asbestos fibers can cause serious bodily harm. Exercise care when servicing brake parts. Do not sand or grind brake lining unless equipment used is designed to contain the dust residue. Do not clean brake parts with compressed air or by dry brushing. To clean, dampen the brake components with a fine mist of water, then wipe the brake components clean with a damp cloth. Dispose of the cloth and all residue containing asbestos fibers in an impermeable container with the appropriate label. Follow practices prescribed by the Occupational Safety and Health Administration (OSHA) and the Environmental Protection Agency (EPA) for the han-

dling, processing, and disposing of dust or debris that may contain asbestos fibers.

BRAKE CALIPER

REMOVAL & INSTALLATION

JH5 and JH6 Brake Hydraulic Power, 4 Wheel Disc, 7,200 lbs and 9,900 lbs

See Figures 17 through 20.

✳✳ WARNING

Refer to the Brakes Precautions.

1. Inspect the fluid level in the brake master cylinder reservoir.

2. If the brake fluid level is midway between the maximum-full point and the minimum allowable level, no brake fluid needs to be removed from the reservoir before proceeding.

3. If the brake fluid level is higher than

REAR DISC BRAKES

midway between the maximum-full point and the minimum allowable level, remove brake fluid to the midway point before proceeding.

4. Raise and support the vehicle.

5. Remove the tire and wheel assembly.

6. Compress the brake caliper pistons.

a. Install a large C-clamp over the top of the caliper housing and

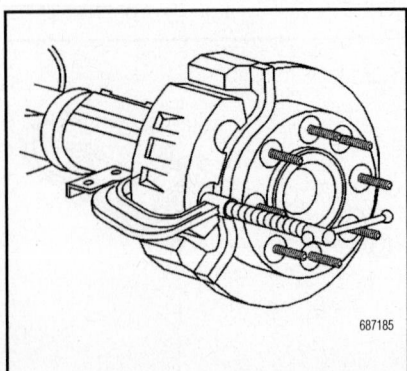

Fig. 17 Rear caliper brake replacement

against the back of the outboard brake pad.

b. Slowly tighten the C-clamp until the caliper pistons are pushed completely into the caliper bores.

c. Remove the C-clamp from the caliper.

7. Clean all dirt and foreign material from the brake hose end.

8. Remove the brake hose fitting bolt from the brake caliper.

9. Cap the brake hose fitting to prevent brake fluid loss and contamination.

10. Remove and discard the 2 copper brake hose gaskets. These gaskets may be stuck to the brake caliper housing or the brake hose end.

11. Remove the caliper guide pin bolts.

12. Remove the brake caliper from the vehicle.

13. Inspect the caliper assembly.

To install:

➡**Use denatured alcohol to clean the outside surface of caliper boots before installing new brake pads.**

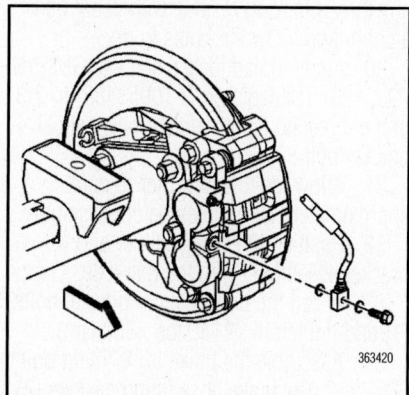

Fig. 18 Compress the brake caliper pistons

14. If you are installing new brake pads use a C-clamp in order to compress the pistons to the bottom of the caliper bores. Use the old brake pad, a metal plate or a wooden block across the face of the pistons in order to protect the pistons and the caliper boots.

➡**Use a small flat-bladed tool and lift the inner edge of the caliper boots next to both pistons to release any trapped air.**

15. Ensure that the caliper boots are below the level of the face of both pistons.

16. Install the brake caliper to the brake caliper mounting bracket.

17. Perform the following procedure before installing the caliper guide pin bolts.

a. Remove all traces of the original adhesive patch.

b. Clean the threads of the bolt with brake parts cleaner or the equivalent and allow to dry.

c. Apply thread locker, such as GM P/N 12345493 (Canadian P/N 10953488) to the threads of the bolt.

d. Install the rear brake caliper guide pin bolts.

18. Tighten the rear brake caliper guide pin bolts; the specifications are different for the JH5 and the JH6:

a. Tighten the bolts to 25 ft. lbs. (34 Nm) for the JH5 (7200 lbs).

b. Tighten the bolts to 53 ft. lbs. (72 Nm) for the JH6 (9,900 lbs).

19. Remove the cap from the brake hose fitting end.

➡**Install 2 NEW copper brake hose gaskets.**

20. Assemble 2 NEW copper brake hose gaskets and the brake hose fitting bolt to the brake hose.

21. Install the brake hose assembly to the brake caliper and tighten the brake hose fitting bolt to 32 ft. lbs. (44 Nm).

22. Bleed the hydraulic brake system.

23. Install the tire and wheel assembly.

24. Fill the master cylinder reservoir to the proper level with clean brake fluid.

JH9 Brake Hydraulic Power, 4 Wheel Disc, 14,050 lbs

See Figures 21 through 27.

✳✳ WARNING

Refer to the Brakes Precautions.

1. Inspect the fluid level in the brake master cylinder reservoir.

2. If the brake fluid level is midway between the maximum-full point and the minimum allowable level, no brake fluid needs to be removed from the reservoir before proceeding.

3. If the brake fluid level is higher than midway between the maximum-full point and the minimum allowable level, remove brake fluid to the midway point before proceeding.

4. Raise and support the vehicle.

5. Remove the tire and wheel assembly.

6. Position a large C-clamp against the outboard disc brake pad backing plate and over the rear of the brake caliper body.

7. Using the C-clamp, slowly and evenly bottom the brake caliper pistons into the brake caliper bores.

8. Remove the brake hose fitting bolt (1).

➡**Do not reuse the brake hose fitting gaskets.**

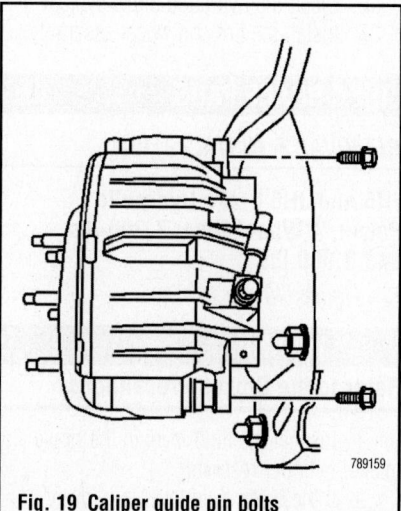

Fig. 19 Caliper guide pin bolts

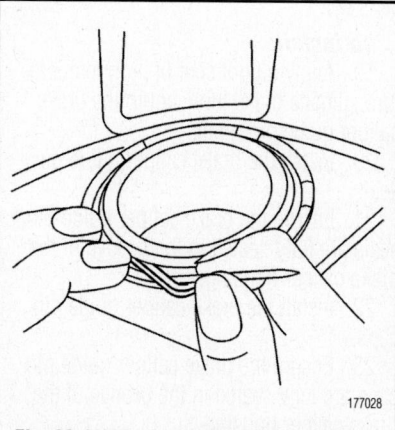

Fig. 20 Lift the inner edge of the caliper boots next to both pistons to release any trapped air

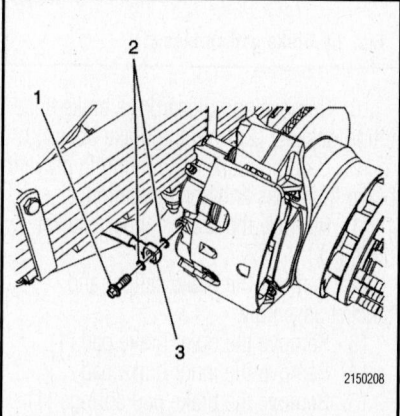

Fig. 21 Brake hose fitting bolt (1), brake hose fitting gaskets (2), and brake hose (3)

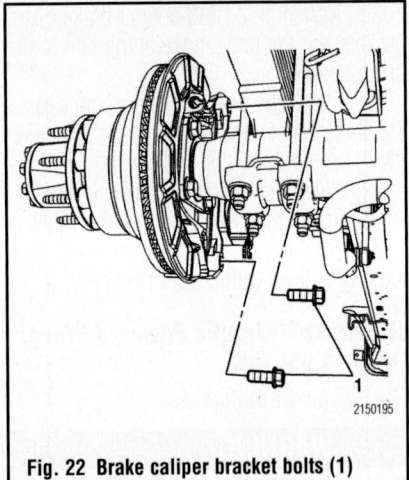

Fig. 22 Brake caliper bracket bolts (1)

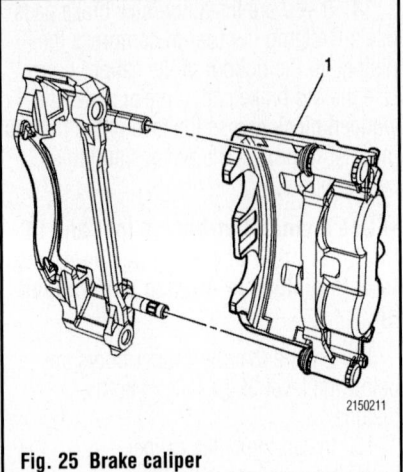

Fig. 25 Brake caliper

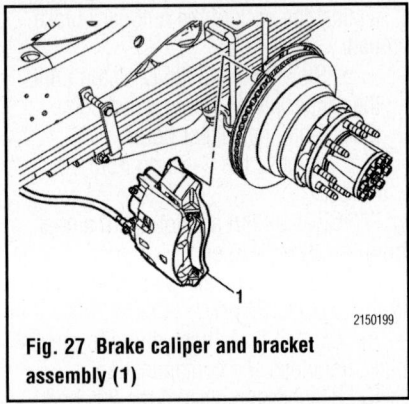

Fig. 27 Brake caliper and bracket assembly (1)

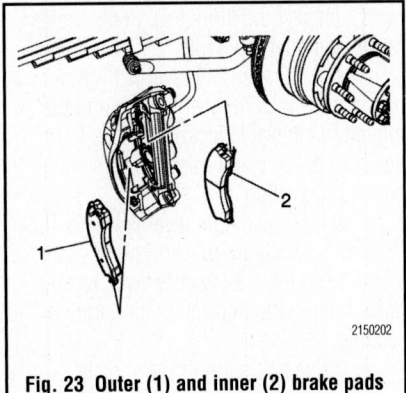

Fig. 23 Outer (1) and inner (2) brake pads

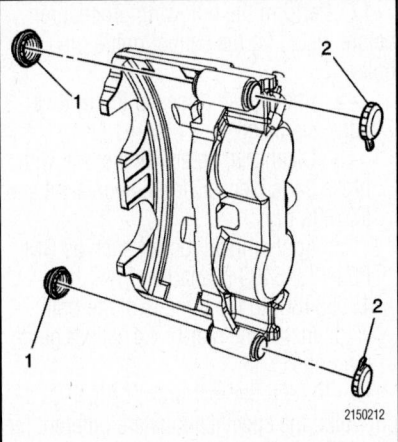

Fig. 26 Brake caliper guide pin seals (1) and the brake caliper guide pin caps (2)

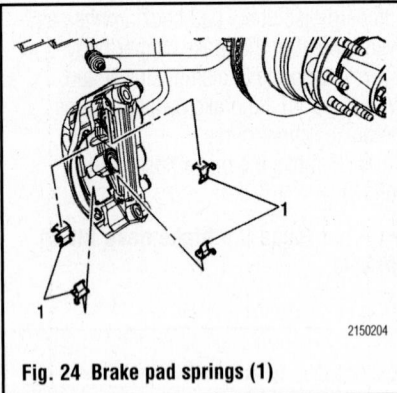

Fig. 24 Brake pad springs (1)

9. Remove and discard the brake hose fitting gaskets (2) from the brake hose (3).

10. Cap the brake hose fitting to prevent brake fluid loss and contamination.

11. Remove the brake caliper bracket bolts (1).

12. Remove the brake caliper and bracket assembly.

13. Remove the outer brake pad (1).

14. Remove the inner brake pad (2).

15. Remove the brake pad springs (1).

➡**Do not remove the brake caliper guide pins unless replacement is required.**

16. Slide the brake caliper (1) off of the brake caliper guide pins and the caliper bracket.

17. Inspect the brake caliper mounting and hardware for damage and wear.

18. Remove the brake caliper guide pin seals (1) and the brake caliper guide pin caps (2).

To install:

19. Apply a light coat of high temperature silicone brake lubricant to the brake caliper guide pin bores.

20. Install the brake caliper guide pin seals.

21. Ensure the brake caliper guide pin seals are fully seated in the groove of the brake caliper housing.

22. Install the brake caliper guide pin caps.

23. Ensure the brake caliper guide pin caps are fully seated in the groove of the brake caliper housing.

➡**Do not remove the brake caliper guide pins unless replacement is required.**

24. Slide the brake caliper onto the brake caliper guide pins and the caliper bracket.

25. Ensure the brake caliper guide pin seals are fully seated in the groove of the brake caliper bracket.

26. Install the brake pad springs.

27. Prepare the brake caliper bracket bolts and the rear axle threaded holes for assembly.

28. Clean the brake caliper bracket bolts of any thread locking residue

29. Clean the rear axle threaded holes of any thread locking residue with denatured alcohol and allow the holes to dry

30. Apply thread locker, such as GM P/N 89021297 (Canadian P/N 10953488) to 2/3 of the threaded length of the brake caliper bracket bolt.

31. Allow the thread locker to cure approximately 10 minutes before assembly.

32. Position the brake caliper and bracket assembly (1) to the rear axle.

33. Install the brake caliper bracket bolts (1) and tighten to 221 ft. lbs. (300 Nm).

34. Assemble the brake hose fitting bolt (1) and 2 new brake hose fitting gaskets (2) to the brake hose (3).

35. Tighten the brake hose fitting bolt to 30 ft. lbs. (40 Nm).

36. Bleed the hydraulic brake system.

37. Install the tire and wheel assembly.

DISC BRAKE PADS

REMOVAL & INSTALLATION

JH5 and JH6 Brake Hydraulic Power, 4 Wheel Disc, 7,200 lbs and 9,900 lbs

See Figures 28 and 29.

✳✳ WARNING

Refer to the Brakes Precautions.

1. Inspect the fluid level in the brake master cylinder reservoir.

2. If the brake fluid level is midway between the maximum-full point and the

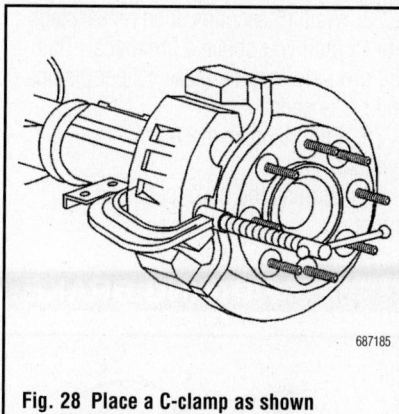

Fig. 28 Place a C-clamp as shown

minimum allowable level, no brake fluid needs to be removed from the reservoir before proceeding.

3. If the brake fluid level is higher than midway between the maximum-full point and the minimum allowable level, remove brake fluid to the midway point before proceeding.

4. Raise and support the vehicle.

5. Remove the tire and wheel assembly.

6. Inspect the caliper operation.

7. Place a C-clamp as shown. Slowly bottom the pistons of the caliper. It may be necessary to reposition the C-clamp to allow both of the pistons to bottom into the caliper bores.

✳✳ CAUTION

Support the brake caliper with heavy mechanic wire, or an equivalent, whenever it is separated from its mount and the hydraulic flexible brake hose is still connected. Failure to support the caliper in this manner will cause the flexible brake hose to bear the weight of the caliper, which may cause damage to the brake hose and in turn may cause a brake fluid leak.

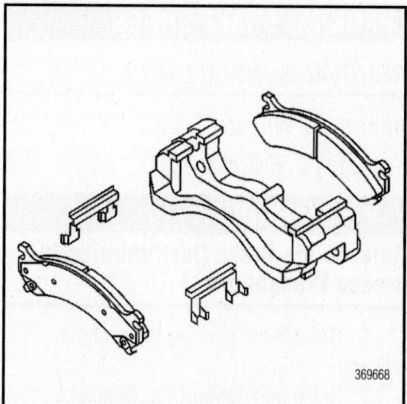

Fig. 29 Brake pad components

8. Remove the caliper from the mounting bracket and support the caliper with heavy mechanic's wire or an equivalent. DO NOT disconnect the hydraulic brake flexible hose from the caliper.

9. Inspect the caliper assembly.

10. Remove the brake pads from the brake caliper bracket. Note the orientation.

11. Remove and discard the anti-rattle clips from the brake caliper mounting bracket.

To install:

12. Install the anti-rattle clips to the brake caliper bracket.

13. Install the brake caliper.

14. Install the brake pads to the brake caliper bracket. Place the new pads in the same orientation as noted during removal.

15. Install the tire and wheel assembly.

16. Lower the vehicle.

17. With the engine OFF, gradually apply the brake pedal to approximately 2/3 of its travel distance.

18. Slowly release the brake pedal.

19. Wait 15 seconds, then repeat steps 6–7 until a firm pedal is obtained. This will properly seat the brake caliper pistons and brake pads.

20. Fill the master cylinder reservoir to the proper level with clean brake fluid.

21. Burnish the brakes pads and rotors as necessary.

JH9 Brake Hydraulic Power, 4 Wheel Disc, 14,050 lbs

See Figures 22 through 24, 27 and 30.

✳✳ WARNING

Refer to the Brakes Precautions.

1. Inspect the fluid level in the brake master cylinder reservoir.

2. If the brake fluid level is midway between the maximum-full point and the minimum allowable level, no brake fluid needs to be removed from the reservoir before proceeding.

3. If the brake fluid level is higher than midway between the maximum-full point and the minimum allowable level, remove brake fluid to the midway point before proceeding.

4. Raise and support the vehicle.

5. Remove the tire and wheel assembly.

➥**Do not remove the brake caliper guide pins unless replacement is required.**

6. Remove the brake caliper bracket bolts (1).

✳✳ CAUTION

Support the brake caliper with heavy mechanic wire, or an equivalent, whenever it is separated from its mount and the hydraulic flexible brake hose is still connected. Failure to support the caliper in this manner will cause the flexible brake hose to bear the weight of the caliper, which may cause damage to the brake hose and in turn may cause a brake fluid leak.

7. Remove the brake caliper and bracket assembly (1) and support it with heavy mechanics wire or an equivalent.

8. Remove the outer brake pad (1).

9. Remove the inner brake pad (2).

10. Remove the brake pad springs (1).

11. Clean the brake pad springs contact areas of the brake caliper bracket of any accumulated corrosion and debris.

To install:

12. Ensure the brake caliper guide pin caps (1) are in good condition and firmly seated on the brake caliper body.

13. Replace any missing or damaged brake caliper guide pin caps.

14. Without disengaging the brake caliper from the brake caliper guide pins, inspect the brake caliper hardware.

15. Install the brake pad springs.

16. Install the outer brake pad.

17. Install the inner brake pad.

18. Prepare the brake caliper bracket bolts and the rear axle threaded holes for assembly.

19. Clean the brake caliper bracket bolts of any thread locking residue.

20. Clean the rear axle threaded holes of any thread locking residue with denatured alcohol and allow the holes to dry

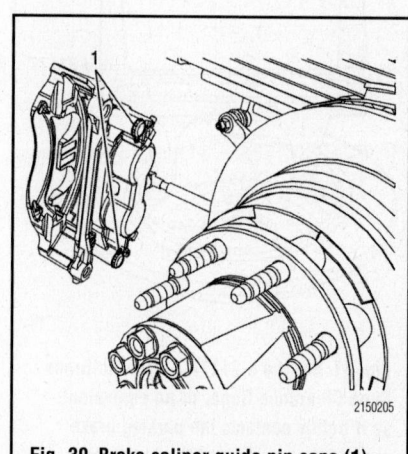

Fig. 30 Brake caliper guide pin caps (1)

21. Apply thread locker, such as GM P/N 89021297 (Canadian P/N 10953488), to 2/3 of the threaded length of the brake caliper bracket bolt.

22. Allow the thread locker to cure approximately 10 minutes before assembly.

23. Position the brake caliper and bracket assembly to the rear axle.

24. Install the brake caliper bracket bolts and tighten to 221 ft. lbs. (300 Nm).

25. Install the tire and wheel assembly.

26. With the engine OFF, gradually apply the brake pedal to approximately 2/3 of its travel distance.

27. Slowly release the brake pedal.

28. Wait 15 seconds, then repeat steps 14–15 until you obtain a firm pedal. This will properly seat the brake caliper pistons and brake pads.

29. Fill the brake master cylinder.

30. Burnish the brake pads and rotors.

BRAKES   PARKING BRAKE

PARKING BRAKE

ADJUSTMENT

Dual Rear Wheels

See Figures 31 and 32.

> ❊❊ **WARNING**
>
> **Refer to the Brake Dust Warning in Brakes Precautions.**

1. Remove the rear disc brake rotor.

2. Set the J-21177-A Drum-to-Brake Shoe Clearance Gage, or an equivalent, so it lightly contacts the parking brake shoe friction surface of the brake rotor.

3. Position the drum-to-brake shoe clearance gauge over the parking brake shoes (1) at the widest point.

4. Rotate the parking brake adjuster until the parking brake shoes just contact the drum-to-brake shoe clearance gauge.

5. Using a feeler gage, set the parking brake shoe clearance to 0.024 in. (0.62 mm).

6. Repeat steps 1–4 for the opposite parking brake assembly.

7. Install the rear disc brake rotor.

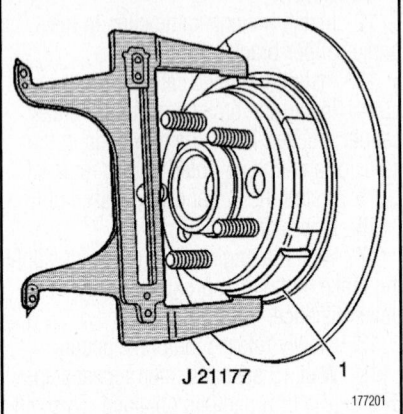

Fig. 32 Position the drum-to-brake shoe clearance gauge over the parking brake shoes (1) at the widest point

Single Rear Wheels

See Figures 33 and 34.

> ❊❊ **WARNING**
>
> **Refer to the Brake Dust Warning in Brakes Precautions.**

➡ **Adjust the park brake shoes before adjusting the park brake pedal.**

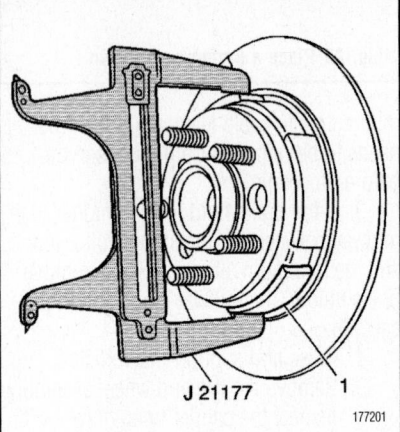

Fig. 34 Position the drum-to-brake shoe clearance gauge over the shoe and the lining at the widest point.

1. Set the J-21177-A Drum-to-Brake Shoe Clearance Gage, or an equivalent, so it contacts the inside diameter of the rotor.

2. Position the drum-to-brake shoe clearance gauge over the shoe and the lining at the widest point.

3. Turn the adjuster nut until the lining just contacts the drum-to-brake shoe clearance gauge.

4. Repeat steps 1–3 for the opposite side.

5. The clearance between the park brake shoe and the rotor is 0.026 in (0.6604 mm).

PARKING BRAKE SHOES

REMOVAL & INSTALLATION

Dual Rear Wheel

See Figures 35 through 41.

> ❊❊ **WARNING**
>
> **Refer to the Brake Dust Warning in Brakes Precautions.**

1. Disable the parking brake cable adjuster.

2. Raise and support the vehicle.

3. Remove the tire and wheel assembly.

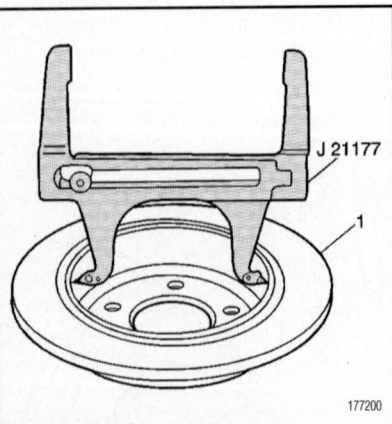

Fig. 31 Set the J-21177-A Drum-to-Brake Shoe Clearance Gage, or an equivalent, so it lightly contacts the parking brake shoe friction surface of the brake rotor

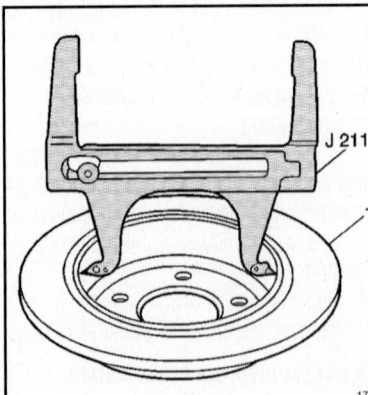

Fig. 33 Set the J-21177-A Drum-to-Brake Shoe Clearance Gage, or an equivalent, so it contacts the inside diameter of the rotor.

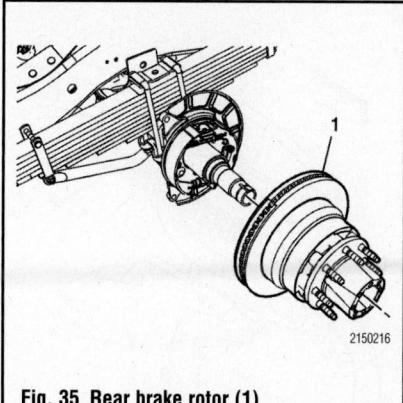

Fig. 35 Rear brake rotor (1)

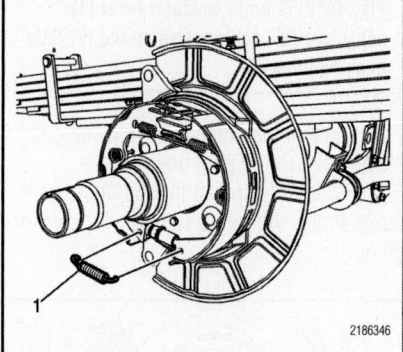

Fig. 36 Parking brake shoe adjuster spring (1)

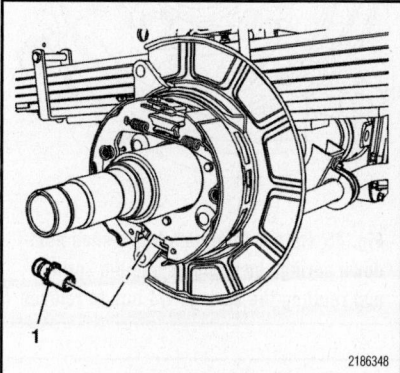

Fig. 37 Parking brake shoe adjuster (1)

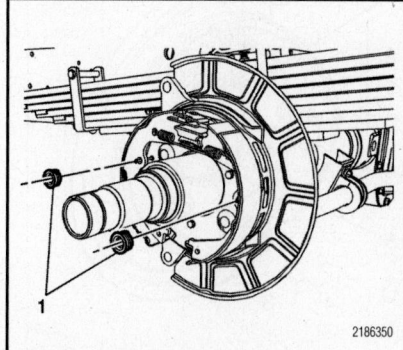

Fig. 38 Parking brake shoe hold-down springs and cups (1)

➡ Do not separate the brake rotor from the wheel hub.

4. Remove the rear brake rotor (1).

5. Remove the parking brake shoe adjuster spring (1).

6. Rotate the parking brake adjuster star wheel to retract the parking brake shoes, if necessary.

7. Remove the parking brake shoe adjuster (1).

8. Disassemble and clean the parking brake shoe adjuster assembly.

9. Apply high-temperature brake lubricant to the threads of the parking brake shoe adjuster.

10. Remove the parking brake shoe hold-down springs and cups (1).

11. Compress the springs and rotate the springs and cups 1/4 turn to disengage the cups from the hold-down spring pins.

12. Remove the parking brake shoe hold-down spring pins (1).

13. Grasp the parking brake shoe (1) and pull out and upward to release the parking brake shoe from the park brake shoe actuator.

14. Pull the parking brake shoe over the parking brake shoe actuator and remove the parking brake shoes as an assembly.

➡ Position the inner parking brake shoe return spring below the outer parking brake shoe return spring.

15. Remove the inner parking brake shoe return spring (1).

16. Remove the outer parking brake shoe return spring (2).

17. Clean the parking brake shoe contact surfaces on the parking brake shield.

To install:

18. Apply high-temperature brake lubricant to the parking brake shoe contact surfaces on the parking brake shield.

➡ Position the inner parking brake shoe return spring below the outer parking brake shoe return spring.

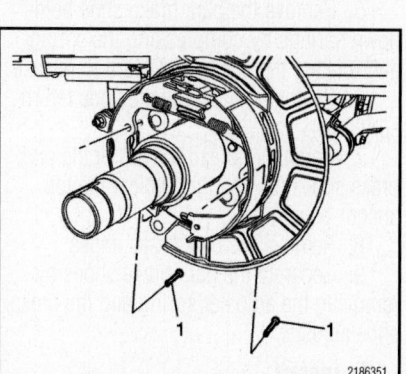

Fig. 39 Parking brake shoe hold-down spring pins (1)

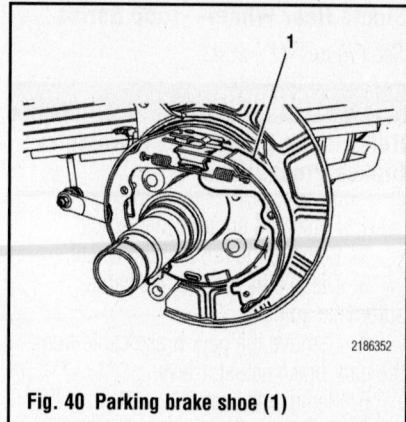

Fig. 40 Parking brake shoe (1)

19. Install the inner parking brake shoe return spring.

20. Install the outer parking brake shoe return spring.

21. Be sure to position the outer parking brake shoe return spring above the inner parking brake shoe return spring.

22. Position the parking brake shoe assembly to the parking brake shield.

23. Grasp the parking brake shoe and pull the parking brake shoe over the parking brake shoe actuator.

24. Install the parking brake shoe hold-down spring pins.

25. Install the parking brake shoe hold-down springs and cups.

26. Compress the springs and rotate the springs and cups 1/4 turn to engage the cups to the hold-down spring pins.

27. Assemble the parking brake shoe adjuster to the fully retracted position.

28. Install the parking brake shoe adjuster.

29. Install the parking brake shoe adjuster spring.

30. Install the rear brake rotor.

31. Install the tire and wheel assembly.

32. Enable the parking brake cable adjuster.

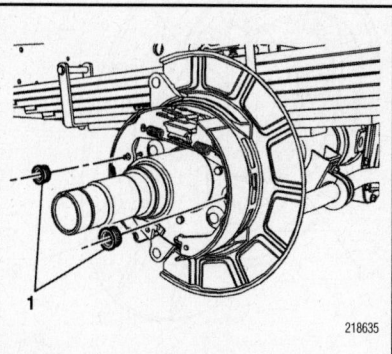

Fig. 41 Inner (1) and outer (2) parking brake shoe return springs

Single Rear Wheel—1500 Series

See Figures 42 and 43.

✳✳ WARNING

Refer to the Brake Dust Warning in Brakes Precautions.

1. Raise and support the vehicle.
2. Remove the tire and the wheel.
3. Disable the park brake cable automatic adjuster.
4. Remove the park brake cable from the park brake actuator lever.
5. Remove the rotor.
6. Turn the adjustment screw (1) to the fully home position in the notched adjustment nut.
7. Remove the park brake shoe assembly from the backing plate:
    a. Remove the tips from the slots
    b. Slide the shoe (2) toward the retaining spring (3) until the shoe disengages from the spring, and
8. Remove the park brake shoe assembly from the vehicle:
    a. Place one of the open ends of the shoe over the axle flange and,
    b. Rotate the shoe until it has cleared the flange.

To install:

9. Align the slots in both the adjusting screw and tappet to be parallel with the backing plate face.
10. Install the park brake shoe assembly to the vehicle by placing one of the open ends of the shoe over the axle flange and rotating the shoe until it is behind the flange.
11. Position the park brake shoe in the inboard side of the actuator.
12. Slide the park brake shoe into position and seat into the retaining spring.

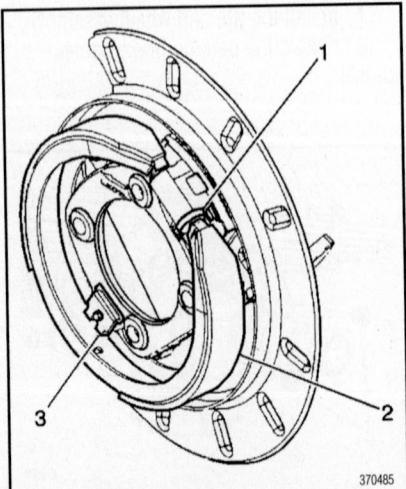

Fig. 42 Adjustment screw (1), shoe (2), and retaining spring (3)

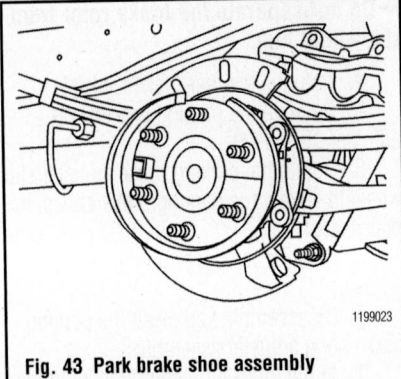

Fig. 43 Park brake shoe assembly

13. Inspect the shoe assembly position. The shoe must be central on the backing plate with both tips located in the slots.
14. Adjust the park brake shoe.
15. Install the rotor.
16. Install the park brake cable to the park brake actuator lever.
17. Enable the park brake automatic cable adjuster.
18. Install the tire and wheel.
19. Remove the safety stands.
20. Lower the vehicle.
21. Adjust park brake cable.

Single Rear Wheel —2500 and 3500 Series

See Figures 44 through 46.

✳✳ WARNING

Refer to the Brake Dust Warning in Brakes Precautions.

1. Disable the park brake cable automatic adjuster.
2. Raise and support the vehicle.
3. Remove the rear brake rotor.
4. Disconnect the park brake cable eye (2) from the park brake actuator lever (1). Compress the park brake cable return spring (3) and release the park brake cable conduit from the backing plate (4) by pressing the locking tabs on the cable conduit.
5. Remove the park brake shoe hold-down springs by compressing the spring and rotating the springs 1/4 turn to release.
6. Remove the park brake shoe return spring (6).
7. Carefully spread the top of the park brake shoes (2) enough to clear the top anchor point.
8. Remove the park brake shoes.
9. Separate the park brake shoes by removing the adjuster spring and the brake shoe adjuster.

To install:

10. Clean the debris and the dust from the park brake components using a clean shop cloth.

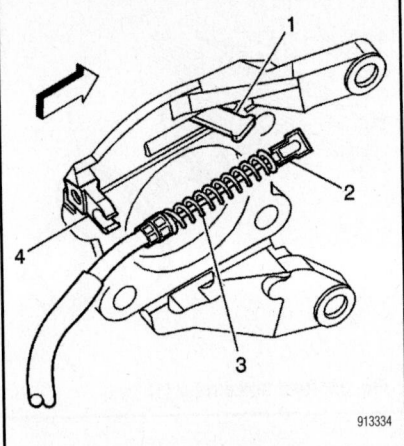

Fig. 44 Park brake actuator lever (1), cable eye (2), cable return spring (3), and backing plate (4)

11. Install the brake shoe adjuster and the adjuster to the park brake shoes.
12. Carefully spread the top of the park brake shoes enough to clear the top anchor point.

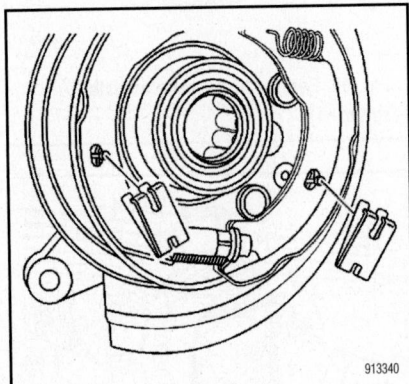

Fig. 45 Remove the park brake shoe hold-down springs by compressing the spring and rotating the springs 1/4 turn to release

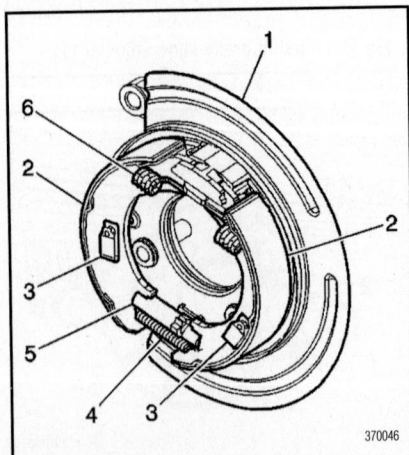

Fig. 46 Park brake shoes (2) and shoe return spring (6)

13. Install the park brake shoe hold-down springs by compressing the spring and rotating the springs 1/4 turn.

14. Install the park brake shoe return spring.

15. Adjust the park brake shoe.

16. Install the disc brake rotor.

17. Install the park brake cable eyelet to the actuator lever.

18. Compress the park brake cable return spring and install the park brake cable conduit to the backing plate.

19. Push the cable conduit into place until the locking tabs are fully

engaged in the park brake cable bracket.

20. Install the tire and wheel.

21. Enable the park brake cable automatic adjuster.

22. Adjust the park brake cable.

CHASSIS ELECTRICAL

AIR BAG (SUPPLEMENTAL RESTRAINT SYSTEM)

GENERAL INFORMATION

✳✳ CAUTION

These vehicles have an airbag system. Disarm the airbag system before performing service on, or around, system components, the steering column, instrument panel components, wiring and sensors. Failure to follow the safety precautions and the disarming procedure could result in accidental airbag deployment, possible injury and unnecessary system repairs.

SERVICE PRECAUTIONS

Disconnect and isolate the battery negative cable before beginning any airbag system component diagnosis, testing, removal, or installation procedures. Allow the system capacitor to discharge for two minutes before beginning any component service. This will disable the airbag system. Failure to disable the airbag system may result in accidental airbag deployment, personal injury, or death. Refer to Battery Negative Cable Disconnect/Connect in the Engine Electrical section in the Engine Electrical section.

Do not place an intact undeployed airbag face down on a solid surface. The airbag will propel into the air if accidentally deployed and may result in personal injury or death.

When carrying or handling an undeployed airbag, point the trim side (face) of the airbag away from the body to minimize possibility of injury if accidental deployment occurs. Failure to do this may result in personal injury or death.

Replace airbag system components with OEM replacement parts. Substitute parts may appear interchangeable, but internal differences may result in inferior occupant protection. Failure to do so may result in occupant personal injury or death.

Wear safety glasses, rubber gloves, and long-sleeved clothing when cleaning powder residue from a vehicle after an airbag deployment. Powder residue emitted from a deployed airbag can cause skin irritation. Flush the affected area with cool water if there

is irritation. For nasal or throat irritation, exit the vehicle for fresh air until the irritation ceases. If irritation continues, see a physician.

Do not use a replacement airbag that is not in the original packaging. This may result in improper deployment, personal injury, or death.

The factory installed fasteners, screws and bolts used to fasten airbag components have a special coating and are specifically designed for the airbag system. Do not use substitute fasteners. Use only original equipment fasteners listed in the parts catalog when fastener replacement is required.

During, and following any child restraint anchor service, due to an impact event or vehicle repair, carefully inspect all mounting hardware, tether straps, and anchors for proper installation, operation, or damage. If a child restraint anchor is found damaged in any way, the anchor must be replaced. Failure to do this may result in personal injury or death.

Deployed and non-deployed airbags may or may not have live pyrotechnic material within the airbag inflator.

Do not dispose of driver/passenger/curtain airbags or seat belt tensioners unless you are sure of complete deployment. Refer to the Hazardous Substance Control System for proper disposal.

Dispose of deployed airbags and tensioners consistent with state, provincial, local, and federal regulations.

After any airbag component testing or service, do not connect the battery negative cable. Personal injury or death may result if the system test is not performed first.

If the vehicle is equipped with the Occupant Classification System (OCS), do not connect the battery negative cable before performing the OCS Verification Test using the scan tool and the appropriate diagnostic information. Personal injury or death may result if the system test is not performed properly.

Never replace both the Occupant Restraint Controller (ORC) and the Occupant Classification Module (OCM) at the same time. If both require replacement, replace one, and then perform the Airbag System test before replacing the other.

Both the ORC and the OCM store Occupant Classification System (OCS) calibration data, which they transfer to one another when one of them is replaced. If both are replaced at the same time, an irreversible fault will be set in both modules and the OCS may malfunction and cause personal injury or death.

If equipped with OCS, the Seat Weight Sensor is a sensitive, calibrated unit—handle it carefully. Do not drop it or handle it roughly. If dropped or damaged, replace it with another sensor. Failure to do so may result in occupant injury or death.

If equipped with OCS, handle the front passenger seat carefully as well. When removing the seat, be careful when setting it on the floor not to drop it. If dropped, the sensor may be inoperative and could result in occupant injury, or possibly death.

If equipped with OCS, when the passenger front seat is on the floor, no one should sit in the front passenger seat. This uneven force may damage the sensing ability of the seat weight sensors. If sat on and damaged, the sensor may be inoperative and could result in occupant injury, or possibly death.

✳✳ WARNING

When performing service on or near the airbag/supplemental restraint system components or the airbag/supplemental restraint system wiring, you must first disable the airbag/supplemental restraint system. Refer to Disarming the System. Failure to observe the correct procedure could cause deployment of the airbag/supplemental restraint components, personal injury, or unnecessary airbag/supplemental restraint system repairs.

The inflatable restraint sensing and diagnostic module (SDM) maintains a reserved energy supply. The reserved energy supply provides deployment power for the air bags. Deployment power is available for as much as 1 minute after disconnecting the vehicle power. Disabling the airbag/supplemental restraint system prevents deployment of the air bags from the reserved energy supply.

General Service Instructions

Follow these instructions in order to properly repair the vehicle and return it to its original integrity:

- Do not expose inflator modules to temperatures above 65°C (150°F).
- Verify the correct replacement part number. Do not substitute a component from a different vehicle.
- Use only original GM replacement parts available from your authorized GM dealer. Do not use salvaged parts for repairs to the airbag/supplemental restraint system.

Discard any of the following inflatable restraint components if it has been dropped from a height of 3 ft (91 cm) or greater:

- Sensing and diagnostic module (SDM)
- Instrument panel module
- Driver steering wheel module
- Driver steering wheel module coil
- Roof side rail modules
- Side impact sensors
- Seat belt retractor pretensioners
- Front end sensors

DISARMING THE SYSTEM/SIR DISABLING

There are several reasons for disabling the SIR system, such as repairs to the SIR system or servicing a component near or attached to an SIR component. There are different ways to disable the SIR system depending on what type of service is being performed. Diagnostic Trouble Codes (DTCs) will be lost when the negative battery cable is disconnected, so follow the diagnostic procedures, which may include removing the airbag fuse.

※ CAUTION
Refer to the SIR Precautions.

※ WARNING
Follow proper inspection procedures when working on a vehicle that has been in an accident.

Disconnect the negative battery cable(s) to disable the system for any of the following conditions:

- If the vehicle was involved in an accident.
- When moving, removing. or replacing an SIR component or a component attached to an SIR component. (Including, anytime you remove fasteners.)
- If you suspect the vehicle has shorted electrical wires.
- For diagnostics of the SIR system as well as electrical diagnostics on other systems, follow the diagnostic procedure, which may include removing the airbag fuse, as DTCs are lost when the negative battery cable is disconnected.

Disabling Procedure—Air Bag Fuse

1. Turn the steering wheel so that the vehicles wheels are pointing straight ahead.
2. Place the ignition in the OFF position.

※ WARNING
The Inflatable Restraint Sensing and Diagnostic Module, or SDM, may have more than one fused power input. To ensure there is no unwanted SIR deployment, personal injury, or unnecessary SIR system repairs, remove all fuses supplying power to the SDM. With all SDM fuses removed and the ignition switch in the ON position, the AIR BAG warning indicator illuminates. This is normal operation, and does not indicate a SIR system malfunction.

3. Locate and remove the fuse(s) supplying power to the SDM.
4. Wait 1 minute before working on the system.

Disabling Procedure—Negative Battery Cable

1. Turn the steering wheel so that the vehicles wheels are pointing straight ahead.
2. Place the ignition in the OFF position.
3. Disconnect the negative battery cable from the battery. Refer to Battery Negative Cable Disconnect/Connect in the Engine Electrical section in the Engine Electrical section.
4. Wait 1 minute before working on system.

➡**DTCs will be lost when you disconnect the negative battery cable.**

ARMING THE SYSTEM/SIR ENABLING

Enabling Procedure—Air Bag Fuse

- Place the ignition in the OFF position.
- Install the fuse(s) supplying power to the Inflatable Restraint Sensing and Diagnostic Module, or SDM.
- Turn the ignition switch to the ON position. The AIR BAG indicator will flash then turn OFF.
- Perform a diagnostic system check of the vehicle if the AIR BAG warning indicator does not operate as described.

Enabling Procedure—Negative Battery Cable

- Place the ignition in the OFF position.
- Connect the negative battery cable to the battery. Refer to Battery Negative Cable Disconnect/Connect in the Engine Electrical section in the Engine Electrical section. •
Turn the ignition switch to the ON position. The AIR BAG indicator will flash then turn OFF.
- Perform a diagnostic system check of the vehicle if the AIR BAG warning indicator does not operate as described.

STEERING WHEEL MODULE COIL/CENTERING

See Figures 47 and 48.

※ CAUTION
The new SIR coil assembly will be centered. Improper alignment of the SIR coil assembly may damage the unit, causing an inflatable restraint malfunction.

1. Verify the following conditions before centering the SIR coil:

    a. The front wheels of the vehicle are in the straight ahead position.

    b. The block tooth (1) of the steering shaft assembly is in the 12 o'clock position.

    c. The ignition switch is in the LOCK position.

➡**If a double wire harness strap is installed onto the wire harness assembly and the column, you must reuse the holder for the wire straps during the installation.**

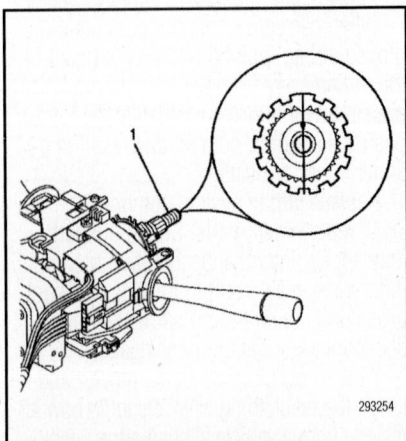

Fig. 47 Verify that block tooth (1) of the steering shaft assembly is in the 12 o'clock position

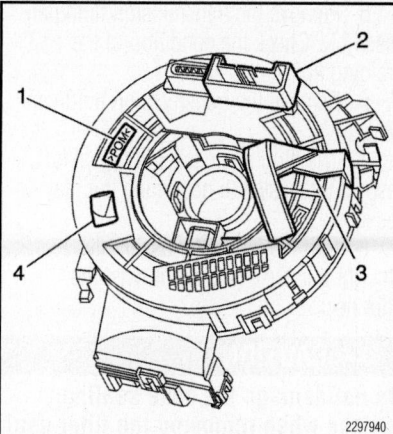

Fig. 48 Look at the side with the letters "POM" (1), place the upload connector (2) in the 12 o'clock position, orange lock pin (if equipped; 3), and centering window (4)

2. Remove the wire harness strap or straps where necessary.

3. Hold the SIR coil and look at the side with the letters "POM" (1).

4. Rotate the coil hub clockwise until the coil ribbon stops.

✳✳ CAUTION

Do not rotate the SIR coil more than 3 turns counterclockwise from the center position. There is no stop in the counterclockwise direction. Rotating the SIR coil more than 3 turns counterclockwise from the center position will damage the SIR coil, causing an inflatable restraint malfunction.

5. From the clockwise stop, rotate the coil hub slowly counterclockwise approximately 3.3 turns. Place the upload connector (2) in the 12 o'clock position. Ensure the flat wire cable loop appears in the centering window (4). This is the CENTER position.

6. If you have the orange lock pin (3), use the lock pin to lock the SIR coil in the center position.

7. If you do not have the orange lock pin, hold the SIR coil in the center position.

8. Align the SIR coil with the horn tower and slide the SIR coil onto the steering shaft assembly.

9. If a double wire harness strap is installed onto the wire harness assembly and the column, you must route the wires up against the steering column. One wire harness strap will surround one lead from the coil to the steering column. The other wire harness strap will surround all other leads to the steering column.

DRIVE TRAIN

AUTOMATIC TRANSMISSION FLUID, FLUID PAN AND/OR FILTER REPLACEMENT

4-SPEED TRANSMISSION

See Figures 49 through 51.

✳✳ WARNING

When the transmission is at operating temperatures, take necessary precautions when removing the drain plug to avoid being burned by draining fluid.

1. Raise and support the vehicle.

2. Place a drain pan under the transmission oil pan.

3. Remove the oil pan drain plug, if equipped.

4. If necessary, remove the bolts and position aside the range selector cable bracket for clearance while lowering the pan. It is not necessary to remove the cable from the lever or bracket.

5. Remove the catalytic converter.

6. Remove the oil pan bolts from the front and sides of the pan only.

7. Loosen the rear oil pan bolts approximately 4 turns.

8. Lightly tap the oil pan with a rubber mallet in order to loosen the pan to allow the fluid to drain.

9. Remove the remaining oil pan bolts.

10. Remove the oil pan and the gasket.

11. To remove the filter, grasp it firmly while pulling down with a twisting motion.

12. Remove the filter seal. The filter seal may be stuck in the pump; if necessary, carefully use pliers or another suitable tool to remove the seal.

13. Discard the seal.

14. Inspect the fluid color.

15. Inspect the filter. Pry the metal crimping away from the top of the filter and pull apart. The filter may contain the following evidence for root cause diagnosis:

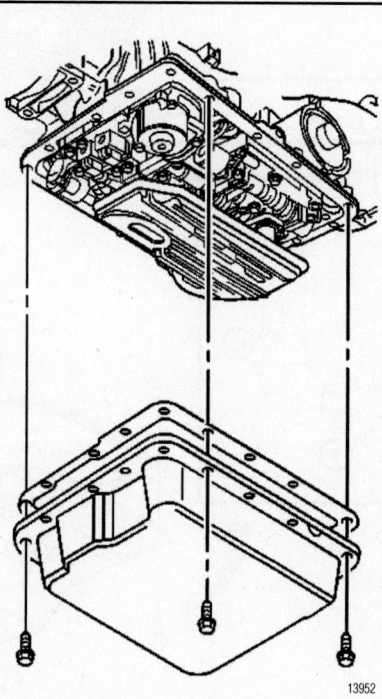

Fig. 49 Oil pan bolts

a. Clutch material

b. Bronze slivers indicating bushing wear

c. Steel particles

16. Clean the transmission case and the oil pan gasket surfaces with solvent, and air dry. You must remove all traces of the old gasket material.

To install:

17. Coat the new filter seal with automatic transmission fluid.

18. Install the new filter seal into the transmission case. Tap the seal into place using a suitable size socket.

19. Install the new filter into the case.

20. Install the oil pan and a new gasket.

21. Install the oil pan bolts and tighten alternately and evenly to 97 inch lbs. (11 Nm).

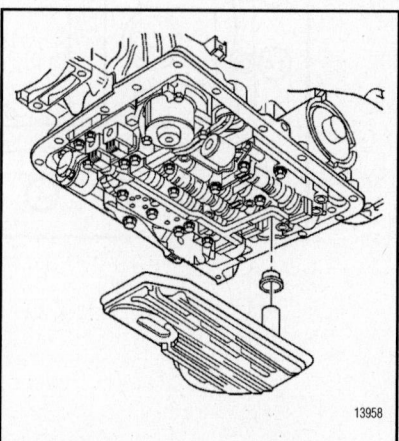

Fig. 50 Grasp the filter firmly while pulling down with a twisting motion

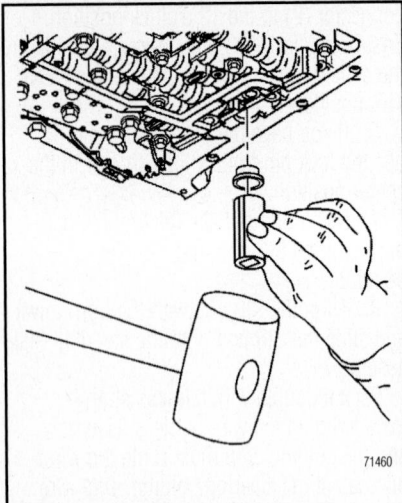

Fig. 51 Tap the seal into place using a suitable size socket

22. Install the catalytic converter.

23. If previously removed, install the range selector cable bracket and bolts and tighten to 18 ft. lbs. (25 Nm).

24. Apply a small amount of sealant GM P/N 12346004 to the threads of the oil pan drain plug, if equipped.

25. Install the oil pan drain plug, if equipped and tighten to 13 ft. lbs. (18 Nm).

26. Lower the vehicle.

27. Fill the transmission to the proper level with DEXRON® VI transmission fluid.

28. Check the COLD fluid level reading for initial fill only.

29. Inspect the oil pan gasket for leaks.

6-SPEED TRANSMISSION

See Figures 52 through 54.

✳✳ WARNING

When the transmission is at operating temperatures, take necessary precautions when removing the drain plug to avoid being burned by draining fluid.

1. Raise and support the vehicle.

2. Disconnect and lower the catalytic converter.

3. Place a suitable drain pan under the transmission.

4. Remove the 18 transmission fluid drain pan bolts.

5. Remove the transmission fluid pan assembly. Check the condition of the draining fluid.

6. Remove the transmission fluid pan gasket.

7. The fluid pan gasket is reusable. Inspect the gasket to determine if it may be reused.

8. Pull the fluid filter assembly straight out. Do not bend or twist the filter neck.

✳✳ CAUTION

Do not damage the case sealing surface when removing the filter seal assembly.

9. Remove the fluid filter seal assembly: Use a screwdriver or snap ring pliers to remove the filter seal.

To install:

10. Tighten the bolts in the sequence shown. Tighten to 80 inch lbs. (9 Nm).

11. Install the transmission fluid pan assembly.

   a. Fill the transmission with the proper fluid.

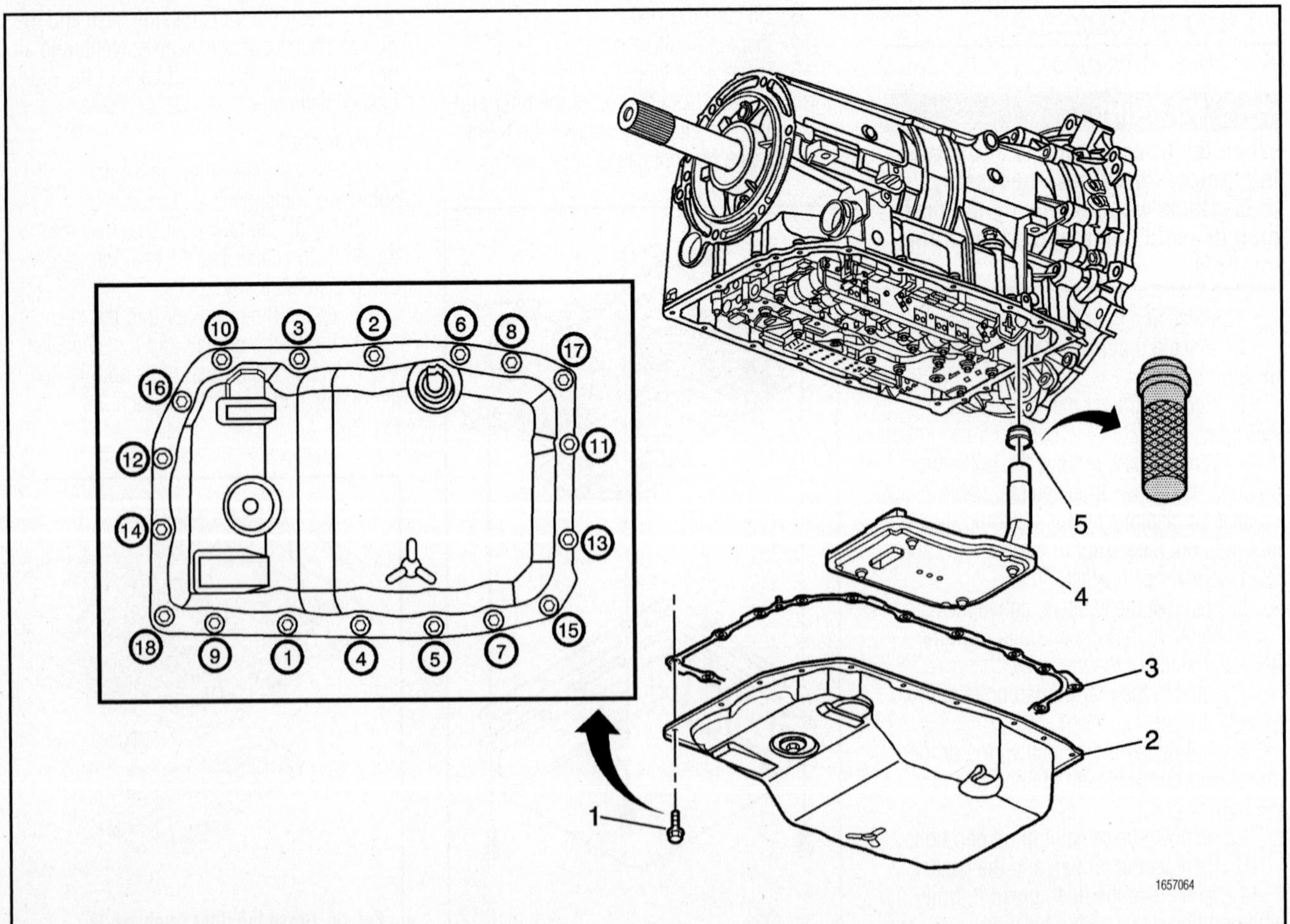

Fig. 52 Eighteen transmission fluid pan bolts (1), pan assembly (2), gasket (3), filter assembly (4), and filter seal assembly

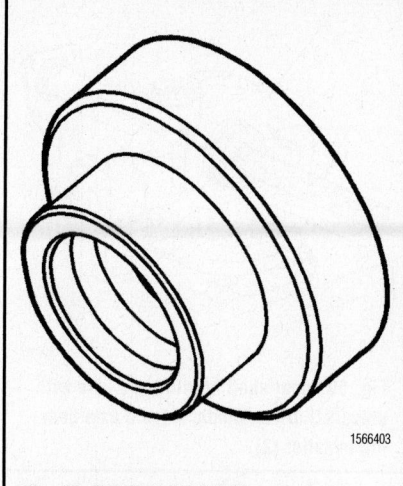

Fig. 53 GM Tool DT 47848, a seal installer

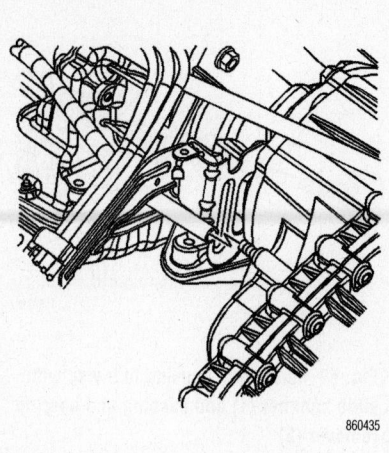

Fig. 55 Remove the vent hose from the transfer case

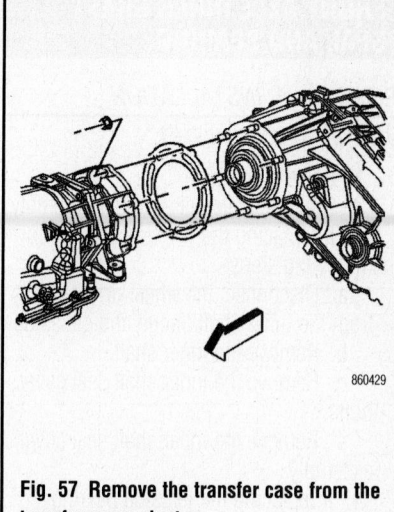

Fig. 57 Remove the transfer case from the transfer case adapter

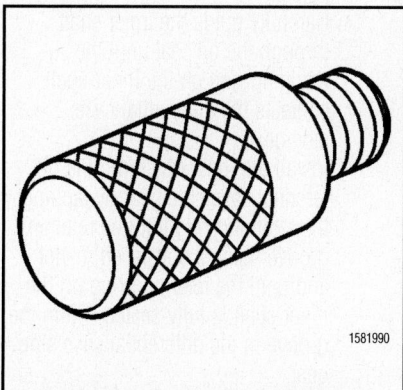

Fig. 54 GM Tool J 42183, a driver handle

b. Fill the transmission with the proper amount of transmission fluid.

12. Install a NEW fluid filter assembly.

13. Use the DT 47848 and the J 42183 (or suitable equivalents) to install a NEW filter seal.

14. Lubricate the filter seal with transmission fluid before installing the filter.

TRANSFER CASE ASSEMBLY

REMOVAL & INSTALLATION

Borg Warner 4473

See Figures 55 through 57.

1. Raise the vehicle.

2. Remove the transmission support crossmember.

3. Drain the transfer case.

4. Remove the rear propeller shaft from the transfer case.

5. Remove the front propeller shaft from the transfer case.

6. Remove the vent hose from the transfer case.

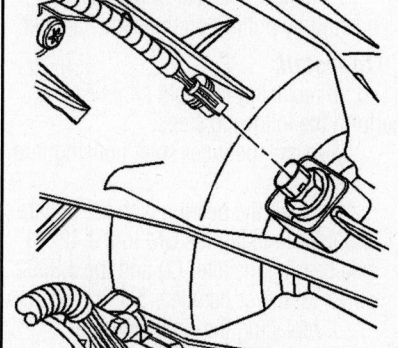

Fig. 56 Disconnect the electrical connector from the speed sensor

7. Disconnect the electrical connector from the speed sensor.

8. Unclip the fuel lines from the fuel line bracket.

9. Install a suitable transmission jack to the transfer case.

10. Remove the nuts from the transfer case to the adapter.

➡**Pull straight back on the transfer case in order to position the transfer case so that the transfer case can be turned parallel to the transmission.**

11. Remove the transfer case from the transfer case adapter.

12. Rotate the transfer case so that the transfer case is perpendicular to the torsion bar mounting bracket.

13. Lower the transfer case.

14. Remove the gasket from the transfer case.

15. Remove the transfer case from the transmission jack.

To install:

16. Install the transfer case on a suitable transmission jack.

➡**When installing a new transfer case gasket, ensure that the locator tab is facing up for proper installation. Install the gasket without the use of any type of sealant or of lubricant.**

17. Install a new transfer case adapter gasket.

18. Rotate the transfer case so that the transfer case is parallel to the torsion bar mounting bracket.

19. Raise the transfer case into position.

20. Rotate the transfer case so that the transfer case is aligned with the adapter.

21. Install the transfer case on the adapter.

22. Install the mounting nuts for the transfer case and tighten to 37 ft. lbs. (50 Nm).

23. Install the transmission support crossmember.

24. Remove the transmission jack.

25. Install the electrical connector to the speed sensor.

26. Install the vent hose to the vent tube.

27. Install the fuel lines to the fuel line bracket.

28. Install the front propeller shaft.

29. Install the rear propeller shaft.

30. Fill the transfer case with the proper transfer case fluid.

31. Lower the vehicle.

FRONT AXLE INNER SHAFT SEAL AND BEARING

REMOVAL & INSTALLATION

See Figures 58 through 61.

1. Raise the vehicle.
2. Drain the differential carrier assembly.
3. If replacing the left side seal, perform the following steps:
   a. Disconnect the wheel driveshaft from the inner shaft flange and set aside.
   b. Remove the inner shaft.
   c. Remove the inner shaft seal cover bolts.
   d. Remove the inner shaft seal cover assembly.
4. If replacing the left side bearing, perform the following steps:
   a. Remove the differential carrier assembly.
   b. Remove the left inner shaft.
   c. Remove the inner shaft seal cover assembly.
   d. Install the bushing and bearing remover (GM tool, J 29369-1; or a suitable equivalent) to the back side of the inner shaft bearing.
   e. Install the GM tool, J 2619-01 slide hammer, to a bushing and bearing remover.
   f. Remove the inner shaft bearing by pulling on the slide hammer.
5. If replacing the right side seal and/or bearing, perform the following steps:
   a. Remove the inner shaft and housing assembly.
   b. Remove the inner shaft from the inner shaft housing.
   c. Install the inner shaft housing into a vise.

Fig. 58 Inner shaft seal cover assembly

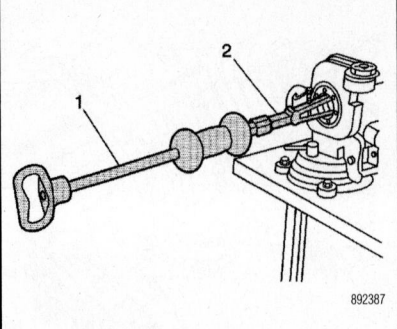

Fig. 59 Inner shaft housing in a vise with slide hammer (1) and bushing and bearing remover (2)

   d. Install the bushing and bearing remover (2) to the back side of the seal or bearing as necessary.
   e. Install the slide hammer (1) to the bushing and bearing remover (2).
   f. Remove the seal or the seal and bearing by pulling on the slide hammer.

To install:

6. If replacing the right side bearing, perform the following steps:
   a. Install the inner shaft housing into a vise.
   b. Install the bearing with the square shoulder in using the GM tool J 42211 axle bearing installer (2) and the J 8092 universal driver handle - 3/4 in - 10 (1).
7. If replacing the right side seal, perform the following steps:
   a. Install the inner shaft housing into a vise.
   b. Install the new inner shaft seal using the GM tool J 42738 seal installer or an equivalent.

➡**Carefully guide the inner shaft through the oil seal so as to not nick or cut the seal.**

   c. Install the inner shaft into the inner shaft housing.
   d. Install the inner shaft and housing assembly.
8. If installing the left side bearing, perform the following steps:
   a. Install the bearing with the square shoulder in using the axle bearing installer and the universal driver handle.
   b. Install the inner shaft seal cover assembly.
9. Install the inner shaft seal cover bolts and tighten to 13 ft. lbs. (18 Nm).

➡**Carefully guide the inner shaft through the oil seal so as to not nick or cut the seal.**

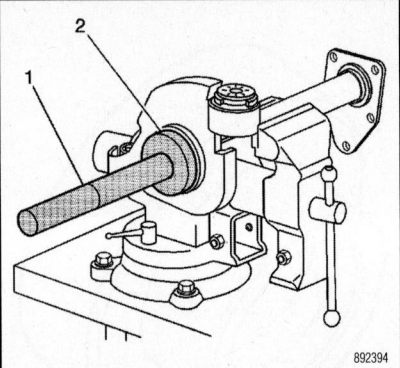

Fig. 60 Inner shaft housing in a vise with universal driver handle (1) and axle bearing installer (2)

10. Install the left inner shaft into the differential carrier assembly by performing the following steps:
    • Carefully guide the inner shaft through the oil seal until the retaining ring on the inner shaft contacts the differential case side gear.
    • Install the inner shaft into the differential case side gear by tapping the retaining ring into the retaining groove using a soft-faced mallet and until the retaining ring on the inner shaft is fully seated within the groove in the differential case side gear.
    • Pull back on the inner shaft to ensure that the inner shaft is properly retained in the differential case side gear.
11. Install the differential carrier assembly.
12. Install the wheel driveshaft to the inner shaft flange.
13. Fill the differential carrier assembly with the proper fluid.
14. Lower the vehicle.

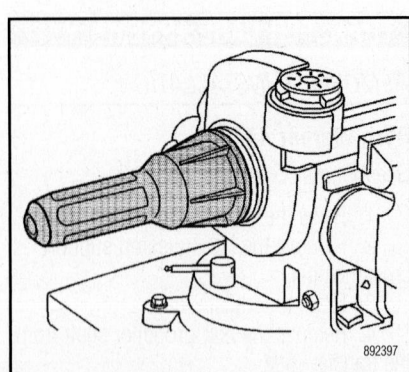

Fig. 61 Put the inner shaft housing in a vise and use a seal installer to install the new inner shaft seal

FRONT DRIVESHAFT/ PROPELLER SHAFT

REMOVAL & INSTALLATION

See Figures 62 through 66.

1. Raise the vehicle.
2. Mark the relationship of the front propeller shaft U-Joint to the differential yoke.
3. Remove the front propeller shaft retainer bolts.
4. Remove the U-Joint retainers.
5. Remove the front propeller shaft from the front differential.

➡ **The following procedure is to ensure that the U-Joint bearings and caps DO NOT become separated.**

6. This will prevent the lost of the needle bearings inside the bearing cap.
7. Tape the U-Joint bearing caps together.
8. Remove the front propeller shaft from the transfer case.

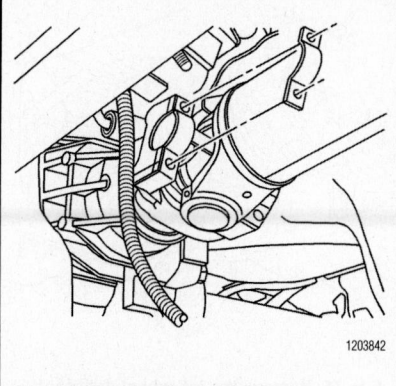

Fig. 64 Remove the U-Joint retainers

To install:

9. Install the front propeller shaft in the transfer case.
10. Remove the tape from the propeller shaft U-Joint.

➡ **Ensure that the alignment marks on the U-Joint and the yoke are aligned for proper installation.**

11. Install the front propeller shaft in the front differential yoke.

12. Install the propeller shaft retainers.
13. Install the propeller shaft retainer bolts and tighten to 18 ft. lbs. (25 Nm).
14. Check the fluid level of the front differential.
15. Inspect the fluid level of the transfer case.
16. Lower the vehicle.

WHEEL DRIVESHAFT

REMOVAL & INSTALLATION

See Figures 67 through 72.

✳✳ WARNING

Do not attempt to move the vehicle with drive axle(s) removed from wheel bearing. Wheel(s) could fall off, dropping vehicle to the ground and causing personal injury or damage to the vehicle.

1. Remove the tire and wheel assembly.
2. Remove the wheel driveshaft nut.
3. Remove the wheel driveshaft retaining bolts.
4. Remove the left wheel driveshaft from the front differential flange.
5. Remove the right wheel driveshaft from the differential flange.

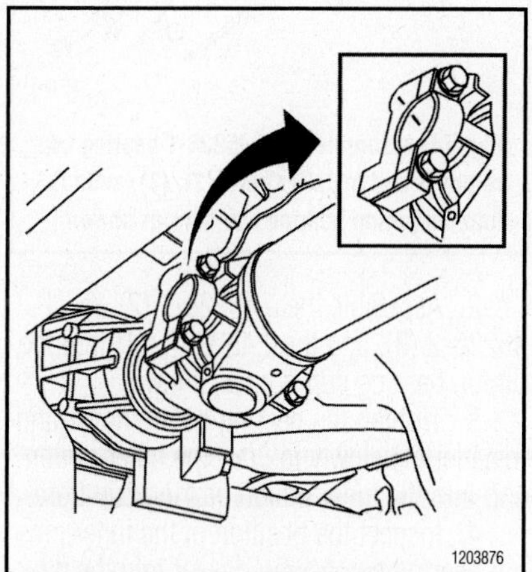

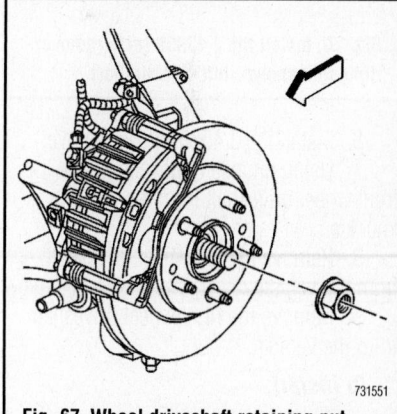

Fig. 67 Wheel driveshaft retaining nut

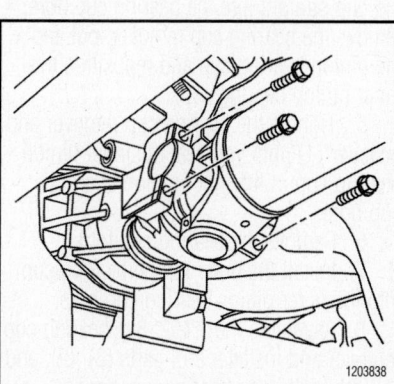

Fig. 62 Mark the relationship of the front propeller shaft U-Joint to the differential yoke

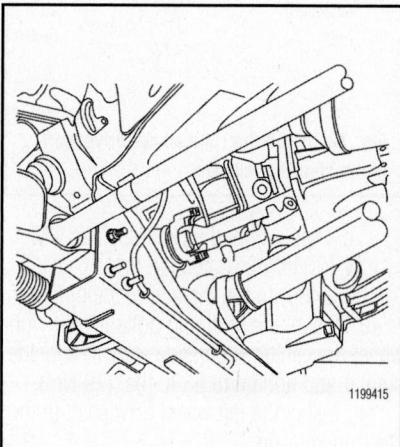

Fig. 65 Tape the U-Joint bearing caps together

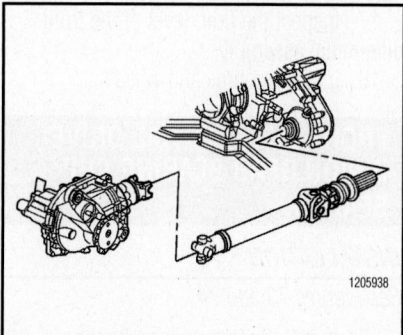

Fig. 63 Front propeller shaft retainer bolts

Fig. 66 Remove the front propeller shaft from the transfer case

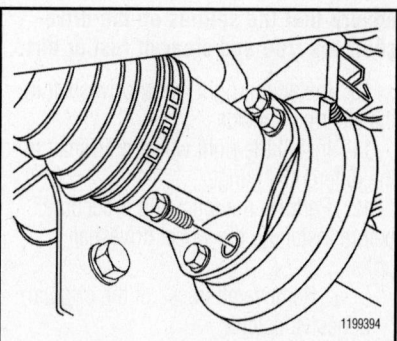

Fig. 68 Wheel driveshaft retaining bolts (right side shown left side similar)

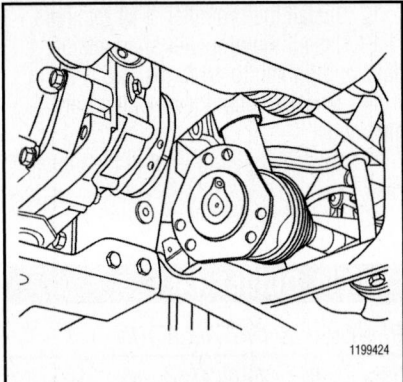

Fig. 69 Remove the left wheel driveshaft from the front differential flange

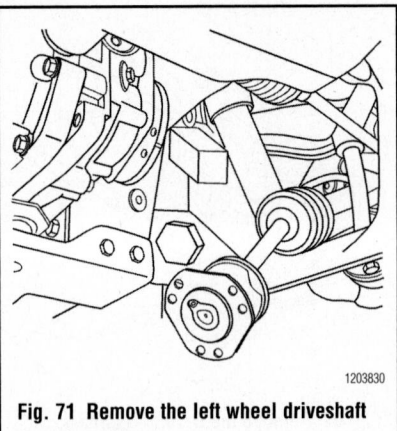

Fig. 71 Remove the left wheel driveshaft from the vehicle

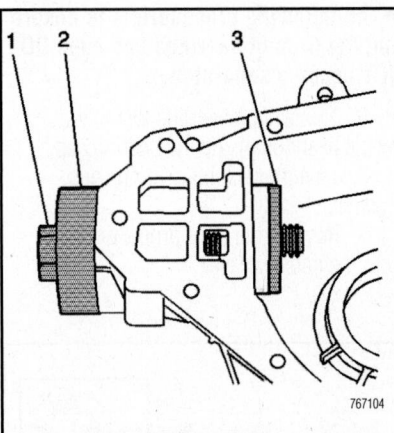

Fig. 73 J 45228 pinion bearing cup remover and installer

Fig. 70 Install the J 45859 (axle remover; right side shown, left side similar)

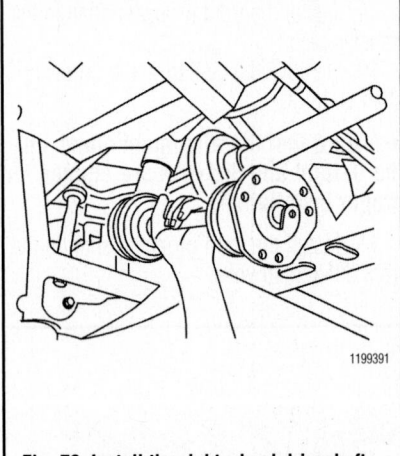
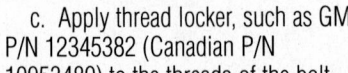

Fig. 72 Install the right wheel driveshaft in the steering knuckle

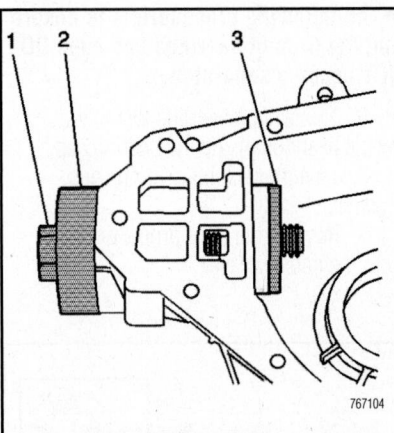

Fig. 74 Assemble the J 45228-1 bearing cup remover and installer parts (2), (3), and (1) into the pinion bearing cup bore as shown

6. Install the J 45859 (axle remover).

7. Using an axle remover, remove the front wheel driveshaft from the steering knuckle.

8. Remove the left wheel driveshaft from the vehicle.

9. Remove the right wheel driveshaft from the vehicle.

To install:

➡ **Before installing the front wheel driveshaft in the steering knuckle, ensure that the splines on the driveshaft are free and clear of rust or dirt.**

10. Install the right wheel driveshaft in the steering knuckle.

11. Install the right wheel driveshaft to the differential flange.

12. Perform the following procedure before installing the wheel driveshaft bolts.

　a. Remove all traces of the original adhesive patch.

　b. Clean the threads of the bolt with denatured alcohol or equivalent and allow to dry.

　c. Apply thread locker, such as GM P/N 12345382 (Canadian P/N 10953489) to the threads of the bolt.

13. Install the retaining bolts for the right wheel driveshaft. Right side shown; left side similar and tighten to 58 ft. lbs. (79 Nm).

14. Install the left wheel driveshaft in the steering knuckle.

15. Install the left wheel driveshaft to the differential flange.

16. Install the wheel driveshaft retaining nuts and tighten to 155 ft. lbs. (210 Nm).

17. Inspect the fluid level of the front differential assembly.

18. Install the tires and wheels.

FRONT DIFFERENTIAL DRIVE PINION GEAR BEARING CUP SEAL

INSTALLATION

See Figures 73 and 74.

1. Install the inner pinion bearing cup into the inner pinion bearing cup bore.

2. Assemble the J 45228-1 (2), the J 45228-2 (3), and the J 45228-5 (1) into the pinion bearing cup bore as shown.

3. Tighten the bearing cup remover and installer (1) slowly to draw the inner pinion cup into the inner pinion bearing cup bore.

4. Inspect the position of the inner pinion bearing cup as you draw it into the pinion bearing cup bore to ensure you pull the bearing cup straight into the pinion bearing cup bore. If you don't pull the pinion bearing cup straight into the bearing cup bore, remove the bearing cup remover tool and the pinion bearing cup and reposition the inner pinion bearing cup.

5. Tighten the bearing cup remover and installer (1) until you seat the inner pinion bearing cup in the inner pinion bearing cup bore.

6. Remove the bearing cup tool.

7. Install the outer pinion bearing cup into the outer pinion bearing cup bore.

8. Assemble the J 45228-1 bearing cup remover and installer tool parts (3), (2), and (1) into the pinion bearing cup bore as shown.

9. Tighten the bearing cup tool (1) slowly to draw the outer pinion cup into the outer pinion bearing cup bore.

10. Inspect the position of the outer pinion bearing cup as it is being drawn into the pinion bearing cup bore to ensure the bearing cup is being pulled straight into the pinion bearing cup bore. If the pinion bearing cup is not being pulled straight into the bearing cup bore, remove the bearing cup tool and the pinion bearing cup and reposition the outer pinion bearing cup.

11. Tighten the bearing cup tool until the outer pinion bearing cup is seated in the outer pinion bearing cup bore.

12. Remove the bearing cup tool.

REAR AXLE FLUID

DIFFERENTIAL OIL REPLACEMENT

8.6-inch Axle

See Figure 75.

1. Raise the vehicle.
2. Clean the area around the rear axle fill plug.
3. Remove the rear axle fill plug.
4. Remove the rear axle cover.
5. Drain the lubricant into a suitable container.

To install:

6. Install the rear axle cover.
7. Fill the rear axle with axle lubricant.
8. Install the rear axle fill plug and tighten to 24 ft. lbs. (33 Nm).
9. Lower the vehicle.

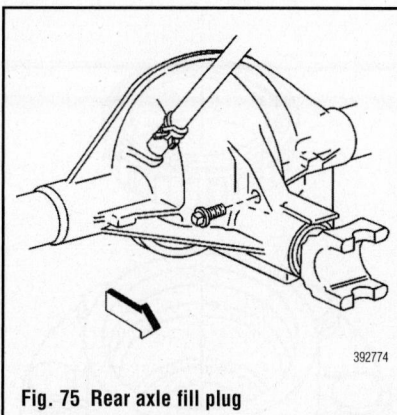

Fig. 75 Rear axle fill plug

9.5LD-inch Axle

See Figures 76 and 77.

1. Raise and support the vehicle.
2. Remove the drain plug.
3. Remove the fill plug.

To install:

4. Install the drain plug and tighten to 24 ft. lbs. (33 Nm).

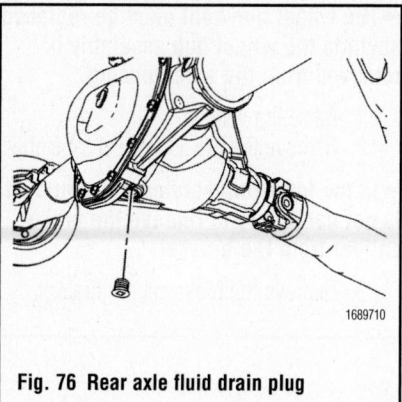

Fig. 76 Rear axle fluid drain plug

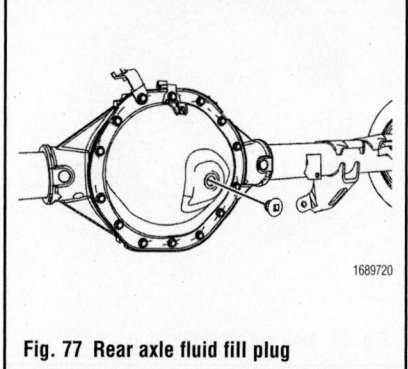

Fig. 77 Rear axle fluid fill plug

5. Fill the rear drive axle.
6. Use the proper fluid in the proper amount. (See Fluid and Capacity specifications.)
7. Install the fill plug and tighten to 24 ft. lbs. (33 Nm).
8. Remove the support and lower the vehicle.

10.5-inch Axle

See Figures 78 and 79.

1. Raise the vehicle.
2. Remove the fill plug (1).
3. Remove the rear axle drain plug (1).
4. Drain the lubricant into a suitable container.

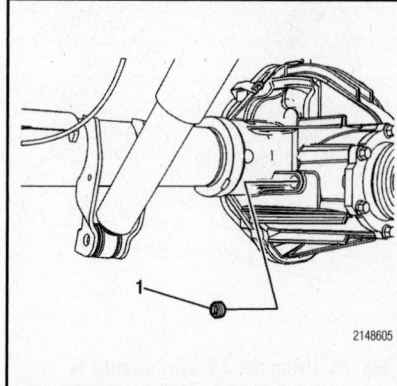

Fig. 78 Rear axle fluid fill plug (1)

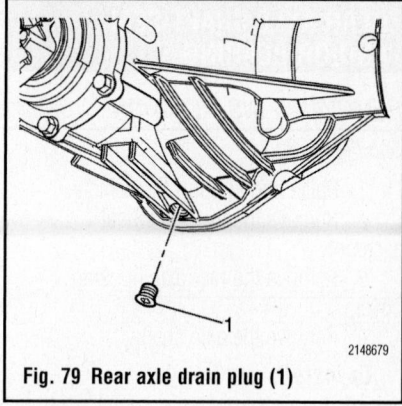

Fig. 79 Rear axle drain plug (1)

To install:

5. Install the rear axle drain plug and tighten to 24 ft. lbs. (33 Nm).
6. Fill the rear axle with the proper fluid in the proper amount. (See Fluid and Capacity specifications.)
7. Install the fill plug and tighten to 24 ft. lbs. (33 Nm).
8. Remove the support and lower the vehicle.

REAR AXLE HOUSING

REMOVAL & INSTALLATION

1. Raise the vehicle.
2. Remove the axle lubricant.
3. Remove the rear axle assembly.
4. Remove the brake caliper brackets.
5. Remove the rear axle cover housing and gasket.
6. Remove the rear brake shield.
7. Remove the axle shafts.
8. Remove the differential.
9. Remove the drive pinion.
10. Remove the drive pinion shaft yoke and the seal.

To install:

11. Install the drive pinion.
12. Install the differential case.
13. Adjust the side bearing preload.
14. Adjust the backlash.
15. Perform a gear tooth contact pattern check.
16. Install the rear brake shield.
17. Install the axle shafts.
18. Install the rear axle housing cover and gasket.
19. Install the brake caliper brackets.
20. Install the rear axle.
21. Fill the axle with lubricant.
22. Lower the vehicle.

REAR AXLE SHAFT SEAL AND/OR BEARING

REMOVAL & INSTALLATION

See Figure 80.

1. Raise and support the vehicle.
2. Remove the tire and wheel assembly.
3. Remove the rear axle housing cover.
4. Remove the axle shaft.

To install:

➡**Ensure that the axle shaft bearing is fully seated in the rear axle shaft housing.**

5. Using the J 23690, an axle bearing installer (1) and the J 8092, a ¾ x 10 inch universal driver handle (2), install the axle shaft bearing.
6. Using the J 21128 axle pinion oil installer, or an equivalent, to install the axle shaft seal.
7. Drive the tool into the bore until the axle shaft seal bottoms flush with the tube.
8. Install the rear axle shaft.
9. Install the rear axle housing cover.
10. Install the tire and wheel assembly.
11. Fill the rear axle.
12. Remove the support and lower the vehicle.

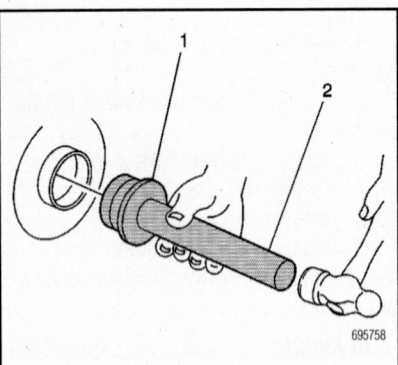

Fig. 80 Using the J 23690, an axle bearing installer (1) and the J 8092, a ¾ x 10 inch universal driver handle (2) to install the axle shaft bearing

REAR AXLE HUB BEARING CUP, AND/OR SEAL

REMOVAL & INSTALLATION

See Figures 81 through 93.

➡**The wheel speed sensor ring is NOT serviced separately. The hub and wheel speed sensor ring are serviced as an assembly.**

➡**The wheel hub seal must be replaced anytime the wheel hub assembly is removed from the axle housing.**

1. Raise the vehicle.
2. Remove the tire and wheel assembly.

➡**In the following service procedure, it is not necessary to remove the brake caliper from the bracket.**

3. Remove the brake caliper bracket.

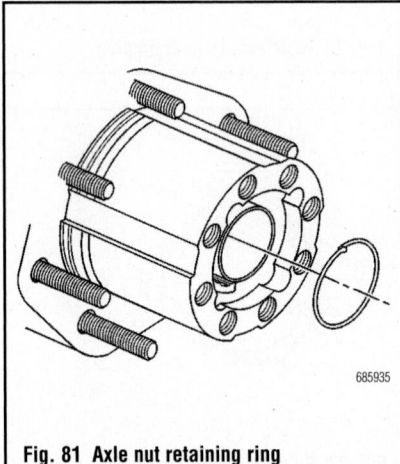

Fig. 81 Axle nut retaining ring

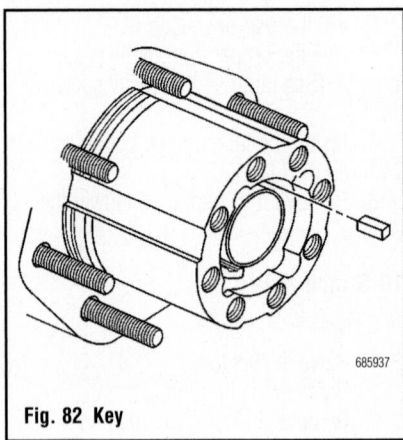

Fig. 82 Key

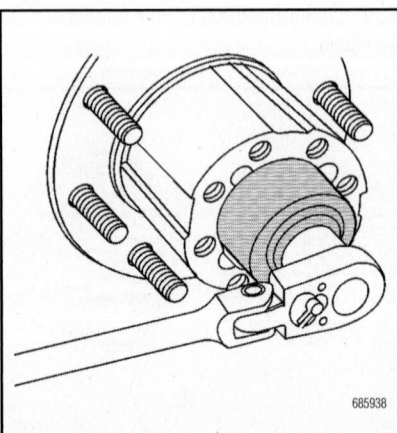

Fig. 83 Using the J 2222-C wrench to loosen the adjusting nut

4. Remove the axle shaft.
5. Remove the axle nut retaining ring.
6. Remove the key.
7. Using the J 2222-C wrench or an equivalent wheel bearing nut wrench, loosen the adjusting nut.
8. Remove the adjusting nut.

➡**If the oil seal remains on the axle hub, remove the seal using a suitable seal removal tool.**

9. Remove the hub from the axle housing.
10. Remove the rotor, if necessary.
11. Using a suitable seal removal tool, remove the oil seal from the wheel hub.
12. Remove the inner hub bearing.

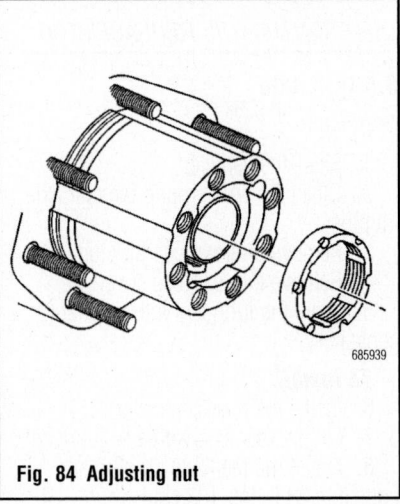

Fig. 84 Adjusting nut

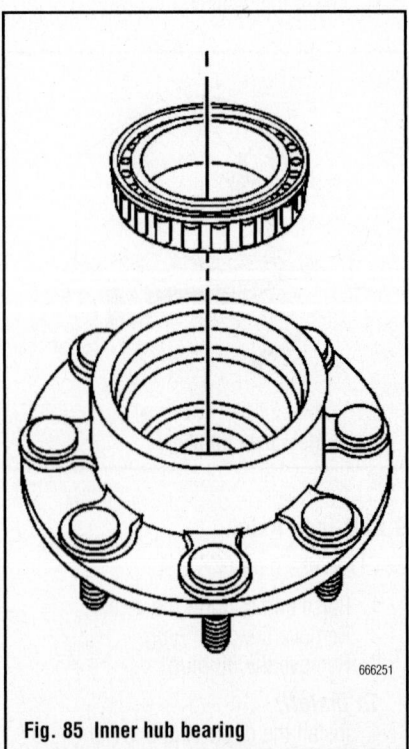

Fig. 85 Inner hub bearing

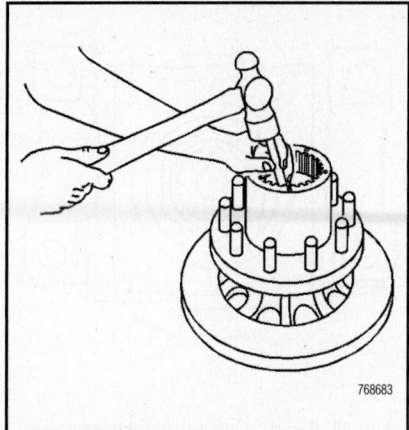

Fig. 86 Using a brass drift and a hammer to remove the inner hub bearing cup

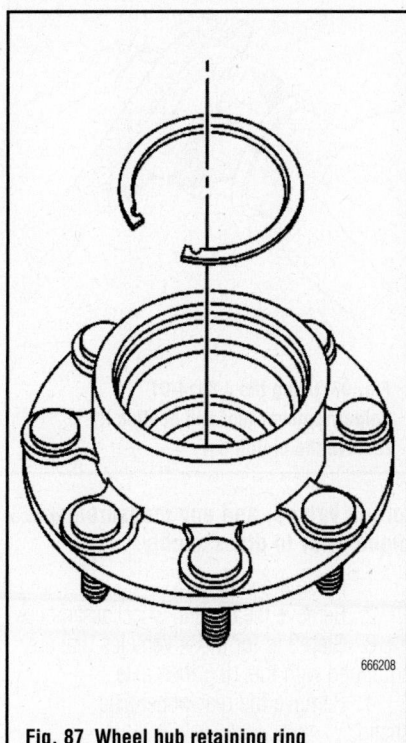

Fig. 87 Wheel hub retaining ring

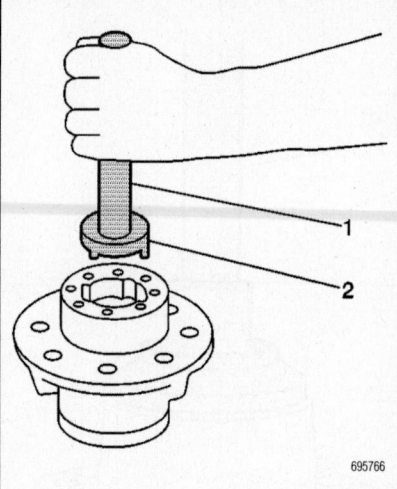

Fig. 88 Using the J 24426, an outer wheel bearing race installer (2), and the J 8092 handle, a 2/4 x 10-inch universal driver (1), to remove the outer hub bearing and bearing cup.

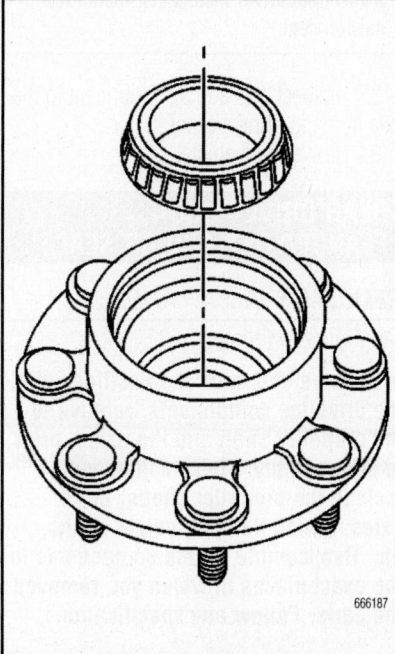

Fig. 89 Install the outer bearing into the wheel hub

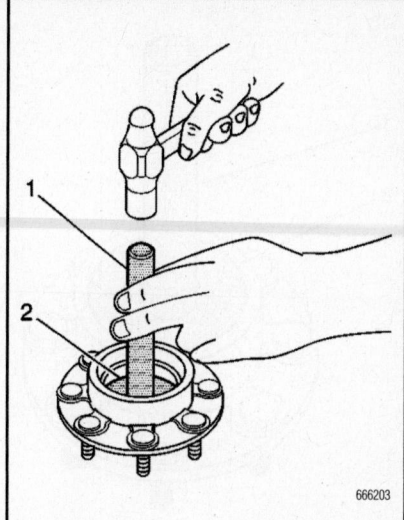

Fig. 90 Using the J 44419 hub bearing installer (2) or an equivalent and a universal driver ¾ x 10-inch handle (1), install the outer bearing cup into the wheel hub

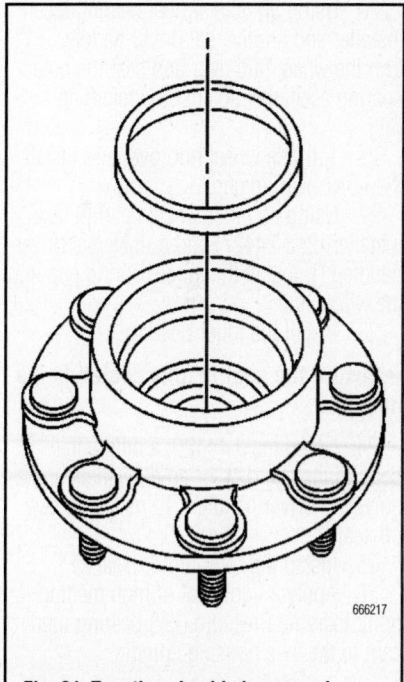

Fig. 91 Turn the wheel hub over and install the inner bearing cup

13. Using a brass drift and a hammer, remove the inner hub bearing cup.

14. Remove the retaining ring from the wheel hub.

15. Using the J 24426, an outer wheel bearing race installer (2) and the J 8092 handle, a 2/4 x 10-inch universal driver (1), remove the outer hub bearing and bearing cup.

To install:

16. Lubricate the following with a light coat of high melting point EP bearing lubricant:

    a. The outer wheel bearing
    b. The inner wheel bearing
    c. The outer wheel bearing cup

    d. The inner wheel bearing cup
    e. The axle hub spindle

17. Install the outer bearing into the wheel hub.

➡**Drive the outer bearing cup into the wheel hub until it is just past the retaining ring groove. Do not bottom out the bearing assembly in the bore.**

18. Using the J 44419 hub bearing installer (2) or an equivalent and a universal

driver 3/4 x 10-inch handle (1), install the outer bearing cup into the wheel hub.

➡**Fully and evenly seat the retaining ring in the groove.**

19. Install the retaining ring into the groove.

➡**Ensure that the outer bearing assembly rotates freely in the hub**

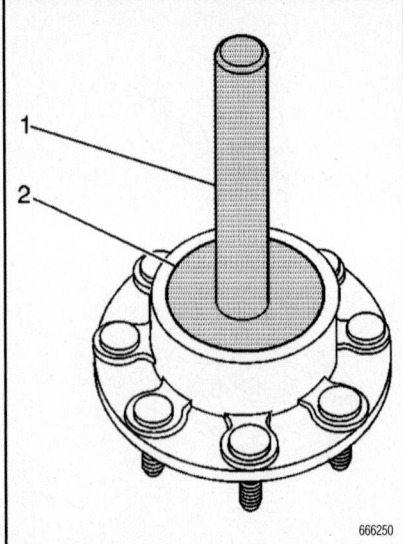

Fig. 92 Using an inner wheel bearing race installer (2; J 24427) and a universal driver handle (1), install the inner bearing cup into the wheel hub

20. Using an outer wheel bearing race installer and a universal driver handle, turn the wheel hub over and seat the outer bearing assembly against the retaining ring.

21. Turn the wheel hub over and install the inner bearing cup.

22. Using an inner wheel bearing race installer (2; J 24427) and a universal driver handle (1), install the inner bearing cup into the wheel hub.

23. Install the inner bearing.

➡**Ensure the seal is fully seated in the hub bore.**

24. Using the J 44420, a differential bearing installer (2), or an equivalent and a universal driver handle (1), install the new oil seal.

25. Install the rotor, if necessary.

26. Apply a light coat of high melting point Extreme Pressure (EP) bearing lubricant to the axle housing spindle.

➡**If the wheel hub assembly does not fully seat itself onto the axle shaft spindle and is removed, the wheel hub seal must be replaced.**

27. Install the wheel hub to the axle housing.

28. Use a wheel bearing nut (J 2222-C) wrench to install the adjusting nut to the hub.

29. Adjust the wheel bearings.
30. Install the axle shaft.
31. Install the brake caliper bracket.
32. Install the tire and wheel assembly.

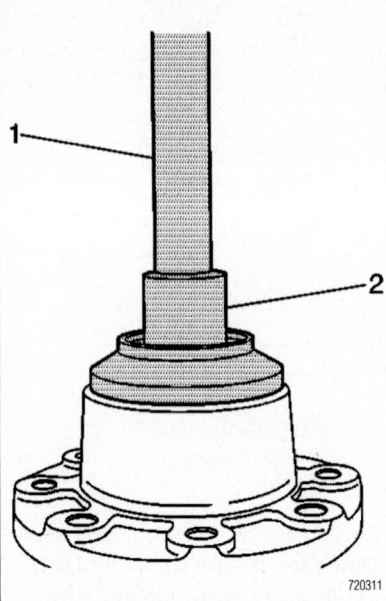

Fig. 93 Using the J 44420, a differential bearing installer (2), or an equivalent and a universal driver handle (1), install the new oil seal

33. Inspect and add axle lubricant to the axle housing, if necessary.

34. Lower the vehicle.

REAR DRIVE PINION FLANGE/YOKE AND/OR SEAL

REMOVAL & INSTALLATION

See Figures 94 through 100.

➡**Observe and mark the positions of all the driveline components, relative to the propeller shaft and the axles, prior to disassembly. These components include the propeller shafts, drive axles, pinion flanges, output shafts, etc. Reassemble all the components in the exact places in which you removed the parts. Follow any specifications,**

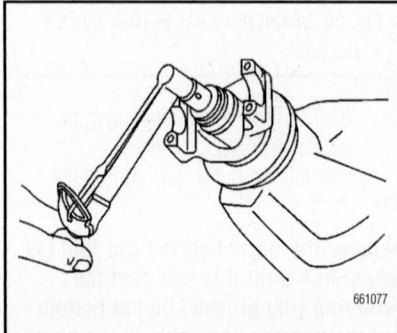

Fig. 94 Measure the amount of torque required to rotate the pinion

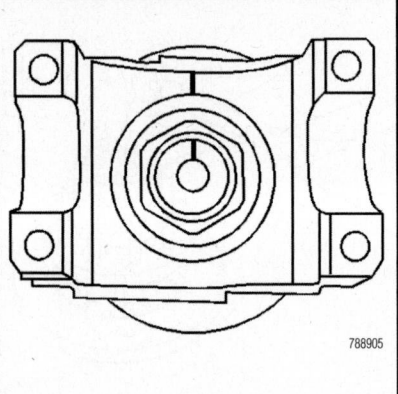

Fig. 95 Place an alignment mark between the pinion and the pinion yoke

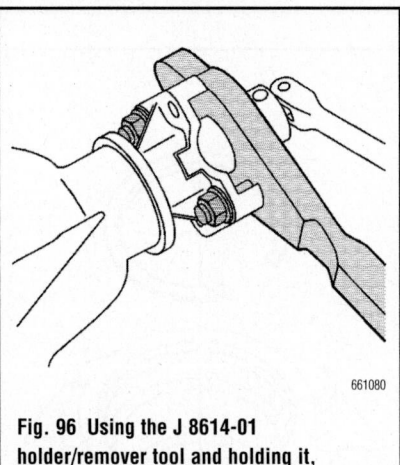

Fig. 96 Using the J 8614-01 holder/remover tool and holding it, remove the pinion nut

torque values, and any measurements made prior to disassembly.

1. Raise the vehicle.
2. Remove the tire and wheel assemblies.
3. Step 3 is for those vehicles that are equipped with the 10.5 inch axle.
4. Remove the rear wheel axle shafts.
5. Step 4 is for those vehicles that are equipped with the 8.6 or 9.5 inch axle.
6. Remove the rear brake rotors.
7. Remove the propeller shaft from the vehicle.

➡**Record the following torque measurement for reassembly.**

8. Using an inch-pound torque wrench, measure the amount of torque required to rotate the pinion.

9. Place an alignment mark between the pinion and the pinion yoke.

10. Using the J 8614-01 holder/remover and holding it, remove the pinion nut.

11. Remove the washer.

12. Rotate the J 8614-3 clockwise to remove the yoke.

13. Using the J 8614-2 (2) and the J 8614-3 (3), remove the pinion yoke.

14. Using a suitable tool, remove the drive pinion seal (1).

To install:

15. Using the J 44414 oil seal installer, install a new pinion oil seal.

16. Apply sealant to the splines of the pinion yoke.

✳✳ CAUTION

Do not hammer the pinion flange/yoke onto the pinion shaft. You may damage pinion components if you hammer the pinion flange/yoke onto the pinion shaft.

➡**Align the reference marks and install the drive pinion yoke.**

17. Using a soft-faced hammer, install the drive flange (1) onto the pinion shaft until a few threads show through the drive flange (1).

18. Install the washer (2) and the nut (3).

➡**If the rotating torque is exceeded, the pinion will have to be removed and a new collapsible spacer installed.**

19. Using and holding the J 8614-01 holder/remover, tighten the pinion nut until the pinion end play is just taken up. Rotate the pinion while tightening the nut to seat the bearing.

➡**Compare this measurement with the rotating torque prior to removing the drive flange.**

20. Using an inch-pound torque wrench, tighten the nut in small increments, as needed, until the rotating torque is 3–5 inch lbs. (0.40–0.57 Nm) greater than the rotating torque recorded during removal.

➡**Recheck the rotating torque and adjust if necessary.**

21. Once the specified torque is obtained, rotate the pinion several times to seat the bearings.

22. Install the propeller shaft in the vehicle.

➡**Step 9 is for those vehicles that are equipped with the 10.5 inch axle.**

23. Install the axle shafts.

➡**Step 10 is for those vehicles that are equipped with the 8.6 or 9.5 inch axle.**

24. Install the rear brake rotors.

25. Install the tire and wheel assemblies.

26. Inspect and add axle lubricant to the axle housing, if necessary.

27. Remove the support and lower the vehicle.

REAR DRIVESHAFT

REMOVAL & INSTALLATION

See Figures 101 through 107.

1. Raise the vehicle.

2. Remove the tire and wheel assembly.

3. Remove the brake caliper mounting bracket.

4. Remove the rear axle housing cover and the gasket.

5. Remove the pinion shaft locking bolt.

6. On axles without a locking differential, remove the pinion shaft.

7. On axles with a locking differential, remove the shaft part way. Rotate the case until the pinion shaft touches the housing.

8. On axles with a locking differential, use a screwdriver, or a similar tool, to enter the differential case and rotate the C-lock

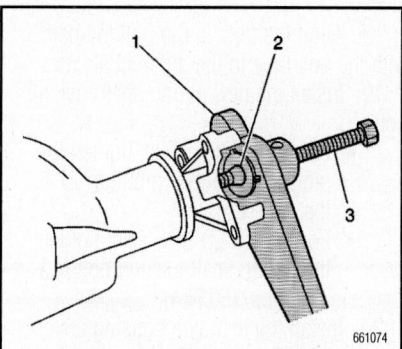

Fig. 97 Removing the pinion yoke with the J8614 (2) and (3)

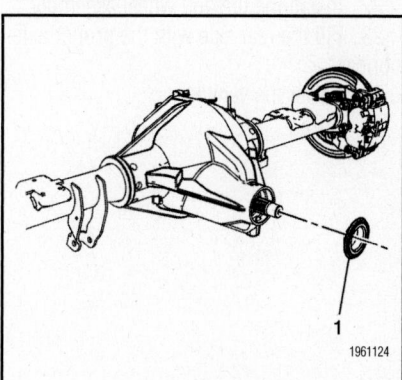

Fig. 98 Remove the drive pinion seal (1)

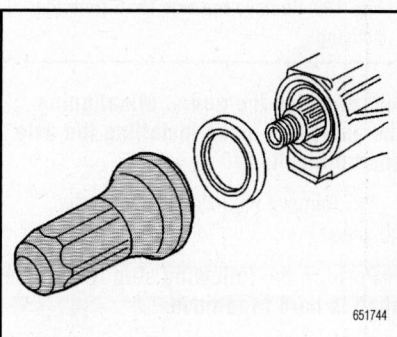

Fig. 99 Install a new pinion oil seal with an oil seal installer

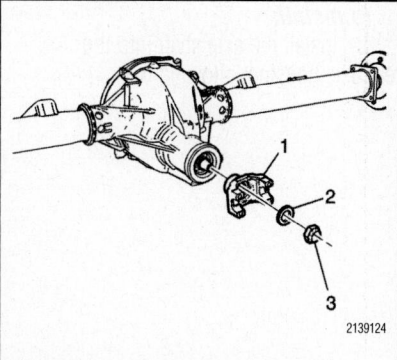

Fig. 100 Drive flange (1), washer (2) and nut (3)

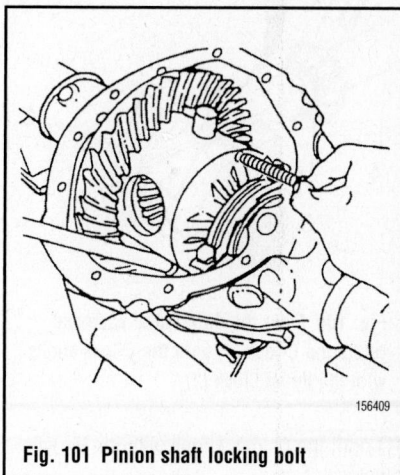

Fig. 101 Pinion shaft locking bolt

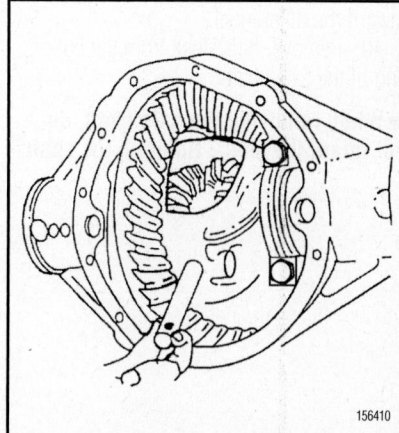

Fig. 102 On axles without a locking differential, remove the pinion shaft

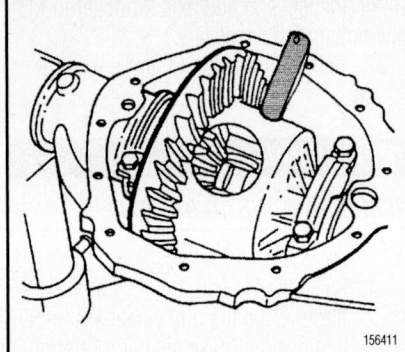

Fig. 103 On axles with a locking differential, remove the shaft part way. Rotate the case until the pinion shaft touches the housing

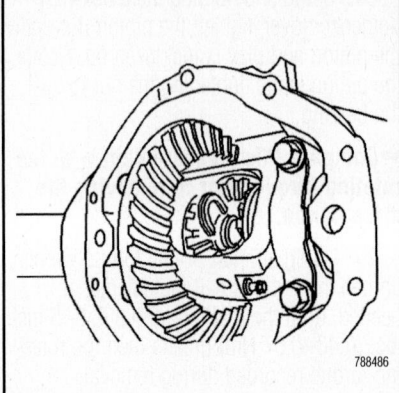

Fig. 105 C-lock at the button end of the axle shaft

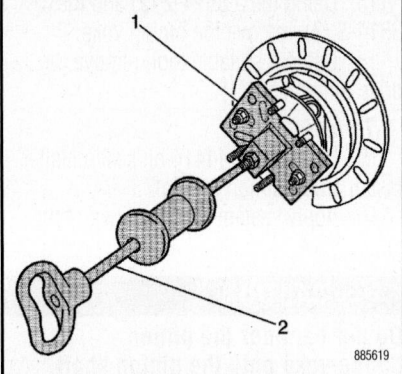

Fig. 107 Use the J 2619-01 slide hammer (1) and the J 45859 remover/installer (2) to remove the axle shaft from the housing

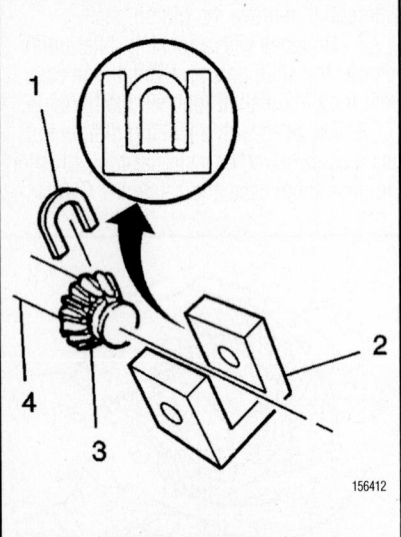

Fig. 104 Enter the differential case and rotate the C-lock (1) until the C-lock aligns with the thrust block (2)

(1) until the C-lock aligns with the thrust block (2).

9. Push the flange of the axle shaft (3) toward the differential.

10. Remove the C-lock from the button end of the axle shaft.

➡**When removing the axle shaft, do not rotate the shaft. Rotating the shaft**

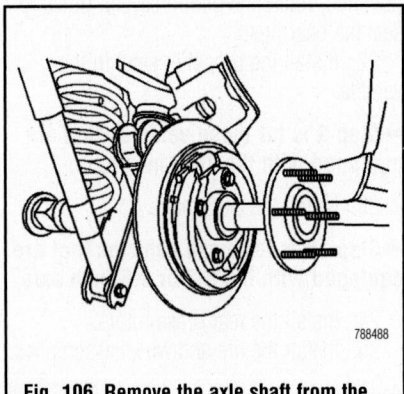

Fig. 106 Remove the axle shaft from the housing

will misalign the gears. Misaligning the gears will make installing the axle shaft difficult.

11. Remove the axle shaft from the housing.

➡**Perform the following step if the axle shaft is hard to remove.**

12. Use the J 2619-01 slide hammer (1) and the J 45859 remover/installer (2) to remove the axle shaft from the housing.

To install:

13. Install the axle shaft into the rear axle housing, allowing the

splines to engage the differential side gear.

14. On axles without a locking differential, place the C-lock on the button end of the axle shaft.

15. On axles with a locking differential, keep the pinion shaft partially withdrawn.

16. On axles with a locking differential, place the C-lock (1) on the axle shaft (3) so that the ends are flush with the thrust block (2).

17. Pull the shaft flange outward in order to seat the C-lock in the differential gear.

18. Align the hole in the pinion shaft with the bolt hole in the differential case.

19. Install the new pinion shaft locking bolt.

- For the 8.6 inch axle, tighten the pinion shaft locking bolt to 27 ft. lbs. (36 Nm).
- For the 9.5 LD inch axle, tighten the pinion shaft locking bolt to 37 ft. lbs. (50 Nm).

20. Install the rear axle housing cover and the gasket.

21. Install the brake caliper mounting bracket.

22. Install the tire and wheel assembly.

23. Fill the rear axle with the proper axle lubricant.

24. Lower the vehicle.

ENGINE COOLING

ENGINE COOLANT

DRAIN & REFILL PROCEDURE

2010 Models—Except Diesel Engines

See Figure 108.

Draining Procedure

✻✻ WARNING

With a pressurized cooling system, the coolant temperature in the radiator can be considerably higher than the boiling point of the solution at atmospheric pressure. Removal of the surge tank cap, while the cooling system is hot and under high pressure, causes the solution to boil instantaneously with explosive force. This will cause the solution to spew out over the engine, the fenders, and the person removing the cap. Serious bodily injury may result.

1. Park the vehicle on a level surface.
2. Remove the coolant pressure cap.
3. Raise and support the vehicle.
4. Place a drain pan under the lower radiator hose.
5. Using the J 38185 or equivalent hose clamp pliers, reposition the lower radiator hose clamp at the radiator.
6. Remove the lower radiator hose from the radiator.
7. Drain the cooling system.
8. If a complete engine block drain is required, remove the engine block drain plug.
9. Inspect the coolant.
10. Follow the appropriate procedure based on the condition of the coolant.

    a. Normal in appearance—Follow the filling procedure.

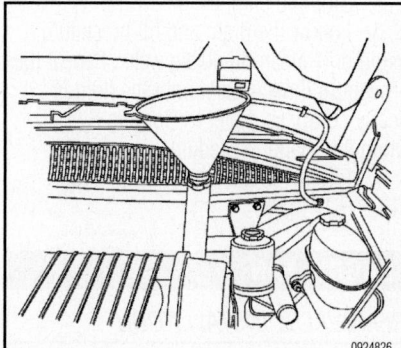

Fig. 108 Place a funnel into the upper radiator hose

    b. Discolored—Follow the flush procedure. Refer to Flushing.
Filling Procedure

✻✻ CAUTION

The procedure below must be followed. Improper coolant level could result in a low or high coolant level condition, causing engine damage.

11. Connect the lower radiator hose.
12. Using hose clamp pliers position the clamp into the original position on the hose.
13. If the engine block drain plug was removed, perform the following:

    a. Apply pipe sealer to the drain plug.

14. Install the drain plug and tighten to 16 ft. lbs. (22 Nm).
15. Lower the vehicle.
16. Using hose clamp pliers, position the upper radiator hose clamp at the radiator.
17. Remove the upper radiator hose from the radiator.
18. Remove the coolant air bleed hose from the radiator.
19. Place a funnel into the upper radiator hose.

➡**Use a 50/50 mixture of DEX-COOL® antifreeze and deionized water.**

20. Slowly fill the cooling system through the upper radiator hose with a 50/50 coolant mixture until the coolant comes out the coolant air bleed hose. Refer to Fluid Capacities.
21. Connect the upper radiator hose to the radiator.
22. Using the hose clamp pliers, position the radiator hose clamp into the original position on the hose.
23. Connect the coolant air bleed hose to the radiator.
24. Fill the radiator with coolant through the filler neck.
25. Install the coolant pressure cap.
26. Fill the coolant overflow bottle to the full line.
27. Start the engine.
28. Run the engine at 2,000—2,500 RPM until the engine reaches normal operating temperature.
29. Allow the engine to idle for 3 minutes.
30. Shut the engine OFF.
31. Allow the engine to cool.
32. Top off the coolant as necessary.
33. Inspect the concentration of the engine coolant, using a coolant tester.

34. Rinse away any excess coolant from the engine and the engine compartment.
35. Inspect the cooling system for leaks.

2011 Models—Except Diesel Engines

Draining Procedure

✻✻ WARNING

With a pressurized cooling system, the coolant temperature in the radiator can be considerably higher than the boiling point of the solution at atmospheric pressure. Removal of the surge tank cap, while the cooling system is hot and under high pressure, causes the solution to boil instantaneously with explosive force. This will cause the solution to spew out over the engine, the fenders, and the person removing the cap. Serious bodily injury may result.

1. Park the vehicle on a level surface.
2. Remove the coolant pressure cap.
3. Raise and support the vehicle.
4. Place a drain pan under the lower radiator hose.
5. Place a drain pan under the lower radiator hose.
6. Using the J 38185 hose clamp pliers or an equivalent, reposition the lower radiator hose clamp at the radiator.
7. Remove the lower radiator hose from the radiator.
8. Drain the cooling system.
9. If a complete engine block drain is required, remove the engine block drain plug.
10. Inspect the coolant.
11. Follow the appropriate procedure based on the condition of the coolant.

    a. Normal in appearance—Follow the filling procedure.

    b. Discolored—Follow the flush procedure. Refer to Flushing.
Filling Procedure

✻✻ CAUTION

You must follow the following procedure. Improper coolant level could result in a low or high coolant level condition, causing engine damage.

12. Connect the lower radiator hose.
13. Using hose clamp pliers, position the clamp into the original position on the hose.
14. If the engine block drain plug was removed, perform the following:

a. Apply pipe sealer to the drain plug.

b. Install the drain plug and tighten to 16 ft. lbs. (22 Nm).

15. Lower the vehicle.

16. Using hose clamp pliers, position the upper radiator hose clamp at the radiator.

➡**Use a 50/50 mixture of DEX-COOL® antifreeze and deionized water.**

17. Slowly fill the cooling system through the surge tank with a 50/50 coolant mixture until the coolant comes out the coolant air bleed hose. Refer to Fluid Capacities.

18. Install the coolant pressure cap.

19. Start the engine.

20. Run the engine at 2,000–2,500 RPM until the engine reaches normal operating temperature.

21. Allow the engine to idle for 3 minutes.

22. Shut the engine OFF.

23. Allow the engine to cool.

24. Top off the coolant as necessary.

25. Inspect the concentration of the engine coolant, using the J 26568 coolant and battery tester or an equivalent.

26. Rinse away any excess coolant from the engine and the engine compartment.

27. Inspect the cooling system for leaks.

Diesel Engines

See Figure 109.

✳✳ WARNING

To avoid being burned, do not remove the radiator cap or surge tank cap while the engine is hot. The cooling system will release scalding fluid and steam under pressure if radiator cap or surge tank cap is removed while the engine and radiator are still hot.

1. Follow the steps below in order to remove the surge tank fill cap:

a. Slowly rotate the cap counterclockwise.

b. Stop rotating and allow the hissing to stop.

c. After all the hissing stops, continue turning counterclockwise in order to remove the cap.

2. Raise and support the vehicle.

3. Place a drain pan under the lower radiator hose and/or drain cock.

4. Remove quick connect snap ring.

5. Reposition the lower radiator hose and/or drain cock from the radiator.

6. Drain the cooling system.

7. If a complete engine block drain is

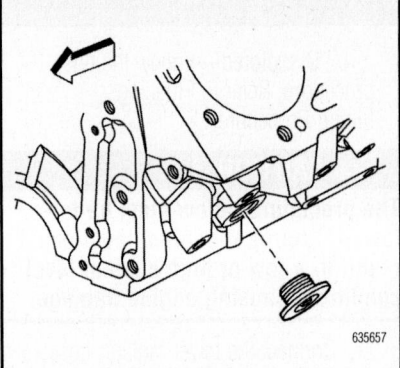

Fig. 109 Left and right engine block coolant drain plugs

635657

required, remove the left and right engine block coolant drain plugs.

8. Remove the engine block coolant heater, if equipped.

9. Inspect the coolant.

10. Follow the appropriate procedure based on the condition of the coolant:

a. Normal in appearance—Follow the filling procedure.

b. Discolored—Follow the flush procedure. Refer to Flushing.

Filling Procedure

✳✳ CAUTION

The procedure below must be followed. Improper coolant level could result in a low or high coolant level condition, causing engine damage.

➡**If a complete engine block was drained, GM recommends Vac-N-Fill.**

11. Install the lower radiator hose and/or drain cock to the radiator.

12. Reposition the lower radiator hose and install quick connect snap ring.

13. If the left and right engine block coolant drain plugs were removed, perform the following:

a. Apply pipe sealer to the drain plugs.

b. Install the drain plugs and tighten them to 44 ft. lbs. (60 Nm).

14. Install the engine block coolant heater, if equipped.

15. Lower the vehicle.

➡**Use a 50/50 mixture of DEX-COOL® antifreeze and clean, drinkable water.**

16. Slowly fill the cooling system with a 50/50 coolant mixture. Refer to Fluid Capacities.

17. Slowly continue filling as the level goes down.

18. Start the engine.

19. Run the engine at 2,000—2,500 RPM until the engine reaches normal operating temperature.

The engine should reach an operating temperature of 90°C (194°F) and the upper radiator hose should be HOT.

20. Continue to run the engine at 2,000—2,500 RPM for 5 more minutes.

21. Slowly add more coolant to the cooling system.

22. Allow the engine to idle for 5 minutes.

23. Slowly add more coolant to the cooling system.

24. Repeat steps 10 and 11.

25. Install the radiator cap.

26. Shut the engine OFF.

27. Allow the engine to cool.

28. Top off the coolant as necessary.

29. Inspect the concentration of the engine coolant using a tester, such as the J 26568 coolant and battery tester.

30. Rinse away any excess coolant from the engine and the engine compartment.

FLUSHING

Note the following:

• Do not use a chemical flush.

• Store used coolant in the proper manner, such as in a used engine coolant holding tank. Do not pour used coolant down a drain. Ethylene glycol antifreeze is a very toxic chemical. Do not dispose of coolant into the sewer system or ground water. This is illegal and ecologically unsound.

• Various methods and equipment can be used to flush the cooling system. If special equipment is used, such as a back flusher, follow the manufacturer's instructions. However, always remove the thermostat before back flushing the system.

1. Block the drive wheels.

2. Place the transmission in park (P) or neutral (N).

3. Engage the park brake.

4. Run the engine until the thermostat opens.

5. Stop the engine.

6. Follow the drain and fill procedure using only clean drinkable water. Repeat the procedure if necessary, until the fluid is nearly colorless. Refer to Cooling System Drain and Refill Procedure.

7. Fill the coolant surge tank to the FULL HOT mark.

ENGINE FAN

REMOVAL & INSTALLATION

See Figure 110.

1. If a fan assembly fails, inspect the hub and the drive components. A fan

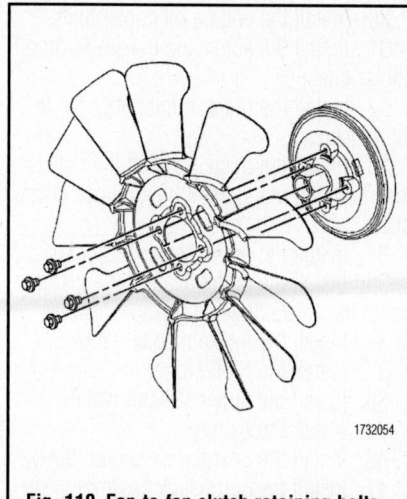

Fig. 110 Fan-to-fan clutch retaining bolts

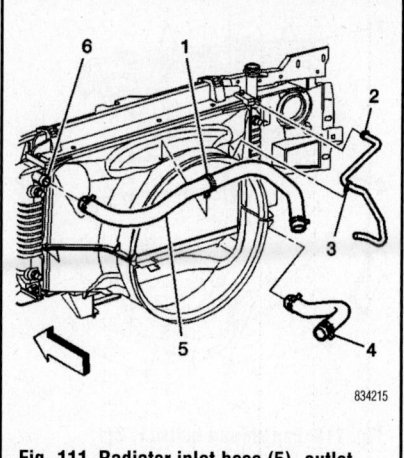

Fig. 111 Radiator inlet hose (5), outlet heater hose (2)

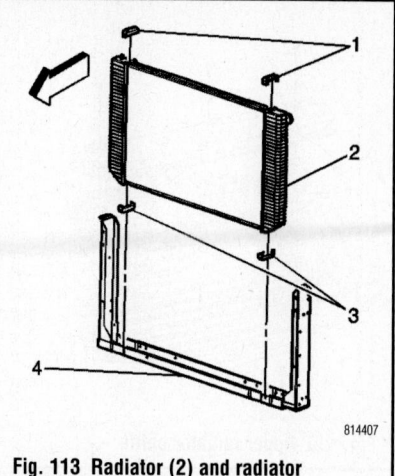

Fig. 113 Radiator (2) and radiator insulators (1, 3)

assembly may fail due to an imbalance in the hub. This type of failure may not be the fault of the blades.

✳✳ CAUTION

If a fan blade is bent or damaged, do not repair and use the damaged part. Replace a bent or damaged fan assembly with a new fan assembly. Using a fan with a different diameter, pitch, number of blades, or type of blade material may affect the cooling efficiency, performance and engine noise level.

2. Remove the fan clutch assembly.
3. Remove the fan-to-fan clutch retaining bolts.
4. Remove the fan from the fan clutch.

To install:

5. Install the fan to the fan clutch.
6. Install the fan to fan clutch retaining bolts and tighten to 17 ft. lbs. (23 Nm).
7. Install the fan clutch assembly.

RADIATOR

REMOVAL & INSTALLATION

Gas Engines

See Figures 111 through 113.

➡**Always install a new set of insulators when replacing a radiator. Used insulators may be worn or too large for the new radiator. These conditions may cause the new radiator to be loose.**

1. Remove the air cleaner assembly.
2. Remove the coolant recovery reservoir.
3. Remove the clamp at the radiator inlet using the J 38185 hose clamp pliers or an equivalent.

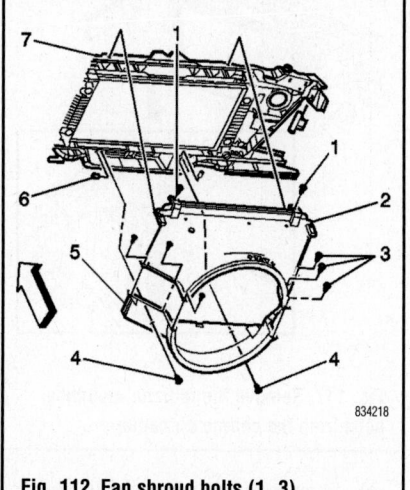

Fig. 112 Fan shroud bolts (1, 3)

4. Remove the radiator inlet hose (5) from the radiator.
5. Remove the outlet heater hose clamp at the radiator using hose clamp pliers.
6. Remove the outlet heater hose (2) from the radiator.
7. Remove the automatic transmission cooler lines.
8. Remove the engine oil cooler lines.
9. Remove the fan shroud bolts (1) from the top of the radiator support.
10. Remove the fan shroud bolts (3) from the sides of the fan shroud.
11. Remove the radiator (2).
12. Remove the radiator insulators (1, 3).
13. Inspect the following components:
   • The radiator
   • The insulators
   • The hoses and clamps
   • The mounting hardware
   • Replace the components as necessary.

To install:

14. Install the radiator insulators.
15. Install the radiator.
16. Install the fan shroud bolts to the top of the radiator support and tighten to 53 inch lbs. (6 Nm).
17. Install the fan shroud bolts to the sides of the fan shroud and tighten to 53 inch lbs. (6 Nm).
18. Install the engine oil cooler lines.
19. Install the automatic transmission oil cooler lines.
20. Install the radiator inlet hose to the radiator.
21. Install the hose clamp at the radiator inlet housing using hose clamp pliers.
22. Install the outlet heater hose.
23. Install the outlet heater hose clamp using J 39529, the wiper linkage installer, or an equivalent.
24. Install the coolant recovery reservoir.
25. Install the air cleaner assembly.
26. Inspect the automatic transmission fluid level. Refer to Fluid Capacities.
27. Inspect the engine oil level. Refer to Fluid Capacities.

Diesel Engines

See Figures 114 through 117.

➡**Always install a new set of insulators when replacing a radiator. Used insulators may be worn or too large for the new radiator. These conditions may cause the new radiator to be loose.**

1. Remove the air cleaner assembly.
2. Remove the upper radiator baffle.
3. Remove the surge tank.
4. Remove the battery.
5. Remove the charged air cooler inlet pipe.

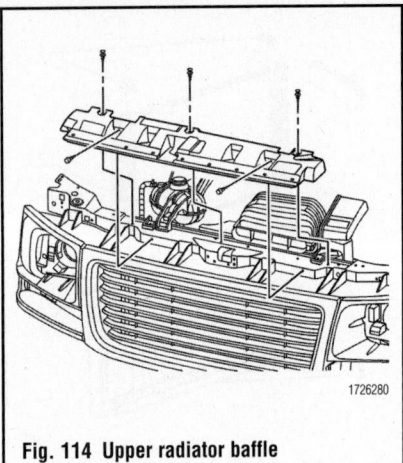

Fig. 114 Upper radiator baffle

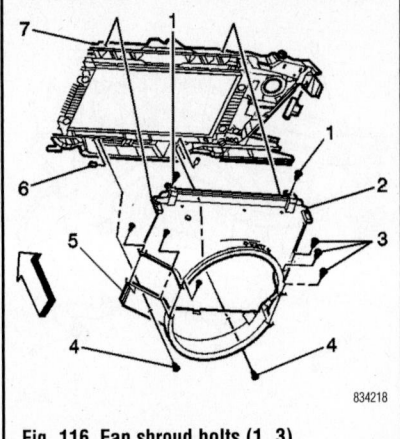

Fig. 116 Fan shroud bolts (1, 3)

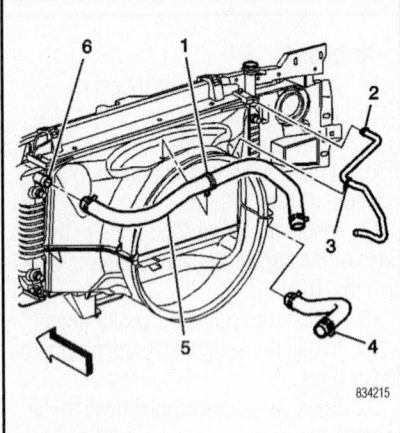

Fig. 115 Radiator inlet hose (5), outlet heater hose (2)

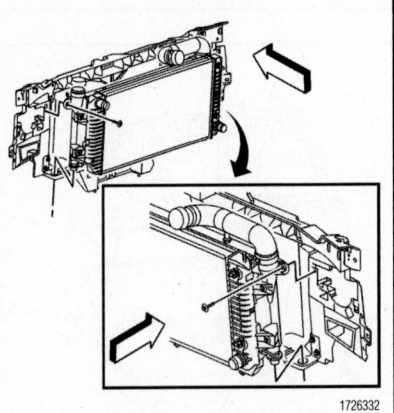

Fig. 117 Remove the radiator mounting bolts from the charge air cooler

6. Remove the clamp at the radiator inlet using the J 38185 hose clamp pliers or an equivalent.

7. Remove the radiator inlet hose (5) from the radiator.

8. Remove the outlet heater hose clamp at the radiator using hose clamp pliers.

9. Remove the outlet heater hose (2) from the radiator.

10. Remove the automatic transmission cooler lines.

11. Remove the engine oil cooler lines.

12. Remove the engine oil fill tube.

13. Remove the intake manifold tube.

14. Remove the upper radiator baffle.

15. Remove the fan shroud bolts (1) from the top of the radiator support.

16. Remove the fan shroud bolts (3) from the sides of the fan shroud.

17. Remove the radiator mounting bolts from the charge air cooler.

18. Remove the charge air cooler bolts to the core support.

19. Remove the radiator and charge air cooler as an assembly.

20. Remove the radiator bolts to the charge air cooler.

21. Remove the radiator insulators.

22. Inspect the following components:
    a. The radiator
    b. The insulators
    c. The hoses and clamps
    d. The mounting hardware

23. Replace the components as necessary.

To install:

24. Install the radiator insulators.

25. Install the radiator to the charge air cooler and tighten the bolts to 53 inch lbs. (6 Nm).

26. Install the radiator and charge air cooler as an assembly.

27. Install the radiator mounting bolts to the charged air cooler and tighten to 53 inch lbs. (6 Nm).

28. Install the fan shroud bolts (1) to the top of the radiator support and tighten to 53 inch lbs. (6 Nm).

29. Install the fan shroud bolts (3) to the sides of the fan shroud and tighten to 53 inch lbs. (6 Nm).

30. Install the engine oil cooler lines.

31. Install the automatic transmission oil cooler lines.

32. Install the radiator inlet hose (5) to the radiator.

33. Install the hose clamp at the radiator inlet housing using the J 38185 hose clamp pliers.

34. Install the outlet heater hose (2).

35. Install the outlet heater hose clamp using the J 39529 wiper linkage installer.

36. Install the intake manifold tube.

37. Install the oil fill tube.

38. Install the upper radiator baffle.

39. Install the battery.

40. Install the charged air cooler pipe.

41. Install the surge tank assembly.

42. Install the air cleaner assembly.

43. Install the upper radiator baffle.

44. Inspect the automatic transmission fluid level. Refer to Fluid Capacities.

45. Inspect the engine oil level. Refer to Fluid Capacities.

THERMOSTAT

REMOVAL & INSTALLATION

V6 Gasoline Engines

See Figures 118 and 119.

1. Remove the air cleaner and the duct assembly.

2. Partially drain the coolant. Refer to Cooling System Drain and Refill.

3. Remove the coolant recovery reservoir.

4. Disconnect the radiator hose from the thermostat housing.

5. Remove the bolts attaching the thermostat housing to the thermostat.

6. Remove the thermostat housing.

7. Remove the thermostat.

8. Clean the gasket mating surfaces.

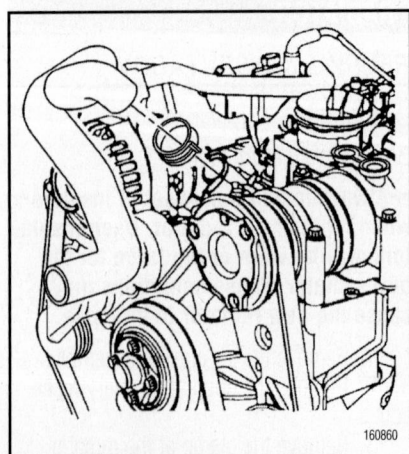

Fig. 118 Disconnect the hose from the thermostat housing.

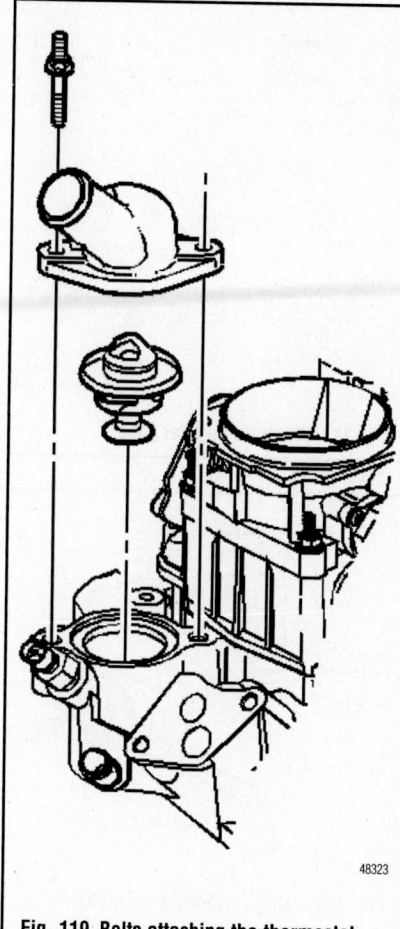

Fig. 119 Bolts attaching the thermostat housing to the thermostat

To install:

9. Install the thermostat.

10. Install the thermostat housing to the intake manifold.

11. Install the bolts to the housing and tighten to 18 ft. lbs. (25 Nm).

12. Connect the radiator hose to the thermostat housing.

13. Install the coolant recovery reservoir.

14. Install the air cleaner and the duct.

15. Refill the cooling system.

16. Bleed the air from the cooling system.

17. Inspect the thermostat housing and the gasket for coolant leaks.

V8 Gasoline Engines

See Figure 120.

➡The thermostat is not serviceable separately. The water pump inlet and thermostat must be replaced as an assembly.

1. Remove the bolt from the coolant recovery reservoir and reposition.

2. Remove the air cleaner assembly.

3. Remove the radiator outlet hose.

4. Remove the water pump inlet bolts.

5. Remove the water pump inlet and thermostat from the water pump.

To install:

6. Install the thermostat and water pump inlet to the water pump.

7. Install the water pump inlet bolts and tighten to 11 ft. lbs. (15 Nm).

8. Install the radiator outlet hose.

9. Install the air cleaner assembly.

10. Install the coolant recovery reservoir and bolt and tighten to 97 inch lbs. (11 Nm).

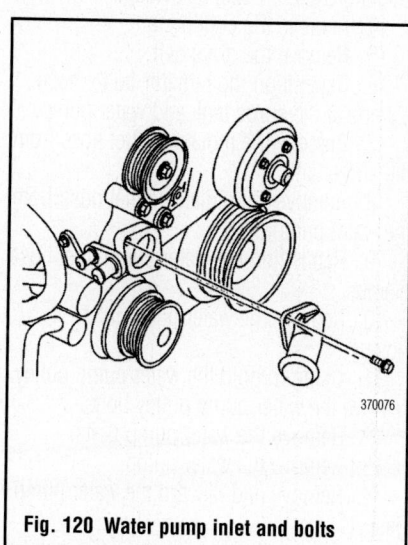

Fig. 120 Water pump inlet and bolts

Diesel Engines

See Figures 121 through 125.

1. Remove the upper fan shroud.

2. Remove the intake manifold.

3. Drain the cooling system. Refer to Cooling System Drain and Refill.

4. Remove the radiator inlet hose.

5. Disconnect the turbocharger coolant feed pipe retaining bracket bolt.

6. Remove the fuel pressure valve bracket bolt (1) and reposition the fuel line (2).

7. Remove the thermostat bolts (1) from the engine coolant outlet pipe/thermostat housing (2).

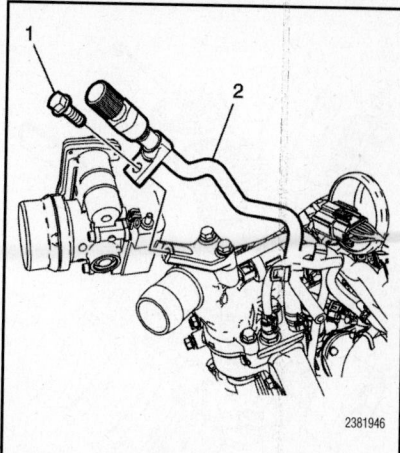

Fig. 121 Fuel pressure valve bracket bolt (1) and fuel line (2)

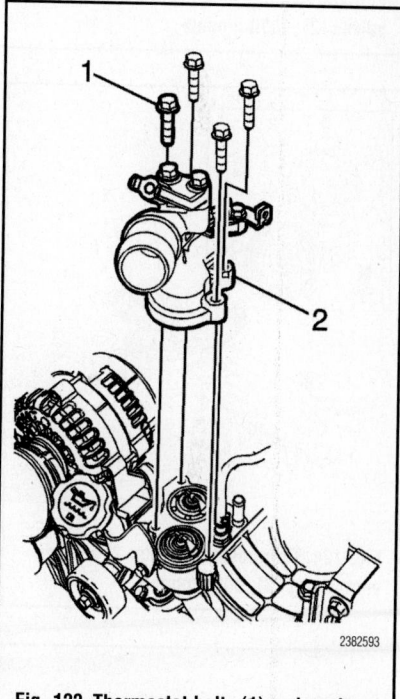

Fig. 122 Thermostat bolts (1) and engine coolant outlet pipe (2)

8. Remove the thermostats from the engine coolant thermostat housing.
Inspection Procedure

9. Inspect the thermostats for sticking, cracks, and/or leakage of wax.

10. Replace the thermostats if you find damage.

11. Clean the thermostat housing and thermostat housing cover sealing surfaces.

To install:

12. Install the thermostats and seals to the thermostat housing.

13. The rear thermostat has 2 vent valves. Install the vent valves towards the rear of the engine.

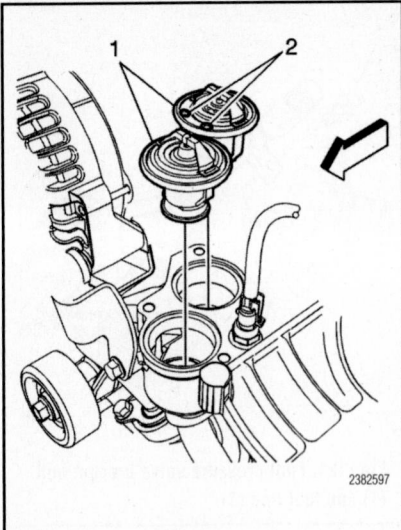

Fig. 123 Thermostats (1) and two vent valves (2), 2010 models

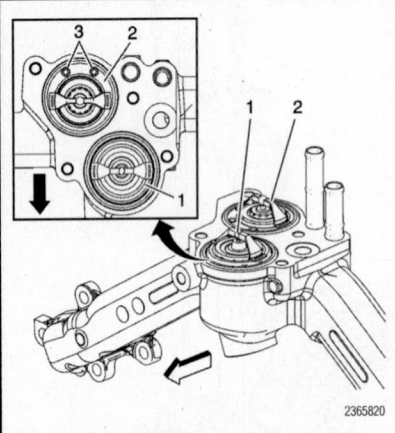

Fig. 124 Thermostats (1-rear, 2) and two vent valves (3), 2011 models

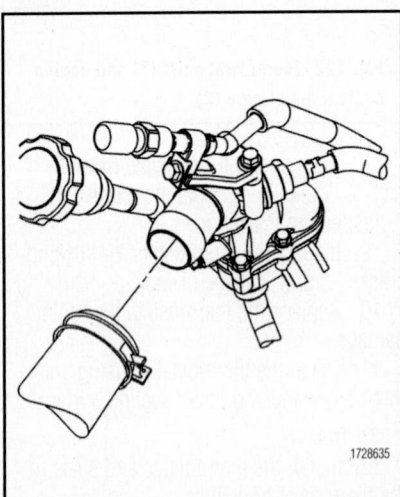

Fig. 125 Compress the clamp and connect the radiator inlet hose to the thermostat housing

14. Position the thermostat housing and install the bolts. Tighten to 17 ft. lbs. (25 Nm).

15. Connect the turbocharger coolant feed pipe retaining bracket bolt.

16. Position the fuel pressure valve bracket bolt and fuel line to the thermostat housing and tighten to 17 ft. lbs. (25 Nm).

17. Compress the clamp and connect the radiator inlet hose to the thermostat housing.

18. Install the intake manifold tube.

19. Install the upper fan shroud.

20. Fill the cooling system.

WATER PUMP

REMOVAL & INSTALLATION

V6 Gasoline Engines

See Figures 126 through 129.

1. Remove the air cleaner assembly.

2. Remove the air cleaner outlet resonator duct.

3. Drain the cooling system. Refer to Cooling System Drain and Refill.

4. Remove the cooling fan.

5. Remove the drive belt.

6. Reposition the radiator outlet hose clamps at the surge tank and water pump.

7. Remove the radiator outlet hose from the surge tank.

8. Remove the radiator outlet hose from the water pump.

9. Reposition the water pump inlet hose clamps.

10. Remove the water pump inlet hose.

11. Using to hold the water pump pulley, remove the water pump pulley bolts.

12. Remove the water pump bolts.

13. Remove the water pump.

14. Remove and discard the water pump gaskets.

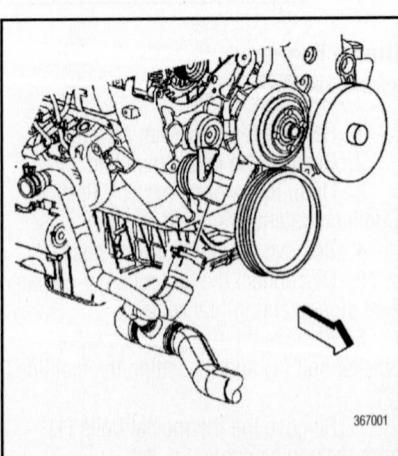

Fig. 126 Radiator outlet hose removal

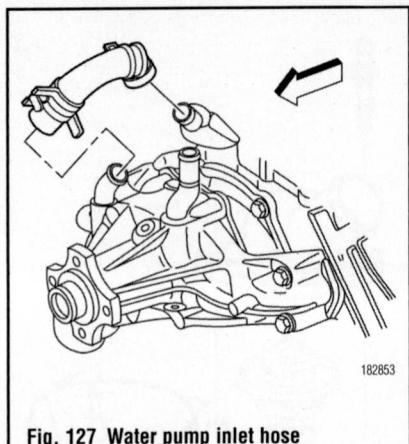

Fig. 127 Water pump inlet hose

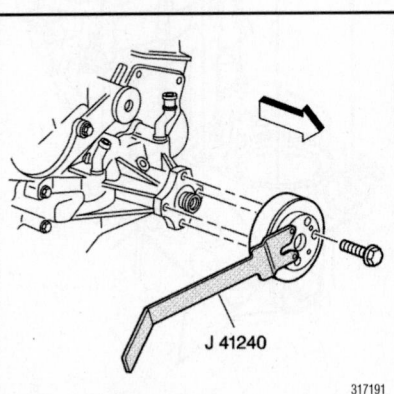

Fig. 128 Using J 41240, a fan clutch remover and installer, or equivalents, to hold the water pump pulley, remove the water pump pulley bolts

15. Clean and inspect the water pump, if necessary.

To install:

16. If reusing the fasteners, apply sealant GM P/N 12346004 (Canadian P/N 10953480), or an equivalent to the threads of the water pump bolts.

17. Install NEW water pump gaskets and the water pump.

18. Install the water pump bolts and tighten to 45 Nm (33 lb ft).

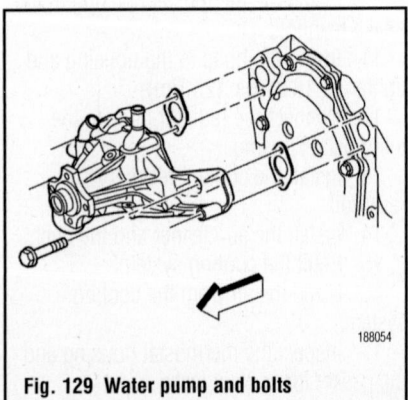

Fig. 129 Water pump and bolts

19. Using a fan clutch remover and installer tool to hold the water pump pulley, install the water pump pulley bolts and tighten to 18 ft. lbs. (25 Nm).

➡️**After assembly, the hose clamp tangs (water pump end) must point forward and the upper tang should be level with the outside diameter of the water pump inlet hose.**

20. Install the water pump inlet hose.

21. Position the water pump inlet hose clamps.

22. Install the radiator outlet hose to the water pump.

23. Install the radiator outlet hose to the surge tank.

24. Position the radiator outlet hose clamps at the surge tank and water pump.

25. Install the drive belt.

26. Install the cooling fan.

27. Install the air cleaner outlet resonator duct.

28. Install the air cleaner assembly.

29. Fill the cooling system. Refer to Cooling System Drain and Refill.

30. Inspect the cooling system for leaks.

V8 Gasoline Engines

See Figures 130 through 135.

1. Remove the air cleaner outlet assembly.

2. Drain the cooling system. Refer to Cooling System Drain and Refill.

3. Reposition the radiator vent inlet hose clamp (1) at the coolant air bleed pipe fitting.

4. Remove the radiator vent inlet hose (2) from the coolant air bleed pipe fitting.

5. Reposition the radiator inlet hose clamp (3) at the water pump.

6. Remove the radiator inlet hose from the water pump.

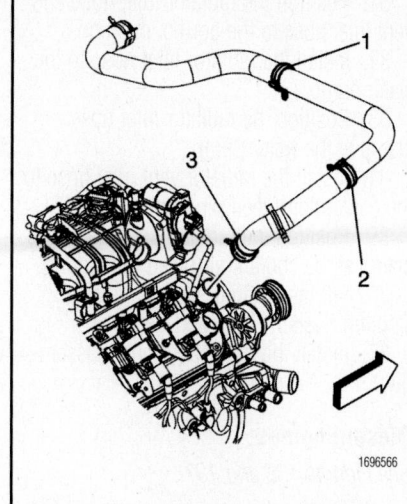

Fig. 131 Radiator inlet hose clamp (3)

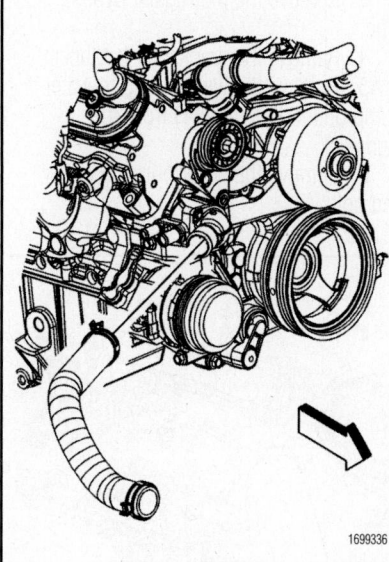

Fig. 132 Radiator outlet hose and hose clamp

7. Reposition the radiator inlet hose and vent inlet hose out of the way.

8. Remove the accessory drive belt.

9. Reposition the radiator outlet hose clamp at the water pump.

10. Remove the radiator outlet hose from the water pump.

11. Reposition the outlet hose out of the way.

12. Reposition the radiator surge tank outlet hose clamp at the water pump (1).

13. Remove the radiator surge tank outlet hose (2) from the water pump.

14. Reposition the outlet hose out of the way.

15. Reposition the heater inlet hose clamp (1) at the water pump.

16. Remove the heater inlet hose (2) from the water pump.

17. Reposition the inlet hose out of the way.

18. Remove the water pump bolts (301).

19. Remove the water pump (300) and gaskets (306). Discard the gaskets.

To install:

❄️ CAUTION

DO NOT use cooling system seal tabs, or similar compounds, unless otherwise instructed. The use of cooling system seal tabs, or similar compounds, may restrict coolant flow through the passages of the cooling system or the engine components. Restricted coolant flow may cause engine overheating and/or damage to the cooling system or the engine components/assembly.

➡️**All gaskets surfaces are to be free of oil or other foreign material during assembly.**

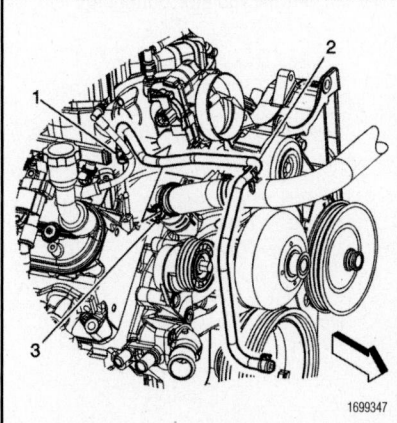

Fig. 130 Radiator vent inlet hose clamp (1) and vent inlet hose (2)

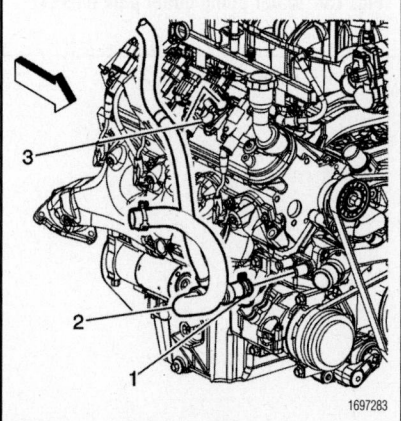

Fig. 133 Radiator surge tank outlet hose clamp (1), outlet hose (2)

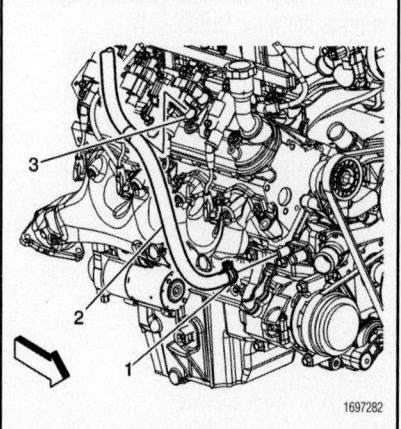

Fig. 134 Heater inlet hose clamp (1) and inlet hose (2)

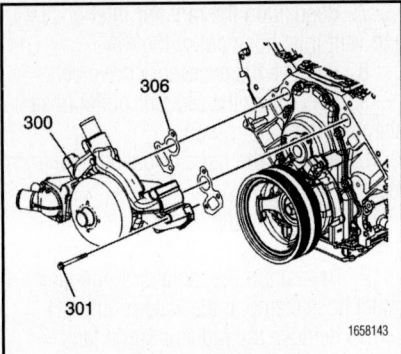

Fig. 135 Water pump bolts (301), water pump (300) and gaskets (309)

20. Inspect the drained coolant for sand or other debris, flush the system as needed. Refer to Flushing.

21. Inspect and clear the radiator vent hose fitting, if necessary.
   • There is a small 0.080 in (2.0 mm) orifice (vent hose fitting) in the neck of the radiator where the coolant vent hose from the engine attaches to the radiator.

22. Position the water pump and NEW gaskets (306) to the engine block.

23. Install the water pump bolts (301).
   a. Tighten the bolts a first pass to 11 ft. lbs. (15 Nm).
   b. Tighten the bolts a final pass to 22 ft. lbs. (30 Nm).

24. Position and install the heater inlet hose to the water pump.

25. Position the heater inlet hose clamp at the water pump.

26. Position and install the radiator surge tank outlet hose to the water pump.

27. Position the radiator surge tank outlet hose clamp at the water pump.

28. Position and install the radiator outlet hose to the water pump.

29. Position the radiator outlet hose clamp at the water pump.

30. Install the accessory drive belt.

31. Position the radiator inlet hose and vent inlet hose to the correct position.

32. Install the radiator inlet hose to the water pump.

33. Position the radiator inlet hose clamp at the water pump.

34. Install the radiator vent inlet hose to the coolant air bleed pipe fitting.

35. Position the radiator vent inlet hose clamp at the coolant air bleed pipe fitting.

36. Fill the cooling system. Refer to Cooling System Drain and Refill.

37. Install the air cleaner outlet assembly.

Diesel Engines

See Figures 136 and 137.

1. Drain the cooling system. Refer to Cooling System Drain and Refill.

2. Remove the radiator outlet pipe.

3. Remove the thermostat bypass pipe.

4. Remove the crankshaft balancer.

5. Remove the water pump to water pump outlet pipe nuts (1) from the studs (2).

6. Remove the water pump nut (1) and bolts (2).

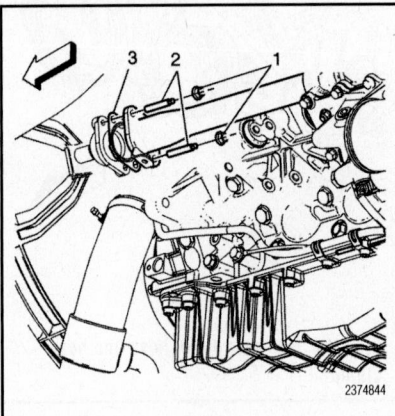

Fig. 136 Water pump outlet pipe nuts (1) and studs (2)

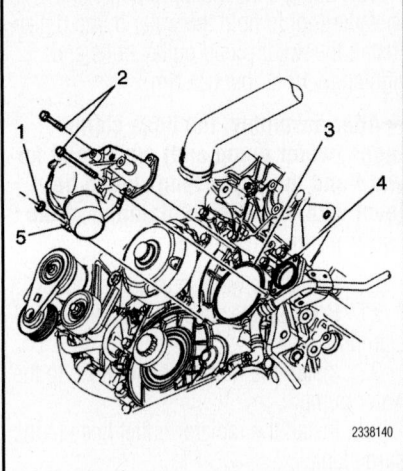

Fig. 137 Water pump nut (1), bolts (2), water pump (5), O-ring (3), and outlet pipe gasket (4)

➡**The 2 bolts are different lengths.**

7. Remove the water pump (5).

8. Remove and discard the water pump O-ring (3) and the water pump outlet pipe gasket (4).

   To install:

9. Lubricate the water pump O-ring with engine oil.

10. Install the water pump outlet pipe gasket and the lubricated water pump O-ring.

11. Install the water pump nut and bolts. Ensure the correct length bolt is used in the proper location and tighten to 18 ft. lbs. (25 Nm).

12. Install the water pump to water pump outlet pipe nuts to the studs and tighten to 18 ft. lbs. (25 Nm).

13. Install the crankshaft balancer.

14. Install the thermostat bypass pipe.

15. Install the radiator outlet pipe.

ENGINE ELECTRICAL

BATTERY SYSTEM

BATTERY

REMOVAL & INSTALLATION

See Figures 138 and 139.

✴✴ CAUTION

Batteries produce explosive gases. Batteries contain corrosive acid. Batteries supply levels of electrical current high enough to cause burns. Therefore, in order to reduce the risk of personal injury while working near a battery, observe the following guidelines:

- Always shield your eyes.
- Avoid leaning over the battery whenever possible.
- Do not expose the battery to open flames or sparks.
- Do not allow battery acid to contact the eyes or the skin.
- Flush any contacted areas with water immediately and thoroughly.
- Get medical help.

✴✴ WARNING

Car batteries contain lead, acid, and plastic, and are dangerous to both you and the environment if disposed of incorrectly. Recycle the battery to conserve natural resources and energy.

1. Remove the fender brace.

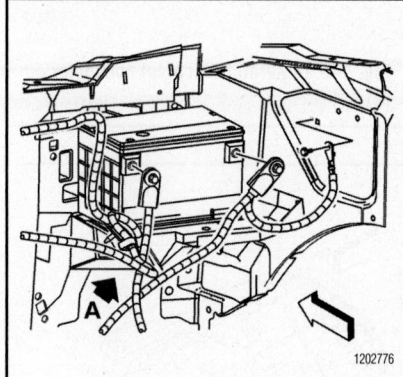

Fig. 138 Battery cables and terminals

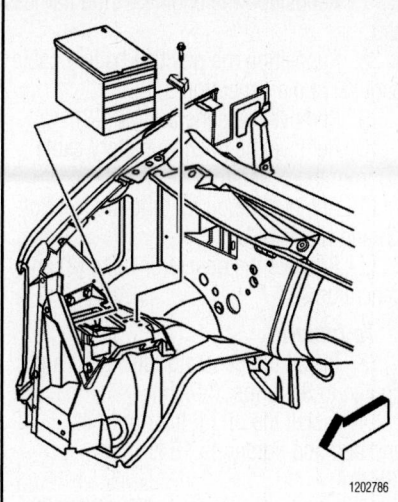

Fig. 139 Battery hold-down retainer bolt and retainer

2. Disconnect the battery negative cable from the negative battery terminal.
3. Disconnect the battery positive cable from the positive battery terminal.
4. Remove the battery hold-down retainer bolt and retainer.
5. Remove the battery from the vehicle.
6. Inspect the battery for the following:
   a. Damage
   b. Worn or corroded cables and connectors
   c. Damage or foreign objects in the battery carrier
7. If damage is noted, find and correct the cause.
8. Clean any corrosion from the battery cables and connectors.
9. Clean the battery tray and remove any foreign objects from the tray.

To install:
10. Install the battery into the battery tray.
11. Install the battery hold-down retainer and bolt and tighten to 12 ft. lbs. (18 Nm).
12. Connect the battery positive cable and the positive battery cable terminal to the battery.

13. Connect the battery negative cable and the negative battery cable terminal to the battery.
14. Install the fender brace.

BATTERY DISCONNECT/CONNECT

See Figure 140.

1. Turn OFF all the lamps and accessories.
2. Turn the ignition OFF.
3. Remove the battery negative cable bolt in order to disconnect the negative battery cable from the battery.
4. Remove the auxiliary negative battery cable bolt (1) and cable (2), from the auxiliary battery.

To install:

➡**Clean any existing corrosion from the battery terminal bolt flange and the battery cable end.**

5. Install the negative cable terminal bolt and cable to the battery and tighten to 14 Nm (123 lb in).

➡**Clean any existing corrosion from the battery terminal bolt flange and the battery cable end.**

6. If applicable, install the auxiliary negative cable terminal bolt (1) and cable (2) to the auxiliary battery and tighten to 14 Nm (123 lb in).

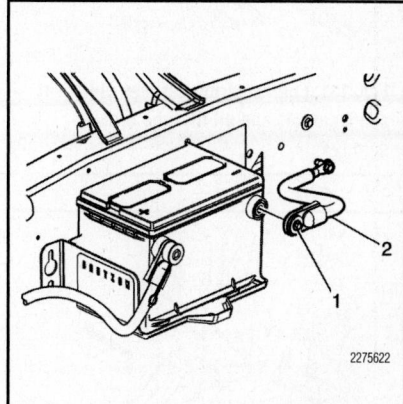

Fig. 140 Auxiliary battery negative cable bolt (1) and cable (2)

ALTERNATOR/ GENERATOR

REMOVAL & INSTALLATION

V6 Gasoline Engines

See Figures 141 through 144.

1. Disconnect the negative battery cable. Refer to Battery Negative Cable Disconnect/Connect in the Engine Electrical section in the Engine Electrical section

2. Remove the drive belt.

3. Unbolt and reposition the oil level indicator tube.

4. Unbolt and reposition the oil fill tube.

5. Disconnect the engine wiring harness electrical connector (1) from the generator.

6. Remove the oil fill tube bracket stud (2).

7. Reposition the engine wiring harness clip.

8. Reposition the positive battery cable boot (2) at the generator.

9. Remove the generator nut (3).

10. Remove the positive battery cable (1) from the generator.

11. Remove the oil fill tube bracket bolt (2) and bracket (1).

12. Remove the generator bolts (2) and generator (1).

To install:

13. Install the generator and bolts and tighten to 37 ft. lbs. (50 Nm).

14. Install the oil fill tube bracket and bolt and tighten to 18 ft. lbs. (25 Nm).

15. Install the positive cable to the generator.

16. Install the generator nut and tighten to 89 inch lbs. (10 Nm)

17. Position the positive cable boot at the generator.

18. Position the engine wiring harness clip to the generator bracket.

19. Install the oil fill tube bracket stud and tighten to 18 ft. lbs. (25 Nm).

20. Connect the engine wiring harness electrical connector to the generator.

21. Position and install the oil fill tube.

22. Position and install the oil level indicator tube.

23. Install the drive belt.

24. Connect the negative battery cable. Refer to Battery Negative Cable Disconnect/Connect in the Engine Electrical section.

V8 Gasoline Engines

See Figures 145 through 147.

1. Disconnect the negative battery cable. Refer to Battery Negative Cable

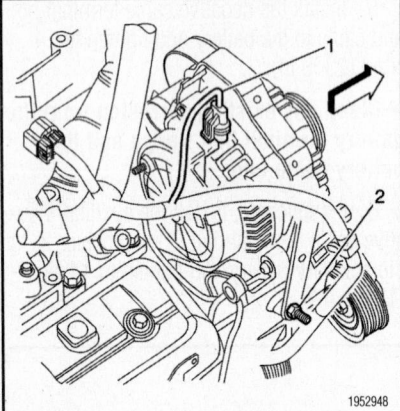

Fig. 141 Engine wiring harness electrical connector (1) and oil fill tube bracket stud (2)

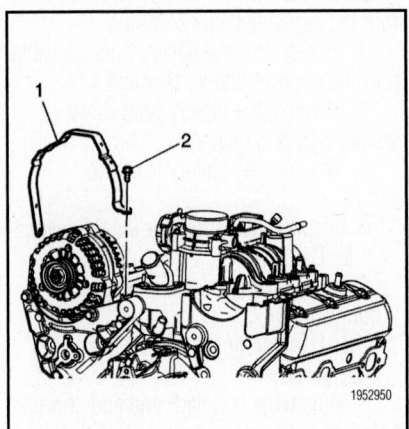

Fig. 143 Oil fill tube bracket bolt (2) and bracket (1)

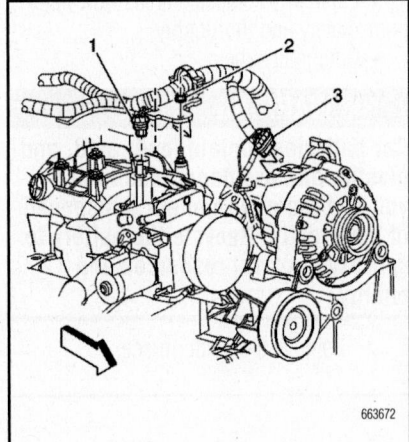

Fig. 145 Generator electrical connector (3)

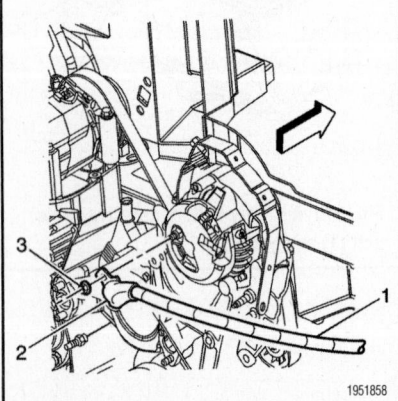

Fig. 142 Positive battery cable boot (2), generator nut (3), and positive battery cable (1)

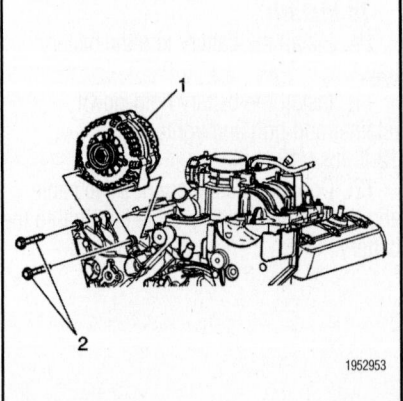

Fig. 144 Remove the generator bolts (2) and generator (1)

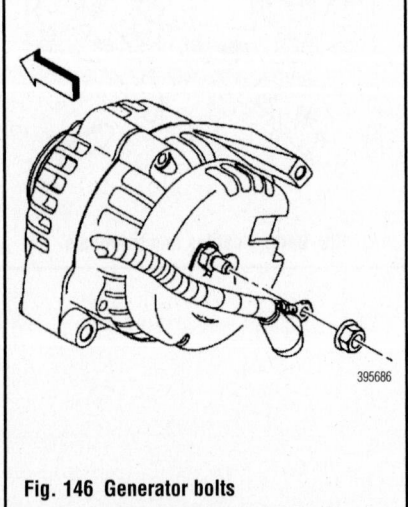

Fig. 146 Generator bolts

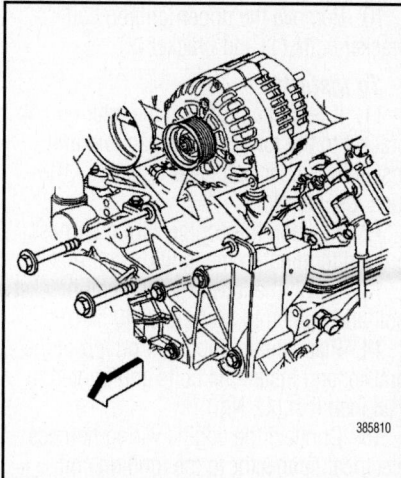

Fig. 147 Generator electrical connector (3)

Disconnect/Connect in the Engine Electrical section in the Engine Electrical section

2. Remove the accessory drive belt.

3. Disconnect the generator electrical connector (3).

4. Remove the generator cable from the generator and then perform the following:

    a. Slide the boot down, revealing the terminal stud.

    b. Remove the generator cable nut from the terminal stud.

    c. Remove the generator cable.

5. Remove the generator bolts.

6. Remove the generator from the bracket.

To install:

7. Install the generator to the bracket.

8. Install the generator bolts and tighten to 37 ft. lbs. (50 Nm).

9. Install the generator cable to the generator and perform the following:

    a. Install the generator cable.

    b. Install the generator cable nut to the terminal stud and tighten to 89 inch lbs. (10 Nm)

    c. Slide the boot over the terminal stud.

10. Connect the generator electrical connector (3).

11. Install the accessory drive belt.

12. Connect the negative battery cable. Refer to Battery Negative Cable Disconnect/Connect in the Engine Electrical section in the Engine Electrical section

Diesel Engines

See Figures 141 and 142.

1. Disconnect the negative battery cable. Refer to Battery Negative Cable Disconnect/Connect in the Engine Electrical section in the Engine Electrical section

2. Remove the upper fan shroud.

3. Remove the drive belt.

4. Uncover the B+ terminal (2) by sliding away the protective boot (1).

5. Remove the generator B+ terminal nut (2) and the electrical connector (4).

6. Remove the generator bolts (1) and generator (2) from the generator bracket.

To install:

7. Install the generator to the generator bracket and tighten the generator mounting bolts (1) to 37 ft. lbs. (50 Nm)

8. Connect the generator electrical connector.

9. Install the battery positive B+ cable terminal to the generator stud and tighten to 89 inch lbs. (10 Nm)

10. Slide the protective boot back onto the terminal stud.

11. Install the drive belt.

12. Install the upper fan shroud.

13. Connect the negative battery cable. Refer to Battery Negative Cable Disconnect/Connect in the Engine Electrical section in the Engine Electrical section

ENGINE ELECTRICAL

FIRING ORDER

V6 Gasoline Engines

The cast iron engine block has six cylinders arranged in a V shape with three cylinders in each bank. Starting at the front side of the engine block, the cylinders in the left bank are numbered 1-3-5 and cylinders in the right bank are numbered 2-4-6, when viewed from the rear. The firing order of the cylinders is 1-6-5-4-3-2.

V8 Gasoline Engines

The firing order of the cylinders is: 1-8-7-2-6-5-4-3.

• Cylinders 1, 3, 5 and 7 are the left bank.

• Cylinder 2, 4, 6 and 8 are the right bank.

Diesel Engines

See Figure 148.

The cylinders are positioned in a 90 degree "V" orientation. The number 1 cylinder is the right front. The firing order of the cylinders is: 1-2-7-8-4-5-6-3.

Fig. 148 Diesel engine block: the number 1 cylinder is the right front

IGNITION SYSTEM

IGNITION COIL

REMOVAL & INSTALLATION

4.3L Engine

See Figures 149 through 152.

1. Remove the engine cover.

2. Disconnect the chassis fuel feed pipe quick connect fitting from the engine fuel feed pipe.

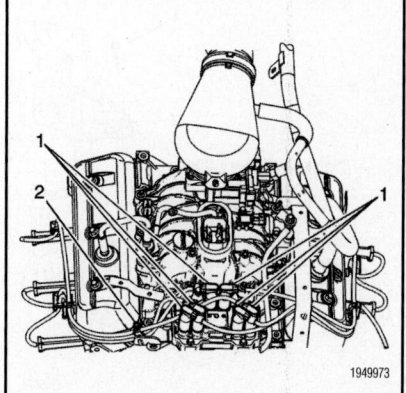

Fig. 149 Spark plug wires (1) and spark plug wire retainer (2)

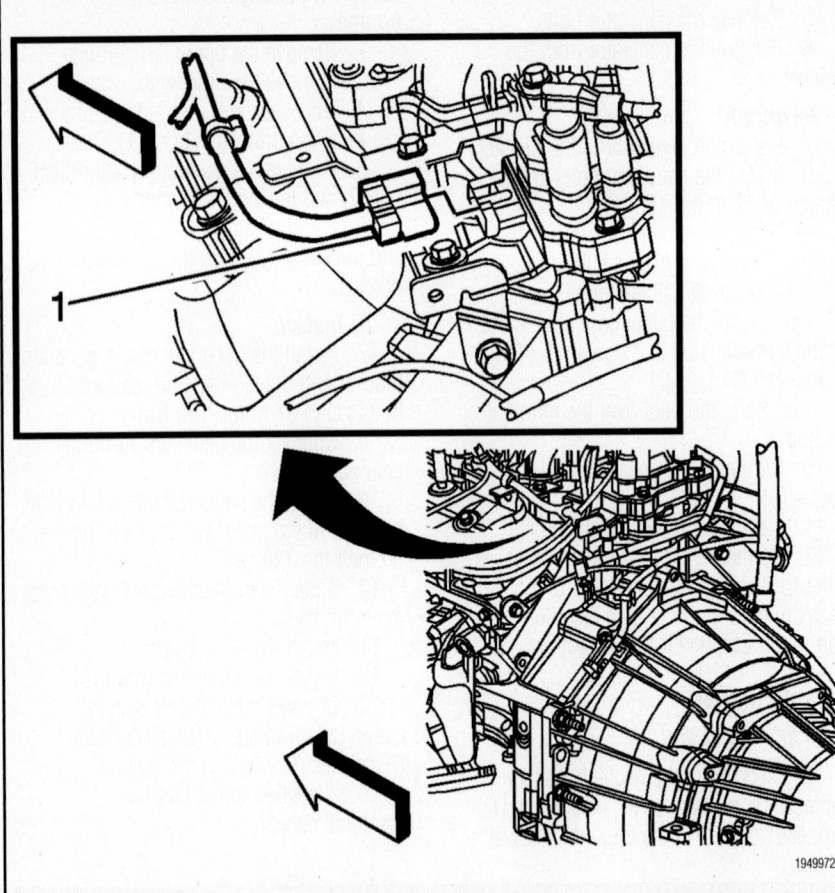

Fig. 150 Engine wiring harness electrical connector (1)

➡**Note the routing of the spark plug wires prior to disconnecting the wires from the ignition coil.**

3. Disconnect the spark plug wires (1) from the ignition coil.

4. Remove the spark plug wire retainer (2) from the ignition coil bracket.

5. Reposition the spark plug wires out of the way.

6. Disconnect engine wiring harness electrical connector (1) from the ignition coil.

7. Remove the ignition coil bolts (1) and ignition coil (2) from the bracket.

8. If required, remove the lower ignition coil bracket bolt (3).

9. Remove the engine wiring harness ground terminal from the ignition coil bracket.

10. Remove the upper ignition coil bracket bolts (1) and bracket (2).

To install:

11. If required, position the ignition coil bracket to the lower intake manifold and install the upper bolts and tighten to 106 inch lbs. (12 Nm).

12. Position the engine wiring harness ground terminal to the ignition coil bracket.

13. Install the lower ignition coil bracket bolt and tighten to 30 ft. lbs. (40 Nm).

14. Place the ignition coil on top of the bracket and install the bolts and tighten to 106 inch lbs. (12 Nm).

15. Connect the engine wiring harness electrical connector to the ignition coil.

16. Position the spark plug wires and install the spark plug wire retainer to the ignition coil bracket.

17. Connect the spark plug wires to the ignition coil as noted during removal.

18. Connect the chassis fuel feed pipe quick connect fitting to the engine fuel feed pipe.

19. Install the engine cover.

4.8L & 5.3L Engines

See Figures 153 through 155.

1. Remove the engine cover.

2. Disconnect the spark plug wires at the ignition coils.

3. Disconnect the ignition coil harness connector.

4. Remove the ignition coil mounting bolts.

5. Remove the ignition coil.

To install:

6. Install the ignition coil to the bracket.

7. Install the ignition coil mounting bolts and tighten to 71 inch lbs. (8 Nm).

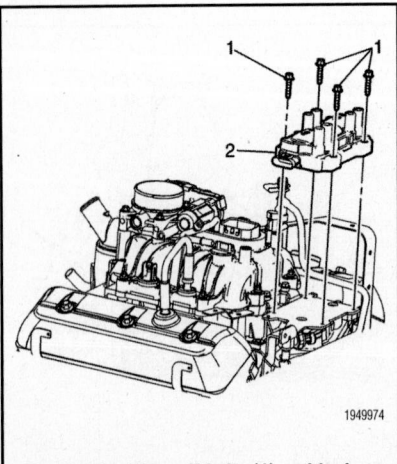

Fig. 151 Ignition coil bolts (1) and ignition coil (2)

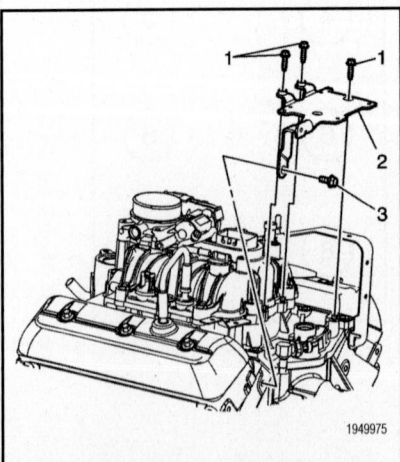

Fig. 152 Upper ignition coil bracket bolts (1) and bracket (2)

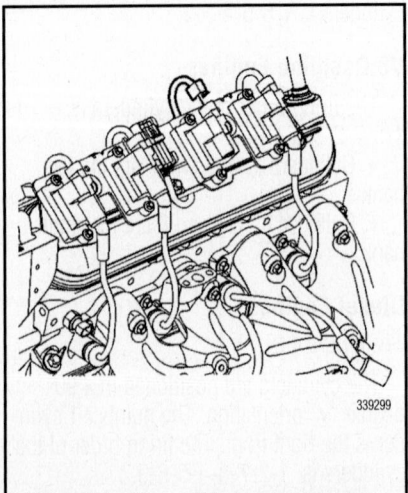

Fig. 153 Ignition coil harness connector

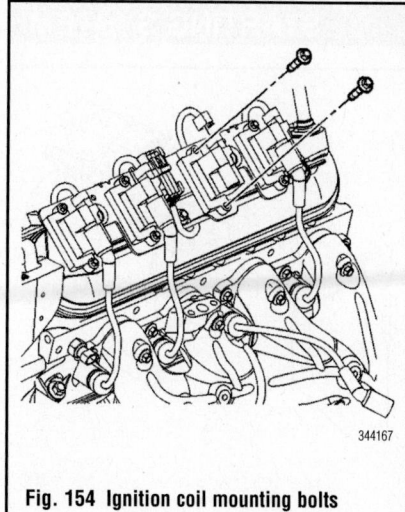

Fig. 154 Ignition coil mounting bolts

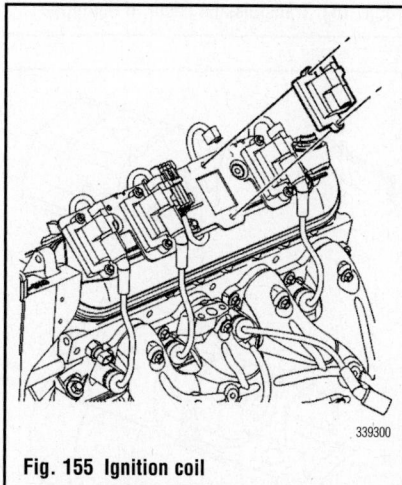

Fig. 155 Ignition coil

8. Connect the ignition coil harness connector.

9. Connect the spark plug wires at the ignition coils.

10. Install the engine cover.

IGNITION TIMING

ADJUSTMENT

Ignition timing is controlled by control modules. No adjustment is necessary or possible. On gas engines, the Knock Sensor (KS) system enables the control module to control ignition timing for the best possible performance while protecting the engine from potentially damaging levels of detonation (spark knock).

SPARK PLUGS

REMOVAL & INSTALLATION

4.3L Engine

See Figure 156.

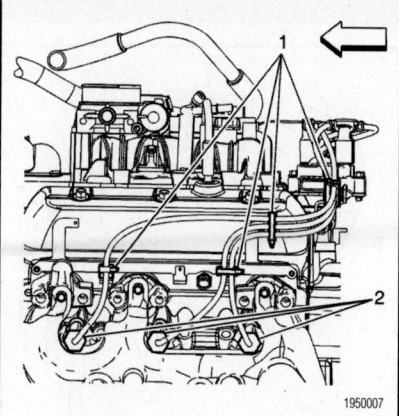

Fig. 156 Left side spark plug wire boots (2); right side similar

1. Remove the engine cover, if required.

2. If required, remove the appropriate left side spark plug wire boot(s) (2) from the spark plug(s) as follows:
   a. Twist the spark plug boot 1/2 turn.
   b. Pull ONLY on the spark plug boot or use a tool designed for this purpose in order to remove the spark plug wire boot from the spark plug.

3. If required, remove the appropriate right side spark plug wire boot(s) from the spark plug(s).
   a. Twist the spark plug boot 1/2 turn.
   b. Pull ONLY on the spark plug boot or use a tool designed for this purpose in order to remove the spark plug wire boot from the spark plug.

4. If required, loosen the appropriate left side spark plug 1 or 2 turns.

5. Brush or air blast away any dirt from around the spark plug.

6. Remove the appropriate left side spark plug. If removing more than 1 plug, place each plug in a tray marked with the corresponding cylinder number.

7. If required, loosen the appropriate right side spark plug 1 or 2 turns.

8. Brush or air blast away any dirt from around the spark plug.

9. Remove the appropriate right side spark plug. If removing more than 1 plug, place each plug in a tray marked with the corresponding cylinder number.

To install:

10. Ensure that the spark plug washer is positioned correctly.

11. Inspect the spark plug gap. Adjust the gap as needed. Specification is: 0.060 in (1.52 mm).

12. Install the appropriate right side spark plug into the cylinder head by hand.

13. Tighten the spark plug to 11 ft. lbs. (15 Nm).

14. Install the appropriate left side spark plug (1) into the cylinder head by hand.

15. Tighten the spark plug to 11 ft. lbs. (15 Nm).

✳✳ WARNING

If the boot to wire movement has occurred, the boot will give a false visual impression of being fully seated. Ensure that the boots have been properly assembled by pushing sideways on the installed boots. Failure to properly seat the terminal onto the spark plug will lead to wire core erosion and result in an engine misfire or crossfire condition, and possible internal damage to the engine.

16. If reinstalling the old spark plug wires, apply dielectric grease (GM PN 12345579; Canadian PN 10953481), or an equivalent to the inside of the spark plug wire boots.

17. Install the appropriate right side spark plug wire boot(s) to the spark plug(s).

18. Install the appropriate left side spark plug wire boot(s) to the spark plug(s).

19. Install the engine cover, if required.

4.8L & 5.3L Engines

1. Remove the spark plug wires.

2. Loosen each spark plug 1 or 2 turns.

3. Brush or air blast away any dirt from around the spark plugs.

4. Remove the spark plugs one at a time. Place each plug in a tray marked with the corresponding cylinder numbers.

To install:

5. Inspect each spark plug gap. Adjust each plug as needed.

6. Spark plug gap specification: 0.040 in (1.01 mm)

7. Hand start the spark plugs in the corresponding cylinders.

8. Tighten the spark plugs for used heads to 11 ft. lbs. (15 Nm). Tighten the spark plugs for new aluminum heads to 15 ft. lbs. (20 Nm). Tighten the spark plugs for new iron heads to 22 ft. lbs. (30 Nm).

9. Install the spark plug wires

STARTER

REMOVAL & INSTALLATION

V6 Gasoline Engines

See Figure 157.

1. Disconnect the negative battery cable. Refer to Battery Negative Cable Disconnect/Connect in the Engine Electrical section.
2. Raise and support the vehicle.
3. Disconnect the S terminal harness connector from the starter.

➡ **Orient the B+ terminal Harness anti rotation tab to the starter orientation slot.**

4. Remove the B+ terminal harness from the starter.

➡ **The starter motor bracket shield snaps into place on the starter solenoid.**

5. Remove the starter motor bracket shield from the starter.
6. Remove the starter (3).

To install:

7. Installation is the reverse of removal.
8. Tighten the 2 starter bolts to 37 ft. lbs. (50 Nm).
9. Tighten the battery terminal nut to 80 inch lbs. (9 Nm).

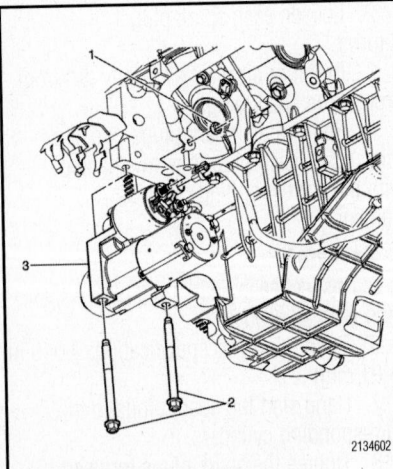

Fig. 157 Battery terminal nut (1), two starter bolts (2), and starter (3)

V8 Gasoline Engines

See Figures 158 through 162.

1. Disconnect the negative battery cable. Refer to Battery Negative Cable

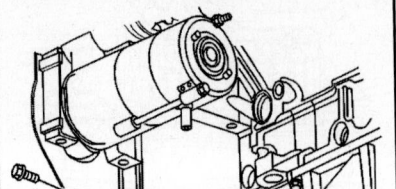

Fig. 158 Right transmission cover bolt, if equipped

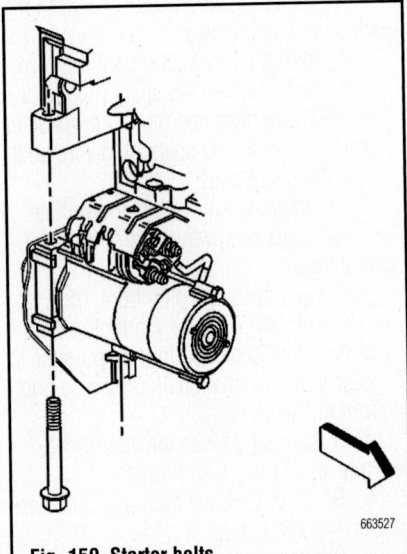

Fig. 159 Starter bolts

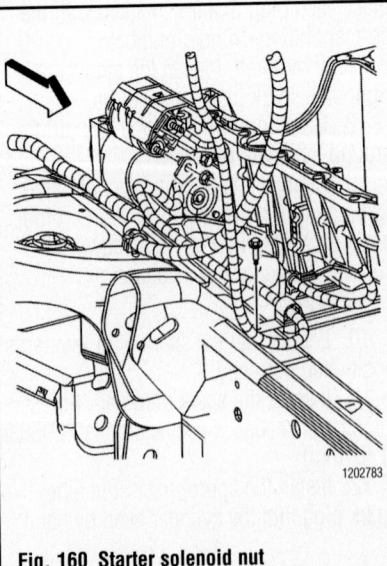

Fig. 160 Starter solenoid nut

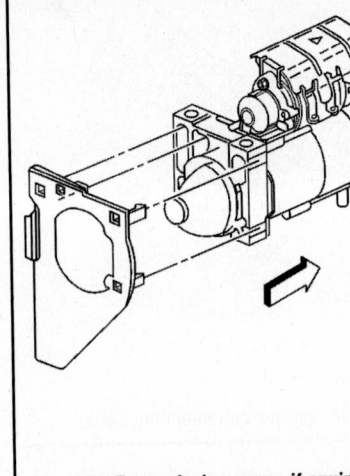

Fig. 161 Transmission cover, if equipped

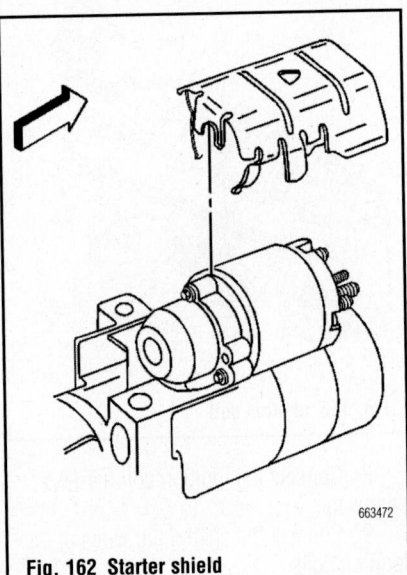

Fig. 162 Starter shield

Disconnect/Connect in the Engine Electrical section.

2. Raise and suitably support the vehicle.
3. Remove the right transmission cover bolt, if equipped.
4. Disconnect the oil level sensor electrical connector.
5. Remove the starter bolts.
6. Slide the starter forward until the starter clears the transmission.
7. Remove the starter solenoid nut.
8. Remove the starter lead from the solenoid stud.
9. Remove the starter lead nut.
10. Remove the positive cable from the starter stud.
11. Place the starter on a workbench.
12. Unsnap the transmission cover from the starter, if equipped.

13. If necessary, remove the starter shield.

To install:

14. If necessary, install the starter shield.

15. Snap the transmission cover to the starter, if equipped.

16. Install the positive cable to the starter stud.

17. Install the starter lead nut and tighten to 89 inch lbs. (10 Nm)

18. Install the starter solenoid lead to the solenoid stud.

19. Install the starter solenoid nut and tighten to 30 inch lbs. (3.4 Nm).

20. Slide the starter rearward.

21. Install the starter bolts and tighten to 37 ft. lbs. (50 Nm).

22. Install the right transmission cover bolt, if equipped and tighten to 80 inch lbs. (9 Nm).

23. Connect the oil level sensor electrical connector.

24. Lower the vehicle.

25. Connect the negative battery cable. Refer to Battery Negative Cable Disconnect/Connect in the Engine Electrical section.

Diesel Engines

See Figure 163.

1. Disconnect the battery negative cable. Refer to Battery Negative Cable Disconnect/Connect in the Engine Electrical section.

2. Remove the starter solenoid cable nut (1).

3. Remove the engine harness starter solenoid nut (2).

4. Remove the engine harness (3).

5. Remove the battery positive cable (4).

6. Remove the 2 starter bolts (5).

7. Remove the starter (6).

To install:

8. Install the starter.

9. Tighten the 2 starter bolts to 63 ft. lbs. (85 Nm).

10. Install the battery positive cable.

11. Install the engine harness.

12. Tighten the engine harness starter solenoid nut to 35 inch lbs. (4 Nm).

13. Tighten the starter solenoid cable nut to 80 inch lbs. (9 Nm).

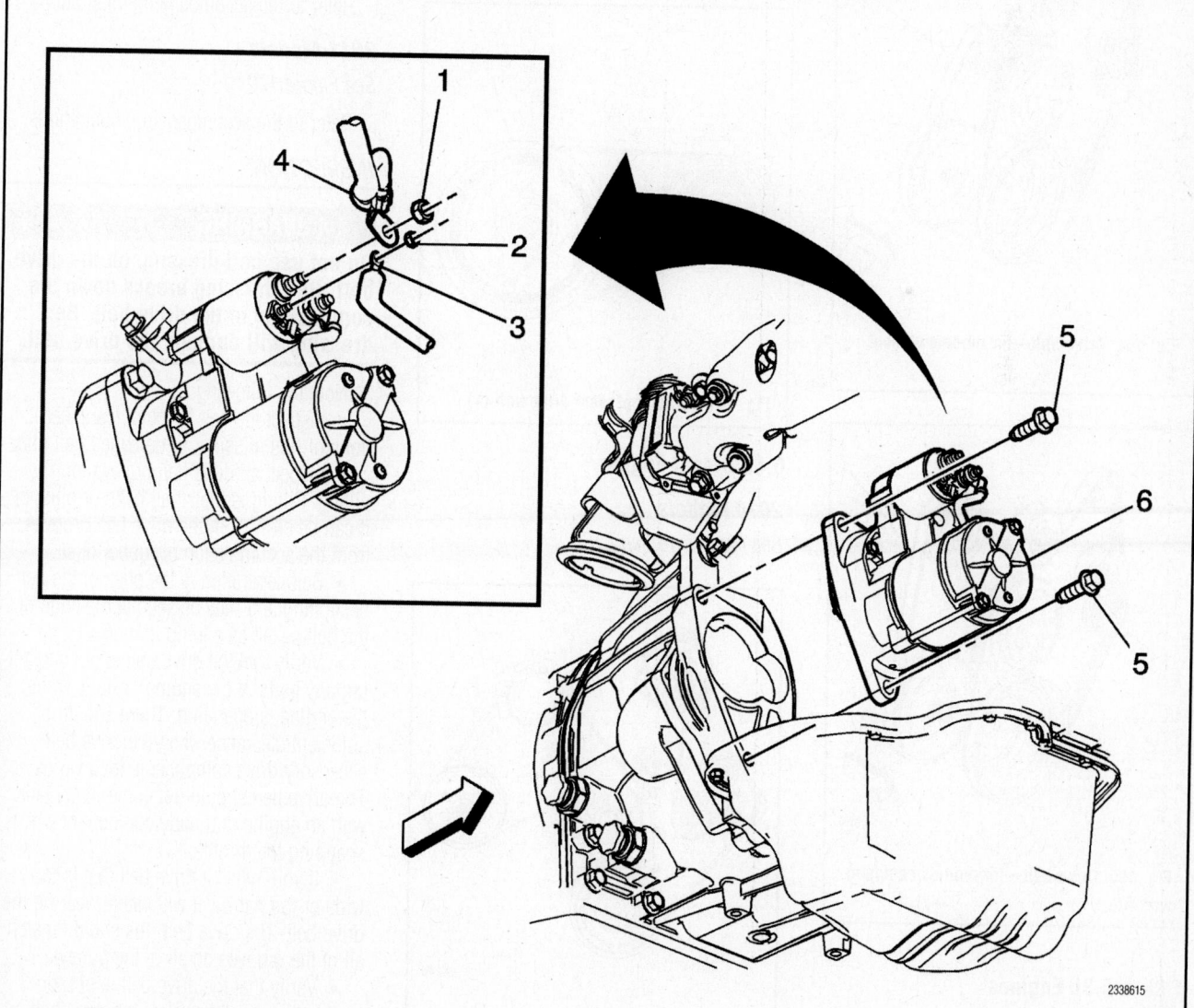

Fig. 163 Starter replacement

ENGINE MECHANICAL

➥Disconnecting the negative battery cable interferes with the functions of the on-board computer systems and requires the computer to undergo a relearning process, once the negative battery cable is reconnected.

ACCESSORY DRIVE BELTS

ACCESSORY BELT ROUTING

4.3L Engine

See Figures 164 and 165.

Refer to the accompanying illustrations.

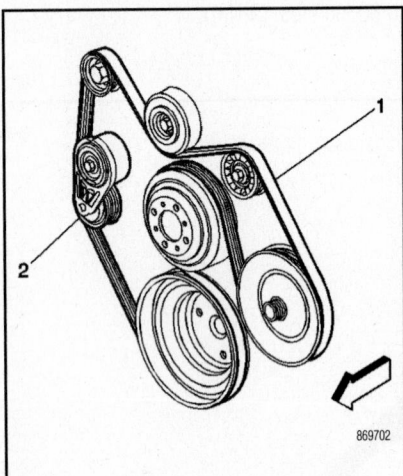

Fig. 164 Drive belt—for models without A/C

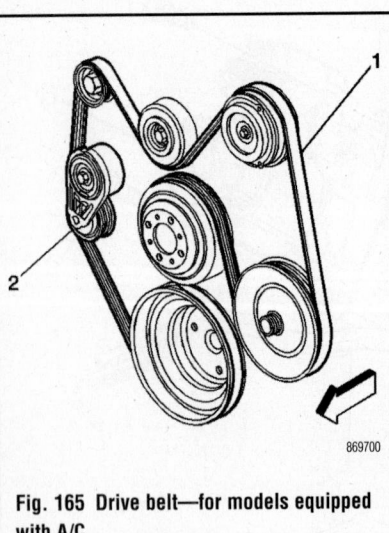

Fig. 165 Drive belt—for models equipped with A/C

4.8L & 5.3L Engines

See Figures 166 and 167.

Refer to the accompanying illustrations.

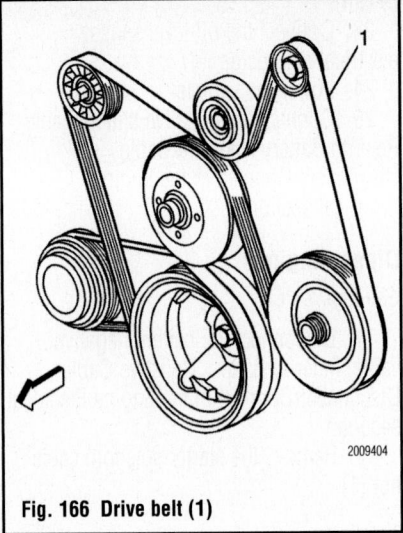

Fig. 166 Drive belt (1)

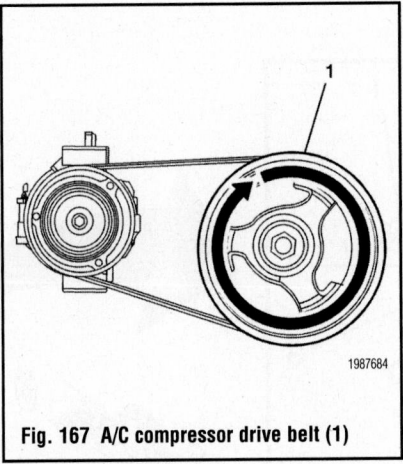

Fig. 167 A/C compressor drive belt (1)

6.6L Diesel Engine

2010 Models

See Figures 168 and 169.

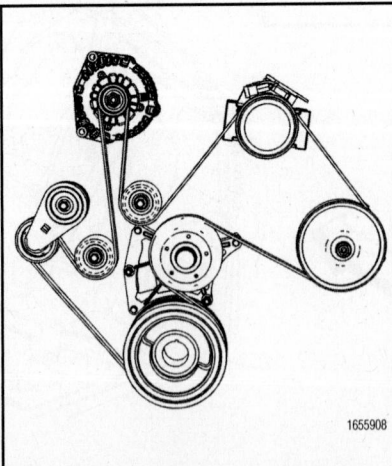

Fig. 168 Drive belt—for models equipped with a single generator

Fig. 169 Drive belt—for models equipped with dual generators

Refer to the accompanying illustrations.

2011 Models

See Figure 170.

Refer to the accompanying illustrations.

INSPECTION

✳✳ WARNING

Do not use belt dressing on the drive belt. Belt dressing breaks down the composition of the drive belt. Belt dressing will damage the drive belt.

Note the following:
- Inspect the belt for cuts, tears, sections of ribs missing, or damaged belt plies.
- Inspect all drive belt pulleys for pilling. Pilling is the small balls or pills, or it can be strings, in the drive belt grooves from the accumulation of rubber dust.
- Belt separation is the plies of the belt separating and may be seen at the edge of the belt or felt as a lump in the belt.
- Verify that the drive belt is not contacting any parts of the engine or body while the engine is operating. There should be sufficient clearance when the drive belt accessory drive components load varies. The drive belt should not come in contact with an engine or a body component when snapping the throttle.
- If you install a drive belt that is too wide or too narrow it will cause wear on the drive belt. The drive belt ribs should match all of the grooves on all of the pulleys.
- Verify that the drive belt is not too long, which would prevent the drive belt tensioner from working properly. Also if an incorrect length drive belt was installed, it

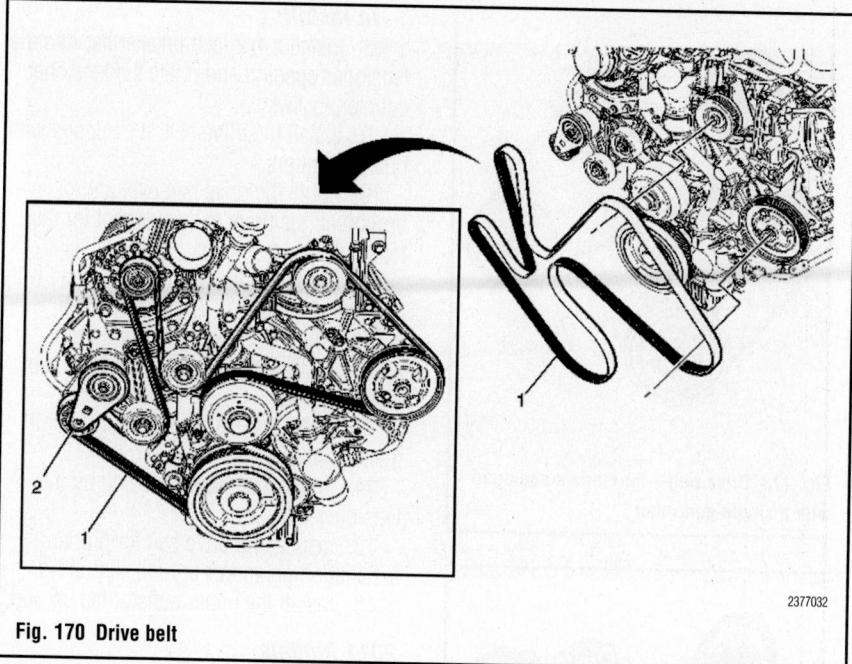

Fig. 170 Drive belt

may not be routed properly and may be turning an accessory drive component in the wrong direction.

• Test for a misaligned pulley using a straight edge in the pulley grooves across two or three pulleys. If you find a misaligned pulley refer to that accessory drive component for the proper installation procedure for that pulley. Misalignment of the pulleys may be caused from improper mounting of the accessory drive component, incorrect installation of the accessory drive component pulley, or the pulley bent inward or outward from a previous repair.

• Look for bent pulleys and include inspect for a dent or other damage to the pulleys that would prevent the drive belt from not seating properly in all of the pulley grooves or on the smooth surface of a pulley when the back side of the belt is used to drive the pulley.

• Verify that the pulleys are the correct diameter or width. Compare the pulley sizes using a known good vehicle.

• Verify that the drive belt tensioner operates properly. If the drive belt tensioner is not operating properly, proper belt tension may not be achieved to keep the drive belt from slipping which could cause a squeal noise.

• Inspect fasteners to eliminate the possibility that a wrong bolt, nut, spacer, or washer was installed.

ADJUSTMENT

These vehicles are equipped with a 1 or 2 belts and a spring loaded tensioner. The

tensioner automatically maintains proper belt adjustment, therefore, no periodic adjustment is needed. If correct belt tension cannot be achieved make sure the correct belt is installed. If the correct tension is still not achieved and check for the proper mounting of all accessory drives.

If equipped, the A/C compressor drive belt cord is made of polyamide; a tensioner is not needed. Polyamid cord, when combined with a more elastic backing compound, ensures the belt is able to maintain the specified tension within the specified range of usage.

REMOVAL & INSTALLATION

4.3L Engine

See Figures 164 and 165.

1. Remove the coolant air cleaner outlet resonator duct.
2. Install a 3/8 inch drive breaker bar to the drive belt tensioner arm.
3. Rotate the drive belt tensioner (2) counterclockwise in order to relieve tension on the belt.
4. If equipped without air conditioning (A/C), remove the belt (1) from the pulleys and the drive belt tensioner.
5. If equipped with A/C, remove the belt (1) from the pulleys and the drive belt tensioner.
6. Slowly release the tension on the drive belt tensioner (2).
7. Remove the breaker bar from the drive belt tensioner.
8. Clean and inspect the belt surfaces of all the pulleys.

To install:

9. Route the belt around all the pulleys except the flat idler pulley.
10. Install a 3/8 inch drive breaker bar to the drive belt tensioner arm.
11. Rotate the belt tensioner counterclockwise in order to relieve the tension on the tensioner.
12. If equipped with A/C, install the belt under the flat idler pulley.
13. If equipped without A/C, install the belt to the pulleys and the drive belt tensioner.
14. Slowly release the tension on the belt tensioner.
15. Remove the breaker bar from the drive belt tensioner.
16. Inspect the drive belt for proper installation and alignment.
17. Install the coolant air cleaner outlet resonator duct.

4.8L & 5.3L Engines

See Figures 171 and 172.

1. Remove the air cleaner assembly. Refer to Air Cleaner Assembly Replacement.
2. Remove the retaining bolt for the coolant recovery reservoir and set the reservoir aside.
3. Install a breaker bar with hex-head socket to the drive belt tensioner bolt.
4. Rotate the drive belt tensioner clockwise in order to relieve tension on the belt.
5. Remove the belt from the pulleys and the drive belt tensioner.
6. Slowly release the tension on the drive belt tensioner.
7. Remove the breaker bar and socket and from the drive belt tensioner bolt.
8. Clean and inspect the belt surfaces of all the pulleys.

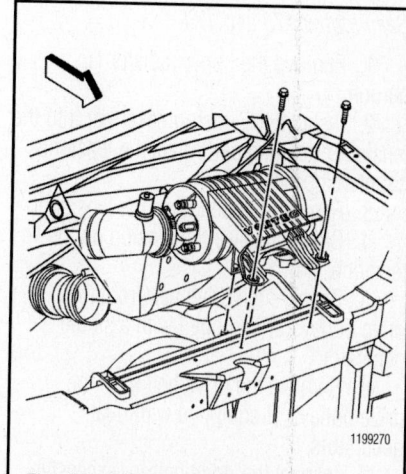

Fig. 171 Coolant recovery reservoir retaining bolt

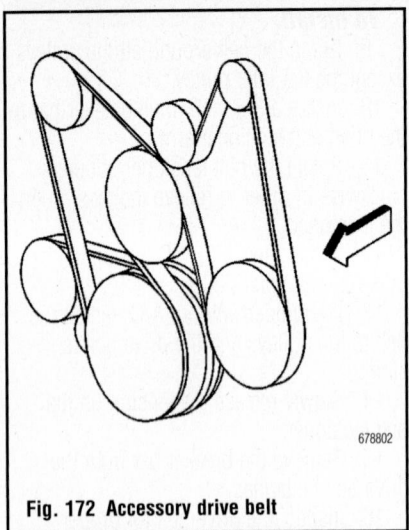

Fig. 172 Accessory drive belt

To install:

9. Route the drive belt around all the pulleys except the idler pulley.

10. Install the breaker bar with hex-head socket to the belt tensioner bolt.

11. Rotate the belt tensioner clockwise in order to relieve the tension on the tensioner.

12. Install the drive belt under the idler pulley.

13. Slowly release the tension on the belt tensioner.

14. Remove the breaker bar and socket from the belt tensioner bolt.

15. Inspect the drive belt for proper installation and alignment.

16. Position the coolant recovery reservoir and install the retaining bolt and tighten to 97 inch lbs. (11 Nm).

17. Install the air cleaner assembly. Refer to Air Cleaner Assembly Replacement.

6.6L Diesel Engine

2010 Models

See Figures 173 and 174.

1. Remove the upper radiator fan shroud.

2. Install a 1/2-inch breaker bar into the tensioner opening and rotate the tensioner counterclockwise.

3. Remove the belt from the tensioner.

4. Slowly release the tension on the tensioner arm.

5. Remove the drive belt from the drive pulleys, if equipped with a single generator.

6. Remove the drive belt from the drive pulleys, if equipped with dual generators.

7. Inspect the drive belt for excessive cracking or any visible damage and replace if necessary.

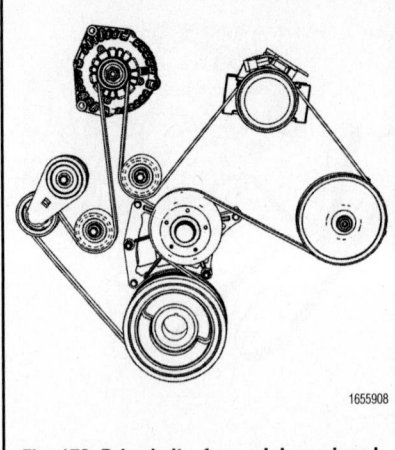

Fig. 173 Drive belt—for models equipped with a single generator

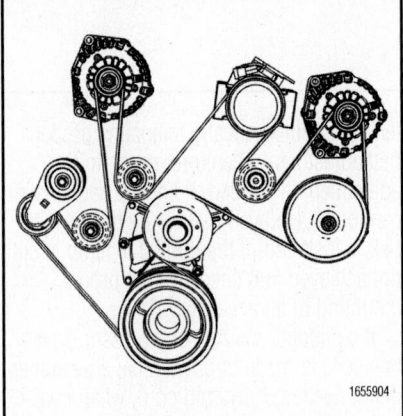

Fig. 174 Drive belt—for models equipped with dual generators

To install:

8. Install a 1/2 inch breaker bar into the tensioner opening and rotate the tensioner counterclockwise.

9. Install the drive belt, if equipped with dual generators.

10. Route the drive belt over and/or around all the drive pulleys except for the tensioner.

11. Install the drive belt, if equipped with a single generator.

12. Route the drive belt over and/or around all the drive pulleys except for the tensioner.

13. Install the belt over and/or around the tensioner.

14. Slowly release the tension on the tensioner arm.

15. Inspect the drive belt for proper installation on and/or around all pulleys.

16. Install the upper radiator fan shroud.

2011 Models

See Figure 175.

1. Remove the engine coolant fan upper shroud.

2. Use the proper tool to rotate the drive belt tensioner.

3. Remove the drive belt from the pulleys and tensioner.

4. Clean and inspect the drive belt surfaces of all the pulleys.

5. Inspect the drive belt for correct alignment.

To install:

6. Installation is the reverse of removal.

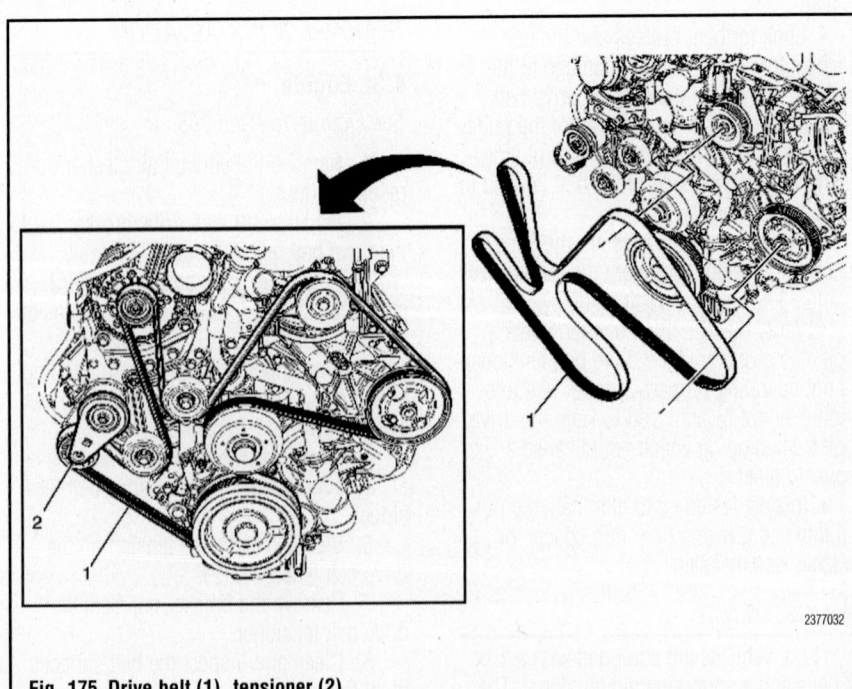

Fig. 175 Drive belt (1), tensioner (2)

AIR CLEANER ASSEMBLY

REMOVAL & INSTALLATION

4.3L Engine

See Figure 176.

1. Loosen the air cleaner outlet duct clamp (1).
2. Remove the air cleaner assembly bolts (2).
3. Remove the air cleaner assembly (3).

To install:

4. Install the air cleaner assembly.
5. Install the air cleaner assembly bolts and tighten to 97 inch lbs. (11 Nm).
6. Tighten the air cleaner outlet duct clamp to 44 inch lbs. (5 Nm).

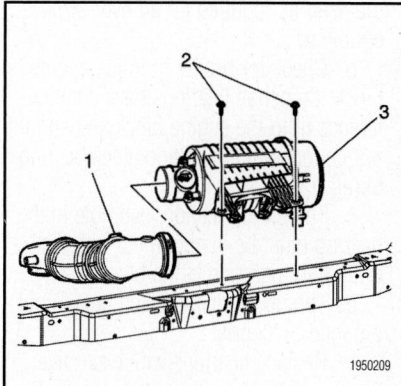

Fig. 176 Air cleaner outlet duct clamp (1), air cleaner assembly bolts (2) and air cleaner assembly (3)

4.8L & 5.3L Engines

See Figure 177.

1. Remove the two air cleaner assembly fasteners (2).
2. Remove the air cleaner assembly. Pull up to disconnect the grommets from the rubber studs.

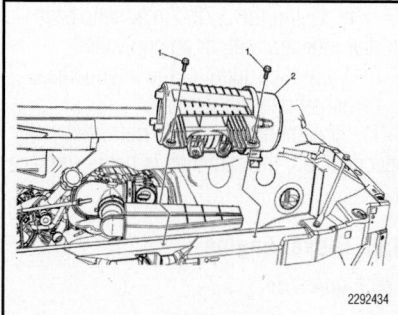

Fig. 177 Two air cleaner assembly fasteners (1), air cleaner assembly (2)

To install:

3. Install the air cleaner assembly.
4. Tighten the two air cleaner assembly fasteners to 89 inch lbs. (10 Nm)

6.6L Diesel Engine

See Figure 178.

1. Disconnect the Mass Air Flow (MAF) harness connector.
2. Remove the air cleaner assembly hold-down screw.
3. Loosen the air cleaner outlet duct hose clamp.
4. Remove the air cleaner assembly.

To install:

5. Install the air cleaner assembly.
6. Tighten the air cleaner outlet duct hose clamp to 35 inch lbs. (4 Nm).
7. Install the air cleaner assembly hold-down screw.
8. Connect the MAF harness connector.

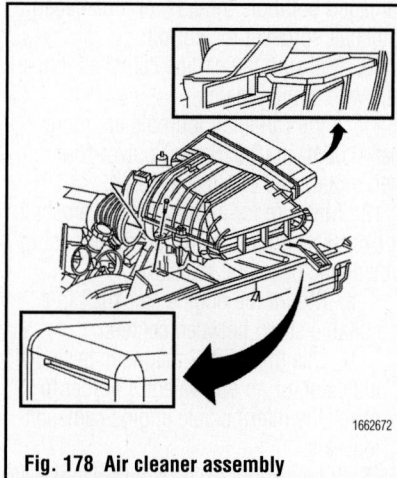

Fig. 178 Air cleaner assembly replacement

FILTER/ELEMENT REPLACEMENT

4.3L Engine

See Figures 179 and 180.

1. Disengage the 2 air cleaner housing cover retainers (1).
2. Remove the air cleaner housing cover (3) from the air cleaner housing.

To install:

3. Install the NEW air filter element.
4. Align the air cleaner housing cover to the house so that the arrow on the air cleaner housing cover aligns with the arrow on the air cleaner housing.
5. Install the air cleaner housing cover to the air cleaner housing.
6. Ensure that the arrow on the housing is still aligned with the arrow on the cover.

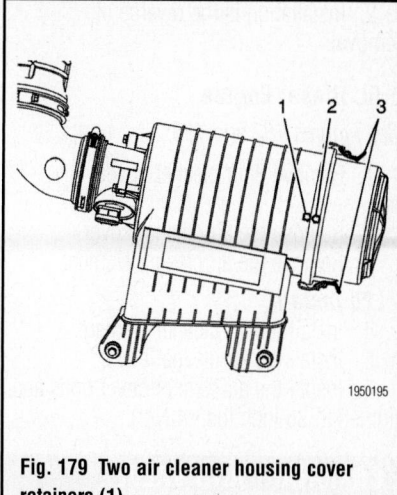

Fig. 179 Two air cleaner housing cover retainers (1)

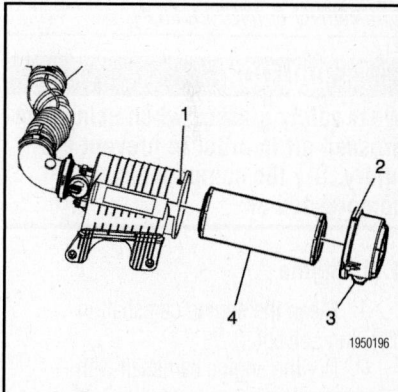

Fig. 180 Air cleaner housing cover (3) and air filter element (4); Arrow on the air cleaner housing cover (2, and arrow (1) on the air cleaner housing.

7. Secure the air cleaner housing cover by engaging the 2 air cleaner housing cover retainers.

4.8L & 5.3L Engines

See Figure 181.

1. Release the retaining clips and remove the air cleaner housing.

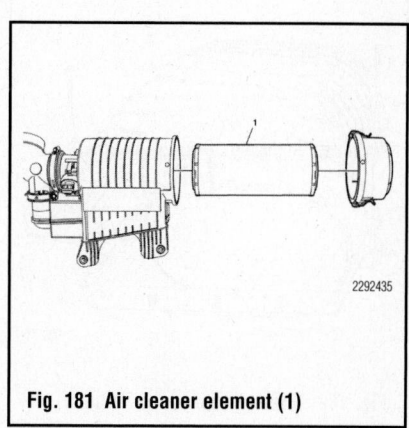

Fig. 181 Air cleaner element (1)

2. Installation is the reverse of removal.

6.6L Diesel Engine

See Figures 182 and 183.

1. Remove 3 air cleaner cover bolts.
2. Remove the air cleaner cover.
3. Remove the air cleaner element.

To install:

4. Install the air cleaner element.
5. Install the air cleaner cover.
6. Install the air cleaner cover bolts and tighten to 35 inch lbs. (4 Nm).

CAMSHAFT AND VALVE LIFTERS

CLEANING & INSPECTION

❄ CAUTION

Wear safety glasses when using compressed air in order to prevent eye injury. Dry the components with compressed air.

4.3L Engine

1. Clean the engine camshaft in cleaning solvent.
2. Dry the engine camshaft with compressed air.
3. Inspect the camshaft retainer plate for damage.
4. If the camshaft retainer plate is damaged, replace as necessary.
5. Inspect the camshaft bearings for correct fit into the engine block camshaft bearing bores.
6. The camshaft bearings have an interference fit to the engine block camshaft bearing bores and must not be loose in the engine block camshaft bearing bores.

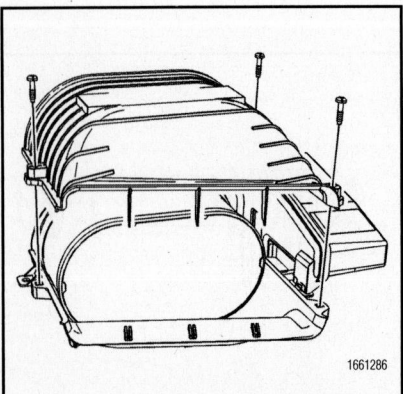

Fig. 182 Three air cleaner cover bolts

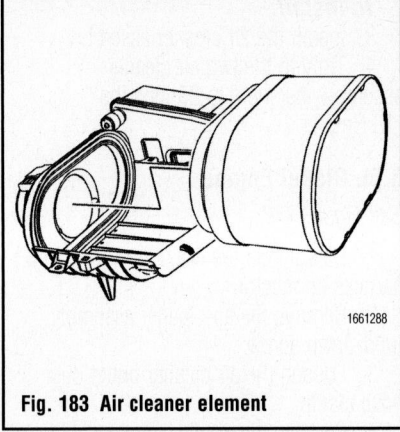

Fig. 183 Air cleaner element

7. If any camshaft bearing is excessively worn or scored, replace all the camshaft bearings.
8. Inspect the camshaft bearings for excessive wear or scoring.
9. Inspect the engine camshaft for the following: worn, scored, or damaged bearing journals, worn engine camshaft lobes, damaged bolt hole threads, or a damaged camshaft sprocket locator pin.
10. Measure the engine camshaft journals with a micrometer.
11. If the camshaft journals are more than 0.0010 in (0.025 mm) out-of-round, then replace the engine camshaft.
12. Measure for a bent engine camshaft or excessive engine camshaft runout using a magnetic base dial indicator:
    a. Mount the engine camshaft in a suitable stand between centers.
    b. Use the J 7872 magnetic base dial indicator, or an equivalent, in order to check the intermediate engine camshaft journals.
13. If the runout exceeds 0.065 mm (0.0026 in), the engine camshaft is bent and must be replaced.
14. Measure the engine camshaft lobe lift using a magnetic base dial indicator:
    a. Place the engine camshaft on the V-blocks.
    b. Use the magnetic base dial indicator to measure the engine camshaft lobe lift.
15. Replace the engine camshaft if the engine camshaft lobe lift is not within specifications.

4.8L & 5.3L Engines

1. Clean the components in solvent.
2. Inspect the camshaft bearing journals and valve lifter lobes for scoring or excessive wear.
3. Inspect the Camshaft Position (CMP) actuator oil passages for restrictions.

4. Inspect the threaded bolt hole in the front of the camshaft for damaged threads or debris.
5. Inspect the camshaft sprocket pin for damage.
6. Inspect the camshaft retainer plate for wear or a damaged sealing gasket.
    a. If the camshaft retainer plate sealing gasket is not cut or damaged, it may be used again.
7. Inspect the camshaft bearings for the following:
    a. Excessive wear, evidence of galling, pitting, scoring, or embedded debris. The bearing material appearing to be different shades of gray is considered normal, and is not a reason for bearing replacement. Measure the bearing inside diameter as required for an over-sized condition.
    b. Check for proper fit in the engine block. Camshaft bearings have an interference fit to the engine block and should not be loose in the engine block bearing bores.
    c. The oil lubrication feed hole in the bearing must be in alignment with the drilled out passage in the block.
    d. The oil lubrication feed hole is not plugged by debris.
    e. Replace bearings with excessive wear or scoring.
    f. Replace bearings with excessive wear, galling, pitting, scoring, or embedded debris.
8. Using a micrometer, measure the camshaft journals for wear and out-of-round.
    a. If the camshaft bearing journals are out-of-round, replace the camshaft.
    b. If the camshaft bearing journal diameter is not within specification, replace the camshaft.
9. Using a micrometer, measure the camshaft lobes for wear.
10. Measure the camshaft runout.
    a. Mount the camshaft in wooden V-blocks or between centers on a fixture.
    b. Using the J 7872 magnetic base dial indicator set, or an equivalent, measure the runout of the intermediate camshaft bearing journals.
11. If camshaft runout is not within specification, the camshaft is bent—replace it.

6.6L Diesel Engine

See Figure 184.

1. Clean the camshaft.

➡**The camshaft bearings are not serviceable. If the camshaft bearings are**

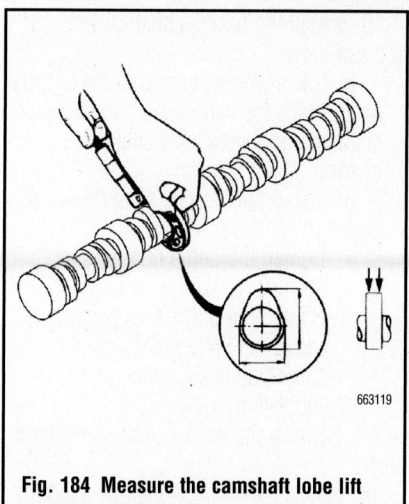

Fig. 184 Measure the camshaft lobe lift

damaged, the engine must be replaced.

2. Visually inspect the camshaft bearings in the engine block for the following conditions: Scoring, nicks, damage caused by lack of lubrication, and misaligned oil feed holes.

3. Measure the camshaft journal diameter.

a. The production value is 2.3990–2.4001 in (60.932–60.962 mm) and service limit is 2.3984 in (60.920 mm).

b. Replace the camshaft if the measured value is less than service limit.

4. Measure the camshaft lobe lift.

a. The production value for intake is 0.2863 in (7.273 mm).

b. The production value for exhaust is 0.2326 in (5.907 mm).

5. Replace the camshaft if the measured value is less than the service limit.

6. Measure the camshaft runout.

7. Mount the camshaft on the V-blocks.

8. Use the J 872 dial indicator set, or an equivalent to measure the camshaft runout.

9. The runout service limit is 0.0020 in (0.05 mm).

10. Replace the camshaft if the runout is over the service limit.

Valve Lifter and Guide Cleaning and Inspection

11. Mark, sort, and organize the components for assembly.

✳✳ WARNING

Warning: Wear safety glasses when using compressed air in order to prevent eye injury.

12. Clean the components in cleaning solvent.

13. Dry the components with compressed air.

14. Inspect the valve lifter pushrod guides for excessive wear.

15. Inspect the valve lifter pushrod guides for cracks or damage.

16. Inspect the valve lifter for the following: Broken or damaged clip, worn pushrod socket, scuffed or worn lifter body (If the valve lifter shows scuffing or wear, inspect the engine block valve lifter bores for wear), worn roller, loose or damaged pin, or a plugged oil hole (6).

REMOVAL & INSTALLATION

4.3L Engine

Valve Lifters

See Figures 185 and 186.

1. Remove the intake manifold.
2. Remove the pushrods.

➡**Place the components in a rack so that the components can be installed to their original location.**

3. Remove the bolts and lifter pushrod guide.

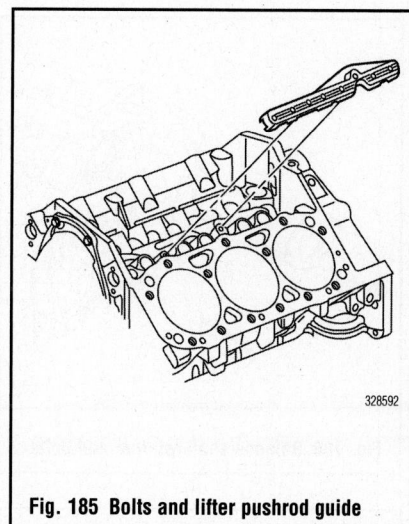

Fig. 185 Bolts and lifter pushrod guide

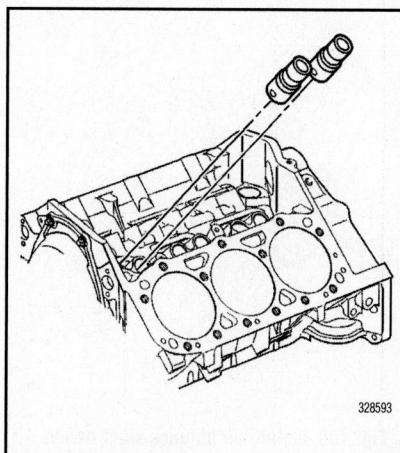

Fig. 186 Valve lifters

➡**Place the valve lifters in the rack in the upright position in order to maintain the oil inside the valve lifters.**

4. Remove the lifters.

➡**Some valve lifters may be stuck in the valve lifter bores because of gum or varnish deposits and may require the use of the J 3049-A, a valve lifter remover tool for removal.**

5. Use a valve lifter removal tool in order to remove the stuck valve lifters.

6. Use a cleaning solvent and a shop towel to clean any varnish from the valve lifter bores.

7. Inspect the lifter bores for excessive wear or scoring. Replace the engine block if there is excessive wear or deep scoring.

8. Inspect the camshaft for wear or damage. If the wear is questionable remove the camshaft and inspect.

9. Refer to Camshaft Cleaning and Inspection.

10. Clean and inspect the lifters, if necessary.

To install:

11. Install the lifters.

12. It is normal for NEW lifters to make a slight ticking noise when the engine is first started. Increasing the engine RPM slightly to raise oil pressure should stop the noise.

13. Apply lubricant to the lifter rollers. GM specifies: Valve Train Component Prelube, part numbers 88862586 (US) and 88862827 (Canada).

➡**If reusing the lifters, install the lifters to their original positions.**

14. Install the lifters.

15. Install the lifter pushrod guides and tighten the bolts to 12 ft. lbs. (16 Nm).

16. Install the pushrods.

17. Install the intake manifold.

Camshaft

See Figures 187 through 191.

1. With the valve lifters removed, remove the timing chain and the camshaft sprocket. Refer to Timing Chain, Sprocket, and Tensioner in this section.

2. Remove the balance shaft drive gear.

3. Remove the camshaft retainer bolts and retainer.

✳✳ CAUTION

All camshaft journals are the same diameter, so use care in removing or installing the camshaft to avoid damage to the camshaft bearings.

4. Remove the engine camshaft as follows:

a. Install the three 5/16-18 x 4.0 inch bolts into the engine camshaft front bolt holes.

b. Using the bolts as a handle, carefully rotate and pull the engine camshaft out of the camshaft bearings.

c. Remove the bolts from the front of the engine camshaft.

d. Clean and inspect the camshaft and/or bearings, if necessary. Refer to Camshaft Cleaning and Inspection.

To install:

5. Whenever a new camshaft is installed, perform the following:

a. Change the engine oil and filter.

b. Add engine oil supplement to the engine oil. (GM part numbers: 1052367 (US) and 992869 (Canada).

c. Apply lubricant or engine oil supplement to the following components:

- The engine camshaft lobes
- The camshaft bearing journals
- The camshaft bearings

6. Install three 5/16-18 x 4.0 inch bolts into the engine camshaft front bolt holes.

✳✳ CAUTION

All camshaft journals are the same diameter, so use care in removing or installing the camshaft to avoid damage to the camshaft bearings.

7. Using the bolts as a handle, install the engine camshaft.

8. Remove the 3 bolts from the front of the engine camshaft.

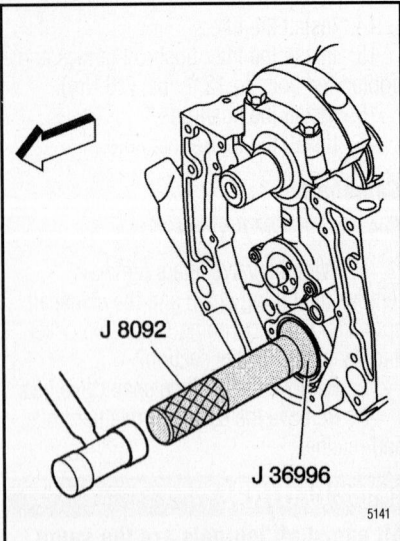

Fig. 187 Use the J 36996 installer and the J 8092 handle, or equivalents, in order to install the balance shaft.

9. If reusing the fasteners, apply thread locker to the threads of the camshaft retainer bolts. GM part numbers: 12345382 (US) and 10953489 (Canada)

10. Install the camshaft retainer and bolts and tighten to 106 inch lbs. (12 Nm).

11. Install the balance shaft drive gear as follows:

➡**Service the balance shaft drive and balance shaft driven gears as a set. The set includes the balance shaft driven gear bolt.**

12. Apply clean engine oil to the balance shaft front bearing.

Using the J 36996 installer and the J 8092 handle, install the balance shaft.

13. Install the balance shaft retainer and bolts and tighten them to 106 inch lbs. (12 Nm).

14. Install the balance shaft driven gear onto the balance shaft.

15. If reusing the fastener, apply thread locker to the threads of the balance shaft driven gear bolt. GM part numbers: 12345382 (US) and 10953489 (Canada)

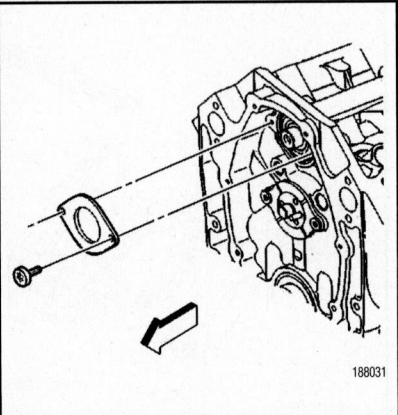

Fig. 188 Balance shaft retainer and bolts

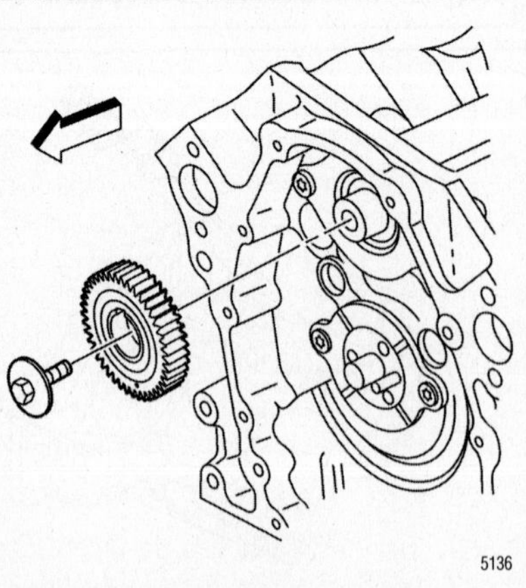

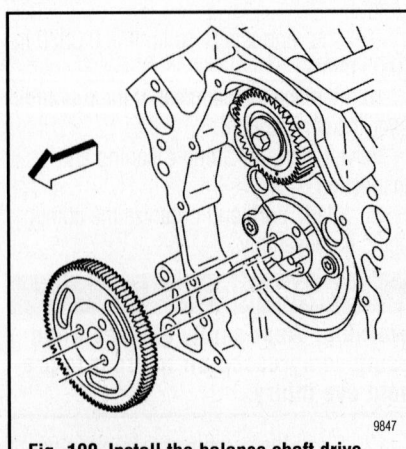

Fig. 189 Install the balance shaft driven gear onto the balance shaft

16. Install the balance shaft driven gear bolt as follows:

a. Use a wrench to secure the balance shaft. Place the wrench onto the balance shaft near to the balance shaft front bearing.

b. Install the balance shaft driven gear bolt.

- Tighten the bolt a first pass to 15 ft. lbs. (20 Nm).
- Tighten the bolt a final pass an additional 35 degrees using J 45059, an angle meter, or an equivalent.

17. Remove the wrench from the balance shaft.

18. Rotate the balance shaft by hand in order to ensure that there is clearance between the balance shaft and the valve lifter pushrod guide. If the balance shaft does not rotate freely, check to ensure that the retaining ring on the balance shaft front bearing is seated on the case.

19. Install the balance shaft drive gear. DO NOT install the camshaft sprocket bolts at this time.

20. Rotate the camshaft so that the timing mark on the balance shaft drive gear is in the 12 o'clock position.

21. Remove the balance shaft drive gear.

22. Rotate the balance shaft so that the timing mark on the balance shaft driven gear is in the 6 o'clock position.

23. Position the balance shaft drive gear onto the engine camshaft.

24. Look to ensure that the balance shaft drive gear and the balance shaft driven gear timing marks are aligned.

25. Install the timing chain and camshaft sprocket. Refer to Camshaft Timing Chain, Sprocket, and Tensioner.

Fig. 190 Install the balance shaft drive gear. DO NOT install the camshaft sprocket bolts at this time

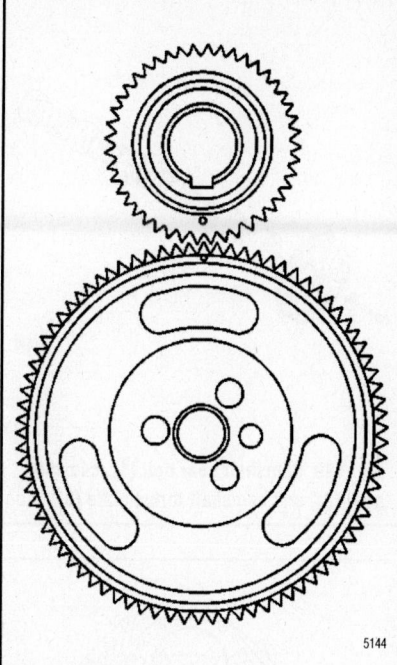

Fig. 191 Position the balance shaft drive gear onto the engine camshaft

4.8L & 5.3L Engines

See Figures 192 and 193.

1. Remove the cylinder head and gasket. Refer to Cylinder Head Replacement—Left Side or Cylinder Head Replacement—Right Side.

2. Remove the valve lifter guide bolts (211).

3. Remove the valve lifters and guide (210).

➡**Some valve lifters may be stuck in their bores because of gum or varnish deposits.**

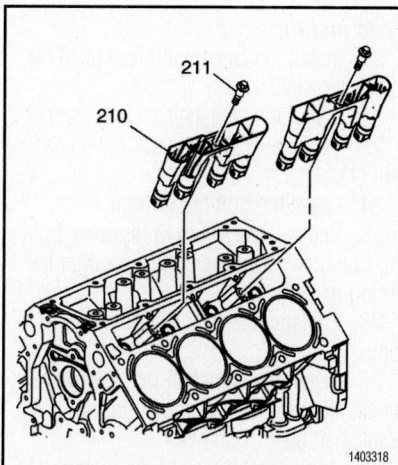

Fig. 192 Valve lifter guide bolts (211) and the valve lifters and guide (210)

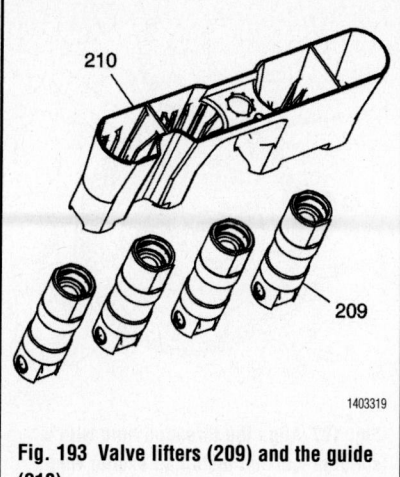

Fig. 193 Valve lifters (209) and the guide (210)

4. Use the J 3049-A, a valve lifter remover or an equivalent in order to remove the valve lifters (if required).

5. Remove the valve lifters (209) from the guide (210).

6. Organize or mark the components to install them in the same location from which you removed them.

7. Clean and inspect the valve lifters.

To install:

➡**When reusing valve lifters, install the lifters to their original locations.**

8. Lubricate the valve lifters and engine block valve lifter bores with clean engine oil.

9. Insert the valve lifters (209) into the lifter guides (210).

10. Align the flat area on the top of the lifter with the flat area in the lifter guide bore. Push the lifter completely into the guide bore.

11. Install the valve lifters (209) and guide (210) to the engine block.

12. Install the valve lifter guide bolts (211).

13. Install the valve lifter guide bolt (211) and tighten it to 106 inch lbs. (12 Nm).

14. Install the cylinder head and gasket. Refer to Cylinder Head Replacement —Left Side or Cylinder Head Replacement—Right Side.

6.6L Diesel Engine

Valve Lifters

See Figure 194.

1. Remove the cylinder head. Refer to Cylinder Head Replacement—Left Side and/or Cylinder Head Replacement —Right Side.

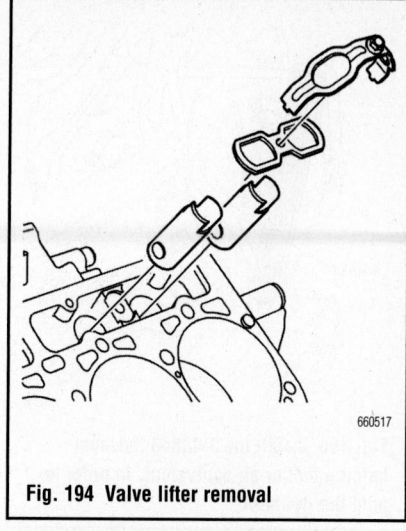

Fig. 194 Valve lifter removal

2. Loosen the valve lifter guide hold-down bracket bolts.

3. Remove the valve lifter guide hold-down brackets.

4. Remove the valve lifter guides.

5. Remove the valve lifters.

To install:

6. Apply clean engine oil to the lifters.

7. Install the valve lifter.

8. Install the valve lifter guides.

9. Install the valve lifter guide hold-down brackets.

10. Install the valve lifter guide hold-down bracket bolt and tighten to 97 inch lbs. (11 Nm).

11. Install the cylinder head. Refer to Cylinder Head Replacement—Left Side and/or Cylinder Head Replacement—Right Side.

Camshaft

See Figures 195 through 201.

1. After removing the valve lifters, remove the starter. Refer to Starter Removal and Installation in the Engine Electrical section.

2. Install the J-44643 flywheel holding tool or an equivalent, in order to hold the flywheel.

3. Remove the engine front cover.

4. Remove the oil pump drive gears and crankshaft reluctor. Refer to Oil Pump Removal and Installation.

5. Remove the oil pump drive gear and crankshaft reluctor.

6. Using J-26900-12 indicator (1) and J-26900-13 base (2), or an equivalent, measure the camshaft end play.

a. The production value is 0.002—0.0045 in (0.050—0.114 mm) and service limit is 0.20 mm (0.008 in).

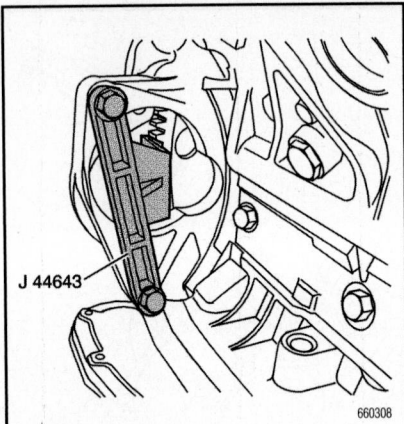

Fig. 195 Install the J-44643 flywheel holding tool or an equivalent, in order to hold the flywheel

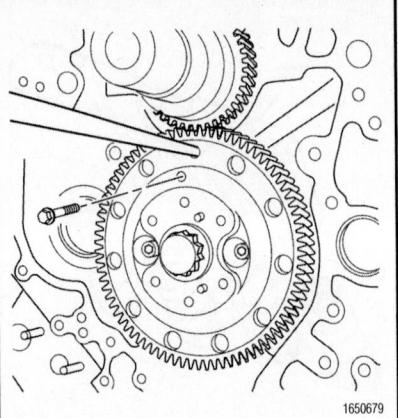

Fig. 197 Align the threaded hole with a suitable tool and install an exciter ring bolt to secure the spring tension

Fig. 199 Camshaft gear bolt (1), camshaft gear (2), and camshaft thrust plate (3)

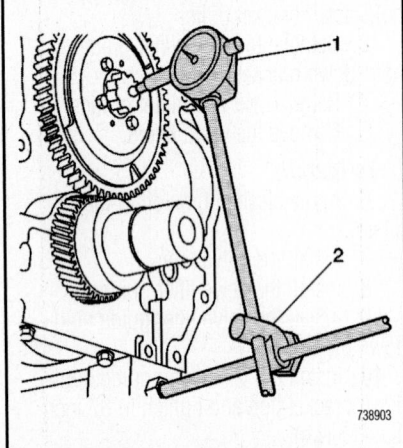

Fig. 196 Using J-26900-12 indicator (1) and J-26900-13 base (2), or an equivalent, measure the camshaft end play

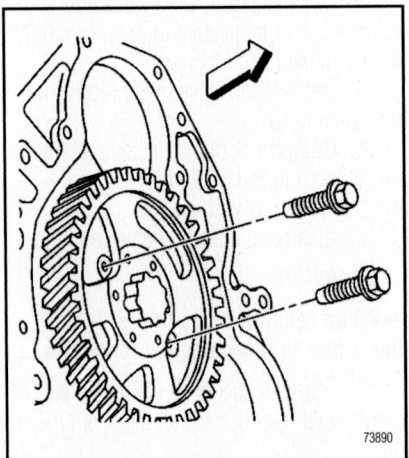

Fig. 198 Remove the camshaft thrust plate bolts through the holes in the camshaft gear

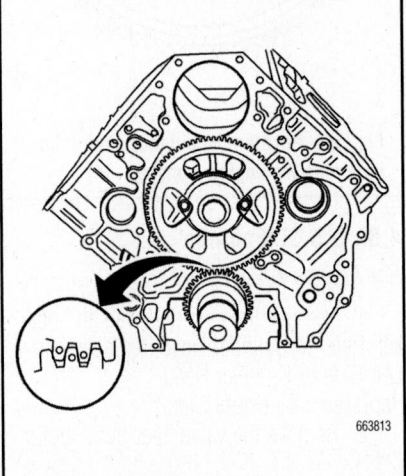

Fig. 200 Camshaft thrust plate (3), driven gear (2), and driven gear bolt (1)

b. Replace the camshaft gear or the camshaft thrust plate if measured value exceeds service limit.

7. Remove the camshaft reluctor screws.

8. Remove the camshaft reluctor.

9. Align the threaded hole with a suitable tool and install an exciter ring bolt to secure the spring tension.

10. Remove the camshaft thrust plate bolts through the holes in the camshaft gear.

11. Loosen the camshaft gear bolt using the J-44643 tool to hold the engine from turning.

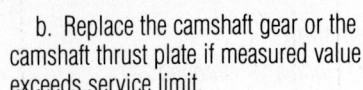

Bolt the two-piece cam gear together to prevent the spring tension from unloading upon removal. Additionally, the two-piece cam gear must remain bolted together until it is re- installed to the camshaft and fully engaged to the crankshaft gear. Failure to do so may result in personal injury.

12. Loosen the camshaft gear bolt and leave the bolt finger tight.

13. Remove the camshaft thrust plate bolts through the holes in the camshaft gear.

14. Remove the camshaft with the camshaft gear attached.

15. Remove the camshaft gear bolt and discard.

16. Remove the camshaft gear bolt (1) and discard.

17. Remove the camshaft gear (2).

18. Remove the camshaft thrust plate (3).

19. Clean and inspect the camshaft and bearings. Refer to Camshaft and Valve Lifters Cleaning and Inspection.

20. If the camshaft bearings are worn or damaged, remove the engine to replace the camshaft bearings.

To install:

21. Install the camshaft thrust plate (3) to the camshaft.

22. Install the camshaft driven gear (2).

23. Install a NEW camshaft driven gear bolt (1).

24. Leave the bolt finger tight.

25. Remove the J-44643, flywheel holding tool then rotate the engine to align the timing marks.

26. Reinstall the flywheel holding tool.

27. Install the camshaft into the cylinder block, align the camshaft gear to the crankshaft gear as shown.

28. Apply thread lock to the threads of the camshaft thrust plate bolts. GM specifies thread lock part number 89021297 (US) and 10953488 (Canada).

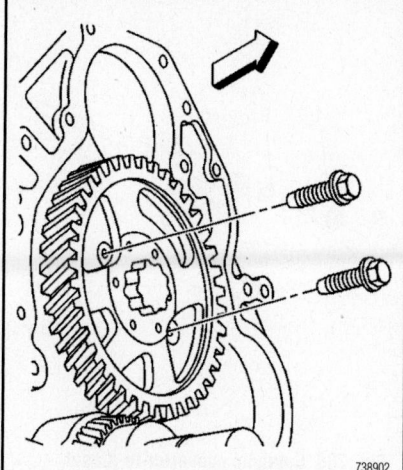

Fig. 201 Install the camshaft into the cylinder block and align the camshaft gear to the crankshaft gear as shown

29. Install the camshaft thrust plate bolts and tighten them to 16 ft. lbs. (22 Nm).

30. Install the camshaft reluctor to the camshaft gear.

31. Install the camshaft reluctor bolts and tighten in a cross-bolt pattern to 80 inch lbs. (9 Nm).

32. Reinstall the flywheel holding tool in the starter opening, if removed.

33. Install a NEW camshaft gear bolt and tighten to 173 ft. lbs. (234 Nm).

34. Using J-26900-12 indicator (1) and J-26900-13 base (2) measure the camshaft end play.

   a. The production value is 0.002—0.0045 in (0.050—0.114 mm) and service limit is 0.008 in (0.20 mm).

   b. Replace the camshaft gear or the camshaft thrust plate if measured value exceeds the service limit.

35. Install the oil pump drive gears and reluctor to the crankshaft. Refer to Oil Pump Removal and Installation.

36. Install the oil pump driven gear.

37. Install the oil pump driven gear nut and tighten to 74 ft. lbs. (100 Nm).

38. Install the engine front cover.

39. Remove the flywheel holder tool.

40. Install the starter.

41. Install the valve lifters.

CATALYTIC CONVERTER

REMOVAL & INSTALLATION

❈❈ CAUTION

In order to avoid being burned, do not service the exhaust system while it is still hot. Service the system when it is cool.

❈❈ CAUTION

Always wear protective goggles and gloves when removing exhaust parts as falling rust and sharp edges from worn exhaust components could result in serious personal injury.

V6 Gasoline Engines

See Figures 202 through 204.

1. Raise and support the vehicle.

2. Remove the heated oxygen sensors (HO2S). Refer to Heated Oxygen Sensor.

3. Remove the exhaust hanger bolts and hanger from the transmission.

4. Remove the catalytic converter to exhaust manifold nuts (1).

5. Remove the muffler to catalytic converter nuts (1).

6. Lower the catalytic converter (3) from the vehicle.

7. Remove and discard the exhaust manifold seals (1 and 2).

To install:

8. Install a NEW exhaust manifold seal (1) into the groove in the left catalytic converter.

9. Install a NEW exhaust manifold seal (2) into the right manifold.

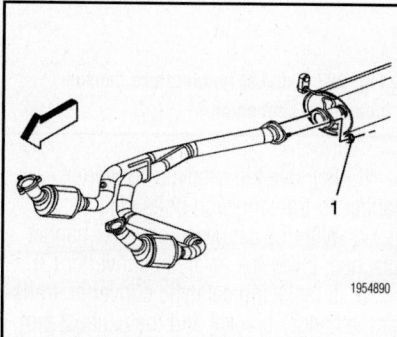

Fig. 202 Catalytic converter to exhaust manifold nuts (1)

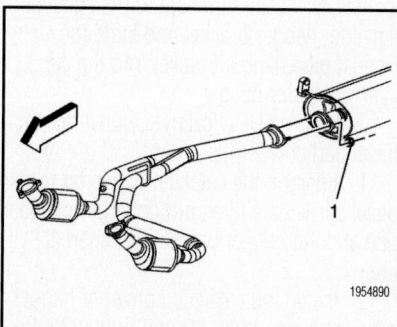

Fig. 203 Muffler to catalytic converter nuts (1)

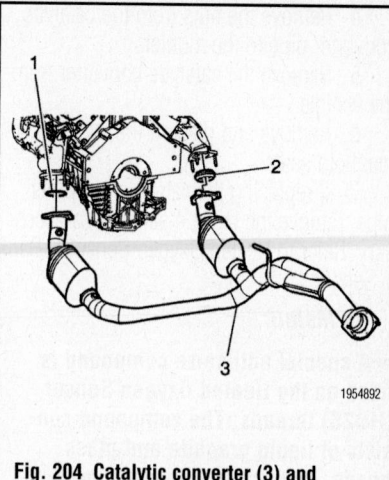

Fig. 204 Catalytic converter (3) and exhaust manifold seals (1 and 2)

10. Position the catalytic converter (3) to the exhaust manifolds.

11. Install the catalytic converter to exhaust manifold nuts (1) and tighten to 37 ft. lbs. (50 Nm).

12. Install the muffler to catalytic converter nuts (1) and tighten to 35 ft. lbs. (48 Nm).

13. Install the exhaust hanger bolts and hanger to the transmission and tighten to 37 ft. lbs. (50 Nm).

14. Install the HO2S. Refer to the Heated Oxygen Sensor.

V8 Gasoline Engines

See Figure 205.

1. Raise and support the vehicle.

2. Disconnect the Heated Oxygen Sensor (HO2S) electrical connectors from the main harness connectors.

3. Remove the nuts (1) from the catalytic converter pipe to the exhaust manifolds.

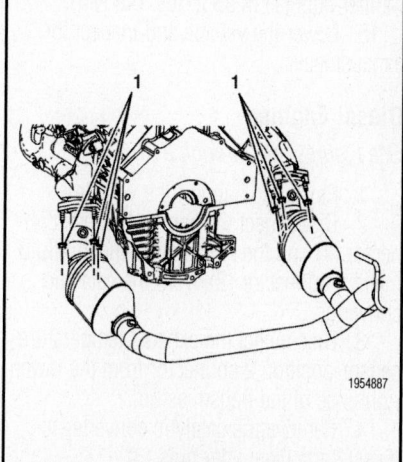

Fig. 205 Catalytic converter pipe-to-exhaust manifolds nuts (1)

4. Remove the nuts from the catalytic converter pipe to the muffler.

5. Remove the catalytic converter from the vehicle.

6. Remove and discard the exhaust manifold seals.

7. If replacing the catalytic converter pipe, remove the oxygen sensors as necessary. Refer to Heated Oxygen Sensor—Bank 1 Sensor 1.

To install:

➡A special anti-seize compound is used on the Heated Oxygen Sensor (HO2S) threads. The compound consists of liquid graphite and glass beads. The graphite tends to burn away, but the glass beads remain, making the sensor easier to remove. New or service replacement sensors already have the compound applied to the threads. If the sensor is removed from an engine and if for any reason the sensors are to be reinstalled, you must reapply anti-seize compound to the threads before the reinstallation.

8. If reusing the old HO2S sensors, coat the threads with ant-seize compound GM P/N 5613695.

9. Install the oxygen sensors to the catalytic converter. Refer to Heated Oxygen Sensor—Bank 1 Sensor 1.

10. Install NEW seals to the exhaust manifolds.

11. Install the catalytic converter to the exhaust manifolds and the muffler.

12. Install the catalytic converter to muffler nuts, but do not completely tighten them.

13. Install the catalytic converter nuts to the exhaust manifold studs and tighten them to 48 ft. lbs. (65 Nm).

14. Tighten the catalytic converter to muffler nuts (1) to 35 ft. lbs. (48 Nm).

15. Lower the vehicle and inspect for exhaust leaks.

Diesel Engines

See Figures 206 through 210.

1. Raise and support the vehicle.

2. Disconnect the engine harness connector (1) and the emission reduction fluid injector connector (2), from the catalytic converter.

3. Disconnect the exhaust temperature sensor-position 2 connector from the lower right side of the transmission.

4. Remove the catalytic converter-to-diesel particulate filter nuts (3).

5. Loosen the turbocharger exhaust pipe-to-catalytic converter clamp (1).

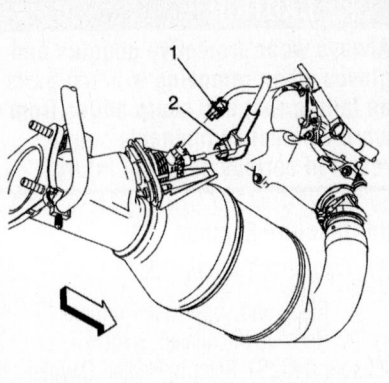

Fig. 206 Engine harness connector (1) and the emission reduction fluid injector connector (2)

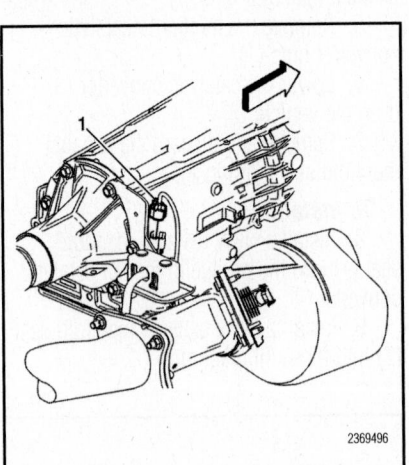

Fig. 207 Exhaust temperature sensor-position 2 connector

6. Remove the catalytic converter hanger-to-transmission bolts (1).

7. With the catalytic converter hanger attached, lower the catalytic converter (2).

8. If replacing catalytic converter, transfer the hanger bracket and the exhaust temperature sensor.

To install:

9. If replacing the catalytic converter, apply water based lubricant to the catalytic converter hanger bracket and slide the exhaust pipe hanger bracket into the catalytic converter hanger.

10. Install a NEW catalytic converter to diesel particulate filter gasket.

11. Position the catalytic converter to the diesel particulate filter, turbocharger exhaust pipe and the hanger bracket to transmission.

12. Install the catalytic converter hanger to transmission bolts (1) and tighten to 43 ft. lbs. (58 Nm).

13. Install the catalytic converter-to-particulate filter nuts (3) until snug.

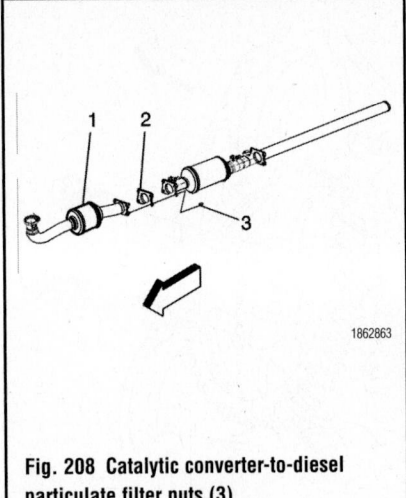

Fig. 208 Catalytic converter-to-diesel particulate filter nuts (3)

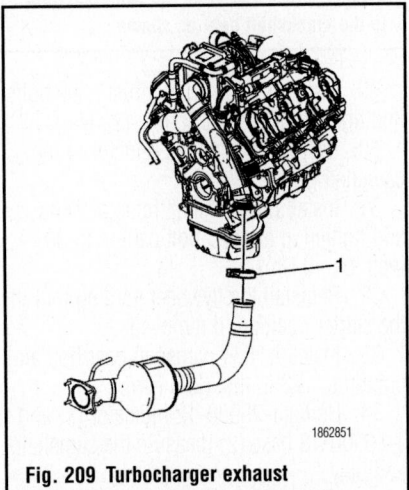

Fig. 209 Turbocharger exhaust pipe-to-catalytic converter clamp (1)

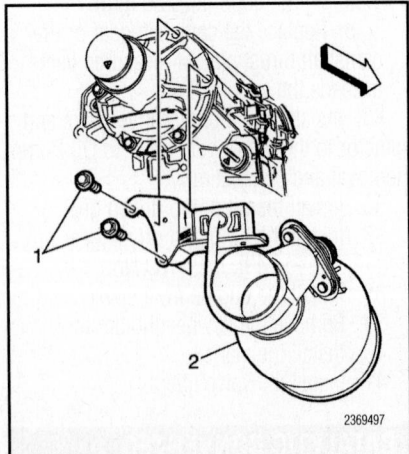

Fig. 210 Catalytic converter hanger-to-transmission bolts (1)

➡Ensure that the manifold pipe is square to the exhaust pipe adapter.

14. Slide the exhaust pipe clamp (1) down and around the pipe connection.

15. Tighten the exhaust pipe clamp and catalytic converter nuts.

16. Tighten the clamp to 106 inch lbs. (12 Nm).

17. Tighten the nuts to 25 ft. lbs. (34 Nm)

18. Connect the exhaust temperature sensor-position 2 connector (1), to the catalytic converter.

19. Connect the emission reduction fluid injector connector (2) and the engine harness connector (1).

20. Lower the vehicle.

CRANKSHAFT FRONT OIL SEAL

REMOVAL & INSTALLATION

4.3L Engine

See Figures 211 and 213.

1. Remove the crankshaft balancer.
2. Inspect the engine front cover seal bore area for damage.
3. Use a suitable seal puller, remove the crankshaft front oil seal.

To install:

4. Lubricate the exterior of the NEW seal with clean engine oil.
5. Using J 35468, a cover aligner and seal installer, or an equivalent, and a hammer, install the crankshaft front oil seal.
6. Ensure the crankshaft front oil seal is flush and square to the engine front cover.
7. Install the crankshaft balancer.

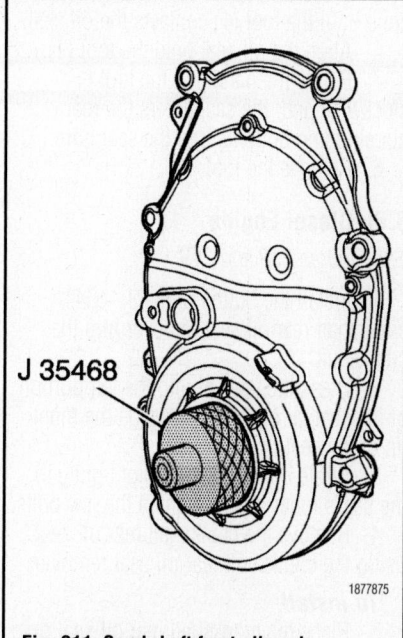

Fig. 211 Crankshaft front oil seal replacement

4.8L & 5.3L Engines

See Figures 212 and 213.

1. Remove the crankshaft balancer.
2. Inspect the engine front cover seal bore area for damage.
3. Use a suitable seal puller, remove the crankshaft front oil seal.

To install:

➡ Note the following:

- Do not lubricate the oil seal sealing surface.
- Do not use the crankshaft front oil seal again.
- Lubricate the outer edge of the oil seal (140) with clean engine oil.

4. Lubricate the front cover oil seal bore with clean engine oil.
5. Install the crankshaft front oil seal (140) onto the J 41478, a crankshaft front oil seal installer, or an equivalent.
6. Install the crankshaft front oil seal installer threaded rod, with nut, washer, guide, and oil seal, into the end of the crankshaft.
7. Use the crankshaft front oil seal installer in order to install the oil seal into the cover bore.

   a. Use a wrench and hold the hex on the installer bolt.

   b. Use a second wrench and rotate the installer nut clockwise until the seal bottoms in the cover bore.

   c. Remove the tool.

   d. Inspect the oil seal for proper installation. The oil seal should be installed evenly and completely into the front cover bore.

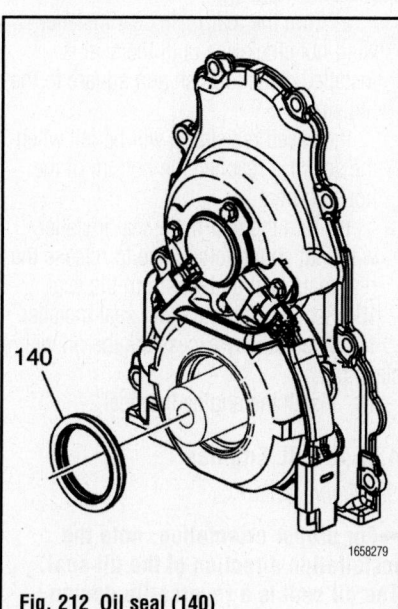

Fig. 212 Oil seal (140)

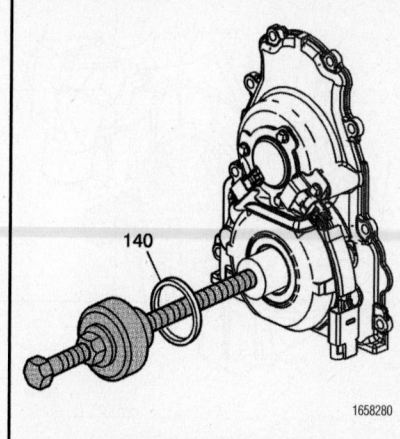

Fig. 213 Installing the oil seal (140) onto the J 41478, a crankshaft front oil seal installer

Diesel Engines

See Figures 214 and 215.

1. Remove the crankshaft balancer.
2. Install the button of the J 44644, a crankshaft front oil seal remover, or an equivalent, into the crankshaft.
3. Press the jaws of into the felt portion of the seal far enough to engage the inner lip of the seal.
4. While holding the jaws of tightly to the seals inner sleeve, tighten the jaw bolts.
5. Using the crankshaft front oil seal remover, remove the crankshaft front oil seal.

To install:

6. Clean the front crankshaft seal bore and the crankshaft.
7. Lubricate the crankshaft sealing surface with clean engine oil.
8. Place the crankshaft front oil seal onto the crankshaft.
9. Install the J 44645, a crankshaft front oil seal installer, or an equivalent, to the crankshaft.

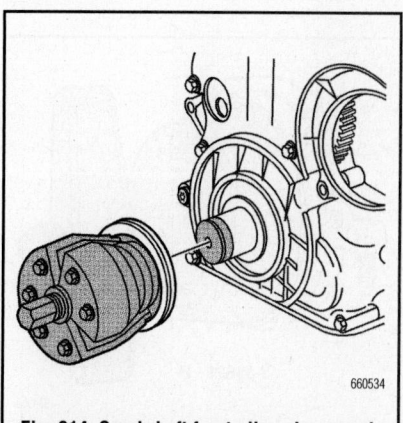

Fig. 214 Crankshaft front oil seal removal with the J 44644, a crankshaft front oil seal remover, or an equivalent

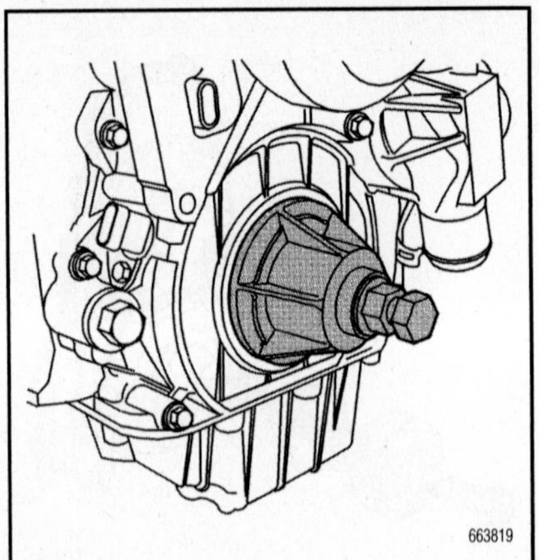

Fig. 215 Crankshaft front oil seal installation

10. Press the crankshaft front oil seal onto the crankshaft using the crankshaft oil seal installer, until the tool bottoms out.
11. Remove the crankshaft front oil seal installer.
12. Install the crankshaft balancer.

CRANKSHAFT REAR OIL SEAL

REMOVAL & INSTALLATION

4.3L Engine

See Figure 216.

1. Remove the flywheel.
2. Insert a flat-tipped screwdriver into the access notches and carefully pry the seal from the housing.
3. Discard the seal.
4. Clean off any dirt or rust in the area.

To install:

5. Apply 2 to 3 drops of clean engine oil to the bore of the housing.
6. Apply 2 to 3 drops of clean engine oil to the outside diameter of the engine flywheel pilot flange.

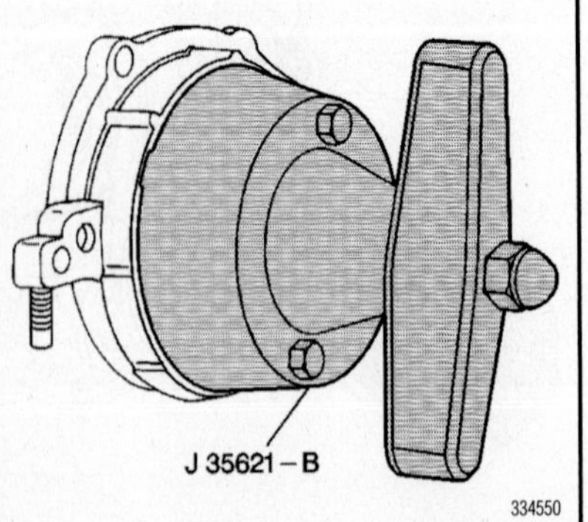

Fig. 216 J 35621-B Rear main seal installer

7. Apply 1 drop of clean engine oil to the outside diameter of the flywheel locator pin.
8. Apply 2 to 3 drops of clean engine oil to the crankshaft seal surface.

➡Notice the direction of the rear oil seal. The new design seal is a reverse style as opposed to what has been used in the past. THIS SIDE OUT has been stamped into the seal.

9. Inspect the J 35621-B rear main seal installer flange for imperfections that may damage the NEW seal.
10. Minor imperfections may be removed with a fine grade emery cloth.

➡DO NOT allow oil or any other lubricants to contact the seal lip surface of the seal.

11. Remove the sleeve from the seal.
12. Apply 2 to 3 drops of clean engine oil to the outside diameter of the seal.
13. Install the seal onto the J 35621-B rear main seal installer.
14. Install the J 35621-B rear main seal installer onto the rear of the crankshaft and hand tighten the tool bolts until snug.

⁂ WARNING

Proper alignment of the crankshaft rear oil seal is critical. Install the crankshaft rear oil seal near to flush and square to the crankshaft rear oil seal housing. Failing to do so may cause the crankshaft rear oil seal or the crankshaft rear oil seal installation tool to fail.

15. Install the seal onto the crankshaft and into the housing:
    a. Turn the rear main seal installer wing nut clockwise until the seal is installed close to flush and square to the housing.

    Increased resistance will be felt when the seal has reached the bottom of the housing bore.

    b. Turn the rear main seal installer wing nut counterclockwise to release the rear main seal installer from the seal.
16. Remove the rear main seal installer.
17. Wipe off any excess engine oil with a clean rag.
18. Install the engine flywheel.

4.8L & 5.3L Engines

See Figure 217.

➡For proper orientation, note the installation direction of the oil seal. The oil seal is a reverse-lip design.

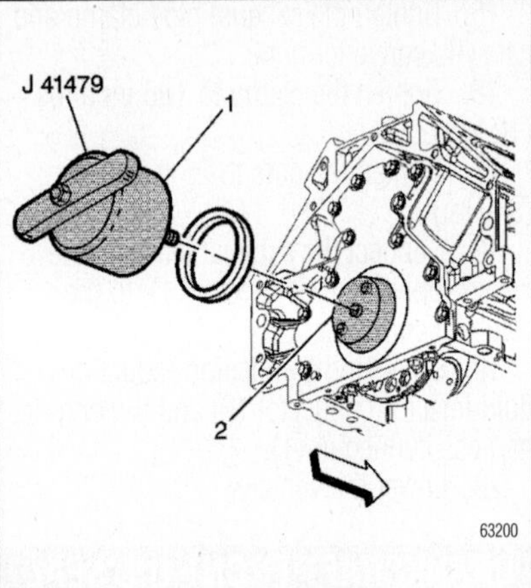

Fig. 217 Crankshaft rear oil seal installation

The part number is applied to the outside face of the seal.

1. Inspect the seal and identify the part number markings for proper orientation.
2. Install the J 41479 crankshaft rear oil seal installer or the J 41479-2A crankshaft rear oil seal installation guide cone (2) and bolts onto the rear of the crankshaft. The J 41479-2A crankshaft rear oil seal installation guide may be required for manual transmission or 5.3L LS4 applications.
3. Tighten the bolts until snug. Do not overtighten them.
4. Install the rear oil seal onto the tapered cone (2) and push the seal to the rear seal bore. Install the oil seal with the part number markings facing away from the engine.
5. Thread the J 41479 crankshaft rear oil seal installer threaded rod into the tapered cone until the tool (1) contacts the oil seal.
6. Align the oil seal onto the tool (1).
7. Rotate the handle of the tool (1) clockwise until the seal enters the rear housing and bottoms into the seal bore.
8. Remove the tool.

6.6L Diesel Engine

See Figures 218 and 219.

1. Install the button of the J 44641 crankshaft rear oil seal remover into the crankshaft.
2. Press the jaws of into the felt portion of the seal far enough to engage the inner lip of the seal.
3. While holding the jaws of tightly to the seal's inner sleeve, tighten the jaw bolts.
4. Remove the crankshaft rear oil seal using the crankshaft rear oil seal remover.

To install:

5. Place the crankshaft rear oil seal onto the crankshaft.

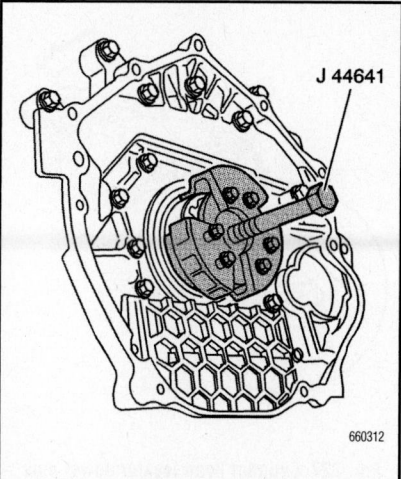

Fig. 218 Crankshaft rear oil seal remover

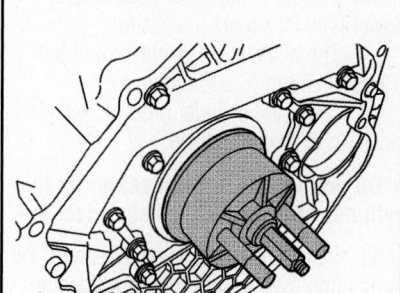

Fig. 219 Install the crankshaft rear oil seal

➡ **The J 44642 crankshaft rear oil seal installer must be fully secured to the crankshaft to ensure proper seal depth.**

6. Install the crankshaft rear oil seal installer to the crankshaft.

7. Press the crankshaft rear oil seal into position using the crankshaft rear oil seal installer. The crankshaft rear oil seal installer will bottom out when the seal reaches the proper depth.

8. Remove the crankshaft rear oil seal installer.

CYLINDER HEAD

❊❊ CAUTION

Wear safety glasses to avoid eye damage.

❊❊ WARNING

Clean all dirt, debris, and coolant from the engine block cylinder head

bolt holes. Failure to remove all foreign material may result in damaged threads, improperly tightened fasteners or damage to components.

REMOVAL & INSTALLATION

4.3L Engine

Left Side

See Figures 220 through 224.

1. Remove the engine coolant temperature sensor, if applicable.

2. Remove the engine coolant temperature gauge sensor, if applicable.

3. Remove the spark plugs.

4. Remove the bolts and the spark plug wire support.

5. Remove the cylinder head bolts and discard.

❊❊ WARNING

After removal, place the cylinder head on 2 wood blocks in order to prevent damage to the sealing surfaces.

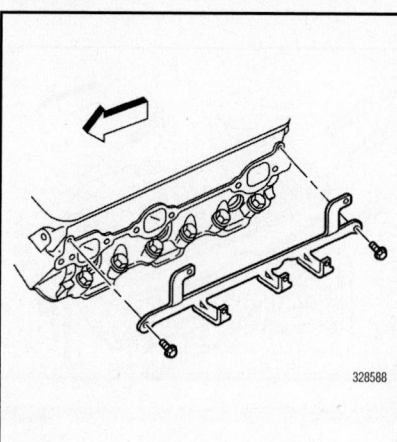

Fig. 220 Spark plug wire support and bolts

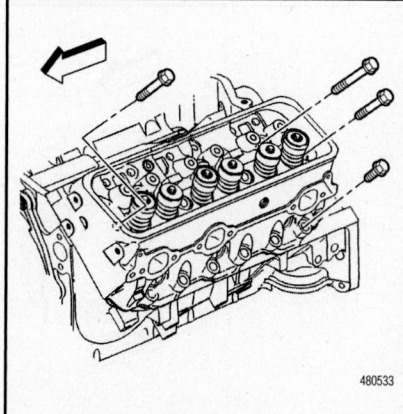

Fig. 221 Cylinder head bolts

6. Remove the cylinder head.

7. Remove and discard the cylinder head gasket.

8. Remove the cylinder head locator dowel pins, if required.

To install:

9. Clean the cylinder head gasket surfaces on the engine block.

10. Inspect the cylinder head locator dowel pins for proper installation.

11. The installation height should be 0.248–0.256 in (6.3–6.5 mm; a).

12. Clean the cylinder head gasket surfaces on the cylinder head.

➡ **Do not use any type of sealer on the cylinder head gasket, unless specified.**

13. Install the NEW cylinder head gasket in position over the cylinder head locator dowel pins.

14. Install the cylinder head onto the engine block.

15. Guide the cylinder head carefully into place over the dowel pins and the cylinder head gasket.

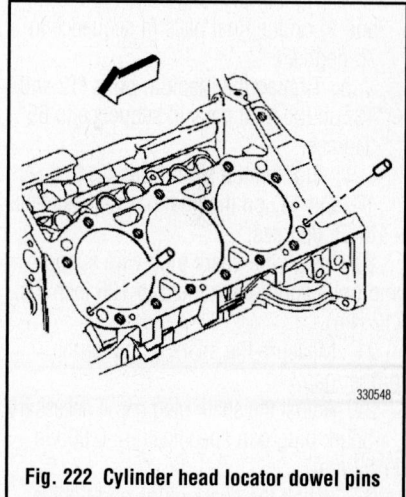

Fig. 222 Cylinder head locator dowel pins

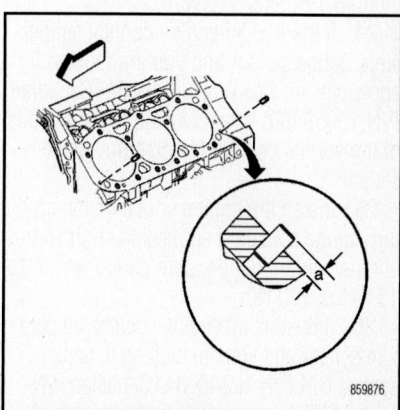

Fig. 223 Cylinder head locator dowel pins proper installation height (a)

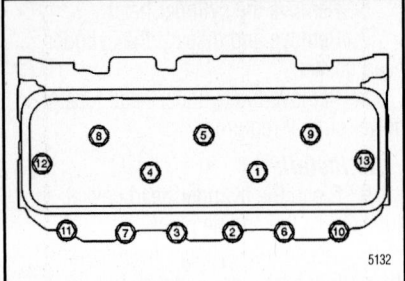

Fig. 224 Tighten the cylinder head bolts in sequence on the first pass to 22 ft. lbs. (30 Nm)

16. Apply sealant GM P/N 12346004 (Canadian P/N 10953480) or an equivalent, to the threads of the NEW cylinder head bolts.

17. Install the NEW cylinder head bolts finger tight.

18. Tighten the cylinder head bolts in sequence on the first pass to 22 ft. lbs. (30 Nm).

19. Use the J 45059 angle meter in order to tighten the cylinder head bolts in sequence on the final pass.

   a. Tighten the long bolts (1, 4, 5, 8, and 9) on the final pass in sequence to 75 degrees.

   b. Tighten the medium bolts (12 and 13) on the final pass in sequence to 65 degrees.

   c. Tighten the short bolts (2, 3, 6, 7, 10, and 11) on the final pass in sequence to 55 degrees.

20. Install the spark plug wire support and bolts and tighten them to 106 inch lbs. (12 Nm).

21. Measure the spark plugs for the proper gap.

22. Adjust the spark plug gap if necessary. Spark plug gap specification: 0.060 in (1.52 mm).

23. Install the spark plugs and tighten them to 11 ft. lbs. (15 Nm).

24. If there is an engine coolant temperature gauge sensor and you are reusing it, apply sealant GM P/N 12346004 (Canadian P/N 10953480) or equivalent, to the threads of the engine coolant temperature gauge sensor.

25. Install the engine coolant temperature gauge sensor, if applicable. Tighten the engine coolant temperature gauge sensor to 15 ft. lbs. (20 Nm).

26. If there is an engine coolant temperature sensor and you are reusing it, apply sealant GM P/N 12346004 (Canadian P/N 10953480) or equivalent, to the threads of the engine coolant temperature gauge sensor.

27. Install the engine coolant temperature sensor, if applicable. Tighten the engine coolant temperature sensor to 15 ft. lbs. (20 Nm).

Right Side

See Figures 224 through 227.

1. Remove the spark plugs.
2. Remove the rear bolt and the spark plug wire support.
3. Remove the cylinder head bolts and discard.

❊❊ WARNING

After removal, place the cylinder head on 2 wood blocks in order to prevent damage to the sealing surfaces.

4. Remove the cylinder head.
5. Remove and discard the cylinder head gasket.
6. Remove the cylinder head locator dowel pins, if required.

To install:

7. Clean the cylinder head gasket surfaces on the engine block.

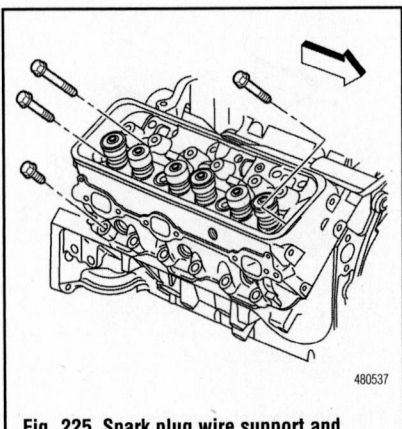

Fig. 225 Spark plug wire support and bolts

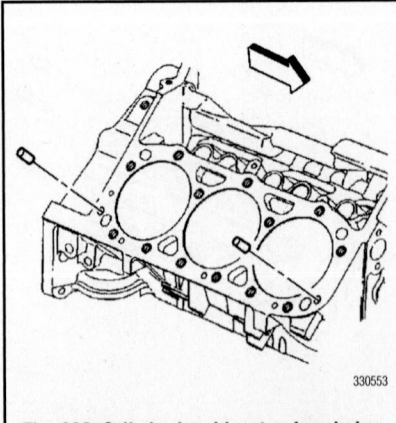

Fig. 226 Cylinder head locator dowel pins

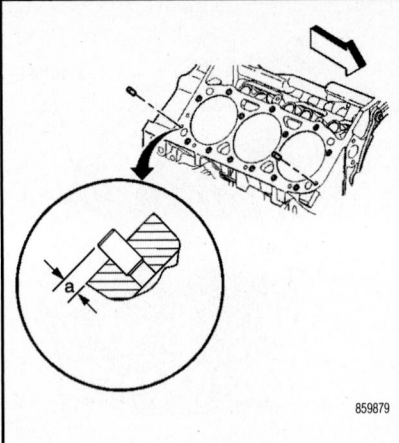

Fig. 227 Cylinder head locator dowel pins proper installation height (a)

8. Inspect the cylinder head locator dowel pins for proper installation.

9. The installation height should be 0.248–0.256 in (6.3–6.5 mm; a).

10. Clean the cylinder head gasket surfaces on the cylinder head.

➡**Do not use any type of sealer on the cylinder head gasket, unless specified.**

11. Install the NEW cylinder head gasket in position over the cylinder head locator dowel pins.

12. Install the cylinder head onto the engine block.

13. Guide the cylinder head carefully into place over the dowel pins and the cylinder head gasket.

14. Apply sealant GM P/N 12346004 (Canadian P/N 10953480) or an equivalent, to the threads of the NEW cylinder head bolts.

15. Install the NEW cylinder head bolts finger tight.

16. Tighten the cylinder head bolts in sequence on the first pass to 22 ft. lbs. (30 Nm).

17. Use the J 45059 angle meter in order to tighten the cylinder head bolts in sequence on the final pass.

   a. Tighten the long bolts (1, 4, 5, and 9) on the final pass in sequence to 75 degrees.

   b. Tighten the medium bolts (12 and 13) on the final pass in sequence to 65 degrees.

   c. Tighten the short bolts (2, 3, 6, 7, 10, and 11) on the final pass in sequence to 55 degrees.

18. Install the spark plug wire support and bolts and tighten them to 106 inch lbs. (12 Nm).

19. Remove the front spark plug wire support bolt.

20. Measure the spark plugs for the proper gap.

21. Adjust the spark plug gap if necessary.

Spark plug gap specification: 0.060 in (1.52 mm).

22. Install the spark plugs and tighten them to 11 ft. lbs. (15 Nm).

4.8L & 5.3L Engines

Left Side

See Figures 228 through 232.

➡The cylinder head bolts are of a torque-to-yield design; do NOT use again. Install NEW cylinder head bolts during assembly.

1. Remove the cylinder head bolts (220, 221).

✳✳ WARNING

After removal, place the cylinder head on 2 wood blocks in order to prevent damage to the sealing surfaces.

2. Remove the cylinder head (218).
3. Remove the gasket (217) and locating pins (230).
4. Discard the gasket and cylinder head bolts.

To install:

➡Note the following:

- Do not use the cylinder head bolts again. Install NEW cylinder head bolts during assembly.
- Do not use any type of sealant on the cylinder head gasket, unless specified.

5. Clean the engine block cylinder head bolt holes, if required.

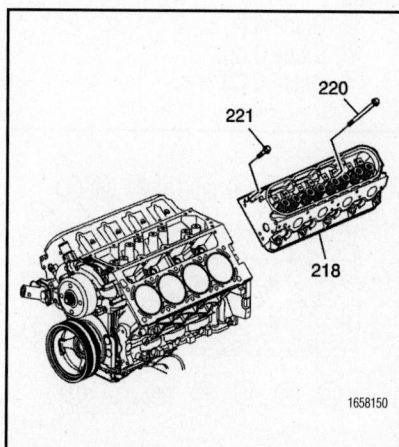

Fig. 228 Cylinder head bolts (220, 221) and cylinder head (218)

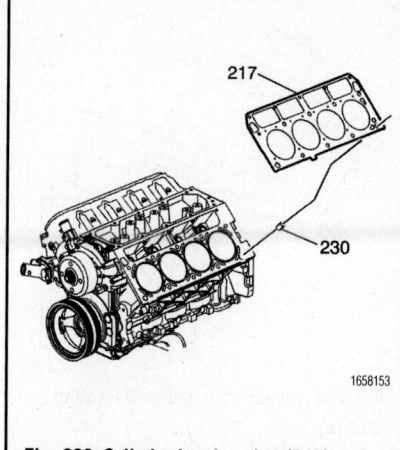

Fig. 229 Cylinder head gasket (217) and locating pins (230)

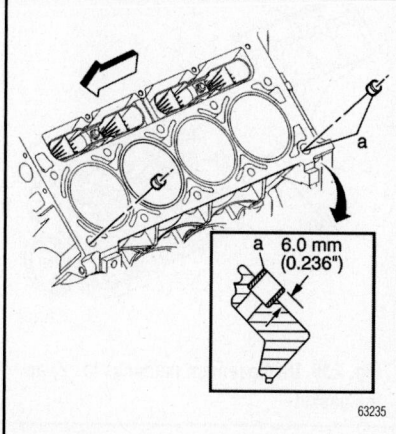

Fig. 230 Proper installation of locating pins (a)

6. Thread repair tool J 42385-107 may be used to clean the threads of old thread locking material.

7. Spray cleaner GM P/N 12346139 (Canadian P/N 10953463), GM P/N 12377981 (Canadian P/N 10953463), or an equivalent, into the hole.

8. Clean the cylinder head bolt holes with compressed air.

9. Install the cylinder head locating pins.

10. Inspect the locating pins for proper installation (a).

11. Inspect the displacement markings (1, 2) on the gasket, for proper usage.

12. Install the NEW cylinder head gasket onto the locating pins.

13. Install the cylinder head onto the locating pins and the gasket.

14. Install the NEW cylinder head bolts.

15. Tighten the cylinder head bolts as follows:

a. Tighten the M11 cylinder head bolts (1–10) a first pass in sequence to 22 ft. lbs. (30 Nm).

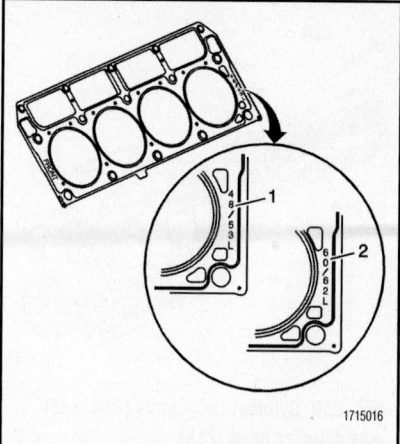

Fig. 231 Displacement markings (1, 2) on the gasket

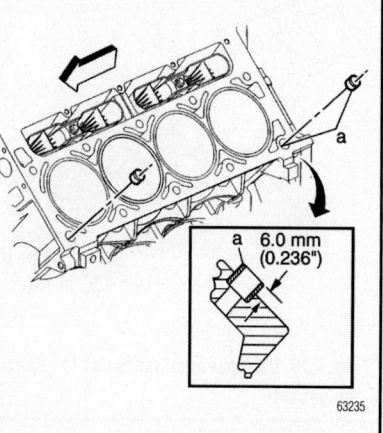

Fig. 232 Tighten the cylinder head bolts

b. Tighten the M11 cylinder head bolts (1–10) a second pass in sequence to 90 degrees using the J 45059 angle meter, or an equivalent.

c. Tighten the M11 cylinder head bolts (1–10) a final pass in sequence to 70 degrees using an angle meter.

d. Tighten the M8 cylinder head bolts (11–15) to 22 ft. lbs. (30 Nm). Begin with the center bolt (11) and alternating side-to-side, work outward, tightening all of the bolts.

Right Side

See Figures 233 through 237.

➡The cylinder head bolts are of a torque-to-yield design; do NOT use again. Install NEW cylinder head bolts during assembly.

1. Remove the cylinder head bolts (220, 221).

✳✳ WARNING

After removal, place the cylinder head on 2 wood blocks in order to prevent damage to the sealing surfaces.

2. Remove the cylinder head (218).

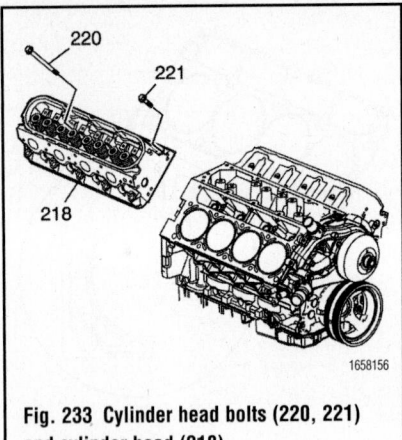

Fig. 233 Cylinder head bolts (220, 221) and cylinder head (218)

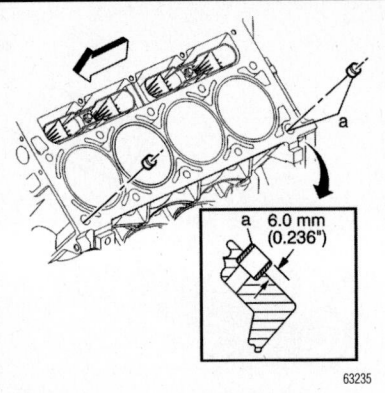

Fig. 235 Proper installation of locating pins (a)

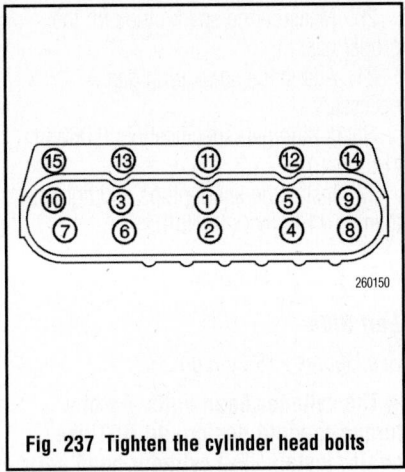

Fig. 237 Tighten the cylinder head bolts

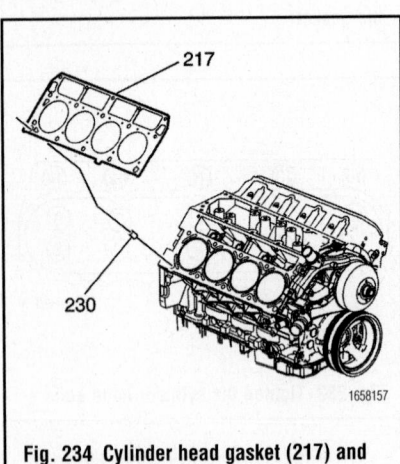

Fig. 234 Cylinder head gasket (217) and locating pins (230)

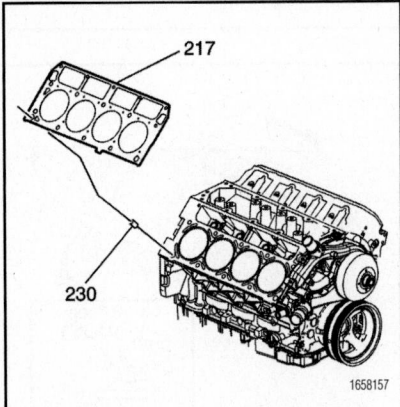

Fig. 236 Displacement markings (1, 2) on the gasket

6.6L Diesel Engine

Left Side

See Figures 238 through 241.

1. Remove the cylinder head bolts in the proper sequence.
2. Discard the large M12 bolts.
3. Remove the left cylinder head assembly.
4. Remove the left cylinder head gasket.

To install:

> **✳✳ WARNING**

The left and right cylinder head gaskets are not interchangeable. Improper placement of the cylinder head gasket will block coolant and oil passages. Blocked coolant and oil passages will cause severe engine damage.

➡ The stamped letter, R or L, must face up. R is the right bank, L is the left bank.

5. The markings on the gasket are as follows:
   a. Grade A (1)
   b. Grade B (2)
   c. Grade C (3)

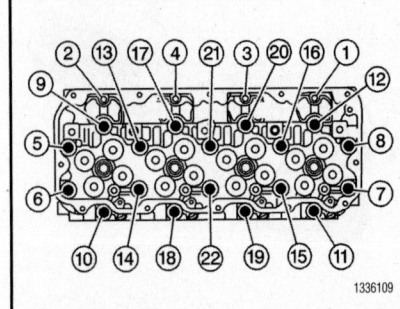

Fig. 238 Remove the cylinder head bolts in the proper sequence

3. Remove the gasket (217) and locating pins (230).
4. Discard the gasket and cylinder head bolts.

To install:

➡ **Note the following:**

- Do not use the cylinder head bolts again. Install NEW cylinder head bolts during assembly.
- Do not use any type of sealant on the cylinder head gasket, unless specified.

5. Clean the engine block cylinder head bolt holes, if required.
6. Thread repair tool J 42385-107 may be used to clean the threads of old thread locking material.
7. Spray cleaner GM P/N 12346139 (Canadian P/N 10953463), GM P/N 12377981 (Canadian P/N 10953463), or an equivalent, into the hole.
8. Clean the cylinder head bolt holes with compressed air.
9. Install the cylinder head locating pins.
10. Inspect the locating pins for proper installation (a).

11. Inspect the displacement markings (1, 2) on the gasket, for proper usage.
12. Install the NEW cylinder head gasket onto the locating pins.
13. Install the cylinder head onto the locating pins and the gasket.
14. Install the NEW cylinder head bolts.
15. Tighten the cylinder head bolts as follows:
   a. Tighten the M11 cylinder head bolts (1–10) a first pass in sequence to 22 ft. lbs. (30 Nm).
   b. Tighten the M11 cylinder head bolts (1–10) a second pass in sequence to 90 degrees using the J 45059 angle meter, or an equivalent.
   c. Tighten the M11 cylinder head bolts (1–10) a final pass in sequence to 70 degrees using an angle meter.
   d. Tighten the M8 cylinder head bolts (11–15) to 22 ft. lbs. (30 Nm). Begin with the center bolt (11) and alternating side-to-side, work outward, tightening all of the bolts.

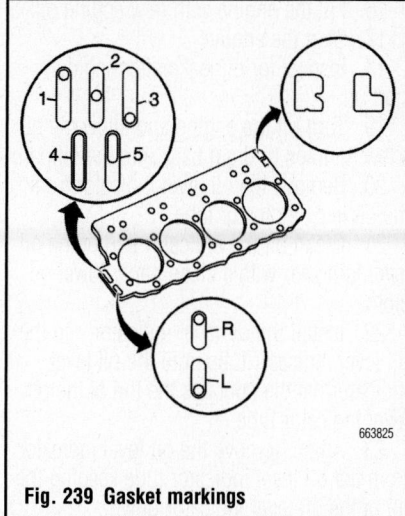

Fig. 239 Gasket markings

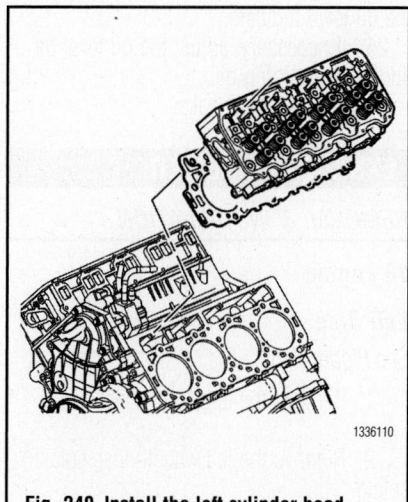

Fig. 240 Install the left cylinder head

d. Block over-bored 0.010—0.030 in (0.254—0.762 mm; 4)

e. Block over-bored 0.010—0.030 in (0.254—0.762 mm) and deck milled 0.008 in (0.203 mm; 5)

6. Install the left cylinder head gasket of the correct grade. The left and right cylinder head gaskets are not interchangeable.

7. Install the left cylinder head.

This component uses bolts with a pre-applied molybdenum disulfide coating for thread lubrication. Do not remove the coating or use any additional lubricant. Improperly lubricated threads will adversely affect the bolt torque and clamp load. Improper bolt torque and clamp load can lead to engine damage.

8. Install the NEW M12 cylinder head bolts and tighten them in four steps:
   a. 1st step: 37 ft. lbs. (50 Nm)

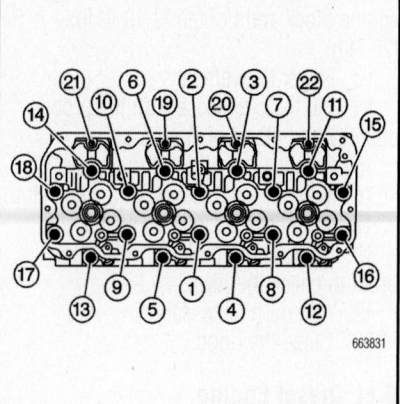

Fig. 241 Tighten the cylinder head bolts in the proper sequence

b. 2nd step: 59 ft. lbs. (80 Nm)

c. 3rd step: tighten 60 degrees using the J 45059 angle meter, or an equivalent.

d. 4th step: tighten 60 degrees using an angle meter

9. Reuse the M8 bolts. Install the M8 bolts and tighten the M8 cylinder head bolts to 18 ft. lbs. (25 Nm).

Right Side

See Figures 238, 239 and 241.

1. Remove the cylinder head bolts in the proper sequence.

2. Discard the large M12 bolts.

3. Remove the right cylinder head assembly.

4. Remove the right cylinder head gasket.

To install:

❊❊ WARNING

The left and right cylinder head gaskets are not interchangeable. Improper placement of the cylinder head gasket will block coolant and oil passages. Blocked coolant and oil passages will cause severe engine damage.

➡The stamped letter, R or L, must face up. R is the right bank, L is the left bank.

5. The markings on the gasket are as follows:
   a. Grade A (1)
   b. Grade B (2)
   c. Grade C (3)
   d. Block over-bored 0.010—0.030 in (0.254—0.762 mm; 4)
   e. Block over-bored 0.010—0.030 in (0.254—0.762 mm) and deck milled 0.008 in (0.203 mm; 5)

6. Install the right cylinder head gasket of the correct grade. The left and right cylinder head gaskets are not interchangeable.

7. Install the right cylinder head.

❊❊ WARNING

This component uses bolts with a pre-applied molybdenum disulfide coating for thread lubrication. Do not remove the coating or use any additional lubricant. Improperly lubricated threads will adversely affect the bolt torque and clamp load. Improper bolt torque and clamp load can lead to engine damage.

8. Install the NEW M12 cylinder head bolts and tighten them in four steps:
   a. 1st step: 37 ft. lbs. (50 Nm)
   b. 2nd step: 59 ft. lbs. (80 Nm)
   c. 3rd step: tighten 60 degrees using the J 45059 angle meter, or an equivalent
   d. 4th step: tighten 60 degrees using an angle meter

9. Reuse the M8 bolts. Install the M8 bolts and tighten the M8 cylinder head bolts to 18 ft. lbs. (25 Nm).

REPLACEMENT

4.3L Engine

See Figure 242.

1. Raise and suitably support the vehicle.

2. Remove the drain plug and drain the engine oil in a suitable container.

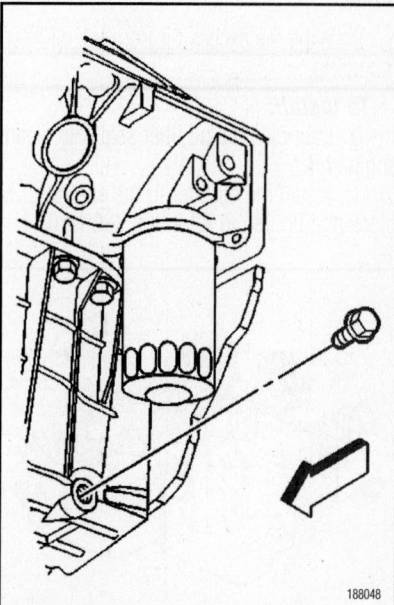

Fig. 242 Remove the drain plug and drain the engine oil in a suitable container

3. Remove the oil filter.

4. Inspect to ensure the engine oil filter gasket is removed.

To install:

5. Lubricate the oil filter gasket with clean engine oil.

6. Install the oil filter and tighten to 22 ft. lbs. (30 Nm).

7. Install the drain plug and tighten to 18 ft. lbs. (25 Nm).

8. Lower the vehicle.

9. Fill the engine with the proper capacity and quality of engine oil.

10. Operate the engine, check for leaks, and oil pressure.

4.8L & 5.3L Engines

See Figure 243.

➡**In order to completely drain the oil from the oil pan internal baffling, the bottom of the oil pan must be level during the oil drain procedure.**

1. Open the hood.

2. Remove the oil fill cap.

3. Raise and suitably support the vehicle.

4. Place an oil drain pan under the oil pan drain plug.

5. Remove the oil pan drain plug.

6. Drain the engine oil.

7. Wipe the excess oil from the drain plug hole and plug.

8. Remove the oil filter from the engine block.

➡**Check the old oil filter to ensure that the filter seal is not left on the engine block.**

9. Wipe the excess oil from the oil filter mounting.

To install:

10. Lubricate the oil filter seal with clean engine oil.

11. Install the oil filter to the engine block and tighten to 22 ft. lbs. (30 Nm).

12. Install the oil drain plug to the engine block and tighten to 18 ft. lbs. (25 Nm).

13. Lower the vehicle.

14. Fill the crankcase with the proper quantity and grade of engine oil.

15. Remove the oil level indicator.

16. Wipe the indicator with a clean cloth.

17. Install the oil level indicator.

18. Remove the oil level indicator in order to check the level.

19. Add oil if necessary.

20. Close the hood.

6.6L Diesel Engine

See Figure 244.

1. Raise and support the vehicle.

2. Position a suitable drain pan under the oil pan drain plug.

3. Remove the oil drain plug.

4. Allow the oil to drain completely.

5. Clean and inspect the oil pan drain plug, replace if necessary.

6. Clean and inspect the oil pan drain plug sealing surface, replace the oil pan if necessary.

7. Wipe any remaining oil from the drain plug hole and reinstall the oil pan drain plug until snug.

8. Position a suitable drain pan under the oil filter

9. Remove the oil filter.

10. Ensure that the oil filter gasket is still on the old oil filter, if not remove the oil filter gasket from the adapter.

To install:

11. Apply clean engine oil to the NEW oil filter gasket.

12. Install the NEW oil filter and tighten after contact plus 1 to 1 1/4 turn.

13. Tighten the oil pan drain plug to 62 ft. lbs. (84 Nm).

14. Remove the oil drain pan from under the vehicle.

15. Lower the vehicle.

16. Fill the engine with new engine oil.

17. Start the engine.

18. Inspect for oil leaks after engine start up.

19. Turn off the engine and allow the oil a few minutes to drain back into the oil pan.

20. Remove the oil level indicator from the oil level indicator tube.

21. Clean off the indicator end of the oil level indicator with a clean paper towel or cloth.

22. Install the oil level indicator into the oil level indicator tube until the oil level indicator handle contacts the top of the oil level indicator tube.

23. Again, remove the oil level indicator from the oil level indicator tube keeping the tip of the oil level indicator down.

24. Check the level of the engine oil on the oil level indicator.

25. If necessary, adjust the oil level be adding or draining oil.

26. Check for oil leaks.

EXHAUST MANIFOLD

REMOVAL & INSTALLATION

V6 Engine

Left Side

See Figure 245.

1. Remove the left front wheel and tire.

2. Remove the left wheelhouse splash shield.

3. Remove the catalytic converter assembly. Refer to Catalytic Converter.

4. Remove the spark plugs. Refer to Spark Plug in the Engine Electrical section.

5. Remove the exhaust manifold bolts (3) and stud (4).

6. Remove the exhaust manifold (2).

7. Remove and discard the exhaust manifold gaskets (1).

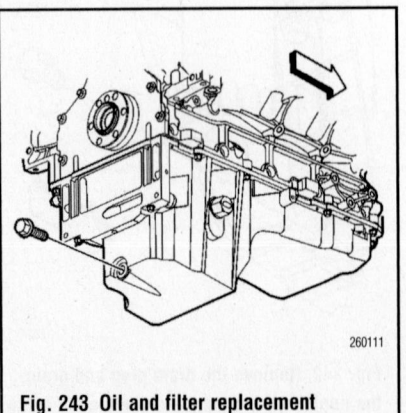

260111

Fig. 243 Oil and filter replacement

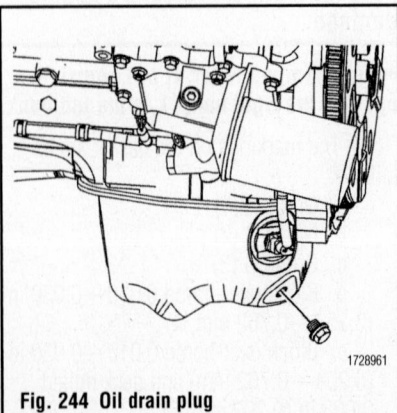

1728961

Fig. 244 Oil drain plug

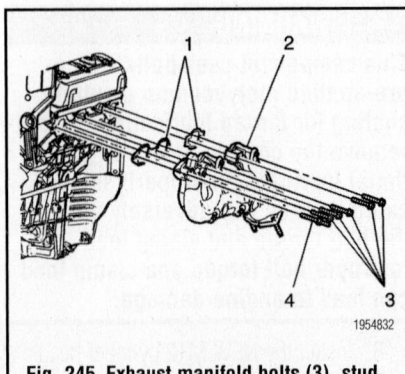

1954832

Fig. 245 Exhaust manifold bolts (3), stud (4), manifold (2) and gaskets (1)

To install:

➡ **To aid in installing the exhaust manifold to the engine, the bolt holes on the NEW exhaust manifold gaskets have tabs that will hold the gasket and the bolts in place.**

8. Install the exhaust manifold bolts and stud to the manifold.

9. Install NEW exhaust manifold gaskets onto the bolt and stud.

10. Position and install the exhaust manifold to the cylinder head.

    a. Tighten the bolts/stud a first pass to 11 ft. lbs. (15 Nm).

    b. Tighten the bolts/stud a final pass to 22 ft. lbs. (30 Nm).

11. Install the spark plugs.

12. Install the catalytic converter assembly.

13. Install the left wheelhouse splash shield.

14. Install the left front wheel and tire.

Right Side

See Figure 000.

1. Remove the right front wheel and tire.

2. Remove the right wheelhouse splash shield.

3. Remove the catalytic converter assembly. Refer to Catalytic Converter.

4. Remove the spark plugs. Refer to Spark Plug in the Engine Electrical section.

5. Remove the exhaust manifold bolts (3).

6. Remove the exhaust manifold (1).

7. Remove and discard the exhaust manifold gaskets (2).

To install:

➡ **To aid in installing the exhaust manifold to the engine, the bolt holes on the NEW exhaust manifold gaskets have tabs that will hold the gasket and the bolts in place.**

8. Install the exhaust manifold bolts (3) to the manifold.

9. Install NEW exhaust manifold gaskets (2) onto the bolt and stud.

10. Position and install the exhaust manifold (1) to the cylinder head.

    a. Tighten the bolts a first pass to 11 ft. lbs. (15 Nm).

    b. Tighten the bolts a final pass to 22 ft. lbs. (30 Nm).

11. Install the spark plugs.

12. Install the catalytic converter assembly.

13. Install the right wheelhouse splash shield.

14. Install the right front wheel and tire.

V8 Engine

Left Side

See Figures 246 and 247.

1. Raise and support the vehicle.

2. Separate the catalytic converter from the exhaust manifold. Refer to Catalytic Converter.

3. Lower the vehicle.

4. Remove the engine cover.

5. Disconnect the exhaust gas recirculation (EGR) pipe from the exhaust manifold, if equipped.

6. Remove the spark plug wires from the spark plugs.

7. Remove the exhaust manifold bolts and remove the exhaust manifold from the vehicle.

8. Discard the gasket and the exhaust manifold to catalytic converter seal.

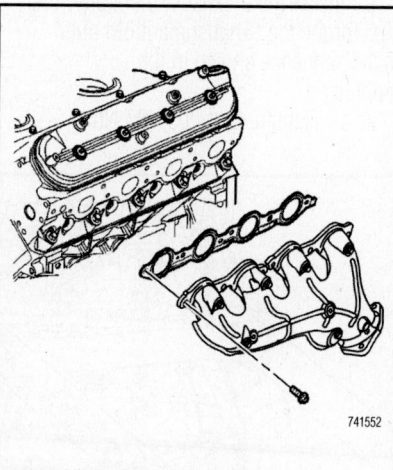

Fig. 246 Separate the catalytic converter from the exhaust manifold

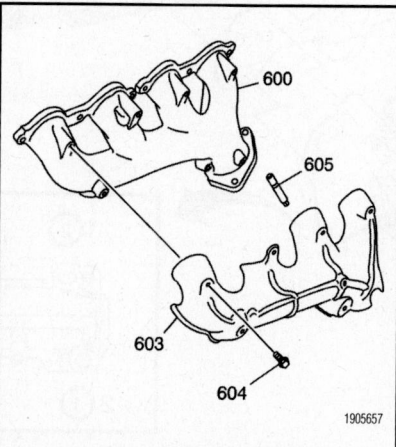

Fig. 247 Heat shield (603), bolts (604), manifold (600), exhaust pipe studs (605)

9. Remove the heat shield (603) and bolts (604) from the manifold (600), as required.

10. Remove the studs (605), as required.

To install:

➡ **Note the following:**

• Tighten the exhaust manifold bolts as specified in the service procedure. Improperly installed and/or leaking exhaust manifold gaskets may affect vehicle emissions and/or on-board diagnostic (OBD) II system performance.

• The cylinder head exhaust manifold bolt hole threads must be clean and free of debris or thread locking material.

• Do not apply sealant to the first 3 threads of the bolt.

11. Install the heat shield (603) and bolts (604) and tighten to 80 inch lbs. (9 Nm).

12. Install the exhaust pipe studs (605) and tighten to 15 ft. lbs. (20 Nm).

13. Apply a 0.2 in (5 mm) wide band of thread lock GM P/N 12345493 (Canadian P/N 10953488), or equivalent, to the threads of the exhaust manifold bolts.

14. Position the exhaust manifold gasket to the manifold with two manifold bolts.

15. Install the exhaust manifold to the cylinder head.

    a. Tighten the manifold bolts a first pass to 11 ft. lbs. (15 Nm). Tighten the manifold bolts beginning with the center 2 bolts. Alternate from side-to-side, and work toward the outside bolts.

    b. Tighten the manifold bolts a final pass to 15 ft. lbs. (20 Nm). Tighten the manifold bolts beginning with the center 2 bolts. Alternate from side-to-side, and work toward the outside bolts.

16. Using a flat punch, bend over the exposed edge of the manifold gasket at the rear of the cylinder head.

17. Connect the EGR pipe to the manifold, if equipped.

18. Install the spark plug wires to the spark plugs.

19. Using a NEW seal, install the catalytic converter to the exhaust manifold.

20. Install the engine cover.

21. Inspect for exhaust leaks.

Right Side

1. Raise and support the vehicle.

2. Separate the catalytic converter from the exhaust manifold. Refer to Catalytic Converter.

3. Lower the vehicle.

4. Remove the engine cover.

5. Remove the oil level indicator tube.

6. Remove the spark plug wires from the spark plugs.

7. Remove the exhaust manifold bolts and remove the exhaust manifold from the vehicle.

8. Discard the exhaust manifold gasket and the exhaust manifold to catalytic converter seal.

9. Remove the exhaust manifold studs.

To install:

10. Install the exhaust manifold studs to the new manifold.

11. Install the new exhaust manifold seal to the new manifold.

12. Position the exhaust manifold to the cylinder head.

    a. Tighten the exhaust manifold bolts—First Pass to 11 ft. lbs. (15 Nm).

    b. Tighten the exhaust manifold bolts—Second Pass to 18 ft. lbs. (25 Nm).

13. Install the oil level indicator tube.

14. Install the spark plug wires.

15. Install the catalytic converter to the exhaust manifold.

16. Install the engine cover.

17. Inspect for exhaust leaks.

Diesel Engines

Left Side

See Figure 248.

1. Remove the left side exhaust pipe.

2. Raise and suitably support the vehicle.

3. Remove the 2 exhaust manifold nuts (1).

4. Remove the 6 exhaust manifold bolts (2).

5. Remove the left side exhaust manifold (3).

To install:

6. Install the left side exhaust manifold:

    a. Transfer the exhaust manifold heat shield.

    b. Replace or transfer the exhaust manifold gasket as needed.

7. Install the 6 exhaust manifold bolts. Tip: Torque the exhaust manifold bolts in the sequence shown in the graphic.

8. Tighten 39 ft. lbs. (53 Nm).

9. Install the 2 exhaust manifold nuts. Tip: Torque the exhaust manifold nuts in the sequence shown in the graphic.

    a. Tighten 42 ft. lbs. (57 Nm).

Right Side

See Figure 249.

1. Remove the right side exhaust pipe.

2. Remove the right front tire and wheel.

3. Remove the right side wheelhouse splash shield.

4. Remove the 2 exhaust manifold nuts (1).

5. Remove the 6 exhaust manifold bolts (2).

6. Remove the right side exhaust manifold bolt (3).

To install:

7. Install the right side exhaust manifold bolt as follows:

    a. Transfer the exhaust manifold gasket.

    b. Replace or transfer the exhaust manifold gasket as needed.

8. Install the 6 exhaust manifold bolts. Tip: Torque the bolts in the sequence shown in the graphic.

9. Tighten to 37 ft. lbs. (50 Nm).

10. Install the 2 exhaust manifold nuts. Tip: Torque the exhaust manifold nuts in the sequence shown in the graphic.

11. Tighten to 42 ft. lbs. (57 Nm).

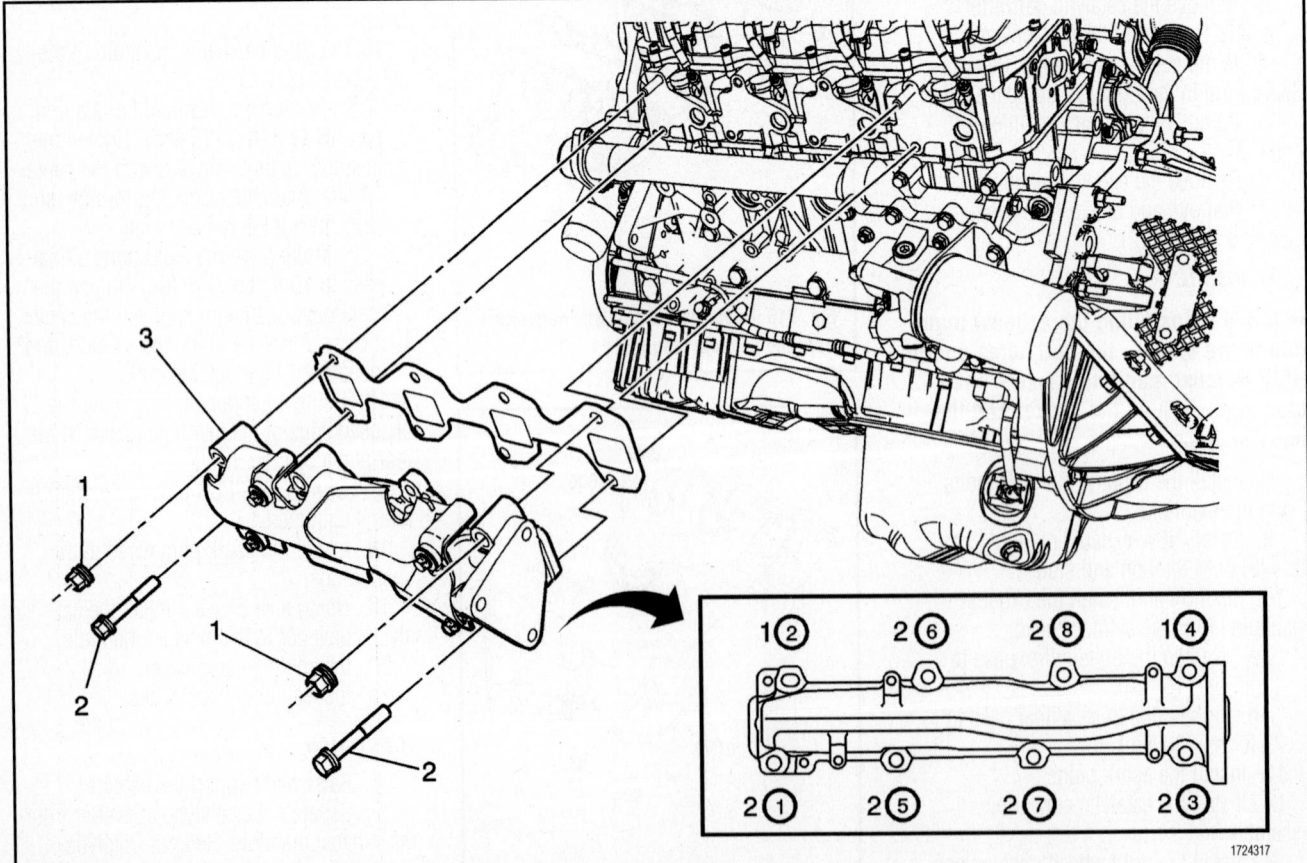

Fig. 248 Two exhaust manifold nuts (1), 6 bolts, and left side exhaust manifold (3)

1724317

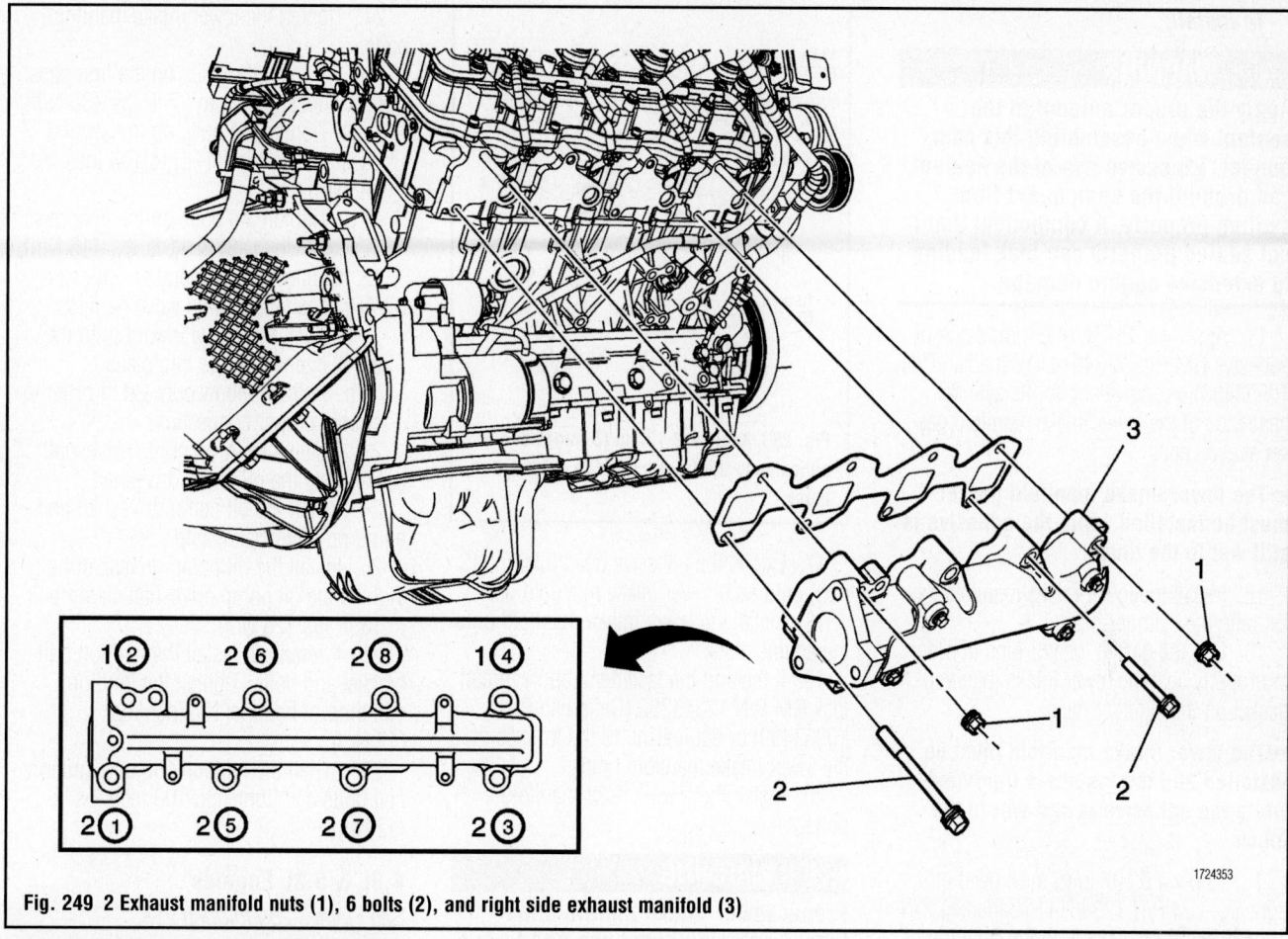

Fig. 249 2 Exhaust manifold nuts (1), 6 bolts (2), and right side exhaust manifold (3)

INTAKE MANIFOLD

REMOVAL & INSTALLATION

4.3L Engine

See Figures 250 through 254.

1. Remove the ignition coil bolts and coil from the bracket.

2. If required, remove the ignition coil bracket bolts and bracket.

3. Remove the oil pump driveshaft bolt.

4. Remove the oil pump driveshaft with clamp.

5. Remove the oil pump driveshaft gasket and discard.

6. Remove the evaporative emission (EVAP) canister purge solenoid valve harness.

   a. Push the quick disconnect clip and hold in place.

   b. Pull outward on the harness elbow.

7. Remove the Engine Coolant Temperature (ECT) sensor wire connector, if equipped, from the engine wiring harness bracket.

8. Remove the lower intake manifold bolts.

➡**Note the following:**

- The intake manifold may be removed as an assembly. Do not remove the specific intake manifold components unless component service is required.

- Do not allow dirt or debris to enter the fuel system. Ensure that the ends of the fuel system are properly sealed.

9. Remove the intake manifold assembly.

10. Remove and discard the lower intake manifold gaskets.

Fig. 250 Oil pump driveshaft

Fig. 251 EVAP canister purge solenoid valve harness

To install:

> ※※ **WARNING**
>
> **Apply the proper amount of the sealant when assembling this component. Excessive use of the sealant can prohibit the component from sealing properly. A component that is not sealed properly can leak leading to extensive engine damage.**

11. Apply a 0.157 in (4.0 mm) patch of adhesive GM P/N 12346141 (Canadian P/N 10953433) or equivalent, to the cylinder head side of the lower intake manifold gasket at each end.

➡ The lower intake manifold gasket must be installed while the adhesive is still wet to the touch.

12. Install the lower intake manifold gasket onto the cylinder head.

13. Use the gasket locator pins in order to properly seat the lower intake manifold gasket on the cylinder head.

➡ The lower intake manifold must be installed and the fasteners tightened while the adhesive is still wet to the touch.

14. Apply a 0.197 in (5 mm) bead of adhesive GM P/N 12346141 (Canadian P/N 10953433) or equivalent, to the front top of the engine block.

15. Extend the adhesive bead 0.50 in (13 mm) onto each lower intake manifold gasket.

16. Apply a 0.197 in (5 mm) bead of adhesive GM P/N 12346141 (Canadian P/N 10953433) or equivalent, to the rear top of the engine block.

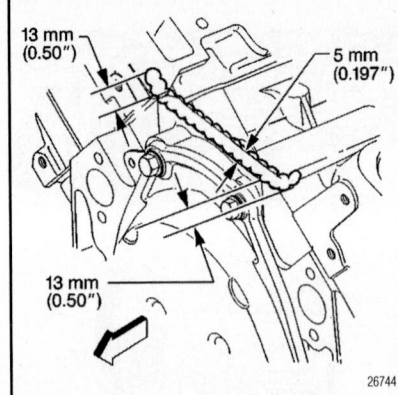

Fig. 253 Apply a 0.197 in (5 mm) bead of adhesive to the front top of the engine block

17. Extend the adhesive bead 0.50 in (13 mm) onto each lower intake manifold gasket.

18. Install the lower intake manifold onto the engine block.

19. If reusing the fasteners, apply thread lock GM P/N 12345382 (Canadian P/N 10953489) or equivalent, to the threads of the lower intake manifold bolts.

20. Install the lower intake manifold bolts.

> ※※ **WARNING**
>
> **Proper lower intake manifold fastener tightening sequence and torque is critical. Always follow the tightening sequence, and torque the intake manifold bolts using the 3 step method. Failing to do so may distort the crankshaft bearing bore alignment and cause damage to the crankshaft bearings.**

21. Tighten the lower intake manifold bolts.

   a. Tighten the bolts on the first pass in sequence (1–8) to 27 ft. lbs. (36 Nm).

   b. Tighten the bolts on the second pass in sequence (1–8) to 106 inch lbs. (12 Nm).

   c. Tighten the bolts on the final pass in sequence (1–8) to 11 ft. lbs. (15 Nm).

22. Connect the evaporative emission (EVAP) canister solenoid valve harness.

   a. Push the elbow inward until the quick connect snaps into place.

   b. Pull the elbow outward in order to ensure proper connection.

23. Install a NEW oil pump driveshaft gasket onto the oil pump driveshaft.

24. Install the oil pump driveshaft and oil pump driveshaft clamp.

25. Install the oil pump driveshaft bolt. Tighten the oil pump driveshaft clamp bolt to 18 ft. lbs. (25 Nm).

26. If required, install the ignition coil bracket and bolts. Tighten the ignition coil bracket bolts to 106 inch lbs. (12 Nm).

27. Install the ignition coil and ignition coil bolts and tighten to 106 inch lbs. (12 Nm).

4.8L & 5.3L Engines

See Figures 255 through 258.

Note the following:

• The intake manifold, throttle body, fuel injection rail, and fuel injectors may be removed as an assembly. If not servicing the individual components, remove the manifold as a complete assembly.

• DO NOT use the intake manifold-to-cylinder head gaskets again.

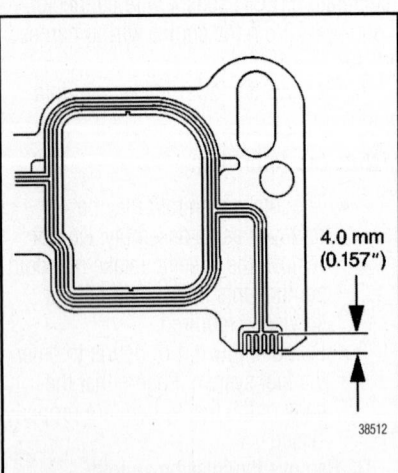

Fig. 252 Apply a 0.157 in (4.0 mm) patch of adhesive to the cylinder head side of the lower intake manifold gasket at each end.

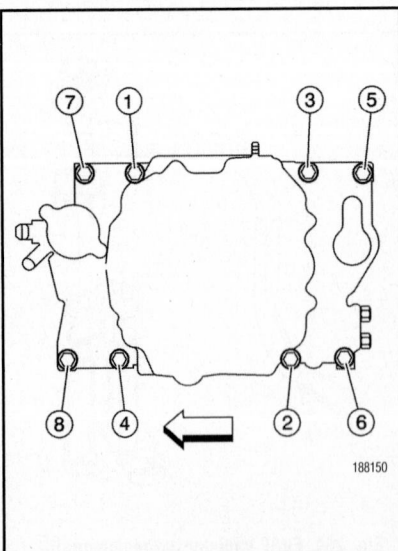

Fig. 254 Lower intake manifold tightening

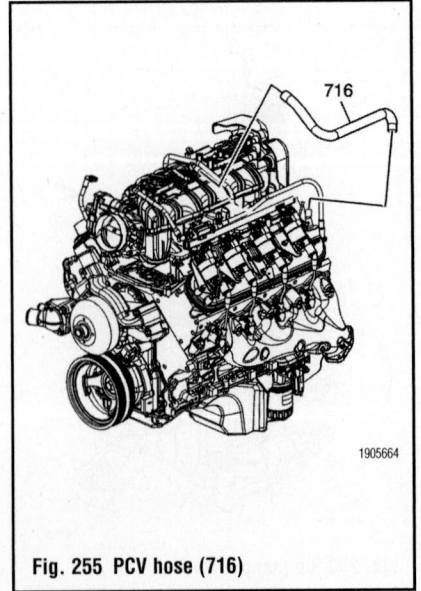

Fig. 255 PCV hose (716)

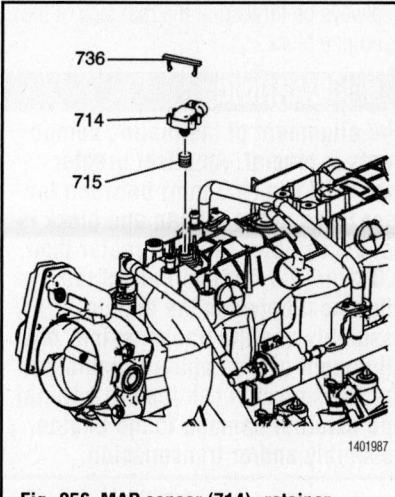

Fig. 256 MAP sensor (714), retainer (736), and O-ring (715)

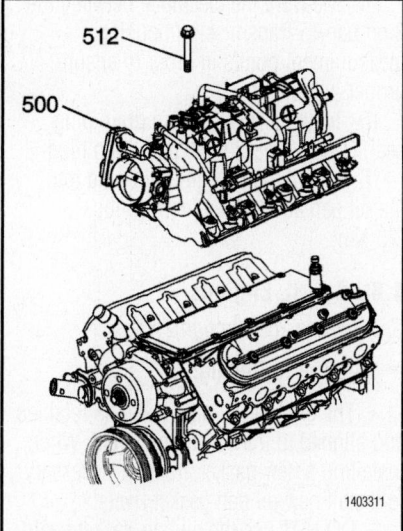

Fig. 257 Intake manifold bolts (512) and manifold (500)

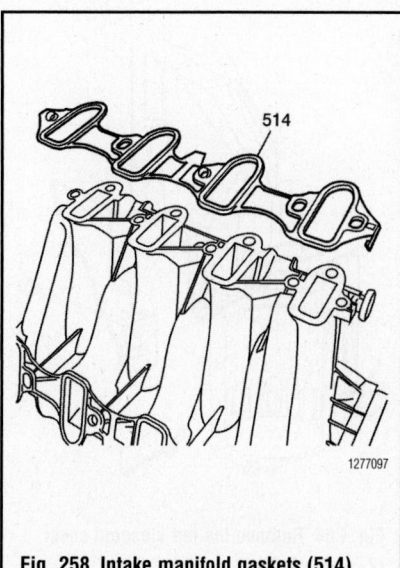

Fig. 258 Intake manifold gaskets (514)

1. Remove the positive crankcase ventilation (PCV) hose—dirty air (716).

2. Remove the Manifold Absolute Pressure (MAP) sensor (714) and retainer (736), as required.

3. Remove the O-ring (715) from the sensor, as required.

4. Remove the intake manifold bolts (512).

5. Remove the intake manifold (500) with gaskets.

6. Remove the intake manifold gaskets (514).

7. Discard the intake manifold gaskets.

6.6L Diesel Engine

See Figures 259 and 260.

1. Remove the fuel return pipe bolt (1) from the top of the intake manifold.

2. Remove the intake manifold bolts (2) and nuts (4).

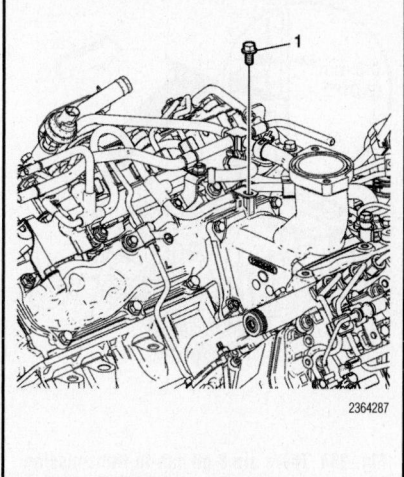

Fig. 259 Fuel return pipe bolt (1)

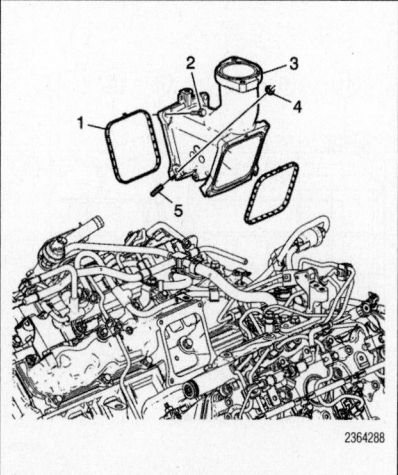

Fig. 260 Intake manifold bolts (2) and nuts (4), manifold (3), gaskets (1), and studs (5)

3. Remove the intake manifold (3).

4. Remove the intake manifold gaskets (1).

5. Remove the intake manifold studs (5).

To install:

➡**Tighten the intake manifold nuts first.**

6. Install the intake manifold studs and tighten to 53 inch lbs. (6 Nm).

7. Install the intake manifold gaskets.

8. Install the intake manifold.

9. Install the intake manifold nuts and tighten to 89 inch lbs. (10 Nm)

10. Install the intake manifold bolts and tighten to 89 inch lbs. (10 Nm)

11. Install the fuel return pipe bolt to the top of the intake manifold and tighten to 89 inch lbs. (10 Nm)

OIL PAN

REMOVAL & INSTALLATION

4.3L Engine

See Figures 261 through 265.

1. Remove the oil pan bolts and nuts.
2. Remove the oil pan.
3. Remove the oil pan gasket.
4. Discard the oil pan gasket.

To install:

5. Apply a 0.197 in (5 mm) wide and 25 mm (1.0 in) long bead of adhesive GM P/N 12346141 (Canadian P/N 10953433) or equivalent, to both the right and left sides of the engine front cover to engine block junction at the oil pan sealing surfaces.

6. Apply a 0.197 in (5 mm) wide and 1.0 in (25 mm) long bead of adhesive GM

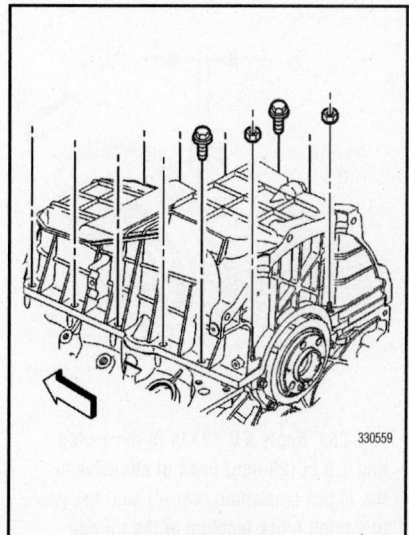

Fig. 261 Oil pan bolts and nuts

P/N 12346141 (Canadian P/N 10953433) or equivalent, to the entire crankshaft rear oil seal housing to engine block junction at the oil pan sealing surfaces.

➡**Always install a NEW oil pan gasket.**

- The oil pan gasket and oil pan must be installed and the fasteners tightened while the adhesive is still wet to the touch.

7. Install the NEW oil pan gasket into the groove in the oil pan.

➡**The oil pan alignment must always be flush or forward no more than 0.011 in (0.3 mm) from the rear face of the engine block.**

8. Install the oil pan onto the engine block.

9. Press the oil pan gasket into the grooves of the engine front cover and crankshaft rear oil seal housing.

10. Slide the oil pan back against a suitable straight edge.

11. Install the oil pan bolts and nuts, but do not tighten.

12. Measure the pan-to-transmission housing clearance using a feeler gauge and a straight edge.

a. Use a feeler gauge to check the clearance between the oil pan-to-transmission housing measurement points.

b. If the clearance exceeds 0.011 in (0.3 mm) at any of the 3 oil pan-to-transmission housing measurement points (1), then repeat the step until the oil pan-to-transmission housing clearance is within the specification. The oil pan must

always be forward of the rear face of the engine block.

❋❋ **WARNING**

The alignment of the mating components is crucial. An offset greater than 0.011 in (0.3 mm) between the rear faces of the oil pan and block is not acceptable. Offsets greater than 0.011 in (0.3 mm) will affect the alignment between the engine assembly and the transmission. Misalignment of the engine assembly to the transmission can lead to internal and external damage to the engine assembly and/or transmission.

13. Tighten the oil pan bolts and nuts in sequence (1–12). Tighten the oil pan bolts to 18 ft. lbs. (25 Nm).

14. Measure the clearance between the 3 oil pan-to-transmission housing measurement points in order to ensure proper alignment.

15. Install a NEW oil pan drain plug seal, O-ring, onto the oil pan drain plug.

16. Install the oil pan drain plug into the oil pan and tighten to 18 ft. lbs. (25 Nm).

4.8L & 5.3L Engines

See Figures 266 through 270.

➡**Note the following:**

- The original oil pan gasket is retained and aligned to the oil pan by rivets. When installing a new gasket, it is not necessary to install new oil pan gasket rivets.
- DO NOT use the oil pan gasket again. When installing the oil pan, install a NEW oil pan gasket.

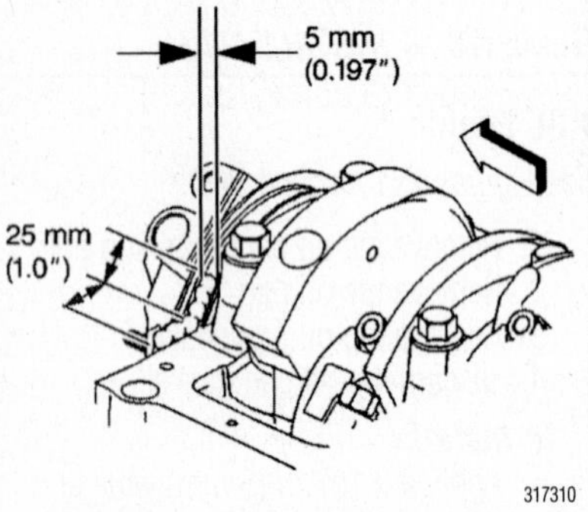

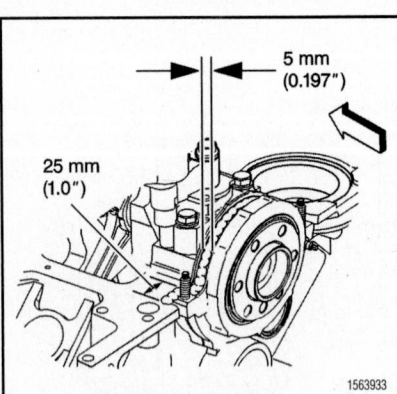

Fig. 262 Apply a 0.197 in (5 mm) wide and 1.0 in (25 mm) long bead of adhesive to both the right and left sides of the engine front cover to engine block junction at the oil pan sealing surfaces

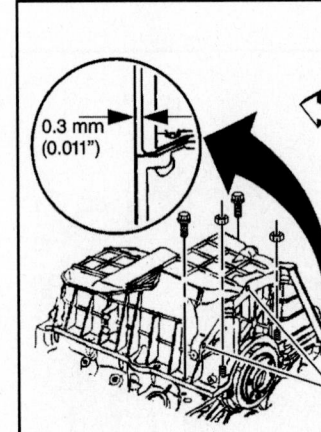

Fig. 264 There are 3 oil pan-to-transmission housing measurement points (1)

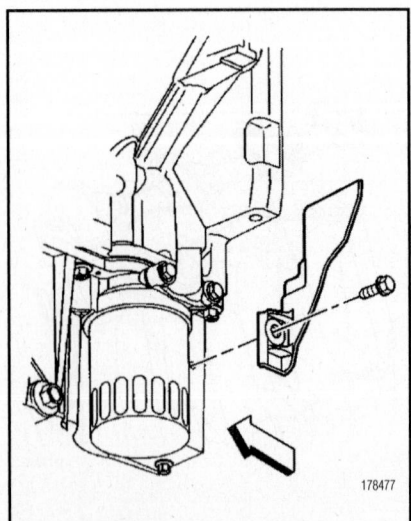

Fig. 266 Remove the left closeout cover (2) and bolt (1)

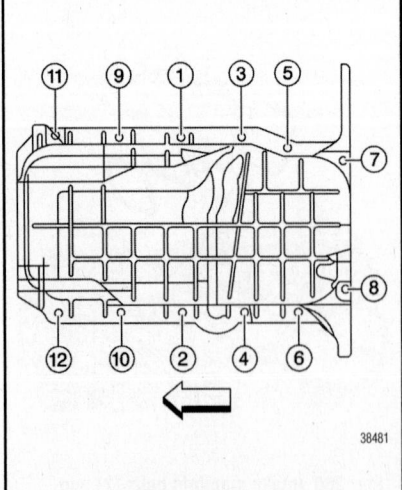

Fig. 263 Apply a 0.197 in (5 mm) wide and 1.0 in (25 mm) bead of adhesive to the entire crankshaft rear oil seal housing to engine block junction at the oil pan sealing surfaces

Fig. 265 Tighten the oil pan bolts and nuts in sequence

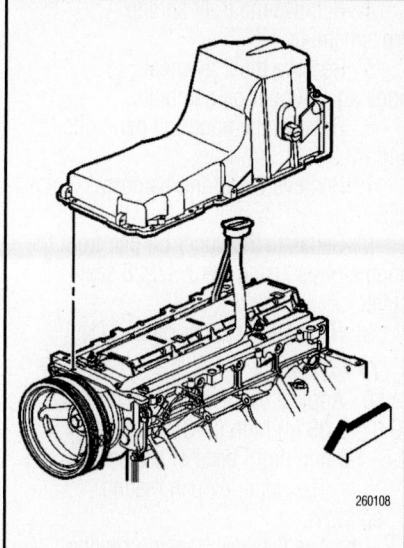

Fig. 267 Remove the right closeout cover and bolt

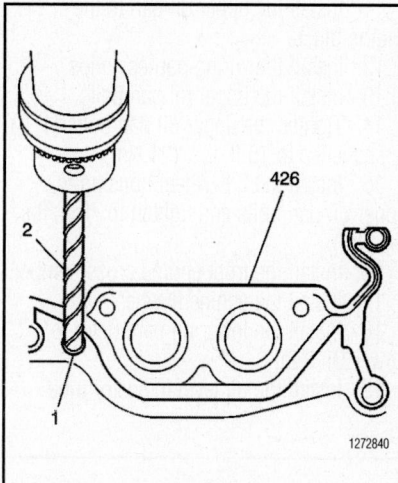

Fig. 268 Drill (2), oil pan gasket retaining rivets (1), and gasket (426)

• It is not necessary to remove the oil level indicator switch prior to oil pan removal. Remove the oil level indicator switch, if applicable and if service is required.

1. Remove the left closeout cover (2) and bolt (1).
2. Remove the right closeout cover and bolt.
3. Remove the oil pan bolts.
4. Remove the oil pan.

➡**Note the following:**

• DO NOT allow foreign material to enter the oil passages of the oil pan. Cap or cover the openings, as required.
• Use care not to gouge, score, or damage the oil pan sealing surface.

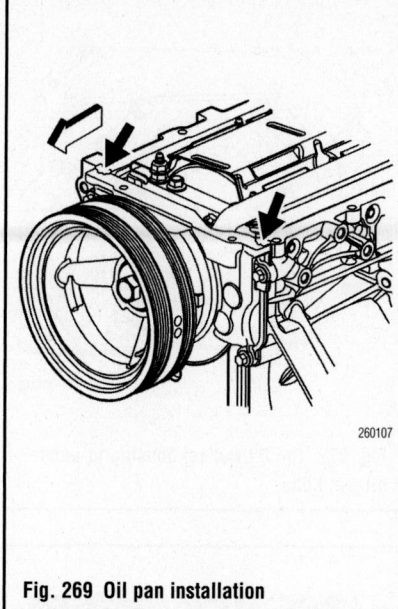

Fig. 269 Oil pan installation

5. Drill (2) out the oil pan gasket retaining rivets (1), if required.
6. Remove the gasket (426) from the pan.
7. Discard the gasket and rivets.

To install:

➡**The alignment of the structural oil pan is critical. The rear bolt hole locations of the oil pan provide mounting points for the transmission housing. To ensure the rigidity of the powertrain and correct transmission alignment, it is important that the rear of the block and the rear of the oil pan are flush or even. The rear of the oil pan must NEVER protrude beyond the engine block and transmission housing plane.**

• Do not use the oil pan gasket again.
• It is not necessary to rivet the NEW gasket to the oil pan.
• It is not necessary to remove the oil level sensor prior to oil pan installation.

8. Apply a 0.2 in (5 mm) bead of sealant GM P/N 12378521 (Canadian P/N 88901148), or equivalent, 0.8 in (20 mm) long to the engine block. Apply the sealant directly onto the tabs of the front cover gasket that protrude into the oil pan surface.
9. Apply a 0.8 in (20 mm) bead of sealant GM P/N 12378521 (Canadian P/N 88901148), or equivalent, 20 mm (0.8 in) long to the engine block. Apply the sealant directly onto the tabs of the rear housing gasket that protrude into the oil pan surface.

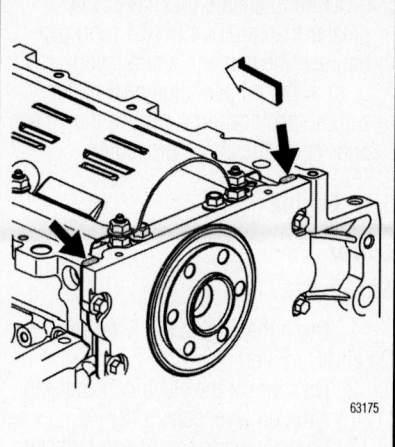

Fig. 270 Apply a 0.2 in (5 mm) bead of sealant 0.8 in (20 mm) long to the engine block. Apply the sealant directly onto the tabs of the rear housing gasket that protrude into the oil pan surface

➡**Be sure to align the oil gallery passages in the oil pan and engine block properly with the oil pan gasket.**

10. Pre-assemble the oil pan gasket to the pan.
   a. Install the gasket onto the oil pan.
   b. Install the oil pan bolts to the pan and through the gasket.
11. Install the oil pan, gasket, and bolts to the engine block.
12. Tighten the bolts finger tight. Do not overtighten them.
13. Place a straight edge across the rear of the engine block and the rear of the oil pan at the transmission housing mounting surfaces.
14. Align the oil pan until the rear of engine block and rear of oil pan are flush or even.
15. Tighten the oil pan-to-block and oil pan-to-front cover bolts to 18 ft. lbs. (25 Nm).
16. Tighten the oil pan-to-rear cover bolts to 106 inch lbs. (12 Nm).
17. Measure the oil pan-to-engine block alignment.
   a. Place a straight edge across the rear of the engine block and rear of oil pan at the transmission housing mounting surfaces.

➡**The rear of the oil pan must NEVER protrude beyond the engine block and transmission housing mounting surfaces.**

   b. Insert a feeler gage between the straight edge and the oil pan transmission housing mounting surface and measure to ensure that there is no greater than a 0.004 in (0.1 mm) gap between the pan and straight edge.

c. If the oil pan alignment is not within specifications, remove the oil pan and repeat the above procedure.

6.6L Engine

Lower

See Figure 271.

1. Drain the engine oil. Refer to Engine Oil and Oil Filter.
2. Disconnect the electrical connector (1) from the oil level sensor (2).
3. Remove the lower oil pan bolts and nuts.
4. Do not damage the sealing surfaces when separating the lower oil pan from the upper oil pan.
5. Separate the lower oil pan from the upper oil pan using the J-37228 seal cutter.
6. Remove the lower oil pan.

To install:

7. Apply a (0.79–0.118 in) wide by (0.02–0.06 in) high (2-3 mm wide by 0.5–1.5 mm high) bead of sealant to the lower oil pan mating surface. GM specifies sealant P/N 12378521 (US) and 88901148 (Canada).
8. Install the lower oil pan.
9. Install the lower oil pan nuts and bolts
10. Tighten the lower oil pan bolts and nuts in sequence to 89 inch lbs. (10 Nm)
11. Connect the oil level sensor.

Upper

See Figures 272 through 274.

1. Remove the oil level indicator tube.
2. Remove the lower oil pan. Refer to Lower Oil Pan.
3. Remove the engine flywheel.

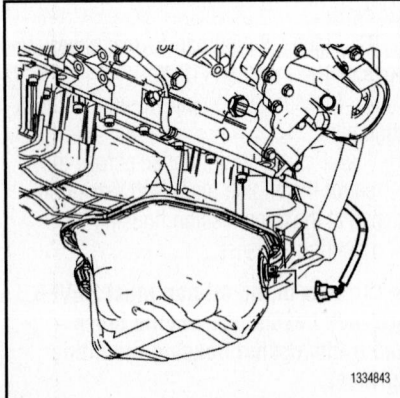

Fig. 271 Disconnect the electrical connector (1) from the oil level sensor (2)

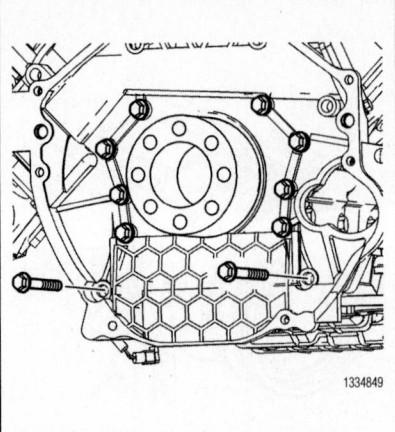

Fig. 272 The 2 flywheel housing-to-upper oil pan bolts

Fig. 273 Upper oil pan bolts (2, 4), wiring harness clips (3), and upper oil pan (1)

4. Remove the front engine crossmember.
5. Remove the 2 flywheel housing-to-upper oil pan bolts.
6. Remove the upper oil pan bolts (2) and (4).
7. Remove the wiring harness clips (3).
8. Separate the upper oil pan from the engine block using the J-37228 seal cutter.
9. Remove the upper oil pan (1).

To install:

10. Apply a (0.79–0.118 in) wide by (0.02–0.06 in) high (2–3 mm wide by 0.5–1.5 mm high) bead of sealant to:

a. The upper oil pan mating surfaces.

b. The flywheel housing sealing surface.

c. GM specifies sealant P/N 12378521 (US) and 88901148 (Canada).

11. Install the upper oil pan to the engine block.
12. Install the wiring harness clips.
13. Install the upper oil pan bolts.
14. Tighten the upper oil pan bolts (1, 2) in sequence to 15 ft. lbs. (21 Nm).
15. Install the 2 flywheel housing to upper oil pan bolts and tighten to 70 ft. lbs. (95 Nm).
16. Install the front engine crossmember.
17. Install the engine flywheel.
18. Install the lower oil pan. Refer to Lower Oil Pan.
19. Install the oil level indicator tube.

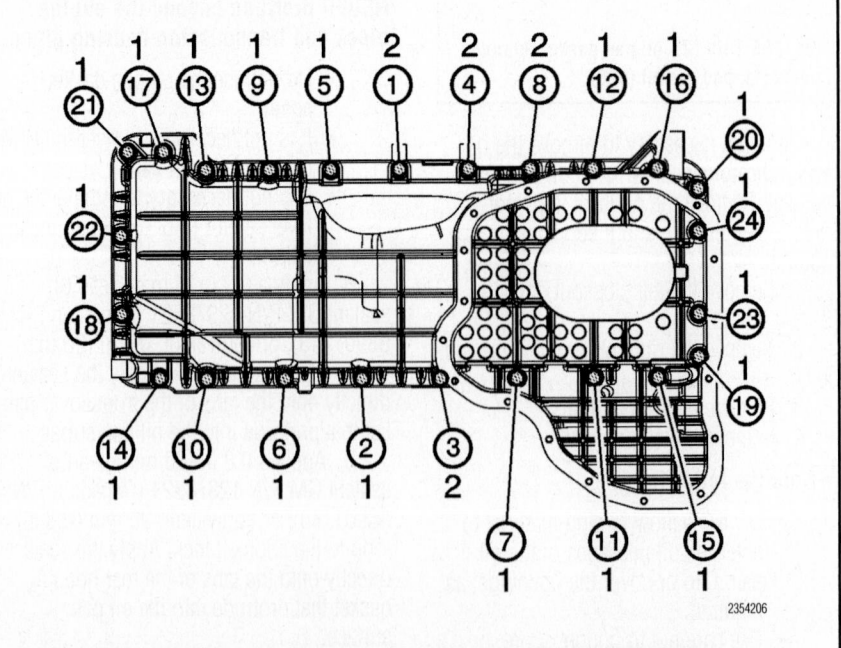

Fig. 274 Tighten the upper oil pan bolts (1, 2) in sequence to 15 ft. lbs. (21 Nm).

OIL PUMP

CLEANING AND INSPECTION

4.3L Engine

See Figure 275.

1. Clean the oil pump components in cleaning solvent.

2. Dry the components with compressed air.

3. Inspect the oil pump for the following conditions:

   a. Scoring on the top of the gears (1)

   b. Damaged gears (2) for chipping, galling, or wear

   c. Scoring, damage, or casting imperfections to the body (3)

   d. Damaged or scored gear shaft (4, 5)

   e. Damaged bolt hole threads

   f. Worn oil pump driveshaft bore

   g. Damaged or sticking oil pump pressure relief valve

   • Minor imperfections may be removed with a fine oil stone.

   h. Collapsed or broken oil pump pressure relief valve spring

4. If the oil pump is to be reused, install a NEW oil pump pressure relief valve spring.

5. During oil pump installation, install a NEW oil pump driveshaft retainer.

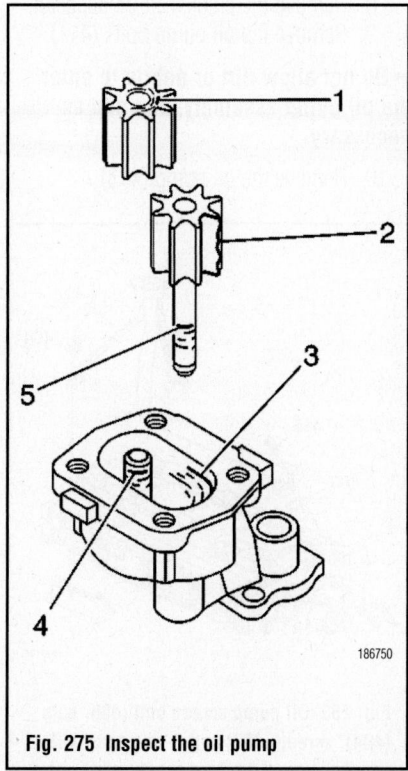

Fig. 275 Inspect the oil pump

4.8L & 5.3L Engines

See Figures 276 and 277.

➡Service the internal components of the oil pump assembly separately, excluding the spring. If the oil pump components are worn or damaged, replace the oil pump as an assembly.

➡Service the oil pump pipe and screen as an assembly. Do not attempt to repair the wire mesh portion of the pump and screen assembly.

1. Clean the parts in solvent.

2. Dry the parts with compressed air.

3. Inspect the oil pump housing (413) and the cover (409) for cracks, excessive wear, scoring, or casting imperfections.

4. Inspect the oil pump housing-to-engine block oil gallery surface for scratches or gouging.

5. Inspect the oil pump housing for damaged bolt hole threads.

6. Inspect the relief valve plug (416) and plug bore for damaged threads.

7. Inspect the oil pump internal oil passages for restrictions.

8. Inspect the drive gear (410) and driven gear (412) for chipping, galling, or wear.

9. Minor burrs or imperfections on the gears may be removed with a fine oil stone.

10. Inspect the drive gear splines for excessive wear.

11. Inspect relief valve spring (415) for cracks, scratches, and wear to coils in spring.

12. Inspect the pressure relief valve (414) and bore for scoring or wear.

13. The valve must move freely in the bore, with no restrictions.

14. Inspect the oil pump screen (407) for debris or restrictions.

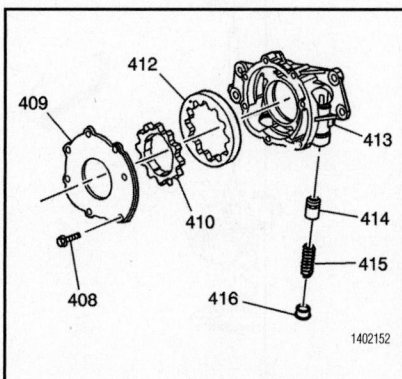

Fig. 276 Oil pump housing (413) and cover (409); relief valve plug (416), drive gear (410), driven gear (412), relief valve spring, and relief pressure valve (414)

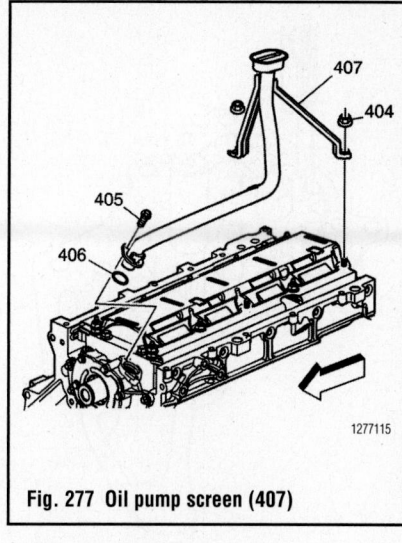

Fig. 277 Oil pump screen (407)

15. Inspect the oil pump screen for broken or loose wire mesh.

6.6L Diesel Engine

See Figures 278 through 280.

1. Remove the oil pump gear cover bolts.

2. Remove the oil pump gear cover.

3. Use a feeler gauge to measure the clearance between the gear teeth and the oil pump housing. The production clearance is 0.0049–0.0087 in (0.125–0.221 mm) and the service limit is 0.0087 in (0.221 mm).

4. Replace the oil pump assembly if the clearance exceeds the service limit.

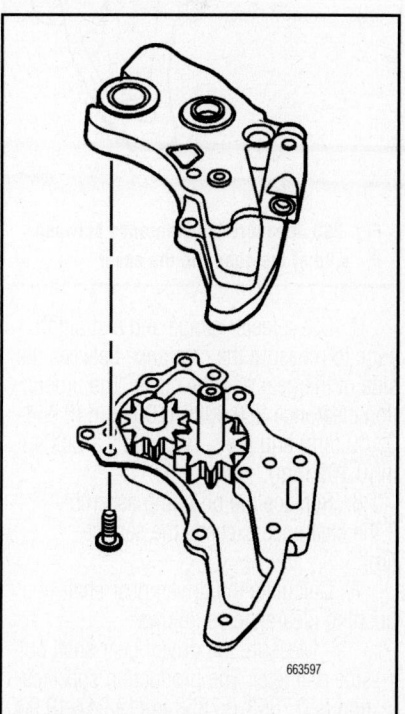

Fig. 278 Oil pump gear cover bolts and gear cover

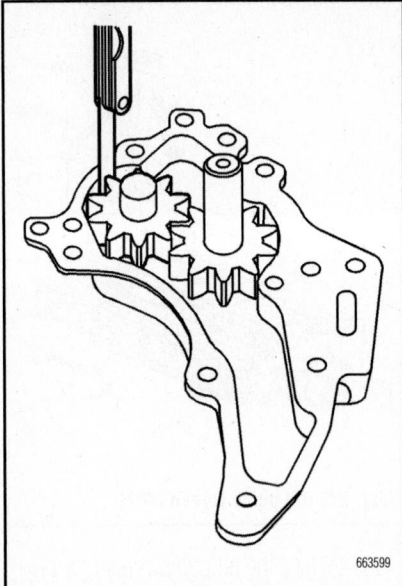

Fig. 279 Measure the clearance between the gear teeth and the oil pump housing

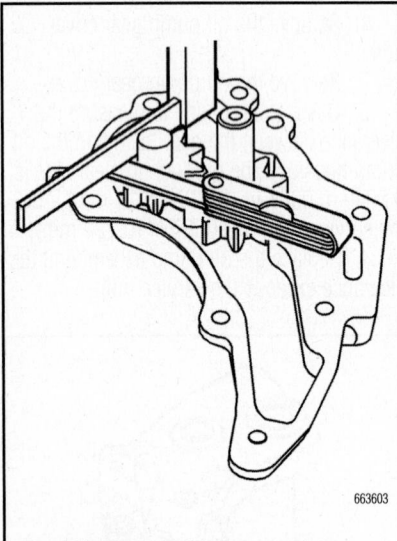

Fig. 280 Measure the clearance between the side of the gear and the cover

5. Use a feeler gauge and a straight-edge to measure the clearance between the side of the gear and the cover. The production clearance is 0.0025-0.0043 in (0.064-0.109 mm) and the service limit is 0.0043 in (0.109 mm).

6. Replace the oil pump assembly if the clearance exceeds the service limit.

7. Calculate the driven gear shaft-to-bushing clearance as follows:

   a. Measure the driven gear shaft outside diameter. The production specification is 0.7853-0.7858 in (19.947-19.960 mm) and the service limit is 0.7819 in (19.86 mm).

   b. Measure the driven gear bushing inside diameter. The production value is 0.7874 in (20 mm).

   c. Calculate the driven gear shaft to bushing clearance. The service limit is 0.0055 in (0.14 mm).

8. Replace the oil pump assembly if the clearance exceeds the service limit.

9. Install the oil pump gear cover to the oil pump assembly.

10. Install the oil pump gear cover bolts and tighten to 15 ft. lbs. (21 Nm).

REMOVAL & INSTALLATION

4.3L Engine

See Figures 281 and 282.

1. Remove the oil pan. Refer to Oil Pan.
2. Remove the oil pump bolt.
3. Remove the oil pump.
4. Inspect the oil pump locator pins for damage, and replace if required.
5. Clean and inspect the oil pump, if necessary.

To install:

6. Inspect for properly installed oil pump locator pins.

➡**Do not reuse the oil pump driveshaft retainer. During assembly, install a NEW oil pump driveshaft retainer.**

7. Install the oil pump. Position the oil pump onto the locator pins.

8. Install the oil pump bolt and tighten to 66 ft. lbs. (90 Nm).

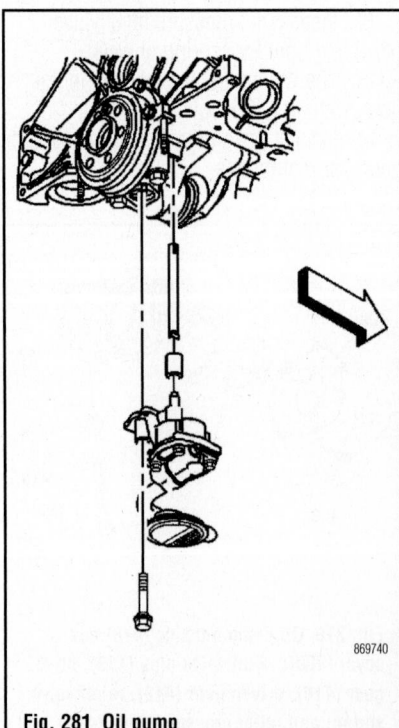

Fig. 281 Oil pump

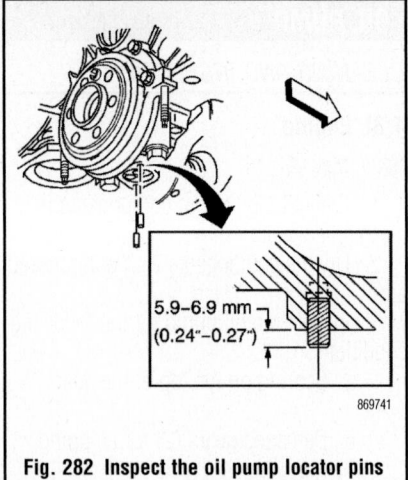

Fig. 282 Inspect the oil pump locator pins for damage, and replace if required

9. Install the oil pan. Refer to Oil Pan.

4.8L & 5.3L Engines

See Figures 283 and 285.

1. Remove the oil pan. Refer to Oil Pan.
2. Remove the engine front cover.
3. Remove the oil pump screen bolt (405) and nuts (404).
4. Remove the oil pump screen (407) with O-ring seal (406).
5. Remove the O-ring seal from the pump screen.
6. Discard the O-ring seal.
7. Remove the remaining crankshaft oil deflector nuts.
8. Remove the crankshaft oil deflector.
9. Remove the oil pump bolts (411).

➡**Do not allow dirt or debris to enter the oil pump assembly, cap end as necessary.**

10. Remove the oil pump (413).

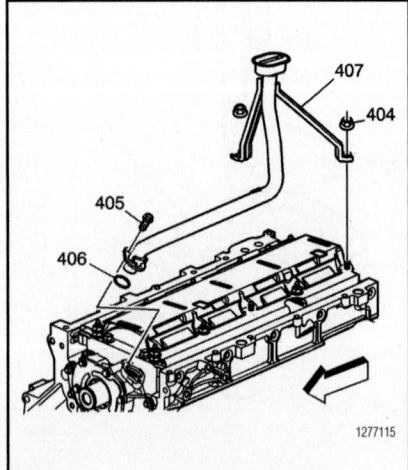

Fig. 283 Oil pump screen bolt (405, nuts (404), screen (407) and O-ring seal (406)

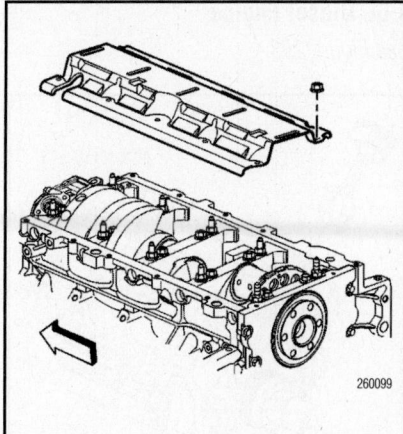

Fig. 284 Crankshaft oil deflector nuts and deflector

11. Clean and inspect the oil pump. Refer to Oil Pump Cleaning and Inspection.

To install:

12. Align the splined surfaces of the crankshaft sprocket and the oil pump drive gear and install the oil pump (413).

13. Install the oil pump onto the crankshaft sprocket until the pump housing contacts the face of the engine block.

14. Install the oil pump bolts (411) and tighten to 18 ft. lbs. (25 Nm).

15. Install the crankshaft oil deflector and nuts until snug.

16. Lubricate a NEW oil pump screen O-ring seal (406) with clean engine oil.

17. Install the NEW O-ring seal onto the oil pump screen.

➡**Push the oil pump screen tube completely into the oil pump prior to tightening the bolt. Do not allow the bolt to pull the tube into the pump.**

18. Align the oil pump screen mounting brackets with the correct crankshaft bearing cap studs.

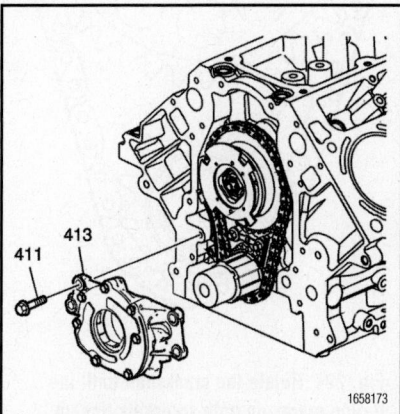

Fig. 285 Oil pump bolts (411) and pump (413),

19. Install the oil pump screen (407).

20. Install the oil pump screen bolt (405) and nuts (404).

21. Tighten the oil pump screen bolt to 106 inch lbs. (12 Nm).

22. Tighten the crankshaft oil deflector/oil pump screen nuts to 18 ft. lbs. (25 Nm).

23. Install the engine front cover.

24. Install the oil pan. Refer to Oil Pan.

6.6L Diesel Engine

See Figures 286 through 290.

1. Remove the upper oil pan. Refer to Oil Pan Removal and Installation—Upper.

2. Remove the engine front cover.

3. Remove the oil pump screen bolts and nuts (1).

4. Remove the oil pump screen.

5. Remove and discard the oil pump screen gasket.

6. Block the crankshaft from turning with a wooden handle.

➡**Look for an "L" on the end of the oil pump shaft. If there is an "L" present, the nut and shaft have left hand threads. Service the nut accordingly.**

7. While holding the secondary oil pump shaft with a hex driver, remove the oil pump driven gear nut.

8. Remove the oil pump driven gear.

➡**Do not damage the crankshaft reluctor. Do not remove the crankshaft reluctor to oil pump drive bolts.**

9. Remove the oil pump drive gear and crankshaft reluctor (1).

10. Use a brass drift.

11. Tap on the back of the reluctor, as close as possible to the center.

12. Remove the hex head and the Allen head bolt (1) in order to remove the oil pump (2).

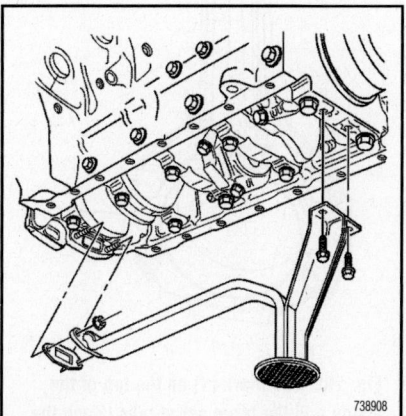

Fig. 286 Oil pump screen bolts and nuts (1)

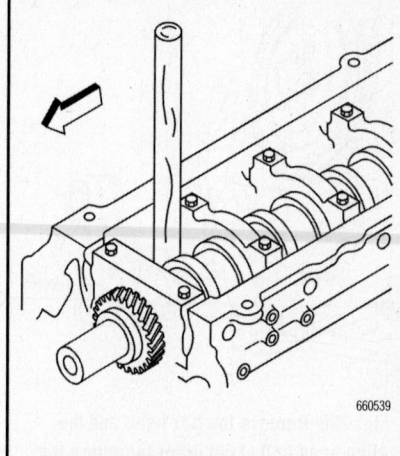

Fig. 287 Block the crankshaft from turning with a wooden handle

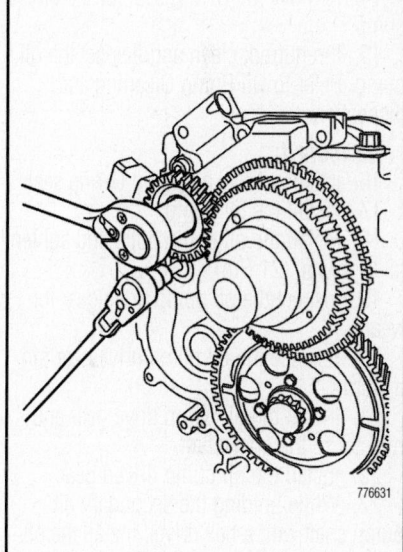

Fig. 288 While holding the secondary oil pump shaft with a hex driver, remove the oil pump driven gear nut

Fig. 289 Remove the oil pump drive gear and crankshaft reluctor (1)

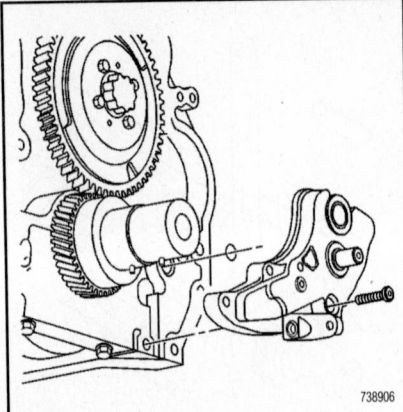

Fig. 290 Remove the hex head and the Allen head bolt (1) in order to remove the oil pump (2)

13. Remove the oil pump.

14. Remove the O-ring seal for the oil pump.

15. If required, clean and inspect the oil pump. Refer to Oil Pump Cleaning and Inspection.

To install:

16. Install a NEW oil pump O-ring seal.

17. Install the oil pump.

18. Install the oil pump bolts and tighten to 15 ft. lbs. (21 Nm).

19. Inspect the oil pump drive gear for wear.

20. Replace the oil pump drive gear pin if worn.

21. Install the oil pump drive gear and reluctor to the crankshaft.

22. Install the oil pump driven gear.

23. While holding the secondary oil pump shaft with a hex driver, install the oil pump driven gear nut and tighten to 74 ft. lbs. (100 Nm).

24. Remove the wooden handle that was used to retain the crankshaft.

25. Install a NEW oil pump screen gasket to the oil pump.

26. Install the oil pump screen.

27. Install the oil pump screen bolts and nuts and tighten to 18 ft. lbs. (25 Nm).

28. Install the engine front cover.

29. Install the upper oil pan.

PISTON AND RING

POSITIONING

4.3L Engine

See Figure 291.

➡When assembling, address the following reference marks: the reference mark on top of the piston (1) must face the front of the engine block. The dim-

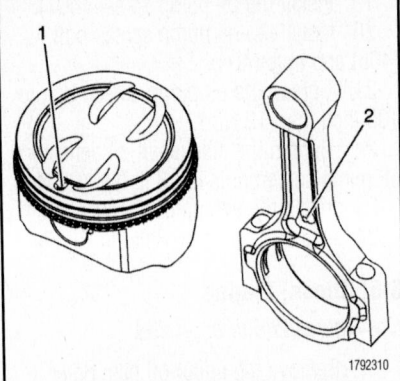

Fig. 291 The reference mark on top of the piston (1) must face the front of the engine block. The dimple on the connecting rod (2) must face the front of the engine block on cylinders 2, 4, and 6, and towards the rear of the engine block on cylinders 1, 3, and 5

ple on the connecting rod (2) must face the front of the engine block on cylinders 2, 4, and 6, and towards the rear of the engine block on cylinders 1, 3, and 5. Wrap a clean, lint free towel around the connecting rod ends when installing the piston into the cylinder so as not to damage the crankshaft journals or cylinder bore.

4.8L & 5.3L Engines

See Figure 292.

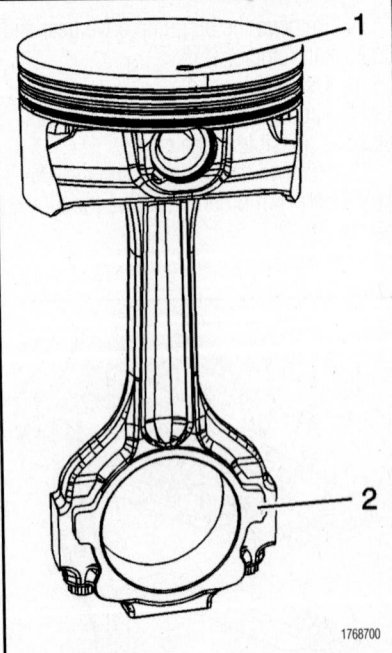

Fig. 292 The mark (1) on the top of the piston and the large set of tabs (2) on the side of the connecting rod should be facing the same direction

6.6L Diesel Engine

See Figure 293.

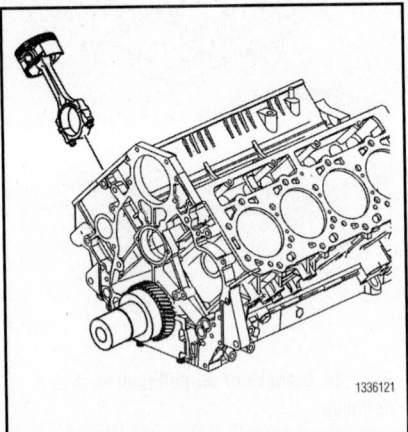

Fig. 293 Orient the piston front mark and the piston inside mark to the engine block

TIMING CHAIN, SPROCKET AND TENSIONER

REMOVAL & INSTALLATION

4.3L Engine

See Figures 294 through 299.

1. Remove the Crankshaft Position (CKP) sensor reluctor ring.

2. Install a 7/16-20 x 1 inch bolt into the end of the crankshaft.

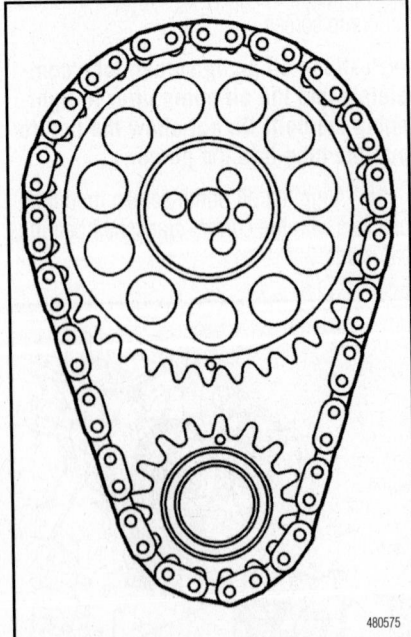

Fig. 294 Rotate the crankshaft until the timing marks on both sprockets line up and the number 4 cylinder is at Top Dead Center (TDC) of the compression stroke.

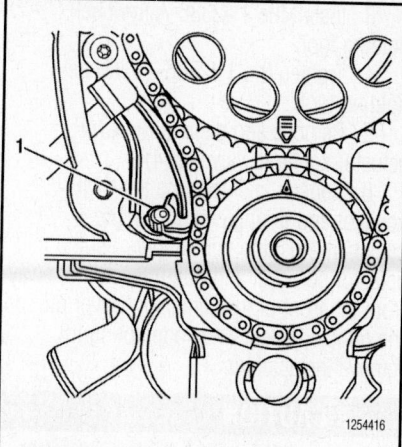

Fig. 295 Unsnap the timing chain tensioner shoe from the pin (1)

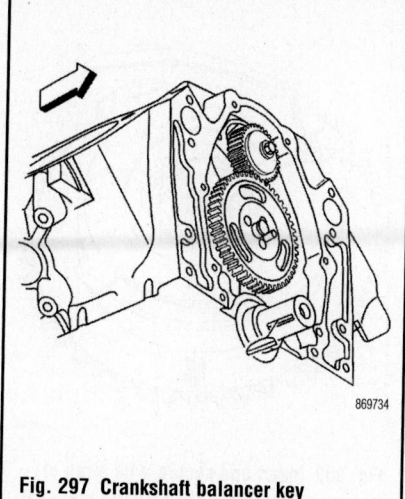

Fig. 297 Crankshaft balancer key

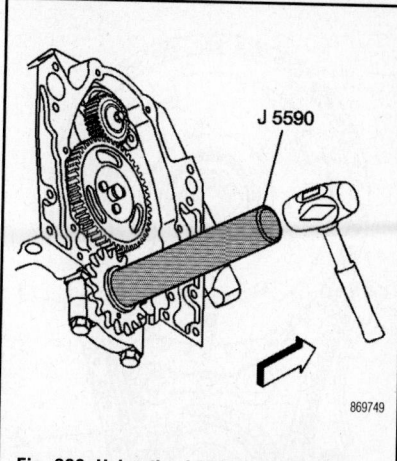

Fig. 299 Using the J 5590 bearing and seal driver, install the crankshaft sprocket

❋❋ WARNING

Align the timing marks before removing the timing chain. If it is necessary to turn either the camshaft or the crankshaft with the timing chain removed, loosen or remove the valve rocker arms. Turning either the crankshaft or camshaft with the timing chain removed may cause the pistons to contact the valves, resulting in damage.

3. Rotate the crankshaft until:
   a. The timing marks on both sprockets line up.
   b. The number 4 cylinder is at Top Dead Center (TDC) of the compression stroke.
4. Unsnap the timing chain tensioner shoe from the pin (1).
5. Remove the camshaft sprocket bolts.

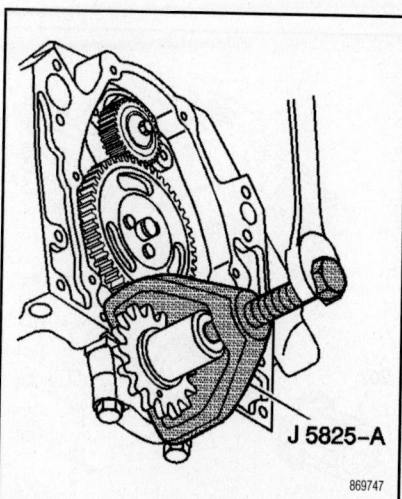

Fig. 296 Using the J 5825-A crankshaft gear remover and an open end wrench, remove the crankshaft sprocket

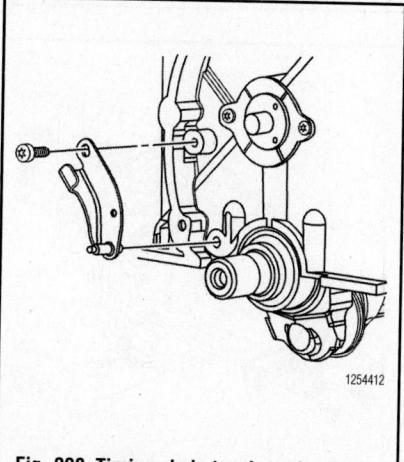

Fig. 298 Timing chain tensioner bracket bolt and bracket

6. Remove the camshaft sprocket and the camshaft timing chain.
7. Using the J 5825-A crankshaft gear remover and an open end wrench, remove the crankshaft sprocket.
8. Remove the crankshaft balancer key.
9. If necessary, remove the timing chain tensioner bracket bolt and bracket.
10. Clean and inspect the timing chain and sprockets, if necessary.

To install:
11. If necessary, install the timing chain tensioner bracket and bolt and tighten the bolt to 106 inch lbs. (12 Nm).
12. Install the key into the crankshaft keyway.
13. The crankshaft balancer key should be parallel to the crankshaft or with a slight incline.
14. Align the keyway of the crankshaft sprocket with the crankshaft balancer key.
15. Using the J 5590 bearing and seal driver, install the crankshaft sprocket.

➡**Install the camshaft sprocket with the alignment mark at the 6 o'clock position.**

16. Install the camshaft sprocket and the camshaft timing chain. Wrap the timing chain around the crankshaft sprocket and position to the driver side of the engine.
17. Install the timing chain tensioner shoe onto the bracket and position the top of the shoe under the tab at the top of the bracket.
18. Insert the camshaft timing chain sprocket into the timing chain and position so when the camshaft timing chain sprocket is installed on the camshaft, the camshaft timing marks will line up.

➡**Do not use a hammer to install the camshaft sprocket onto the camshaft. To do so may dislodge the expansion cup plug.**

19. Install the camshaft sprocket bolts and tighten to 18 ft. lbs. (25 Nm).
20. Ensure that the crankshaft sprocket is aligned at the 12 o'clock position and camshaft sprocket is aligned at the 6 o'clock position.
21. Remove the bolt that you installed in the end of the crankshaft.
22. Install the CKP sensor reluctor ring.

4.8L & 5.3L Engines
See Figures 300 through 311.

1. Remove the oil pump.

➡**Ensure that the teeth of the J 42386-A flywheel holding tool align.**

2. Rotate the crankshaft sprocket until you align the Camshaft Position (CMP) actuator alignment mark (1) with the crankshaft sprocket alignment mark (2).

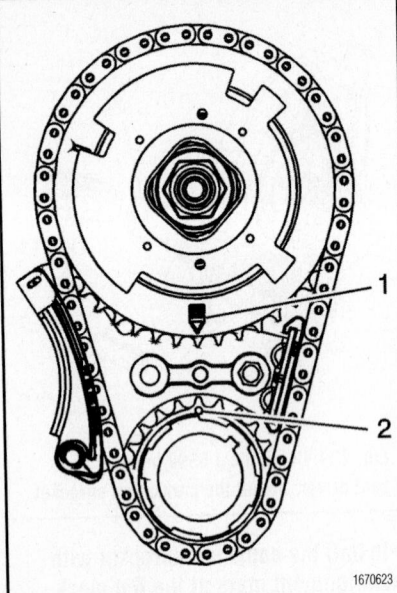

Fig. 300 Rotate the crankshaft sprocket until you align the Camshaft Position (CMP) actuator alignment mark (1) with the crankshaft sprocket alignment mark (2).

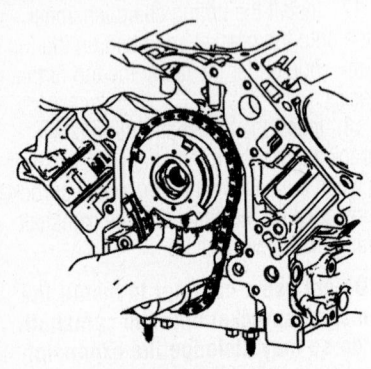

Fig. 301 Loosen and separate the CMP actuator and timing chain from the camshaft. Position your fingers behind the actuator sprocket and pull the actuator away from the front of the camshaft. Never pull on the reluctor wheel when attempting to remove the actuator

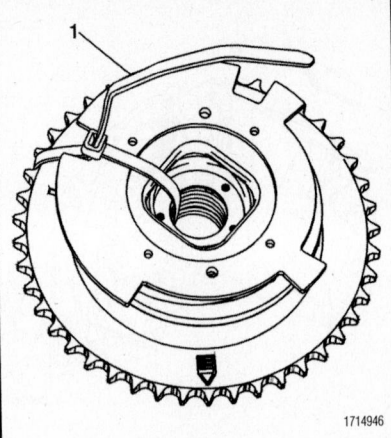

Fig. 302 Insert and secure a tie strap (1) through the center of the actuator and over the reluctor wheel

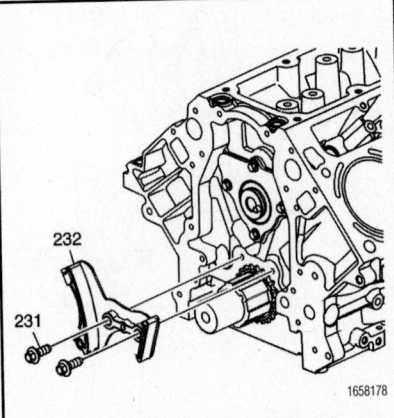

Fig. 303 Timing chain tension bolts (231) and tensioner (232)

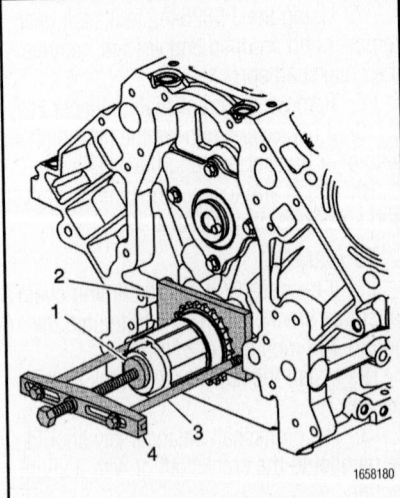

Fig. 304 Use the J 41816-2 (1), the J 41558 (2), bolts (3) and the J 8433 (4) to remove the crankshaft sprocket

3. Install the J 42386-A flywheel holding tool.

4. Tighten the J 42386-A flywheel holding tool.

5. Remove and discard the CMP actuator solenoid valve (234).

6. Loosen and separate the CMP actuator and timing chain from the camshaft. Position your fingers behind the actuator sprocket and pull the actuator away from the front of the camshaft. Never pull on the reluctor wheel when attempting to remove the actuator.

✳✳ CAUTION

Do not turn the crankshaft assembly after the timing chain has been removed in order to prevent damage to the piston assemblies or the valves.

7. Remove the CMP actuator and timing chain.

8. Insert and secure a tie strap (1) through the center of the actuator and over the reluctor wheel.

9. Remove the timing chain tension bolts (231) and tensioner (232).

10. Use the J 41816-2 (1), the J 41558 (2), bolts (3) and the J 8433 (4) to remove the crankshaft sprocket.

11. Remove the crankshaft sprocket (207).

12. Remove the crankshaft sprocket key, if required.

To install:

13. Install the key into the crankshaft keyway, if previously removed.

14. Tap the key into the keyway until both ends of the key bottom onto the crankshaft.

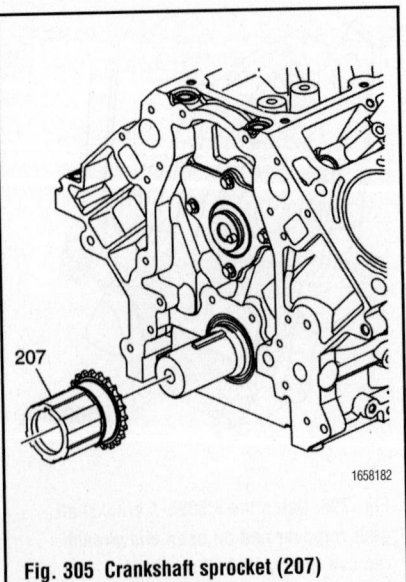

Fig. 305 Crankshaft sprocket (207)

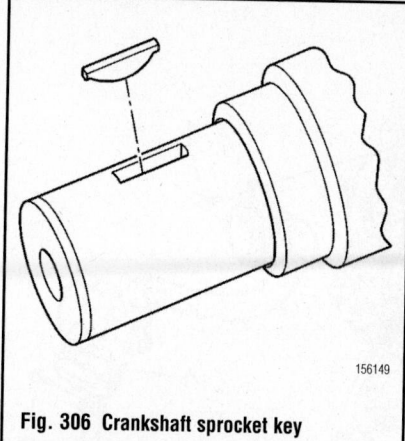

Fig. 306 Crankshaft sprocket key

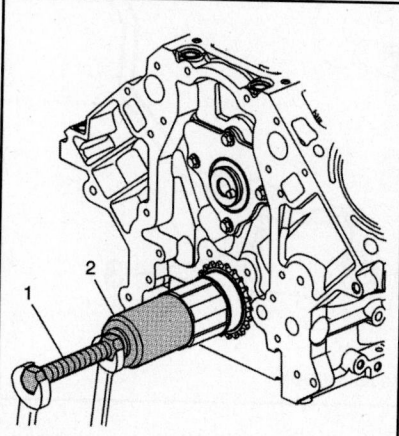

Fig. 307 Use the J 41478 (1) and the J 41665 (2) to install the crankshaft sprocket. Install the sprocket onto the crankshaft until it seats fully against the crankshaft flange

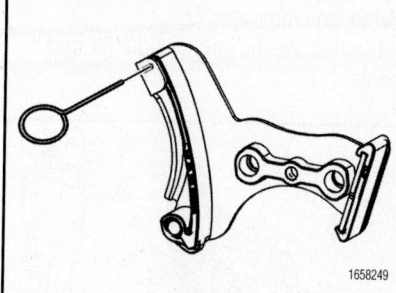

Fig. 308 Compress the timing chain tensioner guide and install the EN 46330 (timing belt tensioner retaining pin)

15. Install the crankshaft sprocket onto the front of the crankshaft. Align the crankshaft key with the crankshaft sprocket keyway.

16. Use the J 41478 (1) and the J 41665 (2) to install the crankshaft sprocket. Install

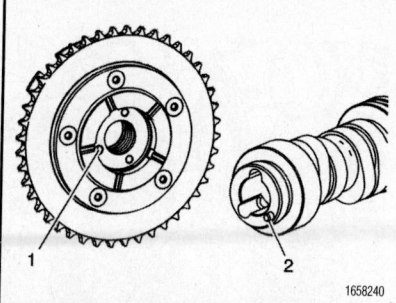

Fig. 309 Identify the alignment hole (1) in the rear face of the CMP actuator and the locating pin (2) on the front face of the camshaft

the sprocket onto the crankshaft until it seats fully against the crankshaft flange.

17. Compress the timing chain tensioner guide and install the EN 46330 (timing belt tensioner retaining pin).

18. Install the timing chain tensioner and bolts.

19. Tighten the bolts to 18 ft. lbs. (25 Nm).

➡**Note the following:**

- Properly locate the CMP actuator onto the locating pin of the camshaft.
- The sprocket teeth and timing chain teeth must mesh.
- The camshaft and the crankshaft sprocket alignment MUST be aligned properly.
- Do not use the CMP solenoid valve again. Install a NEW CMP valve during assembly.

20. Identify the alignment hole (1) in the rear face of the CMP actuator and the locating pin (2) on the front face of the camshaft.

21. Align the CMP actuator so the timing mark is in the 6 o'clock position.

22. Install the CMP actuator and timing chain. Align the hole in the face of the CMP actuator with the locating pin on the front face of the camshaft.

✳✳ CAUTION

Do not push or pull on the reluctor wheel of the Camshaft Position (CMP) actuator during removal or installation. The reluctor wheel is retained to the front of the CMP actuator by 3 roll pins. Pushing or pulling on the wheel may dislodge the wheel from the front of the actuator. The actuator return spring is under tension and may rotate the dislodged reluctor wheel, causing personal injury.

Fig. 310 Install the actuator

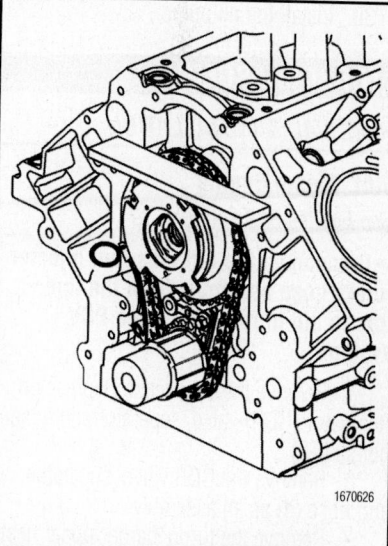

Fig. 311 Inspect for proper installation of the CMP actuator and timing chain

23. Use care to install the actuator completely onto the front of the camshaft. Position your fingers onto the face of the actuator sprocket and push the actuator onto the front of the camshaft. Never push on the reluctor wheel when attempting to install the actuator. The actuator return

spring is under tension and may rotate the dislodged reluctor wheel, causing personal injury.

24. Place a straight edge across the front face of the engine block and inspect for proper installation of the CMP actuator and timing chain. With the CMP actuator properly and completely installed onto the front of the camshaft, the timing chain will not protrude beyond the front face of the engine block.

25. Install a NEW CMP actuator valve. With the CMP actuator properly positioned onto the camshaft, the CMP actuator solenoid valve can be threaded completely into the camshaft using light hand pressure. Tighten by hand until snug.

26. Inspect the sprockets for proper alignment. The mark on the CMP actuator sprocket should be located in the 6 o'clock position and the mark on the crankshaft sprocket should be located in the 12 o'clock position.

27. Remove the EN 46330 (timing belt tensioner retaining pin).

28. Tighten the CMP actuator bolt.

   a. Tighten the bolt a first pass to 48 ft. lbs. (65 Nm).

   b. Tighten the bolt a final pass an additional 90 degrees using J 45059 (angle meter)

29. Remove the J 42386-A flywheel holding tool.

30. Install the oil pump.

TURBOCHARGER

REMOVAL & INSTALLATION

6.6L Diesel Engine

See Figures 312 through 319.

➡**Disconnect the left side fuel injector return hose assembly from the injectors to aid in removal of the PCV system.**

1. Remove the Crankcase Depression Regulator (CDR) valve, separator and hose bolts (1–3).

2. Remove the CDR valve, separator and hose (4) as an assembly.

3. Remove the turbocharger upper heat shield bolts (1).

4. Remove the turbocharger upper heat shield (2).

5. Remove the eye bolt (1) and washers (2) from the turbocharger oil feed pipe.

➡**Use care not to damage this hose during the procedure.**

6. Remove the turbocharger cooling return pipe bolts (3) and (4).

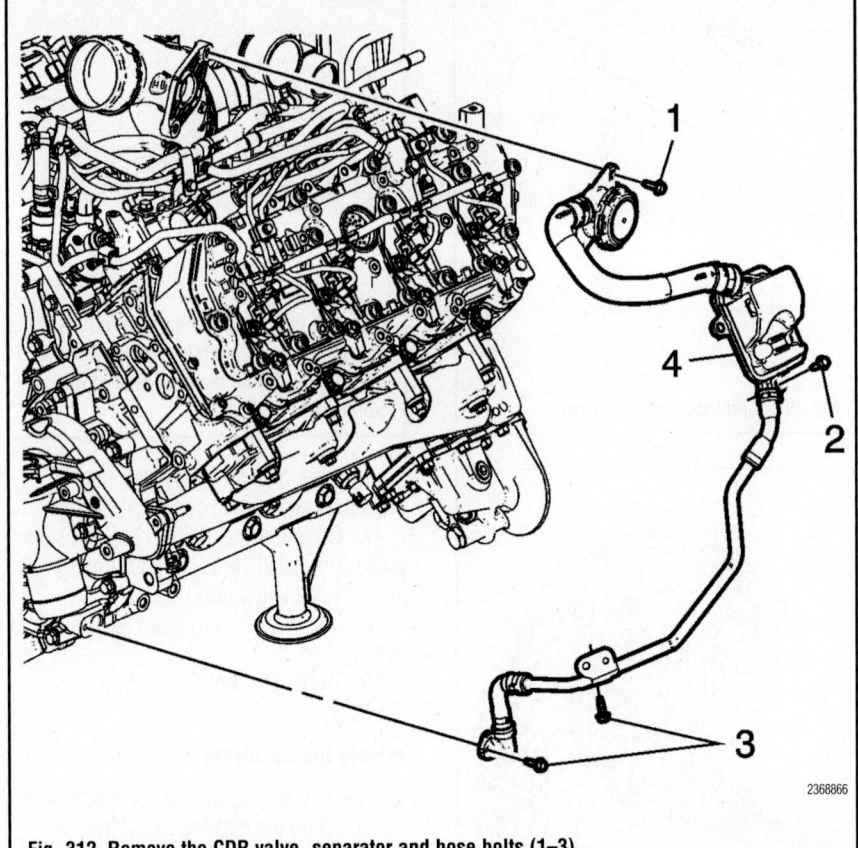

Fig. 312 Remove the CDR valve, separator and hose bolts (1–3).

7. Remove the turbocharger cooling return pipe (2) and the turbocharger cooling return hose (1).

8. Remove the turbocharger cooling feed pipe bolt (4).

9. Remove the turbocharger cooling feed pipe (2) and the turbocharger cooling feed tubes (1) and (3).

10. Remove the turbocharger mounting bolts (1).

11. Remove the turbocharger cooling return pipe bolt (3).

12. Remove the turbocharger assembly (2) with the oil feed pipe, oil return pipe and cooling return pipe.

13. Remove the turbocharger lower heat shield (1).

14. Remove the oil feed pipe eye bolt (1) and washers (2).

15. Remove the oil feed pipe (3).

16. Loosen the turbocharger air inlet adapter holding clamp (2).

17. Remove the turbocharger air inlet adapter (1).

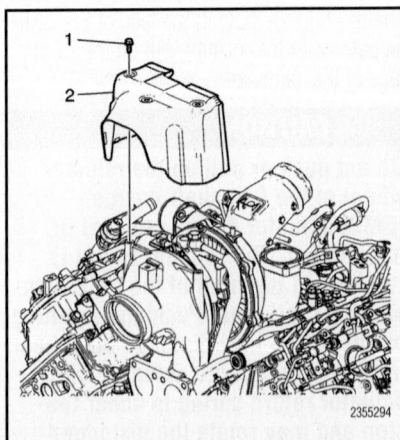

Fig. 313 Turbocharger upper heat shield bolts (1) and shield (2)

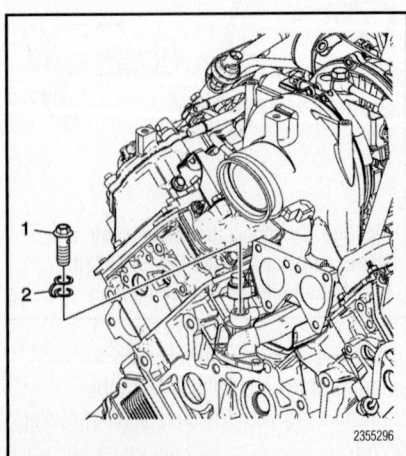

Fig. 314 Turbocharger oil feed pipe eye bolt (1) and washers (2)

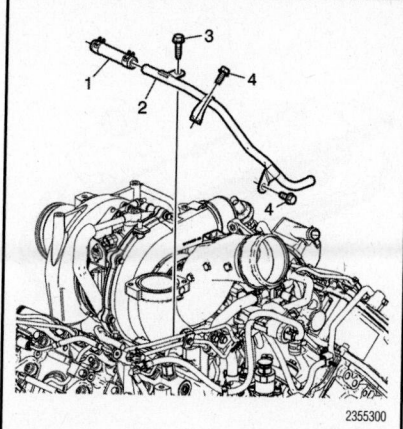

Fig. 315 Turbocharger cooling return pipe bolts (3, 4), return pipe (2) and return hose (1)

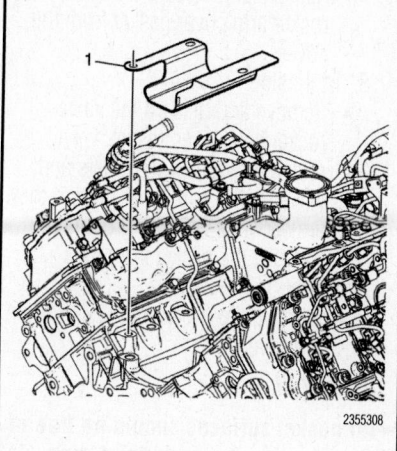

Fig. 317 Turbocharger lower heat shield (1)

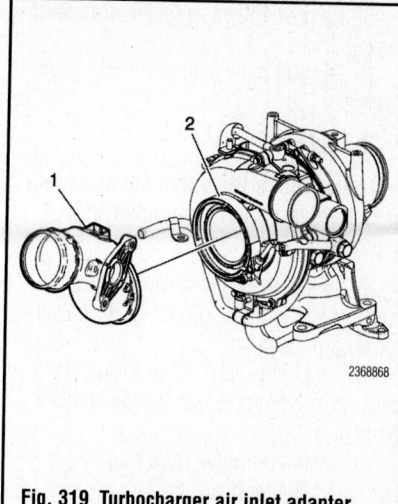

Fig. 319 Turbocharger air inlet adapter holding clamp (2) and adapter (1)

To install:

18. Install the turbocharger air inlet adapter.

19. Tighten the turbocharger air inlet adapter holding clamp to 11 ft. lbs. (15 Nm).

20. Install the turbocharger oil feed pipe.

21. Install the turbocharger oil feed pipe eye bolt and washers. Tighten the eye bolt to 19 ft. lbs. (26 Nm).

22. Install the turbocharger lower heat shield.

23. Install the turbocharger assembly with the oil feed pipe, oil return pipe and cooling return pipe.

24. Install the turbocharger mounting bolts and tighten to 58 ft. lbs. (79 Nm).

25. Install the turbocharger cooling return pipe bolt and tighten to 18 ft. lbs. (25 Nm).

26. Install the turbocharger cooling feed pipe and the turbocharger cooling feed tubes.

27. Install the turbocharger cooling feed pipe bolt and tighten to 18 ft. lbs. (25 Nm).

28. Install the turbocharger cooling return pipe and the turbocharger cooling return hose.

29. Install the turbocharger cooling return pipe bolt and tighten to 18 ft. lbs. (25 Nm).

➡**Lubricate the washers with diesel fuel before installing.**

30. Install the turbocharger oil feed pipe eye bolt and washers. Tighten the eye bolt to 19 ft. lbs. (26 Nm).

31. Install the turbocharger heat shield.

32. Install the turbocharger upper heat shield bolts and tighten to 89 inch lbs. (10 Nm)

➡**Disconnect the left side fuel injector return hose assembly from the injectors to aid in removal of the PCV system.**

33. Install the CDR valve, separator and hose as an assembly.

34. Install the CDR valve, separator and hose bolts and tighten to 89 inch lbs. (10 Nm)

VALVE ROCKER ARM COVERS

REMOVAL & INSTALLATION

4.3L Engine

See Figure 320.

1. Remove the valve rocker arm cover bolts.

2. Remove and discard the valve rocker arm cover gasket, valve rocker arm cover grommets and valve rocker arm cover bolts if they are serviced with the grommet.

3. Remove and discard the valve rocker arm cover bolt grommets.

4. Remove the valve rocker arm cover.

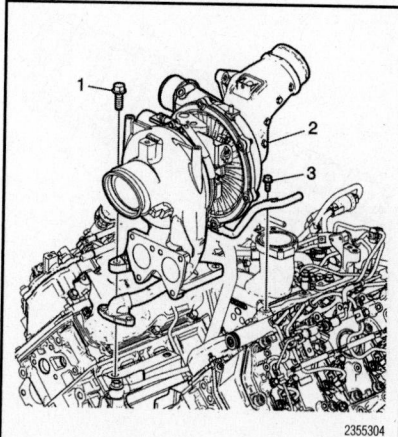

Fig. 316 Turbocharger cooling feed pipe bolt (4), feed pipe (2), and feed tubes (1, 3)

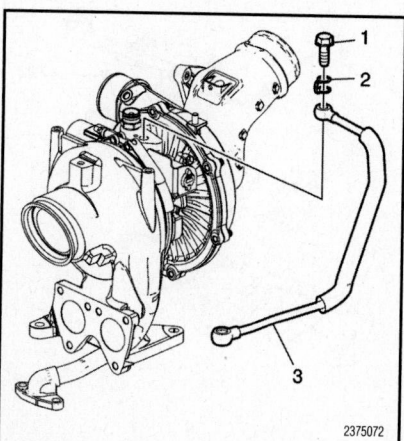

Fig. 318 Remove the oil feed pipe eye bolt (1), washers (2), and pipe (3)

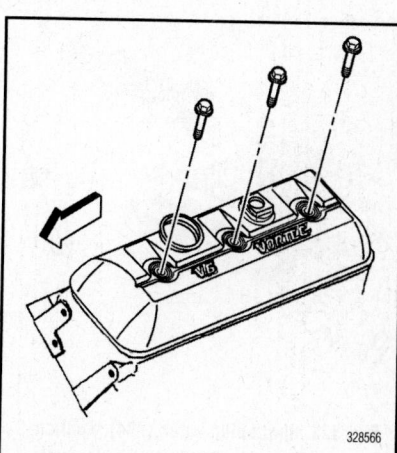

Fig. 320 Valve rocker arm cover bolts—left side shown, right side similar

5. Remove the valve rocker arm cover gasket.

6. Discard the valve rocker arm cover gasket.

To install:

➡**Do not reuse the valve cover gasket or the valve rocker arm cover bolt grommets.**

7. Install the NEW valve rocker arm cover gasket into the groove of the valve rocker arm cover.

8. Install the NEW valve rocker arm cover bolt grommets into the valve rocker arm cover.

9. Install the valve rocker arm cover onto the cylinder head.

10. Install the valve rocker arm cover bolts and tighten to 106 inch lbs. (12 Nm).

4.8L & 5.3L Engines

See Figures 321 through 323.

1. Remove the spark plug wires (724).

2. Remove the ignition coil bracket studs (720).

3. Remove the ignition coil and bracket assembly (719).

4. Disconnect the ignition coil electrical connectors.

5. Remove the bolts (723), coils (722), and wire harness (721) from the bracket (719), as required.

6. Remove the valve rocker arm cover bolts and cover.

7. Left side:
- If the valve rocker arm cover grommets are cracked or damaged, replace the valve rocker arm cover bolts. The grommet is serviced with the rocker arm cover bolt.

- Remove and discard the valve rocker arm cover gasket from the cover.

8. Right side:
- Remove and discard the valve rocker arm cover gasket, valve rocker arm cover grommets and valve rocker arm cover bolts if they are serviced with the grommet.
- Remove the gasket from the cover.
- Remove the grommet (423) from the cover.

To install:

➡**All gasket surfaces should be free of oil or other foreign material during assembly. DO NOT use the valve rocker arm cover gasket again.**

9. Install NEW valve rocker arm cover grommets and use NEW valve rocker arm cover bolts if they are serviced with the grommet.

10. Install a NEW gasket into the valve rocker arm cover.

11. Install the valve rocker arm cover onto the cylinder head.

12. Install the cover bolts with grommets and tighten to 106 inch lbs. (12 Nm).

➡**GM specifies GM P/N 12345382 (Canadian P/N 10953489), or equivalent for thread lock for this procedure.**

13. Apply thread lock to the threads of the ignition coil bolts.

14. Install the ignition coils, wire harness, and bolts to the bracket. Tighten the ignition coil bolts to 89 inch lbs. (10 Nm)

15. Apply thread lock to the threads of the ignition coil bracket studs.

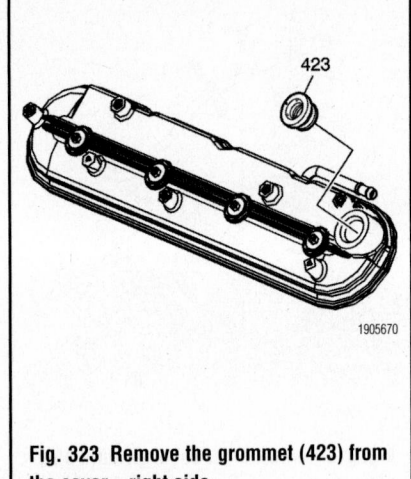

Fig. 323 Remove the grommet (423) from the cover—right side

16. Install the ignition coil and bracket assembly and studs. Tighten the bracket studs to 106 inch lbs. (12 Nm).

6.6L Engine

Lower

See Figures 324 through 326.

1. Remove the lower valve rocker arm cover bolts.

2. Remove the lower valve rocker arm covers.

3. Remove and discard the valve rocker arm cover gasket, valve rocker arm cover grommets and valve rocker arm cover bolts if they are serviced with the grommet.

To install:

4. Install NEW valve rocker arm cover grommets and use NEW valve rocker arm cover bolts if they are serviced with the grommet.

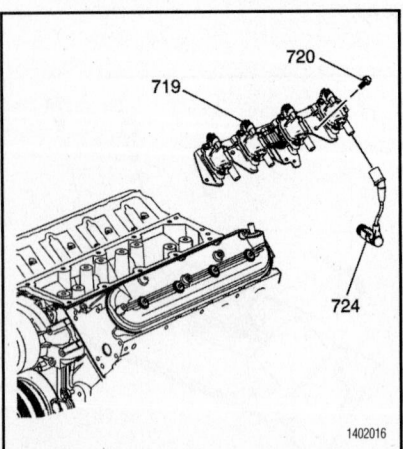

Fig. 321 Spark plug wires (724), ignition coil bracket studs (720) and ignition coil and bracket assembly (719)—left side shown, right side similar

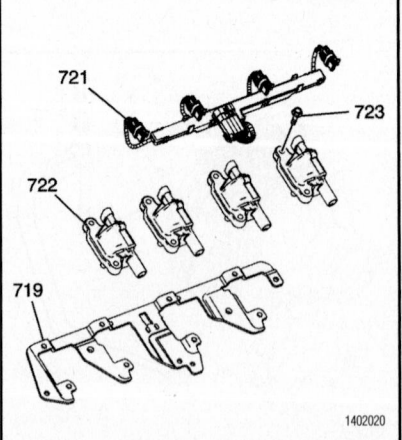

Fig. 322 Bracket bolts (723), coils (722), wire harness (721), and bracket (719)—left side shown, right side similar

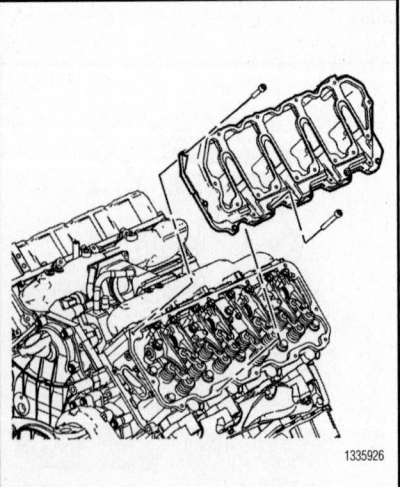

Fig. 324 Left lower valve rocker arm cover and bolts—right side similar

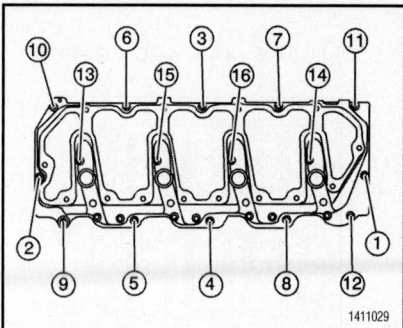

Fig. 325 Tighten the lower valve rocker arm cover bolts in the proper sequence

➡**You may reuse the gasket if it is not torn, cracked, stretched, or swollen.**

5. Install the lower valve rocker arm cover.

6. Install the lower valve rocker arm cover bolts:

    a. Tighten the lower valve rocker arm cover bolts in the proper sequence to 89 inch lbs. (10 Nm)

    b. Retighten the lower valve rocker arm cover bolts in the proper sequence to the same torque, 89 inch lbs. (10 Nm).

Upper

See Figures 326 through 329.

1. Remove the upper valve rocker arm cover bolts.

2. Remove the upper valve rocker arm covers.

3. Remove and discard the valve rocker arm cover gasket, valve rocker arm cover grommets and valve rocker arm cover bolts if they are serviced with the grommet.

4. Install the NEW valve rocker arm cover gasket (1).

To install:

5. Install the NEW valve rocker arm cover gasket (1).

6. Install the NEW valve rocker arm cover grommets (3).

7. Install the upper valve rocker arm cover (2).

8. Install the upper valve rocker arm cover bolts (4).

9. Tighten the upper valve rocker arm cover bolts in sequence to 89 inch lbs. (10 Nm).

VALVE LASH

ADJUSTMENT

4.3L, 4.8L & 5.3L Engines

Valve lash is net build, no valve adjustment is required.

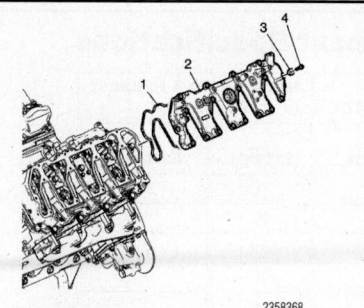

Fig. 326 Valve rocker arm cover gasket (1), grommets (3), cover (2), and bolts (4)—left side

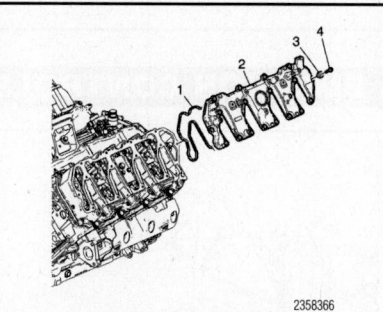

Fig. 327 Valve rocker arm cover gasket (1), grommets (3), cover (2), and bolts (4)—right side

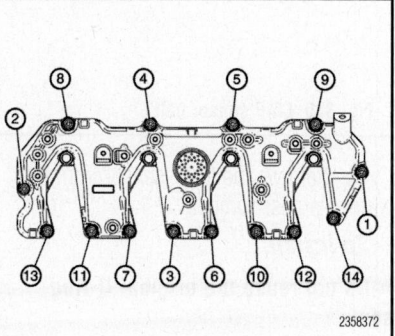

Fig. 328 Tighten the upper valve rocker arm cover bolts in sequence—left side

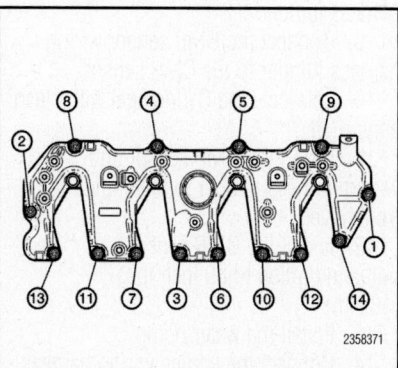

Fig. 329 Tighten the upper valve rocker arm cover bolts in sequence—right side

6.6L Diesel Engine

See Figures 330 through 333.

1. Rotate the crankshaft to bring the number 1 cylinder at the top dead center of the compression stroke.

2. The number 1 cylinder is the front cylinder on the right bank. Align the mark on the crankshaft balancer with the mark on the engine.

3. Loosen the valve adjusting screws.

4. Insert a feeler gauge between the tip of the rocker arm and the valve bridge.

5. Adjust the valve lash to 0.012 in (0.3 mm). Refer to the valve clearance adjustment specifications to determine which valves that can be adjusted when the engine is at Top Dead Center. Tighten the valve lash lock nut to 16 ft. lbs. (22 Nm).

6. Rotate the crankshaft one revolution to bring the number 1 cylinder at Top Dead Center of the exhaust stroke.

7. Adjust the valve lash to 0.012 in (0.3 mm). Refer to the valve clearance adjustment specifications to determine which valves that can be adjusted when the engine is at Top Dead Center. Tighten the valve lash lock nut to 16 ft. lbs. (22 Nm).

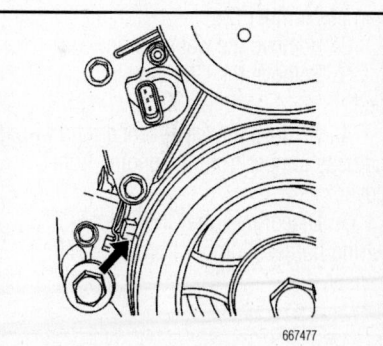

Fig. 330 Rotate the crankshaft to bring the number 1 cylinder at the top dead center of the compression stroke

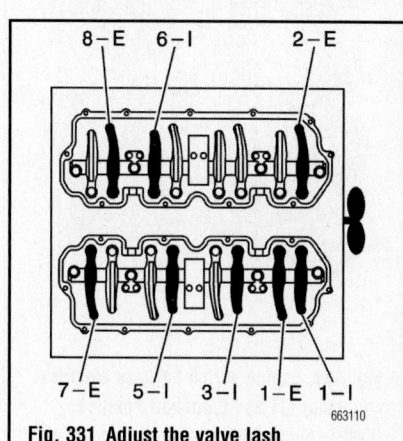

Fig. 331 Adjust the valve lash

Valve Clearance Adjustment Specifications

Cylinder		Adjust at No 1 Compression Stroke TDC		Adjust at No 1 Exhaust Stroke TDC	
Left Bank	Right Bank	Intake	Exhaust	Intake	Exhaust
--	1	X	X	--	--
2	--	--	X	X	--
--	3	X	--	--	X
4	--	--	--	X	X
--	5	X	--	--	X
6	--	X	--	--	X
--	7	--	X	X	--
8	--	--	X	X	--

25742_EXPR_G0001

Fig. 332 Valve clearance adjustment specifications

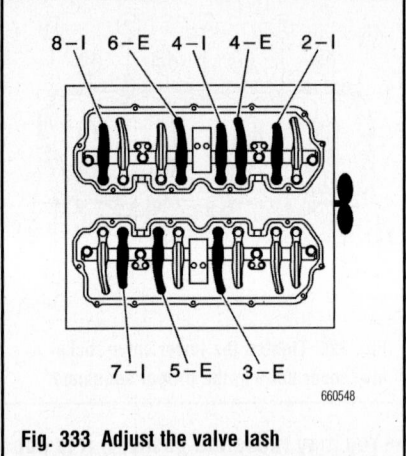

8–I 6–E 4–I 4–E 2–I

7–I 5–E 3–E

660548

Fig. 333 Adjust the valve lash

ENGINE PERFORMANCE & EMISSION CONTROLS

CAMSHAFT POSITION (CMP) SENSOR

REMOVAL & INSTALLATION

4.3L Engine

See Figures 334 and 335.

1. Disconnect the engine wiring harness electrical connector (1) from the Camshaft Position (CMP) sensor wiring harness jumper (2).
2. Remove the water pump.
3. Remove the CMP sensor bolt.
4. Remove the CMP sensor and wiring harness jumper from the engine front cover.
5. Disconnect the CMP sensor wiring harness jumper from the CMP sensor.

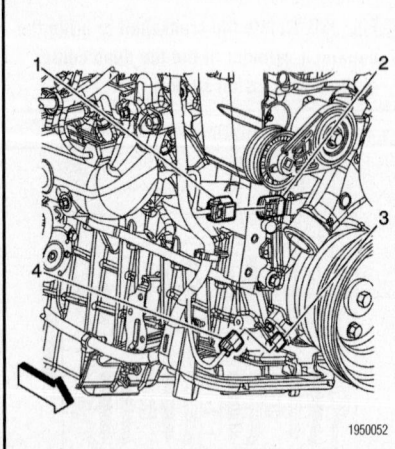

Fig. 334 Engine wiring harness electrical connector (1) and Camshaft Position (CMP) sensor wiring harness jumper (2)

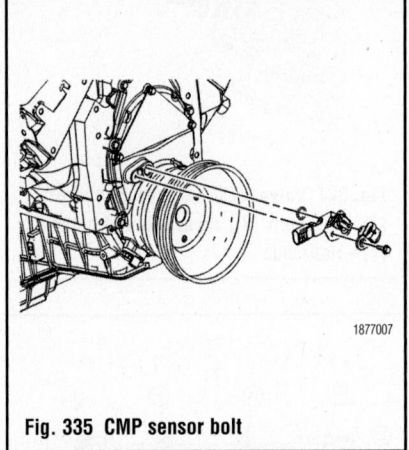

1877007

Fig. 335 CMP sensor bolt

6. Remove the CMP sensor from the wiring harness jumper.

To install:

→**Do not reuse the original O-ring seal.**

7. If you are reinstalling the old CMP sensor, install a NEW O-ring seal onto the sensor.
8. Install the CMP sensor to the wiring harness jumper.
9. Connect the CMP sensor wiring harness jumper to the CMP sensor.
10. Lubricate the O-ring seal with clean engine oil.
11. Install the CMP sensor and wiring harness jumper to the engine front cover.
12. Install the CMP sensor bolt and tighten to 89 inch lbs. (10 Nm).
13. Install the water pump.
14. Connect the engine wiring harness electrical connector (1) to the CMP sensor wiring harness jumper (2).

4.8L & 5.3L Engines

See Figures 336 through 338.

→**Clean the area around the Camshaft Position (CMP) sensor before removal in order to prevent debris from entering the engine.**

1. Raise and support the vehicle.
2. Disconnect the engine wiring harness electrical connector (1) from the CMP sensor wire harness.
3. Remove the 3 CMP sensor wire harness bolts (738).
4. Disconnect the CMP sensor wire harness electrical connectors from the CMP sensor and the CMP actuator magnet.
5. Remove the CMP sensor wire harness (737).
6. Remove the CMP sensor (703) and O-ring seal (704).

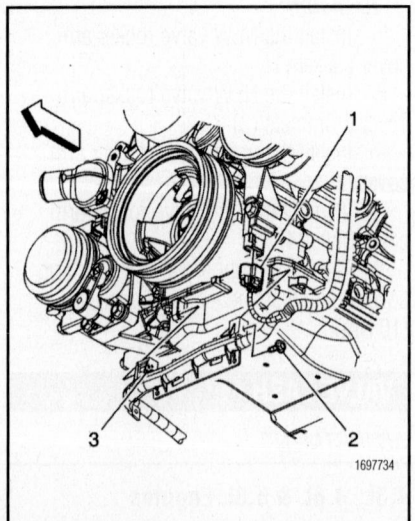

1697734

Fig. 336 Engine wiring harness electrical connector (1)

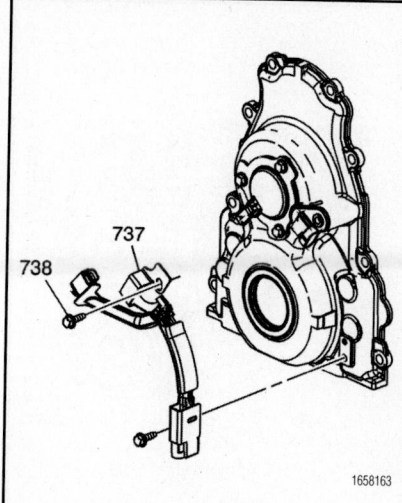

Fig. 337 The 3 CMP sensor wire harness bolts (738) and harness (737)

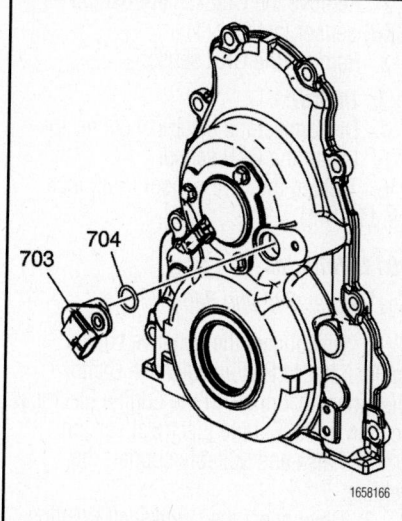

Fig. 338 CMP sensor (703) and O-ring seal (704)

To install:

7. Inspect the CMP O-ring seal for cuts or damage. If the seal is not cut or damaged, it may be used again.

8. Lubricate the O-ring seal with clean engine oil.

9. Install the O-ring seal (704) onto the sensor.

10. Install the CMP sensor (703) to the front cover.

11. Install the CMP sensor wire harness (737).

12. Connect the CMP sensor wire harness electrical connectors to the CMP sensor and the CMP actuator magnet.

13. Install the 3 CMP sensor wire harness bolts (738). Tighten the bolts to 106 inch lbs. (12 Nm).

14. Connect the engine wiring harness electrical connector (1) to the CMP sensor wire harness.

15. Lower the vehicle.

6.6L Diesel Engine

See Figure 339.

1. Disconnect the negative battery cable. Refer to Battery Negative Cable Disconnect/Connect in the Engine Electrical section.

2. Remove the radiator fan and clutch.

3. Remove the Camshaft Position (CMP) sensor electrical connector (1).

4. Remove the Camshaft Position (CMP) sensor bolt (2).

5. Remove the Camshaft Position (CMP) sensor (3).

To install:

6. Lubricate the Camshaft Position (CMP) sensor O-ring with engine oil prior to installation.

7. Install the Camshaft Position (CMP) sensor.

8. Install the Camshaft Position (CMP) sensor bolt; tighten to 89 inch lbs. (10 Nm)

9. Install the Camshaft Position (CMP) sensor electrical connector.

CRANKSHAFT POSITION (CKP) SENSOR

REMOVAL & INSTALLATION

4.3L Engine

See Figures 340 and 341.

1. Raise and suitably support the vehicle.

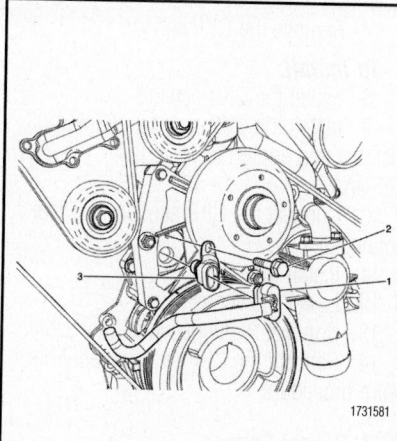

Fig. 339 Camshaft Position (CMP) sensor electrical connector (1)

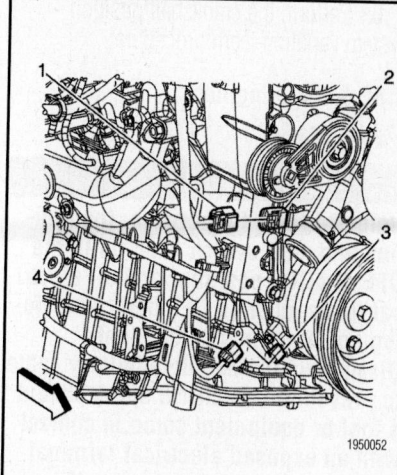

Fig. 340 Engine wiring harness electrical connector (4) and Crankshaft Position (CKP) sensor (3)

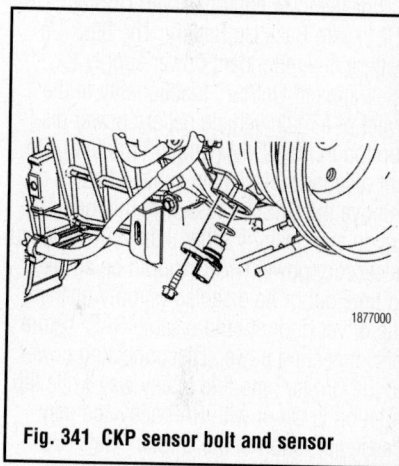

Fig. 341 CKP sensor bolt and sensor

2. Disconnect the engine wiring harness electrical connector (4) from the Crankshaft Position (CKP) sensor (3).

3. Remove the CKP sensor bolt and sensor.

To install:

➡ **When installing the CKP sensor, make sure the sensor is fully seated before tightening the bolt. A poorly seated CKP sensor may perform erratically and may set false diagnostic trouble codes (DTCs).**

➡ **Do not reuse the original O-ring seal.**

4. If you are reinstalling the old CKP sensor, install a NEW O-ring seal onto the sensor.

5. Lubricate the O-ring seal with clean engine oil.

6. Connect the engine wiring harness electrical connector (4) to the CKP sensor (3).

7. Lower the vehicle.

8. Perform the crankshaft position system variation learn procedure.

4.8L & 5.3L Engines

See Figures 342 and 343.

> **❈❈ CAUTION**
>
> **Unless directed otherwise, the ignition and start switch must be in the OFF or LOCK position, and all electrical loads must be OFF before servicing any electrical component. Disconnect the negative battery cable to prevent an electrical spark should a tool or equipment come in contact with an exposed electrical terminal. Failure to follow these precautions may result in personal injury and/or damage to the vehicle or its components.**

For Vehicles equipped with OnStar® (UE1) with Back Up Battery: The Back Up Battery is a redundant power supply to allow limited OnStar® functionality in the event of a main vehicle battery power disruption to the VCIM (OnStar® module). Do not disconnect the main vehicle battery or remove the OnStar® fuse with the ignition key in any position other than OFF. Retained accessory power (RAP) should be allowed to time out or be disabled (simply opening the driver door should disable RAP) before disconnecting power. Disconnecting power to the OnStar® module in any way while the ignition is On or with RAP activated may cause activation of the OnStar® Back-Up Battery (BUB) system and will discharge and permanently damage the back-up battery. Once the Back-Up Battery is activated it

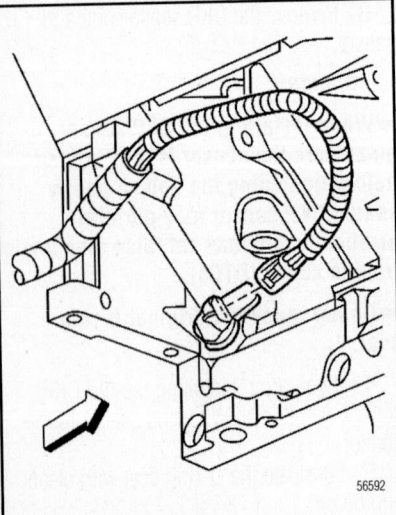

Fig. 342 Crankshaft Position (CKP) sensor electrical connector

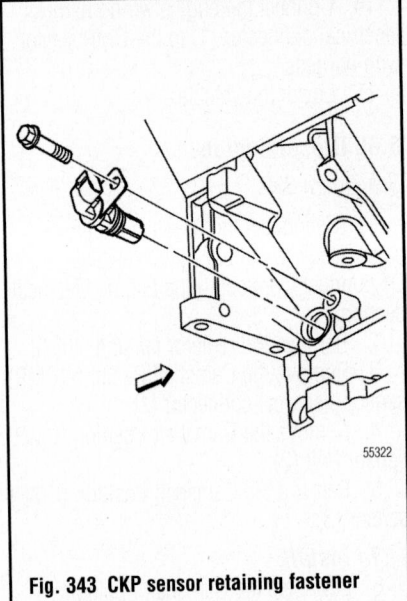

Fig. 343 CKP sensor retaining fastener

will stay on until it has completely discharged. The BUB is not rechargeable and once activated the BUB must be replaced.

➡ **Perform the Crankshaft Position System Variation Learn when the CKP sensor is removed or replaced.**

1. Disconnect the negative battery cable.
2. Raise the vehicle.
3. Remove the starter. Refer to Starter in the Engine Electrical section.
4. Disconnect the Crankshaft Position (CKP) sensor electrical connector.
5. Clean the area around the CKP sensor before removal in order to avoid debris from entering the engine.
6. Remove the CKP sensor retaining fastener.
7. Remove the CKP sensor.

To install:

8. Install the CKP sensor.
9. Install the CKP sensor retaining fastener and tighten to 18 ft. lbs. (25 Nm).
10. Connect the CKP sensor electrical connector.
11. Install the starter.
12. Lower the vehicle.
13. Connect the negative battery cable.
14. Perform the CKP system variation learn procedure.

6.6L Diesel Engine

2010 Vehicles

See Figure 344.

1. Raise and support the vehicle.

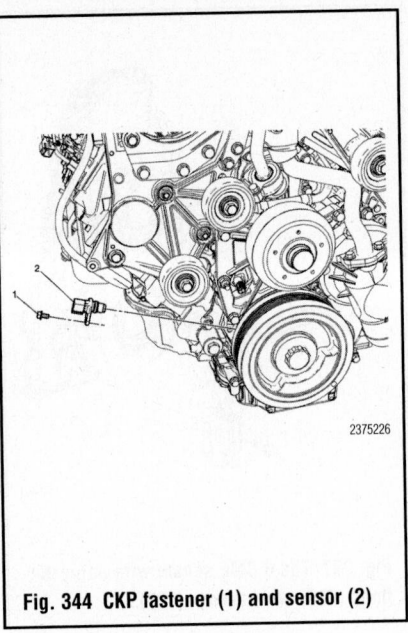

Fig. 344 CKP fastener (1) and sensor (2)

2. Remove the Crankshaft Position (CKP) sensor fastener (1)
3. Remove the CKP sensor.

To install:

4. Disconnect the electrical connector.
5. Install the CKP sensor.
6. Tighten the CKP sensor to 89 inch lbs. (10 Nm).

2011 Vehicles

See Figures 345 and 346.

1. Disconnect the negative battery cable. Refer to Battery Negative Cable Disconnect/Connect in the Engine Electrical section in the Engine Electrical section
2. Raise and suitably support the vehicle.
3. Disconnect the Crankshaft Position (CKP) sensor electrical connector.
4. Remove the CKP sensor bolt.
5. Remove the CKP sensor.
6. If necessary, remove the CKP sensor spacer bolts.
7. If necessary, remove the CKP sensor spacer.

To install:

➡ **The Crankshaft Position (CKP) sensor spacers are machined with different timing positions. However, if the crankshaft position sensor spacer requires replacement, replace with a grade "C" spacer.**

8. If necessary, lubricate a NEW CKP spacer O-ring with clean engine oil.
9. If necessary, install the NEW O-ring to the CKP sensor spacer.
10. If necessary, install the CKP sensor spacer.

Fig. 345 Crankshaft Position (CKP) sensor electrical connector

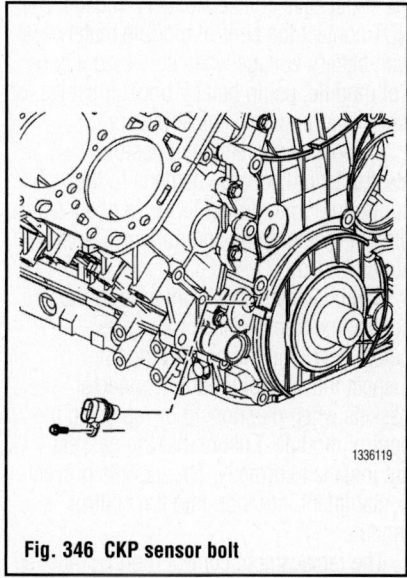

Fig. 346 CKP sensor bolt

11. If necessary, install the CKP sensor spacer bolts and tighten to 89 inch lbs. (10 Nm)

12. Install the CKP sensor.

13. Install the CKP sensor bolt and tighten to 89 inch lbs. (10 Nm)

14. Connect the CKP sensor electrical connector.

15. Lower the vehicle.

16. Connect the negative battery cable.

ELECTRONIC CONTROL MODULE (ECM)

REMOVAL & INSTALLATION

4.3L, 4.8L & 5.3L Engines

See Figures 347 and 348.

Service of the engine control module (ECM) should consist of either replacement of the ECM or programming of the electrically erasable programmable read only memory (EEPROM). If the diagnostic procedures call for the ECM to be replaced, the replacement ECM should be checked to ensure that the correct part is being used. If the correct part is being used, remove the faulty ECM and install the new service ECM.

❋❋ WARNING

Turn the ignition OFF when installing or removing the control module connectors and disconnecting or reconnecting the power to the control module (battery cable, powertrain control module (PCM)/engine control module (ECM)/transaxle control module (TCM) pigtail, control module fuse, jumper cables, etc.) in order to prevent internal control module damage.

Control module damage may result when the metal case contacts battery voltage. DO NOT contact the control module metal case with battery voltage when servicing a control module, using battery booster cables, or when charging the vehicle battery.

In order to prevent any possible electrostatic discharge damage to the control module, do not touch the connector pins or the soldered components on the circuit board.

Remove any debris from around the control module connector surfaces before servicing the control module. Inspect the control module connector gaskets when diagnosing or replacing the control module. Ensure that the gaskets are installed correctly. The gaskets prevent contaminant intrusion into the control module.

The replacement control module must be programmed.

➡**Record the remaining engine oil life. If the replacement module is not programmed with the remaining engine oil life, the engine oil life will default to 100 percent. If the replacement module is not programmed with the remaining engine oil life, the engine oil will need to be changed at 5 000 km (3,000 mi) from the last engine oil change. Use a scan tool to update the new ECM, if you are replacing it.**

1. Using a scan tool, retrieve the percentage of remaining engine oil. Record the remaining engine oil life.

2. Disconnect the negative battery cable. Refer to Battery Negative Cable Disconnect/Connect in the Engine Electrical section.

3. Disconnect the engine wiring harness electrical connectors (2) from the ECM (1).

4. Release the ECM bracket tabs (3).

5. Remove the ECM (4) from the bracket (2).

To install:

6. Install the ECM to the bracket.

7. Ensure that the ECM bracket tabs fully engage the ECM.

8. Connect the engine wiring harness electrical connectors to the ECM.

9. Connect the negative battery cable.

10. If a new ECM was installed, program the ECM.

11. Using a scan tool, set the remaining engine oil life.

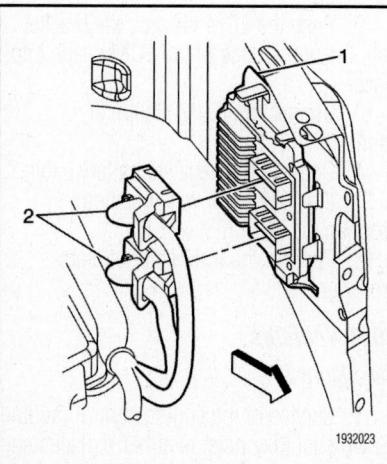

Fig. 347 Engine wiring harness electrical connectors (2) and ECM (1)

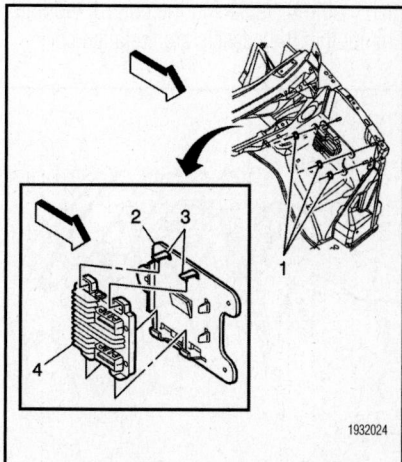

Fig. 348 ECM bracket tabs (3), ECM (4), and bracket (2)

6.6L Diesel Engine

2010 Vehicles

See Figures 349 and 350.

Service of the engine control module (ECM) should consist of either replacement of the ECM or programming of the electrically erasable programmable read only memory (EEPROM). If the diagnostic procedures call for the ECM to be replaced, the replacement ECM should be checked to ensure that the correct part is being used. If the correct part is being used, remove the faulty ECM and install the new service ECM.

> ※※ **WARNING**
>
> **Turn the ignition OFF when installing or removing the control module connectors and disconnecting or reconnecting the power to the control module (battery cable, powertrain control module (PCM)/engine control module (ECM)/transaxle control module (TCM) pigtail, control module fuse, jumper cables, etc.) in order to prevent internal control module damage.**

Control module damage may result when the metal case contacts battery voltage. DO NOT contact the control module metal case with battery voltage when servicing a control module, using battery booster cables, or when charging the vehicle battery.

In order to prevent any possible electrostatic discharge damage to the control module, do not touch the connector pins or the soldered components on the circuit board.

Remove any debris from around the control module connector surfaces before servicing the control module. Inspect the control module connector gaskets when diagnosing or replacing the control module. Ensure that the gaskets are installed cor-

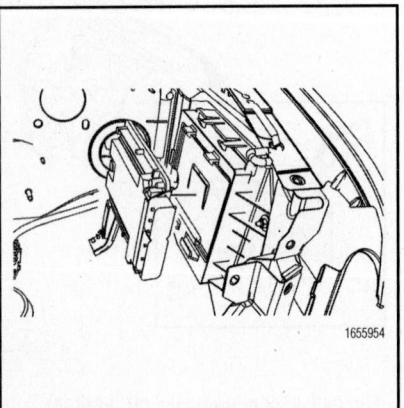

Fig. 349 ECM water deflector

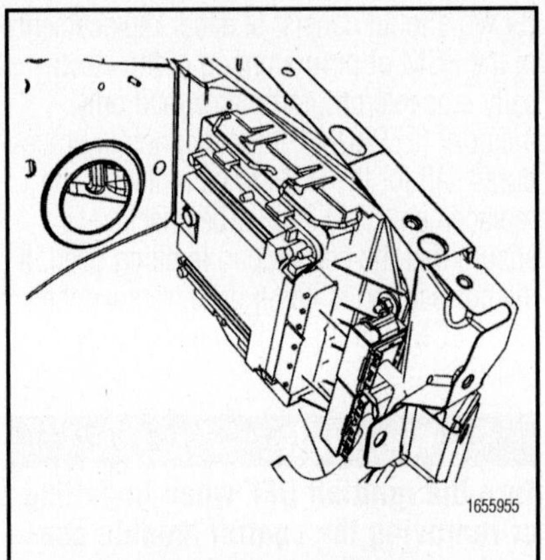

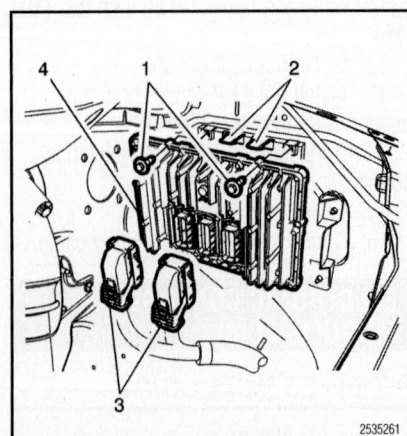

Fig. 350 ECM electrical connectors

rectly. The gaskets prevent contaminant intrusion into the control module.

The replacement control module must be programmed.

➡ **Before removing the engine control module (ECM), use the scan tool to capture the ECM data. This captured data will then need to be restored into the NEW ECM.**

1. Using a scan tool, capture the ECM data.
2. Disconnect the negative battery cable. Refer to Battery Negative Cable Disconnect/Connect in the Engine Electrical section.
3. Remove the ECM water deflector.
4. Release the ECM upper retaining tabs.
5. Disconnect the ECM electrical connectors.
6. Remove the ECM from the bracket.

To install:

7. Place the bottom edge of the ECM into the bracket lower retainers.
8. Install the washer solvent container.
9. Push the ECM towards the bracket until the upper edge of the ECM snaps into place.
10. Connect the ECM electrical connectors.
11. Connect the negative battery cable.
12. If a NEW ECM was installed, program the ECM.
13. Perform the turbocharger learn procedure.

2011 Vehicles

See Figure 351.

1. Service of the engine control module (ECM) should consist of either replacement of the ECM or programming of the electrically erasable programmable read only memory (EEPROM). If the diagnostic

---

procedures call for the ECM to be replaced, the replacement ECM should be checked to ensure that the correct part is being used. If the correct part is being used, remove the faulty ECM and install the new service ECM.

> ※※ **WARNING**
>
> **Turn the ignition OFF when installing or removing the control module connectors and disconnecting or reconnecting the power to the control module (battery cable, powertrain control module (PCM)/engine control module (ECM)/transaxle control module (TCM) pigtail, control module fuse, jumper cables, etc.) in order to prevent internal control module damage.**

Control module damage may result when the metal case contacts battery voltage. DO NOT contact the control module metal case with battery voltage when servicing a control module, using battery booster cables, or when charging the vehicle battery.

In order to prevent any possible electrostatic discharge damage to the control module, do not touch the connector pins or the soldered components on the circuit board.

Remove any debris from around the control module connector surfaces before servicing the control module. Inspect the control module connector gaskets when diagnosing or replacing the control module. Ensure that the gaskets are installed correctly. The gaskets prevent contaminant intrusion into the control module.

The replacement control module must be programmed.

Fig. 351 ECM mounting bolts (1), upper retaining tabs (2), electrical connectors (3), and ECM (4)

→Before removing the engine control module (ECM), use the scan tool to capture the ECM data. This captured data will then need to be restored into the NEW ECM. Refer to Control Module References.

2. Using a scan tool, capture the ECM data.

3. Disconnect the negative battery cable. Refer to Battery Negative Cable Disconnect/Connect in the Engine Electrical section in the Engine Electrical section

4. Reposition the master cylinder without disconnecting the brake lines.

5. Remove the ECM mounting bolts (1).

6. Release the ECM upper retaining tabs (2).

7. Disconnect the ECM electrical connectors (3).

8. Remove the ECM (4) from the bracket.

To install:

9. Place the bottom edge of the ECM into the bracket lower retainers.

10. Push the ECM (4) towards the bracket until the upper edge of the ECM snaps into place.

11. Install the ECM mounting bolts (1).

12. Connect the ECM electrical connectors (3).

13. Install the master cylinder.

14. Connect the negative battery cable.

15. If a NEW ECM was installed, program the ECM.

16. Perform the turbocharger learn procedure.

ENGINE COOLANT TEMPERATURE (ECT) SENSOR

REMOVAL & INSTALLATION

4.3L Engine

See Figures 352 and 353.

1. Remove the engine cover.

2. Drain the cooling system. Refer to Cooling System Drain and Refill in the Engine Cooling section.

3. Disconnect the engine wiring harness electrical connector (1) from the Engine Coolant Temperature (ECT) sensor (2).

☀ WARNING

Use care when handling the coolant sensor. Damage to the coolant sensor will affect the operation of the fuel control system.

Fig. 352 Engine wiring harness electrical connector (1) and ECT sensor (2)

4. Remove the ECT sensor from the cylinder head.

To install:

☀ WARNING

Replacement components must be the correct part number for the application. Components requiring the use of the thread locking compound, lubricants, corrosion inhibitors, or sealants are identified in the service procedure. Some replacement components may come with these coatings already applied. Do not use these coatings on components unless specified. These coatings can affect the final torque, which may affect the operation of the component. Use the correct torque specification when installing components in order to avoid damage.

☀ WARNING

Use care when handling the coolant sensor. Damage to the coolant sensor will affect the operation of the fuel control system.

5. If re-installing the old sensor, coat the threads with sealant GM P/N 12346004 (Canadian P/N 10953480), or equivalent.

6. Install the ECT sensor to the cylinder head and tighten to 15 ft. lbs. (20 Nm).

7. Connect the engine wiring harness electrical connector (1) to the ECT sensor (2).

8. Fill the cooling system. Refer to Cooling System Drain and Refill in the Engine Cooling section.

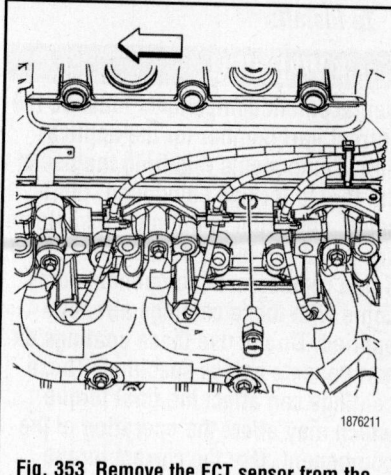

Fig. 353 Remove the ECT sensor from the cylinder head

9. Install the engine cover.

4.8L & 5.3L Engines

See Figure 354.

☀ WARNING

Use care when handling the coolant sensor. Damage to the coolant sensor will affect the operation of the fuel control system.

1. Turn OFF the ignition.

2. Raise the vehicle.

3. Drain the cooling system below the level of the ECT sensor. Refer to Cooling System Drain and Refill in the Engine Cooling section.

4. Lower the vehicle.

5. Disconnect the electrical connector from the Engine Coolant Temperature (ECT) sensor.

6. Remove the ECT sensor.

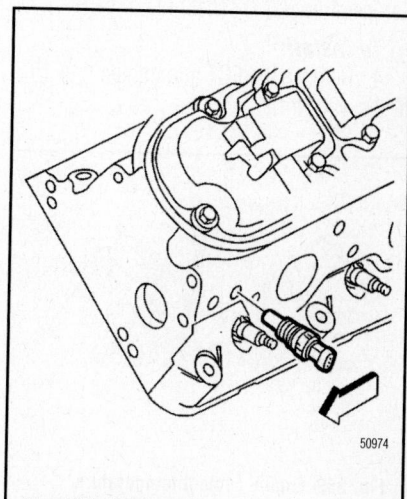

Fig. 354 ECT sensor

To install:

> ### ✳✳ WARNING
>
> **Replacement components must be the correct part number for the application. Components requiring the use of the thread locking compound, lubricants, corrosion inhibitors, or sealants are identified in the service procedure. Some replacement components may come with these coatings already applied. Do not use these coatings on components unless specified. These coatings can affect the final torque, which may affect the operation of the component. Use the correct torque specification when installing components in order to avoid damage.**

> ### ✳✳ WARNING
>
> **Use care when handling the coolant sensor. Damage to the coolant sensor will affect the operation of the fuel control system.**

7. If reusing the ECT sensor, coat the ECT sensor threads with sealer GM P/N 12346004 (Canadian P/N 10953480) or the equivalent.

8. Install the ECT sensor and tighten to 15 ft. lbs. (20 Nm).

9. Connect the ECT sensor electrical connector.

10. Refill the engine coolant.

6.6L Diesel Engines

See Figure 355.

1. Remove the air cleaner outlet duct.

2. Partially drain the cooling system. Refer to Cooling System Drain and Refill in the Engine Cooling section.

3. Remove the Engine Coolant Temperature (ECT) sensor (1).

To install:

4. Remove the ECT and tighten it to 15 ft. lbs. (20 Nm).

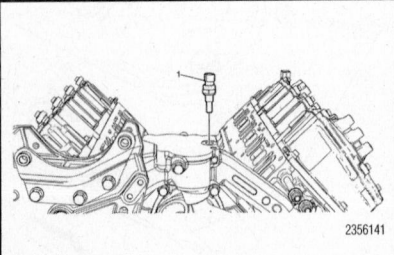

Fig. 355 Engine coolant temperature sensor (1)

5. Disconnect the electrical connector.

HEATED OXYGEN SENSOR (HO2S)

REMOVAL & INSTALLATION

Heated Oxygen and Oxygen Sensor Caution

> ### ✳✳ WARNING
>
> **Do not remove the pigtail from either the Heated Oxygen Sensor (HO2S) or the oxygen sensor (O2S). Removing the pigtail or the connector will affect sensor operation.**

Note the following when working with oxygen sensors:

• Handle the oxygen sensor carefully. Do not drop the HO2S. Keep the in-line electrical connector and the louvered end free of grease, dirt, or other contaminants. Do not use cleaning solvents of any type.

• Do not repair the wiring, connector or terminals. Replace the oxygen sensor if the pigtail wiring, connector, or terminal is damaged.

• This external clean air reference is obtained by way of the oxygen sensor signal and heater wires. Any attempt to repair the wires, connectors, or terminals could result in the obstruction of the air reference and degraded sensor performance.

• Do not apply contact cleaner or other materials to the sensor or vehicle harness connectors. These materials may get into the sensor causing poor performance.

• Do not damage the sensor pigtail and harness wires in such a way that the wires inside are exposed. This could provide a path for foreign materials to enter the sensor and cause performance problems.

• Ensure the sensor or vehicle lead wires are not bent sharply or kinked. Sharp bends or kinks could block the reference air path through the lead wire.

• Do not remove or defeat the oxygen sensor ground wire, where applicable. Vehicles that utilize the ground wired sensor may rely on this ground as the only ground contact to the sensor. Removal of the ground wire will cause poor engine performance.

• Ensure that the peripheral seal remains intact on the vehicle harness connector in order to prevent damage due to water intrusion. The engine harness may be repaired using Packard's Crimp and Splice Seals Terminal Repair Kit. Under no circumstances should repairs be soldered since this could result in the air reference being obstructed.

4.3L Engine

Bank 1 Sensor 1

See Figure 356.

1. Refer to the Heated Oxygen and Oxygen Sensor Caution.

2. Raise and suitably support the vehicle.

3. Remove the connector position assurance (CPA) retainer.

4. Disconnect the HO2S electrical connector (3) from the engine wiring harness electrical connector (4).

5. Remove the HO2S (1).

To install:

➡**A special anti-seize compound is used on the HO2S threads. The compound consists of liquid graphite and glass beads. The graphite tends to burn away, but the glass beads remain, making the sensor easier to remove. New or service replacement sensors already have the compound applied to the threads. If the sensor is removed from an exhaust component and if for any reason the sensor is to be reinstalled, the threads must have anti-seize compound applied before the reinstallation.**

6. If reinstalling the old sensor, coat the threads with special anti-seize compound or equivalent. GM recommends P/N 88862477 (US) and 88862478 (Canada).

7. Install the HO2S and tighten it to 31 ft. lbs. (42 Nm).

8. Connect the HO2S electrical connector to the engine wiring harness electrical connector.

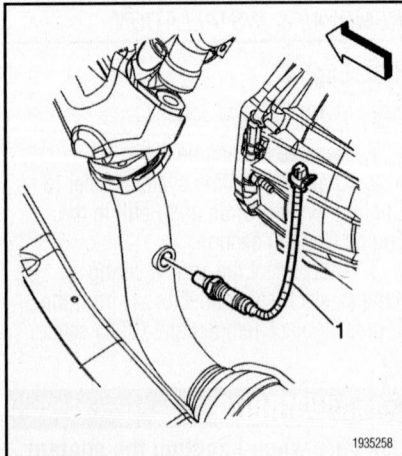

Fig. 356 HO2S electrical connector (3), engine wiring harness electrical connector (4), and HO2S (1)

9. Install the CPA retainer.
10. Lower the vehicle.

Bank 1 Sensor 2

See Figures 357 and 358.

1. Refer to the Heated Oxygen and Oxygen Sensor Caution.
2. Raise and suitably support the vehicle.
3. Remove the connector position assurance (CPA) retainer.
4. Disconnect the HO2S electrical connector (2) from the engine wiring harness electrical connector (1).
5. Remove the HO2S (1).

To install:

➡A special anti-seize compound is used on the HO2S threads. The compound consists of liquid graphite and glass beads. The graphite tends to burn away, but the glass beads remain, making the sensor easier to remove. New, or service replacement sensors already have the compound applied to the threads. If the sensor is removed from an exhaust component and if for any reason the sensor is to be reinstalled, the threads must have anti-

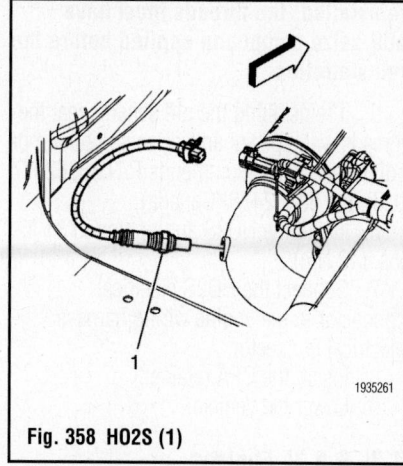

Fig. 358 HO2S (1)

seize compound applied before the reinstallation.

6. If reinstalling the old sensor, coat the threads with special anti-seize compound or equivalent. GM recommends P/N 88862477 (US) and 88862478 (Canada).
7. Install the HO2S (1) and tighten to 31 ft. lbs. (42 Nm).
8. Connect the HO2S electrical connector (2) to the engine wiring harness electrical connector (1).
9. Install the CPA retainer.
10. Lower the vehicle.

Bank 2 Sensor 1

See Figures 359 and 360.

1. Refer to the Heated Oxygen and Oxygen Sensor Caution.
2. Raise and suitably support the vehicle.
3. Remove the connector position assurance (CPA) retainer.
4. Disconnect the HO2S electrical connector (3) from the engine wiring harness electrical connector (2).
5. Remove the HO2S (1).

To install:

➡A special anti-seize compound is used on the HO2S threads. The compound consists of liquid graphite and glass beads. The graphite tends to burn away, but the glass beads remain, making the sensor easier to remove. New or service replacement sensors already have the compound applied to the threads. If the sensor is removed

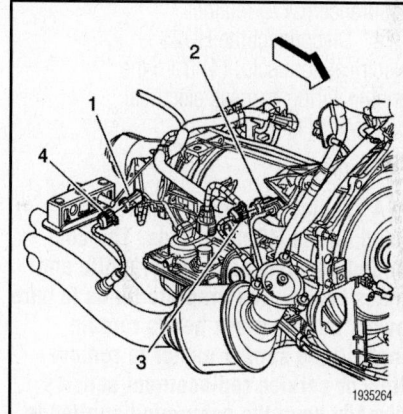

Fig. 359 HO2S electrical connector (3), engine wiring harness electrical connector (2), and HO2S (1)

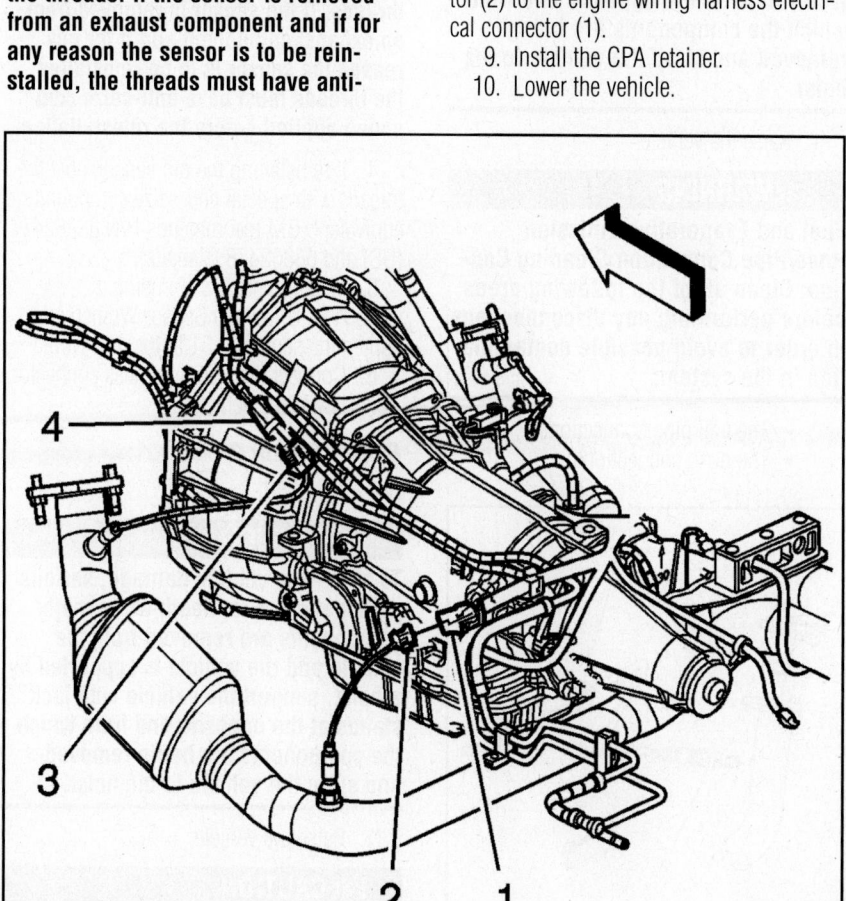

Fig. 357 HO2S electrical connector (2) from the engine wiring harness electrical connector (1)

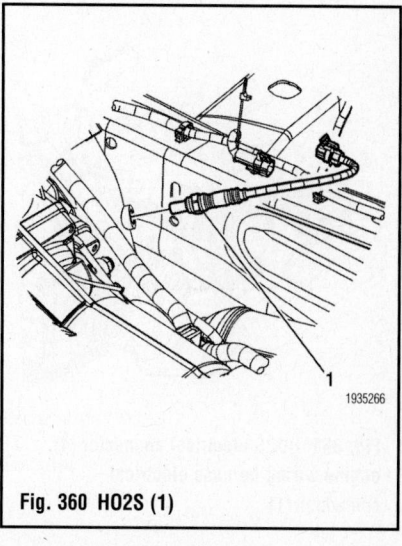

Fig. 360 HO2S (1)

from an exhaust component and if for any reason the sensor is to be reinstalled, the threads must have anti-seize compound applied before the reinstallation.

6. If reinstalling the old sensor, coat the threads with special anti-seize compound or equivalent. GM recommends P/N 88862477 (US) and 88862478 (Canada).

7. Install the HO2S (1) and tighten to 31 ft. lbs. (42 Nm).

8. Connect the HO2S electrical connector (3) to the engine wiring harness electrical connector (2).

9. Install the CPA retainer.

10. Lower the vehicle.

Bank 2 Sensor 2

See Figure 361.

1. Refer to the Heated Oxygen and Oxygen Sensor Caution.

2. Raise and suitably support the vehicle.

3. Remove the connector position assurance (CPA) retainer.

4. Disconnect the HO2S electrical connector (4) from the engine wiring harness electrical connector (1).

To install:

➡A special anti-seize compound is used on the HO2S threads. The compound consists of liquid graphite and glass beads. The graphite tends to burn away, but the glass beads remain, making the sensor easier to remove. New or service replacement sensors already have the compound applied to the threads. If the sensor is removed from an exhaust component and if for any reason the sensor is to be

reinstalled, the threads must have anti-seize compound applied before the reinstallation.

5. If reinstalling the old sensor, coat the threads with special anti-seize compound or equivalent. GM recommends P/N 88862477 (US) and 88862478 (Canada).

6. Install the HO2S and tighten to 31 ft. lbs. (42 Nm).

7. Connect the HO2S electrical connector to the engine wiring harness electrical connector.

8. Install the CPA retainer.

9. Lower the vehicle.

4.8L & 5.3L Engines

Bank 1 Sensor 1 & Bank 2 Sensor 1

See Figure 362.

✸✸ CAUTION

To avoid any vehicle damage, serious personal injury or death when major components are removed from the vehicle and the vehicle is supported by a hoist, support the vehicle with jack stands at the opposite end from which the components are being removed and strap the vehicle to the hoist.

1. Raise the vehicle.

✸✸ WARNING

Fuel and Evaporative Emission Hose/Pipe Connection Cleaning Caution: Clean all of the following areas before performing any disconnections in order to avoid possible contamination in the system:

• The fuel pipe connections
• The hose connections

• The areas surrounding the connections

2. Disconnect the connector (1) for the HO2S.

✸✸ CAUTION

Excessive Force and Oxygen Sensor Caution: The oxygen sensor may be difficult to remove when the engine temperature is below 48°C (120°F). Excessive force may damage threads in the exhaust manifold or the exhaust pipe. Remove the two HO2S using a CH-39194-C Oxygen Sensor Wrench.

3. Remove the two HO2S using a CH-39194-C Oxygen Sensor Wrench.

To install:

➡A special anti-seize compound is used on the HO2S threads. The compound consists of liquid graphite and glass beads. The graphite tends to burn away, but the glass beads remain, making the sensor easier to remove. New or service replacement sensors already have the compound applied to the threads. If the sensor is removed from an exhaust component and if for any reason the sensor is to be reinstalled, the threads must have anti-seize compound applied before the reinstallation.

4. If reinstalling the old sensor, coat the threads with special anti-seize compound or equivalent. GM recommends P/N 88862477 (US) and 88862478 (Canada).

5. Install the HO2S (2) using a CH-39194-C Oxygen Sensor Wrench and tighten the sensor to 31 ft. lbs. (42 Nm).

6. Connect the HO2S harness connector.

7. Lower the vehicle.

Bank 1 Sensor 2

See Figure 363.

✸✸ CAUTION

To avoid any vehicle damage, serious personal injury or death when major components are removed from the vehicle and the vehicle is supported by a hoist, support the vehicle with jack stands at the opposite end from which the components are being removed and strap the vehicle to the hoist.

1. Raise the vehicle.

✸✸ CAUTION

Clean all of the following areas before performing any disconnections in order to avoid possible contamination in the system:

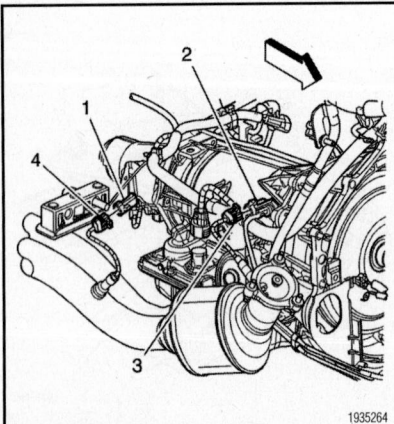

Fig. 361 HO2S electrical connector (4), engine wiring harness electrical connector (1)

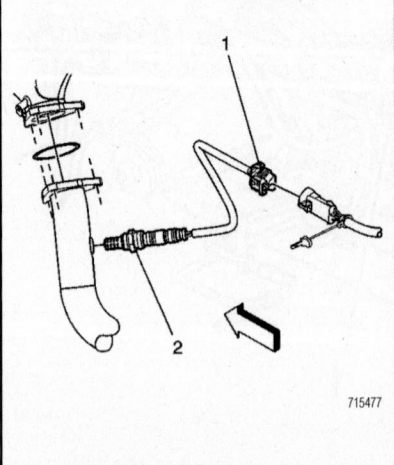

Fig. 362 HO2S connector (1)

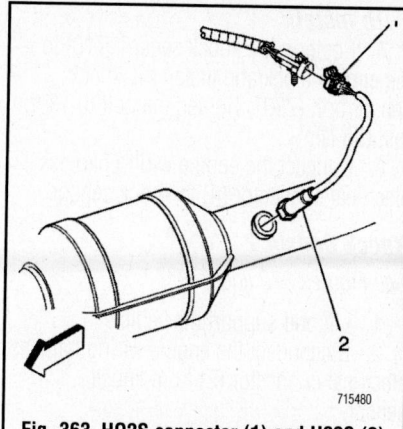

Fig. 363 HO2S connector (1) and HO2S (2)

- The fuel pipe connections
- The hose connections
- The areas surrounding the connections

2. Disconnect the connector (1) for the HO2S.

※ CAUTION

The oxygen sensor may be difficult to remove when the engine temperature is below 48°C (120°F). Excessive force may damage threads in the exhaust manifold or the exhaust pipe. Remove the two HO2S using a CH-39194-C Oxygen Sensor Wrench.

3. Remove the HO2S (2) using a CH-39194-C Oxygen Sensor Wrench.

To install:

➡A special anti-seize compound is used on the HO2S threads. The compound consists of liquid graphite and glass beads. The graphite tends to burn away, but the glass beads remain, making the sensor easier to remove. New or service replacement sensors already have the compound applied to the threads. If the sensor is removed from an exhaust component and if for any reason the sensor is to be reinstalled, the threads must have anti-seize compound applied before the reinstallation.

4. Coat the threads of the oxygen sensor with special anti-seize compound, if necessary. GM recommends P/N 88862477 (US) and 88862478 (Canada).

5. Install the HO2S (2) using a CH-39194-C Oxygen Sensor Wrench and tighten the sensor to 31 ft. lbs. (42 Nm).

6. Connect the HO2S harness connector.

7. Lower the vehicle.

INTAKE AIR TEMPERATURE (IAT) SENSOR 2

REMOVAL & INSTALLATION

6.6L Diesel Engine

See Figure 364.

This model is also equipped with a MAF/IAT sensor, refer also to Manifold Air Flow/Intake Air Temperature Sensor.

1. Remove the Intake Air Temperature (IAT) Sensor.

To install:

2. Tighten to 15 ft. lbs. (20 Nm).
3. Disconnect the electrical connector.

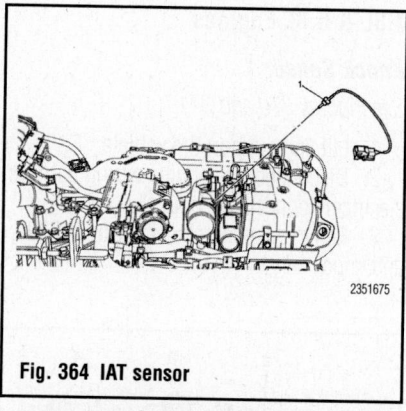

Fig. 364 IAT sensor

INPUT AND OUTPUT SPEED SENSORS

REMOVAL & INSTALLATION

6L45

See Figure 365.

1. Raise the vehicle.

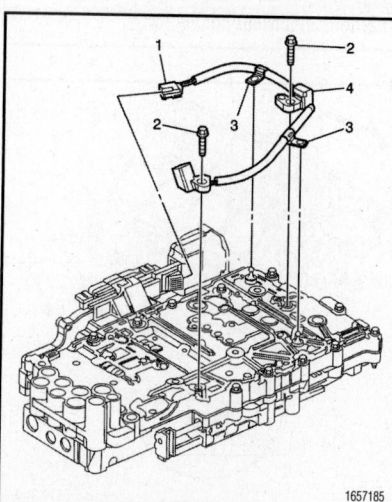

Fig. 365 Speed sensor electrical connector (1), two speed sensor assembly bolts (2), two clips (3) and assembly (4)

2. Remove the transmission fluid pan and filter.
3. Remove the upper and lower valve body assembly.
4. Remove the speed sensor electrical connector (1).
5. Remove the two input and output speed sensor assembly bolts (2).
6. Remove the two input and output speed sensor assembly clips (3).
7. Remove the input and output speed sensor assembly (4).

To install:

8. Installation is the reverse of removal.
9. Tighten the assembly bolts to 106 inch lbs. (12 Nm).
10. Inspect the wiring harness clips for damage replace if necessary.

KNOCK SENSOR (KS)

REMOVAL & INSTALLATION

4.3L Engine

Knock Sensor 1

See Figures 366 and 367.

1. Raise and suitably support the vehicle.
2. Reposition the knock sensor sleeve down, away from the knock sensor, if equipped.
3. Disconnect the engine wiring harness electrical connector (1) from the knock sensor.
4. Remove the knock sensor bolt and sensor.

To install:

5. Position the knock sensor to the engine block and install the bolt. Tighten to 18 ft. lbs. (25 Nm).

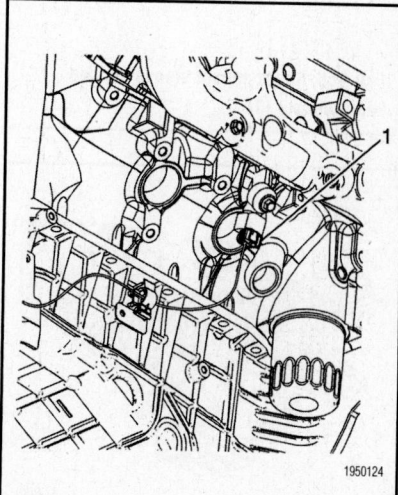

Fig. 366 Knock sensor engine wiring harness electrical connector (1)

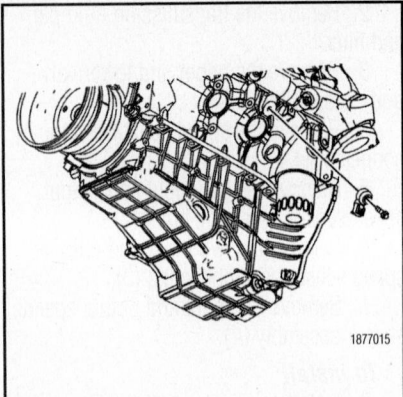

Fig. 367 Knock sensor bolt and sensor

6. Connect the engine wiring harness electrical connector (1) to the knock sensor.

7. Position the knock sensor sleeve up and over the knock sensor, if equipped.

8. Lower the vehicle.

Knock Sensor 2

See Figures 368 and 369.

1. Raise and suitably support the vehicle.

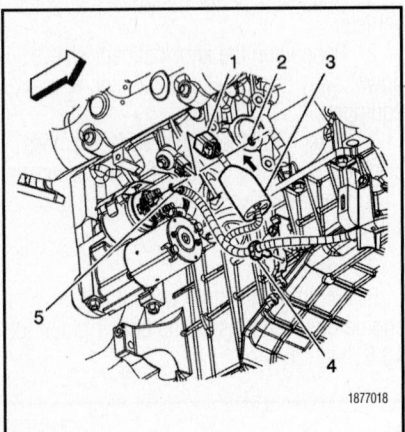

Fig. 368 Knock sensor sleeve (2) and knock sensor (1)

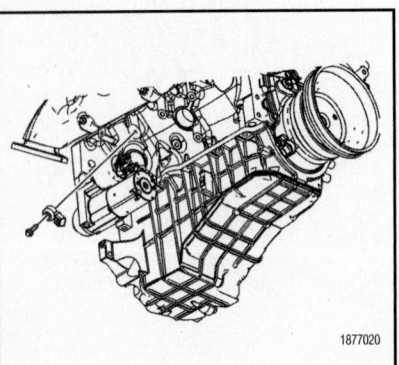

Fig. 369 Knock sensor bolt and sensor

2. Reposition the knock sensor sleeve (2) down, away from the knock sensor.

3. Disconnect the engine wiring harness electrical connector from the knock sensor (1).

4. Remove the knock sensor bolt and sensor.

To install:

5. Position the knock sensor to the engine block and install the bolt and tighten to 18 ft. lbs. (25 Nm).

6. Connect the engine wiring harness electrical connector to the knock sensor (1).

7. Position the knock sensor sleeve (2) up and over the knock sensor.

8. Lower the vehicle.

4.8L & 5.3L Engines

Knock Sensor 1

See Figures 370 and 371.

1. Lift and support the vehicle.

2. Disconnect the engine wiring harness electrical connector (4) from knock sensor.

3. Remove the knock sensor bolt (739) and knock sensor (718).

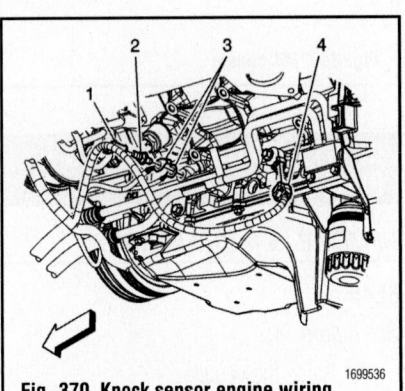

Fig. 370 Knock sensor engine wiring harness electrical connector

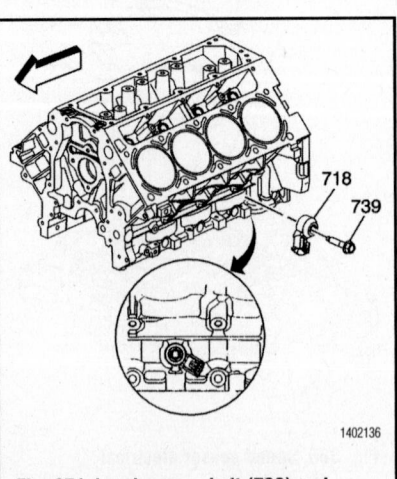

Fig. 371 knock sensor bolt (739) and knock sensor (718)

To install:

4. Position the knock sensor (718) to the engine block and install the knock sensor bolt (739). Tighten the bolt to 18 ft. lbs. (25 Nm).

5. Connect the engine wiring harness electrical connector (4) to knock sensor.

Knock Sensor 2

See Figures 372 and 373.

1. Lift and support the vehicle.

2. Disconnect the engine wiring harness electrical connector (2) from knock sensor.

3. Remove the knock sensor bolt (739) and knock sensor (718).

To install:

4. Position the knock sensor (718) to the engine block and install the knock sensor bolt (739). Tighten the bolt to 18 ft. lbs. (25 Nm).

5. Connect the engine wiring harness electrical connector (2) to the knock sensor.

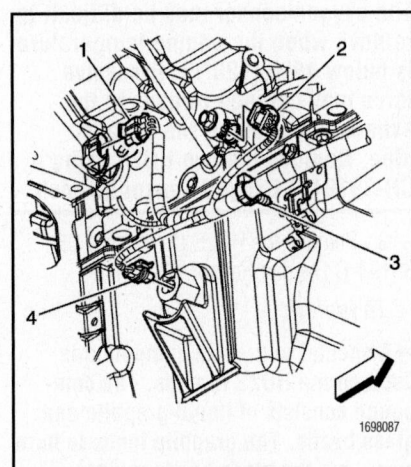

Fig. 372 Knock sensor engine wiring harness electrical connector (2)

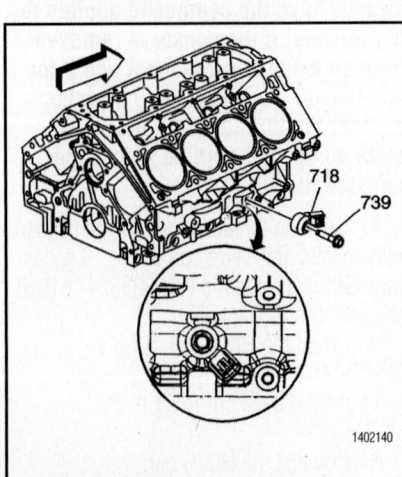

Fig. 373 Knock sensor bolt (739) and knock sensor (718)

MANIFOLD ABSOLUTE PRESSURE (MAP) SENSOR

REMOVAL & INSTALLATION

4.3L Engine

See Figures 374 and 375.

1. Remove the engine cover.
2. Disconnect the engine wiring harness electrical connector (4) from the Manifold Absolute Pressure (MAP) sensor (7).
3. Caution: Do not rotate or pry on the MAP sensor when removing. Damage to the MAP sensor or the intake manifold may result.
4. Remove the MAP sensor bolt (1).
5. Using a slight rocking motion while pulling straight up, remove the MAP sensor (2) from the upper intake manifold.
6. Inspect the MAP sensor seal for damage, replace the seal if necessary.

To install:

7. Install a NEW MAP sensor seal to the MAP sensor, if necessary.

8. Install the MAP sensor (2) to the upper intake manifold.
9. Install the MAP sensor bolt (1) and tighten to 89 inch lbs. (10 Nm)
10. Connect the engine wiring harness electrical connector (4) to the MAP sensor (7).
11. Install the engine cover.

4.8L & 5.3L Engines

See Figure 376.

1. Remove the engine cover.
2. Disconnect the Manifold Absolute Pressure (MAP) sensor electrical connector.
3. Remove the MAP sensor (1) from the intake manifold.

To install:

➡**Lightly coat the MAP sensor seal with clean engine oil before installing the sensor.**

4. Install the MAP sensor to the upper intake manifold.
5. Connect the MAP sensor electrical connector.

6. Install the engine cover.

6.6L Diesel Engine

See Figure 377.

1. Remove the intake air heater.
2. Remove the Manifold Absolute Pressure (MAP) sensor fastener (1).
3. Remove the MAP sensor (2).

To install:

4. Remove the MAP sensor (2).
5. Remove the MAP sensor fastener (1).
6. Tighten to 89 inch lbs. (10 Nm)
7. Disconnect the electrical connector.

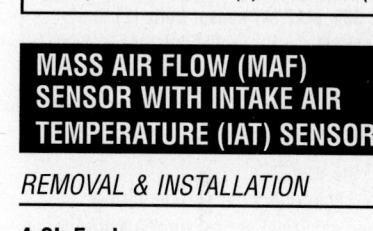

Fig. 377 Manifold Absolute Pressure (MAP) sensor fastener (1) and sensor (2)

MASS AIR FLOW (MAF) SENSOR WITH INTAKE AIR TEMPERATURE (IAT) SENSOR

REMOVAL & INSTALLATION

4.3L Engine

See Figures 378 through 380.

1. Loosen the air cleaner outlet duct clamp (1) at the Mass Air Flow (MAF)/Intake air temperature (IAT) sensor.

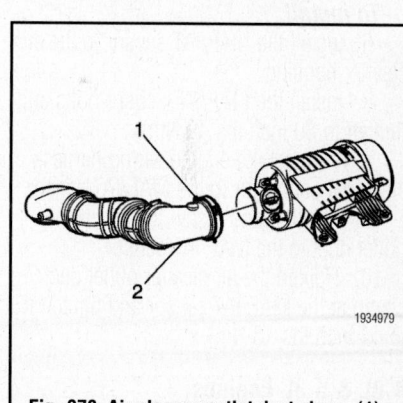

Fig. 378 Air cleaner outlet duct clamp (1) and duct (2)

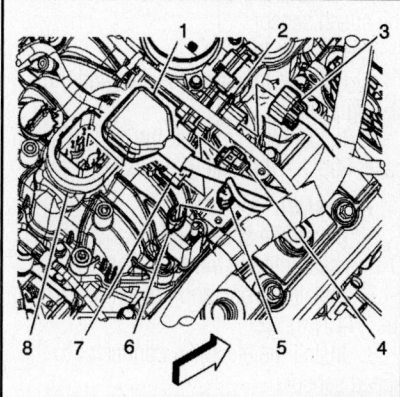

Fig. 374 Engine wiring harness electrical connector (4), Manifold Absolute Pressure (MAP) sensor (7)

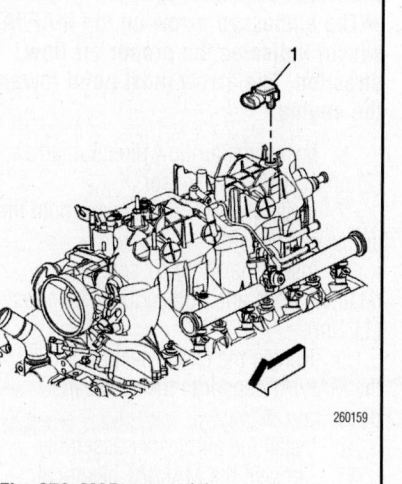

Fig. 376 MAP sensor (1)

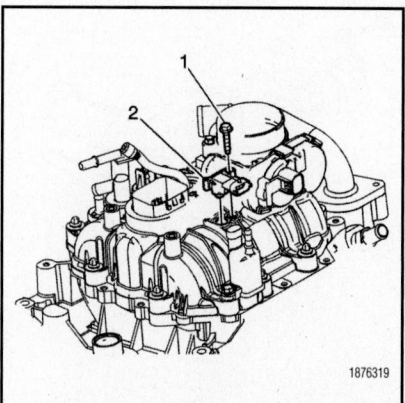

Fig. 375 Remove the MAP sensor bolt (1)

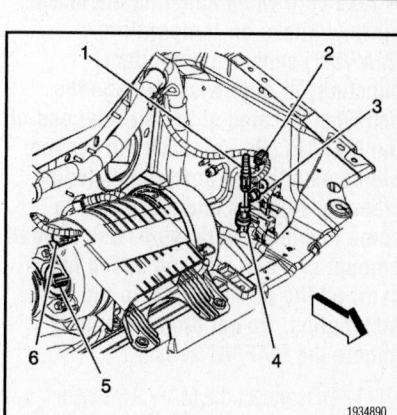

Fig. 379 Engine wiring harness electrical connector (6) and MAF/IAT sensor (5)

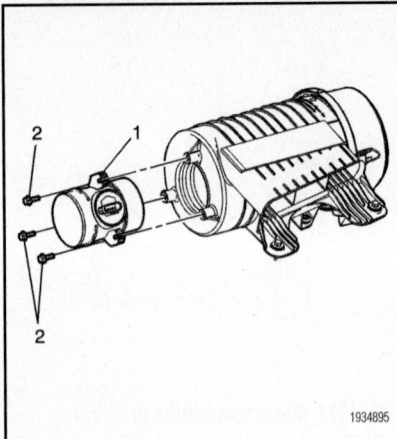

Fig. 380 MAF/IAT sensor bolts (2) and sensor (1)

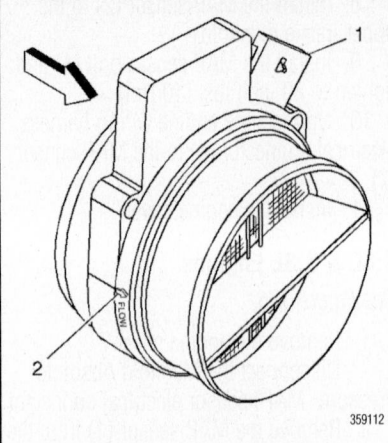

Fig. 381 MAF/IAT sensor electrical connector (1) and air flow direction arrow (2)

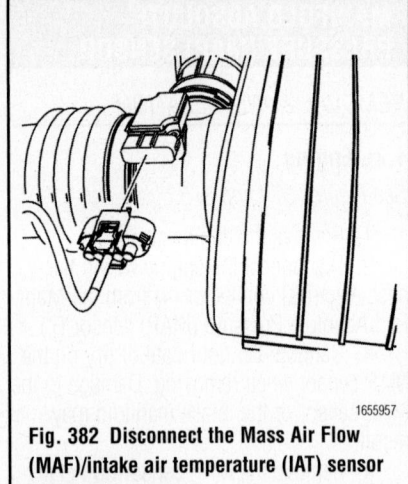

Fig. 382 Disconnect the Mass Air Flow (MAF)/intake air temperature (IAT) sensor electrical connector

2. Remove the air cleaner outlet duct (2) from the MAF/IAT sensor and position it out of the way.

3. Disconnect the engine wiring harness electrical connector (6) from the MAF/IAT sensor (5).

4. Remove the MAF/IAT sensor bolts (2).

5. Remove the MAF/IAT sensor (1) from the air cleaner housing.

To install:

6. Install the MAF/IAT sensor to the air cleaner housing.

7. Install the MAF/IAT sensor bolts and tighten to 80 inch lbs. (9 Nm).

8. Connect the engine wiring harness electrical connector to the MAF/IAT sensor.

9. Position and install the air cleaner outlet duct to the MAF/IAT sensor.

10. Tighten the air cleaner outlet duct clamp at the MAF/IAT sensor and tighten it to 44 inch lbs. (5 Nm).

4.8L & 5.3L Engines

See Figure 381.

➡**Take care when handling the mass air flow/intake air temperature (MAF/IAT) sensor. Do not dent, puncture, or otherwise damage the honeycell located at the air inlet end of the MAF/IAT. Do not touch the sensing elements or allow anything including cleaning solvents and lubricants to come in contact with them. Use a small amount of a non-silicone based lubricant, on the air duct only, to aid in installation. Do not drop or roughly handle the MAF/IAT sensor.**

1. Disconnect the MAF/IAT sensor electrical connector (1).

2. Remove the air cleaner assembly. Refer to Air Cleaner Assembly.

3. Loosen the clamp securing the MAF/IAT sensor to the air cleaner duct.

4. Remove the MAF/IAT sensor bolts from the air cleaner assembly.

5. Remove the MAF/IAT from the air cleaner.

To install:

➡**The embossed arrow on the MAF/IAT sensor indicates the proper air flow direction. The arrow must point toward the engine.**

6. Locate the air flow direction arrow (2) on the MAF/IAT sensor.

7. Install the MAF/IAT sensor onto the air cleaner housing.

8. Install the MAF/IAT sensor retaining bolts and tighten to 97 inch lbs. (11 Nm).

9. Tighten the clamp securing the MAF/IAT sensor to the air cleaner duct.

10. Install the air cleaner assembly.

11. Connect the MAF/IAT electrical connector (1).

6.6L Diesel Engine

See Figure 382.

1. Disconnect the Mass Air Flow (MAF)/intake air temperature (IAT) sensor electrical connector.

2. Remove the MAF/IAT sensor TORX® screws.

3. Remove the MAF/IAT sensor.

To install:

4. Install the MAF/IAT sensor.

5. Install the MAF/IAT sensor TORX® screws and tighten to 70 ft. lbs. (95 Nm).

6. Connect the MAF/IAT sensor electrical connector.

VEHICLE SPEED SENSOR (VSS)

REMOVAL & INSTALLATION

4L60E Transmission

See Figure 383.

1. Raise the vehicle.

2. Remove the electrical connector from the speed sensor.

3. Remove the bolt.

4. Remove the speed sensor and the O-ring seal.

5. Inspect the seal and the transmission case. Replace the seal, if necessary.

To install:

6. Install the speed sensor and the O-ring seal into the transmission.

7. Install the bolt and tighten to 97 inch lbs. (11 Nm).

8. Install the electrical connector to the speed sensor.

9. Lower the vehicle.

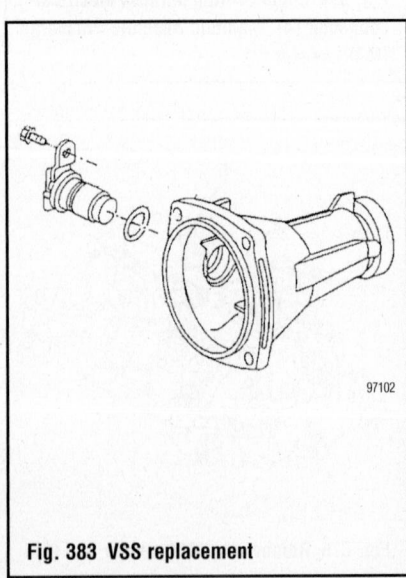

Fig. 383 VSS replacement

FUEL | GASOLINE FUEL INJECTION SYSTEM

FUEL SYSTEM SERVICE PRECAUTIONS

Safety is the most important factor when performing not only fuel system maintenance but any type of maintenance. Failure to conduct maintenance and repairs in a safe manner may result in serious personal injury or death. Maintenance and testing of the vehicle's fuel system components can be accomplished safely and effectively by adhering to the following rules and guidelines.

• To avoid the possibility of fire and personal injury, always disconnect the negative battery cable unless the repair or test procedure requires that battery voltage be applied.

• Always relieve the fuel system pressure prior to disconnecting any fuel system component (injector, fuel rail, pressure regulator, etc.), fitting or fuel line connection. Exercise extreme caution whenever relieving fuel system pressure to avoid exposing skin, face and eyes to fuel spray. Please be advised that fuel under pressure may penetrate the skin or any part of the body that it contacts.

• Always place a shop towel or cloth around the fitting or connection prior to loosening to absorb any excess fuel due to spillage. Ensure that all fuel spillage (should it occur) is quickly removed from engine surfaces. Ensure that all fuel soaked cloths or towels are deposited into a suitable waste container.

• Always keep a dry chemical (Class B) fire extinguisher near the work area.

• Do not allow fuel spray or fuel vapors to come into contact with a spark or open flame.

• Always use a back-up wrench when loosening and tightening fuel line connection fittings. This will prevent unnecessary stress and torsion to fuel line piping.

• Always replace worn fuel fitting O-rings with new Do not substitute fuel hose or equivalent where fuel pipe is installed.

Before servicing the vehicle, make sure to also refer to the precautions in the beginning of this section as well.

FUEL PRESSURE RELIEF

✳✳ WARNING

Gasoline or gasoline vapors are highly flammable. A fire could occur if an ignition source is present.

Never drain or store gasoline or diesel fuel in an open container, due to the possibility of fire or explosion. Have a dry chemical (Class B) fire extinguisher nearby.

✳✳ WARNING

Remove the fuel tank cap and relieve the fuel system pressure before servicing the fuel system in order to reduce the risk of personal injury. After you relieve the fuel system pressure, a small amount of fuel may be released when servicing the fuel lines, the fuel injection pump, or the connections. In order to reduce the risk of personal injury, cover the fuel system components with a shop towel before disconnection. This will catch any fuel that may leak out. Place the towel in an approved container when the disconnection is complete.

1. If the fuel system requires repair, prevent fuel spillage by removing the fuel pump fuse.
2. Loosen the fuel fill cap in order to relieve the fuel tank vapor pressure.
3. Remove the engine cover, if required.
4. Remove the fuel rail service port cap.
5. Wrap a shop towel around the fuel rail service port and using a small flat-bladed tool, depress (open) the fuel rail test port valve.
6. Remove the shop towel from around the fuel rail service port, and place in an approved gasoline container.
7. Install the fuel rail service port cap.
8. Install the engine cover, if required.
9. Tighten the fuel fill cap.

FUEL FILTER

REMOVAL & INSTALLATION

The fuel filter is contained in the fuel sender assembly inside the fuel tank. The paper filter element of the fuel filter traps particles in the fuel that may damage the fuel injection system. The fuel filter housing is made to withstand maximum fuel system pressure, exposure to fuel additives, and changes in temperature. There is no service interval for fuel filter replacement.

FUEL INJECTORS

REMOVAL & INSTALLATION

4.3L Engine

See Figure 384.

➡ The engine oil may be contaminated with fuel if the fuel injectors are leaking.

1. Remove the fuel meter body.
2. Remove the injector retainer lock nuts (4) and retainer (3).

✳✳ WARNING

Use care in removing the fuel injectors to prevent damage to the electrical connector terminals.

• The fuel injector is serviced as a complete assembly only.

• Also since the injectors are electrical components, these injectors should not be immersed in any type of liquid solvent or cleaner as damage may occur. Fuel injector cleaning is not recommended.

3. While pulling the fuel injector downward, push with a small tip punch down between the injector terminals until the injector is removed.

To install:

➡ When ordering new fuel injectors, be sure to order the correct injector for the vehicle.

4. Lubricate the NEW injector O-ring seals with clean engine oil.
5. Install the fuel injector (2) into the fuel meter body injector socket.
6. Install the injector retainer (3) and the injector retainer lock nuts (4), then tighten to 27 ft. lbs. (36 Nm).
7. Install the fuel meter body.

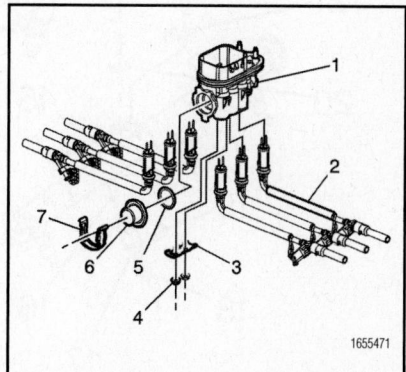

1655471

Fig. 384 Fuel injector retainer lock nuts (4), retainer (3) and injector (2)

4.8L & 5.3L Engines

See Figures 385 through 387.

> ✳✳ **WARNING**
>
> Use care in removing the fuel injectors in order to prevent damage to the fuel injector electrical connector pins or the fuel injector nozzles. Do not immerse the fuel injector in any type of cleaner. The fuel injector is an electrical component and may be damaged by this cleaning method.

➡The Denso fuel injectors that are installed in the 5.3L (L59) E85 application will not have O-rings and retaining clips serviced separately. Therefore, replace the fuel injectors whenever you replace an O-ring or clips.

> ✳✳ **CAUTION**
>
> The engine oil may be contaminated with fuel if the fuel injectors are leaking.

1. Remove the fuel rail.
2. Remove the fuel injector retainer clip (19).
3. Remove the fuel injector (17).
4. Discard the injector retainer clip (1).
5. Remove and discard the fuel injector O-ring seals (2, 4) from the injector.

To install:

➡When ordering new fuel injectors, you must order the correct injector for the vehicle.

6. The fuel injector (1) is stamped with a part number identification (2). A four-digit build date code (3), which indicates the month (4), day (5), year (6), and the shift (7) that built the fuel injector.
7. Lubricate the NEW fuel injector O-ring seals with clean engine oil.
8. Install the NEW injector O-ring seals onto the fuel injector.
9. Install a NEW retainer clip onto the fuel injector.
10. Install the fuel injector into the fuel rail injector socket with the electrical connector facing outward. The retainer clip locks onto a flange on the fuel rail injector socket.
11. Install the fuel rail.

FUEL TANK

DRAINING

> ✳✳ **CAUTION**
>
> Gasoline or gasoline vapors are highly flammable. A fire could occur if an ignition source is present.

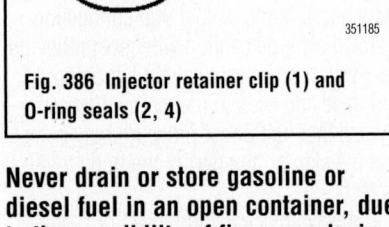

Fig. 386 Injector retainer clip (1) and O-ring seals (2, 4)

Never drain or store gasoline or diesel fuel in an open container, due to the possibility of fire or explosion. Have a dry chemical (Class B) fire extinguisher nearby.

1. Remove the fuel filler cap.
2. Use a hand or air operated pump device in order to drain as much fuel through the fuel tank filler pipe opening as possible.

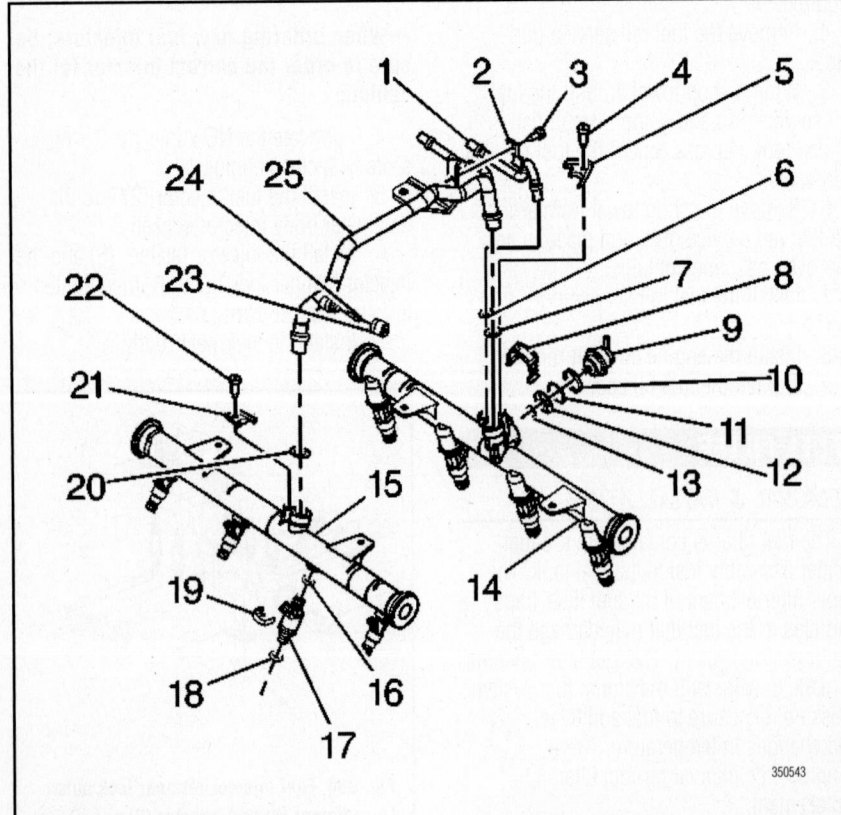

Fig. 385 Fuel injection components

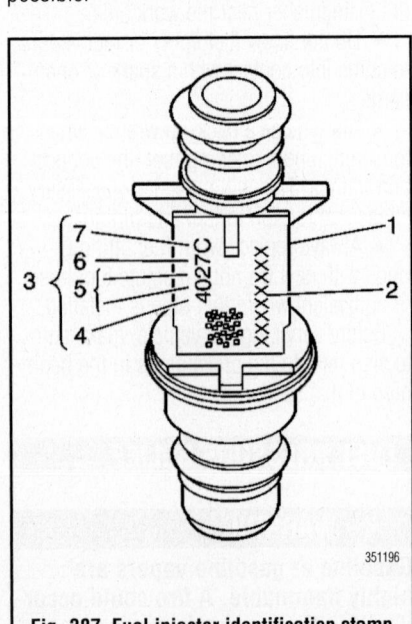

Fig. 387 Fuel injector identification stamp

REMOVAL & INSTALLATION

4.3L Engine

See Figures 388 through 393.

1. Relieve the fuel system pressure. Refer to Fuel Pressure Relief.

2. Drain the fuel tank. Refer to Fuel Tank Draining.

3. Raise and suitably support the vehicle.

4. Disconnect the fuel fill pipe evaporative emission (EVAP) line quick connect fitting (1) from the fuel tank EVAP line.

5. Loosen the fuel fill hose clamp (2) at the fuel tank and remove the hose from the tank.

6. Clean the fuel and EVAP pipe connections and the surrounding areas prior to disconnecting the lines in order to avoid possible contamination of the fuel and or EVAP system.

7. Disconnect the chassis fuel feed pipe quick connect fitting (2) from the fuel tank fuel feed pipe.

8. Disconnect the EVAP canister purge pipe quick connect fitting (1) from the chassis EVAP pipe.

9. Disconnect the chassis wiring harness electrical connector from the EVAP canister vent solenoid valve.

10. Support the fuel tank with an adjustable jack.

11. Remove the fuel tank strap bolts (1).

12. Remove the fuel tank straps (2).

13. With the aid of an assistant, carefully lower the fuel tank (3) until the fuel tank module connections can be accessed.

14. Disconnect the chassis wiring harness electrical connectors from the

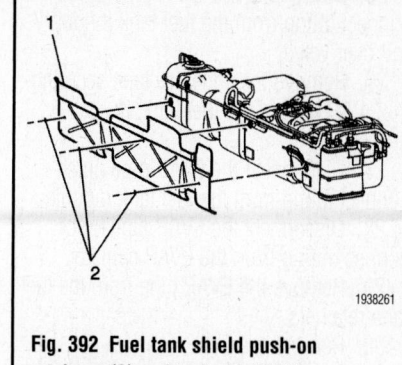

Fig. 392 Fuel tank shield push-on retainers (2) and tank shield (1)

fuel tank pressure sensor and fuel tank module.

15. With the aid of the assistant, completely lower the fuel tank.

16. With the aid of the assistant, place the fuel tank in a suitable work area.

17. If replacing the fuel tank proceed to the next step, otherwise proceed to step 15 in the installation procedure.

18. Remove the fuel tank shield push-on retainers (2).

19. Remove the fuel tank shield (1) from the fuel tank clips.

20. Disconnect the fuel feed pipe quick connect fitting from the fuel tank module.

21. Remove the fuel feed pipe from the fuel tank clips.

22. Remove the fuel feed pipe from under the EVAP front pipe.

23. Disconnect the EVAP front pipe quick connect fittings from the fuel tank module and rollover valve.

24. Remove the EVAP front pipe from under the EVAP pipe.

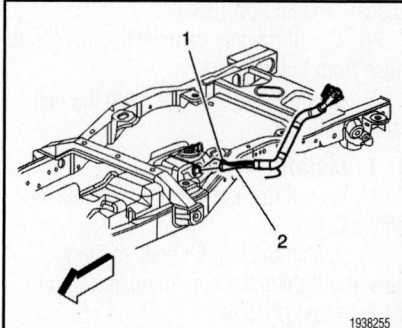

Fig. 388 Disconnect the fuel fill pipe evaporative emission (EVAP) line quick connect fitting (1) from the fuel tank EVAP line and loosen the fuel fill hose clamp (2)—for models with the hinged left rear side door

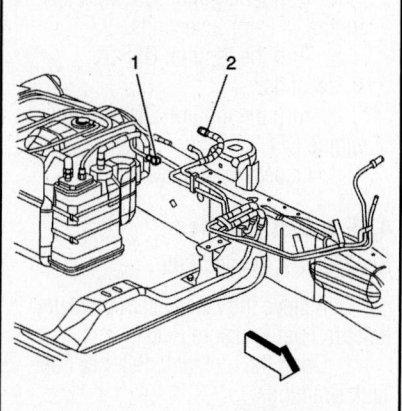

Fig. 390 Chassis fuel feed pipe quick connect fitting (2) and EVAP canister purge pipe quick connect fitting (1)

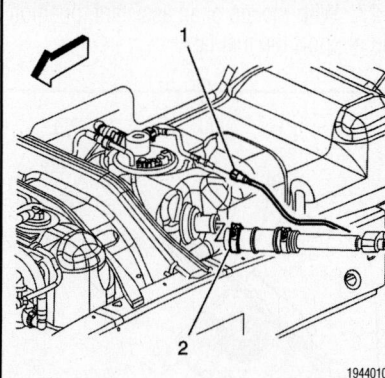

Fig. 389 Disconnect the fuel fill pipe evaporative emission (EVAP) line quick connect fitting (1) from the fuel tank EVAP line and loosen the fuel fill hose clamp (2)—for models without the hinged left rear side door

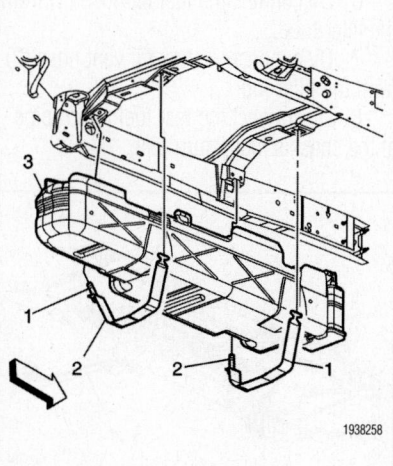

Fig. 391 Fuel tank strap bolts (1), straps (2), and tank (3)

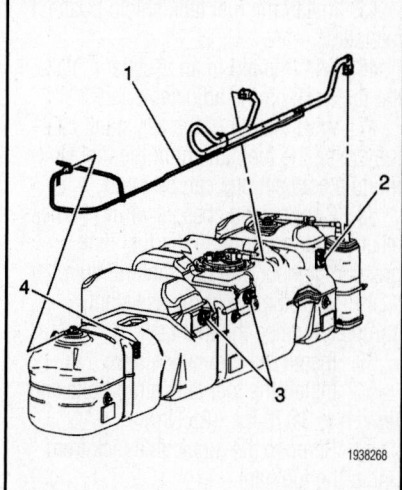

Fig. 393 EVAP pipe (1) and fuel tank retainers (2, 3, and 4)

25. Disconnect the EVAP pipe quick connect fitting from the fuel tank module / roll over valve.

26. Remove the adhesive tape securing the EVAP pipe to the fuel tank, if necessary.

27. Disconnect the EVAP pipe quick connect fitting from the fuel tank module.

28. Disconnect the EVAP pipe quick connect fitting from the EVAP canister.

29. Remove the EVAP pipe from the fuel tank retainers.

30. Remove the EVAP canister.

31. Remove the fuel tank module.

To install:

32. Install the fuel tank module.

33. Install the EVAP canister.

34. Install the EVAP pipe (1) to the fuel tank retainers (2, 3, and 4).

35. Connect the EVAP pipe quick connect fitting to the EVAP canister.

36. Connect the EVAP pipe quick connect fitting to the fuel tank module.

37. Connect the EVAP pipe quick connect fitting to the fuel tank roll over valve.

38. Secure the EVAP pipe to the fuel tank with adhesive tape, if necessary.

39. Install and route the EVAP front pipe under the EVAP line.

40. Connect the EVAP front pipe quick connect fittings to the fuel tank module and roll over valve.

41. Install and route the fuel feed pipe under the EVAP front pipe.

42. Connect the fuel feed pipe quick connect fitting to the fuel tank module.

43. Install the fuel feed pipe to the fuel tank clips.

44. Install the fuel tank shield onto the tank clips.

45. Install the fuel tank shield push on retainers.

46. With the aid of an assistant, place the fuel tank on the adjustable jack.

47. With the aid of the assistant, carefully raise the fuel tank until the fuel tank module connections can be made.

48. Connect the chassis wiring harness electrical connectors to the fuel tank pressure sensor and fuel tank module.

49. With the aid of the assistant, completely raise the fuel tank.

50. Install the fuel tank straps.

51. Install the fuel tank strap bolts and tighten to 18 ft. lbs. (25 Nm).

52. Remove the adjustable jack from under the fuel tank.

53. Connect the chassis wiring harness electrical connector to the EVAP canister vent solenoid valve.

54. Connect the EVAP canister purge pipe quick connect fitting to the chassis EVAP pipe.

55. Connect the fuel feed pipe quick connect fitting to the fuel tank fuel feed pipe.

56. Install the fuel tank fill hose to the fuel tank.

57. Connect the fuel fill pipe EVAP line quick connect fitting to the fuel tank EVAP line.

58. Tighten the fuel fill hose clamp at the fuel tank to 24 inch lbs. (2.75 Nm).

59. Refill the fuel tank.

60. Install the fuel cap.

61. Connect the negative battery cable. Refer to Battery Negative Cable Disconnect/Connect in the Engine Electrical section.

62. Perform the following procedure in order to inspect for leaks:

    a. Turn the ignition ON, with the engine OFF, for 2 seconds.

    b. Turn the ignition OFF for 10 seconds.

    c. Turn the ignition ON, with the engine OFF.

    d. Inspect for fuel leaks.

4.8L & 5.3L Engines

See Figures 394 and 395.

1. Relieve the fuel system pressure. Refer to Fuel Pressure Relief.

2. Drain the fuel tank. Refer to Fuel Tank Draining.

3. Raise the vehicle.

4. Clean all the fuel pipe connections and the surrounding areas before disconnecting the fuel pipes in order to avoid possible contamination of the fuel system.

5. Loosen the fuel fill hose clamp.

6. Disconnect the fuel fill hose (1) from the filler tube.

7. Disconnect the fuel fill vent hose (2) from the filler tube.

8. Disconnect the rear fuel return pipe at the chassis fuel return pipe.

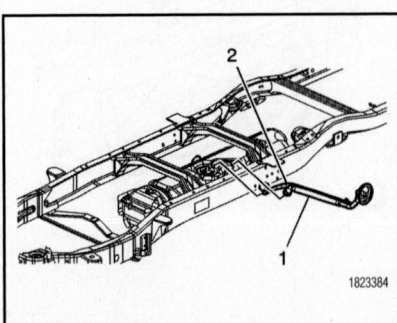

Fig. 394 Fuel fill hose (1) and vent hose (2)

9. Disconnect the rear fuel feed pipe at the chassis fuel feed pipe.

10. With the aid of an assistant, support the fuel tank.

11. Remove and discard the attaching bolts from the fuel tank strap.

12. Remove the fuel tank straps.

13. Carefully lower the fuel tank.

14. Disconnect the fuel tank module and the fuel pump electrical connectors.

15. Remove the fuel tank.

16. Place the fuel tank in a suitable work area.

17. Remove the fuel tank module (1) and the fuel pipes from the fuel tank.

18. Remove the evaporative emission (EVAP) hoses from the fuel tank.

19. On models with EVAP canister mounted to fuel tank, remove two tie down straps from the (EVAP) canister (2) then remove the canister from the fuel tank. Discard the tie down straps.

20. On all models, remove the fuel fill hose from the fuel tank.

21. Remove the fuel tank from the fuel tank shield (3).

To install:

22. Install the fuel tank into the fuel tank shield (3).

23. Install the fuel fill hose to the fuel tank and tighten the fuel fill hose clamp to 24 inch lbs. (2.75 Nm).

24. On models with EVAP canister mounted to fuel tank, place the (EVAP) canister in position on the (EVAP) canister bracket, then install two new tie down straps.

25. On all models, install the (EVAP) hoses to the fuel tank.

26. Install the fuel tank module and the fuel pipes to the fuel tank.

27. With the aid of an assistant, position and support the fuel tank.

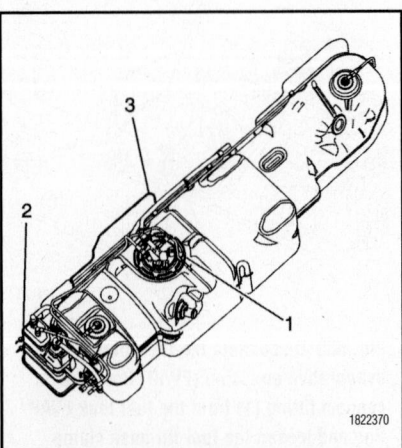

Fig. 395 Fuel tank module (1), EVAP canister (2), and tank shield (3)

28. Raise the fuel tank slightly.
29. Connect the electrical connectors to the fuel tank module and fuel pump.
30. Raise the tank fully.
31. Install the fuel tank straps.

➡When removing or replacing the fuel tank, never reuse the fuel tank support fasteners. Always use new fasteners when installing the fuel tank.

32. Install the new attaching bolts to the fuel tank strap and tighten the bolts to 15 ft. lbs. (20 Nm).
33. Connect the chassis fuel feed pipe to the rear fuel feed pipe.
34. Connect the rear fuel return pipe to the chassis fuel return pipe.
35. Connect the fuel fill vent hose to the filler tube.
36. Connect the fuel fill hose to the fuel tank and tighten the fuel fill hose clamp to 24 inch lbs. (2.75 Nm).
37. Lower the vehicle.
38. Refill the fuel tank.
39. Install the fuel cap.
40. Perform the following procedure in order to inspect for leaks:
   a. Turn the ignition ON for 2 seconds.
   b. Turn the ignition OFF for 10 seconds.
   c. Turn the ignition ON.
   d. Inspect for fuel leaks.

IDLE SPEED

ADJUSTMENT

Idle speed is maintained by the engine control module (ECM); no adjustment is needed or possible.

The ECM learns the airflow through the throttle body to ensure the correct idle. The learned airflow values are stored within the ECM. These values are learned to adjust for production variation and will continuously learn during the life of the vehicle to compensate for reduced airflow due to throttle body coking. Anytime the throttle body airflow rate changes, for example due to cleaning or replacing, the values must be relearned.

An engine that had a heavily coked throttle body that has been cleaned or replaced may take several drive cycles to learn out the coking. To accelerate the process, the scan tool has the ability to reset all learned values back to zero. A new ECM will also have values set to zero.

The idle may be unstable or a DTC may set if the learned values do not match the actual airflow.

THROTTLE BODY ASSEMBLY

REMOVAL & INSTALLATION

4.3L Engine

See Figures 396 and 397.

1. Remove the air cleaner outlet resonator.
2. Disconnect the engine wiring harness electrical connector (3) from the throttle actuator (2).
3. Remove the throttle body bolts (1).
4. Remove the throttle body (2) and gasket (3). Discard the gasket.

To install:

5. Install a NEW throttle body gasket into the upper intake manifold.
6. Place the throttle body onto the upper intake manifold.
7. Install the throttle body bolts and tighten to 89 inch lbs. (10 Nm)
8. Connect the engine wiring harness electrical connector to the throttle actuator.

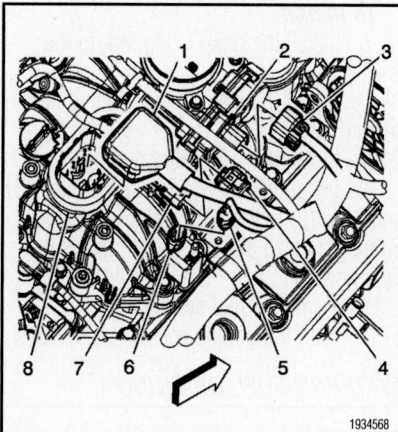

Fig. 396 Engine wiring harness electrical connector (3) and throttle actuator (2)

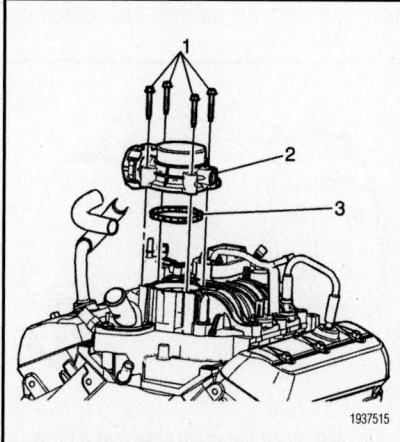

Fig. 397 Throttle body bolts (1), throttle body (2) and gasket (3)

9. Install the air cleaner outlet resonator.
10. Perform the throttle learn procedure.

4.8L & 5.3L Engines

See Figure 398.

1. Before servicing the vehicle, refer to the Precautions Section.
2. Disconnect the negative battery cable.
3. Remove the air cleaner assembly.
4. Disconnect the electrical connector.
5. Disconnect the vacuum hoses.
6. Remove the throttle body retaining nuts.
7. Remove the component from its mounting.

➡Be sure to use new fasteners, as required.

8. Position a new throttle body gasket on the upper intake manifold.
9. Install the throttle body to its mounting.
10. Tighten the retaining nuts to 89 inch lbs. (10 Nm).
11. Continue the installation in the reverse order of the removal procedure.
12. Perform the throttle idle learn procedure.

➡Using the GM diagnostic scan tool, or equivalent, refer to the on-screen reprogramming directions and perform the throttle/idle learn procedure.

13. With the ignition ON and the engine OFF, perform the idle learn reset in mode setup, using the scan tool.
14. Start the engine and monitor the TB Idle Airflow Compensation parameter.
15. The value should equal zero percent and the engine should be idling at a normal idle speed.
16. Clear any DTC's.

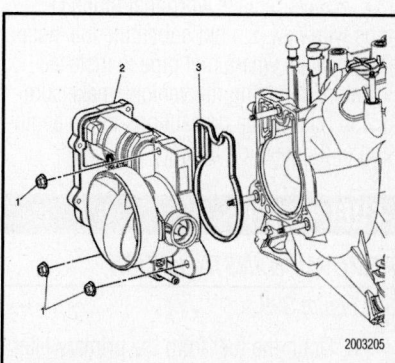

Fig. 398 Three throttle body nuts (1), throttle body assembly (2), and throttle body gasket (3)

FUEL | **DIESEL FUEL INJECTION SYSTEM**

FUEL SYSTEM SERVICE PRECAUTIONS

Safety is the most important factor when performing not only fuel system maintenance but any type of maintenance. Failure to conduct maintenance and repairs in a safe manner may result in serious personal injury or death. Maintenance and testing of the vehicle's fuel system components can be accomplished safely and effectively by adhering to the following rules and guidelines.

• To avoid the possibility of fire and personal injury, always disconnect the negative battery cable unless the repair or test procedure requires that battery voltage be applied.

• Always relieve the fuel system pressure prior to disconnecting any fuel system component (injector, fuel rail, pressure regulator, etc.), fitting or fuel line connection. Exercise extreme caution whenever relieving fuel system pressure to avoid exposing skin, face and eyes to fuel spray. Please be advised that fuel under pressure may penetrate the skin or any part of the body that it contacts.

• Always place a shop towel or cloth around the fitting or connection prior to loosening to absorb any excess fuel due to spillage. Ensure that all fuel spillage (should it occur) is quickly removed from engine surfaces. Ensure that all fuel soaked cloths or towels are deposited into a suitable waste container.

• Always keep a dry chemical (Class B) fire extinguisher near the work area.

• Do not allow fuel spray or fuel vapors to come into contact with a spark or open flame.

• Always use a back-up wrench when loosening and tightening fuel line connection fittings. This will prevent unnecessary stress and torsion to fuel line piping.

• Always replace worn fuel fitting O-rings with new. Do not substitute fuel hose or equivalent where fuel pipe is installed.

Before servicing the vehicle, make sure to also refer to the precautions in the beginning of this section as well.

FUEL FILTER

REMOVAL & INSTALLATION

See Figure 399.

1. Drain the fuel from the primary filter and the secondary fuel filter. Refer to Water-in-Fuel Draining.
2. Unscrew the secondary fuel filter (1).

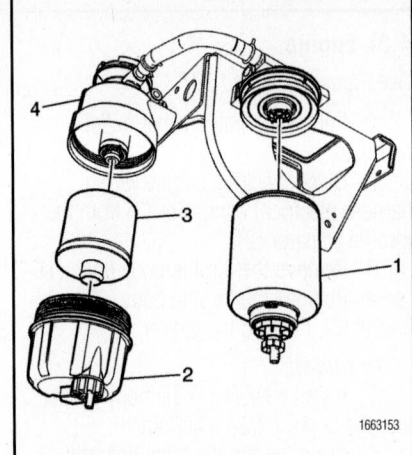

Fig. 399 Secondary fuel filter (1), bowl (2), and filter (3)

3. Unscrew the bowl (2).
4. Remove both filters (1, 3).

To install:

5. Install the new O-ring seal to the bowl (2).
6. Install the new O-ring seals to the secondary filter (1).
7. Install the secondary filter (1).
8. Install the NEW primary fuel filter (3) and bowl (2) to the fuel filter adapter and tighten 1/4 turn after the seal contacts the filter adapter.
9. Prime the fuel system.
10. Start the engine and check for leaks.

WATER-IN-FUEL DRAINING

2011 Models

See Figure 400.

1. Raise and support the vehicle.
2. Attach a small piece of hose to the drain cock onto the water-in-fuel sensor.

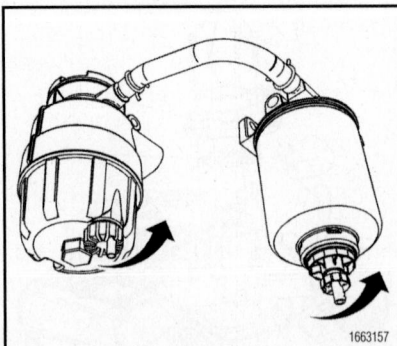

Fig. 400 Open the drain cock 3 or 4 turns or until the water contaminated fuel seeps from the drain cock.

3. Place an approved fuel-resistant container under the fuel filter.
4. Open the drain cock 3 or 4 turns or until the water contaminated fuel seeps from the drain cock.
5. Prime the fuel system until only diesel fuel is visible.
6. Tighten the drain cock.
7. Remove the container and hose.

INJECTION TIMING

ADJUSTMENT

Ignition timing is controlled by the Engine Control Module (ECM). No adjustment is necessary or possible.

FUEL HIGH PRESSURE PIPE

REMOVAL & INSTALLATION

Pump-To-Rail

See Figures 401 and 402.

1. Remove the high pressure fuel pipe fastener (1).
2. Remove the high pressure fuel pipe fitting (2).
3. Remove the turbo charger assembly.
4. Remove the high pressure fuel pipe fitting (1).
5. Remove the high pressure fuel pipes (2) as an assembly.

To install:

6. Install the high pressure fuel pipe fitting (1) and tighten to 28 ft. lbs. (38 Nm).
7. Install the high pressure fuel pipe fitting (2) and tighten to 22 ft. lbs. (30 Nm).
8. Install the high pressure fuel fastener (1) and tighten to 89 inch lbs. (10 Nm)
9. Install the turbo charger assembly.
10. Prime the fuel system.

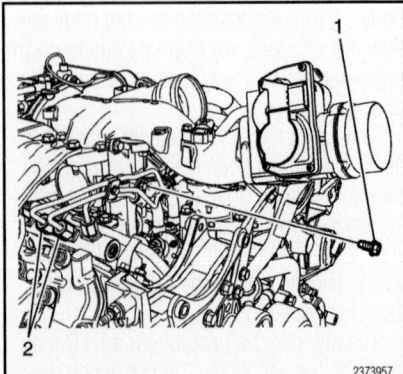

Fig. 401 High pressure fuel pipe fastener (1) and fitting (2)

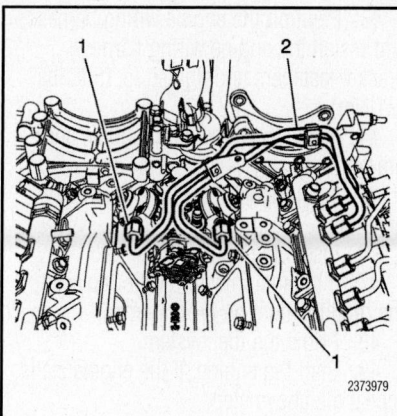

Fig. 402 High pressure fuel pipe fitting (1) and pipes (2) assembly

11. Start the engine.
12. If the engine does not start, repeat the above step.
13. Inspect the fuel system for leaks.

Rail-to-Rail

See Figure 403.

1. Remove the high pressure fuel pipe fastener (1).
2. Remove the high pressure fuel pipe fitting (2).
3. Remove the turbocharger assembly.
4. Remove the high pressure fuel pipe fasteners.
5. Remove the high pressure fuel pipe fitting.
6. Remove the high pressure fuel pipe.

To install:

7. Install the high pressure fuel pipe fitting and tighten to 22 ft. lbs. (30 Nm).
8. Install the high pressure fuel pipe fasteners and tighten to 89 inch lbs. (10 Nm)

9. Install the high pressure fuel pipe fitting and tighten to 22 ft. lbs. (30 Nm).
10. Install the high pressure fuel fastener and tighten to 89 inch lbs. (10 Nm)
11. Install the turbocharger assembly.
12. Prime the fuel system.
13. Start the engine.
14. If the engine does not start, repeat the above step.
15. Inspect the fuel system for leaks.

INJECTORS

REMOVAL & INSTALLATION

Left Side

See Figures 404 through 406.

1. Remove the upper fan shroud.
2. If equipped, remove the auxiliary generator.
3. Remove the glow plug module and bracket.
4. Remove the injector/glow plug wire harness retaining bolt at lower upper valve cover.
5. Disconnect the left engine wiring harness connector.
6. Remove the engine wiring harness bracket fasteners (1) and reposition the wiring harness.
7. Label all the injector electrical connectors before the connectors are removed in order to prevent reconnecting to the wrong injector. Failure to properly connect the injectors in the correct sequence will cause severe engine damage.
8. Disconnect the fuel injector electrical connectors.
9. Disconnect and reposition the fuel return pipes.

➡Prior to removal of the fuel injector pipes, use compressed air to remove

any debris from the injector line and fittings.

• Spray lithium grease, GM P/N 12346293 or equivalent, between the fuel injector line and fittings to assist with removal.

10. Remove the fuel pipe bracket fasteners and fuel injector pipes.
11. Remove the fuel injector bracket bolts (1).
12. Install EN 46954 puller into the bolt hole in the fuel injector bracket.
13. Install a flare nut wrench onto EN 46954 puller, and work the tool outward until the injector releases from its seat.
14. Remove the EN 46954 puller.
15. Remove the fuel injectors with brackets.
16. Remove and discard the copper washer from the fuel injector bore.
17. Remove and discard the fuel injector O-ring from the injector.

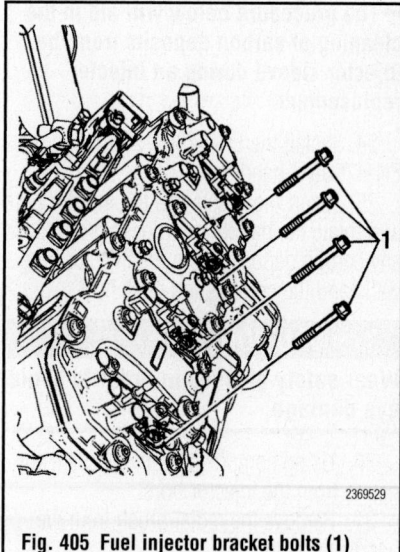

Fig. 405 Fuel injector bracket bolts (1)

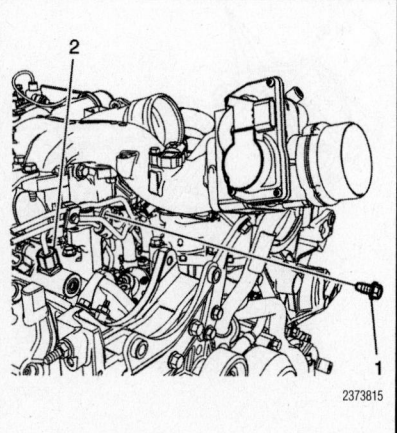

Fig. 403 High pressure fuel pipe fastener (1) and fitting (2)

Fig. 404 Engine wiring harness bracket fasteners (1)

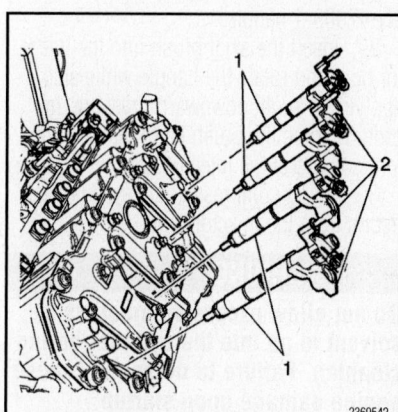

Fig. 406 Install a flare nut wrench onto EN 46954 puller, and work the tool outward until the injector releases from its seat

18. Clean and inspect the fuel injector and injector bore.

Fuel Injector Cleaning and Inspection

➡ **If reusing the old injectors perform the following:**

19. Use a soft bristle non-metallic brush and Top Engine Cleaner, GM P/N 1052626 or equivalent, to remove any deposits from the nozzle tip and the copper washer sealing area (2) before re-installation.

20. Inspect the fuel injector nozzle tip for any signs of discoloration (dark yellow, tan or blue) due to excessive heat.

21. Replace the injector if any damage is found.

22. Clean the fuel injector high pressure line.

23. Inspect the fuel injector line for excessive corrosion or damage to the sealing surfaces. Replace the line if any damage is found.

Injector Bore Cleaning

➡**The procedure below will aid in the cleaning of carbon deposits from the injector sleeve during an injector replacement**

24. Install the EN-47909-2 brush to the EN-47909-1 handle .

25. Insert the brush into the injector bore and rotate the handle in order to break loose any carbon deposits from the injector bore walls and the combustion deck hole.

✳✳ CAUTION

Wear safety glasses in order to avoid eye damage.

26. Using compressed air, evacuate any debris from the injector bore.

27. Remove the radial brush from the handle assembly.

28. Install the EN-47909-3 brush to the EN-47909-1 handle.

29. Insert the axial brush into the injector bore and rotate the handle while also applying a slight downward pressure, in order to force the brush ends into the bottom corners of the injector bore.

30. Using compressed air, evacuate any debris from the injector bore.

✳✳ WARNING

Do not allow excessive amounts of solvent to go into the cylinder during cleaning. Failure to do so may cause engine damage upon startup.

31. Lightly dampen EN-47909-20 swab with Top Engine Cleaner, GM P/N 1052626 (Canadian P/N 993026) or equivalent, and

wipe away any deposits from the injector bore.

32. Inspect the injector bore for any deposits and repeat brushing if necessary.

✳✳ CAUTION

Keep hands and face clear of glow plug holes while cranking. Hot liquid or gases may be expelled during cranking.

33. If necessary, crank the engine in order to expel any solvent before starting the engine.

   a. Remove the glow plugs. Refer to Glow Plug.

   b. Disable the fuel system.

   c. Disconnect the Crankshaft Position (CKP) sensor electrical connector.

   d. Crank the engine in order to expel any excessive solvent.

   e. Using the cotton swabs supplied with the kit, wipe the injector bore clean of any solvent and/or debris.

   f. Connect the CKP sensor electrical connector.

   g. Enable the fuel system.

   h. Reinstall the glow plugs.

To install:

34. Install a NEW copper washer to the fuel injector bore.

35. Install a NEW fuel injector O-ring to the injector.

36. Install the fuel injectors with brackets.

37. Install the fuel injector bracket fasteners and tighten to 22 ft. lbs. (30 Nm).

✳✳ WARNING

Ensure proper torquing of the fuel injector line. An under-torqued fuel injector line will not seal properly and an over-torqued fuel injector line may damage the fuel injector fitting. An improperly sealed or damaged fuel injector line or fuel injector fitting will cause a fuel leak.

38. Install the left fuel injector pipes and tighten to 22 ft. lbs. (30 Nm).

39. Install the fuel pipe bracket fasteners and tighten to 89 inch lbs. (10 Nm)

40. After installing the fuel injector pipes, clean the injector pipes and apply sealant GM P/N 97720043, at the fittings to prevent moisture and debris from collecting between the line and fitting.

41. Reposition and connect and the fuel return pipes.

42. Connect the fuel injector electrical connectors.

43. Position the engine wiring harness, and install the engine wiring harness bracket fasteners and tighten to 15 ft. lbs. (21 Nm).

44. Install the glow plug module and bracket.

45. If equipped, install the auxiliary generator.

46. Install the upper fan shroud.

47. If the fuel injectors were replaced, the module must be programmed.

48. Prime the fuel system.

49. Start the engine. If the engine stalls, repeat the above step.

50. Once the engine starts, inspect for fuel leaks.

Right Side

See Figure 407.

1. Remove the upper fan shroud.

2. Remove the exhaust gas recirculation bracket.

✳✳ WARNING

Label all the injector electrical connectors before you remove them in order to prevent reconnecting to the wrong injector. Failure to properly connect the injectors in the correct sequence will cause severe engine damage.

3. Disconnect the fuel injector electrical connectors.

4. Disconnect and reposition the fuel return pipes.

➡**Prior to removal of the fuel injector pipes, use compressed air to remove any debris from the injector line and fittings.**

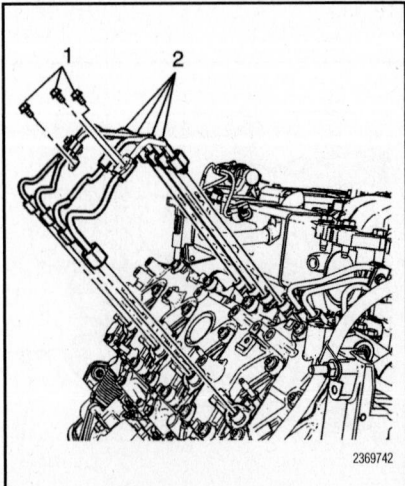

Fig. 407 Fuel pipe bracket fasteners (1) and fuel injector pipes (2)

➡Spray lithium grease, GM P/N 12346293 or equivalent, between the fuel injector line and fittings to assist with removal.

5. Remove the fuel pipe bracket fasteners (1) and fuel injector pipes (2).

6. Remove the fuel injector bracket bolts.

7. Install the EN-46954 puller into the bolt hole in the fuel injector bracket.

8. Install a flare nut wrench onto the EN-46954 puller, and work the tool outward until the injector releases from its seat.

9. Remove the EN-46954 puller.

10. Remove the fuel injectors with brackets.

11. Remove and discard the copper washer from the fuel injector bore.

12. Remove and discard the fuel injector O-ring from the injector.

Fuel Injector Cleaning and Inspection

➡If reusing the old injectors perform the following:

13. Use a soft bristle non-metallic brush and Top Engine Cleaner, GM P/N 1052626 or equivalent, to remove any deposits from the nozzle tip and the copper washer sealing area (2) before re-installation.

14. Inspect the fuel injector nozzle tip for any signs of discoloration (dark yellow, tan or blue) due to excessive heat.

15. Replace the injector if any damage is found.

16. Clean the fuel injector high pressure line.

17. Inspect the fuel injector line for excessive corrosion or damage to the sealing surfaces. Replace the line if any damage is found.

Injector Bore Cleaning

➡The procedure below will aid in the cleaning of carbon deposits from the injector sleeve during an injector replacement

18. Install the EN-47909-2 brush to the EN-47909-1 handle .

19. Insert the brush into the injector bore and rotate the handle in order to break loose any carbon deposits from the injector bore walls and the combustion deck hole.

❈❈ CAUTION

Wear safety glasses in order to avoid eye damage.

20. Using compressed air, evacuate any debris from the injector bore.

21. Remove the radial brush from the handle assembly.

22. Install the EN-47909-3 brush to the EN-47909-1 handle.

23. Insert the axial brush into the injector bore and rotate the handle while also applying a slight downward pressure, in order to force the brush ends into the bottom corners of the injector bore.

24. Using compressed air, evacuate any debris from the injector bore.

❈❈ WARNING

Do not allow excessive amounts of solvent to go into the cylinder during cleaning. Failure to do so may cause engine damage upon startup.

25. Lightly dampen EN-47909-20 swab with Top Engine Cleaner, GM P/N 1052626 (Canadian P/N 993026) or equivalent, and wipe away any deposits from the injector bore.

26. Inspect the injector bore for any deposits and repeat brushing if necessary.

❈❈ CAUTION

Keep hands and face clear of glow plug holes while cranking. Hot liquid or gases may be expelled during cranking.

27. If necessary, crank the engine in order to expel any solvent before starting the engine.

a. Remove the glow plugs. Refer to Glow Plug.

b. Disable the fuel system.

c. Disconnect the Crankshaft Position (CKP) sensor electrical connector.

d. Crank the engine in order to expel any excessive solvent.

e. Using the cotton swabs supplied with the kit, wipe the injector bore clean of any solvent and/or debris.

f. Connect the CKP sensor electrical connector.

g. Enable the fuel system.

h. Reinstall the glow plugs.

To install:

28. Install a NEW copper washer to the fuel injector bore.

29. Install a NEW fuel injector O-ring to the injector.

30. Install the fuel injectors with brackets.

31. Install the fuel injector bracket fasteners and tighten to 22 ft. lbs. (30 Nm).

❈❈ WARNING

Ensure proper torquing of the fuel injector line. An under-torqued fuel injector line will not seal properly and an over-torqued fuel injector line may damage the fuel injector fitting. An improperly sealed or damaged fuel injector line or fuel injector fitting will cause a fuel leak.

32. Install the left fuel injector pipes and tighten to 22 ft. lbs. (30 Nm).

33. Install the fuel pipe bracket fasteners and tighten to 89 inch lbs. (10 Nm)

34. After installing the fuel injector pipes, clean the injector pipes and apply sealant GM P/N 97720043, at the fittings to prevent moisture and debris from collecting between the line and fitting.

35. Reposition and connect and the fuel return pipes.

36. Connect the fuel injector electrical connectors.

37. Position the engine wiring harness, and install the engine wiring harness bracket fasteners and tighten to 15 ft. lbs. (21 Nm).

38. Install the glow plug module and bracket.

39. If equipped, install the auxiliary generator.

40. Install the upper fan shroud.

41. If the fuel injectors were replaced, the module must be programmed.

42. Prime the fuel system.

43. Start the engine. If the engine stalls, repeat the above step.

44. Once the engine starts, inspect for fuel leaks.

FUEL PUMP

REMOVAL & INSTALLATION

See Figure 408.

1. Loosen the fuel cap in order to relieve the fuel system pressure.

2. Raise and support the vehicle.

3. Disconnect the fuel lines.

4. Remove the fuel pump bolt (1).

5. Remove the fuel pump (2).

6. Disconnect the electrical connector.

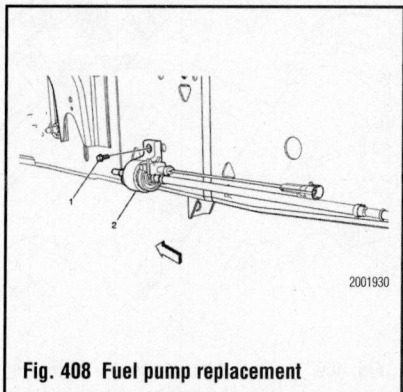

Fig. 408 Fuel pump replacement

To install:

7. Install the fuel pump.

8. Install the fuel pump bolt and tighten to 16 ft. lbs. (22 Nm).

FUEL PRESSURE REGULATOR

REMOVAL & INSTALLATION

See Figure 409.

1. Remove the turbocharger.

2. Disconnect the electrical connector.

3. Remove the two fuel pressure sensor fasteners (1).

4. Remove the fuel pressure regulator.

5. Installation is the reverse of removal. Tighten the two fasteners to 89 inch lbs. (10 Nm)

GLOW PLUGS

REMOVAL & INSTALLATION

See Figure 410.

1. Remove the engine cover.

2. Disconnect the negative battery cable. Refer to Battery Negative Cable Disconnect/Connect in the Engine Electrical section.

3. If necessary, remove the left front wheel and tire.

4. Remove the wheelhouse splash shield.

5. Remove the glow plug harness nut(s).

6. Remove the harness from the glow plug(s).

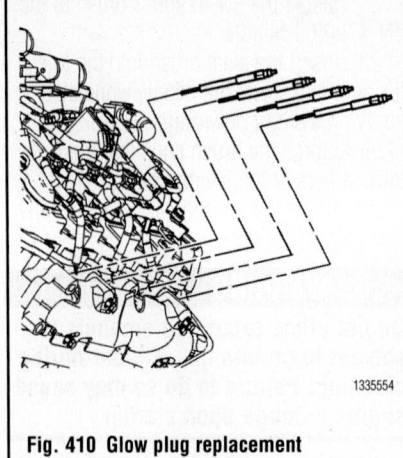

Fig. 410 Glow plug replacement

➡ **If you replace a glow plug is replaced with the tip missing or burned off, you must remove the cylinder head and clean all debris out of the cylinder.**

7. Remove the glow plug(s).

To install:

8. Install the glow plug(s) and tighten to 13 ft. lbs. (18 Nm).

9. Install the harness to the glow plug(s).

10. Install the glow plug harness nut(s) and tighten to 15 inch lbs. (1.7 Nm).

11. Install the left front wheel and tire.

12. Connect the negative battery cable. Refer to Battery Negative Cable Disconnect/Connect in the Engine Electrical section.

13. Install the wheelhouse splash shield.

14. Install the engine cover.

INJECTION PUMP

REMOVAL & INSTALLATION

2010 Models

See Figures 411 through 413.

1. Remove the turbocharger.

2. Remove the high pressure fuel pipes from the fuel injection pump. Refer to Fuel High Pressure Pipe Replacement - Rail to Rail and Fuel High Pressure Pipe Replacement - Pump to Rail.

3. Disconnect the electrical connectors (1).

4. Collapse the hose clamps and remove the fuel return and fuel feed hoses (2).

5. Remove the engine cooling crossover housing.

6. Remove the camshaft gear access hole plug (1).

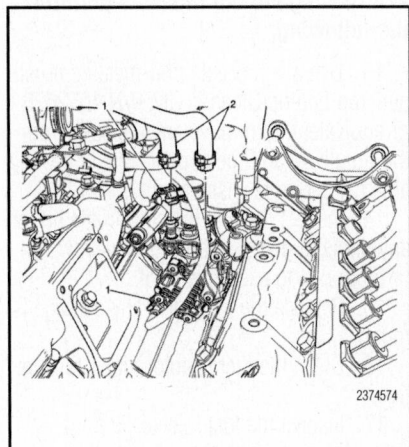

Fig. 411 Electrical connectors (1) and fuel feed hoses (2)

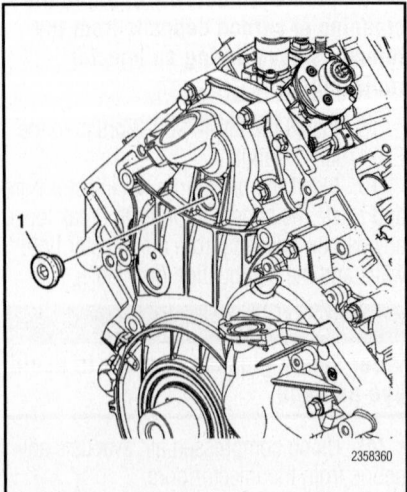

Fig. 412 Camshaft gear access hole plug (1)

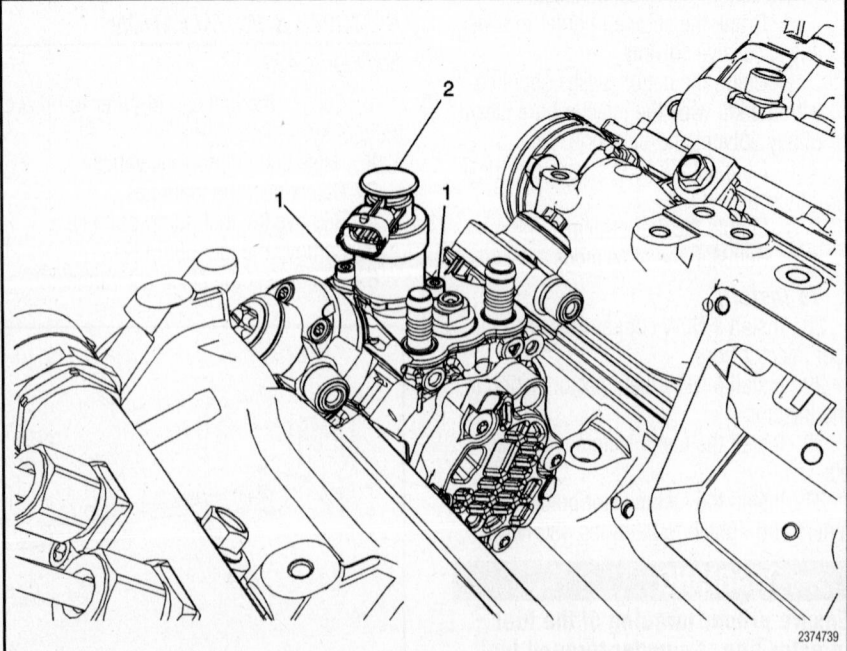

Fig. 409 Two fuel pressure sensor fasteners (1) and fuel pressure regulator (2)

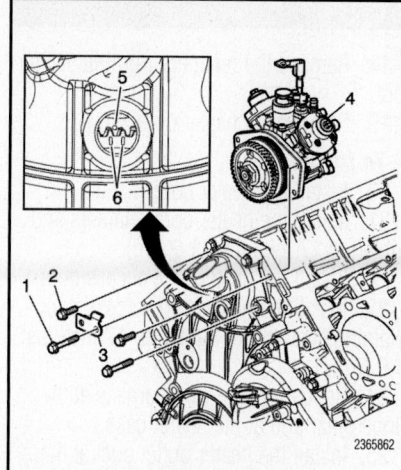

Fig. 413 Fuel injection pump bolts (1, 2), turbocharger cooler return pipe bracket (3), and fuel injection pump (4)

➡**The fuel pump must be correctly timed to the camshaft gear.**

7. Rotate the crankshaft until the fuel injection pump gear timing marks are aligned with camshaft gear timing marks.

8. Remove the fuel injection pump bolts (1) and (2).

9. Remove the turbocharger cooler return pipe bracket (3).

10. Remove the fuel injection pump (4).

11. Preparing the Fuel Injection Pump:

   a. Hold the fuel pump by the drive gear in a vise with copper jaw liners.

   b. Loosen the gear nut until the nut is even with the end of the gear shaft.

   c. Remove the gear from the tapered shaft of the injection pump.

   d. Separate the injection pump and adapter by removing the 3 bolts and spacers.

   e. Inspect the O-ring for damage on the pump adapter and replace, if necessary.

   f. Lubricate the O-ring with clean engine oil.

   g. Clean all mating surfaces.

   h. Install the adapter on the pump.

   i. Install the 3 bolts and spacers and tighten to 15 ft. lbs. (20 Nm).

   j. Install the gear and nut and tighten to 52 ft. lbs. (70 Nm).

To install:

➡**The fuel pump must be correctly timed to the camshaft gear.**

12. Rotate the crankshaft to align the camshaft gear timing marks with the center of the inspection hole

13. Lubricate the O-ring on the fuel injection pump adapter with engine oil.

14. Install the fuel injection pump and adapter assembly (4) so that the timing mark on the fuel pump gear (5) is aligned with the timing marks on the camshaft gear (6).

15. Install the turbocharger cooler return pipe bracket (3).

16. Install the fuel injection pump bolts (1) and (2) and tighten to 18 ft. lbs. (25 Nm).

17. Install the camshaft gear access hole plug (1).

18. Connect the electrical connectors (1).

19. Collapse the hose clamps and install the fuel return and fuel feed hoses (2).

20. Install the engine cooling crossover housing.

21. Install the high pressure fuel pipes from the fuel injection pump.

22. Install the turbocharger.

2011 Models

See Figures 411 through 413.

1. Remove the center intake manifold.

2. Remove the high pressure fuel pipes from the fuel injection pump. Refer to Fuel High Pressure Pipe—Rail to Rail and Fuel High Pressure Pipe Replacement—Pump to Rail.

3. Disconnect the electrical connectors (1).

4. Collapse the hose clamps and remove the fuel return and fuel feed hoses (2).

5. Remove the engine cooling crossover housing.

6. Remove the camshaft gear access hole plug (1).

➡**The fuel pump must be correctly timed to the camshaft gear.**

7. Rotate the crankshaft until the fuel injection pump gear timing marks are aligned with camshaft gear timing marks.

8. Remove the fuel injection pump bolts (1) and (2).

9. Remove the turbocharger cooler return pipe bracket (3).

10. Remove the fuel injection pump (4).

➡**If any metal debris is found, replace the following components: fuel injection pump, fuel rails, fuel injectors, fuel return line assembly, all high pressure fuel pipes, indirect fuel injector, and fuel feed pipes (pump to indirect fuel injector).**

11. Remove the fuel pressure regulator and inspect for metal debris on the end of the regulator tip.

➡**The fuel pump must be correctly timed to the camshaft gear.**

12. Rotate the crankshaft to align the camshaft gear timing marks with the center of the inspection hole

13. Lubricate the O-ring on the fuel injection pump adapter with engine oil.

14. Install the fuel injection pump and adapter assembly (4) so that the timing mark on the fuel pump gear (5) is aligned with the timing marks on the camshaft gear (6).

15. Install the turbocharger cooler return pipe bracket (3).

16. Install the fuel injection pump bolts (1) and (2) and tighten to 18 ft. lbs. (25 Nm).

17. Install the camshaft gear access hole plug (1).

18. Connect the electrical connectors (1).

19. Collapse the hose clamps and install the fuel return and fuel feed hoses (2).

20. Install the engine cooling crossover housing.

21. Install the high pressure fuel pipes from the fuel injection pump.

22. Install the center intake manifold.

HEATING & AIR CONDITIONING SYSTEM

BLOWER MOTOR

REMOVAL & INSTALLATION

See Figure 414.

1. Remove the coolant reservoir.
2. Disconnect the blower motor electrical connector (2).
3. Remove the blower motor cooling tube (3).
4. Remove the blower motor retaining screws (1).
5. Remove the blower motor.
6. Remove the retaining clip from the fan cage.
7. Remove the fan cage from the blower motor.

To install:

8. Install the fan cage to the blower motor.
9. Install the retaining clip to the fan cage.
10. Install the blower motor.
11. Install the blower motor retaining screws and tighten to 18 inch lbs. (2 Nm).
12. Install the blower motor cooling tube.
13. Connect the blower motor electrical connector.
14. Install the coolant reservoir.

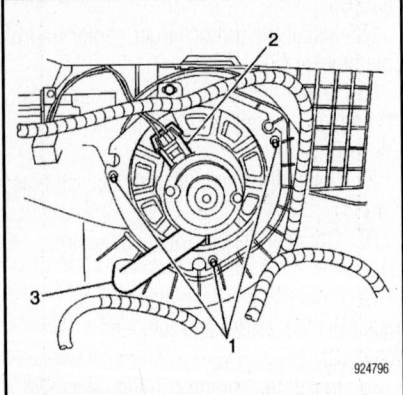

Fig. 414 Blower motor electrical connector (2), cooling tube (3) and retaining screws (1)

HEATER CORE

REMOVAL & INSTALLATION

See Figures 415 and 416.

1. Drain the engine coolant. Refer to Cooling System Drain and Refill in the Engine Cooling section.
2. Remove the A/C accumulator.
3. Remove the engine cover.
4. Remove the right knee bolster bracket.
5. Remove the cowl drain tube bolts.
6. Remove the cowl drain tube.
7. Remove the hose clamps using the J 38185.
8. Remove the inlet and outlet heater hoses from the heater core.
9. Remove the right hinge pillar trim.
10. Remove the ground lead at the right hinge pillar.
11. Remove the harness connector and bracket in the right hinge pillar.
12. Disconnect the radio antenna lead-in cable at the right hinge pillar.
13. Remove the heater outlet duct at the left side of the heater case.
14. Reposition the wire harness at the hinge pillar and at the heater case.
15. Remove the screws from the heater assembly.
16. CAREFULLY open the heater core access door in order to cut the heater core access door.
17. Cut the marked section of the heater core access door and remove the access door.

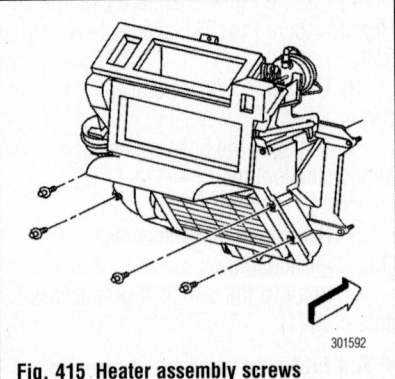

Fig. 415 Heater assembly screws

18. Remove the retainers from the heater core.
19. Remove the heater core.

To install:

20. Install the heater core.
21. Install the heater core retainers and tighten to 17 inch lbs. (1.9 Nm).
22. Install the heater core access door.
23. Install the heater core access door retaining screws and tighten to 17 inch lbs. (1.9 Nm).
24. Reposition the wire harness at the hinge pillar and at the heater case.
25. Install the heater outlet duct at the left side of the heater case.
26. Connect the antenna lead-in cable.
27. Install the harness connector and bracket to the hinge pillar.
28. Install the ground lead at the hinge pillar.
29. Install hinge pillar trim.
30. Install the inlet and outlet heater hoses to the heater core.
31. Install the heater hose clamps using the J 38185.
32. Install the cowl drain tube and bolts.
33. Install the right knee bolster bracket.
34. Install the engine cover.
35. Install the A/C accumulator.
36. Fill the engine coolant. Refer to Cooling System Drain and Refill in the Engine Cooling section.

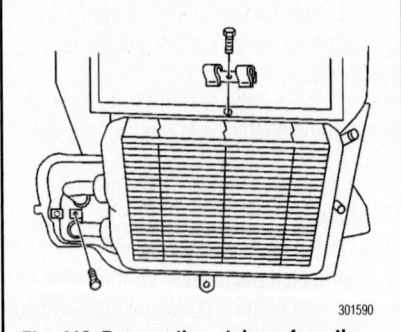

Fig. 416 Remove the retainers from the heater core.

STEERING

POWER STEERING GEAR

REMOVAL & INSTALLATION

Non-Rack & Pinion—2010 Models
See Figures 417 through 421.

✳✳ WARNING

With wheels of the vehicle facing straight ahead, secure the steering wheel utilizing steering column anti-rotation pin, steering column lock, or a strap to prevent rotation. Locking of the steering column will prevent damage and a possible malfunction of the SIR system. The steering wheel must be secured in position before disconnecting the following components:

- The steering column
- The intermediate shaft(s)
- The steering gear

✳✳ WARNING

After disconnecting these components, do not rotate the steering wheel or move the front tires and wheels. Failure to follow this procedure may cause the SIR coil assembly to become un-centered and cause possible damage to the SIR coil. If you think the SIR coil has became un-centered, refer to your specific SIR coil's centering procedure to re-center SIR Coil.

1. Install the J-42640 pin in the steering column lower access hole in order to lock the steering column.

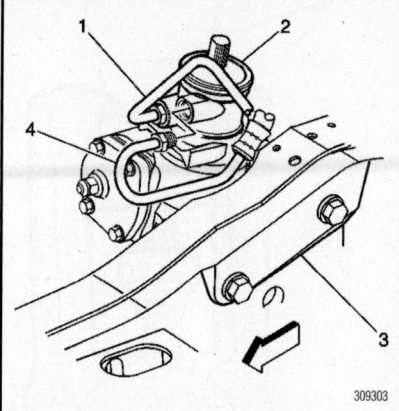

Fig. 418 Power brake booster outlet hose (4), power steering gear outlet hose or the power steering cooler hose (1), power steering gear (2).

2. Raise and support the vehicle.
3. Place a drain pan under the vehicle.
4. Remove the engine protection shield.
5. Disconnect the lower intermediate shaft from the power steering gear.
6. Disconnect the power brake booster outlet hose (4) and power steering gear outlet hose or the power steering cooler hose (1) from the power steering gear (2).
7. Cap the ends of the hoses and the power steering gear fittings in order to prevent the entrance of dirt.
8. Remove the pitman arm to relay rod retaining nut.
9. Disconnect the pitman arm from relay rod using the J-24319-B puller.
10. Disconnect the stabilizer shaft links from the stabilizer shaft.

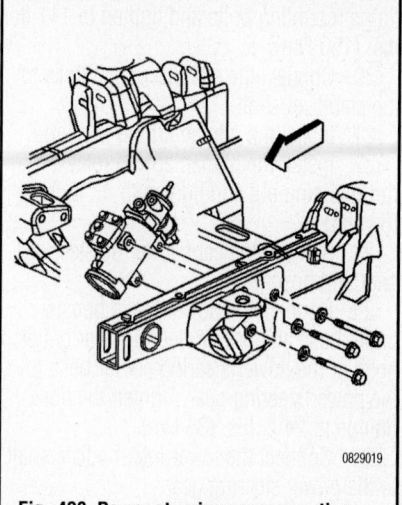

Fig. 420 Power steering gear mounting bolts

11. Move the stabilizer shaft down in order to access the lower steering gear bolts.
12. Remove the power steering gear mounting bolts.
13. Remove the power steering gear from the vehicle.
14. Remove the pitman arm to power steering gear retaining nut and washer.
15. Remove the pitman arm from the power steering gear using the J-6632-01 puller or the J-29107-A puller.

To install:

16. Install the pitman arm to the power steering gear.
17. Install the pitman arm to power steering gear retaining nut and washer and tighten to 184 ft. lbs. (250 Nm).

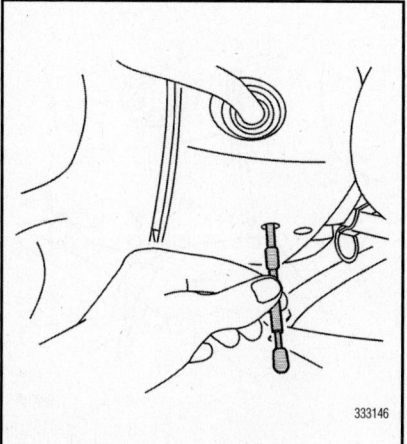

Fig. 417 Install the J-42640 pin in the steering column lower access hole in order to lock the steering column

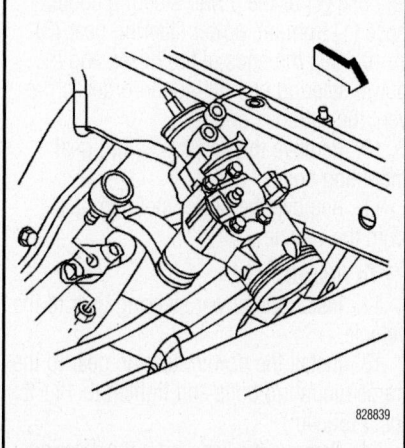

Fig. 419 Disconnect the pitman arm from the relay rod using the J-24319-B puller.

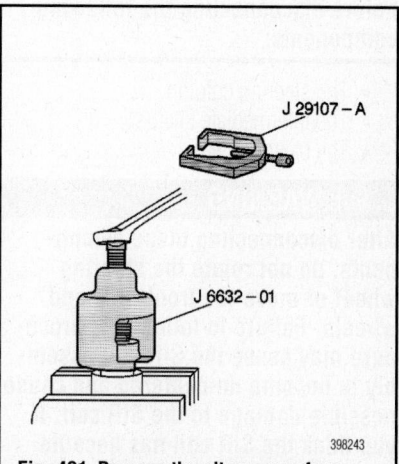

Fig. 421 Remove the pitman arm from the power steering gear using the J-6632-01 puller or the J-29107-A puller

18. Install the power steering gear to the vehicle.

19. Install the power steering gear to the frame mounting bolts and tighten to 111 ft. lbs. (150 Nm).

20. Connect the stabilizer shaft links to the stabilizer shaft.

21. Install the pitman arm to relay rod.

22. Install the pitman arm to relay rod retaining nut and tighten to 47 ft. lbs. (63 Nm).

23. Remove the caps from the steering gear and hoses.

24. Connect the power brake booster outlet hose and power steering gear outlet hose or the power steering cooler hose to the power steering gear. Tighten the hose fittings to 24 ft. lbs. (33 Nm).

25. Connect the lower intermediate shaft to the power steering gear.

26. Install the engine protection shield.

27. Lower the vehicle.

28. Remove the J-42640 pin from the steering column lower access hole.

29. Bleed the power steering system.

30. Remove the drain pan from under the vehicle.

Rack & Pinion

2010 Models

See Figures 422, 423 and 425.

✳✳ WARNING

With wheels of the vehicle facing straight ahead, secure the steering wheel utilizing steering column anti-rotation pin, steering column lock, or a strap to prevent rotation. Locking of the steering column will prevent damage and a possible malfunction of the SIR system. The steering wheel must be secured in position before disconnecting the following components:

- The steering column
- The intermediate shaft(s)
- The steering gear

✳✳ WARNING

After disconnecting these components, do not rotate the steering wheel or move the front tires and wheels. Failure to follow this procedure may cause the SIR coil assembly to become un-centered and cause possible damage to the SIR coil. If you think the SIR coil has became un-centered, refer to your specific SIR coil's centering procedure to re-center SIR Coil.

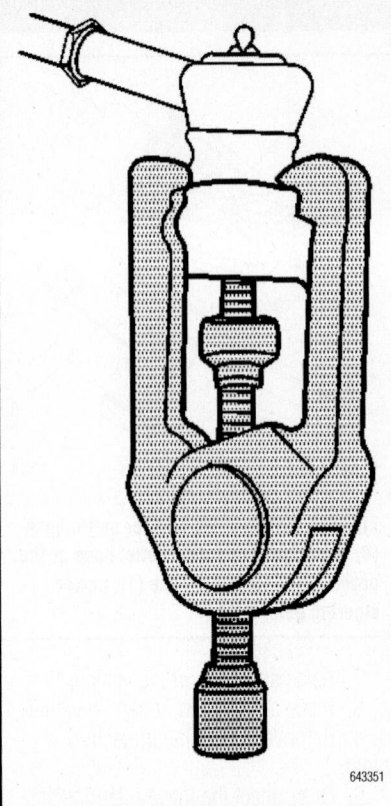

Fig. 422 Disconnect the outer tie rods from the steering knuckles using J 24319-B.

1. Raise and support the vehicle.

2. Place drain pans under the vehicle.

3. Remove the front tires and wheels.

4. Remove the engine protection shield.

5. Remove the outer tie rods retaining nuts.

6. Disconnect the outer tie rods from the steering knuckles using J 24319-B.

7. Disconnect the lower intermediate shaft from the power steering gear.

8. Disconnect the power brake booster outlet hose (2) and power steering gear outlet hose (1) or the power steering cooler hose (1) from the power steering gear (3).

9. Cap the ends of the hoses and the power steering gear fittings in order to prevent the entrance of dirt.

10. Remove the power steering gear mounting bolts.

11. Remove the power steering gear from the vehicle.

To install:

12. Install the power steering gear to the vehicle.

13. Install the power steering gear to the frame mounting bolts and tighten to 111 ft. lbs. (150 Nm).

14. Remove the caps from the steering gear and hoses.

15. Connect the power brake booster

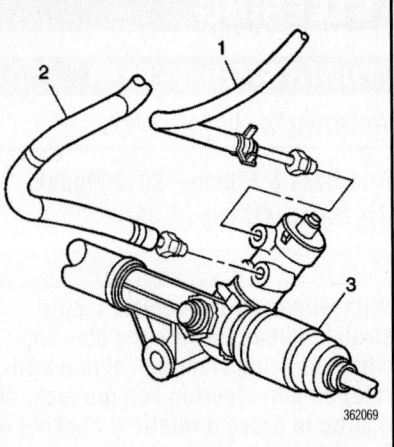

Fig. 423 Disconnect the power brake booster outlet hose (2) and power steering gear outlet hose (1) or the power steering cooler hose (1) from the power steering gear (3)

outlet hose and power steering gear outlet hose or the power steering cooler hose to the power steering gear. Tighten the hose fittings to 24 ft. lbs. (33 Nm).

16. Connect the lower intermediate shaft to the power steering gear.

17. Install the outer tie rods retaining nuts and tighten to 47 ft. lbs. (63 Nm).

18. Install the engine protection shield.

19. Install the front tires and wheels.

20. Lower the vehicle.

21. Bleed the power steering system.

22. Remove the drain pan from under the vehicle.

23. Check the wheel alignment.

2011 Models

See Figures 424 through 426.

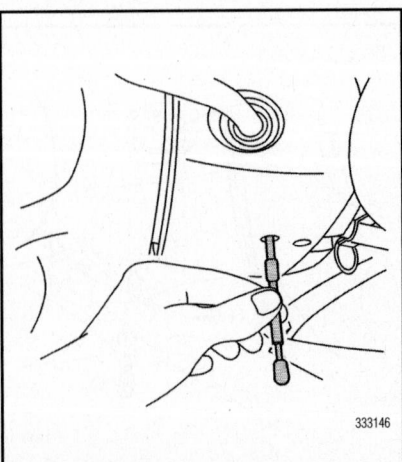

Fig. 424 Install the J-42640 pin in the steering column lower access hole in order to lock the steering column

✳✳ WARNING

With wheels of the vehicle facing straight ahead, secure the steering wheel utilizing steering column anti-rotation pin, steering column lock, or a strap to prevent rotation. Locking of the steering column will prevent damage and a possible malfunction of the SIR system. The steering wheel must be secured in position before disconnecting the following components:

- The steering column
- The intermediate shaft(s)
- The steering gear

✳✳ WARNING

After disconnecting these components, do not rotate the steering wheel or move the front tires and wheels. Failure to follow this procedure may cause the SIR coil assembly to become un-centered and cause possible damage to the SIR coil. If you think the SIR coil has became un-centered, refer to your specific SIR coil's centering procedure to re-center SIR Coil.

1. Install the J-42640 pin in the steering column lower access hole in order to lock the steering column.
2. Raise and support the vehicle.
3. Place drain pans under the vehicle.
4. Remove as much power steering fluid from the reservoir as possible.
5. Raise and support the vehicle.
6. Remove the front tire and wheel assemblies.
7. Remove the engine protection shield.

8. Remove the outer tie rod end retaining nuts.
9. Use the J-24319-B puller in order to disconnect the outer tie rods from the steering knuckles.
10. Disconnect the lower intermediate shaft from the power steering gear.

✳✳ WARNING

Do not start the vehicle with any power steering gear inlet or outlet hoses disconnected. When disconnected, plug or cap all openings of components. Failure to do so could result in contamination or loss of power steering fluid and damage to the system.

11. Disconnect the power brake booster outlet hose (2) and power steering gear outlet hose (1) or the power steering cooler hose (1) from the power steering gear (3).
12. Cap the ends of the hoses and the power steering gear fittings in order to prevent the entrance of dirt.
13. Remove the power steering gear mounting bolts.
14. Remove the power steering gear from the vehicle.

To install:
15. Position the power steering gear in the vehicle.
16. Install the power steering gear to the frame mounting bolts and tighten to 111 ft. lbs. (150 Nm).
17. Remove the caps from the steering gear and hoses.
18. Connect the power brake booster outlet hose and power steering gear outlet hose or the power steering cooler hose to the power steering gear. Tighten the hose fittings to 25 ft. lbs. (34 Nm)

19. Connect the lower intermediate shaft to the power steering gear.
20. Connect the outer tie rods to the steering knuckles.
21. Install the outer tie rods retaining nuts and tighten to 47 ft. lbs. (63 Nm).
22. Install the engine protection shield.
23. Install the front tire and wheel assemblies.
24. Lower the vehicle.
25. Remove the J-42640 pin from the steering column lower access hole.
26. Fill and bleed the power steering system. Refer to Power Steering System Bleeding.
27. Clean any excess power steering fluid from the vehicle.
28. Remove the drain pans from under the vehicle.
29. Measure and adjust the front toe.

Recirculating Ball

2011 Models
See Figures 424 and 427.

✳✳ WARNING

With wheels of the vehicle facing straight ahead, secure the steering wheel utilizing steering column anti-rotation pin, steering column lock, or a strap to prevent rotation. Locking of the steering column will prevent damage and a possible malfunction of the SIR system. The steering wheel must be secured in position before disconnecting the following components:

- The steering column
- The intermediate shaft(s)
- The steering gear

✳✳ WARNING

After disconnecting these components, do not rotate the steering wheel or move the front tires and wheels. Failure to follow this procedure may cause the SIR coil assembly to become un-centered and cause possible damage to the SIR coil. If you think the SIR coil has became un-centered, refer to your specific SIR coil's centering procedure to re-center SIR Coil.

1. Install the J-42640 pin in the steering column lower access hole in order to lock the steering column.
2. Place drain pans under the vehicle.
3. Remove as much power steering fluid from the reservoir as possible.

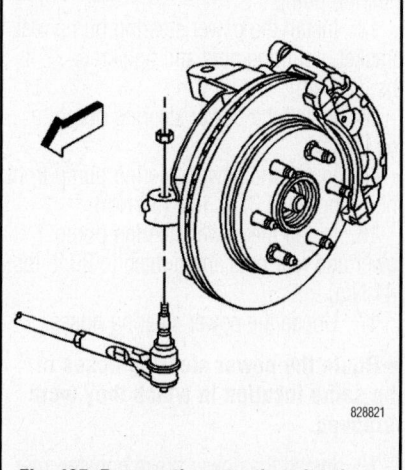

Fig. 425 Remove the outer tie rod end retaining nuts.

828821

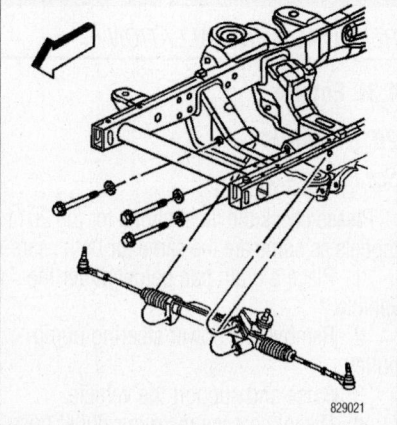

Fig. 426 Power steering gear mounting bolts and the steering gear

829021

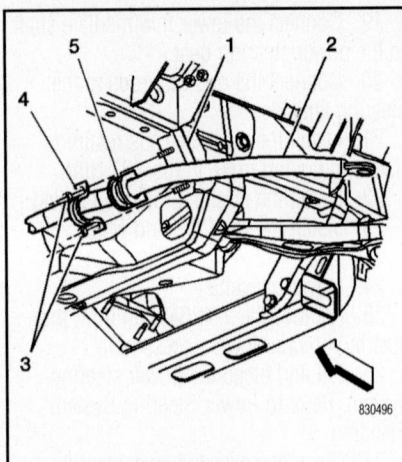

Fig. 427 Stabilizer shaft insulator clamp nuts/studs (3) and shaft (2)

4. Raise and support the vehicle.

5. Remove the engine protection shield.

6. Disconnect the lower intermediate shaft from the power steering gear.

✳✳ WARNING

Do not start the vehicle with any power steering gear inlet or outlet hoses disconnected. When disconnected, plug or cap all openings of components. Failure to do so could result in contamination or loss of power steering fluid and damage to the system.

7. Disconnect the power brake booster outlet hose and power steering gear outlet hose or the power steering cooler hose from the power steering gear.

8. Cap the ends of the hoses and the power steering gear fittings in order to prevent the entrance of dirt.

9. Remove the pitman arm to relay rod retaining nut.

10. Disconnect the pitman arm from the relay rod using the J-24319-B puller.

➡ **The stabilizer shaft insulator stud may come out of the frame while removing the stabilizer shaft insulator clamp nuts.**

11. Remove the stabilizer shaft insulator clamp nuts (3) and/or studs.

12. Move the stabilizer shaft (2) down in order to disconnect the stabilizer shaft from the frame and access the lower steering gear bolts.

13. Support the stabilizer shaft in order to avoid stress on the stabilizer shaft links.

14. Remove the power steering gear mounting bolts.

15. Remove the power steering gear from the vehicle.

16. Remove the pitman arm to power steering gear retaining nut and washer.

17. Remove the pitman arm from the power steering gear using the J-6632-01 puller or the J-29107-A puller.

To install:

18. Install the pitman arm to the power steering gear.

19. Install the pitman arm to power steering gear retaining nut and washer and tighten to 184 ft. lbs. (250 Nm).

20. Position the power steering gear in the vehicle.

21. Install the power steering gear to the frame mounting bolts and tighten to 111 ft. lbs. (150 Nm).

22. Connect the stabilizer shaft and the insulator clamps to the frame.

23. Install the pitman arm to relay rod.

24. Install the pitman arm to relay rod retaining nut and tighten to 47 ft. lbs. (63 Nm).

25. Remove the caps from the steering gear and hoses.

26. Connect the power brake booster outlet hose and power steering gear outlet hose or the power steering cooler hose to the power steering gear. Tighten the hose fittings to 25 ft. lbs. (34 Nm)

27. Connect the lower intermediate shaft to the power steering gear.

28. Install the engine protection shield.

29. Lower the vehicle.

30. Remove the J-42640 pin from the steering column lower access hole.

31. Fill and bleed the power steering system.

32. Clean any excess power steering fluid from the vehicle.

33. Remove the drain pans from under the vehicle.

34. Measure and adjust the front toe.

POWER STEERING PUMP

REMOVAL & INSTALLATION

4.3L Engine

2010 Models

See Figure 428.

Please check the illustrations for the 2011 models as some are the same for both years.

1. Place a drain pan below under the vehicle.

2. Remove the power steering pump pulley.

3. Raise and support the vehicle.

4. Disconnect the reservoir outlet hose from the power steering pump through the wheel well.

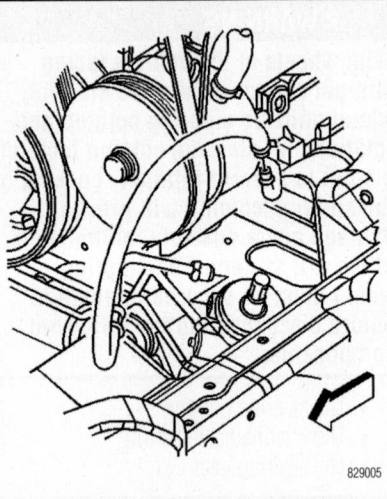

Fig. 428 Disconnect the power steering gear outlet hose or cooler hose from the power steering pump through the wheel well—applies to 4.3L, 4.8L and 5.3L engines

5. Disconnect the power steering gear outlet hose or cooler hose from the power steering pump through the wheel well.

6. Disconnect the power brake booster inlet hose (2) from the power steering pump (1) through the wheel well.

7. Cap the ends of the hose and the power steering pump in order to prevent the entrance of dirt.

8. Remove the power steering pump mounting bolts and the nuts.

9. Remove the power steering pump from the vehicle.

10. Remove the power steering pump rear bracket mounting nuts.

11. Remove the power steering pump rear bracket.

To install:

12. Install the rear bracket to the power steering pump.

13. Install the power steering pump rear bracket mounting nuts and tighten to 37 ft. lbs. (50 Nm).

14. Install the power steering pump to the vehicle.

15. Install the power steering pump front mounting bolts 37 ft. lbs. (50 Nm).

16. Install the power steering pump lower and rear nuts and tighten to 30 ft. lbs. (41 Nm).

17. Uncap the power steering hoses.

➡ **Route the power steering hoses in the same location in which they were removed.**

18. Install the power brake booster inlet hose (2) to the power steering pump

through the wheel well and tighten 24 ft. lbs. (33 Nm).

19. Install the power steering gear outlet hose or cooler hose to the power steering pump through the wheel well.

20. Install the reservoir outlet hose to the power steering pump through the wheel well.

21. Install the power steering pump pulley.

22. Bleed the system. Refer to Power Steering System Bleeding.

23. Remove the drain pan from under the vehicle.

2011 Models

See Figures 429 through 431.

Please check the illustrations for the 2010 models as some are the same for both years.

1. Place drain pans under the vehicle.

2. Remove as much power steering fluid from the reservoir as possible.

3. Remove the power steering pump pulley.

4. Raise and support the vehicle.

※※ WARNING

Do not start the vehicle with any power steering gear inlet or outlet hoses disconnected. When disconnected, plug or cap all openings of components. Failure to do so could result in contamination or loss of power steering fluid and damage to the system.

5. Disconnect the reservoir outlet hose from the power steering pump through the wheel well.

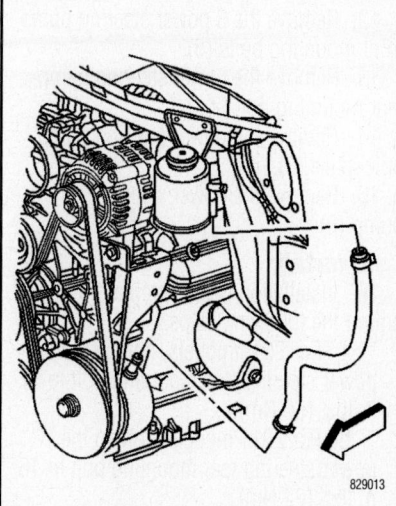

Fig. 429 Disconnect the reservoir outlet hose from the power steering pump through the wheel well—applies to 4.3L, 4.8L, and 5.3L engines

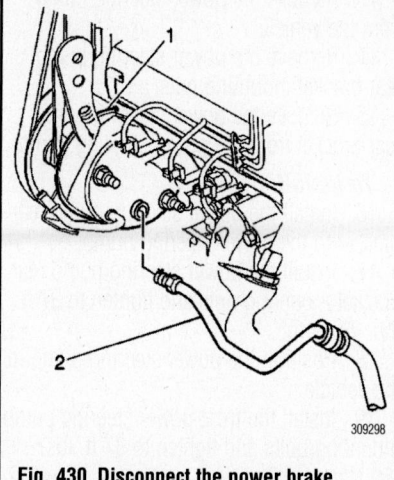

Fig. 430 Disconnect the power brake booster inlet hose (2) from the power steering pump (1) through the wheel well—applies to 4.3L, 4.8L, and 5.3L engines

6. Disconnect the power steering gear outlet hose or the cooler hose from the power steering pump through the wheel well.

7. Disconnect the power brake booster inlet hose (2) from the power steering pump (1) through the wheel well.

8. Cap the ends of the hose and the power steering pump in order to prevent the entrance of dirt.

9. Remove the power steering pump mounting bolts and the nuts.

10. Remove the power steering pump from the vehicle.

11. Remove the power steering pump rear bracket mounting nuts.

12. Remove the power steering pump rear bracket from the power steering pump.

To install:

13. Install the rear bracket to the power steering pump.

14. Install the power steering pump rear bracket mounting nuts and tighten to 37 ft. lbs. (50 Nm).

15. Position the power steering pump in the vehicle.

16. Install the power steering pump front mounting bolts 37 ft. lbs. (50 Nm).

17. Install the power steering pump lower and rear nuts and tighten to 30 ft. lbs. (41 Nm).

18. Uncap the power steering hoses.

※※ WARNING

The inlet and outlet hoses must not be twisted during installation. Do not bend or distort the inlet or outlet hoses to make installation easier. Failure to follow these procedures could result in component damage.

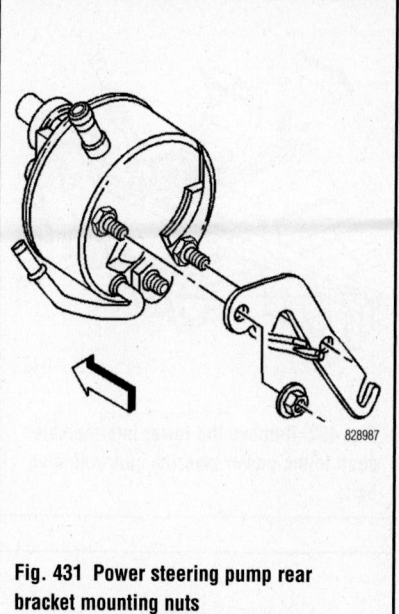

Fig. 431 Power steering pump rear bracket mounting nuts

19. Connect the power brake booster inlet hose (2) to the power steering pump through the wheel well and tighten 25 ft. lbs. (34 Nm)

20. Connect the power steering gear outlet hose or the cooler hose to the power steering pump through the wheel well.

21. Connect the reservoir outlet hose to the power steering pump through the wheel well.

22. Lower the vehicle.

23. Install the power steering pump pulley.

24. Fill and bleed the power steering system. Refer to Power Steering System Bleeding.

25. Clean any excess power steering fluid from the vehicle.

26. Remove the drain pans from under the vehicle.

4.8L & 5.3L Engines

See Figures 432 and 433.

Please check the illustrations for the 4.3L engine as some are the same for both years.

1. Place drain pans under the vehicle.

2. Remove as much power steering fluid from the reservoir as possible.

3. Remove the power steering pump pulley.

4. Remove the lower intermediate shaft to the power steering gear retaining bolt.

5. Disconnect the lower intermediate shaft from the power steering gear.

6. Raise and support the vehicle.

7. Remove the tire and wheel assembly.

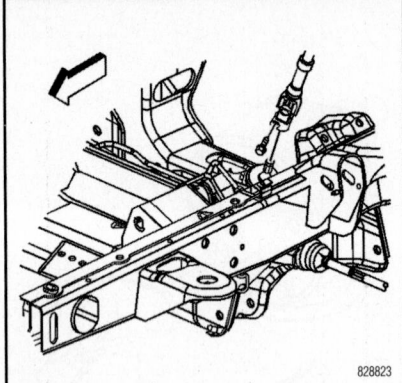

Fig. 432 Remove the lower intermediate shaft to the power steering gear retaining bolt.

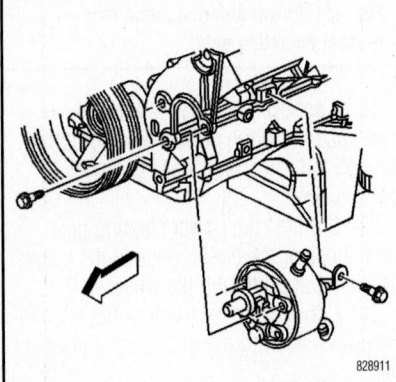

Fig. 433 Power steering pump mounting bolts and pump—applies to 4.3L, 4.8L, and 5.3L engines

✳✳ WARNING

Do not start the vehicle with any power steering gear inlet or outlet hoses disconnected. When disconnected, plug or cap all openings of components. Failure to do so could result in contamination or loss of power steering fluid and damage to the system. Disconnect the reservoir outlet hose from the power steering pump through the wheel well.

8. Disconnect the power steering gear outlet hose or the cooler hose from the power steering pump through the wheel well.

9. Disconnect the power brake booster inlet hose (2) from the power steering pump through the wheel well.

10. Cap the ends of the hose and the pump in order to prevent the entrance of dirt.

11. Remove the rear power steering pump mounting bolt.

12. Remove the front power steering pump mounting bolts.

13. Remove the power steering pump from the vehicle.

14. Remove the power steering pump rear bracket mounting nuts.

15. Remove the power steering pump rear bracket from the power steering pump.

To install:

16. Install the power steering pump rear bracket to the power steering pump.

17. Install the power steering pump rear bracket mounting nuts and tighten to 37 ft. lbs. (50 Nm).

18. Position the power steering pump in the vehicle.

19. Install the front power steering pump mounting bolts and tighten to 37 ft. lbs. (50 Nm).

20. Install the rear power steering pump mounting bolt and tighten to 30 ft. lbs. (41 Nm).

21. Uncap the power steering hoses.

✳✳ WARNING

The inlet and outlet hoses must not be twisted during installation. Do not bend or distort the inlet or outlet hoses to make installation easier. Failure to follow these procedures could result in component damage.

22. Connect the power brake booster inlet hose (2) to the power steering pump through the wheel well and tighten to 25 ft. lbs. (34 Nm)

23. Connect the power steering gear outlet hose or the cooler hose to the power steering pump through the wheel well.

24. Connect the reservoir outlet hose to the power steering pump through the wheel well.

25. Install the tire and wheel assembly.

26. Connect the lower intermediate shaft to the power steering gear.

27. Install the lower intermediate shaft to the power steering gear retaining bolt and tighten to 45 ft. lbs. (61 Nm).

28. Lower the vehicle.

29. Install the power steering pump pulley.

30. Fill and bleed the power steering system. Refer to Power Steering System Bleeding.

31. Clean any excess power steering fluid from the vehicle.

32. Remove the drain pans from under the vehicle.

6.6L Diesel Engine

See Figure 434.

1. Place drain pans under the vehicle.

2. Remove as much power steering fluid from the reservoir as possible.

3. Remove the power steering pump pulley.

4. Raise and support the vehicle.

5. Remove the left front wheelhouse splash shield.

✳✳ WARNING

Do not start the vehicle with any power steering gear inlet or outlet hoses disconnected. When disconnected, plug or cap all openings of components. Failure to do so could result in contamination or loss of power steering fluid and damage to the system.

✳✳ WARNING

The inlet and outlet hoses must not be twisted during installation. Do not bend or distort the inlet or outlet hoses to make installation easier. Failure to follow these procedures could result in component damage.

6. Remove the power steering fluid cooler hose clamp (1).

7. Remove the power steering fluid cooler hose (2).

8. Cap the ends of the hoses and the ports of the pump in order to prevent the entrance of dirt.

9. Remove the power steering fluid reservoir hose clamp (3).

10. Remove the power steering fluid reservoir hose (4).

11. Remove the power brake booster pump inlet hose (5).

12. Remove the 3 power steering pump front mounting bolts (6).

13. Remove the power steering pump rear mounting bolt (7).

14. Remove the power steering pump bolt space (8).

15. Remove the power steering pump (9).

To install:

16. Installation is the reverse of removal, noting the following steps.

   a. For 2010 models, tighten the power steering rear mounting bolt to 37 ft. lbs. (50 Nm).

   b. For 2011 models, tighten the power steering rear mounting bolt to 16 ft. lbs. (22 Nm).

Tighten the 3 power steering pump front mounting bolts to 16 ft. lbs. (22 Nm).

Tighten the power brake booster pump inlet hose to 25 ft. lbs. (34 Nm)

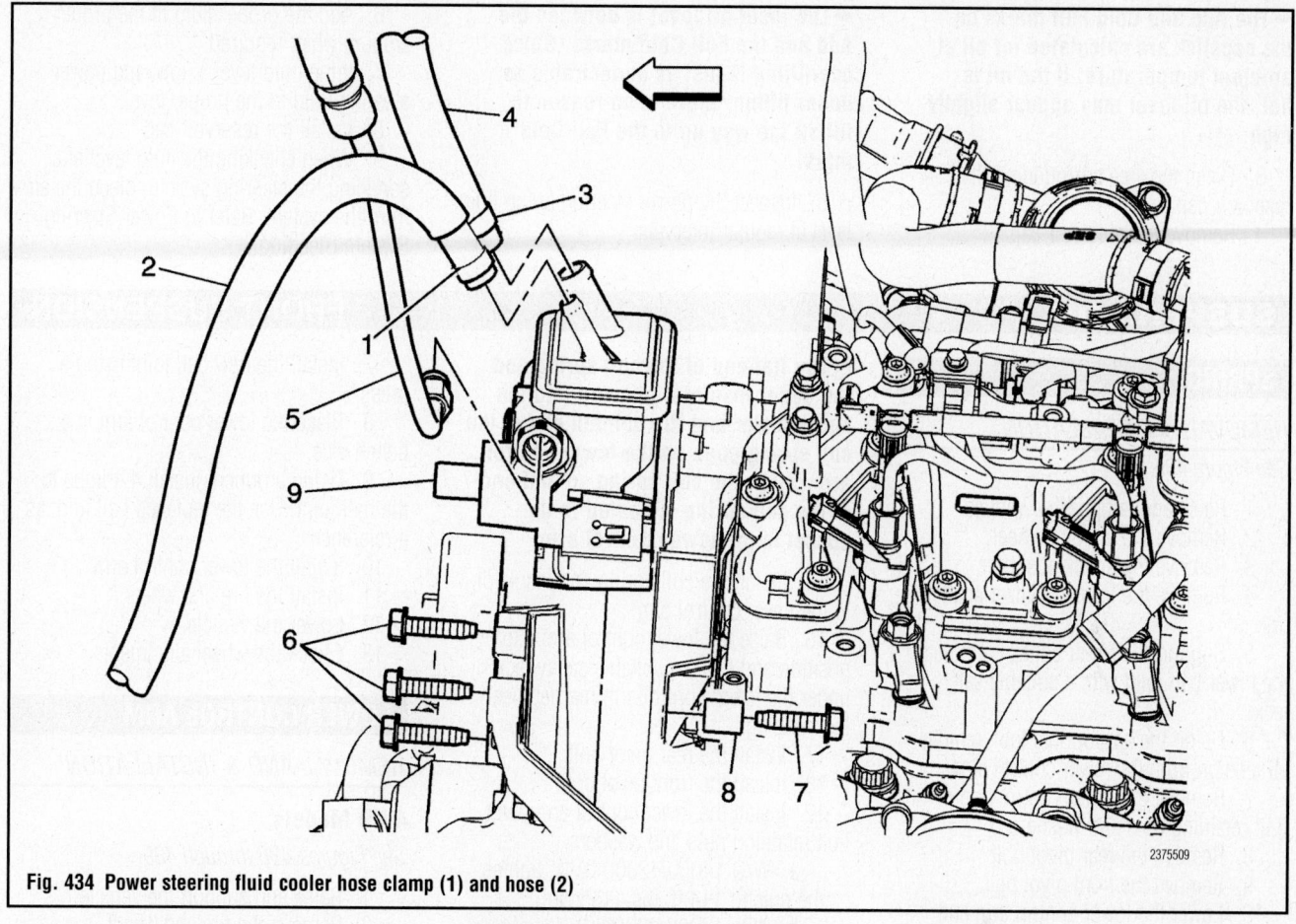

Fig. 434 Power steering fluid cooler hose clamp (1) and hose (2)

2375509

17. If necessary, transfer the lower power steering fluid reservoir.

18. Fill and bleed the power steering system. Refer to Power Steering System Bleeding.

19. Clean any excess power steering fluid from the vehicle.

20. Remove the drain pans from under the vehicle.

BLEEDING

➡Note the following:

• Use clean, new power steering fluid type only. GM Power Steering Fluid GM P/N 89021184 (Canadian P/N 89021186).

• Hoses touching the frame, body or engine may cause system noise. Verify that the hoses do not touch any other part of the vehicle.

• Loose connections may not leak, but could allow air into the steering system. Verify that all hose connections are tight.

➡**Maintain the power steering fluid level throughout the bleed procedure.**

1. Fill pump reservoir with fluid to the minimum system level, FULL COLD level, or the middle of the hash mark on the cap stick fluid level indicator.

➡**With hydro-boost only, the oil level will appear falsely high if the hydro-boost accumulator is not fully charged. Do not apply the brake pedal with the engine OFF. This will discharge the hydro-boost accumulator.**

2. If equipped with hydro-boost, fully charge the hydro-boost accumulator using the following procedure:

   a. Start the engine.

   b. Firmly apply the brake pedal 10–15 times.

   c. Turn the engine OFF.

3. Raise the vehicle until the front wheels are off the ground.

4. Key on engine OFF, turn the steering wheel from stop to stop 12 times.

Vehicles equipped with hydro-boost systems or longer length power steering hoses may require turns up to 15 to 20 stop to stops.

5. Verify the power steering fluid level per operating specification.

6. Start the engine. Rotate the steering wheel from left to right. Check for signs of cavitation or fluid aeration (pump noise/whining).

7. Verify the fluid level. Repeat the bleed procedure, if necessary.

CHECKING AND ADDING POWER STEERING FLUID

✳✳ WARNING

When adding fluid or making a complete fluid change, always use the proper power steering fluid. Failure to use the proper fluid will cause hose and seal damage and fluid leaks.

1. If the power steering system has been serviced, bleed the power steering system to remove any trapped air from the system. Refer to Power Steering System Bleeding.

➡**The oil level will appear falsely high if the hydro-boost accumulator is not fully charged. Do not apply the brake pedal with the engine off, this will discharge the hydro-boost accumulator.**

2. Fully charge the hydro-boost accumulator using the following procedure:

   a. Start the engine.

   b. Firmly apply the brake pedal 2 to 3 times.

   c. Turn the engine Off.

➡The Add and Cold Full marks on the capstick are calculated for oil at ambient temperature. If the oil is hot, the oil level may appear slightly high.

3. Clean the area surrounding the reservoir cap.

4. Remove the reservoir cap.

➡The ideal oil level is between the Add and the Full Cold marks. Since overfilling is just as undesirable as under filling, there is no reason to fill all the way up to the Full Cold mark.

5. Inspect the power steering pump fluid level at regular intervals.

6. Add the proper fluid in the proper amount when required.

7. If the fluid level is low, add power steering fluid to the proper level.

8. Install the reservoir cap.

9. When checking the fluid level after servicing the steering system, bleed the air from the system. Refer to Power Steering System Bleeding.

SUSPENSION

SPRING

REMOVAL & INSTALLATION

See Figure 435.

1. Raise and support the vehicle.
2. Remove the tire and wheel.
3. Remove the shock absorber.
4. Remove the front stabilizer shaft link.
5. Support the lower control arm near the lower ball joint with a suitable safety jack.
6. Using the appropriate tool, remove all tension from the lower control arm.
7. Remove the lower control arm pivot bolt retaining nuts and washers.
8. Remove the rear pivot bolt.
9. Remove the front pivot bolt.
10. Lower the lower control arm and remove the coil spring and insulator.
11. Remove the spring compressor tool from the coil spring.
12. Remove the coil spring insulator from the coil spring.

To install:

13. Install the coil spring insulator to the coil spring.
14. Using the appropriate tool, compress the coil spring.

➡The flat end of the coil spring and the upper insulator goes up into the shock tower and the pointed end of the coil spring goes on the lower control arm. Align the coil spring so that end of the coil spring is seated in the pocket in the lower control arm.

15. Install the coil spring and insulator to the lower control arm.
16. Raise the lower control arm into position and place a suitable safety jack under the lower control arm rear leg near the bushing.
17. Install the rear pivot bolt.
18. Install the front pivot bolt.
19. Install the lower control arm pivot bolt retaining nuts and washers.
   a. W/O 14050/12300 GVW, tighten the nuts to 114 ft. lbs. (155 Nm).
   b. With 14050/12300 GVW, tighten the nuts to 89 ft. lbs. (120 Nm) plus an additional 175°.
   c. With Diesel Engine, tighten the nuts to 89 ft. lbs. (120 Nm) plus an additional 175°.
20. Remove the coil spring compressor tool from the coil spring.
21. Install the front stabilizer shaft link.
22. Install the shock absorber.
23. Install the tire and wheel.
24. Remove the support and lower the vehicle.

LOWER BALL JOINT

REMOVAL & INSTALLATION

1. Raise and support the vehicle.
2. Remove the tire and wheel.
3. Remove the lower control arm.
4. Place the lower control arm in a bench vise.
5. Using a chisel, remove the 4 securing crimps from the ball joint body.
6. Using a press, remove the ball joint from the lower control arm.

To install:

➡Use the outer flange of the ball joint in order to press the ball joint into place.

7. Install the new ball joint using a press.
8. Place the lower control arm in a bench vice.
9. Using a punch, install 4 crimps to the ball joint. Use the replaced ball joint as a reference.
10. Install the lower control arm.
11. Install the tire and wheel.
12. Lower the vehicle.
13. Check the wheel alignment.

LOWER CONTROL ARM

REMOVAL AND & INSTALLATION

4WD Models

See Figures 436 through 439.

1. Raise and support the vehicle.
2. Remove the tire and wheel.
3. Remove the torsion bar.
4. Remove the stabilizer link.
5. Remove the wheel driveshaft.
6. Remove the shock absorber lower retaining nut and bolt.
7. Remove and discard the lower ball joint retaining nut.
8. Using the J 43631 remover and the J 45851 adapters, remove the lower ball joint from the steering knuckle.

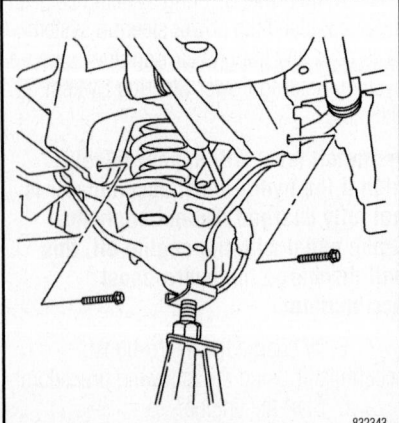

Fig. 435 Lower control arm pivot bolt retaining nuts and washers

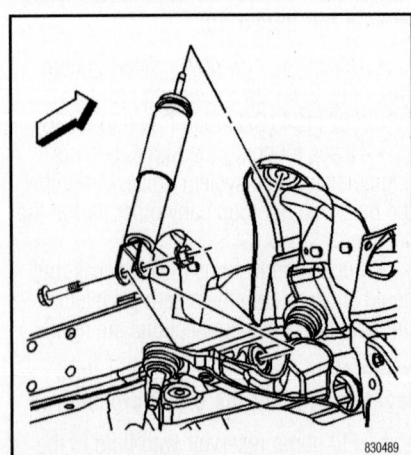

Fig. 436 Shock absorber lower retaining nut and bolt

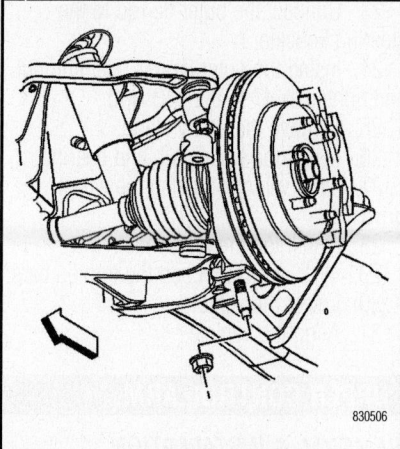

Fig. 437 Lower ball joint retaining nut, applies to both 4WD and RWD models

9. Remove the lower control arm nuts and the washers.

10. Remove the lower control arm bolts.

11. Remove the lower control arm.

To install:

12. Install the lower control arm.

13. Connect the lower ball joint to the steering knuckle.

14. Install the lower control arm mounting bolts.

15. Install the lower control arm mounting nuts and the washers.

　　a. W/O 14050/12300 GVW, tighten the nuts to 114 ft. lbs. (155 Nm).

　　b. With 14050/12300 GVW, tighten the nuts to 89 ft. lbs. (120 Nm) plus 175 degrees.

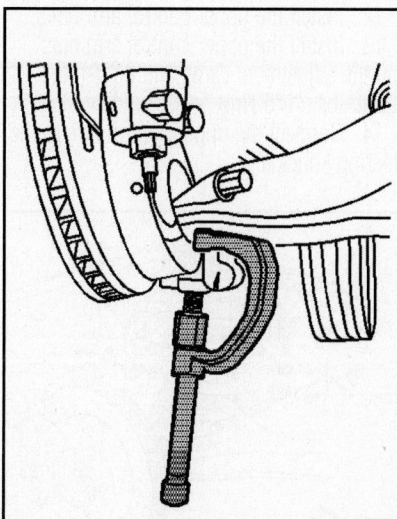

Fig. 438 Using the J 43631 remover and the J 45851 adapters, remove the lower ball joint from the steering knuckle, applies to both 4WD and RWD models

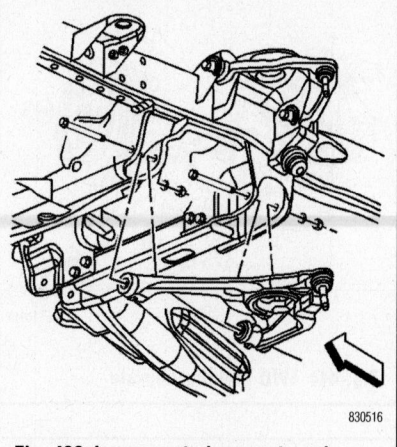

Fig. 439 Lower control arm nuts and washers

　　c. With Diesel Engine, tighten the nuts to 89 ft. lbs. (120 Nm) plus 175 degrees.

16. Install the new lower ball joint retaining nut and tighten to 74 ft. lbs. (100 Nm).

17. Install the shock absorber in the lower control arm.

18. Install the wheel driveshaft.

19. Install the stabilizer link.

20. Install the torsion bar.

21. Install the tire and wheel.

22. Remove the support and lower the vehicle.

23. Check the wheel alignment.

RWD Models

1. Raise and support the vehicle.

2. Remove the tire and wheel.

3. Remove the front coil spring. Refer to Front Springs.

4. Remove and discard the lower ball joint retaining nut (see figure in 4WD).

5. Disconnect the lower ball joint from the steering knuckle using J 43631 and J 45851 (see figure in 4WD).

6. Remove the lower control arm.

To install:

7. Install the lower control arm.

8. Connect the lower ball joint to the steering knuckle.

9. Install the new lower ball joint retaining nut and tighten to 74 ft. lbs. (100 Nm).

10. Install the front coil spring. Refer to Front Springs.

11. Install the tire and wheel.

12. Lower the vehicle.

13. Check the wheel alignment.

STABILIZER SHAFT

REMOVAL & INSTALLATION

See Figure 440.

1. Raise and support the vehicle.

2. Remove the tire and wheel.

3. Remove the stabilizer shaft insulators.

4. Remove the stabilizer shaft link nuts from the stabilizer shaft.

5. Remove the stabilizer shaft.

6. Installation is the reverse of removal.

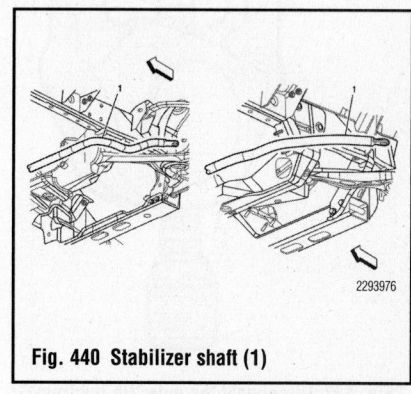

Fig. 440 Stabilizer shaft (1)

STEERING KNUCKLE

REMOVAL & INSTALLATION

See Figures 441 through 445.

1. Raise and support the vehicle.

2. Remove the tire and wheel.

3. 4WD vehicles only: Unload the torsion bars.

4. 4WD vehicles only: Remove the wheel driveshaft.

5. Remove the wheel hub and bearing.

6. Remove the outer tie rod to steering knuckle retaining nut.

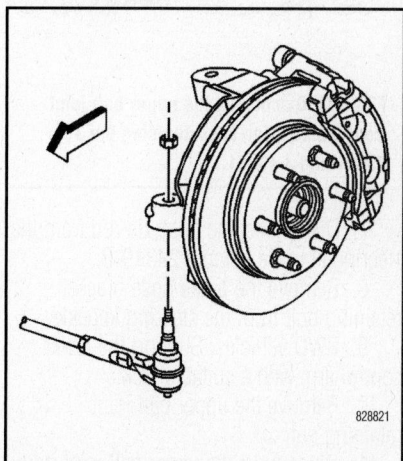

Fig. 441 Outer tie rod-to-steering knuckle retaining nut

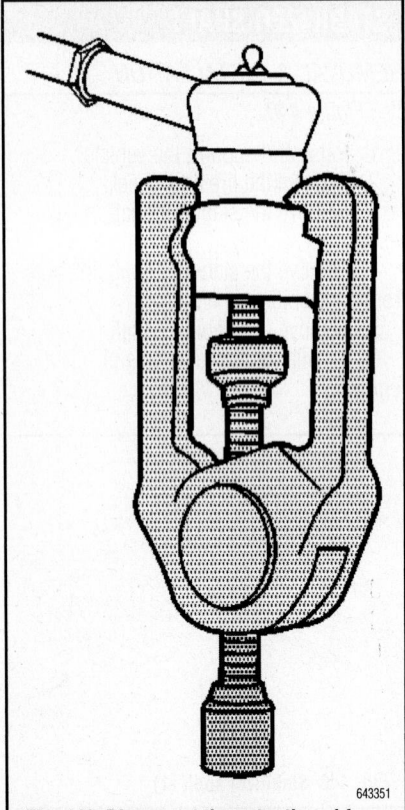

Fig. 442 Disconnect the outer tie rod from the steering knuckle using J 24319-B — 4WD vehicles

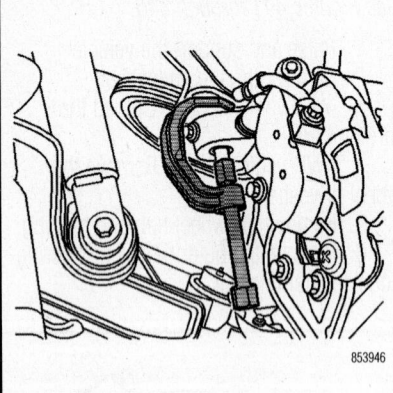

Fig. 443 Disconnect the upper ball joint from the steering knuckle using the J 43631 and J 45851.

7. Disconnect the outer tie rod from the steering knuckle using J 24319-B.

8. Remove the brake hose bracket retaining bolt from the steering knuckle.

9. RWD vehicles: Support the lower control arm with a suitable jack.

10. Remove the upper ball joint retaining nut.

11. Disconnect the upper ball joint from the steering knuckle using the J 43631 and J 45851.

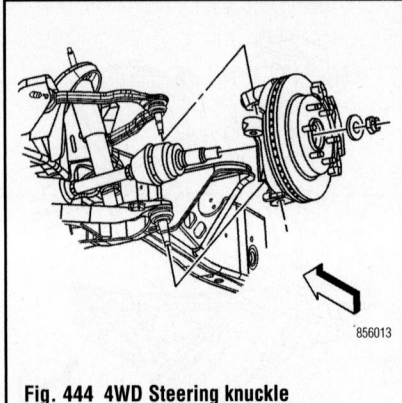

Fig. 444 4WD Steering knuckle

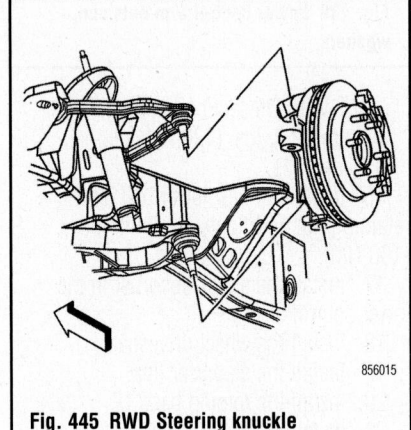

Fig. 445 RWD Steering knuckle

12. 4WD vehicles: Remove the lower control arm retaining nut.

13. RWD vehicles: Remove the lower ball joint retaining nut.

14. Disconnect the lower ball joint from the steering knuckle using the J 43631 and J 45851.

15. Remove the steering knuckle.

To install:

16. Clean all grease and contaminants from the tapered section and the threads of the upper ball joint, the lower ball joint, and the tie rod end.

17. Clean and inspect the taper holes and the mounting surfaces of the steering knuckle. If any of the tapered holes are elongated, out of round, or damaged, replace the steering knuckle.

18. Install the steering knuckle.

19. Install the lower ball joint retaining nut and tighten to 74 ft. lbs. (100 Nm).

20. Install the upper ball joint retaining nut and tighten to 37 ft. lbs. (50 Nm).

21. RWD vehicles: Install the upper ball joint-to steering knuckle retaining nut and tighten to 37 ft. lbs. (50 Nm).

22. Install the brake hose bracket to steering knuckle retaining bolt and tighten to 89 inch lbs. (10 Nm).

23. Connect the outer tie rod to the steering knuckle.

24. Install the outer tie rod retaining nut and tighten to 47 ft. lbs. (63 Nm).

25. Remove the safety stand.

26. Install the wheel hub and bearing.

27. 4WD vehicles: Install the wheel driveshaft.

28. Install the tire and wheel.

29. 4WD vehicles: Load the torsion bars.

30. Lower the vehicle.

31. Align the vehicle.

UPPER CONTROL ARM

REMOVAL & INSTALLATION

See Figures 446 through 448.

1. Raise and support the vehicle.

2. Support lower control arm with a jack stand.

3. Remove the tire and wheel.

4. Remove the retaining bolts for the brake hose and the wheel speed sensor brackets.

5. Remove the wheel driveshaft (4WD only).

6. Remove and discard the upper ball joint retaining nut.

7. Disconnect the upper control arm from the steering knuckle using the J 43631 and J 45851.

8. Remove the upper control arm nuts and the adjustment cams.

9. Remove the upper control arm bolts.

10. Remove the upper control arm.

To install:

11. Install the upper control arm.

12. Install the upper control arm bolts.

13. Install the upper control arm nuts and the adjustment cams and tighten to 129 ft. lbs. (175 Nm).

14. Connect the upper control arm to the steering knuckle.

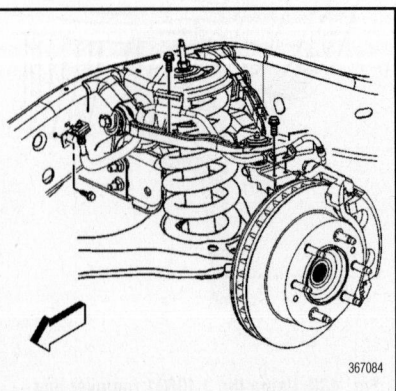

Fig. 446 Remove the retaining bolts for the brake hose and the wheel speed sensor brackets

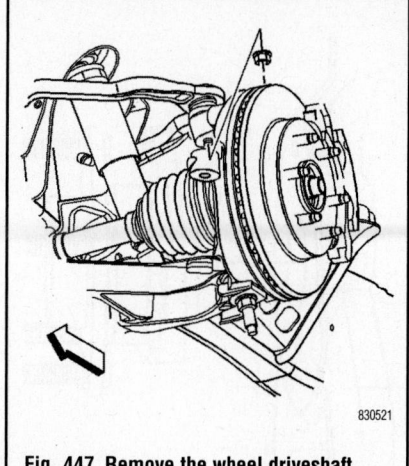

Fig. 447 Remove the wheel driveshaft (4WD only).

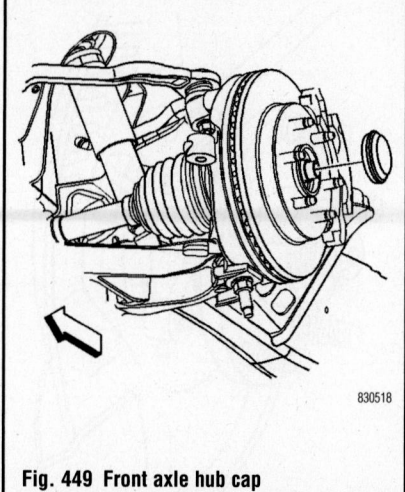

Fig. 449 Front axle hub cap

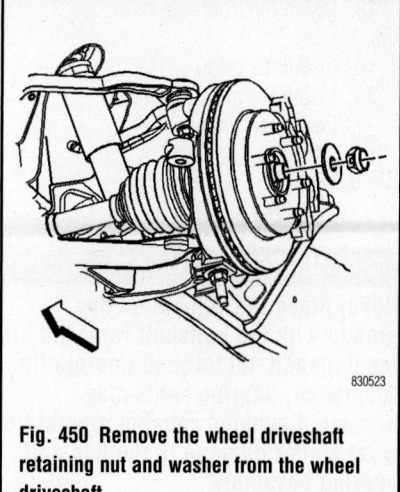

Fig. 450 Remove the wheel driveshaft retaining nut and washer from the wheel driveshaft

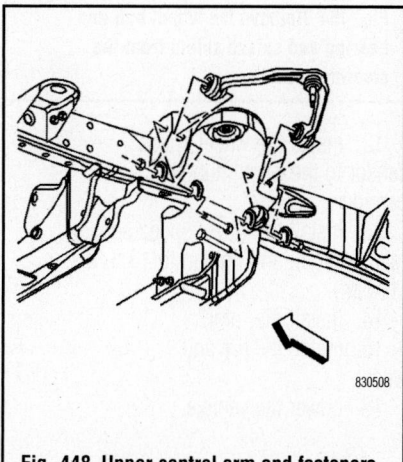

Fig. 448 Upper control arm and fasteners

15. Install the new upper ball joint retaining nut and tighten to 37 ft. lbs. (50 Nm).

16. Install the wheel driveshaft (4WD only).

17. Install the retaining bolts for the brake hose and wheel speed sensor brackets:

    a. Tighten the brake hose bracket to steering knuckle bolt to 89 inch lbs. (10 Nm).

    b. Tighten the brake hose bracket to upper control arm bolt to 89 inch lbs. (10 Nm).

18. Install the tire and wheel.

19. Remove the safety stands.

20. Lower the vehicle.

21. Check the wheel alignment.

WHEEL BEARINGS

REMOVAL & INSTALLATION

4WD Models

See Figures 449 through 452.

☀☀ WARNING

Never place the vehicle on the ground with the halfshaft removed or the halfshaft nut torqued improperly. Otherwise, bearing seals may become dislodged causing premature wear and/or damage to the hub and bearing assembly.

1. Raise and support the vehicle.

2. Remove the tire and wheel.

3. Remove the rotor.

4. Remove the front axle hub cap.

5. Remove the wheel driveshaft retaining nut and washer from the wheel driveshaft.

6. Using the J 45859 or equivalent, disengage the wheel driveshaft from the hub and bearing.

7. Remove the wheel speed sensor mounting bolt from the wheel hub and bearing.

8. Remove the wheel speed sensor from the wheel hub and bearing.

9. Remove the wheel hub and bearing mounting bolts.

10. Remove the wheel hub and bearing and splash shield from the steering knuckle.

To install:

11. Clean all corrosion or contaminates from the steering knuckle bore and the hub and bearing.

12. Lubricate the steering knuckle bore with wheel bearing grease or the equivalent.

13. Install the wheel hub and bearing and splash shield to the steering.

14. Install the wheel hub and bearing mounting bolts and tighten to 133 ft. lbs. (180 Nm).

Fig. 451 Using the J 45859 or equivalent, disengage the wheel driveshaft from the hub and bearing.

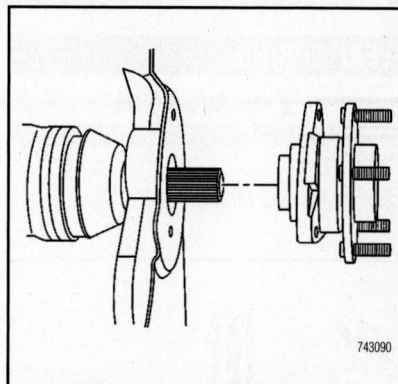

Fig. 452 Remove the wheel hub and bearing and splash shield from the steering knuckle

15. Install the wheel speed sensor to the wheel hub and bearing.

16. Install the wheel speed sensor mounting bolt to the wheel hub and bearing and tighten to 13 ft. lbs. (18 Nm).

17. Install the wheel driveshaft retaining nut and washer and tighten to 155 ft. lbs. (210 Nm).

18. Install the front axle hub cap.
19. Install the rotor.
20. Install the tire and wheel.
21. Lower the vehicle.

RWD Models

See Figures 453 and 454.

> **✳✳ WARNING**
>
> **Never place the vehicle on the ground with the halfshaft removed or the halfshaft nut torqued improperly. Otherwise, bearing seals may become dislodged causing premature wear and/or damage to the hub and bearing assembly.**

1. Raise and support the vehicle.
2. Remove the tire and wheel.
3. Remove the rotor.
4. Remove the wheel speed sensor mounting bolt.
5. Remove the wheel speed sensor from the wheel hub and bearing.
6. Remove the wheel hub and bearing mounting bolts.
7. Remove the wheel hub and bearing and splash shield from the steering knuckle.

To install:

8. Clean all corrosion or contaminates from the steering

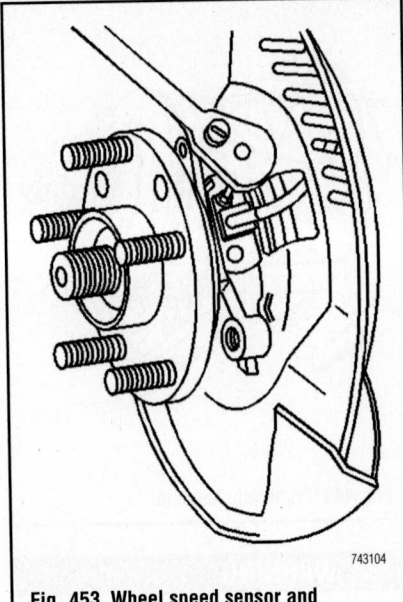

Fig. 453 Wheel speed sensor and mounting

knuckle bore and the hub and bearing.

9. Lubricate the steering knuckle bore with wheel bearing grease or the equivalent.

10. Install the wheel hub and bearing and splash shield to the steering knuckle.

11. Install the wheel hub and bearing mounting bolts and tighten to 133 ft. lbs. (180 Nm).

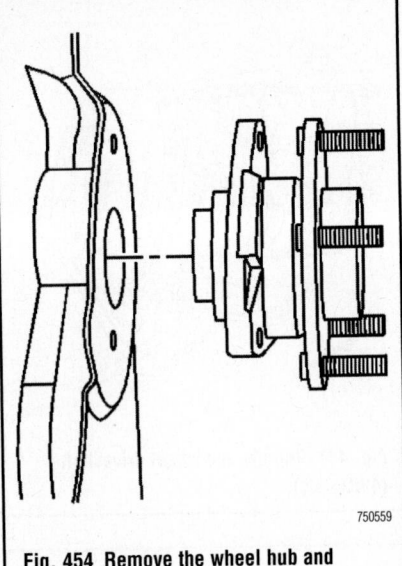

Fig. 454 Remove the wheel hub and bearing and splash shield from the steering knuckle.

12. Install the wheel speed sensor to the wheel hub and bearing.

13. Install the wheel speed sensor retaining bolt and tighten to 13 ft. lbs. (18 Nm).

14. Install the rotor.

15. Install the tire and wheel.

16. Lower the vehicle.

SUSPENSION

LEAF SPRING

REMOVAL & INSTALLATION

1500/3500

See Figures 455 through 458.

REAR SUSPENSION

1. Raise and support the vehicle.
2. Support the rear axle independently in order to relieve the tension on the leaf springs.

3. Remove the leaf spring U-bolt nuts.
4. Remove the leaf spring U-bolts.
5. Remove the leaf spring spacer.

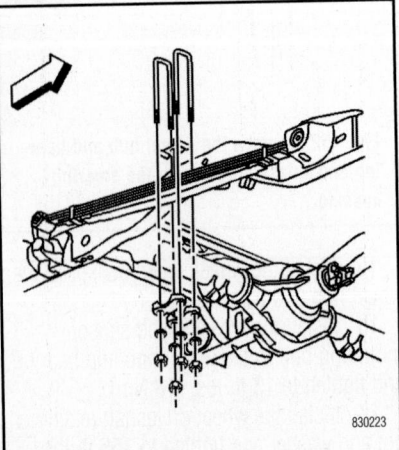

Fig. 455 Leaf spring U-bolts and nuts

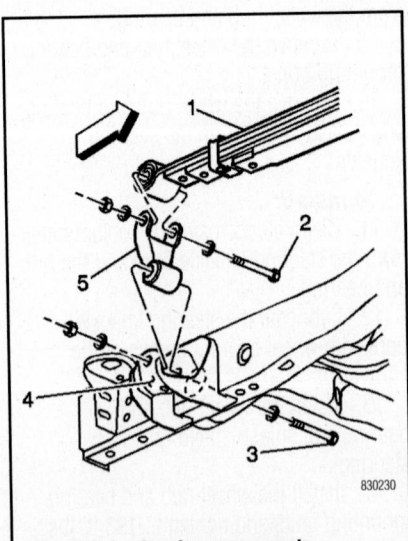

Fig. 456 Leaf spring components

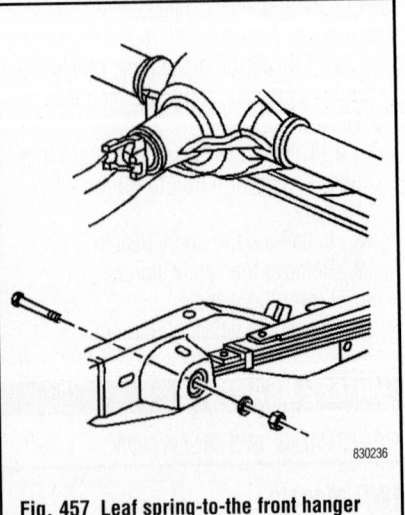

Fig. 457 Leaf spring-to-the front hanger bracket mounting nut and bolt

6. Remove the leaf spring anchor plate.

7. Remove the mounting bolt and nut (3) from the leaf spring mounting bracket (4).

8. Remove the leaf spring (1) and spring shackle (5) as an assembly.

9. Remove the leaf spring-to-the front hanger bracket mounting nut and bolt.

10. Remove the leaf spring from the vehicle.

11. Remove the shackle from the leaf spring.

To install:

➡**Install the front and rear mounting bolts loosely. DO NOT tighten the front and rear mounting bolts until the vehicle is at curb height.**

12. Tighten the U-bolts for the leaf spring before the vehicle is at curb height.

13. Perform the following procedure before installing the front hanger bracket mounting bolt.

   a. Remove all traces of the original adhesive patch.

   b. Clean the threads of the bolt with brake parts cleaner or the equivalent and allow to dry.

   c. Apply Thread locker GM P/N 12345493 (Canadian P/N 10953488) to the threads of the bolt.

14. Install the shackle on the leaf spring.

15. Install the leaf spring to the vehicle.

16. Loosely install the leaf spring to the front hanger bracket mounting bolt and nut.

17. Install the leaf spring to the leaf spring mounting bracket.

18. Note: Do not reuse the leaf spring U-bolts.

19. Install the leaf spring spacer.

20. Install the leaf spring U-bolts.

21. Install the leaf spring anchor plate.

22. Install the leaf spring U-bolt nuts.

23. Tighten the leaf spring U-bolt mounting nuts to 63 ft. lbs. (85 Nm).(All 1500 Series).

24. Tighten the leaf spring U-bolt mounting nuts to 103 inch lbs. (140 Nm), plus 180 degrees (All 2500 and 3500 Series).

25. Tighten the front hanger bracket and spring shackle mounting nuts.

26. Tighten the front hanger bracket mounting nut to 74 ft. lbs. (100 Nm), plus 210 degrees.

27. Tighten the spring shackle to frame mounting nut to 85 ft. lbs. (115 Nm).

28. Tighten the spring shackle to leaf spring mounting nut to 63 ft. lbs. (85 Nm).

29. Remove the rear axle support.

30. Lower the vehicle.

4500

See Figures 455, 456 and 458.

1. Raise and support the vehicle.

2. Support the rear axle independently in order to relieve the tension on the leaf springs.

3. Remove the leaf spring U-bolt nuts.

4. Remove the leaf spring U-bolts.

5. Remove the leaf spring spacer.

6. Remove the leaf spring anchor plate.

7. Remove the mounting bolt and nut (3) from the leaf spring mounting bracket (4).

8. Remove the leaf spring (1) and spring shackle (5) as an assembly.

9. Remove the leaf spring nut (1), washer (2), and the bolt (3).

10. Remove the leaf spring from the vehicle.

11. Remove the shackle from the leaf spring.

To install:

➡**Install the front and rear mounting bolts loosely. DO NOT tighten the front and rear mounting bolts until the vehicle is at curb height.**

12. Tighten the U-bolts for the leaf spring before the vehicle is at curb height.

13. Perform the following procedure before installing the front hanger bracket mounting bolt.

   a. Remove all traces of the original adhesive patch.

   b. Clean the threads of the bolt with brake parts cleaner or the equivalent and allow to dry.

   c. Apply Thread locker GM P/N 12345493 (Canadian P/N 10953488) to the threads of the bolt.

14. Install the shackle on the leaf spring.

15. Install the leaf spring to the vehicle.

16. Loosely install the front leaf spring bolt, washer, and the nut.

17. Install the leaf spring to the leaf spring mounting bracket.

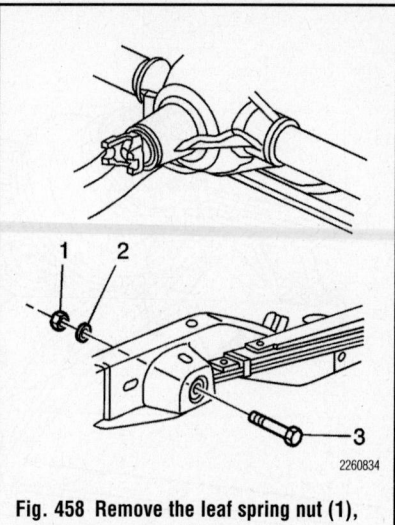

Fig. 458 Remove the leaf spring nut (1), washer (2), and the bolt (3)

➡**Do not reuse the leaf spring U-bolts.**

18. Install the leaf spring spacer.

19. Install the leaf spring U-bolts.

20. Install the leaf spring anchor plate.

21. Install the leaf spring U-bolt nuts and tighten to 103 inch lbs. (140 Nm), plus 180 degrees.

22. Tighten the front hanger bracket and spring shackle mounting nuts.

   a. Tighten the leaf spring to the front hanger bolt to 221 ft. lbs. (300 Nm), plus 140 degrees.

   b. Tighten the spring shackle to frame mounting nut to 85 ft. lbs. (115 Nm), plus 140 degrees.

   c. Tighten the spring shackle to leaf spring mounting nut to 63 ft. lbs. (85 Nm).

23. Remove the rear axle support.

24. Lower the vehicle.

STABILIZER SHAFT

REMOVAL & INSTALLATION

See Figure 459.

1. Raise and support the vehicle.

2. Remove the 2 stabilizer link bolts (1).

3. Remove the 2 stabilizer link nuts (2).

4. Remove the 4 stabilizer shaft insulator clamp bolts (3).

5. Remove the 2 stabilizer shaft insulator clamps (4).

6. Remove the 2 stabilizer shaft insulators (5).

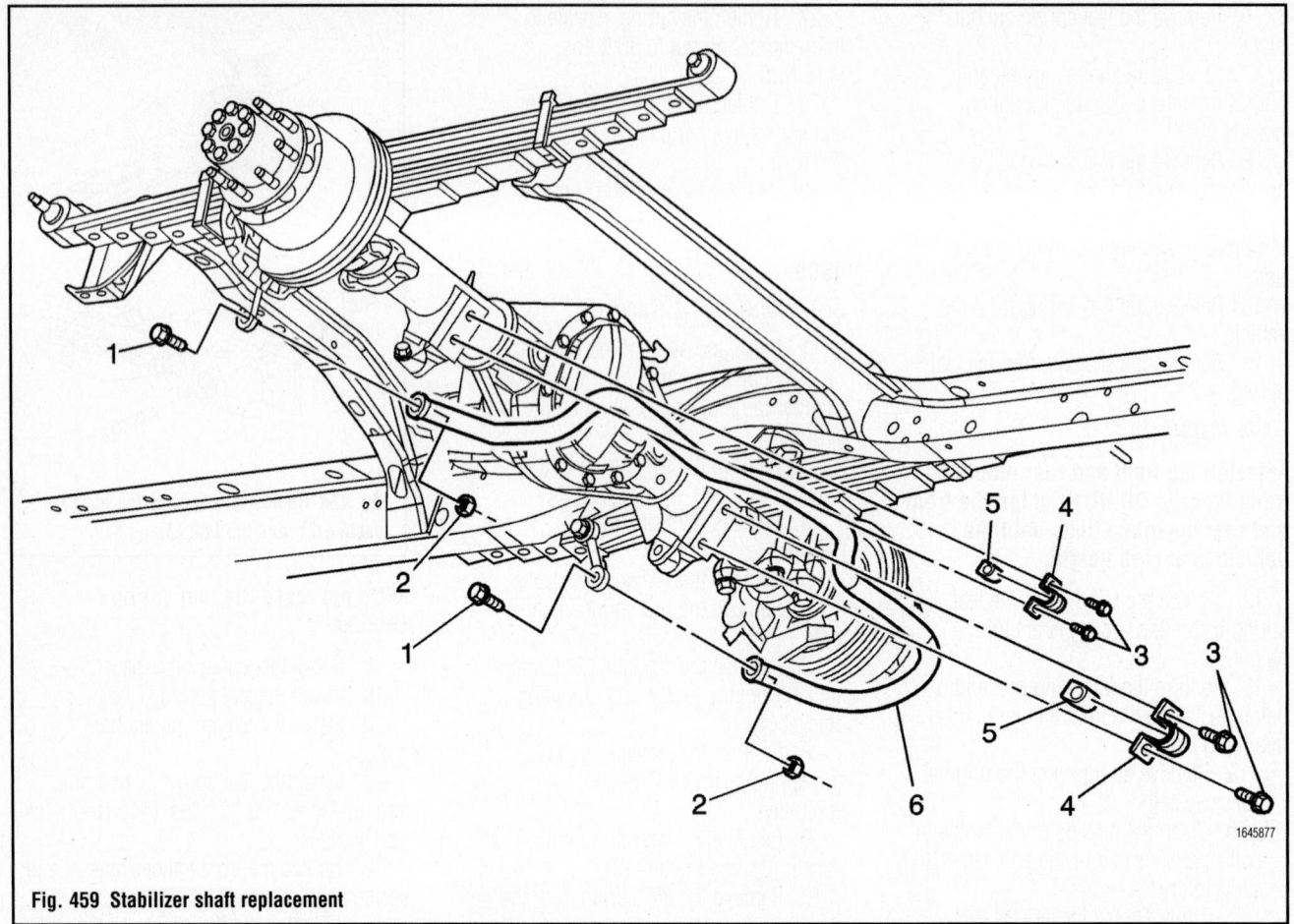

Fig. 459 Stabilizer shaft replacement

7. Remove the stabilizer shaft (6).

To install:

8. Install the stabilizer shaft.
9. Install the 2 stabilizer shaft insulators.

10. Install the 2 stabilizer shaft insulator clamps.
11. Install the 4 stabilizer shaft insulator clamp bolts and tighten to 37 ft. lbs. (50 Nm).

12. Install the 2 stabilizer link nuts and tighten to 52 ft. lbs. (70 Nm).
13. Install the 2 stabilizer link bolts.

PONTIAC

G6

BRAKES 13-10

**ANTI-LOCK BRAKE
SYSTEM (ABS) 13-10**
General Information................. 13-10
Warnings, Cautions,
and Precautions................. 13-10
Speed Sensors 13-11
Removal & Installation....... 13-11
FRONT DISC BRAKES 13-13
Brake Caliper......................... 13-13
Removal & Installation....... 13-13
Disc Brake Pads 13-14
Removal & Installation....... 13-14
**HYDRAULIC BRAKE
SYSTEM BLEEDING......... 13-11**
Bleeding Procedure................ 13-11
Bleeding
Procedure—manual........ 13-11
Bleeding the ABS
System 13-12
Master Cylinder Bench
Bleeding 13-12
Master Cylinder Reservoir
Filling 13-13
PARKING BRAKE............. 13-17
Parking Brake Rear Cable........ 13-17
Adjustment 13-17
REAR DISC BRAKES 13-15
Brake Caliper......................... 13-15
Removal & Installation....... 13-15
Disc Brake Pads 13-16
Removal & Installation....... 13-16

CHASSIS ELECTRICAL 13-17

**AIR BAG (SUPPLEMENTAL
INFLATIBLE RESTRAINT) .. 13-17**
General Information................. 13-17
Disabling the Supplemental
Inflatable Restraint (SIR)
System 13-18
Enabling the System........... 13-18
Inflatable Restraint Steering
Wheel Module Coil
Centering...................... 13-18
Service Precautions 13-17

DRIVE TRAIN 13-19

Driveshaft............................. 13-20
Removal & Installation........ 13-20
Driveshaft Inner Joint and
Boot 13-22
Disassembly & Assembly ... 13-22
Driveshaft Outer Joint and
Boot 13-22
Removal & Installation........ 13-22
Front Wheel Drive
Intermediate Shaft 13-20
Removal & Installation........ 13-20
Transmission Fluid
Replacement 13-19
Fluid, Filter & Seal
Replacement.................... 13-19

ENGINE COOLING 13-24

Engine Coolant....................... 13-24
Best Practices 13-24
Drain & Refill Procedure..... 13-24
Flushing............................ 13-25
Engine Fan & Shroud............. 13-25
Removal & Installation........ 13-25
Radiator................................ 13-26
Removal & Installation........ 13-26
Thermostat 13-28
Removal & Installation........ 13-28
Water Pump 13-29
Removal & Installation........ 13-29

ENGINE ELECTRICAL 13-31

BATTERY SYSTEM............ 13-31
Battery 13-31
Battery Negative Cable
Disconnection and
Connection 13-31
Removal & Installation........ 13-31
CHARGING SYSTEM 13-32
Alternator (Generator)............. 13-32
Removal & Installation........ 13-32
IGNITION SYSTEM 13-33
Firing Order........................... 13-33
Ignition Coil 13-33
Removal & Installation........ 13-33

Ignition Timing...................... 13-35
Adjustment 13-35
Spark Plugs........................... 13-35
Removal & Installation........ 13-35
STARTING SYSTEM 13-37
Starter 13-37
Removal & Installation........ 13-37

ENGINE MECHANICAL...... 13-39

Air Cleaner Assembly.............. 13-41
Element Replacement.......... 13-42
Removal & Installation........ 13-41
Camshaft and Valve Lifters...... 13-44
Cleaning & Inspection 13-44
Removal & Installation........ 13-44
Catalytic Converter 13-48
Removal & Installation........ 13-48
Crankshaft Front Oil Seal 13-52
Removal & Installation........ 13-52
Cylinder Head 13-53
Removal & Installation........ 13-53
Drive Belt 13-39
Adjustment 13-40
Drive Belt Routing.............. 13-39
Inspection 13-39
Removal & Installation........ 13-40
Engine Oil & Oil Filter............. 13-59
Replacement 13-59
Exhaust Manifold 13-61
Removal & Installation........ 13-61
Intake Manifold 13-64
Removal & Installation........ 13-64
Oil Pan 13-72
Removal & Installation......... 13-72
Oil Pump............................... 13-74
Inspection 13-75
Removal & Installation........ 13-74
Piston and Ring..................... 13-76
Positioning 13-76
Rear Oil Seal 13-78
Removal & Installation........ 13-78
Timing Chain & Sprocket
or Tensioner 13-81
Removal & Installation........ 13-81
Valve Cover/Camshaft
Cover 13-89
Removal & Installation........ 13-89

Valve Lash.............................13-92
   Adjustment 13-92

ENGINE PERFORMANCE & EMISSION CONTROLS 13-92

Camshaft Position (CMP)
Sensor 13-92
   Location.............................13-92
   Removal & Installation........13-94
Component Locations 13-92
Crankshaft Position (CKP)
Sensor 13-97
   Location.............................13-97
   Removal & Installation........13-97
Electronic Control Module
(ECM) 13-99
   Location.............................13-99
   Removal & Installation........13-99
Engine Coolant
Temperature (ECT) Sensor ..13-100
   Location.............................13-100
   Removal & Installation......13-100
Heated Oxygen (HO2S)
Sensor 13-101
   Location.............................13-101
   Removal & Installation......13-102
Knock Sensor (KS)...............13-108
   Location.............................13-108
   Removal & Installation......13-108
Manifold Absolute
Pressure (MAP) Sensor 13-109
   Location.............................13-109
   Removal & Installation......13-109
Mass Air Flow (MAF)
Sensor/ Intake Air (IAT)
Temperature Sensor 13-110
   Location.............................13-110
   Removal & Installation......13-110
Vehicle Speed Sensor (VSS) .13-112
   Location.............................13-112
   Removal & Installation......13-112

FUEL.........................13-113

GASOLINE FUEL INJECTION SYSTEM.....................13-113
Fuel Filter/Fuel Strainer.........13-114
   Removal & Installation......13-114
Fuel Rail & Injectors 13-114
   Removal & Installation......13-114
Fuel System Service
Precautions 13-113

Fuel Tank..............................13-118
   Draining.............................13-118
   Removal & Installation......13-118
Fuel Tank Fuel Pump
Module................................13-116
   Removal & Installation......13-116
Fuel Tank Module
Replacement (Fuel Pump)...13-117
   Removal & Installation......13-117
Idle Speed 13-121
   Adjustment 13-121
Relieving Fuel System
Pressure.............................13-123
Throttle Body........................13-121
   Removal & Installation......13-121

HEATING & AIR CONDITIONING SYSTEM....................13-123

Blower Motor 13-123
   Removal & Installation....13-123
Heater Core 13-123
   Removal & Installation......13-123

PRECAUTIONS..............13-10

SPECIFICATIONS AND MAINTENANCE CHARTS.....13-3

Additional Maintenance
Services-Normal 13-9
Additional Maintenance
Services-Severe 13-9
Brake Specifications..................13-7
Camshaft Specifications............13-5
Capacities 13-4
Crankshaft and Connecting
Rod Specifications 13-5
Engine and Vehicle
Identification 13-3
Engine Tune-Up
Specifications 13-3
Fluid Specifications...................13-4
General Engine
Specifications 13-3
Maintenance I and II
Service Schedules..................13-8
Piston and Ring
Specifications 13-6
Tire, Wheel and Ball Joint
Specifications 13-7
Torque Specifications................13-6

Valve Specifications 13-5
Wheel Alignment......................13-7

STEERING 13-124

Power Steering Gear..............13-124
   Removal & Installation......13-124
Power Steering Pump............13-127
   Bleeding 13-127
   Checking and Adding
    Power Steering Fluid......13-128
   Removal & Installation......13-128

SUSPENSION...............13-129

FRONT SUSPENSION.......13-129
Lower Control Arm................13-129
   Bushing Replacement 13-130
   Removal & Installation......13-129
Stabilizer Shaft 13-130
   Removal & Installation......13-130
Stabilizer Shaft Insulator 13-130
   Removal & Installation......13-130
Stabilizer Shaft Link 13-130
   Removal & Installation......13-130
Steering Knuckle 13-131
   Removal & Installation......13-131
Strut Assembly 13-131
   Removal & Installation......13-131
Strut, Strut Component, or
Spring................................13-132
   Disassembly &
    Assembly.......................13-132
   Inspection 13-133
Wheel Bearing & Hub 13-133
   Adjustment 13-134
   Removal & Installation......13-133

REAR SUSPENSION 13-134
Coil Spring...........................13-134
   Removal & Installation......13-134
Rear Axle Lower Control
Arm....................................13-134
   Removal & Installation......13-134
Rear Axle Upper Control
Arm....................................13-134
   Removal & Installation......13-134
Stabilizer Shaft 13-135
   Removal & Installation......13-135
Wheel Bearings & Hub..........13-135
   Adjustment 13-136
   Removal & Installation......13-135

SPECIFICATIONS AND MAINTENANCE CHARTS

ENGINE AND VEHICLE IDENTIFICATION

		Engine						Model Year	
Code ①	Liters	Cu. In.	Cyl.	Fuel Sys.	Engine Type	Eng. Mfg.		Code ②	Year
B	2.4	146	4	MFI	DOHC	General Motors		A	2010
O	2.4	146	4	MFI	DOHC	General Motors			
K	3.5	214	6	SFI	V6 Offset Bore	General Motors			
N	3.5	214	6	SFI	V6 Offset Bore	General Motors			
7	3.6	217	6	SFI	V6 60 degrees	General Motors			
1	3.9	238	6	SFI	V6 Offset Bore	General Motors			

① 8th position of VIN

② 10th position of VIN

MFI: Multi-port Fuel Injection

SFI: Sequential Fuel Injection

25742_GMG6_C0001

GENERAL ENGINE SPECIFICATIONS

All measurements are given in inches.

Year	Model	Engine Disp. Liters	Engine ID/VIN	Fuel System Type	Net Horsepower @ rpm	Net Torque @ rpm (ft. lbs.)	Bore x Stroke (in.)	Com- pression Ratio	Oil Pressure @ rpm
2010	G6	2.4	B, O	MFI	170 @ 6200	158 @ 5200	3.47 x 3.86	10:01	30-70 @ 1000
		3.5	K	SFI	219 @ 5800	221 @ 4000	3.90 x 2.99	9.8:1	30-45 @ 1850
		3.5	N	SFI	211 @ 5800	214 @ 4000	3.90 x 2.99	9.8:1	30-45 @ 1850
		3.6	7	SFI	252 @ 6300	251 @ 3200	3.70 X 3.37	10.2:1	20 @ 2000
		3.9	1	SFI	222 @ 6000	235-242@3000-4800	3.90 x 3.31	9.8:1	30-45 @ 1850

MFI: Multi-port Fuel Injection

SFI: Sequential Fuel Injection

25742_GMG6_C0002

ENGINE TUNE-UP SPECIFICATIONS

Year	Engine Displacement Liters	Engine VIN	Spark Plugs Gap (in.)	Ignition Timing (deg.) MT	AT	Fuel Pump (psi)	Idle Speed (rpm) MT	AT	Valve Clearance In.	Ex.
2010	2.4	B, O	0.035	①	①	50-60	①	①	HYD	HYD
	3.5	K, N	0.040	①	①	56-62	①	①	HYD	HYD
	3.6	7	0.043	①	①	56-62	①	①	HYD	HYD
	3.9	1	0.040	①	①	56-62	①	①	HYD	HYD

NOTE: The Vehicle Emission Control Information label often reflects specification changes changes made during production.

The label figures must be used if they differ from those in this chart.

HYD: Hydraulic

① Controlled by the Powertrain Control Module (PCM) and cannot be manually adjusted.

25742_GMG6_C0003

CAPACITIES

Year	Model	Engine Displacement Liters	Engine ID/VIN	Engine Oil with Filter (qts.)	Transmission (pts.) 4-Spd	Transmission (pts.) 6-Spd	Transmission (pts.) Auto.	Drive Axle Front (pts.)	Drive Axle Rear (pts.)	Fuel Tank (gal.)	Cooling System (qts.)
2010	G6	2.4	B	5.0	—	—	①	—	—	16.3	7.5
		3.5	N	4.0	—	—	①	—	—	16.3	9.7
		3.6	7	5.5	—	—	①	—	—	16.3	9.7
		3.9	1	4.0	—	—	①	—	—	16.3	9.7

NOTE: All capacities are approximate. Add fluid gradually and check to be sure a proper fluid level is obtained.

① **4T45-E:** 14 pts. (bottom pan removal)

19 pts. (complete overhaul)

25.8 pts. (dry)

4T65-E: 14.8 pts. (bottom pan removal)

20 pts. (complete overhaul)

26.8 pts. (dry)

6T40/6T45: 10.6-14.8 pts. (valve body cover removal)

8.4-12.6 pts. (fluid change, drain plug)

17-18 pts. (overhaul)

6T70/6T75: 10.6-14.8 pts. (valve body cover removal)

8.4-12.6 (fluid change)

14.8-19.0 pts. (ovehaul)

25742_GMG6_C0004

FLUID SPECIFICATIONS

Year	Model	Engine Displacement Liters	Engine Oil ①	Auto. Transaxle	Drive Axle Front	Drive Axle Rear	Power Steering Fluid	Brake Master Cylinder	Cooling System
2010	G6	2.4, 3.5, 3.6, 3.9	5W-30	DEXRON®-VI	NS	NS	GM PS Fluid	DOT 3	DEX-COOL®

DOT: Department Of Transpotation

Measurements are approximate.

NS for Not Specified by OEM

① In extreme cold, where the temperature falls below -20 °F (-29 °C), use either an SAE 5W-30 synthetic oil or an SAE 0W-30 engine oil.

25742_GMG6_C0005

VALVE SPECIFICATIONS

Year	Engine Displacement Liters	Engine ID/VIN	Seat Angle (deg.)	Face Angle (deg.)	Spring Load - Closed	Spring Free-Length (in.)	Spring Installed Height - Closed (in.)	Stem-to-Guide Clearance (in.)		Stem Diameter (in.)	
								Intake	Exhaust	Intake	Exhaust
2010	2.4	B, O	45 ①	45	55-61 lbs @ 1.3 in.	1.6299-1.7402	1.2795	0.0012-0.0022	0.0020-0.0026	0.2344-0.2355	0.2344-0.2355
	3.5	K, N	46	45	76.4 lb 1.701 ②	2.08	1.84	0.0009-0.0025	0.0009-0.0025	NA	NA
	3.6	7	45 ①	44.25	55-61 lbs	1.6732-1.7913	1.3779	0.0010-0.0026	0.0014-0.0030	0.2344-0.2352	0.2341-0.2348
	3.9	1	46	45	76.4 lb 1.701②	2.08	1.84	0.0009-0.0025	0.0009-0.0025	NA	NA

NA: Information not available

① Seating surface angle

② Without damper

25742_GMG6_C0006

CAMSHAFT SPECIFICATIONS
All measurements in inches unless noted

Year	Engine Disp.	Engine Code/VIN	Journal Diameter	Bearing Inside Diameter	Shaft Endplay	Journal Out of Round	Journal -to-Bore Clearance	Lobe Height Intake	Lobe Height Exhaust
2010	2.4	B, O	1.0604-1.0614	NS	0.0016-0.0057	NS	NS	NS	NS
	3.5	K, N	2.024-2.025	2.028-2.029	0.0018-0.0085	0.001	NS	0.2727	0.2727
	3.6	7	1.3754-1.3764 ①	1.3779-1.3787 ②	0.0018-0.0085	0.0002	0.0016-0.0033	1.6687-1.6805	1.6703-1.6821
	3.9	1	2.024-2.025	2.028-2.029	NS	0.001	NS	NS	NS

NS for Not Specified by OEM

① Front no. 1. Journal diameter for Middle and Rear Numbers. 2-4: 1.0605-1.0614 in.

② Camshaft Bearing Inside Diameter - Front Number 1. Bearing inside diameter for Middle and Rear Numbers 2-4: 1.0630-1.0638.

25742_GMG6_C0007

CRANKSHAFT AND CONNECTING ROD SPECIFICATIONS
All measurements are given in inches.

Year	Engine Displacement Liters	Engine ID/VIN	Crankshaft Main Brg. Journal Dia.	Crankshaft Main Brg. Clearance	Crankshaft Shaft Endplay	Crankshaft Thrust on No.	Connecting Rod Journal Diameter	Connecting Rod Bearing Clearance	Connecting Rod Side Clearance
2010	2.4	B, O	2.2045-2.2050	0.0012-0.0026	0.0012-0.0150	NS	1.9291-1.9297	0.0011-0.0029	0.0028-0.0146
	3.5	K, N	2.6473-2.6483	0.0008-0.0025 ①	0.0024-0.0083	3	2.2489-2.2495	0.0007-0.0024	0.008-0.009
	3.6	7	2.6768-2.6775	0.0004-0.0024	0.0039-0.0130	NS	NS	0.0004-0.0028	0.0374-0.0140
	3.9	1	NA	0.0008-0.0025 ①	0.0024-0.0083	3	NS	0.0007-0.0024	0.008-0.009

NS for Not Specified by OEM

① Except No. 3. Crankshaft main bearing clearance for the no. 3 thrust bearing is 0.0012-0.0030 in.

25742_GMG6_C0008

PISTON AND RING SPECIFICATIONS
All measurements are given in inches.

Year	Engine Displacement Liters	Engine ID/VIN	Piston Clearance	Ring End Gap			Ring-to-Groove Clearance		
				First Compression	Second Compression	Oil Control	First Compression	Second Compression	Oil Control
2010	2.4	B, O	0.0004-0.0016	0.006-0.012	0.008-0.018	0.006-0.026 ①	0.0015-0.0031	0.0012-0.003	0.0023-0.0081
	3.5	K, N	0.0030 ②	0.007-0.015	0.019-0.029	0.010-0.029	0.046-0.047	0.002-0.003	0.004
	3.6	7	0.0256 ②	0.0059-0.011 ③	0.0110-0.0189	0.0059-0.0236	0.0012-0.0026	0.0006-0.0024	0.0012-0.0067
	3.9	1	0.0030 ②	0.006-0.011	0.009-0.017	0.06-0.025	0.001-0.002	0.0007-0.002	0.0004

① Rails

② Service limit, maximum

③ Nominal

25742_GMG6_C0009

TORQUE SPECIFICATIONS
All readings in ft. lbs.

Year	Engine VIN	Engine Displacement Liters	Cylinder Head Bolts	Main Bearing Bolts	Rod Bearing Bolts	Crankshaft Damper Bolts	Flywheel Bolts	Manifold		Spark Plugs	Oil Pan Drain Plug
								Intake	Exhaust		
2010	2.4	B, O	①	②	③	④	⑤	⑥	⑦	15	18
	3.5	K, N	⑧	⑨	③	⑩	52	⑪	15	11	18
	3.6	7	⑫	⑬	⑭	⑮	⑯	⑰	15	13	18
	3.9	1	⑧	⑨	③	⑩	52	⑱	15	11	18

① Step 1: 22 ft. lbs.

  Step 2: plus 155 degrees

② Step 1: 15 ft. lbs.

  Step 2: plus 70 degrees

③ Step 1: 18 ft. lbs.

  Step 2: plus 110 degrees

④ Step 1: 74 ft. lbs.

  Step 2: plus 125 degrees

⑤ Step 1: 39 ft. lbs.

  Step 2: plus 25 degrees

⑥ Stud 53 INCH lbs.

  Nut/bolts: 89 INCH lbs.

⑦ Step 1: 52 ft. lbs.

  Step 2: plus 72 degrees

⑧ Step 1: 44 ft. lbs.

  Step 2: plus 140 degrees

⑨ Step 1: 37 ft. lbs.

  Step 2: plus 77 degrees

⑩ Step 1: 92 ft. lbs.

  Step 2: plus 130 degrees

⑪ Lower manifold center bolt (first pass): 62 inch lbs.

  Lower manifold center bolt (final pass): 115 inch lbs.

  Lower manifold corner bolt (first pass): 62 inch lbs.

  Lower manifold corner bolt (final pass): 18 ft. lbs.

  Upper manifold: 18 ft. lbs.

⑫ M8: 11 ft. lbs. plus 75 degrees

  M11: 22 ft. lbs. plus 150 degrees

⑬ Inner (Step 1): 15 ft. lbs.

  Inner (Step 2): plus 80 degrees

  Outer (Step 1): 10 ft. lbs.

  Outer (Step 2): plus 110 degrees

  Side (Step 1): 22 ft. lbs.

  Side (Step 2): plus 60 degrees

⑭ Step 1: 22 ft. lbs.

  Step 2: Loosen Bolts

  Step 3: 18 ft. lbs.

  Step 4: plus 110 degrees

⑮ Step 1: 74 ft. lbs.

  Step 2: plus 150 degrees

⑯ Step 1: 22 ft. lbs.

  Step 2: plus 45 degrees

⑰ Lower and Upper manifold bolts: 17 ft. lbs.

⑱ Lower manifold center bolt (first pass): 10 ft. lbs.

  Lower manifold center bolt (final pass): 15 ft. lbs.

  Lower manifold corner bolt (first pass): 10 ft. lbs.

  Lower manifold corner bolt (final pass): 18 ft. lbs.

  Upper manifold: 18 ft. lbs.

25742_GMG6_C0010

WHEEL ALIGNMENT

Year	Model		Caster	Cross Caster	Camber		Total Toe
					Left	**Right**	
2010	G6	F	2.90° ± 0.75°	0.00° ± 0.75°	-1.00° ± 0.75°	-0.70° ± 0.75	+0.20° ± 0.20°
		R	NS	NS	-0.80° ± 0.60°	-0.80° ± 0.60°	+0.20° ± 0.20°

F: Front

R: Rear

NS Not Specified by OEM

25742_GMG6_C0011

TIRE, WHEEL AND BALL JOINT SPECIFICATIONS

Year	Model	OEM Tires	Tire	Wheel		Ball Joint
		Standard	**Pressure**	**Rim Contour**	**Nut (ft. lbs.)** ①	**Inspection**
2010	G6	P215/55R17	②	6J, 6½J, 7J, 7½J	100	③
		P225/50R17	②	6J, 6½J, 7J, 7½J, 8J	100	③
		P225/50R18	②	6½J, 7J, 7½J, 8J, 8½J	100	③

① ALUMINUM WHEELS REQUIRE SPECIAL WHEEL NUTS. Tighten each wheel nut to 100 ft. lbs. using the recommended tightening sequence. Recheck the torque after the first 100 miles.

② Inflate to the tire placard specifications; the tire placard label is located on the driver door.

③ Clean and inspect the ball joint seal for cuts or tears. If the ball joint seal is damaged, replace the lower control arm.

25742_GMG6_C0012

BRAKE SPECIFICATIONS

All measurements in inches unless noted

Year	Model		Brake Disc			Minimum Lining Thickness		Brake Caliper	
			Original Thickness	**Minimum Thickness**	**Maximum Runout**	**Front**	**Rear**	**Mounting Bracket (ft. lbs.)**	**Guide Pin (ft. lbs.)**
2010	G6	F	1.023	0.906	0.002	①	—	96	26
		R	0.551	0.472	0.002	—	①	96	26

① Not available

25742_GMG6_C0013

MAINTENANCE I AND II SERVICE SCHEDULES
G6

When the CHANGE ENGINE OIL light appears, certain services and inspections are required.

Required services are described as Maintenance I and Maintenance II.

The first service of a vehicle should be Maintenance I, and the second service should be Maintenance II.

Alternate between the 2 services thereafter. However, in some cases, Maintenance II may be required more often.

Maintenance I: Use Maintenance I if the CHANGE ENGINE OIL light comes on within 10 months since the vehicle was purchased or, if Maintenance II was performed.

Maintenance II: Use Maintenance II if the previous service performed was Maintenance I. Always use Maintenance II whenever the CHANGE ENGINE OIL light comes on 10 months or more since the last service, or, if the CHANGE ENGINE OIL light has not come on at all for one year.

Service Item	Maintenance I	Maintenance II
Change the engine oil and filter.	✓	✓
Reset the oil life system.	✓	✓
Visually inspect the vehicle for leaks or damage. A fluid loss in the vehicle system could indicate a problem. Inspect, repair and add fluid to the system if necessary.	✓	✓
Inspect the engine air cleaner filter. If necessary, replace the filter.	✓	✓
Rotate the tires. Inspect the tire inflation pressures and the tire wear.	✓	✓
Visually inspect the brake lines and hoses for proper hook-up, binding, leaks, cracks, chafing, etc. Inspect the disc brake pads for wear and the rotors for surface condition. Inspect the drum brake linings for wear or cracks. Inspect other brake parts, including drums, wheel cylinders, calipers, parking brake, etc. Inspect the parking brake adjustment.	✓	✓
Inspect the engine coolant and the windshield washer fluid levels. Add fluid as needed.	✓	✓
Body hinges and latches, key lock cylinders, folding seat hardware, and rear compartment hinges lubrication. See Recommended Fluids and Lubricants. More frequent lubrication may be required when vehicle is exposed to a corrosive environment. Applying silicone grease on weatherstrips with a clean cloth makes them last longer, seal better, and not stick or squeak.	—	✓
Visually inspect the coolant hoses and replace the hoses if they are cracked, swollen or deteriorated. Inspect all pipes, fittings and clamps; replace as needed. To help ensure proper operation, a pressure test of the cooling system and pressure cap and cleaning the outside of the radiator and air conditioning condenser is recommended at least once a year.	—	✓
Inspect the front and rear suspension and the steering system for damaged, loose or missing parts, or signs of wear. Inspect power steering lines and hoses for proper hook-up, binding, leaks, cracks, chafing, etc.	—	✓
Inspect the throttle system for interference or binding and for damaged or missing parts. Replace the parts as needed. Replace any components that have high effort or excessive wear. Do not lubricate the accelerator or the cruise control cables.	—	✓

To reset the CHANGE ENGINE OIL light:

1. Turn the ignition key to the ON/RUN position with the engine OFF.
2. Press and release the stem in the lower center of the instrument cluster until the OIL LIFE message is displayed.
3. Once the alternating OIL LIFE and RESET messages appear, press and hold the stem until several beeps sound.
   This confirms that the oil life system has been reset to 100 percent.
4. Turn the ignition key to the OFF position.
   If the CHANGE ENGINE OIL message comes back on when the vehicle is started, the engine oil life system has not been reset. Repeat the procedure.

25742_GMG6_C0014

ADDITIONAL MAINTENANCE SERVICES - NORMAL
G6

TO BE SERVICED	TYPE OF SERVICE	VEHICLE MILEAGE INTERVAL (x1000)					
		25	50	75	100	125	150
Spark plugs	Replace				✓		
Air cleaner filter	Replace		✓		✓		✓
Engine coolant	Replace						✓
Fuel system	Inspect	✓	✓	✓	✓	✓	✓
Accessory drive belt	Replace				✓		✓
Accessory drive belt	Inspect	✓	✓	✓	✓	✓	✓
Automatic Transmission Fluid (and filter if applicable)	Replace				✓		

25742_GMG6_C0015

ADDITIONAL MAINTENANCE SERVICES - SEVERE
G6

TO BE SERVICED	TYPE OF SERVICE	VEHICLE MILEAGE INTERVAL (x1000)					
		25	50	75	100	125	150
Automatic Transmission Fluid (and filter if applicable)	Replace		✓		✓		✓
Spark plugs	Replace				✓		
Air cleaner filter	Replace		✓		✓		✓
Engine coolant	Replace						✓
Fuel system	Inspect	✓	✓	✓	✓	✓	✓
Accessory drive belt	Inspect		✓		✓		✓
Accessory drive belt	Inspect	✓	✓	✓	✓	✓	✓

25742_GMG6_C0016

PRECAUTIONS

Before servicing any vehicle, please be sure to read all of the following precautions, which deal with personal safety, prevention of component damage, and important points to take into consideration when servicing a motor vehicle:

• Never open, service or drain the radiator or cooling system when the engine is hot; serious burns can occur from the steam and hot coolant.

• Observe all applicable safety precautions when working around fuel. Whenever servicing the fuel system, always work in a well-ventilated area. Do not allow fuel spray or vapors to come in contact with a spark, open flame, or excessive heat (a hot drop light, for example). Keep a dry chemical fire extinguisher near the work area. Always keep fuel in a container specifically designed for fuel storage; also, always properly seal fuel containers to avoid the possibility of fire or explosion. Refer to the additional fuel system precautions later in this section.

• Fuel injection systems often remain pressurized, even after the engine has been turned **OFF**. The fuel system pressure must be relieved before disconnecting any fuel lines. Failure to do so may result in fire and/or personal injury.

• Brake fluid often contains polyglycol ethers and polyglycols. Avoid contact with the eyes and wash your hands thoroughly after handling brake fluid. If you do get brake fluid in your eyes, flush your eyes with clean, running water for 15 minutes. If eye irritation persists, or if you have taken

brake fluid internally, IMMEDIATELY seek medical assistance.

• The EPA warns that prolonged contact with used engine oil may cause a number of skin disorders, including cancer. You should make every effort to minimize your exposure to used engine oil. Protective gloves should be worn when changing oil. Wash your hands and any other exposed skin areas as soon as possible after exposure to used engine oil. Soap and water, or waterless hand cleaner should be used.

• All new vehicles are now equipped with an air bag system, often referred to as a Supplemental Restraint System (SRS) or Supplemental Inflatable Restraint (SIR) system. The system must be disabled before performing service on or around system components, steering column, instrument panel components, wiring and sensors. Failure to follow safety and disabling procedures could result in accidental air bag deployment, possible personal injury and unnecessary system repairs.

• Always wear safety goggles when working with, or around, the air bag system. When carrying a non-deployed air bag, be sure the bag and trim cover are pointed away from your body. When placing a non-deployed air bag on a work surface, always face the bag and trim cover upward, away from the surface. This will reduce the motion of the module if it is accidentally deployed. Refer to the additional air bag system precautions later in this section.

• Clean, high quality brake fluid from a sealed container is essential to the safe and

proper operation of the brake system. You should always buy the correct type of brake fluid for your vehicle. If the brake fluid becomes contaminated, completely flush the system with new fluid. Never reuse any brake fluid. Any brake fluid that is removed from the system should be discarded. Also, do not allow any brake fluid to come in contact with a painted surface; it will damage the paint.

• Never operate the engine without the proper amount and type of engine oil; doing so WILL result in severe engine damage.

• Timing belt maintenance is extremely important. Many models utilize an interference-type, non-freewheeling engine. If the timing belt breaks, the valves in the cylinder head may strike the pistons, causing potentially serious (also time-consuming and expensive) engine damage. Refer to the maintenance interval charts for the recommended replacement interval for the timing belt, and to the timing belt section for belt replacement and inspection.

• Disconnecting the negative battery cable on some vehicles may interfere with the functions of the on-board computer system(s) and may require the computer to undergo a relearning process once the negative battery cable is reconnected.

• When servicing drum brakes, only disassemble and assemble one side at a time, leaving the remaining side intact for reference.

• Only an MVAC-trained, EPA-certified automotive technician should service the air conditioning system or its components.

BRAKES

GENERAL INFORMATION

WARNINGS, CAUTIONS, AND PRECAUTIONS

✳✳ CAUTION

Brake fluid may irritate eyes and skin. In case of contact, take the following actions:

• Eye contact—rinse thoroughly with water.
• Skin contact—wash with soap and water.
• If ingested—consult a physician immediately.

✳✳ WARNING

Avoid spilling brake fluid onto painted surfaces, electrical connec-

tions, wiring, or cables. Brake fluid will damage painted surfaces and cause corrosion to electrical components. If any brake fluid comes in contact with painted surfaces, immediately flush the area with water. If any brake fluid comes in contact with electrical connections, wiring, or cables, use a clean shop cloth to wipe away the fluid.

✳✳ WARNING

Only use products that comply with GM specifications. Follow instructions at all times. The use of any type of fluid other than the recommended type of brake fluid may cause contamination which

ANTI-LOCK BRAKE SYSTEM (ABS)

could result in damage to the internal rubber seals and/or rubber linings of hydraulic brake system components.

• Certain components within the ABS system are not intended to be serviced or repaired individually.

• Do not use rubber hoses or other parts not specifically specified for and ABS system. When using repair kits, replace all parts included in the kit. Partial or incorrect repair may lead to functional problems and require the replacement of components.

• Lubricate rubber parts with clean, fresh brake fluid to ease assembly. Do not use shop air to clean parts; damage to rubber components may result.

- Use only DOT 3 brake fluid from an unopened container.
- If any hydraulic component or line is removed or replaced, it may be necessary to bleed the entire system.
- A clean repair area is essential. Always clean the reservoir and cap thoroughly before removing the cap. The slightest amount of dirt in the fluid may plug an orifice and impair the system function. Perform repairs after components have been thoroughly cleaned; use only denatured alcohol to clean components. Do not allow ABS components to come into contact with any substance containing mineral oil; this includes used shop rags.
- The Anti-Lock control unit is a microprocessor similar to other computer units in the vehicle. Ensure that the ignition switch is **OFF** before removing or installing controller harnesses. Avoid static electricity discharge at or near the controller.
- If any arc welding is to be done on the vehicle, the control unit should be unplugged before welding operations begin.

SPEED SENSORS

REMOVAL & INSTALLATION

See Figure 1.

1. Remove the floor console (1).
2. Remove the two yaw sensor nuts (2).
3. Remove the yaw sensor
   a. Disconnect the electrical connector.
   b. After the installation is complete, reset the yaw rate sensor using the following procedure:
   - Install a scan tool.
   - Using the special functions menu on the scan tool, reset the yaw rate sensor.

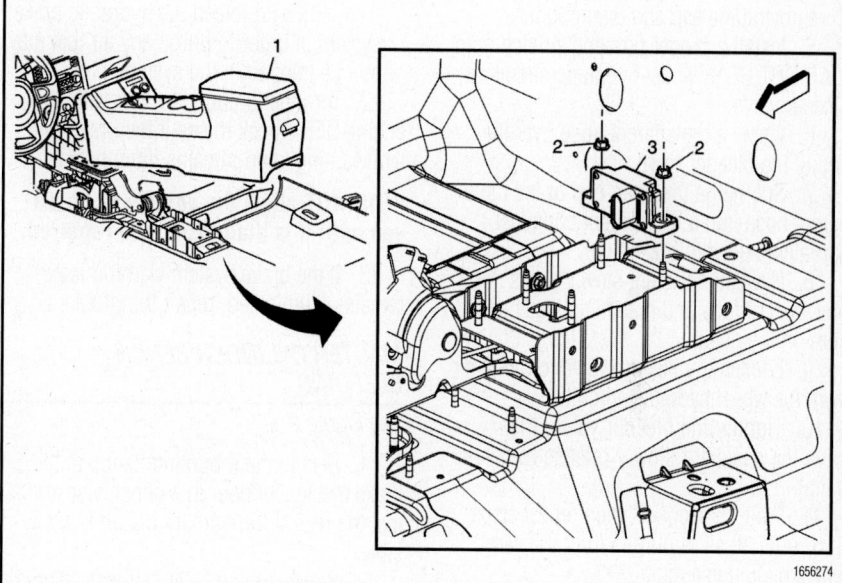

1656274

Fig. 1 Yaw sensor with lateral accelerometer (3), floor console (1), and two yaw sensor nuts (2)

BRAKES

HYDRAULIC BRAKE SYSTEM BLEEDING

BLEEDING PROCEDURE

BLEEDING PROCEDURE—MANUAL

1. Place a clean shop cloth beneath the brake master cylinder to catch brake fluid spills.
2. With the ignition OFF and the brakes cool, apply the brakes 3-5 times, or until the brake pedal effort increases significantly, in order to deplete the brake booster power reserve.
3. If you have performed a brake master cylinder bench bleeding on this vehicle, or if you disconnected the brake pipes from the master cylinder, or if you have disconnected the brake pipes from the proportioning valve assembly or the brake modulator assembly, you must perform the following steps to bleed air at the ports of the hydraulic component:
   - Ensure that the brake master cylinder reservoir is full to the maximum-fill level. If necessary, add Delco Supreme 11®GM P/N 12377967 (Canadian P/N 992667), or an equivalent DOT 3 brake fluid from a clean, sealed brake fluid container.
   - If removal of the reservoir cap and diaphragm is necessary, clean the outside of the reservoir on and around the cap prior to removal.
   a. With the brake pipes installed securely to the master cylinder, proportioning valve assembly, or brake modulator assembly, loosen and separate one of the brake pipes from the port of the component.
   b. For the proportioning valve assembly or the brake modulator assembly, perform these steps in the sequence of system flow; begin with the fluid feed pipes from the master cylinder:
   - a. Allow a small amount of brake fluid to gravity bleed from the open port of the component.
   - b. Connect the brake pipe to the component and tighten securely.
   - c. Have an assistant slowly press the brake pedal fully and maintain steady pressure on the pedal.
   - d. Loosen the same brake pipe to purge air from the open port of the component.
   - e. Tighten the brake pipe, then have the assistant slowly release the brake pedal.
   - f. Wait 15 seconds, then repeat steps a through e, until all air is purged from the same port of the component.
   - g. With the brake pipe installed securely to the master cylinder, proportioning valve assembly, or brake modulator assembly, after all air has been purged from the first port of the component that was bled, loosen and separate the next brake pipe from the component, then repeat steps a through f, until each of the ports on the component has been bled.
   - h. After completing the final component port bleeding procedure, tighten each of the brake pipe-to-component fittings properly.

4. Fill the brake master cylinder reservoir with brake fluid from a clean, sealed brake fluid container:

 a. Ensure that the brake master cylinder reservoir remains at least half-full during this bleeding procedure. Add fluid as needed to maintain the proper level.

 b. Clean the outside of the reservoir on and around the reservoir cap prior to removing the cap and diaphragm.

5. Install a proper box-end wrench onto the RIGHT REAR wheel hydraulic circuit bleeder valve.

6. Install a transparent hose over the end of the bleeder valve.

7. Submerge the open end of the transparent hose into a transparent container partially filled with brake fluid.

8. Have an assistant slowly press the brake pedal fully and maintain steady pressure on the pedal.

9. Loosen the bleeder valve to purge air from the wheel hydraulic circuit.

10. Tighten the bleeder valve, then have the assistant slowly release the brake pedal.

11. Wait 15 seconds, then repeat steps 8-10 until all air is purged from the same wheel hydraulic circuit.

12. With the right rear wheel hydraulic circuit bleeder valve tightened securely, after all air has been purged from the right rear hydraulic circuit, install a proper box-end wrench onto the LEFT FRONT wheel hydraulic circuit bleeder valve.

13. Install a transparent hose over the end of the bleeder valve, and then repeat steps 7-11.

14. With the left front wheel hydraulic circuit bleeder valve tightened securely, after all air has been purged from the left front hydraulic circuit, install a proper box-end wrench onto the LEFT REAR wheel hydraulic circuit bleeder valve.

15. Install a transparent hose over the end of the bleeder valve, and then repeat steps 7-11.

16. With the left rear wheel hydraulic circuit bleeder valve tightened securely, after all air has been purged from the left rear hydraulic circuit, install a proper box-end wrench onto the RIGHT FRONT wheel hydraulic circuit bleeder valve.

17. Install a transparent hose over the end of the bleeder valve, and then repeat steps 7-11.

18. After completing the final wheel hydraulic circuit bleeding procedure, ensure that each of the 4 wheel hydraulic circuit bleeder valves are properly tightened.

19. Fill the brake master cylinder reservoir to the maximum-fill level brake fluid.

20. Slowly press and release the brake pedal. Observe the feel of the brake pedal.

21. If the brake pedal feels spongy, repeat the bleeding procedure again. If the brake pedal still feels spongy after repeating the bleeding procedure, perform the following steps:

 a. Inspect the brake system for external leaks.

 b. Pressure bleed the hydraulic brake system in order to purge any air that may still be trapped in the system.

22. Turn the ignition key ON, with the engine OFF. Check to see if the brake system warning lamp remains illuminated.

➡ **DO NOT allow the vehicle to be driven until it is diagnosed and repaired.**

23. If the brake system warning lamp remains illuminated, repair the problem.

MASTER CYLINDER BENCH BLEEDING

See Figure 2.

1. Secure the mounting flange of the brake master cylinder in a bench vise so that the rear of the primary piston is accessible.

2. Remove the master cylinder reservoir cap and diaphragm.

3. Install suitable fittings to the master cylinder ports that match the type of flare seat required and also provide for hose attachment.

4. Install transparent hoses to the fittings installed to the master cylinder ports, then route the hoses into the master cylinder reservoir.

5. Fill the master cylinder reservoir to at least the half-way point with brake fluid.

6. Ensure that the ends of the transparent hoses running into the master cylinder reservoir are fully submerged in the brake fluid.

7. Using a smooth, round-ended tool, depress and release the primary piston as

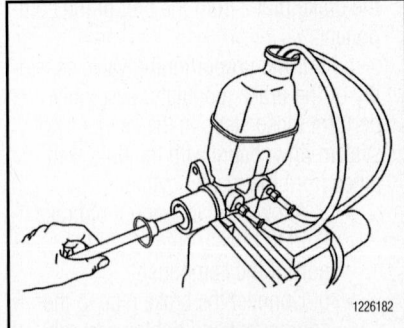

Fig. 2 Secure the mounting flange of the brake master cylinder in a bench vise

far as it will travel, a depth of about 1 in. (25 mm), several times. Observe the flow of fluid coming from the ports. As air is bled from the primary and secondary pistons, the effort required to depress the primary piston will increase and the amount of travel will decrease.

8. Continue to depress and release the primary piston until fluid flows freely from the ports with no evidence of air bubbles.

9. Remove the transparent hoses from the master cylinder reservoir.

10. Install the master cylinder reservoir cap and diaphragm.

11. Remove the fittings with the transparent hoses from the master cylinder ports. Wrap the master cylinder with a clean shop cloth to prevent brake fluid spills.

12. Remove the master cylinder from the vise.

BLEEDING THE ABS SYSTEM

Automated Bleed Procedure

➡ **Before performing the ABS Automated Bleed Procedure, first perform a manual or pressure bleed of the base hydraulic brake system.**

• The automated bleed procedure must be performed when a new brake pressure modulator valve (BPMV) is installed, because the secondary circuits of the new BPMV are not prefilled with brake fluid.

• The automated bleed procedure is recommended when one of the following conditions exist: (1) The base brake system bleeding does not achieve the desired pedal height or feel, (2) An extreme loss of brake fluid has occurred, (3) Air ingestion is suspected in the secondary circuits of the brake modulator assembly.

The ABS Automated Bleed Procedure uses a scan tool to cycle the system solenoid valves and run the pump in order to purge any air from the secondary circuits. These circuits are normally closed off, and are only opened during system initialization at vehicle start up and during ABS operation. The automated bleed procedure opens these secondary circuits and allows any air trapped in these circuits to flow out away from the brake modulator assembly, which is then forced out at the brake corners by the pressure bleeder.

✳✳ WARNING

Terminate the Auto Bleed Procedure at any time during the process by pressing the EXIT button. No further scan tool prompts pertaining to the Auto Bleed procedure will be given.

After exiting the bleed procedure, relieve bleed pressure and disconnect bleed equipment per the manufacturer's instructions. Failure to properly relieve pressure may result in spilled brake fluid causing damage to components and painted surfaces.

1. Raise and support the vehicle.
2. Remove the tire and wheel assemblies.
3. Inspect the brake system for leaks and visual damage.
4. Lower the vehicle.
5. Prepare the brake bleeding equipment and the vehicle for a pressure bleed of the base hydraulic brake system.
6. Inspect the battery state of charge.
7. Install a scan tool.
8. Turn the ignition ON, with the engine OFF.
9. With the scan tool, perform the following steps:
   a. Select Diagnostics
   b. Select the appropriate vehicle information
   c. Select Chassis
   d. Select Electronic Brake Control Module (EBCM)
   e. Select Special Functions
   f. Select Automated Bleed

10. With an assistant ready, raise and support the vehicle. Refer to Lifting and Jacking the Vehicle.
   • Apply the brake pedal when instructed, using moderate effort.
   • Ensure the pedal remains applied until instructed to release by the scan tool.
   • Do not exceed the time period allowed by the scan tool for having the bleeder valves open.
   • The bleed sequence for each corner is as follows: (1) Left front, (2) Right front, (3) Right rear, and (4) Left rear.
11. Perform the automated bleed procedure as instructed by the scan tool.
12. If the automated bleed procedure is aborted, a malfunction exists. If a DTC is detected, diagnose the DTC.
13. After completion of the automated bleed procedure, press and hold the brake pedal to inspect for pedal firmness.
14. If the brake pedal feels spongy, repeat the bleed procedure completely.
15. Remove the scan tool.
16. Install the tire and wheel assemblies.
17. Lower the vehicle.
18. Adjust the brake fluid level.

19. Road test the vehicle while confirming the brake pedal remains high and firm.

MASTER CYLINDER RESERVOIR FILLING

1. Visually inspect the brake fluid level through the brake master cylinder reservoir.
2. If the brake fluid level is at or below the half-full point during routine fluid checks, inspect the brake system for wear and possible brake fluid leaks.
3. If the brake fluid level is at or below the half-full point during routine fluid checks, and an inspection of the brake system did not reveal wear or brake fluid leaks, the brake fluid may be topped-off up to the maximum-fill level.
4. If brake system service was just completed, the brake fluid may be topped-off up to the maximum-fill level.
5. If the brake fluid level is above the half-full point, adding brake fluid is not recommended under normal conditions.
6. If brake fluid is to be added to the master cylinder reservoir, clean the outside of the reservoir on and around the reservoir cap prior to removing the cap and diaphragm. Use only GM-approved brake fluid from a clean, sealed brake fluid container.

BRAKES

FRONT DISC BRAKES

✳✳ WARNING

Dust and dirt accumulating on brake parts during normal use may contain asbestos fibers from production or aftermarket brake linings. Breathing excessive concentrations of asbestos fibers can cause serious bodily harm. Exercise care when servicing brake parts. Do not sand or grind brake lining unless equipment used is designed to contain the dust residue. Do not clean brake parts with compressed air or by dry brushing. Cleaning should be done by dampening the brake components with a fine mist of water, then wiping the brake components clean with a dampened cloth. Dispose of cloth and all residue containing asbestos fibers in an impermeable container with the appropriate label. Follow practices prescribed by the Occupational Safety and Health Administration (OSHA) and the Environmental Protection Agency (EPA) for the handling, processing, and disposing of dust or debris that may contain asbestos fibers.

BRAKE CALIPER

REMOVAL & INSTALLATION
See Figures 3 and 4.

1. Inspect the fluid level in the brake master cylinder reservoir.
2. If the brake fluid level is midway between the maximum-full point and the minimum allowable level, no brake fluid needs to be removed from the reservoir before proceeding.
3. If the brake fluid level is higher than midway between the maximum-full point and the minimum allowable level, remove brake fluid to the midway point before proceeding.
4. Raise and support the vehicle.
5. Remove the tire and wheel assembly.
6. Install and firmly Hand-tighten 2 wheel nuts to opposite wheel studs in order to retain the rotor to the hub.
7. Install a large C-clamp (1) over the body of the brake caliper (2) with the C-clamp ends against the rear of the caliper body and against the outer brake pad.
8. Tighten the C-clamp until the caliper piston is compressed into the caliper bore

enough to allow the caliper to slide past the brake rotor.
9. Remove the C-clamp from the caliper.
10. Remove the brake hose-to-caliper bolt (1) from the brake caliper.

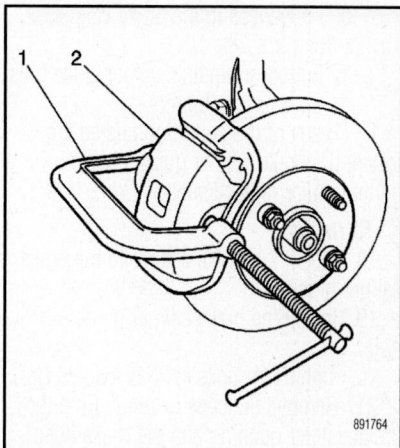
891764

Fig. 3 Install a large C-clamp (1) over the body of the brake caliper (2) with the C-clamp ends against the rear of the caliper body and against the outer brake pad

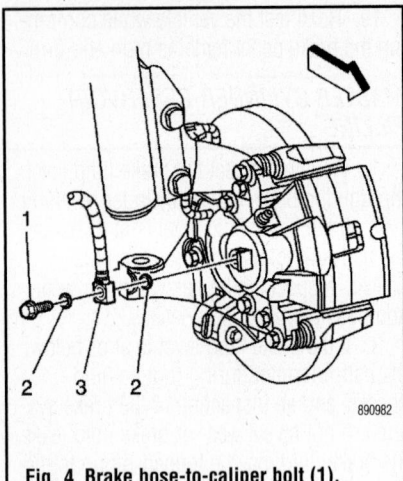

Fig. 4 Brake hose-to-caliper bolt (1), gaskets (2), hose (3) hose

11. Remove the brake hose (3) from the brake caliper.

12. Remove and discard the 2 copper brake hose gaskets (2). These gaskets may be stuck to the brake caliper and/or the brake hose end.

13. Cap or plug the opening in the brake caliper and the brake hose to prevent fluid loss and contamination.

14. Remove the brake caliper guide pin bolts.

15. Remove the brake caliper from the caliper bracket.

16. Inspect the brake caliper guide pins for freedom of movement, and inspect the condition of the guide pin boots. Move the guide pins inboard and outboard within the bracket bores, without disengaging the slides from the boots, and observe for the following:

    a. Restricted caliper guide pin movement

    b. Looseness in the brake caliper mounting bracket

    c. Seized or binding caliper guide pins

    d. Split or torn boots

17. If any of the conditions listed are found, the brake caliper guide pins and/or boots require replacement.

To install:

18. Install the brake caliper to the brake caliper bracket.

19. Install the brake caliper guide pin bolts.

20. Tighten the bolts to 26 ft. lbs. (35 Nm).

21. Remove the caps or plugs from the brake caliper opening and the brake hose.

➡**Do not reuse the copper brake hose gaskets.**

22. Install NEW copper brake hose gaskets to the brake hose-to-caliper bolt and to the brake hose.

23. Install the brake hose and the brake hose-to-brake caliper bolt to the brake caliper.

24. Tighten the bolt to 37 ft. lbs. (50 Nm).

25. Bleed the hydraulic brake system.

26. Remove the wheel nuts retaining the brake rotor to the wheel hub.

27. Install the tire and wheel assembly.

28. Lower the vehicle.

29. With the engine OFF, gradually apply the brake pedal to approximately 2/3 of its travel distance.

30. Slowly release the brake pedal.

31. Wait 15 seconds, then repeat steps 10 and 11 until a firm brake pedal is obtained. This will properly seat the brake caliper piston and brake pads.

DISC BRAKE PADS

REMOVAL & INSTALLATION

See Figures 5 and 6.

1. Inspect the fluid level in the brake master cylinder reservoir.

2. If the brake fluid level is midway between the maximum-full point and the minimum allowable level, no brake fluid needs to be removed from the reservoir before proceeding.

3. If the brake fluid level is higher than midway between the maximum-full point and the minimum allowable level, remove brake fluid to the midway point before proceeding.

4. Raise and support the vehicle.

5. Remove the tire and wheel assembly.

6. Install and firmly Hand-tighten 2 wheel nuts to opposite wheel studs in order to retain the rotor to the hub.

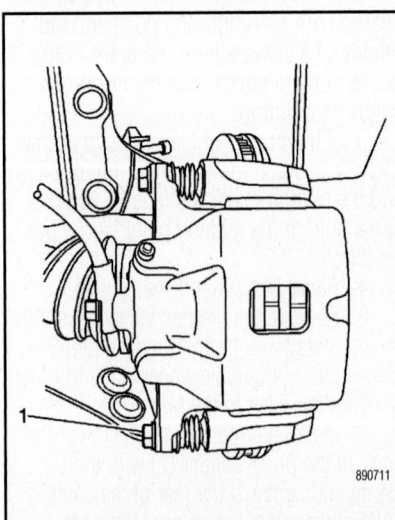

Fig. 5 Brake caliper lower guide pin bolt (1)

7. Remove the brake caliper lower guide pin bolt (1).

✻✻ WARNING

Support the brake caliper with heavy mechanic wire, or equivalent, whenever it is separated from its mount and the hydraulic flexible brake hose is still connected. Failure to support the caliper in this manner will cause the flexible brake hose to bear the weight of the caliper, which may cause damage to the brake hose and in turn may cause a brake fluid leak.

8. Without disconnecting the hydraulic brake flexible hose, pivot the caliper upward and secure the caliper with heavy mechanics wire (1), or equivalent.

9. Remove the brake pads (2) from the caliper mounting bracket.

10. Push the disc brake caliper piston into the caliper bore using an old inner disc brake pad and a disc brake piston installation tool.

11. Remove the brake pad retainers from the caliper bracket.

12. Thoroughly clean the brake pad hardware mating surfaces of the caliper bracket, of any debris and corrosion.

13. Inspect the brake caliper guide pins for freedom of movement, and inspect the condition of the guide pin boots. Move the guide pins inboard and outboard within the

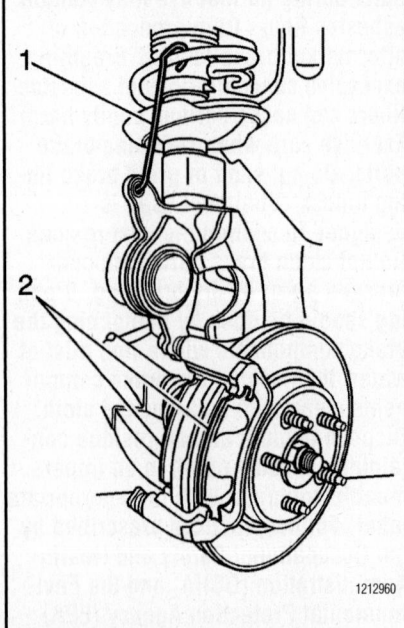

Fig. 6 Secure the caliper with heavy mechanics wire (1) and remove the brake pads (2)

bracket bores, without disengaging the slides from the boots, and observe for the following:

    a. Restricted caliper guide pin movement

    b. Looseness in the brake caliper mounting bracket

    c. Seized or binding caliper guide pins

    d. Split or torn boots

14. If any of the conditions listed are found, the brake caliper guide pins and/or boots require replacement.

To install:

15. Ensure the brake pad hardware mating surfaces are clean.

16. Install the brake pad retainers to the brake caliper bracket.

➡ **Mount the wear sensor-equipped disc brake pad inboard of the rotor with the leading edge of the sensor facing the brake rotor during forward wheel rotation, or at the top of the pad when installed in vehicle position.**

17. Install the brake pads to the caliper bracket.

18. Remove the support and rotate the brake caliper into position over the disc brake pads and to the caliper mounting bracket.

19. Install the lower brake caliper guide pin bolt and tighten to 26 ft. lbs. (35 Nm).

20. Remove the wheel nuts retaining the brake rotor to the hub.

21. Install the tire and wheel assembly.

22. Lower the vehicle.

23. With the engine OFF, gradually apply the brake pedal approximately 2/3 of its travel distance.

24. Slowly release the brake pedal.

25. Wait 15 seconds, then gradually apply the brake pedal approximately 2/3 of its travel distance again until a firm brake pedal apply is obtained. This will properly seat the brake caliper pistons and brake pads.

26. Fill the master cylinder auxiliary reservoir to the proper level.

BRAKES

REAR DISC BRAKES

✳✳ WARNING

Dust and dirt accumulating on brake parts during normal use may contain asbestos fibers from production or aftermarket brake linings. Breathing excessive concentrations of asbestos fibers can cause serious bodily harm. Exercise care when servicing brake parts. Do not sand or grind brake lining unless equipment used is designed to contain the dust residue. Do not clean brake parts with compressed air or by dry brushing. Cleaning should be done by dampening the brake components with a fine mist of water, then wiping the brake components clean with a dampened cloth. Dispose of cloth and all residue containing asbestos fibers in an impermeable container with the appropriate label. Follow practices prescribed by the Occupational Safety and Health Administration (OSHA) and the Environmental Protection Agency (EPA) for the handling, processing, and disposing of dust or debris that may contain asbestos fibers.

BRAKE CALIPER

REMOVAL & INSTALLATION

See Figures 7 and 8.

1. Inspect the fluid level in the brake master cylinder reservoir.

2. If the brake fluid level is midway between the maximum-full point and the minimum allowable level, no brake fluid needs to be removed from the reservoir before proceeding.

3. If the brake fluid level is higher than midway between the maximum-full point and the minimum allowable level, remove brake fluid to the midway point before proceeding.

4. Raise and suitably support the vehicle.

5. Remove the tire and wheel assembly.

6. Install a large C-clamp over the body of the brake caliper with the C-clamp ends against the rear of the caliper body and against the outer brake pad. (See similar image in Front Disc Brakes.)

✳✳ WARNING

When using a large C-clamp to compress a caliper piston into a caliper bore of a caliper equipped with an integral park brake mechanism, do not exceed more than 0.039 in. (1 mm) of piston travel. Exceeding this amount of piston travel will cause damage to the internal adjusting mechanism and/or the integral park brake mechanism.

7. Tighten the C-clamp until the caliper piston is compressed into the caliper bore enough to allow the caliper to slide past the brake rotor.

8. Do not exceed 0.039 in (1 mm) of caliper piston travel.

9. Remove the C-clamp from the caliper.

10. Remove the brake hose to caliper bolt from the brake caliper.

11. Remove the brake hose from the brake caliper.

12. Remove and discard the 2 copper brake hose gaskets. These gaskets may be stuck to the brake caliper and/or the brake hose end.

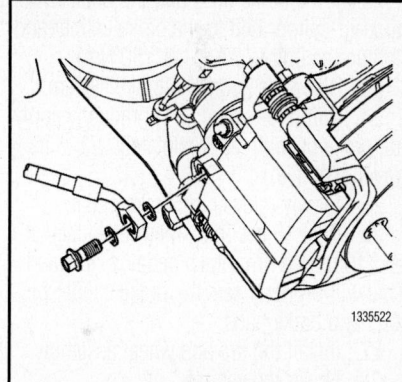

Fig. 7 Remove the brake hose to caliper bolt from the brake caliper

13. Cap or plug the opening in the brake caliper and the brake hose to prevent fluid loss and contamination.

14. Remove the 2 brake caliper pin bolts.

15. Remove the park brake cable from the caliper.

16. Remove the brake caliper from the brake caliper bracket.

To install:

17. Inspect the caliper slide boots for cuts, tears, or deterioration. If damaged, replace the slides and boots.

18. Install the brake caliper to the brake caliper bracket.

19. Install the 2 brake caliper pin bolts and tighten to 26 ft. lbs. (35 Nm).

20. Install the park brake cable to the caliper.

21. Remove the caps or plugs from the brake caliper opening and the brake hose.

➡ **DO NOT reuse the copper brake hose gaskets.**

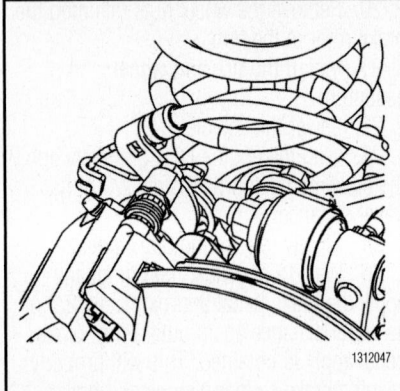

Fig. 8 Remove the park brake cable from the caliper

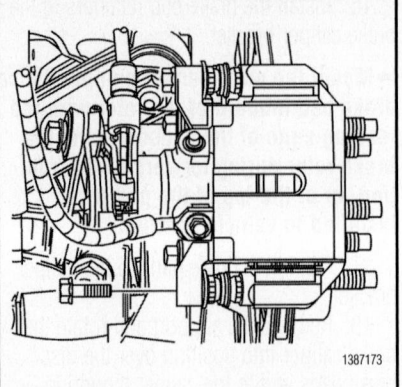

Fig. 9 Remove the lower brake caliper guide pin bolt

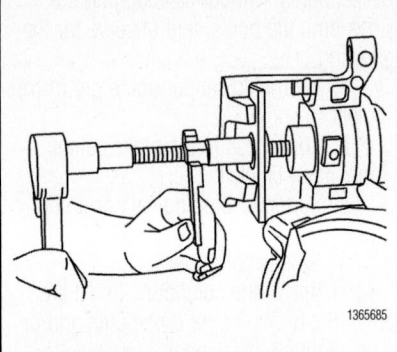

Fig. 11 Remove and the brake pad retainers (2) from the brake caliper mounting bracket (3)

22. Install NEW copper brake hose gaskets to the brake hose-to-caliper bolt and to the brake hose.

Install the brake hose and the brake hose-to-caliper bolt to the brake caliper and tighten the bolt to 37 ft. lbs. (50 Nm).

23. Bleed the hydraulic brake system.

24. With the engine OFF, gradually apply the brake pedal to approximately 2/3 of its travel distance.

25. Slowly release the brake pedal.

26. Wait 15 seconds, then repeat steps 9 and 10 until a firm brake pedal is obtained. This will properly seat the brake caliper pistons and brake pads.

27. Install the tire and wheel assembly.

28. Lower the vehicle.

29. Apply and release the park brake lever 4 times.

DISC BRAKE PADS

REMOVAL & INSTALLATION

See Figures 9 through 11.

1. Inspect the fluid level in the brake master cylinder reservoir.

2. If the brake fluid level is midway between the maximum-full point and the minimum allowable level, no brake fluid needs to be removed from the reservoir before proceeding.

3. Raise and suitably support the vehicle.

4. Remove the tire and wheel assembly.

5. Remove the lower brake caliper guide pin bolt.

❋❋ WARNING

Support the brake caliper with heavy mechanic wire, or equivalent, whenever it is separated from its mount

and the hydraulic flexible brake hose is still connected. Failure to support the caliper in this manner will cause the flexible brake hose to bear the weight of the caliper, which may cause damage to the brake hose and in turn may cause a brake fluid leak.

6. Pivot the brake caliper upward from the caliper bracket and support the caliper out of the way with heavy mechanic's wire or equivalent; ensure that there is no tension on the hydraulic brake flexible hose. Do NOT disconnect the hydraulic brake flexible hose from the caliper.

7. Remove the brake pads (1) from the brake caliper mounting bracket (3).

8. Remove and the brake pad retainers (2) from the brake caliper mounting bracket (3).

9. Inspect the following brake components for damage and corrosion:

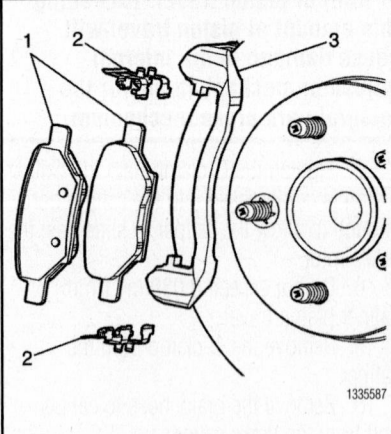

Fig. 10 Brake pads (1), retainers (2), caliper mounting bracket (3)

a. Brake caliper guide pin bolts
b. Brake caliper guide pins
c. Brake caliper guide pin bushing
d. Brake caliper bracket boots
e. Brake caliper bracket

10. Do not attempt to clean away any corrosion. If damaged or corroded replace the necessary components.

11. Inspect the brake caliper piston boot for deterioration, replace if damaged.

12. Use a piston installation tool in order to twist the brake caliper piston into the brake caliper bore.

To install:

13. Install the brake pad retainers to the brake caliper mounting bracket.

14. Install the brake pads to the brake caliper mounting bracket.

15. Pivot the brake caliper downward, over the brake pads and into the caliper bracket.

16. Install the brake caliper guide pin bolt to the brake caliper guide pin and tighten the bolt to 26 ft. lbs. (35 Nm).

17. Install the tire and wheel assembly.

18. Lower the vehicle.

19. With the engine OFF, gradually apply the brake pedal to approximately 2/3 of its travel distance.

20. Slowly release the brake pedal.

21. Wait 15 seconds, then repeat steps 11 and 12 until a firm brake pedal apply is obtained; this will properly seat the brake caliper pistons and brake pads.

22. Fill the brake master cylinder reservoir to the proper level. Refer to Master Cylinder Reservoir Filling.

23. Apply and release the park brake lever 4 times.

24. Burnish the pads and rotors.

BRAKES

PARKING BRAKE

PARKING BRAKE REAR CABLE

ADJUSTMENT

➡ **The G6 uses a self-tensioning, or self-adjusting, park brake cable system. The park brake system does not require adjustment under normal operating conditions. The tension on the park brake cables can be disabled and enabled when necessary during service of the disc brake and/or the park brake system.**

1. Apply and fully release the park brake lever several times. Verify that the park brake lever releases completely.

2. Turn ON the ignition. Verify the red BRAKE warning lamp is not illuminated.

3. If the red BRAKE warning lamp is illuminated, verify the following:

4. The park brake lever is in the fully released position and against the stop.

5. There is no slack in the park brake cables.

6. Turn OFF the ignition.

7. Raise and support the vehicle.

8. With the park brake lever fully released, check the park brake apply levers on the rear calipers. The apply levers should be against the stops on the caliper housings. If the apply levers are not against the stops, binding may exist.

9. Fully apply and release the park brake lever 3-5 times in order for the cable tensioner to take up any slack in the park brake cables.

10. Fully apply the park brake lever, tension should be felt on the lever by pulling the lever less than one full pull.

11. Attempt to rotate the rear brake rotors. There should be no rotation forward or rearward.

12. Fully release the park brake lever.

13. Verify the park brake is released by rotating the rear brake rotors. The rotors should rotate freely and exhibit no brake drag.

14. Lower the vehicle.

CHASSIS ELECTRICAL

AIR BAG (SUPPLEMENTAL INFLATIBLE RESTRAINT)

GENERAL INFORMATION

✳ WARNING

The G6 is equipped with an air bag system. Disarm the system before performing service on, or around, system components, the steering column, instrument panel components, wiring and sensors. Failure to follow the safety precautions and the disarming procedure could result in accidental air bag deployment, possible injury and unnecessary system repairs.

SERVICE PRECAUTIONS

Disconnect and isolate the battery negative cable before beginning any airbag system component diagnosis, testing, removal, or installation procedures. Allow system capacitor to discharge for two minutes before beginning any component service. This will disable the airbag system. Failure to disable the airbag system may result in accidental airbag deployment, personal injury, or death.

Do not place an intact undeployed airbag face down on a solid surface. The airbag will propel into the air if accidentally deployed and may result in personal injury or death.

When carrying or handling an undeployed airbag, the trim side (face) of the airbag should be pointing away from the body to minimize possibility of injury if accidental deployment occurs. Failure to do this may result in personal injury or death.

Replace airbag system components with OEM replacement parts. Substitute parts

may appear interchangeable, but internal differences may result in inferior occupant protection. Failure to do so may result in occupant personal injury or death.

Wear safety glasses, rubber gloves, and long sleeved clothing when cleaning powder residue from vehicle after an airbag deployment. Powder residue emitted from a deployed airbag can cause skin irritation. Flush affected area with cool water if irritation is experienced. If nasal or throat irritation is experienced, exit the vehicle for fresh air until the irritation ceases. If irritation continues, see a physician.

Do not use a replacement airbag that is not in the original packaging. This may result in improper deployment, personal injury, or death.

The factory installed fasteners, screws and bolts used to fasten airbag components have a special coating and are specifically designed for the airbag system. Do not use substitute fasteners. Use only original equipment fasteners listed in the parts catalog when fastener replacement is required.

During, and following, any child restraint anchor service, due to impact event or vehicle repair, carefully inspect all mounting hardware, tether straps, and anchors for proper installation, operation, or damage. If a child restraint anchor is found damaged in any way, the anchor must be replaced. Failure to do this may result in personal injury or death.

Deployed and non-deployed airbags may or may not have live pyrotechnic material within the airbag inflator.

Do not dispose of driver/passenger/curtain airbags or seat belt tensioners unless you are sure of complete deploy-

ment. Refer to the Hazardous Substance Control System for proper disposal.

Dispose of deployed airbags and tensioners consistent with state, provincial, local, and federal regulations.

After any airbag component testing or service, do not connect the battery negative cable. Personal injury or death may result if the system test is not performed first.

If the vehicle is equipped with the Occupant Classification System (OCS), do not connect the battery negative cable before performing the OCS Verification Test using the scan tool and the appropriate diagnostic information. Personal injury or death may result if the system test is not performed properly.

Never replace both the Occupant Restraint Controller (ORC) and the Occupant Classification Module (OCM) at the same time. If both require replacement, replace one, and then perform the Airbag System test before replacing the other.

Both the ORC and the OCM store Occupant Classification System (OCS) calibration data, which they transfer to one another when one of them is replaced. If both are replaced at the same time, an irreversible fault will be set in both modules and the OCS may malfunction and cause personal injury or death.

If equipped with OCS, the Seat Weight Sensor is a sensitive, calibrated unit and must be handled carefully. Do not drop or handle roughly. If dropped or damaged, replace with another sensor. Failure to do so may result in occupant injury or death.

If equipped with OCS, the front passenger seat must be handled carefully as well. When removing the seat, be careful when setting on floor not to drop. If dropped, the sensor may be inoperative, could result in occupant injury, or possibly death.

If equipped with OCS, when the passenger front seat is on the floor, no one should sit in the front passenger seat. This uneven force may damage the sensing ability of the seat weight sensors. If sat on and damaged, the sensor may be inoperative, could result in occupant injury, or possibly death.

DISABLING THE SUPPLEMENTAL INFLATABLE RESTRAINT (SIR) SYSTEM

➡***DTCs will be lost when the negative battery cable is disconnected.**

Note the following:
- If the vehicle was involved in an accident with an air bag deployment, disconnect the negative battery cable(s). Special repairs and inspections are required after a collision.
- When performing SIR diagnostics follow the appropriate SIR service manual diagnostic procedure(s).
- When moving, removing or replacing an SIR component or a component attached to an SIR component and anytime you remove fasteners, disconnect the negative battery cable(s).*
- If the vehicle is suspected of having shorted electrical wires, disconnect the negative battery cable(s).*
- When performing electrical diagnosis on components other than the SIR system, remove the SIR/Airbag fuse(s) when indicated by the diagnostic procedure to disable the SIR system

Disabling Procedure—Air Bag Fuse

1. Turn the steering wheel so that the vehicles wheels are pointing straight ahead.
2. Place the ignition in the OFF position.

✷✷ CAUTION

The SDM may have more than one fused power input. To ensure there is no unwanted SIR deployment, personal injury, or unnecessary SIR system repairs, remove all fuses supplying power to the SDM. With all SDM fuses removed and the ignition switch in the ON position, the AIR BAG warning indicator illuminates. This is normal operation, and does not indicate a SIR system malfunction.

3. Locate and remove the fuse(s) supplying power to the SDM.

4. Wait 1 minute before working on the system.

Disabling Procedure—Negative Battery Cable

1. Turn the steering wheel so that the vehicles wheels are pointing straight ahead.
2. Place the ignition in the OFF position.
3. Disconnect the negative battery cable from the battery.
4. Wait 1 minute before working on system.

ENABLING THE SYSTEM

Enabling Procedure—Air Bag Fuse

1. Place the ignition in the OFF position.
2. Install the fuse(s) supplying power to the SDM.
3. Turn the ignition switch to the ON position. The AIR BAG indicator will flash then turn OFF.
4. Perform the Diagnostic System Check—Vehicle if the AIR BAG warning indicator does not operate as described.

Enabling Procedure—Negative Battery Cable

1. Place the ignition in the OFF position.
2. Connect the negative battery cable to the battery.
3. Turn the ignition switch to the ON position. The AIR BAG indicator will flash then turn OFF.
4. Perform the Diagnostic System Check—Vehicle if the AIR BAG warning indicator does not operate as described.

INFLATABLE RESTRAINT STEERING WHEEL MODULE COIL CENTERING

See Figures 12 and 13.

✷✷ WARNING

The new SIR coil assembly will be centered. Improper alignment of the SIR coil assembly may damage the unit, causing an inflatable restraint malfunction.

1. Verify the following conditions before centering the supplemental inflatable restraint (SIR) steering wheel module coil:

a. The wheels on the vehicle are straight ahead.

b. The block tooth and the centering mark (1) of the steering shaft is in the 12 o'clock position.

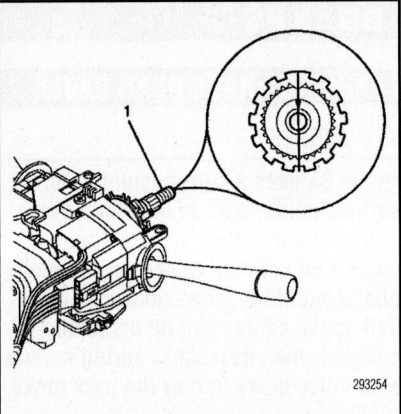

Fig. 12 Verify the block tooth and the centering mark (1) of the steering shaft is in the 12 o'clock position

2. If available, remove the yellow retaining tab (1) from the SIR steering wheel module coil and save the tab for reassembly.
3. Hold the SIR steering wheel module coil face up by the casing (2).

a. Slowly turn the SIR steering wheel module coil hub (3) clockwise until the coil ribbon stops.

b. Slowly rotate the SIR steering wheel module coil hub (3) counterclockwise 2.5 revolutions until the centering window (4) turns yellow. This indicates the CENTER position.

➡**If the retaining tab is not available, the use of tape to secure the SIR steering wheel module coil is recommended for installation to the steering column.**

4. Install the yellow retaining tab (1) to the SIR steering wheel module coil.
5. Slide the centered SIR steering wheel module coil onto the steering shaft.

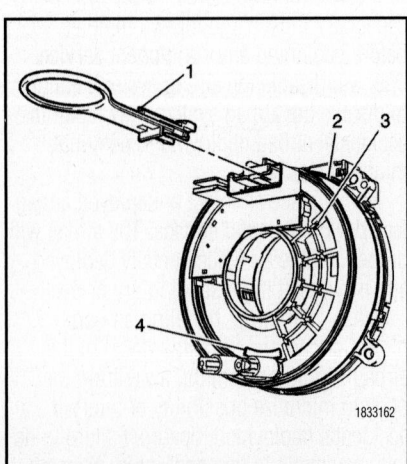

Fig. 13 Yellow retaining tab (1), casing (2), hub (3), and centering window (4)

DRIVE TRAIN

TRANSMISSION FLUID REPLACEMENT

FLUID, FILTER & SEAL REPLACEMENT

4T45E Transaxle

See Figures 14 through 16.

❄❄ CAUTION

Ensure that the vehicle is properly supported and squarely positioned. To help avoid personal injury when a vehicle is on a hoist, provide additional support for the vehicle on the opposite end from which the components are being removed.

1. Position the vehicle on a hoist and raise the vehicle.
2. Place a drain pan under the transaxle oil pan.
3. Remove the oil pan bolts from the front and sides only.
4. Loosen the rear oil pan bolts approximately 4 times.

❄❄ WARNING

Pry the oil pan carefully in order to prevent damage to the transaxle case or the oil pan sealing surfaces.

5. Lightly tap the oil pan with a rubber mallet or carefully pry in order to allow the oil to drain.
6. Remove the AIR.
7. Inspect the fluid color.
8. Remove the remaining oil pan bolts and the oil pan.
9. Remove the oil pan gasket.

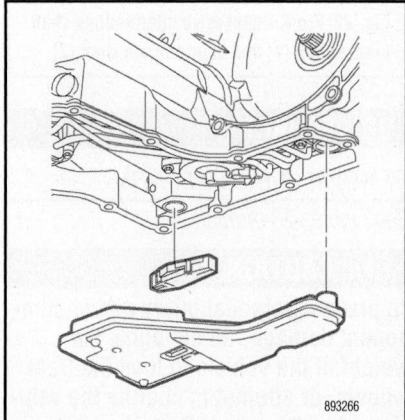
Fig. 14 Remove the oil pan gasket and oil level control valve

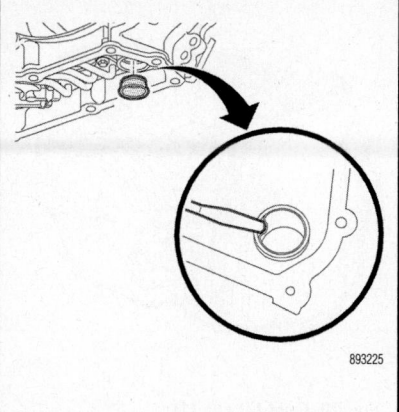
Fig. 15 Remove the oil filter and oil filter O-ring seal

10. Remove the oil level control valve.
11. Remove the oil filter and oil filter O-ring seal. The seal may stay in the case when filter is removed.

➡**Do not score or damage the transaxle case when removing the filter neck seal.**

12. Using a chisel, indent the top of the filter neck seal to relax the press fit.
13. Remove the filter neck seal from the transaxle case and discard.
14. Remove all traces of the old gasket material.
15. Clean the transaxle case and oil pan gasket surfaces with solvent, and allow to air dry.

To install:

❄❄ WARNING

Use petroleum jelly when lubricating the components. Greases other than petroleum jelly will change the transaxle fluid characteristics and will cause undesirable shift conditions or filter clogging.

16. Install a new filter neck seal. A large socket can be used as an installation tool as shown. Two mallets can be used as well.
17. Coat the new filter O-ring seal with a small amount of petroleum jelly, and install the filter into the case.

❄❄ WARNING

Push straight down on the center of the oil level control valve in order to prevent damage to the case bore.

18. Install the oil level control valve.

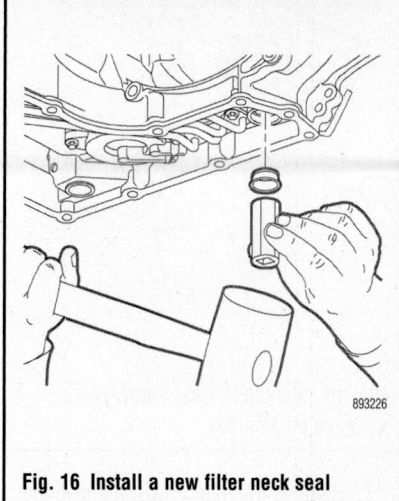
Fig. 16 Install a new filter neck seal

19. Install the oil pan gasket, the oil pan, and hand start the oil pan bolts.
20. Tighten the oil pan bolts to 9 ft. lbs. (12 Nm).
21. Lower the vehicle.
22. Refill the transaxle using DEXRON®VI to the specified refill capacity. Specification
- The bottom pan removal capacity is approximately 6.9 qt (6.5 L).
- The complete overhaul capacity is approximately 9.5 qt (9 L).
- The dry capacity is approximately 12.9 qt (12.2 L).
23. Start the engine. Warm up the transaxle and check for leaks.
24. Check for proper fluid level.

4T65E Transaxle

See Figures 17 and 18.

1. Remove the oil pan (24) and the gasket (25). Refer to Oil Pan replacement.

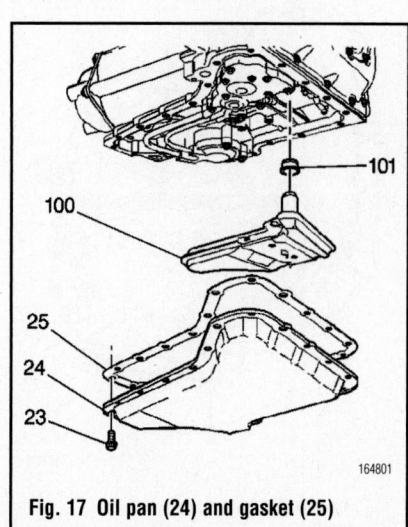
Fig. 17 Oil pan (24) and gasket (25)

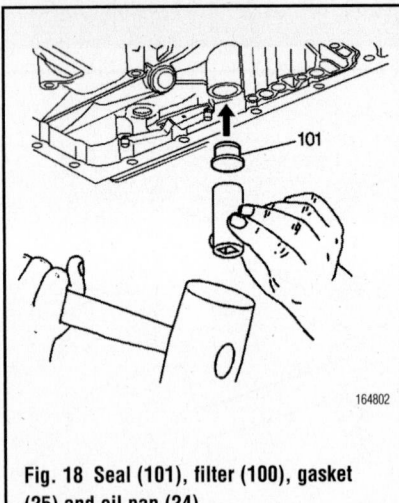

Fig. 18 Seal (101), filter (100), gasket (25) and oil pan (24)

2. Remove the filter (100). Remove the lip ring seal (101) pressed into the case only if replacement is necessary.

3. Inspect the oil pan and the filter for the following foreign material: metal particles, clutch facing material, rubber particles, and engine coolant.

4. Determine the source of the contamination if foreign material is evident.

5. Correct the source of the contamination.

To install:

6. If removed, install a new seal (101).

7. Install the filter (100).

8. Install the gasket (25) and the oil pan (24).

6T40/6T45 Transaxle

See Figures 19 and 20.

1. Raise and support the vehicle.

2. Remove the fluid drain plug (1).

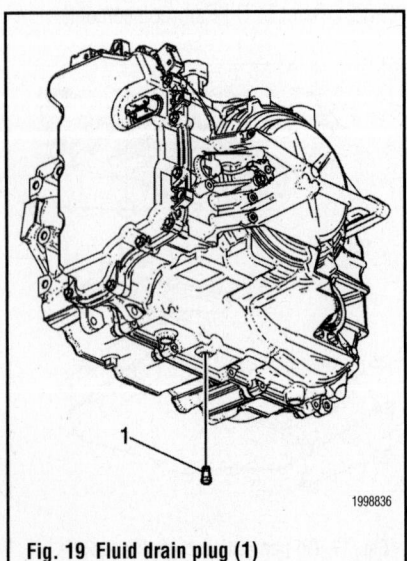

Fig. 19 Fluid drain plug (1)

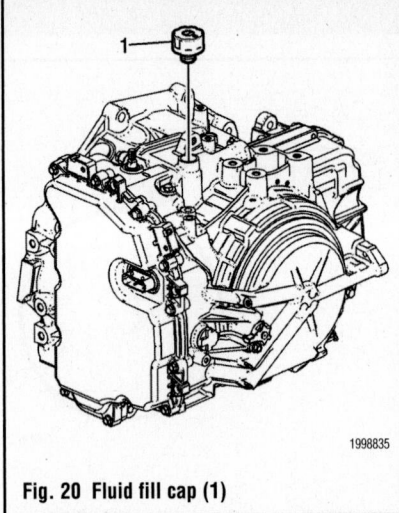

Fig. 20 Fluid fill cap (1)

3. Drain the transmission fluid into a suitable container.

4. Install the fluid drain plug (1) and tighten to 106 inch lbs. (12 Nm).

To install:

5. Lower the vehicle.

6. Remove the fluid fill cap (1).

7. Fill the transmission to the proper level with the correct fluid.

8. Install the fluid fill cap (1).

9. Tighten.

6T70/6T75 Transaxle

See Figure 21.

1. Raise and support the vehicle.

2. Place a drain pan capable of containing more than 5 quarts of fluid under the transmission before removing the plug to drain the fluid.

3. Remove the fluid drain plug (1).

4. Fill the transmission to the proper level with the correct fluid.

5. Install the fluid fill cap.

6. Tighten.

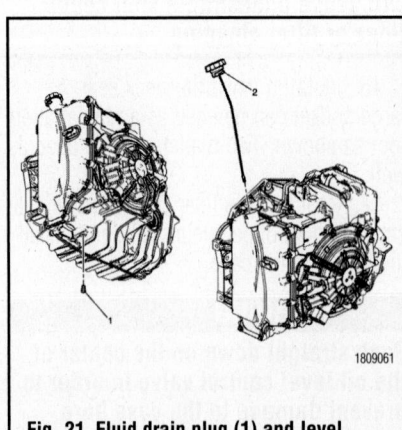

Fig. 21 Fluid drain plug (1) and level indicator (2)

FRONT WHEEL DRIVE INTERMEDIATE SHAFT

REMOVAL & INSTALLATION

3.6L Engine

See Figure 22.

1. Remove the wheel Driveshaft.

2. Remove the 3 front wheel drive intermediate shaft bracket bolts (1).

➡Use care when removing the intermediate Driveshaft from the transmission so as not to damage the seal.

3. Remove the front wheel drive intermediate shaft (2).

➡The J 44394-A seal protector tool must be installed into the differential output shaft seal prior to removing and installing the intermediate shaft. Failure to install the J 44394-A may cause splines of the intermediate shaft to cut the differential output seal.

To install:

Installation is the reverse of assembly. Tighten the intermediate shaft bracket bolts to 16 ft. lbs. (22 Nm).

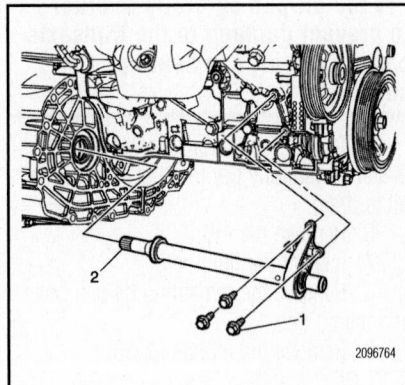

Fig. 22 Front wheel drive intermediate shaft bracket bolt (1) and intermediate shaft (2)

DRIVESHAFT

REMOVAL & INSTALLATION

See Figures 23 through 26.

✼✼ CAUTION

To prevent personal injury and/or component damage, do not allow the weight of the vehicle to load the front wheels, or attempt to operate the vehicle, when the wheel Driveshaft(s) or wheel Driveshaft nut(s) are removed. To do so may cause the inner bearing

race to separate, resulting in damage to brake and suspension components and loss of vehicle control.

Protect wheel Driveshaft boots, seals and clamps from sharp objects any time you are performing service on or near the wheel Driveshaft(s). Damage to the boot(s), the seal(s) or the clamp(s) may cause lubricant to leak from the joint and lead to increased noise and possible failure of the wheel Driveshaft.

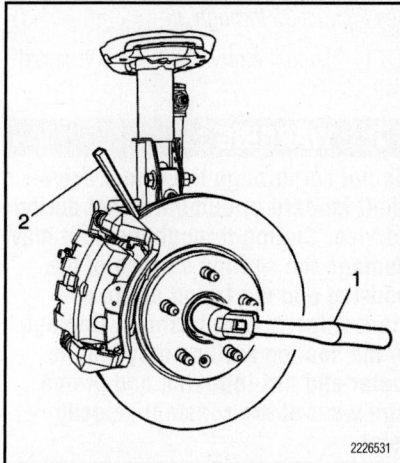

Fig. 23 Insert a brass drift or punch (2) between the brake rotor cooling fins and the brake caliper mounting bracket. Using the appropriate size socket and breaker bar (1), loosen the wheel Driveshaft nut.

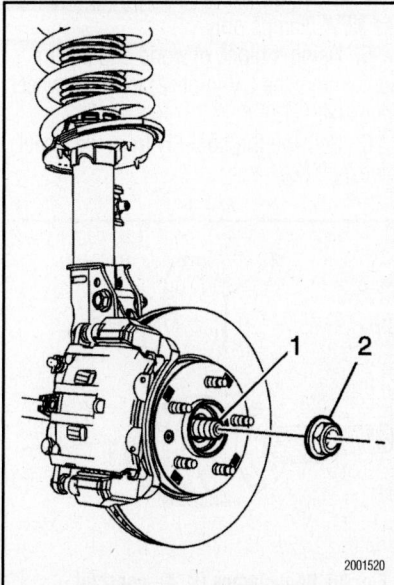

Fig. 24 Wheel Driveshaft nut (2) and Driveshaft (1)

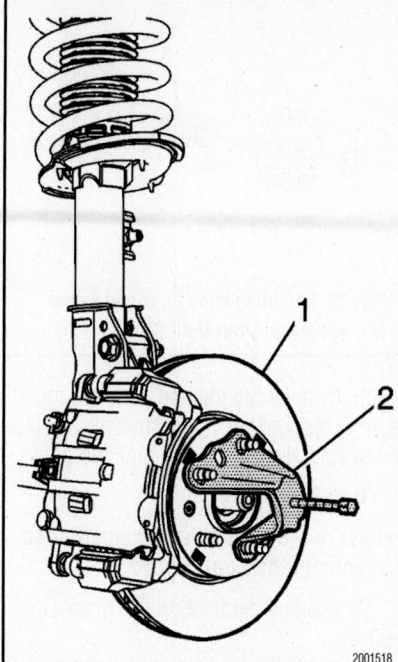

Fig. 25 J 42129 hub spindle remover (2) and the brake rotor and wheel bearing/hub assembly (1)

1. Raise and suitably support the vehicle.
2. Remove the wheel and the tire.
3. Insert a brass drift or punch (2) between the brake rotor cooling fins and the brake caliper mounting bracket.
4. Using the appropriate size socket and breaker bar (1), loosen the wheel Driveshaft nut.

➡**DO NOT re-use the wheel Driveshaft nut. Discard the nut and replace with a NEW one.**

5. Remove the wheel Driveshaft nut (2) from the wheel Driveshaft (1).
6. Using the J 42129 hub spindle remover (2), separate the brake rotor and wheel bearing/hub assembly (1).
7. Remove the outer tie rod assembly from the steering knuckle.
8. Remove the ball joint from the steering knuckle. Refer to Lower Control Arm replacement.

➡**Replace the front axle shaft seal once the wheel Driveshaft has been removed. Replace with a NEW seal only. DO NOT reuse the front axle shaft seal.**

9. Using the J 2619-01 (3), the J 29794 (2), and the J 33008-A (3), remove the wheel Driveshaft (4) from the vehicle.

➡**Remove the front axle shaft seal.**

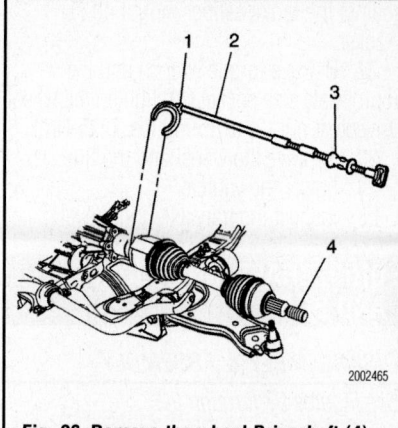

Fig. 26 Remove the wheel Driveshaft (4) from the vehicle

To install:
10. Install the NEW front axle shaft seal.

J-44394 must be installed into the differential output shaft seal prior to removing and installing the wheel Driveshaft. Failure to install J-44394 as indicated may cause the splines of the wheel Driveshaft to cut the differential output seal.

11. Install the J 44394-A into the differential output shaft seal.
➡**In order to prevent lubricant leaks, use care when installing the wheel Driveshaft to the differential.**
12. Do not damage the oil seal. Replace the oil seal if it becomes nicked, distorted, or otherwise damaged.
13. Carefully install the wheel Driveshaft into the differential until the splines are past the J 44394-A.
14. Remove the J 44394-A from the differential output shaft seal.
15. Install the wheel Driveshaft into the differential until the retaining ring is fully seated.
16. Confirm that the front wheel Driveshaft retaining ring is properly seated by holding the inner housing and pull the inner housing outward.
17. Install the front wheel Driveshaft into the front wheel bearing/hub.
18. Install the ball joint to the steering knuckle. Refer to Lower Control Arm replacement.
19. Install the outer tie rod assembly to the steering knuckle.
20. Install the NEW wheel Driveshaft nut (2) on the wheel Driveshaft (1).
21. Insert a drift or punch (5) into the cooling fin of the brake rotor (4) caliper and

against the brake caliper mounting (1) bracket.

22. Using a torque wrench and the appropriate size socket (3), tighten the wheel Driveshaft nut (2) to 159 ft. lbs. (215 Nm).

23. Remove the wheel and the tire.

24. Lower the vehicle.

25. Inspect the transaxle fluid level.

DRIVESHAFT INNER JOINT AND BOOT

DISASSEMBLY & ASSEMBLY

See Figures 27 through 29.

1. Position wheel driveshaft bar in a soft-jawed vise and clamp it securely.

2. Using a flat-bladed tool, remove the boot retaining clamp (2) from the boot (3) for the tripod housing (1).

3. Using side cutters, remove the boot clamp (4) from the boot (3) for the wheel Driveshaft (5).

4. Remove the tripod housing from the wheel Driveshaft.

5. Remove the retaining clip (1) and the tripod spider (2) from the wheel Driveshaft (3).

6. Remove the boot from the wheel Driveshaft.

7. Inspect the wheel Driveshaft inner joint for damage and excessive wear.

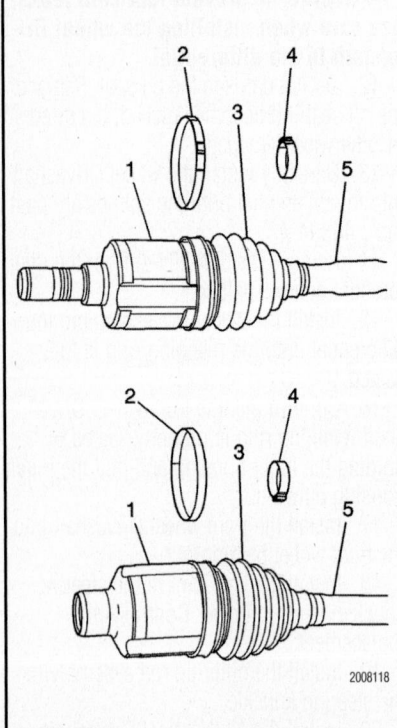

Fig. 27 Boot retaining clamp (2), tripod housing boot (3), tripod housing (1), boot clamp (4), and wheel Driveshaft (5)

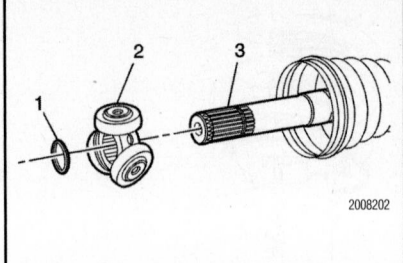

Fig. 28 Retaining clip (1), tripod spider (2), and wheel Driveshaft (3)

8. If any of the internal parts are found to be excessively worn or damaged, replace the wheel Driveshaft inner joint and boot.

To assemble:

➡ **Ensure the seal clamp is positioned correctly in the seal groove.**

9. Position the boot on the wheel Driveshaft.

10. Install the tripod spider assembly (2) to the wheel Driveshaft (3), until seated against shoulder.

11. Install the retaining ring (1) in the wheel Driveshaft.

12. Place approximately half of the grease in the kit to the seal and place the remainder in the tripod housing.

13. Install the tripod housing on the wheel Driveshaft.

14. Install the boot clamp (2) on the boot (3) for the tripod housing (1).

15. Install the boot clamp (4) on the boot (3) for the wheel drive (5).

16. Using the J 35910, crimp the small boot clamp (1).

17. Tighten the boot clamp to 130 ft. lbs. (176 Nm).

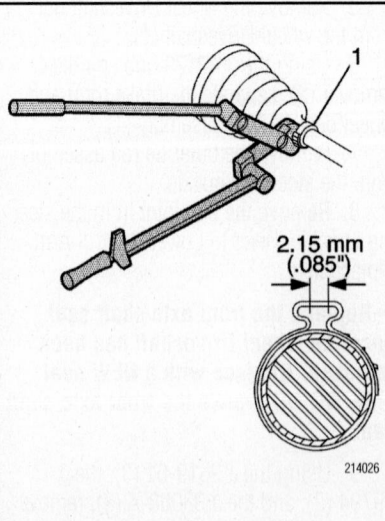

Fig. 29 Using the J 35910, crimp the small boot clamp (1)

18. Measure the clamp gap width. Specification: Clamp gap width should not exceed 0.085 in (2.15 mm).

19. Using the J 35910, crimp the large boot clamp.

20. Measure the clamp gap width (4). Specification: Dimension equals 0.102 in (2.6 mm).

21. Rotate the housing in a circular motion to distribute the grease in the tripod joint.

DRIVESHAFT OUTER JOINT AND BOOT

REMOVAL & INSTALLATION

See Figures 30 through 35.

1. Clamp the driveshaft in a soft-jawed vise.

✳✳ WARNING

Do not cut through the wheel Driveshaft inboard or outboard boot during service. Cutting through the boot may damage the sealing surface of the housing and the tripod or the constant velocity joint bushing. Damage to the sealing surface may lead to water and dirt intrusion and premature wear of the constant velocity joint.

2. Use a flat-bladed tool to remove the boot clamp (2) from the constant velocity (CV) joint (1) and the boot (3).

3. Using a pair of side cutters, remove the boot clamp (4) from the boot (3) and the wheel Driveshaft (5).

4. Discard the boot clamps (2) and (4). Use NEW clamps only.

5. Using a block of wood and a hammer, remove the CV joint (2) from the wheel Driveshaft (1).

6. Remove the boot (1) from the wheel Driveshaft (2).

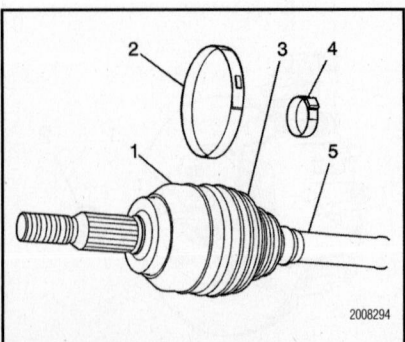

Fig. 30 Boot clamps (2, 4), constant velocity (CV) joint (1), boot (3), and wheel Driveshaft (5)

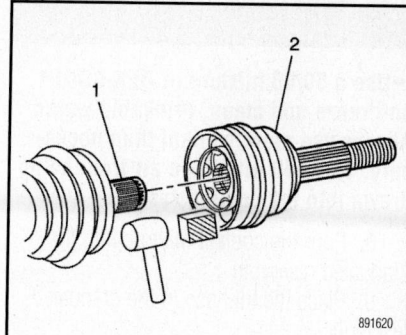

Fig. 31 Using a block of wood and a hammer, remove the CV joint (2) from the wheel Driveshaft (1)

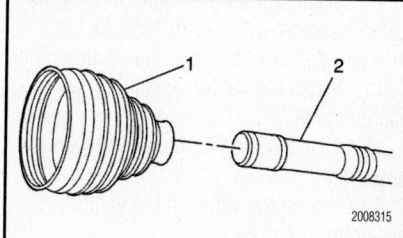

Fig. 32 Remove the boot (1) from the wheel Driveshaft (2)

7. Inspect the outer CV joint for damage and wear. If any of the above items are found to have excessive wear or are damaged, replace the outer CV joint as an assembly.

➡**The internal parts of the CV joint are NOT SERVICED separately. The outer CV joint is serviced as an assembly.**

To install:

8. Position the boot on the wheel Driveshaft.

Ensure that the boot (1) is properly seated in the groove (2) in the wheel Driveshaft (3).

9. Place approximately half the grease from the service kit inside the outboard boot

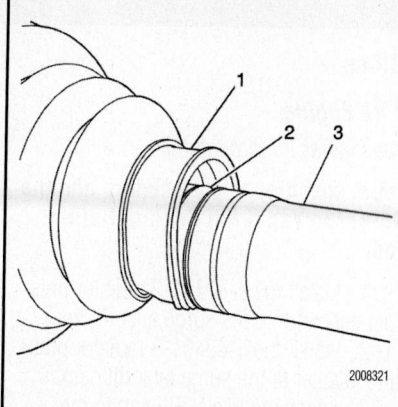

Fig. 33 Ensure that the boot (1) is properly seated in the groove (2) in the wheel Driveshaft (3)

and pack the CV joint with the remaining grease.

10. Using a block of wood and a hammer, install the CV joint on the wheel Driveshaft (1).

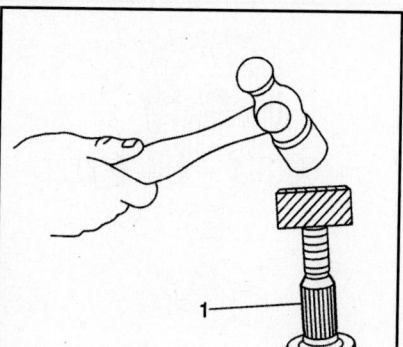

Fig. 34 Using a block of wood and a hammer, install the CV joint on the wheel Driveshaft (1)

11. Install the boot clamp on the boot and the wheel Driveshaft.

12. Install the boot clamp on the boot and the CV joint housing.

➡**Ensure that the boot clamp is properly positioned around the entire circumference of the boot.**

13. Using the J 35910 (3), crimp the boot clamp.

14. Tighten the boot clamp.

15. Tighten the boot clamp to 130 ft. lbs. (174 Nm).

16. Using the CH-48894 boot clamp pliers (1), close the boot clamp (3). Ensure the boot clamp (3) is securely closed and seated properly on the boot (2).

17. Remove the wheel Driveshaft from the bench vise.

18. Distribute the grease within the outer CV joint by rotating the joint in a circular motion four to five times.

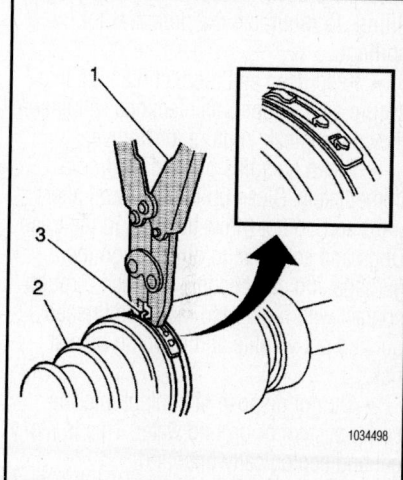

Fig. 35 Using the CH-48894 boot clamp pliers (1), close the boot clamp (3). Ensure the boot clamp (3) is securely closed and seated properly on the boot (2).

ENGINE COOLING

ENGINE COOLANT

BEST PRACTICES

A small amount of antifreeze can kill human beings, pets and wildlife.

• Do not pour used coolant down a drain. Ethylene glycol antifreeze is a very toxic chemical.

• Store used antifreeze in compatible containers that are in good condition and labeled "Used Antifreeze Only" until you recycle it.

• Do not mix used antifreeze with any waste or other material such as solvents, cooling system flushes, used oil, or motor fuels.

• Use antifreeze collection, storage, and transport containers solely for the transfer and storage of antifreeze, to minimize the risk of cross-contamination.

• Keep used antifreeze containers securely closed, except when emptying or filling, to minimize the potential for spillage.

• Keep used antifreeze containers in a secure area. Proper maintenance will ensure they do not leak, rupture, or tip over.

• Clean up spills of used antifreeze immediately. Clean up the area well afterward and do not throw the rags in the trash. Dogs and cats love to dig through the garbage and can become exposed through contact with rags. Also radiators flushed outside put wildlife and roaming pets at risk.

• Do not dispose of coolant into the sewer system or ground water. This is illegal and ecologically unsound.

DRAIN & REFILL PROCEDURE

Draining

1. Unscrew the surge tank cap to remove vacuum when draining the coolant.

2. Raise and support the vehicle.

3. Place a container under the radiator drain.

4. Unscrew the radiator drain plug until coolant flows out the radiator drain.

5. If a complete block drain is required, remove the drain plugs.

6. Follow the appropriate procedure based on the condition of the coolant:

   a. If the coolant is normal in appearance, follow the filling procedure.

   b. If the coolant is discolored, follow the flush procedure. Refer to Flushing.

Filling

2.4L Engine

See Figures 36 through 39.

➥GM specifies this procedure and the GE-47716 Vac N Fill Coolant Refill Tool.

1. Install the J-42401-2 radiator pressure adapter into the surge tank fill neck.

2. Install the J-42401-3 radiator pressure adapter to the surge tank fill neck.

3. Attach the Vac N Fill cap to the J-42401-3.

4. Attach the Vac N Fill cap to the vehicle's coolant fill port.

5. Attach the vacuum gauge assembly to the Vac N Fill cap.

6. Attach the fill hose to the barb fitting on the vacuum gauge assembly.

7. Ensure the valve is closed.

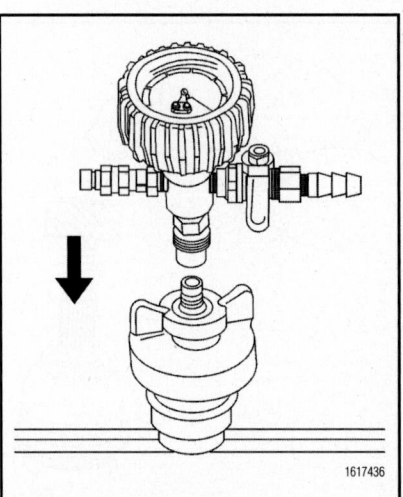

Fig. 36 Attach the Vac N Fill cap to the vehicle's coolant fill port

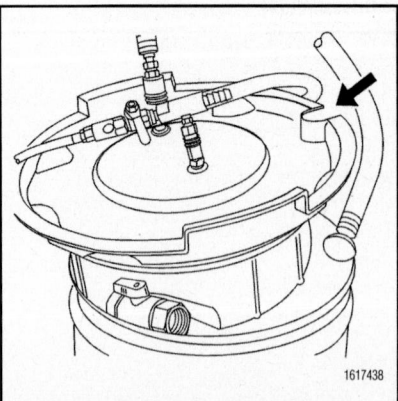

Fig. 37 Attach the fill hose to the barb fitting on the vacuum gauge assembly and ensure the valve is closed

➥Use a 50/50 mixture of DEX-COOL® antifreeze and clean, drinkable water. Always use more coolant than necessary. This will eliminate air from being drawn into the cooling system.

8. Pour the coolant mixture into the graduated reservoir.

9. Place the fill hose in the graduated reservoir.

➥Prior to installing the vacuum tank onto the graduated reservoir, ensure the drain valve located on the bottom of the tank is closed.

10. Install the vacuum tank on the graduated reservoir with the fill hose routed through the cut-out area in the vacuum tank.

11. Attach the venturi assembly to the vacuum tank.

12. Attach a shop air hose to the venturi assembly.

13. Ensure the valve on the venturi assembly is closed.

14. Attach the vacuum hose to the vacuum gauge assembly and the vacuum tank.

15. Open the valve on the venturi assembly. The vacuum gauge will begin to rise and a hissing noise will occur.

16. Continue to draw vacuum until the needle stops rising. This should be 24–26 in Hg (610–660 mm Hg). Cooling hoses may start to collapse. This is normal due to vacuum draw.

17. To aid in the fill process, position the graduated reservoir above the coolant fill port.

18. Slowly open the valve on the vacuum gauge assembly. When the coolant reaches the top of the fill hose, close the valve. This will eliminate air from the fill hose.

19. Close the valve on the venturi assembly.

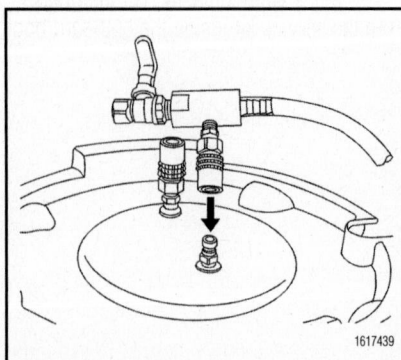

Fig. 38 Install the vacuum tank on the graduated reservoir with the fill hose routed through the cut-out area in the vacuum tank

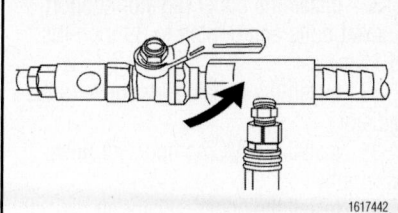

Fig. 39 Attach the vacuum hose to the vacuum gauge assembly and the vacuum tank.

20. If there is a suspected leak in the cooling system, allow the system to stabilize under vacuum and monitor for vacuum loss.

21. If vacuum loss is observed, diagnose and repair the problem.

22. Open the valve on the vacuum gauge assembly. The vacuum gauge will drop as coolant is drawn into the system.

23. Once the vacuum gauge reaches zero, close the valve on the vacuum gauge assembly and repeat steps 11–19.

24. Remove the J-42401-3 from the surge tank fill neck.

25. Remove J-42401-2 from the surge tank fill neck.

26. Detach the Vac N Fill cap from the vehicle's coolant fill port.

27. Add coolant to the system as necessary.

28. Inspect the concentration of the coolant mixture using J 26568.

➡**After filling the cooling system, use the extraction hose to remove excess coolant to achieve the proper coolant level.**

29. Detach the vacuum hose from the vacuum gauge assembly.

30. Attach the extraction hose to the vacuum hose.

31. Open the valve on the venturi assembly to start a vacuum draw.

32. Use the extraction hose to draw out coolant to the proper level.

33. Install the surge tank cap.

34. The vacuum tank has a drain valve on the bottom of the tank. Open the valve to drain coolant from the vacuum tank into a suitable container for disposal.

❈❈ CAUTION

Coolant is very toxic. Refer to Coolant Best Practices.

3.5L, 3.6L & 3.9L Engines

❈❈ WARNING

The procedure below must be followed. Improper coolant level could

result in a low or high coolant level condition, causing engine damage.

1. Ensure coolant drain plugs are closed.
2. Lower the vehicle.
3. Vehicle should be level.
4. Add a mixture of 50/50 DEX-COOL® antifreeze and clean drinkable water until the level stabilizes to approximately 1 inch (25.4 mm) above the weld seam on the surge tank.
5. Install the surge tank cap.

➡**DO NOT exceed 2,200 RPM.**

6. Start the engine and run at 2,000 RPM until the engine cooling fans turn ON.
7. Turn the engine OFF and allow the engine to cool down.
8. Remove the surge tank cap.
9. Refill to approximately 1 inch (25.4 mm) above the weld seam on the surge tank.
10. Install the surge tank cap.
11. Inspect the concentration of the engine coolant using J 26568 or an equivalent coolant tester.
12. Inspect the concentration of the engine coolant using J 26568.
13. Install the surge tank cap.
14. Rinse away any excess coolant from the engine and the engine compartment.

❈❈ CAUTION

Coolant is very toxic. Refer to Coolant Best Practices.

FLUSHING

❈❈ CAUTION

Coolant is very toxic. Refer to Coolant Best Practices.

➡**Do not use a chemical flush. Various methods and equipment can be used to flush the cooling system. If special equipment is used, such as a back flusher, follow the manufacturer's instructions. However, always remove the thermostat before back-flushing the system.**

1. Apply the park brake.
2. Drain the coolant. Refer to Cooling System Draining and Filling.
3. Fill the coolant system with clean drinkable water. Refer to Cooling System Draining and Filling.
4. Start the engine and run at 2,000 RPM until the thermostat opens.
5. Turn OFF the engine.
6. Drain the coolant system. Refer to Cooling System Draining and Filling.

7. Repeat the above procedure until the water from the coolant system is colorless.
8. Drain the coolant system. Refer to Cooling System Draining and Filling.
9. Add 3.8 liters (1.0 gal) of concentrated antifreeze since there will be some water in the system.
10. Add a mixture of 50/50 DEX-COOL® antifreeze and clean drinkable water until the level stabilizes at the weld seam on the surge tank. Refer to Cooling System Draining and Filling.

ENGINE FAN & SHROUD

REMOVAL & INSTALLATION

See Figures 40 through 45.

1. Partially drain the cooling system. Refer to Cooling System Draining and Filling.
2. Remove the air cleaner air duct.
3. Remove the upper radiator air deflector.
4. Remove the transmission oil cooler pipes from the radiator.
5. Loop a rope around each of the upper 2 tabs of the condenser and tie a rope around the upper tie bar.
6. Remove the upper radiator support bracket bolts.

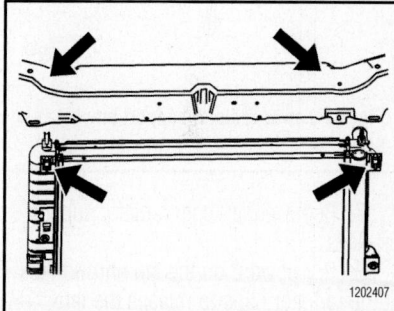

Fig. 40 Loop a rope around each of the upper 2 tabs of the condenser and tie a rope around the upper tie bar

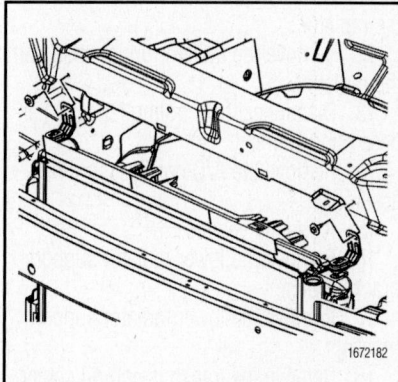

Fig. 41 Upper radiator support bracket bolts

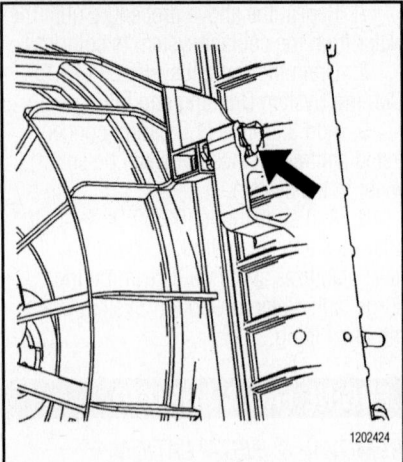

Fig. 42 Pry upward on the fan shroud tabs at the radiator clips to release the fan shroud from the radiator

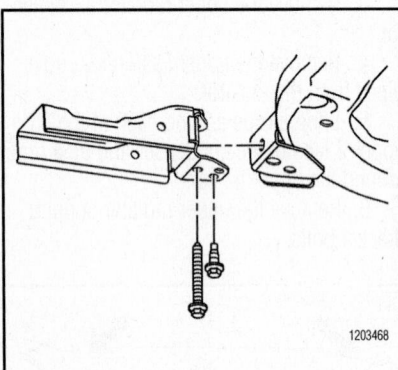

Fig. 43 Lower radiator support bracket bolts

7. Remove the upper radiator support brackets.

8. Pry upward on the fan shroud tabs at the radiator clips to release the fan shroud from the radiator.

9. Remove the lower radiator air deflector.

10. Lower the vehicle.

11. Remove the radiator inlet hose from the radiator.

12. Remove the radiator outlet hose from the radiator.

13. Disconnect the cooling fan wire harness connectors.

14. Remove the A/C compressor hose assembly.

15. Raise the vehicle.

16. Remove the lower radiator support bracket bolts.

17. Remove the lower radiator support brackets.

18. Remove the transmission oil cooler pipe clip from the fan shroud.

19. Remove the fan shroud assembly.

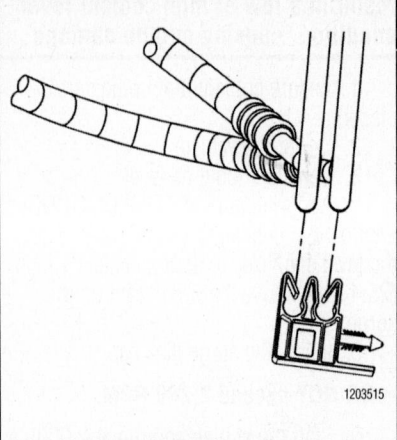

Fig. 44 Transmission oil cooler pipe clip

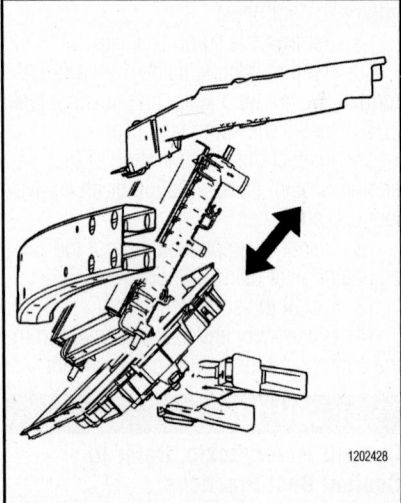

Fig. 45 Remove the fan shroud assembly

To install:

20. Install the fan shroud assembly.

21. Install the transmission oil cooler pipes to the radiator.

22. Install the transmission oil cooler pipe clip to the fan shroud.

23. Install the lower radiator support brackets.

24. Install the lower radiator support bracket bolts and tighten to 44 ft. lbs. (60 Nm).

25. Install the cooling fan wire harness connectors.

26. Install the radiator outlet hose to the radiator.

27. Install the lower radiator air deflector.

28. Lower the vehicle.

29. Snap fan shroud tabs into the radiator clips.

30. Remove the rope attached to the condenser and upper tie bar.

31. Install the upper radiator support brackets.

32. Install the upper radiator support bracket bolts and tighten to 89 inch lbs. (10 Nm).

33. Install the radiator inlet hose to the radiator.

34. Install the A/C compressor hose assembly.

35. Install the upper radiator air deflector.

36. Install the air cleaner air duct.

37. Fill the cooling system. Refer to Cooling System Draining and Filling.

38. Inspect the transmission fluid level.

RADIATOR

REMOVAL & INSTALLATION

3.5L, 3.6L & 3.9L Engines

See Figures 46 through 54.

1. Drain the coolant. Refer to Cooling System Draining and Filling.

2. Loop a rope around each of the upper 2 tabs of the condenser and tie the rope around the upper tie bar. Refer to the first image in Engine Cooling Fan & Shroud Replacement.

3. Remove the upper radiator support brackets.

4. Reposition the radiator inlet hose clamp at the radiator using the J 38185 hose clamp pliers.

5. Remove the radiator inlet hose from the radiator.

6. Remove the front air dam.

7. Remove the right engine splash shield retainers.

8. Remove the right engine splash shield.

9. Remove the left engine splash shield retainers.

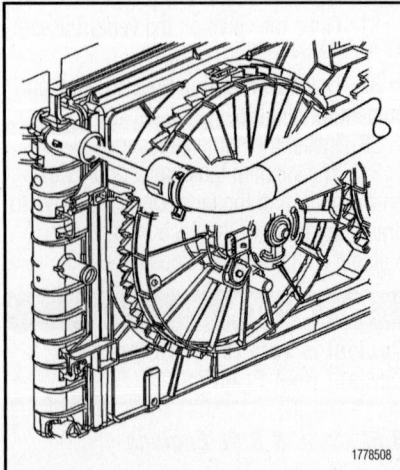

Fig. 46 Reposition the radiator inlet hose clamp at the radiator using the J 38185 hose clamp pliers—3.5L and 3.9L

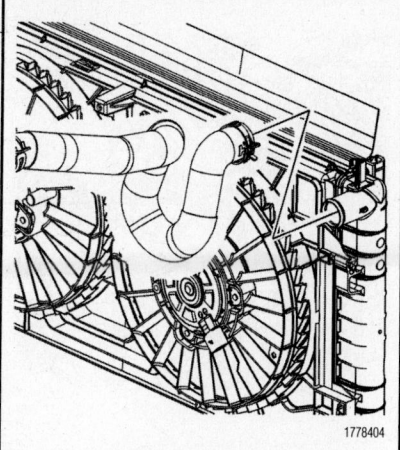

Fig. 47 Reposition the radiator inlet hose clamp at the radiator using the J 38185 hose clamp pliers—3.6L

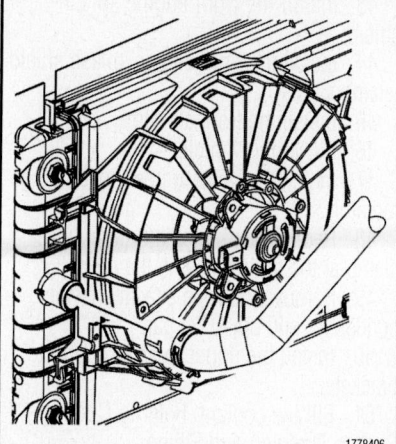

Fig. 50 Reposition the radiator outlet hose clamp at the radiator using the J 38185—3.6L

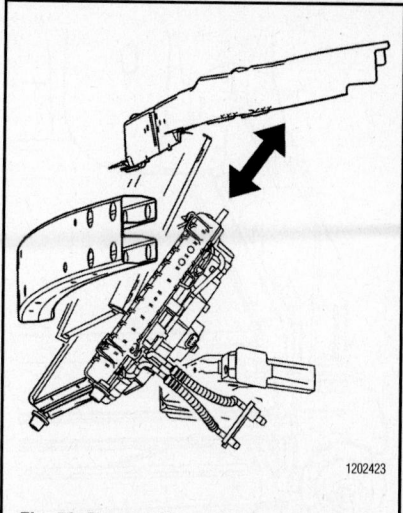

Fig. 52 Remove the radiator and cooling fan shroud assembly from the vehicle

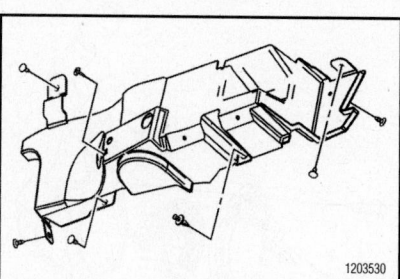

Fig. 48 Right engine splash shield retainers

10. Remove the left engine splash shield.

11. Reposition the radiator outlet hose clamp at the radiator using the J 38185 hose clamp pliers.

12. Remove the radiator outlet hose from the radiator.

13. Remove the transmission oil cooler pipes from the transmission.

14. Remove the lower radiator support bracket bolts.

15. Remove the lower radiator support brackets.

16. Remove the radiator lower mounts.

17. Remove and discard the condenser mounting bolts from the radiator.

18. Push upward on the radiator and downward on the condenser to unsnap the condenser mounting tabs from the radiator clips.

19. Remove and discard the condenser mounting nuts from the radiator.

20. Remove the radiator air side seals.

21. Remove the radiator and cooling fan shroud assembly from the vehicle.

22. Pry upward on the fan shroud tabs at the radiator clips. (Refer to image in Fan & Shroud replacement.)

23. Remove the cooling fan and shroud assembly from the radiator.

To install:
24. Install the cooling fan and shroud assembly to the radiator.

25. Snap the fan shroud tabs into the radiator clips.

26. Install the radiator and cooling fan shroud assembly to the vehicle.

27. Install the radiator air side seals onto the condenser mounting tabs on the radiator.

➡**Replace the condenser mounting bolts and nuts.**

28. Install the condenser mounting nuts to the radiator.

29. Insert the condenser mounting tabs into the radiator clips.

30. Install the condenser to the radiator bolts.

31. Tighten the bolts to 53 inch lbs. (6 Nm).

32. Bend the radiator air side seals and insert the seals into the channel of the intake air splash shields.

33. The radiator air side seals must be in the proper position for proper air flow.

➡**Replace the radiator lower mounts as a pair or vibration may result.**

34. Install the radiator lower mounts.

35. Install the lower radiator support brackets.

36. Install the lower radiator support bracket bolts.

37. Tighten the bolts to 44 ft. lbs. (60 Nm).

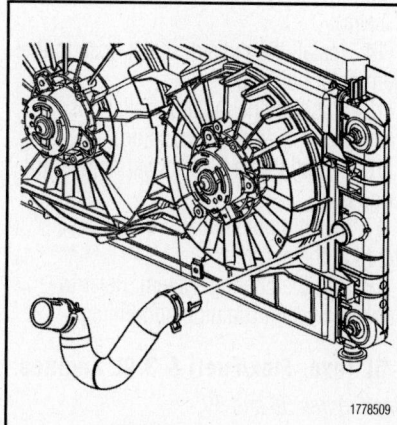

Fig. 49 Reposition the radiator outlet hose clamp at the radiator using the J 38185—3.5L and 3.9L

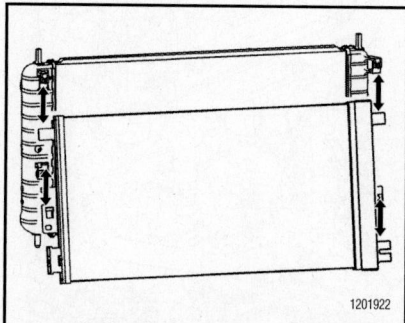

Fig. 51 Push upward on the radiator and downward on the condenser to unsnap the condenser mounting tabs from the radiator clips

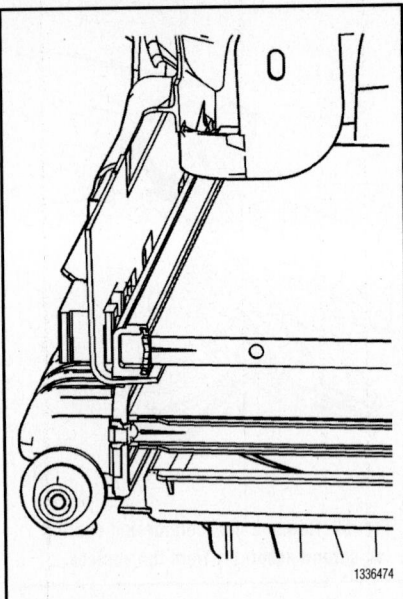

Fig. 53 Bend the radiator air side seals and insert the seals into the channel of the intake air splash shields

38. Install the transmission oil cooler pipes to the transmission.

39. Install the radiator outlet hose to the radiator.

40. Reposition the radiator outlet hose clamp at the radiator using the J 38185.

➡**Engine splash shields must be properly installed or reduced A/C and engine cooling system performance could occur.**

41. Install the left engine splash shield.

42. Install the left engine splash shield retainers.

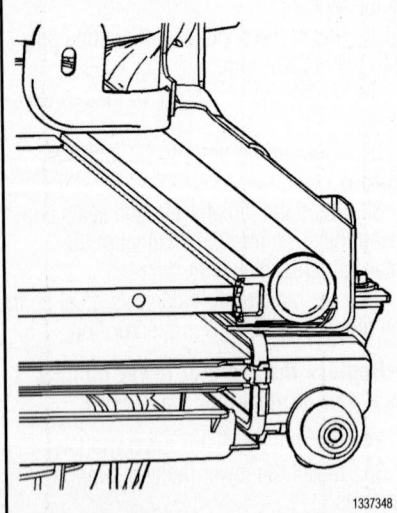

Fig. 54 Bend the radiator air side seals and insert the seals into the channel of the intake air splash shields

43. Install the right engine splash shield.

44. Install the right engine splash shield retainers.

45. Install the front air dam.

46. Lower the vehicle.

47. Install the radiator inlet hose to the radiator.

48. Reposition the radiator inlet hose clamp at the radiator using the J 38185.

49. Remove the rope attached to the condenser and upper tie bar.

50. Install the upper radiator support brackets.

51. Fill the coolant. Refer to Cooling System Draining and Filling.

52. Inspect the transmission fluid level.

THERMOSTAT

REMOVAL & INSTALLATION

2.4L Engine

See Figures 55 through 57.

1. Drain the cooling system. Refer to Cooling System Draining and Filling.

2. Reposition the radiator outlet hose clamp at the surge tank.

3. Remove the radiator outlet hose from the surge tank.

4. Reposition the radiator outlet hose clamp at the thermostat housing.

5. Remove the radiator outlet hose from the thermostat housing.

6. Remove the surge tank outlet hose from the thermostat housing.

7. Remove the thermostat housing cover bolts and cover.

8. Remove the thermostat.

9. Remove and discard the thermostat housing O-ring seal.

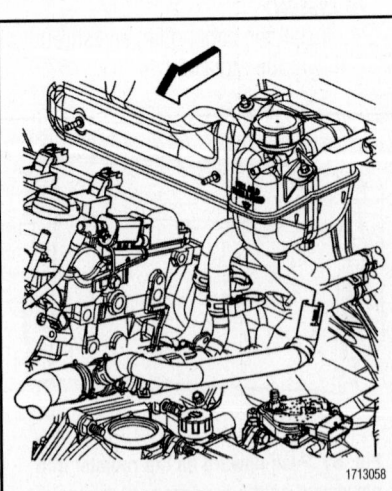

Fig. 55 Remove the radiator outlet hose from the surge tank

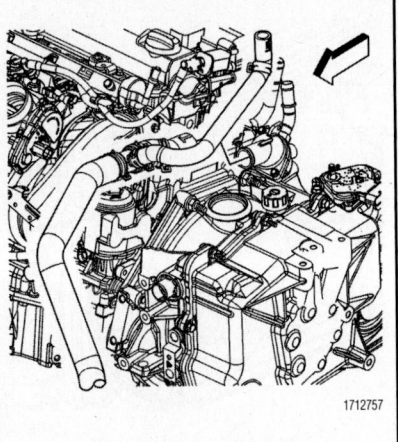

Fig. 56 Remove the surge tank outlet hose from the thermostat housing

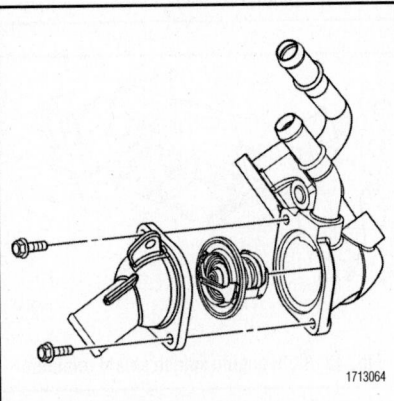

Fig. 57 Remove the thermostat housing cover bolts and cover

To install:

10. Install a NEW thermostat housing cover O-ring seal.

11. Install the thermostat.

12. Install the thermostat housing cover bolts.

13. Tighten the bolts to 89 inch lbs. (10 Nm).

14. Install the radiator outlet hose to the thermostat housing.

15. Position the radiator outlet hose clamp at the thermostat housing.

16. Install the radiator outlet hose to the surge tank.

17. Position the radiator outlet hose clamp at the surge tank.

18. Fill the cooling system. Refer to Cooling System Draining and Filling.

3.5L (exc. Flex/Fuel) & 3.9L Engines

See Figures 58 and 59.

1. Drain the cooling system. Refer to Cooling System Draining and Filling.

2. Remove the air cleaner outlet duct.

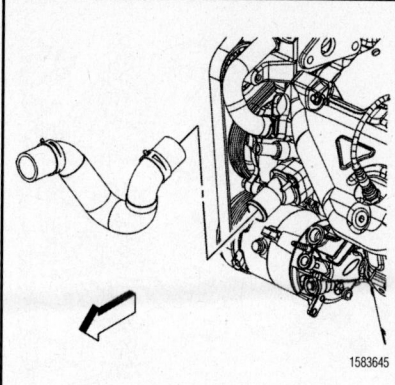

Fig. 58 Remove the radiator outlet hose from the thermostat housing

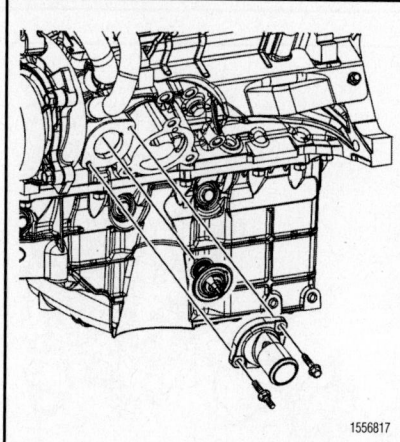

Fig. 59 Remove the thermostat housing bolt/stud.

3. Reposition the radiator outlet hose clamp at the thermostat housing.

4. Remove the radiator outlet hose from the thermostat housing.

5. Remove the thermostat housing bolt/stud.

6. Remove the thermostat housing and gasket.

7. Remove the thermostat.

8. Clean the gasket surfaces.

To install:

9. Install a NEW thermostat.

10. Position a NEW gasket and the thermostat housing to the engine block.

11. Install the thermostat housing bolt/stud.

12. Tighten the bolt/stud to 89 inch lbs. (10 Nm).

13. Install the radiator outlet hose to the thermostat housing.

14. Position the radiator outlet hose clamp at the thermostat housing.

15. Install the air cleaner outlet duct.

16. Fill the cooling system. Refer to Cooling System Draining and Filling.

17. Inspect the system for leaks.

WATER PUMP

REMOVAL & INSTALLATION

2.4L Engine

See Figures 60 through 65.

1. Remove the air cleaner assembly.

2. Remove the exhaust manifold heat shield.

3. If equipped, remove the coolant heater.

4. Remove the catalytic converter.

5. Remove the engine coolant thermostat housing.

6. Remove the water pump cover (2), fasteners (3) and gasket (1) from the engine front cover.

➡**A drain plug has been provided at the bottom of the water pump assembly for additional coolant drainage from the engine block and water pump.**

7. Drain the coolant from the water pump using the plug at the bottom of the pump. Install the plug when finished.

➡**The water pump holding tool supports the sprocket and chain during water pump service. The tool must be used or the balance shaft must be re-timed.**

8. Align the EN-43651 water pump holding tool (1) with the threads on the water pump sprocket. Tighten the water pump holding tool fasteners (2).

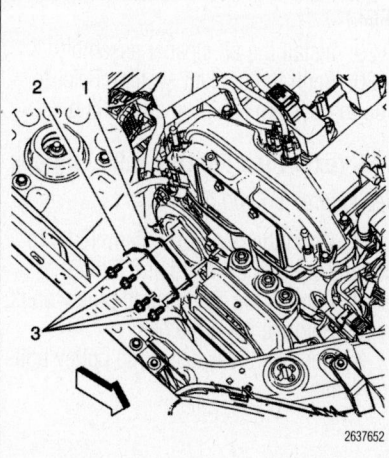

Fig. 60 Remove the water pump cover (2), fasteners (3) and gasket (1) from the engine front cover

Fig. 61 Align the EN-43651 water pump holding tool (1) with the threads on the water pump sprocket. Tighten the water pump holding tool fasteners (2).

9. Secure the water pump holding tool with the previously removed water pump cover fasteners (1) into the engine front cover.

10. Remove the water pump sprocket to water pump fasteners.

➡**Be sure to remove both water pump bolts from the front of the engine block.**

11. Remove the front water pump fasteners (1).

12. Remove the rear water pump fasteners (1).

13. Remove the water pump.

14. If replacing the water pump cover remove the water pump rear cover fasteners (4).

Separate the water pump cover (1) from the water pump (3)

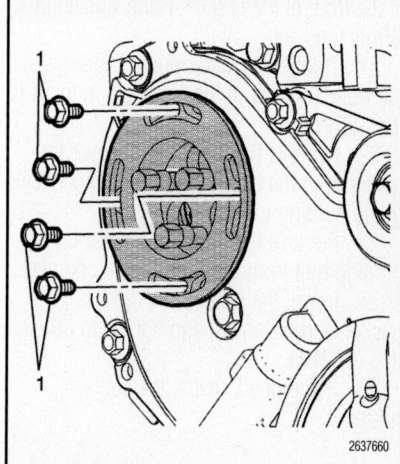

Fig. 62 Secure the water pump holding tool with the previously removed water pump cover fasteners (1) into the engine front cover

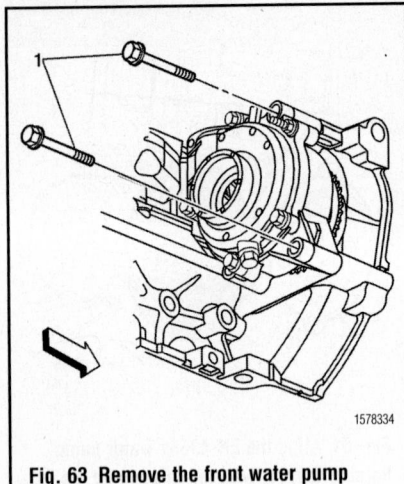

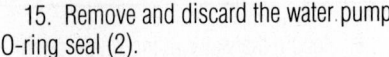

Fig. 63 Remove the front water pump fasteners (1)

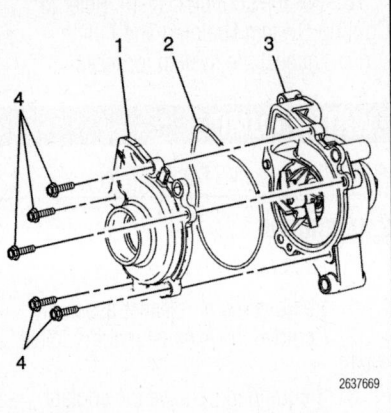

Fig. 64 Water pump cover (1), rear cover fasteners (4), water pump (3), O-ring seal (2)

Fig. 66 Remove the water pump pulley bolts and pulley.

15. Remove and discard the water pump O-ring seal (2).

To install:

16. If replacing the water pump cover (1), install a new O-ring (2) to the water pump (3) and tighten the fasteners (4) to 18 ft. lbs. (25 Nm)

➥**Create a guide pin to aid in water pump alignment: Use an M 6 m x 6 mm x 50.8 mm stud (2 in). Thread the pin into the water pump sprocket.**

17. Using a guide pin (2), align the pin with the water pump holding tool.

18. Position the water pump (1) against the engine block and Hand-tighten the water pump fasteners (3).

19. Install 2 water pump sprocket to water pump fasteners. After the fasteners are snug, remove the guide pin (2) and install the 3rd fastener and tighten to 89 inch lbs. (10 Nm).

20. Install the water pump fasteners (1) at the front of the engine. Hand-tighten them at this time.

21. Tighten the water pump fasteners at the front and rear of the water pump to 18 ft. lbs. (25 Nm).

22. Remove the water pump cover fasteners from the engine front cover and water pump holding tool.

23. Remove the EN-43651 water pump holding tool from the water pump sprocket.

24. Install the water pump access plate, gasket, and fasteners, and tighten to 89 inch lbs. (10 Nm).

25. If equipped, Install the coolant heater.

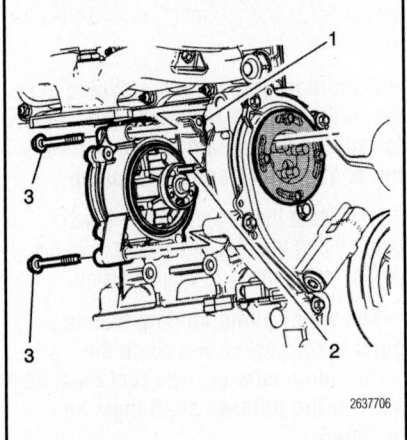

Fig. 65 Guide pin (2), water pump (1), and pump fasteners (3)

26. Install the engine coolant thermostat housing.

27. Install the catalytic converter.

28. Install the exhaust manifold heat shield.

29. Install the air cleaner assembly.

30. Refill the coolant system. Refer to Cooling System Draining and Filling.

3.5L (exc. Flex Fuel) & 3.9L Engines

See Figures 66 and 67.

1. Drain the cooling system. Refer to Cooling System Draining and Filling.

2. Loosen the water pump pulley bolts.

3. Remove the drive belt.

4. Remove the water pump pulley bolts and pulley.

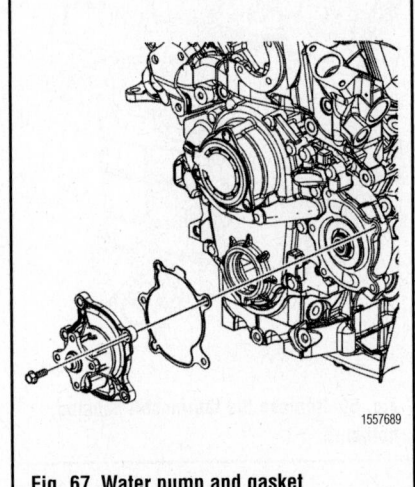

Fig. 67 Water pump and gasket

5. Remove the water pump bolts.

6. Remove the water pump and gasket.

7. Clean the water pump mating surfaces.

To install:

8. Position a NEW water pump gasket and the water pump to the engine front cover.

9. Install the water pump bolts.

10. Tighten the bolts to 18 ft. lbs. (25 Nm).

11. Install the water pump pulley and bolts.

12. Install the drive belt.

13. Tighten the water pump pulley bolts.

14. Tighten the bolts to 18 ft. lbs. (25 Nm).

15. Fill the cooling system. Refer to Cooling System Draining and Filling.

16. Inspect for leaks.

BATTERY

REMOVAL & INSTALLATION

See Figure 68.

1. Disconnect the negative battery cable. Refer to Battery Negative Cable Disconnection and Connection.
2. Disconnect the positive battery cable from the battery.
3. Remove the battery hold-down retainer bolt and retainer.

➡**Do not tip the battery more than 40 degrees during removal.**

4. Remove the battery.

To install:

➡**Do not tip the battery more than 40 degrees during battery installation.**

5. Install the battery.
6. Install the battery hold-down retainer and bolt.
7. Tighten the bolt to 18 ft. lbs. (25 Nm).
8. Connect the positive battery cable to the battery.
9. Tighten the bolt to 13 ft. lbs. (17 Nm).

10. Connect the negative battery cable. Refer to Battery Negative Cable Disconnection and Connection.

BATTERY NEGATIVE CABLE DISCONNECTION AND CONNECTION

See Figures 69 and 70.

> ✳✳ **CAUTION**
> **Refer to SIR Warning in the Preface section.**

> ✳✳ **CAUTION**
> **Refer to Battery Disconnect Warning in the Preface section.**

1. Record each of the vehicle preset radio stations.
2. Make sure the ignition switch is in the OFF position.
3. Remove the battery cover. Disengage the retainers in order to remove the cover.
4. Loosen the battery negative cable clamp nut (1) and remove the negative battery cable (2).

Connect Procedure

➡**Clean any existing oxidation from the contact face of the battery terminal and battery cable using a wire brush before installing the battery cable to the battery terminal.**

5. Connect the negative battery cable (2) to the battery.
6. Tighten the bolt to 13 ft. lbs. (17 Nm).
7. Install the battery cover:
   a. Install the locking tab next to the strut tower first.
   b. Install the locking tab next to the engine second.
   c. Install the locking tab next to the powertrain control module (PCM) last.
8. Reset the radio stations and the clock.
9. For coupe and convertible models, perform the Reinitialization of the Power Windows.

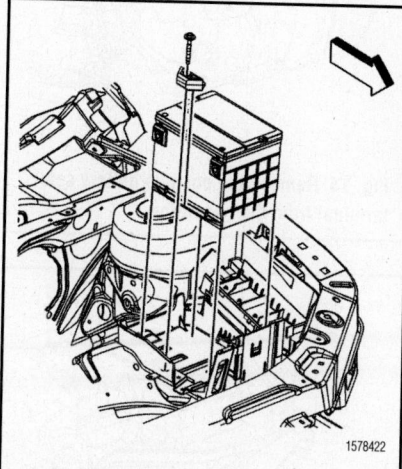

Fig. 68 Remove the battery hold-down retainer bolt and retainer.

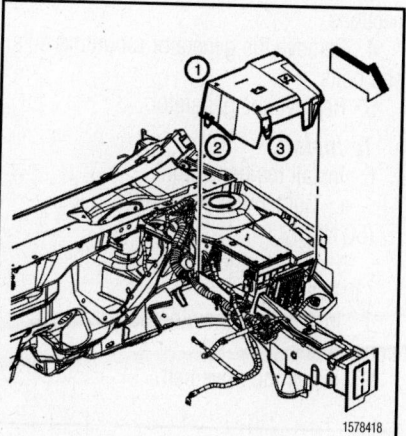

Fig. 69 Remove the battery cover. Disengage the retainers in order to remove the cover

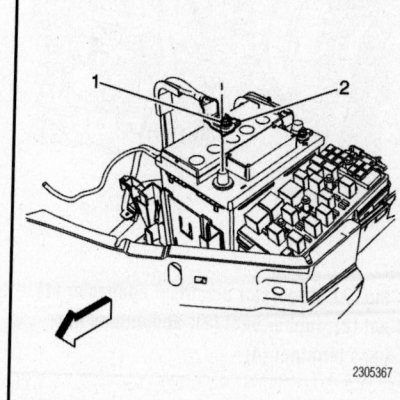

Fig. 70 Loosen the battery negative cable clamp nut (1) and remove the negative battery cable (2)

ALTERNATOR (GENERATOR)

REMOVAL & INSTALLATION

2.4L Engine

See Figures 71 and 72.

1. Disconnect negative battery cable.
2. Remove the drive belt.
3. Disconnect the generator electrical connector (1).
4. Reposition the rubber boot (3).
5. Remove the engine harness terminal lead to generator nut (2).
6. Remove the engine harness terminal (4) from the generator stud.
7. Remove the generator fasteners (1, 3, and 4).
8. Remove the generator.

To install:

9. Position the generator to the engine block.

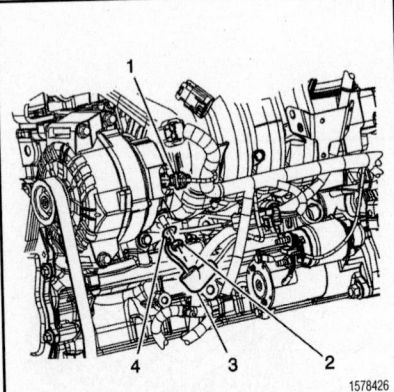

Fig. 71 Generator electrical connector (1), nut (2), rubber boot (3), and engine harness terminal (4)

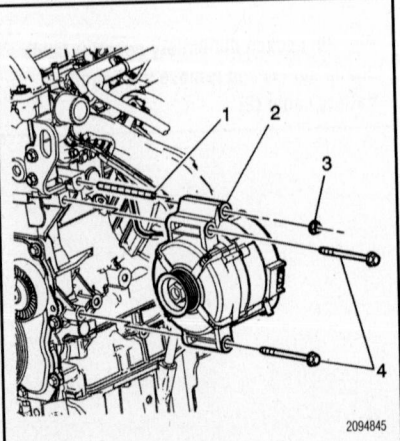

Fig. 72 Generator fasteners (1, 3, 4)

10. Install the generator fasteners (4) loosely.
11. Install the fastener (1) and tighten to 89 inch lbs. (10 Nm).
12. Install the fastener (3) and tighten to 16 ft. lbs. (22 Nm).
13. Tighten the fasteners (4) to 16 ft. lbs. (22 Nm).
14. Install the engine harness terminal (4) to the generator stud.
15. Install the engine harness terminal lead to generator nut (2) and tighten to 15 ft. lbs. (20 Nm).
16. Position the rubber boot (3) over the stud.
17. Connect the generator electrical connector (1).
18. Install the drive belt.
19. Connect negative battery cable.

3.5L Engine

See Figure 73.

➡**Service the generator as a complete unit.**

1. Disconnect the negative battery cable.
2. Remove the drive belt.
3. Remove the generator electrical connections.
4. Remove the generator mounting nuts and bolts.
5. Remove the generator.

To install:

6. Install the generator.
   a. Tighten the bolts to 37 ft. lbs. (50 Nm).
   b. Tighten the nuts to 22 ft. lbs. (30 Nm).
7. Install the generator electrical connections.
8. Install the drive belt.

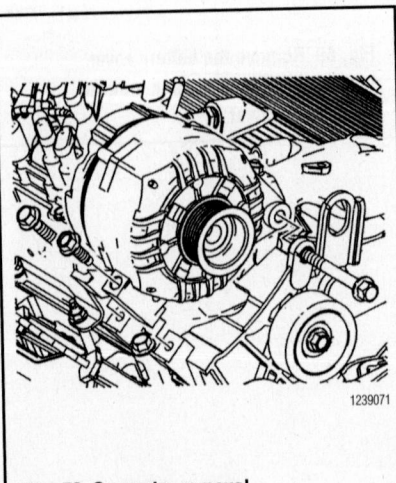

Fig. 73 Generator removal

9. Connect the negative battery cable.

3.6L Engine

See Figures 74 and 75.

1. Disconnect the negative battery cable.
2. Remove the air cleaner outlet duct.
3. Reposition the positive battery cable boot at the generator terminal.
4. Remove the positive battery cable nut at the generator.
5. Remove the positive battery cable terminal from the generator.

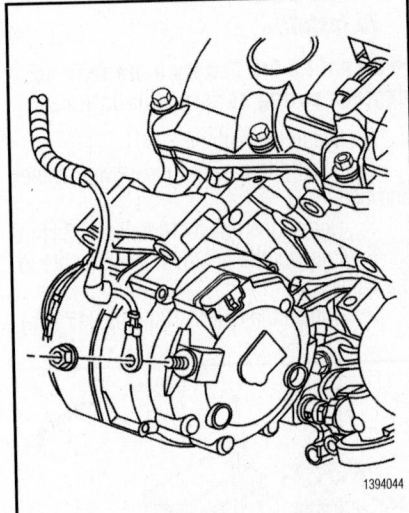

Fig. 74 Remove the positive battery cable terminal from the generator.

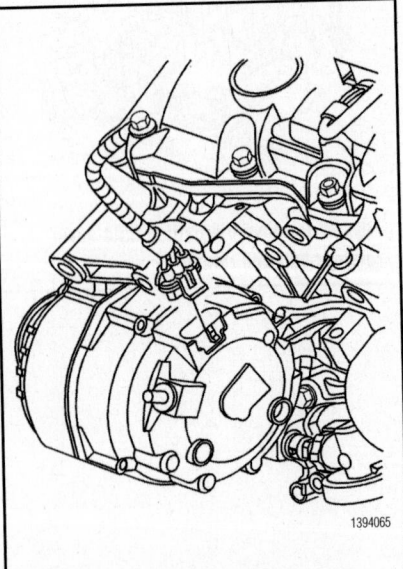

Fig. 75 Disconnect the engine harness electrical connector from the generator

6. Disconnect the engine harness electrical connector from the generator.

7. Remove the drive belt.

8. Remove the idler pulley.

9. Remove the generator bolts.

➡ **When removing the generator from the vehicle, it may be necessary to maneuver the generator to remove it from the vehicle.**

10. Remove the generator.

To install:

11. Position the generator to the engine.

12. Loosely install the generator bolts.

13. Install the idler pulley.

14. Tighten the generator bolts in the sequence shown to 37 ft. lbs. (50 Nm).

15. Install the drive belt.

16. Connect the engine harness electrical connector to the generator.

17. Install the positive battery cable terminal to the generator.

18. Install the positive battery cable nut at the generator and tighten to 15 ft. lbs. (20 Nm).

19. Position the positive battery cable boot at the generator terminal.

20. Connect the negative battery cable.

3.9L Engine

See Figures 76 through 78.

1. Disconnect the negative battery cable.

2. Remove the drive belt.

3. Disconnect the engine harness electrical connector.

4. Reposition the generator rubber boot (3).

5. Remove the engine harness terminal nut (1).

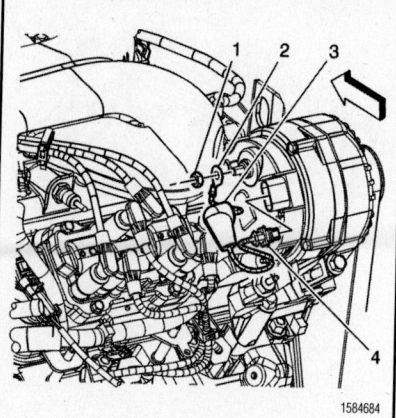

Fig. 76 Generator rubber boot (3), engine harness terminal nut (1), and terminal (2)

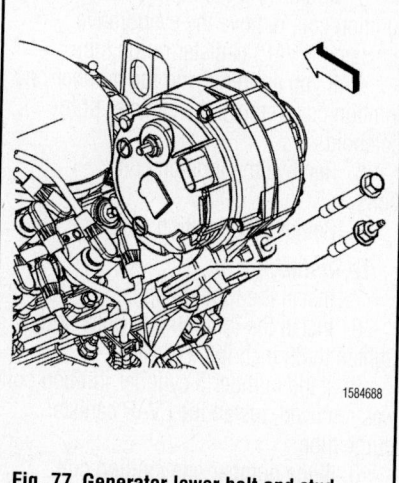

Fig. 77 Generator lower bolt and stud

6. Remove the engine harness terminal (2).

7. Remove the generator lower bolt and stud.

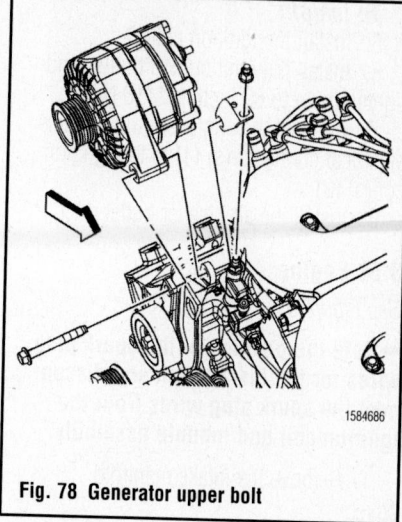

Fig. 78 Generator upper bolt

To install:

8. Install the generator.

9. Install the generator lower bolt and stud until snug.

10. Install the generator upper bolt.

11. Tighten the bolts/stud to 37 ft. lbs. (50 Nm).

12. Install the engine harness terminal (2).

13. Install the engine harness terminal nut (1).

14. Tighten the nut to 22 ft. lbs. (30 Nm).

15. Position the generator rubber boot (3).

16. Connect the engine harness electrical connector.

17. Install the drive belt.

18. Connect the negative battery cable.

ENGINE ELECTRICAL

IGNITION SYSTEM

FIRING ORDER

2.4L engines: 1-3-4-2
3.5L, 3.6L and 3.9L engines: 1-2-3-4-5-6

IGNITION COIL

REMOVAL & INSTALLATION

2.4L Engine

See Figures 79 and 80.

1. Remove the air cleaner outlet duct.

2. Disconnect the engine wiring harness electrical connectors (1) from the ignition coil(s) (2).

3. Remove the ignition coil bolt(s).

4. Remove the ignition coil(s).

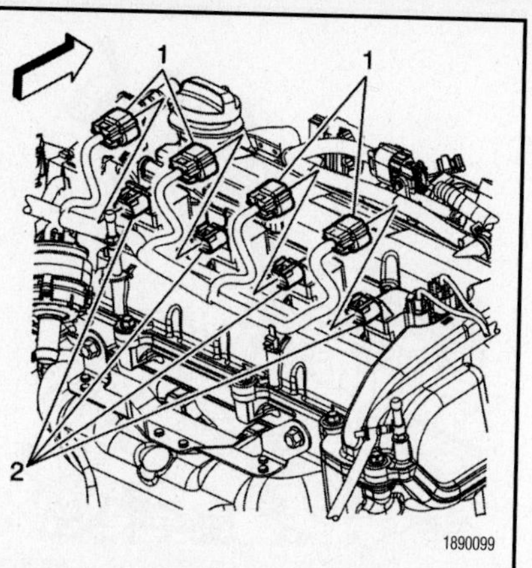

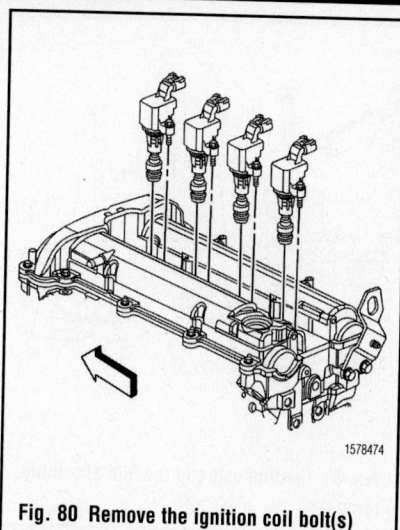

Fig. 79 Disconnect the engine wiring harness electrical connectors (1) from the ignition coil(s) (2)

Fig. 80 Remove the ignition coil bolt(s)

To install:

5. Install the ignition coil(s).

6. Install the ignition coil bolt(s) and tighten them to 89 inch lbs. (10 Nm).

7. Connect the engine wiring harness electrical connector(s) (1) to the ignition coil(s) (2).

8. Install the air cleaner outlet duct.

3.5L Engine

See Figure 81.

➡**Note the position of the spark plug wires for the installation and disconnect the spark plug wires from the ignition coil and module assembly.**

1. Remove the intake manifold cover.

2. Remove the 4 screws securing the ignition coil and module assembly to the bracket.

3. Remove the ignition coil and module assembly.

To install:

4. Install the ignition coil and module assembly to the bracket.

5. Install the ignition coil and module assembly screws.

6. Tighten the screws to 40 inch lbs. (4.5 Nm).

7. Connect the spark plug wires as noted during the removal.

8. Install the intake manifold cover.

3.6L Engine

Bank 1

See Figures 82 and 83.

1. Remove the fuel injector sight shield.

2. Disconnect the engine wiring harness electrical connectors (3) from the ignition coils.

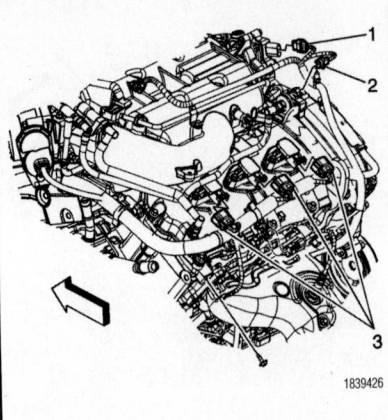

Fig. 82 Engine wiring harness electrical connectors (3)

3. If removing the number 5 cylinder ignition coil, remove the evaporative emission (EVAP) canister purge tube.

4. If you are removing the number one ignition coil, remove the canister purge solenoid.

5. Remove the ignition coil bolts.

6. Remove the ignition coils.

To install:

7. Install the ignition coils.

8. Install the ignition coil bolts and tighten to 89 inch lbs. (10 Nm).

9. If the number 5 cylinder ignition coil was removed, install the EVAP canister purge tube.

10. If the number one ignition coil was removed, install the canister purge solenoid.

11. Connect the engine wiring harness electrical connectors to the ignition coils.

12. Install the fuel injector sight shield.

Bank 2

See Figure 84.

1. Remove the fuel injector sight shield.

2. Disconnect the engine wiring harness electrical connector(s) (2) from the ignition coils.

3. Remove the ignition coil bolts. (See image for 3.6L Bank 1 Ignition Coil removal.)

4. Remove the ignition coils.

To install:

5. Install the ignition coils.

6. Install the ignition coil bolts and tighten to 89 inch lbs. (10 Nm).

7. Connect the engine wiring harness electrical connectors to the ignition coils.

8. Install the fuel injector sight shield.

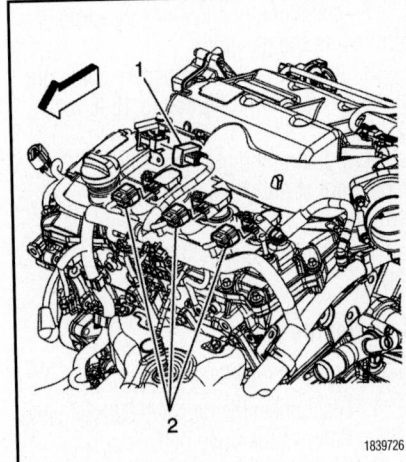

Fig. 84 Disconnect the engine wiring harness electrical connector(s) (2) from the ignition coils

3.9L Engine

See Figures 85 through 88.

Fig. 81 Ignition coil and module assembly removal

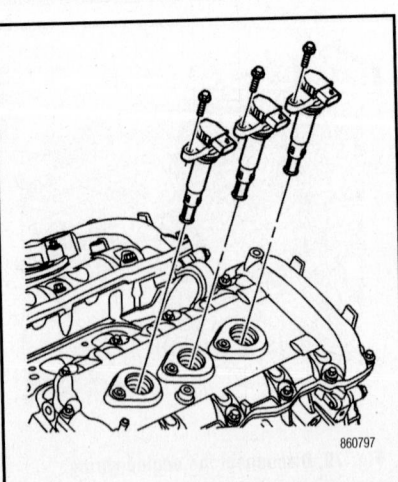

Fig. 83 Remove the ignition coil bolts

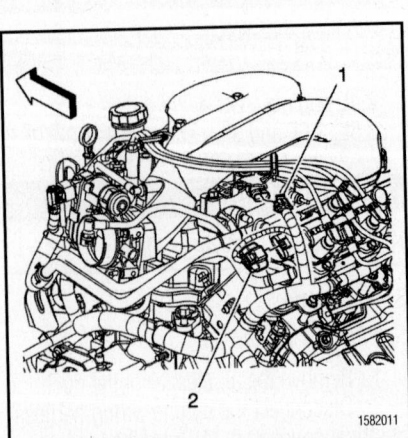

Fig. 85 Disconnect the Manifold Absolute Pressure (MAP) sensor electrical connector (1)

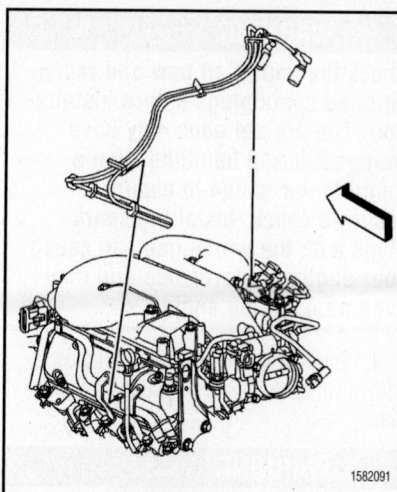

Fig. 86 Disconnect the left side spark plug wires from the ignition coil

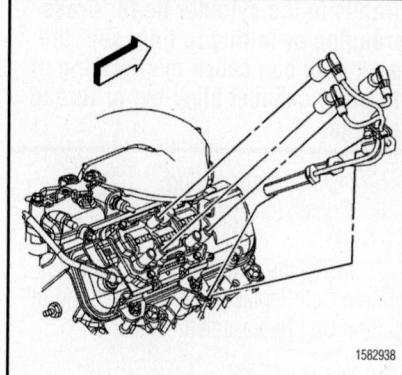

Fig. 87 Disconnect the right side spark plug wires from the ignition coil

1. Remove the intake manifold cover.
2. Disconnect the Manifold Absolute Pressure (MAP) sensor electrical connector (1).
3. Disconnect the ignition coil electrical connector (2).
4. Disconnect the left side spark plug wires from the ignition coil.
5. Disconnect the right side spark plug wires from the ignition coil.
6. Remove the ignition coil bolts (1).
7. Remove the ignition coil nuts (2).
8. Remove the ignition coil (3).
9. Remove the ignition coil studs (4), if necessary.

To install:
10. Install the ignition coil studs (4), if necessary.
11. Tighten the studs to 18 ft. lbs. (25 Nm).
12. Install the ignition coil (3).
13. Install the ignition coil nuts (2).
14. Tighten the nuts to 18 ft. lbs. (25 Nm).

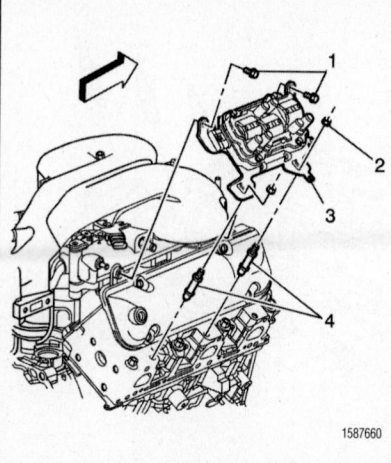

Fig. 88 Ignition coil bolts (1), nuts (2), ignition coil (3), and studs (4)

15. Install the ignition coil bolts (1).
16. Tighten the bolts to 18 ft. lbs. (25 Nm).
17. Connect the right side spark plug wires to the ignition coil.
18. Connect the left side spark plug wires to the ignition coil.
19. Connect the ignition coil electrical connector (2).
20. Connect the MAP sensor electrical connector (1).
21. Install the intake manifold cover.

IGNITION TIMING

ADJUSTMENT

The ignition timing is controlled by the Powertrain Control Module (PCM). No adjustment is necessary or possible.

SPARK PLUGS

REMOVAL & INSTALLATION

2.4L Engine

✳✳ WARNING

This engine has aluminum cylinder heads. Do not remove the spark plugs from a hot engine, allow it to cool first. Removing the spark plugs from a hot engine may cause spark plug thread damage or cylinder head damage.

1. Remove the ignition coil(s). Refer to Ignition Coil replacement.

➡**Make sure that any water and/or debris is blown out of the spark plug holes prior to removing the spark plugs.**

2. Remove the spark plugs using a 5/8 inch spark plug socket.

To install:

✳✳ WARNING

Do not coat spark plug threads with anti-seize compound. If anti-seize compound is used and spark plugs are over-torqued, damage to the cylinder head threads may result.

3. Install the spark plugs.
4. Specification: The spark plug gap is 0.040 in (1.0 mm).
5. Tighten the plugs to 15 ft. lbs. (20 Nm).
6. Install the ignition coil(s). Refer to Ignition Coil Replacement.

3.5L Engine

See Figure 89.

✳✳ WARNING

Observe the following service precautions:

• Allow the engine to cool before removing the spark plugs. Attempting to remove spark plugs from a hot engine can cause the spark plugs to seize. This can damage the cylinder head threads.

• Clean the spark plug recess area before removing the spark plug. Failure to do so can result in engine damage due to dirt or foreign material entering the cylinder head, or in contamination of the cylinder

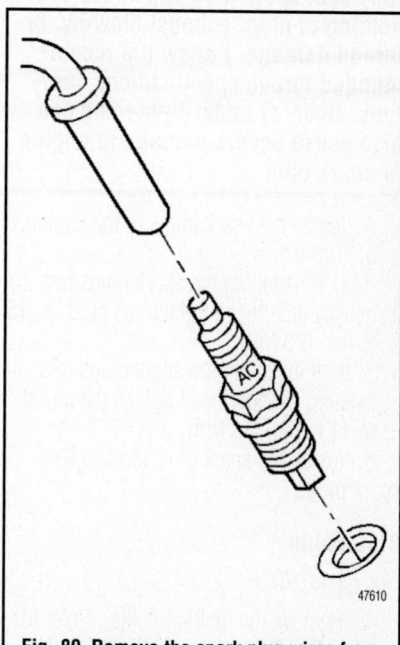

Fig. 89 Remove the spark plug wires from the spark plugs

head threads. Contaminated threads may prevent proper seating of the new spark plug.

• Use only the spark plugs specified for use in the vehicle. Do not install spark plugs that are either hotter or colder than those specified for the vehicle. Installing spark plugs of another type can severely damage the engine.

1. If you are replacing the engine left bank spark plugs; remove the air cleaner outlet duct.

2. Remove the spark plug wires from the spark plugs.

To install:

✳✳ WARNING

It is important to check the gap of all new and reconditioned spark plugs before installation. Pre-set gaps may have changed during handling. Use a round wire feeler gauge to be sure of an accurate check, particularly on used plugs. Installing plugs with the wrong gap can cause poor engine performance and may even damage the engine.

3. Gap the spark plugs to the specifications.

✳✳ WARNING

Be sure the plug threads smoothly into the cylinder head and is fully seated. Use a thread chaser if necessary to clean threads in cylinder head. Cross-threading or failing to fully seat spark plug can cause overheating of plug, exhaust blow-by, or thread damage. Follow the recommended torque specifications carefully. Over- or under-tightening can also cause severe damage to engine or spark plug.

4. Install the spark plugs to the engine.
5. Tighten:
   a. If installing the spark plugs to a new cylinder head tighten the plugs to 15 ft. lbs. (20 Nm).
   b. If installing the spark plugs to an existing cylinder head tighten the plugs to 11 ft. lbs. (15 Nm).
6. Install the spark plug wires to the spark plugs.

3.6L Engine

See Figure 90.

1. Remove the ignition coil(s). Refer to Ignition Coil Replacement - Bank 1 and/or Ignition Coil Replacement - Bank 2.

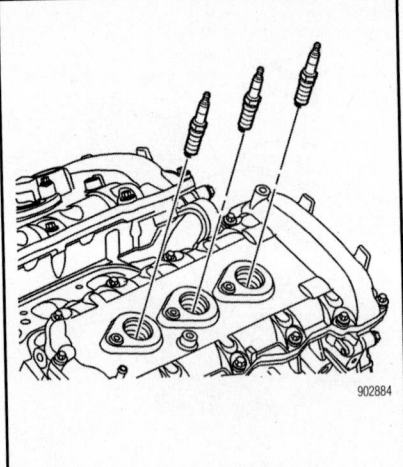

Fig. 90 Remove the ignition coil(s)

✳✳ CAUTION

Wear safety glasses when using compressed air in order to prevent eye injury

✳✳ WARNING

Clean the spark plug recess area before removing the spark plug. Failure to do so could result in engine damage because of dirt or foreign material entering the cylinder head, or by the contamination of the cylinder head threads. The contaminated threads may prevent the proper seating of the new plug. Use a thread chaser to clean the threads of any contamination.

2. Use compressed air in order to remove debris from the spark plug cavity.

✳✳ WARNING

Allow the engine to cool before removing the spark plugs. Attempting to remove the spark plugs from a hot engine may cause the plug threads to seize, causing damage to cylinder head threads.

3. Remove the spark plug.

To install:

✳✳ WARNING

Use only the spark plugs specified for use in the vehicle. Do not install spark plugs that are either hotter or colder than those specified for the vehicle. Installing spark plugs of another type can severely damage the engine.

✳✳ WARNING

Check the gap of all new and reconditioned spark plugs before installation. The pre-set gaps may have changed during handling. Use a round feeler gauge to ensure an accurate check. Installing spark plugs with the wrong gap can cause poor engine performance and may even damage the engine.

4. Ensure that the spark plug gap is equivalent to the spark plug gap specification.

✳✳ WARNING

Be sure that the spark plug threads smoothly into the cylinder head and the spark plug is fully seated. Use a thread chaser, if necessary, to clean threads in the cylinder head. Cross-threading or failing to fully seat the spark plug can cause overheating of the plug, exhaust blow-by, or thread damage.

5. Install the spark plug.
6. Tighten the spark plug to 15 ft. lbs. (20 Nm).
7. Install the ignition coil(s). Refer to Ignition Coil Replacement - Bank 1 and/or Ignition Coil Replacement - Bank 2.

3.9L Engine

See Figure 91.

✳✳ WARNING

Observe the following service precautions:

• Allow the engine to cool before removing the spark plugs. Attempting to remove spark plugs from a hot engine can cause the spark plugs to seize. This can damage the cylinder head threads.

• Clean the spark plug recess area before removing the spark plug. Failure to do so can result in engine damage due to dirt or foreign material entering the cylinder head, or in contamination of the cylinder head threads. Contaminated threads may prevent proper seating of the new spark plug.

• Use only the spark plugs specified for use in the vehicle. Do not install spark plugs that are either hotter or colder than those specified for the vehicle. Installing spark plugs of another type can severely damage the engine.

1. Remove the air cleaner outlet duct, if required.

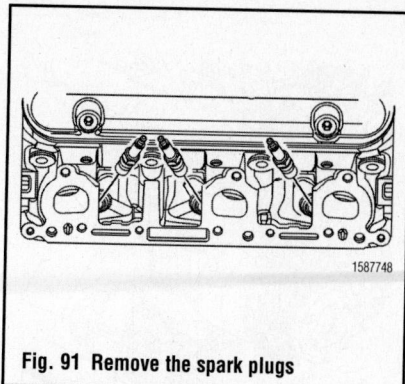

Fig. 91 Remove the spark plugs

2. Remove the intake manifold cover, if required.

3. Remove the left side spark plug wires from the spark plugs, if

required. (See image Ignition Coil replacement.)

4. Remove the right side spark plug wires from the spark plugs, if required. (See image Ignition Coil replacement.)

5. Remove the spark plugs.

To install:

✷✷ WARNING

It is important to check the gap of all new and reconditioned spark plugs before installation. Pre-set gaps may have changed during handling. Use a round wire feeler gauge to be sure of an accurate check, particularly on used plugs. Installing plugs with the

wrong gap can cause poor engine performance and may even damage the engine.

6. Gap the NEW spark plugs.
7. Install the spark plugs.
8. Tighten the plugs to 15 ft. lbs. (20 Nm).
9. Install the right side spark plug wires to the spark plugs, if required.

Install the left side spark plug wires to the spark plugs, if required.

Install the intake manifold cover, if required.

Install the air cleaner outlet duct, if required.

ENGINE ELECTRICAL

STARTER

REMOVAL & INSTALLATION

2.4L Engine

See Figures 92 through 94.

1. Disconnect the negative battery cable.
2. Raise and support the vehicle.
3. Remove the S terminal connector from the starter solenoid.
4. Remove the engine harness lead (2) from the starter.
5. Remove the positive battery cable nut (2) from the starter solenoid.
6. Remove the positive battery cable (3) and engine harness terminal (4) from the starter solenoid.
7. Remove the starter motor bolts.
8. Remove the starter motor.

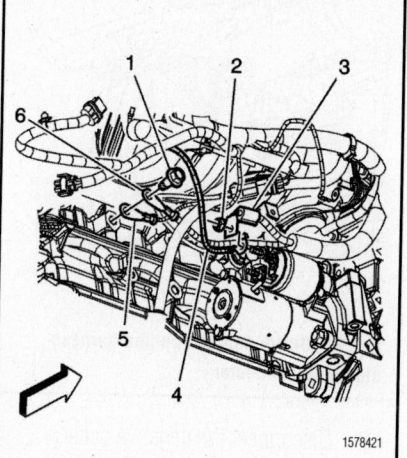

Fig. 93 Remove the positive battery cable nut (2) from the starter solenoid

STARTING SYSTEM

To install:

9. Install the starter motor.
10. Install the starter motor bolts and tighten to 30 ft. lbs. (40 Nm).
11. Install the engine harness terminal and positive battery cable to the starter solenoid.
12. Install the positive battery cable nut to the starter solenoid and tighten to 89 inch lbs. (10 Nm).
13. Install the engine harness lead to the starter.
14. Install the S terminal connector to the starter solenoid.
15. Lower the vehicle.
16. Connect the negative battery cable.

3.5L Engine

See Figures 95 and 96.

1. Disconnect the negative battery cable.

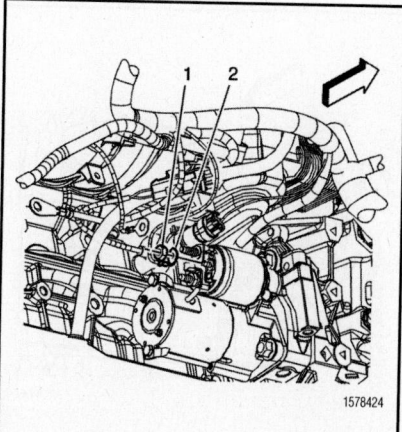

Fig. 92 Remove the engine harness lead (2) from the starter

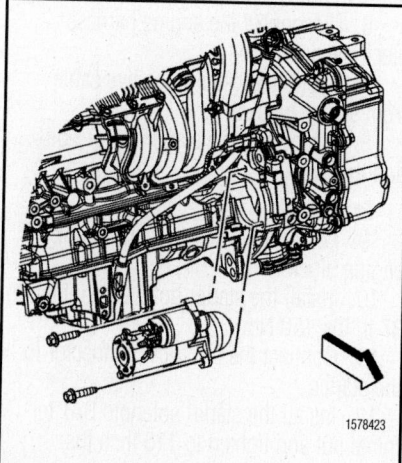

Fig. 94 Remove the starter motor bolts

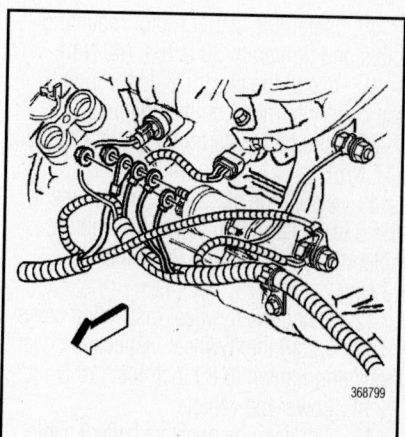

Fig. 95 Remove the electrical connections from the starter motor

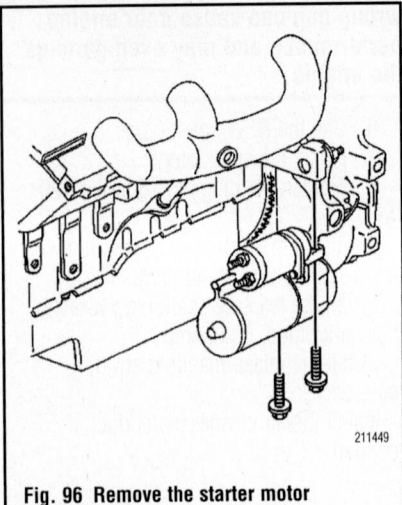

Fig. 96 Remove the starter motor mounting bolts

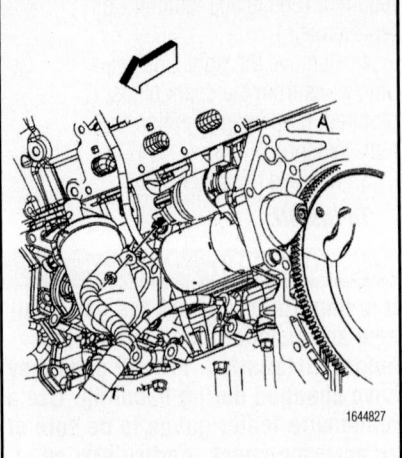

Fig. 97 Remove the starter solenoid BAT terminal nut

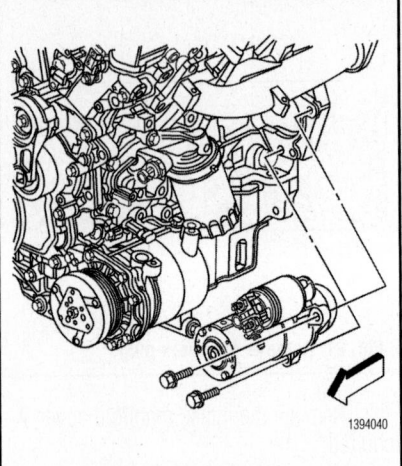

Fig. 99 Unclip battery positive cable from starter bracket

2. Raise the vehicle.

3. Remove the flywheel inspection cover bolts.

4. Remove the flywheel inspection cover.

5. Remove the electrical connections from the starter motor.

6. Remove the starter motor mounting bolts.

7. Remove the starter motor.

To install:

※※ WARNING

Before installing the starter motor to the engine, tighten the nut next to the cap on the solenoid BAT terminal. If this terminal is not tight in the solenoid cap, the cap may be damaged during installation of electrical connections and cause the starter motor to fail later.

8. Install the starter motor to the engine.

9. Install the starter motor mounting bolts and tighten to 30 ft. lbs. (40 Nm).

10. Install the electrical connection to the battery terminal on the solenoid. Tighten the battery terminal nut to 13 ft. lbs. (17 Nm).

11. Install the electrical connections to the S terminal on the solenoid. Tighten solenoid S terminal nut to 27 inch lbs. (3 Nm).

12. Install the flywheel inspection cover.

13. Install the flywheel inspection cover bolts and tighten to 89 inch lbs. (10 Nm).

14. Lower the vehicle.

15. Connect the negative battery cable.

3.6L Engine

See Figures 97 through 99.

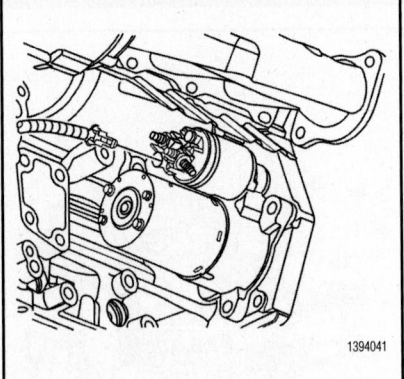

Fig. 98 Disconnect the engine harness electrical connector

1. Disconnect the negative battery cable.

2. Raise and support the vehicle.

3. Remove the left catalytic converter.

4. Remove the knock sensor bank 2.

5. Remove the starter solenoid BAT terminal nut.

6. Disconnect the engine harness electrical connector.

7. Unclip the battery positive cable from starter bracket.

8. Disconnect the starter motor bolts and the starter.

To install:

9. Position the starter motor to the engine block.

10. Install the starter bolts and tighten to 37 ft. lbs. (50 Nm).

11. Connect the electrical connector to the starter.

12. Install the starter solenoid BAT terminal nut and tighten to 115 inch lbs. (13 Nm).

13. Install the knock sensor bank 2.

14. Install the left catalytic converter.

15. Lower the vehicle.

16. Connect the negative battery cable.

3.9L Engine

See Figures 100 through 102.

1. Disconnect the negative battery cable.

2. Raise and support the vehicle.

3. Remove the flywheel inspection cover bolts and cover.

4. Disconnect the engine harness electrical connector from the starter.

5. Remove the engine harness terminal nut (3).

6. Remove the positive battery cable terminal (1) from the starter.

7. Remove the engine harness terminal (2) from the starter.

8. Remove the starter motor bolts.

9. Remove the starter motor.

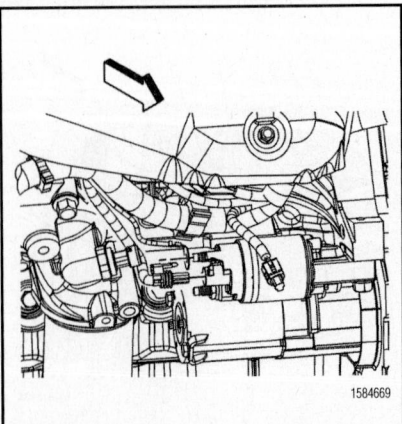

Fig. 100 Disconnect the engine harness electrical connector from the starter

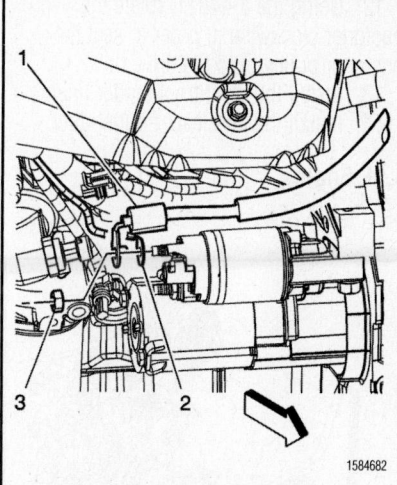

Fig. 101 Engine harness terminal nut (3), positive battery cable terminal (1), and engine harness terminal (2)

To install:

✳✳ WARNING

Before installing the starter motor to the engine, tighten the nut

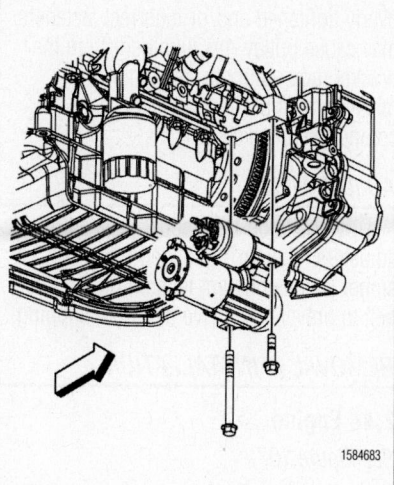

Fig. 102 Positive battery cable terminal (1) and engine harness terminal (2)

next to the cap on the solenoid BAT terminal. If this terminal is not tight in the solenoid cap, the cap may be damaged during installation of electrical connections and

cause the starter motor to fail later.

   10. Install the starter motor.
   11. Install the starter motor bolts.
   12. Tighten the bolts to 30 ft. lbs. (40 Nm).
   13. Install the engine harness terminal to the starter.
   14. Install the positive battery cable terminal to the starter.
   15. Install the engine harness terminal nut.
   16. Tighten the battery terminal nut to 13 ft. lbs. (17 Nm).
   17. Connect the engine harness electrical connector to the starter.
   18. Install the flywheel inspection cover and bolts.
   19. Tighten the bolts to 89 inch lbs. (10 Nm).
   20. Lower the vehicle.
   21. Connect the negative battery cable.

ENGINE MECHANICAL

➡Disconnecting the negative battery cable may interfere with the functions of the onboard computer systems and may require the computer to undergo a relearning process, once the negative battery cable is reconnected. Refer to Battery Negative Cable Disconnection and Connection.

DRIVE BELT

DRIVE BELT ROUTING

See Figures 103 through 106.

Refer to the accompanying illustrations for belt routing.

INSPECTION

✳✳ WARNING

Belt dressing will damage the drive belt. Belt dressing causes the breakdown of the composition of the drive belt.

Note the following:
• Inspect all drive belt pulleys for pilling. Pilling is the small balls or pills, or it can be strings, in the drive belt grooves from the accumulation of rubber dust. Small amounts of pilling is normal condition and acceptable. When the pilling is severe the

drive belt does not have a smooth surface for proper operation.
• Inspect the belt for cuts, tears, sections of ribs missing, or damaged belt plies. *Belt separation* is identified by the plies of the belt separating and may be seen at the edge of the belt our felt as a lump in the belt.
• Verify the drive belt is correctly installed on all of the drive belt pulleys. Wear on the drive belt may be caused by mis-positioning the drive belt by one groove on a pulley.
• The installation of a drive belt that is too wide or too narrow will cause wear on

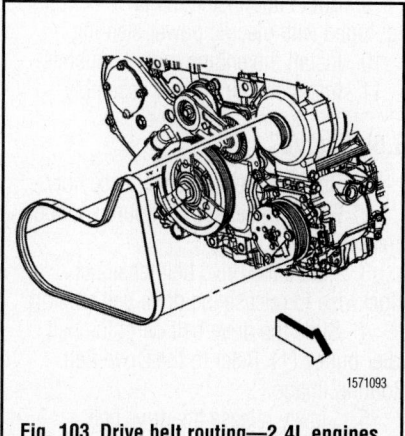

Fig. 103 Drive belt routing—2.4L engines

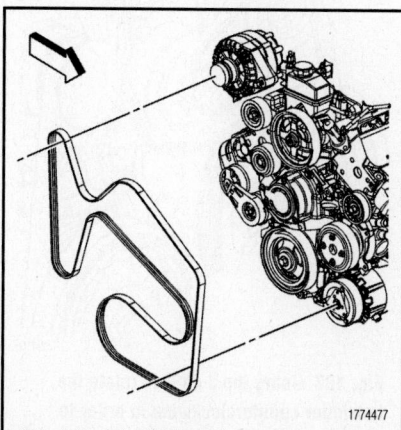

Fig. 104 Drive belt routing—3.5L engines

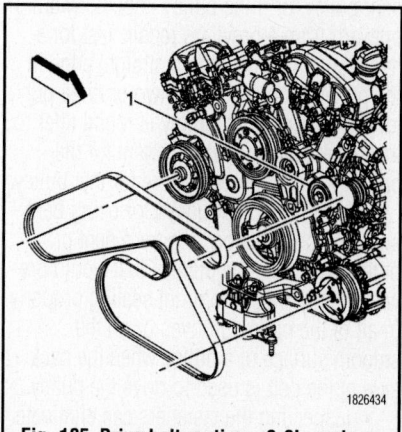

Fig. 105 Drive belt routing—3.6L engines

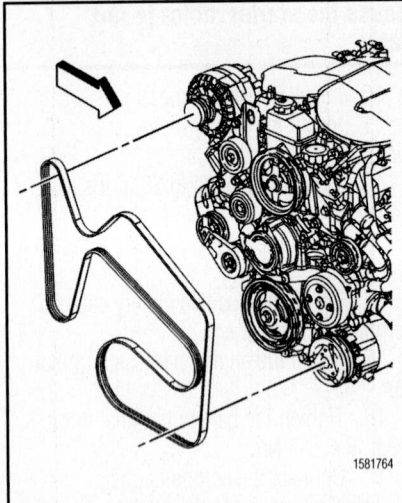

Fig. 106 Drive belt routing—3.9L engines

the drive belt. The drive belt ribs should match all of the grooves on all of the pulleys.

• Verify that the drive belt is not too long, which would prevent the drive belt tensioner from working properly. Also if an incorrect length drive belt was installed, it may not be routed properly and may be turning an accessory drive component in the wrong direction.

• Verify the drive belt is not contacting any parts of the engine or body while the engine is operating. There should be sufficient clearance when the drive belt accessory drive components load varies. The drive belt should not come in contact with an engine or a body component when snapping the throttle.

• Bent, cracked, or loose accessory drive component brackets may put extra strain on that accessory component causing it to vibrate.

• Misalignment of the pulleys may be caused from improper mounting of the accessory drive component, incorrect installation of the accessory drive component pulley, or if the pulley is bent inward or outward from a previous repair. Test for a misaligned pulley using a straight edge in the pulley grooves across two or three pulleys. If a misaligned pulley is found refer to that accessory drive component for the proper installation procedure for that pulley.

• Inspecting the pulleys for being bent should include inspecting for a dent or other damage to the pulleys that would prevent the drive belt from not seating properly in all of the pulley grooves or on the smooth surface of a pulley when the back side of the belt is used to drive the pulley.

• Inspecting the fasteners can eliminate the possibility that a wrong bolt, nut, spacer,

or washer was installed. Missing, loose, overly tightened and/or incorrect fasteners may cause pulley misalignment from the bracket moving under load and/or misalignment of the accessory component bracket.

ADJUSTMENT

Drive belts on this model have automatic adjusters. The spring loaded drive belt tensioner keeps constant tension on the drive belt to prevent the drive belt from slipping.

REMOVAL & INSTALLATION

2.4L Engine

See Figure 107.

1. Remove the air cleaner outlet duct.
2. Remove the right front fender liner.
3. Install the J 44811 belt tensioner unloader to the drive belt tensioner.
4. Using the J 44811, rotate the tensioner counterclockwise in order to release the tensioner from the drive belt.
5. Remove the drive belt. Refer to drive belt routing image.
6. Slowly rotate the J 44811 and the tensioner clockwise in order to allow the tensioner to rest.
7. Remove the J 44811 from the drive belt tensioner.

To install:

8. Install and position the drive belt around all of the pulleys except for the drive belt tensioner.
9. Install the J 44811 to the drive belt tensioner.
10. Using the J 44811, rotate the tensioner counterclockwise.
11. Position the drive belt under the tensioner pulley.

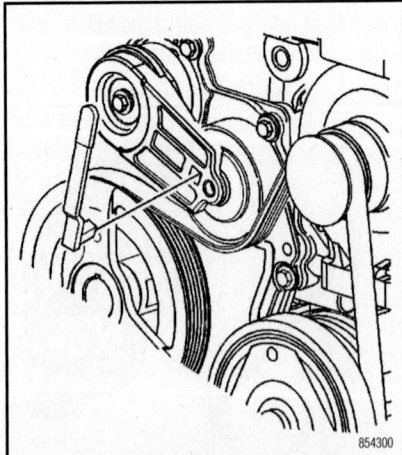

Fig. 107 Using the J 44811, rotate the tensioner counterclockwise in order to release the tensioner from the drive belt

12. Using the J 44811, rotate the tensioner clockwise in order to seat the tensioner pulley onto the drive belt.
13. Install the right front fender liner.
14. Install the air cleaner outlet duct.

3.5L Engine

See Figure 108.

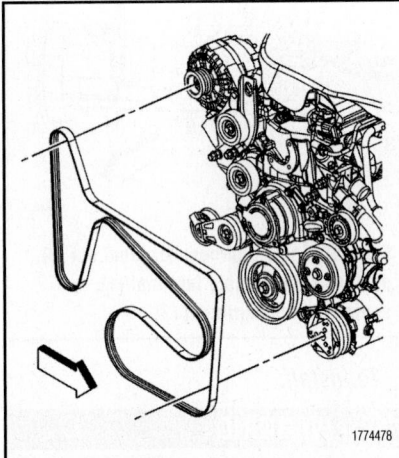

Fig. 108 Rotate the drive belt tensioner counterclockwise to release the spring tension.

1. Remove the air cleaner assembly.
2. Remove the engine mount snubber.
3. Install a breaker bar to the drive belt tensioner.
4. Rotate the drive belt tensioner counterclockwise to release the spring tension. Refer to the Drive Belt Routing image.
5. Remove the drive belt.

To install:

6. Install a breaker bar to the drive belt tensioner.
7. Rotate the drive belt tensioner counterclockwise to release the spring tension.
8. Route and install the drive belt, if equipped with hydraulic power steering.
9. Route and install the drive belt, if equipped with electric power steering.
10. Install the engine mount snubber.
11. Install the air cleaner assembly.

3.6L Engine

1. Remove the air cleaner assembly.
2. Remove the engine mount snubber bracket.
3. Rotate the drive belt tensioner clockwise to release the drive belt tension.
4. Slide the drive belt off of the belt idler pulley (1). Refer to the Drive Belt Routing image.
5. Slowly release the drive belt tensioner.

6. Remove the drive belt from the accessory drive pulleys.

To install:

7. Install the drive belt to the crankshaft pulley, the tensioner and the generator.

8. Rotate the drive belt tensioner clockwise.

9. Install the drive belt to the idler pulley.

➡**Ensure the drive belt is properly aligned and seated into the grooves of the accessory drive pulleys.**

10. Slowly release the drive belt tensioner.

11. Install the engine mount snubber.

12. Install the air cleaner assembly.

3.9L Engine

Coupe

1. Remove the air cleaner.
2. Remove the intake manifold cover.
3. Remove the engine mount snubber.
4. Rotate the drive belt tensioner counterclockwise in order to release the tensioner spring tension. Refer to the Drive Belt Routing image.
5. Remove the drive belt.

To install:

6. Rotate the drive belt tensioner counterclockwise in order to release the tensioner spring tension.

7. Install the drive belt.
8. Install the engine mount snubber.
9. Install the intake manifold cover.
10. Install the air cleaner.

Convertible

See Figure 109.

1. Remove the air cleaner assembly.

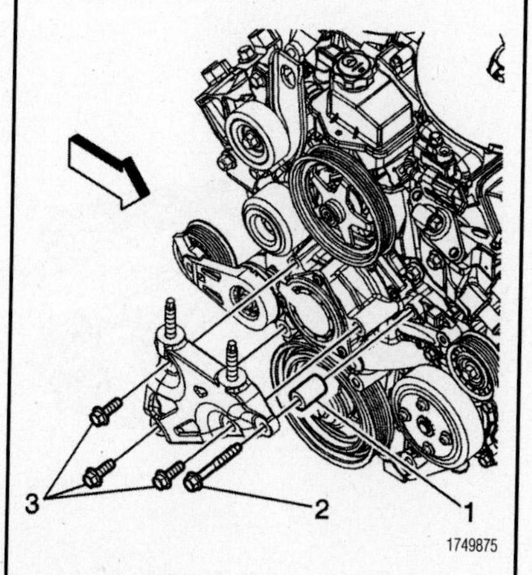

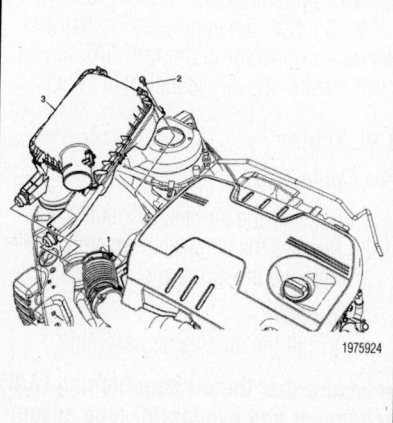

Fig. 109 Engine mount bracket bolt (2) and spacer (1)

2. Remove the intake manifold cover.
3. Remove the engine mount bracket bolt (2).
4. Remove the engine mount bracket spacer (1).
5. Rotate the drive belt tensioner counterclockwise in order to release the tensioner spring tension. Refer to the Drive Belt Routing image.
6. Remove the drive belt.

To install:

7. Rotate the drive belt tensioner counterclockwise in order to release the tensioner spring tension.

8. Install the drive belt.

9. The spacer has a nominal length of 1.42 in (36.0 mm). If the spacer cannot be reinstalled, the spacer will require the ends to be buffed slightly using a crocus cloth or emery paper in order to bring the length to a minimum of 1.41 in (35.80 mm).

10. Install the engine mount bracket spacer.

11. Install the engine mount bracket bolt.
12. Tighten the bolt to 37 ft. lbs. (50 Nm).
13. Install the intake manifold cover.
14. Install the air cleaner assembly.

AIR CLEANER ASSEMBLY

REMOVAL & INSTALLATION

2.4L Engine

See Figure 110.

1. Remove the Mass Air Flow (MAF) sensor. Refer to Mass Airflow Sensor with Intake Air Temperature Sensor replacement.

2. Loosen the clamp (1) in order to slide the duct off.

Fig. 110 Air cleaner outlet duct clamp (1), bolt (2), and assembly (3)

3. Remove the air cleaner bolt (2).
4. Remove the air cleaner assembly (3).
5. Reposition the air conditioning pipe as necessary.

To install:

6. Install the air cleaner assembly.
7. Tighten the air cleaner bolt to 35 inch lbs. (4 Nm).
8. Tighten the air cleaner outlet duct clamp to 89 inch lbs. (10 Nm).

3.5L Engine—Flex Fuel (NU6)

See Figure 111.

1. Disconnect the secondary air injection inlet hose from the air cleaner.

2. Remove the mass airflow senor Refer to Mass Airflow Sensor with Intake Air Temperature Sensor Replacement.

3. Remove the air cleaner assembly bolt (1).

4. Remove the air cleaner assembly (2).

To install:

5. Install the air cleaner assembly.

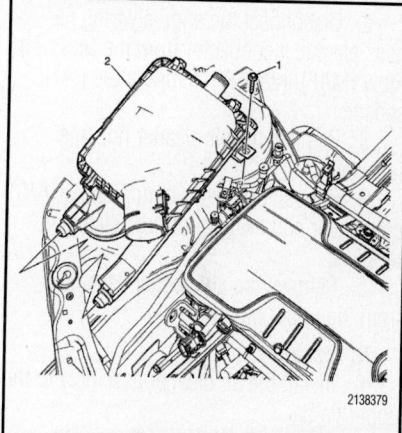

Fig. 111 Air cleaner assembly (2) and bolt (1)

6. Install the air cleaner assembly bolt (1) and tighten to 89 inch lbs. (10 Nm).

3.5L Engine—Gas (NT7)

See Figure 112.

1. Remove the air cleaner outlet duct.
2. Remove the air cleaner assembly bolts.
3. Remove the air cleaner assembly.

To install:

4. Install the air cleaner assembly.
5. Install the air cleaner assembly bolts.
6. Tighten the bolts to 89 inch lbs. (10 Nm).
7. Install the air cleaner outlet duct.

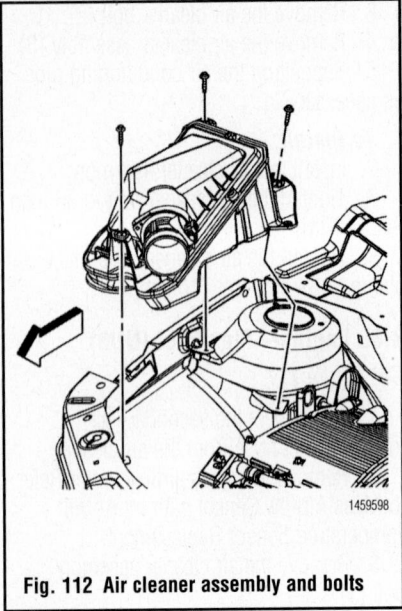

Fig. 112 Air cleaner assembly and bolts

3.6L Engine

See Figures 113 through 115.

1. Remove the air cleaner outlet duct.
2. Disconnect the engine wiring harness electrical connector from the Mass Air Flow (MAF)/Intake Air Temperature (IAT) sensor.
3. Remove the air cleaner housing rear bolt.
4. Reposition the air conditioning (A/C) condenser and evaporator tube clamp as required.
5. Remove the air cleaner assembly from the upper tie bar.

To install:

6. Install the air cleaner assembly to the upper tie bar.
7. Position the A/C condenser and evaporator tube clamp as required.

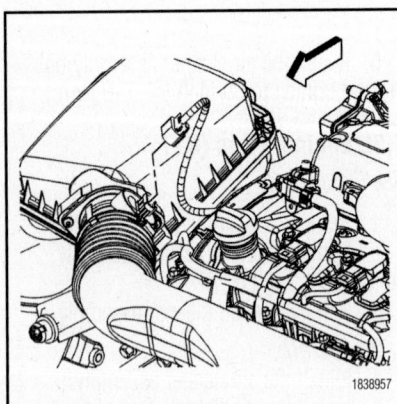

Fig. 113 Disconnect the engine wiring harness electrical connector from the Mass Air Flow (MAF)/Intake Air Temperature (IAT) sensor

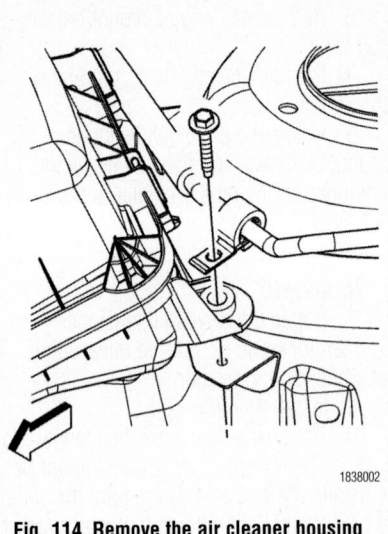

Fig. 114 Remove the air cleaner housing rear bolt

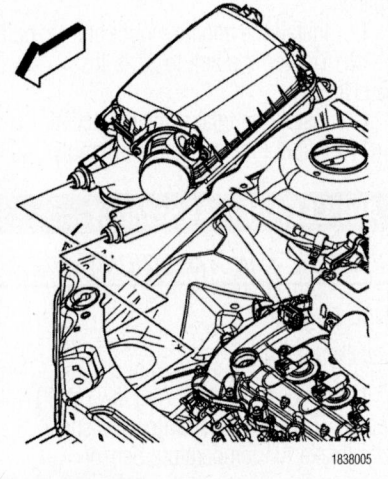

Fig. 115 Remove the air cleaner assembly from the upper tie bar

8. Install the air cleaner housing rear bolt and tighten to 89 inch lbs. (10 Nm).
9. Connect the engine wiring harness electrical connector to the MAF/IAT sensor.
10. Install the air cleaner outlet duct.

3.9L Engine

See Figure 116.

1. Remove the air cleaner outlet duct.
2. Remove the air cleaner assembly bolts.
3. Remove the air cleaner assembly.

To install:

4. Install the air cleaner assembly.

➥**Ensure that the air conditioning (A/C) condenser and evaporator tube assembly is placed on top of the air cleaner at the inboard rear attaching location prior to installing the bolt.**

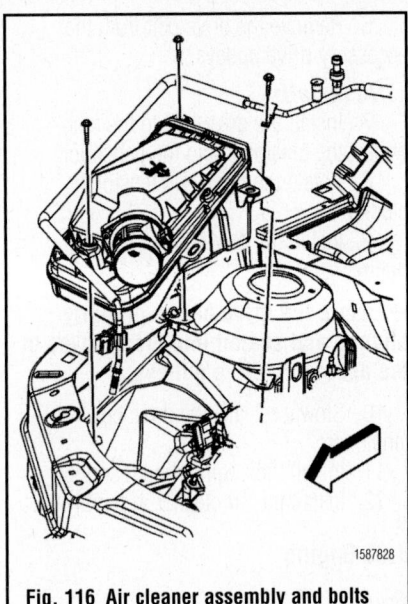

Fig. 116 Air cleaner assembly and bolts

5. Install the air cleaner assembly bolts.
6. Tighten the bolts to 89 inch lbs. (10 Nm).
7. Install the air cleaner outlet duct.

ELEMENT REPLACEMENT

2.4L Engine

See Figures 117 and 118.

1. Disconnect the Mass Air Flow (MAF)/Intake Air Temperature (IAT) sensor electrical connector.
2. Loosen the upper air cleaner cover screws.
3. Remove the upper air cleaner cover.
4. Remove the air cleaner filter from the lower air cleaner housing.
5. Inspect the air cleaner filter for dust, dirt and water contamination.

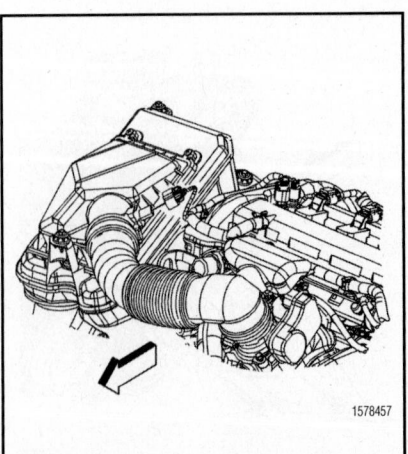

Fig. 117 Disconnect the Mass Air Flow (MAF)/Intake Air Temperature (IAT) sensor electrical connector.

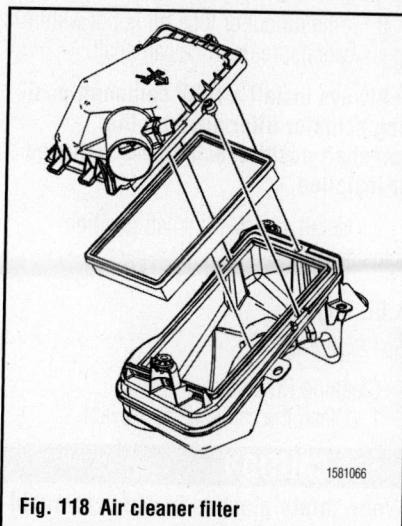

Fig. 118 Air cleaner filter

6. Replace the element as necessary. Refer to the Maintenance Schedule.

To install:

7. Install the air cleaner filter into the lower air cleaner housing.

8. Install the upper air cleaner cover to the lower air cleaner housing.

9. Secure the air cleaner housing cover.

10. Tighten the screws to 44 inch lbs. (5 Nm).

11. Connect the MAF/IAT sensor electrical connector.

3.5L Engine—Flex Fuel (NU6)

See Figure 119.

1. Disconnect the secondary air injection inlet hose from the air cleaner.

2. Disconnect the mass airflow electrical connector.

3. Unlatch the hook retainers.

4. Remove the air cleaner element.

5. Installation is the reverse of removal.

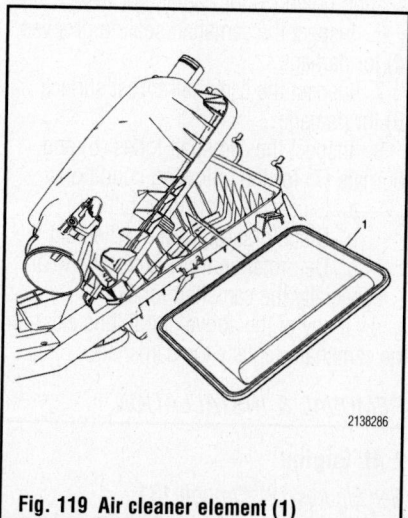

Fig. 119 Air cleaner element (1)

3.5L Engine—Gas (NT7)

See Figure 120.

1. Disconnect the mass air flow (MAF) sensor harness connector.

2. Remove the upper air cleaner cover screws.

3. Remove the upper air cleaner cover.

4. Remove the air cleaner filter from the lower air cleaner housing.

5. Inspect the air cleaner filter for dust, dirt and water contamination.

6. Replace as necessary. Refer to the Maintenance Schedule.

To install:

7. Install the air cleaner filter into the lower air cleaner housing.

8. Install the upper air cleaner cover to the lower air cleaner housing.

9. Secure the air cleaner housing cover.

10. Tighten the air cleaner cover screws to 44 inch lbs. (5 Nm).

11. Connect the MAF sensor harness connector.

Fig. 120 Remove the upper air cleaner cover screws

3.6L Engine

See Figure 121.

1. Disengage the air cleaner cover latches (1).

2. Open the air cleaner cover.

3. Remove and discard the air filter assembly.

To install:

4. Install a NEW air filter assembly.

5. Engage the air cleaner cover retainers to the lower air cleaner housing, and close the cover.

6. Engage the air cleaner cover latches (1).

7. Ensure that the air cleaner cover is secured to the lower air cleaner housing.

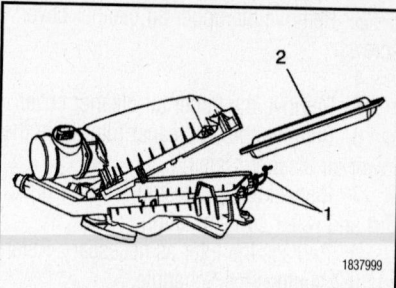

Fig. 121 Disengage the air cleaner cover latches (1)

3.9L Engine

See Figures 122 and 123.

1. Disconnect the Mass Air Flow (MAF)/Intake Air Temperature (IAT) sensor harness connector.

2. Remove the upper air cleaner cover screws. Refer to image for 3.5L Gas Air Cleaner Element Replacement—it is the same.

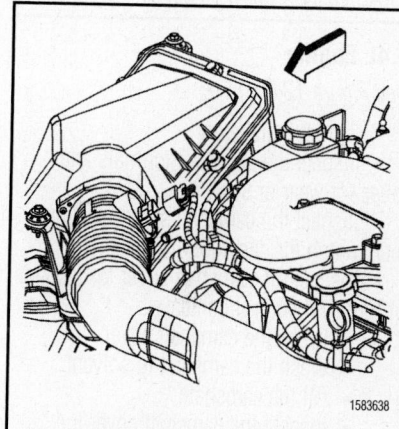

Fig. 122 Disconnect the Mass Air Flow (MAF)/Intake Air Temperature (IAT) sensor harness connector

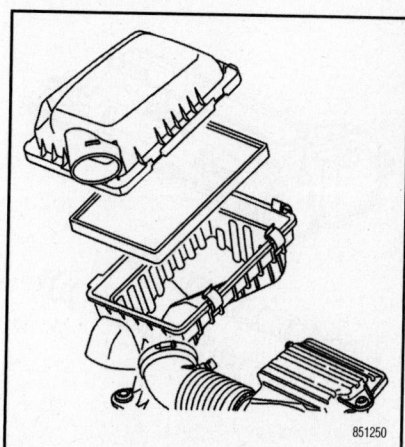

Fig. 123 Install the air cleaner filter into the lower air cleaner housing.

3. Remove the upper air cleaner cover screws.

4.

5. Remove the upper air cleaner cover.

6. Remove the air cleaner filter from the lower air cleaner housing.

7. Inspect the air cleaner filter for dust, dirt and water contamination.

8. Replace the filter as necessary. Refer to the Maintenance Schedule.

To install:

9. Install the air cleaner filter into the lower air cleaner housing.

10. Install the upper air cleaner cover to the lower air cleaner housing.

11. Secure the air cleaner housing cover.

12. Tighten the screws to 44 inch lbs. (5 Nm).

13. Connect the MAF/IAT sensor harness connector.

CAMSHAFT AND VALVE LIFTERS

CLEANING & INSPECTION

2.4L Engine

See Figure 124.

Camshaft Inspection:

• Inspect the camshaft journals and lobes for wear or scoring.

• Inspect the camshaft sprocket alignment notch for damage.

• Inspect the camshaft cover for damage or loose oil control baffles.

  • Clean the camshaft cover.
  • Wash the camshaft in solvent.
  • Oil the camshaft.
  • Inspect the camshaft cover for cracks or other signs of damage.

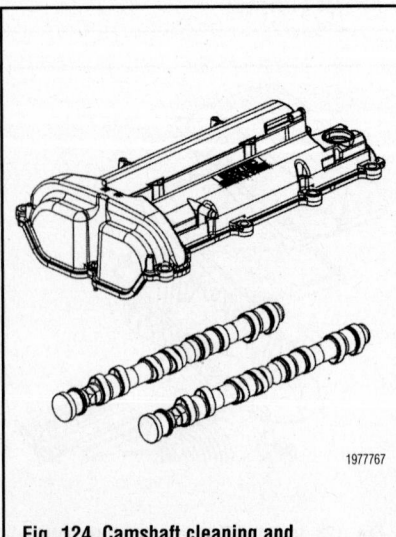

Fig. 124 Camshaft cleaning and inspection

3.5L & 3.9L Engines

See Figure 125.

1. Remove and discard the camshaft position actuator filter (1).

2. Clean the camshaft with cleaning solvent.

> ❄❄ **CAUTION**
>
> **Bodily injury may occur if the cleaning solvent is inhaled or exposed to the skin.**

3. Inspect the camshaft for the following conditions:

   a. Scored camshaft bearing journals (5)

   b. Damaged camshaft lobes (4)

   c. Damaged Camshaft Position (CMP) sensor reluctor area (3)

   d. Damaged threads (2)

4. Measure the camshaft journals using a micrometer.

5. If the camshaft journals are not within specifications, replace the camshaft.

6. Measure the camshaft runout using the J-7872 Magnetic Base Dial Indicator:

   a. Mount the camshaft in V-blocks between the centers.

   b. Use the J-7872 Indicator in order to measure the intermediate camshaft journal.

7. Measure the camshaft lobe lift using the J-7872 Indicator.

   a. Lubricate the camshaft using GM P/N 12345501 (Canadian P/N 992704) or the equivalent.

   b. Set the camshaft on V-blocks.

   c. Use the J-7872 Indicator in order to measure the lobe lift.

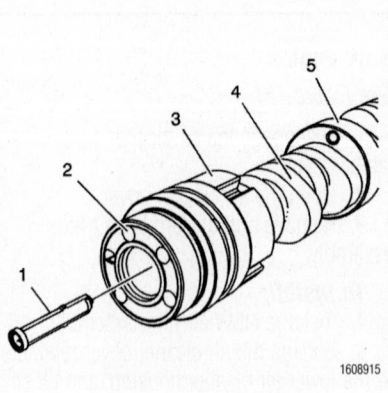

Fig. 125 Camshaft position actuator filter (1), threads (2), Camshaft Position (CMP) sensor reluctor area (3), lobes (4) and bearing journals (5)

8. If the runout or lobe lift is not within specifications, replace the camshaft.

➡ **Always install a NEW camshaft position actuator filter anytime the camshaft position actuator is removed or installed.**

9. Install a NEW camshaft position actuator filter.

3.6L Engine

See Figure 126.

Cleaning Procedure

1. Clean the camshaft in solvent.

> ❄❄ **CAUTION**
>
> **Wear safety glasses in order to avoid eye damage.**

2. Dry the camshaft with compressed air. Visual Inspection

3. Inspect the camshaft oil feed holes (1) to the camshaft position actuator for dirt, debris or blockage.

4. Inspect the threaded hole (2) for damage.

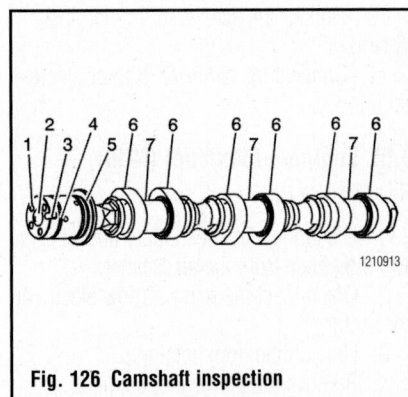

Fig. 126 Camshaft inspection

5. Inspect the camshaft position actuator locating notch (3) for damage or wear.

6. Inspect the camshaft sealing grooves (4) for damage.

7. Inspect the camshaft thrust surface (5) for damage.

8. Inspect the camshaft lobes (6) and journals (7) for the following conditions:

   a. Excessive scoring or pitting

   b. Discoloration from overheating

   c. Deformation from excessive wear, especially the camshaft lobes

9. If any of the above conditions exist on the camshaft, replace the camshaft.

REMOVAL & INSTALLATION

2.4L Engine

See Figures 127 through 131.

Intake & Exhaust Camshaft & Valve Lifter Replacement

➡**Instructions for Intake & Exhaust are combined here, but the procedures are intended to be performed on the intake or exhaust camshaft and lifters separately.**

1. Remove the intake/exhaust camshaft position actuator.

➡**Remove each bolt on each cap one turn at a time until there is no spring tension pushing on the camshaft.**

2. Mark the bearing caps to ensure they are installed in the original position.
3. Remove the bearing cap bolts.
4. Remove the bearing caps.
5. Remove the intake camshaft (1).

➡**Keep all of the roller followers and hydraulic adjusters in order so that they can be reinstalled in their respective locations.**

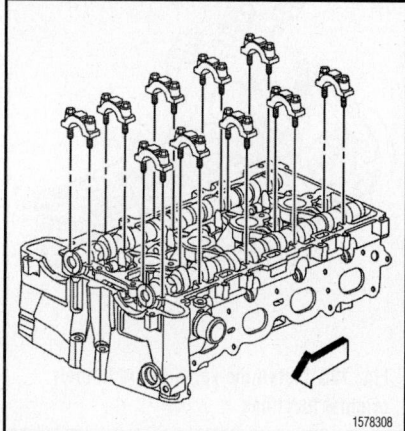

Fig. 127 Remove the bearing cap bolts and caps

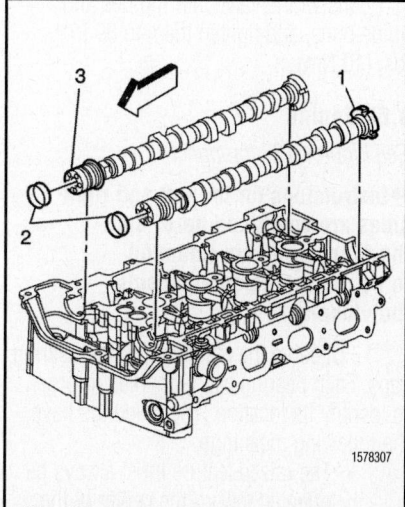

Fig. 128 Remove the intake camshaft (1)

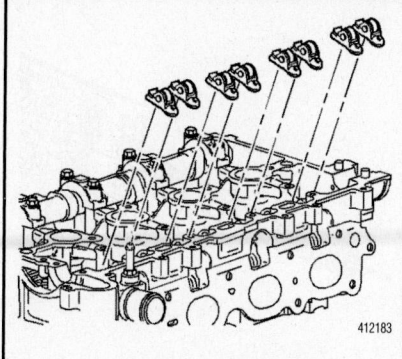

Fig. 129 Remove the camshaft roller followers—Intake shown, exhaust similar

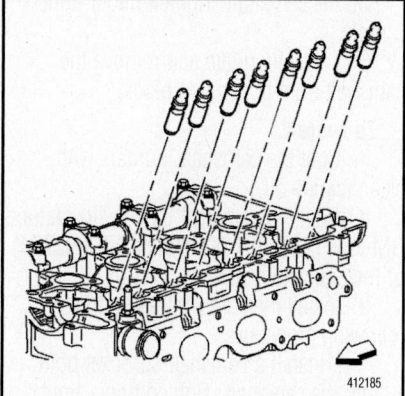

Fig. 130 Remove the hydraulic element adjusters—Intake shown, exhaust similar

6. Remove the camshaft roller followers.
7. Remove the hydraulic element adjusters.

To install:

8. Install the hydraulic element lash adjusters into their bores in the cylinder head.
9. Lubricate the hydraulic lash adjusters with GM PN 12345501 (Canadian PN 992704) or equivalent.
10. Lubricate the valve tips with GM PN 12345501 (Canadian PN 992704) or equivalent.

➡**Used roller followers MUST be returned to their original position on the camshaft. If the camshaft is being replaced, the roller followers actuated by the camshaft must also be replaced.**

11. Position the camshaft roller followers on the tip of the valve stem and on the lash adjuster. Lubricate the roller followers with GM PN 12345501 (Canadian PN 992704) or equivalent.
12. Install the intake camshaft. Lubricate with GM PN 12345501 (Canadian PN 992704) or equivalent.
13. Install the camshaft bearing caps. Hand-tighten the cap bolts.
14. Tighten the bearing cap bolts in increments of 3 turns until they are seated.

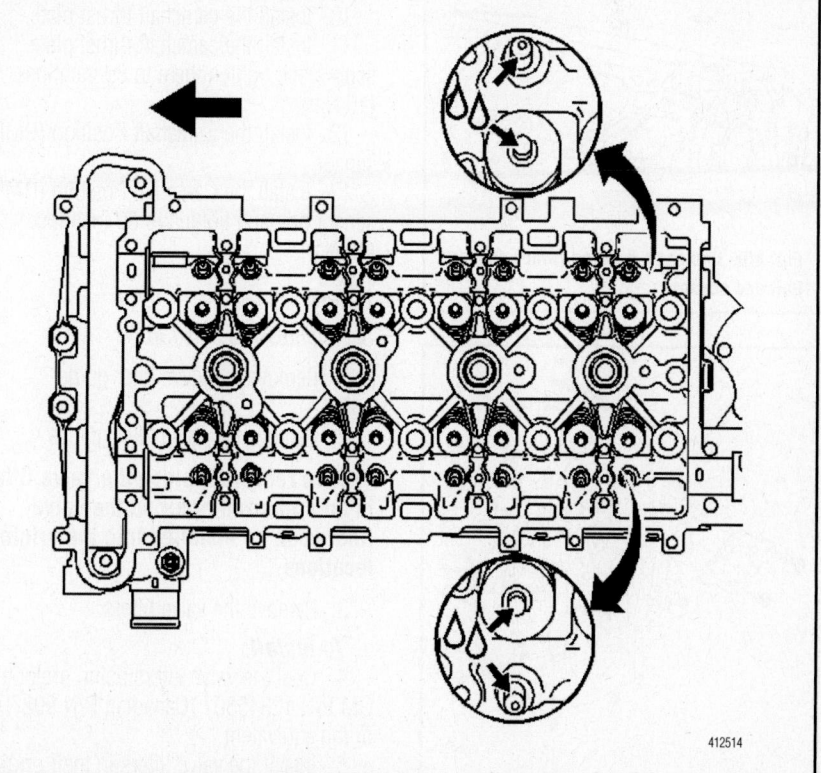

Fig. 131 Lubricate the valve tips with GM PN 12345501 (Canadian PN 992704) or equivalent.

15. Tighten the bolts to 89 inch lbs. (10 Nm).

16. Install the intake camshaft position actuator.

3.5L & 3.9L Engines

Camshaft

See Figures 132 through 134.

1. Remove the Camshaft Position (CMP) sensor bolt.

2. Remove the Camshaft Position (CMP) sensor.

3. Remove the camshaft thrust plate screws.

4. Remove the camshaft thrust plate.

❋❋ WARNING

All camshaft journals are the same diameter, so care must be used in removing or installing the camshaft to avoid damage to the camshaft bearings.

5. Complete the following steps in order to remove the camshaft.

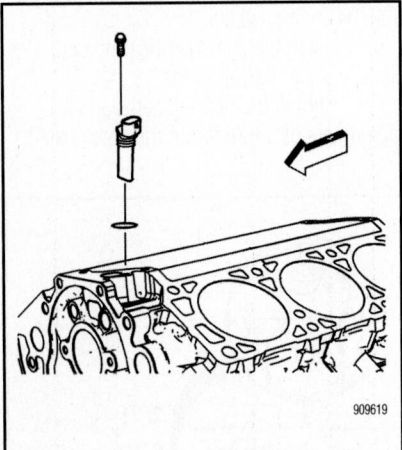

Fig. 132 Camshaft Position (CMP) sensor bolt and sensor

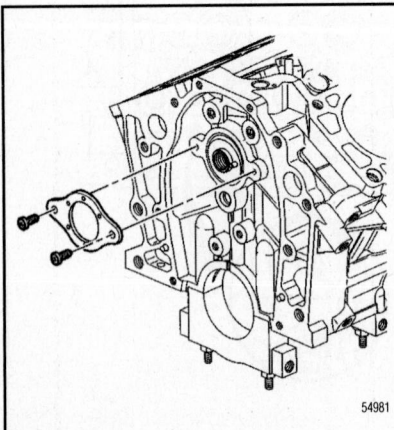

Fig. 133 Camshaft thrust plate screws

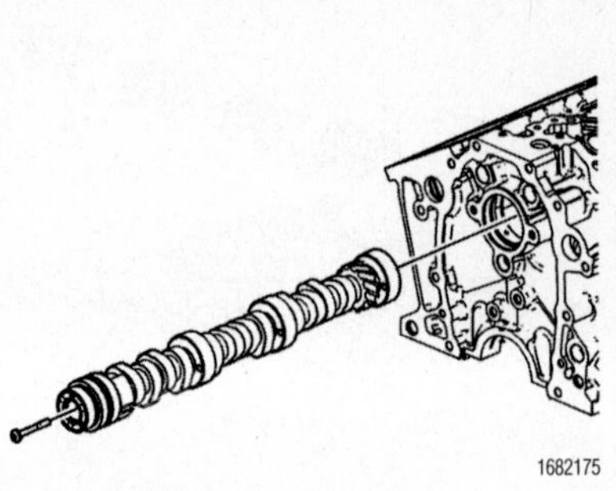

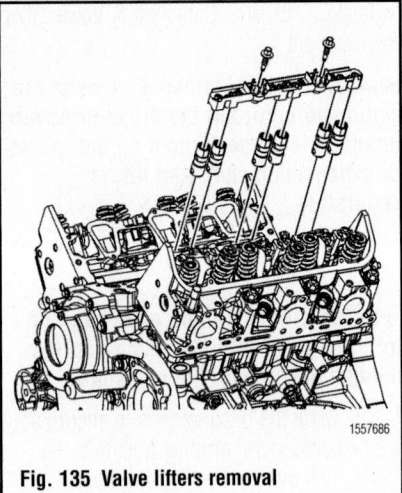

Fig. 134 Camshaft removal

a. Install a camshaft sprocket bolt into the camshaft. Tighten finger tight only.

6. Carefully rotate and remove the camshaft from the engine block.

To install:

7. Coat the camshaft journals with clean engine oil.

8. Coat the camshaft lobes with prelube GM P/N 12345501 (Canadian P/N 992704) or the equivalent.

9. Install the camshaft using the following procedure:

a. Install a camshaft sprocket bolt into the camshaft. Tighten finger tight only.

b. Carefully rotate the camshaft while installing the camshaft into the camshaft bearings.

10. Install the camshaft thrust plate.

11. Install the camshaft thrust plate screws and tighten them to 89 inch lbs. (10 Nm).

12. Install the Camshaft Position (CMP) sensor.

13. Install the Camshaft Position (CMP) sensor bolt and tighten to 89 inch lbs. (10 Nm).

Lifters

See Figures 135 and 136.

1. Remove the valve lifter guide bolts.

2. Remove the valve lifter guides.

➡**Once removed, place the valve lifters in an organized order so the valve lifters can be installed into the original locations.**

3. Remove the valve lifters.

To install:

4. Coat the valve lifters using prelube GM P/N 12345501 (Canadian P/N 992704) or the equivalent.

5. Install the valve lifters in their original locations.

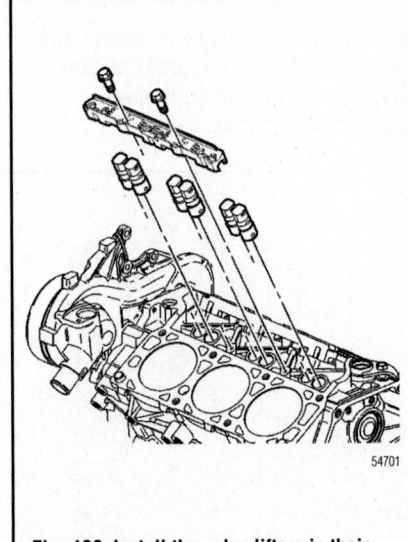

Fig. 135 Valve lifters removal

Fig. 136 Install the valve lifters in their original locations

6. Apply threadlock GM P/N 12345382 (Canadian P/N 10953489) or the equivalent to the threads.

7. Install the valve lifter guides and guide bolts, and tighten them to 89 inch lbs. (10 Nm).

3.6L Engine

See Figures 137 through 142.

➡**Instructions for the left and right sides are combined here, but the procedures are intended to be performed on each side individually.**

1. Observe the markings on the bearing caps. Each bearing cap is marked in order to identify its location. The markings have the following meanings:

- The raised feature must always be oriented toward the center of the cylinder head.

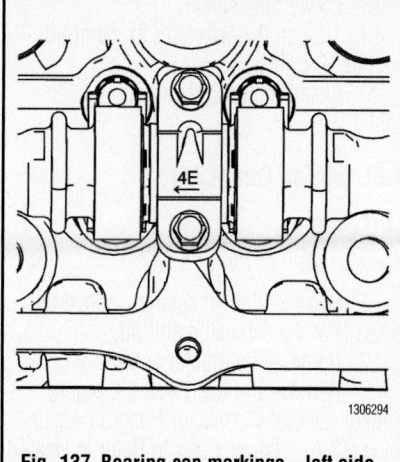

Fig. 137 Bearing cap markings—left side shown

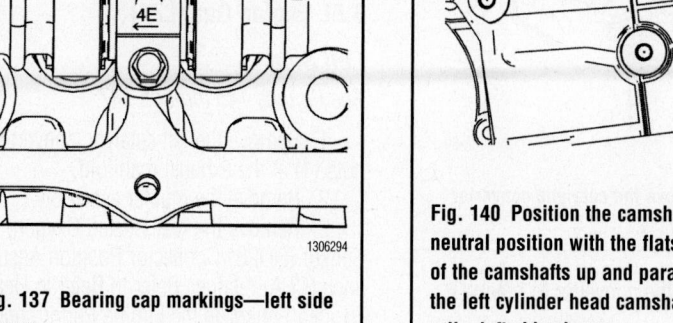

Fig. 140 Position the camshaft lobes in a neutral position with the flats on the back of the camshafts up and parallel (1) with the left cylinder head camshaft cover rail—left side shown

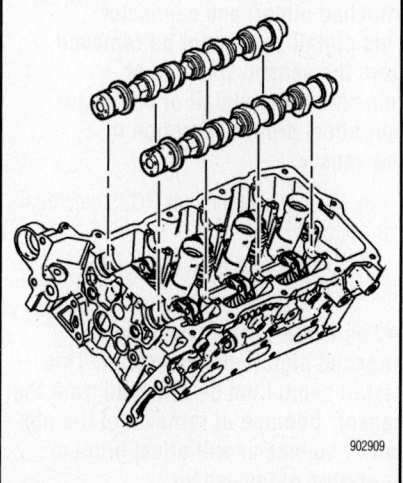

Fig. 138 Remove the camshafts—left side shown

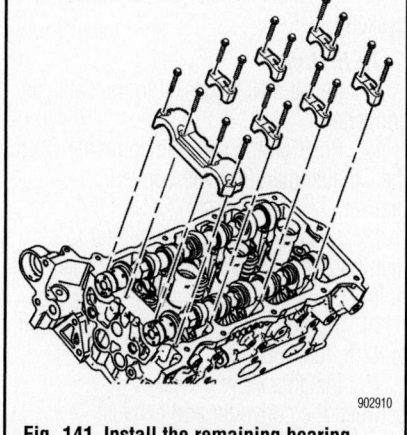

Fig. 141 Install the remaining bearing caps with their orientation mark toward the center of the cylinder head—left side shown

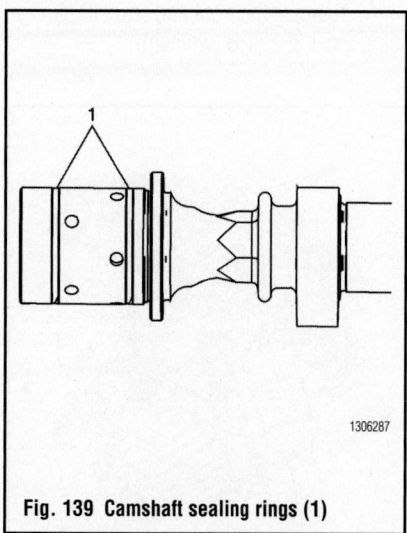

Fig. 139 Camshaft sealing rings (1)

- The I indicates the intake camshaft.
- The E indicates the exhaust camshaft.

- The number indicates the journal position from the front of the engine.
2. Remove the camshaft bearing cap bolts.
3. Remove the camshaft bearing caps.

➡**Mark the camshafts upon removal to ensure installation is in the correct position.**

4. Remove the camshafts.
5. Replace the camshaft bearing caps and bolts.

To install:

6. Ensure that the camshaft sealing rings (1) are in place in the camshaft grooves. Camshaft sealing rings must be in place below the surface of the camshaft journal in order to avoid being pinched between the cylinder head and the camshaft caps.
7. Apply a liberal amount of engine oil to the camshaft journals and the cylinder head camshaft carriers.
8. Left side only: Place the left intake and left exhaust camshafts in position in the left cylinder head.
9. Right side only: Place the right intake and right exhaust camshafts in position in the right cylinder head.
10. Position the camshaft lobes in a neutral position with the flats on the back of the camshafts up and parallel (1) with the left cylinder head camshaft cover rail.
11. Observe the markings on the camshaft bearing caps.

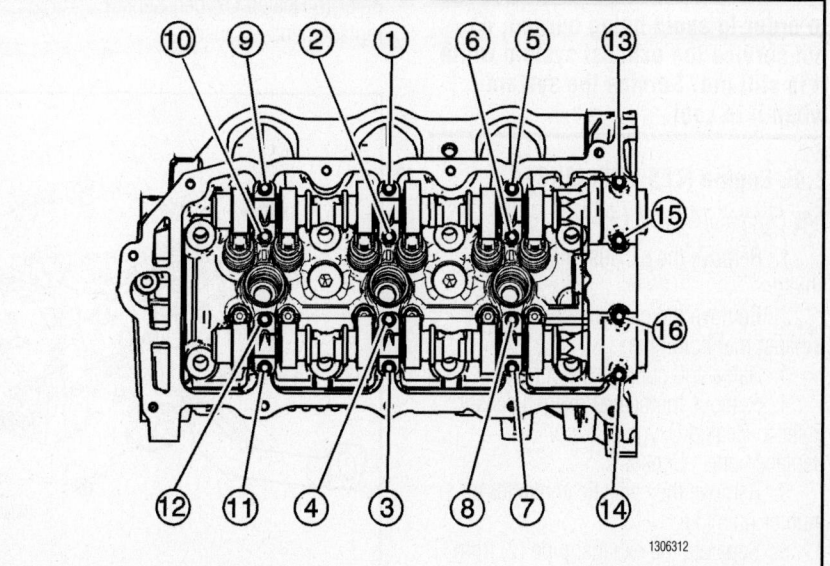

Fig. 142 Tighten the camshaft bearing cap bolts in sequence—right side shown, GM doesn't specify a sequence for the left side

12. Apply a liberal amount of lubricant to the camshaft bearing caps.

13. Left side only: Install the camshaft bearing thrust cap in the first journal of the left cylinder head.

14. Right side only: Install the camshaft bearing thrust cap in the first journal of the right cylinder head.

15. Install the remaining bearing caps with their orientation mark toward the center of the cylinder head.

16. Hand start all the camshaft bearing cap bolts.

17. Tighten the camshaft bearing cap bolts in sequence to 89 inch lbs. (10 Nm).

18. Loosen the center intake camshaft bearing cap bolts 1, 2 and the center exhaust camshaft bearing cap bolts 3, 4.

19. Retighten the center camshaft bearing cap bolts 1, 2, 3, 4 to 89 inch lbs. (10 Nm).

CATALYTIC CONVERTER

REMOVAL & INSTALLATION

> **✸✸ CAUTION**
>
> Always wear protective goggles and gloves when removing exhaust parts as falling rust and sharp edges from worn exhaust components could result in serious personal injury.

> **✸✸ CAUTION**
>
> In order to avoid being burned, do not service the exhaust system while it is still hot. Service the system when it is cool.

2.4L Engine (LE5 With MH8)

See Figures 143 and 144.

1. Remove the exhaust manifold shield.
2. Remove the catalytic converter to exhaust manifold nuts.
3. Raise and support the vehicle.
4. Remove the heated oxygen sensor. Refer to Heated Oxygen Sensor Replacement—Sensor 2.
5. Remove the catalytic converter to muffler nuts (1).
6. Separate the exhaust pipe (2) from the catalytic converter studs.
7. Position and support the exhaust pipe (2) out of the way.

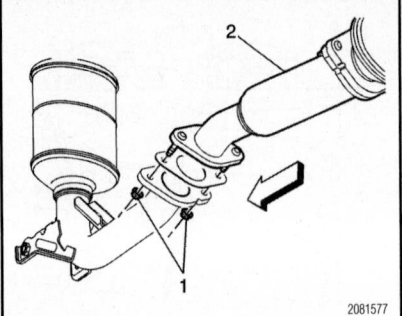

Fig. 143 Remove the catalytic converter to muffler nuts (1).

8. Remove the converter to bracket bolt (1).
9. Remove the catalytic converter (2) and gasket.
10. Discard the Catalytic converter gaskets.

To install:

11. Install a NEW gasket to the catalytic converter.
12. Position the catalytic converter (2) to the exhaust manifold and converter bracket.
13. Loosely install the converter to manifold nuts (3) and converter bracket bolt (1).
14. Tighten the converter to bracket bolt to 42 ft. lbs. (58 Nm).
15. Install a NEW gasket between the converter and exhaust pipe (2).
16. Connect the exhaust pipe to the converter and tighten the nuts (1) to 22 ft. lbs. (30 Nm).
17. Install the heated oxygen sensor. Refer to Heated Oxygen Sensor replacement—Sensor 2.

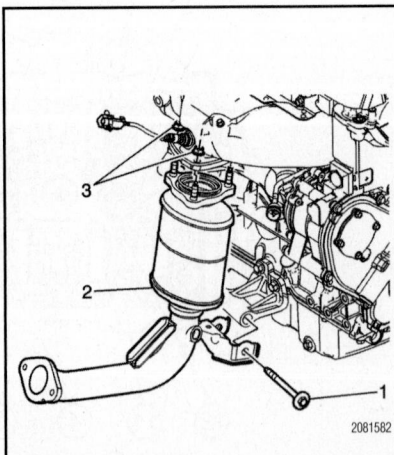

Fig. 144 Remove the converter to bracket bolt (1)

18. Lower the vehicle
19. Tighten the converter to manifold nuts to 18 ft. lbs. (45 Nm).
20. Install the exhaust manifold heat shield.

3.5L Engine Gas (LZ4)

Left Side

See Figures 145 through 147.

1. Remove the left catalytic converter nuts (1) at the exhaust manifold.
2. Remove the muffler assembly.
3. Remove the rear Heated Oxygen Sensor (HO2S) Connector Position Assurance (CPA) retainer. Refer to Refer to Heated Oxygen Sensor in the Engine Performance section.

➡The HO2S uses a permanently attached pigtail and connector. This pigtail should not be removed from the sensor. Damage or removal of the pigtail or connector will affect proper operation of the sensor.

4. Disconnect the rear HO2S electrical connector.
5. Remove the front HO2S CPA retainer (2).

➡The HO2S uses a permanently attached pigtail and connector. This pigtail should not be removed from the sensor. Damage or removal of the pigtail or connector will affect proper operation of the sensor.

➡Disconnect the front HO2S electrical connector.

6. Remove the front and rear HO2S using the J 39194-B (wrench).

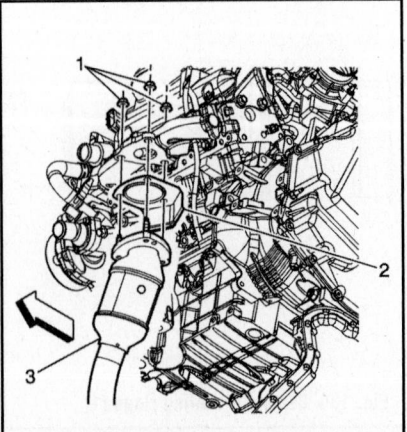

Fig. 145 Remove the left catalytic converter nuts (1) at the exhaust manifold—3.5L and 3.9L left side

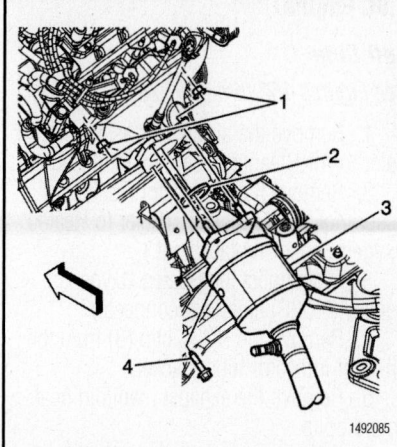

Fig. 146 Remove the right catalytic converter bolt (4) and nuts (1) at the exhaust manifold

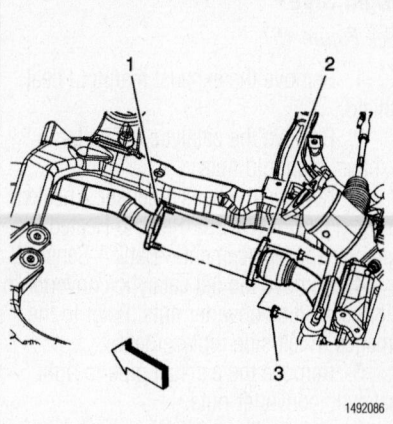

Fig. 147 Remove the left catalytic converter to right catalytic converter nuts (3). (Powertrain shown removed for clarity)

Remove the right catalytic converter bolt (4) and nuts (1) at the exhaust manifold.

7. Remove and discard the gasket (2).

8. Remove the right catalytic converter (3).

9. Remove the left catalytic converter to right catalytic converter nuts (3). (Powertrain shown removed for clarity).

10. Remove the left catalytic converter (1).

11. Remove and discard the left catalytic converter to manifold gasket.

12. Inspect the catalytic converter-to-exhaust manifold flange. Catalytic Converter to Manifold Flange Warpage:
- Service Limit: 0.028 in (0.7 mm) max.
- Standard: 0.028 in (0.7 mm) max.

To install:

13. Install a NEW gasket to the front catalytic converter studs.

14. Install the left catalytic converter.

15. Install a NEW gasket to the right catalytic converter studs.

16. Install the right catalytic converter.

17. Install the right catalytic converter bolt and nuts at the exhaust manifold.

18. Tighten the bolt and nuts to 33 ft. lbs. (45 Nm).

19. Install the left catalytic converter to right catalytic converter nuts.

20. Tighten the nuts to 16 ft. lbs. (22 Nm).

21. Install the front and rear HO2S using the J 39194-B.

22. Tighten the sensor to 31 ft. lbs. (42 Nm).

23. Connect the front HO2S electrical connector.

24. Install the front HO2S CPA retainer.

25. Disconnect the rear HO2S electrical connector.

26. Install the rear HO2S CPA retainer.

27. Install the muffler assembly.

28. Install the left catalytic converter nuts at the exhaust manifold.

29. Tighten the nuts to 33 ft. lbs. (45 Nm).

30. Start the engine, and check for exhaust leaks.

Right Side

➡**Refer to illustrations for left side as they are similar.**

1. Remove the muffler assembly.

2. Remove the Connector Position Assurance (CPA) retainer (1). Refer to Refer to Heated Oxygen Sensor in the Engine Performance section.

➡**The Heated Oxygen Sensor (HO2S) 2 uses a permanently attached pigtail and connector. This pigtail should not be removed from the sensor. Damage or removal of the pigtail or connector will affect proper operation of the sensor.**

3. Disconnect the HO2S electrical connector.

4. Remove the HO2S using the J 39194-B.

5. Remove the left catalytic converter to right catalytic converter nuts.

6. Remove the catalytic converter bolt and nuts at the exhaust manifold allowing the catalytic converter to rest on the cradle.

7. Reposition the frame until the catalytic converter can be removed.

8. Remove and discard the gasket.

To install:

9. Install a NEW gasket to the catalytic converter studs.

10. Install the right catalytic converter.

11. Install the catalytic converter bolt and nuts at the exhaust manifold.

12. Tighten the bolt and nuts to 23 ft. lbs. (31 Nm).

13. Install the left catalytic converter to right catalytic converter nuts.

14. Tighten the nuts to 23 ft. lbs. (31 Nm).

15. Install the HO2S &2) using the J 39194-B.

16. Tighten the sensor to 31 ft. lbs. (42 Nm).

17. Connect the HO2S electrical connector.

18. Install the CPA retainer.

19. Install the muffler assembly.

20. Start the engine, and check for exhaust leaks.

3.6L Engine

Left Side

See Figures 148 through 150.

1. Remove the exhaust manifold heat shield.

2. Remove the left catalytic converter to exhaust manifold nuts (1).

3. Raise and support the vehicle.

4. Disconnect the bank 2 sensor 2 Heated Oxygen Sensor (HO2S) electrical connector from the engine wiring harness electrical connector. Refer to Heated Oxygen Sensor in the Engine Performance section.

5. Remove the left catalytic converter (3) to right catalytic converter (1) nuts (2).

6. Remove the left catalytic converter from the vehicle.

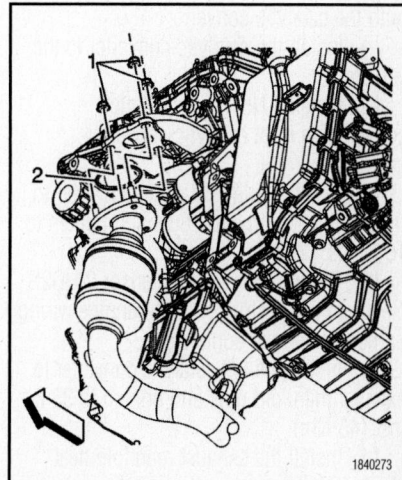

Fig. 148 Remove the left catalytic converter to exhaust manifold nuts (1)

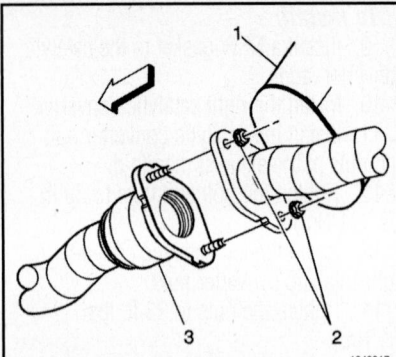

Fig. 149 Remove the left catalytic converter (3) to right catalytic converter (1) nuts (2).

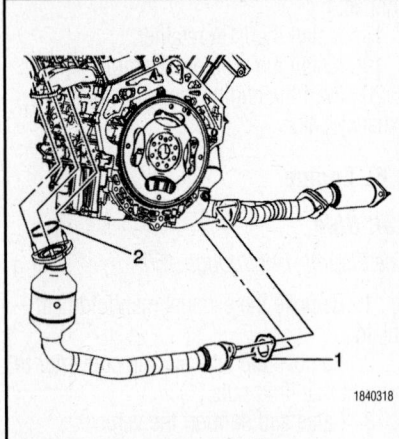

Fig. 150 Remove the left catalytic converter.

Discard the catalytic converter to exhaust manifold gasket (2).

7. Discard the left catalytic converter to right catalytic converter gasket (1).

To install:

8. Install a NEW catalytic converter seal onto the catalytic converter.

9. Install the catalytic converter to the vehicle.

10. Install a NEW left catalytic converter to right catalytic converter gasket.

11. Install the left catalytic converter to right catalytic converter nuts and tighten to 16 ft. lbs. (22 Nm).

12. Connect the bank 2 sensor 2 HO2S electrical connector (3) to the engine wiring harness electrical connector.

13. Install the left catalytic converter to exhaust manifold nuts and tighten to 33 ft. lbs. (45 Nm).

14. Install the exhaust manifold heat shield.

15. Lower the vehicle and inspect for exhaust leaks.

Right Side

See Figure 151.

1. Remove the exhaust manifold heat shield.

2. Remove the catalytic converter to exhaust manifold nuts.

3. Remove the bank 1 sensor 2 heated oxygen sensor (HO2S). Refer to Heated Oxygen Sensor replacement—Bank 1 Sensor 2.

4. Remove the left catalytic converter to right catalytic converter nuts. Refer to the images in left side replacement.

5. Remove the exhaust pipe to right catalytic converter nuts.

6. Remove the catalytic converter from the vehicle.

7. Remove and discard the catalytic converter to exhaust manifold gasket (1).

8. Remove and discard the left catalytic converter to right catalytic converter gasket (2).

To install:

9. Install a NEW catalytic converter to exhaust manifold gasket onto the catalytic converter.

10. Install the catalytic converter to the vehicle.

11. Install a NEW left catalytic converter to right catalytic converter gasket between the converters.

12. Install the left catalytic converter to right catalytic converter nuts and tighten to 16 ft. lbs. (22 Nm).

13. Install the exhaust pipe to right catalytic converter nuts and tighten to 18 ft. lbs. (25 Nm).

14. Install the bank 1 sensor 2 HO2S. Refer to Heated Oxygen Sensor replacement—Bank 1 Sensor 2.

15. Install the catalytic converter to exhaust manifold nuts (1) and tighten to 33 ft. lbs. (45 Nm).

16. Install the exhaust manifold heat shield.

3.9L Engine

Left Side

See Figures 152 through 154.

1. Remove the air cleaner assembly. Refer to Air Cleaner Assembly Replacement.

2. Remove the Connector Position Assurance (CPA) retainer. (Refer to Heated Oxygen Sensor replacement.)

3. Disconnect the Heated Oxygen Sensor (HO2S) electrical connector.

4. Remove the HO2S clip (3) from the oil level indicator tube bracket.

5. Remove the exhaust manifold heat shield bolts.

6. Remove the exhaust manifold heat shield.

7. Remove the left (front) catalytic converter nuts (1) at the exhaust manifold. Refer to the illustration for the 3.5L left side as it is the same.

8. Remove the muffler assembly. Refer to Exhaust Muffler Replacement.

9. Remove the lower right heated oxygen sensor HO2S Connector Position Assurance (CPA) retainer.

10. Disconnect the rear HO2S electrical connector.

11. Remove the lower left HO2S CPA retainer.

12. Disconnect the front HO2S electrical connector.

❄❄❄ WARNING

The oxygen sensor uses a permanently attached pigtail and connector. Do not remove the pigtail from the oxygen sensor. Damage to or removal of the pigtail connector could affect proper operation of the oxygen sensor.

13. Remove the lower right and left HO2S using the J 39194-B wrench.

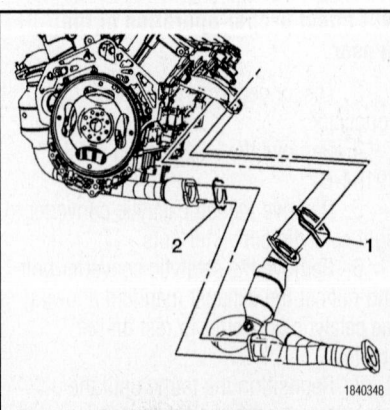

Fig. 151 Remove the catalytic converter from the vehicle

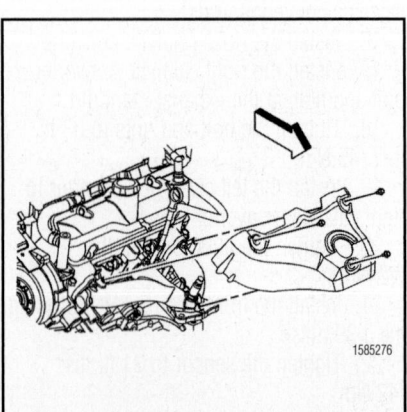

Fig. 152 Remove the exhaust manifold heat shield bolts and shield

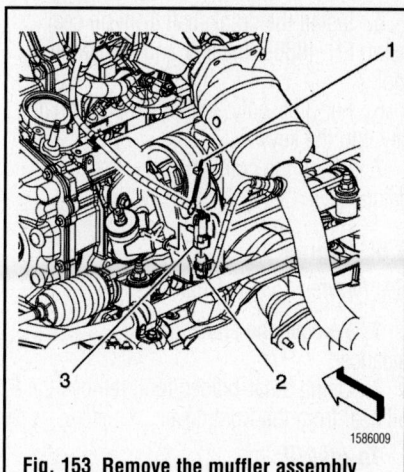

Fig. 153 Remove the muffler assembly

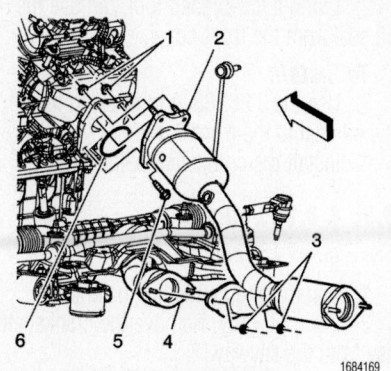

Fig. 154 Remove the left (front) catalytic converter to right (rear) catalytic converter nuts (3)

14. Remove the left (front) catalytic converter to right (rear) catalytic converter nuts (3).

15. Remove the right (rear) catalytic converter bolt (5) and nuts (1) at the exhaust manifold.

16. Remove and discard the gasket (6).

17. Remove the right (rear) catalytic converter (2).

18. Remove the left (front) catalytic converter (4).

19. Remove and discard the left (front) catalytic converter to manifold gasket.

20. Inspect the catalytic converter-to-exhaust manifold flange. Catalytic Converter to Manifold Flange Warpage:
- Service Limit: 0.028 in (0.7 mm) max.
- Standard: 0.028 in (0.7 mm) max.

To install:

21. Install a NEW gasket to the left (front) catalytic converter studs.

22. Install the left (front) catalytic converter (4).

23. Install a NEW gasket (6) to the right (rear) catalytic converter studs.

24. Install the right (rear) catalytic converter (2).

25. Install the right (rear) catalytic converter bolt (5) and nuts (1) at the exhaust manifold.

26. Tighten the bolt and nuts to 33 ft. lbs. (45 Nm).

27. Install the left (front) catalytic converter to right (rear) catalytic converter nuts (3).

28. Tighten the nuts to 16 ft. lbs. (22 Nm).

➡A special anti-seize compound is used on the HO2S threads. The compound consists of liquid graphite and glass beads. The graphite tends to burn away but the beads remain, making the sensor easier to remove. Both new and service replacement sensors already have the compound applied to the threads. If the sensor is removed from an exhaust component and if for any reason the sensor is to be reinstalled, apply anti-seize compound to the threads before the reinstallation.

29. If reinstalling the old HO2S coat the threads with anti-seize compound GM P/N 12377953 or an equivalent.

30. Install the lower right and left HO2S using the J 39194-B.

31. Tighten the sensor to 31 ft. lbs. (42 Nm).

32. Connect the lower left HO2S electrical connector.

33. Install the lower left HO2S CPA retainer.

34. Connect the lower right HO2S electrical connector.

35. Install the lower right HO2S CPA retainer.

36. Install the muffler assembly. Refer to Exhaust Muffler replacement.

37. Install the left (front) catalytic converter nuts at the exhaust manifold.

38. Tighten the nuts to 33 ft. lbs. (45 Nm).

39. Install the exhaust manifold heat shield.

40. Install the exhaust manifold heat shield bolts.

41. Tighten the bolts to 89 inch lbs. (10 Nm).

42. Connect the HO2S electrical connector.

43. Install the CPA retainer.

44. Install the HO2S clip to the oil level indicator tube bracket.

45. Install the air cleaner assembly. Refer to Air Cleaner Assembly Replacement.

46. Perform the engine mount position adjustment procedure.

47. Start the engine, and check for exhaust leaks.

Right Side

See Figure 156.

1. Remove the muffler assembly. Refer to Exhaust Muffler replacement.

2. Remove the rear stabilizer shaft.

3. Remove the Connector Position Assurance (CPA) retainer.

4. Disconnect the lower right Heated Oxygen Sensor (HO2S) electrical connector.

✳✳ WARNING

The oxygen sensor uses a permanently attached pigtail and connector. Do not remove the pigtail from the oxygen sensor. Damage to or removal of the pigtail connector could affect proper operation of the oxygen sensor.

5. Remove the lower right HO2S using the J 39194-B.

6. Remove the left (front) catalytic converter to right (rear) catalytic converter nuts. Refer to image for the left side as it is the same.

7. Remove the right (rear) catalytic converter bolt and nuts at the exhaust manifold.

8. Remove the right catalytic converter.

9. Remove and discard the gasket.

10. Inspect the catalytic converter-to-exhaust manifold flange. Catalytic Converter to Manifold Flange Warpage:
- Service Limit: 0.028 in (0.7 mm) max.
- Standard: 0.028 in (0.7 mm) max.

To install:

11. Install a NEW gasket to the catalytic converter.

12. Install the right (rear) catalytic converter.

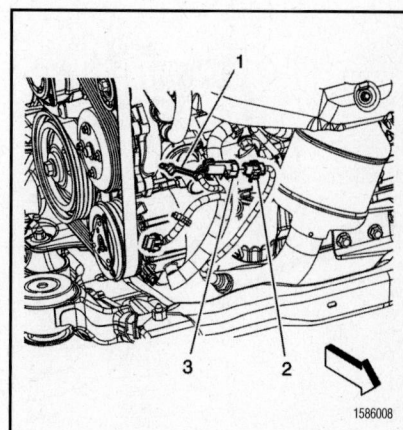

Fig. 155 Remove the muffler assembly. Refer to Exhaust Muffler replacement

13. Install the right (rear) catalytic converter bolt and nuts at the exhaust manifold.

14. Tighten the nuts to 33 ft. lbs. (45 Nm).

15. Install the left (front) catalytic converter to right (rear) catalytic converter nuts.

16. Tighten the nuts to 16 ft. lbs. (22 Nm).

➥A special anti-seize compound is used on the HO2S threads. The compound consists of liquid graphite and glass beads. The graphite tends to burn away but the beads remain, making the sensor easier to remove. Both new and service replacement sensors already have the compound applied to the threads. If the sensor is removed from an exhaust component and if for any reason the sensor is to be reinstalled, apply anti-seize compound to the threads before the reinstallation.

17. If reinstalling the old HO2S coat the threads with anti-seize compound GM P/N 12377953 or an equivalent.

18. Tighten the sensor to 31 ft. lbs. (42 Nm).

19. Connect the lower left HO2S electrical connector.

20. Install the CPA retainer.

21. Ensure that the HO2S connector clip is attached to the stud on the engine.

22. Install the rear stabilizer shaft.

23. Install the muffler assembly. Refer to Exhaust Muffler replacement.

24. Perform the engine mount position adjustment procedure.

25. Start the engine, and check for exhaust leaks.

CRANKSHAFT FRONT OIL SEAL

REMOVAL & INSTALLATION

See Figure 156.

1. Remove the crankshaft balancer.

2. Using a flat-bladed tool, remove the oil seal from the front cover.

To install:

3. Use the J 35268-A in order to install the oil seal to the front cover.

4. Install the crankshaft balancer.

3.5L & 3.9L Engines

See Figures 157 and 158.

1. Remove the crankshaft balancer.

2. For 3.5L only: Remove the crankshaft key from the keyway.

3. Pry out the crankshaft front oil seal using a suitable tool. Use care not to damage the engine front cover or the crankshaft.

To install:

4. Align the EN-48869 installer and the crankshaft front oil seal with the engine front cover and crankshaft.

5. Install the crankshaft front oil seal using EN-48869 installer and a suitable tool.

6. For 3.5L only: Install the crankshaft key into the keyway.

7. Install the crankshaft balancer.

3.6L Engine

See Figures 159 and 160.

1. Remove the crankshaft balancer.

2. Using a flat-bladed tool, remove the oil seal from the front cover.

To install:

➥Do not lubricate the crankshaft front oil seal or the crankshaft balancer sealing surfaces.

3. Use the J 29184 or an equivalent in order to install the oil seal to the front cover.

4. Install the crankshaft balancer.

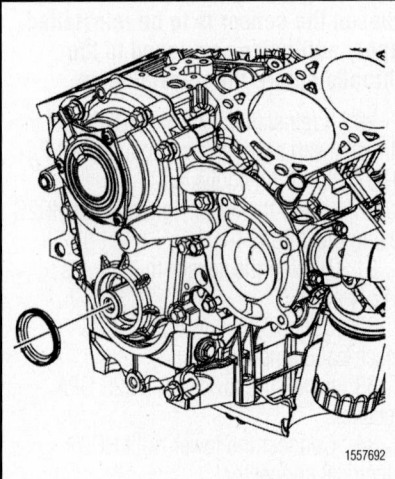

Fig. 157 Pry out the crankshaft front oil seal using a suitable tool. Use care not to damage the engine front cover or the crankshaft

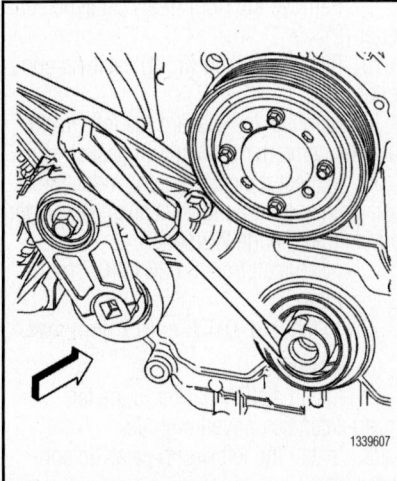

Fig. 159 Using a flat-bladed tool, remove the oil seal from the front cover

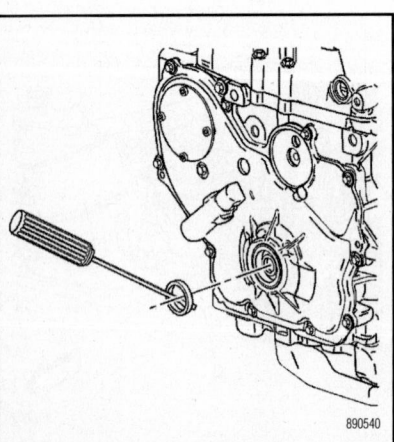

Fig. 156 Using a flat-bladed tool, remove the oil seal from the front cover

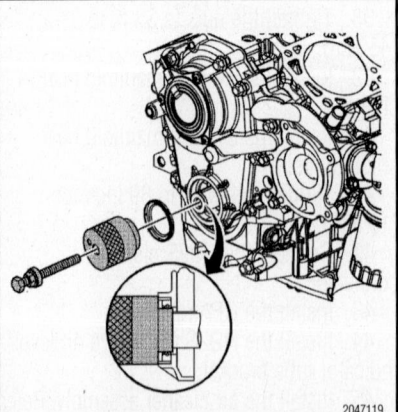

Fig. 158 Install the crankshaft front oil seal (3.9L shown)

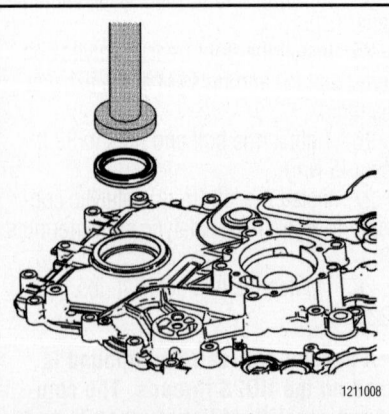

Fig. 160 Use the J 29184 or an equivalent in order to install the oil seal to the front cover

CYLINDER HEAD

REMOVAL & INSTALLATION

2.4L Engine

See Figures 161 through 172.

1. Drain the cooling system. Refer to Cooling System Draining and Filling.
2. Remove the exhaust manifold. Refer to Exhaust Manifold replacement.
3. Remove the intake manifold. Refer to Intake Manifold replacement.
4. Reposition the radiator surge tank air bleed hose clamp.
5. Remove the radiator surge tank air bleed hose from the cylinder head.
6. Reposition the radiator inlet hose clamp using the J 38185.
7. Remove the radiator inlet hose from the cylinder head.
8. Disconnect all electrical connectors as necessary.
9. Remove the spark plugs. Refer to Spark Plug replacement
10. Remove the camshaft cover. Refer to Camshaft Cover replacement.

➡If the intake camshaft actuator is moving independently of the camshaft, this means the camshaft is not locked to the actuator. Rotate the camshaft counter-clockwise while the holding tool is installed and this will lock the camshaft to the actuator.

11. Rotate the crankshaft clockwise to install the camshaft actuator locking tool EN-48953 EGR cooler pressure tester adapter set.
12. Install the EN-48953 (camshaft actuator locking tool; 1).
13. Install the camshaft actuator tool and bolts tighten to 89 inch lbs. (10 Nm).

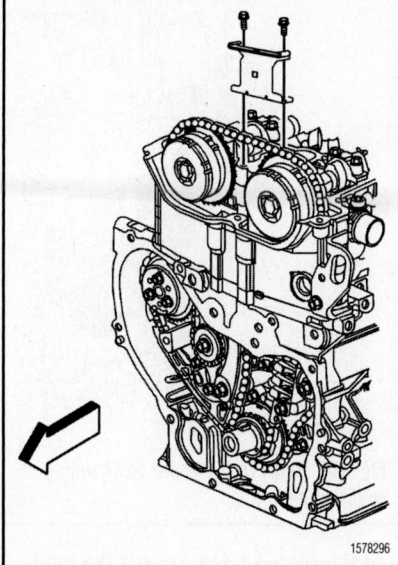

Fig. 162 Upper timing chain guide bolts and guide

14. Remove the upper timing chain guide bolts and guide.
15. Clean the timing chain and gears with solvent.

➡Ensure the timing chain and the camshaft position actuators are marked for proper assembly.

16. Mark the timing gear sprockets and the timing chain. It is recommended that the paint marks are located in the 12 o'clock position.
17. Loosen, but do not remove the intake and exhaust camshaft actuator bolts.
18. Remove the camshaft actuator locking tool, EN-48953.

➡Ensure the tips of the EN-48749 are fully engaged into the timing chain.

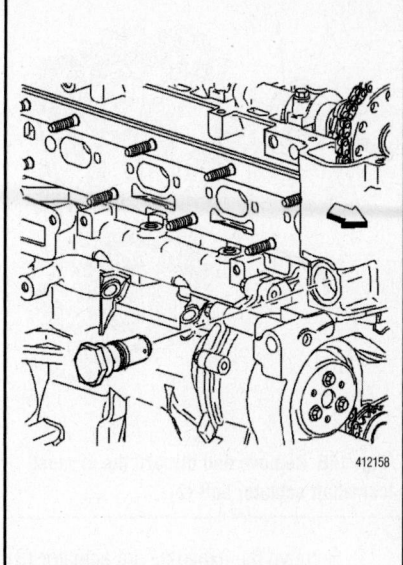

Fig. 164 Remove the timing chain tensioner

The retention tool rod can be used on the back side of the chain to ensure the teeth from the retention tool are engaged.

19. Install the timing chain retention tool EN-48749 (1) to the intake side of the timing chain.
20. Remove the timing chain tensioner.

➡The intake camshaft and actuator should not rotate during the removal or installation.

21. Install the timing chain retention tool EN-48749 (1) to the exhaust side of the timing chain.
22. Remove and discard the exhaust camshaft actuator bolt (2).

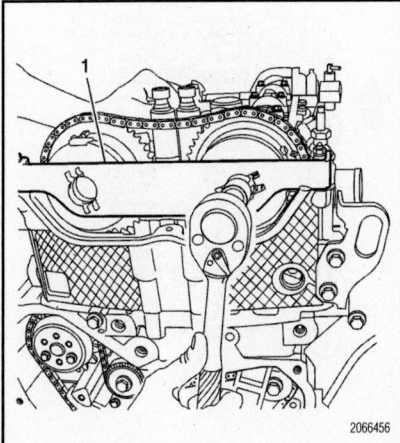

Fig. 161 Install the EN-48953 (camshaft actuator locking tool; 1)

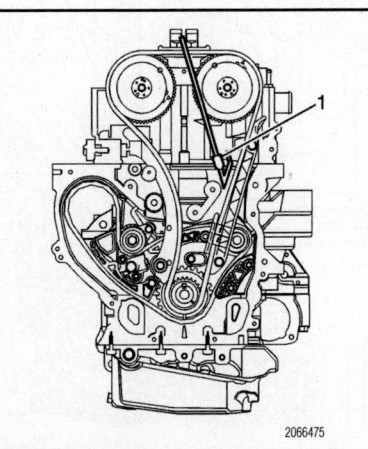

Fig. 163 Install the timing chain retention tool EN-48749 (1) to the intake side of the timing chain.

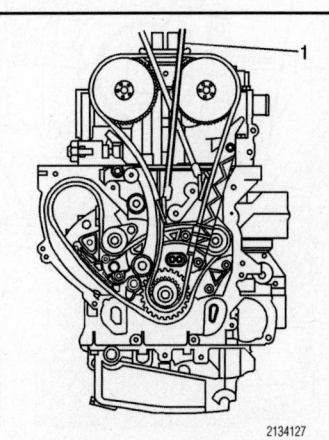

Fig. 165 Install the timing chain retention tool EN-48749 (1) to the exhaust side of the timing chain

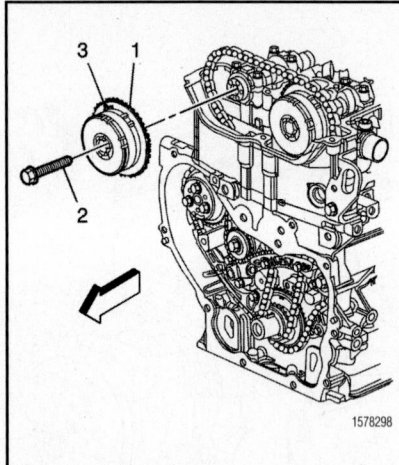

Fig. 166 Remove and discard the exhaust camshaft actuator bolt (2)

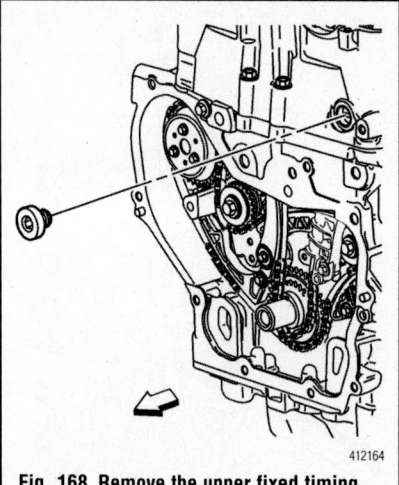

Fig. 168 Remove the upper fixed timing chain guide bolt

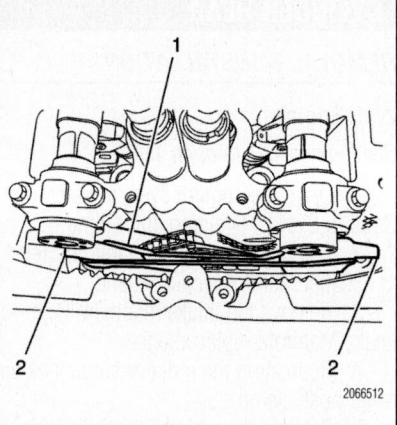

Fig. 169 Install a rubber band (1) around the top of the upper timing chain guides (2) in order to pull the guides together

23. Remove the exhaust cam actuator (3) from the exhaust camshaft while also removing the actuator from the chain.

24. Remove and discard the intake camshaft actuator bolt (refer to image for exhaust camshaft actuator bolt).

25. Remove the intake camshaft actuator from the camshaft while also removing the actuator from the timing chain.

26. Mark the cylinder head (1) in relationship to the camshaft actuator notch is on the camshaft (2).

27. Remove the fixed timing chain guide access plug.

➡**The threaded rod from the timing chain retention tool can be used to help feed the rubber band around the chain guides.**

28. Install a rubber band (1) around the top of the upper timing chain guides (2) in order to pull the guides together.

29. Remove the cylinder head bolts in the sequence shown. Discard the bolts.

30. Remove the cylinder head.

31. Remove the cylinder head gasket.

32. Clean all of the gasket surfaces.

33. Use the following steps when cleaning the cylinder head and cylinder block surfaces:

a. Use a razor blade gasket scraper to clean the cylinder head and cylinder block gasket surfaces. Do not scratch or gouge either surface.

➡**DO NOT use any other method or technique to clean these gasket surfaces.**

b. Use a NEW razor blade on the cylinder head and a NEW blade on the cylinder block.

➡**Be careful not to gouge or scratch the gasket surfaces. DO NOT gouge or scrape the combustion chamber surfaces. The feel of the gasket surface is important, not the appearance. There will be indentations from the gasket left in the cylinder head after all of the gasket material is removed. These small indentations will be filled in by the NEW gasket.**

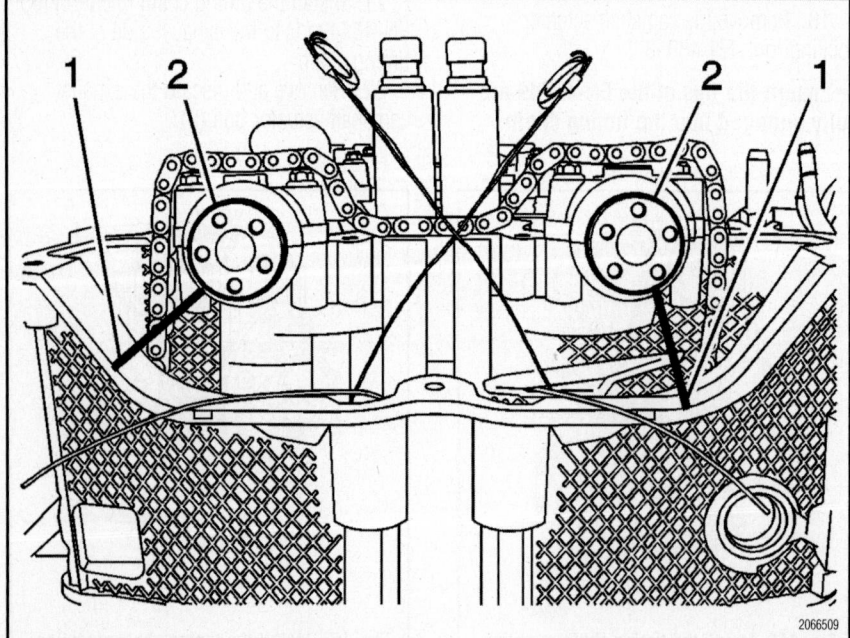

Fig. 167 Mark the cylinder head (1) in relationship to the camshaft actuator notch is on the camshaft (2)

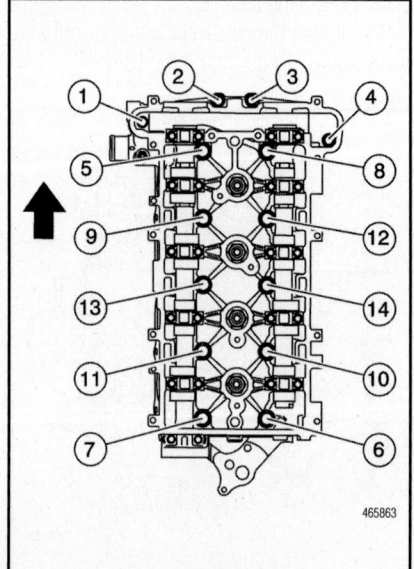

Fig. 170 Remove the cylinder head bolts in the sequence shown. Discard the bolts

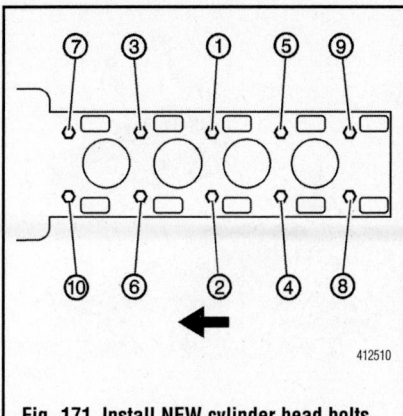

Fig. 171 Install NEW cylinder head bolts

c. Hold the razor blade as parallel to the gasket surface as possible.

34. Clean the old sealer/lube and any dirt from around the bolt holes.

➡ **DO NOT use a tap to clean the cylinder head bolt holes.**

35. Clean the bolts holes with a nylon bristle brush.

36. When cleaning the cylinder head bolt holes use suitable commercial spray liquid solvent and compressed air from an extended-tip blow gun in order to reach the bottom of the holes.

37. If replacing the cylinder head transfer all parts as necessary.

To install:

➡ **DO NOT use any sealing material.**

38. Install the cylinder head gasket.
39. Install the cylinder head.

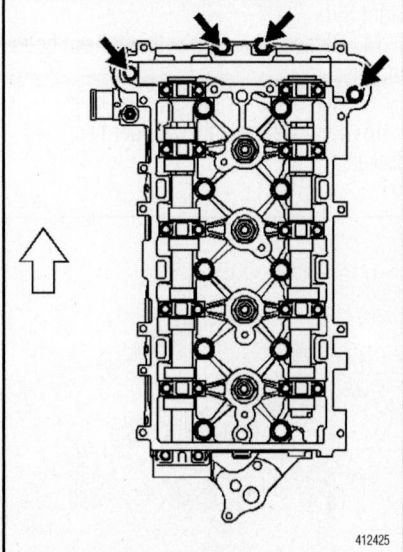

Fig. 172 Install and tighten the cylinder head bolts in the sequence shown to 22 ft. lbs. (30 Nm) plus an additional 155 degrees using the J 45059 (angle meter)

40. Install NEW cylinder head bolts.

41. Install and tighten the cylinder head bolts in the sequence shown to 22 ft. lbs. (30 Nm) plus an additional 155 degrees using the J 45059 (angle meter).

42. Install the NEW front cylinder head bolts and tighten the bolts to 26 ft. lbs. (35 Nm).

43. Ensure the cylinder head (1) and the camshaft (2) are correctly aligned.

44. Remove the rubber band (1) from around the top of the upper timing chain guides (2).

45. Install the fixed guide bolt into the cylinder head and tighten to 106 inch lbs. (12 Nm).

46. Apply sealant compound to thread and install the timing chain guide bolt access hole plug.

47. Install the fixed timing chain guide access plug and tighten the plug to 59 ft. lbs. (90 Nm).

➡ **Ensure that the alignment mark made previously on the intake camshaft actuator is still aligned properly with the mark on the timing chain. If the mark made previously on the intake camshaft actuator is not aligned properly, refer to Camshaft Timing Chain, Sprocket, and Tensioner replacement.**

48. Install the timing chain onto the intake camshaft actuator.

49. Align the intake camshaft actuator alignment mark made previously with the timing chain mark and

50. Install the actuator onto the camshaft.

51. Install a NEW intake camshaft actuator bolt (2) until snug.

52. Remove the timing chain retention tool EN-48749 (1) from the intake side of the timing chain.

➡ **Ensure that the alignment mark made previously on the exhaust camshaft actuator is still aligned properly with the mark on the timing chain. The exhaust cam may have to be rotated clockwise to install the exhaust actuator.**

53. Install the timing chain onto the exhaust camshaft actuator.

54. Align the exhaust camshaft actuator alignment mark made previously with the timing chain mark and install the actuator onto the camshaft.

55. Install a NEW exhaust camshaft actuator bolt (2) until snug.

56. Remove the timing chain retention tool EN-48749 (1) from the exhaust side of the timing chain.

➡ **Failure to reset the chain tensioner will put excess tension on the chain, limiting the chain's life.**

57. Reset and install the timing chain tensioner.

58. Install the EN-48953 (1) to the actuators.

59. Install the camshaft actuator locking tool bolts and tighten to 89 inch lbs. (10 Nm).

60. Tighten the NEW camshaft actuator bolt to 22 ft. lbs. (30 Nm) plus an additional 100 degrees using the J 45059.

61. Release the tensioner by applying a counterclockwise rotational torque of 33 ft. lbs. (45 Nm) to the harmonic balancer bolt.

62. Remove the camshaft actuator locking tool, EN-48953.

63. Install the upper timing chain guide bolts and guide. Tighten the bolts to 89 inch lbs. (10 Nm).

64. Install the camshaft cover.

65. Install the spark plugs. Refer to Spark Plug replacement.

66. Connect all electrical connectors as necessary.

67. Install the radiator inlet hose to the cylinder head.

68. Position the radiator inlet hose clamp using the J 38185.

69. Install the radiator surge tank air bleed hose to the cylinder head.

70. Position the radiator surge tank air bleed hose clamp.

71. Install the exhaust manifold. Refer to Exhaust Manifold replacement.

72. Install the intake manifold. Refer to Intake Manifold replacement.

73. Fill the cooling system. Refer to Cooling System Draining and Filling.

3.5L Engine

Left Side

See Figures 173 through 175.

1. Raise and support the vehicle.
2. Drain the cooling system. Refer to Cooling System Draining and Filling.
3. Drain the engine oil. Refer to Engine Oil and Oil Filter replacement.
4. Lower the vehicle.
5. Remove the lower intake manifold.
6. Remove the valve rocker arms and the pushrods.
7. Remove the exhaust manifold. Refer to Exhaust Manifold replacement—Left Side.
8. Remove the oil level indicator tube.
9. Remove the left spark plug wires from the spark plugs.

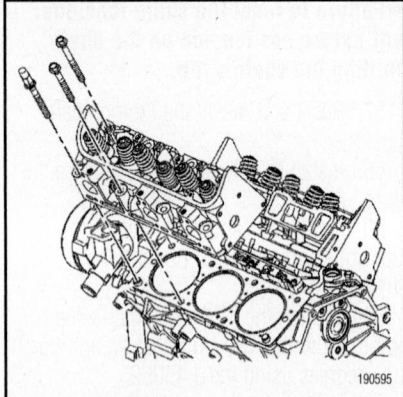

Fig. 173 Remove the left cylinder head bolts and discard.

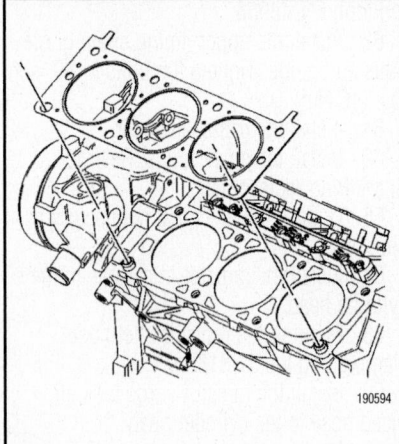

Fig. 174 Remove the left cylinder head gasket

10. Remove the left spark plugs. Refer to Spark Plug replacement.

11. Remove the left exhaust manifold. Refer to Exhaust Manifold replacement—Left Side.

12. Remove the left cylinder head bolts and discard.

13. Remove the left cylinder head.

14. Remove the left cylinder head gasket.

15. Clean and inspect the cylinder head and the gasket mating surfaces.

To install:

16. Install a new left cylinder head gasket.

17. Install the left cylinder head over the locator pins and the gasket.

18. Install the NEW small hex cylinder head bolts (5 and 8).

19. Install the NEW large hex cylinder head bolts (1, 2, 3, 4, 6 and 7).

20. Tighten the cylinder head bolts a first pass in sequence to 44 ft. lbs. (60 Nm).

21. Tighten the cylinder head bolts a final pass in sequence to 140 degrees using the J 45059 (angle meter).

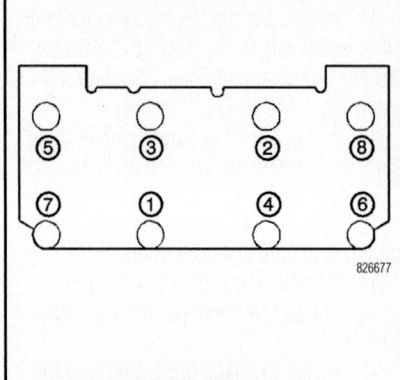

Fig. 175 Install the NEW small hex cylinder head bolts (5 and 8).

22. Install the left exhaust manifold. Refer to Exhaust Manifold replacement—Left Side.

23. Install the left spark plugs. Refer to Spark Plug replacement.

24. Install the left spark plug wires to the spark plugs.

25. Install the oil level indicator tube.

26. Install the exhaust manifold. Refer to Exhaust Manifold replacement—Left Side.

27. Install the valve rocker arms and pushrods.

28. Install the lower intake manifold. Refer to Lower Intake Manifold replacement.

29. Fill the crankcase with engine oil. Refer to Engine Oil and Oil Filter replacement.

30. Fill the cooling system. Refer to Cooling System Draining and Filling.

31. Inspect for leaks.

Right Side

See Figures 176 through 178.

1. Raise and support the vehicle.

2. Drain the cooling system. Refer to Cooling System Draining and Filling.

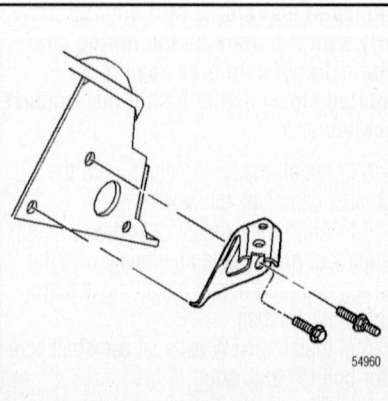

Fig. 176 Remove the fuel line bracket bolt and the stud

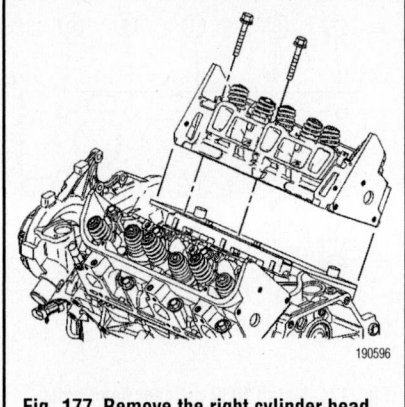

Fig. 177 Remove the right cylinder head bolts and discard

3. Drain the engine oil. Refer to Engine Oil and Oil Filter replacement.

4. Lower the vehicle.

5. Remove the lower intake manifold.

6. Remove the valve rocker arms and push rods.

7. Remove the exhaust manifold. Refer to Exhaust Manifold replacement—Right Side.

8. Remove the right spark plug wires from the spark plugs.

9. Remove the right spark plugs. Refer to Spark Plug replacement.

10. Remove the fuel line bracket bolt and the stud.

11. Remove the fuel line bracket.

12. Remove the alternator (generator). Refer to Alternator replacement.

13. Remove the right exhaust manifold. Refer to Exhaust Manifold replacement—Right Side.

14. Remove the right cylinder head bolts and discard.

15. Remove the right cylinder head.

16. Remove the right cylinder head gasket.

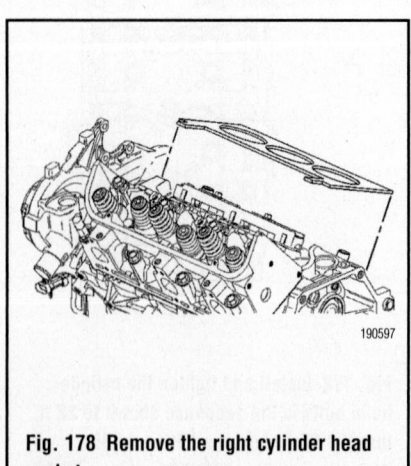

Fig. 178 Remove the right cylinder head gasket

17. Clean and inspect the cylinder head and the gasket mating surfaces.

To install:

18. Install a new right cylinder head gasket.

19. Install the right cylinder head over the locator pins and the gasket.

20. Install the NEW small hex cylinder head bolts (5 and 8; see image for left side—it is the same).

21. Install the NEW large hex cylinder head bolts (1, 2, 3, 4, 6 and 7).

22. Tighten the cylinder head bolts a first pass in sequence to 44 ft. lbs. (60 Nm).

23. Tighten the cylinder head bolts a final pass in sequence to 140 degrees using the J 45059 (angle meter).

24. Install the right exhaust manifold. Refer to Exhaust Manifold replacement—Right Side.

25. Install the alternator (generator). Refer to Alternator replacement.

26. Install the fuel line bracket.

27. Install the fuel line bracket bolt and the stud.

28. Tighten the bolt and the stud to 37 ft. lbs. (50 Nm).

29. Install the right spark plugs. Refer to Spark Plug replacement.

30. Install the right spark plug wires to the spark plugs.

31. Install the exhaust manifold. Refer to Exhaust Manifold replacement—Right Side.

32. Install the push rods and valve rocker arms.

33. Install the lower intake manifold.

34. Fill the crankcase with engine oil. Refer to Engine Oil and Oil Filter replacement.

35. Fill the cooling system. Refer to Cooling System Draining and Filling.

36. Inspect for leaks.

3.6L Engine

Left Side

See Figures 179 through 181.

1. Remove the left bank secondary timing chain.

2. Remove the oil level indicator.

3. Disconnect the coolant temperature sensor electrical connector.

4. Remove the wiring harness ground from the cylinder head.

5. Remove and discard the cylinder head gasket.

6. Clean and inspect the cylinder head and the engine block sealing surfaces.

7. If necessary, perform the following steps:

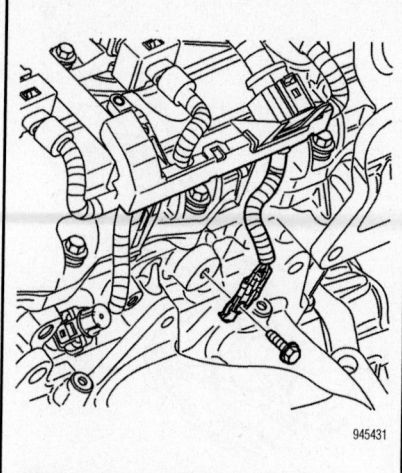

Fig. 179 Remove the wiring harness ground from the cylinder head

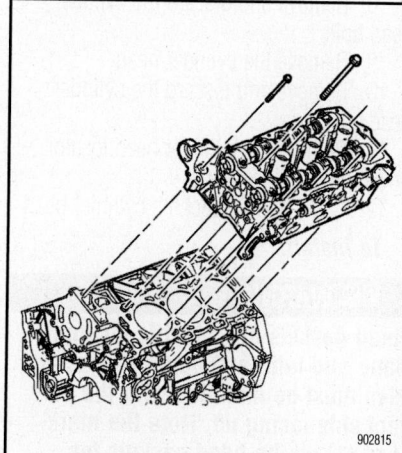

Fig. 180 Remove the cylinder head with the exhaust manifold.

a. Remove the exhaust manifold from the cylinder head. Refer to Exhaust Manifold.

b. Remove the camshaft. Refer to Camshaft removal.

c. Disassemble the cylinder head.

To install:

8. If necessary, perform the following steps:

a. Assemble the cylinder head.

b. Install the camshaft. Refer to Camshaft installation.

c. Install the exhaust manifold to the cylinder head. Refer to Exhaust Manifold installation.

9. Install a NEW cylinder head gasket.

10. Carefully install the cylinder head with the exhaust manifold to the engine.

11. Install the catalytic converter to the exhaust manifold. Refer to Catalytic Converter replacement.

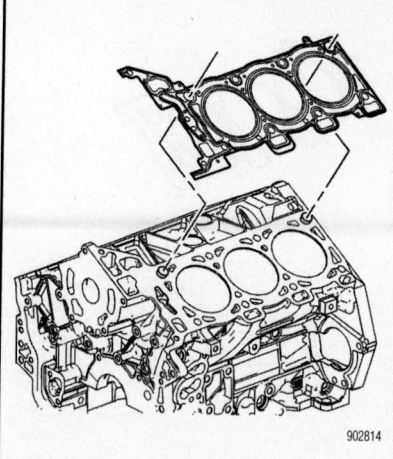

Fig. 181 Remove and discard the cylinder head gasket.

12. Connect the wiring harness electrical connector located at the side of the cylinder head.

13. Install the wiring harness ground to the cylinder head.

14. Tighten the wiring harness ground bolt to 89 inch lbs. (10 Nm).

15. Install the coolant temperature sensor electrical connector.

16. Install the oil level indicator.

17. Install the left bank secondary timing chain.

Right Side

See Figures 182 and 183.

1. Remove the hood.

2. Remove the right bank secondary timing chain.

3. With the aid of an assistant, remove the cylinder head with the exhaust manifold.

4. Remove and discard the cylinder head gasket.

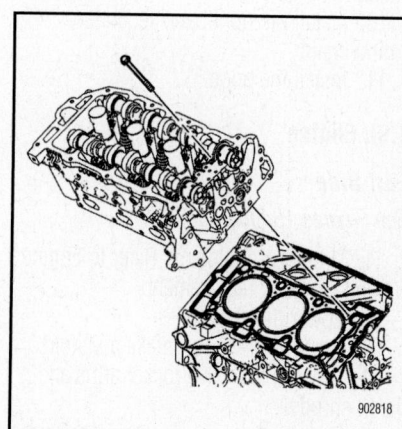

Fig. 182 With the aid of an assistant, remove the cylinder head with the exhaust manifold.

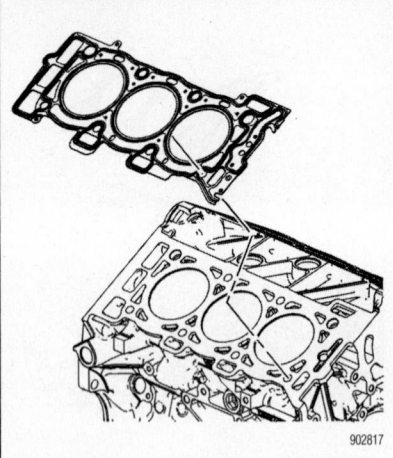

Fig. 183 Remove and discard the cylinder head gasket.

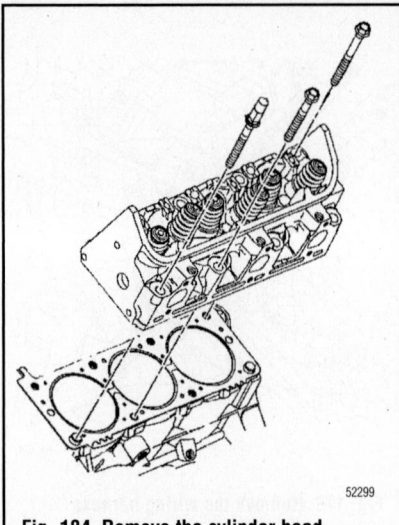

Fig. 184 Remove the cylinder head

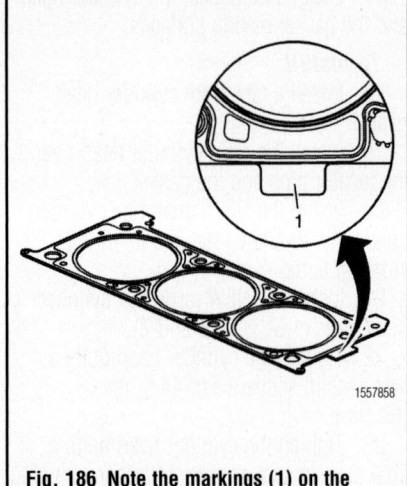

Fig. 186 Note the markings (1) on the head gaskets for proper installation

5. Clean and inspect the cylinder head and the engine block sealing surfaces.

6. If necessary, perform the following steps:

   a. Remove the exhaust manifold from the cylinder head. Refer to Exhaust Manifold.

   b. Remove the camshaft. Refer to Camshaft removal.

   c. Disassemble the cylinder head.

To install:

7. If necessary, perform the following steps:

   a. Assemble the cylinder head.

   b. Install the camshaft. Refer to Camshaft installation.

   c. Install the exhaust manifold to the cylinder head. Refer to Exhaust Manifold installation.

8. Install a NEW cylinder head gasket.

9. With the aid of an assistant, carefully install the cylinder head with the exhaust manifold to the engine.

10. Install the right bank secondary timing chain.

11. Install the hood.

3.9L Engine

Left Side

See Figures 184 through 187.

1. Drain the engine oil. Refer to Engine Oil and Oil Filter replacement.

2. Lower the vehicle.

3. Remove the lower intake manifold.

4. Remove the valve rocker arms and the pushrods.

5. Remove the exhaust manifold. Refer to Exhaust Manifold replacement.

6. Remove the oil level indicator tube.

7. Remove the left spark plugs. Refer to Spark Plug replacement.

8. Remove and discard the cylinder head bolts.

9. Remove the cylinder head.

10. Remove and discard the cylinder head gasket.

11. Remove the cylinder head locator dowel pins, if necessary.

12. Clean and inspect the cylinder head.

To install:

✳✳ WARNING

Head gaskets are specific for right hand and left hand applications, and also must be installed with the correct side facing up. Note the markings (1) on the head gaskets for proper installation. Failure to do so may lead to engine damage.

13. Install the cylinder head locator dowel pins, if necessary.

14. Inspect the cylinder head locator dowel pins for proper installation.

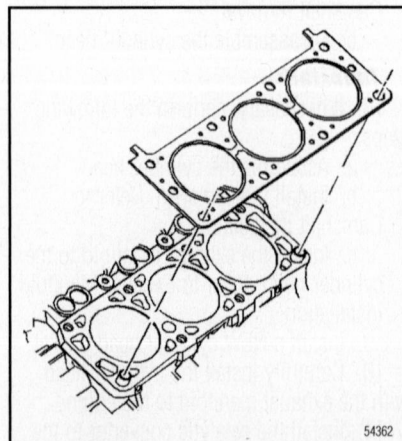

Fig. 185 Remove and discard the cylinder head gasket.

15. Install a NEW cylinder head gasket.

16. Install the cylinder head onto the locator pins and the engine.

✳✳ WARNING

This component uses torque-to-yield bolts. When servicing this component do not reuse the bolts, New torque-to-yield bolts must be installed. Reusing used torque-to-yield bolts will not provide proper bolt torque and clamp load. Failure to install NEW torque-to-yield bolts may lead to engine damage.

17. Install NEW cylinder head bolts finger tight.

18. Install the NEW small hex cylinder head bolts (5 and 8).

19. Install the NEW large hex cylinder head bolts (1, 2, 3, 4, 6 and 7).

20. Tighten the cylinder head bolts a first pass in sequence to 44 ft. lbs. (60 Nm).

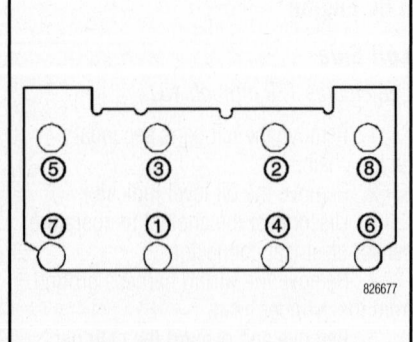

Fig. 187 Install the NEW small hex cylinder head bolts (5 and 8); next install the NEW large hex cylinder head bolts (1, 2, 3, 4, 6 and 7).

21. Tighten the cylinder head bolts a final pass in sequence to 140 degrees using the J 45059 (angle meter).

22. Install the left spark plugs. Refer to Spark Plug replacement.

23. Install the oil level indicator tube.

24. Install the exhaust manifold. Refer to Exhaust Manifold replacement.

25. Install the valve rocker arms and the pushrods.

26. Install the lower intake manifold.

27. Fill the engine with oil. Refer to Engine Oil and Oil Filter replacement.

28. Inspect for leaks.

Right Side

See Figures 188 through 191.

1. Drain the engine oil. Refer to Engine Oil and Oil Filter replacement.

2. Lower the vehicle.

3. Remove the lower intake manifold.

4. Remove the valve rocker arms and push rods.

5. Remove the exhaust manifold. Refer to Exhaust Manifold replacement.

6. Remove the right spark plugs. Refer to Spark Plug replacement.

7. Remove the fuel line bracket bolt and the stud.

8. Remove the fuel line bracket.

9. Remove the alternator (generator). Refer to Alternator replacement.

10. Remove the cylinder head bolts and discard.

11. Remove the right cylinder head.

12. Remove and discard the right cylinder head gasket.

13. Clean and inspect the cylinder head and the gasket mating surfaces.

To install:

☀ WARNING

Head gaskets are specific for right hand and left hand applications, and also must be installed with the

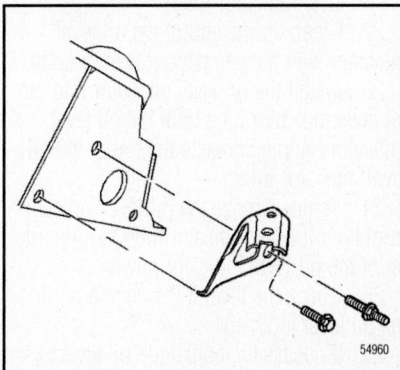

Fig. 188 Remove the fuel line bracket bolt and the stud

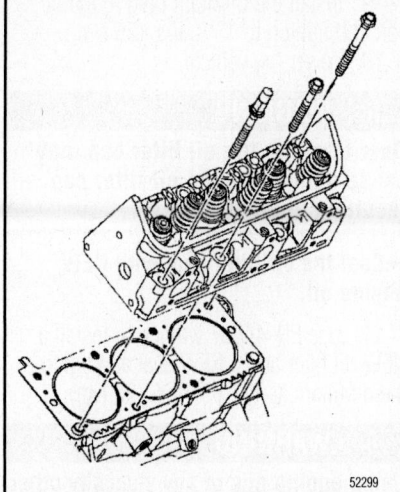

Fig. 189 Remove the cylinder head bolts and discard

correct side facing up. Note the markings (1) on the head gaskets for proper installation. Failure to do so may lead to engine damage.

14. Install the cylinder head locator dowel pins, if necessary.

15. Inspect the cylinder head locator dowel pins for proper installation.

16. Install a new right cylinder head gasket.

17. Install the cylinder head onto the locator pins and the engine.

☀ WARNING

This component uses torque-to-yield bolts. When servicing this component do not reuse the bolts, New torque-to-yield bolts must be installed. Reusing used torque-to-yield bolts will not provide proper bolt torque and clamp load. Failure to install

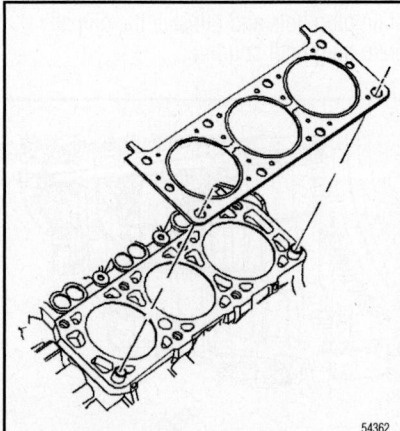

Fig. 190 Remove and discard the right cylinder head gasket

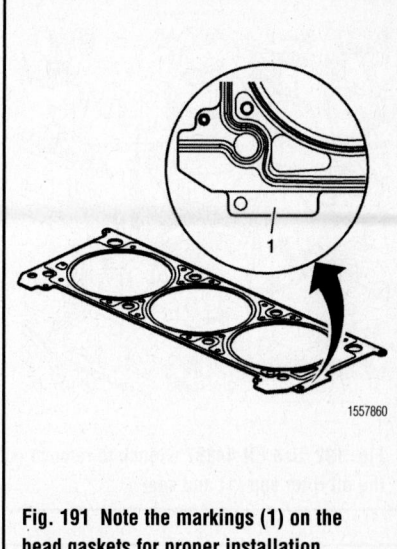

Fig. 191 Note the markings (1) on the head gaskets for proper installation

NEW torque-to-yield bolts may lead to engine damage.

18. Install NEW cylinder head bolts finger tight.

19. Install the NEW small hex cylinder head bolts (5 and 8; see image for left side—it is the same).

20. Install the NEW large hex cylinder head bolts (1, 2, 3, 4, 6 and 7).

21. Tighten the cylinder head bolts a first pass in sequence to 44 ft. lbs. (60 Nm).

22. Tighten the cylinder head bolts a final pass in sequence to 140 degrees using the J 45059 (angle meter).

23. Install the alternator (generator). Refer to Alternator replacement.

24. Position the fuel line bracket to the cylinder head.

25. Install the fuel line bracket bolt and the stud.

26. Tighten the bolt and the stud to 37 ft. lbs. (50 Nm).

27. Install the right spark plugs. Refer to Spark Plug replacement.

28. Install the exhaust manifold. Refer to Exhaust Manifold replacement.

29. Install the push rods and valve rocker arms.

30. Install the lower intake manifold.

31. Fill the engine with oil. Refer to Engine Oil and Oil Filter replacement.

32. Inspect for leaks.

ENGINE OIL & OIL FILTER

REPLACEMENT

2.4L Engine

See Figures 192 and 193.

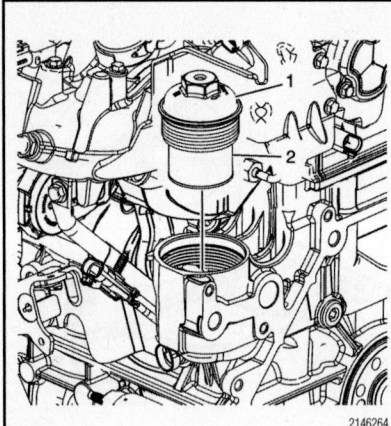

Fig. 192 Use EN-44887 wrench to remove the oil filter cap (1) and seal

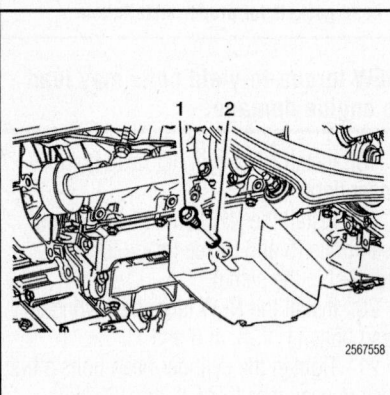

Fig. 193 Remove the oil drain plug (1) and seal (2)

1. Place a collecting pan underneath the oil filter.

2. Use EN-44887 wrench to remove the oil filter cap (1) and seal.

☀☀ WARNING

This engine uses a special high performance oil filter. Use of any other filter may lead to filter failure and/or severe engine damage.

3. Remove and properly dispose of the oil filter insert (2).

4. Raise the vehicle.

5. Place a collecting pan underneath the oil drain plug.

6. Remove the oil drain plug (1) and seal (2).

To install:

7. Clean the oil drain plug thread and the thread in the oil pan.

8. Install a seal (2) to the oil drain plug (1).

9. Install the oil drain plug to the oil pan and tighten to 18 ft. lbs. (25 Nm).

10. Lower the vehicle.

☀☀ WARNING

Over torquing the oil filter cap may cause damage to the oil filter cap resulting in an oil leak.

➡ Coat the oil filter seal with NEW engine oil.

11. Use EN-44887 wrench to Install a NEW oil filter and a NEW seal and tighten the oil filter cap to 16 ft. lbs. (22 Nm).

☀☀ WARNING

Using engine oils of any viscosity other than those viscosities recommended could result in engine damage.

➡ Note the following:

- Use specified volume of engine oil with the specified viscosity class.
- Start the engine and allow it to run until the oil pressure control indicator goes off.
- Inspect the engine oil level.

12. Fill the engine with NEW engine oil. Refer to Engine Mechanical Specifications.

13. Reset the service interval indicator.

3.5L & 3.9L Engines

See Figures 194 and 195.

1. Raise and support the vehicle.

2. Position a suitable drain pan under the oil pan drain plug.

3. Remove the oil pan drain plug.

4. Allow the engine oil to drain completely.

5. Clean and inspect the oil pan drain plug sealing surface, replace the oil pan if necessary.

6. Wipe any remaining oil from the drain plug hole and reinstall the oil pan drain plug until snug.

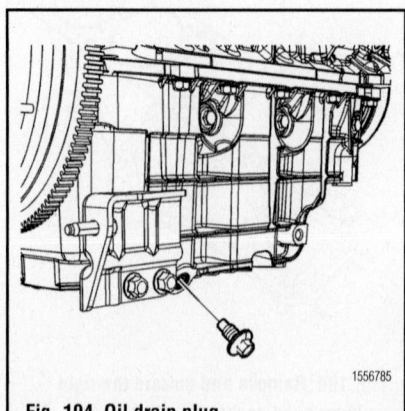

Fig. 194 Oil drain plug

Fig. 195 Oil filter

7. Position a suitable drain pan under the oil filter.

8. Remove the oil filter.

9. Ensure that the oil filter gasket is still on the old filter. If not, remove the oil filter gasket from the adapter.

To install:

10. Apply clean engine oil to the NEW oil filter gasket.

11. Install the NEW oil filter.

12. Tighten the new filter to 3/4 to 1 full turn, after the oil filter gasket contacts the adapter.

13. Tighten the oil pan drain plug.

14. Tighten the oil pan drain plug to 19 ft. lbs. (26 Nm).

15. Remove the oil drain pan from under the vehicle.

16. Lower the vehicle.

17. Fill the engine with new engine oil.

18. Start the engine.

19. Inspect for oil leaks after engine start up.

20. Turn OFF the engine and allow the oil a few minutes to drain back into the oil pan.

21. Remove the oil level indicator from the oil level indicator tube.

22. Clean off the end of the oil level indicator with a clean paper towel or cloth.

23. Install the oil level indicator into the oil level indicator tube until the oil level indicator handle contacts the top of the oil level indicator tube.

24. Again, remove the oil level indicator from the oil level indicator tube keeping the tip of the oil level indicator down.

25. Check the level if the engine oil on the oil level indicator.

26. If necessary, adjust the oil level by adding or draining oil.

27. Check for oil leaks.

3.6L Engine

See Figures 196 and 197.

1. Raise and support the vehicle.
2. Place a drain pan under the oil pan drain plug.
3. Remove the oil pan drain plug (1). Allow the oil to drain completely.
4. Install the oil pan drain plug (1) and tighten it to 15 ft. lbs. (20 Nm).

✳✳ CAUTION

While engine is operating, the exhaust system will become extremely hot. Prevent burns: Avoid contacting a hot exhaust system.

5. Place the drain pan under the oil filter.
6. Remove the oil filter. Allow the oil to drain completely.

To install:

7. Lubricate the NEW oil filter gasket with clean engine oil.
8. Tighten the oil filter to 22 ft. lbs. (30 Nm).
9. Lower the vehicle.
10. Refill the engine oil.
11. Start the engine and inspect for leaks.

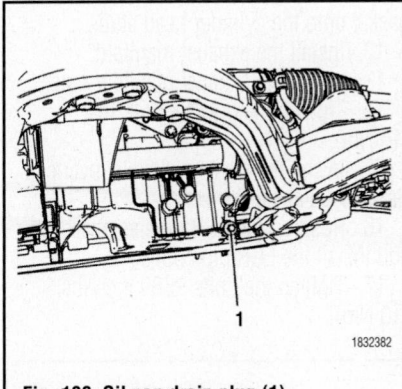

Fig. 196 Oil pan drain plug (1)

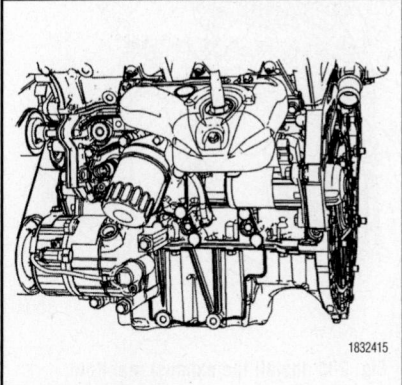

Fig. 197 Oil filter

EXHAUST MANIFOLD

REMOVAL & INSTALLATION

2.4L Engine

See Figures 198 through 201.

1. Remove the Connector Position Assurance (CPA) retainer.
2. Disconnect the Heated Oxygen Sensor (HO2S) electrical connector.
3. The HO2S uses a permanently attached pigtail and connector. This pigtail should not be removed from the sensor. Damage or removal of the pigtail or connector will affect proper operation of the sensor.
4. Remove the HO2S. Refer to Heated Oxygen Sensor 1 replacement.
5. Disconnect the fuel line clip from the bracket.
6. Remove the exhaust manifold heat shield bolts.
7. Remove the heat shield.

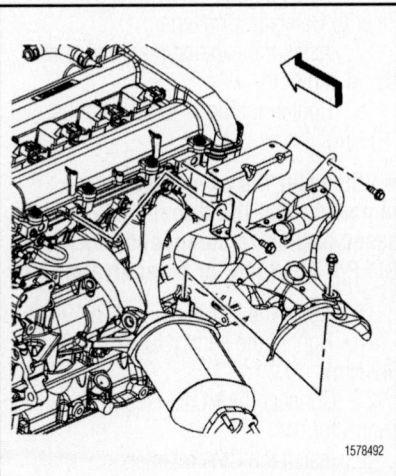

Fig. 198 Disconnect the fuel line clip from the bracket.

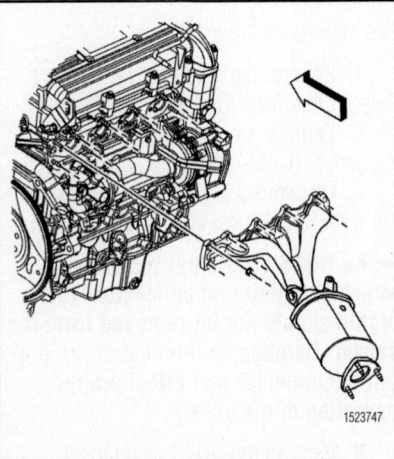

Fig. 199 Remove and discard the exhaust manifold nuts.

8. Remove the exhaust manifold pipe.
9. Remove the upper exhaust manifold brace bolt.
10. Remove and discard the exhaust manifold nuts.
11. Remove the exhaust manifold/catalytic converter assembly.
12. Remove and discard the exhaust manifold gasket.

To install:

13. Install a NEW exhaust manifold gasket on the cylinder head.
14. Install the exhaust manifold/catalytic converter assembly.
15. Install the NEW exhaust manifold nuts finger tight.
16. Install the upper exhaust manifold brace bolt.
17. Tighten the bolt to 18 ft. lbs. (25 Nm).
18. Tighten the exhaust manifold nuts in the sequence shown:
19. Tighten the nuts to 10 ft. lbs. (14 Nm).
20. Install the exhaust manifold pipe.
21. Install the heat shield.
22. Install the exhaust manifold heat shield bolts.

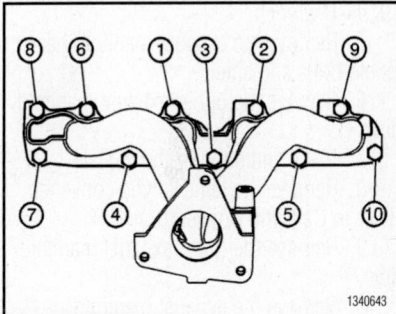

Fig. 200 Exhaust manifold nuts tightening sequence

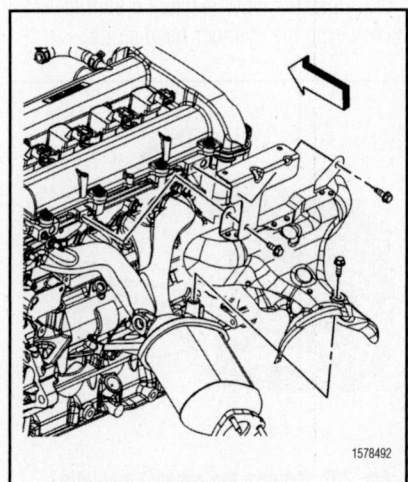

Fig. 201 Install the heat shield

23. Tighten the bolts to 17 ft. lbs. (23 Nm).

24. Connect the fuel line clip to the bracket.

25. Install the HO2S. Refer to Heated Oxygen Sensor 1 Replacement.

26. Connect the HO2S electrical connector.

27. Install the CPA retainer.

28. Start the vehicle and inspect for leaks.

3.5L Engine

Left Side

See Figures 202 and 203.

1. Remove the air cleaner outlet duct.

2. Remove the Connector Position Assurance (CPA) retainer.

3. Disconnect the Heated Oxygen Sensor (HO2S) electrical connector.

➡ **The HO2S uses a permanently attached pigtail and connector. This pigtail should not be removed from the sensor. Damage or removal of the pigtail or connector will affect proper operation of the sensor.**

4. Remove the HO2S using the J 39194-B wrench.

5. Remove the exhaust manifold heat shield bolts and shield.

6. Remove the upper exhaust manifold nuts.

7. Raise and support the vehicle.

8. Remove the left catalytic converter. Refer to Catalytic Converter.

9. Remove the lower exhaust manifold nuts.

10. Remove the exhaust manifold.

11. Remove and discard the exhaust manifold gasket.

To install:

12. Install a NEW exhaust manifold gasket onto the cylinder head studs.

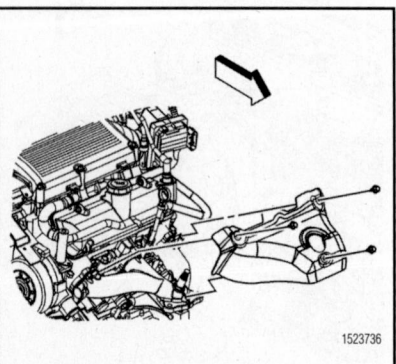

Fig. 202 Remove the exhaust manifold heat shield bolts and shield

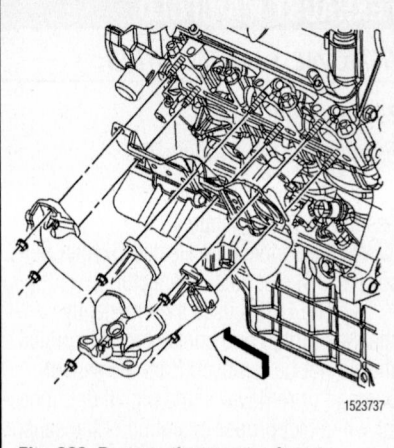

Fig. 203 Remove the upper exhaust manifold nuts

13. Install the exhaust manifold.

14. Install the exhaust manifold nuts.

15. Tighten the nuts to 12 ft. lbs. (16 Nm).

16. Install the left catalytic converter. Refer to Catalytic Converter.

17. Install the exhaust manifold heat shield and bolts.

18. Tighten the bolts to 89 inch lbs. (10 Nm).

➡ **Whenever the oxygen sensor is removed, coat the threads with nickel-based anti-seize compound, such as GM P/N 5613695, or an equivalent.**

19. Install the HO2S using J 39194-B.

20. Tighten the sensor to 31 ft. lbs. (42 Nm).

21. Connect the HO2S electrical connector.

22. Install the CPA retainer.

23. Ensure that the connector rosebud is attached to the clip.

24. Install the air cleaner outlet duct.

Right Side

See Figures 204 and 205.

1. Remove the generator (alternator). Refer to Alternator/Generator replacement.

2. Remove the Connector Position Assurance (CPA) retainer.

3. Disconnect the Heated Oxygen Sensor (HO2S) electrical connector.

➡ **The HO2S uses a permanently attached pigtail and connector. This pigtail should not be removed from the sensor. Damage or removal of the pigtail or connector will affect proper operation of the sensor.**

4. Remove the HO2S using the J 39194-B wrench.

5. Remove the Exhaust Gas Recircula-

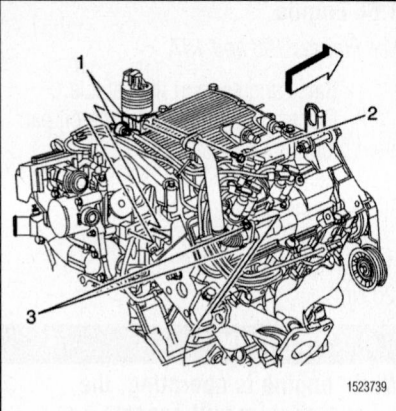

Fig. 204 Remove the Exhaust Gas Recirculation (EGR) pipe bolts (3). Reposition the pipe slightly

tion (EGR) pipe bolts (3). Reposition the pipe slightly.

6. Remove the upper exhaust manifold nuts.

7. Remove the right catalytic converter. Refer to Catalytic Converter.

8. Remove the lower exhaust manifold nuts.

9. Remove the exhaust manifold.

10. Remove and discard the exhaust manifold gasket.

To install:

11. Install a NEW exhaust manifold gasket onto the cylinder head studs.

12. Install the exhaust manifold.

13. Install the exhaust manifold nuts.

14. Tighten the nuts to 12 ft. lbs. (16 Nm).

15. Install the right catalytic converter. Refer to Catalytic Converter.

16. Position the EGR pipe as necessary, and install the EGR pipe bolts.

17. Tighten the bolts to 89 inch lbs. (10 Nm).

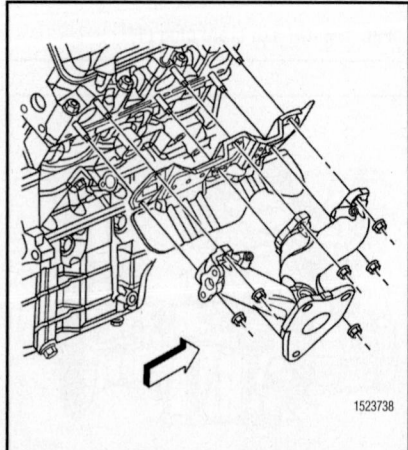

Fig. 205 Install the exhaust manifold nuts.

➡Whenever the oxygen sensor is removed, coat the threads with nickel-based anti-seize compound such as GM P/N 5613695, or an equivalent.

18. Install the HO2S using J 39194-B.

19. Tighten the sensor to 31 ft. lbs. (42 Nm).

20. Connect the HO2S electrical connector.

21. Install the CPA retainer.

22. Ensure that the connector rosebud is attached to the bracket.

23. Install the generator.

3.6L Engine

Left Side

See Figures 206 and 207.

❋❋ **CAUTION**

In order to avoid being burned, do not service the exhaust system while it is still hot. Service the system when it is cool.

❋❋ **CAUTION**

Always wear protective goggles and gloves when removing exhaust parts as falling rust and sharp edges from worn exhaust components could result in serious personal injury.

1. Remove the exhaust manifold heat shield.

2. Remove the oil level indicator.

3. Remove the catalytic converter to exhaust manifold nuts (1).

4. Remove the exhaust manifold bolts (1).

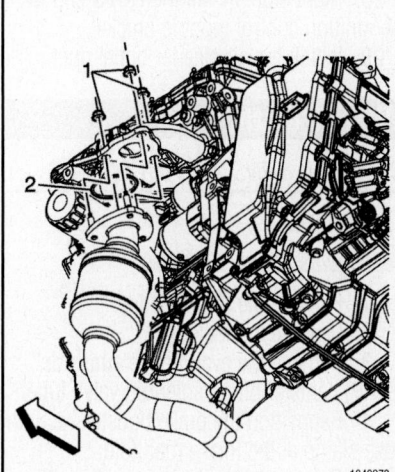
Fig. 206 Remove the catalytic converter to exhaust manifold nuts (1)

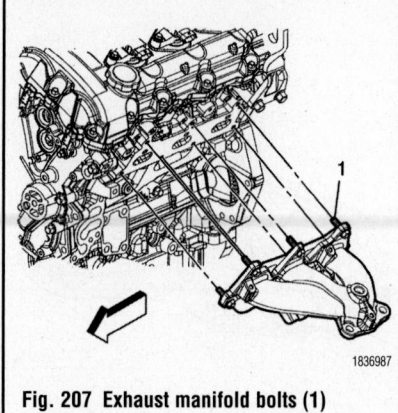
Fig. 207 Exhaust manifold bolts (1)

5. Remove the exhaust manifold and gasket. Discard the gasket.

To install:

6. Install one exhaust manifold bolt to the exhaust manifold.

7. Install the NEW exhaust manifold gasket onto the cylinder head and bolt.

8. Install the exhaust manifold (with gasket) to the catalytic converter and the cylinder head.

9. Install the remaining exhaust manifold bolts and tighten them to 18 ft. lbs. (25 Nm).

10. Install the catalytic converter to exhaust manifold nuts (1) and tighten them to 33 ft. lbs. (45 Nm).

11. Install the oil level indicator.

12. Install the exhaust manifold heat shield.

13. Inspect for exhaust leaks.

Right Side

See Figures 208 through 211.

❋❋ **CAUTION**

In order to avoid being burned, do not service the exhaust system while it is still hot. Service the system when it is cool.

❋❋ **CAUTION**

Always wear protective goggles and gloves when removing exhaust parts as falling rust and sharp edges from worn exhaust components could result in serious personal injury.

1. Remove the catalytic converter.

2. Remove the exhaust manifold lower bolts.

3. Lower the vehicle half way.

4. Remove the exhaust manifold upper bolts.

5. Remove the exhaust manifold. See first image under "To Install."

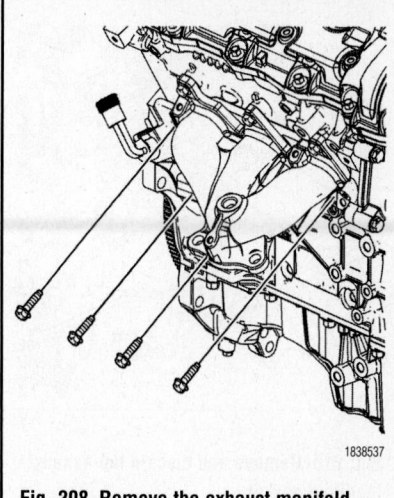
Fig. 208 Remove the exhaust manifold lower bolts

6. Remove and discard the exhaust manifold gasket.

To install:

Install one upper exhaust manifold bolt (1) to the exhaust manifold.

7. Place the NEW exhaust manifold gasket onto the bolt.

8. Position and install the exhaust manifold (with gasket) to the cylinder head.

9. Loosely install the remaining upper exhaust manifold bolts.

10. Raise and support the vehicle.

11. Loosely install the lower exhaust manifold bolts.

12. Tighten the exhaust manifold bolts to 18 ft. lbs. (25 Nm).

13. Install the catalytic converter. Refer to Catalytic Converter.

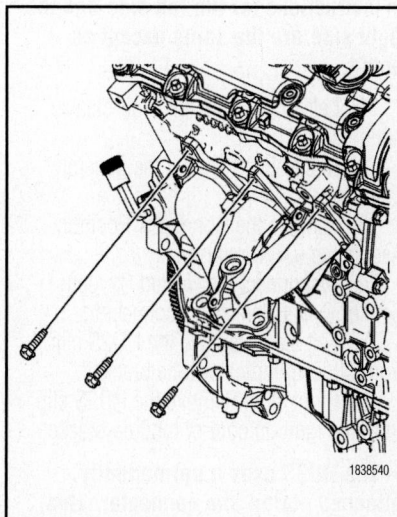
Fig. 209 Remove the exhaust manifold upper bolts

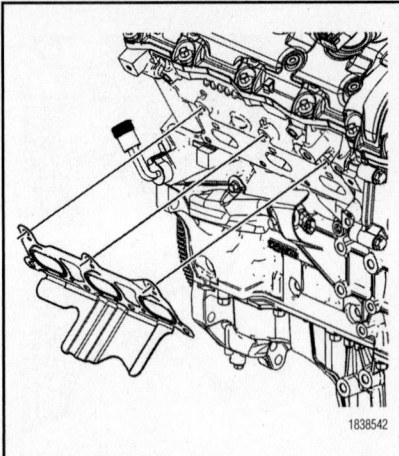

Fig. 210 Remove and discard the exhaust manifold gasket

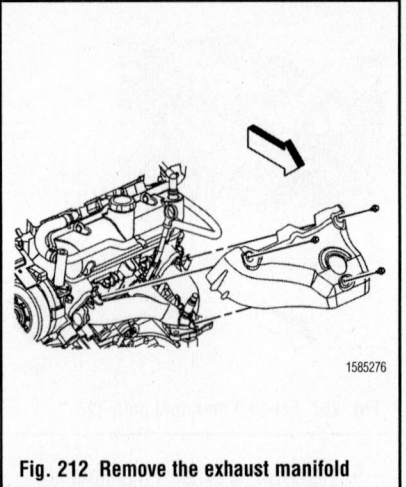

Fig. 212 Remove the exhaust manifold heat shield bolts and shield - left side

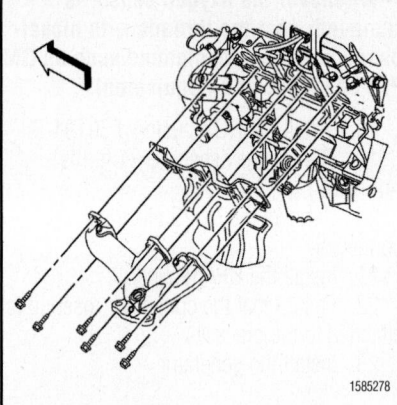

Fig. 214 Remove the upper exhaust manifold bolts, left side shown, right side similar

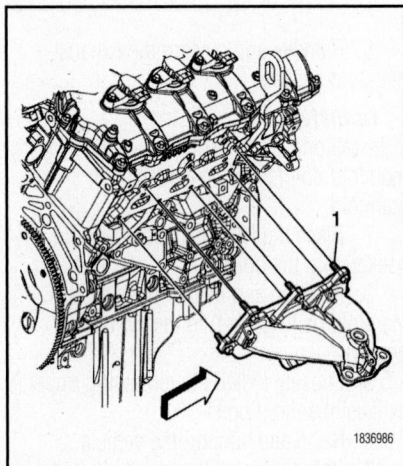

Fig. 211 Install one upper exhaust manifold bolt (1) to the exhaust manifold.

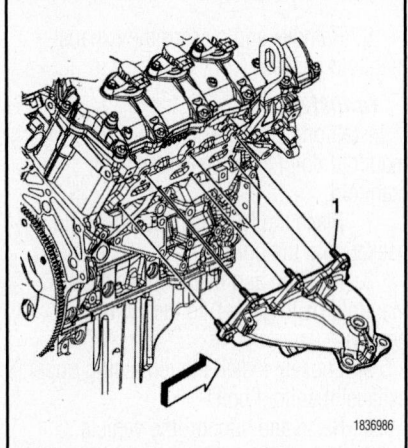

Fig. 213 Remove the exhaust manifold heat shield bolts and shield - right side

3.9L Engine

See Figures 212 through 214.

➡**Instructions for the left side and the right side are the same except as noted.**

1. Left side: Remove the air cleaner outlet duct.
2. Right side: Remove the generator (alternator).
3. Remove the Connector Position Assurance (CPA) retainer.
4. Disconnect the Heated Oxygen Sensor (HO2S) electrical connector.
5. Left side: Remove the HO2S clip from oil level indicator tube bracket.
6. Right side: Remove the HO2S clip from the ignition control module bracket.

➡**The HO2S uses a permanently attached pigtail and connector. This pigtail should not be removed from the sensor. Damage or removal of the**

pigtail or connector will affect proper operation of the sensor.

7. Remove the HO2S using the J 39194-B wrench.
8. Remove the exhaust manifold heat shield bolts and shield.
9. Remove the upper exhaust manifold bolts.
10. Raise and support the vehicle.
11. Depending on what side you are working on, remove the left or right catalytic converter. Refer to Catalytic Converter.
12. Remove the lower exhaust manifold bolts.
13. Remove the exhaust manifold.
14. Remove and discard the exhaust manifold gasket.

To install:

15. Install a NEW exhaust manifold gasket onto the cylinder head studs.
16. Install the exhaust manifold.
17. Install the exhaust manifold bolts.

18. Tighten the nuts to 15 ft. lbs. (20 Nm).
19. Install the left or right catalytic converter. Refer to Catalytic Converter.
20. Lower the vehicle.
21. Install the exhaust manifold heat shield and bolts.
22. Tighten the bolts to 89 inch lbs. (10 Nm).

➡**Whenever the oxygen sensor is removed, coat the threads with nickel-based anti-seize compound, such as GM P/N 5613695, or an equivalent.**

23. Install the HO2S using J 39194-B.
24. Tighten the sensor to 31 ft. lbs. (42 Nm).
25. Connect the HO2S electrical connector.
26. Install the CPA retainer.
27. Left side: Install the HO2S clip to the oil level indicator tube bracket.
28. Right side: Install the HO2S clip to the ignition control module bracket.
29. Install the air cleaner outlet duct.

INTAKE MANIFOLD

REMOVAL & INSTALLATION

2.4L Engine

See Figures 215 through 219.

1. Remove the throttle body.
2. Remove the fuel rail.
3. Remove the evaporative emission (EVAP) canister purge solenoid valve tube.
4. Reposition the brake booster vacuum hose clamp at the intake manifold.
5. Remove the brake booster hose from the intake manifold.
6. Remove the oil level indicator tube bolt.

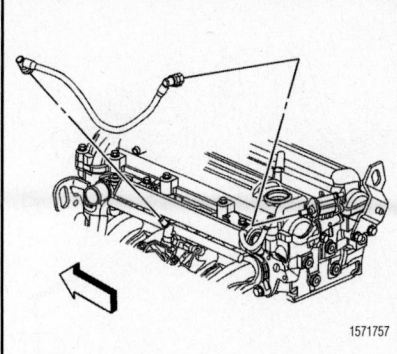

Fig. 215 Remove the evaporative emission (EVAP) canister purge solenoid valve tube

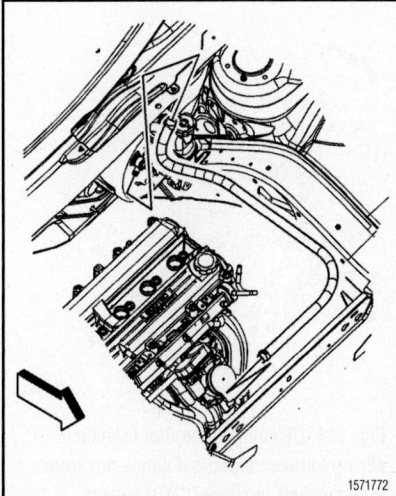

Fig. 216 Reposition the brake booster vacuum hose clamp at the intake manifold

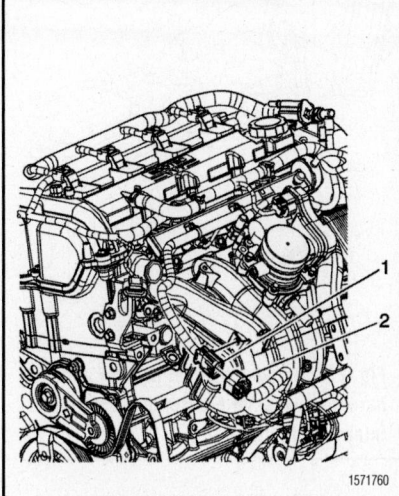

Fig. 217 Disconnect the engine harness electrical connector (1) from the fuel injector inline electrical connector (2)

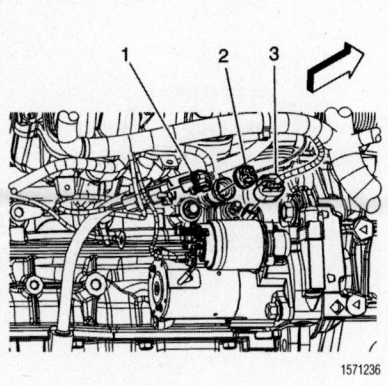

Fig. 218 Disconnect the engine harness electrical connector (1) from the knock sensor harness.

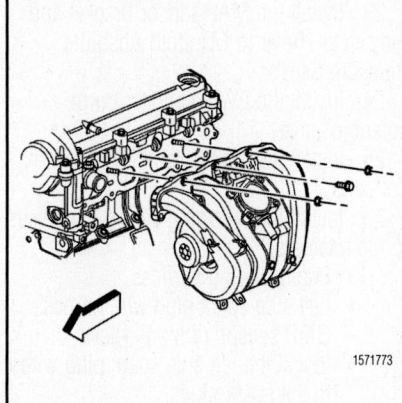

Fig. 219 Remove the intake manifold bolts and nuts.

7. Disconnect the engine harness electrical connector (1) from the fuel injector inline electrical connector (2).

8. Remove the fuel injector inline connector clip from the intake manifold.

9. Disconnect the engine harness electrical connector (1) from the knock sensor harness.

10. Remove the knock sensor connector clip from the oil level indicator tube.

11. Remove the intake manifold bolts and nuts.

12. Remove the intake manifold.

➡The intake manifold gasket is reusable. Only replace the gasket if damage has occurred.

13. Remove the intake manifold gasket, if necessary.

To install:
14. Install the intake manifold gasket, if necessary.

15. Install the intake manifold.

16. Install the intake manifold bolts and nuts.

17. Tighten the bolts and nuts to 89 inch lbs. (10 Nm).

18. Connect the engine harness electrical connector to the knock sensor harness.

19. Install the knock sensor connector clip to the oil level indicator tube.

20. Connect the engine harness electrical connector to the fuel injector inline electrical connector.

21. Install the fuel injector inline connector clip to the intake manifold.

22. Install the oil level indicator tube bolt.

23. Tighten the bolt to 89 inch lbs. (10 Nm).

24. Install the brake booster hose to the intake manifold.

25. Position the brake booster vacuum hose clamp at the intake manifold.

26. Install the EVAP canister purge solenoid valve tube.

27. Install the fuel rail.

28. Install the throttle body.

3.5L Engine

Upper

See Figures 220 through 222.

1. Disconnect the negative battery cable. Refer to Battery Negative Cable Disconnection and Connection.

2. Remove the intake manifold cover.

3. Remove the vacuum hoses from the following:
   • Evaporative emissions (EVAP) canister purge valve
   • Manifold vacuum source
   • Brake booster
   • Heater and air conditioning (A/C) source

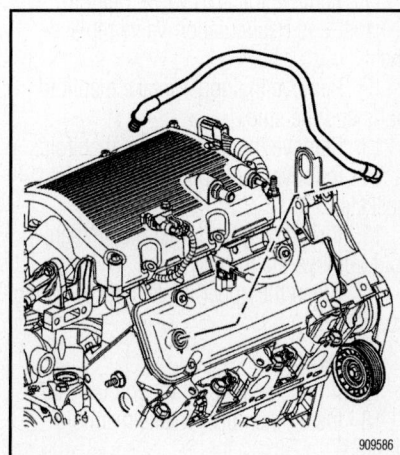

Fig. 220 Upper intake manifold replacement

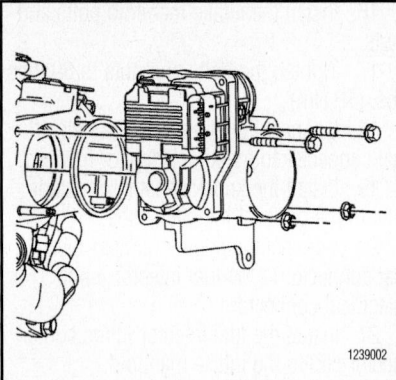

Fig. 221 If replacing the upper intake manifold, remove the throttle body

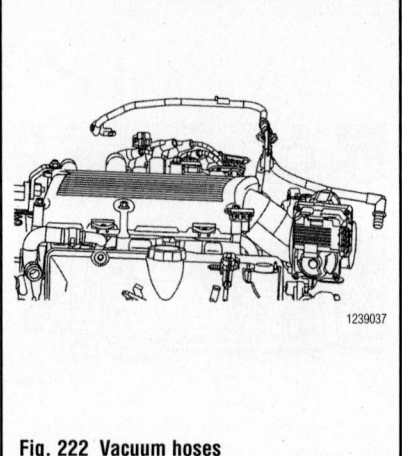

Fig. 222 Vacuum hoses

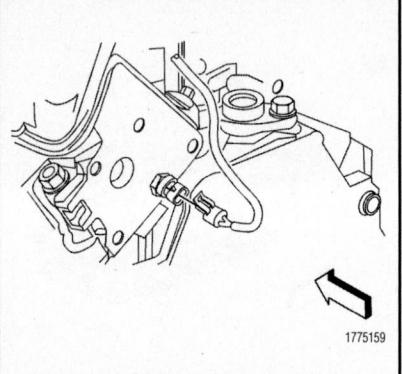

Fig. 223 Disconnect the engine wiring harness electrical connector (2) from the fuel injector inline electrical connector.

4. Disconnect the electrical connectors from the following:
- Exhaust Gas Recirculation (EGR) valve
- Mass air flow (MAF) sensor
- Intake air temperature (IAT) sensor
- Electronic throttle control
- EVAP canister purge valve

5. Remove the air cleaner outlet duct.

6. Remove the left side spark plug wires from the spark plugs.

7. Remove the following wiring harnesses from the retainers:
- Camshaft position (CMP) sensor wiring harness
- Left side spark plug wire harness
- Engine wiring harness

8. Remove the ignition coil bracket with the coils.

9. Remove the EVAP canister purge solenoid valve.

10. Remove the Manifold Absolute Pressure (MAP) sensor and the bracket. Refer to Manifold Absolute Pressure Sensor replacement.

11. Remove the EGR valve. Refer to Exhaust Gas Recirculation Valve replacement.

12. Remove the upper intake manifold bolts and the stud.

13. Remove the upper intake manifold.

14. Remove the upper intake manifold gaskets.

15. If replacing the upper intake manifold, remove the throttle body.

16. Clean the upper intake gasket mating surfaces.

To install:

17. If removed, install the throttle body.

18. Install the upper intake manifold gaskets.

19. Install the upper intake manifold.

20. Install the right upper intake manifold bolts and the stud.

21. Tighten the bolts and the stud to 18 ft. lbs. (25 Nm).

22. Install the EGR valve.

23. Install the MAP sensor bracket and the sensor. Refer to Manifold Absolute Pressure Sensor.

24. Install the EVAP canister purge solenoid valve.

25. Install the ignition coil bracket with the coils.

26. Install the following wiring harnesses to the retainers:
- Engine wiring harness
- Left side spark plug wire harness
- CMP sensor wiring harness
- Install the left side spark plug wires to the spark plugs.
- Install the air cleaner outlet duct.
- Connect the electrical connectors to the following:
- EVAP canister purge valve
- Electronic throttle control
- IAT sensor
- MAF sensor
- EGR valve

27. Install the vacuum hoses to the following components:
- Heater and A/C source
- Brake booster
- EVAP canister purge valve

28. Connect the negative battery cable. Refer to Battery Negative Cable Disconnection and Connection.

29. Install the intake manifold cover.

Lower

See Figures 223 through 230.

➡This engine uses a sequential multi-port fuel injection system. Injector wiring harness connectors must be connected to their appropriate fuel injector or exhaust emissions and engine performance may be seriously affected.

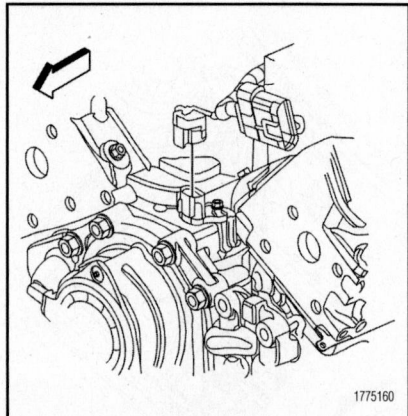

Fig. 224 Disconnect the fuel injector wiring harness electrical connector from the camshaft position (CMP) sensor.

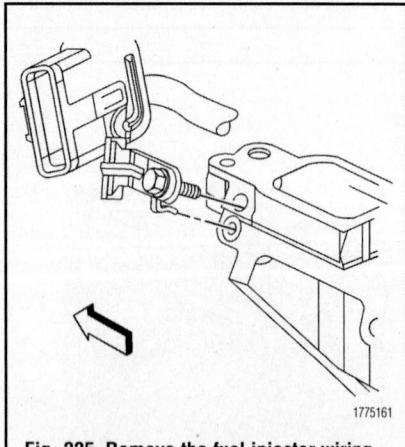

Fig. 225 Remove the fuel injector wiring harness connector bracket bolt from the intake manifold.

1. Remove the upper intake manifold. Refer to Upper Intake Manifold replacement.

2. Drain the cooling system. Refer to Cooling System Draining and Filling.

3. Remove the valve rocker arm covers.

4. Remove the coolant crossover pipe.

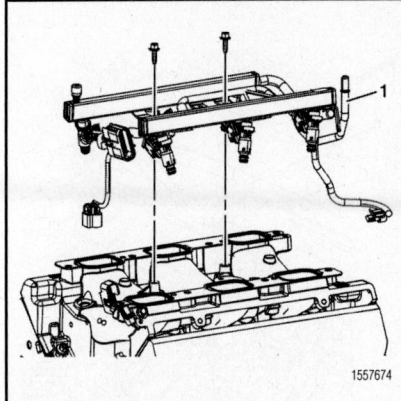

Fig. 226 Remove the fuel rail bolts and rail (1).

5. Disconnect the fuel injector wiring harness electrical connector from the Engine Coolant Temperature (ECT) sensor.

6. Disconnect the engine wiring harness electrical connector (2) from the fuel injector inline electrical connector.

7. Disconnect the fuel injector wiring harness electrical connector from the camshaft position (CMP) sensor.

8. Remove the fuel injector wiring harness connector bracket bolt from the intake manifold.

9. Remove the fuel rail bolts and rail (1).

10. Remove the fuel rail bolts and rail (1).

11. Remove the lower intake manifold bolts.

12. Remove the lower intake manifold.

13. Loosen the rocker arm bolts.

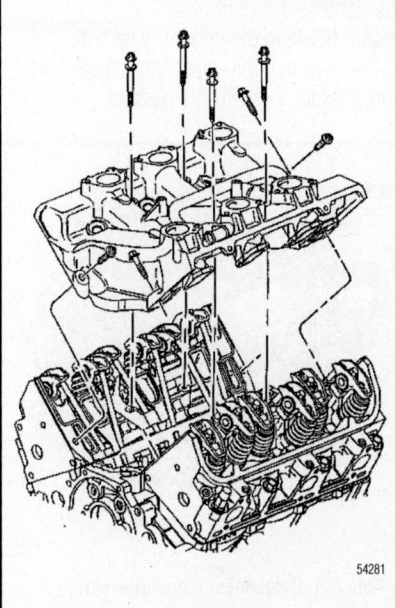

Fig. 227 Lower intake manifold and bolts

Fig. 228 Rocker arm bolts

➡**Place the valve train components in a rack in order to ensure that the components are installed in the same location from which they were removed.**

14. Remove the rocker arms.

15. Remove the push rods.
- The intake push rods measure 5.81 in (147.51 mm).
- The exhaust push rods measure 6.1 in (154.87 mm).

16. Remove the lower intake manifold gaskets and seals.

17. Clean the lower intake manifold gasket and seal surfaces on the cylinder heads and the engine block.

18. Clean the gasket and seal surfaces on the lower intake manifold with degreaser.

19. Remove all the loose room temperature vulcanizing (RTV) sealer.

To install:

➡**All gasket-mating surfaces need to be free of oil and foreign material. Use cleaner to clean the surfaces.**

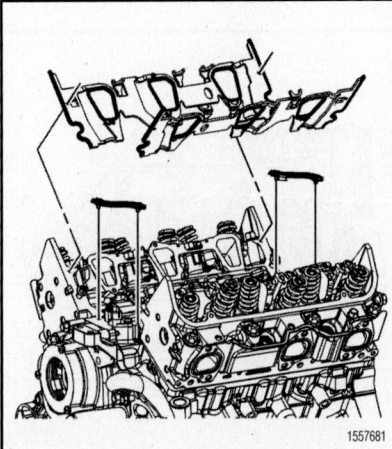

Fig. 229 Lower intake manifold gaskets and seals

➡**RTV sealer is NOT to be placed under the lower intake manifold gaskets.**

20. Install the lower intake manifold gaskets and seals.

21. Coat the ends of the push rods using prelube.

➡**The intake valve push rods measure 5.81 in (147.51 mm) and the exhaust push rods measure 6.1 in (154.87 mm) in length.**

22. Install the push rods in their original location.

23. Coat the rocker arm friction surfaces using prelube.

➡**Shims (P/N 88894006) may be required under the valve rocker arm pedestals if reconditioning has been performed on the cylinder head or its components.**

24. Install the rocker arms in their original locations.

25. Install the rocker arm bolts and tighten them to 25 ft. lbs. (34 Nm).

26. With the NEW gaskets and seals in place, apply a small drop, 0.31–0.39 in (8–10 mm) of RTV sealer to the 4 corners of the intake manifold to block joints.

27. Install the lower intake manifold.

✷✷ WARNING

Maximum gasket performance is achieved when using new fasteners, which contain a thread-locking patch. If the fasteners are not replaced, a thread locking chemical must be applied to the fastener threads. Failure to replace the fasteners or apply a thread-locking chemical MAY reduce gasket sealing capability.

✷✷ WARNING

Failure to tighten vertical bolts before the diagonal bolts may cause an oil leak.

28. Apply sealer to the lower intake manifold bolt threads.

29. Install the lower intake manifold bolts.

30. Tighten the lower intake manifold bolts in the sequence shown.

   a. Tighten the lower intake manifold bolts (1, 2, 3, 4, 5, 8, 6, 7, and 8) in sequence to 62 inch lbs. (7 Nm)

   b. Tighten the center lower intake manifold bolts (1, 2, 3, and 4) in sequence to 12 ft. lbs. (16 Nm).

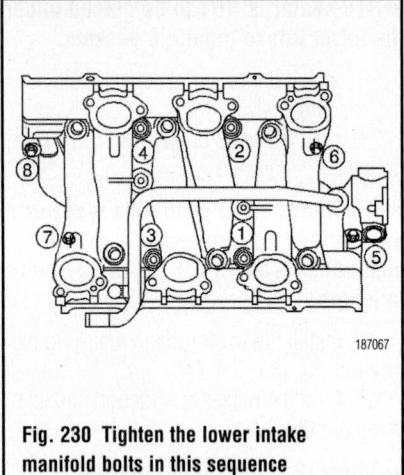

Fig. 230 Tighten the lower intake manifold bolts in this sequence

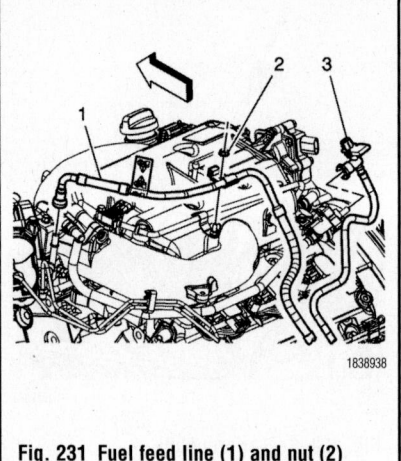

Fig. 231 Fuel feed line (1) and nut (2)

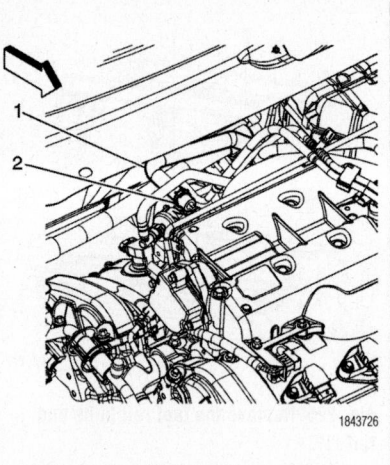

Fig. 233 Brake booster vacuum hose clamp (1) and hose (2) at the upper intake manifold

c. Tighten the visible corner lower intake manifold bolts (5, 8) to 18 ft. lbs. (25 Nm).

d. Tighten the hidden corner lower intake manifold bolts (6, 7) to 18 ft. lbs. (25 Nm).

31. Inspect the fuel rail and fuel injectors for damage and replace as necessary.

32. Lubricate and install NEW injector lower O-rings seals onto the injectors.

33. Install the injector nozzles into the lower intake manifold injector bores.

34. Press on the injector rail using the palms of both hands until the injectors are fully seated.

35. Install the fuel injector rail bolts and tighten them to 89 inch lbs. (10 Nm).

36. Position the fuel injector wiring harness electrical connector bracket to the intake manifold and install the bolt. Tighten the bolt to 10 ft. lbs. (14 Nm).

37. Connect the fuel injector wiring harness electrical connector to the CMP sensor.

38. Connect the engine wiring harness electrical connector (2) to the fuel injector inline electrical connector.

39. Connect the fuel injector wiring harness electrical connector to the ECT sensor.

40. Install the coolant crossover pipe.

41. Install the valve rocker arm covers.

42. Install the upper intake manifold. Refer to Upper Intake Manifold replacement.

43. Fill the coolant system. Refer to Cooling System Draining and Filling.

3.6L Engine

Upper

See Figures 231 through 237.

1. Remove the fuel injector sight shield.

2. Remove the air cleaner outlet duct.

3. Disconnect the fuel feed line (1) quick connect fitting from the fuel rail.

4. Remove the fuel feed pipe line nut (2) and remove the fuel feed line clip from the stud.

5. Reposition the fuel feed line out of the way.

6. Remove the coolant air bleed hose/pipe clip bolt (3) from the upper intake manifold.

7. Reposition the coolant air bleed hose clamp (2) at the water outlet.

8. Remove the coolant air bleed hose from the water outlet.

9. Remove the coolant air bleed hose/pipe clip from the upper intake manifold stud and reposition out of the way.

10. Reposition the brake booster vacuum hose clamp (1) at the upper intake manifold.

11. Remove the brake booster vacuum hose (2) from the upper intake manifold.

12. Disconnect the engine wiring harness electrical connector from the Manifold Absolute Pressure (MAP) sensor.

13. Disconnect the engine wiring harness electrical connector from the electronic throttle control (ETC).

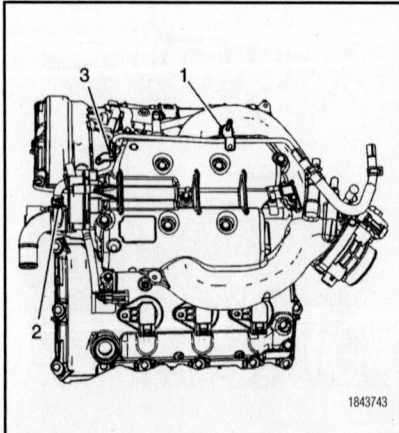

Fig. 232 Coolant air bleed hose/pipe clip bolt (3) and clamp (2)

14. Disconnect the engine wiring harness electrical connector (1) from the intake manifold tuning valve.

15. Disconnect the engine wiring harness electrical connector (2) from the evaporative emission (EVAP) canister purge solenoid.

16. Disconnect the positive crankcase ventilation (PCV) tube from the upper intake manifold and reposition aside.

17. Disconnect the EVAP canister purge solenoid tube quick connect fitting (1) at the upper intake manifold and reposition aside.

18. Remove the fuel rail to bracket bolt (1).

19. Remove the fuel rail wiring harness electrical connector bolt (2) and reposition the harness out of the way.

20. Remove the upper intake bolts (1).

21. Remove the upper intake manifold and gaskets. Discard the gaskets.

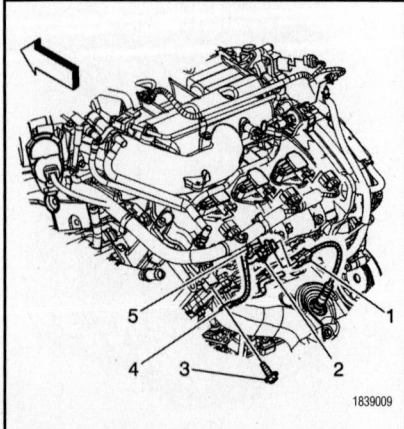

Fig. 234 Disconnect the engine wiring harness electrical connector (1) from the intake manifold tuning valve

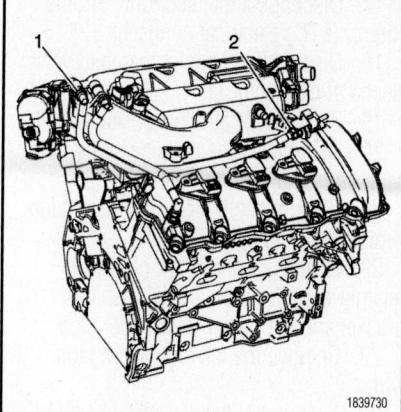

Fig. 235 Disconnect the EVAP canister purge solenoid tube quick connect fitting (1) at the upper intake manifold and reposition aside.

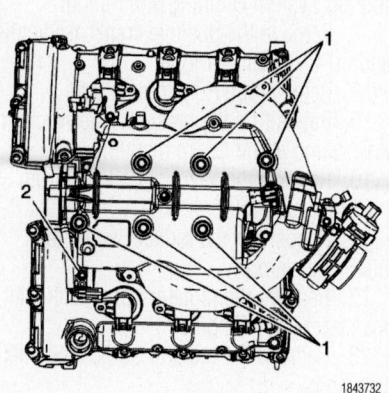

Fig. 237 Remove the fuel rail wiring harness electrical connector bolt (2) and reposition the harness out of the way

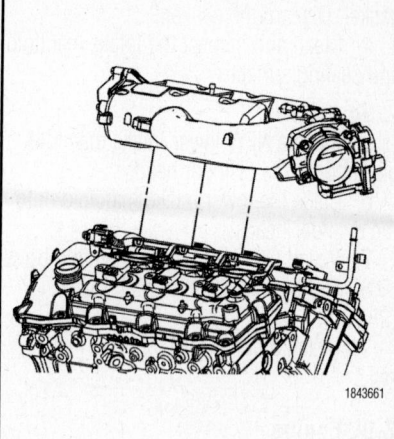

Fig. 238 Remove the upper intake bolts (1)

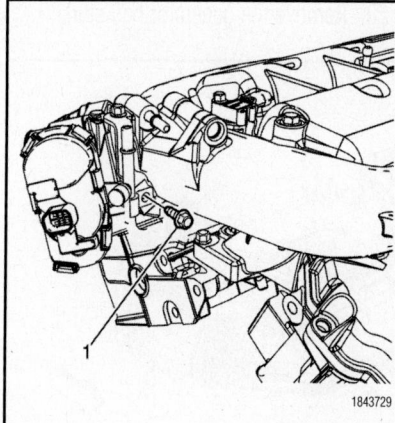

Fig. 236 Remove the fuel rail to bracket bolt (1)

22. If you are replacing the upper intake manifold complete the following steps:

    a. Remove the MAP sensor. Refer to Manifold Absolute Pressure Sensor replacement.

    b. Remove the throttle body.

    c. Remove the EVAP canister purge solenoid valve.

    d. Remove the intake manifold tuning valve. Refer to Intake Manifold Tuning Valve replacement.

To install:

23. If the upper intake manifold was replaced complete the following steps:

    a. Install the MAP sensor. Refer to Manifold Absolute Pressure Sensor replacement.

    b. Install the throttle body.

    c. Install the EVAP canister purge solenoid valve.

    d. Install the intake manifold tuning valve. Refer to Intake Manifold Tuning Valve replacement.

24. Place NEW upper intake manifold gaskets onto the lower intake manifold.

25. Place the upper intake manifold onto the lower intake manifold.

➡**Tighten the intake manifold bolts in an X pattern starting with the inside bolts and moving outward.**

26. Install the upper intake bolts and tighten them to 17 ft. lbs. (23 Nm).

27. Position the fuel rail wiring harness and install the fuel rail wiring harness electrical connector bolt (2). Tighten the bolt to 89 inch lbs. (10 Nm).

28. Install the fuel rail to bracket bolt and tighten it to 89 inch lbs. (10 Nm).

29. Position and install the EVAP canister purge solenoid tube quick connect fitting to the upper intake manifold.

30. Position and install the PCV tube to the upper intake manifold.

31. Connect the engine wiring harness electrical connector to the EVAP canister purge solenoid.

32. Connect the engine wiring harness electrical connector to the intake manifold tuning valve.

33. Connect the engine wiring harness electrical connector to the ETC.

34. Connect the engine wiring harness electrical connector to the MAP sensor.

35. Install the brake booster vacuum hose to the upper intake manifold.

36. Position the brake booster vacuum hose clamp at the upper intake manifold.

37. Position and install the coolant air bleed hose/pipe clip to the upper intake manifold stud.

38. Install the coolant air bleed hose to the water outlet.

39. Position the coolant air bleed hose clamp at the water outlet.

40. Install the coolant air bleed hose/pipe clip bolt to the upper intake manifold. Tighten the bolt to 89 inch lbs. (10 Nm).

41. Position the fuel feed line and install the fuel feed line clip to the stud.

42. Install the fuel feed line nut and tighten it to 89 inch lbs. (10 Nm).

43. Connect the fuel feed line quick connect fitting to the fuel rail.

44. Install the air cleaner outlet duct.

45. Install the fuel injector sight shield.

Lower

See Figure 239.

1. Remove the fuel injectors and fuel rail.

2. Remove the lower intake manifold bolts.

Fig. 239 Intake manifold removal

3. Remove the lower intake manifold and gasket. Discard the gasket.

4. Clean and inspect the intake manifold and sealing surfaces.

To install:

5. Place a NEW lower intake manifold gasket onto the cylinder heads.

6. Place the lower intake manifold onto the cylinder heads.

7. Install the lower intake manifold bolts.

8. Tighten the bolts to 17 ft. lbs. (23 Nm).

9. Install the fuel injectors and fuel rail.

3.9L Engine

See Figures 240 through 252.

1. Remove the intake manifold cover.

2. Relieve the fuel system pressure.

3. Disconnect the fuel feed pipe (3) quick connect fitting from the fuel rail

4. Disconnect the evaporative (EVAP) emission pipe (1) from the purge solenoid.

5. Open the retaining clip (2), and remove the fuel and EVAP pipes from the clip.

6. Drain the cooling system. Refer to Cooling System Draining and Filling.

7. Remove the positive crankcase ventilation (PCV) fresh air tube.

8. Remove the PCV foul air tube.

9. Reposition the brake booster vacuum hose clamp at the intake manifold.

10. Remove the vacuum hose (1) from the intake manifold.

11. Reposition the radiator surge tank inlet hose clamp.

12. Remove the radiator surge tank inlet hose from the inlet pipe.

13. Remove the radiator surge tank inlet pipe bolts.

14. Remove the radiator surge tank inlet pipe.

15. Disconnect the Manifold Absolute Pressure (MAP) sensor electrical connector.

16. Disconnect the evaporative emission (EVAP) canister purge solenoid electrical connector (1).

17. Disconnect the electronic throttle control (ETC) electrical connector (2).

18. Disconnect the inlet manifold valve electrical connector (1).

19. Remove the air cleaner outlet duct.

20. Disconnect the left side spark plug wires from the spark plugs.

21. Disconnect the left side spark plug wires from the ignition coil.

22. Disengage the spark plug wire retainer clips from the intake manifold bracket and the heater inlet/outlet pipe.

23. Remove the left side spark plug wires.

24. Remove the heater inlet and outlet pipe nuts (1) from the throttle body studs.

25. Remove the inlet and outlet pipe (2, 3) from the studs.

26. Remove the 2 ignition coil bolts.

27. Remove the generator (alternator) upper bolt.

28. Remove the generator ball stud.

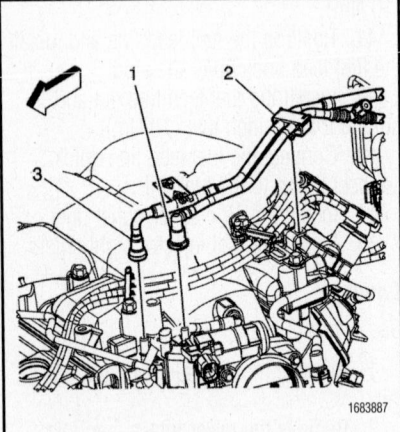

Fig. 240 Fuel feed pipe (3) quick connect fitting at the fuel rail, evaporative (EVAP) emission pipe (1) and retaining clip (2)

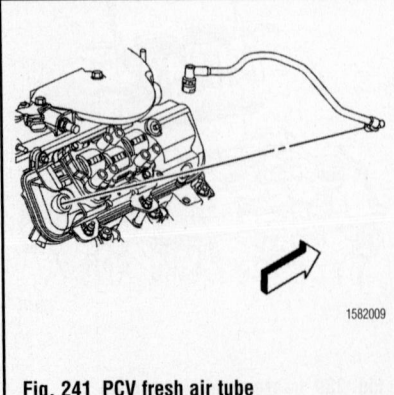

Fig. 241 PCV fresh air tube

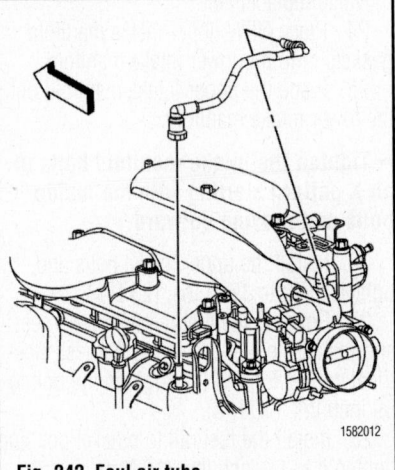

Fig. 242 Foul air tube

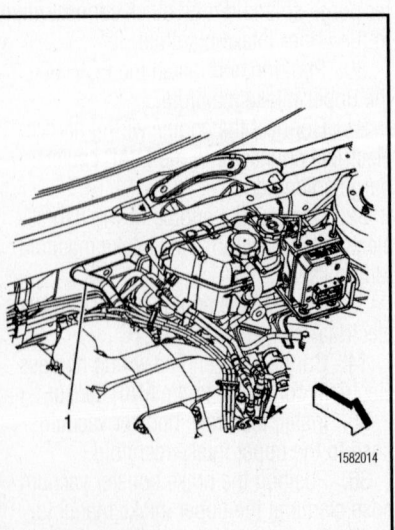
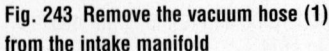

Fig. 243 Remove the vacuum hose (1) from the intake manifold

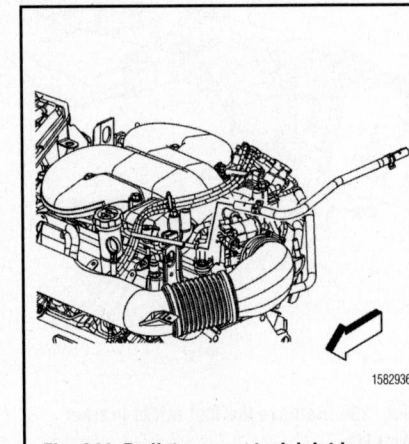

Fig. 244 Radiator surge tank inlet hose, clamp, and pipe

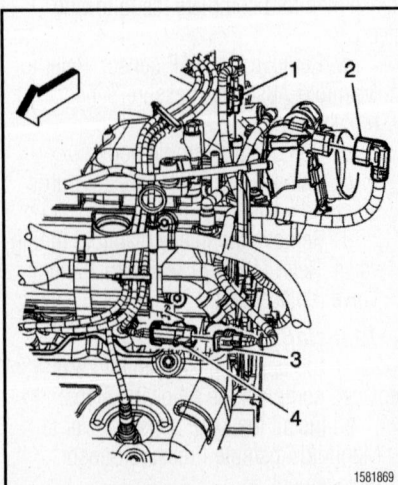

Fig. 245 Disconnect the evaporative emission (EVAP) canister purge solenoid electrical connector (1)

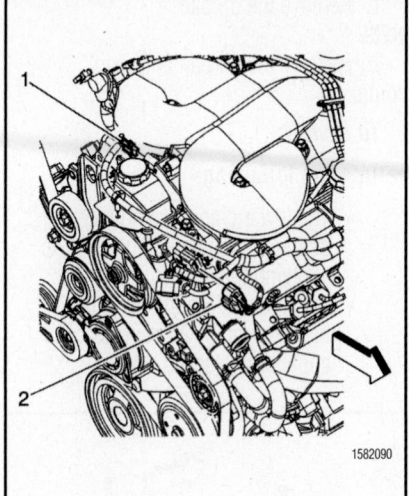
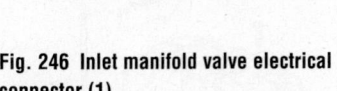

Fig. 246 Inlet manifold valve electrical connector (1)

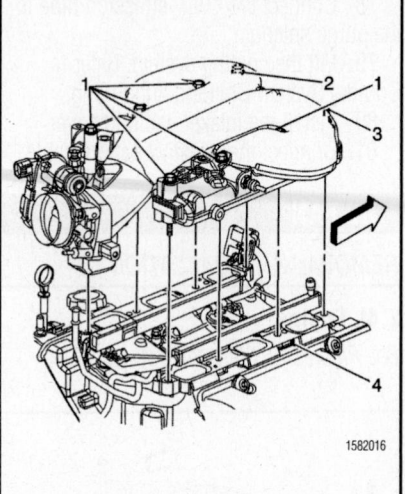

Fig. 248 Upper intake manifold bolts (1, 2) and stud (3)

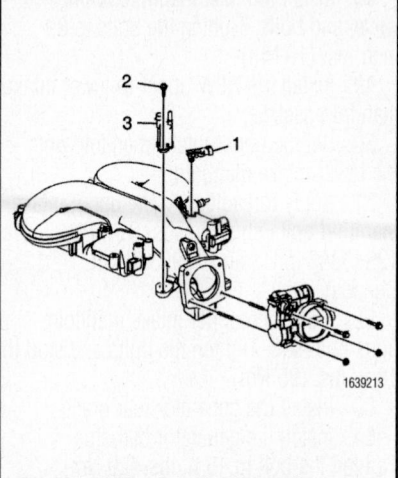

Fig. 251 MAP sensor bracket and sensor (1), and EVAP canister purge solenoid valve bolt (2) and valve (3)

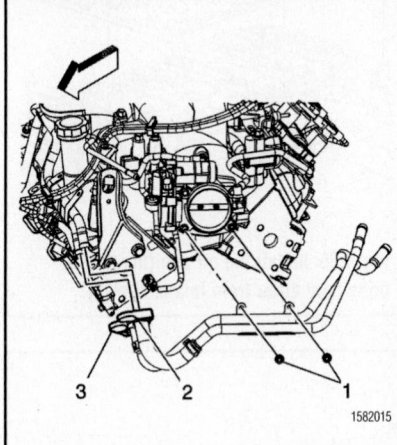

Fig. 247 Remove the heater inlet and outlet pipe nuts (1) from the throttle body studs

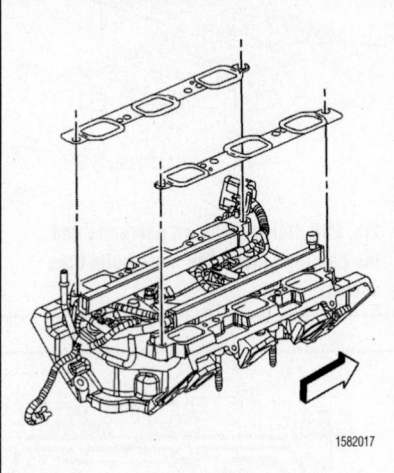

Fig. 249 Upper to lower intake manifold gaskets

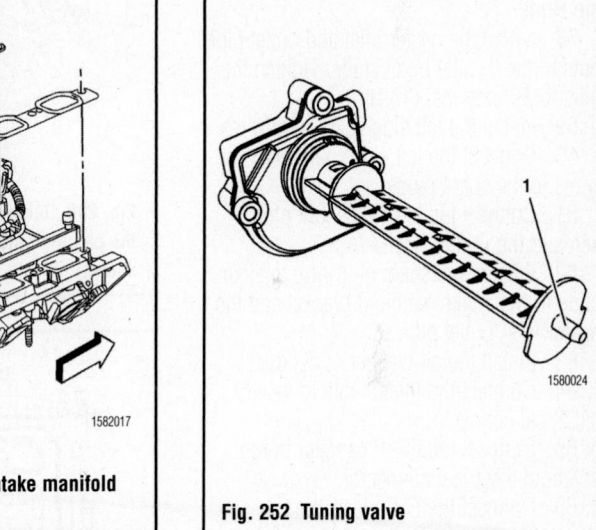

Fig. 252 Tuning valve

29. Remove the generator rear brace.

30. Remove the upper intake manifold bolts (1, 2) and stud (3).

31. Separate and remove the upper intake manifold from the lower intake manifold.

32. Remove the upper to lower intake manifold gaskets.

33. Remove the inlet manifold tuning valve bolts and valve.

34. Remove the throttle body bolts/studs and throttle body.

35. Remove the MAP sensor bracket and sensor (1).

36. Remove the EVAP canister purge solenoid valve bolt (2) and valve (3).

37. Clean the upper intake to lower intake gasket mating surfaces.

38. Inspect the intake manifold tuning valve seal for damage. The tuning valve

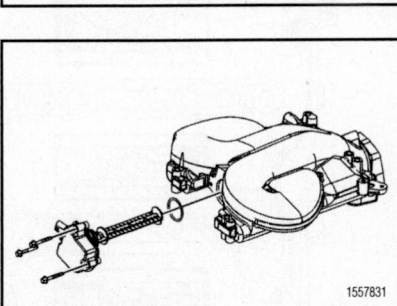

Fig. 250 Inlet manifold tuning valve bolts and valve

blade attachment to the motor should be tight, with no looseness or slack present, Replace as necessary.

39. Apply lubricant to the nose of the valve blade (1). GM recommends PN 1051344 (US) and 993037 (Canada).

To install:

40. Inspect the EVAP canister purge solenoid valve seal for damage, replace as necessary.

41. Install the EVAP canister purge solenoid valve and bolt.

42. Tighten the bolt to 12 ft. lbs. (16 Nm).

43. Inspect the MAP sensor seal for damage, replace as necessary.

44. Install the MAP sensor and bracket.

45. Inspect the throttle body seal for damage, replace as necessary.

46. Apply threadlock to the throttle body bolts/studs threads. (GM PN 12345382 in US and 10953489 in Canada).

47. Install the throttle body and bolts/studs. Tighten the bolts/studs to 89 inch lbs. (10 Nm).

48. Install the inlet manifold tuning valve, and bolts. Tighten the bolts to 89 inch lbs. (10 Nm).

49. Install the NEW upper to lower intake manifold gaskets.

50. Set the upper intake manifold onto the lower intake manifold.

51. Apply threadlock to the upper intake manifold bolts/stud threads. (GM PN 12345382 in US and 10953489 in Canada).

52. Install the upper intake manifold bolts and stud. Tighten the bolts and stud to 18 ft. lbs. (25 Nm).

53. Install the generator rear brace.

54. Install the generator ball stud. Tighten the bolt to 15 ft. lbs. (20 Nm).

55. Install the generator upper bolt. Tighten the bolt to 37 ft. lbs. (50 Nm).

56. Install the 2 ignition coil bolts. Tighten the bolts to 18 ft. lbs. (25 Nm).

57. Install the inlet and outlet pipe to the studs.

58. Install the heater inlet and outlet pipe nuts to the throttle body studs. Tighten the nuts to 89 inch lbs. (10 Nm).

59. Install the left side spark plug wires.

60. Connect the left side spark plug wires to the spark plugs.

61. Connect the left side spark plug wires to the ignition coil.

62. Engage the spark plug wire retainer clips to the intake manifold bracket and the heater inlet/outlet pipe.

63. Install the air cleaner outlet duct.

64. Connect the inlet manifold valve electrical connector.

65. Connect the EVAP canister purge solenoid electrical connector.

66. Connect the ETC electrical connector.

67. Connect the MAP sensor electrical connector.

68. Install the radiator surge tank inlet pipe.

69. Install the radiator surge tank inlet pipe bolts. Tighten the bolts to 89 inch lbs. (10 Nm).

70. Install the radiator surge tank inlet hose to the inlet pipe.

71. Position the radiator surge tank inlet hose clamp.

72. Install the brake booster vacuum hose to the intake manifold.

73. Position the vacuum hose clamp at the intake manifold.

74. Install the PCV foul air tube.

75. Install the PCV fresh air tube.

76. Install the fuel and EVAP pipes to the retainer clip and close the clip.

77. Connect the fuel feed pipe quick connect fitting to the fuel rail.

78. Connect the EVAP emission pipe to the purge solenoid.

79. Fill the cooling system. Refer to Cooling System Draining and Filling.

80. Install the intake manifold cover.

81. Connect the negative battery cable.

OIL PAN

REMOVAL & INSTALLATION

2.4L Engine

See Figures 253 through 256.

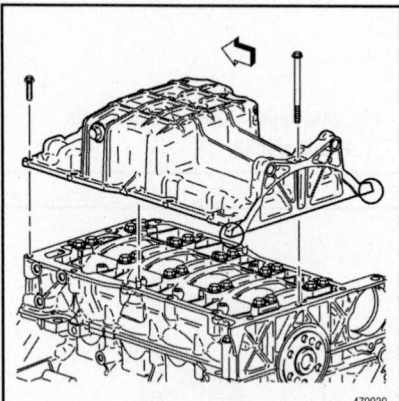

Fig. 253 Remove the oil pan bolts and the pan (pan may have more bolts than shown)

1. Remove the oil pan bolts.

2. Remove the oil pan at the pry points.

To install:

→**Note the following:**

- The lower crankcase surface must be free of contamination prior to applying the sealer.
- Install and align the oil pan to block within 20 minutes of applying the sealer.

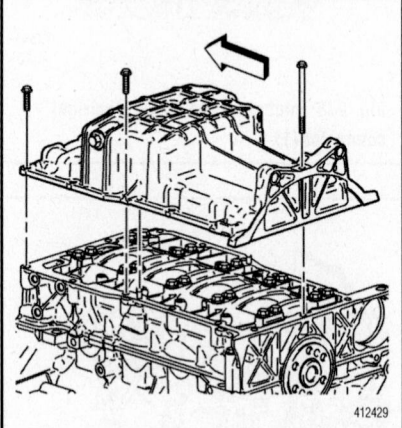

Fig. 255 Install the oil pan (number of bolts may differ from image shown)

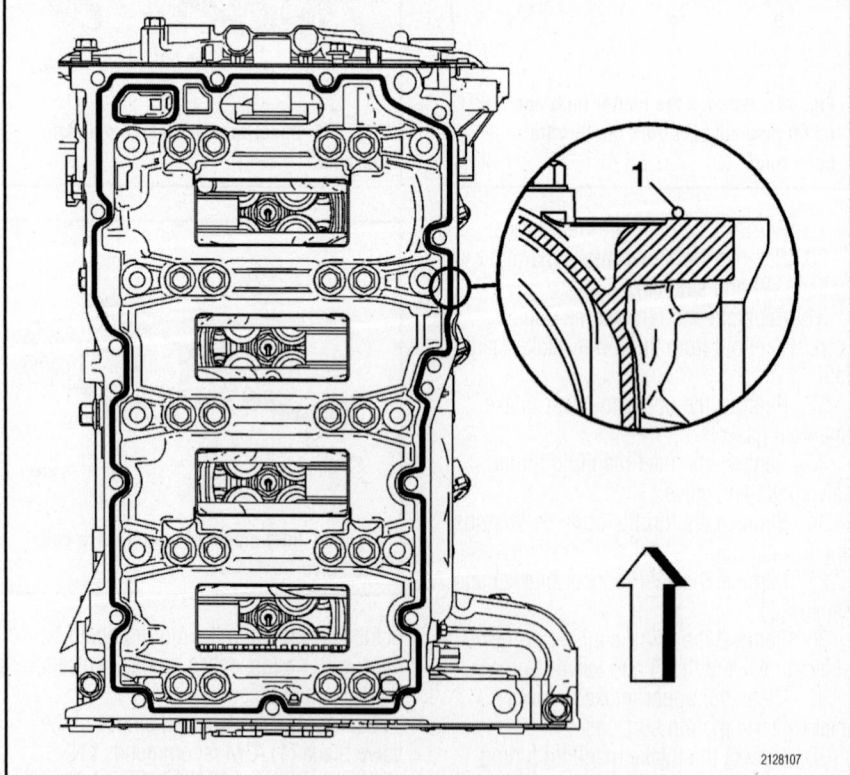

Fig. 254 Apply sealer

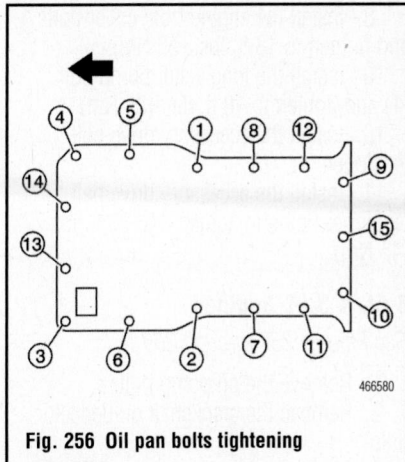

Fig. 256 Oil pan bolts tightening sequence

- The oil pan must be fastened to final torque specification within 60 minutes of applying the sealer.

3. Apply a 0.09 inch (2.25 mm) bead of sealer (1) on the level part of the flange next to the chamfer around the perimeter of the oil pan and the oil suction port opening. (GM PN 12378521 in US and 88901148 in Canada).

4. Install the oil pan.

5. Install the oil pan bolts and tighten to 18 ft. lbs. (25 Nm) in sequence.

3.5L & 3.9L Engines

See Figures 257 through 259.

1. Remove the oil pan support bracket bolts and brackets as needed.

2. Remove the oil pan side bolts.

3. Remove the oil pan bolts.

4. Remove the oil pan.

5. Remove the oil pan gasket.

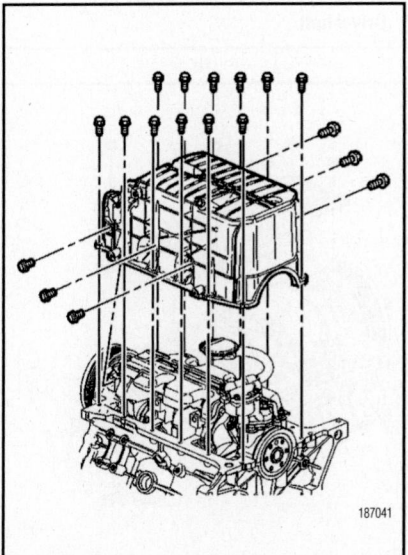

Fig. 257 Oil pan removal

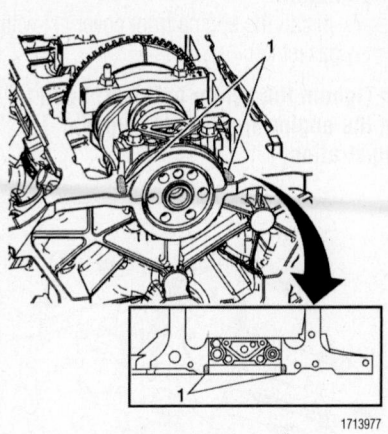

Fig. 258 Apply sealer GM P/N 12378521 (Canadian P/N 88901148) or the equivalent to both sides of the crankshaft rear main bearing cap (1). Press sealer into the gap using a putty knife

To install:

6. Apply sealer GM P/N 12378521 (Canadian P/N 88901148) or the equivalent to both sides of the crankshaft rear main bearing cap (1). Press sealer into gap using a putty knife.

7. Apply sealer GM P/N 12378521 (Canadian P/N 88901148) or the equivalent to both sides of the front cover/block mating area (1).

8. Install the oil pan gasket.

9. Install the oil pan.

10. Install the oil pan bolts and tighten them 18 ft. lbs. (to 25 Nm).

11. Apply sealer GM P/N 12346004 (Canadian P/N 10953480), or an equivalent to the oil pan side bolt threads.

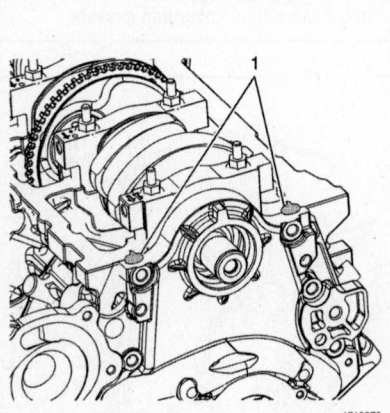

Fig. 259 Apply sealer GM P/N 12378521 (Canadian P/N 88901148) or equivalent to both sides of the front cover/block mating area (1)

12. Install the oil pan side bolts.

13. Tighten the oil pan side bolts a first pass to 37 ft. lbs. (50 Nm).

14. Tighten the oil pan side bolts a second pass to 50 degrees using the J 45059 meter.

15. Install the oil pan drain plug and tighten it to 18 ft. lbs. (to 25 Nm).

3.6L Engine

See Figures 260 through 262.

1. Remove the oil pan bolts (1) and (2).

To install:

Place a 0.118 in (3 mm) bead of RTV sealant, GM P/N 12378521 (Canadian P/N 88901148) or an equivalent, on the block pan rail and the crankshaft rear oil seal housing (1).

2. Position the oil pan onto the block.

3. Loosely install the oil pan bolts.

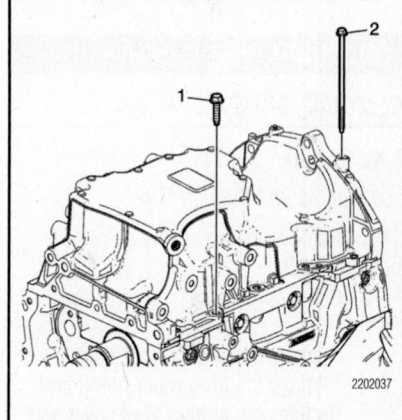

Fig. 260 Remove the oil pan bolts (1) and (2)

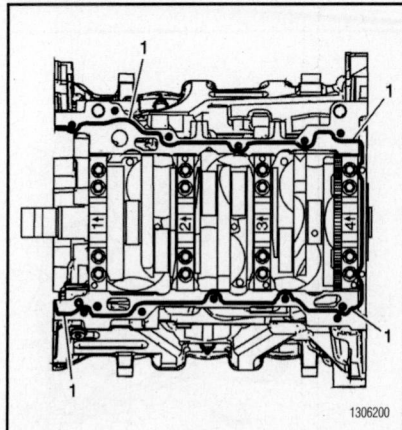

Fig. 261 Place a 0.118 in (3 mm) bead of RTV sealant, GM P/N 12378521 (Canadian P/N 88901148) or an equivalent, on the block pan rail and the crankshaft rear oil seal housing (1)

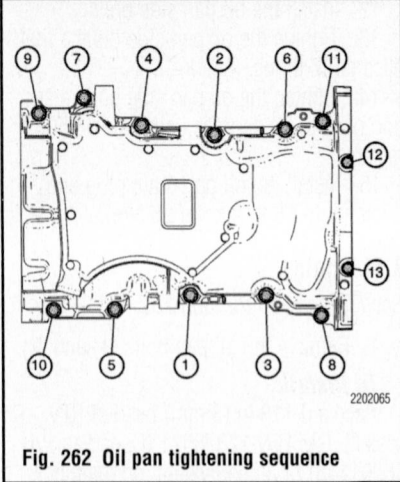

Fig. 262 Oil pan tightening sequence

4. Tighten the oil pan bolts in sequence shown.

    a. Tighten the 8 mm bolts (1–11) to 18 ft. lbs. (25 Nm).

    b. Tighten the 6 mm bolts (12, 13) to 89 inch lbs. (10 Nm).

OIL PUMP

REMOVAL & INSTALLATION

2.4L Engine

See Figures 263 through 266.

1. Remove the accessory drive belt tensioner bolt.

2. Remove the accessory drive belt tensioner.

3. Remove the engine front cover bolts.

4. Remove the long water pump bolt.

5. Remove the engine front cover and gaskets.

6. Remove the crankshaft front cover oil seal with an appropriate tool.

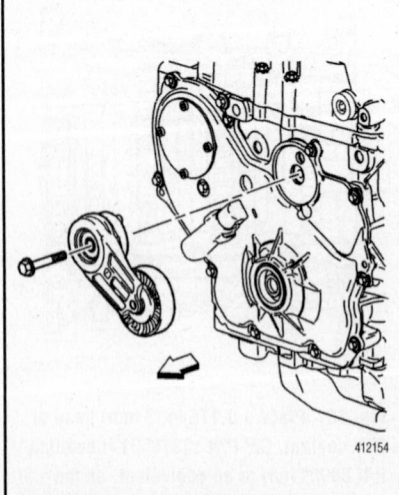

Fig. 263 Accessory drive belt tensioner and bolt

To install:

7. Install the engine front cover (1) with a new gasket (2).

➡**Tighten the center bolt last: See (1) in the engine front cover removal illustration.**

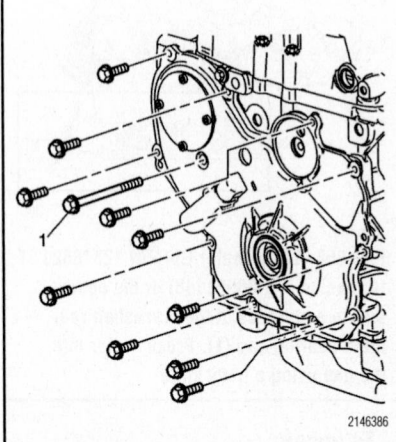

Fig. 264 Remove the engine front cover bolts

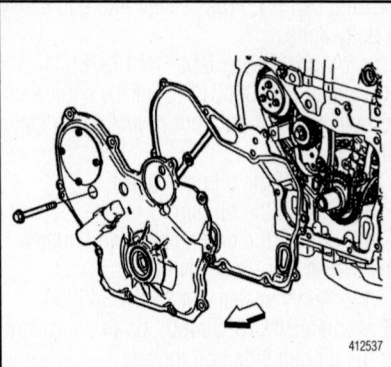

Fig. 265 Remove the long water pump bolt, engine front cover and gaskets

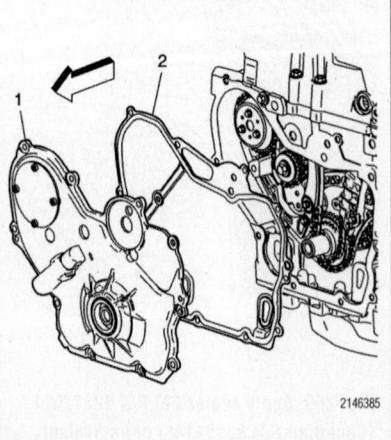

Fig. 266 Install the engine front cover (1) with a new gasket (2)

8. Install the engine front cover bolts and tighten to 18 ft. lbs. (25 Nm).

9. Install the long water pump bolt (1) and tighten to 18 ft. lbs. (25 Nm).

10. Install the accessory drive belt tensioner.

11. Install the accessory drive belt tensioner bolt and tighten it to 33 ft. lbs. (45 Nm).

3.5L & 3.9L Engines

See Figures 267 through 269.

1. Remove the oil pump bolt.

2. Remove the crankshaft oil deflector nuts.

3. Remove the crankshaft oil deflector.

To install:

4. Install the crankshaft oil deflector.

5. Install the crankshaft oil deflector nuts and tighten them to 18 ft. lbs. (25 Nm).

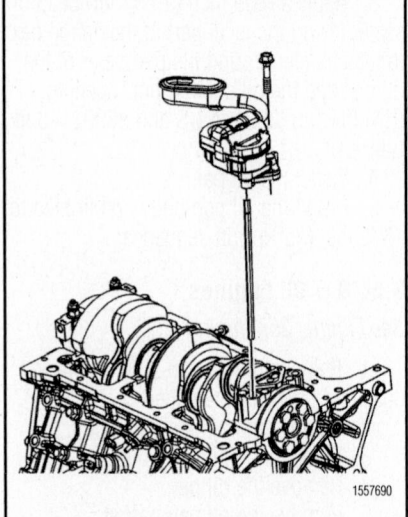

Fig. 267 Oil pump bolt, pump, and Driveshaft

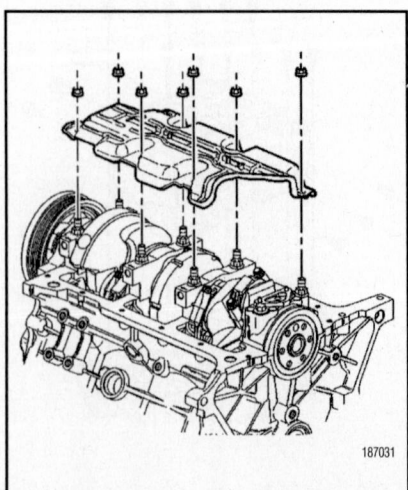

Fig. 268 Crankshaft oil deflector and nuts

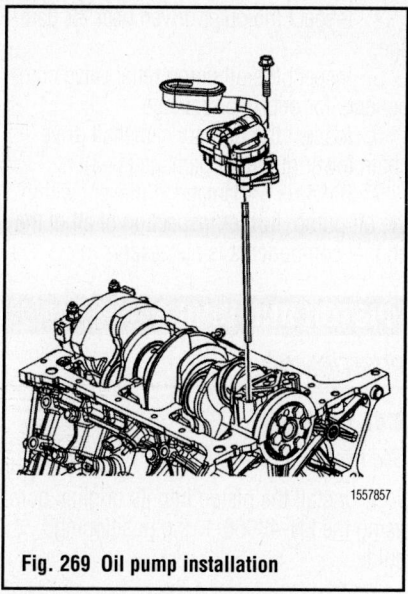

Fig. 269 Oil pump installation

➡**Do not reuse the oil pump driveshaft retainer. During assembly, install a NEW oil pump driveshaft retainer.**

6. Install the oil pump.
7. Position the oil pump onto the pins.
8. Install the oil pump bolt attaching the oil pump to the rear crankshaft bearing cap, and tighten it to 30 ft. lbs. (41 Nm).

3.6L Engine

See Figure 270.

1. Remove the oil pump bolts.
2. Remove the oil pump.

To install:

3. Align the oil pump drive gear with the crankshaft flats and install the oil pump to the engine block.
4. Align the pump body with the mounting holes in the cylinder block.
5. Install the oil pump bolts. Tighten the oil pump bolts to 18 ft. lbs. (25 Nm).

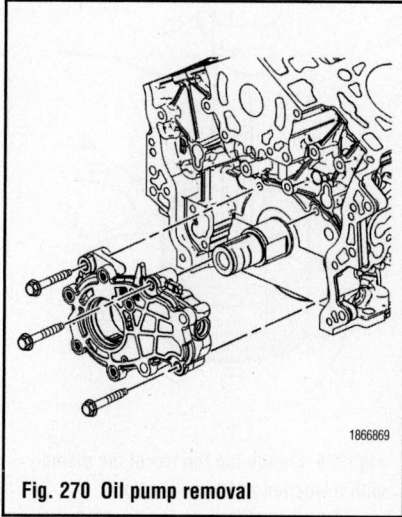

Fig. 270 Oil pump removal

INSPECTION

2.4L Engine

1. Clean all of the parts in cleaning solvent. Remove varnish, sludge and dirt.
2. Inspect the oil pump for wear and scoring. Insure that all components are within specifications. Refer to oil pressure Engine Mechanical Specifications.
3. Replace the front cover and oil pump assembly if it is out of specification or damaged.

3.5L & 3.9L Engines

See Figures 271 through 273.

> **✷✷ CAUTION**
>
> **Bodily injury may occur if the cleaning solvent is inhaled or exposed to the skin.**

1. Clean all parts of sludge, oil, and varnish by soaking in cleaning solvent.
2. Inspect for foreign material and determine the source of the foreign material.
3. Inspect the pump housing and cover for the following conditions:
   - Cracks or casting imperfections
   - Scoring (3)
   - Damaged threads
4. Do not attempt to repair the pump housing. Replace the pump housing.
5. Inspect the oil pump gears for the following conditions:

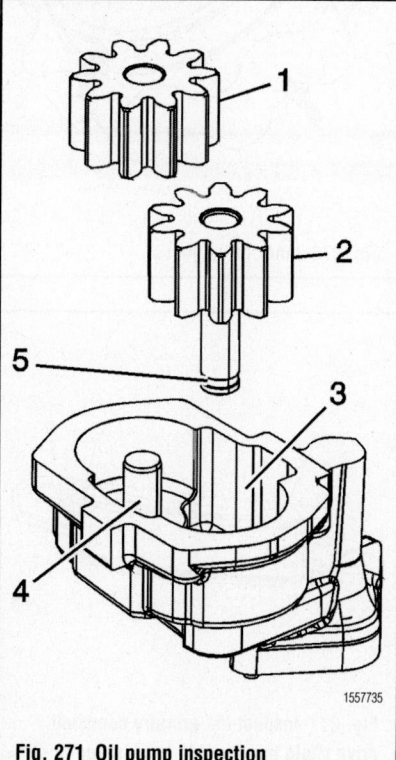

Fig. 271 Oil pump inspection

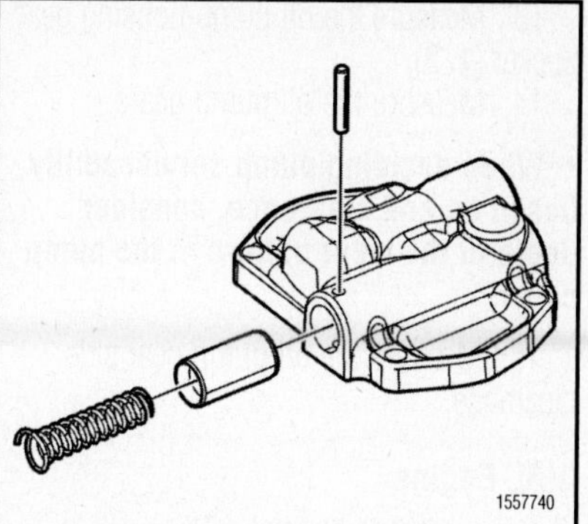

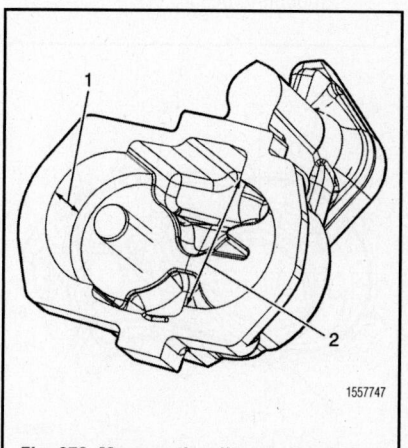

Fig. 272 Pressure regulator valve inspection

   - Scoring (1)
   - Excessive wear (2)
6. Inspect the idler shaft for looseness or scoring (4). If the idler shaft is loose or damaged, replace the oil pump.
7. Inspect the drive gear shaft for looseness or scoring (5).
8. Inspect the pressure regulator valve for the following conditions:
   - Scoring
   - Sticking
9. Burrs may be removed using a fine oil stone.
10. Inspect the pressure regulator valve spring for the following conditions:
   - Loss of tension
   - Bending
11. Inspect the suction pipe and screen assembly for the following conditions:
   - Looseness—If the suction pipe is loose, bent or has been removed, replace the pump body cover and suction pipe.
   - Broken wire mesh or screen
12. Measure the oil pump gear lash. Install the gears, and measure in several places.

Fig. 273 Measure the oil pump housing gear pocket (1, 2)

13. Measure the oil pump housing gear pocket (1, 2).

14. Measure the oil pump gears.

➡ **When deciding pump serviceability based on end clearance, consider depth of the wear pattern in the pump cover.**

15. Measure the oil pump gear side clearance.

3.6L Engine

See Figures 274 through 277.

➡ **There are no serviceable components within the oil pump. Disassemble the pump only to diagnose an oiling concern. A disassembled oil pump must not be reused. A disassembled oil pump must be replaced.**

1. Inspect the oil pump housing for the following:
   - Damage, scoring, or debris on the housing surface for the driven gear (1)
   - Damage to the oil pump mounting bosses (2)
   - Damage, scoring, or debris on the housing surface for the drive gear (3)
   - Damage, scoring, or debris in the oil pump relief valve port (4)
   - Damage, scoring, or debris in the oil pump intake port (5)
   - Damage, scoring, or debris in the oil pump relief valve bore (6)
   - Damage, scoring, or debris in the oil pump output port (7)
   - Damage to the threads in the oil pump housing for the oil pump cover bolts (8)

2. Inspect the oil pump cover for the following conditions:
   - Damage to the oil pump cover mounting bosses (1)

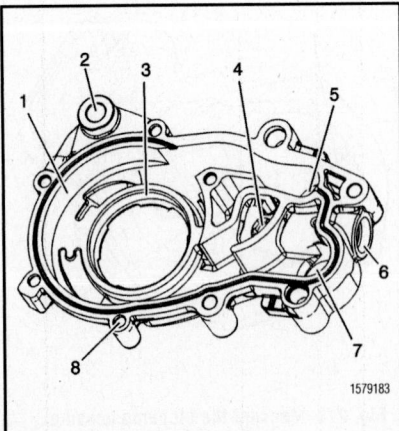

Fig. 274 Oil pump inspection

- Damage, scoring, or debris in the oil pump cover oil passages (2)
- Damage to the sealing surface between the oil pump cover and the oil pump housing (3)

3. Inspect the inner drive gear for damage. If inner diameter damage is found, inspect the crankshaft.

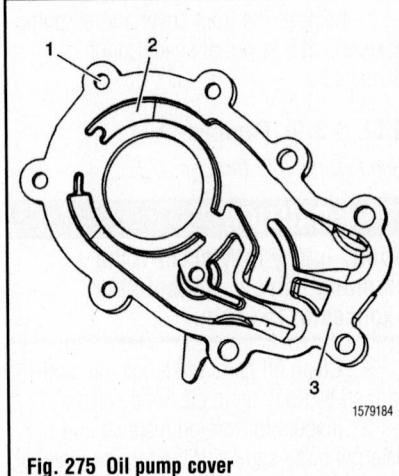

Fig. 275 Oil pump cover

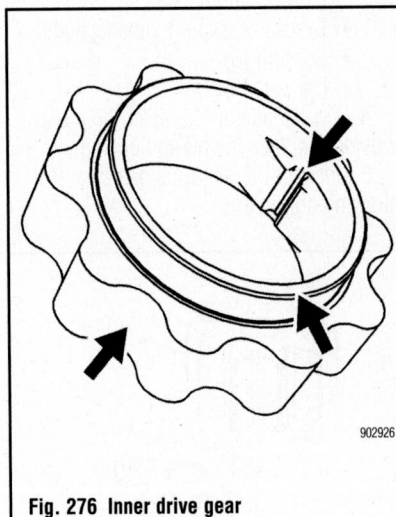

Fig. 276 Inner drive gear

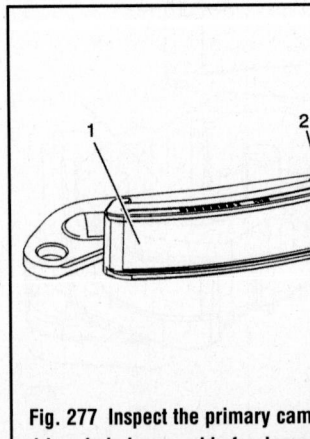

Fig. 277 Inspect the primary camshaft drive chain lower guide for damage (1–3)

4. Inspect the outer driven gear for damage.

5. Inspect the oil pump relief valve components for debris or damage.

6. Inspect the primary camshaft drive chain lower guide for damage (1–3).

7. If debris or damage is present within the oil pump, further inspection of all of the engine components is necessary.

PISTON AND RING

POSITIONING

2.4L Engine

See Figures 278 and 279.

1. Install the piston into its original bore using the EN-43966-1 ring positioning guide.

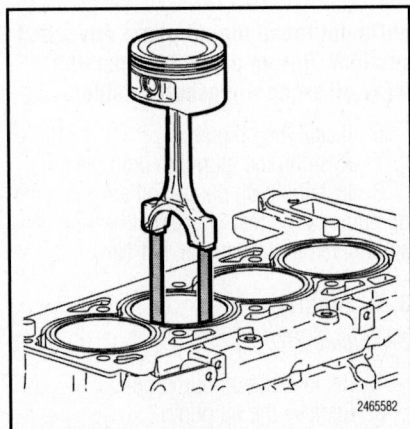

Fig. 278 Install the piston into its original bore using the EN-43966-1 ring positioning guide

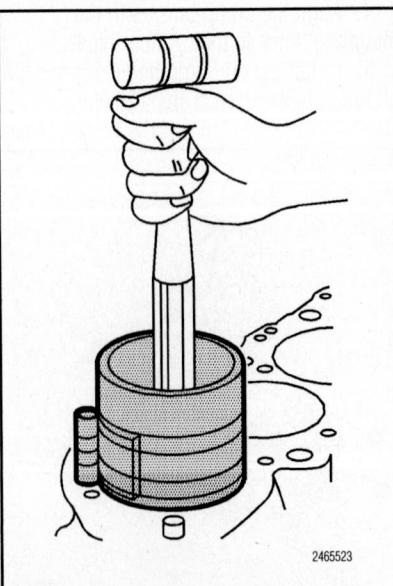

Fig. 279 Lightly tap the top of the piston with a wooden hammer handle

2. Lightly tap the top of the piston with a wooden hammer handle.

3. When installing the piston and the connecting rod, the stamped mark on the piston must point to the front of the engine.

4. Hold the EN-8037 compressor firmly against the engine block until all the piston rings have entered the cylinder bore.

3.5L & 3.9L Engines

See Figures 280 through 283.

There are two styles of pistons in use in the LZ engine, and each piston must use the appropriate matching piston ring set. To identify which make you have, look on the bottom of the piston, in between the piston pin bores (1):

• If there is an "FM" marking, it is a Federal Mogul piston and must use the Federal Mogul piston rings.

• If there is no marking, it is a Mahle piston and must use Mahle piston rings. Failure to do so may result in engine damage.

➡**The tops of the first and second piston rings are marked with light green stripes to insure proper orientation on the piston. The top ring has a light green stripe 180 degrees from the gap,**

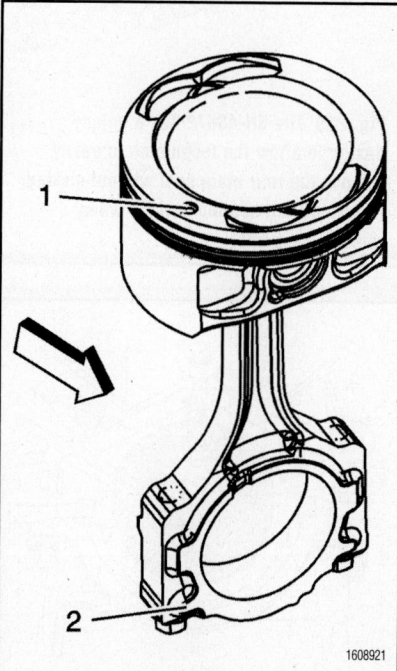

Fig. 280 When assembling the connecting rod to the piston, make sure the connecting rod reference mark (2) is facing towards front of engine, and is in proper correlation with the front of engine piston reference mark (1)

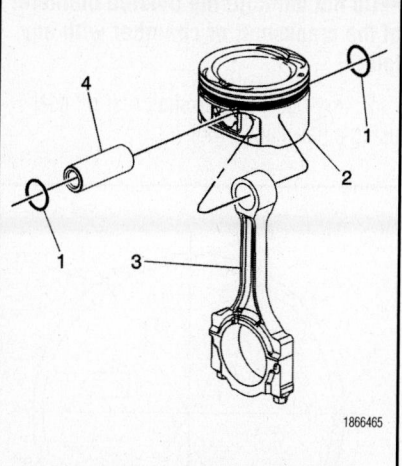

Fig. 281 Slide the piston pin (4) into the piston and the connecting rod (3)—3.5L

and the second ring has a light green stripe 90 degrees from the gap. These stripes must be facing up and in this orientation prior to installing the pistons. This is necessary for proper operation.

1. Stagger the oil control ring end gaps a minimum of 90 degrees.

2. Stagger the compression ring end gaps a minimum of 1 inch (25 mm).

3. Install the J 8037 compressor onto the piston and compress the piston rings.

➡**When assembling the connecting rod to the piston, make sure the connecting rod reference mark (2) is facing towards front of engine, and is in proper correlation with the front of engine piston reference mark (1).**

4. Align the piston pin bore with the connecting rod pin bore.

5. Slide the piston pin (4) into the piston and the connecting rod (3).

➡**Use NEW piston pin retainers. Never reuse the piston pin retainers.**

6. Install NEW piston pin retainers using the J 43654 installer.

7. Ensure that the piston pin retainers are fully seated in their grooves.

8. Repeat these procedures for the remaining pistons.

9. Install the J 41556 guide into the connecting rod.

10. Install the piston and connecting rod assembly into the proper cylinder bore.

11. Hold the piston ring compressor firmly against the engine block. Using a wooden hammer handle, lightly tap the top of the piston until all the piston rings enter the cylinder bore.

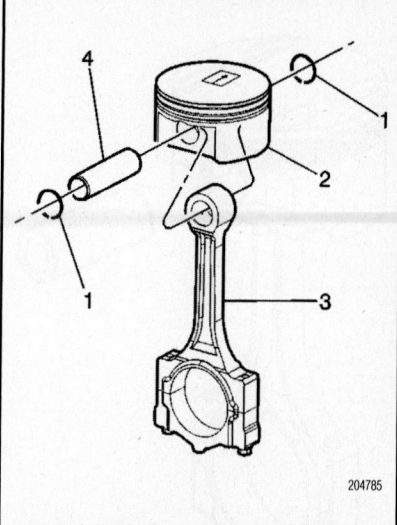

Fig. 282 Slide the piston pin (4) into the piston and the connecting rod (3)—3.9L

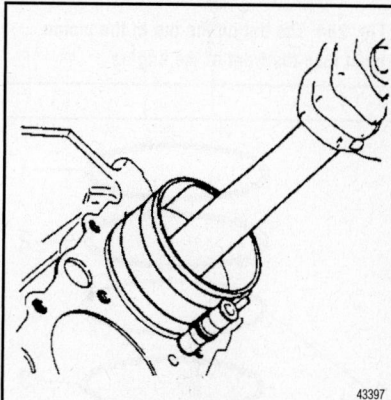

Fig. 283 Hold the piston ring compressor firmly against the engine block. Using a wooden hammer handle, lightly tap the top of the piston until all of the piston rings enter the cylinder bore.

➡**When installing the pistons into the cylinder bore, make sure not to contact the piston oil nozzle with the connecting rod. Failure to do so may damage the piston oil nozzle, resulting in potential engine damage.**

3.6L Engine

See Figures 284 through 286.

➡**The piston is directional and must be installed in the engine block in the proper direction. The dot on the top of the piston must face the front of the engine.**

Once the rings are installed set the ring gaps for the oil control, second and top ring as follows. Use the piston location arrow for reference.

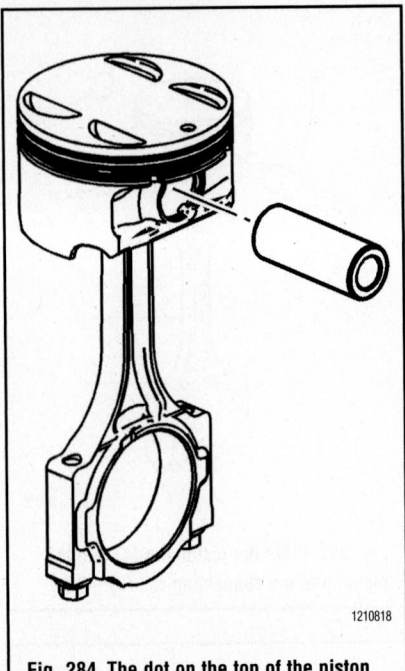

Fig. 284 The dot on the top of the piston must face the front of the engine

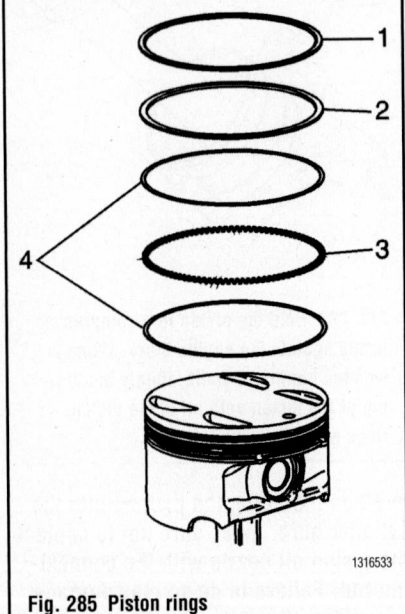

Fig. 285 Piston rings

- Lower oil control ring—position 1
- Upper oil control ring—position 2
- Top Ring—position 3
- Oil control ring expander—position 4
- Second ring—position 5

REAR OIL SEAL

REMOVAL & INSTALLATION

2.4L Engine

See Figures 287 and 288.

1. Remove the flywheel.

➡ **Do not damage the outside diameter of the crankshaft or chamber with any tool.**

2. Pry out the crankshaft rear oil seal using a flat-bladed tool.

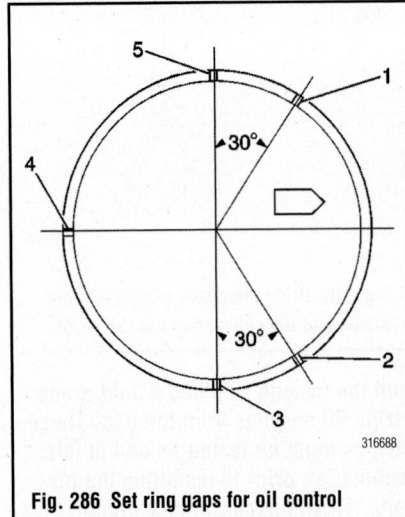

Fig. 286 Set ring gaps for oil control

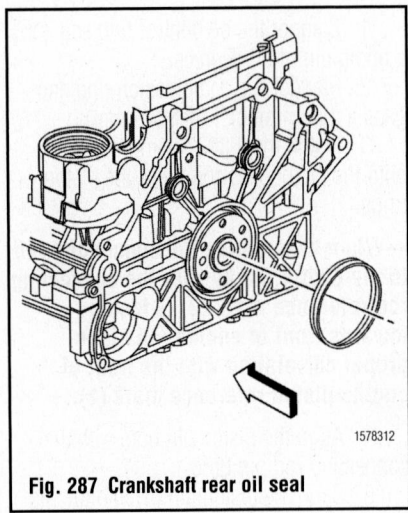

Fig. 287 Crankshaft rear oil seal

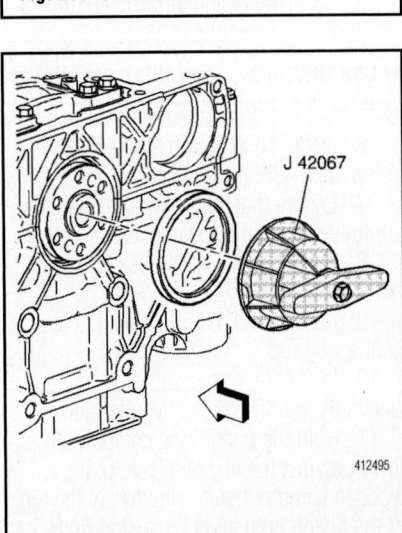

Fig. 288

To install:

3. Using the J 42067 tool, install a NEW crankshaft real oil seal.
4. Install the flywheel.

3.5L & 3.9L Engines

See Figures 289 through 296.

1. The EN-48672 has a unique design to allow the technician to easily remove the rear main seal without nicking the crankshaft sealing surface when removing the seal. Before proceeding with removal, review the illustration to become familiar with the following components:

- Removal Plate (1)
- Threaded Adjustment Pins and Jam Nuts (2)
- Force Screw (3)
- Number 2 Self Drill Screws 1.5 in. (38 mm) long 8 needed (4)

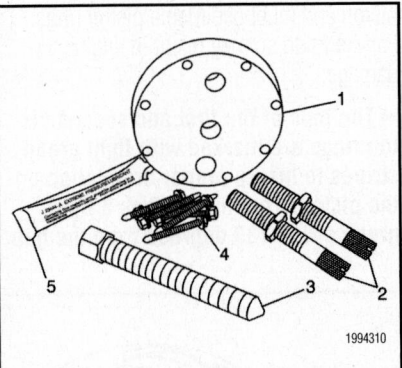

Fig. 289 The EN-48672 has a unique design to allow the technician to easily remove the rear main seal without nicking the crankshaft sealing surface when removing the seal

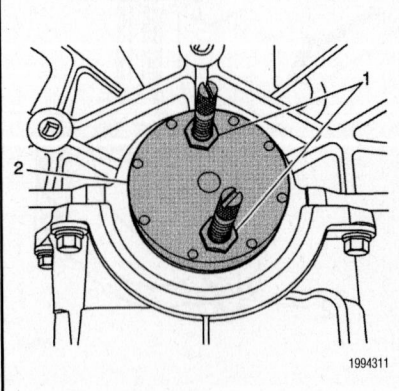

Fig. 290 Install the removal plate (2) and both threaded adjustment pins and jam nuts (1) into the back of the crankshaft flange and secure the plate with adjustment pins and jam nuts

- Extreme Pressure Lubricant (5)
2. Remove the transmission.
3. Remove the engine flywheel.
4. Install the removal plate (2) and both threaded adjustment pins and jam nuts (1) into the back of the crankshaft flange and

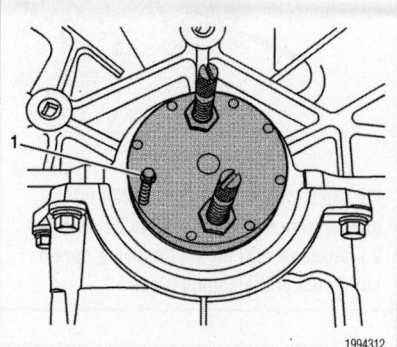

Fig. 291 Install the #2 self drill screws 1.5 in. (38 mm) long, 8 needed (1) and tighten the screws down flush to the plate

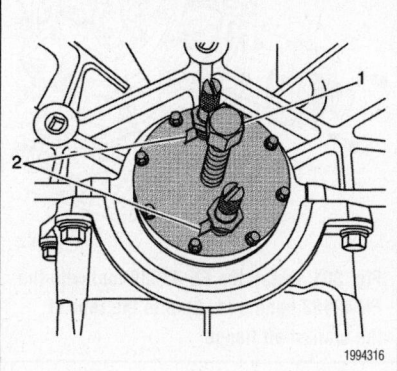

Fig. 292 Install the force screw (1) and back off both jam nuts (2). Continue to turn the force screw (1) into the removal plate in order to remove the seal from the crankshaft

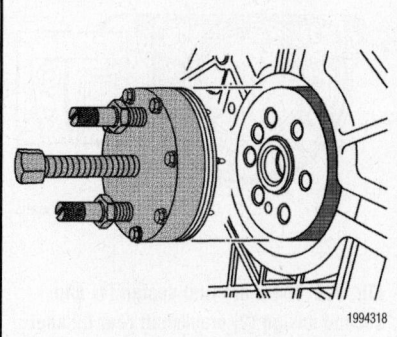

Fig. 293 Once the seal is removed from the crankshaft, remove and save all 8 screws. Discard the old seal

secure the plate with adjustment pins and jam nuts.

5. Install the #2 self drill screws 1.5 in. (38 mm) long, 8 needed (1) and tighten the screws down flush to the plate.

➡ **Before installing the force screw, apply a small amount of the extreme pressure lubricant J 23444-A, provided in the tool kit.**

6. Install the force screw (1) and back off both jam nuts (2). Continue to turn the force screw (1) into the removal plate in order to remove the seal from the crankshaft.

7. Once the seal is removed from the crankshaft, remove and save all 8 screws. Discard the old seal.

To install:

✳✳ WARNING

Do not remove the protective sleeve from the seal. The sleeve assures the seal is installed correctly and protects the seal from damage. If removed, the EN-48108 installation tool will not work.

✳✳ WARNING

Clean the crankshaft sealing surface with a clean, lint-free towel. Inspect lead-in edge of crankshaft for burrs/sharp edges that could damage the rear main oil seal. Remove burrs/sharp edges with crocus cloth before proceeding.

✳✳ WARNING

Do not remove protective nylon sleeve prior to installation. The rear main oil seal installation tool is designed to install the rear main seal with the protective sleeve in place. Never apply or use any oil, lubricants or sealing compounds on the crankshaft rear main oil seal.

➡ **Before replacement of the new design crankshaft rear main oil seal, ensure the positive crankcase ventilation (PCV) system is operating correctly.**

A new design crankshaft rear main oil seal and installation tool, the EN-48108 installer, has been released. This seal incorporates features that improve high mileage durability. Replace the crankshaft rear main oil seal with the new design rear main oil seal, GM P/N 12592195 (Canadian P/N 12592195).

8. The EN-48108 installer has a unique design to allow the technician to easily install the rear main seal squarely to the correct depth and direction. Before proceeding with installation, review the illustration to become familiar with the following components:
- Mandrel (1)
- Drive Drum (2)
- Drive Nut (3)
- Washer (4)
- Bearing (5)
9. Align the mandrel dowel pin to the dowel pin hole in the crankshaft.
10. Using a large flat-blade screwdriver, tighten the 2 mandrel screws to the crankshaft. Ensure the mandrel is snug to the crankshaft hub.

Install the rear main seal (1), with the protective nylon sleeve attached (2), onto the mandrel. The seal, if properly installed, will center on a step that protrudes from the center of the mandrel. As an error proof, the seal will fit only one way onto the mandrel.

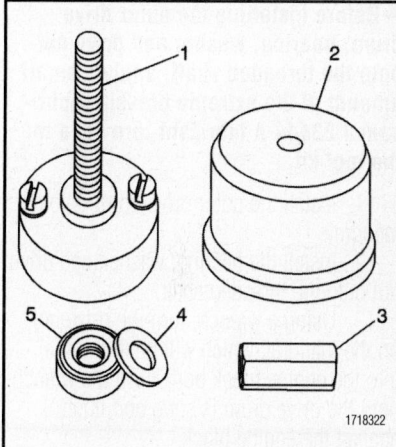

Fig. 294 Installer components: Mandrel (1), Drive Drum (2), Drive Nut (3), Washer (4), and Bearing (5)

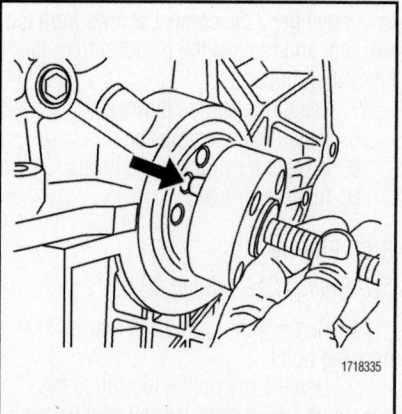

Fig. 295 Align the mandrel dowel pin to the dowel pin hole in the crankshaft

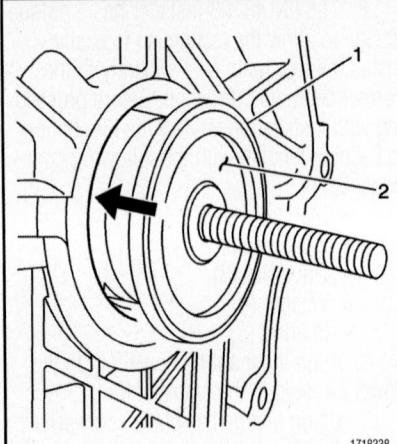

Fig. 296 Install the rear main seal (1), with the protective nylon sleeve attached (2), onto the mandrel. The seal, if properly installed, will center on a step that protrudes from the center of the mandrel. As an error proof, the seal will fit only one way onto the mandrel.

➡Before installing the outer drive drum, bearing, washer and drive nut onto the threaded shaft, apply a small amount of the extreme pressure lubricant J 23444-A lubricant, provided in the tool kit.

11. Install the outer drive drum onto the mandrel.

12. Install the bearing, washer, and drive nut onto the threaded shaft.

13. Using a wrench, turn the drive nut on the mandrel, which will push the seal into the engine block bore. Turn the wrench until the drive drum is snug and flush against the engine block.

14. Loosen and remove the drive nut, washer, bearing, and drive drum. Discard the protective nylon sleeve.

15. Verify that the seal seats properly.

16. Use a flat-blade screwdriver in order to remove the 2 attachment screws from the mandrel and remove the mandrel from the crankshaft hub.

17. Install the engine flywheel.

18. Install the transmission.

19. Inspect for proper fluid levels.

20. Inspect for leaks.

3.6L Engine

See Figures 297 through 302.

1. Remove the crankshaft rear oil seal housing bolts.

2. Use the pry points located at the edge of the crankshaft rear oil seal housing to separate the RTV sealant.

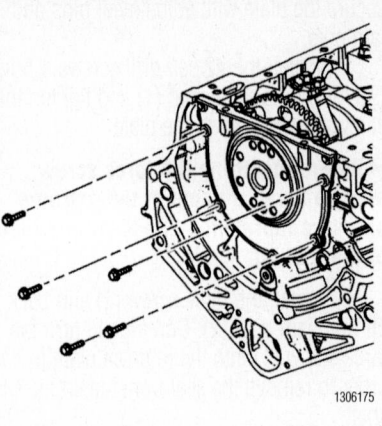

Fig. 297 Crankshaft rear oil seal housing bolts

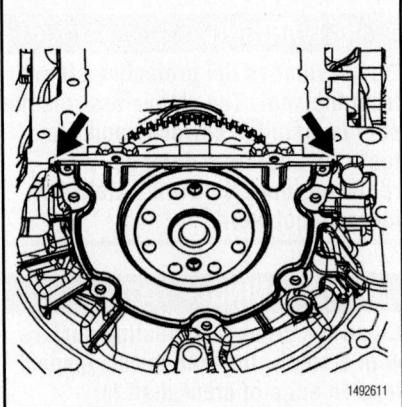

Fig. 298 Use the pry points located at the edge of the crankshaft rear oil seal housing to separate the RTV sealant

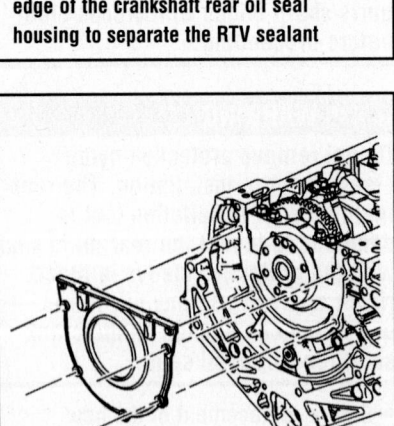

Fig. 299 Remove and discard the crankshaft rear oil seal housing

3. Remove and discard the crankshaft rear oil seal housing.

To install:

4. Install the 6 mm (0.236 in) guides from the EN-46109 pin set into the 2 crankshaft rear oil seal housing

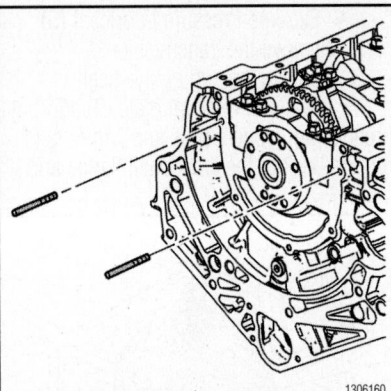

Fig. 300 Install the 6 mm (0.236 in) guides from the EN-46109 pin set into the 2 crankshaft rear oil seal housing corner bolt holes of the engine block.

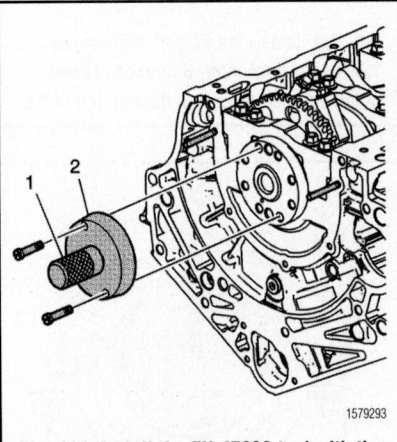

Fig. 301 Install the EN-47839 tool with the EN 42183 handle (1, 2) onto the rear of the crankshaft flange

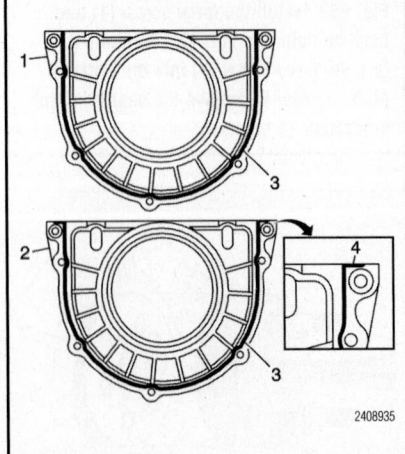

Fig. 302 There are first design (1) and second design (2) crankshaft rear oil seal housings. Second design oil seal housings include additional grooves for RTV sealant near the oil seal housing to oil pan interface (4).

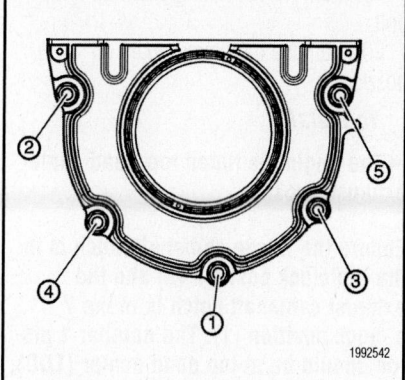

Fig. 303 Tighten the crankshaft rear oil seal housing bolts in sequence and tighten to 89 inch lbs. (10 Nm)

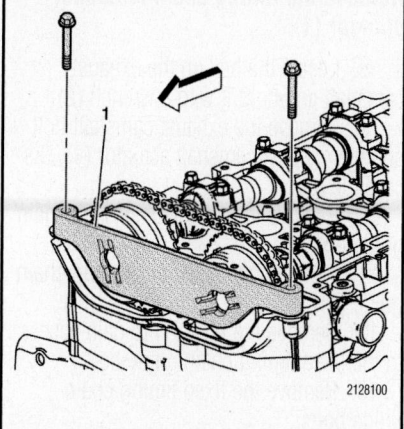

Fig. 304 Rotate the crankshaft to install the EN-48953 locking tool (1)

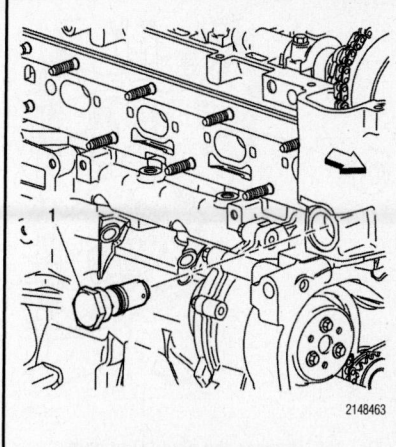

Fig. 306 Remove the timing chain tensioner plunger (1)

corner bolt holes of the engine block.

5. Install the EN-47839 tool with the EN 42183 handle (1, 2) onto the rear of the crankshaft flange.

➡There are first design (1) and second design (2) crankshaft rear oil seal housings. Second design oil seal housings include additional grooves for RTV sealant near the oil seal housing to oil pan interface (4)

6. Place a 3 mm (0.118 in) bead of RTV sealant to the NEW crankshaft rear oil seal housing as shown (3). Sealant recommendation is GM PN 12378521 (US) and 88901148 (Canada).

➡DO NOT allow any engine oil on the area where the crankshaft rear oil seal housing is to be installed.

7. Install the crankshaft rear oil seal housing to the engine block.

8. Remove the EN-46109 pin set 0.236 in. (6 mm) guides from the engine block.

9. Install the crankshaft rear oil seal housing bolts.

10. Tighten the crankshaft rear oil seal housing bolts in sequence and tighten to 89 inch lbs. (10 Nm).

11. Remove the EN-47839 tool and EN 42183 handle from the crankshaft flange.

TIMING CHAIN & SPROCKET OR TENSIONER

REMOVAL & INSTALLATION

2.4L Engine

See Figures 304 through 321.

1. Rotate the crankshaft to install the EN-48953 locking tool (1).

➡It is crucial to mark the chain and actuators. You must remove oil from the surface of the camshaft actuator and timing chain prior to marking both the actuators and the chain.

2. Install the EN-48953 locking tool onto the cylinder head and tighten to 89 inch lbs. (10 Nm). If the intake camshaft actuator is moving independent of the cam and is not locked, rotate the intake camshaft counterclockwise and the tool will hold the actuator, locking the actuator to the cam.

3. Loosen the intake camshaft actuator bolt.

4. Loosen the exhaust camshaft actuator bolt.

5. Remove the EN-48953 locking tool.

6. Remove the upper timing chain guide bolts.

7. Remove the upper timing chain guide (1).

➡Remove the timing chain tensioner to unload chain tension before removing the timing chain.

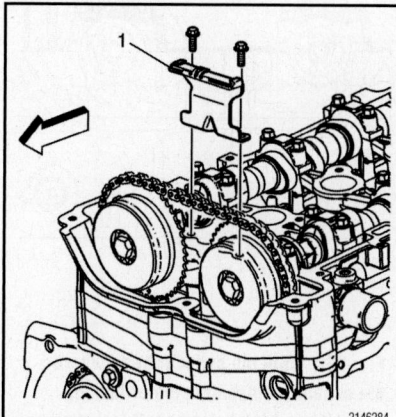

Fig. 305 Upper timing chain guide (1) and bolts

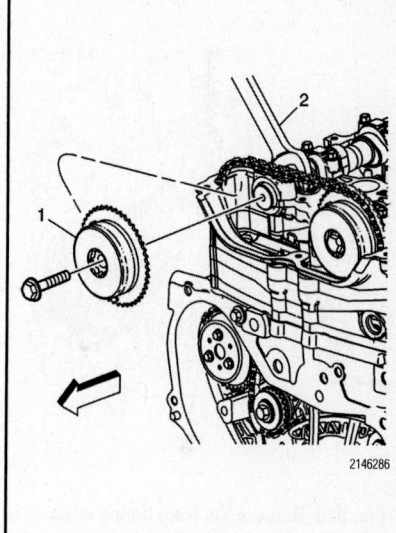

Fig. 307 Locate the hex on the exhaust camshaft and hold it with a wrench (2).

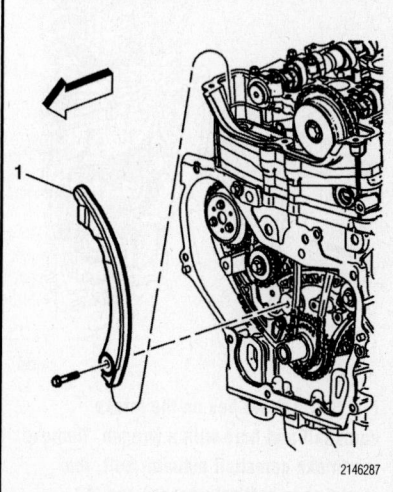

Fig. 308 Remove the adjustable timing chain bolt and guide (1).

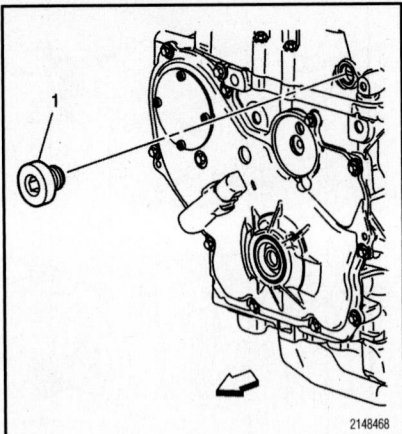

Fig. 309 Remove the plug (1) to gain access to the fixed timing chain guide bolt

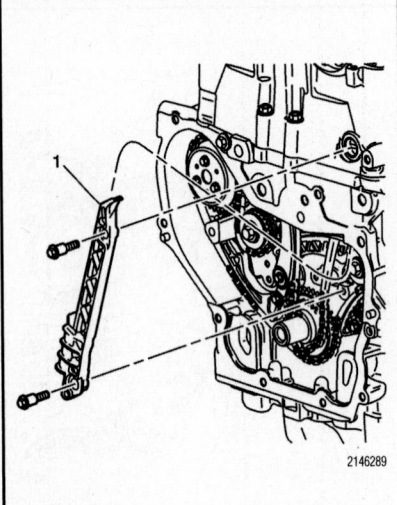

Fig. 310 Remove the fixed timing chain bolts and guide (1).

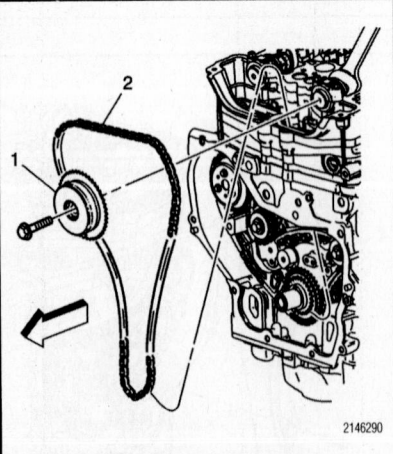

Fig. 311 Locate hex on the intake camshaft and hold with a wrench. Remove the intake camshaft actuator bolt, the intake camshaft actuator (1) and the timing chain (2) through the top of the cylinder head. Discard the bolt.

Remove the timing chain tensioner plunger (1).

8. Locate the hex on the exhaust camshaft and hold it with a wrench (2).

9. Remove the exhaust camshaft bolt and the exhaust camshaft actuator (1). Discard the bolt.

10. Remove the adjustable timing chain guide bolt.

11. Remove the adjustable timing chain guide (1).

12. Remove the plug (1) to gain access to the fixed timing chain guide bolt.

13. Remove the fixed timing chain guide bolts.

14. Remove the fixed timing chain guide (1).

15. Locate the hex on the intake camshaft and hold with a wrench.

16. Remove the intake camshaft actuator bolt, the intake camshaft actuator (1) and the timing chain (2) through the top of the cylinder head. Discard the bolt.

➡**Note the following:**

- The number 3 exhaust valves are open.
- Note the position and direction of the camshafts before removal. Mark the cylinder head in relation to the locking notches before component removal.

17. Mark the cylinder head where the exhaust camshaft actuator locking notch (1) and intake camshaft locking notch (2) are lined up with the cylinder head.

18. Remove the crankshaft sprocket (2) and friction washers (1), if equipped.

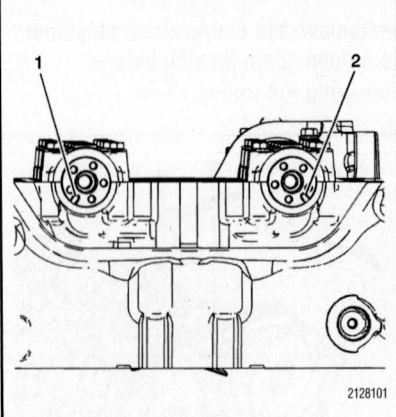

Fig. 312 Mark the cylinder head where the exhaust camshaft actuator locking notch (1) and intake camshaft locking notch (2) are lined up with the cylinder head

19. Remove the timing chain oil nozzle bolt.

20. Remove the timing chain oil nozzle (1).

To install:

➡**The engine is timed top-dead center exhaust stroke.**

Ensure the intake camshaft notch is in the 5 o'clock position (2) and the exhaust camshaft notch is in the 7 o'clock position (1). The number 1 piston should be at top dead center (TDC), crankshaft key at 12 o'clock.

21. Install a friction washer (1), if equipped.

22. Install the timing chain drive sprocket (3) to the crankshaft with the tim-

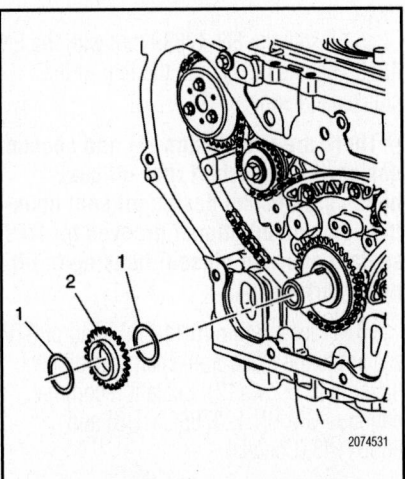

Fig. 313 Remove the crankshaft sprocket (2) and friction washers (1), if equipped

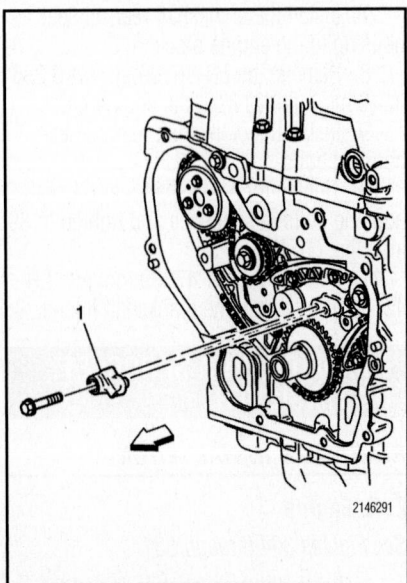

Fig. 314 Remove the timing chain oil nozzle (1) and bolt

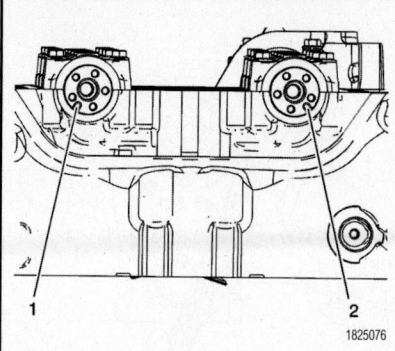

Fig. 315 Ensure the intake camshaft notch is in the 5 o'clock position (2) and the exhaust camshaft notch is in the 7 o'clock position (1). The number 1 piston should be at top dead center (TDC), crankshaft key at 12 o'clock.

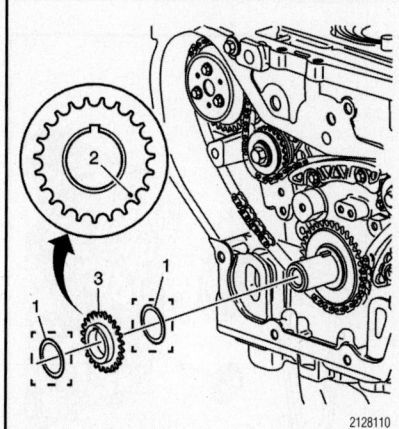

Fig. 316 Install a friction washer (1), if equipped.

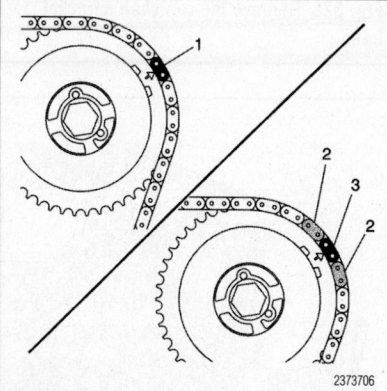

Fig. 317 There are two possible chain configurations for the engine. Both configurations use a unique chain link to line up with the intake camshaft actuator timing mark. The first design uses a unique link color (1). The second design uses a black anodized link (3) with uniquely colored links on either side (2).

ing mark (2) in the 5 o'clock position and the front of the sprocket facing out.

23. Install a second friction washer (1), if equipped.

➡**There are two possible chain configurations for the engine. Both configurations use a unique chain link to line up with the intake camshaft actuator timing mark. The first design uses a unique link color (1).**

24. The second design uses a black anodized link (3) with uniquely colored links on either side (2).

25. Orient the chain so that the colored links are visible.

26. Determine the configuration of the timing chain.

27. For the 1st design timing chain, assemble the intake camshaft actuator into the timing chain with the timing mark lined up with the uniquely colored link (1).

28. For the 2nd design timing chain, assemble the intake camshaft actuator into the timing chain with the timing mark lined up with the black anodized timing link (3) that has uniquely colored links on either side (2).

29. Lower the timing chain through the opening in the cylinder head. Use care to ensure that the chain goes around both sides of the cylinder block bosses (1, 2).

30. Install the intake camshaft actuator onto the intake camshaft while aligning the dowel pin into the camshaft slot.

➡**Always use NEW actuator bolts.**

31. Hand-tighten the new intake camshaft actuator bolt.

32. Route the timing chain around the crankshaft sprocket and line up the colored link (1) with the timing mark on the crankshaft sprocket, in approximately the 5 o'clock position.

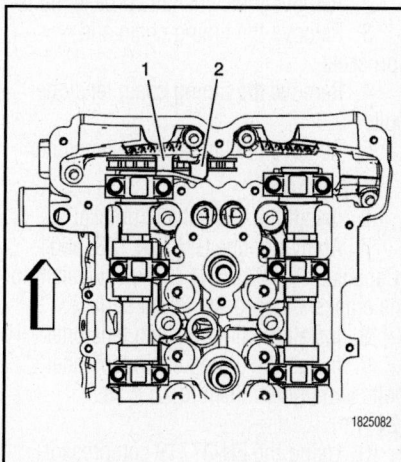

Fig. 318 Cylinder block bosses (1, 2)

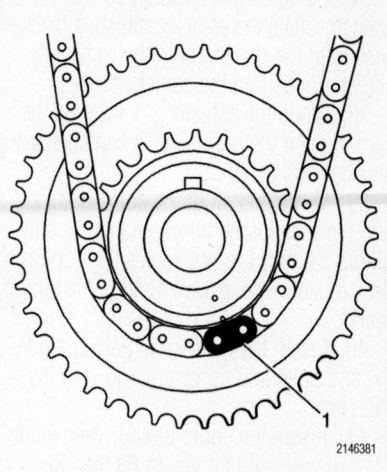

Fig. 319 Route the timing chain around the crankshaft sprocket and line up the colored link (1) with the timing mark on the crankshaft sprocket, in approximately the 5 o'clock position

33. Rotate the crankshaft clockwise to remove all chain slack. Do not rotate the intake camshaft.

34. Install the adjustable timing chain guide (1) down through the opening in the cylinder head and install the adjustable timing chain bolt and tighten to 89 inch lbs. (10 Nm).

35. Install the exhaust camshaft actuator (1) into the timing chain with the timing mark lined up with the colored link.

➡**Always install NEW actuator bolts.**

36. Install the exhaust camshaft actuator (1) onto the exhaust camshaft, aligning the dowel pin into the camshaft slot.

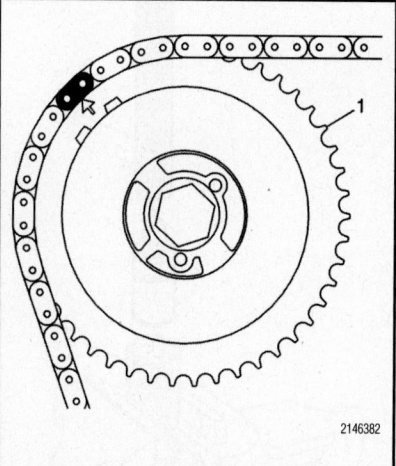

Fig. 320 Install the exhaust camshaft actuator (1) onto the exhaust camshaft, aligning the dowel pin into the camshaft slot

37. Using a 23–24 mm open end wrench, rotate the exhaust camshaft clockwise until the dowel pin in the camshaft actuator goes into the camshaft slot.

38. When the actuator (1) seats on the cam, tighten the new exhaust camshaft actuator bolt Hand-tight.

39. Verify that all of the colored links and the appropriate timing marks are still aligned. If they are not, repeat the portion of the procedure necessary to align the timing marks.

40. Install the fixed timing chain guide (1) and bolts and tighten to 106 inch lbs. (12 Nm).

41. Install the upper timing chain guide (1) and bolts and tighten to 89 inch lbs. (10 Nm).

42. Reset the timing chain tensioner by performing the following steps:

    a. Remove the snap ring.

    b. Remove the piston assembly from the body of the timing chain tensioner.

    c. Install the EN-45027-2 tensioner (2) into a vise.

    d. Install the notch end of the piston assembly into the EN-45027-2 tensioner (2).

    e. Using the EN-45027-1 tensioner (1), turn the ratchet cylinder into the piston.

    f. Reinstall the piston assembly into the body of the tensioner.

    g. Install the snap ring.

43. Inspect the timing chain tensioner seal for damage. If it is damaged, replace the seal.

44. Inspect to ensure all dirt and debris is removed from the timing chain tensioner threaded hole in the cylinder head.

➡ **Ensure the timing chain tensioner seal is centered throughout the torque procedure to eliminate the possibility of an oil leak.**

45. Install the timing chain tensioner assembly and tighten to 55 ft. lbs. (75 Nm).

➡ **The timing chain tensioner is released by compressing it 0.079 in. (2 mm), which will release the locking mechanism in the ratchet.**

46. The crankshaft balancer must be installed in order to release the tensioner. Install the EN-48953 locking tool and tighten the bolts into the cylinder head to 89 inch lbs. (10 Nm).

47. Using a torque wrench, tighten the intake camshaft actuator bolt to 22 ft. lbs. (30 Nm), plus 100 degrees using the EN 45059 meter.

48. Using a torque wrench, tighten the exhaust camshaft actuator bolt to 22 ft. lbs. (30 Nm), plus 100 degrees using the EN 45059 meter.

49. Remove the EN-48953 locking tool.

50. Install the timing chain oiling nozzle and tighten the bolt to 89 inch lbs. (10 Nm).

51. Apply sealant to the thread of the timing chain guide bolt access hole plug. GM recommends PN 12345382 (US) and 10953489 (Canada).

52. Install the timing chain guide bolt access hole plug and tighten it to 66 ft. lbs. (90 Nm).

3.5L & 3.9L Engines

See Figures 322 through 325.

1. Using the EN-47719 fully collapse the tensioner and place the tensioner retaining pin into the retaining hole (1).

2. Remove the camshaft sprocket bolts.

3. Remove the timing chain and sprockets.

4. Remove the timing chain tensioner bolts.

5. Remove the timing chain tensioner.

To install:

6. Install the crankshaft sprocket.

7. Apply prelube GM P/N 12345501 (Canadian P/N 992704) or the equivalent to the crankshaft sprocket thrust surface.

8. Install the timing chain tensioner.

9. Install the timing chain tensioner bolts and tighten them to 15 ft. lbs. (21 Nm).

10. Using the EN-47719 compressor, fully collapse the tensioner, and place the

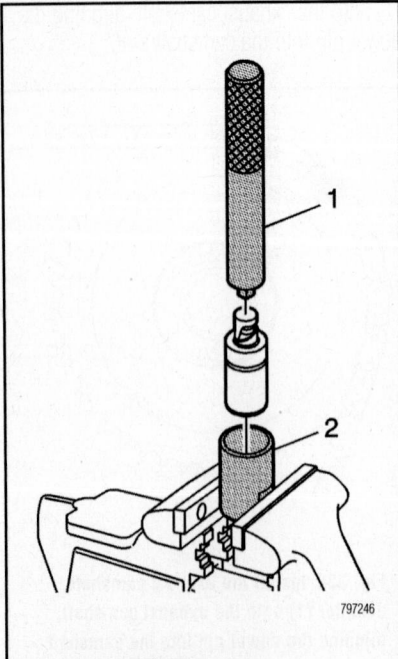

Fig. 321 EN-45027 tensioner

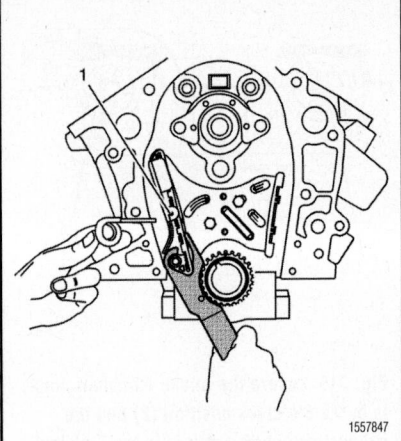

Fig. 322 Using the EN-47719 fully collapse the tensioner and place the tensioner retaining pin into the retaining hole (1).

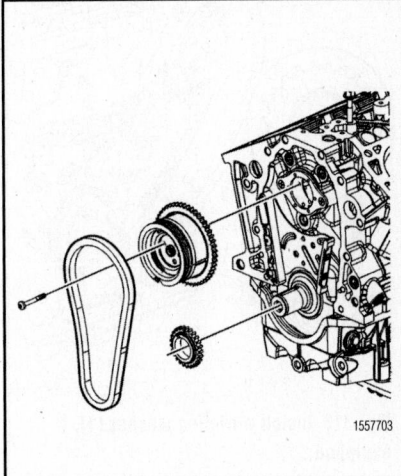

Fig. 323 Remove the camshaft sprocket bolts

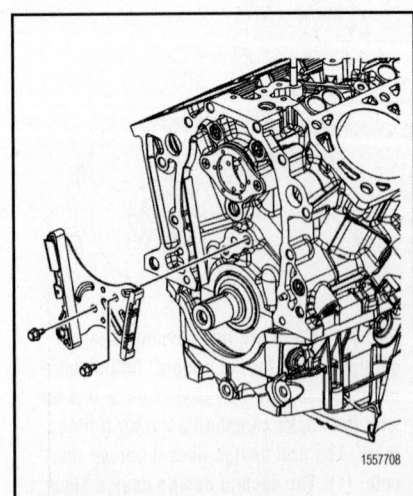

Fig. 324 Remove the timing chain tensioner bolts.

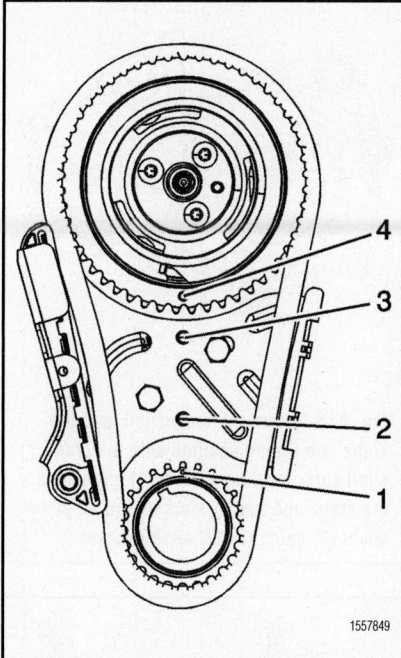

Fig. 325 Align the crankshaft timing mark (1) to the timing mark on the bottom of the timing chain tensioner (2)

tensioner retaining pin into the retaining hole.

➡**Always install a NEW camshaft position actuator filter, located in pilot nose of camshaft, anytime the camshaft position actuator is removed or installed.**

11. Align the crankshaft timing mark (1) to the timing mark on the bottom of the timing chain tensioner (2).

12. Hold the camshaft sprocket with the timing chain hanging down and install the timing chain to the crankshaft gear.

13. Align the timing mark on the camshaft gear (4) with the timing mark on top of the timing chain tensioner (3).

14. Align the dowel in the camshaft position actuator with the dowel hole in the camshaft.

✳✳ WARNING

Use only a Torx Plus® Bit when removing or installing the camshaft position actuator fasteners. The Torx Plus® design differs from typical Torx® fastener. Use of a standard Torx® bit on Torx Plus® fasteners may result in a rounded out fastener head or incorrect faster torque.

➡**DO NOT use any type of threadlocking compound on the camshaft position actuator mounting bolts. Usage of a threadlocking compound on the threads could lead to contamination of the**

camshaft position actuator, possibly resulting in potential damage to the actuator.

15. Draw the camshaft sprocket onto the camshaft using the mounting bolts, and tighten them to 12 ft. lbs. (16 Nm).

16. Remove the tensioner retaining pin.

17. Coat the crankshaft and camshaft sprocket with engine oil.

3.6L Engine

Primary Camshaft Intermediate Drive Chain

See Figures 326 through 330.

1. Remove the primary camshaft drive chain.

To install:

➡**Ensure that the crankshaft is in the stage one timing drive assembly position.**

2. Install the primary camshaft drive chain.

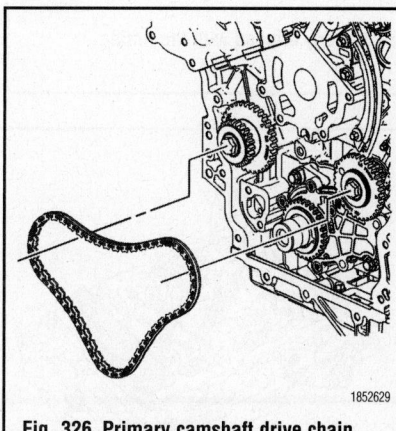

Fig. 326 Primary camshaft drive chain

Fig. 327 Wrap the primary camshaft drive chain around the large sprockets of each camshaft intermediate drive chain idler and the crankshaft sprocket

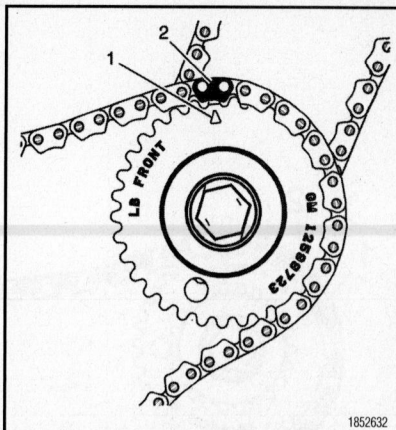

Fig. 328 The left camshaft intermediate drive chain idler timing mark (1) will align with a timing camshaft drive chain link (2)

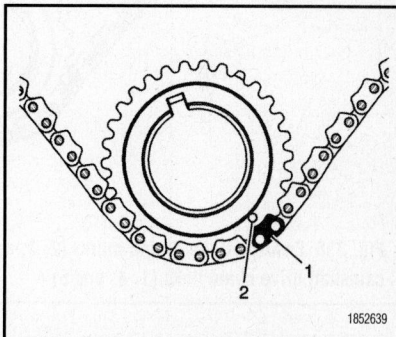

Fig. 329 The crankshaft sprocket timing mark (2) will align with a timing camshaft drive chain link (1)

3. Wrap the primary camshaft drive chain around the large sprockets of each camshaft intermediate drive chain idler and the crankshaft sprocket.

4. The left camshaft intermediate drive chain idler timing mark (1) will align with a timing camshaft drive chain link (2).

5. The right camshaft intermediate drive chain idler timing mark (2) will align with a timing camshaft drive chain link (1).

6. The crankshaft sprocket timing mark (2) will align with a timing camshaft drive chain link (1).

7. Ensure all the timing marks (2, 3, and 6) are properly aligned with the timing camshaft drive chain links (1, 4, and 5).

Secondary Camshaft Intermediate Drive Chain—Left Side

See Figures 331 through 335.

1. Remove the left secondary camshaft drive chain from the left camshaft position actuators and the left camshaft intermediate drive chain idler sprocket.

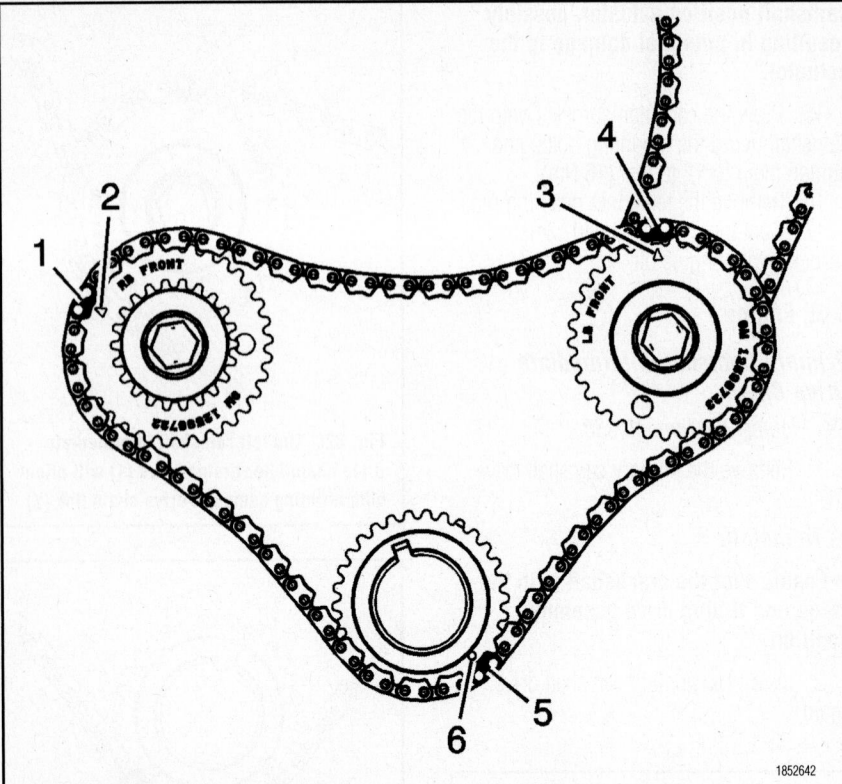

Fig. 330 Ensure all the timing marks (2, 3, and 6) are properly aligned with the timing camshaft drive chain links (1, 4, and 5)

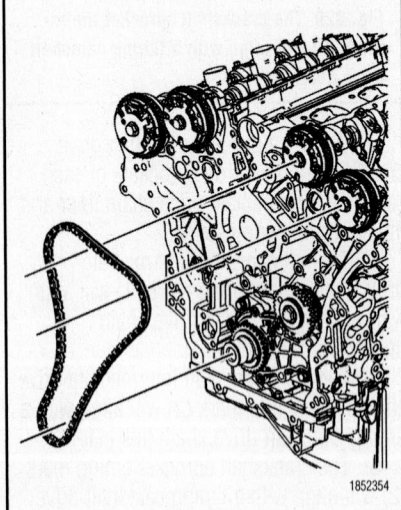

Fig. 331 Remove the left secondary camshaft drive chain from the left camshaft position actuators and the left camshaft intermediate drive chain idler sprocket

To install:

➡There should be no need to rotate the camshaft more than 10 degrees. Using the hex cast into the camshaft, rotate the camshaft in order to install the EN 48383 tools.

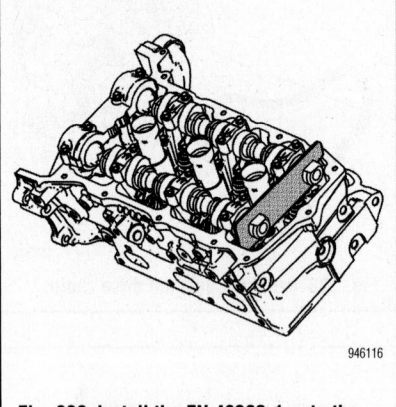

Fig. 332 Install the EN 48383-1 onto the rear of the left camshafts

2. Install the EN 48383-1 onto the rear of the left camshafts.

➡All camshafts must be locked in place before installation of any camshaft drive chains.

3. Ensure that the EN 48383-1 is fully seated onto the camshafts.

4. Ensure the crankshaft is in the stage one timing position with the crankshaft sprocket timing mark (1) aligned to the stage one timing mark on the oil pump cover (2) using the EN 48589 socket. Refer to Timing Chain Alignment Diagrams in this section.

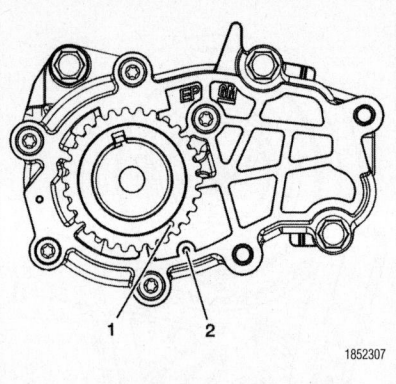

Fig. 333 Ensure the crankshaft is in the stage one timing position with the crankshaft sprocket timing mark (1) aligned to the stage one timing mark on the oil pump cover (2) using the EN 48589 socket

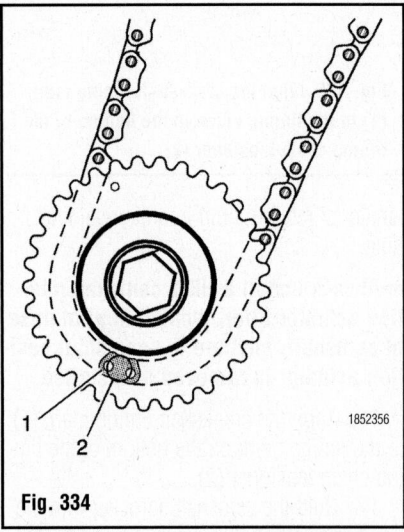

Fig. 334

5. Install the left secondary camshaft drive chain.

6. Place the left secondary camshaft drive chain around the inner sprocket of the left camshaft intermediate drive chain idler with the timing camshaft drive chain link (1) aligned to the alignment access hole (2) made in the left camshaft intermediate drive chain idler outer sprocket.

7. Wrap the secondary camshaft drive chain around both left actuator drive sprockets.

8. Ensure there are 10 links (1) between the timing camshaft drive chain links for the camshaft position actuator sprockets.

9. Align the left exhaust camshaft position actuator sprocket alignment circle mark with the timing camshaft drive chain link.

10. Align the left intake camshaft position actuator sprocket alignment circle mark with the timing camshaft drive chain link.

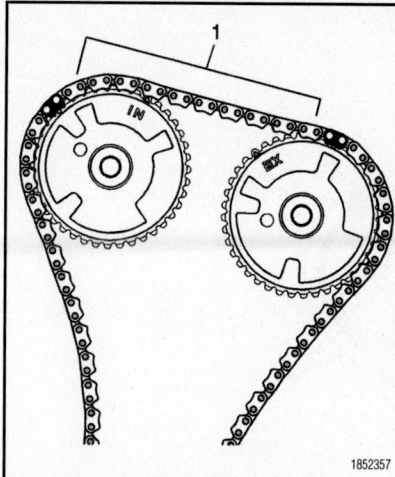

Fig. 335 Ensure there are 10 links (1) between the timing camshaft drive chain links for the camshaft position actuator sprockets

Secondary Camshaft Intermediate Drive Chain—Right Side

See Figures 337 through 339.

1. Remove the right secondary camshaft drive chain from the right camshaft position actuators and the right camshaft intermediate drive chain idler sprocket.

To install:

2. Ensure that the crankshaft is in the stage 2 timing drive assembly position (1).
3. Install the right secondary camshaft drive chain.
4. Place the secondary camshaft drive chain around the right camshaft intermediate drive chain idler outer sprocket, aligning

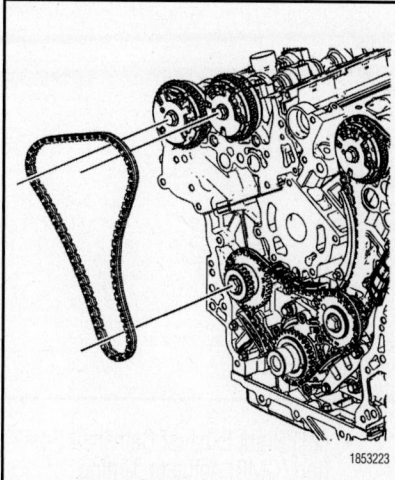

Fig. 336 Remove the right secondary camshaft drive chain from the right camshaft position actuators and the right camshaft intermediate drive chain idler sprocket

Fig. 337 Ensure that the crankshaft is in the stage 2 timing drive assembly position (1).

the timing camshaft drive chain link with the alignment access hole made in the right camshaft intermediate drive chain idler inner sprocket. (See left side illustration, it is similar.)

5. Wrap the secondary camshaft drive chain around both right actuator drive sprockets.

6. Ensure there are 10 links between the timing camshaft drive chain links for the camshaft position actuator sprockets. (See left side illustration, it is similar.)

7. Align the right exhaust camshaft position actuator sprocket alignment triangle mark with the timing camshaft drive

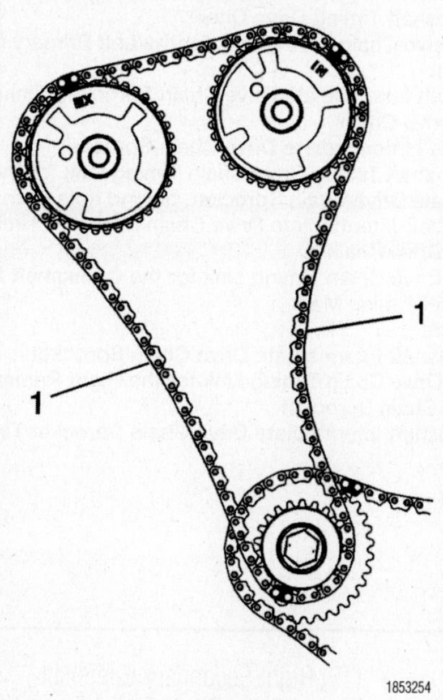

Fig. 338 There will be 22 links (1) between the right camshaft intermediate drive chain idler timing camshaft drive chain link and each right camshaft position actuator sprocket timing camshaft drive chain link

chain link. (See left side illustration, it is similar.)

8. Align the right intake camshaft position actuator sprocket alignment triangle mark with the timing camshaft drive chain link. (See left side illustration, it is similar.)

There will be 22 links (1) between the right camshaft intermediate drive chain idler timing camshaft drive chain link and each right camshaft position actuator sprocket timing camshaft drive chain link.

Timing Chain Alignment Diagrams

See Figures 339 and 340.

Stage one:
• (1) Left Intake Camshaft Position (CMP) Actuator Timing Mark—Circle
• (2) Left Intake Secondary Camshaft Timing Drive Chain Timing Link
• (3) Left Exhaust Secondary Camshaft Timing Drive Chain Timing Link
• (4) Left Exhaust Camshaft Position (CMP) Actuator Timing Mark—Circle

Stage two:
• (1) Left Intake Camshaft Position (CMP) Actuator Timing Mark—Circle
• (2) Left Intake Secondary Camshaft Timing Drive Chain Timing Link
• (3) Left Exhaust Secondary Camshaft Timing Drive Chain Timing Link
• (4) Left Exhaust Camshaft Position (CMP) Actuator Timing Mark—Circle
• (5) Left Secondary Camshaft Timing Drive Chain
• (6) Primary Camshaft Drive Chain Timing Link for the Left Primary Camshaft Intermediate Drive Chain Sprocket
• (7) Left Primary Camshaft Intermediate Drive Chain Sprocket Timing Mark for the Primary Camshaft Drive Chain
• (8) Left Primary Camshaft Intermediate Drive Chain Sprocket
• (9) Left Secondary Camshaft Timing Drive Chain Timing Link for the Left Primary Camshaft Intermediate Drive Chain Sprocket, behind hole in sprocket
• (10) Left Primary Camshaft Intermediate Drive Chain Sprocket Timing Window
• (11) Primary Camshaft Drive Chain
• (12) Primary Camshaft Drive Chain Timing Link for the Crankshaft Sprocket
• (13) Crankshaft Sprocket Timing Mark
• (14) Crankshaft Sprocket
• (15) Right Primary Camshaft Intermediate Drive Chain Sprocket
• (16) Primary Camshaft Drive Chain Timing Link for the Right Primary Camshaft Intermediate Drive Chain Sprocket

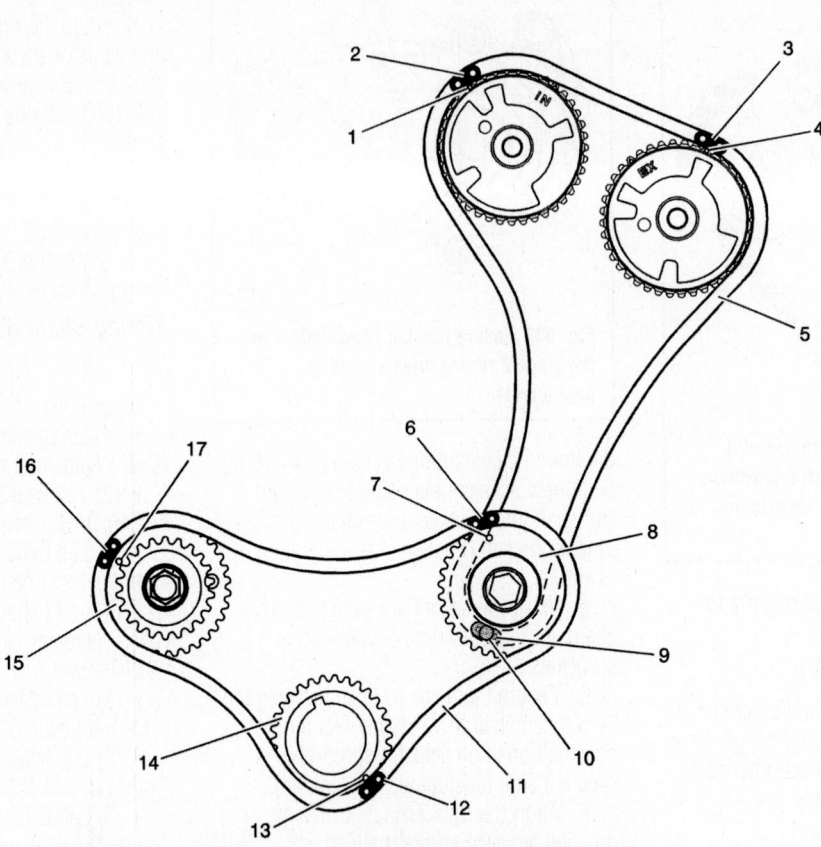

1. Left Intake Camshaft Position (CMP) Actuator Timing Mark - Circle
2. Left Intake Secondary Camshaft Timing Drive Chain Timing Link
3. Left Exhaust Secondary Camshaft Timing Drive Chain Timing Link
4. Left Exhaust Camshaft Position (CMP) Actuator Timing Mark - Circle
5. Left Secondary Camshaft Timing Drive Chain
6. Primary Camshaft Drive Chain Timing Link for the Left Primary Camshaft Intermediate Drive Chain Sprocket
7. Left Primary Camshaft Intermediate Drive Chain Sprocket Timing Mark for the Primary Camshaft Drive Chain
8. Left Primary Camshaft Intermediate Drive Chain Sprocket
9. Left Secondary Camshaft Timing Drive Chain Timing Link for the Left Primary Camshaft Intermediate Drive Chain Sprocket, behind hole in sprocket
10. Left Primary Camshaft Intermediate Drive Chain Sprocket Timing Window
11. Primary Camshaft Drive Chain
12. Primary Camshaft Drive Chain Timing Link for the Crankshaft Sprocket
13. Crankshaft Sprocket Timing Mark
14. Crankshaft Sprocket
15. Right Primary Camshaft Intermediate Drive Chain Sprocket
16. Primary Camshaft Drive Chain Timing Link for the Right Primary Camshaft Intermediate Drive Chain Sprocket
17. Right Primary Camshaft Intermediate Drive Chain Sprocket Timing Mark

1827967

Fig. 339 Stage one

- (17) Right Primary Camshaft Intermediate Drive Chain Sprocket Timing Mark for the Primary Camshaft Drive Chain
- (18) Right Primary Camshaft Intermediate Drive Chain Sprocket Timing Mark/Window for the Right Secondary Camshaft Timing Drive Chain

- (19) Right Secondary Camshaft Timing Drive Chain Timing Link for the Right Primary Camshaft Intermediate Drive Chain Sprocket
- (20) Right Secondary Camshaft Timing Drive Chain

- (21) Right Exhaust Camshaft Position (CMP) Actuator Timing Mark—Triangle
- (22) Right Exhaust Secondary Camshaft Timing Drive Chain Timing Link
- (23) Right Intake Secondary Camshaft Timing Drive Chain Timing Link

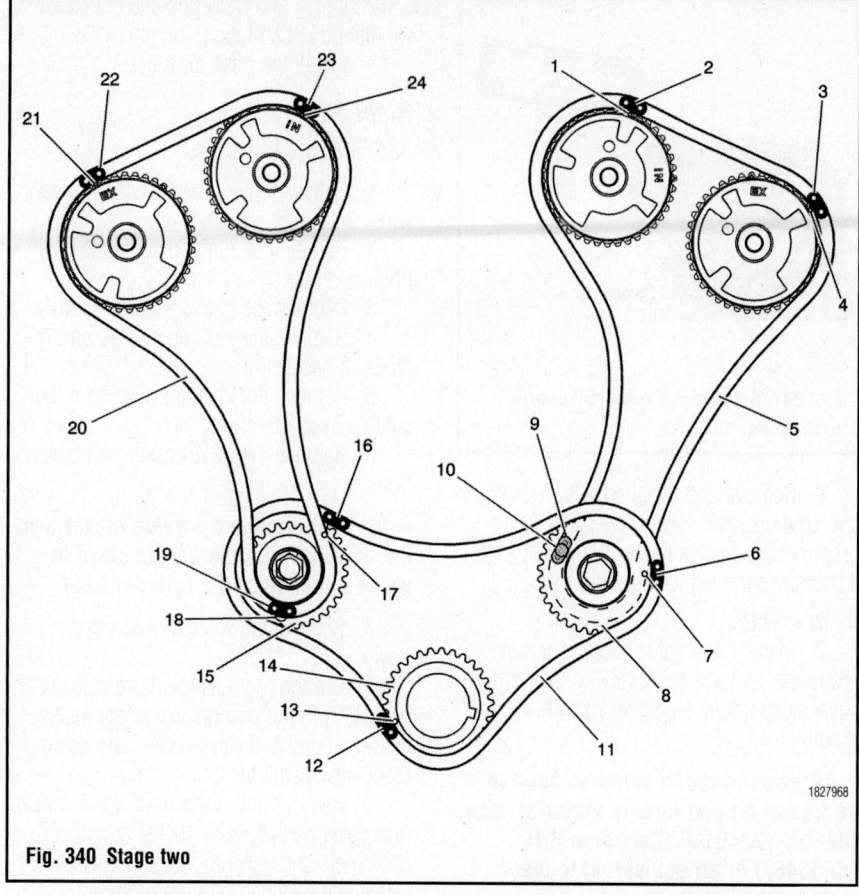

Fig. 340 Stage two

- (24) Right Intake Camshaft Position (CMP) Actuator Timing Mark—Triangle

VALVE COVER/ CAMSHAFT COVER

REMOVAL & INSTALLATION

2.4L Engine

See Figures 341 through 345.

1. Remove the camshaft cover ground strap (1).

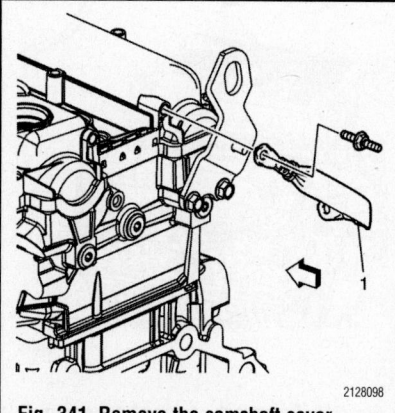

Fig. 341 Remove the camshaft cover ground strap (1)

2. Remove the front lift bracket.
3. Remove the rear lift bracket (1).
4. Remove the bolt and coil (1).
5. Remove the camshaft position actuator solenoid valve bolts.
6. Remove the camshaft position actuator solenoid valves (2).
7. Remove the camshaft cover assembly.
8. Remove and discard the camshaft cover gasket, camshaft cover grommets, and camshaft cover bolts if they are serviced with the grommet.

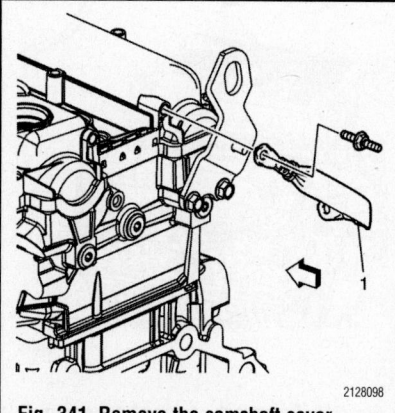

Fig. 342 Remove the front lift bracket

To install:

9. Install NEW camshaft cover grommets and camshaft cover bolts if they are serviced with the grommet.
10. Assemble the camshaft cover and a NEW gasket. Ensure that the gasket is

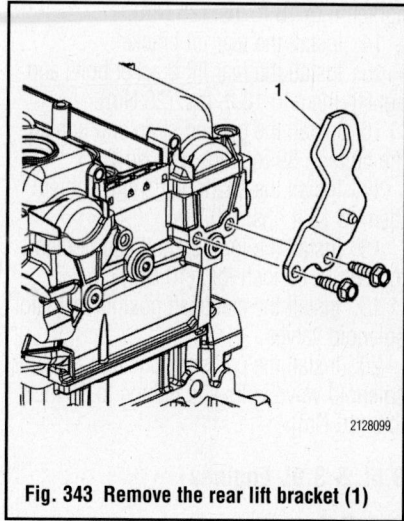

Fig. 343 Remove the rear lift bracket (1)

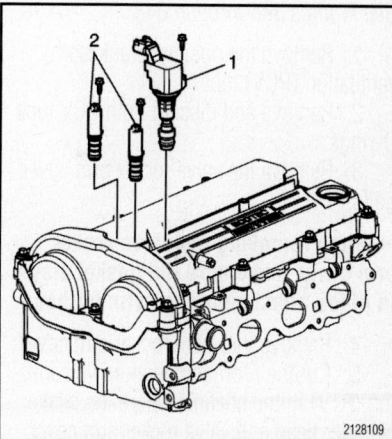

Fig. 344 Remove the bolt and coil (1) and the camshaft position actuator solenoid valves (2)

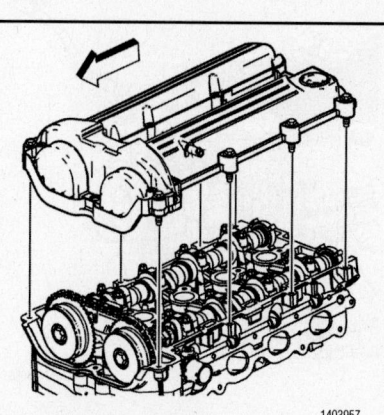

Fig. 345 Remove the camshaft cover assembly

located in the retaining groove in the camshaft cover.

11. Install the cover on the cylinder head and hand start the bolts. Tighten the bolts to 89 inch lbs. (10 Nm).

12. Install the front lift bracket.

13. Install the front lift bracket bolt and tighten it to 18 ft. lbs. (25 Nm).

14. Install the rear lift bracket.

15. Install the rear lift bracket bolts and tighten them to 18 ft. lbs. (25 Nm).

16. Install the ground strap and tighten the bolts to 89 inch lbs. (10 Nm).

17. Install the spark plugs and tighten them to 15 ft. lbs. (20 Nm).

18. Install the ignition coil and tighten the bolt to 89 inch lbs. (10 Nm).

19. Install the camshaft position actuator solenoid valves.

20. Install the camshaft position actuator solenoid valve bolts and tighten to 89 inch lbs. (10 Nm).

3.5L & 3.9L Engines

Left Side

See Figures 346 through 348.

1. Remove the positive crankcase ventilation (PCV) tube.

2. Remove and discard both PCV tube O-rings.

3. Remove the valve rocker arm cover bolts.

➡ **When removing the valve rocker arm cover make sure the gasket stays in place attached to the cylinder head.**

4. Remove the valve rocker arm cover.

5. Cut the room temperature vulcanizing (RTV) in the channel where the intake, cylinder head and valve rocker arm cover meet with a suitable tool.

Fig. 347 Remove the valve rocker arm cover bolts

6. Remove and discard the valve rocker arm cover gasket, valve rocker arm cover grommets and valve rocker arm cover bolts if they are serviced with the grommet.

To install:

7. Install NEW valve rocker arm cover grommets and use NEW valve rocker arm cover bolts if they are serviced with the grommet.

➡ **All gasket-mating surfaces need to be free of oil and foreign material. Use GM P/N 12346139 (Canadian P/N 10953463) or an equivalent to clean surfaces.**

8. Install the valve rocker arm cover gasket into the valve rocker arm cover.

9. Apply sealer GM P/N 12378521 (Canadian P/N 88901148) or an equivalent to the surfaces where the cylinder head and intake manifold meet (1).

10. Install the valve rocker arm cover.

11. Install the valve rocker arm cover bolts, if necessary. Tighten the valve rocker arm cover bolts to 89 inch lbs. (10 Nm).

12. Install two NEW positive crankcase ventilation (PCV) tube O-rings.

13. Install the fresh air tube.

Right Side

See Figures 348 and 349.

1. Remove any remaining spark plug wires from their retainers.

2. Remove the ignition coil assembly bolts and nuts.

3. Remove the ignition coil assembly.

4. Remove the ignition coil assembly studs, if necessary.

5. Remove the fresh air tube from the valve rocker arm cover.

6. Remove the valve rocker arm cover bolts.

➡ **When removing the valve rocker arm cover make sure the gasket stays in place attached to the cylinder head.**

7. Remove the valve rocker arm cover.

8. Cut the room temperature vulcanizing (RTV) in the channel where the intake, cylinder head and valve rocker arm cover meet with a suitable tool.

9. Remove and discard the valve rocker arm cover gasket, valve rocker arm cover grommets and valve rocker arm cover bolts if they are serviced with the grommet.

To install:

10. Install NEW valve rocker arm cover grommets and use NEW valve rocker arm cover bolts if they are serviced with the grommet.

➡ **All gasket-mating surfaces need to be free of oil and foreign material. Use GM P/N 12346139 (Canadian P/N 10953463) or an equivalent to clean surfaces.**

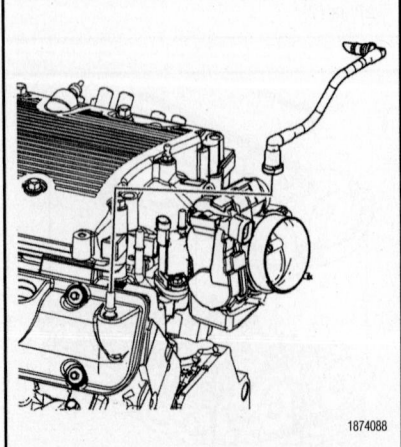

Fig. 346 Remove the positive crankcase ventilation (PCV) tube

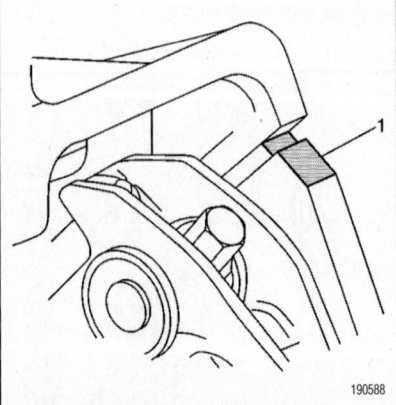

Fig. 348 Apply sealer GM P/N 12378521 (Canadian P/N 88901148) or an equivalent to the surfaces where the cylinder head and intake manifold meet (1)

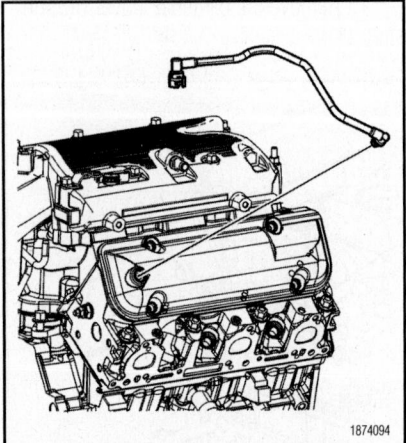

Fig. 349 Remove the fresh air tube from the valve rocker arm cover

11. Install the valve rocker arm cover gasket into the valve rocker arm cover.

12. Apply sealer GM P/N 12378521 (Canadian P/N 88901148) or equivalent to the surfaces where the cylinder head and intake manifold meet (see illustration for left side installation).

13. Install the valve rocker arm cover.

14. Install the valve rocker arm cover bolts, if necessary. Tighten the valve rocker arm cover bolts to 89 inch lbs. (10 Nm).

15. Install the fresh air tube into the valve rocker arm cover.

16. Install the ignition coil assembly studs, if necessary. Tighten the ignition coil assembly studs to 18 ft. lbs. (25 Nm).

17. Install the ignition coil assembly.

18. Install the ignition coil assembly bolts and nuts. Tighten the ignition coil assembly bolts and nuts to 18 ft. lbs. (25 Nm).

3.6L Engine

Left Side

See Figures 350 through 354.

1. Remove the ignition coil bolts.
2. Remove the ignition coils.
3. Remove the left camshaft cover bolts.
4. Remove and discard the camshaft cover grommets and camshaft cover bolts if they are serviced with the grommet.
5. Remove the left camshaft cover from the left cylinder head.

To install:

6. Install the EN 46101 guide onto the spark plug tubes of the left cylinder head.

7. Install the NEW camshaft cover bolt grommets prior to installing the camshaft cover bolts.

8. Wipe the camshaft cover sealing surface on the left cylinder head with a clean, lint-free cloth.

Fig. 350 Remove the left camshaft cover bolts

9. Place a bead 8 mm (0.3150 in) in diameter by 4 mm (0.1575 in) in height of RTV sealant, GM P/N 12378521 (Canadian P/N 88901148) or equivalent, on the engine front cover split lines (1).

10. Place the left camshaft cover into position onto the left cylinder head.

11. Loosely install the left camshaft cover bolts.

12. Tighten the left camshaft cover bolts in the sequence shown to 89 inch lbs. (10 Nm).

Fig. 351 Install the EN 46101 guide onto the spark plug tubes of the left cylinder head

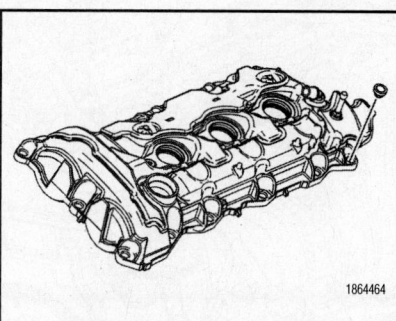

Fig. 352 Install the NEW camshaft cover bolt grommets prior to installing the camshaft cover bolts

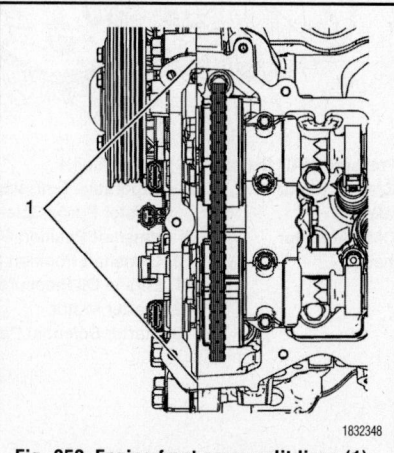

Fig. 353 Engine front cover split lines (1)

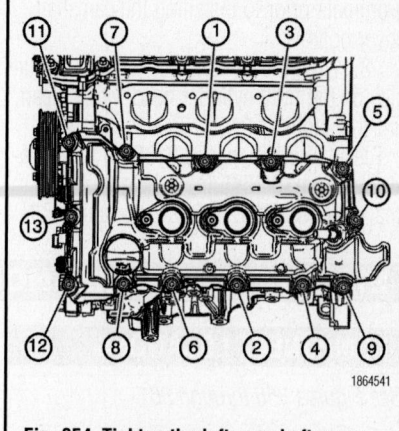

Fig. 354 Tighten the left camshaft cover bolts in the sequence shown

13. Remove the EN 46101 guide from the spark plug tubes of the left cylinder head.

14. Install the NEW spark plugs into the left cylinder head and tighten to 13 ft. lbs. (18 Nm).

15. Install the ignition coils.

16. Install the ignition coil bolts and tighten to 89 inch lbs. (10 Nm).

Right Side

See Figures 352 through 355.

See images for left side, they are similar

1. Remove the ignition coil bolts.
2. Remove the ignition coils.
3. Remove the right camshaft cover bolts.
4. Remove and discard the camshaft cover grommets and camshaft cover bolts if they are serviced with the grommet.
5. Remove the right camshaft cover from the right cylinder head.

To install:

6. Install the EN-46101 guide onto the spark plug tubes of the right cylinder head.

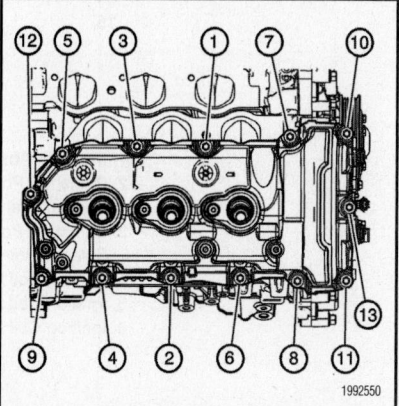

Fig. 355 Tighten the right camshaft cover bolts in the sequence shown

7. Install the NEW camshaft cover bolt grommets prior to installing the camshaft cover bolts.

8. Wipe the camshaft cover sealing surface on the right cylinder head with a clean, lint-free cloth.

Place a bead 8 mm (0.3150 in) in diameter by 4 mm (0.1575 in) in height of RTV sealant, GM P/N 12378521 (Canadian P/N 88901148) or equivalent, on the engine front cover split lines.

9. Loosely install the right camshaft cover bolts.

10. Tighten the right camshaft cover bolts in the sequence shown.

   a. Tighten the right camshaft cover bolts to 89 inch lbs. (10 Nm).

   b. Tighten the right camshaft cover bolts a second pass to 89 inch lbs. (10 Nm).

VALVE LASH

ADJUSTMENT

1. Hydraulic lash adjusters are used on all engines and no adjustment is necessary.

ENGINE PERFORMANCE & EMISSION CONTROLS

COMPONENT LOCATIONS

See Figures 356 through 361.

Refer to the accompanying illustrations.

CAMSHAFT POSITION (CMP) SENSOR

LOCATION

2.4L Exhaust: In the engine compartment on the upper left rear of the engine, near the camshaft cover.

2.4L Intake: In the engine compartment on the upper front of the engine, near the camshaft cover.

3.5L and 3.9L: In the right side of the engine compartment, above the timing chain cover, below the power steering pump.

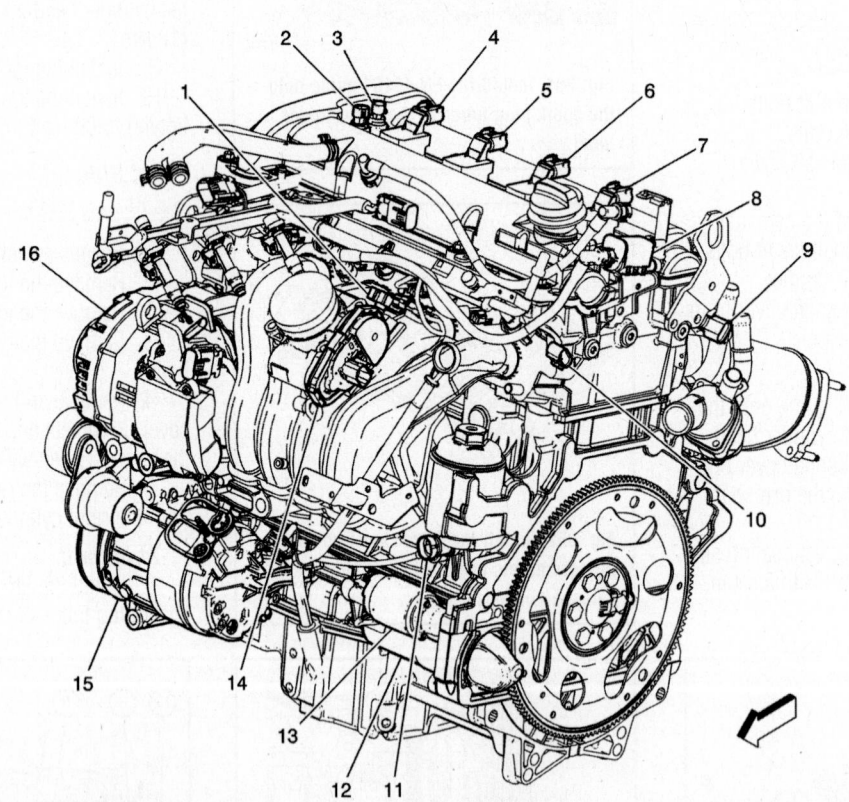

1. Manifold Absolute Pressure MAP Sensor
2. Camshaft Position CMP Actuator Solenoid Valve - Intake
3. Camshaft Position CMP Actuator Solenoid Valve - Exhaust
4. Ignition Coil 1
5. Ignition Coil 2
6. Ignition Coil 3
7. Ignition Coil 4
8. Evaporative Emission EVAP Canister Purge Solenoid Valve
9. Camshaft Position CMP Sensor - Exhaust
10. Camshaft Position CMP Sensor - Intake
11. Engine Oil Pressure EOP Switch
12. Starter Motor
13. Starter Solenoid Part of Starter Motor

2001722

Fig. 356 Component locations—2.4L engine

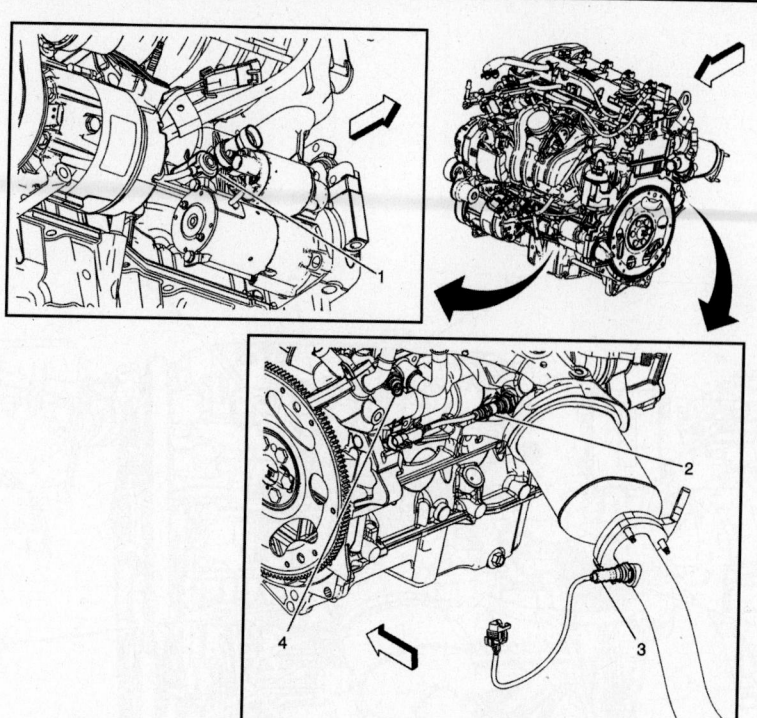

1. Knock Sensor KS
2. Heated Oxygen Sensor HO2S 1
3. Heated Oxygen Sensor HO2S 2
4. Engine Coolant Temperature ECT Sensor

2001746

Fig. 357 Component locations—2.4L engine

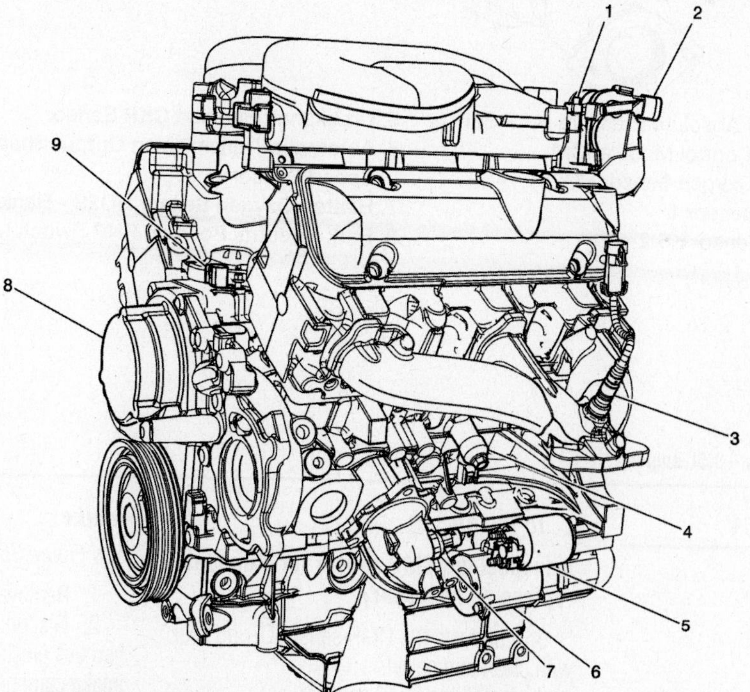

1. Evaporative Emission EVAP Canister
   Purge Solenoid Valve
2. Throttle Body
3. Heated Oxygen Sensor HO2S - Bank 2 Sensor 1
4. Knock Sensor KS 1
5. Starter Solenoid
6. Starter Motor
7. Engine Oil Pressure EOP Sensor
8. Camshaft Position CMP Actuator
   Solenoid Valve
9. Camshaft Position CMP Sensor

2259479

Fig. 358 Component locations—3.5L engine

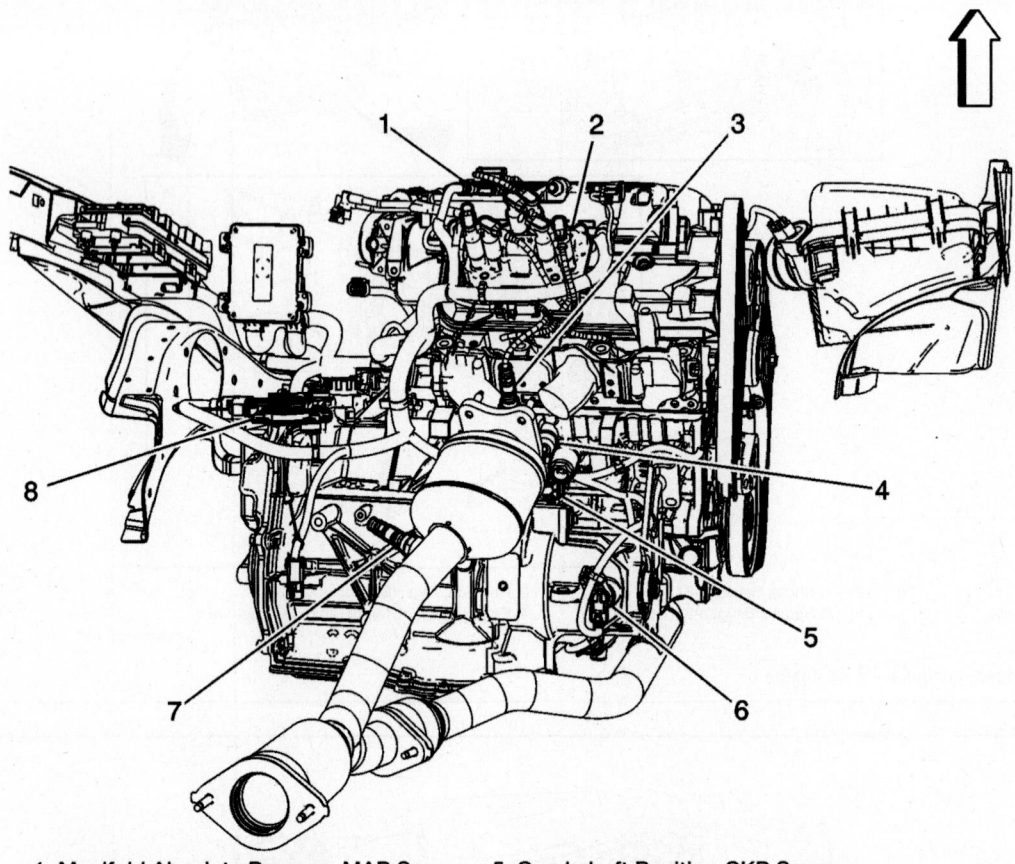

1. Manifold Absolute Pressure MAP Sensor
2. Ignition Control Module ICM
3. Heated Oxygen Sensor HO2S -
   Bank 1 Sensor 1
4. Knock Sensor KS 2
5. Crankshaft Position CKP Sensor
6. Automatic Transmission Output Shaft
   Speed Sensor
7. Heated Oxygen Sensor HO2S - Bank 1 Sensor 2
8. Park / Neutral Position PNP Switch MN5 only

2259484

Fig. 359 Component locations—3.5L engine

REMOVAL & INSTALLATION

2.4L Engine

Exhaust

See Figures 362 and 364.

1. Disconnect the exhaust camshaft position (CMP) sensor electrical connector (2).
2. Remove the CMP sensor bolt. See Intake CMP illustration, the exhaust CMP is similar.
   Remove the CMP sensor.

To install:

➡**Inspect the CMP sensor for damage, replace as necessary.**

3. Lubricate the CMP sensor O-ring seal with clean engine oil.
4. Install the CMP sensor.
5. Install the CMP sensor bolt.
6. Tighten the bolt to 89 inch lbs. (10 Nm).
7. Connect the exhaust CMP sensor electrical connector (2).

Intake

See Figure 363.

1. Remove the air cleaner outlet duct.
2. Disconnect the engine wiring harness electrical connector (7) from the intake camshaft position (CMP) sensor (6).
3. Remove the CMP sensor bolt.
4. Remove the CMP sensor.

To install:

➡**Inspect the CMP sensor for damage, replace as necessary.**

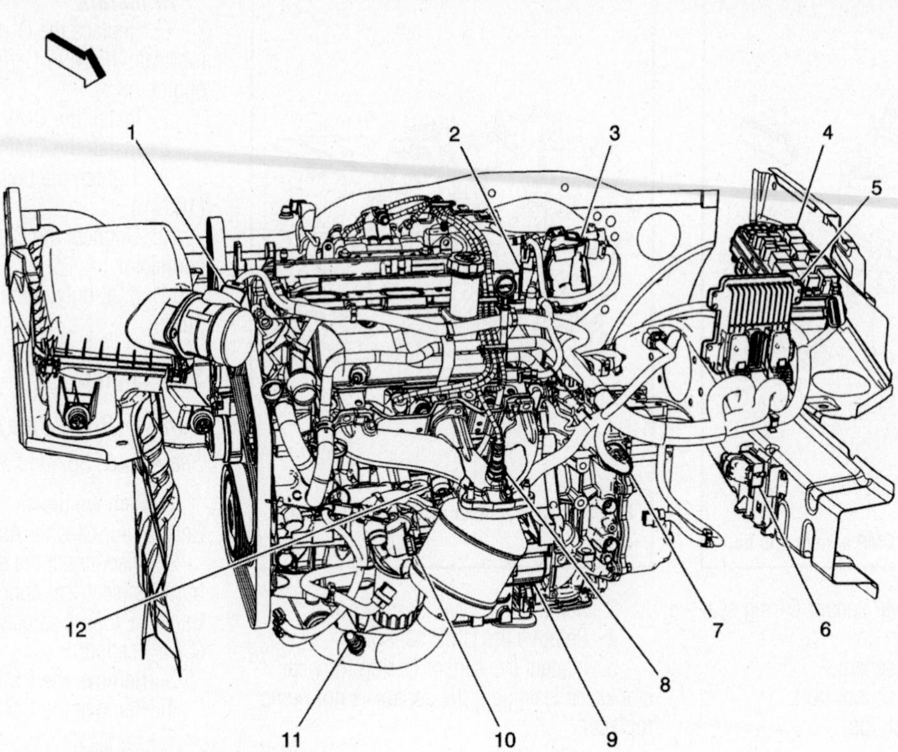

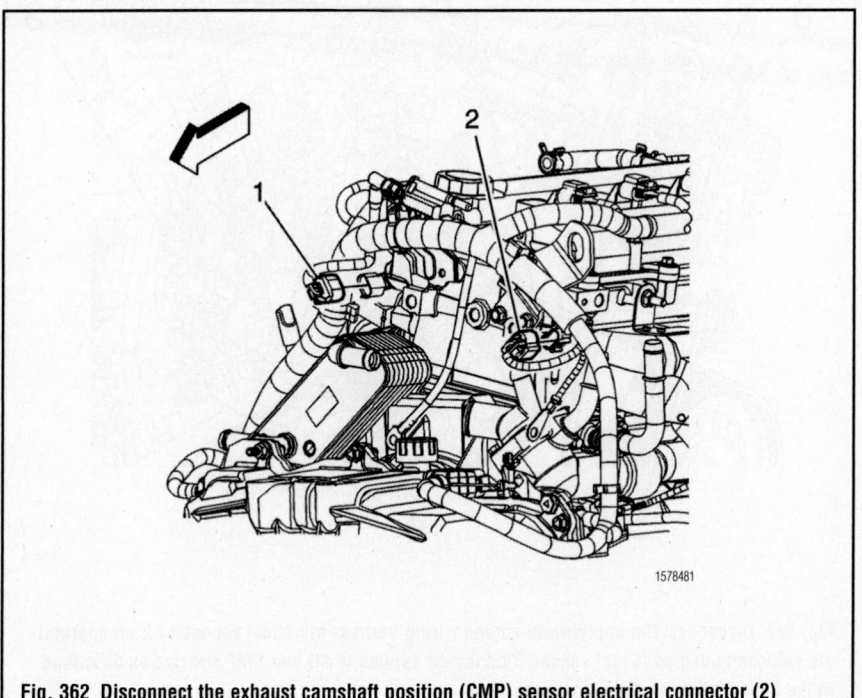

Fig. 360 Component locations—3.5L engine

1. Mass Air Flow MAF/Intake Air Temperature IAT Sensor
2. Evaporative Emission EVAP Canister Purge Solenoid Valve
3. Throttle Body
4. Fuse Block - Underhood
5. Engine Control Module ECM
6. Transmission Control Module TCM MN5 only
7. X100
8. Heated Oxygen Sensor HO2S - Bank 2 Sensor 1
9. Starter Motor
10. Engine Oil Pressure EOP Sensor
11. Heated Oxygen Sensor HO2S - Bank 2 Sensor 2
12. Knock Sensor KS 1

1829705

Fig. 362 Disconnect the exhaust camshaft position (CMP) sensor electrical connector (2)

1578481

Fig. 363 Disconnect the engine wiring harness electrical connector (7) from the intake camshaft position (CMP) sensor (6)

1890093

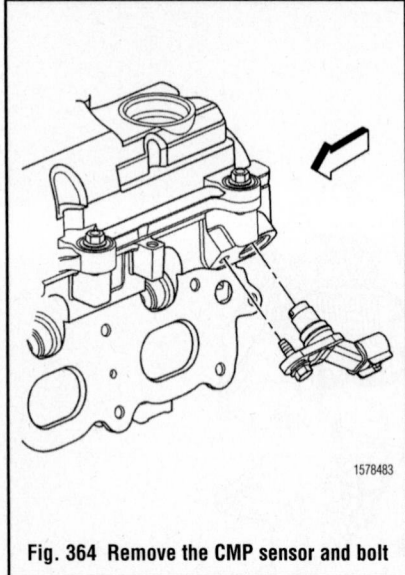

Fig. 364 Remove the CMP sensor and bolt

5. Lubricate the CMP sensor O-ring seal with clean engine oil.

6. Install the CMP sensor.

7. Install the CMP sensor bolt and tighten it to 89 inch lbs. (10 Nm).

8. Connect the engine wiring harness electrical connector (7) to the intake CMP sensor (6).

9. Install the air cleaner outlet duct.

3.5L & 3.9L Engines

See Figures 365 and 366.

1. 3.9L only: Remove the power steering pump.

2. Disconnect the camshaft position (CMP) sensor electrical connector.

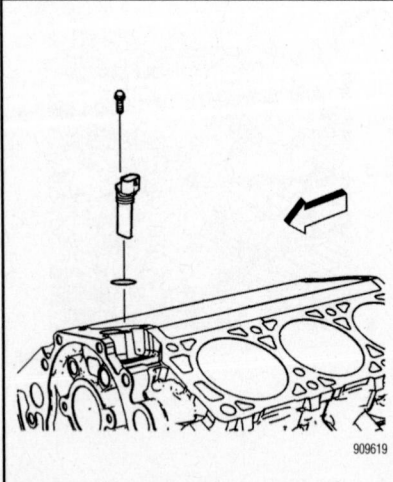

Fig. 365 CMP sensor replacement - 3.5L only

Fig. 366 CMP sensor replacement - 3.9L only

3. Remove the CMP sensor bolt.

4. Remove the CMP sensor.

5. Inspect the sensor O-ring for wear, cracks, or leakage if the sensor is not being replaced.

To install:

6. Replace the O-ring if damaged; lubricate the NEW O-ring with clean engine oil.

7. Install the CMP sensor.

8. Install the CMP sensor bolt.

9. Tighten the bolt to 89 inch lbs. (10 Nm).

10. Connect the CMP sensor electrical connector.

11. 3.9L only: Install the power steering pump.

3.6L Engine

Bank 1 (Right Side) Exhaust

See Figures 367 and 368.

1. Remove the air cleaner assembly. Refer to Air Cleaner Assembly.

2. Disconnect the engine wiring harness electrical connector (6) from the Bank 1 Exhaust camshaft position (CMP) sensor.

3. Remove the CMP sensor bolt.

4. Remove the CMP sensor.

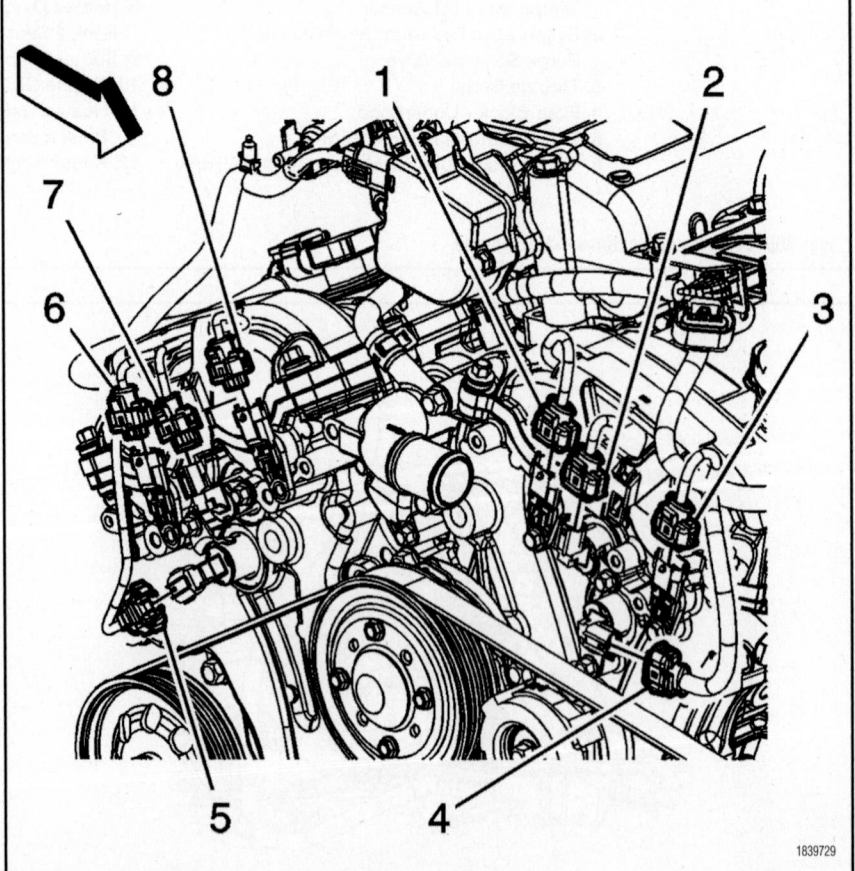

Fig. 367 Disconnect the appropriate engine wiring harness electrical connector from appropriate camshaft position (CMP) sensor. This image applies to all four CMP sensors as described in the individual replacement procedures.

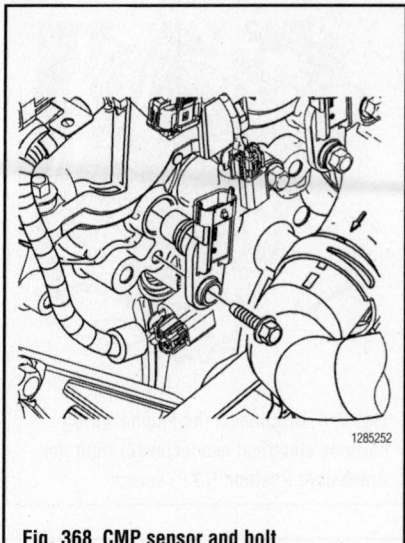

Fig. 368 CMP sensor and bolt

To install:

5. Install the CMP sensor.

6. Install the CMP sensor bolt and tighten to 89 inch lbs. (10 Nm).

7. Connect the engine wiring harness electrical connector (6) to the Bank 1 Exhaust CMP sensor.

8. Install the air cleaner assembly. Refer to Air Cleaner Assembly.

Bank 1 (Right Side) Intake

See Figure 369.

1. Remove the air cleaner assembly. Refer to Air Cleaner Assembly.

2. Disconnect the engine wiring harness electrical connector (8) from the Bank 1 Intake camshaft position (CMP) sensor. (See image for the exhaust, it is the same as the intake.)

3. Remove the CMP sensor bolt.

4. Remove the CMP sensor.

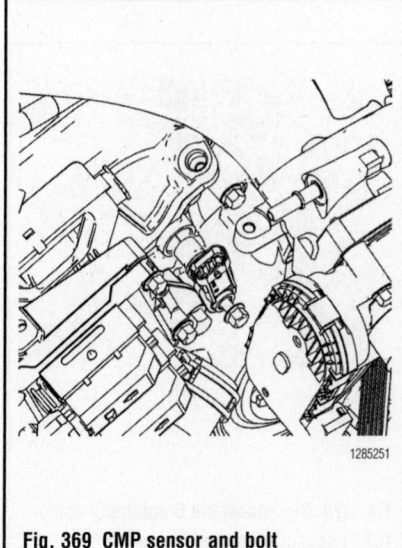

Fig. 369 CMP sensor and bolt

To install:

5. Install the CMP sensor.

6. Install the CMP sensor bolt and tighten to 89 inch lbs. (10 Nm).

7. Connect the engine wiring harness electrical connector (8) to the Bank 1 Intake CMP sensor.

8. Install the air cleaner assembly. Refer to Air Cleaner Assembly.

Bank 2 (Left Side) Exhaust

See Figure 370.

1. Remove the air cleaner assembly. Refer to Air Cleaner Assembly.

2. Disconnect the engine wiring harness electrical connector (3) from the Bank 2 Exhaust camshaft position (CMP) sensor. (See image for the Bank 1 (Right side) Exhaust, it is the same as Bank 2 Exhaust.)

3. Remove the CMP sensor bolt.

4. Remove the CMP sensor.

To install:

5. Install the CMP sensor.

6. Install the CMP sensor bolt and tighten to 89 inch lbs. (10 Nm).

7. Connect the engine wiring harness electrical connector (3) to the Bank 2 Exhaust CMP sensor.

8. Install the air cleaner assembly. Refer to Air Cleaner Assembly.

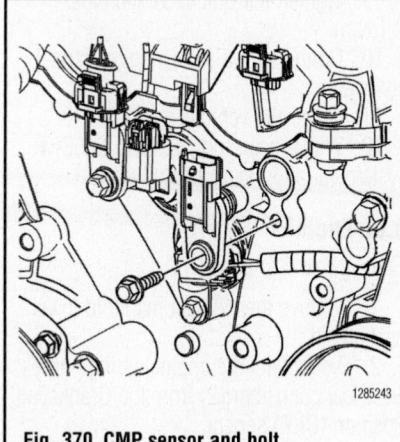

Fig. 370 CMP sensor and bolt

Bank 2 (Left Side) Intake

See Figure 371.

1. Remove the air cleaner assembly. Refer to Air Cleaner Assembly.

2. Disconnect the engine wiring harness electrical connector (1) from the Bank 2 Intake camshaft position (CMP) sensor. (See image for the Bank 1 (Right side) Exhaust, it is the same as Bank 2 Intake.)

3. Remove the CMP sensor bolt.

4. Remove the CMP sensor.

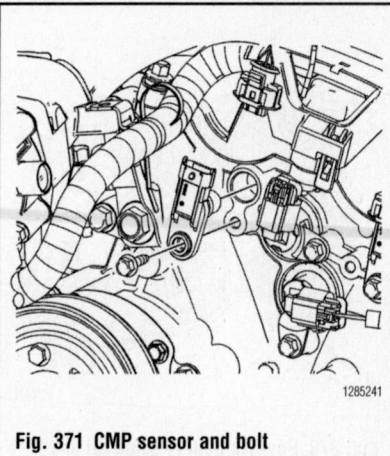

Fig. 371 CMP sensor and bolt

To install:

5. Install the CMP sensor.

6. Install the CMP sensor bolt and tighten to 89 inch lbs. (10 Nm).

7. Connect the engine wiring harness electrical connector (1) to the bank 2 intake CMP sensor.

8. Install the air cleaner assembly. Refer to Air Cleaner Assembly.

CRANKSHAFT POSITION (CKP) SENSOR

LOCATION

2.4L: In the engine compartment, on the left side front of the engine, above the starter motor

3.5L: In the engine compartment, on the right side of the engine, at the end of the crankshaft, behind the harmonic balancer.

REMOVAL & INSTALLATION

2.4L Engine

See Figures 372 through 374.

1. Disconnect the Crankshaft Position (CKP) sensor electrical connector (3).

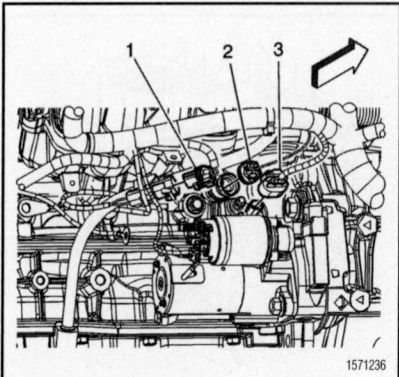

Fig. 372 Crankshaft Position (CKP) sensor electrical connector (3)

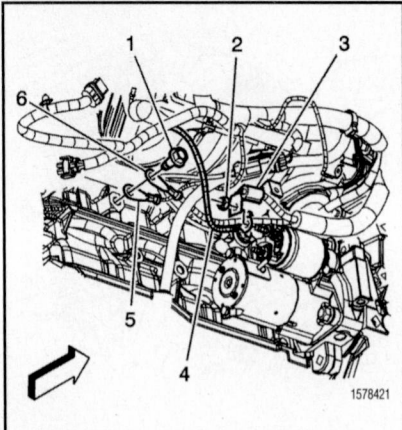

Fig. 373 Positive battery cable (3) and nut (2)

2. Remove the oil level indicator tube.

3. Remove the positive battery cable nut (2) from the starter solenoid.

4. Remove the positive battery cable (3) from the starter solenoid.

5. Remove the CKP sensor bolt.

6. Remove the CKP sensor.

To install:

7. Lubricate the CKP sensor O-ring seal with clean engine oil.

8. Install the CKP sensor.

9. Install the CKP sensor bolt.

10. Tighten the sensor bolt to 89 inch lbs. (10 Nm).

➡**Ensure that the engine harness terminal (4) is still installed on the starter solenoid.**

11. Install the positive battery cable (3) to the starter solenoid.

12. Install the positive battery cable nut (2) to the starter solenoid.

13. Tighten the nut to 89 inch lbs. (10 Nm).

14. Connect the CKP sensor electrical connector (3).

15. Install the oil level indicator tube.

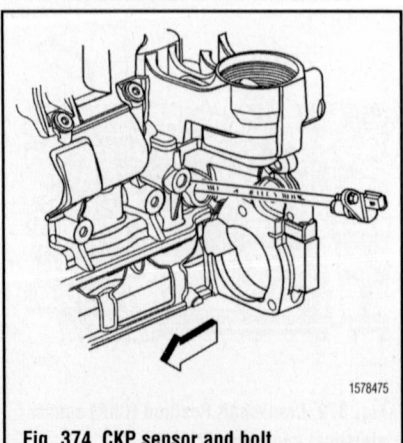

Fig. 374 CKP sensor and bolt

3.5L Engine

See Figure 375.

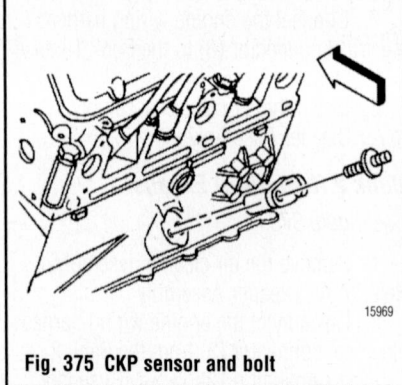

Fig. 375 CKP sensor and bolt

1. Raise and support the vehicle.

2. Disconnect the Crankshaft Position (CKP) sensor electrical connector.

3. Remove the CKP sensor bolt.

4. Remove the CKP sensor.

5. Inspect for wear, cracks, or leakage if the sensor is not being replaced.

To install:

6. Lubricate the O-ring with clean engine oil before installation and replace the O-ring if necessary.

7. Install the CKP sensor.

8. Install the CKP sensor bolt.

9. Tighten the bolt to 97 inch lbs. (11 Nm).

10. Connect the CKP sensor electrical connector.

11. Lower the vehicle.

12. With a scan tool, perform the CKP system variation learn procedure.

3.6L Engine

See Figures 376 and 377.

1. Remove the exhaust manifold lower heat shield.

2. Disconnect the engine wiring harness electrical connector (2) from the Crankshaft Position (CKP) sensor.

3. Remove the crankshaft sensor bolt.

4. Remove the crankshaft sensor.

To install:

5. Install the crankshaft position sensor.

6. Install the crankshaft position sensor bolt and tighten to 89 inch lbs. (10 Nm).

7. Connect the engine wiring harness electrical connector (2) to the CKP sensor.

8. Install the exhaust manifold lower heat shield.

9. With a scan tool, perform the Crankshaft Position System Variation Learn procedure.

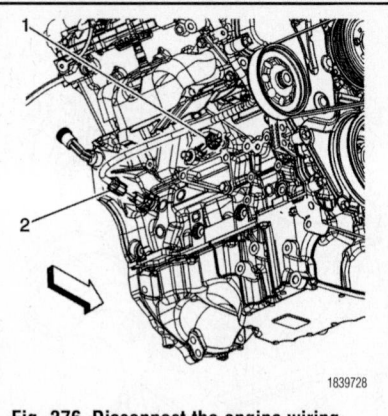

Fig. 376 Disconnect the engine wiring harness electrical connector (2) from the Crankshaft Position (CKP) sensor

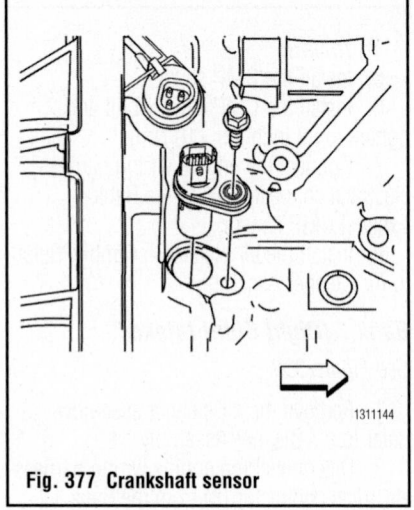

Fig. 377 Crankshaft sensor

3.9L Engine

See Figures 378 and 379.

1. Raise and support the vehicle.

2. Disconnect the Crankshaft Position (CKP) sensor electrical connector (2).

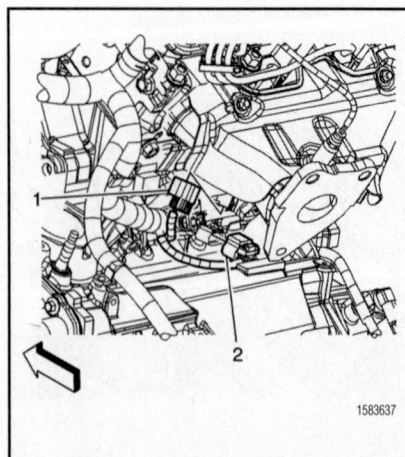

Fig. 378 Disconnect the Crankshaft Position (CKP) sensor electrical connector (2)

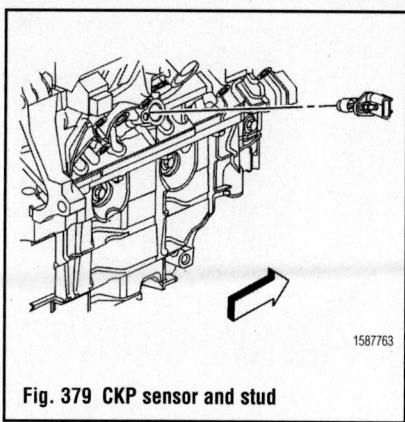

Fig. 379 CKP sensor and stud

3. Remove the CKP sensor stud.

4. Remove the CKP sensor.

To install:

5. Lubricate the CKP sensor O-ring with clean engine oil.

6. Install the CKP sensor.

7. Install the CKP sensor stud.

8. Tighten the stud to 89 inch lbs. (10 Nm).

9. Connect the CKP sensor electrical connector (2).

10. Lower the vehicle.

ELECTRONIC CONTROL MODULE (ECM)

LOCATION

The ECM is located in the left side of the engine compartment, in front of the battery.

REMOVAL & INSTALLATION

✳✳ WARNING

Note the following:

• Turn the ignition OFF when installing or removing the control module connectors and disconnecting or reconnecting the power to the control module (battery cable, powertrain control module (PCM)/engine control module (ECM)/transaxle control module (TCM) pigtail, control module fuse, jumper cables, etc.) in order to prevent internal control module damage.

• Control module damage may result when the metal case contacts battery voltage. DO NOT contact the control module metal case with battery voltage when servicing a control module, using battery booster cables, or when charging the vehicle battery.

• In order to prevent any possible electrostatic discharge damage to the control module do not touch the connector pins or the soldered components on the circuit board.

• Remove any debris from around the control module connector surfaces before servicing the control module. Inspect the control module connector gaskets when diagnosing or replacing the control module.

• Ensure that the gaskets are installed correctly. The gaskets prevent contaminant intrusion into the control module.

• The replacement control module must be programmed.

1. Disconnect the electrical connectors.

2. Release the retaining tab located in the battery box lower half using a small screwdriver or other suitable tool.

3. Program the ECM, if replacing.

➡**It is necessary to record the remaining engine oil life. If the replacement module is not programmed with the remaining engine oil life, the engine oil life will default to 100 percent. If the replacement module is not programmed with the remaining engine oil life, the engine oil will need to be changed at 3,000 miles (5,000 km) from the last engine oil change.**

2.4L & 3.5L Engines

See Figure 380.

1. Disconnect the negative battery cable. Refer to Battery Negative Cable Disconnection and Connection.

3.6L Engine

See Figures 381 and 382.

1. Using a scan tool, retrieve the percentage of remaining engine oil. Record the remaining engine oil life.

2. Record the preset radio stations.

3. Turn the ignition OFF.

4. Disconnect the negative battery cable. Refer to Battery Negative Cable Disconnection and Connection.

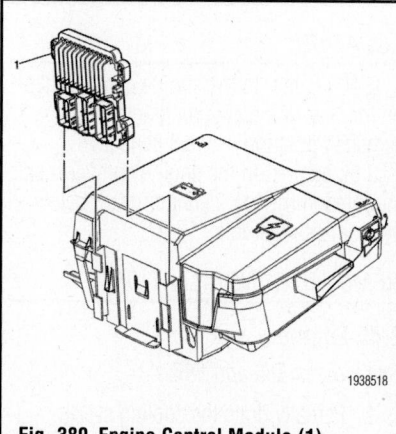

Fig. 380 Engine Control Module (1)

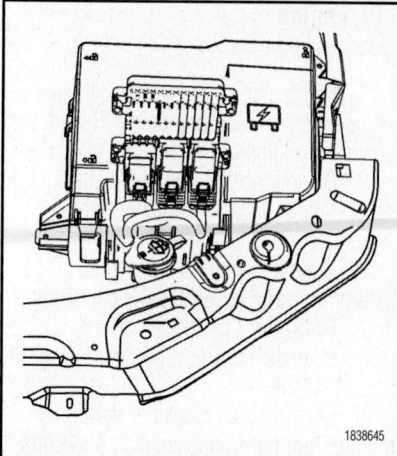

Fig. 381 Lift and gently pull the ECM up and out of the retainer on the battery tray

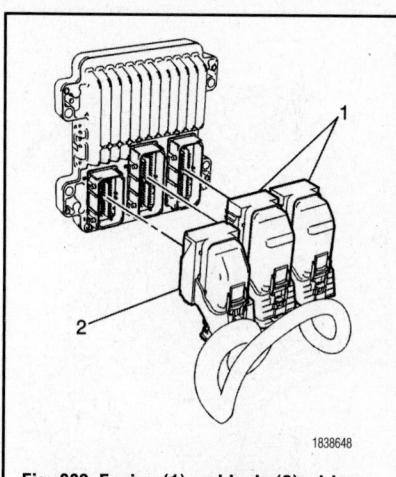

Fig. 382 Engine (1) and body (2) wiring harness electrical connectors

5. Lift and gently pull the ECM up and out of the retainer on the battery tray.

6. Disconnect the engine wiring harness electrical connectors (1) from the ECM.

7. Disconnect the body wiring harness electrical connector (2) from the ECM.

To install:

8. Connect the engine wiring harness electrical connectors (1) to the ECM.

9. Connect the body wiring harness electrical connector (2) to the ECM.

10. Position the ECM above the retainer in the battery tray and slide the ECM down into the retainer.

11. Connect the negative battery cable. Refer to Battery Negative Cable Disconnection and Connection.

12. Reset the clock and preset radio stations.

13. If installing a NEW ECM, program the ECM.

3.9L Engine

See Figures 383 through 385.

1. Using a scan tool, retrieve the percentage of remaining engine oil. Record the remaining engine oil life.

2. Disconnect the negative battery cable. Refer to Battery Negative Cable Disconnection and Connection.

3. Slide the lever lock to the up position in order to release the connector.

4. Disconnect the body harness electrical connector from the engine control module (ECM).

5. Slide the lever locks to the up position in order to release the connectors.

6. Disconnect the engine harness electrical connectors (1) from the ECM.

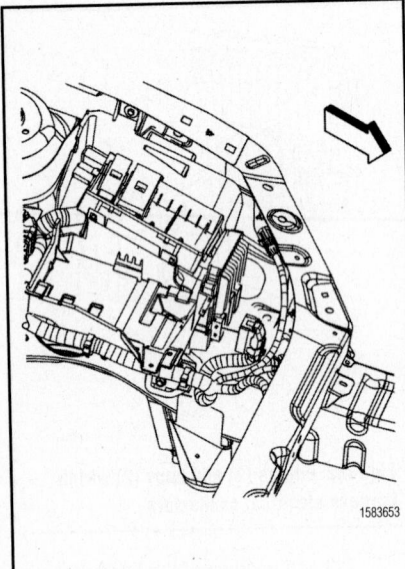

Fig. 383 Slide the lever lock to the up position in order to release the connector

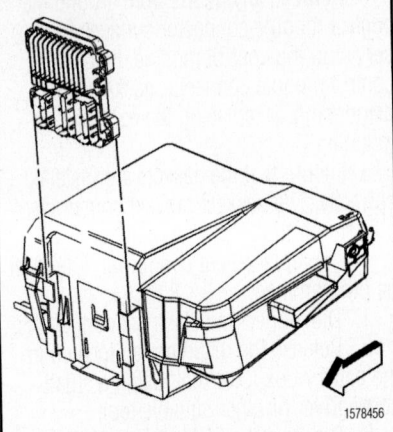

Fig. 385 Release the retaining tab located in the battery box lower half using a small screwdriver or other suitable tool.

7. Release the retaining tab located in the battery box lower half using a small screwdriver or other suitable tool.

8. Remove the ECM by lifting upward after releasing the tab.

To install:

9. Slide the ECM into the ECM bracket on the front of the battery box.

10. Push down on the ECM until the retaining tab snaps into place.

11. Connect the engine harness electrical connectors to the ECM.

12. Slide the lever locks downward to secure the connectors.

13. Connect the body harness electrical connectors to the ECM.

14. Slide the lever lock downward to secure the connector.

15. Connect the negative battery cable. Refer to Battery Negative Cable Disconnection and Connection.

16. If installing a NEW ECM, program the ECM.

ENGINE COOLANT TEMPERATURE (ECT) SENSOR

LOCATION

2.4L engine: In the engine compartment on the rear of the engine, below the camshaft position exhaust sensor.

3.5L engine: In the engine compartment mounted in the rear cylinder head, below the coolant reservoir.

REMOVAL & INSTALLATION

2.4L Engine

See Figures 386 and 387.

1. Partially drain the cooling system. Refer to Cooling System Draining and Filling.

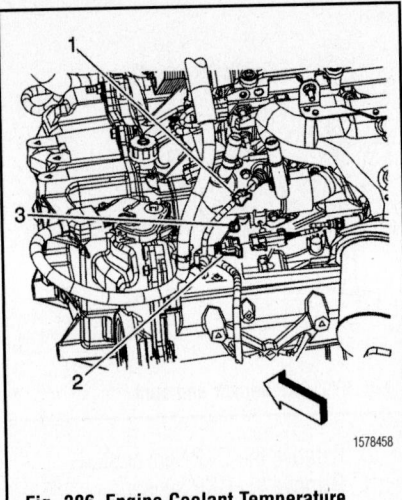

Fig. 386 Engine Coolant Temperature (ECT) sensor electrical connector (1)

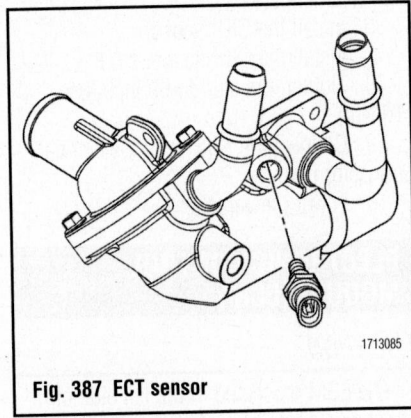

Fig. 387 ECT sensor

2. Disconnect the Engine Coolant Temperature (ECT) sensor electrical connector (1).

3. Remove the ECT sensor.

To install:

➡Use a tap to remove any sealant residue in the sensor hole in the thermostat housing. Clean any sealant residue from the old sensor (if reusing) and apply the room temperature vulcanizing (RTV) sealant to the threads.

4. Apply sealant to the threads of the ECT sensor (GM PN 12378521—US and 88901148—Canada).

5. Install the ECT sensor. Tighten the sensor to 15 ft. lbs. (20 Nm).

6. Connect the ECT sensor electrical connector.

7. Fill the cooling system as needed. Refer to Cooling System Draining and Filling.

3.5L Engine

See Figure 388.

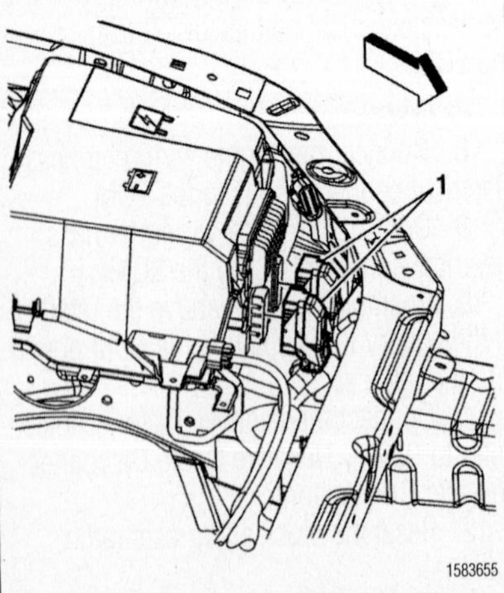

Fig. 384 Disconnect the engine harness electrical connectors (1) from the ECM

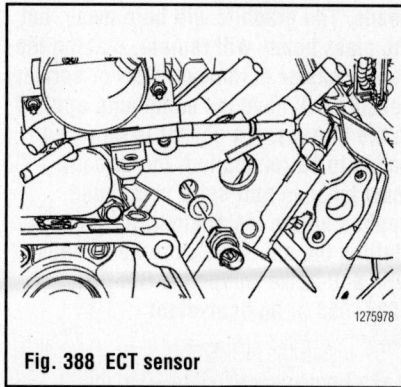

Fig. 388 ECT sensor

> ❊❊ **WARNING**
>
> **Use care when handling the coolant sensor. Damage to the coolant sensor will affect the operation of the fuel control system.**

1. Partially drain the cooling system. Refer to Cooling System Draining and Filling.

2. Disconnect the Engine Coolant Temperature (ECT) sensor electrical connector.

3. Remove the ECT sensor.

To install:

> ❊❊ **WARNING**
>
> **Replacement components must be the correct part number for the application. Components requiring thread locking compound, lubricants, corrosion inhibitors, or sealants are identified. Some replacement components may come with these coatings already applied. Do not use these coatings on components unless specified. These coatings can affect the final torque, which may affect the operation of the component. Use the correct torque specification when installing components in order to avoid damage.**

4. Coat the threads with sealer GM P/N 13246004 (Canadian P/N 10953480) or equivalent.

5. Install the ECT sensor. Tighten the ECT sensor to 15 ft. lbs. (20 Nm).

6. Connect the ECT electrical connector.

7. Fill the cooling system. Refer to Cooling System Draining and Filling.

3.6L Engine

See Figures 389 and 390.

1. Disconnect the engine wiring harness electrical connector (1) from the Engine Coolant Temperature (ECT) sensor.

2. Remove the ECT sensor.

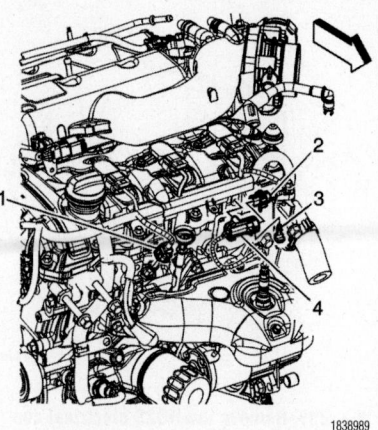

Fig. 389 Disconnect the engine wiring harness electrical connector (1) from the Engine Coolant Temperature (ECT) sensor.

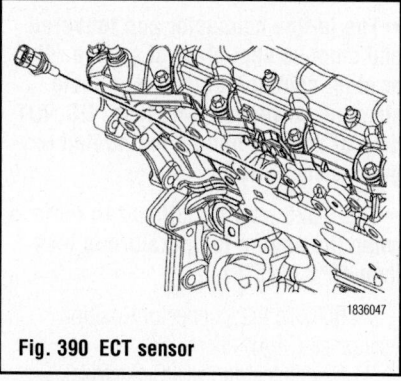

Fig. 390 ECT sensor

To install:

3. Install the ECT sensor and tighten it to 16 ft. lbs. (22 Nm).

Connect the engine wiring harness electrical connector (1) to the ECT sensor.

3.9L Engine

See Figure 391.

> ❊❊ **WARNING**
>
> **Use care when handling the coolant sensor. Damage to the coolant sensor will affect the operation of the fuel control system.**

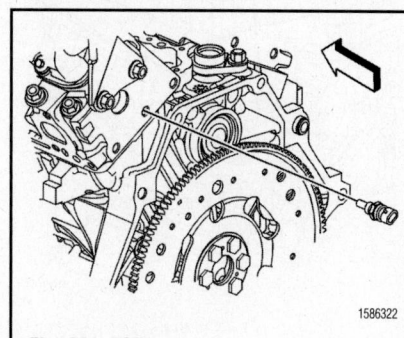

Fig. 391 ECT sensor

1. Drain the cooling system. Refer to Cooling System Draining and Filling.

2. Remove the intake manifold cover, if necessary. Refer to Intake Manifold Cover replacement.

3. Disconnect the Engine Coolant Temperature (ECT) sensor electrical connector.

4. Remove the ECT sensor.

To install:

> ❊❊ **WARNING**
>
> **Replacement components must be the correct part number for the application. Components requiring the use of the thread locking compound, lubricants, corrosion inhibitors, or sealants are identified in the service procedure. Some replacement components may come with these coatings already applied. Do not use these coatings on components unless specified. These coatings can affect the final torque, which may affect the operation of the component. Use the correct torque specification when installing components in order to avoid damage.**

5. Coat the threads of the ECT sensor with sealer GM P/N 13246004 (Canadian P/N 10953480) or equivalent.

6. Install the ECT sensor.

7. Tighten the ECT sensor to 15 ft. lbs. (20 Nm).

8. Connect the ECT electrical connector.

9. Install the intake manifold cover, if necessary. Refer to Intake Manifold Cover replacement.

10. Fill the cooling system. Refer to Cooling System Draining and Filling.

HEATED OXYGEN SENSOR (HO2S)

LOCATION

2.4L HO2S 1: In the engine compartment on the rear of the engine, between the exhaust manifold and the catalytic convertor.

2.4L HO2S 2: In the engine compartment on the rear of the engine, below the catalytic convertor.

3.5L Bank 1 Sensor 1: In the engine compartment center of the rear exhaust manifold.

3.5L Bank 1 Sensor 2: In the engine compartment rear of the engine compartment, after the catalytic converter.

3.5L Bank 2 Sensor 1: In the front of the engine compartment, on the exhaust manifold.

3.5L Bank 2 Sensor 2: In the lower front of the engine compartment, after the catalytic converter.

3.6L Bank 1 and 2 Sensor 1: On the exhaust manifold.

3.6L Bank 1 and 2 Sensor 2: On the catalytic converter.

3.9L Bank 1 Sensor 1: Near the ignition control module bracket.

3.9L Bank 1 and 2 Sensor 2: On the catalytic converter.

REMOVAL & INSTALLATION

2.4L Engine

Sensor 1

See Figures 392 through 394.

> ❊❊ **WARNING**
>
> **The oxygen sensor uses a permanently attached pigtail and connector. Do not remove the pigtail from the oxygen sensor. Damage to or removal of the pigtail connector could affect proper operation of the oxygen sensor.**

> ❊❊ **WARNING**
>
> **The use of excessive force may damage the threads in the exhaust manifold/pipe.**

> ❊❊ **WARNING**
>
> **When replacing the HO2S perform the following:**

- A code clear with a scan tool, regardless of whether or not a DTC is set.
- HO2S heater resistance learn reset with a scan tool, where available.

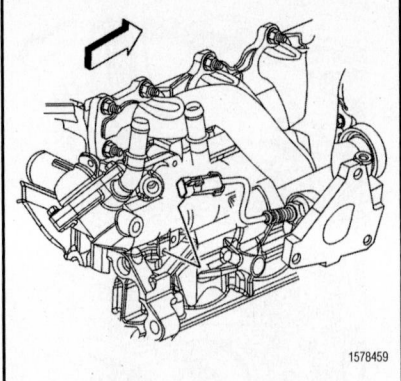

Fig. 393 Remove the HO2S electrical connector clip from the thermostat housing

Perform the above in order to reset the HO2S resistance learned value and avoid possible HO2S failure.

➡The in-line connector and louvered end must be kept clear of grease, dirt or other contaminants. Avoid using cleaning solvents of any type. DO NOT drop or roughly handle the heated oxygen sensor (HO2S).

➡The HO2S may be difficult to remove when the engine temperature is less than 48°C (120°F).

1. Remove the Connector Position Assurance (CPA) retainer (3).
2. Disconnect the HO2S electrical connector (2).
3. Remove the HO2S electrical connector clip from the thermostat housing.
4. Remove the HO2S.

To install:

➡A special anti-seize compound is used on the HO2S threads. The compound consists of a liquid graphite and glass beads. The graphite will burn away, but the glass beads will remain, making the sensor easier to remove. New or service sensors will have the compound applied to the threads. If a sensor is removed and is to be reinstalled, the threads must have an anti-seize compound applied before installation. If reinstalling the old HO2S coat the threads with anti-seize compound GM P/N 12377953 or an equivalent.

5. Install the HO2S.
6. Tighten the HO2S to 30 ft. lbs. (41 Nm).
7. Install the HO2S electrical connector clip to the thermostat housing.
8. Connect the HO2S electrical connector.
9. Install the CPA retainer.

Sensor 2

See Figures 395 and 396.

> ❊❊ **WARNING**
>
> **The oxygen sensor uses a permanently attached pigtail and connector. Do not remove the pigtail from the oxygen sensor. Damage to or removal of the pigtail connector could affect proper operation of the oxygen sensor.**

> ❊❊ **WARNING**
>
> **The use of excessive force may damage the threads in the exhaust manifold/pipe.**

> ❊❊ **WARNING**
>
> **When replacing the HO2S perform the following:**

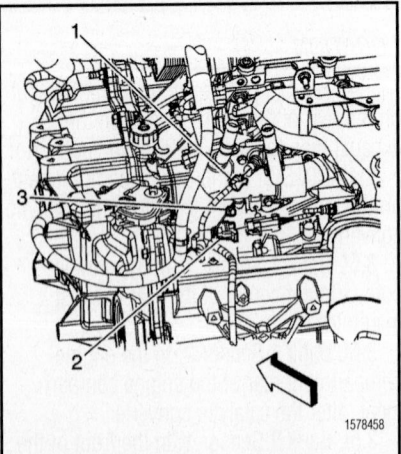

Fig. 392 CPA retainer (3) and HO2S electrical connector (2)

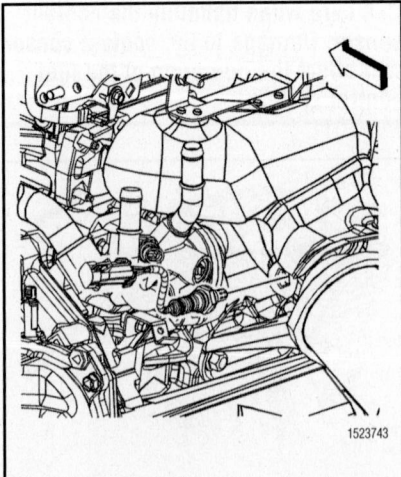

Fig. 394 HO2S sensor

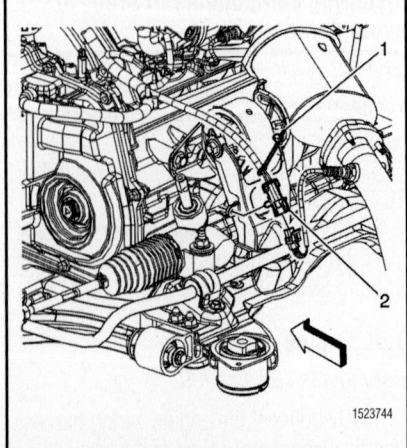

Fig. 395 CPA retainer (1) and HO2S electrical connector (2)

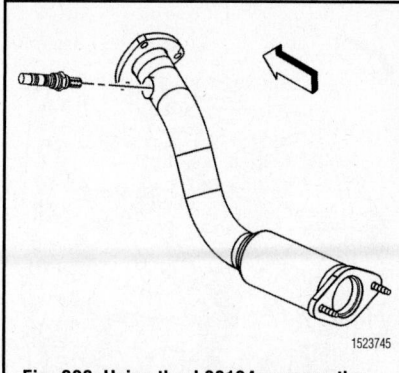

Fig. 396 Using the J 39194, remove the HO2S

• A code clear with a scan tool, regardless of whether or not a DTC is set.

• HO2S heater resistance learn reset with a scan tool, where available.

Perform the above in order to reset the HO2S resistance learned value and avoid possible HO2S failure.

➡The in-line connector and louvered end must be kept clear of grease, dirt or other contaminants. Avoid using cleaning solvents of any type. DO NOT drop or roughly handle the heated oxygen sensor (HO2S).

➡The HO2S may be difficult to remove when the engine temperature is less than 48°C (120°F).

1. Raise and support the vehicle.
2. Remove the Connector Position Assurance (CPA) retainer (1).
3. Disconnect the HO2S electrical connector (2).
4. Remove the HO2S electrical connector clip from the thermostat housing.
5. Using the J 39194, remove the HO2S.

To install:

➡A special anti-seize compound is used on the HO2S threads. The compound consists of a liquid graphite and glass beads. The graphite will burn away, but the glass beads will remain, making the sensor easier to remove. New or service sensors will have the compound applied to the threads. If a sensor is removed and is to be reinstalled, the threads must have an anti-seize compound applied before installation.

If reinstalling the old HO2S coat the threads with anti-seize compound GM P/N 12377953 or an equivalent.

6. If reinstalling the old HO2S coat the threads with anti-seize compound GM P/N 12377953 or an equivalent.

7. Using the J 39194, install the HO2S.
8. Tighten the HO2S to 30 ft. lbs. (41 Nm).
9. Connect the HO2S electrical connector.
10. Install the CPA retainer.
11. Lower the vehicle.

3.5L Engine

Bank 1 Sensor 1

See Figure 397.

✳✳ WARNING

When replacing the HO2S perform the following:

• A code clear with a scan tool, regardless of whether or not a DTC is set.

• HO2S heater resistance learn reset with a scan tool, where available.

Perform the above in order to reset the HO2S resistance learned value and avoid possible HO2S failure.

➡The HO2S may be difficult to remove when the engine temperature is less than 48°C (120°F).

1. Disconnect the HO2S electrical connector (1).
2. Using the J 39194-B, remove the HO2S.

To install:

➡A special anti-seize compound is used on the HO2S threads. The compound consists of a liquid graphite and glass beads. The graphite will burn away, but the glass beads will remain, making the sensor easier to remove. New or service sensors will have the compound applied to the threads. If a sensor is removed and is to be rein-

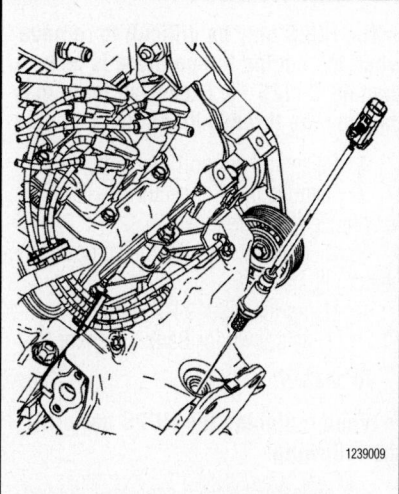

Fig. 397 HO2S electrical connector (1)

stalled, the threads must have an anti-seize compound applied before installation.

3. Coat the threads with anti-seize compound GM P/N 12377953 or an equivalent if necessary.
4. Install the HO2S.
5. Tighten the HO2S to 30 ft. lbs. (41 Nm).
6. Connect the HO2S electrical connector.

Bank 1 Sensor 2

See Figures 398 and 399.

➡The HO2S may be difficult to remove when the engine temperature is less than 48°C (120°F). Excessive force may damage the threads in the exhaust pipe.

1. Raise and support the vehicle.
2. Remove the Connector Position Assurance (CPA) retainer (1).
3. Disconnect the HO2S electrical connector (2).

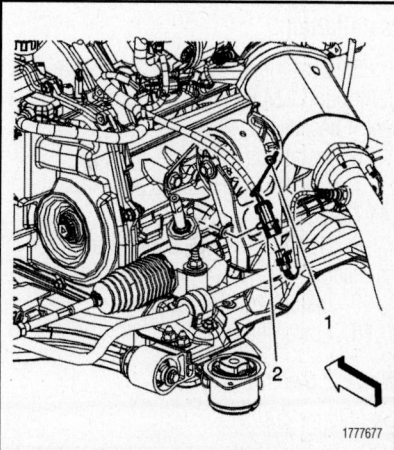

Fig. 398 CPA retainer (1) and HO2S electrical connector (2)

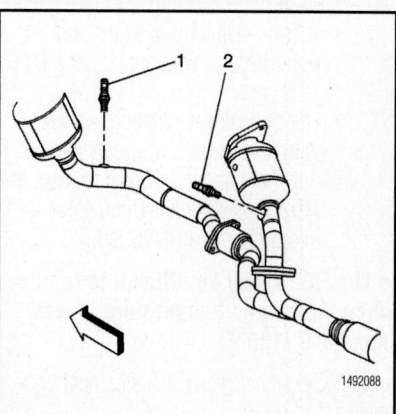

Fig. 399 Using the J 39194-B, remove the HO2S (1)

4. Using the J 39194-B, remove the HO2S (1).

To install:

When replacing the HO2S perform the following:

- A code clear with a scan tool, regardless of whether or not a DTC is set.
- HO2S heater resistance learn reset with a scan tool, where available.

Perform the above in order to reset the HO2S resistance learned value and avoid possible HO2S failure.

➡**A special anti-seize compound is used on the HO2S threads. The compound consists of a liquid graphite and glass beads. The graphite will burn away, but the glass beads will remain, making the sensor easier to remove. New or service sensors will have the compound applied to the threads. If a sensor is removed and is to be reinstalled, the threads must have an anti-seize compound applied before installation.**

5. Coat the threads with anti-seize compound GM P/N 12377953 or an equivalent if necessary.
6. Install the HO2S.
7. Tighten the HO2S to 30 ft. lbs. (41 Nm).
8. Connect the HO2S electrical connector.
9. Install the CPA retainer.
10. Lower the vehicle.

Bank 2 Sensor 1
See Figure 400.

When replacing the HO2S perform the following:

- A code clear with a scan tool, regardless of whether or not a DTC is set.
- HO2S heater resistance learn reset with a scan tool, where available.

Perform the above in order to reset the HO2S resistance learned value and avoid possible HO2S failure.

➡**The HO2S may be difficult to remove when the engine temperature is less than 48°C (120°F).**

1. Disconnect the HO2S electrical connector.
2. Using the J 39194-B, remove the HO2S.

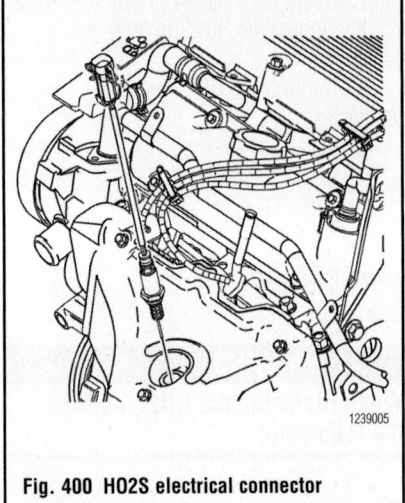

Fig. 400 HO2S electrical connector

To install:

➡**A special anti-seize compound is used on the HO2S threads. The compound consists of a liquid graphite and glass beads. The graphite will burn away, but the glass beads will remain, making the sensor easier to remove. New or service sensors will have the compound applied to the threads. If a sensor is removed and is to be reinstalled, the threads must have an anti-seize compound applied before installation.**

3. Coat the threads with anti-seize compound GM P/N 12377953 or an equivalent if necessary.
4. Install the HO2S.
5. Use the J 39194-B to tighten the sensor to 30 ft. lbs. (41 Nm).
6. Connect the HO2S electrical connector.

Bank 2 Sensor 2
See Figures 399 and 401.

➡**The HO2S may be difficult to remove when the engine temperature is less than 48°C (120°F). Excessive force may damage the threads in the exhaust pipe.**

1. Raise and support the vehicle.
2. Remove the Connector Position Assurance (CPA) retainer (2).
3. Disconnect the HO2S electrical connector (1).
4. Using the J 39194-B, remove the HO2S (1) as shown for Bank 1 Sensor 2.

To install:

➡**When replacing the HO2S perform the following:**

- A code clear with a scan tool, regardless of whether or not a DTC is set.

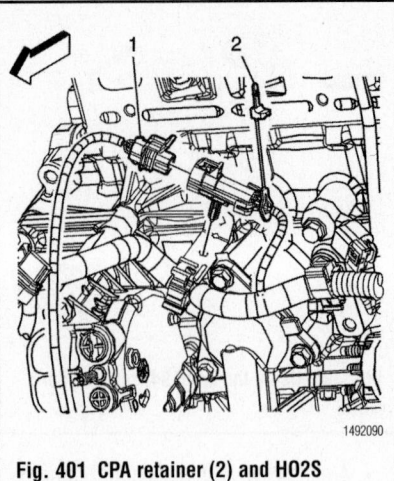

Fig. 401 CPA retainer (2) and HO2S electrical connector (1)

- HO2S heater resistance learn reset with a scan tool, where available.

Perform the above in order to reset the HO2S resistance learned value and avoid possible HO2S failure.

➡**A special anti-seize compound is used on the HO2S threads. The compound consists of a liquid graphite and glass beads. The graphite will burn away, but the glass beads will remain, making the sensor easier to remove. New or service sensors will have the compound applied to the threads. If a sensor is removed and is to be reinstalled, the threads must have an anti-seize compound applied before installation.**

5. Coat the threads with anti-seize compound GM P/N 12377953 or an equivalent if necessary.
6. Install the HO2S.
7. Tighten the HO2S to 30 ft. lbs. (41 Nm).
8. Connect the HO2S electrical connector.
9. Install the CPA retainer.
10. Lower the vehicle.

3.6L Engine

Bank 1 Sensor 1
See Figures 402 and 403.

➡**When replacing the HO2S perform the following:**

- A code clear with a scan tool, regardless of whether or not a DTC is set.
- HO2S heater resistance learn reset with a scan tool, where available.

Perform the above in order to reset the HO2S resistance learned value and avoid possible HO2S failure.

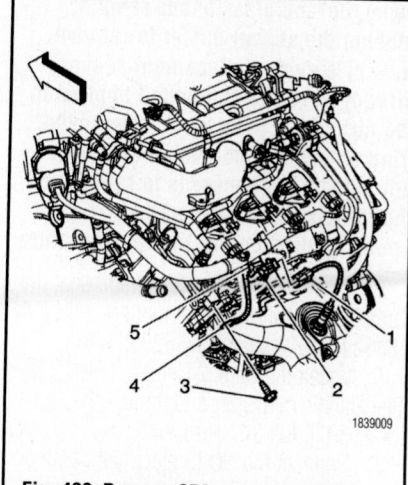

Fig. 402 Remove CPA and connectors

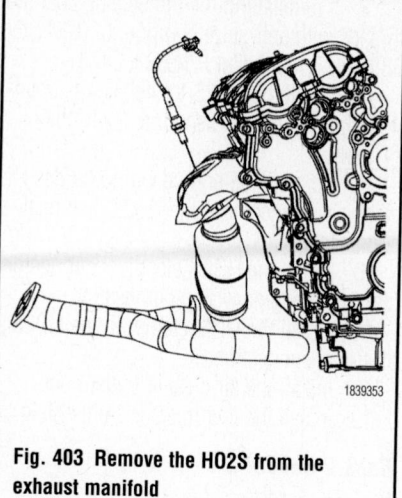

Fig. 403 Remove the HO2S from the exhaust manifold

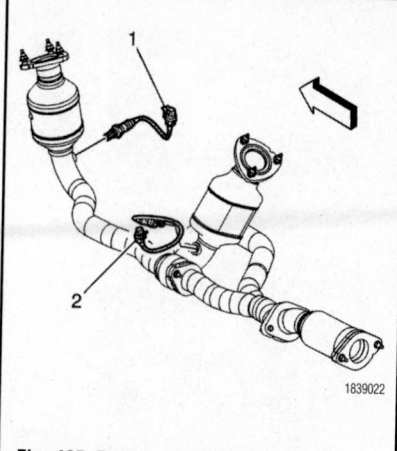

Fig. 405 Remove the bank 1 sensor 2 HO2S (2) from the catalytic converter

1. Raise and support the vehicle.
2. Remove the engine wiring harness Heated Oxygen Sensor (HO2S) electrical connector clip from the engine harness.
3. Remove the Connector Position Assurance (CPA) retainer (5) from the HO2S electrical connection.
4. Disconnect the engine wiring harness electrical connector (2) from the HO2S electrical connector (1).
5. Raise and support the vehicle to an appropriate height to reach the HO2S.
6. Remove the HO2S from the exhaust manifold.

To install:

➡A special anti-seize compound is used in the HO2S threads. The compound consists of liquid graphite and glass beads. The graphite tends to burn away, but the glass beads remain, making the sensor easier to remove. New or service replacement sensors already have the compound applied to the threads. If the sensor is removed from an exhaust component and if for any reason the sensor is to reinstalled, the threads must have anti-seize compound applied before the reinstallation.

7. If reinstalling the old sensor, coat the threads with anti-seize compound: (GM P/N 88862477; Canadian P/N 88862478)
8. Install the HO2S to the exhaust manifold and tighten the sensor to 30 ft. lbs. (41 Nm).
9. Lower the vehicle.
10. Connect the engine wiring harness electrical connector (2) to the HO2S electrical connector (1).
11. Install the engine wiring harness HO2S electrical connector clip to the engine harness.

12. Install the CPA retainer (5) to the HO2S electrical connection.

Bank 1 Sensor 2
See Figures 404 and 405.

➡**When replacing the HO2S perform the following:**

• A code clear with a scan tool, regardless of whether or not a DTC is set.
• HO2S heater resistance learn reset with a scan tool, where available.

Perform the above in order to reset the HO2S resistance learned value and avoid possible HO2S failure.

1. Raise and support the vehicle.
2. Remove the Connector Position Assurance (CPA) retainer from the HO2S electrical connection.
3. Disconnect the Heated Oxygen Sensor (HO2S) electrical connector (2) from the engine wiring harness electrical connector.

Remove the bank 1 sensor 2 HO2S (2) from the catalytic converter.

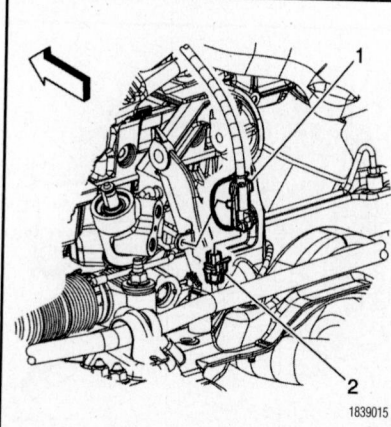

Fig. 404 HO2S electrical connection (2)

To install:

➡A special anti-seize compound is used in the HO2S threads. The compound consists of liquid graphite and glass beads. The graphite tends to burn away, but the glass beads remain, making the sensor easier to remove. New or service replacement sensors already have the compound applied to the threads. If the sensor is removed from an exhaust component and if for any reason the sensor is to reinstalled, the threads must have anti-seize compound applied before the reinstallation.

4. If reinstalling the old sensor, coat the threads with anti-seize compound: (GM P/N 88862477; Canadian P/N 88862478)

Install the bank 1 sensor 2 HO2S (2) to the catalytic converter and tighten the sensor to 30 ft. lbs. (41 Nm).

Connect the HO2S electrical connector (2) to the engine wiring harness electrical connector.

Install the CPA retainer to the HO2S electrical connection.

Lower the vehicle.

Bank 2 Sensor 1
See Figures 406 and 407.

➡**When replacing the HO2S perform the following:**

• A code clear with a scan tool, regardless of whether or not a DTC is set.
• HO2S heater resistance learn reset with a scan tool, where available.

Perform the above in order to reset the HO2S resistance learned value and avoid possible HO2S failure.

1. Remove the fuel injector sight shield.
2. Remove the air cleaner outlet duct.

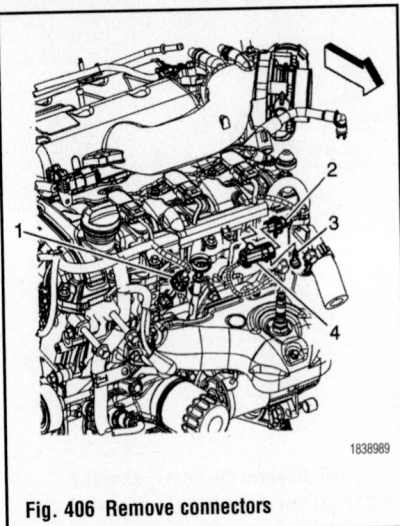

Fig. 406 Remove connectors

3. Remove the Connector Position Assurance (CPA) retainer (3) from the HO2S electrical connection.

4. Disconnect the engine wiring harness electrical connector (2) from the Heated Oxygen Sensor (HO2S) electrical connector (3).

5. Remove the HO2S electrical connector clip from the engine wiring harness tab.

6. Remove the HO2S from the exhaust manifold.

To install:

➡A special anti-seize compound is used in the HO2S threads. The compound consists of liquid graphite and glass beads. The graphite tends to burn away, but the glass beads remain, making the sensor easier to remove. New or service replacement sensors already have the compound applied to the threads. If the sensor is removed from an exhaust component and if for any reason the sensor is to reinstalled, the threads must have anti-seize compound applied before the reinstallation.

7. If reinstalling the old sensor, coat the threads with anti-seize compound: (GM P/N 88862477; Canadian P/N 88862478)

8. Install the HO2S to the exhaust manifold and tighten the sensor to 30 ft. lbs. (41 Nm).

9. Connect the engine wiring harness electrical connector to the HO2S electrical connector.

10. Install the HO2S electrical connector clip to the engine wiring harness tab.

11. Install the CPA retainer to the HO2S electrical connection.

12. Install the air cleaner outlet duct.

13. Install the fuel injector sight shield.

Bank 2 Sensor 2

See Figure 408.

➡**When replacing the HO2S perform the following:**

- A code clear with a scan tool, regardless of whether or not a DTC is set.
- HO2S heater resistance learn reset with a scan tool, where available.

Perform the above in order to reset the HO2S resistance learned value and avoid possible HO2S failure.

1. Raise and support the vehicle.

2. Remove the Connector Position Assurance (CPA) retainer (4) from the HO2S electrical connection.

3. Disconnect the Heated Oxygen Sensor (HO2S) electrical connector (3) from the engine wiring harness electrical connector (2).

4. Remove the Bank 2 Sensor 2 HO2S from the catalytic converter (see image for Bank 1 Sensor 2, it is the same).

To install:

➡A special anti-seize compound is used in the HO2S threads. The compound consists of liquid graphite and glass beads. The graphite tends to burn

away, but the glass beads remain, making the sensor easier to remove. New or service replacement sensors already have the compound applied to the threads. If the sensor is removed from an exhaust component and if for any reason the sensor is to reinstalled, the threads must have anti-seize compound applied before the reinstallation.

5. If reinstalling the old sensor, coat the threads with anti-seize compound: (GM P/N 88862477; Canadian P/N 88862478)

6. Install the Bank 2 Sensor 2 HO2S to the catalytic converter and tighten the sensor to 30 ft. lbs. (41 Nm).

7. Connect the HO2S electrical connector to the engine wiring harness electrical connector.

8. Install the CPA retainer to the HO2S electrical connection.

9. Lower the vehicle.

3.9L Engine

Bank 1 Sensor 1

See Figures 409 and 410.

➡**When replacing the HO2S perform the following:**

- A code clear with a scan tool, regardless of whether or not a DTC is set.
- HO2S heater resistance learn reset with a scan tool, where available.

Perform the above in order to reset the HO2S resistance learned value and avoid possible HO2S failure.

1. Remove the intake manifold cover.

2. Remove the Connector Position Assurance (CPA) retainer (2).

3. Disconnect the Heated Oxygen Sensor (HO2S) (1) electrical connector.

4. Remove the HO2S clip from the ignition control module bracket.

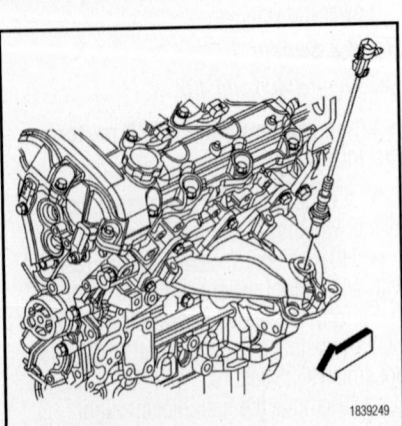

Fig. 407 Remove the HO2S from the exhaust manifold

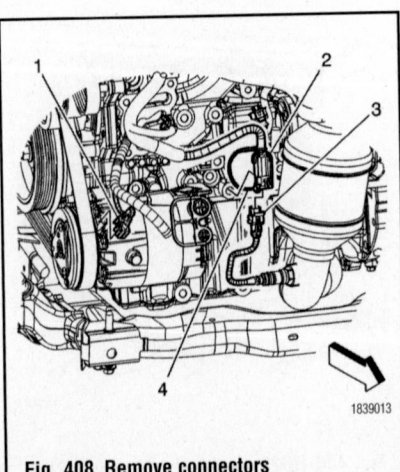

Fig. 408 Remove connectors

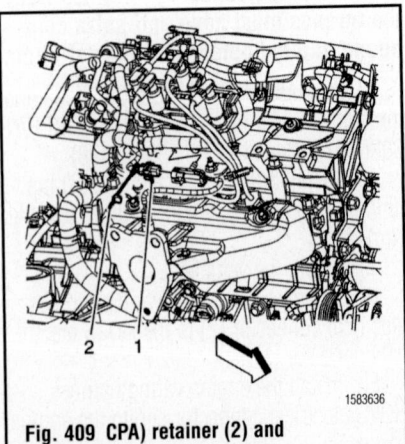

Fig. 409 CPA) retainer (2) and HO2S (1) electrical connector

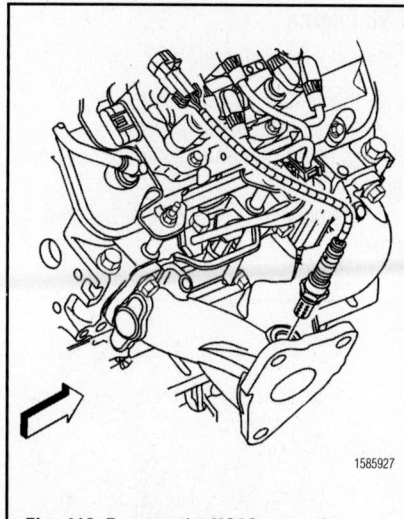

Fig. 410 Remove the HO2S using the J 39194-B

➡The HO2S may be difficult to remove when the engine temperature is less than 48°C (120°F).

5. Excessive force may damage the threads in the exhaust manifold.

6. Remove the HO2S using the J 39194-B.

To install:

➡A special anti-seize compound is used on the HO2S threads. The compound consists of graphite suspended in fluid and glass beads. The graphite will burn away, but the glass beads will remain, making the sensor easier to remove. New or service sensors will already have the compound applied to the threads. If a sensor is removed from an engine and is to be reinstalled, the threads must have anti-seize compound applied before the reinstallation.

7. Coat the threads of the HO2S with anti-seize compound GM P/N 12377953 or equivalent, if necessary.

8. Install the HO2S.

9. Tighten the sensor to 30 ft. lbs. (41 Nm) using the J 39194-B.

10. Connect the HO2S (1) electrical connector.

11. Install the CPA retainer.

12. Install the HO2S clip to the ignition control module bracket.

13. Install the intake manifold cover.

Bank 1 & Bank 2 Sensor 2

See Figures 411 and 412.

1. Raise and support the vehicle.

2. Remove the Connector Position Assurance (CPA) retainer (1).

3. Disconnect the Heated Oxygen Sensor (HO2S) electrical connector (2).

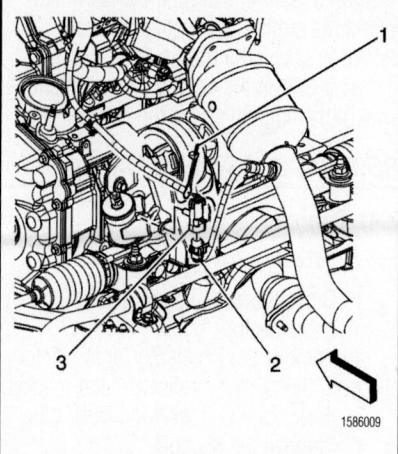

Fig. 411 CPA retainer (1) and HO2S electrical connector (2) and transmission mount connector clip (3)--Bank 1 Sensor 2

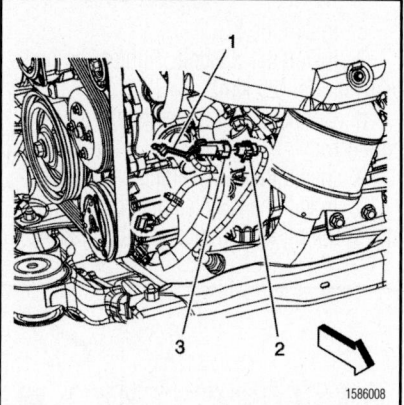

Fig. 412 CPA retainer (1) and HO2S electrical connector (2) and engine stud connector clip (3)—Bank 2 Sensor 2

➡The HO2S may be difficult to remove when the engine temperature is less than 120°F (48°C). Excessive force may damage the threads in the exhaust pipe.

4. Remove the HO2S using the J 39194-B. Refer to the image for 3.5L Bank 1 Sensor 2, it is the same. The sensor labeled HO2S (1) is actually Bank 2 Sensor 2 and HO2S (2) is Bank 1 Sensor 2.

To install:

➡When replacing the HO2S perform the following:

• A code clear with a scan tool, regardless of whether or not a DTC is set.

• HO2S heater resistance learn reset with a scan tool, where available.

Perform the above in order to reset the HO2S resistance learned value and avoid possible HO2S failure.

➡A special anti-seize compound is used on the HO2S threads. The compound consists of graphite suspended in fluid and glass beads. The graphite will burn away, but the glass beads will remain, making the sensor easier to remove. New or service sensors will already have the compound applied to the threads. If a sensor is removed from an engine and is to be reinstalled, the threads must have anti-seize compound applied before reinstallation.

5. Coat the threads of the HO2S with anti-seize compound GM P/N 12377953 or equivalent, if necessary.

6. Install the HO2S.

7. Tighten the sensor to 30 ft. lbs. (41 Nm) using the J 39194-B.

8. Connect the HO2S electrical connector.

9. Install the CPA retainer.

10. Bank 1 Sensor 2: Ensure that the HO2S connector clip is secured to the tab on the transmission mount.

11. Bank 2 Sensor 2: Ensure that the HO2S connector clip is attached to the stud on the engine.

12. Lower the vehicle.

Bank 2 Sensor 1

See Figures 413 and 414.

➡When replacing the HO2S perform the following:

• A code clear with a scan tool, regardless of whether or not a DTC is set.

• HO2S heater resistance learn reset with a scan tool, where available.

Perform the above in order to reset the HO2S resistance learned value and avoid possible HO2S failure.

1. Remove the Connector Position Assurance (CPA) retainer (3).

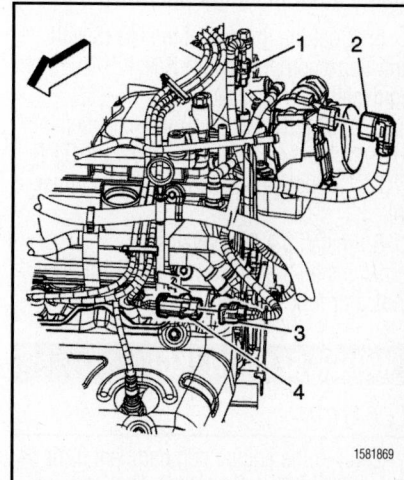

Fig. 413 CPA retainer (3) and HO2S (4)

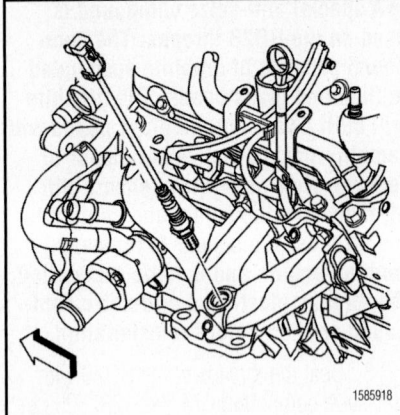

Fig. 414 Remove the HO2S using the J 39194-B

2. Disconnect the Heated Oxygen Sensor (HO2S) (4) electrical connector.

3. Remove the HO2S clip from the oil level indicator tube bracket.

➡ **The HO2S may be difficult to remove when the engine temperature is less than 48°C (120°F). Excessive force may damage the threads in the exhaust manifold.**

4. Remove the HO2S using the J 39194-B.

To install:

➡ **A special anti-seize compound is used on the HO2S threads. The compound consists of graphite suspended in fluid and glass beads. The graphite will burn away, but the glass beads will remain, making the sensor easier to remove. New or service sensors will already have the compound applied to the threads. If a sensor is removed from an engine and is to be reinstalled, the threads must have anti-seize compound applied before the reinstallation.**

5. Coat the threads of the HO2S with anti-seize compound GM P/N 12377953 or equivalent, if necessary.

6. Install the HO2S. Tighten the sensor to 30 ft. lbs. (41 Nm) using the J 39194-B.

7. Connect the HO2S electrical connector.

8. Install the CPA retainer.

9. Install the HO2S clip to the oil level indicator tube bracket.

KNOCK SENSOR (KS)

LOCATION

2.4L: In the engine compartment front of the engine, below the intake manifold.

3.5L KS 1: In the engine compartment rear of the engine, below the exhaust manifold, above the transaxle.

3.5L KS 2: In the engine compartment front of the engine, above the starter.

REMOVAL & INSTALLATION

2.4L Engine

See Figures 415 and 416.

1. Disconnect the knock sensor (KS) electrical connector (1).

2. Remove the KS electrical connector clip from the oil level indicator tube bracket.

3. Remove the oil level indicator tube.

4. Remove the KS bolt.

5. Remove the KS.

To install:

➡ **Rotate the pigtail 90 degrees from vertical before securing the fastener.**

6. Install the KS.

7. Install the KS bolt. Tighten the bolt to 18 ft. lbs. (25 Nm).

8. Connect the KS electrical connector.

9. Install the oil level indicator tube.

10. Install the KS electrical connector clip to the oil level indicator tube bracket.

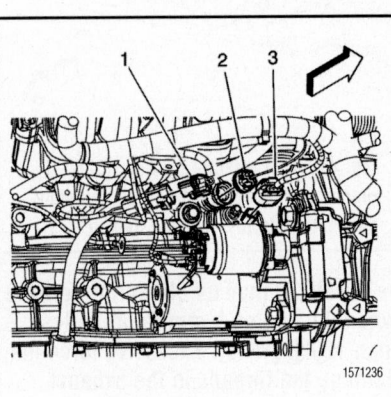

Fig. 415 KS electrical connector (1)

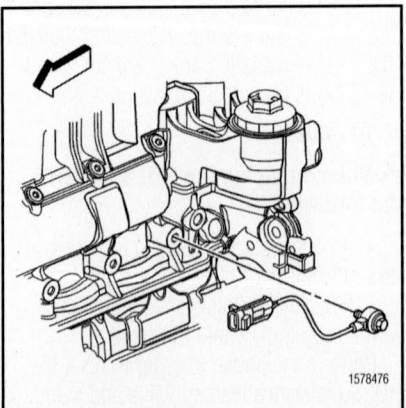

Fig. 416 KS and bolt

3.5L Engine

See Figures 417 through 420.

1. Raise and support the vehicle.

2. Disconnect the engine wiring harness electrical connector from the knock sensor.

3. Remove the knock sensor bolt and sensor.

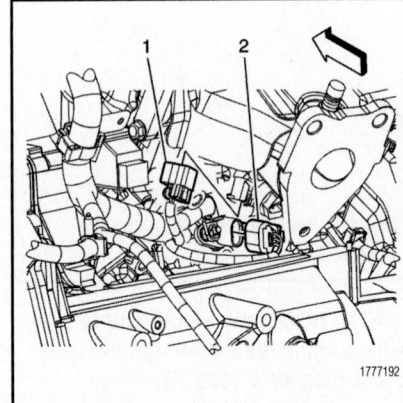

Fig. 417 Engine wiring harness electrical connector (1)—Bank 1

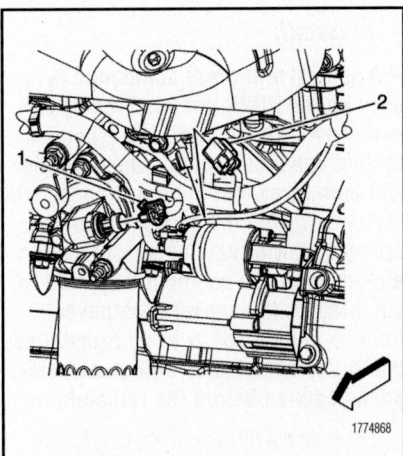

Fig. 418 Engine wiring harness electrical connector (2)—Bank 2

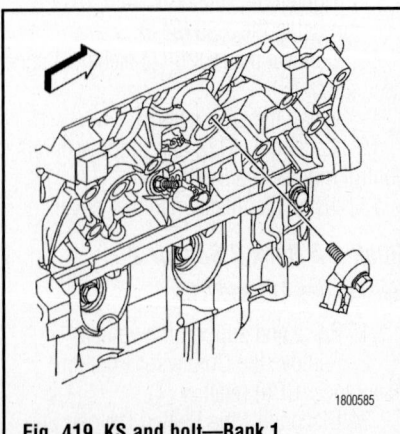

Fig. 419 KS and bolt—Bank 1

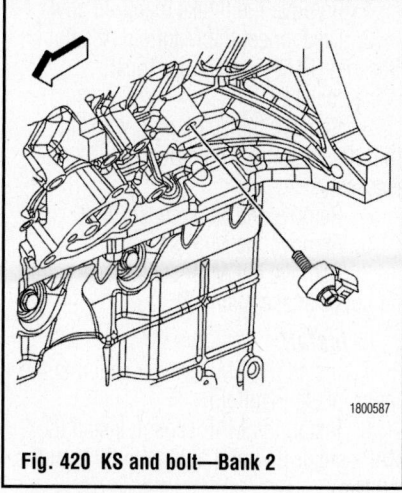

Fig. 420 KS and bolt—Bank 2

Fig. 422 Engine wiring harness electrical connector (2)—Bank 2

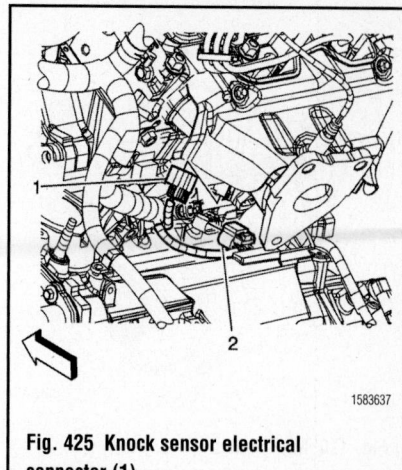

Fig. 425 Knock sensor electrical connector (1)

To install:

4. Position the knock sensor to the engine block and install the knock sensor bolt. Tighten the bolt to 18 ft. lbs. (25 Nm).

5. Connect the engine wiring harness electrical connector to the knock sensor.

6. Lower the vehicle.

3.6L Engine

See Figures 421 through 424.

1. Bank 1: Remove the exhaust manifold lower heat shield.

2. Bank 2: Raise and support the vehicle.

3. Disconnect the engine wiring harness electrical connector from the knock sensor.

4. Loosen the knock sensor bolt and remove the knock sensor.

To install:

5. Position the knock sensor and tighten the knock sensor bolt to 17 ft. lbs. (23 Nm).

6. Connect the engine wiring harness electrical connector to the knock sensor.

7. Install the exhaust manifold lower heat shield.

Fig. 421 Engine wiring harness electrical connector (1)—Bank 1

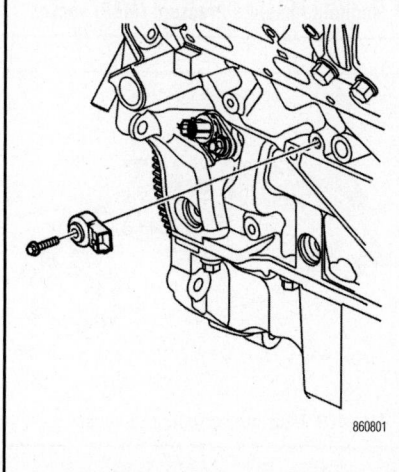

Fig. 423 Knock sensor and bolt—Bank 1

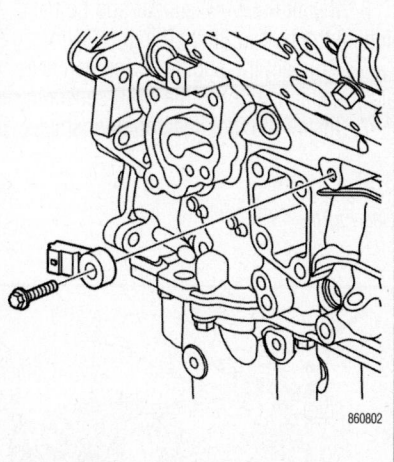

Fig. 424 Knock sensor and bolt—Bank 2

3.9L Engine

See Figure 425.

1. Raise and support the vehicle.

2. Disconnect the knock sensor electrical connector (1).

3. Loosen and remove the knock sensor (1).

To install:

➡ **DO NOT apply thread sealant to the sensor threads. The sensor threads are coated at the factory.**

4. Applying additional sealant affects the sensor's ability to detect detonation.

5. Install and tighten the knock sensor.

6. Tighten the sensor to 18 ft. lbs. (25 Nm).

7. Connect the knock sensor electrical connector.

8. Lower the vehicle.

MANIFOLD ABSOLUTE PRESSURE (MAP) SENSOR

LOCATION

The MAP sensor is located in the engine compartment on the top left of the engine near the throttle body.

REMOVAL & INSTALLATION

2.4L Engine

See Figure 426.

1. Remove the throttle body.

2. Disconnect the Manifold Absolute Pressure (MAP) sensor electrical connector.

3. Remove the MAP sensor and the MAP sensor port seal if it is still retained in the intake manifold.

To install:

4. Install the MAP sensor with the port seal into the intake manifold.

5. Connect the MAP sensor electrical connector.

6. Install the throttle body.

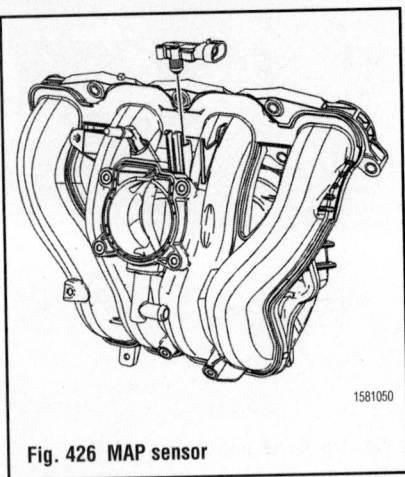

Fig. 426 MAP sensor

3.5L Engine

See Figure 427.

1. Remove the intake manifold cover.
2. Disconnect the Manifold Absolute Pressure (MAP) sensor electrical connector.
3. Remove the MAP sensor attaching screw.
4. Remove the MAP sensor and MAP sensor seal from the upper intake manifold.

To install:

5. Install the MAP sensor and MAP sensor seal into the upper intake manifold.
6. Install the MAP sensor attaching screw.
7. Tighten the attaching screw to 57 inch lbs. (6.5 Nm).
8. Connect the MAP sensor electrical connector.
9. Install the intake manifold cover.

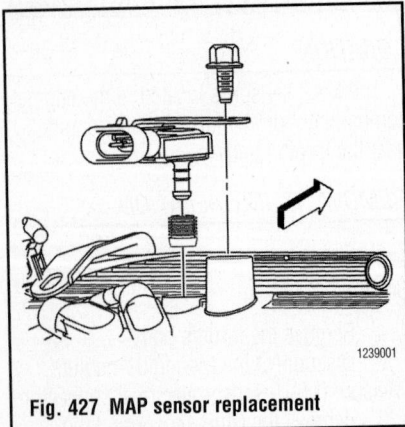

Fig. 427 MAP sensor replacement

3.6L Engine

See Figures 428 and 429.

1. Remove the fuel injector sight shield.
2. Disconnect the engine wiring harness electrical connector (1) from the Manifold Absolute Pressure (MAP) sensor.
3. Remove the MAP sensor bolt and sensor.

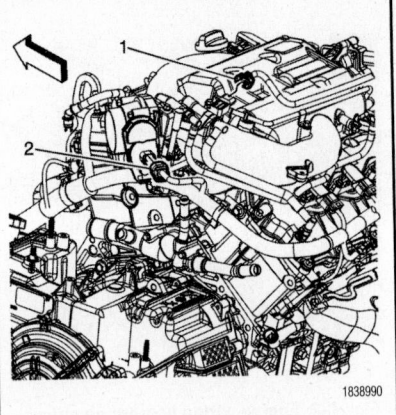

Fig. 428 Disconnect the engine wiring harness electrical connector (1) from the Manifold Absolute Pressure (MAP) sensor

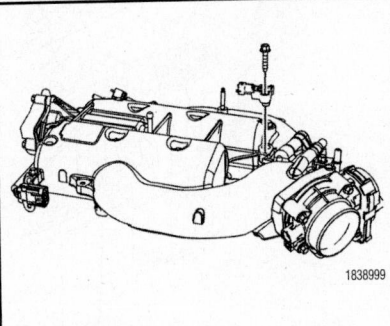

Fig. 429 MAP sensor bolt and sensor

To install:

4. Lubricate the MAP sensor O-ring seal with clean engine oil.
5. Install the MAP sensor and bolt and tighten the bolt to 89 inch lbs. (10 Nm).
6. Connect the engine wiring harness electrical connector to the MAP sensor.
7. Install the fuel injector sight shield.

3.9L Engine

See Figure 430.

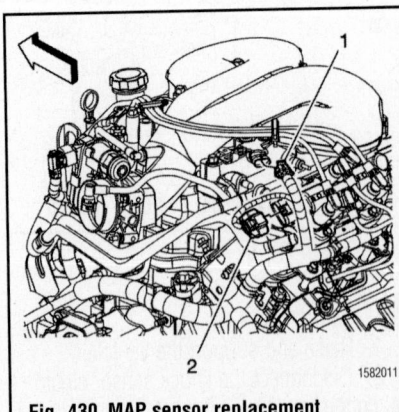

Fig. 430 MAP sensor replacement

1. Remove the intake manifold cover.
2. Disconnect the Manifold Absolute Pressure (MAP) sensor electrical connector (1).
3. Remove the spark plug wire clip from the intake manifold bracket, if necessary.
4. Remove the MAP sensor bolt.
5. Remove the MAP sensor.
6. Remove the MAP sensor seal from the upper intake manifold.

To install:

7. Install the MAP sensor seal into the upper intake manifold.
8. Install the MAP sensor. Install the MAP sensor bolt and tighten to 89 inch lbs. (10 Nm).
9. If required, install the spark plug wire clip to the intake manifold bracket.
10. Connect the MAP sensor electrical connector.
11. Install the intake manifold cover.

MASS AIR FLOW (MAF) SENSOR/ INTAKE AIR (IAT) TEMPERATURE SENSOR

LOCATION

In the engine compartment on the top right side of the engine, at the air cleaner.

REMOVAL & INSTALLATION

2.4L Engine

See Figures 431 and 432.

1. Disconnect the Mass Air Flow (MAF)/Intake Air Temperature (IAT) sensor electrical connector.
2. Using a tamper proof TORX®, remove the MAF/IAT sensor screws.
3. Remove the MAF/IAT sensor.

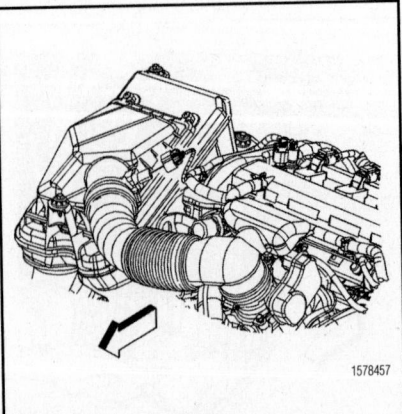

Fig. 431 Disconnect the Mass Air Flow (MAF)/Intake Air Temperature (iAT) sensor electrical connector

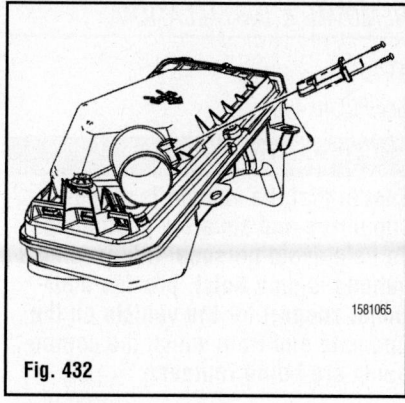

Fig. 432

To install:

4. Install the MAF/IAT sensor.

5. Using a tamper proof TORX®, install the MAF/IAT sensor screws and tighten the screws to 5 inch lbs. (0.6 Nm).

6. Connect the MAF/IAT sensor electrical connector.

3.5L & 3.9L Engines

3.5L Gas & 3.9L Engines

See Figures 433 through 435.

1. Remove the positive crankcase ventilation (PCV) fresh air tube from the air cleaner intake duct.

2. Disconnect the mass air flow/intake air temperature (MAF/IAT) sensor electrical connector (1).

3. Loosen the clamps and remove the air cleaner intake duct with the MAF/IAT sensor from the throttle body and the air cleaner housing cover.

4. Loosen the clamp and remove the MAF/IAT sensor from the air cleaner intake duct.

To install:

5. Install the MAF/IAT sensor to the air cleaner intake duct. Tighten the clamp to 18 inch lbs. (2 Nm).

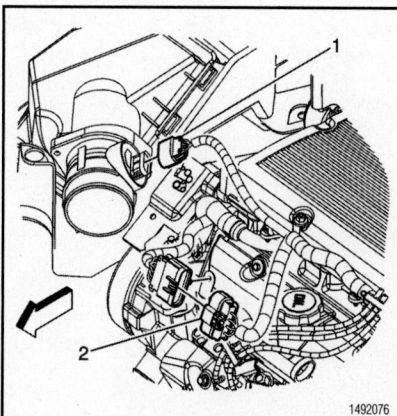

Fig. 433 Disconnect the MAF/IAT sensor electrical connector (1)—3.5L gas only

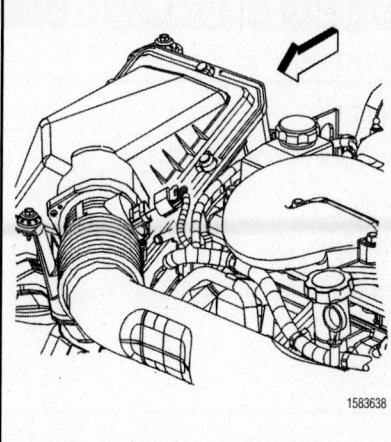

Fig. 434 Disconnect the MAF/IAT sensor electrical connector (1)—3.9L

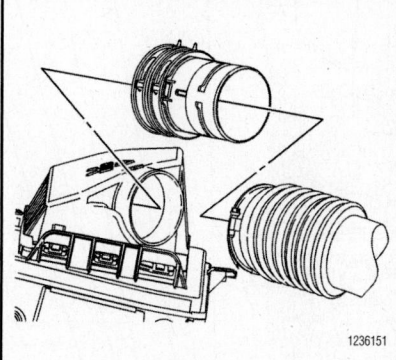

Fig. 435 Loosen the clamps and remove the air cleaner intake duct with the MAF/IAT sensor from the throttle body and the air cleaner housing cover

6. Install the air cleaner intake duct with the MAF/IAT sensor to the throttle body and the air cleaner housing cover. Tighten the clamps to 18 inch lbs. (2 Nm).

7. Connect the MAF/IAT sensor electrical connector.

8. Install the PCV fresh air tube to the air cleaner intake duct.

9. Start and idle the engine.

10. Inspect the air intake duct for leaks.

3.5L Flex Fuel (NU6) Only

See Figure 436.

1. Disconnect the electrical connector.

2. Remove the two MAF/IAT sensor fasteners (1).

3. Remove the sensor (2).

To install:

4. Install the MAF/IAT sensor. Tighten the two fasteners to 22 inch lbs. (2.5 Nm).

5. Attach the electrical connector.

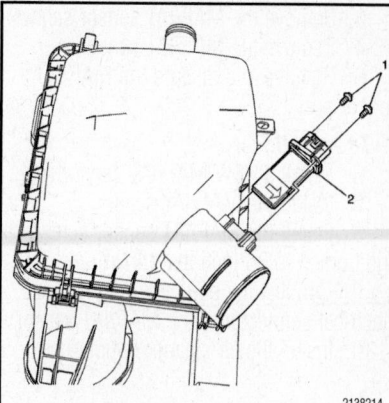

Fig. 436 (1) Mass Airflow Sensor/Intake Air Temperature sensor fasteners and the sensor (2)

3.6L Engine

See Figures 437 and 438.

1. Remove the air cleaner outlet duct.

2. Disconnect the engine wiring harness electrical connector from the Mass Air Flow (MAF)/Intake Air Temperature (IAT) sensor.

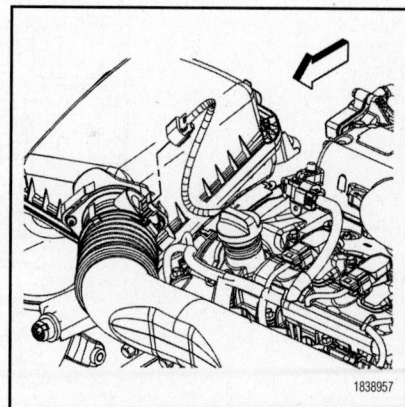

Fig. 437 Disconnect the engine wiring harness electrical connector from the Mass Air Flow (MAF)/Intake Air Temperature (IAT) sensor

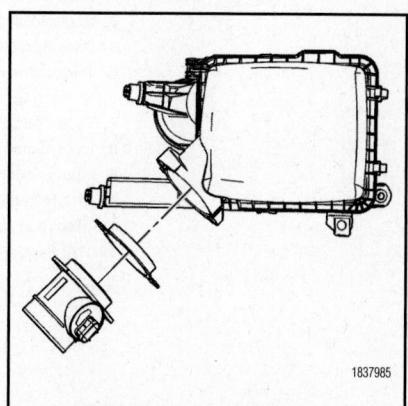

Fig. 438 MAF/IAT sensor replacement

3. Remove the MAF/IAT sensor screws.
4. Remove the MAF/IAT sensor.
5. Remove and discard the MAF/IAT sensor seal.

To install:

6. Install a NEW MAF/IAT sensor seal.
7. Install the MAF/IAT sensor.
8. Install the MAF/IAT sensor screws and tighten to 35 inch lbs. (4 Nm).
9. Connect the engine wiring harness electrical connector to the MAF/IAT sensor.
10. Install the air cleaner outlet duct.

VEHICLE SPEED SENSOR (VSS)

LOCATION

4T45-E

On the transmission case.

4T65-E

See Figure 439.

Refer to the accompanying illustration.

REMOVAL & INSTALLATION

4T45-E

See Figure 440.

⁂ CAUTION

Ensure that the vehicle is properly supported and squarely positioned. To help avoid personal injury when a vehicle is on a hoist, provide additional support for the vehicle on the opposite end from which the components are being removed.

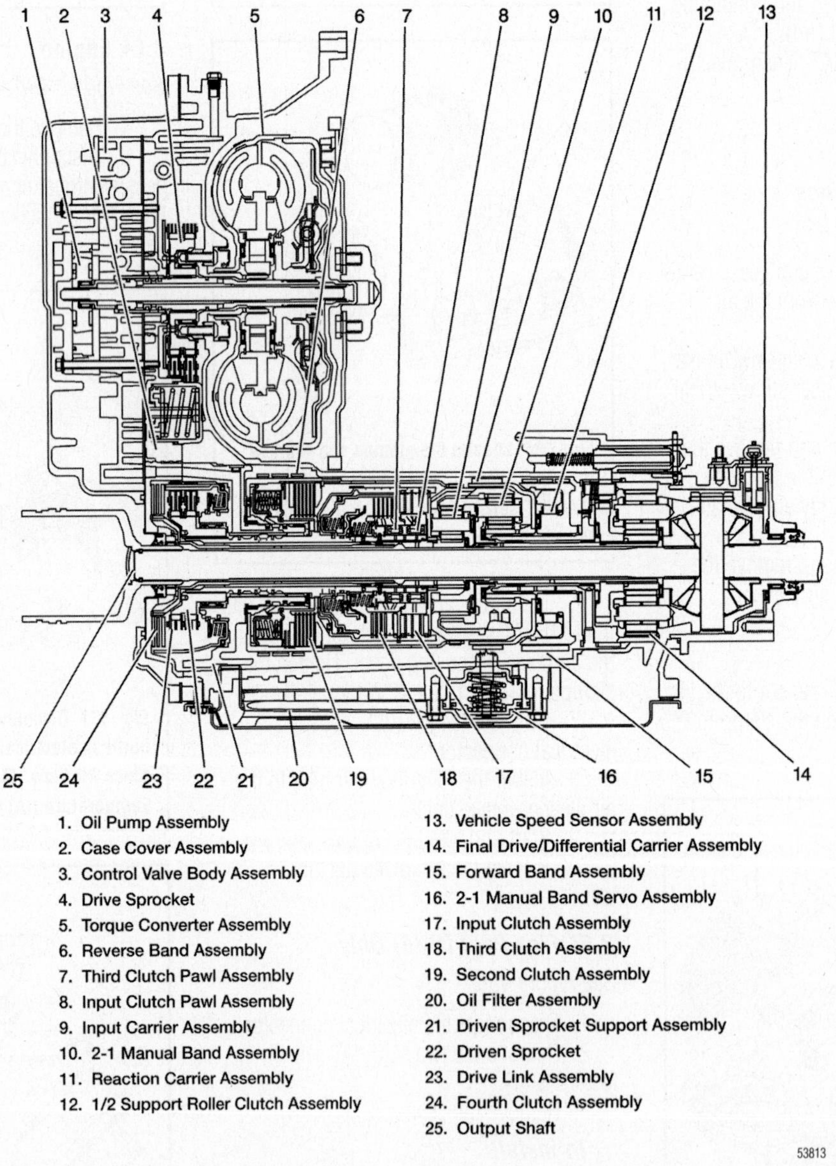
1
2
3
4
5
6
7
8
9
10
11
12
13
14
15
16
17
18
19
20
21
22
23
24
25
1. Oil Pump Assembly
2. Case Cover Assembly
3. Control Valve Body Assembly
4. Drive Sprocket
5. Torque Converter Assembly
6. Reverse Band Assembly
7. Third Clutch Pawl Assembly
8. Input Clutch Pawl Assembly
9. Input Carrier Assembly
10. 2-1 Manual Band Assembly
11. Reaction Carrier Assembly
12. 1/2 Support Roller Clutch Assembly
13. Vehicle Speed Sensor Assembly
14. Final Drive/Differential Carrier Assembly
15. Forward Band Assembly
16. 2-1 Manual Band Servo Assembly
17. Input Clutch Assembly
18. Third Clutch Assembly
19. Second Clutch Assembly
20. Oil Filter Assembly
21. Driven Sprocket Support Assembly
22. Driven Sprocket
23. Drive Link Assembly
24. Fourth Clutch Assembly
25. Output Shaft
53813

Fig. 439 VSS location (13)

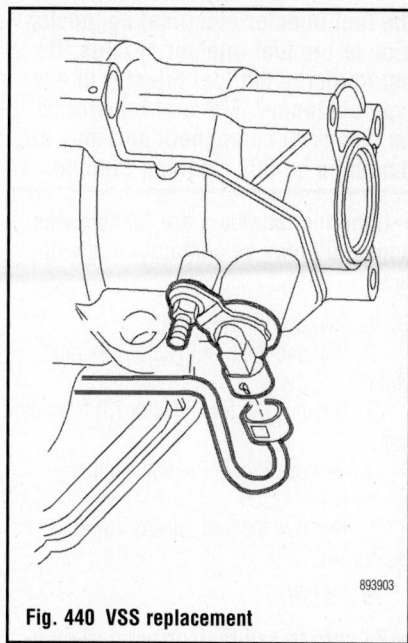

Fig. 440 VSS replacement

1. Position the vehicle on a hoist and raise the vehicle.

2. Disconnect the vehicle speed sensor (VSS) electrical connector.

3. Remove the VSS electrical harness retainer from the VSS stud.

4. Remove the VSS stud.

5. Remove the output VSS from the transmission case.

➡**Inspect the O-ring for damage and replace it if necessary.**

6. Remove the O-ring from the VSS.

To install:

7. Install the O-ring onto the VSS.

8. Install the output VSS into the transmission case.

9. Install the VSS stud and tighten the stud to 106 inch lbs. (12 Nm).

10. Install the VSS electrical harness retainer to the VSS stud.

11. Connect the VSS electrical connector.

12. Lower the vehicle.

4T65-E

See Figure 441.

1. Raise and support the vehicle.

2. Remove the right front tire and wheel.

3. Disconnect the vehicle speed sensor (VSS) electrical connector.

4. Remove the VSS bolt (9).

5. Remove the VSS (10) from the extension case.

6. Remove the O-ring from the VSS.

To install:

7. Install the O-ring to the VSS (10).

8. Install the VSS (10).

9. Install the VSS bolt (9).

10. Tighten the bolt (9) to 106 inch lbs. (12 Nm).

11. Connect the VSS electrical connector.

12. Install the right front tire and wheel.

13. Lower the vehicle.

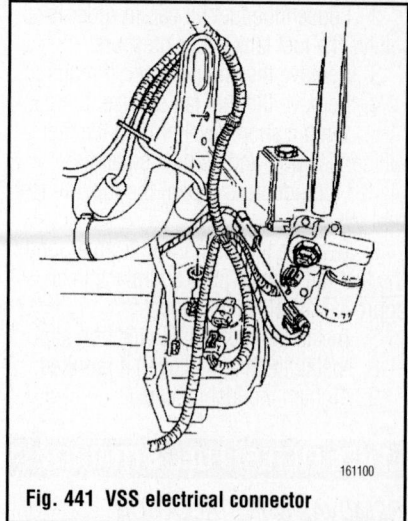

Fig. 441 VSS electrical connector

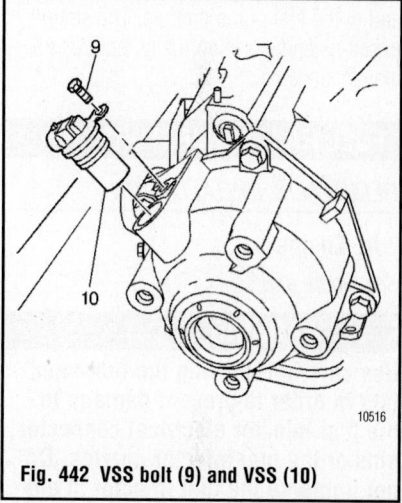

Fig. 442 VSS bolt (9) and VSS (10)

FUEL   **GASOLINE FUEL INJECTION SYSTEM**

FUEL SYSTEM SERVICE PRECAUTIONS

Safety is the most important factor when performing not only fuel system service but any type of service. Failure to conduct maintenance and repairs in a safe manner may result in serious personal injury or death. Servicing and testing of the vehicle's fuel system components can be accomplished safely and effectively by adhering to the following rules and guidelines:

• To avoid the possibility of fire and personal injury, always disconnect the negative battery cable unless the repair or test procedure requires that battery voltage be applied.

• Warning: Gasoline or gasoline vapors are highly flammable. A fire could occur if an ignition source is present. Never drain or store gasoline or diesel fuel in an open con-

tainer, due to the possibility of fire or explosion.

• Always relieve the fuel system pressure prior to disconnecting any fuel system component (injector, fuel rail, pressure regulator, etc.), fitting or fuel line connection. Exercise extreme caution whenever relieving fuel system pressure to avoid exposing skin, face and eyes to fuel spray. Please be advised that fuel under pressure may penetrate the skin or any part of the body that it contacts.

• Always place a shop towel or cloth around the fitting or connection prior to loosening to absorb any excess fuel due to spillage. Ensure that all fuel spillage (should it occur) is quickly removed from engine surfaces. Ensure that all fuel soaked cloths or towels are deposited into a suitable waste container.

• Always keep a dry chemical (Class B) fire extinguisher near the work area.

• Do not allow fuel spray or fuel vapors to come into contact with a spark or open flame.

• Always use a back-up wrench when loosening and tightening fuel line connection fittings. This will prevent unnecessary stress and torsion to fuel line piping.

• Always replace worn fuel fitting O-rings with new ones. Do not substitute fuel hose or equivalent where fuel pipe is installed.

Before servicing the vehicle, make sure to also refer to the precautions in the beginning of this section.

RELIEVING FUEL SYSTEM PRESSURE

1. If the fuel system requires repair, prevent fuel spillage by removing the fuel pump fuse.

2. Loosen the fuel fill cap in order to relieve the fuel tank vapor pressure.

3. Remove the engine cover, if required.

4. Remove the fuel rail service port cap.

5. Wrap a shop towel around the fuel rail service port and using a small flat-bladed tool, depress (open) the fuel rail test port valve.

6. Remove the shop towel from around the fuel rail service port, and place in an approved gasoline container.

7. Install the fuel rail service port cap.

8. Install the engine cover, if required.

9. Tighten the fuel fill cap.

FUEL FILTER/ FUEL STRAINER

REMOVAL & INSTALLATION

A fuel strainer is attached to the lower end of the fuel pump module. The strainer is self-cleaning and normally requires no maintenance.

FUEL RAIL & INJECTORS

REMOVAL & INSTALLATION

2.4L Engine

See Figure 443.

✳✳ WARNING

Use care in removing the fuel injectors in order to prevent damage to the fuel injector electrical connector pins or the fuel injector nozzles. Do not immerse the fuel injector in any type of cleaner. The fuel injector is an electrical component and may be damaged by this cleaning method.

➡**If the fuel injectors are leaking, the engine oil may be contaminated with fuel.**

1. Remove the fuel rail.
2. Remove the fuel injector retainer (1).

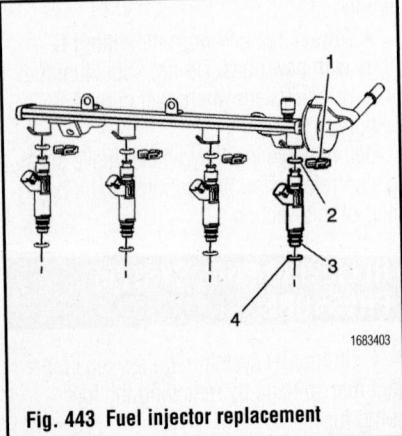

Fig. 443 Fuel injector replacement

3. Remove the fuel injector (3) from the fuel rail.

4. Remove the fuel injector upper O-ring (2).

5. Remove the fuel injector lower O-ring (4).

To install:

➡**The fuel injector assembly is stamped with a part number identification. Be sure to use the correct part number when ordering replacement fuel injectors.**

6. Lubricate the NEW fuel injector O-rings with clean engine oil.

7. Install the NEW fuel injector upper O-ring (2).

8. Install the NEW fuel injector lower O-ring (4).

9. Install the fuel injector (3) to the fuel rail.

10. Install the fuel injector retainer (1).

11. Install the fuel rail.

3.5L Engine

See Figures 444 and 445.

✳✳ WARNING

Use care in removing the fuel injectors in order to prevent damage to

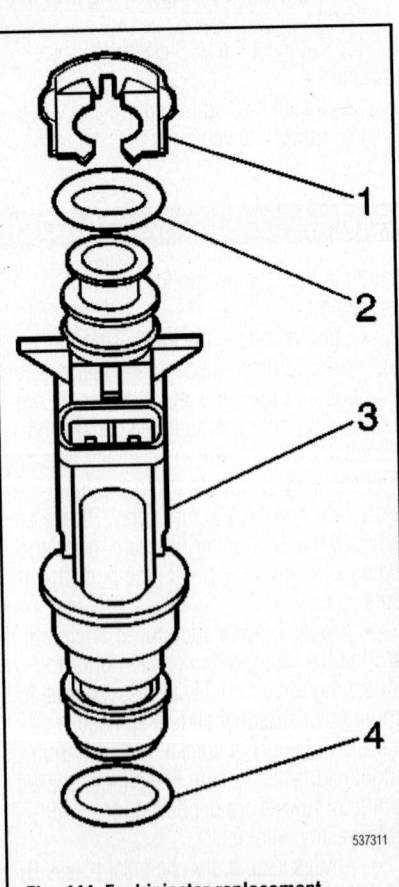

Fig. 444 Fuel injector replacement

the fuel injector electrical connector pins or the fuel injector nozzles. Do not immerse the fuel injector in any type of cleaner. The fuel injector is an electrical component and may be damaged by this cleaning method.

➡**If the fuel injectors are leaking, the engine oil may be contaminated with fuel.**

1. Remove the fuel rail.

2. Remove the fuel injector retaining clip (1).

3. Remove the fuel injector (3) from the fuel rail.

4. Remove the fuel injector upper O-ring (2).

5. Remove the fuel injector lower O-ring (4).

To install:

➡**Be sure to use the correct part number when ordering replacement fuel injectors. The fuel injector assembly (1) is stamped with a part number identification (2).**

6. Lubricate the new injector O-rings with clean engine oil.

7. Install the fuel injector upper O-ring.

8. Install the fuel injector lower O-ring.

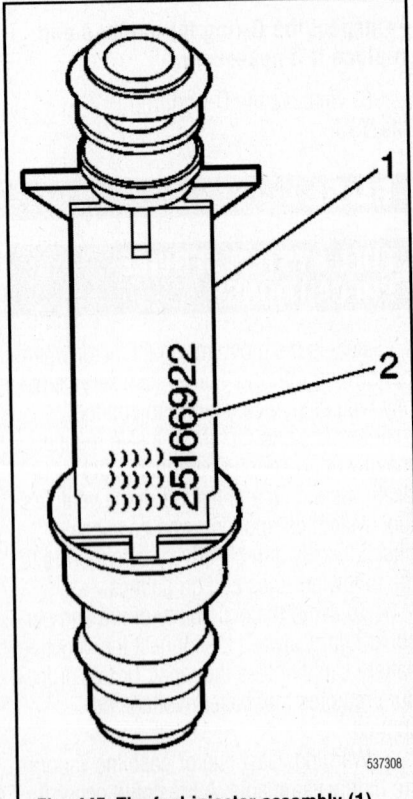

Fig. 445 The fuel injector assembly (1) is stamped with a part number identification (2)

9. Install the fuel injector to the fuel rail.

10. Install the fuel injector retaining clip.

11. Install the fuel rail.

3.6L Engine

See Figures 446 through 449.

1. Remove the fuel injector sight shield.

2. Disconnect the engine wiring harness electrical connector (1) from the fuel injector wiring harness electrical connector.

3. Disconnect the fuel feed pipe quick-connect fitting from the fuel rail.

4. Remove the upper intake manifold.

✳✳ CAUTION

Wear safety glasses when using compressed air in order to prevent eye injury. Use compressed air in order

to remove any debris from the around the area where the fuel injectors enter the lower intake manifold.

5. Remove the fuel rail bolts.

✳✳ WARNING

Note the following:

- Remove the fuel rail assembly carefully in order to prevent damage to the injector electrical connector terminals and the injector spray tips. Support the fuel rail after the fuel rail is removed in order to avoid damaging the fuel rail components.
- Cap the fittings and plug the holes when servicing the fuel system in order to prevent dirt and other contaminants from entering open pipes and passages.

6. Remove the fuel rail with fuel injectors from the lower intake manifold.

7. Lift up the fuel injector electrical connector retainer (2).

8. Push in the fuel injector electrical connector tab (1) in order to disconnect the connector from the injector.

9. Remove the fuel injector retainer clip.

10. Remove the fuel injector.

11. Remove and discard the fuel injector seals.

To install:

12. Install NEW fuel injector seals.

13. Install the fuel injector.

14. Install the fuel injector retainer clip.

15. Install the fuel injector electrical connector.

16. Push down on the fuel injector electrical connector retainer, securing the electrical connector.

17. Install the fuel rail with fuel injectors to the lower intake manifold.

18. Install the fuel rail bolts and tighten them to 89 inch lbs. (10 Nm).

19. Install the upper intake manifold.

20. Connect the fuel feed pipe quick-connect fitting to the fuel rail.

21. Connect the engine wiring harness electrical connector to the fuel injector wiring harness electrical connector.

22. Install the fuel injector sight shield.

3.9L Engine

See Figures 450, 444 and 445.

An 8-digit identification number is stamped on the fuel rail. Refer to this number if servicing or part replacement is required.

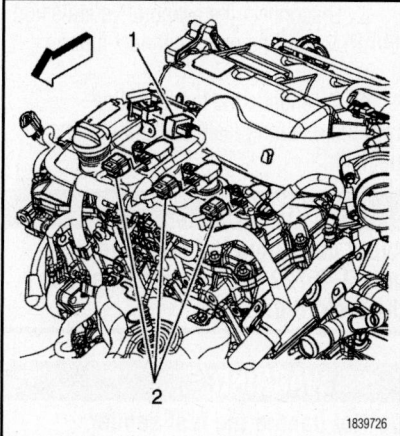

Fig. 446 Disconnect the engine wiring harness electrical connector (1) from the fuel injector wiring harness electrical connector

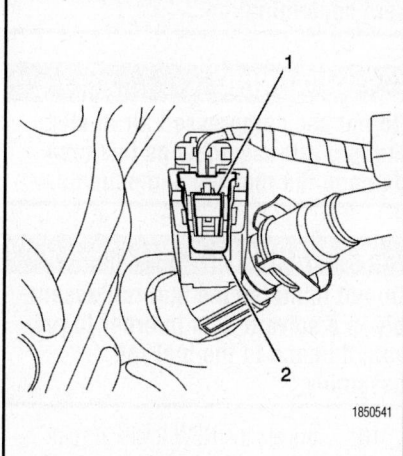

Fig. 448 Fuel injector electrical connector retainer (2) and tab (1)

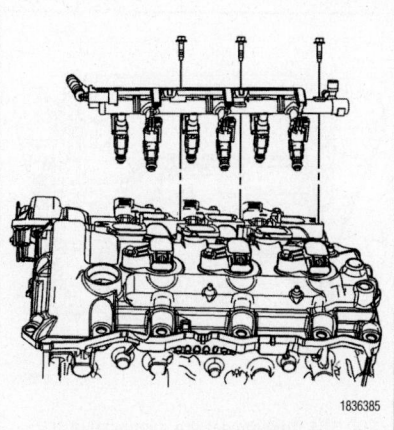

Fig. 447 Remove the fuel rail with fuel injectors from the lower intake manifold

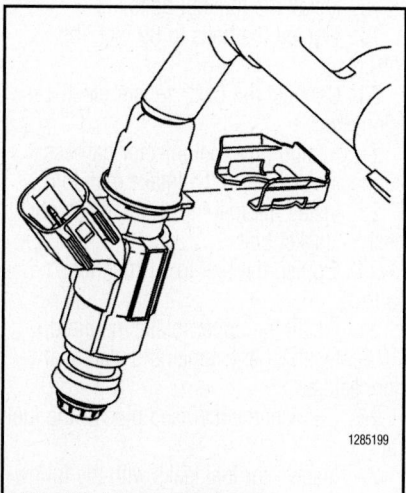

Fig. 449 Injector retainer clip

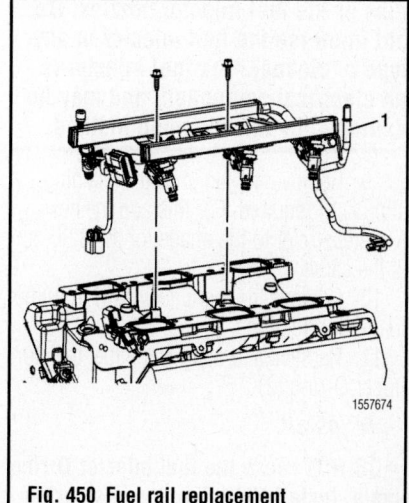

Fig. 450 Fuel rail replacement

In order to reduce the risk of fire and personal injury that may result from a fuel leak, always install the fuel injector O-rings in the proper position. If the upper and lower O-rings are different colors (black and brown), be sure to install the black O-ring in the upper position and the brown O-ring in the lower position on the fuel injector. The O-rings are the same size but are made of different materials.

✳✳ WARNING

Cap the fittings and plug the holes when servicing the fuel system in order to prevent dirt and other contaminants from entering the open pipes and passages.

➡If the fuel injectors leak, the engine oil may be contaminated with fuel.

1. Disconnect the fuel feed pipe from the fuel rail.
2. Disconnect any remaining electrical connectors.
3. Remove the upper intake manifold.
4. Remove the fuel injector harness connector bracket bolt from the intake manifold.
5. Disconnect the camshaft position (CMP) sensor electrical connector.
6. Remove the fuel rail bolts.
7. Remove the fuel rail (1).
8. Remove and discard the O-rings from the spray tip end of each injector.

✳✳ WARNING

Use care in removing the fuel injectors in order to prevent damage to the fuel injector electrical connector pins or the fuel injector nozzles. Do not immerse the fuel injector in any type of cleaner. The fuel injector is an electrical component and may be damaged by this cleaning method.

9. Remove the fuel injector retaining clip (1), if required. For this and the next two steps refer to the image for the 3.5L, it is the same.
10. Remove the fuel injector (3) from the fuel rail, if required.
11. Remove and discard the fuel injector upper O-ring (2).

To install:

➡DO NOT reuse the fuel injector O-ring seals. Install NEW O-ring seals during assembly.

➡Use the correct part number when ordering the replacement fuel injectors.

The fuel injector (1) is stamped with a part number identification (2). Refer to the image for the 3.5L, it is the same.

12. Lubricate the NEW injector O-rings with clean engine oil.
13. Install the NEW fuel injector upper O-ring.
14. Install the fuel injector to the fuel rail, if required.
15. Install the fuel injector retaining clip, if required.

✳✳ WARNING

Use care when servicing the fuel system components, especially the fuel injector electrical connectors, the fuel injector tips, and the injector O-rings. Plug the inlet and the outlet ports of the fuel rail in order to prevent contamination.

✳✳ WARNING

Do not use compressed air to clean the fuel rail assembly as this may damage the fuel rail components.

✳✳ WARNING

Do not immerse the fuel rail assembly in a solvent bath in order to prevent damage to the fuel rail assembly.

16. Lubricate the NEW lower injector O-rings with clean engine oil.
17. Install the fuel rail assembly into the intake manifold. Tilt the fuel rail assembly slightly to install the injectors.
18. Install the fuel rail bolts.
19. Tighten the bolts to 89 inch lbs. (10 Nm).
20. Connect the CMP sensor electrical connector.
21. Position the fuel injector harness connector bracket to the intake manifold.
22. Install the fuel injector harness connector bracket bolt.
23. Tighten the bolt to 71 inch lbs. (8 Nm).
24. Install the upper intake manifold.
25. Connect any remaining electrical connectors.
26. Connect the fuel feed pipe to the fuel rail.
27. Inspect for fuel leaks with the following procedure:
    a. Turn ON the ignition for 2 seconds.

b. Turn OFF the ignition for 10 seconds.
    c. Turn ON the ignition.
    d. Inspect for fuel leaks.

FUEL TANK FUEL PUMP MODULE

REMOVAL & INSTALLATION

2.4L, 3.5L & 3.9L Engines
See Figures 451 through 454.

✳✳ CAUTION

In order to reduce the risk of fire and personal injury that may result from a fuel leak, always replace the fuel sender gasket when reinstalling the fuel sender assembly.

1. Remove the fuel tank. Refer to Fuel Tank Replacement.
2. Disconnect the fuel pressure sensor and sender electrical connections.
3. Disconnect the evaporative emission (EVAP) vapor line quick-connect fittings (1, 2).
4. Disengage the fuel feed line from the retaining features built into the fuel tank.

✳✳ WARNING

Avoid damaging the lock ring. Use only J-45722 to prevent damage to the lock ring.

✳✳ WARNING

Do Not handle the fuel sender assembly by the fuel pipes. The amount of leverage generated by handling the fuel pipes could damage the joints.

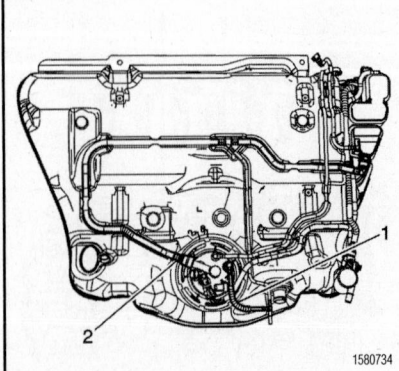

Fig. 451 Disconnect the evaporative emission (EVAP) vapor line quick-connect fittings (1, 2)

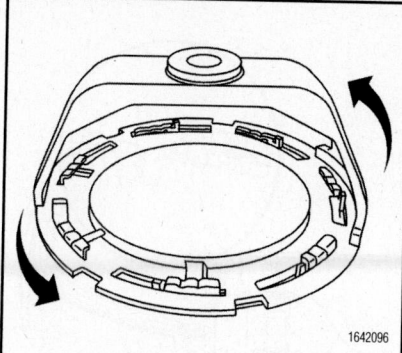

Fig. 452 Use the J-45722 wrench and a long breaker-bar in order to unlock the fuel sender lock ring

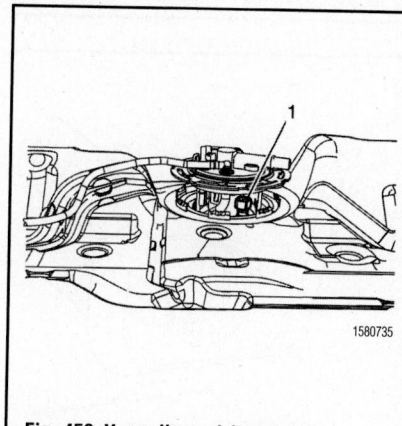

Fig. 453 Vapor line quick-connect fitting (1)

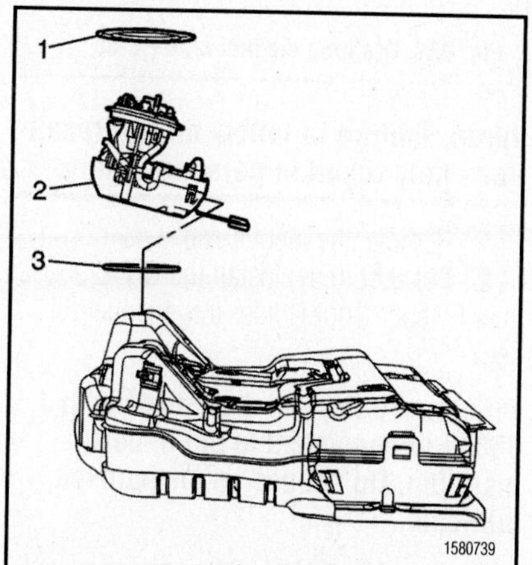

Fig. 454 Fuel sender assembly (2)

➡Do NOT use impact tools. Significant force will be required to release the lock ring. The use of a hammer and screwdriver is not recommended. Secure the fuel tank in order to prevent fuel tank rotation.

5. Use the J-45722 wrench and a long breaker-bar in order to unlock the fuel sender lock ring.

➡The fuel sender assembly may spring up from its position.

➡When removing the fuel sender assembly from the fuel tank, be aware that the reservoir bucket is full of fuel. It must be tipped slightly during removal to avoid damage to the float. Discard the fuel sender assembly O-ring and replace it with a new one. Carefully discard the fuel in the reservoir bucket into an approved container.

6. Raise the fuel sender assembly out of the tank far enough to access the vapor line quick-connect fitting (1) on the underside of the sender cover.

7. Disconnect the vapor line quick-connect fitting (1).

8. Remove the fuel sender assembly (2) from the fuel tank.

To install:

9. Install a NEW O-ring seal (3) onto the fuel sender.

10. Install the fuel sender assembly (2) into the fuel tank far enough to connect the vapor line quick-connect fitting on the underside of the sender cover.

11. Connect the vapor line quick-connect fitting.

12. Align the cover "paddle" or anti-rotation feature with the corresponding feature in the top of the fuel tank.

13. Slowly apply pressure to the top of the spring loaded sender cover until the sender aligns flush with the surface of the tank.

➡Note the following:

• Some lock rings were manufactured with "DO NOT REUSE" stamped into them. These lock rings may be reused if they are not damaged or warped.

• Inspect the lock ring for damage due to improper removal or installation procedures. If damage is found, install a NEW lock ring.

• Check the lock ring for flatness.

➡Always replace the fuel sender seal when installing the fuel sender assembly. Replace the lock ring if necessary. DO NOT apply any type of lubrication in the seal groove.

14. Ensure the lock ring is installed with the correct side facing upward. A correctly installed lock ring will only turn in a clockwise direction.

15. Use the J-45722 wrench in order to install the fuel sender lock ring. Turn the fuel sender lock ring in a clockwise direction.

16. Turn the lock ring until the ring seats on the second detent.

17. Engage the fuel feed line to the retaining features built into the fuel tank.

18. Connect the EVAP vapor line quick-connect fittings.

19. Connect the fuel pressure sensor and sender electrical connections.

20. Install the fuel tank. Refer to Fuel Tank Replacement.

21. Lower the vehicle.

22. Refill the tank.

23. Connect the negative battery cable. Refer to Battery Negative Cable Disconnection and Connection.

24. Inspect for fuel leaks with the following procedure:

a. Turn ON the ignition for 2 seconds.

b. Turn OFF the ignition for 10 seconds.

c. Turn ON the ignition.

d. Inspect for fuel leaks.

FUEL TANK MODULE REPLACEMENT (FUEL PUMP)

REMOVAL & INSTALLATION

3.6L Engine

See Figures 455 through 457.

1. Remove the fuel tank. Refer to Fuel Tank Replacement.

2. Disconnect the fuel tank fuel pump module wiring harness electrical connectors (1, 2) from the fuel pressure sensor and the module.

3. Disconnect the fuel tank vent pipe quick-connect fittings (3, 4) from the module.

4. Install the J 45722 wrench to the fuel pump module lock ring.

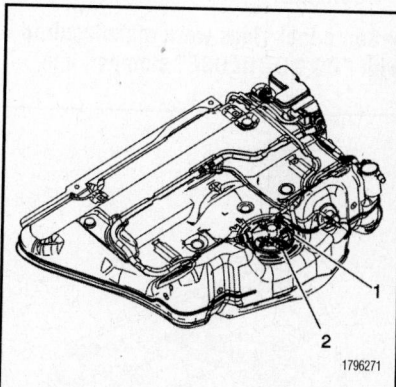

Fig. 455 Fuel tank fuel pump module wiring harness electrical connectors (1, 2) and fuel tank vent pipe quick-connect fittings (3, 4)

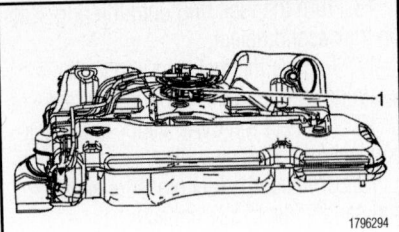

Fig. 456 Lift the fuel pump module up slightly in order to disconnect the fuel tank vent pipe quick-connect fitting (1) from the module cover

➡️Do NOT use impact tools. Significant force will be required to release the lock ring. The use of a hammer and screwdriver is not recommended. Secure the fuel tank in order to prevent fuel tank rotation.

5. Using the J 45722 wrench and a long breaker-bar, rotate the lock ring in a counterclockwise direction in order to unlock the lock ring. Refer to image for 2.4L and 3.5L as it is the same.

6. Remove the J 45722 wrench from the fuel pump module lock ring.

7. Lift the fuel pump module up slightly in order to disconnect the fuel tank vent pipe quick-connect fitting (1) from the module cover.

8. Raise the fuel pump module up from the fuel tank. Tilt the module in order to allow the fuel level sensor arm and float to clear the module opening.

9. Remove the fuel pump module.

10. Remove and discard the fuel pump module seal.

11. Clean the fuel pump module sealing surfaces.

To install:

➡️Some lock rings were manufactured with "DO NOT REUSE" stamped into

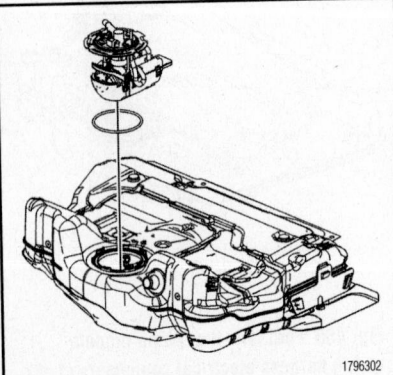

Fig. 457 Exploded view of the fuel pump module and seal

them. These lock rings may be reused if they are not damaged or warped.

- Inspect the lock ring for damage due to improper removal or installation procedures. If damage is found, install a NEW fuel pump module.
- Inspect the lock ring for flatness as best as possible. If the lock ring is warped, replace the fuel pump module.

12. Clean any contamination from the male pipe ends of the fuel pump module.

13. Place a NEW fuel tank module seal onto the fuel tank.

14. Insert the fuel pump module into the fuel tank allowing the sensor arm and float to clear the module opening.

15. Lower the module down into the fuel tank until the fuel tank vent pipe quick-connect fitting can be connected.

16. Connect the fuel tank vent pipe quick-connect fitting at the module cover.

17. Press the fuel tank module downward.

18. Install the J 45722 wrench to the fuel pump module lock ring.

➡️Ensure that the lock ring is installed with the correct side facing upward. A correctly installed lock ring will only turn in a clockwise direction.

19. Using the J 45722 wrench and a long breaker-bar, rotate the lock ring in a clockwise direction in order the lock the lock ring.

20. Connect the fuel tank vent pipe quick-connect fittings to the module.

21. Connect the fuel tank fuel pump module wiring harness electrical connectors to the fuel pressure sensor and the module.

22. Install the fuel tank. Refer to Fuel Tank Replacement.

FUEL TANK

DRAINING

See Figures 458 and 459.

✳️ CAUTION

Never drain or store fuel in an open container. Always use an approved fuel storage container in order to reduce the chance of fire or explosion.

✳️ CAUTION

Place a dry chemical (Class B) fire extinguisher nearby before performing any on-vehicle service proce-

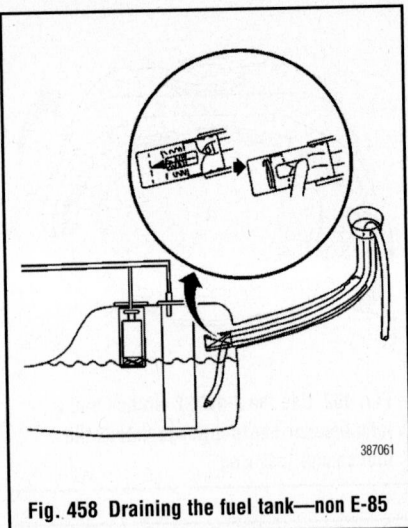

Fig. 458 Draining the fuel tank—non E-85

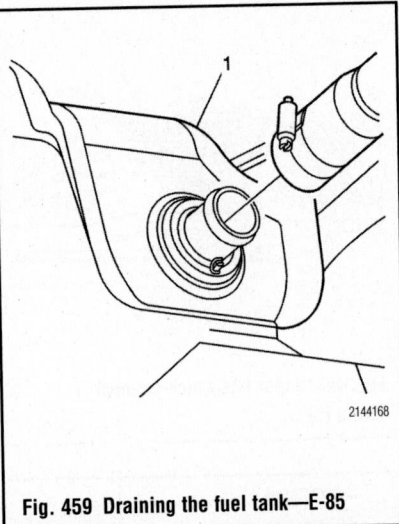

Fig. 459 Draining the fuel tank—E-85

dures. Failure to follow these precautions may result in personal injury.

1. Remove the fuel fill cap.

2. For 3.6L only: Install the CH 42960-2 Fuel Flapper Door Holder into the fuel fill neck.

➡️Lubricate the fuel drain hose with J 36850 or equivalent to aid in hose insertion. Do not use an unapproved lubricant.

3. Insert the CH 45004 or an equivalent fuel drain hose into the fuel tank until the bottom is reached.

4. Use a hand or air operated pump device in order to drain as much fuel through the fuel fill pipe as possible.

REMOVAL & INSTALLATION

2.4L, 3.5L & 3.9L Engines

See Figures 460 through 464.

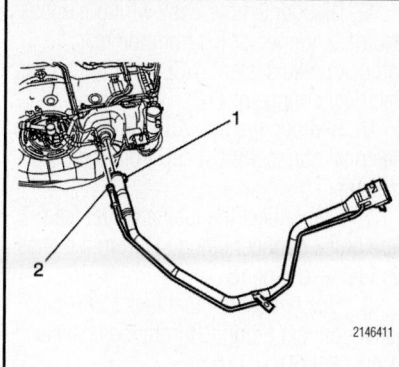

Fig. 460 Loosen the fuel fill pipe hose clamp (1) at the fuel tank

1. Relieve the fuel system pressure. Refer to Fuel Pressure Relief.

2. Drain the fuel tank. Refer to Fuel Tank Draining.

3. Raise and support the vehicle.

4. Loosen the fuel fill pipe hose clamp (1) at the fuel tank.

5. For 2.4L and 3.9L: Disconnect and reposition the rear stabilizer shaft.

6. Disconnect the vapor recirculation line quick-connect fitting (2).

7. Disconnect the fuel fill pipe hose from the fuel tank.

8. Release the exhaust pipe insulators from the underbody hangers.

9. Release the muffler insulator from the underbody hanger and slowly lower the exhaust to rest on a tall jack stand. If this is not possible, remove the rear half of the exhaust system at the take down flange.

10. If applicable, disengage the rear antilock brake system (ABS) wiring harness connector clip from the side of the EVAP canister bracket.

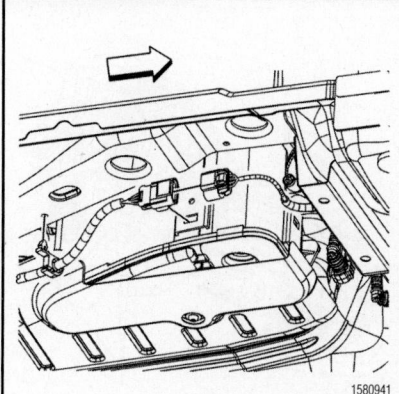

Fig. 461 If applicable, disengage the rear antilock brake system (ABS) wiring harness connector clip from the side of the EVAP canister bracket

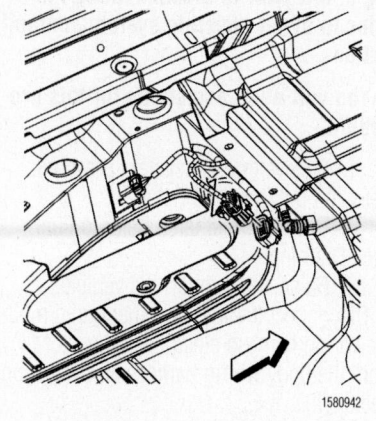

Fig. 462 Disengage the underbody wiring harness connector clip from the EVAP canister bracket

11. Disconnect the fuel tank jumper electrical connector from the underbody wiring harness.

12. Disengage the underbody wiring harness connector clip from the EVAP canister bracket.

13. Use an appropriate adjustable jack to support the fuel tank during removal.

14. Remove the fuel tank strap bolts.

15. Remove the fuel tank straps.

16. For 3.5L: Using the adjustable jack, lower the fuel tank slightly in order to access the fuel line connections.

17. Disconnect the fuel feed (2) and vapor (1) line quick-connect fittings.

18. Cap or plug the fuel feed and vapor lines in order to prevent fuel loss and/or system contamination.

19. In order to clear the exhaust pipe; slowly lower the right side of the fuel tank.

20. Once the tank is clear of the right frame rail, remove the fuel tank down and forward toward the right side of the vehicle.

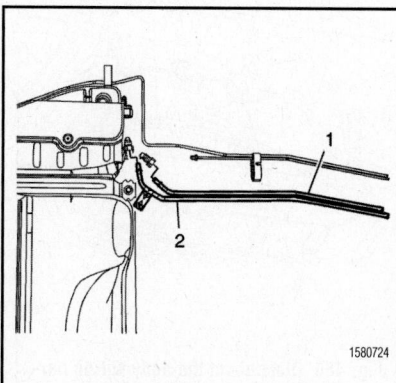

Fig. 463 Disconnect the fuel feed (2) and vapor (1) line quick-connect fittings

21. If the fuel tank is being replaced, disconnect and remove the fuel tank electrical harness.

22. If the fuel tank is being replaced, perform the following:

   a. Disconnect and remove the fuel tank vapor line.

   b. Remove the EVAP canister.

   c. Remove the EVAP canister vent solenoid valve.

   d. Remove the fuel pump module. Refer to Fuel Tank Fuel Pump Module Replacement.

To install:

23. If the fuel tank is being replaced, perform the following:

   a. Install the fuel pump module. Refer to Fuel Tank Fuel Pump Module Replacement.

   b. Install the EVAP canister vent solenoid valve.

   c. Install the EVAP canister.

   d. Install and connect the fuel tank vapor line.

24. If the fuel tank is being replaced, install and connect the fuel tank electrical harness.

25. Begin to install the left side of the fuel tank over the exhaust pipe.

26. Raise the right side of the fuel tank into position inboard of the right frame rail.

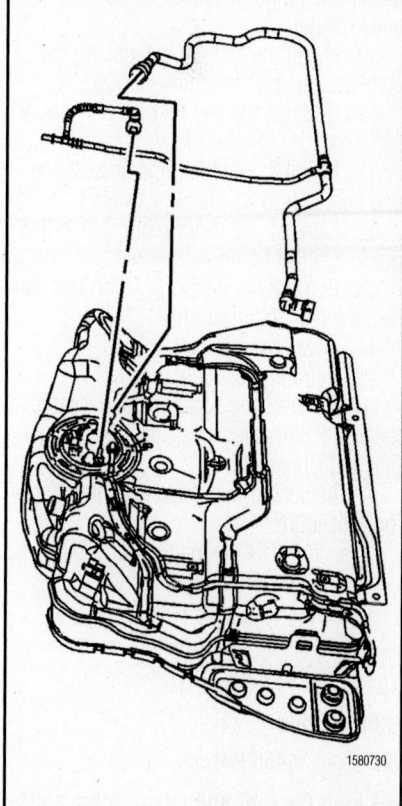

Fig. 464 Fuel pump module replacement

Use care in feeding the fuel feed, EVAP vapor line, and the fuel sender electrical harness over the exhaust system.

27. For 3.5L: Remove the caps or plugs from the fuel feed and vapor lines.

28. For 3.5L: Connect the fuel feed and vapor line quick-connect fittings.

29. Completely raise and install the fuel tank into position.

➡**Ensure that the strap marked with the "L" is installed on the left side and the strap marked "R" is installed on the right side.**

30. Install the fuel tank straps.

31. Install the fuel tank strap bolts and tighten them to 15 ft. lbs. (20 Nm).

32. Remove the adjustable jack from under the fuel tank.

33. For 2.4L and 3.9L: Remove the caps or plugs from the fuel feed and vapor lines.

34. For 2.4L and 3.9L: Connect the fuel feed and vapor line quick-connect fittings.

35. Connect the fuel tank jumper electrical connector to the underbody wiring harness.

36. Engage the underbody wiring harness connector clip to the EVAP canister bracket.

37. If applicable, engage the rear ABS wiring harness connector clip to the side of the EVAP canister bracket.

38. Raise the exhaust into position and install the muffler insulator to the underbody hanger.

39. Install the exhaust extension pipe insulators to the underbody hangers.

40. Connect the fuel fill pipe hose to the fuel tank.

41. Install the fuel fill pipe hose clamp and tighten it to 35 inch lbs. (4 Nm).

42. Connect the vapor recirculation line quick-connect fitting.

43. For 2.4L and 3.9L: Position and connect the rear stabilizer shaft.

44. Lower the vehicle.

45. Refill the fuel tank.

46. Connect the negative battery cable. Refer to Battery Negative Cable Disconnection and Connection.

47. Inspect for fuel leaks with the following procedure:

   a. Turn ON the ignition for 2 seconds.

   b. Turn OFF the ignition for 10 seconds.

   c. Turn ON the ignition.

   d. Inspect for fuel leaks.

3.6L Engine

See Figures 465 through 468.

➡**Clean the fuel and evaporative emission (EVAP) connections and surround-**

ing areas prior to disconnecting the lines to avoid possible system contamination.

➡**You will need assistants for this procedure.**

1. Relieve the fuel system pressure. Refer to Fuel Pressure Relief.

2. Drain the fuel tank. Refer to Fuel Tank Draining.

3. Raise and support the vehicle. Disconnect the fuel tank fuel pump module wiring harness electrical connector (1) from the body wiring harness electrical connector (2).

4. Remove the body wiring harness electrical connector clip (3) from the EVAP canister.

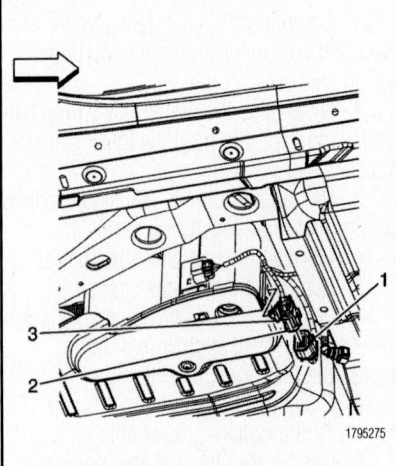

Fig. 465 Disconnect the fuel tank fuel pump module wiring harness electrical connector (1) from the body wiring harness electrical connector (2)

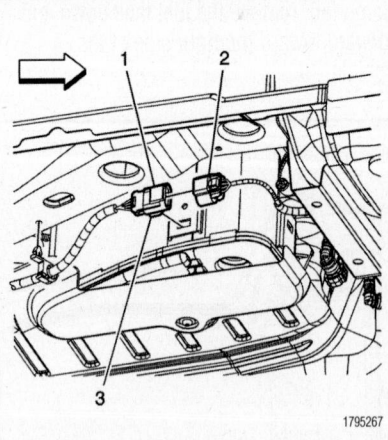

Fig. 466 Disconnect the body wiring harness electrical connector (2) from the rear antilock brake system (ABS) wiring harness electrical connector (1)

5. Disconnect the body wiring harness electrical connector (2) from the rear antilock brake system (ABS) wiring harness electrical connector (1).

6. Remove the rear ABS wiring harness electrical connector (3) clip from the EVAP canister.

7. Disconnect the fuel tank fuel feed pipe quick connect fitting (1) from the chassis fuel feed pipe (3)

8. Disconnect the fuel tank EVAP pipe quick connect fitting (2) from the chassis EVAP pipe (4).

9. Cap the chassis fuel and EVAP pipes in order to prevent possible fuel and/or EVAP system contamination.

10. Loosen the fuel fill pipe hose clamp (1) at the fuel tank.

11. Separate the fuel fill pipe hose from the fuel tank.

12. Disconnect the EVAP canister vent solenoid tube quick connect fitting (2).

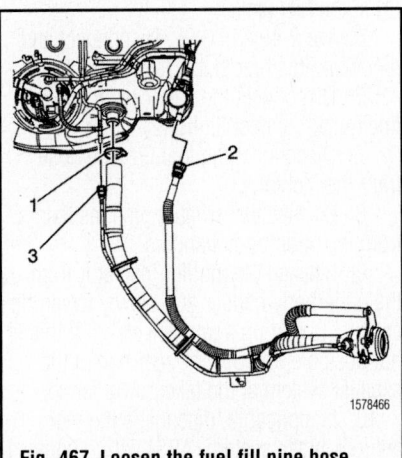

Fig. 467 Loosen the fuel fill pipe hose clamp (1) at the fuel tank.

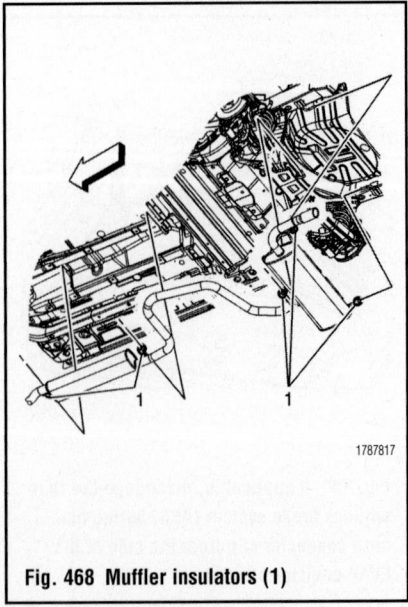

Fig. 468 Muffler insulators (1)

13. Disconnect the vapor recirculation line quick connect fitting (3).

14. Place a jack stand under the muffler assembly.

15. With the aid of an assistant, separate the muffler insulators (1) from the underbody hangers.

16. Slowly lower the muffler assembly allowing it to rest on the jack stand. If this is not possible, remove the muffler assembly.

17. Have assistants support either side of the fuel tank.

18. Remove fuel tank strap bolts and straps.

19. Place a suitable adjustable jack under the fuel tank, and have the assistants rest the fuel tank on the adjustable jack.

20. If applicable, in order to clear the muffler assembly, slowly lower the right side of the fuel tank.

21. Once the tank is clear of the right frame rail, lower the fuel tank down and remove forward toward the right side of the vehicle.

To install:

22. Have assistants support either side of the fuel tank.

23. If applicable, begin to install the right side of the fuel tank over the muffler assembly.

24. If applicable, raise the right side of the fuel tank into position inboard of the right frame rail. Use care in feeding the fuel feed, EVAP line wiring harness over the muffler assembly.

25. If applicable and the muffler assembly was removed, have assistants raise the fuel tank into position.

26. Install fuel tank straps and bolts. Tighten the bolts to 15 ft. lbs. (20 Nm).

27. Raise the muffler assembly into position if applicable, otherwise install the muffler assembly.

28. With the aid of an assistant, install the muffler insulators (1) to the underbody hangers.

29. Remove the jack stand from under the muffler assembly.

30. Install the fuel fill pipe hose to the fuel tank.

31. Connect the vapor recirculation line quick connect fitting (3).

32. Connect the EVAP canister vent solenoid tube quick connect fitting (2).

33. Tighten the fuel fill pipe hose clamp (1) at the fuel tank. Tighten the clamp to 35 inch lbs. (4 Nm).

34. Remove the caps from the fuel and EVAP pipes.

35. Connect the fuel tank EVAP pipe

quick connect fitting (2) to the chassis EVAP pipe (4).

36. Connect the fuel tank fuel feed pipe quick connect fitting (1) to the chassis fuel feed pipe (3).

37. Install the rear ABS wiring harness electrical connector (2) clip to the EVAP canister.

38. Connect the body wiring harness electrical connector (1) to the rear ABS wiring harness electrical connector (2).

39. Install the body wiring harness electrical connector clip (3) to the underbody.

40. Connect the fuel tank fuel pump module wiring harness electrical connector (1) to the body wiring harness electrical connector (2).

41. Lower the vehicle.

42. Refill the fuel tank.

43. Inspect for fuel leaks with the following procedure:

   a. Turn ON the ignition for 2 seconds.

   b. Turn OFF the ignition for 10 seconds.

   c. Turn ON the ignition.

   d. Tighten the fuel fill cap.

   e. Inspect for fuel leaks.

IDLE SPEED

ADJUSTMENT

The engine control module (ECM) controls the air/fuel metering system in order to provide the best possible combination of drivability, fuel economy, and emission control.

THROTTLE BODY

REMOVAL & INSTALLATION

2.4L Engine

See Figures 469 and 470.

❉❉ WARNING

Do not use solvent of any type when cleaning the gasket surfaces on the intake manifold and the throttle body assembly, as damage to the gasket surfaces and throttle body assembly may result.

Use care in cleaning the gasket surfaces on the intake manifold and the throttle body assembly, as sharp tools may damage the gasket surfaces.

❉❉ WARNING

Do not use any solvent that contains Methyl Ethyl Ketene (MEK). This sol-

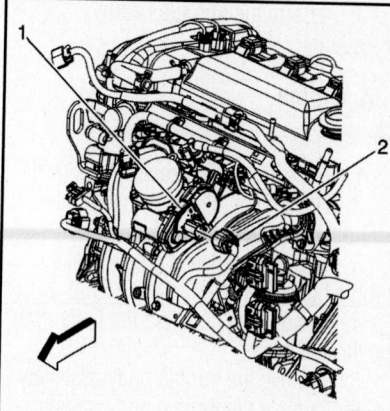

Fig. 469 Disconnect the engine wiring harness electrical connector (2) from the electronic throttle control (1)

vent may damage fuel system components.

➡**DO NOT prop open the throttle blade with the ignition key in the ON position as it may set a diagnostic trouble code (DTC).**

1. Remove the air cleaner outlet duct.

2. Disconnect the engine wiring harness electrical connector (2) from the electronic throttle control (ETC) (1).

3. Remove the throttle body bolts.

4. Remove the throttle body.

5. Inspect the throttle body gasket, and replace if necessary.

To install:

6. Install the throttle body.

7. Install the throttle body bolts and tighten to 89 inch lbs. (10 Nm).

8. Connect the engine wiring harness electrical connector to the ETC.

9. Install the air cleaner outlet duct.

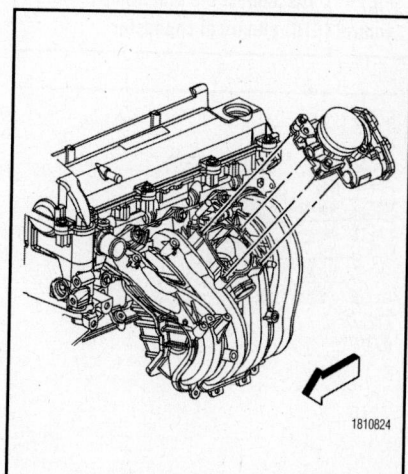

Fig. 470 Throttle body, bolts, and gasket

10. Perform the Throttle Learn procedure.

3.5L Engine

See Figures 471 and 472.

1. Remove the air cleaner outlet duct.
2. Disconnect the electronic throttle control (ETC) electrical connector.
3. Remove the heater pipe nut at the throttle body.
4. Remove the nuts and the bolts from the throttle body.
5. Remove the throttle body assembly.
6. Remove the throttle body gasket.

> ✷✷ **WARNING**
>
> **Do not use solvent of any type when cleaning the gasket surfaces on the intake manifold and the throttle body assembly, as damage to the gasket surfaces and throttle body assembly may result.**

Use care in cleaning the gasket surfaces on the intake manifold and the throttle body assembly, as sharp tools may damage the gasket surfaces.

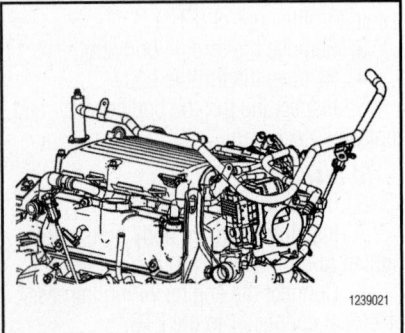

Fig. 471 Disconnect the electronic throttle control (ETC) electrical connector

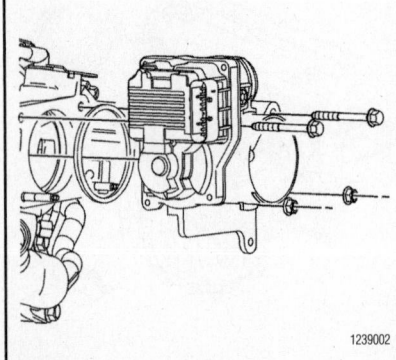

Fig. 472 Throttle body assembly and gasket

7. Clean and inspect the throttle body gasket mating surfaces.

To install:

8. Install a new gasket, if necessary.
9. Install the throttle body assembly.
10. Install the throttle body nuts and the bolts. Tighten the nuts and the bolts to 89 inch lbs. (10 Nm).
11. Install the heater pipe nut to the throttle body. Tighten the nut to 18 inch lbs. (25 Nm).
12. Connect the ETC electrical connector.
13. Install the air cleaner outlet duct.
14. Perform the Throttle Learn Procedure.

3.6L Engine

See Figures 473 and 474.

1. Remove the air cleaner outlet duct.
2. Disconnect the engine wiring harness electrical connector (2) from the electronic throttle control (ETC).

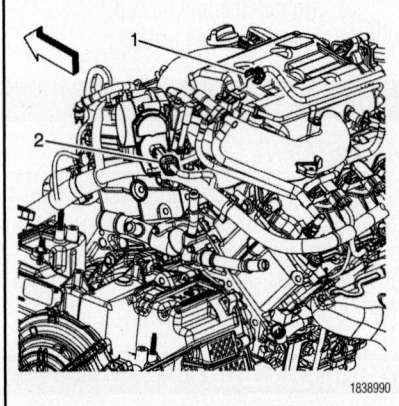

Fig. 473 Disconnect the engine wiring harness electrical connector (2) from the electronic throttle control (ETC)

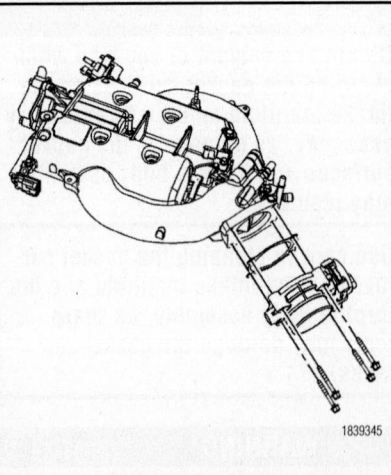

Fig. 474 Throttle body, bolts, and gasket

3. Remove the throttle body bolts.
4. Remove the throttle body and gasket. Discard the gasket.

To install:

5. Position a NEW throttle body gasket to the upper intake manifold.
6. Position the throttle body to the upper intake manifold. Install the throttle body bolts and tighten to 89 inch lbs. (10 Nm).
7. Connect the engine wiring harness electrical connector (2) to the ETC.
8. Install the air cleaner outlet duct.
9. Perform the Throttle Learn Procedure.

3.9L Engine

See Figures 475 and 476.

> ✷✷ **WARNING**
>
> **Do not use solvent of any type when cleaning the gasket surfaces on the intake manifold and the throttle body assembly, as damage to the gasket**

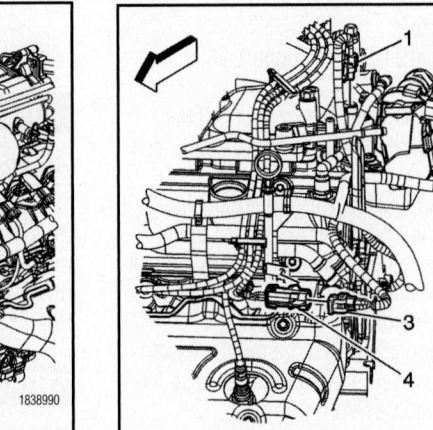

Fig. 475 Disconnect the electronic throttle control (ETC) electrical connector (2)

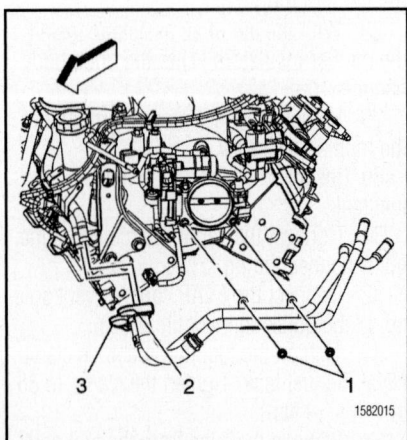

Fig. 476 Remove the heater inlet and outlet pipe nuts (1).

surfaces and throttle body assembly may result.

Use care in cleaning the gasket surfaces on the intake manifold and the throttle body assembly, as sharp tools may damage the gasket surfaces.

1. Remove the intake manifold cover.
2. Remove the air cleaner outlet duct.
3. Disconnect the electronic throttle control (ETC) electrical connector (2).

4. Remove the heater inlet and outlet pipe bracket from the throttle body studs. Reposition the pipes.
5. Remove the throttle body bolts/studs.
6. Remove the throttle body.
7. Remove the throttle body gasket.

To install:
8. Install a new gasket, if necessary.
9. Install the throttle body.
10. Install the throttle body bolts/studs.
11. Tighten the bolts/studs to 89 inch lbs. (10 Nm).

12. Position the heater inlet and outlet pipes and install the pipe bracket to the throttle body studs.
13. Install the heater inlet and outlet pipe nuts.
14. Tighten the nuts to 89 inch lbs. (10 Nm).
15. Connect the ETC electrical connector.
16. Install the air cleaner outlet duct.
17. Install the intake manifold cover.

HEATING & AIR CONDITIONING SYSTEM

BLOWER MOTOR

REMOVAL & INSTALLATION

See Figures 477 through 480.

1. Remove the right closeout panel.
2. Remove the blower motor wire harness connector.

➡Cut through the case as straight as possible because the motor cup must be replaced. In order to prevent damage to the component, do not cut any deeper than necessary to remove the motor cup.

3. Cut out the blower motor using a utility knife in the narrow groove of the lower case.
4. Remove the blower motor.
5. Remove the blower motor nuts.
6. Remove the blower motor from the blower motor cup.

To install:
7. Install the new blower motor to the blower motor cup.
8. Install the blower motor nuts.
9. Tighten the nuts to 21 inch lbs. (2.4 Nm).
10. Install the motor blower seal to the blower motor service ring.

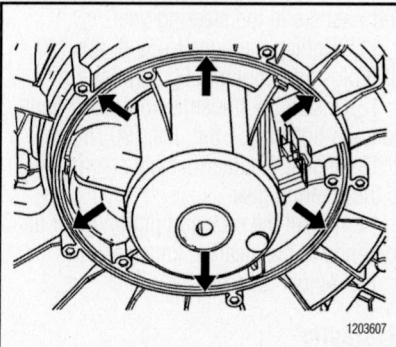
Fig. 477 Remove the blower motor wire harness connector

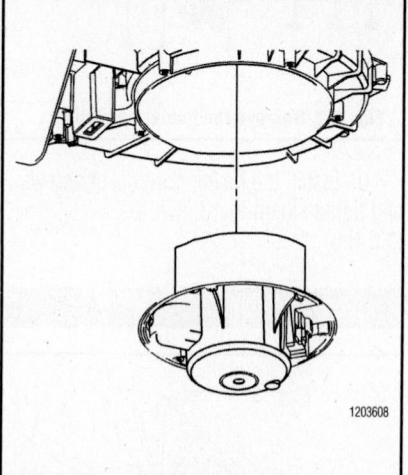
Fig. 478 Remove the blower motor

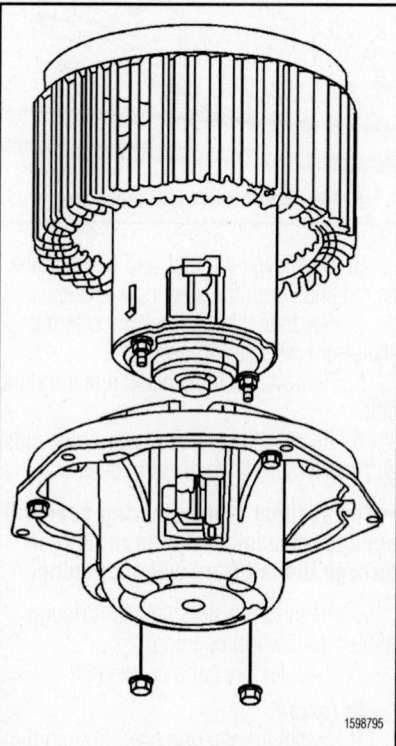
Fig. 479 Remove the blower motor nuts

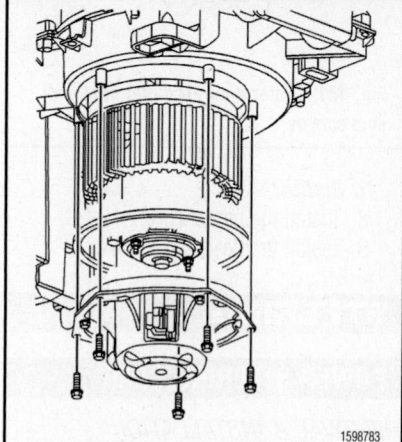
Fig. 480 Install the motor blower seal to the blower motor service ring

11. Install the blower motor.
12. Install the blower motor attachment ring.
13. Install the blower motor screws.
14. Tighten the screws to 13 inch lbs. (1.5 Nm).
15. Install the blower motor wire harness connector.
16. Install the right closeout panel.

HEATER CORE

REMOVAL & INSTALLATION

See Figures 481 through 483.

1. Remove the HVAC module assembly.
2. Remove the center floor air outlet duct screws.
3. Remove the center floor air outlet duct.
4. Drill out the heater core cover heat stakes.
5. Remove the heater core cover screws.
6. Remove the heater core cover.
7. Remove the heater core.

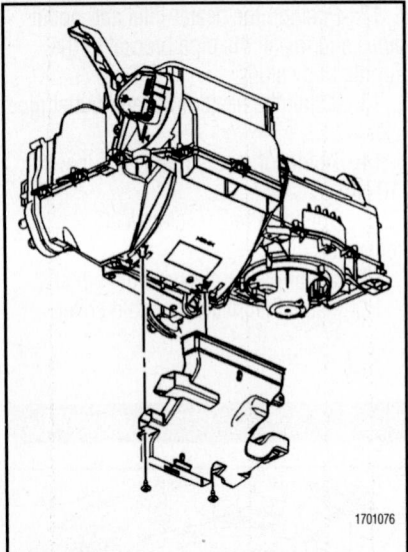

Fig. 481 Center floor air outlet duct and duct screws

To install:

8. Install the heater core.
9. Install the heater core cover.

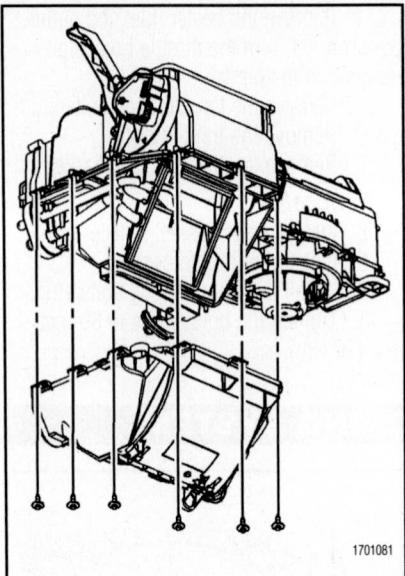

Fig. 482 Remove the heater core cover

10. Install the heater core cover screws and tighten them to 13 inch lbs. (1.5 Nm).

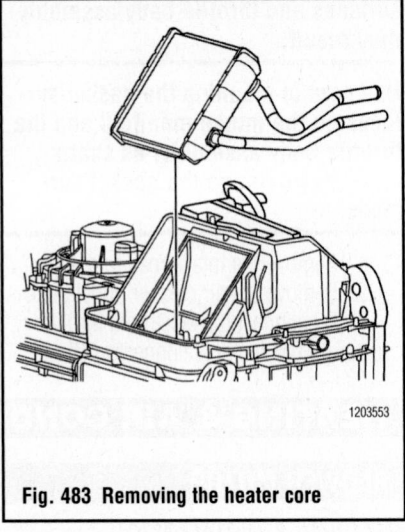

Fig. 483 Removing the heater core

11. Install the center floor air outlet duct.
12. Install the upper floor air outlet duct screws and tighten them to 13 inch lbs. (1.5 Nm).
13. Install the HVAC module assembly.

STEERING

POWER STEERING GEAR

REMOVAL & INSTALLATION

Electronic

See Figures 484 and 485.

❊❊ WARNING

With the vehicle's wheels facing straight ahead, prevent steering wheel rotation with a steering column anti-rotation pin, steering column lock, or a strap. Locking of the steering column will prevent damage and a possible malfunction of the SIR system. Secure the steering wheel in position before disconnecting the following components:

- The steering column
- The intermediate shaft(s)
- The steering gear

1. After disconnecting these components do not rotate the steering wheel or move the front tires and wheels. Failure to follow this procedure may cause the SIR coil assembly to become un-centered and cause possible damage to the SIR coil. If you think the SIR coil has became un-centered, refer to your specific SIR coil's centering procedure to re-center SIR Coil.
2. Turn the front wheels to the straight forward position and secure the steering wheel from moving.

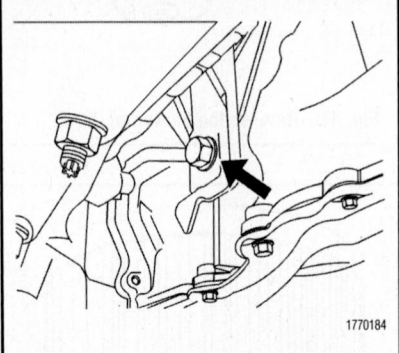

Fig. 484 Transmission rear mount bolt

3. Disengage the rack and pinion outer tie rod ends from the steering knuckles.
4. Separate the intermediate steering shaft from the steering gear.
5. Remove the transmission rear mount bolt.
6. Remove the steering gear bolts, nuts, and washers from the steering gear.

➡**The position of the steering gear will need to be manipulated to remove it through the left front wheel opening.**

7. Remove the steering gear through the left front wheel opening.
8. Transfer any parts as needed.

To install:

9. Install the steering gear through the left front wheel opening.

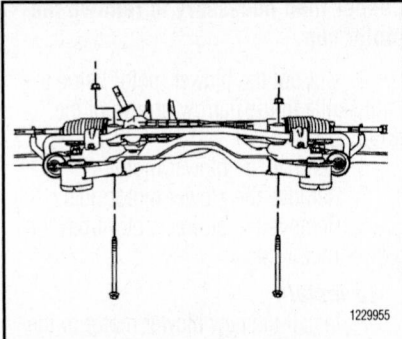

Fig. 485 Remove the steering gear bolts, nuts, and washers from the steering gear

➡**Start all of the bolts and nuts by hand before finalizing any torques.**

10. Install the steering gear bolts, nuts, and washers to the steering gear.
11. Tighten the bolts to 52 ft. lbs. (70 Nm) plus an additional 90 degrees.
12. Install the transmission rear mount bolt and tighten to 66 ft. lbs. (90 Nm).
13. Install the intermediate steering shaft to the steering gear.
14. Install the rack and pinion outer tie rod ends to the steering knuckles.
15. Adjust the front toe.

Hydraulic

3.5L Gas & 3.9L Engines

See Figures 486 through 491.

1. Turn the steering wheel to the straight forward position, support it from movement, and remove the key from the ignition.

2. Raise and support the vehicle.

3. Remove the front tires and wheels.

4. Remove the tie rod end castle nuts.

❊❊ WARNING

Do not free the ball stud by using a pickle fork or a wedge-type tool. Damage to the seal or bushing may result.

5. Using the J 24319-B, separate the tie rod ends from the steering knuckles.

6. Remove the intermediate shaft to steering gear pinch bolt (1). Discard the bolt.

➡**Secure the steering wheel in the straight forward position before separating the intermediate shaft from the steering gear, or damage to the SIR coil will occur.**

7. Separate the intermediate shaft (2) from the steering gear (3).

8. Loosen the transaxle mount through bolt.

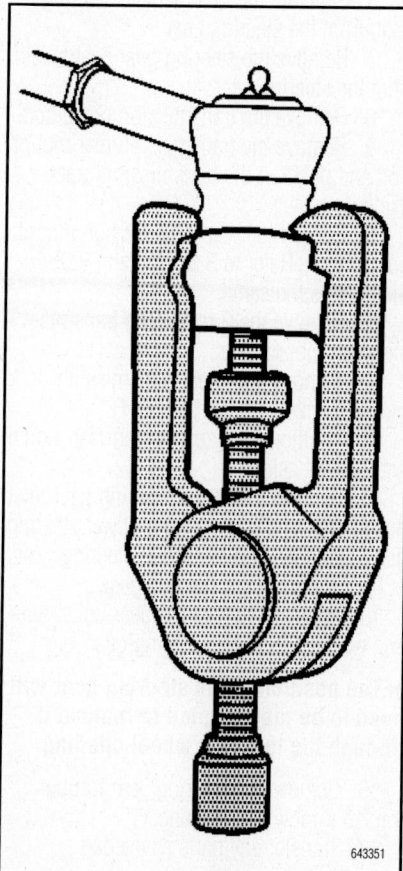

Fig. 486 Using the J 24319-B, separate the tie rod ends from the steering knuckles

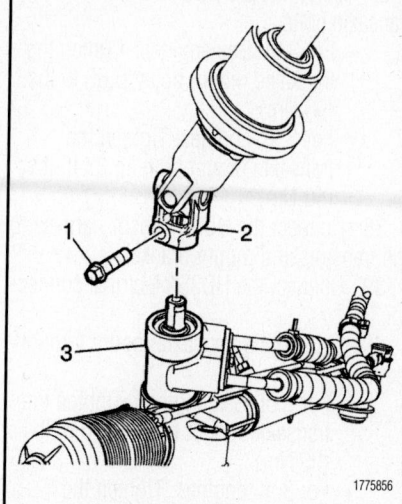

Fig. 487 Remove the intermediate shaft to steering gear pinch bolt (1)

9. Disconnect the Heated Oxygen Sensor (HO2S) electrical connector.

10. Disconnect the HO2S sensor harness from the transmission mount bracket.

11. Remove the 3 transaxle mount to transaxle bolts.

12. Remove the 3 transaxle bracket to frame nuts.

13. Position the transaxle bracket and rear mount aside.

14. Remove the bolt (1) and disconnect the power steering gear inlet (2) and outlet (4) pipe/hoses from the power steering gear (3). Cap off the pipe/hoses and position aside.

15. Remove the power steering gear outlet pipe routing pin-style retainer from the right rear side of the frame.

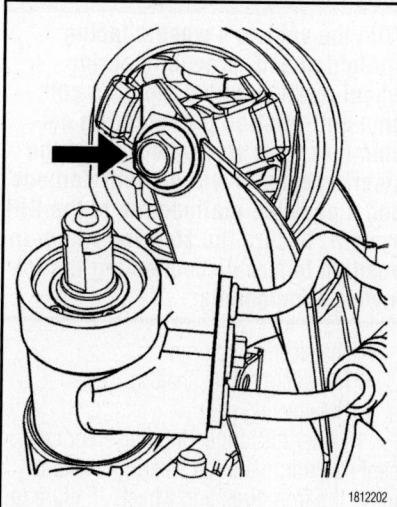

Fig. 488 Loosen the transaxle mount through bolt

➡**Convertible vehicles utilize a cross brace that is installed by sharing the frame mounting bolts. With the rear frame bolts removed, it allows the cross brace to have movement to gain access to the power steering gear mounting bolts.**

16. For convertible vehicles, support the rear of the frame with a suitable jack stand.

17. For convertible vehicles, remove the rear frame mount bolts.

18. Remove the power steering gear mounting bolts, nuts, and washers from the gear.

➡**The power steering gear will need to be rotated while it is removed through the left wheel opening.**

19. Remove the power steering gear through the left wheel opening.

20. If the power steering gear is to be replaced, transfer the outer tie rod ends to the new steering gear.

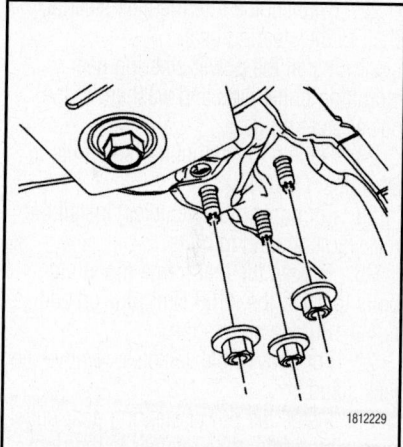

Fig. 489 Remove the 3 transaxle bracket to frame nuts

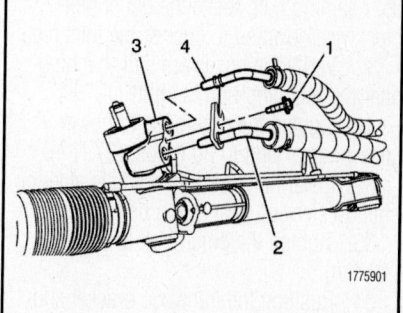

Fig. 490 Remove the bolt (1) and disconnect the power steering gear inlet (2) and outlet (4) pipe/hoses from the power steering gear (3)

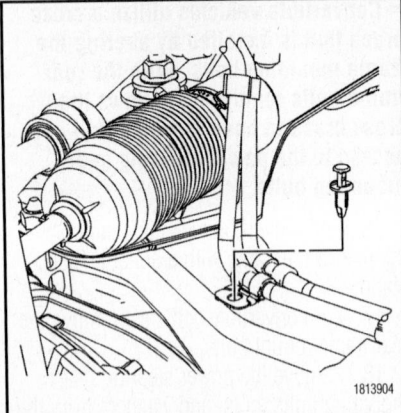

Fig. 491 Remove the power steering gear outlet pipe routing pin-style retainer from the right rear side of the frame

To install:

➡**The power steering gear will need to be rotated while it is installed through the left wheel opening.**

21. Position the power steering gear into the vehicle.

22. Connect the intermediate steering shaft to the steering gear.

23. Install the power steering gear mounting bolts, nuts and washers to the power steering gear.

24. Tighten the mounting bolts/nuts to 81 ft. lbs. (110 Nm).

25. For convertible vehicles, install the rear frame mounting bolts.

26. Tighten the rear frame mounting bolts to 73 ft. lbs. (100 Nm).plus an additional 180 degree rotation.

27. For convertible vehicles, remove the jack stand.

28. Install the power steering gear outlet pipe routing pin-style retainer to the right rear side of the frame.

29. Connect the power steering gear inlet and outlet pipe/hoses to the power steering gear and install the bolt. Prior to tightening the retaining bolt, rotate the outlet pipe clockwise/down so it touches the inlet pipe.

30. Verify the hoses are still touching after the retaining bolt is tight.

31. Tighten the pipe/hose to power steering gear bolt to 20 ft. lbs. (27 Nm).

32. Install the new intermediate steering shaft to steering gear pinch bolt.

33. Tighten the pinch bolt to 36 ft. lbs. (49 Nm).

34. Position the transaxle bracket and rear mount back to their original position.

35. Install the 3 transaxle bracket to frame nuts.

36. Tighten the transaxle bracket to frame nuts to 37 ft. lbs. (50 Nm).

37. Install the 3 transaxle mount to transaxle bolts.
- For 3.5L Gas engines: Tighten the transaxle mount bolts to 66 ft. lbs. (90 Nm).
- For 3.9L engines: Tighten the transaxle mount bolts to 37 ft. lbs. (50 Nm).

38. Connect the HO2S sensor harness to the transmission mount bracket.

39. Connect the HO2S electrical connector.

40. Tighten the transaxle mount through bolt.
- For 3.5L Gas engines: Tighten the transaxle mount bolts to 66 ft. lbs. (90 Nm).
- For 3.9L engines: Tighten the transaxle mount bolts to 37 ft. lbs. (50 Nm).

41. Position the outer tie rod ends into the steering knuckles.

➡**Hold the ball stud from turning during installation of the castle nut.**

42. Install new torque castle nuts to the tie rod end ball studs.

43. Tighten the castle nuts to 18 ft. lbs. (25 Nm) plus an additional 90 degree rotation.

44. Install the front tires and wheels.

45. Lower the vehicle.

46. Fill and bleed the power steering system. Refer to Power Steering System Bleeding.

47. Measure the wheel alignment and adjust as necessary.

3.6L Engines

See Figures 492 through 496.

✳✳ WARNING

With the vehicle's wheels facing straight ahead, prevent steering wheel rotation with a steering column anti-rotation pin, steering column lock, or a strap. Locking of the steering column will prevent damage and a possible malfunction of the SIR system. Secure the steering wheel in position before disconnecting the following components:

- The steering column
- The intermediate shaft(s)
- The steering gear

1. After disconnecting these components do not rotate the steering wheel or move the front tires and wheels. Failure to follow this procedure may cause the SIR coil assembly to become un-centered and cause possible damage to the SIR coil.

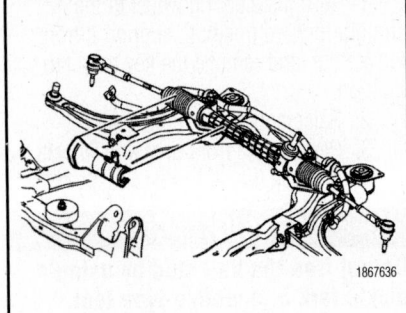

Fig. 492 Remove the steering gear heat shield from the steering gear

If you think the SIR coil has became uncentered, refer to your specific SIR coil's centering procedure to re-center SIR Coil.

2. Turn the front wheels to the straight forward position and secure the steering wheel from moving.

3. Remove as much power steering fluid from the remote power steering fluid reservoir as possible.

4. Place drain pans under the vehicle as needed.

5. Disengage the rack and pinion outer tie rod ends from the steering knuckles.

6. Separate the intermediate steering shaft from the steering gear.

7. Remove the steering gear heat shield from the steering gear.

8. Remove the transmission brace bolt.

9. Remove the transmission rear mount bolt and position the transmission brace aside.

10. Loosen the rear transmission mount bracket bolt. Refer to 3.5L Gas and 3.9L image, it is the same.

11. Remove the 2 remaining transmission rear mount bolts.

12. Remove the 3 rear transmission mount bracket nuts and bolts (1).

13. Position the transmission rear mount and bracket aside.

14. Remove the power steering gear inlet hose bolt and disconnect the power steering gear inlet hose and the power steering gear outlet hose from the steering gear.

15. Remove the steering gear bolts, nuts, and washers from the steering gear.

➡**The position of the steering gear will need to be manipulated to remove it through the left front wheel opening.**

16. Remove the steering gear through the left front wheel opening.

17. Transfer any parts as needed.

To install:

18. Install the steering gear through the left front wheel opening.

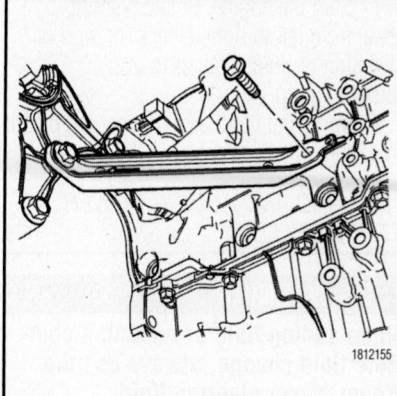

Fig. 493 Remove the transmission brace bolt

➡️**Start all of the bolts and nuts by hand before finalizing any torques.**

19. Install the steering gear bolts, nuts, and washers to the steering gear.

20. Tighten the bolts and nuts to 81 ft. lbs. (110 Nm).

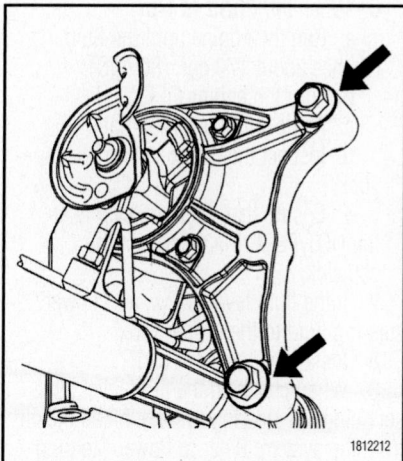

Fig. 494 Transmission rear mount bolts

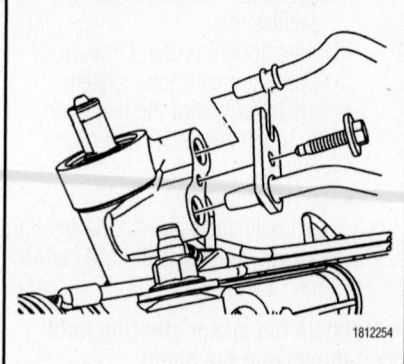

Fig. 496 Remove the power steering gear inlet hose bolt and disconnect the power steering gear inlet hose and the power steering gear outlet hose from the steering gear

21. Connect the power steering gear inlet hose and the power steering gear outlet hose to the steering gear and install the power steering gear inlet hose bolt and tighten to 20 ft. lbs. (27 Nm).

22. Position the transmission rear mount and bracket in place.

23. Install the 3 rear transmission mount bracket bolts and nuts and tighten to 37 ft. lbs. (50 Nm).

24. Install the 2 remaining transmission rear mount bolts.

25. Place the transmission brace in the proper position. Install the bolt in order to secure the transmission brace to the trans-

mission rear mount. Tighten the 3 transmission rear mount bolts to 37 ft. lbs. (50 Nm).

26. Install the transmission brace bolt and tighten to 37 ft. lbs. (50 Nm).

27. Tighten the rear transmission mount bracket bolt and tighten to 37 ft. lbs. (50 Nm).

28. Install the steering gear heat shield to the steering gear.

29. Clean any excess power steering fluid from the vehicle and remove the drain pans.

30. Install the intermediate steering shaft to the steering gear.

31. Install the rack and pinion outer tie rod ends to the steering knuckles.

32. Fill and bleed the power steering system. Refer to Power Steering System Bleeding.

33. Adjust the front toe.

POWER STEERING PUMP

REMOVAL & INSTALLATION

3.5L Gas & 3.9L Engines

See Figure 497.

1. Remove the intake manifold cover.

2. Remove the drive belt and engine mount snubber. Refer to Drive Belt replacement for the 3.5L or 3.9L engine.

3. Remove the drive belt idler pulley.

4. Remove the air cleaner assembly. Refer to Air Cleaner Assembly replacement for the 3.5L or 3.9L.

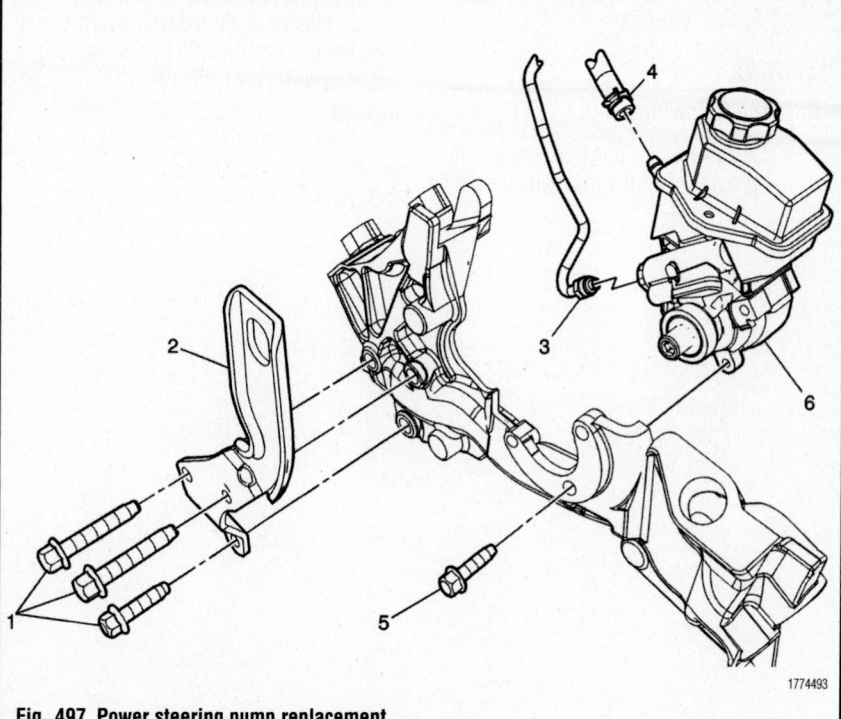

Fig. 497 Power steering pump replacement

Fig. 495 Remove the 3 rear transmission mount bracket nuts and bolts (1)

5. Remove the power steering pump pulley.

6. Remove the 3 engine lift bracket bolts (1).

7. Remove the engine lift bracket (2).

8. Remove the power steering gear inlet pipe/hose fitting (3).

➡**Use an appropriate tool to remove the power steering fluid from the reservoir before removing the hoses from the pump.**

➡**Use a new O-ring seal for installation.**

9. Remove the power steering reservoir inlet pipe/hose (4): compress the clamp to disconnect the return hose from the power steering reservoir.

10. Remove the 3 power steering pump bolts (5).

11. Remove the power steering pump (6).

To install:

12. Tighten the 3 engine lift bracket bolts to 37 ft. lbs. (50 Nm).

13. Install the power steering gear inlet pipe/hose fitting and tighten to 20 ft. lbs. (27 Nm).

14. Install the power steering reservoir inlet pipe/hose.

15. Install the 3 power steering pump bolts and tighten them to 18 ft. lbs. (25 Nm).

16. Install the power steering pump.

17. After installation, fill and bleed the power steering system. Refer to Power Steering System Bleeding.

BLEEDING

➡**Note the following:**

- Use clean, new power steering fluid type only. See the Maintenance and Lubrication subsection for fluid specifications.
- Hoses touching the frame, body or engine may cause system noise. Verify that the hoses do not touch any other part of the vehicle.
- Loose connections may not leak, but could allow air into the steering system. Verify that all hose connections are tight.

➡**Maintain the power steering fluid level throughout the bleed procedure.**

1. Fill the pump reservoir with fluid to the minimum system level, FULL COLD level, or the middle of hash mark on cap stick fluid level indicator.

➡**With hydro-boost only, the oil level will appear falsely high if the hydro-boost accumulator is not fully charged. Do not apply the brake pedal with the engine OFF. This will discharge the hydro-boost accumulator.**

2. If equipped with hydro-boost, fully charge the hydro-boost accumulator using the following procedure:

a. Start the engine.

b. Firmly apply the brake pedal 10-15 times.

c. Turn the engine OFF.

3. Raise the vehicle until the front wheels are off the ground.

4. Key on engine OFF, turn the steering wheel from stop to stop 12 times.

5. Vehicles equipped with hydro-boost systems or longer length power steering hoses may require turns up to 15 to 20 stop to stops.

6. Verify the power steering fluid level per operating specification. Refer to Checking and Adding Power Steering Fluid.

7. Start the engine. Rotate steering wheel from left to right. Check for sign of cavitation or fluid aeration (pump noise/whining).

8. Verify the fluid level. Repeat the bleed procedure, if necessary.

CHECKING AND ADDING POWER STEERING FLUID

> ☀❖☀ **WARNING**
>
> **When adding fluid or making a complete fluid change, always use the proper power steering fluid.**

1. Failure to use the proper fluid will cause hose and seal damage and fluid leaks.

2. Clean the area surrounding the reservoir cap.

3. Remove the reservoir cap.

4. Inspect the power steering pump fluid level at regular intervals. Use the appropriate procedure below.

5. Add fluid when required.

6. When the **Fluid Is Hot**:

a. Run the engine until the fluid reaches about 170;dgF (80;dgC).

b. Turn the engine OFF.

c. Remove the reservoir cap.

d. Inspect the fluid level on the cap-stick.

e. Ensure that the fluid level is at the HOT/FULL/MAX mark on the capstick.

7. If the fluid level is low, add power steering fluid to the proper level.

8. Install the reservoir cap.

9. When checking the fluid level after servicing the steering system, bleed the air from the system. Refer to Power Steering System Bleeding.

LOWER CONTROL ARM

REMOVAL & INSTALLATION

See Figures 498 through 500.

1. Raise and support the vehicle.
2. Remove the tire and wheel.

➡**DO NOT re-use the lower ball joint bolt. Discard and use a NEW bolt only.**

3. Remove the lower ball joint to knuckle nut and bolt.
4. Separate the lower control arm from the knuckle.
5. If removing the left lower control arm, refer to the following:
   - For vehicles equipped with the 4T45-E transmission, remove the left side transmission mount.
   - For vehicles equipped with the 4T65-E transmission, remove the left side transmission mount.
   - For vehicles equipped with the 6T70/6T75 transmission, remove the left side transmission mount.
6. If removing the right lower control arm, refer to the following:
   - For vehicles equipped with the 3.5L engine, remove the right engine mount.
   - For vehicles equipped with the 3.6L engine, remove the right engine mount.
   - For vehicles equipped with the 3.9L engine, remove the right engine mount.
7. Remove the front lower control arm bolt.
8. Remove the rear lower control arm bushing nuts and bolts. Refer to Front Lower Control Arm Bushing Replacement.

Fig. 498 Remove the lower ball joint to knuckle nut and bolt

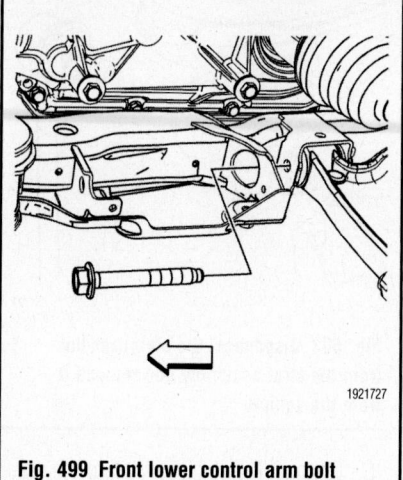

Fig. 499 Front lower control arm bolt

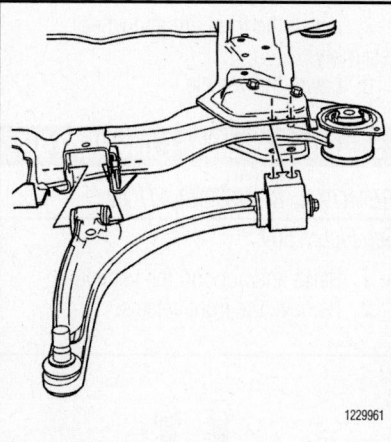

Fig. 500 Remove the lower control arm from the cradle

9. Remove the lower control arm from the cradle.

To install:

10. Position the lower control arm in the cradle.
11. Install and Hand-tighten the rear lower control arm bushing nuts and bolts.
12. Install and Hand-tighten the front lower control arm bolt.
13. Install the ball joint to knuckle bolt and nut.
14. Tighten the ball joint bolt and nut to 37 ft. lbs. (50 Nm). Reverse the nut 3/4 of a turn. Tighten to 37 ft. lbs. (50 Nm) plus 30 degrees.
15. Load the front suspension with the proper jack stand before tightening the bolts to specifications.
16. Tighten the front lower control arm bolt.

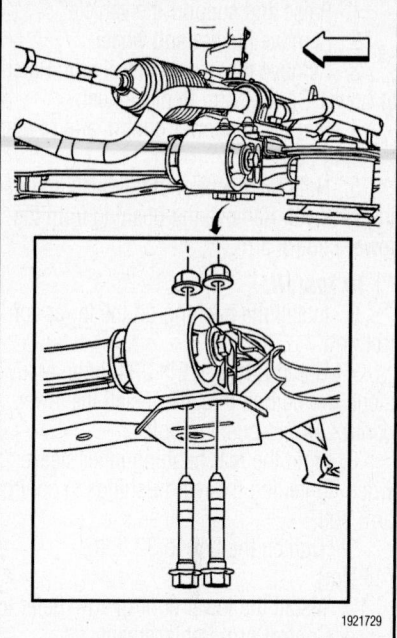

Fig. 501 Rear lower control arm bushing nuts and bolts

17. Tighten the lower control arm bolt to 37 ft. lbs. (50 Nm) plus 90 degrees.
18. Tighten the rear bushing to frame bolts.
19. Tighten the lower control arm bolt to 37 ft. lbs. (50 Nm) plus 90 degrees.
20. Remove the jack stand.
21. If installing the left lower control arm, refer to the following:
   - For vehicles equipped with the 4T45-E transmission, remove the left side transmission mount.
   - For vehicles equipped with the 4T65-E transmission, remove the left side transmission mount.
   - For vehicles equipped with the 6T70/6T75 transmission, remove the left side transmission mount.
22. If installing the right lower control arm, refer to the following:
   - For vehicles equipped with the 3.5L engine, remove the right engine mount.
   - For vehicles equipped with the 3.6L engine, remove the right engine mount.
   - For vehicles equipped with the 3.9L engine, remove the right engine mount.
23. Install the tire and wheel.
24. Verify wheel alignment.
25. Remove the support and lower the vehicle.

BUSHING REPLACEMENT

See Figure 502.

1. Raise and support the vehicle.
2. Remove the tire and wheel.
3. Remove the lower control arm. Refer to Lower Control Arm Replacement.
4. Remove the lower control arm to rear bushing bolt.
5. Note the position of the bushing during removal. Remove the bushing from the lower control arm.

To install:

6. Install the bushing on the lower control arm.
7. Using LOCKTITE™ 234, or an equivalent, on the bolt threads, install the lower control arm to bushing bolt.
8. Hold the rear bushing inner sleeve when tightening the rear bushings to control arm bolt.
9. Tighten the bolt to 32 ft. lbs. (44 Nm).
10. Install the lower control arm. Refer to Lower Control Arm Replacement.
11. Install the tire and wheel.
12. Lower the vehicle.

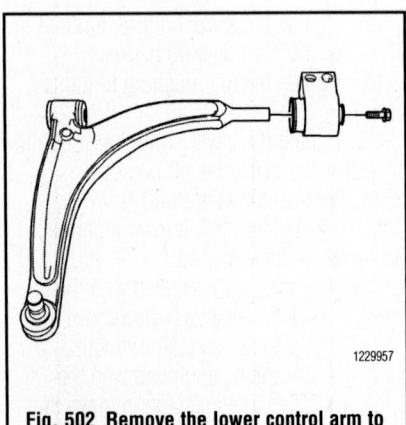

Fig. 502 Remove the lower control arm to rear bushing bolt

STABILIZER SHAFT LINK

REMOVAL & INSTALLATION

See Figure 503.

1. Raise and support the vehicle.
2. Remove the front tire and wheel assembly.
3. Disconnect the stabilizer link from the stabilizer shaft.
4. Disconnect the stabilizer link from the strut assembly and remove it from the vehicle.

To install:

5. Connect the stabilizer link to the strut assembly and tighten to 48 ft. lbs. (65 Nm).

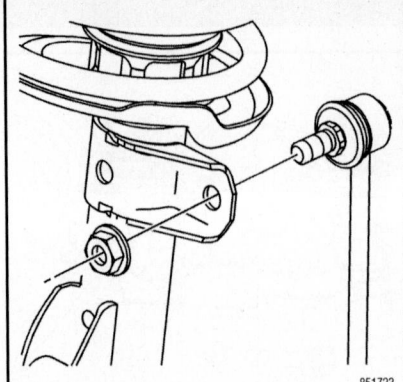

Fig. 503 Disconnect the stabilizer link from the strut assembly and remove it from the vehicle

6. Connect the stabilizer link to the stabilizer shaft and tighten to 48 ft. lbs. (65 Nm).
7. Install the front tire and wheel assembly.
8. Lower the vehicle.

STABILIZER SHAFT INSULATOR

REMOVAL & INSTALLATION

See Figure 504.

1. Raise and support the vehicle.
2. Remove the front wheels.

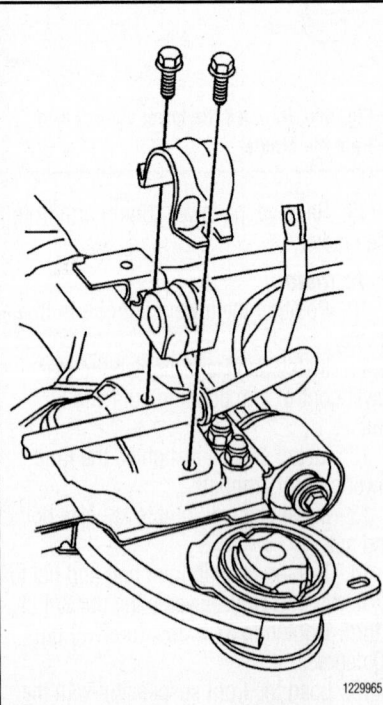

Fig. 504 Remove the stabilizer shaft mounting clamp bolts and clamps from both sides of the vehicle

3. Remove the stabilizer shaft mounting clamp bolts and clamps from both sides of the vehicle.
4. Remove the bushings from the stabilizer shaft.

To install:

5. Install the stabilizer bushings on the stabilizer shaft with the cut line facing rearward.
6. Install the stabilizer shaft clamps and bolts.
7. Tighten the bolts to 18 ft. lbs. (25 Nm).
8. Install the front wheels.
9. Lower the vehicle.

STABILIZER SHAFT

REMOVAL & INSTALLATION

Sedan/Coupe

See Figure 505.

1. Install the engine support fixture.
2. Raise and support the vehicle.
3. Remove the tires and wheels.
4. Disconnect the stabilizer links from the stabilizer shaft. Refer to Stabilizer Shaft Link replacement.
5. Remove the stabilizer bar clamps and insulators. Refer to Stabilizer Shaft Insulator replacement.
6. Remove the catalytic converters (3.5L (LZ4), 3.6L (LY7), and 3.9L (LZ9)).
7. Lower the frame in order to gain clearance to the stabilizer shaft.
8. Remove the stabilizer shaft through the opening between the frame and body.

To install:

9. Position the stabilizer shaft to the frame.
10. Install the stabilizer bar clamps and insulators. Refer to Stabilizer Shaft Insulator replacement.
11. Raise the frame into place.

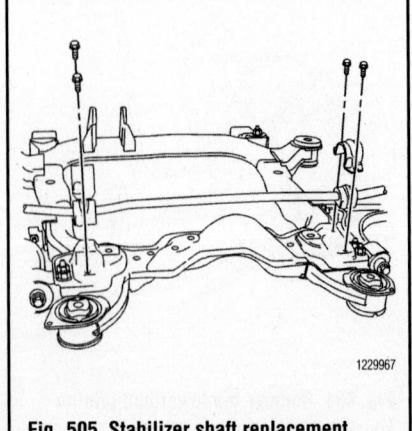

Fig. 505 Stabilizer shaft replacement

12. Remove the jack stand.

13. Connect the stabilizer link to the stabilizer bar. Refer to Stabilizer Shaft Link replacement.

14. Install the catalytic converters [3.5L (LZ4), 3.6L (LY7), and 3.9L (LZ9)].

15. Install the front tires and wheels.

16. Lower the vehicle.

17. Remove the engine support fixture.

Convertible

1. Install the engine support fixture.

2. Raise and support the vehicle.

3. Remove the tires and wheels.

4. Remove the LH and RH reinforcements.

5. Remove the catalytic converters.

6. Disconnect the stabilizer links from the stabilizer shaft. Refer to Stabilizer Shaft Link replacement.

7. Lower the frame in order to gain access to the stabilizer shaft.

8. Support the rear of the frame assembly with a suitable jack stand.

9. Remove the stabilizer bar clamps and insulators. Refer to Stabilizer Shaft Insulator replacement.

10. Remove the stabilizer shaft through the opening between the frame and body.

To install:

11. Position the stabilizer shaft to the vehicle through the opening between the frame and body.

12. Install the stabilizer bar clamps and insulators. Refer to Stabilizer Shaft Insulator replacement.

13. Raise the frame into place.

14. Install the LH and RH reinforcements.

15. Remove the jack stand.

16. Connect the stabilizer link to the stabilizer bar. Refer to Stabilizer Shaft Link replacement.

17. Install the catalytic converters [3.5L (LZ4), 3.6L (LY7), and 3.9L (LZ9)].

18. Install the front tires and wheels.

19. Lower the vehicle.

20. Remove the engine support fixture.

STEERING KNUCKLE

REMOVAL & INSTALLATION

See Figure 506.

1. Raise and support the vehicle.

2. Remove the wheel bearing/hub. Refer to Front Wheel Bearing and Hub replacement.

3. Separate the outer tie rod end from the knuckle.

4. Remove the nuts and bolts from the

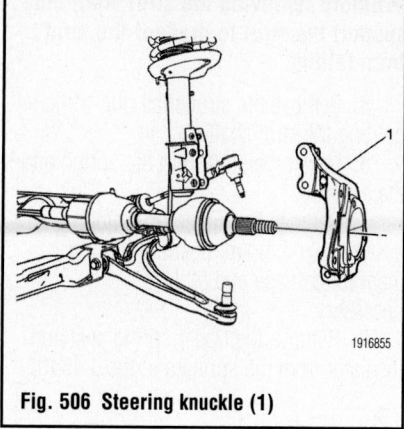

Fig. 506 Steering knuckle (1)

strut to the knuckle. Refer to Strut Assembly Replacement.

5. Separate the lower ball joint from the knuckle. Refer to Lower Control Arm Replacement.

✳✳ WARNING

Do not pry in such a way that the ball joint seal is contacted. Damage to the seal may result.

---

6. Remove the steering knuckle (1).

7. Installation is the reverse of removal.

STRUT ASSEMBLY

REMOVAL & INSTALLATION

See Figures 507 and 508.

1. Raise and support the vehicle.

2. Remove the front wheel.

3. Disconnect the stabilizer link from

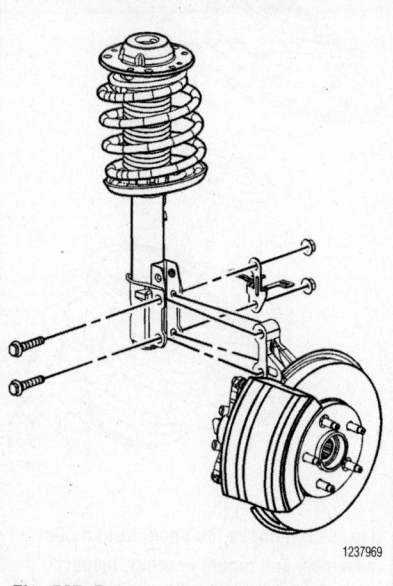

Fig. 507 Remove the strut to steering knuckle nuts

the strut. Refer to image in Stabilizer Shaft Link.

4. Remove the strut to steering knuckle nuts.

5. If applicable, reposition the wheel speed sensor/ABS harness and bracket.

6. Remove the strut to steering knuckle bolts.

7. Remove the upper strut cap to body nuts.

➡In order to prevent damage to the CV joint boot, place a shop towel over the CV joint.

8. Remove the strut from the vehicle.

9. For strut replacement, refer to Strut, Strut Component, & Spring replacement.

To install:

➡It may be necessary to rotate the upper strut mount cover guide to match the hole in the strut tower.

10. Position the strut to the vehicle's strut tower, using the alignment pin as a guide.

11. Install the upper strut cap to body nuts.

12. Tighten the nut to 18 ft. lbs. (25 Nm).

13. Install the strut to steering knuckle bolts, leaving the nuts off.

14. If applicable, place the wheel speed sensor harness and bracket to the bolt end.

15. Install the strut to steering knuckle nuts.

16. Tighten the nuts to 89 ft. lbs. (120 Nm).

17. Connect the stabilizer link to the strut.

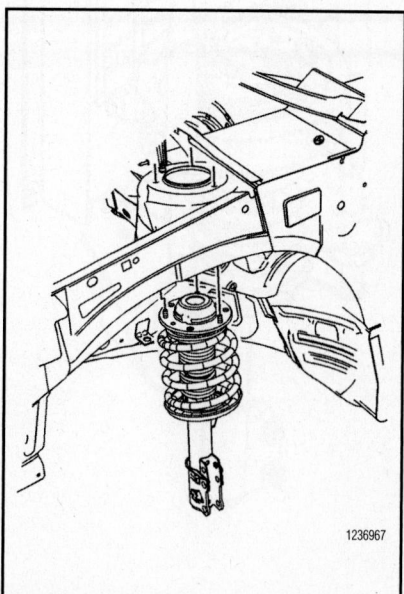

Fig. 508 Remove the upper strut cap to body nuts

18. Tighten the link to 48 ft. lbs. (65 Nm).
19. Install the front wheel.
20. Lower the vehicle.
21. Road test the vehicle and test for leads and pulls.

STRUT, STRUT COMPONENT, OR SPRING

DISASSEMBLY & ASSEMBLY

See Figures 509 through 513.

1. Remove the strut assembly. Refer to Strut Assembly replacement.
2. Place the strut assembly into the J 45400.
3. Adjust the compressing arms to contact the coils farthest away from the center of the spring.
4. Using the J 45400, compress the spring to remove the spring tension from the upper strut mount.

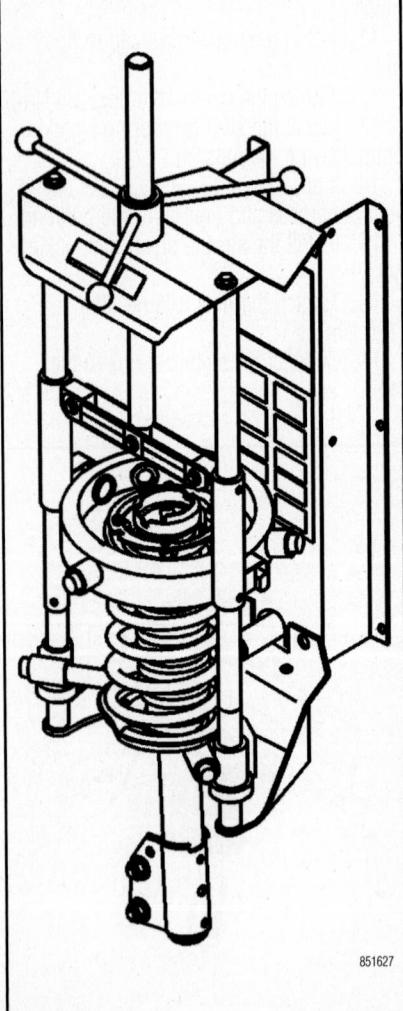

Fig. 509 Place the strut assembly into the J 45400

➡**Before removing the strut shaft nut, support the strut to prevent the strut from falling.**

5. Remove the strut shaft nut, while holding the strut shaft.
6. Lower the strut from the spring and the J 45400.
7. Remove the upper strut mount assembly and mount bearing. Inspect them for damage and replace as necessary.
8. Remove the upper spring seat and insulator from the spring and the J 45400.

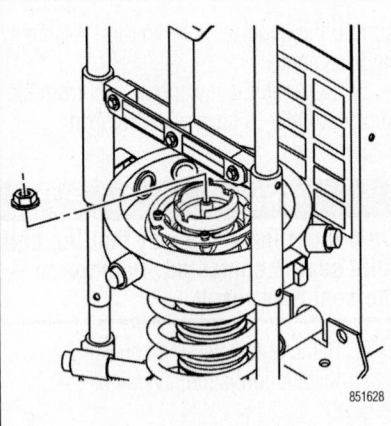

Fig. 510 Remove the strut shaft nut, while holding the strut shaft.

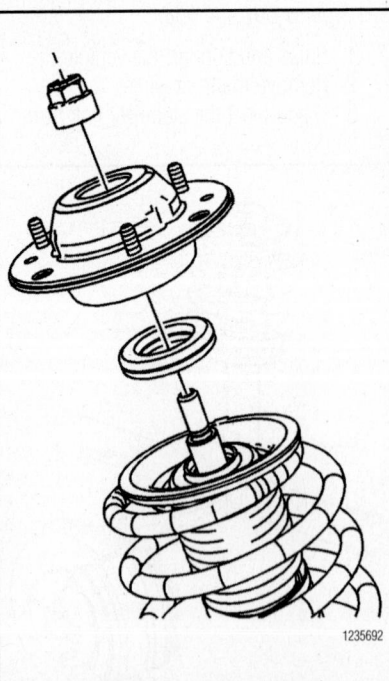

Fig. 511 Remove the upper strut mount assembly and mount bearing. Inspect them for damage and replace as necessary

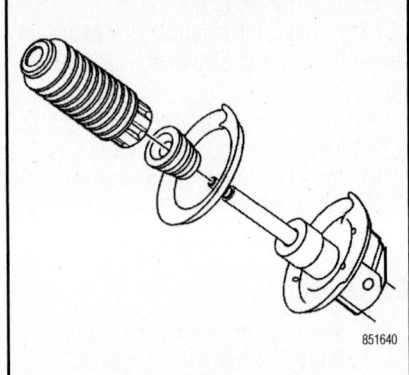

Fig. 512 Remove the dust shield and jounce bumper assembly from the strut shaft. Inspect for damage and replace as necessary

Inspect for damage and replace as necessary.

9. Using the J 45400, remove the spring tension in order to remove the spring. Inspect for damage and replace as necessary.
10. Remove the dust shield and jounce bumper assembly from the strut shaft. Inspect for damage and replace as necessary.
11. Remove the lower spring seat insulator. Inspect for damage and replace as necessary.

To assemble:

12. Install the spring into the J 45400. Make sure the spring is level.
13. Use the J 45400 to compress the spring evenly.
14. Install the lower spring seat insulator.
15. Extend the strut shaft to the upper limit of its travel.
16. Insert the jounce bumper into the dust shield.
17. Slide the dust shield assembly onto the strut shaft.
18. Load the strut through the coil spring and the J 45400.
19. Firmly align the lower spring coil in the spring seat pocket.
20. Place the upper spring insulator and spring seat onto the top of the coil spring.
21. Place the bearing and strut mount on the top of the spring seat.
22. Install the upper strut shaft nut.
23. Tighten the nut to 52 ft. lbs. (70 Nm).
24. Using the J 45400, remove the spring tension.
25. Remove the strut assembly from the J 45400.
26. Install the strut assembly. Refer to Strut Assembly replacement.

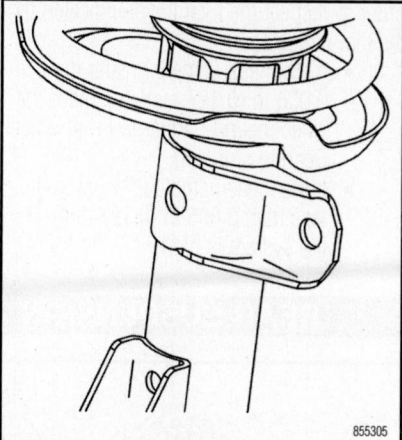

Fig. 513 Firmly align the lower spring coil in the spring seat pocket

INSPECTION

See Figure 514.

➡**You do not have to remove the strut assembly from the vehicle to perform the following inspection procedure.**

➡**A light film of oil on the top portion of the strut is normal. DO NOT replace the strut for this condition.**

Condition 1: Oil or fluid residue only on the bottom of the strut tube or on other strut components and not originating from the shaft seal, is not a strut related problem. DO NOT replace the strut, look for other external leaks.

Condition 2: A light film/residue on the strut tube, but not on the spring seat and originating from the shaft seal, is a NORMAL condition. DO NOT replace the strut.

Condition 3: An oil drip or trail down the strut tube and originating from the shaft seal is an ABNORMAL condition. Replace the strut.

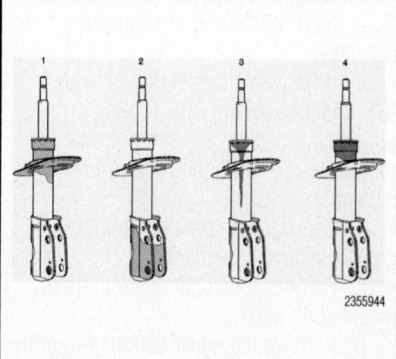

Fig. 514 Strut and Shock Absorber Inspection

Condition 4: An extreme wet film of oil covering the strut tube and pooling in the spring seat and originating from the shaft seal is an ABNORMAL condition. Replace the strut.

Inspection: Verify the concern.

➡**The strut assembly DOES NOT have to be removed from the vehicle to perform the following inspection procedure.**

1. Raise and support the vehicle.
2. Visually inspect each of the shock absorbers or struts for external fluid leaks, referring to Conditions 1, 2, 3, and 4:
   • If Conditions 1 or 2 are found, continue to step 4.
   • If conditions 3 or 4 are found, replace strut. Refer to Strut Assembly replacement.
3. If the G6 is equipped with an electronic suspension control system, ensure that the system is working properly.
4. Use your hands in order to lift up and push down on each corner of the vehicle 3 times. Remove your hands from the vehicle. If the corner motion exceeds 2 cycles, replace the strut. If the strut does not exceed 2 cycles, NO repair is necessary.

WHEEL BEARING & HUB

REMOVAL & INSTALLATION

See Figures 515 through 517.

1. Raise and support the vehicle.
2. Remove the brake rotor.
3. Disconnect the wheel speed sensor electrical connector, if equipped.
4. Remove the wheel speed sensor electrical connector from the mounting bracket, if needed.
5. Loosen the wheel driveshaft from the wheel bearing/hub.
6. Remove the wheel bearing/hub mounting bolts (1).
7. Remove the wheel bearing/hub and backing plate from the steering knuckle.

To install:

8. Position the backing plate and wheel bearing/hub assembly in the steering knuckle.
9. Install the wheel bearing/hub mounting bolts.
10. Tighten the mounting bolts to 85 ft. lbs. (115 Nm).
11. Reconnect the wheel speed senor electrical connector, if needed.
12. Install the wheel speed sensor electrical connector on the retaining bracket, if needed.

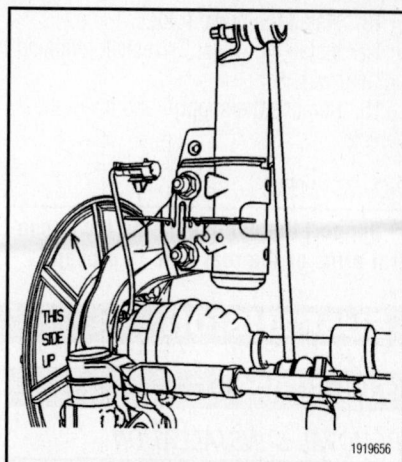

Fig. 515 Loosen the wheel Driveshaft from the wheel bearing/hub

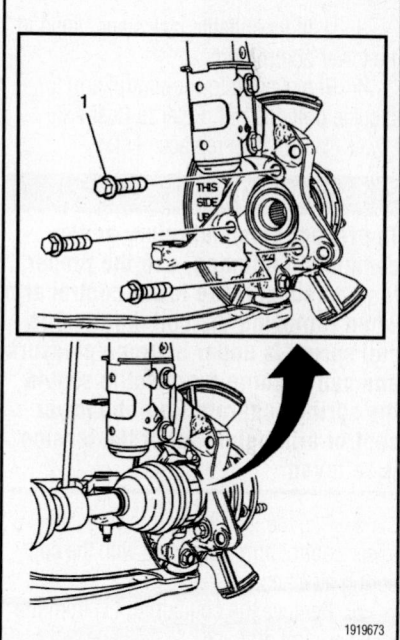

Fig. 516 Wheel bearing/hub mounting bolts (1)

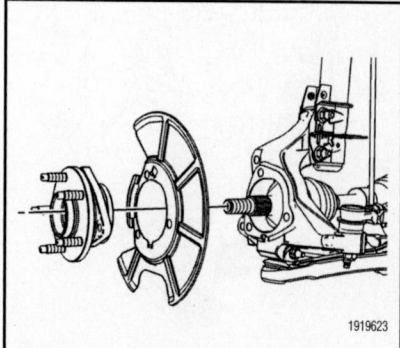

Fig. 517 Remove the wheel bearing/hub and backing plate from the steering knuckle

13. Install the brake rotor.

14. Install the wheel Driveshaft retaining nut and washer.

15. Remove the support and lower the vehicle.

ADJUSTMENT

➡ **Support the vehicle by the lower control arms or the rear axle to prevent** movement during wheel bearing/hub inspection.

1. Mount and secure the J 8001 Dial Indicator.

2. Ensure that the dial indicator contacts the vertical surface of the wheel as close as possible to the top wheel stud.

3. Push and pull on the top of the tire in order to inspect the total travel indicated by the dial indicator.

- If the measurement greater than 0.005 in (0.127 mm)—replace the wheel bearing. Refer to Front Wheel Bearing and Hub.
- If the measurement is equal to or less than 0.005 in (0.127 mm)—the system is okay.

SUSPENSION
REAR SUSPENSION

COIL SPRING

REMOVAL & INSTALLATION

See Figures 518 and 519.

1. Raise and support the vehicle.

2. Remove the rear tire and wheel assembly.

3. Using a suitable jack stand, support the lower control arm.

4. Remove the lower control arm to knuckle bolt and nut. Refer to Rear Axle Lower Control Arm replacement.

✳✳ CAUTION

To prevent personal injury and/or component damage, use the proper tools to support the lower control arm when removing the coil spring. The coil spring is under extreme pressure and can become a projectile should the spring separate from the lower control arm before all of the tension is relieved.

5. Use the jack stand to swing the lower control arm downward with the coil spring attached.

6. Remove the coil spring (1) from the lower control arm.

7. Inspect the coil spring upper (2) and

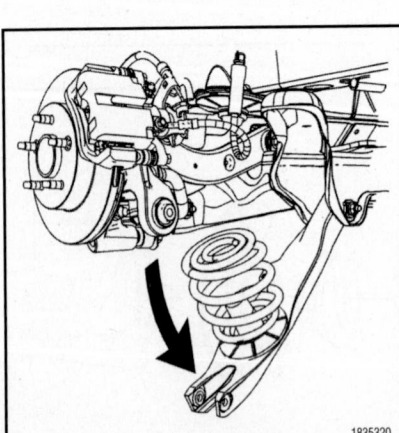

Fig. 518 Use the jack stand to swing the lower control arm downward with the coil spring attached

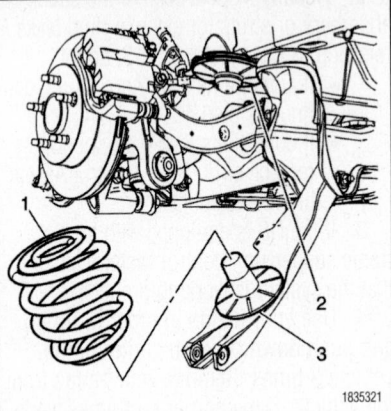

Fig. 519 View of the coil spring (1), and upper (2) and lower (3) insulators

lower (3) insulators for damage, replace as necessary.

To install:

➡ **Be sure that the coil spring upper and lower insulators are properly seated prior to installation of the coil spring.**

8. Position the coil spring onto the lower control arm.

9. Use the jack stand to raise the lower control arm upward into position.

10. Install the lower control arm to knuckle bolt and nut. Refer to Rear Axle Lower Control Arm replacement.

11. Remove the jack stand from under the vehicle.

12. Install the rear tire and wheel assembly.

13. Lower the vehicle.

14. Check the rear wheel alignment.

REAR AXLE LOWER CONTROL ARM

REMOVAL & INSTALLATION

See Figure 520.

1. Raise and suitably support the vehicle.

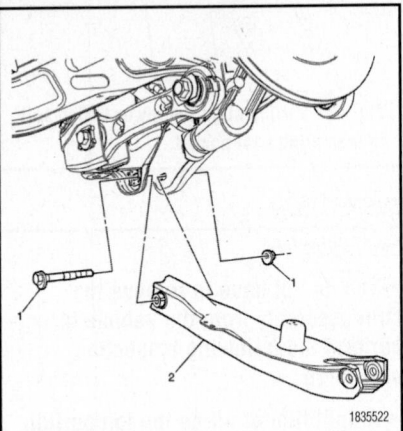

Fig. 520 Remove the lower control arm to support bolt/nut (1)

2. Remove the rear tire and wheel assembly.

3. Remove the coil spring. Refer to Coil Spring replacement.

4. Remove the lower control arm to support bolt/nut (1).

5. Installation is the reverse of removal.

REAR AXLE UPPER CONTROL ARM

REMOVAL & INSTALLATION

See Figures 521 through 523.

1. Raise and support the vehicle.

2. Remove the rear tire and wheel assembly.

3. If the vehicle is equipped with ABS, disconnect the ABS routing harness connectors (1) and position the harness aside. Note the routing for assembly.

4. Remove the upper control arm to support assembly bolt and nut.

5. Remove the upper control arm to knuckle bolt and nut.

6. Remove the upper control arm from the vehicle through the wheelhouse opening.

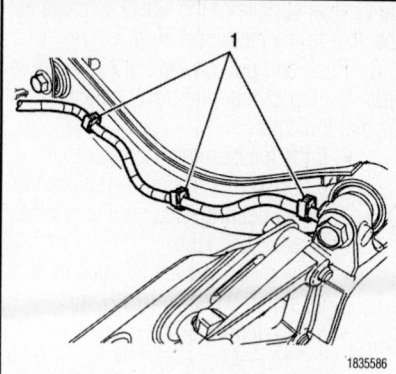

Fig. 521 If the vehicle is equipped with ABS, disconnect the ABS routing harness connectors (1) and position the harness aside. Note the routing for assembly

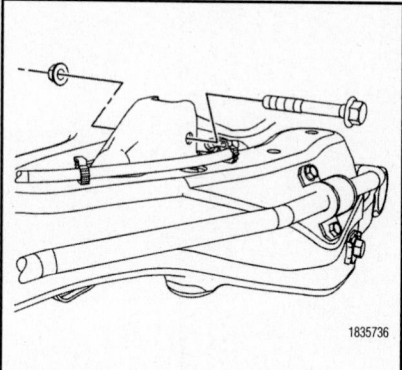

Fig. 522 Remove the upper control arm to support assembly bolt and nut

To install:

7. Position the upper control arm to the support assembly and knuckle through the wheelhouse opening.

8. Install the upper control arm to knuckle bolt and nut. Hand-tighten only.

9. Install the upper control arm to support assembly bolt.

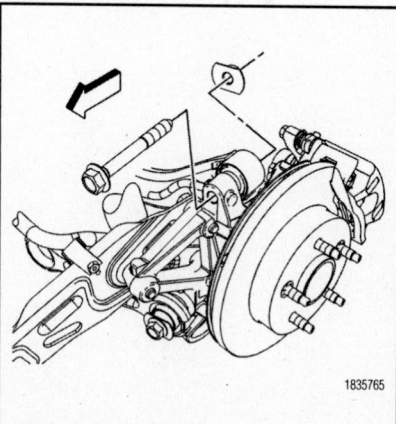

Fig. 523 Remove the upper control arm to knuckle bolt and nut

10. Tighten the upper control arm to support assembly bolt to 44 ft. lbs. (60 Nm) plus 60 degrees.

11. Tighten the upper control arm to knuckle bolt to 81 ft. lbs. (110 Nm) plus 70 degrees.

12. If the vehicle is equipped with ABS, route the harness and connect the ABS routing harness connectors.

13. Install the rear tire and wheel assembly.

14. Lower the vehicle.

STABILIZER SHAFT

REMOVAL & INSTALLATION

See Figures 524 and 525.

1. Raise and support the vehicle.

2. Scribe a line on the rear camber adjustment bolts (both left and right).

3. Remove the rear axle toe link.

4. Remove the rear axle tie rod bracket brace.

Remove the muffler.

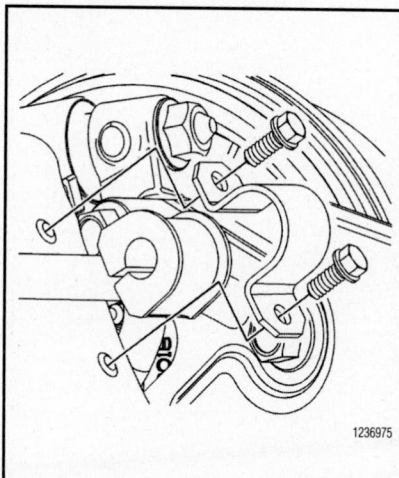

Fig. 524 Stabilizer shaft bracket bolts

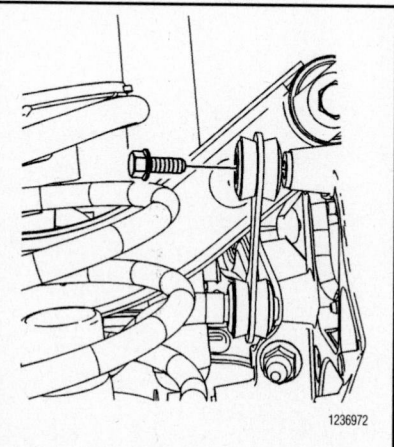

Fig. 525 Stabilizer link to knuckle bolts

Remove the stabilizer shaft bracket bolts.

Remove the stabilizer shaft insulators from the stabilizer shaft.

Remove the stabilizer link to knuckle bolts.

5. Remove the stabilizer shaft.

To install:

6. Install the stabilizer shaft.

7. Install the stabilizer shaft insulators.

8. Install the stabilizer shaft brackets.

9. Install the stabilizer shaft bracket bolts.

10. Tighten the stabilizer shaft insulator bracket retaining bolts to 26 ft. lbs. (35 Nm).

11. Install the stabilizer shaft links to knuckle bolts.

12. Tighten the bolts to 41 ft. lbs. (55 Nm).

13. Install the rear axle toe link.

14. Install the rear axle tie rod bracket brace.

15. Install the muffler.

16. Lower the vehicle.

WHEEL BEARINGS & HUB

REMOVAL & INSTALLATION

See Figure 526.

1. Raise and support the vehicle.

2. Remove the tire and wheel assembly.

3. Remove the brake rotor.

4. Disconnect the electrical connector from the wheel speed sensor, if the G6 is equipped with ABS.

5. Remove the stabilizer link bolt at the knuckle and position the stabilizer link out of the way in order to provide access to the wheel bearing/hub nuts. Refer to Stabilizer Shaft replacement.

6. Remove the 4 wheel bearing/hub assembly nuts.

7. Remove the wheel bearing/hub assembly from the knuckle.

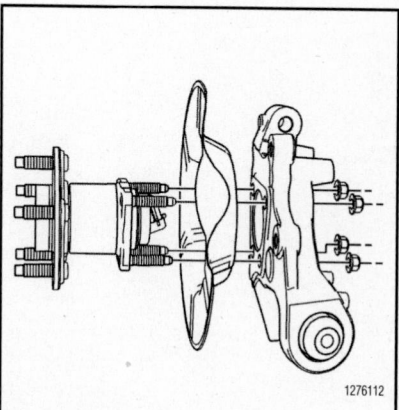

Fig. 526 Wheel bearing/hub assembly replacement

To install:

8. Install the wheel bearing/hub assembly to the knuckle.

9. Install the 4 wheel bearing/hub assembly nuts.

10. Tighten the nuts to 47 ft. lbs. (63 Nm).

11. Connect the stabilizer link bolt at the knuckle. Refer to Stabilizer Shaft replacement.

12. Connect the electrical connector to the wheel speed sensor, if equipped with ABS.

13. Install the brake rotor.

14. Install the tire and wheel assembly.

15. Lower the vehicle.

ADJUSTMENT

→ **Support the vehicle by the lower control arms or the rear axle to prevent movement during wheel bearing/hub inspection.**

1. Mount and secure the J 8001 Dial Indicator.

2. Ensure that the dial indicator contacts the vertical surface of the wheel as close as possible to the top wheel stud.

3. Push and pull on the top of the tire in order to inspect the total travel indicated by the dial indicator:

- If the measurement greater than 0.005 in (0.127 mm)—replace the wheel bearing. Refer to Front Wheel Bearing and Hub.
- If the measurement is equal to or less than 0.005 in (0.127 mm)—the system is okay.

CHEVROLET

14

HHR

BATTERY DISCONNECT WARNING 4-10

BRAKES 4-11

ANTI-LOCK BRAKE SYSTEM (ABS) 4-11
Vehicle Yaw Sensor with Vehicle Lateral Accelerometer 4-11
    Removal & Installation.......... 4-11
BLEEDING THE BRAKE SYSTEM 4-12
Bleeding Procedures 4-12
    ABS System Automated Bleed 4-12
    Hydraulic Brake System Bleeding—manual 4-12
    Master Cylinder Bench Bleeding 4-15
    Master Cylinder Reservoir Filling 4-15

FASTENERS 4-11

FRONT DISC BRAKES 4-16
Brake Caliper 4-16
    Removal & Installation.......... 4-16
Disc Brake Pads 4-16
    Removal & Installation.......... 4-16
PARKING BRAKE 4-22
Parking Brake 4-22
    Adjustment 4-22
PRECAUTIONS 4-11
REAR DISC BRAKES 4-17
Brake Caliper 4-17
    Removal & Installation.......... 4-17
Disc Brake Pads 4-18
    Removal & Installation.......... 4-18
REAR DRUM BRAKES 4-20
Brake Drum 4-20
    Removal & Installation.......... 4-20
Brake Shoes 4-20
    Adjustment 4-21
    Removal & Installation.......... 4-20

CHASSIS ELECTRICAL 14-23
AIR BAG (SUPPLEMENTAL INFLATABLE RESTRAINTS) .. 4-23
General Information.................... 4-23
    Service Precautions 4-23
    SIR Disabling and Enabling .. 4-24
    SIR Identification View.......... 4-24
    Steering Wheel Module Coil Centering 4-25

DRIVE TRAIN 4-25

Automatic Transaxle Fluid 4-25
    Fluid Filter and Seal 4-25
Clutch.................................... 4-29
    Hydraulic Clutch Bleeding 4-29
    Removal & Installation.......... 4-29
Driveshaft 4-31
    Removal & Installation.......... 4-31
Front Wheel Drive Intermediate Shaft 4-30
    Removal & Installation.......... 4-30
Manual Transaxle Assembly 4-26
    Removal & Installation.......... 4-26
Manual Transaxle Fluid 4-27
    Drain and Fill...................... 4-27
Manual Transmission Assembly 4-27
    Removal & Installation.......... 4-27
Manual Transmission Fluid 4-29
    Drain and Fill...................... 4-29
Stub Shaft 4-31
    Removal............................. 4-31

ENGINE COOLING 4-33

Engine Coolant........................ 4-33
    Best Practices 4-33
    Draining & Filling Procedure .. 4-33
    Flushing............................. 4-34
Engine Cooling Fan & Shroud 4-34
    Removal & Installation.......... 4-34
Radiator 4-35
    Removal & Installation.......... 4-35
Thermostat 4-35
    Removal & Installation.......... 4-35

Water Pump 4-36
    Removal & Installation.......... 4-36

ENGINE ELECTRICAL 4-38

BATTERY SYSTEM 4-38
Battery.................................... 4-38
    Battery Negative Cable Disconnection & Connection 4-38
    Removal & Installation.......... 4-38
CHARGING SYSTEM 4-39
Generator (Alternator).............. 4-39
    Removal & Installation.......... 4-39
IGNITION SYSTEM 4-39
Firing Order............................. 4-39
Ignition Coil 4-39
    Removal & Installation.......... 4-39
Ignition Timing......................... 4-40
    Adjustment 4-40
Spark Plugs............................. 4-40
    Removal & Installation.......... 4-40
STARTING SYSTEM 4-40
Starter 4-40
    Removal & Installation.......... 4-40

ENGINE MECHANICAL 4-41

Accessory Drive Belts 4-41
    Accessory Belt Routing........ 4-41
    Adjustment 4-41
    Inspection 4-41
    Removal & Installation.......... 4-41
Air Cleaner 4-42
    Filter/element Replacement 4-42
    Removal & Installation.......... 4-42
Camshaft Front Cover 4-43
    Removal & Installation.......... 4-43
Camshaft Timing Chain Sprocket & Tensioner............ 4-44
    Removal & Installation.......... 4-44
Catalytic Converter 4-51
    Removal & Installation.......... 4-51
Crankshaft Front Oil Seal 4-52
    Removal & Installation.......... 4-52
Crankshaft Rear Oil Seal 4-60
    Removal & Installation.......... 4-60

Cylinder Head 4-53
  Removal & Installation.........4-53
Engine Oil & Filter 4-54
  Drain & Refill.......................4-54
Exhaust Manifold 4-54
  Removal & Installation.........4-54
Intake and Exhaust Camshaft,
  Bearing Cap, and Lash
  Adjuster 4-50
  Camshaft Cleaning &
    Inspection..........................4-50
  Removal & Installation.........4-50
Intake Manifold 4-55
  Removal & Installation.........4-55
Oil Pan 4-58
  Removal & Installation.........4-58
Piston and Ring.........................4-58
  Positioning 4-58
Turbocharger 4-60
  Removal & Installation.........4-60
Valve Lash 4-62
  Adjustment 4-62

ENGINE PERFORMANCE & EMISSION CONTROLS 4-63

Camshaft Position (CMP)
  Sensor 4-63
  Location...............................4-63
  Removal & Installation..........4-63
Crankshaft Position (CKP)
  Sensor 4-63
  Location...............................4-63
  Removal & Installation..........4-63
Electronic Control Module
  (ECM) 4-64
  Location...............................4-64
  Removal & Installation..........4-64
Engine Coolant Temperature
  (ECT) Sensor 4-65
  Location...............................4-65
  Removal & Installation..........4-65
Heated Oxygen (HO2S)
  Sensor..................................4-66
  Location...............................4-66
  Removal & Installation..........4-66
Intake Air Pressure &
  Temperature Sensor 4-69
  Location...............................4-69
  Removal & Installation..........4-69
Knock Sensor (KS) 4-69
  Location...............................4-69
  Removal & Installation..........4-69
Manifold Absolute Pressure
  (MAP) sensor 4-70
  Location...............................4-70
  Removal & Installation..........4-70

Mass Air Flow (MAF) / Intake
  Air Temperature (IAT) Sensor ..4-70
  Location...............................4-70
  Removal & Installation..........4-70
Mass Air Flow (MAF) Sensor 4-69
  Location...............................4-69
  Removal & Installation..........4-70
Vehicle Speed Sensor (VSS) 4-71
  Location...............................4-71
  Removal & Installation..........4-71

FUEL............................4-72

GASOLINE FUEL INJECTION SYSTEM..................4-72

Fuel Injectors...........................4-73
  Removal & Installation..........4-73
Fuel Pressure Relief 4-72
Fuel Pump 4-73
  Removal & Installation..........4-73
Fuel Strainer—2.0L only 4-73
  Inspection & Cleaning..........4-73
Fuel System Service
  Precautions 4-72
Fuel Tank 4-76
  Draining 4-76
  Removal & Installation..........4-76
High Pressure Side Fuel
  Pressure Relief—Additional
  Procedure for 2.0L only 4-72
Idle Speed 4-78
  Adjustment...........................4-78
Throttle Body Assembly 4-79
  Removal & Installation..........4-79
Throttle/Idle Learn 4-79

HEATING & AIR CONDITIONING SYSTEM 4-80

Blower Motor............................4-80
  Removal & Installation..........4-80
Heater Core 4-81
  Removal & Installation..........4-81

PRECAUTIONS..............14-10

BATTERY DISCONNECT WARNING 14-10
FASTENERS 14-11

SPECIFICATIONS AND MAINTENANCE CHARTS.....14-3

Additional Maintenance
  Services-Normal 14-9
Additional Maintenance
  Services-Severe 14-9
Brake Specifications 4-7

Camshaft Specifications 4-5
Capacities.................................4-4
Crankshaft and Connecting
  Rod Specifications 4-5
Engine and Vehicle Identification...4-3
Engine Tune-Up Specifications....4-3
Fluid Specifications 4-4
General Engine Specifications 4-3
Maintenance I and II Service
  Schedules 14-8
Piston and Ring Specifications....4-6
Tire, Wheel and Ball Joint
  Specifications........................4-7
Torque Specifications 4-6
Valve Specifications 4-4
Wheel Alignment 4-7

STEERING 4-81

Power Steering Assist Motor 4-82
  Removal & Installation..........4-82
Power Steering Gear.................4-81
  Removal & Installation..........4-81

SUSPENSION..................4-84

FRONT SUSPENSION 4-84
Lower Control Arm 4-84
  Removal & Installation..........4-84
Stabilizer Shaft 4-84
  Removal & Installation..........4-84
Stabilizer Shaft Insulator 4-85
  Removal & Installation..........4-85
Stabilizer Shaft Link 4-84
  Removal & Installation..........4-84
Steering Knuckle 4-85
  Removal & Installation..........4-85
Strut Assembly 4-85
  Removal & Installation..........4-85
Wheel Bearing & Hub................4-86
  Removal & Installation..........4-86
Wheel Stud 4-86
  Removal & Installation..........4-86
REAR SUSPENSION 4-87
Coil Spring...............................4-87
  Removal & Installation..........4-87
Control Arm Bushing 4-87
  Removal & Installation..........4-87
Rear Spring Insulator 4-88
  Removal & Installation..........4-88
Shock Absorber 4-88
  Removal & Installation..........4-88
Spring Bumper 4-88
  Removal & Installation..........4-88
Wheel Bearing & Hub................4-89
  Removal & Installation..........4-89
Wheel Stud...............................4-89
  Removal & Installation..........4-89

SPECIFICATIONS AND MAINTENANCE CHARTS

ENGINE AND VEHICLE IDENTIFICATION

Code ①	Liters (cc)	Cu. In.	Cyl.	Fuel Sys.	Engine Type	Eng. Mfg.	Code ②	Year
M	2.0 (1998)	122	4	DI	DOHC	GM	A	2010
B	2.2 (2189)	134	4	MFI	DOHC	GM	B	2011
V	2.4 (2384)	146	4	MFI	DOHC	GM		
W	2.2 (2189)	134	4	SFI	DOHC	GM		
U	2.4 (2384)	146	4	SFI	DOHC	GM		

① 8th position of VIN

② 10th position of VIN

25742_CHHR_C0001

GENERAL ENGINE SPECIFICATIONS

All measurements are given in inches.

Year	Model	Engine Disp. Liters	Engine ID/VIN	Fuel System Type	Net Horsepower @ rpm	Net Torque@rpm (ft. lbs.)	Bore x Stroke (in.)	Compression Ratio	Oil Pressure @ rpm ①
2010	HHR SS	2.0	M/LNF	Gas	260@5300	260@2000	3.3880-3.3887x3.388	9.2:1	30-70 psi
	HHR LS, 1LT	2.2	B/LE8	Flex Fuel	155@6100	150@4800	3.4642-3.4649x3.861	10:01	30-70 psi
	HHR 2LT	2.4	V/LE9	Flex Fuel	172@5800	167@4500	3.4642-3.4649x3.861	10:01	30-70 psi
2011	HHR LS, 1LT	2.2	W/LE8	Flex Fuel	155@6100	150@4800	3.3855-3.3861x3.727	10.0:1	30-70 psi
	HHR 2LT	2.4	U/LE9	Flex Fuel	172@5800	167@4500	3.4642-3.4649x3.861	10:01	30-70 psi

PSI Pounds per square inch

① Oil Pressure - Minimum - @1000 RPM @ 194 degrees F

25742_CHHR_C0002

ENGINE TUNE-UP SPECIFICATIONS

Year	Engine Displacement Liters	Engine ID/VIN	Spark Plug Gap (in.)	Ignition Timing (deg.) MT	Ignition Timing (deg.) AT	Fuel Pump (psi)	Idle Speed (rpm) MT	Idle Speed (rpm) AT	Valve Stem-to-Guide Clearance Intake	Valve Stem-to-Guide Clearance Exhaust
2010	2.0	M/ LNF	0.035	①	①	57 - 67	②	②	0.0012-0.0022	0.0020-0.0026
	2.2	B/ LE8	0.043	①	①	50 - 60	②	②	0.0012-0.0022	0.0020-0.0026
	2.4	V/ LE9	0.043	①	①	50 - 60	②	②	0.0012-0.0022	0.0020-0.0026
2011	2.2	W/ LE8	0.043	①	①	50 - 60	②	②	0.0012-0.0022	0.0020-0.0026
	2.4	U/ LE9	0.035	①	①	50 - 60	②	②	0.0012-0.0022	0.0020-0.0026

① The engine control module (ECM) controls all ignition system functions, and constantly corrects the spark timing.

② Idle speed is maintained by the ECM.

25742_CHHR_C0003

CAPACITIES

Year	Model	Engine Displacement Liters	Engine ID/VIN	Engine Oil with Filter	Transaxle (pts.) Auto 4T45-E	Transaxle (pts.) Manual M86	Fuel Tank (gal.)	Cooling System (qts.)
2010	HHR SS	2.0	M/ LNF	5.0 qts.	①	②	16.2	9.2
	HHR	2.2	B/ LE8	5.0 qts.	①	② ③	16.2	7.4
	HHR	2.4	V/ LE9	5.0 qts.	①	②	16.2	⑤
2011	HHR LS, 1LT	2.2	W/ LE8	5.0 qts.	①	④	16.2	7.4
	HHR 2LT	2.4	U/ LE9	5.0 qts.	①	④	16.2	⑤

NOTE: All capacities are approximate. Add fluid gradually and ensure a proper fluid level is obtained.

① Hydra-matic: Bottom Pan Removal: 6.9 qts.; Complete Overhaul: 9.5 qts.; Dry: 12.9 qts

② Manual 5 Speed, Saab,: 2.0 qts. (drain and fill)

③ Hydra-matic: Bottom Pan Removal: 7.0 qts.; Complete Overhaul: 9.5 qts.; Dry: 12.9 qts

④ Getrag 5 Speed: 1.9 qts. (dry); 1.7 qts. (drain and fill)

⑤ Manual transaxle: 8.7 qts.; automatic transaxle: 8.5 qts.

25742_CHHR_C0004

FLUID SPECIFICATIONS

Year	Model	Engine Disp. Liters	Engine Oil	Manual Trans.	Auto. Trans.	Drive Axle Front	Drive Axle Rear	Hydraulic Clutch	Brake Master Cylinder	Cooling System
2010	HHR	2.0	SAE 5W-30 ①	②	Dexron VI®	③	③	DOT 3	DOT 3	DEX-COOL®
	HHR	2.2	SAE 5W-30	Dexron VI®	Dexron VI®	③	③	DOT 3	DOT 3	DEX-COOL®
	HHR	2.4	SAE 5W-30	Dexron VI®	Dexron VI®	③	③	DOT 3	DOT 3	DEX-COOL®
2011	HHR	2.2	SAE 5W-30	Dexron VI®	Dexron VI®	③	③	DOT 3	DOT 3	DEX-COOL®
	HHR	2.4	SAE 5W-30	Dexron VI®	Dexron VI®	③	③	DOT 3	DOT 3	DEX-COOL®

DOT: Department Of Transpotation

① This vehicle's engine requires a special oil meeting GM Standard GM4718M, such as Mobil 1® or equivalent. Oils meeting this standard may be identified as synthetic.

② Manual Transmission fluid (GM Part No. U.S. 88862472, in Canada 88862473).

③ Chassis Lubricant (GM Part No. U.S. 12377985, in Canada 88901242) or lubricant meeting requirements of NLGI #2, Category LB or GC-LB.

25742_CHHR_C0005

VALVE SPECIFICATIONS

Year	Engine Displacement Liters	Engine ID/VIN	Seat Angle (deg.)	Face Angle (deg.)	Spring Test Pressure (lbs. @ in.)	Spring Free-Length (in.)	Spring Installed Height (in.)	Stem-to-Guide Clearance (in.) Intake	Stem-to-Guide Clearance (in.) Exhaust	Stem Diameter (in.) Intake	Stem Diameter (in.) Exhaust
2010	2.0	M/ LNF	NS	45	118-129 @ .09 ①	1.6299-1.7402	closed: 1.2795	0.0012-0.0022	0.0020-0.0026	0.2344-0.2355	0.2337-0.2343
	2.2	B/ LE8	NS	45	118-129 @ .09 ①	1.6299-1.7402	closed: 1.2795	0.0012-0.0022	0.0020-0.0026	0.2344-0.2355	0.2337-0.2343
	2.4	V/ LE9	NS	45	118-129 @ .09 ①	1.6299-1.7402	closed: 1.2795	0.0012-0.0022	0.0020-0.0026	0.2344-0.2355	0.2337-0.2343
2011	2.2	W/ LE8	NS	45	118-129 @ .09 ①	1.6299-1.7402	closed: 1.2795	0.0012-0.0022	0.0020-0.0026	0.2344-0.2355	0.2337-0.2343
	2.4	U/ LE9	NS	45	118-129 @ .09 ①	1.6299-1.7402	closed: 1.2795	0.0012-0.0022	0.0020-0.0026	0.2344-0.2355	0.2337-0.2343

NS: Not specified by Chevrolet/GM

① Valve Spring Load - Open - @ .09 in. (22.5 mm)

25742_CHHR_C0006

WHEEL ALIGNMENT

Year	Model		Caster Range (+/-Deg.)	Caster Preferred Setting (Deg.)	Camber Range (+/-Deg.)	Camber Preferred Setting (Deg.)	Total Toe (in.)
2010	HHR Sport/Soft Ride	F	0.75	3.70	0.75	0.95	+0.20° ± 0.20°
	HHR Performance	F	0.75	3.65	0.75	1.25	+0.20° ± 0.20°
	HHR - all	R	NS	NS	NS	NS	+0.25° ± 0.30°
2011	HHR - all	F	0.75	3.70	0.75	0.95	+0.20° ± 0.20°
		R	NS	NS	NS	NS	+0.25° ± 0.30°

NS: Not specified by Chevrolet/GM

25742_CHHR_C0011

TIRE, WHEEL AND BALL JOINT SPECIFICATIONS

Year	Model	OEM Tires Standard	OEM Tires Optional	Tire Pressures (psi) Front	Tire Pressures (psi) Rear	Wheel Size	Ball Joint Inspection	Lug Nut (ft. lbs.)
2010	HHR SS	P225/45R18-91V	NA	①	①	18 x 7.5	②	100
	HHR LS	P215/55R16-91H	NA	①	①	16 X 6.5	②	100
	HHR 1LT	P215/55R16-91S	NA	①	①	16 X 6.5	②	100
	HHR 2LT	P215/50R17-90S	NA	①	①	17 X 6.5	②	100
2011	HHR LS	P215/55R16-91H	NA	①	①	16 X 6.5	②	100
	HHR 1LT	P215/55R16-91S	NA	①	①	16 X 6.5	②	100
	HHR 2LT	P215/50R17-90S	NA	①	①	17 X 6.5	②	100

OEM: Original Equipment Manufacturer

PSI: Pounds Per Square Inch

NA: Information not available

① Refer to placard on vehicle for proper tire inflation pressure.

② Replace the lower control arm if there is ball joint movement > 0.020 inch

25742_CHHR_C0012

BRAKE SPECIFICATIONS

All measurements in inches unless noted

Year	Model		Brake Disc Original Thickness	Brake Disc Minimum Thickness	Brake Disc Maximum Runout	Brake Drum Diameter Original Inside Diameter	Brake Drum Diameter Max. Wear Limit	Brake Drum Diameter Maximum Machine Diameter	Minimum Lining Thickness	Brake Caliper Bracket Bolts (ft. lbs.)	Brake Caliper Guide Pin Bolts (ft. lbs.)
2010	HHR LS, 1LT	F	1.023	0.898	0.002	NA	NA	NA	0.039	85	26
		R	NA	NA	NA	①	9.079	9.059	0.020	NA	NA
	HHR 2LT	F	1.023	0.898	0.002	NA	NA	NA	0.039	85	26
		R	NA	NA	NA	①	9.079	9.059	0.020	NA	NA
	HHR SS	F	1.023	0.898	0.002	NA	NA	NA	0.039	96	26
		R	0.551	0.465	0.002	NA	NA	NA	0.039	85	26
2011	HHR LS, 1LT	F	1.023	0.898	0.002	NA	NA	NA	0.039	85	26
		R	NA	NA	NA	①	9.079	9.059	0.020	NA	NA
	HHR 2LT	F	1.023	0.898	0.002	NA	NA	NA	0.039	85	26
		R	NA	NA	NA	①	9.079	9.059	0.020	NA	NA

NA: Not Applicable

NS: Information not specified by OEM

① 8.996-9.004

25742_CHHR_C0013

MAINTENANCE I AND II SERVICE SCHEDULES
HHR

When the CHANGE ENGINE OIL light appears, certain services and inspections are required.

Required services are described as Maintenance I and Maintenance II.

The first service of a vehicle should be Maintenance I, and the second service should be Maintenance II.

Alternate between the 2 services thereafter. However, in some cases, Maintenance II may be required more often.

Maintenance I: Use Maintenance I if the CHANGE ENGINE OIL light comes on within 10 months since the vehicle was purchased or, if Maintenance II was performed.

Maintenance II: Use Maintenance II if the previous service performed was Maintenance I. Always use Maintenance II whenever the CHANGE ENGINE OIL light comes on 10 months or more since the last service, or, if the CHANGE ENGINE OIL light has not come on at all for one year.

Service Item	Maintenance I	Maintenance II
Change the engine oil and filter.	✓	✓
Reset the oil life system.	✓	✓
Visually inspect the vehicle for leaks or damage. A fluid loss in the vehicle system could indicate a problem. Inspect, repair and add fluid to the system if necessary.	✓	✓
Inspect the engine air cleaner filter. If necessary, replace the filter.	✓	✓
Rotate the tires. Inspect the tire inflation pressures and the tire wear.	✓	✓
Visually inspect the brake lines and hoses for proper hook-up, binding, leaks, cracks, chafing, etc. Inspect the disc brake pads for wear and the rotors for surface condition. Inspect the drum brake linings for wear or cracks. Inspect other brake parts, including drums, wheel cylinders, calipers, parking brake, etc. Inspect the parking brake adjustment.	✓	✓
Inspect engine coolant and windshield washer fluid levels. Add fluid as needed.	✓	✓
Inspect the suspension and steering components. Inspect the front and rear suspension and the steering system for damaged, loose or missing parts, or signs of wear. Inspect the power steering lines and the hoses for proper hook-up, binding, leaks, cracks,	—	✓
Visually inspect the coolant hoses and replace the hoses if they are cracked, swollen or deteriorated. Inspect all pipes, fittings and clamps; replace with GM parts as needed. To help ensure proper operation, a pressure test of the cooling system and pressure cap and cleaning the outside of the radiator and air conditioning condenser is recommended at least once a year.	—	✓
Body hinges and latches, key lock cylinders, and rear compartment hinges lubrication. More frequent lubrication may be required when the vehicle is exposed to a corrosive environment. Applying silicone grease on weatherstrips with a clean cloth makes them last longer, seal better, and not stick or squeak.	—	✓
Inspect the throttle system for interference or binding and for damaged or missing parts. Replace the parts as needed. Replace any components that have high effort or excessive wear. Do not lubricate the accelerator or the cruise control cables.	—	✓
Replace the passenger compartment air filter.	—	✓

To reset the CHANGE ENGINE OIL light:

1. Turn the ignition key to the ON/RUN position with the engine OFF.
2. Press and release the stem in the lower center of the instrument cluster until the OIL LIFE message is displayed.
3. Once the alternating OIL LIFE and RESET messages appear, press and hold the stem until several beeps sound.
   This confirms that the oil life system has been reset to 100 percent.
4. Turn the ignition key to the OFF position.
   If the CHANGE ENGINE OIL message comes back on when the vehicle is started, the engine oil life system has not been reset. Repeat the procedure.

ADDITIONAL MAINTENANCE SERVICES - NORMAL
HHR

TO BE SERVICED	TYPE OF SERVICE	VEHICLE MILEAGE INTERVAL (x1000)					
		25	50	75	100	125	150
Spark plugs	Replace				✓		
Air cleaner filter	Replace		✓		✓		✓
Engine coolant	Replace						✓
Fuel system	Inspect	✓	✓	✓	✓	✓	✓
Accessory drive belt	Replace						✓
Evaporative control system	Inspect		✓		✓		✓
Passenger compartment air cleaner	Replace	✓	✓	✓	✓	✓	✓

25742_CHHR_C0015

ADDITIONAL MAINTENANCE SERVICES - SEVERE
HHR

TO BE SERVICED	TYPE OF SERVICE	VEHICLE MILEAGE INTERVAL (x1000)					
		25	50	75	100	125	150
Spark plugs	Replace				✓		
Air cleaner filter	Replace		✓		✓		✓
Engine coolant	Replace						✓
Exhaust system & heat shields	Inspect	✓	✓	✓	✓	✓	✓
Fuel system	Inspect	✓	✓	✓	✓	✓	✓
Accessory drive belts	Inspect		✓		✓		✓
Passenger compartment air filter	Replace	✓	✓	✓	✓	✓	✓

25742_CHHR_C0016

PRECAUTIONS

Before servicing any vehicle, please be sure to read all of the following precautions, which deal with personal safety, prevention of component damage, and important points to take into consideration when servicing a motor vehicle:

• Never open, service or drain the radiator or cooling system when the engine is hot; serious burns can occur from the steam and hot coolant.

• Observe all applicable safety precautions when working around fuel. Whenever servicing the fuel system, always work in a well-ventilated area. Do not allow fuel spray or vapors to come in contact with a spark, open flame, or excessive heat (a hot drop light, for example). Keep a dry chemical fire extinguisher near the work area. Always keep fuel in a container specifically designed for fuel storage; also, always properly seal fuel containers to avoid the possibility of fire or explosion. Refer to the additional fuel system precautions later in this section.

• Fuel injection systems often remain pressurized, even after the engine has been turned **OFF**. The fuel system pressure must be relieved before disconnecting any fuel lines. Failure to do so may result in fire and/or personal injury.

• Brake fluid often contains polyglycol ethers and polyglycols. Avoid contact with the eyes and wash your hands thoroughly after handling brake fluid. If you do get brake fluid in your eyes, flush your eyes with clean, running water for 15 minutes. If eye irritation persists, or if you have taken

brake fluid internally, IMMEDIATELY seek medical assistance.

• The EPA warns that prolonged contact with used engine oil may cause a number of skin disorders, including cancer. You should make every effort to minimize your exposure to used engine oil. Protective gloves should be worn when changing oil. Wash your hands and any other exposed skin areas as soon as possible after exposure to used engine oil. Soap and water, or waterless hand cleaner should be used.

• All new vehicles are now equipped with an air bag system, often referred to as a Supplemental Restraint System (SRS) or Supplemental Inflatable Restraint (SIR) system. The system must be disabled before performing service on or around system components, steering column, instrument panel components, wiring and sensors. Failure to follow safety and disabling procedures could result in accidental air bag deployment, possible personal injury and unnecessary system repairs.

• Always wear safety goggles when working with, or around, the air bag system. When carrying a non-deployed air bag, be sure the bag and trim cover are pointed away from your body. When placing a non-deployed air bag on a work surface, always face the bag and trim cover upward, away from the surface. This will reduce the motion of the module if it is accidentally deployed. Refer to the additional air bag system precautions later in this section.

• Clean, high quality brake fluid from a sealed container is essential to the safe and

proper operation of the brake system. You should always buy the correct type of brake fluid for your vehicle. If the brake fluid becomes contaminated, completely flush the system with new fluid. Never reuse any brake fluid. Any brake fluid that is removed from the system should be discarded. Also, do not allow any brake fluid to come in contact with a painted surface; it will damage the paint.

• Never operate the engine without the proper amount and type of engine oil; doing so WILL result in severe engine damage.

• Timing belt maintenance is extremely important. Many models utilize an interference-type, non-freewheeling engine. If the timing belt breaks, the valves in the cylinder head may strike the pistons, causing potentially serious (also time-consuming and expensive) engine damage. Refer to the maintenance interval charts for the recommended replacement interval for the timing belt, and to the timing belt section for belt replacement and inspection.

• Disconnecting the negative battery cable on some vehicles may interfere with the functions of the on-board computer system(s) and may require the computer to undergo a relearning process once the negative battery cable is reconnected.

• When servicing drum brakes, only disassemble and assemble one side at a time, leaving the remaining side intact for reference.

• Only an MVAC-trained, EPA-certified automotive technician should service the air conditioning system or its components.

PRECAUTIONS   BATTERY DISCONNECT WARNING

❋❋ CAUTION

Unless directed otherwise, the ignition and start switch must be in the OFF or LOCK position, and all electrical loads must be OFF before servicing any electrical component. Disconnect the negative battery cable to prevent an electrical spark should a tool or equipment come in contact with an exposed electrical terminal. Failure to follow these precautions may result in personal injury and/or

damage to the vehicle or its components.

For Vehicles equipped with OnStar®(UE1) with Back Up Battery:

The Back Up Battery is a redundant power supply to allow limited OnStar® functionality in the event of a main vehicle battery power disruption to the VCIM (OnStar® module). Do not disconnect the main vehicle battery or remove the OnStar® fuse with the ignition key in any position other than OFF. Retained accessory

power (RAP) should be allowed to time out or be disabled (simply opening the driver door should disable RAP) before disconnecting power. Disconnecting power to the OnStar® module in any way while the ignition is On or with RAP activated may cause activation of the OnStar® Back-Up Battery (BUB) system and will discharge and permanently damage the back-up battery. Once the Back-Up Battery is activated it will stay on until it has completely discharged. The BUB is not rechargeable and once activated the BUB must be replaced.

PRECAUTIONS   FASTENERS

✳✳ WARNING

Use the correct fastener in the correct location. Replacement fasteners must be the correct part number for that application. Do not use paints, lubricants, or corrosion inhibitors on fasteners, or fastener joint surfaces, unless specified. These coatings affect fastener torque and joint clamping force and may damage the fastener. Use the correct tightening sequence and specifications when installing fasteners in order to avoid damage to parts and systems. When using fasteners that are threaded directly into plastic, use extreme care not to strip the mating plastic part(s). Use hand tools only, and do not use any kind of impact or power tools. A fastener should be Hand-tightened, fully seated, and not stripped.

BRAKES   PRECAUTIONS

✳✳ CAUTION

Brake fluid may irritate eyes and skin. In case of contact, take the following actions:

- Eye contact—rinse thoroughly with water.
- Skin contact—wash with soap and water.
- If ingested—consult a physician immediately.

✳✳ WARNING

Avoid spilling brake fluid onto painted surfaces, electrical connections, wiring, or cables. Brake fluid will damage painted surfaces and cause corrosion to electrical components. If any brake fluid comes in contact with painted surfaces, immediately flush the area with water. If any brake fluid comes in contact with electrical connections, wiring, or cables, use a clean shop cloth to wipe away the fluid.

✳✳ WARNING

Only use products that comply with GM specifications. Follow instructions at all times. The use of any type of fluid other than the recommended type of brake fluid may cause contamination which could result in damage to the internal rubber seals and/or rubber linings of hydraulic brake system components.

- Certain components within the ABS system are not intended to be serviced or repaired individually.
- Do not use rubber hoses or other parts not specifically specified for and ABS system. When using repair kits, replace all parts included in the kit. Partial or incorrect repair may lead to functional problems and require the replacement of components.
- Lubricate rubber parts with clean, fresh brake fluid to ease assembly. Do not use shop air to clean parts; damage to rubber components may result.

- Use only DOT 3 brake fluid from an unopened container.
- If any hydraulic component or line is removed or replaced, it may be necessary to bleed the entire system.
- A clean repair area is essential. Always clean the reservoir and cap thoroughly before removing the cap. The slightest amount of dirt in the fluid may plug an orifice and impair the system function. Perform repairs after components have been thoroughly cleaned; use only denatured alcohol to clean components. Do not allow ABS components to come into contact with any substance containing mineral oil; this includes used shop rags.
- The Anti-Lock control unit is a microprocessor similar to other computer units in the vehicle. Ensure that the ignition switch is **OFF** before removing or installing controller harnesses. Avoid static electricity discharge at or near the controller.
- If any arc welding is to be done on the vehicle, unplug the control unit before welding operations begin.

BRAKES   ANTI-LOCK BRAKE SYSTEM (ABS)

VEHICLE YAW SENSOR WITH VEHICLE LATERAL ACCELEROMETER

REMOVAL & INSTALLATION

See Figure 1.

1. Refer to Brake Precautions.
2. Turn OFF the ignition.
3. Remove the right front seat.
4. Remove the right side body hinge pillar trim panel. Tip: To ease access to the yaw rate sensor, it may be necessary to carefully cut a small section of the floor carpeting neat the yaw rate sensor.
5. Disconnect the yaw rate sensor electrical connector.
6. Remove the yaw rate sensor nuts.

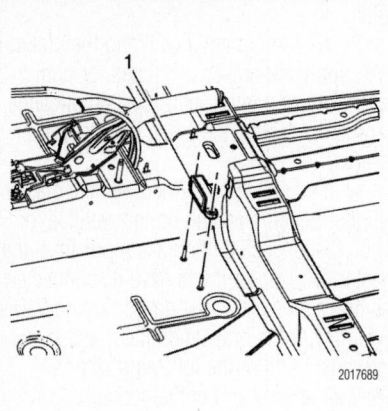

2017689

Fig. 1 Remove the yaw rate nuts and the sensor (1)

7. Remove the yaw rate sensor (1).

To install:

8. Install the yaw rate sensor (1).
9. Install the yaw rate sensor nuts.
10. Tighten the nuts to 89 inch lbs. (10 Nm).
11. Connect the yaw rate sensor electrical connector.
12. Carefully position the floor carpet to the vehicle floor.
13. Install the right side body hinge pillar trim panel.
14. Install the right front seat.
15. Install a scan tool.
16. Using the special functions menu on the scan tool, perform the steering angle sensor calibration.
17. Perform a diagnostic system check.

BLEEDING PROCEDURES

ABS SYSTEM AUTOMATED BLEED

Refer to Brake Precautions.

➡**Before performing the ABS Automated Bleed Procedure, first perform a manual or pressure bleed of the base hydraulic brake system. Refer to Hydraulic Brake System Bleeding.**

The automated bleed procedure is recommended when one of the following conditions exist: (1) The base brake system bleeding does not achieve the desired pedal height or feel, (2) An extreme loss of brake fluid has occurred, (3) Air ingestion is suspected in the secondary circuits of the brake modulator assembly.

The ABS Automated Bleed Procedure uses a scan tool to cycle the system solenoid valves and run the pump in order to purge any air from the secondary circuits. These circuits are normally closed off, and are only opened during system initialization at vehicle start up and during ABS operation. For 2010 models: The automated bleed procedure opens these secondary circuits and allows any air trapped in these circuits to flow out toward the brake corners.

For 2011 models: The automated bleed procedure opens these secondary circuits and allows any air trapped in these circuits to flow out away from the brake modulator assembly, which is then forced out at the brake corners by the pressure bleeder.

Automated Bleed Procedure

✳✳ WARNING

Terminate the Auto Bleed Procedure at any time during the process by pressing the EXIT button. No further scan tool prompts pertaining to the Auto Bleed procedure will be given. After exiting the bleed procedure, relieve bleed pressure and disconnect the bleed equipment per the manufacturer's instructions. Failure to properly relieve pressure may result in spilled brake fluid causing damage to components and painted surfaces.

1. Raise and support the vehicle.
2. Remove all four tire and wheel assemblies.
3. Inspect the brake system for leaks and visual damage.
4. Lower the vehicle.
5. Inspect the battery state of charge.

6. Install a scan tool.
7. Turn the ignition ON, with the engine OFF.
8. With the scan tool, establish communications with the ABS system. Select Special Functions. Select Automated Bleed from the Special Functions menu.
9. Raise and support the vehicle.
10. Following the directions given on the scan tool, pressure bleed the base brake system. Refer to Hydraulic Brake System Bleeding.
11. Follow the scan tool directions until the desired brake pedal height is achieved.
12. If the bleed procedure is aborted, a malfunction exists. Perform the following steps before resuming the bleed procedure:
   a. If a DTC is detected, diagnose the appropriate DTC.
   b. If the brake pedal feels spongy, perform the conventional brake bleed procedure again. Refer to Hydraulic Brake System Bleeding.
13. When the desired pedal height is achieved, press the brake pedal to inspect for firmness.
14. Lower the vehicle.
15. Remove the scan tool.
16. Install the tire and wheel assemblies.
17. Inspect the brake fluid level.
18. Road test the vehicle while confirming the brake pedal remains high and firm.

HYDRAULIC BRAKE SYSTEM BLEEDING —MANUAL

2010 Models

2.0L Engine

1. Refer to Brake Precautions.
2. Place a clean shop cloth beneath the brake master cylinder to catch brake fluid spills.
3. With the ignition OFF and the brakes cool, apply the brakes 3-5 times, or until the brake pedal effort increases significantly, in order to deplete the brake booster power reserve.
4. If you have performed a brake master cylinder bench bleeding on this vehicle, or if you disconnected the brake pipes from the master cylinder, or if you have disconnected the brake pipes from the proportioning valve assembly or the brake modulator assembly, you must perform the following steps to bleed air at the ports of the hydraulic component:
   a. Fill the master cylinder reservoir (combined with the hydraulic clutch (on manual (transmission) to the maximum-

full level with GM approved or equivalent brake fluid from a clean, sealed brake fluid container.

➡**If removal of the reservoir cap and diaphragm is necessary, clean the outside of the reservoir on and around the cap prior to removal.**

   b. With the brake pipes installed securely to the master cylinder, proportioning valve assembly, or brake modulator assembly, loosen and separate one of the brake pipes from the port of the component.

➡**For the brake modulator assembly, perform these steps in the sequence of system flow; begin with the fluid feed pipes on the master cylinder.**

- a. Allow a small amount of brake fluid to gravity bleed from the open port of the component.
- b. Connect the brake pipe to the component and tighten securely.
- c. Have an assistant slowly press the brake pedal fully and maintain steady pressure on the pedal.
- d. Loosen the same brake pipe to purge air from the open port of the component.
- e. Tighten the brake pipe fitting, then have the assistant slowly release the brake pedal.
- f. Wait 15 seconds, then repeat steps a through e, until all air is purged from the same port of the component.
- g. With the brake pipe fitting installed securely to the master cylinder, proportioning valve assembly, or brake modulator assembly after all air been purged from the first port of the component that was bled, loosen and separate the next brake pipe from the component and repeat steps a–f until each of the ports on the component has been bled.
- f. After completing the final component bleeding procedure, ensure each of the brake pipe fittings is properly tightened.

5. Fill the master cylinder reservoir and combined hydraulic clutch, if equipped, to the maximum-full level with GM approved or equivalent brake fluid from a clean, sealed brake fluid container:
   a. Ensure that the brake master cylinder reservoir remains at least half-full during this bleeding procedure.

b. Add fluid as needed to maintain the proper level.

c. Clean the outside of the reservoir on and around the reservoir cap prior to removing the cap and diaphragm.

6. Install a proper box-end wrench onto the RIGHT REAR wheel hydraulic circuit bleeder valve.

7. Install a transparent hose over the end of the bleeder valve.

8. Submerge the open end of the transparent hose into a transparent container partially filled with GM approved or equivalent brake fluid from a clean, sealed brake fluid container.

9. Have an assistant slowly depress the brake pedal fully and maintain steady pressure on the brake pedal.

10. Loosen the bleeder valve to purge air from the wheel hydraulic circuit.

11. Tighten the bleeder valve, then have the assistant slowly release the brake pedal.

12. Wait 15 seconds, the repeat steps 8–10 until all air is purged from the same wheel hydraulic circuit.

13. With the right rear wheel hydraulic circuit bleeder valve tightened securely and after all air has been purged from the right rear wheel hydraulic circuit, install a proper box-end wrench onto the LEFT FRONT wheel hydraulic circuit bleeder valve.

14. Install a proper box-end wrench onto the LEFT FRONT wheel hydraulic circuit INBOARD bleeder valve.

15. Install a transparent hose over the end of the bleeder valve, then repeat steps 7–11.

16. Install a proper box-end wrench onto the LEFT FRONT wheel hydraulic circuit, OUTBOARD bleeder valve.

17. Install a transparent hose over the end of the bleeder valve, then repeat steps 7–11.

18. With the left front wheel hydraulic circuit bleeder valve tightened securely and after all air has been purged from the left front wheel hydraulic circuit, install a proper box-end wrench onto the LEFT REAR wheel hydraulic circuit bleeder valve.

19. Install a transparent hose over the end of the bleeder valve, then repeat steps 7–11.

20. With the left rear wheel hydraulic circuit bleeder valve tightened securely and after all air has been purged from the left rear wheel hydraulic circuit, install a proper box-end wrench onto the RIGHT FRONT wheel hydraulic circuit bleeder valve.

21. Install a proper box-end wrench onto the RIGHT FRONT wheel hydraulic circuit INBOARD bleeder valve.

22. Install a transparent hose over the

end of the bleeder valve, then repeat steps 77–11.

23. Install a proper box-end wrench onto the RIGHT FRONT wheel hydraulic circuit, OUTBOARD bleeder valve.

24. Install a transparent hose over the end of the bleeder valve, then repeat steps 7–11.

25. After completing the final wheel hydraulic circuit bleeding procedure, ensure each of the 4 wheel hydraulic circuit bleeder valves is properly tightened.

26. After completing the final wheel hydraulic circuit bleeding procedure, ensure each of the 6 wheel hydraulic circuit bleeder valves is properly tightened.

27. Fill the brake master cylinder reservoir to the maximum-fill level brake fluid.

28. Slowly depress and release the brake pedal. Observe the feel of the brake pedal.

29. If the brake pedal feels spongy, repeat the bleeding procedure again. If the brake pedal still feels spongy after repeating the bleeding procedure, perform the following steps:

a. Inspect the brake system for external leaks.

b. Pressure bleed the hydraulic brake system in order to purge any air that may still be trapped in the system.

30. Turn the ignition key ON, with the engine OFF. Check to see if the brake system warning lamp remains illuminated.

➡**DO NOT allow the vehicle to be driven until it is diagnosed and repaired.**

31. If the brake system warning lamp remains illuminated, repair the problem.

2.2L & 2.4L Engines

1. Refer to Brake Precautions.

2. Place a clean shop cloth beneath the brake master cylinder to catch brake fluid spills.

3. With the ignition OFF and the brakes cool, apply the brakes 3-5 times, or until the brake pedal effort increases significantly, in order to deplete the brake booster power reserve.

4. If you have performed a brake master cylinder bench bleeding on this vehicle, or if you disconnected the brake pipes from the master cylinder, or if you have disconnected the brake pipes from the proportioning valve assembly or the brake modulator assembly, you must perform the following steps to bleed air at the ports of the hydraulic component:

a. Fill the master cylinder reservoir (combined with the hydraulic clutch (on manual (transmission) to the maximum-full level with GM approved or equivalent

brake fluid from a clean, sealed brake fluid container.

➡**If removal of the reservoir cap and diaphragm is necessary, clean the outside of the reservoir on and around the cap prior to removal.**

b. With the brake pipes installed securely to the master cylinder, proportioning valve assembly, or brake modulator assembly, loosen and separate one of the brake pipes from the port of the component.

c. For the proportioning valve assembly or the brake modulator assembly, perform these steps in the sequence of system flow; begin with the fluid feed pipes from the master cylinder:

- a. Allow a small amount of brake fluid to gravity bleed from the open port of the component.
- b. Connect the brake pipe to the component and tighten securely.
- c. Have an assistant slowly press the brake pedal fully and maintain steady pressure on the pedal.
- d. Loosen the same brake pipe to purge air from the open port of the component.
- e. Tighten the brake pipe, then have the assistant slowly release the brake pedal.
- f. Wait 15 seconds, then repeat steps a through e, until each of the ports on the component has been bled.
- g. After completing the final component bleeding procedure, ensure each of the brake pipe fittings is properly tightened.

5. Fill the master cylinder reservoir and combined hydraulic clutch, if equipped, to the maximum-full level with GM approved or equivalent brake fluid from a clean, sealed brake fluid container:

a. Ensure that the brake master cylinder reservoir remains at least half-full during this bleeding procedure. Add fluid as needed to maintain the proper level.

b. Clean the outside of the reservoir on and around the reservoir cap prior to removing the cap and diaphragm.

6. Install a proper box-end wrench onto the RIGHT REAR wheel hydraulic circuit bleeder valve.

7. Install a transparent hose over the end of the bleeder valve.

8. Submerge the open end of the transparent hose into a transparent container partially filled with brake fluid.

9. Have an assistant slowly press the brake pedal fully and maintain steady pressure on the pedal.

10. Loosen the bleeder valve to purge air from the wheel hydraulic circuit.

11. Tighten the bleeder valve, then have the assistant slowly release the brake pedal.

12. Wait 15 seconds, then repeat steps 8-10 until all air is purged from the same wheel hydraulic circuit.

13. With the right rear wheel hydraulic circuit bleeder valve tightened securely, after all air has been purged from the right rear hydraulic circuit, install a proper box-end wrench onto the LEFT FRONT wheel hydraulic circuit bleeder valve.

14. Install a transparent hose over the end of the bleeder valve, then repeat steps 7-11.

15. With the left front wheel hydraulic circuit bleeder valve tightened securely, after all air has been purged from the left front hydraulic circuit, install a proper box-end wrench onto the LEFT REAR wheel hydraulic circuit bleeder valve.

16. Install a transparent hose over the end of the bleeder valve, then repeat steps 7-11.

17. With the left rear wheel hydraulic circuit bleeder valve tightened securely, after all air has been purged from the left rear hydraulic circuit, install a proper box-end wrench onto the RIGHT FRONT wheel hydraulic circuit bleeder valve.

18. Install a transparent hose over the end of the bleeder valve, then repeat steps 7-11.

19. After completing the final wheel hydraulic circuit bleeding procedure, ensure that each of the 4 wheel hydraulic circuit bleeder valves are properly tightened.

20. Fill the brake master cylinder reservoir to the maximum-fill level brake fluid.

21. Slowly depress and release the brake pedal. Observe the feel of the brake pedal.

22. If the brake pedal feels spongy, repeat the bleeding procedure again. If the brake pedal still feels spongy after repeating the bleeding procedure, perform the following steps:

a. Inspect the brake system for external leaks.

b. Pressure bleed the hydraulic brake system in order to purge any air that may still be trapped in the system.

23. Turn the ignition key ON, with the engine OFF. Check to see if the brake system warning lamp remains illuminated.

➡**DO NOT allow the vehicle to be driven until it is diagnosed and repaired.**

24. If the brake system warning lamp remains illuminated, repair the problem.

2011 Models

1. Place a clean shop cloth beneath the brake master cylinder to catch brake fluid spills.

2. With the ignition OFF and the brakes cool, apply the brakes 3-5 times, or until the brake pedal effort increases significantly, in order to deplete the brake booster power reserve.

3. If you have performed a brake master cylinder bench bleeding on this vehicle, or if you disconnected the brake pipes from the master cylinder, or if you have disconnected the brake pipes from the proportioning valve assembly or the brake modulator assembly, you must perform the following steps to bleed air at the ports of the hydraulic component:

a. Fill the master cylinder reservoir (combined with the hydraulic clutch (on manual (transmission) to the maximum-full level with GM approved or equivalent brake fluid from a clean, sealed brake fluid container.

➡**If removal of the reservoir cap and diaphragm is necessary, clean the outside of the reservoir on and around the cap prior to removal.**

b. With the brake pipes installed securely to the master cylinder, proportioning valve assembly, or brake modulator assembly, loosen and separate one of the brake pipes from the port of the component.

c. For the proportioning valve assembly or the brake modulator assembly, perform these steps in the sequence of system flow; begin with the fluid feed pipes from the master cylinder:

- a. Allow a small amount of brake fluid to gravity bleed from the open port of the component.
- b. Connect the brake pipe to the component and tighten securely.
- c. Have an assistant slowly press the brake pedal fully and maintain steady pressure on the pedal.
- d. Loosen the same brake pipe to purge air from the open port of the component.
- e. Tighten the brake pipe fitting, then have the assistant slowly release the brake pedal.
- f. Wait 15 seconds, then repeat steps a through e, until each of the ports on the component has been bled.
- g. With the brake pipe fitting installed securely to the master cylinder, proportioning valve assembly, or brake modulator

assembly after all air been purged from the first port of the component that was bled, loosen and separate the next brake pipe from the component and repeat steps a through f until each of the ports on the component has been bled.

- h. After completing the final component bleeding procedure, ensure each of the brake pipe fittings is properly tightened.

4. Fill the master cylinder reservoir and combined hydraulic clutch, if equipped, to the maximum-full level with GM approved or equivalent brake fluid from a clean, sealed brake fluid container:

a. Ensure that the brake master cylinder reservoir remains at least half-full during this bleeding procedure.

b. Add fluid as needed to maintain the proper level.

c. Clean the outside of the reservoir on and around the reservoir cap prior to removing the cap and diaphragm.

5. Install a proper box-end wrench onto the RIGHT REAR wheel hydraulic circuit bleeder valve.

6. Install a transparent hose over the end of the bleeder valve.

7. Submerge the open end of the transparent hose into a transparent container partially filled with brake fluid.

8. Have an assistant slowly depress the brake pedal fully and maintain steady pressure on the pedal.

9. Loosen the bleeder valve to purge air from the wheel hydraulic circuit.

10. Tighten the bleeder valve, then have the assistant slowly release the brake pedal.

11. Wait 15 seconds, then repeat steps 8–10 until all air is purged from the same wheel hydraulic circuit.

12. With the right rear wheel hydraulic circuit bleeder valve tightened securely, after all air has been purged from the right rear hydraulic circuit, install a proper box-end wrench onto the LEFT FRONT wheel hydraulic circuit bleeder valve.

13. Install a transparent hose over the end of the bleeder valve, then repeat steps 7–11.

14. With the left front wheel hydraulic circuit bleeder valve tightened securely, after all air has been purged from the left front hydraulic circuit, install a proper box-end wrench onto the LEFT REAR wheel hydraulic circuit bleeder valve.

15. Install a transparent hose over the end of the bleeder valve, then repeat steps 7–11.

16. With the left rear wheel hydraulic circuit bleeder valve tightened securely, after all air has been purged from the left rear

hydraulic circuit, install a proper box-end wrench onto the RIGHT FRONT wheel hydraulic circuit bleeder valve.

17. Install a transparent hose over the end of the bleeder valve, then repeat steps 7–11.

18. After completing the final wheel hydraulic circuit bleeding procedure, ensure that each of the 4 wheel hydraulic circuit bleeder valves are properly tightened.

19. Fill the brake master cylinder reservoir to the maximum-fill level brake fluid.

20. Slowly depress and release the brake pedal. Observe the feel of the brake pedal.

21. If the brake pedal feels spongy, repeat the bleeding procedure again. If the brake pedal still feels spongy after repeating the bleeding procedure, perform the following steps:

a. Inspect the brake system for external leaks.

b. Pressure bleed the hydraulic brake system in order to purge any air that may still be trapped in the system.

22. Turn the ignition key ON, with the engine OFF. Check to see if the brake system warning lamp remains illuminated.

➡**DO NOT allow the vehicle to be driven until it is diagnosed and repaired.**

23. If the brake system warning lamp remains illuminated, repair the problem.

MASTER CYLINDER BENCH BLEEDING

See Figure 2.

1. Refer to Brake Precautions.

2. Secure the mounting flange of the brake master cylinder in a bench vise so that the rear of the primary piston is accessible.

3. Remove the master cylinder reservoir cap and diaphragm.

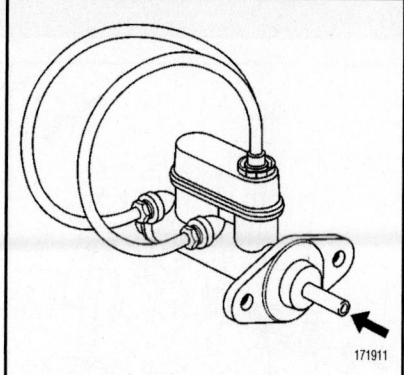

171911

Fig. 2 Secure the mounting flange of the brake master cylinder in a bench vise so that the rear of the primary piston is accessible

4. Install suitable fittings to the master cylinder ports that match the type of flare seat required and also provide for hose attachment.

5. Install transparent hoses to the fittings installed to the master cylinder ports, then route the hoses into the master cylinder reservoir.

6. Fill the master cylinder reservoir to at least the half-way point with brake fluid.

7. Ensure that the ends of the transparent hoses running into the master cylinder reservoir are fully submerged in the brake fluid.

8. Using a smooth, round-ended tool, depress and release the primary piston as far as it will travel, a depth of about 1 in. (25 mm), several times. Observe the flow of fluid coming from the ports. As air is bled from the primary and secondary pistons, the effort required to depress the primary piston will increase and the amount of travel will decrease.

9. Continue to depress and release the primary piston until fluid flows freely from the ports with no evidence of air bubbles.

10. Remove the transparent hoses from the master cylinder reservoir.

11. Install the master cylinder reservoir cap and diaphragm.

12. Remove the fittings with the transparent hoses from the master cylinder ports. Wrap the master cylinder with a clean shop cloth to prevent brake fluid spills.

13. Remove the master cylinder from the vise.

MASTER CYLINDER RESERVOIR FILLING

1. Refer to Brake Precautions.

2. Visually inspect the brake fluid level through the brake master cylinder reservoir.

3. If the brake fluid level is at or below the half-full point during routine fluid checks, inspect the brake system for wear and possible brake fluid leaks.

4. If the brake fluid level is at or below the half-full point during routine fluid checks, and an inspection of the brake system did not reveal wear or brake fluid leaks, the brake fluid may be topped-off up to the maximum-fill level.

5. If brake system service was just completed, the brake fluid may be topped-off up to the maximum-fill level.

6. If the brake fluid level is above the half-full point, adding brake fluid is not recommended under normal conditions.

7. If brake fluid is to be added to the master cylinder reservoir, clean the outside of the reservoir on and around the reservoir cap prior to removing the cap and diaphragm. Use only GM-approved brake fluid from a clean, sealed brake fluid container.

✳✳ WARNING

Dust and dirt accumulating on brake parts during normal use may contain asbestos fibers from production or aftermarket brake linings. Breathing excessive concentrations of asbestos fibers can cause serious bodily harm. Exercise care when servicing brake parts. Do not sand or grind brake lining unless equipment used is designed to contain the dust residue. Do not clean brake parts with compressed air or by dry brushing. Cleaning should be done by dampening the brake components with a fine mist of water, then wiping the brake components clean with a dampened cloth. Dispose of cloth and all residue containing asbestos fibers in an impermeable container with the appropriate label. Follow practices prescribed by the Occupational Safety and Health Administration (OSHA) and the Environmental Protection Agency (EPA) for the handling, processing, and disposing of dust or debris that may contain asbestos fibers.

BRAKE CALIPER

REMOVAL & INSTALLATION

See Figures 3 and 4.

1. Refer to Brake Precautions.
2. Inspect the fluid level in the brake master cylinder reservoir.
3. If the brake fluid level is midway between the maximum-full point and the minimum allowable level, no brake fluid needs to be removed from the reservoir before proceeding.
4. If the brake fluid level is higher than midway between the maximum-full point and the minimum allowable level, remove brake fluid to the midway point before proceeding.
5. Raise and support the vehicle.
6. Remove the tire and wheel assembly.
7. Install and firmly Hand-tighten 2 wheel nuts to opposite wheel studs in order to retain the rotor to the hub.
8. Install a large C-clamp over the body of the brake caliper with the C-clamp ends against the rear of the caliper body and against the outer brake pad.
9. Tighten the C-clamp until the caliper piston is compressed into the caliper bore enough to allow the caliper to slide past the brake rotor.

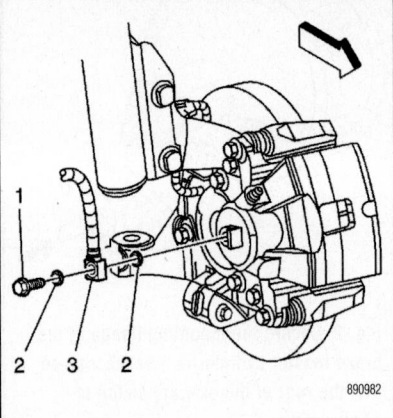

Fig. 3 Brake hose-to-caliper bolt (1), gaskets (2), and (3) hose

10. Remove the C-clamp from the caliper.
11. Remove the brake hose fitting bolt (1).
12. Remove the brake hose fitting gaskets (2) and the brake hose (3) from the brake caliper. Plug the brake hose fitting and the brake caliper inlet port to prevent brake fluid loss and contamination.
13. Discard the brake hose fitting gaskets.
14. Remove the brake caliper guide pin bolts (1).
15. Remove the brake caliper from the caliper bracket.
16. Inspect the brake caliper guide pins for freedom of movement, and inspect the condition of the guide pin boots. Move the guide pins inboard and outboard within the bracket bores, without disengaging the slides from the boots, and observe for the following:

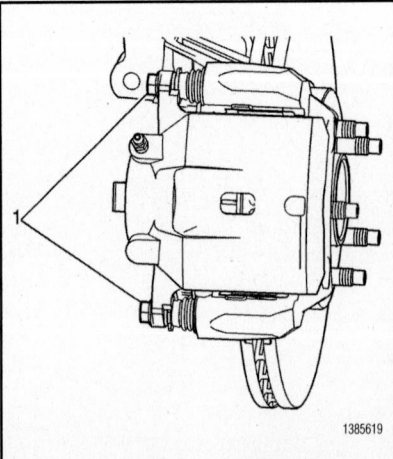

Fig. 4 Brake caliper guide pin bolts (1)

a. Restricted caliper guide pin movement
b. Looseness in the brake caliper mounting bracket
c. Seized or binding caliper guide pins
d. Split or torn boots

17. If any of the conditions listed are found, the brake caliper guide pins and/or boots require replacement.

To install:

18. Install the brake caliper to the brake caliper bracket.
19. Install the brake caliper guide pin bolts and tighten them to 26 ft. lbs. (35 Nm).

➡**Do not reuse the copper brake hose gaskets.**

20. Assemble the brake hose fitting bolt and the brake hose fitting gaskets to the brake hose.
21. Install the brake hose assembly to the brake caliper. Tighten the bolt to 30 ft. lbs. (40 Nm).
22. Bleed the hydraulic brake system.
23. Remove the wheel nuts retaining the brake rotor to the wheel hub.
24. Install the tire and wheel assembly.
25. Lower the vehicle.
26. With the engine OFF, gradually apply the brake pedal to approximately 2/3 of its travel distance.
27. Slowly release the brake pedal.
28. Wait 15 seconds, then repeat steps 9 and 10 until you obtain a firm brake pedal. This will properly seat the brake caliper piston and brake pads.

DISC BRAKE PADS

REMOVAL & INSTALLATION

See Figures 5 and 6.

1. Refer to Brake Precautions.
2. Inspect the fluid level in the master cylinder reservoir:
   • If the brake fluid is midway between the maximum full point and the minimum allowable level, no brake fluid needs to be removed from the reservoir before proceeding.
   • If the brake fluid is higher than midway between the maximum full point and the minimum allowable level, remove brake fluid to the midway point before proceeding.
3. Raise and support the vehicle.
4. Remove the tire and wheel assembly.
5. Install and firmly Hand-tighten 2 wheel nuts to opposite wheel studs in order to retain the rotor to the hub.

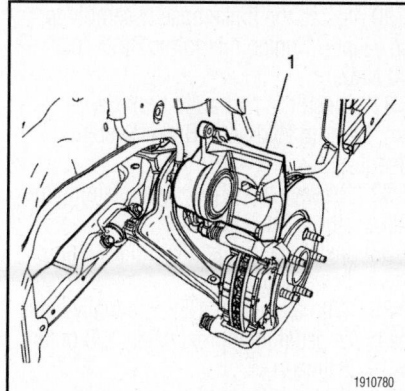

Fig. 5 Pivot the brake caliper (1) upward and support with heavy mechanics wire or equivalent

6. Install a large C-clamp over the body of the brake caliper with the C-clamp ends against the rear of the caliper body and against the outboard brake pad.

7. Tighten the C-clamp evenly until the caliper piston is compressed into the caliper bore.

8. Remove the C-clamp from the brake caliper.

9. Remove the lower brake caliper guide pin bolt.

✷✷ WARNING

Support the brake caliper with heavy mechanic wire, or equivalent, whenever it is separated from its mount and the hydraulic flexible brake hose

is still connected. Failure to support the caliper in this manner will cause the flexible brake hose to bear the weight of the caliper, which may cause damage to the brake hose and in turn may cause a brake fluid leak.

10. Pivot the brake caliper (1) upward and support with heavy mechanics wire or equivalent.

11. Remove the inboard brake pad.

12. Note the location of the brake pad wear sensor.

13. Remove the outboard brake pad.

14. Remove the disc brake pad retainers (1).

15. Inspect the disc brake mounting and hardware.

To install:

16. Apply a very thin coat of high temperature silicone brake lubricant to the brake pad hardware mating surfaces of the caliper bracket.

17. Install the disc brake pad retainers (1).

➡**The wear sensor equipped brake pad must be mounted inboard of the rotor with the leading edge of the sensor facing the brake rotor during forward wheel rotation, or at the top of the pad when installed in vehicle position.**

18. Install the inboard brake pad.

19. Note the location of the brake pad wear sensor.

20. Install the outboard brake pad.

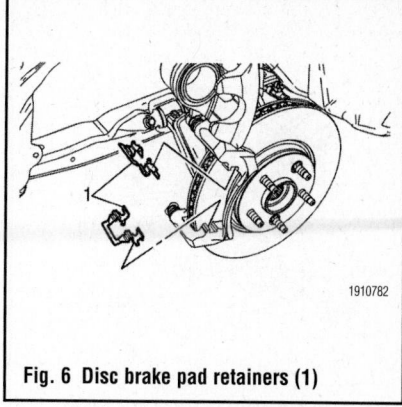

Fig. 6 Disc brake pad retainers (1)

21. Remove the support and pivot the brake caliper to the installed position.

22. Install the lower brake caliper guide pin bolt and tighten it to 26 ft. lbs. (35 Nm).

23. Remove the wheel nuts retaining the brake rotor to the hub.

24. Install the tire and wheel assembly.

25. Lower the vehicle.

26. With the engine OFF, gradually apply the brake pedal approximately 2/3 of its travel distance.

27. Slowly release the brake pedal.

28. Wait 15 seconds then repeat steps 11 and 12 until a firm brake pedal is obtained. This will properly seat the brake caliper pistons and the brake pads.

29. Fill the master cylinder reservoir to the proper level. Refer to Master Cylinder Reservoir Filling.

30. Burnish the brake pads and rotors.

BRAKES

✷✷ WARNING

Dust and dirt accumulating on brake parts during normal use may contain asbestos fibers from production or aftermarket brake linings. Breathing excessive concentrations of asbestos fibers can cause serious bodily harm. Exercise care when servicing brake parts. Do not sand or grind brake lining unless equipment used is designed to contain the dust residue. Do not clean brake parts with compressed air or by dry brushing. Cleaning should be done by dampening the brake components with a fine mist of water, then wiping the brake components clean with a dampened cloth. Dispose of cloth and all residue containing asbestos fibers in an impermeable container with the appropriate label. Follow practices prescribed by

the Occupational Safety and Health Administration (OSHA) and the Environmental Protection Agency (EPA) for the handling, processing, and disposing of dust or debris that may contain asbestos fibers.

BRAKE CALIPER

REMOVAL & INSTALLATION

See Figures 7 and 8.

1. Refer to Brake Precautions.

2. Inspect the fluid level in the brake master cylinder reservoir.

3. If the brake fluid level is midway between the maximum-full point and the minimum allowable level, no brake fluid needs to be removed from the reservoir before proceeding.

4. If the brake fluid level is higher than midway between the maximum-full point

REAR DISC BRAKES

and the minimum allowable level, remove brake fluid to the midway point before proceeding.

a. Inspect the fluid level in the brake master cylinder auxiliary reservoir.

b. If the brake fluid level is midway between the maximum-full point and the minimum allowable level, no brake fluid needs to be removed from the reservoir before proceeding.

c. If the brake fluid level is higher than midway between the maximum-full point and the minimum allowable level, remove brake fluid to the midway point before proceeding.

5. Remove the console rear trim plate.

6. Release the tension from the park brake cables.

7. With the park brake lever in the released position, using ONLY HAND TOOLS, loosen the adjusting nut completely to the end of the front cable threaded rod.

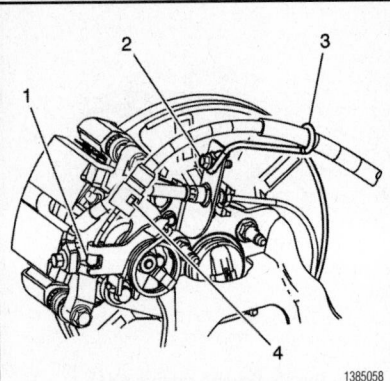

Fig. 7 Park brake cable end (1), brake caliper guide pin bolts (2), and retaining tabs (4)

(Refer to illustration in Parking Brake Adjustment.)

8. Raise and support the vehicle.

9. Remove the tire and wheel assembly.

10. Install and firmly Hand-tighten 2 wheel nuts to opposite wheel studs in order to retain the rotor to the hub.

11. Release the park brake cable end (1) from the lever on the caliper.

12. Release the retaining tabs (4) securing the park brake cable to the bracket on the caliper.

13. Install a large C-clamp over the body of the brake caliper with the C-clamp ends against the rear of the caliper body and against the outer brake pad.

❊❊ WARNING

When using a large C-clamp to compress a caliper piston into a caliper bore of a caliper equipped with an

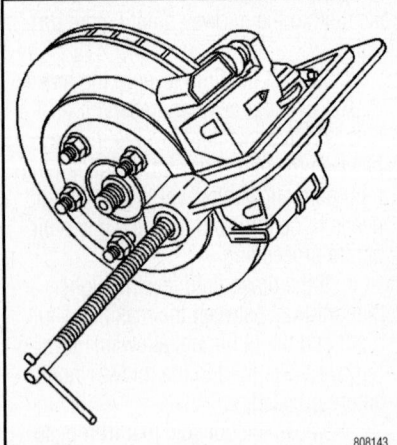

Fig. 8 Install a large C-clamp over the body of the brake caliper with the C-clamp ends against the rear of the caliper body and against the outer brake pad.

integral park brake mechanism, do not exceed more than 0.039 in. (1 mm) of piston travel. Exceeding this amount of piston travel will damage the internal adjusting mechanism and/or the integral park brake mechanism.

14. Tighten the C-clamp just enough to compress the caliper piston 0.039 in. (1 mm) of travel only.

15. Remove the C-clamp from the caliper.

16. Remove the brake hose-to-caliper bolt from the brake caliper.

17. Remove the brake hose from the brake caliper.

18. Remove and discard the 2 brake hose gaskets.

19. Plug the brake hose fitting and the brake caliper inlet port to prevent brake fluid loss and contamination.

20. While using a wrench on the flats of the caliper guide pins, remove the brake caliper guide pin bolts.

21. Remove the brake caliper from the caliper bracket.

22. Inspect the brake caliper guide pins for freedom of movement, and inspect the condition of the guide pin boots. Move the guide pins inboard and outboard within the bracket bores, without disengaging the slides from the boots, and observe for the following conditions:

- Restricted caliper guide pin movement
- Looseness in the brake caliper mounting bracket
- Seized or binding caliper guide pins
- Split or torn boots

23. If any of the conditions listed are found, the brake caliper guide pins and/or boots require replacement.

To install:

24. Install the brake caliper to the caliper bracket.

25. While using a wrench on the flats of the caliper guide pins, install the brake caliper guide pin bolts.

26. Tighten the bolts to 26 ft. lbs. (35 Nm).

27. Press the park brake cable end fitting into the bracket on the caliper to secure the retaining tabs.

28. Secure the park brake cable end to the lever on the caliper.

➡**Do not reuse the copper brake hose gaskets.**

29. Assemble the brake hose fitting bolt and the brake hose fitting gaskets to the brake hose.

30. Install the brake hose assembly to the caliper. Tighten the bolt to 30 ft. lbs. (40 Nm).

31. Bleed the hydraulic brake system. Refer to Hydraulic Brake System Bleeding.

32. Remove the wheel nuts retaining the brake rotor to the wheel hub.

33. Install the tire and wheel assembly.

34. Lower the vehicle.

35. With the engine OFF, gradually apply the brake pedal to approximately 2/3 of its travel distance.

36. Slowly release the brake pedal.

37. Wait 15 seconds, then repeat steps 12 and 13 until you obtain a firm brake pedal. This will properly seat the brake caliper pistons and brake pads.

38. Adjust the park brake cable tension. Refer to Parking Brake Adjustment.

39. Install the console rear trim plate.

DISC BRAKE PADS

REMOVAL & INSTALLATION

See Figures 9 through 11.

1. Refer to Brake Precautions.

2. Inspect the fluid level in the brake master cylinder reservoir.

3. If the brake fluid level is midway between the maximum full point and the minimum allowable level, no brake fluid needs to be removed from the reservoir before proceeding.

4. If the brake fluid level is higher than midway between the maximum full point and the minimum allowable level, remove brake fluid to the midway point before proceeding.

5. Raise and support the vehicle.

6. Remove the tire and wheel assembly.

7. Install and firmly Hand-tighten 2 wheel nuts to opposite wheel studs in order to retain the rotor to the hub.

8. Install a large C-clamp, over the body of the brake caliper with the C-clamp ends against the rear of the caliper body and against the outer brake pad.

❊❊ WARNING

When using a large C-clamp to compress a caliper piston into a caliper bore of a caliper equipped with an integral park brake mechanism, do not exceed more than 0.039 in. (1 mm) of piston travel. Exceeding this amount of piston travel will cause damage to the internal adjusting mechanism and/or the integral park brake mechanism.

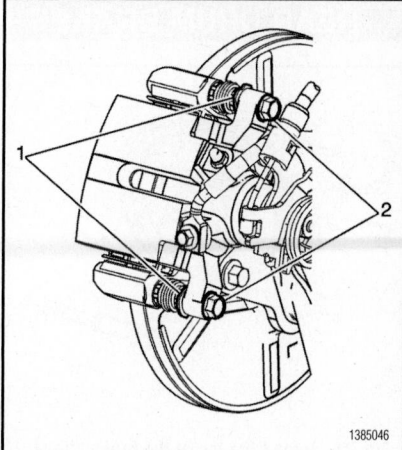

Fig. 9 While using a wrench on the flats of the brake caliper guide pins (1), remove the brake caliper guide pin bolts (2)

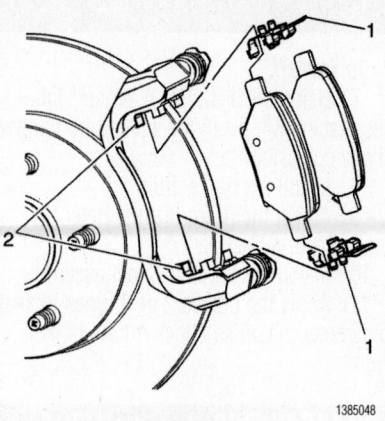

Fig. 10 Remove the brake pad retainers (1) from the caliper bracket and thoroughly clean the brake pad hardware mating surfaces of the caliper bracket (2) of any debris and corrosion

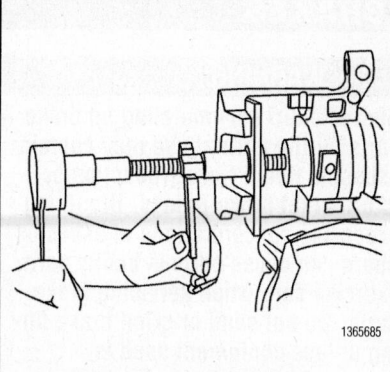

Fig. 11 Using a spanner wrench type caliper piston installer, fully retract the piston into the caliper bore

9. Tighten the C-clamp just enough to compress the caliper piston 0.039 in. (1 mm) of travel only.

10. Remove the C-clamp from the caliper.

11. While using a wrench on the flats of the brake caliper guide pins (1), remove the brake caliper guide pin bolts (2).

✳✳ WARNING

Support the brake caliper with heavy mechanic wire, or equivalent, whenever it is separated from its mount and the hydraulic flexible brake hose is still connected. Failure to support the caliper in this manner will cause the flexible brake hose to bear the weight of the caliper, which may cause damage to the brake hose and in turn may cause a brake fluid leak.

12. Without disconnecting the hydraulic brake flexible hose, remove the caliper from the mounting bracket and secure the caliper with heavy mechanics wire or equivalent.

13. Remove the brake pads from the caliper mounting bracket.

14. Remove the brake pad retainers (1) from the caliper bracket.

15. Thoroughly clean the brake pad

hardware mating surfaces of the caliper bracket (2) of any debris and corrosion.

16. While using a wrench on the flats of the caliper guide pins, remove the brake caliper guide pin bolts.

17. Remove the brake caliper from the caliper bracket.

18. Inspect the brake caliper guide pins for freedom of movement, and inspect the condition of the guide pin boots. Move the guide pins inboard and outboard within the bracket bores, without disengaging the slides from the boots, and observe for the following conditions:

- Restricted caliper guide pin movement
- Looseness in the brake caliper mounting bracket
- Seized or binding caliper guide pins
- Split or torn boots

19. If any of the conditions listed are found, the brake caliper guide pins and/or boots require replacement.

20. Using a spanner wrench type caliper piston installer, fully retract the piston into the caliper bore.

To install:

21. Apply a very thin coating of high temperature silicone brake lubricant to the pad hardware mating surfaces of the caliper bracket only.

22. Install the brake pad retainers to the brake caliper bracket.

➡**The wear sensor equipped disc brake pad must be mounted inboard of the rotor with the leading edge of the sensor facing the brake rotor during forward wheel rotation, or at the bottom of the pad when installed in vehicle position.**

23. Install the brake pads to the caliper bracket.

24. Install the caliper to the caliper mounting bracket.

25. While using a wrench on the flats of the caliper guide pins, install the brake caliper guide pin bolts.

26. Tighten the bolts to 26 ft. lbs. (35 Nm).

27. Remove the wheel nuts retaining the brake rotor to the hub.

28. Install the tire and wheel assembly.

29. Lower the vehicle.

30. With the engine OFF, gradually apply the brake pedal approximately 2/3 of its travel distance.

31. Slowly release the brake pedal.

32. Wait 15 seconds, then repeat steps 10 and 11 until a firm brake pedal is obtained. This will properly seat the brake caliper pistons and brake pads.

33. Fill the master cylinder auxiliary reservoir to the proper level. Refer to Master Cylinder Reservoir Filling.

34. Burnish the pads and rotors.

⚹⚹ WARNING

Dust and dirt accumulating on brake parts during normal use may contain asbestos fibers from production or aftermarket brake linings. Breathing excessive concentrations of asbestos fibers can cause serious bodily harm. Exercise care when servicing brake parts. Do not sand or grind brake lining unless equipment used is designed to contain the dust residue. Do not clean brake parts with compressed air or by dry brushing. Cleaning should be done by dampening the brake components with a fine mist of water, then wiping the brake components clean with a dampened cloth. Dispose of cloth and all residue containing asbestos fibers in an impermeable container with the appropriate label. Follow practices prescribed by the Occupational Safety and Health Administration (OSHA) and the Environmental Protection Agency (EPA) for the handling, processing, and disposing of dust or debris that may contain asbestos fibers.

BRAKE DRUM

REMOVAL & INSTALLATION

See Figure 12.

1. Refer to Brake Precautions.
2. Raise and support the vehicle.
3. Remove the tire and wheel assembly.
4. Remove and discard the brake drum retainers, if equipped.
5. Remove the brake drum (1).
6. If reinstalling the brake drum, use the J-41013 Rotor Resurfacing Kit to clean the wheel hub flange mating surface of the brake drum of any corrosion.

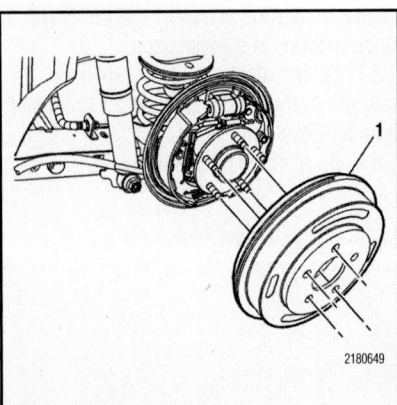

Fig. 12 View of the brake drum (1)

To install:

7. Using the J-42450-A Wheel Hub Resurfacing Kit, clean the wheel hub flange of any corrosion.
8. Install the brake drum.
9. Adjust the drum brakes. Refer to Drum Brake Adjustment.
10. Install the tire and wheel assembly.
11. Apply the brakes 2 or 3 times to seat and center the brake shoes on the brake drum.

BRAKE SHOES

REMOVAL & INSTALLATION

See Figures 13 through 17.

1. Refer to Brake Precautions.
2. Remove the brake drum. Refer to Brake Drum Removal and Installation.
3. Remove the brake adjuster actuator lever spring (1).
4. Remove the brake adjuster actuator lever.

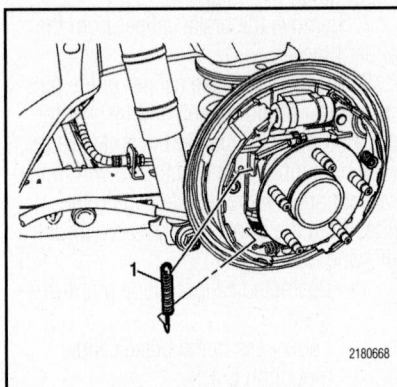

Fig. 13 Remove the brake adjuster actuator lever spring (1)

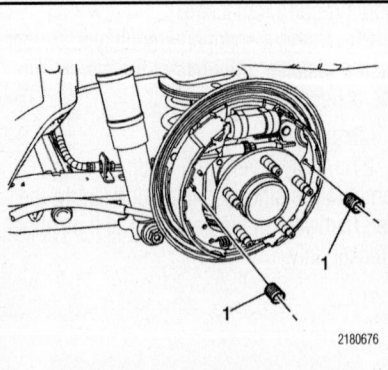

Fig. 14 Remove the brake shoe hold-down spring and cup (1) assemblies by compressing the spring and rotating the assembly ¼ turn

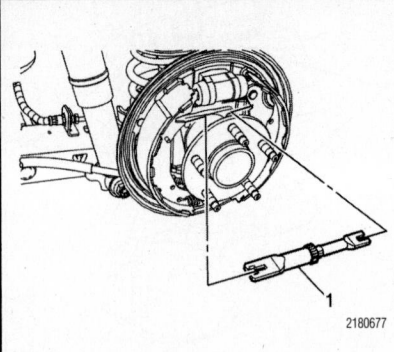

Fig. 15 Spread the top of the brake shoes apart slightly and remove the brake shoe adjuster (1)

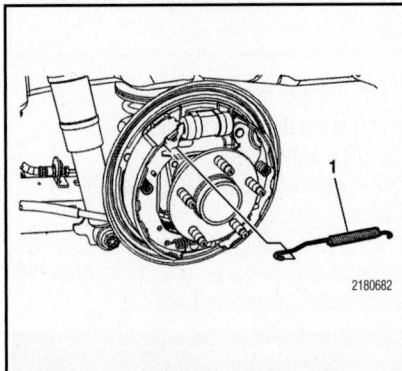

Fig. 16 Remove the upper brake shoe return spring (1)

5. Remove the brake shoe hold-down spring and cup (1) assemblies by compressing the spring and rotating the assembly ¼ turn.
6. Remove the 2 hold-down spring and cup assembly pins.
7. Spread the top of the brake shoes apart slightly and remove the brake shoe adjuster (1).
8. Inspect the drum brake adjusting hardware and replace any components, as necessary.
9. Remove the upper brake shoe return spring (1).
10. Rotate the primary brake shoe toward the wheel hub assembly and release the brake shoe from the lower brake shoe return spring.
11. Remove the lower brake shoe return spring.
12. Inspect the drum brake hardware and replace any components, as necessary.
13. Compress the park brake cable return spring and release the park brake cable fitting (1) from the park brake apply lever and remove the brake shoe (2).

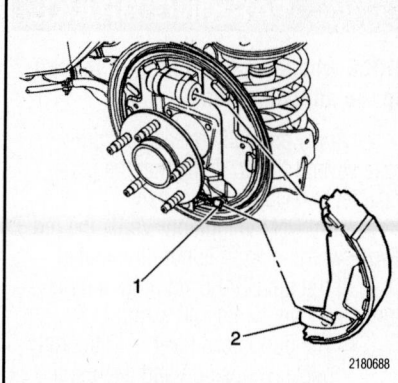

Fig. 17 Compress the park brake cable return spring and release the park brake cable fitting (1) from the park brake apply lever and remove the brake shoe (2)

To install:

14. Clean the drum brake backing plate of any dirt and debris.

15. Apply a light coat of high temperature brake lubricant to the drum brake backing plate brake shoe contact surfaces.

16. Compress the park brake cable return spring and install the park brake cable fitting to the park brake apply lever and position the brake shoe to the drum brake backing plate.

17. Install the lower brake shoe return spring.

18. Position the primary brake shoe to the drum brake backing plate and connect the brake shoe to the lower brake shoe return spring.

19. Install the upper brake shoe return spring.

20. Spread the top of the brake shoes apart slightly and install the brake shoe adjuster.

21. Install the 2 hold-down spring and cup assembly pins.

22. Install the brake shoe hold-down spring and cup assemblies by compressing the spring and rotating the assembly ¼ turn.

23. Install the brake adjuster actuator lever.

24. Install the brake adjuster actuator lever spring.

25. Adjust the drum brakes. Refer to Drum Brake Adjustment.

26. Install the brake drum. Refer to Brake Drum Removal and Installation.

ADJUSTMENT

See Figures 18 and 19.

1. Refer to Brake Precautions.

➡**The park brake cable nut is a nylon lock type. Use ONLY HAND TOOLS when loosening or tightening the adjusting nut.**

2. Remove the console rear trim plate.

3. Ensure that the park brake lever is in the fully released position.

4. With the park brake lever in the released position, loosen the adjusting nut (1) enough to completely relieve tension on the front cable.

5. Raise and support the vehicle.

6. Remove the rear tire and wheel assemblies.

7. Remove the brake drums. Refer to Brake Drum Replacement.

8. Position the J-21177-A Drum to Brake Shoe Clearance Gauge to widest point of the brake drum inside diameter.

9. Firmly Hand-tighten the set screw on the J-21177-A Drum to Brake Shoe Clearance Gauge.

10. Remove the J-21177-A Drum to Brake Shoe Clearance Gauge from the brake drum and position it over the corresponding brake shoe assembly at its widest point.

11. While holding the J-21177-A Drum to Brake Shoe Clearance Gauge in position, insert a 0.015 in. (0.375 mm) feeler gauge between one side of the J-21177-A Drum to Brake Shoe Clearance Gauge, and the corresponding brake shoe lining.

12. Rotate the brake shoe adjuster screw until the brake shoe linings contact the J-21177-A Drum to Brake Shoe Clearance Gauge, and the feeler gauge.

   a. Specification: Brake shoe lining-to-drum clearance: 0.015 in. (0.375 mm).

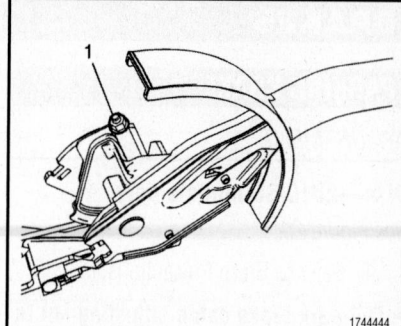

Fig. 18 With the park brake lever in the released position, loosen the adjusting nut (1) enough to completely relieve tension on the front cable

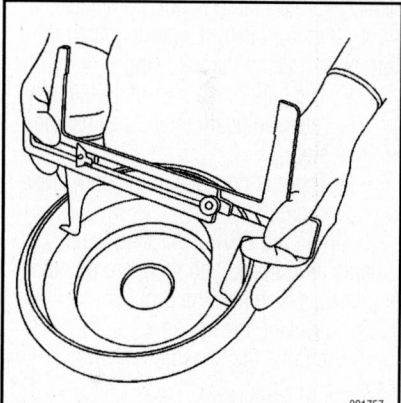

Fig. 19 Position the J-21177-A Drum to Brake Shoe Clearance Gauge to widest point of the brake drum inside diameter

13. Repeat the above steps for the opposite brake drum and brake shoe assembly.

14. Install the brake drums. Refer to Brake Drum Replacement.

15. Adjust the park brake. Refer to Parking Brake Adjustment.

16. Install the rear tire and wheel assemblies.

17. Lower the vehicle.

18. Install the console rear trim plate.

19. Release the park brake lever.

PARKING BRAKE

ADJUSTMENT

Disc—2010 SS models only

See Figure 20.

1. Refer to Brake Precautions.

➡**The park brake cable adjusting nut is a nylon lock type. Use ONLY HAND TOOLS whenever tightening or loosening the adjusting nut.**

2. Apply and fully release the park brake several times. Verify that the park brake lever releases completely.

3. Turn ON the ignition. Verify the red BRAKE warning lamp is not illuminated.

4. If the red BRAKE warning lamp is illuminated, verify the following:
   - The park brake lever is in the fully released position and against the stop.
   - There is no slack in the park brake cables.

5. If the red BRAKE warning lamp remains illuminated and there are no other visible causes, repair the problem.

6. Turn OFF the ignition.

7. Remove the console rear trim plate.

8. With the park brake lever in the released position, loosen the adjusting nut (1) enough to completely relieve tension on the front cable.

9. Raise and support the vehicle. Raise the vehicle just enough to observe the rear calipers and rotate the rear tire and wheel assemblies.

10. With all tension relieved from the park brake cables, rotate the rear tire and wheel assemblies, or the rear brake rotors if the wheels have been removed. Observe the

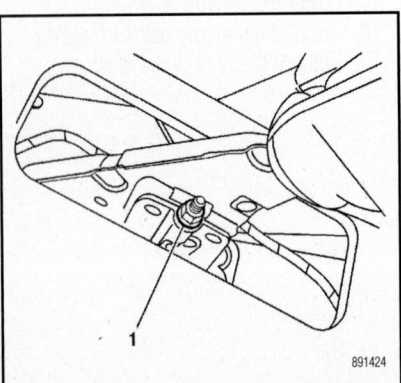

Fig. 20 Park brake cable adjusting nut (1)

891424

amount of effort required for rotation, and the amount of drag if present.

11. Tighten the park brake cable adjusting nut (1) until all slack is taken out of the front cable.

12. Further tighten the adjusting nut (1) until one of the park brake levers on the rear calipers is just lifted off the stop on the caliper housing.

13. Slowly back off the adjusting nut until the park brake lever just rests on the stop.

14. Back off the adjusting nut one full turn.

15. Fully apply and release the park brake lever 3 to 5 times.

16. Raise the park brake lever 3 detent positions and attempt to rotate the rear tire and wheel assemblies, or the rear brake rotors:
   - If rotating the tire and wheel assemblies, they should be difficult to rotate, but should not be locked.
   - If rotating the brake rotors, they should be locked.

17. Raise the park brake lever one additional detent position and attempt to rotate the rear tire and wheel assemblies, or the rear brake rotors. The tire and wheel assemblies, or the rear brake rotors should be locked.

18. Fully release the park brake lever.

19. Verify the park brake is released by rotating the rear tire and wheel assemblies, or the rear brake rotors. The rotors should rotate freely and exhibit no brake shoe drag from the park brake system.

20. With the lever released, if the rotors required more effort to rotate, or exhibited more drag than noted previously when all cable tension was relieved, check the park brake levers on the rear calipers. The levers should be on the stops.

21. If the levers are not against the stops, loosen the adjusting nut just until the levers rest against the stops, then repeat steps 14–18.

22. If the rotors still do not rotate freely, with the park lever fully released, park brake adjustment is not the cause of any drag in the brake system.

23. Lower the vehicle.

24. Install the console rear trim plate.

25. Release the park brake lever.

Drum

1. Refer to Brake Precautions.

➡**The park brake cable adjusting nut is a nylon lock type. Use ONLY HAND**

TOOLS whenever tightening or loosening the adjusting nut.

2. Apply and fully release the park brake several times. Verify that the park brake lever releases completely.

3. Turn ON the ignition. Verify the red BRAKE warning lamp is not illuminated.

4. If the red BRAKE warning lamp is illuminated, verify the following:
   - The park brake lever is in the fully released position and against the stop.
   - There is no slack in the park brake cables.

5. If the red BRAKE warning lamp remains illuminated and there are no other visible causes, repair the problem.

6. Turn OFF the ignition.

7. Remove the console rear trim plate.

8. With the park brake lever in the released position, loosen the adjusting nut enough to completely relieve tension on the front cable. Refer to illustration in Drum Brake Adjustment.

9. Raise and support the vehicle. Raise the vehicle just enough to allow rear tire and wheel assembly removal and rear drum adjustment.

10. Remove the rear tire and wheel assemblies.

11. Adjust the rear drum brakes. Refer to Drum Brake Adjustment.

12. Ensure there is no brake shoe drag after adjustment by rotating the brake drums. If drag exists, re-center the brake shoes and perform the brake shoe adjustment again.

13. Install 2 wheel nuts to the wheel studs and firmly Hand-tighten in order to retain the brake drums.

14. Raise the park brake lever 6 detent positions.

15. Tighten the park brake cable adjusting nut.

16. Tighten the nut to 35 inch lbs. (3.9 Nm).

17. Attempt to rotate the rear brake drums. There should be no rotation forward or rearward.

18. Fully release the park brake lever.

19. Verify the park brake is released by rotating the rear brake drums. The drums should rotate freely and exhibit no brake shoe drag.

20. If the drums do not rotate freely, repeat the park brake cable adjustment procedure.

21. Raise the park brake lever 3 detent positions and attempt to rotate the rear brake drums:

- One of the brake drums should not rotate forward or rearward.
- The other brake drum should not rotate forward or rearward, or should require substantial effort to rotate.

22. Raise the park brake lever one additional detent position and attempt to rotate the rear brake drums.

23. Verify that the left and right brake drums cannot be rotated.

24. Remove the wheel nuts retaining the brake drums.

25. Install the rear tire and wheel assemblies.

26. Lower the vehicle.

27. Install the console rear trim plate.

28. Release the park brake lever.

CHASSIS ELECTRICAL   AIR BAG (SUPPLEMENTAL INFLATABLE RESTRAINTS)

GENERAL INFORMATION

✳✳ WARNING

The Chevrolet HHR is equipped with an air bag system. You must disarm the system before performing service on, or around, system components, the steering column, instrument panel components, wiring and sensors. Failure to follow the safety precautions and the disarming procedure could result in accidental air bag deployment, possible injury and unnecessary system repairs.

SERVICE PRECAUTIONS

✳✳ CAUTION

When performing service on or near the Supplemental Inflatable Restraint (SIR) components or the SIR wiring, disable the SIR system. Refer to SIR Disabling and Enabling. Failure to observe the correct procedure could cause deployment of the SIR components, personal injury, or unnecessary SIR system repairs.

The inflatable restraint sensing and diagnostic module (SDM) maintains a reserved energy supply. The reserved energy supply provides deployment power for the air bags. Deployment power is available for as much as 1 minute after disconnecting the vehicle power. Disabling the SIR system prevents deployment of the air bags from the reserved energy supply.

The following are general service instructions which must be followed in order to properly repair the vehicle and return it to its original integrity:

- Do not handle the inflatable restraint vehicle rollover sensor when connected to vehicle power.
- Do not expose inflator modules to temperatures above 65°C (150°F).
- Verify the correct replacement part number. Do not substitute a component from a different vehicle.

- Use only original GM replacement parts available from your authorized GM dealer. Do not use salvaged parts for repairs to the SIR system.

Discard any of the following components if it has been dropped from a height of 3 ft. (91 cm) or more:

- Inflatable restraint front end sensor
- Inflatable restraint instrument panel (I/P) module
- Inflatable restraint passenger presence system (PPS)
- Inflatable restraint roof rail module
- Inflatable restraint SDM
- Inflatable restraint side impact sensor (SIS)
- Inflatable restraint steering wheel module
- Inflatable restraint steering wheel module coil
- Inflatable restraint vehicle rollover sensor
- Seat belt pretensioner

Do not place an intact undeployed airbag face down on a solid surface. The airbag will propel into the air if accidentally deployed and may result in personal injury or death.

When carrying or handling an undeployed airbag, the trim side (face) of the airbag should be pointing away from the body to minimize possibility of injury if accidental deployment occurs. Failure to do this may result in personal injury or death.

Wear safety glasses, rubber gloves, and long sleeved clothing when cleaning powder residue from vehicle after an airbag deployment. Powder residue emitted from a deployed airbag can cause skin irritation. Flush the affected area with cool water if irritation is experienced. If you experience nasal or throat irritation, exit the vehicle for fresh air until the irritation ceases. If irritation continues, see a physician.

Do not use a replacement airbag that is not in the original packaging. This may result in improper deployment, personal injury, or death.

The factory installed fasteners, screws and bolts used to fasten airbag components have a special coating and are specifically

designed for the airbag system. Do not use substitute fasteners. Use only original equipment fasteners listed in the parts catalog when fastener replacement is required.

During, and following, any child restraint anchor service, due to impact event or vehicle repair, carefully inspect all mounting hardware, tether straps, and anchors for proper installation, operation, or damage. If a child restraint anchor is found damaged in any way, the anchor must be replaced. Failure to do this may result in personal injury or death.

Deployed and non-deployed airbags may or may not have live pyrotechnic material within the airbag inflator.

Do not dispose of driver/passenger/ curtain airbags or seat belt tensioners unless you are sure of complete deployment. Refer to the Hazardous Substance Control System for proper disposal.

Dispose of deployed airbags and tensioners consistent with state, provincial, local, and federal regulations.

After any airbag component testing or service, do not connect the battery negative cable. Personal injury or death may result if the system test is not performed first.

If the vehicle is equipped with the Occupant Classification System (OCS), do not connect the battery negative cable before performing the OCS Verification Test using the scan tool and the appropriate diagnostic information. Personal injury or death may result if the system test is not performed properly.

Never replace both the Occupant Restraint Controller (ORC) and the Occupant Classification Module (OCM) at the same time. If both require replacement, replace one, then perform the Airbag System test before replacing the other.

Both the ORC and the OCM store Occupant Classification System (OCS) calibration data, which they transfer to one another when one of them is replaced. If both are replaced at the same time, an irreversible fault will be set in both modules and the OCS may malfunction and cause personal injury or death.

If equipped with OCS, the Seat Weight Sensor is a sensitive, calibrated unit and must be handled carefully. Do not drop or handle roughly. If dropped or damaged, replace with another sensor. Failure to do so may result in occupant injury or death.

If equipped with OCS, the front passenger seat must be handled carefully as well. When removing the seat, be careful when setting on floor not to drop. If dropped, the sensor may be inoperative, could result in occupant injury, or possibly death.

If equipped with OCS, when the passenger front seat is on the floor, no one should sit in the front passenger seat. This uneven force may damage the sensing ability of the seat weight sensors. If sat on and damaged, the sensor may be inoperative, could result in occupant injury, or possibly death.

SIR IDENTIFICATION VIEW

See Figure 21.

The SIR Identification View illustrates the approximate location of all SIR components available for the vehicle. This will assist in determining the appropriate SIR Disabling and Enabling for a given service procedure, refer to SIR Disabling and Enabling.

SIR DISABLING AND ENABLING

➡ **Select the method of disabling based on the condition as described in the following.**

Disconnect the negative battery cable* as described under "Disabling Procedure" for these conditions:

• If the vehicle was involved in an accident with an air bag deployment.

• When moving, removing or replacing an SIR component or a component attached to an SIR component. (Anytime you remove fasteners.)

• If the vehicle is suspected of having shorted electrical wires.

When performing electrical diagnosis on components other than the SIR system, remove the SIR/Airbag fuse(s) when indicated by the diagnostic procedure to disable the SIR system.

When performing SIR diagnostics, follow the appropriate SIR service manual diagnostic procedure(s).

Disabling Procedure—Airbag Fuse

1. Turn the steering wheel so that the vehicle's wheels are pointing straight ahead.

2. Place the ignition in the OFF position.

❋❋ CAUTION

The SDM may have more than one fused power input. To ensure there is no unwanted SIR deployment, per-

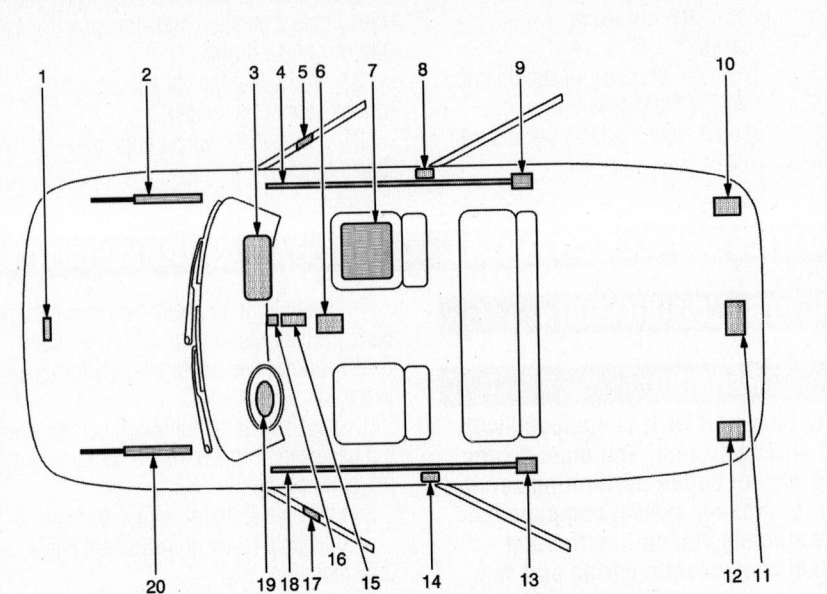

1. Center Front Impact Sensor--Located under the hood at the front of the vehicle
2. Front Hood Assist Rod--A gas shock located under the front hood on the passenger side
3. Passenger Instrument Panel Air Bag--Located at the top right under the instrument panel
4. Right Roof Rail Air Bag--Located under the headliner, extending from the passenger front windshield pillar to the passenger rear windshield pillar
5. Right Front Side Impact Sensor--Located behind door panel on the passenger front door
6. Inflatable Restraint Sensing and Diagnostic Module (SDM)--Located underneath the vehicle carpet under the center console
7. Passenger Presence System--Located on the front passenger seat under the seat bottom trim
8. Passenger Seat Belt Retractor Pretensioner--Located under the trim near the bottom of the center pillar on the passenger side of vehicle
9. Inflator Module for Right Roof Rail Air Bag--Located behind the garnish molding on the upper rear pillar
10. Rear Hood Assist Rod--A gas shock located under the rear truck lid on the passenger side
11. Vehicle Battery--Located in the trunk under the carpet
12. Rear Hood Assist Rod--A gas shock located under the rear truck lid on the driver side
13. Inflator Module for Left Roof Rail Air Bag--Located behind garnish molding on the upper rear pillar
14. Driver Seat Belt Retractor Pretensioner--Located under the trim near the bottom of the center pillar on the driver side of vehicle
15. Body Control Module/Fuse Block-Air Bag and SDM Fuse--Located on RH side of the center console
16. Vehicle Rollover Sensor--Located under the center console
17. Left Front Side Impact Sensor--Located behind door panel on the driver front door
18. Left Roof Rail Air Bag--Located under the headliner, extending from the driver front windshield pillar to the driver rear windshield pillar
19. Driver Steering Wheel Air Bag--Located on the steering wheel
20. Front Hood Assist Rod--A gas shock located under the front hood on the driver side

1615042

Fig. 21 SIR Identification View

sonal injury, or unnecessary SIR system repairs, remove all fuses supplying power to the SDM. With all SDM fuses removed and the ignition switch in the ON position, the AIR BAG warning indicator illuminates. This is normal operation, and does not indicate a SIR system malfunction.

3. Locate and remove the fuse(s) supplying power to the SDM.

4. Wait 1 minute before working on the system.

* DTCs will be lost when the negative battery cable is disconnected.

Disabling Procedure—Negative Battery Cable

5. Turn the steering wheel so that the vehicles wheels are pointing straight ahead.

6. Place the ignition in the OFF position.

7. Disconnect the negative battery cable from the battery. Refer to Battery Negative Cable Disconnection and Connection.

8. Wait 1 minute before working on system.

Enabling Procedure—Airbag Fuse

9. Place the ignition in the OFF position.

10. Install the fuse(s) supplying power to the SDM.

11. Turn the ignition switch to the ON position. The AIR BAG indicator will flash then turn OFF.

12. Check the vehicle's diagnostic systems if the AIR BAG warning indicator does not operate as described.

Enabling Procedure—Negative Battery

13. Place the ignition in the OFF position.

14. Connect the negative battery cable to the battery. Refer to Battery Negative Cable Disconnection and Connection.

15. Turn the ignition switch to the ON position. The AIR BAG indicator will flash then turn OFF.

16. Check the vehicle's diagnostic systems if the AIR BAG warning indicator does not operate as described.

STEERING WHEEL MODULE COIL CENTERING

See Figures 22 and 23.

❄❄ WARNING

The new SIR coil assembly will be centered. Improper alignment of the SIR coil assembly may damage the unit, causing an inflatable restraint malfunction.

1. Verify the following conditions before centering the supplemental inflatable restraint (SIR) steering wheel module coil:
   • The wheels on the vehicle are straight ahead.

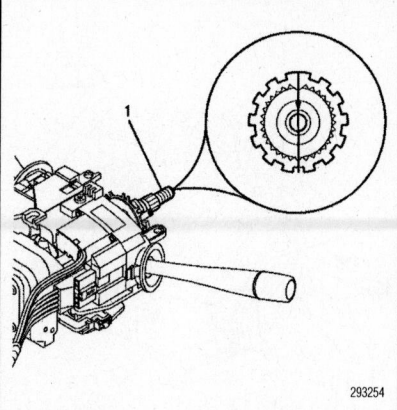

Fig. 22 Verify that the block tooth and the centering mark (1) of the steering shaft is in the 12 o'clock position

   • The block tooth and the centering mark (1) of the steering shaft is in the 12 o'clock position.

2. If available, remove the yellow retaining tab (1) from the SIR steering wheel module coil and save the tab for reassembly.

3. Hold the SIR steering wheel module coil face up by the casing (2).

   a. Slowly turn the SIR steering wheel module coil hub (3) clockwise until the coil ribbon stops.

   b. Slowly rotate the SIR steering

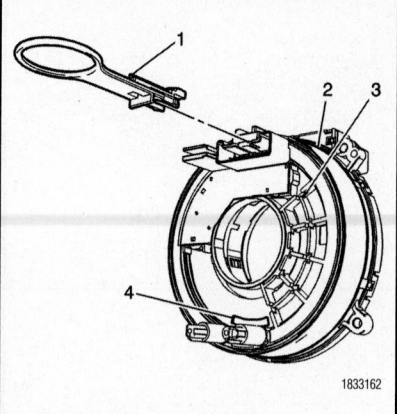

Fig. 23 Yellow retaining tab (1), casing (2), and steering wheel module coil hub (3), and centering window (4)

wheel module coil hub (3) counterclockwise 2.5 revolutions until the centering window (4) turns yellow. This indicates the CENTER position.

➡If the retaining tab is not available, the use of tape to secure the SIR steering wheel module coil is recommended for installation to the steering column.

4. Install the yellow retaining tab (1) to the SIR steering wheel module coil.

5. Slide the centered SIR steering wheel module coil onto the steering shaft.

DRIVE TRAIN

AUTOMATIC TRANSAXLE FLUID

FLUID FILTER AND SEAL

See Figures 24 through 26.

❄❄ CAUTION

To avoid any vehicle damage, serious personal injury, or death when major components are removed from the vehicle and the vehicle is supported by a hoist, support the vehicle with jack stands at the opposite end from which the components are being removed and strap the vehicle to the hoist.

1. Raise and support the vehicle.

2. Place the drain pan under the transaxle oil pan.

❄❄ WARNING

When removing the oil pan bolts, be careful not to damage the oil pan sealing surfaces. Such damage may result in oil leaks in this area.

3. Remove the oil pan bolts from only the front and the sides.

4. Loosen the rear oil pan bolts about 4 turns.

5. Lightly tap the oil pan with a rubber mallet or pry in order to allow the fluid to drain.

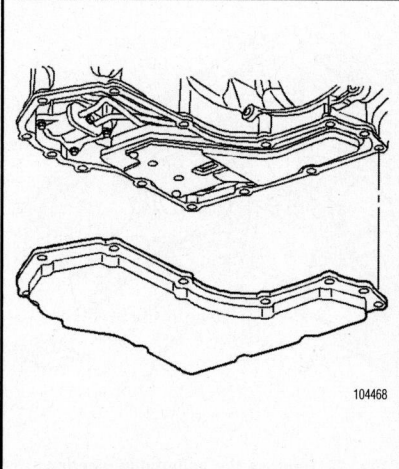

Fig. 24 Oil pan removal

6. Inspect the fluid color.

7. Remove the remaining oil pan bolts.

8. Remove the oil pan.

9. Remove the oil pan gasket.

10. Remove the oil filter. Use a long screwdriver in order to pry the oil filter neck out of the seal.

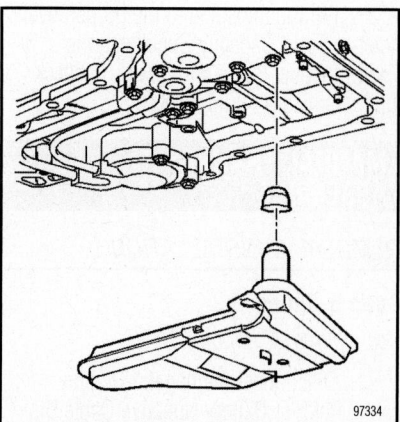

Fig. 25 Remove the oil filter. Use a long screwdriver in order to pry the oil filter neck out of the seal

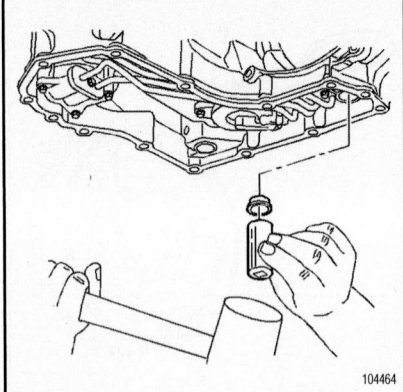

Fig. 26 Install a new seal, as needed. Before installing, coat the new seal with a small amount of J 36850 or petroleum jelly

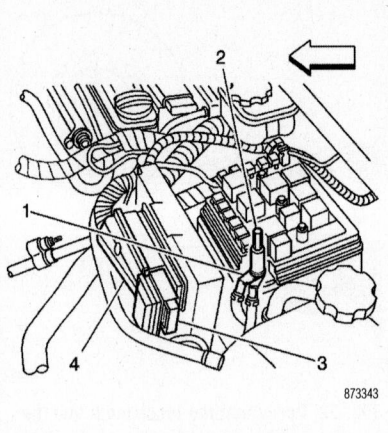

Fig. 27 Remove the positive battery post from the underhood junction block (2)

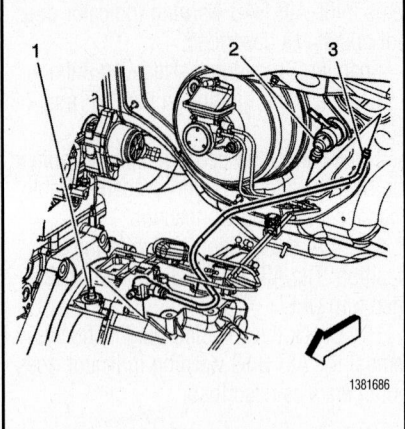

Fig. 29 Disconnect the hydraulic clutch hose (3) from the clutch actuator cylinder (2) and the clutch master cylinder (1)

11. Check the oil filter seal for damage or wear.

12. As needed, remove the seal using the J 6125-1B and the J 23129.

To install:

13. Install a new seal, as needed. Before installing, coat the new seal with a small amount of J 36850 or petroleum jelly.

14. Install a new filter into the case.

15. Install the oil pan gasket. Use a new gasket if the sealing ribs are damaged.

16. Clean and dry the oil pan. Inspect the pan for damage and replace the pan if necessary.

17. Install the oil pan.

18. Clean and dry the oil pan. Inspect the pan for damage and replace the pan if necessary.

19. Install the oil pan.

20. Install the oil pan bolts.

21. Tighten the bolts to 89 inch lbs. (10 Nm).

22. Lower the vehicle.

23. Fill the transaxle to the proper level. Refer to Fluid Capacity Specifications.

24. Inspect the pan for leaks. Recheck the transmission fluid level.

MANUAL TRANSAXLE ASSEMBLY

REMOVAL & INSTALLATION

Saab 5-Speed

See Figures 27 through 31.

1. Disconnect the negative battery cable. Refer to Battery Negative Cable Disconnection and Connection.

2. Remove the positive battery post from the underhood junction block (2).

3. Disconnect the positive cables from the underhood junction block (1).

Remove the underhood junction block bracket nuts (1).

4. Loosen the underhood junction block bracket bolt.

5. Disconnect the front wiring harness from the underhood junction block bracket.

6. Reposition the underhood junction block bracket aside.

7. Disconnect the hydraulic clutch hose (3) from the clutch actuator cylinder (2) and the clutch master cylinder (1).

8. Install the engine support fixture.

9. Secure the cooling module to the upper body structure.

10. Remove the upper transmission to mount bolts.

11. Disconnect the wiring harness retainer from the transmission stud.

12. Remove the upper transmission to engine stud and bolt.

13. Remove the frame.

14. Drain the transaxle. Refer to Transmission Fluid Drain and Fill.

15. Disconnect the drive axle and intermediate shaft from the transmission and secure out of the way.

16. Remove the starter. Refer to Starter Replacement.

17. Disconnect the shift cables (1, 2) from the transmission.

18. Disconnect the backup lamp switch harness connector.

19. Lower the vehicle.

20. Use the engine support fixture rear hook to lower the powertrain enough to allow clearance between the side rail and powertrain.

21. Raise the vehicle.

22. Use a transmission jack to secure the transmission, and remove the transmission to engine bolts.

23. Remove the transmission from the vehicle.

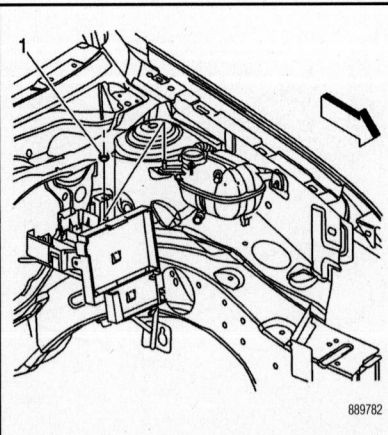

Fig. 28 Remove the underhood junction block bracket nuts (1)

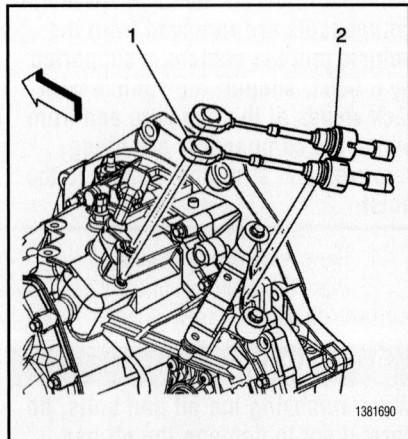

Fig. 30 Disconnect the shift cables (1, 2) from the transmission

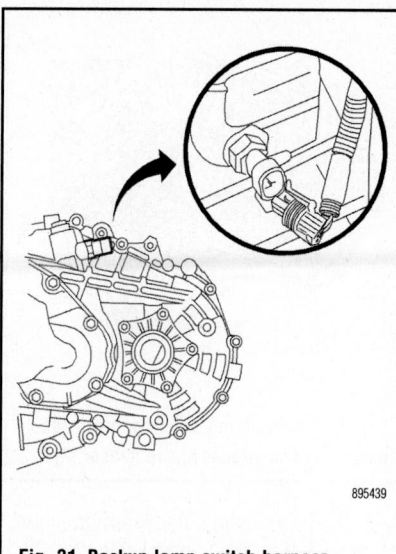

Fig. 31 Backup lamp switch harness connector

24. Remove the front transmission mount from the transmission.

25. Remove the rear transmission mount and bracket from the transmission.

To install:

26. Install the rear transmission mount to the transmission.

27. Install the front transmission mount to the transmission.

28. Use a transmission jack to position the transmission to the vehicle.

29. Secure the transmission to the engine and tighten the bolts to 55 ft. lbs. (75 Nm).

30. Connect the backup lamp switch harness connector.

31. Connect the shift cables to the transmission.

32. Install the starter. Refer to Starter Replacement.

33. Connect the drive axle and intermediate shaft to the transmission.

34. Lower the vehicle.

35. Use the engine support fixture in order to raise the powertrain assembly.

36. Install the left transmission mount.

37. Install the frame.

38. Remove the engine support fixture.

39. Release the cooling module from the upper body structure.

40. Install the top engine to transmission bolt and tighten to 55 ft. lbs. (75 Nm).

41. Install the top engine to transmission stud and tighten to 55 ft. lbs. (75 Nm).

42. Connect the wiring harness retainer to the transmission stud.

43. Connect the hydraulic clutch hose (3) to the clutch actuator cylinder.

44. Bleed the clutch hydraulic system.

45. Connect the front wiring harness to the underhood junction block bracket.

46. Install the junction block bracket, bolt and nuts.
  • Tighten the nuts to 89 inch lbs. (10 Nm).
  • Tighten the bolt to 18 ft. lbs. (25 Nm).

47. Install the front wiring harness to the junction block bracket.

48. Connect the positive battery cables to the junction block bracket.

49. Install the positive battery post to the junction block bracket.

50. Connect the negative battery cable. Refer to Battery Negative Cable Disconnection and Connection.

51. Fill the transmission to the proper level. Refer to Transmission Fluid Drain and Fill.

MANUAL TRANSAXLE FLUID

DRAIN AND FILL

Saab 5-Speed

See Figure 32.

➡**Note the following:**

• The manual transaxle is filled with fluid at the manufacturer and requires no routine oil changes. If it is determined that the fluid needs to be changed due to contamination or a similar issue, follow this procedure.

• To ensure that all sediment within the transaxle is suspended in the fluid, the fluid should only be drained after it has reached a normal operating temperature of 190–200 °F (88–93 °C). (Normal operating temperature is reached

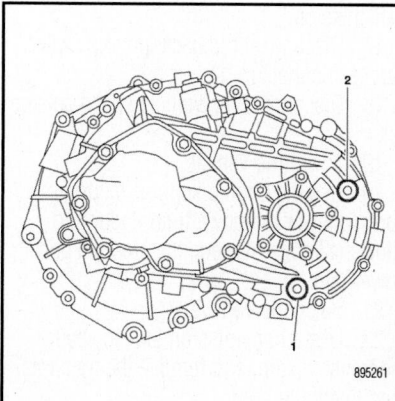

Fig. 32 Transaxle drain plug (1) and level plug (2)

after approximately 15 miles (25 km) of highway driving.)

1. Position the vehicle on a hoist and raise the vehicle.

✳✳ CAUTION

The transmission fluid is hot. Take care to prevent personal injury when the transmission fluid drains from the transmission.

2. Remove the transaxle drain plug (1).

3. Remove the transaxle level plug (2).

4. Clean and apply thread sealant P/N 21485278 to the drain plug (1) and install.

5. Tighten the transaxle drain plug to 37 ft. lbs. (50 Nm).

6. Using a funnel with a flexible spout or a quart bottle hand pump, add manual transaxle lubricant P/N 88862472, (Canadian P/N 88862473) through the level plug (2) opening until fluid flows out. The drain and fill capacity is 1.6 qts. (1.5 L).

7. Clean and apply thread sealant P/N 21485278 to the level plug and install.

8. Tighten the transaxle level plug to 37 ft. lbs. (50 Nm).

MANUAL TRANSMISSION ASSEMBLY

REMOVAL & INSTALLATION

Getrag 5-Speed

See Figures 33 through 39.

1. Disconnect the negative battery cable. Refer to Battery Negative Cable Disconnection and Connection.

2. Remove the positive battery post from the underhood junction block (2).

3. Disconnect the positive cables from the underhood junction block (1).
  Remove the underhood junction block bracket nuts (1).

4. Loosen the underhood junction block bracket bolt.

5. Disconnect the front wiring harness from the underhood junction block bracket.

6. Reposition the underhood junction block bracket aside.

7. Disconnect the hydraulic clutch hose from the clutch actuator cylinder.

8. Install the engine support fixture.

9. Secure the cooling module to the upper body structure.

10. Remove the upper transmission to mount bolts.

11. Remove the upper transmission to engine bolt.

12. Remove the frame.

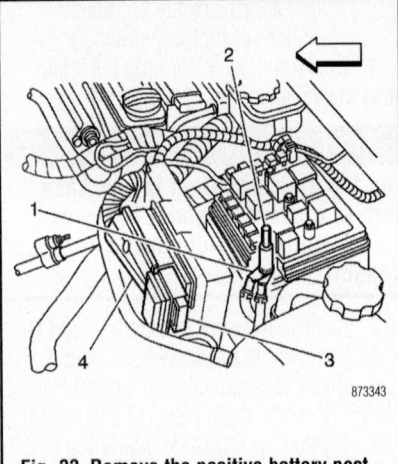

Fig. 33 Remove the positive battery post from the underhood junction block (2)

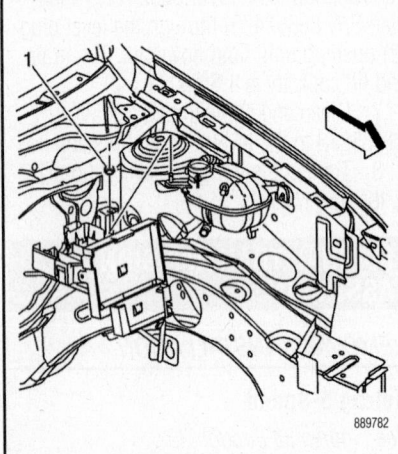

Fig. 34 Remove the underhood junction block bracket nuts (1)

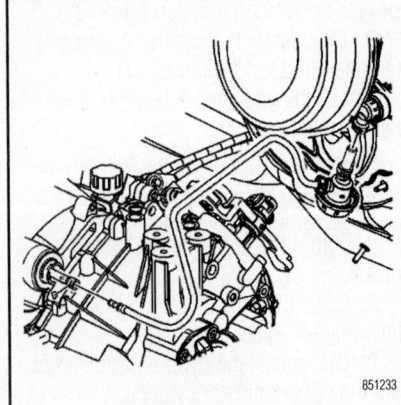

Fig. 35 Disconnect the hydraulic clutch hose from the clutch actuator cylinder

13. Drain the transaxle. Refer to Transmission Fluid Replacement.

14. Disconnect the drive axles from the transmission and secure out of the way.

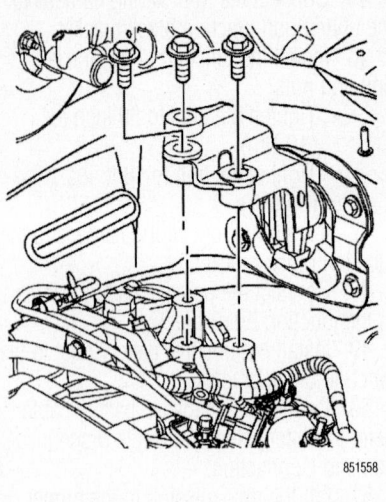

Fig. 36 Remove the upper transmission to mount bolts

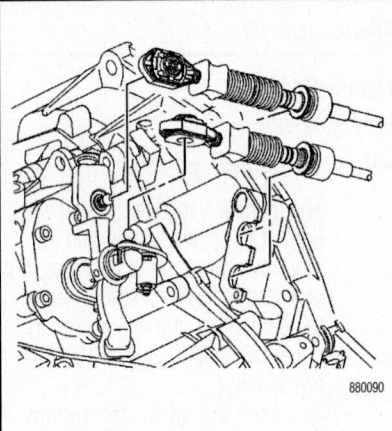

Fig. 37 Disconnect the shift cables from the transmission

15. Remove the starter. Refer to Starter Replacement.

16. Disconnect the shift cables from the transmission.

17. Disconnect the backup lamp switch harness connector (1).

18. Disconnect the vehicle speed sensor (2).

19. Lower the vehicle.

20. Use the engine support fixture rear hook to lower the powertrain enough to allow clearance between the side rail and powertrain.

21. Raise the vehicle.

22. Use a transmission jack to secure the transmission, and remove the transmission to engine bolts.

23. Remove the transmission from the vehicle.

24. Remove the front transmission mount from the transmission.

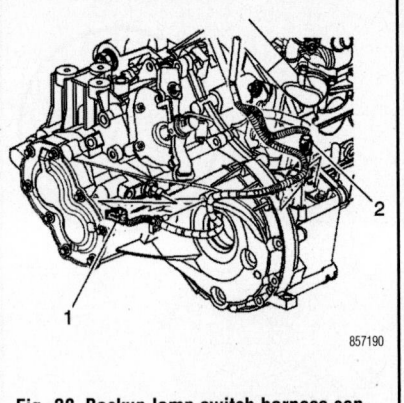

Fig. 38 Backup lamp switch harness connector (1) and vehicle speed sensor (2)

25. Remove the rear transmission mount and bracket from the transmission.

To install:

26. Install the rear transmission mount to the transmission.

27. Install the front transmission mount to the transmission.

28. Use a transmission jack to position the transmission to the vehicle.

➡**The number 3 position does not require a bolt.**

29. Secure the transmission to the engine and tighten the bolts to 55 ft. lbs. (75 Nm).

30. Connect the vehicle speed sensor.

31. Connect the backup lamp switch harness connector.

32. Connect the shift cable to the transmission.

33. Install the starter. Refer to Starter Replacement.

34. Connect the drive axles to the transmission.

35. Lower the vehicle.

36. Use the engine support fixture in order to raise the powertrain assembly.

37. Install the transmission side mount.

38. Position the underhood junction block to the original position.

39. Install the front wiring harness to the junction block bracket.

40. Connect the positive battery cables to the junction block bracket.

41. Install the positive battery post to the junction block bracket.

42. Install the junction block bracket, bolt and nuts.

  a. Tighten the nuts to 89 inch lbs. (10 Nm).

  b. Tighten the bolt to 18 ft. lbs. (25 Nm).

43. Install the frame.

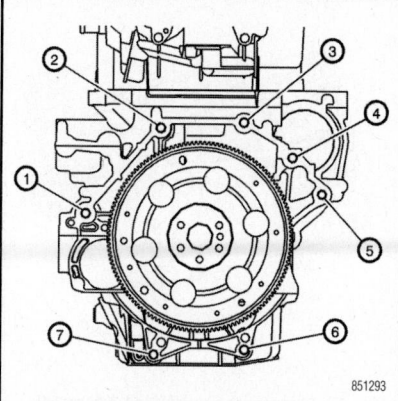

Fig. 39 Secure the transmission to the engine and tighten the bolts to 55 ft. lbs. (75 Nm)

44. Remove the engine support fixture.
45. Install the top engine to transmission bolt and tighten them to 55 ft. lbs. (75 Nm).
46. Connect the hydraulic clutch hose to the clutch actuator cylinder.
47. Bleed the clutch hydraulic system.
48. Release the cooling module from the upper body structure.
49. Connect the negative battery cable. Refer to Battery Negative Cable Disconnection and Connection.
50. Fill the transmission to the proper level.

MANUAL TRANSMISSION FLUID

DRAIN AND FILL

Getrag 5-Speed

See Figure 40.

1. Remove the left front wheel.
2. Raise and suitably support the vehicle.

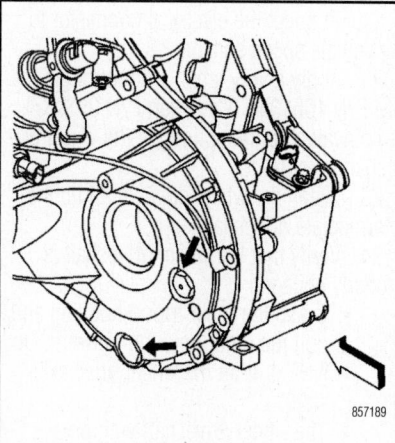

Fig. 40 Transmission fluid drain plug

3. Clean away all dirt and debris from the transmission fluid drain plug area.
4. Remove the drain plug.
5. Allow the system to drain.
6. Install the transmission fluid drain plug, using pipe sealant on the plug threads.
7. Tighten the transmission fluid drain plug to 28 ft. lbs. (38 Nm).
   Filling Procedure
8. Clean away all dirt and debris from the transmission fluid fill plug area.
9. Remove the transmission fluid level check plug.
10. Fill the transmission with the proper fluid until even with the bottom of the fill plug hole.
11. Install the level check plug.
12. Tighten the level check plug to 28 ft. lbs. (38 Nm).
13. Install the left front wheel.

CLUTCH

REMOVAL & INSTALLATION

See Figures 41 and 42.

1. Remove the clutch pedal retainer from the front of the clutch pedal assembly.
2. Pull the clutch pedal upward in order to disengage the clutch master cylinder pushrod from the clutch pedal.
3. Remove the UBEC (Underhood Electrical Center or Junction Block Bracket).

❊❊ WARNING

Avoid spilling brake fluid onto painted surfaces, electrical connections, wiring, or cables. Brake fluid will damage painted surfaces and cause corrosion to electrical components. If any brake fluid comes in contact with painted surfaces,

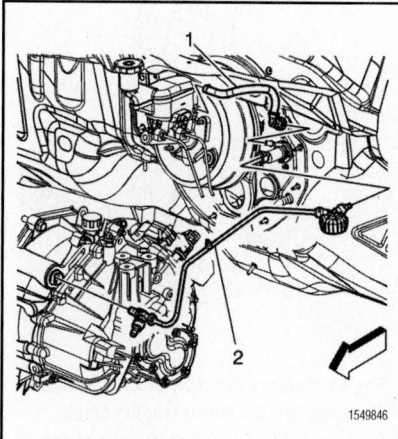

Fig. 41 Clutch hose (1) and line (2)

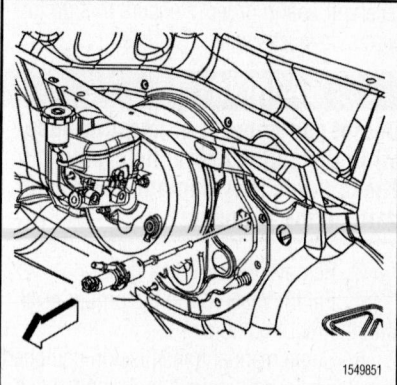

Fig. 42 Rotate the clutch master cylinder one quarter (1/4) turn clockwise and remove the cylinder from the vehicle

immediately flush the area with water. If any brake fluid comes in contact with electrical connections, wiring, or cables, use a clean shop cloth to wipe away the fluid.

4. Place a shop towel under the clutch master cylinder in order to catch any fluid loss.
5. Disconnect the clutch hose (1) from the clutch master cylinder.
6. Disconnect the clutch line (2) from the clutch master cylinder.
7. Cap the reservoir and hydraulic lines in order to prevent fluid loss and contamination.
8. Rotate the clutch master cylinder one quarter (1/4) turn clockwise and remove the cylinder from the vehicle.

To install:

➡**While installing, ensure that the clutch master cylinder pushrod is aligned with the clutch pedal.**

9. Install the clutch master cylinder while rotating one quarter (1/4) turn counterclockwise.
10. Uncap the reservoir and hydraulic lines.
11. Connect the clutch line to the clutch master cylinder.
12. Connect the clutch hose to the clutch master cylinder.
13. Install the UBEC.
14. Connect the clutch master cylinder pushrod to the clutch pedal.
15. Install the clutch pedal retainer.
16. Bleed the clutch hydraulic system. Refer to Hydraulic Clutch Bleeding.

HYDRAULIC CLUTCH BLEEDING

1. Verify that all the lines and fittings are dry and secure.
2. Clean the dirt and grease from the

reservoir cap in order to ensure that no foreign substances enter the system.

❋❋ WARNING

Do not use mineral or paraffin-base oil in the clutch hydraulic system. These fluids may damage the rubber parts in the cylinders.

3. Remove the reservoir cap.

4. Fill the reservoir to the proper level with the required fluid.

5. Some manual transmission equipped vehicles have a combined brake and clutch fluid reservoir.

6. Attach the J 43485 power steering bleeder adapter to the J 35555 metal Mityvac or equivalent tools.

➡**Brake fluid will deteriorate the rubber on the J 43485. Use a clean shop cloth to wipe away the fluid after each use.**

7. Place and hold the adapter on the reservoir filler neck to ensure a tight fit. In some cases, the adapter will fit into the reservoir opening.

8. Apply a vacuum of 51–68 kPa (15–20 hg) and remove the adapter.

9. Refill the reservoir to the proper level.

10. Repeat steps 6 and 7.

11. If needed, refill the reservoir and continue to pull a vacuum until no more bubbles can be seen in the reservoir or until the fluid level no longer drops.

❋❋ CAUTION

The vehicle will move if started in gear before the Actuator Cylinder is refilled and operational. Start the vehicle the first time in neutral to help prevent personal injury from vehicle movement and see if the transmission will shift easily into gear.

12. Pump the clutch pedal until firm (to refill the actuator cylinder).

13. Add additional fluid if needed.

14. Test drive the vehicle to ensure proper operation.

FRONT WHEEL DRIVE INTERMEDIATE SHAFT

REMOVAL & INSTALLATION

2010 Models

See Figures 43 through 45.

1. Raise and support the vehicle.

2. Remove the RH tire and wheel assembly.

3. Disconnect the stabilizer shaft link.

4. Disconnect the outer tie rod assem-

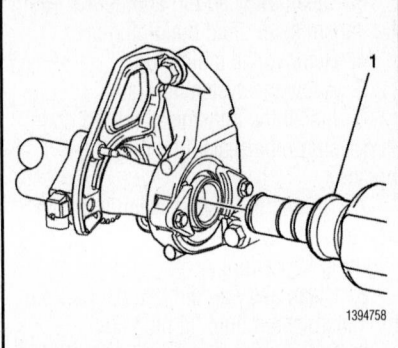

Fig. 43 Inspect the wheel driveshaft-to-intermediate driveshaft seal (1) for excessive wear, damage, and/or contamination

bly from the steering knuckle. Do NOT loosen the tie rod adjustment jamb nut.

5. Rotate the steering knuckle to access the wheel driveshaft inner joint.

6. Assemble the J 45341 and the SA9173G to the wheel driveshaft inner tripod housing assembly.

7. Using the J 45341 and the SA9173G, separate the wheel driveshaft from the intermediate driveshaft.

8. Reposition and support the wheel driveshaft from the intermediate driveshaft.

9. Inspect the wheel driveshaft-to-intermediate driveshaft seal (1) for excessive wear, damage, and/or contamination and replace if necessary.

10. Disconnect the electrical connector from the vehicle speed sensor.

11. Remove the rear, or LH intermediate driveshaft bracket-to-engine block bolts, and remove the vehicle speed sensor with the bracket.

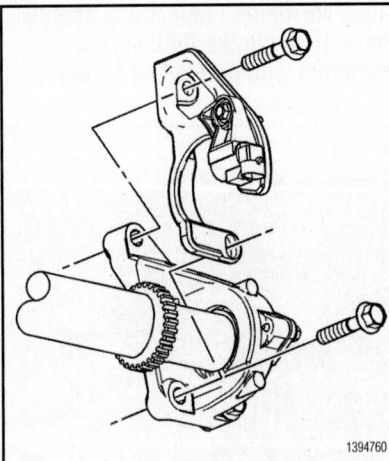

Fig. 44 Remove the rear, or LH intermediate driveshaft bracket-to-engine block bolts, and remove the vehicle speed sensor with the bracket

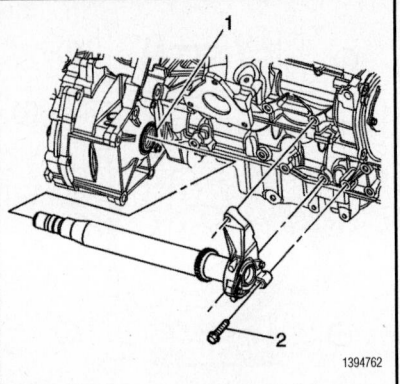

Fig. 45 Remove the remaining intermediate shaft bracket-to-engine block bolt (2)

12. Remove the remaining intermediate shaft bracket-to-engine block bolt (2).

13. Using care to not damage the transaxle output shaft seal (1), remove the intermediate driveshaft assembly.

14. Inspect the transaxle output shaft seal (1) for damage and/or contamination and replace if necessary.

To install:

15. Install the SA91112T into the transaxle output shaft seal.

16. Install the intermediate driveshaft into the transaxle until the driveshaft splines are past the seal, remove the SA91112T, then fully install the driveshaft.

17. Install, but do NOT tighten the intermediate driveshaft bracket-to-engine block forward, or RH bolt.

18. Position the vehicle speed sensor with the bracket to the intermediate driveshaft bracket, and install but do NOT tighten the remaining intermediate driveshaft bracket-to-engine block bolts.

19. Tighten the intermediate driveshaft bracket-to-engine block bolts, beginning with the upper bolt.

20. Tighten the bolts to 37 ft. lbs. (50 Nm).

21. Connect the electrical connector to the vehicle speed sensor.

22. Apply a very small amount of grease, GM P/N 1051344 (Canadian P/N 993037), or equivalent to the splines of the wheel driveshaft inner joint.

23. Install the wheel driveshaft into the intermediate driveshaft.

24. Verify that the wheel driveshaft is properly engaged:

- Grasp the inner tripod housing and pull the inner housing outward. Do NOT pull on the wheel drive axle shaft.

- The wheel driveshaft will remain firmly in place when properly engaged.

25. Connect the outer tie rod assembly to the steering knuckle.

26. Connect the stabilizer shaft link.

27. Install the tire and wheel assembly.

28. Lower the vehicle.

29. Inspect the transaxle fluid level.

2011 Models

1. Raise and support the vehicle.

2. Remove the tire and wheel assembly.

3. Disconnect the stabilizer shaft link.

4. Disconnect the outer tie rod assembly from the steering knuckle. Do NOT loosen the tie rod adjustment jamb nut.

5. Rotate the steering knuckle to access the wheel driveshaft inner joint.

6. Assemble the J 45341 driveshaft removal tool and the SA9173G slide hammer to the wheel driveshaft inner tripod housing assembly.

7. Using the J 45341 and the SA9173G, separate the wheel driveshaft from the intermediate driveshaft.

8. Reposition and support the wheel driveshaft from the intermediate driveshaft.

9. Inspect the wheel driveshaft-to-intermediate driveshaft seal for excessive wear, damage, and/or contamination and replace if necessary. (Refer to image for 2010 models.)

10. Disconnect the electrical connector from the vehicle speed sensor.

11. Remove the intermediate driveshaft bracket-to-engine block bolts, and remove the vehicle speed sensor with the bracket.

12. Remove the remaining intermediate shaft bracket bolt (refer to the image for the 2010 models).

13. Using care to not damage the transaxle output shaft seal, remove the intermediate driveshaft assembly.

14. Inspect the front wheel driveshaft seal for damage and/or contamination and replace if necessary.

To install:

15. Install the SA91112T axle seal protector into the transaxle output shaft seal.

16. Install the intermediate driveshaft into the transaxle until the driveshaft splines are past the seal, remove the SA91112T, and then fully install the driveshaft.

17. Install, but DO NOT tighten the intermediate driveshaft bracket.

18. Position the vehicle speed sensor with the bracket to the intermediate driveshaft bracket, and install but DO NOT tighten the remaining intermediate driveshaft bolts.

➡**Tighten the upper bolt first.**

19. Install the intermediate driveshaft bracket bolts and tighten them to 37 ft. lbs. (50 Nm).

20. Connect the electrical connector to the vehicle speed sensor.

21. Apply a very small amount of grease, GM P/N 1051344 (Canadian P/N 993037), or the equivalent to the splines of the wheel driveshaft inner joint.

22. Install the wheel driveshaft into the intermediate driveshaft.

23. Verify that the wheel driveshaft is properly engaged:

- Grasp the inner tripod housing and pull the inner housing outward. Do NOT pull on the wheel drive axle shaft.
- The wheel driveshaft will remain firmly in place when properly engaged.

24. Connect the outer tie rod assembly to the steering knuckle.

25. Connect the stabilizer shaft link.

26. Install the tire and wheel assembly.

27. Lower the vehicle.

28. Inspect the transaxle fluid level.

STUB SHAFT

REMOVAL

See Figure 46.

➡**Handle the stub shaft carefully. The stub shaft sleeve is reusable if the sleeve is not damaged or removed from the stub shaft. Damage to the stub shaft sleeve will result in a transmission fluid leak.**

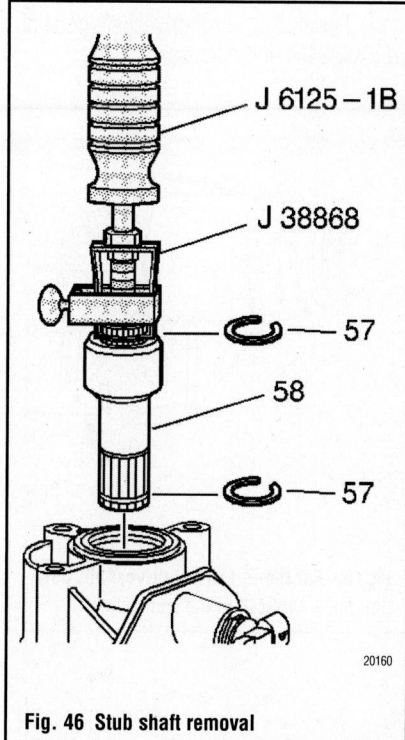

Fig. 46 Stub shaft removal

1. Remove and discard the snapring (57) from the end of the stub shaft (58). The stub shaft snapring is not reusable.

2. Attach the J 6125-1B slide hammer to the J 38868 shaft remover. Install the J 38868 shaft remover into the snapring groove on the stub shaft (58). Tighten the J 38868 shaft remover securely to the stub shaft.

3. Pull lightly on the shaft and rotate it until the stub shaft snapring at the differential seats in the taper on the differential side gear.

✳✳ WARNING

Confirm that the stub shaft snapring (57) is properly seated in the differential side gear. If not, damage may occur to the transmission when you attempt to remove the stub shaft.

4. Pull the stub shaft (58) out with the slide hammer impact.

DRIVESHAFT

REMOVAL & INSTALLATION

2011 Models

See Figures 47 through 50.

1. Raise and support the vehicle.

2. Remove the tire and wheel assembly.

➡**Steps 3, 4 and 5 are for standard disc brakes only. For vehicles equipped with the Brembo brakes, proceed to step 6.**

3. Insert a punch or drift (1) in the cooling fins of the brake rotor (2).

4. Position the punch or drift (1) against the brake caliper mounting bracket (5).

5. Using a breaker bar and the appropriate size socket (4), loosen the wheel driveshaft nut (3).

6. Have an assistant apply the brakes.

7. Remove the wheel driveshaft nut from the wheel driveshaft and discard. DO NOT re-use the wheel driveshaft nut. Use a NEW nut only.

8. Using the J 28733-B (2), separate the wheel driveshaft from the steering knuckle (1).

9. Remove the lower ball joint from the steering knuckle.

➡**The transmission stub staff may be attached to the right wheel driveshaft and be removed at the same time as the wheel driveshaft. Refer to Stub Shaft Removal.**

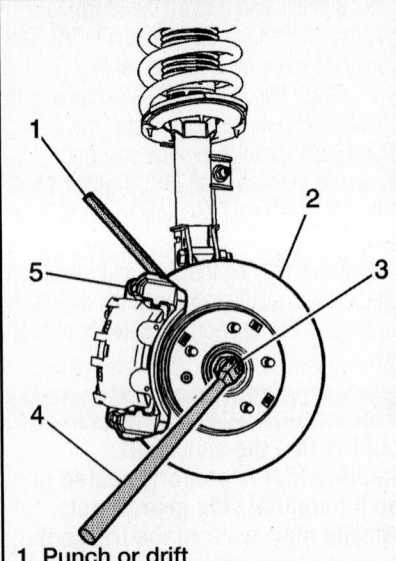

1. Punch or drift
2. Brake rotor
3. Wheel drive shaft nut
4. Socket
5. Brake caliper mounting bracket

2001521

Fig. 47 Insert a punch or drift (1) in the cooling fins of the brake rotor (2)

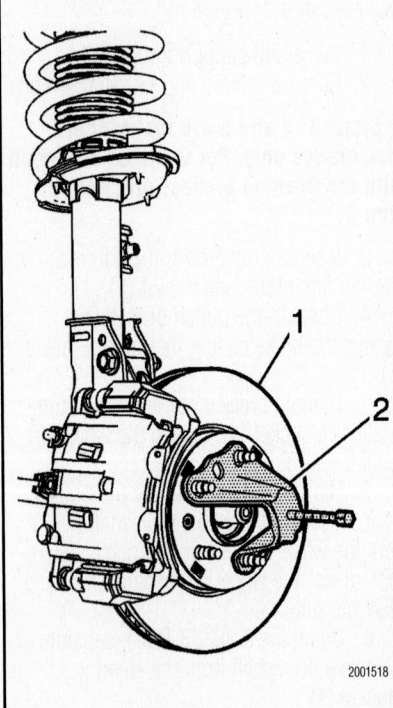

2001518

Fig. 48 Using the J 28733-B (2), separate the wheel driveshaft from the steering knuckle (1)

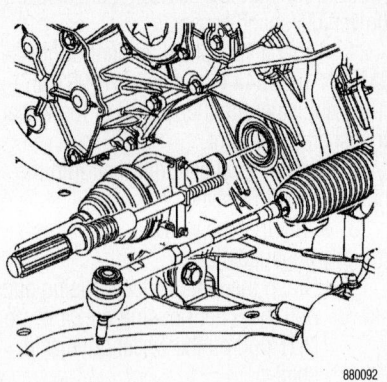

880092

Fig. 49 Using the J-2619-A slide hammer and the J 45341 removal tool, remove the wheel driveshaft

⁜ WARNING

Install a wheel driveshaft seal protector into the differential output shaft seal prior to removing and installing the wheel driveshaft. Failure to install the wheel driveshaft seal protector as indicated may cause the splines of the wheel driveshaft to cut the differential output seal.

10. Using the J-2619-A slide hammer and the J 45341 removal tool, remove the wheel driveshaft.

11. If the wheel driveshaft seal is defective, replace the seal.

To install:

12. For the left wheel driveshaft, position the J 44394-A in the transaxle.

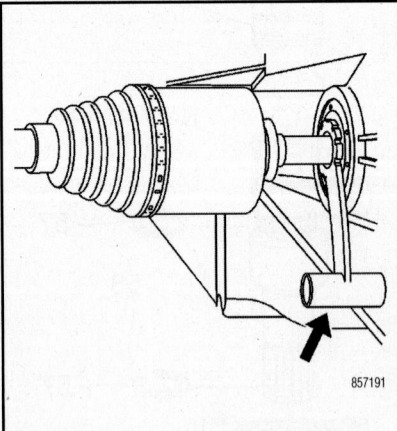

857191

Fig. 50 For the left wheel driveshaft, position the J 44394-A in the transaxle

13. Install the wheel driveshaft until the wheel driveshaft splines are past the axle seal.

14. Remove the J 44394-A from the wheel driveshaft.

➡**The following service procedure is for vehicles equipped with an intermediate shaft.**

15. For the right wheel driveshaft, apply a very small amount of grease to the splines of the wheel driveshaft inner joint. (Wheel driveshaft grease: GM P/N 1051344, Canadian P/N 993037).

16. Install the wheel driveshaft into the intermediate driveshaft.

17. Install the wheel driveshaft until it is fully seated in the transaxle.

18. In the following step, DO NOT pull on the wheel driveshaft. Pull only on the tripod.

19. With the wheel driveshaft installed, grasp the inner tripod housing and pull the tripod outward to ensure that the wheel driveshaft is properly engaged. The wheel driveshaft will remain in place if properly installed.

20. Install the lower ball joint in the steering knuckle.

21. Hand-tighten the NEW wheel driveshaft nut on the wheel driveshaft.

➡**Step 10 is for standard disc brakes only, proceed to step 16 if the vehicle has Brembo brakes.**

Insert a drift or punch in the brake rotor cooling fins and against the brake caliper mounting bracket.

22. Have an assistant apply the brakes.

➡**DO NOT use air tools to tighten the wheel driveshaft nut. Use a torque wrench only.**

23. Using a torque wrench and the appropriate size socket, tighten the wheel driveshaft nut.

24. Tighten the wheel drive nut.

25. Tighten the wheel driveshaft nut to 155 ft. lbs. (210 Nm).

26. Install the tire and wheel assembly.

27. Remove the support and lower the vehicle.

28. Inspect the fluid level of the transaxle.

ENGINE COOLING

ENGINE COOLANT

BEST PRACTICES

A small amount of antifreeze can kill human beings, pets and wildlife.

- Do not pour used coolant down a drain. Ethylene glycol antifreeze is a very toxic chemical.
- Store used antifreeze in compatible containers that are in good condition and labeled "Used Antifreeze Only" until you recycle it.
- Do not mix used antifreeze with any waste or other material such as solvents, cooling system flushes, used oil, or motor fuels.
- Use antifreeze collection, storage, and transport containers solely for the transfer and storage of antifreeze, to minimize the risk of cross-contamination.
- Keep used antifreeze containers securely closed, except when emptying or filling, to minimize the potential for spillage.
- Keep used antifreeze containers in a secure area. Proper maintenance will ensure they do not leak, rupture, or tip over.
- Clean up spills of used antifreeze immediately. Clean up the area well afterward and do not throw the rags in the trash. Dogs and cats love to dig through the garbage and can become exposed through contact with rags. Also radiators flushed outside put wildlife and roaming pets at risk.
- Do not dispose of coolant into the sewer system or ground water. This is illegal and ecologically unsound.

DRAINING & FILLING PROCEDURE

2.0L Engine

See Figures 51 and 52.

Draining Procedure

✳✳ CAUTION

To avoid being burned, do not remove the radiator cap or surge tank cap while the engine is hot. The cooling system will release scalding fluid and steam under pressure if radiator cap or surge tank cap is removed while the engine and radiator are still hot.

➡**Draining the cooling system with the pressure cap installed will siphon the coolant from the overflow tank.**

1. Remove the pressure cap from the radiator fill tube.

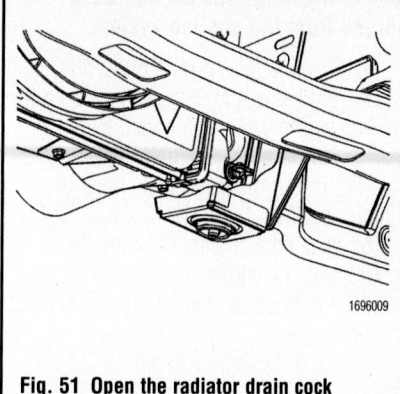

Fig. 51 Open the radiator drain cock

2. Raise and support the vehicle.
3. Place a drain pan under the right side lower radiator mount.
4. Open the radiator drain cock.
5. Drain the cooling system.
6. If a complete block drain is required, place a pan under the water pump drain.
7. Remove the water pump drain plug (1).
8. Drain the cooling system.
9. Inspect the appearance of the engine coolant for discoloration:

- Discolored—Follow the flush procedure. Refer to Coolant System Flushing.
- Normal in appearance—Follow the filling procedure.

Filling Procedure

✳✳ WARNING

Follow the procedure below. Improper coolant level could result in a low or high coolant level condition, causing engine damage.

10. Close the radiator drain cock by hand.
11. Install the water pump drain plug if you removed it during the draining process.

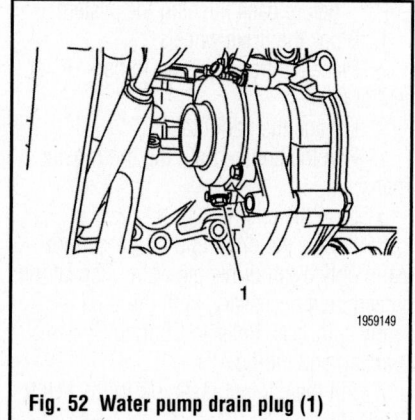

Fig. 52 Water pump drain plug (1)

12. Tighten the drain plug to 16 ft. lbs. (22 Nm).
13. Lower the vehicle.

➡**Use a 50/50 mixture of DEX-COOL® antifreeze and clean, drinkable water.**

14. Slowly add a mixture of 50/50 DEX-COOL® antifreeze and clean, drinkable water to the cooling system until the coolant level reaches the top of the radiator fill tube and stabilizes.
15. Slowly add a mixture of 50/50 DEX-COOL® antifreeze and clean, drinkable water to the overflow bottle until the level reaches the specified mark.
16. Start the engine.
17. Install the pressure cap.
18. Run the engine at idle for 5 minutes in PARK (P) (Automatic) or NEUTRAL (N) (Manual) with the parking brake on.
19. Turn off the engine and allow it to cool and the system pressure to decrease.
20. Remove the surge tank cap.
21. Add coolant to the cooling system until the level reaches the top of the radiator fill tube stabilizes.
22. Install the surge tank cap.
23. Run the engine at idle for an additional 5 minutes.
24. Turn off the engine and allow it to cool.
25. Inspect the cooling system for leaks.
26. Rinse away any excess coolant from the engine and the engine compartment.

2.2L & 2.4L Engines

See Figures 53 and 54.

Draining Procedure

✳✳ CAUTION

To avoid being burned, do not remove the radiator cap or surge tank cap while the engine is hot. The cooling system will release scalding fluid and steam under pressure if radiator cap or surge tank cap is removed while the engine and radiator are still hot.

1. Remove the coolant pressure cap.
2. Raise and support the vehicle.
3. Place a drain pan under the right side lower radiator mount.
4. Open the radiator drain cock.
5. Drain the cooling system.
6. If a complete block drain is required, place a drain pan under the water pump drain.

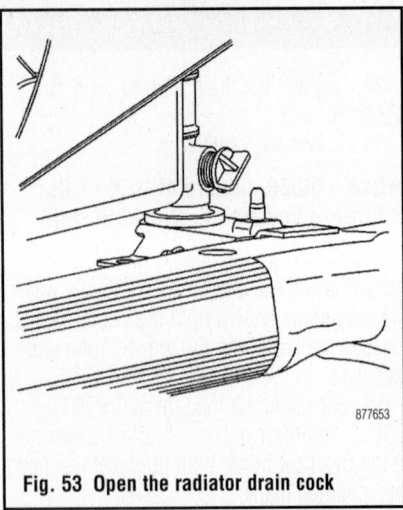

Fig. 53 Open the radiator drain cock

7. Remove the water pump drain plug.

8. Drain the cooling system.

9. Inspect the appearance of the engine coolant for discoloration:

- Discolored—Follow the flush procedure. Refer to Coolant System Flushing.
- Normal in appearance—Follow the filling procedure.

Filling Procedure

✳✳ WARNING

Follow the procedure below. Improper coolant level could result in a low or high coolant level condition, causing engine damage.

10. Close the radiator drain cock by hand.

11. Install the water pump drain plug if you removed it during the draining process.

12. Tighten the plug to 16 inch lbs. (22 Nm).

13. Lower the vehicle.

➡️**Use a 50/50 mixture of DEX-COOL® antifreeze and clean, drinkable water.**

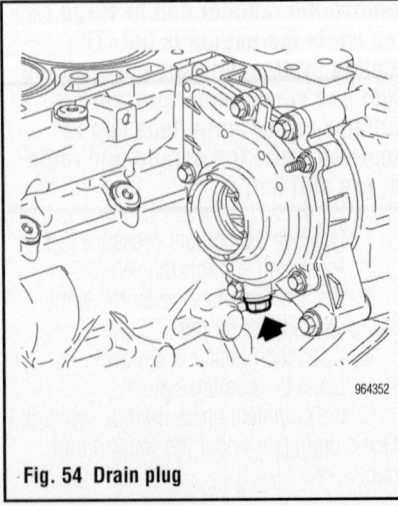

Fig. 54 Drain plug

It is necessary to maintain the coolant level near the cold fill line on the surge tank to insure all the air has been purged from the cooling system.

14. Slowly add a mixture of 50/50 DEX-COOL® antifreeze and deionized water to the cooling system until the coolant level reaches and maintains slightly above the cold fill line on the surge tank. Refer to Fluid Capacities.

15. Install the coolant pressure cap.

16. Start the engine.

17. Run the engine at 2,000–2,500 RPM for 3 minutes.

18. Allow the engine to idle for 30 seconds.

19. Shut the engine off.

20. Top off the coolant as necessary.

21. Fill the coolant reservoir to the cold fill line.

22. Inspect the cooling system for leaks.

23. Inspect the concentration of the coolant mixture using a coolant tester, such as the J 26568.

24. Rinse away any excess coolant from the engine and the engine compartment.

FLUSHING

➡️**Note the following important items:**

- Do not use a chemical flush.
- Store used coolant in the proper manner, such as in a used engine coolant holding tank.
- Do not pour used coolant down a drain.
- Ethylene glycol antifreeze is a very toxic chemical. Do not dispose of coolant into the sewer system or ground water. This is illegal and ecologically unsound.
- Various methods and equipment can be used to flush the cooling system. If special equipment is used, such as a back flusher, follow the manufacturer's instruction. However, always remove the thermostat before back flushing the system.

1. Block the drive wheels.

2. Place the transmission in park (P) or neutral (N).

3. Engage the park brake.

4. Run the engine until the thermostat opens.

5. Stop the engine.

6. Follow the drain and fill procedure using only clean drinkable water. Repeat the procedure if necessary, until the fluid is nearly colorless. Refer to Cooling System Draining and Filling.

7. Fill the coolant reservoir to the FULL COLD mark.

8. Fill the cooling system. Refer to Cooling System Draining and Filling.

ENGINE COOLING FAN & SHROUD

REMOVAL & INSTALLATION

2.0L Engine

See Figure 55.

1. Remove the charge air cooler inlet pipe.

2. Remove the coolant recovery reservoir.

3. Remove the hood latch from the tie bar and set it aside.

4. Remove the radiator inlet hose from the radiator.

5. Remove the upper radiator air baffle.

6. Remove the radiator support brackets.

7. Disconnect the cooling fan motor electrical connector.

8. Remove the transmission line connector from the fan shroud.

9. Lift the radiator out of the support bracket and pull toward the front of the vehicle.

10. Lift up on the fan shroud assembly to release from the radiator.

11. Installation is the reverse of removal.

2.2L & 2.4L Engines

Refer to image of fan and shroud for 2.0L Engine.

1. Remove the air cleaner assembly. Refer to Engine Air Cleaner.

2. Remove the coolant recovery reservoir.

3. Remove the hood latch from the tie bar and set aside.

4. Remove the radiator inlet hose from the radiator.

5. Remove the upper radiator air baffle.

6. Remove the radiator support brackets.

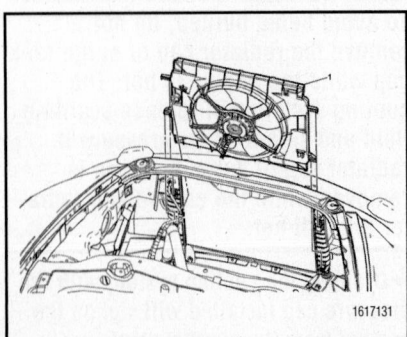

Fig. 55 Engine cooling fan and shroud (1), 2.0L, 2.2L and 2.4L engines

7. Disconnect the cooling fan motor electrical connector.

8. Remove the transmission line connector from the fan shroud.

9. Lift the radiator out of the support bracket and pull toward the front of the vehicle.

10. Lift up on the fan shroud assembly to release from the radiator.

11. Installation is the reverse of removal.

RADIATOR

REMOVAL & INSTALLATION

See Figure 56.

1. Drain the cooling system. Refer to Cooling System Draining and Filling.

2. Remove the air cleaner assembly. Refer to Engine Air Cleaner.

3. Remove the hood latch from the tie bar and set aside.

4. Remove the transmission lines from the radiator.

5. Remove the radiator inlet hose from the radiator.

6. Remove the radiator outlet hose from the radiator.

7. Remove the radiator bracket assembly bolt (1).

8. Remove the radiator bracket assembly.

9. Remove the radiator assembly.

10. Installation is the reverse of removal. Tighten the radiator bracket assembly bolt to 80 inch lbs. (9 Nm).

THERMOSTAT

REMOVAL & INSTALLATION

2.0L Engine

See Figures 57 and 58.

1. Drain the cooling system. Refer to Cooling System Draining and Filling.

2. Reposition the radiator outlet hose clamp at the thermostat housing.

3. Remove the radiator outlet hose from the thermostat housing.

4. Remove the thermostat housing cover bolts and cover.

5. Remove the thermostat.

6. Remove and discard the thermostat housing O-ring seal.

To install:

7. Install a NEW thermostat housing cover O-ring seal.

8. Install the thermostat.

9. Install the thermostat housing cover bolts.

10. Tighten the bolts to 89 inch lbs. (10 Nm).

11. Install the radiator outlet hose to the thermostat housing.

12. Position the radiator outlet hose clamp at the thermostat housing.

13. Fill the cooling system. Refer to Cooling System Draining and Filling.

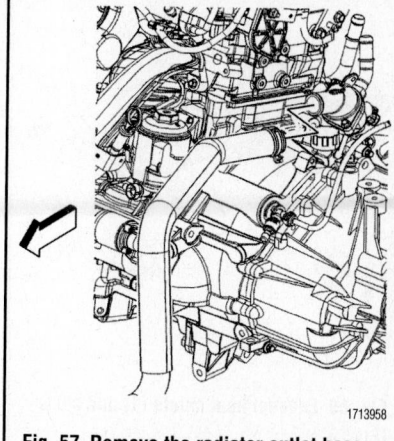

Fig. 57 Remove the radiator outlet hose from the thermostat housing—2.0L, 2.2L & 2.4L engines

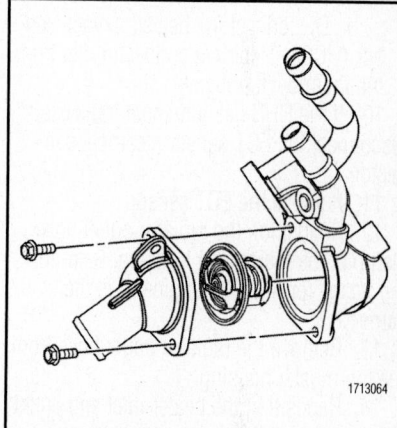

Fig. 58 Thermostat, housing cover bolts, and cover—2.0L, 2.2L & 2.4L engines

2.2L & 2.4L Engines

See Figures 57 through 61.

Engine Coolant Thermostat Housing Replacement

1. Drain the cooling system. Refer to Cooling System Draining and Filling.

2. Remove the air cleaner assembly.

3. Remove the air cleaner bracket nuts.

4. Remove the air cleaner bracket.

5. Remove the exhaust heat shield studs (2).

6. Remove the exhaust heat shield (1).

➡**There is a drain at the bottom of the water pump for engine block coolant drainage.**

7. Drain the coolant from the engine block at the water pump drain. After the coolant has drained, tighten the drain bolt.

8. Lower the vehicle.

9. If the HHR has an automatic transaxle, perform the following steps:

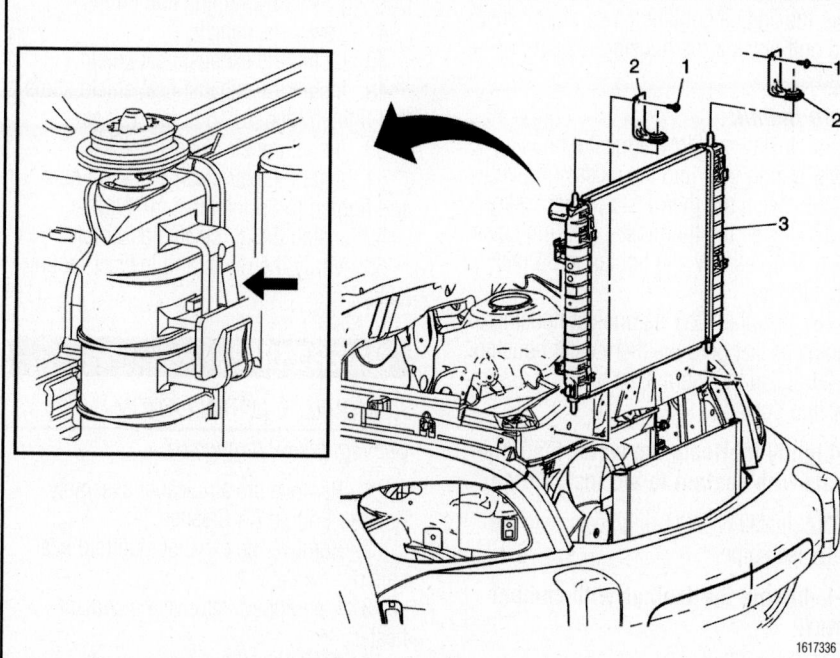

Fig. 56 Radiator bracket assembly bolt (1), bracket assembly (2), and assembly (3)

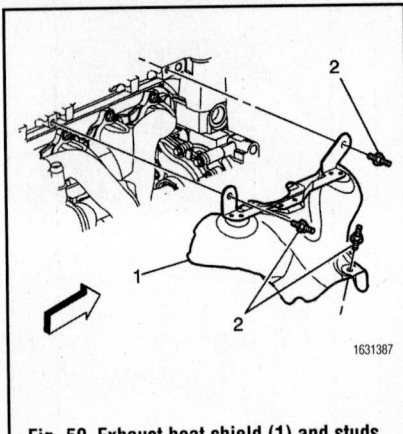

Fig. 59 Exhaust heat shield (1) and studs (2)

a. Disconnect the engine coolant temperature (ECT) sensor electrical connector.

b. Disconnect the heated oxygen sensor (HO2S) electrical connector clip from the thermostat housing.

10. If the HHR has a manual transaxle, disconnect the ECT sensor electrical connector.

11. Remove the ECT sensor.

12. Reposition the radiator outlet hose clamp at the thermostat housing. Refer to the image for the 2.0L engine, it is the same.

13. Remove the radiator outlet hose from the thermostat housing.

14. Reposition the heater inlet and outlet hose clamps at the thermostat housing pipes.

15. Disconnect the heater inlet and outlet hoses from the thermostat housing pipes.

16. Raise and support the vehicle.

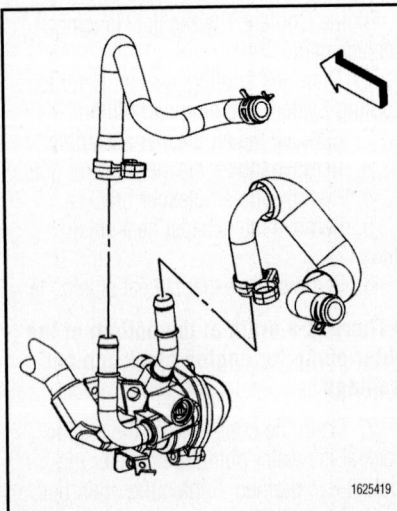

Fig. 60 Heater inlet and outlet hoses and clamps

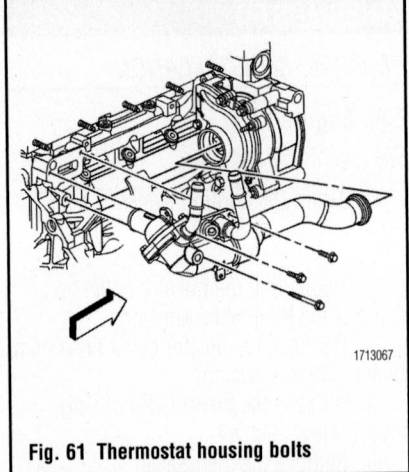

Fig. 61 Thermostat housing bolts

17. Remove the thermostat housing bolts.

➡**Twist the water transfer pipe while pulling in order to remove it from the water pump.**

18. Remove the thermostat housing from the vehicle.

19. Remove the water transfer pipe from the thermostat housing, if necessary.

20. Remove and discard the water transfer pipe O-ring seals, if necessary.

21. Remove the thermostat housing cover bolts and cover, if necessary. Refer to the image for the 2.0L engine, it is the same.

22. Remove the thermostat, if necessary.

23. Remove and discard the thermostat housing O-ring seal, if necessary.

24. Remove all debris and thread sealant from the engine coolant temperature sensor and bolt holes if the housing is being reused.

To install:

25. Install a NEW thermostat housing cover O-ring seal into the recess groove.

26. Install the thermostat, if necessary.

27. Install the thermostat housing cover bolts, if necessary and tighten to 89 inch lbs. (10 Nm).

28. Install a NEW thermostat housing to engine gasket onto the thermostat housing.

29. Load the thermostat housing assembly into position.

➡**Lightly lubricate the water feed pipe seals with coolant to aid installation.**

30. Install NEW O-ring seals onto the water feed pipe.

➡**Lubricate the O-rings with coolant ONLY.**

31. Install the water feed pipe into the thermostat housing aligning locator tab.

32. Align the water pipe to water pump.

33. Seat the water feed O-ring seal by pushing inward toward the water pump. Take care not to tear or damage the O-ring.

34. Position the thermostat housing against the engine.

35. Install the thermostat housing bolts and tighten them to 89 inch lbs. (10 Nm).

36. Lower the vehicle.

37. Connect the heater inlet and outlet hoses to the thermostat housing pipes.

38. Position the heater inlet and outlet hose clamps at the thermostat housing pipes.

39. Install the radiator outlet hose to the thermostat housing.

40. Position the radiator outlet hose clamp at the thermostat housing.

41. If reinstalling the old sensor, coat the threads with sealant (GM P/N 12346004, US and 10953480, Canada).

42. Install the ECT sensor and tighten to 15 ft. lbs. (20 Nm).

43. If equipped with a manual transaxle, connect the ECT sensor electrical connector.

44. If equipped with an automatic transaxle, perform the following steps:

a. Connect the ECT sensor electrical connector.

b. Connect the HO2S electrical connector clip to the thermostat housing.

➡**The vehicle must be level when filling the cooling system.**

45. Verify the drain valves at the radiator and water pump are closed.

46. Fill the cooling system. Refer to Cooling System Draining and Filling.

47. Lower the vehicle.

48. Install the exhaust heat shield.

49. Install the exhaust heat shield studs and tighten them to 16 ft. lbs. (22 Nm).

50. Install the air cleaner bracket.

51. Install the air cleaner bracket nuts and tighten to 89 inch lbs. (10 Nm).

52. Install the air cleaner assembly.

53. Verify the repair and inspect for any leaks.

WATER PUMP

REMOVAL & INSTALLATION

See Figures 62 through 67.

1. Remove the air cleaner assembly. Refer to Engine Air Cleaner.

2. Remove the exhaust manifold heat shield.

3. If equipped, remove the coolant heater.

4. Remove the catalytic converter. Refer to Catalytic Converter Replacement.

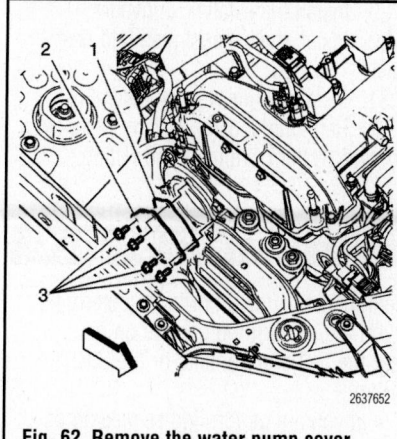

**Fig. 62 Remove the water pump cover
(2), fasteners (3) and gasket (1) from the
engine front cover**

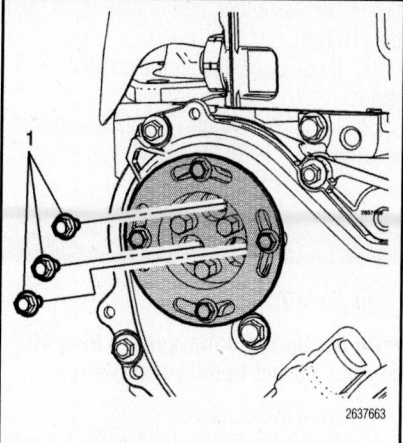

**Fig. 64 Water pump sprocket to water
pump fasteners (1)**

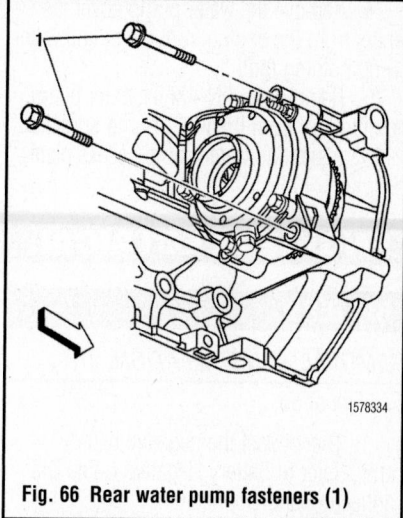

Fig. 66 Rear water pump fasteners (1)

5. Remove the engine coolant thermostat housing.

6. Remove the water pump cover (2), fasteners (3) and gasket (1) from the engine front cover.

➡**There is drain plug at the bottom of the water pump assembly for additional coolant drainage from the engine block and water pump.**

7. Drain the coolant from the water pump using the plug at the bottom of the pump. Install the plug when finished.

➡**The water pump holding tool supports the sprocket and chain during water pump service. The tool must be used or the balance shaft must be re-timed.**

8. Align the EN-43651 water pump holding tool (1) with the threads on the water pump sprocket.

9. Tighten the water pump holding tool fasteners (2).

10. Secure the water pump holding tool with the previously removed water pump cover fasteners into the engine front cover.

11. Remove the water pump sprocket to water pump fasteners (1).

➡**Be sure to remove both water pump bolts from the front of the engine block.**

12. Remove the front water pump fasteners (1).

13. Remove the rear water pump fasteners.

14. Remove the water pump.

15. If replacing the water pump cover remove the water pump rear cover fasteners (4).

16. Separate the water pump cover (1) from the water pump (3)

17. Remove and discard the water pump O-ring seal (2).

To install:

18. If replacing the water pump cover, install a new O-ring to the water pump and tighten the fasteners to 18 ft. lbs. (25 Nm).

➡**A guide pin can be created to aid in water pump alignment. Use an M 6 m x 6 mm x 50.8 mm stud (2 in.). Thread the pin into the water pump sprocket.**

19. Using a guide pin, align the pin with the water pump holding tool.

20. Position the water pump against the engine block and Hand-tighten the water pump fasteners.

21. Install 2 water pump sprocket to water pump fasteners. After the fasteners are snug, remove the guide pin and install the 3rd fastener and tighten to 89 inch lbs. (10 Nm).

22. Install the water pump fasteners at the front of the engine. Hand-tighten them at this time.

23. Tighten the water pump fasteners at the front and rear of the water pump to 18 ft. lbs. (25 Nm).

**Fig. 63 Water pump holding tool (1) and
its fasteners (2)**

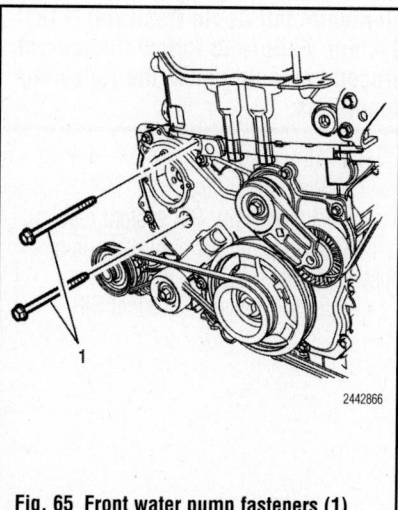

Fig. 65 Front water pump fasteners (1)

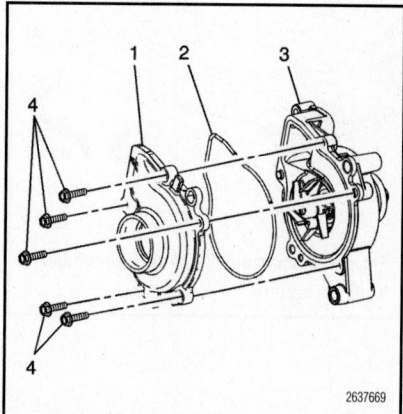

**Fig. 67 Water pump cover (1), O-ring seal
(2), water pump (3), and water pump rear
cover fasteners (4)**

24. Remove the water pump cover fasteners from the engine front cover and water pump holding tool.

25. Remove the EN-43651 water pump holding tool from the water pump sprocket.

26. Install the water pump access plate, gasket, and fasteners, and tighten to 89 inch lbs. (10 Nm).

27. If equipped, Install the coolant heater.

28. Install the engine coolant thermostat housing.

29. Install the catalytic converter.

30. Install the exhaust manifold heat shield.

31. Install the air cleaner assembly.

32. Refill the coolant system. Refer to Cooling System Draining and Filling.

ENGINE ELECTRICAL

BATTERY

REMOVAL & INSTALLATION

See Figure 68.

1. Disconnect the negative battery cable. Refer to Battery Negative Cable Disconnection and Connection.

2. Remove the spare tire.

3. Open the positive battery cable cover.

4. Loosen the positive battery cable nut.

5. Remove the positive battery cable from the battery.

6. Disconnect the battery vent tube from the battery.

7. Remove the battery hold-down retainer bolts.

8. Remove the battery hold-down retainers.

➡**Do not tip the battery more than 40 degrees during removal.**

9. Remove the battery.

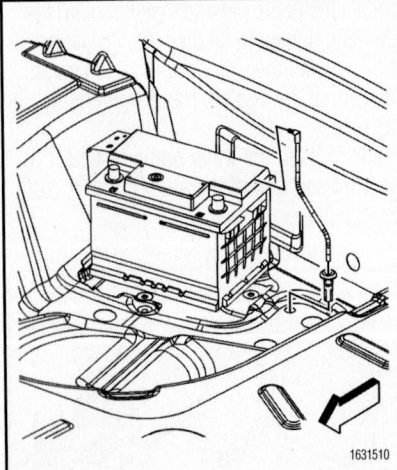

Fig. 68 Disconnect the battery vent tube from the battery

To install:

➡**Do not tip the battery more than 40 degrees during battery installation.**

10. Install the battery.

11. Install the battery hold-down retainers.

12. Install the battery hold-down retainer bolts and tighten them to 18 ft. lbs. (25 Nm).

➡**Replacement batteries may require the vent plug in the battery vent hole to be moved from one end of the battery to the other to permit vent tube installation per the original design.**

13. Connect the battery vent tube to the battery.

14. Install the positive battery cable from the battery.

15. Tighten the positive battery cable nut to 11 ft. lbs. (15 Nm).

16. Close the positive battery cable cover.

17. Install the spare tire.

18. Connect the negative battery cable. Refer to Battery Negative Cable Disconnection and Connection.

BATTERY NEGATIVE CABLE DISCONNECTION & CONNECTION

✳✳ CAUTION

This vehicle is equipped with a Supplemental Inflatable Restraint (SIR) System. Failure to follow the correct procedure could cause the following conditions:

- Air bag deployment
- Personal injury
- Unnecessary SIR system repairs

In order to avoid the above conditions, observe the following guidelines:

- Refer to Chassis Electrical SIR

BATTERY SYSTEM

Identification View in order to determine if you are performing service on or near the SIR components or the SIR wiring.

- If you are performing service on or near the SIR components or the SIR wiring, disable the SIR system. Refer to Disabling the SIR System.

✳✳ CAUTION

Refer to Battery Disconnect Warning in the Precautions at the beginning of the HHR section.

1. Record all of the preset radio stations.

2. Turn OFF all the lamps and the accessories.

3. Make sure the ignition switch is in the OFF position.

4. Remove the rear floor trim plate.

5. Remove the rear compartment trim panel.

6. Loosen the negative battery cable nut.

7. Remove the negative battery cable from the battery.

Connect Procedure

➡**Clean any existing oxidation from the contact face of the battery terminal and battery cable using a wire brush before installing the battery cable to the battery terminal.**

8. Install the negative battery cable to the battery.

9. Tighten the negative battery cable nut to 11 ft. lbs. (15 Nm).

10. Install the rear compartment trim panel.

11. Install the rear floor trim plate.

12. Reset the radio stations and the clock.

ENGINE ELECTRICAL

CHARGING SYSTEM

GENERATOR (ALTERNATOR)

REMOVAL & INSTALLATION

See Figure 69.

1. Disconnect the negative battery cable. Refer to Battery Negative Cable Disconnection and Connection.
2. Remove the drive belt. Refer to Drive Belt Replacement.
3. Remove the engine harness generator connector (1).
4. Remove the engine harness generator terminal boot (2).
5. Remove the generator terminal nut (3).
6. Remove the engine harness generator connector (4).
7. Remove the 3 generator bolts (5).
8. Remove the generator (6).

To install:

9. Installation is the reverse of removal, noting the following:
   a. Tighten the 3 generator bolts to 16 ft. lbs. (22 Nm).
   b. Tighten the generator terminal nut to 15 ft. lbs (20 Nm).

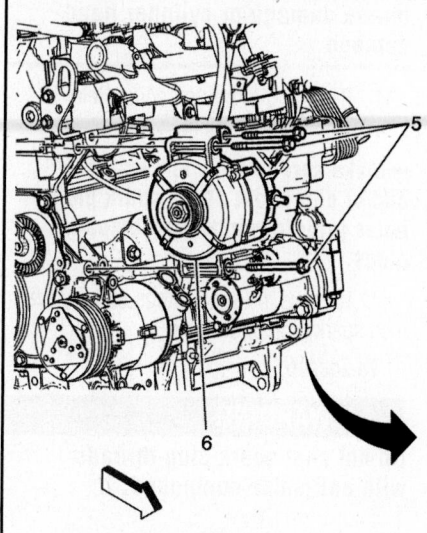
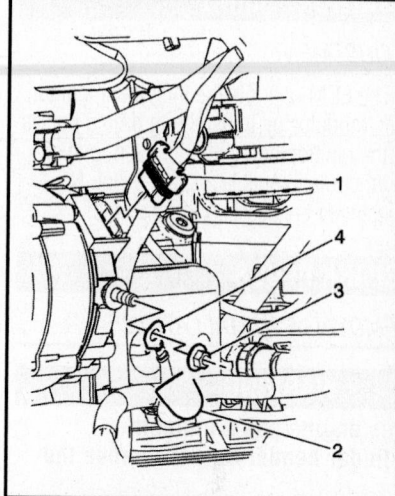

1. Engine harness generator connector
2. Engine harness generator terminal boot
3. Generator terminal nut
4. Engine harness generator connector
5. Generator bolts
6. Generator

2035456

Fig. 69 Generator replacement

ENGINE ELECTRICAL

IGNITION SYSTEM

FIRING ORDER

The firing order for these models is: 1–3–4–2.

IGNITION COIL

REMOVAL & INSTALLATION

2.0L Engine

See Figure 70.

1. Remove the air cleaner assembly. Refer to Engine Air Cleaner.

2. Disconnect the electrical connector.
3. Remove the ignition coil bolt (1).
4. Remove the ignition coil (2).
5. Installation is the reverse of removal. Tighten the ignition coil bolt to 89 inch lbs. (10 Nm).

2.2L, 2.4L

See Figures 71 and 72.

1. Remove the air cleaner assembly. Refer to Engine Air Cleaner.

2. Disconnect the ignition coil electrical connectors (3).
3. Remove the ignition coil bolts.
4. Remove the ignition coils.

To install:

5. Install the ignition coils.
6. Install the ignition coil bolts. Tighten the bolt(s) to 89 inch lbs. (10 Nm).

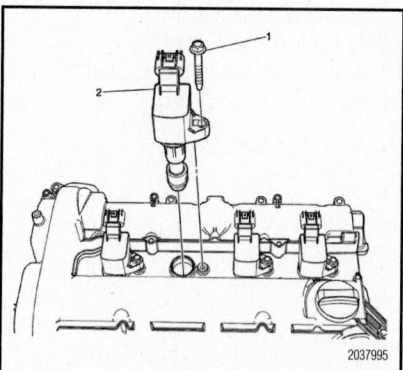

2037995

Fig. 70 Ignition coil bolt (1)

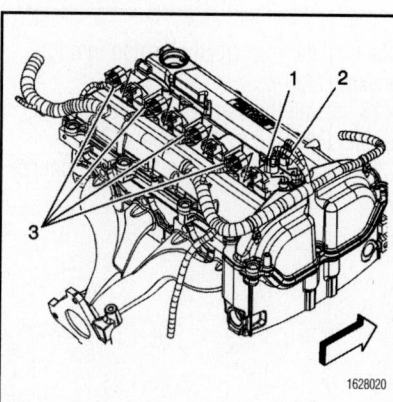

1628020

Fig. 71 Disconnect the ignition coil electrical connectors (3)

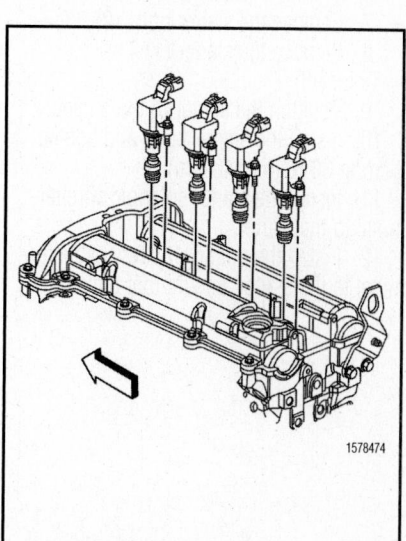

1578474

Fig. 72 Ignition coils and bolts

7. Connect the ignition coil electrical connectors.

8. Install the air cleaner assembly. Refer to Engine Air Cleaner.

IGNITION TIMING

ADJUSTMENT

The ECM controls the individual ignition coils/modules by transmitting timing pulses on the ignition coil circuit of each ignition coil/module to enable a spark event. No adjustment is necessary or possible.

SPARK PLUGS

REMOVAL & INSTALLATION

✷✷ WARNING

This engine has aluminum cylinder heads. Do not remove the spark plugs from a hot engine, allow it to cool first. Removing the spark plugs from a hot engine may cause spark plug thread damage or cylinder head damage.

1. Remove the ignition coils. Refer to Ignition Coil replacement.

➡**Make sure to blow any water and/or debris out of the spark plug holes prior to removing the spark plugs.**

2. Remove the spark plugs using a 5/8 inch spark plug socket.

To install:

✷✷ WARNING

Do not coat spark plug threads with anti-seize compound. If anti-seize compound is used and spark plugs are over-torqued, damage to the cylinder head threads may result.

3. Install the spark plugs, making sure they are properly gapped before installation:

- For 2.0L the spark plug gap is 0.035 in. (0.90 mm).
- For 2.2L and 2.4L the spark plug gap is 0.040 in. (1.00 mm).

4. Tighten the spark plugs to 15 ft. lbs. (20 Nm).

5. Apply dielectric compound to the spark plug boots and make sure no corrosion is present.

6. Install the ignition coils. Refer to Ignition Coil replacement.

ENGINE ELECTRICAL   STARTING SYSTEM

STARTER

REMOVAL & INSTALLATION

See Figures 73 and 74.

1. Disconnect the negative battery cable. Refer to Battery Negative Cable Disconnection and Connection.

2. Raise and support the vehicle.

3. Disconnect the engine harness connector (1) from the starter.

4. Remove the starter solenoid terminal nut (4).

5. Remove the positive battery cable terminal (3) from the starter.

6. Remove the starter solenoid wire terminal (2) from the starter.

7. Remove the starter bolts (2).

8. Remove the starter (1).

To install:

9. Position the starter to the engine.

10. Install the starter bolts and tighten them to 30 ft. lbs. (40 Nm).

11. Install the starter solenoid wire terminal to the starter.

12. Install the positive battery cable terminal to the starter. Ensure that the anti-

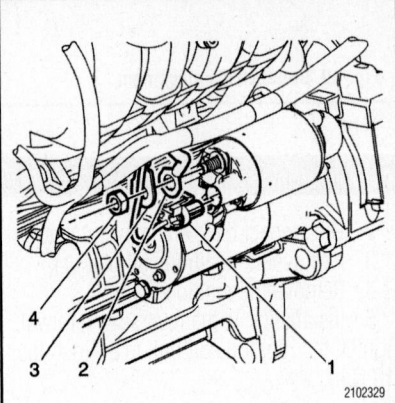

Fig. 73 Engine harness connector (1), starter solenoid wire terminal (2), positive battery cable terminal (3), starter solenoid terminal nut (4)

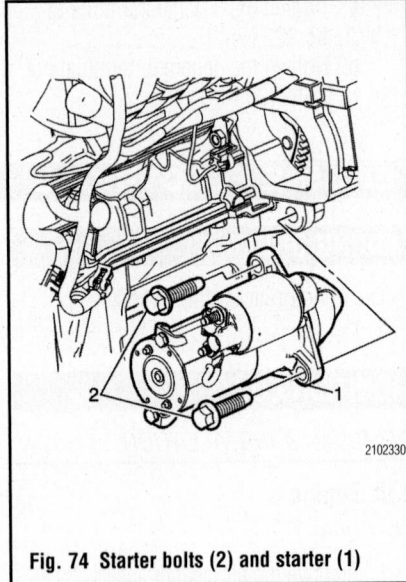

Fig. 74 Starter bolts (2) and starter (1)

rotational tab is correctly located into the indexing slot.

13. Install the starter solenoid terminal nut and tighten it to 13 ft. lbs. (17 Nm).

14. Connect the engine harness connector to the starter.

15. Lower the vehicle.

16. Connect the negative battery cable. Refer to Battery Negative Cable Disconnection and Connection.

ENGINE MECHANICAL

➡ **Disconnecting the negative battery cable may interfere with the functions of the onboard computer systems and may require the computer to undergo a relearning process, once the negative battery cable is reconnected.**

ACCESSORY DRIVE BELTS

ACCESSORY BELT ROUTING

See Figure 75.

Refer to the accompanying illustration.

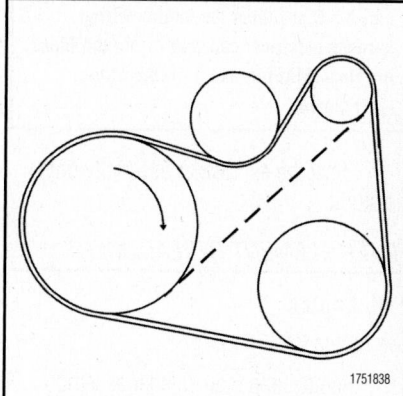

Fig. 75 Engine drive belt routing: Dotted line shows routing for vehicles without air conditioning

INSPECTION

Note the following:
- Inspect all drive belt pulleys for pilling. Pilling is the small balls or pills or it can be strings in the drive belt grooves from the accumulation of rubber dust.
- Inspect the belt for cuts, tears, sections of ribs missing, or damaged belt plies.
- Belt separation is identified by the plies of the belt separating and may be seen at the edge of the belt or felt as a lump in the belt.
- Misaligned pulleys may be caused by improper mounting of an accessory drive component, incorrect installation of the accessory drive component pulley, or a pulley bent inward or outward from a previous repair. Test for a misaligned pulley using a straight edge in the pulley grooves across two or three pulleys. If a misaligned pulley is found refer to that accessory drive component for the proper installation procedure for that pulley.
- Inspecting the pulleys for being bent should include inspecting for a dent or other damage to the pulleys that would prevent the drive belt from not seating properly in all of the pulley grooves or on the

smooth surface of a pulley when the back side of the belt is used to drive the pulley.
- Verify that the drive belt is not too long, which would prevent the drive belt tensioner from working properly. Also if an incorrect length drive belt was installed, it may not be routed properly and may be turning an accessory drive component in the wrong direction.
- A drive belt that is too wide or too narrow will cause wear on the drive belt. The drive belt ribs should match all of the grooves on all of the pulleys.
- Verify that the drive belt is not contacting any parts of the engine or body while the engine is operating. There should be sufficient clearance when the drive belt accessory drive components load varies. The drive belt should not come in contact with an engine or a body component when snapping the throttle.
- Verify that the drive belt tensioner operates properly. If the drive belt tensioner is not operating properly, proper belt tension may not be achieved to keep the drive belt from slipping which could cause a squeal noise.
- Inspect fasteners to eliminate the possibility that a wrong bolt, nut, spacer, or washer was installed.

ADJUSTMENT

The accessory drive belt adjustment is maintained by an automatic tensioner.

REMOVAL & INSTALLATION

2.0L Engine

See Figure 76.

1. Remove the air cleaner assembly. Refer to Engine Air Cleaner.
2. Use a breaker bar to rotate the drive belt tensioner.

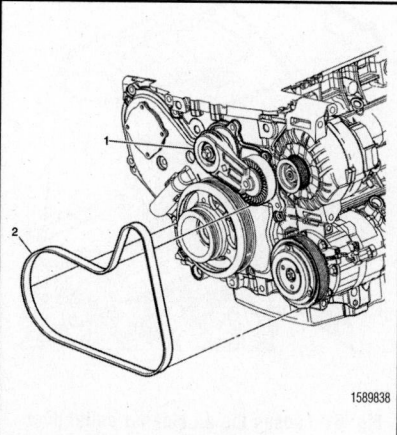

Fig. 76 Drive belt tensioner (1)

3. Remove the drive belt from the pulleys and tensioner.
4. Remove the drive belt tensioner (1).
5. Remove the drive belt (2).
6. Clean and inspect the drive belt surfaces of all the pulleys.
7. Inspect the drive belt for correct alignment.
8. Installation is the reverse of removal.

2.2L & 2.4L Engines

See Figures 77 and 78.

1. Remove the engine splash shield.
2. Install the J 44811 accessory belt tensioner unloader to the drive belt tensioner.
3. Using the J 44811, rotate the drive belt tensioner counter clockwise in order to release the spring tension.
4. Remove the drive belt from under the drive belt tensioner.
5. Remove the drive belt from around the accessory drive pulleys.

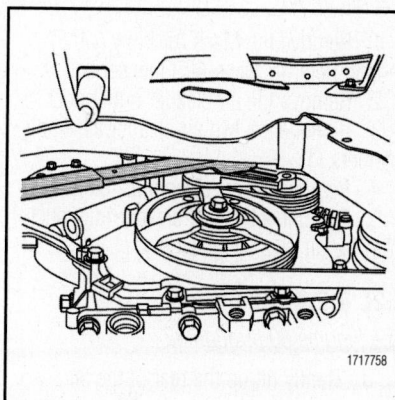

Fig. 77 Releasing the tension with the accessory belt tensioner unloader

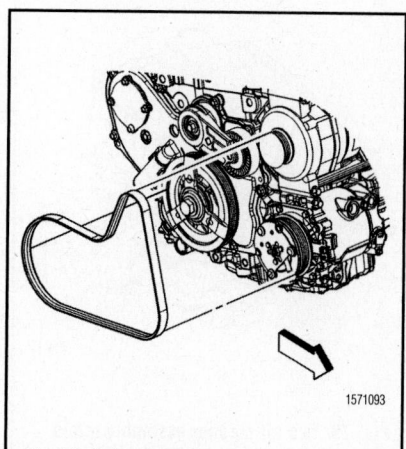

Fig. 78 Drive belt removal

6. Remove the drive belt.

7. Using the J 44811, rotate the drive belt tensioner clockwise in order to release the spring tension.

To install:

8. Position the drive belt around all the accessory drive pulleys, except for the drive belt tensioner.

9. Using the J 44811, rotate the drive belt tensioner counter clockwise in order to release the spring tension.

10. Position the drive belt under the drive belt tensioner.

11. Using the J 44811, rotate the drive belt tensioner clockwise in order to release the spring tension.

12. Remove the J 44811 from the drive belt tensioner.

13. Ensure that the drive belt is properly aligned on the accessory drive pulleys.

14. Install the engine splash shield.

AIR CLEANER

REMOVAL & INSTALLATION

2.0L Engine

See Figure 79.

1. Remove the Mass Air Flow (MAF) sensor. Refer to Mass Air Flow sensor.

2. Remove the air cleaner outlet duct.

3. Remove the two air cleaner assembly retainers (1)

4. Remove the air cleaner assembly (2)

5. Disconnect the air cleaner inlet duct from the air cleaner assembly.

2.2L & 2.4L Engines

See Figures 80 through 82.

1. Gently lift up the rear of the air cleaner assembly in order to disengage the air cleaner from the studs.

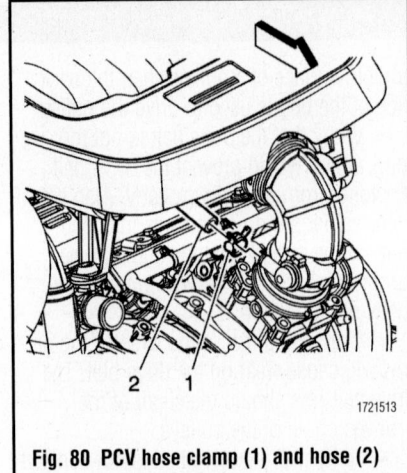

Fig. 80 PCV hose clamp (1) and hose (2)

2. Reposition the air cleaner assembly in order to access the positive crankcase ventilation (PCV) hose and the throttle body duct.

3. Reposition the PCV hose clamp (1) at the air cleaner assembly.

4. Remove the PCV hose (2) from the air cleaner assembly.

5. Loosen the air cleaner outlet duct clamp at the throttle body.

6. Disconnect the engine wiring harness electrical connector from the Mass Air Flow (MAF)/intake air temperature (IAT) sensor.

7. Remove the air cleaner assembly.

To install:

8. Install the air cleaner assembly.

9. Tighten the air cleaner outlet duct clamp at the throttle body.

10. Tighten the clamp to 44 inch lbs. (5 Nm).

11. Connect the engine wiring harness electrical connector to the MAF/IAT sensor.

12. Install the PCV hose to the air cleaner assembly.

13. Position the PCV hose clamp at the air cleaner assembly.

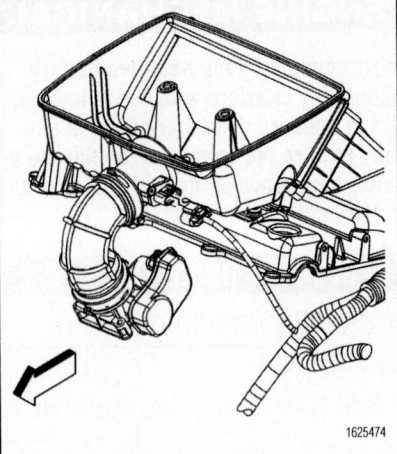

Fig. 82 Disconnect the engine wiring harness electrical connector from the Mass Air Flow (MAF)/intake air temperature (IAT) sensor

14. Seat the air cleaner assembly onto the studs.

FILTER/ELEMENT REPLACEMENT

2.0L Engine

See Figure 83.

1. Remove the 6 air cleaner assembly screws.

2. Remove the air cleaner assembly cover (2).

3. Remove the air cleaner filter (3).

4. Installation is the reverse of removal.

5. Tighten the 6 air cleaner assembly screws to 89 inch lbs. (10 Nm).

2.2L & 2.4L Engines

See Figure 84.

1. Remove the air cleaner assembly. Refer to Engine Air Cleaner.

2. Loosen the air cleaner screws.

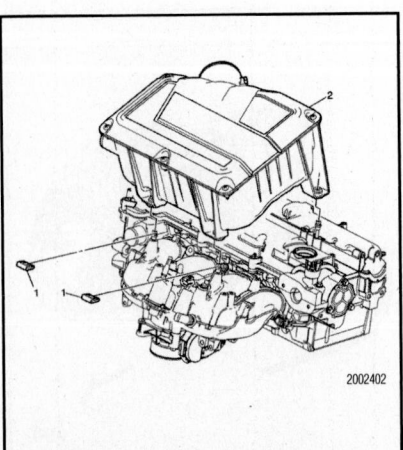

Fig. 79 Two air cleaner assembly retainers (1) and air cleaner assembly (2)

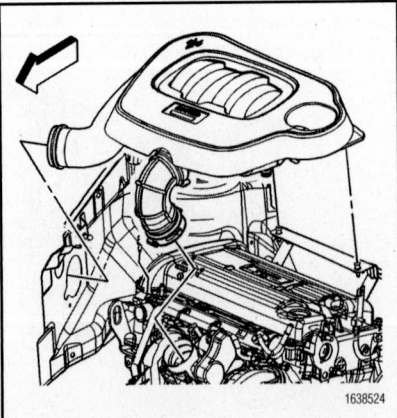

Fig. 81 Loosen the air cleaner outlet duct clamp at the throttle body

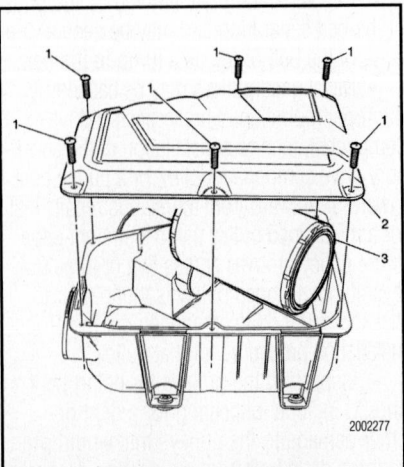

Fig. 83 Air cleaner element replacement

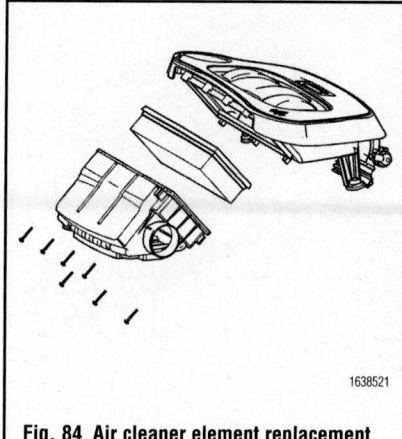

Fig. 84 Air cleaner element replacement

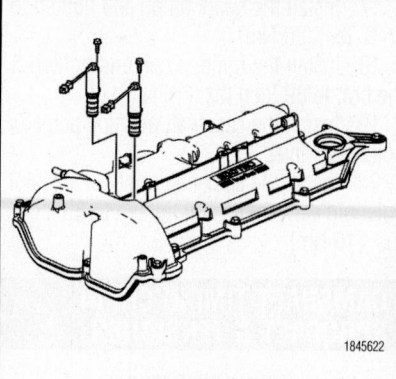

**Fig. 86 Camshaft position actuator sole-
noid valves and valve bolts**

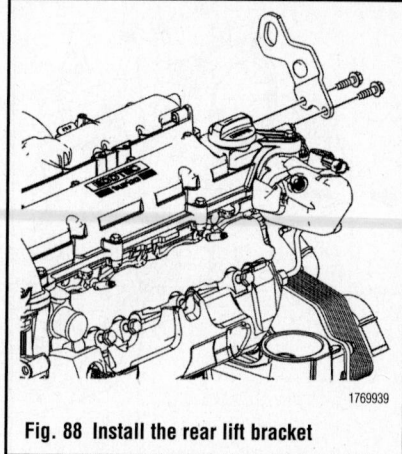

Fig. 88 Install the rear lift bracket

3. Separate the upper and lower portions of the air cleaner assembly.

4. Remove the air cleaner filter from the
lower air cleaner housing.

5. Inspect the air cleaner filter for dust,
dirt, and water contamination.

To install:

6. Install the air cleaner filter into the
lower air cleaner housing.

7. Install the upper air cleaner cover to
the lower air cleaner housing.

8. Tighten the air cleaner screws.

9. Tighten the screws to 35 inch lbs.
(4 Nm).

10. Install the air cleaner assembly. Refer
to Engine Air Cleaner.

CAMSHAFT FRONT COVER

REMOVAL & INSTALLATION

2.0L Engine

See Figures 85 through 88.

1. Remove the bolt and coil.

➡**Do not disconnect the PCV
hose from the camshaft cover.
The PCV hose and the camshaft**

**cover cannot be serviced
individually.**

2. Remove the camshaft cover assembly.

3. Remove and discard the camshaft
cover gasket, camshaft cover grommets,
and camshaft cover bolts if they are serviced with the grommets.

4. Remove the camshaft position actuator solenoid valve bolts.

5. Remove the camshaft position actuator solenoid valves.

To install:

6. Install NEW camshaft cover grommets and camshaft cover bolts if they are
serviced with the grommets.

7. Assemble the camshaft cover and
gasket. Ensure that the gasket is located in
the retaining groove in the camshaft cover.

8. Install the cover on the cylinder head
and hand start the bolts.

9. Install the front lift bracket.

10. Install the front lift bracket bolts and
tighten to 18 ft. lbs. (25 Nm).

11. Install the rear lift bracket.

12. Install the rear lift bracket bolts and
tighten to 18 ft. lbs. (25 Nm).

13. Install the ignition coils (4) and
tighten the bolts (3) to 89 inch lbs.
(10 Nm).

14. Tighten the camshaft cover bolts to
89 inch lbs. (10 Nm).

➡**The solenoid valves are marked
intake and exhaust.**

15. Install the camshaft position actuator
solenoid valves (2).

16. Install the camshaft position actuator
solenoid valve bolts (1) and tighten to
89 inch lbs. (10 Nm).

2.2L & 2.4L Engines

See Figures 89 through 91.

1. Remove the camshaft cover ground
strap (1).

2. Remove the front lift bracket.

3. Remove the rear lift bracket (1).

4. Remove the bolt and coil.

5. Remove the camshaft position actuator solenoid valve bolts.

6. Remove the camshaft position actuator solenoid valves.

7. Remove the camshaft cover
assembly.

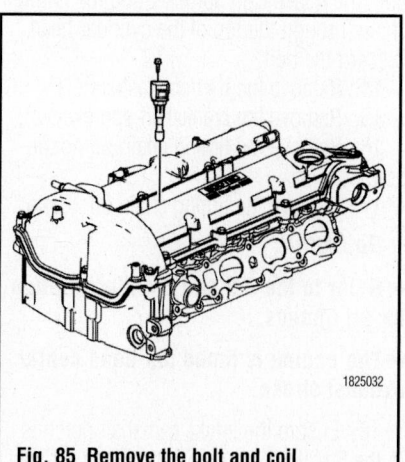

Fig. 85 Remove the bolt and coil

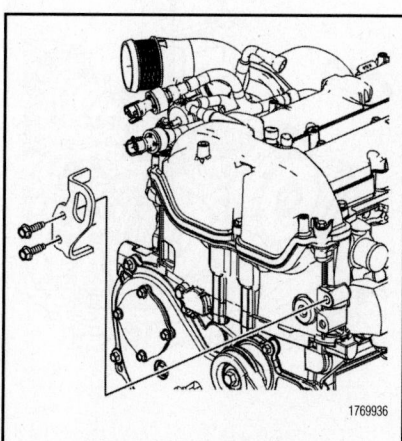

Fig. 87 Install the front lift bracket

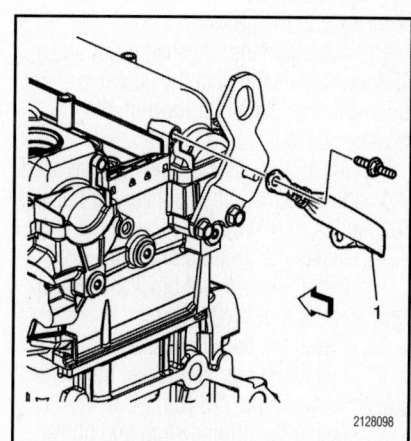

Fig. 89 Camshaft cover ground strap (1)

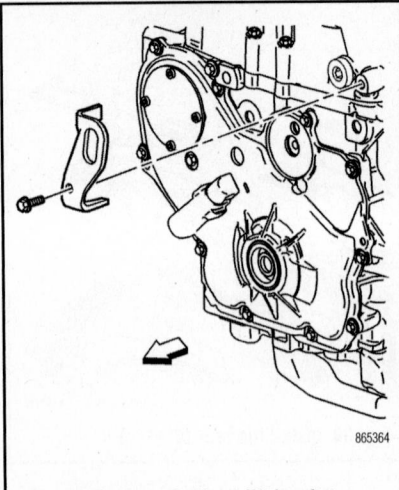

Fig. 90 Remove the front lift bracket

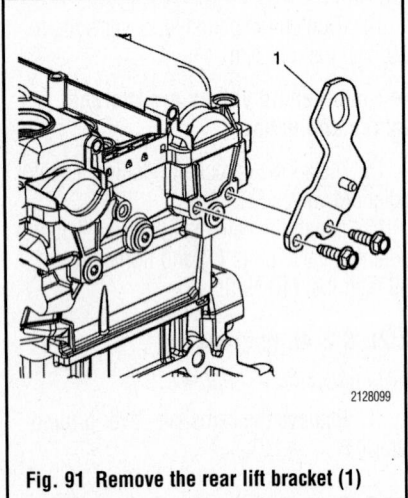

Fig. 91 Remove the rear lift bracket (1)

8. Remove and discard the camshaft cover gasket, camshaft cover grommets, and camshaft cover bolts if they are serviced with the grommet.

To install:

9. Install NEW camshaft cover grommets and camshaft cover bolts if they are serviced with the grommet.

10. Assemble the camshaft cover and a NEW gasket. Ensure that the gasket is located in the retaining groove in the camshaft cover.

11. Install the cover on the cylinder head and hand start the bolts. Tighten the bolts to 89 inch lbs. (10 Nm).

12. Install the front lift bracket.

13. Install the front lift bracket bolt and tighten to 18 ft. lbs. (25 Nm).

14. Install the rear lift bracket.

15. Install the rear lift bracket bolts and tighten to 18 ft. lbs. (25 Nm).

16. Install the ground strap and tighten the bolts to 89 inch lbs. (10 Nm).

17. Install the spark plugs and tighten to 15 ft. lbs. (20 Nm).

18. Install the ignition coil and tighten the bolt to 89 inch lbs. (10 Nm).

19. Install the camshaft position actuator solenoid valves.

20. Install the camshaft position actuator solenoid valve bolts and tighten to 89 inch lbs. (10 Nm).

CAMSHAFT TIMING CHAIN SPROCKET & TENSIONER

REMOVAL & INSTALLATION

2010 Models

2.0L Engine

See Figures 92 through 98.

1. Remove the upper timing chain guide bolts.

2. Remove the upper timing chain guide.

➡**Important: Remove the timing chain tensioner to unload chain tension before the timing chain is removed. If you do not remove the timing chain tensioner first, the timing chain will become cocked and it will be difficult to remove.**

3. Remove the timing chain tensioner.

4. Locate the hex on the exhaust camshaft and hold with a wrench.

5. Remove the exhaust cam bolt and the exhaust cam actuator.

6. Discard the bolt.

7. Remove the adjustable timing chain guide bolt.

8. Remove the adjustable timing chain guide.

9. Remove the plug to gain access to the fixed timing chain guide bolt.

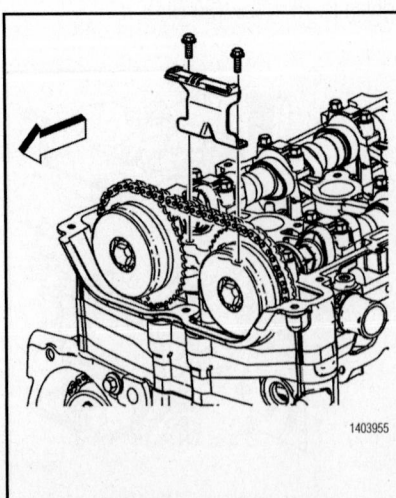

Fig. 92 Upper timing chain guide

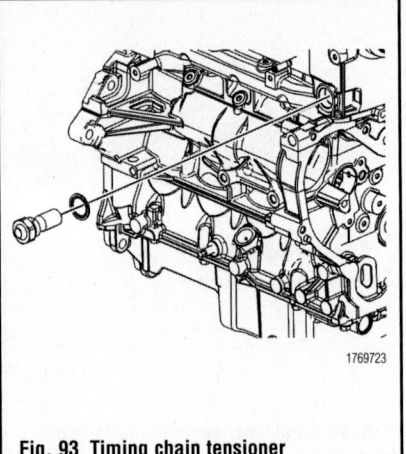

Fig. 93 Timing chain tensioner

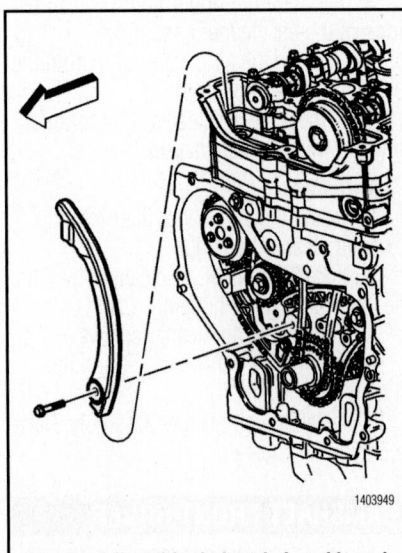

Fig. 94 Adjustable timing chain guide and guide bolt

10. Remove the fixed timing chain guide bolts.

11. Remove the fixed timing chain guide.

12. Locate the hex on the intake camshaft and hold with a wrench.

13. Remove the intake cam sprocket bolt, the intake cam sprocket and the timing chain through the top of the cylinder head. Discard the bolt.

14. Remove the friction washers (1).

15. Remove the crankshaft sprocket (2).

16. Remove the timing chain oil nozzle bolt.

17. Remove the timing chain oil nozzle.

To install:

➡**Refer to the 2.2 and 2.4L installation for all images.**

➡**The engine is timed top-dead center exhaust stroke.**

18. Ensure the intake camshaft notch is in the 5 o'clock position (2) and the exhaust

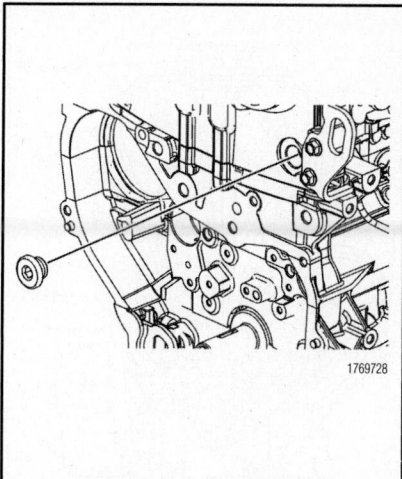

Fig. 95 Remove the plug to gain access to the fixed timing chain guide bolt

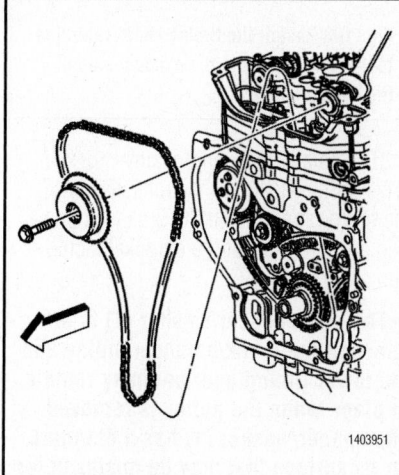

Fig. 96 Remove the intake cam sprocket bolt, the intake cam sprocket and the timing chain through the top of the cylinder head. Discard the bolt

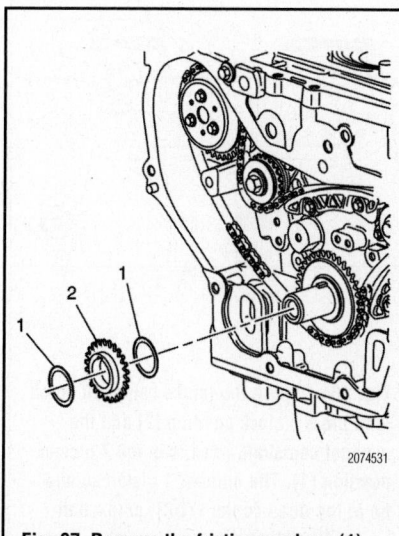

Fig. 97 Remove the friction washers (1)

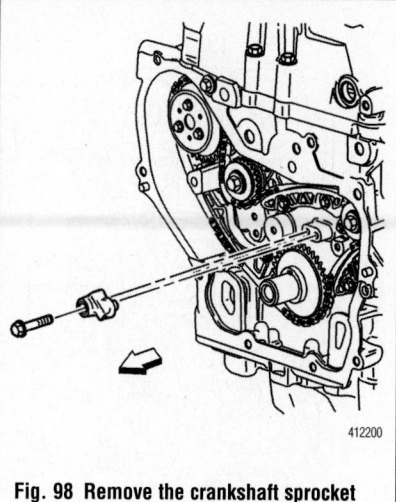

Fig. 98 Remove the crankshaft sprocket (2)

camshaft notch is in the 7 o'clock position (1). The number 1 piston should be at top dead center (TDC), crankshaft key at 12 o'clock.

19. Install a friction washer (1), if equipped.

20. Install the timing chain drive sprocket (3) to the crankshaft with the timing mark (2) in the 5 o'clock position and the front of the sprocket facing out.

➡**The outer spacer/washer (1) is in between the crank/balancer pulley and the lower timing gear and may remain in place when the pulley is removed. The spacer/washer (1) has a dot/mark on its surface that may be mistaken for the lower timing mark, and blocks the proper timing mark on the gear from view. The outer spacer/washer (1) must be removed when timing the engine in order to view the correct timing mark on the lower crank gear.**

21. Install a second friction washer (1), if equipped.

➡**There are 3 colored links on the timing chain. Two links are of matching color, and 1 link is of a unique color. Use the following procedure to line up the links with the actuators. Orient the chain so that the colored links are visible.**

➡**Always use new actuator bolts.**

22. Assemble the intake camshaft actuator into the timing chain with the timing mark lined up with the uniquely colored link (1).

23. Lower the timing chain through the opening in the cylinder head. Use care to ensure that the chain goes around both sides of the cylinder block bosses (1, 2).

24. Install the intake camshaft actuator onto the intake camshaft while

aligning the dowel pin into the camshaft slot.

25. Hand-tighten the new intake camshaft actuator bolt.

26. Route the timing chain around the crankshaft sprocket and line up the first matching colored link with the timing mark on the crankshaft sprocket, in approximately the 5 o'clock position.

27. Rotate the crankshaft clockwise to remove all chain slack. Do not rotate the intake camshaft.

28. Install the adjustable timing chain guide down through the opening in the cylinder head and install the adjustable timing chain bolt. Tighten the adjustable timing chain guide bolt to 89 inch lbs. (10 Nm).

29. Install the exhaust camshaft actuator (1) into the timing chain with the timing mark lined up with the second matching colored link.

➡**Always install NEW actuator bolts.**

30. Install the exhaust camshaft actuator onto the exhaust camshaft, aligning the dowel pin into the camshaft slot.

31. Using a 23 mm open end wrench, rotate the exhaust camshaft approximately 45 degrees until the dowel pin in the camshaft actuator goes into the camshaft slot.

2.2L & 2.4L Engine

See Figures 99 through 113.

1. Remove the camshaft cover. Refer to Camshaft Cover replacement.

➡**If the intake camshaft actuator is moving independently of the camshaft, this means the camshaft is not locked to the actuator. Rotate the camshaft counter-clockwise while the holding tool is installed and this will lock the camshaft to the actuator.**

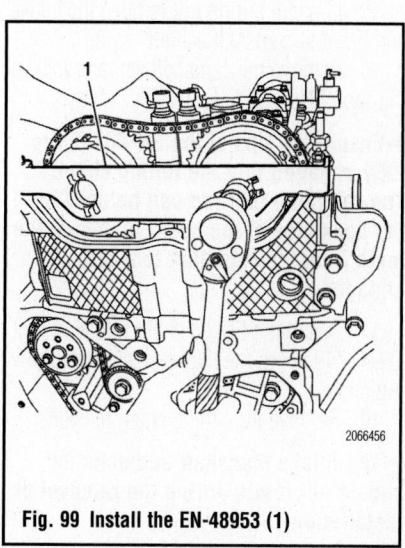

Fig. 99 Install the EN-48953 (1)

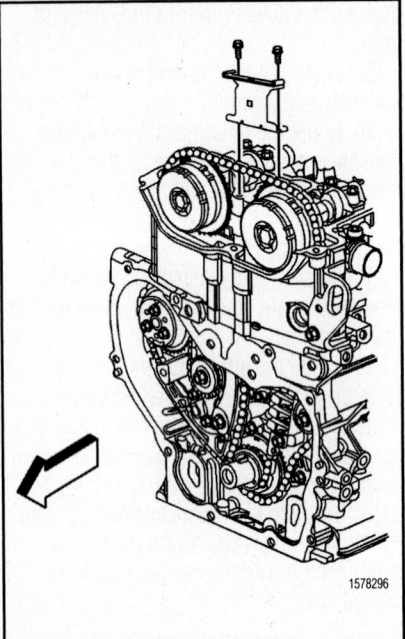

Fig. 100 Remove the upper timing chain guide bolts and guide

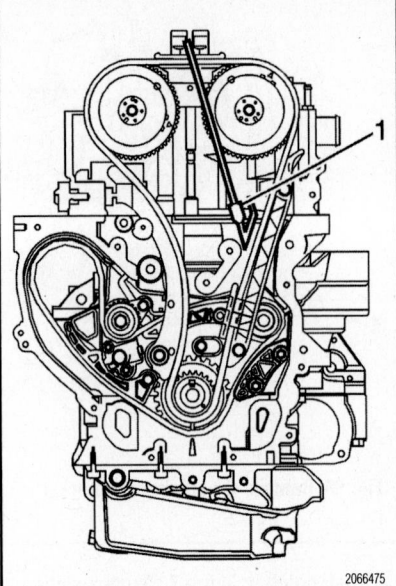

Fig. 101 Install the timing chain retention tool EN-48749 (1) to the intake side of the timing chain

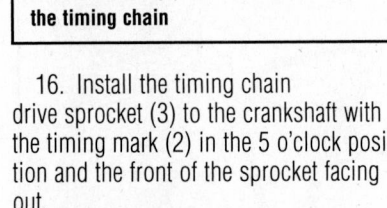

Fig. 103 Install the timing chain retention tool EN-48749 (1) to the exhaust side of the timing chain

2. Rotate the crankshaft clockwise to install the camshaft actuator locking the tool EN-48953 Camshaft Actuator Locking Tool.

3. Install the EN-48953 (1).

4. Install the camshaft actuator locking tool, tightening the bolt to 89 inch lbs. (10 Nm).

5. Remove the upper timing chain guide bolts and guide.

6. Clean the timing chain and gears with solvent.

7. Ensure the timing chain and the camshaft position actuators are marked for proper assembly.

8. Mark the timing gear sprockets and the timing chain. It is recommended that the paint marks are located in the 12 o'clock position.

9. Loosen, but do not remove the intake and exhaust camshaft actuator bolts.

10. Remove the camshaft actuator locking tool, EN-48953.

➡ **Ensure the tips of the EN-48749 are fully engaged into the timing chain. The retention tool rod can be used on the back side of the chain to ensure the teeth from the retention tool are engaged.**

11. Install the timing chain retention tool EN-48749 (1) to the intake side of the timing chain.

12. Remove the timing chain tensioner.

➡ **The intake camshaft and actuator should not rotate during the removal or installation.**

13. Install the timing chain retention tool EN-48749 (1) to the exhaust side of the timing chain.

To install:

➡ **The engine is timed top-dead center exhaust stroke.**

14. Ensure the intake camshaft notch is in the 5 o'clock position (2) and the exhaust camshaft notch is in the 7 o'clock position (1). The number 1 piston should be at top dead center (TDC), crankshaft key at 12 o'clock.

15. Install a friction washer (1), if equipped.

Fig. 102 Remove the timing chain tensioner

16. Install the timing chain drive sprocket (3) to the crankshaft with the timing mark (2) in the 5 o'clock position and the front of the sprocket facing out.

➡ **The outer spacer/washer (1) is in between the crank/balancer pulley and the lower timing gear and may remain in place when the pulley is removed. The spacer/washer (1) has a dot/mark on its surface that may be mistaken for the lower timing mark, and blocks the proper timing mark on the gear from view. The outer spacer/washer (1) must be removed when timing the engine in**

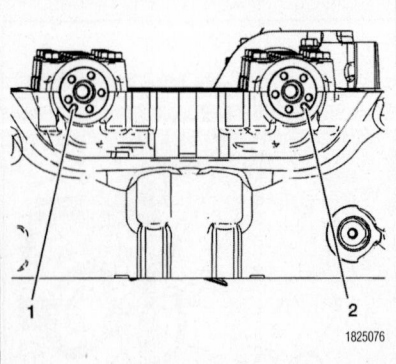

Fig. 104 Ensure the intake camshaft notch is in the 5 o'clock position (2) and the exhaust camshaft notch is in the 7 o'clock position (1). The number 1 piston should be at top dead center (TDC), crankshaft key at 12 o'clock

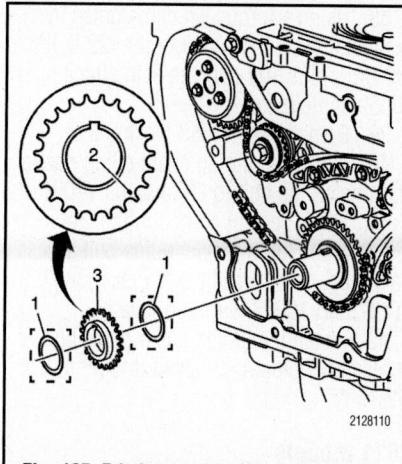

Fig. 105 Friction washer (1), timing mark (2), and timing chain drive sprocket (3)

order to view the correct timing mark on the lower crank gear.

17. Install a second friction washer (1), if equipped.

➡There are 3 colored links on the timing chain. Two links are of matching color, and 1 link is of a unique color. Use the following procedure to line up the links with the actuators. Orient the chain so that the colored links are visible.

❋❋ **WARNING**

Always use new actuator bolts.

18. Assemble the intake camshaft actuator into the timing chain with the timing mark lined up with the uniquely colored link (1).

19. Lower the timing chain through the opening in the cylinder head. Use care to

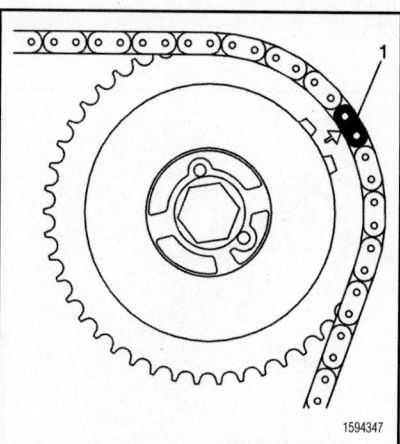

Fig. 106 Assemble the intake camshaft actuator into the timing chain with the timing mark lined up with the uniquely colored link (1)

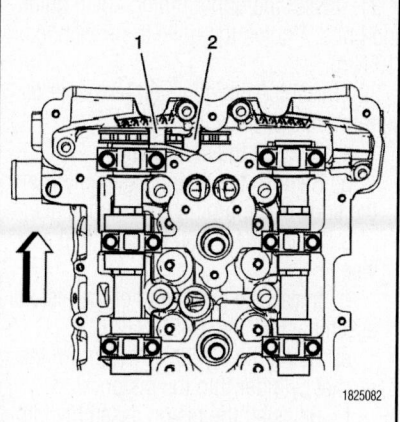

Fig. 107 Lower the timing chain through the opening in the cylinder head. Use care to ensure that the chain goes around both sides of the cylinder block bosses (1, 2)

ensure that the chain goes around both sides of the cylinder block bosses (1, 2).

20. Install the intake camshaft actuator onto the intake camshaft while aligning the dowel pin into the camshaft slot.

21. Hand-tighten the new intake camshaft actuator bolt.

22. Route the timing chain around the crankshaft sprocket and line up the first matching colored link with the timing mark on the crankshaft sprocket, in approximately the 5 o'clock position.

23. Rotate the crankshaft clockwise to

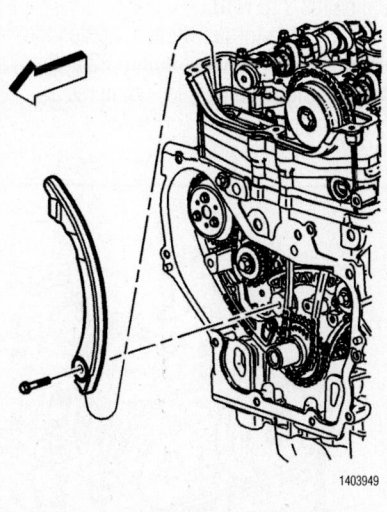

Fig. 108 Install the adjustable timing chain guide down through the opening in the cylinder head and install the adjustable timing chain bolt. Tighten the adjustable timing chain guide bolt to 89 inch lbs. (10 Nm)

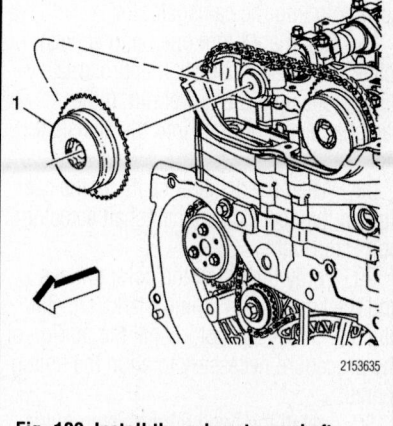

Fig. 109 Install the exhaust camshaft actuator (1) into the timing chain with the timing mark lined up with the second matching colored link

remove all chain slack. Do not rotate the intake camshaft.

24. Install the adjustable timing chain guide down through the opening in the cylinder head and install the adjustable timing chain bolt. Tighten the adjustable timing chain guide bolt to 89 inch lbs. (10 Nm).

25. Install the exhaust camshaft actuator (1) into the timing chain with the timing mark lined up with the second matching colored link.

➡**Always install NEW actuator bolts.**

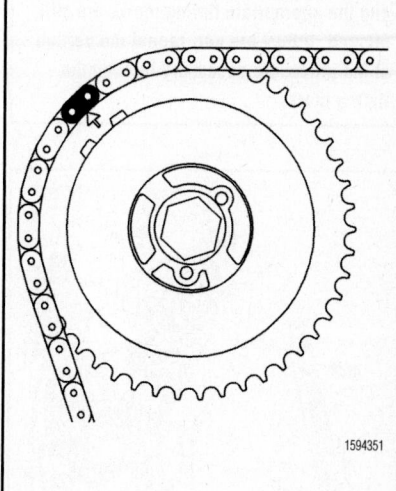

Fig. 110 Using a 23 mm open end wrench, rotate the exhaust camshaft approximately 45 degrees until the dowel pin in the camshaft actuator goes into the camshaft slot

26. Install the exhaust camshaft actuator onto the exhaust camshaft, aligning the dowel pin into the camshaft slot.

27. Using a 23 mm open end wrench, rotate the exhaust camshaft approximately 45 degrees until the dowel pin in the camshaft actuator goes into the camshaft slot.

28. When the actuator seats on the cam, tighten the new exhaust camshaft actuator bolt Hand-tight.

29. Verify that all of the colored links and the appropriate timing marks are still aligned. If they are not, repeat the portion of the procedure necessary to align the timing marks.

30. Install the fixed timing chain guide and bolts and tighten to 106 inch lbs. (12 Nm).

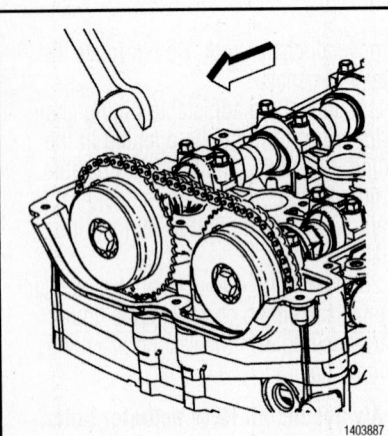

Fig. 111 Verify that all of the colored links and the appropriate timing marks are still aligned. If they are not, repeat the portion of the procedure necessary to align the timing marks

31. Install the upper timing chain guide and bolts. Tighten the bolts to 89 inch lbs. (10 Nm).

32. Reset the timing chain tensioner by performing the following steps:
  a. Remove the snapring.
  b. Remove the piston assembly from the body of the timing chain tensioner.
  c. Install the J-45027-2 (2) into a vise.
  d. Install the notch end of the piston assembly into the J-45027-2 (2).
  e. Using the J-45027-1 (1), turn the ratchet cylinder into the piston.
  f. Reinstall the piston assembly into the body of the tensioner.
  g. Install the snapring.

33. Inspect the timing chain tensioner seal for damage. If damaged, replace the seal.

34. Inspect to ensure all dirt and debris is removed from the timing chain tensioner threaded hole in the cylinder head.

➡**Ensure the timing chain tensioner seal is centered throughout the torque procedure to eliminate the possibility of an oil leak.**

➡**The timing chain tensioner is released by compressing it 0.079 inch (2 mm), which will release the locking mechanism in the ratchet. The crankshaft balancer must be installed in order to release the tensioner.**

35. Install the timing chain tensioner assembly and tighten to 55 ft. lbs. (75 Nm).

36. Install EN-48953 locking tool and tighten the bolts into the cylinder head to 89 inch lbs. (10 Nm).

37. Using a torque wrench, tighten the intake camshaft actuator bolt to 22 ft. lbs. (30 Nm), plus 100 degrees using the J-45059 angle meter.

38. Using a torque wrench, tighten the exhaust camshaft actuator bolt to 22 ft. lbs. (30 Nm), plus 100 degrees using the J-45059 angle meter.

39. Remove EN-48953 locking tool.

40. Install the timing chain oiling nozzle and tighten the bolt to 89 inch lbs. (10 Nm).

41. Apply sealant compound to the thread of the timing chain guide bolt access hole plug. (GM threadlocker P/N 12345382 in US, and 10953489 in Canada.)

42. Install the timing chain guide bolt access hole plug and tighten it to 55 ft. lbs. (75 Nm).

2011 Models

See Figures 114 through 117.

Refer to 2010 2.2L and 2.4L procedure, as many images are the same.

1. Remove the number 1 cylinder spark plug. Refer to Spark Plug replacement.

2. Rotate the crankshaft in the engine rotational direction clockwise, until the number 1 piston is at top dead center (TDC) on the exhaust stroke.

3. Remove the camshaft cover. Refer to Camshaft Cover replacement.

4. Remove the engine front cover.

5. Remove the upper timing chain guide bolts and guide. Refer to image for 2010 2.2L and 2.4L engines.

➡**Important: Remove the timing chain tensioner to unload chain tension before the timing chain is removed. If you do not remove the timing chain tensioner first, the timing chain will become cocked and it will be difficult to remove.**

6. Remove the timing chain tensioner.

7. Install a 24 mm wrench on the hex on the exhaust camshaft in order to hold the camshaft.

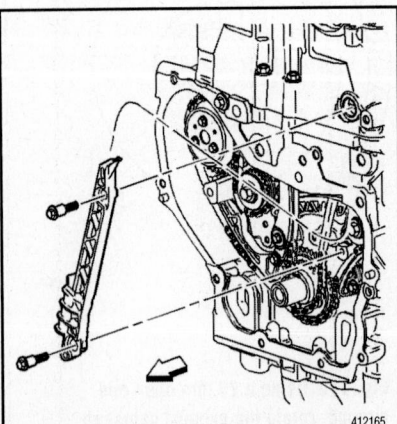

Fig. 112 Install the fixed timing chain guide and bolts and tighten to 106 inch lbs. (12 Nm)

Fig. 113 Install the upper timing chain guide and bolts. Tighten the bolts to 89 inch lbs. (10 Nm)

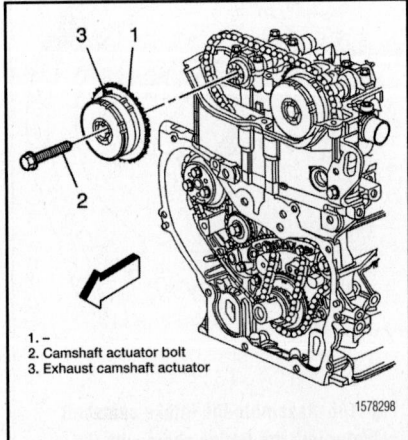

1. –
2. Camshaft actuator bolt
3. Exhaust camshaft actuator

Fig. 114 Exhaust camshaft actuator bolt (2) and actuators (1, 3)

8. Remove and discard the exhaust camshaft actuator bolt (2).

9. Remove the exhaust camshaft actuator (1, 3) from the camshaft and timing chain.

10. Remove the timing chain tensioner guide bolt and guide.

11. Remove the fixed timing chain guide access plug.

12. Remove the fixed timing chain guide bolts and guide.

13. Install a 24 mm wrench on the hex on the intake camshaft in order to hold the camshaft.

14. Remove and discard the intake camshaft actuator bolt.

15. Remove the intake camshaft actuator, and the timing chain through the top of the cylinder head.

➥**Ecotec 4 cylinder engines with SIDI-Direct Injection, the lower timing chain crank gear may be equipped with a second spacing washer installed in front of the lower timing chain crank gear. The outer spacer/washer is in between the crank/balancer pulley and the lower timing gear and may remain in place when the pulley is removed. The spacer/washer has a dot/mark on its surface that may be mistaken for the lower timing mark. If applicable, the washer must be removed in order to view the correct timing mark on the lower crank gear.**

16. Remove the outer friction washer (1) if equipped.

17. Ensure the crankshaft gear timing mark (2) is in the 5 o'clock position

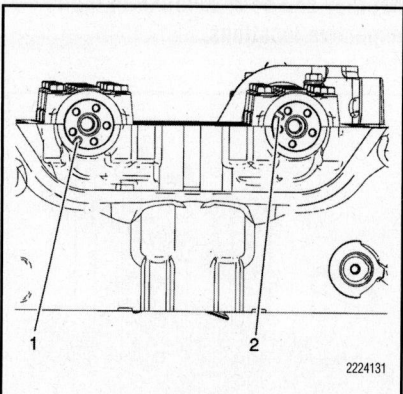

Fig. 115 On 2.2L engines, ensure the intake camshaft notch is in the 10 o'clock position (2) and the exhaust camshaft notch is in the 7 o'clock position (1). The number 1 piston should be at TDC, crankshaft key at 12 o'clock

and crankshaft key is in the 12 o'clock position.

18. Remove the crankshaft sprocket (3).

19. Remove the inner friction washer (1).

To install:

20. On 2.2L engines, ensure the intake camshaft notch is in the 10 o'clock position (2) and the exhaust camshaft notch is in the 7 o'clock position (1). The number 1 piston should be at TDC, crankshaft key at 12 o'clock.

21. On 2.4L engines, ensure the intake camshaft notch is in the 5 o'clock position (2) and the exhaust camshaft notch is in the 7 o'clock position (1). The number 1 piston should be at TDC, crankshaft key at 12 o'clock. (See image for 2010, 2.2L and 2.4L.)

➥**Ecotec 4 cylinder engines with SIDI-Direct Injection, the lower timing chain crank gear may be equipped with a second spacing washer installed in front of the lower timing chain crank gear. The outer spacer/washer is in between the crank/balancer pulley and the lower timing gear and may remain in place when the pulley is removed. The spacer/washer has a dot/mark on its surface that may be mistaken for the lower timing mark. If applicable, the washer must be removed in order to view the correct timing mark on the lower crank gear.**

22. Install the inner friction washer.

23. Install the crankshaft sprocket with the timing mark (2) is in the 5 o'clock position and facing outward.

24. Install the outer friction washer, if equipped.

➥**There are 3 colored links on the timing chain. Two links are of matching color, and 1 link is of a unique color. Use the following procedure to line up the links with the actuators. Orient the chain so that the colored links are visible.**

➥**Always use new actuator bolts.**

25. Assemble the intake camshaft actuator into the timing chain with the timing mark lined up with the uniquely colored link.

26. Lower the timing chain through the opening in the cylinder head. Use care to ensure that the chain goes around both sides of the cylinder block bosses.

27. Install the intake camshaft actuator onto the intake camshaft while aligning the dowel pin into the camshaft slot.

28. Hand-tighten the new intake camshaft actuator bolt.

29. Route the timing chain around the crankshaft sprocket and line up the first matching colored link with the timing mark on the crankshaft sprocket, in approximately the 5 o'clock position.

30. Install the friction washer, if applicable.

31. Rotate the crankshaft clockwise to remove all chain slack. Do not rotate the intake camshaft.

32. Install the adjustable timing chain guide down through the opening in the cylinder head and install the adjustable timing chain bolt. Tighten the adjustable timing chain guide bolt to 89 inch lbs. (10 Nm).

➥**Always install NEW actuator bolts.**

33. Install the exhaust camshaft actuator into the timing chain with the timing mark lined up with the second matching colored link.

34. Install the exhaust camshaft actuator onto the exhaust camshaft, aligning the dowel pin into the camshaft slot.

35. Use 24 mm open ended wrench, rotate the exhaust camshaft approximately 45 degrees until the dowel pin in the camshaft actuator goes into the camshaft slot.

36. When the actuator seats on the cam, tighten the new exhaust camshaft actuator bolt Hand-tight.

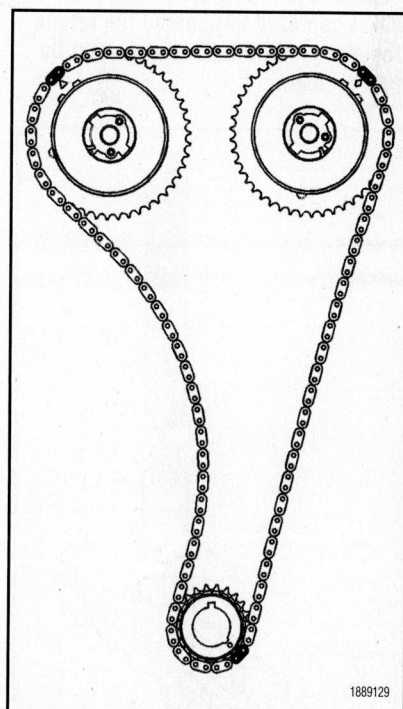

Fig. 116 Verify that all of the colored links and the appropriate timing marks are still aligned. If they are not aligned, repeat the portion of the procedure necessary to align the timing marks

37. Verify that all of the colored links and the appropriate timing marks are still aligned. If they are not aligned, repeat the portion of the procedure necessary to align the timing marks.

38. Install the fixed timing chain guide and bolts. Tighten the fixed timing chain guide bolts to 89 inch lbs. (10 Nm).

39. Install the upper timing chain guide and bolts. Tighten the upper timing chain guide bolts to 89 inch lbs. (10 Nm).

40. Reset the timing chain tensioner by performing the following steps:

 a. Remove the snapring.

 b. Remove the piston assembly from the body of the timing chain tensioner.

 c. Install the EN-45027-2 tool (2) into a vise.

 d. Install the notch end of the piston assembly into the EN-45027-2 tool (2).

 e. Using the EN-45027-1 tool (1), turn the ratchet cylinder into the piston.

 f. Reinstall the piston assembly into the body of the tensioner.

 g. Install the snapring.

41. Inspect the timing chain tensioner seal for damage Replace damaged seals.

42. Inspect to ensure all dirt and debris is removed from the timing chain tensioner threaded hole in the cylinder head.

➡ **Ensure the timing chain tensioner seal is centered throughout the torque procedure to eliminate the possibility of an oil leak.**

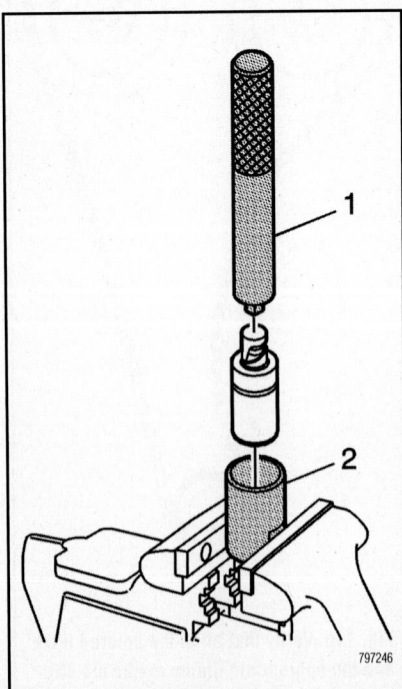

Fig. 117 Reset the timing chain tensioner with the EN-45027

43. Install the timing chain tensioner assembly. Tighten the timing chain tensioner to 55 ft. lbs. (75 Nm).

44. The timing chain tensioner is released by compressing it 0.079 in. (2 mm), which will release the locking mechanism in the ratchet. To release the timing chain tensioner, use a suitable tool with a rubber tip on the end. Feed the tool down through the cam drive chest to rest on the cam chain. Then give a sharp jolt diagonally downwards to release the tensioner.

45. Install EN-48953 locking tool (1) and tighten the bolts into the cylinder head to 89 inch lbs. (10 Nm).

46. Using a torque wrench, tighten the camshaft actuator bolt to 22 ft. lbs. (30 Nm) plus 100 degrees using the EN-45059 angle meter.

47. Remove the EN-48953 locking tool.

48. Install the timing chain oiling nozzle. Tighten the timing chain oiling nozzle bolt to 89 inch lbs. (10 Nm).

49. Apply sealant compound to the thread of the timing chain guide bolt access hole plug. (GM Threadlocker P/N 12345382 in the US and 10953489 in Canada.)

50. Install the timing chain guide bolt access hole plug. Tighten the access hole plug to 66 ft. lbs. (90 Nm).

51. Install the engine front cover.

52. Install the camshaft cover. Refer to Camshaft Cover replacement.

53. Install the number 1 cylinder spark plug. Refer to Spark Plug replacement.

INTAKE AND EXHAUST CAMSHAFT, BEARING CAP, AND LASH ADJUSTER

CAMSHAFT CLEANING & INSPECTION

See Figure 118.

1. Inspect the camshaft journals and lobes for wear or scoring.

2. Inspect the camshaft sprocket alignment notch for damage.

3. Inspect the camshaft cover for damage or loose oil control baffles.

➡ **For 2.0L engines, do not disconnect the PCV hose from the camshaft cover. The PCV hose and camshaft cover cannot be serviced individually.**

4. For 2.0L engines: Inspect the PCV hose attached to the camshaft cover. Replace the camshaft cover if the PCV hose is damaged.

5. Clean the camshaft cover.

6. Wash the camshaft in solvent.

7. Oil the camshaft.

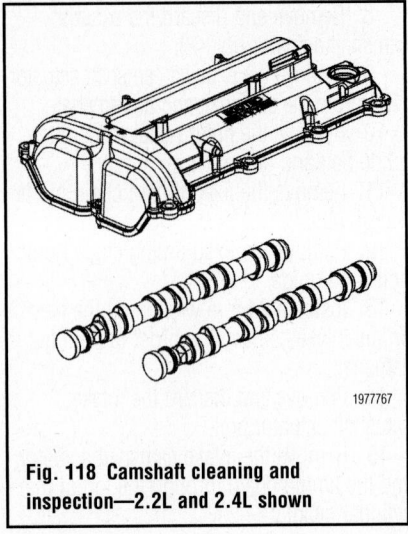

Fig. 118 Camshaft cleaning and inspection—2.2L and 2.4L shown

8. Inspect the camshaft cover for cracks or other signs of damage.

REMOVAL & INSTALLATION

See Figures 119 through 123.

➡ **Remove each bolt on each cap one turn at a time until there is no spring tension pushing on the camshaft.**

1. Mark the camshaft caps to ensure they are installed in the same position.

2. Remove the camshaft cap bolts.

3. For the intake camshaft: Remove the camshaft caps.

4. For the exhaust camshaft: Remove the camshaft caps ensuring they are marked and refitted in the same position on assembly.

5. Remove the camshaft.

➡ **Keep all of the roller finger followers and hydraulic lash adjusters in order so that they can be reinstalled in their respective locations.**

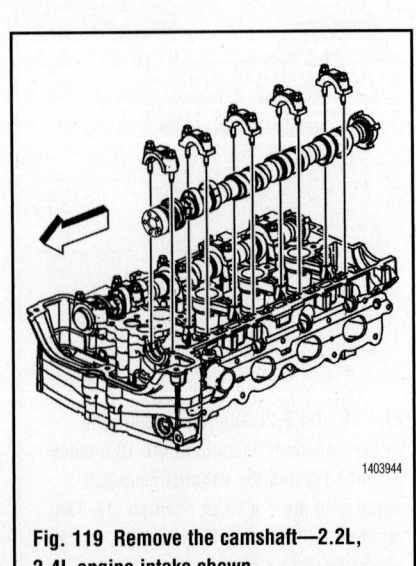

Fig. 119 Remove the camshaft—2.2L, 2.4L engine intake shown

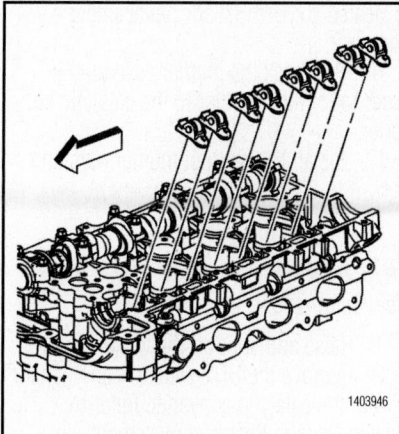

Fig. 120 Remove the camshaft roller finger followers—intake shown

6. Remove the camshaft roller finger followers.

7. Remove the hydraulic lash adjusters.

To install:

8. Install the hydraulic lash adjusters into their bores in the cylinder head. Apply lubricant GM P/N 12345501 (Canadian P/N 992704) or an equivalent.

9. Lubricate the valve tips with GM P/N 12345501 (Canadian P/N 992704) or an equivalent.

➡**Return used roller followers their original position on the camshaft. If you replace the camshaft, you must also replace the roller followers actuated by the camshaft.**

10. Position the roller followers on the tip of the valve stem and on the lash adjuster. Apply lubricant GM P/N 12345501 (Canadian P/N 992704) or equivalent.

➡**The engine is timed top-dead center exhaust stroke.**

Fig. 121 Lubricate the valve tips

11. For 2011 2.2L engines, ensure the intake camshaft notch is in the 10 o'clock position (2) and the exhaust camshaft notch is in the 7 o'clock position (1). The number 1 piston should be at top dead center (TDC), crankshaft key at 12 o'clock.

➡**The engine is timed top-dead center exhaust stroke.**

12. For 2011 2.4L engines, ensure the intake camshaft notch is in the 5 o'clock position and the exhaust camshaft notch is in the 7 o'clock position. The number 1 piston should be at top dead center (TDC), crankshaft key at 12 o'clock.

13. For 2010 engines: When installing the camshafts, ensure the intake camshaft notch is in the 5 o'clock position and the exhaust camshaft notch is in the 7 o'clock position. The number 1 piston should be at top dead center (TDC), crankshaft key at 12 o'clock.

14. Set the camshaft on top of the roller followers in the camshaft bearing journals. Lubricate with GM P/N 12345501 (Canadian P/N 992704) or an equivalent.

15. For the 2010 2.0L only: Rotate the oil seal in the groove of the number one camshaft journal so the split line (1) is at approximately the 12:00 position before installing the camshaft caps.

16. Install the camshaft caps and hand start the camshaft cap bolts.

17. Lubricate and tighten the camshaft cap bolts in increments of 3 turns until they are seated.

18. Tighten the camshaft caps to 89 inch lbs. (10 Nm).

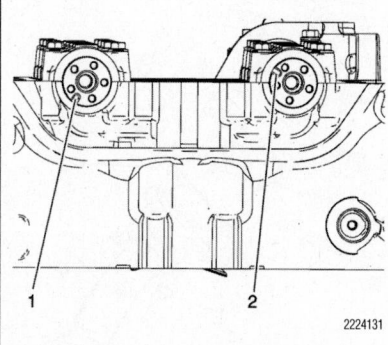

Fig. 122 For 2.2L engines: Ensure the intake camshaft notch is in the 10 o'clock position (2) and the exhaust camshaft notch is in the 7 o'clock position (1). The number 1 piston should be at top dead center (TDC) and the crankshaft key at 12 o'clock - exhaust side shown - 2011 models

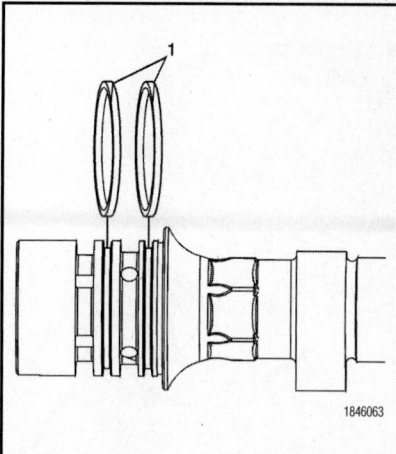

Fig. 123 Rotate the oil seal in the groove of the number one camshaft journal so the split line (1) is at approximately the 12:00 position before installing the camshaft caps—2010 models with 2.0L engine only

CATALYTIC CONVERTER

REMOVAL & INSTALLATION

2.0L Engine

See Figure 124.

1. Disconnect any electrical connectors as needed.

2. Transfer any parts as needed.

3. Raise and support the vehicle.

4. Remove the HO2S Sensor from the Catalytic Converter. Refer to Heated Oxygen Sensor Replacement—Sensor 2.

5. Remove the 4 turbocharger exhaust pipe nuts (1)

6. Remove the 3 catalytic converter nuts (2).

7. Remove the catalytic converter (3).

To install:

8. Installation is the reverse of removal, noting the following:

   a. Tighten the 4 turbocharger exhaust pipe nuts to 37 ft. lbs. (50 Nm).

   b. Tighten the 3 catalytic converter nuts to 34 ft. lbs. (46 Nm)

2.2L & 2.4L Engines

2010 Models

See Figure 125.

❊❊ WARNING

Do not bend the exhaust flex decoupler more than 3 degrees in any direction. Movement of more than 3 degrees will damage the exhaust flex decoupler.

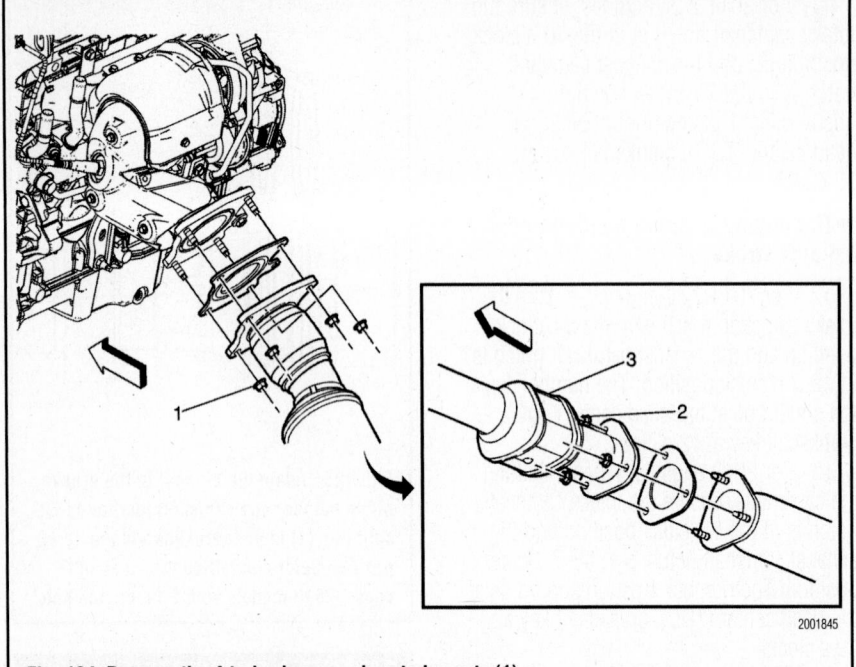

Fig. 124 Remove the 4 turbocharger exhaust pipe nuts (1)

1. Raise and suitably support the vehicle.
2. Remove the exhaust muffler nuts.
3. Pull back the muffler assembly in order to separate the muffler from the catalytic converter.
4. Remove the post catalyst heated oxygen sensor (HO2S). Refer to Heated Oxygen Sensor replacement—Sensor 2.
5. Remove the catalytic converter nuts.
6. Remove the catalytic converter from the exhaust manifold.
7. Remove and discard the catalytic converter to exhaust manifold gasket.

To install:

✷✷ WARNING

Do not bend the exhaust flex decoupler more than 3 degrees in any

direction. Movement of more than 3 degrees will damage the exhaust flex decoupler.

8. Install a NEW gasket to the exhaust manifold studs.
9. Install the catalytic converter to the exhaust manifold.
10. Install the catalytic converter nuts and tighten them to 34 ft. lbs. (46 Nm).
11. Install the post catalyst HO2S. Refer to Heated Oxygen Sensor replacement—Sensor 2.
12. Pull back the muffler assembly in order to join the muffler to the catalytic converter.
13. Install the exhaust muffler nuts and tighten to 34 ft. lbs. (46 Nm).
14. Lower the vehicle.

2011 Models

See Figure 126.

1. Raise and support the vehicle.
2. Remove the HO2 sensor 1 and sensor 2 from the catalytic converter. Refer to Heated Oxygen Sensor replacement.
3. Disconnect any electrical connectors as needed.
4. Transfer any parts as needed.
5. Remove the 3 catalytic converter nuts (1).
6. Remove the gasket (2).
7. Remove the 2 exhaust muffler nuts (3).
8. Remove the catalytic converter (4).
9. Tighten the two exhaust muffler nuts and the 3 catalytic converter nuts to 34 ft. lbs. (46 Nm).

CRANKSHAFT FRONT OIL SEAL

REMOVAL & INSTALLATION

See Figure 127.

1. Remove the crankshaft balancer.
2. Use a flat-bladed tool to remove the seal from the front cover.

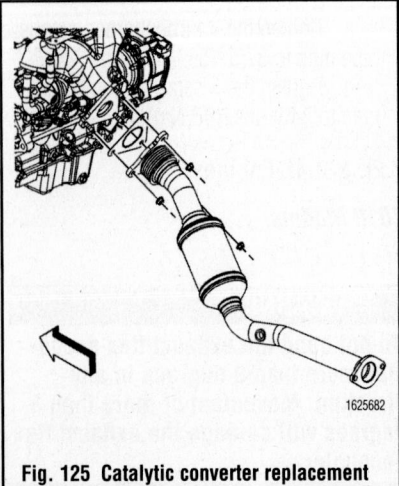

Fig. 125 Catalytic converter replacement

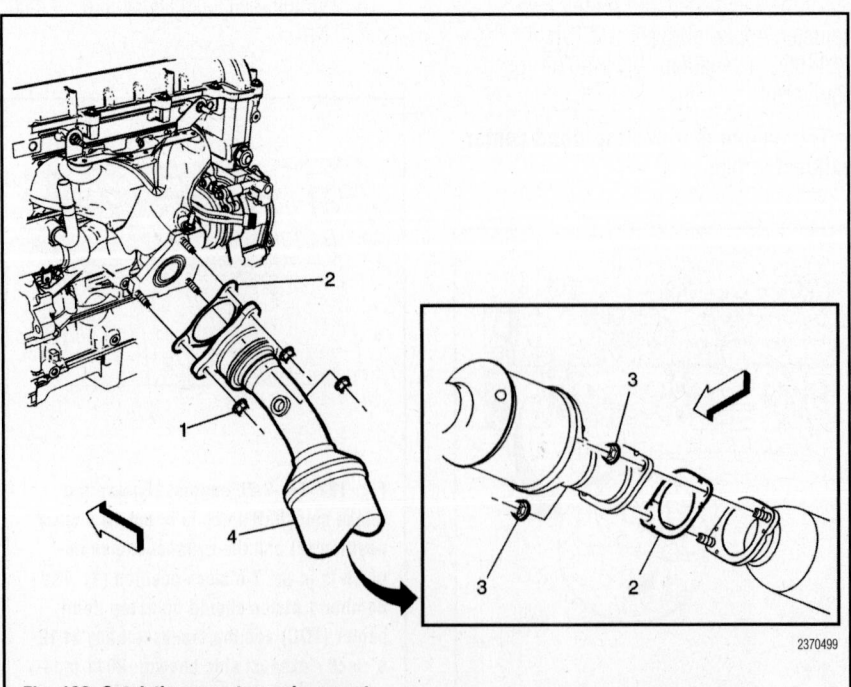

Fig. 126 Catalytic converter replacement

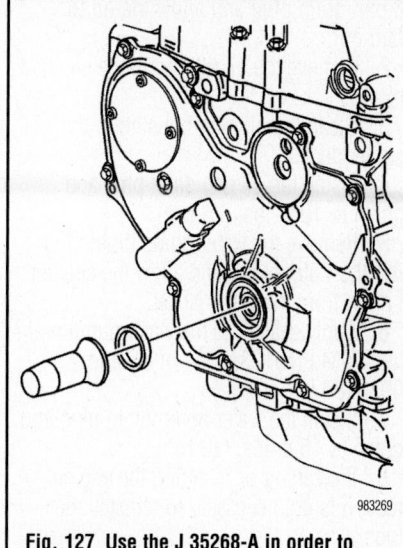

Fig. 127 Use the J 35268-A in order to install the crankshaft front oil seal to the engine front cover

To install:

3. Use the J 35268-A in order to install the crankshaft front oil seal to the engine front cover.

4. Install the crankshaft balancer.

CYLINDER HEAD

REMOVAL & INSTALLATION

See Figures 128 through 132.

At the time of publication, the manufacturer did not provide a procedure for this component. Please note the following when servicing this component.

1. Remove the cylinder head to the block bolts in sequence.

2. Discard the bolts.

✳✳ WARNING

In order to prevent damage to the valves and injectors during cylinder

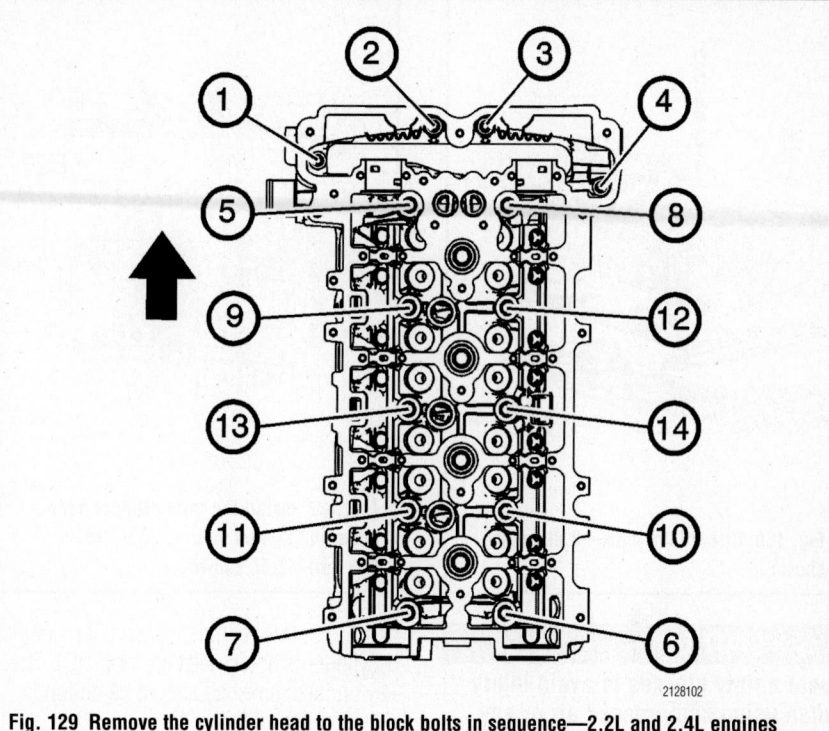

Fig. 129 Remove the cylinder head to the block bolts in sequence—2.2L and 2.4L engines

head removal, set the cylinder head on blocks.

3. Remove the cylinder head.

4. Remove the cylinder head gasket.

5. Clean all of the gasket surfaces.

6. Use the following procedures when cleaning the cylinder head and cylinder block surfaces:

a. Use a razor blade gasket scraper to clean the cylinder head and cylinder block gasket surfaces. Do not scratch or gouge any surface.

➡Do not use any other method or technique to clean these gasket surfaces.

7. Use a new razor blade for each cylinder head and cylinder block.

8. Be careful not to gouge or scratch the gasket surfaces. Do not gouge or scrape the combustion chamber surfaces. The feel of the gasket surface is important, not the appearance. There will be indentations from the gasket left in the cylinder head after all of the gasket material is removed. These small indentations will be filled in by the new gasket.

9. Hold the razor blade as parallel to the gasket surface as possible.

10. Do not use a tap to clean the cylinder head bolt holes.

11. Clean the old sealer/lube and dirt from the bolt holes.

12. Clean the bolt holes with a nylon bristle brush.

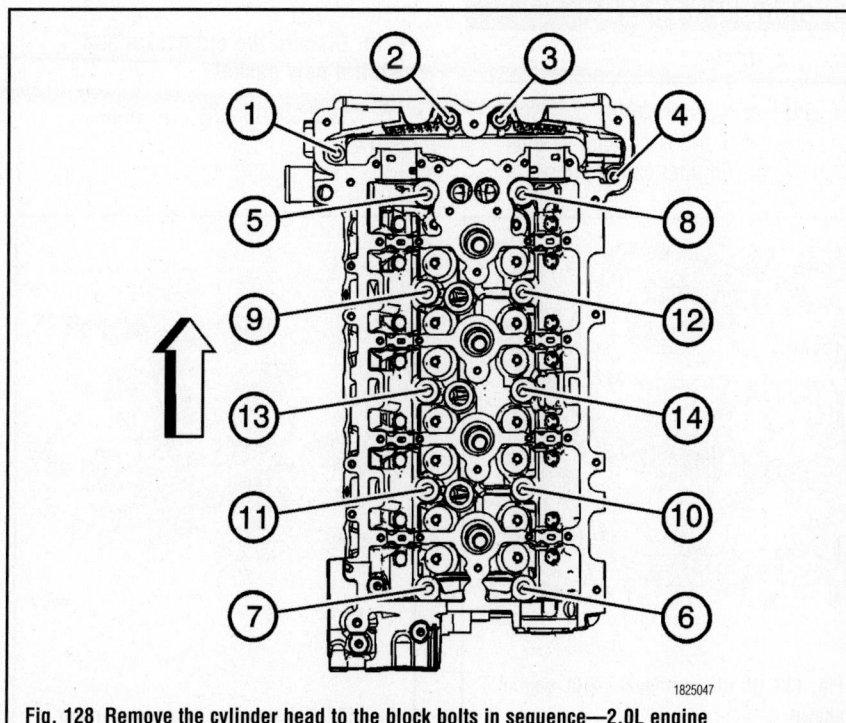

Fig. 128 Remove the cylinder head to the block bolts in sequence—2.0L engine

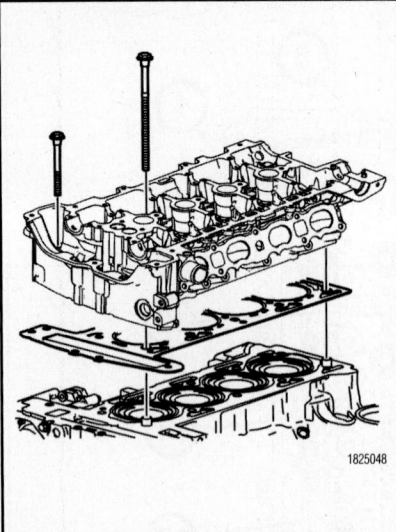

Fig. 130 Discard the bolts—2.0L engine shown

❋❋ CAUTION

Wear safety glasses to avoid injury when using compressed air or any cleaning solvent. Bodily injury may occur if fumes are inhaled or if skin is exposed to chemicals.

13. When cleaning the cylinder head bolt holes use a suitable commercial spray liquid solvent and compressed air from an extended-tip blow gun to reach the bottom of the holes.

14. Remove any broken long cylinder head bolts using the J 38188 kit.

To install:

➡**Do not use any sealing material.**

15. Install the cylinder head gasket to the block.

16. Install the cylinder head.

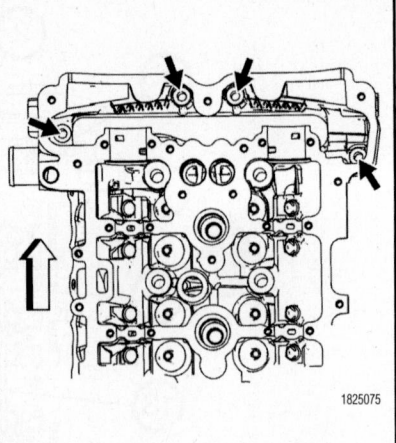

Fig. 132 Install the front cylinder head bolts and tighten them to 26 ft. lbs. (35 Nm)—2.0L shown

17. For 2.0L engines: Ensure the number 1 cylinder is at top dead center (TDC). The key on the crankshaft should be on top in the 12 o'clock position.

➡**Always use NEW cylinder head bolts.**

18. Install the cylinder head bolts.
  a. Tighten the bolts in sequence to 22 ft. lbs. (30 Nm).
  b. Tighten the bolts an additional 155 degrees in sequence using the J 45059 angle meter.

19. Install the front cylinder head bolts and tighten them to 26 ft. lbs. (35 Nm).

ENGINE OIL & FILTER

DRAIN & REFILL

See Figure 133.

1. Use the J 44887 oil filter wrench to remove the oil filter cap. Remove the

oil pan drain plug and allow the oil to drain out.

2. Remove the oil filter from the cap and discard.

3. Clean the oil filter housing in the engine block.

4. Install the oil pan drain plug and tighten to 18 ft. lbs. (25 Nm).

5. Remove the water pump drain plug from the water pump and allow the coolant to drain from the water jacket.

6. Apply sealant to the water pump drain plug. (GM P/N 12346004 in US and 10953480 in Canada.)

7. Install the water pump drain plug and tighten to 15 ft. lbs. (20 Nm).

8. If cleaning or repairing the engine block, it is not necessary to reinstall the plugs.

EXHAUST MANIFOLD

REMOVAL & INSTALLATION

2010 Models

2.0L Engine

See Figure 134.

1. Remove the turbo charger. Refer to Turbocharger replacement.

2. Remove the exhaust manifold heat shield.

3. Remove the 10 exhaust manifold nuts (1).

4. Remove the exhaust manifold (2).

5. Remove the exhaust manifold gasket (3).

➡**Tip: Discard the old gasket and install a new gasket.**

6. Installation is the reverse of removal.

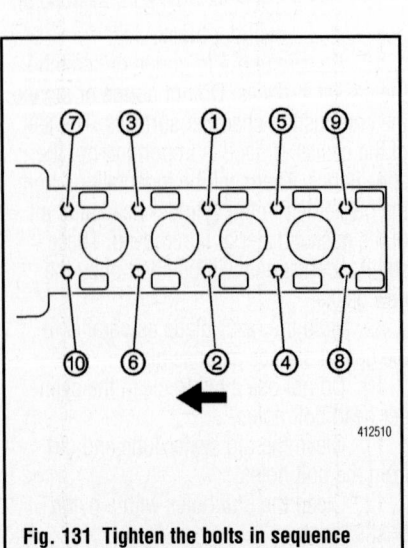

Fig. 131 Tighten the bolts in sequence

Fig. 133 Oil filter removal—2.0L engine shown

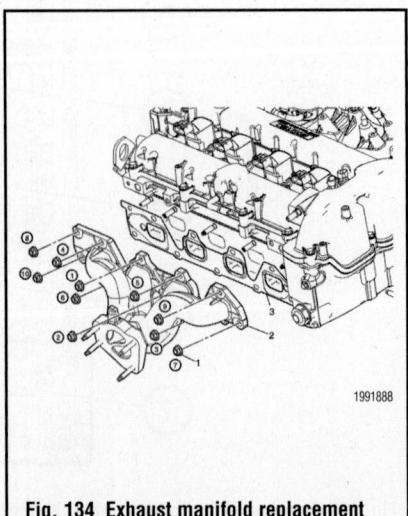

Fig. 134 Exhaust manifold replacement

7. Install 10 NEW exhaust manifold nuts.

8. Tighten them to 124 inch lbs. (14 Nm).

2.2L & 2.4L Engines

See Figures 135 and 136.

1. Remove the exhaust manifold heat shield.

2. Remove the pre catalyst heated oxygen sensor (HO2S). Refer to Heated Oxygen Sensor replacement.

3. Remove the catalytic converter. Refer to Catalytic Converter replacement.

4. Remove and discard the exhaust manifold nuts.

5. Remove the exhaust manifold.

6. Remove and discard the exhaust manifold gasket.

7. Clean the sealing surface of the engine block.

To install:

8. Install a NEW exhaust manifold gasket onto the studs.

9. Install the exhaust manifold.

→**Install the new exhaust nuts.**

10. Install NEW exhaust manifold nuts and tighten in the sequence shown to 10 ft. lbs. (14 Nm).

11. Install the catalytic converter. Refer to Catalytic Converter replacement.

12. Install the pre catalyst HO2S. Refer to Heated Oxygen Sensor replacement—Sensor.

13. Install the exhaust manifold heat shield.

2011 Models

See Figures 137 and 138.

1. Remove the exhaust manifold heat shield.

2. Disconnect the heated oxygen (HO2) sensor 1 and sensor 2. Refer to Heated Oxygen Sensor replacement.

3. Remove the catalytic converter. Refer to Catalytic Converter replacement.

4. Remove and discard the exhaust manifold nuts (1).

5. Remove the exhaust manifold (3).

6. Remove and discard the exhaust manifold gasket (2).

7. Clean the sealing surface of the engine block.

To install:

8. Install a NEW exhaust manifold gasket (2) onto the studs.

9. Install the exhaust manifold (3).

→**Install the new exhaust nuts.**

10. Install NEW exhaust manifold nuts (1) and tighten in the sequence shown to 10 ft. lbs. (14 Nm).

11. Install the catalytic converter. Refer to Catalytic Converter replacement.

12. Connect the heated oxygen (HO2) sensor 1 and sensor 2. Refer to Heated Oxygen Sensor replacement

13. Install the exhaust manifold heat shield.

INTAKE MANIFOLD

REMOVAL & INSTALLATION

2010 Models

2.0L Engine

See Figures 139 through 143.

❊❊ WARNING

Never attempt to remove the intake manifold from a hot engine, allow the engine to cool to ambient temperature. The intake manifold can be damaged if it is removed when the engine is hot.

→**The charger AIR bypass tube assembly connected from the charger AIR bypass valve solenoid to the charger AIR bypass valve tank assembly is permanently attached to the tank assembly. Do not attempt to disconnect the charger AIR bypass tube assembly at the charger AIR bypass valve tank assembly.**

1. Disconnect the charger AIR bypass tube assembly from the intake manifold.

2. Disconnect the charger AIR bypass tube with the retaining clip from the charger AIR bypass valve solenoid.

3. Remove the charger AIR bypass valve tank assembly nut (2).

→**The charger AIR bypass bolt is captured on the bracket and should not be**

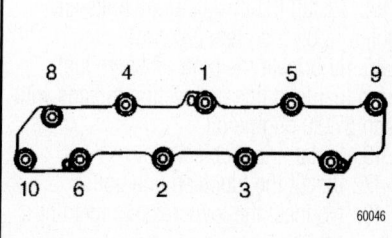

Fig. 135 Exhaust manifold replacement

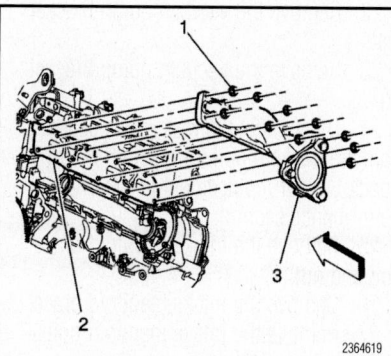

Fig. 137 Exhaust manifold nuts (1), manifold (3), and gasket (2)

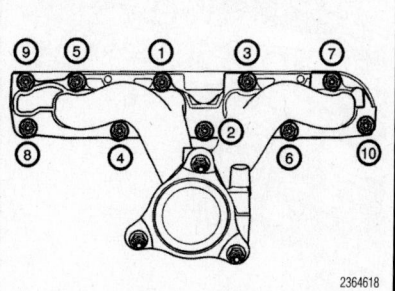

Fig. 136 Install NEW exhaust manifold nuts and tighten in the sequence shown to 10 ft. lbs. (14 Nm)

Fig. 138 Install NEW exhaust manifold nuts (1) and tighten in the sequence shown to 10 ft. lbs. (14 Nm)

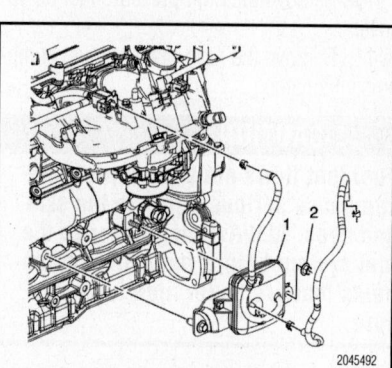

Fig. 139 Charger AIR bypass valve tank assembly nut (2) and assembly (1)

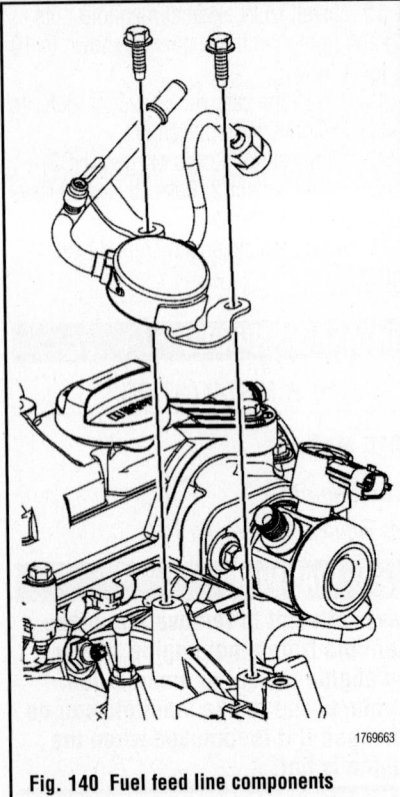

Fig. 140 Fuel feed line components

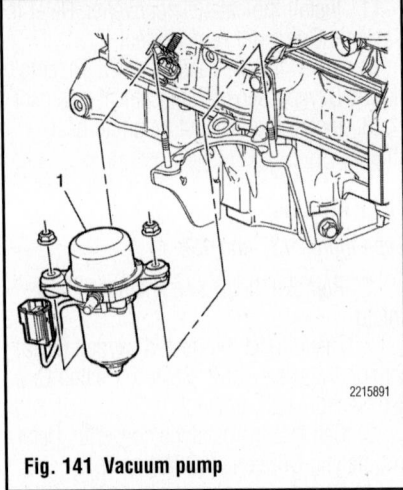

Fig. 141 Vacuum pump

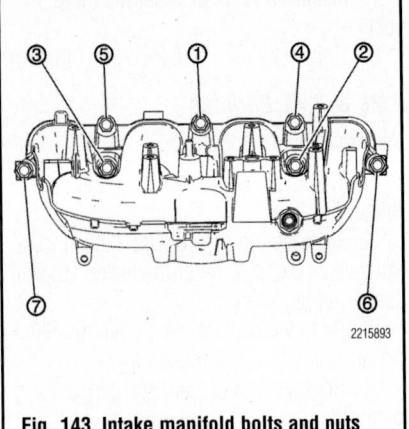

Fig. 143 Intake manifold bolts and nuts installation sequence

removed from the bracket. Loosen the bolt only until it is no longer attached to the block when removing the charger AIR bypass valve tank assembly.

4. Loosen the charger AIR bypass valve tank assembly bolt.

5. Remove the charger AIR bypass valve tank assembly (1).

6. Disconnect the remaining charger AIR bypass tubes at the turbocharger and vehicle.

7. Remove the charger AIR bypass valve solenoid bolts.

8. Remove the charger AIR bypass valve solenoid.

9. Remove the high pressure fuel pump cover bolts.

10. Remove the high pressure fuel pump cover.

11. Remove the high pressure fuel pump noise insulator.

❊❊ CAUTION

Fuel that flows out at high pressure can cause serious injury to the skin and eyes. ALWAYS depressurize the fuel system before removing components that are under high fuel pressure.

12. Loosen and disconnect the fuel feed line tube nut.

13. Remove the fuel feed line bolts.

14. Remove the fuel feed line.

15. Inspect the fuel feed line nut for damaged threads.

16. Inspect the fuel feed line sealing bail for damage or debris.

17. Replace the fuel feed line if any damage is found.

18. Remove the throttle body bolts.

19. Remove the throttle body. Refer to the Fuel section for Throttle Body Removal & Installation.

20. Remove the vacuum pump nuts.

21. Remove the vacuum pump (1).

22. Remove the vacuum pump bracket bolts.

23. Remove the vacuum pump bracket (1).

24. Disconnect the rear knock sensor from the intake manifold brace. Refer to Knock Sensor replacement in the Engine Performance section.

25. Remove the intake manifold brace bolt and nut.

26. Remove the intake manifold brace.

27. Remove the intake manifold bolts and nuts.

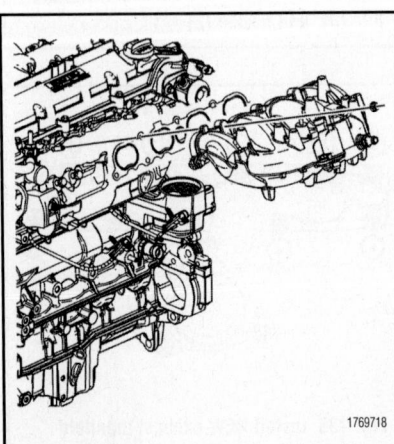

Fig. 142 Intake manifold replacement

28. Remove the intake manifold.

29. Remove the intake manifold gasket.

To install:

30. Install a NEW intake manifold gasket.

31. Install the intake manifold.

32. Install the intake manifold bolts and nuts finger tight.

33. Tighten the intake manifold bolts and nuts in sequence a first pass to 44 inch lbs. (5 Nm).

34. Tighten the intake manifold bolts and nuts in sequence a final pass to 18 ft. lbs. (25 Nm).

35. Install the intake manifold brace.

36. Install the intake manifold brace bolt and nut and tighten to 18 ft. lbs. (25 Nm).

37. Connect the rear knock sensor to the intake manifold brace.

38. Install the vacuum pump bracket.

39. Install the vacuum pump bracket bolt to the lower crankcase. Tighten the bolt to 43 ft. lbs. (58 Nm).

40. Install the vacuum pump bracket bolts to the oil pan. Tighten the bolts to 16 ft. lbs. (22 Nm).

41. Install the vacuum pump onto the vacuum pump bracket.

42. Install the vacuum pump nuts and tighten to 80 inch lbs. (9 Nm).

43. Install the throttle body.

44. Install the throttle body bolts and tighten to 89 inch lbs. (10 Nm).

45. Lubricate the high pressure fuel pump fuel feed line connection threads with clean 5W30 engine oil.

46. Install the fuel feed line.

47. Install the fuel feed line bolts.

48. Connect the low pressure fuel line nut.

    a. Tighten the low pressure fuel line nut to 22 ft. lbs. (30 Nm).

    b. Tighten the fuel feed line bolts to 89 inch lbs. (10 Nm).

49. Install the high pressure fuel pump noise insulator.

50. Install the high pressure fuel pump cover.

51. Install the high pressure fuel pump cover bolts and tighten to 89 inch lbs. (10 Nm).

52. Install the charger AIR bypass valve solenoid with charger AIR bypass tube assemblies.

53. Install the charger AIR bypass valve solenoid bolts and tighten to 89 inch lbs. (10 Nm).

➡**Ensure proper connection of the charger AIR bypass tube assemblies and retaining clips to maintain proper pressure. Connect each tube to the appropriate location.**

54. Connect the charger AIR bypass tube assemblies and clamps from the charger AIR bypass valve solenoid to the turbocharger and vehicle.

55. Install the charger AIR bypass valve tank assembly (1).

56. Tighten the charger AIR bypass valve tank assembly bolt to 18 ft. lbs. (25 Nm).

57. Install the charger AIR bypass valve tank assembly nut (2) and tighten to 18 ft. lbs. (25 Nm).

➡**Ensure proper connection of the charger AIR bypass tube assemblies and retaining clips to maintain proper pressure. Connect each tube to the appropriate location. The tube with retaining clamp located on the charger AIR bypass valve tank assembly left side connects to the charger AIR bypass valve solenoid.**

58. The right side permanently attached tube connects to the intake manifold.

59. Connect the appropriate charger AIR bypass tube assembly to the intake manifold.

60. Connect the final charger AIR bypass tube assembly from the charger AIR bypass valve tank assembly to the charger AIR bypass valve solenoid.

2.2L & 2.4L Engines

See Figures 144 through 148.

❋❋ WARNING

Never attempt to remove the intake manifold from a hot engine, allow the engine to cool to ambient temperature. The intake manifold can be damaged if it is removed when the engine is hot.

1. Remove the evaporative emission (EVAP) canister valve tube (1).

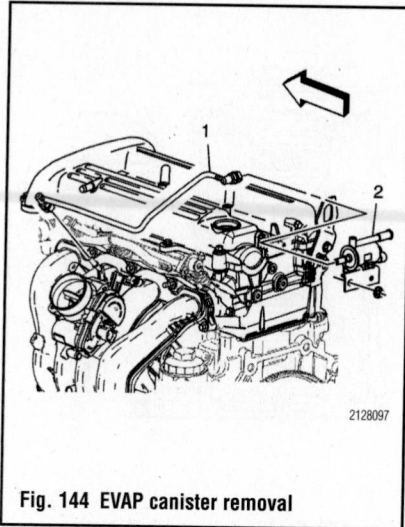

Fig. 144 EVAP canister removal

2. Remove the EVAP canister valve (2).

3. Remove the throttle body bolts.

4. Remove the throttle body.

5. Remove fuel pipes and clip. Remove the fuel rail assembly.

6. Disassemble the fuel rail assembly. Refer to Fuel Injector replacement.

7. Remove the fuel injector tip insulators and discard.

8. Remove the intake manifold retaining nuts and bolts.

9. Remove the intake manifold.

10. Remove the intake manifold gasket, if necessary. The gasket can be used again if it is not damaged.

11. If the intake manifold needs to be replaced, transfer the throttle body to the new intake manifold.

To install:

12. Install the intake manifold studs (1) in the manifold face and tighten them to 53 inch lbs. (6 Nm).

Fig. 145 Fuel rail assembly

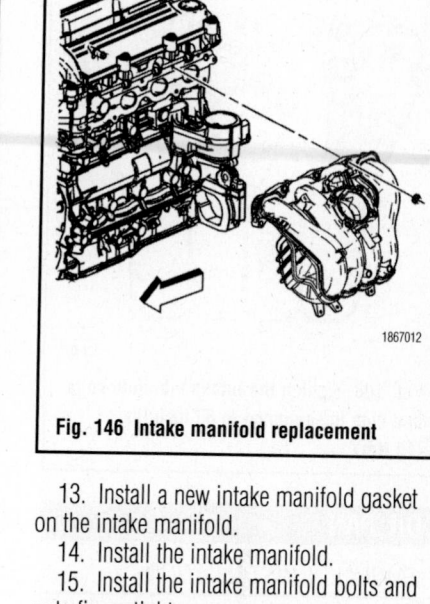

Fig. 146 Intake manifold replacement

13. Install a new intake manifold gasket on the intake manifold.

14. Install the intake manifold.

15. Install the intake manifold bolts and nuts finger tight.

16. Tighten the intake manifold bolts and nuts in sequence to 89 inch lbs. (10 Nm).

17. Lubricate the NEW fuel injector tip insulators with engine oil.

18. Install NEW fuel injector tip insulators.

19. Lubricate the fuel injector oil rings with engine oil.

20. Install the fuel rail assembly.

21. Install the fuel rail fastener and tighten to 89 inch lbs. (10 Nm).

22. Install a new throttle body gasket.

23. Install the throttle body.

24. Install the throttle body bolts and tighten them to 89 inch lbs. (10 Nm).

25. Install the EVAP canister valve and tighten it to 18 ft. lbs. (25 Nm).

26. Install the EVAP canister valve tube.

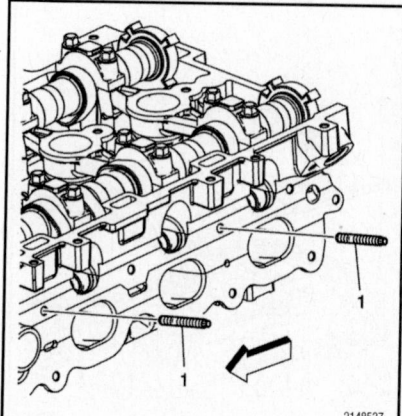

Fig. 147 Install the intake manifold studs (1) in the manifold face and tighten them to 53 inch lbs. (6 Nm).

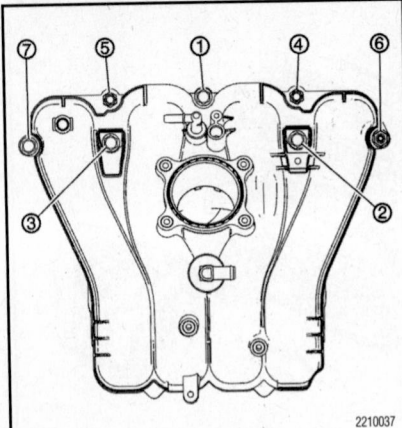

Fig. 148 Tighten the intake manifold bolts and nuts in sequence to 89 inch lbs. (10 Nm)

OIL PAN

REMOVAL & INSTALLATION

See Figures 149 through 151, 000.

At the time of publication, the manufacturer did not provide a procedure for this component. Please note the following when servicing this component:

1. Remove the oil pan bolts.
2. Remove the oil pan at pry points.

To install:

3. Ensure the oil pan and mounting surface on the lower crankcase are free of all oil and debris.

4. For the 2.0L engine: Apply a 3.5 mm bead of sealant around the perimeter of the oil pan and the oil suction port opening.

5. For the 2.2L and 2.4L engines:
- The lower crankcase surface must be free of contamination prior to applying the sealer.

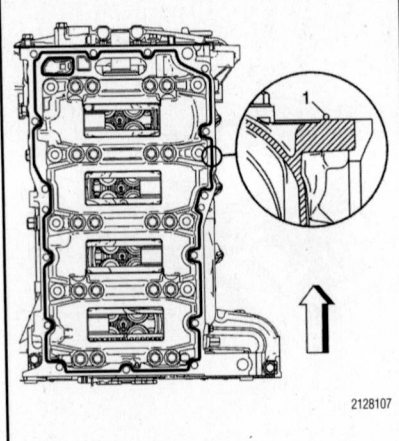

Fig. 150 For the 2.2L and 2.4L engines: Apply a 2.25 mm bead of sealer (1) on the level part of the flange next to the chamfer around the perimeter of the oil pan and the oil suction port opening

- Install and align the oil pan to block within 20 minutes of applying the sealer.
- The oil pan must be fastened to final torque specification within 60 minutes of applying the sealer.

6. For the 2.2L and 2.4L engines: Apply a 2.25 mm bead of sealer (1) on the level part of the flange next to the chamfer around the perimeter of the oil pan and the oil suction port opening.

7. The specified sealant for all engines is GM P/N 12378521 (US) and 88901148 (Canada).

8. Install the oil pan. Install the oil pan bolts and tighten in sequence to 18 ft. lbs. (25 Nm).

PISTON AND RING

POSITIONING

2.0L Engine

See Figures 152 through 154.

Piston and Connecting Rod Assembly

➡**Install the piston onto the connecting rod with the arrow oriented toward the front of the engine.**

1. Assemble the connecting rod and the piston.

✳✳ WARNING

Install the piston pin retainers correctly in the retaining groove during assembly in order to avoid engine damage.

2. Use the following procedure to assemble the piston pin and the retainer:
   a. Coat the piston pin with oil.
   b. Using the EN-46745 remover/installer and the EN-46745-4 adapter, install one side of one piston pin retainer into the retaining groove. Rotate the retainer until it fully seats in the groove.
   c. Install the connecting rod and the piston pin. Push the piston pin until it bottoms in the previously installed retainer.
   d. Using the EN-46745 remover/installer and the EN-46745-4

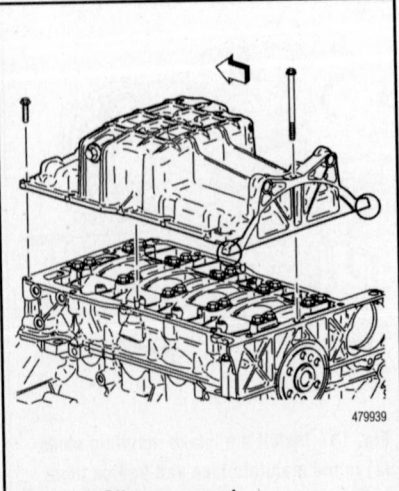

Fig. 149 Oil pan removal

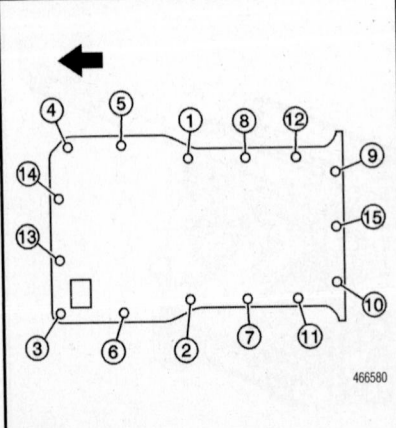

Fig. 151 Install the oil pan bolts and tighten in sequence to 18 ft. lbs. (25 Nm)

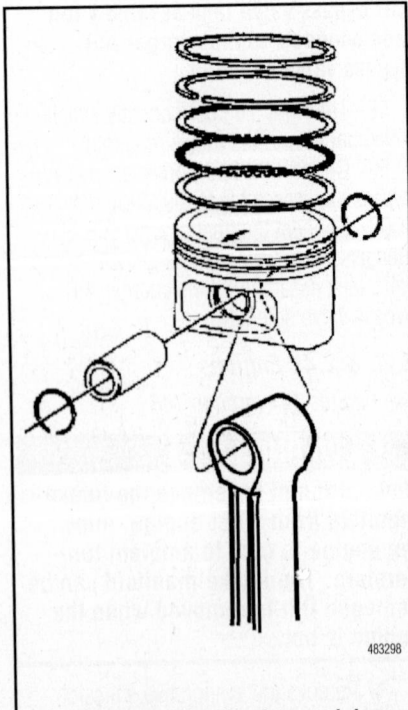

Fig. 152 Assembling the piston and rings

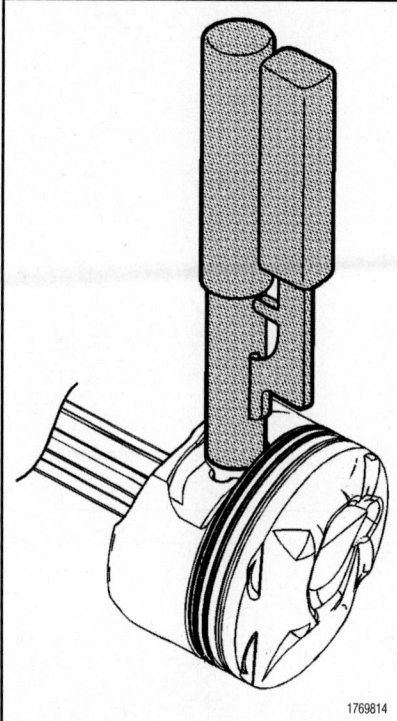

Fig. 153 the EN-46745 remover/installer and the EN-46745-4 adapter , install one side of one piston pin retainer into the retaining groove. Rotate the retainer until it fully seats in the groove

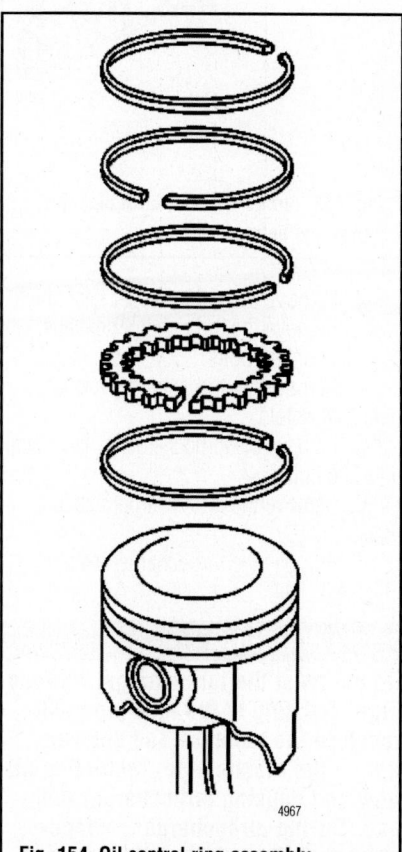

Fig. 154 Oil control ring assembly

adapter, install the second piston pin retainer.

e. Ensure that the piston moves freely.

✱✱ WARNING

Use a piston ring expander to install the piston rings. The rings may be damaged if expanded more than necessary.

3. Install the following components of the oil control ring assembly—bottom ring:

a. The expander
b. The lower oil control ring
c. The upper control ring

4. Install the lower compression ring—second ring. Place the manufacturer's mark facing up.

a. Install the upper compression ring—top ring.

2.2L & 2.4L Engines

See Figures 155 through 158.

➡Install the piston onto the connecting rod with the arrow on top of the piston toward the front oriented toward the front of the engine.

➡The cast boss (1) can be in either or both locations depending on displacement.

1. The cast boss (1), on the underside of the piston, must go to the rear of the block.

2. The larger feature (1), at the split line located on one side of the connecting rod, must go to the front of the block.

3. Assemble the connecting rod and the piston.

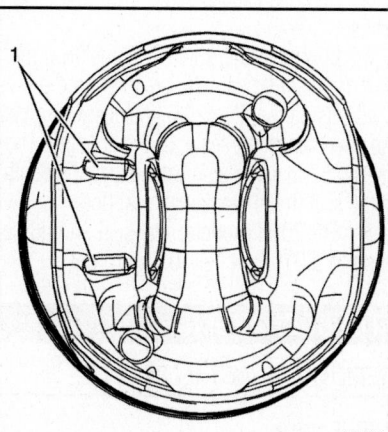

Fig. 155 The cast boss (1) can be in either or both locations depending on displacement

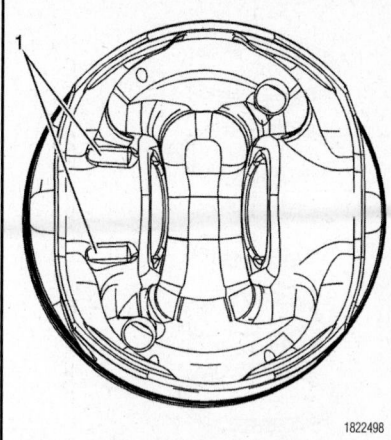

Fig. 156 The cast boss (1), on the underside of the piston, must go to the rear of the block

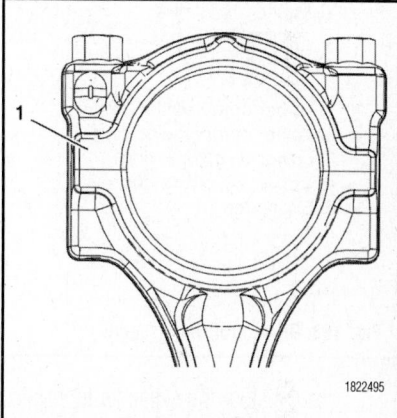

Fig. 157 The larger feature (1), at the split line located on one side of the connecting rod, must go to the front of the block

✱✱ WARNING

Install the piston pin retainers correctly in the retaining groove during assembly in order to avoid engine damage.

4. Use the following procedure to assemble the piston pin and the retainer:

a. Coat the piston pin with oil.
b. Install one side of one piston pin retainer into the retaining groove using EN-46745 installer. Rotate the retainer until it fully seats in the groove.
c. Install the connecting rod and the piston pin. Push the piston pin until it bottoms in the previously installed retainer.
d. Install the second piston pin retainer, using EN-46745 installer.
e. Ensure that the piston moves freely.

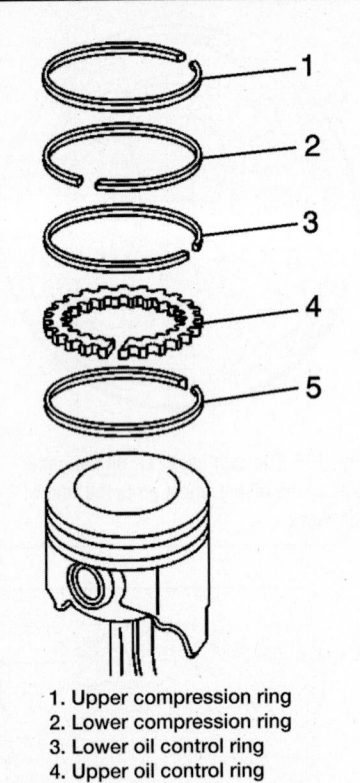

1. Upper compression ring
2. Lower compression ring
3. Lower oil control ring
4. Upper oil control ring
5. Expander

2146346

Fig. 158 Oil control ring assembly

5. Use a piston ring expander to install the piston rings. The rings may be damaged if expanded more than necessary.

6. Install the following components of the oil control ring assembly (bottom ring):

 a. The expander (5)
 b. The lower oil control ring (4)
 c. The upper control ring (3)

7. Install the lower compression ring (2). Place the manufacturer's mark facing up.

8. Install the upper compression ring (1).

CRANKSHAFT REAR OIL SEAL

REMOVAL & INSTALLATION

See Figures 159 and 160.

Crankshaft Rear Oil Seal Replacement
1. Remove the crankshaft (1) from the block.

2. Remove the crankshaft rear oil seal (2).

➡**Do not damage the outside diameter of the crankshaft or chamber with any tool.**

3. Pry out the crankshaft rear oil seal using a flat-bladed tool.

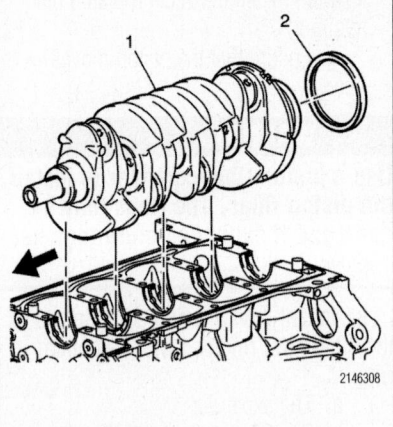

Fig. 159 Crankshaft (1) and crankshaft rear oil seal (2)—2011 shown

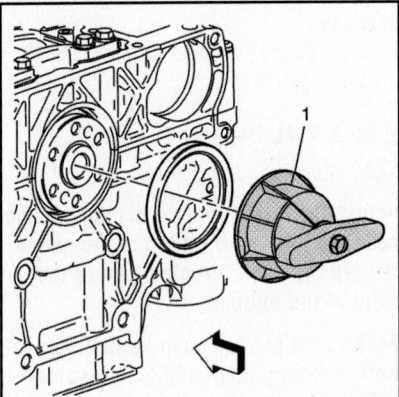

Fig. 160 Using the EN-42067 installer (1), press the new crankshaft seal into the housing. The EN-42067 installer also establishes the depth of the seal in the crankshaft seal bore—2011 shown, 2010 similar

To install:

4. Remove excess sealer from the seal recess.

5. Lubricate the outside diameter of the new crankshaft seal with clean engine oil.

6. Using the EN-42067 installer (1), press the new crankshaft seal into the housing. The EN-42067 installer also establishes the depth of the seal in the crankshaft seal bore.

7. For 2010 models: The seal should be flush to 0.0197 inches (0.5 mm) deep.

TURBOCHARGER

REMOVAL & INSTALLATION

2.0L Engine

See Figures 161 through 170.

1. Remove the turbocharger heat shield bolts.

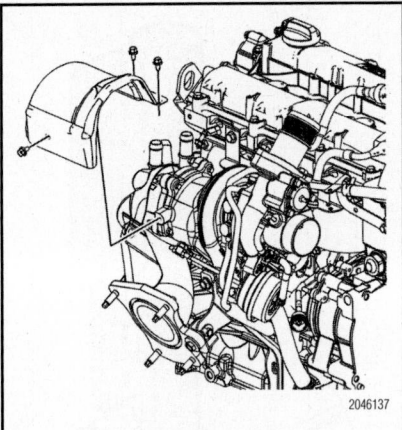

Fig. 161 Turbocharger heat shield and bolts

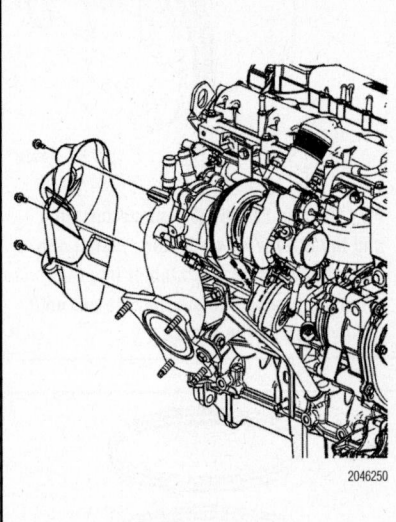

Fig. 162 Turbocharger exhaust pipe heat shield and bolts

2. Remove the turbocharger heat shield.

3. Remove the turbocharger exhaust pipe heat shield bolts.

4. Remove the turbocharger exhaust pipe heat shield.

5. Remove the turbocharger exhaust pipe nuts and bolt.

6. Remove the turbocharger exhaust pipe.

7. Remove the turbocharger exhaust pipe seal.

✳✳ WARNING

Do not twist the turbocharger oil feed pipe. Twisting of the feed pipe will result in the collapse and deformation of the plastic pipe, restricting oil flow and causing turbocharger damage. During turbocharger replacement, gently push the oil feed pipe

Fig. 163 Turbocharger exhaust pipe, pipe nuts and bolt, and seal

towards the front of the engine to clear the turbocharger. Assistance may be required to keep the pipes clear of the turbocharger during removal or installation.

8. Remove the turbocharger oil feed pipe bolts.

9. Remove the turbocharger oil feed pipe gaskets.

10. Remove the turbocharger oil feed pipe.

11. Remove the turbocharger coolant return pipe bolts.

12. Remove the turbocharger coolant return pipe gaskets.

13. Remove the turbocharger coolant return pipe.

14. Remove the turbocharger air cooler outlet pipe bolts.

15. Remove the turbocharger air cooler outlet pipe.

16. Remove the turbocharger coolant feed pipe bolts.

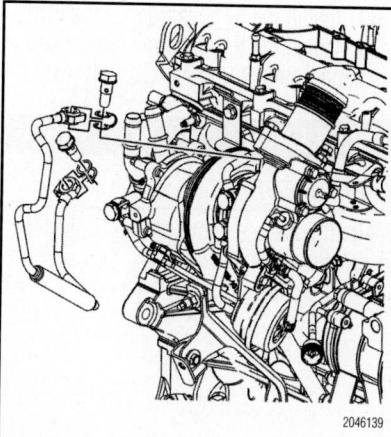

Fig. 164 Oil feed pipe, pipe bolts, and gaskets

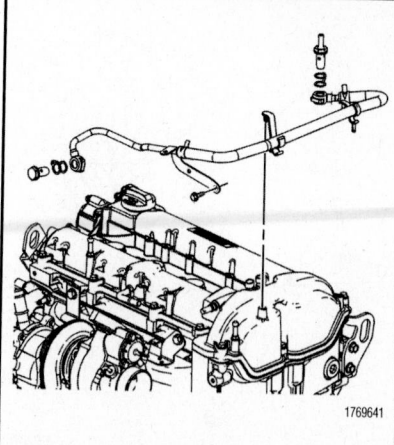

Fig. 165 Turbocharger coolant return pipe, pipe bolts, and gaskets

17. Remove the turbocharger coolant feed pipe gaskets.

18. Remove the turbocharger coolant feed pipe.

19. If necessary, remove the turbocharger brace bracket bolt and turbocharger brace bracket from the turbocharger brace.

20. Remove the turbocharger brace upper and lower nuts.

21. Remove the turbocharger brace bolt.

22. Remove the turbocharger brace.

23. Remove the turbocharger brace bracket bolt.

24. Remove the turbocharger brace bracket.

➡**Do not disconnect the PCV hose from the camshaft cover. The PCV hose and the camshaft cover cannot be serviced individually.**

25. Remove the PCV hose fitting bolt at the turbocharger.

26. Remove the PCV hose fitting from

Fig. 166 Air cooler outlet pipe and bolts

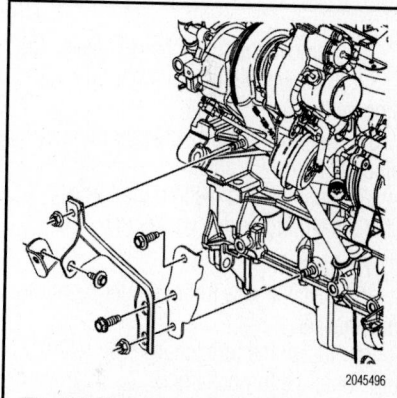

Fig. 167 Turbocharger coolant feed pipe, pipe bolts, and gaskets

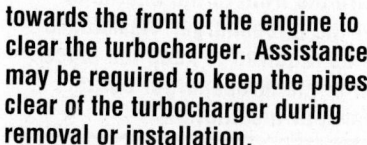

Fig. 168 If necessary, remove the turbocharger brace bracket bolt and turbocharger brace bracket from the turbocharger brace

the turbocharger with the hose still attached to the camshaft cover.

27. Remove the turbocharger nuts (1).

28. Remove the turbocharger (2) with oil return pipe.

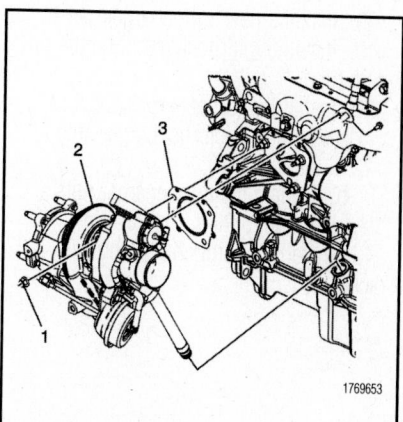

Fig. 169 Turbocharger nuts (1), turbocharger (2), and the turbocharger gasket (3)

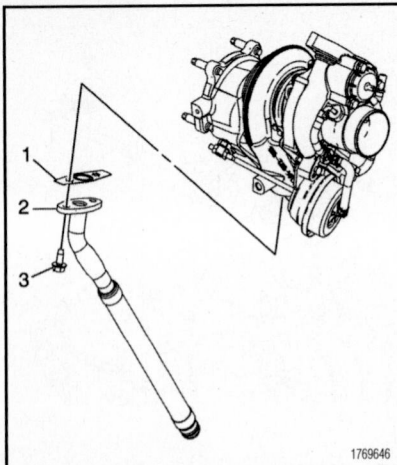

Fig. 170 Turbocharger oil return pipe bolts (3), return pipe (2), and return pipe gasket (1)

29. Remove the turbocharger gasket (3).

30. Remove the turbocharger oil return pipe bolts (3).

31. Remove the turbocharger oil return pipe (2).

32. Remove and discard the turbocharger oil return pipe gasket (1).

To install:

33. Install a new turbocharger oil return pipe gasket.

34. Install the turbocharger oil return pipe onto the turbocharger.

35. Install the turbocharger oil return pipe bolts and tighten to 89 inch lbs. (10 Nm).

36. Attach the positive crankcase ventilation (PCV) hose and fitting with O-ring from the camshaft cover to the turbocharger.

37. Install the PCV hose fitting bolt and tighten to 89 inch lbs. (10 Nm).

38. Lubricate the O-ring on the turbocharger oil return pipe with clean engine oil.

39. Install a new turbocharger gasket.

40. Install the turbocharger and the oil return pipe.

41. Install the turbocharger nuts (1).

    a. Tighten the turbocharger nuts to 22 ft. lbs. (30 Nm).

    b. Tighten the turbocharger nuts a second time to 26 ft. lbs. (35 Nm).

42. Install the turbocharger brace bracket.

43. Install the turbocharger brace bracket bolt and tighten it to 43 ft. lbs. (58 Nm).

44. Install the turbocharger brace.

45. Install the turbocharger brace nuts and tighten them to 37 ft. lbs. (50 Nm).

46. Install the turbocharger brace bolt and tighten to 37 ft. lbs. (50 Nm).

47. Install the turbocharger brace bracket and bolt to the turbocharger brace if necessary. Tighten the turbocharger brace bracket bolt to 16 ft. lbs. (22 Nm).

48. Install the turbocharger coolant feed pipe.

49. Install the turbocharger coolant feed pipe gaskets.

50. Install the turbocharger coolant feed pipe bolts.

    a. Tighten the turbocharger coolant feed pipe bolts to 26 ft. lbs. (35 Nm).

    b. Tighten the turbocharger coolant feed pipe mounting bolt to 37 ft. lbs. (50 Nm).

51. Connect the positive crankcase ventilation (PCV) and hose assembly.

52. Install the turbocharger air cooler outlet pipe.

53. Install the turbocharger air cooler outlet pipe bolts and tighten to 18 ft. lbs. (25 Nm).

❄❄ WARNING

Do not twist the turbocharger oil feed pipe. Twisting of the feed pipe will result in the collapse and deformation of the plastic pipe, restricting oil flow and causing turbocharger damage. During turbocharger replacement, gently push the oil feed pipe towards the front of the engine to clear the turbocharger. Assistance may be required to keep the pipes clear of the turbocharger during removal or installation.

➡The engine block end of the oil feed pipe fitting has an anti-rotation feature. Ensure that the fitting is fully seated against the block when installing the bolt.

54. Install the turbocharger oil feed pipe on the engine block side.

55. Install the turbocharger oil feed pipe gasket on the engine block side.

56. Install the bolt and tighten to 30 ft. lbs. (40 Nm).

57. Install the turbocharger coolant return pipe.

58. Install the turbocharger coolant return pipe gaskets.

59. Install the turbocharger coolant return pipe bolts and tighten to 26 ft. lbs. (35 Nm).

❄❄ WARNING

Do not twist the turbocharger oil feed pipe. Twisting of the feed pipe will result in the collapse and deformation of the plastic pipe, restricting oil flow and causing turbocharger damage. During turbocharger replacement, gently push the oil feed pipe toward the front of the engine to clear the turbocharger. Assistance may be required to keep the pipes clear of the turbocharger during removal or installation.

60. Install the turbocharger oil feed pipe onto the turbocharger.

61. Install the turbocharger oil feed pipe gasket for the turbocharger side.

62. Install the turbocharger oil feed pipe bolt and tighten to 30 ft. lbs. (40 Nm).

63. Install the turbocharger exhaust pipe seal.

64. Install the turbocharger exhaust pipe.

65. Install the turbocharger exhaust pipe bolt and tighten to 16 ft. lbs. (22 Nm).

66. Install the turbocharger exhaust pipe nuts and tighten to 37 ft. lbs. (50 Nm).

67. Install the turbocharger exhaust pipe heat shield.

68. Install the turbocharger exhaust pipe heat shield bolts and tighten to 37 ft. lbs. (50 Nm).

69. Install the turbocharger heat shield.

70. Install the turbocharger heat shield bolts and tighten to 89 inch lbs. (10 Nm).

VALVE LASH

ADJUSTMENT

All engines use hydraulic lash adjusters; no adjustment is necessary.

ENGINE PERFORMANCE & EMISSION CONTROLS

CAMSHAFT POSITION (CMP) SENSOR

LOCATION

Camshaft Position (CMP) Sensor—Exhaust: In the engine compartment, upper rear of the engine, near the camshaft cover.

Camshaft Position (CMP) Sensor—Intake: In the engine compartment, upper front of the engine, near the camshaft cover.

REMOVAL & INSTALLATION

2.0L Engine

See Figure 171.

The HHR 2.0L engine is equipped with both an intake and an exhaust camshaft position sensor.

1. Remove the fuel feed intermediate pipe.
2. Remove the camshaft position sensor bolt (1).
3. Remove the camshaft position sensor O-ring (2).
4. Remove the camshaft position sensor (3):

   a. Disconnect the sensor harness connector.

   b. Inspect the camshaft position sensor for damage; replace as necessary.

5. Installation is the reverse of removal.

➡**Lubricate the camshaft position sensor O-ring seal with clean engine oil.**

Specification: Tighten the camshaft position sensor bolt to 89 inch lbs. (10 Nm).

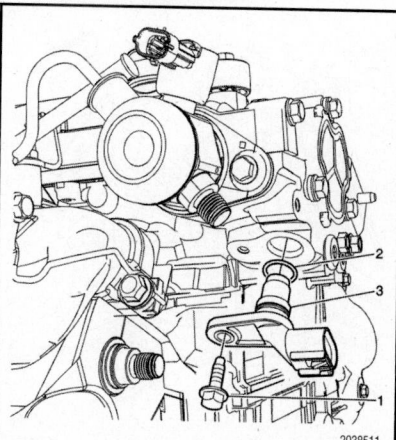

Fig. 171 Camshaft Position (CMP) sensor replacement—Intake sensor shown, exhaust is similar

2.2L & 2.4L Engines

See Figures 172 and 173.

1. Remove the air cleaner assembly. Refer to Engine Air Cleaner.
2. Disconnect the intake Camshaft Position (CMP) sensor electrical connector (2).
3. Remove the CMP sensor bolt.
4. Remove the CMP sensor.

To install:

➡**Inspect the CMP sensor for damage. Replace as necessary.**

5. Lubricate the CMP sensor O-ring seal with clean engine oil.
6. Install the CMP sensor.
7. Install the CMP sensor bolt.
8. Tighten the bolt to 89 inch lbs. (10 Nm).
9. Connect the intake CMP sensor electrical connector (2).

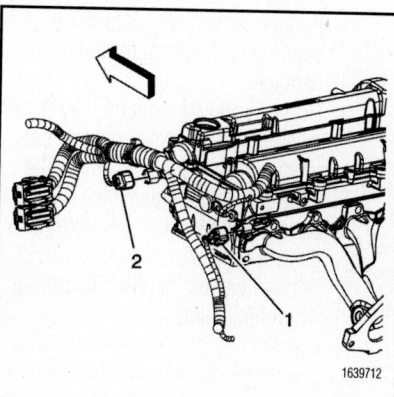

Fig. 172 Intake Camshaft Position (CMP) sensor electrical connector (2)

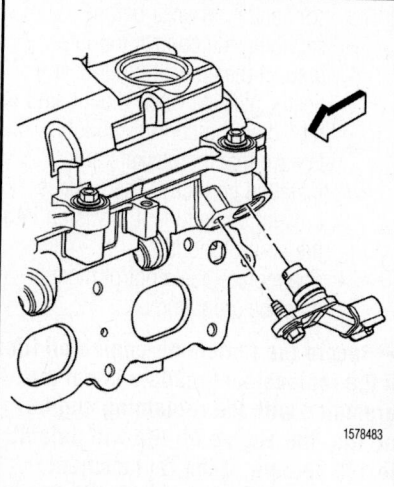

Fig. 173 CMP sensor and bolt

10. Install the air cleaner assembly. Refer to Engine Air Cleaner.

CRANKSHAFT POSITION (CKP) SENSOR

LOCATION

In the engine compartment, on the lower front of the engine, above the starter.

REMOVAL & INSTALLATION

See Figures 174 through 176.

1. Remove the starter. Refer to Starter.
2. For 2.0L engine only: Disconnect the engine wiring harness electrical connector (1) from the Crankshaft Position (CKP) sensor.

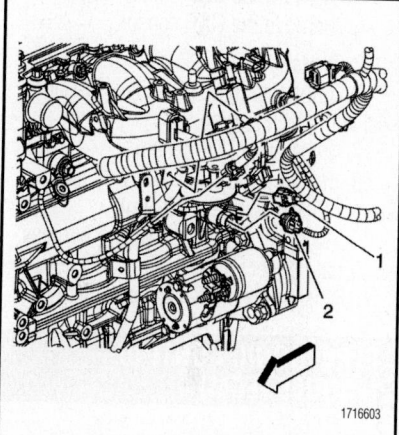

Fig. 174 For 2.0L engine only: Disconnect the engine wiring harness electrical connector (1) from the Crankshaft Position (CKP) sensor

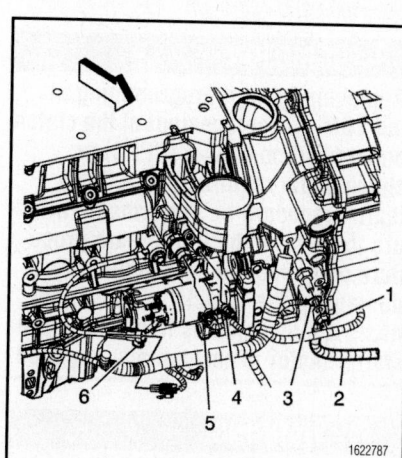

Fig. 175 For 2.2L and 2.4L engines only: Disconnect the Crankshaft Position (CKP) sensor electrical connector (4)

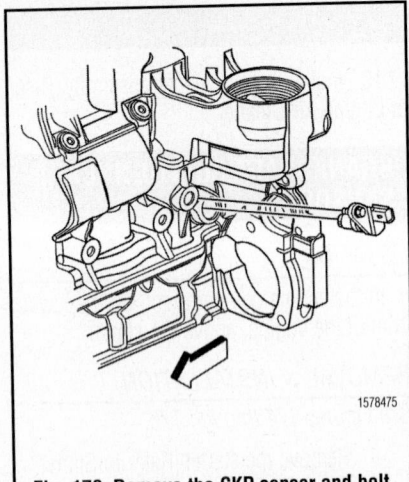

Fig. 176 Remove the CKP sensor and bolt

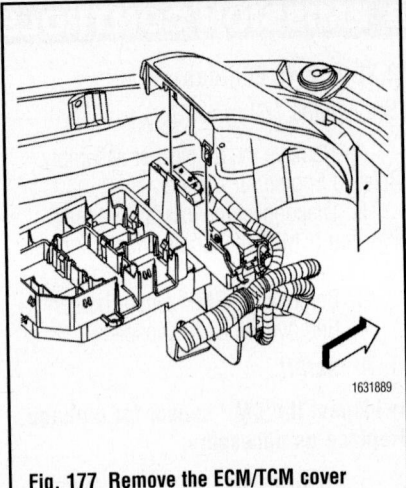

Fig. 177 Remove the ECM/TCM cover

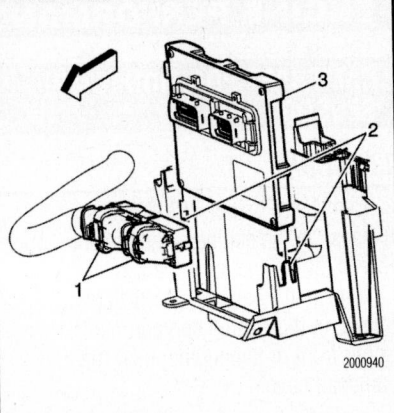

Fig. 178 Disconnect the ECM electrical connectors (1)

3. For 2.2L and 2.4L engines only: Disconnect the Crankshaft Position (CKP)sensor electrical connector (4).

4. Remove the CKP sensor bolt.

5. Remove the CKP sensor.

To install:

6. Lubricate the CKP sensor O-ring seal with clean engine oil.

7. Install the CKP sensor.

8. Install the CKP sensor bolt and tighten to 89 inch lbs. (10 Nm).

9. Connect the engine wiring harness electrical connector (1) to the CKP sensor.

10. Install the starter. Refer to Starter.

ELECTRONIC CONTROL MODULE (ECM)

LOCATION

Left side of the engine compartment, near the left strut tower.

REMOVAL & INSTALLATION

See Figures 177 through 179.

> ✳✳ **CAUTION**
>
> **Replacement or reprogramming of the ECM, or replacement of the clutch pedal position sensor (CPPS) or clutch pedal requires that a CPPS learn procedure be performed. Failure to perform the CPPS learn procedure may result in personal injury or damage to the vehicle or its components if the vehicle is in gear and the starter motor is accidentally engaged.**

> ✳✳ **WARNING**
>
> **Note the following:**
>
> • Turn the ignition OFF when installing or removing the control

module connectors and disconnecting or reconnecting the power to the control module (battery cable, powertrain control module (PCM)/engine control module (ECM)/transaxle control module (TCM) pigtail, control module fuse, jumper cables, etc.) in order to prevent internal control module damage.

• Control module damage may result when the metal case contacts battery voltage. DO NOT contact the control module metal case with battery voltage when servicing a control module, using battery booster cables, or when charging the vehicle battery.

• Prevent any possible electrostatic discharge damage to the control module, do not touch the connector pins or the soldered components on the circuit board.

• Remove any debris from around the control module connector surfaces before servicing the control module. Inspect the control module connector gaskets when diagnosing or replacing the control module. Ensure that the gaskets are installed correctly. The gaskets prevent contaminant intrusion into the control module.

• The replacement control module must be programmed.

➡Record the remaining engine oil life: If the replacement module is not programmed with the remaining engine oil life, the engine oil life will default to 100 percent. If the replacement module is not programmed with the remaining engine oil life, the engine

oil will need to be changed at 3,000 miles (5,000 km) from the last engine oil change.

1. Using a scan tool, retrieve the percentage of remaining engine oil. Record the remaining engine oil life.

2. Disconnect the negative battery cable. Refer to Battery Negative Cable Disconnection and Connection.

3. Remove the ECM/TCM cover.

4. Disconnect the ECM electrical connectors (1).

> ✳✳ **WARNING**
>
> **Control module damage may result when the metal case contacts battery voltage. DO NOT contact the control module metal case with battery voltage when servicing a control module, using battery booster cables or when charging the vehicles battery.**

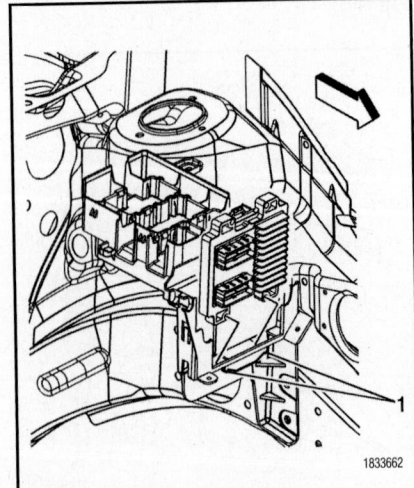

Fig. 179 Release the retaining tab (1) in order to release the ECM from the underhood junction block bracket

5. Disengage the plastic retainer tabs (2) and remove the ECM (3).

6. Release the retaining tab (1) in order to release the ECM from the underhood junction block bracket.

To install:

⁂ **WARNING**

Control module damage may result when the metal case contacts battery voltage. DO NOT contact the control module metal case with battery voltage when servicing a control module, using battery booster cables or when charging the vehicles battery.

7. Install the ECM by pushing straight down until the tabs lock.

8. Connect the ECM electrical connectors.

9. Install the ECM/TCM cover.

10. Connect the negative battery cable. Refer to Battery Negative Cable Disconnection and Connection.

11. Program the ECM with a scan tool.

12. If equipped with a manual transaxle, perform the clutch pedal position sensor learn procedure.

ENGINE COOLANT TEMPERATURE (ECT) SENSOR

LOCATION

In the engine compartment, on the left rear of the engine, near the exhaust manifold.

REMOVAL & INSTALLATION

2.0L Engine

See Figure 180.

1. Partially drain the cooling system. Refer to Cooling System Draining and Filling.

Fig. 180 Disconnect the engine wiring harness electrical connector (3) from the engine coolant temperature (ECT) sensor

2. Remove the heat shield from the around the electrical connector, if necessary.

3. Disconnect the engine wiring harness electrical connector (3) from the engine coolant temperature (ECT) sensor.

4. Remove the ECT. (See image for 2.2L and 2.4L ECT removal.)

To install:

5. Install the ECT and tighten to 15 ft. lbs. (20 Nm).

6. Connect the engine wiring harness electrical connector (3) to the ECT sensor.

7. Install the heat shield around the electrical connector, if necessary.

8. Fill the cooling system as needed. Refer to Cooling System Draining and Filling.

2.2L & 2.4L Engines

See Figures 181 through 183.

⁂ **WARNING**

Use care when handling the coolant sensor. Damage to the coolant sensor will affect the operation of the fuel control system.

1. Drain the coolant system to below the engine coolant temperature (ECT) sensor. Refer to Cooling System Draining and Filling.

2. Reposition the air cleaner assembly from the top of the engine.

3. If the HHR is equipped with an automatic transaxle, disconnect the ECT sensor electrical connector (1).

4. If the HHR is equipped with a manual transaxle, disconnect the ECT sensor electrical connector (1).

5. Remove the ECT sensor.

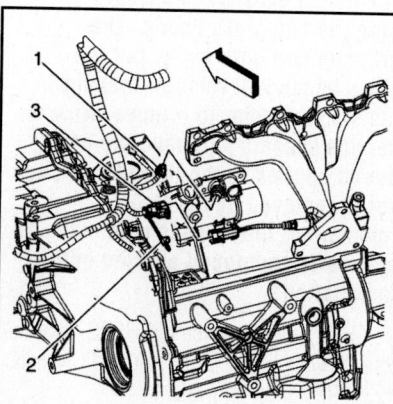

Fig. 181 If the HHR is equipped with an automatic transaxle, disconnect the ECT sensor electrical connector (1)

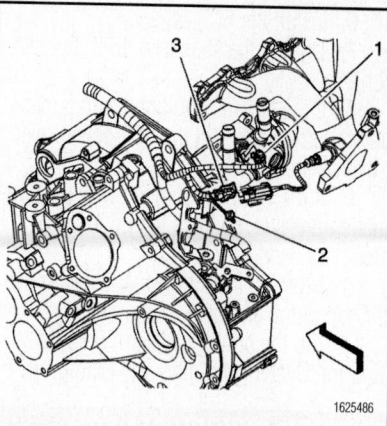

Fig. 182 If the HHR is equipped with a manual transaxle, disconnect the ECT sensor electrical connector (1)

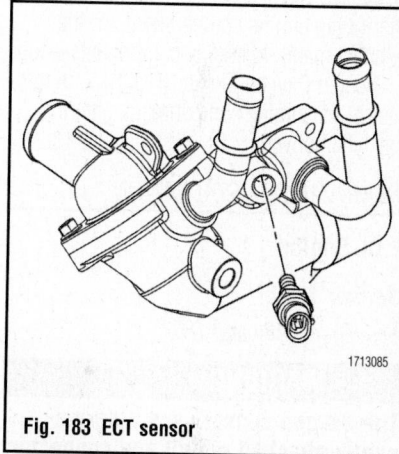

Fig. 183 ECT sensor

To install:

⁂ **WARNING**

Replacement components must be the correct part number for the application. Components requiring the use of the thread locking compound, lubricants, corrosion inhibitors, or sealants are identified in the service procedure. Some replacement components may come with these coatings already applied. Do not use these coatings on components unless specified. These coatings can affect the final torque, which may affect the operation of the component. Use the correct torque specification when installing components in order to avoid damage.

⁂ **WARNING**

Use care when handling the coolant sensor. Damage to the coolant sensor will affect the operation of the fuel control system.

6. Install the ECT sensor.

7. Tighten the sensor to 15 ft. lbs. (20 Nm).

8. If the HHR is equipped with a manual transaxle, connect the ECT sensor electrical connector.

9. If the HHR is equipped with an automatic transaxle, connect the ECT sensor electrical connector.

10. Position the air cleaner assembly to the top of the engine.

11. Fill the cooling system. Refer to Cooling System Draining and Filling.

HEATED OXYGEN SENSOR (HO2S)

LOCATION

Heated Oxygen Sensor (HO2S) 1: In the rear of the engine compartment, on the exhaust manifold engine components—top.

Heated Oxygen Sensor (HO2S) 2: In the rear of the engine compartment, after the catalytic converter

REMOVAL & INSTALLATION

2.0L Engine

Sensor 1

See Figures 184 and 185.

> ❋❋ **WARNING**
>
> **The oxygen sensor uses a permanently attached pigtail and connector. Do not remove the pigtail from the oxygen sensor. Damage to or removal of the pigtail connector could affect proper operation of the oxygen sensor.**

> ❋❋ **WARNING**
>
> **The use of excessive force may damage the threads in the exhaust manifold/pipe.**

➡Note the following:

- The in-line connector and louvered end must be kept clear of grease, dirt or other contaminants. Avoid using cleaning solvents of any type. DO NOT drop or roughly handle the heated oxygen sensor (HO2S).
- The HO2S may be difficult to remove when the engine temperature is less than 120 °F (48 °C).

1. Open the hood.

2. Remove the connector position assurance (CPA) retainer.

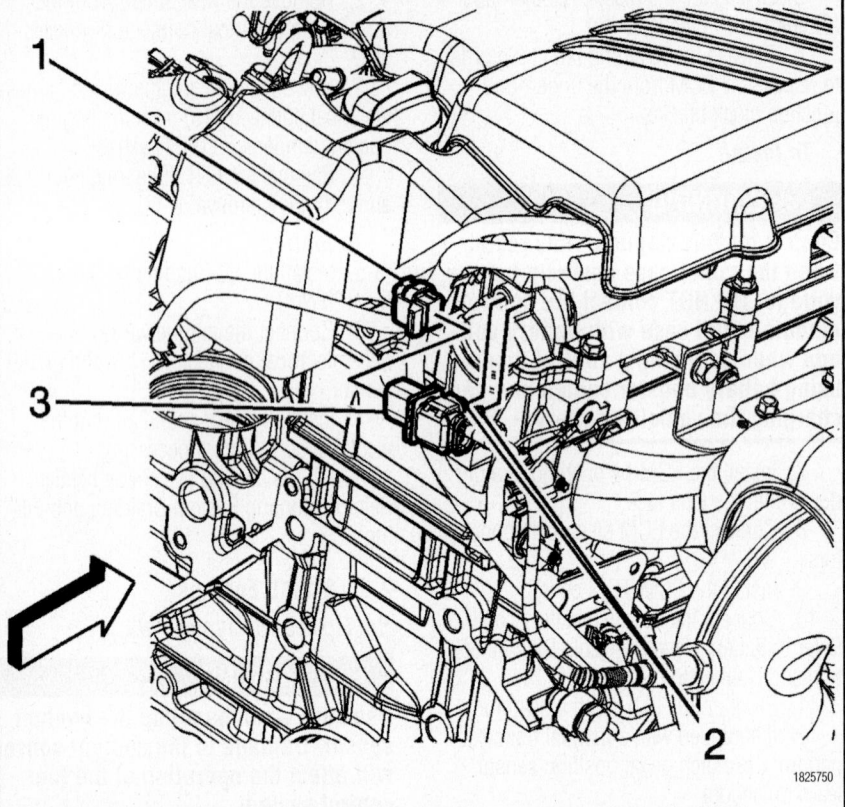

Fig. 184 Disconnect the engine wiring harness electrical connector (1) from the HO2S electrical connector (3)

3. Disconnect the engine wiring harness electrical connector (1) from the HO2S electrical connector (3).

4. Remove the HO2S electrical connector clip (2) from the camshaft cover.

5. Using the J 39194, remove the position 1 HO2S.

To install:

➡**A special anti-seize compound is used on the HO2S threads. The compound consists of a liquid graphite and glass beads. The graphite will burn away, but the glass beads will remain, making the sensor easier to remove. New or service sensors will have the compound applied to the threads. If a sensor is removed and is to be reinstalled, the threads must have an anti-seize compound applied before installation.**

6. If reinstalling the old HO2S, coat the threads with anti-seize compound GM P/N 12377953 or an equivalent.

7. Using the J 39194, install the position 1 HO2S and tighten to 31 ft. lbs. (42 Nm).

8. Connect the engine wiring harness electrical connector (1) to the HO2S electrical connector (3).

9. Install the HO2S electrical connector clip (2) to the camshaft cover.

10. Install the CPA retainer.

11. Close the hood.

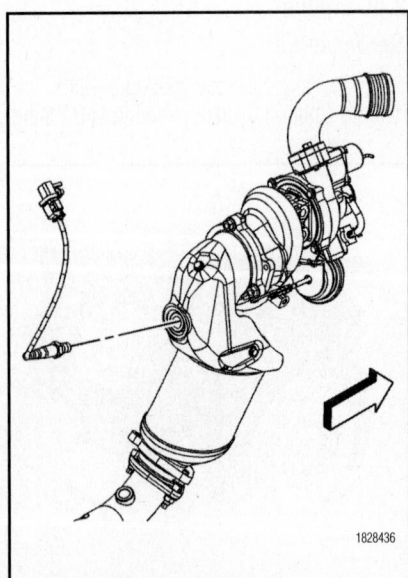

Fig. 185 Disconnect the engine wiring harness electrical connector (1) from the HO2S electrical connector (3)

Sensor 2

See Figure 186.

1. Raise and support the vehicle.

> ❊❊ **WARNING**
>
> **The oxygen sensor uses a permanently attached pigtail and connector. Do not remove the pigtail from the oxygen sensor. Damage to or removal of the pigtail connector could affect proper operation of the oxygen sensor.**

> ❊❊ **WARNING**
>
> **The use of excessive force may damage the threads in the exhaust manifold/pipe.**

➡When replacing the HO2S perform the following:

- A code clear with a scan tool, regardless of whether or not a DTC is set
- HO2S heater resistance learn reset with a scan tool, where available
- Perform the above in order to reset the HO2S resistance learned value and avoid possible HO2S failure.

2. Disconnect the electrical connector.

3. Uncrimp the heat shield from the O2 sensor wiring harness.

➡Note the following:

- Keep the in-line connector and louvered end clear of grease, dirt or other contaminants. Avoid using cleaning solvents of any type. DO NOT drop or roughly handle the heated oxygen sensor (HO2S).
- The HO2S may be difficult to remove when the engine temperature is less than 120 °F (48 °C).
- A special anti-seize compound is used on the HO2S threads. The

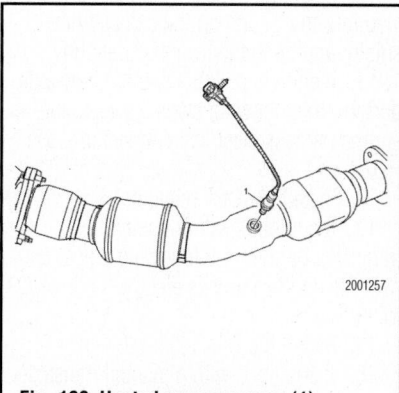

Fig. 186 Heated oxygen sensor (1)

compound consists of a liquid graphite and glass beads. The graphite will burn away, but the glass beads will remain, making the sensor easier to remove. New or service sensors will have the compound applied to the threads. If a sensor is removed and is to be reinstalled, the threads must have an anti-seize compound applied before installation.

4. Remove the heated oxygen sensor (1).

5. Installation is the reverse of removal. Specification: Tighten the sensor to 31 ft. lbs. (42 Nm).

2.2L & 2.4L Engines

Sensor 1

See Figures 187 and 188.

> ❊❊ **WARNING**
>
> **The oxygen sensor uses a permanently attached pigtail and connector. Do not remove the pigtail from the oxygen sensor. Damage to or removal of the pigtail connector could affect proper operation of the oxygen sensor.**

> ❊❊ **WARNING**
>
> **The use of excessive force may damage the threads in the exhaust manifold/pipe.**

➡Note the following:

- The in-line connector and louvered end must be kept clear of grease, dirt or other contaminants. Avoid using cleaning solvents of any type. DO NOT drop or roughly handle the heated oxygen sensor (HO2S).
- The HO2S may be difficult to remove when the engine temperature is less than 120 °F (48 °C).

1. Remove the exhaust manifold heat shield. Refer to Exhaust Manifold replacement.

2. If the HHR is equipped with an automatic transaxle, perform the following steps, remove the connector position assurance (CPA) retainer (2). Refer to image for 2.2L and 2.4L engine ECT removal.

3. Disconnect the engine harness electrical connector (3) from the HO2S.

4. If the HHR is equipped with a manual transaxle, perform the following steps, remove the CPA retainer (2). Refer to image for 2.2L and 2.4L engine ECT removal.

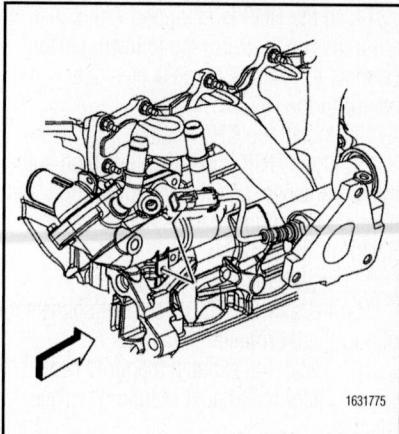

Fig. 187 Remove the HO2S electrical connector clip from the thermostat housing

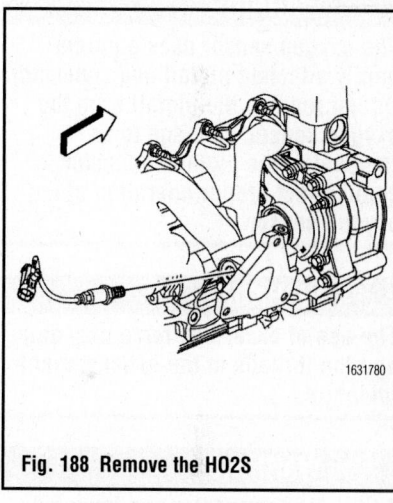

Fig. 188 Remove the HO2S

5. Disconnect the engine harness electrical connector (3) from the HO2S.

6. Remove the HO2S electrical connector clip from the thermostat housing.

7. Remove the HO2S.

To install:

➡**A special anti-seize compound is used on the HO2S threads. The compound consists of a liquid graphite and glass beads. The graphite will burn away, but the glass beads will remain, making the sensor easier to remove. New or service sensors will have the compound applied to the threads. If a sensor is removed and is to be reinstalled, the threads must have an anti-seize compound applied before installation.**

8. If reinstalling the old HO2S, coat the threads with anti-seize compound GM P/N 12377953 or equivalent.

9. Install the HO2S.

10. Tighten the sensor to 31 ft. lbs. (42 Nm).

11. If the HHR is equipped with a manual transaxle, perform the following steps, connect the engine harness electrical connector to the HO2S.

12. Install the CPA retainer.

13. If the HHR is equipped with an automatic transaxle, perform the following steps, connect the engine harness electrical connector to the HO2S.

14. Install the CPA retainer.

15. Install the HO2S electrical connector clip to the thermostat housing.

16. Install the exhaust manifold heat shield. Refer to Exhaust Manifold replacement.

Sensor 2

See Figures 189 through 192.

> ⁕⁕ **WARNING**
>
> The oxygen sensor uses a permanently attached pigtail and connector. Do not remove the pigtail from the oxygen sensor. Damage to or removal of the pigtail connector could affect proper operation of the oxygen sensor.

> ⁕⁕ **WARNING**
>
> The use of excessive force may damage the threads in the exhaust manifold/pipe.

> ⁕⁕ **WARNING**
>
> The in-line connector and louvered end must be kept clear of grease, dirt or other contaminants. Avoid using cleaning solvents of any type. DO NOT drop or roughly handle the heated oxygen sensor (HO2S).

➡ The HO2S may be difficult to remove when the engine temperature is less than 120°F (48°C).

1. If the HHR is equipped with a manual transaxle, remove the wheel driveshaft heat shield.

2. If the HHR is equipped with an automatic transaxle, perform the following steps, remove the connector position assurance (CPA) retainer (2).

3. Disconnect the engine harness electrical connector (3) from the HO2S.

4. If equipped with a manual transaxle, perform the following steps, remove the CPA retainer (3).

5. Disconnect the engine harness electrical connector (4) from the HO2S.

6. Bend down the trough (1) on the exhaust heat shield just enough to remove the HO2S electrical harness lead (2).

7. Remove the HO2S.

To install:

➡ A special anti-seize compound is used on the HO2S threads. The compound consists of a liquid graphite and glass beads. The graphite will burn away, but the glass beads will remain, making the sensor easier to remove. New or service sensors will have the compound applied to the threads. If a sensor is removed and is to be reinstalled, the threads must have an anti-seize compound applied before installation.

8. If reinstalling the old HO2S, coat the threads with anti-seize compound GM P/N 12377953 or equivalent.

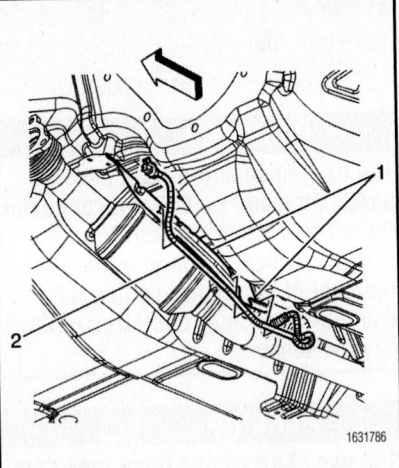

Fig. 191 Bend down the trough (1) on the exhaust heat shield just enough to remove the HO2S electrical harness lead (2)

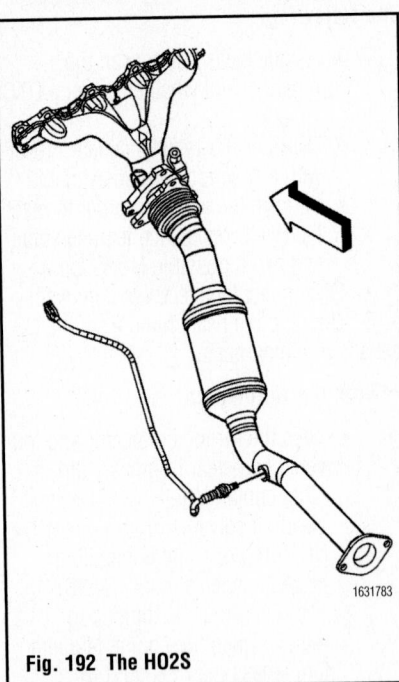

Fig. 192 The HO2S

9. Install the HO2S. Tighten the sensor to 31 ft. lbs. (42 Nm).

10. Install the HO2S electrical harness lead into the trough on the exhaust heat shield, and bend the trough up slightly.

11. If equipped with a manual transaxle, perform the following steps, connect the engine harness electrical connector to the HO2S.

12. Install the CPA retainer.

13. If equipped with a automatic transaxle, perform the following steps, connect the engine harness electrical connector to the HO2S.

14. Install the CPA retainer.

15. If equipped with a manual transaxle, install the wheel driveshaft heat shield.

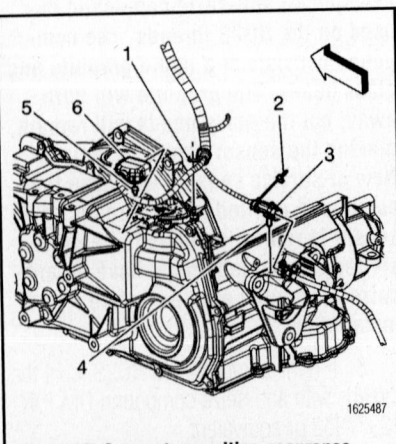

Fig. 189 Connector position assurance (CPA) retainer (2) and engine harness electrical connector (3)

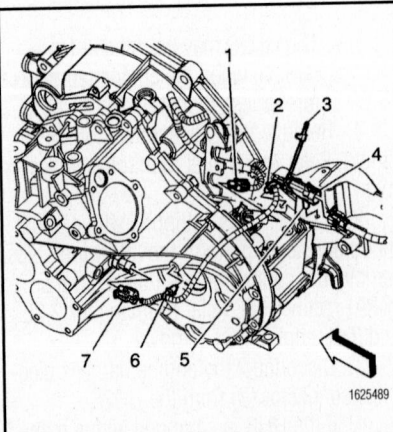

Fig. 190 CPA retainer (3) and engine harness electrical connector (4)

INTAKE AIR PRESSURE & TEMPERATURE SENSOR

LOCATION

2.0L Engine

In the engine compartment, on the intercooler duct, by the air compressor.

REMOVAL & INSTALLATION

2.0L Engine

See Figure 193.

1. Remove the charge air cooler outlet pipe.
2. Disconnect the electrical connector.
3. Remove the 2 sensor screws (1).
4. Remove the intake air temperature and pressure sensor (2).
5. Installation is the reverse of removal.
Specification: Tighten the sensor screws to 80 inch lbs. (9 Nm).

KNOCK SENSOR (KS)

LOCATION

2.0L Engine

Knock Sensor (KS) 1: In the engine compartment, on the lower left front side of the engine

Knock Sensor (KS) 2: In the engine compartment, on the lower right front side of the engine

2.2L & 2.4L Engines

In the engine compartment, on the left lower side of the engine, above the starter.

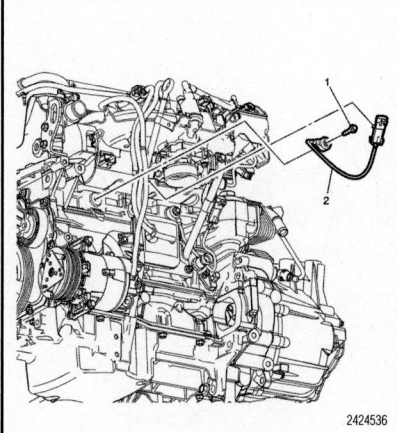

Fig. 193 Remove the intake air temperature and pressure sensor (2) and screws (1)

REMOVAL & INSTALLATION

2.0L Engine

Sensor 1

See Figure 194.

1. Remove the generator. Refer to Generator replacement.
2. Disconnect the electrical connector.
3. Remove the knock sensor fastener (1).
4. Remove the knock sensor (2).
5. Installation is the reverse of removal.
Specification: Tighten the knock sensor fastener to 18 ft. lbs. (25 Nm).

Sensor 2

See Figure 195.

1. Remove the starter. Refer to Starter replacement.
2. Disconnect the electrical connector.
3. Remove the knock sensor fastener (1).
4. Remove the knock sensor (2).
5. Installation is the reverse of removal.
Specification: Tighten the knock sensor fastener to 18 ft. lbs. (25 Nm)

2.2L & 2.4L Engines

See Figure 196.

1. Raise and suitably support the vehicle.
2. Disconnect the knock sensor (KS) electrical connector (6). For the image, refer to Crankshaft Position Sensor removal for 2.2L and 2.4L engines.
3. Remove the KS bolt.
4. Remove the KS.

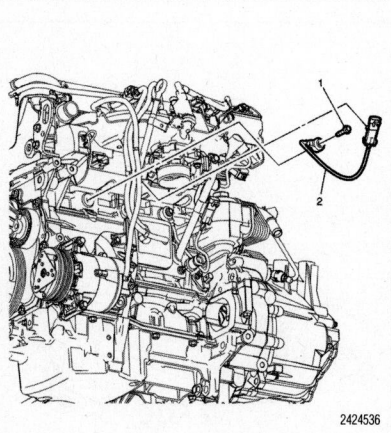

Fig. 194 Remove the knock sensor (2) and fastener (1)

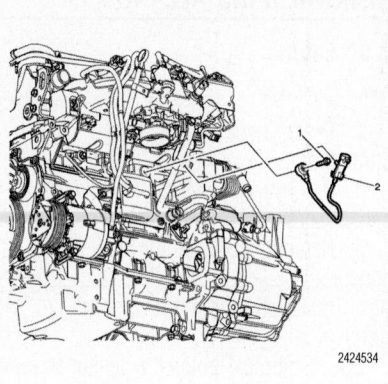

Fig. 195 Remove the knock sensor (2) and fastener (1)

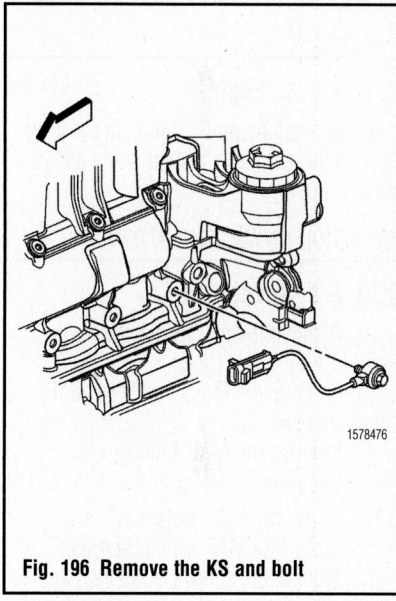

Fig. 196 Remove the KS and bolt

To install:

➡**Rotate the pigtail 90 degrees from vertical before securing the fastener.**

5. Install the KS.
6. Install the KS bolt.
7. Tighten the bolt to 18 ft. lbs. (25 Nm).
8. Connect the KS electrical connector (6).
9. Lower the vehicle.

MASS AIR FLOW (MAF) SENSOR

LOCATION

2.0L Engine

In the engine compartment, at the front right of the engine, attached to the air cleaner outlet.

REMOVAL & INSTALLATION

2.0L Engine

See Figure 197.

1. Disconnect the electrical connector.
2. Remove the 2 Mass Air Flow (MAF) sensor screws (1).
3. Remove the Mass Air Flow (MAF) sensor.
4. Installation is the reverse of removal.

Specification: Tighten the sensor screws to 5 inch lbs. (0.6 Nm)

MASS AIR FLOW (MAF) / INTAKE AIR TEMPERATURE (IAT) SENSOR

LOCATION

2.2L & 2.4L Engines

In the engine compartment, at the front right of the engine, attached to the air cleaner outlet.

REMOVAL & INSTALLATION

2.2L & 2.4L Engines

1. Remove the air cleaner assembly. Refer to Engine Air Cleaner.
2. Remove the Mass Air Flow (MAF) sensor screws.
3. Remove the MAF sensor.

To install:

4. Install the MAF sensor.
5. Install the MAF sensor screws.
6. Tighten the screws to 89 inch lbs. (10 Nm).
7. Install the air cleaner assembly. Refer to Engine Air Cleaner.

MANIFOLD ABSOLUTE PRESSURE (MAP) SENSOR

LOCATION

In the engine compartment, top front of the engine, at the number 3 intake port runner.

REMOVAL & INSTALLATION

2.0L Engine

See Figures 198 and 199.

1. Disconnect the engine wiring harness electrical connector (2) from the Manifold Absolute Pressure (MAP) sensor.
2. Remove the MAP sensor bolts.
3. Remove the MAP sensor and O-ring seal from the intake manifold.

To install:

4. Lubricate the O-ring seal with clean engine oil.

5. Install the MAP sensor to the intake manifold.
6. Install the MAP sensor bolts and tighten to 89 inch lbs. (10 Nm).
7. Connect the engine wiring harness electrical connector to the MAP sensor.

2.2L & 2.4L Engines

See Figures 200 and 201.

1. Remove the throttle body. Refer to Throttle Body in the Fuel section.
2. Disconnect the evaporative emission (EVAP) purge tube from the intake manifold.
3. Disconnect the wiring harness clips from the fuel rail and reposition the harness out of the way.
4. Disconnect the Manifold Absolute Pressure (MAP) sensor electrical connector.
5. Remove the MAP sensor.

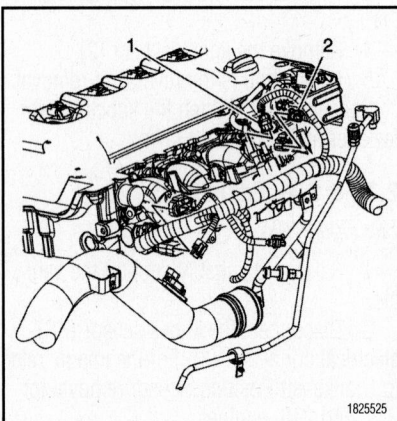

Fig. 198 Disconnect the engine wiring harness electrical connector (2) from the Manifold Absolute Pressure (MAP) sensor

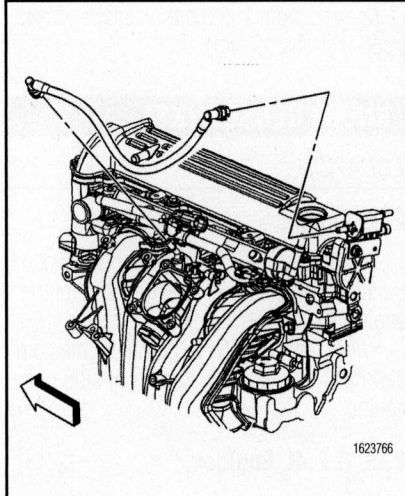

Fig. 200 Disconnect the evaporative emission (EVAP) purge tube from the intake manifold

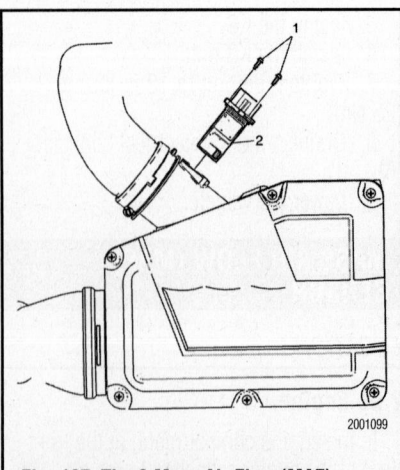

Fig. 197 The 2 Mass Air Flow (MAF) sensor screws (1) and sensor (2)

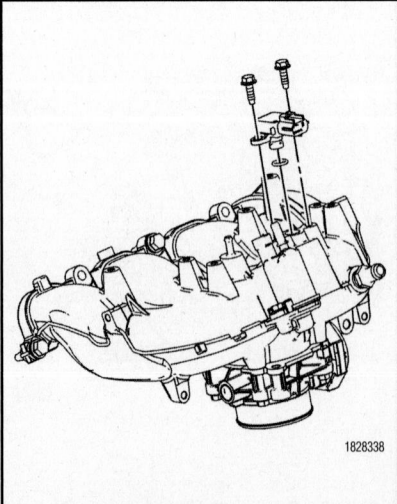

Fig. 199 MAP sensor and bolts

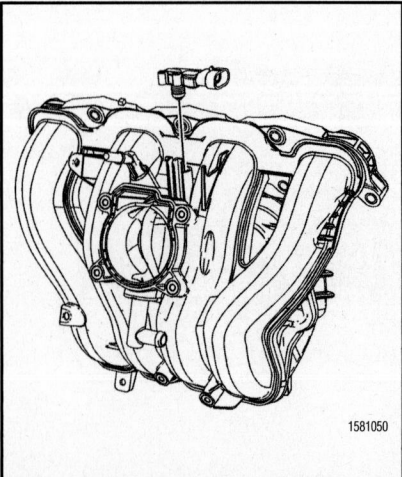

Fig. 201 Manifold Absolute Pressure (MAP) sensor and its electrical connector

→**You must replace damaged MAP sensor seals.**

6. Inspect the seal for damage.

To install:

7. Install the NEW MAP sensor seal, if required.

8. Install the MAP sensor.

9. Connect the MAP sensor electrical connector.

10. Position the wiring harness and connect the harness clips to the fuel rail.

11. Connect the EVAP purge tube to the intake manifold.

12. Install the throttle body. Refer to Throttle Body in the Fuel section.

VEHICLE SPEED SENSOR (VSS)

LOCATION

Manual 5 Speed, Getrag, 5T45-E: In the engine compartment, at the rear of the engine, on top of the transmission.

Automatic 4 Speed, 4T45-E: In the engine compartment, at the rear of the engine, on top of the transmission.

REMOVAL & INSTALLATION

With Automatic Transaxle

See Figure 202.

✳✳ CAUTION

Refer to Battery Disconnect Warning in the Precautions.

1. Disconnect the negative battery cable from the battery negative terminal.

2. Raise and support the vehicle.

3. Remove the electrical connector at the vehicle speed sensor.

4. Remove the retaining stud and the sensor. Pull straight out in order to avoid damage to the case.

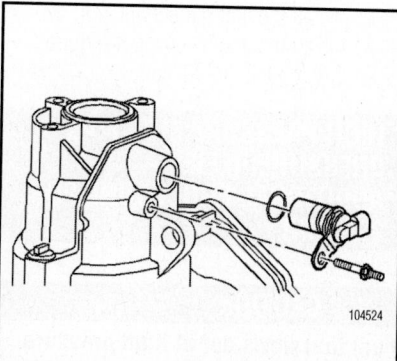

Fig. 202 Remove the retaining stud and the sensor. Pull straight out in order to avoid damage to the case

To install:

5. Clean and dry the vehicle speed sensor.

6. Install the vehicle speed sensor and the retaining bolt.

7. Tighten the stud to 97 inch lbs. (12 Nm).

8. Install the electrical connector at the sensor.

9. Remove the safety stands.

10. Lower the vehicle.

11. Connect the negative battery cable.

12. Tighten the terminal bolt to 11 ft. lbs. (15 Nm).

With 5T45-E Hydramatic Manual Transaxle

See Figures 203 through 206.

1. Disconnect the vehicle speed sensor (VSS) electrical connector.

2. Remove the retainer bolt.

3. Remove the retainer.

4. Pull up on the VSS in order to remove the VSS from the transaxle.

5. Remove the O-ring.

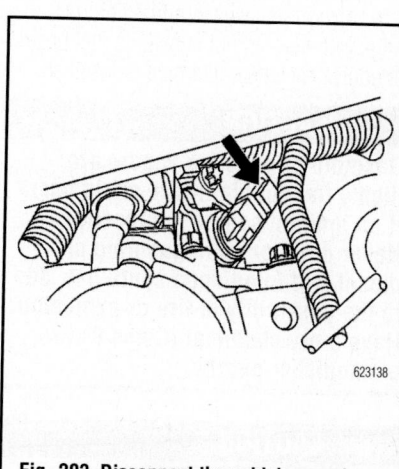

Fig. 203 Disconnect the vehicle speed sensor (VSS) electrical connector

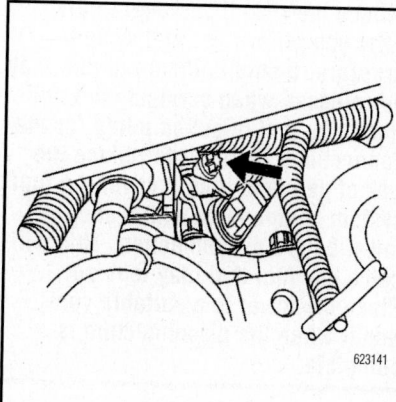

Fig. 204 Remove the retainer and bolt

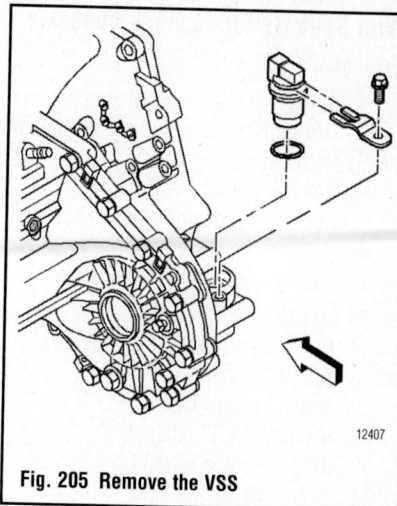

Fig. 205 Remove the VSS

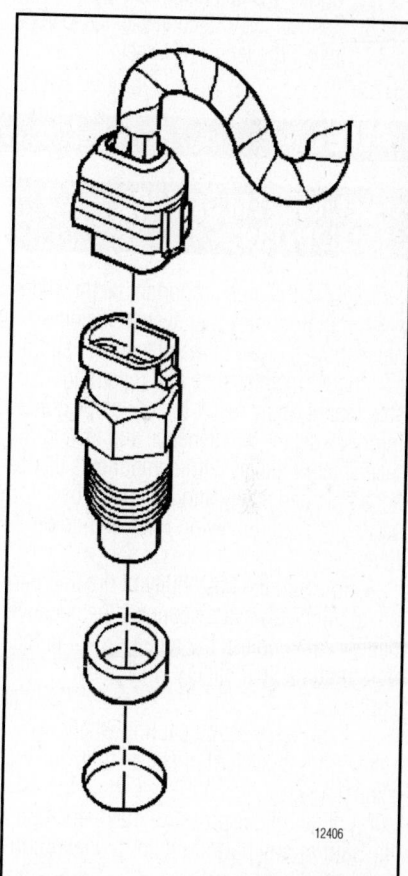

Fig. 206 Connect the VSS connector to the VSS

To install:

6. Lubricate a new O-ring with DEXRON III transmission fluid.

7. Install the new O-ring.

8. Install the VSS assembly.

9. Install the VSS retainer.

10. Install the VSS retainer bolt.

11. Tighten the bolt to 8 ft. lbs. (12 Nm).

12. Connect the VSS connector to the VSS.

13. Lower the vehicle.

With Saab Getrag Manual Transaxle

See Figures 207 and 208.

1. Remove the left front wheel.
2. Disconnect the vehicle speed sensor (VSS) electrical connector (2).
3. Remove the retainer bolt.
4. Remove the retainer.
5. Remove the VSS.
6. Remove and discard the O-ring.

To install:

7. Lubricate a new O-ring with transmission fluid.
8. Install the new O-ring.
9. Install the VSS retainer.
10. Install the VSS assembly.
11. Install the VSS retainer bolt.
12. Tighten the bolt to 80 inch lbs. (9 Nm).
13. Connect the VSS connector to the VSS.
14. Install the left front wheel.

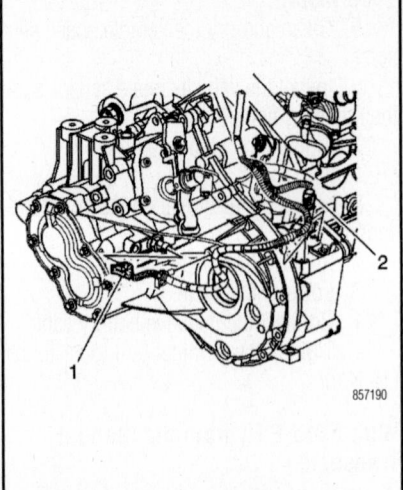

857190

Fig. 207 Disconnect the vehicle speed sensor (VSS) electrical connector (2)

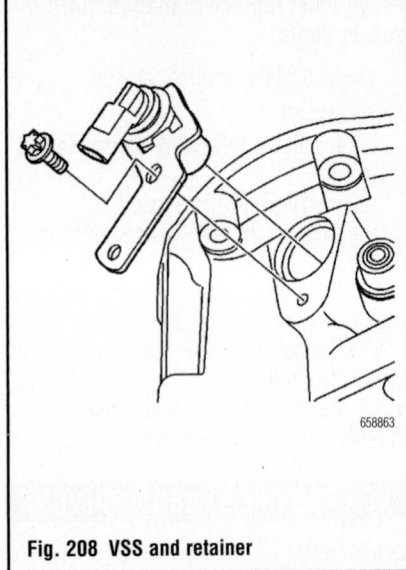

658863

Fig. 208 VSS and retainer

FUEL   GASOLINE FUEL INJECTION SYSTEM

FUEL SYSTEM SERVICE PRECAUTIONS

Safety is the most important factor when performing not only fuel system maintenance but any type of maintenance. Failure to conduct maintenance and repairs in a safe manner may result in serious personal injury or death. Maintenance and testing of the vehicle's fuel system components can be accomplished safely and effectively by adhering to the following rules and guidelines.

• To avoid the possibility of fire and personal injury, always disconnect the negative battery cable unless the repair or test procedure requires that battery voltage be applied.

• Exercise extreme caution whenever relieving fuel system pressure to avoid exposing skin, face and eyes to fuel spray: Fuel under pressure may penetrate the skin or any part of the body that it contacts.

• Always place a shop towel or cloth around the fitting or connection prior to loosening to absorb any excess fuel due to spillage. Ensure that all fuel spillage (should it occur) is quickly removed from engine surfaces.

• Always keep a dry chemical (Class B) fire extinguisher near the work area.

• Do not allow fuel spray or fuel vapors to come into contact with a spark or open flame.

• Always use a back-up wrench when loosening and tightening fuel line connection fittings. This will prevent unnecessary stress and torsion to the fuel line piping.

• Always replace worn fuel fitting O-rings with new Do not substitute fuel hose or equivalent where fuel pipe is installed.

✳✳ CAUTION

Gasoline or gasoline vapors are highly flammable. A fire could occur if an ignition source is present. Never drain or store gasoline or diesel fuel in an open container, due to the possibility of fire or explosion. Have a dry chemical (Class B) fire extinguisher nearby.

✳✳ CAUTION

Remove the fuel tank cap and relieve the fuel system pressure before servicing the fuel system in order to reduce the risk of personal injury. After you relieve the fuel system pressure, a small amount of fuel may be released when servicing the fuel lines, the fuel injection pump, or the connections. In order to reduce the risk of personal injury, cover the fuel system components with a shop towel before disconnection. This will catch any fuel that may leak out. Place the towel in a suitable container when the disconnection is complete.

Before servicing the HHR, make sure to also refer to the precautions in the beginning of this section as well.

FUEL PRESSURE RELIEF

✳✳ CAUTION

Refer to Fuel Precautions.

1. If the fuel system requires repair, prevent fuel spillage by removing the fuel pump fuse.
2. Loosen the fuel fill cap in order to relieve the fuel tank vapor pressure.
3. Remove the engine cover, if required.
4. Remove the fuel rail service port cap.
5. Wrap a shop towel around the fuel rail service port and using a small flat-bladed tool, depress (open) the fuel rail test port valve.
6. Remove the shop towel from around the fuel rail service port, and place in an approved gasoline container.
7. Install the fuel rail service port cap.
8. Install the engine cover, if required.
9. Tighten the fuel fill cap.

HIGH PRESSURE SIDE FUEL PRESSURE RELIEF— ADDITIONAL PROCEDURE FOR 2.0L ONLY

✳✳ CAUTION

Fuel that flows out at high pressure can cause serious injury to the skin and eyes. ALWAYS depressurize the fuel system before removing components that are under high fuel pressure.

1. Install a scan tool to the vehicle and command the fuel pump relay OFF, allowing the low pressure fuel pump to shut off.

2. Start the vehicle and allow the engine to idle until the engine stops. The engine will stop in approximately 20–30 seconds.

3. Turn the ignition OFF.

4. Using the scan tool, verify that there is little to no fuel pressure; if there still is fuel pressure repeat Step 2.

➡️**If a scan tool is not available, WAIT at LEAST 2 hours after the engine has been run, before removing the high pressure fuel line.**

5. Remove the high pressure fuel line.

FUEL STRAINER—2.0L ONLY

INSPECTION & CLEANING

A woven plastic fuel strainer attaches to the lower end of the fuel pump module. The fuel strainer filters contaminants and wicks fuel. The fuel strainer normally requires no maintenance. Fuel stoppage at the strainer indicates that the fuel tank contains an abnormal amount of sediment or contamination.

➡️**If the fuel filter is plugged, internally inspect the fuel tank and clean it if necessary.**

FUEL INJECTORS

REMOVAL & INSTALLATION

See Figures 209 and 210.

✷✷ WARNING

Use care in removing the fuel injectors in order to prevent damage to the fuel injector electrical connector pins or the fuel injector nozzles. Do not immerse the fuel injector in any type of cleaner. The fuel injector is an electrical component and may be damaged by this cleaning method.

➡️**If the fuel injectors are found to be leaking, the engine oil may be contaminated with fuel.**

1. Remove the fuel rail.
2. Remove the fuel injector retaining clip (1).
3. Remove the fuel injector (3) from the fuel rail.
4. Remove and discard the fuel injector lower O-ring (4).
5. Remove and discard the fuel injector upper O-ring (2).

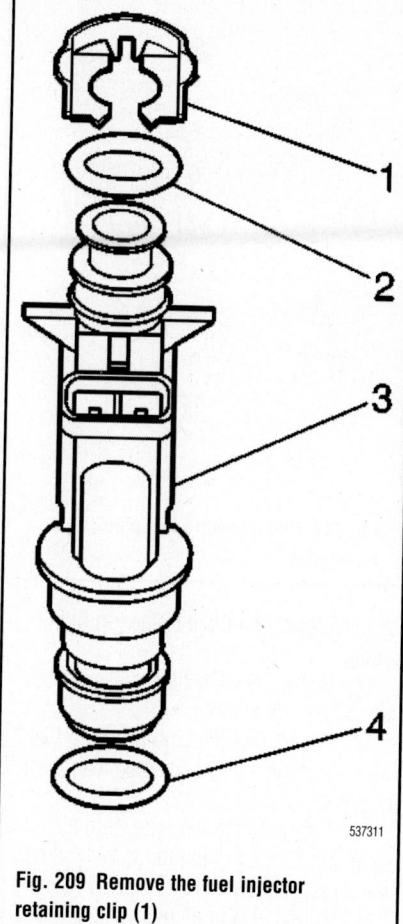

Fig. 209 Remove the fuel injector retaining clip (1)

To install:

➡️**Be sure to use the correct part number when ordering replacement fuel injectors.**

6. The fuel injector assembly (1) is stamped with a part number identification (2).
7. Lubricate the NEW injector O-rings with clean engine oil.
8. Install the fuel injector upper O-ring.
9. Install the fuel injector lower O-ring.
10. Install the fuel injector (3) to the fuel rail.
11. Install the fuel injector retaining clip.
12. Install the fuel rail.

FUEL PUMP

REMOVAL & INSTALLATION

2.0L Engine

See Figures 211 through 215.

1. Relieve the low and high side fuel system pressure. Refer to Fuel Pressure Relief.

2. Disconnect the engine wiring harness electrical connector (1) from the high pressure fuel pump.

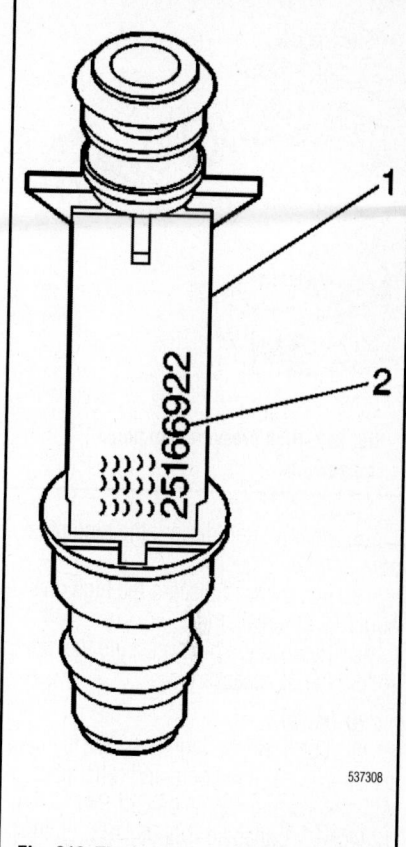

Fig. 210 The fuel injector assembly (1) is stamped with a part number identification (2)

3. Remove the engine wiring harness clip (3) from the high pressure fuel pump cover.
4. Remove the fuel feed intermediate pipe.
5. Remove the fuel feed pipe.
6. Remove and discard the high pressure fuel pump bolts.
7. Remove the high pressure fuel pump.

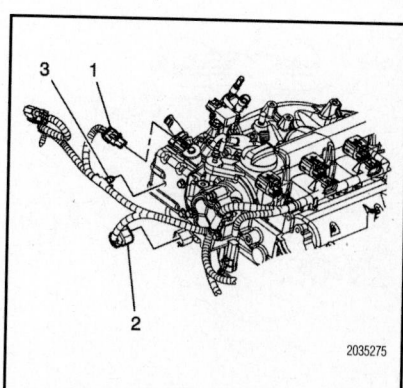

Fig. 211 Disconnect the engine wiring harness electrical connector (1) from the high pressure fuel pump

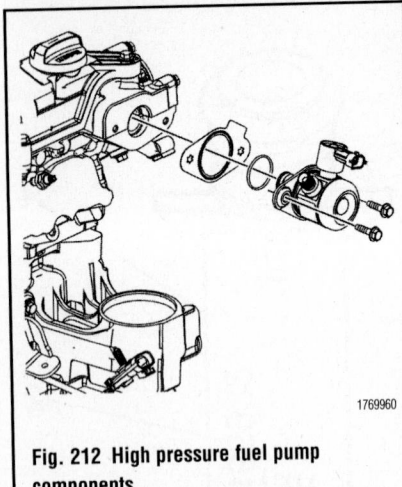

Fig. 212 High pressure fuel pump components

8. Remove and discard the high pressure fuel pump gasket.

9. Remove and discard the high pressure fuel pump O-ring.

10. Remove the high pressure fuel pump roller lifter, if necessary.

To install:

11. Lubricate the high pressure fuel pump cylinder head bore and roller lifter with silicon free engine oil GM P/N 12345610; Canadian P/N 993193) or an equivalent, if necessary.

12. Install the high pressure fuel pump roller lifter, if necessary.

13. Install a NEW high pressure fuel pump O-ring.

14. Position the NEW high pressure fuel pump gasket to the cylinder head.

➡**Ensure the plastic bolt retainers are installed in the high pressure fuel pump mounting holes prior to installing.**

15. Install the high pressure fuel pump. Push the pump into the cylinder head bore

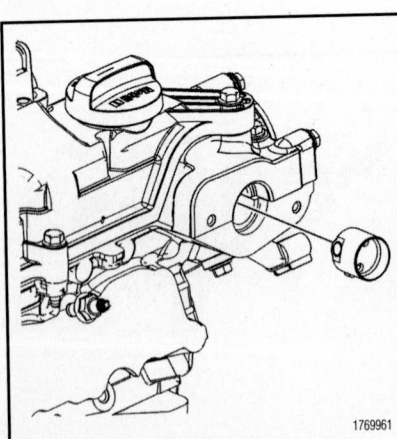

Fig. 213 Remove the high pressure fuel pump roller lifter, if necessary

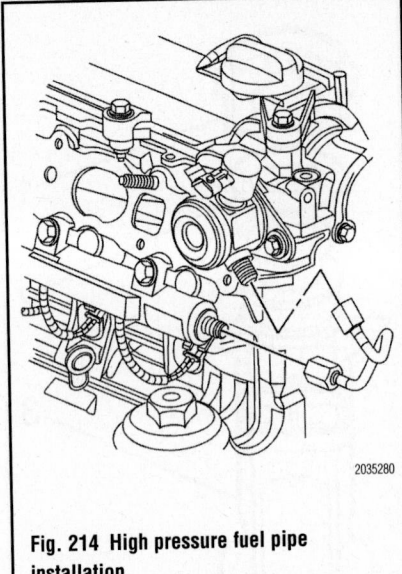

Fig. 214 High pressure fuel pipe installation

by hand, applying force to the top of the pump.

16. Install the NEW high pressure fuel pump bolts Hand-tight.

17. Ensure that the high pressure fuel pump, and fuel rail fittings are clean prior to assembly.

18. Lubricate the high pressure fuel pump, and the fuel rail fittings with silicon free engine oil GM P/N 12345610 (Canadian P/N 993193) or an equivalent.

19. Install the NEW high pressure fuel pipe.

20. Tighten the high pressure fuel pipe fitting to the fuel rail Hand-tight.

21. Tighten the high pressure fuel pipe fitting to the fuel pump Hand-tight.

22. Place the fuel feed pipe onto the intake manifold.

23. Install the fuel feed pipe bolts Hand-tight.

24. Tighten the fuel feed pipe to fuel pump fitting Hand-tight.

   a. Tighten the fuel feed pipe bolts to 89 inch lbs. (10 Nm).

   b. Tighten the fuel feed pipe to fuel pump fitting to 22 ft. lbs. (30 Nm).

   c. Tighten the high pressure fuel pipe fittings to 24 ft. lbs. (32 Nm).

   d. Tighten the high pressure fuel pump bolts evenly to 11 ft. lbs. (15 Nm).

25. Install the high pressure fuel pump insulator.

26. Position the high pressure fuel pump cover.

27. Install the high pressure fuel pump cover bolts.

28. Tighten the bolts to 89 inch lbs. (10 Nm).

29. Connect the engine wiring harness

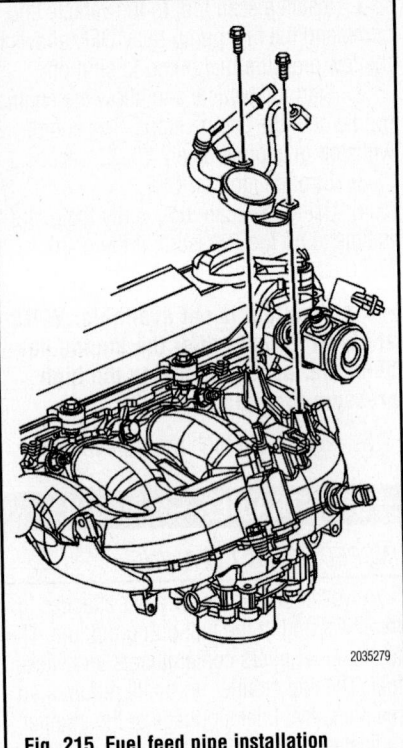

Fig. 215 Fuel feed pipe installation

electrical connector (1) to the high pressure fuel pump.

30. Install the engine wiring harness clip (3) to the fuel pump cover.

31. Inspect for leaks using the following procedure:

   a. Turn ON the ignition, with the engine OFF for 2 seconds.

   b. Turn OFF the ignition, for 10 seconds.

   c. Turn ON the ignition, with the engine OFF.

   d. Inspect for fuel leaks.

32. Install the low side fuel pressure service port cap.

33. Tighten the fuel fill cap.

2.2L & 2.4L Engines

See Figures 216 through 218.

Fuel Pump Module

❋❋ CAUTION

Gasoline or gasoline vapors are highly flammable. A fire could occur if an ignition source is present. Never drain or store gasoline or diesel fuel in an open container, due to the possibility of fire or explosion. Have a dry chemical (Class B) fire extinguisher nearby.

❋❋ CAUTION

To reduce the risk of fire and personal injury that may result from a

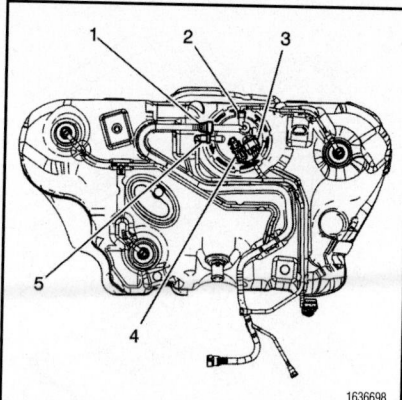

Fig. 216 Disconnect the fuel pressure sensor and fuel pump module electrical connectors (1, 4)

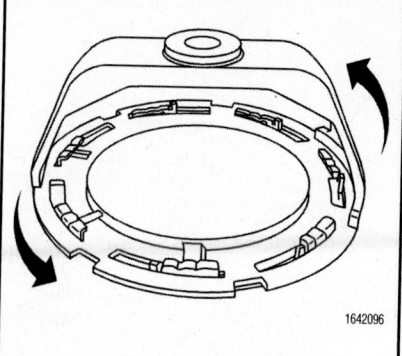

Fig. 217 Use the J 45722 and a long breaker-bar in order to unlock the fuel sender lock ring. Turn the fuel sender lock ring in a counterclockwise direction

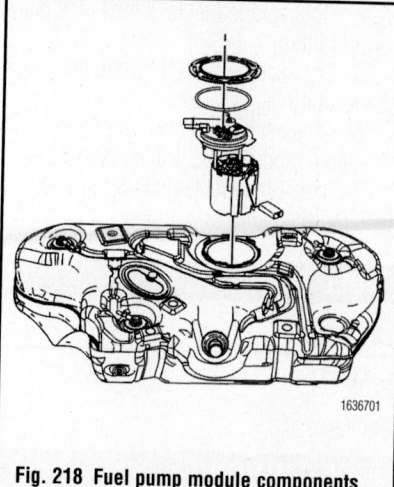

Fig. 218 Fuel pump module components

fuel leak, always replace the fuel sender gasket when reinstalling the fuel sender assembly.

1. Remove the fuel tank. Refer to Fuel Tank replacement.
2. Disconnect the fuel pressure sensor and fuel pump module electrical connectors (1, 4).
3. Disconnect the fuel tank vent pipe quick connect fittings (2, 3).
4. Disconnect the fuel tank feed pipe quick connect fitting (5).
5. Install the J 45722 to the lock ring.

※※ WARNING

Avoid damaging the lock ring. Use only J-45722 to prevent damage to the lock ring.

※※ WARNING

Do not handle the fuel sender assembly by the fuel pipes. The amount of leverage generated by handling the fuel pipes could damage the joints.

➡Note the following:

- The fuel sender assembly may spring up from its position.
- When removing the fuel sender assembly from the fuel tank, be aware that the reservoir bucket is full of fuel. It must be tipped slightly during removal to avoid damage to the float. Discard the fuel sender assembly O-ring and replace it with a new one.
- Carefully discard the fuel in the reservoir bucket into an approved container.

➡Do NOT use impact tools. Significant force will be required to release the

lock ring. The use of a hammer and screwdriver is not recommended. Secure the fuel tank in order to prevent fuel tank rotation.

6. Use the J 45722 and a long breaker-bar in order to unlock the fuel sender lock ring. Turn the fuel sender lock ring in a counterclockwise direction.
7. Remove the module lock ring.
8. Slowly raise the module until the fuel level sensor float arm is just visible. Ensure that the fuel level sensor harness connector clears the tank opening.

➡When removing the module from the fuel tank, be aware that the module reservoir bowl is full of fuel. Tip the module slightly during removal to avoid bending the fuel level sensor float arm.

9. Tilt the module toward the rear of the fuel tank to allow the level sensor float arm to clear the tank opening. Remove the module from the tank.
10. Carefully discard the fuel in the module reservoir bowl into an approved fuel container.
11. DO NOT reuse the old fuel pump module seal.
12. Remove and discard the fuel pump module seal.

➡Some lock ring were manufactured with DO NOT REUSE stamped into them. These lock rings may be reused if they are not damaged or warped. Inspect the lock ring for damage due to improper removal or installation procedures. If damage is found, install a NEW lock ring. Check the lock ring for flatness.

13. Place the lock ring on a flat surface. Measure the clearance between to lock ring

and the flat surface using a feeler gauge at 7 points.

14. If the warpage is less than 0.016 inch (0.41 mm), the lock ring does not require replacement.
15. If the warpage is greater than 0.016 inch (0.41 mm), replace the lock ring.
16. If only replacing the module, remove the fuel level sensor.

To install:

17. Install a NEW fuel pump module seal onto the fuel tank.
18. If installing only the module, install the fuel level sensor.

➡The reservoir must be tipped slightly during installation to avoid bending the fuel level sensor float arm.

19. Tilt the module toward the rear of the fuel tank to allow the fuel level sensor float arm to clear the tank opening. Install the module into the fuel tank.
20. Lower the module assembly into the tank. Ensure that the fuel level sensor harness connector is positioned properly.
21. Install the module lock ring over the module pipes and electrical harness, and into position on the top of the module.

➡Always replace the fuel sender seal when installing the fuel sender assembly. Replace the lock ring if necessary. Do not apply any type of lubrication in the seal groove. Ensure the lock ring is installed with the correct side facing upward. A correctly installed lock ring will only turn in a clockwise direction.

22. Using the J 45722, rotate the fuel sender assembly lock ring clockwise until the ring is locked into place on the fuel tank.
23. Remove the J 45722 from the lock ring.

24. Connect the fuel tank feed pipe quick connect fitting.

25. Connect the fuel tank vent pipe quick connect fittings.

26. Connect the fuel pressure sensor and fuel pump module electrical connectors.

27. Install the fuel tank. Refer to Fuel Tank replacement.

FUEL TANK

DRAINING

E-85

See Figure 219.

> ❋❋ **CAUTION**
>
> **Refer to Fuel System Precautions.**

➡ **Lubricate the fuel drain hose with J 36850 or an equivalent to aid in hose insertion. Do not use an unapproved lubricant.**

1. Insert the J 45004 into the fuel tank (1) until the hose reaches the bottom of the fuel tank.

2. Use a hand or air operated pump device in order to drain as much fuel through the fuel fill pipe as possible.

Non E-85

See Figure 220.

> ❋❋ **CAUTION**
>
> **Refer to Fuel System Precautions.**

1. Remove the fuel filler cap.

2. Install the J 42960-2, or an equivalent, into the fuel fill pipe in order to hold the door open.

3. Insert the J 43290 (2) through the J 42960-2 (1) and into the fill pipe.

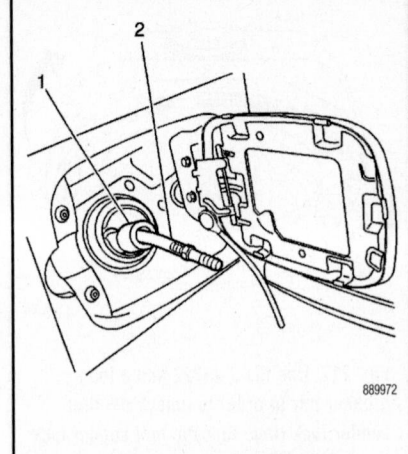

Fig. 220 Insert the J 43290 (2) through the J 42960-2 (1) and into the fill pipe

4. Continue to insert the J 43290 (2) into the fill pipe until the hose exits the valve (1) and reaches the bottom of the tank.

5. Use an air operated pump device in order to drain as much fuel out through the J 43290 (1) as possible.

REMOVAL & INSTALLATION

2.0L Engine

See Figures 221 through 228.

> ❋❋ **CAUTION**
>
> **Refer to Fuel System Precautions.**

> ❋❋ **WARNING**
>
> **Cap the fittings and plug the holes when servicing the fuel system in order to prevent dirt and other contaminants from entering the open pipes and passages.**

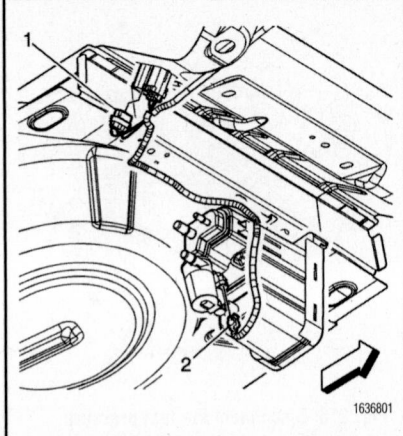

Fig. 222 Disconnect the fuel tank electrical connector (1) from the pass through connector

1. Relieve the fuel system pressure. Refer to Fuel Pressure Relief.

2. Drain the fuel tank. Refer to Fuel Tank Draining.

3. Raise and support the vehicle.

4. Disconnect the fuel tank vent pipe quick connect fittings (1, 4).

5. Loosen the fuel fill pipe hose clamp (2) at the fuel tank.

6. Remove the fuel fill pipe hose from the fuel tank.

7. Disconnect the fuel tank electrical connector (1) from the pass through connector.

8. Remove the exhaust pipe insulators from the underbody hangers.

9. Remove the muffler insulators from the underbody hanger and slowly lower the exhaust in order to allow it to rest on the rear axle beam.

10. Place an adjustable jack under the fuel tank.

11. Remove the fuel tank strap bolts.

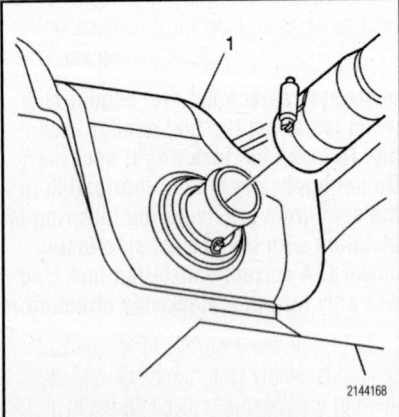

Fig. 219 Insert the J 45004 into the fuel tank (1) until the hose reaches the bottom of the fuel tank

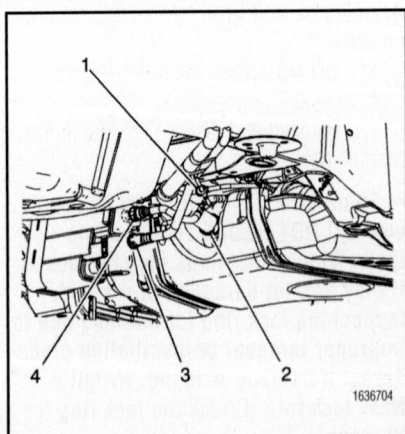

Fig. 221 Disconnect the fuel tank vent pipe quick connect fittings (1, 4)

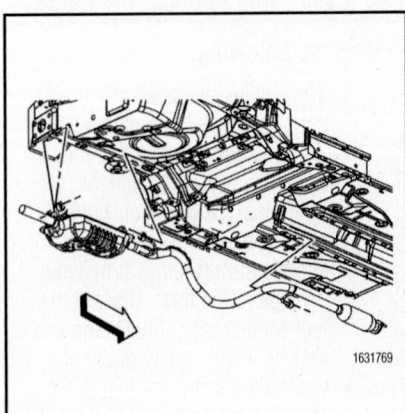

Fig. 223 Remove the insulators and lower the exhaust slowly to allow it to rest on the rear axle beam

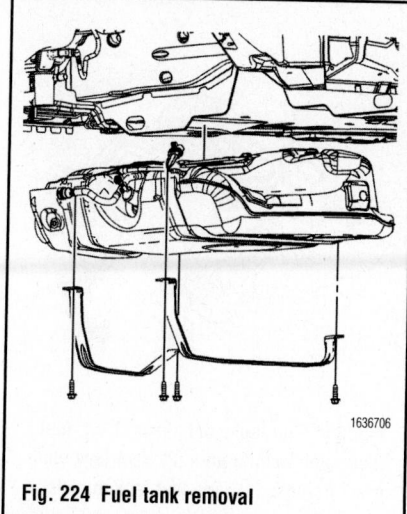

Fig. 224 Fuel tank removal

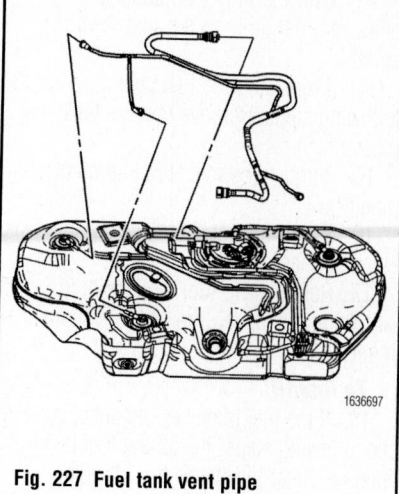

Fig. 227 Fuel tank vent pipe

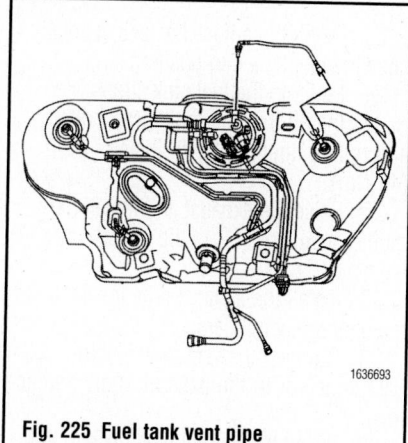

Fig. 225 Fuel tank vent pipe

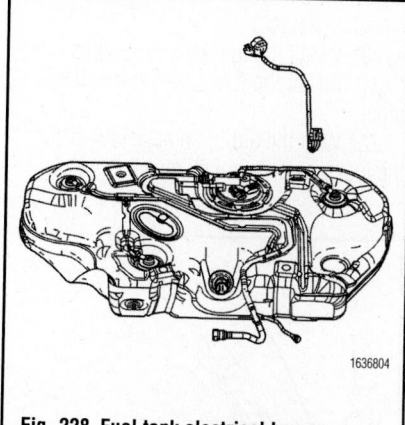

Fig. 228 Fuel tank electrical harness

12. Remove the fuel tank straps.

13. Using the adjustable jack, carefully lower the fuel tank away from the vehicle.

14. With the aid of an assistant, place the fuel tank on a suitable work surface.

15. If replacing the fuel tank, perform the following steps: remove the fuel tank vent pipe.

16. Remove the fuel feed intermediate pipe.

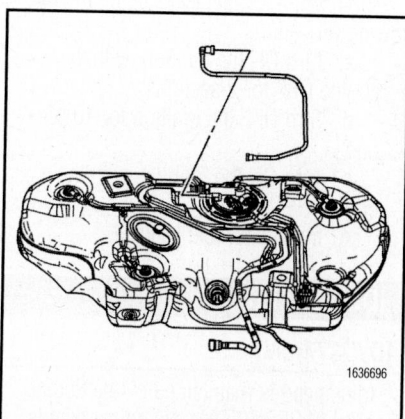

Fig. 226 Fuel feed intermediate pipe

17. Remove the fuel tank vent pipe.

18. Disconnect and remove the fuel tank electrical harness.

19. Remove the fuel tank module. Refer to Fuel Pump Module replacement.

To install:

20. If the fuel tank was replaced perform the following steps: Install the fuel tank module. Refer to Fuel Pump Module replacement.

21. Install the fuel tank vent pipe.

22. Install and connect the fuel tank electrical harness.

23. Install the fuel feed intermediate pipe.

24. Install the fuel tank vent pipe. With the aid of an assistant, place the fuel tank on the suitable jack.

25. Using the adjustable jack, carefully raise the fuel tank into position.

26. Position the fuel tank straps.

27. Install the fuel tank strap bolts and tighten the bolts to 33 ft. lbs. (45 Nm).

28. Remove adjustable jack from under the fuel tank.

29. Raise the exhaust and install the muffler insulators to the underbody hangers.

30. Install the exhaust pipe insulators to the underbody hangers.

31. Connect the fuel tank electrical connector (1) to the pass through connector.

32. Install the fuel fill pipe hose to the fuel tank.

33. Tighten the fuel fill pipe hose clamp (2) at the fuel tank to 40 inch lbs. (4.5 Nm).

34. Connect the fuel tank vent pipe quick connect fittings (1, 4).

35. Lower the vehicle.

36. Refill the fuel tank.

37. Connect the negative battery cable. Refer to Battery Negative Cable Disconnection and Connection.

38. Inspect for fuel leaks using the following procedure:

a. Turn ON the ignition, with the engine OFF for 2 seconds.

b. Turn OFF the ignition for 10 seconds.

c. Turn ON the ignition, with the engine OFF.

d. Inspect for fuel leaks.

2.2L & 2.4L Engines

See Figures 229 through 234.

✳✳ CAUTION

Refer to Fuel System Precautions.

✳✳ WARNING

Cap the fittings and plug the holes when servicing the fuel system in order to prevent dirt and other contaminants from entering the open pipes and passages.

1. Relieve the fuel system pressure. Refer to Fuel Pressure Relief.

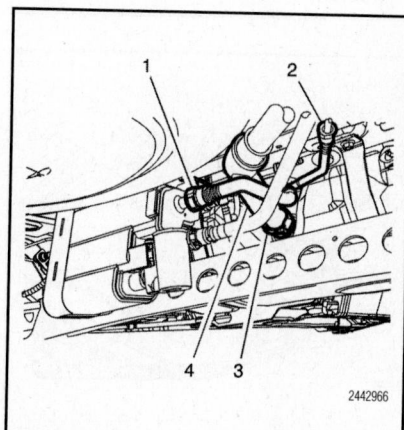

Fig. 229 Disconnect the fuel tank vent pipe quick connect fittings (1)

2. Drain the fuel tank. Refer to Fuel Tank Draining.

3. Raise and support the vehicle.

4. Disconnect the fuel tank vent pipe quick connect fitting (1).

5. Disconnect the fuel tank vent pipe quick connect fitting (2) from the fill tube vent pipe.

6. Loosen the fuel fill pipe hose clamp (3) and remove the hose (4) from the fuel tank.

7. Disconnect the fuel tank electrical connector (1) from the pass through connector.

8. Remove the exhaust pipe insulators (1) from the underbody hangers.

9. Remove the muffler insulators (1) from the underbody hanger and slowly lower the exhaust in order to allow it to rest on the rear axle beam.

10. Place an adjustable jack under the fuel tank.

11. Remove the fuel tank strap bolts (1) and the fuel tank straps (2).

12. Carefully lower the fuel tank away from the vehicle.

13. With the aid of an assistant, place the fuel tank on a suitable work surface.

14. If replacing the fuel tank, perform the following steps: Remove the fuel tank vent pipes (3, 5).

15. Remove the fuel feed intermediate pipe (2).

16. Disconnect and remove the fuel tank electrical harness (1).

17. Remove the fuel tank module (4). Refer to Fuel Pump Module replacement.

To install:

18. If the fuel tank was replaced, perform the following steps: Install the fuel tank module. Refer to Fuel Pump Module replacement.

19. Install and connect the fuel tank electrical harness.

20. Install the fuel tank vent pipes.

21. Install the fuel feed intermediate pipe.

22. With the aid of an assistant, place the fuel tank on a suitable jack.

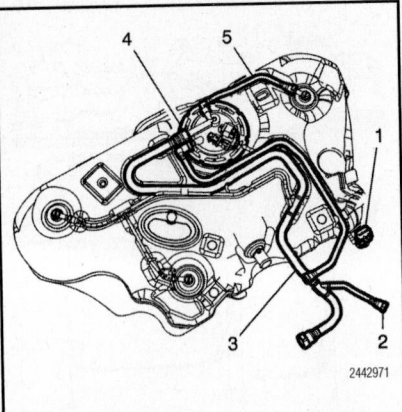

Fig. 234 fuel tank vent pipes (3, 5), fuel feed intermediate pipe (2), fuel tank electrical harness (1), and fuel tank module (4)

23. Using the adjustable jack, carefully raise the fuel tank into position.

24. Position the fuel tank straps.

25. Install the fuel tank strap bolts and tighten them to 33 ft. lbs. (45 Nm).

26. Raise the exhaust and install the muffler insulators (1) to the underbody hangers.

27. Install the exhaust pipe insulators to the underbody hangers.

28. Connect the fuel tank electrical connector to the pass through connector.

29. Install the fuel fill pipe hose to the fuel tank.

30. Tighten the fuel fill pipe hose clamp at the fuel tank to 40 inch lbs. (4.5 Nm).

31. Connect the fuel tank vent pipe quick connect fittings.

32. Lower the vehicle.

33. Refill the fuel tank.

34. Connect the negative battery cable. Refer to Battery Negative Cable Disconnection and Connection.

35. Inspect for fuel leaks using the following procedure:

    a. Turn ON the ignition, with the engine OFF for 2 seconds.

    b. Turn OFF the ignition for 10 seconds.

    c. Turn ON the ignition, with the engine OFF.

    d. Inspect for fuel leaks.

IDLE SPEED

ADJUSTMENT

Idle speed is maintained by the Engine Control Module (ECM). No adjustment is necessary or possible.

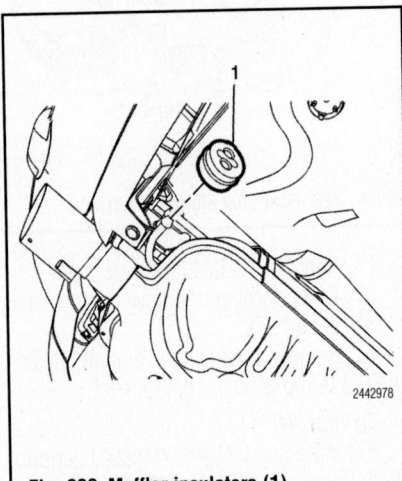

Fig. 230 Disconnect the fuel tank electrical connector (1) from the pass through connector

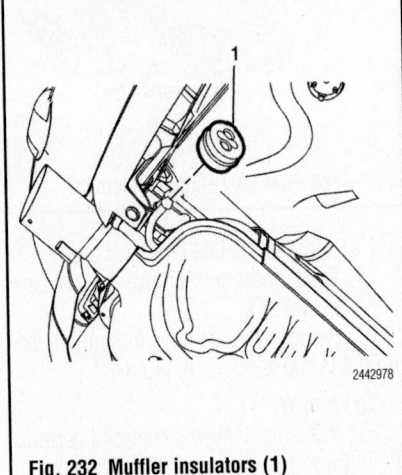

Fig. 232 Muffler insulators (1)

Fig. 231 Exhaust pipe insulators (1)

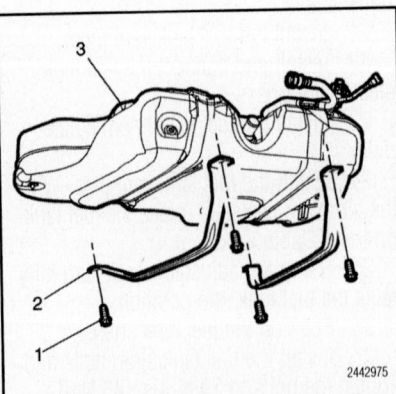

Fig. 233 Remove the fuel tank strap bolts (1) and the fuel tank straps (2).

THROTTLE BODY ASSEMBLY

REMOVAL & INSTALLATION

2.0L Engine

See Figures 235 and 236.

✳✳ WARNING

Do not use solvent of any type when cleaning the gasket surfaces on the intake manifold and the throttle body assembly, as damage to the gasket surfaces and throttle body assembly may result. Use care in cleaning the gasket surfaces on the intake manifold and the throttle body assembly, as sharp tools may damage the gasket surfaces.

✳✳ WARNING

Do not use any solvent that contains Methyl Ethyl Ketone (MEK). This solvent may damage fuel system components.

1. Remove the charge air cooler outlet pipe.
2. Disconnect the engine wiring harness electrical connector (1) from the electronic throttle control (ETC).
3. Remove the throttle body bolts.
4. Remove the throttle body and seal from the intake manifold.

To install:

5. Inspect the throttle body seal, and replace if necessary.
6. Position the throttle body to the intake manifold.
7. Install the throttle body bolts and tighten them to 89 inch lbs. (10 Nm).
8. Connect the engine wiring harness electrical connector to the ETC.

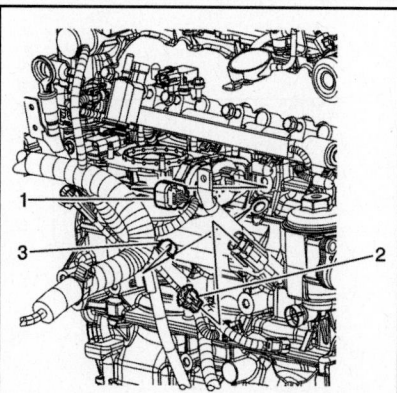

Fig. 235 Disconnect the engine wiring harness electrical connector (1) from the electronic throttle control

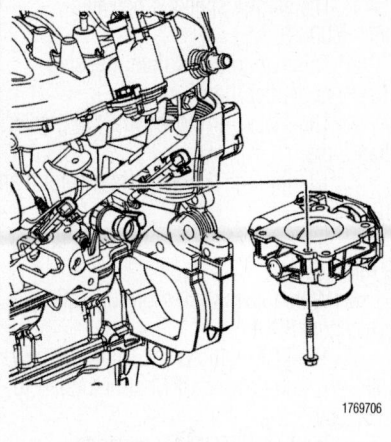

Fig. 236 Remove the throttle body and bolts

9. Install the charge air cooler outlet pipe.

2.2L & 2.4L Engines

See Figures 237 and 238.

✳✳ WARNING

Do not use solvent of any type when cleaning the gasket surfaces on the intake manifold and the throttle body assembly, as damage to the gasket surfaces and throttle body assembly may result. Use care in cleaning the gasket surfaces on the intake manifold and the throttle body assembly, as sharp tools may damage the gasket surfaces.

✳✳ WARNING

Do not use any solvent that contains Methyl Ethyl Ketone (MEK). This sol-

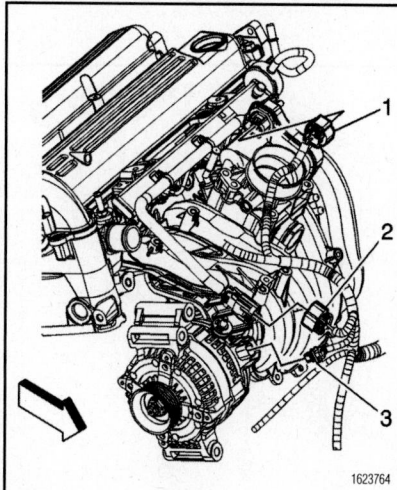

Fig. 237 Disconnect the throttle actuator control (TAC) electrical connector (1)

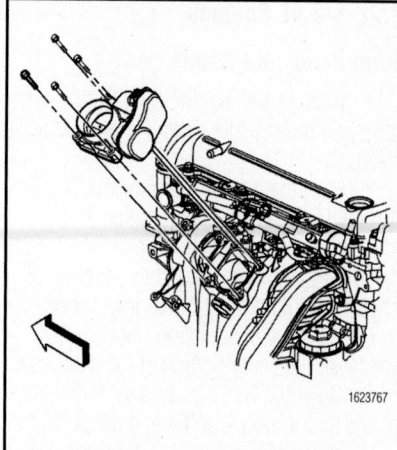

Fig. 238 Remove the throttle body bolts and the throttle body

vent may damage fuel system components.

➡**DO NOT prop open the throttle blade with the ignition key in the ON position as it may set a diagnostic trouble code (DTC).**

1. Remove the air cleaner outlet duct.
2. Disconnect the throttle actuator control (TAC) electrical connector (1).
3. Remove the throttle body bolts.
4. Remove the throttle body.
5. Inspect the throttle body gasket, and replace if necessary.
6. Install the throttle body.
7. Install the throttle body bolts and tighten them to 89 inch lbs. (10 Nm).
8. Connect the TAC electrical connector.
9. Install the air cleaner outlet duct.
10. Perform the throttle learn procedure. Refer to Throttle/Idle Learn.

THROTTLE/IDLE LEARN

2.0L Engine (Turbocharger)

➡**Ensure the following conditions are met before performing with this procedure:**

- Do not perform this procedure if a throttle position sensor or other throttle actuator control (TAC) system DTCs are set other than P2176. The ECM will not perform the idle learn procedure with a DTC set.

1. Turn OFF the ignition for 30 seconds.
2. Turn ON the ignition, with the engine OFF for 60 seconds.
3. Turn OFF the ignition.
4. Turn ON the ignition, with the engine OFF.
5. Clear the DTCs with a scan tool.

2.2L & 2.4L Engines

With Scan Tool-Reset

1. Ignition ON, engine OFF. With a scan tool, perform the Idle Learn Reset in Module Setup.

2. Start the engine, monitor the TB Idle Airflow Compensation parameter. The TB Idle Airflow Compensation parameter value should equal 0 percent and the engine should be idling at a normal idle speed.

If the engine is not idling normally, proceed with the Learn portion of the diagnostic.

3. Clear the DTCs and return to the diagnostic that referred you here, if applicable.

Without Scan Tool-Learn

➡**Do NOT perform the Without Scan Tool-Learn procedure if DTCs are set.**

1. The engine speed is between 450–4,000 RPM.

2. The manifold absolute pressure (MAP) is greater than 5 kPa.

3. The Mass Air Flow (MAF) is greater than 2 g/s.

4. The ignition 1 voltage is greater than 10 volts.

5. Start and idle the engine in Park for 3 minutes.

6. With a scan tool, monitor desired and actual RPM.

7. The ECM will start to learn the new idle cells and desired RPM should start to decrease.

8. Ignition OFF for 60 seconds.

9. Start and idle the engine in Park for 3 minutes.

➡**Important: During the drive cycle the check engine light may come on with idle speed DTCs. If idle speed codes are set, clear the codes so the ECM can continue to learn.**

10. After the 3-minute run time the engine should be idling normal.

11. If the engine idle speed has not been learned the vehicle will need to be driven at speeds above 44 mph (70 km/h) with several decelerations and extended idles.

12. After the drive cycle, the engine should be idling normally.

13. If the engine idle speed has not been learned, turn OFF the ignition for 60 seconds and repeat step 6.

14. Once the engine speed has returned to normal, clear DTCs.

HEATING & AIR CONDITIONING SYSTEM

BLOWER MOTOR

REMOVAL & INSTALLATION

See Figures 239 through 242.

1. Remove the right sound insulator.
2. Remove the Instrument Panel (I/P) compartment.
3. Disconnect the blower motor electrical connector.
4. Remove the lower blower motor cover retaining screws.
5. Remove the lower blower motor cover.
6. Remove the blower motor nuts.

➡**Cut through the case as straight as possible because the motor cup must be reused. In order to prevent damage to the component, do not cut any deeper than necessary to remove the motor cup.**

7. Remove the blower motor and cup from the lower case by cutting through the case between the circular ribs around the motor with a sharp utility knife.

8. Release the blower motor retaining tab and remove the motor from the cup.

To install:

9. Install the blower motor (1) into the motor cup (2) that was cut out of the lower case.

10. Install the blower motor nuts (3).

11. Tighten the nuts to 21 inch lbs. (24 Nm).

12. Attach the service ring (4) to the motor cup (2) with the screws (5) included in the kit.

13. Tighten the screws to 15 inch lbs. (1.8 Nm).

14. Install the blower motor and service ring into the HVAC module using the screws (5) included in the kit. Make certain the blower motor electrical connector is pointing rearward in the vehicle.

15. Tighten the screws to 15 inch lbs. (1.8 Nm).

16. Install the lower blower motor cover.

17. Install the lower blower motor cover retaining screws.

18. Tighten the screws to 15 inch lbs. (1.8 Nm).

19. Connect the blower motor electrical connector.

20. Install the I/P compartment.

21. Install the right sound insulator.

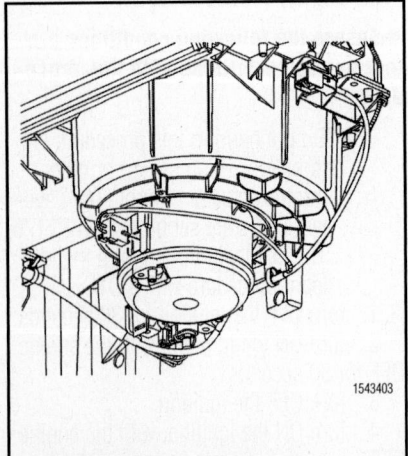

Fig. 239 Blower motor electrical connector

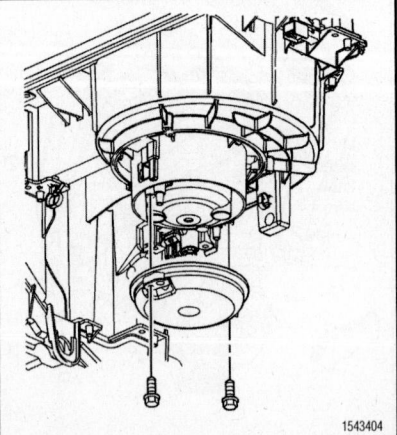

Fig. 240 Blower motor cover and retaining screws

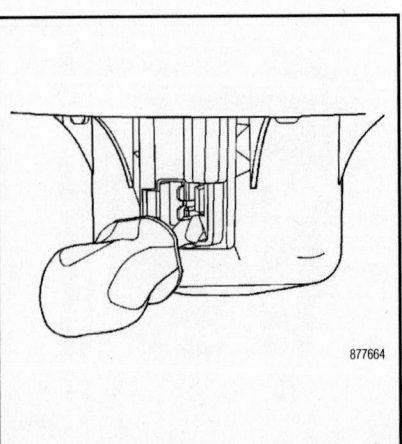

Fig. 241 Release the blower motor retaining tab and remove the motor from the cup

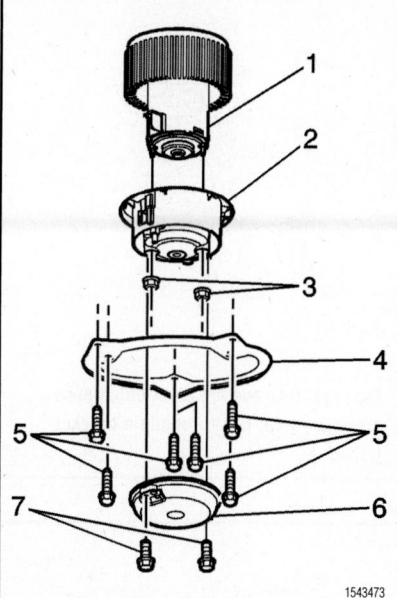

Fig. 242 Install the blower motor (1) into the motor cup (2) that was cut out of the lower case

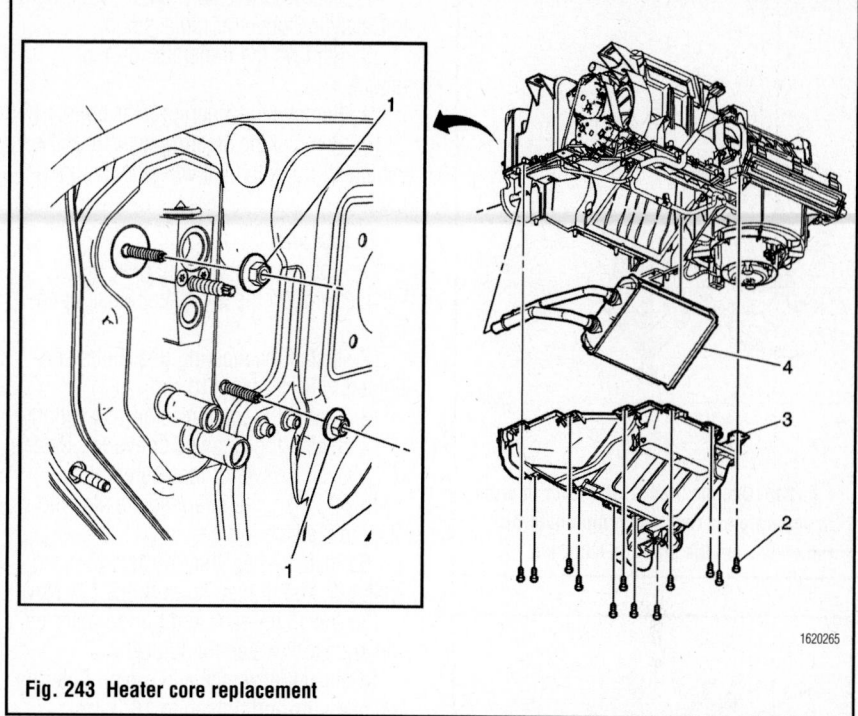

Fig. 243 Heater core replacement

HEATER CORE

REMOVAL & INSTALLATION

See Figure 243.

1. Remove the heater inlet hose from the heater core.
2. Remove the heater outlet hose from the heater core.

3. Remove the instrument panel tie bar.
4. Remove the center floor air outlet duct.
5. Remove the 2 HVAC module to dash panel nuts (1).
6. Remove the 12 cover assembly screws (2).
7. Remove the cover assembly.

8. Remove the heater core assembly.
9. Installation is the reverse of removal, noting the following:
   - Tighten the 12 cover assembly screws to 13 inch lbs. (1.5 Nm)
   - Tighten the HVAC module to dash panel nut to 88 inch lbs. (10 Nm)

STEERING

POWER STEERING GEAR

REMOVAL & INSTALLATION

See Figures 244 through 247.

✳✳ WARNING

With wheels of the vehicle facing straight ahead, secure the steering wheel utilizing steering column anti-rotation pin, steering column lock, or a strap to prevent rotation. Locking of the steering column will prevent damage and a possible malfunction of the SIR system. The steering wheel must be secured in position before disconnecting the following components:

- The steering column
- The intermediate shaft(s)
- The steering gear

✳✳ WARNING

After disconnecting these components, do not rotate the steering wheel or move the front tires and wheels. Failure to follow this procedure may cause the SIR coil assembly to become un-centered and cause possible damage to the SIR coil. If you think the SIR coil has became un-centered, refer to your specific SIR coil's centering procedure to re-center SIR Coil.

1. Turn the steering wheel to the straight ahead position and lock it in place.
2. Remove the front tire and wheel assemblies.
3. Remove both rack and pinion outer tie rod end nuts and discard them.

➡**Do not attempt to separate the rack and pinion outer tie rod ends using a wedge type tool.**

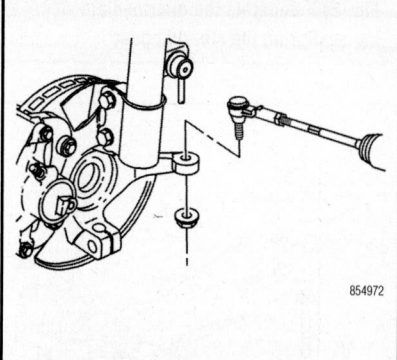

Fig. 244 Remove both rack and pinion outer tie rod end nuts and discard them

4. Use the J 24319-B Puller in order to separate the rack and pinion outer tie rod ends from the steering knuckles.
5. Remove the intermediate steering shaft bolt at the steering gear and discard it.
6. Separate the intermediate steering shaft from the steering gear.

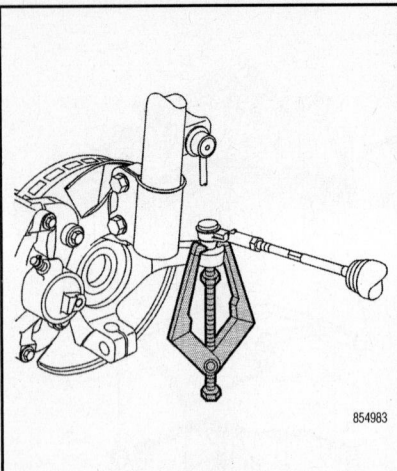

Fig. 245 Use the J 24319-B Puller in order to separate the rack and pinion outer tie rod ends from the steering knuckles

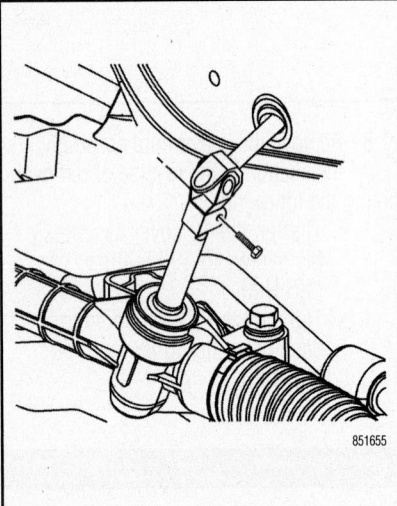

Fig. 246 Separate the intermediate steering shaft from the steering gear

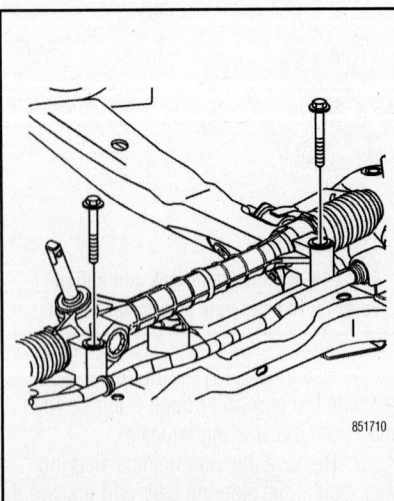

Fig. 247 Steering gear and bolts

7. Remove the catalytic converter. Refer to Catalytic Converter replacement.

8. Remove the transmission rear mount.

9. Remove the steering gear bolts.

10. Remove the steering gear from the vehicle through the left wheelhouse opening.

To install:

11. Position the steering gear in the vehicle through the left wheelhouse opening.

12. Install the steering gear bolts and tighten to 81 ft. lbs (110 Nm).

13. Install the transmission rear mount.

14. Install the catalytic convertor. Refer to Catalytic Converter replacement.

15. Connect the intermediate steering shaft to the steering gear.

16. Install a new intermediate steering shaft bolt and tighten to 25 ft. lbs (34 Nm).

17. Install the rack and pinion outer tie rod ends to the steering knuckles.

18. Install new rack and pinion outer tie rod end nuts and tighten to 18 ft. lbs (25 Nm).

19. Tighten the outer tie rod end nuts an additional 90 degrees.

20. Install the front tire and wheel assemblies.

21. Adjust the front toe. Refer to Wheel Alignment Specifications in the Suspension section.

22. If equipped with Active Brake Control, calibrate the steering angle sensor.

POWER STEERING ASSIST MOTOR

REMOVAL & INSTALLATION

2.0L Engine

See Figures 248 and 249.

Electronic Power Steering Motor Control Module Replacement

1. Position the steering column in the most upward position possible.

2. Disconnect the electronic power steering motor control module electrical connectors.

3. Remove the electronic power steering motor control module bracket bolts (1).

4. Remove the electronic power steering motor control module and bracket together from the vehicle.

5. Remove the electronic power steering motor control module bolts (1).

6. Separate the electronic power steering motor control module and bracket (2).

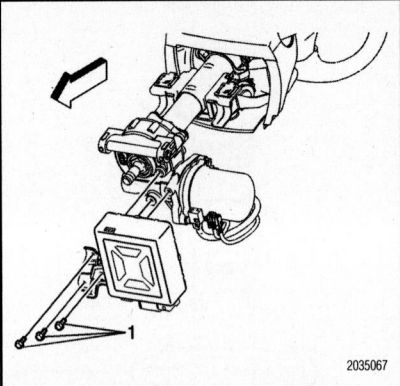

Fig. 248 Remove the electronic power steering motor control module bracket bolts (1)

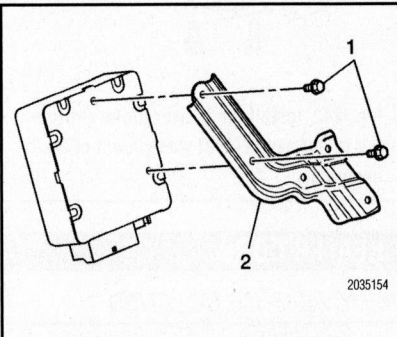

Fig. 249 Remove the electronic power steering motor control module bolts (1)

To install:

7. Position the electronic power steering motor control module and bracket together.

8. Install the electronic power steering motor control module bolts and tighten them to 102 inch lbs. (11.5 Nm).

9. Install the electronic power steering motor control module and bracket to the vehicle.

10. Install the electronic power steering motor control module bracket bolts and tighten them to 102 inch lbs. (11.5 Nm).

11. Connect the electronic power steering motor control module electrical connectors.

2.2L & 2.4L Engines

See Figures 250 through 252.

1. Cover the carpet in order to capture any lubricant that may drip from the steering column or the power steering assist motor.

2. Remove the driver knee bolster reinforcement.

3. Note the location and the routing of the tie strap that holds the power steering assist motor wires to the steering column.

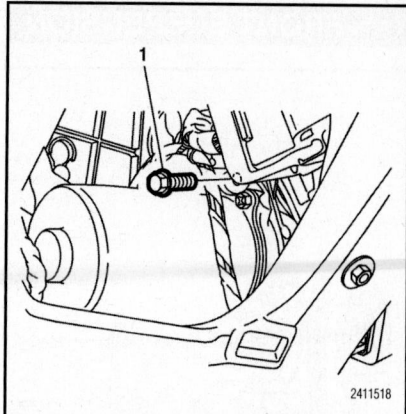

Fig. 250 Use a 12mm socket in order to remove the power steering assist motor upper bolt (1)

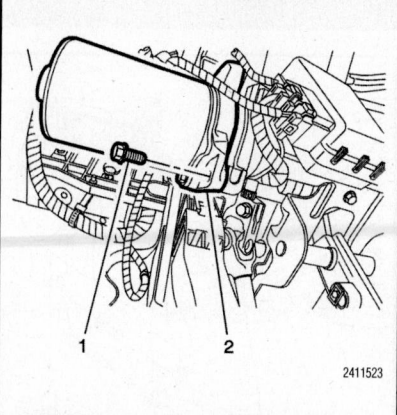

Fig. 251 Use a 12mm socket in order to remove the power steering assist motor lower bolt (1)

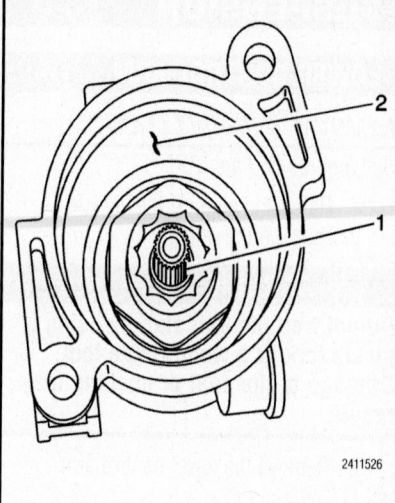

Fig. 252 Use a lint-free cotton cloth or equivalent in order to remove all remaining lubricant from the steering column worm shaft spline (1) and the steering column housing (2)

4. Remove the tie strap from the steering column.

   a. Discard the tie strap.

5. Disconnect the power steering assist motor electrical connector.

6. The bolts that secure the power steering assist motor to the steering column have a 12 mm hex head.

7. Use a 12mm socket in order to remove the power steering assist motor upper bolt (1).

8. Use a 12mm socket in order to remove the power steering assist motor lower bolt (1).

9. Remove the power steering assist motor (2).

➡**The worm shaft spline and the steering column housing must be clean and free from lubricant before continuing the motor service procedure.**

10. Do not use any solvent based cleaners to remove the lubricant. Only use lint free cotton cloth or equivalent to clean the area.

11. Use a lint-free cotton cloth or equivalent in order to remove all remaining lubricant from the steering column worm shaft spline (1) and the steering column housing (2).

12. Use a lint-free cotton cloth or equivalent in order to remove all remaining lubricant from the power steering assist motor.

To install:

➡**Only use the lubricant provided with the new power steering assist motor. Use all of the lubricant supplied with the kit.**

13. Apply the lubricant into the opening of the power steering assist motor shaft. Wipe off any excess lubricant that is not on the inside of the shaft.

14. Ensure that the NEW power steering assist motor O-ring seal is properly seated on the power steering assist motor.

➡**The power steering assist motor should engage evenly and with ease. If the motor will not engage the steering column then remove the motor and try again. Do not force the motor and the steering column together.**

15. Install the power steering assist motor to the steering column with the wire harness facing upwards and towards the front of the vehicle.

16. Do not apply any side load to the power steering assist motor while torquing the bolts, or you may induce a noise or a vibration. If a noise or a vibration emanates from the steering column, remove and install the motor again.

17. While holding the motor in place, install and finger tighten the 2 power steering assist motor bolts.

18. Tighten the 2 power steering assist motor bolts evenly, alternating between the 2 bolts, until you reach 14 ft. lbs. (19 Nm.).

19. Connect the power steering assist motor electrical connector.

20. Install the NEW tie strap in order to hold the power steering assist motor wires to the steering column in the correct location.

21. Install the driver knee bolster reinforcement.

22. Road test the vehicle and ensure that no noise or vibration emanates from the steering column.

SUSPENSION

FRONT SUSPENSION

LOWER CONTROL ARM

REMOVAL & INSTALLATION

See Figures 253 and 254.

1. Raise and support the vehicle.
2. Remove the wheel.

✳✳ WARNING

Do not free the ball stud by using a pickle fork or a wedge-type tool. Damage to the seal or bushing may result.

3. Remove the lower control arm nut (1).
4. Remove the lower control arm bolt (3) from the knuckle (2).
5. Remove the control arm to frame bolt (4).
6. Remove the control arm (3) from the frame (6).
7. Remove the lower control arm bolts (2) and the brackets (5).
8. Remove the lower control arm (1) from the knuckle (1).

To install:

9. Position the lower control arm in the frame.
10. Install the control arm to frame bolt and tighten to 74 ft. lbs. (100 Nm) + 180 degrees.

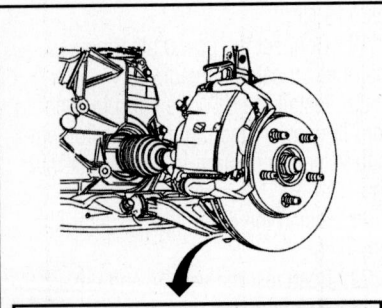
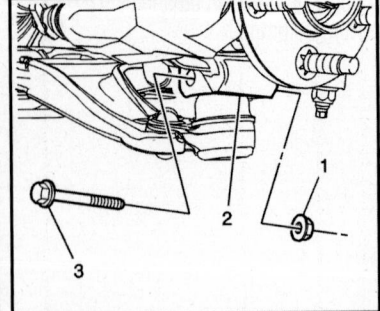

Fig. 253 Remove the lower control arm nut (1)

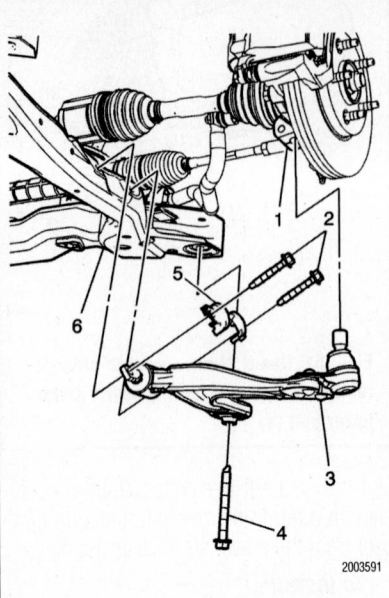

Fig. 254 Remove the control arm to frame bolt (4)

11. Install the lower control arm brackets and bolt and tighten them to 41 ft. lbs. (55 Nm).
12. Install the lower control arm bolt in the knuckle.

➡ **The torque sequence must be followed in the order that is listed.**

13. Install the lower control arm nut and tighten it to 37 ft. lbs. (50 Nm). Reverse the nut 3/4 turn. Then tighten it to 37 ft. lbs. (50 Nm) + 30 degrees.
14. Install the wheel.
15. Lower the vehicle.
16. Road test the vehicle in order to test for leads or pulls.

STABILIZER SHAFT

REMOVAL & INSTALLATION

See Figure 255.

1. Raise and support the vehicle.
2. Remove the tires and wheels.
3. Remove the stabilizer shaft link from the stabilizer shaft. Refer to Stabilizer Shaft Link replacement.
4. Remove the stabilizer shaft insulators from the stabilizer shaft. Refer to Stabilizer Shaft Insulator Replacement.
5. Remove the front stabilizer shaft (1) from the right side of the vehicle.
6. Installation is the reverse of removal.

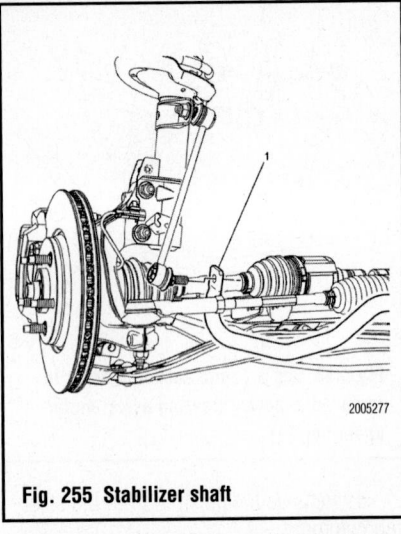

Fig. 255 Stabilizer shaft

STABILIZER SHAFT LINK

REMOVAL & INSTALLATION

See Figure 256.

1. Raise and support the vehicle.
2. Remove the front tire and wheel assembly.
3. Remove the 2 front stabilizer shaft link nuts (1).

➡ **Some models may be equipped with a washer/spacer between the stabilizer link and the shock strut. It will be necessary to transfer the washer/spacer when replacing the stabilizer shaft or the stabilizer link.**

4. Remove the front stabilizer link.
5. Installation is the reverse of removal.

Specification: Tighten the 2 stabilizer shaft link nuts to 59 ft. lbs. (80 Nm)

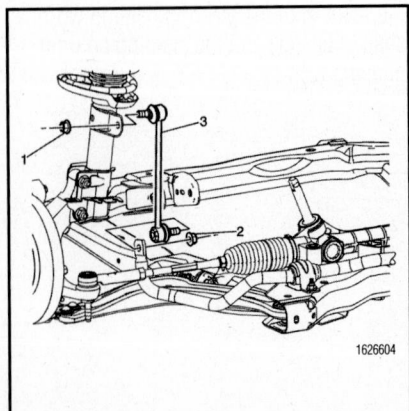

Fig. 256 The 2 front stabilizer link nuts (1) and the stabilizer link (2)

STABILIZER SHAFT INSULATOR

REMOVAL & INSTALLATION

See Figure 257.

1. Raise and support the vehicle.
2. Remove the front stabilizer shaft clamp bolt (1).
3. Remove the front stabilizer shaft clamp nut (2).
4. Remove the front stabilizer shaft clamp (3).
5. Remove the front stabilizer shaft insulator (4).

To install:

➡**Place the cut line of the insulator facing the rear of the vehicle.**

6. Installation is the reverse of removal, noting the following:
   - Tighten the front stabilizer shaft clamp nut to 37 ft. lbs. (50 Nm).
   - Tighten the front stabilizer shaft clamp bolt to 37 ft. lbs. (50 Nm).

STEERING KNUCKLE

REMOVAL & INSTALLATION

See Figure 258.

1. Raise and support the vehicle.
2. Remove the wheel bearing and hub assembly. Refer to Front Wheel Bearing and Hub replacement.
3. Remove the outer tie rod end from the knuckle.
4. Remove the lower control arm from the knuckle. Refer to Lower Control Arm replacement.
5. Remove the 2 bolts (1).
6. Remove the 2 nuts (2).
7. Remove the steering knuckle (3).
8. Installation is the reverse of removal, noting the following:

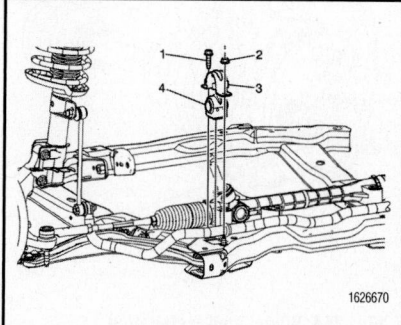

Fig. 257 Stabilizer shaft insulator replacement

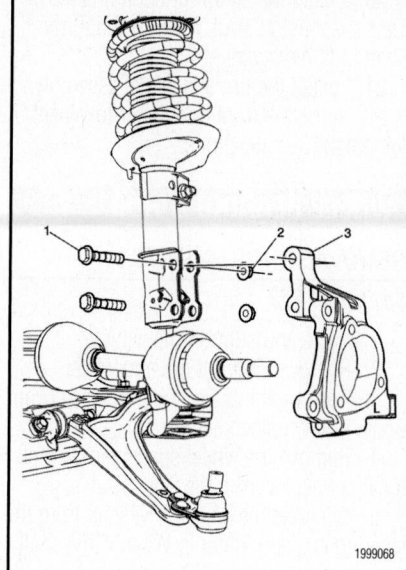

Fig. 258 Steering knuckle bolts (1), nuts (2) and knuckle (3)

- Tighten the 2 nuts to 89 ft. lbs. (120 Nm).
- Check the wheel alignment.

STRUT ASSEMBLY

REMOVAL & INSTALLATION

See Figures 259 through 261.

1. Raise the vehicle just high enough to remove the tire and wheel assembly.

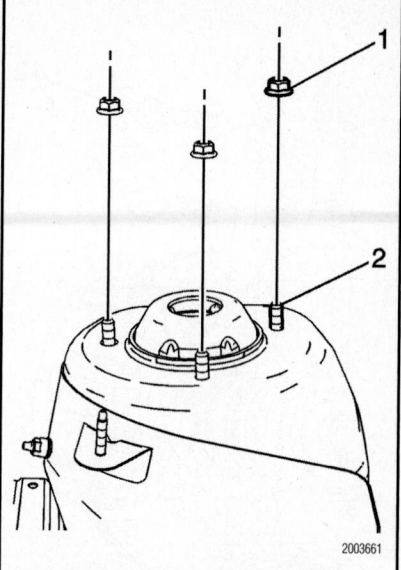

Fig. 259 Remove the front suspension strut mounting nut (1) on the front suspension strut stud (2)

2. Remove the stabilizer shaft link from the front suspension strut. Refer to Stabilizer Shaft Link replacement.
3. Remove the front suspension strut mounting nut (1) on the front suspension strut stud (2).
4. Raise the vehicle high enough to access the lower front suspension strut bolts.
5. Support the lower control arm with an adjustable jack stand.

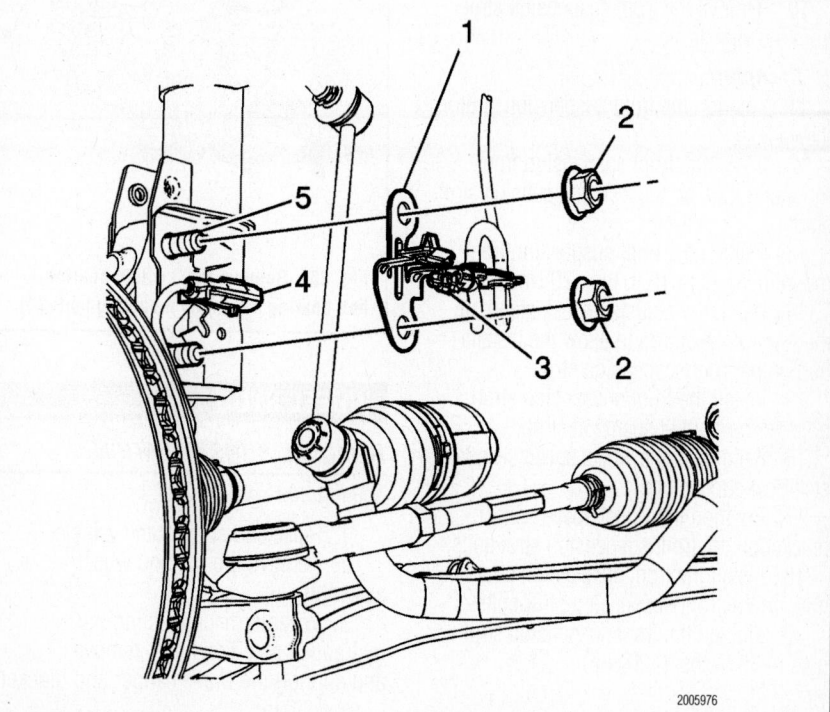

Fig. 260 Remove the front suspension strut nut (2) from the front suspension strut bolts (5)

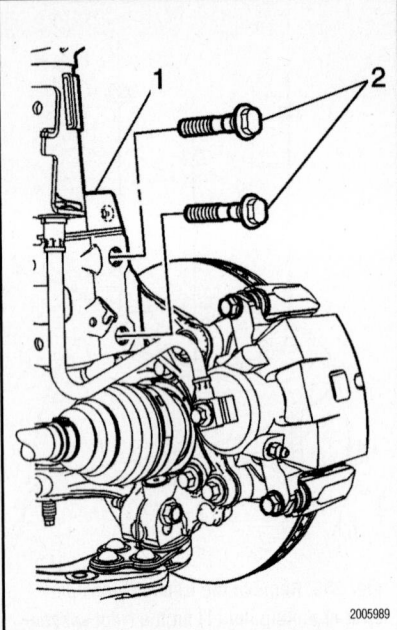

Fig. 261 Remove the front suspension strut bolts (2) from the front suspension strut (1)

6. Remove the front suspension strut nut (2) from the front suspension strut bolts (5).

7. Disconnect the wheel speed sensor electrical connectors (3) and (4).

8. Remove the wheel speed sensor bracket (1), and relocate to the side.

9. Remove the front suspension strut bolts (2) from the front suspension strut (1).

10. Remove the front suspension strut from the vehicle.

To install:

11. Position the front suspension strut in the vehicle.

12. Install the front suspension front mounting nuts on the front suspension strut studs.

13. Tighten the front suspension front mounting nuts to 15 ft. lbs. (20 Nm).

14. Using the adjustable jack stand, lift the lower control arm to allow the installation of the front suspension strut.

15. Install the front suspension strut bolts in the front suspension strut.

16. Reconnect the wheel speed sensor electrical connectors.

17. Position the wheel speed sensor bracket on the front suspension strut bolts.

18. Install the front suspension strut nuts on the front suspension strut bolts.

19. Tighten the front suspension strut nuts to 89 ft. lbs. (120 Nm).

20. Install the stabilizer shaft link the front suspension strut. Refer to Stabilizer Shaft Link replacement .

21. Install the tire and wheel assembly.

22. Align the front end. Refer to Wheel Alignment Specifications.

WHEEL BEARING & HUB

REMOVAL & INSTALLATION

See Figure 262.

1. Raise and support the vehicle.

2. Remove the front tire and wheel.

3. Remove the brake rotor. Refer to Front Brake Rotor replacement.

4. Remove the wheel speed sensor electrical connector from the front strut.

5. Separate the wheel driveshaft from the steering knuckle. Refer to Wheel Driveshaft replacement.

6. Remove the 3 wheel bearing / hub bearing assembly mounting bolts (1).

7. Remove the steering knuckle bearing spacer (2).

8. Remove the wheel bearing / hub bearing assembly (3).

9. Installation is the reverse of removal. Specification: Tighten the 3 wheel bearing / hub assembly mounting bolts to 85 ft. lbs. (115 Nm).

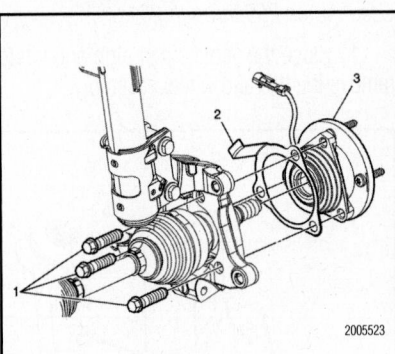

Fig. 262 Remove the 3 wheel bearing / hub bearing assembly mounting bolts (1)

WHEEL STUD

REMOVAL & INSTALLATION

See Figures 263 and 264.

1. Raise and support the vehicle.

2. Remove the tire and wheel assembly.

3. Without disconnecting the hydraulic brake flex hose, remove and support the brake caliper and bracket as an assembly, and remove the brake rotor.

4. Rotate the bearing hub to a position where the least amount of interference between the stud and the steering knuckle exists.

5. Using the J 43631, release the wheel stud from the bearing hub and discard the stud.

To install:

6. Add enough washers (1) in order to draw the stud into the hub.

7. Install the wheel nut (2) with the flat side against the washers.

8. Tighten the wheel nut until the head of the wheel stud is fully seated against the back of the bearing hub flange.

9. Remove the wheel nut and the washers.

10. Install the brake rotor, and install the brake caliper and bracket as an assembly.

11. Install the tire and wheel assembly.

12. Lower the vehicle.

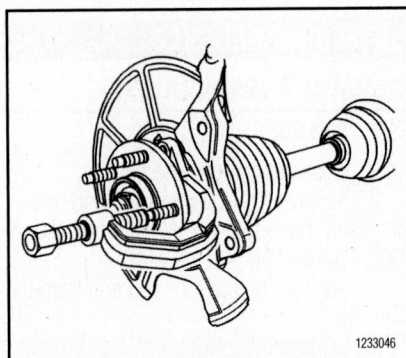

Fig. 263 Using the J 43631, release the wheel stud from the bearing hub and discard the stud

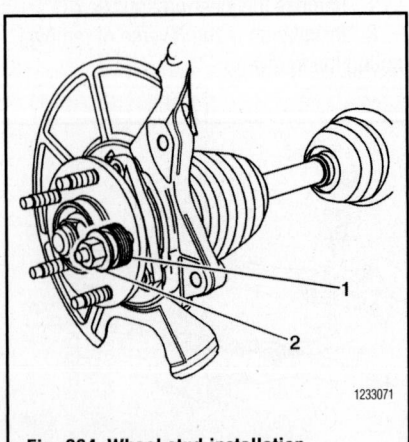

Fig. 264 Wheel stud installation

COIL SPRING

REMOVAL & INSTALLATION

See Figure 265.

1. Raise and support the vehicle.
2. Support the rear axle with tall jack stands near each rear shock absorber.
3. Remove the U-clips from the rear brake hose brackets at the rear axle.
4. Remove the lower shock bolts. Refer to Shock Absorber replacement.
5. Using the tall jack stands, slowly lower the rear axle in order to remove tension from the rear springs.
6. Remove the spring.
7. Remove the upper spring seat/jounce bumper from the spring, while leaving the lower spring seat on the axle.

To install:

➡**Important: The rear springs are indexed with the colored tag toward the rear of the vehicle. No up/down or side to side orientation is required.**

8. Install the upper spring seat/jounce bumper on the spring.
9. Install the spring with the spring tag toward the rear of the vehicle, making sure the lower coil is seated into the lower spring seat.
10. Using the jack stands, raise the rear axle in order to compress the rear springs.
11. Install the lower shock absorber bolts. Refer to Shock Absorber replacement.
12. Reposition the rear brake hoses in the axle brackets.
13. Install the U-clips to secure the brake hoses.
14. Lower the vehicle.

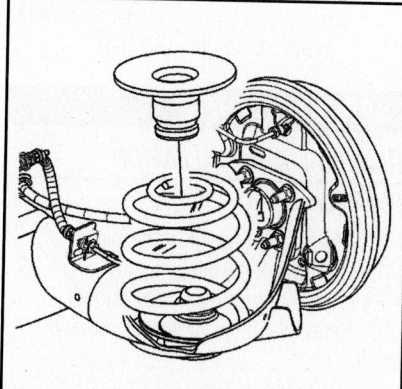

Fig. 265 Remove the upper spring seat/jounce bumper from the spring, while leaving the lower spring seat on the axle

CONTROL ARM BUSHING

REMOVAL & INSTALLATION

See Figures 266 through 270.

➡**It is NOT necessary to remove the rear axle assembly to service the control arm bushings.**

1. Raise and support the vehicle.
2. Remove the rear tire and wheel assembly.
3. Remove the rear coil springs from the vehicle. Refer to Coil Spring replacement .
4. Temporarily re-install the lower rear shock bolts.
5. Disconnect the rear park brake cables from the rear axle mounting brackets (5).
6. Remove the rear suspension trailing arm bracket to body bolts (2).
7. Remove the rear axle bracket to bushing through bolts (1) and nuts (4).
8. Remove the rear suspension control arm bracket support (3).
9. Using the J-44570-1 or the J-44570-4 (2), J-44570-3 (1) and a hammer,

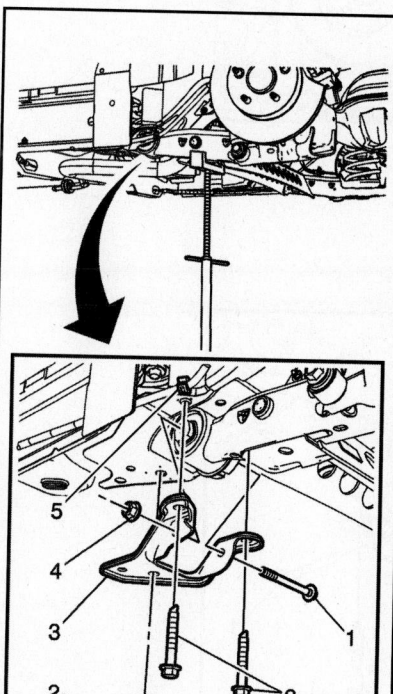

Fig. 266 Disconnect the rear park brake cables from the rear axle mounting brackets (5)

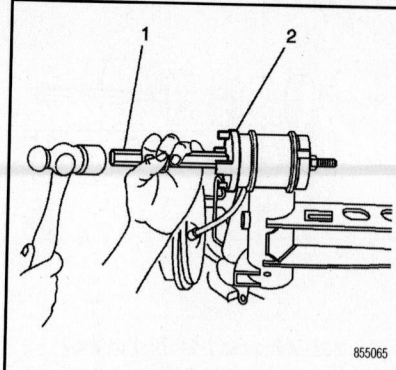

Fig. 267 Using the J-44570-1 or the J-44570-4 (2), J-44570-3 (1) and a hammer, remove the rear suspension insulators from the rear axle

remove the rear suspension insulators from the rear axle.

To install:

➡**Ensure that the orientation of the rear suspension insulators are correct before installation.**

10. Position the NEW insulators into the rear axle with the rubber end (1) facing inboard.

➡**Make sure that the insulators are still properly orientated.**

11. Align the largest notch (2) of the insulator with that of the rear wheel bearing centers (3).
12. Using the J-44570-1 or the J-44570-4 (2), J-44570-3 (3), and the J-44570-2 (1), install the rear suspension insulator.
13. Install the rear suspension control arm bracket support (3) to the rear axle trailing arms, loosely install the through bolt and nut (1, 4).

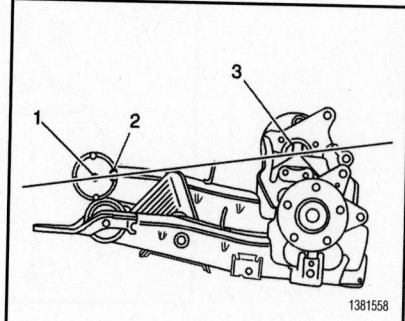

Fig. 268 Position the NEW insulators into the rear axle with the rubber end (1) facing inboard

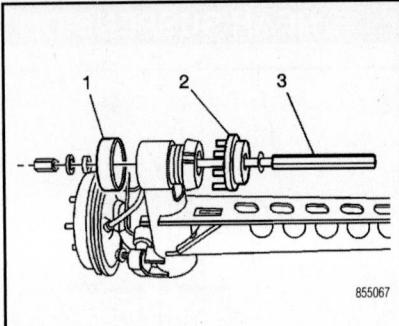

Fig. 269 Using the J-44570-1 or the J-44570-4 (2), J-44570-3 (3), and the J-44570-2 (1), install the rear suspension insulator

➡**Hand-tighten the trailing arm bracket bolts ONLY.**

14. Hand-tighten the axle bracket to body bolts (2) just enough to hold the brackets flush to the body.

15. Raise the rear axle assembly to the D height specifications.

16. Tighten the rear suspension control

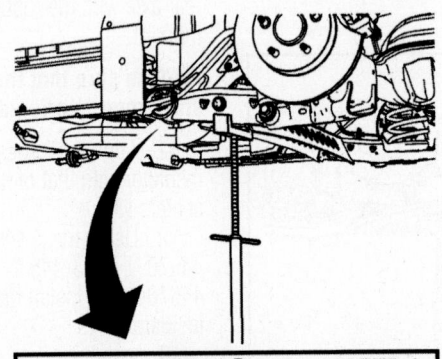

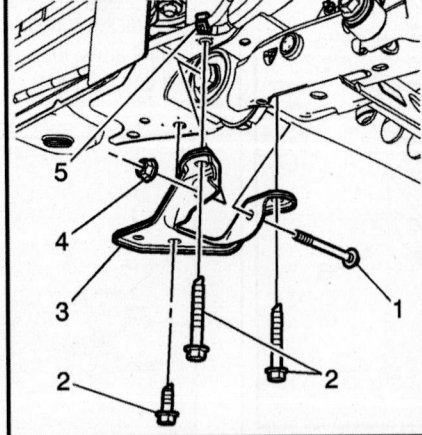

Fig. 270 Install the rear suspension control arm bracket support (3) to the rear axle trailing arms, loosely install the through bolt and nut (1, 4)

arm bracket to bushing through nut (4) to 66 ft. lbs. (90 Nm) plus 60 degrees plus 15 degrees.

17. Using two 12 mm diameter pins, align both rear suspension control arm bracket supports and tighten the trailing arm bracket to body bolts (2) to 66 ft. lbs. (90 Nm) plus + 45 degrees.

18. Install the rear park brake cables to the rear axle mounting brackets (5).

19. Install the rear coil springs in the vehicle. Refer to Coil Spring replacement .

20. Install the rear tire and wheel assembly.

21. Remove the supports and lower the vehicle.

REAR SPRING INSULATOR

REMOVAL & INSTALLATION

See Figure 271.

1. Raise and support the vehicle.
2. Remove the wheel.
3. Remove the lower rear shock bolt. Refer to Shock Absorber replacement.
4. Remove the rear coil spring. Refer to Coil Spring replacement.

Fig. 271 Rear spring insulator (1)

5. Remove the rear spring insulator (1).
6. Installation is the reverse of removal.

SHOCK ABSORBER

REMOVAL & INSTALLATION

See Figure 272.

1. Raise and support the vehicle.
2. Remove the tire and wheel.

➡**Tip: Support the rear axle with a jack stand.**

3. Remove the upper shock absorber bolt (1).
4. Remove the rear shock absorber bolt (2).
5. Remove the rear shock absorber (3).

To install:

6. Installation is the reverse of removal, noting the following:
   - Support the rear axle with a jack stand.
   - Tighten the rear shock absorber bolt to 92 ft. lbs. (125 Nm).
   - Tighten the upper shock absorber bolt to 66 ft. lbs. (90 Nm).

SPRING BUMPER

REMOVAL & INSTALLATION

See Figure 273.

1. Raise and support the vehicle.
2. Remove the wheel.
3. Remove the lower rear shock bolt. Refer to Shock Absorber replacement.
4. Remove the rear coil spring. Refer to Coil Spring replacement.
5. Remove the upper rear spring bumper (1).
6. Installation is the reverse of removal.

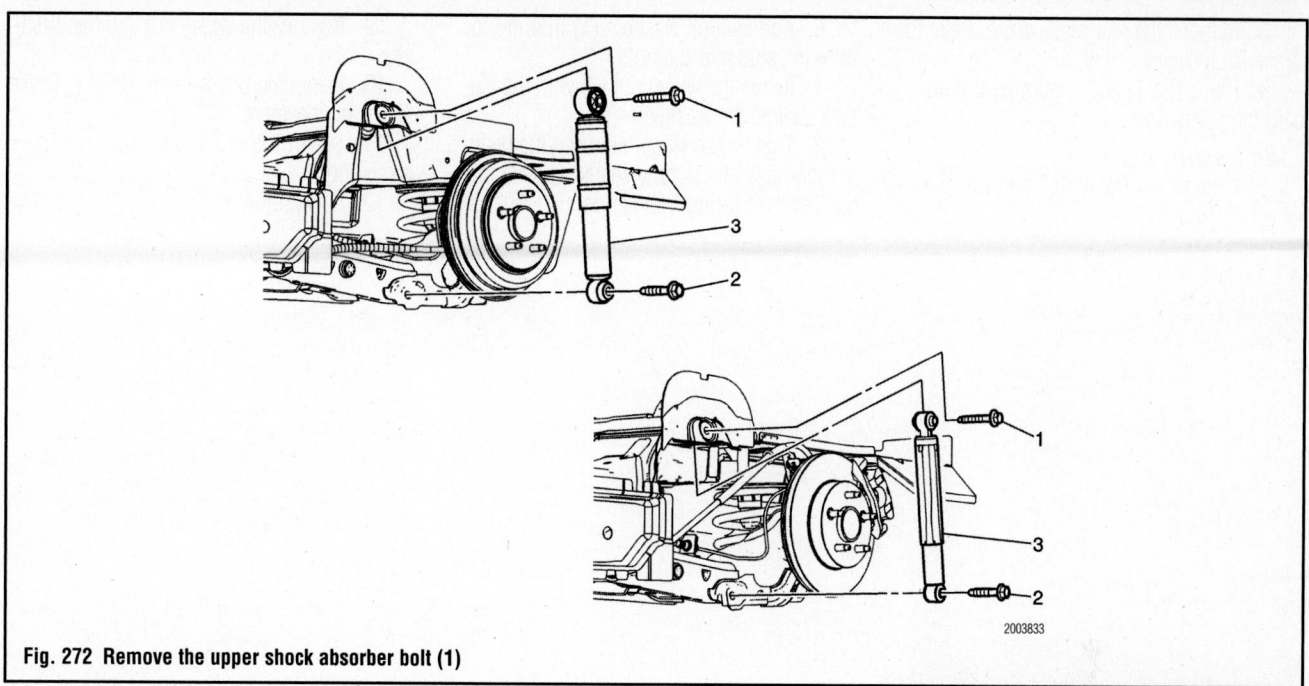

Fig. 272 Remove the upper shock absorber bolt (1)

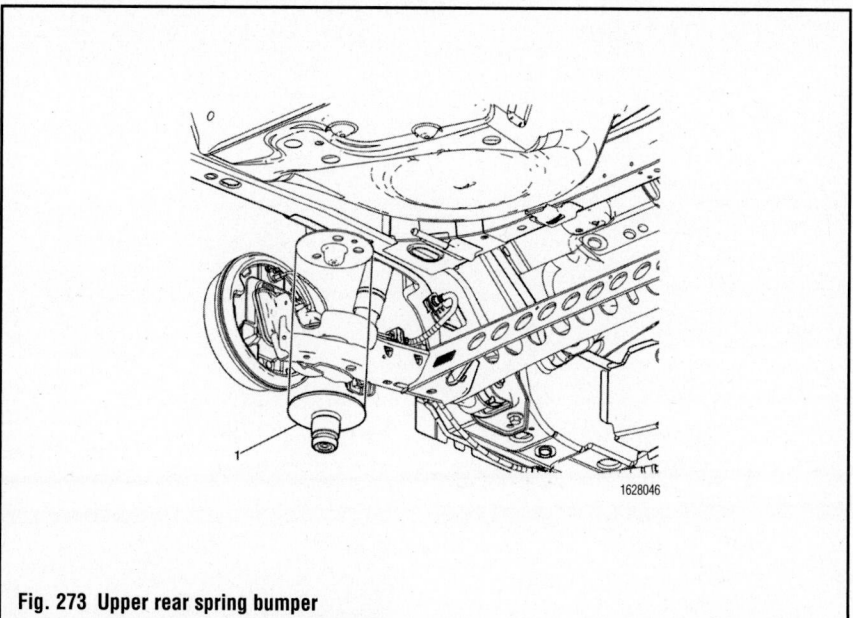

Fig. 273 Upper rear spring bumper

WHEEL BEARING & HUB

REMOVAL & INSTALLATION

See Figure 274.

1. Raise and support the vehicle.
2. Remove the rear tire and wheel assembly.
3. Remove the rear brake drum. Refer to Brake Drum replacement.
4. Remove the 4 rear wheel bearing nuts (1).
5. Remove the rear wheel bearing (2).
6. Installation is the reverse of removal. Tighten the 4 rear wheel bearing nuts to 33 ft. lbs. (45 Nm) plus 30 degrees.

WHEEL STUD

REMOVAL & INSTALLATION

See Figures 275 and 276.

1. Raise and support the vehicle.
2. Remove the rear tire and wheel assembly.

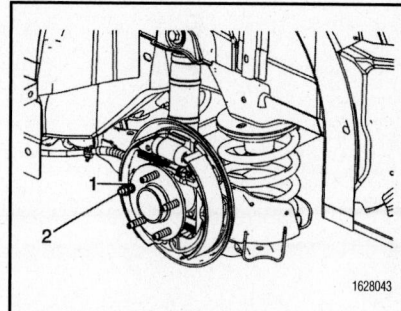

Fig. 276 Add enough washers (1) in order to draw the stud into the hub

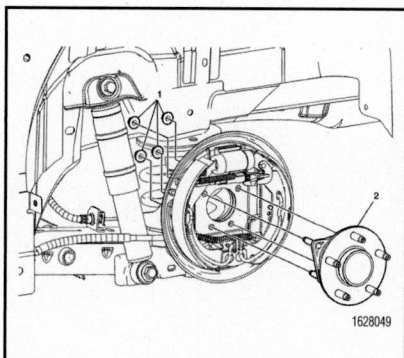

Fig. 274 The 4 rear wheel bearing nuts (1) and the rear wheel bearing (2)

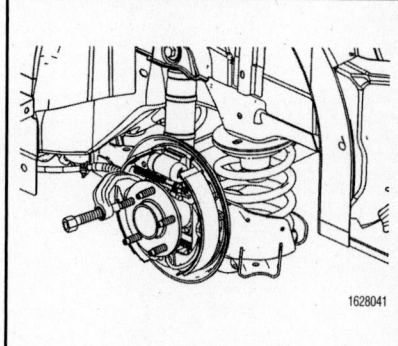

Fig. 275 Using the J 43631, remove and discard the wheel stud

3. Remove the rear brake drum. Refer to Brake Drum replacement.

4. Using the J 43631, remove and discard the wheel stud.

To install:

5. Install the NEW wheel stud into the wheel bearing hub.

6. Add enough washers (1) in order to draw the stud into the hub.

7. Install the wheel nut (2) with the flat side against the washers.

8. Tighten the wheel nut until the head of the wheel stud is fully seated against the back of the bearing hub flange.

9. Remove the wheel nut and the washers.

10. Install the brake drum. Refer to Brake Drum replacement.

11. Install the tire and wheel assembly.

12. Lower the vehicle.

CHEVROLET

15

Impala

BRAKES 15-10

**ANTI-LOCK BRAKE
SYSTEM (ABS) 15-11**
Speed Sensors 15-11
  Removal & Installation........15-11
**BLEEDING THE BRAKE
SYSTEM 15-12**
Bleeding Procedure................15-12
  Master Cylinder
  Reservoir Filling 15-12
  ABS Automated Bleed.........15-14
  Hydraulic Brake
  System Bleeding
  Procedure - Manual..........15-12
  Hydraulic Brake
  System Bleeding
  Procedure - Pressure........15-12
  Master Cylinder Bench
  Bleeding 15-14
FRONT DISC BRAKES 15-15
Brake Caliper.........................15-15
  Removal & Installation........15-15
Disc Brake Pads 15-15
  Removal & Installation........15-15
PARKING BRAKE..............15-17
Parking Brake Cables 15-17
  Adjustment 15-17
Parking Brake Shoes 15-18
  Removal & Installation........15-18
PRECAUTIONS 15-16
REAR DISC BRAKES 15-16
Brake Caliper.........................15-16
  Removal & Installation........15-16
Disc Brake Pads 15-16
  Removal & Installation........15-16

CHASSIS ELECTRICAL 15-19

**AIRBAG (SUPPLEMENTAL
RESTRAINT SYSTEM) 15-19**
General Information.................15-19
  Arming the System/SIR
  Enabling 15-20
  Clockspring Centering........15-20
  Disarming the System/SIR
  Disabling........................15-20
  Service Precautions 15-19

DRIVE TRAIN 15-21

Automatic Transmission
  Fluid...............................15-21
  Drain and Refill...................15-21
  Fluid Filter and Seal
  Replacement 15-22
Drive Axle.............................15-22
  Removal & Installation........15-22

ENGINE COOLING 15-23

Engine Coolant......................15-23
  Drain & Refill Procedure.....15-23
  Flushing............................15-23
Engine Fan 15-24
  Removal & Installation........15-24
Radiator................................15-25
  Removal & Installation........15-25
Thermostat............................15-26
  Removal & Installation........15-26
Water Pump 15-26
  Removal & Installation........15-26

ENGINE ELECTRICAL 15-27

BATTERY SYSTEM............15-27
Battery 15-27
  Battery Disconnect
  Warning..........................15-27
  Battery Negative Cable
  Disconnection and
  Connection 15-27
  Removal & Installation........15-27
CHARGING SYSTEM 15-28
Generator 15-28
  Removal & Installation........15-28
IGNITION SYSTEM 15-29
Firing Order...........................15-29
Ignition Coil 15-29
  Removal & Installation........15-29
Ignition Timing.......................15-29
  Adjustment 15-29
Spark Plugs...........................15-29
  Removal & Installation........15-29
STARTING SYSTEM 15-30
Starter 15-30
  Removal & Installation........15-30

ENGINE MECHANICAL......15-31

Accessory Drive Belts 15-31
  Accessory Belt Routing.......15-31
  Adjustment 15-31
  Inspection 15-31
  Removal & Installation........15-31
Air Cleaner 15-31
  Filter/Element
  Replacement 15-32
  Removal & Installation........15-31
Camshaft..............................15-33
  Cleaning and Inspection 15-33
  Removal & Installation........15-33
Catalytic Converter 15-34
  Removal & Installation........15-34
Crankshaft Front Seal.............15-35
  Removal & Installation........15-35
Cylinder Head 15-34
  Removal & Installation........15-34
Engine Oil & Filter 15-35
  Replacement 15-35
Exhaust Manifold 15-36
  Removal & Installation........15-36
Lower Intake Manifold.............15-36
  Removal & Installation........15-36
Oil Pan 15-38
  Removal & Installation........15-38
Oil Pump..............................15-39
  Cleaning and Inspection 15-39
  Removal & Installation........15-39
Rear Main Seal/ Crankshaft
  Rear Oil Seal 15-40
  Removal & Installation........15-40
Timing Chain & Sprockets 15-41
  Removal & Installation........15-41
Upper Intake Manifold.............15-37
  Removal & Installation........15-37
Valve Covers 15-43
  Removal & Installation........15-43

ENGINE PERFORMANCE &
EMISSION CONTROLS 15-44

Camshaft Position (CMP)
  sensor..............................15-44
  Location............................15-44
  Removal & Installation........15-44

Component Locations 15-44
Crankshaft Position (CKP)
Sensor 15-46
  Location..............................15-46
  Removal & Installation........15-46
Electronic Control
  Module (ECM) 15-47
  Location..............................15-47
  Removal & Installation........15-47
Engine Coolant Temperature
  (ECT) Sensor.......................15-47
  Location..............................15-47
  Removal & Installation........15-47
Heated Oxygen (HO2S)
Sensor 15-47
  Location..............................15-48
  Precautions.........................15-48
  Removal & Installation........15-48
Knock Sensor (KS).................15-49
  Location..............................15-49
  Removal & Installation........15-49
Manifold Absolute Pressure
  (MAP) Sensor 15-50
  Location..............................15-50
  Removal & Installation........15-50
Mass Air Flow (MAF)
  Sensor/Intake Air
  Temperature (IAT) Sensor......15-51
  Location..............................15-51
  Removal & Installation........15-51
Vehicle Speed Sensor (VSS) ...15-51
  Location..............................15-51
  Removal & Installation........15-51

FUEL 15-52

GASOLINE FUEL INJECTION
SYSTEM 15-52
Fuel Injectors 15-52
  Removal & Installation........15-52
Fuel System Service
  Precautions.........................15-52
Fuel Tank...............................15-53
  Draining..............................15-53
  Removal & Installation........15-54

Idle Speed 15-57
  Throttle/Idle Learn 15-57
Relieving Fuel System
  Pressure..............................15-52
Throttle Body.........................15-57
  Removal & Installation........15-57

HEATING & AIR
CONDITIONING SYSTEM...15-58

Blower Motor 15-58
  Removal & Installation........15-58
Heater Core 15-58
  Removal & Installation........15-58

PRECAUTIONS..............15-10

SPECIFICATIONS AND
MAINTENANCE CHARTS.....15-3

Additional Maintenance
  Services-Normal 15-9
Additional Maintenance
  Services-Severe 15-9
Brake Specifications.................15-7
Camshaft Specifications...........15-5
Capacities 15-4
Crankshaft and Connecting
  Rod Specifications 15-5
Engine and Vehicle
  Identification 15-3
Engine Tune-Up
  Specifications 15-3
Fluid Specifications..................15-4
General Engine
  Specifications 15-3
Maintenance I and II Service
  Schedules 15-9
Piston and Ring
  Specifications 15-5
Tire, Wheel and Ball Joint
  Specifications 15-7
Torque Specifications................15-6
Valve Specifications 15-4
Wheel Alignment......................15-6

STEERING 15-59

Power Steering Gear...............15-59
  Removal & Installation........15-59
Power Steering Pump..............15-60
  Bleeding 15-60
  Fluid Fill Procedure 15-61
  Removal & Installation........15-60

SUSPENSION 15-61

FRONT SUSPENSION 15-61
Lower Control Arm..................15-61
  Front Lower Control
  Arm Bushing
  Replacement.....................15-63
  Removal &
  Installation.......................15-61
Lower Control Arm Ball
  Joint..................................15-61
  Removal & Installation........15-61
Stabilizer Shaft 15-64
  Removal & Installation........15-64
Stabilizer Shaft Link 15-65
  Removal & Installation........15-65
Steering Knuckle 15-65
  Removal & Installation........15-65
Strut, Strut Component,
  or Spring............................15-66
  Disassembly &
  Assembly..........................15-66
Wheel Bearing and Hub 15-66
  Removal & Installation........15-66
REAR SUSPENSION 15-67
Stabilizer Shaft 15-67
  Removal & Installation........15-67
Strut, Strut Component,
  or Spring............................15-67
  Disassembly &
  Assembly..........................15-67
Trailing Arm 15-67
  Removal & Installation........15-67
Wheel Bearing and Hub 15-68
  Removal & Installation........15-68

SPECIFICATIONS AND MAINTENANCE CHARTS

ENGINE AND VEHICLE IDENTIFICATION

Engine							Model Year	
Code ①	Liters	Cu. In.	Cyl.	Fuel Sys.	Type	Mfg.	Code ②	Year
K	3.5	214	V6	Flex (Gas/Ethanol)	SFI	LZE	A	2010
N	3.5	214	V6	Gas	SFI	LZ4	B	2011
M	3.9	238	V6	Flex (Gas/Ethanol)	SFI VVT	LGD		

SFI: Sequential Multiport Fuel Injection

VVT: Variable Valve Timing

① 8th position of VIN: Engine code

② 10th position of VIN: Model year

25742_IMPA_C0001

GENERAL ENGINE SPECIFICATIONS

All measurements are given in inches.

Year	Model	Engine Displacement Liters (cu in.)	Engine ID/VIN	Fuel System Type	Net		Bore X Stroke (in.)	Compression Ratio	Oil Pressure @ 1850 rpm
					Horsepower @ rpm	Torque @ rpm (ft. lbs.)			
2010	Impala LS	3.5 (214)	K/LZE	Flex	211 @5800	216 @4000	3.90 X 2.99	9.8:1	30-45 psi
	Impala LT	3.5 (214)	N/LZ4	Gas	211 @5800	216 @4000	3.90 X 2.99	9.8:1	30-45 psi
	Impala LTZ	3.9 (238)	M/LGD	Flex	230 @5700	235 @3200	3.90 X 3.31	9.8:1	30-45 psi
2011	Impala LS	3.5 (214)	K/LZE	Flex	211 @5800	216 @4000	3.90 X 2.99	9.8:1	30-45 psi
	Impala LT	3.5 (214)	N/LZ4	Flex	211 @5800	216 @4000	3.90 X 2.99	9.8:1	30-45 psi
	Impala LTZ	3.9 (238)	M/LGD	Flex	230 @5700	235 @3200	3.90 X 3.31	9.8:1	30-45 psi

25742_IMPA_C0002

ENGINE TUNE-UP SPECIFICATIONS

Year	Engine Displacement Liters	Engine ID/VIN	Ignition: Spark Plug		Wire Resistance Ω per ft	Firing Order	Ignition Timing (deg.)	Fuel Pump (psi)	Idle Speed (rpm)	Thermostat Full Open Temperature
			Gap inches	Torque (ft. lbs.)						
2010	3.5	K/LZE	0.04	11	1.236	1-2-3-4-5-6	①	56-62	②	195 degrees
	3.5	N/LZ4	0.04	11	1.236	1-2-3-4-5-6	①	56-62	②	195 degrees
	3.9	M/LGD	0.04	11	1.236	1-2-3-4-5-6	①	56-62	②	195 degrees
2011	3.5	K/LZE	0.04	11	1.236	1-2-3-4-5-6	①	56-62	②	195 degrees
	3.5	N/LZ4	0.04	11	1.236	1-2-3-4-5-6	①	56-62	②	195 degrees
	3.9	M/LGD	0.04	11	1.236	1-2-3-4-5-6	①	56-62	②	195 degrees

NOTE: The Vehicle Emission Control Information label often reflects specification changes made during production.

Use the label figures if they differ from those in this chart.

① Distributorless Ignition System (DIS) timing is not adjustable

② The Engine Control Module (ECM) maintains idle speed. There is no recommended adjustment procedure.

25742_IMPA_C0003

CAPACITIES

Year	Model	Engine Displacement Liters	Engine ID/VIN	Engine Oil with Filter (qts.)	Auto. Trans. (pts.)	Drive Axle (pints) Front	Rear	Fuel Tank (gal.)	Cooling System (qts.)
2010	Impala LS, LT	3.5	K/LZE	4.0	14.8	NA	NA	17.5	10.1
	Impala LS, LT	3.5	N/LZ4	4.0	14.8	NA	NA	17.5	10.1
	Impala LTZ	3.9	M/LGD	4.0	14.8	NA	NA	17.5	10.1
2011	Impala LS, LT	3.5	K/LZE	4.0	14.8	NA	NA	17.5	10.1
	Impala LS, LT	3.5	N/LZ4	4.0	14.8	NA	NA	17.5	10.1
	Impala LTZ	3.9	M/LGD	4.0	14.8	NA	NA	17.5	10.1

NOTE: All capacities are approximate. Add fluid gradually and ensure a proper fluid level is obtained.

25742_IMPA_C0004

FLUID SPECIFICATIONS

Year	Model	Engine Disp. Liters	Engine Oil	Auto Transaxle	Drive Axle Front	Rear	Power Steering Fluid	Brake Master Cylinder	Cooling System
2010	Impala LS, LT	3.5	5W-30	Dexron® VI	NA	NA	GM Part No. 89021184	DOT 3	Dex-Cool
	Impala LTZ	3.9	5W-30	Dexron® VI	NA	NA	GM Part No. 89021184	DOT 3	Dex-Cool
2011	Impala LS, LT	3.5	5W-30	Dexron® VI	NA	NA	GM Part No. 89021184	DOT 3	Dex-Cool
	Impala LTZ	3.9	5W-30	Dexron® VI	NA	NA	GM Part No. 89021184	DOT 3	Dex-Cool

DOT: Department Of Transpotation

NA: Information not available

25742_IMPA_C0005

VALVE SPECIFICATIONS

Year	Engine Displacement Liters	Engine ID/VIN	Valve Seat Angle (deg.)	Face Angle (deg.)	Stem-to-Guide Clearance (in.)	Seat Width (in.) Intake	Exhaust	Spring Test Pressure (lbs. @ in.)	Free- Length (in.)	Installed Height (in.)
2010	3.5	K/LZE, N/LZ4	46	45	0.0009-0.0025	0.061-0.071	0.067-0.079	78@1.70	2.08	1.84
	3.9	M/LGD	46	45	0.0009-0.0025	0.061-0.071	0.067-0.079	NA	2.08	1.84
2011	3.5	K/LZE, N/LZ4	46	45	0.0009-0.0025	0.061-0.071	0.067-0.079	78@1.70	2.08	1.84
	3.9	M/LGD	46	45	0.0009-0.0025	0.061-0.071	0.067-0.079	NA	2.08	1.84

25742_IMPA_C0006

CAMSHAFT SPECIFICATIONS

All measurements in inches unless noted

Year	Engine Displacement Liters	Engine Code/VIN	Journal		Bearing Inside Diameter	Lobe Lift	
			Diameter	Out-of-Round		Intake	Exhaust
2010	3.5	K/LZE, N/LZ4	2.024-2.025	0.001	2.028-2.029	0.2727	0.2727
	3.9	M/LGD	2.024-2.025	0.001	2.028-2.029	0.2727	0.2727
2011	3.5	K/LZE, N/LZ4	2.024-2.025	0.001	2.028-2.029	0.2727	0.2727
	3.9	M/LGD	2.024-2.025	0.001	2.028-2.029	0.2727	0.2727

25742_IMPA_C0007

CRANKSHAFT AND CONNECTING ROD SPECIFICATIONS

All measurements are given in inches.

Year	Engine Disp. Liters	Engine ID/VIN	CRANKSHAFT						Connecting Rod		
					Main Bearing						
			Main Journal Dia.	Thrust on No.	Clearance		Shaft End-play	Journal Diameter	Bearing Clearance	Side Clearance
					Except No. 3	On No. 3				
2010	3.5	K/LZE, N/LZ4	2.6473-2.6479	3	0.0008-0.0025	0.0012-0.0030	0.0024-0.0083	2.2489-2.2495	0.0007-0.0024	0.008-0.009
	3.9	M/LGD	2.6473-2.6479	3	0.0008-0.0025	0.0012-0.0030	0.0024-0.0083	2.248-2.249	0.0007-0.0024	0.008-0.009
2011	3.5	K/LZE, N/LZ4	2.6473-2.6479	3	0.0008-0.0025	0.0012-0.0030	0.0024-0.0083	2.2489-2.2495	0.0007-0.0024	0.008-0.009
	3.9	M/LGD	2.6473-2.6479	3	0.0008-0.0025	0.0012-0.0030	0.0024-0.0083	2.248-2.249	0.0007-0.0024	0.008-0.009

25742_IMPA_C0008

PISTON AND RING SPECIFICATIONS

All measurements are given in inches.

Year	Engine Disp. Liters	Piston-to-Bore Clearance		Ring End Gap			Ring-to-Groove Clearance		
		Production	Service Limit Max.	First Compression	Second Compression	Oil Control	First Compression	Second Compression	Oil Control
2010	3.5	-0.0011 to 0.011	0.003	0.007-0.0015	0.019-0.029	0.010-0.029	0.001-0.002	0.002-0.003	0.0004
	3.9	-0.0003 to 0.0018	0.003	0.006-0.011	0.009-0.017	0.06-0.025	0.001-0.002	0.0007-0.002	0.0004
2011	3.5	-0.0011 to 0.011	0.003	0.007-0.0015	0.019-0.029	0.010-0.029	0.001-0.002	0.002-0.003	0.0004
	3.9	-0.0003 to 0.0018	0.003	0.006-0.011	0.009-0.017	0.06-0.025	0.001-0.002	0.0007-0.002	0.0004

25742_IMPA_C0009

TORQUE SPECIFICATIONS
All readings in ft. lbs.

Year	Engine Disp. Liters	Engine ID/VIN	Cylinder Head Bolts	Main Bearing Bolts	Rod Bearing Bolts	Crankshaft Damper Bolts	Flywheel Bolts	Manifold Intake	Manifold Exhaust	Spark Plugs	Oil Pan Drain Plug
2010	3.5	K/LZE	①	②	③	④	52	⑤	15	11	18
	3.5	N/LZ4	①	②	③	④	52	⑤	15	11	18
	3.9	M/LGD	①	②	③	④	52	⑥	15	11	18

① Step 1: 44 ft. lbs.

Step 2: plus 140 degrees

② Step 1: 37 ft. lbs.

Step 2: plus 77 degrees

③ Step 1: 18 ft. lbs.

Step 2: plus 110 degrees

④ Step 1: install the OLD bolt and tighten to 92 ft. lbs.

Step 2: install a NEW bolt and tightne to 92 ft. lbs.

Step 3: plus 130 degrees

⑤ Step 1 (Center): 62 INCH lbs.

Step 2 (Center): 12 ft. lbs.

Step 1 (Corner): 62 INCH lbs.

Step 2 (Corner): 18 ft. lbs.

⑥ Step 1 (Center): 62 INCH lbs.

Step 2 (Center): 12 ft. lbs.

Step 1 (Corner): 10 ft. lbs.

Step 2 (Corner): 18 ft. lbs.

25742_IMPA_C0010

WHEEL ALIGNMENT

Year	Model		Caster Range (+/-Deg.)	Caster Preferred Setting (Deg.)	Camber Range (+/-Deg.)	Camber Preferred Setting (Deg.)	Total Toe (in.)
2010	Impala LS, LT	F	+/- 0.75	2.90	+/- 0.75	-0.80	+0.10 +/- 0.20
	RPO FE1, FE2	R	NA	NA	+/- 0.50	-0.65	+0.10 +/- 0.20
	Impala LTZ	F	+/- 0.75	3.15	+/- 0.75	-0.70	+0.10 +/- 0.20
	RPO FE3	R	NA	NA	+/- 0.75	-0.90	+0.10 +/- 0.20
2011	Impala LS, LT	F	+/- 0.75	2.90	+/- 0.75	-0.80	+0.10 +/- 0.20
	RPO FE1, FE2	R	NA	NA	+/- 0.50	-0.65	+0.10 +/- 0.20
	Impala LTZ	F	+/- 0.75	3.15	+/- 0.75	-0.70	+0.10 +/- 0.20
	RPO FE3	R	NA	NA	+/- 0.75	-0.90	+0.10 +/- 0.20

NA - Not available or not applicable

25742_IMPA_C0011

TIRE, WHEEL AND BALL JOINT SPECIFICATIONS

Year	Model	RPO	OEM Tires Standard	OEM Tires Optional	Tire Pressure	Wheel Size Standard	Wheel Size Optional	Lug Nut (ft. lbs.) Aluminum	Lug Nut (ft. lbs.) Steel
2010	Impala LS, LT	QPP	P225/60R16-97V	NA	①	16	17	93	103
		QPX	P225/60R16-97S	NA	①	16	17	93	103
	Impala LTZ	QPG	P235/50R18-97W	NA	①	18	18	93	103
2011	Impala LS, LT	QPP	P225/60R16-97V	NA	①	17	17	93	103
		QPX	P225/60R16-97S	NA	①	17	17	93	103
	Impala LTZ	QPG	P235/50R18-97W	NA	①	18	17	93	103

OEM: Original Equipment Manufacturer

PSI: Pounds Per Square Inch

NA: Information not available

① See placard on vehicle

25742_IMPA_C0012

BRAKE SPECIFICATIONS

All measurements in inches unless noted

Year	Model		Brake Disc Original Thickness	Brake Disc Minimum Thickness	Brake Disc Maximum Runout	Minimum Pad/Lining Thickness Front	Minimum Pad/Lining Thickness Rear	Brake Caliper Bracket Bolts (ft. lbs.)	Brake Caliper Mounting Bolts (ft. lbs.)	Brake Caliper Bleeder Valve (ft. lbs.)
2010	Impala	F	1.181	1.142	0.002	0.030	0.030	133	26	115
		R	0.433	0.368	0.002	0.030	0.030	88	32	97
2011	Impala	F	1.181	1.142	0.002	0.030	0.030	133	26	115
		R	0.433	0.368	0.002	0.030	0.030	88	32	87

F: Front

R: Rear

NA - Not available or not applicable

All brake rotors have a discard dimension cast into them. Replace any rotor that does not meet this specification. After refinishing the rotor, replace any rotor that does not meet the minimum thickness specification.

25742_IMPA_C0013

MAINTENANCE I AND II SERVICE SCHEDULES
IMPALA

When the CHANGE ENGINE OIL light appears, certain services and inspections are required.

Required services are described as Maintenance I and Maintenance II.

The first service of a vehicle should be Maintenance I, and the second service should be Maintenance II.

Alternate between the 2 services thereafter. However, in some cases, Maintenance II may be required more often.

Maintenance I: Use Maintenance I if the CHANGE ENGINE OIL light comes on within 10 months since the vehicle was purchased or, if Maintenance II was performed.

Maintenance II: Use Maintenance II if the previous service performed was Maintenance I. Always use Maintenance II whenever the CHANGE ENGINE OIL light comes on 10 months or more since the last service, or, if the CHANGE ENGINE OIL light has not come on at all for one year.

Service Item	Maintenance I	Maintenance II
Change the engine oil and filter.	✓	✓
Reset the oil life system.	✓	✓
Visually inspect the vehicle for leaks or damage. A fluid loss in the vehicle system could indicate a problem. Inspect, repair and add fluid to the system if necessary.	✓	✓
Inspect the engine air cleaner filter. If necessary, replace the filter.	✓	✓
Rotate the tires. Inspect the tire inflation pressures and the tire wear.	✓	✓
Visually inspect the brake lines and hoses for proper hook-up, binding, leaks, cracks, chafing, etc. Inspect the disc brake pads for wear and the rotors for surface condition. Inspect the drum brake linings for wear or cracks. Inspect other brake parts, including drums, wheel cylinders, calipers, parking brake, etc. Inspect the parking brake adjustment.	✓	✓
Inspect the engine coolant and the windshield washer fluid levels. Add fluid as needed.	✓	✓
Inspect the suspension and steering components. Inspect the front and rear suspension and the steering system for damaged, loose or missing parts, or signs of wear. Inspect the power steering lines and the hoses for proper hook-up, binding, leaks, cracks,	—	✓
Visually inspect the coolant hoses and replace the hoses if they are cracked, swollen or deteriorated. Inspect all pipes, fittings and clamps; replace with GM parts as needed. To help ensure proper operation, a pressure test of the cooling system and pressure cap and cleaning the outside of the radiator and air conditioning condenser is recommended at least once a year.	—	✓
Body hinges and latches, key lock cylinders, folding seat hardware, and rear compartment hinges lubrication. Applying silicone grease on weatherstrips with a clean cloth makes them last longer, seal better, and not stick or squeak.	✓	✓
Inspect the throttle system for interference or binding and for damaged or missing parts. Replace the parts as needed. Replace any components that have high effort or excessive wear. Do not lubricate the accelerator or the cruise control cables.	—	✓
Replace the passenger compartment air filter.	—	✓
Exhaust system and nearby heat shields inspection for loose or damaged components.	✓	✓
Inspect restraint system.	✓	✓

To reset the CHANGE ENGINE OIL light:

1. Turn the ignition key to the ON/RUN position with the engine OFF.
2. Press and release the stem in the lower center of the instrument cluster until the OIL LIFE message is displayed.
3. Once the alternating OIL LIFE and RESET messages appear, press and hold the stem until several beeps sound.
   This confirms that the oil life system has been reset to 100 percent.
4. Turn the ignition key to the OFF position.
   If the CHANGE ENGINE OIL message comes back on when the vehicle is started, the engine oil life system has not been reset. Repeat the procedure.

ADDITIONAL MAINTENANCE SERVICES - NORMAL
IMPALA

TO BE SERVICED	TYPE OF SERVICE	VEHICLE MILEAGE INTERVAL (x1000)					
		25	50	75	100	125	150
Auto. Trans. Fluid and Filter	Replace				✓		
Spark plugs	Replace				✓		
Air cleaner filter	Replace		✓		✓		✓
Engine coolant	Replace						✓
Evaporative control system	Inspect	✓	✓	✓	✓	✓	✓
Accessory drive belts	Replace						✓
Accessory drive belts	Inspect	✓	✓	✓	✓	✓	✓
Passenger compartment air filter	Replace	✓	✓	✓	✓	✓	✓

25742_IMPA_C0015

ADDITIONAL MAINTENANCE SERVICES - SEVERE
IMPALA

TO BE SERVICED	TYPE OF SERVICE	VEHICLE MILEAGE INTERVAL (x1000)					
		25	50	75	100	125	150
Auto. Trans. Fluid and Filter	Replace		✓		✓		✓
Spark plugs	Replace				✓		
Air cleaner filter	Replace	✓	✓	✓	✓	✓	✓
Engine coolant	Replace						✓
Exhaust system & heat shields	Inspect	✓	✓	✓	✓	✓	✓
Cooling system hoses and clamps	Inspect	✓	✓	✓	✓	✓	✓
Evaporative control system	Inspect	✓	✓	✓	✓	✓	✓
Accessory drive belts	Replace						✓
Accessory drive belts	Inspect	✓	✓	✓	✓	✓	✓
Passenger compartment air filter	Replace	✓	✓	✓	✓	✓	✓

25742_IMPA_C0016

PRECAUTIONS

Before servicing any vehicle, please be sure to read all of the following precautions, which deal with personal safety, prevention of component damage, and important points to take into consideration when servicing a motor vehicle:

• Never open, service or drain the radiator or cooling system when the engine is hot; serious burns can occur from the steam and hot coolant.

• Observe all applicable safety precautions when working around fuel. Whenever servicing the fuel system, always work in a well-ventilated area. Do not allow fuel spray or vapors to come in contact with a spark, open flame, or excessive heat (a hot drop light, for example). Keep a dry chemical fire extinguisher near the work area. Always keep fuel in a container specifically designed for fuel storage; also, always properly seal fuel containers to avoid the possibility of fire or explosion. Refer to the additional fuel system precautions later in this section.

• Fuel injection systems often remain pressurized, even after the engine has been turned **OFF**. Relive the fuel system pressure before disconnecting any fuel lines. Failure to relieve the fuel system pressure may result in fire and/or personal injury.

• Brake fluid often contains polyglycol ethers and polyglycols. Avoid contact with the eyes and wash your hands thoroughly after handling brake fluid. If you do get brake fluid in your eyes, flush your eyes with clean, running water for 15 minutes. If eye irritation persists, or if you have taken brake fluid internally, IMMEDIATELY seek medical assistance.

• The EPA warns that prolonged contact with used engine oil may cause a number of skin disorders, including cancer. You should make every effort to minimize your exposure to used engine oil. Protective gloves should be worn when changing oil. Wash your hands and any other exposed skin areas as soon as possible after exposure to used engine oil. Soap and water, or waterless hand cleaner should be used.

• This vehicle is equipped with Air Bags, which are also called Supplemental Inflatable Restraints. Refer to the "Warnings" in Dangers, Warnings and Cautions in the Air Bag/Supplemental Inflatable Restraint section. Refer to Air Bag/Supplemental Inflatable Restraint component and wiring location views before performing a service on or around Supplemental Inflatable Restraint components or wiring. If you fail to follow "Dangers", "Warnings" and "Cautions," you could cause air bag deployment, personal injury, or otherwise unnecessary repairs. In order to help avoid accidental air bag deployment and personal injury, whenever you service a vehicle that requires repair of the Air Bag/Supplemental Inflatable Restraint and another vehicle system, we recommend that you first repair the Air Bag/Supplemental Inflatable Restraint, then go on to the other system.

• Always wear safety goggles when working with, or around, the air bag system. When carrying a non-deployed air bag, be sure the bag and trim cover are pointed away from your body. When placing a non-deployed air bag on a work surface, always face the bag and trim cover upward, away from the surface. This will reduce the motion of the module if it is accidentally deployed. Refer to the additional air bag system precautions later in this section.

• Clean, high quality brake fluid from a sealed container is essential to the safe and proper operation of the brake system. You should always buy the correct type of brake fluid for your vehicle. If the brake fluid becomes contaminated, completely flush the system with new fluid. Never reuse any brake fluid. Any brake fluid that is removed from the system should be discarded. Also, do not allow any brake fluid to come in contact with a painted surface; it will damage the paint.

• Never operate the engine without the proper amount and type of engine oil; doing so WILL result in severe engine damage.

• Timing belt maintenance is extremely important. Many models utilize an interference-type, non-freewheeling engine. If the timing belt breaks, the valves in the cylinder head may strike the pistons, causing potentially serious (also time-consuming and expensive) engine damage. Refer to the maintenance interval charts for the recommended replacement interval for the timing belt, and to the timing belt section for belt replacement and inspection.

• Disconnecting the negative battery cable on some vehicles may interfere with the functions of the on-board computer system(s) and may require the computer to undergo a relearning process once the negative battery cable is reconnected.

• When servicing drum brakes, only disassemble and assemble one side at a time, leaving the remaining side intact for reference.

• Only an MVAC-trained, EPA-certified automotive technician should service the air conditioning system or its components.

BRAKES   PRECAUTIONS

ABS Precautions

• Certain components within the ABS system are not intended to be serviced or repaired individually.

• Do not use rubber hoses or other parts not specifically specified for and ABS system. When using repair kits, replace all parts included in the kit. Partial or incorrect repair may lead to functional problems and require the replacement of components.

• Lubricate rubber parts with clean, fresh brake fluid to ease assembly. Do not use shop air to clean parts; damage to rubber components may result.

• Use only DOT 3 brake fluid from an unopened container.

• If any hydraulic component or line is removed or replaced, it may be necessary to bleed the entire system.

• A clean repair area is essential. Always clean the reservoir and cap thoroughly before removing the cap. The slightest amount of dirt in the fluid may plug an orifice and impair the system function. Perform repairs after components have been thoroughly cleaned; use only denatured alcohol to clean components. Do not allow ABS components to come into contact with any substance containing mineral oil; this includes used shop rags.

• The Anti-Lock control unit is a microprocessor similar to other computer units in the vehicle. Ensure that the ignition switch is **OFF** before removing or installing controller harnesses. Avoid static electricity discharge at or near the controller.

• If any arc welding is to be done on the vehicle, unplug the control unit before welding operations begin.

✷✷ WARNING
Brake Dust Caution

Avoid taking the following actions when you service wheel brake parts:
• Do not grind brake linings.
• Do not sand brake linings.
• Do not clean wheel brake parts with

a dry brush or with compressed air.

Some models or aftermarket brake parts may contain asbestos fibers which can become airborne in dust. Breathing dust with asbestos fibers may cause serious bodily harm. Use a water-dampened cloth in order to remove any dust on brake parts. Use commercial equipment to perform this washing function. These wet methods prevent fibers from becoming airborne.

Brake Fluid and Brake Fluid Handling

✳✳ CAUTION

Brake fluid may irritate eyes and skin. In case of contact, take the following actions:

- Eye contact—rinse thoroughly with water.
- Skin contact—wash with soap and water.
- If ingested—consult a physician immediately.

✳✳ CAUTION

Use only Delco Supreme 11, GM P/N 12377967 (Canadian P/N 992667), or equivalent DOT 3 brake fluid from a clean, sealed container. Do not use fluid from an open container that may be contaminated with water. Improper or contaminated fluid could result in damage to components, or loss of braking, with possible injury.

The use of any type of fluid other than the recommended type of brake fluid, may cause contamination which could result in damage to the internal rubber seals and/or rubber linings of hydraulic brake system components.

✳✳ WARNING

When filling the master cylinder, use only Delco Supreme 11, GM P/N 12377967 (Canadian P/N 992667), or equivalent DOT 3 brake fluid. Do not use a container which has been used for petroleum based fluids, or a container which is wet with water. Petroleum based fluids will cause swelling and distortion of rubber parts in the hydraulic brake system, and water will mix with brake fluid, lowering the boiling point. Keep all fluid containers capped to prevent contamination.

✳✳ WARNING

Brake fluid will damage electrical connections and painted surfaces. Use shop cloths, suitable containers, and fender covers to prevent brake fluid from contacting these areas. Always re-seal and wipe off brake fluid containers to prevent spills.

✳✳ WARNING

Avoid spilling brake fluid on any of the vehicle's painted surfaces, wiring, cables or electrical connectors. Brake fluid will damage paint and electrical connections. If any fluid is spilled on the vehicle, immediately flush the area with water to minimize the potential for damage.

✳✳ WARNING

Power steering fluid, engine oil, brake fluid, or any mineral based fluids cannot be mixed. If brake seals contact power steering fluid or steering seals contact brake fluid, seal damage will result.

➡Note the following:

- Do not reuse the brake fluid collected during the hydraulic brake system bleeding.
- Always store brake fluid in a closed container.
- Reseal brake fluid containers immediately after use.
- Do not use brake fluid left in an open container.
- Do not use brake fluid left in an improperly sealed container.
- Do not use the following fluids in the hydraulic brake system: Power steering fluid, Automatic transmission fluid, DOT 5 silicone hydraulic brake fluid

BRAKES

ANTI-LOCK BRAKE SYSTEM (ABS)

SPEED SENSORS

REMOVAL & INSTALLATION

Vehicle Yaw Sensor with Vehicle Lateral Accelerometer Replacement

1. Turn OFF the ignition.
2. Remove the front floor center console.
3. Disconnect the yaw rate sensor/lateral accelerometer electrical connector.
4. Remove the two yaw rate sensor/lateral accelerometer mounting nuts.
5. Remove the yaw rate sensor/lateral accelerometer.

To install:

➡Install the yaw sensor with lateral accelerometer with the

electrical connection facing forward.

6. Install the yaw sensor with lateral accelerometer.
7. Install the yaw sensor with lateral accelerometer nuts and tighten to 19 inch lbs. (26 Nm).
8. Connect the yaw rate sensor with lateral accelerometer electrical connector.
9. Install the front floor center console.
10. Install a scan tool.
11. Using the special functions menu on the scan tool, reset the yaw rate sensor.
12. Perform a diagnostic system check of the vehicle.

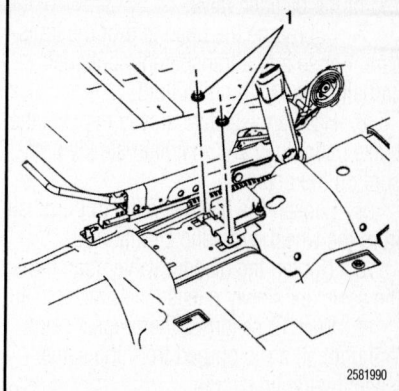

2581990

Fig. 1 Yaw sensor with lateral accelerometer replacement

BLEEDING PROCEDURE

HYDRAULIC BRAKE SYSTEM BLEEDING PROCEDURE - MANUAL

Refer to the Brakes Precautions.

1. Place a clean shop cloth beneath the brake master cylinder to prevent brake fluid spills.

2. With the ignition OFF and the brakes cool, apply the brakes 3-5 times, or until the brake pedal effort increases significantly, in order to deplete the brake booster power reserve.

➡**If you performed a brake master cylinder bench bleeding, disconnected the brake pipes from the master cylinder, replaced the ABS pressure modulator valve, or disconnected the jumper lines from the master cylinder to the ABS pressure valve, you MUST use the pressure bleeding procedure to remove all the air from the system..**

3. Fill the brake master cylinder reservoir with DOT-3 brake fluid from a clean, sealed brake fluid container. Ensure that the brake master cylinder reservoir remains at least half-full during this bleeding procedure. Add fluid as needed to maintain the proper level.

4. Clean the outside of the reservoir on and around the reservoir cap prior to removing the cap and diaphragm.

5. Install a proper box-end wrench onto the RIGHT REAR wheel hydraulic circuit bleeder valve.

6. Install a transparent hose over the end of the bleeder valve.

7. Submerge the open end of the transparent hose into a transparent container partially filled with brake fluid.

8. Have an assistant slowly depress the brake pedal fully and maintain steady pressure on the pedal.

9. Loosen the bleeder valve to purge air from the wheel hydraulic circuit.

10. Tighten the bleeder valve, then have the assistant slowly release the brake pedal.

11. Wait 15 seconds, then repeat steps 7-9 until all air is purged from the same wheel hydraulic circuit.

12. With the right rear wheel hydraulic circuit bleeder valve tightened securely, after all air has been purged from the right rear hydraulic circuit, install a proper box-end wrench onto the LEFT FRONT wheel hydraulic circuit bleeder valve.

13. Install a transparent hose over the end of the bleeder valve, and then repeat steps 6-10.

14. With the left front wheel hydraulic circuit bleeder valve tightened securely, after all air has been purged from the left front hydraulic circuit, install a proper box-end wrench onto the LEFT REAR wheel hydraulic circuit bleeder valve.

15. Install a transparent hose over the end of the bleeder valve, and then repeat steps 6-10.

16. With the left rear wheel hydraulic circuit bleeder valve tightened securely, after all air has been purged from the left rear hydraulic circuit, install a proper box-end wrench onto the RIGHT FRONT wheel hydraulic circuit bleeder valve.

17. Install a transparent hose over the end of the bleeder valve, and then repeat steps 6-10.

18. After you complete the final wheel hydraulic circuit bleeding procedure, ensure that each of the 4 wheel hydraulic circuit bleeder valves are properly tightened.

19. Fill the brake master cylinder reservoir to the maximum-fill level with brake fluid.

20. Slowly depress and release the brake pedal. Observe the feel of the brake pedal.

➡**If you determine that air was inducted into the system upstream of the ABS modulator prior to servicing, you must perform the Antilock Brake System Automated Bleed Procedure.**

21. If the brake pedal feels spongy, repeat the bleeding procedure again. If the brake pedal still feels spongy after repeating the bleeding procedure, perform the following steps:

   a. Inspect the brake system for external leaks.

   b. Pressure bleed the hydraulic brake system in order to purge any air that may still be trapped in the system.

22. Turn the ignition key ON, with the engine OFF. Check to see if the brake system warning lamp remains illuminated.

➡**DO NOT drive or allow the vehicle to be driven until it is diagnosed and repaired.**

HYDRAULIC BRAKE SYSTEM BLEEDING PROCEDURE - PRESSURE

See Figures 2 and 3.

Refer to the Brakes Precautions.

1. Place a clean shop cloth beneath the brake master cylinder to prevent brake fluid spills.

2. With the ignition OFF and the brakes cool, apply the brakes 3-5 times, or until

the brake pedal effort increases significantly, in order to deplete the brake booster power reserve.

3. If you have performed a brake master cylinder bench bleeding on this vehicle, replaced the ABS pressure modulator valve, or disconnected the brake lines between master cylinder and ABS on this vehicle, you must perform the following steps:

   a. Ensure that the brake master cylinder reservoir is full to the maximum-fill level. If necessary, add DOT-3 brake fluid from a clean, sealed brake fluid container. If you need to remove the reservoir cap, clean the outside of the reservoir on and around the cap prior to removal.

   b. With the rear brake pipe installed securely to the master cylinder, loosen and separate the front brake pipe from the front port of the brake master cylinder.

   c. Allow a small amount of brake fluid to gravity bleed from the open port of the master cylinder.

   d. Reconnect the brake pipe to the master cylinder port, and rotate the line at the master cylinder at least 30 degrees, so that the line will be positioned BELOW the MAX fill line on the brake master cylinder reservoir. Tighten the line nut securely.

   e. Have an assistant slowly depress the brake pedal fully and maintain steady pressure on the pedal.

   f. Loosen the same brake pipe to purge air from the open port of the master cylinder.

   g. Tighten the brake pipe, then have an assistant slowly release the brake pedal.

   h. Wait 15 seconds, then repeat steps 5, 6, and 7 until all air is purged from the same port of the master cylinder.

   i. With the front brake pipe installed securely to the master cylinder—after all air has been purged from the front port of the master cylinder—loosen and separate the rear brake pipe from the master cylinder, then repeat steps 5, 6, and 7, ensuring that you rotate the line below the master cylinder MAX fill line.

   j. After completing the final master cylinder port bleeding procedure, ensure that both of the brake pipe-to-master cylinder fittings are properly tightened, and that they remain in their new rotated positions below the MAX fill line of the brake fluid reservoir.

4. Fill the brake master cylinder reservoir to the maximum-fill level with brake fluid.

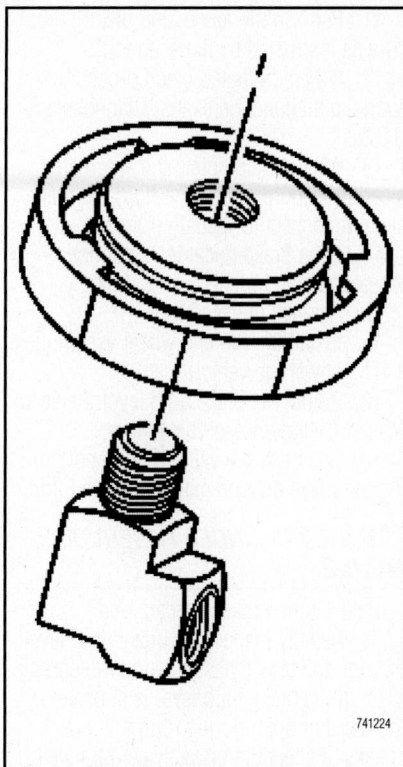

**Fig. 2 GM special tool, J 35589-A, Brake
Pressure Bleeder Adapter**

5. Clean the outside of the reservoir as well as on and around the reservoir cap prior to removing the cap and diaphragm.

6. Install a brake pressure bleeder adapter to the brake master cylinder reservoir.

7. Check the brake fluid level in a diaphragm-type brake pressure bleeder or an equivalent tool. Add brake fluid from as necessary to bring the level to approximately the half-full point.

8. Connect the pressure bleeder, to the pressure bleeder adapter.

9. Charge the pressure bleeder air tank to 25-30 psi (175-205 kPa).

10. Open the pressure bleeder fluid tank valve to allow pressurized brake fluid to enter the brake system.

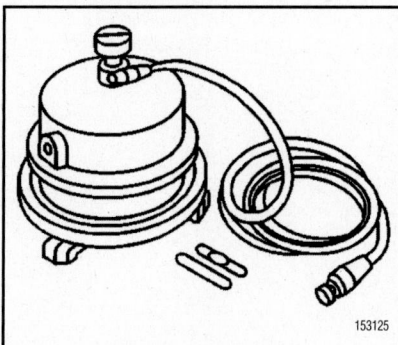

**Fig. 3 GM special tool, J 29532,
Diaphragm Type Brake Pressure Bleeder**

11. Wait approximately 30 seconds, then inspect the entire hydraulic brake system in order to ensure that there are no existing external brake fluid leaks.

12. Repair any brake fluid leaks you identify prior to completing this procedure.

13. Install a proper box-end wrench onto the RIGHT REAR wheel hydraulic circuit bleeder valve.

14. Install a transparent hose over the end of the bleeder valve.

15. Submerge the open end of the transparent hose into a transparent container partially filled with brake fluid.

16. Repeat steps 11-13 for the LEFT FRONT wheel hydraulic circuit bleeder valve.

17. Loosen the bleeder valve to purge air from the wheel hydraulic circuit. It is important that both bleeder valves be open at the same time. Allow fluid to flow until air bubbles stop flowing from the bleeder, then tighten the bleeder valve.

18. With the right rear and left front wheel hydraulic circuit bleeder valve tightened securely - after all air has been purged from the right rear and left front hydraulic circuit - install a proper box-end wrench onto the LEFT REAR and RIGHT FRONT wheel hydraulic circuit bleeder valve.

19. Install a transparent hose over the end of the bleeder valve, then repeat step 15.

20. After completing the final wheel hydraulic circuit bleeding procedure, tighten each of the 4 wheel hydraulic circuit bleeder valves properly.

21. Loosen the rear master cylinder jumper line nut slightly (just enough to rotate the line), and rotate the rear master cylinder hydraulic pipe back to the original position, and tighten the line nut.

22. Reposition the front master cylinder jumper line to the original position in a similar manner to step 19.

23. Close the pressure bleeder fluid tank valve, then disconnect the pressure bleeder from the adapter.

24. Remove the adapter from the brake master cylinder reservoir.

25. Fill the brake master cylinder reservoir to the maximum-fill level with brake fluid.

26. Slowly depress and release the brake pedal. Observe the feel of the brake pedal.

27. If the brake pedal feels spongy perform the following steps:

a. Inspect the brake system for external leaks.

b. Using a scan tool, perform the antilock brake system automated bleed-

ing procedure to remove any air that may have been trapped in the BPMV (Brake Pressure Modulator Valve). Refer to the Antilock Brake System Automated Bleed Procedure.

28. Turn the ignition key ON, with the engine OFF. Check to see if the brake system warning lamp remains illuminated.

➥**DO NOT drive or allow anyone to drive the vehicle until it is diagnosed and repaired.**

MASTER CYLINDER BENCH BLEEDING

Refer to the Brakes Precautions.

1. Secure the mounting flange of the brake master cylinder in a bench vise so that the rear of the primary piston is accessible.

2. Remove the master cylinder reservoir cap and diaphragm.

3. Install suitable fittings to the master cylinder ports that match the type of flare seat required and also provide for hose attachment.

4. Install transparent hoses to the fittings installed to the master cylinder ports, then route the hoses into the master cylinder reservoir.

5. Fill the master cylinder reservoir to at least the half-way point with GM-approved brake fluid from a clean, sealed brake fluid container. Refer to Master Cylinder Reservoir Filling.

6. Ensure that the ends of the transparent hoses running into the master cylinder reservoir are fully submerged in the brake fluid.

7. Using a smooth, round-ended tool, depress and release the primary piston as far as it will travel, a depth of about 1 inch (25 mm), several times. Observe the flow of fluid coming from the ports.

8. As air bleeds from the primary and secondary pistons, the effort required to depress the primary piston will increase and the amount of travel will decrease.

9. Continue to depress and release the primary piston until fluid flows freely from the ports with no evidence of air bubbles.

10. Remove the transparent hoses from the master cylinder reservoir.

11. Install the master cylinder reservoir cap and diaphragm.

12. Remove the fittings with the transparent hoses from the master cylinder ports. Wrap the master cylinder with a clean shop cloth to prevent brake fluid spills.

13. Remove the master cylinder from the vise.

ABS AUTOMATED BLEED

Refer to the Brakes Precautions.

➡ **Before performing the ABS Automated Bleed Procedure, first perform a manual or pressure bleed of the base hydraulic brake system. Refer to Hydraulic Brake System Bleeding.**

The automated bleed procedure must be performed when a new brake pressure modulator valve (BPMV) is installed, because the secondary circuits of the new BPMV are not prefilled with brake fluid.

The automated bleed procedure is recommended when one of the following conditions exist:
• Base brake system bleeding does not achieve the desired pedal height or feel
• Extreme loss of brake fluid has occurred
• Air ingestion is suspected in the secondary circuits of the brake modulator assembly

The ABS Automated Bleed Procedure uses a scan tool to cycle the system solenoid valves and run the pump in order to purge any air from the secondary circuits. These circuits are normally closed off, and are only opened during system initialization at vehicle start up and during ABS operation. The automated bleed procedure opens these secondary circuits and allows any air trapped in these circuits to flow out away from the brake modulator assembly, which is then forced out at the brake corners by the pressure bleeder.

Automated Bleed Procedure

❊❊ WARNING

Terminate the Auto Bleed Procedure at any time during the process by pressing the EXIT button. No further Scan Tool prompts pertaining to the Auto Bleed procedure will be given.

After exiting the bleed procedure, relieve bleed pressure and disconnect bleed equipment per the manufacturer's instructions. Failure to properly relieve pressure may result in spilled brake fluid causing damage to components and painted surfaces.

1. Raise and support the vehicle.
2. Remove the tire and wheel assemblies.
3. Inspect the brake system for leaks and visual damage. Repair or replace components as needed.
4. Lower the vehicle.
5. Prepare the brake bleeding equipment and the vehicle for a pressure bleed of the base hydraulic brake system.
6. Inspect the battery state of charge.
7. Install a scan tool.
8. Turn the ignition ON, with the engine OFF.
9. With the scan tool, perform the following steps:
   a. 9.1. Select Diagnostics
   b. 9.2. Select the appropriate vehicle information
   c. 9.3. Select Chassis
   d. 9.4. Select Electronic Brake Control Module (EBCM)
   e. 9.5. Select Special Functions
   f. 9.6. Select Automated Bleed
10. With an assistant ready, raise and support the vehicle.

➡ **Apply the brake pedal when instructed, using moderate effort, and note the following:**

• Ensure the pedal remains applied until instructed to release by the scan tool.
• Do not exceed the time period allowed by the scan tool for having the bleeder valves open.
• The bleed sequence for each corner is as follows:
• 1. Left front, 2. Right front, 3. Right rear, 4. Left rear

11. Perform the automated bleed procedure as instructed by the scan tool.
12. If the automated bleed procedure aborts, a malfunction exists. Diagnose any DTCs.
13. After you complete the automated bleed procedure, press and hold the brake pedal to inspect for pedal firmness.
14. If the brake pedal feels spongy, repeat the bleed procedure completely.
15. Remove the scan tool.
16. Install the tire and wheel assemblies.
17. Lower the vehicle.
18. Adjust the brake fluid level. Refer to Master Cylinder Reservoir Filling.
19. Road test the vehicle while confirming the brake pedal remains high and firm.

- MASTER CYLINDER RESERVOIR FILLING

Refer to the Brakes Precautions.
1. Visually inspect the brake fluid level through the brake master cylinder reservoir.
2. If the brake fluid level is at or below the half-full point during routine fluid checks, inspect the brake system for wear and possible brake fluid leaks.
3. If the brake fluid level is at or below the half-full point during routine fluid checks, and an inspection of the brake system did not reveal wear or brake fluid leaks, top off the brake fluid up to the maximum-fill level.
4. If brake system service was just completed, the brake fluid may be topped-off up to the maximum-fill level.
5. If the brake fluid level is above the half-full point, adding brake fluid is not recommended under normal conditions.
6. If brake fluid is to be added to the master cylinder reservoir, clean the outside of the reservoir on and around the reservoir cap prior to removing the cap and diaphragm. Use only GM-approved brake fluid from a clean, sealed brake fluid container.

BRAKES   **FRONT DISC BRAKES**

Dust and dirt accumulating on brake parts during normal use may contain asbestos fibers from production or aftermarket brake linings. Breathing excessive concentrations of asbestos fibers can cause serious bodily harm. Exercise care when servicing brake parts. Do not sand or grind brake lining unless equipment used is designed to contain the dust residue. Do not clean brake parts with compressed air or by dry brushing. Cleaning should be done by dampening the brake components with a fine mist of water, then wiping the brake components clean with a dampened cloth. Dispose of cloth and all residue containing asbestos fibers in an impermeable container with the appropriate label. Follow practices prescribed by the Occupational Safety and Health Administration (OSHA) and the Environmental Protection Agency (EPA) for the handling, processing, and disposing of dust or debris that may contain asbestos fibers.

BRAKE CALIPER

REMOVAL & INSTALLATION

See Figure 4.

1. Refer to the Brake Precautions.
2. Raise and support the vehicle.
3. Remove the tire and wheel.
4. Remove the brake hose fitting bolt (1).
5. Remove the two brake hose fitting gaskets (2).
6. Remove and then cap the brake hose

fitting (3) to prevent brake fluid loss and contamination.

7. Remove the two guide pin bolts (4).

❄❄ WARNING

Refer to Fasteners caution in general Precautions section.

8. Remove the brake caliper (5).

To install:

9. Install the brake caliper (5).
10. Tighten the two guide pin bolts (4) to 26 ft. lbs. (36 Nm).
11. Install the brake hose fitting (3).
12. Install two new brake hose fitting gaskets (2). DO NOT reuse the brake hose fitting gaskets.
13. Tighten the brake hose fitting bolt (1) to 40 ft. lbs. (54 Nm).
14. Lower the vehicle.
15. Bleed the hydraulic brake system. Refer to Hydraulic Brake System Bleeding.
16. With the engine OFF, gradually apply the brake pedal to approximately 2/3 of its travel distance.
17. Slowly release the brake pedal.
18. Wait 15 seconds, then repeat steps 8 and 9 until the brake pedal is firm. This will properly seat the brake caliper pistons and brake pads.
19. Fill the master cylinder reservoir to the proper level. Refer to Master Cylinder Reservoir Filling.
20. Burnish the pads and rotors.

DISC BRAKE PADS

REMOVAL & INSTALLATION

See Figure 5.

1. Refer to the Brakes Precautions.

❄❄ WARNING

Support the brake caliper with heavy mechanic wire, or its equivalent, whenever it is separated from its mount and the hydraulic flexible brake hose is still connected. Failure to support the caliper in this manner will cause the flexible brake hose to bear the weight of the caliper, which may cause damage to the brake hose and in turn may cause a brake fluid leak.

2. Inspect the fluid level in the brake master cylinder reservoir:
   a. If the brake fluid level is midway between the maximum-full point and the minimum allowable level, do not remove brake fluid before proceeding.
   b. If the brake fluid level is higher than midway between the maximum-full point and the minimum allowable level, remove brake fluid to the midway point before proceeding.
3. Raise and support the vehicle.
4. Remove the tire and wheel.
5. Remove the guide pin bolt (1).

❄❄ WARNING

Refer to the Fasteners caution in general Precautions section.

6. Brake caliper (2) procedure:
   a. Rotate the brake caliper up and to the rear until it rests on the mounting bracket and support with heavy mechanics wire or equivalent.
   b. Place a block of wood or an old disc brake pad against the brake caliper pistons.
   c. Using a brake pad spreader or an equivalent tool, slowly compress the brake caliper pistons squarely into the caliper bores.
7. Brake pad (3) procedure:
   a. If installing the original brake pads, note the brake pad location for proper installation.
   b. Clean the friction surfaces of the brake rotor with denatured alcohol.
8. Spring retainers (4) procedure:
   a. Remove the two spring retainers.

To install:

9. If replacing the brake pads, DO NOT reuse the two spring retainers (4). Install two NEW spring retainers.
10. Clean the friction surfaces of the brake rotor with denatured alcohol.
11. When replacing the brake pads (3),

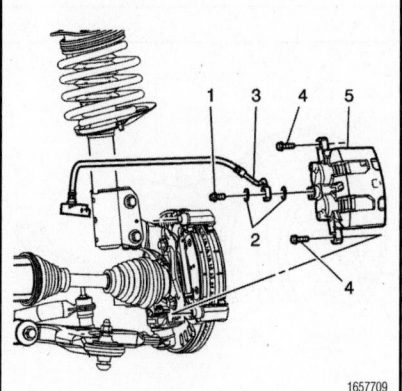

Fig. 4 Front brake caliper replacement

1657709

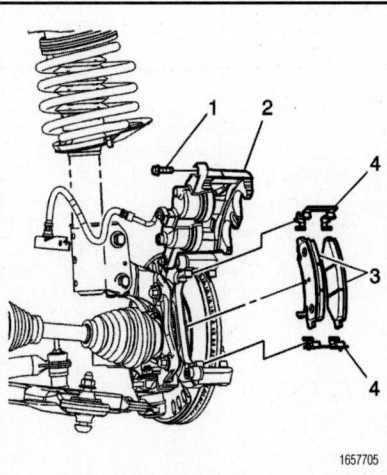

Fig. 5 Front disc brake pads replacement

1657705

position the brake pad with the wear indicator inboard of the brake rotor and pointing down.

12. Install the brake caliper (2).

13. Tighten the guide pin bolt (1) to 26 ft. lbs. (36 Nm).

14. Lower the vehicle.

15. With the engine OFF, gradually apply the brake pedal to approximately 2/3 of its travel distance.

16. Slowly release the brake pedal.

17. Wait 15 seconds, then repeat the two prior steps until you obtain a firm brake pedal. This will properly seat the brake caliper pistons and the brake pads.

18. Fill the master cylinder reservoir to the proper level. Refer to Master Cylinder Reservoir Filling.

19. Burnish the pads and rotors.

BRAKES

❋❋ WARNING

Dust and dirt accumulating on brake parts during normal use may contain asbestos fibers from production or aftermarket brake linings. Breathing excessive concentrations of asbestos fibers can cause serious bodily harm. Exercise care when servicing brake parts. Do not sand or grind brake lining unless equipment used is designed to contain the dust residue. Do not clean brake parts with compressed air or by dry brushing. Cleaning should be done by dampening the brake components with a fine mist of water, then wiping the brake components clean with a dampened cloth. Dispose of cloth and all residue containing asbestos fibers in an impermeable container with the appropriate label. Follow practices prescribed by the Occupational Safety and Health Administration (OSHA) and the Environmental Protection Agency (EPA) for the handling, processing, and disposing of dust or debris that may contain asbestos fibers.

BRAKE CALIPER

REMOVAL & INSTALLATION

See Figure 6.

1. Inspect the fluid level in the brake master cylinder reservoir:

    a. If the brake fluid level is midway between the maximum-full point and the minimum allowable level, do not remove brake fluid before proceeding.

    b. If the brake fluid level is higher than midway between the maximum-full point and the minimum allowable level, remove brake fluid to the midway point before proceeding.

2. Raise and suitably support the vehicle.

3. Remove the rear tire and wheel assembly.

4. Remove the brake hose fitting bolt (1).

❋❋ WARNING

Refer to the Fasteners Caution in the general Precautions section.

5. Remove the brake hose fitting (2).

6. Cap the brake hose fitting and plug the brake caliper inlet port to prevent brake fluid loss and contamination.

7. Remove and discard the two brake hose fitting gaskets (3).

8. Remove the two brake caliper guide pin bolts (4).

9. Remove the brake caliper (5).

To install:

10. Install the brake caliper.

11. Tighten the two brake caliper guide pin bolts (4) to 32 ft. lbs. (44 Nm).

12. Install new brake hose fitting gaskets (3).

13. Install the brake hose fittings (2).

14. Tighten the brake hose fitting bolt (1) to 40 ft. lbs. (54 Nm).

15. Bleed the hydraulic brake system. Refer to Hydraulic Brake System Bleeding.

16. Lower the vehicle.

17. With the engine OFF, gradually apply the brake pedal to approximately 2/3 of its travel distance.

18. Slowly release the brake pedal.

19. Wait 15 seconds, then repeat steps 8 and 9 until the brake pedal is firm. This will properly seat the brake caliper pistons and brake pads.

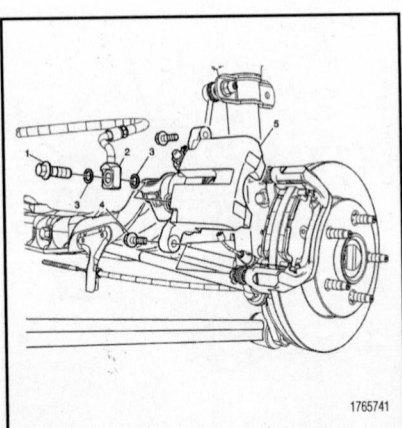

Fig. 6 Front brake caliper replacement

REAR DISC BRAKES

DISC BRAKE PADS

REMOVAL & INSTALLATION

See Figures 7 and 8.

1. Refer to the Brakes Precautions.

2. Inspect the fluid level in the brake master cylinder reservoir:

    a. If the brake fluid level is midway between the maximum-full point and the minimum allowable level, do not remove brake fluid before proceeding.

    b. If the brake fluid level is higher than midway between the maximum-full point and the minimum allowable level, remove brake fluid to the midway point before proceeding.

3. Raise and suitably support the vehicle.

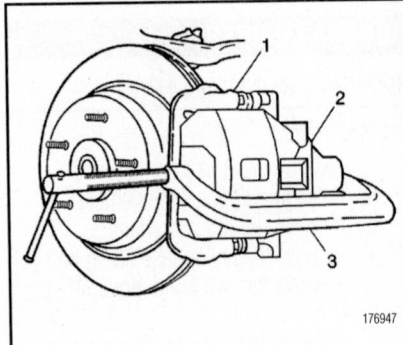

Fig. 7 Use C-clamp to compress the caliper piston

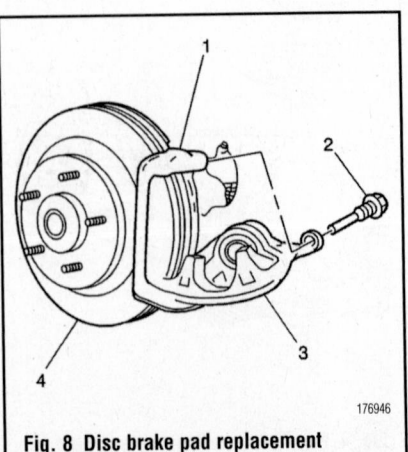

Fig. 8 Disc brake pad replacement

4. Remove the rear tire and wheel assembly.

5. Install a hand-tightened wheel lug nut to retain the rotor to the hub.

6. Compress the caliper piston enough for clearance. Use a C-clamp (3).

7. Remove the upper caliper bolt (2).

❋❋ WARNING

Use care to avoid damaging the pin boot when rotating the caliper.

❋❋ WARNING

Support the brake caliper with heavy mechanic wire, or its equivalent, whenever it is separated from its mount and the hydraulic flexible brake hose is still connected. Failure to support the caliper in this manner will cause the flexible brake hose to bear the weight of the caliper, which may cause damage to the brake hose and in turn may cause a brake fluid leak.

8. Pivot the caliper down in order to access the pads. It is not necessary to remove the caliper.

9. Remove the brake pads from the caliper bracket.

10. Remove the two pad clips from the caliper bracket.

11. Inspect the caliper mounting hardware for cuts, tears, or deterioration.

12. Replace any hardware if damage exists.

13. Inspect the caliper dust boot for cuts, tears, or deterioration.

14. Replace the caliper dust boot if damage exists.

15. Inspect the caliper bolts for corrosion or damage. If corrosion exists, use new caliper bolts when installing the caliper.

To install:

16. Bottom the piston into the caliper bore.

17. Use a C-clamp before installing new brake pads in order to compress the piston. Use an old brake pad or wooden block across the face of the piston to avoid damage to the piston or the caliper boot.

18. Install the pad clips (1) to the caliper bracket.

➡**The wear sensor is on the outside pad. Position the sensor at the trailing or downward edge of the pad during forward wheel rotation.**

19. Install the pads (2) to the caliper bracket.

❋❋ WARNING

Use care to avoid damaging the pin boot when rotating the caliper.

20. Swing the caliper (3) upward in position around the pads.

21. Lubricate the bolt and the bolt boot. Use silicone grease.

22. Install the upper caliper bolt (2).

23. Tighten the caliper bolt to 32 ft. lbs. (44 Nm).

24. Remove the wheel lug nut retaining the rotor to the hub.

25. Install the rear tire and the wheel assembly.

26. Lower the vehicle.

27. With the engine OFF, gradually apply the brake pedal to approximately 2/3 of its travel distance.

28. Slowly release the brake pedal.

29. Wait 15 seconds, then repeat steps 12 and 13 until the brake pedal is firm. This will properly seat the brake caliper pistons and brake pads.

30. Fill the brake master cylinder reservoir to the proper level.

31. Burnish the pads and rotors.

BRAKES

PARKING BRAKE CABLES

ADJUSTMENT

See Figures 9 through 11.

1. Refer to the Brakes Precautions.

2. Apply and fully release the parking brake 6 times.

3. Verify that the parking brake pedal releases completely.

4. Turn ON the ignition. Verify that the BRAKE indicator lamp is off.

5. If the BRAKE indicator lamp is on, ensure that the parking brake pedal is in release mode and fully returned to stop. Remove the slack in the front parking brake cable by pulling downward on the cable.

6. Raise and suitably support the vehicle.

7. Remove the rear tire and wheel assemblies.

8. Remove both rear caliper brackets.

9. Relieve tension on the park brake system at the park brake equalizer.

10. Remove both rear brake rotors.

11. Set a gage inside of the park brake drum (1) at the widest point.

12. Place the contacts on the tool to the widest point of the drum.

13. Tighten the set screw on the tool to ensure the proper measurement when removing the tool from the drum.

14. Position the gage over the park brake shoe (1) at the widest point.

15. Turn the adjuster on the actuator until the park brake shoe just contacts the gage.

16. Repeat these measurements for the opposite side.

PARKING BRAKE

17. Install both rear brake rotors.

18. Install both rear caliper brackets.

19. Install the rear tire and wheel assemblies.

20. Adjust the parking brake by turning the nut at the equalizer (2) while spinning both rear wheels. When either of the rear wheels starts to drag, back off the nut one full turn.

21. Lower the vehicle to curb height.

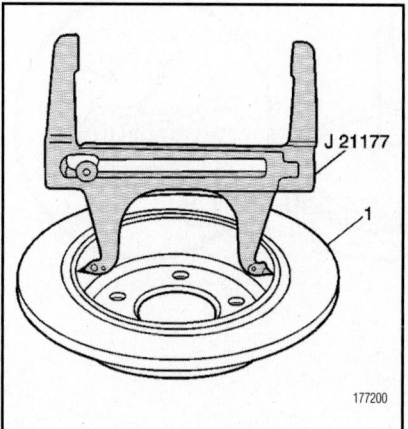

Fig. 9 Drum-to-brake shoe clearance gage set inside the park brake drum

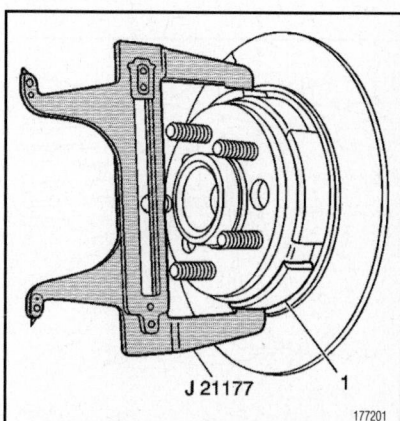

Fig. 10 Drum-to-brake shoe clearance gage positioned over the park brake shoe at the widest point

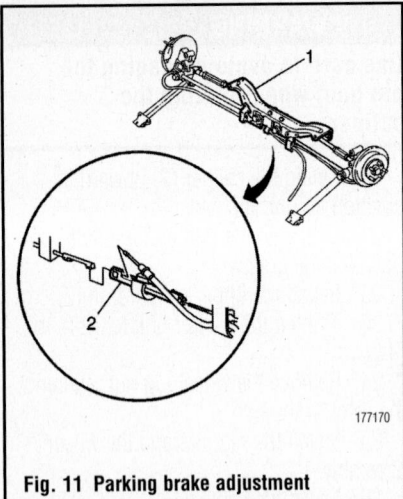

Fig. 11 Parking brake adjustment

22. Apply the parking brake, then inspect for rotation of the rear wheels. If the rear wheels rotate during this inspection, then readjust the parking brake shoes.

23. Release the parking brake. Verify that the wheels rotate freely.

24. Lower the vehicle.

PARKING BRAKE SHOES

REMOVAL & INSTALLATION

See Figures 12 through 14.

1. Refer to the Brakes Precautions.
2. Raise and suitably support the vehicle.
3. Remove the rear tire and wheel assemblies.
4. Relieve the parking brake system tension at the equalizer assembly.
5. Remove the rear caliper bracket.
6. Remove the rear rotor.
7. Disconnect and remove the rear parking brake cable from the bracket at the rear wheel
8. Disconnect the parking brake cable

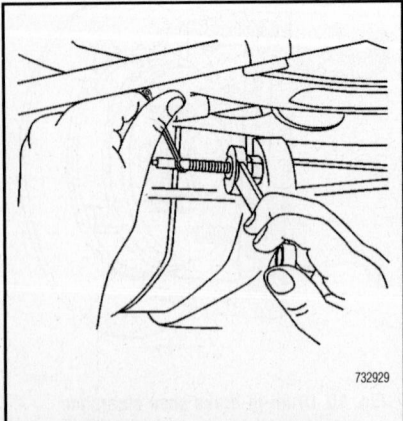

Fig. 12 Relieve the park brake system tension at the equalizer assembly

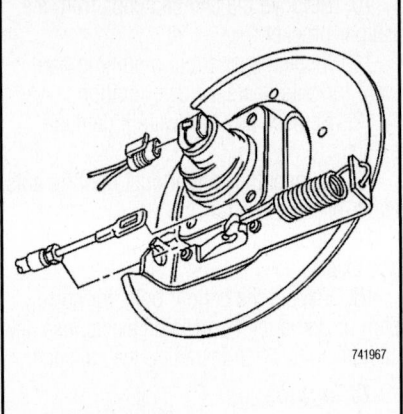

Fig. 13 Disconnect and remove the rear park brake cable

return spring from the park brake actuator and bracket at the rear wheel.

9. Remove the rear hub.

10. The rear hub, backing plate, park brake cable bracket, and park brake actuator will be removed as an assembly.

11. Remove the two retainers (9) and the park brake cable bracket (8) from the park brake actuator (4). Position the rear hub aside.

12. Remove the park brake shoe and actuator (4) from the backing plate (7).

13. Separate the park brake shoe from the actuator.

To install:

14. Assemble the park brake shoe to the actuator (4).

15. Install the park brake shoe and actuator (4) onto the backing plate (7).

16. Position the park brake shoe, actuator (4), and backing plate (7) over the rear hub.

17. Install the park brake cable bracket (8) and the two retainers (9).

18. Tighten the bracket retainers to 124 inch lbs. (14 Nm).

19. Install the rear hub.

20. Install the rear hub, backing plate, park brake cable bracket, and park brake actuator as an assembly.

21. Install and connect the rear park brake cable to the bracket at the rear wheel.

22. Connect the park brake cable return spring to the park brake actuator and bracket at the rear wheel.

23. Install the rear rotor.

24. Install the rear caliper bracket.

25. Install the rear tire and wheel assemblies.

26. Adjust the park brake system.

27. Lower the vehicle.

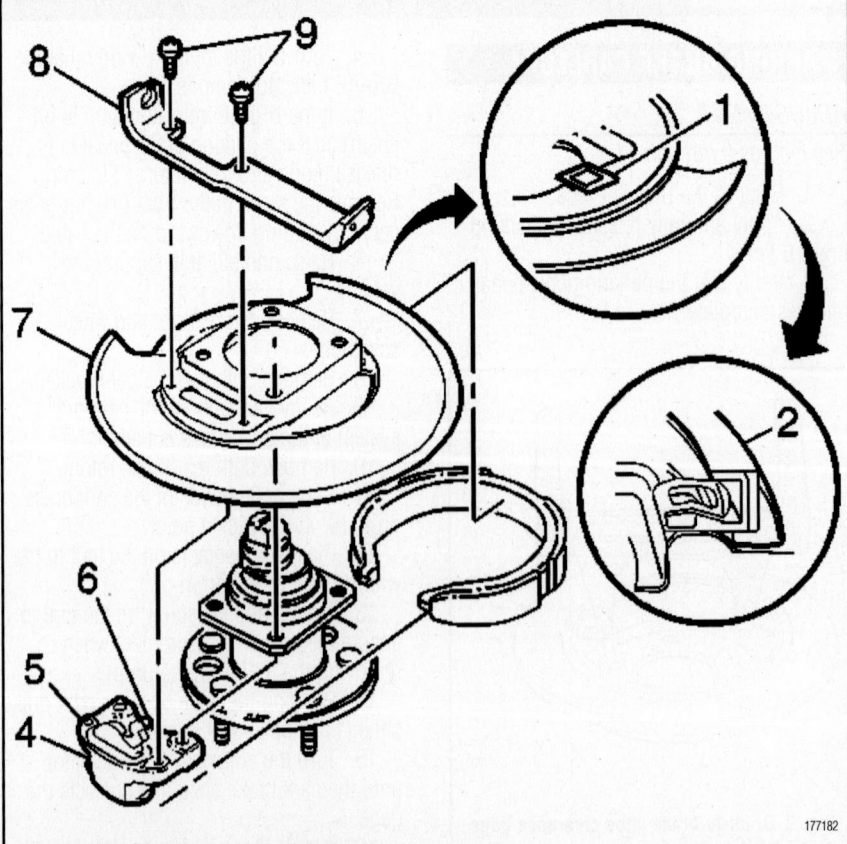

Fig. 14 Hub, bracket, actuator assembly

CHASSIS ELECTRICAL | AIRBAG (SUPPLEMENTAL RESTRAINT SYSTEM)

GENERAL INFORMATION

✳✳ WARNING

Impalas have an airbag system. Disarm the airbag system before performing service on, or around, system components, the steering column, instrument panel components, wiring and sensors. Failure to follow the safety precautions and the disarming procedure could result in accidental airbag deployment, possible injury and unnecessary system repairs.

SERVICE PRECAUTIONS

Disconnect and isolate the battery negative cable before beginning any airbag system component diagnosis, testing, removal, or installation procedures. Allow the system capacitor to discharge for two minutes before beginning any component service. This will disable the airbag system. Failure to disable the airbag system may result in accidental airbag deployment, personal injury, or death.

Do not place an intact undeployed airbag face down on a solid surface. The airbag will propel into the air if accidentally deployed and may result in personal injury or death.

When carrying or handling an undeployed airbag, point the trim side (face) of the airbag away from the body to minimize possibility of injury if accidental deployment occurs. Failure to do this may result in personal injury or death.

Replace airbag system components with OEM replacement parts. Substitute parts may appear interchangeable, but internal differences may result in inferior occupant protection. Failure to do so may result in occupant personal injury or death.

Wear safety glasses, rubber gloves, and long-sleeved clothing when cleaning powder residue from a vehicle after an airbag deployment. Powder residue emitted from a deployed airbag can cause skin irritation. Flush the affected area with cool water if there is irritation. For nasal or throat irritation, exit the vehicle for fresh air until the irritation ceases. If irritation continues, see a physician.

Do not use a replacement airbag that is not in the original packaging. This may result in improper deployment, personal injury, or death.

The factory installed fasteners, screws and bolts used to fasten airbag components have a special coating and are specifically designed for the airbag system. Do not use substitute fasteners. Use only original equipment fasteners listed in the parts catalog when fastener replacement is required.

During, and following any child restraint anchor service, due to an impact event or vehicle repair, carefully inspect all mounting hardware, tether straps, and anchors for proper installation, operation, or damage. If a child restraint anchor is found damaged in any way, the anchor must be replaced. Failure to do this may result in personal injury or death.

Deployed and non-deployed airbags may or may not have live pyrotechnic material within the airbag inflator.

Do not dispose of driver/passenger/curtain airbags or seat belt tensioners unless you are sure of complete deployment. Refer to the Hazardous Substance Control System for proper disposal.

Dispose of deployed airbags and tensioners consistent with state, provincial, local, and federal regulations.

After any airbag component testing or service, do not connect the battery negative cable. Personal injury or death may result if the system test is not performed first.

If the vehicle is equipped with the Occupant Classification System (OCS), do not connect the battery negative cable before performing the OCS Verification Test using the scan tool and the appropriate diagnostic information. Personal injury or death may result if the system test is not performed properly.

Never replace both the Occupant Restraint Controller (ORC) and the Occupant Classification Module (OCM) at the same time. If both require replacement, replace one, and then perform the Airbag System test before replacing the other.

Both the ORC and the OCM store Occupant Classification System (OCS) calibration data, which they transfer to one another when one of them is replaced. If both are replaced at the same time, an irreversible fault will be set in both modules and the OCS may malfunction and cause personal injury or death.

If equipped with OCS, the Seat Weight Sensor is a sensitive, calibrated unit - handle it carefully. Do not drop it or handle it roughly. If dropped or damaged, replace it with another sensor. Failure to do so may result in occupant injury or death.

If equipped with OCS, handle the front passenger seat carefully as well. When removing the seat, be careful when setting it on the floor not to drop it. If dropped, the sensor may be inoperative and could result in occupant injury, or possibly death.

If equipped with OCS, when the passenger front seat is on the floor, no one should sit in the front passenger seat. This uneven force may damage the sensing ability of the seat weight sensors. If sat on and damaged, the sensor may be inoperative and could result in occupant injury, or possibly death.

✳✳ CAUTION

When performing service on or near the airbag/supplemental restraint system components or the airbag/supplemental restraint system wiring, you must first disable the airbag/supplemental restraint system. Refer to Disarming the System/Airbag/SIR Disabling. Failure to observe the correct procedure could cause deployment of the airbag/supplemental restraint components, personal injury, or unnecessary airbag/supplemental restraint system repairs.

➡**The inflatable restraint sensing and diagnostic module (SDM) maintains a reserved energy supply. The reserved energy supply provides deployment power for the air bags. Deployment power is available for as much as 1 minute after disconnecting the vehicle power. Disabling the airbag/supplemental restraint system prevents deployment of the air bags from the reserved energy supply.**

General Service Instructions:
Follow these instructions in order to properly repair the vehicle and return it to its original integrity:

• Do not expose inflator modules to temperatures above 65°C (150°F).

• Verify the correct replacement part number. Do not substitute a component from a different vehicle.

• Use only original GM replacement parts available from your authorized GM dealer. Do not use salvaged parts for repairs to the airbag/supplemental restraint system.

Discard any of the following components if it has been dropped from a height of 3 ft (91 cm) or greater:

• Sensing and diagnostic module (SDM)

• Passenger instrument panel airbag

• Driver steering wheel airbag

- Front seat side airbag
- Driver steering wheel air bag coil
- Roof rail airbags
- Front and/or side impact sensors (SIS)
- Passenger presence module and/or occupant sensor
- Seat belt anchor and/or retractor pretensioners

DISARMING THE SYSTEM/SIR DISABLING

There are several reasons for disabling the SIR system, such as repairs to the SIR system or servicing a component near or attached to an SIR component. There are different ways to disable the SIR system depending on what type of service is being performed. The following information covers the proper procedures for disabling the SIR system.

Disconnect the negative battery cable(s)* to disable the system for any of the following conditions:

- If the vehicle was involved in an accident with an air bag deployment.
- When moving, removing. or replacing an SIR component or a component attached to an SIR component. (Including, anytime you remove fasteners.)
- If you suspect the vehicle has shorted electrical wires.

Follow the appropriate SIR service manual diagnostic procedure(s)*

- When performing SIR diagnostics.

Remove the SIR/Airbag fuse(s) when indicated by the diagnostic procedure to disable the SIR system.

- When performing electrical diagnosis on components other than the SIR system.

❋❋ CAUTION

Refer to Airbag Service Precautions

Disabling Procedure - Air Bag Fuse

1. Turn the steering wheel so that the vehicles wheels are pointing straight ahead.
2. Place the ignition in the OFF position.

❋❋ CAUTION

The Inflatable Restraint Sensing and Diagnostic Module, or SDM, may have more than one fused power input. To ensure there is no unwanted SIR deployment, personal injury, or unnecessary SIR system repairs, remove all fuses supplying power to the SDM. With all SDM fuses removed and the ignition switch in the ON position, the AIR BAG warning indicator illuminates. This is normal

operation, and does not indicate a SIR system malfunction.

3. Locate and remove the fuse(s) supplying power to the SDM.
4. Wait 1 minute before working on the system.

Disabling Procedure - Negative Battery Cable*

1. Turn the steering wheel so that the vehicles wheels are pointing straight ahead.
2. Place the ignition in the OFF position.
3. Disconnect the negative battery cable from the battery.
4. Wait 1 minute before working on system.

➡ ***Diagnostic Trouble Codes (DTCs) will be lost when the negative battery cable is disconnected.**

ARMING THE SYSTEM/SIR ENABLING

Enabling Procedure - Air Bag Fuse

1. Place the ignition in the OFF position.
2. Install the fuse(s) supplying power to the Inflatable Restraint Sensing and Diagnostic Module, or SDM.
3. Turn the ignition switch to the ON position. The AIR BAG indicator will flash then turn OFF.
4. Perform a diagnostic system check of the vehicle if the AIR BAG warning indicator does not operate as described.

Enabling Procedure - Negative Battery Cable

1. Place the ignition in the OFF position.
2. Connect the negative battery cable to the battery.
3. Turn the ignition switch to the ON position. The AIR BAG indicator will flash then turn OFF.
4. Perform a diagnostic system check of the vehicle if the AIR BAG warning indicator does not operate as described.

CLOCKSPRING CENTERING

See Figures 15 through 19.

❋❋ WARNING

The new Supplemental Inflatable Restraint (SIR) coil assembly will be centered. Improper alignment of the SIR coil assembly may damage the unit, causing an inflatable restraint malfunction.

➡ **If a double wire harness strap is installed onto the wire harness assem-**

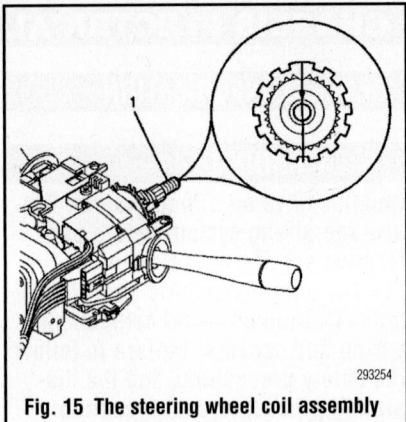

Fig. 15 The steering wheel coil assembly

293254

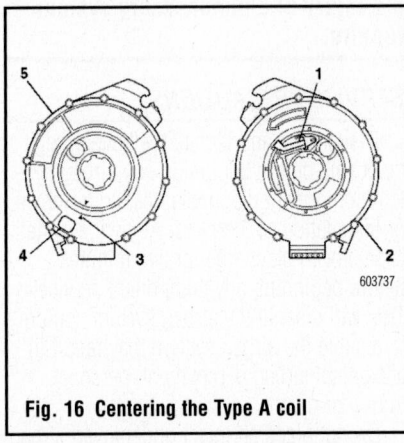

Fig. 16 Centering the Type A coil

603737

bly and column, you must reuse the holder for the wire straps during installation. Remove the wire harness strap(s) where necessary.

1. Verify the following conditions before centering the SIR coil:

   a. The wheels on the vehicle are straight ahead.

   b. The block tooth (1) of the steering shaft assembly is in the 12 o'clock position.

   c. The ignition switch is in the LOCK position.

   Type A Coil

2. If the front (5) of the SIR coil has a centering window (4), and the back side (2) includes a spring service lock (1), perform the following steps:

   a. Hold the SIR coil with the face up.

   b. While depressing the spring service lock, rotate the coil hub clockwise until the coil ribbon stops.

   c. Rotate the coil hub slowly, counterclockwise, until the centering window appears yellow and both arrows (3) line up.

   d. Release the spring service lock between the locking tab. The SIR coil is now centered.

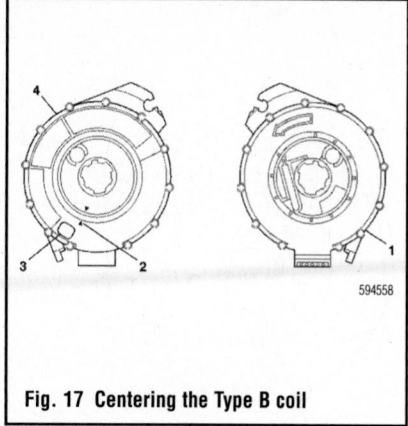

Fig. 17 Centering the Type B coil

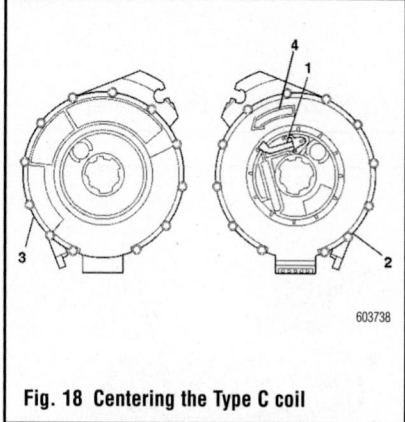

Fig. 18 Centering the Type C coil

e. Align the centered SIR coil with the horn tower and slide onto the steering shaft assembly.

3. If the front (4) of the SIR coil has a centering window (3), and the back side (1)

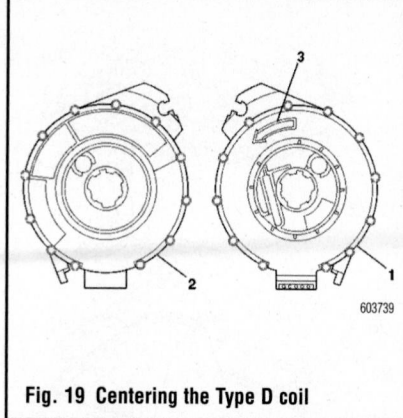

Fig. 19 Centering the Type D coil

includes NO spring service lock, perform the following steps:

a. Hold the SIR coil with the face up.

b. Rotate the coil hub clockwise until the coil ribbon stops.

c. Rotate the coil hub slowly, counterclockwise until the centering window appears yellow and both arrows (2) line up. This is the CENTER position.

d. While holding the coil hub in the CENTER position, align the SIR coil with the horn tower and slide onto the steering shaft assembly.

4. If the front side (3) of the SIR coil has NO centering window, but the back side (2) includes a spring service lock (1), perform the following steps:

a. Hold the SIR coil with the back side up.

b. While depressing the spring service lock, rotate the coil hub in the direction of the arrow (4) until the coil ribbon stops.

c. Still pressing the spring service lock, rotate the coil hub in the opposite direction 2 1/2 revolutions.

d. Release the spring service lock between locking tabs. The SIR coil is now centered.

e. Align the centered SIR coil with the horn tower and slide onto the steering shaft assembly.

5. If the front side (2) of the SIR coil has NO centering window, and the back side (1) includes NO spring service lock, perform the following steps:

a. Hold the SIR coil with the face up.

b. Rotate the coil hub in the direction of the arrow until the coil ribbon stops.

c. Rotate the coil hub, slowly, counterclockwise, for 2 1/2 revolutions. This is the CENTER position.

d. While maintaining the coil hub in the CENTER position, align the centered SIR coil with the horn tower and slide onto the steering shaft assembly.

6. If a double wire harness strap is installed onto the wire harness assembly and column, you must route the wires up against the steering column. One wire harness strap will surround one lead from the coil to the steering column. The other wire harness strap will surround all leads to the steering column.

DRIVE TRAIN

AUTOMATIC TRANSMISSION FLUID

DRAIN AND REFILL

✳✳ WARNING

Check the transmission fluid level immediately after adding fluid and before operating the Impala. Do not overfill the transmission. An overfilled transmission may result in foaming, or fluid may be expelled out the vent tube when the vehicle is operated. Overfilling will result in possible damage to the transmission.

How to Check Automatic Transmission Fluid

✳✳ WARNING

Be sure to follow all the instructions here, or a false reading on the dipstick could result.

➡ **Too much or too little fluid can damage the transmission. Too much can mean that some of the fluid could come out and fall on hot engine parts or exhaust system parts, starting a fire. Too little fluid could cause the transmission to overheat. Be sure to get an accurate reading if checking the transmission fluid.**

1. Wait at least 30 minutes before checking the transmission fluid level if the Impala has been driven under any of these conditions:

• When outside temperatures are above 90 °F (32 °C).

• At high speed for quite a while.

• In heavy traffic—especially in hot weather.

• While pulling a trailer.

2. To get the right reading, the fluid should be at normal operating temperature, which is 180 °F to 200 °F (82 °C to 93 °C).

3. Warm up the Impala by driving about 24 km (15 mi) when outside temperatures are above 50° F (10 °C). If it is colder than 50 °F (10 °C), you may have to drive the Impala longer.

Checking the Fluid Level

1. Prepare your vehicle as follows:

a. Park the vehicle on a level place. Keep the engine running.

b. With the parking brake applied, place the shift lever in P (Park).

c. With your foot on the brake pedal, move the shift lever through each gear range, pausing for about three seconds in each range. Then, position the shift lever in P (Park).

   d. Let the engine run at idle for three to five minutes.

2. Then, without shutting off the engine, follow these steps:

   a. Pull out the dipstick and wipe it with a clean rag or paper towel.

   b. Push the dipstick back in all the way, wait three seconds, and then pull it back out again.

   c. Check both sides of the dipstick, and read the lower level. The fluid level must be in the cross-hatched area.

   d. If the fluid level is in the acceptable range, push the dipstick back in all the way.

How to Add Fluid

GM recommends using DEXRON® -VI automatic transmission fluid.

1. If the fluid level is low, add only enough of the proper fluid to bring the level into the cross-hatched area on the dipstick.

2. Pull out the dipstick.

3. Using a long-neck funnel, add enough fluid at the dipstick hole to bring it to the proper level.

4. It does not take much fluid, generally less than 0.5 L (1 pt). Do not overfill.

➡ **Use of the incorrect automatic transmission fluid may damage the vehicle, and the damages may not be covered by the vehicle warranty. Always use the recommended automatic transmission fluid.**

5. After adding fluid, recheck the fluid level as described under "How to Check Automatic Transmission Fluid," earlier in this section.

6. When the fluid level is correct, push the dipstick back in all the way.

FLUID FILTER AND SEAL REPLACEMENT

See Figures 20 and 21.

1. Remove the oil pan (24) and the gasket (25).

2. Remove the filter (100). Remove the lip ring seal (101) pressed into the case only if replacement is necessary.

3. Inspect the oil pan and the filter for foreign material, such as: metal particles, clutch facing material, rubber particles, and engine coolant.

4. Determine the source of the contamination if foreign material is evident.

5. Correct the source of the contamination.

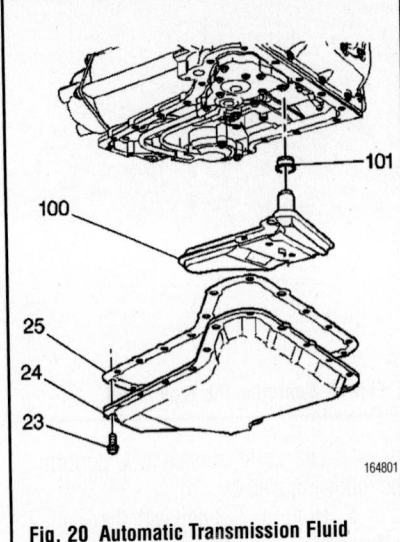

Fig. 20 Automatic Transmission Fluid Filter and Seal Replacement

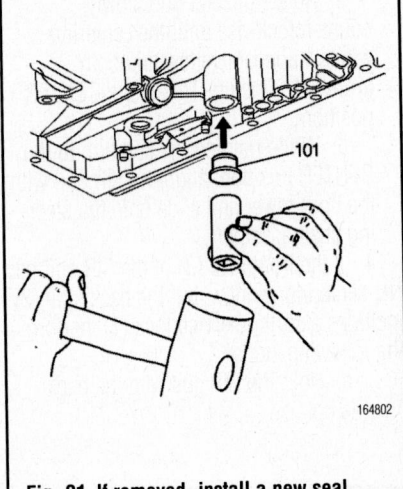

Fig. 21 If removed, install a new seal (101).

To install:

6. If removed, install a new seal (101).

7. Install the filter.

8. Install the gasket (25) and the oil pan (24).

DRIVE AXLE

REMOVAL & INSTALLATION

See Figures 22 and 23.

✳✳ CAUTION

To prevent personal injury and/or component damage, do not allow the weight of the vehicle to load the front wheels, or attempt to operate the vehicle, when the wheel driveshaft(s) or wheel driveshaft nut(s) are removed. To do so may cause the inner bearing race to separate,

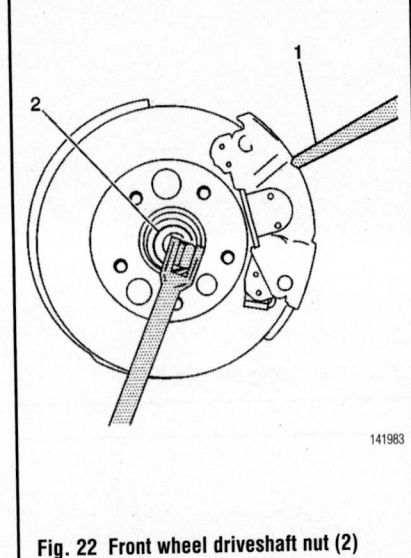

Fig. 22 Front wheel driveshaft nut (2)

Fig. 23 Front wheel driveshaft

resulting in damage to brake and suspension components and loss of vehicle control.

✳✳ WARNING

Protect wheel driveshaft boots, seals and clamps from sharp objects any time service is performed on or near the wheel driveshaft(s). Damage to the boot(s), the seal(s) or the clamp(s) may cause lubricant to leak from the joint and lead to increased noise and possible failure of the wheel driveshaft.

1. Raise and suitably support the vehicle.

2. Remove the wheel and the tire.

3. Remove the stabilizer shaft link.

4. Remove the front wheel drive shaft nut (2). Insert a drift or a flat-bladed tool (1) into the caliper and the rotor to prevent the rotor from turning.

5. Disconnect the outer tie rod assembly from the steering knuckle.

6. Separate the ball joint from the steering knuckle.

7. Separate the front wheel drive axle from the front wheel drive shaft bearing (GM has a special tool for this: J 42129). You can partially re-install the nut to protect the threads.

8. If necessary, remove the left front wheel drive axle (1) from the transaxle.

9. If necessary, remove the right front wheel drive axle (2) from the transaxle.

10. GM's special tools J 33008-A , the J 29794 and the J 2619-01 are available to separate the axle from the transaxle.

To install:

11. Install the front wheel drive axle into the transaxle (1, 2; see Front wheel driveshaft illustration).

12. Verify that the front wheel drive shaft retaining ring is properly seated:

a. Grasp the inner housing and pull the inner housing outward. Do not pull on the front wheel drive axle shaft.

b. The front wheel drive axle will remain in place when the front wheel drive shaft retaining ring is properly seated.

13. Install the front wheel drive axle into the front wheel drive shaft bearing.

14. Connect the ball joint to the steering knuckle.

15. Connect the outer tie rod assembly to the steering knuckle.

16. Install a new front wheel drive shaft nut. Insert a drift or a flat-bladed tool into the caliper and the rotor to prevent the rotor from turning.

17. Tighten the nut to 118 ft. lbs. (160 Nm).

18. Install the stabilizer shaft link.

19. Install the wheel and the tire.

20. Lower the vehicle.

21. Inspect the transaxle fluid level.

22. Inspect the wheel alignment.

ENGINE COOLING

ENGINE COOLANT

DRAIN & REFILL PROCEDURE

Draining Procedure

✶✶ CAUTION

To avoid being burned, do not remove the radiator cap or surge tank cap while the engine is hot. The cooling system will release scalding fluid and steam under pressure if the radiator cap or surge tank cap is removed while the engine and radiator are still hot.

➡**Draining the cooling system with the pressure cap installed will siphon the coolant from the overflow tank.**

1. Remove the coolant pressure cap.
2. Place a drain pan under the drain cock.
3. Open the radiator drain cock.
4. Drain the cooling system.
5. If a complete engine block drain is required, remove the coolant drain plugs from the engine block.
6. Inspect the coolant.
7. Follow the appropriate procedure based on the condition of the coolant:
   - Normal in appearance — follow the filling procedure.
   - Discolored — follow the flush procedure. Refer to Flushing.

Filling Procedure

✶✶ WARNING

You must follow this procedure. Improper coolant level could result in a low- or high-coolant level condition, causing engine damage.

✶✶ WARNING

Use the correct fastener in the correct location. Replacement fasteners must be the correct part number for that application. The service procedure identifies fasteners requiring replacement or fasteners requiring the use of thread locking compound or sealant. Do not use paints, lubricants, or corrosion inhibitors on fasteners or fastener joint surfaces unless specified. These coatings affect fastener torque and joint clamping force and may damage the fastener. Use the correct tightening sequence and specifications when installing fasteners in order to avoid damage to parts and systems.

1. Close the radiator drain cock.
2. If a complete engine block drain was required, install the coolant drain plugs to the engine block.

➡**Use a 50/50 mixture of DEX-COOL® antifreeze and clean, drinkable water.**

3. Slowly fill the cooling system with a 50/50 coolant mixture until the coolant level is visible and stable. Refer to Approximate fluid capacities.

4. Install the pressure cap loosely (threaded on about one turn).

5. Start the engine and raise the engine speed to 2500 rpm and hold it there for 40 seconds, and then shut the engine off.

6. Remove the pressure cap and fill the coolant system until the level is visible and stable.

7. Install the pressure cap loosely (threaded on about one turn).

8. Start the engine and raise the engine speed to 2500 rpm and hold it there for 30 seconds, and then shut the engine off.

9. Remove the pressure cap and fill the coolant system until the level is visible and stable.

10. Install the pressure cap loosely (threaded on about one turn).

11. Start the engine and raise the engine speed to 2500 rpm and hold it there for 20 seconds, and then shut the engine off.

12. Remove the pressure cap and fill the coolant system until the level is visible and stable.

13. Install the pressure cap, fully threaded on.

14. Fill the coolant recovery bottle to the indicator line, and then add 13.5 ounces (400 milliliters) more.

15. Start the engine and run it above 2500 rpm until it is hot enough to open the thermostat, this will allow the trapped air to be purged from the engine.

16. Complete a series of three, 4-second-duration idles with 4-second-duration 3000 rpm cycles.

17. Turn the engine off and allow it to cool down to room temperature.

18. Fill the coolant recovery bottle to the indicator line.

19. Inspect the concentration of the engine coolant using the a coolant tester, such as GM's J 1657924.

20. Rinse away any excess coolant from the engine and the engine compartment.

FLUSHING

➡**Do not use a chemical flush.**

Store used coolant in a properly labeled container. Do not pour used coolant down a drain. Ethylene glycol antifreeze is a very toxic chemical. Do not dispose of coolant into the sewer system or ground water. This is illegal and ecologically unsound.

Various methods and equipment can be used to flush the cooling system. If special equipment is used, such as a back flusher, follow the manufacturer's instruction.

When the cooling system is contaminated, flush the cooling system thoroughly to remove the contaminants before the engine is seriously damaged.

1. Drain the cooling system. Refer to Cooling System Draining and Filling.

2. Remove the coolant recovery reservoir.

3. Clean and flush the coolant recovery reservoir with clean, drinkable water.

4. Install the coolant recovery reservoir.

5. Follow the drain and fill procedure using only clean, drinkable water. Refer to Cooling System Draining and Filling.

6. Run the engine for 20 minutes.

7. Stop the engine.

8. Drain the cooling system. Refer to Cooling System Draining and Filling

9. Repeat the procedure if necessary, until the fluid is nearly colorless.

10. Fill the cooling system. Refer to Cooling System Draining and Filling.

ENGINE FAN

REMOVAL & INSTALLATION
See Figures 24 and 25.

❊❊ CAUTION

An electric fan under the hood can start up even when the engine is not running and can injure you. Keep hands, clothing and tools away from any underhood electric fan.

❊❊ CAUTION

To help avoid personal injury or damage to the vehicle, always replace a bent, cracked, or damaged fan blade or housing.

❊❊ CAUTION

Unless directed otherwise, the ignition and start switch must be in the OFF or LOCK position, and all electrical loads must be OFF before servicing any electrical component. Disconnect the negative battery cable to prevent an electrical spark should a tool or equipment come in contact with an exposed electrical terminal. Failure to follow these precautions

may result in personal injury and/or damage to the vehicle or its components.

For Vehicles equipped with OnStar® (UE1) with Back Up Battery: The Back Up Battery is a redundant power supply to allow limited OnStar® functionality in the event of a main vehicle battery power disruption to the VCIM (OnStar® module). Do not disconnect the main vehicle battery or remove the OnStar® fuse with the ignition key in any position other than OFF. Allow retained accessory power (RAP) to time out or be disabled (simply opening the driver door should disable RAP) before disconnecting power. Disconnecting power to the OnStar® module in any way while the ignition is On or with RAP activated may cause activation of the OnStar® Back-Up Battery (BUB) system and will discharge and permanently damage the back-up battery. Once the Back-Up Battery is activated it will stay on until it has completely discharged. The BUB is not rechargeable and once activated the BUB must be replaced.

1. Remove the fan shroud assembly from the vehicle.

➡**Hold the fan blade to prevent rotation.**

2. Use a socket such as GM tool GE-47827, to turn the fan motor drive plate in the opposite direction of the arrow on the fan blade until the motor drive plate disengages from the fan blade.

❊❊ WARNING

Failure to tape off all of the entry points to the cooling fan motor(s) will allow debris to enter and damage the motor(s).

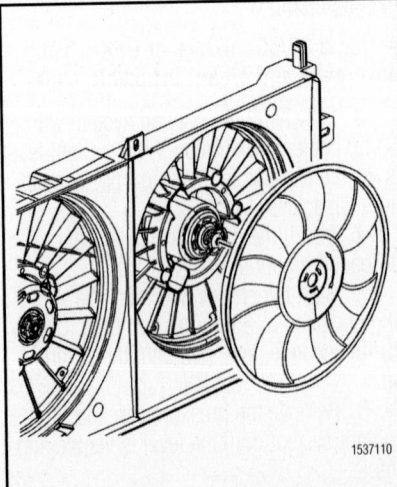

Fig. 24 Fan shroud assembly

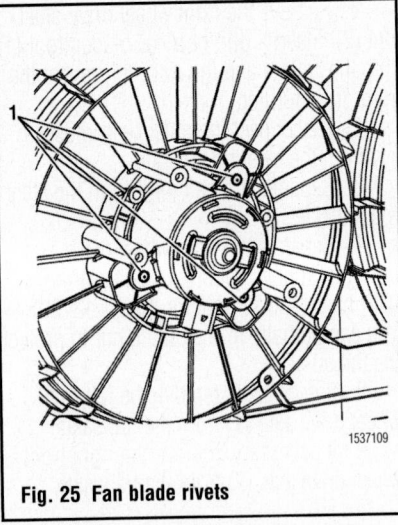

Fig. 25 Fan blade rivets

➡**When reusing the fan motor tape off the front and rear entry points of the fan motor before drilling the rivets.**

3. Center punch each of the rivets (1) from the rear of the motor.

4. Drill the head of the rivets (1) from the fan motor using a 0.25 in (6.35 mm) drill bit.

5. Remove and discard the fan blade.

6. Tap the rivets out of the fan shroud.

7. Remove the fan motor from the fan shroud.

➡**Blow off any excess debris from the fan motor.**

8. Remove the tape covering the entry points from the fan motor.

To install:

9. Install the engine cooling fan motor to the fan shroud.

➡**Position the fan motor to the fan shroud and insert the bolts from the front side.**

10. Install the cooling fan motor bolts.

❊❊ WARNING

Refer to Fastener Caution in the general Precautions section.

11. Install the cooling fan motor nuts and tighten to 53 inch lbs. (6 Nm).

❊❊ WARNING

Failure to heat the fan hub in hot tap water before installation will result in cooling fan failure due to cracking. Allowing the heated fan to cool for more than one minute prior to installation will also result in failure due to cracking.

➡**Using hot tap water at a minimum of 120 °F (49 °C), hold the new fan blade hub under the running water for a minimum of 60 seconds to heat the fan blade to the temperature of the water.**

12. Immediately after heating, position the fan blade on the fan motor drive plate.

13. Install the new engine cooling fan blade.

➡**Hold the fan blade to prevent rotation.**

14. Turn the fan motor drive plate in the same direction as the arrow on the fan blade until the fan motor drive plate engages to the fan blade. It's fully engaged when the motor drive plate fully occupies the three slots in the face of the fan blade.

15. Rotate the cooling fan blade to ensure proper rotation.

16. Install the fan shroud assembly to the vehicle.

RADIATOR

REMOVAL & INSTALLATION

See Figures 26 through 30.

✳✳ CAUTION

Unless directed otherwise, the ignition and start switch must be in the OFF or LOCK position, and all electrical loads must be OFF before servicing any electrical component. Disconnect the negative battery cable to prevent an electrical spark should a tool or equipment come in contact with an exposed electrical terminal. Failure to follow these precautions may result in personal injury and/or damage to the vehicle or its components.

For Vehicles equipped with OnStar® (UE1) with Back Up Battery: The Back Up Battery is a redundant power supply to allow limited OnStar® functionality in the event of a main vehicle battery power disruption to the VCIM (OnStar® module). Do not disconnect the main vehicle battery or remove the OnStar® fuse with the ignition key in any position other than OFF. Retained accessory power (RAP) should be allowed to time out or be disabled (simply opening the driver door should disable RAP) before disconnecting power. Disconnecting power to the OnStar® module in any way while the ignition is On or with RAP activated may cause activation of the OnStar® Back-Up Battery (BUB) system and will discharge and permanently damage the back-up bat-

tery. Once the Back-Up Battery is activated it will stay on until it has completely discharged. The BUB is not rechargeable and once activated the BUB must be replaced.

1. Disconnect the negative battery cable.

2. Remove the air cleaner assembly. Refer to Air Cleaner Assembly.

3. Drain the cooling system. Refer to Cooling System Drain and Refill Procedure.

4. Remove the engine mount struts.

5. Use hose clamp pliers, such as the GM special tool J 38185, to reposition the upper radiator hose clamp from the radiator.

6. Remove the upper radiator hose from the radiator.

7. Remove the powertrain control module (PCM) harness clip from the fan shroud.

8. Remove the condenser tubes bracket bolt from the fan shroud.

9. Remove the bolt that connects the fan shroud to the condenser hold-down bracket.

10. Remove the condenser hold-down bracket from the radiator and condenser.

11. Remove the cooling fan shroud bolts.

12. Remove the radiator upper support brackets and bolts that connect to the fan shroud.

13. Disconnect the engine cooling fan motors' electrical connectors.

14. Remove the cooling fan motors' electrical harness from the fan shroud clips.

15. Remove the cooling fan shroud.

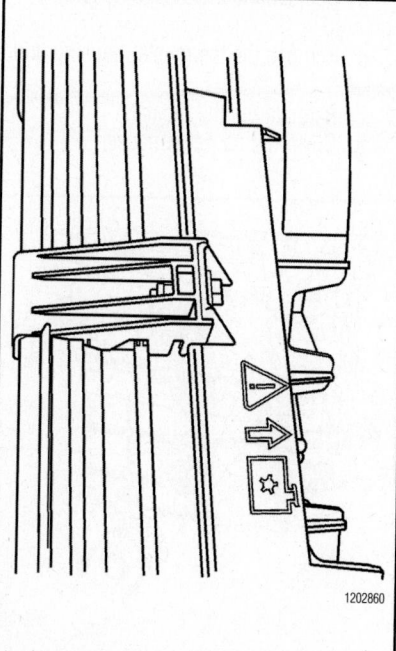

Fig. 26 Condenser hold-down bracket and fan shroud

16. Use hose clamp pliers, such as GM's special tool J 38185, to reposition the lower radiator hose clamp from the radiator.

17. Remove the lower radiator hose from the radiator.

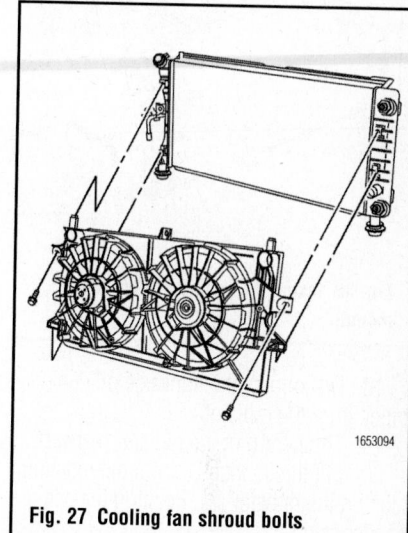

Fig. 27 Cooling fan shroud bolts

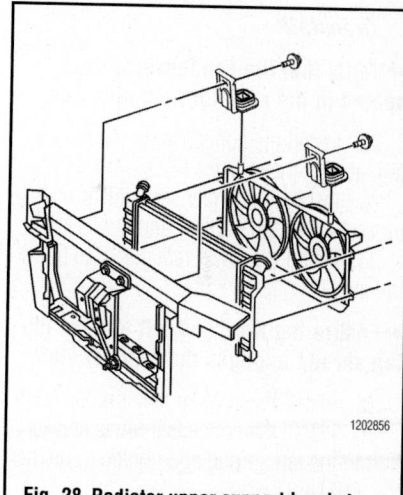

Fig. 28 Radiator upper support brackets and bolts that connect to the fan shroud

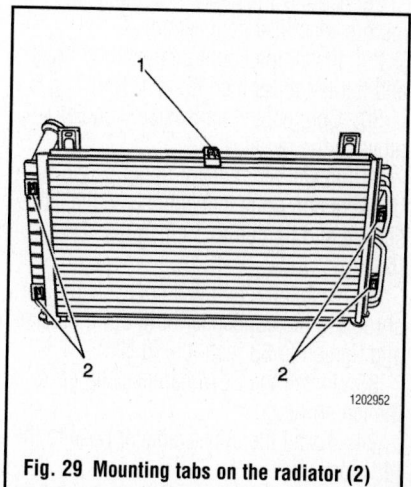

Fig. 29 Mounting tabs on the radiator (2)

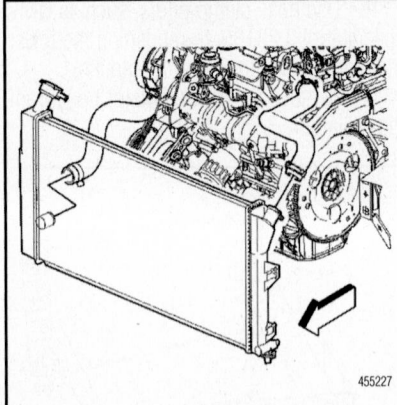

Fig. 30 Install the radiator to the lower mounts

18. Disconnect the transaxle oil cooler pipes from the radiator.

19. Tilt the top of the radiator rearward.

20. Lift the condenser from the mounting tabs on the radiator (2). Position the condenser aside.

21. Remove the radiator.

To install:

→**Verify that the condenser is fully seated in the radiator mounting tabs.**

22. Install the condenser to the mounting tabs on the radiator (2).

23. Install the condenser hold-down bracket (1) to the radiator and condenser.

24. Install the lower radiator hose to the radiator.

→**Ensure the right and left edge of the fan shroud engages the radiator slots.**

25. Install the cooling fan shroud.

26. Install the condenser tubes bracket bolt to the fan shroud and tighten to 89 inch lbs. (10 Nm).

27. Install the cooling fan motors' electrical harness to the fan shroud clips.

28. Connect the engine cooling fan motors' electrical connectors.

29. Install the cooling fan shroud bolts and tighten to 89 inch lbs. (10 Nm)

30. Connect the transaxle oil cooler pipes to the radiator.

31. Install the radiator upper support brackets and bolts that connect to the fan shroud and tighten to 53 inch lbs. (6 Nm).

32. Install the bolt that connects the fan shroud to the condenser hold down bracket and tighten to 53 inch lbs. (6 Nm).

33. Install the PCM harness clip on to the fan shroud.

34. Install the upper radiator hose to the radiator.

35. Use hose clamp pliers to install the upper radiator hose clamp to the radiator.

36. Install the air cleaner assembly.

37. Install the coolant reservoir hose to the fan shroud.

38. Install the radiator vent hose to the right upper radiator tank and fill neck.

39. Install the engine mount struts.

40. Fill the cooling system.

41. Connect the negative battery cable.

✺ WARNING

Do NOT overfill the transaxle. The overfilling of the transaxle causes foaming, loss of fluid, shift complaints, and possible damage to the transaxle.

42. Adjust the transaxle fluid level.

THERMOSTAT

REMOVAL & INSTALLATION

See Figures 31 and 32.

1. Drain the cooling system. Refer to Cooling System Drain and Refill Procedure.

2. Remove the air cleaner outlet duct.

3. Reposition the radiator outlet hose clamp at the thermostat housing.

4. Remove the radiator outlet hose from the thermostat housing (3.5L shown, 3.9L similar).

5. Remove the thermostat housing bolt/stud.

6. Remove the thermostat housing and gasket.

7. Remove the thermostat.

8. Clean the gasket surfaces.

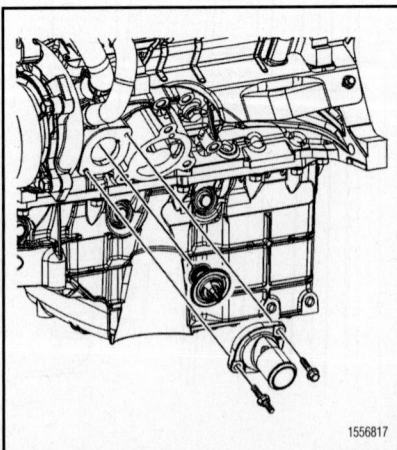

Fig. 31 Thermostat housing—3.5L engine shown, 3.9L similar

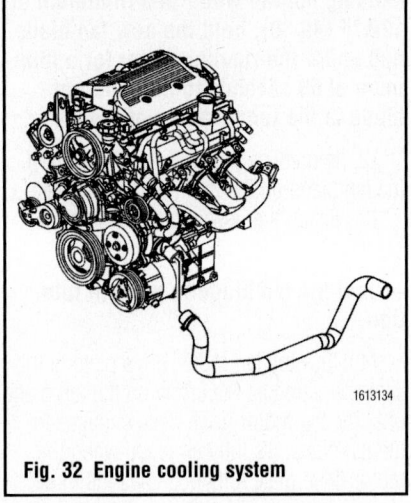

Fig. 32 Engine cooling system

To install:

9. Install a NEW thermostat.

10. Position a NEW gasket and the thermostat housing to the engine block.

11. Install the thermostat housing bolt/stud.

12. Tighten the bolt/stud to 89 inch lbs. (10 Nm).

13. Install the radiator outlet hose to the thermostat housing.

14. Position the radiator outlet hose clamp at the thermostat housing.

15. Install the air cleaner outlet duct.

16. Fill the cooling system. Refer to Cooling System Draining and Filling

17. Inspect the system for leaks.

WATER PUMP

REMOVAL & INSTALLATION

See Figures 33 and 34.

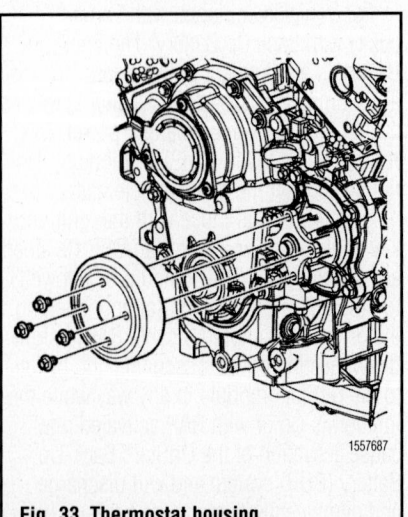

Fig. 33 Thermostat housing

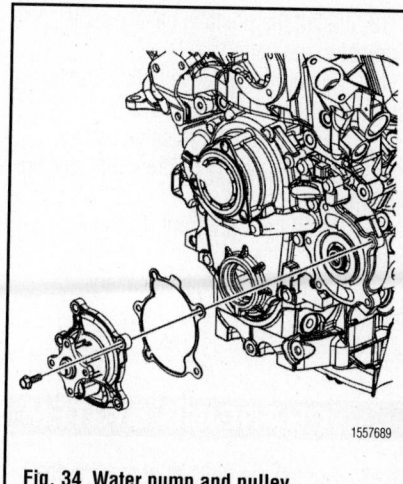

Fig. 34 Water pump and pulley

1557689

1. Drain the cooling system. Refer to Cooling System Drain and Refill Procedure.
2. Loosen the water pump pulley bolts.
3. Remove the drive belt.
4. Remove the water pump pulley bolts and pulley.
5. Remove the water pump bolts.
6. Remove the water pump and gasket.
7. Clean the water pump mating surfaces.

To install:

8. Position a NEW water pump gasket and the water pump to the engine front cover.

9. Install the water pump bolts.
10. Tighten the bolts to 11 ft. lbs. (15 Nm).
11. Install the water pump pulley and bolts.
12. Install the drive belt.
13. Tighten the water pump pulley bolts.
14. Tighten the bolts to 18 ft. lbs. (25 Nm).
15. Fill the cooling system. Refer to Cooling System Drain and Refill Procedure.
16. Inspect for leaks.

ENGINE ELECTRICAL

BATTERY SYSTEM

BATTERY

BATTERY NEGATIVE CABLE DISCONNECTION AND CONNECTION

> ❊❊ **CAUTION**
>
> **Refer to the Airbag/Supplemental restraint system warnings and precautions in the Chassis Electrical section.**

> ❊❊ **CAUTION**
>
> **Refer to the Battery disconnect warning in this section.**

1. Record each one of the vehicle preset radio stations.
2. Turn OFF all lamps and accessories.
3. Turn the ignition switch to the OFF position.
4. Loosen the negative battery cable terminal nut.
5. Remove the negative battery cable terminal from the battery.

To install:

6. Clean any existing oxidation from the contact face of the battery terminal and battery cable using a wire brush before installing the battery cable to the battery terminal.
7. Install the negative battery cable terminal to the battery.
8. Tighten the negative battery cable terminal nut.
9. Tighten the nut to 11 ft. lbs. (15 Nm).
10. Set the clock and program the radio stations back into the radio as recorded at the beginning of the procedure.

BATTERY DISCONNECT WARNING

> ❊❊ **CAUTION**
>
> **Unless directed otherwise, the ignition and start switch must be in the OFF or LOCK position, and all electrical loads must be OFF before servicing any electrical component. Disconnect the negative battery cable to prevent an electrical spark should a tool or equipment come in contact with an exposed electrical terminal. Failure to follow these precautions may result in personal injury and/or damage to the vehicle or its components.**

For Vehicles equipped with OnStar® (UE1) with Back Up Battery:
The Back Up Battery is a redundant power supply to allow limited OnStar® functionality in the event of a main vehicle battery power disruption to the VCIM (OnStar® module). Do not disconnect the main vehicle battery or remove the OnStar® fuse with the ignition key in any position other than OFF. Retained accessory power (RAP) should be allowed to time out or be disabled (simply opening the driver door should disable RAP) before disconnecting power. Disconnecting power to the OnStar® module in any way while the ignition is On or with RAP activated may cause activation of the OnStar® Back-Up Battery (BUB) system and will discharge and permanently damage the back-up battery. Once the Back-Up Battery is activated it will stay on until it has completely discharged. The BUB is not rechargeable and once activated you must replace the BUB.

REMOVAL & INSTALLATION
See Figures 35 and 36.

➡**Do not tip the battery more than 40 degrees during removal.**

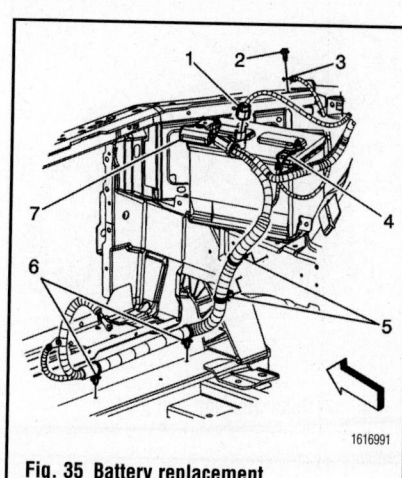

1616991

Fig. 35 Battery replacement

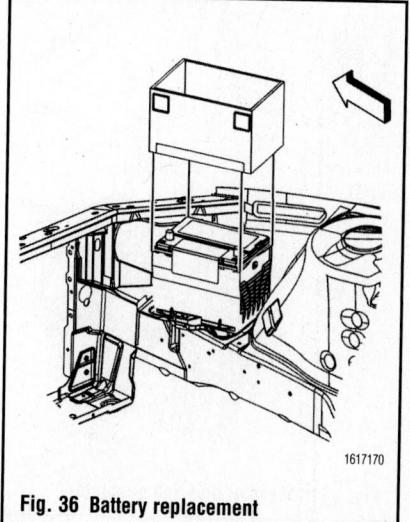

1617170

Fig. 36 Battery replacement

1. Disconnect the negative battery cable.

2. Remove the right front diagonal brace.

3. Open the positive battery cable terminal cover (7).

4. Loosen the positive battery cable terminal nut.

5. Remove the positive battery cable terminal from the battery.

6. Remove the battery insulator.

7. Remove the battery hold down bolt and hold down.

8. Remove the battery.

To install:

➡**Do not tip the battery more than 40 degrees during installation.**

9. Install the battery.

10. Install the battery hold down and bolt.

11. Tighten the battery hold down bolt to 13 ft. lbs. (18 Nm).

12. Install the battery insulator.

13. Install the positive battery cable terminal to the battery.

14. Tighten the positive battery cable terminal nut to 11 ft. lbs. (15 Nm).

15. Snap closed the positive battery cable terminal cover (7; Battery replacement illustration).

16. Install the right front diagonal brace.

17. Connect the negative battery cable.

ENGINE ELECTRICAL

CHARGING SYSTEM

GENERATOR

REMOVAL & INSTALLATION

See Figures 37 through 39.

1. Disconnect the negative battery cable. Refer to Battery Negative Cable Disconnection and Connection.

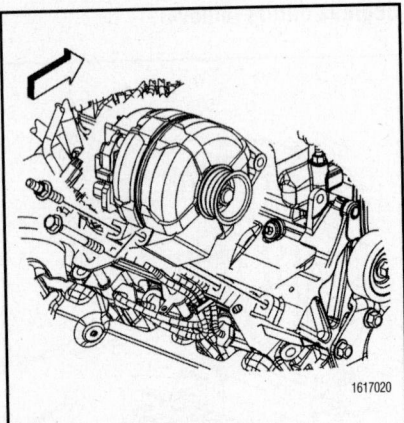

Fig. 37 Generator bolt and stud

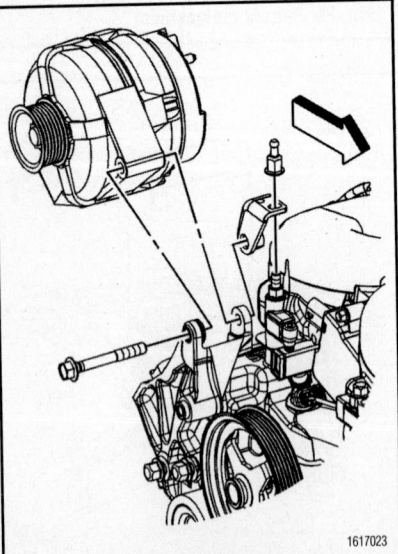

Fig. 38 Generator bolt and generator

2. Remove the drive belt. Refer to Drive Belt Replacement.

3. Reposition the protective boot (2) from the generator output BAT terminal.

4. Remove the generator output BAT terminal nut (5).

5. Remove the engine harness terminal (4) from the generator.

6. Disconnect the generator electrical connector (3).

7. Remove the generator bolt and stud.

8. Remove the generator bolt.

9. Remove the generator.

To install:

10. Install the generator.

11. Install the generator bolt until snug.

12. Install the generator bolt and stud.

13. Tighten the bolts/stud to 37 ft. lbs. (50 Nm).

14. Connect the generator electrical connector (3).

15. Install the engine harness terminal (4) to the generator.

16. Install the generator output BAT terminal nut (5).

17. Tighten the nut to 22 ft. lbs. (30 Nm).

18. Position the protective boot (2) to the generator output BAT terminal.

19. Install the drive belt. Refer to Drive Belt Replacement.

20. Connect the negative battery negative cable. Refer to Battery Negative Cable Disconnection and Connection.

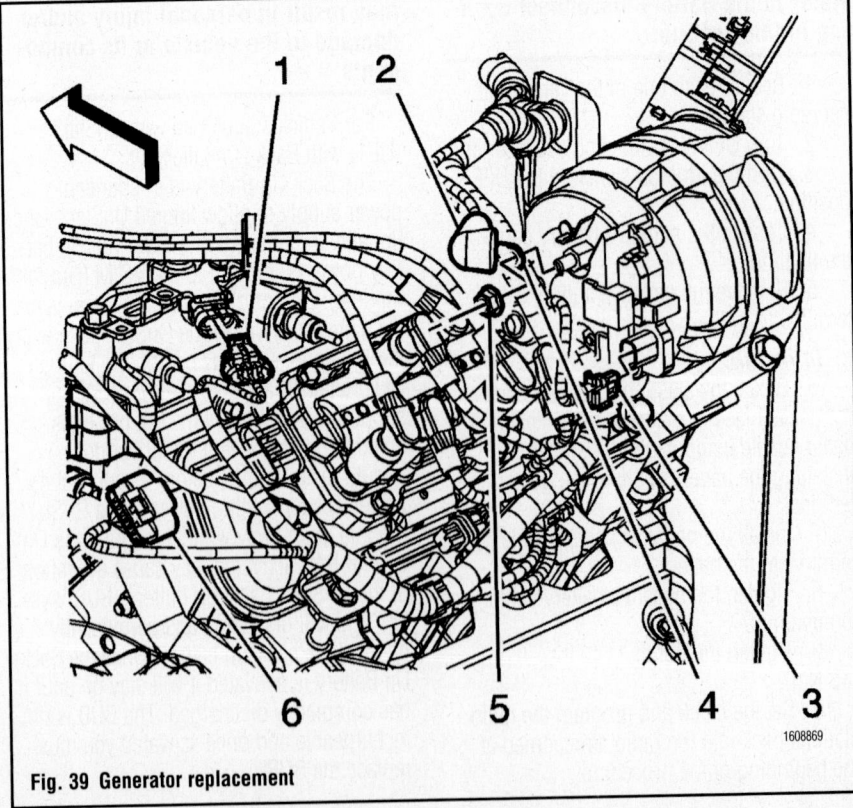

Fig. 39 Generator replacement

ENGINE ELECTRICAL

FIRING ORDER

The left-front bank cylinders are 2, 4, 6. The right-rear bank cylinders are 1, 3, 5. Firing order is 1-2-3-4-5-6.

IGNITION COIL

REMOVAL & INSTALLATION

See Figures 40 through 43.

1. Remove the intake manifold cover.
2. Disconnect the manifold absolute pressure (MAP) sensor electrical connector (1).
3. Disconnect the ignition coil electrical connector (6).
4. Disconnect the left side spark plug wires from the ignition coil.
5. Disconnect the right side spark plug wires from the ignition coil.
6. Remove the ignition coil bolts/nuts.
7. Remove the ignition coil.
8. Remove the ignition coil studs, if necessary.

To install:

9. Install the ignition coil studs, if necessary.
10. Tighten the studs to 15 ft. lbs. (25 Nm).
11. Install the ignition coil bolts/nuts.

12. Tighten the bolts/nuts to 15 ft. lbs. (25 Nm).
13. Connect the right side spark plug wires to the ignition coil.
14. Connect the left side spark plug wires to the ignition coil.
15. Connect the ignition coil electrical connector (6).
16. Connect the MAP sensor electrical connector (1).

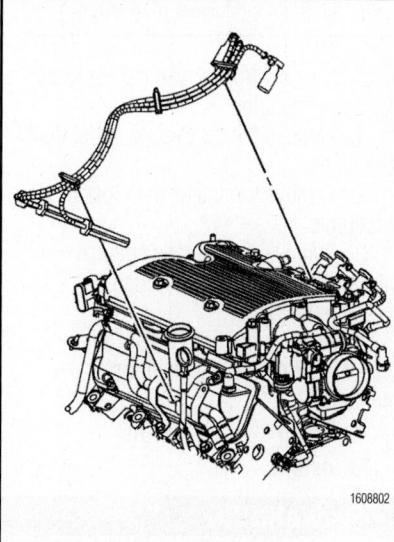

Fig. 41 Left side spark plug wires

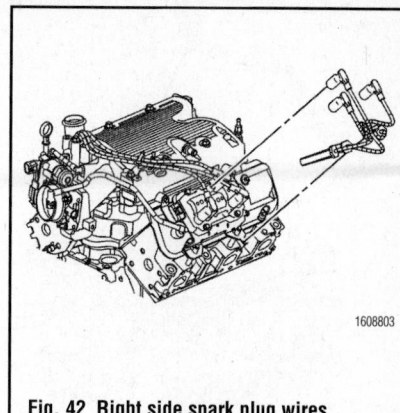

Fig. 42 Right side spark plug wires

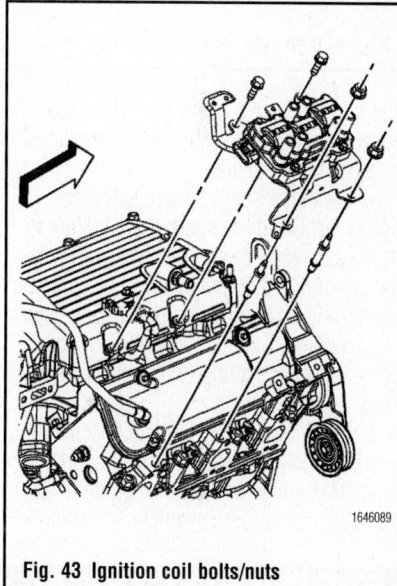

Fig. 43 Ignition coil bolts/nuts

17. Install the intake manifold cover.

IGNITION TIMING

ADJUSTMENT

The Engine Control Module (ECM) control module sets the ignition timing for the best possible performance. No adjustment is necessary or possible.

SPARK PLUGS

REMOVAL & INSTALLATION

See Figures 44 through 46.

✳✳ WARNING

Observe the following service precautions:

• Allow the engine to cool before removing the spark plugs. Attempting to remove

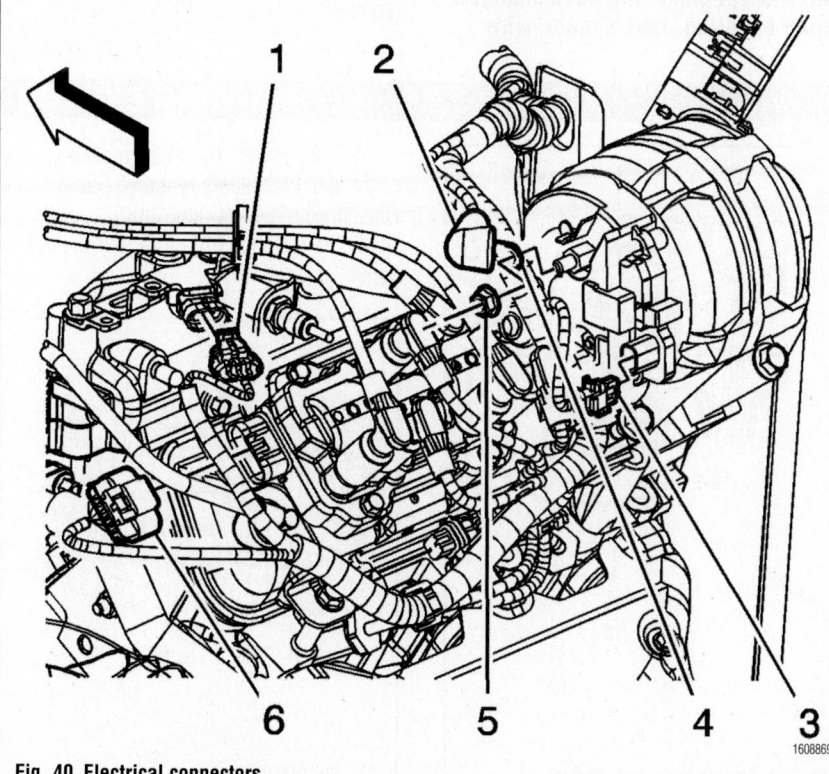

Fig. 40 Electrical connectors

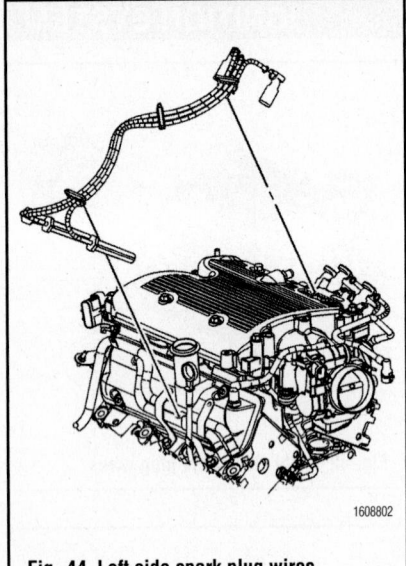

Fig. 44 Left side spark plug wires

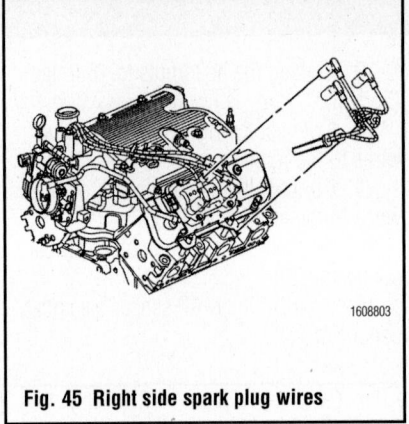

Fig. 45 Right side spark plug wires

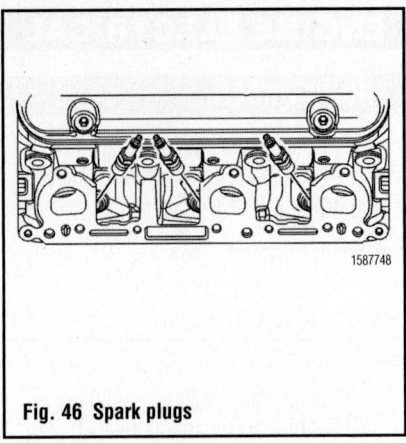

Fig. 46 Spark plugs

spark plugs from a hot engine can cause the spark plugs to seize. This can damage the cylinder head threads.

• Clean the spark plug recess area before removing the spark plug. Failure to do so can result in engine damage due to dirt or foreign material entering the cylinder head, or in contamination of the cylinder head threads. Contaminated threads may prevent proper seating of the new spark plug.

• Use only the spark plugs specified for use in the vehicle. Do not install spark plugs that are either hotter or colder than those specified for the vehicle. Installing

spark plugs of another type can severely damage the engine.

1. Remove the air cleaner outlet duct, if required.
2. Remove the intake manifold cover, if required.
3. Remove the left side spark plug wires from the spark plugs, if required.
4. Remove the right side spark plug wires from the spark plugs, if required.
5. Remove the spark plugs.

To install:

❋❋ WARNING

Check the gap of all new and reconditioned spark plugs before installation. Pre-set gaps may have changed during handling. Use a round wire

feeler gauge to be sure of an accurate check, particularly on used plugs. Installing plugs with the wrong gap can cause poor engine performance and may even damage the engine.

6. Gap the NEW spark plugs. Refer to the Engine Tune-up Specifications Chart.
7. Install the spark plugs.
8. Tighten the spark plugs to 11 ft. lbs. (15 Nm).
9. Install the right side spark plug wires to the spark plugs, if required.
10. Install the left side spark plug wires to the spark plugs, if required.
11. Install the intake manifold cover, if required.
12. Install the air cleaner outlet duct, if required.

ENGINE ELECTRICAL

STARTER

REMOVAL & INSTALLATION

See Figures 47 through 49.

STARTING SYSTEM

1. Disconnect the negative battery cable. Refer to Battery Negative Cable Disconnection and Connection.
2. Remove the front lower air deflector panel.

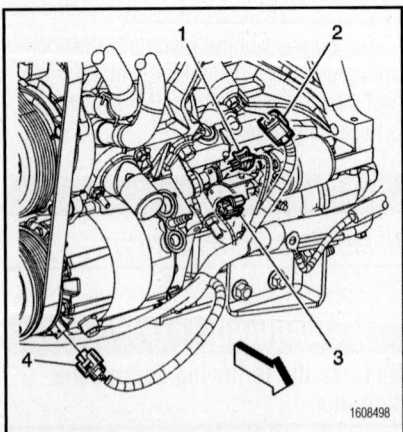

Fig. 47 Starter motor electrical connector (3)

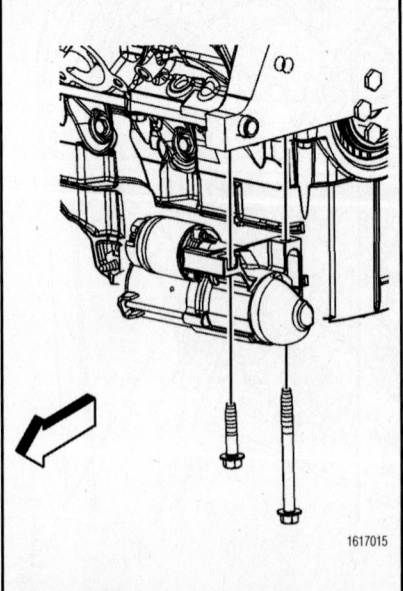

Fig. 48 Starter bolts and starter

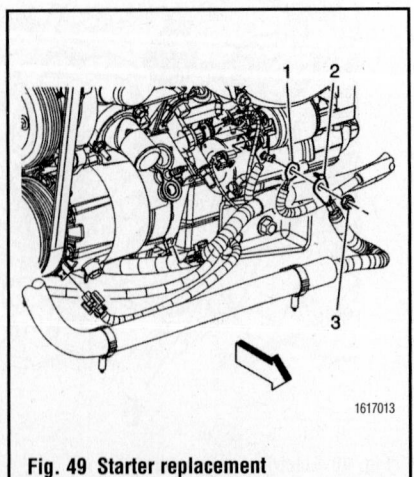

Fig. 49 Starter replacement

3. Remove the torque converter cover.

4. Remove the starter solenoid BAT terminal nut (1) from the starter motor.

5. Remove the positive battery cable terminal (2) and engine harness terminal (3) from the starter.

6. Disconnect the starter motor electrical connector (3).

7. Remove the starter bolts.

8. Remove the starter.

To install:

9. Position the starter motor to the engine.

10. Install the starter bolts.

11. Tighten the bolts to 32 ft. lbs. (43 Nm).

12. Connect the starter motor electrical connector (3).

13. Install the engine harness terminal (1) and positive battery cable terminal (2) to the starter. Be sure to align the positive battery cable terminal anti-rotation feature correctly.

14. Install the starter solenoid BAT terminal nut (3) to the starter motor.

15. Tighten the BAT terminal nut to 89 inch lbs. (10 Nm).

16. Install the torque converter covers.

17. Install the front lower air deflector panel.

18. Connect the negative battery cable.

ENGINE MECHANICAL

➡**Disconnecting the negative battery cable may interfere with the functions of the onboard computer systems and may require the computer to undergo a relearning process when the negative battery cable is reconnected.**

ACCESSORY DRIVE BELTS

✳✳ WARNING

Do not use belt dressing on the drive belt. Belt dressing breaks down the composition of the drive belt. Using belt dressing will damage the drive belt.

ACCESSORY BELT ROUTING

See Figure 50.

Refer to the accompanying illustration.

INSPECTION

• Inspect the drive belt for signs of glazing or cracking. A glazed belt will be perfectly smooth from slippage, while a good belt will have a slight texture of fabric visible. Cracks will usually start at the inner edge of the belt and run outward. Immediately replace all worn or damaged drive belts.

• Inspect all drive belt pulleys for pilling. Pilling is the small balls or pills, or it can be strings in the drive belt grooves from the accumulation of rubber dust. Replacing the drive belt when it is not damaged or there is not excessive pilling will only be a temporary repair.

• Verify that the drive belt is not too long, as it would prevent the drive belt tensioner from working properly. Also if an incorrect length drive belt was installed, it may not be routed properly and may be turning an accessory drive component in the wrong direction.

• The installation of a drive belt that is too wide or too narrow will cause wear on the drive belt. The drive belt ribs should match all of the grooves on all of the pulleys.

• Verify the drive belt is not contacting any parts of the engine or body while the engine operates. There should be sufficient clearance when the drive belt accessory drive components' load varies. The drive belt should not come in contact with an engine or a body component when snapping the throttle.

• Belt separation is identified by the plies of the belt separating and may be seen at the edge of the belt our felt as a lump in the belt.

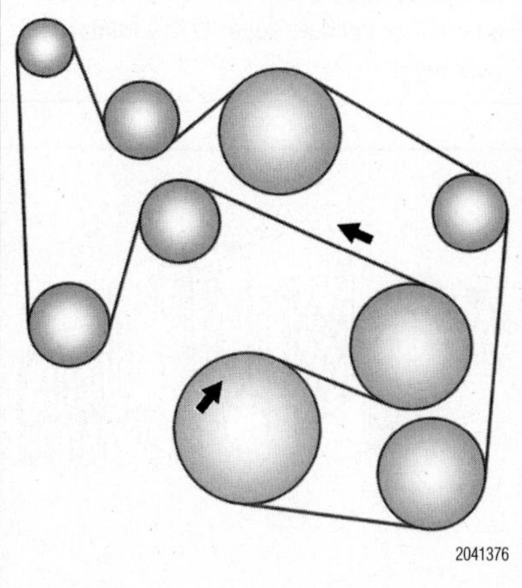

ADJUSTMENT

No adjustment is possible or necessary.

REMOVAL & INSTALLATION

See Figure 51.

1. Remove the intake manifold cover.

2. Rotate the drive belt tensioner clockwise in order to release the spring tension.

3. Remove the drive belt from around the tensioner pulley.

4. Remove the drive belt from around all the other pulleys.

5. Remove the drive belt from the vehicle.

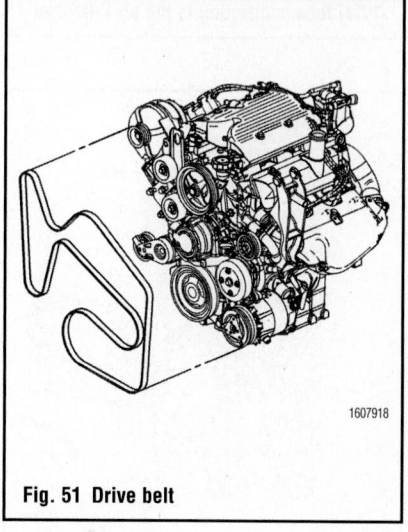

1607918

Fig. 51 Drive belt

To install:

6. Install the drive belt to the vehicle.

7. Starting at the generator, route the drive belt around all of the pulleys, except for the tensioner.

8. Rotate the drive belt tensioner clockwise in order to release the spring tension.

9. Install the drive belt around the tensioner.

10. Install the intake manifold cover.

AIR CLEANER

REMOVAL & INSTALLATION

See Figures 52 through 55.

1. Remove the intake manifold cover.

2. Remove the left inner fender brace.

3. Loosen the air cleaner outlet duct clamp at the throttle body.

4. Remove the air cleaner outlet duct from the throttle body.

5. Disconnect the Positive Crankcase Ventilation (PCV) tube from the air inlet duct.

6. For 2010 model year Impalas only: Remove the secondary air injection (AIR) pump hose quick connect fitting (1) from the air cleaner housing cover.

2041376

Fig. 50 Drive belt routing for 3.5L and 3.9L engines

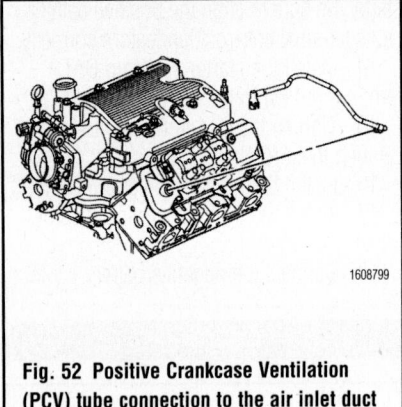

Fig. 52 Positive Crankcase Ventilation (PCV) tube connection to the air inlet duct

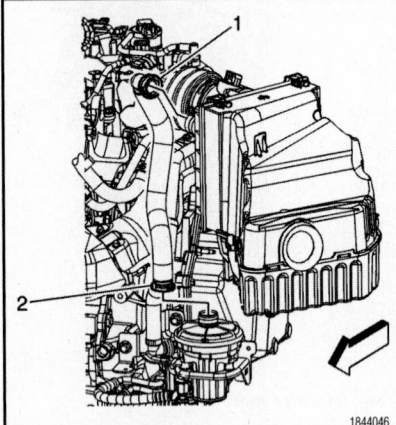

Fig. 53 Secondary air injection (AIR) pump hose quick connect fitting (1) at the air cleaner housing (2010 model year only)

7. Disconnect the mass air flow (MAF) sensor electrical connector.

8. Remove the upper air cleaner housing from the lower housing. Disengage the tabs on the upper housing from the slots on the lower housing.

9. Without disconnecting the powertrain control module (PCM) connectors, remove the PCM and the harness from the lower air cleaner housing.

10. Without disconnecting the transmission control module (TCM) connectors, remove the TCM and the harness from the lower air cleaner housing.

11. Loosen the air cleaner outlet duct clamp at the air cleaner assembly.

12. Remove the air cleaner outlet duct from the air cleaner.

13. Remove the lower air cleaner housing by pulling the housing from the two rubber grommets on the inner rail.

14. Inspect the air cleaner housing assembly for signs of damage and replace if necessary.

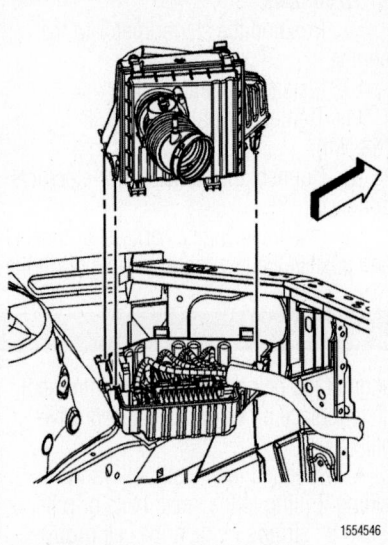

Fig. 54 Upper air cleaner housing

To install:

15. Install the lower air cleaner housing by pushing the housing down, into the two rubber grommets on the inner rail.

16. Install the TCM and the harness to the lower air cleaner housing.

17. Install the PCM and the harness to the lower air cleaner housing.

18. For 2010 models only: Connect the AIR pump hose quick connect fitting (1) to the air cleaner housing cover.

19. Install the air cleaner outlet duct to the air cleaner assembly.

20. Tighten the air cleaner outlet duct clamp at the air cleaner assembly. Tighten the clamp to 27 inch lbs. (3 Nm).

21. Install the upper air cleaner housing to the lower housing. Engage the tabs on the upper housing to the slots on the lower housing.

22. Connect the MAF sensor electrical connector.

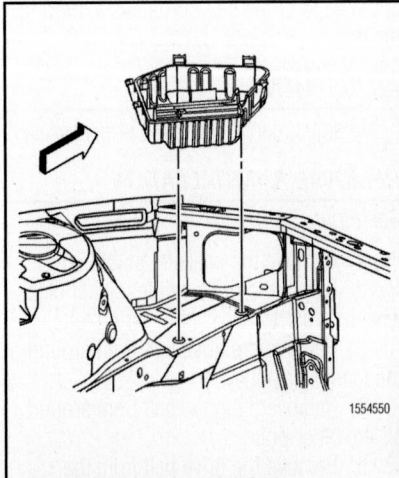

Fig. 55 Air cleaner outlet duct

23. Connect the PCV tube to the air inlet duct.

24. Install the air cleaner outlet duct to the throttle body.

25. Tighten the air cleaner outlet duct clamp at the throttle body. Tighten the clamp to 27 inch lbs. (3 Nm).

26. Install the left inner fender brace.

27. Install the intake manifold cover.

FILTER/ELEMENT REPLACEMENT

See Figures 56 and 57.

1. Remove the air cleaner outlet duct.

2. For 2010 model year Impalas only: Disconnect the secondary air injection (AIR) pump hose quick connect fitting (1) from the air cleaner housing cover.

3. Release the spring clamps on top of the air cleaner housing.

4. Remove the air cleaner housing cover.

5. Remove the air filter element.

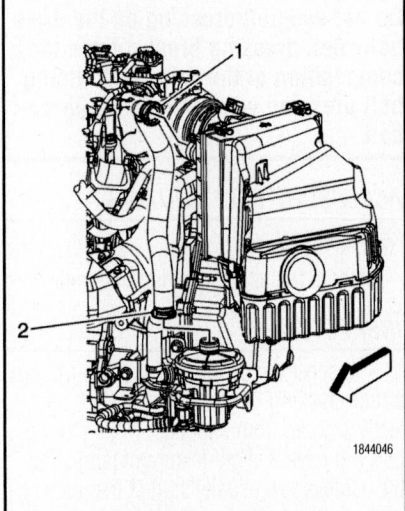

Fig. 56 Secondary air injection (AIR) pump hose quick connect fitting (1) at the air cleaner housing cover (2010 model year only)

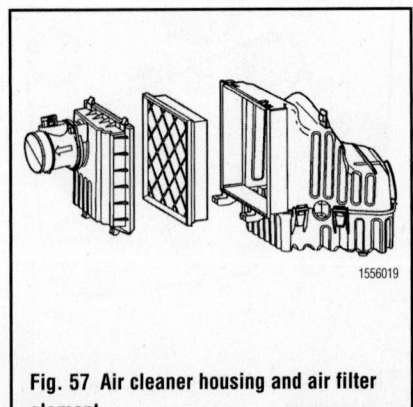

Fig. 57 Air cleaner housing and air filter element

To install:

6. Install a NEW air filter element.

7. Install the air cleaner housing cover.

8. Engage the spring clamps on top of the air cleaner housing.

9. For 2010 models only: Connect the AIR pump hose quick connect fitting (1) to the air cleaner housing cover.

10. Install the air cleaner outlet duct.

CAMSHAFT

CLEANING AND INSPECTION

See Figures 58 through 60.

※ CAUTION

Bodily injury may occur if the cleaning solvent is inhaled or exposed to the skin.

1. Remove and discard the camshaft position actuator filter (1).

2. Clean the camshaft with cleaning solvent.

3. Inspect the camshaft for the following conditions:
   - Scored camshaft bearing journals (5)
   - Damaged camshaft lobes (4)
   - Damaged Camshaft Position (CMP) sensor reluctor area (3)
   - Damaged threads (2)

4. Measure the camshaft journals using a micrometer.

5. If the camshaft journals are not within specifications, replace the camshaft.

   a. Mount the camshaft in V-blocks between the centers.

   b. Use the indicator in order to measure the intermediate camshaft journal.

6. Measure the camshaft lobe lift using a tool such as GM's J-7872 indicator.

   a. Lubricate the camshaft using GM P/N 12345501 (Canadian P/N 992704) or the equivalent.

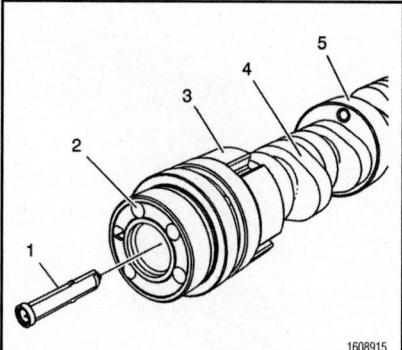

Fig. 58 Camshaft position actuator filter (1)

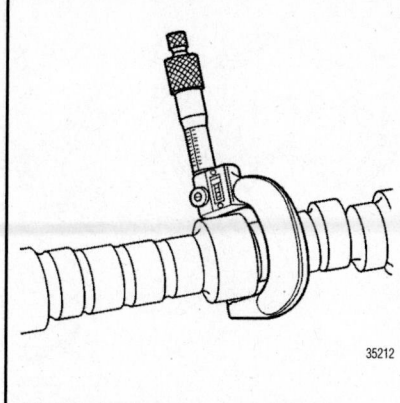

Fig. 59 Measure the camshaft journals using a micrometer

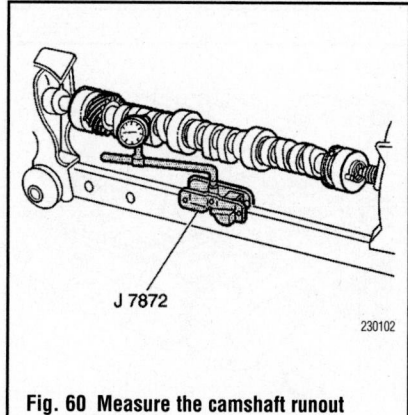

Fig. 60 Measure the camshaft runout

   b. Set the camshaft on V-blocks.

   c. Use the indicator in order to measure the lobe lift.

7. If the runout or lobe lift is not within specifications, replace the camshaft.

➡ **Always install a NEW camshaft position actuator filter anytime the camshaft position actuator is removed or installed.**

8. Install a NEW camshaft position actuator filter (1).

REMOVAL & INSTALLATION

See Figures 61 through 63.

1. Remove the Camshaft Position (CMP) sensor bolt.

2. Remove the camshaft position sensor.

3. Remove the camshaft thrust plate screws.

4. Remove the camshaft thrust plate.

※ WARNING

All camshaft journals are the same diameter, so use care in removing or installing the camshaft to avoid damage to the camshaft bearings.

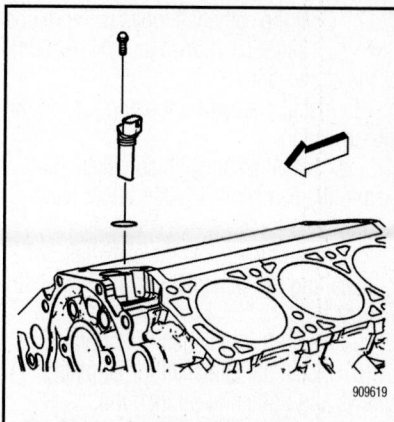

Fig. 61 Camshaft Position (CMP) sensor and bolt

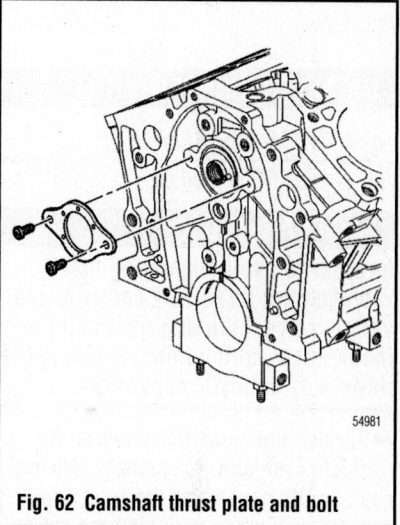

Fig. 62 Camshaft thrust plate and bolt

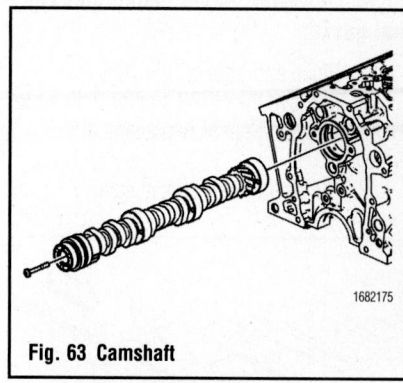

Fig. 63 Camshaft

5. Complete the following steps in order to remove the camshaft.

   a. Install a camshaft sprocket bolt into the camshaft. Tighten finger tight only.

   b. Carefully rotate and remove the camshaft from the engine block.

To install:

6. Coat the camshaft journals with clean engine oil.

7. Coat the camshaft lobes with prelube GM P/N 12345501 (Canadian P/N 992704) or the equivalent.

8. Install the camshaft using the following procedure:

a. Install a camshaft sprocket bolt into the camshaft. Tighten finger tight only.

b. Carefully rotate the camshaft while installing the camshaft into the camshaft bearings.

9. Install the camshaft thrust plate.

10. Install the camshaft thrust plate screws and tighten to 89 inch lbs. (10 Nm).

11. Install the camshaft position sensor.

12. Install the Camshaft Position (CMP) sensor bolt and tighten to 89 inch lbs. (10 Nm).

CATALYTIC CONVERTER

REMOVAL & INSTALLATION

See Figures 64 through 66.

❈❈ WARNING

In order to avoid damaging the replacement three-way catalytic converter, correct the engine misfire or mechanical fault before replacing the three-way catalytic converter.

➥Service the catalytic converter by replacing the entire assembly. Always replace the gaskets at the front and rear flanges when servicing the catalytic converter. Never install the original gasket.

1. Raise and support the vehicle.

2. Remove the HO2S sensor 2. Refer to Heated Oxygen Sensor Replacement - Sensor 2.

3. Support the exhaust system.

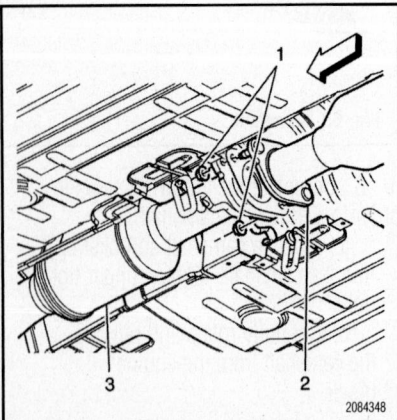

Fig. 64 Catalytic converter-to-muffler nuts (1) and catalytic converter (3)

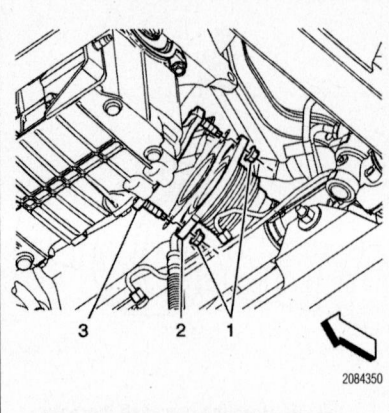

Fig. 65 Catalytic converter-to-exhaust manifold nuts (1) and catalytic converter (2)

Fig. 66 Catalytic converter (1)

4. Remove the catalytic converter (3) to muffler nuts (1).

5. Remove the catalytic converter hanger insulators.

6. Remove the catalytic converter (2) to engine exhaust manifold nuts (1).

7. Reposition the muffler assembly rearward until the catalytic converter can be removed.

8. Remove the catalytic converter (1) from the vehicle.

9. Remove the catalytic converter gaskets.

10. Clean and inspect the exhaust manifold and the exhaust pipe gasket mating surfaces.

To install:

11. Install NEW gaskets to the catalytic converter and muffler assembly.

12. Reposition the muffler assembly rearward in order to position the catalytic converter (1) to the exhaust manifold and muffler assembly.

13. Install the catalytic converter (2) to the engine exhaust manifold nuts (1) and tighten to 26 ft. lbs. (35 Nm).

14. Install the catalytic converter (3) hanger insulators.

15. Install the catalytic converter to muffler nuts (1) and tighten to 44 ft. lbs. (60 Nm).

16. Remove the support from the exhaust system.

17. Install the HO2S sensor 2.

18. Lower the vehicle.

CYLINDER HEAD

REMOVAL & INSTALLATION

See Figures 67 through 71.

➥At the time of publication, the manufacturer does not provide a procedure for this component. Please note the following when servicing this component.

1. Remove the cylinder head bolts and discard them.

2. Remove the cylinder head.

3. Remove the cylinder head gasket.

4. Remove the cylinder head locator dowel pins, if required.

To install:

❈❈ WARNING

Head gaskets are specific for right hand and left hand applications, and also must be installed with the correct side facing up. Note the markings (1) on the head gaskets for proper installation. Failure to do so may lead to engine damage.

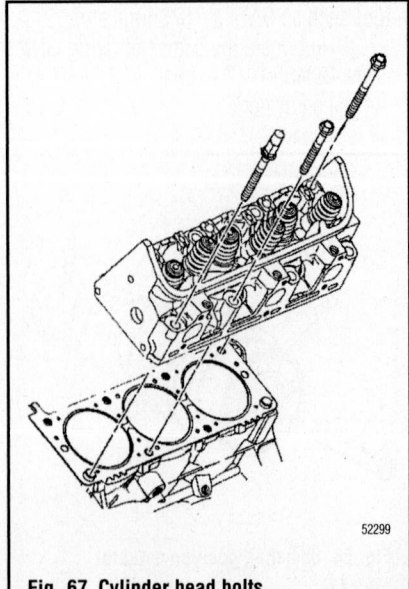

Fig. 67 Cylinder head bolts

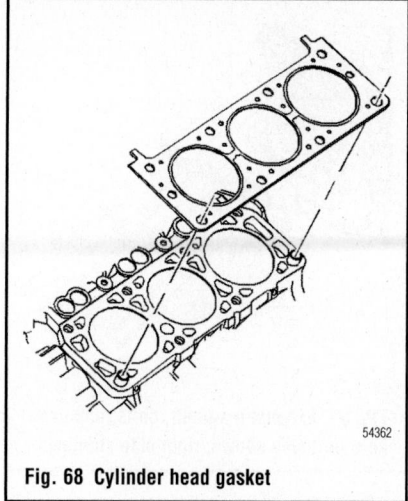

Fig. 68 Cylinder head gasket

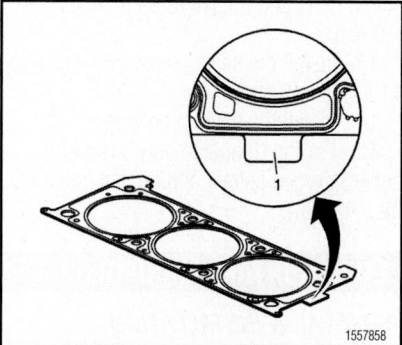

Fig. 69 Markings (1) are on the head gaskets for proper installation - left side cylinder head gasket shown

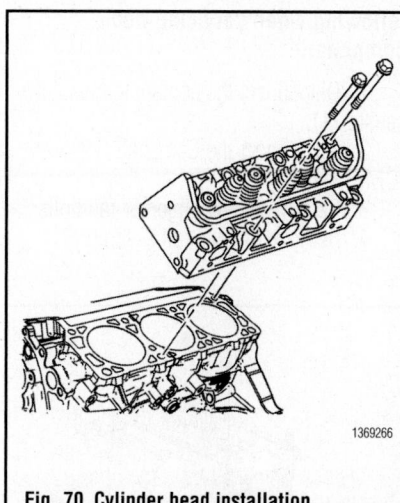

Fig. 70 Cylinder head installation

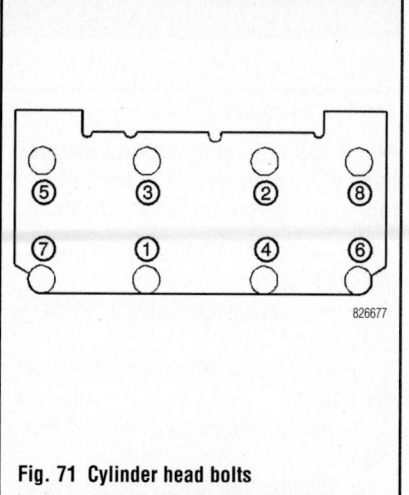

Fig. 71 Cylinder head bolts

Failure to install NEW torque-to-yield bolts may lead to engine damage.

5. Install the cylinder head locator dowel pins, if necessary.
6. Inspect the cylinder head locator dowel pins for proper installation.
7. Install the cylinder head gasket.
8. Install the cylinder head.

➡**The bolt installation step is different for 2010 and 2011 models, but the tightening sequence is the same for both.**

9. For 2010 models only:
  • Install the NEW small hex cylinder head bolts (5 and 8).
  • Install the NEW large hex cylinder head bolts (1, 2, 3, 4, 6 and 7).
10. For 2011 models only:
11. Install the NEW cylinder head bolts and tighten in sequence.

➡**The following steps are for 2010 and 2011 models:**

12. Tighten the cylinder head bolts a first pass in sequence to 44 ft. lbs. (60 Nm).
13. Tighten the cylinder head bolts a final pass in sequence to 140 degrees using a special tool, such as GM's J 45059 angle meter.

CRANKSHAFT FRONT SEAL

REMOVAL & INSTALLATION

See Figure 72.

1. Pry out the crankshaft front oil seal using a suitable tool. Use care not to damage the engine front cover or the crankshaft.

To install:

2. Place the crankshaft front oil seal on a tool, such as GM's front crankshaft oil seal installer (EN-48869) with the lip facing

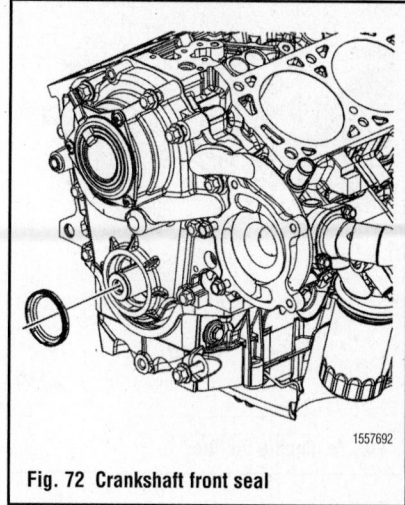

Fig. 72 Crankshaft front seal

inward, aligning the crankshaft keyway to the groove in the installer.
3. Thread the forcing bolt with bearing, washer and nut as shown.
4. Tighten the nut until the seal bottoms, then remove the installer tool.

ENGINE OIL & FILTER

REPLACEMENT

See Figures 73 and 74.

1. Raise and support the vehicle.
2. Position a suitable drain pan under the oil pan drain plug.
3. Remove the oil pan drain plug.
4. Allow the engine oil to drain completely.
5. Clean and inspect the oil pan drain plug sealing surface; replace the oil pan if necessary.
6. Wipe any remaining oil from the drain plug hole and reinstall the oil pan drain plug until snug.
7. Position a suitable drain pan under the oil filter.
8. Remove the oil filter.

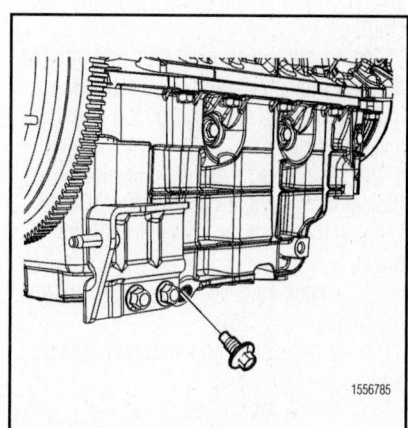

Fig. 73 Engine oil pan drain plug

Fig. 74 Engine oil filter

9. Is the oil filter gasket is still on the old filter? If not, remove the oil filter gasket from the adapter.

To install:

10. Apply clean engine oil to the NEW oil filter gasket.

11. Install the NEW oil filter.

12. Tighten the new filter to 3/4 to 1 full turn, after the oil filter gasket contacts the adapter.

13. Tighten the oil pan drain plug.

14. Tighten the plug to 19 ft. lbs. (26 Nm).

15. Remove the oil drain pan from under the vehicle.

16. Lower the vehicle.

17. Fill the engine with new engine oil. Refer to the Fluid Capacities chart.

18. Start the engine.

19. Inspect for oil leaks after engine start up.

20. Turn the engine OFF and allow the oil a few minutes to drain back into the engine oil pan.

21. Remove the oil level indicator from the oil level indicator tube.

22. Clean the indicator end of the oil level indicator with a clean paper towel or cloth.

23. Install the oil level indicator into the oil level indicator tube until the oil level indicator handle contacts the top of the oil level indicator tube.

24. Again, remove the oil level indicator from the oil level indicator tube keeping the tip of the oil level indicator down.

25. Check the level if the engine oil on the oil level indicator.

26. If necessary, adjust the oil level by adding or draining oil.

27. Check for oil leaks.

EXHAUST MANIFOLD

REMOVAL & INSTALLATION

See Figures 75 through 77.

➡ **Left and right side removal instructions differ slightly due to the HO2S removal required for the right side.**

1. Remove the heated oxygen sensor (right side only).

2. Remove the spark plug wires and spark plugs.

3. Remove the exhaust manifold heat shield bolts.

4. Remove the exhaust manifold heat shield.

5. Remove the exhaust manifold bolts.

6. Remove the exhaust manifold.

7. Remove the exhaust manifold gasket.

To install:

8. Install the exhaust manifold gasket.

9. Install the exhaust manifold.

10. Install the exhaust manifold bolts and tighten to 15 ft. lbs. (20 Nm).

11. Install the exhaust manifold heat shield.

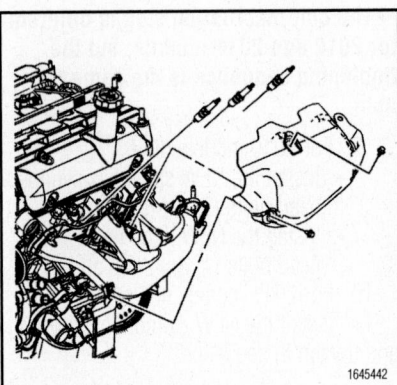

Fig. 75 Spark plugs and wires, heat shield and bolts for left side

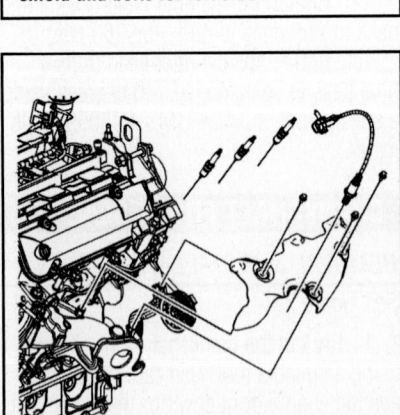

Fig. 76 HO2S sensor, spark plugs and wires, heat shield and bolts for right side

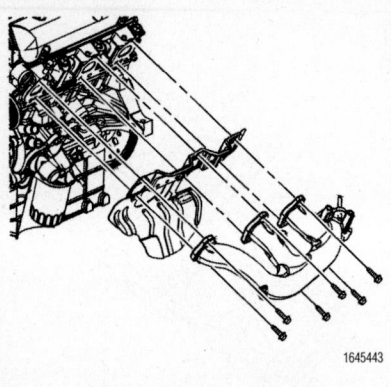

Fig. 77 Exhaust manifold, bolts, and gaskets (left side shown; right side similar)

12. Install the exhaust manifold heat shield bolts and tighten to 89 inch lbs. (10 Nm).

13. Install the spark plugs and tighten to 11 ft. lbs. (15 Nm).

14. Install the spark plug wires.

15. For the right side only, install the heated oxygen sensor and tighten to 31 ft. lbs. (42 Nm).

LOWER INTAKE MANIFOLD

REMOVAL & INSTALLATION

See Figures 78 through 81.

➡ **At the time of publication, the manufacturer does not provide a procedure for this component. Please note the following when servicing this component.**

1. Disconnect the coolant temperature sensor (1).

2. Disconnect the Camshaft Position (CMP) sensor (2).

3. Remove the fuel injector rail bolts.

4. Remove the fuel rail assembly.

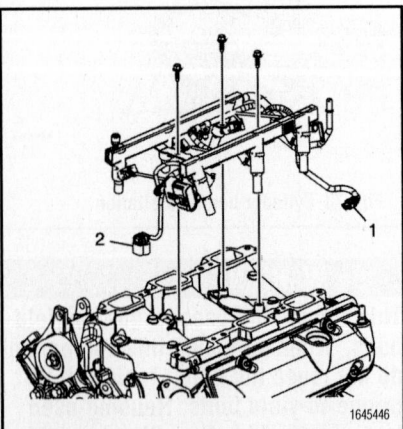

Fig. 78 Coolant temperature sensor (1) and Camshaft Position (CMP) sensor (2)

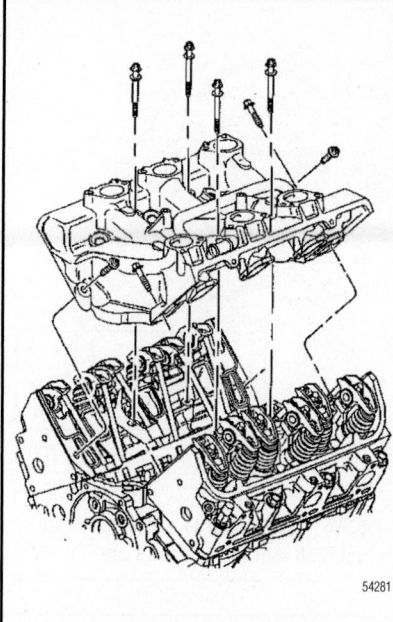

Fig. 79 Lower intake manifold and bolts

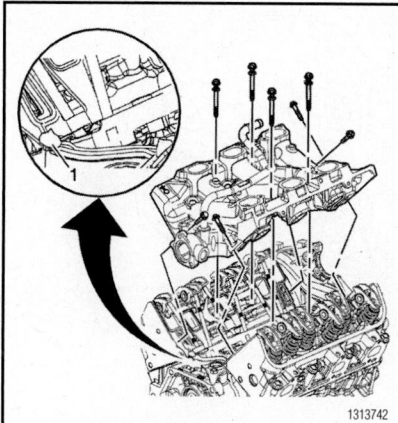

Fig. 80 Apply sealer to the intake manifold-to-block joints (1).

5. Remove the lower intake manifold bolts and discard.

6. Remove the lower intake manifold.

To install:

➡**All gasket-mating surfaces need to be free of oil and foreign material. Clean surfaces with GM P/N 12346139 (Canadian P/N 10953463) or equivalent.**

• With gaskets and seals in place apply a small drop, 0.31-0.39 in (8-10 mm), of room temperature vulcanizing (RTV) sealer (GM P/N 12378521; Canadian P/N 88901148 or equivalent) to the four corners of the intake manifold-to-block joints (1).

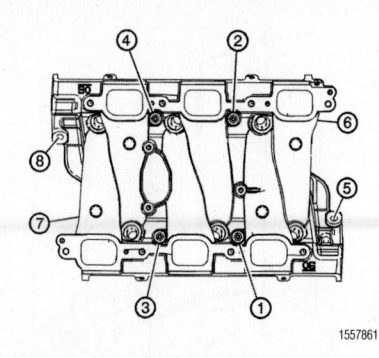

Fig. 81 Install the new lower intake manifold bolts if applicable, in sequence

➡**To ensure proper lower intake manifold orientation during installation, make sure the intake port marked 1 faces the front of the engine.**

7. Install the lower intake manifold.

❋❋ WARNING

Use new fasteners for maximum gasket performance. New fasteners contain a thread-locking patch. Apply a thread locking chemical to the fastener threads if you don't replace the fasteners. Failure to replace the fasteners or apply a thread-locking chemical MAY reduce gasket sealing capability.

❋❋ WARNING

Failure to tighten vertical bolts before the diagonal bolts may cause an oil leak.

8. Apply sealer GM P/N 12345382 (Canadian P/N 10953489) or an equivalent to the lower intake manifold bolt threads.

9. Install the new lower intake manifold bolts if applicable, in sequence.

a. Tighten the lower intake manifold bolts in sequence to 62 inch lbs. (7 Nm) on the first pass.

b. Tighten the lower intake manifold bolts (1, 2, 3, 4) in sequence to 12 ft. lbs. (16 Nm) on the final pass.

10. Tighten the lower intake manifold bolts (5, 6, 7, 8) in sequence to 18 ft. lbs. (25 Nm) on the final pass.

11. Inspect the fuel rail, and fuel injectors for damage and replace if necessary.

12. Install NEW lower fuel injector O-rings.

13. Lubricate the fuel injector O-rings using GM P/N 12345616 (Canadian P/N 993182) or equivalent.

➡**To ensure proper fuel rail orientation during installation, make sure the fuel feed pipe faces the rear of the engine.**

14. Install the injector nozzles into the lower intake manifold injector bores.

15. Press on the injector rail using the palms of both hands until the injectors are fully seated.

16. Install the fuel injector rail bolts and tighten to 89 inch lbs. (10 Nm).

17. Connect the coolant temperature sensor (1).

18. Connect the Camshaft Position (CMP) sensor (2).

UPPER INTAKE MANIFOLD

REMOVAL & INSTALLATION

3.5L Engines

See Figure 82.

➡**At the time of publication, the manufacturer does not provide a procedure for this component. Please note the following when servicing this component.**

1. Remove the upper intake manifold bolts and stud.

2. Remove the manifold absolute pressure (MAP) sensor bracket.

3. Remove the upper intake manifold and gaskets.

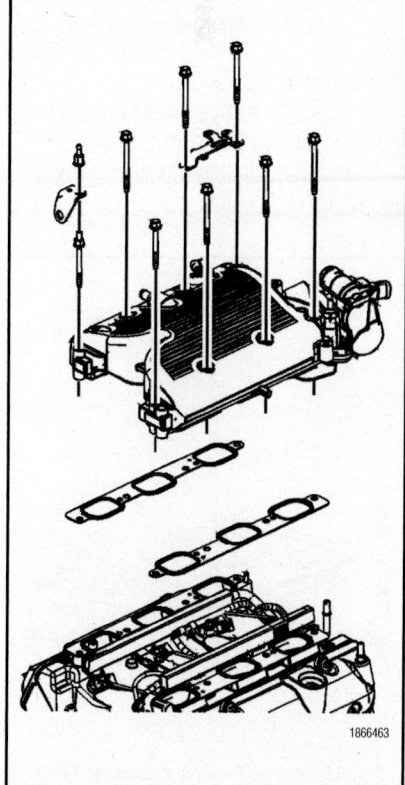

Fig. 82 Upper intake manifold removal

To install:

4. Install the upper intake manifold gaskets and manifold.

5. Apply threadlock, such as GM P/N 12345382 (Canadian P/N 10953489) or an equivalent, to the upper intake manifold bolt threads.

6. Install the MAP sensor bracket, upper intake manifold bolts, and the upper intake manifold stud and tighten the upper intake manifold bolts and stud to 18 ft. lbs. (25 Nm).

3.9L Engines

See Figures 83 and 84.

➡ **At the time of publication, the manufacturer does not provide a procedure for this component. Please note the following when servicing this component.**

1. Remove the foul air Positive Crankcase Ventilation (PCV) tube.

2. Remove the upper intake manifold bolts, stud, and manifold absolute pressure (MAP) sensor bracket.

3. Remove the upper intake manifold and gaskets.

To install:

4. Install the upper intake manifold gaskets and manifold.

5. Apply threadlock, such as GM P/N 12345382 (Canadian P/N 10953489) or an equivalent, to the upper intake manifold bolt threads.

6. Install the upper intake manifold bolts, stud, and manifold absolute pressure (MAP) sensor bracket.

7. Tighten the upper intake manifold bolts and stud to 18 ft. lbs. (25 Nm).

8. Install the foul air Positive Crankcase Ventilation (PCV) tube.

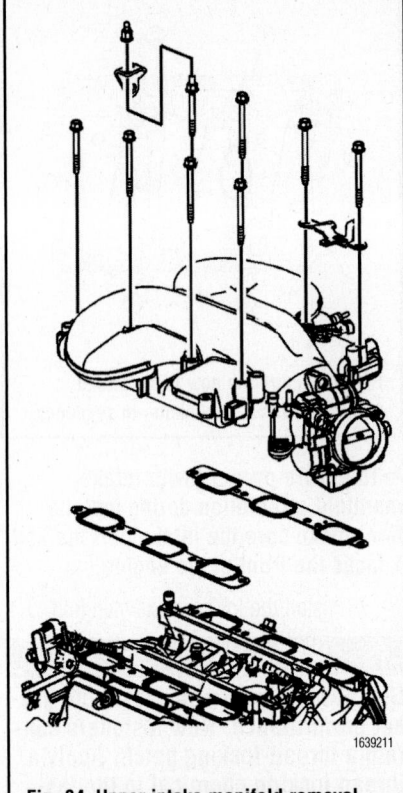

Fig. 84 Upper intake manifold removal

OIL PAN

REMOVAL & INSTALLATION

See Figures 85 through 87.

1. Remove the oil pan support bracket bolts and brackets as needed

2. Remove the oil pan side bolts.

3. Remove the oil pan bolts.

4. Remove the oil pan.

5. Remove the oil pan gasket.

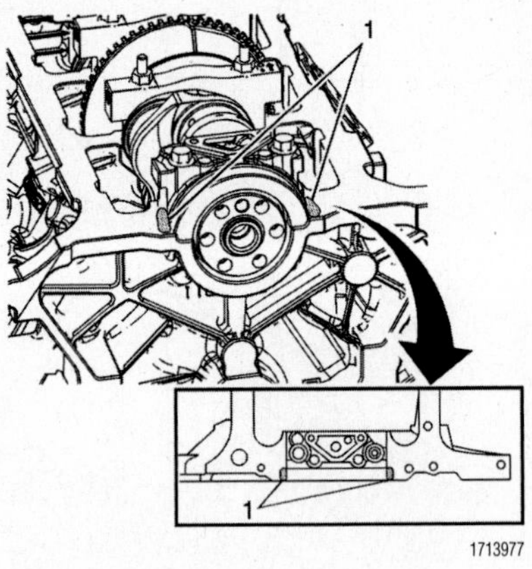

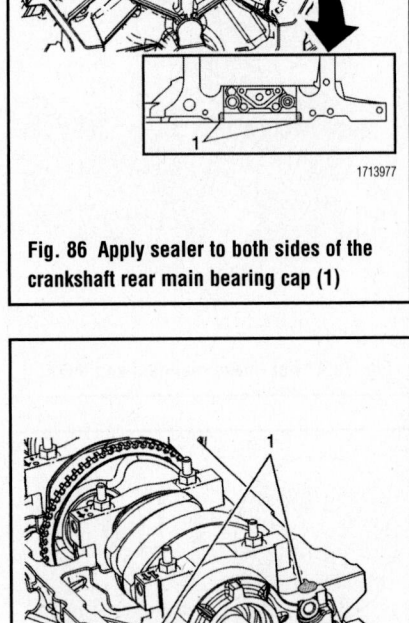

Fig. 86 Apply sealer to both sides of the crankshaft rear main bearing cap (1)

Fig. 87 Apply sealer to both sides of the front cover/block mating area (1)

To install:

6. Apply sealer to both sides of the crankshaft rear main bearing cap (1). Press sealer into the gap using a putty knife.

7. Apply sealer to both sides of the front cover/block mating area (1).

8. Install the oil pan gasket.

9. Install the oil pan.

10. Install the oil pan bolts and tighten to 18 ft. lbs. (25 Nm).

11. Apply sealer to the oil pan side bolt threads.

12. Install the oil pan side bolts.

13. Tighten the oil pan side bolts a first pass to 37 ft. lbs. (50 Nm).

14. Tighten the oil pan side bolts a second pass to 50 degrees using an angle meter, such as GM's tool: J 45059.

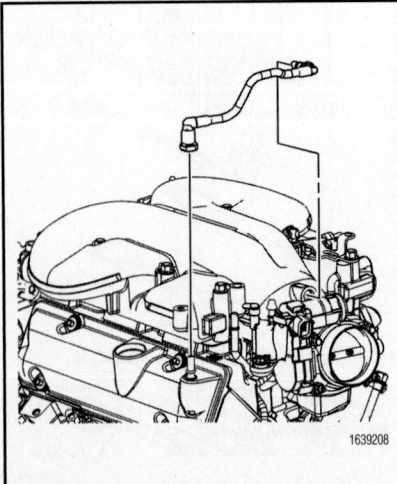

Fig. 83 Foul air Positive Crankcase Ventilation (PCV) tube

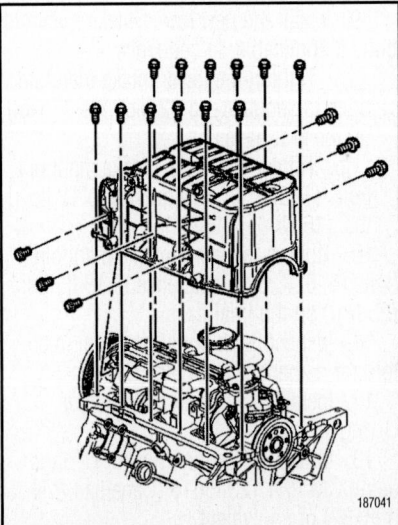

Fig. 85 Oil pan removal

15. Install the oil pan drain plug and tighten to 18 ft. lbs. (25 Nm). (Location shown in Oil Filter procedure.)

OIL PUMP

CLEANING AND INSPECTION

See Figures 88 through 93.

✵ CAUTION

Bodily injury may occur if cleaning solvent is inhaled or exposed to the skin.

1. Clean all parts of sludge, oil, and varnish by soaking in cleaning solvent.
2. Inspect for foreign material and determine the source of the foreign material.
3. Inspect the pump housing and cover for the following conditions:
   a. Cracks or casting imperfections
   b. Scoring (3)
   c. Damaged threads
4. Do not attempt to repair the pump housing.
5. Replace the pump housing.
6. Inspect the oil pump gears for the following conditions:
   a. Scoring (1)
   b. Excessive wear (2)
7. Inspect the idler shaft for looseness or scoring (4).

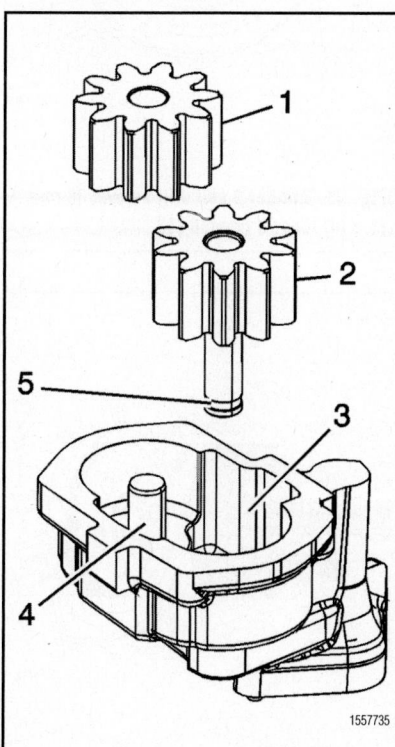

Fig. 88 Pump housing and cover and oil pump gears

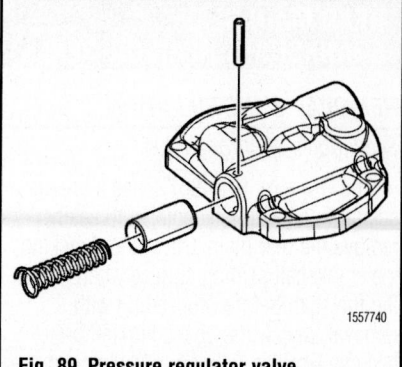

Fig. 89 Pressure regulator valve

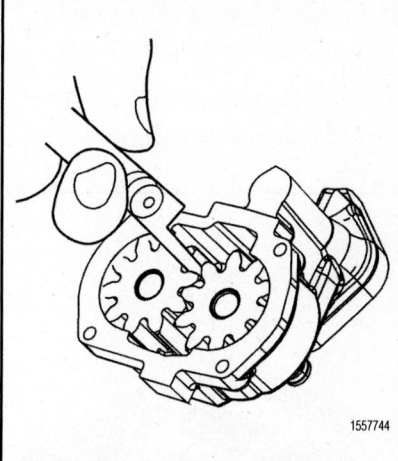

Fig. 90 Measure the oil pump gear lash

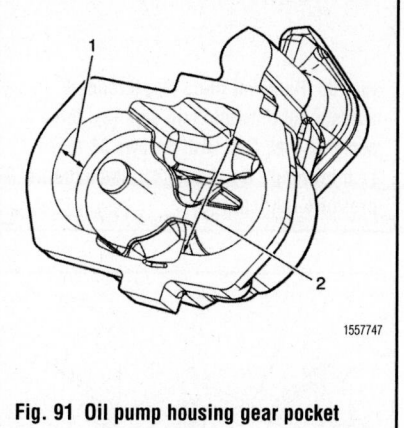

Fig. 91 Oil pump housing gear pocket

8. If it is loose or damaged, replace the oil pump.
9. Inspect the drive gear shaft for looseness or scoring (5).
10. Inspect the pressure regulator valve for the following conditions:
    a. Scoring
    b. Sticking
    c. Remove burrs using a fine oil stone.
11. Inspect the pressure regulator valve spring for the following conditions:

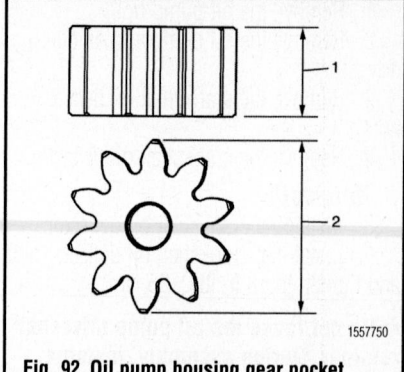

Fig. 92 Oil pump housing gear pocket

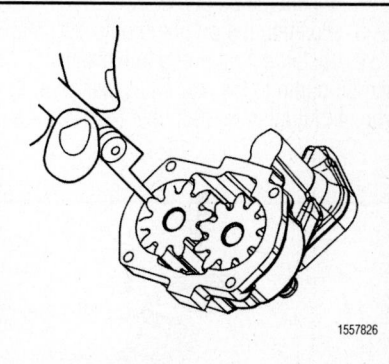

Fig. 93 Measure the oil pump gear side clearance

a. Loss of tension
b. Bending
12. Inspect the suction pipe and screen assembly for the following conditions:
   a. Looseness—If the suction pipe is loose, bent or has been removed, replace the pump body cover and suction pipe.
13. Broken wire mesh or screen
14. Measure the oil pump gear lash. Install the gears, and measure in several places.
15. Measure the oil pump housing gear pocket (1, 2).
16. Measure the oil pump gears (1, 2).

➡**When deciding pump serviceability based on end clearance, consider the depth of the wear pattern in the pump cover.**

17. Measure the oil pump gear side clearance.

REMOVAL & INSTALLATION

See Figures 94 and 95.

➡**At the time of publication, the manufacturer does not provide a procedure for this component. Please note the following when servicing this component.**

1. Remove the oil pump bolt.
2. Remove the oil pump and oil pump driveshaft.
3. Remove the crankshaft oil deflector nuts.
4. Remove the crankshaft oil deflector.

To install:

5. Install the crankshaft oil deflector.
6. Install the crankshaft oil deflector nuts and tighten to 18 ft. lbs. (25 Nm).

➡**Do not reuse the oil pump driveshaft retainer. During assembly, install a NEW oil pump driveshaft retainer.**

7. Install the oil pump.
8. Position the oil pump onto the pins.
9. Install the oil pump bolt attaching the oil pump to the rear crankshaft bearing cap, and tighten to 30 ft. lbs. (41 Nm).

REAR MAIN SEAL/ CRANKSHAFT REAR OIL SEAL

REMOVAL & INSTALLATION

See Figures 96 through 104.

The GM tool, EN-48672, has a unique design to allow the technician to easily remove the rear main seal without nicking the crankshaft sealing surface when removing the seal. Before proceeding with removal, review the above illustration to become familiar with the following components: Removal plate (1), threaded adjustment pins and jam nuts (2), force screw (3), #2 Self Drill Screws 38 mm (1.5 in) long - 8 needed (4), and extreme pressure lubricant (5).

1. Remove the transmission.
2. Remove the engine flywheel.

3. Install the removal plate (2) and both threaded adjustment pins and jam nuts (1) into the back of the crankshaft flange and secure the plate with adjustment pins and jam nuts.
4. Install the #2 self drill screws 38 mm (1.5 in) long, 8 needed (1) and tighten the screws down flush to the plate.

➡**Before installing the force screw, apply a small amount of the extreme pressure lubricant J 23444-A, provided in the tool kit.**

5. Install the force screw (1) and back off both jam nuts (2). Continue to turn the force screw (1) into the removal plate in order to remove the seal from the crankshaft.
6. Once the seal is removed from the crankshaft, remove and save all 8 screws. Discard the old seal.

Fig. 94 Oil pump bolt

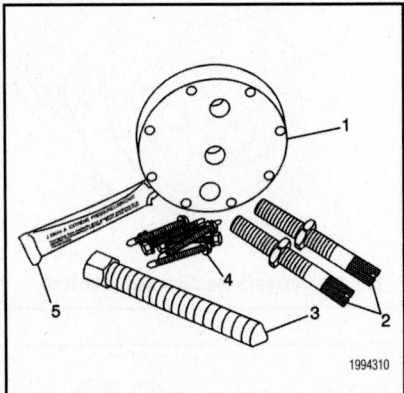

Fig. 96 Removal plate (1), threaded adjustment pins and jam nuts (2), force screw (3), #2 Self Drill Screws 38 mm (1.5 in) long - 8 needed (4), and extreme pressure lubricant (5)

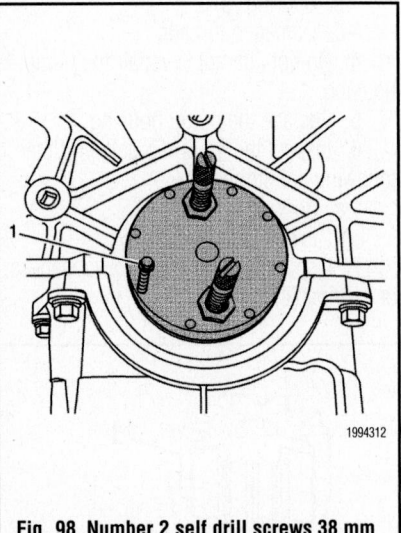

Fig. 98 Number 2 self drill screws 38 mm (1.5 in) long, 8 needed (1)

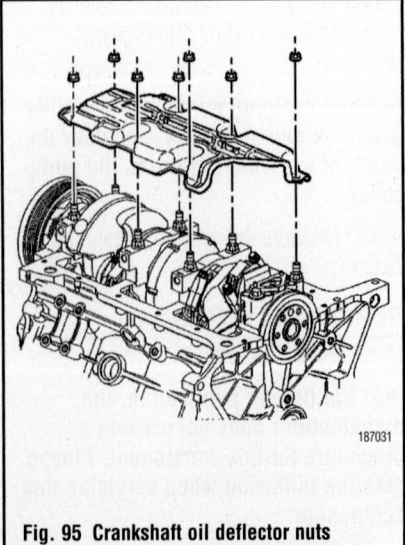

Fig. 95 Crankshaft oil deflector nuts

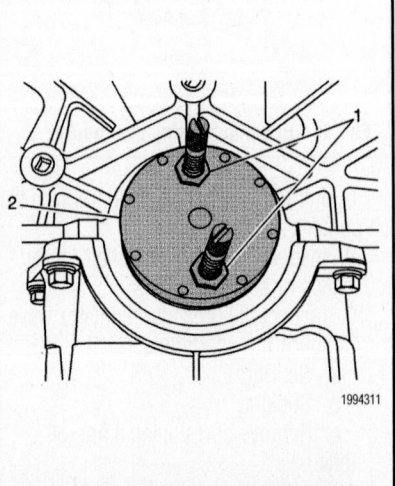

Fig. 97 Removal plate (2) and threaded adjustment pins and jam nuts (1)

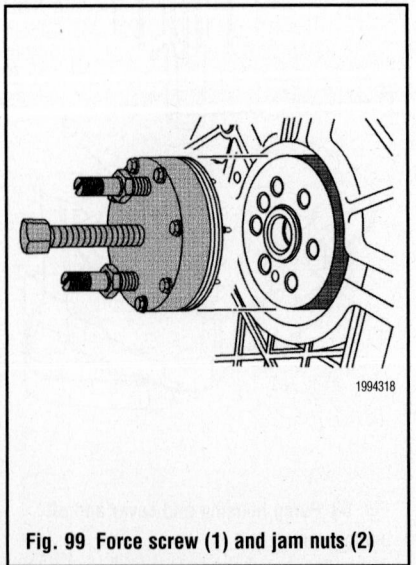

Fig. 99 Force screw (1) and jam nuts (2)

To install:

> ❄❄ **WARNING**
>
> Do not remove the protective sleeve from the seal. The sleeve assures the seal is installed correctly and protects the seal from damage. If removed, the EN-48108 installation tool will not work.

> ❄❄ **WARNING**
>
> Clean the crankshaft sealing surface with a clean, lint-free towel. Inspect lead-in edge of crankshaft for burrs/sharp edges that could damage the rear main oil seal. Remove burrs/sharp edges with crocus cloth before proceeding.

> ❄❄ **WARNING**
>
> Do not remove protective nylon sleeve prior to installation. The rear main oil seal installation tool is designed to install the rear main seal with the protective sleeve in place. Never apply or use any oil, lubricants or sealing compounds on the crankshaft rear main oil seal.

➡Before replacement of the new design crankshaft rear main oil seal, ensure the Positive Crankcase Ventilation (PCV) system is operating correctly.

A new design crankshaft rear main oil seal and installation tool, the EN-48108 installer, incorporates features that improve high mileage durability. Replace the crankshaft rear main oil seal with the new design rear main oil seal, GM P/N 12592195 (Canadian P/N 12592195).

The EN-48108 installer has a unique design to allow the technician to easily install the rear main seal squarely to the correct depth and direction. Before proceeding with installation, review the above illustration to become familiar with the following components: mandrel (1), drive drum (2), drive nut (3), washer (4), and bearing (5).

7. Align the mandrel dowel pin to the dowel pin hole in the crankshaft.

8. Using a large flat-blade screwdriver, tighten the two mandrel screws to the crankshaft. Ensure the mandrel is snug to the crankshaft hub.

9. Install the rear main seal (1), with the protective nylon sleeve attached (2), onto the mandrel. The seal, if properly installed, will center on a step that protrudes from the center of the mandrel. As an error

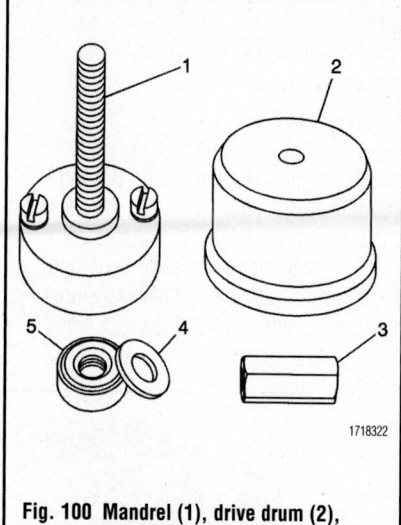

Fig. 100 Mandrel (1), drive drum (2), drive nut (3), washer (4), and bearing (5)

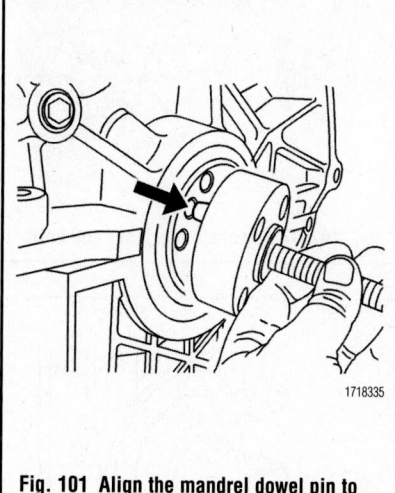
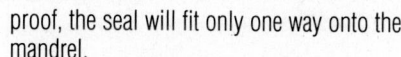

Fig. 101 Align the mandrel dowel pin to the dowel pin hole in the crankshaft

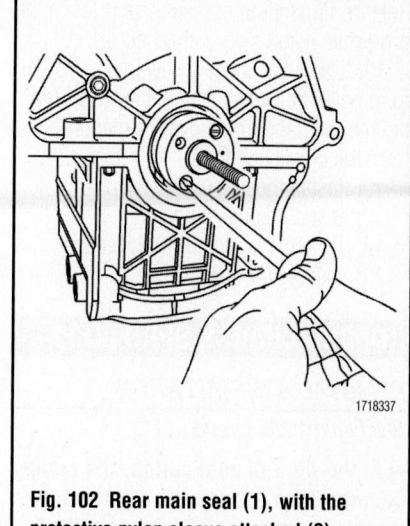

Fig. 102 Rear main seal (1), with the protective nylon sleeve attached (2)

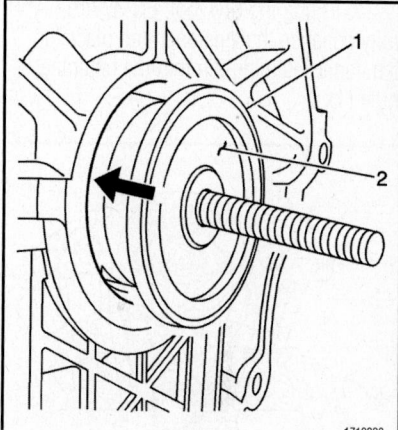

Fig. 103 Install the outer drive drum, bearing, washer, and drive nut onto the threaded shaft

proof, the seal will fit only one way onto the mandrel.

➡Before installing the outer drive drum, bearing, washer, and drive nut onto the threaded shaft, apply a small amount of the extreme pressure lubricant J 23444-A, provided in the tool kit.

10. Install the outer drive drum onto the mandrel.

11. Install the bearing, washer, and drive nut onto the threaded shaft.

12. Using a wrench, turn the drive nut on the mandrel, which will push the seal into the engine block bore. Turn the wrench until the drive drum is snug and flush against the engine block.

13. Loosen and remove the drive nut, washer, bearing, and drive drum. Discard the protective nylon sleeve.

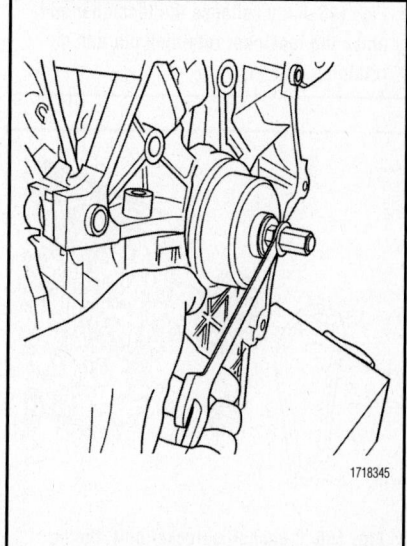

Fig. 104 Turn the drive nut on the mandrel

14. Verify that the seal seats properly. Refer to illustration of main seal (1) with the protective nylon sleeve attached (2).

15. Use a flat-blade screwdriver in order to remove the two attachment screws from the mandrel and to remove the mandrel from the crankshaft hub.

16. Install the engine flywheel.

17. Install the transmission.

18. Inspect for proper fluid levels.

19. Inspect for leaks.

TIMING CHAIN & SPROCKETS

REMOVAL & INSTALLATION

See Figures 105 through 111.

➡️At the time of publication, the manufacturer does not provide a procedure for this component. Please note the following when servicing this component.

1. Using the GM tool, EN-47719, fully collapse the tensioner and place the tensioner retaining pin into the retaining hole (1).

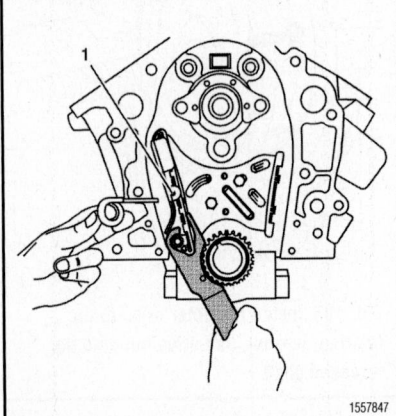

Fig. 105 Fully collapse the tensioner and place the tensioner retaining pin into the retaining hole (1)

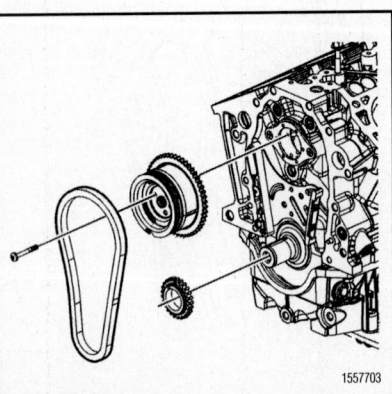

Fig. 106 Camshaft sprocket bolt, timing chain and sprockets

2. Remove the camshaft sprocket bolts.

3. Remove the timing chain and sprockets.

To install:

4. Install the crankshaft sprocket.

5. Apply prelube GM P/N 12345501 (Canadian P/N 992704) or the equivalent to the crankshaft sprocket thrust surface.

6. Install the timing chain tensioner.

7. Install the timing chain tensioner bolts and tighten to 15 ft. lbs. (21 Nm).

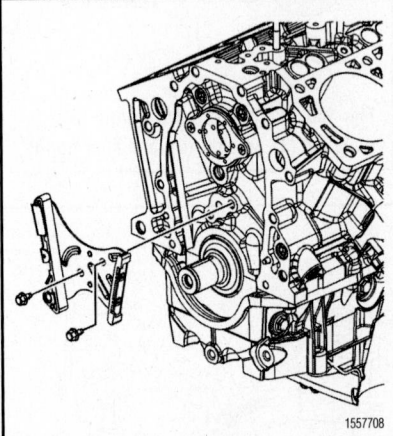

Fig. 107 Timing chain tensioner and bolts

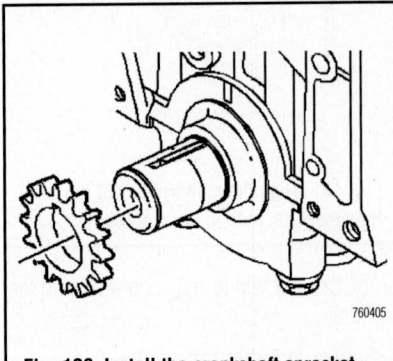

Fig. 108 Install the crankshaft sprocket

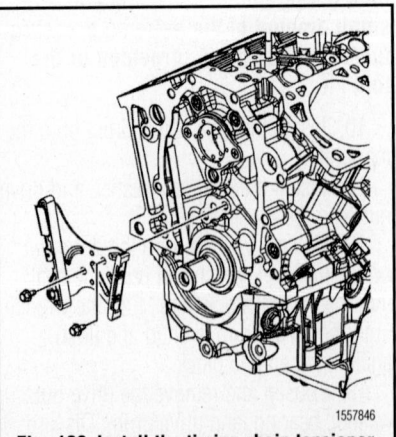

Fig. 109 Install the timing chain tensioner

8. Using the EN-47719 compressor, fully collapse the tensioner, and place the tensioner retaining pin into the retaining hole (1).

9. Align the dowel in the camshaft position actuator with the dowel hole in the camshaft.

✳✳ WARNING

Use only a Torx Plus® Bit when removing or installing the camshaft position actuator fasteners (1). The Torx Plus® design differs from typical Torx® fastener. Use of a standard Torx® bit on Torx Plus® fasteners may result in a rounded out fastener head or incorrect faster torque.

➡️DO NOT use any type of threadlocking compound on the camshaft position actuator mounting bolts. Usage of a thread-

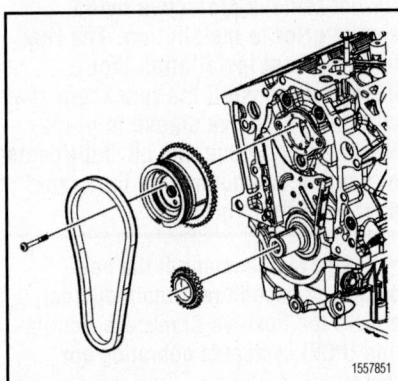

Fig. 110 Align the dowel in the camshaft position actuator with the dowel hole in the camshaft

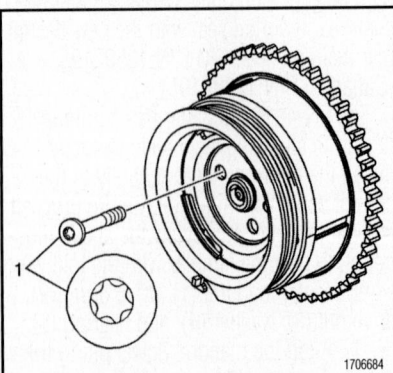

Fig. 111 Use only a Torx Plus® Bit when removing or installing the camshaft position actuator fasteners (1). The Torx Plus® design differs from typical Torx® fastener. Using a standard Torx® bit on Torx Plus® fasteners may result in a rounded out fastener head or incorrect faster torque

locking compound on the threads could lead to contamination of the camshaft position actuator, possibly resulting in potential damage to the actuator.

10. Draw the camshaft sprocket onto the camshaft using the mounting bolts and tighten the bolts to 12 ft. lbs. (16 Nm).

11. Remove the tensioner retaining pin.

12. Coat the crankshaft and camshaft sprocket with engine oil.

VALVE COVERS

REMOVAL & INSTALLATION

Left Side

See Figures 112 through 115.

1. Remove the Positive Crankcase Ventilation (PCV) tube.

2. Remove and discard both PCV tube O-rings.

3. Remove the valve rocker arm cover bolts.

➡**When removing the valve rocker arm cover make sure the gasket stays in place attached to the cylinder head.**

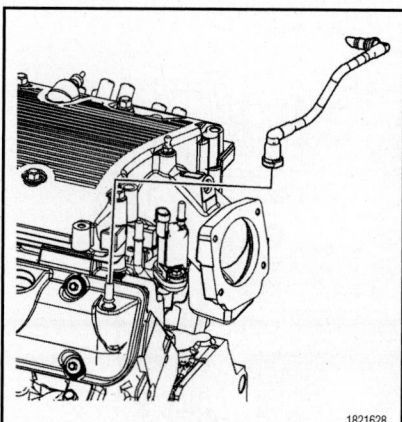

Fig. 112 Positive Crankcase Ventilation (PCV) tube

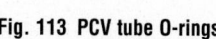

Fig. 113 PCV tube O-rings

4. Remove the valve rocker arm cover.

5. Cut the room temperature vulcanizing (RTV) in the channel where the intake, cylinder head and valve rocker arm cover meet with a suitable tool.

6. Remove and discard the valve rocker arm cover gasket, valve rocker arm cover grommets and valve rocker arm cover bolts if they are serviced with the grommet.

To install:

7. Install NEW valve rocker arm cover grommets and use NEW valve rocker arm cover bolts if they are serviced with the grommet.

Note: All gasket-mating surfaces need to be free of oil and foreign material. Use GM P/N 12346139 (Canadian P/N 10953463) or equivalent to clean surfaces.

8. Install the valve rocker arm cover gasket into the valve rocker arm cover.

9. Apply sealer GM P/N 12378521 (Canadian P/N 88901148) or an equivalent to the surfaces where the cylinder head and intake manifold meet (1).

10. Install the valve rocker arm cover.

11. Install the valve rocker arm cover bolts, if necessary, and tighten to 89 inch lbs. (10 Nm).

12. Install two NEW Positive Crankcase Ventilation (PCV) tube O-rings.

13. Install the fresh air tube.

Fig. 114 Valve rocker arm cover bolts

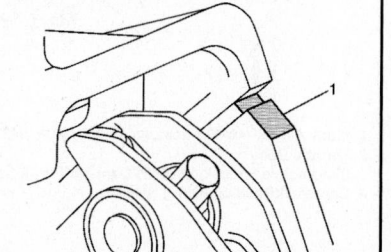

Fig. 115 Apply sealer to the surfaces where the cylinder head and intake manifold meet (1)

Right Side

See Figures 117 through 119.

1. Remove any remaining spark plug wires from their retainers.

2. Remove the ignition coil assembly bolts and nuts.

3. Remove the ignition coil assembly.

4. Remove the ignition coil assembly studs, if necessary.

5. Remove the fresh air tube from the valve rocker arm cover.

➡**When removing the valve rocker arm cover make sure the gasket stays in place attached to the cylinder head.**

6. Remove the valve rocker arm cover.

7. Cut the room temperature vulcanizing (RTV) in the channel where the intake, cylinder head and valve rocker arm cover meet with a suitable tool.

8. Remove and discard the valve rocker arm cover gasket, valve rocker arm cover grommets and valve rocker arm cover bolts if they are serviced with the grommet.

To install:

9. Install NEW valve rocker arm cover grommets and use NEW valve rocker arm cover bolts if they are serviced with the grommet.

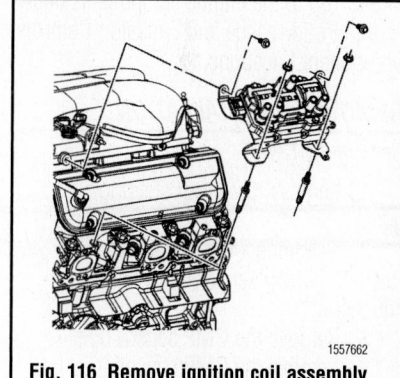

Fig. 116 Remove ignition coil assembly

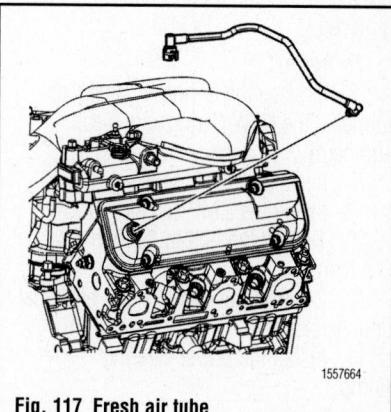

Fig. 117 Fresh air tube

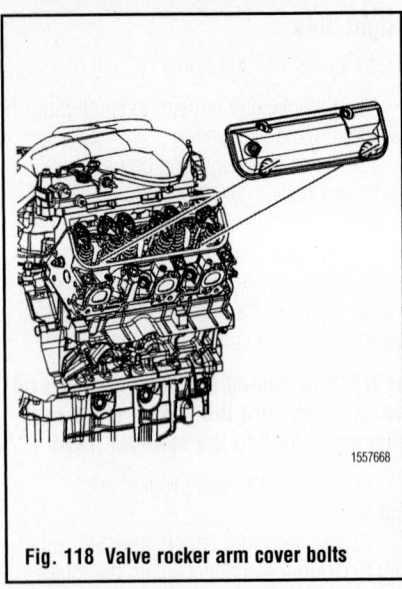

Fig. 118 Valve rocker arm cover bolts

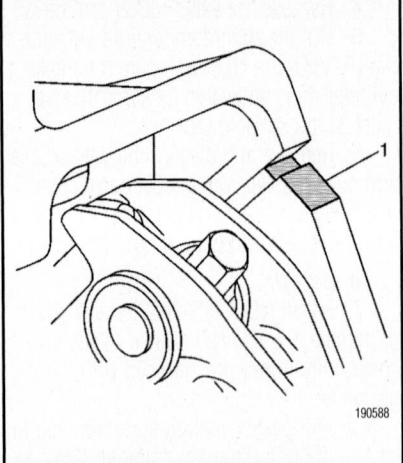

Fig. 119 Apply sealer to the surfaces where the cylinder head and intake manifold meet (1)

Note: All gasket-mating surfaces need to be free of oil and foreign material. Use GM P/N 12346139 (Canadian P/N 10953463) or equivalent to clean surfaces.

10. Install the valve rocker arm cover gasket into the valve rocker arm cover.

11. Apply sealer GM P/N 12378521 (Canadian P/N 88901148) or an equivalent to the surfaces where the cylinder head and intake manifold meet (1).

12. Install the valve rocker arm cover.

13. Install the valve rocker arm cover bolts, if necessary, and tighten to 89 inch lbs. (10 Nm).

14. Install the fresh air tube.

15. Install the ignition coil assembly studs, if necessary, and tighten to 18 ft. lbs. (25 Nm).

16. Install the ignition coil assembly.

17. Install the ignition coil assembly bolts and nuts and tighten to 18 ft. lbs. (25 Nm).

ENGINE PERFORMANCE & EMISSION CONTROLS

COMPONENT LOCATIONS

See Figures 120 through 123.

CAMSHAFT POSITION (CMP) SENSOR

LOCATION

See Top of the engine components under Engine Performance and Emission Controls Component Locations.

REMOVAL & INSTALLATION

See Figure 124.

1. Remove the power steering pump.

2. Disconnect the Camshaft Position (CMP) sensor electrical connector.

3. Remove the CMP sensor bolt.

4. Remove the CMP sensor.

5. Inspect the sensor O-ring for wear, cracks, or leakage if the sensor is not being replaced.

To install:

6. Replace the O-ring if damaged; lubricate the NEW O-ring with clean engine oil.

7. Install the CMP sensor.

8. Install the CMP sensor bolt.

9. Tighten the bolt to 89 inch lbs. (10 Nm).

10. Connect the CMP sensor electrical connector.

11. Install the power steering pump.

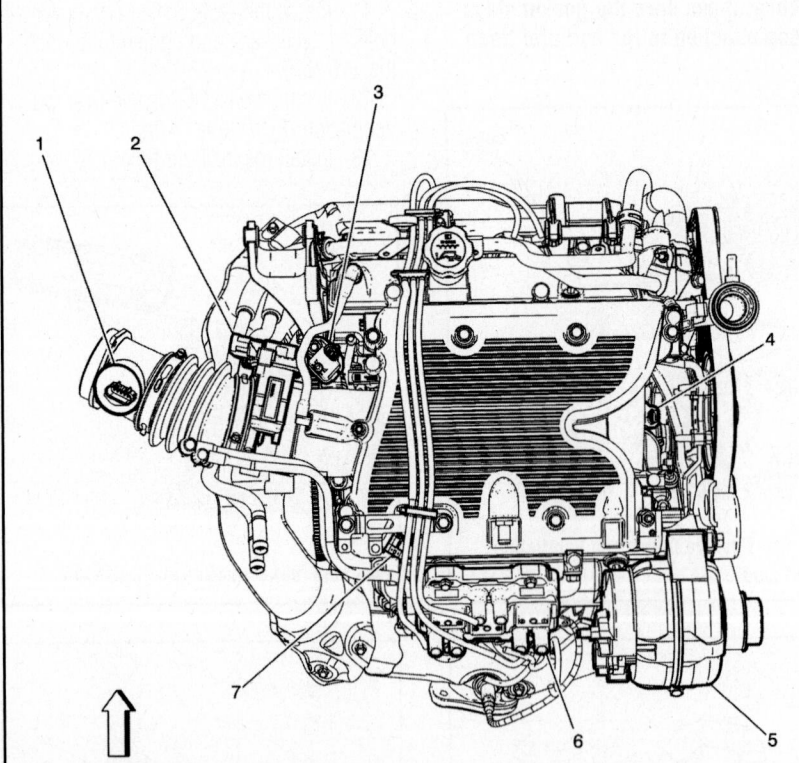

1. Mass Airflow (MAF)/Intake Air Temperature (IAT) Sensor
2. Throttle Body
3. Evaporative Emission (EVAP) Canister Purge Solenoid Valve
4. Camshaft Position (CMP) Sensor
5. Generator
6. Ignition Control Module (ICM)
7. Manifold Absolute Pressure (MAP) Sensor

Fig. 120 Top of the engine components

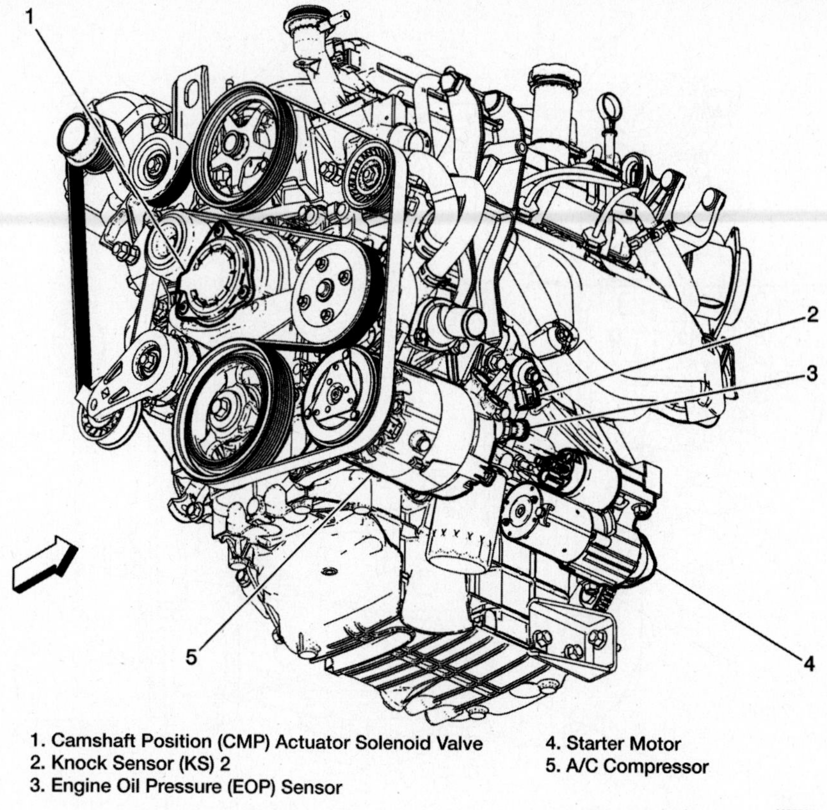
1
2
3
4
5
1. Camshaft Position (CMP) Actuator Solenoid Valve
2. Knock Sensor (KS) 2
3. Engine Oil Pressure (EOP) Sensor
4. Starter Motor
5. A/C Compressor
2330268

Fig. 121 Lower front of the engine components

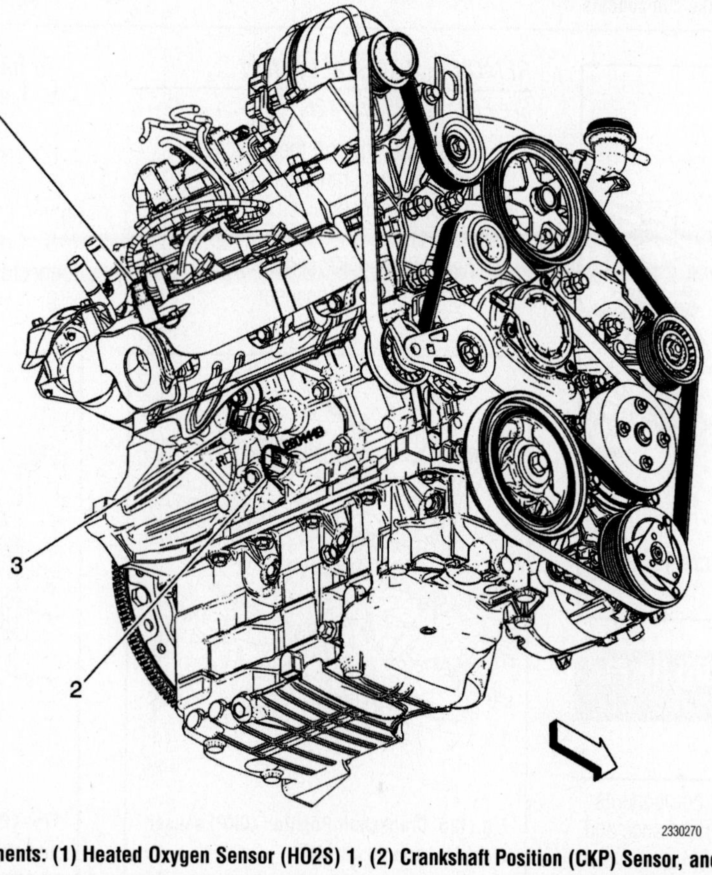
1
2
3
2330270

Fig. 122 Rear of the engine components: (1) Heated Oxygen Sensor (HO2S) 1, (2) Crankshaft Position (CKP) Sensor, and (3) Knock Sensor (KS) 1

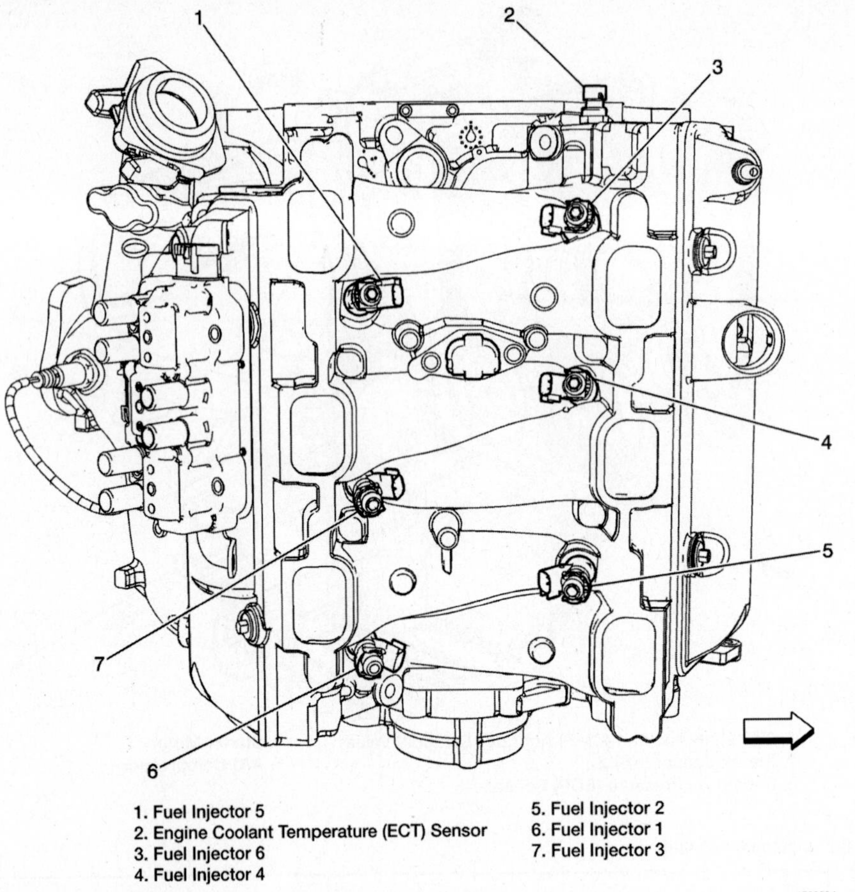

Fig. 123 Under the upper intake components

1. Fuel Injector 5
2. Engine Coolant Temperature (ECT) Sensor
3. Fuel Injector 6
4. Fuel Injector 4
5. Fuel Injector 2
6. Fuel Injector 1
7. Fuel Injector 3

1700294

Fig. 124 Camshaft Position (CMP) sensor bolt

1599076

CRANKSHAFT POSITION (CKP) SENSOR

LOCATION

See the Rear of the engine components illustrations under Engine Performance and Emission Controls Component Locations.

REMOVAL & INSTALLATION

See Figures 125 and 126.

1. Raise and support the vehicle.
2. Remove the Crankshaft Position (CKP) sensor electrical connector (4).
3. Remove the CKP sensor stud.
4. Remove the CKP sensor.

To install:

5. Lubricate the CKP sensor O-ring with clean engine oil.
6. Install the CKP sensor.
7. Install the CKP sensor stud and tighten to 89 inch lbs. (10 Nm).
8. Connect the CKP sensor electrical connector (4).
9. Lower the vehicle.

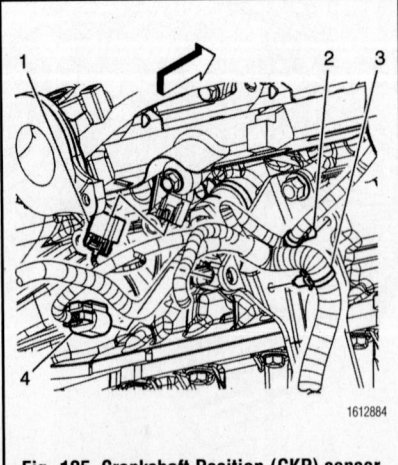

Fig. 125 Crankshaft Position (CKP) sensor electrical connector (4)

1612884

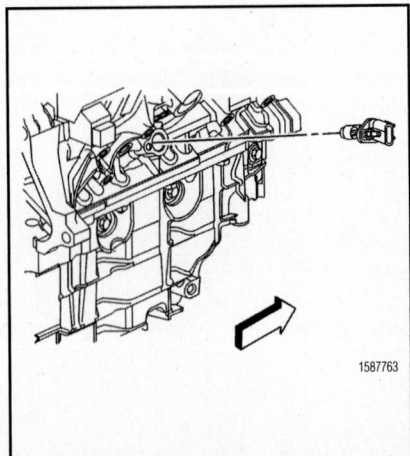

Fig. 126 Crankshaft Position (CKP) sensor and stud

1587763

ELECTRONIC CONTROL MODULE (ECM)

LOCATION

Lower air cleaner housing.

REMOVAL & INSTALLATION

See Figures 127 and 128.

Service of the engine control module (ECM) should normally consist of either replacement of the ECM or electrically erasable programmable read only memory (EEPROM) programming. If the diagnostic procedures call for ECM replacement, inspect the ECM first to see if the replacement is the correct part. If the ECM is faulty, remove the ECM and install the new service ECM.

The new service ECM will not be programmed. You must program the new ECM.

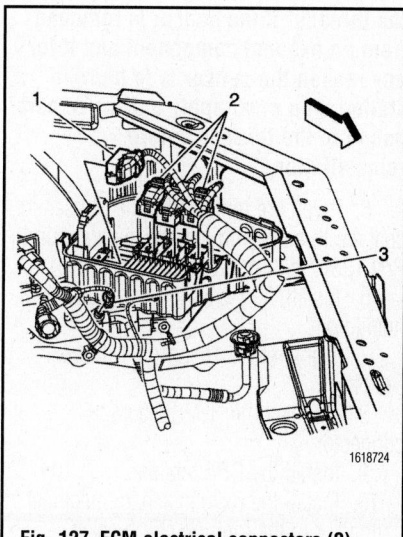

Fig. 127 ECM electrical connectors (2)

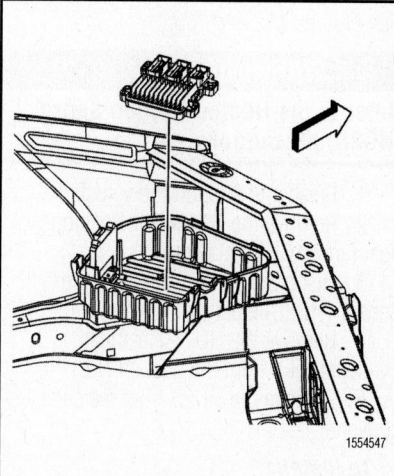

Fig. 128 Remove the ECM from the air cleaner lower housing

DTC P0602 indicates the EEPROM is not programmed or has malfunctioned.

✳✳ WARNING
In order to prevent any possible electrostatic discharge damage to the ECM, do not touch the connector pins or the soldered components on the circuit board.

✳✳ WARNING
Always turn the ignition off when installing or removing the ECM connectors in order to prevent damage to the components.

➡ It is necessary to record the remaining engine oil life. If the replacement module is not programmed with the remaining engine oil life, the engine oil life will default to 100 percent. If the replacement module is not programmed with the remaining engine oil life, the engine oil will need to be changed at 5 000 km (3,000 mi) from the last engine oil change.

1. Using a scan tool, retrieve the percentage of remaining engine oil. Record the remaining engine oil life, if required.
2. Disconnect the negative battery cable. Refer to Battery Negative Cable Disconnection and Connection.
3. Remove the left front inner fender brace.
4. Remove the air cleaner assembly. Refer to Air Cleaner Assembly replacement.
5. Disconnect the ECM electrical connectors (2).
6. Remove the ECM from the air cleaner lower housing.

To install:
7. Install the ECM to the air cleaner lower housing.
8. Connect the ECM electrical connectors (2).
9. Install the air cleaner assembly.
10. Install the left front inner fender brace.
11. Connect the negative battery cable.
12. Program the new ECM.

ENGINE COOLANT TEMPERATURE (ECT) SENSOR

LOCATION

See "Under the upper intake components" illustration under Engine Performance and Emission Controls Component Locations.

REMOVAL & INSTALLATION

See Figure 129.

✳✳ WARNING
Use care when handling the coolant sensor. Damage to the coolant sensor will affect the operation of the fuel control system.

1. Drain the cooling system. Refer to Cooling System Draining and Filling.
2. Remove the intake manifold cover, if necessary. Refer to Intake Manifold Cover Replacement.
3. Remove the exhaust crossover. Refer to Exhaust Crossover Pipe Replacement.
4. Disconnect the Engine Coolant Temperature (ECT) sensor electrical connector.
5. Remove the ECT sensor.

To install:

✳✳ WARNING
Replacement components must be the correct part number for the application. Components requiring the use of the thread locking compound, lubricants, corrosion inhibitors, or sealants are identified in the service procedure. Some replacement components may come with these coatings already applied. Do not use these coatings on components unless specified. These coatings can affect the final torque, which may affect the operation of the component. Use the correct torque specification when installing components in order to avoid damage.

6. Coat the threads of the ECT sensor with sealer GM P/N 13246004 (Canadian P/N 10953480) or an equivalent.

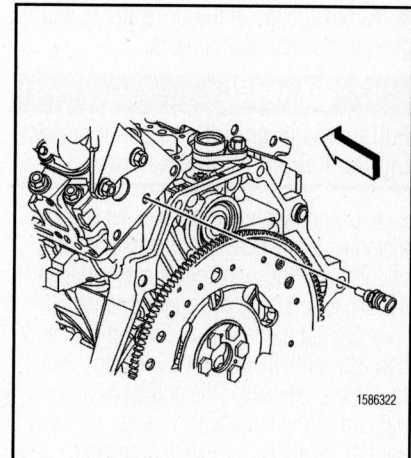

Fig. 129 Engine Coolant Temperature (ECT) sensor and electrical connector.

7. Install the ECT sensor. Tighten the ECT sensor to 15 ft. lbs. (20 Nm).

8. Connect the ECT electrical connector.

9. Install the intake manifold cover, if necessary.

10. Install the exhaust crossover.

11. Fill the cooling system. Refer to Cooling System Draining and Filling.

HEATED OXYGEN (HO2S) SENSOR

LOCATION

For Sensor 1, see Rear of the engine components illustration under Engine Performance and Emission Controls Component Locations. Sensor 2 is on the catalytic converter.

PRECAUTIONS

✳✳ WARNING

Do not remove the pigtail from either the Heated Oxygen Sensor (HO2S) or the oxygen sensor (O2S). Removing the pigtail or the connector will affect sensor operation.

- Handle the oxygen sensor carefully. Do not drop the HO2S. Keep the in-line electrical connector and the louvered end free of grease, dirt, or other contaminants. Do not use cleaning solvents of any type.
- Do not repair the wiring, connector or terminals. Replace the oxygen sensor if the pigtail wiring, connector, or terminal is damaged.
- An external clean air reference is obtained by way of the oxygen sensor signal and heater wires. Any attempt to repair the wires, connectors, or terminals could result in the obstruction of the air reference and degraded sensor performance.

✳✳ WARNING

Follow these guidelines when servicing the heated oxygen sensor:

- Do not apply contact cleaner or other materials to the sensor or vehicle harness connectors. These materials may get into the sensor causing poor performance.
- Do not damage the sensor pigtail and harness wires in such a way that the wires inside are exposed. This could provide a path for foreign materials to enter the sensor and cause performance problems.
- Ensure the sensor or vehicle lead wires are not bent sharply or kinked. Sharp bends or kinks could block the reference air path through the lead wire.

1. Do not remove or defeat the oxygen sensor ground wire, where applicable. Vehicles that utilize the ground wired sensor may rely on this ground as the only ground contact to the sensor. Removal of the ground wire will cause poor engine performance.

2. Ensure that the peripheral seal remains intact on the vehicle harness connector in order to prevent damage due to water intrusion. The engine harness may be repaired using Packard's Crimp and Splice Seals Terminal Repair Kit. Under no circumstances should repairs be soldered since this could result in the air reference being obstructed.

REMOVAL & INSTALLATION

Sensor 1

See Figures 130 and 131.

✳✳ WARNING

Refer to the heated oxygen sensor precautions.

1. Remove the Connector Position Assurance (CPA) retainer (3).

2. Disconnect the Heated Oxygen Sensor (HO2S) electrical connector (2).

3. Remove the oxygen sensor electrical connector from the ignition coil bracket.

4. Remove the HO2S from the exhaust manifold.

To install:

➡ **A special anti-seize compound is used on the HO2S threads. The compound consists of liquid graphite and glass beads. The graphite tends to burn away, but the glass beads remain, making the sensor easier to remove. New or service replacement sensors**

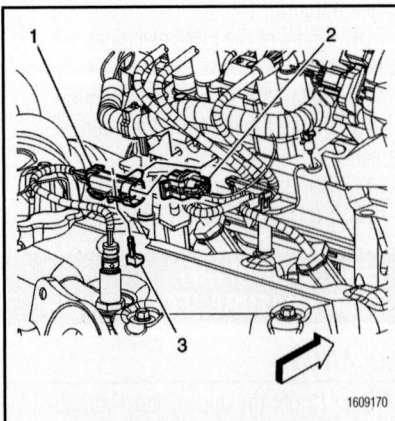

Fig. 130 Connector Position Assurance (CPA) retainer (3) and Heated Oxygen Sensor (HO2S) electrical connector (2)

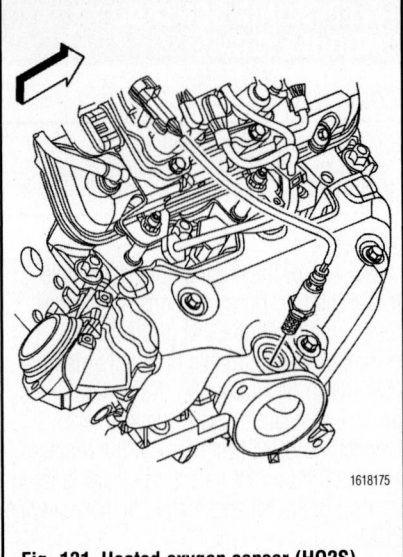

Fig. 131 Heated oxygen sensor (HO2S)

already have the compound applied to the threads. If the sensor is removed from an exhaust component and if for any reason the sensor is to be reinstalled, you must apply anti-seize compound to the threads before reinstallation.

5. If you are reinstalling the old sensor, coat the threads with anti-seize compound P/N 12377953, or an equivalent.

6. Install the HO2S to the exhaust manifold.

7. Tighten the sensor to 31 ft. lbs. (42 Nm).

8. Connect the HO2S electrical connector.

9. Install the CPA retainer.

10. Install the oxygen sensor electrical connector to the ignition coil bracket.

Sensor 2

See Figures 132 and 133.

✳✳ WARNING

Refer to the Heated Oxygen Sensor (HO2S) precautions.

1. Raise and support the vehicle.

2. Remove the Connector Position Assurance (CPA) retainer (1).

3. Disconnect the Heated Oxygen Sensor (HO2S) electrical connector (3).

4. Remove the HO2S electrical connector clip from the heat shield.

5. Remove the HO2S from the catalytic converter.

To install:

➡ **A special anti-seize compound is used on the HO2S threads. The compound consists of liquid graphite and glass**

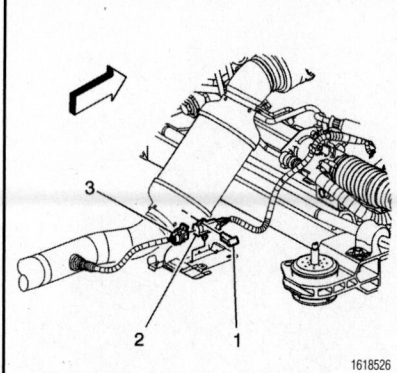

Fig. 132 Connector Position Assurance (CPA) retainer (1) and Heated Oxygen Sensor (HO2S) electrical connector (3)

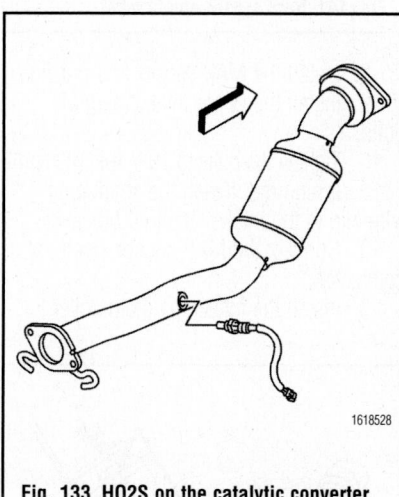

Fig. 133 HO2S on the catalytic converter

beads. The graphite tends to burn away, but the glass beads remain, making the sensor easier to remove. New or service replacement sensors already have the compound applied to the threads. If the sensor is removed from an exhaust component and if for any reason the sensor is to be reinstalled, you must apply anti-seize compound to the threads before reinstallation.

6. If you are reinstalling the old sensor, coat the threads with anti-seize compound P/N 12377953, or an equivalent.
7. Install the HO2S to the exhaust manifold.
8. Tighten the sensor to 31 ft. lbs. (42 Nm).
9. Connect the HO2S electrical connector.
10. Install the CPA retainer.
11. Install the HO2S electrical connector clip to the heat shield.
12. Lower the vehicle.

KNOCK SENSOR (KS)

LOCATION

See both the Lower front of the engine components and the Rear of the engine components illustrations under Engine Performance and Emission Controls Component Locations.

REMOVAL & INSTALLATION

Bank 1

See Figures 134 through 136.

1. Raise and support the vehicle.
2. For 3.9L engines only, remove the catalytic converter. Refer to Catalytic Converter replacement.
3. Disconnect the left knock sensor electrical connector (1).
4. Loosen and remove the knock sensor; 3.5L and 3.9L locations are different, see illustrations.

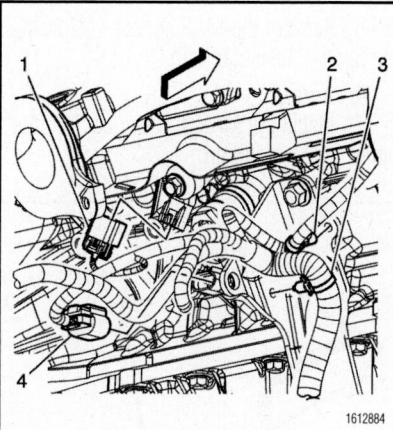

Fig. 134 Left knock sensor electrical connector (1)

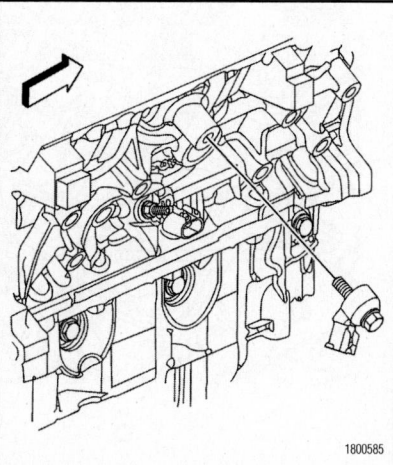

Fig. 135 Knock sensor, bank 1, 3.5L engine only

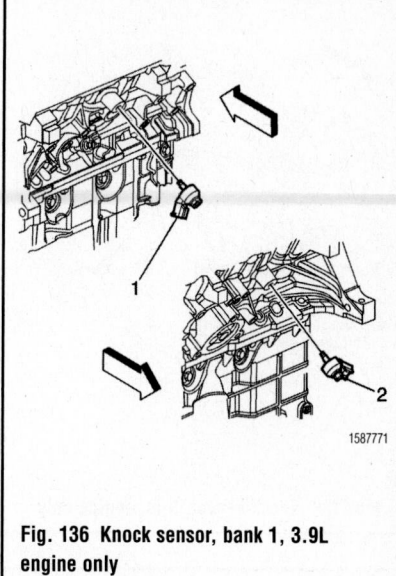

Fig. 136 Knock sensor, bank 1, 3.9L engine only

To install:

➡DO NOT apply thread sealant to the sensor threads. The sensor threads are coated at the factory. Applying additional sealant affects the sensor's ability to detect detonation.

5. Install and tighten the knock sensor.
6. Tighten the sensor to 18 ft. lbs. (25 Nm).
7. Connect the left knock sensor electrical connector (1).
8. For 3.9L engines only: Install the catalytic converter. Refer to Catalytic Converter replacement.
9. Lower the vehicle.

Bank 2

See Figures 137 through 139.

1. Raise and support the vehicle.

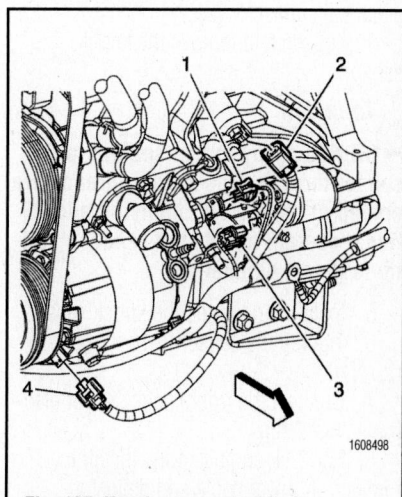

Fig. 137 Knock sensor electrical connector (2).

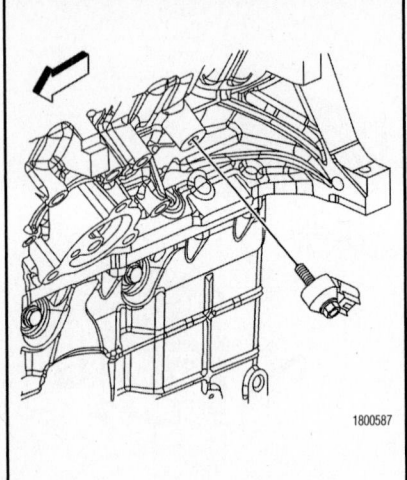

Fig. 138 Knock sensor, 3.5L engine only

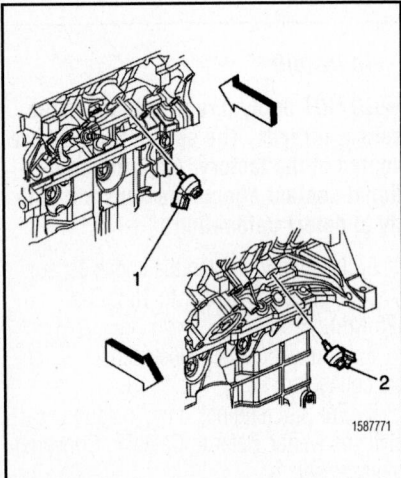

Fig. 139 Knock sensor (2), 3.9L engine only

2. For 3.9L engines only: Remove the radiator air lower baffle and deflector.

3. Disconnect the right knock sensor electrical connector (2).

4. Loosen and remove the knock sensor.

To install:

➡ DO NOT apply thread sealant to the sensor threads. The sensor threads are coated at the factory. Applying additional sealant affects the sensor's ability to detect detonation.

5. Install and tighten the knock sensor.

6. Tighten the sensor to 18 ft. lbs. (25 Nm).

7. Connect the right knock sensor electrical connector.

8. For 3.9L engines only: Install the radiator air lower baffle and deflector.

9. Lower the vehicle.

MANIFOLD ABSOLUTE PRESSURE (MAP) SENSOR

LOCATION

See "Top of the engine components" illustration under Engine Performance and Emission Controls Component Locations.

REMOVAL & INSTALLATION

See Figures 140 and 141.

1. Remove the intake manifold cover. Refer to Intake Manifold Cover Replacement.

2. Disconnect the manifold absolute pressure (MAP) sensor electrical connector (1).

3. Remove the spark plug wire clip from the intake manifold bracket, if necessary.

4. Remove the upper intake manifold bolts.

5. Remove the MAP sensor and bracket.

6. Remove the MAP sensor seal from the upper intake manifold.

To install:

7. Install the MAP sensor seal into the upper intake manifold.

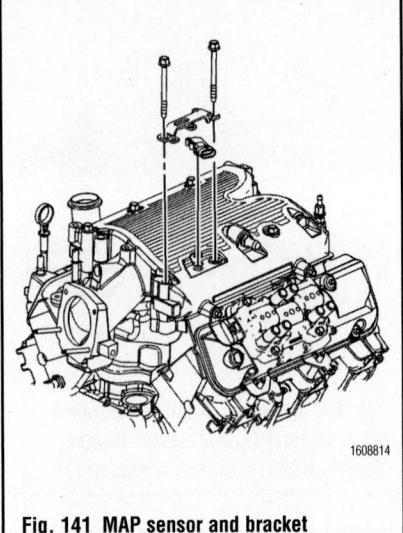

Fig. 141 MAP sensor and bracket

8. Install the MAP sensor and bracket.

9. Install the upper intake manifold bolts.

10. Tighten the bolts to 18 ft. lbs. (25 Nm).

11. If required, install the spark plug wire clip to the intake manifold bracket.

12. Connect the MAP sensor electrical connector.

13. Install the intake manifold cover.

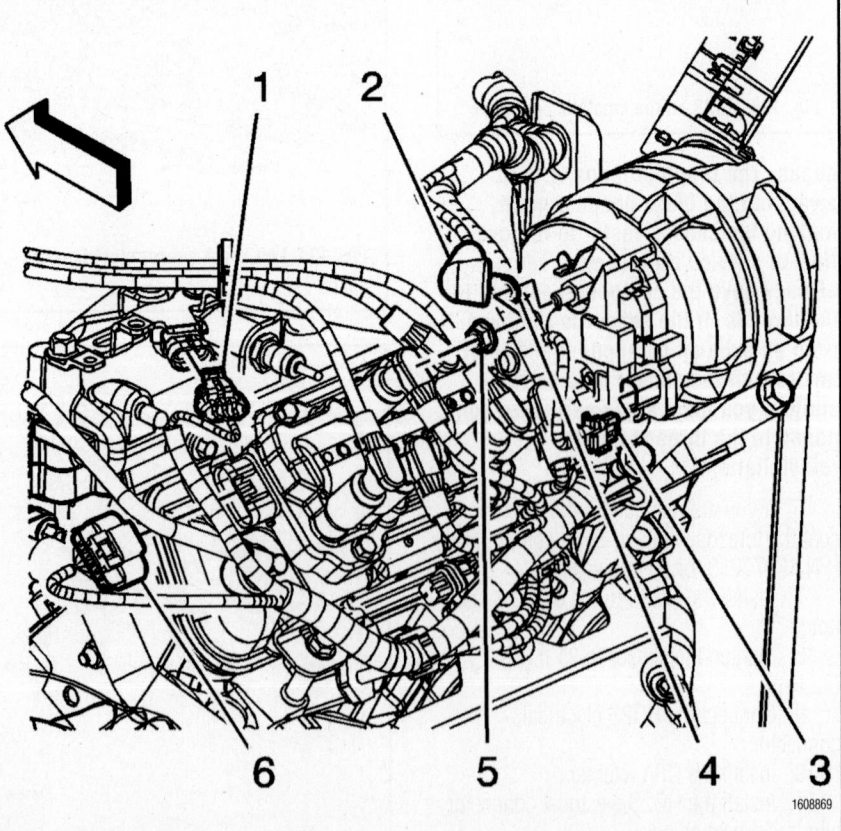

Fig. 140 Manifold Absolute Pressure (MAP) sensor electrical connector (1)

MASS AIR FLOW (MAF) SENSOR/INTAKE AIR TEMPERATURE (IAT) SENSOR

LOCATION

See "Top of the engine components" illustration under Engine Performance and Emission Controls Component Locations.

REMOVAL & INSTALLATION

See Figure 142.

1. Disconnect the electrical connector.
2. Remove the Mass Air Flow (MAF)/Intake Air Temperature (IAT) sensor.

To install:
3. Tighten the MAF/IAT sensor to 18 inch lbs. (2 Nm).
4. Attach the electrical connector.

VEHICLE SPEED SENSOR (VSS)

LOCATION

See "Transaxle components" illustration under Engine Performance and Emission Controls Component Locations.

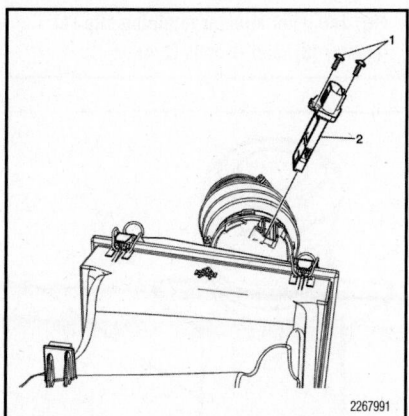

Fig. 142 Mass Air Flow (MAF) Sensor with Intake Air Temperature (IAT) Sensor (2) and two MAF sensor fasteners (1)

REMOVAL & INSTALLATION

See Figures 143 through 145.

1. Raise and support the vehicle.
2. Remove the right front tire and wheel.
3. Disconnect the vehicle speed sensor (VSS) electrical connector.
4. Remove the VSS bolt (9).
5. Remove the VSS (10) from the extension case.
6. Remove the O-ring (11) from the VSS (10).

To install:
7. Install the O-ring to the VSS.
8. Install the VSS.
9. Install the VSS bolt.
10. Tighten the VSS bolt to 106 inch lbs. (12 Nm).
11. Connect the VSS electrical connector.
12. Install the right front tire and wheel. Refer to Tire and Wheel Removal and Installation.
13. Lower the vehicle.

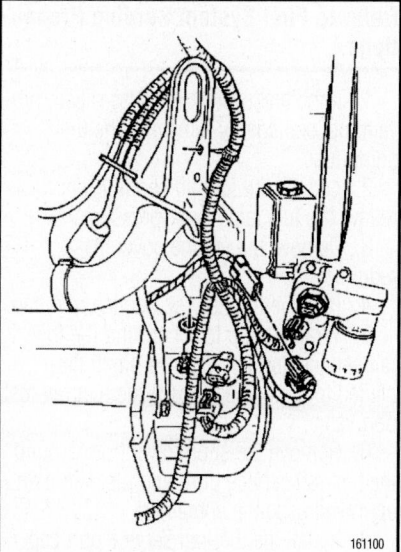

Fig. 143 Disconnect the vehicle speed sensor (VSS) electrical connector

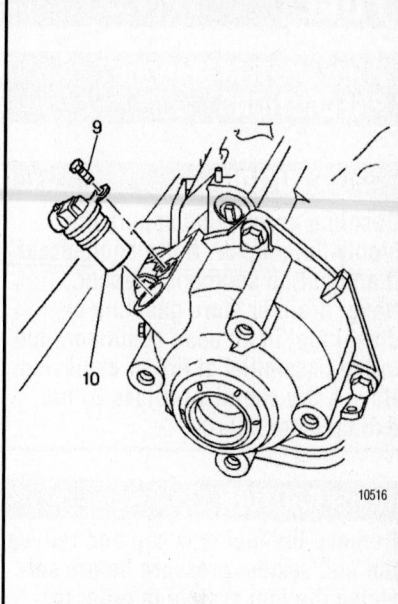

Fig. 144 Vehicle speed sensor (10) and bolt (9)

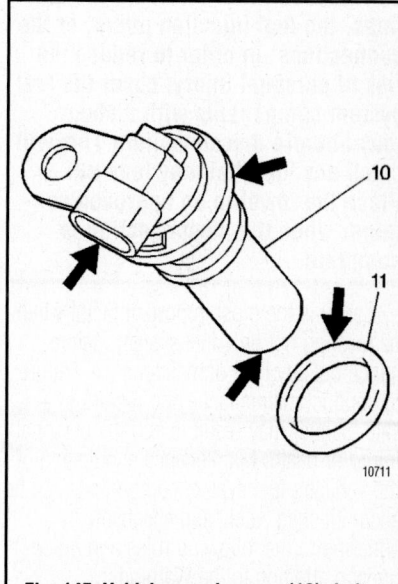

Fig. 145 Vehicle speed sensor (10), bolt (9), and O-ring (11)

FUEL SYSTEM SERVICE PRECAUTIONS

✳✳ CAUTION

Gasoline or gasoline vapors are highly flammable. A fire could occur if an ignition source is present. Never drain or store gasoline or diesel fuel in an open container, due to the possibility of fire or explosion. Have a dry chemical (Class B) fire extinguisher nearby.

✳✳ CAUTION

Remove the fuel tank cap and relieve the fuel system pressure before servicing the fuel system in order to reduce the risk of personal injury. After you relieve the fuel system pressure, a small amount of fuel may be released when servicing the fuel lines, the fuel injection pump, or the connections. In order to reduce the risk of personal injury, cover the fuel system components with a shop towel before disconnection. This will catch any fuel that may leak out. Place the towel in an approved container when the disconnection is complete.

Safety is the most important factor when performing not only fuel system maintenance but any type of maintenance. Failure to conduct maintenance and repairs in a safe manner may result in serious personal injury or death. Maintenance and testing of the vehicle's fuel system components can be accomplished safely and effectively by adhering to the following rules and guidelines in addition to the Warnings:

• To avoid the possibility of fire and personal injury, always disconnect the negative battery cable unless the repair or test procedure requires that battery voltage be applied.

• Always relieve the fuel system pressure prior to disconnecting any fuel system component (injector, fuel rail, pressure regulator, etc.), fitting or fuel line connection. Exercise extreme caution whenever relieving fuel system pressure to avoid exposing skin, face and eyes to fuel spray. Please be advised that fuel under pressure may penetrate the skin or any part of the body that it contacts.

• Always place a shop towel or cloth around the fitting or connection prior to

loosening to absorb any excess fuel due to spillage. Ensure that all fuel spillage (should it occur) is quickly removed from engine surfaces. Ensure that all fuel-soaked cloths or towels are deposited into a suitable waste container.

• Do not allow fuel spray or fuel vapors to come into contact with a spark or open flame.

• Always use a back-up wrench when loosening and tightening fuel line connection fittings. This will prevent unnecessary stress and torsion to fuel line piping.

• Always replace worn fuel fitting O-rings with new ones. Do not substitute fuel hose or equivalent where fuel pipe is installed.

RELIEVING FUEL SYSTEM PRESSURE

✳✳ CAUTION

Refer to Fuel System Service Precautions.

1. If the fuel system requires repair, prevent fuel spillage by removing the fuel pump fuse.
2. Loosen the fuel fill cap in order to relieve the fuel tank vapor pressure.
3. Remove the engine cover, if required.
4. Remove the fuel rail service port cap.
5. Wrap a shop towel around the fuel rail service port and using a small flat-bladed tool, depress (open) the fuel rail test port valve.
6. Remove the shop towel from around the fuel rail service port, and place it in an approved gasoline container.
7. Install the fuel rail service port cap.
8. Install the engine cover, if required.
9. Tighten the fuel fill cap.

FUEL INJECTORS

REMOVAL & INSTALLATION
See Figures 146 and 147.

✳✳ WARNING

Use care in removing the fuel injectors in order to prevent damage to the fuel injector electrical connector pins or the fuel injector nozzles. Do not immerse the fuel injector in any type of cleaner. The fuel injector is an electrical component and may be damaged by this cleaning method.

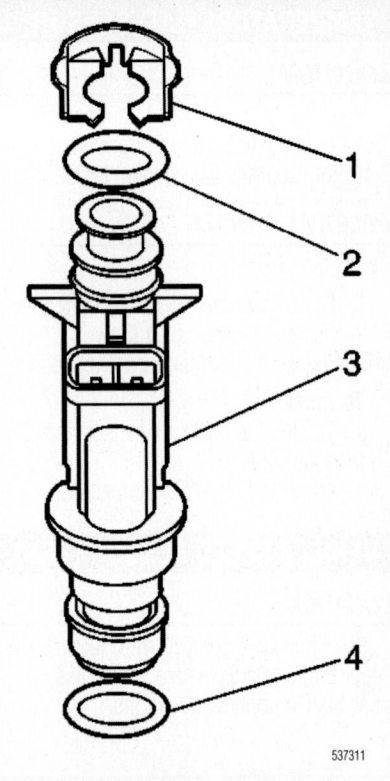

537311

Fig. 146 Fuel injector retaining clip (1), injector (3), and O-rings (2,4)

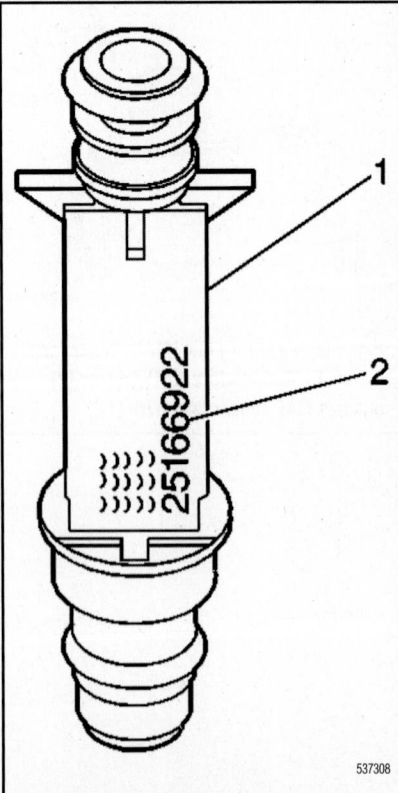

537308

Fig. 147 Fuel injector assembly (1) with part number identification (2)

➡If the fuel injectors are found to be leaking, the engine oil may be contaminated with fuel.

1. Remove the fuel rail.
2. Remove the fuel injector retaining clip (1).
3. Remove the fuel injector (3) from the fuel rail.
4. Remove the fuel injector upper O-ring (2).
5. Remove the fuel injector lower O-ring (4).

To install:

➡Be sure to use the correct part number when ordering replacement fuel injectors. The fuel injector assembly (1) is stamped with a part number identification (2).

The next five steps refer to the illustration in the removal section.

6. Lubricate the new injector O-rings (2, 4) with clean engine oil.
7. Install the fuel injector upper O-ring (2).
8. Install the fuel injector lower O-ring (4).
9. Install the fuel injector (3) to the fuel rail.
10. Install the fuel injector retaining clip (1).
11. Install the fuel rail.

FUEL TANK

DRAINING

2010 3.5L (LZ4) Engine & 2010–11 3.9L non E85 Engine

See Figures 148 and 150.

✷✷ CAUTION

Refer to Fuel System Service Precautions.

1. Remove the fuel fill cap.
2. Install the fuel door flapper holder tool (J 42960-2) into the fuel fill pipe in order to hold the door open.

➡Lubricate the fuel drain hose with or equivalent to aid in hose insertion. Do not use an unapproved lubricant. Use Transjel lubricant (transmission assembly lube from Sealed Power).

3. Insert the fuel tank drain hose tool (J 45004) into the fuel tank until the hose reaches the bottom of the fuel tank.
4. Use a hand- or air-operated pump device in order to drain as much fuel

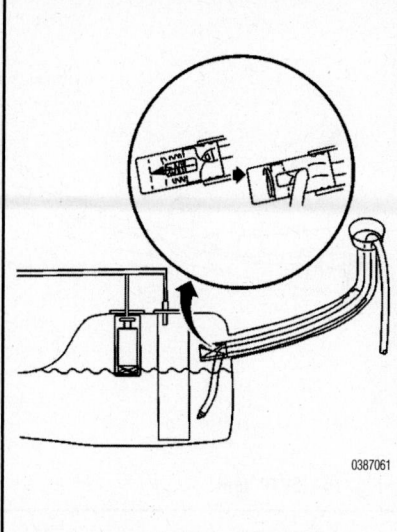

Fig. 148 Fuel tank draining, 2010 model year, 3.5L engine with E85 (flex fuel)

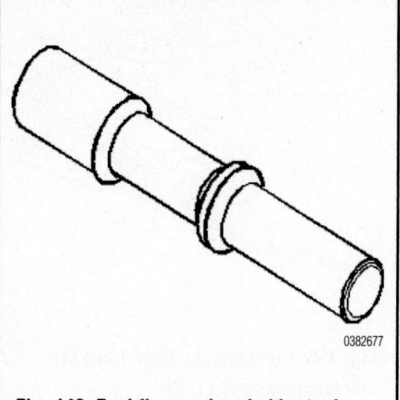

Fig. 149 Fuel flapper door holder tool

through the fuel fill pipe as possible.

2010 3.5L (LZE) Engine with E85 (Flex Fuel)

✷✷ CAUTION

Refer to Fuel System Service Precautions.

1. Loosen the fuel fill cap in order to relieve the fuel tank vapor pressure.
2. Raise and support the vehicle.
3. Loosen the fuel tank fill pipe clamp (1) at the fuel tank.
4. Remove the fuel tank fill pipe/hose (2).
5. Insert a hose into the fuel tank opening.
6. Use a hand- or air-operated pump device in order to drain as much fuel from the fuel tank as possible.

2010 and 2011 model year 3.5L engine with E85 (flex fuel)

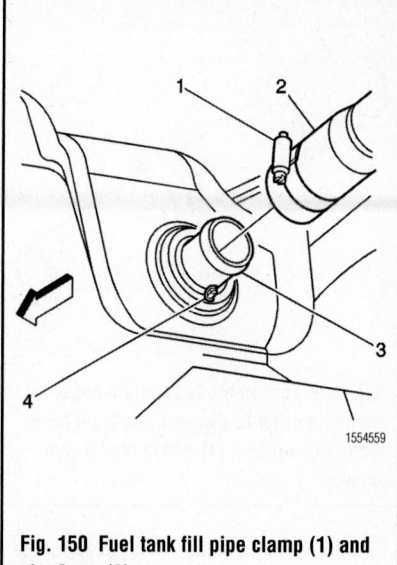

Fig. 150 Fuel tank fill pipe clamp (1) and pipe/hose (2)

See Figures 151 and 152.

✷✷ CAUTION

Refer to Fuel System Service Precautions.

1. Raise and support the vehicle.

➡Lubricate the fuel drain hose with J 36850 Transjel lubricant or equivalent to aid in hose insertion. Do not use an unapproved lubricant.

2. Loosen the lower drain hose clamp in order to separate the drain hose from the fuel tank (1).

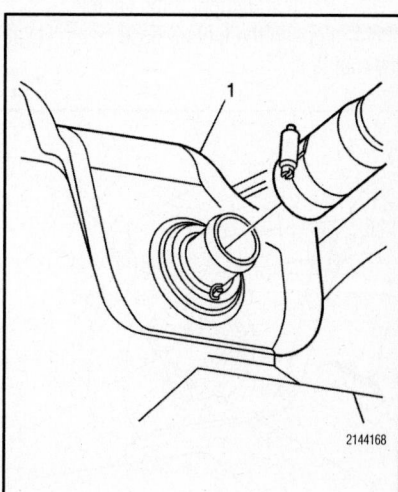

Fig. 151 Loosen the lower drain hose clamp in order to separate the drain hose from the fuel tank (1) - 2010 model year shown

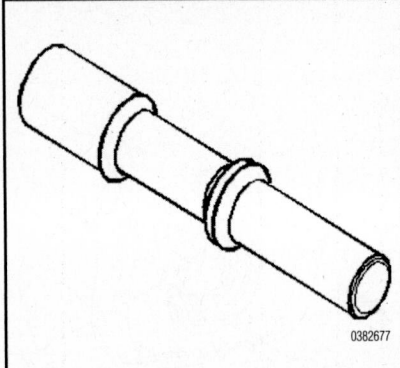

Fig. 152 Loosen the lower drain hose clamp in order to separate the drain hose from the fuel tank (1) - 2011 model year shown

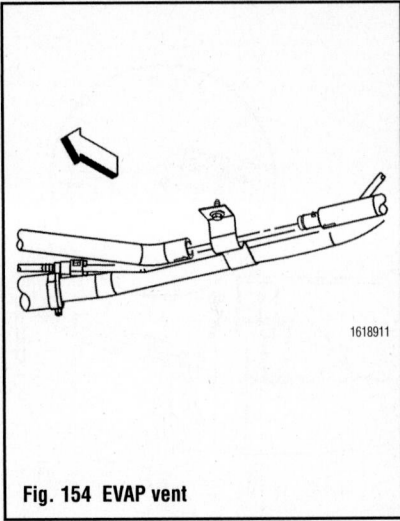

Fig. 154 EVAP vent

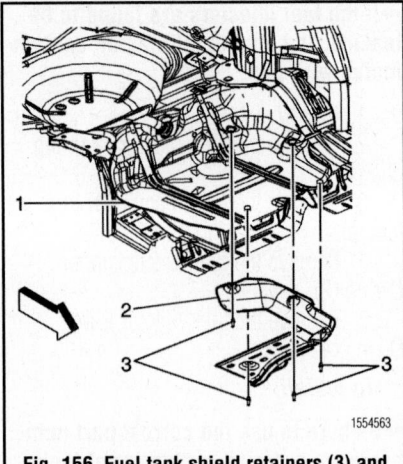

Fig. 156 Fuel tank shield retainers (3) and fuel tank shield (2)

3. Insert the fuel tank drain hose tool (J 45004) into the fuel tank until the hose reaches the bottom of the fuel tank.

4. Use a hand- or air-operated pump device in order to drain as much fuel from the fuel tank as possible.

REMOVAL & INSTALLATION

2010 NC7 Engine & All 2011 Engines

See Figures 153 through 160.

➡**Clean the fuel and Evaporative Emission (EVAP) connections and surrounding areas prior to disconnecting the lines in order to avoid possible system contamination.**

1. Relieve the fuel system fuel pressure. Refer to Fuel Pressure Relief.

2. Drain the fuel tank. Refer to Fuel Tank Draining.

3. Raise and support the vehicle.

4. Loosen the fuel fill hose clamp (1) at the fuel tank.

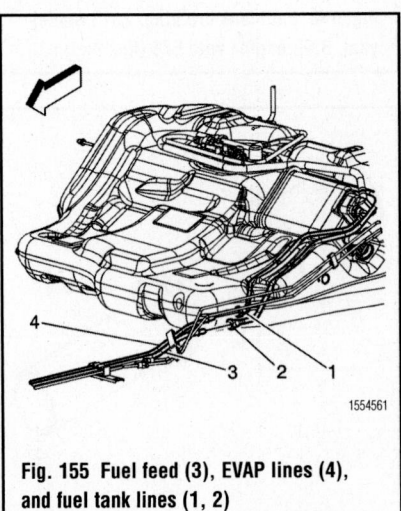

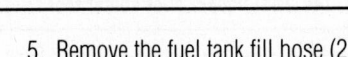

Fig. 155 Fuel feed (3), EVAP lines (4), and fuel tank lines (1, 2)

5. Remove the fuel tank fill hose (2) from the fuel tank (3).

6. Disconnect the EVAP vent pipe quick connect fitting from the fill pipe EVAP vent pipe quick connect fitting.

7. Disconnect the EVAP vent solenoid hose on the tank from the vent valve solenoid hose.

8. Disconnect the fuel feed (3), and the EVAP (4) lines from the fuel tank lines (1, 2). Support the exhaust system.

9. Remove the rubber exhaust pipe hangers in order to allow the exhaust system to drop slightly.

10. Remove the fuel tank shield retainers (3).

11. Remove the fuel tank shield (2).

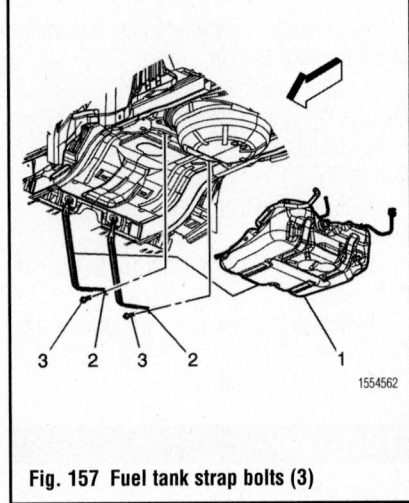

Fig. 157 Fuel tank strap bolts (3)

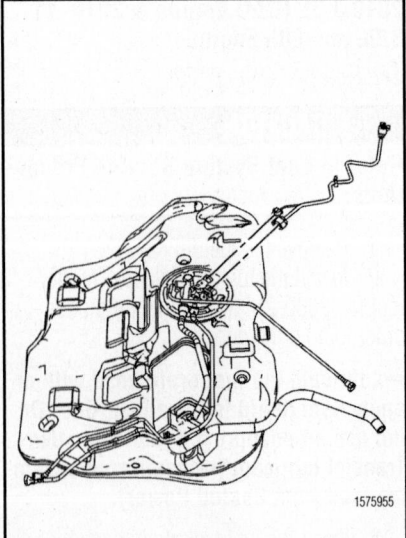

Fig. 158 Fuel pressure sensor and fuel sender jumper harness electrical connectors, 3.5L engine only

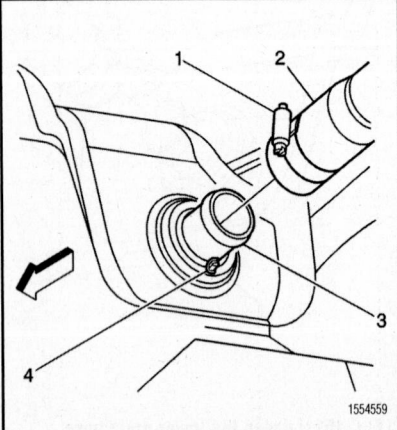

Fig. 153 Fuel fill hose clamp (1), hose (2), tank (3), and orientation feature for installation (4)

❋❋ WARNING

Do not bend the fuel tank straps. Bending the fuel tank straps may damage the straps.

12. Support the fuel tank with a suitable adjustable jack.

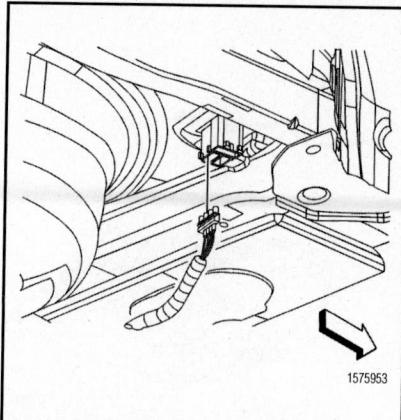

Fig. 159 Fuel sender jumper harness electrical connector, 3.9L engine only

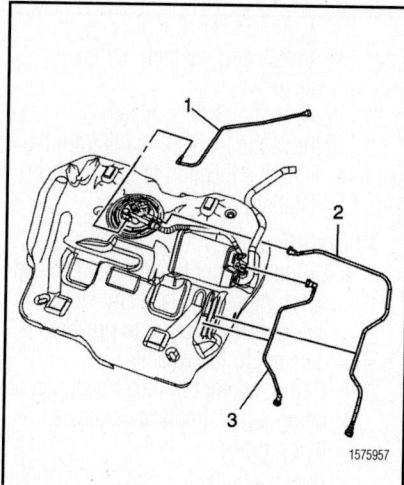

Fig. 160 Fuel feed line (2), and EVAP lines (1, 3)

13. Remove the fuel tank strap bolts (3).
14. Using the jack, lower the fuel tank.
15. For NC7 only: Disconnect the fuel sender jumper harness electrical connector.
16. For NU6 only: Disconnect the fuel tank wiring harness electrical connector from the underbody connector.
17. Remove the fuel tank and place the tank in a suitable work area.
18. For the 3.5L engine only: Disconnect and remove the fuel pressure sensor.
19. Disconnect and remove the fuel sender jumper harness electrical connector(s).

➡**Note the routing of the lines for installation.**

20. Disconnect and remove the fuel feed line (2), and the EVAP lines (1, 3).
21. Remove the EVAP canister.
22. Remove the insulator pads from the fuel tank. Note the location of the insulator pads for installation.

To install:

23. Install the insulator pads to the fuel tank.
24. Install the EVAP canister.
• Do not attempt to straighten kinked nylon pipes. Replace any kinked nylon pipes in order to prevent damage to the vehicle.
• Do not attempt to repair sections of nylon pipes. Replace damaged nylon pipes.
• Replace the vapor pipes with original equipment or parts that meet GM specifications.
• Replace the vapor hoses with original equipment or parts meeting GM specifications. Use only reinforced fuel-resistant hose identified with the word Fluoroelastomer or GM 6163M on the hose.
25. Install and connect the fuel feed line and the EVAP lines.
26. Install and connect the fuel pressure sensor (3.5L engine only) and the fuel sender jumper harness electrical connectors.
27. Install the fuel tank onto a suitable jack.
28. Partially raise the fuel tank until the electrical connection can be made.
29. Connect the fuel sender jumper harness electrical connector.
30. Completely raise the tank.
31. Install the fuel tank strap bolts. Tighten the bolts to 35 ft. lbs. (48 Nm).
32. Remove the jack from the fuel tank.
33. Position the fuel tank shield to the fuel tank.
34. Install the shield retainers.
35. Install the rubber exhaust pipe hangers.
36. Remove the support from the exhaust system.
37. Connect the fuel feed and EVAP lines to the fuel tank lines.
38. Connect the EVAP vent solenoid hose on the tank to the EVAP vent valve solenoid hose.
39. Connect the EVAP vent pipe quick connect fitting to the fill pipe EVAP vent pipe quick connect fitting.
40. Install the fuel tank fill hose onto the fuel tank. Install the hose over the orientation feature (4; see first illustration in Removal procedure) on the tank, until fully seated to the tank.
41. Tighten the fuel fill hose clamp (1) at the fuel tank. Tighten the clamp to 22 inch lbs. (2.5 Nm).
42. Lower the vehicle.
43. Add fuel and install the fuel fill cap.
44. Connect the negative battery cable. Refer to Battery Negative Cable Disconnection and Connection.

45. Inspect the fuel system for leaks by performing the following steps:
a. Turn ON the ignition for 2 seconds.
b. Turn OFF the ignition for 10 seconds.
c. Turn ON the ignition.
d. Inspect for fuel leaks.
46. Install the intake manifold cover.

2010 NU6

See Figures 161 through 167.

➡**Clean the fuel and evaporative emission (EVAP) connections and surrounding areas prior to disconnecting the lines in order to avoid possible system contamination.**

1. Relieve the fuel system fuel pressure. Refer to Fuel Pressure Relief.
2. Drain the fuel tank. Refer to Fuel Tank Draining.
3. Raise and support the vehicle.
4. Loosen the fuel fill hose clamp (1) at the fuel tank.
5. Remove the fuel tank fill hose (2) from the fuel tank (3).

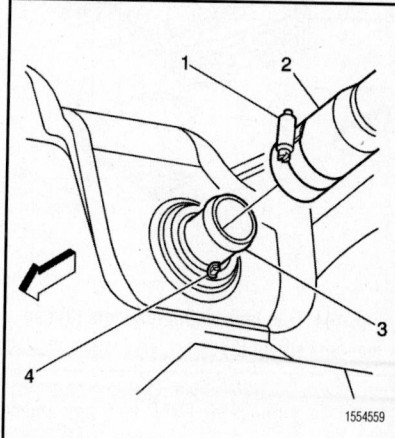

Fig. 161 Fuel fill hose clamp (1), hose (2), tank (3), and orientation feature for installation (4)

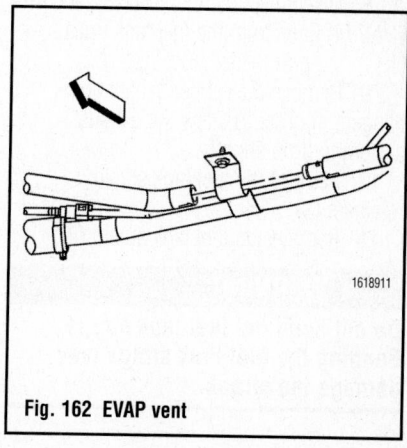

Fig. 162 EVAP vent

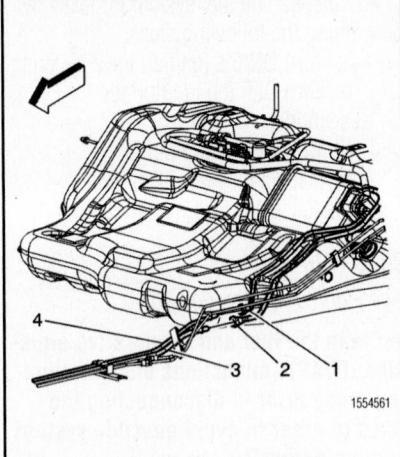

Fig. 163 Fuel feed (3), EVAP lines (4), and fuel tank lines (1, 2)

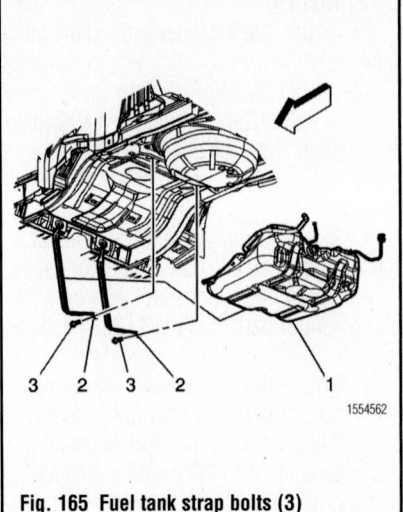

Fig. 165 Fuel tank strap bolts (3)

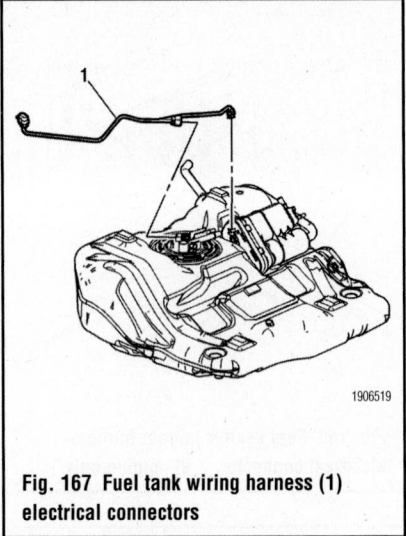

Fig. 167 Fuel tank wiring harness (1) electrical connectors

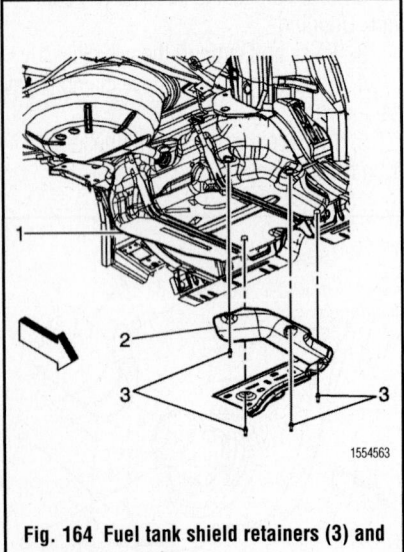

Fig. 164 Fuel tank shield retainers (3) and fuel tank shield (2)

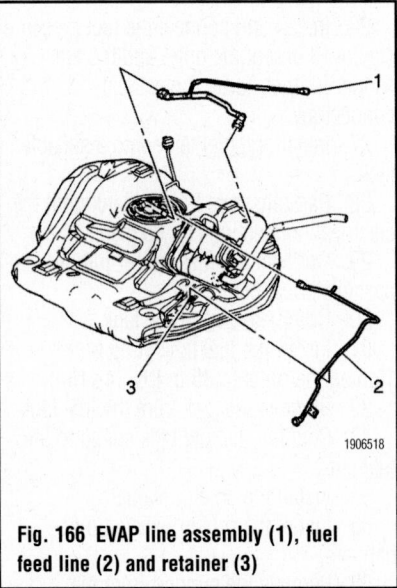

Fig. 166 EVAP line assembly (1), fuel feed line (2) and retainer (3)

6. Disconnect the EVAP vent pipe quick connect fitting from the fill pipe EVAP vent pipe quick connect fitting.

7. Disconnect the EVAP vent solenoid hose on the tank from the vent valve solenoid hose.

8. Disconnect the fuel feed (3), and the EVAP (4) lines from the fuel tank lines (1, 2). Support the exhaust system.

9. Remove the rubber exhaust pipe hangers in order to allow the exhaust system to drop slightly.

10. Remove the fuel tank shield retainers (3).

11. Remove the fuel tank shield (2).

✸✸ WARNING

Do not bend the fuel tank straps. Bending the fuel tank straps may damage the straps.

12. Support the fuel tank with a suitable adjustable jack.

13. Remove the fuel tank strap bolts (3).

14. Using the jack, lower the fuel tank.

15. Disconnect the fuel tank wiring harness electrical connector from the underbody connector.

➥Note the routing of the lines for installation.

16. Disconnect the EVAP line (1) quick connect fittings from the fuel tank module and the EVAP canister.

17. Remove the EVAP line assembly (1).

18. Disconnect the fuel feed line (2) from the fuel tank module.

19. Disengage the fuel feed line from the retaining feature (3) built into the fuel tank and remove the fuel line (2).

20. Disconnect the fuel tank wiring harness (1) electrical connectors from the fuel tank module and the fuel pressure sensor.

21. Remove the EVAP canister.

22. Remove the insulator pads from the fuel tank. Note the location of the insulator pads for installation.

To install:

- Do not attempt to straighten kinked nylon pipes. Replace any kinked nylon pipes in order to prevent damage to the vehicle.
- Do not attempt to repair sections of nylon pipes. Replace damaged nylon pipes.
- Replace the vapor pipes with original equipment or parts that meet GM specifications.
- Replace the vapor hoses with original equipment or parts meeting GM specifications. Use only reinforced fuel-resistant hose identified with the word Fluoroelastomer or GM 6163M on the hose.

23. Install and connect the fuel feed line and the EVAP lines.

24. Install and connect the fuel pressure sensor (3.5L engine only) and the fuel sender jumper harness electrical connectors.

25. Install the insulator pads to the fuel tank.

26. Install the EVAP canister.

27. Connect the fuel tank wiring harness electrical connectors to the fuel tank module and the fuel pressure sensor.

28. Install and connect the fuel feed line to the fuel tank module.

29. Engage the fuel feed line to the retaining feature built into the fuel tank.

30. Install and connect the EVAP line quick connect fittings to the fuel tank module and the EVAP canister.

31. Install the fuel tank onto a suitable jack.

32. Partially raise the fuel tank until the electrical connection can be made.

33. Connect the fuel tank wiring harness electrical connector to the underbody connector.

34. Completely raise the tank.

35. Install the fuel tank strap bolts. Tighten the bolts to 35 ft. lbs. (48 Nm).

36. Remove the jack from the fuel tank.

37. Position the fuel tank shield to the fuel tank.

38. Install the shield retainers.

39. Install the rubber exhaust pipe hangers.

40. Remove the support from the exhaust system.

41. Connect the fuel feed and EVAP lines to the fuel tank lines.

42. Connect the EVAP vent solenoid hose on the tank to the EVAP vent valve solenoid hose.

43. Connect the EVAP vent pipe quick connect fitting to the fill pipe EVAP vent pipe quick connect fitting.

44. Install the fuel tank fill hose onto the fuel tank. Install the hose over the orientation feature (4; see first illustration in Removal procedure) on the tank, until fully seated to the tank.

45. Tighten the fuel fill hose clamp (1) at the fuel tank. Tighten the clamp to 22 inch lbs. (2.5 Nm).

46. Lower the vehicle.

47. Add fuel and install the fuel fill cap.

48. Connect the negative battery cable. Refer to Battery Negative Cable Disconnection and Connection.

49. Inspect the fuel system for leaks by performing the following steps:

  a. Turn ON the ignition for 2 seconds.

  b. Turn OFF the ignition for 10 seconds.

  c. Turn ON the ignition.

  d. Inspect for fuel leaks.

50. Install the intake manifold cover.

IDLE SPEED

THROTTLE/IDLE LEARN

The engine control module (ECM) learns the airflow through the throttle body to ensure the correct idle. The learned airflow values are stored within the ECM. These values are learned to adjust for production variation and will continuously learn during the life of the vehicle to compensate for reduced airflow due to throttle body coking. Anytime the throttle body airflow rate changes, for example due to cleaning or replacing, the values must be relearned.

An engine that had a heavily coked throttle body that has been cleaned or replaced may take several drive cycles to learn out the coking. To accelerate the process, the scan tool has the ability to reset all learned values back to zero. A new ECM will also have values set to zero.

The idle may be unstable or a DTC may set if the learned values do not match the actual airflow.

THROTTLE BODY

REMOVAL & INSTALLATION

See Figures 168 through 170.

✳✳ WARNING

Handle the electronic throttle control components carefully. Use cleanliness in order to prevent damage. Do not drop the electronic throttle control components. Do not roughly handle the electronic throttle control components. Do not immerse the electronic throttle control components in cleaning solvents of any type.

➡**DO NOT for any reason, insert a screwdriver or other small hand tool into the throttle body to hold open the throttle plate as a wedge, as the inside of the throttle body could be damaged.**

➡**An 8-digit part identification number is stamped on the throttle body casting. Refer to this number, if servicing or part replacement is required.**

1. Remove the intake manifold cover.
2. Remove the air cleaner outlet duct.
3. Disconnect the electronic throttle control (ETC) electrical connector (2).

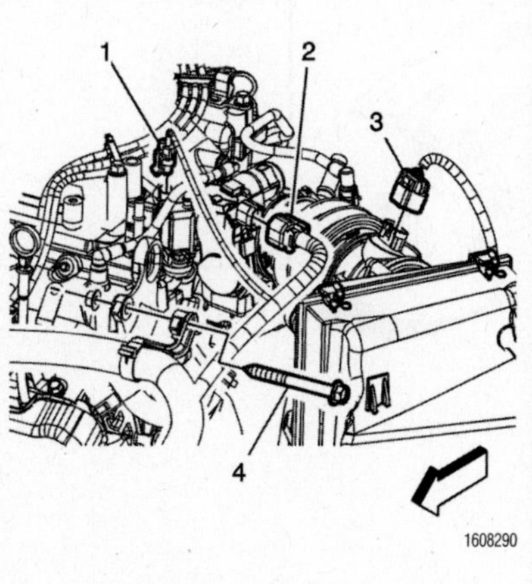

Fig. 168 Electronic throttle control (ETC) electrical connector (2)

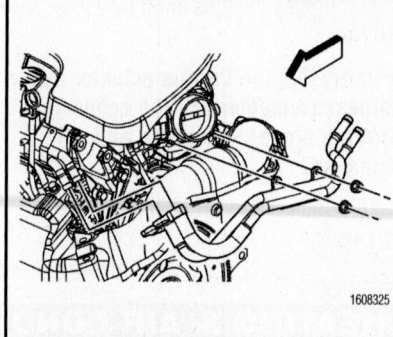

Fig. 169 Remove the heater inlet and outlet pipe clip nuts from the throttle body studs

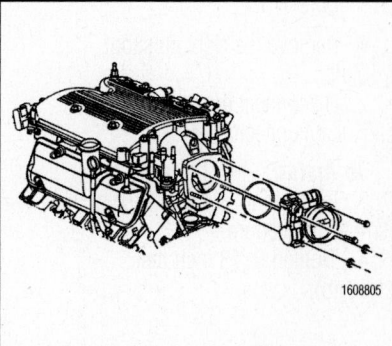

Fig. 170 Throttle body, bolts/studs, and gasket

4. Remove the heater inlet and outlet pipe clip nuts from the throttle body studs.
5. Reposition the heater inlet and outlet hose clamps at the engine pipes.
6. Reposition the heater inlet and outlet hose/pipe.
7. Remove the throttle body bolts/studs.
8. Remove the throttle body.
9. Remove and discard the throttle body gasket.

To install:

➡**DO NOT reuse the throttle body gasket. Install a NEW gasket during assembly.**

10. Install a NEW throttle body gasket. Align the locating tab of the gasket with the notch in the manifold.
11. Position the throttle body to the intake manifold.
12. Install the throttle body bolts.
13. Tighten the bolts to 89 inch lbs. (10 Nm).
14. Position the heater inlet and outlet hose/pipe.
15. Position the heater inlet and outlet hose clamps at the engine pipes.
16. Install the heater inlet and outlet pipe clip nuts to the throttle body studs.

17. Tighten the nuts to 89 inch lbs. (10 Nm).

➡**Verify that the throttle actuator motor harness connector and the connector seal are properly installed and not damaged.**

18. Connect the ETC electrical connector.

19. Install the air cleaner outlet duct.
20. Install the intake manifold cover.
21. Connect a scan tool in order to test for proper throttle opening and throttle closing ranges.
22. Operate the accelerator pedal and monitor the throttle angles. The accelerator pedal should operate freely, without bind-ing, between closed throttle, and Wide Open Throttle (WOT).

23. Verify that the vehicle meets the following conditions:
- The vehicle is not in a reduced engine power mode.
- The ignition is ON.
- The engine is OFF.

HEATING & AIR CONDITIONING SYSTEM

BLOWER MOTOR

REMOVAL & INSTALLATION

See Figure 171.

1. Remove the right closeout insulator.
2. Disconnect the blower motor electrical connector.

To install:

3. Installation is the reverse of the removal procedure.
4. Tighten to 13 inch lbs. (1.5 Nm).

HEATER CORE

REMOVAL & INSTALLATION

See Figure 172.

1. Remove the right closeout panel and then remove the left closeout panel.
2. Remove the rear floor air outlet duct.
3. Remove the seven floor air outlet cover screws (1).

➡**Remove the heat stakes that secure the HVAC module assembly upper case to the HVAC module lower case using a small chisel.**

4. Remove the floor air outlet cover (2).
5. Remove the seven heater core cover screws (3).
6. Remove the heater core cover (4).
7. Remove the heater core (5).

To install:

8. Installation is the reverse of removal.
9. Tighten heater core cover and floor air outlet cover screws to 13 inch lbs. (1.5 Nm).

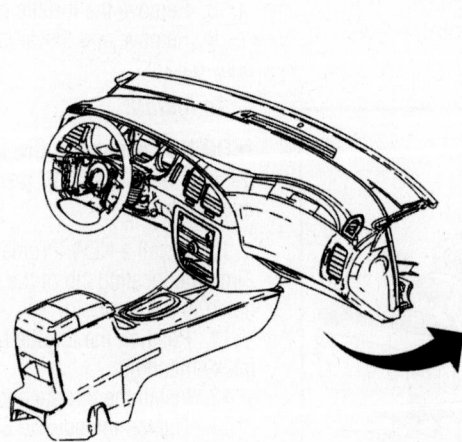
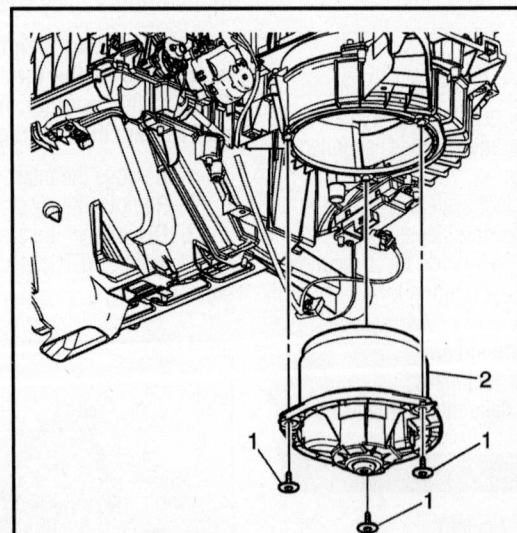

1614119

Fig. 171 Blower motor (2) and two blower motor screws (1)

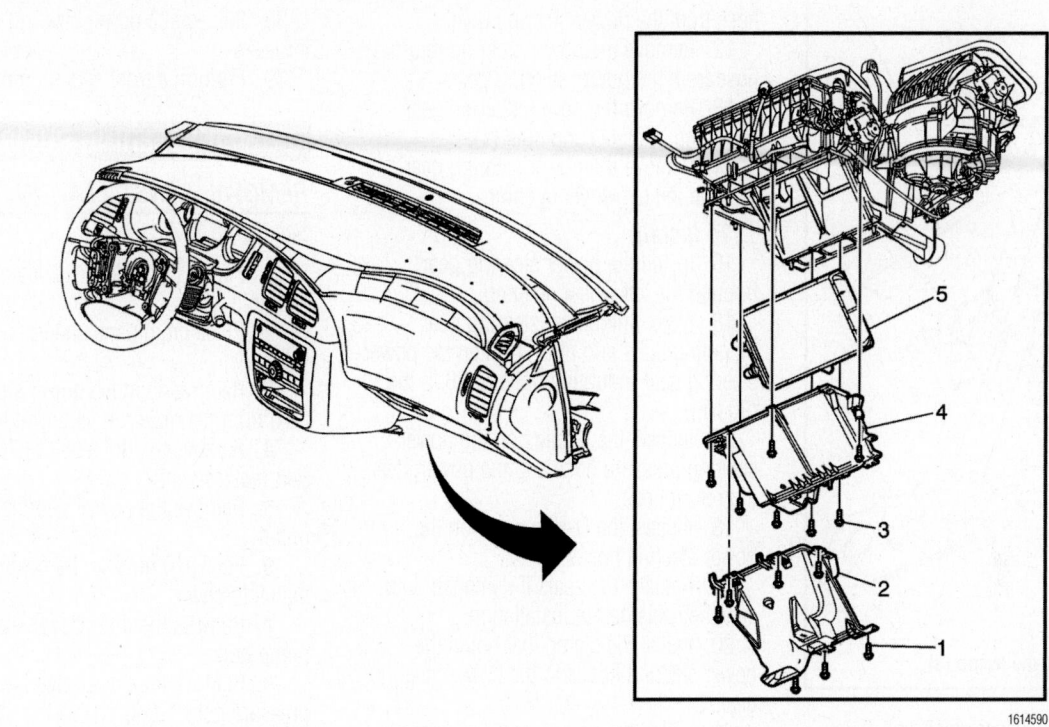

1614590

Fig. 172 Floor air outlet (1), Floor air outlet cover (2), Seven heater core cover screws (3), Heater core cover (4), and Heater core (5)

STEERING

POWER STEERING GEAR

REMOVAL & INSTALLATION

See Figures 173 through 176.

❊❊ WARNING

With the wheels of the vehicle facing straight ahead, secure the steering wheel utilizing steering column anti-rotation pin, steering column lock, or a strap to prevent rotation. Locking the steering column will prevent damage and a possible malfunction of the SIR system. Secure the steering wheel in position before disconnecting the following components:

- The steering column
- The intermediate shaft(s)
- The steering gear

After disconnecting these components, do not rotate the steering wheel or move the front tires and wheels. Failure to follow this procedure may cause the SIR coil assembly to become un-centered and cause possible damage to the SIR coil. If you think the SIR coil

has became un-centered, refer to your specific SIR coil's centering procedure to re-center SIR Coil.

1. Insert a steering column anti-rotation pin, such as GM's J-42640 pin, into the steering column access hole in order to lock the steering column.
2. Raise and support the vehicle.
3. Place a drain pan under the vehicle.
4. Remove the tire and wheel assemblies.

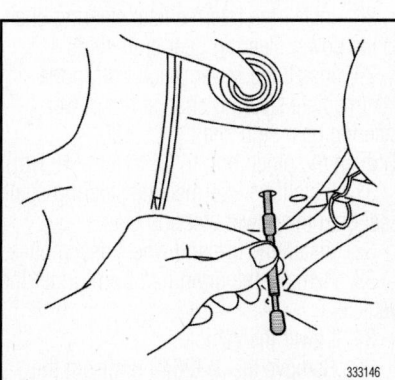

333146

Fig. 173 Insert a steering column anti-rotation pin, such as GM's J-42640 pin, into the steering column access hole in order to lock the steering column

❊❊ CAUTION

Failure to disconnect the intermediate shaft from the rack and pinion steering gear stub shaft can result in damage to the steering gear and/or intermediate shaft. This damage may cause loss of steering control which could result in an accident and possible personal injury.

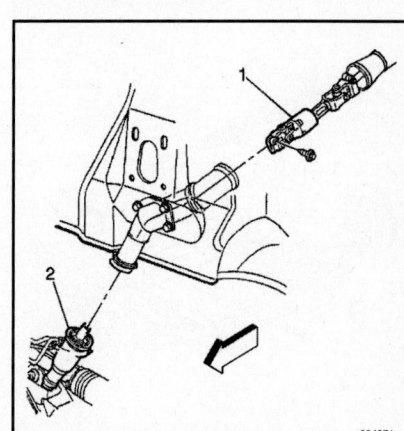

294371

Fig. 174 Remove the lower pinch bolt from the power steering gear stub shaft (2)

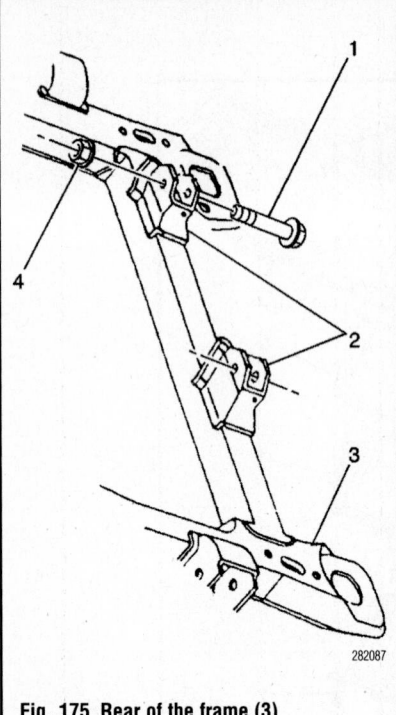

Fig. 175 Rear of the frame (3)

5. Remove the lower pinch bolt from the power steering gear stub shaft (2).

6. Remove the intermediate steering shaft from the power steering gear stub shaft.

7. Remove both of the tie rod ends from the steering knuckles.

8. Support the rear of the frame (3) using jackstands.

9. Remove the frame bolts from the rear of the frame.

✳✳ WARNING

Do not lower the rear of the frame too far as damage to the engine components nearest to the cowl may result.

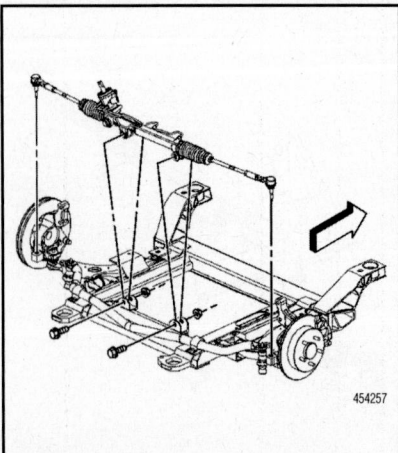

Fig. 176 Power steering gear mounting bolts (1) and nuts (4)

10. Lower the rear of the frame (3).

11. Remove the power steering pressure hose from the power steering gear.

12. Remove the power steering return hose from the power steering gear.

13. Remove the power steering gear mounting bolts (1) and nuts (4).

14. Remove the power steering gear through the left wheel opening.

To install:

15. Install the power steering gear through the left wheel opening.

16. Install the power steering gear mounting bolts and nuts. Tighten the power steering gear mounting bolts to 66 ft. lbs. (90 Nm).

17. Inspect the threads on the power steering pressure hose and the power steering return hose.

18. Inspect the O-ring seals on the power steering hoses.

19. Replace the seals if damaged, lubricate the seals before installation.

20. Install the clamp that holds the power steering hoses to the power steering gear.

21. Install the power steering pressure hose to the power steering gear.

22. Install the power steering return hose to the power steering gear.

23. Raise the frame into position.

24. Install the rear frame bolts.

25. Remove the jackstands.

26. Install the tie rod ends to the steering knuckles.

27. Raise and support the vehicle.

➥**During the installation of the intermediate steering shaft, ensure the steering shaft is seated before you install the pinch bolt. The two mating shafts may disengage if the pinch bolt is inserted into the coupling before the steering shaft installation.**

28. Install the intermediate steering shaft to the power steering gear stub shaft.

29. Install the lower pinch bolt to the intermediate steering shaft at the power steering gear stub shaft.   30. Tighten the pinch bolt to 35 ft. lbs. (48 Nm).

31. Install the intermediate steering shaft seal onto the power steering gear.

32. Install the tire and wheel assemblies.

33. Remove the drain pan from under the vehicle.

34. Lower the vehicle.

35. Remove the J-42640 pin from the steering column.

36. Fill the power steering system with power steering fluid. Refer to Power Steering Fluid Fill Procedure.

37. Bleed the power steering system. Refer to Power Steering System Bleeding.

38. Inspect the power steering system for leaks.

39. Perform a front end alignment.

POWER STEERING PUMP

REMOVAL & INSTALLATION

See Figure 177.

1. For 2011 models: Remove the intake manifold cover.

2. Place drain pans under the vehicle.

3. Remove as much power steering fluid from the reservoir as possible.

4. Remove the drive belt. Refer to Drive Belt replacement.

5. Remove the power steering pump pulley.

6. For 2010 models: Remove the intake manifold cover.

7. Remove the three power steering pump bolts.

8. Remove the power steering high-pressure hose fitting.

9. Remove the power steering return hose clamp (at pump).

Tip: Position the clamp rearward to remove the hose from the pump.

10. Remove the power steering pump.

To install:

11. Installation is the reverse of removal.

12. Tighten the three power steering pump bolts to 18 ft. lbs. (25 Nm).

13. Tighten the high-pressure hose fitting to 24 ft. lbs. (32 Nm).

BLEEDING

➥**Note the following:**

- Use clean, new power steering fluid only.
- Hoses touching the frame, body or engine may cause system noise. Verify that the hoses do not touch any other part of the vehicle.
- Loose connections may not leak, but could allow air into the steering system. Verify that all hose connections are tight.

➥**Maintain the power steering fluid level throughout the bleed procedure.**

1. Fill the pump reservoir with fluid to the minimum system level, FULL COLD level, or middle of hash mark on cap stick fluid level indicator.

➥**With hydro-boost only, the oil level will appear falsely high if the hydro-**

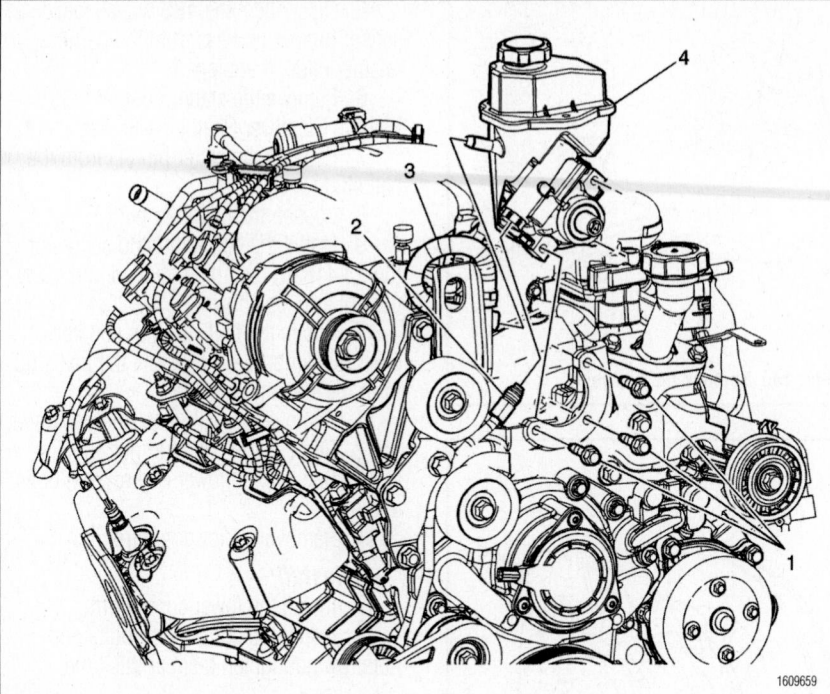

Fig. 177 Three power steering pump bolts (1), high-pressure hose fitting (2), return hose clamp (at pump; 3), and pump

8. Verify the fluid level.

9. Repeat the bleed procedure, if necessary.

FLUID FILL PROCEDURE

☀☀ WARNING

When adding fluid or making a complete fluid change, always use the proper power steering fluid. Failure to use the proper fluid will cause hose and seal damage and fluid leaks.

1. Clean the area surrounding the reservoir cap.

2. Remove the reservoir cap.

3. Inspect the power steering pump fluid level at regular intervals. Use the appropriate procedure below. Add fluid when required. Refer to Fluid recommendations.

4. Fluid Is Hot:
   • Run the engine until the fluid reaches about 170°F (80°C).
   • Turn the engine OFF.
   • Remove the reservoir cap.
   • Inspect the fluid level on the cap-stick.
   • Ensure that the fluid level is at the HOT/FULL/MAX mark on the cap-stick.

5. If the fluid level is low, add power steering fluid to the proper level.

6. Install the reservoir cap.

7. When checking the fluid level after servicing the steering system, bleed the air from the system. Refer to Power Steering System Bleeding.

boost accumulator is not fully charged. **Do not apply the brake pedal with the engine OFF. This will discharge the hydro-boost accumulator.**

2. If equipped with hydro-boost, fully charge the hydro-boost accumulator using the following procedure:
   a. Start the engine.
   b. Firmly apply the brake pedal 10-15 times.
   c. Turn the engine OFF.

3. Raise the vehicle until the front wheels are off the ground.

4. Key on engine OFF, turn the steering wheel from stop to stop 12 times.

5. Vehicles equipped with hydro-boost systems or with longer length power steering hoses may require turns up to 15 to 20 stop to stops.

6. Verify the power steering fluid level per operating specification. Refer to Fluid Fill Procedure.

7. Start the engine. Rotate the steering wheel from left to right. Check for signs of cavitation or fluid aeration (pump noise/whining).

SUSPENSION

FRONT SUSPENSION

LOWER CONTROL ARM BALL JOINT

REMOVAL & INSTALLATION

See Figures 178 through 180.

1. Raise and support the vehicle.

2. Remove the tires and wheels.

3. Remove the lower control arm. Refer to Lower Control Arm replacement.

4. Secure the lower control arm in a suitable vise.

5. Using the appropriate size drill, drill out the rivet heads from the lower control arm.

6. Using a hammer and a drift punch, remove the remaining rivets from the control arm.

7. Remove the ball joint from the lower control arm.

To install:

8. Position the new ball joint in the lower control arm.

➡**Install the NEW ball joint bolts facing downward.**

9. Install the NEW ball joint bolts.

10. Install the NEW ball joint retaining nuts.

11. Tighten the ball joint nuts to 50 ft. lbs. (68 Nm).

12. Install the lower control arm. Refer to Lower Control Arm replacement.

13. Install the tires and wheels.

14. Remove the support and lower the vehicle.

LOWER CONTROL ARM

REMOVAL & INSTALLATION

See Figures 181 through 184.

☀☀ WARNING

Use only the recommended tools for separating the ball joint from the knuckle. Do NOT hammer or pry the ball joint from the knuckle. Failure to use the recommended tools may cause damage to the ball joint and seal.

➡**Use the ignition key in order to unlock the steering column.**

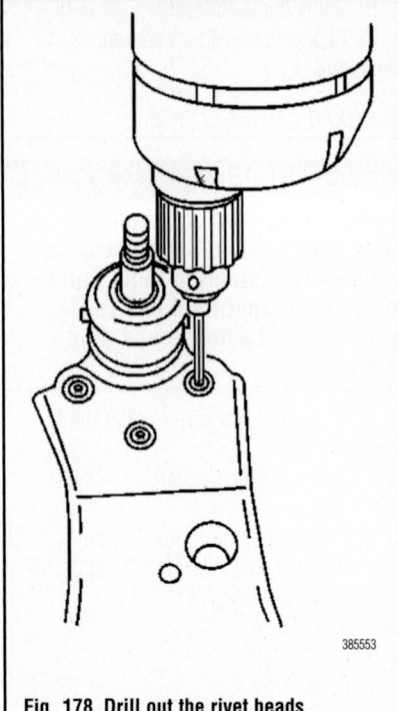

Fig. 178 Drill out the rivet heads

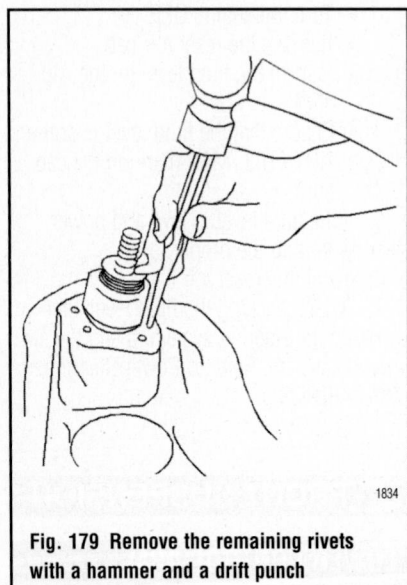

Fig. 179 Remove the remaining rivets with a hammer and a drift punch

1. Turn the steering wheel in order to move the front of the applicable wheel to the outboard most position.

➡ **Use ONLY a frame-contact type vehicle lift or a floor jack at the recommended lift points. Do NOT use a suspension-contact type vehicle lift. Do NOT lift the vehicle by the lower control arms.**

2. Raise and support the vehicle.
3. Remove the tire and wheel.
4. Disconnect the ABS wheel speed sensor connector (2), if equipped.

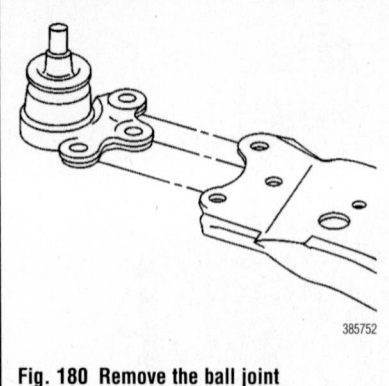

Fig. 180 Remove the ball joint

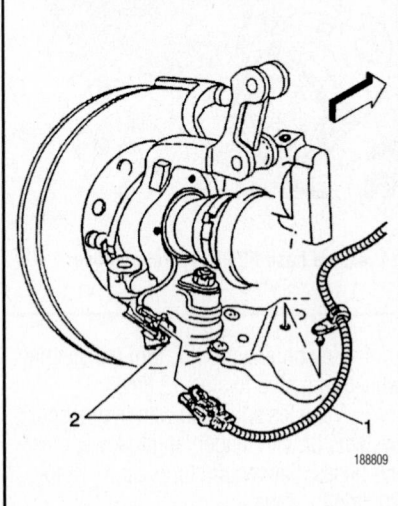

Fig. 181 Disconnect the ABS wheel speed sensor connector (2), if equipped

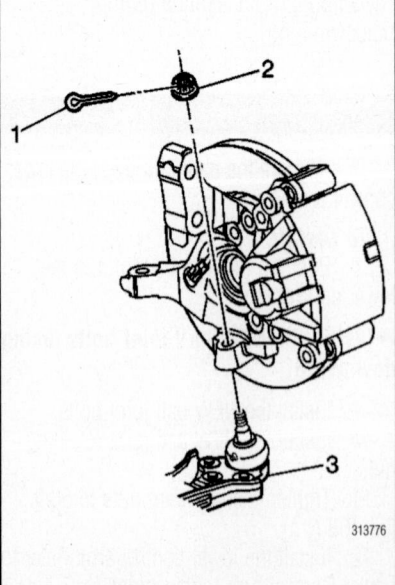

Fig. 182 Cotter pin (1), ball stud (3), and ball stud nut (2)

5. Disconnect the ABS wheel speed sensor jumper harness from the harness retainer clips, if equipped.
6. Remove the stabilizer shaft link. Refer to Stabilizer Shaft Link Replacement.
7. Remove the cotter pin (1) from the ball stud (3).
8. Loosen the ball stud nut (2).
9. Install the ball joint/stud separator tool (J 41820) over the ball stud and lower control arm, as shown.
10. Rotate the ball stud nut counterclockwise in order to separate the ball stud from the steering knuckle.
11. Remove the ball joint/stud separator.
12. Remove the ball stud nut.
13. Remove the lower control arm bolts and nuts.
14. Remove the lower control arm.

To install:
15. Install the lower control arm.
16. Install the control arm bolts and nuts. Do not tighten them at this time.

➡ **Align the ball stud cotter pin hole parallel to the knuckle in order to ease the cotter pin installation.**

17. Install the ball stud to the knuckle.

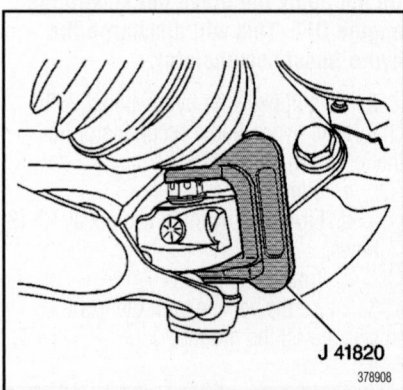

Fig. 183 Install the ball joint/stud separator tool (J 41820) over the ball stud and lower control arm

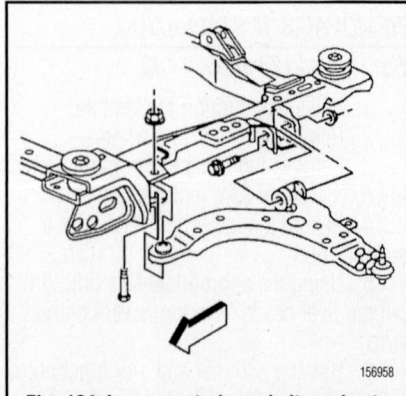

Fig. 184 Lower control arm bolts and nuts

➡**Verify the nut is torqued to a minimum of 41 ft. lbs. (55 Nm).**

18. Install the ball stud castle nut.

19. Tighten the ball stud castle nut to 15 lb ft + 120 degrees (20 Nm + 120 degrees).

➡**Do NOT loosen the ball stud nut in order to align the ball stud nut slots to the ball stud cotter pin hole.**

If necessary, tighten the ball stud castle nut in order to align the ball stud castle nut slot (1) to the ball stud cotter pin hole (2), as shown.

➡**Ensure that the cotter pin ends do NOT contact the ABS wheel speed sensor, the ABS sensor connector, or the drive axle.**

20. Install a NEW cotter pin and bend the ends as shown in either example.

21. Install the stabilizer shaft link. Refer to Stabilizer Shaft Link replacement.

22. Install the ABS wheel speed sensor jumper harness to the harness retainer clips, if equipped.

➡**This is a prevailing torque type fastener. This fastener may be reused ONLY if:**

- The fastener and its counterpart are clean and free from rust.
- The fastener develops 27 inch lbs. (3 Nm) of torque against its counterpart prior to the fastener seating.

If the fastener does not meet these criteria, REPLACE the fastener.

23. Install the lower control arm nuts.

24. Tighten the lower control arm nuts to 92 ft. lbs. (125 Nm).

25. Install the tire and wheel.

26. Lower the vehicle.

FRONT LOWER CONTROL ARM BUSHING REPLACEMENT

Horizontal

See Figure 185.

1. Remove the lower control arm. Refer to Lower Control Arm replacement.

2. Secure the lower control arm in a vise.

➡**Use a 1/2 x 20 in standard thread nut with the puller bolt.**

3. Assemble the bushing removal tools as indicated: The nut (1), the J 21474-01 washer (2), the J 21474-01 bearing (3), the J 21474-5 (4), and the J 21474-01 puller bolt (5).

4. Tighten the puller bolt (5) until the bushing is removed.

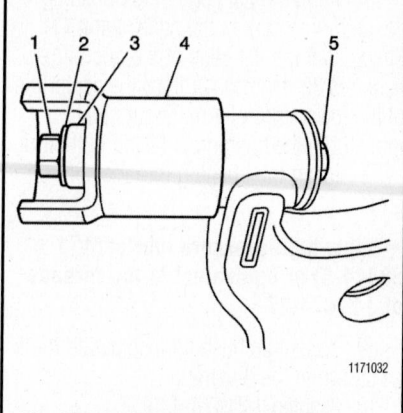

Fig. 185 Bushing removal tools: The nut (1), the J 21474-01 washer (2), the J 21474-01 bearing (3), the J 21474-5 (4), and the J 21474-01 puller bolt (5)

5. Disassemble the J 21474-01 and J 21474-5.

To install:

6. Lubricate the bushing with liquid hand soap or equivalent.

➡**Use a 1/2 x 20 in standard thread nut with the puller bolt.**

7. Assemble the following bushing installation tools: The nut (1), the J 21474-01 washer (2), the J 21474-01 bearing (3), the J 21474-5 (4), and the J 21474-01 puller bolt (5).

8. Tighten the puller bolt (5) until the bushing is installed into the control arm.

9. Disassemble the J 21474-01 and J 21474-5.

10. Remove the control arm from the vise.

11. Install the lower control arm. Refer to Lower Control Arm replacement.

Vertical

See Figures 186 through 190.

1. Remove the lower control arm. Refer to Lower Control Arm replacement.

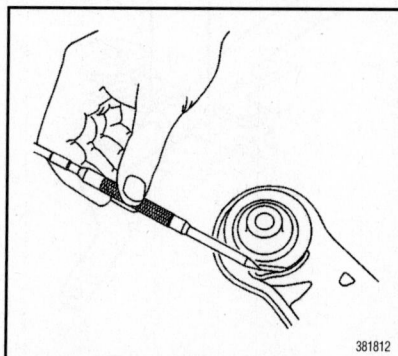

Fig. 186 Mark the lower control arm along the flat edge of the bushing flange

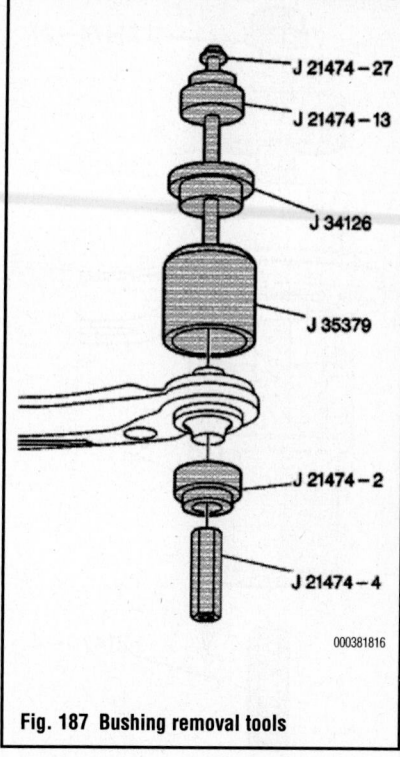

Fig. 187 Bushing removal tools

2. Secure the lower control arm in a vise.

3. Mark the lower control arm along the flat edge of the bushing flange.

➡**Apply high-pressure lubricant (J 23444-A) or equivalent to the threads of J 21474-27.**

4. Assemble bushing removal tools as shown in the illustration.

5. Tighten J 21474-4.

6. Disassemble the bushing removal tools.

To install:

➡**You MUST install the lower control arm vertical bushing in the same position in order to maintain the original vehicle ride, handling, and road feel.**

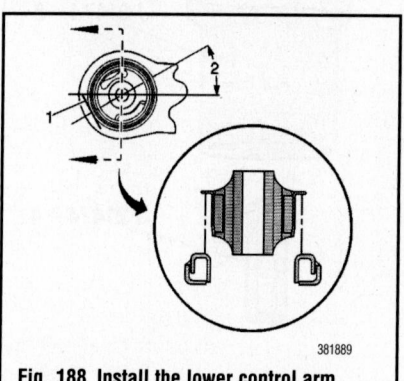

Fig. 188 Install the lower control arm vertical bushing in the same position

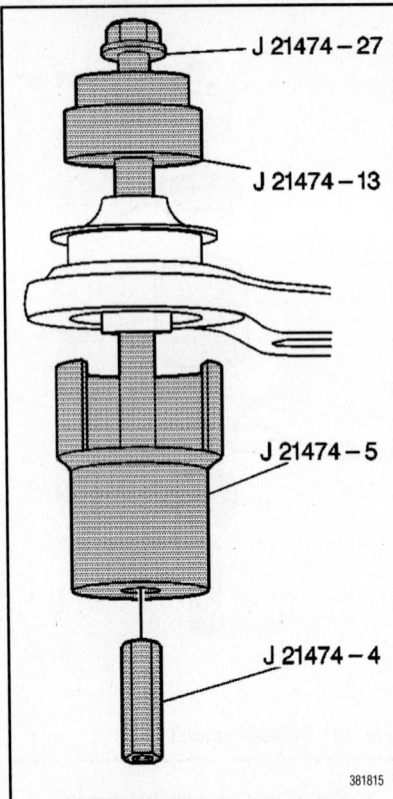

Fig. 189 Apply high-pressure lubricant (J 23444-A) or equivalent to the threads of J 21474-27

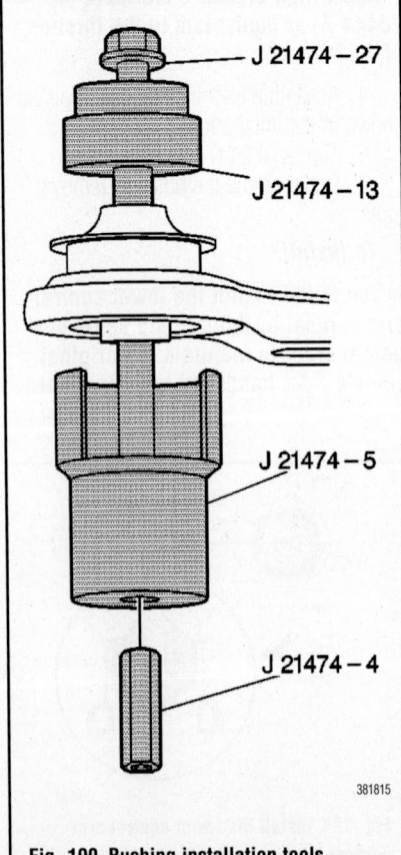

Fig. 190 Bushing installation tools

7. Align the flat edge of the bushing flange to the mark in the control arm (1). Ensure that the flat edge of the bushing flange is 30 degrees (2) from the centerline of the lower control arm. Ensure that the thin slot in the bushing is facing outboard.

8. Insert the bushing into the control arm.

➡ **Apply high-pressure lubricant (J 23444-A) or equivalent to the threads of J 21474-27.**

9. Assemble bushing installation tools as shown in the illustration.

10. Tighten J 21474-4.

11. Disassemble the bushing installation tools.

12. Install the lower control arm. Refer to Lower Control Arm Replacement.

STABILIZER SHAFT

REMOVAL & INSTALLATION

See Figures 191 through 193.

✳ CAUTION

Failure to disconnect intermediate shaft from rack and pinion stub shaft can result in damage to steering gear and/or intermediate shaft. This damage can cause loss of steering con-

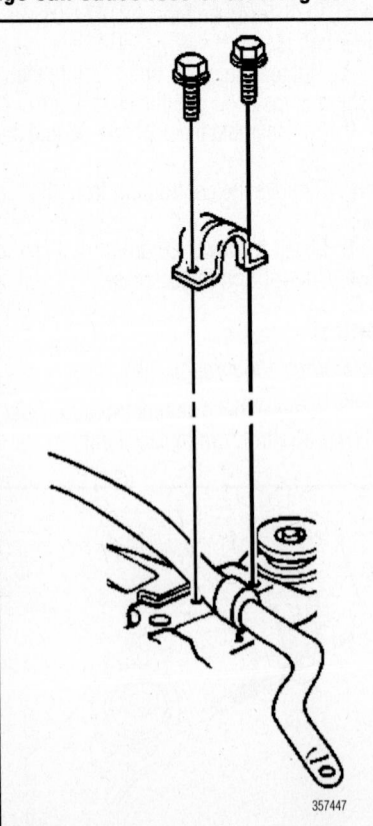

Fig. 191 Insulator clamp bolts and the clamps from the frame

Fig. 192 Remove the insulators from the stabilizer bar

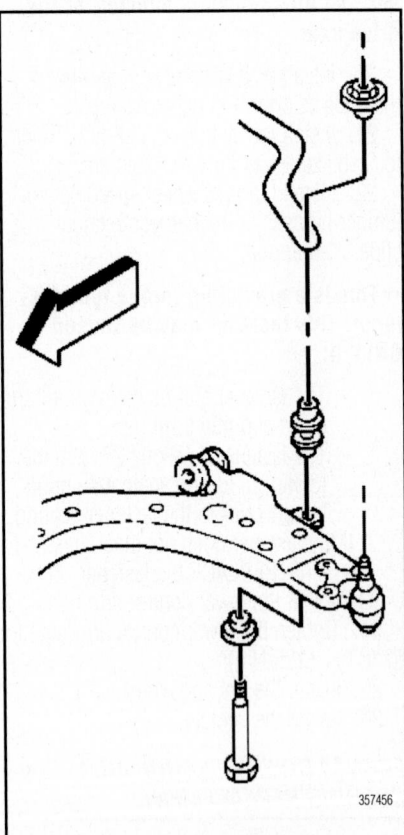

Fig. 193 Remove the stabilizer bar links from the control arms

trol which could result in personal injury.

1. Raise and suitably support the vehicle.

2. Remove the left tire and wheel assembly.

3. Remove the pinch bolt from the lower intermediate steering shaft.

4. Loosen all insulator clamp attaching bolts.

5. Place a jackstand under the center of the rear frame crossmember.

6. Remove the rear frame-to-body bolts.

7. Lower the rear of the frame just enough to gain access to the stabilizer shaft.

8. Remove the insulator clamp bolts and the clamps from the frame.

9. Remove the insulators from the stabilizer bar.

10. Remove the stabilizer bar links from the control arms. Refer to Stabilizer Shaft Link replacement.

11. Pull the stabilizer shaft rearward.

12. Swing the stabilizer shaft down to remove the stabilizer shaft from the left side of the vehicle.

To install:

✳✳ CAUTION

When installing the intermediate shaft make sure that the shaft is seated prior to pinch bolt installation. If the pinch bolt is inserted into the coupling before shaft installation, the two mating shafts may disengage. Disengagement of the two mating shafts will cause loss of steering control which could result in personal injury.

13. Insert the stabilizer shaft to the left side of the vehicle.

➡ **DO NOT tighten the stabilizer link nut at this time. The weight of the vehicle must be supported by the control arms such that you can obtain the vehicle design trim heights before tightening the link nut.**

14. Loosely install the stabilizer shaft link at the control arm.

15. Install the insulators on to the stabilizer bar.

16. Connect the insulator clamps to the frame.

17. Tighten the stabilizer shaft bracket bolt to 31 ft. lbs. (42 Nm).

18. Raise the frame into position while you guide the steering shaft onto the gear.

19. Install the rear frame-to-body attaching bolts.

20. Tighten the frame to body attaching bolts to 118 ft. lbs. (160 Nm).

21. Remove the jackstand.

22. Install the pinch bolt and tighten.

23. Install the left tire and wheel assembly.

24. Lower the vehicle.

25. Support the weight of the vehicle by the control arms.

26. Tighten the stabilizer link nut.

27. Tighten the stabilizer shaft link nut to 17 ft. lbs. (23 Nm).

STABILIZER SHAFT LINK

REMOVAL & INSTALLATION

See Figure 194.

1. Raise the vehicle and suitably support the vehicle.

2. Remove the tire and wheel assembly.

3. Remove the stabilizer shaft link bolt and nut.

4. Remove the stabilizer shaft link from the vehicle.

To install:

5. Install the stabilizer link into the vehicle.

6. Install the stabilizer shaft link bolt and nut.

7. Tighten the stabilizer shaft link nut to 17 ft. lbs. (23 Nm).

8. Install the tire and wheel assembly.

9. Lower the vehicle.

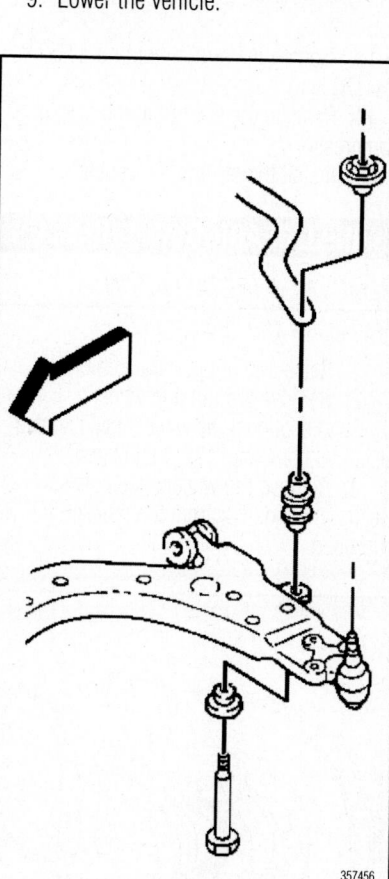

Fig. 194 Stabilizer shaft link bolt and nut

STEERING KNUCKLE

REMOVAL & INSTALLATION

See Figures 195 and 196.

1. Raise and suitably support the vehicle.

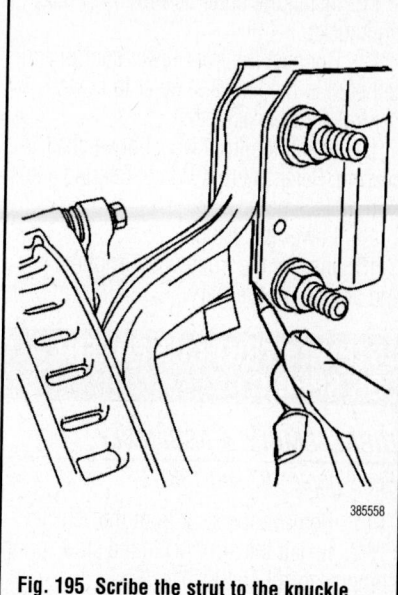

Fig. 195 Scribe the strut to the knuckle

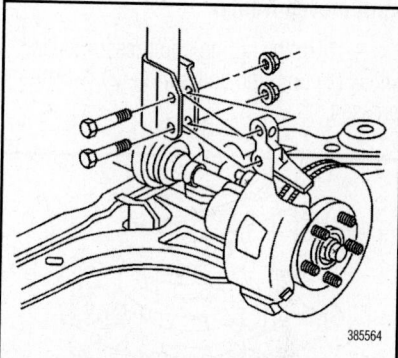

Fig. 196 The bolts and nuts attaching the strut to the knuckle.

2. Remove the bearing/hub assembly. Refer to Front Wheel Bearing and Hub replacement.

3. Remove the front lower control arm ball stud. Refer to Lower Control Arm replacement.

4. Remove the outer tie rod end from the steering knuckle.

5. If removing the knuckle to service other suspension or steering components, perform the following step:

   a. Scribe the strut to the knuckle.

6. Remove the bolts and nuts attaching the strut to the knuckle.

7. Remove the knuckle from the vehicle.

To install:

8. Install the knuckle to the vehicle.

9. Install the bolts and nuts attaching the strut to the knuckle.

10. Tighten the strut to knuckle bolts to 96 ft. lbs. (130 Nm).

11. Install the outer tie rod to the steering knuckle.

12. Connect the front lower control arm ball stud to the knuckle. Refer to Lower Control Arm replacement.

13. Install the front wheel drive shaft bearing. Refer to Front Wheel Bearing and Hub replacement.

14. Lower the vehicle.

15. Inspect the front wheel alignment and adjust, if necessary.

STRUT, STRUT COMPONENT, OR SPRING

DISASSEMBLY & ASSEMBLY

See Figures 197 and 198.

1. Remove the strut from the vehicle.

2. Install the strut (2) in the strut spring compressor (J 45400; 1).

➡**The spring is compressed when the strut moves freely.**

3. Turn the spring compressor forcing screw (1) until the coil spring (2) is compressed.

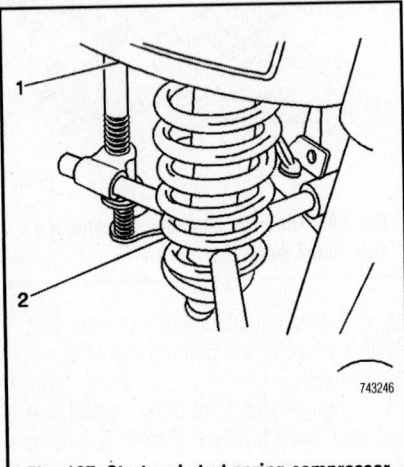

Fig. 197 Strut and strut spring compressor

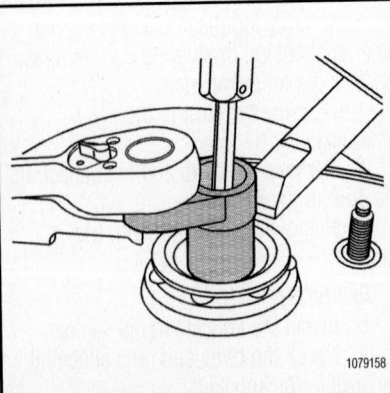

Fig. 198 Spring compressor forcing screw (1) and coil spring (2)

4. Use a 45 TORX® socket in order to hold the strut shaft. Remove the upper strut mount nut by turning with the strut rod nut socket (J 42991).

5. Remove the strut from the spring compressor.

6. Loosen the compressor forcing screw (1) until the upper strut mount and coil spring (2) may be removed.

7. Remove the upper strut mount and the coil spring from the spring compressor.

Assembly Procedure

8. Install the coil spring and upper strut mount to the spring compressor.

9. Turn the spring compressor forcing screw until the coil spring is compressed.

10. Install the strut to the coil spring and upper strut mount.

11. Install the strut retaining nut.

12. Using the strut rod nut socket and a 45 TORX® socket, install the strut mount nut.

13. Tighten the strut mount nut to 52 ft. lbs. (70 Nm).

14. Remove the strut from the spring compressor.

15. Install the strut to the vehicle.

WHEEL BEARING AND HUB

REMOVAL & INSTALLATION

See Figures 199 through 202.

1. Raise and support the vehicle.

2. Remove the tire and wheel.

3. Disconnect the wheel speed sensor electrical connector (2), if equipped.

4. Remove the wheel speed sensor electrical connector from the bracket, if equipped.

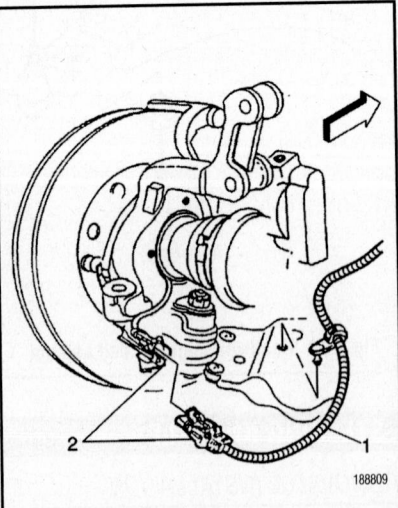

Fig. 199 Wheel speed sensor electrical connector (2)

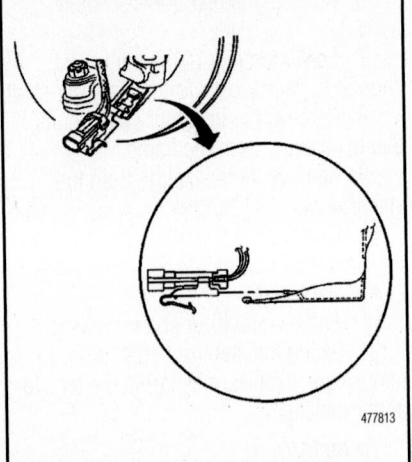

Fig. 200 Remove the wheel speed sensor electrical connector from the bracket

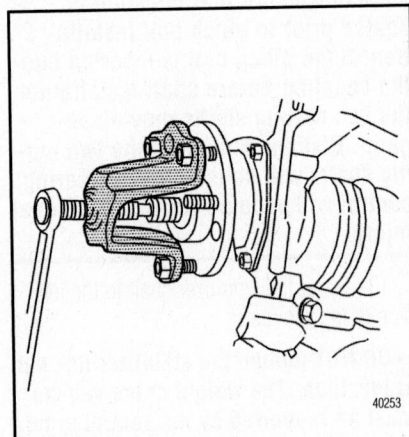

Fig. 201 Use the three wheel nuts in order to attach the wheel hub remover (J 42129) to the wheel bearing/hub

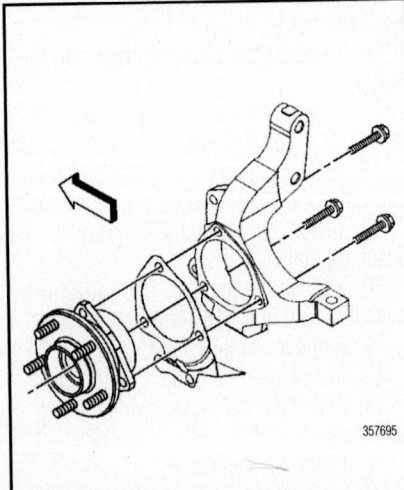

Fig. 202 Remove and DISCARD the wheel bearing/hub bolts. Remove the wheel hub remover from the hub.

5. Remove the front wheel drive shaft nut.

6. Remove the brake rotor. Refer to Front Brake Rotor Replacement.

7. Use the three wheel nuts in order to attach the wheel hub remover (J 42129) to the wheel bearing/hub.

8. Use the wheel hub remover in order to push the wheel drive shaft out of the wheel bearing/hub.

9. Remove and DISCARD the wheel bearing/hub bolts. Remove the wheel hub remover from the hub.

➡Ensure that the wheel drive shaft outer seal/boot is not damaged.

10. Remove the wheel bearing/hub and splash shield-noting the position of the shield for re-installation.

To install:

11. Install the wheel bearing/hub with the splash shield as noted during removal.

✳✳ WARNING

These fasteners MUST be replaced with new fasteners anytime they become loose or are removed.

12. Failure to replace these fasteners after they become loose or are removed may cause loss of vehicle control and personal injury.

13. Install NEW wheel bearing/hub bolts.

14. Tighten the NEW wheel bearing/hub bolts to 96 ft. lbs. (130 Nm).

15. Install the brake rotor and caliper. Refer to Front Brake Rotor Replacement.

16. Install the front wheel drive shaft nut. Refer to Wheel Drive Shaft Replacement.

➡Ensure that the connector clip engages the bracket properly.

17. Install the wheel speed sensor electrical connector to the bracket, if equipped.

18. Connect the wheel speed sensor electrical connector, if equipped.

19. Install the tire and wheel.

20. Lower the vehicle.

SUSPENSION

STABILIZER SHAFT

REMOVAL & INSTALLATION

See Figures 203 and 204.

1. Raise and suitably support the vehicle.

2. Remove the left tire and wheel assembly.

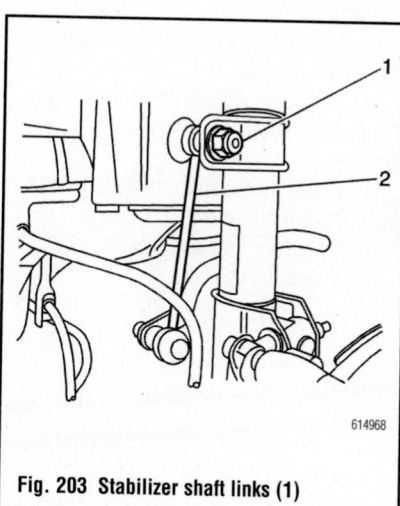

Fig. 203 Stabilizer shaft links (1)

614968

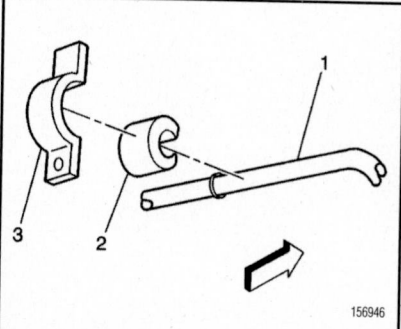

Fig. 204 Insulator brackets (3) and stabilizer shaft (1)

156946

3. Remove the left and right stabilizer shaft link nuts from the stabilizer shaft links (1).

4. Remove the insulator brackets (3) and the bolts from the stabilizer shaft (1).

5. Remove the stabilizer shaft (1) from the rear suspension support.

To install:

6. Install the stabilizer shaft (1) to the rear suspension support.

7. Install the stabilizer shaft insulator brackets (3) and hand-tighten the bolts. Do not tighten the bolts at this time.

8. Install the right and left stabilizer shaft link nuts to the stabilizer shaft links.

9. Tighten the stabilizer shaft link nuts to 38 ft. lbs. (52 Nm).

10. Tighten the stabilizer shaft insulator bracket nuts to 35 ft. lbs. (48 Nm).

11. Install the left tire and wheel assembly.

12. Lower the vehicle.

STRUT, STRUT COMPONENT, OR SPRING

DISASSEMBLY & ASSEMBLY

See Figures 197 and 198.

1. Remove the strut from the vehicle.

2. Install the strut (2) in the strut spring compressor (J 45400; 1).

➡The spring is compressed when the strut moves freely.

3. Turn the spring compressor forcing screw (1) until the coil spring (2) is compressed.

4. Use a 45 TORX® socket in order to hold the strut shaft. Remove the upper strut mount nut by turning with the strut rod nut socket (J 42991).

REAR SUSPENSION

5. Remove the strut from the spring compressor.

6. Loosen the compressor forcing screw (1) until the upper strut mount and coil spring (2) may be removed.

7. Remove the upper strut mount and the coil spring from the spring compressor.

Assembly Procedure

8. Install the coil spring and upper strut mount to the spring compressor.

9. Turn the spring compressor forcing screw until the coil spring is compressed.

10. Install the strut to the coil spring and upper strut mount.

11. Install the strut rod to mount nut.

12. Using the strut rod nut socket and a 45 TORX® socket, install the strut mount nut.

13. Tighten the strut mount nut to 55 ft. lbs. (75 Nm).

14. Remove the strut from the spring compressor.

15. Install the strut to the vehicle.

TRAILING ARM

REMOVAL & INSTALLATION

See Figure 205.

1. Raise and support the vehicle.

2. Remove the bolt (6) and nut (2) from the trailing arm (3) and the knuckle (8).

3. Remove the nut (4) and bolt (7) from the trailing arm (3) and the trailing arm bracket.

4. Remove the trailing arm (3) from the vehicle.

To install:

5. Install the trailing arm (3) to the trailing arm bracket.

6. Install the bolt (7) and nut (4) to the trailing arm (3) and the trailing arm bracket.

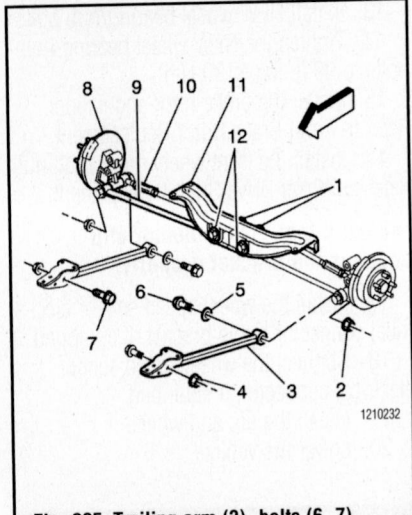

Fig. 205 Trailing arm (3), bolts (6, 7), nuts (2, 4), and knuckle (8)

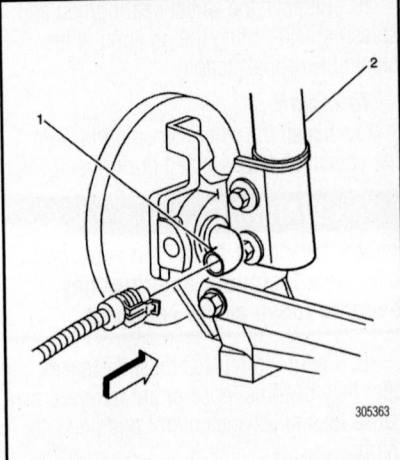

Fig. 206 Remove the ABS electrical connector from the wheel speed sensor (1), if equipped

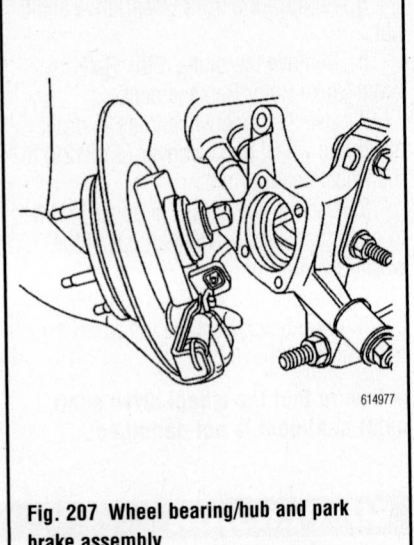

Fig. 207 Wheel bearing/hub and park brake assembly

7. Tighten the bolt and nut to 77 ft. lbs. (105 Nm).

8. Install the trailing arm (3) to the knuckle (8).

9. Install the bolt (6) and nut (2) to the trailing arm (3) and the knuckle (8).

10. Tighten the nut to 177 ft. lbs. (240 Nm).

11. Lower the vehicle.

WHEEL BEARING AND HUB

REMOVAL & INSTALLATION

See Figures 206 and 207.

➡The wheel bearing in the rear wheel hub is integrated into one unit. The hub is non-serviceable. If the hub and/or bearing is damaged, replace the complete hub and bearing assembly.

1. Raise and suitably support the vehicle.

2. Remove the tires and wheels.

3. Remove the brake rotor. Refer to Rear Brake Rotor replacement.

4. Remove the ABS electrical connector from the wheel speed sensor (1), if equipped.

5. Remove the park brake cable from the park brake actuator.

6. Remove the mounting bolts from the rear bearing/hub.

7. Remove the wheel bearing/hub and park brake assembly from the knuckle.

8. Remove the park brake actuator from the rear wheel bearing/hub.

To install:

9. Install the park brake actuator to the rear wheel bearing/hub.

10. Install the wheel bearing/hub and park brake assembly to the knuckle.

11. Install the wheel bearing/hub-to-knuckle bolts.

12. Tighten the bolts to 55 ft. lbs. (75 Nm).

13. Install the park brake cable to the park brake actuator.

14. Install the ABS electrical connector to the wheel speed sensor (1), if equipped.

15. Install the brake rotor. Refer to Rear Brake Rotor replacement.

16. Install the tires and wheels.

17. Lower the vehicle.

BUICK

LaCrosse

16

BRAKES 16-11

**ANTI-LOCK BRAKE
SYSTEM (ABS) 16-11**
General Information.................16-11
  Precautions.........................16-11
Speed Sensors 16-11
  Removal & Installation........16-11
**BLEEDING THE BRAKE
SYSTEM 16-13**
Bleeding Procedure................16-13
  Bleeding Procedure 16-13
  Bleeding the ABS
    System (automated
    Bleed) 16-13
  Master Cylinder Bench
    Bleeding 16-13
  Master Cylinder Fluid Fill
    Procedure........................16-14
FRONT DISC BRAKES 16-14
Brake Caliper........................16-14
  Removal & Installation........16-14
Disc Brake Pads 16-15
  Removal & Installation........16-15
PARKING BRAKE.............16-16
Electronic Parking Brake
  Adjuster 16-16
  Adjuster Disabling 16-16
  Adjuster Enabling 16-17
Electronic Parking Brake
  Module..............................16-17
  EPB Control Module
    Programming 16-17
  Removal & Installation........16-17
Parking Brake Cables 16-17
  Replacement 16-17
REAR DISC BRAKES 16-15
Brake Caliper........................16-15
  Removal & Installation........16-15
Disc Brake Pads 16-16
  Removal & Installation........16-16

CHASSIS ELECTRICAL 16-18

**AIR BAG (SUPPLEMENTAL
RESTRAINT SYSTEM) 16-18**
General Information.................16-18
  Arming the System 16-19

Clockspring Centering........16-19
Disarming the System.........16-18
Service Precautions 16-18

DRIVE TRAIN 16-19

Automatic Transaxle Fluid 16-19
  Drain & Refill.....................16-19
Front Driveshaft....................16-19
  Removal & Installation........16-19
Propeller Shaft 16-20
  Removal & Installation........16-20
Rear Axle (Differential)
  Housing Assembly 16-20
  Removal & Installation........16-20
Rear Axle Fluid.....................16-20
  Drain & Refill.....................16-20
Rear Axle Shaft, Bearing &
  Seal 16-20
  Removal & Installation........16-20

ENGINE COOLING 16-21

Engine Coolant......................16-21
  Drain & Refill Procedure.....16-21
  Flushing............................16-21
Engine Fan 16-21
  Removal & Installation........16-21
Radiator..............................16-21
  Removal & Installation........16-21
Thermostat 16-21
  Removal & Installation........16-21
Water Pump 16-22
  Removal & Installation........16-22

ENGINE ELECTRICAL 16-23

BATTERY SYSTEM.............16-23
Battery.................................16-23
  Removal & Installation........16-23
CHARGING SYSTEM 16-23
Generator 16-23
  Removal & Installation........16-23
IGNITION SYSTEM 16-24
Firing Order..........................16-24
Ignition Coil 16-24
  Removal & Installation........16-24
Ignition Timing 16-24
  Adjustment 16-24

Spark Plugs.........................16-24
  Removal & Installation........16-24
STARTING SYSTEM 16-25
Starter 16-25
  Removal & Installation........16-25

ENGINE MECHANICAL......16-25

Accessory Drive Belts 16-25
  Accessory Belt Routing.......16-25
  Removal & Installation........16-25
Air Cleaner 16-26
  Filter/element
    Replacement 16-26
  Removal & Installation........16-26
Camshaft.............................16-26
  Removal & Installation........16-26
Camshaft Position Actuator.....16-28
  Removal & Installation........16-28
Camshaft Valve Lifters............16-28
  Removal & Installation........16-28
Catalytic Converter................16-30
  Removal & Installation........16-30
Crankshaft Front Seal............16-30
  Removal & Installation........16-30
Cylinder Head 16-30
  Removal & Installation........16-30
Engine Front Cover 16-32
  Removal & Installation........16-32
Engine Oil & Filter 16-34
  Replacement 16-34
Exhaust Manifold 16-35
  Removal & Installation........16-35
Flywheel..............................16-36
  Removal & Installation........16-36
Intake Manifold 16-36
  Removal & Installation........16-36
Oil Pan 16-38
  Removal & Installation........16-38
Oil Pump 16-38
  Removal & Installation........16-38
Piston & Ring.......................16-39
  Positioning 16-39
Rear Main Seal.....................16-39
  Removal & Installation........16-39
Timing Chain &
  Sprockets 16-39
  Removal & Installation........16-39

Valve (Camshaft) Covers.........16-48
  Removal & Installation........16-48
Valve Lash.................................16-49
  Adjustment 16-49

**ENGINE PERFORMANCE &
EMISSION CONTROLS 16-49**

Accelerator Pedal with
  Position Sensor 16-49
  Location.............................16-49
  Removal & Installation........16-49
Camshaft Position (CMP)
  Sensor 16-49
  Location.............................16-49
  Removal & Installation........16-49
Crankshaft Position (CKP)
  Sensor 16-50
  Location.............................16-50
  Removal & Installation........16-50
Crankshaft Position Sensor
  Variation Learn....................16-51
  Procedure 16-51
ECM Programming 16-52
  Information 16-52
Electronic Control Module
  (ECM).................................16-51
  Location.............................16-51
  Removal & Installation........16-51
Engine Coolant Temperature
  (ECT) Sensor 16-52
  Location.............................16-52
  Removal & Installation........16-52
Evaporative Emissions
  (EVAP) Canister 16-53
  Location.............................16-53
  Removal & Installation........16-53
Evaporative Emissions (EVAP)
  Canister Purge Solenoid
  Valve.................................16-53
  Location.............................16-53
  Removal & Installation........16-53
Evaporative Emissions (EVAP)
  Canister Vent Solenoid
  Valve.................................16-54
  Location.............................16-54
  Removal & Installation........16-54
Heated Oxygen (HO2S)
  Sensor 16-54
  Location.............................16-54
  Removal & Installation........16-54
Intake Air Temperature (IAT)
  Sensor 16-55
  Location.............................16-55
Knock Sensor (KS).................16-55
  Location.............................16-55
  Removal & Installation........16-55

Manifold Absolute Pressure
  (MAP) Sensor 16-55
  Location.............................16-55
  Removal & Installation........16-55
Mass Air Flow (MAF)
  Sensor 16-55
  Location.............................16-55
  Removal & Installation........16-56
Secondary Air Injection
  (AIR) Pump 16-56
  Location.............................16-56
  Removal & Installation........16-56

FUEL 16-56

**GASOLINE FUEL INJECTION
SYSTEM 16-56**
Fuel Injectors 16-56
  Removal & Installation........16-56
Fuel Pump..............................16-57
  Removal & Installation........16-57
Fuel Rail.................................16-57
  Removal & Installation........16-57
Fuel System Service
  Precautions 16-56
Fuel Tank................................16-58
  Draining.............................16-58
  Removal & Installation........16-58
Relieving Fuel System
  Pressure............................16-56
Throttle Body..........................16-60
  Removal & Installation........16-60
Throttle/Idle Learn..................16-60
  After ECM Programmed or
  Replaced............................16-60
  After Throttle Body
  Cleaned or Replaced........16-60

**HEATING & AIR
CONDITIONING SYSTEM...16-60**

Auxiliary Heater Core 16-60
  Removal & Installation........16-60
Blower Motor 16-60
  Removal & Installation........16-60
Compressor 16-60
  Removal & Installation........16-60
Heater Core 16-61
  Removal & Installation........16-61

PRECAUTIONS..............16-11

**SPECIFICATIONS AND
MAINTENANCE CHARTS.....16-4**

Additional Maintenance
  Services - Normal 16-10

Additional Maintenance
  Services - Severe.................16-10
Brake Specifications.................16-8
Camshaft Specifications............16-6
Capacities 16-5
Crankshaft & Connecting Rod
  Specifications......................16-6
Engine and Vehicle
  Identification 16-4
Engine Tune-Up
  Specifications......................16-4
Fluid Specifications..................16-5
General Engine
  Specifications......................16-4
Maintenance I and II Service
  Schedules...........................16-9
Piston & Ring Specifications 16-6
Tire, Wheel & Ball Joint
  Specifications......................16-8
Torque Specifications...............16-7
Valve Specifications.................16-5
Wheel Alignment.....................16-7

STEERING 16-62

Power Steering Gear................16-62
  Removal & Installation........16-62
Power Steering Pump..............16-64
  Bleeding 16-64
  Fluid Fill Procedure 16-64
  Removal & Installation........16-64
Steering Column 16-65
  Removal & Installation........16-65

SUSPENSION 16-66

ELECTRONIC SUSPENSION..16-66
Electronic Suspension
  Control Module....................16-66
  Removal & Installation........16-66
Electronic Suspension Rear
  Position Sensor 16-66
  Removal & Installation........16-66
Front Vertical
  Accelerometer 16-66
  Removal & Installation........16-66
FRONT SUSPENSION 16-67
Lower Control Arm..................16-67
  Removal & Installation........16-67
Stabilizer Shaft 16-67
  Removal & Installation........16-67
Stabilizer Shaft Link 16-68
  Removal & Installation........16-68
Steering Knuckle 16-68
  Removal & Installation........16-68
Strut & Spring Assembly 16-68
  Removal & Installation........16-68

Wheel Hub & Bearing 16-69
   Removal & Installation........16-69
REAR SUSPENSION 16-70
Adjust Link.............................16-70
   Removal & Installation........16-70
Coil Spring.............................16-70
   Removal & Installation........16-70

Lower Control Arm..................16-71
   Removal & Installation........16-71
Rear Suspension Link 16-72
   Removal & Installation........16-72
Shock Absorber......................16-72
   Removal & Installation........16-72
Stabilizer Shaft 16-72
   Removal & Installation........16-72

Stabilizer Shaft Link 16-73
   Removal & Installation........16-73
Upper Control Arm..................16-73
   Removal & Installation........16-73
Wheel Hub & Bearings...........16-74
   Removal & Installation........16-74

SPECIFICATIONS AND MAINTENANCE CHARTS

ENGINE AND VEHICLE IDENTIFICATION

			Engine					Model Year	
Code ①	Liters (cc)	Cu. In.	Cyl.	Fuel Sys.	Engine Type	Eng. Mfg.		Code ②	Year
C	2.4 (2392)	146	4	SIDI	DOHC	BOC		B	2011
D	3.6 (3564)	217	6	SIDI	OHC	BOC			

① 8th position of VIN

② 10th position of VIN

25742_LACR_C0001

GENERAL ENGINE SPECIFICATIONS

All measurements are given in inches.

Year	Model	Engine Displacement Liters (cc)	Engine ID/VIN	Fuel System Type	Net Horsepower @ rpm	Net Torque @ rpm (ft. lbs.)	Bore x Stroke (in.)	Compression Ratio	Oil Pressure @ rpm
2011	LaCrosse	2.4 (2392)	C	DI	182@6700	172@4900	3.46x3.86	10.0:01	30-70@1000
		3.6 (3564)	D	SIDI	280@6400	259@5200	3.70x3.37	11.4:1	20@2000

25742_LACR_C0002

ENGINE TUNE-UP SPECIFICATIONS

Year	Engine Displacement Liters	Engine ID/VIN	Spark Plug Gap (in.)	Ignition Timing (deg.) MT	Ignition Timing (deg.) AT	Fuel Pump (psi)	Idle Speed (rpm) MT	Idle Speed (rpm) AT	Valve Clearance Intake	Valve Clearance Exhaust
2011	2.4	C	0.35	—	①	N/A	—	①	②	②
	3.6	D	0.43	—	①	N/A	—	①	②	②

N/A: Information not available.

① Ignition timing is computer controlled; therefore, no adjustment is required.

② Valve lash (clearance) is maintained by hydraulic valve lifters; no adjustment is required.

25742_LACR_C0003

CAPACITIES

Year	Model	Engine Displacement Liters	Engine ID/VIN	Engine Oil with Filter (qts.)	Transmission/axle (pts.) Auto.	Manual	Drive Axle (pts.) Front	Rear	Transfer Case (pts.)	Fuel Tank (gal.)	Cooling System (qts.)
2011	LaCrosse	2.4	C	5.0	①	—	—	②	1.4	③	7.5
		3.6	D	5.5	①	—	—	②	1.4	③	9.9

NOTE: All capacities are approximate. Add fluid gradually and ensure a proper fluid level is obtained.

① Drain & refill: 8.4-12.6 pts.

　Overhaul: 14.8-19.0 pts.

② Rear differential housing: 1.48 pts.

　Differential clutch with Electronic Limited Slip Differential: 0.74 pts.

③ With FWD: 18.6 gal.

　With AWD: 19.5 gal.

25742_LACR_C0004

FLUID SPECIFICATIONS

Year	Model	Engine Disp. Liters	Engine Oil	Auto. Trans.	Drive Axle Front	Rear	Transfer Case	Power Steering Fluid	Brake Master Cylinder	Cooling System
2011	LaCrosse	2.4	Dexos 5W-30	Dexron-VI	—	①	①	Dexron-VI	DOT 3	DEX-COOL
		3.6	Dexos 5W-30	Dexron-VI	—	①	①	Dexron-VI	DOT 3	DEX-COOL

DOT: Department Of Transpotation

① Manufacturer refers to their electronic parts catalog; also see Owner's Manual.

25742_LACR_C0005

VALVE SPECIFICATIONS

Year	Engine Displacement Liters	Engine ID/VIN	Seat Angle (deg.)	Face Angle (deg.)	Spring Test Pressure (lbs. @ in.)	Spring Free-Length (in.)	Spring Installed Height (in.)	Stem-to-Guide Clearance (in.) Intake	Exhaust	Stem Diameter (in.) Intake	Exhaust
2011	2.4	C	45	45	55-61@1.28 ①	1.630-1.740	1.280	0.0012-0.0022	0.0020-0.0026	0.2344-0.2355	0.2337-0.2343
	3.6	D	45	44.25	55-61@1.38 ②	1.6732-1.7913	1.280	0.0010-0.0026	0.0014-0.0030	0.2344-0.2352	0.2341-0.2348

① Valve spring closed measurement.

　With valve spring open: 118-129 lbs. @ 0.89 in.

② Valve spring closed measurement.

　With valve spring open: 134-149 lbs. @ 0.994 in.

25742_LACR_C0006

CAMSHAFT SPECIFICATIONS

All measurements in inches unless noted

Year	Engine Displacement Liters	Engine Code/VIN	Journal Diameter	Brg. Oil Clearance	Shaft End-play	Runout	Journal Bore	Lobe Height Intake	Lobe Height Exhaust
2011	2.4	C	1.0604-1.0614	N/A	N/A	N/A	N/A	N/A	N/A
	3.6	D	①	0.0016-0.0033	0.0018-0.0085	②	N/A	1.6687-1.6805	1.6703-1.6821

N/A: Information not available.

① Front (No. 1): 1.3754-1.3764 in.

   Middle & rear (Nos. 2-4): 1.0605-1.0614 in.

② Front & rear (Nos. 1, 4): 0.0010 in.

   Middle (Nos. 2, 3): 0.0020 in.

25742_LACR_C0007

CRANKSHAFT AND CONNECTING ROD SPECIFICATIONS

All measurements are given in inches.

Year	Engine Displacement Liters	Engine ID/VIN	Crankshaft Main Brg. Journal Dia.	Main Brg. Oil Clearance	Shaft End-play	Thrust on No.	Connecting Rod Journal Diameter	Oil Clearance	Side Clearance
2011	2.4	C	2.2044-2.2051	0.0012-0.0026	0.0012-0.0150	N/A	1.9291-1.9297	0.0011-0.0029	0.0028-0.0146
	3.6	D	2.6768-2.6775	0.0004-0.0024	0.0039-0.0130	N/A	2,2044-2.2050	0.0004-0.0028	0.0374-0.0140

25742_LACR_C0008

PISTON AND RING SPECIFICATIONS

All measurements are given in inches.

Year	Engine Displacement Liters	Engine ID/VIN	Piston Clearance	Ring Gap Top Compression	Ring Gap Bottom Compression	Ring Gap Oil Control	Ring Side Clearance Top Compression	Ring Side Clearance Bottom Compression	Ring Side Clearance Oil Control
2011	2.4	C	0.0004-0.0016	0.006-0.012	0.008-0.018	0.006-0.026	0.0015-0.0031	0.0012-0.0030	0.0023-0.0081
	3.6	D	0.0008-0.0013	0.0059-0.0118	0.0110-0.0189	0.0059-0.0236	0.0012-0.0026	0.0006-0.0024	0.0012-0.0067

25742_LACR_C0009

TORQUE SPECIFICATIONS
All readings in ft. lbs.

Year	Engine Disp. Liters	Engine ID/VIN	Cylinder Head Bolts	Main Bearing Bolts	Rod Bearing Bolts	Crankshaft Damper Bolts	Flywheel Bolts	Manifold (inch lbs.)		Spark Plugs	Oil Pan Drain Plug
								Intake	Exhaust		
2011	2.4	C	22 ①	N/A	18 ②	74 ③	39 ④	89 ⑤	124 ⑥	15	18
	3.6	D	⑦	⑧	⑨	74 ⑩	22 ⑪	18	15	13	18

NOTE: Many component bolts require a specific tightening sequence. Refer to appropriate component in "ENGINE MECHANICAL" section for any specific sequence.

① Second step: an additional 155 degrees, in sequence.

② Second step: an additional 100 degrees.

③ Second step: an additional 125 degrees.

④ Second step: an additional 25 degrees.

⑤ Torque value given in Inch. Lbs.

⑥ Torque value given in Inch. Lbs. Tightening requires two passes, in sequence.

⑦ M8 bolts first step: 11 ft. lbs., in sequence

M8 bolts second step: an additional 75 degrees, in sequence

M11 bolts first step: 22 ft. lbs., in sequence

M11 bolts second step: an additional 150 degrees, in sequence

⑧ Inner bolts first step: 15 ft. lbs., in sequence

Inner bolts second step: an additional 80 degrees, in sequence

Outer bolts first step: 11 ft. lbs., in sequence

Outer bolts second step: an additional 110 degrees, in sequence

Side bolts first step: 22 ft. lbs., in sequence

Side bolts second step: an additional 60 degrees, in sequence

⑨ First step: 22 ft. lbs.

Second step: back off to zero

Third step: 18 ft. lbs.

Final step: an additional 110 degrees.

⑩ Second step: an additional 150 degrees.

⑪ Second step: an additional 45 degrees.

25742_LACR_C0010

WHEEL ALIGNMENT

Year	Model	F/R	Caster		Camber		Toe-in (Deg.)
			Range (+/-Deg.)	Preferred Setting (Deg.)	Range (+/-Deg.)	Preferred Setting (Deg.)	
2011	LaCrosse	F	3.35 to 4.85	4.1	-1.1 to 0.7	-0.35	0.20
		R	—	—	-1.65 to -0.15	-0.90	0.10

25742_LACR_C0011

TIRE, WHEEL AND BALL JOINT SPECIFICATIONS

| Year | Model | OEM Tires | | Tire Pressures (psi) | | Wheel Size | Ball Joint Inspection | Lug Nut (ft. lbs.) |
		Standard	Optional	Front	Rear			
2011	LaCrosse	①	245/40-19	②	②	③	N/A	110

OEM: Original Equipment Manufacturer

PSI: Pounds Per Square Inch

NA: Information not available

① CX with 17" wheels: 245/50-17

   CXL/CXS with 18" wheels: 235/50-18

② See tire placard on door jamb.

③ Varies by tire size application 17", 18" or 19".

25742_LACR_C0012

BRAKE SPECIFICATIONS

All measurements in inches unless noted

| Year | Model | | Brake Disc | | | Brake Drum Diameter | | | Minimum Pad/Lining Thickness | | Brake Caliper | |
			Original Thickness	Minimum Thickness	Max. Runout	Original Inside Diameter	Max. Wear Limit	Maximum Machine Diamter	Front	Rear	Bracket Bolts (ft. lbs.)	Mounting Bolts (ft. lbs.)
2011	LaCrosse	F	1.180	1.070	0.0020	—	—	—	N/A	N/A	111 ①	20
		R	0.905	0.827	0.0020	—	—	—	N/A	N/A	74 ②	20

F: Front

R: Rear

NA: Information not available

① Plus 45 degrees, plus 15 degrees.

② Plus 60 degrees.

25742_LACR_C0013

MAINTENANCE I AND II SERVICE SCHEDULES
LACROSSE

When the CHANGE ENGINE OIL light appears, certain services and inspections are required.

Required services are described as Maintenance I and Maintenance II.

The first service of a vehicle should be Maintenance I, and the second service should be Maintenance II.

Alternate between the 2 services thereafter. However, in some cases, Maintenance II may be required more often.

Maintenance I: Use Maintenance I if the CHANGE ENGINE OIL light comes on within 10 months since the vehicle was purchased or, if Maintenance II was performed.

Maintenance II: Use Maintenance II if the previous service performed was Maintenance I. Always use Maintenance II whenever the CHANGE ENGINE OIL light comes on 10 months or more since the last service, or, if the CHANGE ENGINE OIL light has not come on at all for one year.

Service Item	Maintenance I	Maintenance II
Change the engine oil and filter.	✓	✓
Reset the oil life system.	✓	✓
Visually inspect the vehicle for leaks or damage. A fluid loss in the vehicle system could indicate a problem. Inspect, repair and add fluid to the system if necessary.	✓	✓
Inspect the engine air cleaner filter. If necessary, replace the filter.	✓	✓
Rotate the tires. Inspect the tire inflation pressures and the tire wear.	✓	✓
Visually inspect the brake lines and hoses for proper hook-up, binding, leaks, cracks, chafing, etc. Inspect the disc brake pads for wear and the rotors for surface condition. Inspect the drum brake linings for wear or cracks. Inspect other brake parts, including drums, wheel cylinders, calipers, parking brake, etc. Inspect the parking brake adjustment.	✓	✓
Inspect engine coolant and windshield washer fluid levels. Add fluid as needed.	✓	✓
Inspect the suspension and steering components. Inspect the front and rear suspension and the steering system for damaged, loose or missing parts, or signs of wear. Inspect the power steering lines and the hoses for proper hook-up, binding, leaks, cracks, chafing, etc.	—	✓
Visually inspect the coolant hoses and replace the hoses if they are cracked, swollen or deteriorated. Inspect all pipes, fittings and clamps; replace with GM parts as needed. To help ensure proper operation, a pressure test of the cooling system and pressure cap and cleaning the outside of the radiator and air conditioning condenser is recommended at least once a year.	—	✓
Ensure the safety belt reminder light and all the belts, buckles, latch plates, retractors and anchorages are working properly. Look for any other loose or damaged safety belt system parts. If you see anything that might keep a safety belt system from working correctly, repair or replaced the damaged part. Replace torn or frayed safety belts, refer to Operational and Functional Checks in Seat Belts. Inspect for any opened or broken air bag coverings, and repair or replace as needed. The air bag system does require regular maintenance.	—	✓
Lubricate the body components.	—	✓
Lubricate all key lock cylinders, hood latch assemblies, secondary latches, pivots, spring anchor and release pawl, hood and door hinges, rear folding seats and liftgate hinges. Frequent lubrication may be required when exposed to a corrosive environment, refer to Fluid and Lubricant Recommendations . Applying dielectric silicone grease GM P/N 12345579 (Canadian P/N 1974984) or equivalent on the weatherstrips with a clean cloth.	—	✓
Inspect the transaxle fluid level and add fluid as needed.		✓
Inspect the wiper blades and replace as necessary	✓	✓
Inspect the throttle system.	—	✓
Replace the passenger compartment air filter.	—	✓

To reset the CHANGE ENGINE OIL light:

1. Turn the ignition key to the ON/RUN position with the engine OFF.
2. Press and release the stem in the lower center of the instrument cluster until the OIL LIFE message is displayed.
3. Once the alternating OIL LIFE and RESET messages appear, press and hold the stem until several beeps sound.
    This confirms that the oil life system has been reset to 100 percent.
4. Turn the ignition key to the OFF position.

    If the CHANGE ENGINE OIL message comes back on when the vehicle is started, the engine oil life system has not been reset. Repeat the procedure.

ADDITIONAL MAINTENANCE SERVICES - NORMAL
LACROSSE

TO BE SERVICED	TYPE OF SERVICE	VEHICLE MILEAGE INTERVAL (x1000)					
		25	50	75	100	125	150
Engine coolant	Replace						✓
Air cleaner filter	Replace		✓		✓		✓
Automatic transaxle fluid & filter	Replace				✓		
Spark plugs	Replace				✓		
Exhaust system & heat shields	Service/ Inspect	✓	✓	✓	✓	✓	✓
Cooling system hoses and clamps	Service/ Inspect						✓
Fuel system	Inspect	✓	✓	✓	✓	✓	✓
Accessory drive belt	Replace						✓
Evaporative control system	Inspect		✓		✓		✓

25742_LACR_C0015

ADDITIONAL MAINTENANCE SERVICES - SEVERE
LACROSSE

TO BE SERVICED	TYPE OF SERVICE	VEHICLE MILEAGE INTERVAL (x1000)					
		25	50	75	100	125	150
Engine coolant	Replace						✓
Air cleaner filter	Replace	✓	✓	✓	✓	✓	✓
Automatic transaxle fluid & filter	Replace		✓		✓		✓
Spark plugs	Replace				✓		
Exhaust system & heat shields	Service/ Inspect	✓	✓	✓	✓	✓	✓
Cooling system hoses and clamps	Service/ Inspect						✓
Fuel system	Inspect	✓	✓	✓	✓	✓	✓
Accessory drive belt	Inspect						✓
Evaporative control system	Inspect		✓		✓		✓

25742_LACR_C0016

PRECAUTIONS

Before servicing any vehicle, please be sure to read all of the following precautions, which deal with personal safety, prevention of component damage, and important points to take into consideration when servicing a motor vehicle:

• Never open, service or drain the radiator or cooling system when the engine is hot; serious burns can occur from the steam and hot coolant.

• Observe all applicable safety precautions when working around fuel. Whenever servicing the fuel system, always work in a well-ventilated area. Do not allow fuel spray or vapors to come in contact with a spark, open flame, or excessive heat (a hot drop light, for example). Keep a dry chemical fire extinguisher near the work area. Always keep fuel in a container specifically designed for fuel storage; also, always properly seal fuel containers to avoid the possibility of fire or explosion. Refer to the additional fuel system precautions later in this section.

• Fuel injection systems often remain pressurized, even after the engine has been turned **OFF**. The fuel system pressure must be relieved before disconnecting any fuel lines. Failure to do so may result in fire and/or personal injury.

• Brake fluid often contains polyglycol ethers and polyglycols. Avoid contact with the eyes and wash your hands thoroughly after handling brake fluid. If you do get brake fluid in your eyes, flush your eyes with clean, running water for 15 minutes. If eye irritation persists, or if you have taken brake fluid internally, IMMEDIATELY seek medical assistance.

• The EPA warns that prolonged contact with used engine oil may cause a number of skin disorders, including cancer. You should make every effort to minimize your exposure to used engine oil. Protective gloves should be worn when changing oil. Wash your hands and any other exposed skin areas as soon as possible after exposure to used engine oil. Soap and water, or waterless hand cleaner should be used.

• All new vehicles are now equipped with an air bag system, often referred to as a Supplemental Restraint System (SRS) or Supplemental Inflatable Restraint (SIR) system. The system must be disabled before performing service on or around system components, steering column, instrument panel components, wiring and sensors. Failure to follow safety and disabling procedures could result in accidental air bag deployment, possible personal injury and unnecessary system repairs.

• Always wear safety goggles when working with, or around, the air bag system. When carrying a non-deployed air bag, be sure the bag and trim cover are pointed away from your body. When placing a non-deployed air bag on a work surface, always face the bag and trim cover upward, away from the surface. This will reduce the motion of the module if it is accidentally deployed. Refer to the additional air bag system precautions later in this section.

• Clean, high quality brake fluid from a sealed container is essential to the safe and proper operation of the brake system. You should always buy the correct type of brake fluid for your vehicle. If the brake fluid becomes contaminated, completely flush the system with new fluid. Never reuse any brake fluid. Any brake fluid that is removed from the system should be discarded. Also, do not allow any brake fluid to come in contact with a painted surface; it will damage the paint.

• Never operate the engine without the proper amount and type of engine oil; doing so WILL result in severe engine damage.

• Timing belt maintenance is extremely important. Many models utilize an interference-type, non-freewheeling engine. If the timing belt breaks, the valves in the cylinder head may strike the pistons, causing potentially serious (also time-consuming and expensive) engine damage. Refer to the maintenance interval charts for the recommended replacement interval for the timing belt, and to the timing belt section for belt replacement and inspection.

• Disconnecting the negative battery cable on some vehicles may interfere with the functions of the on-board computer system(s) and may require the computer to undergo a relearning process once the negative battery cable is reconnected.

• When servicing drum brakes, only disassemble and assemble one side at a time, leaving the remaining side intact for reference.

• Only an MVAC-trained, EPA-certified automotive technician should service the air conditioning system or its components.

BRAKES

GENERAL INFORMATION

PRECAUTIONS

• Certain components within the ABS system are not intended to be serviced or repaired individually.

• Do not use rubber hoses or other parts not specifically specified for and ABS system. When using repair kits, replace all parts included in the kit. Partial or incorrect repair may lead to functional problems and require the replacement of components.

• Lubricate rubber parts with clean, fresh brake fluid to ease assembly. Do not use shop air to clean parts; damage to rubber components may result.

• Use only DOT 3 brake fluid from an unopened container.

• If any hydraulic component or line is removed or replaced, it may be necessary to bleed the entire system.

• A clean repair area is essential. Always clean the reservoir and cap thoroughly before removing the cap. The slightest amount of dirt in the fluid may plug an orifice and impair the system function. Perform repairs after components have been thoroughly cleaned; use only denatured alcohol to clean components. Do not allow ABS components to come into contact with any substance containing mineral oil; this includes used shop rags.

• The Anti-Lock control unit is a microprocessor similar to other computer units in the vehicle. Ensure that the ignition switch is **OFF** before removing or installing controller harnesses. Avoid static electricity discharge at or near the controller.

• If any arc welding is to be done on the vehicle, the control unit should be unplugged before welding operations begin.

ANTI-LOCK BRAKE SYSTEM (ABS)

SPEED SENSORS

REMOVAL & INSTALLATION

Front

Without Continuously Variable Real Time Damping Chassis System
See Figure 1.

1. Raise and support the vehicle.
2. Remove the tire and wheel assembly.

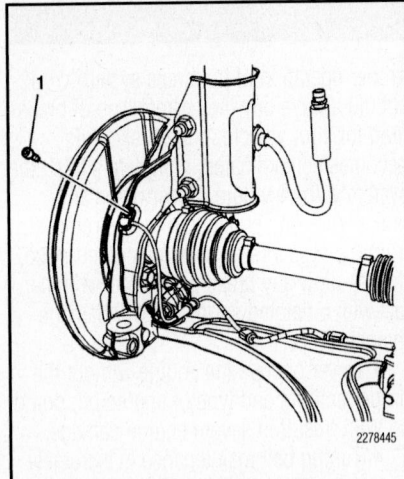

Fig. 1 Remove the wheel speed sensor bolt (1) and remove the wheel speed sensor from the steering knuckle.

3. Disconnect the wheel speed sensor electrical connector and release the connector from the frame. Release the harness clip from the frame. Release the harness clips from the lower control arm.

4. Remove any accumulated dirt and debris from the surrounding the wheel speed sensor.

5. Remove the wheel speed sensor bolt. Remove the wheel speed sensor from the steering knuckle.

6. Release the harness clip from the steering knuckle and remove the wheel speed sensor.

To install:

7. Install the wheel speed sensor to the steering knuckle.

8. Install the harness clip to the steering knuckle. Install the wheel speed sensor bolt and tighten to 80 inch lbs. (9 Nm).

9. Connect the wheel speed sensor electrical connector and secure the connector to the frame. Install the harness clip to the frame. Install the harness clips to the lower control arm.

10. Install the tire and wheel assembly.

With Continuously Variable Real Time Damping Chassis System

See Figure 2.

1. Raise and support the vehicle.
2. Remove the tire and wheel assembly.
3. Disconnect the wheel speed sensor electrical connector.
4. Remove the wheel speed sensor bolt and remove the speed sensor.
5. Installation is the reverse of the removal procedure.
6. Tighten the speed sensor bolt to 80 inch lbs. (9 Nm).

Rear

With 4-Link

1. Raise and support the vehicle.
2. Remove the tire and wheel assembly.
3. Disconnect the wheel speed sensor electrical connector.
4. Remove the wheel speed sensor bolt and remove the speed sensor.
5. Installation is the reverse of the removal procedure.
6. Tighten the speed sensor bolt to 80 inch lbs. (9 Nm).

With H-Arm

1. Raise and support the vehicle.
2. Remove the tire and wheel assembly.
3. Clean the wheel speed sensor mounting area on the suspension knuckle of any accumulated dirt and debris.
4. Remove the wheel speed sensor bolt and remove the wheel speed sensor by pulling the sensor straight out of the rear suspension knuckle.
5. Release the wheel speed sensor harness from the retainers. Disconnect the wheel speed sensor electrical connector. Release the wheel speed sensor electrical connector retainer and remove the wheel speed sensor.

To install:

6. Install the wheel speed sensor connector retainer to the rear suspension cradle.

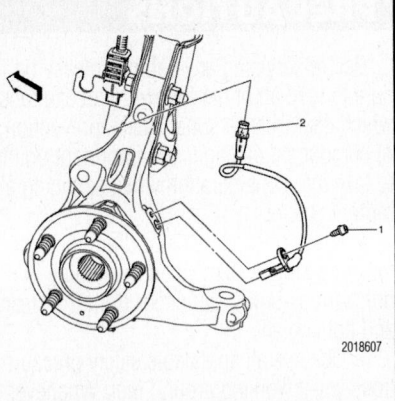

Fig. 2 Removing the wheel speed sensor bolt (1) and electrical connector (2).

7. Connect the wheel speed sensor electrical connector. Install the wheel speed sensor harness to the retainers.

8. Install the wheel speed sensor to the rear suspension knuckle.

9. Install the wheel speed sensor bolt and tighten to 80 inch lbs. (9 Nm).

10. Install the tire and wheel assembly.

11. Perform the Vehicle Diagnostic Repair Verification as follows:

a. Turn ignition OFF.

b. Install any components or connectors that have been removed or replaced during diagnosis.

c. Perform any adjustment, programming or setup procedures that are required when a component or module is removed or replaced.

d. Turn ignition ON.

e. Clear the DTCs.

f. Turn the ignition OFF for 60 seconds.

g. If the repair was related to a DTC, duplicate the Conditions for Running the DTC and use the Freeze Frame/Failure Records, if applicable, in order to verify the DTC does not reset.

h. If the DTC resets or another DTC is present, refer to an applicable DTC List and perform the appropriate diagnostic procedure.

BLEEDING PROCEDURE

BLEEDING PROCEDURE

1. Before servicing the vehicle, refer to the Precautions Section.

2. Place a clean shop cloth beneath the brake master cylinder to prevent brake fluid spills.

3. With the ignition OFF and the brakes cool, apply the brakes 3-5 times, or until the brake pedal effort increases significantly, in order to deplete the brake booster power reserve.

4. If you have performed a brake master cylinder bench bleeding on this vehicle, or if you disconnected the brake pipes from the master cylinder, you must perform the following steps:

a. Ensure that the brake master cylinder reservoir is full to the maximum-fill level. If necessary, add GM approved brake fluid from a clean, sealed brake fluid container. If removal of the reservoir cap and diaphragm is necessary, clean the outside of the reservoir on and around the cap prior to removal.

b. With the rear brake pipe installed securely to the master cylinder, loosen and separate the front brake pipe from the front port of the brake master cylinder.

c. Allow a small amount of brake fluid to gravity bleed from the open port of the master cylinder.

d. Reconnect the brake pipe to the master cylinder port and tighten securely.

e. Have an assistant slowly depress the brake pedal fully and maintain steady pressure on the pedal.

f. Loosen the same brake pipe to purge air from the open port of the master cylinder.

g. Tighten the brake pipe, then have the assistant slowly release the brake pedal.

h. Wait 15 seconds, then repeat the above 5 steps until all air is purged from the same port of the master cylinder.

i. With the front brake pipe installed securely to the master cylinder, after all air has been purged from the front port of the master cylinder, loosen and separate the rear brake pipe from the master cylinder, then repeat the above 6 steps.

j. After completing the final master cylinder port bleeding procedure, ensure that both of the brake pipe-to-master cylinder fittings are properly tightened.

5. Fill the brake master cylinder reservoir with GM approved brake fluid from a clean, sealed brake fluid container. Ensure that the brake master cylinder reservoir remains at least half-full during this bleeding procedure. Add fluid as needed to maintain the proper level. Clean the outside of the reservoir on and around the reservoir cap prior to removing the cap and diaphragm.

6. Install a proper box-end wrench onto the RIGHT REAR wheel hydraulic circuit bleeder valve.

7. Install a transparent hose over the end of the bleeder valve.

8. Submerge the open end of the transparent hose into a transparent container partially filled with GM approved brake fluid from a clean, sealed brake fluid container.

9. Have an assistant slowly depress the brake pedal fully and maintain steady pressure on the pedal.

10. Loosen the bleeder valve to purge air from the wheel hydraulic circuit.

11. Tighten the bleeder valve, then have the assistant slowly release the brake pedal.

12. Wait 15 seconds, then repeat steps 9-11 until all air is purged from the same wheel hydraulic circuit.

13. With the right rear wheel hydraulic circuit bleeder valve tightened securely, after all air has been purged from the right rear hydraulic circuit install a proper box-end wrench onto the LEFT REAR wheel hydraulic circuit bleeder valve.

14. Install a transparent hose over the end of the bleeder valve, then repeat steps 9-13.

15. With the left rear wheel hydraulic circuit bleeder valve tightened securely, after all air purged from the left rear hydraulic circuit, install a proper box-end wrench onto the RIGHT FRONT wheel hydraulic circuit bleeder valve.

16. Install a transparent hose over the end of the bleeder valve, then repeat steps 9-13.

17. With the right front wheel hydraulic circuit bleeder valve tightened securely, after all air has been purged from the right front hydraulic circuit, install a proper box-end wrench onto the LEFT FRONT wheel hydraulic circuit bleeder valve.

18. Install a transparent hose over the end of the bleeder valve, then repeat steps 9-13.

19. After completing the final wheel hydraulic circuit bleeding procedure, ensure that each of the 4 wheel hydraulic circuit bleeder valves are properly tightened.

20. Fill the brake master cylinder reservoir to the maximum-fill level with GM approved brake fluid from a clean, sealed brake fluid container.

21. Slowly depress and release the brake pedal. Observe the feel of the brake pedal.

MASTER CYLINDER BENCH BLEEDING

1. Secure the mounting flange of the brake master cylinder in a bench vise so that the rear of the primary piston is accessible.

2. Remove the master cylinder reservoir cap and diaphragm.

3. Install suitable fittings to the master cylinder ports that match the type of flare seat required and also provide for hose attachment.

4. Install transparent hoses to the fittings installed to the master cylinder ports, then route the hoses into the master cylinder reservoir.

5. Fill the master cylinder reservoir to at least the half-way point with GM approved brake fluid from a clean, sealed brake fluid container.

6. Ensure that the ends of the transparent hoses running into the master cylinder reservoir are fully submerged in the brake fluid.

7. Using a smooth, round-ended tool, depress and release the primary piston as far as it will travel, a depth of about 1 in. (25 mm), several times. Observe the flow of fluid coming from the ports.

➡**As air is bled from the primary and secondary pistons, the effort required to depress the primary piston will increase and the amount of travel will decrease.**

8. Continue to depress and release the primary piston until fluid flows freely from the ports with no evidence of air bubbles.

9. Remove the transparent hoses from the master cylinder reservoir.

10. Install the master cylinder reservoir cap and diaphragm.

11. Remove the fittings with the transparent hoses from the master cylinder ports. Wrap the master cylinder with a clean shop cloth to prevent brake fluid spills.

12. Remove the master cylinder from the vise.

BLEEDING THE ABS SYSTEM (AUTOMATED BLEED)

The ABS Automated Bleed Procedure uses a scan tool to cycle the system solenoid valves and run the pump in order to purge any air from the secondary circuits.

These circuits are normally closed off, and are only opened during system initialization at vehicle start up and during ABS operation. The automated bleed procedure opens these secondary circuits and allows any air trapped in these circuits to flow out toward the brake corners.

❄❄ CAUTION

The Auto Bleed Procedure may be terminated at any time during the process by pressing the EXIT button. No further Scan Tool prompts pertaining to the Auto Bleed procedure will be given. After exiting the bleed procedure, relieve bleed pressure and disconnect bleed equipment per manufacturer's instructions. Failure to properly relieve pressure may result in spilled brake fluid causing damage to components and painted surfaces.

1. Raise and support the vehicle.
2. Remove all four tire and wheel assemblies.
3. Inspect the brake system for leaks and visual damage. Repair or replace components as needed.
4. Lower the vehicle.
5. Inspect the battery state of charge.

6. Install a scan tool.
7. Turn the ignition ON, with the engine OFF.
8. With the scan tool, establish communications with the ABS system. Select Control Functions. Select Automated Bleed from the Control Functions menu.
9. Raise and support the vehicle.
10. Following the directions given on the scan tool, pressure bleed the base brake system.
11. Follow the scan tool directions until the desired brake pedal height is achieved.
12. If the bleed procedure is aborted, a malfunction exists. Perform the following steps before resuming the bleed procedure:

   a. If a DTC is detected, refer to Diagnostic Trouble Code (DTC) List - Vehicle, and diagnose the appropriate DTC.

   b. If the brake pedal feels spongy, perform the conventional brake bleed procedure again. Refer to "Hydraulic Brake System Bleeding" in this section.

13. When the desired pedal height is achieved, press the brake pedal to inspect for firmness.
14. Lower the vehicle.
15. Remove the scan tool.
16. Install the tire and wheel assemblies.
17. Inspect the brake fluid level.

18. Road test the vehicle while inspecting that the pedal remains high and firm.

MASTER CYLINDER FLUID FILL PROCEDURE

1. Visually inspect the brake fluid level through the brake master cylinder reservoir.
2. If the brake fluid level is at or below the half-full point during routine fluid checks, the brake system should be inspected for wear and possible brake fluid leaks.
3. If the brake fluid level is at or below the half-full point during routine fluid checks, and an inspection of the brake system did not reveal wear or brake fluid leaks, the brake fluid may be topped-off up to the maximum-fill level.
4. If brake system service was just completed, the brake fluid may be topped-off up to the maximum-fill level.
5. If the brake fluid level is above the half-full point, adding brake fluid is not recommended under normal conditions.
6. If brake fluid is to be added to the master cylinder reservoir, clean the outside of the reservoir on and around the reservoir cap prior to removing the cap and diaphragm. Use only GM approved brake fluid from a clean, sealed brake fluid container.

BRAKES

❄❄ CAUTION

Dust and dirt accumulating on brake parts during normal use may contain asbestos fibers from production or aftermarket brake linings. Breathing excessive concentrations of asbestos fibers can cause serious bodily harm. Exercise care when servicing brake parts. Do not sand or grind brake lining unless equipment used is designed to contain the dust residue. Do not clean brake parts with compressed air or by dry brushing. Cleaning should be done by dampening the brake components with a fine mist of water, then wiping the brake components clean with a dampened cloth. Dispose of cloth and all residue containing asbestos fibers in an impermeable container with the appropriate label. Follow practices prescribed by the Occupational Safety and Health Administration (OSHA) and the Environmental Protection Agency (EPA) for the handling, processing, and disposing of dust or debris that may contain asbestos fibers.

BRAKE CALIPER

REMOVAL & INSTALLATION
See Figure 3.

1. Raise and support the vehicle.
2. Remove the tire and wheel assembly.
3. Remove the brake hose fitting bolt.

➡**Do not reuse the brake hose fitting gaskets.**

4. Remove and discard the brake hose fitting gaskets from the brake hose fitting.
5. Cap the brake hose fitting to prevent brake fluid loss and contamination.

❄❄ CAUTION

DO NOT use any air tools to remove or install the guide pin bolts. Use hand tools ONLY.

➡**Install an open end wrench to hold the caliper guide pin in line with the brake caliper while removing or installing the caliper guide pin bolt. DO NOT allow the open end wrench to come in contact**

FRONT DISC BRAKES

with the brake caliper. Allowing the open end wrench to come in contact with the brake caliper will cause a pulsation when the brakes are applied.

6. Using a backup wrench to hold the brake caliper guide pin stationary, remove the brake caliper guide pin bolts.
7. Remove the brake caliper.

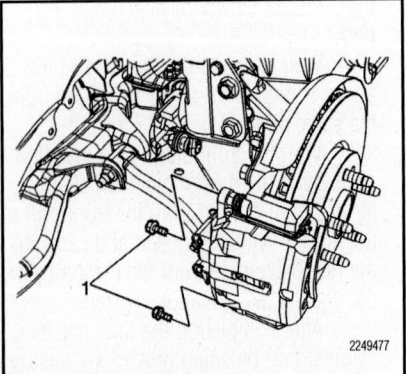

Fig. 3 Removing caliper guide pin bolts (1) for caliper removal

To install:

8. Install the brake caliper.

9. Hold the brake caliper guide pin stationary and install the brake caliper guide pin bolts and tighten to 20 ft. lbs. (27 Nm).

10. Assemble the brake hose fitting bolt and the 2 new brake hose fitting gaskets to the front brake hose fitting.

11. Install the brake hose assembly and tighten the brake hose fitting bolt to 30 ft. lbs. (40 Nm).

12. Bleed the hydraulic brake system.

13. Install the tire and wheel assembly.

DISC BRAKE PADS

REMOVAL & INSTALLATION

1. Inspect the fluid level in the brake master cylinder reservoir.

   a. If the brake fluid level is midway between the maximum-full point and the minimum allowable level, no brake fluid needs to be removed before proceeding.

   b. If the brake fluid level is higher than midway between the maximum-full point and the minimum allowable level, remove brake fluid to the midway point before proceeding.

2. Raise and support the vehicle.

3. Remove the tire and wheel assembly.

4. Place a large C-clamp over the brake caliper body and against the outer brake pad.

5. Using the C-clamp, compress the brake caliper piston fully into the brake caliper bore.

➡ **DO NOT use any air tools to remove or install the guide pin bolts. Use hand tools ONLY.**

➡ **Install an open end wrench to hold the caliper guide pin in line with the brake caliper while removing or installing the caliper guide pin bolt. DO NOT allow the open end wrench to come in contact with the brake caliper. Allowing the open end wrench to come in contact with the brake caliper will cause a pulsation when the brakes are applied.**

6. Using a backup wrench to hold the brake caliper guide pin stationary, remove the lower brake caliper guide pin bolt.

❋❋ CAUTION

Support the brake caliper with heavy mechanic wire, or equivalent, whenever it is separated from its mount and the hydraulic flexible brake hose is still connected. Failure to support the caliper in this manner will cause the flexible brake hose to bear the weight of the caliper, which may cause damage to the brake hose and in turn may cause a brake fluid leak.

7. Pivot the brake caliper upward and support with heavy mechanics wire or equivalent.

8. Note the location of the brake pad wear sensor for correct installation.

9. Remove the inner brake pad and the outer brake pad.

10. Remove the upper and lower brake pad springs.

11. If installing new brake pads, discard the springs.

To install:

➡ **If installing new brake pads, install new springs.**

12. Install the upper and lower brake pad springs.

13. Install the inner brake pad and the outer brake pad.

14. Pivot the brake caliper to the installed position.

15. Using a backup wrench to hold the brake caliper guide pin stationary, install the lower brake caliper guide pin bolt and tighten to 20 ft. lbs. (27 Nm).

16. Install the tire and wheel assembly.

17. With the engine OFF, gradually apply the brake pedal to approximately 2/3 of its travel distance.

Slowly release the brake pedal.

18. Wait 15 seconds, then repeat previous steps until a firm brake pedal is obtained. This will properly seat the brake caliper piston and brake pads.

19. Fill the master cylinder reservoir.

20. Burnish the brake pads and rotors.

BRAKES

❋❋ CAUTION

Dust and dirt accumulating on brake parts during normal use may contain asbestos fibers from production or aftermarket brake linings. Breathing excessive concentrations of asbestos fibers can cause serious bodily harm. Exercise care when servicing brake parts. Do not sand or grind brake lining unless equipment used is designed to contain the dust residue. Do not clean brake parts with compressed air or by dry brushing. Cleaning should be done by dampening the brake components with a fine mist of water, then wiping the brake components clean with a dampened cloth. Dispose of cloth and all residue containing asbestos fibers in an impermeable container with the appropriate label. Follow practices prescribed by the Occupational Safety and Health

Administration (OSHA) and the Environmental Protection Agency (EPA) for the handling, processing, and disposing of dust or debris that may contain asbestos fibers.

BRAKE CALIPER

REMOVAL & INSTALLATION

1. Raise and support the vehicle.

2. Remove the tire and wheel assembly.

3. Disable the parking brake cable adjuster.

4. Remove the brake hose fitting bolt.

5. Remove and discard the brake hose fitting gaskets from the brake hose.

6. Plug the brake hose fitting to prevent brake fluid loss and contamination.

7. Remove the parking brake cable retainer.

8. Disconnect the parking brake cable from the actuator lever.

REAR DISC BRAKES

9. Remove the parking brake cable from the cable bracket and position the parking brake cable end aside.

➡ **DO NOT use any air tools to remove or install the guide pin bolts. Use hand tools ONLY**

➡ **Install an open end wrench to hold the caliper guide pin in line with the brake caliper while removing or installing the caliper guide pin bolt. DO NOT allow the open end wrench to come in contact with the brake caliper. Allowing the open end wrench to come in contact with the brake caliper will cause a pulsation when the brakes are applied.**

10. Using a backup wrench to hold the brake caliper guide pin stationary, remove the brake caliper guide pin bolts.

11. Remove the brake caliper.

To install:

12. Install the brake caliper.

13. Using a backup wrench to hold the brake caliper guide pin stationary, install the brake caliper guide pin bolts and tighten to 20 ft. lbs. (27 Nm).

14. Install the parking brake cable to the cable bracket.

15. Connect the parking brake cable to the actuator lever.

16. Install the parking brake cable retainer.

17. Assemble the brake hose fitting bolt and the new brake hose fitting gaskets to the brake hose.

18. Install the brake hose assembly to the brake caliper and tighten the fitting bolt to 30 ft. lbs. (40 Nm).

19. Bleed the hydraulic brake system.

20. Enable the parking brake cable adjuster.

21. Install the tire and wheel assembly.

DISC BRAKE PADS

REMOVAL & INSTALLATION

1. Inspect the fluid level in the brake master cylinder reservoir.

   a. If the brake fluid level is midway between the maximum-full point and the minimum allowable level, no brake fluid needs to be removed before proceeding.

   b. If the brake fluid level is higher than midway between the maximum-full point and the minimum allowable level, remove brake fluid to the midway point before proceeding.

2. Raise and support the vehicle.

3. Remove the tire and wheel assembly.

➡ **DO NOT use any air tools to remove or install the guide pin bolts. Use hand tools ONLY.**

➡ **Install an open end wrench to hold the caliper guide pin in line with the brake caliper while removing or installing the caliper guide pin bolt. DO NOT allow the open end wrench to come in contact with the brake caliper. Allowing the open end wrench to come in contact with the brake caliper will cause a pulsation when the brakes are applied.**

4. Using a backup wrench to hold the brake caliper guide pin stationary, remove the brake caliper guide pin bolts.

5. Remove the brake caliper from the brake caliper bracket and support with heavy mechanics wire or equivalent.

6. Remove the outer brake pad0.

➡ **The inner brake pad is equipped with the wear sensor.**

7. Remove the inner brake pad.

8. Remove and discard the brake pad springs.

9. Thoroughly clean the brake caliper bracket contact areas of any corrosion.

To install:

10. Install new brake pad springs.

11. Install the outer brake pad.

12. Install the inner brake pad.

13. Using an appropriate brake caliper piston spanner tool, slowly rotate the brake caliper piston clockwise while applying inward pressure to the brake caliper piston until the piston is fully seated in the brake caliper housing.

14. Ensure the notches in the brake caliper piston align correctly with the pins on the inner disc brake pad.

Install the brake caliper to the brake caliper bracket.

15. Using a backup wrench to hold the brake caliper guide pin stationary, install the brake caliper guide pin bolts and tighten to 20 ft. lbs. (27 Nm).

16. Install the tire and wheel assembly.

17. With the engine OFF, gradually apply the brake pedal to approximately 2/3 of its travel distance.

18. Slowly release the brake pedal.

19. Wait 15 seconds, then repeat previous steps until a firm brake pedal is obtained. This will properly seat the brake caliper piston and brake pads.

20. Fill the master cylinder reservoir.

21. Burnish the brake pads and rotors.

BRAKES

ELECTRONIC PARKING BRAKE ADJUSTER

ADJUSTER DISABLING

The park brake cable tension is controlled by the electronic park brake (EPB) module. Tension can be fully released from the park brake cables to allow for service of the park brake system. Perform one of the following three methods to fully release cable tension.

Electronic Parking Brake Cable Tension Release

With Scan Tool - Preferred Method

1. Block the drive wheels.

2. Install a scan tool to the vehicle.

3. Turn the ignition switch to the ON/RUN position with the engine OFF.

4. Select Control Functions from the electronic parking brake control module menu.

5. Follow the instructions on the scan tool.

Without Scan Tool - Optional Method

1. Block the drive wheels.

2. Turn the ignition switch to the ON/RUN position with the engine OFF.

3. Place the automatic transmission in PARK or manual transmission in NEUTRAL, as equipped.

4. Apply and hold the brake pedal. The brake pedal must remain applied throughout the park brake cable tension release process.

5. Press and hold down the electronic park brake (EPB) switch approximately 5 seconds.

6. Observe the PARK BRAKE lamp on the instrument cluster.

7. When the PARK BRAKE lamp flashes, release then immediately press and release the EPB switch.

➡ **The parking brake cable tension is fully released.**

8. Release the brake pedal.

PARKING BRAKE

Manual Parking Brake Cable Tension Release

See Figure 4.

➡ **In the event the above methods to release the parking brake cable tension are unsuccessful, the following procedure may be necessary to release the parking brake cable tension.**

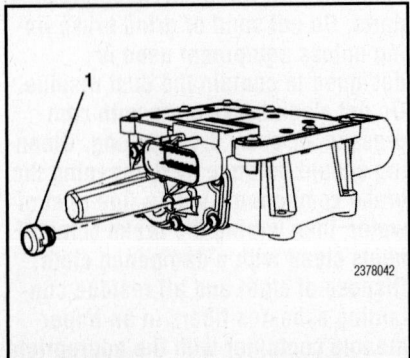

Fig. 4 Showing EPB module protective plug location

1. Raise and support the vehicle.
2. Remove the tire and wheel assembly.
3. Remove the left rear wheelhouse panel liner.

➡**The protective plug for the manual release is located near the electrical connector.**

4. Remove the protective plug from the Electronic Parking Brake (EPB) manual release.
5. Using an appropriate square-drive tool, rotate the mechanism clockwise until the tension is fully released from the parking brake cables.

➡**Up to 50 cycles may be required until the parking brake cable tension is fully released.**

6. Install the protective plug to the EPB module.

ADJUSTER ENABLING

Electronic Parking Brake Cable Tensioning

With Scan Tool—Preferred Method

1. Block the drive wheels.
2. Install a scan tool to the vehicle.
3. Turn the ignition switch to the ON/RUN position with the engine OFF.
4. Select Configuration/Reset Functions from the electronic parking brake control module menu.
5. Follow the instructions on the scan tool.

Without Scan Tool—Optional Method

1. Block the drive wheels.
2. Turn the ignition switch to the ON/RUN position with the engine OFF.
3. Apply the brake pedal.
4. Place the automatic transmission in PARK or manual transmission in NEUTRAL, as equipped.
5. Momentarily lift then release the EPB switch to apply the EPB.
6. Momentarily press down then release the EPB switch to release the EPB.
7. Repeat previous steps to cycle the EPB on then off an additional 4 times.

➡**The EPB module will be calibrated and proper tension will be applied to the parking brake cables.**

ELECTRONIC PARKING BRAKE MODULE

REMOVAL & INSTALLATION

1. Block the drive wheels.
2. Disable the electronic parking brake cable adjuster. See "Electronic

Parking Brake Adjuster" in this section.
3. Turn the ignition to the OFF position.
4. Raise and support the vehicle.
5. Remove the left rear tire and wheel assembly.
6. Remove the left rear wheelhouse panel liner.
7. Remove the following:
   • EPB cable nut
   • EPB rear cable clip
   • EPB module mounting nuts
   • Electronic Parking Brake (EPB) control module
8. Installation is the reverse of the removal procedure.
9. After the installation is complete, program the electronic parking brake control module as described below.
10. After the installation is complete, enable the electronic parking brake cable adjuster. See "Electronic Parking Brake Adjuster" in this section.

EPB CONTROL MODULE PROGRAMMING

Calibration with Scan Tool

1. Verify the rear brakes are clear of any obstacles before starting the calibration procedure.

✳✳ **CAUTION**

During the procedure the rear brakes will cycle several times, stay clear of all moving parts until the process is complete.

2. Perform the "Parking Brake Calibration" procedure in "Module Setup" in the scan tool menu.

Calibration without Scan Tool

1. Turn ignition ON, apply and hold the brake pedal.
2. Push and hold the electric parking brake switch down for 5–6 seconds.
3. Release the electric parking brake switch.
4. Momentarily push the electric parking brake switch down.
5. Remove the EPB module fuse and reinstall.
6. Apply the electric parking brake.
7. Release the electric parking brake.

PARKING BRAKE CABLES

REPLACEMENT

See Figure 5.

1. Release the electric parking brake.
2. Set ignition in Run mode and put your foot on top of the service brake.
3. Press the parking brake switch down and hold for 5 seconds, then a solid yellow telltale is shown on instrument panel.
4. Press the parking brake switch again within 5 seconds, then a flashing yellow telltale is shown on instrument panel.

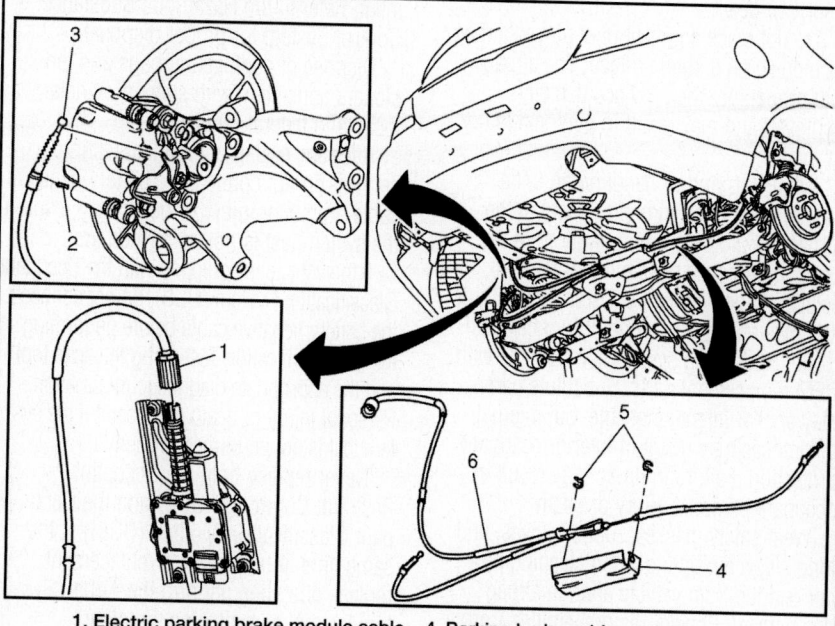

1. Electric parking brake module cable
2. Retainer washer
3. Parking brake cable
4. Parking brake cable protector
5. Retainer washers
6. Rear parking brake cable

Fig. 5 Showing parking brake cable configuration

2018613

5. Raise and support the vehicle.
6. Remove the tire and wheel assembly.
7. Remove the rear wheelhouse panel liner.
8. Remove the following in order:

- Electric Parking Brake Module Cable
a. Retainer Washer
b. Parking Brake Cable
c. Protector, Parking Brake Cable

d. Retainer Washer (Qty: 2)
e. Parking Brake Rear Cable
9. Installation is the reverse of the removal procedure.

CHASSIS ELECTRICAL — AIR BAG (SUPPLEMENTAL RESTRAINT SYSTEM)

GENERAL INFORMATION

✳✳ CAUTION

These vehicles are equipped with an air bag system. The system must be disarmed before performing service on, or around, system components, the steering column, instrument panel components, wiring and sensors. Failure to follow the safety precautions and the disarming procedure could result in accidental air bag deployment, possible injury and unnecessary system repairs.

SERVICE PRECAUTIONS

Disconnect and isolate the battery negative cable before beginning any airbag system component diagnosis, testing, removal, or installation procedures. Allow system capacitor to discharge for two minutes before beginning any component service. This will disable the airbag system. Failure to disable the airbag system may result in accidental airbag deployment, personal injury, or death.

Do not place an intact undeployed airbag face down on a solid surface. The airbag will propel into the air if accidentally deployed and may result in personal injury or death.

When carrying or handling an undeployed airbag, the trim side (face) of the airbag should be pointing away from the body to minimize possibility of injury if accidental deployment occurs. Failure to do this may result in personal injury or death.

Replace airbag system components with OEM replacement parts. Substitute parts may appear interchangeable, but internal differences may result in inferior occupant protection. Failure to do so may result in occupant personal injury or death.

Wear safety glasses, rubber gloves, and long sleeved clothing when cleaning powder residue from vehicle after an airbag deployment. Powder residue emitted from a deployed airbag can cause skin irritation. Flush affected area with cool water if irritation is experienced. If nasal or throat irritation is experienced, exit the vehicle for fresh air until the irritation ceases. If irritation continues, see a physician.

Do not use a replacement airbag that is not in the original packaging. This may result in improper deployment, personal injury, or death.

The factory installed fasteners, screws and bolts used to fasten airbag components have a special coating and are specifically designed for the airbag system. Do not use substitute fasteners. Use only original equipment fasteners listed in the parts catalog when fastener replacement is required.

During, and following, any child restraint anchor service, due to impact event or vehicle repair, carefully inspect all mounting hardware, tether straps, and anchors for proper installation, operation, or damage. If a child restraint anchor is found damaged in any way, the anchor must be replaced. Failure to do this may result in personal injury or death.

Deployed and non-deployed airbags may or may not have live pyrotechnic material within the airbag inflator.

Do not dispose of driver/passenger/curtain airbags or seat belt tensioners unless you are sure of complete deployment. Refer to the Hazardous Substance Control System for proper disposal.

Dispose of deployed airbags and tensioners consistent with state, provincial, local, and federal regulations.

After any airbag component testing or service, do not connect the battery negative cable. Personal injury or death may result if the system test is not performed first.

If the vehicle is equipped with the Occupant Classification System (OCS), do not connect the battery negative cable before performing the OCS Verification Test using the scan tool and the appropriate diagnostic information. Personal injury or death may result if the system test is not performed properly.

Never replace both the Occupant Restraint Controller (ORC) and the Occupant Classification Module (OCM) at the same time. If both require replacement, replace one, then perform the Airbag System test before replacing the other.

Both the ORC and the OCM store Occupant Classification System (OCS) calibration data, which they transfer to one another when one of them is replaced. If both are

replaced at the same time, an irreversible fault will be set in both modules and the OCS may malfunction and cause personal injury or death.

If equipped with OCS, the Seat Weight Sensor is a sensitive, calibrated unit and must be handled carefully. Do not drop or handle roughly. If dropped or damaged, replace with another sensor. Failure to do so may result in occupant injury or death.

If equipped with OCS, the front passenger seat must be handled carefully as well. When removing the seat, be careful when setting on floor not to drop. If dropped, the sensor may be inoperative, could result in occupant injury, or possibly death.

If equipped with OCS, when the passenger front seat is on the floor, no one should sit in the front passenger seat. This uneven force may damage the sensing ability of the seat weight sensors. If sat on and damaged, the sensor may be inoperative, could result in occupant injury, or possibly death.

DISARMING THE SYSTEM

Battery Cable Disarming

1. Turn the steering wheel so that the vehicles wheels are pointing straight ahead.
2. Place the ignition in the OFF position.
3. Disconnect the negative battery cable from the battery.
4. Wait 1 minute before working on system.

➡ **The inflatable restraint sensing and diagnostic module (SDM) maintains a reserved energy supply. The reserved energy supply provides deployment power for the air bags if the SDM loses battery power during a collision. Deployment power is available for as much as 1 minute after disconnecting the vehicle power. Waiting 1 minute before working on the system after disabling the SIR system prevents deployment of the air bags from the reserved energy supply.**

Air Bag Fuse Disabling

1. Turn the steering wheel so that the vehicles wheels are pointing straight ahead.
2. Place the ignition in the OFF position.

✳✳ CAUTION

The SDM may have more than one fused power input. To ensure there is no unwanted SIR deployment, personal injury, or unnecessary SIR system repairs, remove all fuses supplying power to the SDM. With all SDM fuses removed and the ignition switch in the ON position, the AIR BAG warning indicator illuminates. This is normal operation, and does not indicate a SIR system malfunction.

3. Locate and remove the fuse(s) supplying power to the SDM.
4. Wait 1 minute before working on the system.

ARMING THE SYSTEM

Battery Cable Enabling

1. Place the ignition in the OFF position.
2. Connect the negative battery cable to the battery.
3. Turn the ignition switch to the ON position. The AIR BAG indicator will flash then turn OFF.
4. Perform the Diagnostic System Check–Vehicle, if the AIR BAG warning indicator does not operate as described.

Air Bag Fuse Enabling

1. Place the ignition in the OFF position.
2. Install the fuse(s) supplying power to the SDM.
3. Turn the ignition switch to the ON position. The AIR BAG indicator will flash then turn OFF.
4. Perform the Diagnostic System Check–Vehicle, if the AIR BAG warning indicator does not operate as described.

CLOCKSPRING CENTERING

See Figure 6.

✳✳ CAUTION

The new SIR coil assembly will be centered. Improper alignment of the SIR coil assembly may damage the unit, causing an inflatable restraint malfunction.

1. Verify the following conditions before centering the supplemental inflatable restraint (SIR) steering wheel module coil:
   a. The wheels on the vehicle are straight ahead.
   b. The centering mark of the steering shaft is in the 6 o'clock position.
2. Turn the lobe of the clock spring

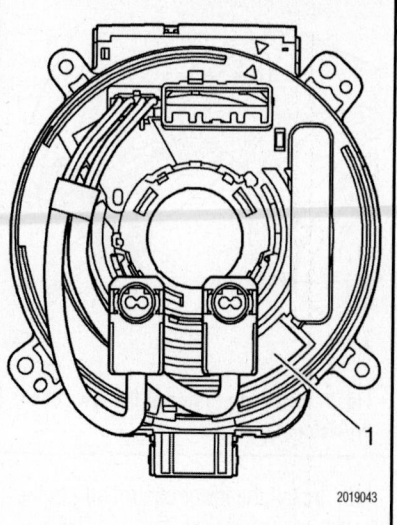

Fig. 6 Properly align until the centering window (1) turns yellow. This indicates the CENTER position.

clockwise until the coil ribbon stops. Do not force.
3. Turn the lobe of the clock spring counterclockwise approximately 3 turns to the Neutral position.
4. Properly align until the centering window turns yellow. This indicates the CENTER position.

DRIVE TRAIN

AUTOMATIC TRANSAXLE FLUID

DRAIN & REFILL

1. Raise the vehicle.
2. Remove the transmission fluid drain plug.

➡**Place a drain pan capable of containing more than 5 quarts of fluid under the transmission before removing the plug to drain the fluid.**

3. Install and tighten the drain plug to 106 inch lbs. (12 Nm).
4. Refill the transmission with fluid.

➡**Transmission will require approximately 5 quarts of fluid.**

FRONT DRIVESHAFT

REMOVAL & INSTALLATION

See Figure 7.

1. Raise and support the vehicle.
2. Remove the tire and wheel assembly.
3. Insert a drift or punch in the cooling fins of the brake rotor.
4. Rotate the brake rotor until the drift

or punch contacts the brake caliper mounting bracket.
5. Using a breaker bar, loosen the wheel drive shaft nut.
6. Using the appropriate tool, separate the wheel drive shaft from the knuckle.
7. Remove the wheel drive shaft nut.
8. Remove the lower control arm from the knuckle.
9. Remove the outer tie rod end from the knuckle.
10. Using a large screw driver, remove the wheel drive shaft from the differential.

➡**It may be necessary to have an assistant hold the knuckle assembly while removing the wheel drive shaft.**

✳✳ CAUTION

If removing the wheel drive shaft to service other suspension or driveline components, use care when removing or installing the wheel drive shaft so as not to damage the wheel drive shaft boots.

11. Remove the wheel drive shaft from the vehicle.

12. Remove and discard the washer from the wheel drive shaft. DO NOT re-use the washer, replace with NEW only.
13. Remove the front axle shaft seal.

To install:
14. Install the NEW front axle shaft seal.

✳✳ CAUTION

Wheel drive shaft seal protector must be installed into the differential output shaft seal prior to removing and installing the wheel drive shaft. Failure to install the wheel drive shaft seal protector as indicated may cause the splines of the wheel drive shaft to cut the differential output seal.

15. Install the drive shaft protector (DT 44394-A or equivalent) into the differential, if removed.
16. Position the wheel drive shaft in the vehicle.
17. Remove the protector from the differential.
18. Insert the wheel drive shaft in the knuckle.

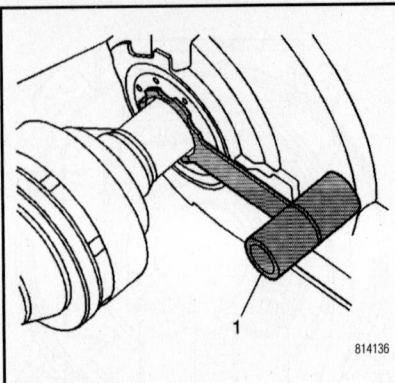

Fig. 7 Installed position of the drive shaft protector (1)

19. Install the lower control arm in the knuckle.

20. Install the outer tie rod end in the knuckle.

21. Install the wheel drive shaft nut.

22. Insert a drift or punch in the cooling fins of the brake rotor.

23. Rotate the brake rotor until the drift or punch contacts the brake caliper mounting bracket.

24. Using a torque wrench, tighten the wheel drive shaft nut to 111 ft. lbs. (150 Nm), then back off 45°, then re-torque to 184 ft. lbs. (250 Nm).

25. Install the tire and wheel assembly.

26. Remove the support and lower the vehicle.

PROPELLER SHAFT

REMOVAL & INSTALLATION

1. Raise and support the vehicle.

2. Remove the 3 rear differential drive flange bolts and retainers.

3. Mark a reference point between the propeller shaft and the flange.

4. Using the appropriate tools, remove the flange bolts and the retainers.

5. Use the puller (DT 49064 or equivalent), if needed to remove the propeller shaft.

6. Remove the 4 support bearing mounting bolts.

7. Lower the evaporator canister to gain access to the center bearing bolts.

8. Support the support bearings with jack stands.

9. Clean threads of all residue of the old thread locker.

10. Apply new thread locker to the bolts.

11. Remove the propeller shaft.

12. Using the fork tool (DT-49030 or equivalent), remove the propeller shaft from the transfer case.

13. It may be necessary to have the help of an assistant to remove the propeller shaft.

14. Apply grease on the spline.

15. Installation is the reverse of the removal procedure.

16. Tighten the support mounting bolts to 43 ft. lbs. (58 Nm).

17. Tighten the flange bolts to 27 ft. lbs. (36 Nm).

REAR AXLE FLUID

DRAIN & REFILL

1. Raise the vehicle. Ensure the vehicle is in level.

2. Inspect the rear axle for leaks, repair if necessary.

3. Remove the lubricant fill plug from the side of the axle housing.

4. Clean the area around the rear axle fill plug.

5. Remove the drain plug and drain the fluid.

6. Install the drain plug and tighten to 19 ft. lbs. (25 Nm).

7. Add new lubricant until the level is even with the bottom edge of the fill plug opening. Use the proper fluid.

8. Install the fill plug and tighten to 19 ft. lbs. (25 Nm).

9. Lower the vehicle.

REAR AXLE (DIFFERENTIAL) HOUSING ASSEMBLY

REMOVAL & INSTALLATION

1. Raise and support the vehicle.

2. If replacing the rear differential assembly, drain the rear differential fluid.

3. Remove the propeller shaft assembly.

4. Remove the rear stabilizer shaft.

5. Remove the rear wheel drive shaft.

6. Disconnect the electrical connectors from the rear differential assembly to the chassis.

✳✳ CAUTION

Ensure that the rear differential is securely fastened to the hydraulic jack stand.

7. Support the rear differential assembly with a hydraulic transmission jack.

8. Remove the rear differential assembly mounting bolts.

9. Remove the front differential mounting bolts.

10. Using the hydraulic jack stand, remove the rear differential assembly from the vehicle.

To install:

11. Using the hydraulic jack stand, position the rear differential assembly in the vehicle.

12. Clean the bolts and apply thread locker on the threads. Install the front differential mounting bolts and tighten to 92 ft. lbs. (125 Nm).

13. Install the rear differential assembly mounting bolts and tighten to 66 ft. lbs. (90 Nm), plus an additional 100 degrees.

14. Remove the hydraulic jack stand.

15. Install the rear wheel drive shafts.

16. Install the rear stabilizer shaft.

17. Reconnect the electrical connectors from the rear differential assembly to the chassis.

18. Install the propeller shaft assembly.

19. Check the fluid level of the rear differential assembly.

20. If installing a NEW rear differential assembly, fill with the proper fluid.

21. Remove the supports and lower the vehicle.

22. Program the rear differential assembly using the GM SPS system, or equivalent.

REAR AXLE SHAFT, BEARING & SEAL

REMOVAL & INSTALLATION

1. Remove the tire and wheel.

2. Remove the knuckle assembly as one unit. Do not remove the caliper bracket, hub or disc.

3. Place drain pans underneath the vehicle as needed.

4. Tap out the rear wheel drive shaft from the rear axle using a brass drift and a mallet.

To install:

5. Installation is the reverse of the removal procedure.

6. On installation, lubricate the rear wheel drive shaft's splines with rear axle lubricant to help ease installation. Press in the shaft until the circlip engages.

7. After repairs, check the rear axle lubricant level.

ENGINE COOLING

ENGINE COOLANT

DRAIN & REFILL PROCEDURE

1. Remove the coolant pressure cap from the radiator surge tank.
2. Raise and support the vehicle.
3. Place a drain pan under the drain cock.
4. Loosen the radiator drain cock, located on the lower side of the radiator.
5. Drain the cooling system.
6. Lower the vehicle.
7. Inspect the coolant.
8. Follow the appropriate procedure based on the condition of the coolant:
   a. If normal in appearance, follow the filling procedure.
   b. If discolored, follow the flushing procedure.

To install:

❈❈ CAUTION

The procedure below must be followed. Improper coolant level could result in a low or high coolant level condition, causing engine damage.

9. Raise and support the vehicle.
10. Tighten the radiator drain cock.
11. Lower the vehicle.
12. Slowly fill the radiator with a 50/50 coolant mixture until the coolant level reaches the base of the radiator surge tank.
13. Allow 30 seconds for the coolant level to stabilize and continue to fill the coolant filler neck until the level stabilizes for at least 2 minutes.
14. Start the engine and allow to the engine to idle in PARK or NEUTRAL with the parking brake engaged.
15. Slowly fill the coolant mixture until the level stabilizes at the base of the radiator surge tank.
16. Install the coolant pressure cap.
17. Raise the engine RPM to 2500 rpm for 30–40 seconds.
18. Shut the engine OFF.
19. Allow the engine to cool, remove coolant fill cap and repeat steps 4-10 until the coolant level has completely stabilized within the radiator surge tank.
20. Inspect the concentration of the engine coolant using a proper Coolant and Battery Fluid Tester.
21. Inspect and if necessary, fill the coolant reservoir bottle as necessary.
22. Rinse away any excess coolant from the engine and the engine compartment.
23. Inspect the cooling system for leaks.

24. Top off the radiator surge tank if necessary.

FLUSHING

➡**Do not use a chemical flush.**

➡**Store used coolant in the proper manner, such as in a used engine coolant holding tank. Do not pour used coolant down a drain. Ethylene glycol antifreeze is a very toxic chemical. Do not dispose of coolant into the sewer system or ground water. This is illegal and ecologically unsound.**

➡**Various methods and equipment can be used to flush the cooling system. If special equipment is used, such as a back flusher, follow the manufacturer's instruction. Always remove the thermostat before flushing the cooling system.**

➡**When the cooling system becomes contaminated, the cooling system should be flushed thoroughly to remove the contaminants before the engine is seriously damaged.**

1. Drain the cooling system.
2. Remove the radiator surge tank.
3. Clean and flush the radiator surge tank with clean, drinkable water.
4. Install the radiator surge tank.
5. Follow the drain and fill procedure using only clean, drinkable water.
6. Run the engine for 20 minutes.
7. Stop the engine.
8. Drain the cooling system.
9. Repeat the procedure if necessary, until the fluid is nearly colorless.
10. Fill the cooling system.

ENGINE FAN

REMOVAL & INSTALLATION

1. Disconnect the engine coolant fan motor electrical connectors.
2. Unclip all wiring harnesses that are connected to the shroud.
3. Push in the tabs at the bottom of the radiator to release the shroud.
4. Pull up to remove the cooling fan shroud assembly from the vehicle.
5. Remove the retainers from the engine coolant fan blades.
6. Remove the fan motor bolts.
7. Remove the engine coolant fan motors.

To install:

8. Install the engine coolant fan motors. Tighten the bolts to 89 inch lbs. (10 Nm).

9. Install the coolant fan blades and the retainers.
10. Install the cooling fan shroud assembly into the vehicle and carefully press into the retaining tabs.
11. Connect the wiring harnesses that were removed from the shroud.
12. Connect the engine coolant fan motor electrical connectors.
13. Check for proper operation of the engine cooling fans.

RADIATOR

REMOVAL & INSTALLATION

1. Drain the cooling system.
2. Remove the radiator inlet hose.
3. Remove the radiator outlet hose.
4. Remove transmission oil cooler lines.
5. Disconnect the engine coolant fan harness electrical connectors.
6. Remove the radiator support brackets.
7. Release the 2 condenser assembly retainers.
8. Remove the engine coolant fan shroud from the radiator.
9. Remove the radiator.
10. Installation is the reverse of the removal procedure.

THERMOSTAT

REMOVAL & INSTALLATION

2.4L Engine

See Figure 8.

1. Raise the vehicle by its full height.
2. Drain the cooling system.

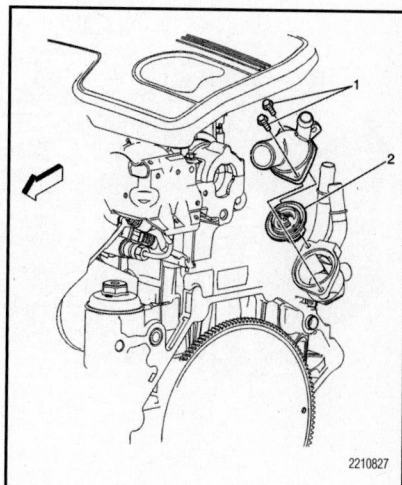

2210827

Fig. 8 Removing the thermostat bolts (1) and thermostat (2)—2.4L engine

3. Disconnect the radiator outlet hose from the water inlet housing.

4. Remove the thermostat bolts.

5. Remove the thermostat and gasket.

To install:

6. Clean the mating surfaces.

7. Install the thermostat and a new gasket.

8. Install the retaining bolts and tighten to 88 inch lbs. (10 Nm).

3.6L Engine

See Figure 9.

1. Remove the fuel injector pipe shield.

2. Reposition engine control module.

3. Drain the cooling system.

4. Remove the intake manifold cover.

5. Remove the heater inlet and outlet hoses.

6. Remove the surge tank hose.

7. Remove the radiator outlet hose.

8. Remove the bolts retaining the engine coolant thermostat housing.

9. Remove the thermostat housing.

10. Remove the thermostat gasket and discard.

11. Remove the engine cooling thermostat from the thermostat housing.

To install:

12. Replace the thermostat gasket and any worn hoses.

13. Clean the engine block and thermostat gasket surfaces.

14. Install the thermostat and a new gasket.

15. Installation is the reverse of the removal procedure.

16. Tighten the thermostat housing bolts to 88 inch lbs. (10 Nm).

17. Fill the cooling system with the proper type and amount of fluid.

18. Run the engine and check for fluid leaks.

WATER PUMP

REMOVAL & INSTALLATION

2.4L Engine

See Figures 10 through 12.

1. Remove the air cleaner assembly.

2. Remove the intake manifold cover.

3. Remove the exhaust manifold heat shield.

4. If equipped, remove the coolant heater.

5. Remove the catalytic converter.

6. Remove the engine coolant thermostat housing.

7. Remove the water pump cover, fasteners and gasket from the engine front cover.

8. Drain the coolant from the water pump using the plug at the bottom of the pump. Install the plug when finished.

➡**The water pump holding tool supports the sprocket and chain during water pump service. The tool must be used or the balance shaft must be re-timed.**

9. Align the water pump holding tool (EN-43651 or equivalent) with the threads on the water pump sprocket. Tighten the water pump holding tool fasteners.

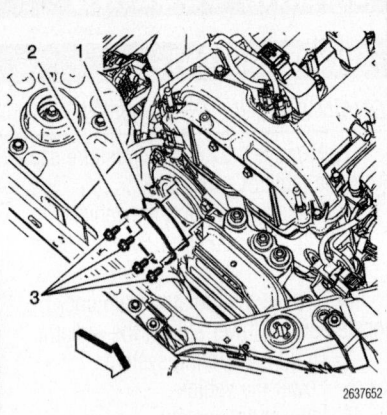

Fig. 10 Remove the water pump cover (2), fasteners (3) and gasket (1) from the engine front cover.

Fig. 11 Align the water pump holding tool (EN-43651 or equivalent) (1) with the threads on the water pump sprocket. Tighten the water pump holding tool fasteners.

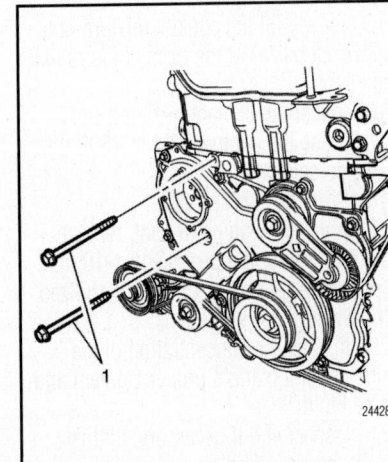

Fig. 12 Remove both water pump bolts (1) from the front of the engine block.

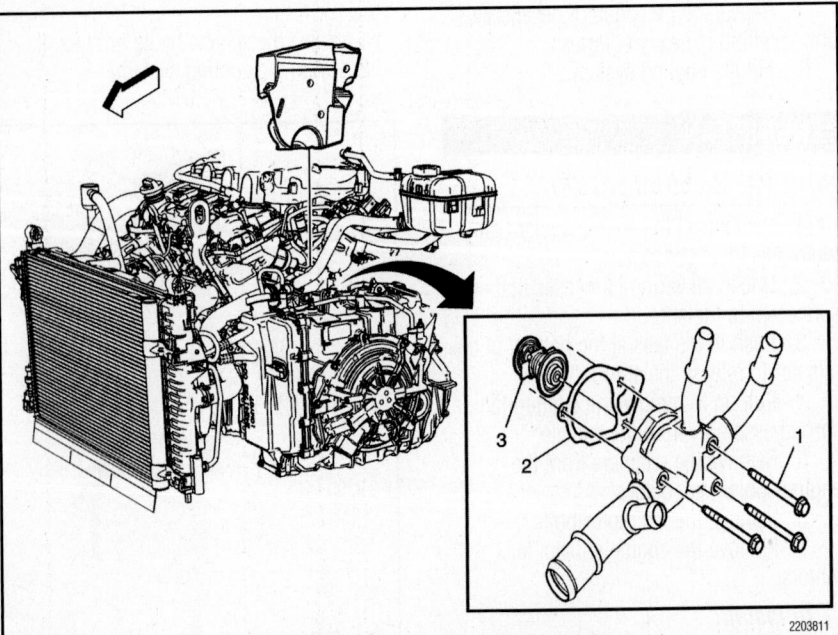

Fig. 9 Removing the bolts (1), gasket (2) and thermostat (3)—3.6L engine

10. Secure the water pump holding tool with the previously removed water pump cover fasteners into the engine front cover.

11. Remove both water pump bolts from the front of the engine block.

12. Remove the front and rear water pump fasteners.

13. Remove the water pump.

14. If replacing the water pump cover remove the water pump rear cover fasteners.

15. Separate the water pump cover from the water pump.

16. Remove and discard the water pump O-ring seal.

To install:

17. If replacing the water pump cover, install a new O-ring to the water pump and tighten the fasteners to 18 ft. lbs. (25 Nm).

➡**A guide pin can be created to aid in water pump alignment. Use a M 6 m x 6 mm x 50.8 mm stud (2 in.). Thread the pin into the water pump sprocket.**

18. Using a guide pin, align the pin with the water pump holding tool.

19. Position the water pump against the engine block and hand tighten the water pump fasteners.

20. Install 2 water pump sprocket to water pump fasteners. After the fasteners are snug, remove the guide pin and install the 3rd fastener and tighten to 89 inch lbs. (10 Nm).

21. Install the water pump fasteners at the front of the engine. Hand tighten at this time.

22. Tighten the water pump fasteners at the front and rear of the water pump to 18 ft. lbs. (25 Nm).

23. Remove the water pump cover fasteners from the engine front cover and water pump holding tool.

24. Remove the water pump holding tool from the water pump sprocket.

25. Install the water pump access plate, gasket and fasteners and tighten to 89 inch lbs. (10 Nm).

26. If equipped, Install the coolant heater.

27. Install the engine coolant thermostat housing.

28. Install the catalytic converter.

29. Install the exhaust manifold heat shield.

30. Install the intake manifold cover.

31. Install the air cleaner assembly.

32. Refill the coolant system.

3.6L Engine

1. Drain the cooling system.
2. Remove the accessory drive belt.

Refer to Accessory Drive Belts in "ENGINE MECHANICAL" section.

3. Use tool EN 46104 in order to retain the water pump pulley.

4. Remove the water pump pulley bolts.

5. Remove the water pump pulley.

6. Remove the water pump bolts.

7. Remove the water pump.

8. Remove and DISCARD the water pump seal.

9. Carefully clean the water pump sealing surfaces.

To install:

10. Install a NEW water pump seal.

11. Install the water pump.

12. Install the water pump bolts. Tighten the water pump bolts to 89 inch lbs. (10 Nm).

13. Install the water pump pulley and the water pump pulley bolts.

14. Install the water pump pulley bolts. Tighten the water pump pulley bolts to 106 inch lbs. (12 Nm).

15. Install the alternator drive belt.

16. Fill the cooling system with the proper type and amount of fluid.

17. Run the engine and check for fluid leaks.

ENGINE ELECTRICAL   BATTERY SYSTEM

BATTERY

REMOVAL & INSTALLATION

1. Remove the battery cover.

2. Disconnect the negative battery cable.

3. Remove the fuse block.

4. Remove the battery retainer fastener and battery retainer bracket.

5. Remove the battery.

6. Installation is the reverse of the removal procedure.

ENGINE ELECTRICAL   CHARGING SYSTEM

GENERATOR

REMOVAL & INSTALLATION

2.4L Engine

1. Disconnect the negative battery cable.

2. Remove the accessory drive belt.

3. Disconnect the engine harness generator connector.

4. Remove the generator battery positive nut.

5. Remove the generator nut.

6. Remove the generator mounting bolts.

7. Remove the generator.

To install:

8. Install the generator and the mounting bolts. Tighten to 16 ft. lbs. (22 Nm).

9. Install and tighten the generator nut to 16 ft. lbs. (22 Nm).

10. Install and tighten the generator battery positive nut to 15 ft. lbs. (20 Nm).

11. Attach the generator engine harness connector.

12. Install the accessory drive belt.

13. Reconnect the negative battery cable.

3.6L Engine

1. Disconnect the negative battery cable.

2. Reposition the positive battery cable boot at the generator terminal.

3. Disconnect the engine harness electrical connector from the generator.

4. Remove the positive battery cable nut at the generator.

5. Remove the positive battery cable terminal from the generator.

6. Remove the drive belt.

7. Remove the idler pulley bolt and idler pulley.

8. Remove the generator mounting bolts.

➡**When removing the generator from the vehicle, it may be necessary to maneuver the generator to remove it from the vehicle.**

9. Remove the generator

To install:

10. Position the generator to the engine. Loosely install the generator bolts.

11. Install the idler pulley.

12. Tighten the generator bolts to 37 ft. lbs. (50 Nm).

13. Install the drive belt.

14. Connect the engine harness electrical connector to the generator.

15. Install the positive battery cable terminal to the generator.

16. Install the positive battery cable nut at the generator and tighten to 15 ft. lbs. (20 Nm).

17. Position the positive battery cable boot at the generator terminal.

18. Connect the negative battery cable.

ENGINE ELECTRICAL

FIRING ORDER

2.4L Engine

1–3–4–2

3.6L Engine

1–2–3–4–5–6

IGNITION COIL

REMOVAL & INSTALLATION

2.4L Engine

1. Remove the intake manifold cover.

2. Disconnect the engine wiring harness electrical connectors from the ignition coil(s).

3. Remove the ignition coil bolt(s) and remove the ignition coil(s).

To install:

4. Install the ignition coil(s).

5. Install the ignition coil bolt(s) and tighten to 89 inch lbs. (10 Nm).

6. Connect the engine wiring harness electrical connector(s) to the ignition coil(s).

7. Install the intake manifold cover.

3.6L Engine

Bank 1

1. Remove the fuel injector sight shield.

2. Disconnect the engine wiring harness electrical connector(s) from the ignition coil(s).

3. If removing the number 5 cylinder ignition coil, remove the Evaporative Emission (EVAP) canister purge tube.

4. If removing the number one ignition coil, remove the canister purge solenoid.

5. Remove the ignition coil bolt(s). Remove the ignition coil(s).

To install:

6. Install the ignition coil(s).

7. Install the ignition coil bolt(s) and tighten to 89 inch lbs. (10 Nm).

8. If the number 5 cylinder ignition coil was removed, install the EVAP canister purge tube.

9. If the number one ignition coil was removed, install the canister purge solenoid.

10. Connect the engine wiring harness electrical connector(s) to the ignition coil(s).

11. Install the fuel injector sight shield.

Bank 2

1. Remove the fuel injector sight shield.

2. Disconnect the engine wiring harness electrical connector(s) from the ignition coil(s).

3. Remove the ignition coil bolt(s).

4. Remove the ignition coil(s).

To install:

5. Installation is the reverse of the removal procedure.

6. Tighten the ignition coil bolts to 89 inch lbs. (10 Nm).

IGNITION TIMING

ADJUSTMENT

➡Ignition timing is computer controlled. No manual adjustment is required.

SPARK PLUGS

REMOVAL & INSTALLATION

2.4L Engine

✴✴ CAUTION

This engine has aluminum cylinder heads. Do not remove the spark plugs from a hot engine, allow it to cool first. Removing the spark plugs from a hot engine may cause spark plug thread damage or cylinder head damage.

1. Remove the ignition coil(s).

2. Make sure that any water and/or debris is blown out of the spark plug holes prior to removing the spark plugs.

3. Remove the spark plugs, using a 5/8 inch spark plug socket.

To install:

✴✴ CAUTION

Do not coat spark plug threads with anti-seize compound. If anti-seize compound is used and spark plugs

IGNITION SYSTEM

are over-torqued, damage to the cylinder head threads may result.

4. Verify the spark plug gap before installing. Gap should be 0.040 in. (1.0 mm).

5. Install the spark plugs. Tighten the plugs to 15 ft. lbs. (20 Nm).

6. Install the ignition coil(s).

3.6L Engine

1. Clean the spark plug recess area before removing the spark plug.

✴✴ CAUTION

Failure to do so could result in engine damage because of dirt or foreign material entering the cylinder head, or by the contamination of the cylinder head threads. The contaminated threads may prevent the proper seating of the new plug. Use a thread chaser to clean the threads of any contamination.

2. Remove the ignition coil(s). Refer to Ignition Coils.

3. Use compressed air in order to remove debris from the spark plug cavity.

✴✴ CAUTION

Allow the engine to cool before removing the spark plugs. Attempting to remove the spark plugs from a hot engine may cause the plug threads to seize, causing damage to cylinder head threads.

4. Remove the spark plug(s).

To install:

✴✴ CAUTION

Use only the spark plugs specified for use in the vehicle. Do not install spark plugs that are either hotter or colder than those specified for the vehicle. Installing spark plugs of another type can severely damage the engine.

5. Check the gap of all new and reconditioned spark plugs before installation.

➡ The pre-set gaps may have changed during handling. Use a round feeler gage to ensure an accurate check. Installing the spark plugs with the wrong gap can cause poor engine perfor-mance and may even damage the engine.

6. Ensure that the spark plug is equivalent to the spark plug gap of 0.0433 inch.
7. Be sure that the spark plug threads smoothly into the cylinder head and the spark plug is fully seated.
8. Install the spark plug. Tighten the spark plug to 15 ft. lbs. (20 Nm).
9. Install the ignition coil(s). Refer to Ignition Coils.

ENGINE ELECTRICAL

STARTER

REMOVAL & INSTALLATION

2.4L Engine

1. Disconnect the negative battery cable.
2. Raise and support the vehicle.
3. Disconnect the engine harness connector from the starter.
4. Remove the starter solenoid terminal nut.
5. Remove the positive battery cable terminal from the starter.
6. Remove the starter solenoid wire terminal from the starter.
7. Remove the starter bolts.
8. Remove the starter.

To install:

9. Position the starter to the engine.
10. Install the starter bolts and tighten to 30 ft. lbs. (40 Nm).
11. Install the starter solenoid wire terminal to the starter.
12. Install the positive battery cable terminal to the starter Ensure that the anti-rotational tab is correctly located into the indexing slot.
13. Install the starter solenoid terminal nut.
14. Connect the engine harness connector to the starter.
15. Lower the vehicle.
16. Connect the negative battery cable.

3.6L Engine

1. Turn OFF the ignition.
2. Disconnect the battery negative cable.
3. Remove the heat shield from the starter.

STARTING SYSTEM

4. Raise and support the vehicle.
5. Disconnect the knock sensor connector.
6. Remove the battery positive nut and the engine harness connector, from the starter solenoid.
7. Remove the starter motor bolts.
8. Remove the starter motor.

To install:

9. Install the starter motor.
10. Install the starter motor mounting bolts. Tighten to 43 ft. lbs. (58 Nm).
11. Install the battery positive cable and engine harness connector to the starter. Tighten the battery positive cable nut to 18 ft. lbs. (25 Nm).
12. Install the engine harness connector to the starter solenoid.
13. Install the starter heat shield and tighten the bolt.
14. Connect the knock sensor connector.

ENGINE MECHANICAL

➡ Disconnecting the negative battery cable may interfere with the functions of the on board computer systems and may require the computer to undergo a relearning process, once the negative battery cable is reconnected.

ACCESSORY DRIVE BELTS

ACCESSORY BELT ROUTING

See Figures 13 and 14.

Refer to the accompanying illustrations.

REMOVAL & INSTALLATION

2.4L Engine

1. Use the proper tool to rotate the drive belt tensioner.
2. Remove the drive belt from the pulleys and tensioner. Remove the drive belt tensioner.
3. Clean and inspect the drive belt surfaces of all the pulleys.
4. Inspect the drive belt for correct alignment.

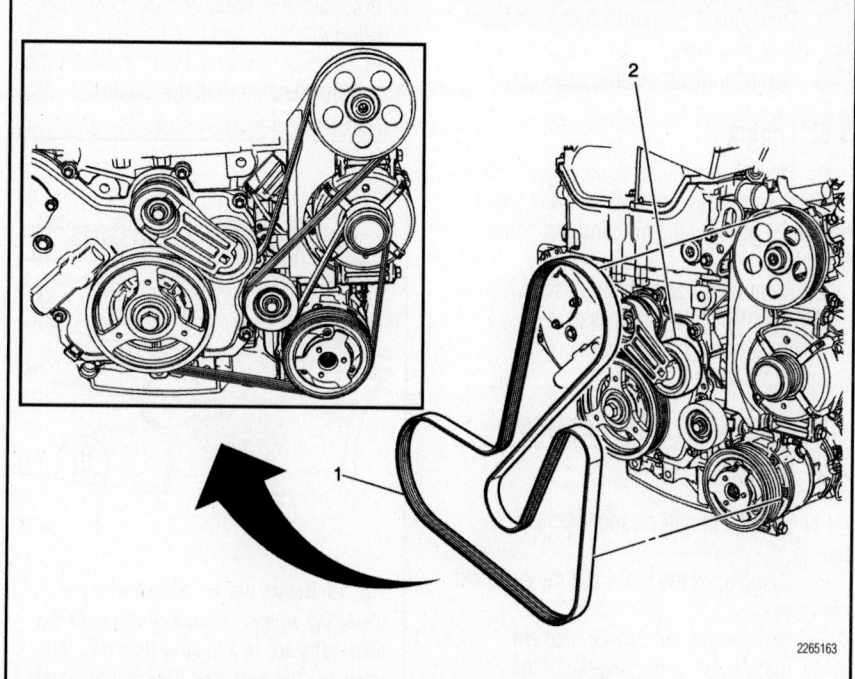

Fig. 13 Accessory belt (1) routing, showing belt tensioner (2)—2.4L engine

2265163

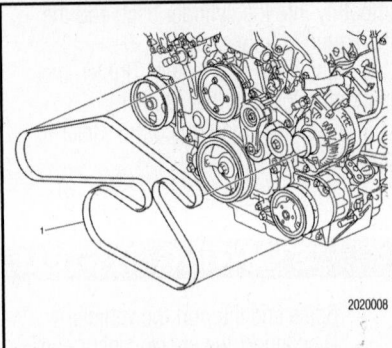

Fig. 14 Accessory belt (1) routing—2.4L engine

5. Installation is the reverse of the removal procedure.

6. Tighten the tensioner bolt to 33 ft. lbs. (45 Nm).

3.6L Engine

1. Rotate the drive belt tensioner clockwise to release the drive belt tension.

2. Slide the drive belt off of the belt idler pulley.

3. Slowly release the drive belt tensioner.

4. Installation is the reverse of the removal procedure.

AIR CLEANER

REMOVAL & INSTALLATION

2.4L Engine

1. Remove the mass airflow sensor.

2. Disconnect the outlet duct from the air cleaner assembly.

3. Remove the air cleaner assembly.

3.6L Engine

1. Disconnect the air cleaner outlet duct.

2. Remove the housing from the retainers, while guiding the housing out of the inlet duct.

3. Remove the air cleaner assembly.

4. Transfer parts as necessary.

5. Installation is the reverse of the removal procedure.

FILTER/ELEMENT REPLACEMENT

2.4L Engine

1. Release the air cleaner element fasteners.

2. Disconnect the mass airflow electrical connector.

3. Remove the air cleaner element.

4. Installation is the reverse of the removal procedure.

3.6L Engine

1. Release the air cleaner housing fasteners.

2. From the left side of the air cleaner cover, tilt the cover upward.

3. Disengage the upper cover tabs from the lower cover.

4. Remove the air cleaner upper cover from the vehicle.

5. Installation is the reverse of the removal procedure.

CAMSHAFT

REMOVAL & INSTALLATION

2.4L Engine

➡**Camshaft cannot be removed until engine is disassembled.**

3.6L Engine

See Figures 15 through 18.

➡**Procedure is the same for left side and right side camshafts.**

1. Remove the intake manifold. See "Intake Manifold" in this section.

2. Remove the fuel pump from the cylinder head. See "FUEL" section.

3. Remove the left bank camshaft cover. See "Valve (Camshaft) Cover" in this section.

4. Remove the camshaft sensors. See "ENGINE PERFORMANCE & EMISSION CONTROLS" section.

5. Remove the camshaft position actuator solenoid and actuator. See "Camshaft Position Actuators" in this section.

6. Remove the crankshaft balancer. See "Crankshaft Damper" in this section.

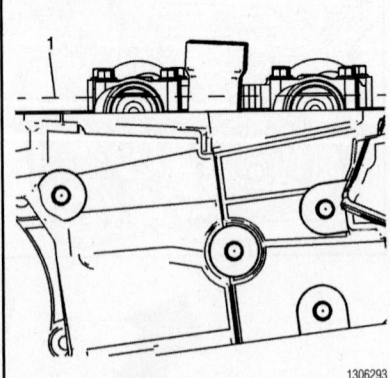

Fig. 15 Rotate the crankshaft with the EN-46111 socket (or equivalent) until the camshafts are in a neutral (low tension) position. The camshaft flats will be parallel with the camshaft cover rail (1).

7. Rotate the crankshaft with the EN-46111 socket (or equivalent) until the camshafts are in a neutral (low tension) position. The camshaft flats will be parallel with the camshaft cover rail.

✴✴ CAUTION

A wrench must be used on the hex of the camshaft when loosening or tightening in order to prevent component damage. Failure to prevent the torque reaction against the timing drive chain can lead to timing drive chain failure.

8. Use an open-end wrench at the camshaft hex to prevent camshaft/engine rotation. DO NOT remove the camshaft position actuator bolt at this time.

9. Loosen the camshaft position actuator bolt.

10. Install the EN-48313 tool (or equivalent) in order to retain the timing chain. Ensure the tips of the tool are fully engaging. Firmly tighten the tool nuts.

➡**Ensure that the camshaft timing chain and the camshaft position actuators are marked for proper assembly.**

11. Mark the timing chain and the respective locations on the camshaft position actuators (1-4).

12. Remove the camshaft position actuator bolt.

13. Remove the left camshaft as follows:

a. Observe the markings on the bearing caps. Each bearing cap is marked in order to identify its location. The markings have the following meanings:

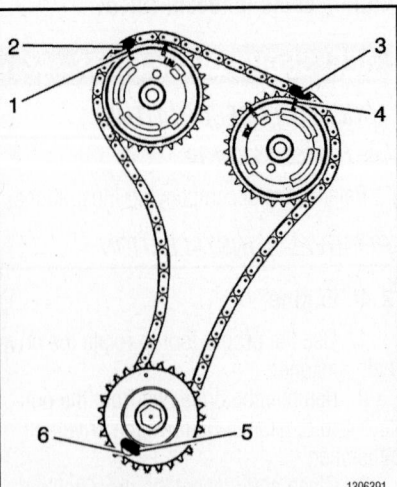

Fig. 16 Mark the timing chain and the respective locations on the camshaft position actuators (1-4).

- The raised feature must always be oriented toward the center of the cylinder head.
- The I indicates the intake camshaft.
- The E indicates the exhaust camshaft.
- The number indicates the journal position from the front of the engine.

b. Remove the camshaft bearing cap bolts and the camshaft bearing caps.

➡ **Mark the camshafts upon removal to ensure installation is in the correct position.**

c. Remove the camshafts.

d. Replace the camshaft bearing caps and bolts.

To install:

14. Ensure that the marks on the camshaft position actuator and the timing chain are aligned.

➡ **DO NOT tighten the camshaft position actuator bolt at this time.**

15. Locate the camshafts to the cylinder head and assemble the camshaft actuators to the camshafts.

16. Install the camshafts and the camshaft bearing caps as follows:

a. Ensure that the camshaft sealing rings are in place in the camshaft grooves.

✳✳ CAUTION

Camshaft sealing rings must be in place below the surface of the camshaft journal in order to avoid being pinched between the cylinder head and the camshaft caps.

17. Apply a liberal amount of lubricant to the camshaft journals and the left cylinder head camshaft carriers.

18. Place the left intake and left exhaust camshafts in position in the left cylinder head.

19. Position the camshaft lobes in a neutral position with the flats on the back of the camshafts up and parallel with the left cylinder head camshaft cover rail.

20. Observe the markings on the left cylinder head camshaft bearing caps. Each bearing cap is marked in order to identify its location. The markings have the following meanings:

- The raised feature must always be oriented toward the center of the cylinder head.
- The I indicates the intake camshaft.
- The E indicates the exhaust camshaft.

- The number 2, 4, 6 indicates the cylinder position from the front of the engine.

a. Apply a liberal amount of lubricant to the camshaft bearing caps.

b. For applications that have a second design camshaft bearing cap, apply a liberal amount of lubricant to the camshaft bearing cap and camshaft thrust surface.

c. Install the camshaft bearing thrust cap in the first journal of the left cylinder head.

d. Install the remaining bearing caps with their orientation mark toward the center of the cylinder head.

e. Hand start all the camshaft bearing cap bolts.

f. Tighten the camshaft bearing cap bolts in the sequence shown and tighten to 89 inch lbs. (10 Nm).

g. Loosen the center intake camshaft bearing cap bolts 1, 2 and the center exhaust camshaft bearing cap bolts 3, 4.

h. Retighten the center camshaft bearing cap bolts 1, 2, 3, 4 and retighten the camshaft bearing cap bolts to 89 inch lbs. (10 Nm).

21. Remove the EN-46108 tool.

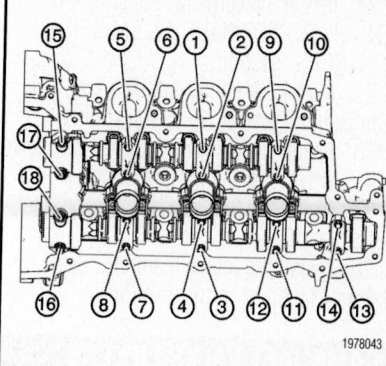

Fig. 18 Camshaft bearing cap bolt tightening sequence

✳✳ CAUTION

A wrench must be used on the hex of the camshaft when loosening or tightening in order to prevent component damage. Failure to prevent the torque reaction against the timing drive chain can lead to timing drive chain failure.

22. Use an open-end wrench at the camshaft hex to prevent camshaft/engine rotation.

23. Install and tighten the camshaft position actuators and actuator solenoid.

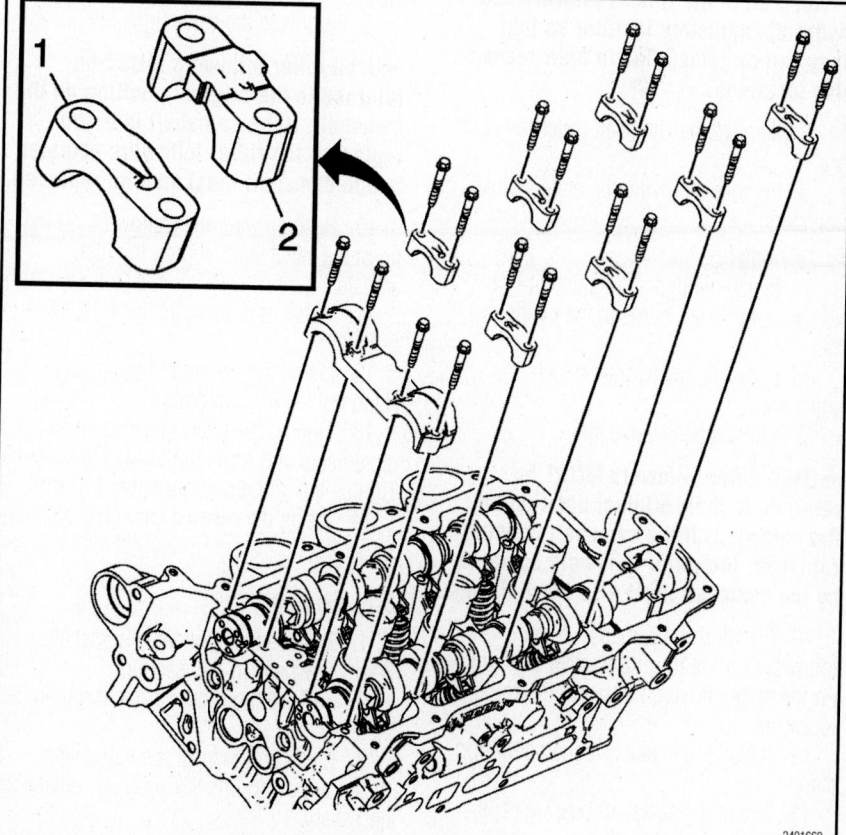

Fig. 17 Showing first (1) and second (2) design bearing caps

24. Install the camshaft sensors. See "ENGINE PERFORMANCE & EMISSION CONTROLS" section.

25. Install the crankshaft balancer. See "Crankshaft Damper" in this section.

26. Install the camshaft cover. See "Valve (Camshaft) Covers" in this section.

27. Install the fuel pump to the cylinder head.

28. Install the intake manifold. See "Intake Manifold" in this section.

CAMSHAFT VALVE LIFTERS

REMOVAL & INSTALLATION

2.4L Engine

Intake

1. Remove the intake camshaft position actuator. See "Camshaft Position Actuator" in this section.

➡**Remove each bolt on each cap one turn at a time until there is no spring tension pushing on the camshaft.**

2. Mark the bearing caps to ensure they are installed in the original position.

3. Remove the bearing cap bolts. Remove the bearing caps.

4. Remove the intake camshaft.

➡**Keep all of the roller followers and hydraulic adjusters in order so that they can be reinstalled in their respective locations.**

5. Remove the camshaft roller followers.

6. Remove the hydraulic element lash adjusters.

To install:

7. Install the hydraulic element lash adjusters into their bores in the cylinder head.

8. Lubricate the hydraulic lash adjusters.

9. Lubricate the valve tips.

➡**Used roller followers MUST be returned to their original position on the camshaft. If the camshaft is being replaced, the roller followers actuated by the camshaft must also be replaced.**

10. Position the camshaft roller followers on the tip of the valve stem and on the lash adjuster. Lubricate the roller followers.

11. Install the intake camshaft and lubricate.

12. Install the camshaft bearing caps. Hand tighten the cap bolts.

13. Tighten the bearing cap bolts in increments of 3 turns until they are seated. Tighten the bolts to 89 inch lbs. (10 Nm).

14. Install the intake camshaft position actuator. See "Camshaft Position Actuator" in this section.

Exhaust

1. Remove the exhaust camshaft position actuator.

➡**Remove each bolt on each cap one turn at a time until there is no spring tension pushing on the camshaft.**

2. Mark the bearing caps to ensure they are installed in the original position.

3. Remove the bearing cap bolts. Remove the bearing caps.

4. Remove the exhaust camshaft.

➡**Keep all of the roller followers and hydraulic adjusters in order so that they can be reinstalled in their respective locations.**

5. Remove the camshaft roller followers.

6. Remove the hydraulic element lash adjusters.

To install:

7. Install the hydraulic element lash adjusters into their bores in the cylinder head.

8. Lubricate the hydraulic lash adjusters.

9. Lubricate the valve tips.

➡**Used roller followers MUST be returned to the original position on the camshaft. If the camshaft is being replaced, the roller followers actuated by the camshaft must also be replaced.**

10. Position the roller followers on the tip of the valve stem and on the lash adjuster.

11. Install and lubricate the exhaust camshaft.

12. Install the camshaft bearing caps. Hand tighten the cap bolts.

13. Tighten the bearing cap bolts in increments of 3 turns until they are seated. Tighten the bolts to 89 inch lbs. (10 Nm).

14. Install the exhaust camshaft position actuator.

3.6L Engine

1. Remove the applicable camshafts. See "Camshaft" in this section.

2. Remove the rocker arms and then the lifters.

3. Clean and inspect the camshafts, rocker arms and lifters. Repair or replace as necessary.

4. Clean and inspect the rocker arm.

To install:

5. Install the lifters and then the rocker arms.

6. Install the camshaft(s). See "Camshaft" in this section.

CAMSHAFT POSITION ACTUATOR

REMOVAL & INSTALLATION

2.4L Engine

See Figures 19 and 20.

➡**Intake camshaft side described in this procedure. Exhaust side similar.**

1. Remove the camshaft cover.

2. Remove the spark plugs.

3. Rotate the crankshaft clockwise and install the EN-48953 retention tool.

4. Install the camshaft actuator retainer bolts and tighten to 89 inch lbs. (10 Nm).

5. Loosen, but DO NOT remove the intake camshaft actuator bolt.

6. Remove the locking tool.

7. Properly remove the timing chain. See "Timing Chain & Sprockets" in this section.

8. Remove and discard the intake camshaft actuator bolt.

9. Rotate the exhaust camshaft clockwise slightly to take the tension off of the timing chain on the intake actuator.

10. Remove the intake camshaft actuator from the camshaft while also removing the actuator from the timing chain.

To install:

11. Ensure that the alignment mark made previously on the intake camshaft actuator is still aligned properly with the mark on the timing chain.

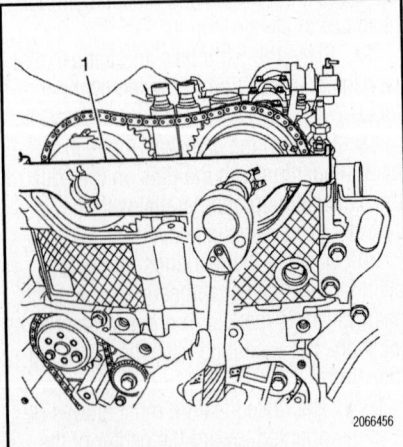

2066456

Fig. 19 Rotate the crankshaft clockwise and install the EN-48953 retention tool (1).

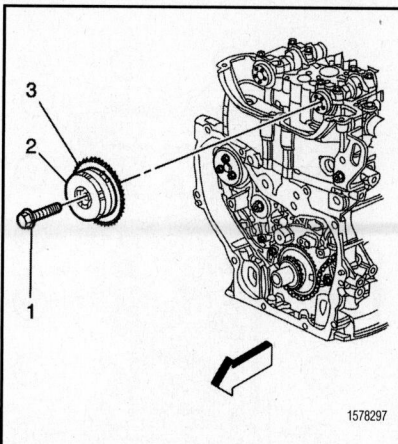

Fig. 20 Remove the bolt (1) and the pulley (2) and intake camshaft actuator (3) from the camshaft while also removing the actuator from the timing chain.

12. Install the timing chain onto the intake camshaft actuator.

13. Align the intake camshaft actuator alignment mark made previously with the timing chain mark and install the actuator onto the camshaft rotating the exhaust camshaft clockwise, if required.

14. Install a NEW intake camshaft actuator bolt until snug.

15. Continue and complete installation of the timing chain. See "Timing Chain & Sprockets" in this section.

16. Install the camshaft actuator retainer bolts and tighten to 89 inch lbs. (10 Nm).

17. Tighten the NEW camshaft actuator bolt to 22 ft. lbs. (30 Nm), plus an additional 100 degrees using the EN-45059 meter.

➡**You must have the EN-48953 retention tool installed to perform this procedure.**

18. To release the tensioner apply a counterclockwise rotational torque to the crankshaft balancer bolt of 33 ft. lbs. (45 Nm).

19. Remove the retention tool.

20. Install the upper timing chain guide and bolts and tighten to 89 inch lbs. (10 Nm).

21. Install the spark plugs.

22. Install the camshaft cover.

3.6L Engine

See Figure 21.

1. Remove the camshaft cover.

2. Remove the camshaft position actuator solenoid valve solenoid (intake).

3. Remove the intake camshaft position sensor.

4. Remove the exhaust camshaft position sensor.

5. Remove the camshaft position actuator solenoid valve solenoid (exhaust).

6. Rotate engine clockwise using crankshaft dampener retaining bolt until the flats at the rear ends of the camshafts are pointing up. This puts the camshafts on "base circle" and will reduce their tendency to rotate from valve spring pressure when the camshaft position actuators/drive chains are removed.

➡**Do NOT remove or back out the camshaft position actuator bolt(s) significantly, simply break them loose from their fully-torqued position. The position actuators must stay firmly attached until the retaining tools are in place, but they should be broken loose while the chain is still tight and in position.**

7. Loosen intake and/or exhaust camshaft position actuator retaining bolts, depending on which camshaft position actuator and/or camshaft you will be servicing. If servicing both camshaft position actuators and/or camshafts, loosen both bolts.

➡**Be certain to clearly mark the position of the chain to the camshaft position actuator(s). Though the engine does not need to be set to a specific timing mark before starting the procedure, the relationship of the chain to the actuator(s) is critical and must be reestablished on assembly.**

8. Mark the position of the chain to the camshaft position actuator (intake).

9. Mark the position of the chain to the camshaft position actuator (exhaust).

10. Remove camshaft front cap bolts.

➡**Do NOT remove or loosen any other camshaft bearing caps at this time, even if you intend to eventually remove the camshaft.**

11. Remove the camshaft front cap.

12. Loosen wing nut to open the clamping area of EN49982-1 retainer.

➡**Do NOT overtighten the thumbscrew. The EN49982-1 retainer should be able to slide slightly via the slot the screw goes through. This fore/aft movement will allow easier removal and installation of the chain later.**

13. Install the retainer tool intake side chain holder onto front cover by screwing in the thumbscrew on the retainer finger-tight.

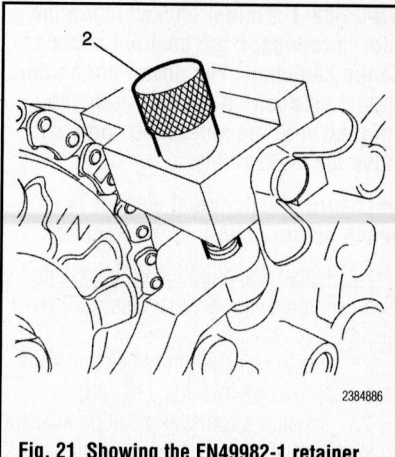

Fig. 21 Showing the EN49982-1 retainer with wing nut and thumbscrew (2)

➡**Do NOT tighten the wing nut with a tool of any kind. Firm finger-tightening is sufficient.**

14. Tighten wing nut so retainer closes over and firmly grasps timing chain.

15. Continue and complete the steps needed to remove the timing chain. See "Timing Chain & Sprockets" in this section.

16. To remove the intake camshaft position actuator, remove the loosened retaining bolt. To remove only the exhaust camshaft position actuator, skip the steps for removing the intake camshaft position actuator. However, the retainer MUST be installed as discussed even if the intake side will not be serviced or the timing of the camshaft chains will be lost.

17. Slide the camshaft position actuator forward and off the end of the intake camshaft. The slot in the retainer will allow the tool to move forward enough to disengage the camshaft position actuator from the front of the camshaft. Remove the plastic thrust washer when removing the camshaft position actuator from the end of the camshaft.

18. Tilt the camshaft position actuator forward and out/away from the engine.

➡**DO NOT remove the EN49982 retainers . They are holding the cam chains to maintain their properly-timed positions.**

19. Allow the chain to rest on the EN49982-1 retainer and EN49982-2 retainer in position during service.

To install:

20. Install plastic camshaft position actuator thrust washer between cylinder head face and camshaft position actuator on assembly.

➡**It may help to carefully pry the camshaft forward and to move the**

EN49982-1 retainer backward via the slot to reengage the position actuator to the camshaft. The dowel pin on the camshaft position actuator must be aligned with the slot in the camshaft nose for reassembly.

➡**Ensure plastic thrust washer is in place before installing the actuator.**

21. Install and align the timing chain. See "Timing Chain & Sprockets" in this section.
22. Install camshaft front cap and bolts and tighten to 89 inch lbs. (10 Nm).
23. Install the camshaft position actuator solenoid valve solenoid (exhaust) and the camshaft position actuator solenoid valve solenoid (intake).
24. Install the intake and exhaust camshaft position sensors.
25. Install the camshaft cover.

CATALYTIC CONVERTER

REMOVAL & INSTALLATION

2.4L Engine

1. Remove the exhaust front pipe.
2. Remove the 3 catalytic converter nuts.
3. Remove and discard the gasket.
4. Remove the catalytic converter.
5. Installation is the reverse of the removal procedure.
6. Install and tighten the 3 catalytic converter nuts to 36 ft. lbs. (50 Nm).

3.6L Engine

1. Remove the exhaust manifold heat shield.
2. Remove the exhaust front pipe.
3. Remove the 2 catalytic converter nuts.
4. Remove the retaining bolt.
5. Remove and discard the seal.
6. Remove the catalytic converter.
7. Installation is the reverse of the removal procedure.
8. Install and tighten the catalytic converter nuts and bolt to 36 ft. lbs. (50 Nm).

CRANKSHAFT FRONT SEAL

REMOVAL & INSTALLATION

1. Remove the crankshaft balancer. See "Crankshaft Damper" in this section.
2. Use a flat-bladed tool to remove the seal from the front cover.

To install:

3. Use the EN-35268-A (or equivalent) installer in order to install the crankshaft front oil seal to the engine front cover.
4. Install the crankshaft balancer.

CYLINDER HEAD

REMOVAL & INSTALLATION

2.4L Engine

See Figures 22 and 23.

1. Drain the cooling system.
2. Remove the exhaust manifold. See "Exhaust Manifold" in this section.
3. Remove the intake manifold. See "Intake Manifold" in this section.
4. Reposition the radiator surge tank air bleed hose clamp.
5. Remove the radiator surge tank air bleed hose from the cylinder head.
6. Reposition the radiator inlet hose clamp.
7. Remove the radiator inlet hose from the cylinder head.
8. Disconnect all electrical connectors as necessary.
9. Remove the camshaft cover.
10. Remove the upper timing chain guide bolts and guide.

➡**If the intake camshaft actuator is moving independently of the camshaft, this means the camshaft is not locked to the actuator. Rotate the camshaft counterclockwise while the holding tool is installed and this will lock the camshaft to the actuator.**

11. Ensure the timing chain and the camshaft position actuators are marked for proper assembly.
12. Rotate the intake camshaft clockwise and install the EN-48953 locking tool (1) to the actuators.
13. Install the camshaft actuator retainer bolts and tighten to 89 inch lbs. (10 Nm).
14. Clean the timing chain and gears with solvent.
15. Mark the timing gear sprockets and the timing chain. It is recommended that the paint marks are located in the 12 o'clock position.
16. Loosen, but do not remove the intake and exhaust camshaft actuator bolts.
17. Remove the locking tool
18. Remove the timing chain. See "Timing Chain & Sprockets" in this section.
19. Install a rubber band around the top of the upper timing chain guides in order to pull the guides together.
20. Remove the cylinder head.
21. Remove the cylinder head gasket.
22. Clean all of the gasket surfaces.
23. Use the following steps when cleaning the cylinder head and cylinder block surfaces:
    a. Use a razor blade gasket scraper to

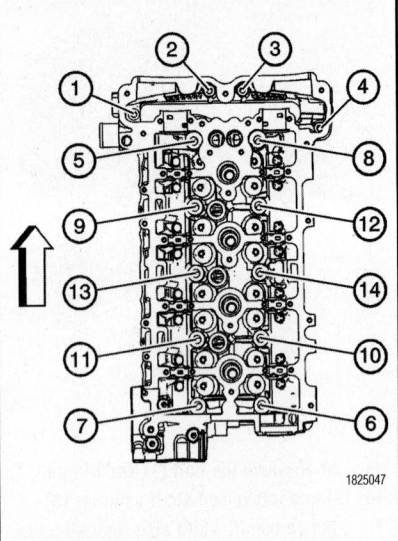

Fig. 22 Cylinder head bolt loosening sequence—2.4L engine

clean the cylinder head and cylinder block gasket surfaces. Do not scratch or gouge either surface.

➡**DO NOT use any other method or technique to clean these gasket surfaces.**

b. Use a NEW razor blade on the cylinder head and a NEW blade on the cylinder block.

➡**Be careful not to gouge or scratch the gasket surfaces. DO NOT gouge or scrape the combustion chamber surfaces. The feel of the gasket surface is important, not the appearance. There will be indentations from the gasket left in the cylinder head after all of the gasket material is removed. These small indentations will be filled in by the NEW gasket.**

c. Hold the razor blade as parallel to the gasket surface as possible.
24. Clean the old sealer/lube and any dirt from around the bolt holes.

➡**DO NOT use a tap to clean the cylinder head bolt holes.**

25. Clean the bolts holes with a nylon bristle brush.
26. When cleaning the cylinder head bolt holes use suitable commercial spray liquid solvent and compressed air from an extended-tip blow gun in order to reach the bottom of the holes.
27. If replacing the cylinder head, transfer all parts as necessary.

To install:

➡**DO NOT use any sealing material.**

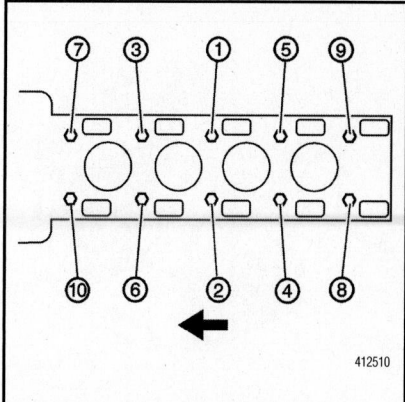

Fig. 23 Cylinder head bolt tightening sequence

28. Install the cylinder head gasket.

29. Install the cylinder head.

30. Install NEW cylinder head bolts.

31. Install and tighten the cylinder head bolts in the sequence shown. Tighten the bolts to 22 ft. lbs. (30 Nm) plus an additional 155 degrees using the EN-45059 meter (or equivalent).

32. Install the NEW front cylinder head bolts and tighten to 26 ft. lbs. (35 Nm).

33. Install the timing chain and sprockets. See "Timing Chain & Sprockets" in this section.

34. Install the camshaft cover.

35. Connect all electrical connectors as necessary.

36. Install the radiator inlet hose to the cylinder head.

37. Position the radiator inlet hose clamp.

38. Install the radiator surge tank air bleed hose to the cylinder head.

39. Position the radiator surge tank air bleed hose clamp.

40. Install the exhaust manifold. See "Exhaust Manifold" in this section.

41. Install the intake manifold. See "Intake Manifold" in this section.

42. Fill the cooling system.

3.6L Engine

Left Side

See Figure 24.

1. Remove the left bank secondary timing chain. Refer to "Timing Chain & Sprockets" in this section.

2. Remove the oil level indicator.

3. Remove the fuel pump. See "FUEL" section.

4. Remove the wiring harness ground from the cylinder head.

5. Disconnect the wiring harness electrical connector located at the side of the cylinder head.

6. Remove the wiring harness connector bracket from the side of the cylinder head.

➡**DO NOT disconnect the power steering pipes and/or hoses.**

7. Remove the generator. See "ENGINE ELECTRICAL" section.

8. Remove the surge tank hose from the bracket at the rear of the cylinder head.

9. Remove the wiring harness bracket from the rear of the cylinder head.

10. Remove the catalytic converter. See "Catalytic Converter" in this section.

➡**Do not remove the oil filter adapter.**

11. Remove the oil filter adapter upper bolt.

12. Remove the left cylinder head with the left exhaust manifold.

13. Remove manifold and transfer other parts as needed.

To install:

14. Carefully reassemble the cylinder head and exhaust manifold as needed.

15. Clean and inspect the cylinder head and the engine block sealing surfaces.

16. Ensure the cylinder head locating pins are securely mounted in the cylinder block deck face.

17. Install a NEW left cylinder head gasket using the deck face locating pins for retention.

18. Install the NEW M11 cylinder head bolts:

    a. Tighten the M11 cylinder head bolts a first pass in sequence to 22 ft. lbs. (30 Nm).

    b. Tighten the M11 cylinder head bolts a second pass in sequence an additional 150 degrees using the J 45059 meter (or equivalent)/

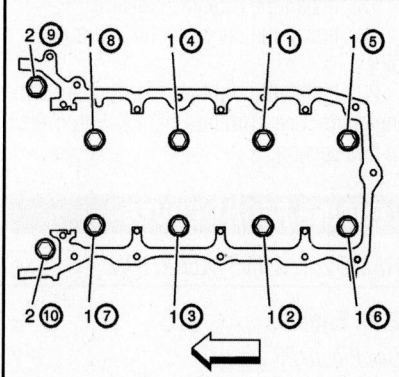

Fig. 24 Left cylinder head bolt tightening sequence, showing the M11 bolts (1) and M8 bolts (2)

19. Install the 2 NEW front M8 left cylinder head bolts:

    a. Tighten the M8 cylinder head bolts a first pass to 11 ft. lbs. (15 Nm).

    b. Tighten the M8 cylinder head bolts a second pass in sequence an additional 75 degrees using the J 45059 meter (or equivalent).

20. Install the oil filter adapter upper bolt.

21. Install the oil level indicator.

22. Install the catalytic converter to the exhaust manifold.

23. Install the wiring harness bracket to the rear of the cylinder head.

24. Install the surge tank hose to the bracket at the rear of the cylinder head.

25. Install the generator.

26. Install the wiring harness connector bracket from the side of the cylinder head.

27. Install the wiring harness ground to the cylinder head and tighten the bolt to 89 inch lbs. (10 Nm).

28. Disconnect the wiring harness electrical connector located at the side of the cylinder head.

29. Install the coolant temperature sensor electrical connector heat shield.

30. Install the fuel pump.

31. Install the oil level indicator.

32. Install the left bank secondary timing chain. See "Timing Chain & Sprockets" in this section.

Right Side

See Figure 25.

1. Remove the right bank secondary timing chain. See "Timing Chain & Sprockets" in this section.

2. Remove the coolant inlet and outlet pipes.

3. Remove the catalytic converter, as described in this section.

4. Remove the wiring harness ground from the side of the cylinder head.

5. Remove the wiring harness conduit upper bolt from the cylinder head and reposition the conduit to provide access.

6. Remove the battery cable from the cylinder head.

7. Remove the cylinder head bolts and remove the cylinder head with the exhaust manifold.

8. Remove and discard the cylinder head gasket.

9. Clean and inspect the cylinder head and the engine block sealing surfaces.

To install:

10. Install a NEW cylinder head gasket.

11. Carefully install the cylinder head with the exhaust manifold to the engine:

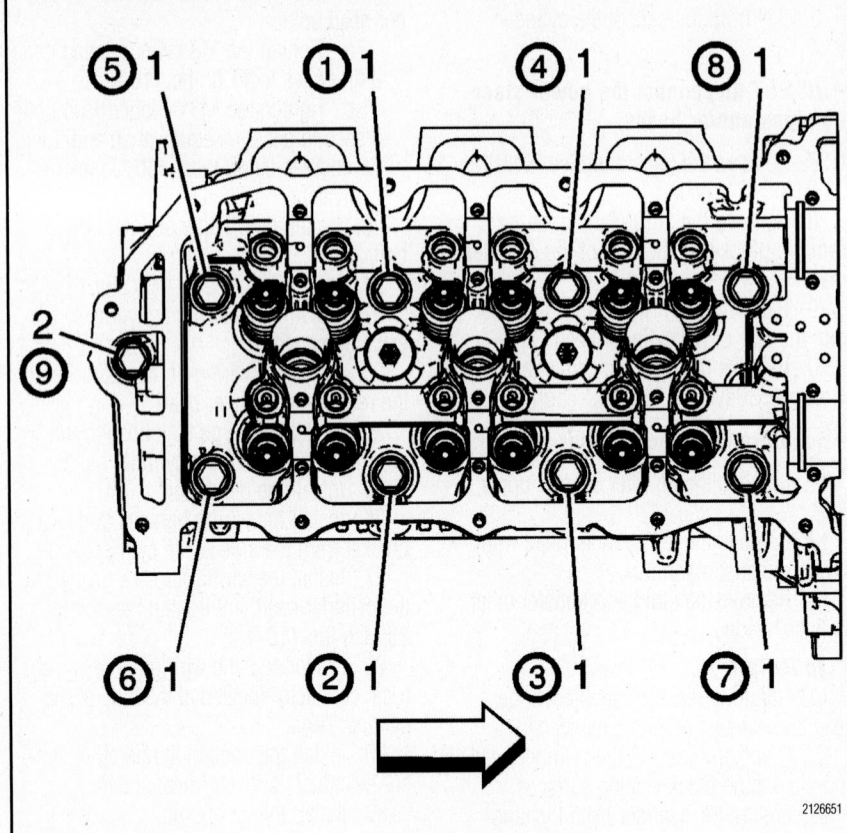

Fig. 25 Right cylinder head bolt tightening sequence, showing M11 bolts (1) and M8 bolts (2)

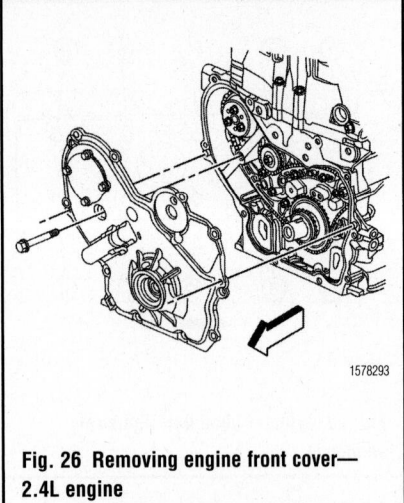

Fig. 26 Removing engine front cover— 2.4L engine

a. Install the lower fuel rail noise shield

b. Ensure the cylinder head locating pins are securely mounted in the cylinder block deck face.

c. Install a NEW right cylinder head gasket using the deck face locating pins for retention.

d. Align the right cylinder head with the deck face locating pins.

e. Place the right cylinder head in position on the deck face.

12. Install the NEW M11 cylinder head bolts:

a. Tighten the M11 cylinder head bolts a first pass in sequence to 22 ft. lbs. (30 Nm).

b. Tighten the M11 cylinder head bolts a second pass in sequence an additional 150 degrees using the J 45059 meter (or equivalent)/

13. Install the 2 NEW front M8 left cylinder head bolts:

a. Tighten the M8 cylinder head bolts a first pass to 11 ft. lbs. (15 Nm).

b. Tighten the M8 cylinder head bolts a second pass in sequence an additional 75 degrees using the J 45059 meter (or equivalent)/

14. Connect the catalytic converter to the exhaust manifold.

15. Install the battery negative cable to the cylinder head.

16. Install the wiring harness conduit to the cylinder head. Tighten the wiring harness upper bolt to 89 inch lbs. (10 Nm).

17. Install the wiring harness ground to the side of the cylinder head. Tighten the wiring harness ground bolt to 89 inch lbs. (10 Nm).

18. Install the catalytic converter.

19. Install the coolant inlet and outlet pipes.

20. Install the right bank secondary timing chain. See "Timing Chain & Sprockets" in this section.

ENGINE FRONT COVER

REMOVAL & INSTALLATION

2.4L Engine

See Figure 26.

1. Remove the engine mount bracket.
2. Remove the drive belt tensioner.
3. Remove the crankshaft balancer. See "Crankshaft Damper" in this section.

4. Remove the engine front cover to water pump bolt.

5. Raise and suitably support the vehicle.

6. Remove the engine front cover bolts and remove the engine front cover.

7. Remove and discard the engine front cover gasket.

To install:

8. Install a NEW engine front cover gasket to the dowel pins.

9. Install the engine front cover. Install the bolts and tighten to 18 ft. lbs. (25 Nm).

10. Lower the vehicle.

11. Install the engine front cover to water pump bolt and tighten to 18 ft. lbs. (25 Nm).

12. Install the crankshaft balancer. See "Crankshaft Damper" in this section.

13. Install the drive belt tensioner.

14. Install the engine mount bracket.

3.6L Engine

See Figures 27 through 31.

1. Remove the intake manifold. See "Intake Manifold" in this section.

2. Remove the camshaft covers.

3. Drain the engine coolant.

4. Remove the water outlet with the radiator hose and reposition aside.

5. Remove the generator. See "ENGINE ELECTRICAL" section.

➡**Do not disconnect the power steering pipes or drain the power steering fluid.**

6. Remove the power steering fluid reservoir and reposition the power steering fluid reservoir in order to provide access.

7. Remove the crankshaft balancer. See "Crankshaft Damper" in this section.

8. Remove the camshaft position sensors.

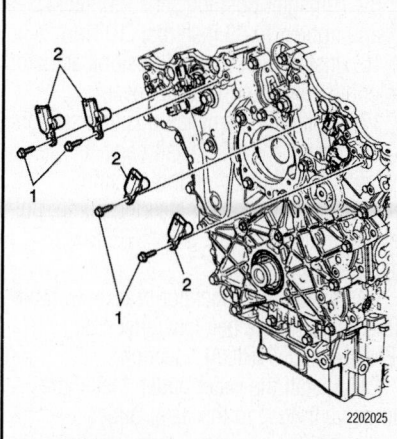

Fig. 27 Remove the camshaft position sensor bolts (1) and the camshaft position sensors (2).

9. Remove the belt tensioner.

10. Remove the camshaft position actuator solenoid valves from the front cover.

11. Remove the engine front cover with the water pump as follows:

a. Remove the camshaft position sensor bolts and the camshaft position sensors.

✳✳ CAUTION

The camshaft position actuator valves must be removed from the front cover prior to front cover removal or damage to the valves may occur.

b. Remove the camshaft position actuator valve bolts and the actuator valves from the front cover.

➡**Engine front cover bolts in the number (3) location are model dependent and may have already been removed.**

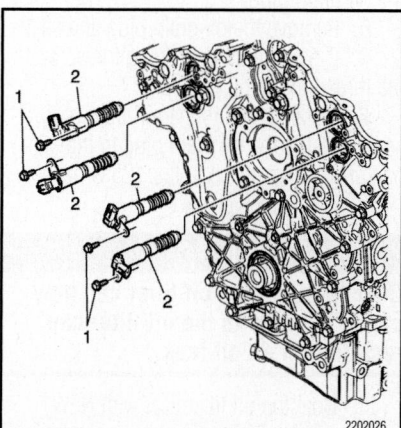

Fig. 28 Remove the camshaft position actuator valve bolts (1) and the actuator valves (2) from the front cover.

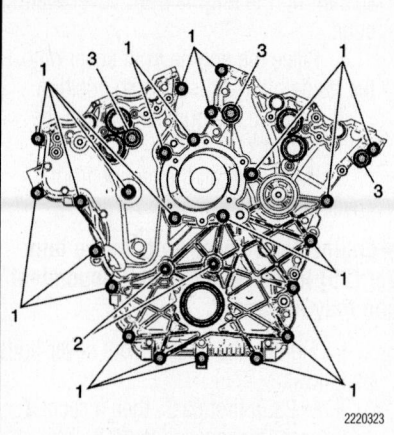

Fig. 29 Remove the engine front cover bolts, including the M8 bolts (1), M6 bolts (2) and M12 bolts (3).

➡**There are a total of 23 M8 bolts and 2 M6 bolts that must be removed, and 3 optional M12 bolts that may need to be removed before the front cover will separate from the engine block.**

c. Remove the engine front cover bolts.

✳✳ CAUTION

Do not use the jackscrew hole without first removing all engine front cover bolts. Failure to remove all engine front cover bolts before using the jackscrew hole could result in damage to components.

✳✳ CAUTION

Do not pry between the engine front cover and the camshaft position sensors or the camshaft position actuators in order to separate the RTV. Use the pry points and a bolt in the jackscrew hole in order to remove the engine front cover. Damage to the camshaft position sensors or the camshaft position actuators may occur if the camshaft position sensors or the camshaft position actuators are used to pry against in order to remove the engine front cover.

d. Loosely install a 10 x 1.5 mm bolt in the jackscrew hole. Using the pry points located at the edge of the front

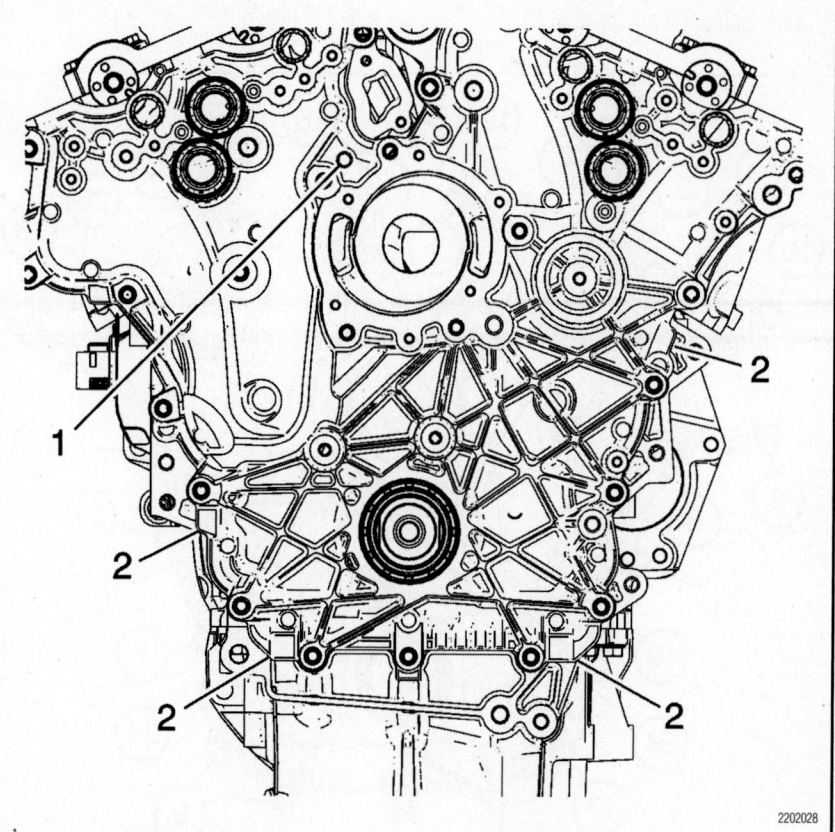

Fig. 30 Loosely install a 10 x 1.5 mm bolt in the jackscrew hole (1). Using the pry points (2) located at the edge of the front cover and the jackscrew, separate the room temperature vulcanizing (RTV) sealant.

cover and the jackscrew, separate the room temperature vulcanizing (RTV) sealant.

e. Remove the engine front cover.

12. Carefully clean the engine front cover sealing surfaces.

➡ **Insert a piece of cardboard between the oil pan front and the oil pump in order to prevent any contaminants from falling into the oil pan.**

13. Carefully clean the engine front cover sealing surfaces.

14. Use compressed air in order to remove any engine coolant from the engine cooling passages and from the top of the oil pan scraper (windage tray).

To install:

15. Use the EN-46109 pins (or equivalent) in order to install the engine front cover as follows:

a. Install the NEW engine front cover to cylinder block seal.

➡ **No RTV sealant should be visible in the M12 bolt holes upon final assembly of front cover to engine.**

b. Apply a 3 mm bead of RTV sealant on the engine front cover mating edge. Apply a 5 mm bead of RTV

sealant on the engine front cover mating edge.

c. Place the engine front cover onto the guide pins and slide into position.

d. Remove the guide pins from the cylinder block.

e. Hand start all the engine front cover bolts.

➡ **Engine front cover bolts in the number (25) location are model dependent and may not apply.**

f. Tighten the engine front cover bolts as follows:

- 1–23: a first pass, then a second pass in sequence to 14 ft. lbs. (20 Nm).
- 1–23: a third pass in sequence an additional 60 degrees.
- 24: 11 ft. lbs. (15 Nm).
- 25: to 48 ft. lbs. (65 Nm).

g. Place the camshaft position actuator valves in position on the front cover. Install the camshaft position actuator valve bolts and tighten to 89 inch lbs. (10 Nm).

h. Install NEW O-rings on the camshaft position sensor.

i. Place the camshaft position sensors in position on the front cover. Install

the camshaft position sensor bolts (1) and tighten to 89 inch lbs. (10 Nm).

16. Install the camshaft position actuator solenoid valves to the front cover.

17. Install the camshaft position sensors.

18. Install the crankshaft balancer. See "Crankshaft Damper" in this section.

19. Install the power steering pump, pulley and fluid reservoir. See "STEERING" section.

20. Install the generator bracket with the generator and the belt tensioner. See "ENGINE ELECTRICAL" section.

21. Install the water outlet. Install the purge vent hose to the water outlet.

22. Fill the cooling system.

23. Install the camshaft covers.

24. Install the intake manifold. See "Intake Manifold" in this section.

25. Install the drive belt tensioner.

26. Fill the cooling system.

ENGINE OIL & FILTER

REPLACEMENT

2.4L Engine

1. Place a collecting pan underneath the oil filter.

2. Use a proper wrench (EN-44887 or equivalent) to remove the oil filter cap and seal.

❊❊ CAUTION

This engine uses a special high performance oil filter. Use of any other filter may lead to filter failure and/or severe engine damage.

3. Remove and properly dispose of the oil filter insert.

4. Raise the vehicle.

5. Place a collecting pan underneath the oil drain plug.

6. Remove the oil drain plug and seal.

7. Clean the oil drain plug thread and the thread in the oil pan.

8. Install a seal to the oil drain plug.

9. Install the oil drain plug to the oil pan and tighten to 18 ft. lbs. (25 Nm).

10. Lower the vehicle.

❊❊ CAUTION

Over torquing the oil filter cap may cause damage to the oil filter cap resulting in an oil leak.

11. Coat the oil filter seal with NEW engine oil.

12. Use the wrench to install a NEW oil filter and a NEW seal and tighten the oil filter cap to 16 ft. lbs. (22 Nm).

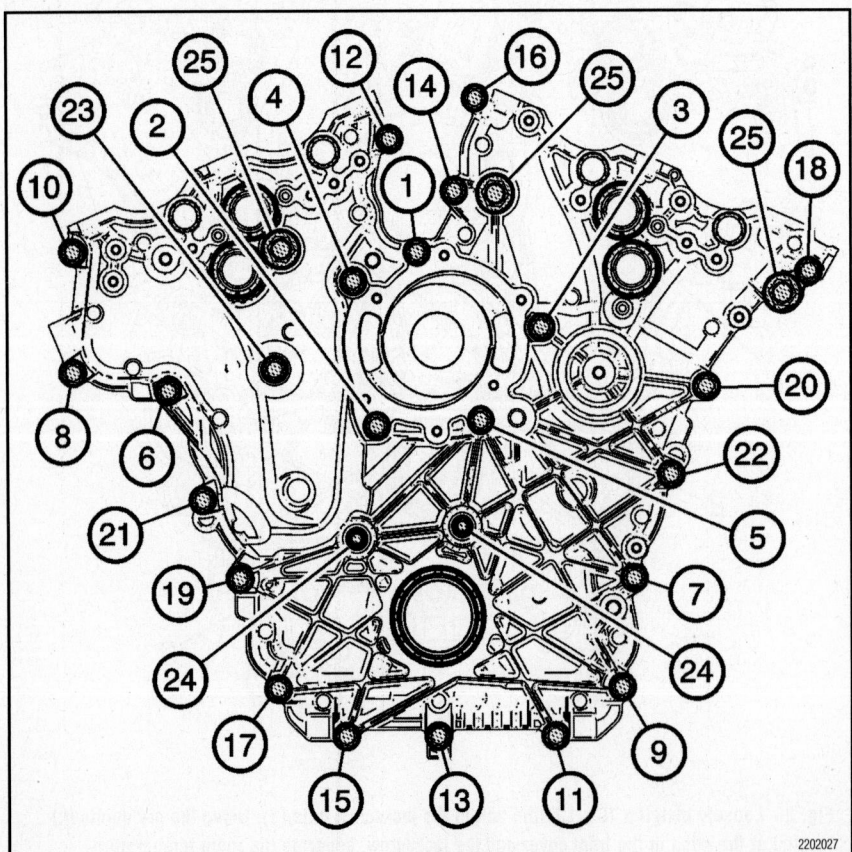

Fig. 31 Engine front cover bolt tightening sequence—3.6L engine

2202027

13. Fill with NEW engine oil.

14. Start the engine and allow it to run until the oil pressure control indicator goes off.

15. Inspect the engine oil level.

16. Reset the service interval indicator.

3.6L Engine

1. Raise and support the vehicle.

2. Place a drain pan under the oil pan drain plug.

3. Remove the oil pan drain plug. Allow the oil to drain completely.

4. Install the oil pan drain plug and tighten to 15 ft. lbs. (20 Nm).

5. Place the drain pan under the oil filter.

6. Remove the oil filter. Allow the oil to drain completely.

7. Lubricate the NEW oil filter gasket with clean engine oil.

8. Tighten the oil filter to 22 ft. lbs. (30 Nm).

9. Lower the vehicle.

10. Refill the engine oil.

11. Start the engine and inspect for leaks.

EXHAUST MANIFOLD

REMOVAL & INSTALLATION

2.4L Engine

See Figure 32.

1. Remove the exhaust front pipe.

2. Remove the exhaust manifold heat shield.

3. Remove the exhaust manifold heated oxygen sensor. See "ENGINE PERFORMANCE & EMISSION CONTROLS" section.

4. Remove 10 exhaust manifold nuts.

5. Remove and discard the exhaust manifold gasket.

6. Clean any exhaust manifold gasket debris from the cylinder head and exhaust manifold.

To install:

7. Install new exhaust manifold gasket.

8. Position the manifold and install the 10 nuts.

9. Tighten the exhaust manifold nuts working from the center out to 10. Install 10 ft. lbs. (14 Nm).

11. Install the oxygen sensor.

12. Install the heat shield.

13. Install the front exhaust pipe.

3.6L Engine

1. Remove the front exhaust pipe.

2. Disconnect the manifold heated oxygen sensor. See "ENGINE PERFORMANCE & EMISSION CONTROLS" section.

3. Remove the exhaust manifold heat shield.

4. Remove the catalytic converter nuts, bolt and seal at the exhaust manifold.

5. Remove the exhaust manifold bolts and gasket from the cylinder head. Discard the old gasket.

6. If reusing the exhaust manifold, clean and inspect the exhaust manifold sealing surfaces.

To install:

7. Inspect the catalytic converter seal/heat shield sealing surface. Replace the seal/heat shield if the sealing surface is worn or damaged.

8. Install a NEW exhaust manifold gasket to the exhaust manifold.

9. Install the exhaust manifold with the gasket to the cylinder head.

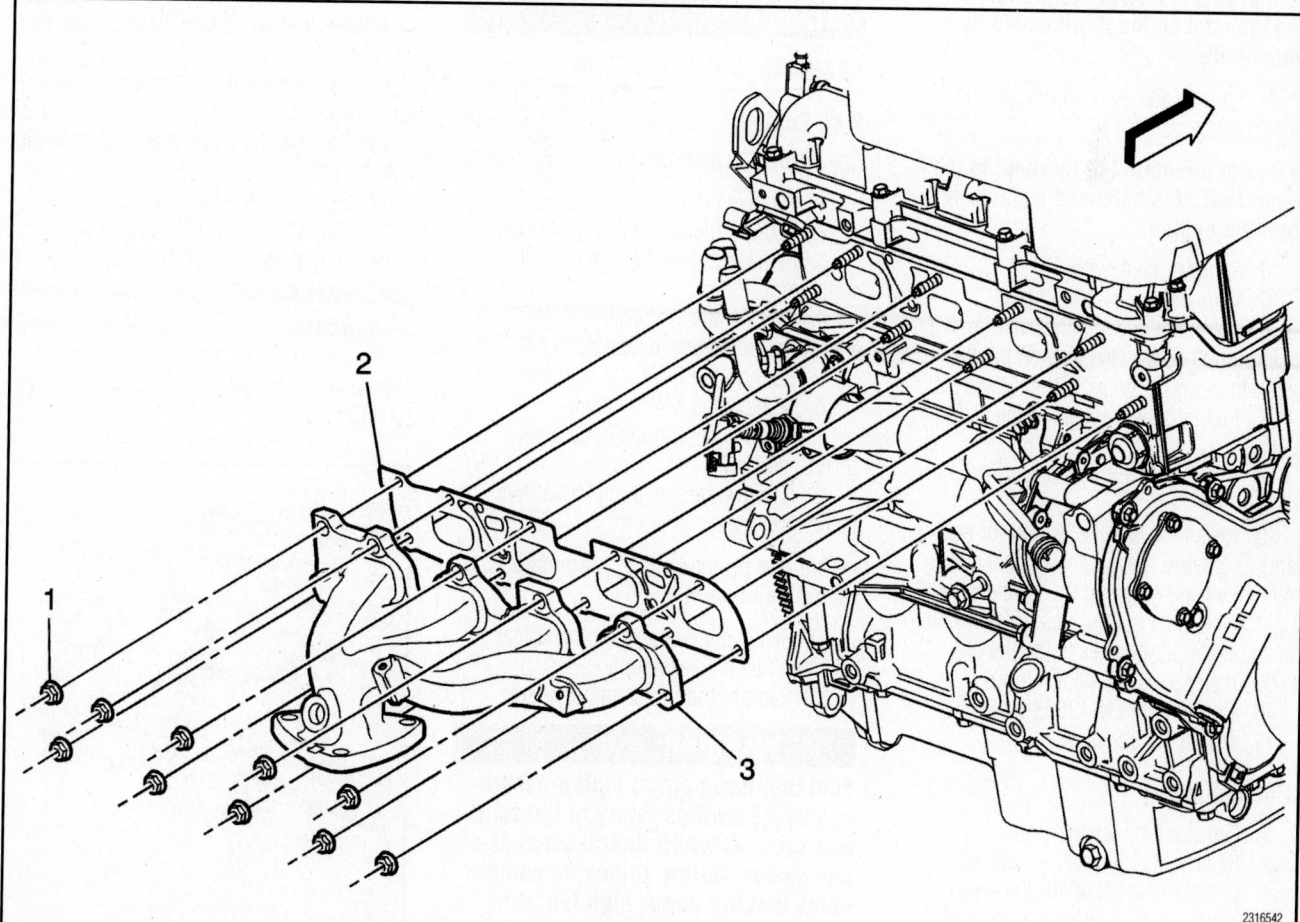

Fig. 32 Showing exhaust manifold mounting

2316542

10. Install the exhaust manifold bolts.

11. Tighten the bolts starting at the center, alternating side-to-side, working outward:

   a. First Pass: 7 ft. lbs. (10 Nm).

   b. Final Pass: 16 ft. lbs. (22 Nm).

12. Install the manifold heat shield.

13. Connect the exhaust manifold heated oxygen sensor.

14. Install the catalytic converter nuts, bolt and gasket. Tighten to 37 ft. lbs. (50 Nm).

15. Install the front exhaust pipe.

16. Connect the heated oxygen sensors.

17. Inspect the exhaust system for leaks.

FLYWHEEL

REMOVAL & INSTALLATION

2.4L Engine

1. Remove the transaxle.

2. Install the EN-43653 tool (or equivalent) in order to prevent the flywheel from rotating when loosening the flywheel bolts.

➡ **It may be necessary to remove the chamfer (bevel) from the edge of an 18 mm socket in order to get full engagement on the thin-headed flywheel bolts.**

3. Loosen, remove and discard the flywheel bolts.

➡ **Do not orientate the flywheel to the crankshaft. It is balanced separately from the engine.**

4. Remove the flywheel.

5. Remove the EN-43653 tool.

6. Clean the thread adhesive from the flywheel bolt holes. Use a nylon bristle brush to clean the holes in the crankshaft.

7. Position the flywheel to the crankshaft.

8. Install the NEW flywheel bolts until snug.

9. Install the EN-43653 tool (or equivalent) in order to prevent the flywheel from rotating when tightening the flywheel bolts. Tighten the bolts to 39 ft. lbs. (53 Nm) plus an additional 25 degrees using the EN-45059 meter (or equivalent).

10. Remove the EN-43653 tool.

11. Install the transaxle.

3.6L Engine

1. Remove the transmission.

2. Remove the flywheel as follows:

   a. Install the EN 46106 (or equivalent) through the starter mounting hole to lock the flywheel from turning.

   b. Remove the engine flywheel bolts and discard.

   c. Remove the engine flywheel from the crankshaft.

   d. Remove the locking tool.

3. Clean and inspect the flywheel. If the flywheel teeth are damaged, inspect the starter for proper operation. Replace the starter if you find excessive wear or damage to the starter drive.

To install:

4. Install the flywheel as follows:

   a. Place the engine flywheel in position on the crankshaft.

   b. Install 2 NEW bolts in location at the top and bottom of the engine flywheel bolt pattern allowing the engine flywheel to hang in position.

   c. Install the locking tool.

   d. Install the remaining NEW engine flywheel bolts. Tighten the NEW engine flywheel bolts to 22 ft. lbs. (30 Nm).

   e. Tighten the NEW engine flywheel bolts an additional 45 degrees using the EN 45059 meter (or equivalent).

5. Remove the locking tool.

6. Install the transmission.

INTAKE MANIFOLD

REMOVAL & INSTALLATION

2.4L Engine

See Figures 33 through 37.

1. Remove the oil fill cap.

2. Remove the intake manifold cover.

3. Remove the oil fill tube assembly and O-ring.

4. Remove the evaporative (EVAP) emission canister valve tube.

5. Remove the EVAP canister valve.

6. Remove the MAP sensor.

7. Remove the throttle body. See "FUEL" section.

8. Remove the fuel pump cover nut, bolts, and cover.

➡ **The low pressure fuel pipe used is model dependent.**

9. Remove the bracket bolt and low pressure fuel pipe assembly.

10. Remove the fuel pump insulator.

✳✳ WARNING

Fuel that flows out at high pressure can cause serious injury to the skin and eyes. ALWAYS depressurize the fuel system before removing components that are under high fuel pressure. See "FUEL" section.

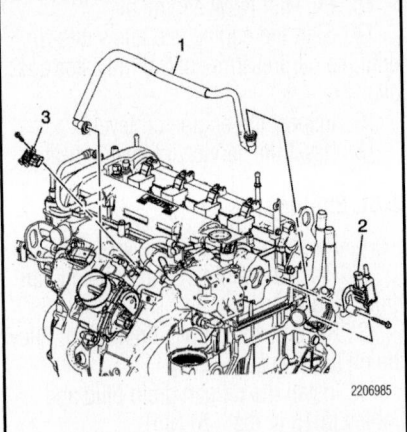

Fig. 33 Remove the evaporative (EVAP) emission canister valve tube (1), the EVAP canister valve (2), and the MAP sensor (3).

11. Remove and discard the high-pressure fuel feed intermediate pipe.

12. Remove the fuel pump assembly. See "FUEL" section.

13. Remove and discard the fuel pump housing O-ring and gasket, and the fuel pump roller lifter.

14. Remove the fuel rail harness connector bracket bolt and intake manifold insulator bolt.

15. Remove the intake manifold insulator.

16. Remove the intake manifold retaining nuts and bolts.

17. Remove the intake manifold.

18. If the intake manifold needs to be replaced, transfer the throttle body to the new intake manifold.

To install:

19. Install the intake manifold studs in the manifold face and tighten to 53 inch lbs. (6 Nm).

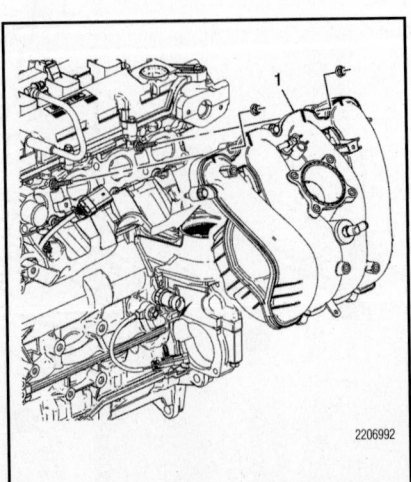

Fig. 34 Removing the intake manifold (1)

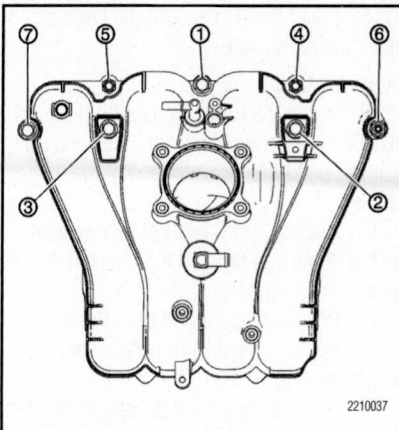

Fig. 35 Intake manifold bolt tightening sequence—2.4L engine

20. Install the intake manifold. Start and hand tighten the intake manifold bolts and nuts. Tighten the bolts and nuts in sequence to 89 inch lbs. (10 Nm).

21. Install the intake manifold insulator shield. Install the insulator bolt and tighten to 89 inch lbs. (10 Nm).

22. Install the fuel rail harness connector bracket to the intake manifold. Tighten the bracket bolt to 89 inch lbs. (10 Nm).

➡**The camshaft must be in the base circle position before the high pressure fuel pump is installed.**

23. Use the EN-48896 alignment gauge (or equivalent) to ensure that the camshaft lobe is in the base circle position. At base circle position, the tool will be flush with the head.

24. Lubricate the high pressure fuel pump cylinder head bore with 5W30 engine oil.

➡**Ensure that the high pressure fuel pump roller lifter is oriented properly, the camshaft is at base circle, and the number 1 piston is at top dead center (TDC) on the exhaust stroke. The distance from the mounting flange surface to the camshaft at base circle should be 2.05 in. (52 mm).**

25. Lubricate the high pressure fuel pump roller lifter with 5W30 engine oil and install into the cylinder head bore.

26. Install a NEW fuel pump housing O-ring and gasket. See "FUEL" section.

➡**Ensure the plastic bolt retainers are installed in the high pressure fuel pump mounting holes before installing.**

27. Install the fuel pump assembly. Start and hand-tighten the fuel pump assembly bolts evenly. Tighten the fuel pump bolts evenly to 11 ft. lbs. (15 Nm).

28. Install and hand-tighten both ends of the NEW high pressure (intermediate) fuel line. Tighten the high pressure fuel line fitting nuts to 22 ft. lbs. (30 Nm).

29. Install the fuel pump cover.

➡**The low pressure fuel pipe used is model dependent.**

30. Install the low pressure fuel pipe assembly.

31. Install the fuel pump cover and nut. Tighten the nut to 89 inch lbs. (10 Nm).

32. Install a new throttle body gasket. Install the throttle body. Install and tighten bolts to 89 inch lbs. (10 Nm).

33. Install the MAP sensor. Tighten the sensor bolt.

34. Install the EVAP canister valve and tighten to 18 ft. lbs. (25 Nm).

35. Install the EVAP canister valve tube.

36. Install the O-ring and oil fill tube assembly.

37. Install the intake manifold cover onto the camshaft cover ball studs.

38. Install the oil fill cap.

3.6L Engine

See Figure 38.

1. Remove the intake manifold cover.
2. Disconnect the coolant hose.
3. Disconnect and remove the positive crankcase ventilation (PCV) tube from the intake manifold and right camshaft cover.
4. Remove the evaporative emission (EVAP) hose from the intake manifold and EVAP solenoid.
5. Loosen the EVAP solenoid bolt. Remove the EVAP solenoid.
6. Remove the fuel pump cover bolt and remove the fuel pump cover.
7. Remove the intake manifold bolts.
8. Remove the intake manifold assembly.
9. Remove and discard the intake manifold gasket.

To install:

10. Install the NEW intake manifold gasket.

11. Install the intake manifold assembly and the intake manifold bolts:

a. Tighten the intake manifold bolts in the sequence shown to 17 ft. lbs. (23 Nm).

b. Tighten the intake manifold bolts a second pass in sequence to 17 ft. lbs. (23 Nm).

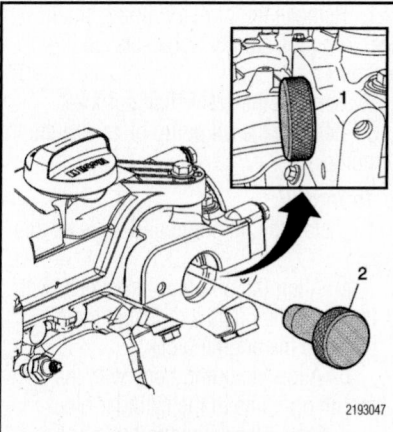

Fig. 36 Use the EN-48896 alignment gauge (or equivalent) (2) to ensure that the camshaft lobe is in the base circle position. At base circle position, the tool will be flush with the head (1).

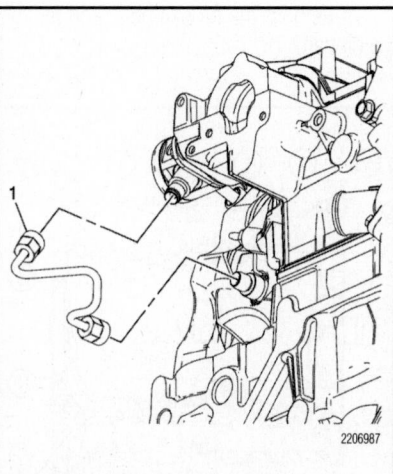

Fig. 37 Install and hand-tighten both ends of the NEW high pressure (intermediate) fuel line (1). Tighten the high pressure fuel line fitting nuts to 22 ft. lbs. (30 Nm).

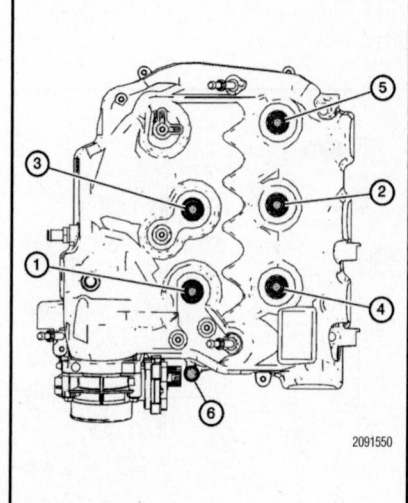

Fig. 38 Intake manifold bolt tightening sequence

12. Install the fuel pump cover and bolt and tighten to 89 inch lbs. (10 Nm).

13. Install the EVAP solenoid and tighten the bolt to 89 inch lbs. (10 Nm).

14. Connect the EVAP hose to the upper intake manifold and EVAP solenoid.

15. Connect the PCV tube assembly (1) to the upper intake manifold and the right camshaft cover.

16. Install coolant hose.

17. Install intake manifold cover.

OIL PAN

REMOVAL & INSTALLATION

2.4L Engine

See Figure 39.

1. Remove the drive belt.

2. Remove the oil level indicator tube.

➡ **The support fixture bar must be installed to provide enough access to remove and properly tighten the oil pan bolts.**

3. Install a proper engine support fixture.

4. Remove engine mount.

5. Using the engine support fixture, raise the engine approximately 3 in. (76 mm).

6. Raise and support the vehicle.

7. Loosen the upper air conditioning (A/C) compressor bolts. Remove the lower A/C compressor bolt.

8. Place a suitable drain pan under the oil pan drain plug.

9. Remove the oil pan drain plug and drain the engine oil.

10. Reinstall the oil pan drain plug until snug.

11. Remove the 4 oil pan to transaxle bolts.

12. Remove the oil pan bolts and remove the oil pan.

13. Remove any old oil pan sealant.

To install:

14. Ensure that the oil pan and the sealing surface on the lower crankcase are free of all oil and debris.

15. Apply a 2 mm bead of sealant (1) around the perimeter of the oil pan and the oil suction port opening. DO NOT over apply the sealant. More than a 2 mm bead is not required.

16. Install the oil pan and the oil pan bolts.

17. Install the 4 oil pan to transaxle bolts and tighten to 55 ft. lbs. (75 Nm).

18. Tighten the oil pan bolts in the sequence shown to 18 ft. lbs. (25 Nm).

19. Lower the vehicle.

20. Using the engine support fixture, lower the engine.

21. Install the engine mount. Tighten the bolts to 46 ft. lbs. (62 Nm).

22. Remove the engine support fixture.

23. Install the oil level indicator tube.

24. Install the drive belt.

25. Fill the engine oil to the proper level.

3.6L Engine

See Figure 40.

1. Raise and support the vehicle.

2. Drain the engine oil and remove the oil filter.

3. Remove the catalytic converter.

4. Remove the air conditioning (A/C) compressor bolts and reposition the compressor (do not disconnect the A/C lines).

5. Remove the front cover. See "Engine Front Cover" in this section.

6. Remove the oil pan to transmission bolts.

7. Remove the oil pan bolts and remove the oil pan.

8. Clean the oil pan and the engine block gasket surface.

To install:

9. Install the 8 mm guides from the EN-46109 set (or equivalent) into the center oil pan rail bolt hole on each side of the engine block.

10. Place a 3 mm bead of RTV sealant, on the block pan rail and the crankshaft rear oil seal housing.

11. Position the oil pan onto the block.

12. Remove the 8 mm guides from the engine block.

13. Loosely install the oil pan bolts, then tighten the oil pan bolts in sequence:

- 1–11: 8 mm bolts to 18 ft. lbs. (25 Nm).
- 12–13: 6 mm bolts to 89 inch lbs. (10 Nm).

14. Install engine front cover. See "Engine Front Cover" in this section.

15. Install the air conditioning (A/C) compressor and tighten bolts to 43 ft. lbs. (58 Nm).

16. Install the catalytic converter. Tighten nuts to 36 ft. lbs. (50 Nm).

17. Lower the vehicle.

18. Refill the engine oil.

OIL PUMP

REMOVAL & INSTALLATION

2.4L Engine

➡ **Oil pump is removed and disassembled after engine is removed for overhaul.**

3.6L Engine

See Figure 41.

1. Remove the primary timing chain. See "Timing Chain & Sprockets" in this section.

2. Remove the crankshaft sprocket.

3. Remove the oil pump bolts and the oil pump.

To install:

4. Install the oil pump and bolts as follows:

   a. Align the oil pump drive gear with the crankshaft flats and install the oil pump to the engine block.

   b. Align the pump body with the mounting holes in the cylinder block.

   c. Install the oil pump bolts and tighten to 18 ft. lbs. (25 Nm).

5. Install the crankshaft sprocket as follows:

   a. Ensure the crankshaft sprocket is installed with the timing mark visible.

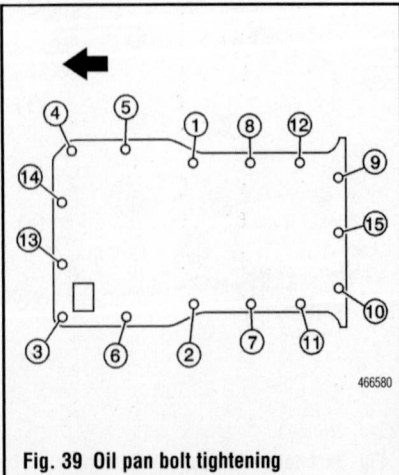

Fig. 39 Oil pan bolt tightening sequence—2.4L engine

466580

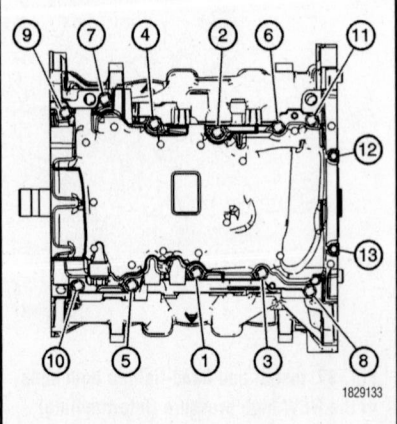

Fig. 40 Oil pan bolt tightening sequence

1829133

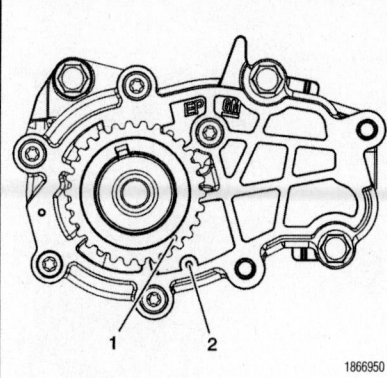

Fig. 41 Ensure the crankshaft is in the stage one timing position with the crankshaft sprocket timing mark (1) aligned to the stage one timing mark on the oil pump cover (2), using the EN-48589 socket (or equivalent).

b. Install the crankshaft sprocket onto the nose of the crankshaft.

c. Align the notch in the crankshaft sprocket with the pin in the crankshaft.

d. Slide the crankshaft sprocket on the crankshaft nose until the crankshaft sprocket contacts the step in the crankshaft.

e. Ensure the crankshaft is in the stage one timing position with the crankshaft sprocket timing mark aligned to the stage one timing mark on the oil pump cover, using the EN-48589 socket (or equivalent).

6. Install the primary timing chain. See "Timing Chain & Sprockets" in this section.

PISTON & RING

POSITIONING

2.4L Engine

See Figure 42.

3.6L Engine

See Figure 43.

REAR MAIN SEAL

REMOVAL & INSTALLATION

See Figures 44 and 45.

1. Remove the engine flywheel. See "Flywheel" in this section.

2. Remove the oil pan. See "Oil Pan" in this section.

3. Remove the crankshaft rear oil seal and housing.

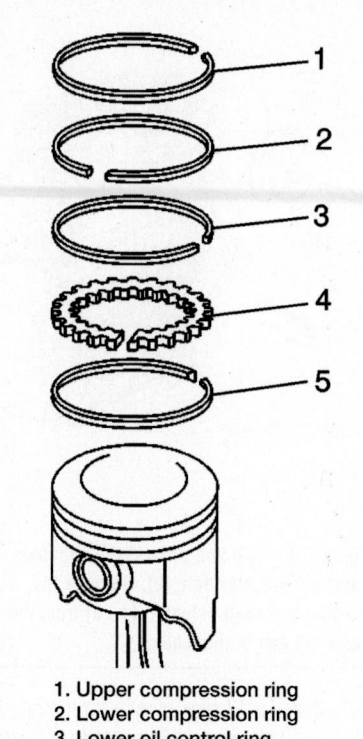

1. Upper compression ring
2. Lower compression ring
3. Lower oil control ring
4. Upper oil control ring
5. Expander

Fig. 42 Showing location and orientation of piston rings

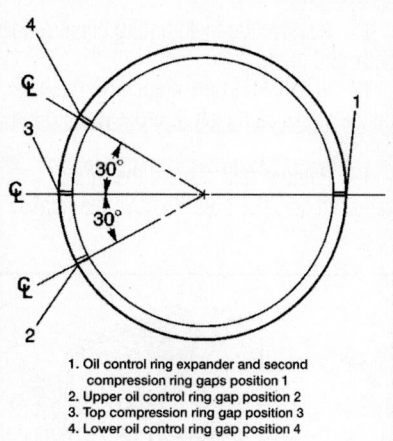

1. Oil control ring expander and second compression ring gaps position 1
2. Upper oil control ring gap position 2
3. Top compression ring gap position 3
4. Lower oil control ring gap position 4

Fig. 43 Showing orientation of piston rings

To install:

4. Install the crankshaft rear oil seal and housing as follows:

a. Install the 6 mm guides from the EN-46109 pin set (or equivalent) into the 2 crankshaft rear oil seal housing corner bolt holes of the engine block.

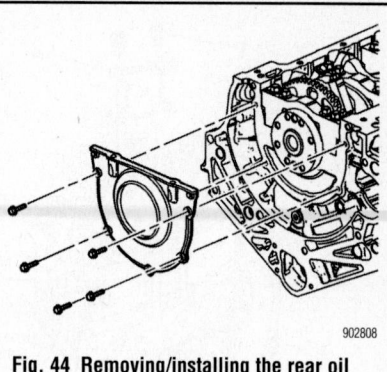

Fig. 44 Removing/installing the rear oil seal

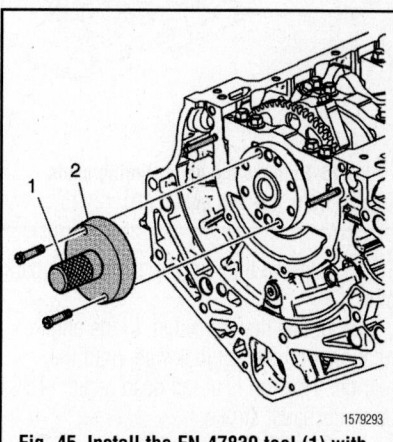

Fig. 45 Install the EN-47839 tool (1) with the EN-42183 handle (2) (or equivalent) onto the rear of the crankshaft flange.

5. Install the EN-47839 tool with the EN-42183 handle (or equivalent) onto the rear of the crankshaft flange.

6. Place a 3 mm bead of RTV sealant around the sealing edge of the seal housing.

7. Install the crankshaft rear oil seal housing to the engine block.

8. Remove the 6 mm pin guides from the engine block.

9. Install the crankshaft rear oil seal housing bolts. Tighten the bolts in a crisscross sequence to 89 inch lbs. (10 Nm).

10. Remove the EN-47839 tool and EN-42183 handle from the crankshaft flange.

11. Install the oil pan. See "Oil Pan" in this section.

12. Install the engine flywheel. See "Flywheel" in this section.

TIMING CHAIN & SPROCKETS

REMOVAL & INSTALLATION

2.4L Engine

See Figures 46 through 61.

1. Remove the camshaft cover. See "Valve (Camshaft) Cover" in this section.

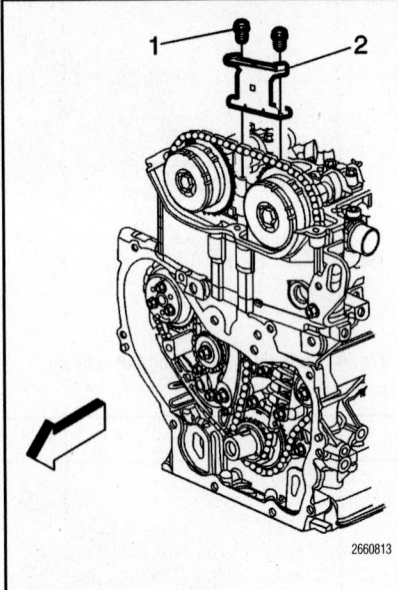

Fig. 46 Remove the upper timing chain guide bolts_(1) and guide_(2).

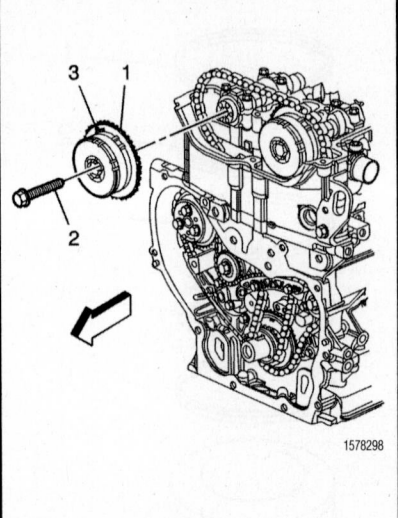

Fig. 48 Remove and discard the exhaust camshaft actuator bolt_(2). Remove the exhaust camshaft actuator_(1,_3) from the camshaft and timing chain.

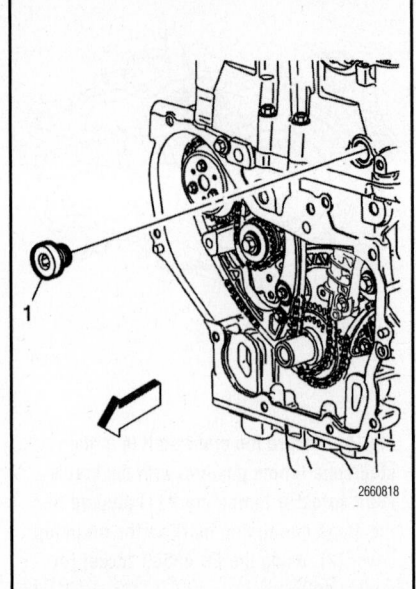

Fig. 50 Remove the fixed timing chain guide access plug_(1).

2. Remove the number 1 cylinder spark plug.

3. Rotate the crankshaft in the engine rotational direction clockwise, until the number 1 piston is at top dead center (TDC) on the exhaust stroke.

4. Remove the engine front cover. See "Engine Front Cover" in this section.

5. Remove the upper timing chain guide bolts and guide.

➡**The timing chain tensioner must be removed to unload chain tension before the timing chain is removed. If it is not, the timing chain will become cocked and it will be difficult to remove.**

6. Remove the timing chain tensioner.

7. Install a 24 mm wrench on the hex on the exhaust camshaft in order to hold the camshaft.

8. Remove and discard the exhaust camshaft actuator bolt. Remove the exhaust camshaft actuator from the camshaft and timing chain.

9. Remove the timing chain tensioner guide bolt and guide.

10. Remove the fixed timing chain guide access plug.

11. Remove the fixed timing chain guide bolts and guide.

12. Install a 24 mm wrench on the hex on the intake camshaft in order to hold the camshaft.

13. Remove and discard the intake camshaft actuator bolt. Remove the intake

camshaft actuator, and the timing chain through the top of the cylinder head.

➡**Ecotec 4 cylinder engines with SIDI-Direct Injection, the lower timing chain crank gear may be equipped with a second spacing washer installed in front of the lower timing chain crank gear. The outer spacer/washer is in between the crank/balancer pulley and the lower timing gear and may remain in place when the pulley is removed. The spacer/washer has a dot/mark on its surface that may be mistaken for the lower timing mark. If applicable, the washer must be removed in order to view the correct timing mark on the lower crank gear.**

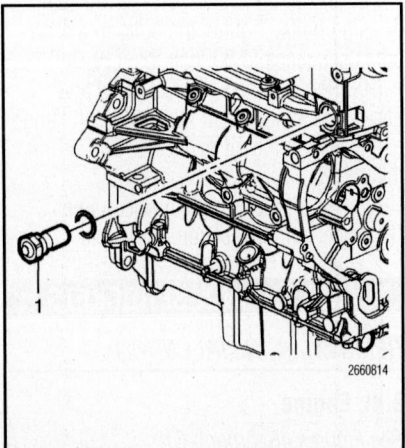

Fig. 47 Remove the timing chain tensioner_(1).

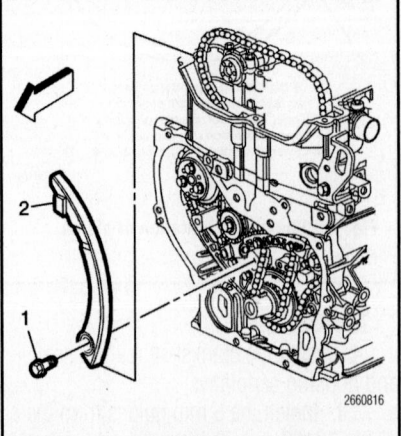

Fig. 49 Remove the timing chain tensioner guide bolt_(1) and guide_(2).

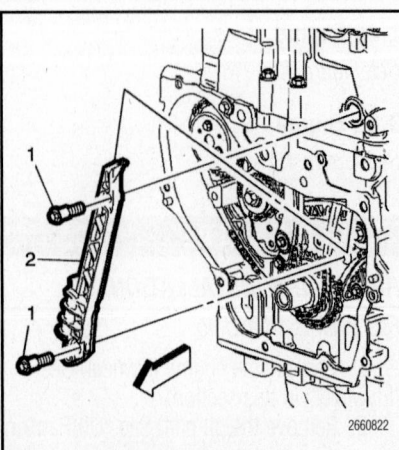

Fig. 51 Remove the fixed timing chain guide bolts_(1) and guide_(2).

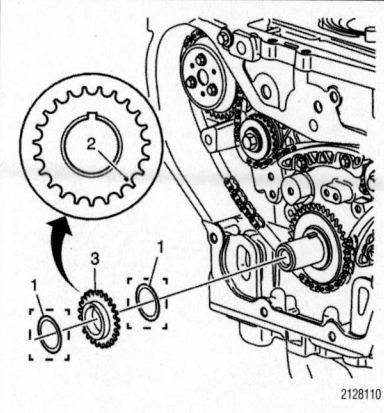

Fig. 52 Remove the outer friction washer (1) if equipped. Ensure the crankshaft gear timing mark (2) is in the 5_o'clock position and crankshaft key is in the 12 o'clock position. Remove the crankshaft sprocket (3). Remove the inner friction washer (1).

14. Remove the outer friction washer if equipped. Ensure the crankshaft gear timing mark is in the 5 o'clock position and crankshaft key is in the 12 o'clock position. Remove the crankshaft sprocket. Remove the inner friction washer.

To install:

15. During installation, ensure the intake camshaft notch is in the 10 o'clock position (2) and the exhaust camshaft notch is in the 7 o'clock position (1). The number 1 piston should be at top dead center (TDC), crankshaft key at 12 o'clock.

16. Install the inner friction washer. Install the crankshaft sprocket with the timing mark is in the 5 o'clock position and

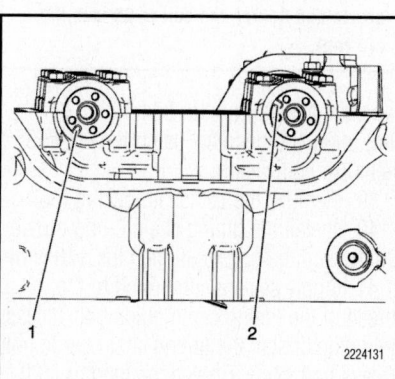

Fig. 53 During installation, ensure the intake camshaft notch is in the 10 o'clock position (2) and the exhaust camshaft notch is in the 7 o'clock position (1). The number 1 piston should be at top dead center (TDC), crankshaft key at 12 o'clock.

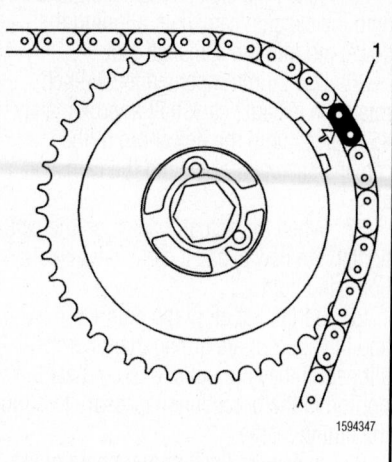

Fig. 54 Assemble the intake camshaft actuator into the timing chain with the timing mark lined up with the uniquely colored link (1).

facing outward. Install the outer friction washer if equipped.

➡**There are 3 colored links on the timing chain. Two links are of matching color, and 1 link is of a unique color. Use the following procedure to line up the links with the actuators. Orient the chain so that the colored links are visible.**

➡**Always use new actuator bolts.**

17. Assemble the intake camshaft actuator into the timing chain with the timing mark lined up with the uniquely colored link.

18. Lower the timing chain through the opening in the cylinder head. Use care to

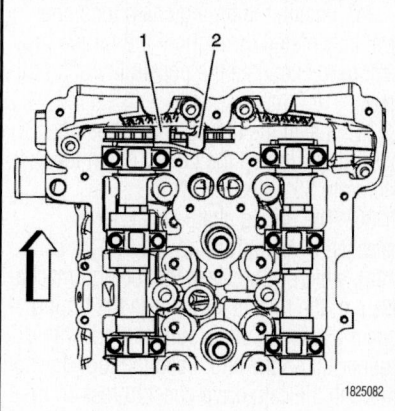

Fig. 55 Lower the timing chain through the opening in the cylinder head. Use care to ensure that the chain goes around both sides of the cylinder block bosses (1, 2).

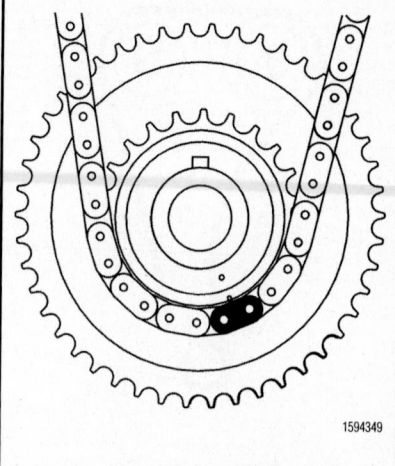

Fig. 56 Route the timing chain around the crankshaft sprocket and line up the first matching colored link with the timing mark on the crankshaft sprocket, in approximately the 5 o'clock position.

ensure that the chain goes around both sides of the cylinder block bosses.

19. Install the intake camshaft actuator onto the intake camshaft while aligning the dowel pin into the camshaft slot. Hand tighten the new intake camshaft actuator bolt.

20. Route the timing chain around the crankshaft sprocket and line up the first matching colored link with the timing mark on the crankshaft sprocket, in approximately the 5 o'clock position.

21. Install the friction washer, if applicable.

22. Rotate the crankshaft clockwise to remove all chain slack. Do not rotate the intake camshaft.

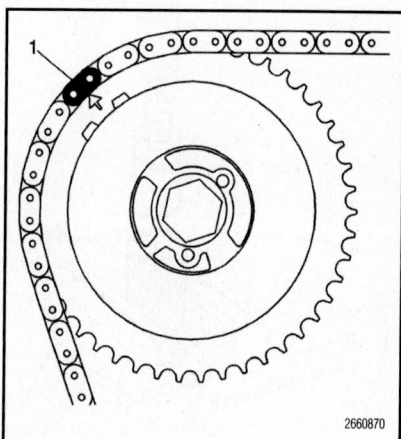

Fig. 57 Install the exhaust camshaft actuator into the timing chain with the timing mark lined up with the second matching colored link.

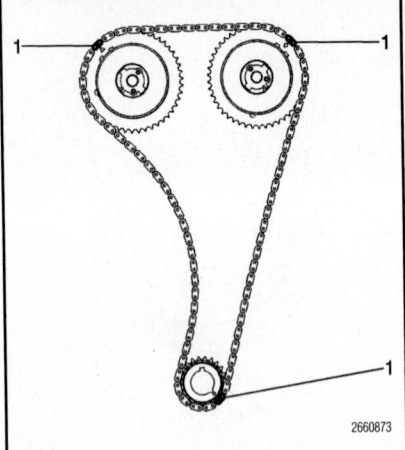

Fig. 58 Verify that all of the colored links (1) and the appropriate timing marks are still aligned. If they are not aligned, repeat the portion of the procedure necessary to align the timing marks.

23. Install the adjustable timing chain guide down through the opening in the cylinder head and install the adjustable timing chain bolt. Tighten the adjustable timing chain guide bolt to 89 inch lbs. (10 Nm). Always install NEW actuator bolts.

24. Install the exhaust camshaft actuator into the timing chain with the timing mark lined up with the second matching colored link.

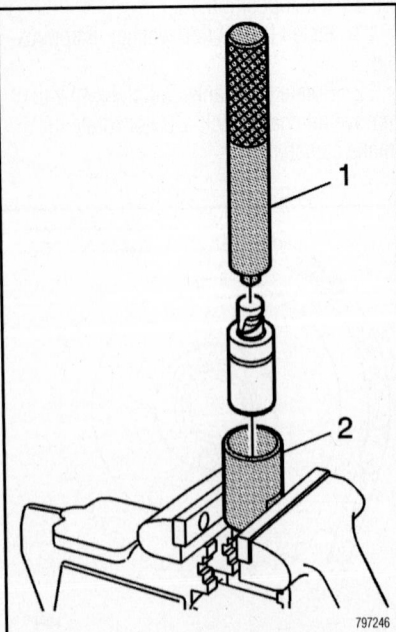

Fig. 59 Install the notch end of the piston assembly into the EN-45027-2 tool (2). With the tool (1), turn the ratchet cylinder into the piston.

25. Install the exhaust camshaft actuator onto the exhaust camshaft, aligning the dowel pin into the camshaft slot.

26. Use 24 mm open ended wrench, rotate the exhaust camshaft approximately 45 degrees until the dowel pin in the camshaft actuator goes into the camshaft slot.

27. When the actuator seats on the cam, tighten the new exhaust camshaft actuator bolt hand tight.

28. Verify that all of the colored links and the appropriate timing marks are still aligned. If they are not aligned, repeat the portion of the procedure necessary to align the timing marks.

29. Install the fixed timing chain guide and bolts. Tighten the fixed timing chain guide bolts to 89 inch lbs. (10 Nm).

30. Install the upper timing chain guide and bolts. Tighten the upper timing chain guide bolts to 89 inch lbs. (10 Nm).

31. Reset the timing chain tensioner by performing the following steps:

 a. Remove the snap ring.

 b. Remove the piston assembly from the body of the timing chain tensioner.

 c. Install the EN-45027-2 tool into a vise.

 d. Install the notch end of the piston assembly into the EN-45027-2 tool. With the tool, turn the ratchet cylinder into the piston.

 e. Reinstall the piston assembly into the body of the tensioner.

 f. Install the snap ring.

32. Inspect the timing chain tensioner seal for damage. If damaged, replace the seal.

33. Inspect to ensure all dirt and debris is removed from the timing chain tensioner threaded hole in the cylinder head.

34. Ensure the timing chain tensioner seal is centered throughout the torque procedure to eliminate the possibility of an oil leak.

35. Install the timing chain tensioner assembly. Tighten the timing chain tensioner to 55 ft. lbs. (75 Nm).

36. The timing chain tensioner is released by compressing it 0.079 in. (2 mm), which will release the locking mechanism in the ratchet. To release the timing chain tensioner, use a suitable tool with a rubber tip on the end. Feed the tool down through the cam drive chest to rest on the cam chain. Then give a sharp jolt diagonally downwards to release the tensioner.

37. Install the EN-48953 locking tool and tighten the bolts into the cylinder head to 89 inch lbs. (10 Nm).

38. Using a torque wrench, tighten the

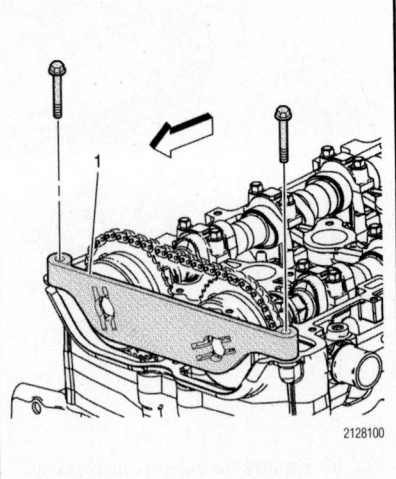

Fig. 60 Install the EN-48953 locking tool (1) and tighten the bolts into the cylinder head to 89 inch lbs. (10 Nm).

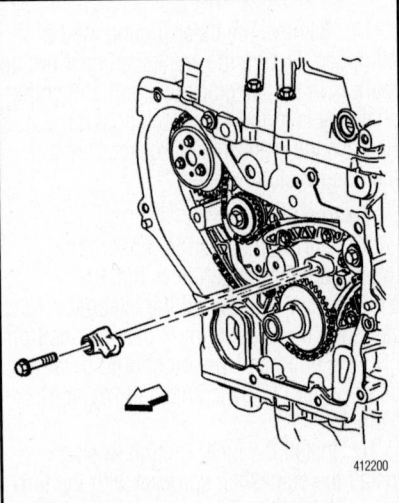

Fig. 61 Install the timing chain oiling nozzle and tighten the bolt to 89 inch lbs. (10 Nm).

camshaft actuator bolt to 22 ft. lbs. (30 Nm), plus 100 degrees, using the EN-45059 meter (or equivalent).

39. Remove the camshaft locking tool.

40. Install the timing chain oiling nozzle and tighten the bolt to 89 inch lbs. (10 Nm).

41. Apply sealant compound to the thread of the timing chain guide bolt access hole plug. Install the timing chain guide bolt access hole plug. Tighten the plug to 66 ft. lbs. (90 Nm).

42. Install the engine front cover. See "Engine Front Cover" in this section.

43. Install the camshaft cover. See "Valve (Camshaft) Cover" in this section.

44. Install the number 1 cylinder spark plug. Tighten to 15 ft. lbs. (20 Nm).

3.6L Engine

Secondary Camshaft Intermediate Timing Chain—Left Side

See Figures 62 through 69.

1. Remove the engine front cover. See "Engine Front Cover" in this section.
2. Remove the secondary camshaft drive chain tensioner as follows:

a. Remove the secondary camshaft drive chain tensioner bolts and drive chain tensioner. Remove and discard the right secondary camshaft drive chain tensioner gasket.

b. Inspect the secondary camshaft drive chain tensioner mounting surface on the cylinder head for burrs or any defects that would degrade the sealing of the NEW secondary camshaft drive chain tensioner gasket.

3. Remove the secondary camshaft drive chain shoe.
4. Remove the secondary camshaft drive chain guide.

5. Remove the secondary camshaft drive chain.
6. Remove the primary camshaft intermediate drive chain tensioner as follows:

a. Remove the primary camshaft drive chain tensioner bolts.

b. Remove the primary camshaft drive chain tensioner.

c. Remove and discard the primary camshaft drive chain tensioner gasket.

d. Inspect the primary camshaft drive chain tensioner mounting surface on the

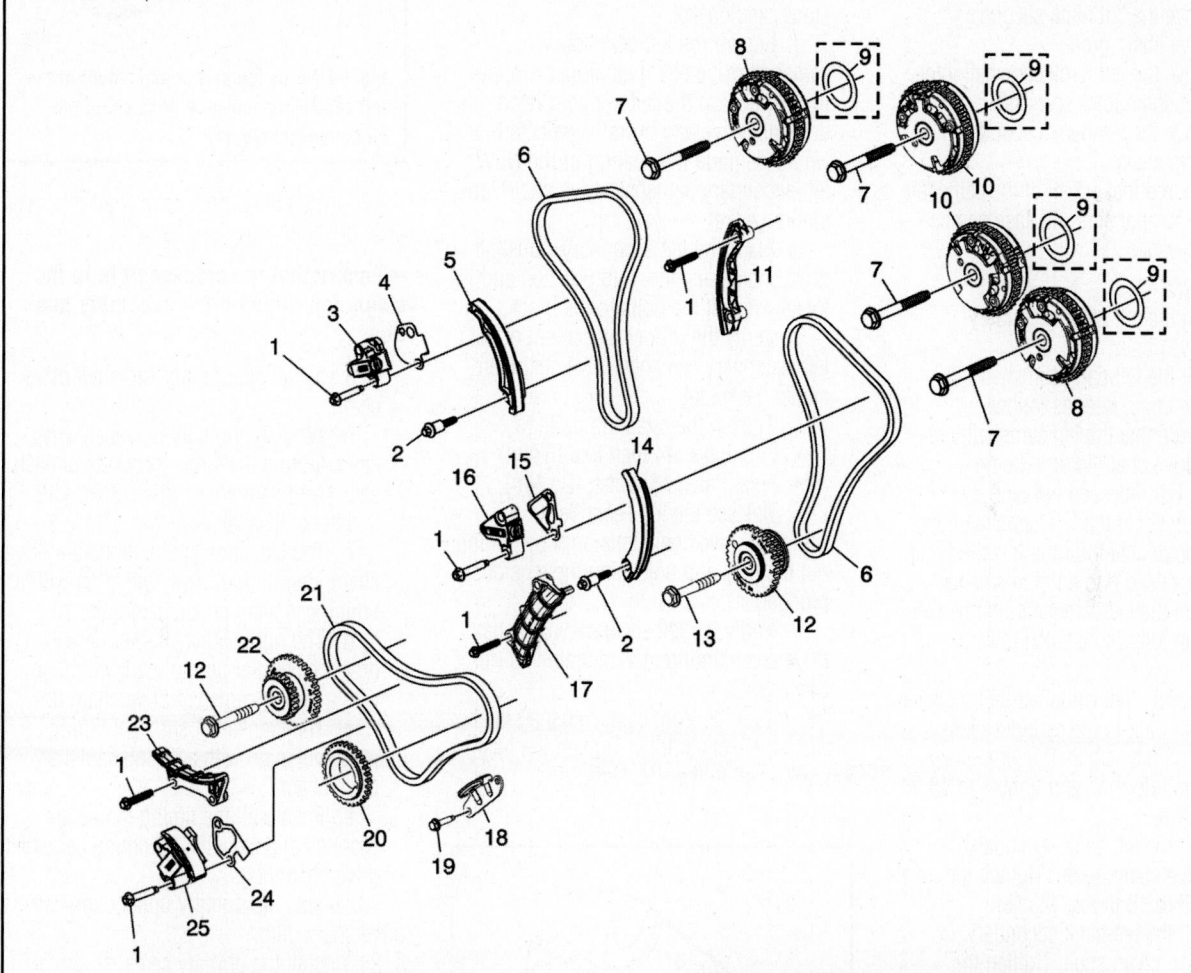

1. Primary Timing Chain Tensioner Bolt
2. Left Secondary Timing Chain Shoe Bolt
3. Right Secondary Timing Chain Tensioner
4. Right Secondary Timing Chain Tensioner Gasket
5. Right Secondary Timing Chain Shoe
6. Secondary Timing Chain
7. Camshaft Position Actuator Bolt
8. Exhaust Camshaft Position Actuator
9. Camshaft Position Actuator Thrust Washer
10. Intake Camshaft Position Actuator
11. Right Secondary Timing Chain Guide
12. Left Camshaft Intermediate Drive Shaft Sprocket
13. Camshaft Intermediate Drive Shaft Sprocket Bolt
14. Left Secondary Timing Chain Shoe
15. Left Secondary Timing Chain Tensioner Gasket
16. Left Secondary Timing Chain Tensioner
17. Left Secondary Timing Chain Guide
18. Lower Primary Timing Chain Guide
19. Lower Primary Timing Chain Guide Bolt
20. Crankshaft Sprocket
21. Primary Timing Chain
22. Right Camshaft Intermediate Drive Shaft Sprocket
23. Upper Primary Timing Chain Guide
24. Primary Timing Chain Tensioner Gasket
25. Primary Timing Chain Tensioner

1826061

Fig. 62 Exploded view of camshaft timing components

engine block for burrs or any defects that would degrade the sealing of the NEW primary camshaft drive chain tensioner gasket.

7. Remove the primary upper camshaft drive chain guide.

8. Remove the primary camshaft drive chain.

9. Remove the right bank camshaft intermediate drive chain sprocket.

10. Remove the left bank secondary camshaft drive chain tensioner.

11. Remove the left bank secondary camshaft drive chain shoe.

12. Remove the left bank secondary camshaft drive chain guide.

13. Remove the left bank camshaft intermediate drive chain idler sprocket.

14. Remove the left bank secondary camshaft drive chain.

15. Clean and inspect all of the camshaft timing drive components. Replace components as necessary.

To install:

16. Install the left bank secondary camshaft drive chain.

17. Install the left bank camshaft intermediate drive chain idler as follows:

a. Ensure that the left camshaft intermediate drive chain idler is being installed. The recessed hub and the larger sprocket of the left camshaft intermediate drive chain idler is installed outward. The raised hub and the smaller sprocket of the left camshaft intermediate drive chain idler is installed towards the block.

b. Place the left camshaft intermediate drive chain idler to the cylinder block.

c. Install the camshaft intermediate drive chain idler bolt and tighten to 43 ft. lbs. (58_Nm).

18. Install the left bank secondary camshaft drive chain guide. Tighten the retaining bolt to 18 ft. lbs. (25 Nm).

19. Install the left bank secondary camshaft drive chain shoe. Tighten the retaining bolt to 18 ft. lbs. (25 Nm).

20. Install the left bank secondary camshaft drive chain tensioner as follows:

a. Using the EN 45027 tool (or equivalent), reset the left secondary camshaft drive chain tensioner plunger.

b. Install the plunger into the left secondary camshaft drive chain tensioner body.

c. Compress the plunger into the body and lock the left secondary camshaft drive chain tensioner by inserting the EN-46112 pins (or equivalent) into the access hole in the side of the left

secondary camshaft drive chain tensioner body.

d. Slowly release pressure on the left secondary camshaft drive chain tensioner. The left secondary camshaft drive chain tensioner should remain compressed.

e. Install a NEW left secondary camshaft drive chain tensioner gasket to the left secondary camshaft drive chain tensioner.

f. Install the left secondary camshaft drive chain tensioner bolts through the left secondary camshaft drive chain tensioner and gasket.

g. Ensure the left secondary camshaft drive chain tensioner mounting surface on the left cylinder head does not have any burrs or defects that would degrade the sealing of the NEW left secondary camshaft drive chain tensioner gasket.

h. Place the left secondary camshaft drive chain tensioner into position and loosely install the bolts to the block.

i. Verify the proper placement of the left secondary camshaft drive chain tensioner gasket tab.

j. Tighten the retaining bolts to:
• First Pass: 44 inch lbs. (5 Nm)
• Final Pass: 18 ft. lbs. (25 Nm)

k. Release the left secondary camshaft drive chain tensioner by pulling out the pins and unlocking the tensioner plunger.

l. Verify the left secondary camshaft drive chain timing mark alignments (for Stage One).

21. Install the right bank camshaft intermediate drive chain idler. Tighten the retaining bolt to 43 ft. lbs. (58 Nm).

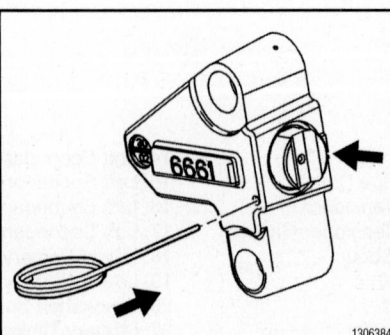

Fig. 63 Compress the plunger into the body and lock the left secondary camshaft drive chain tensioner by inserting the EN-46112 pins (or equivalent) into the access hole in the side of the left secondary camshaft drive chain tensioner body.

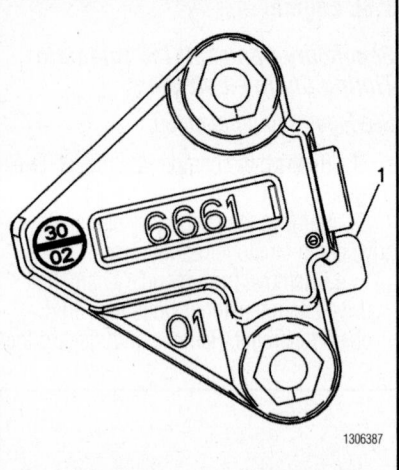

Fig. 64 Verify the proper placement of the left secondary camshaft drive chain tensioner gasket tab_(1).

22. Install the primary camshaft intermediate drive chain as follows:

➡**Ensure that the crankshaft is in the stage one timing drive assembly position.**

a. Install the primary camshaft drive chain.

b. Wrap the primary camshaft drive chain around the large sprockets of each camshaft intermediate drive chain idler and the crankshaft sprocket.

c. The left camshaft intermediate drive chain idler timing mark_will align with a timing camshaft drive chain link.

d. The right camshaft intermediate drive chain idler timing mark will align with a timing camshaft drive chain link.

e. The crankshaft sprocket timing mark will align with a timing camshaft drive chain link.

f. Ensure all the timing marks are properly aligned with the timing camshaft drive chain links.

23. Install the primary upper camshaft drive chain guide.

24. Install the primary camshaft drive chain tensioner as follows:

a. Using the EN-45027 tool (or equivalent), reset the primary camshaft drive chain tensioner plunger.

b. Install the plunger into the primary camshaft drive chain tensioner body.

c. Compress the plunger into the body and lock the primary camshaft drive chain tensioner by inserting the EN-46112 pins into the access hole in the side of the primary camshaft drive chain tensioner body.

d. Slowly release pressure on the primary camshaft drive chain tensioner. The

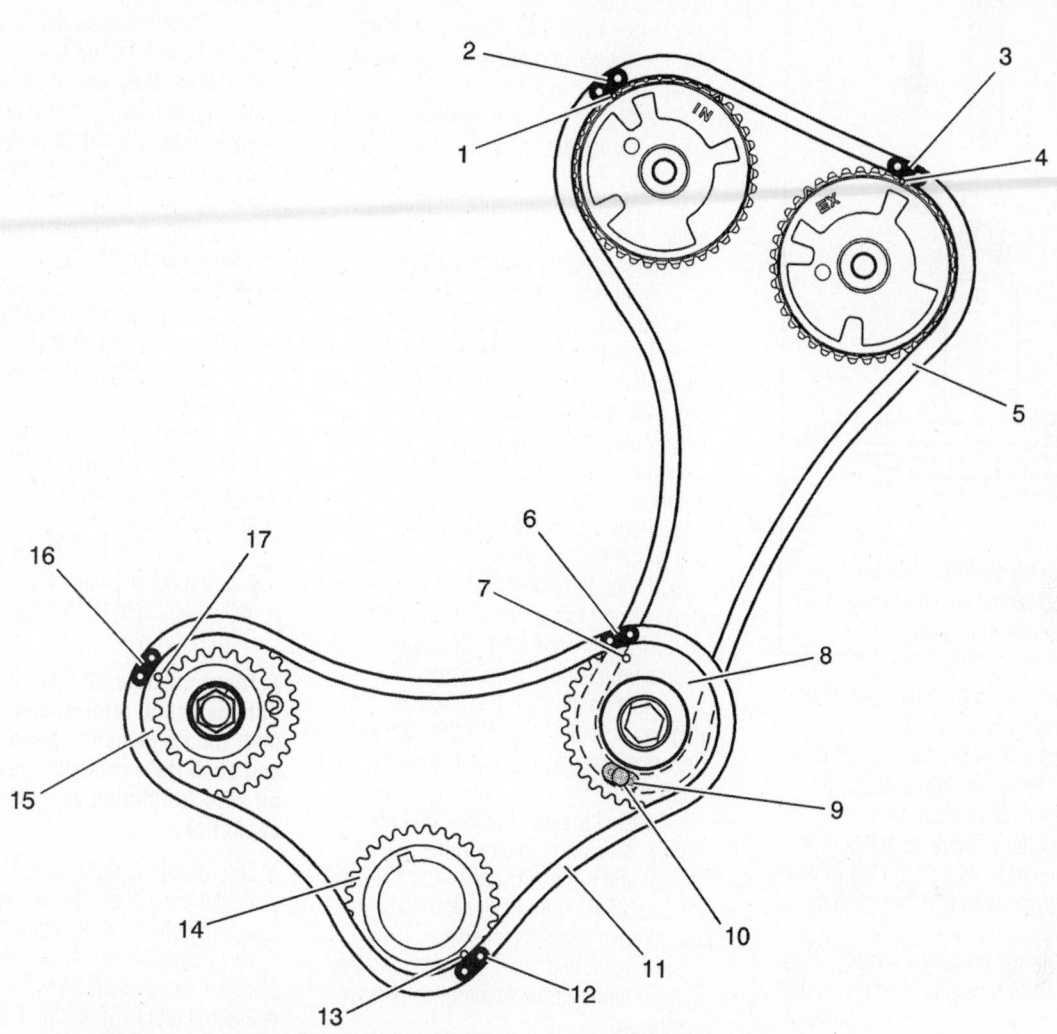

1. Left Intake Camshaft Position (CMP) Actuator Timing Mark - Circle
2. Left Intake Secondary Camshaft Timing Drive Chain Timing Link
3. Left Exhaust Secondary Camshaft Timing Drive Chain Timing Link
4. Left Exhaust Camshaft Position (CMP) Actuator Timing Mark - Circle
5. Left Secondary Camshaft Timing Drive Chain
6. Primary Camshaft Drive Chain Timing Link for the Left Primary Camshaft Intermediate Drive Chain Sprocket
7. Left Primary Camshaft Intermediate Drive Chain Sprocket Timing Mark for the Primary Camshaft Drive Chain
8. Left Primary Camshaft Intermediate Drive Chain Sprocket
9. Left Secondary Camshaft Timing Drive Chain Timing Link for the Left Primary Camshaft Intermediate Drive Chain Sprocket, behind hole in sprocket
10. Left Primary Camshaft Intermediate Drive Chain Sprocket Timing Window
11. Primary Camshaft Drive Chain
12. Primary Camshaft Drive Chain Timing Link for the Crankshaft Sprocket
13. Crankshaft Sprocket Timing Mark
14. Crankshaft Sprocket
15. Right Primary Camshaft Intermediate Drive Chain Sprocket
16. Primary Camshaft Drive Chain Timing Link for the Right Primary Camshaft Intermediate Drive Chain Sprocket
17. Right Primary Camshaft Intermediate Drive Chain Sprocket Timing Mark

1827967

Fig. 65 Stage One timing mark alignment positions—left side shown; right side similar

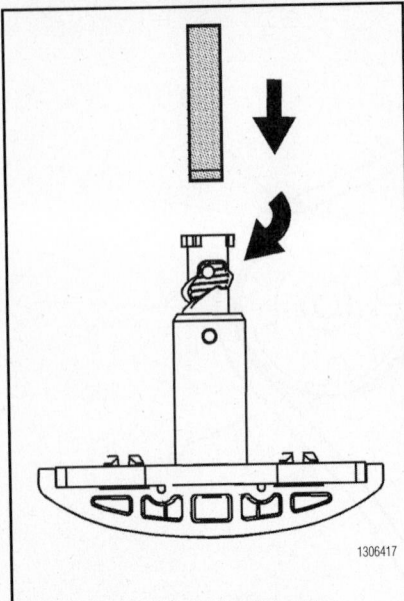

Fig. 66 Using the EN-45027 tool (or equivalent), reset the primary camshaft drive chain tensioner plunger.

primary camshaft drive chain tensioner should remain compressed.

e. Install a NEW primary camshaft drive chain tensioner gasket to the primary camshaft drive chain tensioner.

f. Install the primary camshaft drive chain tensioner bolts through the primary camshaft drive chain tensioner and gasket.

g. Ensure the primary camshaft drive chain tensioner mounting surface on the engine block does not have any burrs or defects that would degrade the sealing of

the NEW primary camshaft drive chain tensioner gasket.

h. Place the primary camshaft drive chain tensioner into position and loosely install the bolts to the block.

i. Verify the proper placement of the primary camshaft drive chain tensioner gasket tab.

j. Tighten the tensioner retaining bolts:
- First Pass: 44 inch lbs. (5 Nm)
- Final Pass: 18 ft. lbs. (25 Nm)

k. Release the primary camshaft drive chain tensioner by pulling out the pins and unlocking the tensioner plunger.

l. Verify the primary and left secondary camshaft drive chain timing mark alignments (stage one—see illustration in this section).

m. Remove the EN-48383-1 from the rear of the left camshafts.

n. Using the EN-48589 (or equivalent) socket , rotate the crankshaft and crankshaft sprocket from the stage 1 alignment position to the Stage Two alignment position, 115 crankshaft degrees, in order to install the right secondary camshaft drive chain components.

o. Install the EN-48383-2 and EN 48383-3 locking tools onto the rear of the left and right camshafts, respectively.

25. Install the right bank secondary camshaft drive chain as follows:

a. Ensure that the crankshaft is in the stage 2 timing drive assembly position as shown.

b. Install the right secondary camshaft drive chain.

c. Place the secondary camshaft drive chain around the right camshaft intermediate drive chain idler outer sprocket, aligning the timing camshaft drive chain link with the alignment access hole made in the right camshaft intermediate drive chain idler inner sprocket.

d. Wrap the secondary camshaft drive chain around both right actuator drive sprockets.

e. Ensure there are 10 links between the timing camshaft drive chain links for the camshaft position actuator sprockets.

f. Align the right exhaust camshaft position actuator sprocket alignment triangle mark with the timing camshaft drive chain link.

g. Align the right intake camshaft position actuator sprocket alignment triangle mark with the timing camshaft drive chain link.

➡ **There must be 22 links between the right camshaft intermediate drive chain idler timing camshaft drive chain link and each right camshaft position actuator sprocket timing camshaft drive chain link.**

26. Install the right bank secondary camshaft drive chain guide. Tighten the retaining bolts to 18 ft. lbs. (25 Nm).

27. Install the right bank secondary camshaft drive chain shoe. Tighten the retaining bolts to 18 ft. lbs. (25 Nm).

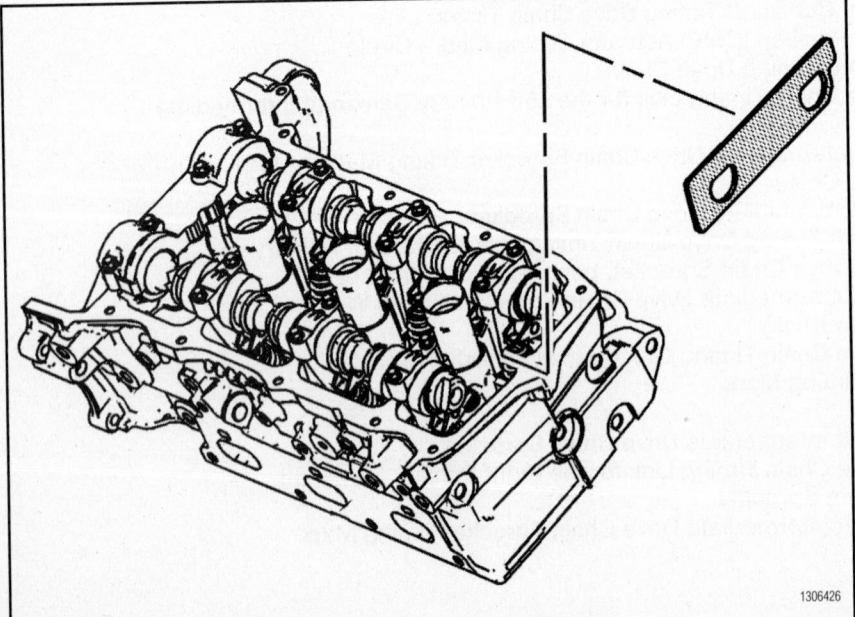

Fig. 67 Remove the EN 48383-1 from the rear of the left camshafts.

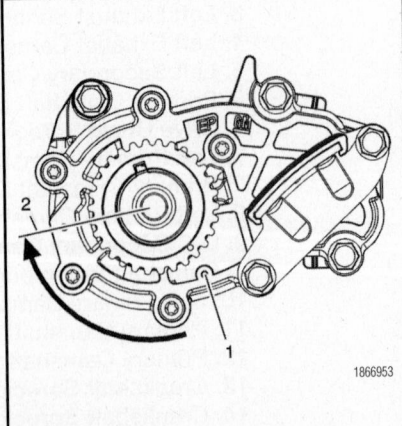

Fig. 68 Using the EN-48589 (or equivalent) socket, rotate the crankshaft and crankshaft sprocket from the stage 1 alignment position (1) to the stage 2 alignment position (2), 115 crankshaft degrees, in order to install the right secondary camshaft drive chain components.

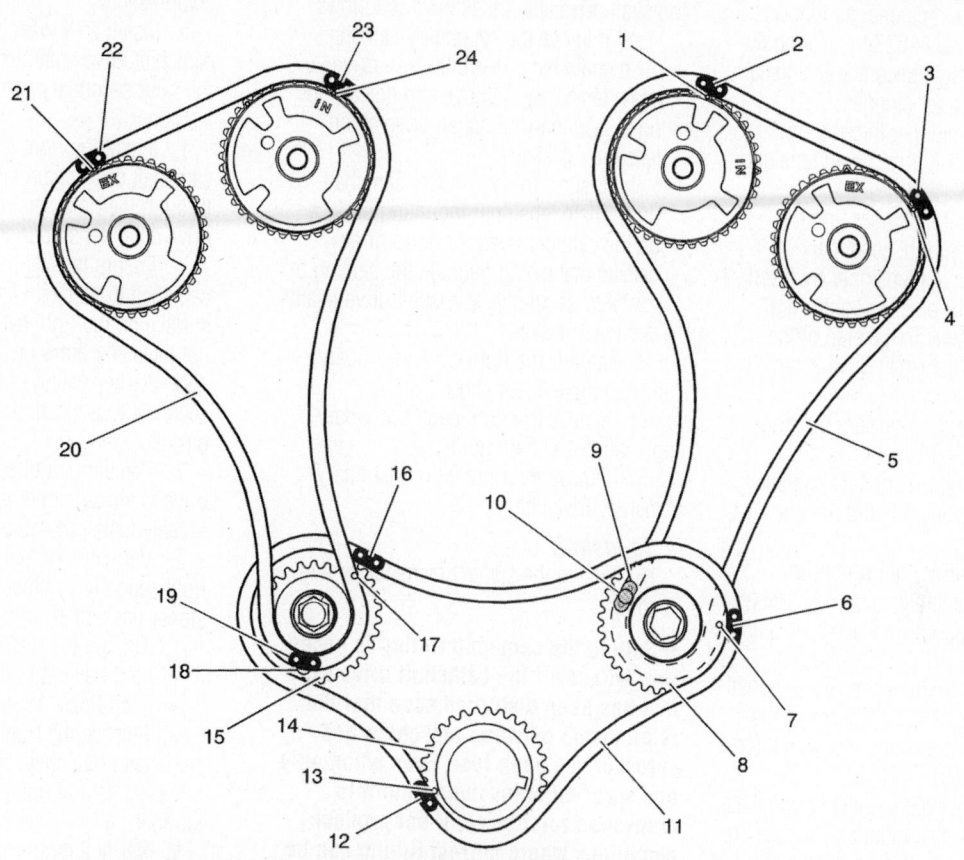

1. Left Intake Camshaft Position (CMP) Actuator Timing Mark - Circle
2. Left Intake Secondary Camshaft Timing Drive Chain Timing Link
3. Left Exhaust Secondary Camshaft Timing Drive Chain Timing Link
4. Left Exhaust Camshaft Position (CMP) Actuator Timing Mark - Circle
5. Left Secondary Camshaft Timing Drive Chain
6. Primary Camshaft Drive Chain Timing Link for the Left Primary Camshaft Intermediate Drive Chain Sprocket
7. Left Primary Camshaft Intermediate Drive Chain Sprocket Timing Mark for the Primary Camshaft Drive Chain
8. Left Primary Camshaft Intermediate Drive Chain Sprocket
9. Left Secondary Camshaft Timing Drive Chain Timing Link for the Left Primary Camshaft Intermediate Drive Chain Sprocket, behind hole in sprocket
10. Left Primary Camshaft Intermediate Drive Chain Sprocket Timing Window
11. Primary Camshaft Drive Chain
12. Primary Camshaft Drive Chain Timing Link for the Crankshaft Sprocket
13. Crankshaft Sprocket Timing Mark
14. Crankshaft Sprocket
15. Right Primary Camshaft Intermediate Drive Chain Sprocket
16. Primary Camshaft Drive Chain Timing Link for the Right Primary Camshaft Intermediate Drive Chain Sprocket
17. Right Primary Camshaft Intermediate Drive Chain Sprocket Timing Mark/Window for the Right Secondary Camshaft Timing Drive Chain
18. Right Primary Camshaft Intermediate Drive Chain Sprocket Timing Mark/Window for the Right Secondary Camshaft Timing Drive Chain
19. Right Secondary Camshaft Timing Drive Chain Timing Link for the Right Primary Camshaft Intermediate Drive Chain Sprocket
20. Right Secondary Camshaft Timing Drive Chain
21. Right Exhaust Camshaft Position (CMP) Actuator Timing Mark - Triangle
22. Right Exhaust Secondary Camshaft Timing Drive Chain Timing Link
23. Right Intake Secondary Camshaft Timing Drive Chain Timing Link
24. Right Intake Camshaft Position (CMP) Actuator Timing Mark - Triangle

1827968

Fig. 69 Stage_Two timing chain mark alignment positions—left side shown; right side similar

28. Install the right bank secondary camshaft drive chain tensioner as follows:

a. Using the EN 45027 tool (or equivalent), reset the right secondary camshaft drive chain tensioner plunger.

b. Install the plunger into the right secondary camshaft drive chain tensioner body.

c. Compress the plunger into the body and lock the right secondary camshaft drive chain tensioner by inserting the EN-46112 pins (or equivalent) into the access hole in the side of the right secondary camshaft drive chain tensioner body.

d. Slowly release pressure on the right secondary camshaft drive chain tensioner. The right secondary camshaft drive chain tensioner should remain compressed.

e. Install a NEW right secondary camshaft drive chain tensioner gasket to the right secondary camshaft drive chain tensioner.

f. Install the right secondary camshaft drive chain tensioner bolts through the right secondary camshaft drive chain tensioner and gasket.

g. Ensure the right secondary camshaft drive chain tensioner mounting surface on the right cylinder head does not have any burrs or defects that would degrade the sealing of the NEW right secondary camshaft drive chain tensioner gasket.

h. Place the right secondary camshaft drive chain tensioner into position and loosely install the bolts to the block.

i. Verify the proper placement of the right secondary camshaft drive chain tensioner gasket tab.

j. Tighten the retaining bolts to:
• First Pass: 44 inch lbs. (5 Nm)
• Final Pass: 18 ft. lbs. (25 Nm)

k. Release the right secondary camshaft drive chain tensioner by pulling out the pins and unlocking the tensioner plunger.

l. Verify the right secondary camshaft drive chain timing mark alignments (for Stage Two—see illustration in this section).

29. Install the engine front cover. See "Engine Front Cover" in this section.

Secondary Camshaft Intermediate Timing Chain—Right Side

➡**Use illustrations under "Left Side" for component references when following this procedure for the right side.**

1. Remove the engine front cover. See "Engine Front Cover" in this section.

2. Remove the right bank secondary camshaft drive chain tensioner as follows:

a. Remove the secondary camshaft drive chain tensioner bolts and drive chain tensioner. Remove and discard the right secondary camshaft drive chain tensioner gasket.

b. Inspect the secondary camshaft drive chain tensioner mounting surface on the cylinder head for burrs or any defects that would degrade the sealing of the NEW secondary camshaft drive chain tensioner gasket.

3. Remove the right bank secondary camshaft drive chain shoe.

4. Remove the right bank secondary camshaft drive chain guide.

5. Remove the right bank secondary camshaft drive chain.

To install:

6. Ensure the stage 1 camshaft timing is correct.

➡**Setting the camshaft timing is necessary whenever the camshaft drive system has been disturbed such that the relationship between any chain and sprocket has been lost. Even when only one sprocket is involved, multiple crankshaft rotations will not produce conditions where correct timing can be confirmed. Follow the left bank secondary camshaft drive chain replacement procedures to reset the camshaft timing in this section.**

7. Install the right bank secondary camshaft drive chain.

8. Install the right bank secondary camshaft drive chain guide. Tighten the bolt to 18 ft. lbs. (25 Nm).

9. Install the right bank secondary camshaft drive chain shoe. Tighten the bolt to 18 ft. lbs. (25 Nm).

10. Install the right bank secondary camshaft drive chain tensioner as follows:

a. Using the EN 45027 tool (or equivalent), reset the right secondary camshaft drive chain tensioner plunger.

b. Install the plunger into the left secondary camshaft drive chain tensioner body.

c. Compress the plunger into the body and lock the right secondary camshaft drive chain tensioner by inserting the EN-46112 pins (or equivalent) into the access hole in the side of the right secondary camshaft drive chain tensioner body.

d. Slowly release pressure on the right secondary camshaft drive chain tensioner. The right secondary camshaft

drive chain tensioner should remain compressed.

e. Install a NEW right secondary camshaft drive chain tensioner gasket to the right secondary camshaft drive chain tensioner.

f. Install the right left secondary camshaft drive chain tensioner bolts through the right secondary camshaft drive chain tensioner and gasket.

g. Ensure the right secondary camshaft drive chain tensioner mounting surface on the right cylinder head does not have any burrs or defects that would degrade the sealing of the NEW right secondary camshaft drive chain tensioner gasket.

h. Place the right secondary camshaft drive chain tensioner into position and loosely install the bolts to the block.

i. Verify the proper placement of the right secondary camshaft drive chain tensioner gasket tab.

j. Tighten the retaining bolts to:
• First Pass: 44 inch lbs. (5 Nm)
• Final Pass: 18 ft. lbs. (25 Nm)

k. Release the right secondary camshaft drive chain tensioner by pulling out the pins and unlocking the tensioner plunger.

l. Verify the right secondary camshaft drive chain timing mark alignments (for Stage Two).

11. Install the engine front cover. See "Engine Front Cover" in this section.

VALVE (CAMSHAFT) COVERS

REMOVAL & INSTALLATION

2.4L Engine

1. Remove the air cleaner outlet duct.

2. Remove the ignition coils. See "ENGINE ELECTRICAL" section.

3. Remove the intake and exhaust Camshaft Position Sensors. See "ENGINE PERFORMANCE & EMISSION CONTROLS" section.

4. Release the camshaft cover fasteners.

5. Remove the camshaft (valve) cover, noting the following:

a. Do not reuse camshaft gasket. Also use a new gasket when removing or replacing camshaft cover.

b. Remove ignition coil wiring harness clips from the camshaft cover.

c. Remove the fuel line bracket from the camshaft cover.

d. Transfer components as necessary.

6. Installation is the reverse of the removal procedure.

3.6L Engine

See Figures 70 and 71.

➡**Procedure specifies left side; however, right side procedure is the same.**

1. Remove the ignition coils. See "ENGINE ELECTRICAL" section.
2. Disconnect and remove the engine harness from the camshaft cover.
3. Remove the intake manifold. See "Intake Manifold" in this section.
4. Remove the power steering reservoir bracket and reposition without disconnecting the hoses.
5. Remove the left camshaft cover bolts. Remove the left camshaft cover from the left cylinder head.
6. Clean the mating surfaces of the cylinder head and the camshaft cover.
7. Install the EN-46101 guide (or equivalent) onto the spark plug tubes of the left cylinder head.

To install:

8. Install new camshaft cover bolt grommets prior to installing the camshaft cover bolts.
9. Place a bead 8 mm in diameter by 4 mm in height of RTV sealant equivalent, on the engine front cover split lines.
10. Place the left camshaft cover into position onto the left cylinder head.

Fig. 70 Install the EN-46101 guide (or equivalent) onto the spark plug tubes of the left cylinder head.

11. Loosely install the left camshaft cover bolts.
12. Tighten the left camshaft cover bolts in the sequence shown to 89 inch lbs. (10_Nm).
13. Install the power steering reservoir bracket.
14. Connect and install the engine harness to the camshaft cover.
15. Install the intake manifold. See "Intake Manifold" in this section.

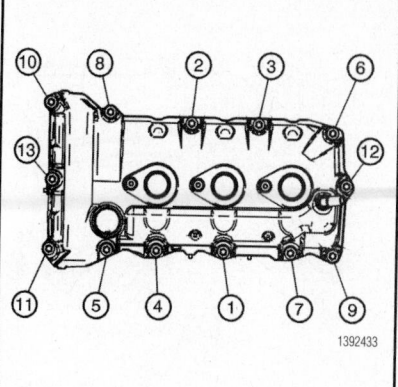

Fig. 71 Left camshaft cover bolt tightening sequence

16. Remove the guides from the spark plug tubes of the left cylinder head.
17. Install the ignition coils. See "ENGINE ELECTRICAL" section.

VALVE LASH

ADJUSTMENT

➡**Valve clearance (lash) is maintained by hydraulic lifters; therefore, no adjustment is required.**

ENGINE PERFORMANCE & EMISSION CONTROLS

ACCELERATOR PEDAL WITH POSITION SENSOR

LOCATION

See Figure 72.

Refer to the accompanying illustration.

REMOVAL & INSTALLATION

1. Remove the accelerator pedal retaining bolt.

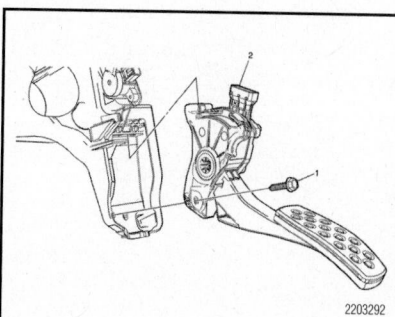

Fig. 72 Showing the accelerator pedal and position sensor—retaining bolt (1) and position sensor (2)

2. Remove the pedal assembly.
3. Disconnect the electrical connector from the position sensor.
4. Installation is the reverse of the removal procedure.
5. Tighten the retaining bolt to 80 inch lbs. (9 Nm).

CAMSHAFT POSITION (CMP) SENSOR

LOCATION

2.4L Engine

See Figures 73 and 74.

Refer to the accompanying illustrations.

3.6L Engine

See Figures 75 through 78.

Refer to the accompanying illustrations.

REMOVAL & INSTALLATION

2.4L Engine

1. Remove the air cleaner outlet duct.

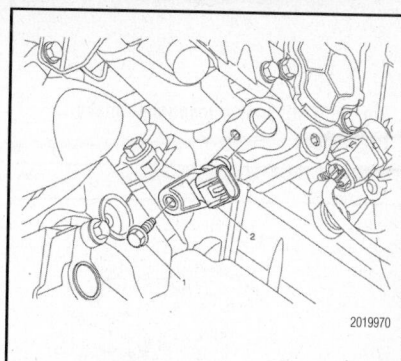

Fig. 73 Camshaft Position (CMP) Sensor location—intake

2. Remove the intake manifold cover (intake side replacement only).
3. Disconnect the engine wiring harness electrical connector from the intake camshaft position (CMP) sensor.
4. Remove the intake CMP sensor bolt. Remove the intake CMP sensor.

To install:

5. Inspect the intake CMP sensor for damage, replace as necessary.

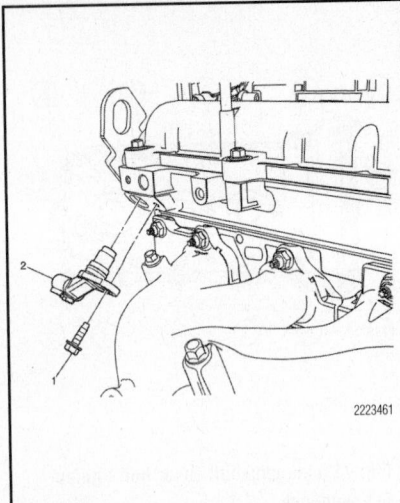

Fig. 74 Camshaft Position (CMP) Sensor location—exhaust

Fig. 77 CMP sensor location—intake (left side)

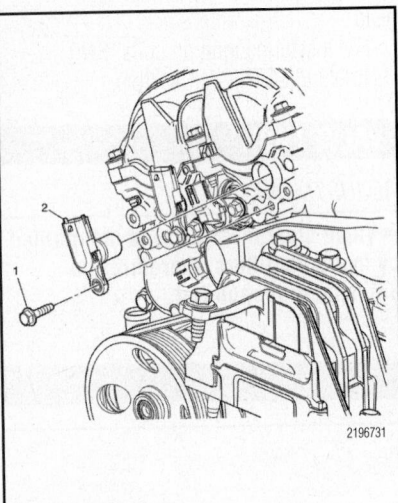

Fig. 75 CMP sensor location—intake (right side)

Fig. 78 CMP sensor location—exhaust (left side)

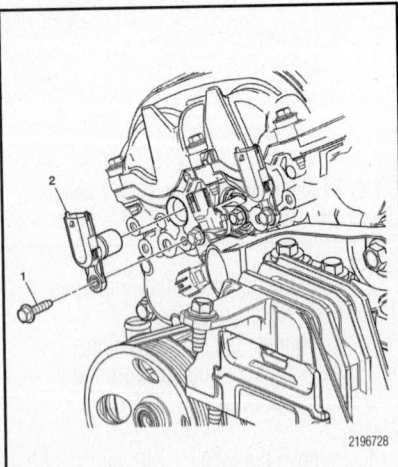

Fig. 76 CMP sensor location—exhaust (right side)

6. Lubricate the intake CMP sensor O-ring seal with clean engine oil.

7. Install the intake CMP sensor.

8. Install the intake CMP sensor bolt. Tighten the bolt to 89 inch lbs. (10 Nm).

3.6L Engine

1. Remove the air cleaner assembly.

2. Remove the CMP sensor fastener

3. Remove the CMP sensor.

4. Disconnect the electrical connector.

5. Installation is the reverse of the removal procedure. Tighten the sensor fastener to 89 inch lbs. (10 Nm).

CRANKSHAFT POSITION (CKP) SENSOR

LOCATION

2.4L Engine

See Figure 79.

Refer to the accompanying illustration.

3.6L Engine

See Figure 80.

Refer to the accompanying illustration.

REMOVAL & INSTALLATION

2.4L Engine

1. Remove the CKP sensor bolt.

2. Remove the CKP sensor.

3. Detach the electrical connector.

4. Installation is the reverse of the removal procedure.

5. Tighten the bolt to 89 inch lbs. (10 Nm).

3.6L Engine

1. If equipped with AWD, remove the right side catalytic converter.

2. Raise and support the vehicle.

3. Remove the heat shield bolts.

4. Remove the exhaust manifold lower heat shield.

5. Remove the CKP sensor bolt.

6. Remove the CKP sensor and disconnect the electrical connector.

7. Installation is the reverse of the removal procedure.

8. Tighten the bolts as follows:
   • CKP sensor bolt: 89 inch lbs. (10 Nm)

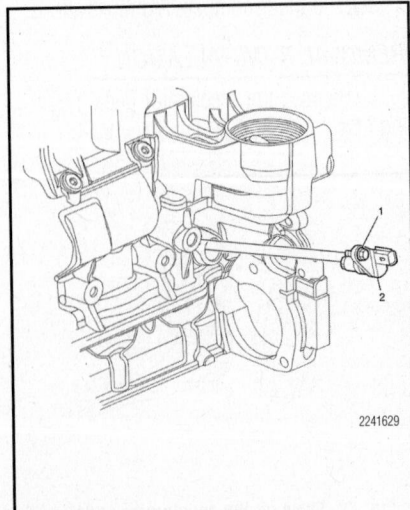

Fig. 79 Location of CKP sensor—2.4L engine

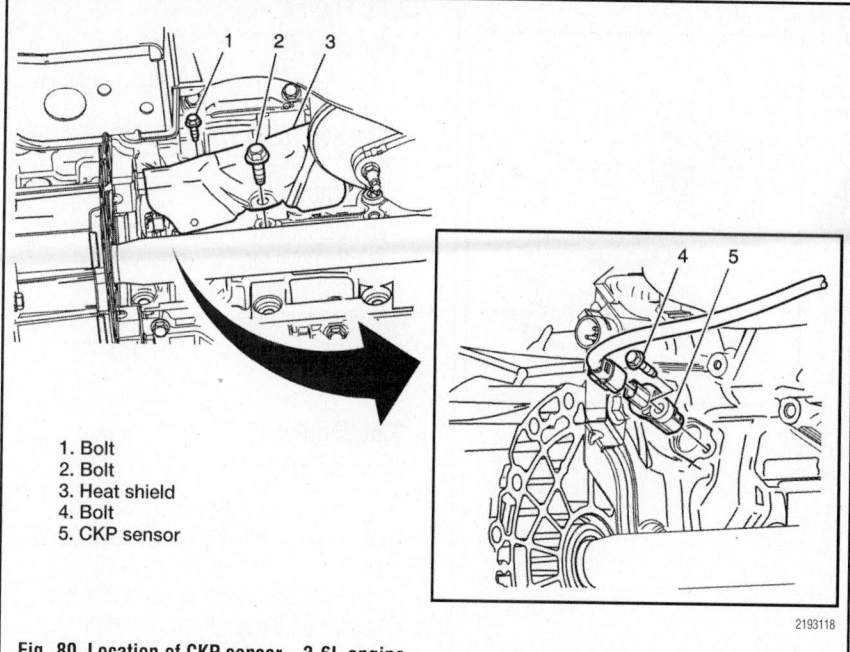

1. Bolt
2. Bolt
3. Heat shield
4. Bolt
5. CKP sensor

Fig. 80 Location of CKP sensor—3.6L engine

- Heat shield bolt (2): 42 ft. lbs. (58 Nm)
- Heat shield bolt (1): 80 inch lbs. (9 Nm)

CRANKSHAFT POSITION SENSOR VARIATION LEARN

PROCEDURE

The Crankshaft Position Variation Learn procedure is also required when the following service procedures have been performed, regardless of whether DTC_P0315 is set. The ECM monitors certain component signals to determine if all the conditions are met to continue with the Crankshaft Position Variation Learn procedure:

- An engine replacement
- An engine control module (ECM) replacement
- A crankshaft balancer replacement
- A crankshaft replacement
- A crankshaft position sensor replacement
- Any engine repairs which disturb the crankshaft to crankshaft position sensor relationship.

1. Turn the ignition ON, observe the DTC information with a scan tool. Verify no other DTCs are set, except DTCs P0300-P0304, or P0315.

2. If DTCs are set, except DTCs P0300-P0304, or P0315.

3. Select the Crankshaft Position Variation Learn Procedure with a scan tool and perform the following:

a. Close the hood.

b. Ensure the engine is at operating temperature.

c. Block drive wheels.

d. Set parking brake (DO NOT apply brake pedal).

e. Turn the air conditioning (A/C) OFF.

f. When directed, apply and hold brake pedal for the duration of the procedure.

➡**While the ignition is ON and the engine running at operating temperature, the vehicle must remain in Park or Neutral.**

g. While the learn procedure is in progress, release the throttle immediately when the engine starts to decelerate. The engine control is returned to the operator and the engine responds to throttle position after the learn procedure is complete.

h. Accelerate to wide open throttle (WOT) and release when the fuel cut-off occurs.

i. Check that the scan tool displays Learn In Progress, then Learn Successful.

j. Verify DTC P0315 ran and passed This Ignition Cycle.

k. If DTC P0315 failed or did not run This Ignition Cycle, or another DTC is present, consult a proper DTC list to diagnose and repair the DTCs in order.

l. Once the Crankshaft Position Variation Learn procedure has successfully

completed, and in order to store the crankshaft position variation values in the ECM, turn OFF the ignition and verify all vehicle systems are OFF. This may take up to 2 minutes.

ELECTRONIC CONTROL MODULE (ECM)

LOCATION

2.4L Engine

See Figure 81.

Refer to the accompanying illustration.

3.6L Engine

See Figure 82.

Refer to the accompanying illustration.

REMOVAL & INSTALLATION

1. Disconnect the negative battery cable.
2. Remove the Electronic Control Module (ECM).

✳✳ CAUTION

Always turn the ignition off when installing or removing the ECM connectors in order to prevent damage to the components.

3. It is necessary to record the remaining engine oil life. If the replacement module is not programmed with the remaining engine oil life, the engine oil life will default to 100%. If the replacement module is not programmed with the remaining engine oil life, the engine oil will need to be changed at 3,000 mi. from the last engine oil change.

4. Using a scan tool, retrieve the percentage of remaining engine oil and the remaining automatic transmission fluid life. Record the remaining engine oil and the remaining automatic transmission fluid life.

5. Disconnect the electrical connectors.

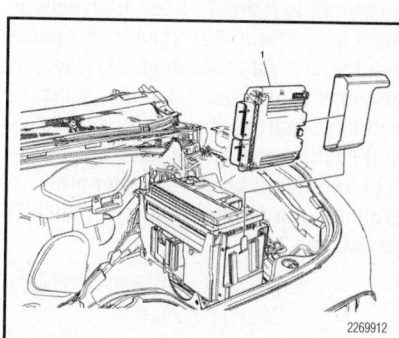

Fig. 81 Removing the Engine Control Module (ECM)

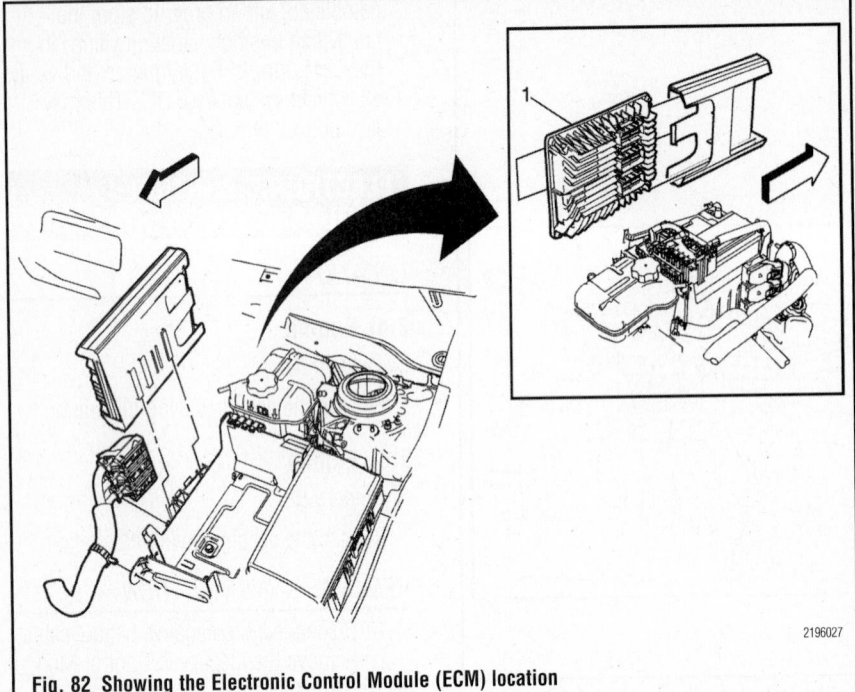

Fig. 82 Showing the Electronic Control Module (ECM) location

6. Release the retaining tab.
7. If replacing, program the ECM.

ECM PROGRAMMING

INFORMATION

→ECM programming requires the use of the GM Service Procedure System (SPS) or an applicable aftermarket equivalent. Consult with an authorized facility if such programming is needed.

If the engine control module (ECM) is replaced, the following procedures must be performed:

- ECM Reprogramming
- Theft Deterrent Programming

→The ECM will learn the incoming fuel continue password immediately upon receipt of a password message. Once a password message is received, and a password is learned, a learn procedure must be performed to change this password again. An ECM which has been previously installed in another vehicle will have learned the other vehicle's fuel continue password, and will require a learn procedure after programming to learn the current vehicle's password.

- Crankshaft Position Variation Learn
- Idle Learn Procedure
- Engine Oil Life Reset
- Transmission Fluid Life Remaining

If any of the following components are replaced, a Crankshaft Position Variation Learn must be performed. See "Crankshaft Position Variation Learn" in this section:

- Engine replacement
- Any engine repair that disturbs the CKP sensor or its relationship with the crankshaft reluctor wheel
- CKP sensor

→If the throttle body is replaced or a throttle body cleaning procedure is completed, the Idle Learn must be performed. See "Throttle/Idle Learn" in "FUEL SYSTEM" section.

ENGINE COOLANT TEMPERATURE (ECT) SENSOR

LOCATION

2.4L Engine

See Figure 83.

Refer to the accompanying illustration.

Fig. 83 Locating the ECT sensor (1)

3.6L Engine

See Figure 84.

Refer to the accompanying illustration.

REMOVAL & INSTALLATION

2.4L Engine

1. Disconnect the electrical connector.
2. Remove the ECT sensor
3. Installation is the reverse of the removal procedure.
4. Tighten the sensor to 15 ft. lbs. (20 Nm).

3.6L Engine

See Figure 85.

1. Turn the ignition OFF.
2. Remove the engine oil dipstick indicator.
3. Slide the electrical connector heat protector off the electrical connector.
4. Disconnect the coolant temperature sensor electrical connector.
5. Remove the coolant temperature sensor.

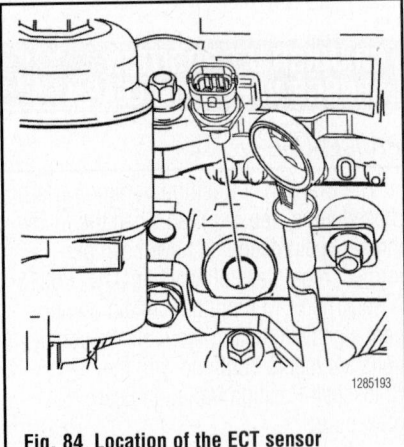

Fig. 84 Location of the ECT sensor

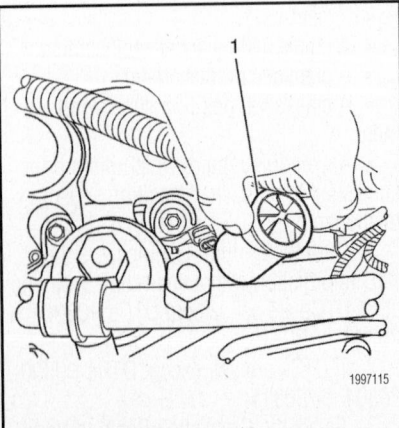

Fig. 85 Slide the electrical connector heat protector (1) off the electrical connector.

To install:

6. Install the coolant temperature sensor and tighten to 16 ft. lbs. (22 Nm).

7. Install the coolant temperature sensor electrical connector.

8. Slide the electrical connector heat protector onto the electrical connector.

9. Inspect and fill the cooling system as necessary.

EVAPORATIVE EMISSIONS (EVAP) CANISTER

LOCATION

2.4L Engine

See Figure 86.

Refer to the accompanying illustration.

3.6L Engine

See Figures 87 and 88.

Refer to the accompanying illustrations.

REMOVAL & INSTALLATION

2.4L Engine

1. Remove the fuel tank. See "FUEL" section.

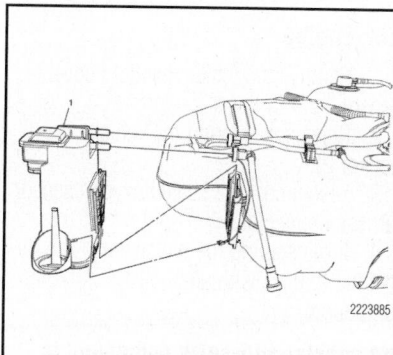

Fig. 86 The EVAP canister is mounted to the side of the fuel tank.

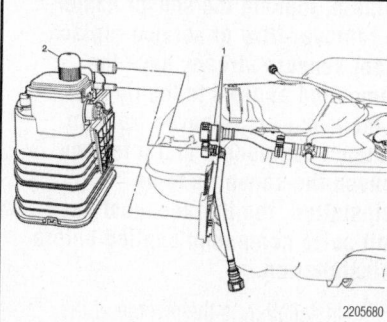

Fig. 87 The EVAP canister (2) is mounted to the side of the fuel tank and joined by quick connects (1)—with FWD

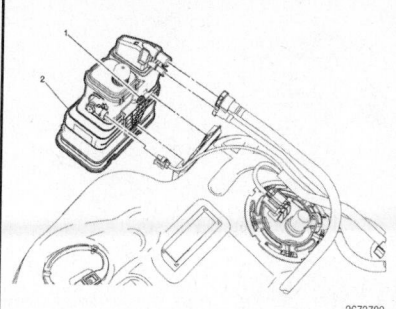

Fig. 88 The EVAP canister (2) is mounted to the side of the fuel tank and joined at the retaining tab (1)—with AWD

2. Remove the EVAP canister as follows:

    a. Disconnect the quick connects.

    b. Disconnect the fuel filter ground cable terminal.

    c. Release the retaining tab and pull upwards to remove.

3. Installation is the reverse of the removal procedure.

3.6L Engine

FWD Vehicles

1. Remove the fuel tank. See "FUEL" section.

2. Remove the EVAP canister as follows:

    a. Disconnect the quick connects.

    b. Disconnect the fuel filter ground cable terminal.

    c. Release the retaining tab and pull upwards to remove.

3. Installation is the reverse of the removal procedure.

AWD Vehicles

1. Lower the fuel tank enough to allow evaporative emission canister removal.

2. Detach the EVAP canister retaining tab: depress the retaining tab in order to release the evaporative emission canister from the fuel tank.

3. Remove the canister as follows:

    a. Release the evaporative emission vent pipe from the evaporative emission canister.

    b. Release the evaporative emission canister purge pipe from the evaporative emission canister.

    c. Disconnect the evaporative emission canister solenoid wiring harness.

4. Installation is the reverse of the removal procedure.

EVAPORATIVE EMISSIONS (EVAP) CANISTER PURGE SOLENOID VALVE

LOCATION

2.4L Engine

See Figure 89.

Refer to the accompanying illustration.

3.6L Engine

See Figure 90.

Refer to the accompanying illustration.

REMOVAL & INSTALLATION

1. Remove the intake manifold cover.

2. Disconnect the evaporative emission pipes.

3. Remove the EVAP canister purge solenoid fastener and remove the solenoid while disconnecting the electrical connector.

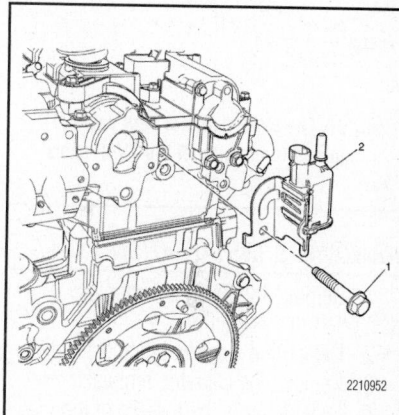

Fig. 89 Showing the mounting fastener (1) and the canister purge solenoid valve (2)

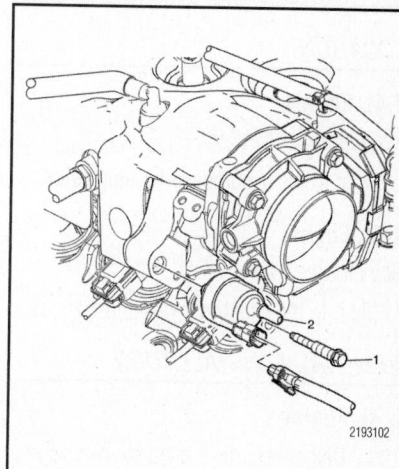

Fig. 90 Showing the mounting fastener (1) and the canister purge solenoid valve (2)

4. Installation is the reverse of the removal procedure.

5. On 3.6L engine, replace the O-ring.

6. Tighten the solenoid fastener to 18 ft. lbs. (25 Nm).

EVAPORATIVE EMISSIONS (EVAP) CANISTER VENT SOLENOID VALVE

LOCATION

See Figure 91.

Refer to the accompanying illustration.

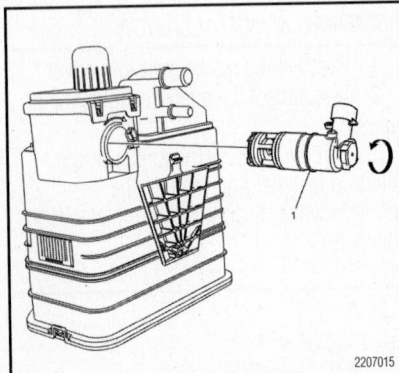

Fig. 91 The EVAP canister vent valve (1) is mounted in the side of the EVAP canister

REMOVAL & INSTALLATION

1. Remove the EVAP canister, as described in this section.

2. Detach the electrical connector.

3. Remove the canister vent valve.

4. Installation is the reverse of the removal procedure.

HEATED OXYGEN (HO2S) SENSOR

LOCATION

2.4L Engine

See Figures 92 and 93.

Refer to the accompanying illustrations.

3.6L Engine

See Figures 94 and 95.

Refer to the accompanying illustrations.

REMOVAL & INSTALLATION

2.4L Engine

1. Disconnect the heated oxygen sensor harness connector.

2. If reinstalling the old sensor, coat the threads with anti-seize compound.

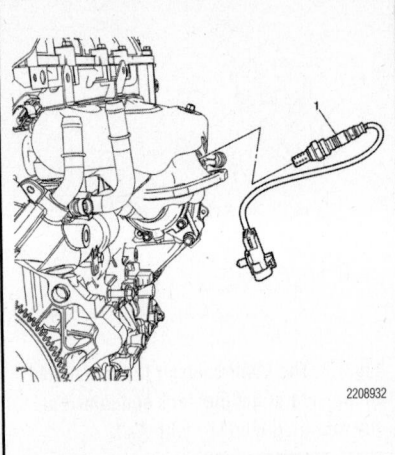

Fig. 92 Location of heated oxygen sensor 1

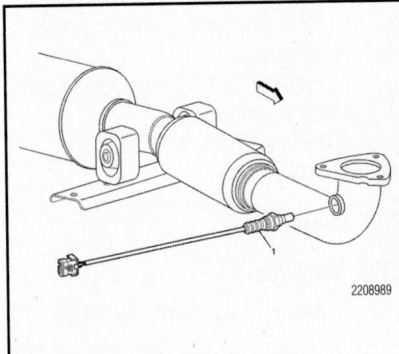

Fig. 93 Location of heated oxygen sensor 2

➡A special anti-seize compound is used in the HO2S threads. The compound consists of liquid graphic and glass beads. The graphic tends to burn away, but the glass beads remain, making the sensor easier to remove. New or service replacement sensors already have the compound applied to the threads.

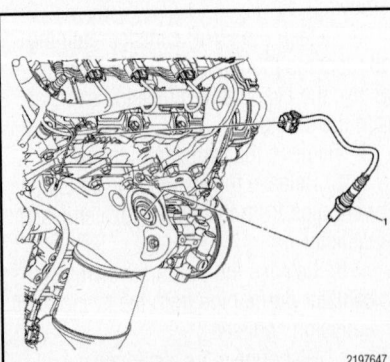

Fig. 94 Showing the location of the heated oxygen sensor—bank 1 sensor 1 (bank 2 sensor 1 similar)

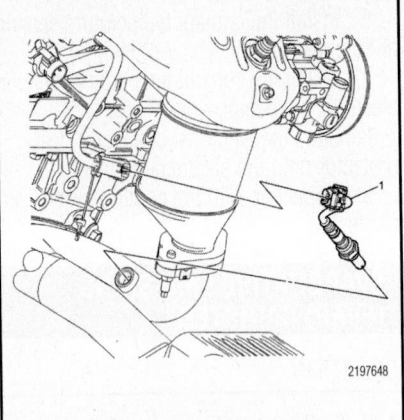

Fig. 95 Showing the location of the heated oxygen sensor—bank 1 sensor 2 (bank 2 sensor 2 similar)

If the sensor is removed from an exhaust component and if for any reason the sensor is to be reinstalled, the threads must have anti-seize compound applied before reinstallation.

3. Installation is the reverse of the removal procedure.

4. Tighten the sensor to 31 ft. lbs. (42 Nm).

3.6L Engine

1. Remove the intake manifold cover (sensor 1).

2. Raise and support the vehicle (sensor 2).

3. Disconnect the heated oxygen sensor harness connector.

4. If reinstalling the old sensor, coat the threads with anti-seize compound.

➡A special anti-seize compound is used in the HO2S threads. The compound consists of liquid graphic and glass beads. The graphic tends to burn away, but the glass beads remain, making the sensor easier to remove. New or service replacement sensors already have the compound applied to the threads. If the sensor is removed from an exhaust component and if for any reason the sensor is to be reinstalled, the threads must have anti-seize compound applied before reinstallation.

5. Installation is the reverse of the removal procedure.

6. Tighten the sensor to 31 ft. lbs. (42 Nm).

INTAKE AIR TEMPERATURE (IAT) SENSOR

LOCATION

➡️ **See "Mass Air Flow (MAF) Sensor" in this section.**

KNOCK SENSOR (KS)

LOCATION

2.4L Engine

See Figure 96.

Refer to the accompanying illustration.

3.6L Engine

See Figures 97 and 98.

Refer to the accompanying illustrations.

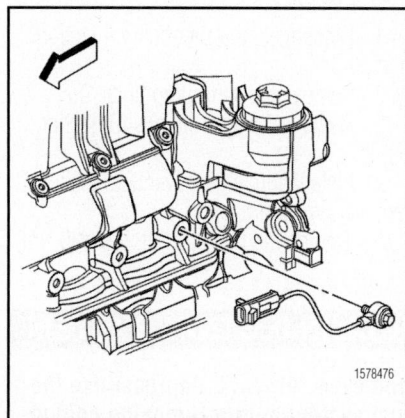

Fig. 96 Removing the knock sensor

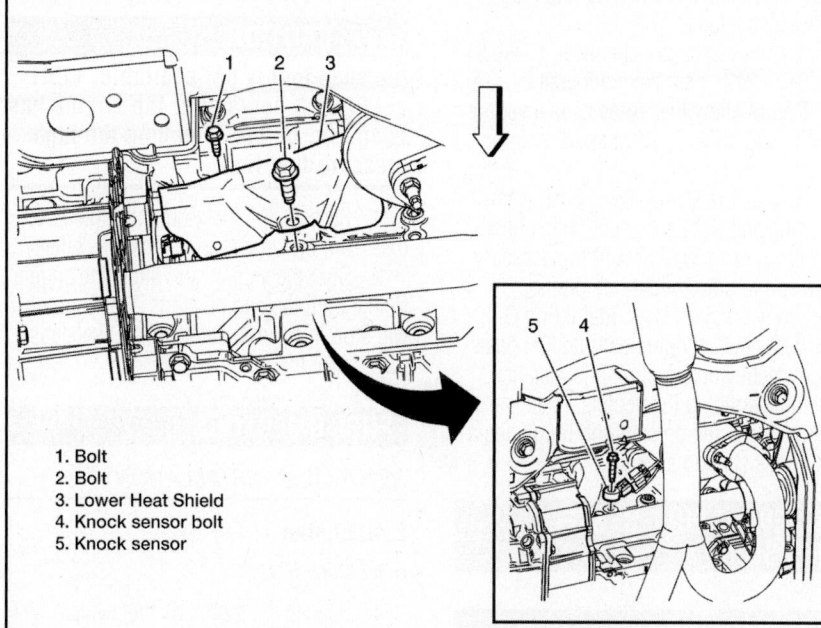

1. Bolt
2. Bolt
3. Lower Heat Shield
4. Knock sensor bolt
5. Knock sensor

Fig. 97 Showing the location of the knock sensor—bank 1

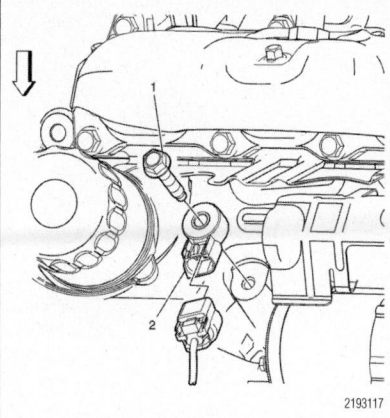

Fig. 98 Showing the location of the knock sensor—bank 1

REMOVAL & INSTALLATION

2.4L Engine

1. Disconnect the engine wiring harness electrical connector from the knock sensor electrical connector.
2. Remove the knock sensor electrical connector from the oil level indicator tube bracket.
3. Remove the knock sensor bolt. Remove the knock sensor.

To install:

4. Installation is the reverse of the removal procedure.
5. Tighten the knock sensor bolt to 18 ft. lbs. (25 Nm).

3.6L Engine

1. Remove the bolts and remove the exhaust manifold heat shield.
2. Disconnect the connector from the knock sensor.
3. Remove the bolt and remove the knock sensor.
4. Installation is the reverse of the removal procedure.
5. Tighten the knock sensor bolt to 18 ft. lbs. (25 Nm).

MANIFOLD ABSOLUTE PRESSURE (MAP) SENSOR

LOCATION

2.4L Engine

See Figure 99.

Refer to the accompanying illustration.

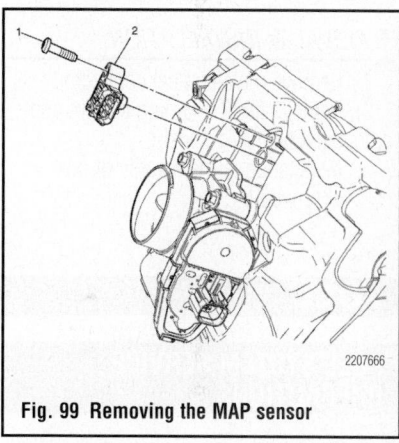

Fig. 99 Removing the MAP sensor

3.6L Engine

➡️**This engine does not use a MAP sensor.**

REMOVAL & INSTALLATION

2.4L Engine

1. Disconnect the MAP sensor electrical connector.
2. Remove the retaining bolt and remove the MAP sensor.
3. Installation is the reverse of the removal procedure.

MASS AIR FLOW (MAF) SENSOR

LOCATION

2.4L Engine

See Figure 100.

Refer to the accompanying illustration.

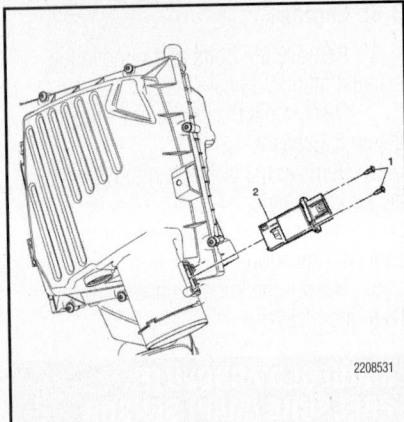

2208531

Fig. 100 Showing the MAF/IAT sensor (2) and retaining screws (1)

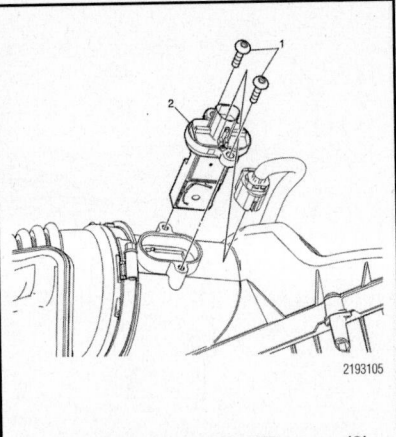

2193105

Fig. 101 Showing the MAF/IAT sensor (2) and retaining screws (1)

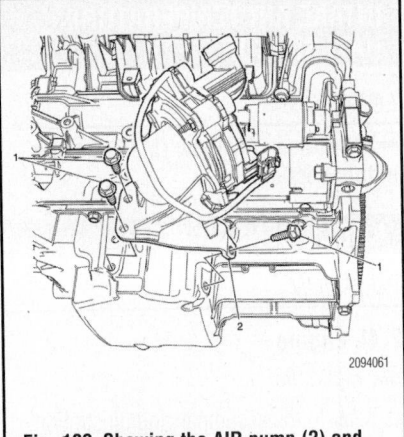

2094061

Fig. 102 Showing the AIR pump (2) and retaining bolt (1)

3.6L Engine

See Figure 101.

Refer to the accompanying illustration.

REMOVAL & INSTALLATION

1. Remove the electrical connector.
2. Remove the 2 retaining screws and remove the MAF/IAT sensor.
3. Installation is the reverse of the removal procedure.

SECONDARY AIR INJECTION (AIR) PUMP

LOCATION

2.4L Engine

See Figure 102.

Refer to the accompanying illustration.

REMOVAL & INSTALLATION

2.4L Engine

1. Disconnect the secondary injection pump hose.
2. Remove the AIR pump bolt.
3. Remove the secondary air injection pump.
4. Installation is the reverse of the removal procedure.
5. Tighten the bolt to 22 ft. lbs. (30 Nm).

FUEL   GASOLINE FUEL INJECTION SYSTEM

FUEL SYSTEM SERVICE PRECAUTIONS

Safety is the most important factor when performing not only fuel system maintenance but any type of maintenance. Failure to conduct maintenance and repairs in a safe manner may result in serious personal injury or death. Maintenance and testing of the vehicle's fuel system components can be accomplished safely and effectively by adhering to the following rules and guidelines.

• To avoid the possibility of fire and personal injury, always disconnect the negative battery cable unless the repair or test procedure requires that battery voltage be applied.

• Always relieve the fuel system pressure prior to disconnecting any fuel system component (injector, fuel rail, pressure regulator, etc.), fitting or fuel line connection. Exercise extreme caution whenever relieving fuel system pressure to avoid exposing skin, face and eyes to fuel spray. Please be advised that fuel under pressure may penetrate the skin or any part of the body that it contacts.

• Always place a shop towel or cloth around the fitting or connection prior to

loosening to absorb any excess fuel due to spillage. Ensure that all fuel spillage (should it occur) is quickly removed from engine surfaces. Ensure that all fuel soaked cloths or towels are deposited into a suitable waste container.

• Always keep a dry chemical (Class B) fire extinguisher near the work area.

• Do not allow fuel spray or fuel vapors to come into contact with a spark or open flame.

• Always use a back-up wrench when loosening and tightening fuel line connection fittings. This will prevent unnecessary stress and torsion to fuel line piping.

• Always replace worn fuel fitting O-rings with new Do not substitute fuel hose or equivalent where fuel pipe is installed.

Before servicing the vehicle, make sure to also refer to the precautions in the beginning of this section as well.

RELIEVING FUEL SYSTEM PRESSURE

✷✷ WARNING

Fuel that flows out at high pressure can cause serious injury to the skin

and eyes. **ALWAYS depressurize the fuel system before removing components that are under high fuel pressure.**

✷✷ CAUTION

If a scan tool is not available, WAIT at LEAST 2 hours after the engine has been run, before removing the high pressure fuel line.

1. Remove the fuel pump module 20A fuse from the underhood electrical center.
2. Start the vehicle and allow the engine to idle until the engine stops. The engine will stop in approximately 20–30 seconds.
3. Turn the ignition OFF.

FUEL INJECTORS

REMOVAL & INSTALLATION

2.4L Engine

See Figure 103.

1. Relieve the high side fuel system pressure. See "Relieving Fuel System Pressure" in this section.

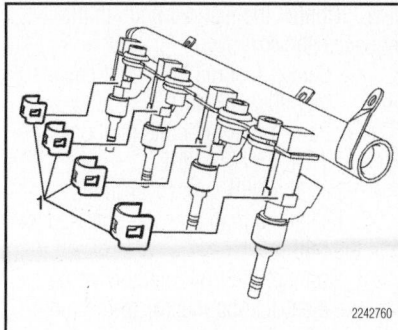

Fig. 103 Remove and discard the fuel injector retainers (1)

➡**The fuel injectors have an alignment feature, note the position of the injectors alignment for installation.**

2. Remove the fuel injection fuel rail assembly. See "Fuel Rail" in this section.

3. Remove and discard the fuel injector retainers.

4. Remove the fuel injectors.

5. Clean and inspect the fuel rail and injectors.

To install:

6. Install the fuel injectors.

7. Install NEW fuel injector retainers.

8. Install the fuel injection fuel rail assembly. See "Fuel Rail" in this section.

3.6L Engine

➡**See "Fuel Rail" in this section.**

FUEL PUMP

REMOVAL & INSTALLATION

See Figures 104 through 106.

1. Relieve the low and high side fuel system pressure. See "Relieving Fuel System Pressure".

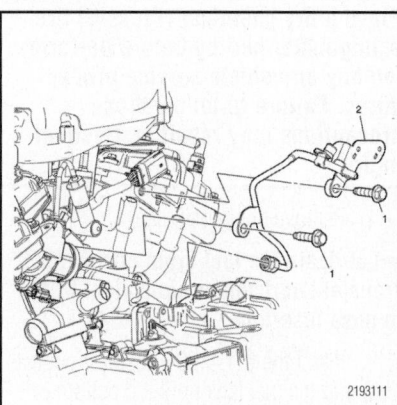

Fig. 104 Remove bolts (1) and remove the low pressure feed pipe (2).

2. Remove the high pressure fuel pump shield.

3. Disconnect the engine wiring harness electrical connector from the high pressure fuel pump.

4. Remove bolts and remove the low pressure feed pipe. Discard the pipe.

5. Remove the high pressure pipe. Discard the pipe.

6. Remove and discard the high pressure fuel pump bolts (1).

7. Remove the high pressure fuel pump (2).

8. Remove and discard the high pressure fuel pump O-ring (3).

9. Remove and discard the high pressure fuel pump gasket (4).

10. Remove the high pressure fuel pump roller lifter (5).

To install:

➡**The camshaft must be in the base circle position before the high pressure fuel pump is installed.**

11. Use the EN-48896 alignment gauge (or equivalent) to ensure that the camshaft lobe is in the base circle position. At base circle the tool will be flush with the head.

12. Lubricate the high pressure fuel pump cylinder head bore and roller lifter with camshaft prelube.

➡**The high pressure fuel pump gasket has a retaining feature to hold the pump retaining bolts in place.**

13. Install the high pressure fuel pump roller lifter.

14. Install a NEW high pressure fuel pump O-ring.

15. Position the NEW high pressure fuel pump gasket and bolts to the fuel pump.

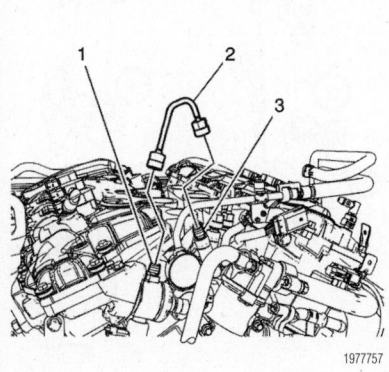

Fig. 105 Disconnect the fittings (1, 3) and remove the high pressure pipe (2). Discard the pipe.

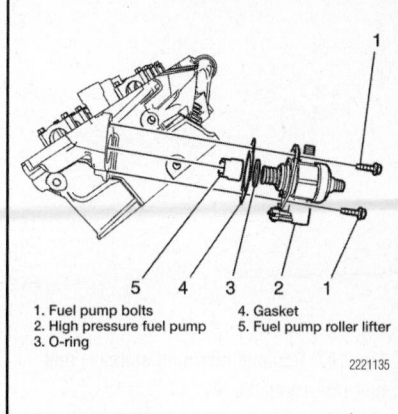

1. Fuel pump bolts
2. High pressure fuel pump
3. O-ring
4. Gasket
5. Fuel pump roller lifter

Fig. 106 Showing components of the high pressure fuel pump.

16. Install the high pressure fuel pump. Force will be required while hand tightening the bolts. Tighten the high pressure fuel pump retaining bolts to 11 ft. lbs. (15_Nm).

17. Ensure the high pressure fuel pump and fuel rail fittings are clean prior to assembly.

18. Install a NEW high pressure fuel pipe. Tighten the fittings:
- First pass: 11 ft. lbs. (15Nm)
- Second pass: 22 ft. lbs. (30 Nm)

19. Install a NEW fuel feed pipe to the high pressure fuel pump. Tighten as follows:
- Line fitting: 21 ft. lbs. (28 Nm)
- Retaining bolts: 28 ft. lbs. (40 Nm)

20. Connect the high pressure fuel pump wiring harness.

21. Install the fuel tank cap.

➡**If a fuel leak accrues at the fuel rail, the fuel rail will need to be replaced.**

22. Inspect for leaks using the following procedure:

a. Turn ON the ignition, with the engine OFF for 2 seconds.

b. Turn OFF the ignition, for 10_seconds.

c. Turn ON the ignition, with the engine OFF.

d. Inspect for fuel leaks.

23. Install the pressure relief cap to the fuel feed pipe.

24. Install the high pressure fuel pump shield.

FUEL RAIL

REMOVAL & INSTALLATION

2.4L Engine

See Figure 107.

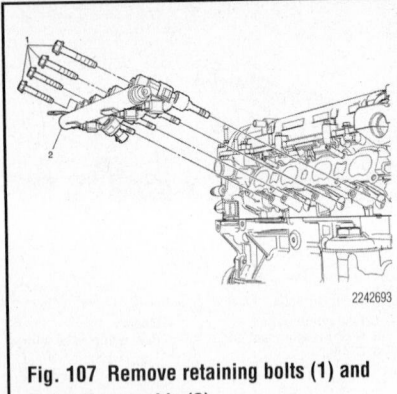

Fig. 107 Remove retaining bolts (1) and fuel rail assembly (2)

1. Relieve the fuel system pressure. See "Relieving Fuel System Pressure".
2. Remove the intake manifold. See "ENGINE MECHANICAL" section.
3. Remove the 4 fuel rail assembly fasteners.
4. Disconnect the electrical connector and remove the fuel rail assembly.

➡ **The direct fuel injectors must be rebuilt whenever the injector has been released from the fuel rail or cylinder head.**

5. Installation is the reverse of the removal procedure.
6. Tighten the 4 fuel rail assembly fasteners to 18 ft. lbs. (25Nm).

3.6L Engine

See Figures 108 and 109.

1. Relieve the fuel system pressure. See "Relieving Fuel System Pressure".
2. Remove the fuel pipe shield.
3. Remove the intake manifold. See "ENGINE MECHANICAL" section.
4. Remove the crossover tube.
5. Remove the foam insulator from the fuel rails.
6. Remove the bank 2 fuel injection rail, as described below.
7. Disconnect the fuel pressure sensor electrical connector and cut the wire harness tie straps.
8. Remove the fuel rail bolts.
9. Remove the fuel pressure sensor.
10. Remove and discard the direct fuel injector hold down clamps.

➡ **The direct fuel injectors must be rebuilt whenever the injector has been released from the fuel rail or cylinder head.**

11. Once the fuel rail is removed, remove the fuel injectors and rebuild them.

Fig. 108 Install the rebuilt direct fuel injectors (1) to the cylinder heads.

To install:

12. Install the rebuilt direct fuel injectors to the cylinder heads.
13. Install NEW direct injector hold down clamps to the injector.
14. On a new fuel rail, lubricate the fuel injector cups with silicon free engine oil.
15. Carefully place the fuel rail into position, placing the front into the fuel rail over the front injector and rotating the rear downward.
16. Install the 2 outer fuel rail bolts first, then the 2 inner bolts, and hand tighten.
17. Install the bank 2 fuel injection rail, as described below.

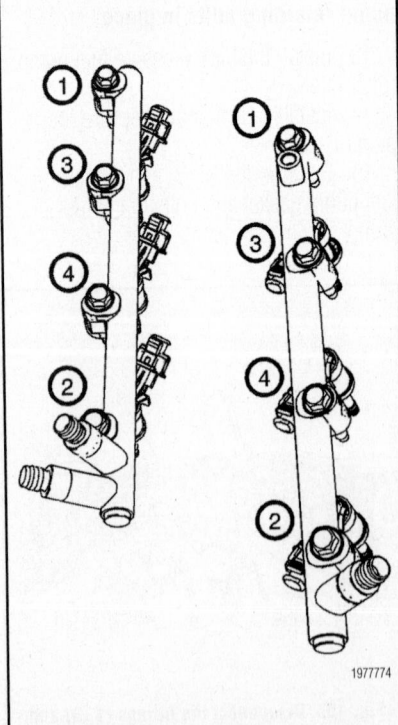

Fig. 109 Tighten the fuel rail bolts in the sequence shown

18. Tighten the fuel rail bolts in the sequence shown:
   - Bank 1 fuel rail bolts first pass: 106 inch lbs. (12 Nm).
   - Bank 1 fuel rail bolts final pass: 17 ft. lbs. (23 Nm).
19. Install a NEW crossover tube.
20. Install the high pressure fuel sensor onto the rail.
21. Connect the fuel injector wiring harness electrical connector to the fuel injectors, fuel rail and fuel pressure sensor.
22. Inspect for fuel leaks using the following procedure:
   a. Turn ON the ignition, with the engine OFF for 2 seconds.
   b. Turn OFF the ignition, for 10 seconds.
   c. Turn ON the ignition, with the engine OFF.
   d. Inspect for fuel leaks.
23. Install the foam insulator from the fuel rails.
24. Install the intake manifold. See "ENGINE MECHANICAL" section.
25. Install the fuel pipe shield.
26. Install the low side fuel pressure service port cap.
27. Install the fuel tank cap.

FUEL TANK

DRAINING

✲✲ CAUTION

Never drain or store fuel in an open container. Always use an approved fuel storage container in order to reduce the chance of fire or explosion.

✲✲ WARNING

Place a dry chemical (Class B) fire extinguisher nearby before performing any on-vehicle service procedures. Failure to follow these precautions may result in personal injury.

1. Remove the fuel fill cap.

➡ **Lubricate the fuel drain hose with Transjel Lubricant or equivalent to aid in hose insertion.**

2. Insert the CH 45004 hose (or equivalent) into the fuel tank until the bottom is reached.
3. Use a hand or air operated pump device in order to drain as much fuel through the fuel fill pipe as possible.

REMOVAL & INSTALLATION

2.4L Engine

1. Relieve the system fuel pressure. See "Relieving Fuel System Pressure."
2. Drain the fuel tank. See "Draining".
3. Disconnect the evaporative emission and fuel pipes.
4. Disconnect the fuel pressure sensor electrical connector.
5. Loosen the hose clamps and remove the filler tube.
6. Disconnect the fuel tank harness electrical connector.
7. Support the fuel tank with a suitable jack.
8. Remove the fuel tank strap bolts. Swing the fuel tank straps out of the way.
9. Remove the fuel tank.
10. Remove the following components if replacing just the fuel tank:
   - Fuel tank fuel pump module.
   - Evaporative emission carbon canister.

➡Transfer components as necessary.

11. Remove the fuel tank protector.

To install:

12. Install indicated components (during removal) if fuel tank replacement was necessary
13. Use a suitable jack and install the fuel tank.
14. Reposition the fuel tank straps. Install the fuel tank strap bolts and tighten to 15 ft. lbs. (20 Nm).
15. Connect the fuel tank harness electrical connector.
16. Install the filler tube and tighten the hose clamps.
17. Connect the evaporative emission line.
18. Connect the evaporative emission and fuel pipes.
19. Connect the fuel pressure sensor electrical connector.
20. Install the fuel tank protector.
21. Refill the fuel tank.
22. Inspect for fuel leaks.

3.6L Engine

FWD Vehicles

➡Use procedure for 2.4L engine.

AWD Vehicles

❄❄ WARNING

Unless directed otherwise, the ignition and start switch must be in the OFF or LOCK position, and all electrical loads must be OFF before servicing any electrical component. Disconnect the negative battery cable to prevent an electrical spark should a tool or equipment come in contact with an exposed electrical terminal. Failure to follow these precautions may result in personal injury and/or damage to the vehicle or its components. For Vehicles equipped with OnStar® (UE1) with Back Up Battery: The Back Up Battery is a redundant power supply to allow limited OnStar functionality in the event of a main vehicle battery power disruption to the VCIM (OnStar module). Do not disconnect the main vehicle battery or remove the OnStar fuse with the ignition key in any position other than OFF. Retained accessory power (RAP) should be allowed to time out or be disabled (simply opening the driver door should disable RAP) before disconnecting power. Disconnecting power to the OnStar module in any way while the ignition is On or with RAP activated may cause activation of the OnStar Back-Up Battery (BUB) system and will discharge and permanently damage the back-up battery. Once the Back-Up Battery is activated it will stay on until it has completely discharged. The BUB is not rechargeable and once activated the BUB must be replaced.

1. Turn the ignition OFF.
2. Disconnect the negative battery cable.
3. Relieve the fuel system pressure. See "Relieving Fuel System Pressure".
4. Drain the fuel tank. See "Draining".
5. Remove the propeller shaft. See "DRIVE TRAIN" section.
6. Remove the exhaust system.
7. Remove the rear wheelhouse panel liner.
8. Disconnect the fuel tank fuel pump module wiring harness.
9. Unclip the fuel tank module wiring harness from the chassis.

❄❄ WARNING

Do not breathe the air through the EVAP component tubes or hoses. The fuel vapors inside the EVAP components may cause personal injury.

10. Disconnect the fuel tank filler vent pipe from the fuel tank filler vent pipe.

11. Disconnect the fuel tank filler tube from the fuel tank.
12. Disconnect the evaporative emission purge and fuel feed pipes.
13. Disconnect the fuel pressure sensor harness connector.
14. Disconnect the wiring harness connector from the fuel pipe.
15. Position a suitable hydraulic lift below the fuel tank.
16. Remove both fuel tank strap fasteners. Remove both fuel tank straps from the fuel tank.

❄❄ WARNING

To help avoid personal injury, always use jack stands when you are working on or under any vehicle that is supported only by a jack. When you are jacking or lifting a vehicle at the frame side rails or other prescribed lift points, be certain that the lift pads do not contact the catalytic converter, the brake pipes or the fuel lines. If such contact occurs, vehicle damage or unsatisfactory vehicle performance may result.

➡Carefully maneuver the fuel tank past the exhaust system.

17. With the aid of an assistant, lower the hydraulic lift to remove the fuel tank from the vehicle.
18. Remove the fuel tank from the hydraulic lift.
19. If replacing the fuel tank transfer the following components:
   - EVAP canister
   - EVAP canister purge pipe
   - Fuel tank feed pipe
   - Sender assembly
   - Tank fuel pump module
   - Fuel tank wiring harness.
20. With the aid of an assistant, position the fuel tank on a hydraulic lift and raise into vehicle position.
21. Install both fuel tank straps to the fuel tank and tighten the fasteners to 20 ft. lbs. (27 Nm).
22. Remove the hydraulic lift from the fuel tank.
23. Connect the following:
   - EVAP purge and fuel pipes
   - Fuel pressure sensor harness connector
   - Fuel tank filler tube (tighten the clamp)
   - Fuel tank filler vent pipe
   - Fuel tank fuel pump module wiring harness

24. Clip the fuel tank module wiring harness to the chassis.

25. Install the rear wheelhouse panel liner.

26. Install the exhaust system.

27. Install the propeller shaft. See "DRIVE TRAIN" section.

28. Connect the negative battery cable.

29. Refill the fuel tank.

THROTTLE BODY

REMOVAL & INSTALLATION

1. Disconnect the negative battery cable.

2. Remove the 4 throttle body bolts and remove the throttle body.

3. Disconnect the electrical connector.

4. Installation is the reverse of the removal procedure.

5. Tighten the bolts to 89 inch lbs. (10 Nm).

6. Perform Throttle/Idle Learn.

THROTTLE/IDLE LEARN

AFTER THROTTLE BODY CLEANED OR REPLACED

1. With ignition ON and engine OFF, perform the Idle Learn Reset in Module Setup with a scan tool.

2. With engine idling, monitor the Throttle Body Idle Airflow Compensation parameter. The Throttle Body Idle Airflow Compensation value should equal 0 % and the engine should be idling at a normal idle speed.

3. Clear the DTCs and return to the diagnostic that referred you here.

AFTER ECM PROGRAMMED OR REPLACED

➡ Do NOT perform this procedure if DTCs are set. Refer to an appropriate Diagnostic Trouble Code (DTC) List.

1. Start engine and idle for 3_minutes.

2. Monitor the Desired Idle Speed and the actual Engine Speed with a scan tool.

3. The ECM will start to learn the new idle cells and Desired Idle Speed should start to decrease.

4. Ignition OFF for 60 s.

5. Engine idling for 3 minutes.

➡ After the 3_minute run time the engine speed should return to normal.

➡ During the drive cycle monitor the DTC information with a scan tool to verify DTC P0506 and P0507 do not set. If DTC P0506 and P0507 set, clear the DTCs so the ECM can continue to learn.

6. If the engine idle speed has not been learned the vehicle will need to be driven at speeds above 44 mph with several decelerations and extended idles.

7. After the drive cycle, the engine speed should return to normal.

8. If the engine idle speed has not been learned, turn OFF the ignition for 60 s and repeat step 6.

9. Once the engine speed has returned to normal, clear DTCs and return to the diagnostic that referred you here.

HEATING & AIR CONDITIONING SYSTEM

AUXILIARY HEATER CORE

REMOVAL & INSTALLATION

See Figure 110.

1. Loosen the carpet in the range of the auxiliary heater core.

2. Use a screw driver to release the snap feature and move the connector from the bracket.

3. Disconnect the electrical connector.

4. Remove the 2 auxiliary heater core fasteners.

5. Remove the auxiliary heater core.

6. Installation is the reverse of the removal procedure.

BLOWER MOTOR

REMOVAL & INSTALLATION

1. Remove the instrument panel (I/P) insulator panel from the right side.

2. Remove the floor air outlet duct.

3. Disconnect the blower motor electrical connector.

4. Remove the blower motor fasteners.

5. Remove the blower motor.

COMPRESSOR

REMOVAL & INSTALLATION

1. Recover the refrigerant.

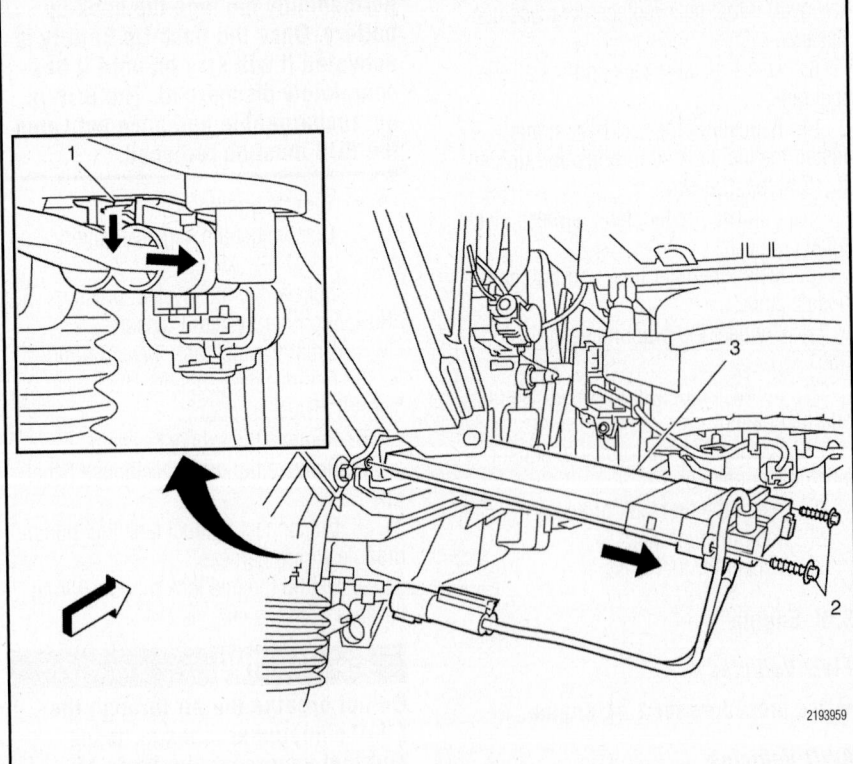

Fig. 110 Remove the wiring harness bracket (1), the auxiliary heater core fasteners (2) and the auxiliary heater core (3).

2. Raise and support the vehicle.

3. Remove front compartment splash shield.

4. Remove the compressor drive belt.

5. Disconnect the A/C compressor electrical connector.

6. Remove the air conditioning compressor and condenser hose.

7. Remove the A/C compressor nut.

8. Remove the A/C compressor stud (2.4L).

9. Remove the 2 A/C compressor bolts.

10. Remove the A/C compressor.

To install:

11. Position the compressor and install the 2 mounting bolts. On 2.4L, tighten to 16 ft. lbs. (22 Nm). On 3.6L, tighten to 43 ft. lbs. (58 Nm).

12. On 2.4L only, install the compressor stud and tighten to 16 ft. lbs. (22 Nm).

13. Install the compressor nut. On 2.4L, tighten to 79 inch lbs. (9 Nm). On 3.6L, tighten to 12 ft. lbs. (22 Nm).

14. Attach the compressor and condenser hoses.

15. Connect the compressor electrical connector.

16. Install the drive belt.

17. Install the splash shield.

18. Lower the vehicle.

19. Check and adjust compressor oil, if needed.

20. Evacuate and recharge the A/C system.

HEATER CORE

REMOVAL & INSTALLATION

See Figure 111.

1. Remove the instrument panel (I/P) insulator panel on the left side.

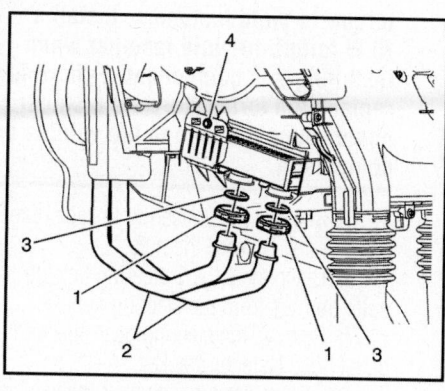
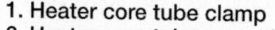
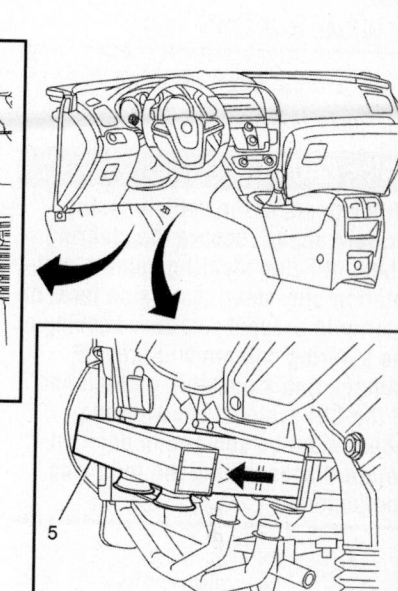

1. Heater core tube clamp
2. Heater core tube assembly
3. Heater core tube seal
4. Heater core bracket bolt
5. Heater core

Fig. 111 Heater core and related components

2. Remove the instrument panel (I/P) lower trim panel.

3. Remove the heater inlet hose from the heater core tube.

4. Remove the heater outlet hose from the heater core tube.

5. Remove the floor air outlet duct on the left side.

6. Remove the 2 heater core tube clamps.

7. Remove the heater core tube assembly.

➡**Coolant may still be in the heater core, collect coolant or blow out heater core with compressed air.**

8. Remove the 2 heater core tube seals.

9. Remove the heater core bracket fastener.

10. Pull out the heater core.

11. Installation is the reverse of the removal procedure.

STEERING

POWER STEERING GEAR

REMOVAL & INSTALLATION

With Variable Effort Steering

See Figure 112.

✳✳ CAUTION

With wheels of the vehicle facing straight ahead, secure the steering wheel utilizing steering column anti-rotation pin, steering column lock, or a strap to prevent rotation. Locking of the steering column will prevent damage and a possible malfunction of the SIR system. The steering wheel must be secured in position before disconnecting the following components:

- The steering column
- The intermediate shaft(s)
- The steering gear

✳✳ CAUTION

After disconnecting these components, do not rotate the steering wheel or move the front tires and wheels. Failure to follow this procedure may cause the SIR coil assembly to become un-centered and cause possible damage to the SIR coil. If you think the SIR coil has became un-centered, refer to your specific SIR coil's centering procedure to re-center SIR Coil.

1. With the wheels of the vehicle in the straight ahead position, LOCK the steering column.

2. Disconnect the intermediate steering shaft from the steering gear.

3. Raise and support the vehicle.

4. Perform the following steps in order to lower the rear part of the frame:

  a. Remove the front tire and wheel assemblies.

  b. Disconnect the 2 stabilizer shaft links from the struts.

  c. Remove the front exhaust pipe.

  d. If equipped with all-wheel drive, remove the propeller shaft.

  e. Support the frame with a jack.

  f. Remove the transmission mount bolts.

  g. Remove the rear frame-to-body bolts.

  h. Lower the rear part of the frame a maximum of 1 in. (50 mm) in order to gain clearance for the steering gear.

✳✳ CAUTION

This component is equipped with torque-to-yield fasteners. Install a NEW torque-to-yield fastener when installing this component. Failure to replace the torque-to-yield fastener could cause damage to the vehicle or component.

5. Remove the 2 steering linkage outer tie rod nuts. Discard the nuts.

6. Disconnect the 2 steering linkage outer tie rods from the steering knuckles.

7. Remove the steering gear inlet and outlet hose fastener bracket:

  a. Place drain pans under the vehicle in order to catch any power steering fluid.

  b. Remove the 2 steering gear seals. Discard the seals.

8. Remove the 2 steering gear nuts and the 2 steering gear bolts. Discard the nuts and the bolts.

9. Remove the steering gear:

  a. Disconnect any electrical connectors as necessary.

  b. Rotate the front stabilizer shaft in order to gain clearance for the steering gear. DO NOT loosen the stabilizer shaft insulator clamp bolts.

  c. Remove the steering gear through the left front wheel opening.

  d. Transfer components if necessary.

10. Position the steering gear into place and mount as follows:

  a. Install 2 NEW steering gear nuts and 2 NEW steering gear bolts. Hold the steering gear nuts while tightening the steering gear bolts to 81 ft. lbs. (110 Nm), plus an additional 150 degrees.

  b. Install 2 NEW steering gear seals.

  c. Install 2 NEW steering linkage outer tie rod nuts and tighten to 26 ft. lbs. (35 Nm), plus an additional 30 degrees.

11. Reposition and install the rear part of the frame:

  a. Install the frame retaining bolts, then tighten the bolts to 118 ft. lbs. (160 Nm).

  b. If removed, install the frame reinforcements with NEW bolts and then tighten the bolts to 44 ft. lbs. (60 Nm) plus 30 degrees.

12. After the installation is complete, fill and bleed the power steering system.

13. Measure and adjust the front toe.

➡**The front stabilizer shaft insulators grip the stabilizer shaft and provide**

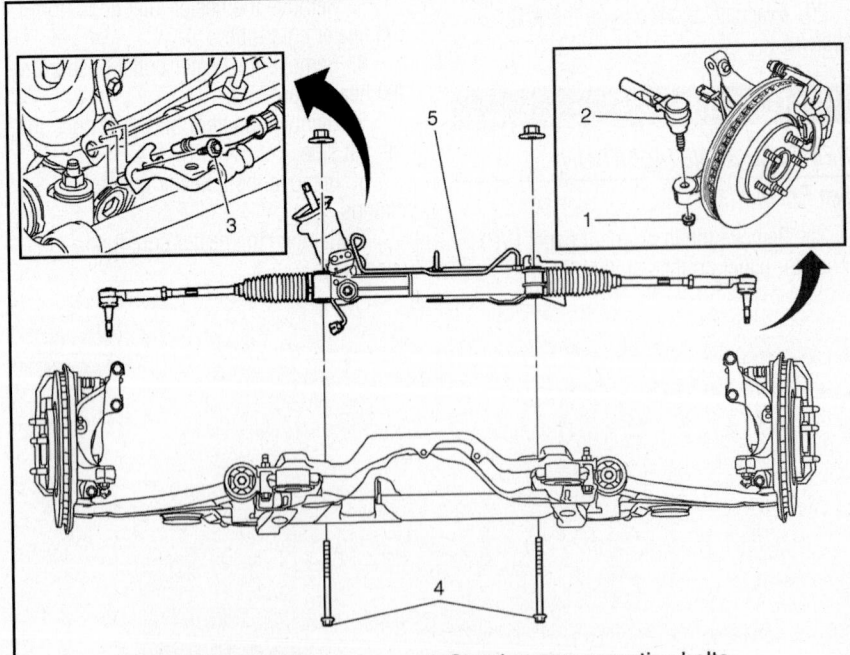

1. Tie rod end nut
2. Tie rod end
3. P/S hose bracket screw
4. Steering gear mounting bolts
5. Power steering gear variable effort)

2018631

Fig. 112 Showing the Variable Effort power steering gear mounting

resistance to rotating the stabilizer shaft.

14. Ensure the steering column dash inner and outer seals are positioned properly on the dash panel.

With Non-Variable Ratio Electronic Assist Steering

See Figure 113.

> ✳ **CAUTION**
>
> **Electrostatic discharge (ESD) can damage many solid-state electrical components. ESD susceptible components may or may not be labeled with the ESD symbol. Handle all electrical components carefully. Use the following precautions in order to avoid ESD damage:**

- Touch a metal ground point in order to remove your body's static charge before servicing any electronic component; especially after sliding across the vehicle seat.
- Do not touch exposed terminals. Terminals may connect to circuits susceptible the ESD damage.
- Do not allow tools to contact exposed terminals when servicing connectors.
- Do not remove components from their protective packaging until required to do so.

> ✳ **CAUTION**
>
> **Avoid the following actions unless required by the diagnostic procedure:**

- Jumping or grounding of the components or connectors.
- Connecting test equipment probes to components or connectors. Connect the ground lead first when using test probes.

> ✳ **CAUTION**
>
> **Ground the protective packaging of any component before opening. Do not rest solid-state components on metal workbenches, or on top of TVs, radios, or other electrical devices.**

> ✳ **CAUTION**
>
> **With wheels of the vehicle facing straight ahead, secure the steering wheel utilizing steering column anti-rotation pin, steering column lock, or a strap to prevent rotation. Locking of the steering column will prevent**

damage and a possible malfunction of the SIR system. The steering wheel must be secured in position before disconnecting the following components:

> ✳ **CAUTION**
>
> **After disconnecting these components, do not rotate the steering wheel or move the front tires and wheels. Failure to follow this procedure may cause the SIR coil assembly to become un-centered and cause possible damage to the SIR coil. If you think the SIR coil has became un-centered, refer to your specific SIR coil's centering procedure to re-center SIR Coil.**

1. With the wheels of the vehicle in the straight ahead position, LOCK the steering column.

2. Disconnect the intermediate steering shaft from the steering gear.

3. Raise and support the vehicle.

4. Disconnect the 2 outer tie rods from the steering knuckles.

5. Perform the following steps in order to lower the rear part of the frame:

a. Remove the front tire and wheel assemblies.

Disconnect the 2 stabilizer shaft links from the struts.
Remove the front exhaust pipe.

b. Support the frame with a jack.

c. Remove the transmission mount bolts.

d. Remove the rear frame-to-body bolts.

g. Lower the rear part of the frame a maximum of 2 in. (50 mm) in order to gain clearance for the steering gear.

6. Remove and discard the 2 steering gear nuts. Remove the 2 washers, then remove and discard the 2 steering gear bolts.

7. Remove the steering gear heat shield.

8. Disconnect the electrical connectors.

9. Rotate the front stabilizer shaft in order to gain clearance for the steering gear. DO NOT loosen the stabilizer shaft insulator clamp bolts.

10. Remove the steering gear from the vehicle.

11. Transfer components if necessary.

To install:

> ✳ **CAUTION**
>
> **This component is equipped with torque-to-yield fasteners. Install a NEW torque-to-yield fastener when**

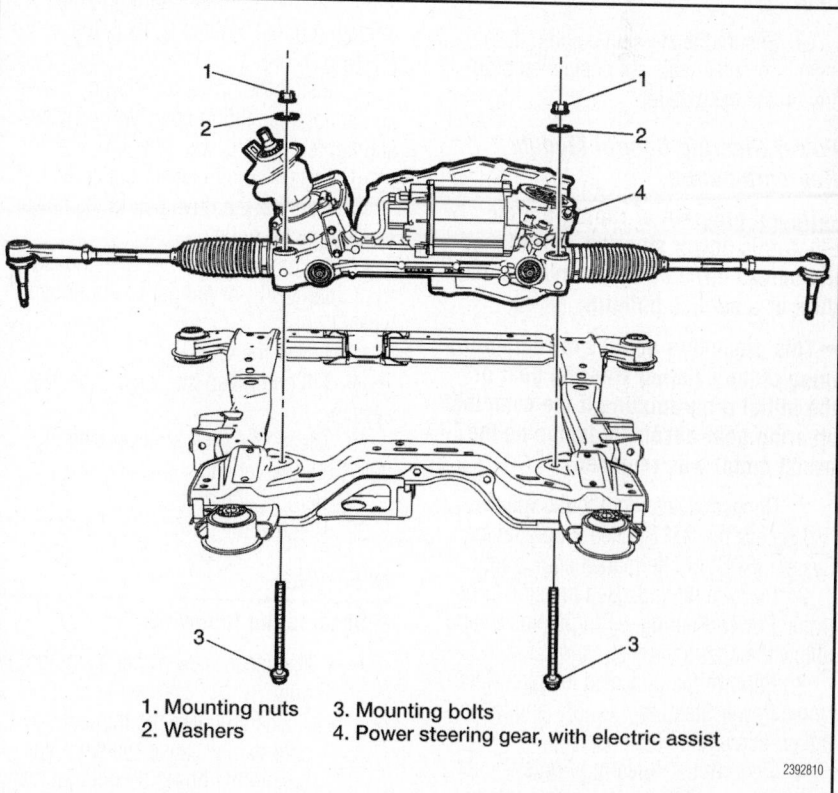

1. Mounting nuts
2. Washers
3. Mounting bolts
4. Power steering gear, with electric assist

2392810

Fig. 113 Showing Non-Variable Ratio Electronic Assist power steering gear mounting

installing this component. **Failure to replace the torque-to-yield fastener could cause damage to the vehicle or component.**

12. Position the steering gear into the vehicle.

13. Install 2 NEW steering gear nuts and washers.

14. Install 2 NEW steering gear bolts. Hold the steering gear nuts while tightening the steering gear bolts to 81 ft. lbs. (110 Nm), plus an additional 150 degrees.

15. Reconnect the electrical connectors and install the heat shield.

16. Reposition and install the rear part of the frame:

   a. Install the frame retaining bolts, then tighten the bolts to 118 ft. lbs. (160 Nm).

   b. If removed, install the frame reinforcements with NEW bolts and then tighten the bolts to 44 ft. lbs. (60 Nm) plus 30 degrees.

17. After the installation is complete, measure and adjust the front toe.

18. Program the power steering control module.

➡**The front stabilizer shaft insulators grip the stabilizer shaft and provide resistance to rotating the stabilizer shaft.**

19. Ensure the steering column dash inner and outer seals are positioned properly on the dash panel.

Power Steering Control Module Reprogramming

➡**Do not program or reprogram the electronic power steering control module unless directed by a service procedure or a service bulletin.**

➡**This procedure applies to reprogramming of the existing steering gear or the initial programming if the complete steering gear assembly including the assist motor was replaced.**

1. Connect a scan tool to the vehicle and access the GM Service Programming System (SPS) or aftermarket equivalent.

2. Perform the indicated function "Electronic Power Steering—Programming" and follow the on-screen instructions.

3. Perform the indicated function "Electronic Power Steering—Setup" and follow the on-screen instructions.

4. Perform the "Steering Angle Sensor Centering and Software Endstop Learning" procedure.

5. Clear DTCs after completing the programming and setup procedures.

POWER STEERING PUMP

REMOVAL & INSTALLATION

1. Cover the generator in order to prevent power steering fluid from dripping on the generator.

2. Place drain pans under the vehicle.

3. Remove as much power steering fluid from the reservoir as possible.

4. Remove the air cleaner outlet duct.

5. Raise and support the vehicle.

6. Remove the right front wheelhouse front liner (2.4L) or the right front tire and wheel (3.6L).

7. Disconnect the drive belt only from the power steering pump pulley.

8. Disconnect the power steering fluid reservoir outlet hose from the power steering pump.

9. Remove the power steering gear inlet hose fitting bolt. Remove the power steering gear inlet hose.

10. Remove the 3 power steering pump mounting bolts.

11. Remove the power steering pump.

12. If needed, transfer the power steering pump pulley to the replacement pump.

To install:

13. Position the power steering pump and install the 3 power steering pump mounting bolts. Tighten to 16 ft. lbs. (22 Nm).

14. Install the power steering gear inlet and outlet hose fitting bolts, with new seals, and tighten to 28 ft. lbs. (38 Nm).

15. Install the air cleaner outlet duct.

16. Connect the drive belt to the power steering pump pulley.

17. Install the right front wheelhouse front liner (2.4L) or the right front tire and wheel (3.6L).

18. Lower the vehicle.

19. Fill and bleed the power steering system.

20. Clean any excess power steering fluid from the vehicle.

21. Remove the drain pans.

22. Remove the cover from the generator.

BLEEDING

➡**Observe the following:**

- Use clean, new power steering fluid only.
- Hoses touching the frame, body or engine may cause system noise. Ensure the hoses do not touch any other part of the vehicle.
- Loose connections may not leak, but could allow air into the steering system. Ensure all hose connections are tight.
- Maintain the power steering fluid level throughout the bleeding procedure.

1. Fill the power steering fluid reservoir with fluid to the minimum system level, the FULL COLD level, or the middle of the hash mark on the cap stick fluid level indicator, as applicable.

2. Raise the vehicle until the front wheels are off the ground.

3. With the key in the ON position and with the engine OFF, turn the steering wheel from stop to stop 12 times.

4. If the vehicle is equipped with longer length power steering hoses, turn the steering wheel from stop to stop 15 to 20 times.

5. Verify the power steering fluid level.

6. Start the engine. Rotate the steering wheel from left to right. Inspect the power steering system for signs of cavitation or fluid aeration, like pump noise or whining.

7. Verify the fluid level. Repeat the bleed procedure, if necessary.

8. Lower the vehicle.

FLUID FILL PROCEDURE

1. Run the engine until the power steering fluid reaches about 170°F (80°C).

2. Turn the engine OFF.

3. If the power steering fluid reservoir is covered by a shield or a cover, remove the shield or the cover, as applicable.

4. Clean the power steering fluid reservoir and the reservoir cap.

5. Remove the reservoir cap.

➡**Inspect the power steering pump fluid level at regular intervals.**

6. Inspect the power steering fluid level in the reservoir or on the cap stick, as applicable. Ensure that the fluid level is at the HOT/FULL/MAX mark on the cap stick or on the reservoir, as applicable.

✳✳ CAUTION

When adding fluid or making a complete fluid change, always use the proper power steering fluid. Failure to use the proper fluid will cause hose and seal damage and fluid leaks.

7. Add power steering fluid if necessary.

8. Install the reservoir cap.

9. Install the shield or the cover, as applicable.

STEERING COLUMN

REMOVAL & INSTALLATION
See Figure 114.

✳✳ CAUTION

With wheels of the vehicle facing straight ahead, secure the steering wheel utilizing steering column anti-rotation pin, steering column lock, or a strap to prevent rotation. Locking of the steering column will prevent damage and a possible malfunction of the SIR system. The steering wheel must be secured in position before disconnecting the following components:

- The steering column
- The steering shaft coupling
- The intermediate shaft(s)

✳✳ CAUTION

After disconnecting these components, do not rotate the steering wheel or move the front tires and wheels. Failure to follow this procedure may cause the SIR coil assembly to become un-centered and cause possible damage to the SIR coil. If you think the SIR coil has became un-centered, refer to your specific SIR coil's centering procedure to re-center SIR Coil.

1. Lock the steering column and verify the front wheels are in the straight ahead position.
2. Remove the left side instrument panel lower trim panel.
3. Remove the instrument panel insulator panel.
4. Remove the steering column trim covers.
5. Use paint in order to place match marks on the steering column shaft and on the intermediate shaft.
6. Disconnect the intermediate steering shaft from the steering column.
7. Remove the 4 steering column nuts and remove the steering column.

✳✳ CAUTION

Once the steering column is removed from the vehicle, the column is extremely susceptible to damage. Dropping the column assembly on the end could collapse the steering shaft or loosen the plastic injections, which maintain column rigidity. Leaning on the column assembly could cause the jacket to bend or deform. Any of the above damage could impair the columns collapsible design. Do NOT hammer on the end of the shaft, because hammering could loosen the plastic injections, which maintain column rigidity. If you need to remove the steering wheel, refer to the Steering Wheel Replacement procedure in this section.

8. Disconnect any electrical connectors as needed.
9. If replacing the steering column, copy the match marks from the old steering column to the new steering column.
10. Transfer any parts as necessary.

To install:

11. Installation is the reverse of the removal procedure.
12. Tighten the steering column mounting nuts to 16 ft. lbs. (22 Nm), plus an additional 30 degrees.
13. After installation, center the steering angle sensor.

Steering Angle Sensor Centering

➡The external, column mounted, steering angle sensor does not require centering very often. Centering of the external steering angle sensor might be required after certain service procedures are performed. Some of these procedures are as follows:

- Electronic brake control module (EBCM) replacement
- Steering angle sensor replacement
- Steering gear replacement
- Steering column replacement

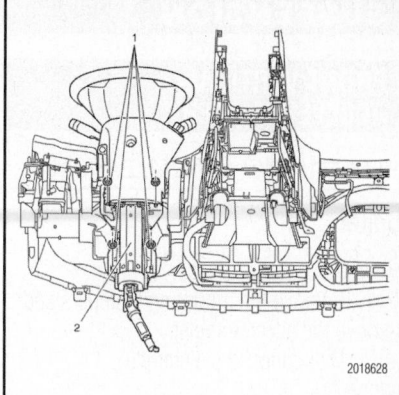

Fig. 114 Removing retaining bolts (1) and steering column (2)

- Collision or other physical damage
1. The external steering angle sensor centering procedure can be completed with a scan tool using the following steps:

a. Using the steering wheel, align the front wheels forward.
b. Apply the parking brake, or set the transmission in the P position.
c. Install the scan tool to the data link connector.
d. Ignition ON, engine OFF
e. Select "Steering Wheel Angle Sensor Reset in the Steering Wheel Angle Sensor Module Configuration/Reset Functions" list. Follow the scan tool directions to complete the learn procedure.
f. Select "Steering Wheel Angle Sensor Learn in the Steering Wheel Angle Sensor Module Configuration/Reset Functions" list. Follow the scan tool directions to complete the learn procedure.
g. Select "Steering Wheel Angle Sensor Learn in the EBCM Configuration/Reset Functions" list. Follow the scan tool directions to complete the learn procedure.
h. If the vehicle is equipped with electronic power steering, perform the "Software Endstop Learning" procedure.
i. Clear any DTCs that may be set.

SUSPENSION   **ELECTRONIC SUSPENSION**

FRONT VERTICAL ACCELEROMETER

REMOVAL AND & INSTALLATION

Upper

See Figure 115.

1. Remove the mounting fasteners and remove the accelerometer.
2. Disconnect the electrical connector.
3. Installation is the reverse of the removal procedure.
4. Tighten the fasteners to 80 inch lbs. (9 Nm).

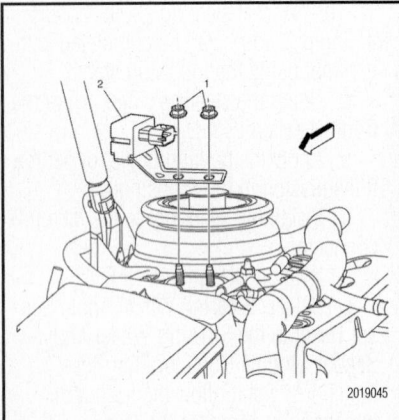

Fig. 115 Remove the mounting nuts (1) and remove the upper front vertical accelerometer (2)

Lower

See Figure 116.

1. Raise and support the vehicle.
2. Remove the front tire and wheel assemblies.
3. Remove the accelerometer fastener and remove the accelerometer as follows:

Fig. 116 Showing the lower vertical accelerometer (2) location, with mounting fastener (1)

   a. Remove the connector from the strut.
   b. Disconnect the connector from the sensor (the connector has a secondary locking that should be released before turning and releasing the connector).
4. Installation is the reverse of removal procedure.
5. Tighten the fasteners to 80 inch lbs. (9 Nm).

ELECTRONIC SUSPENSION CONTROL MODULE

REMOVAL & INSTALLATION

See Figure 117.

1. Remove the left side luggage compartment trim.
2. Remove the electronic suspension control module fasteners.
3. Remove the bracket from the control module. Slide the control module down from the bracket.
4. Remove the control module. Disconnect the connectors.
5. Installation is the reverse of removal procedure.

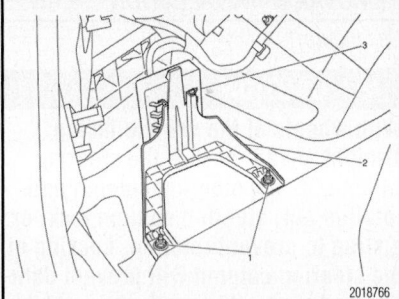

Fig. 117 Electronic suspension control module mounting nuts (1), bracket (2) and control module (3)

ELECTRONIC SUSPENSION REAR POSITION SENSOR

REMOVAL AND & INSTALLATION

See Figure 118.

1. Fold the back on left side of the backseat.
2. Lift the front left side of the luggage compartment trim floor panel and also the damping material.
3. Remove the fasteners and remove the sensor.
4. Installation is the reverse of the removal procedure.

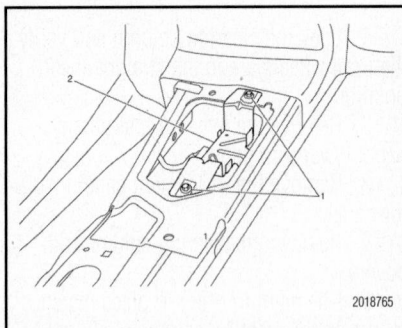

Fig. 118 Remove the mounting fasteners (1) and remove the sensor (2)

LOWER CONTROL ARM

REMOVAL & INSTALLATION

Without Performance Suspension

See Figure 119.

1. Raise and support the vehicle.
2. Remove the tire and wheel assembly.
3. Remove the steering knuckle nut at the ball joint.
4. Support the knuckle with the proper jack stand.
5. Using the CH 43631 remover (or equivalent), separate the ball joint from the knuckle.
6. Remove the steering knuckle bolt and discard.
7. Remove the lower control arm front bolt. Discard the bolt.
8. Remove the lower control arm rear nuts and bolts. Discard the bolts.
9. Remove the lower control arm.

To install:

➡This component is equipped with torque-to-yield fasteners. Install a NEW torque-to-yield fastener when installing this component. Failure to replace the torque-to-yield fastener could cause damage to the vehicle or component.

10. Position the lower control arm.

11. Install new rear nuts and bolts. Tighten as follows:
- First Pass: 74 ft. lbs. (100 Nm)
- Final Pass: plus 75 degrees
12. Install a new lower control arm front bolt. Tighten the bolt as follows:
- First Pass: 74 ft. lbs. (100 Nm)
- Final Pass: plus 90 degrees
13. Install the ball joint for the lower control arm into the steering knuckle and tighten the new nut as follows:
- First Pass: 37 ft. lbs. (50 Nm)
- Final Pass: plus 30 degrees
14. Verify the wheel alignment.

With Performance Suspension

1. Raise and support the vehicle.
2. Remove the tire and wheel assembly.
3. Remove the lower control arm nut.
4. Remove the lower control arm bolt.
5. Remove and discard the lower control arm nut and bolt at the steering knuckle.
6. Remove and discard the lower control arm nut and bolt at the frame.
7. Remove the lower control arm from the vehicle.

To install:

➡This component is equipped with torque-to-yield fasteners. Install a NEW torque-to-yield fastener when installing this component. Failure to replace the torque-to-yield fastener could cause damage to the vehicle or component.

8. Position the lower control arm in the frame and the steering knuckle. Install the front lower control arm bolts to hold the lower control arm in place.
9. Install the NEW lower control arm bolt and tighten the bolt to 74 ft. lbs. (100 Nm), plus 90 degrees.
10. Install the NEW lower control arm bolt and tighten the bolt to 78 ft. lbs. (115 Nm), plus 125 degrees.
11. Install the NEW lower control arm bolts and tighten to 75 ft. lbs. (100 Nm), plus 75 degrees.
12. Install the tire and wheel assembly.
13. Remove the support and lower the vehicle.

STABILIZER SHAFT

REMOVAL & INSTALLATION

1. Raise and support the vehicle.
2. Remove the tire and wheel assembly.
3. For AWD, remove the propeller shaft. See "DRIVE TRAIN" section.
4. Support the front cradle with the proper jackstands.
5. Remove the stabilizer links from the stabilizer shaft.
6. Remove rear transmission bolt.
7. Lower the rear front cradle to gain enough clearance to remove the stabilizer shaft.
8. Remove and discard the bolts. DO NOT reuse, replace with NEW only.
9. Remove the stabilizer shaft.

To install:

10. Installation is the reverse of the removal procedure.
11. Tighten the stabilizer shaft bolts as follows:
- First Pass: 16 ft. lbs. (22 Nm)
- Second Pass: plus 30 degrees
- Final Pass: plus 15 degrees

✳✳ CAUTION

This component is equipped with torque-to-yield fasteners. Install a NEW torque-to-yield fastener when installing this component. Failure to replace the torque-to-yield fastener could cause damage to the vehicle or component.

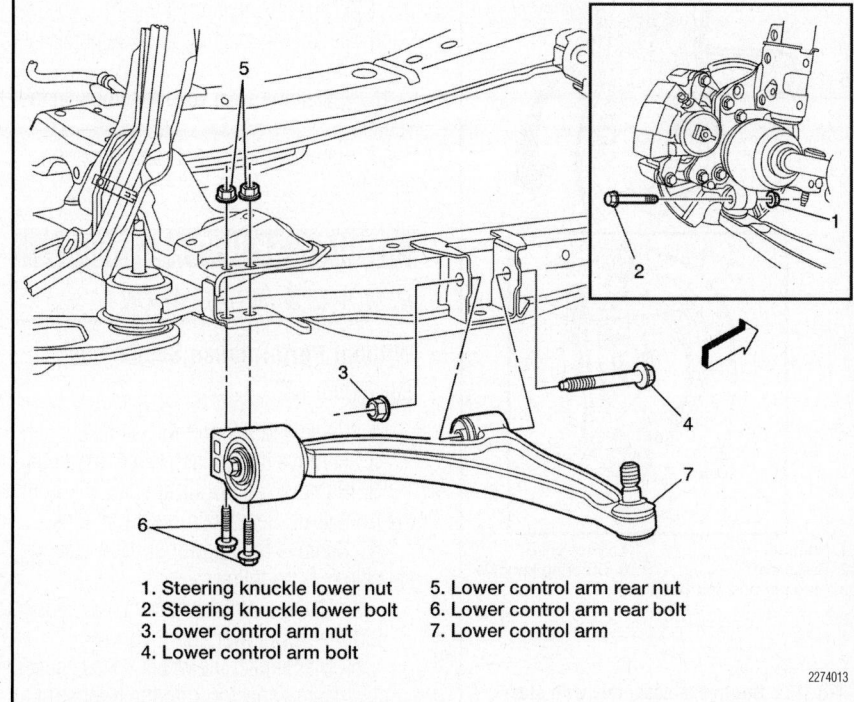

1. Steering knuckle lower nut	5. Lower control arm rear nut
2. Steering knuckle lower bolt	6. Lower control arm rear bolt
3. Lower control arm nut	7. Lower control arm
4. Lower control arm bolt	

2274013

Fig. 119 Showing the lower control arm assembly

STABILIZER SHAFT LINK

REMOVAL & INSTALLATION

See Figure 120.

1. Raise and support the vehicle.
2. Remove the tire and wheel assembly.
3. Remove the 2 stabilizer shaft link nuts.
4. Remove the stabilizer shaft link.
5. Installation is the reverse of the removal procedure.
6. Tighten the stabilizer shaft link nuts to 48 ft. lbs. (65 Nm).

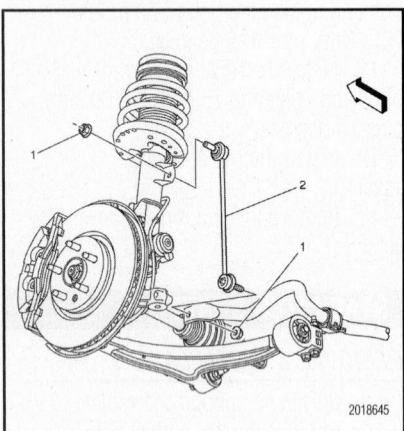

Fig. 120 Showing stabilizer shaft link (2) and retainers (1)

STEERING KNUCKLE

REMOVAL & INSTALLATION

Without Performance Suspension

➡For specific procedures on related components in these steps, see respective component heading in this section.

1. Raise and support the vehicle.
2. Remove the tire and wheel assembly.
3. Remove the steering knuckle as follows:

✳✳ CAUTION

Do not pry in such a way that the ball joint seal is contacted. Damage to the seal may result.

   a. Remove the wheel bearing/hub.
   b. Separate the outer tie rod end from the knuckle.
   c. Remove the nuts and bolts from the strut to the knuckle.
   d. Separate the lower ball joint from the knuckle.
4. Installation is the reverse of the removal procedure.

5. Tighten the nuts and bolts, as applicable, as follows:
- Lower ball joint-to-steering knuckle nut: 37 ft. lbs. (50 Nm), plus 30 degrees
- Strut lower mounting bolts/nuts-to-knuckle: 63ft. lbs. (85 Nm), plus 60 degrees
- Outer tie rod-to-knuckle ball joint nut: 26ft. lbs. (35 Nm), plus 30 degrees
- Wheel bearing bolts: 74 ft. lbs. (100 Nm), plus 75 degrees
6. Check wheel alignment.

With Performance Suspension

See Figure 121.

➡For specific procedures on related components in these steps, see respective component heading in this section.

1. Raise and support the vehicle.
2. Remove the tire and wheel assembly.
3. Remove the strut yoke assembly from the vehicle.

➡The upper ball stud DOES NOT have to be removed from the yoke assembly to perform the following step.

4. Separate the steering knuckle upper ball stud from the steering knuckle.

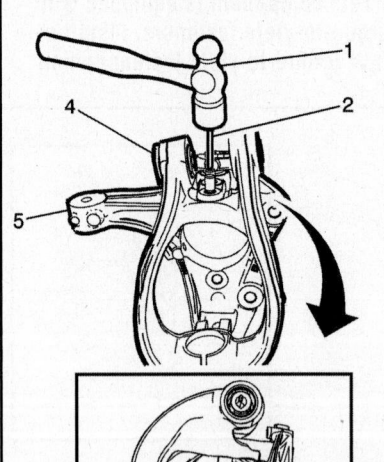

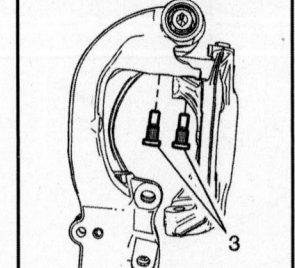

1. Hammer   4. Strut yoke
2. Brass drift   5. Steering knuckle
3. King pin bushing bolts

Fig. 121 Strut yoke assembly with steering knuckle

5. Remove the king pin bushing nuts.
6. If servicing the strut yoke, perform the following after the king pin bushing nuts have been removed:
   a. Using a brass drift and a hammer, remove the steering king pin bushing bolts from the strut yoke.
   b. Remove the steering knuckle from the strut yoke.
7. If servicing the steering knuckle, loosen the king pin bushing nuts until they are even with the studs or two or three of threads of the king pin nut are exposed.

➡It may be necessary to rotate the steering knuckle to gain enough room to position the punch on the king pin bushing.

8. Position a punch on the king pin bushing.
9. Using a hammer, remove the king pin and knuckle from the yoke.
10. Remove the steering knuckle from the strut yoke.

To install:

11. Ensure to that the steering knuckle upper ball stud is properly aligned in the steering knuckle.
12. Position the steering knuckle in the strut yoke.
13. When tightening the king pin bushing nuts, tighten them in small increments until the king pin bushing bolts are drawn into evenly into the front suspension yoke.
14. Tighten the king pin bushing nuts in small increments until the torque of 52 ft. lbs. (70 Nm) is reached.
15. Install the steering knuckle upper ball stud nut.
16. Install the strut yoke assembly in the vehicle.
17. Remove the support and lower the vehicle.

STRUT & SPRING ASSEMBLY

REMOVAL & INSTALLATION

Without Performance Suspension

See Figure 122.

1. Raise and support the vehicle.
2. Remove the tire and wheel assembly.
3. Remove the stabilizer shaft link from the front strut. See "Stabilizer Shaft Link".
4. Remove the 2 lower strut-to-steering knuckle nuts as follows:
   a. Using a suitable jack stand, support the front lower control arm.
   b. Disconnect the wheel speed sensor electrical connector from the front strut, if equipped.

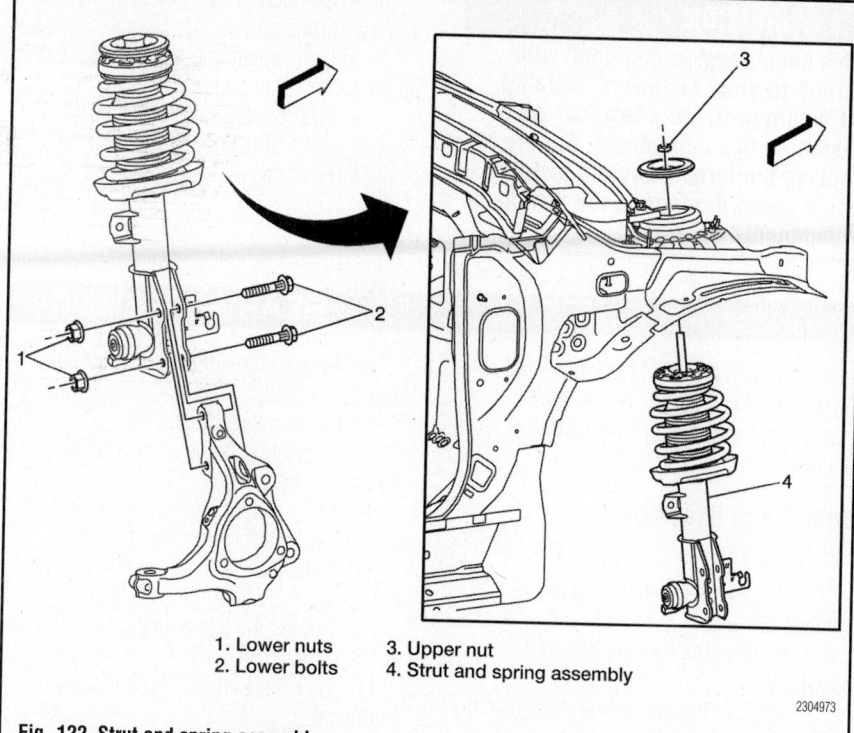

1. Lower nuts
2. Lower bolts
3. Upper nut
4. Strut and spring assembly

2304973

Fig. 122 Strut and spring assembly

c. Remove brake hose, connector and clip from the strut.

d. Remove the 2 lower nuts.

5. Remove the 2 lower steering knuckle-to-strut bolts and discard.

6. Remove the upper strut mount nut:

a. Remove the plastic cap, if equipped.

b. Using the CH-49375 wrench (or equivalent), remove the nut.

7. Remove the front suspension strut.

To install:

➡**This component is equipped with torque-to-yield fasteners. Install a NEW torque-to-yield fastener when installing this component. Failure to replace the torque-to-yield fastener could cause damage to the vehicle or component.**

8. Position the strut and spring assembly to the vehicle.

9. Install the upper strut mount nut and tighten to 40 ft. lbs. (55 Nm).

10. Install new bolts and nuts to the lower knuckle-to-strut mounting and tighten to 63 ft. lbs. (85 Nm), plus 60 degrees.

With Performance Suspension

1. Remove the front compartment sight shields.

2. Remove the tire and wheel assembly.

3. Remove the wheel drive shaft nut from the steering knuckle.

4. Remove the brake rotor from the steering knuckle. See "BRAKES" section.

5. Remove the steering linkage outer tie rod from the steering knuckle.

6. Remove the stabilizer shaft link from the stabilizer shaft from the steering knuckle. See "Stabilizer Shaft Link".

7. Remove the brake hose and wheel speed sensor.

8. Support the lower control arm with hydraulic jack stand.

9. Remove the lower control arm bolt.

10. Remove strut mount cover.

➡**Use the proper Torx® bit to hold the strut shaft while removing the strut mount nut.**

11. Remove the strut mount nut and bumper.

12. Remove the strut assembly.

13. Remove the shock absorber yoke nut.

14. Remove the brake hose bracket and the shock absorber yoke bolt.

15. Remove shock assembly.

To install:

16. Install the shock assembly in the suspension yoke.

17. Install the brake hose bracket and the shock absorber yoke bolt.

18. Install the shock absorber yoke nut and tighten the nut to 52 ft. lbs. (70 Nm).

19. Install the strut assembly.

20. Install the strut mount.

21. Install the strut mount nut and tighten to 41 ft. lbs. (55 Nm).

22. Install the strut mount cover.

23. Install the lower control arm bolt.

24. Install the wheel speed sensor on the yoke, the brake rotor on the steering knuckle, and the brake hose in the mounting bracket. See "BRAKES" section.

25. Install the stabilizer shaft link in the stabilizer shaft. See "Stabilizer Shaft Link".

26. Install the steering linkage outer tie rod in the steering knuckle. Tighten the new nut to 26 ft. lbs. (35 Nm), plus 30 degrees.

27. Install the wheel drive shaft nut in the steering knuckle. Tighten the nut as follows:

- First step: 111 ft. lbs. (150 Nm)
- Second step: back off 45 degrees
- Final step: 184 ft. lbs. (250 Nm)

28. Install the tire and wheel assembly.

29. Remove the support stand and lower the vehicle.

WHEEL HUB & BEARING

REMOVAL & INSTALLATION

Without Performance Suspension

1. Raise and support the vehicle.

2. Remove the tire and wheel assembly.

3. Remove the brake rotor. See "BRAKES" section.

4. Separate the wheel drive shaft from the wheel bearing assembly. See "DRIVE TRAIN" section.

5. Front wheel bearing bolts.

➡**DO NOT re-use the wheel bearing bolt. Replace with NEW only.**

6. Remove the wheel bearing assembly.

✳✳ CAUTION

This component is equipped with torque-to-yield fasteners. Install a NEW torque-to-yield fastener when installing this component. Failure to replace the torque-to-yield fastener could cause damage to the vehicle or component.

7. Installation is the reverse of the removal procedure.

8. Tighten the wheel bearing bolts as follows:

- First Pass: 74 ft. lbs. (100 Nm)
- Final Pass: plus 75 degrees

Without Performance Suspension

1. Raise and support the vehicle.

2. Remove the steering knuckle assem-

bly from the vehicle. See "Steering Knuckle".

3. Remove the front wheel bearing bolts.

➡ **Remove and discard the bolts. Do not re-use, replace with new only.**

4. Remove the brake shield.
5. Remove the wheel hub and bearing.

✳✳ CAUTION

This component is equipped with torque-to-yield fasteners. Install a NEW torque-to-yield fastener when installing this component. Failure to replace the torque-to-yield fastener could cause damage to the vehicle or component.

6. Installation is the reverse of the removal procedure.
7. Tighten wheel hub bolts as follows:
   - First pass: 74 ft. lbs. (100 Nm)
   - Final pass: plus 60 degrees

SUSPENSION

ADJUST LINK

REMOVAL & INSTALLATION

With 4-Link Rear Axle

See Figure 123.

1. Raise and suitably support the vehicle.
2. Remove the adjust link inner nut.
3. Remove the adjust link cam washer.
4. Remove the adjust link inner bolt.
5. Remove and discard the bolt. Replace with NEW only.
6. Remove the adjust link outer nut and bolt. Discard the bolt.
7. Remove the adjust link.
8. Installation is the reverse of the removal procedure.
9. Tighten the adjust link outer bolt to 85 ft. lbs. (115 Nm), plus 90 degrees.

10. Tighten the adjust link inner nut to 66 ft. lbs. (90 Nm), plus 60 degrees.
11. After installation, check the rear alignment.

With H-Arm Rear Axle

See Figure 124.

1. Raise and suitably support the vehicle.
2. Remove the rear tire and wheel assembly.
3. Remove the adjust link inner cam nut and washer as follows:
   a. Support the fuel tank using a proper jack stand.
   b. Remove fuel tank strap and loosen the other fuel tank strap fastener.
   c. Lower the fuel tank to get access to rear suspension adjust link nut.
4. Remove the adjust link inner bolt.

REAR SUSPENSION

5. Remove the adjust link outer bolt. Discard the bolt.
6. Remove the adjust link.
7. Installation is the reverse of the removal procedure.
8. Use a proper jack stand to load the knuckle when tightening the fasteners.
9. Tighten the adjust link outer bolt to 111 ft. lbs. (150 Nm), plus 60 degrees.
10. Tighten the adjust link inner cam nut to 111ft. lbs. (150 Nm).
11. After installation, check the rear alignment.

COIL SPRING

REMOVAL & INSTALLATION

✳✳ CAUTION

To prevent personal injury and/or component damage, use the proper tools to support the lower control arm when removing the coil spring. The coil spring is under extreme pressure and can become a projectile should the spring separate from the lower control arm before all of the tension is relieved.

1. Raise and support the vehicle.
2. Remove the rear tire and wheel.
3. Remove the rear brake caliper and relocate to the side, if needed. See "BRAKES" section.
4. Remove the rear coil spring as follows:
   a. Use the proper jack stand to support the lower control arm.
   b. Disconnect the lower control arm from the rear wheel hub bracket or from the stabilizer shaft link. See "Lower Control Arm" and/or "Stabilizer Shaft Link".
   c. Carefully lower the control arm on the jack stand until tension is removed from coil spring.
   d. Remove the coil spring.
5. Remove the upper and lower spring insulators, if needed.
6. Installation is the reverse of the removal procedure.

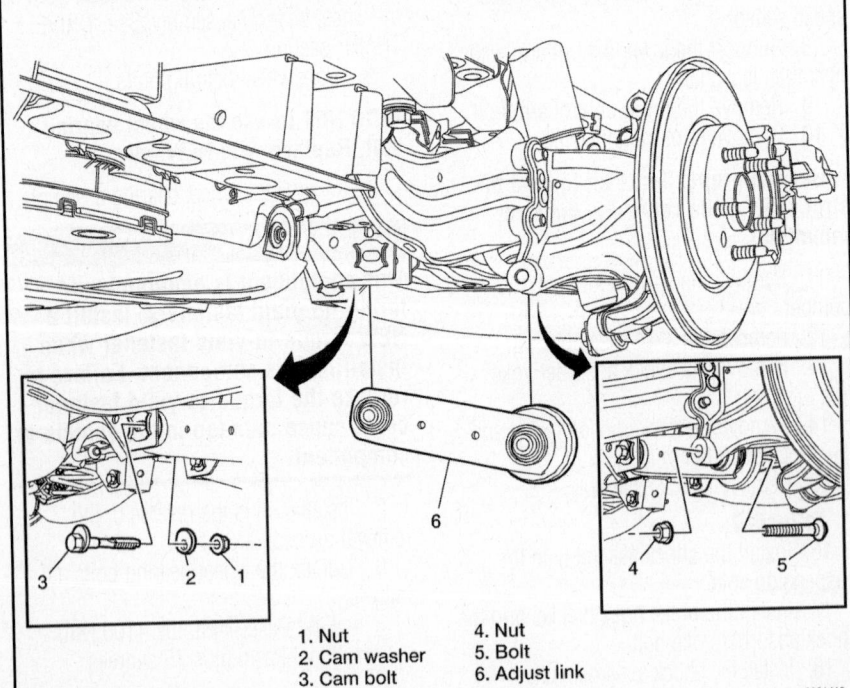

1. Nut
2. Cam washer
3. Cam bolt
4. Nut
5. Bolt
6. Adjust link

2321410

Fig. 123 Showing the adjust link

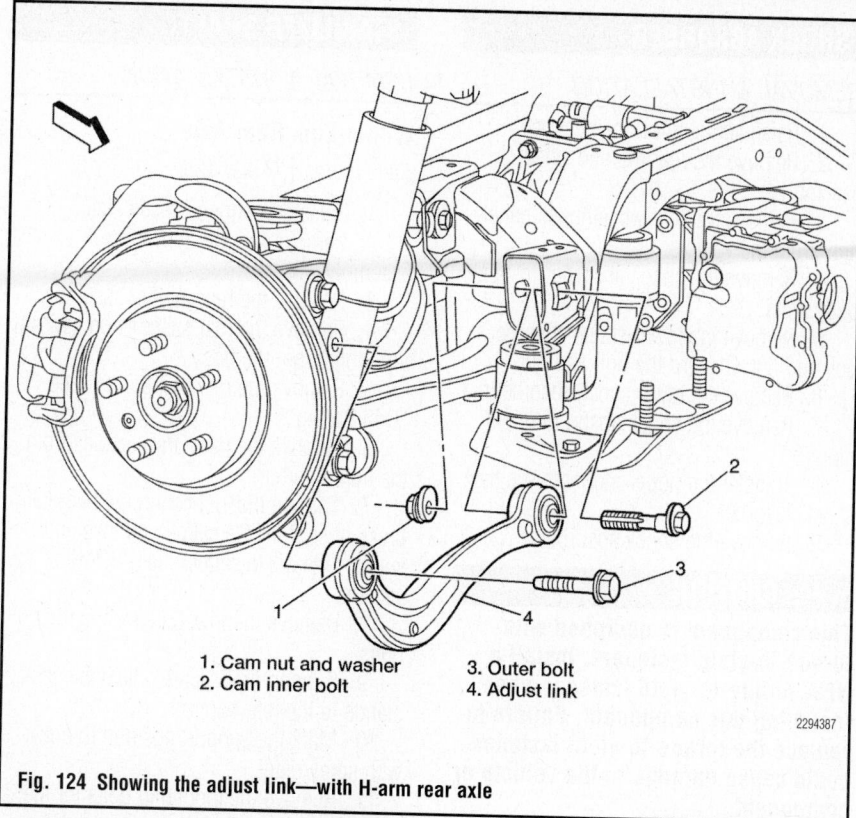

1. Cam nut and washer
2. Cam inner bolt
3. Outer bolt
4. Adjust link

2294387

Fig. 124 Showing the adjust link—with H-arm rear axle

LOWER CONTROL ARM

REMOVAL & INSTALLATION

With 4-Link Rear Axle

1. Raise and support the vehicle.
2. Remove the tire and wheel assembly.
3. Remove the rear spring. See "Coil Spring".
4. Remove the lower control arm inner nut, washer and bolt. Discard the bolt.
5. Remove the control arm outer nut and bolt. Discard the bolt.
6. Remove the lower control arm.

✳✳ CAUTION

This component is equipped with torque-to-yield fasteners. Install a NEW torque-to-yield fastener when installing this component. Failure to replace the torque-to-yield fastener could cause damage to the vehicle or component.

7. Installation is the reverse of the removal procedure.
8. Tighten the outer bolt to 51 ft. lbs. (70 Nm), plus 90 degrees.
9. Tighten the control arm inner nut to 66 ft. lbs. (90 Nm), plus 60 degrees.
10. Check the rear alignment after installation.

With H-Arm Rear Axle

See Figure 125.

1. Raise and support the vehicle.
2. Remove the tire and wheel assembly.
3. Remove the rear spring. See "Coil Spring".
4. Remove the shock absorber lower bolt at the rear wheel hub bracket.
5. Remove the control arm inner forward nut and bolt. Discard the bolt.
6. Remove the control arm inner rear nut and bolt. Discard the bolt.
7. Remove the control arm outer bolt. Discard the bolt.
8. Remove the lower control arm as follows:

   a. Lower the fuel tank so as to gain enough clearance to remove the lower control arm from the vehicle. See "FUEL" section.

✳✳ CAUTION

This component is equipped with torque-to-yield fasteners. Install a NEW torque-to-yield fastener when installing this component. Failure to

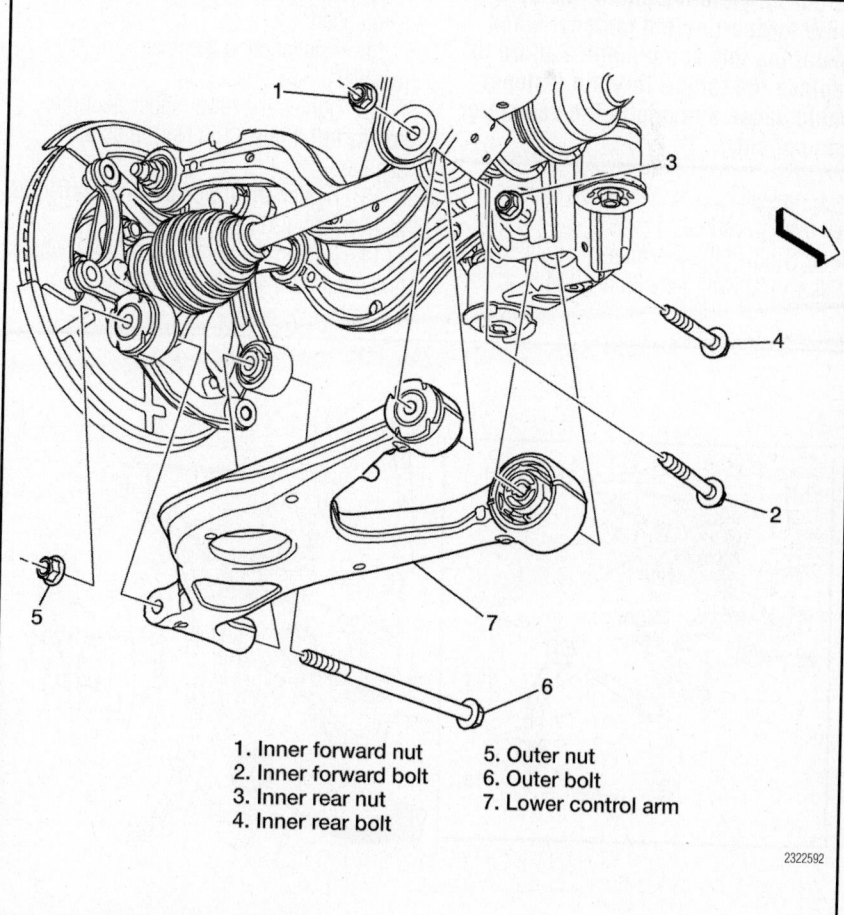

1. Inner forward nut
2. Inner forward bolt
3. Inner rear nut
4. Inner rear bolt
5. Outer nut
6. Outer bolt
7. Lower control arm

2322592

Fig. 125 Showing the lower control arm

replace the torque-to-yield fastener could cause damage to the vehicle or component.

9. Installation is the reverse of the removal procedure.

10. Use a proper jack stand to load the control arm when tightening the bolts.

11. Tighten the inner and outer nuts and new bolts to 111 ft. lbs. (150 Nm), plus 90 degrees.

REAR SUSPENSION LINK

REMOVAL & INSTALLATION

See Figure 126.

With H-Arm Rear Axle

1. Raise and support the vehicle.
2. Remove the tire and wheel assembly.
3. Remove the rear suspension link nuts and bolts. Discard the nuts and bolts.
4. Remove the rear suspension link while supporting the rear suspension lower control arm with the proper jack stand.

✳✳ CAUTION

This component is equipped with torque-to-yield fasteners. Install a NEW torque-to-yield fastener when installing this component. Failure to replace the torque-to-yield fastener could cause damage to the vehicle or component.

5. Installation is the reverse of the removal procedure.
6. Tighten the link nuts and bolts to 111 ft. lbs. (150 Nm), plus 60 degrees.

SHOCK ABSORBER

REMOVAL & INSTALLATION

1. Raise and support the vehicle.
2. Remove the rear tire and wheel assembly.
3. Remove the rear wheelhouse panel liner from the vehicle.
4. Remove the shock absorber-to-upper body bolts.
5. Remove the lower shock absorber bolt and nut. Discard the bolt and nut.
6. Remove the lower shock absorber nut
7. Remove the shock absorber upper mount.
8. Transfer the upper mount to the new shock absorber.
9. Remove the shock absorber.

✳✳ CAUTION

This component is equipped with torque-to-yield fasteners. Install a NEW torque-to-yield fastener when installing this component. Failure to replace the torque-to-yield fastener could cause damage to the vehicle or component.

10. Disconnect any electrical connectors, if equipped.
11. Installation is the reverse of the removal procedure.
12. Tighten the lower shock absorber bolt to 110 ft. lbs. (150 Nm), plus 60 degrees.
13. Tighten the lower shock absorber nut to 15 ft. lbs. (20 Nm).
14. Tighten the shock absorber-to-upper body bolts to 74 ft. lbs. (100 Nm).

STABILIZER SHAFT

REMOVAL & INSTALLATION

With 4-Link Rear Axle

See Figures 127 and 128.

1. Raise and support the vehicle.
2. Remove the tire and wheel assembly.
3. Remove the rear muffler assembly.
4. Remove the rear suspension control arm bolts from the body.
5. Remove the rear coil spring. See "Coil Spring".
6. Remove the park brake cables from the trailing arms.
7. Without disconnecting the hydraulic brake hose from the caliper, remove and support the brake caliper. See "BRAKES" section.
8. Remove the lower shock absorber bolts.
9. Support and secure adjustable jack stands to the rear support.
10. Mark the support position to body with spray paint.
11. Remove the mounting bolts for the support.
12. Lower the support enough to gain access to the rear stabilizer shaft insulator clamps mounting bolts.
13. Remove the stabilizer shaft from the stabilizer shaft link.
14. Remove and discard the stabilizer shaft bolts from the retaining clamps. Replace with NEW only.
15. Remove the stabilizer shaft assembly_from the support.

To install:

➡Load the suspension with the proper jack stand before tightening the bolts to specifications.

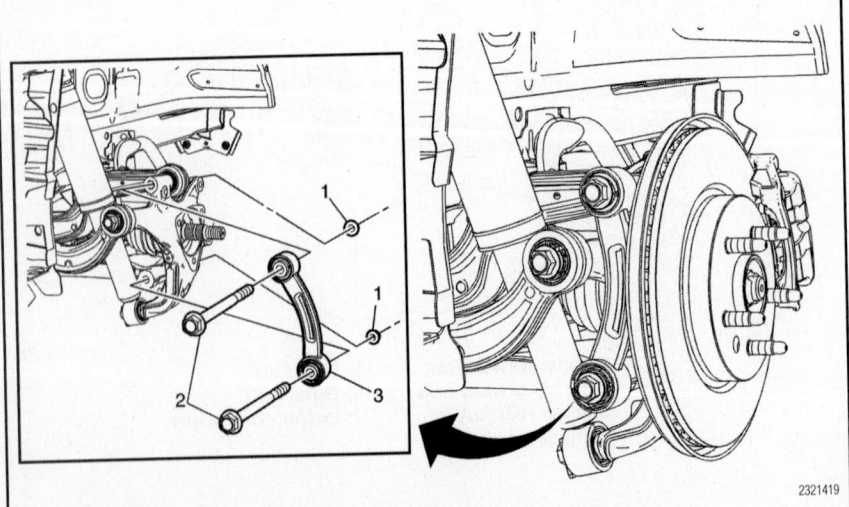

Fig. 126 Remove the nuts (1), bolts (2), and the suspension link (3)

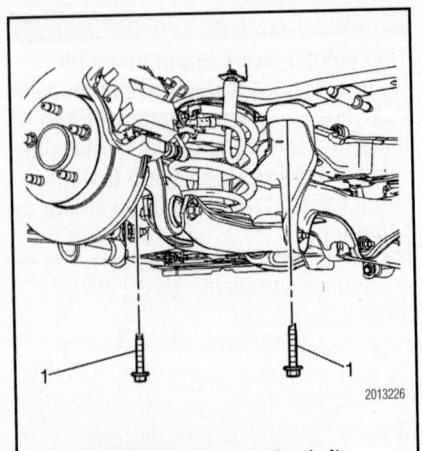

Fig. 127 Remove the mounting bolts (1)_for the support.

16. Install the stabilizer shaft on the support. Install NEW clamp bolts and tighten to 16 ft. lbs. (22 Nm), plus 30 degrees.

17. Install the stabilizer shaft to stabilizer shaft link. Tighten the nuts and bolts to 37 ft. lbs. (50 Nm).

18. Raise the rear support back into position.

19. Install the rear support bolts. Tighten the bolts to 66 ft. lbs. (90 Nm), plus an additional 120 degrees, then a final 15 degrees.

20. Install the lower shock absorber mounting bolts. Tighten the bolts to 110 ft. lbs. (150 Nm), plus 60 degrees.

21. Install the rear brake calipers. See "BRAKES" section.

22. Install the rear suspension control

arm bolts to the body. Tighten the bolts to 111 ft. lbs. (150 Nm), plus 30 degrees.

23. Install the rear springs. See "Coil Springs".

24. Remove the adjustable jack stands from the rear support.

25. Install the park brake cables on the trailing arms.

26. Install the rear muffler assembly.

27. Install the tire and wheel assemblies.

28. Lower the vehicle.

With H-Arm Rear Axle

1. Raise and support the vehicle.
2. Remove the tire and wheel assembly.
3. Remove the stabilizer links from the stabilizer shaft. See "Stabilizer Shaft Link".
4. Remover the stabilizer shaft insulators.
5. Remove the rear stabilizer shaft.
6. Installation is the reverse of the removal procedure.

STABILIZER SHAFT LINK

REMOVAL & INSTALLATION

With 4-Link Rear Axle

See Figure 129.

1. Raise and support the vehicle.
2. Remove the tire and wheel assembly.
3. Remove the rear stabilizer shaft link bolt and nut.
4. Remove the stabilizer shaft link.
5. Installation is the reverse of the removal procedure.
6. Tighten the shaft link nut and bolt to 37 ft. lbs. (50 Nm) each.
7. Remove the stabilizer shaft link.

With H-Arm Rear Axle

See Figure 130.

1. Raise and support the vehicle.
2. Remove the tire and wheel assembly.
3. Remove the stabilizer shaft link nuts and remove the shaft link.
4. Installation is the reverse of the removal procedure.
5. Tighten the shaft link nuts to 37 ft. lbs. (50 Nm).

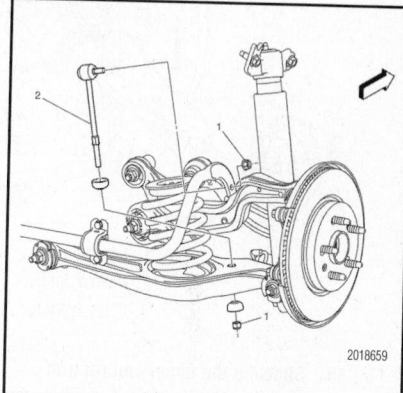

Fig. 130 Remove the stabilizer shaft link nuts (1) and remove the shaft link (2).

UPPER CONTROL ARM

REMOVAL & INSTALLATION

With 4-Link Rear Axle

See Figure 131.

1. Raise and suitably support the vehicle.
2. Remove the rear tire and wheel assembly.

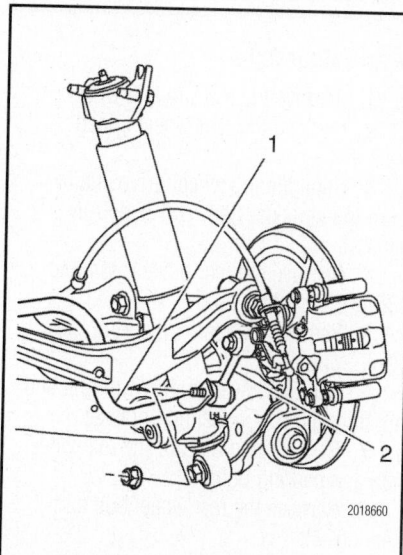

Fig. 128 Remove the stabilizer shaft (1) from the stabilizer shaft link (2).

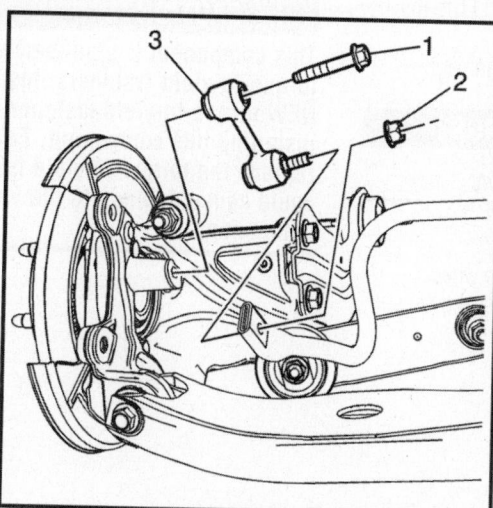
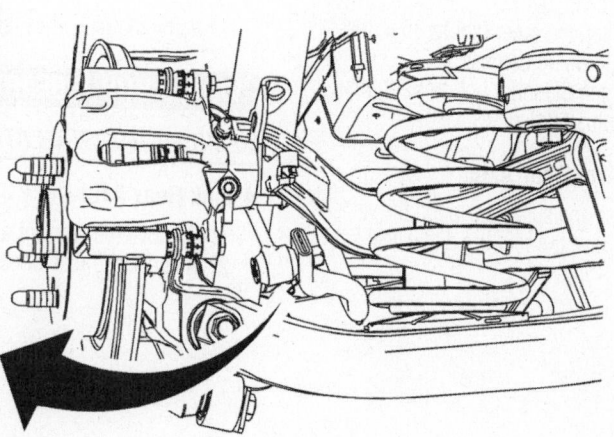

Fig. 129 Remove the rear stabilizer shaft link bolt (1), nut (2) and shaft link (3).

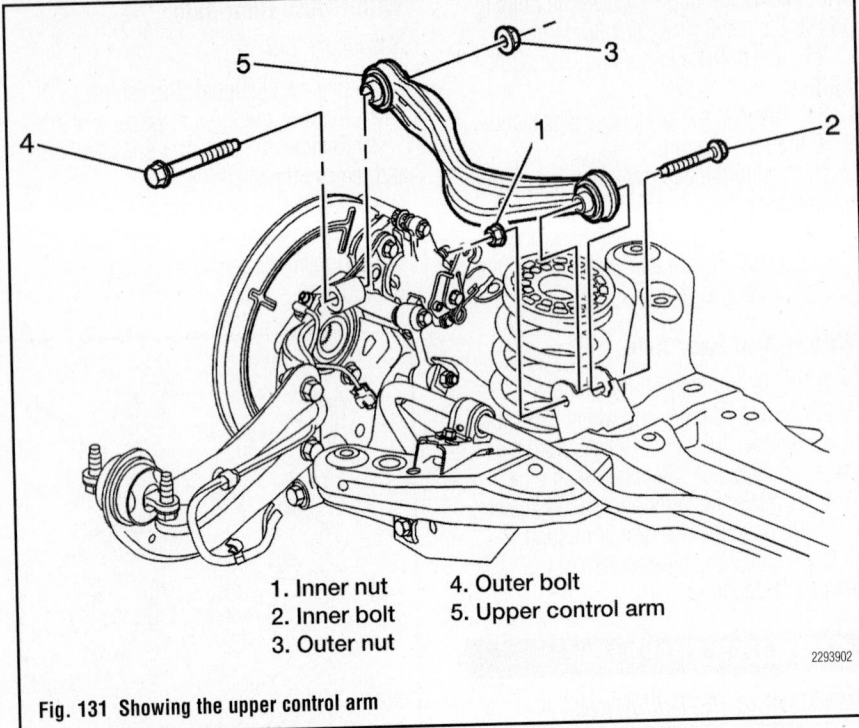

1. Inner nut
2. Inner bolt
3. Outer nut
4. Outer bolt
5. Upper control arm

2293902

Fig. 131 Showing the upper control arm

3. Remove the upper control arm inner nut and bolt. Discard the bolt.

4. Remove the upper control arm outer nut and bolt. Discard the bolt.

5. Remove the upper control arm.

✳✳ CAUTION

This component is equipped with torque-to-yield fasteners. Install a NEW torque-to-yield fastener when installing this component. Failure to replace the torque-to-yield fastener could cause damage to the vehicle or component.

6. Installation is the reverse of the removal procedure.

7. Tighten the outer bolt to 85 ft. lbs. (150 Nm), plus 90 degrees.

8. Tighten the inner bolt to 52 ft. lbs. (70 Nm), plus 60 degrees.

With H-Arm Rear Axle

1. Raise and suitably support the vehicle.

2. Remove the rear tire and wheel assembly.

3. Remove the upper control arm inner nut and washer.

4. Remove the upper control arm inner bolt.

5. Remove the upper control arm as follows:

  a. Use a proper jack stand, support the lower control arm and the rear wheel bracket.

  b. Remove the bolt from the upper control to the lower control arm.

  c. Remove cable harness clips from control arm.

6. Installation is the reverse of the removal procedure.

7. Tighten the inner nut to 111 ft. lbs. (150 Nm).

8. Verify the rear wheel alignment.

WHEEL HUB & BEARINGS

REMOVAL & INSTALLATION

4-Link Rear Axle

1. Remove the rear tire and wheel.

2. Remove the rear wheel speed sensor

and the rear brake rotor. See "BRAKES" section.

3. Remove and discard the rear wheel bearing bolts. DO NOT reuse, replace with NEW only.

4. Remove the rear wheel hub and bearing.

5. Installation is the reverse of the removal procedure.

6. Tighten the rear wheel bearing bolts to 66 ft. lbs. (90 Nm) plus 75 degrees.

✳✳ CAUTION

This component is equipped with torque-to-yield fasteners. Install a NEW torque-to-yield fastener when installing this component. Failure to replace the torque-to-yield fastener could cause damage to the vehicle or component.

H-Arm Rear Axle

1. Remove the rear tire and wheel.

2. Remove the rear wheel speed sensor.

3. Separate the wheel drive shaft from the knuckle. See "DRIVE TRAIN" section.

4. Remove the rear brake rotor. See "BRAKES" section.

5. Remove the rear coil spring. See "Coil Spring".

6. Remove lower control arm bolt and nut from the rear wheel hub bracket.

7. Remove and discard the rear wheel hub and bearing bolts.

8. Remove the rear wheel hub and bearing.

9. Installation is the reverse of the removal procedure.

10. Tighten the rear wheel bearing bolts to 66 ft. lbs. (90 Nm) plus 75 degrees.

✳✳ CAUTION

This component is equipped with torque-to-yield fasteners. Install a NEW torque-to-yield fastener when installing this component. Failure to replace the torque-to-yield fastener could cause damage to the vehicle or component.

BUICK

Lucerne

17

BRAKES 17-11

ANTI-LOCK BRAKE SYSTEM (ABS).........................17-11
Electronic Brake Control
Module (EBCM) 17-11
EBCM Programming...........17-12
Removal & Installation.......17-11
Electronic Traction Control
Switch 17-12
Removal & Installation.......17-12
General Information...............17-11
Precautions.....................17-11
Speed Sensors 17-13
Removal & Installation.......17-13
Vehicle Yaw Rate Sensor
with Vehicle Lateral
Accelerometer 17-13
Removal & Installation.......17-13
BLEEDING THE BRAKE SYSTEM 17-13
Bleeding Procedure............17-13
Anti-lock Brake System
Automated Bleed 17-14
Fluid Fill Procedure 17-15
Manual Bleeding Procedure..17-13
Master Cylinder Bench
Bleeding 17-14
FRONT DISC BRAKES 17-15
Brake Caliper....................17-15
Removal & Installation.......17-15
Disc Brake Pads 17-15
Burnishing Pads & Rotors ..17-16
Removal & Installation.......17-15
REAR DISC BRAKES 17-16
Brake Caliper....................17-16
Removal & Installation.......17-16
Disc Brake Pads 17-16
Burnishing Pads & Rotors ..17-16
Removal & Installation.......17-16

CHASSIS ELECTRICAL 17-17

AIR BAG (SUPPLEMENTAL RESTRAINT SYSTEM) 17-17
General Information...............17-17
Arming the System 17-18
Clockspring Centering........17-19

Component Locations.........17-18
Disarming the System.........17-18
Service Precautions 17-17

DRIVE TRAIN 17-19

Automatic Transaxle Fluid 17-19
Fluid & Filter Replacement..17-19
Front Drive Shaft Inner Seal 17-20
Removal & Installation.......17-20
Front Halfshaft (Front Drive
Shaft) 17-20
Removal & Installation.......17-20
Range Selector Cable 17-19
Adjustment 17-19

ENGINE COOLING 17-21

Engine Coolant....................17-21
Drain & Refill Procedure.....17-21
Flushing.........................17-22
Engine Coolant Crossover
Pipe.............................17-22
Removal & Installation.......17-22
Engine Fan 17-24
Removal & Installation.......17-24
Engine Fan Shroud..............17-24
Removal & Installation.......17-24
Radiator...........................17-24
Removal & Installation.......17-24
Thermostat 17-25
Removal & Installation.......17-25
Water Pump 17-25
Removal & Installation.......17-25

ENGINE ELECTRICAL 17-26

BATTERY SYSTEM............17-26
Battery............................17-26
Removal & Installation.......17-26
CHARGING SYSTEM 17-26
Generator 17-26
Removal & Installation.......17-26
IGNITION SYSTEM 17-27
Firing Order......................17-27
Ignition Coil 17-27
Removal & Installation.......17-27
Ignition Timing...................17-27
Adjustment 17-27

Spark Plugs.......................17-27
Removal & Installation........17-27
STARTING SYSTEM 17-28
Starter 17-28
Removal & Installation.......17-28

ENGINE MECHANICAL......17-28

Accessory Drive Belts 17-28
Accessory Belt Routing.......17-28
Adjustment 17-29
Removal & Installation.......17-29
Air Cleaner Assembly.............17-29
Filter/Element
Replacement...................17-30
Removal & Installation.......17-29
Camshaft..........................17-30
Removal & Installation.......17-30
Catalytic Converter 17-32
Removal & Installation.......17-32
Crankshaft Front Seal............17-32
Removal & Installation.......17-32
Cylinder Head 17-33
Removal & Installation.......17-33
Engine Front Cover 17-35
Removal & Installation.......17-35
Engine Mount Strut &
Bracket..........................17-35
Removal & Installation.......17-35
Engine Oil & Filter 17-36
Engine Pre-lube
Procedure.......................17-36
Replacement 17-36
Exhaust Manifold 17-36
Removal & Installation.......17-36
Intake Manifold 17-38
Removal & Installation.......17-38
Oil Pan 17-41
Removal & Installation.......17-41
Oil Pump..........................17-42
Removal & Installation.......17-42
Piston & Rings 17-43
Positioning 17-43
Rear Main Seal...................17-43
Removal & Installation.......17-43
Timing Chain &
Sprockets.......................17-43
Removal & Installation.......17-43

Valve (Camshaft)Covers 17-44
  Removal & Installation........17-44
Valve Lash 17-47
  Adjustment 17-47

ENGINE PERFORMANCE & EMISSION CONTROLS 17-47

Accelerator Pedal Position
  (APP) Sensor 17-47
  Location 17-47
  Removal & Installation........17-47
Barometric (BARO) Pressure
  Sensor 17-47
  Location 17-47
  Removal & Installation........17-47
Camshaft Position (CMP)
  Sensor 17-47
  Location 17-47
  Removal & Installation........17-48
Crankshaft Position (CKP)
  Sensor 17-48
  CKP System Variation
   Learn Procedure 17-48
  Location 17-48
  Removal & Installation........17-48
Electronic Control Module
  (ECM) 17-49
  Location 17-49
  Removal & Installation........17-49
Engine Coolant Temperature
  (ECT) Sensor 17-50
  Location 17-50
  Removal & Installation........17-50
Heated Oxygen (HO2S)
  Sensor 17-51
  Location 17-51
  Removal & Installation........17-51
Intake Air Temperature (IAT)
  Sensor 17-53
  Location 17-53
Knock Sensor (KS) 17-53
  Location 17-53
  Removal & Installation........17-53
Manifold Absolute Pressure
  (MAP) Sensor 17-53
  Location 17-53
  Removal & Installation........17-54
Mass Air Flow/Intake Air
  Sensor (MAF/IAT)
  Sensor 17-54
  Location 17-54
  Removal & Installation........17-54
Vehicle Speed Sensor
  (VSS) 17-54
  Location 17-54
  Removal & Installation........17-54

FUEL 17-55

GASOLINE FUEL INJECTION SYSTEM 17-55

Fuel Injectors 17-56
  Removal & Installation........17-56
Fuel Rail Assembly.................17-57
  3.9L Engine 17-57
  Removal & Installation........17-57
Fuel Sender Module................17-56
  Removal & Installation........17-56
Fuel System Service
  Precautions 17-55
Fuel Tank 17-58
  Draining 17-58
  Removal & Installation........17-58
Idle Speed 17-59
  Throttle Learn Procedure 17-59
Relieving Fuel System
  Pressure............................17-55
Throttle Body...........................17-60
  Removal & Installation........17-60

HEATING & AIR CONDITIONING SYSTEM 17-61

Blower Motor 17-61
  Removal & Installation........17-61
Compressor 17-61
  Removal & Installation........17-61
Evaporator Core 17-62
  Removal & Installation........17-62
Heater Core 17-62
  Removal & Installation........17-62
HVAC Module 17-62
  Removal & Installation........17-62
Thermal Expansion Valve
  (TXV) 17-63
  Removal & Installation........17-63

PRECAUTIONS 17-11

SPECIFICATIONS AND MAINTENANCE CHARTS 17-4

Additional Maintenance
  Services - Normal 17-10
Additional Maintenance
  Services - Severe................17-10
Brake Specifications 17-8
Camshaft Specifications............17-6
Capacities 17-5
Crankshaft & Connecting Rod
  Specifications 17-6
Engine & Vehicle
  Identification 17-4

Engine Tune-Up
  Specifications 17-4
Fluid Specifications..................17-5
General Engine
  Specifications 17-4
Maintenance I and II Service
  Schedules 17-9
Piston & Ring
  Specifications 17-7
Tire, Wheel & Ball Joint
  Specifications 17-8
Torque Specifications...............17-7
Valve Specifications 17-5
Wheel Alignment......................17-8

STEERING 17-64

Power Steering Gear...............17-64
  Removal & Installation........17-64
Power Steering Pump..............17-65
  Bleeding 17-66
  Fluid Fill Procedure 17-66
  Removal & Installation........17-65

SUSPENSION 17-66

AUTOMATIC LEVEL CONTROL 17-66

Air Compressor.......................17-67
  Removal & Installation........17-67
Air Tubes 17-66
  Removal & Installation........17-66
Automatic Level Control (ALC)
  Trimset Procedure 17-66
Automatic Level Control
  Sensor...............................17-66
  Removal & Installation........17-66

ELECTRONIC SUSPENSION..17-68

Control Module.......................17-68
  Removal & Installation........17-68
Position Sensor.......................17-68
  Removal & Installation........17-68

FRONT SUSPENSION 17-69

Lower Ball Joint 17-69
  Removal & Installation........17-69
Lower Control Arm..................17-69
  Removal & Installation........17-69
Stabilizer Shaft 17-69
  Removal & Installation........17-69
Stabilizer Shaft Link 17-70
  Removal & Installation........17-70
Steering Knuckle 17-70
  Removal & Installation........17-70
Strut & Spring Assembly 17-70
  Removal & Installation........17-70
Wheel Hub & Bearing 17-71
  Removal & Installation........17-71

REAR SUSPENSION **17-71**
  Adjustment Link 17-71
    Removal & Installation........17-71
  Coil Spring...........................17-71
    Removal & Installation........17-71
  Lower Control Arm.................17-72
    Removal & Installation........17-72

  Rear Suspension
    Support..............................17-72
      Removal & Installation........17-72
  Shock Absorber.....................17-73
    Removal & Installation........17-73
  Stabilizer Shaft 17-73
    Removal & Installation........17-73

  Stabilizer Shaft Link 17-73
    Removal & Installation........17-73
  Wheel Hub & Bearing 17-74
    Removal & Installation........17-74

SPECIFICATIONS AND MAINTENANCE CHARTS

ENGINE AND VEHICLE IDENTIFICATION

	Engine							Model Year	
Code ①	Liters (cc)	Cu. In.	Cyl.	Fuel Sys.	Engine Type	Eng. Mfg.		Code ②	Year
1	3.9 (3880)	238	6	SFI	DOHC	BOC		A	2010
M	3.9 (3880)	238	6	Flex Fuel SFI	DOHC	BOC		B	2011
L	4.6 (4565)	281	8	MFI	DOHC	BOC			

① 8th position of VIN

② 10th position of VIN

25742_LUCE_C0001

GENERAL ENGINE SPECIFICATIONS

All measurements are given in inches.

Year	Model	Engine Displacement Liters (cc)	Engine ID/VIN	Fuel System Type	Net Horsepower @ rpm	Net Torque @ rpm (ft. lbs.)	Bore x Stroke (in.)	Compression Ratio	Oil Pressure @ rpm
2010	Lucerne	3.9 (3880)	M	Flex Fuel SFI	227@5700	237@5200	3.90x3.31	9.8:1	30-45 @1850
2011	Lucerne	4.6 (4565)	L	MFI	292@6300	288@4500	3.66x3.31	10.0:1	35@2000

25742_LUCE_C0002

ENGINE TUNE-UP SPECIFICATIONS

Year	Engine Displacement Liters	Engine ID/VIN	Spark Plug Gap (in.)	Ignition Timing (deg.) MT	Ignition Timing (deg.) AT	Fuel Pump (psi)	Idle Speed (rpm) MT	Idle Speed (rpm) AT	Valve Clearance Intake	Valve Clearance Exhaust
2010	3.9	1	0.040	—	①	N/A	—	②	③	③
	3.9	M	0.040	—	①	N/A	—	②	③	③
	4.6	L	0.050	—	①	N/A	—	②	③	③
2011	3.9	1	0.040	—	①	N/A	—	②	③	③
	3.9	M	0.040	—	①	N/A	—	②	③	③
	4.6	L	0.050	—	①	N/A	—	②	③	③

N/A: Information no available.

① Ignition timing is computer controlled; no manual adjustment is required.

② Idle speed is computer controlled; no manual adjustment is required.

③ Valve clearance (valve lash) is automatically maintained by the hydraulic valve lifters; no manual adjustment is required.

25742_LUCE_C0003

CAPACITIES

Year	Model	Engine Displacement Liters	Engine ID/VIN	Engine Oil with Filter	Transmission/axle (pts.)		Drive Axle (pts.)		Transfer Case (pts.)	Fuel Tank (gal.)	Cooling System (qts.)
					Auto.	Manual	Front	Rear			
2010	Lucerne	3.9	M	4.0 qts.	14.8 ①	—	N/A	N/A	—	18.6 ②	③
2011	Lucerne	4.6	L	7.4 qts.	14.8 ①	—	N/A	N/A	—	18.6	③

NOTE: All capacities are approximate. Add fluid gradually and ensure a proper fluid level is obtained.

N/A: Information not available.

① Specification shown is with bottom pan removal; drain and refill.

   With complete overhaul: 4T60-E = 20.0 pts.; 4T80-E = 25.2 pts.

② Specification shown is with federal emission (Tier 2) level

   With California emission (PZEV): 18.3 gal.

③ Consult owner's manual or fill following procedure in "ENGINE COOLING" section.

25742_LUCE_C0004

FLUID SPECIFICATIONS

Year	Model	Engine Disp. Liters	Engine Oil	Auto. Trans.	Drive Axle		Power Steering Fluid	Brake Master Cylinder	Cooling System
					Front	Rear			
2010	Lucerne	3.9	①	Dexron® III	N/A	N/A	①	DOT 3	Dex-Cool
2011	Lucerne	4.6	①	Dexron® III	N/A	N/A	①	DOT 3	Dex-Cool

① The Recommended Fluids and Lubricants information is found in the Owner's Manual. Refer to the Maintenance Schedule subsection of the Owner's Manual.

25742_LUCE_C0005

VALVE SPECIFICATIONS

Year	Engine Displacement Liters	Engine ID/VIN	Seat Angle (deg.)	Face Angle (deg.)	Spring Test Pressure (lbs. @ in.) ①	Spring Free-Length (in.)	Spring Installed Height (in.)	Stem-to-Guide Clearance (in.)		Stem Diameter (in.)	
								Intake	Exhaust	Intake	Exhaust
2010	3.9	1	46	45	76.4@ 1.701	2.080	1.840	0.0009-0.0025	0.0009-0.0025	N/A	N/A
	3.9	M	46	45	76.4@ 1.701	2.080	1.840	0.0009-0.0025	0.0009-0.0025	N/A	N/A
	4.6	L	45.75	45	47.5-52.4@ 1.378	1.6059-1.72.01	1.378 ①	0.0011-0.0027	0.0020-0.0039	0.2331-0.2339	0.2331-0.2339
2011	3.9	1	46	45	76.4@ 1.701	2.080	1.840	0.0009-0.0025	0.0009-0.0025	N/A	N/A
	3.9	M	46	45	76.4@ 1.701	2.080	1.840	0.0009-0.0025	0.0009-0.0025	N/A	N/A
	4.6	L	45.75	45	47.5-52.4@ 1.378	1.6059-1.72.01	1.378 ①	0.0011-0.0027	0.0020-0.0039	0.2331-0.2339	0.2331-0.2339

N/A: Information not available.

① Closed

25742_LUCE_C0006

CAMSHAFT SPECIFICATIONS

All measurements in inches unless noted

Year	Engine Displacement Liters	Engine Code/VIN	Journal Diameter	Brg. Oil Clearance	Shaft End-play	Runout	Journal Bore	Lobe Height Intake	Lobe Height Exhaust
2010	3.9	1	2.024-2.025	0.0004	N/A	0.001	①	0.2727	0.2727
	3.9	M	2.024-2.025	0.0004	N/A	0.001	①	0.2727	0.2727
	4.6	L	1.0610-1.0619	0.0020-0.0030	0.0050-0.0087	0.002	N/A	0.2421	0.2339
2011	3.9	1	2.024-2.025	0.0004	N/A	0.001	①	0.2727	0.2727
	3.9	M	2.024-2.025	0.0004	N/A	0.001	①	0.2727	0.2727
	4.6	L	1.0610-1.0619	0.0020-0.0030	0.0050-0.0087	0.002	N/A	0.2421	0.2339

N/A: Information not available.

① Front and rear bore diameter: 2.175-2.177

Middle #2 & #3 bore diameter: 2.155-2.157

25742_LUCE_C0007

CRANKSHAFT AND CONNECTING ROD SPECIFICATIONS

All measurements are given in inches.

Year	Engine Displacement Liters	Engine ID/VIN	Crankshaft Main Brg. Journal Dia.	Crankshaft Main Brg. Oi Clearance	Crankshaft Shaft End-play	Thrust on No.	Connecting Rod Journal Diameter	Connecting Rod Oil Clearance	Connecting Rod Side Clearance
2010	3.9	1	N/A	0.0008-0.0025 ①	0.0024-0.0083	3	2.248-2.249	0.0007-0.0024	0.008-0.009
	3.9	M	N/A	0.0008-0.0025 ①	0.0024-0.0083	3	2.248-2.249	0.0007-0.0024	0.008-0.009
	4.6	L	2.5335-2.5341	0.0006-0.0022	0.0020-0.0197	3	2.1239-2.1245	0.0010-0.0030	0.0079-0.0197
2011	3.9	1	N/A	0.0008-0.0025 ①	0.0024-0.0083	3	2.248-2.249	0.0007-0.0024	0.008-0.009
	3.9	M	N/A	0.0008-0.0025 ①	0.0024-0.0083	3	2.248-2.249	0.0007-0.0024	0.008-0.009
	4.6	L	2.5335-2.5341	0.0006-0.0022	0.0020-0.0197	3	2.1239-2.1245	0.0010-0.0030	0.0079-0.0197

N/A: Information not available.

① Except #3 thrust bearing clearance shown

#3 thrust bearing clearance: 0.0012-0.0030

25742_LUCE_C0008

PISTON AND RING SPECIFICATIONS

All measurements are given in inches.

Year	Engine Displacement Liters	Engine ID/VIN	Piston Clearance	Ring Gap			Ring Side Clearance		
				Top Compression	Bottom Compression	Oil Control	Top Compression	Bottom Compression	Oil Control
2010	3.9	1	0.0003-0.0018	0.006-0.011	0.009-0.017	0.060-0.025	0.001-0.002	0.0007-0.0020	0.0004
	3.9	M	0.0003-0.0018	0.006-0.011	0.009-0.017	0.060-0.025	0.001-0.002	0.0007-0.0020	0.0004
	4.6	L	0.0008-0.0020	0.0098-0.0157	0.0138-0.0020	0.0098-0.0299	0.0016-0.0037	0.0016-0.0037	①
2011	3.9	1	0.0003-0.0018	0.006-0.011	0.009-0.017	0.060-0.025	0.001-0.002	0.0007-0.0020	0.0004
	3.9	M	0.0003-0.0018	0.006-0.011	0.009-0.017	0.060-0.025	0.001-0.002	0.0007-0.0020	0.0004
	4.6	L	0.0008-0.0020	0.0098-0.0157	0.0138-0.0020	0.0098-0.0299	0.0016-0.0037	0.0016-0.0037	①

① No clearance; self-sealing

25742_LUCE_C0009

TORQUE SPECIFICATIONS

All readings in ft. lbs.

Year	Engine Disp. Liters	Engine ID/VIN	Cylinder Head Bolts	Main Bearing Bolts	Rod Bearing Bolts	Crankshaft Damper Bolts	Flywheel Bolts	Manifold		Spark Plugs	Oil Pan Drain Plug
								Intake	Exhaust		
2010	3.9	1	①	②	③	④	52	⑤	15	11	18
	3.9	M	①	②	③	④	52	⑤	15	11	18
	4.6	L	⑥	⑦	⑧	⑨	⑩	⑪	18	11	15
2011	3.9	1	①	②	③	④	52	⑤	15	11	18
	3.9	M	①	②	③	④	52	⑤	15	11	18
	4.6	L	⑥	⑦	⑧	⑨	⑩	⑪	18	11	15

① 1st pass: 44 ft. lbs., in sequence

  2nd pass: additional 140 degrees, in sequence

② 1st pass: 37 ft. lbs., in sequence

  2nd pass: additional 77 degrees, in sequence

③ 1st pass: 18 ft. lbs., in sequence

  2nd pass: additional 110 degrees, in sequence

④ 1st pass, 92 ft. lbs.

  2nd pass: additional 130 degrees

⑤ Lower manifold, center: 1st pass, 62 inch. lbs.

  Lower manifold, center: 2nd pass: 12 ft. lbs.

  Lower manifold, corner: 1st pass, 10 ft. lbs.

  Lower manifold, corner: 2nd pass: 18 ft. lbs.

  Upper manifold, stud/nut: 18 ft. lbs.

⑥ M11 bolts:

  1st pass: 30 ft. lbs., in sequence

  2nd pass: additional 70 degrees, in sequence

  3rd pass: additional 60 degrees, in sequence

  4th pass: additional 45 degrees, in sequence

  M6 bolts: 106 inch. lbs.

⑦ 1st pass, 15 ft. lbs., in sequence

  2nd pass: additional 65 degrees, in sequence

⑧ 1st pass, 22 ft. lbs.

  2nd pass: back off to zero

  3rd pass: 18 ft. lbs.

  4th pass: additional 110 degrees

⑨ 1st pass: 37 ft. lbs.

  2nd pass: additional 120 degrees.

⑩ To crankshaft:

  1st pass: 22 ft. lbs.

  2nd pass: additional 50 degrees

  To torque converter: 44 ft. lbs.

⑪ 89 inch. lbs.

25742_LUCE_C0010

WHEEL ALIGNMENT

Year	Model		Caster Range (+/-Deg.)	Caster Preferred Setting (Deg.)	Camber Range (+/-Deg.)	Camber Preferred Setting (Deg.)	Toe-in (Deg.)
2010	Lucerne	F	0.75	5.40	0.75	0.00	0.20
		R	—	—	—	—	0.20
2011	Lucerne	F	0.75	5.40	0.75	0.00	0.20
		R	—	—	—	—	0.20

25742_LUCE_C0011

TIRE, WHEEL AND BALL JOINT SPECIFICATIONS

Year	Model	OEM Tires Standard	OEM Tires Optional	Tire Pressures (psi) Front	Tire Pressures (psi) Rear	Wheel Size	Ball Joint Inspection	Lug Nut (ft. lbs.)
2010	Lucerne	①	①	②	②	①	③	100
2011	Lucerne	①	①	②	②	①	③	100

OEM: Original Equipment Manufacturer

PSI: Pounds Per Square Inch

NA: Information not available

① Tire and wheel sizes and options vary according to model trim level and equipment. Consult owner's manual, dealership or local tire dealer for size information.

② For the correct inflation pressures refer to the vehicle's tire placard.

③ See "Suspension" section for ball joint information. Ball joint lash is measured with a dial gauge.

25742_LUCE_C0012

BRAKE SPECIFICATIONS

All measurements in inches unless noted

Year	Model		Brake Disc Original Thickness	Brake Disc Minimum Thickness	Brake Disc Max. Runout	Brake Drum Diameter Original Inside Diameter	Brake Drum Diameter Max. Wear Limit	Brake Drum Diameter Maximum Machine Diamter	Minimum Pad/Lining Thickness Front	Minimum Pad/Lining Thickness Rear	Brake Caliper Bracket Bolts (ft. lbs.)	Brake Caliper Mounting Bolts (ft. lbs.)
2010	Lucerne	F	1.181	1.126	0.0020	—	—	—	①	—	133	27 ②
		R	0.472	0.413	0.0020	—	—	—	—	①	94	25 ②
2011	Lucerne	F	1.181	1.126	0.0020	—	—	—	①	—	133	27 ②
		R	0.472	0.413	0.0020	—	—	—	—	①	94	25 ②

F: Front

R: Rear

NA: Information not available

① Pads use built-in wear indicators; when indicators are exposed, squealing indicates pads require replacement.

② Caliper guide pin bolts.

25742_LUCE_C0013

MAINTENANCE I AND II SERVICE SCHEDULES
LUCERNE

When the CHANGE ENGINE OIL light appears, certain services and inspections are required.

Required services are described as Maintenance I and Maintenance II.

The first service of a vehicle should be Maintenance I, and the second service should be Maintenance II.

Alternate between the 2 services thereafter. However, in some cases, Maintenance II may be required more often.

Maintenance I: Use Maintenance I if the CHANGE ENGINE OIL light comes on within 10 months since the vehicle was purchased or, if Maintenance II was performed.

Maintenance II: Use Maintenance II if the previous service performed was Maintenance I. Always use Maintenance II whenever the CHANGE ENGINE OIL light comes on 10 months or more since the last service, or, if the CHANGE ENGINE OIL light has not come on at all for one year.

Service Item	Maintenance I	Maintenance II
Change the engine oil and filter.	✓	✓
Reset the oil life system.	✓	✓
Visually inspect the vehicle for leaks or damage. A fluid loss in the vehicle system could indicate a problem. Inspect, repair and add fluid to the system if necessary.	✓	✓
Inspect the engine air cleaner filter. If necessary, replace the filter.	✓	✓
Rotate the tires. Inspect the tire inflation pressures and the tire wear.	✓	✓
Visually inspect the brake lines and hoses for proper hook-up, binding, leaks, cracks, chafing, etc. Inspect the disc brake pads for wear and the rotors for surface condition. Inspect the drum brake linings for wear or cracks. Inspect other brake parts, including drums, wheel cylinders, calipers, parking brake, etc. Inspect the parking brake adjustment.	✓	✓
Inspect engine coolant and windshield washer fluid levels. Add fluid as needed.	✓	✓
Inspect the suspension and steering components. Inspect the front and rear suspension and the steering system for damaged, loose or missing parts, or signs of wear. Inspect the power steering lines and the hoses for proper hook-up, binding, leaks, cracks, chafing, etc.	—	✓
Visually inspect the coolant hoses and replace the hoses if they are cracked, swollen or deteriorated. Inspect all pipes, fittings and clamps; replace with GM parts as needed. To help ensure proper operation, a pressure test of the cooling system and pressure cap and cleaning the outside of the radiator and air conditioning condenser is recommended at least once a year.	—	✓
Ensure the safety belt reminder light and all the belts, buckles, latch plates, retractors and anchorages are working properly. Look for any other loose or damaged safety belt system parts. If you see anything that might keep a safety belt system from working correctly, repair or replaced the damaged part. Replace torn or frayed safety belts, refer to Operational and Functional Checks in Seat Belts. Inspect for any opened or broken air bag coverings, and repair or replace as needed. The air bag system does require regular maintenance.	—	✓
Lubricate the body components.	—	✓
Lubricate all key lock cylinders, hood latch assemblies, secondary latches, pivots, spring anchor and release pawl, hood and door hinges, rear folding seats and liftgate hinges. Frequent lubrication may be required when exposed to a corrosive environment, refer to Fluid and Lubricant Recommendations . Applying dielectric silicone grease GM P/N 12345579 (Canadian P/N 1974984) or equivalent on the weatherstrips with a clean cloth.	—	✓
Inspect the transaxle fluid level and add fluid as needed.	—	✓
Inspect the wiper blades and replace as necessary	✓	✓
Inspect the throttle system.	—	✓
Replace the passenger compartment air filter.	—	✓

To reset the CHANGE ENGINE OIL light:

1. Turn the ignition key to the ON/RUN position with the engine OFF.

2. Press and release the stem in the lower center of the instrument cluster until the OIL LIFE message is displayed.

3. Once the alternating OIL LIFE and RESET messages appear, press and hold the stem until several beeps sound.
   This confirms that the oil life system has been reset to 100 percent.

4. Turn the ignition key to the OFF position.
   If the CHANGE ENGINE OIL message comes back on when the vehicle is started, the engine oil life system has not been reset. Repeat the procedure.

ADDITIONAL MAINTENANCE SERVICES - NORMAL
LUCERNE

TO BE SERVICED	TYPE OF SERVICE	VEHICLE MILEAGE INTERVAL (x1000)					
		25	50	75	100	125	150
Engine coolant	Replace						✓
Air cleaner filter	Replace		✓		✓		✓
Automatic transaxle fluid	Replace				✓		
Spark plugs	Replace				✓		
Exhaust system & heat shields	Service/Inspect	✓	✓	✓	✓	✓	✓
Fuel system	Inspect	✓	✓	✓	✓	✓	✓
Accessory drive belt	Replace						✓
Evaporative control system	Inspect		✓		✓		✓

25742_LUCE_C0015

ADDITIONAL MAINTENANCE SERVICES - SEVERE
LUCERNE

TO BE SERVICED	TYPE OF SERVICE	VEHICLE MILEAGE INTERVAL (x1000)					
		25	50	75	100	125	150
Engine coolant	Replace						✓
Air cleaner filter	Replace	✓	✓	✓	✓	✓	✓
Automatic transaxle fluid & filter	Replace		✓		✓		✓
Spark plugs	Replace				✓		
Exhaust system & heat shields	Service/Inspect	✓	✓	✓	✓	✓	✓
Fuel system	Inspect	✓	✓	✓	✓	✓	✓
Accessory drive belt	Inspect						✓
Evaporative control system	Inspect		✓		✓		✓

25742_LUCE_C0016

PRECAUTIONS

Before servicing any vehicle, please be sure to read all of the following precautions, which deal with personal safety, prevention of component damage, and important points to take into consideration when servicing a motor vehicle:

• Never open, service or drain the radiator or cooling system when the engine is hot; serious burns can occur from the steam and hot coolant.

• Observe all applicable safety precautions when working around fuel. Whenever servicing the fuel system, always work in a well-ventilated area. Do not allow fuel spray or vapors to come in contact with a spark, open flame, or excessive heat (a hot drop light, for example). Keep a dry chemical fire extinguisher near the work area. Always keep fuel in a container specifically designed for fuel storage; also, always properly seal fuel containers to avoid the possibility of fire or explosion. Refer to the additional fuel system precautions later in this section.

• Fuel injection systems often remain pressurized, even after the engine has been turned **OFF**. The fuel system pressure must be relieved before disconnecting any fuel lines. Failure to do so may result in fire and/or personal injury.

• Brake fluid often contains polyglycol ethers and polyglycols. Avoid contact with the eyes and wash your hands thoroughly after handling brake fluid. If you do get brake fluid in your eyes, flush your eyes with clean, running water for 15 minutes. If eye irritation persists, or if you have taken

brake fluid internally, IMMEDIATELY seek medical assistance.

• The EPA warns that prolonged contact with used engine oil may cause a number of skin disorders, including cancer. You should make every effort to minimize your exposure to used engine oil. Protective gloves should be worn when changing oil. Wash your hands and any other exposed skin areas as soon as possible after exposure to used engine oil. Soap and water, or waterless hand cleaner should be used.

• All new vehicles are now equipped with an air bag system, often referred to as a Supplemental Restraint System (SRS) or Supplemental Inflatable Restraint (SIR) system. The system must be disabled before performing service on or around system components, steering column, instrument panel components, wiring and sensors. Failure to follow safety and disabling procedures could result in accidental air bag deployment, possible personal injury and unnecessary system repairs.

• Always wear safety goggles when working with, or around, the air bag system. When carrying a non-deployed air bag, be sure the bag and trim cover are pointed away from your body. When placing a non-deployed air bag on a work surface, always face the bag and trim cover upward, away from the surface. This will reduce the motion of the module if it is accidentally deployed. Refer to the additional air bag system precautions later in this section.

• Clean, high quality brake fluid from a sealed container is essential to the safe and

proper operation of the brake system. You should always buy the correct type of brake fluid for your vehicle. If the brake fluid becomes contaminated, completely flush the system with new fluid. Never reuse any brake fluid. Any brake fluid that is removed from the system should be discarded. Also, do not allow any brake fluid to come in contact with a painted surface; it will damage the paint.

• Never operate the engine without the proper amount and type of engine oil; doing so WILL result in severe engine damage.

• Timing belt maintenance is extremely important. Many models utilize an interference-type, non-freewheeling engine. If the timing belt breaks, the valves in the cylinder head may strike the pistons, causing potentially serious (also time-consuming and expensive) engine damage. Refer to the maintenance interval charts for the recommended replacement interval for the timing belt, and to the timing belt section for belt replacement and inspection.

• Disconnecting the negative battery cable on some vehicles may interfere with the functions of the on-board computer system(s) and may require the computer to undergo a relearning process once the negative battery cable is reconnected.

• When servicing drum brakes, only disassemble and assemble one side at a time, leaving the remaining side intact for reference.

• Only an MVAC-trained, EPA-certified automotive technician should service the air conditioning system or its components.

BRAKES   ANTI-LOCK BRAKE SYSTEM (ABS)

GENERAL INFORMATION

PRECAUTIONS

• Certain components within the ABS system are not intended to be serviced or repaired individually.

• Do not use rubber hoses or other parts not specifically specified for and ABS system. When using repair kits, replace all parts included in the kit. Partial or incorrect repair may lead to functional problems and require the replacement of components.

• Lubricate rubber parts with clean, fresh brake fluid to ease assembly. Do not use shop air to clean parts; damage to rubber components may result.

• Use only DOT 3 brake fluid from an unopened container.

• If any hydraulic component or line is

removed or replaced, it may be necessary to bleed the entire system.

• A clean repair area is essential. Always clean the reservoir and cap thoroughly before removing the cap. The slightest amount of dirt in the fluid may plug an orifice and impair the system function. Perform repairs after components have been thoroughly cleaned; use only denatured alcohol to clean components. Do not allow ABS components to come into contact with any substance containing mineral oil; this includes used shop rags.

• The Anti-Lock control unit is a microprocessor similar to other computer units in the vehicle. Ensure that the ignition switch is **OFF** before removing or installing controller harnesses. Avoid static electricity discharge at or near the controller.

• If any arc welding is to be done on the vehicle, the control unit should be unplugged before welding operations begin.

ELECTRONIC BRAKE CONTROL MODULE (EBCM)

REMOVAL & INSTALLATION

See Figure 1.

✳✳ CAUTION

Always connect or disconnect the wiring harness connector from the EBCM/EBTCM with the ignition switch in the OFF position. Failure to observe this precaution could result in damage to the EBCM/EBTCM.

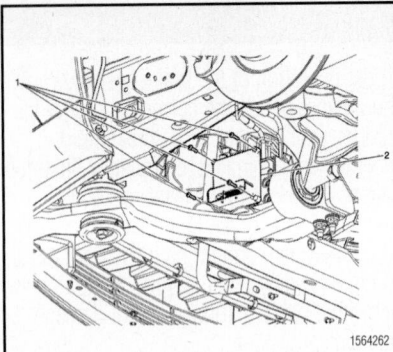

Fig. 1 Removing the bolts (1) and the EBCM (2)

1. Raise and support the vehicle.
2. Remove the left front tire and wheel.
3. Remove the left front inner wheelhouse liner.
4. Thoroughly clean the area around the electronic brake control module (EBCM) of all dirt and debris.
5. Remove the EBCM bolts and the EBCM from the vehicle.
6. Disconnect the electrical connector from the electronic brake control module.

To install:

7. Clean the sealing surfaces of the EBCM and the brake pressure modulator valve with denatured alcohol and a clean shop cloth.
8. Position the EBCM and connect the electrical connector.

➡️**If a new electronic brake control module is installed, program the EBCM.**

9. After the installation is complete, tighten the bolts in a cross pattern beginning with the upper left bolt. Tighten to 27 inch lbs. (3 Nm).

EBCM PROGRAMMING

1. Note the following before starting the programming:
   - DO NOT program a control module unless you are directed by a service procedure or you are directed by a General Motors service bulletin. Programming a control module at any other time will not permanently correct a customer's concern.
   - It is essential that the TIS terminal, MDI, and/or Scan Tool, is equipped with the latest software before performing service programming.
   - Due to the time requirements of programming a controller, install EL-49642 SPS Programming Support Tool (or equivalent) to maintain system voltage. Stable battery voltage is critical during programming. Any fluctuation, spiking, over voltage or loss of voltage will interrupt programming. If the above tool is not available, DO NOT connect a battery charger, connect a fully charged 12V jumper or booster pack disconnected from the AC voltage supply.
   - Some modules will require additional programming/setup events to be performed before or after programming.
   - Some vehicles may require the use of a CANDi or MDI module for programming.
   - Review the appropriate service information for these procedures.
   - DTCs may set during programming. Clear DTCs after programming is complete.
   - Clearing powertrain DTCs will set the Inspection/Maintenance (I/M) system status indicators to NO.
2. Ensure the following conditions are met before programming a control module:
   a. Ensure there is not a charging system concern. All charging system concerns must be repaired before programming a control module.
   b. Battery voltage is greater than 12 volts but less than 16 volts. The battery must be fully charged before programming the control module.
3. Turn OFF or disable any system that may put a load on the vehicles battery, such as the following components:
   - Interior lights
   - Exterior lights including daytime running lights (DRL)—Applying the parking brake, on most vehicles, disables the DRL system
   - Heating, ventilation, and air conditioning (HVAC) systems
   - Engine cooling fans
   - Radio, etc.
4. The ignition switch must be in the proper position. SPS prompts you to turn ON the ignition, with the engine OFF. DO NOT change the position of the ignition switch during the programming procedure, unless instructed to do so.
5. Make certain all tool connections are secure, including the following components and circuits:
   - Scan Tool
   - The RS-232 communication cable port
   - The connection at the data link connector (DLC)
   - The voltage supply circuits
   - MDI
   - The USB, Ethernet or Wireless communication port
   - The connection at the data link connector (DLC)

✳️✳️ CAUTION

DO NOT disturb the tool harnesses while programming. If an interruption occurs during the programming procedure, programming failure or control module damage may occur.

6. In the event of an interrupted or unsuccessful programming event, perform the following steps:
   a. DO NOT turn the ignition OFF. Ensure that all control module and DLC connections are secure and the TIS terminal operating software is up to date.
   b. Attempt to reprogram the control module.
   c. If the control module can still not be programmed, turn the ignition OFF for at least one minute.
   d. Turn the ignition ON and attempt to reprogram the control module. The control module should program.
7. If the control module still cannot be programmed, replace the control module.

ELECTRONIC TRACTION CONTROL SWITCH

REMOVAL & INSTALLATION

See Figure 2.

➡️**The traction control switch on column shift equipped vehicles is integral to the shift lever.**

1. Remove the floor shift control knob.
2. Remove the front floor console trim.
   a. Lift the rear edge of the front floor console trim plate using a flat-bladed, plastic tool to release the 4 retaining clips.
3. Detach the electrical connector.
4. Remove the traction control switch.
   a. Press the retaining tabs to release the traction control switch from the front floor console trim plate.

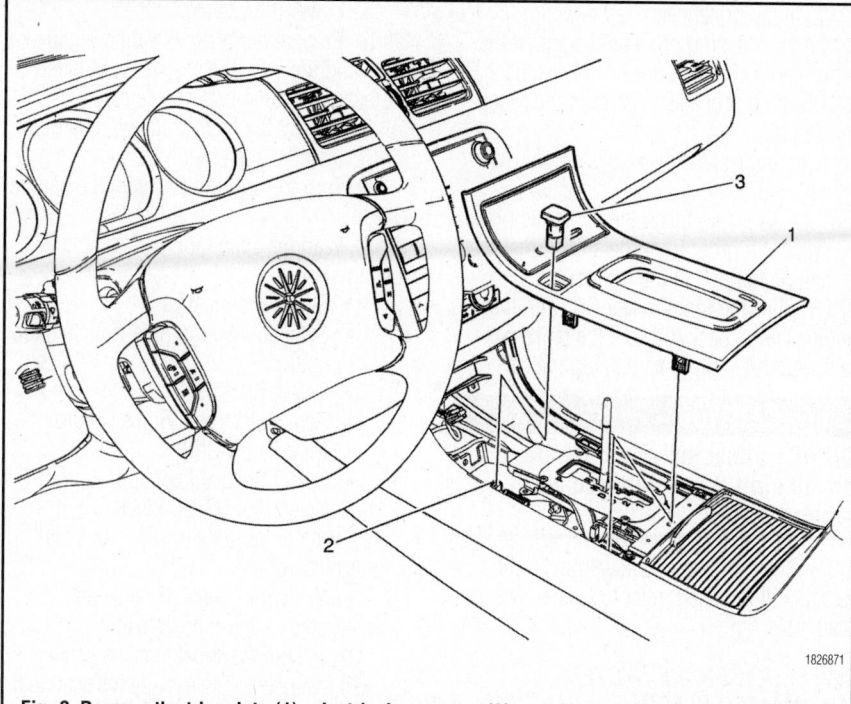

Fig. 2 Remove the trim plate (1), electrical connector (2) and the traction control switch (3)

REMOVAL & INSTALLATION

See Figure 3.

1. Remove the driver's seat.
2. Disconnect the yaw rate sensor/lateral accelerometer electrical connector.
3. Remove the nuts and remove the yaw rate sensor/lateral accelerometer.
4. Installation is the reverse of the removal procedure.
5. During installation use the special functions menu on the scan tool, reset the yaw sensor.

Perform the "Diagnostic System Check— Vehicle", following scan tool instructions.

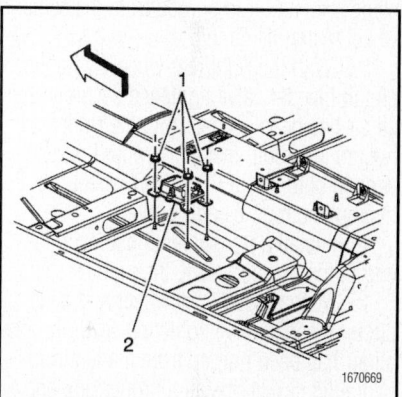

Fig. 3 Showing vehicle yaw rate sensor mounting

5. Installation is the reverse of the removal procedure.

SPEED SENSORS

REMOVAL & INSTALLATION

Passive wheel speed sensors— Each wheel speed sensor receives a 5V reference voltage from the Electronic Brake Control Module (EBCM) and provides an alternating current square wave signal to the EBCM. As the wheel spins, the wheel speed sensor produces an AC signal. The EBCM uses this AC signal to calculate wheel speed.

➡**The wheel speed sensors are replaceable only as part of the wheel hub and bearing assemblies. See "SUSPENSION" section.**

BRAKES

BLEEDING THE BRAKE SYSTEM

BLEEDING PROCEDURE

MANUAL BLEEDING PROCEDURE

1. Place a clean shop cloth beneath the brake master cylinder to prevent brake fluid spills.
2. With the ignition OFF and the brakes cool, apply the brakes 3–5 times, or until the brake pedal effort increases significantly, in order to deplete the brake booster power reserve.
3. If you have performed a brake master cylinder bench bleeding on this vehicle, or if you disconnected the brake pipes from the master cylinder, you must perform the following steps:

  a. Ensure that the brake master cylinder reservoir is full to the maximum-fill level. If necessary, add GM approved brake fluid from a clean, sealed brake fluid container.

  b. If removal of the reservoir cap and diaphragm is necessary, clean the outside of the reservoir on and around the cap prior to removal.

  c. With the rear brake pipe installed securely to the master cylinder, loosen and separate the front brake pipe from the front port of the brake master cylinder.

  d. Allow a small amount of brake fluid to gravity bleed from the open port of the master cylinder.

  e. Reconnect the brake pipe to the master cylinder port and tighten securely.

  f. Have an assistant slowly depress the brake pedal fully and maintain steady pressure on the pedal.

  g. Loosen the same brake pipe to purge air from the open port of the master cylinder.

  h. Tighten the brake pipe, then have the assistant slowly release the brake pedal.

  i. Wait 15 seconds, then repeat the above steps until all air is purged from the same port of the master cylinder.

  j. With the front brake pipe installed securely to the master cylinder, after all air has been purged from the front port of the master cylinder, loosen and separate the rear brake pipe from the master cylinder, then repeat the previous steps.

  k. After completing the final master cylinder port bleeding procedure, ensure that both of the brake pipe-to-master cylinder fittings are properly tightened.

4. Fill the brake master cylinder reservoir with GM approved brake fluid from a clean, sealed brake fluid container. Ensure that the brake master cylinder reservoir remains at least half-full during this bleeding procedure. Add fluid as needed to maintain the proper level.

5. Clean the outside of the reservoir on and around the reservoir cap prior to removing the cap and diaphragm.

6. Install a proper box-end wrench onto the RIGHT REAR wheel hydraulic circuit bleeder valve.

7. Install a transparent hose over the end of the bleeder valve.

8. Submerge the open end of the transparent hose into a transparent container partially filled with GM approved brake fluid from a clean, sealed brake fluid container.

9. Have an assistant slowly depress the brake pedal fully and maintain steady pressure on the pedal.

10. Loosen the bleeder valve to purge air from the wheel hydraulic circuit.

11. Tighten the bleeder valve, then have the assistant slowly release the brake pedal.

12. Wait 15 seconds, then repeat these steps until all air is purged from the same wheel hydraulic circuit.

13. With the right rear wheel hydraulic circuit bleeder valve tightened securely, after all air has been purged from the right rear hydraulic circuit, install a proper box-end wrench onto the LEFT FRONT wheel hydraulic circuit bleeder valve.

14. Install a transparent hose over the end of the bleeder valve, then repeat steps.

15. With the left front wheel hydraulic circuit bleeder valve tightened securely, after all air has been purged from the left front hydraulic circuit, install a proper box-end wrench onto the LEFT REAR wheel hydraulic circuit bleeder valve.

16. Install a transparent hose over the end of the bleeder valve, then repeat steps.

17. With the left rear wheel hydraulic circuit bleeder valve tightened securely, after all air has been purged from the left rear hydraulic circuit, install a proper box-end wrench onto the RIGHT FRONT wheel hydraulic circuit bleeder valve.

18. Install a transparent hose over the end of the bleeder valve, then repeat steps.

19. After completing the final wheel hydraulic circuit bleeding procedure, ensure that each of the 4 wheel hydraulic circuit bleeder valves are properly tightened.

20. Fill the brake master cylinder reservoir to the maximum-fill level with GM approved brake fluid from a clean, sealed brake fluid container.

21. Slowly depress and release the brake pedal. Observe the feel of the brake pedal.

➡**If it is determined that air was induced into the system upstream of the ABS modulator prior to servicing, the "Antilock Brake System Automated Bleed" must be performed.**

22. If the brake pedal feels spongy, repeat the bleeding procedure again. If the brake pedal still feels spongy after repeating the bleeding procedure, perform the following steps:

a. Inspect the brake system for external leaks.

b. Pressure bleed the hydraulic brake system in order to purge any air that may still be trapped in the system.

23. Turn the ignition key ON, with the engine OFF. Check to see if the brake system warning lamp remains illuminated.

✳✳ CAUTION

DO NOT allow the vehicle to be driven until it is diagnosed and repaired.

24. If the brake system warning lamp remains illuminated, refer to further system diagnosis.

ANTI-LOCK BRAKE SYSTEM AUTOMATED BLEED

➡**Before performing the ABS Automated Bleed Procedure, first perform a manual or pressure bleed of the base hydraulic brake system. See "Manual Bleed Procedure".**

The automated bleed procedure must be performed when a new brake pressure modulator valve (BPMV) is installed, because the secondary circuits of the new BPMV are not prefilled with brake fluid.

The automated bleed procedure is recommended when one of the following conditions exist:

• Base brake system bleeding does not achieve the desired pedal height or feel.

• Extreme loss of brake fluid has occurred.

• Air ingestion is suspected in the secondary circuits of the brake modulator assembly

The ABS Automated Bleed Procedure uses a scan tool to cycle the system solenoid valves and run the pump in order to purge any air from the secondary circuits. These circuits are normally closed off, and are only opened during system initialization at vehicle start up and during ABS operation. The automated bleed procedure opens these secondary circuits and allows any air trapped in these circuits to flow out away from the brake modulator assembly, which is then forced out at the brake corners by the pressure bleeder.

1. Raise and support the vehicle.
2. Remove the tire and wheel assemblies.
3. Inspect the brake system for leaks and visual damage.

4. Lower the vehicle.

5. Prepare the brake bleeding equipment and the vehicle for a pressure bleed of the base hydraulic brake system.

6. Inspect the battery state of charge.

7. Install a scan tool.

8. Turn the ignition ON, with the engine OFF.

9. With the scan tool, perform the following steps:

• Select Diagnostics
• Select the appropriate vehicle information
• Select Chassis
• Select Electronic Brake Control Module (EBCM)
• Select Special Functions
• Select Automated Bleed

10. With an assistant ready, raise and support the vehicle.

a. Apply the brake pedal when instructed, using moderate effort.

b. Ensure the pedal remains applied until instructed to release by the scan tool.

c. Do not exceed the time period allowed by the scan tool for having the bleeder valves open.

11. The bleed sequence for each corner is as follows:

• Left front
• Right front
• Right rear
• Left rear

12. Perform the automated bleed procedure as instructed by the scan tool.

13. If the automated bleed procedure is aborted, a malfunction exists. If a DTC is detected, diagnose the DTC.

14. After completion of the automated bleed procedure, press and hold the brake pedal to inspect for pedal firmness.

15. If the brake pedal feels spongy, repeat the bleed procedure completely.

16. Remove the scan tool.

17. Install the tire and wheel assemblies.

18. Lower the vehicle.

19. Adjust the brake fluid level.

20. Road test the vehicle while confirming the brake pedal remains high and firm.

MASTER CYLINDER BENCH BLEEDING

1. Secure the mounting flange of the brake master cylinder in a bench vise so that the rear of the primary piston is accessible.

2. Remove the master cylinder reservoir cap and diaphragm.

3. Install suitable fittings to the master cylinder ports that match the type of flare seat required and also provide for hose attachment.

4. Install transparent hoses to the fittings installed to the master cylinder ports, then route the hoses into the master cylinder reservoir.

5. Fill the master cylinder reservoir to at least the half-way point with GM approved brake fluid from a clean, sealed brake fluid container.

6. Ensure that the ends of the transparent hoses running into the master cylinder reservoir are fully submerged in the brake fluid.

7. Using a smooth, round-ended tool, depress and release the primary piston as far as it will travel, a depth of about 1 in. (25 mm), several times. Observe the flow of fluid coming from the ports.

8. As air is bled from the primary and secondary pistons, the effort required to depress the primary piston will increase and the amount of travel will decrease.

9. Continue to depress and release the primary piston until fluid flows freely from the ports with no evidence of air bubbles.

10. Remove the transparent hoses from the master cylinder reservoir.

11. Install the master cylinder reservoir cap and diaphragm.

12. Remove the fittings with the transparent hoses from the master cylinder ports. Wrap the master cylinder with a clean shop cloth to prevent brake fluid spills.

13. Remove the master cylinder from the vise.

FLUID FILL PROCEDURE

1. Visually inspect the brake fluid level through the brake master cylinder reservoir.

2. If the brake fluid level is at or below the half-full point during routine fluid checks, the brake system should be inspected for wear and possible brake fluid leaks.

3. If the brake fluid level is at or below the half-full point during routine fluid checks, and an inspection of the brake system did not reveal wear or brake fluid leaks, the brake fluid may be topped-off up to the maximum-fill level.

4. If brake system service was just completed, the brake fluid may be topped-off up to the maximum-fill level.

5. If the brake fluid level is above the half-full point, adding brake fluid is not recommended under normal conditions.

6. If brake fluid is to be added to the master cylinder reservoir, clean the outside of the reservoir on and around the reservoir cap prior to removing the cap and diaphragm. Use only GM approved brake fluid from a clean, sealed brake fluid container.

BRAKES

❄ CAUTION

Dust and dirt accumulating on brake parts during normal use may contain asbestos fibers from production or aftermarket brake linings. Breathing excessive concentrations of asbestos fibers can cause serious bodily harm. Exercise care when servicing brake parts. Do not sand or grind brake lining unless equipment used is designed to contain the dust residue. Do not clean brake parts with compressed air or by dry brushing. Cleaning should be done by dampening the brake components with a fine mist of water, then wiping the brake components clean with a dampened cloth. Dispose of cloth and all residue containing asbestos fibers in an impermeable container with the appropriate label. Follow practices prescribed by the Occupational Safety and Health Administration (OSHA) and the Environmental Protection Agency (EPA) for the handling, processing, and disposing of dust or debris that may contain asbestos fibers.

BRAKE CALIPER

REMOVAL & INSTALLATION

1. Remove the tire and wheel assembly.
2. Remove the brake hose from the brake caliper.

3. Remove the guide pin bolts.
   a. Use a backup wrench on the brake caliper guide to hold the guide pin stationary.
4. Remove the brake caliper. Cap or plug the brake hose to prevent the contamination of the brake system and fluid leaks.

To install:

➡**DO NOT re-use the gaskets for the brake hose bolt. Use NEW gaskets only.**

5. Install the caliper and tighten the guide pin bolts to 27 ft. lbs. (36 Nm).
6. Install the brake hose to the caliper.
7. Bleed the brake system.
8. With the engine OFF, gradually apply the brake pedal to approximately 2/3 of its travel distance. Slowly release the brake pedal. Wait 15 seconds, then repeat until a firm brake pedal is obtained. This will properly seat the brake caliper pistons and brake pads.
9. Fill the master cylinder reservoir to the proper level.

DISC BRAKE PADS

REMOVAL & INSTALLATION

1. Inspect the fluid level in the brake master cylinder reservoir:
   a. If the brake fluid level is midway between the maximum-full point and the minimum allowable level, no brake fluid needs to be removed from the reservoir before proceeding.

FRONT DISC BRAKES

   b. If the brake fluid level is higher than midway between the maximum-full point and the minimum allowable level, remove brake fluid to the midway point before proceeding.
2. Raise and support the vehicle.
3. Remove the tire and wheel.
4. Remove the guide pin bolts. Use a backup wrench on the brake caliper guide to hold the guide pin stationary and remove the brake caliper.
   a. Rotate the brake caliper up and to the rear until it rests on the mounting bracket and support with heavy mechanics wire or equivalent.
5. Place a block of wood or an old disc brake pad against the brake caliper pistons.
6. Using a suitable tool, slowly compress the brake caliper pistons squarely into the caliper bores.
7. Remove the brake pads.
8. Remove the spring retainers.

To install:

9. Install the brake pads and spring retainers.

➡**If replacing the brake pads, DO NOT reuse the spring retainers. Use NEW spring retainers only.**

10. Install the caliper and the guide pin bolts. Tighten to 27 ft. lbs. (36 Nm).
11. With the engine OFF, gradually apply the brake pedal to approximately 2/3 of its travel distance. Slowly release the brake pedal. Wait 15 seconds, then repeat steps until a firm brake pedal is obtained. This

will properly seat the brake caliper pistons and brake pads.

12. Fill the master cylinder reservoir to the proper level.

13. Burnish the pads and rotors. See "Burnishing Pads & Rotors".

BURNISHING PADS & ROTORS

※※ WARNING

Road test a vehicle under safe conditions and while obeying all traffic laws. Do not attempt any maneuvers that could jeopardize vehicle control.

BRAKES

※※ CAUTION

Dust and dirt accumulating on brake parts during normal use may contain asbestos fibers from production or aftermarket brake linings. Breathing excessive concentrations of asbestos fibers can cause serious bodily harm. Exercise care when servicing brake parts. Do not sand or grind brake lining unless equipment used is designed to contain the dust residue. Do not clean brake parts with compressed air or by dry brushing. Cleaning should be done by dampening the brake components with a fine mist of water, then wiping the brake components clean with a dampened cloth. Dispose of cloth and all residue containing asbestos fibers in an impermeable container with the appropriate label. Follow practices prescribed by the Occupational Safety and Health Administration (OSHA) and the Environmental Protection Agency (EPA) for the handling, processing, and disposing of dust or debris that may contain asbestos fibers.

BRAKE CALIPER

REMOVAL & INSTALLATION

See Figure 4.

1. Raise and support the vehicle.
2. Remove the tire and wheel.
3. Disconnect the park brake cable from the brake caliper.
4. Disconnect the brake hose from the rear brake caliper. Cap or plug the brake hose to prevent brake fluid loss or contamination.
5. Remove the guide pin bolts and the rear brake caliper.

Failure to adhere to these precautions could lead to serious personal injury and vehicle damage.

➡Burnishing the brake pads and brake rotors is necessary in order to ensure that the braking surfaces are properly prepared after service has been performed on the disc brake system. This procedure should be performed whenever the disc brake rotors have been refinished or replaced, and/or whenever the disc brake pads have been replaced.

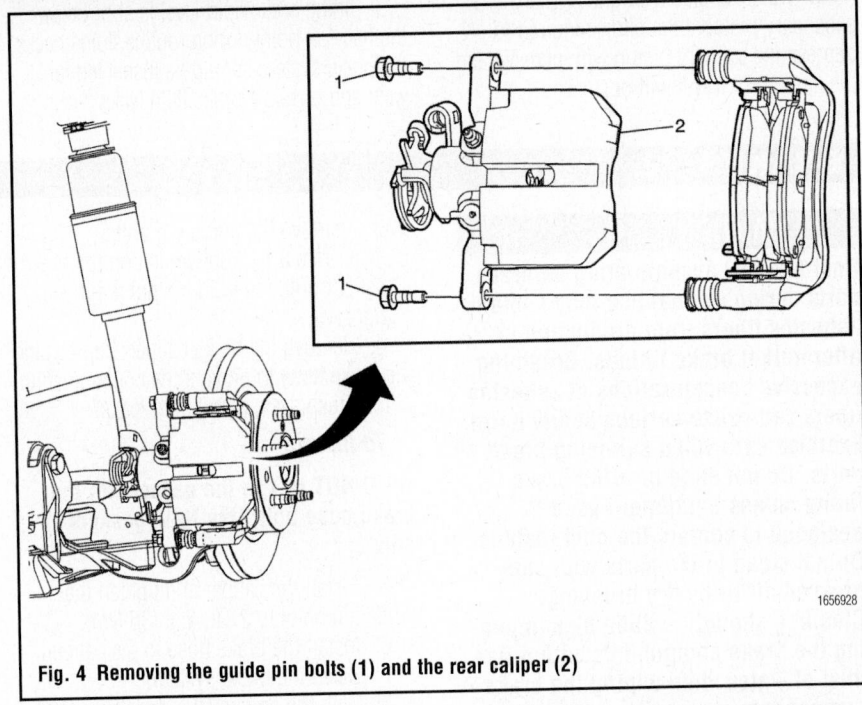

Fig. 4 Removing the guide pin bolts (1) and the rear caliper (2)

6. Cap or plug the brake hose to prevent brake fluid loss or contamination.

To install:

➡DO NOT re-use the gaskets for the brake hose bolt. Use NEW gaskets only.

7. Position the caliper to the rotor and install the guide pin bolts. Tighten to 25 ft. lbs. (34 Nm).
8. Connect the rear brake hose and the park brake cable.
9. Bleed the brake system, as described in this section.
10. With the engine OFF, gradually apply the brake pedal to approximately 2/3 of its travel distance. Slowly release the brake pedal. Wait 15 seconds, then repeat steps until a firm brake pedal is obtained. This will properly seat the brake caliper pistons and brake pads.

1. Select a smooth road with little or no traffic.
2. Accelerate the vehicle to 30 mph.

➡Use care to avoid overheating the brakes while performing this step.

3. Using moderate to firm pressure, apply the brakes to bring the vehicle to a stop. Do not allow the brakes to lock.
4. Repeat steps until approximately 20 stops have been completed. Allow sufficient cooling periods between stops in order to properly burnish the brake pads and rotors.

REAR DISC BRAKES

11. Fill the master cylinder reservoir to the proper level.

DISC BRAKE PADS

REMOVAL & INSTALLATION

※※ CAUTION

Support the brake caliper with heavy mechanic wire, or equivalent, whenever it is separated from its mount and the hydraulic flexible brake hose is still connected. Failure to support the caliper in this manner will cause the flexible brake hose to bear the weight of the caliper, which may cause damage to the brake hose and in turn may cause a brake fluid leak.

1. Inspect the fluid level in the brake master cylinder reservoir.

   a. If the brake fluid level is midway between the maximum-full point and the minimum allowable level, no brake fluid needs to be removed from the reservoir before proceeding.

   b. If the brake fluid level is higher than midway between the maximum-full point and the minimum allowable level, remove brake fluid to the midway point before proceeding.

2. Raise the vehicle.

3. Remove the tire and wheel.

4. Remove the guide pin bolts.

5. Remove the park brake cables from the retainers on the lower control arms.

6. Using a spanner wrench type caliper piston installer, fully retract the piston into the caliper bore.

7. Remove the brake caliper.

   a. Remove the lower brake caliper guide pin bolt and pivot the brake caliper upward.

   b. Support the brake caliper with heavy mechanics wire or equivalent.

8. Remove the rear brake pads and spring clips.

To install:

➡**When replacing the brakes pads, ensure that the wear indicators are on the inside pad on the bottom.**

9. Position the near brake pads and spring clips.

10. Install the brake caliper. Tighten the guide pin bolts to 25 ft. lbs. (34 Nm).

11. Connect the park brake cables to the retainers on the lower control arms.

12. After the installation is complete and with the engine OFF, gradually apply the brake pedal to approximately 2/3 of its travel distance. Slowly release the brake pedal. Wait 15 seconds, then repeat steps until a firm brake pedal is obtained. This will properly seat the brake caliper piston and the brake pads.

13. Fill the master cylinder.

14. Burnish the brake pads and rotors.

BURNISHING PADS & ROTORS

✳✳ WARNING

Road test a vehicle under safe conditions and while obeying all traffic laws. Do not attempt any maneuvers that could jeopardize vehicle control. Failure to adhere to these precautions could lead to serious personal injury and vehicle damage.

➡**Burnishing the brake pads and brake rotors is necessary in order to ensure that the braking surfaces are properly prepared after service has been performed on the disc brake system. This procedure should be performed whenever the disc brake rotors have been refinished or replaced, and/or whenever the disc brake pads have been replaced.**

1. Select a smooth road with little or no traffic.

2. Accelerate the vehicle to 30 mph.

➡**Use care to avoid overheating the brakes while performing this step.**

3. Using moderate to firm pressure, apply the brakes to bring the vehicle to a stop. Do not allow the brakes to lock.

4. Repeat steps until approximately 20 stops have been completed. Allow sufficient cooling periods between stops in order to properly burnish the brake pads and rotors.

CHASSIS ELECTRICAL   AIR BAG (SUPPLEMENTAL RESTRAINT SYSTEM)

GENERAL INFORMATION

✳✳ CAUTION

These vehicles are equipped with an air bag system. The system must be disarmed before performing service on, or around, system components, the steering column, instrument panel components, wiring and sensors. Failure to follow the safety precautions and the disarming procedure could result in accidental air bag deployment, possible injury and unnecessary system repairs.

SERVICE PRECAUTIONS

Disconnect and isolate the battery negative cable before beginning any airbag system component diagnosis, testing, removal, or installation procedures. Allow system capacitor to discharge for two minutes before beginning any component service. This will disable the airbag system. Failure to disable the airbag system may result in accidental airbag deployment, personal injury, or death.

Do not place an intact undeployed airbag face down on a solid surface. The airbag will propel into the air if accidentally deployed and may result in personal injury or death.

When carrying or handling an undeployed airbag, the trim side (face) of the airbag should be pointing away from the body to minimize possibility of injury if accidental deployment occurs. Failure to do this may result in personal injury or death.

Replace airbag system components with OEM replacement parts. Substitute parts may appear interchangeable, but internal differences may result in inferior occupant protection. Failure to do so may result in occupant personal injury or death.

Wear safety glasses, rubber gloves, and long sleeved clothing when cleaning powder residue from vehicle after an airbag deployment. Powder residue emitted from a deployed airbag can cause skin irritation. Flush affected area with cool water if irritation is experienced. If nasal or throat irritation is experienced, exit the vehicle for fresh air until the irritation ceases. If irritation continues, see a physician.

Do not use a replacement airbag that is not in the original packaging. This may result in improper deployment, personal injury, or death.

The factory installed fasteners, screws and bolts used to fasten airbag components have a special coating and are specifically designed for the airbag system. Do not use substitute fasteners. Use only original equipment fasteners listed in the parts catalog when fastener replacement is required.

During, and following, any child restraint anchor service, due to impact event or vehicle repair, carefully inspect all mounting hardware, tether straps, and anchors for proper installation, operation, or damage. If a child restraint anchor is found damaged in any way, the anchor must be replaced. Failure to do this may result in personal injury or death.

Deployed and non-deployed airbags may or may not have live pyrotechnic material within the airbag inflator.

Do not dispose of driver/passenger/curtain airbags or seat belt tensioners unless you are sure of complete deployment. Refer to the Hazardous Substance Control System for proper disposal.

Dispose of deployed airbags and tensioners consistent with state, provincial, local, and federal regulations.

After any airbag component testing or service, do not connect the battery negative cable. Personal injury or death may result if the system test is not performed first.

If the vehicle is equipped with the Occupant Classification System (OCS), do not connect the battery negative cable before performing the OCS Verification Test using the scan tool and the appropriate diagnostic information. Personal injury or death may result if the system test is not performed properly.

Never replace both the Occupant Restraint Controller (ORC) and the Occupant Classification Module (OCM) at the same time. If both require replacement, replace one, then perform the Airbag System test before replacing the other.

Both the ORC and the OCM store Occupant Classification System (OCS) calibration data, which they transfer to one another when one of them is replaced. If both are replaced at the same time, an irreversible fault will be set in both modules and the OCS may malfunction and cause personal injury or death.

If equipped with OCS, the Seat Weight Sensor is a sensitive, calibrated unit and must be handled carefully. Do not drop or handle roughly. If dropped or damaged, replace with another sensor. Failure to do so may result in occupant injury or death.

If equipped with OCS, the front passenger seat must be handled carefully as well. When removing the seat, be careful when setting on floor not to drop. If dropped, the sensor may be inoperative, could result in occupant injury, or possibly death.

If equipped with OCS, when the passenger front seat is on the floor, no one should sit in the front passenger seat. This uneven force may damage the sensing ability of the seat weight sensors. If sat on and damaged, the sensor may be inoperative, could result in occupant injury, or possibly death.

COMPONENT LOCATIONS

See Figure 5.

Refer to the accompanying illustration.

DISARMING THE SYSTEM

The inflatable restraint sensing and diagnostic module (SDM) maintains a reserved energy supply. The reserved energy supply provides deployment power for the air bags if the SDM loses battery power during a collision. Deployment power is available for as much as 1 minute after disconnecting the vehicle power. Waiting 1 minute before working on the system after disabling the SIR system prevents deployment of the air bags from the reserved energy supply.

1. Turn the steering wheel so that the vehicles wheels are pointing straight ahead.
2. Place the ignition in the OFF position.

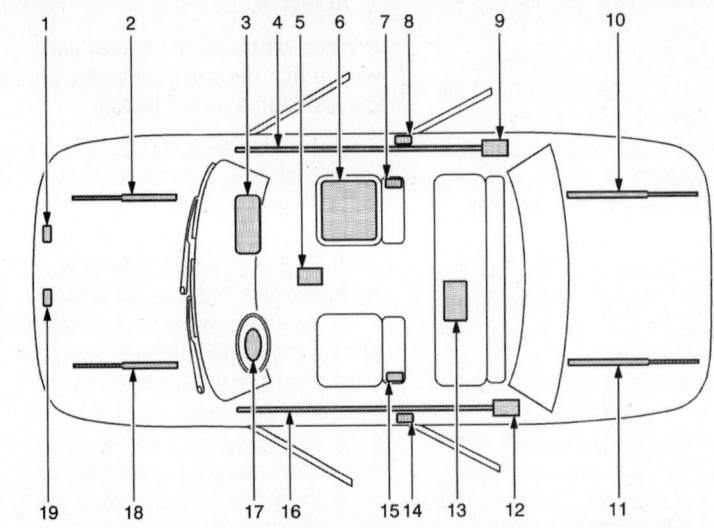

1. Right Front Impact Sensor--Located on the front of the vehicle in the engine compartment
2. Front Hood Assist Rod--A gas shock located under the front hood on the passenger side
3. Passenger Instrument Panel Air Bag--Located at the top right under the instrument panel
4. Right Roof Rail Air Bag--Located under the headliner, extending from the passenger front windshield pillar to the passenger rear windshield pillar
5. Inflatable Restraint Sensing and Diagnostic Module SDM)--Located underneath the center console
6. Passenger Presence System PPS)--Located on the passenger front seat underneath the seat bottom trim
7. Passenger Seat Side Air Bag--Located on the seat back of passenger seat
8. Passenger Seat Belt Retractor Pretensioner and Right Front Side Impact Sensor SIS)--Located under the center pillar trim near the bottom on the passenger side
9. Inflator Module for Right Roof Rail Air Bag--Located near rear pillar on passenger side
10. Rear Compartment Lid Assist Rod--A gas shock is located under the rear trunk lid on the passenger side
11. Rear Compartment Lid Assist Rod--A gas shock is located under the rear trunk lid on the driver side
12. Inflator Module for Left Roof Rail Air Bag--Located near rear pillar on driver side
13. Vehicle Battery--Located under the rear seat bottom cushion
14. Driver Seat Belt Retractor Pretensioner and Left Front Side Impact Sensor SIS)--Located under the center pillar trim near the bottom on the driver side
15. Driver Seat Side Air Bag--Located on the seat back of driver seat
16. Left Roof Rail Air Bag--Located under the headliner, extending from the driver front windshield pillar to the driver rear windshield pillar
17. Driver Steering Wheel Air Bag--Located on the steering wheel
18. Front Hood Assist Rod--A gas shock located under the front hood on the driver side
19. Left Front Impact Sensor--Located on the front of the vehicle in the engine compartment

1613908

Fig. 5 Showing the location of Supplemental Restraint System components

⁎⁑ WARNING

The SDM may have more than one fused power input. To ensure there is no unwanted SIR deployment, personal injury, or unnecessary SIR system repairs, remove all fuses supplying power to the SDM. With all SDM fuses removed and the ignition switch in the ON position, the AIR BAG warning indicator illuminates. This is normal operation, and does not indicate a SIR system malfunction.

Disabling Procedure—Air Bag Fuse

1. Locate and remove the fuse(s) supplying power to the SDM.
2. Wait 1 minute before working on the system.

Disabling Procedure—Negative Battery Cable

1. Turn the steering wheel so that the vehicles wheels are pointing straight ahead.
2. Place the ignition in the OFF position.
3. Disconnect the negative battery cable from the battery.
4. Wait 1 minute before working on system.

ARMING THE SYSTEM

Enabling Procedure—Air Bag Fuse

1. Place the ignition in the OFF position.
2. Install the fuse(s) supplying power to the SDM.
3. Turn the ignition switch to the ON position. The AIR BAG indicator will flash then turn OFF.
4. Perform the Diagnostic System Check.

Enabling Procedure—Negative Battery Cable

1. Place the ignition in the OFF position.
2. Connect the negative battery cable to the battery.
3. Turn the ignition switch to the ON position. The AIR BAG indicator will flash then turn OFF.
4. Perform the Diagnostic System Check

CLOCKSPRING CENTERING

See Figures 6 and 7.

❊❊ **CAUTION**

The new SIR coil assembly will be centered. Improper alignment of the SIR coil assembly may damage the unit, causing an inflatable restraint malfunction.

1. Verify the following conditions before centering the SIR coil:
   • The wheels on the vehicle are straight ahead.

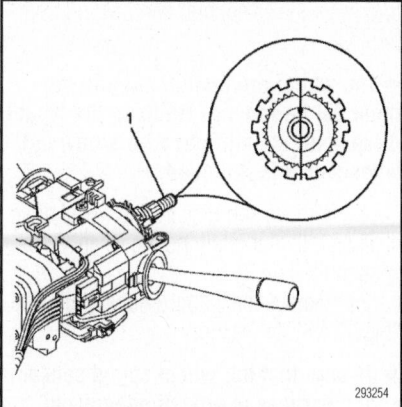

Fig. 6 Centering the steering wheel module coil (clockspring) and noting position of block tooth (1)

   • The block tooth of the steering shaft assembly is in the 12 o'clock position.
   • The ignition switch assembly is in the LOCK position.
2. Hold the coil with the face up.
3. Rotate the coil hub in the direction of the arrow until the coil ribbon stops.

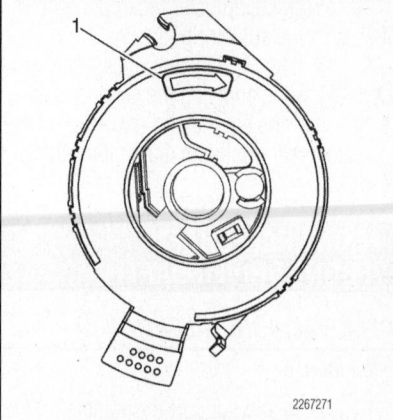

Fig. 7 Rotate the coil hub in the direction of the arrow (1) until the coil ribbon stops.

4. Rotate the coil hub, slowly, counter-clockwise, for 2 1/2 revolutions. This is the CENTER position.
5. While maintaining the coil hub in the CENTER position, align the centered coil with the horn tower and slide the coil onto the steering shaft assembly.

DRIVE TRAIN

AUTOMATIC TRANSAXLE FLUID

FLUID & FILTER REPLACEMENT

1. Raise and support the vehicle.
2. Place the drain pan under the transaxle oil pan.

❊❊ **CAUTION**

When removing the oil pan bolts, be careful not to damage the oil pan sealing surfaces. Such damage may result in oil leaks in this area.

3. Remove the oil pan bolts from only the front and the sides.
4. Loosen the rear oil pan bolts about 4 turns.
5. Lightly tap the oil pan with a rubber mallet or pry in order to allow the fluid to drain.
6. Inspect the fluid color.
7. Remove the remaining oil pan bolts.
8. Remove the oil pan and the gasket.
9. Remove the oil filter. Use a long screwdriver in order to pry the oil filter neck out of the seal.
10. Check the oil filter seal for damage or wear.
11. As needed, remove the seal.

To install:
12. Install a new seal, as needed. Before installing, coat the new seal with a small amount of petroleum jelly.
13. Install a new filter into the case.

➡**Oil pan gaskets are reusable. Only replace if sealing surface is damaged.**

14. Install the oil pan and the gasket at the same time.
15. Install the oil pan bolts. Tighten the bolts to 125 inch lbs. (14 Nm).
16. Lower the vehicle.
17. Fill the transaxle to the proper level.
18. Inspect the transmission fluid level.
19. Inspect the oil pan gasket for leaks.

RANGE SELECTOR CABLE

ADJUSTMENT

❊❊ **CAUTION**

Adjust the shift control cable only while the transaxle and the gear selector are in NEUTRAL. Failure to do so may cause misadjustment.

1. Set the parking brake and chock the wheels.
2. Remove the shift cable terminal from the transmission manual shaft lever pin.

3. Pry on the shift cable terminal at the manual shaft lever pin with an appropriate tool.

❊❊ **CAUTION**

Prying or pulling up on any other part of the shift cable may result in damage to the shift cable.

4. Fully lift the adjuster lock button. Ensure that the adjuster is free to move.
5. Place the transmission manual shaft lever in (N) Neutral. In order to find (N) Neutral, rotate the lever fully counterclockwise to (P) Park, and then clockwise 2 clicks into (N) Neutral.
6. Place the gear shifter inside the car to the (N) Neutral position. Use the transmission shift indicator on the console to find (N) Neutral.
7. From under the hood, grasp the shift cable terminal and pull it toward the pin on the manual shaft lever. The shift cable adjuster spring should compress as the terminal is moved toward the pin.
8. Attach the pin to the lever by pushing down carefully until it snaps.

❊❊ **CAUTION**

Do not pull the terminal beyond the pin and then push back. This action could move the shifter out of (N) Neutral.

9. Press the adjuster lock button down flush with the adjuster body.

10. Shift to (P) Park and release the parking brake while applying the service brake.

11. Start the engine and assure all of the indicated gear positions match the vehicle response.

FRONT HALFSHAFT (FRONT DRIVE SHAFT)

REMOVAL & INSTALLATION

See Figure 8.

1. Raise and support the vehicle.
2. Remove the tire and wheel assembly.

➡ **Do NOT loosen the tie rod end jam nut.**

3. Disconnect the outer tie rod end from the steering knuckle.

4. Insert a drift or punch into the brake rotor and against the brake caliper in order to prevent the wheel hub and bearing from turning.

➡ **The wheel drive shaft spindle nut must not be reused. Replace the wheel drive shaft spindle nut with a new nut whenever it is removed.**

5. Remove and discard the wheel drive shaft spindle nut retaining the wheel drive shaft to the hub.

6. Remove the stabilizer shaft link. See "SUSPENSION" section.

➡ **Be sure that the wheel speed sensor wiring harness is repositioned away from the ball joint after disconnecting the electrical connector from the sensor.**

7. Disconnect the electrical connector from the wheel speed sensor and reposition the wiring harness away from the ball joint.

8. Disconnect the lower ball joint from the steering knuckle. See "SUSPENSION" section.

9. Install the proper puller (J 42129 or equivalent) onto the wheel hub and secure with wheel nuts.

➡ **Be sure to support the wheel drive shaft until it is fully removed from the vehicle.**

10. Using the puller, disengage the wheel drive shaft from the wheel hub and bearing and support the wheel drive shaft.

11. Using a proper tool set (J 2619-01, the J 29794, and the J 33008-A or equivalent), disengage the wheel drive shaft from the transaxle.

12. Remove the wheel drive shaft from the vehicle.

To install:

13. Install the wheel drive shaft to the transaxle.

14. Verify that the wheel drive shaft is properly engaged to the transaxle by grasping the inner tripot housing and pulling outward. Do not pull on the wheel drive shaft bar. The wheel drive shaft will remain firmly in place when properly engaged.

15. Install the wheel drive shaft to the hub and bearing.

16. Connect the ball joint to the steering knuckle. See "FRONT SUSPENSION" section.

17. Connect the wheel speed sensor electrical connector.

18. Install the stabilizer shaft link. See "FRONT SUSPENSION" section.

19. Insert a drift or punch into the rotor and against the caliper in order to prevent the hub and bearing from turning.

20. Install a new wheel drive shaft spindle nut to the wheel drive shaft. Tighten the wheel drive shaft spindle nut to 118 ft. lbs. (160 Nm).

21. Connect the outer tie rod end to the steering knuckle. See "FRONT SUSPENSION" section.

22. Install the tire and wheel assembly.

23. Lower the vehicle.

FRONT DRIVE SHAFT INNER SEAL

REMOVAL & INSTALLATION

4T65-E

See Figure 9.

1. Raise and suitably support the vehicle.

2. Remove the front tire and wheel.

3. Remove the stabilizer shaft link from the lower control arm. See "FRONT SUSPENSION" section.

4. Remove the tie rod end from the steering knuckle. See "FRONT SUSPENSION" section.

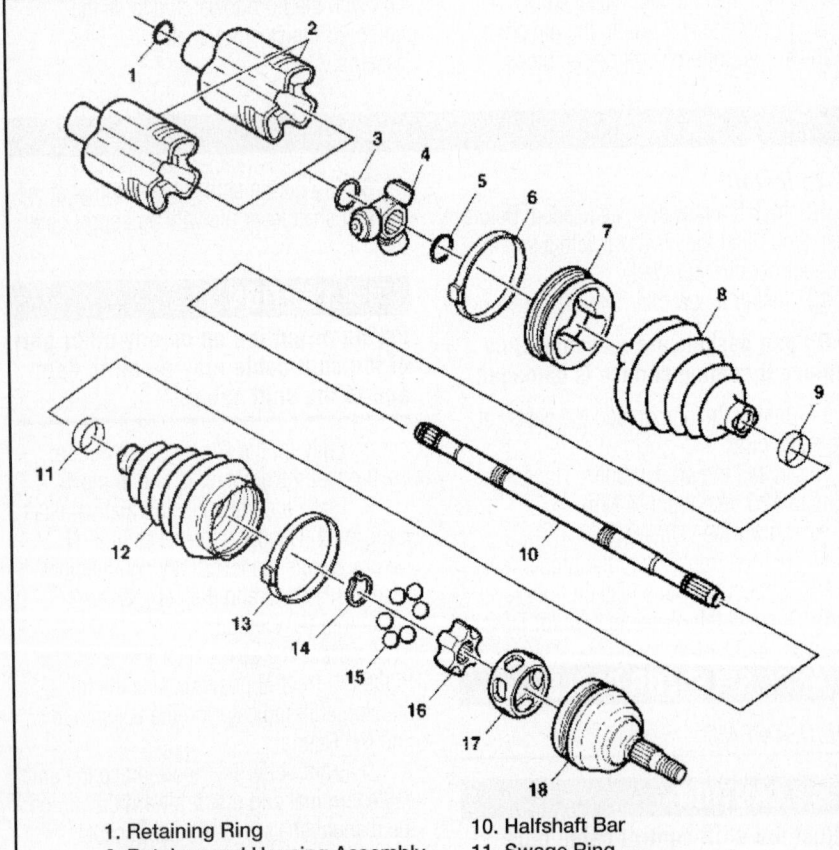

1. Retaining Ring
2. Retainer and Housing Assembly
3. Spacer Ring
4. Tripot Spider Assembly
5. Spacer Ring
6. Seal Retaining Clamp
7. Tripot Trilobal Bushing
8. Inboard Seal
9. Swage Ring
10. Halfshaft Bar
11. Swage Ring
12. Outboard Seal
13. Seal Retaining Clamp
14. Race Retaining Ring
15. Chrome Alloy Balls
16. CV Joint Inner Race
17. CV Joint Cage
18. CV Joint Outer Race

228645

Fig. 8 Exploded view of the front drive shaft

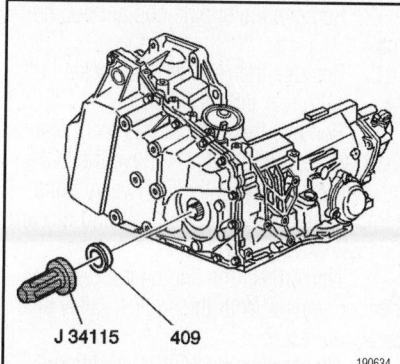

Fig. 9 Use a proper tool set to remove the seal—left side shown; right side similar

5. Remove the lower ball joint from the steering knuckle. See "FRONT SUSPENSION" section.

6. Disconnect the drive axle from the transaxle. See "Front Wheel Drive Shaft" in this section.

7. Secure the drive axle to the left steering knuckle and strut.

8. Use a proper tool set to remove the seal.

To install:

9. Use a light wipe of transaxle fluid to lubricate the seal lip. Use the seal installer tool to install a new seal.

> ❋❋ **CAUTION**
>
> **Carefully guide the axle shaft past the lip seal. Do NOT allow the shaft splines to contact any portion of the seal lip surface.**

10. Connect the drive axle to the transaxle. See "Front Wheel Drive Shaft" in this section.

11. Install the lower ball joint to the steering knuckle. See "FRONT SUSPENSION" section.

12. Install the tie rod end to the steering knuckle. See "FRONT SUSPENSION" section.

13. Install the stabilizer shaft link to the lower control arm. See "FRONT SUSPENSION" section.

14. Install the front tire and wheel.

15. Lower the vehicle.

16. Fill the transaxle to the proper level.

17. Inspect the transaxle fluid level.

18. Inspect for fluid leaks.

4T80-E

See Figures 10 and 11.

1. Remove the applicable drive axle, as described in this section.

> ❋❋ **CAUTION**
>
> **Be careful not to damage the transmission case extension when removing the seal with a screwdriver.**

2. Remove the drive axle seal with a screwdriver to pry the seal from the transaxle and then pliers to remove the remaining housing of the seal from the transaxle bore.

3. Inspect the drive axle seal mating surface on the drive axle housing for corrosion, grooves or nicks.

4. Clean the drive axle seal mating surface on the drive axle housing with crocus cloth.

To install:

> ❋❋ **CAUTION**
>
> **Be careful not to damage the transmission case extension**

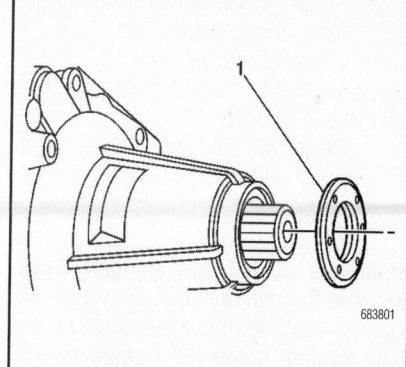

Fig. 10 Removing the right front drive shaft seal (1)

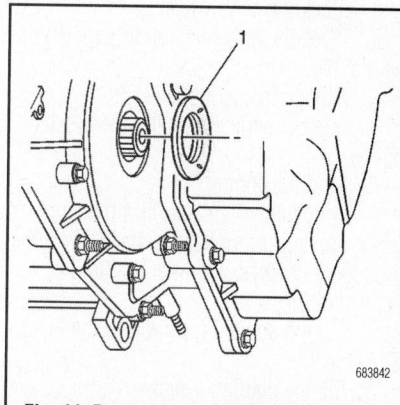

Fig. 11 Removing the left front drive shaft seal (1)

when installing the drive axle seal.

5. Install the axle seal using a proper seal driver (J 39051-1 or equivalent).

6. Install the drive axle.

ENGINE COOLING

ENGINE COOLANT

DRAIN & REFILL PROCEDURE

Draining Procedure

➡ **Do not use coolant system sealers in this cooling system.**

1. Park the vehicle on a level surface.

2. Remove the surge tank cap.

3. Remove the air cleaner box.

4. Raise and support the vehicle.

5. Remove the air deflector.

6. Lower the vehicle.

7. Place a drain pan under the lower radiator hose connection.

8. Using hose clamp pliers, reposition the lower radiator hose clamp away from the radiator. Slowly remove the lower radiator hose. Drain the coolant into the drain pan.

9. Inspect the engine coolant for the following conditions:

- Discolored appearance—Follow the flush procedure. See "Flushing" in this section.
- Normal in appearance—Follow the filling procedure.

Filling Procedure

> ❋❋ **CAUTION**
>
> **The procedure below must be followed. Improper coolant level could result in a low or high coolant level condition, causing engine damage.**

1. Install the lower radiator hose.

2. Reposition the lower radiator hose clamp to the radiator.

3. Lower the vehicle.

4. Slowly add a mixture of 50/50 DEX-COOL® antifreeze and de-ionized water to the cooling system through the top of the surge tank opening.

5. Fill the surge tank to the FULL COLD level.

6. Install the surge tank cap.

7. Idle the engine for 2 minutes and occasionally raise the throttle to 3000–3500 RPM.

8. Turn off the engine and allow the engine to cool.

9. Repeat the previous steps.

10. Install the front air deflector.

11. Install the air cleaner box.

12. Allow the engine to cool.

13. Remove the surge tank cap and fill to the FULL COLD level.

14. Rinse away any excess coolant from the engine and the engine compartment.

FLUSHING

→ Various methods and equipment can be used to flush the cooling system. If special equipment is used, such as a back flusher, follow the manufacturer's instruction. However, always remove the thermostat before back flushing the system.

1. Block the drive wheels.

2. Place the transmission in park (P) or neutral (N).

3. Engage the park brake.

4. Run the engine until the thermostat opens.

5. Stop the engine.

6. Follow the drain and fill procedure using only clean drinkable water. Repeat the procedure if necessary, until the fluid is nearly colorless.

7. Fill the coolant reservoir to the FULL COLD mark.

8. Fill the cooling system.

ENGINE COOLANT CROSSOVER PIPE

REMOVAL & INSTALLATION

4.6L Engine

See Figures 12 through 17.

1. Drain the cooling system.

2. Remove the air cleaner. See "Air Cleaner Assembly" in "ENGINE MECHANICAL" section.

3. Remove the fuel injector sight shield.

4. Remove the water pump drive belt.

5. Reposition the brake booster vacuum hose clamp at the water pump housing. Remove the brake booster vacuum hose from the water pump housing.

6. Remove the oil level indicator tube nut. Reposition the oil level indicator tube.

7. Remove the transaxle vent hose clip from the bracket.

8. Remove the throttle body bolts. Remove the bracket. Remove the throttle body. Remove and discard the throttle body seal. See "FUEL SYSTEMS" section.

9. Loosen the throttle body plenum duct clamp. Remove and discard the throttle body plenum duct.

10. Remove the fuel rail bracket nut at the rear left lift bracket.

11. Reposition the surge tank inlet hose clamp at the fitting. Remove the surge tank inlet hose from the fitting.

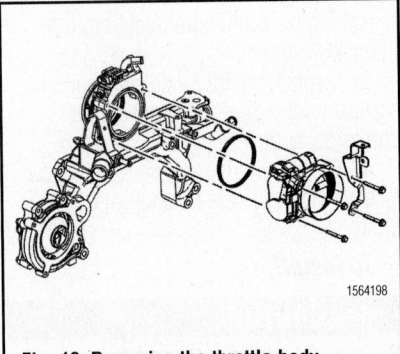

Fig. 13 Removing the throttle body

12. Remove the engine coolant outlet fitting.

13. Remove the rear left lift bracket bolt. Remove the rear left lift bracket.

14. Remove the exhaust gas recirculation (EGR) valve shield nuts. Remove the EGR valve shield. Remove the EGR valve bolts. Remove the EGR valve. Remove and discard the EGR valve gasket.

15. Disconnect the engine harness electrical connector from the engine valley electrical connector.

16. Disconnect the EGR inlet pipe nut from the exhaust manifold front pipe.

✳✳ CAUTION

The EGR valve inlet pipe incorporates a crush seal connection at the water pump housing. The EGR valve inlet pipe must be replaced if disconnected from the water pump housing.

17. Remove the EGR inlet pipe bolt from the water pump housing. Remove and discard the EGR inlet pipe.

18. Remove the evaporative emission (EVAP) canister purge solenoid valve bolt. Remove the EVAP canister purge solenoid valve.

19. Remove the manifold absolute pressure (MAP) sensor bracket bolt. Remove the MAP sensor bracket. Remove the MAP sensor.

20. Reposition the radiator inlet hose clamp at the water pump housing. Remove the radiator inlet hose from the water pump housing.

21. Reposition the radiator outlet hose clamp at the thermostat housing. Remove the radiator outlet hose from the thermostat housing.

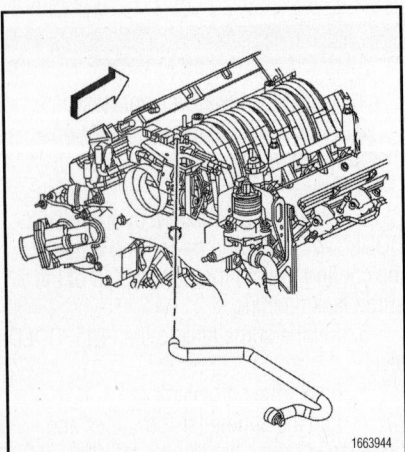

Fig. 12 Reposition the brake booster vacuum hose clamp at the water pump housing. Remove the brake booster vacuum hose from the water pump housing.

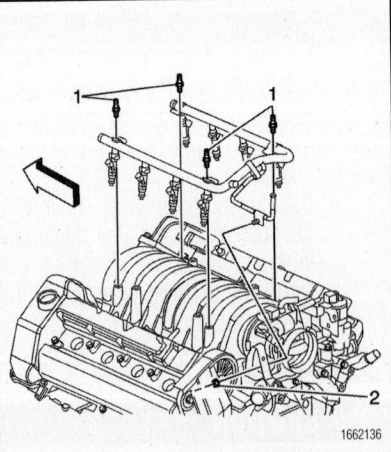

Fig. 14 Remove the fuel rail bracket nut (2) at the rear left lift bracket—fuel rail studs (1) do not apply to this procedure

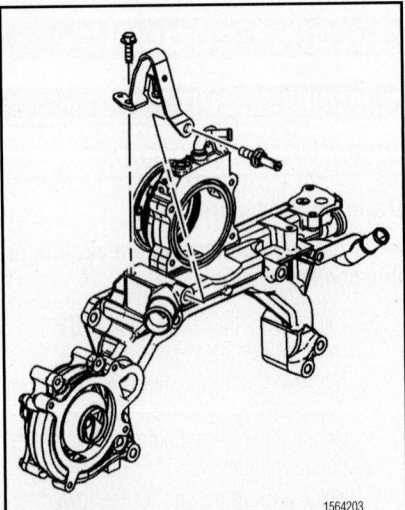

Fig. 15 Remove the rear left lift bracket bolt. Remove the rear left lift bracket.

22. Remove the water pump belt tensioner studs. Remove the water pump belt tensioner.

23. Reposition the heater outlet hose clamp at the heater pipe. Remove the heater outlet hose from the heater pipe.

24. Remove the water pump cover bolt and studs. Remove the water pump cover. Loosen the water pump housing bolts. Remove the water pump housing. See "Water Pump" in this section. Remove the water pump housing gaskets and bolts.

25. With the water pump housing on the bench, remove the water pump bolts. Remove the water pump from the water pump housing. Remove and discard the water pump O-ring.

To install:

26. Install a NEW water pump O-ring to the water pump. Install the water pump. Install the water pump bolts and tighten the bolts to 89 inch lbs. (10 Nm).

27. With the water pump housing on the bench, install the bolts in the locations shown.

- Bolt (1) length 1.6024 in. (40.7 mm).
- Bolts (2) length 3.6220 in. (92.0 mm).
- Bolts (3) length 4.2913 in. (109.0 mm).

- Bolts (4) length 4.5276 in. (115.0 mm).

28. With the housing still on the bench, install the NEW water pump housing gasket onto the bolts.

29. Position the water pump housing to the engine and hand start the bolts.

30. Tighten the water pump housing bolts in the sequence shown to 18 ft. lbs. (25 Nm).

31. Install the water pump cover.

32. Ensure the water pump cover bolt is installed in the lower inboard position and the studs are installed in the remaining position. Tighten the bolt/studs to 89 inch lbs. (10 Nm).

33. Install the heater outlet hose to the heater pipe. Position the heater outlet hose clamp at the heater pipe.

34. Position the water pump belt tensioner. Install the water pump belt tensioner studs. Tighten the studs to 89 inch lbs. (10 Nm).

35. Install the radiator outlet hose to the thermostat housing. Install the radiator outlet hose clamp at the thermostat housing.

36. Install the radiator inlet hose to the water pump housing. Install the radiator inlet hose clamp at the water pump housing.

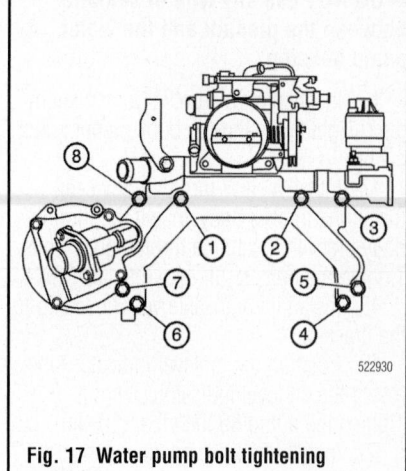

Fig. 17 Water pump bolt tightening sequence

37. Install the MAP sensor. Install the MAP sensor bracket. Install the MAP sensor bracket bolt. Tighten the bolt to 89 inch lbs. (10 Nm).

38. Install the EVAP canister purge solenoid valve. Install the EVAP canister purge solenoid valve bolt. Tighten the bolt to 89 inch lbs. (10 Nm).

➡ **The EGR valve inlet pipe incorporates a crush seal connection at the water pump housing. The EGR valve inlet pipe must be replaced if disconnected from the water pump housing.**

39. Hand start the NEW EGR inlet pipe nut at the exhaust manifold front pipe. Install the EGR inlet pipe and bolt to the water pump housing. Tighten the nut to 44 ft. lbs. (60 Nm). Tighten the bolt to 18 ft. lbs. (25 Nm).

40. Connect the engine harness electrical connector to the engine valley electrical connector.

41. Install the NEW EGR valve gasket. Install the EGR valve. Install the EGR valve bolts. Tighten the bolts to 18 ft. lbs. (25 Nm).

Install the EGR valve shield. Install the EGR valve shield nuts. Tighten the nuts to 89 inch lbs. (10 Nm).

42. Position the rear left lift bracket to the water pump housing. Install the rear left lift bracket bolt. Tighten the bolt to 18 ft. lbs. (25 Nm).

43. Install the engine coolant outlet fitting. Tighten the fitting to 35 ft. lbs. (47 Nm).

44. Install the surge tank inlet hose to the fitting. Position the surge tank inlet hose clamp at the fitting.

45. Install the fuel rail bracket nut at the rear left lift bracket. Tighten the nut to 89 inch lbs. (10 Nm).

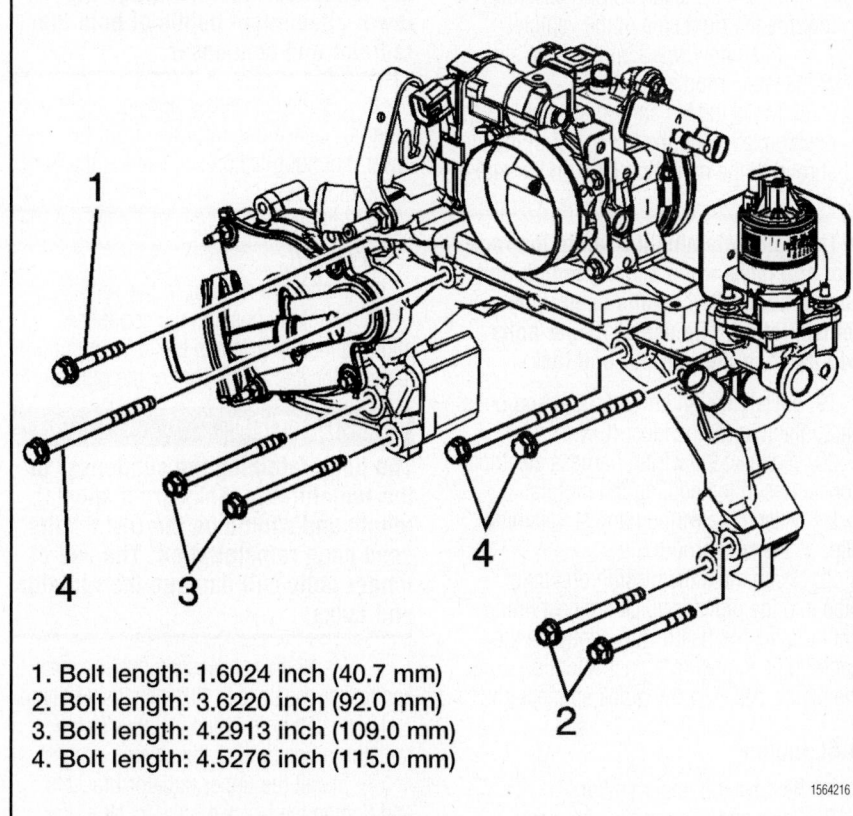

1. Bolt length: 1.6024 inch (40.7 mm)
2. Bolt length: 3.6220 inch (92.0 mm)
3. Bolt length: 4.2913 inch (109.0 mm)
4. Bolt length: 4.5276 inch (115.0 mm)

Fig. 16 Installation locations of water pump bolts

→**DO NOT use any type of sealant between the plenum and the water pump housing.**

46. Install a NEW throttle body plenum duct. Tighten the throttle body plenum duct clamp.

47. Install a NEW throttle body seal. Install the throttle body. Install the throttle body bracket. Install the throttle body bolts. Tighten the bolts to 89 inch lbs. (10 Nm).

48. Install the transaxle vent hose clip to the bracket.

49. Position the oil level indicator tube. Install the oil level indicator tube nut. Tighten the nut to 89 inch lbs. (10 Nm).

50. Install the brake booster vacuum hose to the water pump housing. Position the brake booster vacuum hose clamp at the water pump housing.

51. Install the water pump drive belt.

52. Install the air cleaner.

53. Fill the cooling system.

54. Install the fuel injector sight shield.

ENGINE FAN

REMOVAL & INSTALLATION

1. Remove the cooling fan shroud assembly, as described in this section.

2. Remove the cooling fan blade retaining nut.

3. Remove the cooling fan blade.

To install:

4. Install the cooling fan blade.

5. Install the cooling fan retaining nut and tighten to 53 inch lbs. (6 Nm).

6. Install the cooling fan shroud assembly.

ENGINE FAN SHROUD

REMOVAL & INSTALLATION

3.9L Engine

1. Disconnect the battery negative cable.

2. Remove the condenser.

3. Remove the upper tie bar.

4. Drain the cooling system, as described in this section.

5. Raise and support the vehicle.

6. Remove the front air deflector.

7. Remove the radiator outlet hose (lower) from the radiator.

8. Remove the transmission oil cooler pipe retaining bolts from the fan shroud.

9. Lower the vehicle.

10. Disconnect the radiator inlet hose from the radiator.

11. Slide the transmission oil cooler line caps reward to access the lines to the radiator. Remove the transmission oil cooler lines from the radiator.

12. Disconnect the wiring harness electrical connectors from the cooling fan motors.

13. Remove the clips attaching the harness to the fan shroud.

14. Remove the fan shroud mounting bolts.

→**Care should be taken when removing the fan shroud assembly not to damage the lower attachment points of both the fan shroud assembly and the radiator.**

15. Remove the fan shroud assembly from the vehicle by positioning the fan shroud assembly toward the left side of the vehicle, the pull upward on the right side of the fan shroud assembly. Pull upward on the fan shroud assembly removing the fan shroud assembly from the vehicle.

16. Remove the cooling fan motors when replacing the fan shroud assembly.

To install:

17. Install the cooling fan motors when replacing the fan shroud assembly.

18. Install the fan shroud assembly to the vehicle in the following order:

   a. Position the fan shroud assembly behind the radiator.

   b. Position the fan shroud assembly towards the right side of the vehicle.

   c. Push downward on the right side of the fan shroud assembly.

   d. Move the fan shroud assembly into position, aligning the lower feet of the fan shroud to the mounting tabs on the radiator.

→**The bolts retaining the fan to the radiator end tanks are a special length and should be the ONLY bolts used upon reinstallation. The use of longer bolts will damage the radiator end tanks.**

19. Install the fan shroud mounting bolts and tighten to 53 inch lbs. (6 Nm).

20. Connect the wiring harness electrical connectors to the cooling fan motors.

21. Attach the wiring harness retaining clips to the fan shroud.

22. Push the transmission oil cooler pipe into the radiator quick connect fitting, until a "click" is heard. Tug gently on the cooler pipe to ensure proper retention. Slide the plastic cap over the quick connect joint

4.6L Engine

1. Remove the upper tie bar.

2. Raise and support the vehicle.

3. Remove the front air deflector.

4. Remove the radiator inlet hose.

5. Disconnect the wiring harness electrical connectors from the cooling fan motors.

6. Remove the transmission oil cooler pipes.

7. Remove the shroud retaining bolts.

8. Remove the fan shroud.

9. Installation is the reverse of the removal procedure.

RADIATOR

REMOVAL & INSTALLATION

3.9L Engine

1. Partially drain the cooling system.

2. Remove the cooling fan shroud assembly. See "Engine Fan Shroud".

3. Remove the condenser line to radiator retaining bolt.

4. Remove the radiator outlet hose (lower) from the radiator.

5. Remove the radiator inlet hose (upper) from the radiator.

6. Remove the upper radiator bracket bolts and remove the upper radiator brackets.

7. Remove the condenser mounting bolts on the sides of the condenser.

✸✸ CAUTION

Care should be taken when removing the condenser not to damage the lower attachment points of both the radiator and condenser.

8. Lift the condenser upward slightly in order to release the lower feet from the lower mounting features located at the front of the radiator.

9. Lift the radiator up and out the vehicle.

To install:

10. Install the radiator to the vehicle.

11. Carefully position the condenser, aligning the lower feet to the lower mounting features located at the front of the radiator.

✸✸ CAUTION

The bolts retaining the condenser to the radiator end tanks are a special length and should be the ONLY bolts used upon reinstallation. The use of longer bolts will damage the radiator end tanks.

12. Install the condenser mounting bolts and tighten the bolts to 115 inch lbs. (13 Nm).

13. Install both radiator hoses to the radiator, repositioning the clamps properly.

14. Install the upper radiator brackets and tighten the bracket bolts to 18 ft. lbs. (25 Nm).

15. Install the condenser line to radiator retaining bolt and tighten to 53 inch lbs. (6 Nm).

16. Install the cooling fans.

17. Fill the cooling system.

4.6L Engine

1. Partially drain the cooling system.

2. Remove the cooling fan shroud assembly. See "Engine Fan Shroud".

3. Discharge the A/C system and remove the condenser.

4. Remove the radiator support bracket.

5. Remove the radiator inlet and outlet hoses.

6. Remove the radiator.

7. Installation is the reverse of the removal procedure.

8. Recharge the A/C system.

THERMOSTAT

REMOVAL & INSTALLATION

3.9L Engine

1. Drain the cooling system.

2. Remove the air cleaner outlet duct.

3. Disconnect the radiator outlet hose from the thermostat housing.

4. Remove the bolts and the thermostat housing.

5. Remove the thermostat and gasket.

6. Clean the water inlet and engine block surfaces.

7. Installation is the reverse of the removal procedure.

8. Install a new gasket.

9. Tighten thermostat housing bolts to 89 inch lbs. (10 Nm).

4.6L Engine

1. Remove the air cleaner.

2. Drain the cooling system.

3. Remove the radiator outlet hose from the thermostat housing.

4. Remove the thermostat housing bolts. Remove the thermostat housing, thermostat, and gasket from the water pump housing.

5. Discard the old thermostat housing gasket.

To install:

6. Install a NEW thermostat housing gasket into the water pump housing. Install the thermostat into the water pump housing.

Install the thermostat housing. Install the thermostat housing bolts. Tighten the bolts to 89 inch lbs. (10 Nm).

7. Install the radiator outlet hose to the thermostat housing.

8. Fill the cooling system.

9. Install the air cleaner.

WATER PUMP

REMOVAL & INSTALLATION

3.9L Engine

See Figure 18.

1. Drain the cooling system.

2. Remove the drive belt. See "Accessory Drive Belt" in "ENGINE MECHANICAL" section.

3. Remove the pulley bolts. The pulley bolts may be loosened before the drive belt is removed. Remove the water pump pulley.

4. Remove the water pump bolts and remove the water pump.

To install:

➡**Always use the NEW gasket supplied with the water pump.**

5. Install the water pump and tighten the bolts to 18 ft. lbs. (25 Nm).

6. Install the water pump pulley and tighten the bolts to 18 ft. lbs. (25 Nm).

7. Install the accessory drive belt.

8. Refill the cooling system.

4.6L Engine

➡**See "Engine Coolant Crossover Pipe" in this section.**

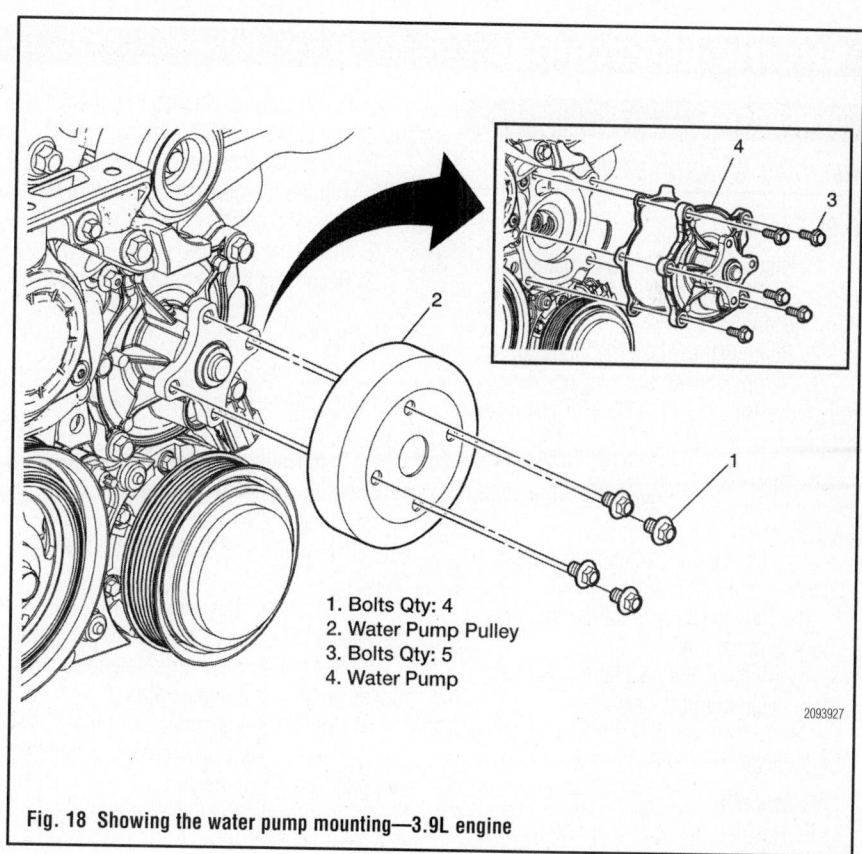

1. Bolts Qty: 4
2. Water Pump Pulley
3. Bolts Qty: 5
4. Water Pump

2093927

Fig. 18 Showing the water pump mounting—3.9L engine

ENGINE ELECTRICAL

BATTERY

REMOVAL & INSTALLATION

✱✱ WARNING

Unless directed otherwise, the ignition and start switch must be in the OFF or LOCK position, and all electrical loads must be OFF before servicing any electrical component. Disconnect the negative battery cable to prevent an electrical spark should a tool or equipment come in contact with an exposed electrical terminal. Failure to follow these precautions may result in personal injury and/or damage to the vehicle or its components.

➡For Vehicles equipped with OnStar® (UE1) with Back Up Battery:

- The Back Up Battery is a redundant power supply to allow limited OnStar functionality in the event of a main vehicle battery power disruption to the VCIM (OnStar module).
- Do not disconnect the main vehicle battery or remove the OnStar fuse with the ignition key in any position other than OFF. Retained accessory power (RAP) should be allowed to time out or be disabled (simply opening the driver door should disable RAP) before disconnecting power.
- Disconnecting power to the OnStar module in any way while the ignition is On or with RAP activated may cause activation of the OnStar Back-Up Battery (BUB) system and will discharge and permanently damage the back-up battery.

BATTERY SYSTEM

- Once the Back-Up Battery is activated it will stay on until it has completely discharged. The BUB is not rechargeable and once activated the BUB must be replaced.

1. Disconnect the negative battery cable:

    a. Turn all lamps and accessories OFF.

    b. Turn the Ignition to the OFF position.

    c. Remove the rear seat cushion.

2. Remove the battery terminal nut and remove the cable terminal.

3. Remove the battery hold down bolts. Remove the hold down retainer.

4. Remove the battery vent tube.

5. Remove the battery.

6. Installation is the reverse of the removal procedure.

ENGINE ELECTRICAL

GENERATOR

REMOVAL & INSTALLATION

3.9L Engine

1. Disconnect the negative battery cable. See "Battery" in "ENGINE ELECTRICAL" section.

2. Remove the intake manifold cover.

3. Remove the drive belt. See "Accessory Drive Belt" in "ENGINE MECHANICAL" section.

4. Remove both generator mounting bolts and remove the generator while doing the following:

    a. Reposition the generator output battery terminal protective boot.

    b. Remove the generator output battery terminal nut.

    c. Remove the generator output battery cable from the generator.

    d. Disconnect the generator electrical connector.

To install:

5. Position the generator and loosely install the mounting bolts.

6. Reconnect the electrical connector and output battery cable to the generator.

7. Install the accessory drive belt.

8. Tighten the generator mounting bolts to 37 ft. lbs. (50 Nm).

9. Install the manifold cover.

10. Reconnect the negative battery cable.

4.6L Engine

1. Disconnect the negative battery cable. See "Battery" in "ENGINE ELECTRICAL" section.

2. Remove the radiator. See "Radiator" in "ENGINE COOLING" section.

3. Remove the drive belt. See "Accessory Drive Belt" in "ENGINE MECHANICAL" section.

4. Disconnect the engine wiring harness electrical connector from the generator.

5. Reposition the starter solenoid cable protective boot at the generator.

6. Remove the generator terminal nut.

7. Remove the starter solenoid cable terminal from the generator.

8. Remove the generator mounting bolts.

CHARGING SYSTEM

9. Reposition the engine ground cable.

10. Remove the generator.

To install:

11. Position the generator to the engine.

12. Install the generator bolts finger tight in the following sequence:

- Upper bolt
- Side bolt
- Lower bolt

13. Tighten the generator bolts to 37 ft. lbs. (50 Nm).

14. Install the starter solenoid cable terminal to the generator.

15. Install the generator terminal nut. Tighten the nut to 106 inch lbs. (12 Nm).

16. Position the starter solenoid cable protective boot at the generator.

17. Connect the engine wiring harness electrical connector to the generator.

18. Install the drive belt.

19. Install the radiator.

20. Connect the negative battery cable.

ENGINE ELECTRICAL

FIRING ORDER

3.9L Engine

Firing order: 1–2–3–4–5–6

4.6L Engine

Firing order: 1–2–7–3–4–5–6–8

IGNITION COIL

REMOVAL & INSTALLATION

3.9L Engine

See Figure 19.

1. Remove the intake manifold cover.
2. Disconnect the manifold absolute pressure (MAP) sensor electrical connector.
3. Disconnect the ignition coil electrical connector.
4. Disconnect the left side spark plug wires from the ignition coil.
5. Disconnect the right side spark plug wires from the ignition coil.
6. Remove the ignition coil bolts/nuts and remove the ignition coil.
7. Remove the ignition coil studs, if necessary.

To install:

8. Install the ignition coil studs, if necessary. Tighten the studs to 15 ft. lbs. (25 Nm).
9. Install the ignition coil bolts/nuts. Tighten to 15 ft. lbs. (25 Nm).
10. Connect the right side spark plug wires to the ignition coil.

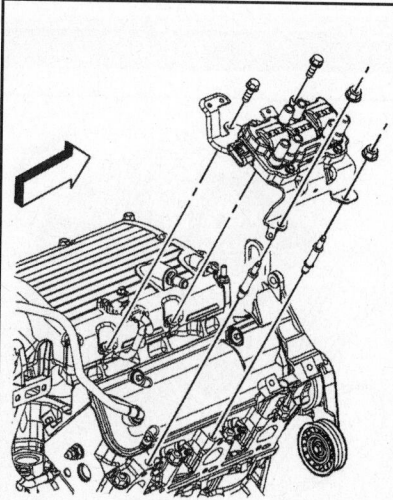

Fig. 19 Remove the ignition coil bolts/nuts and remove the ignition coil.

11. Connect the left side spark plug wires to the ignition coil.
12. Connect the ignition coil electrical connector.
13. Connect the MAP sensor electrical connector.
14. Install the intake manifold cover.

4.6L Engine

1. Remove both of the fuel injector sight shields.
2. Disconnect the engine harness electrical connector from the ignition coil assembly.
3. Remove the fuel injector sight shield studs.
4. Remove the ignition coil assembly bolts. Remove the ignition coil assembly.

To install:

a. Install the ignition coil assembly.
b. Install the ignition coil assembly bolts. Tighten the bolts to 89 inch lbs. (10 Nm).
5. Install the fuel injector sight shield studs. Tighten the studs to 89 inch lbs. (10 Nm).
6. Connect the engine harness electrical connector to the ignition coil assembly.
7. Install both of the fuel injector sight shields.

IGNITION TIMING

ADJUSTMENT

➡ Ignition timing is computer-controlled; therefore, no manual adjustment is required.

SPARK PLUGS

REMOVAL & INSTALLATION

3.9L Engine

✳ CAUTION

Observe the following service precautions:

- Allow the engine to cool before removing the spark plugs. Attempting to remove spark plugs from a hot engine can cause the spark plugs to seize. This can damage the cylinder head threads.
- Clean the spark plug recess area before removing the spark plug. Failure to do so can result in engine damage due to dirt or foreign material entering the cylinder

head, or in contamination of the cylinder head threads. Contaminated threads may prevent proper seating of the new spark plug.

- Use only the spark plugs specified for use in the vehicle. Do not install spark plugs that are either hotter or colder than those specified for the vehicle. Installing spark plugs of another type can severely damage the engine.

1. Remove the air cleaner outlet duct, if required.
2. Remove the intake manifold cover, if required.
3. Remove the left side spark plug wires from the spark plugs, if required.
4. Remove the right side spark plug wires from the spark plugs, if required.
5. Remove the spark plugs.

To install:

✳ CAUTION

It is important to check the gap of all new and reconditioned spark plugs before installation. Pre-set gaps may have changed during handling. Use a round wire feeler gauge to be sure of an accurate check, particularly on used plugs. Installing plugs with the wrong gap can cause poor engine performance and may even damage the engine.

6. Gap the NEW spark plugs to 0.040 in.
7. Install the spark plugs. Tighten the plugs to 11 ft. lbs. (15 Nm).
8. Install the right side spark plug wires to the spark plugs, if required.
9. Install the left side spark plug wires to the spark plugs, if required.
10. Install the intake manifold cover, if required.
11. Install the air cleaner outlet duct, if required.

4.6L Engine

1. Remove the appropriate ignition coil. See "Ignition Coil" in this section.

✳ CAUTION

Allow the engine to cool before removing the spark plugs. Attempting to remove the spark plugs from a hot engine may cause the plug threads to seize, causing damage to cylinder head threads.

❊❊ CAUTION

Clean the spark plug recess area before removing the spark plug. Failure to do so could result in engine damage because of dirt or foreign material entering the cylinder head, or by the contamination of the cylinder head threads. The contaminated threads may prevent the proper seating of the new plug. Use a thread chaser to clean the threads of any contamination.

2. Remove the spark plug(s) from the engine.
3. Inspect the spark plugs.

To install:

❊❊ CAUTION

Use only the spark plugs specified for use in the vehicle. Do not install spark plugs that are either hotter or colder than those specified for the vehicle. Installing spark plugs of another type can severely damage the engine.

4. Check the gap of all new and reconditioned spark plugs before installation. The pre-set gaps may have changed during handling. Use a round feeler gauge to ensure an accurate check. Installing the spark plugs with the wrong gap can cause poor engine performance and may even damage the engine.

Measure the spark plug gap on the spark plug(s) to be installed. It should be 0.050 in.

❊❊ CAUTION

Be sure that the spark plug threads smoothly into the cylinder head and the spark plug is fully seated.

5. Use a thread chaser, if necessary, to clean threads in the cylinder head. Cross-threading or failing to fully seat the spark plug can cause overheating of the plug, exhaust blow-by, or thread damage.
6. Install the spark plug(s) to the engine. Tighten the plug(s) to 11 ft. lbs. (15 Nm).
7. Install the appropriate ignition coil, as removed.

ENGINE ELECTRICAL

STARTER

REMOVAL & INSTALLATION

3.9L Engine

1. Disconnect the negative battery cable.
2. Remove the torque converter cover.
3. Remove the starter solenoid BAT terminal nut from the starter motor.
4. Remove the positive battery cable terminal and engine harness terminal from the starter.
5. Disconnect the starter motor electrical connector.
6. Remove the transmission brace.
7. Remove the starter bolts and starter.

To install:

8. Position the starter motor to the engine. Install the starter bolts and tighten to 32 ft. lbs. (43 Nm).

9. Install the transmission brace.
10. Connect the starter motor electrical connector.
11. Install the engine harness terminal and positive battery cable terminal to the starter. Ensure that the positive battery cable terminal anti-rotation feature is aligned correctly.
12. Install the starter solenoid BAT terminal nut to the starter motor and tighten to 89 inch lbs. (10 Nm).
13. Install the torque converter covers.
14. Connect the negative battery cable.

4.6L Engine

1. Disconnect the negative battery cable. See "Battery" in "ENGINE ELECTRICAL" section.
2. Remove the intake manifold. See "Intake Manifold" in "ENGINE MECHANICAL" section.

STARTING SYSTEM

3. Remove the "BAT" terminal nut, "S" terminal nut, and solenoid cable from the starter.
4. Remove the starter motor bolts and remove the starter motor.

To install:

5. Install the starter motor. Tighten the bolts to 18 ft. lbs. (25 Nm).

➡**Ensure that the large terminal locator tab is placed into the starter solenoid retention slot.**

6. Install the starter solenoid cable, "S" terminal nut, and the "BAT" terminal nut to the starter. Tighten "BAT" terminal nut to 89 inch lbs. (10 Nm).
7. Install the intake manifold.
8. Connect the negative battery cable.

ENGINE MECHANICAL

➡**Disconnecting the negative battery cable may interfere with the functions of the on board computer systems and may require the computer to undergo a relearning process, once the negative battery cable is reconnected.**

ACCESSORY DRIVE BELTS

ACCESSORY BELT ROUTING

3.9L Engine

See Figure 20.

Refer to the accompanying illustration.

4.6L Engine

See Figure 21.

Refer to the accompanying illustration.

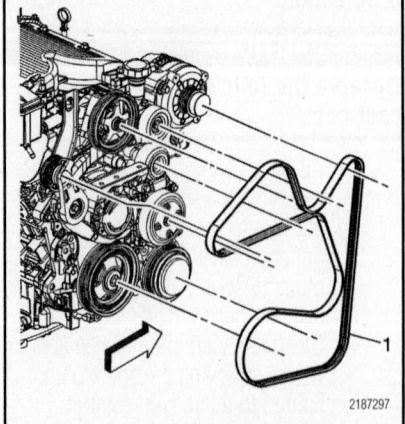

Fig. 20 Accessory drive belt routing— 3.9L engine

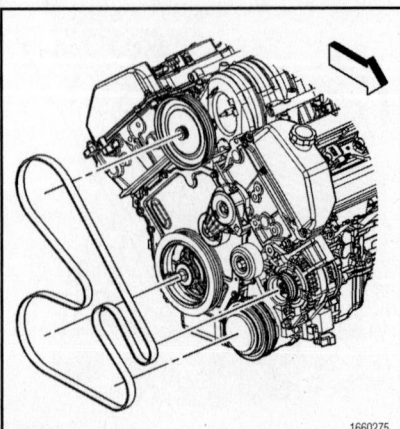

Fig. 21 Accessory drive belt routing— 4.6L engine

➡**Accessory drive belt tension is maintained via an automatic tensioner and pulley. No manual adjustment is required.**

REMOVAL & INSTALLATION

3.9L Engine

1. Remove the intake manifold cover.
2. Rotate the drive belt tensioner clockwise in order to release the tensioner spring tension.
3. Remove the drive belt from around the tensioner pulley.
4. Release the drive belt tensioner.
5. Remove the drive belt from around all the other pulleys.

To install:

6. Install the drive belt around the pulleys except for the tensioner pulley.
7. Rotate the drive belt tensioner clockwise in order to release the tensioner spring tension.
8. Install the drive belt around the tensioner pulley.
9. Release the drive belt tensioner.
10. Install the intake manifold cover.

4.6L Engine

1. Remove the right front wheelhouse liner.
2. Install a 1/2-inch drive breaker to the drive belt tensioner.
3. Push down on the breaker bar in order to release the tension.
4. Remove the drive belt from the power steering pump.
5. Slowly return the tensioner to the original position.
6. Remove the belt from the lower pulley and idlers.

To install:

7. Partially raise the vehicle.
8. Route the drive belt around all the pulleys except for the power steering pump.
9. Lower the vehicle.
10. Install a 1/2 inch drive breaker bar to the drive belt tensioner.
11. Push down on the breaker bar in order to release the tension and route the belt around the power steering pump pulley.
12. Ensure the belt is seated on all pulleys.
13. Slowly return the tensioner to its original position.
14. After drive belt installation, inspect the drive belt for the proper routing and correct alignment.

15. Install the right front wheelhouse liner.
16. Start the engine and check for proper belt and accessory operation.

AIR CLEANER ASSEMBLY

REMOVAL & INSTALLATION

3.9L Engine

1. Disconnect the engine harness electrical connector from the mass air flow (MAF)/intake air temperature (IAT) sensor.
2. Disconnect the positive crankcase ventilation (PCV) tube quick connect fitting from the air cleaner outlet duct.
3. Disconnect the secondary air injection (AIR) hose quick connect fitting from the air cleaner, if equipped.
4. Loosen the air cleaner outlet duct clamp at the throttle body.
5. Remove the air cleaner outlet duct from the throttle body.
6. Disengage the 3 integral clips on the lower housing from the upper housing.
7. Remove the air cleaner upper housing.
8. If replacing the air cleaner lower housing also, perform the following steps if not proceed to step 12.
9. Remove the engine harness and powertrain control module (PCM) from the lower housing.
10. Pull up firmly on the lower housing in order to disengage the grommets from the studs. Remove the air cleaner lower housing.

✳✳ CAUTION

Note the following precautions:

- Handle the MAF sensor carefully.
- Do not drop the MAF sensor in order to prevent damage to the MAF sensor.
- Do not damage the screen located on the air inlet end of the MAF.
- Do not touch the sensing elements.
- Do not allow solvents and lubricants to come in contact with the sensing elements.

11. If replacing the air cleaner upper housing only perform the following steps, loosen the air cleaner outlet duct clamp at the MAF/IAT sensor.
12. Remove the air cleaner outlet duct.
13. Remove the MAF/IAT sensor bolts and sensor.

To install:

➡**Use a small amount of a soap based solution in order to aid in the installation.**

14. If the upper air cleaner housing was replaced only perform the following steps, otherwise proceed to step 6.
15. Install the MAF/IAT sensor.
16. Install the air cleaner outlet duct.
17. Place the lower air cleaner housing over the studs and push down firmly in order to engage the grommets to the studs.
18. Install the engine harness and PCM to the lower housing.
19. Install the air cleaner upper housing.
20. Engage the 3 integral clips on the lower housing to the upper housing.
21. Install the air cleaner outlet duct to the throttle body.
22. Connect the AIR hose quick connect fitting to the air cleaner, if equipped.
23. Connect the PCV tube quick connect fitting to the air cleaner outlet duct.
24. Connect the engine harness electrical connector to the MAF/IAT sensor.

4.6L Engine

See Figure 22.

1. Disconnect the engine harness electrical connector from the mass air flow (MAF)/intake air temperature (IAT) sensor.
2. Disconnect the positive crankcase ventilation (PCV) fresh air tube quick connect fitting from the air cleaner outlet duct.
3. Disconnect the secondary air injection (AIR) pump inlet hose quick connect fitting from the air cleaner.
4. Loosen the air cleaner outlet duct clamp at the throttle body. Remove the air cleaner outlet duct from the throttle body.
5. Disengage the 3 integral clips on the lower housing from the upper housing. Remove the air cleaner upper housing.

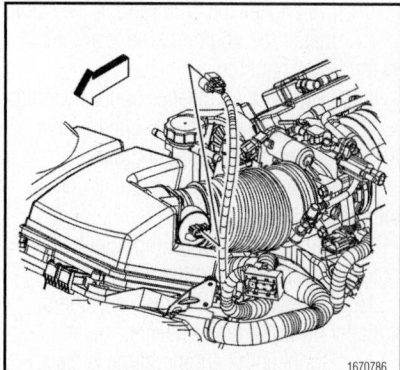

1670786

Fig. 22 Disconnect the engine harness electrical connector from the mass air flow (MAF)/intake air temperature (IAT) sensor.

6. If replacing the air cleaner lower housing also, perform the following steps if not proceed to step 9.

7. Remove the engine harness and engine control module (ECM) from the lower housing.

8. Pull up firmly on the lower housing in order to disengage the grommets from the studs. Remove the air cleaner lower housing.

⁕⁕ CAUTION

Observe the following precautions:

- Handle the MAF sensor carefully.
- Do not drop the MAF sensor in order to prevent damage to the MAF sensor.
- Do not damage the screen located on the air inlet end of the MAF.
- Do not touch the sensing elements.
- Do not allow solvents and lubricants to come in contact with the sensing elements.

9. If replacing the air cleaner upper housing only perform the following steps, loosen the air cleaner outlet duct clamp at the MAF/IAT sensor:

a. Remove the air cleaner outlet duct.

b. Remove the MAF/IAT sensor bolts.

c. Remove the MAF/IAT sensor.

To install:

➡**Use a small amount of a soap based solution in order to aid in the installation.**

10. If the upper air cleaner housing was replaced only, perform the following steps, otherwise proceed to step 6:

a. Install the MAF/IAT sensor.

b. Install the air cleaner outlet duct.

c. Place the lower air cleaner housing over the studs and push down firmly in order to engage the grommets to the studs.

11. Install the engine harness and ECM to the lower housing.

12. Install the air cleaner upper housing.

13. Engage the 3 integral clips on the lower housing to the upper housing.

14. Install the air cleaner outlet duct to the throttle body.

15. Connect the AIR pump inlet hose quick connect fitting to the air cleaner.

16. Connect the PCV fresh air tube quick connect fitting to the air cleaner outlet duct.

17. Connect the engine harness electrical connector to the MAF/IAT sensor.

FILTER/ELEMENT REPLACEMENT

➡**DO NOT remove the screws from the upper air cleaner cover.**

1. Loosen the air cleaner cover screws.

2. Open the air cleaner cover and remove the air filter from the air cleaner.

➡**For the LZ9 engine (3.9L flex fuel), the air cleaner cover has a hydrocarbon absorber that is not serviceable. If the absorber shows any kind of physical damage the cover must be replaced.**

3. Inspect the air cleaner housing assembly for damage. If a problem is found, replace as necessary.

To install:

4. Install the air filter to the air cleaner.

5. Close the air cleaner cover. Ensure that the inboard hinges are engaged prior to tightening the screws.

CAMSHAFT

REMOVAL & INSTALLATION

3.9L Engine

See Figure 23.

1. Remove the valve (camshaft) cover. See "Valve (Camshaft) Cover" in this section.

➡**Camshaft removal is with engine removed from vehicle.**

2. Remove the camshaft position sensor bolt. Remove the camshaft position sensor.

3. Remove the camshaft thrust plate screws. Remove the camshaft thrust plate.

⁕⁕ CAUTION

All camshaft journals are the same diameter, so care must be used in removing or installing the camshaft to avoid damage to the camshaft bearings.

4. Complete the following steps in order to remove the camshaft.

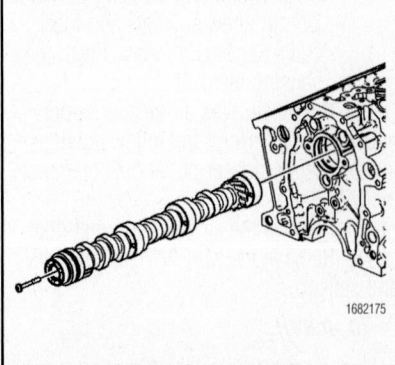

Fig. 23 Removing the camshaft—3.9L engine

a. Install a camshaft sprocket bolt into the camshaft. Tighten finger tight only.

b. Carefully rotate and remove the camshaft from the engine block.

To install:

5. Coat the camshaft journals with clean engine oil.

6. Coat the camshaft lobes with prelube (GM P/N 12345501 or equivalent).

7. Install the camshaft using the following procedure:

a. Install a camshaft sprocket bolt into the camshaft. Tighten finger tight only.

b. Carefully rotate the camshaft while installing the camshaft into the camshaft bearings.

8. Install the camshaft thrust plate. Install the camshaft thrust plate screws and tighten to 89 inch lbs. (10 Nm).

9. Install the camshaft position sensor. Install the camshaft position sensor bolt and tighten to 89 inch lbs. (10 Nm).

10. Install the valve (camshaft) cover. See "Valve (Camshaft) Cover" in this section.

4.6L Engine

Exhaust Camshaft

See Figures 24 and 25.

➡**Camshaft removal is the same for either bank.**

1. Remove the valve (camshaft) cover for the left side. See "Valve (Camshaft) Cover" in this section.

➡**Bearing caps must remain with their original cylinder head and in their original location. Do not mix bearing caps.**

2. Observe the markings on the bearing caps. Each bearing cap is marked in order to identify its location. The markings have the following meanings:

- The arrow points toward the front of the engine.
- The "E" indicates the exhaust camshaft.
- The number indicates the journal position from the front of the engine.

3. Remove the left exhaust camshaft bearing caps. Store the bearing caps in a clean shop towel.

4. Remove the left exhaust camshaft. Place the camshaft in a secure location. Cover the camshaft with an oil soaked towel in order to prevent corrosion.

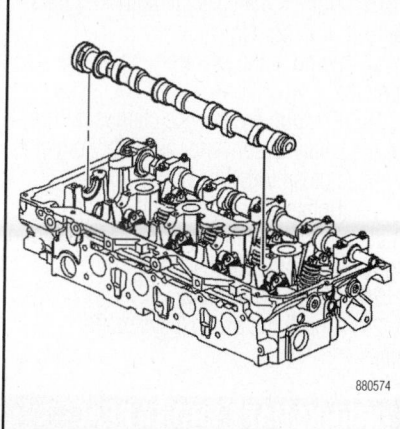

Fig. 24 Removing the left side exhaust camshaft—4.6L engine

To install:

5. Clean the camshaft journals, camshaft and the camshaft caps with a clean, lint-free cloth.

6. Apply a liberal amount of lubricant (GM P/N 12345001 or equivalent) to the camshaft lobes and journals.

➡Ensure each valve rocker arm is properly aligned to the valve tip, the valve lifter and the camshaft lobe. Inspect the alignment prior to and after the camshaft caps are tightened to specifications.

7. Place the camshaft in the camshaft journals with the camshaft sprocket drive pins near the top of their rotation and the camshaft lobes in a neutral position. The camshaft can be identified by a stamping near the rear journal. For example: L-EXH is defined as left bank exhaust.

8. Observe the markings on the bearing caps. Each bearing cap is marked in order to identify its location. The markings have the following meanings:
   • The arrow points toward the front of the engine.
   • The "E" indicates the exhaust camshaft.
   • The number indicates the journal position from the front of the engine.

9. Apply a liberal amount of lubricant to the left exhaust camshaft bearing cap journals.

10. Install the left exhaust camshaft bearing caps according to the identifications marks.

11. Hand start all the left exhaust camshaft bearing cap bolts.

➡Ensure each valve rocker arm is properly aligned to the valve tip, the

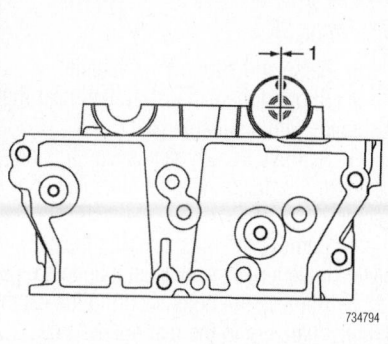

Fig. 25 Place the camshaft in the camshaft journals with the camshaft sprocket drive pins near the top of their rotation (1) and the camshaft lobes in a neutral position.

valve lifter and the camshaft lobe. Inspect the alignment prior to and after the camshaft caps are tightened to specifications.

12. Install the left cylinder head exhaust camshaft bearing cap bolts, front to back:
   a. Tighten the camshaft bearing cap bolts to 44 inch lbs. (5 Nm).
   b. Tighten the camshaft bearing cap bolts an additional 30 degrees.

13. Install the valve (camshaft) cover. See "Valve (Camshaft) Cover" in this section.

Intake Camshaft

See Figure 26.

➡Camshaft removal is the same for either bank.

1. Remove the valve (camshaft) cover. See "Valve (Camshaft) Cover" in this section.

➡Bearing caps must remain with their original cylinder head and in their original location. Do not mix bearing caps.

2. Observe the markings on the bearing caps. Each bearing cap is marked in order to identify its location. The markings have the following meanings:
   • The arrow points toward the front of the engine.
   • The "I" indicates the exhaust camshaft.
   • The number indicates the journal position from the front of the engine.

3. Remove the left intake camshaft bearing cap bolts. Remove the left intake camshaft bearing caps. Store the bearing caps in a clean shop towel.

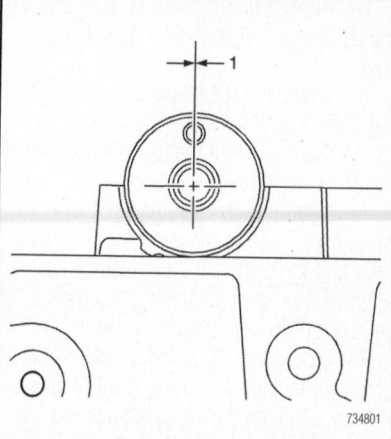

Fig. 26 Place the camshaft in the camshaft journals with the camshaft sprocket drive pins near the top of their rotation (1) and the camshaft lobes in a neutral position.

4. Remove the left intake camshaft. Place the camshaft in a secure location. Cover the camshaft with an oil soaked towel in order to prevent corrosion.

To install:

5. Clean the camshaft journals, camshaft and the camshaft caps with a clean, lint-free cloth.

6. Apply a liberal amount of lubricant (GM P/N 12345001 or equivalent) to the camshaft journals.

7. Apply a liberal amount of lubricant to the camshaft lobes and the camshaft journals.

➡Ensure each valve rocker arm is properly aligned to the valve tip, the valve lifter and the camshaft lobe. Inspect the alignment prior to and after the camshaft caps are tightened to specifications.

8. Place the camshaft in the camshaft journals with the camshaft sprocket drive pins near the top of their rotation and the camshaft lobes in a neutral position. The camshaft can be identified by a stamping near the rear journal. For example: L-INT is defined as left bank intake.

9. Observe the markings on the bearing caps. Each bearing cap is marked in order to identify its location. The markings have the following meanings:
   • The arrow points toward the front of the engine.
   • The "I" indicates the exhaust camshaft.
   • The number indicates the journal position from the front of the engine.

10. Apply a liberal amount of lubricant to the left intake camshaft bearing cap journals.

11. Install the left intake camshaft bearing caps according to the identifications marks. Hand start all the left intake camshaft bearing cap bolts.

12. Ensure each valve rocker arm is properly aligned to the valve tip, the valve lifter and the camshaft lobe. Inspect the alignment prior to and after the camshaft caps are tightened to specifications.

13. Install the left cylinder head intake camshaft bearing cap bolts, front to back:

    a. Tighten the camshaft bearing cap bolts to 44 inch lbs. (5 Nm).

    b. Tighten the camshaft bearing cap bolts an additional 30 degrees.

14. Install the valve (camshaft) cover. See "Valve (Camshaft) Cover" in this section.

CATALYTIC CONVERTER

REMOVAL & INSTALLATION

3.9L Engine

See Figure 27.

1. Raise and support the vehicle.
2. Remove the forward flange nuts.
3. Remove the rear flange nuts.
4. Remove the 3-way catalytic converter:
    a. Move the muffler assembly rearward in order to clear the studs.

To install:

5. Installation is the reverse of the removal procedure.

➡**Use new gaskets during reassembly.**

6. Install new rear flange nuts. Tighten to 35 ft. lbs. (47 Nm).

7. Install new forward flange nuts. Tighten to 37 ft. lbs. (50 Nm).

4.6L Engine

See Figure 28.

1. Raise and support the vehicle.
2. Support the exhaust system near the resonator with a suitable jack.
3. Remove the oxygen sensor. It is not necessary to disconnect the electrical connector.
4. Remove the nuts securing the catalytic converter to the exhaust manifold pipe.
5. Remove the bolts securing the center exhaust hangers to the rear suspension support brackets.
6. Remove the catalytic converter from the manifold pipe.
7. Lower the exhaust system.
8. Remove the catalytic converter gasket. Do not reuse the gasket.
9. Cut the intermediate pipe 1.3 in. (34 mm) from the resonator weld.

To install:

10. Slide 2 service clamps over the catalytic converter assembly outlet pipe. Do not tighten at this time.

➡**Ensure the O2 sensor boss is facing the right side of the vehicle.**

11. Slide the catalytic converter assembly outlet pipe over the intermediate pipe.

12. Place a NEW catalytic converter gasket over the catalytic converter studs.

13. Raise the exhaust system into position, aligning the catalytic converter with the exhaust manifold pipe.

14. Install the nuts securing the catalytic converter to the exhaust manifold pipe. Do not tighten at this time.

15. Install the bolts securing the center exhaust hangers to the rear suspension support brackets and tighten to 20 ft. lbs. (30 Nm).

16. Tighten the catalytic converter nuts to 18 ft. lbs. (25 Nm).

17. Remove the jack from under the vehicle.

18. Position the service clamps midway on the catalytic converter assembly outlet pipe, as close together as possible.

19. Rotate the clamps so the fastening ends are pointing in opposite directions and tighten to 40 ft. lbs. (54 Nm).

20. Lower the vehicle.

21. Check the exhaust system for leaks.

CRANKSHAFT FRONT SEAL

REMOVAL & INSTALLATION

3.9L Engine

See Figure 29.

1. Remove the crankshaft balancer. See "Crankshaft Balancer" in this section.

2. Pry out the crankshaft front oil seal using a suitable tool. Use care not to damage the engine front cover or the crankshaft.

To install:

3. Lubricate the NEW oil seal with clean engine oil.

4. Align the installer tool (EN-48869 or equivalent) and the crankshaft front oil seal with the engine front cover and crankshaft. Install the crankshaft front oil seal.

5. Install the crankshaft balancer. See "Crankshaft Balancer" in this section.

4.6L Engine

➡**Do not remove the crankshaft front oil seal. The crankshaft front oil seal is**

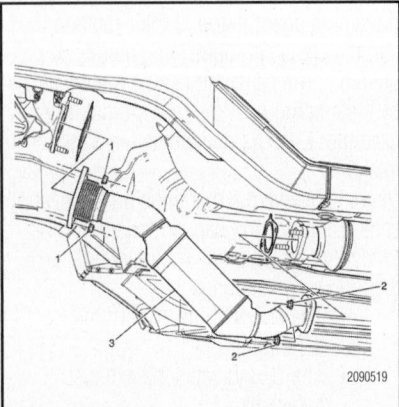

Fig. 27 Remove the forward flange nuts (1), the rear flange nuts (2), and the 3-way catalytic converter (3)

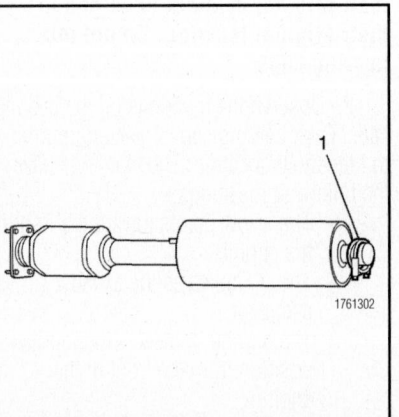

Fig. 28 Slide 2 service clamps over the catalytic converter assembly outlet pipe. Do not tighten at this time.

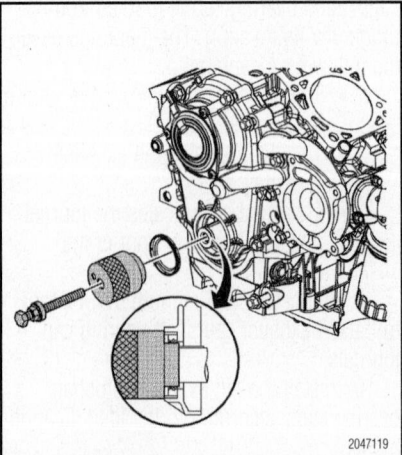

Fig. 29 Align the installer tool (EN-48869 or equivalent) and the crankshaft front oil seal with the engine front cover and crankshaft. Install the crankshaft front oil seal.

not serviced as an individual component. When replacing the crankshaft front oil seal, install a NEW engine front cover. In order to precisely align the crankshaft front oil seal to the crankshaft balancer and crankshaft balancer dust shield, the engine front cover and the crankshaft front oil seal are sold as an assembly. See "Engine Front Cover" in this section.

CYLINDER HEAD

REMOVAL & INSTALLATION

3.9L Engine

See Figure 30.

1. Drain the cooling system.
2. Drain the engine oil.
3. Lower the vehicle.
4. If removing the left side head, remove the generator. See "ENGINE ELECTRICAL" section.
5. Remove the lower intake manifold. See "Intake Manifold" in this section.
6. Remove the valve rocker arms and the pushrods. See "Rocker Arms & Pushrods" in this section.
7. Remove the exhaust manifold.
8. If removing the left side head, remove the oil level indicator tube.
9. Disconnect the spark plug wires from the spark plugs. Remove the spark plug wire clips from the brackets. Disconnect and remove the spark plug wires from the ignition coil. Remove the spark plugs.
10. If removing the right side head, remove the power steering fluid reservoir. See "STEERING" section.
11. If removing the right side head, remove the drive belt tensioner and drive belt.
12. Remove and discard the cylinder head bolts. Remove the cylinder head.
13. Remove and discard the cylinder head gasket.

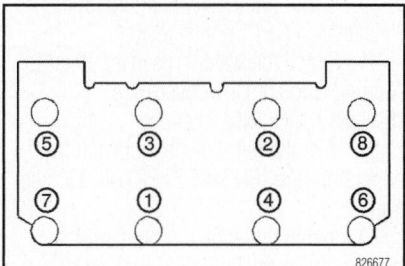

Fig. 30 Cylinder head bolt tightening sequence—left head on 3.9L engine

14. Remove the cylinder head locator dowel pins, if necessary.

To install:

> **CAUTION**
>
> **Head gaskets are specific for right hand and left hand applications, and also must be installed with the correct side facing up. Note the markings on the head gaskets for proper installation. Failure to do so may lead to engine damage.**

15. Install the cylinder head locator dowel pins, if necessary.
16. Inspect the cylinder head locator dowel pins for proper installation.
17. Install a NEW cylinder head gasket.
18. Install the cylinder head onto the locator pins and the engine.

> **CAUTION**
>
> **This component uses torque-to-yield bolts. When servicing this component do not reuse the bolts, new torque-to-yield bolts must be installed. Reusing used torque-to-yield bolts will not provide proper bolt torque and clamp load. Failure to install NEW torque-to-yield bolts may lead to engine damage.**

19. Install NEW cylinder head bolts finger tight.
20. Install the cylinder head bolts as follows:
    a. Tighten the cylinder head bolts a first pass in sequence to 44 ft. lbs. (60 Nm).
    b. Tighten the cylinder head bolts a final pass in sequence an additional 140 degrees, using the proper torque meter (J 45059 or equivalent).
21. For the right side head, install the drive belt tensioner and drive belt.
22. For the right side head, install the power steering fluid reservoir. See "STEERING" section.
23. Install the left spark plugs.
24. Install and connect the left spark plug wires to the ignition coil.
25. Install the spark plug wire clips to the brackets. Connect the left spark plug wires to the spark plugs.
26. For the left side head, install the oil level indicator tube.
27. Install the exhaust manifold. See "Exhaust Manifold" in this section.
28. Install the valve rocker arms and the pushrods. See "Rocker Arms & Pushrods" in this section.

29. Install the lower intake manifold. See "Intake Manifold" in this section.
30. For the left side head, install the generator. See "ENGINE ELECTRICAL" section.
31. Fill the engine with oil.
32. Fill the cooling system.
33. Inspect for leaks.

4.6L Engine

See Figures 31 through 33.

1. Remove the exhaust manifold. See "Exhaust Manifold" in this section.
2. Remove the engine mount strut bracket. See "Engine Mount Strut Bracket" in this section.
3. For the left side head, remove the generator. See "ENGINE ELECTRICAL" section.
4. Remove the water crossover. See "Engine Coolant Crossover Pipe" in "ENGINE COOLING" section.
5. Remove the intake manifold. See "Intake Manifold" in this section.
6. Remove the camshaft cover.
7. Remove the engine front cover. See "Engine Front Cover" in this section.
8. Remove the left or right secondary camshaft drive chain (depending on side of head). See "Timing Chain & Sprockets" in this section.
9. For the right cylinder head, do the following:
    a. Disconnect the engine harness electrical connector from the engine coolant temperature (ECT) sensor.
    b. Remove the engine harness ground terminal nut.
    c. Remove the engine harness ground terminal.
    d. Remove the stud attaching the exhaust manifold front pipe to the cylinder head.
    e. Raise and support the vehicle.
    f. Remove the stud attaching the right engine mount bracket to the cylinder head.
    g. Loosen the bolts attaching the engine mount bracket to the transaxle. Remove the bolt attaching the transaxle brace to the transaxle.
    h. Lower the vehicle.
    i. Remove the nuts attaching the transaxle brace to the lift bracket studs. Remove the transaxle brace.
    j. Remove the rear lift bracket studs. Remove the rear lift bracket.
10. Remove the 3 M6 cylinder head bolts.
11. Remove and discard the 10 M11 cylinder head bolts.

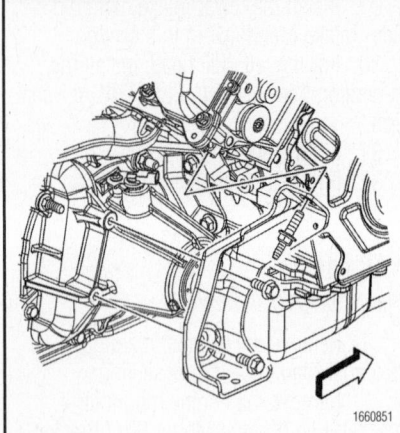

Fig. 31 Loosen the bolts attaching the engine mount bracket to the transaxle. Remove the bolt attaching the transaxle brace to the transaxle.

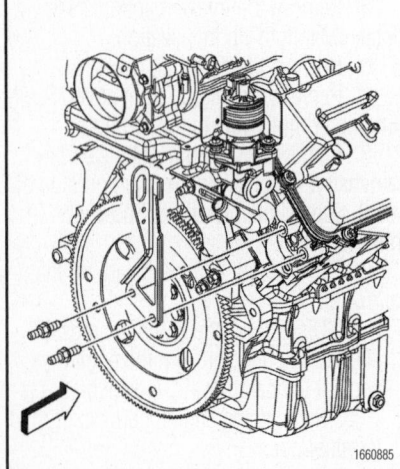

Fig. 32 Remove the nuts attaching the transaxle brace to the lift bracket studs. Remove the transaxle brace.

12. Remove the cylinder head. Make sure that no locating pins are stuck in the cylinder head.

✷✷ CAUTION

You must clean the thread sealant material from the cylinder head bolt holes in the cylinder block. Failure to do so could cause false torque readings during reassembly.

13. After removing the cylinder head, remove any remaining bolt thread sealant material from the threaded cylinder block holes.

14. Remove and discard the cylinder head gasket.

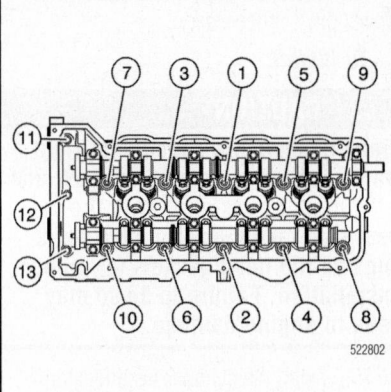

Fig. 33 Cylinder head bolt tightening sequence—left head shown; right head same, but opposite, sequence

15. Remove all remaining gasket material from the cylinder head and cylinder block.

16. Place the cylinder head on a clean, flat surface with the combustion chambers face-up in order to prevent damage to the deck face.

17. Clean and inspect the cylinder head.

To install:

18. Make sure all the cylinder head locating pins are securely installed in the cylinder block deck face.

✷✷ CAUTION

Failure to remove all the old thread sealant material from the cylinder block could cause false torque readings.

19. Make sure all old thread sealant material is removed from the cylinder head bolt holes in the cylinder block.

20. Install a NEW cylinder head gasket using the locating pins for retention.

21. Align the cylinder head with the locating pins. Place the cylinder head in position on the cylinder block.

22. Install 10 NEW M11 cylinder head bolts until snug.

23. Install the 3 M6 cylinder head bolts until snug.

➡A proper torque meter may be required when tightening bolts to additional degrees (J 45059 or equivalent).

24. Tighten the 10 M11 cylinder head bolts as follows:

a. Tighten the bolts a first pass in the sequence shown to 22 ft. lbs. (30 Nm).

b. Tighten the bolts a second pass in the sequence shown an additional 70 degrees.

c. Tighten the bolts a third pass in the sequence shown an additional 60 degrees.

d. Tighten the bolts a final pass in the sequence shown an additional 45 degrees (total 175 degrees).

25. Tighten the 3 M6 bolts cylinder head as follows:

a. Tighten the bolts to 106 inch lbs. (12 Nm).

26. For the right cylinder head, do the following:

a. Install the rear lift bracket studs. Remove the rear lift bracket.

b. Install the nuts attaching the transaxle brace to the lift bracket studs. Remove the transaxle brace.

c. Raise and support the vehicle.

d. Install the bolt attaching the transaxle brace to the transaxle.

e. Tighten the bolts attaching the engine mount bracket to the transaxle.

f. Lower the vehicle.

g. Install the stud attaching the right engine mount bracket to the cylinder head.

h. Install the stud attaching the exhaust manifold front pipe to the cylinder head.

i. Install the engine harness ground terminal.

j. Install the engine harness ground terminal nut.

k. Connect the engine harness electrical connector from the engine coolant temperature (ECT) sensor.

27. Install the left or right secondary camshaft drive chain (depending on side of head). See "Timing Chain & Sprockets" in this section.

28. Install the engine front cover. See "Engine Front Cover" in this section.

29. Install the camshaft cover.

30. Install the intake manifold. See "Intake Manifold" in this section.

31. Install the water crossover. Refer to "Engine Coolant Crossover Pipe" in "ENGINE COOLING" section.

32. For the left side head, install the generator. See "ENGINE ELECTRICAL" section.

33. Install the engine mount strut bracket. Refer to "Engine Mount Strut Bracket" in this section.

34. Install the left exhaust manifold. See "Exhaust Manifold" in this section.

ENGINE FRONT COVER

REMOVAL & INSTALLATION

3.9L Engine

See Figure 34.

1. Drain the cooling system. See "ENGINE COOLING" section.
2. Remove the drive belt tensioner. See "Accessory Drive Belt" in this section.
3. Remove the oil pan. See "Oil Pan" in this section.
4. Remove the crankshaft balancer. See "Crankshaft Balancer" in this section.
5. Remove the crankshaft position actuator magnet.
6. Remove the thermostat housing.
7. Remove the water pump. See "ENGINE COOLING" section.
8. Remove the engine front cover bolts.
9. Remove coolant hose from front cover
10. Remove the engine front cover.
11. Remove the engine front cover gasket.

To install:

12. Install the engine front cover gasket.
13. Install the engine front cover. Install the engine front cover bolts and tighten to 18 ft. lbs. (25 Nm).
14. Install the water pump.
15. Install the thermostat housing.
16. Install the crankshaft position actuator magnet.
17. Install the crankshaft balancer.
18. Install the oil pan.
19. Install the drive belt tensioner.
20. Fill the cooling system.

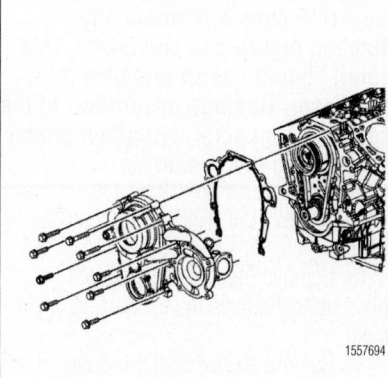

Fig. 34 Removing/installing front engine cover

4.6L Engine

See Figure 35.

1. Remove the drive belt idler pulley.
2. Remove the crankshaft balancer. See "Crankshaft Balance" in this section.
3. Remove the engine front cover bolts.
4. Remove the engine front cover and gasket.

➡**The gasket is reusable. Do not discard unless it is damaged.**

To install:

5. Place a small amount of sealant at the split line of the upper and lower crankcases.
6. Place the engine front cover gasket over the crankcase dowel pins.
7. Place the engine front cover in position on the crankcase.
8. Apply threadlock to the engine front cover bolts.
9. Install the engine front cover bolts until snug.
10. Tighten the engine front cover bolts in the sequence to 89 inch lbs. (10 Nm).
11. Install the crankshaft balancer.
12. Install the drive belt idler pulley.

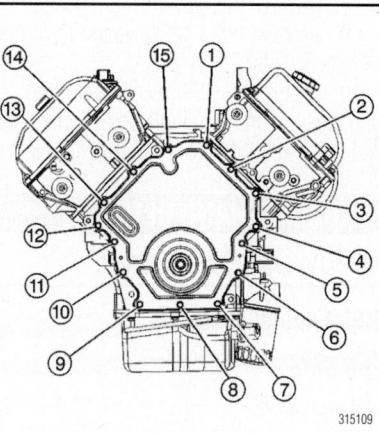

Fig. 35 Engine front cover bolt tightening sequence—4.6L engine

ENGINE MOUNT STRUT & BRACKET

REMOVAL & INSTALLATION

4.6L Engine

See Figure 36.

1. Remove the engine mount strut as follows:
   a. Remove the surge tank nuts and push pin retainer. Remove the surge tank from the studs and position the tank aside.

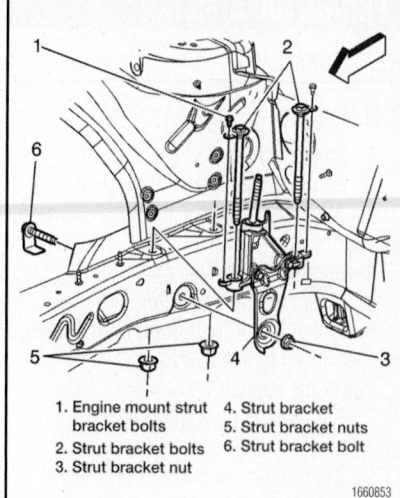

1. Engine mount strut bracket bolts
2. Strut bracket bolts
3. Strut bracket nut
4. Strut bracket
5. Strut bracket nuts
6. Strut bracket bolt

Fig. 36 Removing engine mount strut bracket and retainers

   b. Remove the engine mount strut brace nut.
   c. Remove the engine mount strut bolt.
   d. Remove the engine mount strut.
2. Remove the right front wheel and tire.
3. Remove the engine mount strut bracket bolts and nuts as indicated in the illustration.
4. Remove the engine mount strut bracket to engine bolts.
5. Remove the engine mount strut bracket.

To install:

6. Position the engine mount strut bracket to the cylinder head. Install the engine mount strut bracket to engine bolts. Tighten the bolts to 37 ft. lbs. (50 Nm).
7. Position the engine mount strut bracket to the front compartment rail.
8. Install the strut bracket bolts and nuts. Tighten to 52 ft. lbs. (70 Nm), except the bolt which is tightened to 80 inch lbs. (9 Nm).
9. Install the right front wheel and tire.
10. Install the engine mount strut as follows:
    a. Install the engine mount strut.
    b. Install the engine mount strut bolt. Tighten the bolt to 52 ft. lbs. (70 Nm).
11. Install the engine mount strut nut. Tighten the nut to 52 ft. lbs. (70 Nm).
12. Position the surge tank to the studs. Install the surge tank nuts and push pin retainer. Tighten the nuts to 53 inch lbs. (6 Nm).

ENGINE OIL & FILTER

REPLACEMENT

3.9L Engine

1. Raise and support the vehicle.
2. Remove the oil pan drain plug.
3. Allow the engine oil to drain completely.
4. Remove the oil filter.
5. Install the new oil filter.
6. Install the oil pan drain bolt. Tighten the bolt to 19 ft. lbs. (26 Nm).
   Lower the vehicle.
7. Fill the engine with oil to the appropriate level.
8. Start engine and inspect for leaks.

4.6L Engine

1. Raise and support the vehicle.
2. Position the oil drain pan under the engine oil drain plug.
3. Remove the engine oil drain plug.
4. Clean and inspect the engine oil drain plug, replace if necessary.
5. Clean and inspect the engine oil drain plug sealing surface on the oil pan, repair or replace oil pan if necessary.
6. Remove the oil filter.
7. Clean and inspect the oil filter sealing area on the oil filter adapter, repair or replace if necessary.
8. Fill the oil filter with oil. Lightly oil the replacement oil filter gasket with clean oil. Install the new oil filter. Tighten the new oil filter to 3/4 to 1 full turn, after the oil filter gasket contacts the oil filter mounting surface.
9. Install the engine oil drain plug. Tighten the engine oil drain plug to 15 ft. lbs. (20 Nm).
10. Lower the vehicle.
11. Fill the engine with new engine oil.
12. Inspect for oil leaks after engine start up.

ENGINE PRE-LUBE PROCEDURE

4.6L Engine

See Figure 37.

1. Remove the engine oil filter.
2. Install a proper tester (J 42907 or equivalent) onto the oil filter adapter. Install the 1/8 NPT fitting into the port on the tester .
3. Install the pre-lube flexible hose to the fitting.
4. Open the valve of the J 45299 preluber.

➡A constant and continuous flow of clean engine oil is required in order to properly prime the engine. Use the

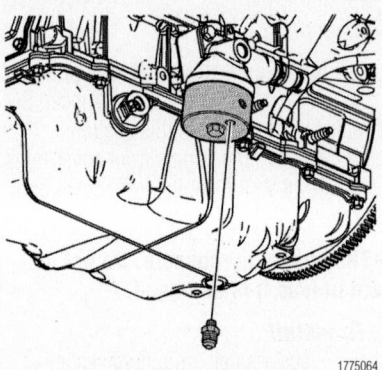

Fig. 37 Install a proper tester (J 42907 or equivalent) onto the oil filter adapter. Install the 1/8 NPT fitting into the port on the tester.

approved engine oil as specified in the owner's manual.

5. Pump the handle of the preluber in order to flow a minimum of 1–2 qts. (1–1.9 liters) of fresh clean engine oil. Observe the flow of engine oil through the flexible hose and into the engine assembly.
6. Close the valve of the preluber .
7. Remove the preluber flexible hose.
8. Remove the fitting from the tester.
9. Remove the J 42907 tester from the oil filter adapter.
10. Ensure the NEW oil filter is filled with clean fresh engine oil. Install the NEW oil filter and tighten to 24 ft. lbs. (32 Nm).

EXHAUST MANIFOLD

REMOVAL & INSTALLATION

3.9L Engine

Left Side

See Figure 38.

1. Remove the air cleaner outlet duct.
2. Remove the exhaust crossover pipe heat shield bolts. Remove the exhaust crossover pipe heat shield.
3. Remove the exhaust manifold heat shield bolts. Remove the exhaust manifold heat shield.
4. Remove the exhaust crossover pipe to left exhaust manifold nuts.
5. Remove the exhaust manifold bolts.
6. Remove the exhaust manifold.
7. Remove and discard the exhaust manifold gasket.

To install:

8. Install a NEW exhaust manifold gasket onto the cylinder head studs.
9. Install the exhaust manifold. Install

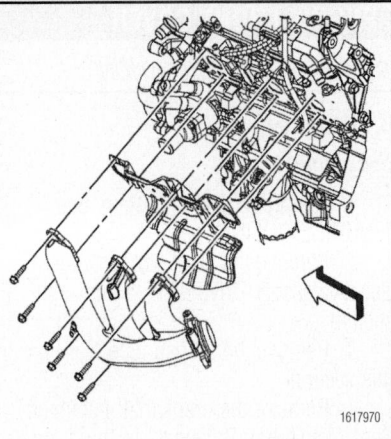

Fig. 38 Exhaust manifold mounting—left side 3.9L engine

the exhaust manifold bolts and tighten to 15 ft. lbs. (20 Nm).
10. Install the exhaust crossover pipe to left exhaust manifold nuts and tighten to 15 ft. lbs. (20 Nm).
11. Install the exhaust manifold heat shield. Install the exhaust manifold heat shield bolts and tighten to 89 inch lbs. (10 Nm).
12. Install the engine front mount bracket.
13. Install the exhaust crossover pipe heat shield. Install the exhaust crossover pipe heat shield bolts and tighten to 89 inch lbs. (10 Nm).
14. Install the air cleaner outlet duct.

Right Side

See Figures 39 and 40.

1. Remove the connector position assurance (CPA) retainer. Disconnect the heated oxygen sensor (HO2S) electrical connector. Remove the HO2S clip from the ignition coil bracket.

✳✳ CAUTION

The HO2S uses a permanently attached pigtail and connector. This pigtail should not be removed from the sensor. Damage or removal of the pigtail or connector will affect proper operation of the sensor.

2. Remove the HO2S using a proper wrench.
3. Remove the exhaust manifold shield bolts. Remove the exhaust manifold shield.
4. Remove the exhaust crossover pipe heat shield bolts. Remove the exhaust crossover pipe heat shield.
5. Remove the exhaust crossover pipe to right exhaust manifold nuts.

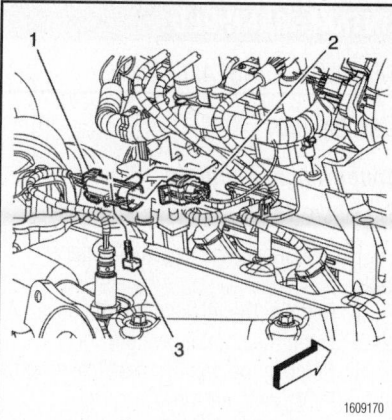

Fig. 39 Remove the connector position assurance (CPA) retainer (3). Disconnect the heated oxygen sensor (HO2S) electrical connector (2). Remove the HO2S clip (1) from the ignition coil bracket.

6. Remove the upper exhaust manifold bolts.

7. Remove the catalytic converter.

8. Remove the lower exhaust manifold bolts.

9. Remove the exhaust manifold from the bottom of the vehicle.

10. Remove and discard the exhaust manifold gasket.

To install:

11. Install a NEW exhaust manifold gasket onto the cylinder head studs.

12. Install the exhaust manifold.

13. Install the lower exhaust manifold bolts and tighten to 15 ft. lbs. (20 Nm).

14. Install the catalytic converter. See "Catalytic Converter" in this section.

15. Lower the vehicle.

16. Install the upper exhaust manifold bolts and tighten to 15 ft. lbs. (20 Nm).

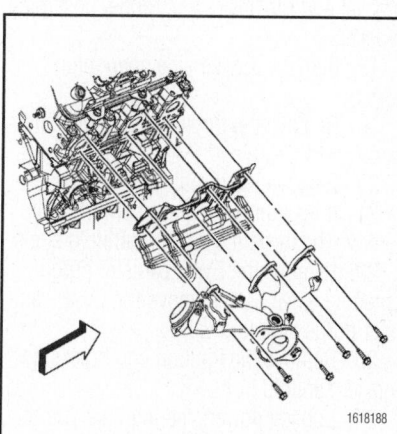

Fig. 40 Showing the exhaust manifold mounting—3.9L engine

17. Install the exhaust crossover pipe to right exhaust manifold nuts.

18. Install the exhaust crossover pipe heat shield. Install the exhaust crossover pipe heat shield bolts.

19. Install the exhaust manifold shield. Install the exhaust manifold shield bolts and tighten to 89 inch lbs. (10 Nm).

➡️**Whenever the oxygen sensor is removed, coat the threads with nickel-based anti-seize compound such as GM P/N 5613695 (or equivalent).**

20. Install the HO2S using a proper Heated Oxygen Sensor Wrench and tighten to 31 ft. lbs. (42 Nm).

21. Connect the HO2S electrical connector. Install the CPA retainer. Install the HO2S clip to the ignition coil bracket.

22. Install the power steering reservoir.

4.6L Engine

Left Side

See Figures 41 and 42.

1. Remove the front engine mount bracket.

2. Remove the connector position assurance (CPA) retainer. Disconnect the engine harness electrical connector from the heated oxygen sensor (HO2S).

3. Remove the HO2S.

4. Remove the exhaust manifold front pipe bolts at the exhaust manifold flange.

5. Remove the exhaust manifold bolts.

6. Remove the exhaust manifold.

7. Remove and discard the exhaust manifold gasket.

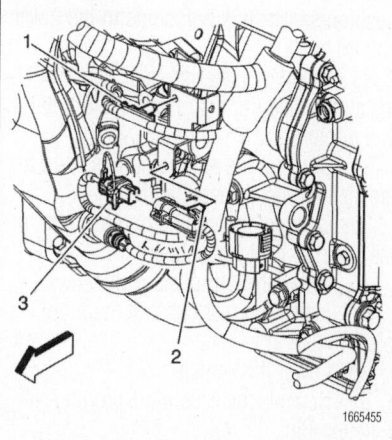

Fig. 41 Remove the connector position assurance (CPA) retainer (2). Disconnect the engine harness electrical connector (3) from the heated oxygen sensor (HO2S)—retainer (1) shown; not applicable for this procedure.

8. Remove and discard the front exhaust manifold pipe seal.

9. Remove the front exhaust manifold pipe flange.

To install:

10. Install the front exhaust manifold pipe flange and a NEW seal onto the exhaust manifold.

11. Insert the upper right exhaust manifold bolt to the manifold in location shown.

12. Place the NEW exhaust manifold gasket over the bolt and against the manifold.

13. Insert the exhaust manifold into the front exhaust manifold pipe and against the cylinder head.

14. Finger start the exhaust manifold bolt.

15. Install the remaining exhaust manifold bolts and tighten all exhaust manifold bolts starting from right to left beginning with the bolt in upper right location. Tighten the bolts 18 ft. lbs. (25 Nm).

16. Install the exhaust manifold front pipe bolts.

17. If reusing the old HO2S, coat the threads with anti-seize compound, GM P/N 12377953 or equivalent.

18. Install the HO2S and tighten to 30 ft. lbs. (40 Nm).

19. Connect the engine harness electrical connector to the HO2S. Install the CPA retainer.

20. Install the front engine mount bracket.

Right Side

1. Remove the connector position assurance (CPA) retainer. Disconnect the engine harness electrical connector from the

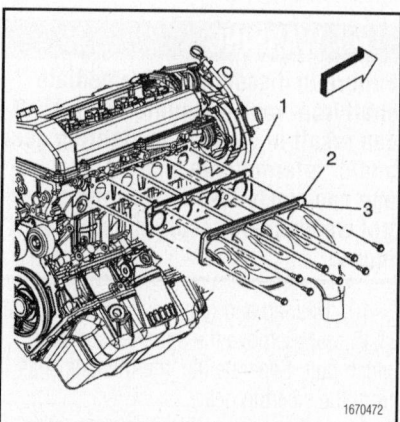

Fig. 42 Left side exhaust manifold mounting—gasket (1), upper right bolt location (2), and exhaust manifold (3).

heated oxygen sensor (HO2S). Remove the HO2S clip from the secondary air injection (AIR) valve hose bracket.

2. With wheels of the vehicle facing straight ahead, secure the steering wheel utilizing steering column anti-rotation pin, steering column lock, or a strap to prevent rotation. Locking of the steering column will prevent damage and a possible malfunction of the SIR system. The steering wheel must be secured in position before disconnecting the following components:

- The steering column
- The intermediate shaft(s)
- The steering gear

❊❊ CAUTION

After disconnecting these components, do not rotate the steering wheel or move the front tires and wheels. Failure to follow this procedure may cause the SIR coil assembly to become un-centered and cause possible damage to the SIR coil. If you think the SIR coil has became un-centered, refer to your specific SIR coil's centering procedure to re-center SIR Coil.

3. Lock the steering column by installing the Steering Column Anti-Rotation Pin into the underside of the steering column.

4. Raise and support the vehicle.

5. Remove the rear exhaust manifold pipe.

6. Remove the AIR check valve.

7. Disconnect the engine harness clips from the steering gear heat shield.

8. Remove the steering gear heat shield bolts. Remove the steering gear heat shield.

9. Disconnect the electronic suspension position sensor link ball studs from the lower control arms.

❊❊ WARNING

Failure to disconnect intermediate shaft from rack and pinion stub shaft can result in damage to steering gear and/or intermediate shaft. This damage can cause loss of steering control which could result in personal injury.

10. Unsnap and remove the intermediate shaft seal. Remove the intermediate shaft pinch bolt. Separate the intermediate shaft from the steering gear.

11. Remove the right engine mount to frame nut.

12. Remove the left engine mount to frame nut.

13. Remove the transaxle mount to frame nuts.

14. Support the rear of the frame with a tall screw type jack.

15. Remove the 4 rearward engine frame-to-body bolts.

16. Lower the screw type jack approximately 1.5 in. (4 cm), allowing the rear of the engine frame to lower.

17. Remove the HO2S.

18. Remove the exhaust manifold nuts.

19. Remove the exhaust manifold.

20. Remove and discard the exhaust manifold gasket.

To install:

21. Install a NEW exhaust manifold gasket onto the cylinder head studs.

22. Install exhaust manifold. Install the exhaust manifold nuts and tighten to 18 ft. lbs. (25 Nm).

23. If reusing the old HO2S, coat the threads with anti-seize compound, GM P/N 12377953 or equivalent.

24. Install the HO2S and tighten to 30 ft. lbs. (40 Nm).

25. Raise the engine frame into position. Install the 4 rearward engine frame-to-body bolts and tighten to 141 ft. lbs. (191 Nm).

26. Remove the screw type jack.

27. Install the transaxle mount to frame nuts and tighten to 37 ft. lbs. (50 Nm).

28. Install the left engine mount to frame nut and tighten to 59 ft. lbs. (80 Nm).

29. Install the right engine mount to frame nut and tighten to 59 ft. lbs. (80 Nm).

30. Connect the intermediate shaft to the steering gear. Install the intermediate shaft pinch bolt and tighten to 33 ft. lbs. (45 Nm).

31. Install the intermediate shaft seal.

32. Connect the electronic suspension position sensor link ball studs to the lower control arms.

33. Install the steering gear heat shield. Install the steering gear heat shield bolts and tighten.

34. Connect the engine harness clip to the steering gear heat shield.

35. Connect the engine harness clip to the steering gear heat shield.

36. Install the AIR check valve.

37. Install the rear exhaust manifold pipe.

38. Lower the vehicle.

39. Remove the Steering Column Anti-Rotation Pin.

40. Connect the engine harness electrical connector to the HO2S.

41. Install the HO2S clip to the AIR valve hose bracket.

42. Install the CPA retainer.

INTAKE MANIFOLD

REMOVAL & INSTALLATION

3.9L Engine

Upper Intake Manifold

See Figure 43.

1. Disconnect the negative battery cable.

2. Remove the intake manifold cover.

3. Drain the cooling system.

4. Remove the positive crankcase ventilation (PCV) fresh air tube.

5. Remove the PCV foul air tube.

6. Remove the brake booster vacuum hose from the intake manifold fitting.

7. Remove the heater inlet and outlet hose/pipe clamp nuts from the throttle body studs.

8. Remove the heater inlet and outlet hoses/pipes from the engine pipes and the throttle body studs. Reposition the hoses/pipes out of the way.

9. Remove the fuel line and evaporative emission (EVAP) line clip from the manifold absolute pressure (MAP) sensor bracket.

10. Disconnect the MAP sensor electrical connector.

11. Disconnect the EVAP canister purge solenoid electrical connector.

12. Disconnect the chassis EVAP line quick connect fitting from the purge solenoid.

13. Disconnect the electronic throttle control (ETC) electrical connector.

14. Remove the air cleaner outlet duct.

15. Disconnect the left side spark plug wires from the spark plugs.

16. Disconnect the left side spark plug wires from the ignition coil.

17. Disengage the spark plug wire retainer clips from the intake manifold bracket and the heater inlet/outlet hose/pipe bracket.

18. Remove the left side spark plug wires.

19. Remove the throttle body bolts and nuts.

20. Remove the throttle body and gasket.

21. If installing a replacement manifold, remove the throttle body-to-manifold studs.

22. Remove the EVAP canister purge solenoid valve bolt. Remove the EVAP canister purge solenoid valve.

23. Remove the ignition coil bracket to intake manifold bolts.

24. Loosen power steering reservoir to intake manifold bolt and reposition.

25. Remove generator to intake manifold bracket bolt.

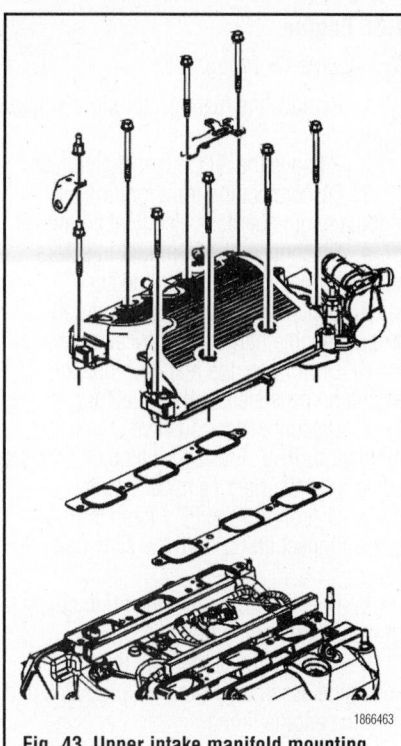

Fig. 43 Upper intake manifold mounting

26. Remove the intake manifold cover ball stud nut from the intake manifold stud.

27. Remove the upper intake manifold bolts and stud.

28. Separate and remove the upper intake manifold from the lower intake manifold.

29. Remove the upper to lower intake manifold gaskets.

30. Clean the upper intake to lower intake gasket mating surfaces.

To install:

31. Install the upper intake manifold onto the lower intake manifold.

32. Apply threadlock to the upper intake manifold bolts/stud threads.

33. Install the upper intake manifold bolts and stud and tighten the bolts to 18 ft. lbs. (25 Nm).

34. Install the intake manifold cover ball stud nut to the intake manifold stud and tighten the nut.

35. Install the ignition coil bracket to intake manifold bolts and tighten the bolts to 18 ft. lbs. (25 Nm).

36. Install the MAP sensor and bracket. Install the MAP sensor bracket/upper intake manifold bolts and tighten to 18 ft. lbs. (25 Nm).

37. Install the EVAP canister purge solenoid valve. Install the EVAP canister purge solenoid valve bolt and tighten to 12 ft. lbs. (16 Nm).

38. Inspect the throttle body seal for damage. Replace as necessary.

39. Apply threadlock to the throttle body bolts/studs threads.

40. Position the throttle body gasket and throttle body to the intake:

 a. Install the throttle body studs, if required and tighten to 53 inch lbs. (6 Nm).

 b. Install the throttle body bolts and nuts and tighten to 89 inch lbs. (10 Nm).

41. Install the left side spark plug wires.

42. Engage the spark plug wire retainer clips to the intake manifold bracket and the heater inlet/outlet hose/pipe bracket.

43. Connect the left side spark plug wires to the ignition coil.

44. Connect the left side spark plug wires to the spark plugs.

45. Install the air cleaner outlet duct.

46. Connect the EVAP canister purge solenoid electrical connector.

47. Connect the chassis EVAP line quick connect fitting to the purge solenoid.

48. Connect the ETC electrical connector.

49. Connect the MAP sensor electrical connector.

50. Install the fuel feed and EVAP line clip to the MAP sensor bracket.

51. Position the hoses/pipes:

 a. Install the heater inlet and outlet hoses/pipes to the engine pipes and the throttle body studs.

 b. Install the heater inlet and outlet hose/pipe clamp nuts to the throttle body studs and tighten the nuts to 89 inch lbs. (10 Nm).

52. Position the heater inlet and outlet hose/pipe clamps at the engine pipes.

53. Install the brake booster vacuum hose to the intake manifold.

54. Install the PCV foul air tube.

55. Install the PCV fresh air tube.

56. Fill the cooling system.

57. Install the intake manifold cover.

58. Connect the negative battery cable.

Lower Intake Manifold

See Figures 44 and 45.

➡**This procedure also involves removal of the rocker arms and pushrods.**

✳✳ CAUTION

This engine uses a sequential multiport fuel injection system. Injector wiring harness connectors must be connected to their appropriate fuel injector or exhaust emissions and engine performance may be seriously affected.

1. Disconnect the negative battery cable.

2. Remove the upper intake manifold, as described in this section.

3. Remove the valve rocker arm covers.

4. Disconnect the fuel feed line from the fuel rail.

5. Disconnect fuel injector inline electrical multi-pin connector.

6. Remove the fuel injector harness connector bracket retainer from the intake manifold.

7. Disconnect the engine coolant temperature (ECT) electrical connector.

8. Disconnect the camshaft position (CMP) sensor electrical connector.

9. Remove two Lifter Oil Manifold Assembly (LOMA) electrical connector bolts from the lower intake manifold if equipped.

10. Remove the fuel injector rail bolts (2).

11. Remove power steering pump.

12. Remove the fuel rail and LOMA.

13. Remove the lower intake manifold bolts. Remove the lower intake manifold.

14. Loosen the valve rocker arm bolts.

15. Place the valve train components in a rack in order to ensure that the components are installed in the same location from which they were removed.

16. Remove the valve rocker arms.

17. Remove the pushrods (exhaust pushrods are slightly longer than the intake pushrods).

18. Remove the lower intake manifold gaskets and seals.

19. Clean the lower intake manifold gasket and seal surfaces on the cylinder heads and the engine block.

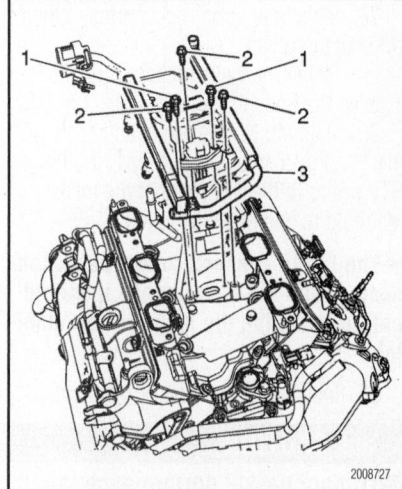

Fig. 44 Remove the LOMA connector bolts (1), fuel injector rail bolts (2) and the fuel rail (3)

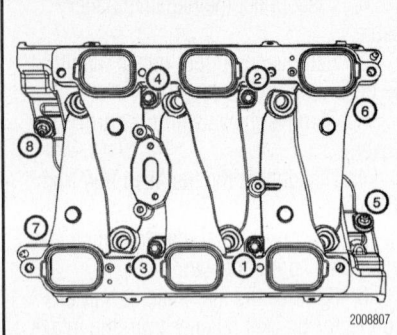

Fig. 46 Showing lower intake manifold bolt locations for tightening reference

20. Clean the gasket and seal surfaces on the lower intake manifold with degreaser.

21. Remove all the loose room temperature vulcanizing (RTV) sealer.

To install:

22. All gasket mating surfaces need to be free of oil and foreign material. Use cleaner to clean the surfaces.

23. RTV sealer must NOT be placed under the lower intake manifold gaskets.

24. Install the lower intake manifold gaskets and seals.

25. Coat the ends of the pushrods using prelube.

26. Install the pushrods in their original location.

27. Coat the rocker arm friction surfaces using prelube.

➡**Shims (P/N 88894006) may be required under the valve rocker arm pedestals if reconditioning has been performed on the cylinder head or its components.**

28. Install the valve rocker arms in their original positions.

29. Install the valve rocker arm bolts. Tighten the bolts to 25 ft. lbs. (34 Nm).

30. With the NEW gaskets and seals in place, apply a small drop, 0.031–0.39 in. of RTV sealer to the 4 corners of the intake manifold to engine block joints.

➡**The LOMA connector must be disconnected from the lower intake manifold before installing the lower intake manifold.**

31. Install the lower intake manifold.

✳✳ CAUTION

Maximum gasket performance is achieved when using new fasteners, which contain a thread-locking patch. If the fasteners are not replaced, a

thread locking chemical must be applied to the fastener threads. Failure to replace the fasteners or apply a thread-locking chemical MAY reduce gasket sealing capability.

✳✳ CAUTION

Failure to tighten vertical bolts before the diagonal bolts may cause an oil leak.

32. Apply sealer to the lower intake manifold bolt threads.

33. Install the lower intake manifold bolts. Tighten the lower intake manifold bolts in the sequence shown:

a. Tighten the lower intake manifold bolts (1, 2, 3, 4, 5, 8, 6, 7, 8) in sequence to 62 inch lbs. (7 Nm).

b. Tighten the center lower intake manifold bolts (1, 2, 3, 4) in sequence to 12 ft. lbs. (16 Nm).

c. Tighten the visible corner lower intake manifold bolts (5, 8) to 18 ft. lbs. (25 Nm).

d. Tighten the hidden corner lower intake manifold bolts (6, 7) to 18 ft. lbs. (25 Nm).

34. Inspect the fuel rail, fuel injectors, and fuel injector O-rings for damage and replace as necessary.

35. Lubricate the fuel injector O-rings using engine oil.

36. Install the injector nozzles into the lower intake manifold injector bores.

37. Install the LOMA then press on the injector rail using the palms of both hands until the injector are fully seated. Install the fuel injector rail bolts. Tighten the bolts to 89 inch lbs. (10 Nm).

38. Connect the CMP sensor electrical connector and the ECT electrical connector.

39. Position the fuel injector harness connector bracket to the intake manifold.

40. Install the fuel injector harness connector bracket bolt. Tighten the bolt to 71 inch lbs. (8 Nm).

41. Install two LOMA electrical connector bolts to the lower intake manifold. Tighten the bolts to 89 inch lbs. (10 Nm).

42. Connect fuel injector inline electrical connector.

43. Connect the fuel feed line to the fuel rail.

44. Install the right and left valve rocker arm covers.

45. Install the upper intake manifold, as described in this section.

46. Connect the negative battery cable.

4.6L Engine

See Figures 46 through 48.

1. Remove the fuel injector sight shield cover.

2. Remove the air cleaner outlet duct.

3. Disconnect the front ignition coil module engine harness electrical connector.

4. Disconnect the front fuel injectors engine harness electrical connectors.

5. Disconnect the rear ignition coil module engine harness electrical connector.

6. Disconnect the rear fuel injectors engine harness electrical connectors.

7. Disconnect the positive crankcase ventilation (PCV) foul air tube quick connect fitting from the right camshaft cover.

8. Disconnect the PCV fresh air tube quick connect fitting from the camshaft cover.

9. Disconnect the fuel feed line quick connect fitting at the fuel rail.

10. Remove the surge tank inlet hose/pipe assembly from the surge tank and from the engine fitting.

11. Remove the 2 push nuts securing the surge tank inlet hose/pipe to the fuel rail studs.

12. Remove the surge tank inlet hose/pipe from the fuel rail studs.

13. Remove the engine harness retainer from the fuel rail stud.

14. Remove the coolant heater cord tabs from the fuel rail studs, if equipped.

15. Remove the fuel rail bracket nut at the rear left lift bracket. Remove the fuel rail studs. Remove the fuel rail.

16. Loosen the plenum duct clamp screw at the water pump housing.

17. Remove intake manifold bolts.

18. Position the power steering pump aside.

19. Remove the intake manifold.

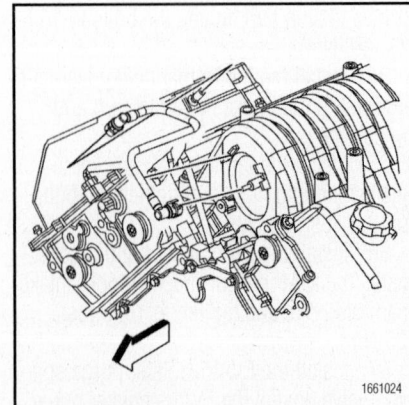

Fig. 46 Disconnect the positive crankcase ventilation (PCV) foul air tube quick connect fitting from the right camshaft cover.

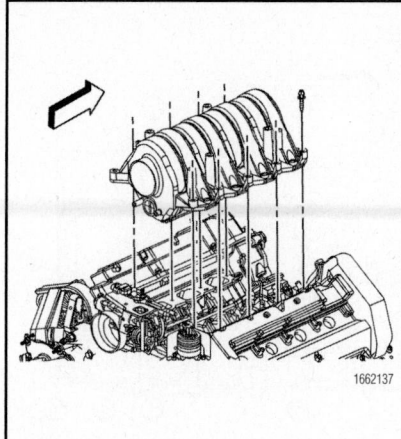

Fig. 47 Removing the intake manifold—4.6L engine

20. Disconnect the PCV foul air tube quick connect fitting at the intake manifold. Remove the PCV foul air tube from the retaining features on the intake manifold.

21. Remove and discard the old seals.

22. Clean and inspect the intake manifold.

To install:

23. Install the new intake manifold seals.

24. Connect the PCV foul air tube quick connect fitting at the intake manifold.

25. Install the PCV foul air tube to the retaining features on the intake manifold.

26. Lightly grease the inside edge of the rubber plenum duct on the water pump housing.

27. Install the intake manifold. Install intake manifold bolts until snug.

28. Tighten the intake manifold bolts. Tighten the bolts in the sequence shown to 89 ft. lbs. (10 Nm).

29. Ensure that the intake manifold is fully installed into the plenum duct on the water pump housing.

30. Install the power steering pump.

31. Tighten the plenum duct clamp screw at the water pump housing.

32. Lubricate the fuel injector lower O-ring seals with clean engine oil. Install the fuel rail. Install the fuel rail studs. Tighten the studs to 89 inch lbs. (10 Nm).

33. Install the fuel rail bracket nut at the rear left lift bracket. Tighten the nut to 89 inch lbs. (10 Nm).

34. Install the coolant heater cord tabs to the fuel rail studs, if equipped.

35. Install the engine harness retainer to the fuel rail stud. Install the surge tank inlet hose/pipe to the fuel rail studs. Install the 2 push nuts securing the surge tank inlet hose/pipe to the fuel rail studs.

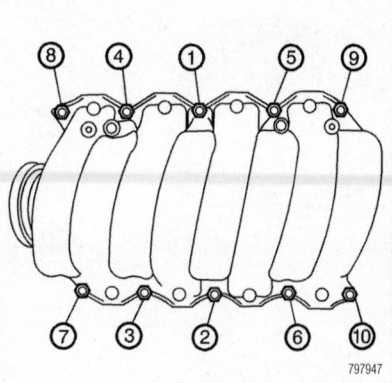

Fig. 48 Intake manifold bolt tightening sequence—4.6L engine

36. Install the surge tank inlet hose/pipe to the engine fitting. Position the radiator surge tank inlet hose/pipe clamp at the engine.

37. Install the surge tank inlet hose/pipe to the surge tank. Position the radiator surge tank inlet hose/pipe clamp at the surge tank.

38. Connect the fuel feed line quick connect fitting at the fuel rail.

39. Connect the PCV fresh air tube quick connect fitting to the camshaft cover.

40. Connect the PCV foul air tube quick connect fitting to the right camshaft cover.

41. Connect the rear fuel injectors engine harness electrical connectors and the rear ignition coil module engine harness electrical connector.

42. Connect the front fuel injectors engine harness electrical connectors and the front ignition coil module engine harness electrical connector.

43. Install the air cleaner outlet duct.

44. Install the fuel injector sight shield cover.

OIL PAN

REMOVAL & INSTALLATION

3.9L Engine

See Figures 49 through 52.

1. Disconnect the negative battery cable.

2. Remove the engine mount struts. See "Engine Mount Strut & Bracket" in this section.

3. Install the engine support fixture.

4. Remove the oil pan drain plug. Drain the crankcase. Reinstall the oil pan drain plug.

5. Remove the right front tire and wheel.

6. Remove the front wheelhouse liner.

7. Remove the accessory drive belt. See "Accessory Drive Belt" in this section.

8. Remove the oil filter and adapter.

9. Remove the starter. See "ENGINE ELECTRICAL" section.

10. Remove the air conditioning (A/C) compressor nut and bolt. Remove the A/C compressor rear bolt and position the compressor aside.

➡️**Do not disconnect A/C hoses/pipes and do not discharge the system.**

11. Disconnect the oil level sensor electrical connector.

12. Remove the engine harness clips from the oil pan and the transaxle brace.

13. Remove the front transaxle brace to engine bolts and the brace.

14. Loosen the transaxle mount lower nuts.

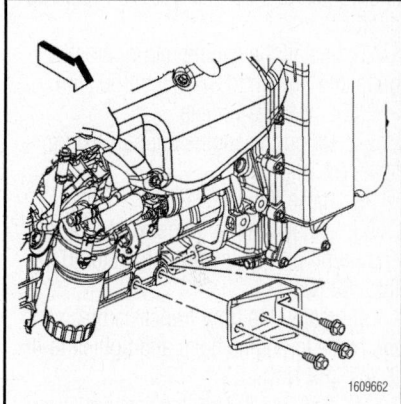

Fig. 49 Remove the front transaxle brace to engine bolts and the brace—3.9L engine

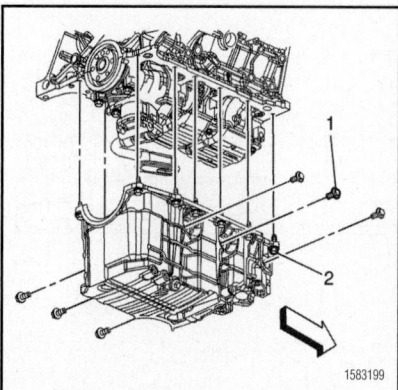

Fig. 50 Remove the right side oil pan side bolts, then the left side oil pan side bolts. Remove the oil pan retaining bolts. Remove the oil pan.

15. Remove the rear transaxle brace to engine/oil pan bolts.

16. Lower the vehicle.

17. Using the engine support fixture, raise the engine.

18. Remove the right side oil pan side bolts, then the left side oil pan side bolts. Remove the oil pan retaining bolts. Remove the oil pan.

19. Remove the oil pan gasket.

20. Clean the pan and all related parts.

To install:

21. Apply sealer to both sides of the crankshaft rear main bearing cap and to the front cover/block mating area. Press the sealer into the gap using a putty knife.

22. Install a NEW oil pan gasket. Position the oil pan to the engine.

23. Install the oil pan retaining bolts and tighten to 18 ft. lbs. (25 Nm).

24. Install the left side oil pan side bolts and install the right side oil pan side bolts and tighten to 37 ft. lbs. (50 Nm), plus 50 degrees.

25. Install the engine mount bracket bolts and tighten to 37 ft. lbs. (50 Nm).

26. Lower the vehicle.

27. Using the engine support fixture, lower the engine.

28. Raise the vehicle.

29. Install the rear transaxle brace to engine/oil pan bolts and tighten to 46 ft. lbs. (63 Nm).

30. Install the front transaxle brace and the brace to engine bolts and tighten to 46 ft. lbs. (63 Nm).

31. Connect the oil level sensor electrical connector.

32. Install the engine harness clips to the oil pan and the transaxle brace.

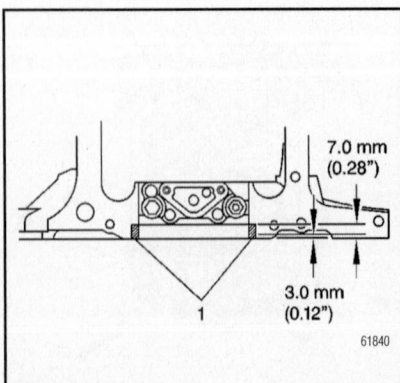

Fig. 51 Apply sealer to both sides of the crankshaft rear main bearing cap and to the front cover/block mating area.

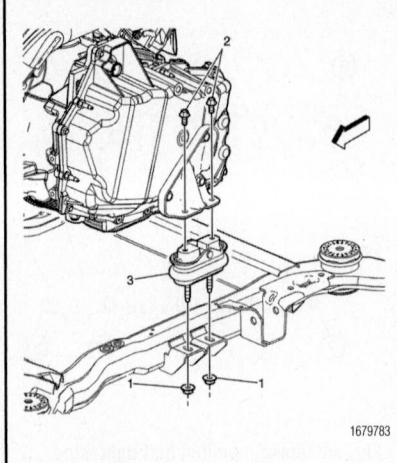

Fig. 52 Showing the rear transaxle mount (3), lower nuts (1) and bolts (2)

33. Tighten the transaxle mount lower nuts. Tighten the nuts to 37 ft. lbs. (50 Nm).

34. Position the A/C compressor, and install the A/C compressor nut and bolt and the rear bolt and tighten to 37 ft. lbs. (50 Nm).

35. Install the starter. See "ENGINE ELECTRICAL" section.

36. Install the oil filter and adapter.

37. Install the accessory drive belt.

38. Install the front wheelhouse liner.

39. Install the right front tire and wheel.

40. Remove the engine support fixture.

41. Install the engine mount struts. See "Engine Mount Strut & Bracket" in this section.

42. Fill the crankcase with new engine oil.

43. Connect the negative battery cable.

4.6L Engine

See Figure 53.

1. Drain the engine oil.

2. Remove the front exhaust manifold pipe.

3. Disconnect the engine harness electrical connector from the oil level sensor at the oil filter adapter.

4. Loosen the oil pan bolts Remove the oil pan and discard the oil pan gasket.

5. Clean and inspect the oil pan, if necessary.

To install:

6. Completely fill and slightly overfill the oil pan seal groove with a continuous bead of RTV sealant. Ensure the RTV sealant is higher than the oil pan sealing surface by 0.118 in. (3 mm).

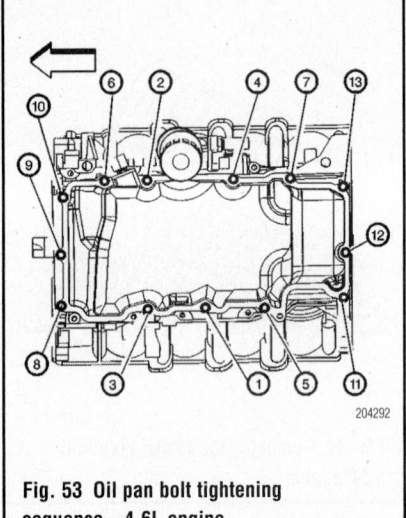

Fig. 53 Oil pan bolt tightening sequence—4.6L engine

7. To prevent shifting of the oil pan, install one guide pin (EN 46109 or equivalent) into the bolt hole in each side of the lower crankcase.

8. Position the oil pan to the lower crankcase and finger start the oil pan bolts.

9. Tighten the oil pan bolts.

  a. Tighten the bolts, in sequence, a first pass to 71 inch lbs. (8 Nm).

  b. Tighten the bolts a final pass to 106 inch lbs. (12 Nm).

10. Connect the engine harness electrical connector to the oil level sensor.

11. Install the front exhaust manifold pipe. Tighten the nuts, studs and bolts to 18 ft. lbs. (25 Nm).

12. Fill the engine oil.

OIL PUMP

REMOVAL & INSTALLATION

3.9L Engine

See Figure 54.

1. Remove the oil pan, as described in this section.

2. Remove the oil pump bolt.

3. Remove the oil pump and the oil pump drive shaft.

To install:

4. Rotate the oil pump drive shaft as necessary in order to obtain the engagement with the oil pump drive unit.

5. Install the oil pump drive shaft and the oil pump.

6. Install the oil pump bolt. Tighten the bolt to 30 ft. lbs. (41 Nm).

7. Install the oil pan, as described in this section.

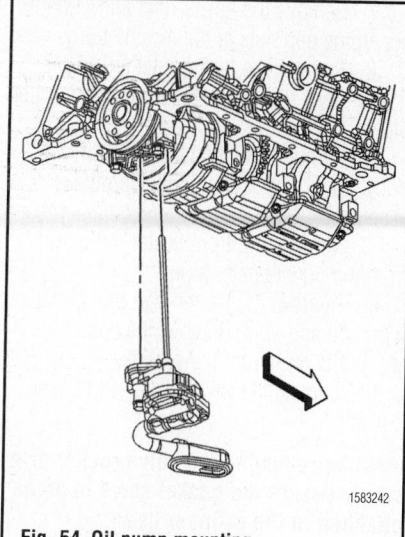

Fig. 54 Oil pump mounting

4.6L Engine

See Figure 55.

1. Remove the engine front cover. See "Engine Front Cover" in this section.

2. Remove the 3 oil pump assembly retaining bolts identified by the larger head size.

3. Slide the oil pump assembly off the nose of the crankshaft with the drive collar in place.

4. Clean and inspect the oil pump.

To install:

5. Install the oil pump drive spacer into the oil pump so that the drive flat engages the pump rotor.

6. Position the oil pump on the crankshaft.

7. Install the retaining bolts. Apply

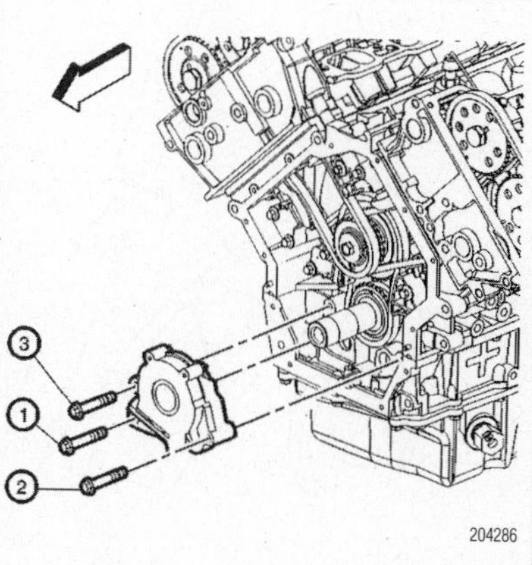

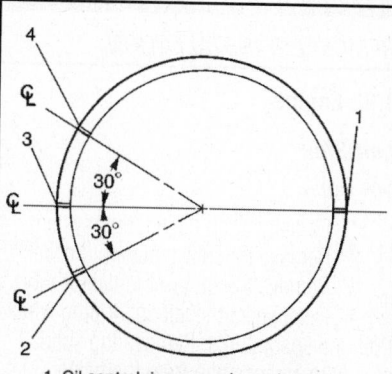

Fig. 55 Oil pump bolt tightening sequence

---

upward pressure on the pump while tightening the three retaining bolts. Tighten the bolts in the sequence shown.

　　a. First Pass: Tighten the oil pump mounting bolts in sequence to 89 inch lbs. (10 Nm).

　　b. Final Pass: Tighten the oil pump mounting bolts in sequence an additional 35 degrees.

8. Install the engine front cover.

PISTON & RINGS

POSITIONING

3.9L Engine

Piston rings should be positioned as follows:

• Stagger the oil control ring end gaps a minimum of 90 degrees.

• Stagger the compression ring end gaps a minimum of 1 in. (25 mm).

4.6L Engine

See Figure 56.

REAR MAIN SEAL

REMOVAL & INSTALLATION

1. Remove the flywheel. See "Flywheel" in 'AUTOMATIC TRANSAXLE' section.

2. Remove the crankshaft rear oil seal.

To install:

3. Install the rear main seal.

4. Install the engine flywheel. See "Flywheel" in 'AUTOMATIC TRANSAXLE' section.

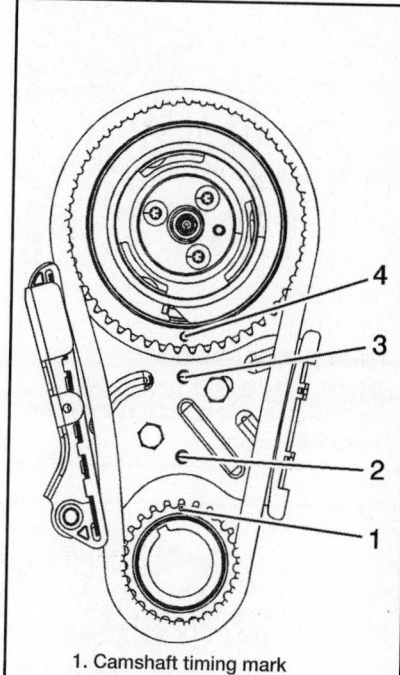

1. Oil control ring expander and second compression ring gaps position 1
2. Upper oil control ring gap position 2
3. Top compression ring gap position 3
4. Lower oil control ring gap position 4

Fig. 56 Showing piston ring end gap positions—4.6L engine

TIMING CHAIN & SPROCKETS

REMOVAL & INSTALLATION

3.9L Engine

See Figures 57 through 60.

1. Remove the engine front cover. See "Engine Front Cover" in this section.

2. Align the crankshaft timing mark to the timing mark on the bottom of the timing chain tensioner. Align the timing mark on the camshaft gear with the timing mark on top of the timing chain tensioner.

3. Using the tensioner compressor tool (EN-47719 or equivalent), collapse the tensioner and place the tensioner retaining pin into the retaining hole.

4. Remove the camshaft sprocket/actuator bolts. Remove the timing chain, camshaft sprocket/actuator, and crankshaft sprockets.

5. Remove the timing chain tensioner bolts. Remove the timing chain tensioner.

1. Camshaft timing mark
2. Timing chain tensioner
3. Camshaft gear
4. Timing chain tensioner

Fig. 57 Align the crankshaft timing mark (1) to the timing mark on the bottom of the timing chain tensioner (2). Align the timing mark on the camshaft gear (3) with the timing mark on top of the timing chain tensioner (4).

To install:

6. Install the crankshaft sprocket. Apply prelube to the crankshaft sprocket thrust surface.

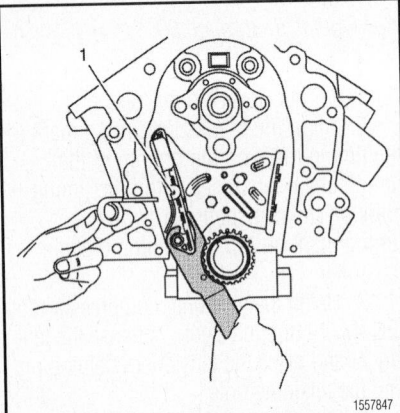

Fig. 58 Using the tensioner compressor tool (EN-47719 or equivalent), collapse the tensioner and place the tensioner retaining pin into the retaining hole (1)

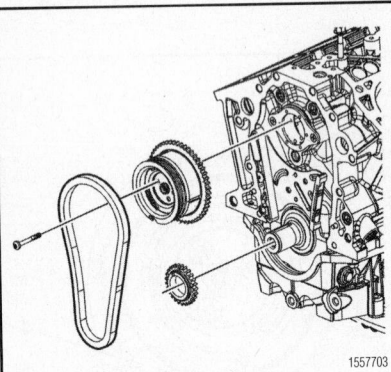

Fig. 59 Remove the camshaft sprocket/actuator bolts. Remove the timing chain, camshaft sprocket/actuator, and crankshaft sprockets.

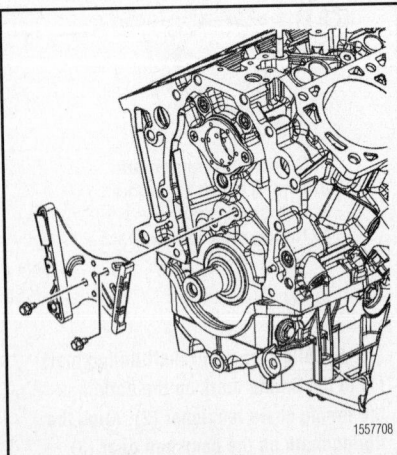

Fig. 60 Remove the timing chain tensioner bolts. Remove the timing chain tensioner.

7. Install the timing chain tensioner. Install the timing chain tensioner bolts and tighten to 15 ft. lbs. (21 Nm).

8. Using the tensioner compressor tool, fully collapse the tensioner, and place the tensioner retaining pin into the retaining hole.

➡ **Always install a NEW camshaft position actuator filter (located in the camshaft pilot nose) anytime the camshaft position actuator is removed or installed.**

9. Align the crankshaft timing mark to the timing mark on the bottom of the timing chain tensioner. Hold the camshaft sprocket with the timing chain hanging down and install the timing chain to the crankshaft gear. Align the timing mark on the camshaft gear with the timing mark on top of the timing chain tensioner.

10. Align the dowel in the camshaft sprocket with the dowel hole in the camshaft.

➡ **DO NOT use any type of threadlocking compound on the camshaft position actuator mounting bolts. Usage of a threadlocking compound on the threads could lead to contamination of the camshaft position actuator, possibly resulting in potential damage to the actuator.**

11. Draw the camshaft sprocket onto the camshaft using the mounting bolts and tighten the bolts to 12 ft. lbs. (16 Nm).

12. Coat the crankshaft and camshaft sprockets with clean engine oil.

13. Install the engine front cover. See "Engine Front Cover" in this section.

VALVE (CAMSHAFT)COVERS

REMOVAL & INSTALLATION

3.9L Engine

Left Side

See Figure 61.

1. Partially drain the cooling system.
2. Remove the intake manifold cover.
3. Remove the oil level indicator tube.
4. Disconnect the left spark plug wires from the spark plugs. Remove the spark plug wire harness clip from the heater inlet and outlet front pipe bracket. Reposition the spark plug harness.
5. Remove the positive crankcase ventilation (PCV) foul air tube.
6. Reposition the heater inlet and outlet hose/pipe clamps at the engine inlet and outer pipes.

7. Remove the heater inlet and outlet hose/pipe clip nuts at the throttle body.
8. Remove the heater inlet and outer hoses/pipes from the engine inlet and outlet pipes.
9. Remove the clips from the throttle body studs. Reposition the hose/pipe assembly.
10. Remove the front heater outlet hose from the outlet heater pipe.
11. Remove the heater inlet and outlet pipe bolt and stud. Remove the heater inlet and outlet pipe from the vehicle.
12. Loosen the valve rocker arm cover bolts.

➡ **When removing the valve rocker arm cover, ensure the gasket stays in place attached to the cylinder head.**

13. Remove the valve rocker arm cover. If necessary, bump the end of the cover with the palm of your hand or a soft rubber mallet if the cover adheres to the cylinder head.
14. Cut the RTV in the channel where the intake, cylinder head and valve rocker arm cover meet with a suitable tool.
15. Remove the valve cover gasket.
16. Clean the sealing surface on the cylinder head with degreaser.

To install:

➡ **All gasket mating surfaces need to be free of oil and foreign material. Use cleaner to clean the surfaces.**

17. Install a NEW valve rocker arm cover gasket into the groove in the valve rocker arm cover. Ensure that the gasket is properly seated in the groove of the valve rocker arm cover.
18. Apply sealant at the cylinder head to the surfaces where the cylinder head and intake manifold meet.
19. Install the valve rocker arm cover.

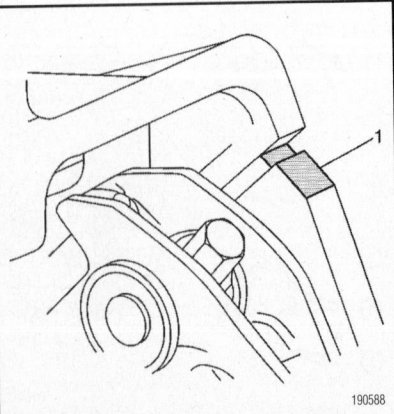

Fig. 61 Apply sealant at the cylinder head to the surfaces where the cylinder head and intake manifold meet (1).

➡️**Use an alternating criss-cross pattern when tightening the valve rocker cover bolts. Failure to do so may result in oil leakage from the valve cover due to improper seating of the gasket.**

20. Install the valve rocker arm cover bolts.

21. Install the heater inlet and outlet pipe to the vehicle.

22. Install the heater inlet and outlet pipe bolt and stud:

   a. Tighten the bolt to 18 ft. lbs. (25 Nm).

   b. Tighten the stud to 89 inch lbs. (10 Nm).

23. Install the front heater outlet hose to the outlet heater pipe.

24. Position the hose/pipe assembly. Install the clips to the throttle body studs. Install the heater inlet and outer hoses/pipes to the engine inlet and outlet pipes. Install the heater inlet and outlet hose/pipe clip nuts at the throttle body and tighten the nuts to 89 inch lbs. (10 Nm).

25. Position the heater inlet and outlet hose/pipe clamps at the engine inlet and outer pipes.

26. Install the PCV foul air tube.

27. Position the spark plug harness. Install the spark plug wire harness clip to the heater inlet and outlet front pipe bracket. Connect the left spark plug wires to the spark plugs.

28. Install the oil level indicator tube.

29. Install the intake manifold cover.

30. Fill the cooling system.

Right Side

See Figures 62 through 64.

1. Remove power steering reservoir.

2. Disconnect the positive crankcase ventilation (PCV) fresh air tube from the air cleaner outlet duct.

3. Remove the PCV fresh air tube from the right side valve rocker arm cover.

4. Disconnect the left side spark plug wires from the ignition coil.

5. Disconnect the right side spark plug wires from the spark plugs.

6. Disconnect the right side spark plug wires from the ignition coil. Remove the right side spark plug harness clip from the ignition coil bracket. Remove the spark plug harness.

7. Disconnect the manifold absolute pressure (MAP) sensor electrical connector. Disconnect the ignition coil electrical connector.

8. Remove the engine harness clip from the ignition coil bracket.

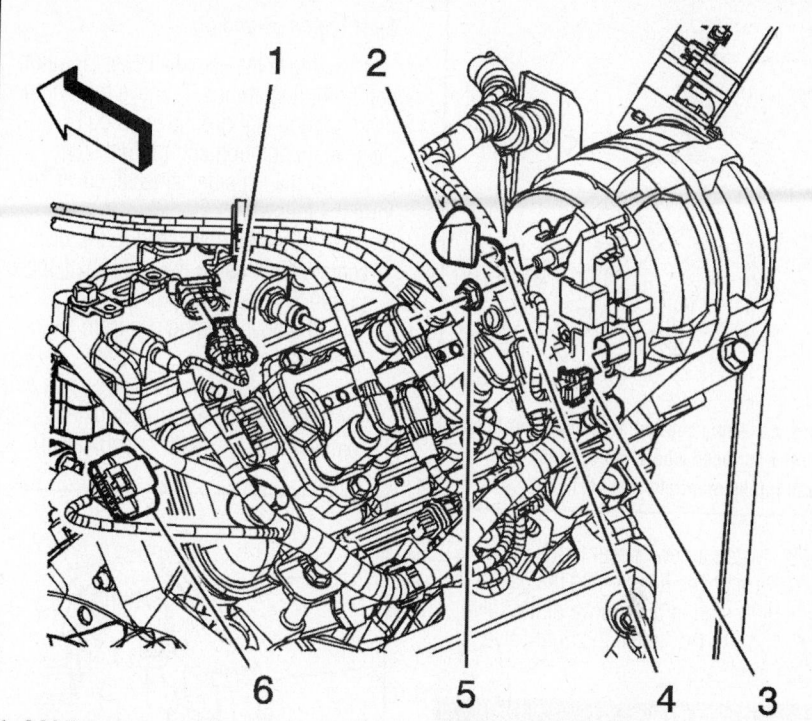

1. MAP sensor electrical connector
2. Boot
3. Generator connector
4. Electrical connector
5. Nut
6. Ignition coil electrical connector

1608869

Fig. 62 Disconnect the manifold absolute pressure (MAP) sensor electrical connector (1). Disconnect the ignition coil electrical connector (6).

9. Remove the heated oxygen sensor (HO2S) electrical connector clip from the ignition coil bracket by removing the retainer.

10. Remove the ignition coil bracket nuts. Remove the ignition coil bracket bolts. Remove the ignition coil.

11. Loosen the valve rocker arm cover bolts.

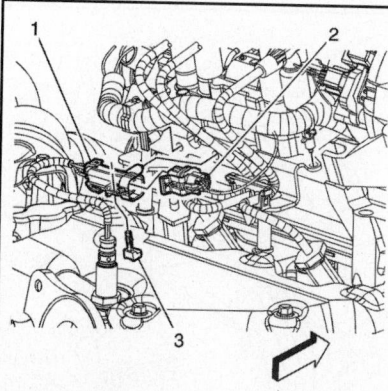

1609170

Fig. 63 Remove the heated oxygen sensor (HO2S) electrical connector clip (1) from the ignition coil bracket (2) by removing the retainer (3).

➡️**When removing the valve rocker arm cover, ensure the gasket stays in place attached to the cylinder head.**

12. Remove the valve rocker arm cover. Bump the end of the cover with the palm of your hand or a soft rubber mallet if the cover adheres to the cylinder head.

13. Cut the room temperature vulcanizing (RTV) sealer in the channel where the intake, cylinder head and valve rocker arm cover meet with a suitable tool.

14. Remove the valve cover gasket.

15. Clean the sealing surface on the cylinder head with degreaser.

To install:

➡️**All gasket mating surfaces need to be free of oil and foreign material. Use cleaner to clean the surfaces.**

16. Install a NEW valve rocker arm cover gasket into the groove in the valve rocker arm cover. Ensure that the gasket is properly seated in the groove of the valve rocker arm cover.

17. Apply sealant at the cylinder head to the surfaces where the cylinder head and intake manifold meet.

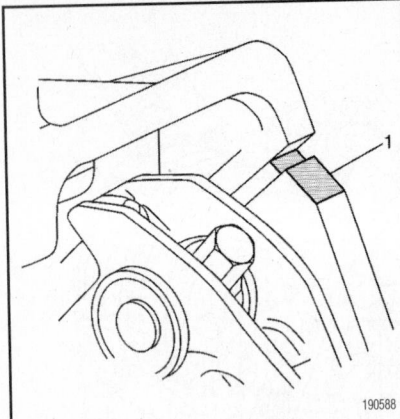

Fig. 64 Apply sealant at the cylinder head to the surfaces where the cylinder head and intake manifold meet (1).

18. Install a new gasket to the valve rocker arm cover. Ensure that the gasket is properly seated in the groove of the valve rocker arm cover. Install the right valve rocker arm cover.

⁂ CAUTION

Use an alternating criss-cross pattern when tightening the valve rocker cover bolts. Failure to do so may result in oil leakage from the valve cover due to improper seating of the gasket.

19. Install the valve rocker arm cover bolts. Tighten the bolts, in a criss-cross pattern, to 89 inch lbs. (10 Nm).
20. Install the ignition coil. Install the ignition coil bracket bolts. Install the ignition coil bracket nuts. Tighten the bolts/nuts to 18 ft. lbs. (25 Nm).
21. Install the HO2S electrical connector clip to the ignition coil bracket. Install the engine harness clip to the ignition coil bracket.
22. Connect the ignition coil electrical connector. Connect the MAP sensor electrical connector.
23. Install the spark plug harness. Connect the right side spark plug wires to the spark plugs.
24. Connect the right side spark plug wires to the ignition coil.
25. Install the right side spark plug harness clip to the ignition coil bracket.
26. Connect the left side spark plug wires to the ignition coil.
27. Install the PCV fresh air tube to the right side valve rocker arm cover. Connect the PCV fresh air tube to the air cleaner outlet duct.
28. Install the power steering reservoir.

4.6L Engine

See Figures 65 and 66.

1. Remove the camshaft cover ignition coil ground strap bolt. Remove the cylinder head ignition coil ground strap bolt. Remove the ignition coil ground strap.
2. For the left side camshaft cover, perform the following:
   a. Align the crankshaft to top dead center (TDC) using the crankshaft socket (J 39946 or equivalent).
   b. Remove the end cap from the intake camshaft.
   c. Remove the water pump drive pulley from the intake camshaft using pulley remover tool (J 38825 or equivalent).

Fig. 65 Remove the camshaft cover ignition coil ground strap bolt. Remove the cylinder head ignition coil ground strap bolt. Remove the ignition coil ground strap.

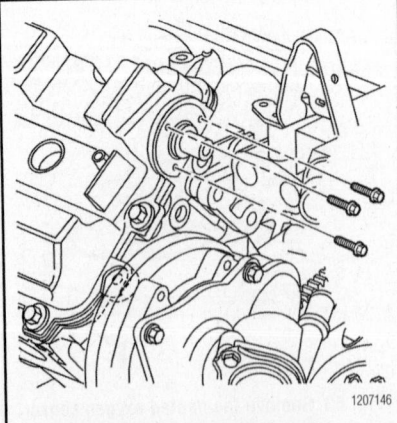

Fig. 66 Remove the camshaft seal screws. Slide the seal off the end of the camshaft—left side

   d. Remove the camshaft seal screws. Slide the seal off the end of the camshaft.

➡ **DO NOT reuse the camshaft seal.**

   e. Loosen the camshaft cover bolts. Remove and discard the camshaft cover grommets and camshaft cover bolts if they are serviced with the grommet.
   f. Lift up the front of the cover approximately 10 in. (250 mm). Swing the front of the cover over the intake manifold while sliding the entire cover over the end of the camshaft.

➡ **The camshaft cover seals, perimeter and sparkplug, should be reused unless they are damaged or if the perimeter seal is pulled from its groove during removal.**

3. For the right side camshaft cover, perform the following:
   a. Remove the camshaft cover bolts.
   b. Remove and discard the camshaft cover grommets and camshaft cover bolts if they are serviced with the grommet.
   c. Lift the camshaft cover from the cylinder head.

To install:

4. Ensure new camshaft cover seals are installed. Place the camshaft cover in position on the cylinder head.
5. For the left side camshaft cover, perform the following:
   a. Insert the intake camshaft end through the hole in the end of the camshaft cover.
   b. Using your fingers, guide the camshaft cover up over the edge of the cylinder head. Be careful not to damage the exposed section of the camshaft cover seal on the edge of the cylinder head.
   c. Work the camshaft cover into position by pivoting the cover down and to the left allowing the cover to clear the camshaft drive chain and then aligning the bolt holes.
   d. Install the NEW camshaft cover bolt grommets prior to installing the camshaft cover bolts.
   e. Install the camshaft cover bolts and tighten to 89 inch lbs. (10 Nm).
   f. Install a new camshaft seal: Lubricate the lips of the camshaft seal with engine oil. Push the camshaft seal into position around the intake camshaft using the protective sleeve supplied with

the seal. Coat the seal screws with sealant (GM P/N 1052080 or equivalent). Install the screws. Tighten the camshaft cover seal screws to 27 inch lbs. (3 Nm).

g. Place the water pump drive pulley in position on the intake camshaft.

h. Install the water pump pulley on the intake camshaft using the J 38823 installer. During installation, the tool will bottom out on the camshaft at the proper depth.

i. Install the camshaft end cap in the camshaft.

j. Install the ignition coil ground

strap to the cylinder head and camshaft cover. Install the cylinder head ignition coil ground strap bolt and tighten. Install the camshaft cover ignition coil ground strap bolt and tighten to 89 inch lbs. (10 Nm).

6. For the right side camshaft cover, perform the following:

a. Ensure new camshaft cover seals are installed.

b. Place the right camshaft cover in position on the cylinder head by aligning the bolt holes.

c. Install the NEW camshaft cover bolt grommets prior to installing the camshaft cover bolts.

d. Install the camshaft cover bolts and tighten to 89 inch lbs. (10 Nm).

e. Install the ignition coil ground strap to the cylinder head and camshaft cover. Install the cylinder head ignition coil ground strap bolt and tighten. Install the camshaft cover ignition coil ground strap bolt and tighten to 89 inch lbs. (10 Nm).

VALVE LASH

ADJUSTMENT

➡**Valve clearance is maintained by hydraulic valve lifters. No manual adjustment is required.**

ENGINE PERFORMANCE & EMISSION CONTROLS

✳✳ CAUTION

Replacement components must be the correct part number for the application. Components requiring the use of the thread locking compound, lubricants, corrosion inhibitors, or sealants are identified in the service procedure. Some replacement components may come with these coatings already applied. Do not use these coatings on components unless specified. These coatings can affect the final torque, which may affect the operation of the component. Use the correct torque specification when installing components in order to avoid damage.

ACCELERATOR PEDAL POSITION (APP) SENSOR

LOCATION

See Figure 67.

Refer to the accompanying illustration.

REMOVAL & INSTALLATION

1. Remove the left instrument panel (I/P) sound insulator.
2. Disconnect the body harness electrical connector from the accelerator pedal position (APP) sensor.
3. Remove the accelerated pedal nuts. Remove the accelerator pedal.

To install:

4. Install the accelerator pedal. Install the accelerated pedal nuts. Tighten the nuts to 89 inch lbs. (10 Nm).

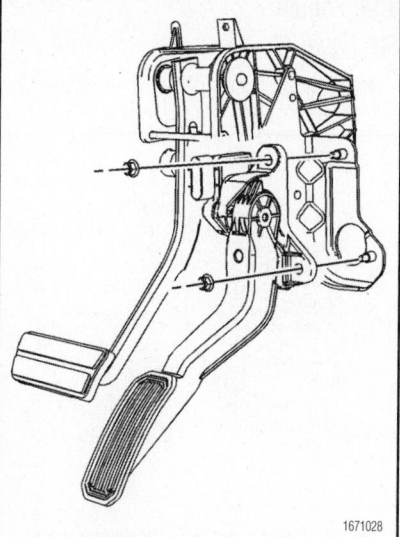

Fig. 67 The APP sensor is an integral part of the accelerator pedal assembly—all engines

5. Connect the body harness electrical connector to the APP sensor.
6. Install the left I/P sound insulator.

BAROMETRIC (BARO) PRESSURE SENSOR

LOCATION

3.9L Engine

See Figure 68.

Refer to the accompanying illustration.

REMOVAL & INSTALLATION

3.9L Engine

1. Remove the intake manifold cover.
2. Disconnect the engine wiring harness

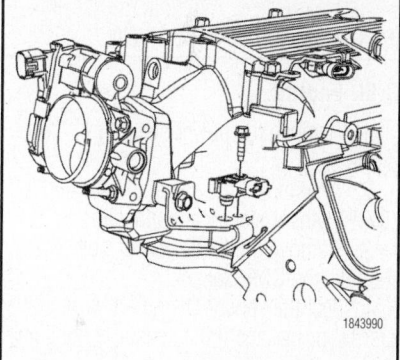

Fig. 68 Location of BARO sensor—3.9L engine

electrical connector from the barometric (BARO) pressure sensor.

3. Remove the BARO sensor bolt. Remove the BARO sensor.

To install:

4. Lubricate the BARO sensor O-ring seal with clean engine oil.
5. Install the BARO sensor to the bracket. Install the BARO sensor bolt. Tighten the bolt to 89 inch lbs. (10 Nm).
6. Connect the engine wiring harness electrical connector to the BARO sensor.
7. Install the intake manifold cover.

CAMSHAFT POSITION (CMP) SENSOR

LOCATION

3.9L Engine

See Figure 69.

Refer to the accompanying illustration.

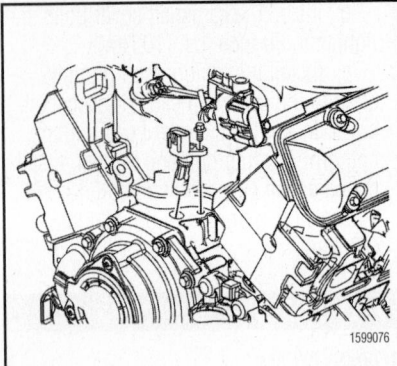

Fig. 69 Location of the CMP sensor—3.9L engine

4.6L Engine

See Figure 70.

Refer to the accompanying illustration.

REMOVAL & INSTALLATION

3.9L Engine

1. Remove the power steering pump.
2. Disconnect the camshaft position (CMP) sensor electrical connector.
3. Remove the CMP sensor bolt. Remove the CMP sensor.

Inspect the sensor O-ring for wear, cracks, or leakage if the sensor is not being replaced.

To install:
4. Replace the O-ring if damaged, lubricate the NEW O-ring with clean engine oil.
5. Install the CMP sensor.

Install the CMP sensor bolt. Tighten the bolt to 89 inch lbs. (10 Nm).
6. Connect the CMP sensor electrical connector.
7. Install the power steering pump. See "STEERING" section.

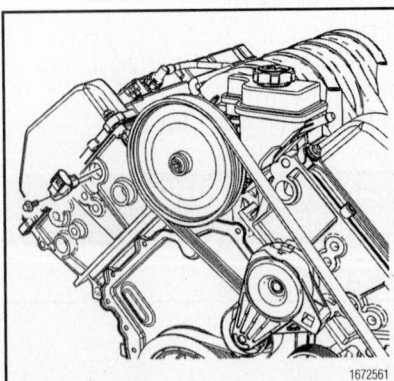

Fig. 70 Location of the CMP sensor—4.6L engine

4.6L Engine

1. Disconnect the electrical connector from the camshaft position (CMP) sensor.
2. Remove the CMP sensor bolt. Remove the CMP sensor.

To install:
3. Lubricate the CMP sensor O-ring seal with clean engine oil.
4. Install the CMP sensor.
5. Install the CMP sensor bolt. Tighten the bolt to 89 inch lbs. (10 Nm).
6. Connect the electrical connector to the CMP sensor.

CRANKSHAFT POSITION (CKP) SENSOR

LOCATION

3.9L Engine

See Figure 71.

Refer to the accompanying illustration.

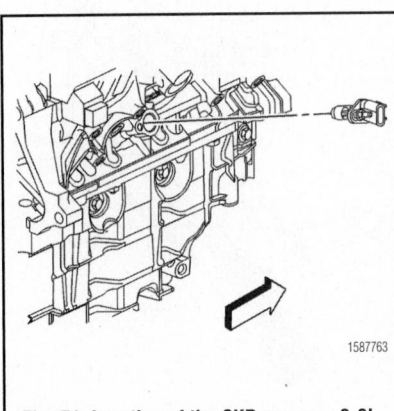

Fig. 71 Location of the CKP sensor—3.9L engine

4.6L Engine

See Figure 72.

Refer to the accompanying illustration.

REMOVAL & INSTALLATION

3.9L Engine

1. Raise and support the vehicle.
2. Remove the catalytic converter.
3. Disconnect the crankshaft position (CKP) sensor electrical connector.
4. Remove the CKP sensor stud. Remove the CKP sensor.

To install:
5. Lubricate the CKP sensor O-ring with clean engine oil.
6. Install the CKP sensor. Install the CKP sensor stud and tighten to 89 inch lbs. (10 Nm).

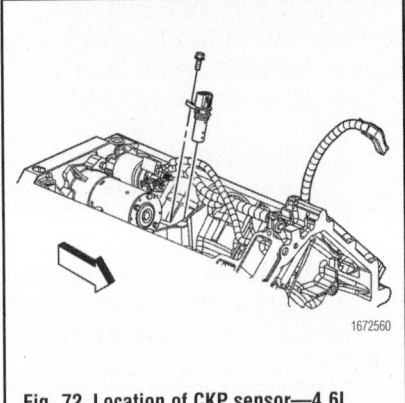

Fig. 72 Location of CKP sensor—4.6L engine

7. Connect the CKP sensor electrical connector.
8. Install the catalytic converter.
9. Lower the vehicle.

4.6L Engine

1. Remove the intake manifold. See "Intake Manifold" in "ENGINE MECHANICAL" section.
2. Disconnect the crankshaft position (CKP) sensor wiring harness electrical connector from the CKP sensor.
3. Remove the CKP sensor bolt. Remove the CKP sensor.

To install:
4. Lubricate the crankshaft sensor O-ring seal with clean engine oil.
5. Install the CKP sensor.
6. Install the CKP sensor bolt. Tighten the bolt to 89 inch lbs. (10 Nm).
7. Connect the CKP sensor wiring harness electrical connector to the CKP sensor.
8. Install the intake manifold. See "Intake Manifold" in "ENGINE MECHANICAL" section.
9. Perform the CKP system variation learn procedure, as described below.

CKP SYSTEM VARIATION LEARN PROCEDURE

The crankshaft position (CKP) system variation learn procedure is required when the following service procedures have been performed, regardless of whether DTC P0315 is set:

- Engine replacement
- Engine control module (ECM) replacement
- Crankshaft damper replacement
- Crankshaft replacement
- CKP sensor replacement
- Any engine repairs which disturb the crankshaft to CKP sensor relationship

The scan tool monitors certain component signals to determine if all the conditions are met to continue with the CKP system variation learn procedure. The scan tool only displays the condition that inhibits the procedure. The scan tool monitors the following components:

- CKP sensor activity—If there is a CKP sensor condition, refer to the applicable DTC that set.
- Camshaft position (CMP) signal activity—If there is a CMP signal condition, refer to the applicable DTC that set.
- Engine coolant temperature (ECT)—If the engine coolant temperature is not warm enough, idle the engine until the engine coolant temperature reaches the correct temperature.

1. Install a scan tool.
2. Monitor the ECM for DTCs with a scan tool. If other DTCs are set, except DTC P0315. Perform any diagnosis for other DTCs that set.
3. With a scan tool, select the CKP system variation learn procedure within the Module Setup menu and perform the following:

    a. Observe the fuel cut-off for the applicable engine.
    b. Block the drive wheels.
    c. Set the parking brake.
    d. Place the vehicle's transmission in Park or Neutral.
    e. Turn the air conditioning (A/C) OFF.
    f. Cycle the ignition from OFF to ON.
    g. Apply and hold the brake pedal for the duration of the procedure.
    h. Start and idle the engine.
    i. Accelerate to wide open throttle (WOT). The engine should not accelerate beyond the calibrated fuel cut-off RPM value noted in the first sub-step. Release the throttle immediately if the value is exceeded.

➡ While the learn procedure is in progress, release the throttle immediately when the engine starts to decelerate. The engine control is returned to the operator and the engine responds to throttle position after the learn procedure is complete.

    j. Release the throttle when fuel cut-off occurs.
4. The scan tool displays Learn Status: Learned this Ignition. If the scan tool indicates that DTC P0315 ran and passed, the CKP variation learn procedure is complete. If the scan tool indicates DTC P0315 failed or did not run, or if any other DTCs set, perform diagnostics for the applicable DTC that set.

5. Turn OFF the ignition for 30 seconds after the learn procedure is completed successfully.

ELECTRONIC CONTROL MODULE (ECM)

LOCATION

3.9L Engine

See Figure 73.

Refer to the accompanying illustration.

4.6L Engine

See Figure 74.

Refer to the accompanying illustration.

REMOVAL & INSTALLATION

3.9L Engine

1. Disconnect the negative battery cable.
2. Remove the air cleaner assembly upper housing.
3. Remove the Engine Control Module (ECM) as follows:

    a. Disconnect the electrical connectors.
    b. Pull straight up to release the ECM from its retainers.

➡ It is necessary to record the remaining engine oil life. If the replacement module is not programmed with the

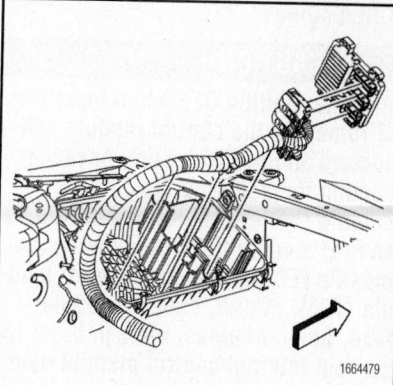

Fig. 74 ECM is located inside air cleaner housing—4.6L engine

remaining engine oil life, the engine oil life will default to 100 percent. If the replacement module is not programmed with the remaining engine oil life, the engine oil will need to be changed at 3000 miles from the last engine oil change.

4. Installation is the reverse of the removal procedure.
5. Program the ECM, if replacing.

➡ ECM programming is accomplished through the General Motors Service Programming System. If aftermarket equipment is used, it must comply with OE specifications in order to properly program the ECM.

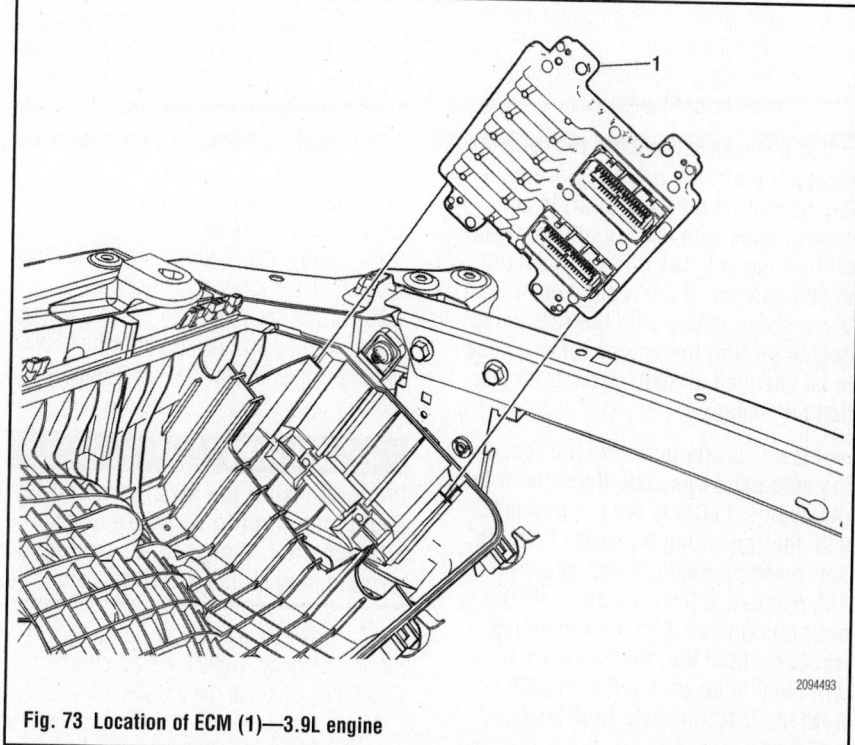

Fig. 73 Location of ECM (1)—3.9L engine

4.6L Engine

✳✳ CAUTION

Turn the ignition OFF when installing or removing the control module connectors and disconnecting or reconnecting the power to the control module (battery cable, powertrain control module (PCM)/engine control module (ECM)/transaxle control module (TCM) pigtail, control module fuse, jumper cables, etc.) in order to prevent internal control module damage.

- Control module damage may result when the metal case contacts battery voltage. DO NOT contact the control module metal case with battery voltage when servicing a control module, using battery booster cables, or when charging the vehicle battery.
- In order to prevent any possible electrostatic discharge damage to the control module, do not touch the connector pins or the soldered components on the circuit board.
- Remove any debris from around the control module connector surfaces before servicing the control module. Inspect the control module connector gaskets when diagnosing or replacing the control module. Ensure that the gaskets are installed correctly. The gaskets prevent contaminant intrusion into the control module.
- The replacement control module must be programmed.

➡It is necessary to record the remaining engine oil life. If the replacement engine control module (ECM) is not programmed with the remaining engine oil life, the engine oil life will default to 100 percent. If the replacement ECM is not programmed with the remaining engine oil life, the engine oil will need to be changed at 3000 miles from the last oil change.

➡It is necessary to record the remaining automatic transaxle fluid life. If the replacement ECM is not programmed with the remaining transaxle fluid life, the transaxle fluid life will default to 100 percent. If the replacement ECM is not programmed with the remaining transaxle fluid life, the transaxle fluid will need to be changed at 50,000 mi. from the last transaxle fluid change.

1. Using a scan tool, retrieve the percentage of remaining engine oil and automatic transaxle fluid life. Record the remaining engine oil and transaxle fluid life.
2. Ensure that the ignition is in the OFF position.
3. Disconnect the negative battery cable.
4. Disconnect the engine harness electrical connector from the mass air flow/intake air temperature (MAF/IAT) sensor.
5. Disconnect the positive crankcase ventilation (PCV) fresh air tube quick connect fitting from the air duct.
6. Disconnect the secondary air injection (AIR) pump inlet tube quick connect fitting from the air cleaner upper housing.
7. Loosen the air cleaner outlet duct clamp at the throttle body. Remove the air cleaner outlet duct from the throttle body.
8. Disengage the lower housing clips. Disengage the upper housing front tabs from the lower housing. Remove the air cleaner upper housing.
9. Disengage the engine harness electrical connector lever locks at the ECM.
10. Remove the engine harness electrical connectors from the ECM.
11. Remove the ECM from the air cleaner lower housing.

To install:
12. Inspect the following areas prior to installing the ECM:
  a. No debris in the air filter/ECM housing assembly, or the MAF/IAT sensor inlet screen that may distort the air flow.
  b. No signs of damage to the air filter/ECM housing assembly, or the intake air duct. If a problem is found, replace the components as necessary.
13. Install the ECM to the lower air cleaner housing.
14. Install the engine harness electrical connectors to the ECM.
15. Engage the engine harness electrical connector lever locks at the ECM.
16. Install the air cleaner upper housing. Engage the upper housing front tabs to the lower housing. Engage the lower housing clips.

✳✳ CAUTION

Properly install the air cleaner outlet duct to the throttle body. An improperly installed, distorted, or damaged air duct may cause a DTC to set.

17. Install the air cleaner outlet duct to the throttle body. Tighten the air cleaner outlet duct clamp at the throttle body.
18. Connect the AIR pump inlet tube

quick connect fitting to the air cleaner upper housing.
19. Connect the PCV fresh air tube quick connect fitting to the air duct.
20. Connect the engine harness electrical connector to the MAF/IAT sensor.
21. Connect the negative battery cable.
22. Program the ECM.

➡ECM programming is accomplished through the General Motors Service Programming System. If aftermarket equipment is used, it must comply with OE specifications in order to properly program the ECM.

ENGINE COOLANT TEMPERATURE (ECT) SENSOR

LOCATION

3.9L Engine
See Figure 75.

Refer to the accompanying illustration.

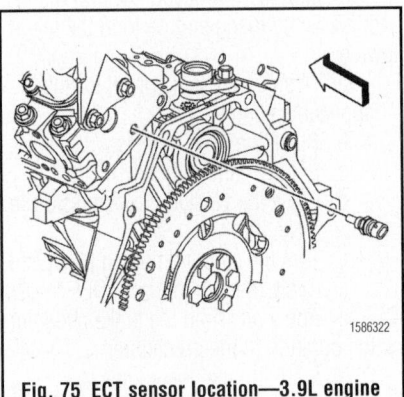

Fig. 75 ECT sensor location—3.9L engine

4.6L Engine
See Figure 76.

Refer to the accompanying illustration.

REMOVAL & INSTALLATION

3.9L Engine
1. Drain the cooling system.
2. Remove the intake manifold cover, if necessary.
3. Disconnect the engine coolant temperature (ECT) sensor electrical connector.
4. Remove the ECT sensor.

To install:
5. Coat the threads of the ECT sensor with sealer (GM P/N 13246004 or equivalent).
6. Install the ECT sensor and tighten to 15 ft. lbs. (20 Nm).
7. Connect the ECT electrical connector.
8. Install the intake manifold cover.
9. Fill the cooling system.

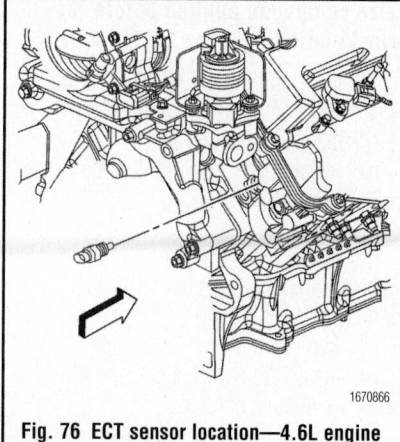

Fig. 76 ECT sensor location—4.6L engine

4.6L Engine

1. Remove the fuel injector sight shield.
2. Drain the cooling system.
3. Disconnect the engine harness electrical connector (6) from the engine coolant temperature (ECT) sensor.
4. Remove the ECT sensor.

To install:

5. Apply sealant (GM P/N 12346004 or equivalent) to the threads of the ECT sensor.
6. Install the ECT sensor. Tighten the sensor to 15 ft. lbs. (20 Nm).
7. Connect the engine harness electrical connector to the ECT sensor.
8. Fill the cooling system.
9. Install the fuel injector sight shield.

HEATED OXYGEN (HO2S) SENSOR

LOCATION

3.9L Engine

See Figures 77 and 78.

Refer to the accompanying illustrations.

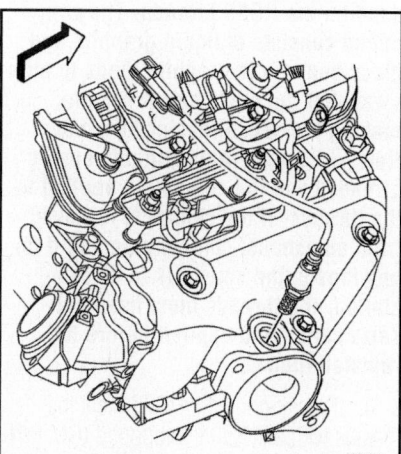

Fig. 77 Location of heated oxygen sensor 1—3.9L engine

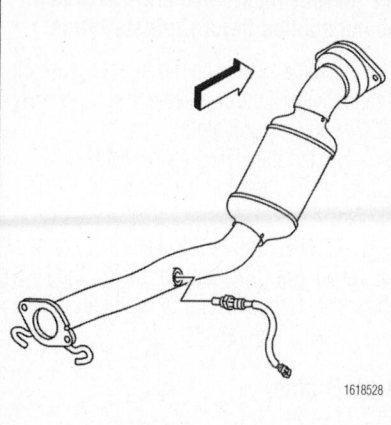

Fig. 78 Location of heated oxygen sensor 2—3.9L engine

4.6L Engine

See Figures 79 through 81.

Refer to the accompanying illustrations.

REMOVAL & INSTALLATION

3.9L Engine

HO2S-1

See Figure 82.

1. Remove the connector position assurance (CPA) retainer. Disconnect the heater oxygen sensor (HO2S) electrical connector. Remove the oxygen sensor electrical connector from the ignition coil bracket.
2. Remove the HO2S from the exhaust manifold.

To install:

➡**A special anti-seize compound is used on the HO2S threads. The compound consists of liquid graphite and**

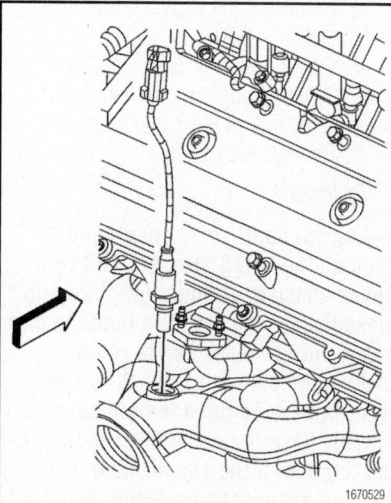

Fig. 79 Location of heated oxygen sensor 1 on bank 1—4.6L engine

glass beads. The graphite tends to burn away, but the glass beads remain, making the sensor easier to remove. New or service replacement sensors

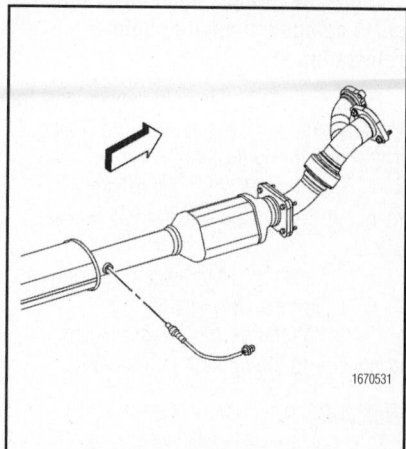

Fig. 80 Location of heated oxygen sensor 2 on bank 1—4.6L engine

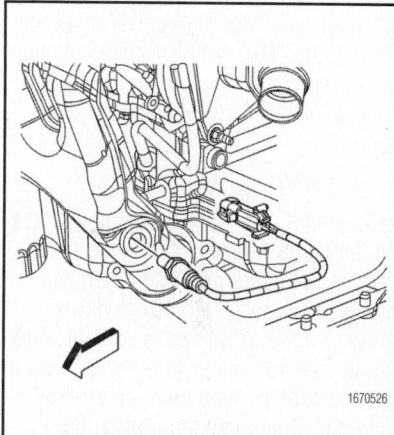

Fig. 81 Location of heated oxygen sensor 1 on bank 2—4.6L engine

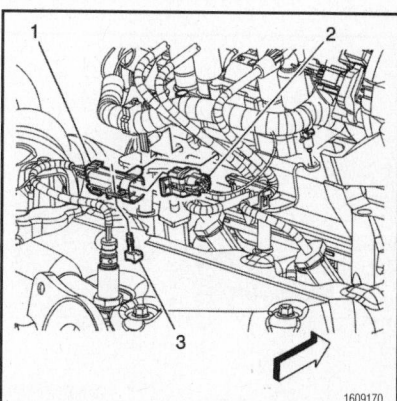

Fig. 82 Remove the connector position assurance (CPA) retainer (3). Disconnect the heater oxygen sensor (HO2S) electrical connector (2). Remove the oxygen sensor electrical connector from the ignition coil bracket (1).

already have the compound applied to the threads. If the sensor is removed from an exhaust component and if for any reason the sensor is to be reinstalled, the threads must have anti-seize compound applied before reinstallation.

3. If re-installing the old sensor, coat the threads with anti-seize compound (P/N 12377953, or equivalent).

4. Install the HO2S to the exhaust manifold. Tighten the sensor to 31 ft. lbs. (42 Nm).

5. Connect the HO2S electrical connector.

6. Install the CPA retainer.

7. Install the oxygen sensor electrical connector to the ignition coil bracket.

HO2S-2

See Figure 83.

1. Raise and support the vehicle.

2. Remove the connector position assurance (CPA) retainer. Disconnect the heated oxygen sensor (HO2S) electrical connector. Remove the HO2S electrical connector clip from the heat shield.

3. Remove the HO2S from the catalytic converter.

To install:

➡A special anti-seize compound is use on the HO2S threads. The compound consists of liquid graphite and glass beads. The graphite tends to burns away, but the glass beads remain, making the sensor easier to remove. New or service replacement sensors already have the compound applied to the threads. If the sensor is removed from an exhaust component and if for any reason the sensor is to be reinstalled,

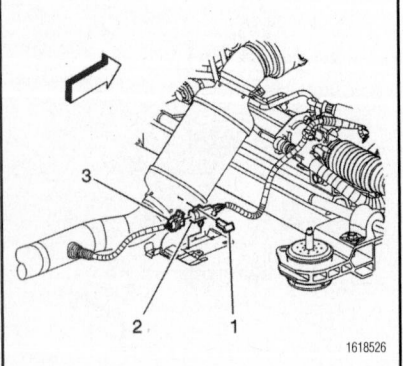

Fig. 83 Remove the connector position assurance (CPA) retainer (1). Disconnect the heated oxygen sensor (HO2S) electrical connector (3). Remove the HO2S electrical connector clip from the heat shield (2).

the threads must have anti-seize compound applied before reinstallation.

4. If reinstalling the old sensor, coat the threads with the anti-seize compound (P/N 12377953, or equivalent).

5. Install the HO2S to the catalytic converter. Tighten the sensor to 31 ft. lbs. (42 Nm).

6. Connect the HO2S electrical connector. Install the CPA retainer. Install the HO2S electrical connector clip to the heat shield.

7. Lower the vehicle.

4.6L Engine

HO2S 1 Bank 1

✳✳ CAUTION

Handle the oxygen sensors carefully in order to prevent damage to the component. Keep the electrical connector and the exhaust inlet end free of contaminants. Do not use cleaning solvents on the sensor. Do not drop or mishandle the sensor.

➡Remove the heated oxygen sensors (HO2S) with the engine temperature above 120°F (48°C). Otherwise the HO2S may be difficult to remove.

1. Remove the fuel injector sight shield.

2. Remove the connector position assurance (CPA) retainer. Disconnect the engine harness electrical connector from the heated oxygen sensor (HO2S).

3. Remove the HO2S clip from the secondary air injection (AIR) check valve hose bracket.

4. Raise and support the vehicle.

5. Support the rear of the frame with a tall screw type jack.

6. Remove the 4 rearward frame to body bolts.

7. Lower the screw type jack approximately 1.5 in., but not more than 3 in., allowing the rear of the frame to lower.

8. Remove the HO2S.

To install:

➡A special anti-seize compound is used on the HO2S threads. The compound consists of liquid graphite and glass beads. the graphite tends to burn away, but the glass beads remain, making the sensor easier to remove. New, or service replacement sensors already have the compound applied to the threads. If the sensor is removed from an exhaust components and if for any reason the sensor is to be reinstalled, the threads must have anti-

seize compound applied before the reinstallation

9. If reusing the old HO2S, coat the threads with anti-seize compound (GM P/N 12377953 or equivalent).

10. Install the HO2S. Tighten the sensor to 30 ft. lbs. (41 Nm).

11. Raise the engine frame into position.

12. Install the 4 rearward frame to body bolts. Tighten the bolts to 141 ft. lbs. (191 Nm).

13. Remove the screw type jack.

14. Install the HO2S clip to the AIR check valve hose bracket.

15. Connect the engine harness electrical connector to the HO2S. Install the CPA retainer.

16. Install the fuel injector sight shield.

HO2S 2 Bank 1

✳✳ CAUTION

Handle the oxygen sensors carefully in order to prevent damage to the component. Keep the electrical connector and the exhaust inlet end free of contaminants. Do not use cleaning solvents on the sensor. Do not drop or mishandle the sensor.

➡Remove the heated oxygen sensors (HO2S) with the engine temperature above 120°F (48°C). Otherwise the HO2S may be difficult to remove.

1. Remove the oxygen sensor wiring harness heat shield.

2. Disconnect the engine harness electrical connector from the heated oxygen sensor (HO2S).

3. Remove the HO2S.

To install:

➡A special anti-seize compound is used on the HO2S threads. The compound consists of liquid graphite and glass beads. the graphite tends to burn away, but the glass beads remain, making the sensor easier to remove. New, or service replacement sensors already have the compound applied to the threads. If the sensor is removed from an exhaust components and if for any reason the sensor is to be reinstalled, the threads must have anti-seize compound applied before the reinstallation

4. If reusing the old HO2S, coat the threads with anti-seize compound (GM P/N 12377953 or equivalent.

5. Install the HO2S. Tighten the sensor to 30 ft. lbs. (41 Nm).

6. Connect the engine harness electrical connector to the HO2S.

7. Install the oxygen sensor wiring harness heat shield.

HO2S 1 Bank 2

> ※※ **CAUTION**
>
> Handle the oxygen sensors carefully in order to prevent damage to the component. Keep the electrical connector and the exhaust inlet end free of contaminants. Do not use cleaning solvents on the sensor. Do not drop or mishandle the sensor.

➡ Remove the heated oxygen sensors (HO2S) with the engine temperature above 120°F (48°C). Otherwise the HO2S may be difficult to remove.

1. Remove the air deflector.
2. Remove the connector position assurance (CPA) retainer. Disconnect the engine harness electrical connector from the heated oxygen sensor (HO2S). Remove the HO2S clip from the engine bracket.
3. Remove the HO2S.

To install:

➡ A special anti-seize compound is used on the HO2S threads. The compound consists of liquid graphite and glass beads. the graphite tends to burn away, but the glass beads remain, making the sensor easier to remove. New, or service replacement sensors already have the compound applied to the threads. If the sensor is removed from an exhaust components and if for any reason the sensor is to be reinstalled, the threads must have anti-seize compound applied before the reinstallation

4. If reusing the old HO2S, coat the threads with anti-seize compound (GM P/N 12377953 or equivalent).
5. Install the HO2S. Tighten the sensor to 30 ft. lbs. (41 Nm).
6. Connect the engine harness electrical connector to the HO2S. Install the CPA retainer. Install the HO2S clip to the engine bracket.
7. Install the air deflector.

INTAKE AIR TEMPERATURE (IAT) SENSOR

LOCATION

➡ See "Mass Air Flow/Intake Air Temperature (MAF/IAT) Sensor" in this section.

KNOCK SENSOR (KS)

LOCATION

3.9L Engine

See Figure 84.

Refer to the accompanying illustration.

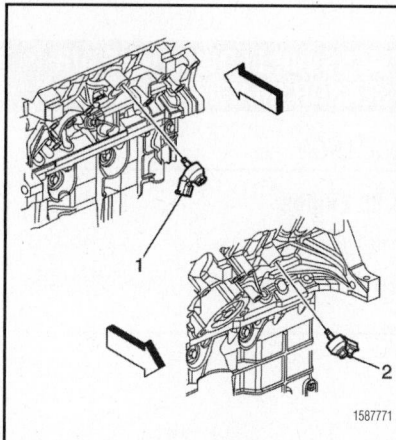
1587771

Fig. 84 Knock sensor locations bank 1 (1) and bank 2 (2)—3.9L engine

4.6L Engine

See Figure 85.

Refer to the accompanying illustration.

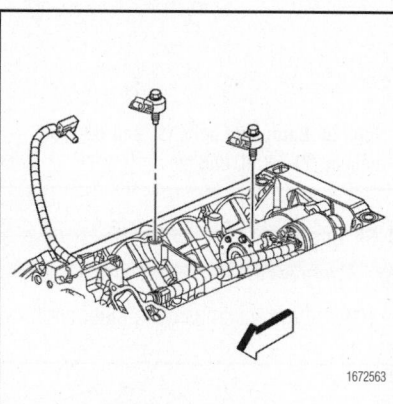
1672563

Fig. 85 Both knock sensors are located under the intake manifold on top of the block—4.6L engine

REMOVAL & INSTALLATION

3.9L Engine

1. For the knock sensor on bank 1, do the following:
   a. Raise and support the vehicle.
   b. Remove the catalytic converter.
2. Disconnect the knock sensor electrical connector.
3. Loosen and remove the knock sensor.

To install:

> ※※ **CAUTION**
>
> DO NOT apply thread sealant to the sensor threads. The sensor threads are coated at the factory. Applying additional sealant affects the sensors ability to detect detonation.

4. Install and tighten the knock sensor to 18 ft. lbs. (25 Nm).
5. Connect the knock sensor electrical connector.
6. For the knock sensor on bank 1, do the following:
   a. Install the catalytic converter.
   b. Lower the vehicle.

4.6L Engine

1. Remove the intake manifold. See "Intake Manifold" in "ENGINE MECHANICAL" section.
2. Disconnect the electrical connector from the knock sensor(s), as required.
3. Remove the appropriate knock sensor(s).
4. Install the appropriate knock sensor and tighten the sensor to 18 ft. lbs. (25 Nm).
5. Connect the electrical connector to the appropriate knock sensor.
6. Install the intake manifold. See "Intake Manifold" in "ENGINE MECHANICAL" section.

MANIFOLD ABSOLUTE PRESSURE (MAP) SENSOR

LOCATION

3.9L Engine

See Figure 86.

Refer to the accompanying illustration.

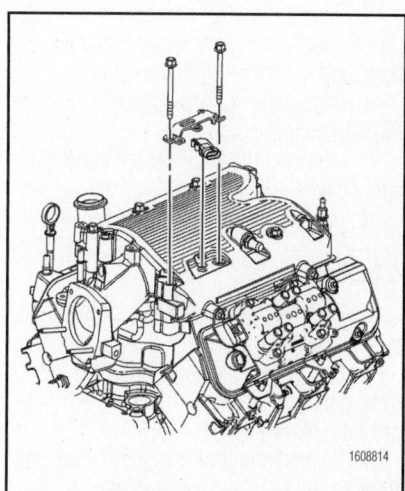
1608814

Fig. 86 MAP sensor location—3.9L engine

4.6L Engine

See Figure 87.

Refer to the accompanying illustration.

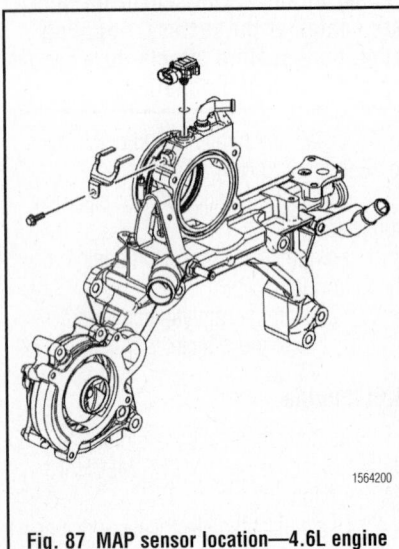

1564200

Fig. 87 MAP sensor location—4.6L engine

REMOVAL & INSTALLATION

3.9L Engine

1. Remove the intake manifold cover.
2. Disconnect the manifold absolute pressure (MAP) sensor electrical connector.
3. Remove the spark plug wire clip from the intake manifold bracket, if necessary.
4. Remove the upper intake manifold bolts.
5. Remove the MAP sensor and bracket.
6. Remove the MAP sensor seal from the upper intake manifold.

To install:
7. Install the MAP sensor seal into the upper intake manifold.
8. Install the MAP sensor and bracket.
9. Install the upper intake manifold bolts and tighten to 18 ft. lbs. (25 Nm).
10. Install the spark plug wire clip to the intake manifold bracket.
11. Connect the MAP sensor electrical connector.
12. Install the intake manifold cover.

4.6L Engine

1. Remove the fuel injector sight shield, if necessary.
2. Disconnect the engine harness electrical connector from the manifold absolute pressure (MAP) sensor.
3. Remove the MAP sensor bracket bolt. Remove the MAP sensor bracket.
4. Remove the MAP sensor.

To install:
5. Install the MAP sensor.
6. Install the MAP sensor bracket. Install the MAP sensor bracket bolt. Tighten the bolt to 89 inch lbs. (10 Nm).
7. Connect the engine harness electrical connector to the MAP sensor.
8. Install the fuel injector sight shield, if necessary.

MASS AIR FLOW/INTAKE AIR SENSOR (MAF/IAT) SENSOR

LOCATION

3.9L Engine

See Figure 88.

Refer to the accompanying illustration.

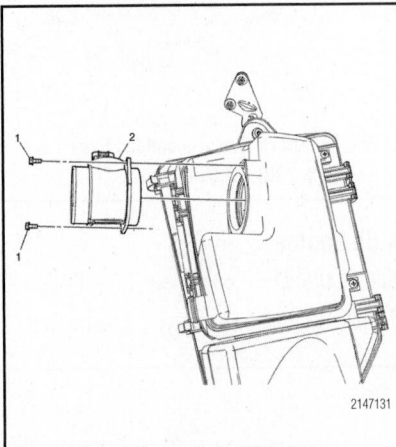

2147131

Fig. 88 Removing bolts (1) and MAF/IAT sensor (2)—3.9L engine

4.6L Engine

See Figure 89.

Refer to the accompanying illustration.

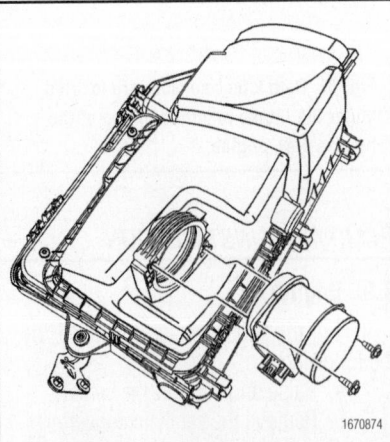

1670874

Fig. 89 Removing the MAF/IAT sensor—4.6L engine

REMOVAL & INSTALLATION

3.9L Engine

1. Disconnect the air outlet duct from the mass air flow sensor.
2. Remove the Mass Airflow Sensor/Intake Air Temperature (MAF/IAT) sensor.
3. Installation is the reverse of the removal procedure.

4.6L Engine

✳✳ CAUTION

Note the following precautions:

- Handle the MAF sensor carefully.
- Do not drop the MAF sensor in order to prevent damage to the MAF sensor.
- Do not damage the screen located on the air inlet end of the MAF.
- Do not touch the sensing elements.
- Do not allow solvents and lubricants to come in contact with the sensing elements.
- Use a small amount of a soap based solution in order to aid in the installation.

1. Disconnect the engine harness electrical connector from the mass air flow/intake air temperature (MAF/IAT) sensor.
2. Remove the air cleaner outlet duct.
3. Remove the MAF/IAT sensor bolts. Remove the MAF/IAT sensor.

To install:
4. Install the MAF/IAT sensor. Install the MAF/IAT sensor bolts.
5. Install the air cleaner outlet duct. Tighten the air cleaner duct clamps.
6. Connect the engine harness electrical connector to the MAF/IAT sensor.

VEHICLE SPEED SENSOR (VSS)

LOCATION

3.9L Engine with 4T65-E A/T

See Figure 90.

Refer to the accompanying illustration.

4.6L Engine with 4T80-E A/T

See Figure 91.

Refer to the accompanying illustration.

REMOVAL & INSTALLATION

3.9L Engine with 4T65-E A/T

1. Raise and support the vehicle.
2. Disconnect the electrical connector at the vehicle speed sensor.

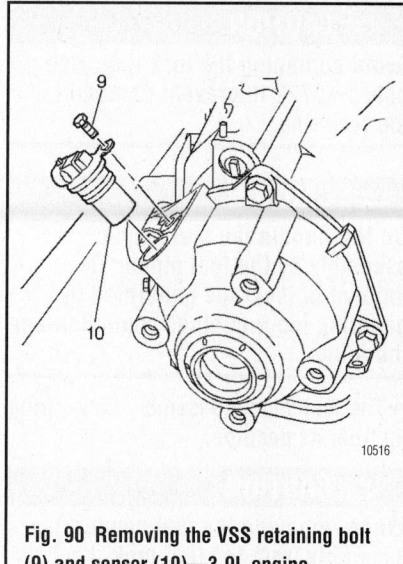

Fig. 90 Removing the VSS retaining bolt (9) and sensor (10)—3.9L engine

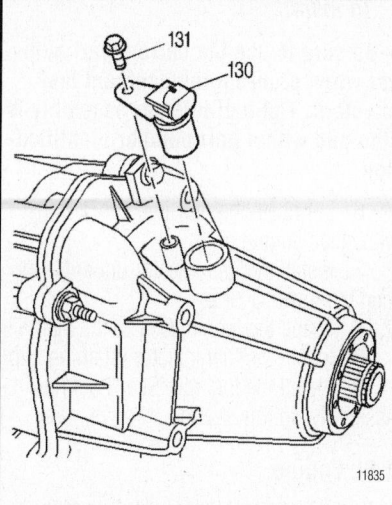

Fig. 91 Removing the VSS retaining bolt (131) and sensor (130)—4.6L engine

4.6L Engine with 4T80-E A/T

1. Raise the vehicle.
2. Remove the bolts securing the front transaxle brace to the transaxle and right cylinder head.
3. Remove the electrical connector at the vehicle speed sensor.
4. Remove the retaining bolt and the sensor.

➡**Twisting the sensor while pulling outward will aid in removal.**

To install:

5. Install a new O-ring seal on sensor if necessary.
6. Install the vehicle speed sensor and the retaining bolt. Tighten the bolt to 89 inch lbs. (10 Nm).
7. Install the electrical connector at the sensor.
8. Install the bolts securing the front transaxle brace to the transaxle and right cylinder head.
9. Lower the vehicle.

3. Remove the retaining bolt and the sensor.

To install:

4. Inspect the O-ring. If damaged, replace as necessary.

5. Install the vehicle speed sensor and the retaining bolt. Tighten the bolt to 106 inch lbs. (12 Nm).
6. Connect the electrical connector to the sensor.
7. Lower the vehicle.

FUEL

GASOLINE FUEL INJECTION SYSTEM

FUEL SYSTEM SERVICE PRECAUTIONS

Safety is the most important factor when performing not only fuel system maintenance but any type of maintenance. Failure to conduct maintenance and repairs in a safe manner may result in serious personal injury or death. Maintenance and testing of the vehicle's fuel system components can be accomplished safely and effectively by adhering to the following rules and guidelines.

• To avoid the possibility of fire and personal injury, always disconnect the negative battery cable unless the repair or test procedure requires that battery voltage be applied.

• Always relieve the fuel system pressure prior to disconnecting any fuel system component (injector, fuel rail, pressure regulator, etc.), fitting or fuel line connection. Exercise extreme caution whenever relieving fuel system pressure to avoid exposing skin, face and eyes to fuel spray. Please be advised that fuel under pressure may penetrate the skin or any part of the body that it contacts.

• Always place a shop towel or cloth around the fitting or connection prior to loosening to absorb any excess fuel due to

spillage. Ensure that all fuel spillage (should it occur) is quickly removed from engine surfaces. Ensure that all fuel soaked cloths or towels are deposited into a suitable waste container.

• Always keep a dry chemical (Class B) fire extinguisher near the work area.

• Do not allow fuel spray or fuel vapors to come into contact with a spark or open flame.

• Always use a back-up wrench when loosening and tightening fuel line connection fittings. This will prevent unnecessary stress and torsion to fuel line piping.

• Always replace worn fuel fitting O-rings with new Do not substitute fuel hose or equivalent where fuel pipe is installed.

Before servicing the vehicle, make sure to also refer to the precautions in the beginning of this section as well.

RELIEVING FUEL SYSTEM PRESSURE

✳✳ CAUTION

Remove the fuel tank cap and relieve the fuel system pressure before servicing the fuel system in order to reduce the risk of personal injury. After you relieve the fuel system

pressure, a small amount of fuel may be released when servicing the fuel lines, the fuel injection pump, or the connections. In order to reduce the risk of personal injury, cover the fuel system components with a shop towel before disconnection. This will catch any fuel that may leak out. Place the towel in an approved container when the disconnection is complete.

1. If the fuel system requires repair, prevent fuel spillage by removing the fuel pump fuse.
2. Loosen the fuel fill cap in order to relieve the fuel tank vapor pressure.
3. Remove the engine cover, if required.
4. Remove the fuel rail service port cap.
5. Wrap a shop towel around the fuel rail service port and using a small flat-bladed tool, depress (open) the fuel rail test port valve.
6. Remove the shop towel from around the fuel rail service port, and place in an approved gasoline container.
7. Install the fuel rail service port cap.
8. Install the engine cover, if required.
9. Tighten the fuel fill cap.

FUEL INJECTORS

REMOVAL & INSTALLATION

3.9L Engine

See Figure 92.

> ※※ **CAUTION**
>
> Use care in removing the fuel injectors in order to prevent damage to the fuel injector electrical connector pins or the fuel injector nozzles. Do not immerse the fuel injector in any type of cleaner. The fuel injector is an electrical component and may be damaged by this cleaning method.

➡ If the fuel injectors are found to be leaking, the engine oil may be contaminated with fuel.

1. Remove the fuel rail. See "Fuel Rail Assembly" in this section.
2. Remove the fuel injector retaining clip.
3. Remove the fuel injector from the fuel rail.
4. Remove the fuel injector upper O-ring.
5. Remove the fuel injector lower O-ring.

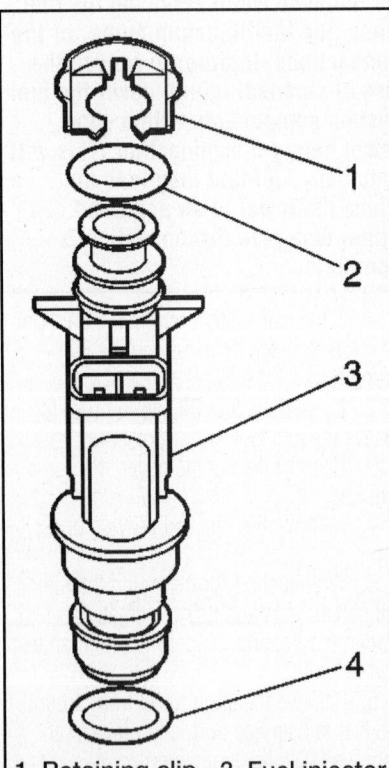

1. Retaining clip   3. Fuel injector
2. O-ring   4. O-ring

537311

Fig. 92 Exploded view of the injector

To install:

➡ Be sure to use the correct part number when ordering replacement fuel injectors. The fuel injector assembly is stamped with a part number identification.

6. Lubricate the new injector O-rings with clean engine oil.
7. Install the fuel injector upper O-ring, then the lower O-ring.
8. Install the fuel injector to the fuel rail.
9. Install the fuel injector retaining clip.
10. Install the fuel rail. See "Fuel Rail Assembly" in this section.

4.6L Engine

➡ See "Fuel Rail Assembly" in this section.

FUEL SENDER MODULE

REMOVAL & INSTALLATION

See Figure 93.

1. Relieve the fuel system pressure.
2. Remove the rear compartment liner.
3. Remove the fuel sender access hole cover bolts. Remove the fuel sender access hole cover.
4. Disconnect the fuel feed rear pipe quick connect fitting from the sender.
5. Disconnect the evaporative emission (EVAP) pipe quick connect fitting from the sender.
6. Disconnect the fuel level sensor wiring harness electrical connectors from the sender.
7. Reposition the fuel feed pipe, EVAP pipe, and harness connector out of the way.
8. Install the wrench (J 45722) to the lock ring.

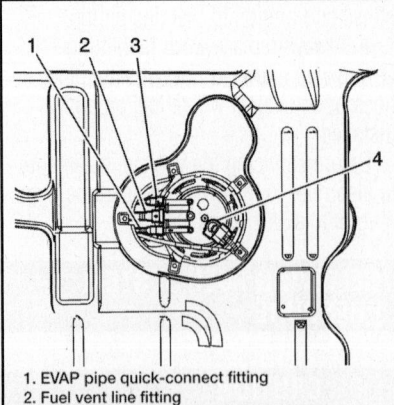

1. EVAP pipe quick-connect fitting
2. Fuel vent line fitting
3. Fuel feed rear pipe quick-connect fitting
4. Fuel level sensor wiring harness connector

1755108

Fig. 93 Disconnecting components from the fuel sender

> ※※ **CAUTION**
>
> Avoid damaging the lock ring. Use only J-45722 to prevent damage to the lock ring.

> ※※ **CAUTION**
>
> Do Not handle the fuel sender assembly by the fuel pipes. The amount of leverage generated by handling the fuel pipes could damage the joints.

➡ The fuel sender assembly may spring up from its position.

> ※※ **CAUTION**
>
> When removing the fuel sender assembly from the fuel tank, be aware that the reservoir bucket is full of fuel. It must be tipped slightly during removal to avoid damage to the float. Discard the fuel sender assembly O-ring seal and replace it with a new one.

➡ Carefully discard the fuel in the reservoir bucket into an approved container.

➡ Do NOT use impact tools. Significant force will be required to release the lock ring. The use of a hammer and screwdriver is not recommended. Secure the fuel tank in order to prevent fuel tank rotation.

9. Use the wrench and a long breaker-bar in order to unlock the fuel sender lock ring. Rotate the lock ring in a counterclockwise direction. Remove the wrench.
10. Raise the sender slightly from the fuel tank and disconnect the vent line quick connect fitting from the sender.
11. Remove the fuel sender lock ring.
12. Slowly raise the module until the vapor line quick connect fittings are visible.
13. In order to prevent the internal vent lines from dropping into the raw gasoline, tie a string to the lines and secure.
14. Disconnect the vapor line quick connect fittings from the module flange.
15. Slowly raise the sender until the fuel level sensor float arm is just visible.

➡ When removing the sender from the fuel tank, be aware that the sender reservoir bucket is full of fuel. The sender must be tipped slightly during removal to avoid bending the fuel level sensor float arm.

16. Tilt the sender toward the rear of the fuel tank to allow the level sensor float arm

to clear the tank opening. Remove the sender from the tank.

17. Remove and discard the fuel pump sender O-ring seal.

➡**Some lock ring were manufactured with DO NOT REUSE stamped into them. These lock rings may be reused if they are not damaged or warped.**

18. Inspect the lock ring for damage due to improper removal or installation procedures. If damage is found, install a NEW lock ring.

19. Check the lock ring for flatness.

20. Place the lock ring on a flat surface. Measure the clearance between to lock ring and the flat surface using a feeler gauge at 7 different points.

a. If the warpage is less than 0.016 in. (0.41 mm), the lock ring does not require replacement.

b. If the warpage is greater than 0.016 in. (0.41 mm), the lock ring must be replaced.

To install:

21. Place a NEW fuel pump sender O-ring seal onto the fuel tank.

22. Tilt the sender toward the rear of the fuel tank to allow the fuel level sensor float arm to clear the tank opening. Install the sender into the fuel tank.

23. Lower the sender assembly into the tank.

24. Connect the internal vent line quick connect fittings to the sender.

25. Remove the string securing the internal vent lines.

26. Install the sender lock ring, and move it into position on the top of the sender.

27. Connect the vent line quick connect fitting to the sender.

28. Install the wrench (J 45722 or equivalent) to the lock ring.

29. Ensure the lock ring is installed with the correct side facing upward. A correctly installed lock ring will only turn in a clockwise direction.

30. Using the wrench and a breaker bar, rotate the fuel sender lock ring clockwise until the ring is locked into place on the fuel tank. Remove the wrench.

31. Position the fuel feed pipe and harness connector.

32. Connect the EVAP line quick connect fitting to the sender.

33. Connect the fuel feed rear pipe quick connect fitting to the sender.

34. Connect the fuel level sensor wiring harness electrical connector to the sender.

35. Connect the negative battery cable.

36. Perform the following procedure in order to inspect for leaks:

a. Turn ON the ignition, with the engine OFF for 2 seconds.

b. Turn OFF the ignition for 10 seconds.

c. Turn ON the ignition, with the engine OFF.

d. Inspect for fuel leaks.

37. Install the fuel sender access hole cover.

38. Install the fuel sender access hole cover bolts and tighten.

39. Install the rear compartment liner.

40. Install the intake manifold cover.

FUEL RAIL ASSEMBLY

REMOVAL & INSTALLATION

3.9L Engine

➡**An 8-digit identification number is stamped on the fuel rail. Refer to this number if servicing or part replacement is required.**

✳✳ WARNING

In order to reduce the risk of fire and personal injury that may result from a fuel leak, always install the fuel injector O-rings in the proper position. If the upper and lower O-rings are different colors (black and brown), be sure to install the black O-ring in the upper position and the brown O-ring in the lower position on the fuel injector. The O-rings are the same size but are made of different materials.

✳✳ CAUTION

Cap the fittings and plug the holes when servicing the fuel system in order to prevent dirt and other contaminants from entering the open pipes and passages.

➡**If the fuel injectors are found to be leaking, the engine oil may be contaminated with fuel.**

1. Disconnect the fuel feed pipe from the fuel rail.

2. Disconnect any remaining electrical connectors.

3. Remove the upper intake manifold. See "Intake Manifold" in "ENGINE MECHANICAL" section.

4. Remove the fuel injector harness connector bracket bolt from the intake manifold.

5. Disconnect the camshaft position (CMP) sensor electrical connector.

6. Disconnect the engine coolant temperature (ECT) sensor electrical connector.

7. Remove the fuel rail bolts. Remove the fuel rail.

8. Remove the fuel injectors, if needed. See "Fuel Injectors" in this section.

To install:

9. Install the fuel injectors, if removed. See "Fuel Injectors" in this section.

10. Install the fuel rail assembly into the intake manifold. Tilt the fuel rail assembly slightly to install the injectors. Install the fuel rail bolts. Tighten the bolts to 89 inch lbs. (10 Nm).

11. Connect the CMP sensor electrical connector.

12. Disconnect the ECT sensor electrical connector.

13. Position the fuel injector harness connector bracket to the intake manifold.

14. Install the fuel injector harness connector bracket bolt. Tighten the bolt to 71 inch lbs. (8 Nm).

15. Install the upper intake manifold. See "Intake Manifold" in "ENGINE MECHANICAL" section.

16. Connect any remaining electrical connectors.

17. Connect the fuel feed pipe to the fuel rail.

18. Connect the negative battery cable.

19. Inspect for fuel leaks with the following procedure:

a. Turn ON the ignition for 2 seconds.

b. Turn OFF the ignition for 10 seconds.

c. Turn ON the ignition.

d. Inspect for fuel leaks.

4.6L Engine

See Figure 94.

✳✳ CAUTION

Remove the fuel rail assembly carefully in order to prevent damage to the injector electrical connector terminals and the injector spray tips. Support the fuel rail after the fuel rail is removed in order to avoid damaging the fuel rail components.

1. Cap the fittings and plug the holes when servicing the fuel system in order to prevent dirt and other contaminants from entering open pipes and passages.

2. Relieve the fuel system pressure, as described in this section.

3. Clean the fuel rail assembly with a spray type engine cleaner, if necessary.

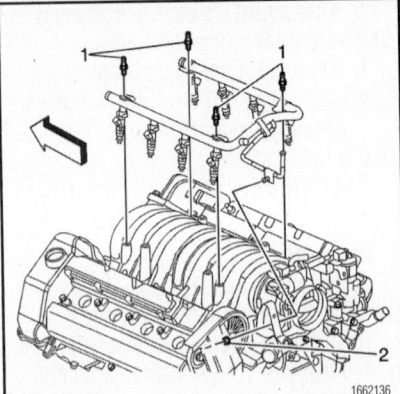

Fig. 94 Removing the fuel rail studs (1) and bracket nut (2) to remove the fuel rail assembly.

4. Disconnect the fuel feed pipe quick connect fitting from the fuel rail.

5. Disconnect the positive crankcase ventilation (PCV) air tube quick connect fitting from the camshaft cover.

6. Remove the surge tank inlet pipe hose from the surge tank.

7. Remove the surge tank inlet pipe hose from the engine fitting.

8. Remove the surge tank inlet pipe nuts. Remove the surge tank inlet pipe from the fuel rail studs.

9. Disconnect the engine harness electrical connector from the starter solenoid cable electrical connector.

10. Disconnect the engine harness electrical connectors from the front fuel injectors.

11. Disconnect the engine harness electrical connectors from the rear fuel injectors.

12. Remove the engine harness clip from the fuel rail stud. Lay the harness aside.

13. Remove the fuel rail bracket retainer nut.

14. Remove the fuel rail studs. Remove the fuel rail.

15. Remove and discard the O-ring seals from the spray tip end of each fuel injector.

16. If replacing the fuel rail, remove the fuel injectors.

To install:

✳✳ CAUTION
Note the following precautions:

- Use care when servicing the fuel system components, especially the fuel injector electrical connectors, the fuel injector tips, and the injector O-rings. Plug the inlet and the outlet ports of the fuel rail in order to prevent contamination.

- Do not use compressed air to clean the fuel rail assembly as this may damage the fuel rail components.
- Do not immerse the fuel rail assembly in a solvent bath in order to prevent damage to the fuel rail assembly.

17. If the fuel rail was replaced, install the fuel injectors.

18. Install NEW O-ring seals to the spray tip end of each fuel injector.

19. Lubricate the NEW lower injector O-ring seals with clean engine oil.

20. Install the fuel rail. Install the fuel rail studs. Tighten the studs to 89 inch lbs. (10 Nm). Install the fuel rail bracket retainer nut. Tighten the nut to 89 inch lbs. (10 Nm).

21. Position the harness over the engine. Install the engine harness clip to the fuel rail stud.

22. Connect the engine harness electrical connectors to the rear fuel injectors.

23. Connect the engine harness electrical connectors to the front fuel injectors.

24. Connect the engine harness electrical connector to the starter solenoid cable electrical connector.

25. Install the surge tank inlet pipe to the fuel rail studs. Install the surge tank inlet pipe nuts.

26. Install the surge tank inlet pipe hose and clamp to the engine fitting.

27. Install the surge tank inlet pipe hose and clamp to the surge tank.

28. Connect the PCV air tube quick connect fitting to the camshaft cover.

29. Connect the fuel feed pipe quick connect fitting to the fuel rail.

30. Connect the negative battery cable.

31. Inspect for fuel leaks with the following procedure:
   a. Turn ON the ignition for 2 seconds.
   b. Turn OFF the ignition for 10 seconds.
   c. Turn ON the ignition.
   d. Inspect for fuel leaks.

32. Install the fuel injector sight shield.

FUEL TANK

DRAINING

✳✳ WARNING

Never drain or store fuel in an open container. Always use an approved fuel storage container in order to reduce the chance of fire or explosion. Place a dry chemical (Class B) fire extinguisher nearby before performing any on-vehicle service procedures. Failure to follow these

precautions may result in personal injury.

1. Insert the fuel tank drain hose into the fuel tank until the hose reaches the bottom of the fuel tank.

2. Use a hand or air operated pump device in order to drain as much fuel through the fuel fill pipe as possible.

REMOVAL & INSTALLATION

See Figures 95 through 99.

1. Relieve the fuel system pressure, as described in this section.

2. Drain the fuel tank.

3. Remove the left rear wheelhouse liner.

4. Using compressed air, blow any dirt and/or debris from around the fuel fill pipe and evaporative emission (EVAP) line connections.

5. Loosen the fuel fill hose clamp at the fill pipe.

6. Disconnect the fuel fill hose from the fuel fill pipe.

7. Disconnect the fuel tank EVAP recirculation line quick connect fitting from the fill pipe line.

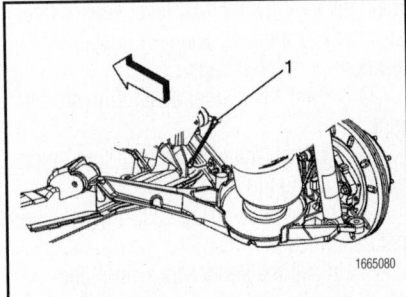

Fig. 95 Disconnect the left and right electronic position sensor links (1) from the ball studs.

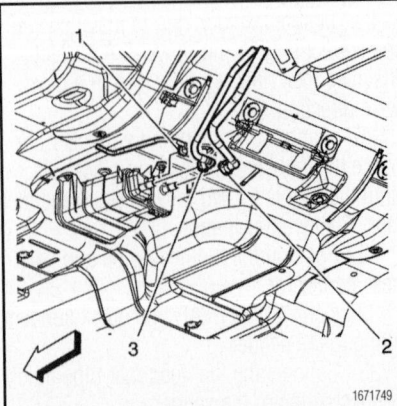

Fig. 96 Disconnect the fill pipe vent line and the fuel tank vapor line quick connect fittings from the EVAP canister.

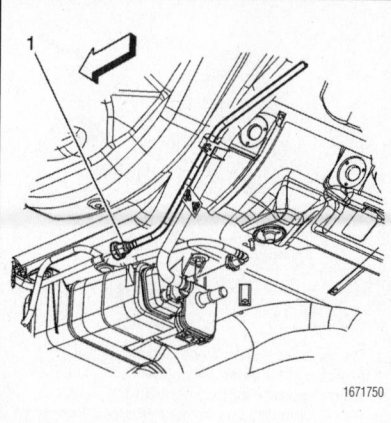

Fig. 97 Disconnect the fuel feed line quick connect fitting (1) from the chassis line.

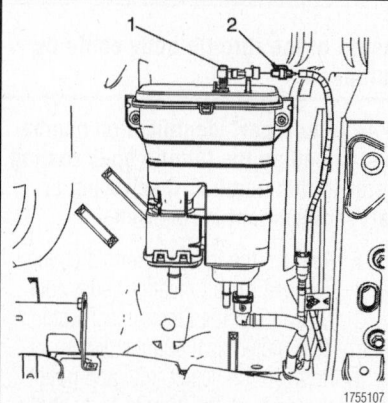

Fig. 98 Disconnect the fuel tank wiring harness electrical connector (2) from the fuel tank pressure sensor.

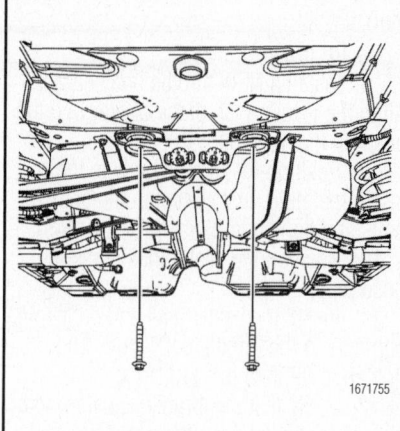

Fig. 99 Remove the rear suspension crossmember bolts.

8. Disconnect the left and right electronic position sensor links from the ball studs.

9. Disconnect the fill pipe vent line and the fuel tank vapor line quick connect fittings from the EVAP canister.

10. Disconnect the fuel feed line quick connect fitting from the chassis line.

11. Disconnect the fuel tank wiring harness electrical connector from the fuel tank pressure sensor.

12. Remove the fuel and EVAP line retainer from the side rail.

13. Disconnect the body harness electrical connector from the fuel tank harness electrical connector.

14. Remove the fuel tank harness clips from the rear compartment side rail.

15. Remove the exhaust system.

16. Loosen the left and right rear brake hose bracket nut and slide the stud out of the keyhole slot in the side rail.

17. Remove the rear shock lower bolts.

18. Support the front of the vehicle with a jack stand at the engine cradle.

19. Support the rear suspension crossmember with a suitable adjustable jack.

20. Remove the rear suspension crossmember bolts.

21. Using the adjustable jack, slowly lower the rear suspension crossmember allowing the crossmember to pivot at the front bolts, until the rear springs can be removed. Remove the rear coil springs.

22. Remove the fuel tank strap bolts. Remove the fuel tank straps.

23. Remove the fuel tank.

24. Place the fuel tank on a suitable work surface.

To install:

25. Place the fuel tank onto the rear suspension crossmember.

26. Install the fuel tank straps. Install the fuel tank strap bolts and tighten to 34 ft. lbs. (46 Nm).

27. Install the rear coil springs while slowly raising the rear suspension crossmember using the adjustable jack.

28. Install the rear suspension crossmember bolts and tighten to 141 ft. lbs. (191 Nm).

29. Remove the adjustable jack from the rear suspension crossmember.

30. Remove the jack stand from the front of the vehicle.

31. Install the rear shock bolts and tighten to 18 ft. lbs. (25 Nm).

32. Connect the body harness electrical connector to the fuel tank harness electrical connector.

33. Install the fuel tank harness clips to the rear compartment side rail.

34. Install the fuel and EVAP line retainer to the side rail.

35. Connect the fuel tank wiring harness electrical connector to the fuel tank pressure sensor.

36. Connect the fuel feed line quick connect fitting to the chassis line.

37. Connect the fill pipe vent line and the fuel tank vapor line quick connect fittings to the EVAP canister.

38. Install the left and right rear brake hose bracket studs into the keyhole slots. Tighten the nuts to 89 inch lbs. (10 Nm).

39. Install the exhaust system.

40. Connect the left and right electronic position sensor links to the ball studs.

41. Clean the fill pipe or any dirt or debris. Ensure the fill pipe is installed to the original depth to the fill hose. The fill pipe bead must be inserted into the hose past the clamp position.

42. Connect the fuel tank EVAP recirculation line quick connect fitting to the fill pipe line.

43. Connect the fuel fill hose to the fuel fill pipe.

44. Tighten the fuel fill hose clamp at the fill pipe.

45. Install the left rear wheelhouse liner.

46. Fill the fuel tank.

47. Connect the negative battery cable.

48. Inspect for fuel leaks with the following procedure:

   a. Turn ON the ignition for 2 seconds.

   b. Turn OFF the ignition for 10 seconds.

   c. Turn ON the ignition.

   d. Inspect for fuel leaks.

IDLE SPEED

THROTTLE LEARN PROCEDURE

Description

The engine control module (ECM) learns the airflow through the throttle body to ensure the correct idle. The learned airflow values are stored within the ECM. These values are learned to adjust for production variation and will continuously learn during the life of the vehicle to compensate for reduced airflow due to throttle body coking. Anytime the throttle body airflow rate changes, for example due to cleaning or replacing, the values must be relearned.

An engine that had a heavily coked throttle body that has been cleaned or replaced may take several drive cycles to learn out the coking. To accelerate the process, the scan tool has the ability to reset all learned values back to zero. A new ECM will also have values set to zero.

The idle may be unstable or a DTC may set if the learned values do not match the actual airflow.

Conditions for Running the Throttle Learn Procedure

1. For the reset procedure, check that none of the following are set:
- DTCs P0068, P0101, P0102, P0103, P0106, P0107, P0108, P0116, P0117, P0118, P0120, P0122, P0123, P0128, P0171, P0172, P0174, P0175, P0201, P0202, P0203, P0204, P0205, P0206, P0220, P0222, P0223, P0300, P0351, P0352, P0353, P0496, P0601, P0604, P0606, P060D, P0641, P0651, P1516, P2101, P2119, P2120, P2122, P2123, P2125, P2127, P2128, P2135, P2138, or P2176.

2. Turn ignition ON, engine OFF.
3. Ensure the Vehicle Speed Sensor (VSS) is 0 mph.
4. For the learn procedure, check that none of the following are set:
- DTCs P0068, P0101, P0102, P0103, P0106, P0107, P0108, P0116, P0117, P0118, P0120, P0122, P0123, P0128, P0171, P0172, P0174, P0175, P0201, P0202, P0203, P0204, P0205, P0206, P0220, P0222, P0223, P0300, P0351, P0352, P0353, P0496, P0601, P0604, P0606, P060D, P0641, P0651, P1516, P2101, P2119, P2120, P2122, P2123, P2125, P2127, P2128, P2135, P2138, or P2176.

5. Ensure the following conditions:
- The engine speed is between 450–4000 RPM.
- The manifold absolute pressure (MAP) is greater than 5 kPa.
- The mass air flow (MAF) is greater than 2 g/s.
- The ignition voltage is greater than 10 volts.

Throttle Learn

➥ The following reset procedure is performed after the throttle body is cleaned or replaced.

1. Turn ignition ON, engine OFF.
2. Perform the Idle Learn Reset in Module Setup with a scan tool.
3. Start the engine and monitor the TB Idle Airflow Compensation parameter. The TB Idle Airflow Compensation value should equal 0 percent and the engine should be idling at a normal idle speed.
4. Clear the DTCs and return to the original diagnostic that referred you here.

➥ The following learn procedure is performed after the ECM is flashed or replaced.

➥ Do NOT perform this procedure if DTCs are set.

5. Start and idle the engine for 3 minutes.
6. With a scan tool, monitor the Desired Idle Speed and the actual Engine Speed.
7. The ECM will start to learn the new idle cells and Desired Idle Speed should start to decrease.
8. Turn ignition OFF for 60 seconds.
9. Start and idle the engine for 3 minutes.
10. After the 3 minute run time the engine should be idling normal.
11. During the drive cycle the check engine light may come on with idle speed DTCs. If idle speed codes are set, clear codes so the ECM can continue to learn.
   a. If the engine idle speed has not been learned the vehicle will need to be driven at speeds above 70 km/h (44 mph) with several decelerations and extended idles.
12. After the drive cycle, the engine should be idling normally.
   a. If the engine idle speed has not been learned, turn OFF the ignition for 60 seconds and repeat step 6.
13. Once the engine speed has returned to normal, clear DTCs and return to the diagnostic that referred you here.

THROTTLE BODY

REMOVAL & INSTALLATION

3.9L Engine

See Figure 100.

> ※※ **CAUTION**
>
> **Handle the electronic throttle control components carefully. Use cleanliness in order to prevent damage. Do not drop the electronic throttle control components. Do not roughly handle the electronic throttle control components. Do not immerse the electronic throttle control components in cleaning solvents of any type.**

> ※※ **CAUTION**
>
> **DO NOT for any reason, insert a screwdriver or other small hand tool into the throttle body to hold open the throttle plate as a wedge, as the**

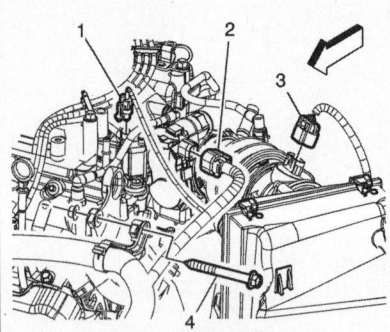

1. Oil pressure sensor electrical connector
2. Knock sensor electrical connector
3. Starter motor electrical connector
4. Air conditioning compressor electrical connector

1608290

Fig. 100 Disconnect the Electronic Throttle control (ETC) electrical connector (2).

inside of the throttle body could be damaged.

➥ An 8-digit part identification number is stamped on the throttle body casting. Refer to this number, if servicing or part replacement is required.

1. Remove the intake manifold cover.
2. Remove the air cleaner outlet duct.
3. Disconnect the Electronic Throttle control (ETC) electrical connector.
4. Remove the heater inlet and outlet pipe clip nuts from the throttle body studs.
5. Reposition the heater inlet and outlet hose/pipe.
6. Remove the throttle body bolts/studs. Remove the throttle body.
7. Remove and discard the throttle body gasket.

To install:

8. Install a NEW throttle body gasket. Align the locating tab of the gasket with the notch in the manifold.
9. Position the throttle body to the intake manifold. Install the throttle body bolts and tighten to 89 inch lbs. (10 Nm).
10. Position the heater inlet and outlet hose/pipe.
11. Install the heater inlet and outlet pipe clip nuts to the throttle body studs and tighten to 89 inch lbs. (10 Nm).
12. Verify that the throttle actuator motor harness connector and the connector seal are properly installed and not damaged.
13. Connect the ETC electrical connector on the throttle body.
14. Install the air cleaner outlet duct.
15. Install the intake manifold cover.
16. Connect a scan tool in order to test for proper throttle opening and throttle closing ranges.

a. Operate the accelerator pedal and monitor the throttle angles.

b. The accelerator pedal should operate freely, without binding, between closed throttle, and wide open throttle (WOT).

c. Verify that the vehicle meets the following conditions:

- The vehicle is not in a reduced engine power mode.
- The ignition is ON.
- The engine is OFF.

17. Perform the Throttle Learn Procedure, as described in this section.

4.6L Engine

See Figure 101.

✳✳ CAUTION

Handle the electronic throttle control components carefully. Use cleanliness in order to prevent damage. Do not drop the electronic throttle control components. Do not roughly handle the electronic throttle control components. Do not immerse the electronic throttle control components in cleaning solvents of any type.

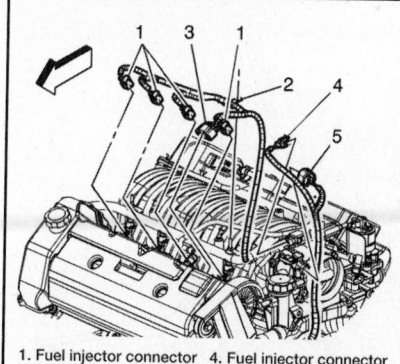

1. Fuel injector connector
2. Fuel injector harness
3. Fuel injector connector
4. Fuel injector connector
5. Throttle actuator electrical connector

1662120

Fig. 101 Disconnect the engine harness electrical connector from the throttle actuator.

1. Remove the fuel injector sight shield.
2. Remove the air cleaner outlet duct.
3. Disconnect the positive crankcase ventilation (PCV) fresh air tube quick connect fittings at the camshaft cover and the air cleaner outlet duct.
4. Disconnect the engine harness electrical connector from the throttle actuator.
5. Remove the transaxle vent hose clip from the shift cable bracket.

6. Remove the transaxle shift cable clip from the shift cable bracket.
7. Remove the throttle body bolts. Remove the shift cable bracket. Remove the throttle body.
8. Remove and discard the throttle body seal.

To install:

9. Install a NEW throttle body seal.
10. Position the throttle body. Position the shift cable bracket. Install the throttle body bolts. Tighten the bolts to 89 inch lbs. (10 Nm).
11. Install the transaxle shift cable clip to the shift cable bracket.
12. Install the transaxle vent hose clip to the shift cable bracket.
13. Connect the engine harness electrical connector to the throttle actuator.
14. Route the PCV fresh air tube under the vacuum brake booster hose and the evaporative emission (EVAP) purge valve.
15. Install the PCV fresh air tube.
16. Connect the PCV fresh air tube quick connect fittings at the camshaft cover and the air cleaner outlet duct.
17. Install the air cleaner outlet duct.
18. Install the fuel injector sight shield.
19. Perform the Throttle Learn procedure.

HEATING & AIR CONDITIONING SYSTEM

BLOWER MOTOR

REMOVAL & INSTALLATION

See Figure 102.

1. Remove the right hand closeout insulator panel.

2. Disconnect the blower motor electrical connector.
3. Remove the blower motor screws, and remove the blower motor.
4. Installation is the reverse of the removal procedure.

COMPRESSOR

REMOVAL & INSTALLATION

See Figures 103 and 104.

➥As A/C system connections are opened, cap openings immediately to prevent excess entry of air, moisture and dirt into system.

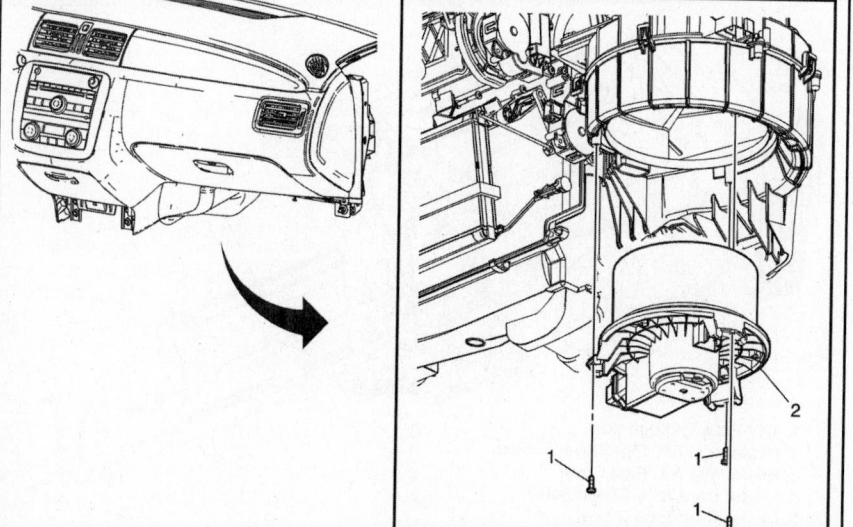

Fig. 102 Removing retaining screws (1) and blower motor (2)

1674210

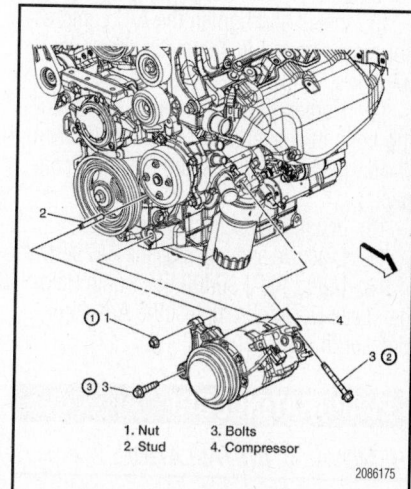

1. Nut
2. Stud
3. Bolts
4. Compressor

2086175

Fig. 103 Showing compressor mounting— 3.9L engine

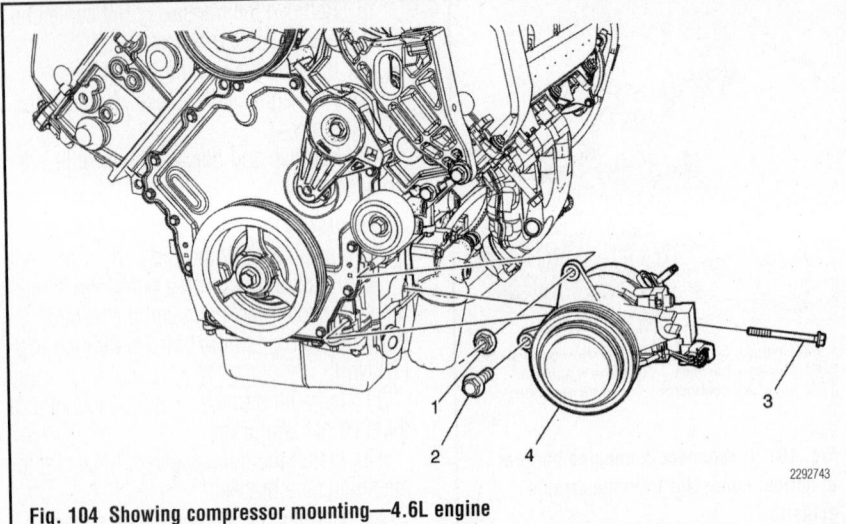

Fig. 104 Showing compressor mounting—4.6L engine

1. Recover the refrigerant.
2. Remove the accessory drive belt.
3. Raise and support the vehicle.
4. Disconnect the compressor electrical connector.
5. Remove the A/C compressor and condenser hose.
6. Remove the A/C compressor hose.
7. Remove the A/C compressor nut.
8. Remove the A/C compressor stud.
9. Remove the 2 A/C compressor bolts.
10. Remove the compressor.

To install:

→**When replacing the A/C compressor, balance the compressor oil. Use a low viscosity, polyalkylene glycol (PAG) oil. Use of the incorrect oil can result in compressor failure.**

11. Position the compressor and install the bolts snugly.
12. Install and tighten the A/C compressor stud to 71 inch lbs. (8 Nm).
13. Install and tighten the A/C compressor mounting nut in sequence shown to 37 ft. lbs. (50 Nm).
14. Tighten the A/C compressor mounting bolts in sequence to 37 ft. lbs. (50 Nm).
15. Install the hoses and electrical connector.
16. Install the accessory drive belt.
17. Evacuate and recharge the A/C system.
18. Using the J 39400 Electronic Halogen Leak Detector leak test the A/C compressor fittings.

EVAPORATOR CORE

REMOVAL & INSTALLATION

See Figure 105.

1. Remove the HVAC module assembly. See "HVAC Module Assembly" in this section.

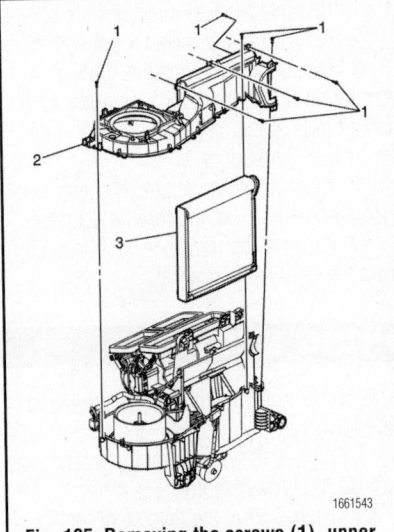

Fig. 105 Removing the screws (1), upper case half (2) and the evaporator core (3)

2. Remove the heater core. See "Heater Core" in this section.
3. Remove the thermal expansion valve. See "Thermal Expansion Valve" in this section.
4. Remove the air inlet housing assembly.
5. Remove the 7 A/C evaporator case screws.
6. Remove the upper half of the case and remove the evaporator core.
7. Installation is the reverse of the removal procedure.

HEATER CORE

REMOVAL & INSTALLATION

See Figure 106.

1. Remove the HVAC module assembly. See "HVAC Module" in this section.
2. Remove the left hand floor duct.
3. Remove the TXV pass-through seal.
4. Remove the pipe screws and the pipe cover.
5. Remove the heater core tube clamp screw and clamp.
6. Slide the heater core out of the HVAC housing.
7. Installation is the reverse of the removal procedure.

HVAC MODULE

REMOVAL & INSTALLATION

See Figures 107 and 108.

1. Drain the cooling system.
2. Recover the refrigerant.

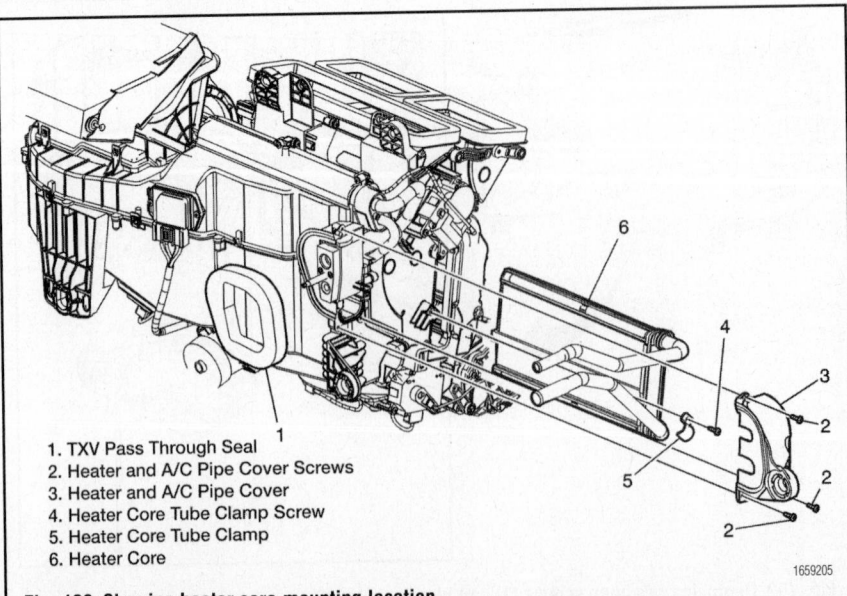

1. TXV Pass Through Seal
2. Heater and A/C Pipe Cover Screws
3. Heater and A/C Pipe Cover
4. Heater Core Tube Clamp Screw
5. Heater Core Tube Clamp
6. Heater Core

Fig. 106 Showing heater core mounting location

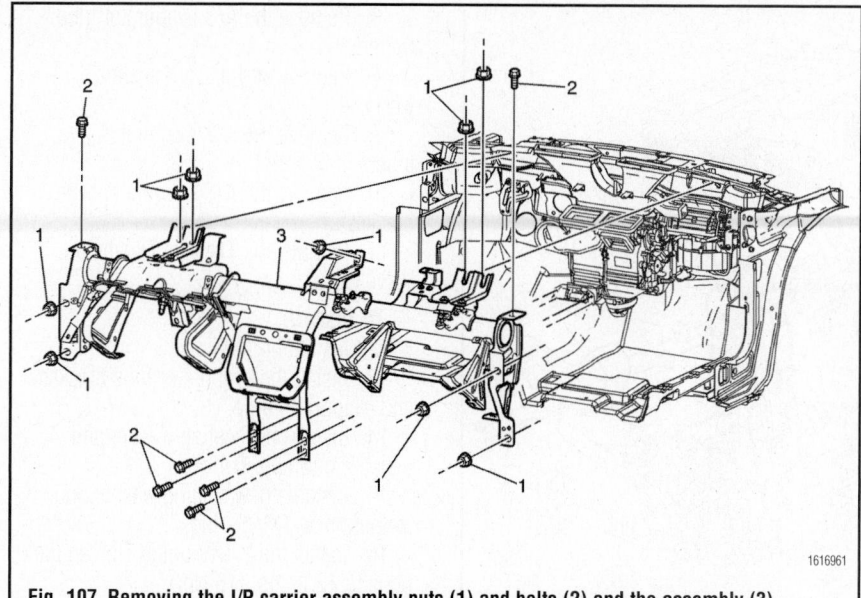

Fig. 107 Removing the I/P carrier assembly nuts (1) and bolts (2) and the assembly (3)

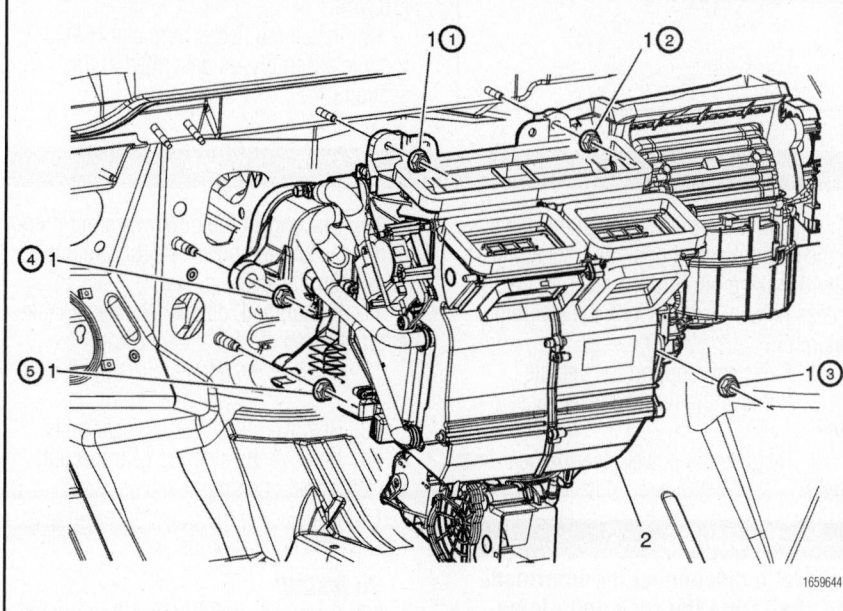

Fig. 108 Removing the nuts (1) and the HVAC assembly module (2)—showing nut tightening sequence

→Note the routing of the electric harness prior to removal of the carrier to aid in the reinstallation.

   j. Disconnect the electrical harness connections.

   k. With the aid of an assistant, remove the carrier from the vehicle.

10. Disconnect the HVAC module assembly electrical connectors.

11. Remove the 5 module assembly nuts.

12. Remove the HVAC assembly module.

To install:

13. Position the HVAC assembly to the vehicle and install the 5 retaining nuts. Tighten the nuts in sequence to 80 inch lbs. (9 Nm).

14. Attach the electrical connectors.

15. Install the I/P carrier assembly as follows:

   a. Position the I/P carrier to the vehicle.

   b. Attach the electrical connectors.

   c. Install the 6 I/P carrier assembly bolts. Tighten to 18 ft. lbs. (25 Nm).

   d. Install the 9 instrument panel carrier assembly nuts. Tighten to 18 ft. lbs. (25 Nm).

   e. Install the air ducts in reverse of the removal sequence.

   f. Install the I/P lower trim panel.

16. Reposition the auxiliary air distribution duct.

17. Install the lower instrument panel (I/P) support brace.

18. Reposition the carpet.

19. Install the brake pedal bracket assembly.

20. Reattach the heater hoses to the heater core.

21. Install the evaporator tube to the thermal expansion valve (TXV).

22. Evacuate and recharge the A/C system.

23. Refill the cooling system.

THERMAL EXPANSION VALVE (TXV)

REMOVAL & INSTALLATION

See Figure 109.

1. Remove the HVAC Module. See "HVAC Module Assembly" in this section.

2. Remove the heater core. See "Heater Core" in this section.

3. Remove the 2 A/C evaporator tube bolts.

4. Remove the 2 TXV bolts.

5. Remove the TXV O-ring.

6. Remove and discard sealing washer.

3. Remove the evaporator tube from the thermal expansion valve.

4. Remove the heater hoses from the heater core.

5. Remove the brake pedal bracket assembly.

6. Pull back and reposition the carpet.

7. Remove the lower instrument panel (I/P) support brace.

8. Reposition the auxiliary air distribution duct.

9. Remove the instrument panel carrier as follows:

   a. Remove the instrument panel lower trim panel.

   b. Remove the left and right air distribution ducts.

   c. Remove the center air outlet duct.

   d. Remove the floor air outlet duct.

   e. Remove the left and right side window defroster outlet ducts.

   f. Remove the screws securing the windshield defroster nozzle duct to the carrier.

   g. Remove the 9 instrument panel carrier assembly nuts.

   h. Remove the 6 I/P carrier assembly bolts.

   i. Remove the I/P carrier assembly.

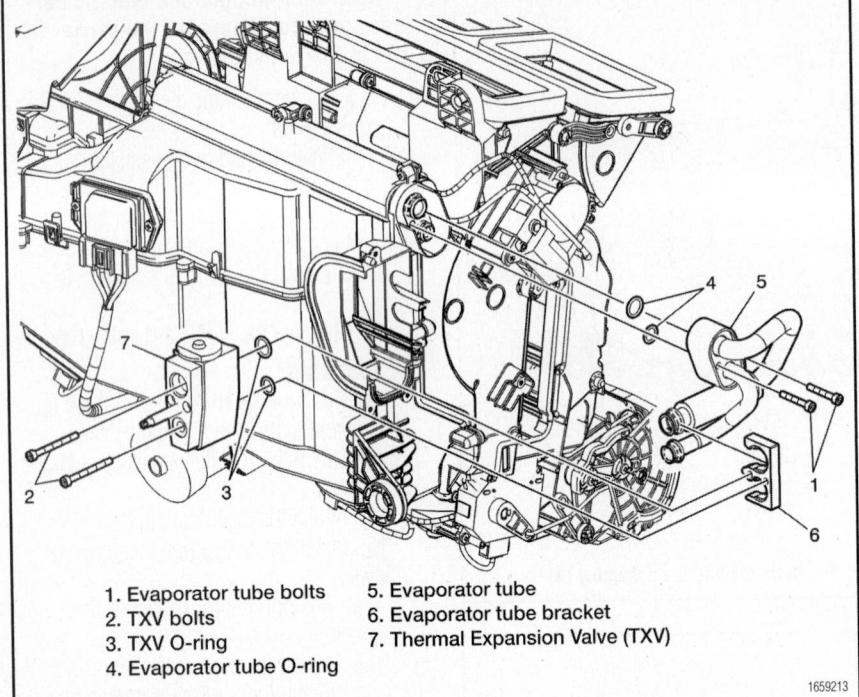

1. Evaporator tube bolts
2. TXV bolts
3. TXV O-ring
4. Evaporator tube O-ring
5. Evaporator tube
6. Evaporator tube bracket
7. Thermal Expansion Valve (TXV)

1659213

Fig. 109 Removing the thermal expansion valve

7. Remove the A/C evaporator tube O-ring.

8. Remove and discard sealing washer.

9. Remove the A/C evaporator tube.

10. Remove the A/C evaporator tube bracket.

11. Remove the Thermal Expansion Valve (TXV).

To install:

12. Install the TXV.

13. Install the evaporator tube bracket and evaporator tube.

14. Install new sealing washer and install a new tube O-ring.

15. Install a new sealing washer and install a new TXV O-ring.

16. Install the 2 TXV bolts. Tighten the bolts to 12 ft. lbs. (16 Nm).

17. Install the 2 A/C evaporator tube bolts. Tighten the bolts to 12 ft. lbs. (16 Nm).

18. Install the heater core and HVAC module assembly, as described in this section.

STEERING

POWER STEERING GEAR

REMOVAL & INSTALLATION
See Figure 110.

✳✳ CAUTION

With wheels of the vehicle facing straight ahead, secure the steering wheel utilizing steering column anti-rotation pin, steering column lock, or a strap to prevent rotation. Locking of the steering column will prevent damage and a possible malfunction of the SIR system. The steering wheel must be secured in position before disconnecting the following components:

- The steering column
- The intermediate shaft(s)
- The steering gear
- After disconnecting these components, do not rotate the steering wheel or move the front tires and wheels. Failure to follow this procedure may cause the SIR coil assembly to become un-centered and cause possible damage to the SIR coil. If you think the SIR coil has became un-centered, refer to your specific SIR coil's centering procedure to re-center SIR Coil.

1. With the front wheels of the vehicle in the straight ahead position, install the J-42640 locking pin into the steering column access hole in order to lock the steering column.

2. Raise and support the vehicle.

3. Remove the tire and wheel assemblies.

4. Remove the power steering gear heat shield.

✳✳ WARNING

Failure to disconnect the intermediate shaft from the rack and pinion steering gear stub shaft can result in damage to the steering gear and/or intermediate shaft. This damage may cause loss of steering control which could result in an accident and possible personal injury.

5. Remove the intermediate shaft lower pinch bolt.

6. Disconnect the intermediate shaft from the power steering gear.

7. Remove the outer tie rod retaining nuts.

8. Use a puller (J-24319-B) in order to disconnect the outer tie rod from the steering knuckle.

9. Place a drain pan under the vehicle.

10. Disconnect the power steering pressure hose and the power steering return hose from the steering gear.

11. If equipped, disconnect the variable effort steering electrical connector.

12. Remove the left stabilizer shaft insulator.

13. Remove the 2 steering gear bolts.

14. Remove the steering gear through the left wheel opening.

15. If replacing the power steering gear, transfer the outer tie rods.

To install:

16. Install the steering gear through the left wheel opening.

17. Install the 2 steering gear bolts and tighten to 89 ft. lbs. (120 Nm).

18. Install the left stabilizer shaft insulator.

19. Connect the power steering return hose and pressure hose to the steering gear and tighten the fittings to 25 ft. lbs. (34 Nm).

20. Remove the drain pan from under the vehicle.

21. If equipped, connect the variable effort steering electrical connector.

22. Connect the outer tie rods to the steering knuckles:

    a. Install the outer tie rod retaining nuts and tighten to 22 ft. lbs. (30 Nm).

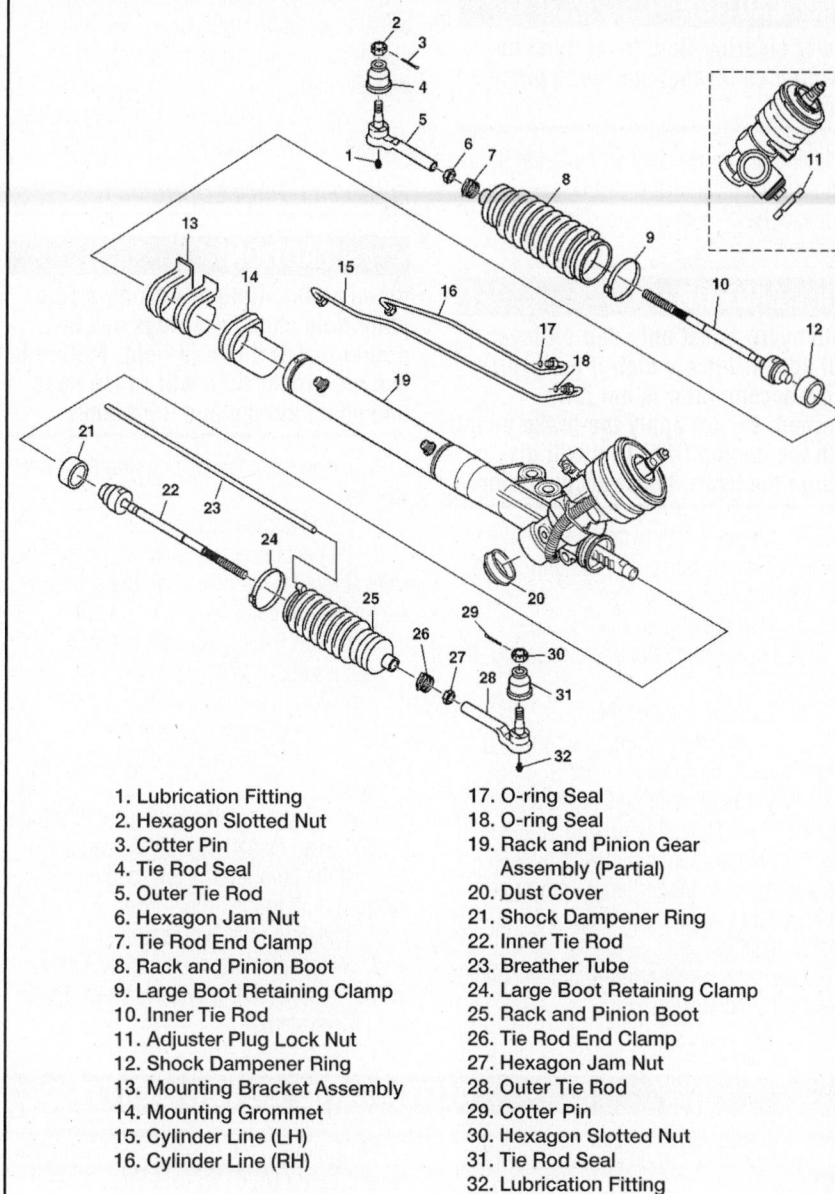

Fig. 110 Exploded view of the power steering gear

1. Lubrication Fitting
2. Hexagon Slotted Nut
3. Cotter Pin
4. Tie Rod Seal
5. Outer Tie Rod
6. Hexagon Jam Nut
7. Tie Rod End Clamp
8. Rack and Pinion Boot
9. Large Boot Retaining Clamp
10. Inner Tie Rod
11. Adjuster Plug Lock Nut
12. Shock Dampener Ring
13. Mounting Bracket Assembly
14. Mounting Grommet
15. Cylinder Line (LH)
16. Cylinder Line (RH)

17. O-ring Seal
18. O-ring Seal
19. Rack and Pinion Gear
    Assembly (Partial)
20. Dust Cover
21. Shock Dampener Ring
22. Inner Tie Rod
23. Breather Tube
24. Large Boot Retaining Clamp
25. Rack and Pinion Boot
26. Tie Rod End Clamp
27. Hexagon Jam Nut
28. Outer Tie Rod
29. Cotter Pin
30. Hexagon Slotted Nut
31. Tie Rod Seal
32. Lubrication Fitting

483378

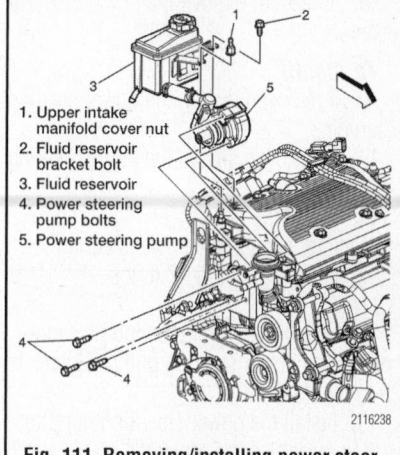

1. Upper intake
   manifold cover nut
2. Fluid reservoir
   bracket bolt
3. Fluid reservoir
4. Power steering
   pump bolts
5. Power steering pump

2116238

Fig. 111 Removing/installing power steering pump—3.9L engine

b. Tighten the outer tie rod retaining nuts an additional 180 degrees.

23. Connect the intermediate shaft to the steering gear. Install the intermediate shaft lower pinch bolt and tighten to 37 ft. lbs. (47 Nm).

24. Install the power steering gear heat shield.

25. Install the tire and wheel assemblies.

26. Lower the vehicle.

27. Remove the locking pin from the steering column access hole.

28. Bleed the power steering system. See "Power Steering Pump" in this section.

29. Inspect the power steering system for leaks.

30. Measure and adjust the front toe.

POWER STEERING PUMP

REMOVAL & INSTALLATION

3.9L Engine

See Figure 111.

1. Remove the intake manifold cover. Remove the upper intake manifold cover nut.

2. Remove the accessory drive belt.

3. Remove the power steering fluid reservoir bracket bolt.

4. Remove the reservoir.

   a. Remove as much power steering fluid from the remote power steering fluid reservoir as possible.

b. Disconnect the power steering reservoir inlet hose from the remote power steering fluid reservoir.

5. Remove the power steering pump bolts and remove the pump.

   a. Disconnect the power steering pressure hose from the power steering pump.

6. Transfer any parts as needed.

To install:

7. Position the pump and snugly install the mounting bolts.

8. Connect the power steering pressure hose to the pump.

9. Install the accessory drive belt.

10. Tighten the power steering pump mounting bolts to 18 ft. lbs. (25 Nm).

11. Connect the inlet hose to the fluid reservoir.

12. Install the reservoir and tighten the bracket bolt to 16 ft. lbs. (22 Nm).

13. After repairs, fill and bleed the power steering system, as described below.

14. After repairs, clean any excess power steering fluid from the vehicle and remove the drain pans.

15. Install the manifold cover.

4.6L Engine

1. Remove the drive belt.

2. Install a drain pan under the vehicle.

3. Disconnect the power steering return hose from the power steering reservoir.

4. Remove the power steering pressure hose from the power steering pump.

5. Remove the power steering pump mounting bolt.

6. Remove the power steering pump from the vehicle.

7. If needed, remove the power steering pulley.

8. If needed, remove the power steering reservoir.

To install:

9. If removed, install the power steering reservoir.

10. If removed, install the power steering pulley.

11. Install the power steering pump to the vehicle. Tighten the power steering pump mounting bolt to 37 ft. lbs. (50 Nm).

12. Install the power steering pressure hose to the power steering pump. Tighten to 25 ft. lbs. (34 Nm).

13. Install the power steering return hose to the power steering reservoir.

14. Remove the drain pan from under vehicle.

15. Install the drive belt.

16. Bleed the power steering system, as described below.

BLEEDING

➡ Use clean, new power steering fluid type only.

✳✳ CAUTION

Hoses touching the frame, body or engine may cause system noise. Verify that the hoses do not touch any other part of the vehicle. Loose connections may not leak, but could allow air into the steering system. Verify that all hose connections are tight.

✳✳ CAUTION

Power steering fluid level must be maintained throughout bleed procedure.

1. Fill pump reservoir with fluid to minimum system level, FULL COLD level, or middle of hash mark on cap stick fluid level indicator.

✳✳ CAUTION

With hydro-boost only, the oil level will appear falsely high if the hydro-boost accumulator is not fully charged. Do not apply the brake pedal with the engine OFF. This will discharge the hydro-boost accumulator.

2. If equipped with hydro-boost, fully charge the hydro-boost accumulator using the following procedure:
  a. Start the engine.
  b. Firmly apply the brake pedal 10-15 times.
  c. Turn the engine OFF.

3. Raise the vehicle until the front wheels are off the ground.

4. With key on, engine OFF, turn the steering wheel from stop to stop 12 times.

5. On vehicles equipped with hydro-boost systems or longer length power steering hoses may require turns up to 15 to 20 stop to stops.

6. Verify power steering fluid level per operating specification.

7. Start the engine. Rotate steering wheel from left to right. Check for sign of cavitation or fluid aeration (pump noise/whining).

8. Verify the fluid level. Repeat the bleed procedure, if necessary.

FLUID FILL PROCEDURE

✳✳ CAUTION

When adding fluid or making a complete fluid change, always use the proper power steering fluid. Failure to use the proper fluid will cause hose and seal damage and fluid leaks.

1. Clean the area surrounding the reservoir cap.

2. Remove the reservoir cap.

3. Inspect the power steering pump fluid level at regular intervals. Use the appropriate procedure below:
  a. Run the engine until the fluid reaches about 170°F (80°C).
  b. Turn the engine OFF.
  c. Remove the reservoir cap.
  d. Inspect the fluid level on the cap stick.
  e. Ensure that the fluid level is at the HOT/FULL/MAX mark on the cap stick.

4. If the fluid level is low, add power steering fluid to the proper level.

5. Install the reservoir cap.

6. When checking the fluid level after servicing the steering system, bleed the air from the system.

SUSPENSION

AUTOMATIC LEVEL CONTROL (ALC) TRIMSET PROCEDURE

If the system is functioning abnormally, performing the ALC Trimset recalibration procedure may correct the condition. When a system component has been replaced, ALC Trimset calibration must be performed. In the scan tool Special Functions menu, select ALC Trimset and follow the screen prompts to perform the procedure. Once the process has been completed, the system should be fully functional.

AUTOMATIC LEVEL CONTROL SENSOR

REMOVAL & INSTALLATION

1. Raise the vehicle.
2. Remove the wheel from the vehicle.

3. Disconnect the height sensor connector.

4. Disconnect the sensor link from the ball stud.

5. Loosen the sensor mounting nut.

6. Disengage the anti-rotation tab and slide the sensor downward.

7. Remove the sensor from the vehicle.

To install:

8. Insert head of the sensor mounting stud into the key hole.

9. Slide the sensor upward until the anti-rotation tab engages in the lower hole. Tighten the sensor mounting nut to 80 inch lbs. (9 Nm).

10. Connect the sensor link on the ball stud.

11. Connect the height sensor connector.

12. Install the wheel on the vehicle.

13. Lower the vehicle.

AUTOMATIC LEVEL CONTROL

14. Calibrate the trimset. See "Automatic Level Control (ALC) Trimset Procedure" in this section.

➡ Other programming of the level control module requires access to or use of equivalent dealer service programming, such as Service Programming System.

AIR TUBES

REMOVAL & INSTALLATION

At the rear shock absorbers, the air tube connectors are held on with spring clips which snap into the grooves of the shock absorber air fittings. Air tube connectors are sealed using 2 O-rings.

1. Before disconnecting any air tube, clean the connector and the surrounding area to prevent dirt and other foreign material from entering the ELC system.

a. To disconnect an air tube from a shock absorber, rotate the spring clip 90 degrees out of the slots, and pull the connector from the shock absorber.

b. To connect an air tube to a shock absorber, lubricate the 2 O-rings using silicone lubricant, rotate the spring clip 90 degrees into the slots, and push the air tube connector on the shock absorber fitting until spring clip snaps into fitting groove.

2. Raise the vehicle.

3. Remove the air tube from the air dryer.

4. Remove the bolt and the harness tie from the air compressor bracket.

5. Remove both rear wheels.

6. Disconnect the air tube from the left and right rear shock absorbers.

7. Remove the 2 metal clips from the air tube and the vehicle.

8. Remove the air tube with the 3 clips from the vehicle.

To install:

9. Connect the air tube to the air dryer.

10. Install the air tube with the harness tie and the bolt on the air compressor bracket.

11. Install the air tube on the vehicle with 3 clips.

12. Connect the air tube to the left and right rear shock absorbers.

13. Install 2 metal clips on the air tube and the vehicle. Place each clip immediately forward of the wheel house fold-over tabs on the LH and RH side of the vehicle.

14. Install both rear wheels.

15. Before driving the vehicle, turn the ignition on and wait approximately 45 seconds. This will ensure that the air adjustable shock absorbers are filled with residual pressure.

16. Lower the vehicle.

AIR COMPRESSOR

REMOVAL & INSTALLATION

See Figures 112 and 113.

1. Raise the vehicle.

2. Before disconnecting the air hose from the intake air filter or the air compressor, clean the components and the surrounding area to prevent dirt and other foreign material from entering the ALC system.

3. Disconnect the air tube from the air dryer.

4. Remove the bolt and the harness tie with the air tube from the air compressor bracket.

5. Remove the intake air filter from the vehicle.

6. Remove the vehicle harness connector from the air compressor connector.

7. Remove the 2 nuts, 2 bolts, and the air compressor assembly from the vehicle.

8. Slide the air compressor connector off of the connector anchor.

9. Remove 2 bolts and the heat shield from the air compressor bracket.

To install:

10. Install the heat shield on the air compressor bracket with 3 bolts.

➡ **Do not install the fourth heat shield bolt. It must be installed after the air tube is connected.**

11. Install the air compressor connector to the connector anchor.

12. Install the air compressor assembly on the vehicle with 2 nuts and 2 bolts. Tighten to 80 inch lbs. (9 Nm).

13. Connect the harness connector to the air compressor connector.

14. Install the intake air filter on the vehicle.

15. Connect the air tube to the air dryer.

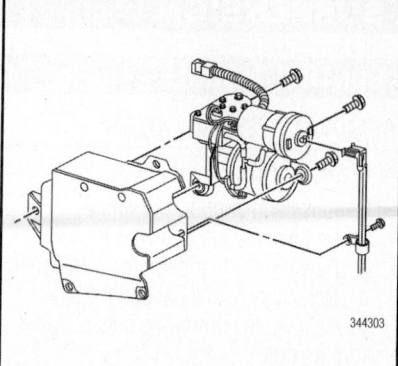

Fig. 112 Removing/installing the air compressor

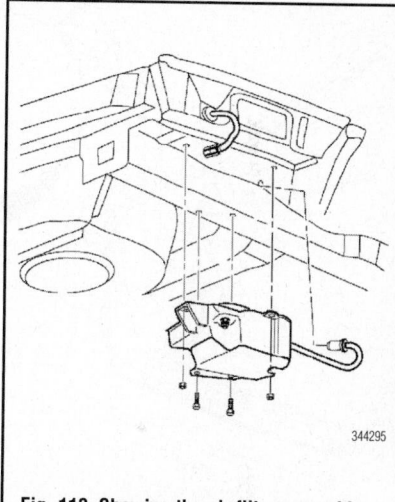

Fig. 113 Showing the air filter assembly mounting

16. Connect the air tube and the harness tie to the air compressor bracket with the bolt.

17. Before driving the vehicle, turn the ignition on and wait approximately 45 seconds. This will ensure that the air adjustable shock absorbers are filled with residual pressure.

18. Lower the vehicle.

CONTROL MODULE

REMOVAL & INSTALLATION

See Figure 114.

1. Raise and support the vehicle.
2. Remove the tire and wheel.
3. Remove the compartment trim panel.
4. Detach the electrical connector.
5. Remove the mounting nuts and the control module.

5. Loosen the sensor mounting nut.
6. Remove the sensor from the vehicle.

To install:

7. Insert head of the sensor mounting stud into the key hole.
8. Tighten the sensor mounting nut to 80 inch lbs. (9 Nm).
9. Connect the sensor link on the ball stud.
10. Connect the height sensor connector.

11. Install the wheel on the vehicle.
12. Lower the vehicle.

Rear

See Figure 116.

1. Raise the vehicle.
2. Remove the wheel from the vehicle.
3. Disconnect the height sensor electrical connector.
4. Disconnect the sensor link from the ball stud.
5. Loosen the sensor mounting nut.
6. Disengage the anti-rotation tab and slide the sensor downward.
7. Remove the sensor from the vehicle.

To install:

8. Insert head of the sensor mounting stud into the key hole.
9. Slide the sensor upward until the anti-rotation tab engages in the lower hole.
10. Tighten the sensor mounting nut to 80 inch lbs. (9 Nm).
11. Connect the sensor link on the ball stud.
12. Connect the height sensor electrical connector.
13. Install the wheel on the vehicle.
14. Lower the vehicle.

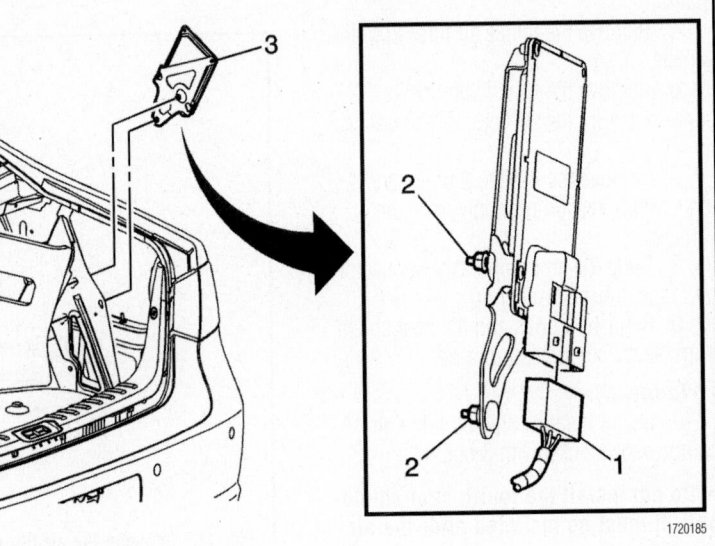

Fig. 114 Electronic suspension control module (3), showing the electrical connector (1) and mounting bolts (2)

➡ **If a replacement control module is installed, program the module.**

6. Installation is the reverse of the removal procedure.

POSITION SENSOR

REMOVAL & INSTALLATION

Front

See Figure 115.

1. Raise the vehicle.
2. Remove the wheel from the vehicle.
3. Disconnect the height sensor connector.
4. Disconnect the sensor link from the ball stud.

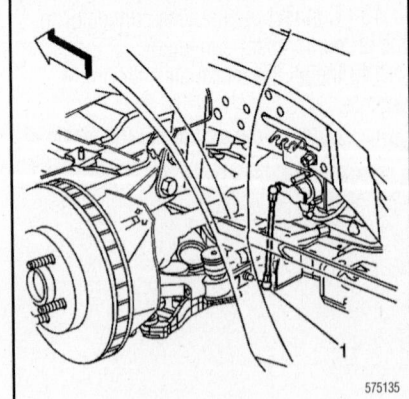

Fig. 115 Showing electronic suspension front position sensor (1)

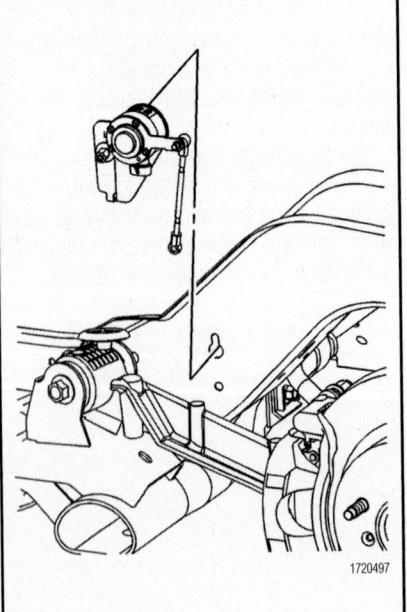

Fig. 116 Removing/installing the rear position sensor

LOWER BALL JOINT

REMOVAL & INSTALLATION

➡**The lower ball joint is serviced as part of the lower control arm.**

LOWER CONTROL ARM

REMOVAL & INSTALLATION

See Figure 117.

1. Raise and support the vehicle.
2. Remove the front tire and wheel assembly.
3. Remove the front stabilizer shaft link.
4. Remove the lower ball joint nut.

➡**Always replace the ball joint nut after it has been used.**

5. Separate the ball joint stud from the control arm.
6. Remove the 2 lower control arm front nuts.
7. Remove the 2 lower control arm front bolts.

8. Remove the lower control arm rear nut.
9. Remove the lower control arm rear bolt.
10. Remove the lower control arm.

To install:

11. Install the lower control arm.
12. Install all bolts and nuts snugly, but do not fully tighten.

➡**Do not tighten the control arm retainers until the weight of the vehicle is supported by the control arm. The vehicle needs to be sitting at normal trim height.**

13. When vehicle is resting on the ground, tighten lower control arm rear nut to 116 ft. lbs. (157 Nm).
14. When vehicle is resting on the ground, tighten lower control arm front nuts to 111 ft. lbs. (150 Nm).
15. Install lower ball joint nut and tighten to 22 ft. lbs. (30 Nm), plus an additional 210 degrees.

STABILIZER SHAFT

REMOVAL & INSTALLATION

See Figure 118.

1. Raise and support the vehicle.
2. Remove the front tires and wheels.
3. Remove the stabilizer shaft links. See "Stabilizer Shaft Links" in this section.
4. Remove the stabilizer shaft insulators.
5. Remove the left outer tie rod retaining nut. Use a proper puller (J 24319-B or equivalent) in order to remove the left tie rod end from the steering knuckle.
6. Remove the exhaust manifold pipe.
7. Turn the left strut completely to the left. Guide the stabilizer shaft out the left side of the vehicle between the body and the strut.
8. Remove the stabilizer shaft from the vehicle.

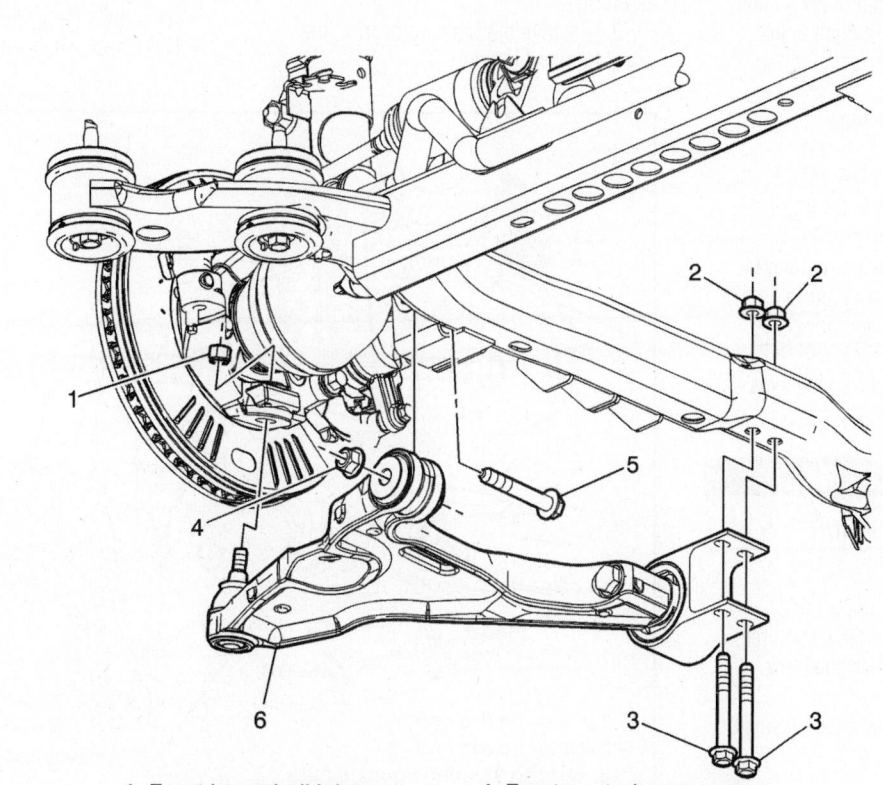

1. Front lower ball joint nut
2. Front control arm front nuts
3. Front control arm front bolts
4. Front control arm rear nut
5. Front control arm rear bolt
6. Front control arm

1659533

Fig. 117 Removing the lower control arm

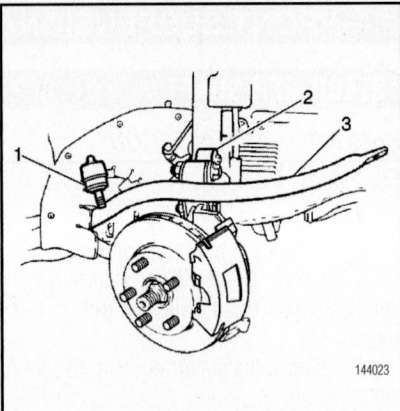

Fig. 118 Remove the stabilizer shaft (3) from the vehicle after disconnecting the tie rod end (1) from the steering knuckle (2)

To install:

10. Install the stabilizer shaft to the vehicle.

11. Install the exhaust manifold pipe.

12. Loosely install the following components:

- The left and right stabilizer shaft insulators
- The stabilizer shaft insulator brackets
- The stabilizer shaft bracket bolts

13. Install the stabilizer shaft links.

14. Install the left tie rod end to the steering knuckle.

15. Tighten the following components.

a. Tighten the stabilizer shaft insulator bracket bolts to 37 ft. lbs. (50 Nm).

b. Tighten the outer tie rod end to steering knuckle retaining nut to 22 ft. lbs. (30 Nm), plus an additional 200 degrees.

16. Install the front tires and wheels.

17. Lower the vehicle.

STABILIZER SHAFT LINK

REMOVAL & INSTALLATION

See Figure 119.

1. Raise and support the vehicle.

2. Remove the front wheels and tires.

3. Remove the stabilizer shaft link bolt.

4. Remove the stabilizer shaft insulators and spacers.

To install:

5. Loosely install the stabilizer link components. Tighten the stabilizer link bolt to 13 ft. lbs. (17 Nm).

6. Install the front wheels and tires.

7. Lower the vehicle.

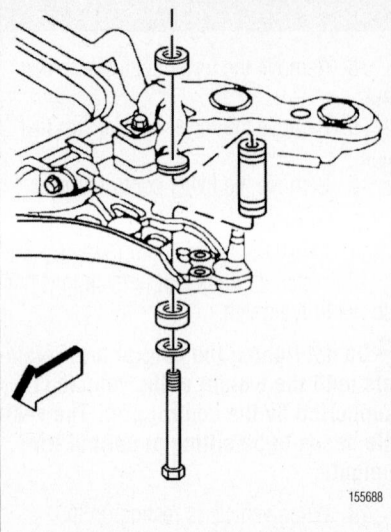

Fig. 119 Remove the stabilizer shaft link bolt.

STEERING KNUCKLE

REMOVAL & INSTALLATION

See Figure 120.

1. Raise and support the vehicle.

2. Remove the front tire and wheel assembly.

3. Remove the brake rotor from the wheel hub and bearing.

4. Remove the wheel hub and bearing. See "Wheel Hub & Bearing" in this section.

5. Remove the outer tie rod end nut. Separate the tie rod end from the steering knuckle. Discard the nut.

6. Remove the 2 strut to steering knuckle nuts.

7. Remove the 2 strut to steering knuckle bolts.

8. Remove and discard the lower control arm ball joint nut and separate the ball joint from the control arm.

9. Remove the steering knuckle from the vehicle.

To install:

10. Position the steering knuckle to the vehicle.

11. Install the lower control arm ball joint to the control arm and install new nuts. Tighten to 22 ft. lbs. (30 Nm), plus an additional 210 degrees

12. Install new strut to steering knuckle nuts. Tighten to 108 ft. lbs. (147 Nm).

13. Connect the outer tie rod end and install a new nut. Tighten nut to 22 ft. lbs. (30 Nm), plus an additional 200 degrees.

14. Install the wheel hub and bearing.

15. Install the front wheel and tire.

16. Lower the vehicle.

17. Check wheel alignment.

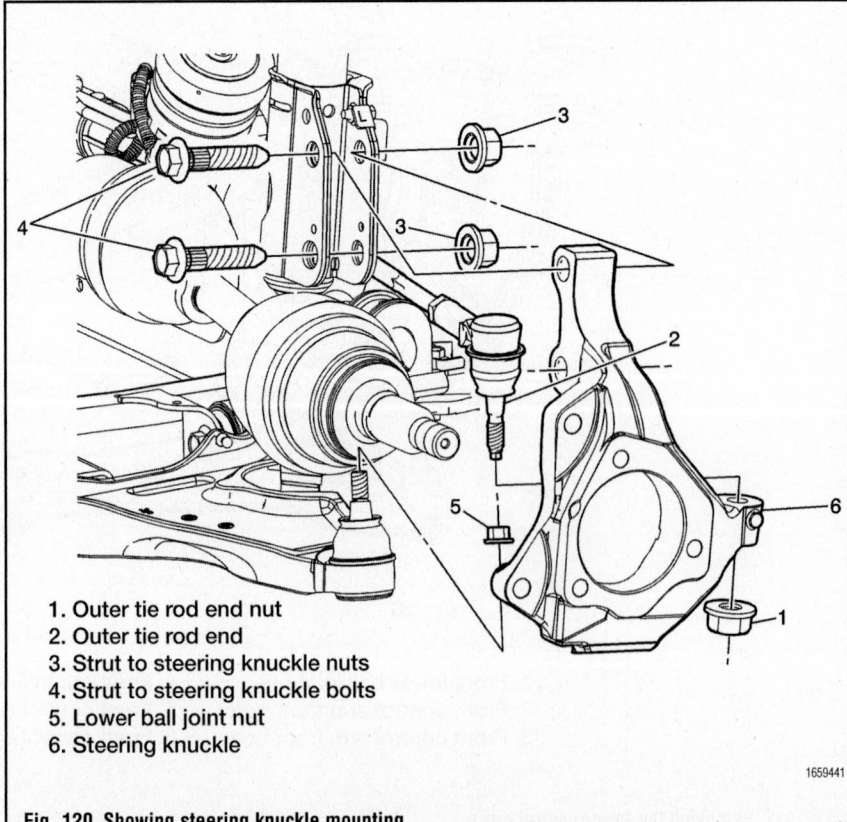

1. Outer tie rod end nut
2. Outer tie rod end
3. Strut to steering knuckle nuts
4. Strut to steering knuckle bolts
5. Lower ball joint nut
6. Steering knuckle

Fig. 120 Showing steering knuckle mounting

STRUT & SPRING ASSEMBLY

REMOVAL & INSTALLATION

1. Remove the strut mount retaining bolts.
2. Raise and support the vehicle.
3. Remove the tire and wheel.
4. Disconnect the ABS front wheel speed sensor harness connector.
5. If applicable, remove the speed sensor bracket from the strut.

✳✳ CAUTION

The knuckle must be retained after the strut-to-knuckle bolts have been removed. Failure to observe this may cause ball joint and/or wheel drive shaft damage.

6. Remove the brake line bracket from the strut on the left side.
7. Remove the strut to knuckle bolts and the nuts.
8. Remove the strut from the vehicle.

To install:

9. Lower the vehicle.
10. Install the strut to the vehicle.
11. Install the strut mount to body retaining bolts. Tighten the strut mount to body bolts to 35 ft. lbs. (47 Nm).
12. Raise the vehicle.
13. Install the strut to steering knuckle bolts and the nuts.
14. Tighten the strut to knuckle nuts to 108 ft. lbs. (147 Nm).
15. Connect the brake line and retaining bolt to the strut.
16. If applicable, connect the speed sensor bracket and retaining bolt to the strut.
17. Tighten the brake line and the speed sensor bracket bolts to 13 ft. lbs. (17 Nm).
18. Connect the ABS front wheel speed sensor harness connector.

19. Install the tire and wheel assembly.
20. Lower the vehicle.
21. Perform a front wheel alignment.

WHEEL HUB & BEARING

REMOVAL & INSTALLATION

See Figure 121.

1. Raise and support the vehicle.
2. Remove the tire and wheel.
3. Clean the drive axle threads of all dirt.
4. Insert a drift punch or a screwdriver into the caliper and the rotor in order to prevent the rotor from turning.
5. Remove the drive axle nut.
6. Remove the brake rotor. See "BRAKES" section.
7. Disconnect the antilock brake system (ABS) front wheel speed sensor connector. Unclip the connector from the dust shield.
8. Remove the wheel hub and bearing retaining bolts.

➡**Replace the hub and bearing only as an assembly.**

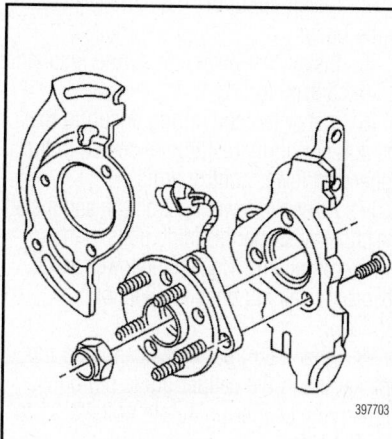

Fig. 121 Removing the wheel hub and bearing assembly

9. Remove the wheel hub and bearing from the steering knuckle.
10. Remove the dust shield.
11. Use the puller (J 28733-B) in order to separate the hub and bearing from the drive axle.
12. Clean the rust and the foreign material from the following components in order to allow proper seating of the bearing into the knuckle:
   • The knuckle mounting face
   • The bore
   • The chamber

To install:

13. Remove the protective plastic cover before installation.

➡**Do not handle the knuckle or hub assembly by the ABS sensor wire.**

14. Carefully install the dust shield.

➡**Do not damage the bearing outboard lip seal, or the hub and bearing bolts.**

15. Apply a thin layer of grease to the steering knuckle bore.
16. Install the wheel hub and bearing assembly and dust shield to the steering knuckle. Install the retaining bolts and tighten to 96 ft. lbs. (130 Nm).
17. Install the new drive axle nut, draw wheel hub and bearing onto the axle.
18. Connect the ABS front wheel speed sensor connector. Clip the connector to the dust shield.
19. Install the brake rotor. See "BRAKES" section.
20. Insert a drift punch or a screwdriver into the caliper and rotor in order to prevent the rotor from turning. Tighten the drive axle nut to 118 ft. lbs. (160 Nm).
21. Install the tire and wheel.
22. Lower the vehicle.

ADJUSTMENT LINK

REMOVAL & INSTALLATION

See Figure 122.

1. Raise and support the vehicle.
2. Remove the nut from the adjustment link.
3. Separate the adjustment link from the control arm.
4. Remove the exhaust system.
5. Remove the rear suspension support. See "Rear Suspension Support" in this section.
6. Remove the cam lock nut and the bolt. Remove the adjustment link from the support assembly.

To install:

7. Install the adjustment link to the support assembly. See "Rear Suspension Support" in this section.
8. Install the cam lock nut, washer and bolt. Tighten the cam lock nut to 67 ft. lbs. (91 Nm).
9. Connect the adjustment link to the control arm. Install the adjustment link nut. Tighten the nut to 22 ft. lbs. (30 Nm), then tighten an additional 180 degrees.
10. Install the rear suspension support. See "Rear Suspension Support" in this section.
11. Install the exhaust.
12. Lower the vehicle.
13. Check the rear toe adjustment.

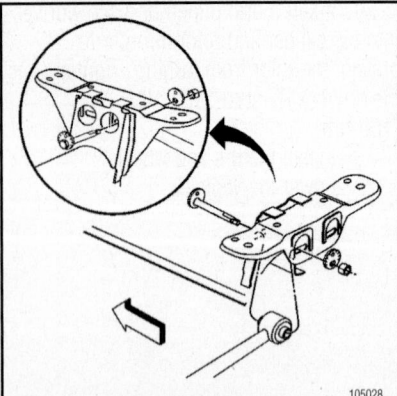

Fig. 122 Remove the cam lock nut and the bolt. Remove the adjustment link from the support assembly.

105028

COIL SPRING

REMOVAL & INSTALLATION

1. Raise and support the vehicle.
2. Remove the tire and wheel.

3. Support the control arm with a suitable jack.
4. Remove the automatic level control sensor link from the control arm.
5. Remove the lower shock absorber retaining bolts.
6. Disconnect the stabilizer link from the control arm. See "Stabilizer Link" in this section.
7. Remove the rear caliper pin bolts.
8. Using heavy wire, hang the rear brake caliper.
9. Remove the adjustment link retaining nut. Separate the adjustment link from the lower control arm.
10. Slowly lower the lower control arm until it bottoms on the support assembly.
11. Using a pry bar, pry under the lower coil spring insulator and remove the coil spring with the insulator.
12. Remove the upper coil spring insulator by pulling downward.
13. Separate the lower control arm insulator from the coil spring.

To install:

14. Install the upper coil spring insulator to the body.
15. Install the lower coil spring insulator in the control arm.
16. Install the coil spring ensuring that the coil spring insulators are seated in the upper and lower control arms.
17. Raise the lower control arm and install the shock absorber retaining bolts in the lower control arm. Tighten the lower shock absorber retaining bolts to 18 ft. lbs. (25 Nm).
18. Attach the rear brake caliper to the bracket using the caliper guide pin bolts. Tighten the caliper guide pin bolts to 25 ft. lbs. (34 Nm).
19. Install the stabilizer link. See "Stabilizer Link" in this section.
20. Install the adjustment link to the control arm. Tighten adjustment link retaining nut to 22 ft. lbs. (30 Nm), plus 180 degrees.
21. Connect the automatic level control sensor link to the control arm.
22. Install the tire and wheel.
23. Lower the vehicle.

LOWER CONTROL ARM

REMOVAL & INSTALLATION

See Figure 123.

1. Raise and support the vehicle.
2. Remove the rear tire and wheel assembly.

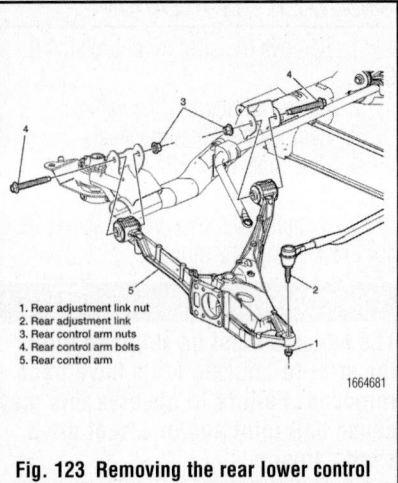

1. Rear adjustment link nut
2. Rear adjustment link
3. Rear control arm nuts
4. Rear control arm bolts
5. Rear control arm

1664681

Fig. 123 Removing the rear lower control arm

3. Remove the wheel hub and bearing assembly. See "Wheel Hub & Bearing" in this section.
4. Remove the rear leveling sensor link from the control arm, if equipped.
5. Remove the stabilizer shaft link. See "Stabilizer Shaft Link" in this section.
6. Remove the rear suspension support. See "Rear Suspension Support" in this section.
7. Remove the rear adjusting link nut and the rear adjustment link.
8. Remove the rear control arm nuts.
9. Remove the rear control arm bolts.
   a. Support the control arm before removing the bolts.
10. Remove the rear control arm.

To install:

11. Installation is the reverse of the removal procedure.
   a. Tighten the rear control arm nuts to 67 ft. lbs. (91 Nm).
   b. Tighten the rear adjusting link nut to 22 ft. lbs. (30 Nm), plus an additional 180 degrees

REAR SUSPENSION SUPPORT

REMOVAL & INSTALLATION

See Figures 124 and 125.

1. Raise and support the vehicle.
2. Remove the rear tires and the wheels.
3. Remove the exhaust system.
4. Remove the coil springs. See "Coil Springs" in this section.
5. Disconnect the electrical connector from each wheel speed sensor and remove the wire from the rear support.

6. Remove the electronic level control link from the ball stud on the lower control arm.

7. Disconnect the park brake cables from both calipers and remove cables from suspension support assembly. Remove the brake calipers and support calipers from vehicle underbody. See "BRAKES" section.

8. Support the rear suspension support assembly with a transmission jack.

9. Remove the 6 suspension support reinforcement brace bolts, the 4 suspension support assembly bolts, the 2 suspension support reinforcement braces, remove the transmission jack, and remove the suspension support assembly.

10. Transfer all necessary parts from the old support to the new support.

To install:

11. Raise the suspension support assembly into position with the transmission jack.

12. Install the 2 suspension support reinforcement braces. Loosely install the 6 suspension support reinforcement brace bolts.

13. Align the suspension support assembly utilizing the alignment gauge holes.

14. Install the 4 suspension support assembly bolts. Tighten the bolts to 141 ft. lbs. (191 Nm).

15. Finish securing the 6 suspension support reinforcement brace bolts. Tighten the bolts to 63 ft. lbs. (86 Nm).

16. Install the brake calipers. See "BRAKES" section.

17. Install the park brake cables to the suspension support assembly and connect

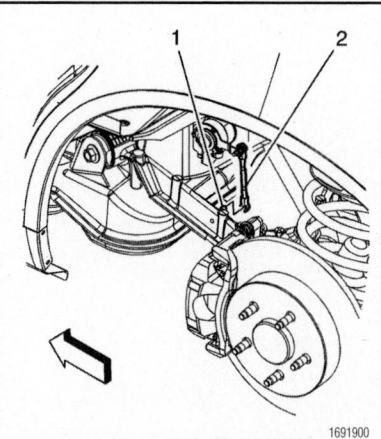

Fig. 124 Remove the electronic level control link (2) from the ball stud (1) on the lower control arm.

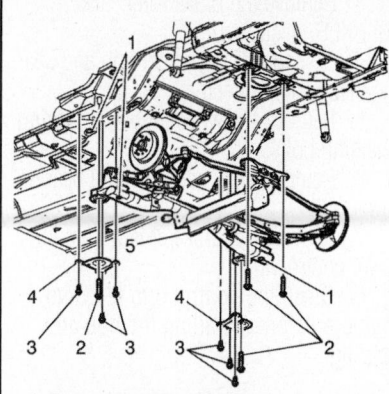

1. Rear suspension alignment gauge holes
2. Rear suspension support bolts
3. Reinforcement brace bolts
4. Reinforcement braces
5. Rear suspension support assembly

1690811

Fig. 125 Exploded view of the suspension support

the cables to both calipers. See "BRAKES" section.

18. Install the electronic level control link to the ball stud on the lower control arm.

19. Attach the wheel speed sensor wire to the rear support and connect the electrical connector to each wheel speed sensor.

20. Install the coil springs. See "Coil Springs" in this section.

21. Install the exhaust system.

22. Install the tires and the wheels.

STABILIZER SHAFT

REMOVAL & INSTALLATION

1. Raise and support the vehicle.

2. Remove the stabilizer shaft links. See "Stabilizer Shaft Links" in this section.

3. Remove the stabilizer shaft insulator bracket bolt, bend the open end of the clamp upward, and remove the stabilizer shaft insulators.

4. Remove the stabilizer shaft.

To install:

5. Install the stabilizer shaft to the vehicle.

6. Install the stabilizer shaft insulators to the stabilizer shaft with the slits forward. Bend the stabilizer shaft insulator brackets downward.

7. Install the stabilizer shaft bracket retaining bolt. Tighten the stabilizer shaft bracket retaining bolts to 24 ft. lbs. (33 Nm).

8. Install the stabilizer shaft links, as described below.

9. Lower the vehicle.

STABILIZER SHAFT LINK

REMOVAL & INSTALLATION

See Figure 126.

1. Raise and support the vehicle.

2. Remove the stabilizer shaft link bolts.

3. Remove the stabilizer shaft link insulators and spacer.

To install:

4. Loosely install the stabilizer link insulators, spacer, nut and bolt. Tighten the stabilizer shaft link nut to 11 ft. lbs. (15 Nm).

5. Lower the vehicle.

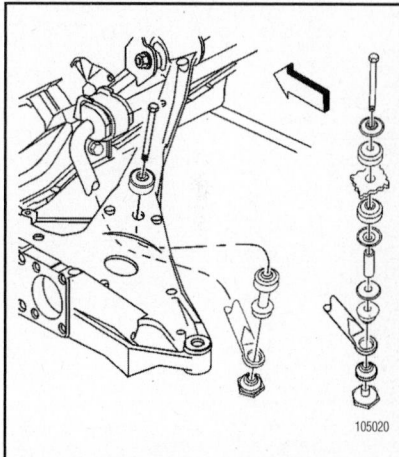

105020

Fig. 126 Exploded view of the stabilizer shaft link and connecting components

SHOCK ABSORBER

REMOVAL & INSTALLATION

1. Raise and support the vehicle.

2. Remove the tire and wheel.

3. Support the control arm with a jack stand.

4. Disconnect the automatic level control air tube from the shock.

5. Remove the lower shock absorber retaining bolts.

6. Remove the trunk trim to gain access to the shock absorber upper mounting nuts.

7. Remove the upper shock absorber cover and the shock retaining nuts.

8. Remove the upper shock absorber reinforcement.

9. Remove the shock from the vehicle.

To install:

10. Install the shock, reinforcement, and the retaining nuts. Tighten the upper shock absorber retaining nuts to 18 ft. lbs. (25 Nm).

11. Install the upper shock absorber cover.

12. Install the trunk trim.

13. Install the lower shock absorber retaining bolts. Tighten the lower shock absorber retaining bolts to 18 ft. lbs. (25 Nm).

14. Connect the automatic level control air tube to the shock.

15. Install the tire and wheel.

16. Lower the vehicle.

WHEEL HUB & BEARING

REMOVAL & INSTALLATION

1. Raise and support the vehicle.
2. Remove the tire and wheel.
3. Remove the brake rotor. See "BRAKES" section.
4. Disconnect the wheel hub and bearing electrical connector.
5. Remove the wheel hub and bearing retaining bolts.
6. Remove the wheel hub and bearing lower.
7. Remove the brake shield from the lower control arm.
8. Clean the control arm face and the bore before installing the hub and bearing.

To install:

9. Install the brake shield and the wheel hub and bearing to the control arm.
10. Install the wheel hub and bearing retaining bolts. Tighten the wheel hub and bearing bolts to 50 ft. lbs. (68 Nm).
11. Connect the wheel/hub electrical connector.
12. Install the brake rotor.
13. Install the tire and wheel.
14. Lower the vehicle.

GENERAL MOTORS

Diagnostic Trouble Codes

DIAGNOSTIC TROUBLE CODES **DTC-1**

OBD II Trouble Code List (xxxx Codes)..DTC-2
OBD II Trouble Code List (P0xxx Codes)...DTC-2
OBD II Trouble Code List (P1xxx Codes)...DTC-77
OBD II Trouble Code List (P2xxx Codes)...DTC-90
OBD II Vehicle Applications...DTC-1
    General Motors DTC-1
GM Reference Introduction DTC-1
    OBD II Trouble Code List..DTC-1

DIAGNOSTIC TROUBLE CODES

OBD II VEHICLE APPLICATIONS

GENERAL MOTORS

Cruze
2011
- 1.4L . . . . VIN 9
- 1.8L . . . . VIN H

Equinox
2010–2011
- 2.4L . . . . VIN C
- 3.0L . . . . VIN 5

Express
2010–2011
- 4.3L . . . . VIN X
- 4.8L . . . . VIN A
- 5.3L . . . . VIN 4
- 6.0L . . . . VIN G
- 6.6L . . . . VIN 6
- 6.6L . . . . VIN L

G6
2010
- 2.4L . . . . VIN B
- 2.4L . . . . VIN O
- 3.5L . . . . VIN N
- 3.5L . . . . VIN K
- 3.6L . . . . VIN 7
- 3.9L . . . . VIN 1

HHR
2010–2011
- 2.0L . . . . VIN M

- 2.2L . . . . VIN B
- 2.2L . . . . VIN W
- 2.4L . . . . VIN U
- 2.4L . . . . VIN V

Impala
2010–2011
- 3.5L . . . . VIN K
- 3.5L . . . . VIN N
- 3.9L . . . . VIN M

LaCrosse
2010–2011
- 2.4L . . . . VIN C
- 3.6L . . . . VIN D

Lucerne
2010–2011
- 3.9L . . . . VIN 1
- 3.9L . . . . VIN M
- 4.6L . . . . VIN L

Savana
2010–2011
- 4.3L . . . . VIN X
- 4.8L . . . . VIN A
- 5.3L . . . . VIN 4
- 6.0L . . . . VIN G
- 6.6L . . . . VIN 6
- 6.6L . . . . VIN L

Terrain
2010–2011
- 2.4L . . . . VIN C
- 3.0L . . . . VIN 5

GM REFERENCE INFORMATION

OBD II TROUBLE CODE LIST

To use this information, first read and record All codes in memory along with Freeze Frame data. *If a ECM Reset function is done prior to recording this data, All codes and freeze frame data are lost!*

Look up the appropriate trouble code in the list on the following pages. The left hand column includes the code number, the number of trips to set the code (e. g. , **1T or 2T**), the year, model description and type of OBD II Monitor that failed (e. g. , **CCM or O2S**). This data can be used to determine how to drive a vehicle after a repair in order to validate the repair has been completed.

The **(N/MIL)** designator in the left hand column indicates the trouble code does not turn on the Malfunction Indicator Lamp or MIL. The **(STS Lamp)** indicator in the left column indicates a code that turns on the Service Transmission Soon lamp. This code may or may not turn "on" the MIL.

OBD II Trouble Code List (xxxx Codes)

DTC	Trouble Code Title, Conditions, Possible Causes
DTC: 1380	**Misfire Detected - Rough Road Data Not Available:** The vehicle speed is greater than 8 km/h (5 mph). The engine speed is less than 8,192 RPM. The engine load is less than 60 percent. Engine misfire is detected and DTC P0300 sets with the MIL illuminated. DTCs P1380 and P1381 run continuously when the above conditions are met.
DTC: 1381	**Misfire Detected - No Communication with Brake Control Module:** The vehicle speed is greater than 8 km/h (5 mph). The engine speed is less than 8,192 RPM. The engine load is less than 60 percent. Engine misfire is detected and DTC P0300 sets with the MIL illuminated. DTCs P1380 and P1381 run continuously when the above conditions are met.

OBD II Trouble Code List (P0xxx Codes)

DTC	Trouble Code Title, Conditions, Possible Causes
DTC: P0002 00	**Fuel Pressure Regulator 1 Circuit Resistance Too High:** The ignition is ON, or the engine is running. The ignition voltage is less than 16 V. These DTCs runs continuously once the above conditions are met.
DTC: P0003 00	**Fuel Pressure Regulator 1 Control Circuit Low Current:** The ignition is ON, or the engine is running. The ignition voltage is less than 16 V. These DTCs runs continuously once the above conditions are met.
DTC: P0004 00	**Fuel Pressure Regulator 1 Control Circuit High Current:** The ignition is ON, or the engine is running. The ignition voltage is less than 16 V. These DTCs runs continuously once the above conditions are met.
DTC: P0008	**Engine Position System Performance Bank 1:** DTC P0010, P0011, P0013, P0014, P0020, P0021, P0023, P0024, P0341, P0342, P0343, P0346, P0347, P0348, P0366, P0367, P0368, P0391, P0392, P0393, P2088, P2089, P2090, P2091, P2092, P2093, P2094, or P2095 is not set. The engine is operating for greater than 50 seconds. The engine coolant temperature is between 0-95°C (32-203°F). The calculated engine oil temperature is colder than 120°C (248°F). The engine must accelerate such that the CMP actuator system is commanded from the park position to the phased position. This is considered a cam control cycle. There must be a minimum of 2 cam control cycles for at least 2. 5 seconds each, in the phased position. DTC P0008 and P0009 run continuously once the above conditions are met, approximately 600 seconds.
DTC: P0009	**Engine Position System Performance Bank 2:** DTC P0010, P0011, P0013, P0014, P0020, P0021, P0023, P0024, P0341, P0342, P0343, P0346, P0347, P0348, P0366, P0367, P0368, P0391, P0392, P0393, P2088, P2089, P2090, P2091, P2092, P2093, P2094, or P2095 is not set. The engine is operating for greater than 50 seconds. The engine coolant temperature is between 0-95°C (32-203°F). The calculated engine oil temperature is colder than 120°C (248°F). The engine must accelerate such that the CMP actuator system is commanded from the park position to the phased position. This is considered a cam control cycle. There must be a minimum of 2 cam control cycles for at least 2. 5 seconds each, in the phased position. DTC P0008 and P0009 run continuously once the above conditions are met, approximately 600 seconds.
DTC: P000A	**Intake Camshaft Position System Slow Response Bank 1:** Before the ECM can report DTC P000A, P000B, P000C, P000D, P0011, P0014, P0021, or P0024 failed, DTCs P0010, P0013, P0020, P0023, P0341, P0342, P0343, P0346, P0347, P0348, P0366, P0367, P0368, P0391, P0392, P0393, P2088, P2089, P2090, P2091, P2092, P2093, P2094, and P2095 must run and pass. DTC P0016, P0017, P0018, P0019, P0335, P0336, or P0338 is not set. The engine is operating for greater than 1 seconds. The engine speed is greater than 520 RPM. The engine must accelerate such that the CMP actuator system is commanded from the park position to the phased position. This is considered a cam control cycle. There must be a minimum of 2 cam control cycles for at least 2. 5 seconds each in the phased position. DTCs P000A, P000B, P000C, P000D, P0011, P0014, P0021, and P0024 run continuously once the above conditions are met for greater than 600 seconds.
DTC: P000A 00	**Intake Camshaft Position System Slow Response:** The engine speed is between 736-6016 RPM. The engine oil temperature is between -10 to +130°C (14-266°F). The commanded camshaft position is stable. The battery voltage is between 10-16 VDTCs P000A 00, P000B 00, P0010 00, P0013 00, P0014 00, P0016 00, P0017 00, P0335 00, P0336 00, P0340 00, P0341 00, P0365 00, P0366 00, P2088 00, P2089 00, P2090 00, P2091 00 are not set.
DTC: P000B	**Exhaust Camshaft Position System Slow Response Bank 1:** Before the ECM can report DTC P000A, P000B, P000C, P000D, P0011, P0014, P0021, or P0024 failed, DTCs P0010, P0013, P0020, P0023, P0341, P0342, P0343, P0346, P0347, P0348, P0366, P0367, P0368, P0391, P0392, P0393, P2088, P2089, P2090, P2091, P2092, P2093, P2094, and P2095 must run and pass. DTC P0016, P0017, P0018, P0019, P0335, P0336, or P0338 is not set. The engine is operating for greater than 1 seconds. The engine speed is greater than 520 RPM. The engine must accelerate such that the CMP actuator system is commanded from the park position to the phased position. This is considered a cam control cycle. There must be a minimum of 2 cam control cycles for at least 2. 5 seconds each in the phased position. DTCs P000A, P000B, P000C, P000D, P0011, P0014, P0021, and P0024 run continuously once the above conditions are met for greater than 600 seconds.

DTC	Trouble Code Title, Conditions, Possible Causes
DTC: P000B 00	**Exhaust Camshaft Position System Slow Response:** The engine speed is between 736-6016 RPM. The engine oil temperature is between -10 to +130°C (14-266°F). The commanded camshaft position is stable. The battery voltage is between 10-16 VDTCs P000A 00, P000B 00, P0010 00, P0013 00, P0014 00, P0016 00, P0017 00, P0335 00, P0336 00, P0340 00, P0341 00, P0365 00, P0366 00, P2088 00, P2089 00, P2090 00, P2091 00 are not set.
DTC: P000C	**Intake Camshaft Position System Slow Response Bank 2:** Before the ECM can report DTC P000A, P000B, P000C, P000D, P0011, P0014, P0021, or P0024 failed, DTCs P0010, P0013, P0020, P0023, P0341, P0342, P0343, P0346, P0347, P0348, P0366, P0367, P0368, P0391, P0392, P0393, P2088, P2089, P2090, P2091, P2092, P2093, P2094, and P2095 must run and pass. DTC P0016, P0017, P0018, P0019, P0335, P0336, or P0338 is not set. The engine is operating for greater than 1 seconds. The engine speed is greater than 520 RPM. The engine must accelerate such that the CMP actuator system is commanded from the park position to the phased position. This is considered a cam control cycle. There must be a minimum of 2 cam control cycles for at least 2. 5 seconds each in the phased position. DTCs P000A, P000B, P000C, P000D, P0011, P0014, P0021, and P0024 run continuously once the above conditions are met for greater than 600 seconds.
DTC: P000D	**Exhaust Camshaft Position System Slow Response Bank 2:** Before the ECM can report DTC P000A, P000B, P000C, P000D, P0011, P0014, P0021, or P0024 failed, DTCs P0010, P0013, P0020, P0023, P0341, P0342, P0343, P0346, P0347, P0348, P0366, P0367, P0368, P0391, P0392, P0393, P2088, P2089, P2090, P2091, P2092, P2093, P2094, and P2095 must run and pass. DTC P0016, P0017, P0018, P0019, P0335, P0336, or P0338 is not set. The engine is operating for greater than 1 seconds. The engine speed is greater than 520 RPM. The engine must accelerate such that the CMP actuator system is commanded from the park position to the phased position. This is considered a cam control cycle. There must be a minimum of 2 cam control cycles for at least 2. 5 seconds each in the phased position. DTCs P000A, P000B, P000C, P000D, P0011, P0014, P0021, and P0024 run continuously once the above conditions are met for greater than 600 seconds.
DTC: P0010	**Intake Camshaft Position Actuator Solenoid Valve Control Circuit Bank 1:** The ignition voltage is between 11-32 V. The ignition switch is in the Crank or Run position. The ECM commanded the Camshaft Position Actuator Solenoid Valve ON. DTCs P0010, P0013, P0020, and P0023 run continuously when the above conditions are met.
DTC: P0010	**Camshaft Position (CMP) Actuator Solenoid Control Circuit:** The ignition is in Crank or Run. The system voltage is between 11-18 volts. DTC P0010 runs continuously when the above conditions are met.
DTC: P0010	**Intake Camshaft Position Actuator Solenoid Control Circuit:** The engine speed is greater than 80 RPM. The ignition voltage is between 10-18 volts. The ECM has commanded the CMP actuator solenoid ON and OFF at least once during the ignition cycle. DTCs P0010, P0013, P2088, P2089, P2090, and P2091 run continuously once the above conditions are met.
DTC: P0010 00	**Intake Camshaft Position Actuator Solenoid Valve Control Circuit:** The engine speed is greater than 80 RPM. DTC P0606 00 is not set. The ignition voltage is between 10-18 V. The ECM has commanded the camshaft position actuator intake or camshaft position actuator exhaust solenoid ON and OFF at least once during the ignition cycle. DTCs P0010 00, P0013 00, P2088 00, P0289 00, P2090 00, and P2091 00 run continuously once the above conditions are met for greater than 1 s.
DTC: P0010 00	**Intake Camshaft Position Actuator Solenoid Valve Control Circuit:** The engine is running. The ignition voltage is between 11-18 V. The camshaft position actuator is commanded on. The DTCs run continuously when the above conditions are met.
DTC: P0011	**Intake Camshaft Position (CMP) System Performance:** Before the ECM can report DTC P000A, P000B, P0011, or P0014 failed, DTCs P0010, P0013, P0341, P0342, P0343, P0366, P0367, P0368, P2088, P2089, P2090, and P2091 must run and pass. DTC P0016, P0017, P0335, P0336, or P0338 is not set. The engine is operating for greater than 2 seconds. The engine speed is greater than 480 RPM. The engine must accelerate such that the CMP actuator system is commanded from the park position to the phased position. This is considered a cam control cycle. There must be a minimum of 2 cam control cycles for at least 2. 5 seconds each in the phased position. DTC P000A, P000B, P0011, and P0014 run continuously once the above conditions are met for greater than 20 seconds.
DTC: P0011	**Intake Camshaft Position System Performance:** DTC P0010, P0013, P0016, P0017, P0335, P0336, P0340, P0341, P0365, or P0366 is not set. The ignition voltage is greater than 11 V. The engine is operating. The desire camshaft position is not changing greater than 4. 5 degrees for at least 1 s. Both of the desired and actual camshaft position actuator values cannot be greater than 25 degrees or less than 5 degrees. DTCs P0011 and P0014 run continuously once the above conditions are met.
DTC: P0011 00	**Camshaft Position System Performance:** The ignition is ON, or the engine is running. The ignition voltage is less than 16 V. DTCs P0336 00, P0339 00, or P0344 00 are not set. This DTC runs continuously once the above conditions are met.
DTC: P0013	**Exhaust Camshaft Position Actuator Solenoid Valve Control Circuit Bank 1:** The ignition voltage is between 11-32 V. The ignition switch is in the Crank or Run position. The ECM commanded the Camshaft Position Actuator Solenoid Valve ON. DTCs P0010, P0013, P0020, and P0023 run continuously when the above conditions are met.

DTC	Trouble Code Title, Conditions, Possible Causes
DTC: P0013	**Exhaust Camshaft Position Actuator Solenoid Control Circuit:** The engine speed is greater than 80 RPM. The ignition voltage is between 10-18 volts. The ECM has commanded the CMP actuator solenoid ON and OFF at least once during the ignition cycle. DTCs P0010, P0013, P2088, P2089, P2090, and P2091 run continuously once the above conditions are met.
DTC: P0013 00	**Exhaust Camshaft Position Actuator Solenoid Valve Control Circuit:** The engine is running. The ignition voltage is between 11-18 V. The camshaft position actuator is commanded on. The DTCs run continuously when the above conditions are met.
DTC: P0013 00	**Exhaust Camshaft Position Actuator Solenoid Valve Control Circuit:** The engine speed is greater than 80 RPM. DTC P0606 00 is not set. The ignition voltage is between 10-18 V. The ECM has commanded the camshaft position actuator intake or camshaft position actuator exhaust solenoid ON and OFF at least once during the ignition cycle. DTCs P0010 00, P0013 00, P2088 00, P0289 00, P2090 00, and P2091 00 run continuously once the above conditions are met for greater than 1 s.
DTC: P0014	**Exhaust Camshaft Position System Performance Bank 1:** Before the ECM can report DTC P000A, P000B, P000C, P000D, P0011, P0014, P0021, or P0024 failed, DTCs P0010, P0013, P0020, P0023, P0341, P0342, P0343, P0346, P0347, P0348, P0366, P0367, P0368, P0391, P0392, P0393, P2088, P2089, P2090, P2091, P2092, P2093, P2094, and P2095 must run and pass. DTC P0016, P0017, P0018, P0019, P0335, P0336, or P0338 is not set. The engine is operating for greater than 1 seconds. The engine speed is greater than 520 RPM. The engine must accelerate such that the CMP actuator system is commanded from the park position to the phased position. This is considered a cam control cycle. There must be a minimum of 2 cam control cycles for at least 2. 5 seconds each in the phased position. DTCs P000A, P000B, P000C, P000D, P0011, P0014, P0021, and P0024 run continuously once the above conditions are met for greater than 600 seconds.
DTC: P0014 00	**Exhaust Camshaft Position System Performance:** DTC P0010 00, P0013 00, P0016 00, P0017 00, P0335 00, P0336 00, P0340 00, P0341 00, P0365 00, or P0366 00 is not set. The engine is running. The ignition voltage is between 11-18 V. The camshaft position actuator is enabled. The rate of change in the camshaft position is less than 5° for 4 s.
DTC: P0014 00	**Exhaust Camshaft Position System Performance:** The engine speed is between 736-6016 RPM. The engine oil temperature is between -10 to +130°C (14-266°F). The commanded camshaft position is stable. The battery voltage is between 10-16 VDTCs P000A 00, P000B 00, P0010 00, P0013 00, P0014 00, P0016 00, P0017 00, P0335 00, P0336 00, P0340 00, P0341 00, P0365 00, P0366 00, P2088 00, P2089 00, P2090 00, P2091 00 are not set.
DTC: P0016	**Crankshaft Position - Intake Camshaft Position Not Plausible Bank 1:** P0016 DTC P0040, P0041, P0335, P0336, P0641, and P0651 are not set. The engine is cranking or running. The crankshaft and camshaft position signals are synchronized. The camshaft position actuator is in the parked position. DTC P0016, P0017, P0018, and P0019 run continuously when the above conditions are met.
DTC: P0016	**Crankshaft Position (CKP) Camshaft Position (CMP) Correlation:** DTCs P0191 and P0315 are not set. The engine speed is greater than 600 RPM. DTC P0016 runs continuously when the above conditions are met.
DTC: P0016	**Crankshaft Position (CKP) Camshaft Position (CMP) Correlation:** DTC P0335, P0336, P0340, P0341, P0641, or P0651 is not set. The engine is running. The engine speed is less than 2,000 RPM. The CMP actuator is commanded to the parked position - if equipped. DTC P0016 runs continuously when the above conditions are met.
DTC: P0016	**Crankshaft Position - Intake Camshaft Position Not Plausible Bank 1:** Before the ECM can report DTC P0016, P0017, P0018, or P0019 failed, DTCs P0010, P0011, P0013, P0014, P0020, P0021, P0023, P0024, P0335, P0336, P0338, P0341, P0342, P0343, P0346, P0347, P0348, P0366, P0367, P0368, P0391, P0392, P0393, P2088, P2089, P2090, P2091, P2092, P2093, P2094, and P2095 must run and pass. The engine is operating for greater than 50 s. The engine coolant temperature is between 0-95°C (32-203°F). The calculated engine oil temperature is less than 120°C (248°F). DTC P0016, P0017, P0018, and P0019 run continuously once the above conditions are met for approximately 10 minutes.
DTC: P0016 00	**Crankshaft Position - Intake Camshaft Position Not Plausible:** DTCs P000A 00, P000B 00, P0010 00, P0013 00, P0014 00, P0335 00, P0336 00, P0340 00, P0341 00, P0365 00, P0366 00, P2088 00, P2089 00, P2090 00, or P2091 00 are not set. The ignition is ON. The engine is running. The engine speed is between 672-4 000 RPM. The battery voltage is between 10-16 V. The engine oil temperature is more than -10°C (14°F). The engine coolant temperature (ECT) is more than -9. 8°C (14. 4°F). These DTCs run continuously when the above conditions are met.
DTC: P0016 00	**Crankshaft Position - Intake Camshaft Position Not Plausible:** DTC P0335 00, P0336 00, P0340 00, P0341 00, P0365 00, P0366 00, P0641 00, or P0651 00 is not set. The engine is cranking or running. The camshaft position actuator solenoid valves are in the parked position. The DTCs run continuously when the above conditions are met.

DTC	Trouble Code Title, Conditions, Possible Causes
DTC: P0016 5A	**Crankshaft Position-Camshaft Position Not Plausible:** DTCs P0335 and P0336 are not set. The engine is running. The engine speed is greater than 50 RPM. The DTC runs continuously once the above conditions are met.
DTC: P0017	**Crankshaft Position - Exhaust Camshaft Position Not Plausible Bank 1:** Before the ECM can report DTC P0016, P0017, P0018, or P0019 failed, DTCs P0010, P0011, P0013, P0014, P0020, P0021, P0023, P0024, P0335, P0336, P0338, P0341, P0342, P0343, P0346, P0347, P0348, P0366, P0367, P0368, P0391, P0392, P0393, P2088, P2089, P2090, P2091, P2092, P2093, P2094, and P2095 must run and pass. The engine is operating for greater than 50 s. The engine coolant temperature is between 0-95°C (32-203°F). The calculated engine oil temperature is less than 120°C (248°F). DTC P0016, P0017, P0018, and P0019 run continuously once the above conditions are met for approximately 10 minutes.
DTC: P0017	**Crankshaft Position - Exhaust Camshaft Position Not Plausible Bank 1:** P0017 DTC P0335, P0336, P0365, P0366, P0641, and P0651 are not set. The engine is cranking or running. The crankshaft and camshaft position signals are synchronized. The camshaft position actuator is in the parked position. DTC P0016, P0017, P0018, and P0019 run continuously when the above conditions are met.
DTC: P0017	**Crankshaft Position (CKP) - Exhaust Camshaft Position (CMP) Correlation Bank 1:** DTC P0335, P0336, P0340, P0341, P0345, P0346, P0365, P0366, P0390, P0391, P0641, or P0651 is not set. The engine speed is less than 1,200 RPM and the CMP actuator is commanded to the home or parked position. The engine is running. DTC P0016, P0017, P0018, and P0019 run continuously once the above conditions are met.
DTC: P0017 00	**Crankshaft Position - Exhaust Camshaft Position Not Plausible:** DTCs P000A 00, P000B 00, P0010 00, P0013 00, P0014 00, P0335 00, P0336 00, P0340 00, P0341 00, P0365 00, P0366 00, P2088 00, P2089 00, P2090 00, or P2091 00 are not set. The ignition is ON. The engine is running. The engine speed is between 672-4 000 RPM. The battery voltage is between 10-16 V. The engine oil temperature is more than -10°C (14°F). The engine coolant temperature (ECT) is more than -9. 8°C (14. 4°F). These DTCs run continuously when the above conditions are met.
DTC: P0018	**Crankshaft Position - Intake Camshaft Position Not Plausible Bank 2:** P0018 or P0019 DTC P0018, P0019, P0335, P0336, P0345, P0346, P0390, P0391, P0641, and P0651 are not set. The engine is cranking or running. The crankshaft and camshaft position signals are synchronized. The camshaft position actuator is in the parked position. DTC P0016, P0017, P0018, and P0019 run continuously when the above conditions are met.
DTC: P0018	**Crankshaft Position - Intake Camshaft Position Not Plausible Bank 2:** Before the ECM can report DTC P0016, P0017, P0018, or P0019 failed, DTCs P0010, P0011, P0013, P0014, P0020, P0021, P0023, P0024, P0335, P0336, P0338, P0341, P0342, P0343, P0346, P0347, P0348, P0366, P0367, P0368, P0391, P0392, P0393, P2088, P2089, P2090, P2091, P2092, P2093, P2094, and P2095 must run and pass. The engine is operating for greater than 50 s. The engine coolant temperature is between 0-95°C (32-203°F). The calculated engine oil temperature is less than 120°C (248°F). DTC P0016, P0017, P0018, and P0019 run continuously once the above conditions are met for approximately 10 minutes.
DTC: P0019	**Crankshaft Position - Exhaust Camshaft Position Not Plausible Bank 2:** Before the ECM can report DTC P0016, P0017, P0018, or P0019 failed, DTCs P0010, P0011, P0013, P0014, P0020, P0021, P0023, P0024, P0335, P0336, P0338, P0341, P0342, P0343, P0346, P0347, P0348, P0366, P0367, P0368, P0391, P0392, P0393, P2088, P2089, P2090, P2091, P2092, P2093, P2094, and P2095 must run and pass. The engine is operating for greater than 50 s. The engine coolant temperature is between 0-95°C (32-203°F). The calculated engine oil temperature is less than 120°C (248°F). DTC P0016, P0017, P0018, and P0019 run continuously once the above conditions are met for approximately 10 minutes.
DTC: P0019	**Crankshaft Position - Exhaust Camshaft Position Not Plausible Bank 2:** P0018 or P0019 DTC P0018, P0019, P0335, P0336, P0345, P0346, P0390, P0391, P0641, and P0651 are not set. The engine is cranking or running. The crankshaft and camshaft position signals are synchronized. The camshaft position actuator is in the parked position. DTC P0016, P0017, P0018, and P0019 run continuously when the above conditions are met.
DTC: P0020	**Intake Camshaft Position (CMP) Actuator Solenoid Control Circuit Bank 2:** The ignition is in the Crank or Run position. The ECM has commanded the Camshaft Position Actuator Solenoid Valve ON. The ignition voltage is between 11-18 volts. DTCs P0010, P0013, P0020, and P0023 run continuously once the above conditions are met.
DTC: P0021	**Intake Camshaft Position System Performance Bank 2:** Before the ECM can report DTC P000A, P000B, P000C, P000D, P0011, P0014, P0021, or P0024 failed, DTCs P0010, P0013, P0020, P0023, P0341, P0342, P0343, P0346, P0347, P0348, P0366, P0367, P0368, P0391, P0392, P0393, P2088, P2089, P2090, P2091, P2092, P2093, P2094, and P2095 must run and pass. DTC P0016, P0017, P0018, P0019, P0335, P0336, or P0338 is not set. The engine is operating for greater than 1 seconds. The engine speed is greater than 520 RPM. The engine must accelerate such that the CMP actuator system is commanded from the park position to the phased position. This is considered a cam control cycle. There must be a minimum of 2 cam control cycles for at least 2. 5 seconds each in the phased position. DTCs P000A, P000B, P000C, P000D, P0011, P0014, P0021, and P0024 run continuously once the above conditions are met for greater than 600 seconds.

DTC	Trouble Code Title, Conditions, Possible Causes
DTC: P0021	**Intake Camshaft Position System Performance Bank 2:** DTC P0010, P0013, P0020, P0023, P0016, P0017, P0018, P0019, P0335, P0336, P0340, P0341, P0345, P0346, P0365, P0366, P0390, and P0391 is not set. The ignition voltage is between 11-32 V. The engine is running. The desired camshaft position is not changing greater than 4. 5° for at least 1 s. Both of the desired and actual camshaft position actuator values cannot be greater than 20° or less than 5°. DTCs P0011, P0014, P0021, and P0024 run continuously when the above conditions are met.
DTC: P0023	**Exhaust Camshaft Position Actuator Solenoid Valve Control Circuit Bank 2:** The ignition voltage is between 11-32 V. The ignition switch is in the Crank or Run position. The ECM commanded the Camshaft Position Actuator Solenoid Valve ON. DTCs P0010, P0013, P0020, and P0023 run continuously when the above conditions are met.
DTC: P0023	**Exhaust Camshaft Position (CMP) Actuator Solenoid Control Circuit Bank 2:** The ignition is in the Crank or Run position. The ECM has commanded the Camshaft Position Actuator Solenoid Valve ON. The ignition voltage is between 11-18 volts. DTCs P0010, P0013, P0020, and P0023 run continuously once the above conditions are met.
DTC: P0024	**Exhaust Camshaft Position System Performance Bank 2:** DTC P0010, P0013, P0020, P0023, P0016, P0017, P0018, P0019, P0335, P0336, P0340, P0341, P0345, P0346, P0365, P0366, P0390, and P0391 is not set. The ignition voltage is between 11-32 V. The engine is running. The desired camshaft position is not changing greater than 4. 5° for at least 1 s. Both of the desired and actual camshaft position actuator values cannot be greater than 20° or less than 5°. DTCs P0011, P0014, P0021, and P0024 run continuously when the above conditions are met.
DTC: P0024	**Exhaust Camshaft Position System Performance Bank 2:** Before the ECM can report DTC P000A, P000B, P000C, P000D, P0011, P0014, P0021, or P0024 failed, DTCs P0010, P0013, P0020, P0023, P0341, P0342, P0343, P0346, P0347, P0348, P0366, P0367, P0368, P0391, P0392, P0393, P2088, P2089, P2090, P2091, P2092, P2093, P2094, and P2095 must run and pass. DTC P0016, P0017, P0018, P0019, P0335, P0336, or P0338 is not set. The engine is operating for greater than 1 seconds. The engine speed is greater than 520 RPM. The engine must accelerate such that the CMP actuator system is commanded from the park position to the phased position. This is considered a cam control cycle. There must be a minimum of 2 cam control cycles for at least 2. 5 seconds each in the phased position. DTCs P000A, P000B, P000C, P000D, P0011, P0014, P0021, and P0024 run continuously once the above conditions are met for greater than 600 seconds.
DTC: P0030	**HO2S Heater Control Circuit Sensor 1:** P0030 or P0036The ignition voltage is between 11-32 V. The engine speed is greater than 400 RPM. The DTCs run continuously once the above conditions are met for 10 s.
DTC: P0030	**HO2S Heater Control Circuit Bank 1 Sensor 1:** P0030, P0036, P0050, or P0056The ignition 1 voltage is between 11-18 V. The engine speed is greater than 400 RPM. The DTCs run continuously when the above conditions are met.
DTC: P0030 00	**HO2S Heater Control Circuit Sensor 1:** P0030 00, P0031 00, and P0030 02The ignition is ON. The ignition signal parameter is more than 9 V. DTC P0030 00, P0031 00, and P0032 00 run continuously when the above conditions are met for 1 s. P0135 00 DTCs P0030 00, P0031 00, P0032 00, are not set. The ignition is ON. The ignition signal parameter is more than 9 V. DTC P0135 00 runs continuously.
DTC: P0031	**HO2S Heater Control Circuit Low Voltage Sensor 1:** P0030, P0031, P0032The engine is running The Ignition 1 Signal parameter is 10. 5-18. 1 volts.
DTC: P0031	**HO2S Heater Control Circuit Low Voltage Bank 1 Sensor 1:** P0030, P0031, P0032, P0050, P0051, P0052The ignition voltage is between 10-18 volts. The engine speed is greater than 240 RPM. The HO2S heater is commanded ON. The DTCs run continuously once the above conditions are met for 5 seconds.
DTC: P0031 00	**HO2S Heater Control Circuit Low Voltage Sensor 1:** P0030 00, P0031 00, and P0030 02The ignition is ON. The ignition signal parameter is more than 9 V. DTC P0030 00, P0031 00, and P0032 00 run continuously when the above conditions are met for 1 s. P0135 00 DTCs P0030 00, P0031 00, P0032 00, are not set. The ignition is ON. The ignition signal parameter is more than 9 V. DTC P0135 00 runs continuously.
DTC: P0032	**HO2S Heater Control Circuit High Voltage Bank 1 Sensor 1:** P0030, P0031, P0032, P0050, P0051, P0052The ignition voltage is between 10-18 volts. The engine speed is greater than 240 RPM. The HO2S heater is commanded ON. The DTCs run continuously once the above conditions are met for 5 seconds.
DTC: P0032	**HO2S Heater Control Circuit High Voltage Sensor 1:** P0030, P0031, P0032The engine is running. The Ignition 1 Signal parameter is 10. 5-18. 1 volts.
DTC: P0032 00	**HO2S Heater Control Circuit High Voltage Sensor 1:** P0030 00, P0031 00, and P0030 02The ignition is ON. The ignition signal parameter is more than 9 V. DTC P0030 00, P0031 00, and P0032 00 run continuously when the above conditions are met for 1 s. P0135 00 DTCs P0030 00, P0031 00, P0032 00, are not set. The ignition is ON. The ignition signal parameter is more than 9 V. DTC P0135 00 runs continuously.
DTC: P0033	**Turbocharger Bypass Valve Solenoid Control Circuit:** The engine speed is greater than 80 RPM. The battery voltage is between 10-18 volts. The bypass valve must be activated in order to set the open and short to ground faults. This DTC runs continuously within the enabling conditions.

DTC	Trouble Code Title, Conditions, Possible Causes
DTC: P0033 00	**Turbocharger Bypass Solenoid Valve Control Circuit:** The engine speed is greater than 40 RPM. The ignition voltage is between 8-16 V. The bypass valve must be activated in order to set the open and short to ground faults. These DTCs runs continuously within the enabling conditions.
DTC: P0034	**Turbocharger Bypass Valve Solenoid Control Circuit Low Voltage:** The engine speed is greater than 80 RPM. The battery voltage is between 10-18 V. The bypass valve must be activated in order to set the open and short to ground faults. This DTC runs continuously within the enabling conditions.
DTC: P0034 00	**Turbocharger Bypass Solenoid Valve Control Circuit Low Voltage:** The engine speed is greater than 40 RPM. The ignition voltage is between 8-16 V. The bypass valve must be activated in order to set the open and short to ground faults. These DTCs runs continuously within the enabling conditions.
DTC: P0035	**Turbocharger Bypass Valve Solenoid Control Circuit High Voltage:** The engine speed is greater than 80 RPM. The battery voltage is between 10-18 V. The bypass valve must be activated in order to set the open and short to ground faults. This DTC runs continuously within the enabling conditions.
DTC: P0035 00	**Turbocharger Bypass Solenoid Valve Control Circuit High Voltage:** The engine speed is greater than 40 RPM. The ignition voltage is between 8-16 V. The bypass valve must be activated in order to set the open and short to ground faults. These DTCs runs continuously within the enabling conditions.
DTC: P0036	**HO2S Heater Control Circuit Sensor 2:** P0036, P0037, and P0038The Ignition 1 Signal parameter is between 10-18 volts. The engine speed is more than 80 RPM. DTC P0036, P0037, and P0038 run continuously when the above conditions are met for 1 second.
DTC: P0036	**HO2S Heater Control Circuit Sensor 2:** P0030 and P0036The engine is cranking or running. The system voltage is between 11-18V.
DTC: P0036	**HO2S Heater Control Circuit Sensor 2:** P0030 or P0036The ignition voltage is between 11-32 V. The engine speed is greater than 400 RPM. The DTCs run continuously once the above conditions are met for 10 s.
DTC: P0036 00	**HO2S Heater Control Circuit Sensor 2:** P0036 00, P0037 00, and P0038 00The ignition is ON. The Ignition Signal parameter is more than 9 V. DTC P0036 00, P0037 00, and P0038 00 run continuously when the above conditions are met for 1 s.
DTC: P0037	**HO2S Heater Control Circuit Low Voltage Bank 1 Sensor 2:** P0036, P0037, P0038, P0056, P0057, P0058The ignition voltage is between 10-18 volts. The engine speed is greater than 80 RPM. The HO2S heater is commanded ON and OFF at least once during the ignition cycle. The HO2S 2 is at operating temperature. The DTCs run continuously once the above conditions are met.
DTC: P0037	**HO2S Heater Control Circuit Low Voltage Sensor 2:** P0036, P0037, and P0038The Ignition 1 Signal parameter is between 10-18 volts. The engine speed is more than 80 RPM. DTC P0036, P0037, and P0038 run continuously when the above conditions are met for 1 second.
DTC: P0037 00	**HO2S Heater Control Circuit Low Voltage Sensor 2:** P0037 00, and P0038 00The engine is running. The ignition voltage is between 11-16 V. DTC P0037 00, and P0038 00 run continuously when the above conditions are met for 1 s.
DTC: P0037 00	**HO2S Heater Control Circuit Low Voltage Sensor 2:** P0036 00, P0037 00, and P0038 00The ignition is ON. The Ignition Signal parameter is more than 9 V. DTC P0036 00, P0037 00, and P0038 00 run continuously when the above conditions are met for 1 s.
DTC: P0038	**HO2S Heater Control Circuit High Voltage Sensor 2:** P0036, P0037, and P0038The Ignition 1 Signal parameter is between 10-18 volts. The engine speed is more than 80 RPM. DTC P0036, P0037, and P0038 run continuously when the above conditions are met for 1 second.
DTC: P0038	**HO2S Heater Control Circuit High Voltage Bank 1 Sensor 2:** P0036, P0037, P0038, P0056, P0057, P0058The ignition voltage is between 10-18 volts. The engine speed is greater than 80 RPM. The HO2S heater is commanded ON and OFF at least once during the ignition cycle. The HO2S 2 is at operating temperature. The DTCs run continuously once the above conditions are met.
DTC: P0038 00	**HO2S Heater Control Circuit High Voltage Sensor 2:** P0036 00, P0037 00, and P0038 00The ignition is ON. The Ignition Signal parameter is more than 9 V. DTC P0036 00, P0037 00, and P0038 00 run continuously when the above conditions are met for 1 s.
DTC: P0038 00	**HO2S Heater Control Circuit High Voltage Sensor 2:** P0037 00, and P0038 00The engine is running. The ignition voltage is between 11-16 V. DTC P0037 00, and P0038 00 run continuously when the above conditions are met for 1 s.

DTC	Trouble Code Title, Conditions, Possible Causes
DTC: P003A	**Turbocharger Vane Position Not Learned:** The ECM is commanding the turbocharger vanes open or closed during a position learn procedure. The engine speed is between 640-850 RPM. DTC P003A runs once per key cycle when the above conditions are met.
DTC: P003A	**Turbocharger Boost Control Position Not Learned:** DTCs P0107, P0108, P0117, P0118, P2563, P2564, P2565, P2228, P2229 are not set. The battery voltage is equal to or greater than 11 V. The ECM is commanding the turbocharger vanes open or closed during a position learn process. The engine speed is between 600-750 RPM. The engine coolant temp (ECT) is between 73-96°C (163-205°F). The calculated fuel rate is less than 30 mm ;. DTC P003A runs once per key cycle when the above conditions are met.
DTC: P003A 00	**Turbocharger Vane Position Not Learned:** The battery voltage is equal to or greater than 11 V. The ECM is commanding the turbocharger vanes open or closed during a position learn process. The engine speed is between 750-850 RPM. The engine coolant temperature (ECT) is between 73-96°C (163-205°F). DTC P003A 00 runs once per key cycle when the above conditions are met.
DTC: P0045	**Turbocharger Boost Control Solenoid Control Circuit:** P0045, P0047, P0048 and P006EThe battery voltage is greater than 11 V. The engine is running. DTCs P0045, P0047, P0048 and P006E run continuously when the above conditions are met.
DTC: P0045 00	**Turbocharger Boost Control Solenoid Control Circuit Malfunction:** The ignition is ON or the engine is running. The ignition voltage is greater than 16. 5 V. The ECM has commanded the turbocharger boost control solenoid ON and OFF at least once during the ignition cycle. The DTCs run continuously once the above conditions are met.
DTC: P0045 01	**Turbocharger Boost Control Solenoid Control Circuit Short to Battery:** The ignition is ON or the engine is running. The ignition voltage is greater than 11 V. The ECM has commanded the turbocharger boost control solenoid ON and OFF at least once during the ignition cycle. The DTCs run continuously once the above conditions are met.
DTC: P0045 02	**Turbocharger Boost Control Solenoid Control Circuit Short to Ground:** The ignition is ON or the engine is running. The ignition voltage is greater than 11 V. The ECM has commanded the turbocharger boost control solenoid ON and OFF at least once during the ignition cycle. The DTCs run continuously once the above conditions are met.
DTC: P0045 04	**Turbocharger Boost Control Solenoid Control Circuit Open:** The ignition is ON or the engine is running. The ignition voltage is greater than 11 V. The ECM has commanded the turbocharger boost control solenoid ON and OFF at least once during the ignition cycle. The DTCs run continuously once the above conditions are met.
DTC: P0045 54	**Turbocharger Boost Control Solenoid Control Circuit High Temperature:** The ignition is ON or the engine is running. The ignition voltage is greater than 11 V. The ECM has commanded the turbocharger boost control solenoid ON and OFF at least once during the ignition cycle. The DTCs run continuously once the above conditions are met.
DTC: P0047	**Turbocharger Boost Control Solenoid Control Circuit Low Voltage:** The engine run time is greater than 60 seconds. DTCs P0047 and P0048 run continuously when the above condition is met.
DTC: P0047	**Turbocharger Boost Control Solenoid Control Circuit Low Voltage:** P0045, P0047, P0048 and P006EThe battery voltage is greater than 11 V. The engine is running. DTCs P0045, P0047, P0048 and P006E run continuously when the above conditions are met.
DTC: P0047 00	**Turbocharger Boost Control Solenoid Control Circuit Low Voltage:** The ignition is ON or the engine is running. The ignition voltage is greater than 16. 5 V. The ECM has commanded the turbocharger boost control solenoid ON and OFF at least once during the ignition cycle. The DTCs run continuously once the above conditions are met.
DTC: P0048	**Turbocharger Boost Control Solenoid Control Circuit High Voltage:** P0045, P0047, P0048 and P006EThe battery voltage is greater than 11 V. The engine is running. DTCs P0045, P0047, P0048 and P006E run continuously when the above conditions are met.
DTC: P0048	**Turbocharger Boost Control Solenoid Control Circuit High Voltage:** The engine run time is greater than 60 seconds. DTCs P0047 and P0048 run continuously when the above condition is met.
DTC: P0048 00	**Turbocharger Boost Control Solenoid Control Circuit High Voltage:** The ignition is ON or the engine is running. The ignition voltage is greater than 16. 5 V. The ECM has commanded the turbocharger boost control solenoid ON and OFF at least once during the ignition cycle. The DTCs run continuously once the above conditions are met.
DTC: P0050	**HO2S Heater Control Circuit Bank 2 Sensor 1:** P0030, P0031, P0032, P0050, P0051, P0052The ignition voltage is between 10-18 volts. The engine speed is greater than 240 RPM. The HO2S heater is commanded ON. The DTCs run continuously once the above conditions are met for 5 seconds.

DTC	Trouble Code Title, Conditions, Possible Causes
DTC: P0051	**HO2S Heater Control Circuit Low Voltage Bank 2 Sensor 1:** P0030, P0031, P0032, P0050, P0051, P0052 The ignition voltage is between 10-18 volts. The engine speed is greater than 240 RPM. The HO2S heater is commanded ON. The DTCs run continuously once the above conditions are met for 5 seconds.
DTC: P0052	**HO2S Heater Control Circuit High Voltage Bank 2 Sensor 1:** P0030, P0031, P0032, P0050, P0051, P0052 The ignition voltage is between 10-18 volts. The engine speed is greater than 240 RPM. The HO2S heater is commanded ON. The DTCs run continuously once the above conditions are met for 5 seconds.
DTC: P0053	**HO2S Heater Resistance Sensor 1:** P0053 or P0054 DTCs P0112, P0113, P0116, P0117, P0118, P2610 are not set. The engine is started. The ignition is OFF for more than 8 hours. The ECT Sensor parameter is between -30 to +45°C (-22 to +113°F) at engine start-up. The ECT Sensor parameter minus the IAT Sensor parameter is less than 8°C (14°F) at engine start-up. The Ignition Voltage parameter is less than 18 volts. DTCs P0053 and P0054 run once per drive cycle when the above conditions are met.
DTC: P0053	**HO2S Heater Resistance Bank 1 Sensor 1:** P0053, P0054, or P0059 DTCs P0112, P0113, P0117, P0118, or P2610 are not set. The engine run time is greater than 3 seconds. The ignition voltage is less than 18 volts. The ignition is OFF for greater than 8 hours. The engine coolant temperature (ECT) is between -30 to +45°C (-22 to +113°F) at engine start-up. The ECT and the intake air temperature (IAT) are within 8°C (14°F) at engine start-up. The DTCs run once per drive cycle when the above conditions are met.
DTC: P0053	**HO2S Heater Resistance Sensor 1:** P0053 The engine is started. The Ignition 1 Signal parameter is 10. 5-18. 1 volts. DTC P0053 runs once per drive cycle when the above conditions are met.
DTC: P0054	**HO2S Heater Resistance Bank 1 Sensor 2:** P0053, P0054, or P0059 DTCs P0112, P0113, P0117, P0118, or P2610 are not set. The engine run time is greater than 3 seconds. The ignition voltage is less than 18 volts. The ignition is OFF for greater than 8 hours. The engine coolant temperature (ECT) is between -30 to +45°C (-22 to +113°F) at engine start-up. The ECT and the intake air temperature (IAT) are within 8°C (14°F) at engine start-up. The DTCs run once per drive cycle when the above conditions are met.
DTC: P0054	**HO2S Heater Resistance Sensor 2:** P0053 and P0054 DTC P2610 has run and passed. The ignition is OFF for more than 10 hours. The ECT Sensor parameter is between -30 and +45°C (-22 and +113°F) at engine start-up. The system voltage is less than 18V. This diagnostic runs one time per valid cold start when the above conditions are met.
DTC: P0056	**HO2S Heater Control Circuit Bank 2 Sensor 2:** P0036, P0037, P0038, P0056, P0057, P0058 The ignition voltage is between 10-18 volts. The engine speed is greater than 80 RPM. The HO2S heater is commanded ON and OFF at least once during the ignition cycle. The HO2S 2 is at operating temperature. The DTCs run continuously once the above conditions are met.
DTC: P0057	**HO2S Heater Control Circuit Low Voltage Bank 2 Sensor 2:** P0036, P0037, P0038, P0056, P0057, P0058 The ignition voltage is between 10-18 volts. The engine speed is greater than 80 RPM. The HO2S heater is commanded ON and OFF at least once during the ignition cycle. The HO2S 2 is at operating temperature. The DTCs run continuously once the above conditions are met.
DTC: P0058	**HO2S Heater Control Circuit High Voltage Bank 2 Sensor 2:** P0036, P0037, P0038, P0056, P0057, P0058 The ignition voltage is between 10-18 volts. The engine speed is greater than 80 RPM. The HO2S heater is commanded ON and OFF at least once during the ignition cycle. The HO2S 2 is at operating temperature. The DTCs run continuously once the above conditions are met.
DTC: P0059	**HO2S Heater Resistance Bank 2 Sensor 1:** P0053, P0054, or P0059 DTCs P0112, P0113, P0117, P0118, or P2610 are not set. The engine run time is greater than 3 seconds. The ignition voltage is less than 18 volts. The ignition is OFF for greater than 8 hours. The engine coolant temperature (ECT) is between -30 to +45°C (-22 to +113°F) at engine start-up. The ECT and the intake air temperature (IAT) are within 8°C (14°F) at engine start-up. The DTCs run once per drive cycle when the above conditions are met.
DTC: P0060	**HO2S Heater Resistance Bank 2 Sensor 2:** P0053, P0054, P0059, or P0060 DTCs P0112, P0113, P0117, P0118, or P2610 are not set. The engine run time is greater than 20 s. The ignition voltage is less than 18 V. The ignition is OFF for greater than 8 h. The engine coolant temperature (ECT) is between -30 to +45°C (-22 to +113°F) at engine start-up. The ECT and the intake air temperature (IAT) are within 8°C (14°F) at engine start-up. The DTCs run once per drive cycle when the above conditions are met.
DTC: P0068	**Throttle Body Airflow Performance:** P0068 DTCs P0122, P0123, P0220, P0221, P0222, P0223, P0601, P0602, P0603, P0604, P060D, P062F, P0606, P0652, P0653, P1516, P2101, P2119, P2135, P2176 are not set. The engine is running. DTC P0068 runs continuously when the above conditions are met.
DTC: P0068 00	**Throttle Body Air Flow Performance:** DTCs P0106 00, P0107 00, P0108 00, and P0112 00 are not set. The engine is running. The DTC runs continuously when the above conditions are met.

DTC	Trouble Code Title, Conditions, Possible Causes
DTC: P0068 00	**Throttle Body Air Flow Performance:** DTCs P000A 00, P000B 00, P0016 00, P0017 00, P0111 00, P0112 00, P0113 00, P0114 00, P0116 00, P0117 00, P0118 00, P0119 00, P0122 00, P0123 00, P0222 00, P0223 00, P0121 00, P0221 00, P0340 00, P0341 00, P0365 00, P0366 00, P0458 00, P0459 00, P0642 00, P0643 00, P0652 00, P0653 00, P065B 00 are not set. The engine is running. DTCs P0068 00, P0642 00, P0643 00 are not set.
DTC: P0069 00	**Manifold Absolute Pressure (MAP) - Barometric Pressure (BARO) Not Plausible:** DTCs P010 007, or P0108 00 are not set. The ignition is ON. The DTC runs continuously when the above conditions are met.
DTC: P0069 5A	**Manifold Absolute Pressure (MAP) - Barometric Pressure (BARO) Not Plausible:** DTCs P0105, P0107, or P0108 are not set. The ignition is ON. The DTC runs continuously when the above conditions are met.
DTC: P006E	**Turbocharger Boost Control Solenoid High Control Circuit Low Voltage:** P0045, P0047, P0048 and P006EThe battery voltage is greater than 11 V. The engine is running. DTCs P0045, P0047, P0048 and P006E run continuously when the above conditions are met.
DTC: P006F	**Turbocharger Boost Control Solenoid High Control Circuit High Voltage:** P006FThe battery voltage is greater than 11 V. The ignition is OFF. The engine is in after-run. DTC P006F runs continuously when the above conditions are met.
DTC: P007C	**Charge Air Cooler (CAC) Temperature Sensor Circuit Low Voltage:** P007C or P007DThe engine is running for longer than 10 s. The DTCs run continuously when the enabling condition is met.
DTC: P007D	**Charge Air Cooler (CAC) Temperature Sensor Circuit High Voltage:** P007C or P007DThe engine is running for longer than 10 s. The DTCs run continuously when the enabling condition is met.
DTC: P0087	**Fuel Rail Low Pressure:** DTCs P0090, P0091, P0092, P0191, P0192, P0193 are not set. The ignition 1 signal parameter is less than 18. 1 V. The relative injected fuel mass is between 5. 016-500 %. The deceleration fuel cut-off is inactive. The engine speed is greater than 25 RPM. The engine start temperature is greater than -48°C (-54. 4°F). The DTCs run continuously when the above conditions are met for 2 s.
DTC: P0087	**Fuel Rail Pressure (FRP) Too Low:** Fuel tank level is greater than 15 %. Engine is in crank or run mode. Ambient air temperature is greater than -7°C (+19°F). Ambient pressure is greater than 74. 8 kPa.
DTC: P0087 00	**Fuel Rail Low Pressure:** The engine is running. The DTCs runs continuously once the above conditions are met.
DTC: P0088	**Fuel Rail High Pressure:** DTCs P0090, P0091, P0092, P0191, P0192, P0193 are not set. The ignition 1 signal parameter is less than 18. 1 V. The relative injected fuel mass is between 5. 016-500 %. The deceleration fuel cut-off is inactive. The engine speed is greater than 25 RPM. The engine start temperature is greater than -48°C (-54. 4°F). The DTCs run continuously when the above conditions are met for 2 s.
DTC: P0088	**Fuel Rail Pressure (FRP) Too High:** Fuel tank level is greater than 15 %. Engine is in crank or run mode. Ambient air temperature is greater than -7°C (+19°F). Ambient pressure is greater than 74. 8 kPa.
DTC: P0088 00	**Fuel Rail High Pressure:** The engine is running. The DTCs runs continuously once the above conditions are met.
DTC: P0089	**Fuel Pressure Regulator Performance:** P0089, P228C, or P228DDTC P0016, P0017, P0018, P0019, P0090, P0091, P0092, P00C8, P00C9, P00CA, P0111, P0112, P0113, P0116, P0117, P0118, P0128, P0192, P0193, P0335, P0336, P0340, P0341, P0345, P0346, P0365, P0366, P0390, P0391, P0627, P0628, or P0629 is not set. The ignition voltage is greater than 8 V. The low side fuel pressure is greater than 275 kPa (40 psi). The engine is running. The DTCs run continuously when the above conditions are met for 10 s.
DTC: P0089 00	**Fuel Pressure Regulator Performance Malfunction:** The engine is running. The DTCs runs continuously once the above conditions are met.
DTC: P0089 11	**Fuel Pressure Regulator Performance High Input:** The engine is running. The DTCs runs continuously once the above conditions are met.
DTC: P0089 12	**Fuel Pressure Regulator Performance Low Input:** The engine is running. The DTCs runs continuously once the above conditions are met.
DTC: P0089 18	**Fuel Pressure Regulator Performance Low Signal Amplitude:** The engine is running. The DTCs runs continuously once the above conditions are met.
DTC: P0089 19	**Fuel Pressure Regulator Performance High Signal Amplitude:** The engine is running. The DTCs runs continuously once the above conditions are met.

DTC	Trouble Code Title, Conditions, Possible Causes
DTC: P008F	**Engine Coolant Temperature (ECT) Fuel Temperature Not Plausible:** DTC P0016, P0112, P0113, P0117, P0118, P0182, P0183, P0335, P0336, P0340 or P0341 is not set. Condition 1Ignition has been OFF for 8 hours or more. The ambient temperature is greater than -60°C (-76°F). The engine is running. OR Condition 2Ignition has been OFF for 8 hours or more. The ambient temperature is greater than -60°C (-76°F). The engine is running. In the first 60 s of engine run time, the ECM determines the block heater is OFF. DTC P008F will only run once per ignition cycle until a Pass, Fail or Disable condition exists.
DTC: P0090	**Fuel Pressure Regulator 1 Control Circuit:** The ignition 1 signal parameter is between 6-18. 1 V. The DTCs run continuously within the enabling condition.
DTC: P0090	**Fuel Pressure Regulator Solenoid 1 Control Circuit:** Engine speed is greater than 600 RPM. Battery voltage is greater than 11 V.
DTC: P0090 00	**Fuel Pressure Regulator Control Circuit:** The ignition is ON, or the engine is running. The ignition voltage is less than 16 V. These DTCs runs continuously once the above conditions are met.
DTC: P0090 01	**Fuel Pressure Regulator Control Circuit Short to Battery:** The ignition is ON, or the engine is running. The ignition voltage is less than 16 V. The DTCs runs continuously once the above conditions are met.
DTC: P0090 02	**Fuel Pressure Regulator Control Circuit Short to Ground:** The ignition is ON, or the engine is running. The ignition voltage is less than 16 V. The DTCs runs continuously once the above conditions are met.
DTC: P0090 04	**Fuel Pressure Regulator Control Circuit Open:** The ignition is ON, or the engine is running. The ignition voltage is less than 16 V. The DTCs runs continuously once the above conditions are met.
DTC: P0090 54	**Fuel Pressure Regulator Control Circuit High Temperature:** The ignition is ON, or the engine is running. The ignition voltage is less than 16 V. The DTCs runs continuously once the above conditions are met.
DTC: P0091	**Fuel Pressure Regulator Solenoid 1 Control Circuit Low Voltage:** Engine speed is greater than 600 RPM. Battery voltage is greater than 11 V.
DTC: P0091	**Fuel Pressure Regulator Control Circuit Low Voltage:** The ignition voltage is between 11-18 V. The DTCs run continuously within the enabling conditions.
DTC: P0091 00	**Fuel Pressure Regulator Control Circuit Low Voltage:** The ignition is ON, or the engine is running. The ignition voltage is less than 16 V. These DTCs runs continuously once the above conditions are met.
DTC: P0092	**Fuel Pressure Regulator Solenoid 1 Control Circuit High Voltage:** Engine speed is greater than 600 RPM. Battery voltage is greater than 11 V.
DTC: P0092	**Fuel Pressure Regulator 1 Control Circuit High Voltage:** The ignition 1 signal parameter is between 6-18. 1 V. The DTCs run continuously within the enabling condition.
DTC: P0092	**Fuel Pressure Regulator Control Circuit High Voltage:** The ignition voltage is between 11-18 V. The DTCs run continuously within the enabling conditions.
DTC: P0092 00	**Fuel Pressure Regulator Control Circuit High Voltage:** The ignition is ON, or the engine is running. The ignition voltage is less than 16 V. These DTCs runs continuously once the above conditions are met.
DTC: P0093 00	**Fuel System Large Leak Detected:** The engine is running. The DTCs runs continuously once the above conditions are met.
DTC: P0095 03	**Intake Air Temperature (IAT) Sensor 2 Circuit Low Voltage:** The ignition is ON, or the engine is running. The DTCs run continuously once the above conditions are met.
DTC: P0095 07	**Intake Air Temperature (IAT) Sensor 2 Circuit High Voltage:** The ignition is ON, or the engine is running. The DTCs run continuously once the above conditions are met.
DTC: P0096	**Intake Air Temperature (IAT) Sensor 2 Performance:** DTC P0097, P0098, or P0099 is not set. The engine coolant temperature (ECT) at start-up is colder than 88°C (190°F). The ECT reaches a target temperature that is warmer than 60°C (140°F). The engine is idling. The mass air flow (MAF) is less than 8 g/s. The vehicle speed is less than 16 km/h (10 mph). Drive period. DTC P0097, P0098, or P0099 is not set. The mass air flow (MAF) is between 6-111 g/s. The vehicle speed is greater than 35 km/h (22 mph). This DTC runs continuously within the enabling conditions.

DTC	Trouble Code Title, Conditions, Possible Causes
DTC: P0096 00	**Intake Air Temperature (IAT) Sensor 2 Performance:** The ignition is ON or the engine is running. The ignition voltage is greater than 8.5 V. The DTCs run continuously once the above conditions are met.
DTC: P0097	**Intake Air Temperature (IAT) Sensor 2 Circuit Low Voltage:** The ignition is ON or the engine is running. The DTCs run continuously when the enabling conditions are met.
DTC: P0097 00	**Intake Air Temperature (IAT) Sensor 2 Circuit Low Voltage:** The ignition is ON or the engine is running. The ignition voltage is greater than 8.5 V. The DTCs run continuously once the above conditions are met.
DTC: P0098	**Intake Air Temperature (IAT) Sensor 2 Circuit High Voltage:** P0097 or P0098 The engine is running for longer than 10 s. The DTCs run continuously when the enabling condition is met.
DTC: P0098	**Intake Air Temperature (IAT) Sensor 2 Circuit High Voltage:** The ignition is ON or the engine is running. The DTCs run continuously when the enabling conditions are met.
DTC: P0098	**Intake Air Temperature (IAT) Sensor 2 Circuit High Voltage:** P0098 The engine is running. This DTC runs continuously within the enabling conditions.
DTC: P0098 00	**Intake Air Temperature (IAT) Sensor 2 Circuit High Voltage:** The ignition is ON or the engine is running. The ignition voltage is greater than 8.5 V. The DTCs run continuously once the above conditions are met.
DTC: P0099	**Intake Air Temperature (IAT) Sensor 2 Circuit Intermittent:** P0099 The ignition is ON or the engine is running. This DTC runs continuously within the enabling conditions.
DTC: P0099 00	**Intake Air Temperature (IAT) Sensor 2 Circuit Intermittent:** The ignition is ON or the engine is running. The ignition voltage is greater than 8.5 V. The DTCs run continuously once the above conditions are met.
DTC: P00B3	**Radiator Coolant Temperature (RCT) Sensor Circuit Low Voltage:** The ignition is ON, or the engine is running. The battery voltage is greater than 9 V. The intake air temperature (IAT) is warmer than -30°C (-22°F) or the IAT is colder than -30°C (-22°F) and the engine run time is greater than 120 s. This DTC runs continuously within the enabling conditions.
DTC: P00B3 00	**Radiator Coolant Temperature (RCT) Sensor Circuit Low Voltage:** The ignition is ON, or the engine is running. The battery voltage is greater than 9 V. The intake air temperature (IAT) is warmer than -30°C (-22°F) or the IAT is colder than -30°C (-22°F) and the engine run time is greater than 120 s. This DTC runs continuously within the enabling conditions.
DTC: P00B4	**Radiator Coolant Temperature (RCT) Sensor Circuit High Voltage:** The ignition is ON, or the engine is running. The battery voltage is greater than 9 V. The intake air temperature (IAT) is warmer than -30°C (-22°F) or the IAT is colder than -30°C (-22°F) and the engine run time is greater than 120 s. This DTC runs continuously within the enabling conditions.
DTC: P00B4 00	**Radiator Coolant Temperature (RCT) Sensor Circuit High Voltage:** The ignition is ON, or the engine is running. The battery voltage is greater than 9 V. The intake air temperature (IAT) is warmer than -30°C (-22°F) or the IAT is colder than -30°C (-22°F) and the engine run time is greater than 120 s. This DTC runs continuously within the enabling conditions.
DTC: P00B6	**Radiator Coolant Temperature (RCT) - Engine Coolant Temperature (ECT) Correlation:** DTCs P00B3, P00B4, P0112, P0113, P0117, P0118 or P2610 are not set. The ignition has been off for greater than 8 h before vehicle is started. The ignition is ON, or the engine is running. The intake air temperature (IAT) is greater than -7°C (19°F). The fuel level is greater than 10%. The DTC runs once per ignition cycle when the above conditions are met.
DTC: P00B6 00	**Radiator Coolant Temperature (RCT) - Engine Coolant Temperature (ECT) Not Plausible:** DTCs P00B3 00, P00B4 00, P0112 00, P0113 00, P0117 00, or P0118 00 are not set. The ignition has been off for greater than 8 h before vehicle is started. The ignition is ON, or the engine is running. The intake air temperature (IAT) is greater than -7°C (19°F). The fuel level is greater than 10%. The DTC runs once per ignition cycle when the above conditions are met.
DTC: P00C6	**Fuel Rail Pressure Low During Engine Cranking:** P00C6 DTC P0016, P0017, P0090, P0091, P0092, P00C8, P00C9, P00CA, P0112, P0113, P0116, P0117, P0118, P0128, P0192, P0193, P0335, P0336, P0340, P0341, P0365, P0366, P0627, P0628, P0629 or P1682 is not set. The ignition voltage is more than 8 V. The engine coolant temperature is between -100 and +80°C (-148 and +176°F). The low side fuel pressure is more than 300 kPa (43.5 psi). The engine is not running. The DTC runs once for each engine start.
DTC: P00C7 00	**Intake Air Pressure Measurement System - Multiple Sensors Not Plausible:** The engine is running. This DTC runs continuously within the enabling conditions.

DTC	Trouble Code Title, Conditions, Possible Causes
DTC: P00C8	**Fuel Pressure Regulator High Control Circuit:** The ignition voltage is between 11-18 V. The DTCs run continuously within the enabling conditions.
DTC: P00C9	**Fuel Pressure Regulator High Control Circuit Low Voltage:** The ignition voltage is between 11-18 V. The DTCs run continuously within the enabling conditions.
DTC: P00C9	**Fuel Pressure Regulator 1 High Control Circuit Low Voltage:** Engine speed is greater than 600 RPM. Battery voltage is greater than 11 V.
DTC: P00CA	**Fuel Pressure Regulator 1 High Control Circuit High Voltage:** Engine speed is greater than 600 RPM. Battery voltage is greater than 11 V.
DTC: P00CA	**Fuel Pressure Regulator High Control Circuit High Voltage:** The ignition voltage is between 11-18 V. The DTCs run continuously within the enabling conditions.
DTC: P0100	**Mass Air Flow (MAF) Sensor Circuit:** The engine is running. The engine speed is greater than 300 RPM. The ignition 1 voltage signal is greater than 10 V. The above conditions are met for greater than 1 s. This DTC runs continuously within the enabling conditions.
DTC: P0100	**Mass Air Flow (MAF) Sensor Circuit:** The ignition is ON, or the engine is operating. The ignition voltage is greater than 10. 5 V. DTC P0100, P0102 and P0103 run continuously once the above conditions are met for 200 mS.
DTC: P0100 00	**Mass Air Flow (MAF) Sensor Circuit Malfunction:** The ignition is ON. The battery voltage is greater than 8. 5 V. The engine speed is between 1 000-4 000 RPM.
DTC: P0101	**Mass Air Flow (MAF) Sensor Performance:** DTCs P0102, P0103, P0107, P0108, P0112, P0113, P0116, P0117, P0118, P0128, P0335 or P0336 are not set. The engine is running. The engine coolant is between 69-127°C (156-261°F). The intake air temperature is between -20 and +125°C (-4 and +257°F). The DTC runs continuously when the above conditions are met.
DTC: P0101	**Mass Air Flow (MAF) Sensor Circuit Performance:** Before the ECM can report DTC P0101 failed, DTCs P0010, P0011, P0013, P0014, P0020, P0021, P0023, P0024, P0100, P0102, P0103, P0111, P0112, P0113, P0121, P0122, P0123, P0221, P0222, P0223, P0335, P0336, P0338, P2088, P2089, P2090, P2091, P2092, P2093, P2094, P2095, P2227, P2228, or P2229 must run and pass. DTC P2176 is not set. The engine is operating for greater than 1 s. The MAF signal is greater than 0. 00 g/s and steady. The ignition voltage is greater than 10. 5 V. The engine coolant temperature (ECT) is greater than 10°C (50°F). The long term fuel trim is enabled. The throttle angle is steady +/-2 %. The ECM detects greater than 150 revolutions of the crankshaft. DTC P0101 runs continuously once the above conditions are met for greater than 2 s.
DTC: P0101 00	**Mass Air Flow (MAF) Sensor Performance:** The ignition is ON. The battery voltage is greater than 8. 5 V. The engine speed is between 1 000-4 000 RPM.
DTC: P0101 00	**Mass Air Flow (MAF) Sensor Performance:** DTCs P0102 00, P0103 00, P0106 00, P0107 00, P0108 00, P0112 00, P0113 00, P0117 00, P0118 00, P0335 00, P0336 00 are not set. The engine speed is between 400-6 500 RPM. The IAT sensor is between -20 to +125°C (-4 to +257°F). The engine coolant temperature (ECT) sensor is between 70-125°C (158-257°F). The DTC runs continuously when the above conditions are met.
DTC: P0101 11	**Mass Air Flow (MAF) Sensor Performance High Input:** The ignition is ON. The battery voltage is greater than 8. 5 V. The engine speed is between 1 000-4 000 RPM.
DTC: P0101 12	**Mass Air Flow (MAF) Sensor Performance Low Input:** The ignition is ON. The battery voltage is greater than 8. 5 V. The engine speed is between 1 000-4 000 RPM.
DTC: P0102	**Mass Air Flow (MAF) Sensor Circuit Low Frequency:** The engine is running for greater than 1 s. The ignition 1 signal is greater than 8 V. The above conditions are met for greater than 0. 5 s. The DTC runs continuously when the above conditions are met.
DTC: P0102 00	**Mass Air Flow (MAF) Sensor Circuit Low Frequency:** The ignition is ON. The battery voltage is greater than 8. 5 V. The engine speed is between 1 000-4 000 RPM.
DTC: P0102 00	**Mass Air Flow (MAF) Sensor Circuit Low Frequency:** The engine is running for greater than 1 s. The engine speed is greater than 300 RPM. The ignition voltage is greater than 10 V. The DTCs run continuously when the above conditions are met for greater than 1 s.
DTC: P0103	**Mass Air Flow (MAF) Sensor Circuit High Frequency:** The ignition is ON, or the engine is operating. The ignition voltage is greater than 10. 5 V. DTC P0100, P0102 and P0103 run continuously once the above conditions are met for 200 mS.
DTC: P0103 00	**Mass Air Flow (MAF) Sensor Circuit High Frequency:** The ignition is ON. The battery voltage is greater than 8. 5 V. The engine speed is between 1 000-4 000 RPM.

DTC	Trouble Code Title, Conditions, Possible Causes
DTC: P0103 00	**Mass Air Flow (MAF) Sensor Circuit High Frequency:** The engine is running for greater than 1 s. The engine speed is greater than 300 RPM. The ignition voltage is greater than 10 V. The DTCs run continuously when the above conditions are met for greater than 1 s.
DTC: P0105 03	**Manifold Absolute Pressure (MAP) Sensor Circuit Low Voltage:** DTCs P0069, P0652, P2226, P2228, and P2229 are not set. The ignition is ON.
DTC: P0105 07	**Manifold Absolute Pressure (MAP) Sensor Circuit High Voltage:** DTCs P0069, P0652, P2226, P2228, and P2229 are not set. The ignition is ON.
DTC: P0105 5A	**Manifold Absolute Pressure (MAP) Sensor Circuit Not Plausible:** DTCs P0069, P0652, P2226, P2228, and P2229 are not set. The ignition is ON.
DTC: P0106	**Manifold Absolute Pressure (MAP) Sensor Performance:** DTCs P0102, P0103, P0107, P0108, P0112, P0113, P0116, P0117, P0118, P0128, P0335, P0336 are not set. The engine is running. The IAT Sensor parameter is between -20 and +125°C (-4 and 257°F). The ECT Sensor parameter is between -20 and +125°C (-4 and 257°F). This DTC runs continuously when the above conditions are met.
DTC: P0106	**Manifold Absolute Pressure (MAP) Sensor Performance:** DTCs P0016, P0102, P0103, P0107, P0108, P0112, P0113, P0116, P0117, P0118, P0128, P0335, or P0336 are not set. The engine is running. The engine coolant is between 70-125°C (158-257°F). The intake air temperature is between -7 and +125°C (+19.4 and +257°F). This DTC runs continuously when the above conditions are met.
DTC: P0106	**Manifold Absolute Pressure (MAP) Sensor Performance:** P0106 - Engine Cranking DTCs P0096, P0097, P0098, P0099, P0107, P0108, P0121, P0122, P0123, P0221, P0222, P0223, P0236, P0237, P0238, P0455, P0496, P2176, P2227, P2228, P2229 are not set. The engine OFF timer is greater than 4 seconds before cranking begins. The engine is cranking at less than 400 RPM for at least 200 ms. This DTC runs once per key cycle within the enabling conditions. P0106 - Engine Running DTCs P0010, P0011, P0013, P0014, P0107, P0108, P0121, P0122, P0123, P0221, P0222, P0223, P0236, P0237, P0238, P0341, P0342, P0343, P0366, P0367, P0368, P2088, P2089, P2090, P2091, P2227, P2228, P2229 are not set. The engine is running and the ECM has counted greater than 200 RPM. The engine speed is greater than 1,500 RPM once during the drive cycle. If start-up ECT is colder than -8°C (+18°F), then the diagnostic is disabled until the ECT reaches 30°C (86°F). The change in the MAP Sensor parameter is greater than 10 kPa once during the drive cycle. The TP Sensor parameter is less than 25 percent once during the drive cycle. This DTC runs continuously within the enabling conditions.
DTC: P0106 00	**Manifold Absolute Pressure (MAP) Sensor Performance:** P0106 00 DTCs P0107 00, P0108 00, P0111 00, P0112 00, P0113 00, P0114 00, P0116 00, P0117 00, P0118 00, P0119 00, P0128 00, P0335 00, P0336 00 are not set. The engine speed is between 400-6 500 RPM. The engine coolant temperature (ECT) sensor is between 70-125°C (158-257°F). The intake air temperature (IAT) sensor is between -20 to +125°C (-4 to +257°F). This DTC runs continuously when the above conditions are met.
DTC: P0106 00	**Manifold Absolute Pressure (MAP) Sensor Performance:** P0106 00 DTCs P0107 00, P0108 00, P0112 00, P0113 00, P0117 00, P0118 00, P0335 00, P0336 00 are not set. The engine is running greater than or equal to 400 RPM. The intake air temperature (IAT) Sensor parameter is between -7 to +125°C (19-257°F). The engine coolant temperature (ECT) Sensor parameter is between 70-125°C (158-257°F). This DTC runs continuously when the above conditions are met.
DTC: P0106 00	**Manifold Absolute Pressure (MAP) Sensor Performance:** DTCs P0102 00, P0103 00, P0107 00, P0108 00, P0112 00, P0113 00, P0117 00, P0118 00, P0335 31, or P0335 31 are not set. The engine speed is between 400-6 500 RPM. The engine coolant temperature (ECT) sensor is between 70-125°C (158-257°F). The intake air temperature (IAT) sensor is between -20 to +125°C (-4 to +257°F). The DTC runs continuously when the above conditions are met.
DTC: P0106 00	**Manifold Absolute Pressure (MAP) Sensor Performance:** P0106 00 DTCs P0107 00, P0108 00, P0111 00, P0112 00, P0113 00, P0114 00, P0116 00, P0117 00, P0118 00, P0119 00, P0128 00, P0335 00, P0336 00 are not set. The engine is running greater than or equal to 400 RPM. The intake air temperature (IAT) Sensor parameter is between -7 to +125°C (19-257°F). The engine coolant temperature (ECT) Sensor parameter is between 70-125°C (158-257°F). This DTC runs continuously when the above conditions are met.
DTC: P0107	**Manifold Absolute Pressure (MAP) Sensor Circuit Low Voltage:** P0107 DTCs P0120, P0121, P0122, P0123, P0220, P0221, P0222, P0223, P0641, or P0651 are not set. The throttle angle is greater than 0 percent when the engine speed is less than 800 RPM. OR The throttle angle is greater than 12 percent when the engine speed is more than 800 RPM. This DTC runs continuously when the above enabling conditions are met.
DTC: P0107 00	**Manifold Absolute Pressure (MAP) Sensor Circuit Low Voltage:** P0107 00 DTCs P0120 00, P0121 00, P0122 00, P0123 00, P0220 00, P0221 00, P0222 00, P0223 00 or P0641 00 are not set. The engine speed is between 400-6 500 RPM. The throttle position is greater than or equal to 0% when the engine speed is less than or equal to 1 000 RPM or The throttle position is greater than or equal to 12.5% when the engine speed is greater than 1 000 RPM. This DTC runs continuously when the above conditions are met.

DTC	Trouble Code Title, Conditions, Possible Causes
DTC: P0108	**Manifold Absolute Pressure (MAP) Sensor Circuit High Voltage:** P0108The engine has been running for a length of time that is determined by the start-up coolant temperature. The length of time ranges from 5. 5 minutes at colder than -30°C (-22°F) to 10 seconds at greater than +30°C (+86°F). DTCs P0120, P0121, P0122, P0123, P0220, P0222, P0223, or P2135 are not set. The throttle position is less than or equal to one percent when the engine speed is less than or equal to 1,200 RPM. OR The throttle position is less than or equal to 20 percent when the engine speed is greater than 1,200 RPM. The DTC runs continuously when the above conditions are met.
DTC: P0108 00	**Manifold Absolute Pressure (MAP) Sensor Circuit High Voltage:** P0108 00The engine has been running for a length of time that is determined by the start-up coolant temperature. The length of time ranges from 5. 5 min at colder than -30°C (-22°F) to 10 s at greater than 30°C (+86°F). DTCs P0120 00, P0121 00, P0122 00, P0123 00, P0220 00, P0221 00, P0222 00, P0223 00 or P0641 00 are not set. The throttle position is less than or equal to 1% when the engine speed is less than or equal to 1 200 RPM. OR The throttle position is less than or equal to 20% when the engine speed is greater than 1 200 RPM. The DTC runs continuously when the above conditions are met.
DTC: P0110 00	**Intake Air Temperature (IAT) Sensor 1 Circuit Malfunction:** The ignition is ON or the engine is running. The ignition voltage is greater than 8. 5 V. The DTCs run continuously once the above conditions are met.
DTC: P0110 03	**Intake Air Temperature (IAT) Sensor 1 Circuit Low Voltage:** The ignition is ON or the engine is running. The ignition voltage is greater than 8. 5 V. The DTCs run continuously once the above conditions are met.
DTC: P0110 07	**Intake Air Temperature (IAT) Sensor 1 Circuit High Voltage:** The ignition is ON or the engine is running. The ignition voltage is greater than 8. 5 V. The DTCs run continuously once the above conditions are met.
DTC: P0110 09	**Intake Air Temperature (IAT) Sensor 1 Circuit Too Fast Transitions:** The ignition is ON or the engine is running. The ignition voltage is greater than 8. 5 V. The DTCs run continuously once the above conditions are met.
DTC: P0110 0A	**Intake Air Temperature (IAT) Sensor 1 Circuit Too Slow Transitions:** The ignition is ON or the engine is running. The ignition voltage is greater than 8. 5 V. The DTCs run continuously once the above conditions are met.
DTC: P0110 11	**Intake Air Temperature (IAT) Sensor 1 Circuit High Input:** The ignition is ON or the engine is running. The ignition voltage is greater than 8. 5 V. The DTCs run continuously once the above conditions are met.
DTC: P0110 12	**Intake Air Temperature (IAT) Sensor 1 Circuit Low Input:** The ignition is ON or the engine is running. The ignition voltage is greater than 8. 5 V. The DTCs run continuously once the above conditions are met.
DTC: P0111	**Intake Air Temperature (IAT) Sensor Circuit Performance:** P0111 Idle Test Before the ECM can report DTC P0111 failed, DTC P0101 must run and pass. DTC P0112, P0113, P0116, P0117, P0118, P0119, P0125, or P0128 is not set. The engine coolant temperature (ECT) at engine start is less than 110°C (230°F). The ECT is warmer than 66°C (151°F). The vehicle speed is less than 5 km/h (3 mph). The MAF is less than 8 g/s. DTC P0111 runs continuously when the above conditions are met for greater than 300 s. P0111 Cruise Test Before the ECM can report DTC P0111 failed, DTC P0101 must run and pass. DTC P0112, P0113, P0116, P0117, P0118, P0119, or P0128 is not set. The ECT at engine start is less than 110°C (230°F). The vehicle speed is greater than 29 km/h (18 mph). The MAF is between 7-67 g/s. Decel fuel cut-off is not active. DTC P0111 runs continuously when the above conditions are met for greater than 300 s.
DTC: P0111	**Intake Air Temperature (IAT) Sensor Performance:** DTCs P0112, P0113, P0117, P0118 are not set. The ignition has been OFF at least 8 hours. The ignition is ON. This DTC runs once per ignition cycle when the enabling conditions are met.
DTC: P0111 00	**Intake Air Temperature (IAT) Sensor Performance:** P0111 00 DTCs P0501 00, P0116 00, P0117 00, P0118 00, P0119 00, P0112 00, P0113 00, P0114 00, P0107 00 or P0108 00 are not set. The engine run time is greater than 10 min.
DTC: P0111 00	**Intake Air Temperature (IAT) Sensor 1 Performance:** The ignition is ON or the engine is running. The ignition voltage is greater than 8. 5 V. The DTCs run continuously once the above conditions are met.
DTC: P0112	**Intake Air Temperature (IAT) Sensor Circuit Low Voltage:** P0112 DTC P0116, P0117, P0118, or P0128 are not set. The engine is running for greater than 10 s. The engine coolant temperature (ECT) is colder than 150°C (302°F). This DTC runs continuously within the enabling conditions.

DTC	Trouble Code Title, Conditions, Possible Causes
DTC: P0112 00	**Intake Air Temperature (IAT) Sensor Circuit Low Voltage:** P0112 00 DTCs P0117 00, P0118 00 or P0501 00 are not set. The engine run time is greater than 10 s. The engine coolant temperature (ECT) sensor is less than 150°C (302°F). The vehicle speed is greater than 80 km/h (50 MPH). The DTC runs continuously once the above conditions are met.
DTC: P0112 00	**Intake Air Temperature (IAT) Sensor 1 Circuit Low Voltage:** The ignition is ON or the engine is running. The ignition voltage is greater than 8. 5 V. The DTCs run continuously once the above conditions are met.
DTC: P0113	**Intake Air Temperature (IAT) Sensor Circuit High Voltage:** P0113 DTC P0101, P0102, P0103, P0116, P0117, P0118, P0128, P0502 or P0503 is not set. The engine is running for greater than 10 s. The ECT is warmer than -40°C (-40°F). This DTC runs continuously within the enabling conditions.
DTC: P0113 00	**Intake Air Temperature (IAT) Sensor Circuit High Voltage:** P0113 00 DTCs P0107 00, P0108 00, P0117 00, P0118 00 or P0501 00 are not set. The engine run time is greater than 10 s. The airflow into the engine is less than 512 g/s. The engine coolant temperature (ECT) sensor is greater than -40°C (-40°F). The vehicle speed is less than 25 km/h (40 MPH). The DTC runs continuously once the above conditions are met.
DTC: P0114	**Intake Air Temperature (IAT) Sensor Circuit Intermittent:** P0114The ignition is ON or the engine is running. This DTC runs continuously within the enabling conditions.
DTC: P0114 00	**Intake Air Temperature (IAT) Sensor Circuit Intermittent:** P0114 00 DTC P0112 00, or P0113 00 is not set. The ignition is ON, or the engine is running. The battery voltage is greater than 9 V.
DTC: P0115 03	**Engine Coolant Temperature (ECT) Sensor Circuit Low Voltage:** The ignition is ON.
DTC: P0115 07	**Engine Coolant Temperature (ECT) Sensor Circuit High Voltage:** The ignition is ON.
DTC: P0116	**Engine Coolant Temperature (ECT) Sensor Performance:** Condition 1Before the ECM can report DTC P0116 failed, DTC P0101 must run and pass. DTC P0112, P0113, P0117, P0118 or P2610 is not set. The engine run time of the previous ignition cycle was greater than 10 min. The calculated engine cool down of the previous test was greater than 50°C (120°F). The ignition was OFF for greater than 330 min after the previous engine shut down. The accumulated air mass of the previous ignition cycle was greater than 6,000 grams. The DTC runs once an ignition cycle when the above conditions are met for greater than 35 s. Condition 2Before the ECM can report DTC P0116 failed, DTC P0101 must run and pass. DTCs P0112, P0113, P0117, P0118 are not set. The ECT at the previous engine shut down is warmer than 82°C (180°F). The block heater is not detected. The ignition was OFF for greater than 330 min after the previous engine shut down. DTC runs once an ignition cycle when the above conditions are met.
DTC: P0116 00	**Engine Coolant Temperature (ECT) Sensor Performance:** DTCs P0112 00, P0113 00, P0117 00, P0118 00, and P2610 00 are not set. The ignition has been off for greater than 8 h before the engine is started. The engine is running. This DTC runs once per ignition cycle when the above conditions are met.
DTC: P0117	**Engine Coolant Temperature (ECT) Sensor Circuit Low Voltage:** P0117 DTCs P0106, P0191, P0234, P0263, P0266, P0269, P0272, P0275, P0278, P0281, P0284, P0299, P0300, P0301, P0302, P0303, P0304, P0305, P0306, P0307, P0308, P0401, P0402, P0506, P0507, P2080, P2084, P242B or P246F are not set. The ignition is ON. DTC P0117 runs continuously within the enabling condition.
DTC: P0117 00	**Engine Coolant Temperature (ECT) Sensor Circuit Low Voltage:** P0117 00 and P0118 00The ignition is ON, or the engine is running. The battery voltage is greater than 9 V. The intake air temperature (IAT) is warmer than -30°C (-22°F) or the IAT is colder than -30°C (-22°F) and the engine run time is greater than 120 s. This DTC runs continuously within the enabling conditions.
DTC: P0118	**Engine Coolant Temperature (ECT) Sensor Circuit High Voltage:** P0118 DTCs P0106, P0191, P0234, P0263, P0266, P0269, P0272, P0275, P0278, P0281, P0284, P0299, P0300, P0301, P0302, P0303, P0304, P0305, P0306, P0307, P0308, P0401, P0402, P0506, P0507, P2080, P2084, P242B or P246F are not set. The ignition is ON. DTC P0118 runs continuously within the enabling condition.
DTC: P0118 00	**Engine Coolant Temperature (ECT) Sensor Circuit High Voltage:** P0117 00 and P0118 00The ignition is ON, or the engine is running. The battery voltage is greater than 9 V. The intake air temperature (IAT) is warmer than -30°C (-22°F) or the IAT is colder than -30°C (-22°F) and the engine run time is greater than 120 s. This DTC runs continuously within the enabling conditions.
DTC: P0119	**Engine Coolant Temperature (ECT) Sensor Circuit Intermittent:** The ignition is ON. The engine speed is greater than 1 000 RPM. These DTCs run continuously once the above conditions are met.
DTC: P0119 00	**Engine Coolant Temperature (ECT) Sensor Circuit Intermittent:** P0119 00The ignition is ON, or the engine is running. The battery voltage is greater than 9 V. DTC P0117 00 or P0118 00 are not set

DTC	Trouble Code Title, Conditions, Possible Causes
DTC: P0120	**Throttle Position (TP) Sensor 1 Circuit:** P0120, P0122, P0123, P0220, P0222, and P0223 DTC P0601, P0602, P0603, P0604, P0606, P0607, P0641, or P0651 is not set. The system voltage is greater than 5. 23 V. The ignition is in the Unlock/Accessory or Run position. The DTCs run continuously when the above conditions are met.
DTC: P0121	**Throttle Position (TP) Sensor Performance:** P0121 DTCs P0102, P0103, P0107, P0108, P0112, P0113, P0117, P0118, P0116, P0128, P0122, P0123, P0220, P0221, P0222, P0223, P0335, P0336, P0401, P0405, P0601, P0602, P0603, P0604, P060D, P062F, P0606, P0652, P0653, P1404, P1516, P2101, P2119, P2135, P2176 are not set. The engine coolant temperature (ECT) is between 70-125°C (158-257°F). The engine IAT is between -7 and +100°C (+19 and +212°F). The engine speed is between 550-5,000 RPM. DTC P0121 runs continuously when the above conditions are met.
DTC: P0121 00	**Throttle Position Sensor 1 Performance:** P0121 00 DTCs P0102 00, P0103 00, P0107 00, P0108 00, P0112 00, P0113 00, P0117 00, P0118 00, P0335 00, or P0336 00 are not set. The engine speed is between 400-6 500 RPM. The engine coolant temperature (ECT) is between 70-125°C (158-257°F). The intake air temperature (IAT) is between -20 to +125°C (-4 to +257°F). The DTC runs continuously when the above conditions are met.
DTC: P0121 00	**Throttle Position Sensor 1 Performance:** DTCs P000A 00, P000B 00, P0016 00, P0017 00, P0111 00, P0112 00, P0113 00, P0114 00, P0116 00, P0117 00, P0118 00, P0119 00, P0122 00, P0123 00, P0222 00, P0223 00, P0121 00, P0221 00, P0340 00, P0341 00, P0365 00, P0366 00, P0458 00, P0459 00, P0642 00, P0643 00, P0652 00, P0653 00, P065B 00 are not set. The engine is running. DTCs P0068 00, P0642 00, P0643 00 are not set.
DTC: P0121 00	**Throttle Position Sensor Performance:** DTC P0641 00 or P0651 00 are not set. The run/crank or powertrain relay voltage is greater than 6 V and reduced power is not active. The ignition is ON or the engine is operating. DTC P0122 00, P0123 00, P0222 00, P0223 00, and P2135 00 run continuously when the above conditions are met.
DTC: P0122	**Throttle Position (TP) Sensor 1 Circuit Low Voltage:** P0120, P0122, P0123, P0220, P0222, or P0223 DTCs P0601, P0602, P0603, P0604, P0606, P060D, P062F, P0641, P0651 are not set. The system voltage is greater than 5. 23 V. The ignition is in the Unlock/Accessory or Run position. The DTCs run continuously when the above conditions are met.
DTC: P0122 00	**Throttle Position Sensor 1 Circuit Low Voltage:** DTC P0641 00 or P0651 00 are not set. The run/crank or powertrain relay voltage is greater than 6 V and reduced power is not active. The ignition is ON or the engine is operating. DTC P0122 00, P0123 00, P0222 00, P0223 00, and P2135 00 run continuously when the above conditions are met.
DTC: P0122 00	**Throttle Position Sensor 1 Circuit Low Voltage:** P0122 00, P0123 00, P0222 00, P0223 00The system voltage is more than 6 V. The ignition is in the unlock/accessory or run position. DTC P0641 00 or P06A3 00 are not set. DTCs P0122 00, P0123 00, P0222 00, P0223 00 run continuously when the above conditions are met.
DTC: P0123	**Throttle Position (TP) Sensor 1 Circuit High Voltage:** P0120, P0122, P0123, P0220, P0222, and P0223 DTC P0641 or P0651 are not set. The run/crank or powertrain relay voltage is greater than 6 V and reduced power is not active. The ignition is ON or the engine is running. DTC P0120, P0122, P0123, P0220, P0222, P0223 run continuously when the above conditions are met.
DTC: P0123 00	**Throttle Position Sensor 1 Circuit High Voltage:** P0122 00, P0123 00, P0222 00, P0223 00The system voltage is more than 6 V. The ignition is in the unlock/accessory or run position. DTC P0641 00 or P06A3 00 are not set. DTCs P0122 00, P0123 00, P0222 00, P0223 00 run continuously when the above conditions are met.
DTC: P0128	**Engine Coolant Temperature (ECT) Below Thermostat Regulating Temperature:** DTCs P0068, P0101, P0102, P0103, P0106, P0107, P0108, P0111, P0112, P0113, P0116, P0117, P0118, P0121, P0122, P0123, P0223, P0502, P0503, P1516, P2101, P2135 are not set. The start-up IAT is warmer than -7°C (+19°F). The start-up ECT is colder than 70°C (158°F), when the IAT is above 10°C (50°F). OR The start-up ECT is colder than 50°C (122°F), when the IAT is below 10°C (50°F). The engine run time is between 90 s and 22 min. The vehicle has traveled greater than 2. 4 kilometers (1. 5 miles) at greater than 8 km/h (5 mph). The accumulated airflow is between 20-75 g/s, with the minimum average airflow greater than 10 g/s. The fuel ethanol percentage is less than 87 %. This DTC runs once per ignition cycle when the above conditions are met.
DTC: P0128 00	**Engine Coolant Temperature (ECT) Below Thermostat Regulating Temperature:** DTC P0102 00, P0103 00, P0111 00, P0112 00, P0113 00, P0114 00, P0116 00, P0117 00, P0118 00, P0119 00, P0121 00, P0122 00, P0123 00, P0221 00, P0222 00, P0223 00, P0335 00, P0336 00, or P0501 00 are not set. The ignition voltage is greater than 10 V. The startup ECT is between -10 to +75°C (+14 to +167°F). The startup IAT is warmer than -10°C (+14°F). The engine run time at minimum load is less than 50%. The engine run time at maximum load is less than 90%. The engine idle time is less than 40%.

DTC	Trouble Code Title, Conditions, Possible Causes
DTC: P0130	**HO2S Circuit Closed Loop (CL) Performance Sensor 1:** P0130The engine is running. The Ignition 1 Signal parameter is between 11-18 volts. DTC P0130 runs continuously when the above conditions are met.
DTC: P0131	**HO2S Circuit Low Voltage Sensor 1:** P0131 and P0137 DTCs P0068, P0101, P0102, P0103, P0107, P0108, P0112, P0113, P0116, P0117, P0118, P0120, P0121, P0122, P0123, P0128, P0201, P0202, P0203, P0204, P0205, P0206, P0220, P0222, P0223, P0442, P0443, P0446, P0449, P0451, P0452, P0453, P0454, P0455, P0496, P1516, P2101, P2119, P2135, P2176 are not set. The system voltage is between 10-18V. The scan tool special functions are not active. The Air Fuel Ratio parameter is between 0. 9-1. 1. The TP Indicated Angle parameter is between 3-45 percent. The Loop Status parameter is closed. The ECT parameter is less than 131°C (268°F). All fuel injectors are ON. The traction control is not active.
DTC: P0131 00	**HO2S Circuit Low Voltage Sensor 1:** DTCs P0031 00, P0032 00, P0037 00, P0038 00, P0106 00, P0107 00, P0108 00, P0112 00, P0113 00, P0117 00, P0118 00, P0122 00, P0123 00, P0135 00, P0141 00, P0171 00, P0172 00, P0261 00, P0262 00, P0264 00, P0265 00, P0267 00, P0268 00, P0260 00, P0271 00, P0300 00, P0335 00, P0336 00, P0351 00, P0352 00, P0401 00, P0402 00, P0404 00, P0405 00, P0406 00, P0458 00, P0459 00, P0502 00,P0506 00, P0507 00, P0562 00, P0563 00, or P2110 00 are not set. The engine has been operating for greater than 60 s. The calculated airflow into the engine is greater than 9 g/s. The engine coolant temperature is greater than 60°C (140°F). The ignition voltage is between 11-18 V. The fuel system is in closed loop. The vehicle is not decelerating. These DTCs run continuously when the above conditions are met for 3 s.
DTC: P0132	**HO2S Circuit High Voltage Sensor 1:** P0132 DTCs P0068, P0101, P0102, P0103, P0106, P0107, P0108, P0120, P0121, P0122, P0123, P0201, P0202, P0203, P0204, P0220, P0222, P0223, P0442, P0443, P0446, P0449, P0451, P0452, P0453, P0454, P0455, P0496, P1516, P2101, P2119, P2135, P2176 are not set. The Loop Status parameter is Closed. The Ignition 1 Signal parameter is between 10-18V. The Fuel Level Sensor parameter is more than 10 percent. The Throttle Position (TP) Sensor parameter is between 0-50 percent. DTC P0132 runs continuously when the above conditions are met for 5 seconds.
DTC: P0132 00	**HO2S Circuit High Voltage Sensor 1:** DTCs P0031 00, P0032 00, P0037 00, P0038 00, P0106 00, P0107 00, P0108 00, P0112 00, P0113 00, P0117 00, P0118 00, P0122 00, P0123 00, P0135 00, P0141 00, P0171 00, P0172 00, P0261 00, P0262 00, P0264 00, P0265 00, P0267 00, P0268 00, P0260 00, P0271 00, P0300 00, P0335 00, P0336 00, P0351 00, P0352 00, P0401 00, P0402 00, P0404 00, P0405 00, P0406 00, P0458 00, P0459 00, P0502 00,P0506 00, P0507 00, P0562 00, P0563 00, or P2110 00 are not set. The engine has been operating for greater than 60 s. The calculated airflow into the engine is greater than 9 g/s. The engine coolant temperature is greater than 60°C (140°F). The ignition voltage is between 11-18 V. The fuel system is in closed loop. The vehicle is not decelerating. These DTCs run continuously when the above conditions are met for 3 s.
DTC: P0133	**HO2S Slow Response Sensor 1:** P0133 DTCs P0068, P0101, P0102, P0103, P0106, P0107, P0108, P0112, P0113, P0116, P0117, P0118, P0120, P0121, P0122, P0123, P0128, P0131, P0132, P0134, P0201, P0202, P0203, P0204, P0220, P0222, P0223, P0300, P0442, P0443, P0446, P0449, P0451, P0452, P0453, P0454, P0455, P0496, P1516, P2101, P2119, P2135, P2176 are not set. The Engine Coolant Temperature (ECT) Sensor parameter is more than 70°C (158°F). The Ignition 1 Signal parameter is between 10-18 volts. The Fuel Level Sensor parameter is more than 10 percent. The Engine Run Time parameter is more than 120 seconds. The Engine Speed parameter is between 1,000-3,500 RPM. The barometric pressure (BARO) is more than 70 kPa. The Mass Airflow (MAF) Sensor parameter is between 13-40 g/s. The intake air temperature is more than -40°C (-40°F). The Loop Status parameter is Closed. The Throttle Position (TP) Indicated Angle parameter is more than 4 percent. DTC P0133 runs once per drive cycle when the above conditions are met for 3 seconds.
DTC: P0133 00	**HO2S Slow Response Sensor 1:** DTCs P0106 00, P0107 00, P0108 00, P0112 00, P0113 00, P0116 00, P0117 00, P0118 00, P0121 00, P0122 00, P0123 00, P0131 00, P0132 00, P0134 00, P0201 00, P0202 00, P0203 00, P0204 00, P0300 00, P0315 00, P0335 00, P0336 00, P044 00, P0443 00, P0446 00, P0449 00, P0451 00, P0452 00, P0453 00, and P0496 00 are not set. The calculated airflow into the engine is between 10-45 g/s. The engine speed is between 1 100-3 500 RPM. The engine coolant temperature is greater than 60°C (140°F). The Barometric Pressure (BARO) is greater than 70 kPa (10 PSI). The ignition voltage is between 10-18 V. The fuel system is in closed loop. The evaporative emissions (EVAP) purge is less than 20%. The EVAP purge is not changing states. The engine run time is greater than 3 min. The fuel level is greater than 10%. The long term fuel trim is enabled. The HO2S heater is enabled for greater than 40 s. The vehicle is not decelerating. The vehicle is not operating in power enrichment. The DTCs run once per ignition cycle when the above conditions are met for greater than 1 s.
DTC: P0134	**HO2S Circuit Insufficient Activity Sensor 1:** P0134 DTCs P0030, P0053, P0068, P0101, P0102, P0103, P0107, P0108, P0112, P0113, P0116, P0117, P0118, P0120, P0121, P0122, P0123, P0128, P0201, P0202, P0203, P0204, P0205, P0206, P0220, P0222, P0223, P0442, P0443, P0446, P0449, P0451, P0452, P0453, P0454, P0455, P0496, P1516, P2101, P2119, P2135, P2176 are not set. The system voltage is between 10-18 volts. The scan tool special functions are not active. The HO2S Sensor 1 Heater command parameter is ON. The Fuel Alcohol Content parameter is less than 87 percent for 3. 9L (RPO LGD), VIN code M, E85 compatible engines only. The Engine Run Time parameter is more than 2 minutes.

DTC	Trouble Code Title, Conditions, Possible Causes
DTC: P0134 00	**HO2S Circuit Insufficient Activity Sensor 1:** DTCs P0031 00, P0032 00, P0037 00, P0038 00, P0106 00, P0107 00, P0108 00, P0112 00, P0113 00, P0117 00, P0118 00, P0122 00, P0123 00, P0135 00, P0141 00, P0171 00, P0172 00, P0261 00, P0262 00, P0264 00, P0265 00, P0267 00, P0268 00, P0260 00, P0271 00, P0300 00, P0335 00, P0336 00, P0351 00, P0352 00, P0401 00, P0402 00, P0404 00, P0405 00, P0406 00, P0458 00, P0459 00, P0502 00,P0506 00, P0507 00, P0562 00, P0563 00, or P2110 00 are not set. The engine has been operating for greater than 60 s. The calculated airflow into the engine is greater than 9 g/s. The engine coolant temperature is greater than 60°C (140°F). The ignition voltage is between 11-18 V. The fuel system is in closed loop. The vehicle is not decelerating. These DTCs run continuously when the above conditions are met for 3 s.
DTC: P0135	**HO2S Heater Performance Sensor 1:** P0135 DTCs P0030, P0053, P0068, P0101, P0102, P0103, P0106, P0107, P0108, P0112, P0113, P0116, P0117, P0118, P0120, P0121, P0122, P0123, P0128, P0135, P0141, P0201, P0202, P0203, P0204, P0205, P0206, P0220, P0222, P0223, P0442, P0443, P0446, P0449, P0451, P0452, P0453, P0454, P0455, P0496, P1516, P2101, P2135, P2176 are not set. The system voltage is between 10-18V. The scan tool special functions are not active. The Engine Run Time parameter is more than 180 seconds. The ECT Sensor parameter is at least 65°C (149°F). The MAF Sensor parameter is between 5-30 g/s. The Engine Speed parameter is between 500-3,000 RPM. The above conditions have been met for more than 6 seconds.
DTC: P0135 00	**HO2S Heater Performance Sensor 1:** P0030 00, P0031 00, and P0030 02The ignition is ON. The ignition signal parameter is more than 9 V. DTC P0030 00, P0031 00, and P0032 00 run continuously when the above conditions are met for 1 s. P0135 00 DTCs P0030 00, P0031 00, P0032 00, are not set. The ignition is ON. The ignition signal parameter is more than 9 V. DTC P0135 00 runs continuously.
DTC: P0136 00	**HO2S Circuit Sensor 2:** P0136 00 DTC P0031 00, P0032 00, P0037 00, P0038 00, P0112 00, P0113 00, P0117 00, P0118 00, P0121 00, P0122 00, P0123 00, P0125 00, P0171 00, P0172 00, P0300 00 - P0304 00, P0335 00, P0340 00, P0341 00, P0455 00, P0456 00, P0500 00, P2A00 00 are not set. The battery voltage is greater than 11 V. The engine coolant temperature (ECT) is greater than or equal to 75°C (167°F). The engine speed is between 1600-4000 RPM. The engine is operating in closed loop fuel control. DTC P0136 00 runs once per drive cycle when the above conditions are met for 2 s.
DTC: P0137	**HO2S Circuit Low Voltage Sensor 2:** P0131 and P0137 DTCs P0068, P0101, P0102, P0103, P0107, P0108, P0112, P0113, P0116, P0117, P0118, P0120, P0121, P0122, P0123, P0128, P0201, P0202, P0203, P0204, P0205, P0206, P0220, P0222, P0223, P0442, P0443, P0446, P0449, P0451, P0452, P0453, P0454, P0455, P0496, P1516, P2101, P2119, P2135, P2176 are not set. The system voltage is between 10-18V. The scan tool special functions are not active. The Air Fuel Ratio parameter is between 0. 9-1. 1. The TP Indicated Angle parameter is between 3-45 percent. The Loop Status parameter is closed. The ECT parameter is less than 131°C (268°F). All fuel injectors are ON. The traction control is not active.
DTC: P0137 00	**HO2S Circuit Low Voltage Sensor 2:** DTCs P0031 00, P0032 00, P0037 00, P0038 00, P0106 00, P0107 00, P0108 00, P0112 00, P0113 00, P0117 00, P0118 00, P0122 00, P0123 00, P0135 00, P0141 00, P0171 00, P0172 00, P0261 00, P0262 00, P0264 00, P0265 00, P0267 00, P0268 00, P0260 00, P0271 00, P0300 00, P0335 00, P0336 00, P0351 00, P0352 00, P0401 00, P0402 00, P0404 00, P0405 00, P0406 00, P0458 00, P0459 00, P0502 00,P0506 00, P0507 00, P0562 00, P0563 00, or P2110 00 are not set. The engine has been operating for greater than 60 s. The calculated airflow into the engine is greater than 2 g/s. The engine coolant temperature is greater than 60°C (140°F). The ignition voltage is between 11-18 V. The fuel system is in closed loop. The vehicle is not decelerating. These DTCs run continuously when the above conditions are met for 3 s.
DTC: P0138	**HO2S Circuit High Voltage Bank 1 Sensor 2:** P0132, P0138, P0152, or P0158 DTCs P0068, P0101, P0102, P0103, P0106, P0107, P0108, P0112, P0113, P0116, P0117, P0118, P0120, P0121, P0122, P0123, P0128, P0201, P0202, P0203, P0204, P0205, P0206, P0207, P0208, P0220, P0222, P0223, P0442, P0443, P0446, P0449, P0455, P0496, P1516, P2101, P2119, P2135, P2176 are not set. The engine is operating in Closed Loop. The Ignition 1 voltage is between 10-32 V. The fuel level is greater than 10 %. The throttle position (TP) is between 0-70 %. The DTCs run continuously when the above conditions are met for 3 s.
DTC: P0138 00	**HO2S Circuit High Voltage Sensor 2:** DTCs P0031 00, P0032 00, P0037 00, P0038 00, P0106 00, P0107 00, P0108 00, P0112 00, P0113 00, P0117 00, P0118 00, P0122 00, P0123 00, P0135 00, P0141 00, P0171 00, P0172 00, P0261 00, P0262 00, P0264 00, P0265 00, P0267 00, P0268 00, P0260 00, P0271 00, P0300 00, P0335 00, P0336 00, P0351 00, P0352 00, P0401 00, P0402 00, P0404 00, P0405 00, P0406 00, P0458 00, P0459 00, P0502 00,P0506 00, P0507 00, P0562 00, P0563 00, or P2110 00 are not set. The engine has been operating for greater than 60 s. The calculated airflow into the engine is greater than 2 g/s. The engine coolant temperature is greater than 60°C (140°F). The ignition voltage is between 11-18 V. The fuel system is in closed loop. The vehicle is not decelerating. These DTCs run continuously when the above conditions are met for 3 s.

DTC	Trouble Code Title, Conditions, Possible Causes
DTC: P0139 00	**HO2S Slow Response Sensor 2:** P0139 00 DTCs P000A 00, P000B 00, P0010 00, P0011 00, P0013 00, P0014 00, P0016 00, P0017 00, P0107 00, P0108 00, P0117 00, P0118 00, P0119 00, P0121 00, P0122 00, P0123 00, P0136 00, P0137 00, P0138 00, P0141 00, P0171 00, P0172 00, P0201 00, P0202 00, P0203 00, P0204 00, P0221 00, P0222 00, P0223 00, P0261 00, P0262 00, P0264 00, P0265 00, P0267 00, P0268 00, P0270 00, P0271 00, P0300 00, P030 001, P0302 00, P0303 00, P0304 00, P0313 00, P0335 00, P0336 00, P0340 00, P0341 00, P0365 00, P0366 00, P0443 00, P0458 00, P0459 00, P0496 00, P0501 00, P2088 00, P2089 00, P2090 00, P2091 00, P2100 00, P2101 00, P2176 00, P2270 00, P2271 00, P2A01 00 are not set. The ignition is ON. The engine coolant is hotter than 60°C (140°F). The heated oxygen sensor (HO2S) 2 signal voltage is more than 552 mV. The vehicle speed is between 19-31 km/h (12-93 MPH). DTC P0140 00 runs continuously when the above conditions are met for 60 min.
DTC: P013A	**HO2S Slow Response Rich to Lean Bank 1 Sensor 2:** P013A P013C, P013E, or P014ABefore the ECM can report DTC P013A, or P013C failed, DTCs P013E, P014A, P2270, and P2272 must run and pass. Before the ECM can report DTC P013E, or P014A failed, DTCs P2270 and P2272 must run and pass. DTCs P0030, P0036, P0053, P0054, P0101, P0102, P0103, P0106, P0107, P0108, P0120, P0121, P0122, P0123, P0131, P0132, P0133, P0134, P0135, P0137, P0138, P013A, P013B, P013E, P013F, P0140, P0141, P0171, P0172, P0201, P0202, P0203, P0204, P0220, P0222, P0223, P0300, P0442, P0443, P0446, P0449, P0455, P0496, P1133, P1174, P1516, P2101, P2119, P2135, P2176, P2270, P2271, P2A00 are not set. The ignition 1 voltage is between 10-32 V. The learned heater resistance is valid. The fuel level is greater than 10%. The engine run time is equal to or greater than 5 minutes. The accelerator pedal (APP) is steady. The torque converter clutch (TCC) is applied. The DTCs run once per ignition cycle, during decel fuel cut-off (DFCO), when the above conditions are met.
DTC: P013A 00	**HO2S Slow Response Rich to Lean Sensor 2:** P013A 00 DTCs P0030 00, P0036 00, P0053 00, P0054 00, P0101 00, P0102 00, P0103 00, P0106 00, P0107 00, P0108 00, P0120 00, P0121 00, P0122 00, P0123 00, P0131 00, P0132 00, P0133 00, P0134 00, P0135 00, P0137 00, P0138 00, P013A 00, P013B 00, P013E 00, P013F 00, P0140 00, P0141 00, P0171 00, P0172 00, P0201 00, P0202 00, P0203 00, P0204 00, P0220 00, P0222 00, P0223 00, P0300 00, P0443 00, P1133 00, P1516 00, P2101 00, P2119 00, P2135 00, P2176 00, P2270 00, P2271 00, P2A00 00 are not set. The system voltage is between 10-18 V. The fuel level is more than 10%. Engine run time is equal to or more than 40 s. The engine coolant is hotter than 50. 25°C (122. 45°F). The Deceleration fuel cut-off is active. The accelerator pedal position (APP) is stable. The torque converter clutch (TCC) is locked. DTC P013E 00 and P2270 00 have run and passed. DTC P013A 00 runs once per trip.
DTC: P013B	**HO2S Slow Response Lean to Rich Bank 1 Sensor 2:** P013B P013D, P013F, or P014BBefore the ECM can report DTC P013B, or P013D failed, DTCs P013A, P013C, P013E, P013F, P014A, P014B, P2270, P2271, P2272, and P2273 must run and pass. Before the ECM can report DTC P013F, or P014B failed, DTCs P013A, P013C, P013E, P014A, P2270, P2271, P2272, and P2273 must run and pass. DTCs P0030, P0036, P0053, P0054, P0101, P0102, P0103, P0106, P0107, P0108, P0120, P0121, P0122, P0123, P0131, P0132, P0133, P0134, P0135, P0137, P0138, P013A, P013B, P013E, P013F, P0140, P0141, P0171, P0172, P0201, P0202, P0203, P0204, P0220, P0222, P0223, P0300, P0442, P0443, P0446, P0449, P0455, P0496, P1133, P1174, P1516, P2101, P2119, P2135, P2176, P2270, P2271, P2A00 are not set. The ignition 1 voltage is between 10-32 V. The learned heater resistance is valid. The fuel level is greater than 10 %. The engine run time is equal to or greater than 5 min. The DTCs run once per ignition cycle when the above conditions are met.
DTC: P013B 00	**HO2S Slow Response Lean to Rich Sensor 2:** P013B 00 and P013F 00 DTCs P0068 00, P0101 00, P0102 00, P0103 00, P0106 00, P0107 00, P0108 00, P0112 00, P0113 00, P0116 00, P0117 00, P0118 00, P0121 00, P0122 00, P0123 00, P0128 00, P013B 00, P013E 00, P013F 00, P0171 00, P0172 00, P0201 00, P0202 00, P0203 00, P0204 00, P0222 00, P0223 00, P0300 00, P1516 00, P2101 00, P2119 00, P2135 00, P2176 00, P2270 00, P2271 00 are not set. The system voltage is between 10-32 V. The fuel level is more than 10%. Engine run time is equal to or more than 40 s. DTCs P013A 00, P013E 00, P013F 00, P2270 00, and P2271 00 have run and passed. DTCs P013B 00 and P013F 00 run once per trip.
DTC: P013C	**HO2S Slow Response Rich to Lean Bank 2 Sensor 2:** P013A P013C, P013E, or P014ABefore the ECM can report DTC P013A, or P013C failed, DTCs P013E, P014A, P2270, and P2272 must run and pass. Before the ECM can report DTC P013E, or P014A failed, DTCs P2270 and P2272 must run and pass. DTCs P0030, P0036, P0053, P0054, P0101, P0102, P0103, P0106, P0107, P0108, P0120, P0121, P0122, P0123, P0131, P0132, P0133, P0134, P0135, P0137, P0138, P013A, P013B, P013E, P013F, P0140, P0141, P0171, P0172, P0201, P0202, P0203, P0204, P0220, P0222, P0223, P0300, P0442, P0443, P0446, P0449, P0455, P0496, P1133, P1174, P1516, P2101, P2119, P2135, P2176, P2270, P2271, P2A00 are not set. The ignition 1 voltage is between 10-32 V. The learned heater resistance is valid. The fuel level is greater than 10%. The engine run time is equal to or greater than 5 minutes. The accelerator pedal (APP) is steady. The torque converter clutch (TCC) is applied. The DTCs run once per ignition cycle, during decel fuel cut-off (DFCO), when the above conditions are met.
DTC: P013D	**HO2S Slow Response Lean to Rich Bank 2 Sensor 2:** P013B P013D, P013F, or P014BBefore the ECM can report DTC P013B, or P013D failed, DTCs P013A, P013C, P013E, P013F, P014A, P014B, P2270, P2271, P2272, and P2273 must run and pass. Before the ECM can report DTC P013F, or P014B failed, DTCs P013A, P013C, P013E, P014A, P2270, P2271, P2272, and P2273 must run and pass. DTCs P0030, P0036, P0053, P0054, P0101, P0102, P0103, P0106, P0107, P0108, P0120, P0121, P0122, P0123, P0131, P0132, P0133, P0134, P0135, P0137, P0138, P013A, P013B, P013E, P013F, P0140, P0141, P0171, P0172, P0201, P0202, P0203, P0204, P0220, P0222, P0223, P0300, P0442, P0443, P0446, P0449, P0455, P0496, P1133, P1174, P1516, P2101, P2119, P2135, P2176, P2270, P2271, P2A00 are not set. The ignition 1 voltage is between 10-32 V. The learned heater resistance is valid. The fuel level is greater than 10%. The engine run time is equal to or greater than 5 minutes. The DTCs run once per ignition cycle when the above conditions are met.

DTC	Trouble Code Title, Conditions, Possible Causes
DTC: P013E	**HO2S Delayed Response Rich to Lean Bank 1 Sensor 2:** P013A P013C, P013E, or P014ABefore the ECM can report DTC P013A, or P013C failed, DTCs P013E, P014A, P2270, and P2272 must run and pass. Before the ECM can report DTC P013E, or P014A failed, DTCs P2270 and P2272 must run and pass. DTCs P0030, P0036, P0053, P0054, P0101, P0102, P0103, P0106, P0107, P0108, P0120, P0121, P0122, P0123, P0131, P0132, P0133, P0134, P0135, P0137, P0138, P013A, P013B, P013E, P013F, P0140, P0141, P0171, P0172, P0201, P0202, P0203, P0204, P0220, P0222, P0223, P0300, P0442, P0443, P0446, P0449, P0455, P0496, P1133, P1174, P1516, P2101, P2119, P2135, P2176, P2270, P2271, P2A00 are not set. The ignition 1 voltage is between 10-32 V. The learned heater resistance is valid. The fuel level is greater than 10 %. The engine run time is equal to or greater than 5 min. The accelerator pedal (APP) is steady. The torque converter clutch (TCC) is applied. The DTCs run once per ignition cycle, during decel fuel cut-off (DFCO), when the above conditions are met.
DTC: P013E 00	**HO2S Delayed Response Rich to Lean Sensor 2:** P013E 00 DTCs P0030 00, P0036 00, P0053 00, P0054 00, P0101 00, P0102 00, P0103 00, P0106 00, P0107 00, P0108 00, P0120 00, P0121 00, P0122 00, P0123 00, P0131 00, P0132 00, P0133 00, P0134 00, P0135 00, P0137 00, P0138 00, P013A 00, P013B 00, P013E 00, P013F 00, P0140 00, P0141 00, P0171 00, P0172 00, P0201 00, P0202 00, P0203 00, P0204 00, P0220 00, P0222 00, P0223 00, P0300 00, P0443 00, P1133 00, P1516 00, P2101 00, P2119 00, P2135 00, P2176 00, P2270 00, P2271 00, P2A00 00 are not set. The system voltage is between 10-18 V. The fuel level is more than 10%. Engine run time is equal to or more than 40 s. The engine coolant is hotter than 50. 25°C (122. 45°F). The Deceleration fuel cut-off is active. The accelerator pedal position (APP) is stable. The torque converter clutch (TCC) is locked. DTCs P2270 00 has run and passed. DTC P013E 00 runs once per trip.
DTC: P013F	**HO2S Delayed Response Lean to Rich Bank 1 Sensor 2:** P013B P013D, P013F, or P014BBefore the ECM can report DTC P013B, or P013D failed, DTCs P013A, P013C, P013E, P013F, P014A, P014B, P2270, P2271, P2272, and P2273 must run and pass. Before the ECM can report DTC P013F, or P014B failed, DTCs P013A, P013C, P013E, P014A, P2270, P2271, P2272, and P2273 must run and pass. DTCs P0030, P0036, P0053, P0054, P0101, P0102, P0103, P0106, P0107, P0108, P0120, P0121, P0122, P0123, P0131, P0132, P0133, P0134, P0135, P0137, P0138, P013A, P013B, P013E, P013F, P0140, P0141, P0171, P0172, P0201, P0202, P0203, P0204, P0220, P0222, P0223, P0300, P0442, P0443, P0446, P0449, P0455, P0496, P1133, P1174, P1516, P2101, P2119, P2135, P2176, P2270, P2271, P2A00 are not set. The ignition 1 voltage is between 10-32 V. The learned heater resistance is valid. The fuel level is greater than 10 %. The engine run time is equal to or greater than 5 min. The DTCs run once per ignition cycle when the above conditions are met.
DTC: P013F 00	**HO2S Delayed Response Lean to Rich Sensor 2:** P013F 00 DTCs P0030 00, P0036 00, P0053 00, P0054 00, P0101 00, P0102 00, P0103 00, P0106 00, P0107 00, P0108 00, P0120 00, P0121 00, P0122 00, P0123 00, P0131 00, P0132 00, P0133 00, P0134 00, P0135 00, P0137 00, P0138 00, P013A 00, P013B 00, P013E 00, P013F 00, P0140 00, P0141 00, P0171 00, P0172 00, P0201 00, P0202 00, P0203 00, P0204 00, P0220 00, P0222 00, P0223 00, P0300 00, P0443 00, P1133 00, P1516 00, P2101 00, P2119 00, P2135 00, P2176 00, P2270 00, P2271 00, P2A00 00 are not set. The system voltage is between 10-18 V. The fuel level is more than 10%. Engine run time is equal to or more than 40 s. The DTCs P013A 00, P013E 00, P2270 00, and P2271 00 have run and passed. DTC P013F 00 runs once per trip.
DTC: P0140	**HO2S Circuit Insufficient Activity Bank 1 Sensor 2:** DTCs P0068, P0101, P0102, P0103, P0106, P0107, P0108, P0112, P0113, P0116, P0117, P0118, P0120, P0121, P0122, P0123, P0128, P0201, P0202, P0203, P0204, P0205, P0206, P0207, P0208, P0220, P0222, P0223, P0442, P0443, P0446, P0449, P0455, P0496, P1516, P2101, P2119, P2135, P2176 are not set. The ignition 1 voltage is between 10-32 V. The engine run time is greater than 300 s. The fuel system is in Closed Loop. The DTCs run continuously when the above conditions are met.
DTC: P0140	**HO2S Circuit Insufficient Activity Sensor 2:** P0140 DTCs P0068, P0101, P0102, P0103, P0120, P0121, P0122, P0123, P0220, P0222, P0223, P1516, P2101, P2119, P2135, P2176 are not set. The ECT Sensor parameter is more than 70°C (158°F). The Ignition 1 Signal parameter is between 10-18 volts. The Engine Run Time parameter is more than 200 seconds. The Loop Status parameter is closed. DTC P0140 runs once per drive cycle when the above conditions are met.
DTC: P0140	**HO2S Circuit Insufficient Activity Sensor 2:** P0140 - Regular Test DTCs P0036, P0054, P0068, P0101, P0102, P0103, P0107, P0108, P0112, P0113, P0116, P0117, P0118, P0120, P0121, P0122, P0123, P0128, P0201, P0202, P0203, P0204, P0205, P0206, P0220, P0222, P0223, P0442, P0443, P0446, P0449, P0451, P0452, P0453, P0454, P0455, P0496, P1516, P2101, P2119, P2135, P2176 are not set. The system voltage is between 10-18 volts. The scan tool special functions are not active. The Engine Run Time parameter is more than 2 minutes. The TP Indicated Angle parameter has changed more than 3 percent at least 1 time. The Fuel Alcohol Content parameter is more than 87 percent for 3. 9L (RPO LGD), VIN code M, E85 compatible engines only. The Loop Status parameter is closed. P0140 - Fast Pass Test DTCs P0036, P0054, P0068, P0101, P0102, P0103, P0107, P0108, P0112, P0113, P0116, P0117, P0118, P0120, P0121, P0122, P0123, P0128, P0201, P0202, P0203, P0204, P0205, P0206, P0220, P0222, P0223, P0442, P0443, P0446, P0449, P0451, P0452, P0453, P0454, P0455, P0496, P1516, P2101, P2119, P2135, P2176 are not set. The system voltage is between 10-18 volts. The Fuel Alcohol Content parameter is more than 87 percent for 3. 9L (RPO LGD), VIN code M, E85 compatible engines only. The scan tool special functions are not active. The Engine Run Time parameter is less than 90 seconds.

DTC	Trouble Code Title, Conditions, Possible Causes
DTC: P0140 00	**HO2S Circuit Insufficient Activity Sensor 2:** DTCs P0031 00, P0032 00, P0037 00, P0038 00, P0106 00, P0107 00, P0108 00, P0112 00, P0113 00, P0117 00, P0118 00, P0122 00, P0123 00, P0135 00, P0141 00, P0171 00, P0172 00, P0261 00, P0262 00, P0264 00, P0265 00, P0267 00, P0268 00, P0260 00, P0271 00, P0300 00, P0335 00, P0336 00, P0351 00, P0352 00, P0401 00, P0402 00, P0404 00, P0405 00, P0406 00, P0458 00, P0459 00, P0502 00, P0506 00, P0507 00, P0562 00, P0563 00, or P2110 00 are not set. The engine has been operating for greater than 60 s. The calculated airflow into the engine is greater than 2 g/s. The engine coolant temperature is greater than 60°C (140°F). The ignition voltage is between 11-18 V. The fuel system is in closed loop. The vehicle is not decelerating. These DTCs run continuously when the above conditions are met for 3 s.
DTC: P0140 00	**HO2S Circuit Insufficient Activity Sensor 2:** P0140 00 DTCs P000A 00, P000B 00, P0010 00, P0011 00, P0013 00, P0014 00, P0016 00, P0017 00, P0030 00, P0031 00, P0032 00, P0107 00, P0108 00, P0117 00, P0118 00, P0119 00, P0121 00, P0122 00, P0123 00, P0130 00, P0131 00, P0132 00, P0133 00, P0137 00, P0138 00, P0139 00, P0141 00, P0171 00, P0172 00, P0221 00, P0222 00, P0223 00, P0300 00, P0301 00, P0302 00, P0303 00, P0304 00, P0313 00, P0335 00, P0336 00, P0340 00, P0341 00, P0365 00, P0366 00, P0443 00, P0458 00, P0459 00, P0496 00, P2088 00, P2089 00, P2090 00, P2091 00, P2176 00, P2270 00, P2271 00, P2297 00, P2A01 00 are not set. The engine has been running for more than 5 min. The engine coolant is greater than 75°C (167°F). The engine run time parameter is less than 90 s.
DTC: P0141	**HO2S Heater Performance Sensor 2:** P0141 DTCs P0036, P0054, P0068, P0101, P0102, P0103, P0107, P0108, P0112, P0113, P0116, P0117, P0118, P0120, P0121, P0122, P0123, P0128, P0201, P0202, P0203, P0204, P0205, P0206, P0220, P0222, P0223, P0442, P0443, P0446, P0449, P0451, P0452, P0453, P0454, P0455, P0496, P1516, P2101, P2135, P2176 are not set. The system voltage is between 10-18V. The scan tool special functions are not active. The Engine Run Time parameter is at least 180 seconds. The ECT parameter is at least 65°C (149°F). The MAF Sensor parameter is between 5-30 g/s. The Engine Speed parameter is between 500-3,000 RPM. The above conditions have been met for more than 6 seconds.
DTC: P0141	**HO2S Heater Performance Bank 1 Sensor 2:** P0135, P0141, or P0155 DTCs P0068, P0101, P0102, P0103, P0106, P0107, P0108, P0112, P0113, P0116, P0117, P0118, P0120, P0121, P0122, P0123, P0125, P0128, P0201, P0202, P0203, P0204, P0220, P0222, P0223, P0442, P0443, P0446, P0449, P0455, P0496, P1101, P1516, P2101, P2119, P2135, P2176 are not set. The engine coolant temperature (ECT) is greater than 60°C (140°F). The ignition 1 voltage is between 10-18 volts. The mass air flow (MAF) is between 5-45 g/s. The engine run time is greater than 180 seconds. The engine speed is between 500-3,000 RPM. The DTCs run twice per drive cycle when the above conditions are met for 2 seconds.
DTC: P0141 00	**HO2S Heater Performance Sensor 2:** P0141 00 Heater Resistance Test DTCs P0036 00, P0037 00, or P0038 00, are not set. The ignition is ON. The Ignition Signal parameter is more than 9 V. DTC P0141 00 runs continuously.
DTC: P0141 00	**HO2S Heater Performance Sensor 2:** P0141 00 DTCs P0037 00, or P0038 00, are not set. The engine is running. The ignition voltage is between 11-18 V. The engine is not in deceleration fuel cut-off. DTC P0141 00 runs continuously.
DTC: P014A	**HO2S Delayed Response Rich to Lean Bank 2 Sensor 2:** P014A DTCs P0030, P0036, P0053, P0054, P0101, P0102, P0103, P0106, P0107, P0108, P0120, P0121, P0122, P0123, P0131, P0132, P0133, P0134, P0135, P0137, P0138, P013A, P013B, P013E, P013F, P0140, P0141, P0171, P0172, P0201, P0202, P0203, P0204, P0220, P0222, P0223, P0300, P0442, P0443, P0446, P0449, P0455, P0496, P1133, P1174, P1516, P2101, P2119, P2135, P2176, P2270, P2271, P2A00, P2A03 are not set. The system voltage is between 10-18 volts. The learned heater resistance is valid. The fuel level is more than 10 percent. The engine run time is equal to or more than 5 minutes. THENDFCO is active. The accelerator pedal position (APP) is stable. The torque converter clutch (TCC) is locked. DTCs P2270 and P2272 have run and passed. This DTC runs once per trip.
DTC: P014B	**HO2S Delayed Response Lean to Rich Bank 2 Sensor 2:** P013B P013D, P013F, or P014B Before the ECM can report DTC P013B, or P013D failed, DTCs P013A, P013C, P013E, P013F, P014A, P014B, P2270, P2271, P2272, and P2273 must run and pass. Before the ECM can report DTC P013F, or P014B failed, DTCs P013A, P013C, P013E, P014A, P2270, P2271, P2272, and P2273 must run and pass. DTCs P0030, P0036, P0053, P0054, P0101, P0102, P0103, P0106, P0107, P0108, P0120, P0121, P0122, P0123, P0131, P0132, P0133, P0134, P0135, P0137, P0138, P013A, P013B, P013E, P013F, P0140, P0141, P0171, P0172, P0201, P0202, P0203, P0204, P0220, P0222, P0223, P0300, P0442, P0443, P0446, P0449, P0455, P0496, P1133, P1174, P1516, P2101, P2119, P2135, P2176, P2270, P2271, P2A00 are not set. The ignition 1 voltage is between 10-32 V. The learned heater resistance is valid. The fuel level is greater than 10 %. The engine run time is equal to or greater than 5 min. The DTCs run once per ignition cycle when the above conditions are met.
DTC: P0151	**HO2S Circuit Low Voltage Bank 2 Sensor 1:** P0131, P0137, P0151, or P0157 DTCs P0068, P0101, P0102, P0103, P0106, P0107, P0108, P0112, P0113, P0116, P0117, P0118, P0120, P0121, P0122, P0123, P0128, P0201, P0202, P0203, P0204, P0205, P0206, P0207, P0208, P0220, P0222, P0223, P0442, P0443, P0446, P0449, P0455, P0496, P1516, P2101, P2119, P2135, P2176 are not set. The engine is operating in Closed Loop. The Ignition 1 voltage is between 10-32 V. The fuel level is greater than 10 %. The throttle position (TP) is between 3-70 %. The DTCs run continuously when the above conditions are met for 2 s.

DTC	Trouble Code Title, Conditions, Possible Causes
DTC: P0152	**HO2S Circuit High Voltage Bank 2 Sensor 1:** P0152 DTCs P0068, P0101, P0102, P0103, P0106, P0107, P0108, P0112, P0113, P0116, P0117, P0118, P0120, P0121, P0122, P0123, P0128, P0201, P0202, P0203, P0204, P0205, P0206, P0207, P0208, P0220, P0222, P0223, P0442, P0443, P0446, P0449, P0455, P0496, P1516, P2101, P2119, P2135, P2176 are not set. The Loop Status parameter is Closed. The Ignition 1 Signal parameter is between 10-18 volts. The Fuel Level Sensor parameter is more than 10 percent. The Throttle Position (TP) Sensor parameter is between 0-70 percent. DTC P0152 runs continuously when the above conditions are met.
DTC: P0153	**HO2S Slow Response Bank 2 Sensor 1:** P0133, P0153, P1133, or P1153 DTCs P0068, P0101, P0102, P0103, P0106, P0107, P0108, P0112, P0113, P0116, P0117, P0118, P0120, P0121, P0122, P0123, P0128, P0201, P0202, P0203, P0204, P0205, P0206, P0207, P0208, P0220, P0222, P0223, P0442, P0443, P0446, P0449, P0455, P0496, P1516, P2101, P2119, P2135, P2176 are not set. The engine coolant temperature (ECT) is greater than 71°C (159°F). The intake air temperature (IAT) is warmer than -40°C (-40°F)The ignition 1 voltage is between 10-32 V. The fuel level is greater than 10 %. The engine run time is greater than 60 s. The engine speed is between 1,000-3,000 RPM. The barometric (BARO) pressure is greater than 70 kPa. The mass airflow (MAF) is between 15-55 g/s. The fuel system is in Closed Loop. The throttle position (TP) is greater than 5 %. The DTCs run once per drive cycle when the above conditions are met.
DTC: P0153	**HO2S Slow Response Bank 2 Sensor 1:** P0153 DTCs P0068, P0101, P0102, P0103, P0106, P0107, P0108, P0112, P0113, P0116, P0117, P0118, P0120, P0121, P0122, P0123, P0128, P0201, P0202, P0203, P0204, P0205, P0206, P0207, P0208, P0220, P0222, P0223, P0442, P0443, P0446, P0449, P0455, P0496, P1516, P2101, P2119, P2135, P2176 are not set. The Engine Coolant Temperature (ECT) Sensor parameter is more than 60°C (140°F). The Intake Air Temperature (IAT) Sensor parameter is more than -40°C (-40°F). The Ignition 1 Signal parameter is between 10-18 volts. The Fuel Level Sensor parameter is more than 10 percent. The Engine Run Time parameter is more than 160 seconds. The Engine Speed parameter is between 1,200-3,000 RPM. The Barometric (BARO) Pressure parameter is more than 70 kPa. The Mass Airflow (MAF) Sensor parameter is between 20-55 g/s. The Loop Status parameter is Closed. The Throttle Position (TP) Indicated Angle parameter is more than 5 percent. DTC P0153 runs once per drive cycle when the above conditions are met for 1 second.
DTC: P0154	**HO2S Circuit Insufficient Activity Bank 2 Sensor 1:** DTCs P0068, P0101, P0102, P0103, P0106, P0107, P0108, P0112, P0113, P0116, P0117, P0118, P0120, P0121, P0122, P0123, P0128, P0201, P0202, P0203, P0204, P0205, P0206, P0207, P0208, P0220, P0222, P0223, P0442, P0443, P0446, P0449, P0455, P0496, P1516, P2101, P2119, P2135, or P2176 are not set. The ignition 1 voltage is between 10-18 volts. The engine run time is greater than 101 seconds. The fuel system is in Closed Loop. The DTCs run continuously when the above conditions are met.
DTC: P0155	**HO2S Heater Performance Bank 2 Sensor 1:** P0135, P0141, or P0155 DTCs P0068, P0101, P0102, P0103, P0106, P0107, P0108, P0112, P0113, P0116, P0117, P0118, P0120, P0121, P0122, P0123, P0125, P0128, P0201, P0202, P0203, P0204, P0220, P0222, P0223, P0442, P0443, P0446, P0449, P0455, P0496, P1101, P1516, P2101, P2119, P2135, P2176 are not set. The engine coolant temperature (ECT) is greater than 60°C (140°F). The ignition 1 voltage is between 10-18 volts. The mass air flow (MAF) is between 5-45 g/s. The engine run time is greater than 180 seconds. The engine speed is between 500-3,000 RPM. The DTCs run twice per drive cycle when the above conditions are met for 2 seconds.
DTC: P0157	**HO2S Circuit Low Voltage Bank 2 Sensor 2:** P0131, P0137, P0151, or P0157 DTCs P0068, P0101, P0102, P0103, P0106, P0107, P0108, P0112, P0113, P0116, P0117, P0118, P0120, P0121, P0122, P0123, P0128, P0201, P0202, P0203, P0204, P0205, P0206, P0207, P0208, P0220, P0222, P0223, P0442, P0443, P0446, P0449, P0455, P0496, P1516, P2101, P2119, P2135, P2176 are not set. The engine is operating in Closed Loop. The Ignition 1 voltage is between 10-32 V. The fuel level is greater than 10 %. The throttle position (TP) is between 3-70 %. The DTCs run continuously when the above conditions are met for 2 s.
DTC: P0158	**HO2S Circuit High Voltage Bank 2 Sensor 2:** P0132, P0138, P0152, or P0158 DTCs P0068, P0101, P0102, P0103, P0106, P0107, P0108, P0112, P0113, P0116, P0117, P0118, P0120, P0121, P0122, P0123, P0128, P0201, P0202, P0203, P0204, P0205, P0206, P0207, P0208, P0220, P0222, P0223, P0442, P0443, P0446, P0449, P0455, P0496, P1516, P2101, P2119, P2135, P2176 are not set. The engine is operating in Closed Loop. The Ignition 1 voltage is between 10-32 V. The fuel level is greater than 10 %. The throttle position (TP) is between 0-70 %. The DTCs run continuously when the above conditions are met for 3 s.
DTC: P0158	**HO2S Circuit High Voltage Bank 2 Sensor 2:** P0158 DTCs P0068, P0101, P0102, P0103, P0106, P0107, P0108, P0112, P0113, P0116, P0117, P0118, P0120, P0121, P0122, P0123, P0128, P0201, P0202, P0203, P0204, P0205, P0206, P0207, P0208, P0220, P0222, P0223, P0442, P0443, P0446, P0449, P0455, P0496, P1516, P2101, P2119, P2135, P2176 are not set. The Loop Status parameter is Closed. The Ignition 1 Signal parameter is between 10-18 volts. The Fuel Alcohol Content parameter is less than 87 percent. The Fuel Level Sensor parameter is more than 10 percent. The TP Sensor parameter is between 3-70 percent. DTC P0158 runs the rich test continuously when the above conditions are met.

DTC	Trouble Code Title, Conditions, Possible Causes
DTC: P015A 00	**HO2S Delayed Response Rich to Lean Bank 1 Sensor 1:** P015A 00 DTCs P0030 00, P0036 00, P0053 00, P0054 00, P0101 00, P0102 00, P0103 00, P0106 00, P0107 00, P0108 00, P0120 00, P0121 00, P0122 00, P0123 00, P0131 00, P0132 00, P0133 00, P0134 00, P0135 00, P0137 00, P0138 00, P013A 00, P013B 00, P013E 00, P013F 00, P0140 00, P0141 00, P0171 00, P0172 00, P0201 00, P0202 00, P0203 00, P0204 00, P0220 00, P0222 00, P0223 00, P0300 00, P0443 00, P1133 00, P1516 00, P2101 00, P2119 00, P2135 00, P2176 00, P2270 00, P2271 00, P2A00 00 are not set. The system voltage is between 10-18 V. The fuel level is more than 10%. Engine run time is equal to or more than 40 s. The engine coolant is hotter than 50. 25°C (122. 45°F). The Deceleration fuel cut-off is active. The accelerator pedal position (APP) is stable. The torque converter clutch (TCC) is locked. DTC P013E 00 and P2270 00 have run and passed. DTC P015A 00 runs once per trip.
DTC: P015B 00	**HO2S Delayed Response Lean to Rich Bank 1 Sensor 1:** P015B 00 DTCs P0030 00, P0036 00, P0053 00, P0054 00, P0101 00, P0102 00, P0103 00, P0106 00, P0107 00, P0108 00, P0120 00, P0121 00, P0122 00, P0123 00, P0131 00, P0132 00, P0133 00, P0134 00, P0135 00, P0137 00, P0138 00, P013A 00, P013B 00, P013E 00, P013F 00, P0140 00, P0141 00, P0171 00, P0172 00, P0201 00, P0202 00, P0203 00, P0204 00, P0220 00, P0222 00, P0223 00, P0300 00, P0443 00, P1133 00, P1516 00, P2101 00, P2119 00, P2135 00, P2176 00, P2270 00, P2271 00, P2A00 00 are not set. The system voltage is between 10-18 V. The fuel level is more than 10%. Engine run time is equal to or more than 40 s. The engine coolant is hotter than 50. 25°C (122. 45°F). The DTCs P013A 00, P013E 00, P013F 00, P2270 00, and P2271 00 have run and passed. DTC P015B 00 runs once per trip.
DTC: P0160	**HO2S Circuit Insufficient Activity Bank 2 Sensor 2:** P0160 DTCs P0068, P0101, P0102, P0103, P0106, P0107, P0108, P0112, P0113, P0116, P0117, P0118, P0120, P0121, P0122, P0123, P0128, P0201, P0202, P0203, P0204, P0205, P0206, P0207, P0208, P0220, P0222, P0223, P0442, P0443, P0446, P0449, P0455, P0496, P1516, P2101, P2119, P2135, P2176 are not set. The Ignition 1 Signal parameter is between 10-18 volts. The Engine Run Time parameter is more than 200 seconds. The Loop Status parameter is closed. DTC P0160 runs once per drive cycle when the above conditions are met.
DTC: P0161	**HO2S Heater Performance Bank 2 Sensor 2:** P0135, P0141, P0155, or P0161 DTCs P0116, P0117, P0118, P0125, or P0128 are not set. The ignition 1 voltage is between 10-32 V. The HO2S is at operating temperature. The HO2S is commanded ON. The DTCs run once per drive cycle when the above conditions are met for 120 s.
DTC: P0168	**Engine Fuel Over-Temperature:** The ignition is ON. DTC P0168 runs continuously within the enabling conditions.
DTC: P0171	**Fuel Trim System Lean:** DTCs P0030, P0036, P0053, P0054, P0068, P0101, P0102, P0103, P0107, P0108, P0112, P0113, P0116, P0120, P0121, P0122, P0123, P0128, P0131, P0132, P0133, P0134, P0135, P0137, P0138, P013A, P013B, P013E, P013F, P0140, P0141, P0201-P0206, P0220, P0222, P0223, P0300, P0442, P0443, P0446, P0449, P0451, P0452, P0453, P0454, P0455, P0461, P0462, P0463, P0464, P0496, P0506, P0507, P1133, P1516, P2101, P2119, P2120, P2122, P2123, P2125, P2127, P2128, P2135, P2138, P2176, P2270, P2271, P2A00 are not set. The engine is in Closed Loop status. The Fuel Trim Learn is enabled. The engine coolant temperature (ECT) is between -38 and +150°C (-36. 4 and +302°F). The intake air temperature (IAT) is between -38 and +150°C (-36. 4 and +302°F). The manifold absolute pressure (MAP) is between 10-105 kPa. OR The MAP is between 10-255 kPa for vehicles equipped with secondary air injection (AIR) reaction systems. The vehicle speed is less than 300 km/h (186 mph). The engine speed is between 400-7,000 RPM. The mass airflow (MAF) is between 1-510 g/s. The barometric pressure (BARO) is more than 70 kPa. The fuel level is more than 10 percent. DTC P0171 and P0172 run continuously when the above conditions have been met.
DTC: P0171	**Fuel Trim System Lean Bank 1:** DTCs P0030, P0036, P0050, P0053, P0054, P0056, P0059, P0060, P0068, P0101, P0102, P0103, P0107, P0108, P0112, P0113, P0116, P0120, P0121, P0122, P0123, P0128, P0131, P0132, P0133, P0134, P0135, P0137, P0138, P0140, P0141, P0151, P0152, P0153, P0154, P0155, P0157, P0158, P0160, P0161, P0201-P0206, P0220, P0222, P0223, P0300-P0306, P0442, P0443, P0446, P0449, P0451, P0452, P0453, P0454, P0455, P0461, P0462, P0463, P0464, P0496, P0506, P0507, P1133, P1153, P1516, P2101, P2119, P2120, P2122, P2123, P2125, P2127, P2128, P2135, P2138, P2176, P2A00, P2A03 are not set. Where applicable DTCs P2270, P2271, P2272, P2273, P2A01, P2A04 are not set. The Loop Status parameter indicates Closed. The Fuel Trim Learn is enabled. The engine coolant temperature (ECT) is between -38 and +150°C (-36. 4 and +302°F). The intake air temperature (IAT) is between -38 and +150°C (-36. 4 and +302°F). The manifold absolute pressure (MAP) is between 5-255 kPa. The vehicle speed is less than 134 km/h (83 mph). The engine speed is between 400-6,000 RPM. The mass air flow (MAF) is between 1-510 g/s. The barometric pressure (BARO) is more than 70 kPa. The scan tool special functions are not active. DTCs P0171, P0172, P0174, and P0175 run continuously when the above conditions have been met.

DTC	Trouble Code Title, Conditions, Possible Causes
DTC: P0171 00	**Fuel Trim System Lean:** P0171 00 DTCs P0030 00, P0031 00, P0032 00, P0107 00, P0108 00, P0112 00, P0113 00, P0121 00, P0122 00, P0123 00, P0128 00, P0131 00, P0132 00, P0133 00, P0134 00, P0135 00, P0137 00, P0138 00, P0140 00, P0141 00, P0201 00 - P0204 00, P0220 00, P0222 00, P0223 00, P0300 00 - P0304 00, P0442 00, P0443 00, P0446 00, P0451 00, P0452 00, P0453 00, P0454 00, P0455 00, P0461 00, P0462 00, P0463 00, P0496 00, P0506 00, P0507 00, P2101 00, P2119 00, P2122 00, P2123 00, P2127 00, P2128 00, P2138 00, P2176 00, P2A00 00 are not set. Where applicable DTCs P2270 00, P2271 00, P2272 00, P2A01 00 are not set. The loop status parameter indicates closed. The fuel trim learn is enabled. The engine coolant temperature (ECT) is between -38 to +150°C (-36. 4 to +302°F). The intake air temperature (IAT) is between -38 to +150°C (-36. 4 to +302°F). The manifold absolute pressure (MAP) is between 5-255 kPa (0. 73-37 PSI). The vehicle speed is less than 134 km/h (83 MPH). The engine speed is between 400-6 000 RPM. The barometric pressure (BARO) is more than 70 kPa (10 PSI). DTCs P0171 00 and P2096 00 run continuously when the above conditions have been met.
DTC: P0172	**Fuel Trim System Rich:** DTCs P0030, P0036, P0053, P0054, P0068, P0101, P0102, P0103, P0107, P0108, P0112, P0113, P0116, P0120, P0121, P0122, P0123, P0128, P0131, P0132, P0133, P0134, P0135, P0137, P0138, P0140, P0141, P0201-P0206, P0220, P0222, P0223, P0300, P0442, P0443, P0446, P0449, P0451, P0452, P0453, P0454, P0455, P0461, P0462, P0463, P0464, P0496, P0506, P0507, P1133, P1516, P2101, P2119, P2120, P2122, P2123, P2125, P2127, P2128, P2135, P2138, P2176, P2A00, P2270, P2271 are not set. The Loop Status parameter indicates Closed. The Fuel Trim Learn is enabled. The engine coolant temperature (ECT) is between -38 and +150°C (-36. 4 and +302°F). The intake air temperature (IAT) is between -38 and +150°C (-36. 4 and +302°F). The manifold absolute pressure (MAP) is between 10-255 kPa. The vehicle speed is less than 300 km/h (186 mph). The engine speed is between 400-7,000 RPM. The mass air flow (MAF) is between 1-510 g/s. The barometric pressure (BARO) is more than 70 kPa. The fuel level is more than 10 percent. DTC P0171 or P0172 runs continuously when the above conditions have been met.
DTC: P0172 00	**Fuel Trim System Rich:** P0172 00 DTCs P0030 00, P0031 00, P0032 00, P0111 00, P0112 00, P0113 00, P0114 00, P0117 00, P0118 00, P0119 00, P0122 00, P0123 00, P0130 00, P0131 00, P0132 00, P0133 00, P0134 00, P0135 00, P0201 00, P0202 00, P0203 00, P0204 00, P0222 00, P0223 00, P0261 00, P0262 00, P0264 00, P0265 00, P0267 00, P0268 00, P0270 00, P0271 00, P0301 00, P0302 00, P0303 00, P0304 00, P0335 00, P0336 00, P0340 00, P0341 00, P0365 00, P0366 00, P0443 00, P0458 00, P0459 00, P0496 00, P2227 00, P2228 00, P2229 00, P2297 00, P2A00 00 are not set. The loop status parameter indicates closed. The engine coolant temperature (ECT) is between -38 to +150°C (-36. 4 to +302°F). The intake air temperature (IAT) is between -38 to +150°C (-36. 4 to +302°F). The manifold absolute pressure (MAP) is between 5-255 kPa (0. 73-37 PSI). The engine speed is between 400-6 000 RPM. The barometric pressure (BARO) is more than 70 kPa (10 PSI). DTCs P0172 00 and P2097 00 run continuously when the above conditions have been met.
DTC: P0174	**Fuel Trim System Lean Bank 2:** DTCs P0101, P0102, P0103, P0106, P0107, P0108, P0178, P0179, P0201-P0206, P0261, P0262, P0264, P0265, P0267, P0268, P0270, P0271, P0273, P0274, P0275, P0277, P0300-P0306, P0442, P0443, P0446, P0449, P0451-P0455, P0496, P0506, P0507, P1248, P1249, P124A, P124B, P124C, P124D, P2147, P2148, P2150, P2151, P2153, P2154, P2156, P2157, P216B, P216C, P216E, P216F, P2227-P2230, P2269 are not set. The engine is in Closed Loop status. The catalyst monitor diagnostic intrusive test, post 02 diagnostic intrusive test, device control, and EVAP diagnostic Tank Pull Down test are not active. The engine coolant temperature (ECT) is between -38 and +150°C (-36 and +302°F). The intake air temperature (IAT) is between -38 and +150°C (-36 and +302°F). The manifold absolute pressure (MAP) is between 5-255 kPa (1. 45-37 psi). The engine speed is between 400-6,600 RPM. The mass air flow (MAF) is between 0. 5-510 g/s. The barometric pressure (BARO) is greater than 70 kPa (10. 2 psi). The fuel level is greater than 10 %. This diagnostic runs continuously when the above conditions have been met.
DTC: P0175	**Fuel Trim System Rich Bank 2:** DTCs P0101, P0102, P0103, P0106, P0107, P0108, P0178, P0179, P0201-P0206, P0261, P0262, P0264, P0265, P0267, P0268, P0270, P0271, P0273, P0274, P0275, P0277, P0300-P0306, P0442, P0443, P0446, P0449, P0451-P0455, P0496, P0506, P0507, P1248, P1249, P124A, P124B, P124C, P124D, P2147, P2148, P2150, P2151, P2153, P2154, P2156, P2157, P216B, P216C, P216E, P216F, P2227-P2230, P2269 are not set. The engine is in Closed Loop status. The catalyst monitor diagnostic intrusive test, post 02 diagnostic intrusive test, device control, and EVAP diagnostic Tank Pull Down test are not active. The engine coolant temperature (ECT) is between -38 and +150°C (-36 and +302°F). The intake air temperature (IAT) is between -38 and +150°C (-36 and +302°F). The manifold absolute pressure (MAP) is between 5-255 kPa (1. 45-37 psi). The engine speed is between 400-6,600 RPM. The mass air flow (MAF) is between 0. 5-510 g/s. The barometric pressure (BARO) is greater than 70 kPa (10. 2 psi). The fuel level is greater than 10 %. This diagnostic runs continuously when the above conditions have been met.
DTC: P0180 03	**Fuel Temperature Sensor Circuit Low Voltage:** The ignition is ON or the engine is running. The DTCs run continuously once the above condition is met
DTC: P0180 07	**Fuel Temperature Sensor Circuit High Voltage:** The ignition is ON or the engine is running. The DTCs run continuously once the above condition is met
DTC: P0181 00	**Fuel Temperature Sensor Performance:** The ignition is ON or the engine is running. The DTCs run continuously once the above condition is met.

DTC	Trouble Code Title, Conditions, Possible Causes
DTC: P0182	**Fuel Temperature Sensor 1 Circuit Low:** P0182 or P0187Engine speed is greater than 600 RPM. Engine has been running for greater than 10 seconds. DTCs P0182 and P0187 run continuously within the enabling conditions.
DTC: P0183	**Fuel Temperature Sensor 1 Circuit High:** P0183 or P0188Engine speed is greater than 600 RPM. Engine has been running for greater than 10 seconds. DTCs P0183 and P0188 run continuously within the above enabling conditions.
DTC: P0187	**Fuel Temperature Sensor 2 Circuit Low:** P0182 or P0187Engine speed is greater than 600 RPM. Engine has been running for greater than 10 seconds. DTCs P0182 and P0187 run continuously within the enabling conditions.
DTC: P0188	**Fuel Temperature Sensor 2 Circuit High:** P0183 or P0188Engine speed is greater than 600 RPM. Engine has been running for greater than 10 seconds. DTCs P0183 and P0188 run continuously within the above enabling conditions.
DTC: P018B	**Fuel Pressure Sensor Performance:** The engine is running. DTC P018C, P018D, P0231, P0232, P023F, P064A, P1255 or P06A6 are not active. DTC P0641 has not failed this ignition cycle. Fuel pump control is enabled and the fuel pump control state is normal. The engine has been running for at least 5 seconds.
DTC: P018C	**Fuel Pressure Sensor Circuit Low Voltage:** The engine is running. DTC P018C, P018D, P0231, P0232, P023F, P064A, P1255 or P06A6 are not active. DTC P0641 has not failed this ignition cycle. Fuel pump control is enabled and the fuel pump control state is normal. The engine has been running for at least 5 seconds.
DTC: P018D	**Fuel Pressure Sensor Circuit High Voltage:** The engine is running. DTC P018C, P018D, P0231, P0232, P023F, P064A, P1255 or P06A6 are not active. DTC P0641 has not failed this ignition cycle. Fuel pump control is enabled and the fuel pump control state is normal. The engine has been running for at least 5 seconds.
DTC: P0190 00	**Fuel Rail Pressure Sensor Performance:** The engine is running. DTC P0651 00 is not set. The DTCs run continuously when the above conditions are met.
DTC: P0190 03	**Fuel Rail Pressure Sensor Circuit Low Voltage:** The ignition is ON or the engine is running. The DTCs run continuously once the above condition is met.
DTC: P0190 07	**Fuel Rail Pressure Sensor Circuit High Voltage:** The ignition is ON or the engine is running. The DTCs run continuously once the above condition is met.
DTC: P0191	**Fuel Rail Pressure Sensor Performance:** Condition 1 DTC P0016, P0017, P0068, P0090, P0091, P0092, P00C8, P00C9, P00CA, P0101, P0102, P0103, P0106, P0107, P0108, P0112, P0113, P0117, P0118, P0121, P0122, P0123, P0128, P0192, P0193, P0201, P0202, P0203, P0204, P0222, P0223, P0261, P0262, P0264, P0265, P0267, P0268, P0270, P0271, P0300, P0301, P0302, P0303, P0304, P0335, P0336, P0340, P0341, P0351-P0354, P0365, P0366, P0506, P0507, P0627, P0628, P0629, P0722, P0723, P1248, P1249, P124A, P124B, P1682, P16F3, P2101, P2122, P2123, P2127, P2128, P2135, P2147, P2148, P2150, P2151, P2153, P2154, P2156, P2157 is not set. The engine is not cranking. The ignition voltage is greater than 11 V. The vehicle speed is less than or equal to 1 km/h (0. 62 mph). The low side fuel pressure is greater than or equal to 275 kPa (40 psi). The Accelerator Pedal Position is 0 percent for 12. 5s. DTC P0191 runs continuously when the above conditions have been met. Condition 2 and 3 DTC P0016, P0017, P0068, P0090, P0091, P0092, P00C8, P00C9, P00CA, P0101, P0102, P0103, P0106, P0107, P0108, P0112, P0113, P0117, P0118, P0121, P0122, P0123, P0128, P0192, P0193, P0201, P0202, P0203, P0204, P0222, P0223, P0261, P0262, P0264, P0265, P0267, P0268, P0270, P0271, P0300, P0301, P0302, P0303, P0304, P0335, P0336, P0340, P0341, P0351-P0354, P0365, P0366, P0506, P0507, P0627, P0628, P0629, P0722, P0723, P1248, P1249, P124A, P124B, P1682, P16F3, P2101, P2122, P2123, P2127, P2128, P2135, P2147, P2148, P2150, P2151, P2153, P2154, P2156, P2157 is not set. The engine is not cranking. The ignition voltage is greater than 11 V. The engine speed is between 1,000-2,200 RPM. The vehicle speed is greater than or equal to 45 km/h (27. 96 mph). The low side fuel pressure is greater than or equal to 275 kPa (40 psi). The Desired Fuel Rail Pressure is between 7-8 MPa (1,015-1,160 psi). DTC P0191 runs continuously when the above conditions have been met. Condition 4 DTC P0016, P0017, P0068, P0090, P0091, P0092, P00C8, P00C9, P00CA, P0101, P0102, P0103, P0106, P0107, P0108, P0112, P0113, P0117, P0118, P0121, P0122, P0123, P0128, P0192, P0193, P0201, P0202, P0203, P0204, P0222, P0223, P0261, P0262, P0264, P0265, P0267, P0268, P0270, P0271, P0300, P0301, P0302, P0303, P0304, P0335, P0336, P0340, P0341, P0351-P0354, P0365, P0366, P0506, P0507, P0627, P0628, P0629, P0722, P0723, P1248, P1249, P124A, P124B, P1682, P16F3, P2101, P2122, P2123, P2127, P2128, P2135, P2147, P2148, P2150, P2151, P2153, P2154, P2156, P2157 is not set. The engine is not cranking. The vehicle speed is greater than or equal to 30 km/h (18. 64 mph). The engine speed is greater than or equal to 2,000 RPM. DTC P0191 runs continuously when the above conditions have been met.
DTC: P0191 00	**Fuel Rail Pressure Sensor Performance:** The engine is running. DTC P0651 00 is not set. The DTCs run continuously when the above conditions are met.

DTC	Trouble Code Title, Conditions, Possible Causes
DTC: P0191 11	**Fuel Rail Pressure Sensor Performance High Input:** The ignition is ON or the engine is running. The DTCs run continuously once the above condition is met.
DTC: P0191 12	**Fuel Rail Pressure Sensor Performance Low Input:** The ignition is ON or the engine is running. The DTCs run continuously once the above condition is met.
DTC: P0192	**Fuel Rail Pressure Sensor Circuit Low Voltage:** The engine is running. The ignition voltage is between 11-18 V. The DTCs run continuously within the enabling conditions.
DTC: P0192 00	**Fuel Rail Pressure Sensor Circuit Low Voltage:** The engine is running. DTC P0651 00 is not set. The DTCs run continuously when the above conditions are met.
DTC: P0193	**Fuel Rail Pressure Sensor Circuit High Voltage:** The engine is running. The ignition voltage is between 11-18 V. The DTCs run continuously within the enabling conditions.
DTC: P0193 00	**Fuel Rail Pressure Sensor Circuit High Voltage:** The engine is running. DTC P0651 00 is not set. The DTCs run continuously when the above conditions are met.
DTC: P0201	**Cylinder 1 Injector Control Circuit:** The engine speed is greater than 80 RPM. The ignition 1 signal parameter is between 10-18 V. The injector has been commanded ON and OFF at least once. The DTCs run continuously once the above conditions are met.
DTC: P0201 00	**Cylinder 1 Injector Control Circuit:** DTCs P0607 00, P0628 00, P0629 00 are not set. The battery voltage is greater than 9 V. The engine is running. The engine speed is between 320-6016 RPM. All fuel injectors are active. These DTCs run continuously when the above conditions are met
DTC: P0202	**Cylinder 2 Injector Control Circuit:** The engine is running. The ignition voltage is between 11-18 V. The DTCs run continuously once the above conditions are met.
DTC: P0202 00	**Cylinder 2 Injector Control Circuit:** DTCs P0607 00, P0628 00, P0629 00 are not set. The battery voltage is greater than 9 V. The engine is running. The engine speed is between 320-6016 RPM. All fuel injectors are active. These DTCs run continuously when the above conditions are met
DTC: P0203	**Injector 3 Control Circuit:** The engine is running. The ignition voltage is more than 11 volts. DTCs P0201-P0208 runs continuously when the above conditions are met.
DTC: P0203 00	**Cylinder 3 Injector Control Circuit:** DTCs P0607 00, P0628 00, P0629 00 are not set. The battery voltage is greater than 9 V. The engine is running. The engine speed is between 320-6016 RPM. All fuel injectors are active. These DTCs run continuously when the above conditions are met
DTC: P0204	**Cylinder 4 Injector Control Circuit:** The engine speed is greater than 80 RPM. The ignition 1 signal parameter is between 8-18. 1 V. The DTCs run continuously within the enabling conditions.
DTC: P0204 00	**Cylinder 4 Injector Control Circuit:** DTCs P0607 00, P0628 00, P0629 00 are not set. The battery voltage is greater than 9 V. The engine is running. The engine speed is between 320-6016 RPM. All fuel injectors are active. These DTCs run continuously when the above conditions are met
DTC: P0205	**Injector 5 Control Circuit:** The engine is running. The ignition voltage is more than 11 V for 5 seconds. DTCs P0201-P0206 run continuously when the above conditions are met.
DTC: P0205	**Cylinder 5 Injector Control Circuit:** The engine speed is greater than 80 RPM. The ignition 1 signal parameter is between 10-18 V. The injector has been commanded ON and OFF at least once. The DTCs run continuously once the above conditions are met.
DTC: P0206	**Injector 6 Control Circuit:** The engine is running. The ignition voltage is more than 11 volts. DTCs P0201-P0208 runs continuously when the above conditions are met.
DTC: P0206	**Cylinder 6 Injector Control Circuit:** The engine speed is greater than 80 RPM. The ignition 1 signal parameter is between 10-18 V. The injector has been commanded ON and OFF at least once. The DTCs run continuously once the above conditions are met.
DTC: P0207	**Injector 7 Control Circuit:** The engine is running. The ignition voltage is greater than 11 V. DTC P0201-P0208 runs continuously when the above conditions are met.
DTC: P0208	**Fuel Injector 8 Control Circuit:** The engine is running. The charging system voltage is between 10-18 V.

DTC	Trouble Code Title, Conditions, Possible Causes
DTC: P0208	**Injector 8 Control Circuit:** The engine is running. The ignition voltage is greater than 11 V. DTC P0201-P0208 runs continuously when the above conditions are met.
DTC: P0218	**Transmission Fluid Over temperature:** Ignition voltage is 8. 6 volts or greater. The TFT is -39 to +149°C (-38 to +300°F) for 5 seconds.
DTC: P0219	**Engine Overspeed Condition:** The engine is running.
DTC: P0219 00	**Engine Overspeed:** The engine is running. The DTC runs continuously once the above condition is met.
DTC: P0220	**Throttle Position (TP) Sensor 2 Circuit:** P0120, P0122, P0123, P0220, P0222, or P0223 DTCs P0601, P0602, P0603, P0604, P0606, P060D, P062F, P0641, P0651 are not set. The system voltage is greater than 5. 23 V. The ignition is in the Unlock/Accessory or Run position. The DTCs run continuously when the above conditions are met.
DTC: P0221	**Throttle Position Sensor 2 Performance:** The ignition voltage is greater than 7 V. The ignition is ON, with the engine OFF, or the engine is operating. DTC P0121 runs continuously once the above conditions are met.
DTC: P0221	**Throttle Position Sensor 2 Performance:** The ignition is ON, with the engine OFF, or the engine is operating. The ignition voltage is greater than 7 volts. DTCs run continuously once the above conditions are met.
DTC: P0221 00	**Throttle Position Sensor 2 Performance:** DTCs P000A 00, P000B 00, P0016 00, P0017 00, P0111 00, P0112 00, P0113 00, P0114 00, P0116 00, P0117 00, P0118 00, P0119 00, P0122 00, P0123 00, P0222 00, P0223 00, P0121 00, P0221 00, P0340 00, P0341 00, P0365 00, P0366 00, P0458 00, P0459 00, P0642 00, P0643 00, P0652 00, P0653 00, P065B 00 are not set. The engine is running. DTCs P0068 00, P0642 00, P0643 00 are not set.
DTC: P0222	**Throttle Position (TP) Sensor 2 Circuit Low Voltage:** P0120, P0122, P0123, P0220, P0222, and P0223 DTC P0641 or P0651 are not set. The run/crank or powertrain relay voltage is greater than 6 V and reduced power is not active. The ignition is ON or the engine is running. DTC P0120, P0122, P0123, P0220, P0222, P0223 run continuously when the above conditions are met.
DTC: P0222 00	**Throttle Position Sensor 2 Circuit Low Voltage:** P0122 00, P0123 00, P0222 00, P0223 00 The ignition is ON, or the engine is running. The engine is not operating in reduced power mode. The ignition voltage is greater than 6 V. The DTCs runs continuously when the above condition is met.
DTC: P0223	**Throttle Position (TP) Sensor 2 Circuit High Voltage:** P0120, P0122, P0123, P0220, P0222, and P0223 DTC P0601, P0602, P0603, P0604, P0606, P0607, P0641, or P0651 is not set. The system voltage is greater than 5. 23 V. The ignition is in the Unlock/Accessory or Run position. The DTCs run continuously when the above conditions are met.
DTC: P0223 00	**Throttle Position Sensor 2 Circuit High Voltage:** DTC P0641 00 or P0651 00 are not set. The run/crank or powertrain relay voltage is greater than 6 V and reduced power is not active. The ignition is ON or the engine is operating. DTC P0122 00, P0123 00, P0222 00, P0223 00, and P2135 00 run continuously when the above conditions are met.
DTC: P0230	**Fuel Pump Relay Control Circuit:** The ignition voltage is between 9-18 V. DTC P0230 runs continuously once the above conditions are met.
DTC: P0230	**Fuel Pump Relay Control Circuit:** The ignition voltage is between 11-32 volts. Engine speed is greater than 0 RPM. DTC P0230 runs continuously when the above conditions are met.
DTC: P0230 00	**Fuel Pump Relay Control Circuit:** The ignition is ON. The ignition voltage is between 11-18 V. The DTCs run continuously once the above conditions are met.
DTC: P0231	**Fuel Pump Control Circuit Low Voltage:** P0231, P023F The ignition voltage is between 9-18 V.
DTC: P0232	**Fuel Pump Control Circuit High Voltage:** P0232 The control enable voltage signal supplied for the ECM to fuel pump control module is inactive for 4 seconds after engine has been shut off.
DTC: P0234	**Turbocharger Engine Overboost:** DTCs P0106, P0563, P2564 or P2565 are not set. The engine speed is between 800-3,600 RPM. DTC P0234 runs continuously when the above conditions are met.

DTC	Trouble Code Title, Conditions, Possible Causes
DTC: P0234	**Turbocharger Engine Overboost:** DTC P0045, P0047, P0048, P006E, P006F, P007C, P007D, P0102, P0103, P0106, P0107, P0108, P0117, P0118, P0200, P02E0, P02E3, P02E8, P02E9, P02EB, P0403, P046C, P0489, P0490, P122B, P122C, P122F, P1407, P140B, P140D, P140E, P140F, P2228, P2229, P2263, P2453, P2494, P2495, P2564, or P2565 is not set. The engine speed is stable between 1,600-3,000 RPM. Fuel injector delivery rate is greater than 45 mm ; and stable. Ambient air temperature is greater than -7°C (19. 4°F). BARO is greater than 75 kPa (11 psi). Turbocharger actuator position sensor offset learning is not active. Turbocharger vane cleaning, wiping, procedure is not active. DTC P0234 runs continuously when the above conditions are met.
DTC: P0234 00	**Engine Overboost:** P0234 00 DTCs P0237 00, or P0238 00 are not set. The driver requested boost pressure level exceeds the level of the base boost pressure. This DTC runs continuously within the enabling conditions.
DTC: P0234 00	**Engine Overboost Malfunction:** The engine is running. The DTCs run continuously when the above conditions are met.
DTC: P0236	**Turbocharger Boost System Performance:** P0236 - Engine Cranking DTCs P0107, P0108, P0121, P0122, P0123, P0221, P0222, P0223, P0237, P0238, P2227, P2228, or P2229 are not set. The engine OFF timer is greater than 4 s. The engine is cranking at less than 400 RPM for at least 200 ms. This DTC runs during engine cranking only. P0236 - Engine Idling. DTCs P0121, P0122, P0123, P0221, P0222, P0223, P0237, P0238, P2227, P2228, or P2229 are not set. The engine is running and the ECM has counted greater than three revolutions. The engine speed is less than 1000 RPM. The Throttle Position Sensor parameter is less than 24 %. The ECM is not in limp home mode. This DTC runs continuously within the enabling conditions.
DTC: P0236 00	**Turbocharger Boost Sensor Performance:** The ignition is ON or the engine is running. These DTCs runs continuously within the enabling conditions.
DTC: P0237	**Turbocharger Boost Sensor Circuit Low Voltage:** P0237The ignition is ON or the engine is running. This DTC runs continuously within the enabling conditions.
DTC: P0237 00	**Turbocharger Boost Sensor Circuit Low Voltage:** The ignition is ON or the engine is running. These DTCs runs continuously within the enabling conditions.
DTC: P0238	**Turbocharger Boost Sensor Circuit High Voltage:** P0238The ignition is ON or the engine is running. This DTC runs continuously within the enabling conditions.
DTC: P0238 00	**Turbocharger Boost Sensor Circuit High Voltage:** The ignition is ON or the engine is running. These DTCs runs continuously within the enabling conditions.
DTC: P023F	**Fuel Pump Control Circuit:** P0231, P023FThe ignition voltage is between 9-18 V.
DTC: P023F	**Fuel Pump Control Circuit:** P0231, P023FThe ignition voltage is between 9-18 V.
DTC: P0243	**Turbocharger Wastegate Solenoid Control Circuit:** The engine speed is greater than 80 RPM. The battery voltage is between 10-18 V. This DTC runs continuously within the enabling conditions.
DTC: P0243 00	**Turbocharger Wastegate Solenoid Valve Control Circuit:** The engine speed is greater than 40 RPM. The battery voltage is between 10-18 V. This DTC runs continuously within the enabling conditions.
DTC: P0245	**Turbocharger Wastegate Solenoid Control Circuit Low Voltage:** The engine speed is greater than 80 RPM. The battery voltage is between 10-18 V. This DTC runs continuously within the enabling conditions.
DTC: P0245 00	**Turbocharger Wastegate Solenoid Valve Control Circuit Low Voltage:** The engine speed is greater than 40 RPM. The battery voltage is between 10-18 V. This DTC runs continuously within the enabling conditions.
DTC: P0246	**Turbocharger Wastegate Solenoid Control Circuit High Voltage:** The engine speed is greater than 80 RPM. The battery voltage is between 10-18 V. This DTC runs continuously within the enabling conditions.
DTC: P0246 00	**Turbocharger Wastegate Solenoid Valve Control Circuit High Voltage:** The engine speed is greater than 40 RPM. The battery voltage is between 10-18 V. This DTC runs continuously within the enabling conditions.
DTC: P0253 00	**Fuel Pressure Regulator Control Circuit Low Voltage:** The ignition is ON, or the engine is running. The ignition voltage is less than 16 V. The DTCs runs continuously once the above conditions are met.

DTC	Trouble Code Title, Conditions, Possible Causes
DTC: P0254 00	**Fuel Pressure Regulator Control Circuit High Voltage:** The ignition is ON, or the engine is running. The ignition voltage is less than 16 V. The DTCs runs continuously once the above conditions are met.
DTC: P025A	**Fuel Pump Control Module Enable Circuit:** The ignition is ON.
DTC: P0261	**Cylinder 1 Injector Control Circuit Low Voltage:** The engine speed is greater than 80 RPM. The ignition 1 signal parameter is between 10-18 V. The injector has been commanded ON and OFF at least once. The DTCs run continuously once the above conditions are met.
DTC: P0261 00	**Cylinder 1 Injector Control Circuit Low Voltage:** The battery voltage is greater than 9 V. The engine speed is greater than 40 RPM. All fuel injectors are active. These DTCs run continuously when the above conditions are met.
DTC: P0262	**Cylinder 1 Injector Control Circuit High Voltage:** The engine speed is greater than 80 RPM. The ignition 1 signal parameter is between 10-18 V. The injector has been commanded ON and OFF at least once. The DTCs run continuously once the above conditions are met.
DTC: P0262	**Cylinder 1 Injector Control Circuit High Voltage:** The engine speed is greater than 80 RPM. The ignition 1 signal parameter is between 8-18. 1 V. The DTCs run continuously within the enabling conditions.
DTC: P0262 00	**Cylinder 1 Injector Control Circuit High Voltage:** The battery voltage is greater than 9 V. The engine speed is greater than 40 RPM. All fuel injectors are active. These DTCs run continuously when the above conditions are met.
DTC: P0263	**Cylinder 1 Balance System:** DTCs P0117, P0118, P0335, P0336, P2146, P2149, P2152, P2155 and P062C are not set. The ECT is more than 40°C (104°F). The engine is running at idle for more than 10 s. The engine RPM is between 600-1,500 RPM. The calculated fuel rate is between 15 mm; and 50 mm;. DTC will run once per ignition cycle when the above conditions are met.
DTC: P0263 00	**Cylinder 1 Injector Control Performance:** The engine is running. The DTCs run continuously when the above conditions are met.
DTC: P0264	**Cylinder 2 Injector Control Circuit Low Voltage:** The engine speed is greater than 80 RPM. The ignition 1 signal parameter is between 10-18 V. The injector has been commanded ON and OFF at least once. The DTCs run continuously once the above conditions are met.
DTC: P0264 00	**Cylinder 2 Injector Control Circuit Low Voltage:** The battery voltage is greater than 9 V. The engine speed is greater than 40 RPM. All fuel injectors are active. These DTCs run continuously when the above conditions are met.
DTC: P0265	**Cylinder 2 Injector Control Circuit High Voltage:** The engine speed is greater than 80 RPM. The ignition 1 signal parameter is between 10-18 V. The injector has been commanded ON and OFF at least once. The DTCs run continuously once the above conditions are met.
DTC: P0265 00	**Cylinder 2 Injector Control Circuit High Voltage:** The battery voltage is greater than 9 V. The engine speed is greater than 40 RPM. All fuel injectors are active. These DTCs run continuously when the above conditions are met.
DTC: P0266	**Cylinder 2 Balance System:** DTCs P0117, P0118, P0335, P0336, P2146, P2149, P2152, P2155 and P062C are not set. The ECT is more than 40°C (104°F). The engine is running at idle for more than 10 s. The engine RPM is between 600-1,500 RPM. The calculated fuel rate is between 15 mm ; and 50 mm ;. DTC will run once per ignition cycle when the above conditions are met.
DTC: P0266 00	**Cylinder 2 Injector Control Performance:** The engine is running. The DTCs run continuously when the above conditions are met.
DTC: P0267	**Cylinder 3 Injector Control Circuit Low Voltage:** The engine speed is greater than 80 RPM. The ignition 1 signal parameter is between 10-18 V. The injector has been commanded ON and OFF at least once. The DTCs run continuously once the above conditions are met.
DTC: P0267 00	**Cylinder 3 Injector Control Circuit Low Voltage:** The battery voltage is greater than 9 V. The engine speed is greater than 40 RPM. All fuel injectors are active. These DTCs run continuously when the above conditions are met.
DTC: P0268	**Cylinder 3 Injector Control Circuit High Voltage:** The engine speed is greater than 80 RPM. The ignition 1 signal parameter is between 10-18 V. The injector has been commanded ON and OFF at least once. The DTCs run continuously once the above conditions are met.

DTC	Trouble Code Title, Conditions, Possible Causes
DTC: P0268 00	**Cylinder 3 Injector Control Circuit High Voltage:** The battery voltage is greater than 9 V. The engine speed is greater than 40 RPM. All fuel injectors are active. These DTCs run continuously when the above conditions are met.
DTC: P0269	**Cylinder 3 Balance System:** DTCs P0117, P0118, P0335, P0336, P2146, P2149, P2152, P2155 and P062C are not set. The ECT is more than 40°C (104°F). The engine is running at idle for more than 10 s. The engine RPM is between 600-1,500 RPM. The calculated fuel rate is between 15 mm ; and 50 mm ;. DTC will run once per ignition cycle when the above conditions are met.
DTC: P0269 00	**Cylinder 3 Injector Control Performance:** The engine is running. The DTCs run continuously when the above conditions are met.
DTC: P026A	**Charge Air Cooler (CAC) Low Efficiency:** Engine speed is greater than 600 to 850 RPM, depending on engine coolant temperature (ECT) and BARO, for at least 10 s. The ECT is between 70-123°C (158-253°F). The Ambient Air Temperature is warmer than -7°C (+19. 4°F). The difference between the CAC Inlet Temperature and the Ambient Air Temperature is at least 40°C (72°F). The Intake Air Flow (IAF) Valve Position is 5 % or less. The MAF signal is between 83. 33-152. 77 g/s. The vehicle speed is at least 60 Km/h (37 mph). The BARO is greater than 75 kPa. The calculated fuel rate is between 20 mm ; and 50 mm ;. This DTC runs once per key cycle when the above conditions exist.
DTC: P0270	**Cylinder 4 Injector Control Circuit Low Voltage:** The engine is running. The ignition voltage is between 11-18 V. The DTCs run continuously once the above conditions are met.
DTC: P0270	**Cylinder 4 Injector Control Circuit Low Voltage:** The engine speed is greater than 80 RPM. The ignition 1 signal parameter is between 10-18 V. The injector has been commanded ON and OFF at least once. The DTCs run continuously once the above conditions are met.
DTC: P0270 00	**Cylinder 4 Injector Control Circuit Low Voltage:** The battery voltage is greater than 9 V. The engine speed is greater than 40 RPM. All fuel injectors are active. These DTCs run continuously when the above conditions are met.
DTC: P0271	**Cylinder 4 Injector Control Circuit High Voltage:** The engine speed is greater than 80 RPM. The ignition 1 signal parameter is between 10-18 V. The injector has been commanded ON and OFF at least once. The DTCs run continuously once the above conditions are met.
DTC: P0271	**Cylinder 4 Injector Control Circuit High Voltage:** The engine is running. The ignition voltage is between 11-18 V. The DTCs run continuously once the above conditions are met.
DTC: P0271	**Cylinder 4 Injector Control Circuit High Voltage:** The engine speed is greater than 80 RPM. The ignition 1 signal parameter is between 8-18. 1 V. The DTCs run continuously within the enabling conditions.
DTC: P0271 00	**Cylinder 4 Injector Control Circuit High Voltage:** DTCs P0607 00, P0628 00, P0629 00 are not set. The battery voltage is greater than 9 V. The engine is running. The engine speed is between 320-6016 RPM. All fuel injectors are active. These DTCs run continuously when the above conditions are met
DTC: P0271 00	**Cylinder 4 Injector Control Circuit High Voltage:** The battery voltage is greater than 9 V. The engine speed is greater than 40 RPM. All fuel injectors are active. These DTCs run continuously when the above conditions are met.
DTC: P0272	**Cylinder 4 Balance System:** DTCs P0117, P0118, P0335, P0336, P2146, P2149, P2152, P2155 and P062C are not set. The ECT is more than 40°C (104°F). The engine is running at idle for more than 10 s. The engine RPM is between 600-1,500 RPM. The calculated fuel rate is between 15 mm ; and 50 mm ;. DTC will run once per ignition cycle when the above conditions are met.
DTC: P0272 00	**Cylinder 4 Injector Control Performance:** The engine is running. The DTCs run continuously when the above conditions are met.
DTC: P0273	**Cylinder 5 Injector Control Circuit Low Voltage:** The engine speed is greater than 80 RPM. The ignition 1 signal parameter is between 10-18 V. The injector has been commanded ON and OFF at least once. The DTCs run continuously once the above conditions are met.
DTC: P0274	**Cylinder 5 Injector Control Circuit High Voltage:** The engine speed is greater than 80 RPM. The ignition 1 signal parameter is between 10-18 V. The injector has been commanded ON and OFF at least once. The DTCs run continuously once the above conditions are met.
DTC: P0275	**Cylinder 5 Balance System:** DTCs P0117, P0118, P0335, P0336, P2146, P2149, P2152, P2155 and P062C are not set. The ECT is more than 40°C (104°F). The engine is running at idle for more than 10 s. The engine RPM is between 600-1,500 RPM. The calculated fuel rate is between 15 mm ; and 50 mm ;. DTC will run once per ignition cycle when the above conditions are met.

DTC	Trouble Code Title, Conditions, Possible Causes
DTC: P0276	**Cylinder 6 Injector Control Circuit Low Voltage:** The engine speed is greater than 80 RPM. The ignition 1 signal parameter is between 10-18 V. The injector has been commanded ON and OFF at least once. The DTCs run continuously once the above conditions are met.
DTC: P0277	**Cylinder 6 Injector Control Circuit High Voltage:** The engine speed is greater than 80 RPM. The ignition 1 signal parameter is between 10-18 V. The injector has been commanded ON and OFF at least once. The DTCs run continuously once the above conditions are met.
DTC: P0278	**Cylinder 6 Balance System:** DTCs P0117, P0118, P0335, P0336, P2146, P2149, P2152, P2155 and P062C are not set. The ECT is more than 40°C (104°F). The engine is running at idle for more than 10 s. The engine RPM is between 600-1,500 RPM. The calculated fuel rate is between 15 mm ; and 50 mm ;. DTC will run once per ignition cycle when the above conditions are met.
DTC: P0281	**Cylinder 7 Balance System:** DTCs P0117, P0118, P0335, P0336, P2146, P2149, P2152, P2155 and P062C are not set. The ECT is more than 40°C (104°F). The engine is running at idle for more than 10 s. The engine RPM is between 600-1,500 RPM. The calculated fuel rate is between 15 mm ; and 50 mm ;. DTC will run once per ignition cycle when the above conditions are met.
DTC: P0284	**Cylinder 8 Balance System:** DTCs P0117, P0118, P0335, P0336, P2146, P2149, P2152, P2155 and P062C are not set. The ECT is more than 40°C (104°F). The engine is running at idle for more than 10 s. The engine RPM is between 600-1,500 RPM. The calculated fuel rate is between 15 mm ; and 50 mm ;. DTC will run once per ignition cycle when the above conditions are met.
DTC: P0299	**Turbocharger Engine Underboost:** DTC P0045, P0047, P0048, P006E, P006F, P007C, P007D, P0102, P0103, P0107, P0108, P0117, P0118, P02E0, P02E8, P02E9, P02EB, P0403, P122D, P140F, P2228, P2229, P2453, P2494, P2495, P2564, P2565, or P268A is not set. The engine speed is stable between 1400-3000 RPM. Fuel injector delivery rate is stable. Ambient air temperature is greater than -7°C (19. 4°F). BARO is greater than 75 kPa (11 psi). Turbocharger actuator position sensor offset learning is not active. Turbocharger vane cleaning, wiping, procedure is not active. DTC P0299 runs continuously when the above conditions are met.
DTC: P0299 00	**Engine Underboost Malfunction:** The engine is running. The DTCs run continuously when the above conditions are met.
DTC: P029C	**Cylinder 1 Injector Stuck Closed:** The engine is running. The ECM monitors for a condition once per camshaft revolution.
DTC: P029D	**Injector 1 Leak:** Engine has been running for more than 10 seconds. Engine coolant is more than 45°C (113°F). DTCs P0201-P0208, P1224, P1227, P122A, P1233, P1236, P1239, P1242, P1247, P2146, P2149, P2152 or P2155 are not set. The vehicle speed is in Park or Neutral. Engine speed is between 600-850 RPM. This diagnostic runs once per ignition cycle once the above criteria has been met.
DTC: P02A0	**Cylinder 2 Injector Stuck Closed:** The engine is running. The ECM monitors for a condition once per camshaft revolution.
DTC: P02A1	**Injector 2 Leak:** Engine has been running for more than 10 seconds. Engine coolant is more than 45°C (113°F). DTCs P0201-P0208, P1224, P1227, P122A, P1233, P1236, P1239, P1242, P1247, P2146, P2149, P2152 or P2155 are not set. The vehicle speed is in Park or Neutral. Engine speed is between 600-850 RPM. This diagnostic runs once per ignition cycle once the above criteria has been met.
DTC: P02A4	**Cylinder 3 Injector Stuck Closed:** The engine is running. The ECM monitors for a condition once per camshaft revolution.
DTC: P02A5	**Injector 3 Leak:** Engine has been running for more than 10 seconds. Engine coolant is more than 45°C (113°F). DTCs P0201-P0208, P1224, P1227, P122A, P1233, P1236, P1239, P1242, P1247, P2146, P2149, P2152 or P2155 are not set. The vehicle speed is in Park or Neutral. Engine speed is between 600-850 RPM. This diagnostic runs once per ignition cycle once the above criteria has been met.
DTC: P02A8	**Cylinder 4 Injector Stuck Closed:** The engine is running. The ECM monitors for a condition once per camshaft revolution.
DTC: P02A9	**Injector 4 Leak:** Engine has been running for more than 10 seconds. Engine coolant is more than 45°C (113°F). DTCs P0201-P0208, P1224, P1227, P122A, P1233, P1236, P1239, P1242, P1247, P2146, P2149, P2152 or P2155 are not set. The vehicle speed is in Park or Neutral. Engine speed is between 600-850 RPM. This diagnostic runs once per ignition cycle once the above criteria has been met.
DTC: P02AD	**Injector 5 Leak:** Engine has been running for more than 10 seconds. Engine coolant is more than 45°C (113°F). DTCs P0201-P0208, P1224, P1227, P122A, P1233, P1236, P1239, P1242, P1247, P2146, P2149, P2152 or P2155 are not set. The vehicle speed is in Park or Neutral. Engine speed is between 600-850 RPM. This diagnostic runs once per ignition cycle once the above criteria has been met.

DTC	Trouble Code Title, Conditions, Possible Causes
DTC: P02B1	**Injector 6 Leak:** Engine has been running for more than 10 seconds. Engine coolant is more than 45°C (113°F). DTCs P0201-P0208, P1224, P1227, P122A, P1233, P1236, P1239, P1242, P1247, P2146, P2149, P2152 or P2155 are not set. The vehicle speed is in Park or Neutral. Engine speed is between 600-850 RPM. This diagnostic runs once per ignition cycle once the above criteria has been met.
DTC: P02B5	**Injector 7 Leak:** Engine has been running for more than 10 seconds. Engine coolant is more than 45°C (113°F). DTCs P0201-P0208, P1224, P1227, P122A, P1233, P1236, P1239, P1242, P1247, P2146, P2149, P2152 or P2155 are not set. The vehicle speed is in Park or Neutral. Engine speed is between 600-850 RPM. This diagnostic runs once per ignition cycle once the above criteria has been met.
DTC: P02B9	**Injector 8 Leak:** Engine has been running for more than 10 seconds. Engine coolant is more than 45°C (113°F). DTCs P0201-P0208, P1224, P1227, P122A, P1233, P1236, P1239, P1242, P1247, P2146, P2149, P2152 or P2155 are not set. The vehicle speed is in Park or Neutral. Engine speed is between 600-850 RPM. This diagnostic runs once per ignition cycle once the above criteria has been met.
DTC: P02CC	**Cylinder 1 Injector Exceeded Minimum Learning Limit:** The engine is running. The ECM monitors for a condition once per camshaft revolution.
DTC: P02CD	**Cylinder 1 Injector Exceeded Maximum Learning Limit:** The engine is running. The ECM monitors for a condition once per camshaft revolution.
DTC: P02CE	**Cylinder 2 Injector Exceeded Minimum Learning Limit:** The engine is running. The ECM monitors for a condition once per camshaft revolution.
DTC: P02CF	**Cylinder 2 Injector Exceeded Maximum Learning Limit:** The engine is running. The ECM monitors for a condition once per camshaft revolution.
DTC: P02D0	**Cylinder 3 Injector Exceeded Minimum Learning Limit:** The engine is running. The ECM monitors for a condition once per camshaft revolution.
DTC: P02D1	**Cylinder 3 Injector Exceeded Maximum Learning Limit:** The engine is running. The ECM monitors for a condition once per camshaft revolution.
DTC: P02D2	**Cylinder 4 Injector Exceeded Minimum Learning Limit:** The engine is running. The ECM monitors for a condition once per camshaft revolution.
DTC: P02D3	**Cylinder 4 Injector Exceeded Maximum Learning Limit:** The engine is running. The ECM monitors for a condition once per camshaft revolution.
DTC: P02E0	**Diesel Intake Air (IA) Flow Control Circuit:** The ECM is powered up for more than 0. 5 second. The IA valve duty cycle is greater than 10 percent. DTC P02E0 runs continuously.
DTC: P02E0	**Intake Air (IA) Flow Valve Control Circuit:** P02E0The ignition is OFF. The engine is in after-run. The battery voltage is greater than 11 V. The throttle valve motor control circuit is active. The DTC runs continuously whenever the above conditions are met.
DTC: P02E0 00	**Intake Air Flow Valve Control Circuit:** The ignition is ON, or the engine is running. The throttle actuator motor is commanded ON or OFF. The ignition voltage is less than 16 V. The DTCs run continuously when the above conditions are met.
DTC: P02E0 01	**Intake Air Flow Valve Control Circuit Short to Battery:** The ignition is ON, or the engine is running. The throttle actuator motor is commanded ON or OFF. The ignition voltage is less than 16 V. The DTCs run continuously when the above conditions are met.
DTC: P02E0 02	**Intake Air Flow Valve Control Circuit Short to Ground:** The ignition is ON, or the engine is running. The throttle actuator motor is commanded ON or OFF. The ignition voltage is less than 16 V. The DTCs run continuously when the above conditions are met.
DTC: P02E0 04	**Intake Air Flow Valve Control Circuit Open:** The ignition is ON, or the engine is running. The throttle actuator motor is commanded ON or OFF. The ignition voltage is less than 16 V. The DTCs run continuously when the above conditions are met.
DTC: P02E0 54	**Intake Air Flow Valve Control Circuit High Temperature:** The ignition is ON, or the engine is running. The throttle actuator motor is commanded ON or OFF. The ignition voltage is less than 16 V. The DTCs run continuously when the above conditions are met.
DTC: P02E1 00	**Intake Air Flow Valve Control Performance:** The ignition is ON, or the engine is running. The throttle actuator motor is commanded ON or OFF. The ignition voltage is less than 16 V. The DTCs run continuously when the above conditions are met.

DTC	Trouble Code Title, Conditions, Possible Causes
DTC: P02E2	**Intake Air (IA) Flow Valve Control Circuit Low Voltage:** P02E2, P02E3, P02EB, P122C, P122E and P122FThe battery voltage is greater than 11 V. The Engine is running. The throttle valve motor control circuit is active. The DTCs run continuously whenever the above conditions are met.
DTC: P02E2 00	**Intake Air Flow Valve Control Circuit Low Voltage:** The ignition is ON, or the engine is running. The throttle actuator motor is commanded ON or OFF. The ignition voltage is less than 16 V. The DTCs run continuously when the above conditions are met.
DTC: P02E3	**Intake Air (IA) Flow Valve Control Circuit High Voltage:** P02E2, P02E3, P02EB, P122C, P122E and P122FThe battery voltage is greater than 11 V. The Engine is running. The throttle valve motor control circuit is active. The DTCs run continuously whenever the above conditions are met.
DTC: P02E3 00	**Intake Air Flow Valve Control Circuit High Voltage:** The ignition is ON, or the engine is running. The throttle actuator motor is commanded ON or OFF. The ignition voltage is less than 16 V. The DTCs run continuously when the above conditions are met.
DTC: P02E7	**Intake Air (IA) Flow Valve Position Sensor Performance:** P02E7The engine speed is greater than 600 RPM for greater than 10 s. The engine is not in afterrun mode. The charge air cooler temperature is less than 199°C (390°F). DTC P02E7 runs continuously when the above conditions are met.
DTC: P02E7	**Diesel Intake Air (IA) Flow Position Sensor Performance:** DTCs P02E0, P02E8, P02E9, P0642 or P0643 are not set. DTC P02E7 runs continuously while the IA valve is actively being controlled.
DTC: P02E8	**Diesel Intake Air (IA) Flow Position Sensor Circuit Low Voltage:** P02E8 and P02E9 DTCs P0698 or P0699 are not set. The ignition is ON. DTCs P02E8 and P02E9 run continuously.
DTC: P02E8	**Intake Air (IA) Flow Valve Position Sensor Circuit Low Voltage:** P02E8 and P02E9The engine speed is greater than 600 RPM for greater than 10 s. The engine is not in afterrun mode. DTC P02E8 and P02E9 run continuously when the above conditions are met.
DTC: P02E8 00	**Intake Air Flow Valve Position Sensor Circuit Low Voltage:** The ignition is ON, or the engine is running. The throttle actuator motor is commanded ON or OFF. The ignition voltage is less than 16 V. The DTCs run continuously when the above conditions are met.
DTC: P02E9	**Diesel Intake Air (IA) Flow Position Sensor Circuit High Voltage:** P02E8 and P02E9 DTCs P0698 or P0699 are not set. The ignition is ON. DTCs P02E8 and P02E9 run continuously.
DTC: P02E9	**Intake Air (IA) Flow Valve Position Sensor Circuit High Voltage:** P02E8 and P02E9The engine speed is greater than 600 RPM for greater than 10 s. The engine is not in afterrun mode. DTC P02E8 and P02E9 run continuously when the above conditions are met.
DTC: P02E9 00	**Intake Air Flow Valve Position Sensor Circuit High Voltage:** The ignition is ON, or the engine is running. The throttle actuator motor is commanded ON or OFF. The ignition voltage is less than 16 V. The DTCs run continuously when the above conditions are met.
DTC: P02EB	**Intake Air (IA) Flow Valve Control Motor Current Performance:** P02E2, P02E3, P02EB, P122C, P122E and P122FThe battery voltage is greater than 11 V. The Engine is running. The throttle valve motor control circuit is active. The DTCs run continuously whenever the above conditions are met.
DTC: P02EB 00	**Intake Air Flow Valve Control Motor Current Performance:** The ignition is ON, or the engine is running. The throttle actuator motor is commanded ON or OFF. The ignition voltage is less than 16 V. The DTCs run continuously when the above conditions are met.
DTC: P0300	**Engine Misfire Detected:** DTC P0010, P0011, P0013, P0014, P0016, P0017, P0018, P0019, P0020, P0021, P0023, P0024, P0068, P0101, P0102, P0103, P0106, P0107, P0108, P0112, P0113, P0117, P0118, P0120, P0121, P0122, P0123, P0220, P0222, P0223, P0335, P0336, P0606, P0641, P0651, P1516, P2101, P2122, P2123, P2127, P2128 or P2176 is not set. The engine speed is between 450-6,600 RPM. The evaporative emissions (EVAP) leak detection is not active. The delivered torque signal is greater than 5 % at idle. The delivered torque signal is between 6-29 % with the transmission in drive. The engine coolant temperature (ECT) is between -7 and +127°C (+19 and +261°F). The ECM is not receiving a rough road signal. The fuel level is greater than 11 %. The antilock brake system (ABS) and the traction control system (TCS) are not active or detecting rough road. Torque Converter Clutch (TCC) is not applied/active. The ECM is not in fuel cut-off or decel fuel cut-off mode. DTCs P0300 through P0306 run continuously when the above conditions exist for greater than 1,000 engine revolutions. 200 revolutions after the first failure.

DTC	Trouble Code Title, Conditions, Possible Causes
DTC: P0300 00	**Engine Misfire Detected:** DTCs P0016 00, P0121 00, P0122 00, P0123 00, P0222 00, P0223 00, P0335 00, P0336 00 or P0502 00 are not set. The engine speed is between 520-6 200 RPM. The ignition voltage is between 11-18 V. The engine coolant temperature (ECT) is between -7 to +120°C (+19 to +248°F). The A/C compressor clutch is not changing states. The fuel tank level is more than 15%. The ECM is not in fuel cut-off or deceleration fuel cut-off mode. The ECM is not receiving a rough road signal. The throttle angle is steady within 10%. The throttle angle is less than 4% when the vehicle speed is more than 10 km/h (6 MPH). The transmission is not changing gears. DTCs P0300 00 - P0304 00 run continuously when the above conditions are met.
DTC: P0301	**Cylinder 1 Misfire Detected:** DTCs P0016, P0101, P0102, P0103, P0107, P0108, P0116, P0117, P0118, P0120, P0121, P0122, P0123, P0125, P0128, P0220, P0222, P0223, P0335, P0336, P0608, P1516, P2101, P2119, P2120, P2122, P2123, P2125, P2135, or P2138 are not set. DTC P0315 is not set and the engine speed is between 525-6,000 RPM. ORDTC P0315 is set and the engine speed is less than 1,000 RPM. The ignition voltage is between 9-18 V. The engine coolant temperature (ECT) parameter is between -7 and +126°C (+19 and +259°F). If the ECT is less than -7°C (+19°F) at engine start-up, this diagnostic is disabled until the ECT is more than +21°C (+69°F). The fuel level is more than 10 %. The antilock brake system (ABS) and the traction control system (TCS) are not active or detecting rough road. The ECM is not in fuel shut-off or decel fuel cut-off mode. The power management is not active. Excessive drive wheel slip is not detected. DTC P0300 runs continuously when the above conditions are met.
DTC: P0301 00	**Cylinder 1 Misfire Detected:** DTCs P0016 00, P0121 00, P0122 00, P0123 00, P0222 00, P0223 00, P0335 00, P0336 00 or P0502 00 are not set. The engine speed is between 520-6 200 RPM. The ignition voltage is between 11-18 V. The engine coolant temperature (ECT) is between -7 to +120°C (+19 to +248°F). The A/C compressor clutch is not changing states. The fuel tank level is more than 15%. The ECM is not in fuel cut-off or deceleration fuel cut-off mode. The ECM is not receiving a rough road signal. The throttle angle is steady within 10%. The throttle angle is less than 4% when the vehicle speed is more than 10 km/h (6 MPH). The transmission is not changing gears. DTCs P0300 00 - P0304 00 run continuously when the above conditions are met.
DTC: P0302	**Cylinder 2 Misfire Detected:** DTC P0010, P0011, P0016, P0068, P0101, P0102, P0103, P0106, P0107, P0108, P0112, P0113, P0116, P0117, P0118, P0120, P0122, P0123, P0128, P0220, P0222, P0223, P0335, P0336, P0606, P0641, P0651, P1516, P2101, P2119, P2120, P2122, P2123, P2125, P2127, P2128, P2135, P2138, P2176, P3401, P3425, P3441, and P3449 are not set. The engine speed is between 375-5,800 RPM and DTC P0315 is not set. OR The engine speed is greater than 1,000 rpm and DTC P0315 is set. The ignition voltage is between 9-18 volts. The engine coolant temperature (ECT) is between -7 and +130°C (+19 and +266°F). If the ECT is less than -7°C (+19°F) at startup this diagnostic will not run until the ECT is more than +21°C (+69°F). The fuel level is more than 10 percent. The antilock brake system (ABS) and the traction control system (TCS) are not active or detecting rough road. Torque Converter Clutch (TCC) is not applied/active. The power management is not active. The ECM is not in fuel shut-off, or decel fuel cut-off mode. Excessive drive wheel slip is not detected. The power take-off (PTO) is disabled; where applicable. The cylinder deactivation is not in progress; where applicable. A manual transmission with a throttle position less than 95 percent. DTCs P0300-P0308 run continuously when the above conditions are met.
DTC: P0302 00	**Cylinder 2 Misfire Detected:** DTCs P0010 00, P0011 00, P0013 00, P0014 00, P0016 00, P0017 00, P0101 00, P0102 00, P0103 00, P0112 00, P0113 00, P0117 00, P0118 00, P0121 00, P0122 00, P0123 00, P0222 00, P0223 00, P0315 00, P0335 00, P0336 00, P0502 00, P0651 00, and P2135 00 are not set. The engine speed is between 600-6 528 RPM. The ignition voltage is between 11-18 V. The engine coolant temperature (ECT) sensor is between -7 to +125°C (+19 to +257°F). The A/C compressor clutch is not changing states. The fuel tank level is greater than 15%. The ECM is not in fuel cut-off or deceleration fuel cut-off mode. The ECM is not receiving a rough road signal. The throttle angle is steady within 5%. The throttle angle is greater than 3% when the vehicle speed is greater than 5 km/h (3 MPH). The transmission is not changing gears. The antilock brake system (ABS) and the traction control system , if equipped, is not active. DTCs P0300 00, P0301 00, P0302 00, P0303 00, and P0304 00 run continuously when the above conditions are met.
DTC: P0303	**Cylinder 3 Misfire Detected:** DTC P0010, P0011, P0016, P0068, P0101, P0102, P0103, P0106, P0107, P0108, P0112, P0113, P0116, P0117, P0118, P0120, P0122, P0123, P0128, P0220, P0222, P0223, P0335, P0336, P0606, P0641, P0651, P1516, P2101, P2119, P2120, P2122, P2123, P2125, P2127, P2128, P2135, P2138, P2176, P3401, P3425, P3441, and P3449 are not set. The engine speed is between 375-5,800 RPM and DTC P0315 is not set. OR The engine speed is greater than 1,000 rpm and DTC P0315 is set. The ignition voltage is between 9-18 volts. The engine coolant temperature (ECT) is between -7 and +130°C (+19 and +266°F). If the ECT is less than -7°C (+19°F) at startup this diagnostic will not run until the ECT is more than +21°C (+69°F). The fuel level is more than 10 percent. The antilock brake system (ABS) and the traction control system (TCS) are not active or detecting rough road. The power management is not active. The ECM is not in fuel shut-off, or decel fuel cut-off mode. Excessive drive wheel slip is not detected. Power Take Off (PTO) is disabled. Cylinder Deactivation is not in progress. A manual transmission with a throttle position less than 95 percent. DTC P0300-P0306 runs continuously when the above conditions are met.

DTC	Trouble Code Title, Conditions, Possible Causes
DTC: P0303 00	**Cylinder 3 Misfire Detected:** DTCs P0010 00, P0011 00, P0013 00, P0014 00, P0016 00, P0017 00, P0101 00, P0102 00, P0103 00, P0112 00, P0113 00, P0117 00, P0118 00, P0121 00, P0122 00, P0123 00, P0222 00, P0223 00, P0315 00, P0335 00, P0336 00, P0502 00, P0651 00, and P2135 00 are not set. The engine speed is between 600-6 528 RPM. The ignition voltage is between 11-18 V. The engine coolant temperature (ECT) sensor is between -7 to +125°C (+19 to +257°F). The A/C compressor clutch is not changing states. The fuel tank level is greater than 15%. The ECM is not in fuel cut-off or deceleration fuel cut-off mode. The ECM is not receiving a rough road signal. The throttle angle is steady within 5%. The throttle angle is greater than 3% when the vehicle speed is greater than 5 km/h (3 MPH). The transmission is not changing gears. The antilock brake system (ABS) and the traction control system , if equipped, is not active. DTCs P0300 00, P0301 00, P0302 00, P0303 00, and P0304 00 run continuously when the above conditions are met.
DTC: P0304	**Cylinder 4 Misfire Detected:** DTCs P0016, P0068, P0101, P0102, P0103, P0106, P0107, P0108, P0111, P0112, P0113, P0117, P0118, P0119, P0120, P0122, P0123, P0220, P0222, P0223, P0335, P0336, P0606, P0641, P0651, P1516, P2101, P2120, P2122, P2123, P2125, P2127, P2128, P2135, P2138, and P2176 are not set. DTCs P0010 and P0011 are not set – without LU3. When DTC P0315 is set, the engine speed must be greater than 1,000 RPM. Engine run time is greater than 2 crankshaft revolutions. The engine speed is between 375-5,600 RPM. The ignition voltage is between 9-32 volts. The engine coolant temperature (ECT) is between -7 and +130°C (+19 and +266°F). When the startup ECT is colder than -7°C (+19°F), this diagnostic will be delayed until the ECT is warmer than +21°C (+69°F). The fuel level is greater than 10 percent. The ECM is not in fuel shut-off, or decel fuel cut-off mode. The electronic brake control module (EBCM) and the traction control system (TCS) are not active or detecting rough road. An automatic transmission shift with a throttle position greater than 95 percent is not occurring. The power management is not active. Excessive drive wheel slip is not detected. The power take-off (PTO) is disabled, where applicable. The cylinder deactivation is not in progress, where applicable. DTCs P0300-P0308 run continuously when the above conditions are met.
DTC: P0304 00	**Cylinder 4 Misfire Detected:** DTCs P0010 00, P0011 00, P0013 00, P0014 00, P0016 00, P0017 00, P0101 00, P0102 00, P0103 00, P0112 00, P0113 00, P0117 00, P0118 00, P0121 00, P0122 00, P0123 00, P0222 00, P0223 00, P0315 00, P0335 00, P0336 00, P0502 00, P0651 00, and P2135 00 are not set. The engine speed is between 600-6 528 RPM. The ignition voltage is between 11-18 V. The engine coolant temperature (ECT) sensor is between -7 to +125°C (+19 to +257°F). The A/C compressor clutch is not changing states. The fuel tank level is greater than 15%. The ECM is not in fuel cut-off or deceleration fuel cut-off mode. The ECM is not receiving a rough road signal. The throttle angle is steady within 5%. The throttle angle is greater than 3% when the vehicle speed is greater than 5 km/h (3 MPH). The transmission is not changing gears. The antilock brake system (ABS) and the traction control system , if equipped, is not active. DTCs P0300 00, P0301 00, P0302 00, P0303 00, and P0304 00 run continuously when the above conditions are met.
DTC: P0305	**Cylinder 5 Misfire Detected:** DTC P0010, P0011, P0016, P0068, P0101, P0102, P0103, P0106, P0107, P0108, P0112, P0113, P0116, P0117, P0118, P0120, P0122, P0123, P0128, P0220, P0222, P0223, P0335, P0336, P0606, P0641, P0651, P1516, P2101, P2119, P2120, P2122, P2123, P2125, P2127, P2128, P2135, P2138, P2176, P3401, P3425, P3441, and P3449 are not set. The engine speed is between 375-5,800 RPM and DTC P0315 is not set. OR The engine speed is greater than 1,000 rpm and DTC P0315 is set. The ignition voltage is between 9-18 volts. The engine coolant temperature (ECT) is between -7 and +130°C (+19 and +266°F). If the ECT is less than -7°C (+19°F) at startup this diagnostic will not run until the ECT is more than +21°C (+69°F). The fuel level is more than 10 percent. The antilock brake system (ABS) and the traction control system (TCS) are not active or detecting rough road. The power management is not active. The ECM is not in fuel shut-off, or decel fuel cut-off mode. Excessive drive wheel slip is not detected. Power Take Off (PTO) is disabled. Cylinder Deactivation is not in progress. A manual transmission with a throttle position less than 95 percent. DTC P0300-P0306 runs continuously when the above conditions are met.
DTC: P0306	**Cylinder 6 Misfire Detected:** DTC P0010, P0011, P0013, P0014, P0016, P0017, P0018, P0019, P0020, P0021, P0023, P0024, P0068, P0101, P0102, P0103, P0106, P0107, P0108, P0112, P0113, P0117, P0118, P0120, P0121, P0122, P0123, P0220, P0222, P0223, P0335, P0336, P0606, P0641, P0651, P1516, P2101, P2122, P2123, P2127, P2128 or P2176 is not set. The engine speed is between 450-6,600 RPM. The evaporative emissions (EVAP) leak detection is not active. The delivered torque signal is greater than 5 % at idle. The delivered torque signal is between 6-29 % with the transmission in drive. The engine coolant temperature (ECT) is between -7 and +127°C (+19 and +261°F). The ECM is not receiving a rough road signal. The fuel level is greater than 11 %. The antilock brake system (ABS) and the traction control system (TCS) are not active or detecting rough road. Torque Converter Clutch (TCC) is not applied/active. The ECM is not in fuel cut-off or decel fuel cut-off mode. DTCs P0300 through P0306 run continuously when the above conditions exist for greater than 1,000 engine revolutions. 200 revolutions after the first failure.

DTC	Trouble Code Title, Conditions, Possible Causes
DTC: P0307	**Cylinder 7 Misfire Detected:** DTC P0010, P0011, P0016, P0068, P0101, P0102, P0103, P0106, P0107, P0108, P0112, P0113, P0116, P0117, P0118, P0120, P0122, P0123, P0128, P0220, P0222, P0223, P0335, P0336, P0606, P0641, P0651, P1516, P2101, P2119, P2120, P2122, P2123, P2125, P2127, P2128, P2135, P2138, P2176, P3401, P3425, P3441, and P3449 are not set. The engine speed is between 375-5,800 RPM and DTC P0315 is not set. OR The engine speed is greater than 1,000 rpm and DTC P0315 is set. The ignition voltage is between 9-18 volts. The engine coolant temperature (ECT) is between -7 and +130°C (+19 and +266°F). If the ECT is less than -7°C (+19°F) at startup this diagnostic will not run until the ECT is more than +21°C (+69°F). The fuel level is more than 10 percent. The antilock brake system (ABS) and the traction control system (TCS) are not active or detecting rough road. Torque Converter Clutch (TCC) is not applied/active. The power management is not active. The ECM is not in fuel shut-off, or decel fuel cut-off mode. Excessive drive wheel slip is not detected. The power take-off (PTO) is disabled; where applicable. The cylinder deactivation is not in progress; where applicable. A manual transmission with a throttle position less than 95 percent. DTCs P0300-P0308 run continuously when the above conditions are met.
DTC: P0308	**Cylinder 8 Misfire Detected:** DTCs P0016, P0068, P0101, P0102, P0103, P0106, P0107, P0108, P0111, P0112, P0113, P0117, P0118, P0119, P0120, P0122, P0123, P0220, P0222, P0223, P0335, P0336, P0606, P0641, P0651, P1516, P2101, P2120, P2122, P2123, P2125, P2127, P2128, P2135, P2138, and P2176 are not set. DTCs P0010 and P0011 are not set – without LU3. When DTC P0315 is set, the engine speed must be greater than 1,000 RPM. Engine run time is greater than 2 crankshaft revolutions. The engine speed is between 375-5,600 RPM. The ignition voltage is between 9-32 volts. The engine coolant temperature (ECT) is between -7 and +130°C (+19 and +266°F). When the startup ECT is colder than -7°C (+19°F), this diagnostic will be delayed until the ECT is warmer than +21°C (+69°F). The fuel level is greater than 10 percent. The ECM is not in fuel shut-off, or decel fuel cut-off mode. The electronic brake control module (EBCM) and the traction control system (TCS) are not active or detecting rough road. An automatic transmission shift with a throttle position greater than 95 percent is not occurring. The power management is not active. Excessive drive wheel slip is not detected. The power take-off (PTO) is disabled, where applicable. The cylinder deactivation is not in progress, where applicable. DTCs P0300-P0308 run continuously when the above conditions are met.
DTC: P0313 00	**Misfire Detected With Low Fuel Level:** DTCs P0016 00, P0121 00, P0122 00, P0123 00, P0221 00, P0222 00, P0223 00, P0335 00 or P0336 00 are not set. The engine speed is between 600-6528 RPM. The ECM is not in fuel cut-off mode. DTCs P0300 00, P0304 00, and P0313 00 run continuously when the above conditions are met.
DTC: P0315	**Crankshaft Position System Variation Not Learned:** DTCs P0016, P0335, P0336, P0340, and P0341 are not set. The engine speed is between 900-1,900 RPM. The ECM is in fuel shut-off, or decel fuel cut-off mode. The Crankshaft Position Reluctor Wheel Learn has not learned successfully. The diagnostic runs continuously when the above conditions are met.
DTC: P0315	**Crankshaft Position System Variation Not Learned:** The engine is running. The DTC runs continuously.
DTC: P0315 00	**Crankshaft Position System Variation Not Learned:** The engine is running. DTC P0315 00 runs continuously once the above conditions are met.
DTC: P0318 00	**Rough Road Sensor Circuit:** The ignition is ON or the engine is operating. DTC P0318 00 runs continuously once the above conditions are met.
DTC: P0324	**Knock Sensor System Performance:** P0324 and P0326–Excessive Knock Detection Mode. Engine speed is between 400-8,500 RPM. The engine coolant temperature (ECT) is warmer than -40°C (-40°F). The intake air temperature (IAT) is warmer than -40°C (-40°F). The DTCs run continuously when the above conditions are met. P0324 and P0326–Abnormal Noise Detection Mode–Improperly Bolted Knock Sensor. Engine speed is between 2,200-8,500 RPM. The ECT is greater than -40°C (-40°F). The IAT is greater than -40°C (-40°F). The DTCs run continuously when the above conditions are met.
DTC: P0324 00	**Knock Sensor System Performance:** P0324 00, and P0326 00 Excessive Knock Detection Mode. Engine speed is between 400-8 500 RPM. The ECT is greater than -40°C (-40°F). The IAT is greater than -40°C (-40°F). The DTCs run continuously when the above conditions are met. P0324 00 and P0326 00 Abnormal Noise Detection Mode, Improperly Bolted Knock Sensor. Engine speed is between 2 200-8 500 RPM. The ECT is greater than -40°C (-40°F). The IAT is greater than -40°C (-40°F). The DTCs run continuously when the above conditions are met.
DTC: P0325	**Knock Sensor (KS) Circuit Bank 1:** DTC P0324 runs continuously when the engine speed is greater than 2,000 RPM and the engine load is greater than a calibrated amount. DTC P0326 runs continuously when: The engine speed is greater than or equal to 800 RPM. The MAP is greater than 42 kPa. DTCs P0120, P0121, P0122, or P0123 are not set. DTC P0325, P0330, P0327, P0328, P0332, P0333 run continuously when: The engine coolant temperature (ECT) is greater than 75°C (167°F). The engine run time is greater than 90 s.
DTC: P0325 00	**Knock Sensor Circuit:** DTCs P0106 00, P0107 00, and P0108 00 are not set. The engine speed is greater than 1 600 RPM. The engine coolant temperature (ECT) is more than 50°C (122°F). The manifold absolute pressure (MAP) is between 10-50 kPa (1. 4-7. 2 PSI) which depends on engine speed. This DTC runs continuously within the enabling conditions.

DTC	Trouble Code Title, Conditions, Possible Causes
DTC: P0326	**Knock Sensor Performance:** P0324 and P0326—Excessive Knock Detection Mode. Engine speed is between 400-8,500 RPM. The engine coolant temperature (ECT) is warmer than -40°C (-40°F). The intake air temperature (IAT) is warmer than -40°C (-40°F). The DTCs run continuously when the above conditions are met. P0324 and P0326—Abnormal Noise Detection Mode—Improperly Bolted Knock Sensor. Engine speed is between 2,200-8,500 RPM. The ECT is greater than -40°C (-40°F). The IAT is greater than -40°C (-40°F). The DTCs run continuously when the above conditions are met.
DTC: P0326 00	**Knock Sensor Performance:** The engine speed is greater than 700 RPM. The engine speed is between 700-2 500 RPM for DTC P06B6 00. The airflow into the engine is between 40-2 000 mg/cylinder. This DTC runs continuously within the enabling conditions. DTCs P0324 00, P0326 00 and P06B6 00 run continuously once the above conditions are met.
DTC: P0326 00	**Knock Sensor 1 Performance:** The engine is running. The ignition voltage is less than 16 V. These DTC runs continuously once the above conditions are met.
DTC: P0327	**Knock Sensor (KS) Circuit Low Frequency Bank 1:** P0327, P0328, P0332, and P0333 DTC P0112, P0113, P0116, P0117, P0118, or P0128 is not set. The engine coolant temperature (ECT) is greater than -40°C (-40°F). The engine oil temperature is less than 256°C (492. 8°F). The engine run time is greater than 2 minutes. DTCs P0327, P0328, P0332, and P0333 run continuously when the above conditions are met.
DTC: P0327 00	**Knock Sensor Circuit Low Voltage:** P0325 00, P0327 00, and P0328 00Engine speed is between 400-8 500 RPM. The engine coolant temperature (ECT) is greater than -40°C (-40°F). The intake air temperature (IAT) is greater than -40°C (-40°F). The DTCs run continuously when the above conditions are met.
DTC: P0328	**Knock Sensor (KS) Circuit High Frequency Bank 1:** P0327, P0328, P0332, and P0333 DTC P0112, P0113, P0116, P0117, P0118, or P0128 is not set. The engine coolant temperature (ECT) is greater than -40°C (-40°F). The engine oil temperature is less than 256°C (492. 8°F). The engine run time is greater than 2 minutes. DTCs P0327, P0328, P0332, and P0333 run continuously when the above conditions are met.
DTC: P0328	**Knock Sensor (KS) Circuit High Bank 1:** P0325, P0326, and P0330The engine is idling. The manifold absolute pressure (MAP) is greater than 19 kPa. The DTCs run continuously when the above conditions are met. P0324, P0327, P0328, and P0333The ignition is ON. The DTCs run continuously when the above condition is met.
DTC: P0328 00	**Knock Sensor Circuit High Voltage:** The engine speed is greater than 700 RPM. The engine speed is between 700-2 500 RPM for DTC P06B6 00. The airflow into the engine is between 40-2 000 mg/cylinder. This DTC runs continuously within the enabling conditions. DTCs P0324 00, P0326 00 and P06B6 00 run continuously once the above conditions are met.
DTC: P0330	**Knock Sensor (KS) Circuit Bank 2:** DTC P0324 runs continuously when the engine speed is greater than 2,000 RPM and the engine load is greater than a calibrated amount. DTC P0326 runs continuously when: The engine speed is greater than or equal to 800 RPM. The MAP is greater than 42 kPa. DTCs P0120, P0121, P0122, or P0123 are not set. DTC P0325, P0330, P0327, P0328, P0332, P0333 run continuously when: The engine coolant temperature (ECT) is greater than 75°C (167°F). The engine run time is greater than 90 s.
DTC: P0330	**Knock Sensor (KS) Circuit Bank 2:** P0325 and P0330 DTC P0324, P0325, P0326, P0327, P0328, P0330, P0332, or P0333 is not set. The engine speed is greater than 400 RPM. The engine coolant temperature (ECT) is greater than -40°C (-40°F). The engine run time is greater than 2 minutes. The power take-off (PTO) is not active. DTCs P0325 and P0330 run continuously when the above conditions are met.
DTC: P0331	**Knock Sensor Performance Bank 2:** P0324, P0326 and P0331—Excessive Knock Detection Mode. Engine speed is between 400-8,500 RPM. The engine coolant temperature (ECT) is warmer than -40°C (-40°F). The intake air temperature (IAT) is warmer than -40°C (-40°F). The DTCs run continuously when the above conditions are met. P0324, P0326 and P0331—Abnormal Noise Detection Mode—Improperly Bolted Knock Sensor. Engine speed is between 2,200-8,500 RPM. The ECT is warmer than -40°C (-40°F). The IAT is warmer than -40°C (-40°F). The DTCs run continuously when the above conditions are met.
DTC: P0331 00	**Knock Sensor 2 Performance:** The engine is running. The ignition voltage is less than 16 V. These DTC runs continuously once the above conditions are met.
DTC: P0332	**Knock Sensor Circuit Low Bank 2:** P0324, P0327, P0328, P0332, and P0333The ignition is ON. The DTCs run continuously when the above condition is met.
DTC: P0332	**Knock Sensor (KS) Circuit Low Bank 2:** P0325, P0326, and P0330The engine is idling. The manifold absolute pressure (MAP) is greater than 19 kPa. The DTCs run continuously when the above conditions are met. P0324, P0327, P0328, and P0333The ignition is ON. The DTCs run continuously when the above condition is met.

DTC	Trouble Code Title, Conditions, Possible Causes
DTC: P0332	**Knock Sensor (KS) Circuit Low Voltage Bank 2:** DTC P0324 runs continuously when the engine speed is greater than 2,000 RPM and the engine load is greater than a calibrated amount. DTC P0326 runs continuously when: The engine speed is greater than or equal to 800 RPM. The MAP is greater than 42 kPa. DTCs P0120, P0121, P0122, or P0123 are not set. DTC P0325, P0330, P0327, P0328, P0332, P0333 run continuously when: The engine coolant temperature (ECT) is greater than 75°C (167°F). The engine run time is greater than 90 s.
DTC: P0332	**Knock Sensor (KS) Circuit Low Frequency Bank 2:** P0327, P0328, P0332, and P0333 DTC P0112, P0113, P0116, P0117, P0118, or P0128 is not set. The engine coolant temperature (ECT) is greater than -40°C (-40°F). The engine oil temperature is less than 256°C (492. 8°F). The engine run time is greater than 2 minutes. DTCs P0327, P0328, P0332, and P0333 run continuously when the above conditions are met.
DTC: P0333	**Knock Sensor Circuit High Bank 2:** P0327, P0328, P0332, and P0333The ignition is ON. The DTCs run continuously when the above condition is met.
DTC: P0333	**Knock Sensor (KS) Circuit High Frequency Bank 2:** P0327, P0328, P0332, and P0333 DTC P0112, P0113, P0116, P0117, P0118, or P0128 is not set. The engine coolant temperature (ECT) is greater than -40°C (-40°F). The engine oil temperature is less than 256°C (492. 8°F). The engine run time is greater than 2 minutes. DTCs P0327, P0328, P0332, and P0333 run continuously when the above conditions are met.
DTC: P0333	**Knock Sensor (KS) Circuit High Voltage Bank 2:** DTC P0324 runs continuously when the engine speed is greater than 2,000 RPM and the engine load is greater than a calibrated amount. DTC P0326 runs continuously when: The engine speed is greater than or equal to 800 RPM. The MAP is greater than 42 kPa. DTCs P0120, P0121, P0122, or P0123 are not set. DTC P0325, P0330, P0327, P0328, P0332, P0333 run continuously when: The engine coolant temperature (ECT) is greater than 75°C (167°F). The engine run time is greater than 90 s.
DTC: P0335	**Crankshaft Position Sensor Circuit:** The engine is cranking or running. The camshaft position sensor signal is present. DTC P0335 runs continuously when the above conditions are met.
DTC: P0335	**Crankshaft Position Sensor Circuit:** P0335 Condition 1The engine cranking starter is engaged. DTC P0101, P0102 and P0103, are not set. Engine Air Flow is greater than 3. 0 grams/second. Condition 2Engine is running and starter is not engaged. DTC P0651 not active. Condition 3The engine is running or starter is engaged. DTCs P0365, P0366, P0641, or P0651 are not set. P0336 Condition 1Engine Air Flow is greater than 3. 0 grams/second. Engine speed is greater than 450 RPM. DTC P0335 or P0651 is not set. Condition 2Engine is running, starter is not engaged P0651 is not set. Condition 3Starter is engaged. DTC P0101, P0102, or P0103 are not set. Engine Air Flow is greater than 3. 0 grams/second. Condition 4Engine is running or starter is engaged. DTC P0365, P0366, P0641, or P0651 is not set.
DTC: P0335 00	**Crankshaft Position Sensor Circuit:** DTC P0016 00, P0201 00, P0202 00, P0203 00, P0204 00, P0261 00, P0262 00, P0264 00, P0265 00, P0267 00, P0268 00, P0270 00, P0271 00, P0340 00, P0341 00, P0365 00, P0366 00, P0443 00, P0453 00, P0458 00 are not set. The engine is running. The DTC runs continuously.
DTC: P0335 00	**Crankshaft Position Sensor Circuit Malfunction:** The engine is cranking or running. The DTCs run continuously once the above condition is met for greater than 5 s.
DTC: P0335 00	**Crankshaft Position Sensor Circuit:** DTCs P0101 00, P0102 00, P0103 00, P0365 00, P0366 00, P0641 00, and P0651 00 are not set. The engine is cranking or running. The airflow into the engine is greater than 3 g/s. The DTCs run continuously once the above conditions are met.
DTC: P0335 28	**Crankshaft Position Sensor Circuit Incorrect Frequency:** The engine is cranking or running. The DTCs run continuously once the above condition is met for greater than 5 s.
DTC: P0335 29	**Crankshaft Position Sensor Circuit Too Few Pulses:** The engine is cranking or running. The DTCs run continuously once the above condition is met for greater than 5 s.
DTC: P0336	**Crankshaft Position (CKP) Sensor Performance:** The engine is cranking or running. DTC P0336 runs continuously when the above condition is met. DTCs P0642 or P0643 are not set.
DTC: P0336	**Crankshaft Position Sensor Performance:** DTC P0101, P0102, P0103, P0641, or P0651 is not set. The engine is cranking or running. The airflow into the engine is greater than 3 g/s. The DTCs run continuously when the above conditions are met.
DTC: P0336	**Crankshaft Position Sensor Performance:** DTCs P0340, P0341, P0345, P0346, P0365, P0366, P0380, P0381, P0641 or P0651 are not set. The engine is cranking or running. The DTC runs continuously when the above conditions are met.

DTC	Trouble Code Title, Conditions, Possible Causes
DTC: P0336	**Crankshaft Position Sensor Performance:** P0335 Condition 1The engine cranking starter is engaged. DTC P0101, P0102 and P0103, are not set. Engine Air Flow is greater than 3. 0 grams/second. Condition 2Engine is running and starter is not engaged. DTC P0651 not active. Condition 3The engine is running or starter is engaged. DTCs P0365, P0366, P0641, or P0651 are not set. P0336 Condition 1Engine Air Flow is greater than 3. 0 grams/second. Engine speed is greater than 450 RPM. DTC P0335 or P0651 is not set. Condition 2Engine is running, starter is not engaged P0651 is not set. Condition 3Starter is engaged. DTC P0101, P0102, or P0103 are not set. Engine Air Flow is greater than 3. 0 grams/second. Condition 4Engine is running or starter is engaged. DTC P0365, P0366, P0641, or P0651 is not set.
DTC: P0336 00	**Crankshaft Position Sensor Performance:** The engine is cranking or operating. The engine control module detects no or wrong signal. The DTC runs continuously once the above conditions are met.
DTC: P0336 00	**Crankshaft Position Sensor Performance:** DTC P0016 00 and P0340 00 are not set. The engine is cranking or running. These DTCs runs continuously once the above conditions are met.
DTC: P0336 00	**Crankshaft Position Sensor Performance:** DTC P0016 00, P0201 00, P0202 00, P0203 00, P0204 00, P0261 00, P0262 00, P0264 00, P0265 00, P0267 00, P0268 00, P0270 00, P0271 00, P0340 00, P0341 00, P0365 00, P0366 00, P0443 00, P0453 00, P0458 00 are not set. The engine is running. The DTC runs continuously.
DTC: P0336 00	**Crankshaft Position Sensor Performance:** DTCs P0101 00, P0102 00, P0103 00, P0365 00, P0366 00, P0641 00, and P0651 00 are not set. The engine is cranking or running. The airflow into the engine is greater than 3 g/s. The DTCs run continuously once the above conditions are met.
DTC: P0338	**Crankshaft Position Sensor Circuit High Duty Cycle:** P0335 Condition 1The engine cranking starter is engaged. DTC P0101, P0102 and P0103, are not set. Engine Air Flow is greater than 3. 0 grams/second. Condition 2Engine is running and starter is not engaged. DTC P0651 not active. Condition 3The engine is running or starter is engaged. DTCs P0365, P0366, P0641, or P0651 are not set. P0336 Condition 1Engine Air Flow is greater than 3. 0 grams/second. Engine speed is greater than 450 RPM. DTC P0335 or P0651 is not set. Condition 2Engine is running, starter is not engaged P0651 is not set. Condition 3Starter is engaged. DTC P0101, P0102, or P0103 are not set. Engine Air Flow is greater than 3. 0 grams/second. Condition 4Engine is running or starter is engaged. DTC P0365, P0366, P0641, or P0651 is not set.
DTC: P0338	**Crankshaft Position Sensor Circuit High Duty Cycle:** The engine is cranking or operating. The ECM has detected greater than 12 camshaft revolutions. The DTCs run continuously once the above conditions are met for greater than 5 s.
DTC: P0339 00	**Crankshaft Position Sensor Performance:** The engine is cranking or operating. The engine control module detects no or wrong signal. The DTC runs continuously once the above conditions are met.
DTC: P0340	**Camshaft Position Sensor Circuit:** The ignition is ON. The engine is turning faster than 50 RPM. DTC P0340 runs continuously when the above conditions are met. DTCs P0335, P0336 are not set.
DTC: P0340	**Camshaft Position Sensor Circuit:** The mass air flow (MAF) is greater than 3 grams per second. DTC P0101, P0102, P0103, P0641, or P0651 is not set. The engine is cranking or running. DTC P0340 runs continuously when the above conditions are met.
DTC: P0340	**Intake Camshaft Position Sensor Circuit Bank 1:** DTC P0335, 0336, P0641 or P0651 is not set. The engine is cranking or running. The DTCs run continuously when the above conditions are met.
DTC: P0340	**Intake Camshaft Position Sensor Circuit Bank 1:** NOTE: The ECM detects engine movement by sensing the airflow through the MAF sensor when airflow is greater than 3 g/s, or by sensing crankshaft position sensor pulses. DTC P0102, P0103, P0335, P0336, P0641, P0651, or P0697 is not set. The engine is cranking or running. The DTC runs continuously when the above conditions are met.
DTC: P0340 00	**Intake Camshaft Position Sensor Circuit:** DTC P0101 00, P0102 00, P0103 00, P0335 00, P0336 00, P0641 00, or P0651 00 are not set. The engine is cranking or running. The mass air flow (MAF) is greater than 3 g/s. The DTCs run continuously when the above conditions are met.
DTC: P0340 00	**Camshaft Position Sensor Circuit Malfunction:** DTCs P0016, P0335 and P0336 are not set. The engine is running. The engine speed is greater than 50 RPM. The DTCs run continuously once the above conditions are met.
DTC: P0340 00	**Camshaft Position Sensor Circuit:** DTCs P0335 00 and P0336 00 are not set. The engine is running. This DTC run continuously when the above conditions are met.

DTC	Trouble Code Title, Conditions, Possible Causes
DTC: P0340 28	**Camshaft Position Sensor Circuit Incorrect Frequency:** DTCs P0016, P0335 and P0336 are not set. The engine is running. The engine speed is greater than 50 RPM. The DTCs run continuously once the above conditions are met.
DTC: P0340 29	**Camshaft Position Sensor Circuit Too Few Pulses:** DTCs P0016, P0335 and P0336 are not set. The engine is running. The engine speed is greater than 50 RPM. The DTCs run continuously once the above conditions are met.
DTC: P0341	**Intake Camshaft Position Sensor Performance Bank 1:** DTCs P0335, P0336, P0641, P0651, or P0697 are not set. The engine is cranking or running. The DTC runs continuously when the above conditions are met.
DTC: P0341	**Camshaft Position Sensor Performance:** DTC P0641, or P0651 is not set. The engine is cranking or running. DTCs run continuously when the above conditions are met.
DTC: P0341	**Intake Camshaft Position Sensor Performance:** The engine is running. DTCs P0341, P0342 and P0343 run continuously when the above condition is met.
DTC: P0341	**Intake Camshaft Position Sensor Performance:** P0341 - Near Engine Start, Camshaft Position Fast Event Based Test. The engine is cranking. The medium resolution is less than or equal to 10 counts. P0341 - After Engine Start, Camshaft Position Slow Event Based Test. The engine is running. DTCs P0335, P0336, and P0340 are not set. DTC P0341 runs continuously when the above conditions are met.
DTC: P0341 00	**Intake Camshaft Position Sensor Performance:** The engine is cranking or running. The DTC runs continuously.
DTC: P0341 00	**Intake Camshaft Position Sensor Performance:** DTC P0335 00, P0336 00, P0641 00, or P0651 00 are not set. The engine is cranking or running. The mass air flow (MAF) is greater than 3 g/s. The DTCs run continuously when the above conditions are met.
DTC: P0341 00	**Camshaft Position Sensor Performance Malfunction:** DTCs P0016, P0335 and P0336 are not set. The engine is running. The engine speed is greater than 50 RPM. The DTCs run continuously once the above conditions are met.
DTC: P0342	**Intake Camshaft Position Sensor Circuit Low Voltage:** The engine is running. DTCs P0341, P0342 and P0343 run continuously when the above condition is met.
DTC: P0343	**Intake Camshaft Position Sensor Circuit High Voltage:** The engine is running. DTCs P0341, P0342 and P0343 run continuously when the above condition is met.
DTC: P0344 00	**Camshaft Position Sensor Performance:** DTC P0016 00, P0336 00 or P0339 00 are not set. The engine is running. The engine speed is greater than 50 RPM. The DTC run continuously once the above conditions are met.
DTC: P0345	**Intake Camshaft Position Sensor Circuit Bank 2:** DTC P0335, P0336, P0641 or P0651 is not set. The engine is cranking or running. The DTCs run continuously when the above conditions are met.
DTC: P0345	**Intake Camshaft Position Sensor Circuit Bank 2:** **NOTE: The ECM detects engine movement by sensing the airflow through the MAF sensor when airflow is greater than 3 g/s, or by sensing crankshaft position sensor pulses.** DTC P0102, P0103, P0335, P0336, P0641, P0651, or P0697 is not set. The engine is cranking or running. The DTC runs continuously when the above conditions are met.
DTC: P0346	**Intake Camshaft Position Sensor Performance Bank 2:** DTCs P0335, P0336, P0641, P0651, or P0697 are not set. The engine is cranking or running. The DTC runs continuously when the above conditions are met.
DTC: P0351	**Ignition Coil 1 Control Circuit:** The engine speed is less than 6,000 RPM. The ignition 1 voltage signal is between 9-18 volts. DTCs P0351, P0352, P0353, P0354 run continuously when the above conditions are met.
DTC: P0351 00	**Ignition Coil 1 Control Circuit:** The engine is running. The ignition voltage is greater than 6 V. The DTC runs continuously once the above condition is met.
DTC: P0352	**Ignition Coil 2 Control Circuit:** Engine running. Ignition voltage greater than 6V. DTC P0351-P0358 runs continuously when the above condition is met.
DTC: P0352	**Ignition Coil 2 Control Circuit:** The engine speed is less than 6,000 RPM. The ignition 1 voltage signal is between 9-18 volts. DTCs P0351, P0352, P0353, P0354 run continuously when the above conditions are met.

DTC	Trouble Code Title, Conditions, Possible Causes
DTC: P0352 00	**Ignition Coil 2 Control Circuit:** The engine is running. The ignition voltage is greater than 6 V. The DTC runs continuously once the above condition is met.
DTC: P0353	**Ignition Coil 3 Control Circuit:** The engine speed is less than 6,000 RPM. The ignition 1 voltage signal is between 9-18 volts. DTCs P0351, P0352, P0353, P0354 run continuously when the above conditions are met.
DTC: P0353	**Ignition Coil 3 Control Circuit:** The engine is running. DTCs P0351-P0354 run continuously when the above condition is met.
DTC: P0353 00	**Ignition Coil 3 Control Circuit:** The engine is running. The ignition voltage is greater than 6 V. The DTC runs continuously once the above condition is met.
DTC: P0354	**Ignition Coil 4 Control Circuit:** The engine speed is less than 6,000 RPM. The ignition 1 voltage signal is between 9-18 volts. DTCs P0351, P0352, P0353, P0354 run continuously when the above conditions are met.
DTC: P0354	**Ignition Coil 4 Control Circuit:** The engine is running. The ignition voltage is greater than 6 V. DTC P0351-P0356 runs continuously when the above conditions are met.
DTC: P0354 00	**Ignition Coil 4 Control Circuit:** The engine is running. The ignition voltage is greater than 6 V. The DTC runs continuously once the above condition is met.
DTC: P0355	**Ignition Coil 5 Control Circuit:** Engine running. Ignition voltage greater than 6V. DTC P0351-P0358 runs continuously when the above condition is met.
DTC: P0355	**Ignition Coil 5 Control Circuit:** The engine is cranking or running. The DTCs run continuously when the above condition is met.
DTC: P0356	**Ignition Coil 6 Control Circuit:** The engine is running. The ignition voltage is greater than 6 V. DTC P0351-P0356 runs continuously when the above conditions are met.
DTC: P0357	**Ignition Coil 7 Control Circuit:** Engine running. Ignition voltage greater than 6V. DTC P0351-P0358 runs continuously when the above condition is met.
DTC: P0358	**Ignition Coil 8 Control Circuit:** Engine running. Ignition voltage greater than 6V. DTC P0351-P0358 runs continuously when the above condition is met.
DTC: P0365	**Exhaust Camshaft Position Sensor Circuit Bank 1:** **NOTE: The ECM detects engine movement by sensing the airflow through the MAF sensor when airflow is greater than 3 g/s, or by sensing crankshaft position sensor pulses.** DTC P0102, P0103, P0335, P0336, P0641, P0651, or P0697 is not set. The engine is cranking or running. The DTC runs continuously when the above conditions are met.
DTC: P0365	**Exhaust Camshaft Position Sensor Circuit:** DTCs P0101, P0102, P0103, P0340 and P0365 are not set. The engine is cranking or running. The mass air flow (MAF) is greater than 3 grams per s. The DTCs run continuously when the above condition is met.
DTC: P0365	**Exhaust Camshaft Position Sensor Circuit Bank 1:** DTC P0335, P0336, P0641 or P0651 is not set. The engine is cranking or running. The DTCs run continuously when the above conditions are met.
DTC: P0365 00	**Exhaust Camshaft Position Sensor Circuit:** The engine is cranking or running. The DTC runs continuously.
DTC: P0366	**Exhaust Camshaft Position Sensor Performance Bank 1:** DTC P0335, P0336, P0641 or P0651 is not set. The engine is cranking or running. The DTCs run continuously when the above conditions are met.
DTC: P0366	**Exhaust Camshaft Position Sensor Performance:** P0366 - Near Engine Start, Camshaft Position Fast Event Based Test. The engine is cranking. The medium resolution is less than or equal to 10 counts. P0366 - After Engine Start, Camshaft Position Slow Event Based Test. The engine is running. DTCs P0335, P0336, and P0365 are not set. DTC P0366 runs continuously when the above conditions are met.
DTC: P0366 00	**Exhaust Camshaft Position Sensor Performance:** The engine is cranking or running. The DTC runs continuously.
DTC: P0367	**Exhaust Camshaft Position Sensor Circuit Low Voltage:** The engine is running. DTCs P0366, P0367 and P0368 run continuously when the above condition is met.

DTC	Trouble Code Title, Conditions, Possible Causes
DTC: P0368	**Exhaust Camshaft Position Sensor Circuit High Voltage:** The engine is running. DTCs P0366, P0367 and P0368 run continuously when the above condition is met.
DTC: P037E 00	**Glow Plug Control Module Feedback Circuit Low Voltage:** The ignition is ON. The ignition voltage is between 9-16 V. The DTCs run once per ignition cycle when the above conditions are met.
DTC: P037F 00	**Glow Plug Control Module Feedback Circuit High Voltage:** The ignition is ON. The ignition voltage is between 9-16 V. The DTCs run once per ignition cycle when the above conditions are met.
DTC: P0381	**Wait to Start Lamp Control Circuit:** Battery voltage is greater than 11 V. DTC P0381 runs continuously when the ignition is ON.
DTC: P0383 00	**Glow Plug Control Module Control Circuit Low Voltage:** The ignition is ON. The ignition voltage is between 9-16 V. The DTCs run once per ignition cycle when the above conditions are met.
DTC: P0384 00	**Glow Plug Control Module Control Circuit High Voltage:** The ignition is ON. The ignition voltage is between 9-16 V. The DTCs run once per ignition cycle when the above conditions are met.
DTC: P0390	**Exhaust Camshaft Position Sensor Circuit Bank 2:** **NOTE: The ECM detects engine movement by sensing the airflow through the MAF sensor when airflow is greater than 3 g/s, or by sensing crankshaft position sensor pulses.** DTC P0102, P0103, P0335, P0336, P0641, P0651, or P0697 is not set. The engine is cranking or running. The DTC runs continuously when the above conditions are met.
DTC: P0390	**Exhaust Camshaft Position Sensor Circuit Bank 2:** DTC P0335, P0336, P0641 or P0651 is not set. The engine is cranking or running. The DTCs run continuously when the above conditions are met.
DTC: P0391	**Exhaust Camshaft Position Sensor Performance Bank 2:** DTCs P0335, P0336, P0641, P0651, or P0697 are not set. The engine is cranking or running. The DTC runs continuously when the above conditions are met.
DTC: P0391	**Exhaust Camshaft Position Sensor Performance Bank 2:** DTC P0335, P0336, P0641 or P0651 is not set. The engine is cranking or running. The DTCs run continuously when the above conditions are met.
DTC: P0400	**Exhaust Gas Recirculation (EGR) Flow Incorrect:** DTC P0045, P0047, P0048, P006E, P006F, P007C, P007D, P0101, P0102, P0103, P0106, P0107, P0108, P0112, P0113, P0117, P0118, P02E0, P02E7, P02E8, P02E9, P02EB, P0403, P0405, P0406, P0489, P0490, P122C, P122E, P122F, P1407, P140D, P140E, P140F, P1411, P1412, P1413, P1414, P16A0, P16A1, P16A2, P2228, P2229, P2263, P2453, P245A, P245C, P245D, P2493, P2494, P2495, P2564, P2565, P2598, or P2599 is not set. The engine is running. The DTC runs continuously when the above conditions are met.
DTC: P0400 00	**Exhaust Gas Recirculation (EGR) Current Performance:** The ignition is ON, or the engine is running. The DTCs run continuously when the above conditions are met.
DTC: P0401	**Exhaust Gas Recirculation (EGR) Flow Insufficient:** DTCs P0101, P0102, P0103, P0403, P0405, P0406, P046C are not set. The engine is running. The engine coolant temperature (ECT) is greater than 60°C (140°F). The EGR valve is active. DTCs P0401 and P0402 run continuously when the above conditions are met.
DTC: P0401	**Exhaust Gas Recirculation (EGR) Flow Insufficient:** P0401 DTC P0045, P0047, P0048, P006E, P006F, P007C, P007D, P0101, P0102, P0103, P0106, P0107, P0108, P0112, P0113, P0117, P0118, P02E0, P02E7, P02E8, P02E9, P02EB, P0403, P0405, P0406, P0489, P0490, P122C, P122E, P122F, P1407, P140D, P140E, P140F, P1411, P1412, P1413, P1414, P16A0, P16A1, P16A2, P2228, P2229, P2263, P2453, P245A, P245C, P245D, P2493, P2494, P2495, P2564, P2565, P2598, or P2599 is not set. The engine speed is between 500-950 RPM. The calculated fuel rate is between 1-15 mm ;The ambient air temperature is greater than -7°C (19. 4°F). The engine coolant temperature is greater than 70°C (158°F). The Barometric Pressure is greater than 74. 8 kPa (10. 9 psi). The system is not in Diesel Particulate Filter (DPF) regeneration. The EGR valve position is greater than 5 %. The throttle valve position is less than 5 %. The DTC runs continuously when the above conditions are met.
DTC: P0401 00	**Exhaust Gas Recirculation (EGR) Flow Insufficient:** P0401 00 DTCs P0106 00, P0107 00, P0108 00, P0112 00, P0113 00, P0117 00, P0118 00, P0122 00, P0123 00, P0351 00, P0352 00, P0402 00, P0404 00, P0405 00, P0406 00, P0502 00, P0506 00, and P0507 00 are not set. The EGR flow test is ran in deceleration fuel cut-off mode with the following conditions present before deceleration occurs: The A/C compressor clutch does not change state during deceleration. The intake air temperature (IAT) sensor is between -3 to +120°C (+27 to +248°F). The barometric pressure (BARO) is greater than 82 kPa (11. 89 PSI). The vehicle speed is greater than 30 km/h (19 MPH) before deceleration. The throttle position is less than 1. 5%. The EGR flow test is ran when the following conditions are met during deceleration fuel cut-off mode: The EGR position is less than 1%. The MAP is between 11-55 kPa (1. 5-7. 9 PSI). The engine speed is between 1 600-3 200 RPM. The MAP does not vary greater than 3 kPa (0. 4 PSI). The EGR flow test is performed once per ignition cycle. This DTC runs multiple times on the first ignition cycle after the DTC is cleared from the ECM memory.

DTC	Trouble Code Title, Conditions, Possible Causes
DTC: P0402	**Exhaust Gas Recirculation (EGR) Flow Excessive:** DTCs P0101, P0102, P0103, P0403, P0405, P0406, P046C are not set. The engine is running. The engine coolant temperature (ECT) is greater than 60°C (140°F). The EGR valve is active. DTCs P0401 and P0402 run continuously when the above conditions are met.
DTC: P0402	**Exhaust Gas Recirculation (EGR) Flow Excessive:** P0402 DTC P0045, P0047, P0048, P006E, P006F, P007C, P007D, P0101, P0102, P0103, P0106, P0107, P0108, P0112, P0113, P0117, P0118, P02E0, P02E7, P02E8, P02E9, P02EB, P0403, P0405, P0406, P0489, P0490, P122C, P122E, P122F, P1407, P140D, P140E, P140F, P1411, P1412, P1413, P1414, P16A0, P16A1, P16A2, P2228, P2229, P2263, P2453, P245A, P245C, P245D, P2493, P2494, P2495, P2564, P2565, P2598, or P2599 is not set. The engine speed is between 1,200-1,400 RPM. The calculated fuel rate is greater than 40mm ;. The ambient air temperature is greater than -7°C (19. 4°F). The Barometric Pressure is greater than 74. 8 kPa (10. 9 psi). The system is not in Diesel Particulate Filter (DPF) regeneration. The EGR valve is active. The DTC runs continuously when the above conditions are met.
DTC: P0402 00	**Exhaust Gas Recirculation (EGR) Flow Excessive:** The ignition is ON, or the engine is running. The DTCs run continuously when the above conditions are met.
DTC: P0403	**Exhaust Gas Recirculation (EGR) Motor Control Circuit:** P0403The Ignition is OFF. The engine is in after-run. The battery voltage is greater than 11 V. The EGR valve offset learning procedure is active. The starter is not cranking. The DTC runs continuously when the above conditions are met. OR The Ignition is ON. The battery voltage is greater than 11 V. The EGR control circuit is active. The starter is not cranking. The DTC runs continuously when the above conditions are met.
DTC: P0403	**Exhaust Gas Recirculation (EGR) Solenoid Control Circuit:** P0403The engine is running for more than 0. 5 second. The EGR duty cycle is more than 10 percent. DTC P0403 runs continuously when the above conditions are met.
DTC: P0403 00	**Exhaust Gas Recirculation (EGR) Control Circuit:** P0403 00, P0404 00, and P042EDTCs P0112 00, P0113 00, P0405 00, P0406 00, P0502 00, P0562 00, and P0563 00 are not set. The engine is running. The intake air temperature (IAT) is between 3-80°C (37-176°F). The ignition voltage is between 11-16 V. The Desired EGR position is greater than 0% and does not change more than 3%. These DTCs run continuously when the above conditions are met. P0405 00 and P0406 00The engine is running. The ignition voltage is between 11-16 V. This DTC runs continuously when the above conditions are met.
DTC: P0403 01	**Exhaust Gas Recirculation (EGR) Control Circuit Short to Battery:** The engine is running. The ignition voltage is less than 16. 5 v. The EGR is commanded ON. The DTCs run continuously when the above conditions are met.
DTC: P0403 02	**Exhaust Gas Recirculation (EGR) Control Circuit Short to Ground:** The engine is running. The ignition voltage is less than 16. 5 v. The EGR is commanded ON. The DTCs run continuously when the above conditions are met.
DTC: P0403 04	**Exhaust Gas Recirculation (EGR) Control Circuit Open:** The engine is running. The ignition voltage is less than 16. 5 v. The EGR is commanded ON. The DTCs run continuously when the above conditions are met.
DTC: P0403 54	**Exhaust Gas Recirculation (EGR) Control Circuit High Temperature:** The engine is running. The ignition voltage is less than 16. 5 v. The EGR is commanded ON. The DTCs run continuously when the above conditions are met.
DTC: P0404 00	**Exhaust Gas Recirculation (EGR) Open Position Performance:** P0403 00, P0404 00, and P042EDTCs P0112 00, P0113 00, P0405 00, P0406 00, P0502 00, P0562 00, and P0563 00 are not set. The engine is running. The intake air temperature (IAT) is between 3-80°C (37-176°F). The ignition voltage is between 11-16 V. The Desired EGR position is greater than 0% and does not change more than 3%. These DTCs run continuously when the above conditions are met. P0405 00 and P0406 00The engine is running. The ignition voltage is between 11-16 V. This DTC runs continuously when the above conditions are met.
DTC: P0404 00	**Exhaust Gas Recirculation (EGR) Open Position Performance:** The ignition is ON, or the engine is running. The DTCs run continuously when the above conditions are met.
DTC: P0405	**Exhaust Gas Recirculation (EGR) Position Sensor Circuit Low Voltage:** Engine speed is greater than 600 RPM for 10s. The DTCs run continuously when the above conditions are met.
DTC: P0405 00	**Exhaust Gas Recirculation (EGR) Position Sensor Circuit Low Voltage:** The ignition is ON, or the engine is running. The DTCs run continuously when the above conditions are met.

DTC	Trouble Code Title, Conditions, Possible Causes
DTC: P0405 00	**Exhaust Gas Recirculation (EGR) Position Sensor Circuit Low Voltage:** P0403 00, P0404 00, and P042EDTCs P0112 00, P0113 00, P0405 00, P0406 00, P0502 00, P0562 00, and P0563 00 are not set. The engine is running. The intake air temperature (IAT) is between 3-80°C (37-176°F). The ignition voltage is between 11-16 V. The Desired EGR position is greater than 0% and does not change more than 3%. These DTCs run continuously when the above conditions are met. P0405 00 and P0406 00The engine is running. The ignition voltage is between 11-16 V. This DTC runs continuously when the above conditions are met.
DTC: P0406	**Exhaust Gas Recirculation (EGR) Position Sensor Circuit High Voltage:** Engine speed is greater than 600 RPM for 10 s. The DTCs run continuously when the above conditions are met.
DTC: P0406 00	**Exhaust Gas Recirculation (EGR) Position Sensor Circuit High Voltage:** P0403 00, P0404 00, and P042EDTCs P0112 00, P0113 00, P0405 00, P0406 00, P0502 00, P0562 00, and P0563 00 are not set. The engine is running. The intake air temperature (IAT) is between 3-80°C (37-176°F). The ignition voltage is between 11-16 V. The Desired EGR position is greater than 0% and does not change more than 3%. These DTCs run continuously when the above conditions are met. P0405 00 and P0406 00The engine is running. The ignition voltage is between 11-16 V. This DTC runs continuously when the above conditions are met.
DTC: P0406 00	**Exhaust Gas Recirculation (EGR) Position Sensor Circuit High Voltage:** The ignition is ON, or the engine is running. The DTCs run continuously when the above conditions are met.
DTC: P040C	**Exhaust Gas Recirculation (EGR) Temperature Sensor 1 Circuit Low Voltage:** P040CThe engine is running for 30 seconds or longer. The engine coolant temperature is 60°C (140°F) or warmer. The engine is not in diesel particulate filter (DPF) regeneration. This DTC runs continuously when the above conditions are met. The EGR valve is open more than 4 percent.
DTC: P040C	**Exhaust Gas Recirculation (EGR) Temperature Sensor 2 Circuit Low Voltage:** The engine speed is greater than 600 RPM for 10 s. The DTCs run continuously when the above conditions are met.
DTC: P040D	**Exhaust Gas Recirculation (EGR) Temperature Sensor 2 Circuit High Voltage:** The engine speed is greater than 600 RPM for 10 s. The DTCs run continuously when the above conditions are met.
DTC: P040F	**Exhaust Gas Recirculation (EGR) Temperature Sensor 1-2 Correlation:** The engine has been OFF for more than 5 hours. The ambient temperature is warmer than -7°C (+20°F). DTC P040F runs once per key cycle within the above enabling conditions.
DTC: P040F	**Exhaust Gas Recirculation (EGR) Temperature Sensor 1-2 Correlation:** Condition 1 DTC P0016, P0112, P0113, P0335, P0336, P0340, P0341, P040C, P040D, P041C, or P041D is not set. The ignition has been OFF for greater than 8 hours. The engine is running. The ambient air temperature is greater than -60°C (-76°F). OR Condition 2 DTC P0016, P0112, P0113, P0335, P0336, P0340, P0341, P040C, P040D, P041C, or P041D is not set. The ignition has been OFF for greater than 8 hours. The engine is running. The ambient air temperature is greater than -60°C (-76°F). In the first 60 s of engine run time, the ECM determines the block heater is OFF. AND In the first 10 minutes of engine run time, the vehicle speed as been at least 24 km/h (15 mph) for at least 5 minutes and the ECM determines there is no Sunload. DTC P040F runs once per key cycle when Condition 1 or Condition 2 above is met.
DTC: P0411	**Secondary Air Injection (AIR) System Incorrect Air Flow Detected:** DTC P0101, P0102, P0103, P0107, P0108, P0112, P0113, P0116, P0117, P0118, P0201, P0202, P0203, P0204, P0205, P0206, P0300, P0301, P0302, P0303, P0304, P0305, P0306, P0412, P0418, P0420, P0606, P2430, P2431, P2432, or P2433 is not set. Greater than 120 minutes has elapsed since the last cold start. The ignition voltage is between 9-18 V. The start-up intake air temperature (IAT) is between 5-60°C (41-140°F). The barometric pressure (BARO) is greater than 60 kPa (8. 7 psi). The mass air flow (MAF) is between 3-24 g/s. The engine coolant temperature (ECT) is between 5-60°C (41-140°F). The secondary air injection system is commanded ON. DTC P0411 runs once per trip start up when the above conditions are met for greater than 5 s.
DTC: P0411	**Secondary Air Injection System Incorrect Air Flow Detected:** DTCs P0101, P0102, P0103, P0106, P0107, P0108, P0112, P0113, P0114, P0116, P0117, P0118, P0121, P0122, P0123, P0128, P0201, P0202, P0203, P0204, P0222, P0223, P0261, P0262, P0264, P0265, P0267, P0268, P0270, P0271, P0300, P0301, P0302, P0303, P0304, P0351, P0352, P0353, P0354, P0412, P0418, P0420, P0606, P0641, P0651, P1248, P1249, P124A, P124B, P2147, P2148, P2150, P2151, P2153, P2154, P2156, P2157, P2430, P2431, P2432 or P2433 are not set. The ignition voltage is between 10-32 V. The intake air temperature (IAT) is greater than -11°C (+12°F). The barometric pressure (BARO) is greater than 60 kPa (8. 7 psi). The engine coolant temperature (ECT) is between -11 to +60°C (12-140°F). The manifold absolute pressure (MAP) sensor is greater than 20 kPa (2. 9 psi). The engine speed is less than 5,000 RPM. The mass air flow (MAF) is less than 50 g/s. Greater than 60 min has elapsed since the last cold start. The Secondary Air Injection system is commanded ON. DTC P0411 runs once per trip at start up when the above conditions are met.
DTC: P0412	**Secondary Air Injection (AIR) Solenoid Control Circuit:** The ignition is ON, or the engine is operating. The ignition voltage is between 9-18 V. The ECM has commanded the air system ON and OFF at least once during the ignition cycle. The DTCs run continuously once the above conditions are met.
DTC: P0412	**Secondary Air Injection Valve Control Circuit:** The ignition voltage is between 10-32 V. The DTCs run continuously once the above conditions are met.

DTC	Trouble Code Title, Conditions, Possible Causes
DTC: P0418	**Secondary Air Injection (AIR) Pump Control Circuit:** The ignition is ON, or the engine is operating. The ignition voltage is between 9-18 V. The ECM has commanded the air system ON and OFF at least once during the ignition cycle. The DTCs run continuously once the above conditions are met.
DTC: P0418	**Secondary Air Injection Pump Relay Control Circuit:** The ignition voltage is between 10-32 V. The DTCs run continuously once the above conditions are met.
DTC: P0418	**Secondary Air Injection (AIR) Pump Control Circuit:** The engine speed is greater than 80 RPM. The ignition voltage is between 10-18 V. The ECM has commanded the air system ON and OFF at least once during the ignition cycle. The DTCs run continuously once the above conditions are met.
DTC: P041C	**Exhaust Gas Recirculation (EGR) Temperature Sensor 2 Circuit Low Voltage:** P041CThe engine is running for 30 seconds or longer. The engine coolant temperature is 60°C (140°F) or warmer. The engine is not in regeneration. This DTC runs continuously when the above conditions are met. The EGR valve is open more than 4 percent.
DTC: P041C	**Exhaust Gas Recirculation (EGR) Temperature Sensor 1 Circuit Low Voltage:** The engine speed is greater than 600 RPM for 10 s. The DTCs run continuously when the above conditions are met.
DTC: P041D	**Exhaust Gas Recirculation (EGR) Temperature Sensor 1 Circuit High Voltage:** The engine speed is greater than 600 RPM for 10 s. The DTCs run continuously when the above conditions are met.
DTC: P041D	**Exhaust Gas Recirculation (EGR) Temperature Sensor 2 Circuit High Voltage:** P041DThe engine is running for 30 seconds or longer. The engine coolant temperature is 60°C (140°F) or warmer. This DTC runs continuously when the above conditions are met. The EGR valve is open more than 4 percent.
DTC: P0420	**Catalyst System Low Efficiency Bank 1:** DTCs P0030, P0036, P0050, P0053, P0054, P0056, P0059, P0060, P0068, P0101, P0012, P0103, P0107, P0108, P0112, P0113, P0116, P0117, P0118, P0120, P0121, P0122, P0128, P0131, P0132, P0133, P0134, P0135, P0137, P0138, P0140, P0141, P0151, P0152, P0153, P0154, P0155, P0156, P0157, P0158, P0160, P0161, P0171, P0172, P0174, P0175, P0201, P0202, P0203, P0204, P0205, P0206, P0220, P0222, P0223, P0300-P0306, P0325, P0327, P0332, P0335, P0336, P0340, P0341, P0442, P0443, P0446, P0449, P0455, P0496, P0506, P0507, P1133, P1153, P1258, P1516, P2101, P2119, P2120, P2122, P2123, P2125, P2127, P2128, P2135, P2138, P2176, P2270, P2271, P2272, P2273, P2A00, or P2A03 are not set. Before the ECM performs the idle test, the vehicle must be driven under the following conditions: The engine speed is greater than 1,000 RPM. The condition exists for greater than 1 minute. The engine run time is greater than 10 minutes. The engine is operating in Closed Loop. The engine coolant temperature (ECT) is between 70-125°C (156-257°F). The barometric pressure (BARO) is greater than 70 kPa. The catalytic converter (TWC) calculated temperature is greater than 450°C (842°F). The intake air temperature (IAT) is between -20 to +85°C (-4 to +185°F). The ignition voltage is greater than 11 volts. The vehicle speed is less than 2 km/h (1 mph). The throttle position is in the rest position. The short term fuel trim (FT) is between -10 and +10 percent. The transmission is not in P/N (automatic transmission only). This diagnostic attempts one test during each valid idle period once the above conditions have been met. This diagnostic attempts up to 6 tests during each drive cycle.
DTC: P0420	**Catalyst System Low Efficiency:** The hydrocarbon converted in the diesel oxidation catalyst is greater than 115 g and the hydrocarbon mass flow is greater than 0. 0009 g/s. The ECM is commanding a regeneration. The exhaust gas temperature sensor 1 is greater than 250°C (482°F). The engine speed is between 700-3,400 RPM. The barometric pressure (BARO) is greater than 74. 8 kPa (10. 8 psi). The ambient air temperature is greater than -7°C (19. 4°F). DTC P0420 runs once per driving cycle when the above conditions are met.
DTC: P0420 00	**Catalyst System Low Efficiency:** DTCs P000A 00, P000B 00, P0010 00, P0013 00, P0016 00, P0017 00, P0030 00, P0031 00, P0032 00, P0036 00, P0038 00, P0117 00, P0118 00, P0119 00, P0121 00, P0122 00, P0123 00, P0131 00, P0132 00, P0133 00, P0134 00, P0135 00, P0136 00, P0137 00, P0138 00, P0139 00, P0140 00, P0141 00, P0171 00, P0201 00, P0202 00, P0203 00, P0204 00, P0221 00, P0222 00, P0223 00, P0261 00, P0262 00, P0264 00, P0265 00, P0267 00, P0268 00, P0270 00, P0271 00, P0301 00, P0302 00, P0303 00, P0304 00, P0335 00, P0336 00, P0340 00, P0365 00, P0366 00, P0443 00, P0446 00, P0458 00, P0459 00, P0496 00, P0562 00, P0563 00, P0642 00, P0643 00, P0652 00, P0653 00, P0661 00, P0662 00, P2088 00, P2089 00, P2090 00, P2091 00, P2096 00, P2097 00, P2100 00, P2101 00, P2122 00, P2123 00, P2127 00, P2128 00, P2176 00, P2297 00, P2301 00, P2303 00, P2304 00, P2306 00, P2307 00, P2309 00, P2310 00, P2A00 00, or P2A0 001 are not set. The engine speed is between 1 040-2 760 RPM. The engine load is between 15-50%. The vehicle is in closed loop. The calculated exhaust mass gas flow is between 5-55. 56 g/s, and stable. The calculated catalyst temperature is between 400-850°C (852-1 562°F), and stable. The rear heated oxygen sensor (HO2S) has exceeded the dew point for more than 60 s. This diagnostic attempts one test during each period when the above conditions have been met. This diagnostic attempts up to 4 tests during each drive cycle.
DTC: P042E 00	**Exhaust Gas Recirculation (EGR) Closed Position Performance:** P0403 00, P0404 00, and P042EDTCs P0112 00, P0113 00, P0405 00, P0406 00, P0502 00, P0562 00, and P0563 00 are not set. The engine is running. The intake air temperature (IAT) is between 3-80°C (37-176°F). The ignition voltage is between 11-16 V. The Desired EGR position is greater than 0% and does not change more than 3%. These DTCs run continuously when the above conditions are met. P0405 00 and P0406 00The engine is running. The ignition voltage is between 11-16 V. This DTC runs continuously when the above conditions are met.

DTC	Trouble Code Title, Conditions, Possible Causes
DTC: P0430	**Catalyst System Low Efficiency Bank 2:** LF1 DTCs P000A, P000B, P000C, P000D, P0010, P0011, P0013, P0014, P0020, P0021, P0023, P0024, P0030, P0031, P0032, P0050, P0051, P0052, P0100, P0101, P0102, P0103, P0116, P0117, P0118, P0119, P0121, P0122, P0123, P0128, P0130, P0131, P0132, P0133, P0135, P0137, P0138, P013A, P013C, P013E, P0140, P0141, P014A, P0150, P0151, P0152, P0153, P0155, P0157, P0158, P0160, P0161, P0221, P0222, P0223, P0300, P0301-P0306, P0443, P0455, P0458, P0459, P0496, P2088, P2089, P2090, P2091, P2092, P2093, P2094, P2095, P2096, P2097, P2098, P2099, P2100, P2101, P2107, P2119, P2122, P2123, P2127, P2128, P2138, P2176, P2177, P2178, P2179, P2180, P2187, P2188, P2189, P2190, P2232, P2235, P2270, P2271, P2272, or P2273 is not set. Before the ECM performs the idle test, the vehicle must be driven under the following conditions: The engine speed is greater than 915 RPM. The engine run time is greater than a calibrated value. Both conditions exist for greater than 15 seconds. The throttle is in the rest position. The intake air temperature (IAT) is between -20 to +250°C (-4 to +482°F). The ignition voltage is greater than 11 volts. The engine coolant temperature (ECT) is between 40-127°C (104-261°F). The barometric pressure (BARO) is greater than 70 kPa. The engine has been idling less than 50 seconds. The vehicle speed is less than 2 km/h (1 mph). The short term fuel trim is learned. The air flow into the engine is between 3-13 g/s. The EVAP purge concentration is learned. The catalytic converter (TWC) calculated temperature is between 450-250°C (842-1,742°F). The engine is operating in Closed Loop. The transmission is not in P/N (automatic transmission only). This diagnostic attempts one test during each valid idle period once the above conditions have been met. This diagnostic attempts up to 8 tests during each drive cycle. Before the ECM can report DTC P0420 or P0430 failed, DTCs P0030, P0031, P0032, P0036, P0037, P0038, P0050, P0051, P0052, P0056, P0057, P0058, P0100, P0101, P0102, P0103, P0121, P0122, P0123, P0131, P0132, P0133, P0135, P0137, P0138, P0140, P0141, P0151, P0152, P0153, P0155, P0157, P0158, P0160, P0161, P0221, P0222, P0223, P0335, P0336, P0338, P2096, P2097, P2098, P2099, P2195, P2196, P2197, P2198, P2232, P2235, P2237, P2240, P2243, P2247, P2251, P2254, P2270, P2271, P2272, P2273, P2297, P2298, P2626, and P2629 must run and pass. DTC P0010, P0011, P0013, P0014, P0020, P0021, P0023, P0024, P0030, P0031, P0032, P0050, P0051, P0052, P0100, P0101, P0102, P0103, P0116, P0117, P0118, P0119, P0121, P0122, P0123, P0128, P013A, P013C, P013E, P0130, P0131, P0132, P0133, P0135, P0137, P0138, P014A P0140, P0141, P0150, P0151, P0152, P0153, P0155, P0157, P0158, P0160, P0161, P0221, P0222, P0223, P0300, P0301-P0306, P0443, P0455, P0458, P0459, P0496, P0497, P2088, P2089, P2090, P2091, P2092, P2093, P2094, P2095, P2096, P2097, P2098, P2099, P2100, P2101, P2107, P2119, P2122, P2123, P2127, P2128, P2138, P2176, P2177, P2178, P2179, P2180, P2187, P2188, P2189, P2190, P2232, P2235, P2270, P2271, P2272, or P2273 is not set. The engine speed is between 1,160-2,440 RPM. The engine load is between 13-80 percent. The air flow into the engine is between 3-28 g/s and steady. The ambient air temperature is warmer than -30°C (-22°F). The HO2S 2 is at operating temperature for greater than a range of 140-210 seconds. The engine is operating in Closed Loop. The calculated TWC temperature is between 500-900°C (932-1,652°F) and steady. The above conditions exist for approximately 17 minutes. This diagnostic attempts one test during each period when the above conditions have been met. This diagnostic attempts up to 3 tests during each drive cycle.
DTC: P0430	**Catalyst System Low Efficiency Bank 2:** DTC P0016, P0017, P0018, P0019, P0053, P0054, P0059, P0060, P0068, P0090, P0091, P0092, P00C8, P00C9, P00CA, P0101, P0102, P0103, P0112, P0113, P0116, P0117, P0118, P0119, P0121, P0122, P0123, P0128, P0131, P0132, P0133, P0135, P0137, P0138, P013A, P013B, P013C, P013D, P013E, P013F, P0140, P0141, P014A, P014B, P0151, P0152, P0153, P0155, P0157, P0158, P0160, P0161, P0171, P0172, P0174, P0175, P0191, P0192, P0193, P0222, P0223, P0300, P0301. P0302, P0303, P0304, P0305, P0306, P0335, P0336, P0341, P0345, P0346, P0365, P0366, P0390, P0391, P0443, P0506, P0507, P0606, P1153, P16F3, P2101, P2122, P2123, P2127, P2128, P2135, P2138, P2227, P2228, P2229, P2230, P2270, P2271, P2272, or P2273 is not set. Before the ECM performs the idle test, the vehicle must be driven under the following conditions: The engine speed is greater than 965 RPM. The engine run time is greater than a calibrated value. Both conditions exist for greater than 15s. The throttle is in the rest position. The Intake Air Temperature (IAT) is between -20 to +250°C (-4 to +482°F). The ignition voltage is greater than 11 V. The Engine Coolant Temperature (ECT) is between 40-127°C (104-261°F). The Barometric Pressure (BARO) is greater than 70 kPa. The engine has been idling less than 50s. The vehicle speed is less than 2 km/h (1 mph). The short term fuel trim is learned. The air flow into the engine is between 3-13 g/s. The Evaporative Emission (EVAP) purge concentration is learned. The catalytic converter calculated temperature is between 450-850°C (842-1,562°F). The engine is operating in Closed Loop. The transmission is not in P/N (automatic transmission only). This diagnostic attempts one test during each valid idle period once the above conditions have been met. This diagnostic attempts up to 8 tests during each drive cycle.
DTC: P0442	**Evaporative Emission (EVAP) System Small Leak Detected:** Important: The following conditions must be met prior to ignition OFF. DTCs P0106, P0107, P0108, P0112, P0113, P0117, P0118, P0122, P0128, P0446, P0452, P0453, P0455, P0496, P0502, P0562, P0563, P0601, P0602, P0606, P2610 are not set. The diagnostic runs once after a cold start drive cycle. The start-up intake air temperature (IAT) is between 2-32°C (36-90°F). The start-up engine coolant temperature (ECT) is colder than 42°C (108°F). The start-up IAT and ECT are within 9°C (16°F). The barometric pressure (BARO) is more than 68 kPa. The ambient air temperature is between 2-32°C (36-90°F). The engine run time minimum is 10 minutes. The vehicle has traveled more than 8 km (5 mi) this trip. The shut-down ECT is warmer than 74°C (165°F). The fuel level is between 12-88 percent. The ignition is OFF. A refueling event is not detected. DTC P0442 runs once per drive cycle when the above conditions are met. One test occurs at ignition OFF after a drive cycle and may require up to 45 minutes to complete. No more than 2 tests per day are allowed.

DTC	Trouble Code Title, Conditions, Possible Causes
DTC: P0442 00	**Evaporative Emission (EVAP) System Small Leak Detected:** DTCs P000A 00, P000B 00, P0010 00, P0013 00, P0016 00, P0017 00, P0030 00, P0031 00, P0032 00, P0111 00, P0112 00, P0113 00, P0114 00, P0117 00, P0118 00, P0119 00, P0121 00, P0122 00, P0123 00, P0131 00, P0132 00, P0133 00, P0134 00, P0135 00, P0171 00, P0172 00, P0201 00, P0202 00, P0203 00, P0204 00, P0221 00, P0222 00, P0223 00, P0261 00, P0262 00, P0264 00, P0265 00, P0267 00, P0268 00, P0270 00, P0271 00, P0300 00, P0301 00, P0302 00, P0303 00, P0304 00, P0335 00, P0336 00, P0340 00, P0341 00, P0365 00, P0366 00, P0442 00, P0443 00, P0446 00, P0451 00, P0452 00, P0453 00, P0454 00, P0455 00, P0456 00, P0458 00, P0459 00, P0496 00, P0498 00, P0499 00, P0501 00, P0506 00, P0507 00, P0562 00, P0563 00, P0601 00, P0602 00, P0604 00, P0606 00, P0607 00, P061A 00, P0642 00, P0643 00, P2088 00, P2089 00, P2090 00, P2091 00, P2100 00, P2101 00, P2119 00, P2176 00, P2297 00, P2301 00, P2304 00, P2307 00, P2310 00, P2610 00, and P2A00 00 are not set. The barometric pressure (BARO) is more than 75 kPa (11 PSI). The engine has been running between 1-10 min. The engine is idling. The fuel level is between 6-40 L (2-10 gal). The fuel tank pressure is between -3 to +1 kPa (-0. 4 to +0. 1 PSI). The vehicle speed is 0 km/h (0 MPH). The intake air temperature (IAT) is between -8 to +70°C (+17 to +158°F). The battery voltage is more than 10 V. The engine is operating in closed loop fuel control. DTC P0442 00 runs once per drive cycle when the above conditions have been met.
DTC: P0443	**Evaporative Emission (EVAP) Purge Solenoid Control Circuit:** The engine RPM is greater than 80. The system voltage is between 10-18 volts. DTCs P0443, P0449, P0458, P0459, P0498, or P0499 run continuously when the above conditions are met.
DTC: P0443	**Evaporative Emission (EVAP) Purge Solenoid Control Circuit:** The ignition is ON. The system voltage is greater than 11 V. DTCs P0443 and P0449 run continuously when the above conditions are met.
DTC: P0443 00	**Evaporative Emission (EVAP) Purge Solenoid Valve Control Circuit:** Engine is running. DTCs P0606 00, P0628 00, or P0629 00 are not set. The battery voltage is greater than 9 V.
DTC: P0446	**Evaporative Emissions (EVAP) Vent System Performance:** Before the ECM can report DTC P0446 failed, DTCs P0450, P0451, P0452, and P0453 must run and pass. DTC P0100, P0101, P0102, P0103, P0111, P0112, P0113, P0116, P0117, P0118, P0119, P0121, P0122, P0123, P0128, P0221, P0222, P0223, P0443, P0449, P0451, P0452, P0453, P0458, P0459, P0496, P0497, P0498, P0499, P0560, P0562, P0563, P0700, P2122, P2123, P2127, P2128 or P2138 is not set. The ignition voltage is 10-18 volts. The Closed Loop fuel control is enabled. The engine run time is greater than 10 minutes or the fuel trim is stable. The engine is idling. The Fuel Tank Pressure is between -18. 7 and +9. 8 mm Hg (-10. 0 and +5. 2 in. H2O). The ambient air temperature (AAT) is between 2-32°C (35-90°F). The ECT and the IAT are within 10°C (18°F) of each other at engine start-up. The barometric pressure (BARO) is greater than 68 kPa. The long term fuel trim remains steady, less than 3 percent change in 200 ms over a period of 8 seconds. The fuel level is between 11-88 percent. The vehicle speed sensor (VSS) is less than 3 km/h (2 mph). The above conditions exist for greater than 5 seconds. DTC P0446 will attempt to run up to 10 times or until the test completes successfully once per ignition cycle.
DTC: P0446	**Evaporative Emissions (EVAP) Vent System Performance:** DTCs P0107, P0108, P0112, P0113, P0116, P0117, P0118, P0125, P0128, P0502, P1106, P1107, P1111, P1112, P1114, P1115, P1125, P1516, P2101, P2108, P2119, P2120, P2125, P2138 are not set. The ignition voltage is between 10-18 volts. The barometric pressure (BARO) is more than 75 kPa. The fuel level is between 15-85 percent. The start-up engine coolant temperature (ECT) is between 4-30°C (39-86°F). The start-up intake air temperature (IAT) is between 4-30°C (39-86°F). The start-up ECT and IAT are within 9°C (16°F) of each other. The vehicle speed sensor (VSS) is less than 129 km/h (80 mph). DTC P0446 runs once per trip when the above conditions have been met.
DTC: P0446 00	**Evaporative Emission (EVAP) Vent System Performance:** DTCs P0449 00, P0451 00, P0452 00, P0453 00, P0454 00, P0498 00, P0499 00, P0562 00, P0563 00, P0642 00, P0643 00 are not set. The ignition voltage is between 10-18 V. The EVAP system is purging. DTC P0446 00 runs once per trip when the above conditions have been met.
DTC: P0446 00	**Evaporative Emission (EVAP) Vent System Performance:** **NOTE: The following conditions must be met prior to ignition OFF:** DTCs P0106 00, P0107 00, P0108 00, P0112 00, P0113 00, P0114 00, P0116 00, P0117 00, P0118 00, P0122 00, P0123 00, P0222 00, P0223 00, P0443 00, P0449 00, P0451 00, P0452 00, P0453 00, P0454 00, P0502 00, and P2135 00 are not set. The ignition voltage is greater than 11 V. The barometric pressure (BARO) is greater than 70 kPa (10. 15 PSI). The startup Engine Coolant Temperature (ECT) is less than 35°C (95°F). The startup Intake Air Temperature (IAT) is between 4-30°C (40-86°F). The purge enable time is less than predetermined value based on startup ECT. The fuel level is between 10-90%. The engine run time is between 1-360 s plus purge enable time. The DTC run once an ignition cycle when the above conditions are met.
DTC: P0449	**Evaporative Emission (EVAP) Vent Solenoid Control Circuit:** The engine RPM is greater than 80. The system voltage is between 10-18 volts. DTCs P0443, P0449, P0458, P0459, P0498, or P0499 run continuously when the above conditions are met.
DTC: P0449	**Evaporative Emission (EVAP) Vent Solenoid Control Circuit:** The ignition is ON. The system voltage is greater than 11 V. DTCs P0443 and P0449 run continuously when the above conditions are met.

DTC	Trouble Code Title, Conditions, Possible Causes
DTC: P0449 00	**Evaporative Emission (EVAP) Vent Solenoid Valve Control Circuit:** The ignition is ON. The system voltage is between 9-18 V. DTCs P0443 and P0449 run continuously when the above conditions are met.
DTC: P0450	**Fuel Tank Pressure (FTP) Sensor Circuit:** P0450The engine is running. The estimated ambient air temperature is warmer than -7°C (+19. 4°F). The EVAP canister vent valve has been open for more than 3 seconds. The vehicle speed is less than 29 km/h (18 mph). DTC P0450 runs continuously when the above conditions have been met.
DTC: P0451	**Fuel Tank Pressure Sensor Performance:** P0451 Condition 1 DTC P0100, P0101, P0102, P0103, P0116, P0117, P0118, P0119, P0443, P0449, P0458, P0459, P0498, P0499, P050A, P0506, P0507, P0700, P2227, P2228, or P2229 is not set. The engine is operating for greater than 1 second. The engine is idling. The ambient air temperature is warmer than -7°C (+19°F). The vehicle speed is less than 10 km/h (6 mph) for greater than 30 seconds. The BARO is greater than 68 kPa. The fuel level is between 11-88 percent. The ECM has commanded the EVAP canister purge solenoid ON. The ECM has commanded the EVAP canister vent valve closed for greater than 4 seconds. DTC P0451 runs continuously once the above conditions are met for approximately 25 seconds. P0451 Condition 2 DTC P0100, P0101, P0102, P0103, P0116, P0117, P0118, P0119, P0443, P0449, P0458, P0459, P0498, P0499, P050A, P0506, P0507, P0700, P2227, P2228, or P2229 is not set. The engine is operating. The BARO is greater than 68 kPa. The ECM has commanded the EVAP canister purge solenoid OFF. The ECM has commanded the EVAP canister vent valve open. OR The vehicle speed is between 10-76 km/h (6-47 mph) for greater than 30 seconds. The fuel level is between 11-73 percent. The EVAP purge solenoid is commanded ON. OR The calculated ambient air temperature is 4-35°C (39-95°F) for greater than 3 seconds. DTC P0451 runs continuously once the above conditions are met for approximately 7 seconds.
DTC: P0451	**Fuel Tank Pressure (FTP) Sensor Performance:** P0451 DTC P0451 runs only when the engine-off natural vacuum small leak test, P0442, executes. The number of times this test runs can range from 0-2 per engine-off period. The length of the test can be up to 10 minutes.
DTC: P0451	**Fuel Tank Pressure (FTP) Sensor Performance:** P0451 - Part 1The engine is running. The vehicle speed is greater than 0 km/h (0 mph). The ambient pressure is greater than 68 kPa. The estimated ambient air temperature is warmer than -7°C (+19. 4°F). The fuel level is between 12-88 percent. DTC P0451 runs continuously when the above conditions have been met. P0451 - Part 2The EVAP canister purge solenoid valve is closed and the EVAP canister vent solenoid valve is open. The vehicle speed is between 10-75 km/h (6-46 mph). The time since engine start is greater than 450 seconds. DTC P0451 runs whenever the above conditions have been met.
DTC: P0451 00	**Fuel Tank Pressure Sensor Performance:** P0451 00This diagnostic runs when the engine off natural vacuum small leak test, DTC P0442 00, is in progress. This diagnostic can be tested 2 times during the engine off period.
DTC: P0451 00	**Fuel Tank Pressure Sensor Performance:** P0451 00 DTCs P0452 00, P0453 00, P0642 00, P0643 00 are not set. The engine has been running for more than 10 s. The fuel tank pressure sensor signal is between 0. 2-4. 9 V. The vehicle speed reached once during drive cycle of 20 km/h (14. 2 MPH). The evaporative emission (EVAP) system has reached full purge and no purge once during drive cycle. The EVAP system is purging. DTC P0451 00 runs continuously when the above conditions have been met.
DTC: P0452	**Fuel Tank Pressure (FTP) Sensor Circuit Low Voltage:** P0452 and P0453 DTC P0452 and P0453 run continuously when the ignition is ON.
DTC: P0452 00	**Fuel Tank Pressure Sensor Circuit Low Voltage:** P0452 00 and P0453 00 DTCs P0642 00 and P0643 00 are not set. The average fuel level is between 6-40 L (0-10 gal). DTCs P0452 00 and P0453 00 run continuously when the ignition is ON.
DTC: P0452 00	**Fuel Tank Pressure Sensor Circuit Low Voltage:** The ignition is ON or the engine is running. The DTCs run continuously once the above condition is met.
DTC: P0453	**Fuel Tank Pressure Sensor Circuit High Voltage:** P0452 and P0453 DTC P0452 and P0453 run continuously when the ignition is ON.
DTC: P0453 00	**Fuel Tank Pressure Sensor Circuit High Voltage:** P0452 00 and P0453 00 DTCs P0642 00 and P0643 00 are not set. The average fuel level is between 6-40 L (0-10 gal). DTCs P0452 00 and P0453 00 run continuously when the ignition is ON.
DTC: P0453 00	**Fuel Tank Pressure Sensor Circuit High Voltage:** The ignition is ON or the engine is running. The DTCs run continuously once the above condition is met.
DTC: P0454 00	**Fuel Tank Pressure Sensor Circuit Intermittent:** P0454 00This diagnostic runs when the engine off natural vacuum small leak test, DTC P0442 00, is in progress. This diagnostic can be tested 1 time during the engine off period. The ECM does not detect a refueling event.

DTC	Trouble Code Title, Conditions, Possible Causes
DTC: P0454 00	**Fuel Tank Pressure Sensor Circuit Intermittent:** P0454 00 DTCs P000A 00, P000B 00, P0010 00, P0013 00, P0016 00, P0017 00, P0030 00, P0031 00, P0032 00, P011 001, P0112 00, P0113 00, P0114 00, P0117 00, P0118 00, P0119 00, P0121 00, P0122 00, P0123 00, P0131 00, P0132 00, P0133 00, P0134 00, P0135 00, P0171 00, P0172 00, P0201 00, P0202 00, P0203 00, P0204 00, P0221 00, P0222 00, P0223 00, P0261 00, P0262 00, P0264 00, P0265 00, P0267 00, P0268 00, P0270 00, P0271 00, P0300 00, P0301 00, P0302 00, P0303 00, P0304 00, P0335 00, P0336 00, P0340 00, P0341 00, P0365 00, P0366 00, P0442 00, P0443 00, P0446 00, P0451 00, P0452 00, P0453 00, P0454 00, P0455 00, P0456 00, P0458 00, P0459 00, P0496 00, P0498 00, P0499 00, P0500 00, P0501 00, P0506 00, P0507 00, P0562 00, P0563 00, P0601 00, P0602 00, P0603 00, P0604 00, P0605 00, P0606 00, P0607 00, P061A 00, P0642 00, P0643 00, P2088 00, P2089 00, P2090 00, P2091 00, P2100 00, P2101 00, P2119 00, P2176 00, P2297 00, P2301 00, P2304 00, P2307 00, P2310 00, and P2A00 00 are not set. The ignition is ON. The barometric pressure (BARO) is more than 75 kPa (11 PSI). The engine coolant temperature (ECT) sensor is less than 110°C (230°F). The engine is idling. The vehicle speed is 0 km/h (0 MPH). The fuel level is between 6-40 L (2-10 gal). The fuel tank pressure sensor is between -3 to +1 kPa (-0. 4 to +0. 1 PSI). The intake air temperature (IAT) is between -8. 25 to +70°C (+17 to +158°F). The battery voltage is more than 10 V. The engine is operating in closed loop fuel control. DTC P045 004 runs once per drive cycle when the above conditions have been met.
DTC: P0455	**Evaporative Emission System Large Leak Detected:** DTCs P00C8, P00C9, P16F3, P0068, P0101, P0102, P0103, P010C, P010D, P0106, P0107, P0108, P0111, P0112, P0113, P0114, P0116, P0117, P0118, P0120, P0121, P0122, P0123, P0125, P0128, P160E, P160D, P0191, P0192, P0193, P0220, P0222, P0223, P0442, P0443, P0449, P0451, P0452, P0453, P0454, P0464, P0496, P0502, P0503, P0606, P0608, P0609, P0641, P0651, P0722, P0723, P1104, P1516, P2100, P2101, P2102, P2103, P2119, P2120, P2122, P2123, P2125, P2127, P2128, P2135, P2138, P2227, P2228, P2229, P2230 is not set. The ignition voltage is greater than 11 V. The barometric pressure (BARO) is more than 70 kPa. The fuel level is between 10-90 percent. The engine coolant temperature (ECT) at start-up is less than 35°C (95°F). The intake air temperature (IAT) is between 4-30°C (39-86°F). DTC P0455 runs once per cold start when the above conditions are met.
DTC: P0455	**Evaporative Emission (EVAP) System Large Leak:** DTCs P0106, P0107, P0108, P0112, P0113, P0116, P0117, P0118, P0121, P0122, P0123, P0222, P0223, P0128, P0443, P0449, P0452, P0453, P0454, P0502, P0503 are not set. The engine is running. The ignition voltage is between 10-18 volts. The barometric pressure (BARO) is more than 74 kPa. The fuel level is between 15-85 percent. The start-up intake air temperature (IAT) is between 4-30°C (39-86°F). The start-up engine coolant temperature (ECT) is less than 30°C (86°F). The start-up ECT and IAT are within 8°C (14. 4°F) of each other. DTC P0455 runs once per cold start within 17 minutes of start-up.
DTC: P0455 00	**Evaporative Emission (EVAP) System Large Leak Detected:** DTCs P0106 00, P0107 00, P0108 00, P0112 00, P0113 00, P0116 00, P0117 00, P0118 00, P0442 00, P0443 00, P0446 00, P0449 00, P0452 00, P0453 00, P0454 00, and P0502 00 are not set. One of the following conditions is met: The ignition is off for greater than 12 h. or The start-up intake air temperature (IAT) and the start-up engine coolant temperature (ECT) are within 8°C (14°F). The ignition voltage is between 11-18 V. The barometric pressure (BARO) is more than 75 kPa (10. 87 PSI). The fuel level is between 15-85%. The startup engine coolant temperature (ECT) is between 4-30°C (39-86°F). The startup intake air temperature (IAT) is between 4-30°C (39-86°F). The EVAP purge is greater than 2%. The fuel level is between 10-90%. The engine run time is less than 17 min. The DTC run once an ignition cycle when the above conditions are met.
DTC: P0455 00	**Evaporative Emission (EVAP) System Large Leak Detected:** DTCs P000A 00, P000B 00, P0010 00, P0013 00, P0016 00, P0017 00, P0030 00, P0031 00, P0032 00, P0111 00, P0112 00, P0113 00, P0114 00, P0117 00, P0118 00, P0119 00, P0121 00, P0122 00, P0123 00, P0130 00, P013 001, P0132 00, P0133 00, P0134 00, P0135 00, P0171 00, P0172 00, P0201 00, P0202 00, P0203 00, P0204 00, P0221 00, P0222 00, P0223 00, P0261 00, P0262 00, P0264 00, P0265 00, P0267 00, P0268 00, P0270 00, P0271 00, P0300 00, P0301 00, P0302 00, P0303 00, P0304 00, P0335 00, P0336 00, P0340 00, P0341 00, P0365 00, P0366 00, P0436 00, P0442 00, P0443 00, P0446 00, P0449 00, P0451 00, P0452 00, P0453 00, P0454 00, P0456 00, P0458 00, P0459 00, P0496 00, P0498 00, P0499 00, P0500 00, P0506 00, P050 007, P0562 00, P0563 00, P0601 00, P0602 00, P0604 00, P0606 00, P0607 00, P061A 00, P0642 00, P0643 00, P2088 00, P2089 00, P2090 00, P2091 00, P2100 00, P2101 00, P2119 00, P2176 00, P2297 00, P2301 00, P2304 00, P2307 00, P2310 00, P2610 00, and P2A00 00 are not set. The engine is running. The ignition voltage is between 10-18 V. The barometric pressure (BARO) is more than 75 kPa (11 PSI). The engine coolant temperature (ECT) sensor is less than 110°C (230°F). The fuel level is between 6-40 L (2-10 gal). The vehicle speed is 0 km/h (0 MPH). The intake air temperature (IAT) sensor is between -8 to +70°C (+17 to +158°F). The engine is operating in closed loop fuel control. DTC P0455 00 runs once per cold start within 10 min of start-up.
DTC: P0458	**Evaporative Emission (EVAP) Purge Solenoid Control Circuit Low Voltage:** The engine RPM is greater than 80. The system voltage is between 10-18 volts. DTCs P0443, P0449, P0458, P0459, P0498, or P0499 run continuously when the above conditions are met.
DTC: P0458 00	**Evaporative Emission (EVAP) Purge Solenoid Valve Control Circuit Low Voltage:** The engine is running. The ignition voltage is between 1-16 V. These DTCs runs continuously once the above conditions are met.
DTC: P0458 00	**Evaporative Emission (EVAP) Purge Solenoid Valve Control Circuit Low Voltage:** Engine is running. DTCs P0606 00, P0628 00, or P0629 00 are not set. The battery voltage is greater than 9 V.
DTC: P0459	**Evaporative Emission (EVAP) Purge Solenoid Control Circuit High Voltage:** The engine RPM is greater than 80. The system voltage is between 10-18 volts. DTCs P0443, P0449, P0458, P0459, P0498, or P0499 run continuously when the above conditions are met.

DTC	Trouble Code Title, Conditions, Possible Causes
DTC: P0459 00	**Evaporative Emission (EVAP) Purge Solenoid Valve Control Circuit High Voltage:** The engine is running. The ignition voltage is between 1-16 V. These DTCs runs continuously once the above conditions are met.
DTC: P0459 00	**Evaporative Emission (EVAP) Purge Solenoid Valve Control Circuit High Voltage:** Engine is running. DTCs P0606 00, P0628 00, or P0629 00 are not set. The battery voltage is greater than 9 V.
DTC: P0460	**Fuel Level Sensor Circuit:** The engine is running. The system voltage is between 11-16 V.
DTC: P0461	**Fuel Level Sensor 1 Performance:** The engine is running. The system voltage is between 11-16 V.
DTC: P0462	**Fuel Level Sensor 1 Circuit Low Voltage:** The engine is running. The system voltage is between 11-16 V.
DTC: P0463	**Fuel Level Sensor Circuit High Voltage:** The engine is running. The system voltage is between 11-16 V
DTC: P0464	**Fuel Level Sensor Circuit Intermittent:** The engine is running. The system voltage is between 11-16 V.
DTC: P046C	**Exhaust Gas Recirculation (EGR) Position Sensor Performance:** Engine speed is greater than 600 RPM. The Battery voltage is greater than 11 V. The Air Intake Heater duty cycle is less than 5 %. The EGR Valve is active. The EGR Valve offset learning from the previous drive cycle is complete. EGR offset learning is not active. DTC P046C runs continuously when the above conditions are met.
DTC: P046C	**Exhaust Gas Recirculation (EGR) Position Sensor Performance:** P046CDTCs P0401, P0402, P0403, P0642, or P0643 are not set. The EGR valve is actively being controlled. DTC P046C runs continuously when the above conditions have been met.
DTC: P0480	**Cooling Fan Relay 1 Control Circuit:** The ignition voltage is between 10-26 volts. The engine speed is greater than 80 RPM. The ECM driver transitions from ON to OFF or from OFF to ON. DTC P0480, P0481, P0691, P0692, P0693, and P0694 run continuously when the conditions above are met.
DTC: P0480	**Cooling Fan Speed Output Circuit:** The ignition voltage is greater than 11 volts. The engine is operating. The engine speed is greater than 600 RPM. DTC P0480 runs continuously when the conditions above exist for greater than 3 seconds.
DTC: P0480	**Cooling Fan Relay 1 Control Circuit:** The engine speed is greater than 400 RPM. The ignition voltage is between 11-18 volts. The relay control circuit is commanded from OFF to ON, or ON to OFF. DTC P0480 and P0481 run continuously when the conditions above are met.
DTC: P0480	**Cooling Fan Relay 1 Control Circuit:** The ignition voltage is between 10-18 volts. The engine speed is greater than 80 RPM. The ECM driver transitions from ON to OFF or from OFF to ON. DTC P0480, P0481, P0691, P0692, P0693, and P0694 run continuously when the conditions above are met.
DTC: P0480 00	**Cooling Fan Relay 1 Control Circuit:** The engine is running. The ignition voltage is between 11-16 V. The ECM driver transitions from ON to OFF or from OFF to ON.
DTC: P0480 01	**Cooling Fan Relay 1 Control Circuit Short to Battery:** The ignition is ON, or the engine is running. The ignition voltage is greater than 10 V. The DTCs run continuously once the above conditions are met.
DTC: P0480 02	**Cooling Fan Relay 1 Control Circuit Short to Ground:** The ignition is ON, or the engine is running. The ignition voltage is greater than 10 V. The DTCs run continuously once the above conditions are met.
DTC: P0480 04	**Cooling Fan Relay 1 Control Circuit Open:** The ignition is ON, or the engine is running. The ignition voltage is greater than 10 V. The DTCs run continuously once the above conditions are met.
DTC: P0480 54	**Cooling Fan Relay 1 Control Circuit High Temperature:** The ignition is ON, or the engine is running. The ignition voltage is greater than 10 V. The DTCs run continuously once the above conditions are met.
DTC: P0481	**Cooling Fan Relay 2 and 3 Control Circuit:** The engine speed is greater than 400 RPM. The ignition voltage is between 11-18 volts. The relay control circuit is commanded from OFF to ON, or ON to OFF. DTC P0480 and P0481 run continuously when the conditions above are met.
DTC: P0481 00	**Cooling Fan Relay 2 Control Circuit:** The engine is running. The ignition voltage is between 11-16 V. The ECM driver transitions from ON to OFF or from OFF to ON.

DTC	Trouble Code Title, Conditions, Possible Causes
DTC: P0481 01	**Cooling Fan Relay 2 Control Circuit Short to Battery:** The ignition is ON, or the engine is running. The ignition voltage is greater than 10 V. The DTCs run continuously once the above conditions are met.
DTC: P0481 02	**Cooling Fan Relay 2 Control Circuit Short to Ground:** The ignition is ON, or the engine is running. The ignition voltage is greater than 10 V. The DTCs run continuously once the above conditions are met.
DTC: P0481 04	**Cooling Fan Relay 2 Control Circuit Open:** The ignition is ON, or the engine is running. The ignition voltage is greater than 10 V. The DTCs run continuously once the above conditions are met.
DTC: P0481 54	**Cooling Fan Relay 2 Control Circuit High Temperature:** The ignition is ON, or the engine is running. The ignition voltage is greater than 10 V. The DTCs run continuously once the above conditions are met.
DTC: P0482 01	**Cooling Fan Relay 3 Control Circuit Short to Battery:** The ignition is ON, or the engine is running. The ignition voltage is greater than 10 V. The DTCs run continuously once the above conditions are met.
DTC: P0482 02	**Cooling Fan Relay 3 Control Circuit Short to Ground:** The ignition is ON, or the engine is running. The ignition voltage is greater than 10 V. The DTCs run continuously once the above conditions are met.
DTC: P0482 04	**Cooling Fan Relay 3 Control Circuit Open:** The ignition is ON, or the engine is running. The ignition voltage is greater than 10 V. The DTCs run continuously once the above conditions are met.
DTC: P0482 54	**Cooling Fan Relay 3 Control Circuit High Temperature:** The ignition is ON, or the engine is running. The ignition voltage is greater than 10 V. The DTCs run continuously once the above conditions are met.
DTC: P0483	**Cooling Fan System Performance:** DTC P0016, P007C, P007D, P0112, P0113, P0117, P0118, P0335, P0336, P0340, P0341, P0480, P0495, or P0526 is not set. The engine is operating for greater than 10 seconds. The engine speed is between 1,200-3,429 RPM. The BARO is greater than 75 kPa. The engine coolant temperature is warmer than 70°C (158°F). The ECM commanded fan clutch solenoid duty cycle is greater than 36 percent. The cooling fan input shaft speed is steady. DTC P0483 runs continuously every 100 mS when the conditions above exist.
DTC: P0483	**Cooling Fan System Performance:** The engine coolant temperature is warmer than 70°C (158°F). The engine RPM is greater than 1,200 RPM. The fan duty cycle is greater than 36 percent. The engine speed variation is less than 250 RPM.
DTC: P0489	**Exhaust Gas Recirculation (EGR) Motor Control Circuit 1 Low Voltage:** P0489, P0490, P1407, P140D, P140E and P140FThe Ignition is ON. The battery voltage is greater than 11 V. The EGR control circuit is active. The starter is not cranking. The DTCs run continuously when the above conditions are met.
DTC: P0490	**Exhaust Gas Recirculation (EGR) Motor Control Circuit 1 High Voltage:** P0489, P0490, P1407, P140D, P140E and P140FThe Ignition is ON. The battery voltage is greater than 11 V. The EGR control circuit is active. The starter is not cranking. The DTCs run continuously when the above conditions are met.
DTC: P0495	**Cooling Fan Speed High:** The engine is running.
DTC: P0495	**Cooling Fan Speed High:** DTC P0016, P0112, P0113, P0117, P0118, P0335, P0336, P0340, P0341, P0480, P0483, P0526, P2228, or P2229 is not set. The engine is operating for greater than 10 seconds. The engine speed is greater than 1,071 RPM. The engine OFF time after the previous ignition cycle was greater than 0 seconds. The ambient air temperature (AAT) is warmer than -40°C (-40°F). The BARO is greater than 55 kPa. The ECM commanded fan clutch solenoid duty cycle is less than 36 percent. DTC P0495 runs continuously when the conditions above exist.
DTC: P0496	**Evaporative Emission System Flow During Non-Purge:** DTCs P0107, P0108, P0112, P0113, P0117, P0118, P0125, P0128, P0442, P0443, P0446, P0449, P0452, P0453, P0445, P1106, P1107, P1111, P1112, P1114, P1115, P1516 are not set. The ignition voltage is between 10-18 volts. The barometric pressure (BARO) is more than 74 kPa. The fuel level is between 15-85 percent. The engine coolant temperature (ECT) is between 4-30°C (39-86°F). The intake air temperature (IAT) is between 4-30°C (39-86°F). DTC P0496 runs once per cold start for 96 seconds.

DTC	Trouble Code Title, Conditions, Possible Causes
DTC: P0496	**Evaporative Emissions (EVAP) System Flow During Non-Purge:** Before the engine control module (ECM) can report DTC P0496 failed, DTCs P0450, P0451, P0452, and P0453 must run and pass. DTC P0100, P0101, P0102, P0103, P0111, P0112, P0113, P0116, P0117, P0118, P0119, P0443, P0446, P0449, P0450, P0451, P0452, P0453, P0458, P0459, P0498, P0499, P0560, P0562, P0563, P0700, P2122, P2123, P2127, P2128, P2138, P2227, P2228, or P2229 is not set. The fuel system is in closed loop. The engine run time is greater than 10 minutes, or the long term fuel trim is stable. The vehicle speed sensor (VSS) is less than 3 km/h (2 mph). The engine is idling. The ignition voltage is between 10-18 volts. The Closed Loop fuel control is enabled. The fuel tank pressure (FTP) is between -10. 0 and +5. 0 in. H2O (-18. 7 and +9. 8 mm Hg). The ambient air temperature is between 2-32°C (36-90°F). The start-up engine coolant temperature (ECT) is within 10°C (18°F) of ambient air temperature. The fuel tank level is between 11-88 percent. The barometric pressure (BARO) is greater than 68 kPa. The above conditions are met for greater than 30 seconds. DTC P0496 will attempt to run up to 10 times or the test completes successfully once per ignition cycle.
DTC: P0496 00	**Evaporative Emission (EVAP) System Flow During Non-Purge:** DTCs P0106 00, P0107 00, P0108 00, P0112 00, P0113 00, P0116 00, P0117 00, P0118 00, P0442 00, P0443 00, P0446 00, P0449 00, P0452 00, P0453 00, P0454 00, and P0502 00 are not set. The ECM is not commanding reduced engine power. The ignition voltage is between 11-18 V. The barometric pressure (BARO) is more than 75 kPa (10. 87 PSI). The fuel level is between 15-85%. The startup engine coolant temperature (ECT) is between 4-30°C (39-86°F). The startup intake air temperature (IAT) is between 4-30°C (39-86°F). The ignition is OFF for greater than 8 h. The fuel level is between 10-90%. The EVAP canister purge and EVAP vent valves are closed. The DTC run once an ignition cycle when the above conditions are met.
DTC: P0496 00	**Evaporative Emission (EVAP) System Flow During Non-Purge:** DTCs P000A 00, P000B 00, P0010 00, P001 003, P0016 00, P0017 00, P0030 00, P003 001, P0032 00, P0111 00, P0112 00, P0113 00, P0114 00, P0116 00, P0117 00, P0118 00, P0119 00, P0121 00, P0122 00, P0123 00, P0131 00, P0132 00, P0133 00, P0134 00, P0135 00, P0171 00, P0172 00, P0201 00, P0202 00, P0203 00, P0204 00, P0261 00, P0262 00, P0264 00, P0265 00, P0267 00, P0268 00, P0270 00, P0271 00, P0301 00, P0302 00, P0303 00, P0304 00, P0335 00, P0336 00, P0340 00, P0341 00, P0365 00, P0366 00, P0442 00, P0443 00, P0446 00, P0451 00, P0452 00, P0453 00, P0454 00, P0455 00, P0456 00, P0458 00, P0459 00, P0496 00, P0498 00, P0499 00, P0501 00, P0506 00, P0507 00, P0562 00, P0563 00, P061A 00, P0642 00, P0643 00, P2088 00, P2089 00, P2090 00, P2091 00, P2100 00, P2101 00, P2119 00, P2176 00, P2297 00, P2301 00, P2304 00, P2307 00, P2310 00, P2610 00, and U0073 00 are not set. The ignition voltage is between 10-18 V. The barometric pressure (BARO) is more than 75 kPa (11 PSI). The fuel level is between 15-85%. The engine coolant temperature (ECT) is less than 110°C (230°F). The intake air temperature (IAT) is between 4-30°C (39-86°F). The start-up ECT and IAT are within 9°C (16°F) of each other. The vehicle speed sensor (VSS) is less than 121 km/h (75 MPH). The fuel tank pressure sensor is less than -0. 6 kPa (-4. 3 PSI) at ignition ON. DTC P0496 00 runs once per cold start for 96 s.
DTC: P0497	**Evaporative Emission System Low Purge Flow:** DTCs P0030, P0031, P0032, P0053, P0100, P0101, P0102, P0103, P0106, P0107, P0108, P0112, P0113, P0114, P0117, P0118, P0119, P0122, P0123, P0128, P0130, P0131, P0132, P0133, P0135, P0221, P0222, P0223, P0443, P0449, P0450, P0451, P0452, P0453, P0458, P0459, P0498, P0499, P0501, P0502, P2122, P2123, P2127, P2128, P2138, P2177, P2178, P2187, P2188, P2195, P2196, P2199, P2227, P2228, P2229, P2243, P2251, P2297, P2626 are not set. The ignition voltage is between 11-18 volts. The barometric pressure (BARO) is more than 68 kPa. The fuel level is between 15-85 percent. The fuel tank pressure is between -2. 5 and +1. 3 kPa (-10 and +5 in H2O). The engine coolant temperature (ECT) is between 4-30°C (39-86°F). The intake air temperature is between 2-32°C (35. 6-90°F). The start-up ECT and IAT are within 9°C (14. 4°F) of each other. The vehicle speed sensor (VSS) is less than 1. 7 km/h (2 mph). DTC P0497 will attempt to run up to 10 times until it successfully completes. DTC P0497 completes one test per cold start within 10 minutes of start-up.
DTC: P0497	**Evaporative Emission (EVAP) System No Flow During Purge:** Before the engine control module (ECM) can report DTC P0455 or DTC P0497 failed, DTCs P0446 and P0496 must run and pass. DTC P0100, P0101, P0102, P0103, P0111, P0112, P0113, P0116, P0117, P0118, P0119, P0443, P0446, P0449, P0450, P0451, P0452, P0453, P0458, P0459, P0496, P0498, P0499, P0560, P0562, P0563, P0700, P2122, P2123, P2127, P2128, P2138, P2227, P2228, or P2229 is not set. The ignition voltage is between 10-18 volts. The engine run time is greater than 10 minutes or the fuel trim is stable. The FTP is between -18. 7 and +9. 8 mm Hg (-10. 0 and +5. 2 in. H2O). The Closed Loop fuel control is enabled. The engine is idling. The barometric pressure (BARO) is greater than 68 kPa. The fuel level is between 11-88 percent. The ambient air temperature (IAT) is between 2-32°C (36-90°F). The engine coolant temperature (ECT) is within 10°C (18°F) of the ambient air temperature at engine start. The vehicle speed sensor (VSS) is less than 3 km/h (2 mph). The above conditions are met for greater than 30 seconds. DTC P0455 or DTC P0497 will attempt to run up to 10 times or until the test completes successfully once per ignition cycle.
DTC: P0498	**Evaporative Emission (EVAP) Vent Solenoid Control Circuit Low Voltage:** The engine RPM is greater than 80. The system voltage is between 10-18 volts. DTCs P0443, P0449, P0458, P0459, P0498, or P0499 run continuously when the above conditions are met.
DTC: P0499	**Evaporative Emission (EVAP) Vent Solenoid Control Circuit High Voltage:** The engine RPM is greater than 80. The system voltage is between 10-18 volts. DTCs P0443, P0449, P0458, P0459, P0498, or P0499 run continuously when the above conditions are met.

DTC	Trouble Code Title, Conditions, Possible Causes
DTC: P049D	**Exhaust Gas Recirculation (EGR) Position Not Learned:** DTC P0403, P0405, P0406, or P140F is not set. The ignition is OFF and the engine is in after-run/post drive. The EGR Valve offset learning procedure is active or complete for current drive cycle. The Engine Coolant Temperature (ECT) is between 5-123°C (41-253°F). Battery voltage is greater than 10 V. The DTC runs continuously when the above conditions are met.
DTC: P049D 00	**Exhaust Gas Recirculation (EGR) Position Not Learned:** DTC P0404 00, P0405 00, P0406 00, or P1407 00 are not set. The ignition is OFF and the engine is in after run/post drive. The EGR Valve offset learning procedure is active or complete for current drive cycle. The engine coolant temperature (ECT) is between 5-123°C (41-253°F). Battery voltage is greater than 10 V. This DTCs run continuously when the above conditions are met.
DTC: P0500 08	**Vehicle Speed Sensor (VSS) Circuit Signal Invalid:** The engine is running. The DTCs run continuously once the above condition is met.
DTC: P0500 11	**Vehicle Speed Sensor (VSS) Circuit Above Maximum Threshold:** The engine is running. The DTCs run continuously once the above condition is met.
DTC: P0502	**Vehicle Speed Sensor (VSS) Circuit Low Voltage:** P0502 DTCs P0117, P0118, P0119, P0128, P0335, P0336, P0338 or P0501 are not set. The diesel fuel cut-off (DFCO) is active. The engine coolant temperature is more than 40°C (104°F). The engine speed is 1,440-3,520 RPM.
DTC: P0506	**Idle Speed Low:** The engine is operating for greater than 180 s. The engine speed is greater than 300 RPM. The engine coolant temperature (ECT) is between -7 to +123°C (19-253°F). The vehicle speed is less than 3 km/h (2 mph). DTC P0506 and P0507 run continuously when the above conditions are met.
DTC: P0506	**Idle Speed Low:** DTCs P0068, P0101, P0102, P0103, P0106, P0107, P0108, P0116, P0117, P0118, P0120, P0122, P0123, P0128, P0171, P0172, P0174, P0175, P0201, P0202, P0203, P0204, P0205, P0206, P0220, P0222, P0223, P0300, P0351, P0352, P0353, P0496, P0601, P0604, P0606, P060D, P0641, P0651, P1516, P2101, P2119, P2120, P2122, P2123, P2125, P2127, P2128, P2135, P2138, or P2176 are not set. The engine has been running for greater than 60 seconds. The engine is idling for greater than 10 seconds. The intake air temperature (IAT) is more than -40°C (-40°F). The AC mode state has not changed. The barometric pressure (BARO) is greater than 72 kPa. The power steering load state has not changed. The transmission gear selector state has not changed. The engine coolant temperature (ECT) is greater than -40°C (-40°F). The system voltage is between 9-18 volts. The vehicle speed is less than 4.8 km/h (3 mph). The DTCs run continuously when the above conditions are met.
DTC: P0506	**Idle Speed Low:** DTCs P0068, P0101, P0102, P0103, P0106, P0107, P0108, P0112, P0113, P0116, P0117, P0118, P0120, P0121, P0122, P0123, P0128, P0171, P0172, P0174, P0175, P0201-P0208, P0220, P0222, P0223, P0300- P0308, P0336, P0462, P0463, P0496, P0606, P0722, P0723, P1516, P2101, P2120, P2122, P2123, P2125, P2127, P2128, P2135, P2176 are not set. The engine is operating for at least 60 s. The engine is idling for greater than 10 s. The barometric pressure (BARO) is greater than 70 kPa (11 psi). The engine coolant temperature (ECT) is between 60-125°C (140-257°F). The intake air temperature (IAT) is warmer than -20°C (-4°F). The system voltage is between 11-32 V. The vehicle speed is less than 1.9 km/h (1.2 mph). The fuel level is greater than 10 percent. The commanded engine speed is steady within 25 RPM. The transmission is not changing gears. The torque converter clutch (TCC) is not changing states. The transfer case is not in 4WD Low - If equipped. The power take-off (PTO) is not active - If equipped. The manual transmission clutch pedal position top of travel is greater than 5 percent - If equipped. The manual transmission clutch pedal position bottom of travel is less than 5 percent - If equipped. The manual transmission clutch is not depressed - If equipped. A scan tool output control is not active. DTC P0506 and P0507 run continuously once the above conditions are met.
DTC: P0506 00	**Idle Speed Low:** DTCs P0016 00, P0068 00, P0106 00, P0107 00, P0108 00, P0117 00, P0118 00, P0122 00, P0123 00, P0171 00, P0172 00, P0222 00, P0223 00, P0261 00, P0262 00, P0264 00, P0265 00, P0267 00, P0268 00, P0270 00, P0271 00, P0335 00, P0336 00, P0340 00, P0341 00, P0458 00, P0459 00, P0502 00, P2101 00, P2122 00, P2123 00, P2127 00, P2128 00 or P2138 00 are not set. The engine has been running for more than 60 s. The long term fuel trim is learned. The vehicle speed is less than 3 km/h (2 MPH). The engine coolant temperature (ECT) is between 70-109°C (160-228°F). The intake air temperature (IAT) is between -7 to +105°C (+19 to +221°F). The barometric pressure (BARO) is more than 72 kPa (10.4 PSI). The ignition voltage is between 11-18 V. DTC P0506 00 and P0507 00 run continuously when the above conditions are met.
DTC: P0506 00	**Idle Speed Low:** DTCs P0107 00, P0108 00, P0117 00, P0118 00, P0120 00, P0122 00, P0123 00, P0128 00, P0171 00, P0172 00, P0201 00, P0202 00, P0203 00, P0204 00, P0222 00, P0223 00, P0300 00, P0496 00, P0601 00, P0604 00, P0606 00, P061A 00, P0641 00, P2101 00, P2119 00, P2122 00, P2123 00, P2127 00, P2128 00, P2138 00, or P2176 00 are not set. The engine has been running for greater than 60 s. The engine is idling for greater than 10 s. The intake air temperature (IAT) is greater than -40°C (-40°F). The transmission gear selector state has not changed. The engine coolant temperature (ECT) is greater than 50°C (122°F). The system voltage is between 9-18 V. The vehicle speed is less than 4.8 km/h (3 MPH). DTCs P0506 00 or P0507 00 run continuously when the above conditions are met.

DTC	Trouble Code Title, Conditions, Possible Causes
DTC: P0507	**Idle Speed High:** DTCs P0068, P0101, P0102, P0103, P0106, P0107, P0108, P0112, P0113, P0116, P0117, P0118, P0120, P0121, P0122, P0123, P0128, P0171, P0172, P0174, P0175, P0201-P0208, P0220, P0222, P0223, P0300- P0308, P0336, P0462, P0463, P0496, P0606, P0722, P0723, P1516, P2101, P2120, P2122, P2123, P2125, P2127, P2128, P2135, P2176 are not set. The engine is operating for at least 60 s. The engine is idling for greater than 10 s. The barometric pressure (BARO) is greater than 70 kPa (11 psi). The engine coolant temperature (ECT) is between 60-125°C (140-257°F). The intake air temperature (IAT) is warmer than -20°C (-4°F). The system voltage is between 11-32 V. The vehicle speed is less than 1. 9 km/h (1. 2 mph). The fuel level is greater than 10 percent. The commanded engine speed is steady within 25 RPM. The transmission is not changing gears. The torque converter clutch (TCC) is not changing states. The transfer case is not in 4WD Low - If equipped. The power take-off (PTO) is not active - If equipped. The manual transmission clutch pedal position top of travel is greater than 5 percent - If equipped. The manual transmission clutch pedal position bottom of travel is less than 5 percent - If equipped. The manual transmission clutch is not depressed - If equipped. A scan tool output control is not active. DTC P0506 and P0507 run continuously once the above conditions are met.
DTC: P0507 00	**Idle Speed High:** DTCs P0107 00, P0108 00, P0117 00, P0118 00, P0120 00, P0122 00, P0123 00, P0128 00, P0171 00, P0172 00, P0201 00, P0202 00, P0203 00, P0204 00, P0222 00, P0223 00, P0300 00, P0496 00, P0601 00, P0604 00, P0606 00, P061A 00, P0641 00, P2101 00, P2119 00, P2122 00, P2123 00, P2127 00, P2128 00, P2138 00, or P2176 00 are not set. The engine has been running for greater than 60 s. The engine is idling for greater than 10 s. The intake air temperature (IAT) is greater than -40°C (-40°F). The transmission gear selector state has not changed. The engine coolant temperature (ECT) is greater than 50°C (122°F). The system voltage is between 9-18 V. The vehicle speed is less than 4. 8 km/h (3 MPH). DTCs P0506 00 or P0507 00 run continuously when the above conditions are met.
DTC: P0507 00	**Idle Speed High:** DTCs P0016 00, P0068 00, P0106 00, P0107 00, P0108 00, P0117 00, P0118 00, P0122 00, P0123 00, P0171 00, P0172 00, P0222 00, P0223 00, P0261 00, P0262 00, P0264 00, P0265 00, P0267 00, P0268 00, P0270 00, P0271 00, P0335 00, P0336 00, P0340 00, P0341 00, P0458 00, P0459 00, P0502 00, P2101 00, P2122 00, P2123 00, P2127 00, P2128 00 or P2138 00 are not set. The engine has been running for more than 60 s. The long term fuel trim is learned. The vehicle speed is less than 3 km/h (2 MPH). The engine coolant temperature (ECT) is between 70-109°C (160-228°F). The intake air temperature (IAT) is between -7 to +105°C (+19 to +221°F). The barometric pressure (BARO) is more than 72 kPa (10. 4 PSI). The ignition voltage is between 11-18 V. DTC P0506 00 and P0507 00 run continuously when the above conditions are met.
DTC: P050A	**Cold Start Idle Air Control System Performance:** P050ADTC P0111, P0112, P0113, P0116, P0117, P0118, P0119, P0121, P0122, P0123, P0221, P0222, P0223, P0442, P0443, P0446, P0455, P0458, P0459, P0496, or P0700 is not set. The engine load is between 70-90 percent, for under speed or manual transmission only. The vehicle speed is 0 km/h (0 mph) and accelerator pedal position (APP) input is at 0 percent. The engine coolant temperature (ECT) is colder than 65°C (149°F). The catalyst cold start heating strategy is active. DTC P050A runs once an ignition cycle when the conditions above have been met for 7 s.
DTC: P050A	**Cold Start Idle Air Control System Performance:** DTCs P0096, P0097, P0098, P0099, P0117, P0118, P0121, P0122, P0123, P0300, P0336, P0446, P0455, P0496, P2101, P2176 are not set. The startup engine coolant temperature (ECT) is between -10 and +40°C (+14 and +104°F). The barometric pressure (BARO) is more than 65 kPa. The engine is running. DTC P050A runs continuously when the above conditions are met.
DTC: P050A 00	**Cold Start Idle Air Control System Performance:** DTCs P000A 00, P0010 00, P0016 00, P0068 00, P0106 00, P0107 00, P0108 00, P0116 00, P0117 00, P0118 00, P0119 00, P0121 00, P0123 00, P0171 00, P0172 00, P0201 00, P0202 00, P0203 00, P0204 00, P0222 00, P0261 00, P0262 00, P0264 00, P0265 00, P0267 00, P0268 00, P0270 00, P0271 00, P0335 00, P0336 00, P0340 00, P0341 00, P0365 00, P0366 00, P0443 00, P0459 00, P0496 00, P2088 00, P2089 00, P2100 00, P2101 00, P2122 00, P2123 00, P2127 00, P2128 00, P2138 00 are not set. The battery voltage is greater than 10 V. The engine speed is at idle. The engine coolant temperature (ECT) is greater than -9. 75°C (14. 45°F). DTC P050A 00 runs continuously when the above conditions are met.
DTC: P050B 00	**Cold Start Ignition Timing Performance:** DTCs P0010 00, P0016 00, P0068 00, P0106 00, P0107 00, P0108 00, P0116 00, P0117 00, P0118 00, P0119 00, P0121 00, P0123 00, P0171 00, P0172 00, P0201 00, P0202 00, P0203 00, P0204 00, P0222 00, P0261 00, P0262 00, P0264 00, P0265 00, P0267 00, P0268 00, P0270 00, P0271 00, P0335 00, P0336 00, P0340 00, P0341 00, P0365 00, P0366 00, P0443 00, P0459 00, P0496 00, P2088 00, P2089 00, P2100 00, P2101 00, P2122 00, P2123 00, P2127 00, P2128 00, P2138 00 are not set. The battery voltage is greater than 10 V. The engine speed is at idle. The engine coolant temperature (ECT) is greater than -9. 75°C (14. 45°F). DTC P050B 00 runs continuously when the above conditions are met.

DTC	Trouble Code Title, Conditions, Possible Causes
DTC: P050D	**Cold Start Rough Idle:** DTCs P0010, P0011, P0013, P0014, P0016, P0017, P0018, P0019, P0020, P0021, P0023, P0024, P0089, P0090-P0092, P00C6, P00C8, P00C9, P00CA, P0101-P0103, P0106-P0108, P0112-P0114, P0116-P0118, P0121-P0123, P0128, P0192, P0193, P0201-P0206, P0222, P0223, P0261, P0262, P0264, P0265, P0267, P0268, P0270, P0271, P0273, P0274, P0276, P0277, P0315, P0335, P0336, P0351-P0356, P0627-P0629, P069E, P0716, P0717, P0722, P0723, P0850-P0852, P1248, P1249, P124A, P124B, P124C, P124D, P1258, P135A, P135B, P150C, P163A, P1762, P1763, P1915, P2122, P2123, P2127, P2128, P2135, P2138, P2147, P2148, P2150, P2151, P2153, P2154, P2156, P2157, P216B, P216C, P216E, P216F, P228C, P228D, U0109 are not set. The catalyst temperature is less than 100°C (212°F). The engine coolant temperature is warmer than 10°C (14°F). The barometric pressure is greater than 70 kPa. The engine speed is between 450-1800 RPM. The engine is running and a cold start has been detected. DTC P050D runs once per cold start.
DTC: P050D	**Cold Start Rough Idle:** DTCs P0101, P0102, P0103, P0106, P0107, P0108, P0112, P0113, P0116, P0117, P0118, P0121, P0122, P0123, P0128, P0171, P0172, P0191, P0192, P0193, P0201, P0202, P0203, P0204, P0205, P0206, P0220, P0223, P0231, P0232, P0315, P0335, P0336, P0340, P0341, P0345, P0346, P1682 are not set. The engine is running and a cold start has been detected. DTC P050D runs once per cold start.
DTC: P050E 00	**Cold Start Exhaust Low Temperature:** DTCs P0010 00, P0016 00, P0068 00, P0106 00, P0107 00, P0108 00, P0116 00, P0117 00, P0118 00, P0119 00, P0121 00, P0123 00, P0171 00, P0172 00, P0201 00, P0202 00, P0203 00, P0204 00, P0222 00, P0261 00, P0262 00, P0264 00, P0265 00, P0267 00, P0268 00, P0270 00, P0271 00, P0335 00, P0336 00, P0340 00, P0341 00, P0365 00, P0366 00, P0443 00, P0459 00, P0496 00, P2088 00, P2089 00, P2100 00, P2101 00, P2122 00, P2123 00, P2127 00, P2128 00, P2138 00 are not set. The battery voltage is greater than 10 V. The engine speed is at idle. The engine coolant temperature (ECT) is between 2-37°C (35-100°F) at start. The catalyst temperature is between 2-52°C (35-125°F) at start. The fuel level is greater than 15%.
DTC: P0513	**Immobilizer Key Incorrect:** Ignition is in the ACCESSORY or RUN position.
DTC: P0520	**Engine Oil Pressure Switch Circuit Malfunction:** The engine is running.
DTC: P0521	**Engine Oil Pressure Sensor Performance Malfunction:** The engine is running.
DTC: P0521	**Engine Oil Pressure (EOP) Sensor Performance:** The engine is running.
DTC: P0524 00	**Engine Oil Pressure Too Low:** The engine is running.
DTC: P0526	**Cooling Fan Speed Sensor Circuit:** The engine is operating for greater than 10 S. The engine speed is greater than 550 RPM. The ECM commanded fan clutch solenoid duty cycle is greater than 45 percent. DTC P0526 runs continuously when the conditions above exist for greater than 30 S.
DTC: P0526	**Cooling Fan Speed Sensor Circuit:** The engine is running at a minimum of 550 RPM.
DTC: P0530 03	**Air Conditioning (A/C) Refrigerant Pressure Sensor Circuit Low Voltage:** Engine is running.
DTC: P0530 07	**Air Conditioning (A/C) Refrigerant Pressure Sensor Circuit High Voltage:** Engine is running.
DTC: P0531 00	**Air Conditioning (A/C) Refrigerant Pressure Sensor Performance:** Engine is running.
DTC: P0532	**Air Conditioning A/C Refrigerant Pressure Sensor Circuit Low Voltage:** The engine is running. The battery voltage is between 11-18 volts.
DTC: P0532 00	**Air Conditioning (A/C) Refrigerant Pressure Sensor Circuit Low Voltage:** Engine is running.
DTC: P0532 00	**Air Conditioning (A/C) Refrigerant Pressure Sensor Circuit Low Voltage:** Engine is running.
DTC: P0533	**Air Conditioning A/C Refrigerant Pressure Sensor Circuit High Voltage:** The engine is running. The battery voltage is between 11-18 volts.
DTC: P0533 00	**Air Conditioning (A/C) Refrigerant Pressure Sensor Circuit High Voltage:** Engine is running.

DTC	Trouble Code Title, Conditions, Possible Causes
DTC: P0544 03	**Exhaust Gas Temperature Sensor 1 Circuit Low Voltage:** The ignition is ON. The DTCs run continuously when the above condition is met.
DTC: P0544 07	**Exhaust Gas Temperature Sensor 1 Circuit High Voltage:** The ignition is ON. The DTCs run continuously when the above condition is met.
DTC: P0545	**Exhaust Gas Temperature Sensor 1 Circuit Low Voltage:** The ignition is ON or the engine is running. The DTCs run continuously when the above conditions are met.
DTC: P0545	**Exhaust Temperature Sensor 1 (EGT-1) Circuit Low Voltage:** The ignition is ON. This DTC runs continuously when the above condition is met.
DTC: P0545 00	**Exhaust Gas Temperature Sensor 1 Circuit Low Voltage:** The ignition is ON. The DTCs run continuously when the above condition is met.
DTC: P0546	**Exhaust Gas Temperature Sensor 1 Circuit High Voltage:** The ignition is ON or the engine is running. The DTCs run continuously when the above conditions are met.
DTC: P0546	**Exhaust Temperature Sensor 1 (EGT-1) Circuit High Voltage:** The ignition is ON. This DTC runs continuously when the above condition is met.
DTC: P0546 00	**Exhaust Gas Temperature Sensor 1 Circuit High Voltage:** The ignition is ON. The DTCs run continuously when the above condition is met.
DTC: P0560	**System Voltage Low:** The engine is running.
DTC: P0560 00	**System Voltage - ECM:** The ignition is ON.
DTC: P0562	**System Voltage Low:** P0562The engine speed is 1,200 RPM or greater for 5 seconds.
DTC: P0562	**System Voltage Low:** The system voltage is between 9. 5-18 V.
DTC: P0562	**System Voltage Low:** Engine Control Module. The engine is running. The system voltage is between 9. 5-18 V. Fuel Pump Control Module. The engine is running. Transmission Control Module. Engine speed is 1200 RPM or greater. The system voltage is between 8. 6-18 V.
DTC: P0562	**System Voltage Low - ECM:** The vehicle speed is greater than 8 km/h (5 mph). Engine speed is above 600 RPM
DTC: P0563	**System Voltage High:** The vehicle speed is above 8 km/h (5 mph). The system voltage is between 9. 5-18. 0 V.
DTC: P0563	**System Voltage High:** Engine Control Module. The vehicle speed is above 8 km/h (5 mph). The system voltage is between 9. 5-18 V. Fuel Pump Control Module. The ignition is ON. Transmission Control Module. The system voltage is between 8. 6-18. 0 V.
DTC: P0564	**Cruise Control Multifunction Switch Circuit:** The engine is running. The cruise switch is ON.
DTC: P0565 00	**Cruise Control Switch Circuit Malfunction:** The ignition is ON. The cruise switch is ON.
DTC: P0567	**Cruise Control Resume Switch Circuit:** The cruise switch is ON. The ignition is ON.
DTC: P0567 00	**Cruise Control Resume Switch Circuit Malfunction:** The cruise switch is ON. The ignition is ON.
DTC: P0568	**Cruise Control Set Switch Circuit:** The cruise switch is ON. The ignition is ON.
DTC: P0568 00	**Cruise Control Set Switch Circuit Malfunction:** The cruise switch is ON. The ignition is ON.
DTC: P056C 00	**Cruise Control Cancel Switch Circuit Malfunction:** The cruise switch is ON. The ignition is ON.

DTC	Trouble Code Title, Conditions, Possible Causes
DTC: P0571	**Cruise Control Brake Switch Circuit:** The engine speed is greater than 700 RPM. The traction control system or the antilock brake system are not active and have not failed. The vehicle speed is greater than 48 km/h (30 mph). The diagnostic will disable when the wheel speed is less than 16 km/h (10 mph).
DTC: P0571	**Cruise Control Brake Switch Circuit:** The engine is running. Battery voltage is greater than 11. 5 volts.
DTC: P0572	**Brake Switch Circuit 1 Low Voltage:** The engine is running. Battery voltage is greater than 11. 5 volts.
DTC: P0573	**Brake Switch Circuit 1 High Voltage:** The engine is ON. Battery voltage is greater than 11. 5 volts.
DTC: P0575	**Cruise Control Switch Signal Circuit:** The ignition is ON. The cruise switch is ON.
DTC: P057B 00	**Brake Pedal Position Sensor Performance:** Battery voltage must be between 9-16 V. Brakes APPLIED.
DTC: P057B 00	**Brake Pedal Position Sensor Performance:** The engine is ON.
DTC: P057C	**Brake Pedal Position Sensor Circuit Low Voltage:** P057C and P057DIgnition voltage is greater than 10 Volts.
DTC: P057C 00	**Brake Pedal Position Sensor Circuit Low Voltage:** The engine is ON.
DTC: P057C 00	**Brake Pedal Position Sensor Circuit Low Voltage:** Battery voltage must be between 9-16 V. Brakes APPLIED.
DTC: P057D	**Brake Pedal Position Sensor Circuit High Voltage:** P057C and P057DIgnition voltage is greater than 10 Volts.
DTC: P057D 00	**Brake Pedal Position Sensor Circuit High Voltage:** Battery voltage must be between 9-16 V. Brakes APPLIED.
DTC: P057E 00	**Brake Pedal Position Sensor Circuit Erratic:** The engine is ON.
DTC: P057E 00	**Brake Pedal Position Sensor Circuit Erratic:** Battery voltage must be between 9-16 V. Brakes APPLIED.
DTC: P0580 00	**Cruise Control Multifunction Switch Circuit Low Voltage:** The cruise switch is ON. The ignition is ON.
DTC: P0581 00	**Cruise Control Multifunction Switch Circuit High Voltage:** The cruise switch is ON. The ignition is ON.
DTC: P0597 00	**Engine Coolant Thermostat Heater Control Circuit:** The ignition is ON, or the engine is running. The ignition voltage is greater than 9 V. DTC P0597 00, P0598 00, and P0599 00 run continuously once the above conditions are met.
DTC: P0598 00	**Engine Coolant Thermostat Heater Control Circuit Low Voltage:** The ignition is ON, or the engine is running. The ignition voltage is greater than 9 V. DTC P0597 00, P0598 00, and P0599 00 run continuously once the above conditions are met.
DTC: P0599 00	**Engine Coolant Thermostat Heater Control Circuit High Voltage:** The ignition is ON, or the engine is running. The ignition voltage is greater than 9 V. DTC P0597 00, P0598 00, and P0599 00 run continuously once the above conditions are met.
DTC: P059F 00	**Active Grille Air Shutter Performance:** Engine running. The ignition voltage is greater than 10 V. The DTC runs continuously when the above conditions are met. If the ambient temperature is below 2. 5°C (36°F) when the vehicle is first started, this DTC will be disabled.
DTC: P059F 00	**Active Grille Air Shutter Performance:** Engine running. The ignition voltage is greater than 10 V. The DTC runs continuously when the above conditions are met.
DTC: P0601	**Transmission Control Module (TCM) Read Only Memory (ROM):** The TCM runs the program to detect an internal fault when the engine is running. The only requirements are voltage and ground. This program runs even if the voltage is out of the valid operating range.

DTC	Trouble Code Title, Conditions, Possible Causes
DTC: P0601 00	**Control Module Read Only Memory Performance:** P0601 00, P0605 00The ignition switch is in run or crank. The system voltage is more than 5. 23 V. The check sum calculation at power down in the last drive cycle had completely finished. DTC P0601 00 and DTC P0605 run once per ignition cycle when the above condition is met. P0602 00The ignition switch is in run or crank. DTC P0602 00 runs once per ignition cycle. P0604 00The ignition switch is in run or crank. The read/write test at power down in the last drive cycle had completely finished. DTC P0604 00 runs once per ignition cycle when the above condition is met. P0606 00The ignition switch is in the unlock, accessory, run, or crank positions. DTC P0606 00 runs continuously when the above conditions are met. P0607 00The engine is running or cranking. DTC P0607 00 runs continuously when the above condition is met. . P061B 00The ignition is ON or the engine is running. The system voltage is more than 5. 23 V. DTC P061B 00 runs continuously when the above conditions are met. P061C 00The ignition is ON or the engine is running. The system voltage is more than 5. 23 V. DTC P061C 00 runs continuously when the above conditions are met. P2610 00The ECM is powered down. DTC P2610 00 runs once per ignition cycle. or The ECM is powered up with the ignition switch in the run or crank position. The engine OFF timer value is less than or greater than an internal reference counter during an 2 s interval. DTC P2610 00 runs continuously when the above conditions are met.
DTC: P0602	**Transmission Control Module (TCM) Not Programmed:** The TCM runs the program to detect an internal fault when the engine is running. The only requirements are voltage and ground. This program runs even if the voltage is out of the valid operating range.
DTC: P0602 00	**Control Module Not Programmed:** P0601 00, P0605 00The ignition switch is in run or crank. The system voltage is more than 5. 23 V. The check sum calculation at power down in the last drive cycle had completely finished. DTC P0601 00 and DTC P0605 run once per ignition cycle when the above condition is met. P0602 00The ignition switch is in run or crank. DTC P0602 00 runs once per ignition cycle. P0604 00The ignition switch is in run or crank. The read/write test at power down in the last drive cycle had completely finished. DTC P0604 00 runs once per ignition cycle when the above condition is met. P0606 00The ignition switch is in the unlock, accessory, run, or crank positions. DTC P0606 00 runs continuously when the above conditions are met. P0607 00The engine is running or cranking. DTC P0607 00 runs continuously when the above condition is met. . P061B 00The ignition is ON or the engine is running. The system voltage is more than 5. 23 V. DTC P061B 00 runs continuously when the above conditions are met. P061C 00The ignition is ON or the engine is running. The system voltage is more than 5. 23 V. DTC P061C 00 runs continuously when the above conditions are met. P2610 00The ECM is powered down. DTC P2610 00 runs once per ignition cycle. or The ECM is powered up with the ignition switch in the run or crank position. The engine OFF timer value is less than or greater than an internal reference counter during an 2 s interval. DTC P2610 00 runs continuously when the above conditions are met.
DTC: P0602 46	**Control Module Not Programmed Configuration Not Programmed:** P0602, P0606, P0607, P060A, P060B, P061C, and P062FThe ignition is ON. The DTCs run continuously once the above condition is met. P062BThe engine is running. The DTC runs continuously once the above condition is met.
DTC: P0603	**Control Module Long Term Memory Reset:** Ignition voltage is between 9. 0 and 18. 0 volts.
DTC: P0603	**Control Module Long Term Memory Reset:** P0601, P0602, P0603, P0604The ignition switch is in Run or Crank. These DTCs run once per ignition cycle.
DTC: P0603	**Transmission Control Module (TCM) Long Term Memory Reset:** The TCM runs the program to detect an internal condition at key ON. The only requirements are voltage and ground. This program runs even if the voltage is out of the valid operating range. Ignition voltage is between 8. 0 and 18. 0 volts - DTC P062F only.
DTC: P0604	**Transmission Control Module (TCM) Random Access Memory (RAM):** The TCM runs the program to detect an internal condition at ignition ON. The only requirements are voltage and ground. This program runs even if the voltage is out of the valid operating range. Ignition voltage is between 8. 0 and 18. 0 volts – DTC P062F only.
DTC: P0604	**Control Module Random Access Memory Performance:** P0601, P0604, P0606The ignition switch is in Run or Crank. These DTCs run continuously when the above condition is met.
DTC: P0604 00	**Control Module Random Access Memory Performance:** P0601 00, P0602 00, P0604 00The ignition is ON, or the engine is operating. . The check sum calculation at power-down in the last drive cycle had completely finished. DTCs P0601 00, P0602 00, P0604 00 runs once per ignition cycle when the above condition is met.
DTC: P0604 00	**Control Module Random Access Memory Performance:** The ignition is ON. This DTCs run continuously once the above condition is met.

DTC	Trouble Code Title, Conditions, Possible Causes
DTC: P0604 00	**Control Module Random Access Memory Performance:** P0601 00, P0605 00The ignition switch is in run or crank. The system voltage is more than 5. 23 V. The check sum calculation at power down in the last drive cycle had completely finished. DTC P0601 00 and DTC P0605 run once per ignition cycle when the above condition is met. P0602 00The ignition switch is in run or crank. DTC P0602 00 runs once per ignition cycle. P0604 00The ignition switch is in run or crank. The read/write test at power down in the last drive cycle had completely finished. DTC P0604 00 runs once per ignition cycle when the above condition is met. P0606 00The ignition switch is in the unlock, accessory, run, or crank positions. DTC P0606 00 runs continuously when the above conditions are met. P0607 00The engine is running or cranking. DTC P0607 00 runs continuously when the above condition is met. . P061B 00The ignition is ON or the engine is running. The system voltage is more than 5. 23 V. DTC P061B 00 runs continuously when the above conditions are met. P061C 00The ignition is ON or the engine is running. The system voltage is more than 5. 23 V. DTC P061C 00 runs continuously when the above conditions are met. P2610 00The ECM is powered down. DTC P2610 00 runs once per ignition cycle. or The ECM is powered up with the ignition switch in the run or crank position. The engine OFF timer value is less than or greater than an internal reference counter during an 2 s interval. DTC P2610 00 runs continuously when the above conditions are met.
DTC: P0605 00	**Control Module Programming Read Only Memory Performance:** P0601 00, P0605 00The ignition switch is in run or crank. The system voltage is more than 5. 23 V. The check sum calculation at power down in the last drive cycle had completely finished. DTC P0601 00 and DTC P0605 run once per ignition cycle when the above condition is met. P0602 00The ignition switch is in run or crank. DTC P0602 00 runs once per ignition cycle. P0604 00The ignition switch is in run or crank. The read/write test at power down in the last drive cycle had completely finished. DTC P0604 00 runs once per ignition cycle when the above condition is met. P0606 00The ignition switch is in the unlock, accessory, run, or crank positions. DTC P0606 00 runs continuously when the above conditions are met. P0607 00The engine is running or cranking. DTC P0607 00 runs continuously when the above condition is met. . P061B 00The ignition is ON or the engine is running. The system voltage is more than 5. 23 V. DTC P061B 00 runs continuously when the above conditions are met. P061C 00The ignition is ON or the engine is running. The system voltage is more than 5. 23 V. DTC P061C 00 runs continuously when the above conditions are met. P2610 00The ECM is powered down. DTC P2610 00 runs once per ignition cycle. or The ECM is powered up with the ignition switch in the run or crank position. The engine OFF timer value is less than or greater than an internal reference counter during an 2 s interval. DTC P2610 00 runs continuously when the above conditions are met.
DTC: P0606	**Control Module Processor Performance:** P0601, P0604, P0606The ignition switch is in Run or Crank. These DTCs run continuously when the above condition is met.
DTC: P0606	**Control Module Internal Performance:** P0606The ignition switch is in the Unlock/Accessory, Run, or Crank positions. DTC P0606 runs continuously.
DTC: P0606	**Control Module Internal Performance:** P0606 DTCs P1224, P1227, P122A, P1233, P1236, P1239, P1242, P1244, P1247, P2146, P2149, P2152, P2155 are not set. The engine speed is greater than 1,200 RPM. The engine run time is greater than 10 s. The battery voltage is greater than 8 V. DTC P0606 runs continuously when the above conditions are met.
DTC: P0606 00	**Control Module Processor Performance Malfunction:** P0602, P0606, P0607, P060A, P060B, P061C, and P062FThe ignition is ON. The DTCs run continuously once the above condition is met. P062BThe engine is running. The DTC runs continuously once the above condition is met.
DTC: P0606 00	**Control Module Processor Performance:** P0601 00, P0605 00The ignition switch is in run or crank. The system voltage is more than 5. 23 V. The check sum calculation at power down in the last drive cycle had completely finished. DTC P0601 00 and DTC P0605 run once per ignition cycle when the above condition is met. P0602 00The ignition switch is in run or crank. DTC P0602 00 runs once per ignition cycle. P0604 00The ignition switch is in run or crank. The read/write test at power down in the last drive cycle had completely finished. DTC P0604 00 runs once per ignition cycle when the above condition is met. P0606 00The ignition switch is in the unlock, accessory, run, or crank positions. DTC P0606 00 runs continuously when the above conditions are met. P0607 00The engine is running or cranking. DTC P0607 00 runs continuously when the above condition is met. . P061B 00The ignition is ON or the engine is running. The system voltage is more than 5. 23 V. DTC P061B 00 runs continuously when the above conditions are met. P061C 00The ignition is ON or the engine is running. The system voltage is more than 5. 23 V. DTC P061C 00 runs continuously when the above conditions are met. P2610 00The ECM is powered down. DTC P2610 00 runs once per ignition cycle. or The ECM is powered up with the ignition switch in the run or crank position. The engine OFF timer value is less than or greater than an internal reference counter during an 2 s interval. DTC P2610 00 runs continuously when the above conditions are met.
DTC: P0606 11	**Control Module Processor Performance High Input:** P0602, P0606, P0607, P060A, P060B, P061C, and P062FThe ignition is ON. The DTCs run continuously once the above condition is met. P062BThe engine is running. The DTC runs continuously once the above condition is met.
DTC: P0606 12	**Control Module Processor Performance Low Input:** P0602, P0606, P0607, P060A, P060B, P061C, and P062FThe ignition is ON. The DTCs run continuously once the above condition is met. P062BThe engine is running. The DTC runs continuously once the above condition is met.
DTC: P0606 31	**Control Module Processor Performance Internal Checksum Error:** P0602, P0606, P0607, P060A, P060B, P061C, and P062FThe ignition is ON. The DTCs run continuously once the above condition is met. P062BThe engine is running. The DTC runs continuously once the above condition is met.

DTC	Trouble Code Title, Conditions, Possible Causes
DTC: P0606 33	**Control Module Processor Performance Special Memory Malfunction:** P0602, P0606, P0607, P060A, P060B, P061C, and P062FThe ignition is ON. The DTCs run continuously once the above condition is met. P062BThe engine is running. The DTC runs continuously once the above condition is met.
DTC: P0606 37	**Control Module Processor Performance Software Malfunction:** P0602, P0606, P0607, P060A, P060B, P061C, and P062FThe ignition is ON. The DTCs run continuously once the above condition is met. P062BThe engine is running. The DTC runs continuously once the above condition is met.
DTC: P0606 3C	**Control Module Processor Performance Internal Communication Malfunction:** P0602, P0606, P0607, P060A, P060B, P061C, and P062FThe ignition is ON. The DTCs run continuously once the above condition is met. P062BThe engine is running. The DTC runs continuously once the above condition is met.
DTC: P0606 5A	**Control Module Processor Performance Not Plausible:** P0602, P0606, P0607, P060A, P060B, P061C, and P062FThe ignition is ON. The DTCs run continuously once the above condition is met. P062BThe engine is running. The DTC runs continuously once the above condition is met.
DTC: P0607	**Control Module Performance:** P0606, P0607, P060DThe ignition switch is in Run or Crank. Reduced engine power is not active. The system voltage is more than 6 V. These DTCs run continuously when the above conditions are met.
DTC: P0607 00	**Control Module Performance:** P0601 00, P0605 00The ignition switch is in run or crank. The system voltage is more than 5. 23 V. The check sum calculation at power down in the last drive cycle had completely finished. DTC P0601 00 and DTC P0605 run once per ignition cycle when the above condition is met. P0602 00The ignition switch is in run or crank. DTC P0602 00 runs once per ignition cycle. P0604 00The ignition switch is in run or crank. The read/write test at power down in the last drive cycle had completely finished. DTC P0604 00 runs once per ignition cycle when the above condition is met. P0606 00The ignition switch is in the unlock, accessory, run, or crank positions. DTC P0606 00 runs continuously when the above conditions are met. P0607 00The engine is running or cranking. DTC P0607 00 runs continuously when the above condition is met. . P061B 00The ignition is ON or the engine is running. The system voltage is more than 5. 23 V. DTC P061B 00 runs continuously when the above conditions are met. P061C 00The ignition is ON or the engine is running. The system voltage is more than 5. 23 V. DTC P061C 00 runs continuously when the above conditions are met. P2610 00The ECM is powered down. DTC P2610 00 runs once per ignition cycle. or The ECM is powered up with the ignition switch in the run or crank position. The engine OFF timer value is less than or greater than an internal reference counter during an 2 s interval. DTC P2610 00 runs continuously when the above conditions are met.
DTC: P0607 39	**Control Module Performance Internal Malfunction:** P0602, P0606, P0607, P060A, P060B, P061C, and P062FThe ignition is ON. The DTCs run continuously once the above condition is met. P062BThe engine is running. The DTC runs continuously once the above condition is met.
DTC: P0609	**Vehicle Speed Output Circuit:** Ignition ON. Ignition voltage is greater than 10 volts.
DTC: P060A 07	**Control Module Monitoring Processor Performance High Voltage:** P0602, P0606, P0607, P060A, P060B, P061C, and P062FThe ignition is ON. The DTCs run continuously once the above condition is met. P062BThe engine is running. The DTC runs continuously once the above condition is met.
DTC: P060B	**Control Module Analog to Digital Performance:** P060B, P062FThese DTCs run continuously when the ignition is ON.
DTC: P060B	**Control Module Analog to Digital Performance:** P060BThe engine speed is more than 650 RPM. The ECM is powered up. DTC P060B runs continuously when the above conditions are met.
DTC: P060B 03	**Control Module Analog to Digital Converter Performance Low Voltage:** P0602, P0606, P0607, P060A, P060B, P061C, and P062FThe ignition is ON. The DTCs run continuously once the above condition is met. P062BThe engine is running. The DTC runs continuously once the above condition is met.
DTC: P060B 07	**Control Module Analog to Digital Converter Performance High Voltage:** P0602, P0606, P0607, P060A, P060B, P061C, and P062FThe ignition is ON. The DTCs run continuously once the above condition is met. P062BThe engine is running. The DTC runs continuously once the above condition is met.
DTC: P060B 08	**Control Module Analog to Digital Converter Performance - Signal Invalid:** P0602, P0606, P0607, P060A, P060B, P061C, and P062FThe ignition is ON. The DTCs run continuously once the above condition is met. P062BThe engine is running. The DTC runs continuously once the above condition is met.
DTC: P060B 11	**Control Module Analog to Digital Converter Performance High Input:** P0602, P0606, P0607, P060A, P060B, P061C, and P062FThe ignition is ON. The DTCs run continuously once the above condition is met. P062BThe engine is running. The DTC runs continuously once the above condition is met.

DTC	Trouble Code Title, Conditions, Possible Causes
DTC: P060D	**Control Module Accelerator Pedal (APP) Position System Circuitry Performance:** P0606, P0607, P060DThe ignition voltage is more than 6. 0 V. Reduced Engine Power is not active. These DTCs run continuously when the above conditions are met.
DTC: P060D	**Control Module Accelerator Pedal (APP) Position System Circuitry Performance:** P060DDTC P0606 is not set. The ignition switch is in the Unlock, Accessory, Run, or Crank position. The system voltage is more than 5. 23 V. DTC P060D runs continuously when the above conditions are met.
DTC: P0615	**Starter Relay Control Circuit:** The ignition is ON. The system voltage is between 9. 5-18 volts.
DTC: P0615 01	**Starter Relay Control Circuit Short to Battery:** The Ignition is in the START position. The system voltage is between 9. 5-18 V.
DTC: P061A 00	**Control Module Torque System Circuitry Performance:** P0601 00, P0605 00The ignition switch is in run or crank. The system voltage is more than 5. 23 V. The check sum calculation at power down in the last drive cycle had completely finished. DTC P0601 00 and DTC P0605 run once per ignition cycle when the above condition is met. P0602 00The ignition switch is in run or crank. DTC P0602 00 runs once per ignition cycle. P0604 00The ignition switch is in run or crank. The read/write test at power down in the last drive cycle had completely finished. DTC P0604 00 runs once per ignition cycle when the above condition is met. P0606 00The ignition switch is in the unlock, accessory, run, or crank positions. DTC P0606 00 runs continuously when the above conditions are met. P0607 00The engine is running or cranking. DTC P0607 00 runs continuously when the above condition is met. . P061B 00The ignition is ON or the engine is running. The system voltage is more than 5. 23 V. DTC P061B 00 runs continuously when the above conditions are met. P061C 00The ignition is ON or the engine is running. The system voltage is more than 5. 23 V. DTC P061C 00 runs continuously when the above conditions are met. P2610 00The ECM is powered down. DTC P2610 00 runs once per ignition cycle. or The ECM is powered up with the ignition switch in the run or crank position. The engine OFF timer value is less than or greater than an internal reference counter during an 2 s interval. DTC P2610 00 runs continuously when the above conditions are met.
DTC: P061A 00	**Control Module Torque System Circuitry Performance:** P061A 00The ignition voltage is between 11-18 V. The ignition is in the unlock, accessory, run, or crank position. DTC P0601 00, P0602 00, P0604 00, P0606 00, P0641 00, P2610 00 are not set.
DTC: P061B 00	**Control Module Torque Calculation Performance:** P0601 00, P0605 00The ignition switch is in run or crank. The system voltage is more than 5. 23 V. The check sum calculation at power down in the last drive cycle had completely finished. DTC P0601 00 and DTC P0605 run once per ignition cycle when the above condition is met. P0602 00The ignition switch is in run or crank. DTC P0602 00 runs once per ignition cycle. P0604 00The ignition switch is in run or crank. The read/write test at power down in the last drive cycle had completely finished. DTC P0604 00 runs once per ignition cycle when the above condition is met. P0606 00The ignition switch is in the unlock, accessory, run, or crank positions. DTC P0606 00 runs continuously when the above conditions are met. P0607 00The engine is running or cranking. DTC P0607 00 runs continuously when the above condition is met. . P061B 00The ignition is ON or the engine is running. The system voltage is more than 5. 23 V. DTC P061B 00 runs continuously when the above conditions are met. P061C 00The ignition is ON or the engine is running. The system voltage is more than 5. 23 V. DTC P061C 00 runs continuously when the above conditions are met. P2610 00The ECM is powered down. DTC P2610 00 runs once per ignition cycle. or The ECM is powered up with the ignition switch in the run or crank position. The engine OFF timer value is less than or greater than an internal reference counter during an 2 s interval. DTC P2610 00 runs continuously when the above conditions are met.
DTC: P061C	**Control Module Engine Speed Performance:** P061CThe ignition is ON. The engine speed is less than 1,300 RPM. DTC P061C runs continuously when the above conditions are met.
DTC: P061C 00	**Control Module Engine Speed System Circuitry Performance:** P0601 00, P0605 00The ignition switch is in run or crank. The system voltage is more than 5. 23 V. The check sum calculation at power down in the last drive cycle had completely finished. DTC P0601 00 and DTC P0605 run once per ignition cycle when the above condition is met. P0602 00The ignition switch is in run or crank. DTC P0602 00 runs once per ignition cycle. P0604 00The ignition switch is in run or crank. The read/write test at power down in the last drive cycle had completely finished. DTC P0604 00 runs once per ignition cycle when the above condition is met. P0606 00The ignition switch is in the unlock, accessory, run, or crank positions. DTC P0606 00 runs continuously when the above conditions are met. P0607 00The engine is running or cranking. DTC P0607 00 runs continuously when the above condition is met. . P061B 00The ignition is ON or the engine is running. The system voltage is more than 5. 23 V. DTC P061B 00 runs continuously when the above conditions are met. P061C 00The ignition is ON or the engine is running. The system voltage is more than 5. 23 V. DTC P061C 00 runs continuously when the above conditions are met. P2610 00The ECM is powered down. DTC P2610 00 runs once per ignition cycle. or The ECM is powered up with the ignition switch in the run or crank position. The engine OFF timer value is less than or greater than an internal reference counter during an 2 s interval. DTC P2610 00 runs continuously when the above conditions are met.
DTC: P061C 00	**Control Module Engine Speed System Circuitry Performance Malfunction:** P0602, P0606, P0607, P060A, P060B, P061C, and P062FThe ignition is ON. The DTCs run continuously once the above condition is met. P062BThe engine is running. The DTC runs continuously once the above condition is met.

DTC	Trouble Code Title, Conditions, Possible Causes
DTC: P0621 00	**Generator L-Terminal Circuit:** The ignition ON, engine OFF for ignition on test. The engine is running for the run test.
DTC: P0621 58	**Generator L-Terminal Circuit Performance:** The ignition ON, engine OFF for ignition on test. The engine is running for the run test.
DTC: P0621 59	**Generator L-Terminal Circuit Protection Time Out:** The ignition ON, engine OFF for ignition on test. The engine is running for the run test.
DTC: P0622	**Generator F-Terminal Circuit:** No generator, crankshaft position (CKP) sensor, or camshaft (CMP) sensor DTCs are set. Ignition ON engine OFF, for the Ignition ON test. Engine running, engine speed less than 3,000 RPM for the RUN test.
DTC: P0622 00	**Generator F-Terminal Circuit:** Ignition ON engine OFF, for the Ignition ON test. Engine running, engine speed less than 3 000 RPM for the RUN test.
DTC: P0622 11	**Generator F-Terminal Circuit High Input:** Ignition ON engine OFF, for the Ignition ON test. Engine running, engine speed less than 3 000 RPM for the RUN test.
DTC: P0622 12	**Generator F-Terminal Circuit Low Input:** Ignition ON engine OFF, for the Ignition ON test. Engine running, engine speed less than 3 000 RPM for the RUN test.
DTC: P0625	**Generator F-Terminal Circuit Low Voltage:** P0625The engine is running. The engine speed is less than 3 000 RPM.
DTC: P0626	**Generator F-Terminal Circuit High Voltage:** P0626The engine is not running. The ignition is in the ON position.
DTC: P0627	**Fuel Pump Enable Circuit:** The engine speed is greater than 80 RPM. The ignition 1 signal parameter is 10-18 V. The ECM has commanded the fuel pump enable circuit ON and OFF at least once during the ignition cycle. The DTCs run continuously when the conditions above are met.
DTC: P0627	**Fuel Pump Enable Circuit:** The engine speed is greater than 0 RPM. The ignition voltage is between 11-18 V. The DTCs run continuously when the conditions above are met.
DTC: P0627 00	**Fuel Pump Relay Control Circuit Open:** P0627 00 and P0629 00The ignition voltage is between 10-18 V. The ECM has commanded the fuel pump OFF. The above conditions are met for greater than 1 s. The DTCs run continuously when the above conditions are met.
DTC: P0627 01	**Fuel Pump Relay Control Circuit Short to Battery:** P0627 01 and P0627 54The ignition is ON, or the engine is running. The power stage is active. The DTCs run continuously once the above conditions are met
DTC: P0627 02	**Fuel Pump Relay Control Circuit Short to Ground:** P0627 02 and P0627 04The ignition is ON. The power stage is not active. The DTCs run continuously once the above conditions are met
DTC: P0627 04	**Fuel Pump Relay Control Circuit Open:** P0627 02 and P0627 04The ignition is ON. The power stage is not active. The DTCs run continuously once the above conditions are met
DTC: P0627 54	**Fuel Pump Relay Control Circuit High Temperature:** P0627 01 and P0627 54The ignition is ON, or the engine is running. The power stage is active. The DTCs run continuously once the above conditions are met
DTC: P0628	**Fuel Pump Enable Circuit Low Voltage:** The engine speed is greater than 80 RPM. The ignition 1 signal parameter is 10-18 V. The ECM has commanded the fuel pump enable circuit ON and OFF at least once during the ignition cycle. The DTCs run continuously when the conditions above are met.
DTC: P0628	**Fuel Pump Relay Control Circuit Low Voltage:** P0628The engine speed is greater than 80 RPM. The ignition voltage is between 10-18. 1 V. The ECM has commanded the fuel pump relay ON. The above conditions are met for greater than 1 second. The DTC runs continuously once the above conditions are met.
DTC: P0628 00	**Fuel Pump Relay Control Circuit Low Voltage:** P0628 00The ignition voltage is between 10-18 V. The ECM has commanded the fuel pump ON. The above conditions are met for greater than 1 s. The DTC runs continuously when the above conditions are met.
DTC: P0628 00	**Fuel Pump Relay Control Circuit Low Voltage:** The engine speed is greater than 80 RPM. The ignition voltage is 10-18 V. The ECM has commanded the fuel pump relay ON and OFF at least once during the ignition cycle. The above conditions are met for less than 1 s. DTCs P0628 00 or P0629 00 runs continuously once the above conditions are met.

DTC	Trouble Code Title, Conditions, Possible Causes
DTC: P0629	**Fuel Pump Relay Control Circuit High Voltage:** P0627 and P0629The engine speed is greater than 80 RPM. The ignition voltage is between 10-18. 1 V. The ECM has commanded the fuel pump relay OFF. The above conditions are met for greater than 1 second. The DTCs run continuously once the above conditions are met.
DTC: P0629 00	**Fuel Pump Relay Control Circuit High Voltage:** P0627 00 and P0629 00The ignition voltage is between 10-18 V. The ECM has commanded the fuel pump OFF. The above conditions are met for greater than 1 s. The DTCs run continuously when the above conditions are met.
DTC: P0629 00	**Fuel Pump Relay Control Circuit High Voltage:** The engine speed is greater than 80 RPM. The ignition voltage is 10-18 V. The ECM has commanded the fuel pump relay ON and OFF at least once during the ignition cycle. The above conditions are met for less than 1 s. DTCs P0628 00 or P0629 00 runs continuously once the above conditions are met.
DTC: P062B	**Control Module Fuel Injector Control Performance:** The engine is running or cranking. The system voltage is between 8-18. 1 V. DTC P062B runs continuously when the above conditions are met.
DTC: P062B 00	**Control Module Fuel Injector Control Performance Malfunction:** P0602, P0606, P0607, P060A, P060B, P061C, and P062FThe ignition is ON. The DTCs run continuously once the above condition is met. P062BThe engine is running. The DTC runs continuously once the above condition is met.
DTC: P062B 00	**Control Module Fuel Injector Control Performance:** The ignition is ON. This DTCs run continuously once the above condition is met.
DTC: P062B 03	**Control Module Fuel Injector Control Performance Low Voltage:** P0602, P0606, P0607, P060A, P060B, P061C, and P062FThe ignition is ON. The DTCs run continuously once the above condition is met. P062BThe engine is running. The DTC runs continuously once the above condition is met.
DTC: P062B 32	**Control Module Fuel Injector Control Performance General Memory Malfunction:** P0602, P0606, P0607, P060A, P060B, P061C, and P062FThe ignition is ON. The DTCs run continuously once the above condition is met. P062BThe engine is running. The DTC runs continuously once the above condition is met.
DTC: P062B 39	**Control Module Fuel Injector Control Performance Internal Malfunction:** P0602, P0606, P0607, P060A, P060B, P061C, and P062FThe ignition is ON. The DTCs run continuously once the above condition is met. P062BThe engine is running. The DTC runs continuously once the above condition is met.
DTC: P062B 3B	**Control Module Fuel Injector Control Performance Self-Test Malfunction:** P0602, P0606, P0607, P060A, P060B, P061C, and P062FThe ignition is ON. The DTCs run continuously once the above condition is met. P062BThe engine is running. The DTC runs continuously once the above condition is met.
DTC: P062B 3C	**Control Module Fuel Injector Control Performance Internal Communication Malfunction:** P0602, P0606, P0607, P060A, P060B, P061C, and P062FThe ignition is ON. The DTCs run continuously once the above condition is met. P062BThe engine is running. The DTC runs continuously once the above condition is met.
DTC: P062B 59	**Control Module Fuel Injector Control Performance Protection Time-Out:** P0602, P0606, P0607, P060A, P060B, P061C, and P062FThe ignition is ON. The DTCs run continuously once the above condition is met. P062BThe engine is running. The DTC runs continuously once the above condition is met.
DTC: P062B 73	**Control Module Fuel Injector Control Performance Parity Error:** P0602, P0606, P0607, P060A, P060B, P061C, and P062FThe ignition is ON. The DTCs run continuously once the above condition is met. P062BThe engine is running. The DTC runs continuously once the above condition is met.
DTC: P062C	**Control Module Vehicle Speed Performance:** P062C, P2610These DTCs run continuously when the ignition is ON.
DTC: P062F	**Transmission Control Module (TCM) Long Term Memory Performance:** The TCM runs the program to detect an internal fault when the engine is running. The only requirements are voltage and ground. This program runs even if the voltage is out of the valid operating range.
DTC: P062F	**Control Module Long Term Memory Performance:** P0602, P0603, P062FThe ignition switch is in ON. These DTCs run once per ignition cycle.
DTC: P062F 00	**Control Module Long Term Memory Performance Malfunction:** P0602, P0606, P0607, P060A, P060B, P061C, and P062FThe ignition is ON. The DTCs run continuously once the above condition is met. P062BThe engine is running. The DTC runs continuously once the above condition is met.
DTC: P062F 36	**Control Module Long Term Memory Performance EEPROM Performance/Malfunction:** P0602, P0606, P0607, P060A, P060B, P061C, and P062FThe ignition is ON. The DTCs run continuously once the above condition is met. P062BThe engine is running. The DTC runs continuously once the above condition is met.

DTC	Trouble Code Title, Conditions, Possible Causes
DTC: P062F 41	**Control Module Long Term Memory Performance Not Programmed:** P0602, P0606, P0607, P060A, P060B, P061C, and P062FThe ignition is ON. The DTCs run continuously once the above condition is met. P062BThe engine is running. The DTC runs continuously once the above condition is met.
DTC: P0630	**VIN Not Programmed or Mismatched – Engine Control Module (ECM):** P0601, P0606, P062B, P0630, P16F3These DTCs run continuously when the ignition is ON.
DTC: P0634	**Transmission Control Module (TCM) Over temperature:** The ignition voltage is greater than 8. 6 volts. The TCM temperature is between 0-170°C (32-338°F) for 0. 25 second or greater. DTC P0634 has not set this ignition cycle.
DTC: P0638	**Throttle Actuator Control (TAC) Command Performance:** P0638 and P2101The engine is operating. The ignition voltage is greater than 7 V. DTCs P0638 and P2101 run continuously once the above conditions are met for greater than 5 s.
DTC: P0640	**Intake Air (IA) Heater Control Circuit:** The intake air heater is commanded OFF. DTC P0640 runs continuously when the above condition is met.
DTC: P0641	**5 V Reference 1 Circuit:** Reduced engine power is not active. The ignition voltage is more than 6 V. DTCs P0641 and P0651 run continuously when the above conditions are met.
DTC: P0641 00	**5 V Reference 1 Circuit:** The ignition is ON. The ECM is not commanding reduced engine power. The ignition voltage is greater than 6 V. These DTCs run continuously when the above conditions are met.
DTC: P0641 03	**5V Reference 1 Circuit Low Voltage:** The ignition is ON. The DTCs run continuously when the above condition is met.
DTC: P0641 07	**5V Reference 1 Circuit High Voltage:** The ignition is ON. The DTCs run continuously when the above condition is met.
DTC: P0642	**5-Volt Reference 1 Circuit Low Voltage:** The ignition is ON. The diagnostics run continuously.
DTC: P0642 00	**5V Reference 1 Circuit Low Voltage:** DTCs P0601 00, P0602 00, P0604 00, P0606 00, P0607 00, and P2610 00 are not set. The ignition is in unlock, accessory, run, or crank. DTCs P0642 00, P0643 00, P0652 00 and P0653 00 run continuously when the above conditions are met.
DTC: P0643	**5-Volt Reference 1 Circuit High Voltage:** The ignition is ON. The diagnostics run continuously.
DTC: P0643 00	**5V Reference 1 Circuit High Voltage:** DTCs P0601 00, P0602 00, P0604 00, P0606 00, P0607 00, and P2610 00 are not set. The ignition is in unlock, accessory, run, or crank. DTCs P0642 00, P0643 00, P0652 00 and P0653 00 run continuously when the above conditions are met.
DTC: P0645	**Air Conditioning (A/C) Clutch Relay Control Circuit:** The ignition voltage is between 9 and 18 volts. The engine speed is more than 800 RPM. The ECM/PCM A/C compressor clutch relay control transitions between ON to OFF or from OFF to ON.
DTC: P0646	**Air Conditioning (A/C) Clutch Relay Control Circuit Low Voltage:** The ignition voltage is between 9 and 18 volts. The engine speed is more than 800 RPM. The ECM/PCM A/C compressor clutch relay control transitions between ON to OFF or from OFF to ON.
DTC: P0647	**Air Conditioning (A/C) Clutch Relay Control Circuit High Voltage:** The ignition voltage is between 9 and 18 volts. The engine speed is more than 800 RPM. The ECM/PCM A/C compressor clutch relay control transitions between ON to OFF or from OFF to ON.
DTC: P0649 01	**Cruise Engaged Indicator Control Circuit Short to Battery:** The engine is operating. The ignition 1 voltage is between 7. 5-16 V. The DTCs run continuously once the above conditions are met.
DTC: P0649 02	**Cruise Engaged Indicator Control Circuit Short to Ground:** The engine is operating. The ignition 1 voltage is between 7. 5-16 V. The DTCs run continuously once the above conditions are met.
DTC: P0649 04	**Cruise Engaged Indicator Control Circuit Open:** The engine is operating. The ignition 1 voltage is between 7. 5-16 V. The DTCs run continuously once the above conditions are met.
DTC: P0649 54	**Cruise Engaged Indicator Control Circuit High Temperature:** The engine is operating. The ignition 1 voltage is between 7. 5-16 V. The DTCs run continuously once the above conditions are met.
DTC: P064A	**Fuel Pump Control Module Performance:** The engine is running.

DTC	Trouble Code Title, Conditions, Possible Causes
DTC: P064C	**Glow Plug Module Control Performance:** The ignition is ON. DTC P064C runs continuously.
DTC: P064C	**Glow Plug Module Control Performance:** The ignition is ON. DTC P064C runs continuously.
DTC: P064C 00	**Glow Plug Control Module Performance Malfunction:** The ignition is ON. The battery voltage is between 9-16 V. The DTC runs once per ignition cycle when the above condition is met.
DTC: P064D	**Control Module HO2S 1 System Performance:** P064DThe ignition switch is in Run or Crank. The system voltage is between 10. 7-18. 1 V. DTC P064D runs continuously when the above conditions are met.
DTC: P064D 00	**Control Module HO2S 1 System Circuitry Performance:** The ignition voltage is between 10-18 V. The engine speed is greater than 80 RPM. The HO2S heater is commanded ON and OFF at least once during the ignition cycle. The DTCs run continuously once the above conditions are met for 2 s.
DTC: P0650	**Malfunction Indicator Lamp (MIL) Control Circuit:** The ignition is in the Run or Crank position. The ignition voltage is between 11-32 V. The ECM has commanded the MIL ON and OFF at least once during the ignition cycle. The DTC runs continuously when the above conditions are met.
DTC: P0650	**Malfunction Indicator Lamp (MIL) Control Circuit:** DTC P0650 runs continuously when the ignition is ON and the ignition voltage is between 9-18 volts.
DTC: P0650 00	**Malfunction Indicator Lamp (MIL) Control Circuit:** DTCs P0601 00, P0604 00, P0605 00, P0606 00, P0607 00, and P2610 00 are not set. DTC P0650 00 runs continuously when the ignition is ON.
DTC: P0650 01	**Malfunction Indicator Lamp (MIL) Control Circuit Short to Battery:** DTCs P0601 00, P0604 00, P0605 00, P0606 00, P0607 00, and P2610 00 are not set. DTC P0650 runs continuously when the ignition is ON.
DTC: P0650 02	**Malfunction Indicator Lamp (MIL) Control Circuit Short to Ground:** DTCs P0601 00, P0604 00, P0605 00, P0606 00, P0607 00, and P2610 00 are not set. DTC P0650 runs continuously when the ignition is ON.
DTC: P0650 04	**Malfunction Indicator Lamp (MIL) Control Circuit Open:** DTCs P0601 00, P0604 00, P0605 00, P0606 00, P0607 00, and P2610 00 are not set. DTC P0650 runs continuously when the ignition is ON.
DTC: P0650 54	**Malfunction Indicator Lamp (MIL) Control Circuit High Temperature:** DTCs P0601 00, P0604 00, P0605 00, P0606 00, P0607 00, and P2610 00 are not set. DTC P0650 runs continuously when the ignition is ON.
DTC: P0651	**5 V Reference 2 Circuit:** Reduced engine power is not active. The ignition voltage is more than 6 V. DTCs P0641 and P0651 run continuously when the above conditions are met.
DTC: P0651	**5 V Reference 2 Circuit:** The ignition is in Unlock, Accessory, Run, or Crank. The ignition voltage is more than 5. 23 V. DTCs P0641 and P0651 run continuously when the above conditions are met.
DTC: P0651	**5 V Reference 2 Circuit:** DTCs P0601, P0602, P0603, P0604, P0605, P0606, P0607, P060D, P062F and P2610 are not set. The ignition is ON. The ignition voltage is greater than 5. 23 V. The DTCs run continuously when the above conditions are met.
DTC: P0651 00	**5 V Reference 2 Circuit:** The ignition is ON. The ECM is not commanding reduced engine power. The ignition voltage is greater than 6 V. These DTCs run continuously when the above conditions are met.
DTC: P0651 03	**5 V Reference 2 Circuit Low Voltage:** The ignition is ON. The DTCs run continuously when the above condition is met.
DTC: P0651 07	**5 V Reference 2 Circuit High Voltage:** The ignition is ON. The DTCs run continuously when the above condition is met.
DTC: P0652	**5 Volt Reference 2 Circuit Low Voltage:** The ignition is ON. The diagnostics run continuously.
DTC: P0652 00	**5V Reference 2 Circuit Low Voltage:** DTCs P0601 00, P0602 00, P0604 00, P0606 00, P0607 00, and P2610 00 are not set. The ignition is in unlock, accessory, run, or crank. DTCs P0642 00, P0643 00, P0652 00 and P0653 00 run continuously when the above conditions are met.

DTC	Trouble Code Title, Conditions, Possible Causes
DTC: P0653	**5 Volt Reference 2 Circuit High Voltage:** The ignition is ON. The diagnostics run continuously.
DTC: P0653 00	**5V Reference 2 Circuit High Voltage:** DTCs P0601 00, P0602 00, P0604 00, P0606 00, P0607 00, and P2610 00 are not set. The ignition is in unlock, accessory, run, or crank. DTCs P0642 00, P0643 00, P0652 00 and P0653 00 run continuously when the above conditions are met.
DTC: P0658	**Actuator High Control Circuit Group 1 Low Voltage:** P0658High side driver 1 is enabled. DTC P0658 is not set.
DTC: P0658	**Solenoid High Control Circuit Group 1 Low Voltage:** P0658High side driver 1 is enabled. DTC P0658 has not set this ignition cycle.
DTC: P0658	**Solenoid High Control Circuit Group 1 Low Voltage:** P0658The engine speed is greater than 500 RPM for 5 seconds. Ignition voltage is 8. 6 volts or greater. High side driver 1 is enabled. DTC P0658 has not set this ignition.
DTC: P0659	**Solenoid High Control Circuit Group 1 High Voltage:** P0659 DTC P0659 is not set. The ignition transitions from OFF to ON.
DTC: P0659	**Solenoid High Control Circuit Group 1 High Voltage:** P0659 DTC P0659 has not set this ignition. Ignition voltage is 8. 6 volts or greater. Ignition switch transitions from OFF to run position.
DTC: P0659	**Actuator High Control Circuit Group 1 High Voltage:** P0659 DTC P0659 is not set. Ignition transitions from OFF to ON.
DTC: P0661 00	**Intake Manifold Tuning Control Valve Control Circuit Low Voltage:** DTC P0606 00 is not set. The ignition is ON, or the engine is running. The battery voltage is greater than 9 V. DTCs P0661 00 and P0662 00 run continuously when the above conditions are met.
DTC: P0662 00	**Intake Manifold Tuning Control Valve Control Circuit High Voltage:** DTC P0606 00 is not set. The ignition is ON, or the engine is running. The battery voltage is greater than 9 V. DTCs P0661 00 and P0662 00 run continuously when the above conditions are met.
DTC: P0667	**Control Module Temperature Sensor Performance:** P0667 DTC P0101, P0102, P0103, P0106, P0107, P0108, P0171, P0172, P0174, P0175, P0201, P0202, P0203, P0204, P0205, P0206, P0207, P0208, P0300, P0301, P0302, P0303, P0304, P0305, P0306, P0307, P0308, P0401, P042E, P0658, P0667, P0668, P0669, P06AD, P06AE, P0712, P0713, P0716, P0717, P0722, P0723, P0962, P0963, P0966, P0967, P0970, P0971, P215C, P2720, P2721, P2729, or P2730 is not set. Brake torque is not active. The engine speed is 400 RPM or greater for 5 seconds. The ignition voltage is 8. 6 volts or greater. The engine torque signal is valid. The throttle position signal is valid.
DTC: P0667	**Transmission Control Module (TCM) Temperature Sensor Performance:** P0667No DTCs P0101, P0102, P0103, P0106, P0107, P0108, P0171, P0172, P0174, P0175, P0201, P0202, P0203, P0204, P0205, P0206, P0207, P0208, P0300, P0301, P0302, P0303, P0304, P0305, P0306, P0307, P0308, P0401, P042E, P0658, P0668, P0669, P06AD, P06AE, P0712, P0713, P0716, P0717, P0722, P0723, P0962, P0963, P0966, P0967, P0970, P0971, P215C, P2720, P2721, P2729, or P2730. Brake torque is not active. The engine speed is greater than 400 RPM for 5 seconds or greater. The ignition voltage is 8. 6 volts or greater.
DTC: P0668	**Transmission Control Module (TCM) Temperature Sensor Circuit Low Voltage:** DTC P0667, P0668, or P0669 DTCs P0667, P0716, P0717, P0722, or P0723 are not set. The TCM internal temperature is between -55°C and +150°C (-67°F and +302°F). The engine speed is 500 RPM or more for 5 seconds. The ignition voltage is 8. 6V or greater.
DTC: P0668	**Transmission Control Module (TCM) Temperature Sensor Circuit Low Voltage:** P0668The ignition voltage is 9. 0 volts or greater. The engine speed is greater than 500 RPM for 5 seconds or greater. DTC P0668 has not set.
DTC: P0669	**Transmission Control Module (TCM) Temperature Sensor Circuit High Voltage:** P0669No ISS DTCs P0716 or P0717. No OSS DTCs P0722 or P0723. The ignition voltage is 9. 0 volts or greater. The engine speed is greater than 500 RPM for 5 seconds or greater. DTC P0669 has not set.
DTC: P0669	**Control Module Temperature Sensor Circuit High Voltage:** P0669 DTC P0669, P0716, P0717, P0722, or P0723 is not set. The ignition voltage is 9. 0 volts or greater. The engine speed is greater than 400 RPM for 5 seconds or greater.
DTC: P0669	**Transmission Control Module (TCM) Temperature Sensor Circuit High Voltage:** P0669No ISS DTCs P0716 or P0717. No OSS DTCs P0722 or P0723. The transmission output shaft speed is 200 RPM or greater for 200 seconds or more. The engine speed is greater than 400 RPM for 5 seconds. The ignition voltage is 8. 6 volts or greater.

DTC	Trouble Code Title, Conditions, Possible Causes
DTC: P0670 00	**Glow Plug Control Module Control Circuit:** The ignition is ON, or the engine is running. The ignition voltage is between 9-16 V. The DTCs run once per ignition cycle when the above conditions are met.
DTC: P0670 01	**Glow Plug Control Module Control Circuit Short to Battery:** P0670 01 or P0670 54The ignition is ON, or the engine is running. The ignition voltage is between 9-16 V. The DTCs run once per ignition cycle when the above conditions are met. P0670 02 or P0670 44The ignition is ON. The ignition voltage is between 9-16 V. The DTCs run once per ignition cycle when the above conditions are met.
DTC: P0670 02	**Glow Plug Control Module Control Circuit Short to Ground:** P0670 01 or P0670 54The ignition is ON, or the engine is running. The ignition voltage is between 9-16 V. The DTCs run once per ignition cycle when the above conditions are met. P0670 02 or P0670 44The ignition is ON. The ignition voltage is between 9-16 V. The DTCs run once per ignition cycle when the above conditions are met.
DTC: P0670 04	**Glow Plug Control Module Control Circuit Open:** P0670 01 or P0670 54The ignition is ON, or the engine is running. The ignition voltage is between 9-16 V. The DTCs run once per ignition cycle when the above conditions are met. P0670 02 or P0670 44The ignition is ON. The ignition voltage is between 9-16 V. The DTCs run once per ignition cycle when the above conditions are met.
DTC: P0670 54	**Glow Plug Control Module Control Circuit High Temperature:** P0670 01 or P0670 54The ignition is ON, or the engine is running. The ignition voltage is between 9-16 V. The DTCs run once per ignition cycle when the above conditions are met. P0670 02 or P0670 44The ignition is ON. The ignition voltage is between 9-16 V. The DTCs run once per ignition cycle when the above conditions are met.
DTC: P0671	**Cylinder #1 Glow Plug Control Circuit:** The ignition is ON. DTCs P0671-P0678 run continuously.
DTC: P0671 00	**Cylinder 1 Glow Plug Control Circuit:** The ignition is ON, or the engine is running. The ignition voltage is less than 16 V. These DTCs run once per ignition cycle when the above conditions are met.
DTC: P0671 02	**Cylinder 1 Glow Plug Control Circuit Short to Ground:** The ignition is ON, or the engine is running. The ignition voltage is less than 16 V. The DTCs run once per ignition cycle when the above conditions are met.
DTC: P0671 04	**Cylinder 1 Glow Plug Control Circuit Open:** The ignition is ON, or the engine is running. The ignition voltage is less than 16 V. The DTCs run once per ignition cycle when the above conditions are met.
DTC: P0672	**Cylinder #2 Glow Plug Control Circuit:** The ignition is ON. DTCs P0671-P0678 run continuously.
DTC: P0672 00	**Cylinder 2 Glow Plug Control Circuit:** The ignition is ON, or the engine is running. The ignition voltage is less than 16 V. These DTCs run once per ignition cycle when the above conditions are met.
DTC: P0672 02	**Cylinder 2 Glow Plug Control Circuit Short to Ground:** The ignition is ON, or the engine is running. The ignition voltage is less than 16 V. The DTCs run once per ignition cycle when the above conditions are met.
DTC: P0672 04	**Cylinder 2 Glow Plug Control Circuit Open:** The ignition is ON, or the engine is running. The ignition voltage is less than 16 V. The DTCs run once per ignition cycle when the above conditions are met.
DTC: P0673	**Cylinder #3 Glow Plug Control Circuit:** The ignition is ON. DTCs P0671-P0678 run continuously.
DTC: P0673 00	**Cylinder 3 Glow Plug Control Circuit:** The ignition is ON, or the engine is running. The ignition voltage is less than 16 V. These DTCs run once per ignition cycle when the above conditions are met.
DTC: P0673 02	**Cylinder 3 Glow Plug Control Circuit Short to Ground:** The ignition is ON, or the engine is running. The ignition voltage is less than 16 V. The DTCs run once per ignition cycle when the above conditions are met.
DTC: P0673 04	**Cylinder 3 Glow Plug Control Circuit Open:** The ignition is ON, or the engine is running. The ignition voltage is less than 16 V. The DTCs run once per ignition cycle when the above conditions are met.
DTC: P0674	**Cylinder #4 Glow Plug Control Circuit:** The ignition is ON. DTCs P0671-P0678 run continuously.

DTC	Trouble Code Title, Conditions, Possible Causes
DTC: P0674 00	**Cylinder 4 Glow Plug Control Circuit:** The ignition is ON, or the engine is running. The ignition voltage is less than 16 V. These DTCs run once per ignition cycle when the above conditions are met.
DTC: P0674 02	**Cylinder 4 Glow Plug Control Circuit Short to Ground:** The ignition is ON, or the engine is running. The ignition voltage is less than 16 V. The DTCs run once per ignition cycle when the above conditions are met.
DTC: P0674 04	**Cylinder 4 Glow Plug Control Circuit Open:** The ignition is ON, or the engine is running. The ignition voltage is less than 16 V. The DTCs run once per ignition cycle when the above conditions are met.
DTC: P0675	**Cylinder #5 Glow Plug Control Circuit:** The ignition is ON. DTCs P0671-P0678 run continuously.
DTC: P0676	**Cylinder #6 Glow Plug Control Circuit:** The ignition is ON. DTCs P0671-P0678 run continuously.
DTC: P0677	**Cylinder #7 Glow Plug Control Circuit:** The ignition is ON. DTCs P0671-P0678 run continuously.
DTC: P0678	**Cylinder #8 Glow Plug Control Circuit:** The ignition is ON. DTCs P0671-P0678 run continuously.
DTC: P0683 00	**Glow Plug Control Module Communication Circuit Malfunction:** The ignition is ON, or the engine is running. The ignition voltage is greater than 9 V. The DTCs run continuously once the above conditions are met.
DTC: P0683 3A	**Glow Plug Control Module Communication Circuit Incorrect Component Installed:** The ignition is ON, or the engine is running. The ignition voltage is greater than 9 V. The DTCs run continuously once the above conditions are met.
DTC: P0683 71	**Glow Plug Control Module Communication Circuit Invalid Data:** The ignition is ON, or the engine is running. The ignition voltage is greater than 9 V. The DTCs run continuously once the above conditions are met.
DTC: P0685	**Engine Controls Ignition Relay Control Circuit:** P0685, P0686, and P0687The ignition voltage is between 10-18 V. The engine speed is greater than 80 RPM. The engine control module relay has been commanded ON and OFF. The DTCs run continuously when the above conditions are met.
DTC: P0685 00	**Engine Controls Ignition Relay Control Circuit:** The ignition is ON, or the engine is running. The ignition voltage is between 11-18 V. This DTCs run continuously once the above conditions are met.
DTC: P0686	**Engine Controls Ignition Relay Control Circuit Low Voltage:** P0685 and P0686The battery voltage is between 10. 5-18 V. The ignition is ON. The relay has been commanded ON. These DTCs run continuously when the above conditions have been met.
DTC: P0686 00	**Engine Controls Ignition Relay Control Circuit Low Voltage:** P0686 00 and P0687 00The ignition is ON, or the engine is running. DTC P0606 00 is not set. P0688 00 and P0689 00The ignition is ON. DTC P0686 00 or P0687 00 is not set. P068BThe ignition is switched OFF. The DTC runs continuously until the ECM powers down.
DTC: P0687	**Engine Controls Ignition Relay Control Circuit High Voltage:** P0687, P0689, and P0690The battery voltage is between 10. 5-18 V. The ignition is OFF. The powertrain relay has been commanded OFF. These DTCs run continuously when the above conditions have been met.
DTC: P0687	**Engine Controls Ignition Relay Control Circuit High Voltage:** P0685, P0686, and P0687The ignition voltage is between 10-18 V. The engine speed is greater than 80 RPM. The engine control module relay has been commanded ON and OFF. The DTCs run continuously when the above conditions are met.
DTC: P0687 00	**Engine Controls Ignition Relay Control Circuit High Voltage:** P0686 00 and P0687 00The ignition is ON, or the engine is running. DTC P0606 00 is not set. P0688 00 and P0689 00The ignition is ON. DTC P0686 00 or P0687 00 is not set. P068BThe ignition is switched OFF. The DTC runs continuously until the ECM powers down.
DTC: P0688 00	**Engine Controls Ignition Relay Feedback Circuit:** P0686 00 and P0687 00The ignition is ON, or the engine is running. DTC P0606 00 is not set. P0688 00 and P0689 00The ignition is ON. DTC P0686 00 or P0687 00 is not set. P068BThe ignition is switched OFF. The DTC runs continuously until the ECM powers down.
DTC: P0688 00	**Engine Controls Ignition Relay Feedback Circuit:** P0688 00 and P0689 00The ignition is ON. DTC P0686 00 or P0687 00 is not set.

DTC	Trouble Code Title, Conditions, Possible Causes
DTC: P0689	**Engine Controls Ignition Relay Feedback Circuit Low Voltage:** The ignition is ON. The ignition voltage is between 11-18 V. The DTCs run continuously when the above conditions are met.
DTC: P0689 00	**Engine Controls Ignition Relay Feedback Circuit Low Voltage:** The ignition is ON, or the engine is running. The ignition voltage is between 11-18 V. These DTCs run continuously once the above conditions are met.
DTC: P0689 00	**Engine Controls Ignition Relay Feedback Circuit Low Voltage:** P0686 00 and P0687 00The ignition is ON, or the engine is running. DTC P0606 00 is not set. P0688 00 and P0689 00The ignition is ON. DTC P0686 00 or P0687 00 is not set. P068BThe ignition is switched OFF. The DTC runs continuously until the ECM powers down.
DTC: P068A 00	**Engine Controls Ignition Relay De-Energized Too Early:** The ignition is ON, or the engine is running. The ignition voltage is between 11-18 V. These DTCs run continuously once the above conditions are met.
DTC: P068B 00	**Engine Controls Ignition Relay De-Energized Too Late:** The ignition is ON, or the engine is running. The ignition voltage is between 11-18 V. These DTCs run continuously once the above conditions are met.
DTC: P0690	**Engine Controls Ignition Relay Feedback Circuit High Voltage:** P0689 and P0690The ignition voltage is between 10-18 V. The ignition is ON. The DTCs runs continuously when the above conditions are met.
DTC: P0690	**Engine Controls Ignition Relay Feedback Circuit High Voltage:** P0689, P0690The ignition voltage is greater than 11 V. The engine control module relay is commanded ON. DTC P0685 is not set. These DTCs run continuously when the above conditions are met.
DTC: P0690	**Engine Controls Relay Feedback Circuit High Voltage:** P0690This DTC will run with the ignition ON or OFF. This DTC will run when the powertrain relay is commanded ON or OFF. DTC P0685 is not set.
DTC: P0690 00	**Engine Controls Ignition Relay Feedback Circuit High Voltage:** The ignition is ON, or the engine is running. The ignition voltage is between 11-18 V. These DTCs run continuously once the above conditions are met.
DTC: P0691	**Cooling Fan Relay 1 Control Circuit Low Voltage:** The ignition voltage is between 10-26 volts. The engine speed is greater than 80 RPM. The ECM driver transitions from ON to OFF or from OFF to ON. DTC P0480, P0481, P0691, P0692, P0693, and P0694 run continuously when the conditions above are met.
DTC: P0691 00	**Cooling Fan Relay 1 Control Circuit Low Voltage:** The ignition voltage is between 8-18 V. The engine is running greater than or equal to 400 RPM.
DTC: P0692	**Cooling Fan Relay 1 Control Circuit High Voltage:** The ignition voltage is between 10-26 volts. The engine speed is greater than 80 RPM. The ECM driver transitions from ON to OFF or from OFF to ON. DTC P0480, P0481, P0691, P0692, P0693, and P0694 run continuously when the conditions above are met.
DTC: P0692 00	**Cooling Fan Relay 1 Control Circuit High Voltage:** The ignition voltage is between 8-18 V. The engine is running greater than or equal to 400 RPM.
DTC: P0693	**Cooling Fan Relays 2 and 3 Control Circuit Low Voltage:** The ignition voltage is between 10-18 volts. The engine speed is greater than 80 RPM. The ECM driver transitions from ON to OFF or from OFF to ON. DTC P0480, P0481, P0691, P0692, P0693, and P0694 run continuously when the conditions above are met.
DTC: P0693	**Cooling Fan Relays 2 and 3 Control Circuit Low Voltage:** The ignition voltage is between 10-26 volts. The engine speed is greater than 80 RPM. The ECM driver transitions from ON to OFF or from OFF to ON. DTC P0480, P0481, P0691, P0692, P0693, and P0694 run continuously when the conditions above are met.
DTC: P0693 00	**Cooling Fan Relay 2 Control Circuit Low Voltage:** The ignition voltage is between 8-18 V. The engine is running greater than or equal to 400 RPM.
DTC: P0694	**Cooling Fan Relays 2 and 3 Control Circuit High Voltage:** The ignition voltage is between 10-26 volts. The engine speed is greater than 80 RPM. The ECM driver transitions from ON to OFF or from OFF to ON. DTC P0480, P0481, P0691, P0692, P0693, and P0694 run continuously when the conditions above are met.
DTC: P0694 00	**Cooling Fan Relay 2 Control Circuit High Voltage:** The ignition voltage is between 8-18 V. The engine is running greater than or equal to 400 RPM.
DTC: P0697	**5 V Reference 3 Circuit:** DTCs P0641, P0651, P0697, P06A3 run continuously when the ignition is ON.

DTC	Trouble Code Title, Conditions, Possible Causes
DTC: P0697	**5 V Reference 3 Circuit:** Ignition voltage is greater than 6. 4 V. Reduced engine power is not active. DTCs P0641, P0651, P0697, P06A3 run continuously when the above conditions are met.
DTC: P0697 00	**5V Reference 3 Circuit:** The ignition is ON, or the engine is running. The ignition voltage is between 9-16 V. The DTCs run continuously when the above condition is met.
DTC: P0697 03	**5V Reference 3 Circuit Low Voltage:** The ignition is ON. The DTCs run continuously when the above condition is met.
DTC: P0697 07	**5V Reference 3 Circuit High Voltage:** The ignition is ON. The DTCs run continuously when the above condition is met.
DTC: P069E	**Fuel Pump Control Module Requested MIL Illumination:** The ignition is ON, or the engine is running for greater than 3 s.
DTC: P069E	**Fuel Pump Control Module Requested MIL Illumination:** The ignition is ON, or the engine is running.
DTC: P069E 00	**Fuel Pump Control Module Requested MIL Illumination:** The ignition is ON, or the engine is running. The ignition voltage is between 11-18 V. DTC P069E 00 runs continuously once the above condition is met.
DTC: P06A3	**5 V Reference 4 Circuit:** DTCs P0641, P0651, P0697, P06A3 run continuously when the ignition is ON.
DTC: P06A6	**5 V Reference Performance:** The ignition is ON.
DTC: P06AC	**Control Module Power Up Temperature Sensor Performance:** P06ACDTC P0101, P0102, P0103, P0106, P0107, P0108, P0171, P0172, P0174, P0175, P0201, P0202, P0203, P0204, P0205, P0206, P0207, P0208, P0300, P0301, P0302, P0303, P0304, P0305, P0306, P0307, P0308, P0401, P042E, P0658, P0668, P0669, P06AC, P06AD, P06AE, P0712, P0713, P0716, P0717, P0722, P0723, P0962, P0963, P0966, P0967, P0970, P0971, P215C, P2720, P2721, P2729, or P2730 is not set. The engine speed is 400 RPM or greater for 5 seconds. The ignition voltage is 8. 6 volts or greater. Brake torque is not active. The engine torque signal is valid. The throttle position signal is valid.
DTC: P06AD	**Transmission Control Module (TCM) Power Up Temperature Sensor Circuit Low Voltage:** P06ADDTCs P06AD, P0716, P0717, P0722, or P0723 are not set. The transmission output shaft speed is 200 RPM or greater for 4 minutes. The torque converter clutch (TCC) slip speed is 120 RPM or greater for 4 minutes. The engine speed is 500 RPM or greater for 5 seconds. The ignition voltage is 8. 6 volts or greater.
DTC: P06AE	**Transmission Control Module (TCM) Power Up Temperature Sensor Circuit High Voltage:** P06AEThe engine speed is 500 RPM or greater for 5 seconds. The ignition voltage is 8. 6 volts or greater. DTC P06AE has not failed set this ignition.
DTC: P06B6	**Control Module Knock Sensor Processor 1 Performance:** P06B6Engine speed is between 400-4,000 RPM. The engine coolant temperature (ECT) is warmer than -40°C (-40°F). The intake air temperature (IAT) is warmer than -40°C (-40°F). The DTC runs continuously when the above conditions are met.
DTC: P06B6 00	**Control Module Knock Sensor Processor 1 Performance:** P06B6 00Engine speed is between 400-4 000 RPM. The ECT is greater than -40°C (-40°F). The IAT is greater than -40°C (-40°F). The DTC runs continuously when the above conditions are met.
DTC: P06B6 00	**Control Module Knock Sensor Processor 1 Performance:** The engine speed is greater than 700 RPM. The engine speed is between 700-2 500 RPM for DTC P06B6 00. The airflow into the engine is between 40-2 000 mg/cylinder. This DTC runs continuously within the enabling conditions. DTCs P0324 00, P0326 00 and P06B6 00 run continuously once the above conditions are met.
DTC: P06B7	**Control Module Knock Sensor Processor 2 Performance:** P06B6 and P06B7Engine speed is between 400-4,000 RPM. The ECT is warmer than -40°C (-40°F). The IAT is warmer than -40°C (-40°F). The DTCs run continuously when the above conditions are met.
DTC: P06B8 00	**Control Module Random Access Memory Performance:** The ignition is ON. This DTCs run continuously once the above condition is met.
DTC: P0700	**Transmission Control Module (TCM) Requested MIL Illumination:** The ignition is ON or the engine is operating. DTC P0700 runs continuously.

DTC	Trouble Code Title, Conditions, Possible Causes
DTC: P0700 00	**Transmission Control Module Requested MIL Illumination:** The ignition is ON, or the engine is running. The ignition voltage is between 11-18 V. This DTCs run continuously once the above conditions are met.
DTC: P0703	**Brake Switch Circuit 2:** The engine is ON.
DTC: P0705	**Transmission Range (TR) Switch Circuit:** The engine is running for 5 seconds.
DTC: P0711	**Transmission Fluid Temperature Sensor Performance:** P0711 DTC P0101, P0102, P0103, P0106, P0107, P0108, P0171, P0172, P0174, P0175, P0201, P0202, P0203, P0204, P0205, P0206, P0207, P0208, P0300, P0301, P0302, P0303, P0304, P0305, P0306, P0307, P0308, P0401, P042E, P0658, P0668, P0669, P06AD, P06AE, P0711, P0712, P0713, P0716, P0717, P0722, P0723, P0962, P0963, P0966, P0967, P0970, P0971, P215C, P2720, P2721, P2729, or P2730 is not set. The engine speed is 400 RPM or greater for 5 seconds. The ignition voltage is 8. 6 volts or greater. Brake torque is not active. The engine torque signal is valid. The throttle position signal is valid.
DTC: P0711	**Transmission Fluid Temperature (TFT) Sensor Performance:** No ECT DTC P0117 or P0118. No input speed sensor (ISS) DTCs P0716 or P0717. No output speed sensor (OSS) DTCs P0722 or P0723. DTC P0711 has not passed in the current ignition cycle. The transmission fluid temperature is -40 to +150°C (-40 to +302°F). Condition 1The engine coolant temperature (ECT) is at least 70°C (158°F) and has changed by 55°C (131°F) since start up. The vehicle speed is 8 km/h (5 mph) or more for at least 5 minutes cumulative. The torque converter clutch (TCC) slip is 120 RPM or more for at least 5 minutes cumulative. Condition 2The engine coolant temperature is at least 70°C (158°F) and has changed by 55°C (131°F) since start up. The vehicle speed is 8 km/h (5 mph) or more for at least 5 minutes cumulative. Condition 3The calc. throttle position is between 8 and 90 percent. The engine torque is 37 ft. lbs. (50 Nm) or more. The vehicle speed is 8 km/h (5 mph) or more. The engine speed is greater than 500 RPM.
DTC: P0711	**Transmission Fluid Temperature (TFT) Sensor Performance:** P0711No DTCs P0101, P0102, P0103, P0106, P0107, P0108, P0171, P0172, P0174, P0175, P0201, P0202, P0203, P0204, P0205, P0206, P0207, P0208, P0300, P0301, P0302, P0303, P0304, P0305, P0306, P0307, P0308, P0401, P042E, P0658, P0668, P0669, P06AD, P06AE, P0711, P0712, P0713, P0716, P0717, P0722, P0723, P0962, P0963, P0966, P0967, P0970, P0971, P215C, P2720, P2721, P2729, or P2730. The engine speed is greater than 400 RPM for 5 seconds. The ignition voltage is 8. 6 volts or greater. Brake torque is not active. The engine torque signal is valid. The throttle position signal is valid.
DTC: P0712	**Transmission Fluid Temperature (TFT) Sensor Circuit Low Voltage:** P0712The engine speed is greater than 500 RPM for 5 seconds. The ignition voltage is greater than 9. 0 volts. DTC P0712 has not set this ignition cycle. No DTCs P0716, P0717, P0722, or P0723.
DTC: P0713	**Transmission Fluid Temperature (TFT) Sensor Circuit High Voltage:** P0713No input speed sensor (ISS) DTCs P0716 or P0717. No output speed sensor (OSS) DTCs P0722 or P0723. The output shaft speed is greater than 200 RPM for 200 seconds (3 minutes and 20 seconds) cumulative. The TCC slip speed is greater than 120 RPM for 200 seconds (3 minutes and 20 seconds) cumulative.
DTC: P0713	**Transmission Fluid Temperature (TFT) Sensor Circuit High Voltage:** P0713 DTCs P0716, P0717, P0722 or P0723. The ignition voltage is between 8-18 volts. The engine speed is between 500-6,500 RPMs for 5 seconds. The transmission output shaft speed is 64 RPM or greater for 200 seconds cumulatively. The TCC slip speed is 120 RPM or greater for 200 seconds cumulatively.
DTC: P0716	**Input Speed Sensor Performance:** P0716 DTC P0101, P0102, P0103, P0121, P0122, P0123, P0716, P0717, P0752, P0973, or P0974 is not set. Vehicle speed is 10 km/h (6 mph) or greater. The engine speed is greater than 400 RPM for 5 seconds. The ignition voltage is 9. 0 volts or greater. The engine torque signal is valid. Throttle position signal is valid. P0717 DTC P0717 is not set. The engine speed is greater than 400 RPM for 5 seconds. The ignition voltage is 9. 0 volts or greater. The vehicle speed is 16 km/h (10 mph) or greater. The engine torque is 37 ft. lbs. (50 Nm) or greater. P07BF or P070CThe ignition voltage is 9. 0 volts or greater.
DTC: P0717	**Input Speed Sensor Circuit No Signal:** P0716 DTC P0101, P0102, P0103, P0121, P0122, P0123, P0716, P0717, P0752, P0973, or P0974 is not set. Vehicle speed is 10 km/h (6 mph) or greater. The engine speed is greater than 400 RPM for 5 seconds. The ignition voltage is 9. 0 volts or greater. The engine torque signal is valid. Throttle position signal is valid. P0717 DTC P0717 is not set. The engine speed is greater than 400 RPM for 5 seconds. The ignition voltage is 9. 0 volts or greater. The vehicle speed is 16 km/h (10 mph) or greater. The engine torque is 37 ft. lbs. (50 Nm) or greater. P07BF or P070CThe ignition voltage is 9. 0 volts or greater.
DTC: P071A	**Transmission Tow Mode Switch Circuit:** DTC P1762 is not set. The engine speed is greater than 400 RPM for 5 seconds. The ignition voltage is 8. 6 volts or greater.
DTC: P071D	**Transmission Sport Mode Switch circuit:** The engine speed is greater than 500 RPM for 5 seconds. Ignition voltage is between 9. 0 volts and 19. 0 volts.

DTC	Trouble Code Title, Conditions, Possible Causes
DTC: P0722	**Output Speed Sensor (OSS/VSS) Circuit Low Voltage:** P0722No ISS DTC P0716 or P0717. No OSS/VSS DTC P0723. No TPS DTC P0120, P0121, P0122, P0123, P0220, P0221, P0222, P0223, P0225, P0226, P0227, P0228, P1120, P1121, P1122, P1125, P1280, P1281, P1282, P1283, P1285, P1286, P1287 or P1288. Ignition voltage is 8. 0-18. 0 V. The transmission is not in PARK or NEUTRAL. The engine speed is greater than 500 RPM for 5 seconds. The engine torque is greater than 37 ft. lbs. (50 Nm). The calc. throttle position is 8 percent or greater. The input shaft speed is greater than 1,500 RPM. The torque converter clutch (TCC) slip speed is -20 RPM or greater. The transmission fluid temperature (TFT) is -40°C (-40°F) or greater.
DTC: P0723	**Output Speed Sensor (OSS) Intermittent:** P0723 DTCs P0101, P0102, P0103, P0121, P0122, P0123, P0716, P0717, P0722, P0723, P0973, P0974, P0976, or P0977 are not set. Ignition voltage is 8. 6 volts or greater. The engine speed is 3200 RPM or greater for 5 seconds. Greater than 5 seconds since last range change. The TCM must receive a valid torque signal from the ECM. Accelerator pedal position signal is valid.
DTC: P0741	**Torque Converter Clutch (TCC) - Stuck Off:** P0741 DTCs P0101, P0102, P0103, P0121, P0122, P0123, P0716, P0717, P0722, P0723, P0742, P2762, P2763, or P2764 are not set. Ignition voltage is 8. 6 volts or greater. The engine run time is greater than 5 seconds. The transmission fluid temperature (TFT) is 20-130°C (68-266°F). The accelerator pedal position signal is valid. The throttle position is greater than 8 percent. The TCM must receive a valid torque signal from the ECM. The engine torque is greater than 37 ft. lbs. (50 Nm). The TCC is commanded ON and PWM duty cycle is greater than 60 percent for 5 seconds. The following 6L80/6L90 gear ratios are achieved in the specified gear range while the TCC is commanded On: The 2nd gear ratio is between 2. 19-2. 52. The 3rd gear ratio is between 1. 42-1. 63. The 4th gear ratio is between 1. 07-1. 23. The 5th gear is between 0. 79-0. 91. The 6th gear is between 0. 62-0. 71. The following 6L50 gear ratios are achieved in the specified gear range while the TCC is commanded On: The 2nd gear ratio is between 2. 20-2. 53. The 3rd gear ratio is between 1. 44-1. 65. The 4th gear ratio is between 1. 07-1. 23. The 5th gear is between 0. 79-0. 91. The 6th gear is between 0. 62-0. 72.
DTC: P0742	**Torque Converter Clutch (TCC) System Stuck On:** P0742 DTC P0101, P0102, P0103, P0106, P0107, P0108, P0171, P0172, P0174, P0175, P0201, P0202, P0203, P0204, P0205, P0206, P0207, P0208, P0300, P0301, P0302, P0303, P0304, P0305, P0306, P0307, P0308, P0401, P042E, P0716, P0717, P0722, P0723, P0741, P0742, P2763, or P2764 is not set. The engine speed is greater than 400 RPM for 5 seconds. The ignition voltage is 9. 0 volts or greater. The TFT is 20-130°C (68-266°F). The calculated throttle position is greater than 8 percent. The engine torque is greater than 59 ft. lbs. (80 Nm). The vehicle speed greater than 16 km/h (10 mph). Commanded gear is 2nd or greater. The gear ratio is between 0. 69-1. 97. Solenoid A is enabled.
DTC: P0751	**1-2 Shift solenoid (SS) Valve Performance - No First or Fourth Gear:** P0751 and P0756 DTCs P0120, P0121, P0122, P0123, P0220, P0221, P0222, P0223, P0225, P0226, P0227, P0228, P0716, P0717, P0722, P0723, P0742, P0842, P0843, P0973, P0974, P0976, P0977, P1120, P1121, P1122, P1125, P1280, P1281, P1282, P1283, P1285, P1286, P1287, or P1288 are not set. The ignition voltage is between 8 and 18 volts. The engine speed is between 500 and 6,500 RPM for 5 seconds. The transmission fluid temperature (TFT) is between 20-130°C (68-266°F). The engine torque is between 37-1,100 ft. lbs. (50-1,492 Nm). The calc. throttle position is 8 percent or greater. The transmission input speed sensor (ISS) is between 150-6,500 RPM. The transmission output speed sensor (OSS) is 64 RPM or greater. The time since the last gear change is 1 second.
DTC: P0752	**1-2 Shift Solenoid (SS) Valve Performance - No Second or Third Gear:** P0752No TP sensor DTC P0120 or P0220. No ISS DTC P0716 or P0717. No OSS DTC P0722 or P0723. No TCC system stuck ON DTC P0742. The engine speed is greater than 500 RPM for 5 seconds. The TFT is between 20-130°C (68-266°F). No TCC system stuck ON DTC P0742. No 1-2 SS valve electrical DTC P0973 or P0974. No 2-3 SS valve electrical DTC P0976 or P0977. The calc. throttle position is 8 percent or greater. The transmission ISS is 150 RPM or greater. The transmission OSS is 160 RPM or greater. The engine torque is greater than 37 ft. lbs. (50 Nm). The time since the last gear change is 1. 5 seconds.
DTC: P0752	**1-2 Shift solenoid (SS) Valve Performance - No Second or Third Gear:** P0752 and P0757 DTCs P0120, P0121, P0122, P0123, P0220, P0221, P0222, P0223, P0225, P0226, P0227, P0228, P0716, P0717, P0722, P0723, P0742, P0842, P0843, P0973, P0974, P0976, P0977, P1120, P1121, P1122, P1125, P1280, P1281, P1282, P1283, P1285, P1286, P1287, or P1288 are not set. The ignition voltage is between 8 and 18 volts. The engine speed is between 500 and 6,500 RPM for 5 seconds. The transmission fluid temperature (TFT) is between 20-130°C (68-266°F). The engine torque is between 37-1,100 ft. lbs. (50-1,492 Nm). The calc. throttle position is 8 percent or greater. The transmission input speed sensor (ISS) is between 150-6,500 RPM. The transmission output speed sensor (OSS) is 64 RPM or greater. The time since the last gear change is 1 second.
DTC: P0752	**1-2 Shift solenoid (SS) Valve Performance - No Second or Third Gear:** P0752No TP sensor DTCs P0121, P0122, or P0123. No ISS DTCs P0716 or P0717. No OSS DTCs P0722 or P0723. No TCC system stuck ON DTC P0742. No 1-2 SS valve electrical DTCs P0973 or P0974. No 2-3 SS valve electrical DTCs P0976 or P0977. The calc. throttle position is 8 percent or more. The transmission ISS is 150 RPM or more. The transmission OSS is 200 RPM or more. The engine torque is greater than 50 N·m (37 lb ft). The time since the last gear change is 1 second. The engine speed is greater than 500 RPM for 5 seconds. The transmission fluid temperature is between 20-130°C (68-266°F).
DTC: P0756	**Shift Solenoid Valve 2 Performance - Stuck Off:** No DTCs P0101, P0102, P0103, P0106, P0107, P0108, P0171, P0172, P0174, P0175, P0201, P0202, P0203, P0204, P0205, P0206, P0207, P0208, P0300, P0301, P0302, P0303, P0304, P0305, P0306, P0307, P0308, P0401, P042E, P0716, P0717, P0722, P0723, or P182E. The engine speed is 400 RPM or greater for 5 seconds. The high side driver (HSD) is enabled. The ignition voltage is 8. 6 volts or greater. Throttle position signal is valid. Transmission fluid temperature (TFT) is 0°C (32°F) or greater.

DTC	Trouble Code Title, Conditions, Possible Causes
DTC: P0756	**2-3 Shift Solenoid (SS) Valve Performance - No First or Second Gear:** No input speed sensor (ISS) DTCs P0716 or P0717. No output speed sensor (OSS) DTCs P0722 or P0723. No torque converter clutch (TCC) performance DTCs P0741 or P0742. No shift solenoid electrical DTCs P0973, P0974, P0976, or P0977. No internal mode switch (IMS) DTCs P1820, P1822, P1823, P1825, P1826 or P1915. No torque converter clutch pulse width module (TCC PWM) DTCs P2763 or P2764. No torque converter clutch enable DTCs P2769 or P2770. The engine torque is greater than 50 N·m (37 lb ft). The engine run time is greater than 5 seconds. The engine is not in fuel cutoff. The gear range is D4. The throttle position is 8 percent or greater. The input shaft speed is 50 RPM or greater. The output shaft speed is 50 RPM or greater. The transmission fluid temperature is 20-130°C (68-266°F).
DTC: P0757	**2-3 Shift Solenoid (SS) Valve Performance - No Third, Fourth or Fifth Gear:** No input speed sensor (ISS) DTCs P0716 or P0717. No output speed sensor (OSS) DTCs P0722 or P0723. No torque converter clutch (TCC) performance DTCs P0741 or P0742. No shift solenoid electrical DTCs P0973, P0974, P0976, or P0977. No internal mode switch (IMS) DTCs P1820, P1822, P1823, P1825, P1826 or P1915. No torque converter clutch pulse width module (TCC PWM) DTCs P2763 or P2764. No torque converter clutch enable DTCs P2769 or P2770. The engine torque is greater than 50 N·m (37 lb ft). The engine run time is greater than 5 seconds. The engine is not in fuel cutoff. The gear range is D4. The throttle position is 8 percent or greater. The input shaft speed is 50 RPM or greater. The output shaft speed is 50 RPM or greater. The transmission fluid temperature is 20-130°C (68-266°F).
DTC: P0776	**Clutch Pressure Control (PC) Solenoid 2 - Stuck Off:** P0776No ISS DTCs P0101, P0102, P0103, P0106, P0107, P0108, P0171, P0172, P0174, P0175, P0201, P0202, P0203, P0204, P0205, P0206, P0207, P0208, P0300, P0301, P0302, P0303, P0304, P0305, P0306, P0307, P0308, P0401, P042E, P0716, P0717, P0722, P0723, or P182E. The engine speed is greater than 500 RPM for 5 seconds. The ignition voltage is 9. 0 volts or greater. The transmission fluid temperature is 0°C (32°F) or greater. The transmission output speed is 650 RPM or greater or the throttle position is 0. 5 percent or greater. The throttle position signal is valid. The high side driver (HSD) is enabled.
DTC: P0777	**Clutch Pressure Control (PC) Solenoid 2 - Stuck On:** P0777No DTCs P0101, P0102, P0103, P0106, P0107, P0108, P0171, P0172, P0174, P0175, P0201, P0202, P0203, P0204, P0205, P0206, P0207, P0208, P0300, P0301, P0302, P0303, P0304, P0305, P0306, P0307, P0308, P0401, P042E, P0716, P0717, P0722, P0723, or P182E. The transmission fluid temperature is 0°C (32°F) or greater. The transmission output shaft speed is 350 RPM or greater. The transmission input speed is 200 RPM or greater. The commanded gear is not 1st range. The HSD is enabled.
DTC: P077C	**Output Speed Sensor Circuit Low Voltage:** P077CDTC P077D is not set. The ignition voltage is 9. 0 volts or greater.
DTC: P077D	**Output Speed Sensor Circuit High Voltage:** P077DDTC P077C is not set. The ignition voltage is 9. 0 volts or greater.
DTC: P0796	**Clutch Pressure Control Solenoid 3 - Stuck Off:** P0796 DTC P0101, P0102, P0103, P0106, P0107, P0108, P0171, P0172, P0174, P0175, P0201, P0202, P0203, P0204, P0205, P0206, P0207, P0208, P0300, P0301, P0302, P0303, P0304, P0305, P0306, P0307, P0308, P0401, P042E, P0716, P0717, P0722, P0723, or P182E is not set. The engine speed is greater than 500 RPM for 5 seconds. The transmission output speed is 650 RPM or greater or the throttle position is 0. 5 percent or greater. The ignition voltage is 9. 0 volts or greater. The transmission fluid temperature is 0°C (32°F) or greater. The high side driver (HSD) is enabled. The throttle position signal is valid.
DTC: P0797	**Clutch Pressure Control (PC) Solenoid 3 - Stuck On:** P0796 or P0797No ISS DTCs P0101, P0102, P0103, P0106, P0107, P0108, P0171, P0172, P0174, P0175, P0201, P0202, P0203, P0204, P0205, P0206, P0207, P0208, P0300, P0301, P0302, P0303, P0304, P0305, P0306, P0307, P0308, P0401, P042E, P0716, P0717, P0722, P0723, or P182E. The ignition voltage is greater than 8. 6 volts. The engine speed is greater than 400 RPM for 5 seconds. The output speed is 16 RPM or greater, or the throttle position is 0. 4 percent or greater. The throttle position signal is valid. The high side driver is commanded on. The transmission fluid temperature is 0°C (32°F) or greater.
DTC: P07BF	**Input Speed Sensor Circuit Low Voltage:** P0716 DTC P0101, P0102, P0103, P0121, P0122, P0123, P0716, P0717, P0752, P0973, or P0974 is not set. Vehicle speed is 10 km/h (6 mph) or greater. The engine speed is greater than 400 RPM for 5 seconds. The ignition voltage is 9. 0 volts or greater. The engine torque signal is valid. Throttle position signal is valid. P0717 DTC P0717 is not set. The engine speed is greater than 400 RPM for 5 seconds. The ignition voltage is 9. 0 volts or greater. The vehicle speed is 16 km/h (10 mph) or greater. The engine torque is 50 N·m (37 lb ft) or greater. P07BF or P070CThe ignition voltage is 9. 0 volts or greater.
DTC: P07C0	**Input Speed Sensor Circuit High Voltage:** P0716 DTC P0101, P0102, P0103, P0121, P0122, P0123, P0716, P0717, P0752, P0973, or P0974 is not set. Vehicle speed is 10 km/h (6 mph) or greater. The engine speed is greater than 400 RPM for 5 seconds. The ignition voltage is 9. 0 volts or greater. The engine torque signal is valid. Throttle position signal is valid. P0717 DTC P0717 is not set. The engine speed is greater than 400 RPM for 5 seconds. The ignition voltage is 9. 0 volts or greater. The vehicle speed is 16 km/h (10 mph) or greater. The engine torque is 50 N·m (37 lb ft) or greater. P07BF or P070CThe ignition voltage is 9. 0 volts or greater.
DTC: P0806	**Clutch Pedal Position (CPP) Sensor Performance:** P0806, P0807 and P0808 DTCs P0641 or P0651 are not set. The system voltage is more than 9 V. The ignition is in the RUN position.

DTC	Trouble Code Title, Conditions, Possible Causes
DTC: P0807	**Clutch Pedal Position (CPP) Sensor Circuit Low Voltage:** P0806, P0807 and P0808 DTCs P0641 or P0651 are not set. The system voltage is more than 9 V. The ignition is in the RUN position.
DTC: P0808	**Clutch Pedal Position (CPP) Sensor Circuit High Voltage:** P0806, P0807 and P0808 DTCs P0642, P0643, P0335, P0336, P0607 or P080A are not set. The system voltage is more than 9 V. The ignition is in the RUN position.
DTC: P0815	**Upshift Switch Circuit:** P0815 or P0816The engine speed is greater than 500 RPM for at least 5 seconds. The ignition voltage is between 9. 0 volts and 19. 0 volts. No TAP system DTC P0826. No IMS DTCs P1825 or P1915. The time since the last gear selector range change is greater than 6 seconds.
DTC: P0816	**Downshift Switch Circuit:** P0815 or P0816The engine speed is greater than 400 RPM for at least 5 seconds. The ignition voltage is 9. 0 volts or greater. DTC P0815, P0816, P0826, P182E, P1761, P1876, P1877, or P1915 is not set. The time since the last gear range change is greater than 1 second.
DTC: P0826	**Up and Down Shift Switch Circuit:** P0826The engine speed is 400 RPM or greater for 5 seconds. The ignition voltage is 8. 6 volts or greater. DTC P0826 or P1761 is not set.
DTC: P0833 03	**Clutch Pedal Position (CPP) Sensor Circuit Low Voltage:** P0833 DTCs P0641 is not set. The system voltage is more than 9 V. The ignition is in the RUN position.
DTC: P0833 07	**Clutch Pedal Position (CPP) Sensor Circuit High Voltage:** P0833 DTCs P0641 is not set. The system voltage is more than 9 V. The ignition is in the RUN position.
DTC: P0833 08	**Clutch Pedal Position (CPP) Sensor Circuit Performance - Signal Invalid:** P0833 DTC P0641 is not set. The system voltage is more than 9 V. The ignition is in the RUN position.
DTC: P0833 58	**Clutch Pedal Position (CPP) Sensor Circuit Performance:** P0833 DTC P0641 is not set. The system voltage is more than 9 V. The ignition is in the RUN position.
DTC: P0842	**Transmission Fluid Pressure (TFP) Sensor Circuit Low Voltage:** P0842No ISS DTC P0716 or P0717. No TCC performance DTC P0741 or P0742. No TCC PWM solenoid valve electrical DTC P2763 or P2764. The engine speed is greater than 500 RPM for 5 seconds. The transmission fluid temperature (TFT) is between 20-130°C (68-266°F). The engine torque is 50 N·m (37 lb ft) or greater. The TCC is commanded OFF. the TCC slip speed is greater than 80 RPM. The vehicle speed is 16 km/h (10 mph) or greater.
DTC: P0843	**Transmission Fluid Pressure (TFP) Switch 1 Circuit High Voltage:** P0842 or P0843 DTCs P0751, P0752, P0756, P0757, P0973, P0974, P0977, P1825 or P1915 are not set. Ignition voltage is 8. 6 volts or greater. The transmission fluid temperature (TFT) is 0-120°C (32-248°F). Engine speed is 500 RPM or greater for 5 seconds.
DTC: P0843	**Transmission Fluid Pressure (TFP) Switch Circuit High Voltage:** P0843No ISS DTCs P0716 or P0717. No TCC performance DTCs P0741 or P0742. No TCC PWM solenoid valve electrical DTCs P2763 or P2764. The TCC is commanded ON. The TCC slip speed is -20 to +60 RPM. The engine speed is greater than 500 RPM for 5 seconds. The transmission fluid temperature is between 20-130°C (68-266°F). The engine torque is 50 N·m (37 lb ft) or more.
DTC: P0850	**Park/Neutral Position (PNP) Switch Circuit:** Ignition voltage is between 8-18 volts. Engine speed is greater than 1,000 RPM.
DTC: P0851	**Park/Neutral Position (PNP) Switch Circuit Low Voltage:** P0851Ignition voltage is between 9-18 volts. No TCM DTC P0601, P0602, P0603, or P0604. No IMS DTC P1825 or P1915. No Communication DTC U0073, U0100, U0121, or U0140.
DTC: P0852	**Park/Neutral Position (PNP) Switch Circuit High Voltage:** P0852Ignition voltage is between 9-18 volts. No TCM DTC P0601, P0602, P0603, or P0604. No IMS DTC P1825 or P1915. No Communication DTC U0073, U0100, U0121, or U0140. No TP DTC P0121, P0122, or P0123. No OSS DTC P0722 or P0723. No MAF DTC P0101, P0102, or P0103. No MAP DTC P0106, P0107, or P0108. Engine speed is greater than 400 RPM.
DTC: P0856	**Traction Control Torque Request Circuit:** The ignition is ON. The DTCs run continuously once the above condition is met.
DTC: P0856	**Engine Control Module (ECM) Traction Control Torque Request Circuit:** Engine Running.
DTC: P0856	**Traction Control Torque Request Circuit Malfunction:** Engine running.
DTC: P0856 00	**Traction Control Torque Request Circuit:** The ignition is ON. Ignition voltage is greater than 8 volts.

DTC	Trouble Code Title, Conditions, Possible Causes
DTC: P0864	**Invalid Data Received From Transmission Control Module:** Battery voltage is between 9-16 V and data link communications operate normally.
DTC: P0872	**Transmission Fluid Pressure Switch 3 Circuit Low Voltage:** No DTCs P0711, P0712, P0713, P0716, P0717, P0722, P0723, P0742, P0751, P0756, P0757, P0973, P0974, P0976, P0977, P182E, or P1915. The engine speed is 500 RPM or greater for 5 seconds. Ignition voltage is 9. 0 volts or greater. The transmission fluid temperature (TFT) is 0-110°C (32-230°F). The High Side Driver is ON. The engine speed is 550 RPM or greater.
DTC: P0873	**Transmission Fluid Pressure Switch 3 Circuit High Voltage:** No DTCs P0711, P0712, P0713, P0716, P0717, P0722, P0723, P0742, P0751, P0756, P0757, P0973, P0974, P0976, P0977, P182E, or P1915. The engine speed is 500 RPM or greater for 5 seconds. Ignition voltage is 9. 0 volts or greater. The transmission fluid temperature (TFT) is 0-110°C (32-230°F). The High Side Driver is ON. The engine speed is 550 RPM or greater.
DTC: P0877	**Transmission Fluid Pressure Switch 4 Circuit Low Voltage:** P0877 or P0878 DTC P0711, P0712, P0713, P0716, P0717, P0722, P0723, P0742, P0751, P0756, P0757, P0973, P0974, P0976, P0977, P1915, P182E is not set. The engine speed is 400 RPM or greater for 5 seconds. The engine speed is 550 RPM or greater. Ignition voltage is 8. 6 volts or greater. The transmission fluid temperature (TFT) is 0-120°C (32-248°F).
DTC: P0878	**Transmission Fluid Pressure Switch 4 Circuit High Voltage:** P0877 or P0878 DTC P0711, P0712, P0713, P0716, P0717, P0722, P0723, P0742, P0751, P0756, P0757, P0973, P0974, P0976, P0977, P1915, or P182E is not set. The high side driver is enabled. The engine speed is 400 RPM or greater for 5. 0 seconds. The engine speed is 550 RPM or greater. The ignition voltage is 8. 6 volts or greater. The transmission fluid temperature (TFT) is -7 to +120°C (19-248°F).
DTC: P0878	**Transmission Fluid Pressure (TFP) Switch 4 Circuit High Voltage:** No DTCs P0711, P0712, P0713, P0973, P0974, P0976, P0977, P182E or P1915. The engine speed is 500 RPM or greater for 5 seconds. Ignition voltage is between 9. 0 volts and 18. 0 volts. The transmission fluid temperature (TFT) is 0-120°C (32-248°F).
DTC: P0897	**Transmission Fluid Life:** DTCs P0711, P0712, or P0713 are not set. The ignition voltage is between 8 and 18 volts.
DTC: P0961	**Line Pressure Control (PC) Solenoid System Performance:** The engine speed is greater than 400 RPM for 5 seconds. The ignition voltage is 8. 6 volts or greater.
DTC: P0962	**Line Pressure Control Solenoid Valve Control Circuit Low Voltage:** P0961, P0962, or P0963The engine speed is 500 RPM or greater for 5 seconds. The ignition voltage is 9. 0 volts or greater.
DTC: P0963	**Line Pressure Control Solenoid Valve Control Circuit High Voltage:** P0961, P0962, or P0963The engine speed is 400 RPM or greater for 5 seconds. The ignition voltage is 9. 0 volts or greater.
DTC: P0965	**Clutch Pressure Control (PC) Solenoid 2 System Performance:** P0965, P0966, or P0967 DTCs P0965, P0966, or P0967 have not set this ignition. The ignition voltage is 8. 6 volts or greater. The engine run time is greater than 5 seconds. The clutch PC solenoid 2 is commanded ON.
DTC: P0966	**Clutch Pressure Control (PC) Solenoid 2 Control Circuit Low Voltage:** P0965, P0966, or P0967 DTCs P0965, P0966, or P0967 have not set this ignition. The ignition voltage is 8. 6 volts or greater. The clutch PC solenoid 2 is commanded ON. The engine speed is greater than 400 RPM for 5 seconds.
DTC: P0967	**Clutch Pressure Control (PC) Solenoid 2 Control Circuit High Voltage:** P0965, P0966, or P0967 DTCs P0965, P0966, or P0967 have not set this ignition. The ignition voltage is 8. 6 volts or greater. The clutch PC solenoid 2 is commanded ON. The engine speed is greater than 400 RPM for 5 seconds.
DTC: P0969	**Clutch Pressure Control (PC) Solenoid 3 System Performance:** P0969, P0970, or P0971 DTCs P0969, P0970, or P0971 have not set this ignition. The ignition voltage is 8. 6 volts or greater. The engine speed is 500 RPM or greater for 5 seconds. The clutch PC solenoid 3 is commanded ON.
DTC: P0970	**Clutch Pressure Control (PC) Solenoid 3 Control Circuit Low Voltage:** P0969, P0970, or P0971 DTCs P0969, P0970, or P0971 have not set this ignition. The ignition voltage is 8. 6 volts or greater. The engine speed is 500 RPM or greater for 5 seconds. The clutch PC solenoid 3 is commanded ON.
DTC: P0971	**Clutch Pressure Control (PC) Solenoid 3 Control Circuit High Voltage:** P0969, P0970, or P0971 DTCs P0969, P0970, or P0971 have not set this ignition. The ignition voltage is 8. 6 volts or greater. The engine speed is 500 RPM or greater for 5 seconds. The clutch PC solenoid 3 is commanded ON.
DTC: P0973	**Shift Solenoid Valve 1 Control Circuit Low Voltage:** P0973The engine speed is 400 RPM or greater for 5 seconds. The ignition voltage is 8. 6 volts or greater. DTC P0973 is not set.
DTC: P0973	**1-2 Shift Solenoid (SS) Control Circuit Low Voltage:** No DTC P0335, P0336, P0340, P0345, P0346, P0365, P0366, P0390 or P0391. The engine speed is greater than 500 RPM for 5 seconds. The ignition voltage is greater than 8. 0 V.

DTC	Trouble Code Title, Conditions, Possible Causes
DTC: P0974	**Shift Solenoid (SS) 1 Control Circuit High Voltage:** P0973 or P0974The engine speed is 500 RPM or greater for 5 seconds. The ignition voltage is between 9. 0 volts and 18. 0 volts.
DTC: P0974	**1-2 Shift Solenoid (SS) Control Circuit High Voltage:** No DTC P0335, P0336, P0340, P0345, P0346, P0365, P0366, P0390 or P0391. The engine speed is greater than 500 RPM for 5 seconds. The ignition voltage is greater than 8. 0 V.
DTC: P0976	**2-3 Shift Solenoid (SS) Control Circuit Low Voltage:** No DTC P0335, P0336, P0340, P0345, P0346, P0365, P0366, P0390 or P0391. The engine speed is greater than 500 RPM for 5 seconds. The ignition voltage is greater than 8. 0 V.
DTC: P0976	**Shift Solenoid (SS) 2 Control Circuit Low Voltage:** P0976 or P0977 DTCs P0976 or P0977 have not set this ignition. The ignition voltage is 8. 6 volts or greater. The engine speed is 500 RPM or greater for 5 seconds. The SS 2 is commanded ON or OFF.
DTC: P0977	**2-3 Shift Solenoid (SS) Control Circuit High Voltage:** No DTC P0335, P0336, P0340, P0345, P0346, P0365, P0366, P0390 or P0391. The engine speed is greater than 500 RPM for 5 seconds. The ignition voltage is greater than 8. 0 V.
DTC: P0977	**2-3 Shift Solenoid (SS) Control Circuit High Voltage:** The engine speed is 500 RPM for 5 seconds. The 2-3 SS is commanded ON.
DTC: P0990	**Transmission Fluid Pressure Switch 5 Circuit High Voltage:** DTC P0989 or P0990 DTC P0711, P0712, P0713, P0716, P0717, P0722, P0723, P0742, P0751, P0756, P0757, P0973, P0974, P0976, P0977, P1915, or P182E is not set. The engine speed is 400 RPM or greater for 5 seconds. The engine speed is 550 RPM or greater. Ignition voltage is 8. 6 volts or greater. The transmission fluid temperature (TFT) is 0-120°C (32-248°F).

OBD II Trouble Code List (P1xxx Codes)

DTC	Trouble Code Title, Conditions, Possible Causes
DTC: Pw1043	**Reductant Pump High Control Circuit Low Voltage:** DTCs P204F, P20A1, or P2510 are not set. The battery voltage is greater than 11 V. The engine speed is greater than 600 RPM. The engine run time is greater than 10 s. The DTCs run continuously once the above conditions are met.
DTC: P1044	**Reductant Pump High Control Circuit High Voltage:** DTCs P204F, P20A1, or P2510 are not set. The battery voltage is greater than 11 V. The engine speed is greater than 600 RPM. The engine run time is greater than 10 s. The DTCs run continuously once the above conditions are met.
DTC: P1045	**Reductant Purge Valve High Control Circuit Low Voltage:** The battery voltage is greater than 11 V. The engine speed is greater than 600 RPM. The engine run time is greater than 10 s. The DTCs run continuously when the above conditions are met.
DTC: P1048	**Reductant Injector High Control Circuit Low Voltage:** The engine is running. The battery voltage is greater than 11 V. The ECM is commanding the reductant injector duty cycle greater than 0 %. The Reductant Injection Inhibit Reason displays None. The DTCs run continuously once the above conditions are met.
DTC: P1049	**Reductant Injector High Control Circuit High Voltage:** The engine is running. The battery voltage is greater than 11 V. The ECM is commanding the reductant injector duty cycle greater than 0 %. The Reductant Injection Inhibit Reason displays None. The DTCs run continuously once the above conditions are met.
DTC: P1082	**Fuel Filter Pressure Switch Performance:** ECM monitors the circuit 30 s into the after-run mode.
DTC: P10CC	**Exhaust Aftertreatment Fuel Injector Control Circuit Shorted:** Battery Voltage is greater than 11 V. Engine speed is greater than 600 RPM.
DTC: P10CD	**Exhaust Aftertreatment Fuel Injector High Control Circuit Low Voltage:** Battery Voltage is greater than 11 V. Engine speed is greater than 600 RPM.
DTC: P10CE	**Exhaust Aftertreatment Fuel Injector High Control Circuit High Voltage:** Battery Voltage is greater than 11 V. Engine speed is greater than 600 RPM.
DTC: P1101	**Intake Air Flow System Performance:** DTC P0102, P0103, P0107, P0108, P0112, P0113, P0116, P0117, P0118, P0128, P0335, or P0336 are not set. The engine speed is between 400-7,192 RPM. The IAT Sensor parameter is between -7 to +125°C (+19 to +257°F). The Engine Coolant Temperature (ECT) Sensor parameter is between 70-125°C (158-257°F). This DTC runs continuously within the enabling conditions.

DTC	Trouble Code Title, Conditions, Possible Causes
DTC: P1101 00	**Intake Air Flow System Performance:** P1101 00 DTCs P0102 00, P0103 00, P0106 00, P0107 00, P0108 00, P0112 00, P0113 00, P0117 00, P0118 00, P0335 00, P0336 00 are not set. The engine speed is between 400-6 500 RPM. The engine coolant temperature (ECT) Sensor is between 70-125°C (158-257°F). The intake air temperature (IAT) Sensor is between -20 to +125°C (-4 to +257°F). DTC P1101 00 run continuously when the above conditions are met.
DTC: P1104 00	**Throttle Actuator Control (TAC) Motor Control Circuit Shorted:** P1104 00The ignition is ON or the engine is operating. The ignition voltage is greater than 7 V. The system is not in battery safe mode. DTC P0068 00 is not set. DTCs P1516 00 and P2101 00 run continuously once the above conditions are met for greater than 5 s.
DTC: P111C	**Charge Air Cooler (CAC) Temperature - Intake Air Temperature (IAT) Sensor 2 Correlation:** Condition 1 DTCs P0016, P007C, P0097, P0098, P0112, P0113, P0335, P0336, P0340, or P0341 are not set. Ignition has been OFF for 8 hours or more. The engine is running. OR Condition 2 DTCs P0016, P007C, P0097, P0098, P0112, P0113, P0335, P0336, P0340, or P0341 are not set. . Ignition has been OFF for 8 hours or more. The engine is running. In the first 60 s of engine run time, the ECM determines the block heater is OFF. AND In the first 60 s of engine run time, the ECM determines the block heater is OFF. AND In the first 10 minutes of engine run time, the vehicle speed as been at least 24 km/h (15 mph) for at least 5 minutes and the ECM determines there is no Sunload. This DTC runs once per key cycle when the conditions in 1 or 2 are met.
DTC: P111D	**Intake Air Temperature (IAT) Sensor 1-Fuel Temperature Sensor 2 Correlation:** Condition 1 DTCs P0016, P0112, P0113, P0187, P0188, P0335, P0336, P0340, or P0341 are not set. Ignition has been OFF for 8 hours or more. The ambient temperature is warmer than -60°C (-76°F). The engine is running. OR Condition 2 DTCs P0016, P0112, P0113, P0187, P0188, P0335, P0336, P0340, or P0341 are not set. Ignition has been OFF for 8 hours or more. The ambient temperature is warmer than -60°C (-76°F). The engine is running. In the first 60 s of engine run time, the ECM determines the block heater is OFF. AND In the first 10 minutes of engine run time, the vehicle speed as been at least 24 km/h (15 mph) for at least 5 minutes and the ECM determines there is no Sunload. This DTC runs once per key cycle when the conditions in 1 or 2 are met.
DTC: P1125 00	**Accelerator Pedal Position (APP) System:** DTCs P0641 00, P0651 00, or P0697 00 are not set. The ignition is ON or the engine is operating. The DTCs run continuously once the above conditions are met.
DTC: P1133	**HO2S Insufficient Switching Sensor 1:** P0133 and P1133 DTCs P0101, P0102, P0103, P0106, P0107, P0108, P0116, P0117, P0118, P0128, P0131, P0132, P0134, P0201, P0202, P0203, P0204, P0300, P0411, P0412, P0418, P0442, P0443, P0446, P0449, P0451, P0452, P0453, P0454, P0455, P0496 are not set. The Engine Coolant Temperature (ECT) Sensor parameter is more than 70°C (158°F). The Ignition 1 Signal parameter is between 10-32 V. The Fuel Level Sensor parameter is more than 10 percent. The Engine Run Time parameter is more than 120 s. The Engine Speed parameter is between 1,000-3,500 RPM. The EGR device control is not active. The idle speed device control is not active. The fuel device control is not active. The AIR device control is not active. The HO2S heaters have been ON for more than 40 s. The learned HO2S heater resistance is valid. The IAT parameter is more than -40°C (-40°F). The fuel composition is less than 87 percent ethanol. The BARO parameter is more than 70 kPa. The fuel control is not in power enrichment. DFCO is not active. The Mass Airflow (MAF) Sensor parameter is between 14-40 g/s. The Loop Status parameter is Closed. DTCs P0133 and P1133 run once per drive cycle when the above conditions are met for 3 s.
DTC: P1133	**HO2S Insufficient Switching Bank 1 Sensor 1:** P0133, P0153, P1133, or P1153 DTCs P0068, P0101, P0102, P0103, P0106, P0107, P0108, P0112, P0113, P0116, P0117, P0118, P0120, P0121, P0122, P0123, P0128, P0201, P0202, P0203, P0204, P0205, P0206, P0207, P0208, P0220, P0222, P0223, P0442, P0443, P0446, P0449, P0455, P0496, P1516, P2101, P2119, P2135, P2176 are not set. The engine coolant temperature (ECT) is greater than 71°C (159°F). The intake air temperature (IAT) is warmer than -40°C (-40°F)The ignition 1 voltage is between 10-32 V. The fuel level is greater than 10 %. The engine run time is greater than 60 s. The engine speed is between 1,000-3,000 RPM. The barometric (BARO) pressure is greater than 70 kPa. The mass airflow (MAF) is between 15-55 g/s. The fuel system is in Closed Loop. The throttle position (TP) is greater than 5 %. The DTCs run once per drive cycle when the above conditions are met.
DTC: P1133 00	**HO2S Insufficient Switching Sensor 1:** DTCs P0106 00, P0107 00, P0108 00, P0112 00, P0113 00, P0116 00, P0117 00, P0118 00, P0121 00, P0122 00, P0123 00, P0131 00, P0132 00, P0134 00, P0201 00, P0202 00, P0203 00, P0204 00, P0300 00, P0315 00, P0335 00, P0336 00, P044 00, P0443 00, P0446 00, P0449 00, P0451 00, P0452 00, P0453 00, and P0496 00 are not set. The calculated airflow into the engine is between 10-45 g/s. The engine speed is between 1 100-3 500 RPM. The engine coolant temperature is greater than 60°C (140°F). The Barometric Pressure (BARO) is greater than 70 kPa (10 PSI). The ignition voltage is between 10-18 V. The fuel system is in closed loop. The evaporative emissions (EVAP) purge is less than 20%. The EVAP purge is not changing states. The engine run time is greater than 3 min. The fuel level is greater than 10%. The long term fuel trim is enabled. The HO2S heater is enabled for greater than 40 s. The vehicle is not decelerating. The vehicle is not operating in power enrichment. The DTCs run once per ignition cycle when the above conditions are met for greater than 1 s.
DTC: P113A	**Exhaust Gas Temperature Sensors 3-4 Not Plausible:** P113ADTC P0112, P0113, P242C, P242D, P2470, or P2471 is not set. The ignition has been OFF for greater than 8 hours. The engine is running. The ambient air temperature is greater than -60°C (-76°F). DTC P113A runs once per key cycle when the above conditions are met.

DTC	Trouble Code Title, Conditions, Possible Causes
DTC: P1153	**HO2S Insufficient Switching Bank 2 Sensor 1:** P0133, P0153, P1133, or P1153 DTCs P0068, P0101, P0102, P0103, P0106, P0107, P0108, P0112, P0113, P0116, P0117, P0118, P0120, P0121, P0122, P0123, P0128, P0201, P0202, P0203, P0204, P0205, P0206, P0207, P0208, P0220, P0222, P0223, P0442, P0443, P0446, P0449, P0455, P0496, P1516, P2101, P2119, P2135, or P2176 are not set. The engine coolant temperature (ECT) is greater than 70°C (158°F). The intake air temperature (IAT) is warmer than -40°C (-40°F)The ignition 1 voltage is between 10-18 volts. The fuel level is greater than 10 percent. The engine run time is greater than 202 seconds. The engine speed is between 1,100-2,500 RPM. The barometric (BARO) pressure is greater than 70 kPa. The mass airflow (MAF) is between 20-40 g/s. The fuel system is in Closed Loop. The throttle position (TP) is greater than 3 percent. The DTCs run once per drive cycle when the above conditions are met.
DTC: P1159 00	**Exhaust Gas Recirculation (EGR) Control Circuit:** The ignition is ON, or the engine is running. The DTCs run continuously when the above conditions are met.
DTC: P1161 00	**Exhaust Gas Recirculation (EGR) Control Circuit Low Voltage:** The ignition is ON, or the engine is running. The DTCs run continuously when the above conditions are met.
DTC: P1166 00	**HO2S Circuit Low Voltage During Power Enrichment Sensor 1:** The startup engine coolant temperature is greater than 60°C (140°F). The ignition voltage is greater than 10 V. The engine has been operating greater than 60 s. The engine is in power enrichment mode. The DTCs run continuously when the above conditions are met for 2 s.
DTC: P1168 00	**Exhaust Gas Recirculation (EGR) Control Circuit High Voltage:** The ignition is ON, or the engine is running. The DTCs run continuously when the above conditions are met.
DTC: P1174	**Air Fuel Imbalance Bank 1:** DTCs P0053, P0059, P0068, P0101, P0102, P0103, P0106, P0107, P0108, P0117, P0118, P0120, P0122, P0123, P0128, P0131, P0132, P0133, P0134, P0135, P0151, P0152, P0153, P0154, P0155, P0201-P0206, P0220, P0222, P0223, P0300, P0301-P0306, P0442, P0443, P0446, P0449, P0452, P0453, P0455, P0496, P0606, P0641, P0651, P1133, P1516, P2101, P2120, P2122, P2123, P2125, P2127, P2128, P2135, P2176, P2A00 are not set. The device control is not active. The intrusive diagnostics are not active. The engine overspeed protection is not active. Reduced engine power is not active. The traction control is not active. The engine is in Closed Loop status. The system voltage is between 10-32 V for greater than 4 s. The engine run time is greater than 50 seconds. The engine coolant temperature (ECT) is warmer than -20°C (-4°F). The engine speed is between 500-4,000 RPM. The mass air flow is between 5-600 g/s.
DTC: P1174	**Fuel Trim Cylinder Balance:** DTCs P0030, P0053, P0068, P0101, P0102, P0103, P0106, P0107, P0108, P0116, P0117, P0118, P0120, P0121, P0122, P0123, P0128, P0131, P0132, P0133, P0134, P0135, P0201-P0204, P0220, P0222, P0223, P0300, P0442, P0443, P0446, P0449, P0451, P0452, P0453, P0454, P0455, P0496, P060D, P1133, P1516, P2101, P2119, P2120, P2122, P2123, P2125, P2127, P2128, P2135, P2138, P2176, P2A00 are not set. The device control is not active. The intrusive diagnostics are not active. The engine overspeed protection is not active. The traction control is not active. The fuel control is in air-fuel Closed Loop. The system voltage is greater than 10 volts, or less than 18 volts. The engine run time is greater than 50 seconds. The engine coolant temperature (ECT) is greater than 10°C (50°F). The engine speed is greater than 1,000 RPM, but less than 4,000 RPM. The mass air flow is greater than 7 g/s, but less than 400 g/s. This DTC runs continuously when the above conditions are met.
DTC: P1175	**Fuel Trim Cylinder Balance Bank 2:** DTCs P0030, P0036, P0050, P0053, P0059, P0101, P0102, P0103, P0106, P0107, P0108, P0117, P0118, P0128, P0131, P0132, P0133, P0134, P0135, P0151, P0152, P0153, P0154, P0155, P0201-P0206, P0300, P0301-P0306, P0411, P0412, P0418, P0442, P0443, P0446, P0449, P0452, P0453, P0454, P0455, P0496, P1133, P1153, P1516, P2101, P2119, P2120, P2125, P2135, P2138, P2176, P2431, P2432, P2433, P2440, P2A00, P2A03 are not set. The device control is not active. The intrusive diagnostics are not active. The engine overspeed protection is not active. The power take-off (PTO) is not active. The traction control is not active. The fuel control is in air-fuel Closed Loop. The system voltage is more than 10 volts, or less than 18 volts. The engine run time is greater than 100 seconds. The engine coolant temperature (ECT) is greater than -20°C (-4°F). The engine speed is greater than 425 RPM, but less than 6,000 RPM. The mass air flow is greater than 25 g/s, but less than 510 g/s.
DTC: P11AF	**HO2S Performance - Signal High During Moderate Load Sensor 2:** P11AF or P11B2The engine run time is greater than 10 s. The engine speed is between 1,300 and 2,600 RPM. The intake air temperature is between -43 to +123°C (-45 to +253°F). The BARO pressure is between 75-110 kPa (11-16 psi). The battery voltage is greater than 11 V. The EGR is commanded ON and the exhaust gas temperature sensor 2 is between 100-1,000°C (212-1,832° F). The DPF regeneration is not active. The fuel level is greater than 15 percent. The DTCs run continuously once the above conditions are met.
DTC: P11B2	**HO2S Performance - Signal Low During Moderate Load Sensor 2:** P11AF or P11B2The engine run time is greater than 10 s. The engine speed is between 1,300 and 2,600 RPM. The intake air temperature is between -43 to +123°C (-45 to +253°F). The BARO pressure is between 75-110 kPa (11-16 psi). The battery voltage is greater than 11 V. The EGR is commanded ON and the exhaust gas temperature sensor 2 is between 100-1,000°C (212-1,832° F). The DPF regeneration is not active. The fuel level is greater than 15 percent. The DTCs run continuously once the above conditions are met.

DTC	Trouble Code Title, Conditions, Possible Causes
DTC: P11B5	**HO2S Current Performance Sensor 2:** P11B5The engine speed is greater than 600 RPM. The battery voltage is greater than 11 V. The engine run time is greater than 10 s. The NOx sensor is at operating temperature. The DTC runs continuously once the above conditions are met.
DTC: P11CB	**NOx Sensor 1 Performance - Signal High:** P11CB or P11CCDTCs P0101, P0234, P0299, P0401, P0402, P140B, P140C, P2228, or P2229 are not set. The DPF Regeneration is not active. The BARO is between 75-106 kPa (11-15 psi). The ambient air temperature is between -7 to +38°C (19-100°F). The engine run time is greater than 30 s. The engine coolant temperature is between -7 to +123°C (19-253°F). The engine speed is greater than 600 RPM. The battery voltage is greater than 11 V. The NOx sensor is at operating temperature. The DTCs run once per drive cycle when the above conditions are met.
DTC: P11CC	**NOx Sensor 1 Performance - Signal Low:** P11CB or P11CCDTCs P0101, P0234, P0299, P0401, P0402, P140B, P140C, P2228, or P2229 are not set. The DPF Regeneration is not active. The BARO is between 75-106 kPa (11-15 psi). The ambient air temperature is between -7 to +38°C (19-100°F). The engine run time is greater than 30 s. The engine coolant temperature is between -7 to +123°C (19-253°F). The engine speed is greater than 600 RPM. The battery voltage is greater than 11 V. The NOx sensor is at operating temperature. The DTCs run once per drive cycle when the above conditions are met.
DTC: P11DB	**NOx Sensor 1 Current Performance:** P11DBDTCs P064C, P163C, P2200, P2205, P220A, P220B, U029D and U029E are not set. The exhaust temperature sensor 2 is greater than 95°C (203° F). The engine speed is greater than 600 RPM. The battery voltage is greater than 11 V. The DPF regeneration is not active. The DTCs run continuously when the above conditions are met.
DTC: P11DC	**NOx Sensor 2 Current Performance:** P11DCThe exhaust temperature sensor 4 is greater than 95°C (203°F). The engine speed is greater than 600 RPM. The battery voltage is greater than 11 V. The DPF regeneration is not active. The DTC runs continuously when the above conditions are met.
DTC: P1224	**Fuel Injector 1 Control Circuit Shorted:** The engine is running. The charging system voltage is between 10-18 volts.
DTC: P1224 00	**Cylinder 1 Injector Control Circuit Malfunction:** The engine is running. The ECM monitors for a condition once per camshaft revolution.
DTC: P1227	**Fuel Injector 2 Control Circuit Shorted:** Engine speed is greater than 600 RPM. The charging system voltage is between 10-18 V.
DTC: P1227 00	**Cylinder 2 Injector Control Circuit Malfunction:** The engine is running. The ECM monitors for a condition once per camshaft revolution.
DTC: P122A	**Fuel Injector 3 Control Circuit Shorted:** Engine speed is greater than 600 RPM. The charging system voltage is between 10-18 V.
DTC: P122A 00	**Cylinder 3 Injector Control Circuit Malfunction:** The engine is running. The ECM monitors for a condition once per camshaft revolution.
DTC: P122B 00	**Intake Air Flow Valve Control Circuit Low Voltage:** The ignition is ON, or the engine is running. The throttle actuator motor is commanded ON or OFF. The ignition voltage is less than 16 V. The DTCs run continuously when the above conditions are met.
DTC: P122C	**Intake Air (IA) Flow Valve Control Circuit Shorted:** P02E2, P02E3, P02EB, P122C, P122E and P122FThe battery voltage is greater than 11 V. The Engine is running. The throttle valve motor control circuit is active. The DTCs run continuously whenever the above conditions are met.
DTC: P122C 00	**Intake Air Flow Valve Control Circuit Shorted:** P122C 00The ignition is ON, or the engine is running. The throttle valve motor control circuit is active. The ignition voltage is less than 16 V. This DTCs run continuously when the above conditions are met.
DTC: P122D	**Intake Air (IA) Flow Position Sensor Exceeded Learning Limit:** DTC P02E0 or P02EB is not set. The ignition is ON. Offset learning for the throttle valve was successful in the previous driving cycle. The battery voltage is greater than 8 V. DTC P122D runs continuously when the above conditions are met.
DTC: P122D 00	**Intake Air Flow Position Sensor Exceeded Learning Limit:** P122D 00The ignition is ON, or the engine is running. DTC P02E0 00 or P02EB 00 is not set. Offset learning for the throttle valve was successful in the previous driving cycle. The ignition voltage is less than 16 V. This DTCs run continuously when the above conditions are met.
DTC: P122E	**Intake Air (IA) Flow Valve Control Circuit 2 Low Voltage:** P02E2, P02E3, P02EB, P122C, P122E and P122FThe battery voltage is greater than 11 V. The Engine is running. The throttle valve motor control circuit is active. The DTCs run continuously whenever the above conditions are met.

DTC	Trouble Code Title, Conditions, Possible Causes
DTC: P122F	**Intake Air (IA) Flow Valve Control Circuit 2 High Voltage:** P02E2, P02E3, P02EB, P122C, P122E and P122FThe battery voltage is greater than 11 V. The Engine is running. The throttle valve motor control circuit is active. The DTCs run continuously whenever the above conditions are met.
DTC: P1233	**Fuel Injector 4 Control Circuit Shorted:** The engine is running. The charging system voltage is between 10-18 volts.
DTC: P1233 00	**Cylinder 4 Injector Control Circuit Malfunction:** The engine is running. The ECM monitors for a condition once per camshaft revolution.
DTC: P1236	**Fuel Injector 5 Control Circuit Shorted:** The engine is running. The charging system voltage is between 10-18 volts.
DTC: P1239	**Fuel Injector 6 Control Circuit Shorted:** Engine speed is greater than 600 RPM. The charging system voltage is between 10-18 V.
DTC: P1242	**Fuel Injector 7 Control Circuit Shorted:** Engine speed is greater than 600 RPM. The charging system voltage is between 10-18 V.
DTC: P1247	**Fuel Injector 8 Control Circuit Shorted:** The engine is running. The charging system voltage is between 10-18 volts.
DTC: P1248	**Cylinder 1 Injector High Control Circuit Shorted to Control Circuit:** The engine is running. The ignition voltage is between 11-18 V. The DTCs run continuously when the above conditions are met.
DTC: P1248 00	**Cylinder 1 Injector High Control Circuit Shorted to Control Circuit:** The engine is running. The ECM monitors for a condition once per camshaft revolution.
DTC: P1249	**Cylinder 2 Injector High Control Circuit Shorted to Control Circuit:** The engine is running. The ignition voltage is between 11-18 V. The DTCs run continuously when the above conditions are met.
DTC: P1249 00	**Cylinder 2 Injector High Control Circuit Shorted to Control Circuit:** The engine is running. The ECM monitors for a condition once per camshaft revolution.
DTC: P124A	**Cylinder 3 Injector High Control Circuit Shorted to Control Circuit:** The engine is running. The ignition voltage is between 11-18 V. The DTCs run continuously when the above conditions are met.
DTC: P124A 00	**Cylinder 3 Injector High Control Circuit Shorted to Control Circuit:** The engine is running. The ECM monitors for a condition once per camshaft revolution.
DTC: P124B	**Cylinder 4 Injector High Control Circuit Shorted to Control Circuit:** The engine is running. The ignition voltage is between 11-18 V. The DTCs run continuously when the above conditions are met.
DTC: P124B 00	**Cylinder 4 Injector High Control Circuit Shorted to Control Circuit:** The engine is running. The ECM monitors for a condition once per camshaft revolution.
DTC: P124C	**Cylinder 5 Injector High Control Circuit Shorted to Control Circuit:** The engine is running. The ignition voltage is between 11-18 V. The DTCs run continuously when the above conditions are met.
DTC: P124D	**Cylinder 6 Injector High Control Circuit Shorted to Control Circuit:** The engine is running. The ignition voltage is between 11-18 V. The DTCs run continuously when the above conditions are met.
DTC: P1255	**Fuel Pump Control Module Driver Over-temperature:** The engine is running.
DTC: P1258	**Engine Coolant Over temperature - Protection Mode Active:** The engine is operating for greater than 30 seconds. DTC P1258 runs continuously when the condition above is met.
DTC: P1258	**Engine Coolant Over temperature - Protection Mode Active:** The engine is operating.
DTC: P125A	**Fuel Pressure Regulator 2 High Control Circuit Low Voltage:** Engine speed is greater than 600 RPM. Battery voltage is greater than 11 V.
DTC: P125B	**Fuel Pressure Regulator 2 High Control Circuit High Voltage:** Engine speed is greater than 600 RPM. Battery voltage is greater than 11 V.
DTC: P128E	**Fuel Rail Pressure Performance:** Fuel tank level is greater than 15 %Engine is in crank or run mode

DTC	Trouble Code Title, Conditions, Possible Causes
DTC: P12B3	**Cylinder 1 Injection Timing Retarded:** Ambient air temperature is above -5° C (23° F). Fuel temperature is between 0-80° C (32-176° F). Engine temperature is greater the 50° C (122° F). Battery voltages is greater than 10 V. Time since last combustion event is between 10-30 s. Vehicle is in decel fuel shut off mode. Engine speed is between 950-1850 RPM. The difference between the Desired Fuel Rail Pressure and the Actual Fuel Rail Pressure is less than 2. 2 MPa (320 psi). No gear change has occurred. Lambda sensors are adapted. Vehicle is not in 4WD (if equipped). Exhaust brake is not ON (if equipped). No other DTCs are present. The DTC runs when the above conditions exists.
DTC: P12B4	**Cylinder 1 Injection Timing Advanced:** Ambient air temperature is above -5° C (23° F)Fuel temperature is between 0-80° C (32-176° F)Engine temperature is greater the 50° C (122° F)Battery voltages is greater than 10 V. Time since last combustion event is between 10-30 s. Vehicle is in decel fuel shut off mode. Engine speed is between 950-1850 RPM. The difference between the Desired Fuel Rail Pressure and the Actual Fuel Rail Pressure is less than 2. 2 MPa (320 psi)No gear change has occurred. Lambda sensors are adapted. Vehicle is not in 4WD (if equipped). Exhaust brake is not ON (if equipped). No other DTCs are present. The DTC runs when the above conditions exists
DTC: P12B5	**Cylinder 2 Injection Timing Retarded:** Ambient air temperature is above -5° C (23° F). Fuel temperature is between 0-80° C (32-176° F). Engine temperature is greater the 50° C (122° F). Battery voltages is greater than 10 V. Time since last combustion event is between 10-30 s. Vehicle is in decel fuel shut off mode. Engine speed is between 950-1850 RPM. The difference between the Desired Fuel Rail Pressure and the Actual Fuel Rail Pressure is less than 2. 2 MPa (320 psi). No gear change has occurred. Lambda sensors are adapted. Vehicle is not in 4WD (if equipped). Exhaust brake is not ON (if equipped). No other DTCs are present. The DTC runs when the above conditions exists.
DTC: P12B6	**Cylinder 2 Injection Timing Advanced:** Ambient air temperature is above -5° C (23° F)Fuel temperature is between 0-80° C (32-176° F)Engine temperature is greater the 50° C (122° F)Battery voltages is greater than 10 V. Time since last combustion event is between 10-30 s. Vehicle is in decel fuel shut off mode. Engine speed is between 950-1850 RPM. The difference between the Desired Fuel Rail Pressure and the Actual Fuel Rail Pressure is less than 2. 2 MPa (320 psi)No gear change has occurred. Lambda sensors are adapted. Vehicle is not in 4WD (if equipped)Exhaust brake is not ON (if equipped)No other DTCs are present. The DTC runs when the above conditions exists
DTC: P12B7	**Cylinder 3 Injection Timing Retarded:** Ambient air temperature is above -5° C (23° F). Fuel temperature is between 0-80° C (32-176° F). Engine temperature is greater the 50° C (122° F). Battery voltages is greater than 10 V. Time since last combustion event is between 10-30 s. Vehicle is in decel fuel shut off mode. Engine speed is between 950-1850 RPM. The difference between the Desired Fuel Rail Pressure and the Actual Fuel Rail Pressure is less than 2. 2 MPa (320 psi). No gear change has occurred. Lambda sensors are adapted. Vehicle is not in 4WD (if equipped). Exhaust brake is not ON (if equipped). No other DTCs are present. The DTC runs when the above conditions exists.
DTC: P12B8	**Cylinder 3 Injection Timing Advanced:** Ambient air temperature is above -5° C (23° F)Fuel temperature is between 0-80° C (32-176° F)Engine temperature is greater the 50° C (122° F)Battery voltages is greater than 10 V. Time since last combustion event is between 10-30 s. Vehicle is in decel fuel shut off mode. Engine speed is between 950-1850 RPM. The difference between the Desired Fuel Rail Pressure and the Actual Fuel Rail Pressure is less than 2. 2 MPa (320 psi)No gear change has occurred. Lambda sensors are adapted. Vehicle is not in 4WD (if equipped)Exhaust brake is not ON (if equipped)No other DTCs are present. The DTC runs when the above conditions exists
DTC: P12B9	**Cylinder 4 Injection Timing Retarded:** Ambient air temperature is above -5° C (23° F). Fuel temperature is between 0-80° C (32-176° F). Engine temperature is greater the 50° C (122° F). Battery voltages is greater than 10 V. Time since last combustion event is between 10-30 s. Vehicle is in decel fuel shut off mode. Engine speed is between 950-1850 RPM. The difference between the Desired Fuel Rail Pressure and the Actual Fuel Rail Pressure is less than 2. 2 MPa (320 psi). No gear change has occurred. Lambda sensors are adapted. Vehicle is not in 4WD (if equipped). Exhaust brake is not ON (if equipped). No other DTCs are present. The DTC runs when the above conditions exists.
DTC: P12BA	**Cylinder 4 Injection Timing Advanced:** Ambient air temperature is above -5° C (23° F)Fuel temperature is between 0-80° C (32-176° F)Engine temperature is greater the 50° C (122° F)Battery voltages is greater than 10 V. Time since last combustion event is between 10-30 s. Vehicle is in decel fuel shut off mode. Engine speed is between 950-1850 RPM. The difference between the Desired Fuel Rail Pressure and the Actual Fuel Rail Pressure is less than 2. 2 MPa (320 psi)No gear change has occurred. Lambda sensors are adapted. Vehicle is not in 4WD (if equipped)Exhaust brake is not ON (if equipped)No other DTCs are present. The DTC runs when the above conditions exists
DTC: P12BB	**Cylinder 5 Injection Timing Retarded:** Ambient air temperature is above -5° C (23° F). Fuel temperature is between 0-80° C (32-176° F). Engine temperature is greater the 50° C (122° F). Battery voltages is greater than 10 V. Time since last combustion event is between 10-30 s. Vehicle is in decel fuel shut off mode. Engine speed is between 950-1850 RPM. The difference between the Desired Fuel Rail Pressure and the Actual Fuel Rail Pressure is less than 2. 2 MPa (320 psi). No gear change has occurred. Lambda sensors are adapted. Vehicle is not in 4WD (if equipped). Exhaust brake is not ON (if equipped). No other DTCs are present. The DTC runs when the above conditions exists.

DTC	Trouble Code Title, Conditions, Possible Causes
DTC: P12BC	**Cylinder 5 Injection Timing Advanced:** Ambient air temperature is above -5° C (23° F)Fuel temperature is between 0-80° C (32-176° F)Engine temperature is greater the 50° C (122° F)Battery voltages is greater than 10 V. Time since last combustion event is between 10-30 s. Vehicle is in decel fuel shut off mode. Engine speed is between 950-1850 RPM. The difference between the Desired Fuel Rail Pressure and the Actual Fuel Rail Pressure is less than 2. 2 MPa (320 psi)No gear change has occurred. Lambda sensors are adapted. Vehicle is not in 4WD (if equipped)Exhaust brake is not ON (if equipped)No other DTCs are present. The DTC runs when the above conditions exists
DTC: P12BD	**Cylinder 6 Injection Timing Retarded:** Ambient air temperature is above -5° C (23° F). Fuel temperature is between 0-80° C (32-176° F). Engine temperature is greater the 50° C (122° F). Battery voltages is greater than 10 V. Time since last combustion event is between 10-30 s. Vehicle is in decel fuel shut off mode. Engine speed is between 950-1850 RPM. The difference between the Desired Fuel Rail Pressure and the Actual Fuel Rail Pressure is less than 2. 2 MPa (320 psi). No gear change has occurred. Lambda sensors are adapted. Vehicle is not in 4WD (if equipped). Exhaust brake is not ON (if equipped). No other DTCs are present. The DTC runs when the above conditions exists.
DTC: P12BE	**Cylinder 6 Injection Timing Advanced:** Ambient air temperature is above -5° C (23° F)Fuel temperature is between 0-80° C (32-176° F)Engine temperature is greater the 50° C (122° F)Battery voltages is greater than 10 V. Time since last combustion event is between 10-30 s. Vehicle is in decel fuel shut off mode. Engine speed is between 950-1850 RPM. The difference between the Desired Fuel Rail Pressure and the Actual Fuel Rail Pressure is less than 2. 2 MPa (320 psi)No gear change has occurred. Lambda sensors are adapted. Vehicle is not in 4WD (if equipped)Exhaust brake is not ON (if equipped)No other DTCs are present. The DTC runs when the above conditions exists
DTC: P12BF	**Cylinder 7 Injection Timing Retarded:** Ambient air temperature is above -5° C (23° F). Fuel temperature is between 0-80° C (32-176° F). Engine temperature is greater the 50° C (122° F). Battery voltages is greater than 10 V. Time since last combustion event is between 10-30 s. Vehicle is in decel fuel shut off mode. Engine speed is between 950-1850 RPM. The difference between the Desired Fuel Rail Pressure and the Actual Fuel Rail Pressure is less than 2. 2 MPa (320 psi). No gear change has occurred. Lambda sensors are adapted. Vehicle is not in 4WD (if equipped). Exhaust brake is not ON (if equipped). No other DTCs are present. The DTC runs when the above conditions exists.
DTC: P12C0	**Cylinder 7 Injection Timing Advanced:** Ambient air temperature is above -5° C (23° F)Fuel temperature is between 0-80° C (32-176° F)Engine temperature is greater the 50° C (122° F)Battery voltages is greater than 10 V. Time since last combustion event is between 10-30 s. Vehicle is in decel fuel shut off mode. Engine speed is between 950-1850 RPM. The difference between the Desired Fuel Rail Pressure and the Actual Fuel Rail Pressure is less than 2. 2 MPa (320 psi)No gear change has occurred. Lambda sensors are adapted. Vehicle is not in 4WD (if equipped)Exhaust brake is not ON (if equipped)No other DTCs are present. The DTC runs when the above conditions exists
DTC: P12C1	**Cylinder 8 Injection Timing Retarded:** Ambient air temperature is above -5° C (23° F). Fuel temperature is between 0-80° C (32-176° F). Engine temperature is greater the 50° C (122° F). Battery voltages is greater than 10 V. Time since last combustion event is between 10-30 s. Vehicle is in decel fuel shut off mode. Engine speed is between 950-1850 RPM. The difference between the Desired Fuel Rail Pressure and the Actual Fuel Rail Pressure is less than 2. 2 MPa (320 psi). No gear change has occurred. Lambda sensors are adapted. Vehicle is not in 4WD (if equipped). Exhaust brake is not ON (if equipped). No other DTCs are present. The DTC runs when the above conditions exists.
DTC: P12C2	**Cylinder 8 Injection Timing Advanced:** Ambient air temperature is above -5° C (23° F)Fuel temperature is between 0-80° C (32-176° F)Engine temperature is greater the 50° C (122° F)Battery voltages is greater than 10 V. Time since last combustion event is between 10-30 s. Vehicle is in decel fuel shut off mode. Engine speed is between 950-1850 RPM. The difference between the Desired Fuel Rail Pressure and the Actual Fuel Rail Pressure is less than 2. 2 MPa (320 psi)No gear change has occurred. Lambda sensors are adapted. Vehicle is not in 4WD (if equipped)Exhaust brake is not ON (if equipped)No other DTCs are present. The DTC runs when the above conditions exists
DTC: P135B	**Ignition Coil Supply Voltage Circuit Bank 2:** The ignition is ON. The ignition module supply voltage is less than 2. 5 V. The DTCs run continuously when the above condition is met.
DTC: P1392 00	**Left Rough Road Sensor Circuit Low Voltage:** DTC P0502 00 is not set. The vehicle speed is more than 5 km/h (3 MPH). The engine coolant temperature (ECT) is between 70-109°C (160-228°F). The ignition voltage is between 11-18 V. These DTCs run continuously when the above conditions are met.
DTC: P1393 00	**Left Rough Road Sensor Circuit High Voltage:** DTC P0502 00 is not set. The vehicle speed is more than 5 km/h (3 MPH). The engine coolant temperature (ECT) is between 70-109°C (160-228°F). The ignition voltage is between 11-18 V. These DTCs run continuously when the above conditions are met.

DTC	Trouble Code Title, Conditions, Possible Causes
DTC: P1400	**Cold Start Emission Reduction Control System:** The engine is running, and a cold start has been detected. The vehicle speed is less than 2 km/h (1 mph). The catalyst temperature is greater than 1,000°C (1,832°F). The coolant temperature is greater than 56°C (133°F). The engine run time is greater than 18 s. The engine is at idle with no input from the accelerator pedal for greater than 5 s. DTCs P0101, P0102, P0103, P0106, P0107, P0108, P0112, P0113, P0116, P0117, P0118, P0120, P0121, P0122, P0123, P0220, P0222, P0223, P0201, P0202, P0203, P0204, P0300, P0335, P0336, P0351, P0352, P0353, P0506, P0507, P0601, P0602, P0603, P0604, P0606, P0607, P062F, P0641, P0651, P1516, P1682, P2101, P2119, P2120, P2122, P2123, P2125, P2127, P2128, P2135, P2138, P2176, P2610 are not set. This DTC runs within 15 seconds within the first 2 minutes of start-up. This diagnostic runs once per trip when a cold start has been determined.
DTC: P1400	**Cold Start Injection Monitoring:** Engine is in Exhaust Warm-up mode. DTC runs continuously when the above condition exists.
DTC: P1400 00	**Cold Start Emission Reduction Control System:** DTCs P0101 00, P0102 00, P0103 00, P0106 00, P0107 00, P0108 00, P0112 00, P0113 00, P0114 00, P0116 00, P0117 00, P0118 00, P0121 00, P0122 00, P0123 00, P0222 00, P0223 00, P0201 00, P0202 00, P0203 00, P0204 00, P0300 00, P0301 00, P0302 00, P0303 00, P0304 00, P0335 00, P0336 00, P0351 00, P0352 00, P0353 00, P0354 00, P0502 00, P0503 00, P0506 00, P0507 00, P0641 00, P0651 00, P0697 00, P06A3 00, P0806 00, P0807 00, P080A 00, P2122 00, P2123 00, P2125 00, P2127 00, P2128 00, P2135 00, and P2138 00 are not set. The engine is idling less than 30 s. The Engine Coolant Temperature (ECT) sensor is greater than -10°C (14°F). The calculated three way catalyst temperature is less than 350°C (662°F). The ECM will exit the diagnostic if the calculated three way catalyst temperature is greater than 420°C (788°F) when the engine run time is greater than 30 s. The ECM will exit the diagnostic if the engine run time is greater than 90 s. The vehicle speed is less than 2 km/h (1 MPH). The engine is at idle with no input from the accelerator pedal. The clutch pedal position switch is less than 10% or greater than 80%, manual transmissions only. This DTC runs within the first 90 s of start up. This diagnostic runs once per trip when a cold start has been determined.
DTC: P1402 00	**Exhaust Gas Recirculation (EGR) Control Circuit Low Voltage:** The ignition is ON, or the engine is running. The DTCs run continuously when the above conditions are met.
DTC: P1407	**Exhaust Gas Recirculation (EGR) Motor Control Circuit Shorted:** P0489, P0490, P1407, P140D, P140E and P140FThe Ignition is ON. The battery voltage is greater than 11 V. The EGR control circuit is active. The starter is not cranking. The DTCs run continuously when the above conditions are met.
DTC: P1407 00	**Exhaust Gas Recirculation (EGR) Control Circuit Shorted:** The ignition is ON, or the engine is running. The DTCs run continuously when the above conditions are met.
DTC: P140B	**Exhaust Gas Recirculation (EGR) Flow Insufficient:** DTC P0045, P0047, P0048, P006E, P006F, P007C, P007D, P008F, P0101, P0102, P0103, P0106, P0107, P0108, P0112, P0113, P0117, P0118, P0128, P0200, P02E0, P02E7, P02E8, P02E9, P02EB, P0400, P0403, P0405, P0406, P0489, P0490, P122C, P122E, P122F, P140D, P140E, P140F, P1407, P1411, P1412, P1413, P1414, P168C, P168D, P16A0, P16A1, P16A2, P2228, P2229, P2263, P2453, P245A, P245C, P245D, P2493, P2494, P2495, P2564, P2565, P2598, or P2599, is not set. The engine speed is between 1,300-2,000 RPM. The calculated fuel rate is between 28-55 mm 3The ambient air temperature is greater than -7°C (19. 4°F). The engine coolant temperature is greater than 70°C (158°F)The Barometric Pressure is greater than 74. 8 kPa (10. 9 psi). The MAF rate is not in a steady state condition. The EGR valve is in closed loop and active. The DTCs run continuously when the above conditions are met.
DTC: P140C	**Exhaust Gas Recirculation (EGR) Flow Excessive:** DTC P0045, P0047, P0048, P006E, P006F, P007C, P007D, P008F, P0101, P0102, P0103, P0106, P0107, P0108, P0112, P0113, P0117, P0118, P0128, P0200, P02E0, P02E7, P02E8, P02E9, P02EB, P0400, P0403, P0405, P0406, P0489, P0490, P122C, P122E, P122F, P140D, P140E, P140F, P1407, P1411, P1412, P1413, P1414, P168C, P168D, P16A0, P16A1, P16A2, P2228, P2229, P2263, P2453, P245A, P245C, P245D, P2493, P2494, P2495, P2564, P2565, P2598, or P2599, is not set. The engine speed is between 1,300-2,000 RPM. The calculated fuel rate is between 28-55 mm 3The ambient air temperature is greater than -7°C (19. 4°F). The engine coolant temperature is greater than 70°C (158°F)The Barometric Pressure is greater than 74. 8 kPa (10. 9 psi). The MAF rate is not in a steady state condition. The EGR valve is in closed loop and active. The DTCs run continuously when the above conditions are met.
DTC: P140D	**Exhaust Gas Recirculation (EGR) Motor Control Circuit 2 Low Voltage:** P0489, P0490, P1407, P140D, P140E and P140FThe Ignition is ON. The battery voltage is greater than 11 V. The EGR control circuit is active. The starter is not cranking. The DTCs run continuously when the above conditions are met.
DTC: P140E	**Exhaust Gas Recirculation (EGR) Motor Control Circuit 2 High Voltage:** P0489, P0490, P1407, P140D, P140E and P140FThe Ignition is ON. The battery voltage is greater than 11 V. The EGR control circuit is active. The starter is not cranking. The DTCs run continuously when the above conditions are met.
DTC: P140F	**Exhaust Gas Recirculation (EGR) Motor Current Performance:** P0489, P0490, P1407, P140D, P140E and P140FThe Ignition is ON. The battery voltage is greater than 11 V. The EGR control circuit is active. The starter is not cranking. The DTCs run continuously when the above conditions are met.
DTC: P1446 00	**Pre-Catalyst Low Temperature During Regeneration Malfunction:** The DTC runs during the DPF regeneration process.

DTC	Trouble Code Title, Conditions, Possible Causes
DTC: P1447 00	**Pre-Catalyst High Temperature During Regeneration Malfunction:** The DTC runs during the DPF regeneration process.
DTC: P1448	**Diesel Particulate Filter Regeneration Frequency Too Low:** The engine is running. DTC P1448 runs continuously when the above condition is met.
DTC: P144B	**Closed Loop Diesel Particulate Filter (DPF) Regeneration Control At Limit - Stage 1 Temperature Too Low:** P144B or P144CThe engine run time is greater than 10 s. The engine speed is greater than 600 RPM. The ignition voltage is greater than 11 V. The ECM is commanding a DPF regeneration. The vehicle speed is between 0-200 km/h (0-124 mph). The exhaust temperature sensor 1 is between 100-650°C (212-1,200°F). The exhaust temperature sensor 1 and 4 is less than 650°C (1,200°F). The DTCs run continuously once the above conditions are met for 10 minutes.
DTC: P144C	**Closed Loop Diesel Particulate Filter (DPF) Regeneration Control At Limit - Stage 1 Temperature Too High:** P144B or P144CThe engine run time is greater than 10 s. The engine speed is greater than 600 RPM. The ignition voltage is greater than 11 V. The ECM is commanding a DPF regeneration. The vehicle speed is between 0-200 km/h (0-124 mph). The exhaust temperature sensor 1 is between 100-650°C (212-1,200°F). The exhaust temperature sensor 1 and 4 is less than 650°C (1,200°F). The DTCs run continuously once the above conditions are met for 10 minutes.
DTC: P144E	**Closed Loop Diesel Particulate Filter (DPF) Regeneration Control At Limit - Stage 2 Temperature Too Low:** P144E or P144FThe engine run time is greater than 10 s. The engine speed is greater than 600 RPM. The ignition voltage is greater than 11 V. The ECM is commanding a DPF regeneration. The vehicle speed is between 24-200 km/h (15-124 mph). The exhaust temperature sensor 1 and 4 is greater than 230°C (446°F). The exhaust temperature sensor 1 and 4 is less than 750°C (1,382°F). The DTCs run continuously once the above conditions are met for 10 minutes.
DTC: P144F	**Closed Loop Diesel Particulate Filter (DPF) Regeneration Control At Limit - Stage 2 Temperature Too High:** P144E or P144FThe engine run time is greater than 10 s. The engine speed is greater than 600 RPM. The ignition voltage is greater than 11 V. The ECM is commanding a DPF regeneration. The vehicle speed is between 24-200 km/h (15-124 mph). The exhaust temperature sensor 1 and 4 is greater than 230°C (446°F). The exhaust temperature sensor 1 and 4 is less than 750°C (1,382°F). The DTCs run continuously once the above conditions are met for 10 minutes.
DTC: P150A	**Transmission Output Speed Signal Circuit:** P150AThe TCM indicates the transmission output speed signal is valid. Transmission output speed is 1,200 RPM or greater.
DTC: P150B	**Transmission Output Speed Sensor Circuit Intermittent:** P150BThe ignition voltage is greater than 18 volts. The engine speed is greater than 500 RPM. The transmission output speed is greater than 1200 RPM.
DTC: P150C	**Transmission Control Module Engine Speed Request Signal Message Counter Incorrect:** The engine run time is greater than 5 seconds. No other CAN errors are present.
DTC: P150C	**Transmission Control Module Engine Speed Request Signal Message Counter Incorrect:** The ignition switch is in Unlock, Accessory, Run or Crank. The system voltage is more than 5. 23 V. DTCs P0601, P0602, P0603, P0604, P0606, P0607, P062F, P0641, P0651, P2610 and U0101 are not set.
DTC: P150C	**Transmission Control Module Engine Speed Request Signal Message Counter Incorrect:** The engine is running. No other CAN errors are present.
DTC: P1516	**Throttle Actuator Control (TAC) Module Throttle Actuator Position Performance:** P1516 and P2101 DTC P0606 and P1682 is not set. The run/crank or powertrain relay voltage is greater than 6 V and reduced power is not active. The engine is running or the following conditions are met: The engine is not running. The ignition voltage is greater than 11 V. The TAC system is not in the Battery Saver mode. The ECM is commanding the throttle. The ECM has learned the minimum throttle position. DTC P1516 and P2101 run continuously when the above conditions are met.
DTC: P1516 00	**Throttle Actuator Control (TAC) Module Throttle Actuator Position Performance:** P1516 00 or P2101 00The ignition is ON or the engine is operating. The ignition voltage is greater than 7 V. The system is not in battery safe mode. DTC P0068 00 is not set. DTCs P1516 00 and P2101 00 run continuously once the above conditions are met for greater than 5 s.
DTC: P1516 00	**Throttle Actuator Control (TAC) Module Throttle Actuator Position Performance:** P1516 00The engine is running. The throttle angle does not change greater than 2%. DTC P1516 00 runs continuously when the above conditions are met.
DTC: P1516 00	**Throttle Actuator Control (TAC) Module Throttle Actuator Position Performance:** P1516 00 or P2101 00 DTC P1682 00 is not set. The engine is running. The ECM has learned the minimum throttle position. The ignition voltage is greater than 6 volts and reduced power is not active. DTCs P1516 00 and P2101 00 run continuously when the above conditions are met.
DTC: P154A	**Intake Air (IA) Heater Feedback Circuit:** Engine speed is greater than 600 RPM. The intake air heater is commanded ON. The battery voltage is more than 8. 6 V. DTCs P154A runs continuously when the above conditions exists.

DTC	Trouble Code Title, Conditions, Possible Causes
DTC: P154B	**Intake Air (IA) Heater Voltage Signal Circuit:** The intake air heater is commanded ON. The glow plug control module battery voltage is between 9.5-15 V. DTC P154B runs continuously when the above condition is met.
DTC: P154C	**Intake Air (IA) Heater Current Signal Circuit:** The intake air heater is commanded ON. The intake air heater battery voltage is more than 6.9 V. Glow plug control module ignition voltage is more than 6.9 V. DTC P154C runs continuously when the above conditions are met.
DTC: P154D	**Intake Air (IA) Heater Temperature Signal Circuit:** The intake air heater is commanded ON. The intake air heater battery voltage is between 6.9-16 V. DTC P154D runs continuously when the above conditions are met.
DTC: P1551	**Throttle Valve Rest Position Not Reached During Learn:** The vehicle speed is 0 km/h (0 mph). The engine speed is 0 RPM. The engine coolant temperature (ECT) is between 5-100°C (41-212°F). The intake air temperature (IAT) is between 5-144°C (41-291°F). The ignition voltage is greater than 10 volts. The accelerator pedal position (APP) is less than 15 percent. DTC P1551 runs when the conditions above have been met for greater than 5 seconds.
DTC: P159F	**Fuel Economy Mode Switch Circuit Low Voltage:** Ignition key must be turned to ON. DTCs P159F and P15A0 run continuously when the above condition is met.
DTC: P15A0	**Fuel Economy Mode Switch Circuit High Voltage:** Ignition key must be turned to ON. DTCs P159F and P15A0 run continuously when the above condition is met.
DTC: P15A1	**Fuel Economy Mode Switch Performance:** The ignition key is turned to ON. DTC P15A1 runs continuously when the above condition is met.
DTC: P160C	**Engine Calibration Information Not Programmed - GPCM:** The ignition is ON.
DTC: P161A	**Glow Plug Control Module Not Programmed:** DTC P161A runs continuously when the ignition is ON.
DTC: P161C 00	**Tire Size Not Programmed Malfunction:** The ignition is ON. The DTC runs continuously once the above condition is met.
DTC: P161E 00	**Glow Plug Control Module Control Circuit Malfunction:** The ignition is ON, or the engine is running. The ignition voltage is between 9-16 V. The DTC runs once per ignition cycle when the above conditions are met.
DTC: P161F 32	**Assembly Plant Mode Counter Not Programmed General Memory Malfunction:** The ignition is ON. The DTC runs continuously once the above condition is met.
DTC: P161F 36	**Assembly Plant Mode Counter Not Programmed EEPROM Performance/Malfunction:** The ignition is ON. The DTC runs continuously once the above condition is met.
DTC: P161F 44	**Assembly Plant Mode Counter Not Programmed Security Access Not Activated:** The ignition is ON. The DTC runs continuously once the above condition is met.
DTC: P1629	**Immobilizer Fuel Enable Signal Not Received:** Ignition is in the ACCESSORY or RUN position.
DTC: P162B	**Remote Vehicle Speed Limiting Signal Message Counter Incorrect:** The engine run time is greater than 5 seconds. A remote slow-down request is sent from OnStar
DTC: P1630 00	**Immobilizer Learn Mode Active Malfunction:** The ECM is in immobilizer learn mode.
DTC: P1631	**Immobilizer Fuel Enable Signal Not Correct:** Ignition is in the ACCESSORY or RUN position.
DTC: P1631	**Theft Deterrent Fuel Enable Signal Not Correct:** Ignition is in the ACCESSORY or RUN position.
DTC: P1632	**Immobilizer Fuel Disable Signal Received:** Ignition is in the RUN position.
DTC: P163A	**Control Module Fuel Pressure Regulator 1 Control System Circuitry Performance:** DTCs P0016, P0017, P0090, P0091, P0092, P00C8, P00C9, P00CA, P0112, P0113, P0116, P0117, P0118, P0128, P0192, P0193, P0335, P0336, P0340, P0341, P0365, P0366, P0627-P0629, P1682 are not set. The engine is running. The ignition voltage is greater than 11 V. The low side fuel pressure is greater than 275 kPa (40 psi). DTC P163A runs continuously when the conditions are met for greater than 500 mS.

DTC	Trouble Code Title, Conditions, Possible Causes
DTC: P163A	**Control Module Fuel Pressure Regulator 1 Control System Circuitry Performance:** The engine is running or cranking. The ignition voltage is between 8-18 V. DTC P163A runs continuously when the conditions are met for greater than 500 mS.
DTC: P163C	**Glow Plug Module Primary Circuit:** The ignition is ON. DTC P163C runs continuously.
DTC: P163D	**Glow Plug Control Module Secondary Circuit:** The ignition is ON. DTC P163D runs continuously.
DTC: P163E	**Glow Plug Control Module Over temperature:** The ignition is ON. DTC P163E runs continuously.
DTC: P1649	**Immobilizer Security Code Not Programmed:** The ECM is in learn mode.
DTC: P1668	**Generator L-Terminal Control Circuit:** The engine is running.
DTC: P166B	**Intake Air (IA) Heater Over Temperature:** The IAH is commanded ON. The engine is running for more than 40 seconds.
DTC: P166B	**Intake Air (IA) Heater Over Temperature:** The intake air heater is commanded ON. The engine is running for more than 40 seconds. Engine coolant temperature is less than 60°C (140°F).
DTC: P166C	**Intake Air (IA) Heater Resistance:** The IAH is commanded ON.
DTC: P1678	**Immobilizer System - Incorrect Engine Control Module (ECM) Identification:** Ignition is in the ACCESSORY or RUN position.
DTC: P167D	**Control Module Ignition Coil Internal Circuit:** P167DThe engine is operating. The ignition voltage is between 10-18 V. The engine speed is less than 6,000 RPM. DTC P167D runs continuously when the above conditions are met.
DTC: P1682	**Ignition 1 Switch Circuit 2:** P1682The powertrain relay is commanded on. Ignition 1 Signal voltage is greater than 5. 5 V. The DTC runs continuously when the above conditions are met.
DTC: P1682	**Ignition 1 Switch Circuit 2:** P1682The ignition is ON. The system voltage is greater than 6 V. The engine control module relay is commanded ON. DTC P1682 runs continuously when the above conditions are met.
DTC: P1682 00	**Ignition 1 Switch Circuit 2:** The ignition is ON. System voltage is more than 6 V. Powertrain relay is commanded ON. DTC P1682 00 runs continuously when the above conditions are met.
DTC: P1684	**Transmission Control Module (TCM) Power Up Temperature Sensor Performance:** P1684 - Fail Case 1 and 2No TFT DTCs P0711, P0712, or P0713. No ISS DTCs P0716 or P0717. No OSS DTCs P0722 or P0723. DTC P1684 has not passed this key ON. The engine speed is 500 RPM or greater for 5 seconds. The ignition voltage is between 8. 6 volts and 19. 0 volts. The TCM power up temperature is between -39 and +149°C (-38 and +300°F). P1684 - Fail Case 3The engine speed is 500 RPM or greater for 5 seconds. The ignition voltage is between 8. 6 volts and 19. 0 volts.
DTC: P1685	**Transmission Control Module (TCM) Power Up Temperature Sensor Circuit Low Voltage:** P1685No ISS DTCs P0716 or P0717. No OSS DTCs P0722 or P0723. The transmission output shaft speed is 200 RPM or greater for 200 seconds or more. The torque converter clutch (TCC) slip speed is 120 RPM or greater for 200 seconds or more. DTC P1686 has not failed this ignition cycle. The engine speed is 500 RPM or greater for 5 seconds. The ignition voltage is between 8. 6 volts and 19. 0 volts.
DTC: P1686	**Transmission Control Module (TCM) Power Up Temperature Sensor Circuit High Voltage:** P1686The engine speed is 500 RPM or greater for 5 seconds. The ignition voltage is between 8. 6 volts and 19. 0 volts. DTC P1686 has not failed this ignition cycle.
DTC: P168C	**Turbocharger Boost Control Position Slow Response - Increasing Position:** DTC P0045, P0047, P0048, P006E, P007C, P007D, P008F, P0117, P0118, P02E8, P02E9, P0401, P0402, P128E, P140B, P140C, P16A0, P16A1, P16A2, P2228, or P2229 is not set. The coolant temperature is greater than 70°C (158°F). The engine speed is between 1,000-1,800 RPM. The barometric pressure (BARO) is greater than 74. 8 kPa (10. 85 psi). The ambient air temperature is greater than -7°C (19. 4°F). The throttle position is less than 5 %. The turbocharger actuator position sensor offset learning is not active. The turbocharger vane cleaning/ wiping, procedure is not active. DTC P168C and P168D run continuously whenever the above conditions are met.

DTC	Trouble Code Title, Conditions, Possible Causes
DTC: P168D	**Turbocharger Boost Control Position Slow Response - Decreasing Position:** DTC P0045, P0047, P0048, P006E, P007C, P007D, P008F, P0117, P0118, P02E8, P02E9, P0401, P0402, P128E, P140B, P140C, P16A0, P16A1, P16A2, P2228, or P2229 is not set. The coolant temperature is greater than 70°C (158°F). The engine speed is between 1,000-1,800 RPM. The barometric pressure (BARO) is greater than 74. 8 kPa (10. 85 psi). The ambient air temperature is greater than -7°C (19. 4°F). The throttle position is less than 5 %. The turbocharger actuator position sensor offset learning is not active. The turbocharger vane cleaning/ wiping, procedure is not active. DTC P168C and P168D run continuously whenever the above conditions are met.
DTC: P16F3	**Control Module Redundant Memory Performance:** P0601, P0606, P062B, P0630, P16F3These DTCs run continuously when the ignition is ON.
DTC: P16F3	**Control Module Redundant Memory Performance:** P16F3 DTCs P0101, P0102, P0103, P0106, P0107, P0108 are not set. Engine speed is greater than 750 RPM. DTC P16F3 runs continuously when the above conditions have been met.
DTC: P16F3 00	**Control Module Redundant Memory Performance:** The ignition is in the unlock, accessory, run, or crank position. The system voltage is more than 5. 23 VDTCs P16F3 00 runs continuously when the above conditions are met.
DTC: P1750	**1-2 Shift Valve Performance:** No ISS DTCs P0716 or P0717. No OSS DTCs P0722 or P0723. The engine is running for 5 seconds or more. The vehicle speed is greater than 24 km/h (15 mph). The calc. throttle position is greater than 8 percent. The transmission fluid temperature (TFT) is 20°C (68°F) or more. The engine torque is greater than 50 N·m (37 lb ft). The time since the last gear change is 2 seconds.
DTC: P1751	**Shift Valve 1 Performance:** DTCs P0716, P0717, P0722, P0723, P0741, P0742, P1751, P2762, P2763, or P2764 are not set. The engine speed is 500 RPM or greater for 5 seconds or greater. The transmission fluid temperature (TFT) is 20-130°C (68-266°F). The calculated throttle position is between 8-90 percent. The engine torque is greater than 50 N·m (36 lb ft). No upshift or downshift in process. The attained gear slip is 70 RPM or greater.
DTC: P1751	**Shift Valve 1 Performance:** No ISS DTCs P0716 or P0717. No OSS DTCs P0722 or P0723. No TCC Performance DTCs P0741 or P0742. No TCC Electrical DTCs P2763, P2763, or P2764. DTC 1751 has not failed this ignition cycle. The engine run time is greater than 5 seconds. The ignition voltage is between 8. 6 volts and 19. 0 volts. The transmission fluid temperature (TFT) is 20-130°C (68-266°F). The calc. throttle position is 8 percent or greater. The engine torque is greater than 59 ft. lbs. (80 Nm). No upshift or downshift in process. The attained gear slip is equal to or greater than 100 RPM. The TCC is commanded OFF. Vehicle speed is greater than 16 km/h (20 mph). The TISS is equal to or greater than 1,100 RPM. Commanded gear is 2nd or greater. The gear ratio is between 0. 69-1. 97. Solenoid A is enabled.
DTC: P1761	**Up and Down Shift Switch Signal Circuit:** The engine speed is 400 RPM or greater for 5 seconds.
DTC: P1761	**Up and Down Shift Switch Signal Message Counter:** The TCM rolling counter diagnostic is enabled. The Tap Up and Tap Down message health is received from the BCM. The engine speed is 400 RPM or greater for 5 seconds.
DTC: P1762	**Transmission Mode Switch Signal Message:** The engine run time is greater than 5 seconds. No other CAN errors are present.
DTC: P1762	**Trans Mode Switch Signal Circuit:** The engine speed is greater than 500 RPM for 5 seconds. Ignition voltage is between 9. 0 volts and 19. 0 volts.
DTC: P1763	**Trans Mode Switch C circuit:** The engine speed is greater than 500 RPM for 5 seconds. Ignition voltage is between 9. 0 volts and 19. 0 volts.
DTC: P1793 71	**Vehicle Speed Sensor Performance Invalid Data:** The ignition is ON.
DTC: P1811	**Maximum Adapt and Long Shift:** The shift is adaptable. The 1-2, 2-3, or 3-4 shift adapt cell has reached the limit.
DTC: P1820	**Internal Mode Switch A Circuit Low Voltage:** P1820, P1822, P1823, P1825The engine is running for 5 seconds. The IMS indicates PARK for 1 second or greater. The engine torque is 50 N·m (37 lb ft) or greater. No engine torque malfunction.
DTC: P1822	**Internal Mode Switch B Circuit High Voltage:** P1820, P1822, P1823, P1825The engine is running for 5 seconds. The IMS indicates PARK for 1 second or greater. The engine torque is 50 N·m (37 lb ft) or greater. No engine torque malfunction.

DTC	Trouble Code Title, Conditions, Possible Causes
DTC: P1823	**Internal Mode Switch P Circuit Low Voltage:** P1820, P1822, P1823, P1825The engine is running for 5 seconds. The IMS indicates PARK for 1 second or greater. The engine torque is 50 N·m (37 lb ft) or greater. No engine torque malfunction.
DTC: P1825	**Internal Mode Switch - Invalid Range:** P1825 or P182EThe engine speed is 500 RPM or greater for 5 seconds. The ignition voltage is between 9. 0 volts and 18. 0 volts. Either the C1234 or CB26 pressure switch is pressurized. DTC P0101, P0102, P0103, P0121, P0122, P0123, P0722, P0723, or P182E is not set.
DTC: P1826	**Internal Mode Switch C Circuit High Voltage:** P1826No OSS DTC P0722 or P0723. DTC P1826 has not passed this key cycle. The engine is running for 5 seconds. The IMS indicates PARK for 1 second or greater. The engine torque is 50 N·m (37 lb ft) or greater. Vehicle speed is 16 km/h (10 mph) or greater. No engine torque malfunction.
DTC: P182A	**Internal Mode Switch A Circuit Low Voltage:** P182A, P182C or P182DThe ignition voltage is between 8 and 18 volts. The engine speed is between 500 and 6,500 RPMs for 5 seconds. The IMS indicates PARK for at least 1 second. No engine torque malfunction. The engine torque is between 37-1,100 ft. lbs. (50-1,492 Nm).
DTC: P182C	**Internal Mode Switch B Circuit High Voltage:** P182A, P182C or P182DThe ignition voltage is between 8 and 18 volts. The engine speed is between 500 and 6,500 RPMs for 5 seconds. The IMS indicates PARK for at least 1 second. No engine torque malfunction. The engine torque is between 37-1,100 ft. lbs. (50-1,492 Nm).
DTC: P182D	**Internal Mode Switch P Circuit Low Voltage:** P182A, P182C or P182DThe ignition voltage is between 8 and 18 volts. The engine speed is between 500 and 6,500 RPMs for 5 seconds. The IMS indicates PARK for at least 1 second. No engine torque malfunction. The engine torque is between 37-1,100 ft. lbs. (50-1,492 Nm).
DTC: P182E	**Internal Mode Switch - Invalid Range:** P182EDTC P0101, P0102, P0103, P0106, P0107, P0108, P0171, P0172, P0174, P0175, P0201, P0202, P0203, P0204, P0205, P0206, P0207, P0208, P0300, P0301, P0302, P0303, P0304, P0305, P0306, P0307, P0308, P0401, P042E, P0722, or P0723 is not set. The engine speed is 400 RPM or greater for 5 seconds. The ignition voltage is 8. 6 volts or greater. The engine torque signal is valid.
DTC: P182F	**Internal Mode Switch C Circuit High Voltage:** P182FNo output speed sensor (OSS) DTCs P0722 or P0723. No engine torque signal DTC P2637. Vehicle speed is greater than 16 km/h (10 mph). The engine torque is greater than 50 N·m (37 lb ft). The IMS indicates Park/Neutral for at least 1 second. DTC P1826 has not passed during the current ignition cycle. The gear ratio is within one of the following ranges:3. 33:1 to 3. 50:1 for first gear2. 16:1 to 2. 27:1 for second gear1. 56:1 to 1. 64:1 for third gear0. 98:1 to 1. 03:1 for fourth gear
DTC: P1831	**Pressure Control (PC)/Shift Lock Solenoid Control Circuit Low Voltage:** P1831The engine speed is greater than 500 RPM for 5 seconds. Ignition voltage is between 8. 6-19. 0 volts. High side driver 1 is enabled. DTC P1831 has not failed this ignition cycle.
DTC: P1832	**Pressure Control (PC)/Shift Lock Solenoid Control Circuit High Voltage:** P1832 DTC P1832 has not failed this ignition cycle.
DTC: P1876	**Up and Down Shift Enable Switch Circuit Low Voltage:** The engine speed is 400 RPM or greater for 5 seconds. The ignition voltage is 9. 0 volts or greater. No DTCs P0815, P0816, P0826, P1761, P1825, P1876, P1877, P1915, or U0100.
DTC: P1876	**Up and Down Shift Enable Switch Circuit Low Voltage:** P1876To TR switch DTC P0705. No TAP system DTCs P0815, P0816, or P0826. No TFP DTCs P1810, P1816, or P1818. No DTC P1877. No Communication DTC U0100. The engine speed is greater than 500 RPM for 5 seconds. The ignition is ON.
DTC: P1877	**Up and Down Shift Enable Switch Circuit High Voltage:** P1877To TR switch DTC P0705. No TAP system DTCs P0815, P0816, or P0826. No TFP DTCs P1810, P1816, or P1818. No DTC P1876. No Communication DTC U0100. The engine speed is greater than 500 RPM for 5 seconds. The ignition is ON.
DTC: P1915	**Internal Mode Switch Does Not Indicate Park/Neutral (P/N) During Start:** P1915The engine is cranking for more than 2. 5 seconds. The engine speed is greater than 500 RPM. 1st gear request for 7 minutes.
DTC: P1915	**Internal Mode Switch Does Not Indicate Park/Neutral During Start:** P1915 DTC P0722, P0723, or P1915 is not set. The transmission output shaft speed is 90 RPM or less. The ignition voltage is 6. 0 volts or greater.
DTC: P1915	**Internal Mode Switch Does Not Indicate Park/Neutral (P/N) During Start:** P1915 DTC P0722, P0723, or P1915 is not set. The transmission output shaft speed is less than 90 RPM or less. The ignition voltage is between 9. 0 volts and 18. 0 volts. The IMS does not indicate park or neutral.

OBD II Trouble Code List (P2xxx Codes)

DTC	Trouble Code Title, Conditions, Possible Causes
DTC: P2002	**Diesel Particulate Filter Efficiency:** DTCs P0101, P2228, P2229, P2453, P2454, and P2455 are not set. The engine speed is greater than 600 RPM. The ambient air temperature is greater than -7°C (19°F). The BARO is greater than 75 kPa (11 psi). The engine run time is greater than 10 s. A regeneration event must be complete. The DPF inlet and outlet temperatures are between 100-400°C (212-752°F). The time since last DPF regeneration is less than 20 minutes. The distance since last DPF regeneration is less than 48 km (30 mi). The Soot Mass is less than 44 grams. DTC P2002 runs once when the above conditions are met.
DTC: P2002 00	**Diesel Particulate Filter (DPF) Low Efficiency Malfunction:** The engine is running. The DTC runs continuously when the above condition is met.
DTC: P2008	**Intake Manifold Runner Control Valve Control Circuit:** Engine is running
DTC: P2008 00	**Intake Manifold Runner Control Valve Control Circuit:** The engine is operating. The ignition voltage is between 11-16 V. The DTCs run continuously once the above condition is met.
DTC: P2009	**Intake Manifold Runner Control Valve Control Circuit Low Voltage:** Engine is running
DTC: P200A	**Intake Manifold Runner Control Valve Control Circuit Performance:** Engine is running
DTC: P2010	**Intake Manifold Runner Control Valve Control Circuit High Voltage:** Engine is running
DTC: P2016	**Intake Manifold Runner Control Valve Feedback Circuit Low Voltage:** Engine is running
DTC: P2017	**Intake Manifold Runner Control Valve Feedback Circuit High Voltage:** Engine is running
DTC: P202E	**Reductant Injector Performance:** P202EDTCs P1048, P1049, P2047, P2048, or P2049 are not set. SCR reductant level not in restriction or empty level state. The engine speed is greater than 600 RPM. The battery voltage is greater than 11 V. The ambient air and emission reduction fluid tank temperatures are warmer than -7°C (19°F). The engine run time is greater than 10 s. The calculated reductant injector temperature is between -7 to +100°C (19-212°F). The reductant pressure is between 350-650 kPa (51-94 psi). The BARO pressure is between 75-130 kPa (11-19 psi). The DTC runs continuously once the above conditions are met.
DTC: P2031 03	**Exhaust Gas Temperature Sensor 2 Circuit Low Voltage:** The ignition is ON. The DTCs run continuously when the above condition is met.
DTC: P2031 07	**Exhaust Gas Temperature Sensor 2 Circuit High Voltage:** The ignition is ON. The DTCs run continuously when the above condition is met.
DTC: P2032	**Exhaust Gas Temperature Sensor 2 Circuit Low Voltage:** The ignition is ON or the engine is running. The DTCs run continuously when the above conditions are met.
DTC: P2032 00	**Exhaust Gas Temperature Sensor 2 Circuit Low Voltage:** The ignition is ON. The DTCs run continuously when the above condition is met.
DTC: P2033	**Exhaust Gas Temperature Sensor 2 Circuit High Voltage:** The ignition is ON or the engine is running. The DTCs run continuously when the above conditions are met.
DTC: P2033 00	**Exhaust Gas Temperature Sensor 2 Circuit High Voltage:** The ignition is ON. The DTCs run continuously when the above condition is met.
DTC: P203B	**Reductant Level Sensor Performance:** The engine speed is greater than 600 RPM. The battery voltage is greater than 11 V. The ambient air and emission reduction fluid tank temperatures are warmer than -7°C (19°F) - DTC P203B only. The engine run time is greater than 10 s. The DTCs run continuously once the above conditions are met.
DTC: P203C	**Reductant Level Sensor 1 Circuit Low Voltage:** The engine speed is greater than 600 RPM. The battery voltage is greater than 11 V. The ambient air and emission reduction fluid tank temperatures are warmer than -7°C (19°F) - DTC P203B only. The engine run time is greater than 10 s. The DTCs run continuously once the above conditions are met.
DTC: P203D	**Reductant Level Sensor 1 Circuit High Voltage:** The engine speed is greater than 600 RPM. The battery voltage is greater than 11 V. The ambient air and emission reduction fluid tank temperatures are warmer than -7°C (19°F) - DTC P203B only. The engine run time is greater than 10 s. The DTCs run continuously once the above conditions are met.

DTC	Trouble Code Title, Conditions, Possible Causes
DTC: P2047	**Reductant Injector Control Circuit:** The engine is running. The battery voltage is greater than 11 V. The ECM is commanding the reductant injector duty cycle greater than 0 %. The Reductant Injection Inhibit Reason displays None. The DTCs run continuously once the above conditions are met.
DTC: P2048	**Reductant Injector Control Circuit Low Voltage:** The engine is running. The battery voltage is greater than 11 V. The ECM is commanding the reductant injector duty cycle greater than 0 %. The Reductant Injection Inhibit Reason displays None. The DTCs run continuously once the above conditions are met.
DTC: P2049	**Reductant Injector Control Circuit High Voltage:** The engine is running. The battery voltage is greater than 11 V. The ECM is commanding the reductant injector duty cycle greater than 0 %. The Reductant Injection Inhibit Reason displays None. The DTCs run continuously once the above conditions are met.
DTC: P204B	**Reductant Pressure Sensor Performance:** DTCs P204C or P204D are not set. The ignition is ON. The BARO pressure is greater than 75 kPa (11 psi). The ambient air temperatures is warmer than -7°C (+19°F). The exhaust temperature sensor 2 is less than 170°C (338° F). The DTC runs continuously when the above conditions are met.
DTC: P204C	**Reductant Pressure Sensor Circuit Low Voltage:** The engine speed is greater than 600 RPM. The battery voltage is greater than 11 V. The DTCs run continuously when the above condition is met.
DTC: P204D	**Reductant Pressure Sensor Circuit High Voltage:** The engine speed is greater than 600 RPM. The battery voltage is greater than 11 V. The DTCs run continuously when the above condition is met.
DTC: P204F	**Reductant System Performance:** DTCs P204B, P204C, P204D, P208A, P208D, P20A0, P20A2, or P20A3, are not set. The engine speed is greater than 600 RPM. The battery voltage is greater than 11 V. The engine run time is greater than 10 s. The DTC runs continuously once the above conditions are met.
DTC: P205B	**Reductant Tank Temperature Sensor Performance:** DTC P205D is not set. - for P205B only. The ignition is OFF for 8 hours. The ECM monitors the ECT, EGT 2, and EGT 4 for the coldest and warmest of the three sensors. The difference between the coldest and warmest should be less than 7°C (45°F). The engine speed is greater than 600 RPM. The battery voltage is greater than 11 V. The DTCs run once per drive cycle when the above conditions are met for greater than 20 s.
DTC: P205C	**Reductant Tank Temperature Sensor Circuit Low Voltage:** DTC P205D is not set. - for P205B only. The ignition is OFF for 8 hours. The ECM monitors the ECT, EGT 2, and EGT 4 for the coldest and warmest of the three sensors. The difference between the coldest and warmest should be less than 7°C (45°F). The engine speed is greater than 600 RPM. The battery voltage is greater than 11 V. The DTCs run once per drive cycle when the above conditions are met for greater than 20 s.
DTC: P205D	**Reductant Tank Temperature Sensor Circuit High Voltage:** DTC P205D is not set. - for P205B only. The ignition is OFF for 8 hours. The ECM monitors the ECT, EGT 2, and EGT 4 for the coldest and warmest of the three sensors. The difference between the coldest and warmest should be less than 7°C (45°F). The engine speed is greater than 600 RPM. The battery voltage is greater than 11 V. The DTCs run once per drive cycle when the above conditions are met for greater than 20 s.
DTC: P2066	**Fuel Level Sensor 2 Performance:** The engine is running. The system voltage is between 11-16 V.
DTC: P2067	**Fuel Level Sensor 2 Circuit Low Voltage:** The engine is running. The system voltage is between 11-16 V.
DTC: P2068	**Fuel Level Sensor 2 Circuit High Voltage:** The engine is running. The system voltage is between 11-16 V.
DTC: P2070 00	**Intake Manifold Tuning Control Valve Stuck Open:** The ignition is ON or the engine is operating. The intake manifold tuning valve solenoid has been commanded ON and OFF at least once during the ignition cycle. These DTCs run continuously once the above condition is met.
DTC: P2071 00	**Intake Manifold Tuning Control Valve Stuck Closed:** The ignition is ON or the engine is operating. The intake manifold tuning valve solenoid has been commanded ON and OFF at least once during the ignition cycle. These DTCs run continuously once the above condition is met.
DTC: P2076 00	**Intake Manifold Tuning Control Valve Position Sensor Performance:** The ignition is ON or the engine is operating. The intake manifold tuning valve solenoid has been commanded ON and OFF at least once during the ignition cycle. These DTCs run continuously once the above condition is met.

DTC	Trouble Code Title, Conditions, Possible Causes
DTC: P2077 00	**Intake Manifold Tuning Control Valve Position Sensor Circuit Low Voltage:** The ignition is ON or the engine is operating. The intake manifold tuning valve solenoid has been commanded ON and OFF at least once during the ignition cycle. These DTCs run continuously once the above condition is met.
DTC: P2078 00	**Intake Manifold Tuning Control Valve Position Sensor Circuit High Voltage:** The ignition is ON or the engine is operating. The intake manifold tuning valve solenoid has been commanded ON and OFF at least once during the ignition cycle. These DTCs run continuously once the above condition is met.
DTC: P207F	**Incorrect Reductant Composition:** The BARO pressure is greater than 75 kPa (11 psi). The ambient air and reductant temperatures are warmer than -7°C (19°F). The engine speed is between 1,000-3,000 RPM. The average SCR temperature is between 240-290°C (464-554°F). The emission reduction fluid tank level is not empty. The battery voltage is greater than 11 V. The engine run time is greater than 10 s. The DTCs run once per drive cycle when the above conditions are met.
DTC: P2080	**Exhaust Gas Temperature Sensor 1 Performance:** P2080 DTC P007C, P007D, P0097, P0098, P0101, P0102, P0103, P0107, P0108, P0112, P0113, P0401, P0402, P0403, P0405, P0406, P046C, P0545, P0546, P111C, P111D, P20E2, P2032, P2033, P2228 or P2229 is not set. The engine is running for at least 327 s. The engine speed is between 700-3000 RPM for 60 s. The calculated fuel rate is between 5-80mm ; for 60 s. DPF regeneration or exhaust gas temperature monitoring has not been active in the last 25 minutes. Exhaust gas temperature sensor 1 has changed less than 7°C (12. 6°F) in 5 s. The DTC runs continuously when the above conditions are met.
DTC: P2080 08	**Exhaust Gas Temperature Sensor 1 Performance Signal Invalid:** The ignition is ON, or the engine is running. The DTCs run continuously when the above conditions are met.
DTC: P2080 13	**Exhaust Gas Temperature Sensor 1 Performance Low Voltage/High Temperature:** The ignition is ON, or the engine is running. The DTCs run continuously when the above conditions are met.
DTC: P2080 14	**Exhaust Gas Temperature Sensor 1 Performance High Voltage/Low Temperature:** The ignition is ON, or the engine is running. The DTCs run continuously when the above conditions are met.
DTC: P2081 00	**Exhaust Gas Temperature Sensor 1 Circuit Intermittent:** The ignition is ON. The DTCs run continuously when the above condition is met.
DTC: P2084	**Exhaust Gas Temperature Sensor 2 Performance:** P2084 DTC P007C, P007D, P0097, P0098, P0101, P0102, P0103, P0107, P0108, P0112, P0113, P0401, P0402, P0403, P0405, P0406, P046C, P0545, P0546, P111C, P111D, P20E2, P2032, P2033, P2228 or P2229 is not set. The engine is running for at least 327 s. The engine speed is between 700-3000 RPM for 60 s. The calculated fuel rate is between 5-80mm ; for 60 s. DPF regeneration or exhaust gas temperature monitoring has not been active in the last 25 minutes. Exhaust gas temperature sensor 2 has changed less than 7°C (12. 6°F) in 5 s. The DTC runs continuously when the above conditions are met.
DTC: P2084 08	**Exhaust Gas Temperature Sensor 2 Performance Signal Invalid:** The ignition is ON, or the engine is running. The DTCs run continuously when the above conditions are met.
DTC: P2084 13	**Exhaust Gas Temperature Sensor 2 Performance Low Voltage/High Temperature:** The ignition is ON, or the engine is running. The DTCs run continuously when the above conditions are met.
DTC: P2084 14	**Exhaust Gas Temperature Sensor 2 Performance High Voltage/Low Temperature:** The ignition is ON, or the engine is running. The DTCs run continuously when the above conditions are met.
DTC: P2085 00	**Exhaust Gas Temperature Sensor 2 Circuit Intermittent:** The ignition is ON. The DTCs run continuously when the above condition is met.
DTC: P2088	**Intake Camshaft Position Actuator Solenoid Control Circuit Low Voltage:** The engine speed is greater than 80 RPM. The ignition voltage is between 10-18 volts. The ECM has commanded the CMP actuator solenoid ON and OFF at least once during the ignition cycle. DTCs P0010, P0013, P2088, P2089, P2090, and P2091 run continuously once the above conditions are met.
DTC: P2088 00	**Intake Camshaft Position Actuator Solenoid Valve Control Circuit Low Voltage:** The engine speed is greater than 80 RPM. DTC P0606 00 is not set. The ignition voltage is between 10-18 V. The ECM has commanded the camshaft position actuator intake or camshaft position actuator exhaust solenoid ON and OFF at least once during the ignition cycle. DTCs P0010 00, P0013 00, P2088 00, P0289 00, P2090 00, and P2091 00 run continuously once the above conditions are met for greater than 1 s.
DTC: P2089	**Intake Camshaft Position Actuator Solenoid Control Circuit High Voltage:** The engine speed is greater than 80 RPM. The ignition voltage is between 10-18 volts. The ECM has commanded the CMP actuator solenoid ON and OFF at least once during the ignition cycle. DTCs P0010, P0013, P2088, P2089, P2090, and P2091 run continuously once the above conditions are met.

DTC	Trouble Code Title, Conditions, Possible Causes
DTC: P2089 00	**Intake Camshaft Position Actuator Solenoid Valve Control Circuit High Voltage:** The engine speed is greater than 80 RPM. DTC P0606 00 is not set. The ignition voltage is between 10-18 V. The ECM has commanded the camshaft position actuator intake or camshaft position actuator exhaust solenoid ON and OFF at least once during the ignition cycle. DTCs P0010 00, P0013 00, P2088 00, P0289 00, P2090 00, and P2091 00 run continuously once the above conditions are met for greater than 1 s.
DTC: P208A	**Reductant Pump Control Circuit:** DTCs P204F, P20A1, or P2510 are not set. The battery voltage is greater than 11 V. The engine speed is greater than 600 RPM. The engine run time is greater than 10 s. The DTCs run continuously once the above conditions are met.
DTC: P208B	**Reductant Pump Performance:** The engine speed is greater than 600 RPM. The engine run time is greater than 10 s. The reductant remaining defrost time is less than 120 s. The reductant motor operating for greater than 2 s. The BARO is greater than 75 kPa (11 psi). The emission reduction fluid tank is not empty. The ambient air and the emission reduction fluid tank is warmer than -7°C (19°F). The DTC runs continuously once the above conditions are met.
DTC: P208D	**Reductant Pump Control Circuit High Voltage:** DTCs P204F, P20A1, or P2510 are not set. The battery voltage is greater than 11 V. The engine speed is greater than 600 RPM. The engine run time is greater than 10 s. The DTCs run continuously once the above conditions are met.
DTC: P2090	**Exhaust Camshaft Position Actuator Solenoid Control Circuit Low Voltage:** The engine speed is greater than 80 RPM. The ignition voltage is between 10-18 volts. The ECM has commanded the CMP actuator solenoid ON and OFF at least once during the ignition cycle. DTCs P0010, P0013, P2088, P2089, P2090, and P2091 run continuously once the above conditions are met.
DTC: P2090 00	**Exhaust Camshaft Position Actuator Solenoid Valve Control Circuit Low Voltage:** The engine speed is greater than 80 RPM. DTC P0606 00 is not set. The ignition voltage is between 10-18 V. The ECM has commanded the camshaft position actuator intake or camshaft position actuator exhaust solenoid ON and OFF at least once during the ignition cycle. DTCs P0010 00, P0013 00, P2088 00, P0289 00, P2090 00, and P2091 00 run continuously once the above conditions are met for greater than 1 s.
DTC: P2091	**Exhaust Camshaft Position Actuator Solenoid Control Circuit High Voltage:** The engine speed is greater than 80 RPM. The ignition voltage is between 10-18 volts. The ECM has commanded the CMP actuator solenoid ON and OFF at least once during the ignition cycle. DTCs P0010, P0013, P2088, P2089, P2090, and P2091 run continuously once the above conditions are met.
DTC: P2091 00	**Exhaust Camshaft Position Actuator Solenoid Valve Control Circuit High Voltage:** The engine speed is greater than 80 RPM. DTC P0606 00 is not set. The ignition voltage is between 10-18 V. The ECM has commanded the camshaft position actuator intake or camshaft position actuator exhaust solenoid ON and OFF at least once during the ignition cycle. DTCs P0010 00, P0013 00, P2088 00, P0289 00, P2090 00, and P2091 00 run continuously once the above conditions are met for greater than 1 s.
DTC: P2096	**Post Catalyst Fuel Trim System Low Limit Bank 1:** Before the ECM can report DTC P2096 or P2098 failed, DTCs P0030, P0031, P0032, P0036, P0037, P0038, P0050, P0051, P0052, P0056, P0057, P0058, P013A, P013C, P013E, P0130, P0131, P0132, P0133, P0135, P0137, P0138, P014A, P0140, P0141, P0150, P0151, P0152, P0153, P0155, P0157, P0158, P0160, P0161, P2232, P2235, P2270, P2271, P2272, and P2273 must run and pass. DTC P0100, P0101, P0102, P0103, P0420, P0430, P0442, P0443, P0455, P0458, P0459, P2177, P2178, P2179, P2180, P2187, P2188, P2189 or P2190 is not set. The engine speed is 1,280-3,480 RPM. The engine load is 17-65 percent and steady. The closed loop fuel control is active for greater than 1 second. The calculated exhaust gas temperature is greater than 250°C (482°F). DTC P2096 and P2098 run continuously when the conditions above have been met for greater than 130 seconds.
DTC: P2096 00	**Post Catalyst Fuel Trim System Low Limit Bank 1:** The engine is running. The ignition voltage is greater than 10 V. The barometric pressure is greater than 72 kPa (10. 44 PSI). The intake air temperature (IAT) sensor parameter is less than -40°C (-40°F).
DTC: P2096 00	**Post Catalyst Fuel Trim System Low Limit:** P2096 00 DTCs P000A 00, P000B 00, P0010 00, P0011 00, P0013 00, P0016 00, P0017 00, P0030 00, P0031 00, P0032 00, P0106 00, P0107 00, P0108 00, P0117 00, P0118 00, P0119 00, P0121 00, P0122 00, P0123 00, P0131 00, P0132 00, P0133 00, P0137 00, P0138 00, P0139 00, P0140 00, P0141 00, P0171 00, P0172 00, P0201 00, P0202 00, P0203 00, P0204 00, P0221 00, P0222 00, P0223 00, P0261 00, P0262 00, P0264 00, P0265 00, P0267 00, P0268 00, P0270 00, P0271 00, P0300 00, P0301 00, P0302 00, P0303 00, P0304 00, P0313 00, P0335 00, P0336 00, P0340 00, P0341 00, P0365 00, P0366 00, P0420 00, P0443 00, P0458 00, P0459 00, P1106 00, P2088 00, P2089 00, P2090 00, P2091 00, P2100 00, P2101 00, P2176 00, P2270 00, P2271 00, P2297 00, P2300 00, P2301 00, P2303 00, P2304 00, P2306 00, P2307 00, P2309 00, P2310 00, P2A00 00, P2A01 00 are not set. The ignition is ON. The evaporative emission (EVAP) system is not purging. The post catalyst fuel trim is enabled. These DTCs run continuously when the above conditions have been met.

DTC	Trouble Code Title, Conditions, Possible Causes
DTC: P2097	**Post Catalyst Fuel Trim System High Limit Bank 1:** Before the ECM can report DTC P2097 or P2099 failed, DTCs P0030, P0031, P0032, P0036, P0037, P0038, P0050, P0051, P0052, P0056, P0057, P0058, P013A, P013C, P013E, P0130, P0131, P0132, P0133, P0135, P0137, P0138, P014A, P0140, P0141, P0150, P0151, P0152, P0153, P0155, P0157, P0158, P0160, P0161, P2232, P2235, P2270, P2271, P2272, and P2273 must run and pass. DTC P0100, P0101, P0102, P0103, P0420, P0430, P0442, P0443, P0455, P0458, P0459, P2177, P2178, P2179, P2180, P2187, P2188, P2189 or P2190 is not set. The engine speed is 1,280-3,480 RPM. The engine load is 17-65 percent and steady. The closed loop fuel control is active for greater than 1 second. The calculated exhaust gas temperature is greater than 250°C (482°F). DTC P2097 and P2099 run continuously when the conditions above have been met for greater than 130 seconds.
DTC: P2097	**Post Catalyst Fuel Trim System High Limit Bank 1:** P2097 DTCs P0030, P0031, P0032, P0053, P0130, P0131, P0132, P0133, P0135, P0137, P0138, P0140, P2231, P2232, P2243, P2251, P2270, P2271, P2297, P2626 are not set. The engine speed is between 1,200-2,900 RPM. The engine load is between 16-21 percent. The engine is in Closed Loop for 3 seconds. The DTC runs continuously when the above conditions have been met for 1 second.
DTC: P2097 00	**Post Catalyst Fuel Trim System High Limit Bank 1:** The engine is running. The ignition voltage is greater than 10 V. The barometric pressure is greater than 72 kPa (10. 44 PSI). The intake air temperature (IAT) sensor parameter is less than -40°C (-40°F).
DTC: P2097 00	**Post Catalyst Fuel Trim System High Limit:** P2097 00 DTCs P000A 00, P000B 00, P0010 00, P0011 00, P0013 00, P0016 00, P0017 00, P0030 00, P0031 00, P0032 00, P0117 00, P0118 00, P0119 00, P0121 00, P0122 00, P0123 00, P0131 00, P0132 00, P0133 00, P0137 00, P0138 00, P0139 00, P0140 00, P0141 00, P0171 00, P0172 00, P0201 00, P0202 00, P0203 00, P0204 00, P0221 00, P0222 00, P0223 00, P0261 00, P0262 00, P0264 00, P0265 00, P0267 00, P0268 00, P0270 00, P0271 00, P0300 00, P0301 00, P0302 00, P0303 00, P0304 00, P0313 00, P0335 00, P0336 00, P0340 00, P0341 00, P0365 00, P0366 00, P0420 00, P0443 00, P0458 00, P0459 00, P2088 00, P2089 00, P2090 00, P2091 00, P2100 00, P2101 00, P2176 00, P2270 00, P2271 00, P2297 00, P2300 00, P2301 00, P2303 00, P2304 00, P2306 00, P2307 00, P2309 00, P2310 00, P2A00 00, P2A01 00 are not set. The ignition is ON. The evaporative emission (EVAP) system is not purging. The post catalyst fuel trim is enabled. This DTC P2097 00 runs continuously when the above conditions have been met.
DTC: P2098	**Post Catalyst Fuel Trim System Low Limit Bank 2:** Before the ECM can report DTC P2096 or P2098 failed, DTCs P0030, P0031, P0032, P0036, P0037, P0038, P0050, P0051, P0052, P0056, P0057, P0058, P013A, P013C, P013E, P0130, P0131, P0132, P0133, P0135, P0137, P0138, P014A, P0140, P0141, P0150, P0151, P0152, P0153, P0155, P0157, P0158, P0160, P0161, P2232, P2235, P2270, P2271, P2272, and P2273 must run and pass. DTC P0100, P0101, P0102, P0103, P0420, P0430, P0442, P0443, P0455, P0458, P0459, P2177, P2178, P2179, P2180, P2187, P2188, P2189 or P2190 is not set. The engine speed is 1,280-3,480 RPM. The engine load is 17-65 percent and steady. The closed loop fuel control is active for greater than 1 second. The calculated exhaust gas temperature is greater than 250°C (482°F). DTC P2096 and P2098 run continuously when the conditions above have been met for greater than 130 seconds.
DTC: P2099	**Post Catalyst Fuel Trim System High Limit Bank 2:** Before the ECM can report DTC P2097 or P2099 failed, DTCs P0030, P0031, P0032, P0036, P0037, P0038, P0050, P0051, P0052, P0056, P0057, P0058, P013A, P013C, P013E, P0130, P0131, P0132, P0133, P0135, P0137, P0138, P014A, P0140, P0141, P0150, P0151, P0152, P0153, P0155, P0157, P0158, P0160, P0161, P2232, P2235, P2270, P2271, P2272, and P2273 must run and pass. DTC P0100, P0101, P0102, P0103, P0420, P0430, P0442, P0443, P0455, P0458, P0459, P2177, P2178, P2179, P2180, P2187, P2188, P2189 or P2190 is not set. The engine speed is 1,280-3,480 RPM. The engine load is 17-65 percent and steady. The closed loop fuel control is active for greater than 1 second. The calculated exhaust gas temperature is greater than 250°C (482°F). DTC P2097 and P2099 run continuously when the conditions above have been met for greater than 130 seconds.
DTC: P20A0	**Reductant Purge Valve Control Circuit:** The battery voltage is greater than 11 V. The engine speed is greater than 600 RPM. The engine run time is greater than 10 s. The DTCs run continuously when the above conditions are met.
DTC: P20A1	**Reductant Purge Valve Performance:** DTCs P1045, P204C, P204D, P208A, P208D, P20A0, P20A2, or P20A3 are not set. The battery voltage is greater than 11 V. The engine speed is greater than 600 RPM. The engine run time is greater than 10 s. The initial reductant system pressure is greater than 350 kPa (51 psi). The ambient and DEF temperature is warmer than -7°C (19°F). The DTCs run continuously when the above conditions are met.
DTC: P20A2	**Reductant Purge Valve Control Circuit Low Voltage:** The battery voltage is greater than 11 V. The engine speed is greater than 600 RPM. The engine run time is greater than 10 s. The DTCs run continuously when the above conditions are met.
DTC: P20A3	**Reductant Purge Valve Control Circuit High Voltage:** The battery voltage is greater than 11 V. The engine speed is greater than 600 RPM. The engine run time is greater than 10 s. The DTCs run continuously when the above conditions are met.

DTC	Trouble Code Title, Conditions, Possible Causes
DTC: P20B9	**Reductant Heater 1 Control Circuit:** P20B9, P20BD, or P20C1 DTC P220B is not set. The DEF heater is commanded ON. The glow plug control module temperature is less than 123°C (254°F). The glow plug control module battery voltage is between 7-16 V. The DTCs run continuously once the above conditions are met.
DTC: P20BA	**Reductant Heater 1 Performance:** P20BADTC P205B, P205C, and P205D are not set. The emission reduction fluid tank heaters are active for 1,000-3,000 s. The emission reduction fluid tank level is greater than 20 %. The emission reduction fluid tank temperature is colder than -16°C (3°F) or hotter than 3003°C (5437°F). The vehicle speed is greater than 5 km/h (3 mph). The battery voltage is greater than 11 V. The engine speed is greater than 600 RPM.
DTC: P20BB	**Reductant Heater 1 Control Circuit Low Voltage:** P20BB, P20BF, or P20C3 DTC P220B is not set. The DEF heater is commanded ON. The glow plug control module temperature is less than 123°C (254°F). The glow plug control module battery voltage is between 7-16. 5 V. The DTCs run continuously once the above conditions are met.
DTC: P20BC	**Reductant Heater 1 Control Circuit High Voltage:** P20BC, P20C0, or P20C4The DEF heater is commanded OFF.
DTC: P20BD	**Reductant Heater 2 Control Circuit:** P20B9, P20BD, or P20C1 DTC P220B is not set. The DEF heater is commanded ON. The glow plug control module temperature is less than 123°C (254°F). The glow plug control module battery voltage is between 7-16 V. The DTCs run continuously once the above conditions are met.
DTC: P20BF	**Reductant Heater 2 Control Circuit Low Voltage:** P20BB, P20BF, or P20C3 DTC P220B is not set. The DEF heater is commanded ON. The glow plug control module temperature is less than 123°C (254°F). The glow plug control module battery voltage is between 7-16. 5 V. The DTCs run continuously once the above conditions are met.
DTC: P20C0	**Reductant Heater 2 Control Circuit High Voltage:** P20BC, P20C0, or P20C4The DEF heater is commanded OFF.
DTC: P20C1	**Reductant Heater 3 Control Circuit:** P20B9, P20BD, or P20C1 DTC P220B is not set. The DEF heater is commanded ON. The glow plug control module temperature is less than 123°C (254°F). The glow plug control module battery voltage is between 7-16 V. The DTCs run continuously once the above conditions are met.
DTC: P20C3	**Reductant Heater 3 Control Circuit Low Voltage:** P20BB, P20BF, or P20C3 DTC P220B is not set. The DEF heater is commanded ON. The glow plug control module temperature is less than 123°C (254°F). The glow plug control module battery voltage is between 7-16. 5 V. The DTCs run continuously once the above conditions are met.
DTC: P20C4	**Reductant Heater 3 Control Circuit High Voltage:** P20BC, P20C0, or P20C4The DEF heater is commanded OFF.
DTC: P20CB	**Exhaust Aftertreatment Fuel Injector Control Circuit:** Battery Voltage is greater than 11 V. Engine speed is greater than 600 RPM.
DTC: P20CC	**Exhaust Aftertreatment Fuel Injector Performance:** Engine speed is greater than 600 RPM. Exhaust temperature is greater than 300° C (572° F). Time since last completed regeneration is greater than 15 minutes. Time since last indirect fuel injector nozzle cleaning request is greater than 5 minutes.
DTC: P20CD	**Exhaust Aftertreatment Fuel Injector Control Circuit Low Voltage:** Battery Voltage is greater than 11 V. Engine speed is greater than 600 RPM.
DTC: P20CE	**Exhaust Aftertreatment Fuel Injector Control Circuit High Voltage:** Battery Voltage is greater than 11 V. Engine speed is greater than 600 RPM.
DTC: P20E2	**Exhaust Temperature Sensor 1-2 Correlation:** DTCs P0545, P0546, P2032, P2033 are not set. The engine has been OFF for greater than 5 hours. The engine is running. The ambient temperature is greater than 10°C (50°F). DTC P20E2 runs once per key cycle within the above enabling conditions.
DTC: P20E2	**Exhaust Gas Temperature Sensors 1-2 Not Plausible:** P20E2Condition 1 DTC P0016, P0112, P0113, P0335, P0336, P0340, P0341, P0545, P0546, P2032, or P2033 is not set. The ignition has been OFF for greater than 8 hours. The engine is running. The ambient air temperature is greater than -60°C (-76°F). OR Condition 2 DTC P0016, P0112, P0113, P0335, P0336, P0340, P0341, P0545, P0546, P2032, or P2033 is not set. The ignition has been OFF for greater than 8 hours. The engine is running. The ambient air temperature is greater than -60°C (-76°F). In the first 60 s of engine run time, the ECM determines that the engine block heater is OFF. DTC P02E0 runs once per key cycle when condition 1 or condition 2 above is met.

DTC	Trouble Code Title, Conditions, Possible Causes
DTC: P20EE	**NOx Catalyst Efficiency Below Threshold:** The BARO pressure is greater than 75 kPa (11 psi). The ambient air and reductant temperatures are warmer than -7°C (19°F). The engine speed is between 1,000-3,000 RPM. The average SCR temperature is between 240-290°C (464-554°F). The emission reduction fluid tank level is not empty. The battery voltage is greater than 11 V. The engine run time is greater than 10 s. The DTCs run once per drive cycle when the above conditions are met.
DTC: P2100	**Throttle Actuator Control (TAC) Motor Control Circuit:** P2100The ECM is active. DTC P2100 runs continuously once the above conditions are met.
DTC: P2100 00	**Throttle Actuator Control (TAC) Motor Control Circuit:** P2100 00The ignition is ON or the engine is operating. The ignition voltage is greater than 7 V. DTCs P210 001 run continuously once the above conditions are met for greater than 5 s.
DTC: P2101	**Throttle Actuator Position Performance:** P1516 and P2101 DTC P0606 and P1682 is not set. The run/crank or powertrain relay voltage is greater than 6 V and reduced power is not active. The engine is running or the following conditions are met: The engine is not running. The ignition voltage is greater than 11 V. The TAC system is not in the Battery Saver mode. The ECM is commanding the throttle. The ECM has learned the minimum throttle position. DTC P1516 and P2101 run continuously when the above conditions are met.
DTC: P2101 00	**Throttle Actuator Position Performance:** P1516 00 or P2101 00The ignition is ON or the engine is operating. The ignition voltage is greater than 7 V. The system is not in battery safe mode. DTC P0068 00 is not set. DTCs P1516 00 and P2101 00 run continuously once the above conditions are met for greater than 5 s.
DTC: P2101 00	**Throttle Actuator Position Performance:** P1516 00 or P2101 00 DTC P1682 00 is not set. The engine is running. The ECM has learned the minimum throttle position. The ignition voltage is greater than 6 volts and reduced power is not active. DTCs P1516 00 and P2101 00 run continuously when the above conditions are met.
DTC: P2101 00	**Throttle Actuator Position Performance:** P2101 00The engine is running. The ignition voltage is between 11-18 V. DTC P2101 00 runs continuously when the above conditions are met.
DTC: P2101 00	**Throttle Actuator Position Performance:** P2101 00, P2119 00, P2176 00The ignition is ON or the engine is operating. DTC P2101 00, P2119 00, and P2176 00 runs continuously once the above conditions are met.
DTC: P2104 00	**Throttle Actuator Control (TAC) System - Forced Engine Idle Speed:** The ignition is ON or the engine is running.
DTC: P2105	**Throttle Actuator Control (TAC) System - Forced Engine Shutdown:** The ECM power down process in the last drive cycle was completely finished. DTC P2105 runs continuously once the above condition is met.
DTC: P2105 00	**Throttle Actuator Control (TAC) System - Forced Engine Shutdown:** The ignition is ON or the engine is running.
DTC: P2106 00	**Throttle Actuator Control System - Throttle Limitation Active:** The ignition is ON or the engine is running.
DTC: P2108 00	**Throttle Actuator Position Performance:** P2108 00 DTCs P0111 00, P0112 00, P0113 00, P0117 00, P0118 00, P0119 00, P0700 00, P2122 00, P2123 00, P2127 00, P2128 00, or P2138 00 is not set. DTCs P0121 00, P0122 00, P0123 00, P0221 00, P0222 00, P0223 00, P2176 00 are not set. DTC P2176 00 run continuously when the above conditions are met.
DTC: P2110 00	**Throttle Actuator Control (TAC) System - Forced Limited Engine Speed:** The ignition is ON or the engine is running.
DTC: P2119	**Throttle Closed Position Performance:** P2119 DTC P0111, P0112, P0113, P0116, P0117, P0118, P0119, P0700, P2122, P2123, P2127, P2128, or P2138 is not set. The ignition is ON. The vehicle speed is 0 km/h (0 mph). The engine speed is less than 40 RPM. The engine coolant temperature (ECT) is 5-100°C (41-212°F). The intake air temperature (IAT) is 5-143°C (41-290°F). The ignition voltage is greater than 10 volts. The accelerator pedal position (APP) is less than 15 percent. DTC P2119 runs once per ignition cycle when the above conditions are met for less than 1 second.
DTC: P2119 00	**Throttle Closed Position Performance:** P2119 00 DTCs P0121 00, P0122 00, P0123 00, P0222 00, P0223 00, P0641 00, P0651 00, P0697 00, P06A3 00, or P2135 00 are not set. The ignition voltage is greater than 8 V. DTC P2119 00 runs when the ignition is turned to the OFF position, when the above conditions are met.

DTC	Trouble Code Title, Conditions, Possible Causes
DTC: P2120	**Accelerator Pedal Position (APP) Sensor 1 Circuit:** P2120, P2122, P2123, P2125, P2127, P2128 DTC P0641 and P0651 are not set. The ignition is ON or the engine is running. The run/crank or powertrain relay voltage is greater than 6. 0 V and reduced power is not active. DTC 2120, P2122, P2123, P2125, P2127, P2128 run continuously when the above conditions are met.
DTC: P2120 03	**Accelerator Pedal Position (APP) Sensor 1 Circuit Low Voltage:** The ignition is ON or the engine is operating. The DTCs run continuously once the above conditions are met.
DTC: P2120 07	**Accelerator Pedal Position (APP) Sensor 1 Circuit High Voltage:** The ignition is ON or the engine is operating. The DTCs run continuously once the above conditions are met.
DTC: P2122	**Accelerator Pedal Position (APP) Sensor 1 Circuit Low Voltage:** P2120, P2122, P2123, P2125, P2127, P2128 DTC P0641 and P0651 are not set. The ignition is ON or the engine is running. The run/crank or powertrain relay voltage is greater than 6. 0 V and reduced power is not active. DTC 2120, P2122, P2123, P2125, P2127, P2128 run continuously when the above conditions are met.
DTC: P2122 00	**Accelerator Pedal Position (APP) Sensor 1 Circuit Low Voltage:** P2122 00, P2123 00, P2127 00, P2128 00 DTC P06A3 00 or P0697 00 are not set. The ignition is ON or the engine is operating. The ignition voltage is greater than 6 V. The ECM is not commanding reduced power. The DTCs run continuously when the above conditions are met.
DTC: P2123	**Accelerator Pedal Position (APP) Sensor 1 Circuit High Voltage:** P2120, P2122, P2123, P2125, P2127, P2128 DTC P0641 and P0651 are not set. The ignition is ON or the engine is running. The run/crank or powertrain relay voltage is greater than 6. 0 V and reduced power is not active. DTC 2120, P2122, P2123, P2125, P2127, P2128 run continuously when the above conditions are met.
DTC: P2123 00	**Accelerator Pedal Position (APP) Sensor 1 Circuit High Voltage:** P2122 00, P2123 00, P2127 00, P2128 00 DTC P06A3 00 or P0697 00 are not set. The ignition is ON or the engine is operating. The ignition voltage is greater than 6 V. The ECM is not commanding reduced power. The DTCs run continuously when the above conditions are met.
DTC: P2125	**Accelerator Pedal Position (APP) Sensor 2 Circuit:** P2120, P2122, P2123, P2125, P2127, P2128 DTC P0641 and P0651 are not set. The ignition is ON or the engine is running. The run/crank or powertrain relay voltage is greater than 6. 0 V and reduced power is not active. DTC 2120, P2122, P2123, P2125, P2127, P2128 run continuously when the above conditions are met.
DTC: P2125 03	**Accelerator Pedal Position (APP) Sensor 2 Circuit Low Voltage:** The ignition is ON or the engine is operating. The DTCs run continuously once the above conditions are met.
DTC: P2125 07	**Accelerator Pedal Position (APP) Sensor 2 Circuit High Voltage:** The ignition is ON or the engine is operating. The DTCs run continuously once the above conditions are met.
DTC: P2127	**Accelerator Pedal Position (APP) Sensor 2 Circuit Low Voltage:** P2120, P2122, P2123, P2125, P2127, P2128 DTC P0641 and P0651 are not set. The ignition is ON or the engine is running. The run/crank or powertrain relay voltage is greater than 6. 0 V and reduced power is not active. DTC 2120, P2122, P2123, P2125, P2127, P2128 run continuously when the above conditions are met.
DTC: P2127 00	**Accelerator Pedal Position (APP) Sensor 2 Circuit Low Voltage:** P2122 00, P2123 00, P2127 00, P2128 00 DTC P06A3 00 or P0697 00 are not set. The ignition is ON or the engine is operating. The ignition voltage is greater than 6 V. The ECM is not commanding reduced power. The DTCs run continuously when the above conditions are met.
DTC: P2128	**Accelerator Pedal Position (APP) Sensor 2 Circuit High Voltage:** P2120, P2122, P2123, P2125, P2127, P2128 DTC P0641 and P0651 are not set. The ignition is ON or the engine is running. The run/crank or powertrain relay voltage is greater than 6. 0 V and reduced power is not active. DTC 2120, P2122, P2123, P2125, P2127, P2128 run continuously when the above conditions are met.
DTC: P2128 00	**Accelerator Pedal Position (APP) Sensor 2 Circuit High Voltage:** P2122 00, P2123 00, P2127 00, P2128 00 DTC P06A3 00 or P0697 00 are not set. The ignition is ON or the engine is operating. The ignition voltage is greater than 6 V. The ECM is not commanding reduced power. The DTCs run continuously when the above conditions are met.
DTC: P2135	**Throttle Position (TP) Sensor 1-2 Correlation:** P2135 DTC P0120, P0122, P0123, P0220, P0222, P0223, P0641, or P0651 are not set. The ignition is ON or the engine is running. The run/crank or powertrain relay voltage is greater than 6. 0 V and reduced power is not active. DTC P2135 runs continuously when the above conditions are met.

DTC	Trouble Code Title, Conditions, Possible Causes
DTC: P2135 00	**Throttle Position Sensors 1-2 Not Plausible:** DTC P0641 00 or P0651 00 are not set. The run/crank or powertrain relay voltage is greater than 6 V and reduced power is not active. The ignition is ON or the engine is operating. DTC P0122 00, P0123 00, P0222 00, P0223 00, and P2135 00 run continuously when the above conditions are met.
DTC: P2135 00	**Throttle Position Sensors 1-2 Not Plausible:** P2135 00 DTCs P0122 00, P0123 00, P0222 00, or P0223 00 are not set. The ignition is ON, or the engine is running. The engine is not operating in reduced power mode. The ignition voltage is greater than 6 V. The DTCs runs continuously when the above condition is met.
DTC: P2138	**Accelerator Pedal Position (APP) Sensor 1-2 Correlation:** P2138 DTC P0641, P0651, P2120, P2122, P2123, P2125, P2127, and P2128 are not set. The ignition is ON or the engine is running. The run/crank or powertrain relay voltage is greater than 6. 0 V and reduced power is not active. DTC P2138 runs continuously when the above conditions are met.
DTC: P2138	**Accelerator Pedal Position (APP) Sensor 1-2 Correlation:** P2138 DTC P0641, P0651, P2120, P2122, P2123, P2125, P2127, and P2128 are not set. The ignition is ON or the engine is running. The run/crank or powertrain relay voltage is greater than 6. 0 V and reduced power is not active. DTC P2138 runs continuously when the above conditions are met.
DTC: P2138 00	**Accelerator Pedal Position (APP) Sensors 1-2 Not Plausible:** P2138 00 DTCs P06A3 00, P0697 00, P2122 00, P2123 00, P2127 00, or P2128 00 are not set. The ignition is ON or the engine is operating. The ignition voltage is greater than 6 V. The ECM is not commanding reduced power. The DTC runs continuously when the above conditions are met.
DTC: P2138 5A	**Accelerator Pedal Position (APP) Sensor 1-2 Not Plausible:** The ignition is ON or the engine is operating. The DTCs run continuously once the above conditions are met.
DTC: P2146	**Cylinder 1 Injector High Control Circuit:** The engine speed is greater than 80 RPM. The ignition 1 signal parameter is between 10-18 V. The injector has been commanded ON and OFF at least once. The DTCs run continuously once the above conditions are met.
DTC: P2146	**Cylinder 1 Injector High Control Circuit:** The engine speed is greater than 80 RPM. The ignition 1 signal parameter is between 8-18. 1 V. The DTCs run continuously within the enabling conditions.
DTC: P2146 00	**Injector High Control Circuit Group 1 Malfunction:** The engine is running. The ECM monitors for a condition once per camshaft revolution.
DTC: P2147	**Cylinder 1 Injector High Control Circuit Low Voltage:** The engine is running. The ignition voltage is between 11-18 V. The DTCs run continuously when the above conditions are met.
DTC: P2147 00	**Injector High Control Circuit Group 1 Low Voltage:** The engine is running. The ECM monitors for a condition once per camshaft revolution.
DTC: P2148	**Cylinder 1 Injector High Control Circuit High Voltage:** The engine is running. The ignition voltage is between 11-18 V. The DTCs run continuously when the above conditions are met.
DTC: P2148 00	**Injector High Control Circuit Group 1 High Voltage:** The engine is running. The ECM monitors for a condition once per camshaft revolution.
DTC: P2149	**Cylinder 2 Injector High Control Circuit:** The engine speed is greater than 80 RPM. The ignition 1 signal parameter is between 10-18 V. The injector has been commanded ON and OFF at least once. The DTCs run continuously once the above conditions are met.
DTC: P2149 F0	**Injector High Control Circuit Group 2 Malfunction:** The engine is running. The ECM monitors for a condition once per camshaft revolution.
DTC: P2150	**Cylinder 2 Injector High Control Circuit Low Voltage:** The engine is running. The ignition voltage is between 11-18 V. The DTCs run continuously when the above conditions are met.
DTC: P2150 00	**Injector High Control Circuit Group 2 Low Voltage:** The engine is running. The ECM monitors for a condition once per camshaft revolution.
DTC: P2151	**Cylinder 2 Injector High Control Circuit High Voltage:** The engine is running. The ignition voltage is between 11-18 V. The DTCs run continuously when the above conditions are met.
DTC: P2151 00	**Injector High Control Circuit Group 2 High Voltage:** The engine is running. The ECM monitors for a condition once per camshaft revolution.

DTC	Trouble Code Title, Conditions, Possible Causes
DTC: P2152	**Cylinder 3 Injector High Control Circuit:** The engine speed is greater than 80 RPM. The ignition 1 signal parameter is between 10-18 V. The injector has been commanded ON and OFF at least once. The DTCs run continuously once the above conditions are met.
DTC: P2153	**Cylinder 3 Injector High Control Circuit Low Voltage:** The engine is running. The ignition voltage is between 11-18 V. The DTCs run continuously when the above conditions are met.
DTC: P2154	**Cylinder 3 Injector High Control Circuit High Voltage:** The engine is running. The ignition voltage is between 11-18 V. The DTCs run continuously when the above conditions are met.
DTC: P2155	**Cylinder 4 Injector High Control Circuit:** The engine speed is greater than 80 RPM. The ignition 1 signal parameter is between 10-18 V. The injector has been commanded ON and OFF at least once. The DTCs run continuously once the above conditions are met.
DTC: P2156	**Cylinder 4 Injector High Control Circuit Low Voltage:** The engine is running. The ignition voltage is between 11-18 V. The DTCs run continuously when the above conditions are met.
DTC: P2157	**Cylinder 4 Injector High Control Circuit High Voltage:** The engine is running. The ignition voltage is between 11-18 V. The DTCs run continuously when the above conditions are met.
DTC: P216A	**Cylinder 5 Injector High Control Circuit:** The engine speed is greater than 80 RPM. The ignition 1 signal parameter is between 10-18 V. The injector has been commanded ON and OFF at least once. The DTCs run continuously once the above conditions are met.
DTC: P216B	**Cylinder 5 Injector High Control Circuit Low Voltage:** The engine is running. The ignition voltage is between 11-18 V. The DTCs run continuously when the above conditions are met.
DTC: P216C	**Cylinder 5 Injector High Control Circuit High Voltage:** The engine is running. The ignition voltage is between 11-18 V. The DTCs run continuously when the above conditions are met.
DTC: P216D	**Cylinder 6 Injector High Control Circuit:** The engine speed is greater than 80 RPM. The ignition 1 signal parameter is between 10-18 V. The injector has been commanded ON and OFF at least once. The DTCs run continuously once the above conditions are met.
DTC: P216E	**Cylinder 6 Injector High Control Circuit Low Voltage:** The engine is running. The ignition voltage is between 11-18 V. The DTCs run continuously when the above conditions are met.
DTC: P216F	**Cylinder 6 Injector High Control Circuit High Voltage:** The engine is running. The ignition voltage is between 11-18 V. The DTCs run continuously when the above conditions are met.
DTC: P2176	**Minimum Throttle Position Not Learned:** The engine speed is less than 40 RPM. The vehicle speed is 0 km/h (0 mph). The engine coolant temperature (ECT) is between 5-101°C (41-214°F). The intake air temperature (IAT) is between 5-144°C (41-291°F). The accelerator pedal position (APP) sensor angle is less than 15 percent. The ignition voltage is greater than 10 volts. DTC P2176 runs once per ignition cycle, when the ignition is ON and the above conditions are met for greater than 1 second.
DTC: P2176 00	**Minimum Throttle Position Not Learned:** P2101 00, P2119 00, P2176 00The ignition is ON or the engine is operating. DTC P2101 00, P2119 00, and P2176 00 runs continuously once the above conditions are met.
DTC: P2176 00	**Minimum Throttle Position Not Learned:** P2176 00The ignition voltage is greater than 8 V. DTC P2176 00 runs once per ignition cycle when the above conditions are met.
DTC: P2177	**Fuel Trim System Lean at Cruise or Acceleration Bank 1:** P2177 or P2179Before the ECM can report DTC P2177 or P2179, failed, DTCs P000A, P000B, P000C, P000D, P0008, P0009, P0010, P0011, P0013, P0014, P0016, P0017, P0018, P0019, P0020, P0021, P0023, P0024, P0201, P0202, P0203, P0204, P0205, P0206, P0261, P0262, P0264, P0265, P0267, P0268, P0270, P0271, P0273, P0274, P0276, P0277, P0300, P0301, P0302, P0303, P0304, P0305, P0306, P0461, P0462, P0463, P2068 P2088, P2089, P2090, P2091, P2092, P2093, P2094, P2095 P2146, P2149, P2152, P2155, P216A, and P216D must run and pass. The engine speed is between 1,200-3,400 RPM. The engine load is between 13-50 %. The throttle angle is less than 100 %. The cold start fuel control is not active. The Closed Loop fuel control is enabled. The engine is not in decel fuel cut-off. The engine coolant temperature is warmer than 60°C (140°F). The intake air temperature (IAT) is colder than 60°C (140°F). DTC P2177 and P2179 run continuously once the above conditions are met for approximately 300 s, after Closed Loop fuel control is enabled.

DTC	Trouble Code Title, Conditions, Possible Causes
DTC: P2178	**Fuel Trim System Rich at Cruise or Acceleration Bank 1:** P2178 or P2180Before the ECM can report DTC P2178 or P2180, failed, DTCs P000A, P000B, P000C, P000D, P0008, P0009, P0010, P0011, P0013, P0014, P0016, P0017, P0018, P0019, P0020, P0021, P0023, P0024, P0201, P0202, P0203, P0204, P0205, P0206, P0221, P0222, P0223, P0261, P0262, P0264, P0265, P0267, P0268, P0270, P0271, P0273, P0274, P0276, P0277, P0300, P0301, P0302, P0303, P0304, P0305, P0306, P0461, P0462, P0463, P2068 P2088, P2089, P2090, P2091, P2092, P2093, P2094, P2095 P2146, P2149, P2152, P2155, P216A, and P216D must run and pass. The engine speed is between 1,200-3,400 RPM. The engine load is between 13-50 %. The throttle angle is less than 100 %. The cold start fuel control is not active. The Closed Loop fuel control is enabled. The engine is not in decel fuel cut-off. The engine coolant temperature is warmer than 60°C (140°F). The intake air temperature (IAT) is colder than 60°C (140°F). DTCs P2178 and P2180 run continuously when the above conditions are met for approximately 300 s, after Closed Loop fuel control is enabled.
DTC: P2179	**Fuel Trim System Lean at Cruise or Acceleration Bank 2:** P2177 or P2179Before the ECM can report DTC P2177 or P2179, failed, DTCs P000A, P000B, P000C, P000D, P0008, P0009, P0010, P0011, P0013, P0014, P0016, P0017, P0018, P0019, P0020, P0021, P0023, P0024, P0201, P0202, P0203, P0204, P0205, P0206, P0261, P0262, P0264, P0265, P0267, P0268, P0270, P0271, P0273, P0274, P0276, P0277, P0300, P0301, P0302, P0303, P0304, P0305, P0306, P0461, P0462, P0463, P2068 P2088, P2089, P2090, P2091, P2092, P2093, P2094, P2095 P2146, P2149, P2152, P2155, P216A, and P216D must run and pass. The engine speed is between 1,200-3,400 RPM. The engine load is between 13-50 %. The throttle angle is less than 100 %. The cold start fuel control is not active. The Closed Loop fuel control is enabled. The engine is not in decel fuel cut-off. The engine coolant temperature is warmer than 60°C (140°F). The intake air temperature (IAT) is colder than 60°C (140°F). DTC P2177 and P2179 run continuously once the above conditions are met for approximately 300 s, after Closed Loop fuel control is enabled.
DTC: P2180	**Fuel Trim System Rich at Cruise or Acceleration Bank 2:** P2178 or P2180Before the ECM can report DTC P2178 or P2180, failed, DTCs P000A, P000B, P000C, P000D, P0008, P0009, P0010, P0011, P0013, P0014, P0016, P0017, P0018, P0019, P0020, P0021, P0023, P0024, P0201, P0202, P0203, P0204, P0205, P0206, P0221, P0222, P0223, P0261, P0262, P0264, P0265, P0267, P0268, P0270, P0271, P0273, P0274, P0276, P0277, P0300, P0301, P0302, P0303, P0304, P0305, P0306, P0461, P0462, P0463, P2068 P2088, P2089, P2090, P2091, P2092, P2093, P2094, P2095 P2146, P2149, P2152, P2155, P216A, and P216D must run and pass. The engine speed is between 1,200-3,400 RPM. The engine load is between 13-50 %. The throttle angle is less than 100 %. The cold start fuel control is not active. The Closed Loop fuel control is enabled. The engine is not in decel fuel cut-off. The engine coolant temperature is warmer than 60°C (140°F). The intake air temperature (IAT) is colder than 60°C (140°F). DTCs P2178 and P2180 run continuously when the above conditions are met for approximately 300 s, after Closed Loop fuel control is enabled.
DTC: P2181	**Engine Cooling System Performance:** DTCs P00B3, P00B4, P0101, P0102, P0103, P0112, P0113, or P0114 are not set. The engine run time is between 70 s and 22 m. The engine coolant temperature (ECT) sensor at start-up is between -20°C to +75°C (19 to 140°F). The intake air temperature (IAT) sensor is between -7°C to +75°C (-4°F to +167°F). The airflow into the engine is between 11 to 100 g/s. The DTC runs once per ignition cycle when the above conditions are met.
DTC: P2181 00	**Engine Cooling System Performance:** DTCs P00B3 00, P00B4 00, P0101 00, P0102 00, P0103 00, P0112 00, P0113 00, or P0114 00 are not set. The engine run time is between 70 s and 22 min. The engine coolant temperature (ECT) sensor at start-up is between -20 to +75°C (19-140°F). The intake air temperature (IAT) sensor is between -7 to +75°C (-4 to +167°F). The engine coolant thermostat heater command is greater than 50%. The airflow into the engine is between 11-100 g/s. The DTC runs once per ignition cycle when the above conditions are met.
DTC: P2186 00	**Engine Coolant Temperature (ECT) Sensor 2 Circuit Erratic:** DTCs P00B3 00, P00B4 00, P0101 00, P0102 00, P0103 00, P0112 00, P0113 00, or P0114 00 are not set. The engine run time is between 70 s and 22 m. The engine coolant temperature (ECT) sensor at start up is between -20 to +75°C (19-140°F). The intake air temperature (IAT) sensor is between -7 to +75°C (-4 to +167°F). The engine coolant thermostat heater command is greater than 50%. The airflow into the engine is between 11-100 g/s. The DTC runs once per ignition cycle when the above conditions are met.
DTC: P2187	**Fuel Trim System Lean at Idle Bank 1:** P2187 or P2189Before the ECM can report DTC P2187 or P2189, failed, DTCs P000A, P000B, P000C, P000D, P0008, P0009, P0010, P0011, P0013, P0014, P0016, P0017, P0018, P0019, P0020, P0021, P0023, P0024, P0201, P0202, P0203, P0204, P0205, P0206, P0261, P0262, P0264, P0265, P0267, P0268, P0270, P0271, P0273, P0274, P0276, P0277, P0300, P0301, P0302, P0303, P0304, P0305, P0306, P0461, P0462, P0463, P2068 P2088, P2089, P2090, P2091, P2092, P2093, P2094, P2095 P2146, P2149, P2152, P2155, P216A, and P216D must run and pass. The engine speed is between 520-1,000 RPM. The engine load is between 0-23 %. The throttle angle is less than 100 %. The cold start fuel control is not active. The Closed Loop fuel control is enabled. The engine is not in decel fuel cut-off. The engine coolant temperature (ECT) is warmer than 60°C (140°F). The intake air temperature (IAT) is colder than 60°C (140°F). DTC P2187 and P2189 run continuously once the above conditions are met for approximately 600 s, after Closed Loop fuel control is enabled.

DTC	Trouble Code Title, Conditions, Possible Causes
DTC: P2187 00	**Fuel Trim System Lean at Idle:** DTCs P0031 00, P0032 00, P0112 00, P0113 00, P0117 00, P0118 00, P0122 00, P0123 00, P0131 00, P0132 00, P0133 00, P0134 00, P0135 00, P0261 00, P0262 00, P0264 00, P0265 00, P0267 00, P0268 00, P0270 00, P0271 00, P0300 00, P0335 00, P0336 00, P0458 00, P0459 00, P0562 00, and P0563 00 are not set. The fuel system is in closed loop. The engine speed is between 700-6 000 RPM. The engine coolant temperature (ECT) is between 70-115°C (158-239°F). The intake air temperature (IAT) sensor is between -40 to +120°C (-40 to +248°F). The throttle position is between 0-95%. The manifold absolute pressure (MAP) is between 25-99. 7 kPa (3. 6-14. 46 PSI). The barometric pressure (BARO) is greater than 72 kPa (10. 44 PSI). The engine airflow is between 1. 5-45 g/s. The vehicle speed is less than 140 km/h (87 MPH). The ignition voltage is greater than 11 V. The DTCs run continuously when the above conditions are met.
DTC: P2188	**Fuel Trim System Rich at Idle Bank 1:** P2188 or P2190Before the ECM can report DTC P2188 or P2190, failed, DTCs P000A, P000B, P000C, P000D, P0008, P0009, P0010, P0011, P0013, P0014, P0016, P0017, P0018, P0019, P0020, P0021, P0023, P0024, P0201, P0202, P0203, P0204, P0205, P0206, P0261, P0262, P0264, P0265, P0267, P0268, P0270, P0271, P0273, P0274, P0276, P0277, P0300, P0301, P0302, P0303, P0304, P0305, P0306, P0461, P0462, P0463, P2068 P2088, P2089, P2090, P2091, P2092, P2093, P2094, P2095 P2146, P2149, P2152, P2155, P216A, and P216D must run and pass. The engine speed is between 520-1,000 RPM. The engine load is between 0-23 %. The throttle angle is less than 100 %. The cold start fuel control is not active. The Closed Loop fuel control is enabled. The engine is not in decel fuel cut-off. The engine coolant temperature (ECT) is warmer than 60°C (140°F). The intake air temperature (IAT) is colder than 60°C (140°F). DTCs P2188 and P2190 run continuously when the above conditions are met for approximately 600 s, after Closed Loop fuel control is enabled.
DTC: P2188 00	**Fuel Trim System Rich at Idle:** DTCs P0031 00, P0032 00, P0112 00, P0113 00, P0117 00, P0118 00, P0122 00, P0123 00, P0131 00, P0132 00, P0133 00, P0134 00, P0135 00, P0261 00, P0262 00, P0264 00, P0265 00, P0267 00, P0268 00, P0270 00, P0271 00, P0300 00, P0335 00, P0336 00, P0458 00, P0459 00, P0562 00, and P0563 00 are not set. The fuel system is in closed loop. The engine speed is between 700-6 000 RPM. The engine coolant temperature (ECT) is between 70-115°C (158-239°F). The intake air temperature (IAT) sensor is between -40 to +120°C (-40 to +248°F). The throttle position is between 0-95%. The manifold absolute pressure (MAP) is between 25-99. 7 kPa (3. 6-14. 46 PSI). The barometric pressure (BARO) is greater than 72 kPa (10. 44 PSI). The engine airflow is between 1. 5-45 g/s. The vehicle speed is less than 140 km/h (87 MPH). The ignition voltage is greater than 11 V. The DTCs run continuously when the above conditions are met.
DTC: P2189	**Fuel Trim System Lean at Idle Bank 2:** P2187 or P2189Before the ECM can report DTC P2187 or P2189, failed, DTCs P000A, P000B, P000C, P000D, P0008, P0009, P0010, P0011, P0013, P0014, P0016, P0017, P0018, P0019, P0020, P0021, P0023, P0024, P0201, P0202, P0203, P0204, P0205, P0206, P0261, P0262, P0264, P0265, P0267, P0268, P0270, P0271, P0273, P0274, P0276, P0277, P0300, P0301, P0302, P0303, P0304, P0305, P0306, P0461, P0462, P0463, P2068 P2088, P2089, P2090, P2091, P2092, P2093, P2094, P2095 P2146, P2149, P2152, P2155, P216A, and P216D must run and pass. The engine speed is between 520-1,000 RPM. The engine load is between 0-23 %. The throttle angle is less than 100 %. The cold start fuel control is not active. The Closed Loop fuel control is enabled. The engine is not in decel fuel cut-off. The engine coolant temperature (ECT) is warmer than 60°C (140°F). The intake air temperature (IAT) is colder than 60°C (140°F). DTC P2187 and P2189 run continuously once the above conditions are met for approximately 600 s, after Closed Loop fuel control is enabled.
DTC: P2190	**Fuel Trim System Rich at Idle Bank 2:** P2188 or P2190Before the ECM can report DTC P2188 or P2190, failed, DTCs P000A, P000B, P000C, P000D, P0008, P0009, P0010, P0011, P0013, P0014, P0016, P0017, P0018, P0019, P0020, P0021, P0023, P0024, P0201, P0202, P0203, P0204, P0205, P0206, P0261, P0262, P0264, P0265, P0267, P0268, P0270, P0271, P0273, P0274, P0276, P0277, P0300, P0301, P0302, P0303, P0304, P0305, P0306, P0461, P0462, P0463, P2068 P2088, P2089, P2090, P2091, P2092, P2093, P2094, P2095 P2146, P2149, P2152, P2155, P216A, and P216D must run and pass. The engine speed is between 520-1,000 RPM. The engine load is between 0-23 %. The throttle angle is less than 100 %. The cold start fuel control is not active. The Closed Loop fuel control is enabled. The engine is not in decel fuel cut-off. The engine coolant temperature (ECT) is warmer than 60°C (140°F). The intake air temperature (IAT) is colder than 60°C (140°F). DTCs P2188 and P2190 run continuously when the above conditions are met for approximately 600 s, after Closed Loop fuel control is enabled.
DTC: P2195	**HO2S Signal Biased Lean Sensor 1:** P2195 DTCs P0030, P0031, P0032, P0036, P0037, P0038, P0053, P0130, P0131, P0132, P0133, P0135, P0137, P0138, P0140, P0141, P2232, P2237, P2243, P2251, P2297, P2626 are not set. The engine is running. The Loop Status parameter is Closed. DTC P2195 runs continuously when the above conditions are met.
DTC: P2195 00	**HO2S Signal Biased Lean Sensor 1:** The engine coolant temperature (ECT) is greater than 60°C (140°F). The ignition 1 voltage is greater than 10 V. The DTC runs continuously once the above conditions are met for 2 s.
DTC: P2196	**HO2S Signal Biased Rich Sensor 1:** P2196 DTCs P0030, P0031, P0032, P0036, P0037, P0038, P0053, P0130, P0131, P0132, P0133, P0135, P0137, P0138, P0140, P0141, P2232, P2237, P2243, P2251, P2297, P2626 are not set. The engine is running. The Loop Status parameter is Closed. DTC P2196 runs continuously when the above conditions are met.

DTC	Trouble Code Title, Conditions, Possible Causes
DTC: P219A	**Fuel Trim Cylinder Balance Bank 1:** DTCs P0030, P0036, P0050, P0053, P0059, P0101, P0102, P0103, P0106, P0107, P0108, P0117, P0118, P0128, P0131, P0132, P0133, P0134, P0135, P0151, P0152, P0153, P0154, P0155, P0201-P0206, P0300, P0301-P0306, P0411, P0412, P0418, P0442, P0443, P0446, P0449, P0452, P0453, P0454, P0455, P0496, P1133, P1153, P1516, P2101, P2119, P2120, P2125, P2135, P2138, P2176, P2431, P2432, P2433, P2440, P2A00, P2A03 are not set. The device control is not active. The intrusive diagnostics are not active. The engine overspeed protection is not active. The power take-off (PTO) is not active. The traction control is not active. The fuel control is in air-fuel Closed Loop. The system voltage is more than 10 V, or less than 18 V. The engine run time is greater than 100 s. The engine coolant temperature (ECT) is greater than -20°C (-4°F). The engine speed is greater than 425 RPM, but less than 6,000 RPM. The mass air flow is greater than 25 g/s, but less than 510 g/s.
DTC: P219A	**Air Fuel Imbalance:** DTCs P0068, P0101, P0102, P0103, P0106, P0107, P0108, P0116, P0117, P0118, P0121, P0122, P0123, P0128, P0131, P0132, P0133, P0134, P0135, P0137, P0138, P013A-P013B, P013E-P013F, P0140, P0141, P0201-P0204, P0261-P0262, P0264-P0265, P0267-P0268, P0270-P0271, P0300, P0301-P0304 P0442, P0443, P0446, P0449, P0451, P0452, P0453, P0454, P0455, P0496, P1101, P1133, P1248, P1249, P124A, P124B, P1516, P2101, P2119, P2122, P2123, P2127-P2128, P2135, P2138, P2147-P2148, P2150-P2151, P2153-P2154, P2156-P2157, P2176, P219A, P2270, P2271, P2A00 are not set. The device control is not active. The intrusive diagnostics are not active. The engine overspeed protection is not active. Reduced power mode, ETC DTC, is not active. The traction control is not active. The fuel control is in air-fuel Closed Loop. The system voltage is more than 10 V, or less than 32 V for more than 4 s. The engine coolant temperature (ECT) is greater than -20°C (-4°F). The engine speed is greater than 1,100 RPM, but less than 4,000 RPM. The mass air flow is greater than 13 g/s, but less than 600 g/s.
DTC: P219B	**Fuel Trim Cylinder Balance Bank 2:** DTCs P0030, P0036, P0050, P0053, P0059, P0101, P0102, P0103, P0106, P0107, P0108, P0117, P0118, P0128, P0131, P0132, P0133, P0134, P0135, P0151, P0152, P0153, P0154, P0155, P0201-P0206, P0300, P0301-P0306, P0411, P0412, P0418, P0442, P0443, P0446, P0449, P0452, P0453, P0454, P0455, P0496, P1133, P1153, P1516, P2101, P2119, P2120, P2125, P2135, P2138, P2176, P2431, P2432, P2433, P2440, P2A00, P2A03 are not set. The device control is not active. The intrusive diagnostics are not active. The engine overspeed protection is not active. The power take-off (PTO) is not active. The traction control is not active. The fuel control is in air-fuel Closed Loop. The system voltage is more than 10 V, or less than 18 V. The engine run time is greater than 100 s. The engine coolant temperature (ECT) is greater than -20°C (-4°F). The engine speed is greater than 425 RPM, but less than 6,000 RPM. The mass air flow is greater than 25 g/s, but less than 510 g/s.
DTC: P219B	**Air Fuel Imbalance Bank 2:** DTCs P0053, P0059, P0068, P0090, P0091, P0092, P00C8, P00C9, P00CA, P0101, P0102, P0103, P0106, P0107, P0108, P0116, P0117, P0118, P0122, P0123, P0128, P0131, P0132, P0133, P0134, P0135, P0151, P0152, P0153, P0154, P0155, P0191, P0192, P0193, P0201-P0206, P0222, P0223, P0261, P0262, P0264, P0265, P0267, P0268, P0270, P0271, P0273, P0274, P0276, P0277, P0300, P0301-P0306, P0442, P0443, P0446, P0449, P0452, P0453, P0455, P0496, P0606, P1133, P1153, P1248, P1249, P124A, P124B, P124C, P124D, P16F3, P2101, P2122, P2123, P2127, P2128, P2135, P2147, P2148, P2150, P2151, P2153, P2154, P2156, P2157, P216B, P216C, P216E, P216F, P228C, P228D, P2A00, P2A03 are not set. Device controls are not active. The intrusive diagnostics are not active. The engine overspeed protection is not active. Reduced power mode is not active. The traction control is not active. The engine is in Closed Loop status. The system voltage is between 10-32 V for greater than 4 s. The engine coolant temperature (ECT) is warmer than -20°C (-4°F). The engine speed is between 950-2750 RPM. The mass air flow is between 1-600 g/s.
DTC: P21AA	**Reductant Level Sensor 2 Circuit Low Voltage:** The engine speed is greater than 600 RPM. The battery voltage is greater than 11 V. The ambient air and emission reduction fluid tank temperatures are warmer than -7°C (19°F) - DTC P203B only. The engine run time is greater than 10 s. The DTCs run continuously once the above conditions are met.
DTC: P21AB	**Reductant Level Sensor 2 Circuit High Voltage:** The engine speed is greater than 600 RPM. The battery voltage is greater than 11 V. The ambient air and emission reduction fluid tank temperatures are warmer than -7°C (19°F) - DTC P203B only. The engine run time is greater than 10 s. The DTCs run continuously once the above conditions are met.
DTC: P21AF	**Reductant Level Sensor 3 Circuit Low Voltage:** The engine speed is greater than 600 RPM. The battery voltage is greater than 11 V. The ambient air and emission reduction fluid tank temperatures are warmer than -7°C (19°F) - DTC P203B only. The engine run time is greater than 10 s. The DTCs run continuously once the above conditions are met.
DTC: P21B0	**Reductant Level Sensor 3 Circuit High Voltage:** The engine speed is greater than 600 RPM. The battery voltage is greater than 11 V. The ambient air and emission reduction fluid tank temperatures are warmer than -7°C (19°F) - DTC P203B only. The engine run time is greater than 10 s. The DTCs run continuously once the above conditions are met.

DTC	Trouble Code Title, Conditions, Possible Causes
DTC: P2200	**NOx Sensor 1 Circuit:** P2200, P2202, P2203, P22A0, and P22A1 DTCs P2205, P2209, P22A3, or P22A7 are not set. The battery voltage is greater than 11 V for greater than 3 s. The engine speed is greater than 600 RPM. The engine run time is greater than 20 s. The exhaust gas temperature Sensor 2 is between 95-3,004°C (203-5,439°F). The NOx sensor is at operating temperature. The DTCs run continuously once the above conditions are met.
DTC: P2201	**NOx Sensor 1 Performance:** P2201The engine run time is greater than 10 s. The engine speed is greater than 600 RPM. The battery voltage is greater than 11 V. The DPF regeneration is not active. The DTC runs continuously when the above conditions are met.
DTC: P2202	**NOx Sensor 1 Circuit Low Voltage:** P2200, P2202, P2203, P22A0, and P22A1 DTCs P2205, P2209, P22A3, or P22A7 are not set. The battery voltage is greater than 11 V for greater than 3 s. The engine speed is greater than 600 RPM. The engine run time is greater than 20 s. The exhaust gas temperature Sensor 2 is between 95-3,004°C (203-5,439°F). The NOx sensor is at operating temperature. The DTCs run continuously once the above conditions are met.
DTC: P2203	**NOx Sensor 1 Circuit High Voltage:** P2200, P2202, P2203, P22A0, and P22A1 DTCs P2205, P2209, P22A3, or P22A7 are not set. The battery voltage is greater than 11 V for greater than 3 s. The engine speed is greater than 600 RPM. The engine run time is greater than 20 s. The exhaust gas temperature Sensor 2 is between 95-3,004°C (203-5,439°F). The NOx sensor is at operating temperature. The DTCs run continuously once the above conditions are met.
DTC: P2205	**NOx Sensor 1 Heater Control Circuit:** DTC P2205 or P22A3The battery voltage is greater than 11 V. The engine speed is greater than 600 RPM for greater than 10 s. The Exhaust Gas Temperature Sensor 1 is greater than 95°C (203°F). The DTCs run continuously once the above conditions are met.
DTC: P2209	**NOx Sensor 1 Heater Feedback Performance:** DTC P2209 or P22A7 DTC P064C, P163C, P220A, or P220B are not set. The battery voltage is greater than 11 V. The engine speed is between 600-5,000 RPM. The Exhaust Gas Temperature Sensor 1 is greater than 95°C (203°F). The DTCs run continuously once the above conditions are met.
DTC: P220A	**NOx Sensor 1 Supply Voltage Circuit:** The ignition is ON. The DTCs run continuously once the above conditions are met.
DTC: P220B	**NOx Sensor 2 Supply Voltage Circuit:** The ignition is ON. The DTCs run continuously once the above conditions are met.
DTC: P2226 03	**Barometric Pressure (BARO) Sensor Circuit Low Voltage:** The ignition is ON or the engine is running.
DTC: P2226 07	**Barometric Pressure (BARO) Sensor Circuit High Voltage:** The ignition is ON or the engine is running.
DTC: P2227	**Barometric Pressure (BARO) Sensor Performance:** P2227 - Engine Cranking DTCs P0121, P0122, P0123, P0221, P0222, P0223, P0335, P0336, P2176, P2228, or P2229 is not set. The engine is cranking. The engine OFF timer is greater than 4 s before cranking begins. This DTC runs once per ignition cycle within the enabling conditions. P2227 - Engine Running Rationality Test DTCs P0121, P0122, P0123, P0221, P0222, P0223, P0335, P0336, P2176, P2228, or P2229 is not set. The engine speed is less than 1000 RPM. The Throttle Position Sensor parameter is less than 24 %. The engine has been running for greater than 5 s. This DTC runs continuously within the enabling conditions. P2227 - Engine Running Range Test DTCs P0121, P0122, P0123, P0221, P0222, P0223, P0335, P0336, P2176, P2228, or P2229 is not set. The engine has been running for greater than 5 s. This DTC runs continuously within the enabling conditions.
DTC: P2228	**Barometric Pressure (BARO) Sensor Circuit Low Voltage:** P2228 or P2229The engine is operating. The DTCs run continuously once the above conditions are met for 2 s.
DTC: P2229	**Barometric Pressure (BARO) Sensor Circuit High Voltage:** P2228 or P2229The engine is running. The DTCs run continuously when the above condition is met. .
DTC: P2230	**Barometric Pressure (BARO) Sensor Circuit Erratic:** P2230The engine is running. DTCs P0068, P0101, P0102, P0103, P0106, P0107, P0108, P0112, P0113, P0117, P0118, P0121, P0122, P0123, P0222, P0223, P1516, P2135, P2228 and P2229 are not set. DTC P2230 runs continuously when the above conditions are met.
DTC: P2232	**HO2S Signal Circuit Shorted to Heater Circuit Sensor 2:** P2232The engine is running. The HO2S 2 heater is stable, and the estimated exhaust temperature was more than 250°C (482°F) for more than 90 seconds. The ignition voltage is more than 10. 5 volts. The estimated exhaust temperature is less than 800°C (1,472°F). DTC P2232 runs continuously when the above conditions are met.

DTC	Trouble Code Title, Conditions, Possible Causes
DTC: P2237	**HO2S Pumping Current Control Circuit Sensor 1:** P2237 DTCs P0121, P0122, P0123, P0221, P0222, P0223, P0335, P0336, P0338 are not set. The ignition voltage is between 10. 7-18. 1 V. The engine is running. HO2S 1 voltage is between 1. 48-1. 52 V. HO2S 1 heater is at operating temperature. HO2S 1 Closed Loop is active. The catalyst temperature is stable. DTC P2237 runs continuously when the above conditions are met for 2 s.
DTC: P2237 00	**HO2S Pump Current Control Circuit Sensor 1:** P2237 00The ignition voltage is between 10. 7-18. 1 V. The engine is running. HO2S 1 voltage is between 1. 48-1. 52 V. HO2S 1 heater is at operating temperature. HO2S 1 Closed Loop is active. The catalyst temperature is stable. DTC P2237 runs continuously when the above conditions are met for 2 s.
DTC: P2238	**HO2S Pump Current Control Circuit Low Voltage Sensor 1:** P2238 and P2239The ignition voltage is between 10. 7-18. 1 V. The engine is running. DTCs P2238 and P2239 run continuously when the above conditions have been met for 1. 5 s.
DTC: P2238 00	**HO2S Pump Current Control Circuit Low Voltage Sensor 1:** P2238 00The ignition voltage is between 10. 7-18. 1 V. The engine is running. DTCs P2238 runs continuously when the above conditions have been met for 1. 5 s.
DTC: P2239	**HO2S Pump Current Control Circuit High Voltage Sensor 1:** P2238 and P2239The ignition voltage is between 10. 7-18. 1 V. The engine is running. DTCs P2238 and P2239 run continuously when the above conditions have been met for 1. 5 s.
DTC: P2243	**HO2S Reference Voltage Circuit Sensor 1:** P2243 DTCs P0030, P0031, P0032 are not set. The ignition voltage is between 10. 7-18. 1 V. The engine is running. HO2S 1 heater is at operating temperature for at least 20 s. HO2S 1 internal resistance is more than 570 Ω. DTC P2243 runs continuously when the above conditions are met for 2 s.
DTC: P2245 00	**HO2S Reference Voltage Circuit Low Voltage Sensor 1:** P2245 00 or P2246 00 DTCs P0030, P0031, P0032 are not set. The ignition voltage is between 10-18 V. The engine speed is greater than 80 RPM. The HO2S 1 heater is at operating temperature. DTC P2243 runs continuously when the above conditions are met for 2 s.
DTC: P2246 00	**HO2S Reference Voltage Circuit High Voltage Sensor 1:** P2245 00 or P2246 00 DTCs P0030, P0031, P0032 are not set. The ignition voltage is between 10-18 V. The engine speed is greater than 80 RPM. The HO2S 1 heater is at operating temperature. DTC P2243 runs continuously when the above conditions are met for 2 s.
DTC: P2251	**HO2S Low Reference Circuit Sensor 1:** P2251 DTCs P0030, P0031, P0032 are not set. The ignition voltage is between 10. 7-18. 1 V. The engine is running. The estimated exhaust temperature is less than 900°C (1,652°F). The HO2S 1 voltage is between 1. 47-1. 53 V. The HO2S 1 heater temperature has been within the normal range for more than 20 s. HO2S 1 internal resistance is more than 570 Ω. The following are true for more than 30 s. The HO2S 1 heater is ready. The engine is running. The ignition voltage is more than 11 V. DTC P2251 runs continuously when the above conditions are met for 10 minutes.
DTC: P2251 00	**HO2S Low Reference Circuit Sensor 1:** P2251 00 DTCs P0030, P0031, P0032 are not set. The ignition voltage is between 10. 7-18. 1 V. The engine is running. The estimated exhaust temperature is less than 900°C (1 652°F). The HO2S 1 voltage is between 1. 47-1. 53 V. The HO2S 1 heater temperature has been within the normal range for more than 20 s. HO2S 1 internal resistance is more than 570 Ω. The following are true for more than 30 s. The HO2S 1 heater is ready. The engine is running. The ignition voltage is more than 11 V. DTC P2251 runs continuously when the above conditions are met for 10 min.
DTC: P2261	**Turbocharger Bypass Valve Stuck Closed:** DTCs P0033, P0034, P0035, P0096, P0097, P0098, P0099, P0100, P0101, P0102, P0103, P0106, P0107, P0108, P0121, P0122, P0123, P0221, P0222, P0223, P0234, P0236, P0237, P0238, P0299, P2227, P2228, or P2229, is not set. The boost pressure versus the BARO pressure ratio is between 1. 1-3. 3. The charge air bypass valve has been commanded ON for greater than 1 s immediately after an abrupt closed throttle has occurred and the resulting pressure ratio across the compressor exceeds the calibrated pressure ratio limit. The battery voltage is between 10-18 V. This DTC runs continuously within the enabling conditions.
DTC: P2261 00	**Turbocharger Bypass Valve Stuck:** DTCs P0033 00, P0034 00, P0035 00, P0097 00, P0098 00, P0100 00, P0101 00, P0102 00, P0103 00, P0121 00, P0122 00, P0123 00, P0221 00, P0222 00, P0223 00, P0234 00, P0237 00, P0238 00, P0299 00, P2228 00, or P2229 00, are not set. The boost pressure versus the Barometric Pressure (BARO) ratio is between 1. 1-3. 3. The charge air bypass valve has been commanded ON for greater than 1 s immediately after an abrupt closed throttle has occurred and the resulting pressure ratio across the compressor exceeds the calibrated pressure ratio limit. The battery voltage is between 10-18 V. The engine coolant temperature is above 39°C (102°F). The intake air temperature is above 4. 5°C (40°F). This DTC runs continuously within the enabling conditions.
DTC: P2263	**Turbocharger Boost System Performance:** DTC P0107 or P0108 is not set. The engine is running. DTC P2263 runs continuously when the above conditions are met.

DTC	Trouble Code Title, Conditions, Possible Causes
DTC: P2264	**Water in Fuel Sensor Circuit:** The ignition is ON. The DTC runs continuously once the above condition is met.
DTC: P2264 00	**Water In Fuel Sensor Circuit Malfunction:** The ignition is ON. The DTC runs continuously once the above condition is met.
DTC: P2266	**Water in Fuel Sensor Circuit Low Voltage:** The engine is running. This diagnostic runs continuously.
DTC: P2269	**Water in Fuel:** The engine is running. The diagnostic runs continuously.
DTC: P2269 00	**Water in Fuel Malfunction:** The ignition is ON. The DTC runs continuously once the above condition is met.
DTC: P2270	**HO2S Signal Stuck Lean Sensor 2:** P2270 DTCs P0068, P0101, P0102, P0103, P0106, P0107, P0108, P0112, P0113, P0116, P0117, P0118, P0120, P0121, P0122, P0123, P0128, P013A, P013B, P013E, P013F, P0171, P0172, P0201, P0202, P0203, P0204, P0220, P0222, P0223, P0300, P1174, P1516, P2101, P2119, P2135, P2176, P2270, P2271 are not set. The system voltage is between 10-18 V. The fuel level is more than 10 percent. Engine run time is equal to or more than 40 seconds. The engine speed is between 1,250-1,950 RPM. Airflow is equal to or more than 3 g/s and equal to or less than 12 g/s. The vehicle speed is equal to or more than 55 km/h (34. 2 mph) and equal to or less than 120 km/h (74. 6 mph). The short term fuel trim is equal to or more than 0. 9 and equal to or less than 1. 065. The fuel state is in closed loop. The EVAP diagnostics are not in control of purge. The Ethanol Estimate is not in progress. The Post Cell Enabled. The Power Take-Off is not active. The EGR diagnostic is not intrusive. The Heater Warm-up Delay is more than 120 seconds. The catalytic converter temperature is equal to or more than 650°C (1,202°F), and equal to less than 900°C (1,652°F). This DTC runs once per trip when all of the above conditions have been met for 1 second.
DTC: P2270 00	**HO2S Signal Stuck Lean Sensor 2:** P2270 00 DTCs P0030 00, P0036 00, P0053 00, P0054 00, P0101 00, P0102 00, P0103 00, P0106 00, P0107 00, P0108 00, P0120 00, P0121 00, P0122 00, P0123 00, P0131 00, P0132 00, P0133 00, P0134 00, P0135 00, P0137 00, P0138 00, P013A 00, P013B 00, P013E 00, P013F 00, P0140 00, P0141 00, P0171 00, P0172 00, P0201 00, P0202 00, P0203 00, P0204 00, P0220 00, P0222 00, P0223 00, P0300 00, P0443 00, P1133 00, P1516 00, P2101 00, P2119 00, P2135 00, P2176 00, P2270 00, P2271 00, P2A00 00 are not set. The system voltage is between 10-18 V. The fuel level is more than 10%. Engine run time is equal to or more than 255 s. Then The engine speed is between 1 100-3 200 RPM. The airflow is equal to or more than 0 g/s and equal to or less than 25 g/s. The vehicle speed is equal to or more than 45 km/h (28 MPH) and equal to or less than 129 km/h (80 MPH). The short term fuel trim is equal to or more than 0. 9, and equal to or less than 1 065. The loop status parameter is closed. The evaporative emission (EVAP) diagnostics are not in control of purge. The heater warm-up delay is more than 120 s. The catalyst temperature is equal to or more than 650°C (1 202°F), and equal to less than 900°C (1 652°F). DTC P2270 00 runs once per trip when all of the above conditions have been met for 2 s.
DTC: P2271	**HO2S Signal Stuck Rich Bank 1 Sensor 2:** Before the ECM can report DTC P2271 or P2273 failed, DTCs P0036, P0037, P0038, P0056, P0057, P0058, P013A, P013C, P013E, P0137, P0138, P014A, P0140, P0141, P0157, P0158, P0160, P0161, P0443, P0458, P0459, P2097, P2099, P2178, P2180, P2188, and P2190 must run and pass. DTC P0461, P0462, P0463, P2066, P2067, or P2068 is not set. The engine is operating. The ignition voltage is greater than 10 volts. The HO2S 2 is at operating temperature for greater than 10 seconds. The long term fuel control is enabled. The engine is not in decel fuel cut-off (DEFCO). The mass air flow (MAF) sensor is greater than 10 g/s. The MAF sensor is between 6-33 g/s for greater than 3 seconds during the intrusive test. DTC P2271 and P2273 run continuously once the above conditions are met for approximately 10 minutes, or 20 minutes if the fuel level is less than 12 percent.
DTC: P2271 00	**HO2S Signal Stuck Rich Sensor 2:** P2271 00 DTCs P000A 00, P000B 00, P0010 00, P0011 00, P0013 00, P0014 00, P0016 00, P0017 00, P0030 00, P0031 00, P0032 00, P0107 00, P0108 00, P0117 00, P0118 00, P0119 00, P0121 00, P0122 00, P0123 00, P0130 00, P0131 00, P0132 00, P0133 00, P0137 00, P0138 00, P0139 00, P0141 00, P0171 00, P0172 00, P0221 00, P0222 00, P0223 00, P0300 00, P0301 00, P0302 00, P0303 00, P0304 00, P0313 00, P0335 00, P0336 00, P0340 00, P0341 00, P0365 00, P0366 00, P0443 00, P0458 00, P0459 00, P0496 00, P2088 00, P2089 00, P2090 00, P2091 00, P2176 00, P2270 00, P2271 00, P2297 00, P2A01 00 are not set. The engine has been running for more than 5 min. The engine coolant is hotter than 75°C (167°F). DTC P2271 00 runs continuously when the above conditions are met for 10 min.
DTC: P2271 00	**HO2S Signal Stuck Rich Sensor 2:** P2271 00 DTCs P0030 00, P0036 00, P0053 00, P0054 00, P0101 00, P0102 00, P0103 00, P0106 00, P0107 00, P0108 00, P0120 00, P0121 00, P0122 00, P0123 00, P0131 00, P0132 00, P0133 00, P0134 00, P0135 00, P0137 00, P0138 00, P013A 00, P013B 00, P013E 00, P013F 00, P0140 00, P0141 00, P0171 00, P0172 00, P0201 00, P0202 00, P0203 00, P0204 00, P0220 00, P0222 00, P0223 00, P0300 00, P0443 00, P1133 00, P1516 00, P2101 00, P2119 00, P2135 00, P2176 00, P2270 00, P2271 00, P2A00 00 are not set. The system voltage is between 10-18 V. The fuel level is more than 10%. Engine run time is equal to or more than 255 s. The Deceleration fuel cut-off is active. The accelerator pedal position (APP) is stable. The torque converter clutch (TCC) is locked. DTCs P013A 00, P013E 00, and P2270 00 have run and passed. DTC P2271 00 runs once per trip.

DTC	Trouble Code Title, Conditions, Possible Causes
DTC: P2272	**HO2S Signal Stuck Lean Bank 2 Sensor 2:** P2272 DTCs P0050, P0059, P0068, P0101, P0102, P0103, P0107, P0108, P0112, P0113, P0117, P0118, P0120, P0121, P0122, P0123, P0128, P0151, P0152, P0153, P0154, P0155, P0171, P0172, P0174, P0175, P0201, P0202, P0203, P0204, P0205, P0206, P0220, P0222, P0223, P0442, P0443, P0446, P0449, P0451, P0452, P0453, P0454, P0455, P0496, P1153, P1516, P2101, P2119, P2135, P2176, P2A03 are not set. The system voltage is between 10-18V. The learned heater resistance is valid. The fuel level is more than 10 percent or the fuel level data fault is active. Engine run time is equal to or more than 40 seconds. THEN The engine speed is between 1,100-2,100 RPM. Airflow is equal to or more than 3 g/s and equal to or less than 12 g/s. The vehicle speed is equal to or more than 73 km/h (45. 4 mph) and equal to or less than 120 km/h (74. 6 mph). The short term fuel trim is equal to or more than 0. 9 and equal to or less than 1. 065. The fuel state is in closed loop. The EVAP diagnostics are not in control of purge. The Post Cell Enabled. The EGR diagnostic is not intrusive. The Heater Warm-up Delay is more than 120 seconds. The catalytic converter temperature is equal to or more that 650°C (1,202°F), and equal to less than 900°C (1,652°F). This DTC runs once per trip when all of the above conditions have been met for 2 seconds.
DTC: P2273	**HO2S Signal Stuck Rich Bank 2 Sensor 2:** Before the ECM can report DTC P2271 or P2273 failed, DTCs P0036, P0037, P0038, P0056, P0057, P0058, P013A, P013C, P013E, P0137, P0138, P014A, P0140, P0141, P0157, P0158, P0160, P0161, P0443, P0458, P0459, P2097, P2099, P2178, P2180, P2188, and P2190 must run and pass. DTC P0461, P0462, P0463, P2066, P2067, or P2068 is not set. The engine is operating. The ignition voltage is greater than 10 volts. The HO2S 2 is at operating temperature for greater than 10 seconds. The long term fuel control is enabled. The engine is not in decel fuel cut-off (DEFCO). The mass air flow (MAF) sensor is greater than 10 g/s. The MAF sensor is between 6-33 g/s for greater than 3 seconds during the intrusive test. DTC P2271 and P2273 run continuously once the above conditions are met for approximately 10 minutes, or 20 minutes if the fuel level is less than 12 percent.
DTC: P228C	**Fuel Pressure Regulator 1 Control Performance - Low Pressure:** P0089, P228C, or P228DDTC P0016, P0017, P0090, P0091, P0092, P00C8, P00C9, P00CA, P0112, P0113, P0116, P0117, P0118, P0128, P0192, P0193, P0335, P0336, P0340, P0341, P0365, P0366, P0627, P0628, P0629 or P1682 is not set. The ignition voltage is more than 11 V. The engine is running. The low side fuel pressure is more than 275 kPa (40 psi). The DTC runs continuously when the above conditions are met for 60 s.
DTC: P228C 00	**Fuel Pressure Regulator 1 Control Performance - Low Pressure:** The ignition is ON, or the engine is running. The ignition voltage is less than 16 V. These DTCs runs continuously once the above conditions are met.
DTC: P228D	**Fuel Pressure Regulator 1 Control Performance – High Pressure:** P0089, P228C, or P228DDTC P0016, P0017, P0018, P0019, P0090, P0091, P0092, P00C8, P00C9, P00CA, P0111, P0112, P0113, P0116, P0117, P0118, P0128, P0192, P0193, P0335, P0336, P0340, P0341, P0345, P0346, P0365, P0366, P0390, P0391, P0627, P0628, or P0629 is not set. The ignition voltage is greater than 8 V. The low side fuel pressure is greater than 275 kPa (40 psi). The engine is running. The DTCs run continuously when the above conditions are met for 10 s.
DTC: P228D 00	**Fuel Pressure Regulator 1 Control Performance - High Pressure:** The ignition is ON, or the engine is running. The ignition voltage is less than 16 V. These DTCs runs continuously once the above conditions are met.
DTC: P2294	**Fuel Pressure Regulator 2 Control Circuit:** Engine speed is greater than 600 RPM. Battery voltage is greater than 11 V.
DTC: P2295	**Fuel Pressure Regulator Solenoid 2 Control Circuit Low Voltage:** Engine speed is greater than 600 RPM. Battery voltage is greater than 11 V.
DTC: P2296	**Fuel Pressure Regulator Solenoid 2 Control Circuit High Voltage:** Engine speed is greater than 600 RPM. Battery voltage is greater than 11 V.
DTC: P2297	**HO2S Performance During Decel Fuel Cut-Off (DFCO) Sensor 1:** P2297The engine is running. The HO2S 1 heater is at operating temperature. Lambda is less than 1. 6. All fuel injectors are active. DTC P2297 runs continuously when the above conditions are met.
DTC: P2297 00	**HO2S Performance During Deceleration Fuel Cut-Off Sensor 1:** DTCs P0106 00, P0107 00, P0108 00, P0117 00, P0118 00, P0122 00, P0123 00, P0171 00, P0172 00, P0300 00, P0336 00, P0337 00, P0351 00, P0352 00, P0401 00, P0402 00, P0404 00, P0405 00, P0406 00, P042E 00, P0502 00, P0506 00, P0507 00, and P1404 00 are not set. The engine has been running for greater than 60 s. The engine is in deceleration fuel cut off mode. The startup engine coolant temperature is greater than 60°C (140°F). The ignition voltage is between 10-16 V. The DTCs run continuously when the above conditions are met for 2 s.
DTC: P2299 00	**Brake Pedal Position - Accelerator Pedal Position Not Plausible:** The ignition is ON or the engine is running. The DTC runs continues once the above conditions are met.
DTC: P229E	**NOx Sensor 2 Circuit:** P229EThe battery voltage is greater than 11 V for greater than 3 s. The engine speed is greater than 600 RPM. The engine run time is greater than 20 s. The exhaust gas temperature sensor 4 is between 95-3,004°C (203-5,439°F). The NOx sensor is at operating temperature. The DTCs run continuously once the above conditions are met.

DTC	Trouble Code Title, Conditions, Possible Causes
DTC: P229F	**NOx Sensor 2 Performance:** P229FThe ambient air temperature is greater than -7°C (19°F)The BARO pressure is greater than 75 kPa (11 psi). The average SCR temperature is greater than 200°C (392° F). The DPF regeneration is not active. The DTC runs once per drive cycle after the above conditions are met.
DTC: P22A0	**NOx Sensor 2 Circuit Low Voltage:** P2200, P2202, P2203, P22A0, and P22A1 DTCs P2205, P2209, P22A3, or P22A7 are not set. The battery voltage is greater than 11 V for greater than 3 s. The engine speed is greater than 600 RPM. The engine run time is greater than 20 s. The exhaust gas temperature Sensor 2 is between 95-3,004°C (203-5,439°F). The NOx sensor is at operating temperature. The DTCs run continuously once the above conditions are met.
DTC: P22A1	**NOx Sensor 2 Circuit High Voltage:** P2200, P2202, P2203, P22A0, and P22A1 DTCs P2205, P2209, P22A3, or P22A7 are not set. The battery voltage is greater than 11 V for greater than 3 s. The engine speed is greater than 600 RPM. The engine run time is greater than 20 s. The exhaust gas temperature Sensor 2 is between 95-3,004°C (203-5,439°F). The NOx sensor is at operating temperature. The DTCs run continuously once the above conditions are met.
DTC: P22A3	**NOx Sensor 2 Heater Control Circuit:** DTC P2205 or P22A3The battery voltage is greater than 11 V. The engine speed is greater than 600 RPM for greater than 10 s. The Exhaust Gas Temperature Sensor 1 is greater than 95°C (203°F). The DTCs run continuously once the above conditions are met.
DTC: P22A7	**NOx Sensor 2 Heater Feedback Performance:** DTC P2209 or P22A7 DTC P064C, P163C, P220A, or P220B are not set. The battery voltage is greater than 11 V. The engine speed is between 600-5,000 RPM. The Exhaust Gas Temperature Sensor 1 is greater than 95°C (203°F). The DTCs run continuously once the above conditions are met.
DTC: P2300 00	**Ignition Coil 1 Control Circuit Low Voltage:** The engine speed is less than 6000 RPM. The ignition voltage is between 9-18 V. DTCs P2300 00, P2301 00, P2303, P2304 00, P2306 00, P2307 00, P2309 00, P2310 00 run continuously when the above conditions are met.
DTC: P2301 00	**Ignition Coil 1 Control Circuit High Voltage:** The engine speed is less than 6000 RPM. The ignition voltage is between 9-18 V. DTCs P2300 00, P2301 00, P2303, P2304 00, P2306 00, P2307 00, P2309 00, P2310 00 run continuously when the above conditions are met.
DTC: P2303 00	**Ignition Coil 2 Control Circuit Low Voltage:** The engine speed is less than 6000 RPM. The ignition voltage is between 9-18 V. DTCs P2300 00, P2301 00, P2303, P2304 00, P2306 00, P2307 00, P2309 00, P2310 00 run continuously when the above conditions are met.
DTC: P2304 00	**Ignition Coil 2 Control Circuit High Voltage:** The engine speed is less than 6000 RPM. The ignition voltage is between 9-18 V. DTCs P2300 00, P2301 00, P2303, P2304 00, P2306 00, P2307 00, P2309 00, P2310 00 run continuously when the above conditions are met.
DTC: P2306 00	**Ignition Coil 3 Control Circuit Low Voltage:** The engine speed is less than 6000 RPM. The ignition voltage is between 9-18 V. DTCs P2300 00, P2301 00, P2303, P2304 00, P2306 00, P2307 00, P2309 00, P2310 00 run continuously when the above conditions are met.
DTC: P2307 00	**Ignition Coil 3 Control Circuit High Voltage:** The engine speed is less than 6000 RPM. The ignition voltage is between 9-18 V. DTCs P2300 00, P2301 00, P2303, P2304 00, P2306 00, P2307 00, P2309 00, P2310 00 run continuously when the above conditions are met.
DTC: P2309 00	**Ignition Coil 4 Control Circuit Low Voltage:** The engine speed is less than 6000 RPM. The ignition voltage is between 9-18 V. DTCs P2300 00, P2301 00, P2303, P2304 00, P2306 00, P2307 00, P2309 00, P2310 00 run continuously when the above conditions are met.
DTC: P2310 00	**Ignition Coil 4 Control Circuit High Voltage:** The engine speed is less than 6000 RPM. The ignition voltage is between 9-18 V. DTCs P2300 00, P2301 00, P2303, P2304 00, P2306 00, P2307 00, P2309 00, P2310 00 run continuously when the above conditions are met.
DTC: P2413	**Exhaust Gas Recirculation (EGR) System Performance:** DTC P0045, P0047, P0048, P006E, P006F, P007C, P007D, P0101, P0102, P0103, P0106, P0107, P0108, P0112, P0113, P0117, P0118, P0200, P02E0, P02E7, P02E8, P02E9, P02EB, P0403, P0405, P0406, P0489, P0490, P122C, P122E, P122F, P1407, P140D, P140E, P140F, P1411, P1412, ,P1413, P1414, P16A0, P16A1, P16A2, P2228, P2229, P2263, P2453, P245A, P245C, P245D, P2493, P2494, P2495, P2564, P2565, P2598, or P2599 is not set. The engine is running at idle. The DTC runs continuously when the above conditions are met.

DTC	Trouble Code Title, Conditions, Possible Causes
DTC: P242B	**Exhaust Gas Temperature Sensor 3 Performance:** P242BDTC P007C, P007D, P0097, P0098, P0101, P0102, P0103, P0107, P0108, P0112, P0113, P0401, P0402, P0403, P0405, P0406, P046C, P111C, P111D, P113A, P20E2, P2032, P2033, P2228, P2229, P242C, or P242D is not set. The engine is running for at least 327 s. The engine speed is between 700-3000 RPM for 60 s. The calculated fuel rate is between 5-80mm ; for 60 s. DPF regeneration or exhaust gas temperature monitoring has not been active in the last 25 minutes. Exhaust gas temperature sensor 3 has changed less than 7°C (12. 6°F) in 5 s. The DTC runs continuously when the above conditions are met.
DTC: P242B 00	**Exhaust Gas Temperature Sensor 3 Performance:** The ignition is ON. The DTCs run continuously when the above condition is met.
DTC: P242C	**Exhaust Gas Temperature Sensor 3 Circuit Low Voltage:** The ignition is ON or the engine is running. The DTCs run continuously when the above conditions are met.
DTC: P242C 00	**Exhaust Gas Temperature Sensor 3 Circuit Low Voltage:** The ignition is ON. The DTCs run continuously when the above condition is met.
DTC: P242D	**Exhaust Gas Temperature Sensor 3 Circuit High Voltage:** The ignition is ON or the engine is running. The DTCs run continuously when the above conditions are met.
DTC: P242D 00	**Exhaust Gas Temperature Sensor 3 Circuit High Voltage:** The ignition is ON. The DTCs run continuously when the above condition is met.
DTC: P242E 00	**Exhaust Gas Temperature Sensor 3 Circuit Intermittent:** The ignition is ON. The DTCs run continuously when the above condition is met.
DTC: P2430	**Secondary Air Injection (AIR) System Pressure Sensor Stuck in Range Bank 1:** DTC P2430 DTCs P0412, P0418, P0606, P2432, P2433, P2437, or P2438 are not set. Greater than 120 min has elapsed since the last cold start. The start-up intake air temperature (IAT) is between 5-60°C (41-140°F). The start-up engine coolant temperature (ECT) is between 5-50°C (41-122°F). DTC P2430 runs continuously when the above conditions are met.
DTC: P2430	**Secondary Air Injection (AIR) System Pressure Sensor Circuit:** DTC P2430 DTC P0411, P0412, P0418, P0601, P0602, P0603, P0604, P0606, P0607, P062F, P0641, or P0651 is not set. Greater than 60 min has elapsed since the last cold start. The Barometric Pressure (BARO) is greater than 60 kPa (8. 7 psi). The Intake Air Temperature (IAT) is warmer than -11°C (12°F). The Engine Coolant Temperature (ECT) is between -11 to +60°C (12-140°F). The ignition voltage is between 10-18 V. The Manifold Absolute Pressure (MAP) sensor is greater than 20 kPa (2. 9 psi). The engine speed is less than 5,000 RPM. The Mass Air Flow (MAF) is less than 50 g/s. The secondary air injection pump is commanded ON. DTC P2430 runs continuously when the above conditions are met.
DTC: P2431	**Secondary Air Injection System Pressure Sensor Performance:** DTC P2431 DTCs P0101, P0102, P0103, P0300, P0301, P0302, P0304, P0412, P0418, P0606, P0641 or P0651 are not set. The barometric pressure (BARO) is greater than 60 kPa (8. 7 psi). The intake air temperature (IAT) is warmer than -11°C (12°F). The engine coolant temperature (ECT) is between -11 to +60°C (12-140°F). The ignition voltage is between 10-32 V. The manifold absolute pressure (MAP) sensor is greater than 20 kPa (2. 9 psi). Run/Crank is not active. The engine speed is less than 5,000 RPM. The mass air flow (MAF) is less than 50 g/s. Greater than 60 minutes has elapsed since the last cold start. DTC P2431 runs continuously when the above conditions are met.
DTC: P2432	**Secondary Air Injection System Pressure Sensor Circuit Low Voltage:** P2432 and P2433 DTCs P0606, P0641, or P0651 are not set. The ignition is ON or the engine is running. DTC P2432 and P2433 run continuously when the above conditions are met.
DTC: P2433	**Secondary Air Injection (AIR) System Pressure Sensor Circuit High Voltage:** P2432 and P2433 DTC P0601, P0602, P0603, P0604, P0606, P0607, P062F, P0641, or P0651 is not set. The ignition is ON or the engine is running. DTC P2432 and P2433 run continuously when the above conditions are met.
DTC: P2435	**Secondary Air Injection (AIR) System Pressure Sensor Stuck in Range Bank 2:** DTC P2435 DTCs P0412, P0418, P0606, P2432, P2433, P2437, or P2438 are not set. Greater than 120 min has elapsed since the last cold start. The start-up intake air temperature (IAT) is between 5-60°C (41-140°F). The start-up engine coolant temperature (ECT) is between 5-50°C (41-122°F). DTC P2435 runs continuously when the above conditions are met.
DTC: P2436	**Secondary Air Injection (AIR) System Pressure Sensor Performance Bank 2:** DTC P2436 DTCs P0107, P0108, P0412, P0418, P0606, P0641, P0651, P2432, P2433, P2437, or P2438 are not set. The ignition is ON. DTC P2436 runs continuously when the above conditions are met.
DTC: P2437	**Secondary Air Injection (AIR) System Pressure Sensor Circuit Low Voltage Bank 2:** P2437 and P2438 DTCs P0606, P0641, or P0651 are not set. The ignition is ON, or the engine is operating. DTC P2432 and P2433 run continuously when the above conditions are met.
DTC: P2438	**Secondary Air Injection (AIR) System Pressure Sensor Circuit High Voltage Bank 2:** P2437 and P2438 DTCs P0606, P0641, or P0651 are not set. The ignition is ON, or the engine is operating. DTC P2432 and P2433 run continuously when the above conditions are met.

DTC	Trouble Code Title, Conditions, Possible Causes
DTC: P2440	**Secondary Air Injection System Shut-Off Valve Stuck Open:** DTCs P0101, P0102, P0103, P0106, P0107, P0108, P0112, P0113, P0114, P0116, P0117, P0118, P0121, P0122, P0123, P0128, P0201, P0202, P0203, P0204, P0222, P0223, P0261, P0262, P0264, P0265, P0267, P0268, P0270, P0271, P0300, P0301, P0302, P0303, P0304, P0351, P0352, P0353, P0354, P0411, P0412, P0418, P0420, P0606, P0641, P0651, P1248, P1249, P124A, P124B, P2147, P2148, P2150, P2151, P2153, P2154, P2156, P2157, P2430, P2431, P2432 or P2433 are not set. Greater than 60 min has elapsed since the last cold start. The ignition voltage is between 10-32 V. The barometric pressure (BARO) is greater than 60 kPa (8. 7 psi). The engine coolant temperature (ECT) is between -11 to +60°C (12-140°F). The intake air temperature (IAT) is warmer than -11°C (+12°F). The manifold absolute pressure (MAP) sensor is greater than 20 kPa (2. 9 psi). The mass air flow (MAF) is less than 50 g/s. The engine speed is less than 5,000 RPM. The AIR system is commanded ON. The DTC runs continuously once the above conditions are met for greater than 3 s.
DTC: P2444	**Secondary Air Injection System Pump Stuck ON:** DTCs P0101, P0102, P0103, P0106, P0107, P0108, P0112, P0113, P0114, P0116, P0117, P0118, P0121, P0122, P0123, P0128, P0201, P0202, P0203, P0204, P0222, P0223, P0261, P0262, P0264, P0265, P0267, P0268, P0270, P0271, P0300, P0301, P0302, P0303, P0304, P0351, P0352, P0353, P0354, P0411, P0412, P0418, P0420, P0606, P0641, P0651, P1248, P1249, P124A, P124B, P2147, P2148, P2150, P2151, P2153, P2154, P2156, P2157, P2430, P2431, P2432 or P2433 are not set. Greater than 60 min has elapsed since the last cold start. The ignition voltage is between 10-32 V. The barometric pressure (BARO) is greater than 60 kPa (8. 7 psi). The engine coolant temperature (ECT) is between -11 to +60°C (12-140°F). The intake air temperature (IAT) is warmer than -11°C (+12°F). The manifold absolute pressure (MAP) sensor is greater than 20 kPa (2. 9 psi). The engine speed is less than 5,000 RPM. The mass air flow (MAF) is less than 50 g/s. The AIR system is commanded ON. The DTC runs continuously once the above conditions are met for greater than 4 s.
DTC: P244B 11	**Diesel Particulate Filter (DPF) High Differential Pressure High Input:** The ignition is ON. The DTC run continuously when the above condition is met. OR The ignition is switched from ON to OFF. The DTC runs after a 2 s delay when the above condition is met.
DTC: P244C	**Catalyst Temperature Too Low During Regeneration:** The engine control system is in an active regeneration. DTC P244C runs continuously when the above condition is met.
DTC: P244C 00	**Catalyst Low Temperature During Regeneration Malfunction:** The DTC runs during the DPF regeneration process.
DTC: P244D	**Catalyst High Temperature During Regeneration:** DTC P0545, P0546, P2032, P2033, P2080, P2084, P242B, P242C, P242D, P246F, P2470 and P2471 are not set. The engine speed is greater than 600 RPM. The DTCs run continuously once the above conditions are met.
DTC: P2452 03	**Diesel Particulate Filter (DPF) Differential Pressure Sensor Circuit Low Voltage:** The ignition is ON, or the engine is running. The DTCs run continuously when the above condition is met.
DTC: P2452 07	**Diesel Particulate Filter Differential (DPF) Pressure Sensor Circuit High Voltage:** The ignition is ON, or the engine is running. The DTCs run continuously when the above condition is met.
DTC: P2453	**Diesel Particulate Filter (DPF) Differential Pressure Sensor Performance:** DTC P0101, P2454, or P2455 are not set. The engine run time is greater than 10 s. The engine speed is greater than 600 RPM. The battery voltage is greater than 11 V. The exhaust gas flow is stable. The DTC runs continuously when the above conditions are met.
DTC: P2453	**Particulate Matter Trap Differential Pressure Sensor Signal Performance:** The engine has been running and then turned off for at least 60 seconds. ORDTC P2453 runs continuously when the engine is running. ANDDTC P2453 runs once after the ignition has been turned OFF.
DTC: P2453 00	**Diesel Particulate Filter (DPF) Differential Pressure Sensor Performance:** P2453 DTC P0101, P2454, or P2455 are not set. The engine has been running and then turned off for at least 60 s. The engine speed is greater than 600 RPM. The battery voltage is greater than 11 V. The exhaust gas flow is stable. The DTC runs continue when the above conditions are met. and DTC P2453 runs once after the ignition has been turned OFF. P2454 DTC P2454 is not set. Engine run time is greater than 10 s. The engine speed is greater than 600 RPM. The DTC runs continuously when the above conditions are met. P2455 DTC P2455 is not set. Engine run time is greater than 10 s. The engine speed is greater than 600 RPM. The DTC runs continuously when the above conditions are met.
DTC: P2453 08	**Diesel Particulate Filter (DPF) Differential Pressure Sensor Performance - Signal Invalid:** P244B, P2453 08, P2453 11, P2453 12, P2453 55, P2453 58, or P2453 09The ignition is ON. The DTCs run continuously when the above condition is met. P244B, P2453 08, P2453 11, P2453 12, P2453 55The ignition is switched from ON to OFF. The DTCs run after a 2 s delay when the above condition is met. P2453 58The ignition is ON. The intake air temperature sensor is less than 0°C (32°F). The DTC runs continuously when the above condition is met.
DTC: P2453 11	**Diesel Particulate Filter (DPF) Differential Pressure Sensor Performance High Input:** P244B, P2453 08, P2453 11, P2453 12, P2453 55, P2453 58, or P2453 09The ignition is ON. The DTCs run continuously when the above condition is met. P244B, P2453 08, P2453 11, P2453 12, P2453 55The ignition is switched from ON to OFF. The DTCs run after a 2 s delay when the above condition is met. P2453 58The ignition is ON. The intake air temperature sensor is less than 0°C (32°F). The DTC runs continuously when the above condition is met.

DTC	Trouble Code Title, Conditions, Possible Causes
DTC: P2453 12	**Diesel Particulate Filter (DPF) Differential Pressure Sensor Performance Low Input:** P244B, P2453 08, P2453 11, P2453 12, P2453 55, P2453 58, or P2453 09The ignition is ON. The DTCs run continuously when the above condition is met. P244B, P2453 08, P2453 11, P2453 12, P2453 55The ignition is switched from ON to OFF. The DTCs run after a 2 s delay when the above condition is met. P2453 58The ignition is ON. The intake air temperature sensor is less than 0°C (32°F). The DTC runs continuously when the above condition is met.
DTC: P2453 18	**Diesel Particulate Filter (DPF) Differential Pressure Sensor Performance Low Signal Amplitude:** P244B, P2453 08, P2453 11, P2453 12, P2453 55, P2453 58, or P2453 09The ignition is ON. The DTCs run continuously when the above condition is met. P244B, P2453 08, P2453 11, P2453 12, P2453 55The ignition is switched from ON to OFF. The DTCs run after a 2 s delay when the above condition is met. P2453 58The ignition is ON. The intake air temperature sensor is less than 0°C (32°F). The DTC runs continuously when the above condition is met.
DTC: P2453 55	**Diesel Particulate Filter (DPF) Differential Pressure Sensor Performance Too Few Transitions:** P244B, P2453 08, P2453 11, P2453 12, P2453 55, P2453 58, or P2453 09The ignition is ON. The DTCs run continuously when the above condition is met. P244B, P2453 08, P2453 11, P2453 12, P2453 55The ignition is switched from ON to OFF. The DTCs run after a 2 s delay when the above condition is met. P2453 58The ignition is ON. The intake air temperature sensor is less than 0°C (32°F). The DTC runs continuously when the above condition is met.
DTC: P2453 58	**Diesel Particulate Filter (DPF) Differential Pressure Sensor Performance:** P244B, P2453 08, P2453 11, P2453 12, P2453 55, P2453 58, or P2453 09The ignition is ON. The DTCs run continuously when the above condition is met. P244B, P2453 08, P2453 11, P2453 12, P2453 55The ignition is switched from ON to OFF. The DTCs run after a 2 s delay when the above condition is met. P2453 58The ignition is ON. The intake air temperature sensor is less than 0°C (32°F). The DTC runs continuously when the above condition is met.
DTC: P2453 59	**Diesel Particulate Filter (DPF) Differential Pressure Sensor Performance Protection Time-Out:** P244B, P2453 08, P2453 11, P2453 12, P2453 55, P2453 58, or P2453 09The ignition is ON. The DTCs run continuously when the above condition is met. P244B, P2453 08, P2453 11, P2453 12, P2453 55The ignition is switched from ON to OFF. The DTCs run after a 2 s delay when the above condition is met. P2453 58The ignition is ON. The intake air temperature sensor is less than 0°C (32°F). The DTC runs continuously when the above condition is met.
DTC: P2454	**Diesel Particulate Filter Differential Pressure Sensor Circuit Low Voltage:** P2454 DTC P2455 is not set. The engine run time is greater than 10 s. The engine speed is greater than 600 RPM. The DTC runs continuously when the above conditions are met.
DTC: P2454	**Diesel Particulate Filter Differential Pressure Sensor Circuit Low Voltage:** The engine is running for greater than 4 seconds. The ignition 1 voltage is greater than 11V. The above conditions are met for greater than 2 seconds. DTCs P2454 and P2455 run continuously within the above enabling conditions.
DTC: P2454 00	**Diesel Particulate Filter (DPF) Differential Pressure Sensor Circuit Low Voltage:** P2453 DTC P0101, P2454, or P2455 are not set. The engine has been running and then turned off for at least 60 s. The engine speed is greater than 600 RPM. The battery voltage is greater than 11 V. The exhaust gas flow is stable. The DTC runs continue when the above conditions are met. and DTC P2453 runs once after the ignition has been turned OFF. P2454 DTC P2454 is not set. Engine run time is greater than 10 s. The engine speed is greater than 600 RPM. The DTC runs continuously when the above conditions are met. P2455 DTC P2455 is not set. Engine run time is greater than 10 s. The engine speed is greater than 600 RPM. The DTC runs continuously when the above conditions are met.
DTC: P2455	**Diesel Particulate Filter Differential Pressure Sensor Circuit High Voltage:** P2455 DTC P2454 is not set. The engine run time is greater than 10 s. The engine speed is greater than 600 RPM. The DTC runs continuously when the above conditions are met.
DTC: P2455	**Diesel Particulate Filter Differential Pressure Sensor Circuit High Voltage:** The engine is running for greater than 4 seconds. The ignition 1 voltage is greater than 11V. The above conditions are met for greater than 2 seconds. DTCs P2454 and P2455 run continuously within the above enabling conditions.
DTC: P2455 00	**Diesel Particulate Filter (DPF) Differential Pressure Sensor Circuit High Voltage:** P2453 DTC P0101, P2454, or P2455 are not set. The engine has been running and then turned off for at least 60 s. The engine speed is greater than 600 RPM. The battery voltage is greater than 11 V. The exhaust gas flow is stable. The DTC runs continue when the above conditions are met. and DTC P2453 runs once after the ignition has been turned OFF. P2454 DTC P2454 is not set. Engine run time is greater than 10 s. The engine speed is greater than 600 RPM. The DTC runs continuously when the above conditions are met. P2455 DTC P2455 is not set. Engine run time is greater than 10 s. The engine speed is greater than 600 RPM. The DTC runs continuously when the above conditions are met.
DTC: P2457	**Exhaust Gas Recirculation (EGR) Cooler Low Efficiency:** Engine speed is between 1,000-2,200 RPM. The engine is not in Diesel Particulate Filter (DPF) regeneration. The calculated fuel rate is greater than 20 mm ;. The engine coolant temperature is less than 123°C (253°F). The difference between the upstream EGR cooler temperature and the Engine Coolant Temperature (ECT) is greater than 40°C (72°F). The ambient air temperature is greater than -7°C (19°F). The EGR valve position is greater than 10 %. The Barometric Pressure (BARO) is greater than 74. 8 kPa (10. 9 psi). DTC P2457 runs once per driving cycle when the above conditions are met.

DTC	Trouble Code Title, Conditions, Possible Causes
DTC: P2458 59	**Diesel Particulate Filter (DPF) Regeneration Time Protection Time-Out:** The DTC runs during the DPF regeneration process.
DTC: P2459	**Diesel Particulate Filter Regeneration Too Often:** The engine is running. One active regeneration event has completed. DTC P2459 runs continuously when the above condition is met.
DTC: P2459	**Diesel Particulate Filter Regeneration Too Often:** DTC P0101, P0401, P0402, P2002, P2229, P2453, P2454, or P2455, are not set. The engine is running. The Intake Air Temperature is warmer than -7°C (19°F)The BARO pressure is greater than 75 kPa (11 psi). One active regeneration event has completed. DTC P2459 runs continuously when the above condition are met.
DTC: P245C 00	**Exhaust Gas Recirculation (EGR) Cooler Bypass Solenoid Valve Control Circuit Low Voltage:** Ignition is on.
DTC: P245D 00	**Exhaust Gas Recirculation (EGR) Cooler Bypass Solenoid Valve Control Circuit High Voltage:** Ignition is on.
DTC: P2463	**Diesel Particulate Filter Soot Level Accumulation:** The ignition is ON. DTC P2463 runs continuously when the above condition is met.
DTC: P2463 00	**Diesel Particulate Filter (DPF) Soot Accumulation:** The engine is running. The DTC runs continuously when the above condition is met.
DTC: P2463 00	**Diesel Particulate Filter (DPF) Soot Accumulation Malfunction:** The engine is running. The DTC runs continuously when the above condition is met.
DTC: P2463 11	**Diesel Particulate Filter (DPF) Soot Accumulation High Input:** The engine is running. The DTC runs continuously when the above condition is met.
DTC: P246C 00	**Diesel Particulate Filter (DPF) Restriction - Not Regenerable:** The engine is running. The DTC runs continuously when the above condition is met.
DTC: P246F	**Exhaust Gas Temperature Sensor 4 Performance:** P246FDTC P007C, P007D, P0097, P0098, P0101, P0102, P0103, P0107, P0108, P0112, P0113, P0401, P0402, P0403, P0405, P0406, P046C, P111C, P111D, P113A, P20E2, P2228, P2229, P242C, P242D, P2470 or P2471 is not set. The engine is running for at least 327 s. The engine speed is between 700-3000 RPM for 60 s. The calculated fuel rate is between 5-80mm ; for 60 s. DPF regeneration or exhaust gas temperature monitoring has not been active in the last 25 minutes. Exhaust gas temperature sensor 4 has changed less than 7°C (12. 6°F) in 5 s. The DTC runs continuously when the above conditions are met.
DTC: P2470	**Exhaust Gas Temperature Sensor 4 Circuit Low Voltage:** The ignition is ON or the engine is running. The DTCs run continuously when the above conditions are met.
DTC: P2471	**Exhaust Gas Temperature Sensor 4 Circuit High Voltage:** The ignition is ON or the engine is running. The DTCs run continuously when the above conditions are met.
DTC: P249D	**Closed Loop Reductant Injection Control At Limit - Flow Too Low:** DTCs P0101, P0401, P0402, P0420, P11DB, P11DC, P140B, P140C, P207F, P2200, P2202, P2203, P2205, P2209, P229E, P229F, P22A3, P22A7, or U029D, or U029E are not set. SCR reductant level not in restriction or empty level state. The engine speed is greater than 600 RPM. The battery voltage is greater than 11 V. The ambient air and emission reduction fluid tank temperatures are warmer than -7°C (19°F). The engine run time is greater than 10 s. The DTCs run continuously once the above conditions are met.
DTC: P249E	**Closed Loop Reductant Injection Control At Limit - Flow Too High:** DTCs P0101, P0401, P0402, P0420, P11DB, P11DC, P140B, P140C, P207F, P2200, P2202, P2203, P2205, P2209, P229E, P229F, P22A3, P22A7, or U029D, or U029E are not set. SCR reductant level not in restriction or empty level state. The engine speed is greater than 600 RPM. The battery voltage is greater than 11 V. The ambient air and emission reduction fluid tank temperatures are warmer than -7°C (19°F). The engine run time is greater than 10 s. The DTCs run continuously once the above conditions are met.
DTC: P24A0	**Closed Loop Diesel Particulate Filter (DPF) Regeneration Control At Limit - Temperature Too Low:** P24A0 or P24A1The engine run time is greater than 10 s. The engine speed is greater than 600 RPM. The ECM is commanding a DPF regeneration. The vehicle speed is between 24-200 km/h (15-124 mph). The exhaust temperature sensor 1 and 4 is greater than 230°C (446°F). The exhaust temperature sensor 1 and 4 is less than 750°C (1,382°F). The DTCs run continuously once the above conditions are met for 10 minutes.
DTC: P24A1	**Closed Loop Diesel Particulate Filter (DPF) Regeneration Control At Limit - Temperature Too High:** P24A0 or P24A1The engine run time is greater than 10 s. The engine speed is greater than 600 RPM. The ECM is commanding a DPF regeneration. The vehicle speed is between 24-200 km/h (15-124 mph). The exhaust temperature sensor 1 and 4 is greater than 230°C (446°F). The exhaust temperature sensor 1 and 4 is less than 750°C (1,382°F). The DTCs run continuously once the above conditions are met for 10 minutes.
DTC: P2500	**Generator L-Terminal Circuit Low:** The engine is running.

DTC	Trouble Code Title, Conditions, Possible Causes
DTC: P2501	**Generator L-Terminal Circuit High:** The ignition is ON. The engine is OFF.
DTC: P2510	**Engine Control Module Relay Circuit:** DTCs P006F, P02E0, P0403, P1049, P2049, P208D, P20A3, P245A are not set. DTC P2510 runs once per ignition cycle.
DTC: P2510 58	**Engine Controls Ignition Relay Feedback Circuit Performance:** P2510 58The ignition is ON, or the engine is running. The DTCs run continuously once the above condition is met.
DTC: P2510 59	**Engine Controls Ignition Relay Feedback Circuit Protection Time-Out:** P2510 59The ignition is switched OFF. The DTC runs continuously until the ECM powers down.
DTC: P2534	**Ignition 1 Switch Circuit Low Voltage:** The engine speed is greater than 500 RPM for 5 seconds. Ignition voltage is between 9. 0 volts and 19. 0 volts.
DTC: P2534	**Ignition On/Start Switch Circuit Low Voltage:** The engine control module (ECM) communicates that the engine is running through the controller area network (CAN).
DTC: P2544	**Transmission Torque Request Signal Message Counter Incorrect:** The ignition is ON. The DTCs run continuously once the above condition is met.
DTC: P2544	**Transmission Torque Request Circuit:** The engine run time is greater than 0. 5 s. No other CAN errors are present.
DTC: P2544 72	**Transmission Torque Request Circuit Message Counter Incorrect:** The ignition is ON. The DTCs run continuously once the above condition is met.
DTC: P2544 74	**Transmission Torque Request Circuit Bus Signal Checksum Error:** The ignition is ON. The DTCs run continuously once the above condition is met.
DTC: P2563	**Turbocharger Boost Control Position Sensor Performance:** DTCs P0047, P0048, P2564, or P2565 are not set. The engine has been running for greater than 30 seconds. DTC P2563 runs continuously when the above conditions are met.
DTC: P2564	**Turbocharger Boost Control Position Sensor Circuit Low Voltage:** The engine has been running for more than 10 s. DTC P2564 and P2565 run continuously when the above conditions are met.
DTC: P2564 00	**Turbocharger Vane Position Sensor Circuit Low Voltage:** The ignition is ON or engine is running.
DTC: P2565	**Turbocharger Boost Control Position Sensor Circuit High Voltage:** The engine has been running for more than 10 s. DTC P2564 and P2565 run continuously when the above conditions are met.
DTC: P2565 00	**Turbocharger Vane Position Sensor Circuit High Voltage:** The ignition is ON or engine is running.
DTC: P2598	**Turbocharger Boost Control Position Performance - Low Position:** DTC P003A, P006E, P006F, P0045, P0047, P0048, P2564, or P2565 is not set. The engine coolant temperature is between 70-123°C (158-253°F). The engine is running for greater than 30-210 s, depending on the engine coolant temperature at start. The turbocharger vane position learn procedure is not active and has completed and passed since the last clearing of fault code memory. The ambient air temperature is greater than -15°C (5°F). DTC P2598 and P2599 run continuously whenever the above conditions are met.
DTC: P2599	**Turbocharger Boost Control Position Performance - High Position:** DTC P003A, P006E, P006F, P0045, P0047, P0048, P2564, or P2565 is not set. The engine coolant temperature is between 70-123°C (158-253°F). The engine is running for greater than 30-210 s, depending on the engine coolant temperature at start. The turbocharger vane position learn procedure is not active and has completed and passed since the last clearing of fault code memory. The ambient air temperature is greater than -15°C (5°F). DTC P2598 and P2599 run continuously whenever the above conditions are met.
DTC: P2610	**Control Module Ignition Off Timer Performance:** P2610The engine speed is greater than 240 RPM. DTC P2610 runs continuously when the engine is operating and the real time clock is active.
DTC: P2610	**Control Module Ignition Off Timer Performance:** P062C, P2610These DTCs run continuously when the ignition is ON.
DTC: P2610 00	**Control Module Ignition Off Timer Performance:** P2610 00The engine is running for at least 10 s. The ignition voltage is between 11-18 V. DTC P2610 00 runs once per ignition cycle.

DTC	Trouble Code Title, Conditions, Possible Causes
DTC: P2610 00	**Control Module Ignition Off Timer Performance:** P0601 00, P0605 00The ignition switch is in run or crank. The system voltage is more than 5. 23 V. The check sum calculation at power down in the last drive cycle had completely finished. DTC P0601 00 and DTC P0605 run once per ignition cycle when the above condition is met. P0602 00The ignition switch is in run or crank. DTC P0602 00 runs once per ignition cycle. P0604 00The ignition switch is in run or crank. The read/write test at power down in the last drive cycle had completely finished. DTC P0604 00 runs once per ignition cycle when the above condition is met. P0606 00The ignition switch is in the unlock, accessory, run, or crank positions. DTC P0606 00 runs continuously when the above conditions are met. P0607 00The engine is running or cranking. DTC P0607 00 runs continuously when the above condition is met. . P061B 00The ignition is ON or the engine is running. The system voltage is more than 5. 23 V. DTC P061B 00 runs continuously when the above conditions are met. P061C 00The ignition is ON or the engine is running. The system voltage is more than 5. 23 V. DTC P061C 00 runs continuously when the above conditions are met. P2610 00The ECM is powered down. DTC P2610 00 runs once per ignition cycle. or The ECM is powered up with the ignition switch in the run or crank position. The engine OFF timer value is less than or greater than an internal reference counter during an 2 s interval. DTC P2610 00 runs continuously when the above conditions are met.
DTC: P2615	**Camshaft Position Signal Output Circuit Low:** The ignition is ON, engine running.
DTC: P2616	**Camshaft Position Signal Output Circuit High:** The ignition is ON, engine running.
DTC: P2626	**HO2S Pumping Current Trim Circuit Sensor 1:** P2626 DTCs P0121, P0122, P0123, P0221, P0222, P0223, P0335, P0336, P0338 are not set. The ignition voltage is between 10. 7-8. 1 V. The engine is running. Fuel cut-off is true. The estimated exhaust temperature is less than 750°C (1,382°F). The HO2S 1 heater is at operating temperature. DTC P2626 runs continuously when the above conditions are met for 4 s, or when the above conditions are met for 10 minutes if the fuel level is low.
DTC: P2635	**Fuel Pump Flow Performance:** DTC P018B, P018C, P018D, P0231, P0232, P023F, P064A, P1255 or P06A6 are not active. DTC P0641 has not failed this ignition cycle. Fuel pump control is enabled and the fuel pump control state is normal. The system voltage is greater than 11 V. The engine has been running for more than 30 s. Low fuel level warning not present.
DTC: P2687 01	**Fuel Heater Relay Control Circuit Short to Battery:** The ignition is ON. The ignition voltage is less than 16. 5 V. The DTC runs continuously once the above conditions are met
DTC: P2687 02	**Fuel Heater Relay Control Circuit Short to Ground:** The ignition is ON. The ignition voltage is less than 16. 5 V. The DTC runs continuously once the above conditions are met
DTC: P2687 04	**Fuel Heater Relay Control Circuit Open:** The ignition is ON. The ignition voltage is less than 16. 5 V. The DTC runs continuously once the above conditions are met
DTC: P2687 54	**Fuel Heater Relay Control Circuit High Temperature:** The ignition is ON. The ignition voltage is less than 16. 5 V. The DTC runs continuously once the above conditions are met
DTC: P268A	**Fuel Injector Calibration Data Not Programmed:** The ignition is ON.
DTC: P268A 00	**Fuel Injector Calibration Not Programmed Malfunction:** The ignition is ON.
DTC: P268C	**Injector 1 Calibration Incorrect:** The ignition is ON.
DTC: P268C 00	**Cylinder 1 Injector Calibration Incorrect:** The ignition is ON.
DTC: P268D	**Injector 2 Calibration Incorrect:** The ignition is ON.
DTC: P268D 00	**Cylinder 2 Injector Calibration Incorrect:** The ignition is ON.
DTC: P268E	**Injector 3 Calibration Incorrect:** The ignition is ON.
DTC: P268E 00	**Cylinder 3 Injector Calibration Incorrect:** The ignition is ON.
DTC: P268F	**Injector 4 Calibration Incorrect:** The ignition is ON.

DTC	Trouble Code Title, Conditions, Possible Causes
DTC: P268F 00	**Cylinder 4 Injector Calibration Incorrect:** The ignition is ON.
DTC: P2690	**Injector 5 Calibration Incorrect:** The ignition is ON.
DTC: P2691	**Injector 6 Calibration Incorrect:** The ignition is ON.
DTC: P2692	**Injector 7 Calibration Incorrect:** The ignition is ON.
DTC: P2693	**Injector 8 Calibration Incorrect:** The ignition is ON.
DTC: P2714	**Pressure Control Solenoid Valve 4 Stuck Off:** P2714 DTC P0101, P0102, P0103, P0106, P0107, P0108, P0171, P0172, P0174, P0175, P0201, P0202, P0203, P0204, P0205, P0206, P0207, P0208, P0300, P0301, P0302, P0303, P0304, P0305, P0306, P0307, P0308, P0401, P042E, P0716, P0717, P0722, P0723, or P182E is not set. The ignition voltage is 8. 6 volts or greater. The output speed is 16 RPM or greater, or the throttle position is 0. 5 percent or greater. The throttle position signal is valid. The engine speed is 400 RPM or greater for 5 seconds. The transmission fluid temperature is -7°C (19°F) or greater. The 2-6 clutch is commanded ON. The high side driver (HSD) is enabled.
DTC: P2714	**Clutch Pressure Control (PC) Solenoid 4 - Stuck Off:** P2714No ISS DTCs P0716 or P0717. No OSS DTCs P0722 or P0723. No IMS DTCs P1825 or P1915. The ignition voltage is between 9. 0 volts and 19. 0 volts. The transmission fluid temperature is 0°C (32°F) or greater. The transmission input shaft speed is 80 RPM or greater. The 2-6 clutch is commanded ON.
DTC: P2715	**Clutch Pressure Control Solenoid Valve 4 Stuck On:** P2715 DTC P0101, P0102, P0103, P0106, P0107, P0108, P0171, P0172, P0174, P0175, P0201, P0202, P0203, P0204, P0205, P0206, P0207, P0208, P0300, P0301, P0302, P0303, P0304, P0305, P0306, P0307, P0308, P0401, P042E, P0716, P0717, P0722, P0723, or P182E is not set. The ignition voltage is 8. 6 volts or greater. The HSD is enabled. The transmission fluid temperature is 0°C (32°F) or greater. The transmission output shaft speed is 350 RPM or greater. The transmission input shaft speed is 200 RPM or greater. The 2-6 clutch is commanded OFF. The commanded and attained gear is not 1st.
DTC: P2715	**Pressure Control Solenoid Valve 4 Stuck On:** P2715 DTC P0101, P0102, P0103, P0106, P0107, P0108, P0171, P0172, P0174, P0175, P0201, P0202, P0203, P0204, P0205, P0206, P0207, P0208, P0300, P0301, P0302, P0303, P0304, P0305, P0306, P0307, P0308, P0401, P042E, P0716, P0717, P0722, P0723, or P182E is not set. The ignition voltage is 9. 0 volts or greater. The transmission output shaft speed is 200 RPM or greater. The 2-6 clutch is commanded OFF. The TFT is 0°C (32°F) or greater. The attained range is not 1st gear. The HSD is enabled. The transmission input speed is 200 RPM or greater.
DTC: P2719	**Clutch Pressure Control (PC) Solenoid 4 System Performance:** P2719, P2720, or P2721 DTCs P2719, P2720, or P2721 have not set this ignition. The ignition voltage is 8. 6 volts or greater. The engine speed is 500 RPM or greater, for 5 seconds. The clutch PC solenoid 4 is commanded ON.
DTC: P2720	**Pressure Control Solenoid Valve 4 Control Circuit Low Voltage:** P2720The engine speed is 400 RPM or greater for 5 seconds. The ignition voltage is 8. 6 volts or greater. DTC P2720 is not set.
DTC: P2720	**Clutch Pressure Control (PC) Solenoid 4 Control Circuit Low Voltage:** P2719, P2720, or P2721 DTCs P2719, P2720, or P2721 have not set this ignition. The ignition voltage is 8. 6 volts or greater. The engine speed is 500 RPM or greater, for 5 seconds. The clutch PC solenoid 4 is commanded ON.
DTC: P2721	**Clutch Pressure Control (PC) Solenoid 4 Control Circuit High Voltage:** P2719, P2720, or P2721 DTCs P2719, P2720, or P2721 have not set this ignition. The ignition voltage is 8. 6 volts or greater. The engine speed is 500 RPM or greater, for 5 seconds. The clutch PC solenoid 4 is commanded ON.
DTC: P2721	**Pressure Control Solenoid Valve 4 Control Circuit High Voltage:** P2721The engine speed is 400 RPM or greater for 5 seconds. The ignition voltage is 8. 6 volts or greater. DTC P2721 is not set.
DTC: P2723	**Pressure Control Solenoid Valve 5 Stuck Off:** P2723 DTC P0101, P0102, P0103, P0106, P0107, P0108, P0171, P0172, P0174, P0175, P0201, P0202, P0203, P0204, P0205, P0206, P0207, P0208, P0300, P0301, P0302, P0303, P0304, P0305, P0306, P0307, P0308, P0401, P042E, P0716, P0717, P0722, P0723, or P182E is not set. The ignition voltage is 8. 6 volts or greater. The high side driver (HSD) is enabled. The output speed is 16 RPM or greater, or the throttle position is 0. 4 percent or greater. The throttle position signal is valid. The engine speed is greater than 400 RPM for 5 seconds. The transmission fluid temperature (TFT) is 0°C (32°F) or greater.
DTC: P2723	**Clutch Pressure Control (PC) Solenoid 5 - Stuck Off:** P2723No ISS DTCs P0716 or P0717. No OSS DTCs P0722 or P0723. No IMS DTCs P1825 or P1915. The transmission input shaft speed is 60 RPM or greater. 1-2-3-4 clutch is commanded ON.

DTC	Trouble Code Title, Conditions, Possible Causes
DTC: P2724	**Pressure Control Solenoid Valve 5 - Stuck On:** P2724 DTC P0101, P0102, P0103, P0106, P0107, P0108, P0171, P0172, P0174, P0175, P0201, P0202, P0203, P0204, P0205, P0206, P0207, P0208, P0300, P0301, P0302, P0303, P0304, P0305, P0306, P0307, P0308, P0401, P042E, P0716, P0717, P0722, P0723, or P182E is not set. The transmission fluid temperature is 0°C (32°F) or greater. The high HSD is ON. The transmission output shaft speed is 200 RPM or greater. The transmission input shaft speed is 200 RPM or greater. The commanded range is not 1st gear.
DTC: P2724	**Clutch Pressure Control (PC) Solenoid 5 - Stuck On:** P2724No DTCs P0101, P0102, P0103, P0106, P0107, P0108, P0171, P0172, P0174, P0175, P0201, P0202, P0203, P0204, P0205, P0206, P0207, P0208, P0300, P0301, P0302, P0303, P0304, P0305, P0306, P0307, P0308, P0401, P042E, P0716, P0717, P0722, P0723, or P182E. The ignition voltage is 8. 6 volts or greater. The high side driver is enabled. The TFT is 0°C (32°F) or greater. The transmission output shaft speed is 350 RPM or greater. The transmission input speed is 200 RPM or greater. 1-2-3-4 clutch is commanded OFF.
DTC: P2728	**Pressure Control Solenoid Valve 5 System Performance:** P2728, P2729, or P2730The engine speed is 400 RPM or greater for 5 seconds. The ignition voltage is 9. 0 volts or greater.
DTC: P2728	**Clutch Pressure Control (PC) Solenoid 5 System Performance:** P2728 DTC P2728 has not set this ignition cycle. The engine speed is 400 RPM or greater for 5 seconds. The ignition voltage is 8. 6 volts or greater.
DTC: P2729	**Pressure Control Solenoid Valve 5 Control Circuit Low Voltage:** P2729 DTC P2729 is not set. The engine speed is 400 RPM or greater for 5 seconds. The ignition voltage is 8. 6 volts or greater.
DTC: P2729	**Clutch Pressure Control (PC) Solenoid 5 Control Circuit Low Voltage:** P2728, P2729, or P2730 DTCs P2728, P2729, or P2730 have not set this ignition. The ignition voltage is 8. 6 volts or greater. The engine speed is 400 RPM or greater for 5 seconds. The clutch PC solenoid 5 is commanded ON.
DTC: P2730	**Pressure Control Solenoid Valve 5 Control Circuit High Voltage:** P2730 DTC P2730 is not set. The engine speed is 400 RPM or greater for 5 seconds. The ignition voltage is 8. 6 volts or greater.
DTC: P2730	**Clutch Pressure Control (PC) Solenoid 5 Control Circuit High Voltage:** P2728, P2729, or P2730 DTCs P2728, P2729, or P2730 have not set this ignition. The ignition voltage is 8. 6 volts or greater. The engine speed is 400 RPM or greater for 5 seconds. The clutch PC solenoid 5 is commanded ON.
DTC: P2762	**Torque Converter Clutch (TCC) Pressure Control Solenoid System Performance:** P2762 DTC P2762 has not set this ignition cycle. The engine speed is 400 RPM or greater for 5 seconds. The ignition voltage is 8. 6 volts or greater. Transmission fluid temperature is 140°C (284°F) or greater.
DTC: P2763	**Torque Converter Clutch (TCC) Pressure Control Solenoid Valve Control Circuit High Voltage:** P2763 or P2764The engine speed is 500 RPM or greater for 5 seconds. The ignition voltage is 9. 0 volts or greater. No DTCs P0658 or P0659. The high side driver is enabled.
DTC: P2764	**Torque Converter Clutch (TCC) Pressure Control (PC) Solenoid Control Circuit Low Voltage:** P2764No DTC P0335, P0336, P0340, P0345, P0346, P0365, P0366, P0390 or P0391. The engine speed is greater than 500 RPM for 5 seconds. The ignition voltage is greater than 8. 0 V.
DTC: P2769	**Torque Converter Clutch (TCC) Enable Solenoid Control Circuit Low Voltage:** P2769The system voltage is 8-18 volts. The engine speed is greater than 475 RPM for 5 seconds. Vehicle speed is less than 200 km/h (124 mph).
DTC: P2770	**Torque Converter Clutch (TCC) Enable Solenoid Control Circuit High Voltage:** P2770The system voltage is 8-18 volts. The engine speed is greater than 475 RPM for 5 seconds. Vehicle speed is less than 200 km/h (124 mph).
DTC: P2A00	**HO2S Circuit Closed Loop Performance Bank 1 Sensor 1:** P2A00 or P2A03 DTCs P0030, P0036, P0053, P0054, P0068, P0101, P0102, P0103, P0106, P0107, P0108, P0112, P0113, P0116, P0117, P0118, P0120, P0121, P0122, P0123, P0128, P0131, P0132, P0133, P0134, P0135, P0137, P0138, P0140, P0141, P0171, P0172, P0174, P0175, P0201, P0202, P0203, P0204, P0205, P0206, P0207, P0208, P0220, P0222, P0223, P0300, P0301, P0302, P0303, P0304, P0305, P0306, P0307, P0308, P0442, P0443, P0446, P0449, P0455, P0496, P1133, P1516, P2101, P2119, P2135, P2176 are not set. The engine is running. The system voltage is between 10-32 V. The ECT Sensor parameter is more than 0°C (32°F). DTCs P2A00 and P2A03 run continuously when the above conditions are met.
DTC: P2A00	**HO2S Circuit Closed Loop (CL) Performance Sensor 1:** P2A00 DTCs P0068, P0106, P0107, P0108, P0116, P0117, P0118, P0120, P0121, P0122, P0123, P0128, P0131, P0201, P0202, P0203, P0204, P0220, P0222, P0223, P1516, P2101, P2119, P2135, P2176 are not set. The Engine Run Time parameter is more than 100 s. The Engine speed parameter is between 500-3,400 RPM. The Ignition 1 Signal parameter is between 10-32 V. The Mass Airflow (MAF) Sensor parameter is between 3. 2-30 g/s. The ECT Sensor parameter is more than 70°C (158°F). DTC P2A00 runs continuously when the above conditions are met for 5 s.

DTC	Trouble Code Title, Conditions, Possible Causes
DTC: P2A00 00	**HO2S Circuit Closed Loop Performance Sensor 1:** Ignition voltage is between 10-18 V. Engine speed is between 1 000-3 400 RPM. Airflow into the engine is between 4-30 g/s. Engine coolant temperature (ECT) is greater than 70°C (158°F). Engine run time is greater than 100 s. DTC P2A00 runs continuously when the above conditions are met for greater than 5 s.
DTC: P2A01	**HO2S Performance Bank 1 Sensor 2:** DTC P2A01 DTC P2A01 runs a passive test and intrusive test when the following conditions are met. DTCs P0030, P0036, P0053, P0054, P0068, P0101, P0102, P0103, P0106, P0107, P0108, P0112, P0113, P0116, P0117, P0118, P0120, P0121, P0122, P0123, P0125, P0128, P0131, P0132, P0133, P0134, P0135, P0137, P0138, P0140, P0141, P0201, P0202, P0203, P0204, P0205, P0206, P0207, P0208, P0220, P0222, P0223, P0442, P0443, P0446, P0449, P0455, P0496, P1133, P1516, P2101, P2119, P2135, P2176, or P2A00 are not set.
DTC: P2A01 00	**HO2S Performance Sensor 2:** P2A01 00 DTCs P0107 00, P0108 00, P0136 00, P0137 00, P0138 00, P0139 00, P0140 00, P0141 00, P0171 00, P0172 00, P0201 00, P0202 00, P0203 00, P0204 00, P0261 00, P0262 00, P0264 00, P0265 00, P0267 00, P0268 00, P0270 00, P0271 00, P0300 00, P0301 00, P0302 00, P0303 00, P0304 00, P0313 00, P0443 00, P0458 00, P0459 00, P0496 00, P2270 00, P2271 00 are not set. The ignition is ON. The deceleration fuel cut-off is active. DTC P2A01 00 runs continuously when the above conditions are met.
DTC: P2A03	**HO2S Circuit Closed Loop Performance Bank 2 Sensor 1:** P2A00 or P2A03 DTCs P0030, P0036, P0053, P0054, P0068, P0101, P0102, P0103, P0106, P0107, P0108, P0112, P0113, P0116, P0117, P0118, P0120, P0121, P0122, P0123, P0128, P0131, P0132, P0133, P0134, P0135, P0137, P0138, P0140, P0141, P0171, P0172, P0174, P0175, P0201, P0202, P0203, P0204, P0205, P0206, P0207, P0208, P0220, P0222, P0223, P0300, P0301, P0302, P0303, P0304, P0305, P0306, P0307, P0308, P0442, P0443, P0446, P0449, P0455, P0496, P1133, P1516, P2101, P2119, P2135, P2176 are not set. The engine is running. The system voltage is between 10-32 V. The ECT Sensor parameter is more than 0°C (32°F). DTCs P2A00 and P2A03 run continuously when the above conditions are met.
DTC: P2A03	**HO2S Performance Bank 2 Sensor 1:** DTCs P2A00 or P2A03 DTCs P0068, P0101, P0102, P0103, P0106, P0107, P0108, P0112, P0113, P0116, P0117, P0118, P0120, P0121, P0122, P0123, P0125, P0128, P0201, P0202, P0203, P0204, P0205, P0206, P0207, P0208, P0220, P0222, P0223, P0442, P0443, P0446, P0449, P0455, P0496, P1516, P2101, P2119, P2135, or P2176 are not set. The engine run time is greater than 100 seconds. The engine speed is between 500-5,000 RPM. The Ignition 1 voltage is between 10-18 volts. The mass air flow (MAF) sensor is between 3-50 g/s. The engine coolant temperature (ECT) is greater than 70°C (158°F). The DTCs run continuously when the above conditions are met for 5 seconds.

GLOSSARY

ABS: Anti-lock braking system. An electro-mechanical braking system which is designed to minimize or prevent wheel lock-up during braking.

ABSOLUTE PRESSURE: Atmospheric (barometric) pressure plus the pressure gauge reading.

ACCELERATOR PUMP: A small pump located in the carburetor that feeds fuel into the air/fuel mixture during acceleration.

ACCUMULATOR: A device that controls shift quality by cushioning the shock of hydraulic oil pressure being applied to a clutch or band.

ACTUATING MECHANISM: The mechanical output devices of a hydraulic system, for example, clutch pistons and band servos.

ACTUATOR: The output component of a hydraulic or electronic system.

ADVANCE: Setting the ignition timing so that spark occurs earlier before the piston reaches top dead center (TDC).

ADAPTIVE MEMORY (ADAPTIVE STRATEGY): The learning ability of the TCM or PCM to redefine its decision-making process to provide optimum shift quality.

AFTER TOP DEAD CENTER (ATDC): The point after the piston reaches the top of its travel on the compression stroke.

AIR BAG: Device on the inside of the car designed to inflate on impact of crash, protecting the occupants of the car.

AIR CHARGE TEMPERATURE (ACT) SENSOR: The temperature of the airflow into the engine is measured by an ACT sensor, usually located in the lower intake manifold or air cleaner.

AIR CLEANER: An assembly consisting of a housing, filter and any connecting ductwork. The filter element is made up of a porous paper, sometimes with a wire mesh screening, and is designed to prevent airborne particles from entering the engine through the carburetor or throttle body.

AIR INJECTION: One method of reducing harmful exhaust emissions by injecting air into each of the exhaust ports of an engine. The fresh air entering the hot exhaust manifold causes any remaining fuel to be burned before it can exit the tailpipe.

AIR PUMP: An emission control device that supplies fresh air to the exhaust manifold to aid in more completely burning exhaust gases.

AIR/FUEL RATIO: The ratio of air-to-gasoline by weight in the fuel mixture drawn into the engine.

ALDL (assembly line diagnostic link): Electrical connector for scanning ECM/PCM/TCM input and output devices.

ALIGNMENT RACK: A special drive-on vehicle lift apparatus/measuring device used to adjust a vehicle's toe, caster and camber angles.

ALL WHEEL DRIVE: Term used to describe a full time four wheel drive system or any other vehicle drive system that continuously delivers power to all four wheels. This system is found primarily on station wagon vehicles and SUVs not utilized for significant off road use.

ALTERNATING CURRENT (AC): Electric current that flows first in one direction, then in the opposite direction, continually reversing flow.

ALTERNATOR: A device which produces AC (alternating current) which is converted to DC (direct current) to charge the car battery.

AMMETER: An instrument, calibrated in amperes, used to measure the flow of an electrical current in a circuit. Ammeters are always connected in series with the circuit being tested.

AMPERAGE: The total amount of current (amperes) flowing in a circuit.

AMPLIFIER: A device used in an electrical circuit to increase the voltage of an output signal.

AMP/HR. RATING (BATTERY): Measurement of the ability of a battery to deliver a stated amount of current for a stated period of time. The higher the amp/hr. rating, the better the battery.

AMPERE: The rate of flow of electrical current present when one volt of electrical pressure is applied against one ohm of electrical resistance.

ANALOG COMPUTER: Any microprocessor that uses similar (analogous) electrical signals to make its calculations.

ANODIZED: A special coating applied to the surface of aluminum valves for extended service life.

ANTIFREEZE: A substance (ethylene or propylene glycol) added to the coolant to prevent freezing in cold weather.

ANTI-FOAM AGENTS: Minimize fluid foaming from the whipping action encountered in the converter and planetary action.

ANTI-WEAR AGENTS: Zinc agents that control wear on the gears, bushings, and thrust washers.

ANTI-LOCK BRAKING SYSTEM: A supplementary system to the base hydraulic system that prevents sustained lock-up of the wheels during braking as well as automatically controlling wheel slip.

ANTI-ROLL BAR: See stabilizer bar.

ARC: A flow of electricity through the air between two electrodes or contact points that produces a spark.

ARMATURE: A laminated, soft iron core wrapped by a wire that converts electrical energy to mechanical energy as in a motor or relay. When rotated in a magnetic field, it changes mechanical energy into electrical energy as in a generator.

ATDC: After Top Dead Center.

ATF: Automatic transmission fluid.

ATMOSPHERIC PRESSURE: The pressure on the Earth's surface caused by the weight of the air in the atmosphere. At sea level, this pressure is 14.7 psi at 32°F (101 kPa at 0°C).

ATOMIZATION: The breaking down of a liquid into a fine mist that can be suspended in air.

AUXILIARY ADD-ON COOLER: A supplemental transmission fluid cooling device that is installed in series with the heat exchanger (cooler), located inside the radiator, to provide additional support to cool the hot fluid leaving the torque converter.

AUXILIARY PRESSURE: An added fluid pressure that is introduced into a regulator or balanced valve system to control valve movement. The auxiliary pressure itself can be either a fixed or a variable value. (See balanced valve; regulator valve.)

AWD: All wheel drive.

AXIAL FORCE: A side or end thrust force acting in or along the same plane as the power flow.

AXIAL PLAY: Movement parallel to a shaft or bearing bore.

AXLE CAPACITY: The maximum load-carrying capacity of the axle itself, as specified by the manufacturer. This is usually a higher number than the GAWR.

AXLE RATIO: This is a number (3.07:1, 4.56:1, for example) expressing the ratio between driveshaft revolutions and wheel revolutions. A low numerical ratio allows the engine to work easier because it doesn't have to turn as fast. A high numerical ratio means that the engine has to turn more rpm's to move the wheels through the same number of turns.

BACKFIRE: The sudden combustion of gases in the intake or exhaust system that results in a loud explosion.

BACKLASH: The clearance or play between two parts, such as meshed gears.

BACKPRESSURE: Restrictions in the exhaust system that slow the exit of exhaust gases from the combustion chamber.

BAKELITE®: A heat resistant, plastic insulator material commonly used in printed circuit boards and transistorized components.

BALANCED VALVE: A valve that is positioned by opposing auxiliary hydraulic pressures and/or spring force. Examples include mainline regulator, throttle, and governor valves. (See regulator valve.)

BAND: A flexible ring of steel with an inner lining of friction material. When tightened around the outside of a drum, a planetary member is held stationary to the transmission/transaxle case.

BALL BEARING: A bearing made up of hardened inner and outer races between which hardened steel balls roll.

BALL JOINT: A ball and matching socket connecting suspension components (steering knuckle to lower control arms). It permits rotating movement in any direction between the components that are joined.

BARO (BAROMETRIC PRESSURE SENSOR): Measures the change in the intake manifold pressure caused by changes in altitude.

BAROMETRIC MANIFOLD ABSOLUTE PRESSURE (BMAP) SENSOR: Operates similarly to a conventional MAP sensor; reads intake manifold pressure and is also responsible for determining altitude and barometric pressure prior to engine operation.

BAROMETRIC PRESSURE: (See atmospheric pressure.)

BALLAST RESISTOR: A resistor in the primary ignition circuit that lowers voltage after the engine is started to reduce wear on ignition components.

BATTERY: A direct current electrical storage unit, consisting of the basic active materials of lead and sulfuric acid, which converts chemical energy into electrical energy. Used to provide current for the operation of the starter as well as other equipment, such as the radio, lighting, etc.

BEAD: The portion of a tire that holds it on the rim.

BEARING: A friction reducing, supportive device usually located between a stationary part and a moving part.

BEFORE TOP DEAD CENTER (BTDC): The point just before the piston reaches the top of its travel on the compression stroke.

BELTED TIRE: Tire construction similar to bias-ply tires, but using two or more layers of reinforced belts between body plies and the tread.

BEZEL: Piece of metal surrounding radio, headlights, gauges or similar components; sometimes used to hold the glass face of a gauge in the dash.

BIAS-PLY TIRE: Tire construction, using body ply reinforcing cords which run at alternating angles to the center line of the tread.

BI-METAL TEMPERATURE SENSOR: Any sensor or switch made of two dissimilar types of metal that bend when heated or cooled due to the different expansion rates of the alloys. These types of sensors usually function as an on/off switch.

BLOCK: See Engine Block.

BLOW-BY: Combustion gases, composed of water vapor and unburned fuel, that leak past the piston rings into the crankcase during normal engine operation. These gases are removed by the PCV system to prevent the buildup of harmful acids in the crankcase.

BOOK TIME: See Labor Time.

BOOK VALUE: The average value of a car, widely used to determine trade-in and resale value.

BOOST VALVE: Used at the base of the regulator valve to increase mainline pressure.

BORE: Diameter of a cylinder.

BRAKE CALIPER: The housing that fits over the brake disc. The caliper holds the brake pads, which are pressed against the discs by the caliper pistons when the brake pedal is depressed.

BRAKE HORSEPOWER (BHP): The actual horsepower available at the engine flywheel as measured by a dynamometer.

BRAKE FADE: Loss of braking power, usually caused by excessive heat after repeated brake applications.

BRAKE HORSEPOWER: Usable horsepower of an engine measured at the crankshaft.

BRAKE PAD: A brake shoe and lining assembly used with disc brakes.

BRAKE PROPORTIONING VALVE: A valve on the master cylinder which restricts hydraulic brake pressure to the wheels to a specified amount, preventing wheel lock-up.

BREAKAWAY: Often used by Chrysler to identify first-gear operation in D and 2 ranges. In these ranges, first-gear operation depends on a one-way roller clutch that holds on acceleration and releases (breaks away) on deceleration, resulting in a freewheeling coast-down condition.

BRAKE SHOE: The backing for the brake lining. The term is, however, usually applied to the assembly of the brake backing and lining.

BREAKER POINTS: A set of points inside the distributor, operated by a cam, which make and break the ignition circuit.

BRINNELLING: A wear pattern identified by a series of indentations at regular intervals. This condition is caused by a lack of lube, overload situations, and/or vibrations.

BTDC: Before Top Dead Center.

BUMP: Sudden and forceful apply of a clutch or band.

BUSHING: A liner, usually removable, for a bearing; an anti-friction liner used in place of a bearing.

CALIFORNIA ENGINE: An engine certified by the EPA for use in California only; conforms to more stringent emission regulations than Federal engine.

CALIPER: A hydraulically activated device in a disc brake system, which is mounted straddling the brake rotor (disc). The caliper contains at least one piston and two brake pads. Hydraulic pressure on the piston(s) forces the pads against the rotor.

CAPACITY: The quantity of electricity that can be delivered from a unit, as from a battery in ampere-hours, or output, as from a generator.

CAMBER: One of the factors of wheel alignment. Viewed from the front of the car, it is the inward or outward tilt of the wheel. The top of the tire will lean outward (positive camber) or inward (negative camber).

CAMSHAFT: A shaft in the engine on which are the lobes (cams) which operate the valves. The camshaft is driven by the crankshaft, via a belt, chain or gears, at one half the crankshaft speed.

CAPACITOR: A device which stores an electrical charge.

CARBON MONOXIDE (CO): A colorless, odorless gas given off as a normal byproduct of combustion. It is poisonous and extremely dangerous in confined areas, building up slowly to toxic levels without warning if adequate ventilation is not available.

CARBURETOR: A device, usually mounted on the intake manifold of an engine, which mixes the air and fuel in the proper proportion to allow even combustion.

CASTER: The forward or rearward tilt of an imaginary line drawn through the upper ball joint and the center of the wheel. Viewed from the sides, positive caster (forward tilt) lends directional stability, while negative caster (rearward tilt) produces instability.

CATALYTIC CONVERTER: A device installed in the exhaust system, like a muffler, that converts harmful byproducts of combustion into carbon dioxide and water vapor by means of a heat-producing chemical reaction.

CENTRIFUGAL ADVANCE: A mechanical method of advancing the spark timing by using flyweights in the distributor that react to centrifugal force generated by the distributor shaft rotation.

CENTRIFUGAL FORCE: The outward pull of a revolving object, away from the center of revolution. Centrifugal force increases with the speed of rotation.

CETANE RATING: A measure of the ignition value of diesel fuel. The higher the cetane rating, the better the fuel. Diesel fuel cetane rating is roughly comparable to gasoline octane rating.

CHECK VALVE: Any one-way valve installed to permit the flow of air, fuel or vacuum in one direction only.

CHOKE: The valve/plate that restricts the amount of air entering an engine on the induction stroke, thereby enriching the air/fuel ratio.

CHUGGLE: Bucking or jerking condition that may be engine related and may be most noticeable when converter clutch is engaged; similar to the feel of towing a trailer.

CIRCLIP: A split steel snapring that fits into a groove to hold various parts in place.

CIRCUIT BREAKER: A switch which protects an electrical circuit from overload by opening the circuit when the current flow exceeds a pre-determined level. Some circuit breakers must be reset manually, while most reset automatically.

CIRCUIT: Any unbroken path through which an electrical current can flow. Also used to describe fuel flow in some instances.

CIRCUIT, BYPASS: Another circuit in parallel with the major circuit through which power is diverted.

CIRCUIT, CLOSED: An electrical circuit in which there is no interruption of current flow.

CIRCUIT, GROUND: The non-insulated portion of a complete circuit used as a common potential point. In automotive circuits, the ground is composed of metal parts, such as the engine, body sheet metal, and frame and is usually a negative potential.

CIRCUIT, HOT: That portion of a circuit not at ground potential. The hot circuit is usually insulated and is connected to the positive side of the battery.

CIRCUIT, OPEN: A break or lack of contact in an electrical circuit, either intentional (switch) or unintentional (bad connection or broken wire).

CIRCUIT, PARALLEL: A circuit having two or more paths for current flow with common positive and negative tie points. The same voltage is applied to each load device or parallel branch.

CIRCUIT, SERIES: An electrical system in which separate parts are connected end to end, using one wire, to form a single path for current to flow.

CIRCUIT, SHORT: A circuit that is accidentally completed in an electrical path for which it was not intended.

CLAMPING (ISOLATION) DIODES: Diodes positioned in a circuit to prevent self-induction from damaging electronic components.

CLEARCOAT: A transparent layer which, when sprayed over a vehicle's paint job, adds gloss and depth as well as an additional protective coating to the finish.

CLUTCH: Part of the power train used to connect/disconnect power to the rear wheels.

CLUTCH, FLUID: The same as a fluid coupling. A fluid clutch or coupling performs the same function as a friction clutch by utilizing fluid friction and inertia as opposed to solid friction used by a friction clutch. (See fluid coupling.)

CLUTCH, FRICTION: A coupling device that provides a means of smooth and positive engagement and disengagement of engine torque to the vehicle powertrain. Transmission of power through the clutch is accomplished by bringing one or more rotating drive members into contact with complementing driven members.

COAST: Vehicle deceleration caused by engine braking conditions.

COEFFICIENT OF FRICTION: The amount of surface tension between two contacting surfaces; identified by a scientifically calculated number.

COIL: Part of the ignition system that boosts the relatively low voltage supplied by the car's electrical system to the high voltage required to fire the spark plugs.

COMBINATION MANIFOLD: An assembly which includes both the intake and exhaust manifolds in one casting.

COMBINATION VALVE: A device used in some fuel systems that routes fuel vapors to a charcoal storage canister instead of venting them into the atmosphere. The valve relieves fuel tank pressure and allows fresh air into the tank as the fuel level drops to prevent a vapor lock situation.

COMBUSTION CHAMBER: The part of the engine in the cylinder head where combustion takes place.

COMPOUND GEAR: A gear consisting of two or more simple gears with a common shaft.

COMPOUND PLANETARY: A gearset that has more than the three elements found in a simple gearset and is constructed by combining members of two planetary gearsets to create additional gear ratio possibilities.

COMPRESSION CHECK: A test involving removing each spark plug and inserting a gauge. When the engine is cranked, the gauge will record a pressure reading in the individual cylinder. General operating condition can be determined from a compression check.

COMPRESSION RATIO: The ratio of the volume between the piston and cylinder head when the piston is at the bottom of its stroke (bottom dead center) and when the piston is at the top of its stroke (top dead center).

COMPUTER: An electronic control module that correlates input data according to prearranged engineered instructions; used for the management of an actuator system or systems.

CONDENSER: An electrical device which acts to store an electrical charge, preventing voltage surges.

2. A radiator-like device in the air conditioning system in which refrigerant gas condenses into a liquid, giving off heat.

CONDUCTOR: Any material through which an electrical current can be transmitted easily.

CONNECTING ROD: The connecting link between the crankshaft and piston.

CONSTANT VELOCITY JOINT: Type of universal joint in a halfshaft assembly in which the output shaft turns at a constant angular velocity without variation, provided that the speed of the input shaft is constant.

CONTINUITY: Continuous or complete circuit. Can be checked with an ohmmeter.

CONTROL ARM: The upper or lower suspension components which are mounted on the frame and support the ball joints and steering knuckles.

CONVENTIONAL IGNITION: Ignition system which uses breaker points.

CONVERTER: (See torque converter.)

CONVERTER LOCKUP: The switching from hydrodynamic to direct mechanical drive, usually through the application of a friction element called the converter clutch.

COOLANT: Mixture of water and anti-freeze circulated through the engine to carry off heat produced by the engine.

CORROSION INHIBITOR: An inhibitor in ATF that prevents corrosion of bushings, thrust washers, and oil cooler brazed joints.

COUNTERSHAFT: An intermediate shaft which is rotated by a mainshaft and transmits, in turn, that rotation to a working part.

COUPLING PHASE: Occurs when the torque converter is operating at its greatest hydraulic efficiency. The speed differential between the impeller and the turbine is at its minimum. At this point, the stator freewheels, and there is no torque multiplication.

CRANKCASE: The lower part of an engine in which the crankshaft and related parts operate.

CRANKSHAFT: Engine component (connected to pistons by connecting rods) which converts the reciprocating (up and down) motion of pistons to rotary motion used to turn the driveshaft.

CURB WEIGHT: The weight of a vehicle without passengers or payload, but including all fluids (oil, gas, coolant, etc.) and other equipment specified as standard.

CURRENT: The flow (or rate) of electrons moving through a circuit. Current is measured in amperes (amp).

CURRENT FLOW CONVENTIONAL: Current flows through a circuit from the positive terminal of the source to the negative terminal (plus to minus).

CURRENT FLOW, ELECTRON: Current or electrons flow from the negative terminal of the source, through the circuit, to the positive terminal (minus to plus).

CV-JOINT: Constant velocity joint.

CYCLIC VIBRATIONS: The off-center movement of a rotating object that is affected by its initial balance, speed of rotation, and working angles.

CYLINDER BLOCK: See engine block.

CYLINDER HEAD: The detachable portion of the engine, usually fastened to the top of the cylinder block and containing all or most of the combustion chambers. On overhead valve engines, it contains the valves and their operating parts. On overhead cam engines, it contains the camshaft as well.

CYLINDER: In an engine, the round hole in the engine block in which the piston(s) ride.

DATA LINK CONNECTOR (DLC): Current acronym/term applied to the federally mandated, diagnostic junction connector that is used to monitor ECM/PC/TCM inputs, processing strategies, and outputs including diagnostic trouble codes (DTCs).

DEAD CENTER: The extreme top or bottom of the piston stroke.

DECELERATION BUMP: When referring to a torque converter clutch in the applied position, a sudden release of the accelerator pedal causes a forceful reversal of power through the drivetrain (engine braking), just prior to the apply plate actually being released.

DELAYED (LATE OR EXTENDED): Condition where shift is expected but does not occur for a period of time, for example, where clutch or band engagement does not occur as quickly as expected during part throttle or wide open throttle apply of accelerator or when manually downshifting to a lower range.

DETENT: A spring-loaded plunger, pin, ball, or pawl used as a holding device on a ratchet wheel or shaft. In automatic transmissions, a detent mechanism is used for locking the manual valve in place.

DETENT DOWNSHIFT: (See kickdown.)

DETERGENT: An additive in engine oil to improve its operating characteristics.

DETONATION: An unwanted explosion of the air/fuel mixture in the combustion chamber caused by excess heat and compression, advanced timing, or an overly lean mixture. Also referred to as "ping".

DEXRON®: A brand of automatic transmission fluid.

DIAGNOSTIC TROUBLE CODES (DTCs): A digital display from the control module memory that identifies the input, processor, or output device circuit that is related to the powertrain emission/driveability malfunction detected. Diagnostic trouble codes can be read by the MIL to flash any codes or by using a handheld scanner.

DIAPHRAGM: A thin, flexible wall separating two cavities, such as in a vacuum advance unit.

DIESELING: The engine continues to run after the car is shut off; caused by fuel continuing to be burned in the combustion chamber.

DIFFERENTIAL: A geared assembly which allows the transmission of motion between drive axles, giving one axle the ability to rotate faster than the other, as in cornering.

DIFFERENTIAL AREAS: When opposing faces of a spool valve are acted upon by the same pressure but their areas differ in size, the face with the larger area produces the differential force and valve movement. (See spool valve.)

DIFFERENTIAL FORCE: (See differential areas)

DIGITAL READOUT: A display of numbers or a combination of numbers and letters.

DIGITAL VOLT OHMMETER: An electronic diagnostic tool used to measure voltage, ohms and amps as well as several other functions, with the readings displayed on a digital screen in tenths, hundredths and thousandths.

DIODE: An electrical device that will allow current to flow in one direction only.

DIRECT CURRENT (DC): Electrical current that flows in one direction only.

DIRECT DRIVE: The gear ratio is 1:1, with no change occurring in the torque and speed input/output relationship.

DISC BRAKE: A hydraulic braking assembly consisting of a brake disc, or rotor, mounted on an axle shaft, and a caliper assembly containing, usually two brake pads which are activated by hydraulic pressure. The pads are forced against the sides of the disc, creating friction which slows the vehicle.

DISPERSANTS: Suspend dirt and prevent sludge buildup in a liquid, such as engine oil.

DOUBLE BUMP (DOUBLE FEEL): Two sudden and forceful applies of a clutch or band.

DISPLACEMENT: The total volume of air that is displaced by all pistons as the engine turns through one complete revolution.

DISTRIBUTOR: A mechanically driven device on an engine which is responsible for electrically firing the spark plug at a pre-determined point of the piston stroke.

DOHC: Double overhead camshaft.

DOUBLE OVERHEAD CAMSHAFT: The engine utilizes two camshafts mounted in one cylinder head. One camshaft operates the exhaust valves, while the other operates the intake valves.

DOWEL PIN: A pin, inserted in mating holes in two different parts allowing those parts to maintain a fixed relationship.

DRIVELINE: The drive connection between the transmission and the drive wheels.

DRIVE TRAIN: The components that transmit the flow of power from the engine to the wheels. The components include the clutch, transmission, driveshafts (or axle shafts in front wheel drive), U-joints and differential.

DRUM BRAKE: A braking system which consists of two brake shoes and one or two wheel cylinders, mounted on a fixed backing plate, and a brake drum, mounted on an axle, which revolves around the assembly.

DRY CHARGED BATTERY: Battery to which electrolyte is added when the battery is placed in service.

DVOM: Digital volt ohmmeter

DWELL: The rate, measured in degrees of shaft rotation, at which an electrical circuit cycles on and off.

DYNAMIC: An application in which there is rotating or reciprocating motion between the parts.

EARLY: Condition where shift occurs before vehicle has reached proper speed, which tends to labor engine after upshift.

EBCM: See Electronic Control Unit (ECU).

ECM: See Electronic Control Unit (ECU).

ECU: Electronic control unit.

ELECTRODE: Conductor (positive or negative) of electric current.

ELECTROLYSIS: A surface etching or bonding of current conducting transmission/transaxle components that may occur when grounding straps are missing or in poor condition.

ELECTROLYTE: A solution of water and sulfuric acid used to activate the battery. Electrolyte is extremely corrosive.

ELECTROMAGNET: A coil that produces a magnetic field when current flows through its windings.

ELECTROMAGNETIC INDUCTION: A method to create (generate) current flow through the use of magnetism.

ELECTROMAGNETISM: The effects surrounding the relationship between electricity and magnetism.

ELECTROMOTIVE FORCE (EMF): The force or pressure (voltage) that causes current movement in an electrical circuit.

ELECTRONIC CONTROL UNIT: A digital computer that controls engine (and sometimes transmission, brake or other vehicle system) functions based on data received from various sensors. Examples used by some manufacturers include Electronic Brake Control Module (EBCM), Engine Control Module (ECM), Powertrain Control Module (PCM) or Vehicle Control Module (VCM).

ELECTRONIC IGNITION: A system in which the timing and firing of the spark plugs is controlled by an electronic control unit, usually called a module. These systems have no points or condenser.

ELECTRONIC PRESSURE CONTROL (EPC) SOLENOID: A specially designed solenoid containing a spool valve and spring assembly to control fluid mainline pressure. A variable current flow, controlled by the ECM/PCM, varies the internal force of the solenoid on the spool valve and resulting mainline pressure. (See variable force solenoid.)

ELECTRONICS: Miniaturized electrical circuits utilizing semiconductors, solid-state devices, and printed circuits. Electronic circuits utilize small amounts of power.

ELECTRONIFICATION: The application of electronic circuitry to a mechanical device. Regarding automatic transmissions, electrification is incorporated into converter clutch lockup, shift scheduling, and line pressure control systems.

ELECTROSTATIC DISCHARGE (ESD): An unwanted, high-voltage electrical current released by an individual who has taken on a static charge of electricity. Electronic components can be easily damaged by ESD.

ELEMENT: A device within a hydrodynamic drive unit designed with a set of blades to direct fluid flow.

ENAMEL: Type of paint that dries to a smooth, glossy finish.

END BUMP (END FEEL OR SLIP BUMP): Firmer feel at end of shift when compared with feel at start of shift.

END-PLAY: The clearance/gap between two components that allows for expansion of the parts as they warm up, to prevent binding and to allow space for lubrication.

ENERGY: The ability or capacity to do work.

ENGINE: The primary motor or power apparatus of a vehicle, which converts liquid or gas fuel into mechanical energy.

ENGINE BLOCK: The basic engine casting containing the cylinders, the crankshaft main bearings, as well as machined surfaces for the mounting of other components such as the cylinder head, oil pan, transmission, etc.

ENGINE BRAKING: Use of engine to slow vehicle by manually downshifting during zero-throttle coast down.

ENGINE CONTROL MODULE (ECM): Manages the engine and incorporates output control over the torque converter clutch solenoid. (Note: Current designation for the ECM in late model vehicles is PCM.)

ENGINE COOLANT TEMPERATURE (ECT) SENSOR: Prevents converter clutch engagement with a cold engine; also used for shift timing and shift quality.

EP LUBRICANT: EP (extreme pressure) lubricants are specially formulated for use with gears involving heavy loads (transmissions, differentials, etc.).

ETHYL: A substance added to gasoline to improve its resistance to knock, by slowing down the rate of combustion.

ETHYLENE GLYCOL: The base substance of antifreeze.

EXHAUST MANIFOLD: A set of cast passages or pipes which conduct exhaust gases from the engine.

FAIL-SAFE (BACKUP) CONTROL: A substitute value used by the PCM/TCM to replace a faulty signal from an input sensor. The temporary value allows the vehicle to continue to be operated.

FAST IDLE: The speed of the engine when the choke is on. Fast idle speeds engine warm-up.

FEDERAL ENGINE: An engine certified by the EPA for use in any of the 49 states (except California).

FEEDBACK: A circuit malfunction whereby current can find another path to feed load devices.

FEELER GAUGE: A blade, usually metal, of precisely predetermined thickness, used to measure the clearance between two parts.

FILAMENT: The part of a bulb that glows; the filament creates high resistance to current flow and actually glows from the resulting heat.

FINAL DRIVE: An essential part of the axle drive assembly where final gear reduction takes place in the powertrain. In RWD applications and north-south FWD applications, it must also change the power flow direction to the axle shaft by ninety degrees. (Also see axle ratio).

FIRING ORDER: The order in which combustion occurs in the cylinders of an engine. Also the order in which spark is distributed to the plugs by the distributor.

FIRM: A noticeable quick apply of a clutch or band that is considered normal with medium to heavy throttle shift; should not be confused with harsh or rough.

FLAME FRONT: The term used to describe certain aspects of the fuel explosion in the cylinders. The flame front should move in a controlled pattern across the cylinder, rather than simply exploding immediately.

FLARE (SLIPPING): A quick increase in engine rpm accompanied by momentary loss of torque; generally occurs during shift.

FLAT ENGINE: Engine design in which the pistons are horizontally opposed. Porsche, Subaru and some old VW are common examples of flat engines.

FLAT RATE: A dealership term referring to the amount of money paid to a technician for a repair or diagnostic service based on that particular service versus dealership's labor time (NOT based on the actual time the technician spent on the job).

FLAT SPOT: A point during acceleration when the engine seems to lose power for an instant.

FLOODING: The presence of too much fuel in the intake manifold and combustion chamber which prevents the air/fuel mixture from firing, thereby causing a no-start situation.

FLUID: A fluid can be either liquid or gas. In hydraulics, a liquid is used for transmitting force or motion.

FLUID COUPLING: The simplest form of hydrodynamic drive, the fluid coupling consists of two look-alike members with straight radial varies referred to as the impeller (pump) and the turbine. Input torque is always equal to the output torque.

FLUID DRIVE: Either a fluid coupling or a fluid torque converter. (See hydrodynamic drive units.)

FLUID TORQUE CONVERTER: A hydrodynamic drive that has the ability to act both as a torque multiplier and fluid coupling. (See hydrodynamic drive units; torque converter.)

FLUID VISCOSITY: The resistance of a liquid to flow. A cold fluid (oil) has greater viscosity and flows more slowly than a hot fluid (oil).

FLYWHEEL: A heavy disc of metal attached to the rear of the crankshaft. It smoothes the firing impulses of the engine and keeps the crankshaft turning during periods when no firing takes place. The starter also engages the flywheel to start the engine.

FOOT POUND (ft. lbs., lbs. ft. or sometimes, ft. lb.): The amount of energy or work needed to raise an item weighing one pound, a distance of one foot.

FREEZE PLUG: A plug in the engine block which will be pushed out if the coolant freezes. Sometimes called expansion plugs, they protect the block from cracking should the coolant freeze.

FRICTION: The resistance that occurs between contacting surfaces. This relationship is expressed by a ratio called the coefficient of friction (CL).

FRICTION, COEFFICIENT OF: The amount of surface tension between two contacting surfaces; expressed by a scientifically calculated number.

FRONT END ALIGNMENT: A service to set caster, camber and toe-in to the correct specifications. This will ensure that the car steers and handles properly and that the tires wear properly.

FRICTION MODIFIER: Changes the coefficient of friction of the fluid between the mating steel and composition clutch/band surfaces during the engagement process and allows for a certain amount of intentional slipping for a good "shift-feel".

FRONTAL AREA: The total frontal area of a vehicle exposed to air flow.

FUEL FILTER: A component of the fuel system containing a porous paper element used to prevent any impurities from entering the engine through the fuel system. It usually takes the form of a canister-like housing, mounted in-line with the fuel hose, located anywhere on a vehicle between the fuel tank and engine.

FUEL INJECTION: A system replacing the carburetor that sprays fuel into the cylinder through nozzles. The amount of fuel can be more precisely controlled with fuel injection.

FULL FLOATING AXLE: An axle in which the axle housing extends through the wheel giving bearing support on the outside of the housing. The front axle of a four-wheel drive vehicle is usually a full floating axle, as are the rear axles of many larger (1 ton and over) pick-ups and vans.

FULL-TIME FOUR-WHEEL DRIVE: A four-wheel drive system that continuously delivers power to all four wheels. A differential between the front and rear driveshafts permits variations in axle speeds to control gear wind-up without damage.

FULL THROTTLE DETENT DOWNSHIFT: A quick apply of accelerator pedal to its full travel, forcing a downshift.

FUSE: A protective device in a circuit which prevents circuit overload by breaking the circuit when a specific amperage is present. The device is constructed around a strip or wire of a lower amperage rating than the circuit it is designed to protect. When an amperage higher than that stamped on the fuse is present in the circuit, the strip or wire melts, opening the circuit.

FUSIBLE LINK: A piece of wire in a wiring harness that performs the same job as a fuse. If overloaded, the fusible link will melt and interrupt the circuit.

FWD: Front wheel drive.

GAWR: (Gross axle weight rating) the total maximum weight an axle is designed to carry.

GCW: (Gross combined weight) total combined weight of a tow vehicle and trailer.

GARAGE SHIFT: initial engagement feel of transmission, neutral to reverse or neutral to a forward drive.

GARAGE SHIFT FEEL: A quick check of the engagement quality and responsiveness of reverse and forward gears. This test is done with the vehicle stationary.

GEAR: A toothed mechanical device that acts as a rotating lever to transmit power or turning effort from one shaft to another. (See gear ratio.)

GEAR RATIO: A ratio expressing the number of turns a smaller gear will make to turn a larger gear through one revolution. The ratio is found by dividing the number of teeth on the smaller gear into the number of teeth on the larger gear.

GEARBOX: Transmission

GEAR REDUCTION: Torque is multiplied and speed decreased by the factor of the gear ratio. For example, a 3:1 gear ratio changes an input torque of 180 ft. lbs. and an input speed of 2700 rpm to 540 Ft. lbs. and 900 rpm, respectively. (No account is taken of frictional losses, which are always present.)

GEARTRAIN: A succession of intermeshing gears that form an assembly and provide for one or more torque changes as the power input is transmitted to the power output.

GEL COAT: A thin coat of plastic resin covering fiberglass body panels.

GENERATOR: A device which produces direct current (DC) necessary to charge the battery.

GOVERNOR: A device that senses vehicle speed and generates a hydraulic oil pressure. As vehicle speed increases, governor oil pressure rises.

GROUND CIRCUIT: (See circuit, ground.)

GROUND SIDE SWITCHING: The electrical/electronic circuit control switch is located after the circuit load.

GVWR: (Gross vehicle weight rating) total maximum weight a vehicle is designed to carry including the weight of the vehicle, passengers, equipment, gas, oil, etc.

HALOGEN: A special type of lamp known for its quality of brilliant white light. Originally used for fog lights and driving lights.

HARD CODES: DTCs that are present at the time of testing; also called continuous or current codes.

HARSH(ROUGH): An apply of a clutch or band that is more noticeable than a firm one; considered undesirable at any throttle position.

HEADER TANK: An expansion tank for the radiator coolant. It can be located remotely or built into the radiator.

HEAT RANGE: A term used to describe the ability of a spark plug to carry away heat. Plugs with longer nosed insulators take longer to carry heat off effectively.

HEAT RISER: A flapper in the exhaust manifold that is closed when the engine is cold, causing hot exhaust gases to heat the intake manifold providing better cold engine operation. A thermostatic spring opens the flapper when the engine warms up.

HEAVY THROTTLE: Approximately three-fourths of accelerator pedal travel.

HEMI: A name given an engine using hemispherical combustion chambers.

HERTZ (HZ): The international unit of frequency equal to one cycle per second (10,000 Hertz equals 10,000 cycles per second).

HIGH-IMPEDANCE DVOM (DIGITAL VOLT-OHMMETER): This styled device provides a built-in resistance value and is capable of limiting circuit current flow to safe milliamp levels.

HIGH RESISTANCE: Often refers to a circuit where there is an excessive amount of opposition to normal current flow.

HORSEPOWER: A measurement of the amount of work; one horsepower is the amount of work necessary to lift 33,000 lbs. one foot in one minute. Brake horsepower (bhp) is the horsepower delivered by an engine on a dynamometer. Net horsepower is the power remaining (measured at the flywheel of the engine) that can be used to turn the wheels after power is consumed through friction and running the engine accessories (water pump, alternator, air pump, fan etc.)

HOT CIRCUIT: (See circuit, hot; hot lead.)

HOT LEAD: A wire or conductor in the power side of the circuit. (See circuit, hot.)

HOT SIDE SWITCHING: The electrical/electronic circuit control switch is located before the circuit load.

HUB: The center part of a wheel or gear.

HUNTING (BUSYNESS): Repeating quick series of up-shifts and downshifts that causes noticeable change in engine rpm, for example, as in a 4-3-4 shift pattern.

HYDRAULICS: The use of liquid under pressure to transfer force of motion.

HYDROCARBON (HC): Any chemical compound made up of hydrogen and carbon. A major pollutant formed by the engine as a by-product of combustion.

HYDRODYNAMIC DRIVE UNITS: Devices that transmit power solely by the action of a kinetic fluid flow in a closed recirculating path. An impeller energizes the fluid and discharges the high-speed jet stream into the turbine for power output.

HYDROMETER: An instrument used to measure the specific gravity of a solution.

HYDROPLANING: A phenomenon of driving when water builds up under the tire tread, causing it to lose contact with the road. Slowing down will usually restore normal tire contact with the road.

HYPOID GEARSET: The drive pinion gear may be placed below or above the centerline of the driven gear; often used as a final drive gearset.

IDLE MIXTURE: The mixture of air and fuel (usually about 14:1) being fed to the cylinders. The idle mixture screw(s) are sometimes adjusted as part of a tune-up.

IDLER ARM: Component of the steering linkage which is a geometric duplicate of the steering gear arm. It supports the right side of the center steering link.

IMPELLER: Often called a pump, the impeller is the power input (drive) member of a hydrodynamic drive. As part of the torque converter cover, it acts as a centrifugal pump and puts the fluid in motion.

INCH POUND (inch lbs.; sometimes in. lb. or in. lbs.): One twelfth of a foot pound.

INDUCTANCE: The force that produces voltage when a conductor is passed through a magnetic field.

INDUCTION: A means of transferring electrical energy in the form of a magnetic field. Principle used in the ignition coil to increase voltage.

INITIAL FEEL: A distinct firmer feel at start of shift when compared with feel at finish of shift.

INJECTOR: A device which receives metered fuel under relatively low pressure and is activated to inject the fuel into the engine under relatively high pressure at a predetermined time.

INPUT: In an automatic transmission, the source of power from the engine is absorbed by the torque converter, which provides the power input into the transmission. The turbine drives the input(turbine)shaft.

INPUT SHAFT: The shaft to which torque is applied, usually carrying the driving gear or gears.

INTAKE MANIFOLD: A casting of passages or pipes used to conduct air or a fuel/air mixture to the cylinders.

INTERNAL GEAR: The ring-like outer gear of a planetary gearset with the gear teeth cut on the inside of the ring to provide a mesh with the planet pinions.

ISOLATION (CLAMPING) DIODES: Diodes positioned in a circuit to prevent self-induction from damaging electronic components.

IX ROTARY GEAR PUMP: Contains two rotating members, one shaped with internal gear teeth and the other with external gear teeth. As the gears separate, the fluid fills the gaps between gear teeth, is pulled across a crescent-shaped divider, and then is forced to flow through the outlet as the gears mesh.

IX ROTARY LOBE PUMP: Sometimes referred to as a gerotor type pump. Two rotating members, one shaped with internal lobes and the other with external lobes, separate and then mesh to cause fluid to flow.

JOURNAL: The bearing surface within which a shaft operates.

JUMPER CABLES: Two heavy duty wires with large alligator clips used to provide power from a charged battery to a discharged battery mounted in a vehicle.

JUMPSTART: Utilizing the sufficiently charged battery of one vehicle to start the engine of another vehicle with a discharged battery by the use of jumper cables.

KEY: A small block usually fitted in a notch between a shaft and a hub to prevent slippage of the two parts.

KICKDOWN: Detent downshift system; either linkage, cable, or electrically controlled.

KILO: A prefix used in the metric system to indicate one thousand.

KNOCK: Noise which results from the spontaneous ignition of a portion of the air-fuel mixture in the engine cylinder caused by overly advanced ignition timing or use of incorrectly low octane fuel for that engine.

KNOCK SENSOR: An input device that responds to spark knock, caused by over advanced ignition timing.

LABOR TIME: A specific amount of time required to perform a certain repair or diagnostic service as defined by a vehicle or after-market manufacturer .

LACQUER: A quick-drying automotive paint.

LATE: Shift that occurs when engine is at higher than normal rpm for given amount of throttle.

LIGHT-EMITTING DIODE (LED): A semiconductor diode that emits light as electrical current flows through it; used in some electronic display devices to emit a red or other color light.

LIGHT THROTTLE: Approximately one-fourth of accelerator pedal travel.

LIMITED SLIP: A type of differential which transfers driving force to the wheel with the best traction.

LIMP-IN MODE: Electrical shutdown of the transmission/ transaxle output solenoids, allowing only forward and reverse gears that are hydraulically energized by the manual valve. This permits the vehicle to be driven to a service facility for repair.

LIP SEAL: Molded synthetic rubber seal designed with an outer sealing edge (lip) that points into the fluid containing area to be sealed. This type of seal is used where rotational and axial forces are present.

LITHIUM-BASE GREASE: Chassis and wheel bearing grease using lithium as a base. Not compatible with sodium-base grease.

LOAD DEVICE: A circuit's resistance that converts the electrical energy into light, sound, heat, or mechanical movement.

LOAD RANGE: Indicates the number of plies at which a tire is rated. Load range B equals four-ply rating; C equals six-ply rating; and, D equals an eight-ply rating.

LOAD TORQUE: The amount of output torque needed from the transmission/transaxle to overcome the vehicle load.

LOCKING HUBS: Accessories used on part-time four-wheel drive systems that allow the front wheels to be disengaged from the drive train when four-wheel drive is not being used. When four-wheel drive is desired, the hubs are engaged, locking the wheels to the drive train.

LOCKUP CONVERTER: A torque converter that operates hydraulically and mechanically. When an internal apply plate (lockup plate) clamps to the torque converter cover, hydraulic slippage is eliminated.

LOCK RING: See Circlip or Snapring

MAGNET: Any body with the property of attracting iron or steel.

MAGNETIC FIELD: The area surrounding the poles of a magnet that is affected by its attraction or repulsion forces.

MAIN LINE PRESSURE: Often called control pressure or line pressure, it refers to the pressure of the oil leaving the pump and is controlled by the pressure regulator valve.

MALFUNCTION INDICATOR LAMP (MIL): Previously known as a check engine light, the dash-mounted MIL illuminates and signals the driver that an emission or driveability problem with the powertrain has been detected by the ECM/PCM. When this occurs, at least one diagnostic trouble code (DTC) has been stored into the control module memory.

MANIFOLD ABSOLUTE PRESSURE (MAP) SENSOR: Reads the amount of air pressure (vacuum) in the engine's intake manifold system; its signal is used to analyze engine load conditions.

MANIFOLD VACUUM: Low pressure in an engine intake manifold formed just below the throttle plates. Manifold vacuum is highest at idle and drops under acceleration.

MANIFOLD: A casting of passages or set of pipes which connect the cylinders to an inlet or outlet source.

MANUAL LEVER POSITION SWITCH (MLPS): A mechanical switching unit that is typically mounted externally to the transmission/transaxle to inform the PCM/ECM which gear range the driver has selected.

MANUAL VALVE: Located inside the transmission/transaxle, it is directly connected to the driver's shift lever. The position of the manual valve determines which hydraulic circuits will be charged with oil pressure and the operating mode of the transmission.

MANUAL VALVE LEVER POSITION SENSOR (MVLPS): The input from this device tells the TCM what gear range was selected.

MASS AIR FLOW (MAF) SENSOR: Measures the airflow into the engine.

MASTER CYLINDER: The primary fluid pressurizing device in a hydraulic system. In automotive use, it is found in brake and hydraulic clutch systems and is pedal activated, either directly or, in a power brake system, through the power booster.

MacPherson STRUT: A suspension component combining a shock absorber and spring in one unit.

MEDIUM THROTTLE: Approximately one-half of accelerator pedal travel.

MEGA: A metric prefix indicating one million.

MEMBER: An independent component of a hydrodynamic unit such as an impeller, a stator, or a turbine. It may have one or more elements.

MERCON: A fluid developed by Ford Motor Company in 1988. It contains a friction modifier and closely resembles operating characteristics of Dexron.

METAL SEALING RINGS: Made from cast iron or aluminum, their primary application is with dynamic components involving pressure sealing circuits of rotating members. These rings are designed with either butt or hook lock end joints.

METER (ANALOG): A linear-style meter representing data as lengths; a needle-style instrument interfacing with logical numerical increments. This style of electrical meter uses relatively low impedance internal resistance and cannot be used for testing electronic circuitry.

METER (DIGITAL): Uses numbers as a direct readout to show values. Most meters of this style use high impedance internal resistance and must be used for testing low current electronic circuitry.

MICRO: A metric prefix indicating one-millionth (0.000001).

MILLI: A metric prefix indicating one-thousandth (0.001).

MINIMUM THROTTLE: The least amount of throttle opening required for upshift; normally close to zero throttle.

MISFIRE: Condition occurring when the fuel mixture in a cylinder fails to ignite, causing the engine to run roughly.

MODULE: Electronic control unit, amplifier or igniter of solid state or integrated design which controls the current flow in the ignition primary circuit based on input from the pick-up coil. When the module opens the primary circuit, high secondary voltage is induced in the coil.

MODULATED: In an electronic-hydraulic converter clutch system (or shift valve system), the term modulated refers to the pulsing of a solenoid, at a variable rate. This action controls the buildup of oil pressure in the hydraulic circuit to allow a controlled amount of clutch slippage.

MODULATED CONVERTER CLUTCH CONTROL (MCCC): A pulse width duty cycle valve that controls the converter lockup apply pressure and maximizes smoother transitions between lock and unlock conditions.

MODULATOR PRESSURE (THROTTLE PRESSURE): A hydraulic signal oil pressure relating to the amount of engine load, based on either the amount of throttle plate opening or engine vacuum.

MODULATOR VALVE: A regulator valve that is controlled by engine vacuum, providing a hydraulic pressure that varies in relation to engine torque. The hydraulic torque signal functions to delay the shift pattern and provide a line pressure boost. (See throttle valve.)

MOTOR: An electromagnetic device used to convert electrical energy into mechanical energy.

MULTIPLE-DISC CLUTCH: A grouping of steel and friction lined plates that, when compressed together by hydraulic pressure acting upon a piston, lock or unlock a planetary member.

MULTI-WEIGHT: Type of oil that provides adequate lubrication at both high and low temperatures.

needed to move one amp through a resistance of one ohm.

MUSHY: Same as soft; slow and drawn out clutch apply with very little shift feel.

MUTUAL INDUCTION: The generation of current from one wire circuit to another by movement of the magnetic field surrounding a current-carrying circuit as its ampere flow increases or decreases.

NEEDLE BEARING: A bearing which consists of a number (usually a large number) of long, thin rollers.

NITROGEN OXIDE (NOx): One of the three basic pollutants found in the exhaust emission of an internal combustion engine. The amount of NOx usually varies in an inverse proportion to the amount of HC and CO.

NONPOSITIVE SEALING: A sealing method that allows some minor leakage, which normally assists in lubrication.

O2 SENSOR: Located in the engine's exhaust system, it is an input device to the ECM/PCM for managing the fuel delivery and ignition system. A scanner can be used to observe the fluctuating voltage readings produced by an O2 sensor as the oxygen content of the exhaust is analyzed.

O-RING SEAL: Molded synthetic rubber seal designed with a circular cross-section. This type of seal is used primarily in static applications.

OBD II (ON-BOARD DIAGNOSTICS, SECOND GENERATION): Refers to the federal law mandating tighter control of 1996 and newer vehicle emissions, active monitoring of related devices, and standardization of terminology, data link connectors, and other technician concerns.

OCTANE RATING: A number, indicating the quality of gasoline based on its ability to resist knock. The higher the number, the better the quality. Higher compression engines require higher octane gas.

OEM: Original Equipment Manufactured. OEM equipment is that furnished standard by the manufacturer.

OFFSET: The distance between the vertical center of the wheel and the mounting surface at the lugs. Offset is positive if the center is outside the lug circle; negative offset puts the center line inside the lug circle.

OHM'S LAW: A law of electricity that states the relationship between voltage, current, and resistance. Volts = amperes x ohms

OHM: The unit used to measure the resistance of conductor-to-electrical flow. One ohm is the amount of resistance that limits current flow to one ampere in a circuit with one volt of pressure.

OHMMETER: An instrument used for measuring the resistance, in ohms, in an electrical circuit.

ONE-WAY CLUTCH: A mechanical clutch of roller or sprag design that resists torque or transmits power in one direction only. It is used to either hold or drive a planetary member.

ONE-WAY ROLLER CLUTCH: A mechanical device that transmits or holds torque in one direction only.

OPEN CIRCUIT: A break or lack of contact in an electrical circuit, either intentional (switch) or unintentional (bad connection or broken wire).

ORIFICE: Located in hydraulic oil circuits, it acts as a restriction. It slows down fluid flow to either create back pressure or delay pressure buildup downstream.

OSCILLOSCOPE: A piece of test equipment that shows electric impulses as a pattern on a screen. Engine performance can be analyzed by interpreting these patterns.

OUTPUT SHAFT: The shaft which transmits torque from a device, such as a transmission.

OUTPUT SPEED SENSOR (OSS): Identifies transmission/transaxle output shaft speed for shift timing and may be used to calculate TCC slip; often functions as the VSS (vehicle speed sensor).

OVERDRIVE: (1.) A device attached to or incorporated in a transmission/transaxle that allows the engine to turn less than one full revolution for every complete revolution of the wheels. The net effect is to reduce engine rpm, thereby using less fuel. A typical overdrive gear ratio would be .87:1, instead of the normal 1:1 in high gear. (2.) A gear assembly which produces more shaft revolutions than that transmitted to it.

OVERDRIVE PLANETARY GEARSET: A single planetary gearset designed to provide a direct drive and overdrive ratio. When coupled to a three-speed transmission/transaxle configuration, a four-speed/overdrive unit is present.

OVERHEAD CAMSHAFT (OHC): An engine configuration in which the camshaft is mounted on top of the cylinder head and operates the valve either directly or by means of rocker arms.

OVERHEAD VALVE (OHV): An engine configuration in which all of the valves are located in the cylinder head and the camshaft is located in the cylinder block. The camshaft operates the valves via lifters and pushrods.

OVERRUNCLUTCH: Another name for a one-way mechanical clutch. Applies to both roller and sprag designs.

OVERSTEER: The tendency of some vehicles, when steering into a turn, to over-respond or steer more than required, which could result in excessive slip of the rear wheels. Opposite of under-steer.

OXIDATION STABILIZERS: Absorb and dissipate heat. Automatic transmission fluid has high resistance to varnish and sludge buildup that occurs from excessive heat that is generated primarily in the torque converter. Local temperatures as high as 6000F (3150C) can occur at the clutch plates during engagement, and this heat must be absorbed and dissipated. If the fluid cannot withstand the heat, it burns or oxidizes, resulting in an almost immediate destruction of friction materials, clogged filter screen and hydraulic passages, and sticky valves.

OXIDES OF NITROGEN: See nitrogen oxide (NOx).

OXYGEN SENSOR: Used with a feedback system to sense the presence of oxygen in the exhaust gas and signal the computer which can use the voltage signal to determine engine operating efficiency and adjust the air/fuel ratio.

PARALLEL CIRCUIT: (See circuit, parallel.)

PARTS WASHER: A basin or tub, usually with a built-in pump mechanism and hose used for circulating chemical solvent for the purpose of cleaning greasy, oily and dirty components.

PART-TIME FOUR WHEEL DRIVE: A system that is normally in the two wheel drive mode and only runs in four-wheel drive when the system is manually engaged because more traction is desired. Two or four wheel drive is normally selected by a lever to engage the front axle, but if locking hubs are used, these must also be manually engaged in the Lock position. Otherwise, the front axle will not drive the front wheels.

PASSIVE RESTRAINT: Safety systems such as air bags or automatic seat belts which operate with no action required on the part of the driver or passenger. Mandated by Federal regulations on all vehicles sold in the U.S. after 1990.

PAYLOAD: The weight the vehicle is capable of carrying in addition to its own weight. Payload includes weight of the driver, passengers and cargo, but not coolant, fuel, lubricant, spare tire, etc.

PCM: Powertrain control module.

PCV VALVE: A valve usually located in the rocker cover that vents crankcase vapors back into the engine to be reburned.

PERCOLATION: A condition in which the fuel actually "boils," due to excessive heat. Percolation prevents proper atomization of the fuel causing rough running.

PICK-UP COIL: The coil in which voltage is induced in an electronic ignition.

PING: A metallic rattling sound produced by the engine during acceleration. It is usually due to incorrect ignition timing or a poor grade of gasoline.

PINION: The smaller of two gears. The rear axle pinion drives the ring gear which transmits motion to the axle shafts.

PINION GEAR: The smallest gear in a drive gear assembly.

PISTON: A disc or cup that fits in a cylinder bore and is free to move. In hydraulics, it provides the means of converting hydraulic pressure into a usable force. Examples of piston applications are found in servo, clutch, and accumulator units.

PISTON RING: An open-ended ring which fits into a groove on the outer diameter of the piston. Its chief function is to form a seal between the piston and cylinder wall. Most automotive pistons have three rings: two for compression sealing; one for oil sealing.

PITMAN ARM: A lever which transmits steering force from the steering gear to the steering linkage.

PLANET CARRIER: A basic member of a planetary gear assembly that carries the pinion gears.

PLANET PINIONS: Gears housed in a planet carrier that are in constant mesh with the sun gear and internal gear. Because they have their own independent rotating centers, the pinions are capable of rotating around the sun gear or the inside of the internal gear.

PLANETARY GEAR RATIO: The reduction or overdrive ratio developed by a planetary gearset.

PLANETARY GEARSET: In its simplest form, it is made up of a basic assembly group containing a sun gear, internal gear, and planet carrier. The gears are always in constant mesh and offer a wide range of gear ratio possibilities.

PLANETARY GEARSET (COMPOUND): Two planetary gearsets combined together.

PLANETARY GEARSET (SIMPLE): An assembly of gears in constant mesh consisting of a sun gear, several pinion gears mounted in a carrier, and a ring gear. It provides gear ratio and direction changes, in addition to a direct drive and a neutral.

PLY RATING: A. rating given a tire which indicates strength (but not necessarily actual plies). A two-ply/four-ply rating has only two plies, but the strength of a four-ply tire.

POLARITY: Indication (positive or negative) of the two poles of a battery.

PORT: An opening for fluid intake or exhaust.

POSITIVE SEALING: A sealing method that completely prevents leakage.

POTENTIAL: Electrical force measured in volts; sometimes used interchangeably with voltage.

POWER: The ability to do work per unit of time, as expressed in horsepower; one horsepower equals 33,000 ft. lbs. of work per minute, or 550 ft. lbs. of work per second.

POWER FLOW: The systematic flow or transmission of power through the gears, from the input shaft to the output shaft.

POWER-TO-WEIGHT RATIO: Ratio of horsepower to weight of car.

POWERTRAIN: See Drivetrain.

POWERTRAIN CONTROL MODULE (PCM): Current designation for the engine control module (ECM). In many cases, late model vehicle control units manage the engine as well as the transmission. In other settings, the PCM controls the engine and is interfaced with a TCM to control transmission functions.

Ppm: Parts per million; unit used to measure exhaust emissions.

PREIGNITION: Early ignition of fuel in the cylinder, sometimes due to glowing carbon deposits in the combustion chamber. Preignition can be damaging since combustion takes place prematurely.

PRELOAD: A predetermined load placed on a bearing during assembly or by adjustment.

PRESS FIT: The mating of two parts under pressure, due to the inner diameter of one being smaller than the outer diameter of the other, or vice versa; an interference fit.

PRESSURE: The amount of force exerted upon a surface area.

PRESSURE CONTROL SOLENOID (PCS): An output device that provides a boost oil pressure to the mainline regulator valve to control line pressure. Its operation is determined by the amount of current sent from the PCM.

PRESSURE GAUGE: An instrument used for measuring the fluid pressure in a hydraulic circuit.

PRESSURE REGULATOR VALVE: In automatic transmissions, its purpose is to regulate the pressure of the pump output and supply the basic fluid pressure necessary to operate the transmission. The regulated fluid pressure may be referred to as mainline pressure, line pressure, or control pressure.

PRESSURE SWITCH ASSEMBLY (PSA): Mounted inside the transmission, it is a grouping of oil pressure switches that inputs to the PCM when certain hydraulic passages are charged with oil pressure.

PRESSURE PLATE: A spring-loaded plate (part of the clutch) that transmits power to the driven (friction) plate when the clutch is engaged.

PRIMARY CIRCUIT: The low voltage side of the ignition system which consists of the ignition switch, ballast resistor or resistance wire, bypass, coil, electronic control unit and pick-up coil as well as the connecting wires and harnesses.

PROFILE: Term used for tire measurement (tire series), which is the ratio of tire height to tread width.

PROM (PROGRAMMABLE READ-ONLY MEMORY): The heart of the computer that compares input data and makes the engineered program or strategy decisions about when to trigger the appropriate output based on stored computer instructions.

PULSE GENERATOR: A two-wire pickup sensor used to produce a fluctuating electrical signal. This changing signal is read by the controller to determine the speed of the object and can be used to measure transmission/transaxle input speed, output speed, and vehicle speed.

PSI: Pounds per square inch; a measurement of pressure.

PULSE WIDTH DUTY CYCLE SOLENOID (PULSE WIDTH MODULATED SOLENOID): A computer-controlled solenoid that turns on and off at a variable rate producing a modulated oil pressure; often referred to as a pulse width modulated (PWM) solenoid. Employed in many electronic automatic transmissions and transaxles, these solenoids are used to manage shift control and converter clutch hydraulic circuits.

PUSHROD: A steel rod between the hydraulic valve lifter and the valve rocker arm in overhead valve (OHV) engines.

PUMP: A mechanical device designed to create fluid flow and pressure buildup in a hydraulic system.

QUARTER PANEL: General term used to refer to a rear fender. Quarter panel is the area from the rear door opening to the tail light area and from rear wheel well to the base of the trunk and roof-line.

RACE: The surface on the inner or outer ring of a bearing on which the balls, needles or rollers move.

RACK AND PINION: A type of automotive steering system using a pinion gear attached to the end of the steering shaft. The pinion meshes with a long rack attached to the steering linkage.

RADIAL TIRE: Tire design which uses body cords running at right angles to the center line of the tire. Two or more belts are used to give tread strength. Radials can be identified by their characteristic sidewall bulge.

RADIATOR: Part of the cooling system for a water-cooled engine, mounted in the front of the vehicle and connected to the engine with rubber hoses. Through the radiator, excess combustion heat is dissipated into the atmosphere through forced convection using a water and glycol based mixture that circulates through, and cools, the engine.

RANGE REFERENCE AND CLUTCH/BAND APPLY CHART: A guide that shows the application of clutches and bands for each gear, within the selector range positions. These charts are extremely useful for understanding how the unit operates and for diagnosing malfunctions.

RAVIGNEAUX GEARSET: A compound planetary gearset that features matched dual planetary pinions (sets of two) mounted in a single planet carrier. Two sun gears and one ring mesh with the carrier pinions.

REACTION MEMBER: The stationary planetary member, in a planetary gearset, that is grounded to the transmission/transaxle case through the use of friction and wedging devices known as bands, disc clutches, and one-way clutches.

REACTION PRESSURE: The fluid pressure that moves a spool valve against an opposing force or forces; the area on which the opposing force acts. The opposing force can be a spring or a combination of spring force and auxiliary hydraulic force.

REACTOR, TORQUE CONVERTER: The reaction member of a fluid torque converter, more commonly called a stator. (See stator.)

REAR MAIN OIL SEAL: A synthetic or rope-type seal that prevents oil from leaking out of the engine past the rear main crankshaft bearing.

RECIRCULATING BALL: Type of steering system in which recirculating steel balls occupy the area between the nut and worm wheel, causing a reduction in friction.

RECTIFIER: A device (used primarily in alternators) that permits electrical current to flow in one direction only.

REDUCTION: (See gear reduction.)

REGULATOR VALVE: A valve that changes the pressure of the oil in a hydraulic circuit as the oil passes through the valve by bleeding off (or exhausting) some of the volume of oil supplied to the valve.

REFRIGERANT 12 (R-12) or 134 (R-134): The generic name of the refrigerant used in automotive air conditioning systems.

REGULATOR: A device which maintains the amperage and/or voltage levels of a circuit at predetermined values.

RELAY: A switch which automatically opens and/or closes a circuit.

RELAY VALVE: A valve that directs flow and pressure. Relay valves simply connect or disconnect interrelated passages without restricting the fluid flow or changing the pressure.

RELIEF VALVE: A spring-loaded, pressure-operated valve that limits oil pressure buildup in a hydraulic circuit to a predetermined maximum value.

RELUCTOR: A wheel that rotates inside the distributor and triggers the release of voltage in an electronic ignition.

RESERVOIR: The storage area for fluid in a hydraulic system; often called a sump.

RESIN: A liquid plastic used in body work.

RESIDUAL MAGNETISM: The magnetic strength stored in a material after a magnetizing field has been removed.

RESISTANCE: The opposition to the flow of current through a circuit or electrical device, and is measured in ohms. Resistance is equal to the voltage divided by the amperage.

RESISTOR SPARK PLUG: A spark plug using a resistor to shorten the spark duration. This suppresses radio interference and lengthens plug life.

RESISTOR: A device, usually made of wire, which offers a preset amount of resistance in an electrical circuit.

RESULTANT FORCE: The single effective directional thrust of the fluid force on the turbine produced by the vortex and rotary forces acting in different planes.

RETARD: Set the ignition timing so that spark occurs later (fewer degrees before TDC).

RHEOSTAT: A device for regulating a current by means of a variable resistance.

RING GEAR: The name given to a ring-shaped gear attached to a differential case, or affixed to a flywheel or as part of a planetary gear set.

ROADLOAD: grade.

ROCKER ARM: A lever which rotates around a shaft pushing down (opening) the valve with an end when the other end is pushed up by the pushrod. Spring pressure will later close the valve.

ROCKER PANEL: The body panel below the doors between the wheel opening.

ROLLER BEARING: A bearing made up of hardened inner and outer races between which hardened steel rollers move.

ROLLER CLUTCH: A type of one-way clutch design using rollers and springs mounted within an inner and outer cam race assembly.

ROTARY FLOW: The path of the fluid trapped between the blades of the members as they revolve with the rotation of the torque converter cover (rotational inertia).

ROTOR: (1.) The disc-shaped part of a disc brake assembly, upon which the brake pads bear; also called, brake disc. (2.) The device mounted atop the distributor shaft, which passes current to the distributor cap tower contacts.

ROTARY ENGINE: See Wankel engine.

RPM: Revolutions per minute (usually indicates engine speed).

RTV: A gasket making compound that cures as it is exposed to the atmosphere. It is used between surfaces that are not perfectly machined to one another, leaving a slight gap that the RTV fills and in which it hardens. The letters RTV represent room temperature vulcanizing.

RUN-ON: Condition when the engine continues to run, even when the key is turned off. See dieseling.

SEALED BEAM: A automotive headlight. The lens, reflector and filament from a single unit.

SEATBELT INTERLOCK: A system whereby the car cannot be started unless the seatbelt is buckled.

SECONDARY CIRCUIT: The high voltage side of the ignition system, usually above 20,000 volts. The secondary includes the ignition coil, coil wire, distributor cap and rotor, spark plug wires and spark plugs.

SELF-INDUCTION: The generation of voltage in a current-carrying wire by changing the amount of current flowing within that wire.

SEMI-CONDUCTOR: A material (silicon or germanium) that is neither a good conductor nor an insulator; used in diodes and transistors.

SEMI-FLOATING AXLE: In this design, a wheel is attached to the axle shaft, which takes both drive and cornering loads. Almost all solid axle passenger cars and light trucks use this design.

SENDING UNIT: A mechanical, electrical, hydraulic or electromagnetic device which transmits information to a gauge.

SENSOR: Any device designed to measure engine operating conditions or ambient pressures and temperatures. Usually electronic in nature and designed to send a voltage signal to an on-board computer, some sensors may operate as a simple on/off switch or they may provide a variable voltage signal (like a potentiometer) as conditions or measured parameters change.

SERIES CIRCUIT: (See circuit, series.)

SERPENTINE BELT: An accessory drive belt, with small multiple v-ribs, routed around most or all of the engine-powered accessories such as the alternator and power steering pump. Usually both the front and the back side of the belt comes into contact with various pulleys.

SERVO: In an automatic transmission, it is a piston in a cylinder assembly which converts hydraulic pressure into mechanical force and movement; used for the application of the bands and clutches.

SHIFT BUSYNESS: When referring to a torque converter clutch, it is the frequent apply and release of the clutch plate due to uncommon driving conditions.

SHIFT VALVE: Classified as a relay valve, it triggers the automatic shift in response to a governor and a throttle signal by directing fluid to the appropriate band and clutch apply combination to cause the shift to occur.

SHIM: Spacers of precise, predetermined thickness used between parts to establish a proper working relationship.

SHIMMY: Vibration (sometimes violent) in the front end caused by misaligned front end, out of balance tires or worn suspension components.

SHORT CIRCUIT: An electrical malfunction where current takes the path of least resistance to ground (usually through damaged insulation). Current flow is excessive from low resistance resulting in a blown fuse.

SHUDDER: Repeated jerking or stick-slip sensation, similar to chuggle but more severe and rapid in nature, that may be most noticeable during certain ranges of vehicle speed; also used to define condition after converter clutch engagement.

SIMPSON GEARSET: A compound planetary gear train that integrates two simple planetary gearsets referred to as the front planetary and the rear planetary.

SINGLE OVERHEAD CAMSHAFT: See overhead camshaft.

SKIDPLATE: A metal plate attached to the underside of the body to protect the fuel tank, transfer case or other vulnerable parts from damage.

SLAVE CYLINDER: In automotive use, a device in the hydraulic clutch system which is activated by hydraulic force, disengaging the clutch.

SLIPPING: Noticeable increase in engine rpm without vehicle speed increase; usually occurs during or after initial clutch or band engagement.

SLUDGE: Thick, black deposits in engine formed from dirt, oil, water, etc. It is usually formed in engines when oil changes are neglected.

SNAP RING: A circular retaining clip used inside or outside a shaft or part to secure a shaft, such as a floating wrist pin.

SOFT: Slow, almost unnoticeable clutch apply with very little shift feel.

SOFTCODES: DTCs that have been set into the PCM memory but are not present at the time of testing; often referred to as history or intermittent codes.

SOHC: Single overhead camshaft.

SOLENOID: An electrically operated, magnetic switching device.

SPALLING: A wear pattern identified by metal chips flaking off the hardened surface. This condition is caused by foreign particles, overloading situations, and/or normal wear.

SPARK PLUG: A device screwed into the combustion chamber of a spark ignition engine. The basic construction is a conductive core inside of a ceramic insulator, mounted in an outer conductive base. An electrical charge from the spark plug wire travels along the conductive core and jumps a preset air gap to a grounding point or points at the end of the conductive base. The resultant spark ignites the fuel/air mixture in the combustion chamber.

SPECIFIC GRAVITY (BATTERY): The relative weight of liquid (battery electrolyte) as compared to the weight of an equal volume of water.

SPLINES: Ridges machined or cast onto the outer diameter of a shaft or inner diameter of a bore to enable parts to mate without rotation.

SPLIT TORQUE DRIVE: In a torque converter, it refers to parallel paths of torque transmission, one of which is mechanical and the other hydraulic.

SPONGY PEDAL: A soft or spongy feeling when the brake pedal is depressed. It is usually due to air in the brake lines.

SPOOLVALVE: A precision-machined, cylindrically shaped valve made up of lands and grooves. Depending on its position in the valve bore, various interconnecting hydraulic circuit passages are either opened or closed.

SPRAG CLUTCH: A type of one-way clutch design using cams or contoured-shaped sprags between inner and outer races. (See one-way clutch.)

SPRUNG WEIGHT: The weight of a car supported by the springs.

SQUARE-CUT SEAL: Molded synthetic rubber seal designed with a square- or rectangular-shaped cross-section. This type of seal is used for both dynamic and static applications.

SRS: Supplemental restraint system

STABILIZER (SWAY) BAR: A bar linking both sides of the suspension. It resists sway on turns by taking some of added load from one wheel and putting it on the other.

STAGE: The number of turbine sets separated by a stator. A turbine set may be made up of one or more turbine members. A three-element converter is classified as a single stage.

STALL: In fluid drive transmission/transaxle applications, stall refers to engine rpm with the transmission/transaxle engaged and the vehicle stationary; throttle valve can be in any position between closed and wide open.

STALL SPEED: In fluid drive transmission/transaxle applications, stall speed refers to the maximum engine rpm with the transmission/transaxle engaged and vehicle stationary, when the throttle valve is wide open. (See stall; stall test.)

STALL TEST: A procedure recommended by many manufacturers to help determine the integrity of an engine, the torque converter stator, and certain clutch and band combinations. With the shift lever in each of the forward and reverse positions and with the brakes firmly applied, the accelerator pedal is momentarily pressed to the wide open throttle (WOT) position. The engine rpm reading at full throttle can provide clues for diagnosing the condition of the items listed above.

STALL TORQUE: The maximum design or engineered torque ratio of a fluid torque converter, produced under stall speed conditions. (See stall speed.)

STARTER: A high-torque electric motor used for the purpose of starting the engine, typically through a high ratio geared drive connected to the flywheel ring gear.

STATIC: A sealing application in which the parts being sealed do not move in relation to each other.

STATOR (REACTOR): The reaction member of a fluid torque converter that changes the direction of the fluid as it leaves the turbine to enter the impeller vanes. During the torque multiplication phase, this action assists the impeller's rotary force and results in an increase in torque.

STEERING GEOMETRY: Combination of various angles of suspension components (caster, camber, toe-in); roughly equivalent to front end alignment.

STRAIGHT WEIGHT: Term designating motor oil as suitable for use within a narrow range of temperatures. Outside the narrow temperature range its flow characteristics will not adequately lubricate.

STROKE: The distance the piston travels from bottom dead center to top dead center.

SUBSTITUTION: Replacing one part suspected of a defect with a like part of known quality.

SUMP: The storage vessel or reservoir that provides a ready source of fluid to the pump. In an automatic transmission, the sump is the oil pan. All fluid eventually returns to the sump for recycling into the hydraulic system.

SUN GEAR: In a planetary gearset, it is the center gear that meshes with a cluster of planet pinions.

SUPERCHARGER: An air pump driven mechanically by the engine through belts, chains, shafts or gears from the crankshaft. Two general types of supercharger are the positive displacement and centrifugal type, which pump air in direct relationship to the speed of the engine.

SUPPLEMENTAL RESTRAINT SYSTEM: See air bag.

SURGE: Repeating engine-related feeling of acceleration and deceleration that is less intense than chuggle.

SWITCH: A device used to open, close, or redirect the current in an electrical circuit.

SYNCHROMESH: A manual transmission/transaxle that is equipped with devices (synchronizers) that match the gear speeds so that the transmission/transaxle can be downshifted without clashing gears.

SYNTHETIC OIL: Non-petroleum based oil.

TACHOMETER: A device used to measure the rotary speed of an engine, shaft, gear, etc., usually in rotations per minute.

TDC: Top dead center. The exact top of the piston's stroke.

TEFLON SEALING RINGS: Teflon is a soft, durable, plastic-like material that is resistant to heat and provides excellent sealing. These rings are designed with either scarf-cut joints or as one-piece rings. Teflon sealing rings have replaced many metal ring applications.

TERMINAL: A device attached to the end of a wire or cable to make an electrical connection.

TEST LIGHT, CIRCUIT-POWERED: Uses available circuit voltage to test circuit continuity.

TEST LIGHT, SELF-POWERED: Uses its own battery source to test circuit continuity.

THERMISTOR: A special resistor used to measure fluid temperature; it decreases its resistance with increases in temperature.

THERMOSTAT: A valve, located in the cooling system of an engine, which is closed when cold and opens gradually in response to engine heating, controlling the temperature of the coolant and rate of coolant flow.

THERMOSTATIC ELEMENT: A heat-sensitive, spring-type device that controls a drain port from the upper sump area to the lower sump. When the transaxle fluid reaches operating temperature, the port is closed and the upper sump fills, thus reducing the fluid level in the lower sump.

THROTTLE POSITION (TP) SENSOR: Reads the degree of throttle opening; its signal is used to analyze engine load conditions. The ECM/PCM decides to apply the TCC, or to disengage it for coast or load conditions that need a converter torque boost.

THROTTLE PRESSURE/MODULATOR PRESSURE: A hydraulic signal oil pressure relating to the amount of engine load, based on either the amount of throttle plate opening or engine vacuum.

THROTTLE VALVE: A regulating or balanced valve that is controlled mechanically by throttle linkage or engine vacuum. It sends a hydraulic signal to the shift valve body to control shift timing and shift quality. (See balanced valve; modulator valve.)

THROW-OUT BEARING: As the clutch pedal is depressed, the throwout bearing moves against the spring fingers of the pressure plate, forcing the pressure plate to disengage from the driven disc.

TIE ROD: A rod connecting the steering arms. Tie rods have threaded ends that are used to adjust toe-in.

TIE-UP: Condition where two opposing clutches are attempting to apply at same time, causing engine to labor with noticeable loss of engine rpm.

TIMING BELT: A square-toothed, reinforced rubber belt that is driven by the crankshaft and operates the camshaft.

TIMING CHAIN: A roller chain that is driven by the crankshaft and operates the camshaft.

TIRE ROTATION: Moving the tires from one position to another to make the tires wear evenly.

TOE-IN (OUT): A term comparing the extreme front and rear of the front tires. Closer together at the front is toe-in; farther apart at the front is toe-out.

TOP DEAD CENTER (TDC): The point at which the piston reaches the top of its travel on the compression stroke.

TORQUE: Measurement of turning or twisting force, expressed as foot-pounds or inch-pounds.

TORQUE CONVERTER: A turbine used to transmit power from a driving member to a driven member via hydraulic action, providing changes in drive ratio and torque. In automotive use, it links the driveplate at the rear of the engine to the automatic transmission.

TORQUE CONVERTER CLUTCH: The apply plate (lockup plate) assembly used for mechanical power flow through the converter.

TORQUE PHASE: Sometimes referred to as slip phase or stall phase, torque multiplication occurs when the turbine is turning at a slower speed than the impeller, and the stator is reactionary (stationary). This sequence generates a boost in output torque.

TORQUE RATING (STALL TORQUE): The maximum torque multiplication that occurs during stall conditions, with the engine at wide open throttle (WOT) and zero turbine speed.

TORQUE RATIO: An expression of the gear ratio factor on torque effect. A 3:1 gear ratio or 3:1 torque ratio increases the torque input by the ratio factor of 3. Input torque (100 ft. lbs.) x 3 = output torque (300 ft. lbs.)

TRACTION: The amount of usable tractive effort before the drive wheels slip on the road contact surface.

TORSION BAR SUSPENSION: Long rods of spring steel which take the place of springs. One end of the bar is anchored and the other arm (attached to the suspension) is free to twist. The bars' resistance to twisting causes springing action.

TRACK: Distance between the centers of the tires where they contact the ground.

TRACTION CONTROL: A control system that prevents the spinning of a vehicle's drive wheels when excess power is applied.

TRACTIVE EFFORT: The amount of force available to the drive wheels, to move the vehicle.

TRANSAXLE: A single housing containing the transmission and differential. Transaxles are usually found on front engine/front wheel drive or rear engine/rear wheel drive cars.

TRANSDUCER: A device that changes energy from one form to another. For example, a transducer in a microphone changes sound energy to electrical energy. In automotive air-conditioning controls used in automatic temperature systems, a transducer changes an electrical signal to a vacuum signal, which operates mechanical doors.

TRANSMISSION: A powertrain component designed to modify torque and speed developed by the engine; also provides direct drive, reverse, and neutral.

TRANSMISSION CONTROL MODULE (TCM): Manages transmission functions. These vary according to the manufacturer's product design but may include converter clutch operation, electronic shift scheduling, and mainline pressure.

TRANSMISSION FLUID TEMPERATURE (TFT) SENSOR: Originally called a transmission oil temperature (TOT) sensor, this input device to the ECM/PCM senses the fluid temperature and provides a resistance value. It operates on the thermistor principle.

TRANSMISSION INPUT SPEED (TIS) SENSOR: Measures turbine shaft (input shaft) rpm's and compares to engine rpm's to determine torque converter slip. When compared to the transmission output speed sensor or VSS, gear ratio and clutch engagement timing can be determined.

TRANSMISSION OIL TEMPERATURE (TOT) SENSOR: (See transmission fluid temperature (TFT) sensor.)

TRANSMISSION RANGE SELECTOR (TRS) SWITCH: Tells the module which gear shift position the driver has chosen.

TRANSFER CASE: A gearbox driven from the transmission that delivers power to both front and rear driveshafts in a four-wheel drive system. Transfer cases usually have a high and low range set of gears, used depending on how much pulling power is needed.

TRANSISTOR: A semi-conductor component which can be actuated by a small voltage to perform an electrical switching function.

TREAD WEAR INDICATOR: Bars molded into the tire at right angles to the tread that appear as horizontal bars when 1/16 in. of tread remains.

TREAD WEAR PATTERN: The pattern of wear on tires which can be "read" to diagnose problems in the front suspension.

TUNE-UP: A regular maintenance function, usually associated with the replacement and adjustment of parts and components in the electrical and fuel systems of a vehicle for the purpose of attaining optimum performance.

TURBINE: The output (driven) member of a fluid coupling or fluid torque converter. It is splined to the input (turbine) shaft of the transmission.

TURBOCHARGER: An exhaust driven pump which compresses intake air and forces it into the combustion chambers at higher than atmospheric pressures. The increased air pressure allows more fuel to be burned and results in increased horsepower being produced.

TURBULENCE: The interference of molecules of a fluid (or vapor) with each other in a fluid flow.

TYPE F: Transmission fluid developed and used by Ford Motor Company up to 1982. This fluid type provides a high coefficient of friction.

TYPE 7176: The preferred choice of transmission fluid for Chrysler automatic transmissions and transaxles. Developed in 1986, it closely resembles Dexron and Mercon. Type 7176 is the recommended service fill fluid for all Chrysler products utilizing a lockup torque converter dating back to 1978.

U-JOINT (UNIVERSAL JOINT): A flexible coupling in the drive train that allows the driveshafts or axle shafts to operate at different angles and still transmit rotary power.

UNDERSTEER: The tendency of a car to continue straight ahead while negotiating a turn.

UNIT BODY: Design in which the car body acts as the frame.

UNLEADED FUEL: Fuel which contains no lead (a common gasoline additive). The presence of lead in fuel will destroy the functioning elements of a catalytic converter, making it useless.

UNSPRUNG WEIGHT: The weight of car components not supported by the springs (wheels, tires, brakes, rear axle, control arms, etc.).

UPSHIFT: A shift that results in a decrease in torque ratio and an increase in speed.

VACUUM: A negative pressure; any pressure less than atmospheric pressure.

VACUUM ADVANCE: A device which advances the ignition timing in response to increased engine vacuum.

VACUUM GAUGE: An instrument used for measuring the existing vacuum in a vacuum circuit or chamber. The unit of measure is inches (of mercury in a barometer).

VACUUM MODULATOR: Generates a hydraulic oil pressure in response to the amount of engine vacuum.

VALVES: Devices that can open or close fluid passages in a hydraulic system and are used for directing fluid flow and controlling pressure.

VALVE BODY ASSEMBLY: The main hydraulic control assembly of the transmission/transaxle that contains numerous valves, check balls, and other components to control the distribution of pressurized oil throughout the transmission.

VALVE CLEARANCE: The measured gap between the end of the valve stem and the rocker arm, cam lobe or follower that activates the valve.

VALVE GUIDES: The guide through which the stem of the valve passes. The guide is designed to keep the valve in proper alignment.

VALVE LASH (clearance): The operating clearance in the valve train.

VALVE TRAIN: The system that operates intake and exhaust valves, consisting of camshaft, valves and springs, lifters, pushrods and rocker arms.

VAPOR LOCK: Boiling of the fuel in the fuel lines due to excess heat. This will interfere with the flow of fuel in the lines and can completely stop the flow. Vapor lock normally only occurs in hot weather.

VARIABLE DISPLACEMENT (VARIABLE CAPACITY) VANE PUMP: Slipper-type vanes, mounted in a revolving rotor and contained within the bore of a movable slide, capture and then force fluid to flow. Movement of the slide to various positions changes the size of the vane chambers and the amount of fluid flow. **Note:** GM refers to this pump design as variable displacement, and Ford terms it variable capacity.

VARIABLE FORCE SOLENOID (VFS): Commonly referred to as the electronic pressure control (EPC) solenoid, it replaces the cable/linkage style of TV system control and is integrated with a spool valve and spring assembly to control pressure. A variable computer-controlled current flow varies the internal force of the solenoid on the spool valve and resulting control pressure.

VARIABLE ORIFICE THERMAL VALVE: Temperature-sensitive hydraulic oil control device that adjusts the size of a circuit path opening. By altering the size of the opening, the oil flow rate is adapted for cold to hot oil viscosity changes.

VARNISH: Term applied to the residue formed when gasoline gets old and stale.

VCM: See Electronic Control Unit (ECU).

VEHICLE SPEED SENSOR (VSS): Provides an electrical signal to the computer module, measuring vehicle speed, and affects the torque converter clutch engagement and release.

VESPEL SEALING RINGS: Hard plastic material that produces excellent sealing in dynamic settings. These rings are found in late versions of the 4T60 and in all 4T60-E and 4T80-E transaxles.

VISCOSITY: The ability of a fluid to flow. The lower the viscosity rating, the easier the fluid will flow. 10 weight motor oil will flow much easier than 40 weight motor oil.

VISCOSITY INDEX IMPROVERS: Keeps the viscosity nearly constant with changes in temperature. This is especially important at low temperatures, when the oil needs to be thin to aid in shifting and for cold-weather starting. Yet it must not be so thin that at high temperatures it will cause excessive hydraulic leakage so that pumps are unable to maintain the proper pressures.

VISCOUS CLUTCH: A specially designed torque converter clutch apply plate that, through the use of a silicon fluid, clamps smoothly and absorbs torsional vibrations.

VOLT: Unit used to measure the force or pressure of electricity. It is defined as the pressure needed to move one amp through the resistance of one ohm.

VOLTAGE: The electrical pressure that causes current to flow. Voltage is measured in volts (V).

VOLTAGE, APPLIED: The actual voltage read at a given point in a circuit. It equals the available voltage of the power supply minus the losses in the circuit up to that point.

VOLTAGE DROP: The voltage lost or used in a circuit by normal loads such as a motor or lamp or by abnormal loads such as a poor (high-resistance) lead or terminal connection.

VOLTAGE REGULATOR: A device that controls the current output of the alternator or generator.

VOLTMETER: An instrument used for measuring electrical force in units called volts. Voltmeters are always connected parallel with the circuit being tested.

VORTEX FLOW: The crosswise or circulatory flow of oil between the blades of the members caused by the centrifugal pumping action of the impeller.

WANKEL ENGINE: An engine which uses no pistons. In place of pistons, triangular-shaped rotors revolve in specially shaped housings.

WATER PUMP: A belt driven component of the cooling system that mounts on the engine, circulating the coolant under pressure.

WATT: The unit for measuring electrical power. One watt is the product of one ampere and one volt (watts equals amps times volts). Wattage is the horsepower of electricity (746 watts equal one horsepower).

WHEEL ALIGNMENT: Inclusive term to describe the front end geometry (caster, camber, toe-in/out).

WHEEL CYLINDER: Found in the automotive drum brake assembly, it is a device, actuated by hydraulic pressure, which, through internal pistons, pushes the brake shoes outward against the drums.

WHEEL WEIGHT: Small weights attached to the wheel to balance the wheel and tire assembly. Out-of-balance tires quickly wear out and also give erratic handling when installed on the front.

WHEELBASE: Distance between the center of front wheels and the center of rear wheels.

WIDE OPEN THROTTLE (WOT): Full travel of accelerator pedal.

WORK: The force exerted to move a mass or object. Work involves motion; if a force is exerted and no motion takes place, no work is done. Work per unit of time is called power. Work = force x distance = ft. lbs. 33,000 ft. lbs. in one minute = 1 horsepower

ZERO-THROTTLE COAST DOWN: A full release of accelerator pedal while vehicle is in motion and in drive range.

Commonly Used Abbreviations

2
2WD	Two Wheel Drive

4
4WD	Four Wheel Drive

A
A/C	Air Conditioning
ABDC	After Bottom Dead Center
ABS	Anti-lock Brakes
AC	Alternating Current
ACL	Air cleaner
ACT	Air Charge Temperature
AIR	Secondary Air Injection
ALCL	Assembly Line Communications Link
ALDL	Assembly Line Diagnostic Link
AT	Automatic Transaxle/Transmission
ATDC	After Top Dead Center
ATF	Automatic Transmission Fluid
ATS	Air Temperature Sensor
AWD	All Wheel Drive

B
BAP	Barometric Absolute Pressure
BARO	Barometric Pressure
BBDC	Before Bottom Dead Center
BCM	Body Control Module
BDC	Bottom Dead Center
BPT	Backpressure Transducer
BTDC	Before Top Dead Center
BVSV	Bimetallic Vacuum Switching Valve

C
CAC	Charge Air Cooler
CARB	California Air Resources Board
CAT	Catalytic Converter
CCC	Computer Command Control
CCCC	Computer Controlled Catalytic Converter
CCCI	Computer Controlled Coil Ignition
CCD	Computer Controlled Dwell
CDI	Capacitor Discharge Ignition
CEC	Computerized Engine Control
CFI	Continuous Fuel Injection
CIS	Continuous Injection System
CIS-E	Continuous Injection System - Electronic
CKP	Crankshaft Position
CL	Closed Loop
CMP	Camshaft Position
CPP	Clutch Pedal Position
CTOX	Continuous Trap Oxidizer System
CTP	Closed Throttle Position
CVC	Constant Vacuum Control
CYL	Cylinder

D
DBC	Dual Bed Catalyst
DC	Direct Current
DFI	Direct Fuel Injection
DIS	Distributorless Ignition System
DLC	Data Link Connector
DMM	Digital Multimeter
DOHC	Double Overhead Camshaft
DRB	Diagnostic Readout Box
DTC	Diagnostic Trouble Code
DTM	Diagnostic Test Mode
DVOM	Digital Volt/Ohmmeter

E
EBCM	Electronic Brake Control Module
ECM	Engine Control Module
ECT	Engine Coolant Temperature
ECU	Engine Control Unit or Electronic Control Unit
EDIS	Electronic Distributorless Ignition System
EEC	Electronic Engine Control
EEPROM	Electrically Erasable Programmable Read Only Memory
EFE	Early Fuel Evaporation
EGR	Exhaust Gas Recirculation
EGRT	Exhaust Gas Recirculation Temperature
EGRVC	EGR Valve Control
EPROM	Erasable Programmable Read Only Memory
EVAP	Evaporative Emissions
EVP	EGR Valve Position

F
FBC	Feedback Carburetor
FEEPROM	Flash Electrically Erasable Programmable Read Only Memory
FF	Flexible Fuel
FI	Fuel Injection
FT	Fuel Trim
FWD	Front Wheel Drive

G
GND	Ground

H
HAC	High Altitude Compensation
HEGO	Heated Exhaust Gas Oxygen sensor
HEI	High Energy Ignition
HO2 Sensor	Heated Oxygen Sensor

I
IAC	Idle Air Control
IAT	Intake Air Temperature
ICM	Ignition Control Module
IFI	Indirect Fuel Injection
IFS	Inertia Fuel Shutoff
ISC	Idle Speed Control
IVSV	Idle Vacuum Switching Valve

Commonly Used Abbreviations

K

KOEO	Key On, Engine Off
KOER	Key ON, Engine Running
KS	Knock Sensor

M

MAF	Mass Air Flow
MAP	Manifold Absolute Pressure
MAT	Manifold Air Temperature
MC	Mixture Control
MDP	Manifold Differential Pressure
MFI	Multiport Fuel Injection
MIL	Malfunction Indicator Lamp or Maintenance
MST	Manifold Surface Temperature
MVZ	Manifold Vacuum Zone

N

NVRAM	Nonvolatile Random Access Memory

O

O2 Sensor	Oxygen Sensor
OBD	On-Board Diagnostic
OC	Oxidation Catalyst
OHC	Overhead Camshaft
OL	Open Loop

P

P/S	Power Steering
PAIR	Pulsed Secondary Air Injection
PCM	Powertrain Control Module
PCS	Purge Control Solenoid
PCV	Positive Crankcase Ventilation
PIP	Profile Ignition Pick-up
PNP	Park/Neutral Position
PROM	Programmable Read Only Memory
PSP	Power Steering Pressure
PTO	Power Take-Off
PTOX	Periodic Trap Oxidizer System

R

RABS	Rear Anti-lock Brake System
RAM	Random Access Memory
ROM	Read Only Memory
RPM	Revolutions Per Minute
RWAL	Rear Wheel Anti-lock Brakes
RWD	Rear Wheel Drive

S

SBC	Single Bed Converter
SBEC	Single Board Engine Controller
SC	Supercharger
SCB	Supercharger Bypass
SFI	Sequential Multiport Fuel Injection
SIR	Supplemental Inflatable Restraint
SOHC	Single Overhead Camshaft
SPL	Smoke Puff Limiter
SPOUT	Spark Output
SRI	Service Reminder Indicator
SRS	Supplemental Restraint System
SRT	System Readiness Test
SSI	Solid State Ignition
ST	Scan Tool
STO	Self-Test Output

T

TAC	Thermostatic Air Cleaner
TBI	Throttle Body Fuel Injection
TC	Turbocharger
TCC	Torque Converter Clutch
TCM	Transmission Control Module
TDC	Top Dead Center
TFI	Thick Film Ignition
TP	Throttle Position
TR Sensor	Transaxle/Transmission Range Sensor
TVV	Thermal Vacuum Valve
TWC	Three-way Catalytic Converter

V

VAF	Volume Air Flow, or Vane Air Flow
VAPS	Variable Assist Power Steering
VRV	Vacuum Regulator Valve
VSS	Vehicle Speed Sensor
VSV	Vacuum Switching Valve

W

WOT	Wide Open Throttle
WU-TWC	Warm Up Three-way Catalytic Converter

ENGLISH TO METRIC CONVERSION: TORQUE

To convert foot-pounds (ft. lbs.) to Newton-meters (Nm), multiply the number of ft. lbs. by 1.36
To convert Newton-meters (Nm) to foot-pounds (ft. lbs.), multiply the number of Nm by 0.7376

ft. lbs.	Nm	ft. lbs.	Nm	ft. lbs.	Nm	ft. lbs.	Nm
0.1	0.1	34	46.2	76	103.4	118	160.5
0.2	0.3	35	47.6	77	104.7	119	161.8
0.3	0.4	36	49.0	78	106.1	120	163.2
0.4	0.5	37	50.3	79	107.4	121	164.6
0.5	0.7	38	51.7	80	108.8	122	165.9
0.6	0.8	39	53.0	81	110.2	123	167.3
0.7	1.0	40	54.4	82	111.5	124	168.6
0.8	1.1	41	55.8	83	112.9	125	170.0
0.9	1.2	42	57.1	84	114.2	126	171.4
1	1.4	43	58.5	85	115.6	127	172.7
2	2.7	44	59.8	86	117.0	128	174.1
3	4.1	45	61.2	87	118.3	129	175.4
4	5.4	46	62.6	88	119.7	130	176.8
5	6.8	47	63.9	89	121.0	131	178.2
6	8.2	48	65.3	90	122.4	132	179.5
7	9.5	49	66.6	91	123.8	133	180.9
8	10.9	50	68.0	92	125.1	134	182.2
9	12.2	51	69.4	93	126.5	135	183.6
10	13.6	52	70.7	94	127.8	136	185.0
11	15.0	53	72.1	95	129.2	137	186.3
12	16.3	54	73.4	96	130.6	138	187.7
13	17.7	55	74.8	97	131.9	139	189.0
14	19.0	56	76.2	98	133.3	140	190.4
15	20.4	57	77.5	99	134.6	141	191.8
16	21.8	58	78.9	100	136.0	142	193.1
17	23.1	59	80.2	101	137.4	143	194.5
18	24.5	60	81.6	102	138.7	144	195.8
19	25.8	61	83.0	103	140.1	145	197.2
20	27.2	62	84.3	104	141.4	146	198.6
21	28.6	63	85.7	105	142.8	147	199.9
22	29.9	64	87.0	106	144.2	148	201.3
23	31.3	65	88.4	107	145.5	149	202.6
24	32.6	66	89.8	108	146.9	150	204.0
25	34.0	67	91.1	109	148.2	151	205.4
26	35.4	68	92.5	110	149.6	152	206.7
27	36.7	69	93.8	111	151.0	153	208.1
28	38.1	70	95.2	112	152.3	154	209.4
29	39.4	71	96.6	113	153.7	155	210.8
30	40.8	72	97.9	114	155.0	156	212.2
31	42.2	73	99.3	115	156.4	157	213.5
32	43.5	74	100.6	116	157.8	158	214.9
33	44.9	75	102.0	117	159.1	159	216.2

METRIC TO ENGLISH CONVERSION: TORQUE

To convert foot-pounds (ft. lbs.) to Newton-meters (Nm), multiply the number of ft. lbs. by 1.36
To convert Newton-meters (Nm) to foot-pounds (ft. lbs.), multiply the number of Nm by 0.7376

Nm	ft. lbs.	Nm	ft. lbs.	Nm	ft. lbs.	Nm	ft. lbs.	Nm	ft. lbs.
0.1	0.1	34	25.0	76	55.9	118	86.8	160	117.6
0.2	0.1	35	25.7	77	56.6	119	87.5	161	118.4
0.3	0.2	36	26.5	78	57.4	120	88.2	162	119.1
0.4	0.3	37	27.2	79	58.1	121	89.0	163	119.9
0.5	0.4	38	27.9	80	58.8	122	89.7	164	120.6
0.6	0.4	39	28.7	81	59.6	123	90.4	165	121.3
0.7	0.5	40	29.4	82	60.3	124	91.2	166	122.1
0.8	0.6	41	30.1	83	61.0	125	91.9	167	122.8
0.9	0.7	42	30.9	84	61.8	126	92.6	168	123.5
1	0.7	43	31.6	85	62.5	127	93.4	169	124.3
2	1.5	44	32.4	86	63.2	128	94.1	170	125.0
3	2.2	45	33.1	87	64.0	129	94.9	171	125.7
4	2.9	46	33.8	88	64.7	130	95.6	172	126.5
5	3.7	47	34.6	89	65.4	131	96.3	173	127.2
6	4.4	48	35.3	90	66.2	132	97.1	174	127.9
7	5.1	49	36.0	91	66.9	133	97.8	175	128.7
8	5.9	50	36.8	92	67.6	134	98.5	176	129.4
9	6.6	51	37.5	93	68.4	135	99.3	177	130.1
10	7.4	52	38.2	94	69.1	136	100.0	178	130.9
11	8.1	53	39.0	95	69.9	137	100.7	179	131.6
12	8.8	54	39.7	96	70.6	138	101.5	180	132.4
13	9.6	55	40.4	97	71.3	139	102.2	181	133.1
14	10.3	56	41.2	98	72.1	140	102.9	182	133.8
15	11.0	57	41.9	99	72.8	141	103.7	183	134.6
16	11.8	58	42.6	100	73.5	142	104.4	184	135.3
17	12.5	59	43.4	101	74.3	143	105.1	185	136.0
18	13.2	60	44.1	102	75.0	144	105.9	186	136.8
19	14.0	61	44.9	103	75.7	145	106.6	187	137.5
20	14.7	62	45.6	104	76.5	146	107.4	188	138.2
21	15.4	63	46.3	105	77.2	147	108.1	189	139.0
22	16.2	64	47.1	106	77.9	148	108.8	190	139.7
23	16.9	65	47.8	107	78.7	149	109.6	191	140.4
24	17.6	66	48.5	108	79.4	150	110.3	192	141.2
25	18.4	67	49.3	109	80.1	151	111.0	193	141.9
26	19.1	68	50.0	110	80.9	152	111.8	194	142.6
27	19.9	69	50.7	111	81.6	153	112.5	195	143.4
28	20.6	70	51.5	112	82.4	154	113.2	196	144.1
29	21.3	71	52.2	113	83.1	155	114.0	197	144.9
30	22.1	72	52.9	114	83.8	156	114.7	198	145.6
31	22.8	73	53.7	115	84.6	157	115.4	199	146.3
32	23.5	74	54.4	116	85.3	158	116.2	200	147.1
33	24.3	75	55.1	117	86.0	159	116.9	201	147.8

ENGLISH/METRIC CONVERSION: TEMPERATURE

To convert Fahrenheit (F°) to Celsius (C°), take F° temperature and subtract 32, multiply the result by 5 and divide the result by 9

To convert Celsius (C°) to Fahrenheit (F°), take C° temperature and multiply it by 9, divide the result by 5 and add 32

F°	C°	F°	C°	C°	F°	C°	F°
-40	-40.0	150	65.6	-38	-36.4	46	114.8
-35	-37.2	155	68.3	-36	-32.8	48	118.4
-30	-34.4	160	71.1	-34	-29.2	50	122
-25	-31.7	165	73.9	-32	-25.6	52	125.6
-20	-28.9	170	76.7	-30	-22	54	129.2
-15	-26.1	175	79.4	-28	-18.4	56	132.8
-10	-23.3	180	82.2	-26	-14.8	58	136.4
-5	-20.6	185	85.0	-24	-11.2	60	140
0	-17.8	190	87.8	-22	-7.6	62	143.6
1	-17.2	195	90.6	-20	-4	64	147.2
2	-16.7	200	93.3	-18	-0.4	66	150.8
3	-16.1	205	96.1	-16	3.2	68	154.4
4	-15.6	210	98.9	-14	6.8	70	158
5	-15.0	212	100.0	-12	10.4	72	161.6
10	-12.2	215	101.7	-10	14	74	165.2
15	-9.4	220	104.4	-8	17.6	76	168.8
20	-6.7	225	107.2	-6	21.2	78	172.4
25	-3.9	230	110.0	-4	24.8	80	176
30	-1.1	235	112.8	-2	28.4	82	179.6
35	1.7	240	115.6	0	32	84	183.2
40	4.4	245	118.3	2	35.6	86	186.8
45	7.2	250	121.1	4	39.2	88	190.4
50	10.0	255	123.9	6	42.8	90	194
55	12.8	260	126.7	8	46.4	92	197.6
60	15.6	265	129.4	10	50	94	201.2
65	18.3	270	132.2	12	53.6	96	204.8
70	21.1	275	135.0	14	57.2	98	208.4
75	23.9	280	137.8	16	60.8	100	212
80	26.7	285	140.6	18	64.4	102	215.6
85	29.4	290	143.3	20	68	104	219.2
90	32.2	295	146.1	22	71.6	106	222.8
95	35.0	300	148.9	24	75.2	108	226.4
100	37.8	305	151.7	26	78.8	110	230
105	40.6	310	154.4	28	82.4	112	233.6
110	43.3	315	157.2	30	86	114	237.2
115	46.1	320	160.0	32	89.6	116	240.8
120	48.9	325	162.8	34	93.2	118	244.4
125	51.7	330	165.6	36	96.8	120	248
130	54.4	335	168.3	38	100.4	122	251.6
135	57.2	340	171.1	40	104	124	255.2
140	60.0	345	173.9	42	107.6	126	258.8
145	62.8	350	176.7	44	111.2	128	262.4

LENGTH CONVERSION

To convert inches (in.) to millimeters (mm), multiply the number of inches by 25.4
To convert millimeters (mm) to inches (in.), multiply the number of millimeters by 0.04

Inches	Millimeters	Inches	Millimeters	Inches	Millimeters	Inches	Millimeters
0.0001	0.00254	0.005	0.1270	0.09	2.286	4	101.6
0.0002	0.00508	0.006	0.1524	0.1	2.54	5	127.0
0.0003	0.00762	0.007	0.1778	0.2	5.08	6	152.4
0.0004	0.01016	0.008	0.2032	0.3	7.62	7	177.8
0.0005	0.01270	0.009	0.2286	0.4	10.16	8	203.2
0.0006	0.01524	0.01	0.254	0.5	12.70	9	228.6
0.0007	0.01778	0.02	0.508	0.6	15.24	10	254.0
0.0008	0.02032	0.03	0.762	0.7	17.78	11	279.4
0.0009	0.02286	0.04	1.016	0.8	20.32	12	304.8
0.001	0.0254	0.05	1.270	0.9	22.86	13	330.2
0.002	0.0508	0.06	1.524	1	25.4	14	355.6
0.003	0.0762	0.07	1.778	2	50.8	15	381.0
0.004	0.1016	0.08	2.032	3	76.2	16	406.4

ENGLISH/METRIC CONVERSION: LENGTH

To convert inches (in.) to millimeters (mm), multiply the number of inches by 25.4
To convert millimeters (mm) to inches (in.), multiply the number of millimeters by 0.04

Inches		Millimeters	Inches		Millimeters	Inches		Millimeters
Fraction	Decimal	Decimal	Fraction	Decimal	Decimal	Fraction	Decimal	Decimal
1/64	0.016	0.397	11/32	0.344	8.731	11/16	0.688	17.463
1/32	0.031	0.794	23/64	0.359	9.128	45/64	0.703	17.859
3/64	0.047	1.191	3/8	0.375	9.525	23/32	0.719	18.256
1/16	0.063	1.588	25/64	0.391	9.922	47/64	0.734	18.653
5/64	0.078	1.984	13/32	0.406	10.319	3/4	0.750	19.050
3/32	0.094	2.381	27/64	0.422	10.716	49/64	0.766	19.447
7/64	0.109	2.778	7/16	0.438	11.113	25/32	0.781	19.844
1/8	0.125	3.175	29/64	0.453	11.509	51/64	0.797	20.241
9/64	0.141	3.572	15/32	0.469	11.906	13/16	0.813	20.638
5/32	0.156	3.969	31/64	0.484	12.303	53/64	0.828	21.034
11/64	0.172	4.366	1/2	0.500	12.700	27/32	0.844	21.431
3/16	0.188	4.763	33/64	0.516	13.097	55/64	0.859	21.828
13/64	0.203	5.159	17/32	0.531	13.494	7/8	0.875	22.225
7/32	0.219	5.556	35/64	0.547	13.891	57/64	0.891	22.622
15/64	0.234	5.953	9/16	0.563	14.288	29/32	0.906	23.019
1/4	0.250	6.350	37/64	0.578	14.684	59/64	0.922	23.416
17/64	0.266	6.747	19/32	0.594	15.081	15/16	0.938	23.813
9/32	0.281	7.144	39/64	0.609	15.478	61/64	0.953	24.209
19/64	0.297	7.541	5/8	0.625	15.875	31/32	0.969	24.606
5/16	0.313	7.938	41/64	0.641	16.272	63/64	0.984	25.003
21/64	0.328	8.334	21/32	0.656	16.669	1/1	1.000	25.400
			43/64	0.672	17.066			